W9-AVH-738

HARRAP'S SLANG

DICTIONARY/DICTIONNAIRE

HARRAP'S SLANG

DICTIONARY/DICTIONNAIRE

English-French
Français-Anglais

Edited by
Georgette A Marks
Charles B Johnson

Completely revised and edited by
Helen Knox

Consultant Editor
Fabrice Antoine

First published in Great Britain in 1984
by Harrap Books Ltd
43–45 Annandale Street, Edinburgh EH7 4AZ, UK

© Chambers Harrap Publishers Ltd 1993

Reprinted 1994

ISBN 0 245 60495 2 (UK)
ISBN 0 245 50246 7 (France)
ISBN 0 671 88346 1 (USA)

Reprinted 1984 (twice), 1985, 1986, 1987 (twice),
1988 (twice), 1989 (twice), 1991, 1992
New edition 1993

Library of Congress Cataloging-in-Publication Data

Harrap's slang French dictionary / H. Knox, editor and reviser. – Rev. ed.
p.   cm.
English and French
ISBN 0–671–88346–1
1. French language – Slang – Dictionaries – English.
1. Knox, Helen

PC3741.H37   1994
447′.09–dc20

92–20848
CIP

Dépôt légal: août 1993
Printed in England by Clays Ltd, St Ives plc

Preface
to the 1st Edition

Informal language is both ephemeral and subject to rapid change and no dictionary can claim to contain an exhaustive record of everyday slang and colloquialisms. The aim of this dictionary is to allow greater access to the daily languages of English and French speaking cultures. We hope that the work will be of interest to academics and the general public whilst, at the same time, providing an entertaining selection of the more light-hearted and racy aspects of the English and French languages.

The dictionary features a broad selection of terms and expressions ranging from the almost standard and colloquial to the *very* vulgar. In order to make the text as readable as possible, the layout has been simplified and abbreviations and other such devices have been kept to a minimum. Many examples of usage are given. Readers are referred to the section on *'How to use this dictionary'* for any guidance they may need.

One of the major features of the dictionary is the inclusion of the Indexes of Slang Synonyms, to be found at the end of each section. Each contains a comprehensive list of slang and colloquial synonyms for each of the key words asterisked in the text, and several other sections, which it was not possible to indicate in the text, but which should prove of interest to the reader.

This dictionary is a revised edition of *Harrap's Dictionary of Slang and Colloquialisms* and the Editor owes a great debt to the care and attention which Marks and Johnson gave to their work on the previous editions. Their work has been continued by many contributors from various parts of the world.

Grateful thanks are due to the following people who, in many different ways, gave advice and assistance during the compilation of this edition:

Fabrice Antoine	Diana Giese	Geneviève Talon
JP Bean	Anne Gruneberg	Jef Tombeur
Fiona Clarke	Paul Janssen	Elisabeth Turner
Françoise Clarke	Janet Kernachan	Sarah Wallis
Peter Collin	Helen Knox	Edward Wilson
Karen George	Gabriel Otman	

JEP

Préface
de la Première Édition

La langue familière est à la fois éphémère et sujette à une évolution rapide: aucun dictionnaire ne peut donc prétendre offrir une compilation exhaustive des expressions familières et de l'argot communément employés. L'objectif de ce dictionnaire est de permettre un meilleur accès à la langue quotidienne de la culture parlée anglaise et française. Nous souhaitons que l'ouvrage intéresse les linguistes professionnels aussi bien que le grand public, tout en montrant la langue anglaise et la langue française sous leur jour le plus amusant et plus savoureux.

On trouvera dans le dictionnaire un large choix de termes et d'expressions variant de l'acceptable et du familier au *très* vulgaire. Pour rendre le texte aussi lisible que possible, la mise en pages a été simplifiée et le recours aux abréviations et autres procédés similaires a été réduit au minimum. L'usage est largement illustré par l'exemple. Les lecteurs peuvent se reporter à la section *'Comment utiliser ce dictionnaire'* s'ils ont besoin de conseils quelconques.

L'une des principales caractéristiques du dictionnaire, ce sont les Répertoires de synonymes populaires qui se trouvent à la fin de chaque section. Chaque index offre une liste complète de synonymes familiers et argotiques pour chacun des mots-clefs marqués d'un astérisque dans le texte, ainsi que quelques autres sections qu'il n'était pas possible de mentionner dans le texte, mais qui devraient intéresser le lecteur.

Ce dictionnaire est une édition revue et corrigée du *Harrap's Dictionary of Slang and Colloquialisms* et la tâche de l'Editeur a été grandement facilitée par le soin et l'attention que Marks et Johnson ont apportés aux éditions précédentes. Leur travail a été poursuivi par de nombreux collaborateurs venus de divers pays.

Nous tenons à exprimer notre reconnaissance aux personnes suivantes, dont l'aide et les conseils, de façon très variée, ont été précieux lors de la compilation de cette édition:

Fabrice Antoine	Diana Giese	Geneviève Talon
JP Bean	Anne Gruneberg	Jef Tombeur
Fiona Clarke	Paul Janssen	Elisabeth Turner
Françoise Clarke	Janet Kernachan	Sarah Wallis
Peter Collin	Helen Knox	Edward Wilson
Karen George	Gabriel Otman	

JEP

Preface
to the 2nd Edition

It is now almost ten years since the *Harrap's Slang Dictionary* was last revised and in that time slang and colloquialisms have inevitably changed. The language heard in the school playground and on radio and television, the language read in the papers and in teenage and other magazines is now enriched with new slang and colloquial expressions from all parts of the English- and French-speaking worlds. What was *super* and *groovy* is now *wicked* and *crucial*; what was *sensass* and *dans le vent* has become *géant* and *branché*. But who can tell for how long? For informal language is ephemeral, and what is an accepted and common expression today may be out of fashion, 'square', or indeed completely forgotten, tomorrow. Taboos are also disappearing, and terms which were not acceptable on radio and television ten years ago are now commonly heard.

Words and expressions have been gleaned from numerous sources, covering subjects as wide-ranging as schools, teenagers, students, the police, crime and the underworld, racing, music, drugs, sex and many more.

It is hoped that this work will be of interest to a wide range of people, academics and the general public alike: it is meant to be a tool for the translator as well as a work any curious person might use to discover and explore the world of slang and colloquialisms. The latest and most up-to-date words and expressions have been included; however, it was felt necessary to retain some of the obsolescent or archaic terms. Those that have been deleted can still be found in the comprehensive Index of Synonyms at the end of each section of the dictionary.

The general layout of the dictionary has not been much altered in this edition, but a few changes have been made to make the dictionary more accessible and easier to use. A large number of glosses in italics have been added, thus avoiding the ambiguities and misunderstandings that might otherwise occur and confuse the user. Certain abbreviations such as *esp* (especially) and *O* (old-fashioned) have been translated into French (*surt* and *Vieilli*).

Credit must be given to the many people who were involved in the first edition of the *Harrap's Slang Dictionary* and not least to Jane Pratt whose dedication and care contributed to the success of this dictionary and made my task that much easier. I would particularly like to thank Fabrice Antoine for his invaluable help and advice during the compilation of this revision. Grateful thanks are also due to the following people whose contributions have greatly enhanced and enriched this edition:

Mulan Bartholomew	Stuart Fortey	Chris Martinez
Y Andrew Bartholomew	Alischia Hatcher	Kendra Thomas
Hazel Curties	Robert Knox	Donovan Worland
Martine Da Silva		

HEK

Préface
de la Deuxième Édition

Voilà bientôt dix ans que le *Harrap's Slang Dictionary* a été révisé et, depuis, l'argot et la langue familière ont forcément évolué. La langue qui se parle dans les cours d'écoles et à la radio ou à la télévision, mais aussi celle qui s'écrit dans les journaux ou dans les magazines, destinés aux jeunes ou non, s'est enrichie d'expressions et de mots argotiques ou familiers qui proviennent des quatre coins du monde anglophone ou francophone. Ce qui était *super* ou *groovy* est devenue *wicked* et *crucial*; ce qui était *sensass* ou *dans le vent* est devenu *géant* et *branché*. Mais qui sait pour combien de temps? Car la langue familière est par nature éphémère et une expression aujourd'hui comprise et couramment utilisée sera peut-être demain démodée, 'ringarde', voire totalement oubliée. Par ailleurs, des tabous disparaissent, et des mots que l'on n'aurait osé prononcer à la radio ou à la télévision il y a dix ans s'entendent tout à fait couramment maintenant.

On a recueilli quantité de mots et expressions à de multiples sources, pour rendre compte de vocabulaires aussi divers que ceux des écoles, des adolescents, des étudiants, de la police, de la pègre et du milieu, des courses, des musiciens, de la drogue, de la sexualité et bien d'autres encore.

Le présent ouvrage s'adresse aussi bien à l'universitaire et au chercheur qu'à l'étudiant et au grand public: il veut être à la fois un outil pour le traducteur et un ouvrage que l'on consulte par curiosité, pour découvrir la langue verte. On y a donc fait figurer les mots et expressions les plus récents et les plus à la mode; cependant, on a jugé nécessaire d'y maintenir un certain nombre de termes vieillis ou archaïques. Ceux qui ont été supprimés des articles se trouvent toutefois encore dans les répertoires alphabétiques de synonymes très complets qui figurent à la suite de chacune des parties du dictionnaire.

On n'a pas jugé bon, dans cette édition, de modifier de façon notable la présentation générale de ce dictionnaire; on a cependant procédé à quelques modifications pour le rendre encore plus clair et plus facile à consulter; on a ajouté de très nombreuses paraphrases explicatives en italique pour éviter les ambiguïtés ou les fausses interprétations qui pourraient entraîner le lecteur sur de mauvaises pistes. Certains abréviations, comme *esp* (pour *especially*) ou *O* (pour *Old-fashioned*) ont été traduites en français (*surt* et *Vieilli*).

Il faut rendre ici hommage à ceux, nombreux, qui ont collaboré à la première édition du *Harrap's Slang Dictionary*, et tout d'abord, à Jane Pratt, dont la rigueur et la persévérance ont assuré le succès de ce dictionnaire et rendu ma tâche encore plus aisée. Je souhaite tout particulièrement adresser mes remerciements à Fabrice Antoine pour sa précieuse collaboration et ses conseils éclairés tout au long de la révision de l'ouvrage. Je tiens enfin à exprimer ma reconnaissance aux personnes suivantes, dont les suggestions sont venues améliorer et enrichir la présente édition:

Mulan Bartholomew	Stuart Fortey	Chris Martinez
Y Andrew Bartholomew	Alischia Hatcher	Kendra Thomas
Hazel Curties	Robert Knox	Donovan Worland
Martine Da Silva		

HEK

How to use this dictionary

headword in bold sans serif

archaic expression

bint [bɪnt] *n P* **1.** *Pej* femme*/gonzesse *f*; she's a silly bint, c'est une connasse, celle-là **2.** *A Pej* petite amie/poule *f*.

entrée en Linéales grasses

archaïsme

---

phonetics in IPA

*: headword in the Index of Slang Synonyms

RS: rhyming slang

cross references

plural noun

Australianism

gender of French nouns

daisy ['deɪzɪ] *n* **1.** *F* qn/qch d'excellent*/ d'épatant/d'impec; she's a daisy, c'est une perle; elle est sensass **2.** *F* to be kicking/ pushing up the daisies, être enterré/bouffer les pissenlits par la racine **3.** *P* daisy roots/ daisies, (*RS = boots*) chaussures*/godillots *mpl*/godasses *fpl* **4.** (*a*) homosexuel*/pédé *m* (*b*) homme efféminé/gâcheuse *f* **5.** *P* daisy chain, partouze *f* (à la bague). (*See* **oops-a-daisy!**; **ups-a-daisy!**; **upsy-daisy!**; **whoops-a-daisy!**)

daks [dæks] *npl Austr P* pantalon*/falzar *m*/ futal *m*.

transcription phonétique selon l'API

*: entrée dans le Répertoire de Synonymes Argotiques

RS: argot dont les mots ont leur sens non pas en eux-mêmes mais dans le mot avec lequel ils riment

renvois

nom pluriel

mot australien

genre des noms communs

---

superior numbers distinguish nouns from verbs

NAm: Americanism

P: slang expression

V: vulgar expression

F: colloquial expression

field label

hammer[1] ['hæmə] *n* **1.** *NAm P* belle fille*/ belle nana/beau petit lot **2.** *P* (*CB*) accélérateur *m*/champignon *m* **3.** *NAm V* pénis*/défonceuse *f*/sabre *m*.

hammer[2] ['hæmə] *vtr* **1.** *F* (*Stock Exchange*) déclarer (un agent) en défaut **2.** *F* to hammer s.o. into the ground, battre qn à plate(s) couture(s)/tailler qn en pièces **3.** *F* to hammer a play/a film, démolir/éreinter une pièce/un film **4.** *P* to hammer (and nail), (*RS = tail*) suivre (qn)/filer (qn)/prendre (qn) en filature.

chiffres supérieurs distinguant le nom du verbe

NAm: américanisme

P: expression argotique

V: expression vulgaire

F: expression familière

champ sémantique

---

phrasal verb

pipe up ['paɪp'ʌp] *vi F* se faire entendre/ l'ouvrir tout d'un coup.

verbe à particule

---

adverb

screamingly ['skriːmɪŋlɪ] *adv F* screamingly funny, tordant/crevant/à se rouler par terre.

adverbe

---

alternative spelling

O: old-fashioned/dated expression

coalie, coaly ['kəʊlɪ] *n O F* charbonnier *m*/carbi *m*.

orthographe différente

O: emploi vielli

Comment utiliser ce dictionnaire

débaucher [deboʃe] *F* **I** *vi* to knock off (after a day's work) **II** *vtr* est-ce que je peux te débaucher et t'inviter au cinéma? can I tempt you with a film? c'est lui qui m'a débauché hier soir, (*il m'a emmené au cinéma, etc*) he led me astray last night **III** *vpr* **se débaucher** *F* laissez là vos livres et débauchez-vous un peu, put your books away and have a bit of fun/let yourself go a little.

quétaine [ketɛn] *a FrC P* 1. old-fashioned/dated; past it 2. cheap and nasty/rubbishy.

ficelle [fisɛl] **I** *a F* cunning/wily/smart **II** *nf* 1. *F* une grosse/vieille ficelle, an old hand/a wily (old) bird; a smooth operator 2. *F (a) (truc)* on voit bien là la ficelle, it's easy to see how it's done; la ficelle est un peu grosse, that's too obvious; I'm not falling for that *(b)* connaître les ficelles, to know the ropes/to know the tricks of the trade *(c)* tirer les ficelles, to pull the strings/to run the show 3. *F Mil (galon)* (NCO's *or* officer's) stripes/gold braid 4. *F* casser la ficelle, to get a divorce/to get unhitched 5. *pl P* handcuffs*/bracelets 6. *F* bootlace tie 7. *F* tirer sur la ficelle, to exaggerate*/to stretch it a bit.

chevreuil [ʃəvrœj] *nm P Péj* informer*/grass/squealer.

fieu, *pl* **-eux** [fjø] *nm (surt Dial)* son/sonny; lad; c'est un bon fieu, he's a good sort/a nice chap.

bâfreur, -euse [bɑfrœr, -øz] *n P* glutton/hog/pig/greedy-guts/guzzler.

Trafalgar [trafalgar] *Prnm F* un (coup de) Trafalgar, a difficult and violent situation; *(bataille)* a punch-up; *(échec)* a failure*/bomb; *(désastre)* a sudden catastrophe/an unexpected disaster.

Abbreviations - Abréviations

a	adjective	adjectif
A	archaic; in former use	archaïque; vieux
abbr, abbrév	abbreviation	abréviation
adv	adverb	adverbe
adv phr	adverbial phrase	locution adverbiale
Anat	anatomy	anatomie
a phr	adjectival phrase	locution adjective
approx	approximately	approximativement
attrib	attributive	attributif
Austr	Australianism	expression australienne
Aut	motoring; motoring industry	automobiles; industrie automobile
Belg	Belgian	mot belge
Br	British	britannique
Can	Canadian	canadien
CB	Citizens Band Radio	jargon des cibistes
Cin	cinema, films	cinéma, films
Comptr	computing	informatique
conj	conjunction	conjonction
Dial	dialect	dialecte
Ecc	ecclesiastical	ecclésiastique
eg	for example	par exemple
esp	especially	surtout
etc	et cetera	et cetera; et cætera
Euph	euphemism	euphémisme
excl	exclamation	exclamation
f	feminine	féminin
F	familiar; colloquial	familier
Fig	figurative	figuratif
FrC	French Canadian	franco-canadien
Hist	historical	historique
Hum	humorous	humoristique
impers	impersonal	impersonnel
indef	indefinite	indéfini
int	interjection	interjection
interr	interrogative	interrogatif
inv	invariable	invariable
Iron	ironical	ironique
Journ	journalism	journalisme
Jur	law, legal	juridique, droit
m	masculine	masculin
Med, Méd	medical, medicine	médical, médecine
Mil	military	militaire
Mus	music	musique
n	noun	nom
NAm	North American	de l'Amérique du Nord
O	old-fashioned, dated	vieilli
occ	occasionally	parfois

P	popular; slang	populaire; argotique
Pej, Péj	pejorative	péjoratif
Phot	photography	photographie
pl	plural	pluriel
Pol	politics	politique
poss	possessive	possessif
pp	past participle	participe passé
pref, préf	prefix	préfixe
prep, prép	preposition	préposition
Prn	proper noun	nom propre
pron	pronoun	pronom
qch	something	quelque chose
qn	someone	quelqu'un
qv	quod vide; which see	se reporter à ce mot
rel	relative	relatif
RS	rhyming slang	mots composés qui ont leur sens non pas en eux-mêmes mais dans le mot avec lequel ils riment
RTM	registered trade mark	marque déposée
Scot	Scottish	écossais
sing	singular	singulier
Sl	slang	expression argotique
s.o.	someone	quelqu'un
souv	often	souvent
sth	something	quelque chose
surt	especially	surtout
TV	television	télévision
US	United States	États-Unis
usu	usually	d'ordinaire
v	verb	verbe
V	vulgar	trivial
vi	intransitive verb	verbe intransitif
Vieilli	old-fashioned	
vpr	reflexive verb	verbe pronominal
vtr	transitive verb	verbe transitif
VV	very vulgar; taboo	obscène; ordurier
WInd	West Indian	antillais
WWI	World War One	première guerre mondiale
WWII	World War Two	deuxième guerre mondiale

Part 1

English-French

Table of Phonetic Symbols

Vowels and Vowel Combinations

[æ]	bat gander	[ə]	china goner balon(e)y bolony
[ɑ:]	cart bar nark hooha	[ɜ:]	burn learn nerd whirl
[e]	get dead belly	[aɪ]	aisle high kite fly hypo
[ɪ]	bit undies system dimwitted	[aʊ]	down mouse kraut
[i:]	bee peter tea spiel	[eɪ]	mate lay fey bait weight
[ɒ]	hot what-for Aussie Oz cough	[eə]	bear spare there airy-fairy
[ɔ:]	all haul rorty jaw war walk	[ɪə]	queer gear real
[ʊ]	wool bull pussy	[ɔɪ]	boil boy
[u:]	loo move shoes	[əʊ]	go snow soap dope dough
[ʌ]	nut bun ton some cover rough	[ʊə]	poorly sure

Consonants and Semi-Consonants

[b]	bat boob job nabbed	[dz]	reds odds
[d]	dab bad fiddle	[dʒ]	ginger age edge juice
[f]	fat fifty syph rough	[ks]	extras expect accident mixer
[g]	gherkin gag guy egg agony	[kʃ]	ructions
[h]	hat behind	[lj]	million
[k]	cat chronic kittens make tick plonk	[nj]	onion
[l]	lid all tumble dildo chisel	[tʃ]	chick bitch rich chunder
[m]	mug jammy ram jism	[θ]	meths
[n]	nab bun tenner knob gnashers pancake	[ð]	feather with that
[p]	pan crap napper	[ʃ]	shark dish chassis machine
[r]	rat around jerry	[ʒ]	usual
[s]	sausage scene mouse sassy psycho ceiling	[ŋ]	bang sing conk anchors
[t]	top pot batter Thames trip	[ŋg]	finger angle danglers
[v]	ever rave savvy vibes	[j]	yack yob used putrid euchre few queue
[z]	zip buzz lousy pansy breeze tizwas business eggs	[w]	wire wank sweep away
		[χ]	loch chutzpah

A

A [eɪ] *abbr* P 1. (*drugs*) (= *amphetamine*) amphétamine(s)*/amphés *fpl*/amphètes *fpl* 2. = **acid 2** 3. A over T (= *arse over tip/tit(s)*) cul par-dessus tête. (*See* **arse 4**)

ab [æb], **AB** ['eɪbiː] (*abbr of abscess*) P (*abscess caused by an unsterilized needle or by impure drugs*) caramel *m*/fondant *m*/puant *m*. (*See* **ABC 3**)

ABC ['eɪbiːsiː] *n* 1. F it's (as) easy as ABC, c'est simple comme bonjour/c'est l'enfance de l'art/c'est bête comme chou. (*See* **easy I 6**) 2. F the ABC/*NAm* the ABCs of sth, le b.a.-ba de qch 3. P = **ab, AB** 4. (*abbr of Australian-born Chinese*) Chinois, -oise né(e) en Australie; (*abbr of American-born Chinese*) Chinois, -oise né(e) aux États-Unis.

abdabs ['æbdæbz] *npl* P to have the screaming abdabs, (*delirium tremens*) piauler à la bit(t)ure/voir les rats bleus; (*enraged frustration*) piquer une crise/voir rouge.

abo, Abo ['æbəʊ] *n* *Austr* F *Pej* (= *aborigine*) aborigène *mf*.

about [ə'baʊt] *adv* F that's about the size of it, c'est à peu près ça/ça se résume à peu près à ça.

above board [əbʌv'bɔːd] *a* F it's all above board, c'est réglo.

absoballylutely! ['æbsəʊbælɪ'l(j)uːtlɪ] *excl* O F ça colle, Anatole!/je veux, mon neveu!/un peu, mon neveu!

absobloodylutely! ['æbsəʊblʌdɪ'l(j)uːtlɪ] *excl* O P = **absoballylutely!**

abysmal [ə'bɪzməl] *a* F affreux/exécrable; abysmal ignorance, ignorance *f* crasse; an abysmal memory, une mémoire épouvantable.

ACAB ['eɪsiː'eɪbiː] *abbr* P (= *all coppers are bastards*) (*approx*) = mort aux vaches!/mort aux keufs!

accident ['æksɪdənt] *n* F *Euph* 1. to have an accident, s'oublier; he's had an accident, il a fait pipi dans sa culotte 2. their first child was an accident, leur premier enfant n'était pas

prévu au programme 3. arrestation *f*; he had an accident, il s'est fait coffrer/alpaguer/gauler.

accidentally [æksɪ'dentəlɪ] *adv* F often *Hum* accidentally on purpose, exprès; he did it accidentally on purpose, il ne l'a pas fait sans le faire exprès.

AC-DC, AC/DC, ac-dc, ac/dc ['eɪsiː'diːsiː] *a* P bisexuel; he's a bit AC-DC, il est/il marche/il va à voile et à vapeur; il est jazz-tango.

ace¹ [eɪs] I *a* F excellent*/formid(able)/super/hyper; we had an ace time, on s'est drôlement amusés/on s'est éclatés; he's an ace guy, c'est un mec super/un mec comme ça; an ace idea, une idée superchouette/un super bon plan II *adv & excl* F d'accord*/dac/OK III *n* 1. F as *m*/crack *m* 2. F to have an ace up one's sleeve, avoir un atout dans sa manche/avoir des atouts en réserve 3. F to hold all the aces, avoir tous les atouts (en main) 4. ace in the hole, avantage *m*/atout *m* (*gardé en réserve*) 5. *NAm* P billet* d'un dollar 6. F (*a*) individu* loyal/bon/généreux (*b*) individu* chouette/chic type *m* 7. *Austr* P anus*/as *m* de pique 8. P (*drugs*) marijuana*/marie-jeanne *f*.

ace² [eɪs] *vtr & i* *NAm* P 1. (*to kill*) tuer*/descendre/liquider 2. (*to win, succeed*) gagner; réussir; décrocher la timbale.

ace of spades [eɪsəv'speɪdz] *n* 1. *v* sexe* de la femme/fente *f*/as *m* de pique 2. P noir(e)*/boule *f* de neige.

acid ['æsɪd] *n* P 1. (*not common*) to put the acid on/to come the acid/to go the old acid, la faire à la pose/se payer la tête de qn 2. P (*drugs*) LSD*/acide *m*; acid freak/acid head, habitué(e) du LSD*/acidulé(e); acid cube, dose de LSD* déposée sur un morceau de sucre; acid funk, dépression due au LSD*/trouille acidulée; to drop/to take/to use acid, prendre du LSD*/de l'acide; acid trip, trip *m*. (*See* **freak 4; trip¹**)

acid house ['æsɪd'haʊs] *n* F (*cult*) acid-house *m*; acid house party, = acid-party *f*.

ackers ['ækəz] *npl* P argent*/fric *m*/pèze *m*.

across [ə'krɒs] *prep* F to get sth across, se faire comprendre; did you get it across to him? il t'a compris?/il a pigé?

act [ækt] *n* F 1. to put on an act/a big act, frimer/faire du cinéma; it's his little act, c'est son petit numéro 2. to get in on the act, se mettre dans le bain; to let s.o. in on the act, mettre qn dans le coup; he wanted to be in on the act, il a voulu être dans le coup/y être pour qch 3. to get one's act together, s'éclaircir les idées/se reprendre en main. (*See* **get together**; **sob-act**)

action ['ækʃən] *n Euph* F 1. (*excitement*) where's the action? où est-ce qu'on va pour se marrer?/où est-ce que ça bouge? 2. (*share*) I want a piece of the action, je veux une part du gâteau/je veux être de fade 3. (*sex*) baise *f*; let's go where the action is, où sont les nanas/les nénettes?

actress ['æktrɪs] *n* F (*catchphrase*) as the actress said to the bishop, soit dit en tout bien tout honneur/soit dit sans penser à mal.

ad [æd] *n* 1. (*abbr* = *advertisement*) annonce *f*/pub *f*; small ads, petites annonces; ad agency, agence *f* de pub. (*See* **advert**) 2. P = **AD**.

AD ['eɪ'diː] *n* P (*abbr* = (*drug*) *addict*) drogué(e)*/camé(e) *mf*/toxico *mf*.

adam[1] ['ædəm] *n* P (*drugs*) = **ecstasy**.

Adam[2] ['ædəm] *Prn* F 1. I don't know him from Adam, je ne le connais ni d'Ève ni d'Adam 2. Adam and Eve on a raft, œufs servis sur un toast.

Adam and Eve ['ædəməni:v] *vtr* P 1. (*RS* = *believe*) you'll never Adam and Eve it! tu ne vas pas le croire! 2. (*RS* = *leave*) partir*/ se barrer/se casser.

addict ['ædɪkt] *n* F mordu(e) *m(f)*/fana *mf*/ accro *mf*; he's a real comic addict, c'est un fana de BD; jazz addict, dingue *mf* de jazz/ accro de jazz.

add up [æd'ʌp] *vi* F it (just) doesn't add up, ça n'a ni queue ni tête/ça ne tient pas debout/ ça n'a ni rime ni raison.

ad-lib[1] ['æd'lɪb] *a* F (*a*) à volonté/à dis-crétion (*b*) improvisé/impromptu; all his jokes were ad-lib, toutes ses blagues étaient improvisées/spontanées.

ad-lib[2] ['æd'lɪb] *vi* F improviser; I just had to ad-lib in the meeting, j'ai dû improviser dans la réunion.

ad-man ['ædmæn], *pl* **ad-men** *n* F agent *m* de publicité/de pub.

admirer [əd'maɪərə] *n O* F soupirant *m*.

adrift [ə'drɪft] *adv* F 1. to be (all) adrift, dérailler/perdre le nord; the project went adrift, le projet est tombé à l'eau 2. the button has come adrift, le bouton est tombé/ s'est décousu/s'est barré 3. a lot of my books went adrift, beaucoup de mes livres ont disparu.

advert ['ædvɜːt] *n* F (*abbr* = *advertisement*) annonce *f*/pub *f*. (*See* **ad 1**)

aer(e)ated ['ɛər(ɪ)eɪtɪd] *a* P fâché/vexé; don't get (all) aer(e)ated, ne prends pas la mouche!/te fâche pas!

after ['ɑːftə] *prep* F 1. *O* after you, Claude. — no, after you, Cecil, (*catchphrase*) après vous, Marquis. — non, après vous, Prince 2. what are you after? qu'est-ce que tu cherches?/où veux-tu en venir? 3. after a fashion, tant bien que mal 4. *Austr* (*abbr of afternoon*) après-midi *m* or *f*/aprème *m*/ aprèm' *m*.

afterbird ['ɑːftəbɜːd] *n* P to do (some) afterbird, boire après la fermeture du pub/du bar.

afterbirth ['ɑːftəbɜːθ] *n Br* P (*schools*) compote *f* de rhubarbe.

afternoon [ɑːftə'nuːn] *excl Br* F (*short for good afternoon!*) = m'sieu-dames!

afters ['ɑːftəz] *npl* F dessert *m*.

afto ['ɑːftəʊ, 'æftəʊ] *n* F (*regional*) (*abbr of afternoon*) après-midi *m* or *f*/aprème *m*/ aprèm' *m*; this afto, cet aprèm'/c't'aprèm'.

age [eɪdʒ] *n* F 1. act your age! (ne) fais pas l'enfant!/sois (un peu) adulte! 2. it took us an age/ages to get there, ça nous a pris un temps fou pour y arriver; I saw that film ages ago, il y a une éternité/un siècle que j'ai vu ce film 3. the age to catch 'em: see **bingo 17**. (*See* **awkward**)

aggravate ['ægrəveɪt] *vtr & i* F exaspérer/ assommer/taper sur le système à (qn).

aggravating ['ægrəveɪtɪŋ] *a* F exaspérant/ assommant; it's really aggravating! c'est exaspérant à la fin!

aggravation [ægrə'veɪʃ(ə)n] *n* F = **aggro**.

aggro ['ægrəʊ] *n* P (*a*) (*trouble*) histoires *fpl*/tracas *mpl*; leave out the aggro! laisse tomber!/écrase! I can't stand all this aggro you're giving me! tu m'épuises à la fin! (*b*) (*physical violence*) baston *f*/grabuge *m*; I never go there because of all the aggro, y a tellement de grabuge que j'y mets jamais les pieds; there'll be some aggro tonight, ça va barder/y aura du grabuge/de la baston ce soir.

agin [ə'gɪn] *prep & adv O F* contre; I'm not agin it, je (ne) suis pas contre/je (ne) dis pas non.

agony ['ægənɪ] *n F* 1. it was agony! j'en ai bavé! 2. to pile on the agony, forcer la dose 3. *Journ* agony column, courrier *m* du cœur; agony aunt, journaliste *mf* qui tient la rubrique du/qui répond au courrier du cœur.

agriculture ['ægrɪkʌltʃə] *n P (police slang)* le fait de cacher des drogues, de l'argent, etc sur un suspect/fabriquer de faux témoignages contre qn.

agro ['ægrəʊ] *n P* = **aggro.**

ahoy! [ə'hɔɪ] *excl F (used to announce sth or s.o.)* Mark and Andy hunks ahoy! Marc et Andy, beaux mecs en vue/à l'horizon!

aid [eɪd] *n F* what's all this in aid of then? à quoi ça rime?

AIDS [eɪdz] *abbr F (= acquired immune deficiency syndrome)* syndrome immunodéficitaire acquis/SIDA *m.*

ain't [eɪnt] *P = am not, is not, are not;* ain't got *= has not (got),* have not (got); I ain't seen it, je l'ai pas vu, moi.

air [ɛə] *n* 1. *F* to go up in the air, se mettre en colère*/se mettre en rogne; he flew straight up in the air when he heard of it, il a sauté au plafond/ça l'a fait bondir quand il l'a su 2. *F* to float/to tread/to walk on air, être au septième ciel/voir les anges/planer 3. *F* to live on (fresh) air, vivre d'amour et d'eau fraîche/vivre de l'air du temps 4. *P* to give s.o. the air, se débarrasser* de qn/envoyer promener qn/envoyer paître qn 5. *F* hot air, platitudes *fpl*/foutaises *fpl*; that's all hot air, tout ça c'est du vent 6. *P* airs and graces, (*RS = faces*) visages*/tronches *fpl* 7. *F* to put on airs and graces/to give oneself airs, faire l'intéressant/minauder/frimer.

airhead ['ɛəhed] *n F* imbécile*/cruche *f*/gourde *f.*

airy-fairy ['ɛərɪ'fɛərɪ] *a F* vasouillard/du bidon; he's full of airy-fairy ideas, il déborde d'idées farfelues/bidon.

aisle [aɪl] *n* 1. *F* to walk down the aisle, se marier/se marida; passer devant Monsieur le curé/Monsieur le maire 2. *P* that'll have 'em rolling in the aisles, ça fera crouler la baraque/ça fera un malheur.

a.k.a., aka [eɪkeɪ'eɪ] *abbr & prep esp NAm F (= also known as)* alias/autrement dit/autrement nommé; (*in other words*) en d'au-

tres termes.

akkers ['ækəz] *npl P* = **ackers.**

Aladdin's cave [ə'lædɪnzkeɪv] *n* cache *f* d'objets volés.

alarming [ə'lɑːmɪŋ] *adv O F* she went off at me something alarming, elle m'est tombée dessus comme une furie.

Alec, alec(k) ['ælɪk] *n* 1. *F* smart alec, (*racketeer*) finaud *m*/combinard *m*; (*clever person*) bêcheur, -euse/m'as-tu-vu *mf*/je-sais-tout *m*; he's a smart alec, c'est un petit malin 2. *NAm Austr P* pigeon *m*/poire *f*/cave *m.*

alfalfa [æl'fælfə] *n NAm P* 1. tabac*/perle *m* 2. argent*/oseille *f* 3. marijuana*/foin *m*/herbe *f.*

alive [ə'laɪv] *a F* 1. alive and kicking, en pleine forme; I'm still alive and kicking, je ne suis pas mort/je suis bien en vie 2. look alive! réveille-toi! / secoue-toi! / grouille-toi! (*See* **dead-and-alive; Jack 12; bingo 5**)

alkie, alky ['ælkɪ] *n P* ivrogne*/alcoolique *mf*/alcoolo *mf*/poivrot *m.*

all [ɔːl] I *adv F* 1. to be all for sth, être tout à fait pour qch; I'm all for it, je ne demande que ça 2. to go all out for sth, (*be enthusiastic about*) être emballé par qch; (*put all one's effort in*) mettre tout le paquet pour faire qch/se donner à fond pour faire qch 3. that's him all over, c'est lui tout craché, je le reconnais bien là! 4. to be all in, être fatigué*/vanné/claqué/à plat 5. to be all there, avoir les yeux en face des trous; he's not quite all there, il lui manque une case, il n'est pas très net. (*See* **there 2**) 6. to be all over s.o., faire de la lèche à qn. (*See* **all right**) II *n F* 1. it's all over/up with him, (*ruined*) il est fichu/à sec; (*found out*) il est grillé/cuit; (*dying*) il est fichu. (*See* **up¹ II 3**) 2. I'm tired. – aren't we all? je suis fatigué.* – (il n')y a pas que toi! 3. all but one: *see* **bingo 89.** (*See* **bugger-all; damn-all; fuck-all; know-all; sod-all**)

all-American ['ɔːlə'merɪkən] *a F* américain jusqu'au bout des ongles/cent pour cent américain; the all-American hero, le héros américain par excellence.

all-clear [ɔːl'klɪə] *n F* to give (s.o.) the all-clear, donner le feu vert (à qn).

alley ['ælɪ] *n F* that's right up my alley, c'est tout à fait mon rayon/mon truc. (*See* **doodle-alley; street 2; tin-pan alley**)

alley cat ['ælɪkæt] *n P* personne *f* qui traîne dans les rues (*surt la nuit*)/dragueur *m*/racoleuse *f*; she's a bit of an alley cat, elle est un peu pute sur les bords/elle couche à droite et à gauche.

alleycat ['ælɪkæt] *vi esp NAm P* to alleycat around, draguer/faire du racolage/racoler*.

alligator ['ælɪgeɪtə] *n F (catchphrase)* see you later, alligator! − in a while, crocodile! à tout à l'heure, voltigeur! − à bientôt, mon oiseau.

all-nighter [ɔːl'naɪtə] *n P* 1. spectacle *m*, boum *f*, etc qui dure toute la nuit/qui se fait jusqu'au petit matin; cafétéria *f*, bar *m*, etc ouvert(e) toute la nuit 2. *(prostitute's client)* client *m*/clille *m* de nuit, couché *m* 3. *NAm (of student)* to **pull an all-nighter**, passer la nuit à étudier/potasser/bûcher.

all right ['ɔːl'raɪt] **I** *a* he's all right/*esp NAm* he's an all(-)right guy, c'est quelqu'un de correct/c'est un type bien **II** *adv F* 1. d'accord*/OK; ça va 2. it's all right for you, you don't have to get up early, ça t'est bien égal, t'es pas obligé de te lever de bonne heure 3. don't worry about him, he's all right, t'en fais pas pour lui 4. to see s.o. all right, *(ensure)* veiller à ce que qn ait son dû; *(help)* donner un coup de main à qn; *(pay)* payer qn grassement **III** *n P* a bit of all right, qn qui a du chien/qui jette du jus; *esp* une fille* séduisante/un beau petit lot; she's a bit of all right, c'est une jolie pépée/elle est bien roulée/elle est mettable; he's a bit of all right, il est beau mec/il est mettable/il en jette.

all-star ['ɔːl'stɑː] *a F* an all-star cast, rien que des têtes d'affiche/des vedettes.

all-time ['ɔːl'taɪm] *a F* sans précédent/ inouï; all-time high, record absolu; his sex life had reached an all-time low, sa vie sexuelle n'avait jamais été aussi déprimante. *(See* **great III***)*

almighty [ɔːl'maɪtɪ] *a* 1. *F* formidable; an almighty row, un boucan de tous les diables 2. *P* God Almighty! Bon Dieu de Bon Dieu!

Alphonse [æl'fɒns] *Prn P (RS = ponce)* souteneur*/mac *m*/Jules *m*.

alright ['ɔːl'raɪt] *adv & n F =* **all right**.

also-ran ['ɔːlsəʊræn] *n F (a)* perdant *m*; to be an also-ran, être dans les choux *(b)* nullité *f*/nullard *m*.

altogether ['ɔːltə'geðə] *n F* in the altogether, nu*/à poil; dans le costume d'Adam/d'Ève.

amber fluid ['æmbə'fluːɪd], **amber nectar** ['æmbə'nektə] *n F Euph* bière *f (en général) ou* bière blonde Australienne/ mousse *f*.

ambidextrous ['æmbi'dekstrəs] *a P* bisexuel/qui marche à voile et à vapeur/qui joue sur les deux tableaux.

ambulance chaser ['æmbjʊləns'tʃeɪsə] *n NAm F* avocat* qui fréqente les lieux d'accidents et les hôpitaux à la recherche de clients.

ammo ['æməʊ] *n F (abbr = ammunition)* munitions *fpl*/bastos *f*.

amp [æmp] *n F* 1. *(abbr = ampoule) (drugs)* ampoule *f* 2. *(abbr = amplifier)* amplificateur *m*/ampli *m*.

amscray ['æm'skreɪ] *vi A P (backslang of scram)* partir*/décamper/se débiner; amscray! décampe!/casse-toi!

amster ['æmstə] *n Austr O P =* **shill(aber)**.

amy ['eɪmɪ] *n (pl amys) P (drugs)* nitrite *m* d'amyle (en capsule)/amyl(e) *m*.

amy-john ['eɪmɪ'dʒɒn] *n P* lesbienne*/ gougnot(t)e *f*/gouine *f*.

amyl ['æmɪl] *n P (drugs) =* **amy**.

anchors ['æŋkəz] *npl O F* to slam on the anchors/put the anchors on, freiner à mort.

ancient ['eɪnʃənt] *a F* 1. croulant/décati; she's ancient, elle est croulante/elle n'est plus cotée à l'argus 2. antédiluvien; that's ancient history, c'est du réchauffé/c'est de l'histoire ancienne.

Andrew ['ændruː] *Prn A P (navy)* Andrew (Miller), la marine nationale.

angel ['eɪndʒəl] *n* 1. *F* you're no angel! te prends pas pour un enfant de chœur!/t'es pas un prix de vertu! 2. *P* white angel, *(nurse who provides drug addicts with unprescribed drugs)* ange blanc 3. *P (a) (theatre)* commanditaire *m (b) NAm* commanditaire *m*/sponsor *m* d'un parti politique 4. *P* victime *f* d'un voleur *ou* d'un escroc*; pigeon *m* 5. *P* homosexuel*/pédé *m*/homo *m*. *(See* **hell 15***)*

angel dust ['eɪndʒəldʌst] *n P (drugs)* phéncyclidine *f*/PCP *f*. *(See* **dust¹ 2***)*

angel-face ['eɪndʒəlfeɪs] *n F (term of affection) (to woman)* ma toute belle/ma gueule; *(to man)* mon chéri/mon chou/mon lapin.

angle ['æŋgl] *n F* 1. what's your angle? quel est ton point de vue?/comment vois-tu la chose? 2. to know all the angles, connaître la musique.

animal ['ænɪməl] *n F* salaud*/dur *m*/peau *f* de vache.

ankle-biter ['æŋkl'baɪtə] *n esp Austr P* enfant*/môme *mf*/têtard *m*.

Anne [æn] *Prn F* Queen Anne's dead *(a)* ta

anno domini (*See* **charlie 2**; **snow² 2**) (*b*) *O* (*old news*) c'est du réchauffé/y'a rien de nouveau là-dedans.

anno domini ['ænəʊ'dɒmɪnaɪ] *n F Hum* vieillesse *f*; she's very anno domini, elle est pas mal décatie; he's suffering from anno domini, il commence à se décatir.

another [ə'nʌðə] *pron F* tell me another! arrête ton charre/tes salades! ask me another, tu me fais rigoler; et après?

AN Other ['eɪ'en'ʌðə] *n F* (*occ Hum*) un illustre inconnu.

answer ['ɑːnsə] *n F* the answer to a maiden's prayer, (*ideal husband*) le mari/l'homme rêvé; (*ideal lover*) un bon coup/une affaire (au lit).

ante ['æntɪ] *n esp NAm F* to up/to raise the ante, (*poker*) augmenter la mise; (*increase price, offer*) augmenter le prix/donner un coup de pouce/allonger le tir.

ante (up) ['æntɪ('ʌp)] *vi F* payer*/les lâcher/cracher/casquer.

anti ['æntɪ, *NAm* 'æntaɪ] *adv & prep F* to be anti s.o./sth, être contre qn/qch; I'm rather anti that sort of thing, je suis plutôt contre (ce genre de truc).

antics ['æntɪks] *npl F* to be up to one's antics again, refaire le même cinéma/le même cirque.

ants [ænts] *npl F* to have ants in one's pants, avoir la bougeotte/ne pas tenir en place.

antsy ['æntsɪ] *a NAm F* énervé/agité/sur des charbons ardents.

any ['enɪ] I *a F* 1. any more for any more? qui veut du rab? any amount, beaucoup 2. any day, n'importe quand; I can do better than that any day, je peux faire mieux quand ça me chante II *pron F* he wasn't having any, il n'a pas marché; I'm not having any! rien à faire!/ça ne prend pas! III *adv F* that didn't help it any, ça ne nous a pas servi à grand-chose.

anybody ['enɪbɒdɪ], **anyone** ['enɪwʌn] *pron & n F* it's anybody's/anyone's guess, qui sait?/vous en savez autant que moi!

anyhow ['enɪhaʊ], **anyoldhow** ['enɪəʊldhaʊ] *adv F* n'importe comment/tant bien que mal; to do sth all anyhow, faire qch n'importe comment/à la six-quatre-deux; they left the bedroom all anyoldhow, ils ont laissé la chambre en pagaille.

anyplace ['enɪpleɪs] *adv esp NAm F* n'importe où.

anyroad(s) ['enɪrəʊd(z)] *adv F* (= *anyway*) de toute façon/quand même; that's what I think anyroad(s), en tout cas, c'est ce que je pense, moi.

Anzac ['ænzæk] *n F* soldat* australien *ou* néo-zélandais.

ape [eɪp] I *a P* to go ape, (*lose self-control*) perdre les pédales; (*go wild*) se déchaîner; to go ape over s.o., s'enticher/s'amouracher de qn II *n F* you big ape! grosse brute!/espèce de gorille!

apeshit ['eɪpʃɪt] *a P* = **ape I**.

apology [ə'pɒlədʒɪ] *n F* an apology for ..., un vague semblant de....

apparatchik [æpə'rɑːtʃɪk] *n F Pej* apparatchik *m*.

apple ['æpl] *n P* 1. apples (and pears), (*RS* = *stairs*) escalier *m* 2. *NAm* individu*/type *m*/mec *m*; smooth apple, individu* mielleux/onctueux. (*See* **apple-polish**; **apple polisher**) 3. the Big Apple, New York *m* 4. *pl Austr* she's apples, (*all right, fine*) ça va/c'est OK/ça colle 5. *pl* (*a*) seins*/oranges *fpl* 6. *pl* testicules*/olives *fpl*.

apple-cart ['æplkɑːt] *n F* to upset s.o.'s apple-cart, chambouler les plans de qn; that's upset the apple-cart, ça a tout chamboulé/ça a tout fichu en l'air/ça a tout fichu par terre.

apple(-)pie ['æpl'paɪ] I *a attrib F* in apple-pie order, en ordre parfait/soi-soi/soin-soin II *n F* as American as apple pie, typiquement amerloque/amerloque comme l'oncle Sam.

apple-polish ['æpl'pɒlɪʃ] *vi P* flatter*/lécher les bottes à (qn). (*See* **apple 3**)

apple polisher ['æpl'pɒlɪʃə] *n P* flatteur, -euse/lèche-bottes *m*.

apple sauce ['æpl'sɔːs] *n NAm P* 1. (*nonsense*) bêtises*/foutaises *fpl*/bidon *m* 2. (*flattery*) flatterie *f*/pommade *f*.

apple tree ['æpltriː] *n P* (*not common*) to fall off the apple tree, (*of girl*) perdre sa virginité/voir le loup/casser sa cruche.

appro ['æprəʊ] *n F* (*abbr* = *approval*) on appro, à condition/à l'essai.

apron-strings ['eɪprənstrɪŋz] *npl F* tied to his mother's apron strings, dans les jupons/jupes de sa mère.

arf [ɑːf] *adv & n P* = **half**.

arf-an'-arf ['ɑːfən'ɑːf] *adv & n P* = **half and half**. (*See* **half I 5**; **half II 2**)

Argie ['ɑːdʒɪ] *n P* Argentin(e) *m(f)*.

argie-bargie ['ɑːdʒɪ'bɑːdʒɪ] *n F* = **argy-bargy**.

argle-bargle ['ɑːglˈbɑːgl] *n F* = **argy-bargy**.

argufy ['ɑːgjʊfaɪ] *vi P* discuter le bout de gras.

Argy ['ɑːdʒɪ] *n P* = **Argie**.

argy-bargy ['ɑːdʒɪˈbɑːdʒɪ] *n F* chicane *f*/ prise *f* de bec; discutailleries *fpl*; they had a bit of an argy-bargy, ils ont eu une prise de bec.

aris ['ærɪs] *n P* = **Aristotle 2**.

Aristotle ['ærɪstɒtl] *n P* 1. (*RS* = *bottle*) (*courage*) sang-froid *m*/cran *m*; (*nerve*) culot *m*. (*See also* **bottle¹**) 2. (*RS* = *bottle and glass* = **arse**) (*buttocks*) fesses*/cul *m*/derche *m*; (*anus*) anus*/trou *m* de balle.

arm [ɑːm] *n* 1. *F* to chance one's arm, tenter le coup 2. *NAm P* to put the arm on s.o., mettre le grappin sur qn 3. *P* on the arm, (*on credit*) à crédit/à la gagne/à croum(e); (*free*) gratuit*/gratis/à l'œil 4. *F* the long arm of the law, la justice. (*See* **short I 3**; **shot II 3**; **strong-arm¹,²**)

army ['ɑːmɪ] *n P* 1. you and whose army? (*in defiance of a threat*) j'espère que tu as des renforts! 2. *O* the (old) army game, escroquerie*/coup *m* d'arnaque.

around [əˈraʊnd] *adv F* 1. I've been around, je connais la vie/j'ai roulé ma bosse 2. she around? elle est là?

Arris, arris ['ærɪs] *n P* = **Aristotle 2**.

arse [ɑːs], *NAm* **ass** [æs] *n V* I 1. (*bottom, buttocks*) cul *m*; (*anus*) anus*/trou *m* du cul 2. my arse! mon cul! twenty-five my arse! she's forty if she's a day, vingt-cinq ans je t'en fiche/mon cul, elle a quarante ans au bas mot! 3. he doesn't know his arse from his elbow/from a hole in the ground, (*stupid*) il est vraiment cul/il est con comme un manche 4. arse over tip/tit(s), cul par-dessus tête; to go arse over tip/tit(s), tomber cul par-dessus tête. (*See* **A 3**) 5. arse about face, sens devant derrière/le derrière devant 6. to sit on one's arse (**and do nothing**), ne pas se magner le cul; get up off your arse! tire ton cul de là! get your arse/ass in(to) gear! remue-toi le cul! démerde-toi un peu! 7. you can kiss my arse!/you can stick it up your arse! tu peux te le foutre au cul! (*See* **shove**) 8. to be out on one's arse/*Austr* to get the arse, être flanqué/foutu à la porte; *Austr* to give s.o. the arse, flanquer/foutre qn à la porte 9. (*sexual intercourse*) coït*/baisage *m* 10. to shag one's arse off, faire l'amour* fréquemment/baiser non-stop 11. to work/shag one's arse off,

travailler dur*/se casser/se crever (le cul) 12. (he/she thinks) the sun shines out of his/her arse, (*he/she is wonderful*) il/elle se prend pour le nombril du monde; il/elle se gobe; il/elle ne se prend pas pour de la merde 13. to talk out of one's arse, raconter/débiter des conneries. (*See* **ass I**; **kick¹ 5**; **lead¹ 4**; **pain**; **shit-arse**; **short-arse**; **split-arse**; **tear-arse**) II idiot*/imbécile*; he's a stupid arse, c'est un vrai cul/connard; il est complètement bouché. (*See* **ass II**)

arse about, arse around ['ɑːsəˈbaʊt, 'ɑːsəˈraʊnd], *NAm* **ass about, ass around** *vi V* faire le con/déconner; don't go arsing about in there! va pas faire le con là-dedans! stop arsing about! déconne pas!

arse-bandit ['ɑːsbændɪt], *NAm* **ass-bandit** *n V* homosexuel* actif/pointeur *m*/ enculeur *m*.

arse-crawl ['ɑːskrɔːl], *NAm* **ass-crawl** *vi V* = **arse-lick**.

arse crawler ['ɑːskrɔːlə], *NAm* **ass crawler** *n V* = **arse-licker**.

arse-end ['ɑːsend] *n P* fin fond; the arse-end of nowhere, un trou perdu.

arsehole ['ɑːs(h)əʊl] *n V* 1. anus*/anneau *m*/trou *m* du cul/trou de balle/troufignon *m* 2. (*term of abuse*) (you) arsehole! trouduc!/ enculé!/connard! 3. pissed as an arsehole, ivre* mort/bourré à mort/rond comme une bille. (*See* **asshole**)

arseholed ['ɑːshəʊld] *a V* ivre* mort/ bourré à mort.

arse-kisser ['ɑːskɪsə], *NAm* **ass-kisser** *n V* = **arse-licker**.

arse-lick ['ɑːslɪk], *NAm* **ass-lick** *vi V* faire de la lèche.

arse-licker ['ɑːslɪkə], *NAm* **ass-licker** *n V* lèche-cul *m*.

arse-licking ['ɑːslɪkɪŋ], *NAm* **ass-licking** *n V* la lèche.

arse-man ['ɑːsmæn] *n* 1. *P* homme* qui préfère les fesses* d'une femme à tout autre partie du corps 2. *V* = **arse-bandit**.

arse up ['ɑːsˈʌp] *vtr V* (*a*) mettre en désordre/chambouler; he completely arsed it up, il y a foutu le mardier/il a tout foutu en l'air (*b*) abîmer*/amocher.

arsy ['ɑːsɪ] *a Austr V* qui a de la chance*/du cul.

artic ['ɑːtɪk] *n F* (= *articulated (lorry)*) semi-remorque *m*; semi *m*; poids lourd *m*.

article ['ɑːtɪkl] *n F* homme*/femme*/ individu*; nosy article, curieux, -euse/fouine *f*/fouille-merde *m*.

artillery [ɑː'tɪlərɪ] *n P* 1. (*drugs*) (**light**) artillery, attirail* de camé/kit *m*/artillerie *f* 2. (*hand weapons in general*) armes *fpl* à main; artillerie *f*; (*pistol*) revolver*; (*knife*) couteau*.

artist ['ɑːtɪst] *n F* (*expert*) expert *m*; (*devotee*) fanatique *mf*/fana *mf*. (*See* **con¹ 1**; **piss artist**; **ripoff**; **sack 4**)

arty ['ɑːtɪ] *a F* to be arty, se prendre pour un artiste/se prétendre artiste; he's very arty, il fait très bohème.

arty-crafty ['ɑːtɪ'krɑːftɪ], **arty-farty** ['ɑːtɪ'fɑːtɪ] *a F* artiste/bohème.

arvo ['ɑːvəʊ] *n Austr F* après-midi *m or f*/aprème *m*/aprèm' *m*.

asap, ASAP [eɪ'eseɪ'piː] *abbr F* (= *as soon as possible*) aussitôt que possible/dès que possible/le plus tôt possible.

ashes ['æʃɪz] *npl* 1. *F* (*cricket*) the Ashes, trophée symbolique des matchs Angleterre-Australie 2. *NAm P* to get/*Br* have one's ashes hauled, faire l'amour*/se l'envoyer/tirer un coup. (*See* **green I 1**)

ask [ɑːsk] *vtr & i* 1. to ask for it, chercher des ennuis *mpl*/des histoires *fpl*; you asked for it! tu l'as cherché!/tu l'as voulu! you're asking for it, and you'll get it if you're not careful! tu me cherches, et tu vas me trouver! 2. *F* don't ask me! est-ce que je sais, moi? he wasn't asking you! il ne t'a pas sonné! I ask you! je vous demande un peu! 3. *F* (*catchphrase*) ask a silly/daft question and you'll get a silly/daft answer, à question idiote, réponse idiote. (*See* **another**)

ass [æs] *n I NAm V* 1. (= **arse**) to chew s.o.'s ass out, engueuler qn/passer un savon à qn. (*For all compounds of* **ass** *see* **arse**) 2. piece of ass (*a*) acte sexuel/partie *f* de jambes en l'air (*b*) (*Pej*) (*considered sexually*) femme*/gonzesse *f*/fendue *f* (*c*) (*occ*) sexe de la femme*; to peddle ass, racoler*/faire le tapin 3. big ass man, coureur *m* de jupons/cavalier *m* 4. to do sth ass backwards, faire qch à rebours/brider l'âne par la queue 5. to have one's ass in a sling, avoir le cafard/broyer du noir 6. out on one's ass, flanqué/foutu à la porte 7. you don't know your ass from a hole in the ground, (*stupid*) t'es un manche!/t'es vraiment cul! (*See* **asshole**; **green-ass**; **kiss-ass**; **lead¹ 4**; **ream out**; **ride² 2**; **shit-ass**; **suckass**) II *Br P* (you) silly ass! espèce d'idiot!/espèce d'andouille!

asshole ['æshəʊl] *n V* 1. *NAm* = **arsehole**

1 2. (*very stupid person*) trouduc *m*/cul *m*/enculé *m*.

ass-kicker ['æskɪkə] *n NAm P* personne agressive; personne à cheval sur la discipline. (*See* **kick ass**)

association [əsəʊsɪ'eɪʃ(ə)n] *n P* (*prisons*) (l'heure *f* de) la promenade.

assy ['æsɪ] *a NAm P* 1. (*stingy*) radin/rapiat; (*nasty*) méchant; (*stubborn*) têtu/buté; (*despicable*) vil 2. (*seat of trousers, etc*) luisant/lustré.

at [æt] *prep F* 1. where it's at, où ça se passe/où il faut aller 2. to be at it (*a*) être au boulot (*b*) (*crime*) être sur un coup (*c*) être en train de faire l'amour*; (*prostitute*) être avec un client.

attaboy ['ætəbɔɪ] *excl esp NAm F* vas-y, mon grand!

attagirl ['ætəgɜːl] *excl esp NAm F* vas-y, fifille!/vas-y, ma grande!

attic ['ætɪk] *n F* he's a bit queer in the attic, il est un peu fou*/il a une araignée au plafond. (*See* **bat¹ 7**)

attitude ['ætɪtjuːd] *n NAm F* mauvaise attitude/comportement anti-social/hostilité *f*; he has a total attitude, il est vraiment antipathique.

Audi 5000! ['aʊdɪfaɪv'θaʊzənd] *excl NAm P* au revoir!/salut!/salutas!/ciao!

aunt, Aunt [ɑːnt] *n* 1. *F* my Aunt Fanny! et ta sœur! 2. *O F* Aunt Jane, WC*/goguenots *mpl* 3. *P* patronne* d'un bordel/taulière *f*/mère-maquerelle *f*/mère-maca *f* 4. *NAm F* Aunt Jemima, noire *f* qui s'insinue dans les bonnes grâces des blancs 5. Aunt Maria, (*RS* = *fire*) feu *m*/incendie *m*.

auntie¹, aunty¹ ['ɑːntɪ] *n P* homosexuel* vieillissant/tantouse *f*.

Auntie², Aunty² ['ɑːntɪ] *n F* 1. *O Auntie* (Beeb), la BBC (*British Broadcasting Corporation*). (*See* **Beeb**) 2. *Austr* l'ABC *f* (*Australian Broadcasting Corporation*)

Aussie ['ɒzɪ] I *a F* (*abbr* = *Australian*) australien(ne) II *n F* (*abbr* = *Australian*) Australien(ne)/kangourou *m*. (*See* **ozzy 2**)

auto-pilot ['ɔːtəʊpaɪlət] *n F* to be on auto-pilot, marcher au radar.

away [ə'weɪ] *adv F* 1. *Euph* en prison*/à l'ombre; they put him away, ils l'ont flanqué en taule 2. well away, ivre*/pompette/parti 3. he's well away, le voilà lancé/il est bien parti. (*See* **have 1, 2, 3**)

awesome ['ɔːsəm] *a NAm F* excellent*/super/terrible.

awful ['ɔːfʊl] *a F* terrible/affreux; **an awful bore,** (*thing*) qch d'ennuyeux/d'assommant/de canulant; (*person*) casse-burettes *m*/casse-pieds *m*; **he's an awful bore,** il est sacrément rasoir; **it's an awful bore!** c'est une vraie barbe!/ce que c'est rasoir! **awful weather,** un temps de chien/de cochon. (*See* **god-awful**)

awkward ['ɔːkwəd] *a F* **1. the awkward age,** l'âge ingrat **2. an awkward customer,** un type pas commode/un mauvais coucheur.

awol, AWOL ['eɪ'dʌbljuː'əʊ'el, 'eɪwɒl] (*abbr* = *absent without leave*) *F Mil* absent sans permission/avec fausse-perm(e); **Lizzy's gone awol, she disappeared three days ago,** Lizzy a décampé/s'est éclipsée, ça fait trois jours qu'elle a disparu.

axe¹ [æks], *NAm* **ax** [æks] *n* **1.** *F* (*expenditure, personnel, etc*) coupe *f* sombre; **to get the axe/ax,** se faire virer; **to give s.o. the axe/ax,** se débarrasser* de qn/sacquer qn/virer qn/balancer qn **2.** *F* **to have an axe/ax to grind,** prêcher pour son saint **3.** *P* axe, guitare*/gratte *f*/râpe *f*.

axe² [æks], *NAm* **ax** [æks] *vtr F* **to axe/to ax expenditure,** faire des coupes *fpl* sombres dans le budget; **to axe/to ax s.o.,** virer/sacquer/balancer qn.

axeman ['æksmæn] *n P* guitariste *m*/gratteur *m*.

B

b [biː] *abbr P* 1. = **bloody**; BF, bf = bloody fool 2. = **bastard** 3. (*drugs*) Benzédrine *f* (*RTM*) 4. B (flat), punaise *f*/bardane *f*.

b & b ['biːən'biː] (*abbr* = *bed and breakfast*) F chambre *f* avec petit déjeuner; (*in Brittany*) café-couette *m*.

babbling ['bæblɪŋ] *a F* babbling brook, jacteuse *f*/pie *f* borgne.

babe [beɪb] *n P* 1. *esp NAm* pépée *f*/poupée *f*/poule *f*; petite amie; hi babe! salut beauté/bébé! 2. *NAm* a hot babe, (*sexy*) un beau petit lot; (*aroused*) une ravageuse; she's a hot babe, elle est drôlement mettable; elle a le feu au cul.

baby ['beɪbɪ] *n* 1. P = **babe 1** 2. P un homme*/un mec; this baby's really tough, c'est un dur à cuire 3. F to be left holding the baby, porter le chapeau/payer les pots cassés/rester en plan 4. F that's my baby, c'est mon affaire/c'est mon blot; that's your baby, c'est ton business/c'est tes oignons *mpl*; débrouille-toi tout seul 5. P to (nearly) have a baby (*a*) avoir peur*/chier dans son froc (*b*) être en colère*/être à cran 6. P (*drugs*) marijuana*/douce *f* 7. baby blues, yeux*/agates *fpl*/mirettes *fpl*. (*See* **bathwater**; **blue¹** II 3; **cry-baby**; **jelly-baby**; **scare-baby**)

baby factory ['beɪbɪ'fæktərɪ] *n F Hum* maternité *f*.

baby-juice ['beɪbɪdʒuːs] *n P* sperme*/jus *m* de cyclope/purée *f*.

baby-kisser ['beɪbɪkɪsə] *n F Hum* politicien *m* en campagne (électorale).

Babylon ['bæbɪlɒn] *n P* (*Black Slang*) 1. police*/flicaille *f*/la maison poulaga 2. la Grande-Bretagne 3. (*white people*) les blancs *mpl*.

baby-snatcher ['beɪbɪsnætʃə] *n* 1. (*a*) F kidnappeur, -euse (d'enfants) (*b*) P homme*/femme* qui épouse *ou* qui sort avec une femme*/un homme beaucoup plus jeune que lui/qu'elle; he/she is a baby-snatcher, il/elle

les prend au berceau/au biberon 2. P baby-snatchers, brigade *f* de répression du proxénétisme des mineurs*/= les Mœurs *fpl*/= la Mondaine. (*See* **cradle-snatcher**)

baccy ['bækɪ] *n F* tabac*/perle *m*.

back [bæk] I *a* 1. F to take a back seat, être la cinquième roue du carrosse/passer au second plan/céder le pas aux autres. (*See* **backseat**) 2. F the back end, l'automne *m* 3. P back door, anus*/trou *m* du cul/trou de balle. (*See* **fed up** (*a*)) II *n* 1. F to get s.o.'s back up, mettre qn en colère*/prendre qn à rebrousse-poil/braquer qn 2. P to get off s.o.'s back, ficher/foutre la paix à qn; get off my back! fous-moi la paix!/lâche-moi! 3. F to be on s.o.'s back (about sth), casser les pieds à qn/tanner qn (pour qch) 4. F you scratch my back and I'll scratch yours, soyez sympa avec moi, je vous renverrai l'ascenseur. (*See* **backscratcher**) 5. F to put one's back into sth, en mettre un coup; come on, put your back into it! allons, un petit effort! 6. F to have one's back to the wall, en être réduit à la dernière extrémité/être au pied du mur 7. F he's at the back of all our problems, il est la cause/il est à l'origine de tous nos ennuis 8. F the back of beyond, en plein bled/au diable (vau)vert; he lives at the back of beyond, il habite dans un trou/un bled/un coin perdu *ou* paumé. (*See* **boondocks**) 9. F to be (laid) on one's back, être malade*/être mal fichu 10. F to break the back of sth, faire le plus dur/gros de qch 11. F I'll be glad to see the back of him, ça me ferait plaisir d'être débarrassé de lui 12. F I know it like the back of my hand, je le connais comme le fond de ma poche 13. F she's got a face like the back of a bus, c'est une mocheté; elle est moche comme un pou/à faire peur 14. P she earns her living on her back, elle fait l'horizontale. (*See* **greenback**; **greybacks**; **piggyback**; **shellback**)

backasswards [bæk'æswədz] *adv NAm P*

9

= ass backwards (**ass I 4**).

backchat ['bæktʃæt] *n* F insolence *f*/impertinence *f*; **less of this backchat!** assez de mauvais esprit!

backdoor man ['bækdɔː'mæn] *n NAm* P (*secret lover*) amant*/coquin *m*/jules *m*.

back down ['bæk'daʊn] *vi* F caler/caner/lâcher pied; se dégonfler.

back-end ['bækend] *n* F **she looks like the back-end of a bus**, c'est une mocheté; elle est moche comme un pou/à faire peur. (*See* **back II 13**).

backfire ['bæk'faɪə] *vi* 1. F rater/mal tourner/merder; **his plan backfired**, son projet a foiré 2. *esp Austr* P péter*/lâcher une perle.

backhanded ['bæk'hændɪd] *a* F **backhanded compliment**, compliment *m* équivoque/à double tranchant.

backhander [bæk'hændə] *n* P 1. (*bribe*) graissage *m* de patte/pot-de-vin *m* 2. (*heavy slap*) calotte *f*/baffe *f*.

backlash ['bæklæʃ] *n* F retour *m* de flamme/effet *m* boomerang.

back-number ['bæknʌmbə] *n* F (*a*) objet démodé (*b*) (*person*) croulant *m*/périmé *m*/PPH *m*.

back off ['bæk'ɒf] *vi* P **back off!** fiche-moi la paix!/lâche-moi!

back out ['bæk'aʊt] *vi* F (*a*) se dédire/se dérober/se dégonfler (*b*) sortir d'une position difficile/faire marche arrière.

backpack ['bækpæk] *vi* F (*to hitchhike*) faire de l'autostop/du stop (*en emportant son matériel de couchage, etc sur le dos*); (*to hike*) faire de la randonnée (avec son sac à dos).

backpacker ['bækpækə] *n* F (*hitchiker*) autostoppeur, -euse/stoppeur, -euse; (*hiker*) randonneur, -euse.

backpacking ['bækpækɪŋ] *n* F **to go backpacking** (*to hitchhike*) faire de l'autostop; (*to hike*) faire de la randonnée (*avec son sac à dos*).

back-pedal ['bæk'pedl] *vi* F faire marche arrière/faire machine arrière.

backroom ['bækruːm] *a* F confidentiel/secret; **the backroom boys**, les experts *mpl*/les techniciens *mpl*, etc qui restent dans les coulisses.

backscratcher ['bækskrætʃə] *n* F flatteur *m*/lèche-cul *m*/lèche-bottes *m*/lécheur *m*. (*See* **back II 4**)

backscratching ['bækskrætʃɪŋ] *n* F flatterie *f*/lèche *f*.

backseat ['bæksiːt] *a attrib* F 1. **backseat driver**, passager *m* qui donne des conseils au chauffeur 2. *NAm* P **backseat Betty**, (*slut*) salope *f*/Marie-couche-toi-là *f*.

backsheesh, backshish [bæk'ʃiːʃ] *n* F bakchich *m*.

backside [bæk'saɪd] *n* F fesses*/postérieur *m*/derche *m*.

backslang ['bækslæŋ] *n* F = verlan *m*/lanvère *m*.

backslapper ['bækslæpə] *n* F **he's a bit of a backslapper**, il est à tu et à toi avec tout le monde.

backslapping ['bækslæpɪŋ] *n* F bruyante démonstration d'amitié.

backstairs ['bækstɛəz] *a* F **backstairs gossip**, cancan *m*/ragots *mpl* de domestiques; **backstairs politics**, intrigues *fpl* politiques/magouilles politiciennes.

backtrack ['bæktræk] *vi* 1. F (*a*) rebrousser chemin (*b*) faire machine arrière/faire marche arrière/se dégonfler 2. P = **back up 2** (*b*).

back-up ['bækʌp] *n* 1. F appui *m*/soutien *m*/aide *f*; **media back-up**, supports-média *mpl* 2. P (*drugs*) (*a*) piqûre* (*dans une veine déjà gonflée*) (*b*) (*practice of drawing blood into syringe before injecting drug*) tirette *f* et poussette *f* 3. O P enculage (hétérosexuel).

back up ['bæk'ʌp] *vtr & i* 1. F **to back s.o. up**, seconder qn/prendre les patins de qn 2. P (*drugs*) (*a*) dilater la veine avant une piqûre de drogues (*b*) aspirer le sang dans la seringue pendant une piqûre pour le mélanger à la drogue avant de le réinjecter 3. F faire machine arrière/faire marche arrière.

backward ['bækwəd] *a* F **he's not backward in coming forward**, il n'a pas froid aux yeux/il n'est pas gêné.

backwards ['bækwədz] *adv* F 1. **to bend/to fall/to lean over backwards for s.o.**, se mettre en quatre/se décarcasser pour qn. (*See* **fall 3**) 2. **to know sth backwards**, comprendre qch parfaitement; savoir/connaître qch par cœur; **I know the way home backwards**, je connais mon chemin sur le bout du doigt/les yeux fermés.

backwoodsman ['bækwʊdzmən] *n* F 1. rustre *m*/péquenaud *m*/plouc *m* 2. *Pol* pair *m* qui fréquente peu la Chambre des Lords.

bacon ['beɪkən] *n* F 1. **to bring home the bacon** (*a*) faire bouillir la marmite/gagner sa croûte/gagner son bifteck (*b*) remporter le pompon/décrocher la timbale 2. **to save one's**

bacon, sauver sa peau.

bad [bæd] I *a* 1. *F* that's too bad! (*what a pity!*) dommage!/manque de pot! (*that's a bit much!*) c'est un peu fort! that's not half bad, c'est pas mal du tout; that's not so bad, c'est pas si mal que ça 2. *F* she's not bad! elle est pas mal!/elle est bien roulée!/elle est bien foutue! 3. *F* he's in a bad way, il est dans le pétrin/dans de mauvais draps; il file un mauvais coton 4. *F* I'm in his bad books, il ne m'a pas à la bonne/je ne suis pas dans ses petits papiers 5. *F* she's bad news, il faut se méfier d'elle 6. *F* to turn up like a bad penny, venir comme un cheveu/des cheveux sur la soupe 7. *F* a bad lot/*O* bad egg/*O* bad hat/*O* bad 'un, une canaille/un salaud; he's a bad lot, c'est un sale type/une canaille 8. *P* to give someone the bad eye, regarder qn avec méfiance; regarder qn d'un œil noir 9. *F* I feel bad about it, ça m'embête 10. *F* (*in films, etc*) the bad guys and the good guys, les bons *mpl* et les méchants *mpl* 11. *P* excellent*/super/terrible; well bad, super/géant; trainers are badder than before, les trainers sont plus formides qu'avant. (*See* **dude 1**) II *adv F* (= *badly*) 1. to have it bad for s.o., aimer qn/en pincer pour qn/être dingue de qn 2. I need it real bad, j'en ai vachement besoin 3. (*obsession*) he's got it bad, c'est une manie chez lui/il en est dingue III *n F* 1. to go to the bad, être sur la mauvaise pente/mal tourner; he's gone to the bad, il a mal tourné 2. to the bad, dans le rouge; to be £5 to the bad, en être de £5.

baddie, baddy ['bædɪ] *n F* (*in films, etc*) le vilain/le méchant. (*See* **goodies 2**)

bad-eye ['bædaɪ] *vtr P* to bad-eye s.o., regarder qn avec méfiance; regarder qn d'un œil noir.

badge [bædʒ] *n O P* (*drugs*) quantité de drogues insuffisante pour le prix payé.

badger ['bædʒə] *n* 1. *NAm P* the badger game, escroquerie*/arnaque *f*; moyens employés pour compromettre un homme avec une femme afin de lui soutirer de l'argent; chantage *m* 2. *NAm F* habitant, -ante de l'état de Wisconsin.

bad-looking ['bæd'lʊkɪŋ] *a F* she's not bad-looking, elle est pas mal/elle est pas désagréable à regarder/elle est bien balancée.

badmouth ['bædmaʊθ] *vtr NAm F* dire du mal de (qn/qch)/casser du sucre sur le dos de (qn).

bag¹ [bæg] *n* 1. *P Pej* femme* laide/

acariâtre; (you) old bag! vieille chouette!/vieille bique!/vieille pouffiasse! 2. bag of wind (*a*) vantard*/esbrouf(f)eur, -euse (*b*) bavard*/baratineur, -euse 3. *F* there's bags of it, il y en a en abondance*/il y en a à gogo/à tire-larigot/en pagaille; there's bags of room, la place ne manque pas 4. *F* it's in the bag, c'est dans le sac/c'est du tout cuit 5. *F* the whole bag of tricks, tout le Saint-Frusquin/tout le bataclan 6. *V* (*rare*) bag (of tricks), testicules*/bijoux *mpl* de famille 7. *F* he's got huge bags under his eyes, il a des valises sous les yeux 8. *F* she's nothing but a bag of bones, elle est maigre* comme un clou/elle n'a que la peau sur les os 9. *pl F* pantalon*/falz(ar) *m*/froc *m* 10. *NAm P* (*drugs*) dose *f*/sachet *m* de drogue (*surt* héroïne*). (*See* **dime**; **nickel 2**) 11. *NAm F* to be left holding the bag = to be left holding the baby (**baby 3**) 12. *NAm O P* (*a*) préservatif*/capote (anglaise) (*b*) diaphragme *m* 13. *NAm P* he's in the bag, il est ivre*/soûl/beurré 14. *esp NAm F* penchant *m*/goût *m*; rock's not my bag, le rock, c'est pas mon genre/mon truc 15. bag lady/man, clocharde *f*/clochard *m* (*qui trimbale des sacs pleins d'effets*). (*See* **bagman**) (*See* **cat 14**; **doggy bag**; **fag 2** (*c*); **fleabag**; **gasbag**; **moneybags**; **nosebag**; **ragbag**; **ratbag**; **scumbag**; **shagbag**; **shitbag**)

bag² [bæg] *vtr P* 1. arrêter*/coffrer 2. mettre le grappin sur (qch); to bag the best seat, rafler la meilleure place 3. voler*/piquer/chauffer 4. bags I go first! à moi/pour bibi le premier tour! 5. (*dismiss, fire*) sacquer/mettre à la porte 6. *NAm* (*give up*) abandonner*/laisser tomber/larguer 7. *Austr* critiquer*/débiner 8. *NAm* to bag some z's, dormir*/piquer un roupillon. (*See* **z's**)

baggage ['bægɪdʒ] *n O F* 1. fille* effrontée/garce *f*/coquine *f*/gisquette *f* 2. prostituée*/traînée *f*/roulure *f*.

bagged [bægd] *a* 1. *NAm P* ivre*/blindé/chargé 2. *Austr P* emprisonné*/en cage/en taule.

bagman ['bægmæn] *n esp NAm P* racketteur *m*.

bag-snatcher ['bægsnætʃə] *n F* voleur *m* à l'arraché (de sacs à main).

bag-snatching ['bæg'snætʃɪŋ] *n* vol à l'arraché (de sacs à main).

bail out ['beɪl'aʊt] *vtr F* to bail s.o. out (*help s.o. financially or otherwise*) aider qn à remonter le courant/la pente.

bait [beɪt] *n P* homme* beau et efféminé qui

attire des homosexuels*. (See **jail-bait**)

bakshee ['bækʃiː] *a & n* = **buckshee**.

ball¹ [bɔːl] *n* 1. *F* to be on the ball (*alert, aware*) être dans le coup/savoir nager/ connaître la musique; (*trendy*) être à la page/à la coule; (*capable, efficient*) être capable/être malin*/être dégourdi; get on the ball, kid! à l'attaque, mon vieux! 2. *P* to have (oneself) a ball, s'en payer une tranche/ prendre son pied; faire la java; we're gonna have ourselves a ball! on va s'en payer! it was a ball, c'était le pied 3. *F* to play ball with s.o., coopérer avec qn/entrer dans le jeu de qn 4. *F* to set the ball rolling, mettre les choses en branle/ouvrir le bal; to keep the ball rolling, continuer une activité/une conversation, etc 5. *P* pilule *f ou* dose *f* de drogue. (See **goofball 3, 4; speedball**) 6. *F* ball of fire, individu* dynamique/plein d'énergie; he's a ball of fire, il pète le feu/des flammes. (See **fireball**) 7. *F Hum* ball and chain, épouse*/bourgeoise *f*/bobonne *f* 8. *F* the ball is in your court, (c'est) à vous de jouer/la balle est dans votre camp 9. *O P* that's the way the ball bounces, c'est la vie, que veux-tu? (See **cookie 1; mop; onion 1**) 10. *V* testicule*/bille *f*/balloche *f*. (See **balls¹; chalk 4; eight 2; fly-ball; oddball; patball; pinball; screwball; snowball¹**)

ball² [bɔːl] *vtr* 1. *P* = to have (oneself) a ball (**ball¹ 2**) 2. *NAm V* faire l'amour* avec qn/ baiser qn/s'envoyer qn/se faire qn. (See **jack¹ 6; snowball²**)

ball-breaker ['bɔːlbreɪkə], **ball-buster** ['bɔːlbʌstə] *n P* 1. femme* agressive 2. (*hard taskmaster*) tyran *m*/casse-couilles *m* 3. boulot *m* extrêmement difficile/casse-gueule *m*.

ball game ['bɔːlgeɪm] *n esp NAm F* it's a whole new ball game, c'est une autre paire de manches/ce n'est plus la même histoire/le vent a changé de direction.

balling-out [bɔːlɪŋ'aut] *n esp NAm P* = **bawling out**.

ball-off ['bɔːlɒf] *n V* branlage *m*; to have a ball-off, se masturber*/se branler.

ball off ['bɔːl'ɒf] *vi V* se masturber*/se branler/s'astiquer.

balloon [bə'luːn] *n* 1. *F* when the balloon goes up ..., quand on découvrira le pot aux roses.../quand la chose éclatera 2. *P* (*drugs*) sachet *m* d'héroïne*/ballon *m*.

ball out ['bɔːl'aut] *vtr esp NAm P* = **bawl out**.

ball-park ['bɔːlpɑːk] *a esp NAm F* a ball-park figure, un chiffre approximatif; in ball-park figures, à peu près.

ball park ['bɔːl'pɑːk] *n esp NAm F* in the right ball park, bien placé.

balls¹ [bɔːlz] *npl V* 1. testicules*/couilles *fpl*/ balloches *fpl*; he kicked him in the balls, il lui a flanqué un coup de pied dans les couilles 2. balls! merde! balls to you! je t'emmerde! balls to that! quelle couillonnade! that's a load of balls/that's all balls! c'est de la couille!/c'est que des conneries! 3. he's got a lot of balls, il a un de ces culots!/il a des couilles au cul 4. it's enough to freeze the balls off a brass monkey, on (se) caille/on se les gèle/on se caille les miches/on pèle de froid. (See **brass monkey(s)**) 5. he made a real balls of it, il y a foutu un de ces merdiers 6. to have s.o. by the balls, avoir qn à sa pogne; she's got him by the balls, elle le tient par la queue/par là 7. to chew s.o.'s balls off, réprimander* qn/engueuler qn/passer un savon à qn/bouffer la tête à qn 8. to work one's balls off, bosser comme un dingue/se crever (le cul) au boulot 9. I'll have his balls for this, j'aurai sa peau.

balls² [bɔːlz], *NAm* **ball** [bɔːl] *vtr V* to balls sth/*NAm* to ball sth, saloper qch/se foutre dedans; he ballsed it/*NAm* he balled it, il s'est foutu dedans/il a tout foutu en l'air.

balls-ache ['bɔːlzeɪk] *n V* you give me balls-ache, tu me casses les couilles/tu me fais chier.

ballsey ['bɔːlzɪ] *a P* = **ballsy**.

balls-up ['bɔːlzʌp], *NAm* **ball-up** ['bɔːlʌp] *n V* to make a balls-up of sth, foutre la merde dans qch; he made a real/a right balls-up of that, il y a foutu le merdier/il a tout foutu en l'air/il a foutu une de ces salades.

balls up ['bɔːlz'ʌp], *NAm* **ball up** ['bɔːl'ʌp] *vtr V* to balls sth up/*NAm* to ball sth up, foutre la merde/le bordel dans qch; he ballsed it up/*NAm* he balled it up, il a foutu le merdier; it's all ballsed up/*NAm* it's all balled up, c'est complètement foutu.

ballsy ['bɔːlzɪ] *a P* viril et courageux*/qui en a des couilles/qui en a.

bally ['bælɪ] *a O F* (*Euph for* bloody) satané/ sacré/fichu.

ballyhoo ['bælɪhuː] *n F* 1. publicité tapageuse/battage *m*/ramdam *m*/tamtam *m* 2. balivernes *fpl*/bourrage *m* de crâne/boniments *mpl*.

balmy ['bɑːmɪ] *a P* = **barmy**.

balon(e)y [bə'ləʊnɪ] *n F* = **boloney**.

bam [bæm] *n P* (*drugs*) amphétamine*/amphés *fpl*/amphètes *fpl*.

bamboo [bæm'buː] *n* 1. *P* pipe *f* à opium*/bambou *m*; **to suck the bamboo,** sucer le bambou 2. *Pol F* **the bamboo curtain,** le rideau de bambou.

bamboozle [bæm'buːzl] *vtr F* duper*/empaumer/embobiner/rouler.

banana [bə'nɑːnə] *n* 1. *V* (*rare*) **to have one's banana peeled/to have a banana (with s.o.),** faire l'amour* (avec qn)/arracher son copeau 2. *Mil F* **banana boat,** péniche *f* de débarquement; *F* **he's come off/come in with a banana boat,** il est entré (dans ce pays) illégalement 3. *NAm O F* comédien *m*/acteur *m* de burlesque; **top banana,** vedette *f* 4. *F* **banana republic,** république bananière 5. *NAm P* course (de chevaux) truquée.

bananas [bə'nɑːnəz] *a P* fou*/maboul/toqué/cinglé; **I'll go bananas in here on my own,** je vais devenir dingue à rester seul ici; **she drives me bananas,** elle me rend dingue.

band [bænd] *n Austr* prostituée*/racoleuse *f*.

B and D ['biːən'diː] *n Br F* (*abbr* = *bondage and discipline*) sadomasochisme *m*.

bandit ['bændɪt] *n F* **one-armed bandit,** machine *f* à sous/bandit manchot. (*See* **arse-bandit; beef-bandit; bum-bandit**)

bandwagon ['bændwægən] *n F* **to jump/to climb/to get on the bandwagon,** prendre le train en marche/se mettre du côté du manche.

bang¹ [bæŋ] **I** *a F* **the whole bang lot/the whole bang shoot,** tout le bataclan/tout le tremblement **II** *adv F* 1. **to arrive bang on time,** arriver pile à l'heure 2. **to be bang up-to-date,** être à jour/à la dernière heure; (*person*) être à la coule/à la page 3. **to be caught bang to rights,** être pris sur le fait/en flagrant délit/en flag 4. *int* **bang went another fiver!** et voilà un autre (billet* de) cinq livres de perdu; **bang goes that idea,** cette idée est (tombée) à l'eau. (*See* **slap-bang(-wallop); wallop**) **III** *n* 1. *P* **l'acte sexuel/baise *f*/coup *m*; **she's a good bang,** elle baise bien/c'est une sacrée baiseuse. (*See* **gang bang**) 2. *F* coup*/gnon *m*; **he gave it a bang with the hammer,** il lui a donné un coup de marteau 3. *F* **to go with a bang** (*go smoothly*) aller comme sur des roulettes; (*be a great success*) faire très fort/marcher du tonnerre; **the party went with a real bang,** ça a été une boum du tonnerre/ça a chauffé à la boum 4. *P*

I got a real bang out of it, ça m'a vraiment fait qch/j'ai trouvé ça vachement chié 5. *P* = **bhang** 6. *esp NAm P* **to have a bang at sth,** tenter/risquer le coup 7. *P* (*drugs*) piqûre*/piquouze *f*/fixe *m* 8. *P* impression *f* de plénitude *ou* sensation *f* de plaisir intense qui suit une injection intraveineuse de drogue/flash *m*. (*See* **whizz-bang**)

bang² [bæŋ] *vtr V* 1. (*usu of a man*) faire l'amour* (avec qn)/s'envoyer (qn)/bourrer (qn); **they banged all night,** ils ont baisé toute la nuit 2. *F* **to bang into s.o.,** se taper dans qn; **I banged into Charlie in town,** je suis tombé sur Charlie en ville 3. **it's like banging your head against a brick wall, trying to talk to him!** inutile d'essayer de lui parler, autant pisser en l'air/dans un violon 4. *P* (*drugs*) se piquer*/piquouser/se faire un fixe.

banged up ['bæŋd'ʌp] *a P* en prison*/en taule/bouclé.

banger ['bæŋə] *n F* 1. (vieille) voiture*/guimbarde *f*/caisse *f*; **my old banger,** ma vieille bagnole/tire *f*/chiotte *f* 2. saucisse *f*; **bangers and mash,** saucisses-purée (de pommes de terre).

bang-on ['bæŋ'ɒn] *adv F* **bang-on!** recta!/au poil!

bang on ['bæŋ'ɒn] *vi Br F* parler* incessamment/jacter/déblatérer; **oh, do stop banging on!** oh, la ferme!/écrase!

bang-up ['bæŋ'ʌp] *a F* excellent*/soin-soin; **a bang-up meal,** un repas fameux/un gueuleton. (*See* **slap-up**)

banjaxed ['bændʒækst] *a Irish* (*broken*) bousillé/pété/démoli; (*amazed*) étonné*/baba.

bank¹ [bæŋk] *n NAm F* liasse *f* de billets* (de banque)/mille-feuille *m*.

bank² [bæŋk] *vi NAm F* (*make a lot of money*) faire du pognon/du fric.

bank on ['bæŋk'ɒn] *vtr F* compter sur (qch); **don't bank on it!** compte pas dessus!

bankroll ['bæŋkrəʊl] *vtr esp NAm F* fournir les frais d'une entreprise; financer/parrainer (qch); **he bankrolled that film,** il a financé ce film.

bar [bɑː] *n* 1. *F* **to be behind bars,** être emprisonné*/être bouclé/être en taule 2. *A P* billet* d'une livre 3. *V* **to have a bar (on),** être en érection*/avoir la trique. (*See* **handlebar**)

barbie ['bɑːbɪ] *n esp Austr F* barbecue *m*.

barbies ['bɑːbɪz] *npl P* = **barbs**.

barbs [bɑːbz] *n P* (*abbr* = *barbiturates*) (*drugs*) barbituriques*/barbitos *mpl*.

bare-arsed ['bɛər'ɑːst], *NAm* **bare-**

ass(ed) ['bɛər'æst] *a P* nu*/le cul à l'air.

bareback ['bɛəbæk] *adv P* (*not common*) to ride bareback, to go bareback riding (*have sex without contraceptive*) faire l'amour* sans préservatif*; cracher dans le bénitier.

barf [bɑːf] *vi NAm P* vomir*/dégueuler/ gerber.

bar-fly ['bɑːflaɪ] *n esp NAm F* 1. pilier *m* de bistrot 2. ivrogne* qui se fait offrir des tournées.

barge in ['bɑːdʒ'ɪn] *vi F* 1. to barge in on a party, s'inviter à une réception/une boum 2. to barge in on s.o.'s conversation, mettre son grain de sel 3. to barge in where you're not wanted, se mêler de ce qui ne vous regarde pas; piétiner les plate-bandes (à qn)/marcher sur les pieds de qn.

barge into ['bɑːdʒ'ɪntuː] *vtr F* to barge into s.o., se taper dans qn/bousculer qn/entrer dans qn.

barge-pole ['bɑːdʒpəʊl] *n F* I wouldn't touch it with a barge-pole, je ne le prendrais pas avec des pincettes.

bar-girl ['bɑːgɜːl] *n P* hôtesse *f*/entraîneuse *f*.

bar-happy ['bɑːhæpɪ] *a NAm F* (légèrement) ivre*/éméché.

barhop ['bɑːhɒp] *vi esp NAm F* faire la tournée des bars/dérouler.

barhopping ['bɑːhɒpɪŋ] *n esp NAm F* to go barhopping, faire la tournée des bars/ dérouler.

bark [bɑːk] *vi F* to bark up the wrong tree, se tromper d'adresse/faire fausse route/se mettre le doigt dans l'œil.

barker ['bɑːkə] *n A P* revolver*/pétard *m*/ flingue *m*.

barking ['bɑːkɪŋ] *a* barking (mad), fou*/ détraqué/siphonné.

barmpot ['bɑːmpɒt] *n P* individu bête*/ cruche *f*/baluche *m*/bas-de-plafond *m*.

barmy ['bɑːmɪ] *a P* fou*/toqué/loufoque.

barn [bɑːn] *n F* were you born/*NAm* raised in a barn? t'es né sous les ponts?/on t'a pas appris à fermer les portes?

Barnaby Rudge ['bɑːnəbɪ'rʌdʒ] *Prn P* (*RS = judge*) juge *m*/gerbier *m*/curieux *m*.

barnet ['bɑːnɪt] *n P* (*RS = Barnet Fair = hair*) cheveux*/tifs *mpl*/cresson *m*.

barney¹ ['bɑːnɪ] *n P* a bit of a barney, querelle*/prise *f* de bec/accrochage *m*.

barney² ['bɑːnɪ] *vi P* avoir une prise de bec (avec qn).

baron ['bærən] *n* 1. *P* prisonnier *m* qui a de

l'argent, du tabac, etc; baron *m*. (*See* **snout** 2) 2. *F* (*in industry, business*) magnat *m*/gros bonnet; the press barons, les grands manitous de la presse.

barrack-room ['bærəkruːm] *a F* barrack-room lawyer (*quarrelsome person*) chicaneur, -euse/râleur, -euse/mauvais coucheur/ emmerdeur, -euse.

barrel¹ ['bærəl] *n P* 1. to be over a barrel, être coincé/dans le pétrin/dans la merde 2. to get/to have s.o. over a barrel, avoir qn dans sa poche/à sa pogne 3. beaucoup/en abondance*; to have a barrel of money, être riche*/plein aux as; he's a barrel of fun, (*funny*) il est rigolo/il est marrant; *Iron* quel rabat-joie! (*See* **scrape²** 1)

barrel² ['bærəl] *vi also NAm* barrel ass, *P* aller vite*/rouler à plein(s) tube(s)/gazer/aller à fond la caisse.

barrelhouse ['bærəlhaʊs] *n NAm O P* cabaret *m* populaire qui sert aussi d'hôtel dans un quartier pauvre.

barrelled up ['bærəld'ʌp] *a P* (*not common*) ivre*/bit(t)uré.

base [beɪs] *n* 1. *NAm F* (*a*) he won't even make first base, il claquera au départ (*b*) baisers *mpl*; (*necking*) papouilles *fpl*/pelotage *m*; he couldn't get to first base with her, il a raté son coup avec elle 2. *F* base over apex, cul par-dessus tête; he went base over apex, il a fait une belle culbute 3. *NAm F* to be off base, se tromper/se gour(r)er/se fourrer le doigt dans l'œil 4. *P* (*drugs*) cocaïne* purifiée/cristallisée; crack *m*. (*See* **freebase**)

bash¹ [bæʃ] *n* 1. *P* coup*/châtaigne *f* 2. *F* to have a bash at sth/to give sth a bash, tenter le coup/sa chance; I'll have a bash at it, je vais essayer un coup 3. *F* réjouissances*/boum *f*/ surboum *f*/fête *f*/fiesta *f*.

bash² [bæʃ] *vtr P* 1. battre*/cogner; to bash s.o. about, passer qn à tabac/tabasser qn 2. *P Austr* to bash it, (*drink heavily*) caresser la bouteille/picoler. (*See* **bishop**; **square-bash**)

basher ['bæʃə] *n P* 1. (*See* **pak(k)i-basher**; **queer-basher**; **spud-basher**; **square-basher**) 2. petite cabane en carton/en papier/en plastique (*habitée par un clochard*).

bash in ['bæʃ'ɪn] *vtr P* to bash s.o.'s head/ face in, abîmer le portrait à qn/passer qn à tabac.

bashing ['bæʃɪŋ] *n P* 1. coups*/raclée *f*/ trempe *f*; Spurs took a bashing from Liverpool, Spurs a été écrasé/laminé par

Liverpool; the platoon took a bashing, la section s'est fait amocher 2. la prostitution/le truc/le trottoir. (See **pak(k)i-bashing**; **queer-bashing**; **spud-bashing**; **square-bashing**)

bash on ['bæʃ'ɒn] vi F to bash on regardless, aller envers et contre tout.

bash out ['bæʃ'aʊt] vr F to bash out a tune, tapoter un air.

bash up ['bæʃ'ʌp] vtr P battre*/filer une avoine à qn/passer qn à tabac/tabasser qn.

basinful ['beɪsnfʊl] n P to have (had) a basinful, en avoir assez*/en avoir marre/en avoir par-dessus la tête; I've had a basinful, j'en ai ras le bol/la casquette.

basket ['bɑːskɪt] n P 1. (Euph for **bastard**) salaud*/saligaud m; you silly basket! espèce de débile, va! 2. basket case, invalide mf/ handicapé(e) physique/mental(e). (See **bread-basket**)

bastard ['bɑːstəd, 'bæstəd] n P 1. salaud*/ canaille f/salopard m; you bastard! (espèce de) salaud!/connard! 2. lucky bastard! le veinard! 3. emmerdement m; that's a bastard! ça c'est chiant!/quelle chiotte! that job's a real bastard! ce boulot est vraiment chiant! (See **rotten 1**)

bat¹ [bæt] n 1. P an old bat, une vieille bique/ une vieille chouette; you daft bat, espèce de nouille! 2. NAm P prostituée*/grue f 3. F like a bat out of hell, vite*/à tout berzingue/comme un zèbre 4. F NAm right off the bat, du premier coup/illico presto 5. F off one's own bat, de son propre chef/sans rien demander à personne 6. NAm P réjouissances*/noce f/ bombe f 7. F to have bats in the belfry/attic, être fou*/avoir une araignée au plafond.

bat² [bæt] vtr 1. O P battre*/frapper/rosser 2. F he didn't bat an eyelid/NAm an eye, il n'a pas sourcillé/bronché/pipé 3. F to bat first, tirer le premier. (See **sticky 4**)

batcave ['bætkeɪv] n (club) boîte f de nuit/ discothèque f.

batch [bætʃ] vtr NAm F to batch it, vivre en célibataire.

bathwater ['bɑːθwɔːtə] n F to throw the baby out with the bathwater, jeter le bébé avec l'eau du bain.

bats [bæts] a P 1. fou*/timbré; to go bats, devenir fou*/perdre la boule 2. to be bats about s.o./sth, aimer*/être toqué de qn/qch; he's bats about it, il en est fou*/dingue.

batter ['bætə] vtr F battre*/cogner qn; I'll batter you if you don't stop! arrête, ou je

t'assomme! battered baby/wife, enfant/femme martyr(e).

battleaxe, NAm **battleax** ['bætlæks] n F femme* acariâtre aux manières autoritaires/ harpie f/dragon m/virago f.

battle cruiser ['bætl'kruːzə] n P (RS = **boozer**) (pub) café*/bistrot m/troquet m.

battler ['bætlə] n A P bagarreur m.

batty ['bætɪ] a F fou*/timbré/toqué/givré.

bawling out ['bɔːlɪŋ'aʊt] n P engueulade f/savon m.

bawl out ['bɔːl'aʊt] vtr P injurier*/ engueuler qn.

bayonet ['beɪənɪt] n P pénis*/arbalète f; to have bayonet practice, faire l'amour*/tirer un coup/filer un coup d'arbalète.

bazoo [bə'zuː] n NAm P bouche*/bec m.

bazooka [bə'zuːkə] n P 1. pénis*/arbalète f 2. pl seins*/doudounes fpl.

bazookaed [bə'zuːkəd] a O P sabordé/ bousillé.

bazoomas, bazumas [bə'zuːməz] npl P = **bazookas** (See **bazooka 2**).

beach [biːtʃ] n NAm F 1. to be on the beach, être chômeur/chômer/être au chômedu 2. you're not the only pebble on the beach, tu n'es pas tout seul/il n'y a pas que toi au monde.

beak [biːk] n P 1. magistrat m/allumeur m/ curieux m; to be up before the beak, paraître devant le juge/au parquet 2. (headmaster) dirlo m 3. nez* (crochu)/pif m/tarin m. (See **stickybeak**)

beam [biːm] n F 1. on the beam, (having similar views) sur la même longueur d'ondes; (in the right direction) dans la bonne direction/sur la bonne voie 2. to be off (the) beam (a) ne pas comprendre/ne rien piger (b) faire fausse route/se tromper; you're way off beam, tu t'es gouré sur toute la ligne/tu débloques (à pleins tubes) 3. to be broad in the beam, être large des hanches fpl/joufflu du pétard.

beam-ends ['biːm'endz] npl F to be on one's beam-ends, être pauvre*/être dans la dèche.

beaming up ['biːmɪŋ'ʌp] n NAm F (drugs) beaming up to Scottie, fumer du crack; (getting high) planer/voyager.

bean [biːn] n 1. P tête*/caboche f 2. O F usu Hum old bean, vieux pote/vieille branche f 3. F he hasn't got a bean, il n'a pas le sou*/il n'a pas un radis 4. F it's not worth a bean, it doesn't amount to a hill of beans, ça ne vaut pas grand-chose/ça ne vaut pas tripette 5. *F to spill the beans*, (*give away secret, etc*) vendre/éventer la mèche; (*confess*) avouer*/manger le morceau. (*See* **spill**) 6. *F to be full of beans*, être d'attaque; être plein d'entrain/péter le feu 7. *P* (*drugs*) Benzédrine* (*RTM*) **jolly beans**, amphétamines*/bonbons *mpl* 8. *NAm P Pej* **bean** (*eater*), Mexicain, -aine. (*See* **bean-pole; string-bean**)

beanery ['biːnərɪ] *n NAm P* restaurant *m* de mauvaise qualité/gargote *f*/bouiboui *m*.

beanfeast ['biːnfiːst] *n F* (*meal*) gueuleton *m*/balthazar *m*; (*party, celebration*) bombe *f*/fête*/nouba *f*.

beano ['biːnəʊ] *n O P* réjouissances*/bombe *f*/fête*/nouba *f*.

bean-pole ['biːnpəʊl] *n F* (*person*) grande perche/asperge (montée).

bear [beə] *n NAm P* agent* de police/flic *m*/poulet *m*.

bear-garden ['beəˈɡɑːdn] *n F* pétaudière *f*; *to turn the place into a bear-garden*, mettre le désordre partout/foutre la pagaille.

beast [biːst] *n P* 1. *Br* agent* de police/flic *m*/poulet *m* 2. *Br* (*prisons*) délinquant sexuel/violeur *m* 3. *NAm* femme*/nana *f*.

beastly ['biːstlɪ] *a & adv F* abominable/infect; *what beastly weather!* quel sale temps!/quel temps de cochon!/quel fichu temps!

beat[1] [biːt] I *a F* 1. (*dead*) beat, très fatigué*/claqué/vanné/crevé 2. (*baffled*) dérouté; *I'm beat*, j'y pige que dalle 3. *the beat generation*, la génération des beatniks. (*See* **downbeat; upbeat**) II *n* 1. *O P* beatnik *m* 2. *F* (*jazz*) le rythme/le beat 3. *F that's off my beat*, ce n'est pas mon rayon 4. *V* to have a beat on, être en érection*/avoir le gourdin/bander. (*See* **dead-beat**)

beat[2] [biːt] *vtr* 1. *P to beat it*, s'enfuir*/se tirer; *beat it!* file!/décampe!/tire-toi!/fous le camp! 2. *F that beats everything/that takes some beating*, c'est le comble/c'est le bouquet 3. *F can you beat it!* ça alors!/faut le faire! 4. *F* (*it*) *beats me*, ça me dépasse/*P* j'en sais foutre rien! *it beats me how you can do that!* je ne comprends pas que tu puisses faire ça! 5. *F to beat about the bush*, s'égarer/tourner autour du pot; *let's not beat about the bush!* ne nous égarons pas; allons droit au but/aux faits. (*See* **dummy 5; meat 3**)

beat-box ['biːtbɒks] *n F* magnéto (stéréo) portatif.

beat off ['biːt'ɒf] *vi V* se masturber*/se

branler.

beat-up ['biːtʌp] *a F* usé jusqu'à la corde; *a beat-up old car*, une vieille voiture*/une vieille guimbarde/un tas de ferraille.

beat up ['biːt'ʌp] *vtr F* 1. battre*/rosser/tabasser (qn); *he was beaten up by the cops*, les flics l'ont passé à tabac 2. *to beat it up*, faire les quatre cents coups.

beaut [bjuːt] I *a Austr F* beau*/bath; *the weather was beaut*, il faisait un temps super; *it's been beaut*, ça a été génial/merveilleux II *n esp Austr F* (= *beauty*) 1. qch *ou* qn de beau*; *she's a beaut!* quelle belle poupée! *it's a beaut!* c'est chouette/super! 2. coup* bien employé par un boxeur.

beauty ['bjuːtɪ] *n F* 1. *what a beauty!* quelle merveille! *that's a beauty of a black eye*, c'est un beau coquard qu'il a 2. *the beauty of this job is that...*, le plus beau de l'affaire c'est que...; *that's the beauty of it*, c'est ça le plus beau/c'est ça qui est formidable 3. *O* (*form of address*) *my beauty!* ma beauté!/ma jolie! *often Hum well, my old beauty!* alors, ma vieille! 4. *Euph Hum* **a pair of beauties**, une belle paire (de seins*)/des nénés *mpl* superbes.

beaver ['biːvə] *n* 1. *F* barbe*/barbouze *f* 2. *V* (*of woman*) poils *mpl* du pubis/barbu *m*; **beaver shot**, photo *f* du sexe* de la femme (*surt en gros plan*). (*See* **eager**)

bed[1] [bed] *n F* 1. *bed of roses*, la vie de château; *it's not exactly a bed of roses*, ce n'est pas tout du miel/du gâteau/de la tarte 2. *you got out of bed on the wrong side this morning*, tu t'es levé du pied gauche ce matin 3. *to go to bed with s.o.*, coucher/faire l'amour* avec qn; *all he ever thinks of is bed*, il ne pense qu'à faire l'amour*/il ne pense qu'à ça 4. *bed and breakfast: see* **bingo 26**. (*See* **feather-bed**)

bed[2] [bed] *vtr O P to bed s.o.*, faire l'amour* avec qn; *she's all right for bedding*, c'est une sacrée baiseuse.

beddable ['bedəbl] *a F* baisable.

bed-house ['bedhaʊs] *n esp NAm P* (*rare*) bordel*/boxon *m*.

bedsit ['bed'sɪt] *n F* (= *bedsitter*) garni *m*/meublé *m*; studio *m*.

bedworthy ['bedwɜːðɪ] *a O P* she's bed-worthy, elle est bonne à baiser/elle est baisable.

bee [biː] *n* 1. *P* (*Euph for* **bastard, bugger**) salaud*/salopard *m* 2. *F he thinks he's the bee's knees*, il ne se prend pas pour de la petite bière/pour de la crotte/pour de la merde. (*See* **cat** 6) 3. *P* bees and honey/ bees, (*RS = money*) argent*/fric *m*/flouse *m* 4. *F* to have a bee in one's bonnet, (*be obsessed with an idea*) avoir une idée fixe/une marotte; *O* (*be slightly mad*) être un peu timbré/avoir une araignée au plafond 5. *A P* to put the bee on s.o., taper qn pour de l'argent. (*See* **bird** 7; **queen**¹ 3)

Beeb [bi:b] *n F* the Beeb, la BBC (*British Broadcasting Corporation*). (*See* **Auntie**²)

beef¹ [bi:f] *n* 1. *F* to have plenty of beef, être fort* comme un bœuf/être costaud 2. *P* réclamation *f*/rouspétance *f*; he had a beef about the bill, il a fait un scandale/du foin pour l'addition.

beef² [bi:f] *vi P* grogner*/rouspéter/ ronchonner; stop beefing and get on with it! arrête de râler et remets-toi au boulot.

beef-bandit ['bi:fbændɪt] *n V =* **arse-bandit**.

beefcake ['bi:fkeɪk] *n P* beau mâle/beau mec. (*See* **cheesecake**)

beefer ['bi:fə] *n F* rouspéteur, -euse/râleur, -euse.

beef up ['bi:f'ʌp] *vtr F* corser (qch).

beefy ['bi:fɪ] *a F* (*a*) costaud/fort/balaise/ solide (*b*) bien en chair.

beer [bɪə] *n* 1. *P* to go on the beer, boire*/ picoler 2. *F* small beer, peu de chose/de la petite bière; he's small beer, really, il compte pour rien/pour du beurre, celui-là 3. *Br F* beer tokens/vouchers, (*one pound coins*) pièces *fpl* d'une livre; (*money*) argent*/fric *m*/pognon *m*.

beer belly ['bɪə'belɪ], **beer gut** ['bɪə'gʌt] *n F* gros ventre*/grosse brioche; what a huge beer gut he's got! qu'est-ce qu'il tient comme bide!

beer joint ['bɪə'dʒɔɪnt] *n NAm F* débit *m* de bière/brasserie *f*.

beer-up ['bɪərʌp] *n P* beuverie *f* (de bière)/ soûlerie *f*.

beeswax ['bi:zwæks] *n P* (*racing*) (*RS = betting tax*) taxe *f*/impôt *m* sur les paris.

beetle ['bi:tl] *vi F* to beetle (along), se dépêcher*/se grouiller/se trotter.

Beetle ['bi:tl] *n F* (*RTM*) (*small car manufactured by Volkswagen*) coccinelle *f*.

beetle-crushers ['bi:tl'krʌʃəz] *npl F* grosses chaussures*/écrase-merde *mpl*.

beetle off ['bi:tl'ɒf] *vi F* partir*/déguerpir/ ficher le camp.

beezer ['bi:zə] *n A P* 1. nez*/blair *m*/pif *m* 2.

visage*/tête*/fiole *f*.

beggar ['begə] *n* (*Euph for* **bugger**) *F* individu*; silly beggar! espèce d'imbécile/ d'abruti! poor beggar! pauvre type!/pauvre con! lucky beggar! le veinard!

beggar-my-neighbour ['begəmaɪ'neɪbə] *n P* (*RS = Labour (Exchange)*) on the beggar-my-neighbour, au chômage/au chômedu.

begob! [bɪ'gɒb], **begorra(h)!** [bɪ'gɒrə] *int F* (*considered to be characteristic of the Irish = by God*) bon Dieu!/nom de Dieu!

behind [bɪ'haɪnd, bə'haɪnd] *n F* fesses*/ postérieur *m*; to sit on one's behind (and do nothing), ne pas se manier/se magner le cul; come on, get up off your behind! allez, magne-toi le train/le popotin!

bejabbers! [bɪ'dʒæbəz], **bejabers!** [bɪ'dʒeɪbəz] *int Irish F =* **begob!**

bejesus! [bɪ'dʒi:zəs, bɪ'dʒeɪzəs] I *int Irish F =* **begob!** II *n NAm P* to knock the bejesus out of s.o., battre* qn comme plâtre/envoyer dormir qn.

belch [beltʃ] *vi esp NAm P* avouer*/cracher/ s'allonger.

bell¹ [bel] *n F* 1. that rings a bell, ça me dit quelque chose/ça me rappelle quelque chose 2. (*catchphrase*) pull the other one (*= leg*), it's got bells on! à d'autres! ça ne prend pas! 3. coup de téléphone*; give me a bell in the morning, passe-moi un coup de fil demain matin. (*See* **dumb-bell**)

bell² [bel] *vtr A P* to bell s.o., téléphoner qn/ passer un coup de fil à qn/bigophoner à qn.

bell-bottoms ['belbɒtəmz] *npl F* (*= bell-bottomed trousers*) pantalon* à pattes d'éléphant/à pattes d'éph'.

belly ['belɪ] *n F* 1. ventre*/panse *f*/bedaine *f* 2. Delhi belly/Bangkok belly, *Austr* Bali Belly, diarrhée*/chiasse *f*/courante *f*. (*See* **beer belly**; **go**² 6; **yellow-belly**)

bellyache¹ ['belieɪk] *n F* mal *m* au ventre/ au bide.

bellyache² ['belieɪk] *vi P* grogner*/ réclamer/ronchonner/rouspéter; he's always belly-aching, il râle toujours.

bellyacher ['belieɪkə] *n P* ronchonneur, -euse/rouspéteur, -euse/râleur, -euse.

bellyaching ['belieɪkɪŋ] *n P* rouspétance *f*.

bellybutton ['belɪ'bʌtn] *n F* nombril *m*.

bellyflop ['belɪflɒp] *n F* 1. (*swimming*) to do a belly-flop, faire un plat (ventre) 2. échec* total/bide *m*/fiasc *m*.

bellyful ['belɪfʊl] *n P* to have had a bellyful,

en avoir assez*/en avoir marre/en avoir ras le bol; **I've had a bellyful of your advice**, j'en ai plein le dos/le cul de tes conseils. (*See* **gutful**)

belly laugh ['belɪlɑːf] *n F* gros rire.

belt¹ [belt] *n* 1. *P* **to give s.o. a belt**, frapper/cogner qn; filer un gnon/une mandale/un pain à qn 2. *F* (*a*) **to hit s.o. below the belt**, donner un coup bas à qn (*b*) **his tactics were a bit below the belt**, sa tactique était plutôt déloyale; **that's a bit below the belt**, c'est un peu salaud 3. *F* **to tighten one's belt**, se serrer la ceinture/se l'accrocher 4. *P* (*not common*) l'acte sexuel/baise *f*/baisage *m* 5. *P* (*not common*) **endless belt**, fille* *ou* femme* de mœurs faciles/qui fait de l'abattage 6. *P* **to have a belt at sth**, s'attaquer à qch/tenter l'aventure.

belt² [belt] *vtr* 1. *P* attaquer* (qn)/sauter sur (qn) 2. *P* battre*/filer une raclée à (qn) 3. *P* faire l'amour* avec (qn)/sauter (qn) 4. *V* (*rare*) **to belt one's batter**, se masturber*/se taper la colonne 5. *NAm P* **to belt the grape**, boire* beaucoup/comme un trou; picoler.

belt along, down ['beltə'lɒŋ, 'daʊn] *vi F* aller à toute vitesse; **to belt down the motorway**, rouler à pleins gaz sur l'autoroute.

belting ['beltɪŋ] *n P* 1. volée *f* de coups*/raclée *f*/dérouillée *f* 2. défaite écrasante/raclée *f*.

belt off ['belt'ɒf] *vi P* s'enfuir*/se tirer/se carapater.

belt out ['belt'aʊt] *vtr F* **to belt out a song**, gueuler/beugler une chanson; chanter à pleins poumons.

belt up ['belt'ʌp] *vi P* se taire*/la boucler/la fermer; **belt up, will you!** la ferme!/boucle-la!/ta gueule!

bend¹ [bend] *n P* 1. **to go round the bend**, devenir fou*/perdre la boule; **that kid drives me round the bend**, ce gosse me rend fou*; **I'm driven round the bend by her incessant chatter**, son bavardage incessant me fait perdre la boule 2. **to go on a bend** = **to go on a bender**. (*See* **bender 1**)

bend² [bend] *vtr F* 1. **to bend the rules**, faire une une entorse au règlement 2. **to bend over backwards to please s.o.**, se mettre en quatre/se décarcasser (pour faire plaisir à qn). (*See* **bent 1; elbow 3**)

bender ['bendə] *n P* 1. soûlerie *f*; **to go on a bender**, aller se cuiter/se soûler; **he went on a real bender**, il a pris une sacrée cuite 2. (*RS = suspender = suspended sentence*)

condamnation* avec sursis; **six month bender**, (condamnation *f* à) six mois *mpl* (de prison) avec sursis. (*See* **hell-bender; mind-bender**)

bennie, benny ['benɪ] *n P* (*drugs*) cachet *m*/pilule *f* de Benzédrine* (*RTM*).

bent [bent] *a P* 1. malhonnête/pourri; **a bent copper**, un flic pourri/un ripou 2. (*stolen*) volé/fauché 3. homosexuel*; **did you know he was bent?** tu savais qu'il était pédé, toi? (*See* **cop¹ 1; nine-bob note**)

benz [benz] *n P* (*abbr = Benzedrine*) (*drugs*) Benzédrine* (*RTM*). (*See* **bennie**)

berk [bɜːk] *n P* (*also abbr of* **Berkeley Hunt**) individu bête*/gourde *f*/andouille *f*/ducon *m*; **what a berk!** quel crétin!/quelle nouille! (*See* **Berkeley Hunt**)

Berkeley Hunt ['bɜːklɪ-, 'bɑːklɪ'hʌnt] *n P* (*RS = cunt*) individu bête*/crétin, -ine/con *m*, conne *f*/connard, -arde/connasse *f*.

bernice ['bɜːnɪs] *n*, **bernies** ['bɜːnɪz] *npl P* (*drugs*) cocaïne*/coco *f*/poudre *f*/neige *f*.

berth [bɜːθ] *n* 1. *F* **to give s.o. a wide berth**, passer au large de qn/éviter qn à tout prix 2. *P* **soft/safe berth**, boulot *m* pépère/planque *f*/filon *m*.

Bertie ['bɜːtɪ] *Prn Br P* **to do a Bertie**, témoigner contre ses complices.

best [best] *n F* (*Iron catchphrase*) **and the best of British (luck) (to you)**, je te souhaite (bien) du plaisir.

bet [bet] *vtr & i F* 1. **you bet!** pour sûr!/tu parles!/(il) y a des chances!/un peu! 2. **I bet you don't!** tu parles (que tu le feras)! 3. **bet you I will!** tu paries (que je le fais)! 4. **you can bet your boots/your bottom dollar/your life**, tu peux y aller/je te fous mon billet que...; **I'll bet anything you like that...**, je te parie tout ce que tu veux que.../je te fous mon billet que... 5. **I bet!** je t'en fiche mon billet! 6. **want to/wanna bet?** tu t'alignes?/(qu'est-ce que) tu paries? (*See* **sweet 2**)

better ['betə] *a F* **better half**, (*wife*) épouse*/moitié *f*; (*husband*) mari*/moitié.

betty¹ ['betɪ] *n A P* passe-partout *m*/crochet *m*/rossignol *m*.

Betty² ['betɪ] *n O F* **that's all my eye and Betty Martin**, tout ça c'est des foutaises/de la blague. (*See* **eye 2**)

betwixt [bɪ'twɪkst] *adv F* **betwixt and between**, ni l'un ni l'autre/ni chèvre ni chou/mi-figue, mi-raisin.

bevvied up ['bevɪd'ʌp] *a P* **to get bevvied up**, boire* beaucoup/se soûler/se cuiter.

bevvy ['bevɪ] n P (beer, wine, etc) pot m/ verre m/coup m; we had a bevvy in the pub, on a été boire un coup/prendre un pot au bistrot; he had a few bevvies first, d'abord, il a bu un bon coup.

b.f., BF ['biː'ef] abbr F Euph for bloody fool. (See **bloody** I)

B-girl ['biːgɜːl] n NAm P = **bar-girl**.

bhang [bæŋ] n P (drugs) baby bhang/bhang ganja(h), marijuana*.

bi [baɪ] a P (= bisexual) bisexuel/à voile et à vapeur/jazz-tango. (See **ambidextrous**)

bib [bɪb] n F in one's best bib and tucker, sur son trente et un/tiré à quatre épingles/bien sapé.

bible-basher ['baɪblbæʃə], **bible-puncher** ['baɪblpʌntʃə] n F évangéliste m de carrefour/prêcheur agressif.

biccy, bicky ['bɪkɪ] n Br F (= biscuit) gâteau sec/biscuit m.

bicycle ['baɪsɪkl] n P = **bike** 4.

biddy ['bɪdɪ] n 1. F old biddy, vieille poule/ mémé f 2. P (red) biddy, vin rouge additionné d'alcool à brûler.

biff¹ [bɪf] n F coup* de poing/gnon m/beigne f/baffe f/mandale f.

biff² [bɪf] vtr F to biff s.o., frapper qn/ flanquer un gnon à qn; to biff s.o. on the nose, flanquer un coup de poing sur la figure de qn/ abîmer le portrait à qn.

big [bɪg] I a F 1. big bug/cheese/gun/hitter/ noise/potato/shot/wheel, personnage important/caïd m/grosse légume/gros bonnet/ (grosse) huile; he's the big man around here, c'est lui la grosse tête/le cerveau du coin; Mr Big/the big white chief, le grand manitou; Big Brother, grand frère 2. big mouth, gueulard m/grande gueule; why can't you keep your big mouth shut? pas moyen que tu la fermes/ boucles? 3. he's a big name in the music industry, il est très connu dans le monde de la musique 4. she's hit the big time, elle est arrivée/elle a bien réussi; she's made it big, elle a fait un triomphe/un malheur 5. to give s.o. a big hand, applaudir qn; they gave him a big hand, ils ont applaudi bien fort/ils l'ont acclamé 6. what's the big idea? à quoi ça rime?/ça ne va pas, non? 7. to earn big money, gagner un max/se faire plein de fric 8. big deal! et alors! that's no big deal, c'est pas dramatique/c'est pas bien difficile/c'est pas sorcier; that's big of you! on nous a gâtés, hein? 9. you big dummy/stiff/twit! gros bêta, va! 10. to be too big for one's boots, péter plus

haut que son derrière. (See **bloke** 3; **chief** 1; **house** 4; **smoke¹** 2; **stick¹** 2; **stink¹** 1; **way** II 2) II adv F 1. to talk big, faire l'important/se faire mousser/crâner 2. to go down big/to go over big, réussir/avoir un succès fou; his idea went down big with the boss, le patron a été emballé par son idée/a trouvé son idée géniale 3. to think big, viser haut/voir grand.

Big Band ['bɪgbænd] n F orchestre m de jazz (comportant vingt musiciens au maximum). (See **one-man**)

Big C ['bɪg'siː] n P (drugs) cocaïne*/coco f/ neige f.

Big D ['bɪg'diː] n P (drugs) LSD*/acide m.

biggie, biggy ['bɪgɪ] n F 1. NAm that's a biggie, c'est vachement dur 2. NAm he's a biggy, c'est un type important/un gros bonnet 3. he's got a biggy, il est en érection*/il bande/il a la trique.

Big H ['bɪg'eɪtʃ] n P (drugs) héroïne*/H f.

bighead ['bɪghed] n P crâneur, -euse; he's such a bighead, il ne se prend pas pour de la merde.

big-headed ['bɪg'hedɪd] a P prétentieux*/ vaniteux/suffisant/crâneur.

big-note¹ ['bɪg'nəʊt] a Austr F 1. big-note man, richard m/rupin m 2. big-note artist, (smooth talker) baratineur, -euse; (one who talks nonsense) déconneur, -euse.

big-note² ['bɪg'nəʊt] vtr Austr F chanter les louanges de (qn)/faire mousser (qn); to big-note oneself, se vanter/se faire mousser.

big P ['bɪg'piː] n P (= parole) Jur liberté conditionnelle.

big-time ['bɪg'taɪm] a F 1. big-time operator, gros(se) trafiquant(e)/gros bonnet 2. big-time racketeer, chef m de bande/caïd m. (See **big I 4**; **small-time**)

big-timer ['bɪg'taɪmə] n F 1. = big noise (**big I 1**); to be a big-timer, être bien lancé. (See **small-timer**) 2. (sport, etc) joueur, -euse professionnel(le)/pro mf.

bigwig ['bɪgwɪg] n F personnage important/gros bonnet/grosse légume/huile f.

big Z's ['bɪg'ziːz] npl P (sleep) sommeil m; time for the big Z's, l'heure d'aller au dodo/au pieu.

bike [baɪk] n 1. F bicyclette f/vélo m 2. F motocyclette f/moto f/meule f 3. P on your bike!/on yer bike! (go away!) tire-toi!/fiche le camp!/casse-toi!/barre-toi! (hurry up!) magne-toi!/grouille-toi! 4. P (loose woman) grue f/salope f/Marie-couche-toi-là f. (See town bike)

biker ['baɪkə], **bikie** ['baɪkɪ] *n P* motocycliste *mf*/motard *m*.

bilge [bɪldʒ] *n P* 1. bêtises*/foutaises *fpl*/eau *f* de bidet/sornettes *fpl*; **to talk bilge,** dire des bêtises; **you do talk a lot of bilge,** tu débloques 2. boisson *f* insipide/pipi *m* de chat/bibine *f*.

bilge-water ['bɪldʒwɔːtə] *n P* = **bilge 2.**

bill¹ [bɪl] *n* 1. *F* **to top the bill/to be top of the bill,** *(of actor)* avoir la vedette/être en haut de l'affiche; *(be wonderful)* être sensass/super 2. *F* **to fit/to fill the bill,** remplir toutes les conditions/faire l'affaire 3. *P* **the Bill:** *see* **Bill² 4.** *NAm P* nez*/pif *m*/blair *m*. *(See* **foot² 1)**

Bill² [bɪl] *Prn P* **the Bill, old Bill,** agent* de police/flic *m*/poulet *m*; la police*/la flicaille/la maison poulaga. *(See* **Uncle 9)**

billet ['bɪlɪt] *n F* 1. *(wartime)* **to get a safe billet,** s'embusquer 2. *(not common)* emploi *m*; **to get a cushy billet,** se dégoter une bonne planque.

Billingsgate ['bɪlɪŋzgeɪt] *Prn F (London fish market)* langage *m* de poissarde; **to talk Billingsgate,** parler comme une poissarde.

billio ['bɪlɪəʊ] *n F* = **billy-o.**

billy ['bɪlɪ] *n* 1. *A P* mouchoir*/blave *m* 2. *Austr F (a)* (= *billycan*) gamelle *f*/bouilloire *f* (à thé).

billy-o, billy-oh ['bɪlɪəʊ] *n O F* **like billy-o,** très fort; avec acharnement; **it's raining like billy-o,** il pleut des cordes/à vache qui pisse; **he's rushing around like billy-o,** il se démène comme un (beau) diable.

bimbo ['bɪmbəʊ] *n P* 1. individu*/gus *m*/oiseau *m* 2. individu bête*/andouille *f*/schnock *m* 3. *(a)* (jolie) jeune femme* (qui n'a rien dans la tête)/minette *f (b)* petite amie d'un homme plus âgé/môme *f*.

bin¹ [bɪn] *n P* = **loony-bin.**

bin² [bɪn] *vtr Br* jeter*/balancer/ficher en l'air.

bind [baɪnd] *n F* 1. *(person)* crampon *m*/casse-pieds *m*/scie *f* 2. *(thing)* scie *f*; **what a bind!** quelle corvée! **it's an awful bind having to do that,** c'est casse-pieds/quelle barbe d'avoir à faire ça 3. **to be in a bit of a bind,** être dans le pétrin.

bindle ['bɪndl] *n NAm P* 1. *A* baluchon *m* (de clochard) 2. *O (drugs)* sachet *m* ou paquet *m* d'héroïne* 3. *O* **bindle stiff,** clochard*/clodo(t) *m*.

bing [bɪŋ] *n NAm A P* cachot *m* (de

prison*)/mitard *m*.

binge¹ [bɪndʒ] *n F* réjouissances*/bombe *f*; **to go on a binge,** faire la foire/la bombe.

binge² [bɪndʒ] *vi F* manger abondamment*/s'empiffrer; **to binge on junk food,** se bourrer de cochonneries.

bingo ['bɪŋgəʊ] *n* sorte *f* de loto public. *The following terms are used in this game:* **Kelly's eye/Little Jimmy** = 1; **buckle my shoe/**O **dirty old Jew/Little Boy Blue** = 2; **dearie me!** = 3; **knock at the door** = 4; **Jack's alive** = 5; **Tom Mix** = 6; **lucky seven** = 7; **one fat lady** = 8; **doctor's orders** = 9; **Downing Street** = 10; **legs eleven** = 11; **one doz** = 12; **unlucky for some** = 13; **she's lovely** *or* **never been kissed** = 16; **the age to catch 'em** = 17; **key of the door** = 21; **all the twos/dinky-doo** = 22; **bed and breakfast/**A **half-a-crown/**A **half-a-dollar** = 26; **you're doing fine** = 29; **all the threes** = 33; **dirty whore** = 34; **all the steps** = 39; **life begins** = 40; **life's begun** = 41; **all the fours/droopy-drawers** = 44; **halfway** = 45; **bullseye/bunghole** = 50; **all the varieties/Heinz** = 57; **Brighton line** = 59; **old-age pension** = 65; **clickety-click** = 66; **any way round** = 69; **was she worth it?** = 76; **sunset strip** = 77; **two fat ladies** = 88; **all but one/nearly there** = 89; **top of the shop/as far as we go** = 99; **bingo!** jeu!/gagné!

bin(n)s [bɪnz] *npl P* 1. lunettes*/binocles *fpl* 2. *(binoculars)* jumelles *fpl* 3. yeux*/mirettes *fpl*.

bint [bɪnt] *n P* 1. *Pej* femme*/gonzesse *f*; **she's a silly bint,** c'est une connasse, celle-là 2. *A Pej* petite amie/poule *f*.

bird [bɜːd] *n* 1. *F* individu*/type *m*/oiseau *m*/moineau *m*; **who's that old bird?** qu'est-ce que c'est que ce vieux type? **he's a queer old bird,** c'est un drôle de vieux numéro 2. *O F (a)* jeune femme*/nana *f*/gonzesse *f (b)* compagne *f*/petite amie; minette *f*; **who was that bird I saw you with?** qui c'était la nana avec qui je t'ai vu/qui t'accompagnait? 3. *F* **to get the bird,** *(be dismissed from one's job)* être renvoyé/sacqué; *(in theatre)* se faire siffler 4. *F* **to give s.o. the bird,** *(dismiss)* envoyer promener qn/envoyer qn au bain; *(dismiss s.o. from post)* renvoyer qn/sacquer qn; *(in theatre)* huer qn/siffler qn 5. *P* **to do bird,** faire de la prison*/faire de la taule; **he's done bird,** il a fait de la taule/c'est un ancien taulard. *(See* **birdlime)** 6. *F* **it's (strictly) for the birds,** c'est seulement pour les cruches 7. **the birds and the bees,** éléments sexuels de base/les papillons et les petits oiseaux; to learn all about the birds and the bees, apprendre que les enfants ne naissent pas dans les choux 8. *F* a little bird told me, mon petit doigt me l'a dit 9. *F* the bird has flown, l'oiseau s'est envolé. (*See* **dicky-bird; dolly-bird; early; feather**[1] **1; gallowsbird; home-bird; jailbird; jaybird; lovebird; night-bird; snowbird; whirlybird; yardbird**)

birdbrain ['bɜːdbreɪn] *n F* individu bête*/ tête de linotte.

birdbrained ['bɜːdbreɪnd] *a F* bête*/ farfelu; écervelé/évaporé.

bird-cage ['bɜːdkeɪdʒ] *n P* cellule *f* de prison*/cellotte *f*.

bird-fancier ['bɜːdfænsɪə] *n P* juponnard *m*/coureur *m* de filles/dragueur *m*.

birdie ['bɜːdɪ] *n P* watch the birdie! (*for photograph*) un beau sourire!/attention, le petit oiseau va sortir!

birdie-powder ['bɜːdɪpaʊdə] *n O P* (*drugs*) héroïne* *ou* morphine* en poudre.

birdlime ['bɜːdlaɪm] *n P* (*RS = time*) 1. *O* how's the bird-lime? quelle heure est-il?/quai d'Orsay? 2. = **bird 5**.

bird's-eye ['bɜːdzaɪ] *n P* (*drugs*) petite quantité de drogue.

bird-watcher ['bɜːdwɒtʃə] *n P* = **birdfancier**.

birthday ['bɜːθdeɪ] *n F* to be in one's birthday suit, être nu*/être à poil/être dans le costume d'Adam.

biscuit ['bɪskɪt] *n* 1. *F* you take the biscuit, tu as/tu remportes la palme! that takes the biscuit! ça c'est le comble!/le bouquet! 2. *NAm P* revolver*/flingue *m*/pétard *m*.

bish [bɪʃ] *n* 1. (*abbr of bishop*) évêque *m* 2. *O F* bévue*/bourde *f*/gaffe *f*.

bishop ['bɪʃəp] *n V* to flog/to bash the bishop, se masturber*/se secouer le bonhomme/faire sauter la cervelle de Charles-le-Chauve. (*See* **actress**)

bit [bɪt] I *a F* (*films, theatre*) a bit part, un rôle secondaire/un panne; a bit player, un(e) figurant(e) II *n* 1. *P* a (nice) bit of all right/ **crumpet/fluff/skirt/stuff/tail** (*pretty young woman*) un beau brin de fille/un beau petit lot/un prix de Diane; (*making love*) l'acte sexuel/baisage *m*; he's only after a bit of **crumpet/tail**, il ne s'intéresse qu'à baiser 2. to have a bit on the side, (*have a lover*) avoir une maîtresse/un amant quelque part; (*be unfaithful*) tromper sa femme/son mari/

donner des coups de canif dans le contrat 3. *F* a bit much, (*expensive*) un peu cher*; (*exaggerated*) un peu exagéré/un peu fort; it was a bit much, all the same! c'était un peu fort, tout de même!/faut pas charrier, quand même! it was all a bit of a laugh really, c'était plutôt une rigolade 4. *F* he's a bit of an idiot, il est un peu bête*/ce n'est pas une lumière; he's a bit of a lad, c'est un chaud lapin/un sacré dragueur 5. *NAm F* two bits, pièce *f* de 25 cents. (*See* **two-bit**) 6. *NAm F* condamnation* à la prison/purge *f* 7. *F* to be thrilled to bits, être ravi/être aux anges; I was thrilled to bits by it, je trouvais ça extra/ génial. (*See* **bum**[1] **II 2; rude 1; side 1, 2; spare II; stray; threepenny-bits; treybits**)

bitch[1] [bɪtʃ] *n P* 1. *Pej* femme*/salope *f*/ garce *f*/tordue *f*/chameau *m*/peau *f* de chien; you bitch! salope!/garce! what a bitch she can be! ce qu'elle peut être vache! his mother is a real bitch! sa mère est une vraie peau de chien! 2. this job is a real bitch! quelle saloperie de boulot! that bitch of a car! cette putain de bagnole! (*See* **s.o.b.; son of a bitch**) 3. *NAm* it's a bitch! (*excellent*) c'est super!/c'est chié!

bitch[2] [bɪtʃ] *vi & tr P* 1. (*grumble*) grogner*/rouspéter/râler; stop bitching! arrête de rouspéter! 2. (*trick, deceive*) tromper*/entuber/rouler (qn); to bitch s.o. out of sth, refaire qn de qch 3. = **bitch up**.

bitchiness ['bɪtʃɪnɪs] *n P* saloperie *f*/coup *m* en vache/vacherie *f*.

bitch up ['bɪtʃʌp] *vtr P* saboter/bousiller (qch); you've bitched that up nicely! tu l'as joliment salopé!/c'est du joli travail!/c'est du beau travail!

bitchy ['bɪtʃɪ] *a P* (*a*) (*grumbling*) rouspéteur/râleur (*b*) (*unpleasant*) moche/ rosse/vache; a bitchy remark, une vanne/une pique/une vacherie.

bite[1] [baɪt] *n* 1. *O P* to put the bite on s.o., (*borrow*) emprunter* à qn/taper qn; (*blackmail*) faire chanter qn; (*pressurize*) serrer la vis à qn 2. *F* to have a bite to eat, manger* un morceau/casser la croûte. (*See* **cherry 2; fleabite**)

bite[2] [baɪt] I *vtr* 1. *F* (*fig*) to get bitten, se faire avoir; I've been badly bitten, (*deceived, tricked, fooled*) j'ai été roulé/eu; on m'a mis dedans; once bitten twice shy, (*catchphrase*) chat échaudé craint l'eau froide 2. *F* what's biting you? quelle mouche te pique?/qu'est-ce qui te prend? **3.** *P* **to bite s.o. for money,** taper/torpiller qn **II** *vi NAm P* copier; **he's bitin'**, il a piqué l'idée de qn d'autre. (*See* **dust¹ 4**)

bite off ['baɪt'ɒf] *F* **1. to bite s.o.'s head off**, injurier* qn/rembarrer qn **2. to bite off more than one can chew**, avoir les yeux plus grands que le ventre.

bitser ['bɪtsə] *n Austr F* chien* bâtard/ corniaud *m*/klebs *m*.

bitsy-witsy ['bɪtsɪ'wɪtsɪ] *n F* = **itsy-bitsy**.

bitty ['bɪtɪ] *a F* (*book, play, etc*) décousu/ hétéroclite/de bric et de broc.

bivvy¹ ['bɪvɪ] *n Br P* (= *bivouac*) (*Scouts & Armed forces*) bivouac *m*.

bivvy² ['bɪvɪ] *vi Br P* (= *to bivouac*) bivouaquer.

biz [bɪz] *n* **1.** *P* (= *business*) **the biz**, le bisness/le truc. (*See* **showbiz**) **2.** (*drugs*) artillerie *f*/kit *m*.

bizzie ['bɪzɪ] *n P* agent* de police/flic *m*/ poulet *m*. (*See* **busy**)

blab (off) ['blæb('ɒf)] *vtr & i P* **1. to blab one's mouth off**, révéler un secret/lâcher le morceau **2.** bavarder*/jaser/jacter.

blabbermouth ['blæbəmaʊθ] *n F* (*a*) personne *f* qui laisse échapper un secret/ cafardeur, -euse qui ne sait pas tenir sa langue (*b*) bavard*/jaspineur *m*.

black¹ [blæk] **I** *a* **1.** *F* **a black mark**, un mauvais point **2. black spot** (*a*) *F* (*on the roads*) endroit dangereux/point noir (*b*) *A P* fumerie *f* d'opium* **3.** *P* **black stuff** (*a*) (*drugs*) opium*/noir *m* (*b*) *Br* macadam (gou-dronné) **4. black and tan** (*a*) *F* (*beer*) pana-ché *m* de bière brune et blonde (*b*) *P* (*drugs*) amphétamine* (*c*) *Hist F* **Black and Tans**, milice chargée de l'ordre en Irlande (*c.* 1920) **5.** *F* **black diamonds**, charbon *m* **6.** *P Pej* **black as a nigger**/*Austr* **as black as an abo's arsehole**, noir comme dans le trou du cul d'un nègre. (*See* **velvet 2**) **II** *n* **1.** *F occ Pej* Noir(e)*/nègre *m*/bougnoul *m* **2.** *A P* chantage *m*; **to put the black on s.o.**, faire du chantage **3.** *F* **in the black**, à l'actif *m*; **my account is in the black**, mon compte est en crédit **4.** *F* **in black and white**, noir sur blanc **5.** *P* (*drugs*) opium*/noir *m*; haschisch* (noir)/shit *m*.

black² [blæk] *vtr F* = **blacklist**.

blackbirding ['blækbɜːdɪŋ] *n Hist P* trafic *m* d'esclaves noirs.

blackbirds ['blækbɜːdz] *npl P* **1.** *Hist* esclaves noirs **2.** (*drugs*) amphétamines*/ speed *m*.

black box ['blæk'bɒks] *n F* (*aviation*) (= *flight recorder*) enregistreur *m* de vol/boîte noire.

blackleg¹ ['blækleg] *n F* briseur, -euse de grève/jaune *mf*.

blackleg² ['blækleg] *vi F* briser une grève.

blacklist ['blæklɪst] *vtr F* mettre sur la liste noire.

Black Maria ['blækmə'raɪə] *n F* car* de police/panier *m* à salade.

black-out ['blækaʊt] *n F* **1.** évanouissement *m* **2.** (*a*) panne *f* d'électricité/de secteur (*b*) (*wartime*) camouflage *m* des lumières/black-out *m*.

black out ['blæk'aʊt] *vtr & i F* **1.** s'évanouir*/tourner de l'œil/tomber dans les pommes **2.** couper l'électricité (dans un quartier, un immeuble, etc); **to be blacked out**, être en panne d'électricité/de secteur; se trouver dans le noir.

blag¹ [blæg] *n P* (*armed robbery*) vol* à main armée/braquage *m*/hold-up *m*.

blag² [blæg] *vtr P* (*to rob with violence*) voler* à main armée/braquer.

blagger ['blægə] *n P* (*armed robber*) braqueur *m*.

blah(-blah) ['blɑː('blɑː)] *n F* blabla(bla) *m*/boniment *m*/baratin *m*.

blank¹ [blæŋk] *n F* **to draw a blank**, échouer/faire chou blanc; **we've looked, but up to now we've drawn a complete blank**, on a bien cherché, mais jusqu'à présent c'est le bide complet.

blank² [blæŋk] *vtr Br F* (*snub*) snober; **she blanked me**, elle a fait semblant de ne pas me voir.

blankety(-blank) ['blæŋkɪtɪ('blæŋk)] *a & n O F Euph for* **damn(ed), bloody,** *etc*.

blarney¹ ['blɑːnɪ] *n F* flatterie *f*/cajolerie *f*/ boniment *m*/pommade *f*; **he's full of the blarney/he's kissed the blarney stone**, il a la langue bien pendue/il sait baratiner.

blarney² ['blɑːnɪ] *vi F* flatter*/cajoler/ bonimenter/passer de la pommade.

blast¹ [blɑːst] *n P* **1.** (*drugs*) piqûre*/ piquouse *f*/shoot *m*/fixe *m* **2.** longue bouffée d'une cigarette* de marijuana/taffe *f*; **here, have a blast of this joint**, tiens, tire-toi une bouffée de ce joint **3.** effet puissant d'une drogue/flash *m* **4.** (*party*) boum *f* **5.** (*enjoy-able experience*) **we had a blast at that party!** on s'est vachement bien marrés/super éclatés à cette boum!

blast² [blɑːst] *vtr & i P* **1.** (*esp sport*) battre

à plate(s) couture(s)/écrabouiller 2. (*drugs*) (*a*) se piquer*/se shooter (*b*) to blast (on) a joint, fumer de la marijuana*/tirer sur un stick 3. **blast (it)!** zut!/la barbe!/merde! **blast you!** va te faire voir! **blast him!** ce qu'il est chiatique/chiant! **damn and blast!** merde (alors)!/bordel!

blasted ['blɑːstɪd] *a P* 1. fichu/sacré/ maudit; **it's a blasted nuisance,** c'est sa- crément embêtant/enquiquinant/casse-pieds; **he's a blasted nuisance,** il est méchamment enquiquinant; **a blasted idiot,** le roi des imbéciles 2. drogué*/envapé/défoncé.

blather¹ ['blæðə] *n F* bêtises*/fadaises *fpl*/ blablabla *m*.

blather² ['blæðə] *vi F* dire des bêtises*/ débloquer; **to go blathering on,** raconter n'importe quoi; débloquer à pleins tubes.

blazes ['bleɪzɪz] *npl O F* 1. **go to blazes!** aller au diable!/va te faire voir! 2. **what the blazes...!** que diable...! 3. **to run like blazes,** courir très vite*/comme si on avait le feu au derrière.

bleat [bliːt] *vi F* dénoncer*/moucharder.

bleed ['bliːd] *vi F Iron* **my heart bleeds (for you)!** tu me fais pleurer!/tu me fends le cœur!

bleeder ['bliːdə] *n P* 1. salaud *m*; **poor bleeder!** pauvre type! **silly bleeder!** espèce de con! 2. **wait till I catch the little bleeder!** le petit morveux ne perd rien pour attendre!

bleeding, bleedin' ['bliːdɪŋ, 'bliːdn] *a P* (*intensifier*) 1. **don't be a bleeding fool!** ne fais pas le con! 2. **it's bleeding/bleedin' beautiful,** c'est vachement beau/c'est super chouette 3. **it's bleeding marvellous, isn't it!** super, hein! 4. **that bleeding car!** cette putain de bagnole!

blessed *a F* 1. [blest] **well I'm blessed!** ça par exemple!/ça alors! **I'm/I'll be blessed if I know,** comment veux-tu que je le sache! 2. ['blesɪd] **what a blessed nuisance!** quel fichu embêtement! **that blessed boy!** il est enquiquinant/empoisonnant, ce gamin! **the whole blessed day,** toute la sainte journée.

blest [blest] *a F* = **blessed 1.**

blether ['bleðə] *n & v* (*Scottish*) *F* = **bla-ther¹,².**

blighter ['blaɪtə] *n F* individu*/type *m*/zèbre *m*; **poor blighter!** pauvre type!/pauvre diable! **lucky blighter!** le veinard! **you rotten blight-er!** salopard, va!

Blighty ['blaɪtɪ] *n F* (*Mil wartime*) l'An-gleterre *f*/le pays.

blimey! ['blaɪmɪ] *excl P* zut alors!/mince alors!/merde alors! (*See* **cor!** (*b*); **gor-blimey!**)

blimp [blɪmp] *n F* 1. (*also* **Colonel Blimp**) vieille culotte de peau 2. (*fat person*) bouboule *mf*/patapouf *m*.

blind¹ [blaɪnd] **I** *a* 1. *F* **blind date,** rendez-vous*/rancart *m* avec qn qu'on ne connaît pas 2. *F* **blind (drunk),** complètement ivre*/ rétamé 3. *F* **to turn a blind eye (to sth),** fermer les yeux (sur qch) 4. *F* **he didn't take a blind bit of notice,** il n'a même pas fait attention/il n'a même pas remarqué. (*See* **eye 9**) **II** *n* 1. *F* couverture*/couverte *f*/couvrante *f* 2. *P* soûlerie *f*; **to go on a blind,** aller se soûler 3. *P* **to put the blinds on s.o.,** mettre un bandeau sur les yeux de qn.

blind² [blaɪnd] *vi P* 1. jurer/sacrer 2. conduire avec insouciance; **blind and brake driver,** chauffard *m*.

blinder ['blaɪndə] *n* 1. *P* (*celebrations*) réjouissances*/bamboche *f*; (*drunken bout*) soûlerie *f* 2. (*racing*) cheval dopé.

blinders ['blaɪndəz] *a O P* (Harry) **blinders,** complètement ivre*/rétamé/bituré.

blindside ['blaɪndsaɪd] *vtr NAm P* (*catch unawares*) surprendre/piéger; (*astonish*) scier/souffler.

blink [blɪŋk] *n F* **on the blink,** qui ne marche pas/qui est en rade/qui déconne; **my phone's on the blink,** mon téléphone est détraqué.

blinkers ['blɪŋkəz] *npl O F* yeux*/quinquets *mpl*.

blinking ['blɪŋkɪŋ] *a F* (*Euph for* **bloody** I, II) 1. **blinking idiot!** espèce d'idiot!/de crétin! 2. **blinking heck!** mince alors! 3. a **blinking cheek/nerve,** un sacré culot 4. a **blinking good film,** un film vachement chouette.

blister ['blɪstə] *n NAm A P* prostituée*/pute *f*. (*See* **skin¹ 11**)

blithering ['blɪðərɪŋ] *a F* **you blithering idiot!** bougre d'idiot!/espèce d'abruti!

blitz [blɪts] *n F* grand nettoyage; **I had a blitz on the bedroom,** j'ai nettoyé la chambre de fond en comble.

blitzed [blɪtst] *a F* ivre*/beurré/raide.

blob [blɒb] *n P* 1. (*cricket*) zéro *m*; **to score a blob,** ne pas marquer de points 2. (*corpse*) refroidi *m*/macchab *m*/viande (froide) 3. ulcère *m*/gros bouton.

block [blɒk] *n P* 1. tête*/caboche *f*; **to knock s.o.'s block off,** casser/amocher la figure à qn; **I'll knock your block off if you do that!** je te casserai la gueule si tu fais ça! **off one's block**, fou*/toqué 2. **to do one's block**, se mettre en colère*/en rogne/en pétard 3. *O* (*drugs*) (*a*) paquet *m* de morphine* (*b*) semelle *f* de haschisch* 4. *V* **block and tackle**, sexe de l'homme*/service *m* trois pièces 5. (*prisons*) **the block**, (*solitary confinement*) isolement *m* (cellulaire). (*See* **chip 6**)

blockbust ['blɒkbʌst] *vi NAm P* (*real estate*) persuader les Blancs de vendre leurs maisons de peur que des Noirs s'installent dans leur quartier.

blockbuster ['blɒk'bʌstə] *n P* 1. bombe très puissante/marmite *f* 2. (*a*) (*person*) personne très efficace et pleine de dynamisme; **she's a real blockbuster**, elle est d'un dynamisme à tout casser/c'est un véritable ouragan, cette femme (*b*) idée *f ou* discours *m*, *etc* percutant(e) *ou* qui a un succès fou; film *m ou* spectacle *m* à gros budget; 'Brideshead Revisited' **was one of ITV's blockbusters**, 'Brideshead Revisited" était une des superproductions de la ITV 3. *NAm* agent immobilier qui achète des propriétés des Blancs dans un quartier résidentiel pour les revendre ensuite à des Noirs qui cherchent à s'y installer.

blocked [blɒkt] *a P* drogué*/camé/défoncé.

blockhead ['blɒk'hed] *n F* imbécile*/crétin, -ine; **you blockhead!** espèce de nouille!

bloke [bləʊk] *n* 1. *F* individu*/type *m*/mec *m*; **a good bloke**, un brave type/un bon zigue; **he's a great bloke**, c'est un type sensass/génial 2. *O F* (*Navy*) **the Bloke**, le Patron 3. *O P* (*drugs*) **big bloke**, cocaïne*.

blood [blʌd] *n* 1. *F* **to be after s.o.'s blood**, vouloir la peau de qn 2. *F* **to get s.o.'s blood up/to make s.o.'s blood boil**, mettre qn en colère*/faire fulminer qn; **to have one's blood up**, être en colère*/voir rouge; **it gets my blood up/it makes my blood boil**, ça me rend furax 3. *F* **to make s.o.'s blood run cold**, glacer le sang à qn 4. **to sweat blood**, suer sang et eau; **travailler dur*** 5. *F* **blood (brother)** = **soul brother**. (*See* **Nelson**)

bloody ['blʌdɪ] I *a P* fichu/foutu; **you bloody fool!** espèce de couillon! **to play the bloody fool**, faire le con; **he's a bloody nuisance**, il est vachement chiant; **stop that bloody row!** arrêtez ce bordel!/arrêtez ce ramdam! **the bloody car's broken down again!** cette putain de bagnole est encore tombée en panne; **bosses are all the bloody same!** ces foutus patrons/ces putains de patrons, c'est toujours

la même histoire!/c'est toujours le même tabac! **the bloody limit**, la fin des haricots. (*See* **Mary 4**) II *adv P* vachement; **I feel bloody**, j'ai pas la frite!/j'ai pas la pêche! **not bloody likely!** pas de danger!/tu te fous de ma gueule? **it's bloody hot!** il fait une chaleur à crever! **bloody awful weather!** fichu temps!

bloody-minded ['blʌdɪ'maɪndɪd] *a P* pas commode; **he's a bloody-minded sod**, c'est un mauvais coucheur/c'est un emmerdeur/il emmerde tout le monde.

bloody-mindedness ['blʌdɪ'maɪndɪdnɪs] *n P* sale caractère *m*/caractère de cochon; **he did it out of sheer bloody-mindedness**, il ne l'a fait que pour emmerder/faire chier le monde.

bloomer ['bluːmə] *n F* bévue*/gaffe *f*/bourde *f*; **he's made a real bloomer**, il s'est complètement gour(r)é/il s'est complètement fichu dedans.

blooming ['bluːmɪŋ] *a & adv F* (*Euph for* **bloody I, II**) **you're a blooming genius!** t'es super doué, toi!

blooper ['bluːpə] *n NAm F* erreur *f*/gaffe *f*.

blotto ['blɒtəʊ] *a F* complètement ivre*/rétamé; **he's completely blotto**, il est complètement paf/bourré à zéro/beurré comme un petit Lu.

blow¹ [bləʊ] *n P* 1. (*drugs*) (*a*) cannabis*/kif *m*/shit *m* (*b*) cocaïne*/coke *f*/neige *f* 2. tabac*/perle *f*.

blow² [bləʊ] *vtr & i* 1. *F* (*Euph for* **blast² 3**) **blow the expense!** au diable l'avarice! **blow me!/well I'm blowed!** ça par exemple!/ça alors! (*See* **blessed 1**); **generous be blowed**, **he's as mean as they come!** généreux, mon œil! il est radin comme tout/comme pas un! **I'll be blowed if I'll do it!** pas question que je le fasse! **blow it!** zut!/la barbe!/merde! 2. *F* **to blow one's top/lid/stack/a fuse**, se mettre en colère*/piquer une crise/sortir de ses gonds/disjoncter 6. *P* **to blow the gaff**, vendre la mèche; lâcher le morceau; **to blow the gaff on**, dénoncer*/donner/balancer (qn); exposer publiquement (un scandale, etc); **to blow s.o.'s cover**, révéler la véritable identité de qn 7. *P* dépenser*/gaspiller (de l'argent); **he blew fifty quid on that**, il a claqué cinquante livres pour ça 8. *P* bousiller/saboter/louper; **we**

should have won but we blew it, on aurait dû gagner mais on a tout raté/on s'est planté 9. *P* priser une drogue/(s)chnouffer; **to blow a joint**, fumer un joint 10. *P* **to blow s.o.'s mind** (*a*) (*esp under hallucinogenic drug*) faire planer qn (*b*) donner à qn une sensation de plaisir et d'euphorie (*c*) secouer qn; **their new album will really blow your mind!** leur nouvel album c'est le super-pied! 11. *P* **se masturber***/se branler 12. *V* faire une **fellation*** à (qn)/sucer (qn)/tailler une pipe à (qn). (*See* **gaff 3**; **lid 2**; **stack 2**; **tank 1**; **top¹ 2**)

blow away ['bləʊə'weɪ] *vtr P* tuer*/descendre/flinguer (qn); ficher/flanquer/foutre (qn) en l'air.

blower ['bləʊə] *n P* téléphone*/ronfleur *m*/tube *m*; **to get on the blower to s.o.**, passer un coup de bigophone à qn. (*See* **mind-blower**)

blowhard ['bləʊhɑːd] *n NAm P* vantard*/crâneur, -euse; gueulard, -arde.

blow in ['bləʊ'ɪn] *vtr & i P* arriver* en coup de vent/s'amener à l'improviste; **look what the wind's blown in!** regarde qui se ramène/s'amène!

blow-job ['bləʊ'dʒɒb] *n V* fellation*/pipe *f*; **she gave him a blow-job**, elle lui a taillé une pipe/elle lui a taillé une plume/elle lui a fait un pompier.

blown away [bləʊnə'weɪ] *a P* 1. tué/démoli/effacé 2. étonné/époustouflé.

blow off ['bləʊ'ɒf] *P* **I** *vi* péter*/cloquer **II** *vtr* **to blow one's mouth off**, parler* trop/dégoiser/dévider/trop l'ouvrir. (*See* **steam 1**)

blow-out ['bləʊaʊt] *n F* gueuleton *m*/ripaille *f*/balthazar *m*/grande bouffe; **to have a good blow-out**, manger* abondamment/gueuletonner/se faire un gueuleton.

blow-up ['bləʊʌp] *n F* 1. (accès *m* de) colère*/engueulade *f*/prise *f* de bec 2. *Phot* agrandissement *m*.

blow up ['bləʊ'ʌp] *F* **I** *vi* se mettre en colère*/exploser **II** *vtr* 1. réprimander*/passer un savon à (qn)/engueuler (qn) 2. *Phot* faire un agrandissement.

blub [blʌb] *vi F* pleurer*/chialer/pleurnicher.

bludge [blʌdʒ] *Austr P* **I** *vi* flâner/fainéanter/tirer au flanc **II** *vtr* taper/torpiller (qch à qn).

bludger ['blʌdʒə] *n Austr P* 1. fainéant, -ante/flemmard, -arde/tire-au-flanc *m* 2. (*parasite, scrounger*) parasite *m*/pique-assiette *mf*/torpilleur *m* 3. (*pimp*) souteneur*/mangeur *m* de blanc/Jules *m*. (*See* **dole-bludger**)

blue¹ [bluː] **I** *a* 1. *F* **blue film/movie**, film *m* porno/film de cul 2. *F* **to scream blue murder**, crier*/gueuler au charron 3. *F* **you can talk till you're blue in the face, I'm not going**, cause toujours, j'irai pas 4. *F* **(the) boys in blue**, agents *mpl* de police* (*en uniforme*)/les habillés 5. *P* **blue house**, bordel*/maison *f* de passe 6. *F* **once in a blue moon**, la semaine des quatre jeudis/tous les 36 du mois 7. *F* triste/cafardeux; **to feel blue**, avoir le cafard. (*See* **devil¹ 17**) 8. *F* (*politics*) **true blue**, Conservateur/de droite. (*See* **funk¹ 1**; **velvet 1**) **II** *n* 1. *P* (*drugs*) bleue *f*; **double blue**, mélange *m* d'amphétamine* et de barbiturique*; *pl* **blues**, préparation artisanale d'amphétamines*/bleues *fpl*; **heavenly blues**, graines *fpl* de volubilis (*utilisées comme drogues*). (*See* **pearly**) 2. *F* **to turn up out of the blue**, arriver* à l'improviste/venir comme un cheveu sur la soupe/débouler 3. *pl F* **to have the blues**, avoir le cafard/broyer du noir; baby blues, cafard *m*/bourdon *m* des accouchées 4. *A P* agent* de police/poulet *m*. (*See* **bluebottle**) 5. *F* **the blues**, (*music*) le blues; **to sing the blues**, chanter le blues 6. *Austr P* querelle*/prise *f* de bec 7. *Austr P* rouquin, -ine/poil *m* de carotte.

blue² [bluː] *vi P* 1. **to blue one's money**, dépenser*/bouffer/claquer son argent 2. **he blued his lot**, il a tout paumé/il a mangé la ferme.

blue balls ['bluː'bɔːlz] *npl P* **to have blue balls**, être bloqué (sexuellement).

bluebottle ['bluːbɒtl] *n O P* agent* de police/flic *m*/poulet *m*.

blue-eyed ['bluːaɪd] *a F* innocent/candide; **to be s.o.'s blue-eyed boy**, être le chouchou/le petit chéri de qn.

blue heaven ['bluː'hevən] *n P* (*drugs*) (*a*) LSD*/acide *m* (*b*) *pl* **blue heavens**, barbituriques*/barbital *m*.

bluey ['bluːɪ] *n P* 1. billet* de cinq livres 2. *pl* **blueys**, (*also* **blueies**) (*drugs*) drinamyl *m*.

B.O. ['biː'əʊ] *n F* (*abbr* = *body odour*) odeur corporelle; **she's got B.O.**, elle ne connaît pas le savon/le déodorant.

bo [bəʊ] *n NAm Austr F* clochard*/clodot *m*.

boat [bəʊt] *n* 1. *F* **to push the boat out** (*a*) payer* une tournée (*b*) faire la fête*/la noce/la foire 2. *F* **to miss the boat**, passer à côté/manquer le coche 3. *F* **to be in the same boat**, être dans le même bateau/être logé(s) à la même enseigne 4. *F* **I haven't just got off the**

boat, je ne suis pas né d'hier/je ne sors pas de l'œuf/je ne suis pas tombé de la dernière pluie **5.** *pl F* grandes chaussures*/bateaux *mpl*/ péniches *fpl* **6.** *P (RS = boat race = face)* visage*/gueule *f. (See* **dreamboat**; **little 2**; **rock² 2)**

bob¹ [bɒb] *n A F* shilling *m*/= cinq pence; ten bob, dix shillings/= cinquante pence.

Bob² [bɒb] *Prn P* Bob's your uncle, ça y est/ c'est dans le sac/le tour est joué; take the next right and, Bob's your uncle, there it is staring you in the face! prends la première rue à droite, et le voilà, juste devant ton nez. *(See* **Uncle 9)**

bobby ['bɒbɪ] *n F* agent* de police/flic *m.*

bobby-dazzler ['bɒbɪdæzlə] *n O F (a)* qch de voyant/de tapageur *(b)* beau brin de fille*/ beau petit lot.

bobbysocks ['bɒbɪsɒks] *npl O F* socquettes *fpl.*

bobbysoxer ['bɒbɪsɒksə] *n O F* jeune fille*/minette *f.*

bo-bo ['bəʊbəʊ] *n P (drugs)* marijuana*/kif *m. (See* **bush 2)**

bod [bɒd] *n F* **1.** individu*; he's a bit of an odd bod, c'est un drôle de type/de zèbre **2.** *NAm (abbr of body)* she's got a great bod, elle est bien roulée.

bodge-up ['bɒdʒʌp] *n F* gâchis · *m*/ bousillage *m*/bâclage *m*; to make a right bodge-up (of sth), tout saloper; foutre le bordel/la merde (dans qch).

bodge (up) ['bɒdʒ('ʌp)] *vtr F* gâcher/ bousiller/saloper.

bodgie ['bɒdʒɪ] *n Austr O P* jeune voyou *m.*

body ['bɒdɪ] *n P* **1.** individu*/mec *m*/ gonzesse *f* **2.** suspect, -e **3.** *(detainee)* détenu, -ue/tôlard, -arde.

boff [bɒf] *vtr & i P* to boff (s.o.), faire l'amour* (avec qn)/baiser (qn).

boffin ['bɒfɪn] *n F (a)* chercheur, -euse/tête *f* d'œuf *(b) (schools) (diligent pupil)* bûcheur, -euse/potasseur *m.*

bog [bɒg] *n P* **1.** WC*/gogues *mpl*/chiottes *fpl*; to go to the bog, aller aux chiottes **2.** to make a bog of sth, bousiller/saloper qch.

bogey, bogie ['bəʊgɪ] *n P* **1.** *(detective)* policier* en civil/perdreau *m*/poulet *m* **2.** *(snot)* morve *f*/crotte *f* de nez.

bog off ['bɒg'ɒf] *vi P* partir*/se débiner/ foutre le camp.

bog-trotter ['bɒg'trɒtə] *n Pej F* Irlandais, -aise.

bogue [bəʊg] *a P (drugs) (rare) (a)* en état

de manque *(b)* souffrant d'un sevrage.

bog-up ['bɒgʌp] *n P* gâchis *m*/bousillage *m*/ bâclage *m.*

bog (up) ['bɒg('ʌp)] *vtr P* bousiller/saloper (qch); he really bogged it (up), il a tout salopé; il y a foutu le bordel/la merde.

bogy ['bəʊgɪ] *n P =* **bogey 1, 2.**

bohunk, Bohunk ['bəʊhʌŋk] *n NAm P* **1.** immigrant, -ante d'Europe centrale **2.** individu *m* bête* et gauche/empoté, -ée/patate *f.*

boil [bɔɪl] *n F* to go off the boil, *(sexually)* ne plus être excité(e)/ne plus avoir envie.

boiled [bɔɪld] *a esp NAm P* ivre*/rétamé. *(See* **hard-boiled**; **shirt 5)**

boiler ['bɔɪlə] *n Pej P* femme*/gonzesse *f*/ poule *f.*

boiling ['bɔɪlɪŋ] **I** *a & adv F* I'm absolutely boiling, je crève de chaleur **II** *n O P* the whole boiling, (et) tout le bazar/(et) tout le bataclan/(et) tout le tremblement. *(See* **caboodle**; **shebang 1**; **shoot¹ 1**; **shooting-match)**

boing! [bɔɪŋ] *excl F* boum!/pan!/vlan!

boink [bɔɪŋk] *vtr NAm P* faire l'amour* avec (qn)/baiser (qn).

boko ['bəʊkəʊ] *n A P* nez*/blair *m.*

bollix ['bɒlɪks] *n V =* **bollocks.**

bollix (up) ['bɒlɪks('ʌp)] *vtr V =* **bollocks (up).**

bollock ['bɒlək] *n V* **1.** testicule*/couille *f. (See* **bollocks)** **2.** to drop a bollock, faire une bévue*/une cagade/une connerie.

bollocking ['bɒləkɪŋ] *n V* engueulade *f*/ savon *m*; to get a bollocking, se faire engueuler; to give s.o. a bollocking, en faire voir des vertes et des pas mûres à qn; passer un savon à qn.

bollock-naked ['bɒlək'neɪkɪd] *a V* nu*/à poil/le cul à l'air.

bollocks ['bɒləks] *npl V* **1.** testicules*/ balloches *fpl*/couilles *fpl*; he kicked him in the bollocks, il lui a flanqué un coup de pied dans les couilles **2.** bollocks!/what a load of bollocks! quelles conneries!/quelle couillon- nade!/c'est de la couille! **3.** bollocks to you! je t'emmerde!/va te faire foutre! **4.** to make a bollocks of sth, saloper qch/foutre le bor- del dans qch; he made a right bollocks of it, il a tout foutu en l'air/il y a foutu le mer- dier.

bollocks (up) ['bɒləks('ʌp)] *vtr V* foutre le bordel dans (qch)/saloper (qch); he really bollocksed it (up), il s'est complètement foutu dedans.

Bolly ['bɒlɪ] *n F* (= *Bollinger champagne*) champ' *m*/champe *m*.

boloney [bə'ləʊnɪ] *n F* bêtises*/foutaises *fpl*; **that's a lot of boloney!** c'est des histoires de con!

bolshie, bolshy ['bɒlʃɪ] I *F a* 1. bolcho/ coco/rouge 2. râleur/enquiquineur; **he's a bolshy sod,** c'est un mauvais coucheur/il emmerde le monde; **don't get bolshy with me!** ne la ramène pas avec moi!/commence pas à me les gonfler!/m'emmerde pas! II *n* coco *mf*/bolcho *mf*. (See **commie**)

bolt [bəʊlt] *vi NAm F* partir*/se barrer/ décamper.

bolted up ['bəʊltɪd'ʌp] *a P* en prison*/en taule/bouclé.

bomb¹ [bɒm] *n* 1. *F* **to cost a bomb,** coûter cher*/coûter les yeux de la tête/coûter la peau des fesses** 2. *F* **to make a bomb,** gagner* beaucoup d'argent/faire du fric/tomber sur un champ d'osier 3. *F* **to go like a bomb,** ronfler/ gazer/boumer; **his car goes like a bomb,** sa voiture, c'est une petite bombe; **it went like a bomb last night,** ça a super bien marché hier soir 4. *NAm P* échec*/fiasc *m*/four *m* 5. *Austr F* vieille voiture*/guimbarde *f* 6. *P* (*schools*) **to drop a bomb,** péter*/lâcher une fusée. (See **sex-bomb; stinkbomb**)

bomb² [bɒm] *vi NAm F* échouer*; **the play bombed on Broadway,** la pièce a été/a fait un four complet à Broadway.

bombed (out) ['bɒmd('aʊt)] *a P* (*drunk*) ivre*/bourré; (*drugged*) drogué*/camé; **he was bombed out of his mind/skull,** il était complètement défoncé.

bomber ['bɒmə] *n P* (*a*) black bomber, (*amphetamine*) bonbon *m*; brown bomber, (*beer*) panaché *m* de bière brune et blonde. (See **black*** 4) (*b*) cigarette* de marijuana/ joint *m*/bombardier *m*.

bombida [bɒm'biːdə], **bombido** [bɒm'biːdəʊ] *n P* (*drugs*) mélange *m* d'amphétamines* pour injection.

bombshell ['bɒmʃel] *n F* 1. a blonde bombshell, une blonde sensass/une super blonde 2. the news hit us like a bombshell, la nouvelle est tombée comme une bombe/a fait l'effet d'une bombe.

bonce [bɒns] *n P* tête*/caboche *f*.

bondage ['bɒndɪdʒ] *n NAm P* in bondage, endetté/déficitaire/dans le rouge.

bone¹ [bəʊn] *n* 1. *F* **to make no bones about sth,** ne pas y aller par quatre chemins; **she**

made no bones about it, elle y est allée carrément/elle n'a pas fait de mystères 2. *F* **to pick a bone with s.o.,** chercher querelle*/ des crosses/des poux à qn; **to have a bone to pick with s.o.,** avoir un petit compte à régler avec qn 3. *F* **close to/near the bone,** (*esp joke*) risqué; **that's a bit near the bone!** ça, c'est un peu osé!/salé!/raide! 4. *pl F* (*dice*) dés*; **to roll the bones,** pousser les bobs 5. *pl F* (*not common*) (*surgeon*) chirurgien *m*/charcutier *m* 6. *V* **to have a bone,** être en érection*/avoir l'os/avoir la trique/bander. (See **bone-on; boner** 2; **dry** 1; **marrowbones; sawbones**)

bone² [bəʊn] *vtr & i P* 1. (*not common*) voler*/chiper 2. *NAm* ennuyer*/barber/ canuler (qn) 3. *esp NAm* **to bone (up on) a subject,** piocher/potasser un sujet 4. *NAm* faire l'amour* (avec qn)/baiser (qn).

bonehead ['bəʊnhed] *n F* imbécile*/crétin, -ine/bûche *f*.

bone-on ['bəʊnɒn] *n V* érection*/bandaison *f*/trique *f*. (See **bone¹** 6)

bone-orchard ['bəʊnɔːtʃəd] *n P* cimetière*/le boulevard des allongés.

boner ['bəʊnə] *n NAm* 1. *F* bévue*/bourde *f*/ gaffe *f* 2. *V* = **bone¹** 6; **bone-on.**

boneshaker ['bəʊnʃeɪkə] *n F* (*a*) vieille voiture*/vieille guimbarde/tape-cul *m* (*b*) (*bike*) vélocipède *m*.

boneyard ['bəʊnjɑːd] *n P* = **bone-orchard.**

bonk¹ [bɒŋk] *n* 1. *F* coup*/gnon *m* 2. *P* coït*/ baise *f*/nique *f*.

bonk² [bɒŋk] I *vtr F* **to bonk s.o. on the head,** donner un coup* sur la tête de qn/ assommer qn II *vtr & i P* faire l'amour*/ baiser/faire des galipettes (avec qn).

bonkers ['bɒŋkəz] *a P* bonkers/O Harry bonkers, dingue/cinglé; stark raving bonkers, fou* à lier/complètement givré.

bonking ['bɒŋkɪŋ] *n V* coït*/baise *f*/nique *f*.

bonzer ['bɒnzə] *a Austr O F* excellent*/ sensass/super.

boo [buː] *n P* (*drugs*) marijuana*/kif *m*.

boob¹ [buːb] *n* 1. *F* (*idiot, fool*) individu bête*/ballot *m*/crétin, -ine; nigaud, -aude/ ducon *m* 2. *F* bévue*/gaffe *f* 3. *pl P* boobs, seins*/nénés *mpl*/nichons *mpl*/lolos *mpl*; she's got huge boobs, elle a de gros nénés 4. *P* (*a*) prison*/trou *m* (*b*) = poste *m* de police/ gendarmerie *f*.

boob² [buːb] *vi F* faire une bévue*/une gaffe; **I really boobed there,** je me suis gouré/je me suis foutu dedans/je me suis planté.

boobies ['bu:bɪz] *npl P* seins*/nénés *mpl.*

booboo ['bu:bu:] *n F* bévue*/bourde *f.*

boob tube ['bu:b'tju:b] *n F* 1. *NAm* télévision *f*/télé *f*/téloche *f.* (*See* **tube 3**) 2. bustier *m.*

booby ['bu:bɪ] *n O F* imbécile*/nigaud, -aude.

booby-hatch ['bu:bɪhætʃ] *n P* 1. *NAm* maison *f* de fous/cabanon *m* 2. *esp Austr* = **boob**[1] **4**.

boodle ['bu:dl] *n P* (*a*) *esp NAm* (*illicit spoils, profits, etc*) butin*/fade *m* (*b*) argent*/fric *m*/oseille *f.*

boofhead ['bu:fhed] *n Austr A F* individu *m* bête*.

boogie[1] ['bu:gɪ] *n* 1. *esp NAm P* sorte *f* de blues sur lequel on danse; **to dance to the boogie,** danser/faire le boogie-woogie 2. *NAm A P Pej* Noir(e)*/nègre *m*/bougnoul *m.*

boogie[2] ['bu:gɪ] *vi esp NAm P* **to boogie (on down),** (aller) danser/faire le boogie-woogie.

boogie-box ['bu:gɪbɒks] *n P* magnéto(phone) *m* stéréo portable. (*See* **ghetto-blaster**)

boogie-pack ['bu:gɪpæk] *n P* (*personal stereo*) baladeur *m*/Walkman (*RTM*) *m.*

book[1] [bʊk] *n F* 1. **to throw the book at s.o.,** (*to give s.o. the maximum sentence*) donner la peine maximum à qn; (*to tell s.o. off*) engueuler qn; **the judge threw the book at him,** le juge l'a fadé; **he got the book thrown at him,** il a attrapé/chopé le maxi; **my mother threw the book at me,** ma mère m'a secoué les bretelles/lavé la tête 2. **to be in s.o.'s good books,** être dans les petits papiers de qn; **I'm not in his good books,** il ne m'a pas à la bonne 3. **it suits my book,** ça me va/ça me botte. (*See* **cook**[2] **2**; **turn-up 1**)

book[2] [bʊk] *vtr F* **to book s.o.,** dresser une contravention à qn/mettre/coller un PV (= procès-verbal) à qn; **to get booked,** (*speeding, parking*) se faire coller un PV; (*sport*) recevoir un avertissement; **the ref booked him,** l'arbitre lui a sorti un carton jaune.

bookie, booky ['bʊkɪ] *n F* book *m.*

boom ['bu:m] *vi NAm P* faire le trafic de drogues.

boom box ['bu:m'bɒks] *n P* magnéto(phone) *m* stéréo portable. (*See* **ghetto-blaster**)

boomer ['bu:mə] *n Austr F* (*a*) qch d'énorme/de géant/de maousse (*b*) qch

d'extraordinaire/de super.

boondocks ['bu:ndɒks], **boonies** ['bu:nɪz] *npl NAm P* le bled/le trou.

boondoggle[1] ['bu:ndɒgl] *n NAm P* objet *m* ou surt travail *m* sans grande valeur/nul.

boondoggle[2] ['bu:ndɒgl] *vi NAm P* perdre son temps en choses inutiles et sans importance; peigner la girafe.

boong [bu:ŋ] *n Austr F Pej* personne *f* de couleur/bronzé, -ée.

boost [bu:st] *vi NAm P* voler* (*surt* à l'étalage)/piquer.

boot[1] [bu:t] *n* 1. *P* **to give s.o. the (order of the) boot,** congédier qn/flanquer qn à la porte; **he got the boot from his job,** il s'est fait sacquer de son boulot 2. *P* **to put the boot in,** donner un coup de pied vicieux (à qn)/tabasser (qn)/passer (qn) à tabac; (*attack, criticize*) critiquer*/démolir qn 3. *F* **to be too big for one's boots,** péter plus haut que son derrière/se prendre trop au sérieux 4. *F* **to lick s.o.'s boots,** flatter* qn/lécher les bottes à qn/lécher le cul à qn/faire de la lèche à qn 5. *P* **to splash one's boots,** uriner*/lancequiner/mouiller une ardoise 6. *NAm F Mil* **boot camp,** camp *m* d'entraînement. (*See* **bet 4**; **bovver-boots**; **slyboots**)

boot[2] [bu:t] *vi NAm P* vomir*/dégueuler/gerber.

bootlick ['bu:tlɪk] *vtr F* (*to toady*) lécher les bottes à/les pieds à (qn).

bootlicker ['bu:tlɪkə] *n F* (*toady*) lèche-bottes *m*/lécheur, -euse (de bottes).

boot out ['bu:t'aut] *vtr P* se débarrasser* de/sacquer/vider/virer (qn); **he got booted out of the army,** il a été viré de l'armée.

booze[1] [bu:z] *n P* alcool*/pinard *m*; **to be on the/to hit the booze,** boire* beaucoup/picoler/se biturer; **must cut down on the booze,** faut que j'arrête de picoler.

booze[2] [bu:z] *vi P* boire*/lever le coude/picoler/biberonner.

boozed (up) ['bu:zd('ʌp)] *a P* ivre*/soûl/bourré.

boozer ['bu:zə] *n P* 1. ivrogne*/poivrot, -ote/soûlaud, -aude/soûlographe *m* 2. (*pub*) café*/bistrot *m*/troquet *m.*

booze-up ['bu:zʌp] *n P* soûlerie *f*; **let's have a booze-up!** on va se payer une bonne cuite!

boozy ['bu:zɪ] *a P* ivrogne/soûlard; **we had a boozy evening,** on a passé la soirée à boire/picoler.

bop[1] [bɒp] *n F* (*dance*) bal *m*/baluche *m*/

gambille *f*.
bop² [bɒp] *vi* danser*/gambiller.
bo-peep ['bəʊ'piːp] *n P* (*RS = sleep*) dodo *m*.
boppy ['bɒpɪ] *a F* rythmé.
boracic [bə'ræsɪk, 'bræsɪk] *a P* (*RS = boracic lint = skint*) très pauvre*/dans la dèche/ sans un/fauché/raide. (*See* **skint**)
born [bɔːn] *a & pp F* 1. in all my born days, de toute ma vie; never in all my born days have I heard so much rubbish! jamais je n'ai entendu tant de conneries! 2. I wasn't born yesterday, je ne suis pas né d'hier/je ne suis pas tombé de la dernière pluie. (*See* **one 7**)
bosh [bɒʃ] *n F* bêtises*/boniments *mpl*/ sornettes *fpl*; what bosh! n'importe quoi!
boss¹ [bɒs] I *a esp NAm P* excellent*/ chouette/extra; we had a boss time, on s'est éclatés/vachement amusés II *n F* patron*/ singe *m*/boss *m*/chef *m*; he's the boss around here, c'est lui qui commande ici.
boss² [bɒs] *vtr P* mener/diriger; to boss the show, être le manitou de l'affaire/tenir la barre/faire marcher la machine.
boss about ['bɒsə'baʊt], **boss around** ['bɒsə'raʊnd] *vtr F* to boss s.o. about, mener qn par le bout du nez/faire marcher qn/faire la loi à qn.
boss-eyed ['bɒsaɪd] *a P* qui louche*/qui a un œil* qui dit merde à l'autre.
boss-man ['bɒsmæn] *n F* = **boss¹** II.
bossy ['bɒsɪ] *a F* autoritaire; he's (too) bossy, c'est un Monsieur Jordonne.
bossy-boots ['bɒsɪbuːts] *n F* individu* autoritaire/grand manitou; she's a real bossy-boots, c'est un vrai gendarme, celle-là.
bot [bɒt] *n F* (*abbr of bottom*) = **bottom** II 1.
bother ['bɒðə] I *excl F* zut!/flûte!/la barbe! II *n P* bagarre*/baston *f*/grabuge *m*. (*See* **bovver; in bother**)
botheration! [bɒðə'reɪʃ(ə)n] *excl F* = **bother** I.
bottle¹ ['bɒtl] *n P* 1. to hit/to be on the bottle, caresser la bouteille/biberonner/picoler 2. (*courage*) sang-froid *m*/cran *m*; (*cheek, nerve*) culot *m*/toupet *m*; lost your bottle? t'as le trac?/t'as la pétoche? he lost his bottle, il s'est dégonflé. (*See* **bluebottle; titty-bottle**)
bottle² ['bɒtl] *P* I *vtr* (*not common*) taper (qn) à coups de bouteille II *vtr & i* avoir peur*/se dégonfler/avoir le trouillomètre à zéro; he bottled it/out, il s'est dégonflé; il a la

chiasse/les chocottes III *vi* sentir* mauvais/ schlinguer.
bottled ['bɒtld] *a P* 1. ivre*/bourré 2. poltron*/froussard.
bottler ['bɒtlə] *n P* voiture *f* difficile à vendre; rossignol *m*. (*See* **square-wheeler**)
bottle-washer ['bɒtlwɒʃə] *n see* **cook¹** 1.
bottom ['bɒtəm] I *a F* to bet one's bottom dollar, risquer le paquet; you can bet your bottom dollar that..., je te fiche/fous mon billet que.... (*See* **bet 4**) II *n F* 1. fesses*/ derrière *m*/postérieur *m* 2. bottoms up! videz vos verres!/cul sec! (*See* **bell-bottoms; bot; botty; burp¹ 2; heap 2; rock¹ 4; scrape² 1**)
botty ['bɒtɪ] *n F* (*esp child's language*) = **bottom** II 1. (*See* **smack-botty**)
bounce [baʊns] *vtr* 1. *P* congédier*/flanquer (qn) à la porte (*d'une boîte de nuit, etc*)/vider 2. *F* to bounce a cheque, renvoyer un chèque sans provision; he paid with a cheque that bounced, il m'a filé un chèque en bois.
bouncer ['baʊnsə] *n P* 1. videur *m* (*d'une boîte de nuit, etc*); (*who refuses entry*) physionomiste *m* 2. *pl* (*not common*) seins*/ rotoplots *mpl* 3. chèque *m* en bois.
bovver ['bɒvə] *n P* (= *bother*) bagarre*/ grabuge *m*; don't give us any bovver! pas d'histoires, hein!/pas de grabuge ici!
bovver-boots ['bɒvə'buːts] *npl P* chaussures* des *bovver-boys*/rangers *mpl*/= Dr Martens (*RTM*) *mpl*. (*See* **DM's**)
bovver-boy ['bɒvəbɔɪ] *n P* jeune voyou *m surt* aux cheveux tondus ras/= skinhead *m*/ skin *m*.
bowl over ['bəʊl'əʊvə] *vtr F* épater/ sidérer; he was bowled over by our present, notre cadeau l'a rendu tout chose/l'a sidéré; I was bowled over by that, j'en ai été soufflé; j'en suis resté assis/baba.
box¹ [bɒks] *n* 1. *V* sexe* de la femme/boîte *f* à ouvrage 2. *F* (*television*) télé *f*/téloche *f*; what's on the box? qu'est-ce qu'il y a à la téloche? (*See* **gogglebox; idiot-box**) 3. *P* cercueil*/boîte *f* à dominos; to go home in a box, mourir*/s'en aller les pieds devant 4. *P* coffre-fort *m*/coffiot *m* 5. *P* (*RS = box of fruit = suit*) costume *m*/complet *m* 6. *P* guitare*/ gratte *f* 7. *NAm F* magnéto(phone) *m* stéréo portatif 8. *P* to be off one's box, = **boxed 1** (*a*), (*b*). (*See* **boogie-box; boom box; brainbox; jack-in-the-box; out I 3; saucebox; squeezebox; think-box**)
box² [bɒks] *vtr P* mettre (qn) en prison*/en

taule; coffrer (qn).

boxed [bɒkst] *a P* 1. (*a*) ivre*/rétamé/ bourré (*b*) drogué*/camé/défoncé 2. emprisonné*/bloqué/bouclé/coffré.

boy [bɔɪ] I *excl F* 1. oh boy!/boy oh boy! chouette alors!/oh là là! 2. boy, did she tear me off a strip! mes enfants! qu'est-ce qu'elle m'a passé!/ce qu'elle m'a passé, je vous dis pas! II *n* 1. *F* hello, old boy! salut, vieille branche/mon pote! 2. *P* (*drugs*) héroïne*/héro *f*/boy *m*. (*See* **backroom**; **bovver-boy**; **bum-boy**; **doughboy**; **glamour-boy**; **jayboy**; **J-boy**; **jewboy**; **job 11**; **K-boy**; **lover-boy**; **old-boy**; **playboy**; **rude 2**; **sandboy**; **wide 1**)

boyo ['bɔɪjəʊ] *n P* fiston *m*; listen boyo! écoute mon gars!

bozack ['bəʊzæk] *n NAm P* pénis*/bite *f*/ queue *f*.

bracelets ['breɪslɪts] *npl F* menottes*/ bracelets *mpl*/cadènes *fpl*.

bracer ['breɪsə] *n F* (*drink*) remontant *m*/ tonique *m*.

Brahms 'n' Liszt ['brɑːmzən'lɪst] *a* (*RS = pissed*) ivre*/bourré/raide.

braille [breɪl] *n Austr P* (bit of) braille, renseignement*/tuyau *m*/info *f*.

brain¹ [breɪn] *n F* 1. to have brains, être intelligent*/une grosse tête 2. he's the brains of the outfit, c'est le cerveau de la bande 3. to have s.o./sth on the brain, être obsédé par qn/ qch; faire une fixation sur qn/qch; he's got it on the brain, il ne pense qu'à ça 4. to beat/to rack one's brains, se creuser la cervelle/les méninges. (*See* **birdbrain**; **featherbrain**; **lamebrain**; **scatterbrain**)

brain² [breɪn] *vtr F* battre*/casser la figure à (qn); if you don't shut up I'll brain you! ferme-la ou je t'assomme!

brainbox ['breɪnbɒks] *n F* (*intelligent person*) grosse tête/tête *f* d'œuf/bête *f*.

brainchild ['breɪntʃaɪld] *n F* idée originale; this model is his brainchild, c'est son invention(, ce modèle).

brain drain ['breɪn'dreɪn] *n F* fuite *f* des cerveaux.

brainwave ['breɪnweɪv] *n F* inspiration *f*/ idée *f* de génie; and then he had a real brainwave, et alors, il a eu l'inspiration/ça a fait tilt.

brainy ['breɪnɪ] *a F* intelligent*/doué/calé/ débrouillard.

brass [brɑːs] I *a F* (*a*) to get down to brass tacks, parler de choses sérieuses/parler

sérieusement (*b*) a brass balls job, un travail difficile*/emmerdant. (*See* **balls¹ 4**) II *n* 1. *P* argent*/pognon *m*/pèze *m*; where there's muck there's brass, (*catchphrase*) il y a toujours du fric dans les ordures 2. *P* (*cheek, nerve*) culot *m*/toupet *m*; he's got the brass to do it, il est assez culotté pour le faire 3. *F* top brass, les huiles *fpl* 4. *P* (*not common*) prostituée*/pute *f*/tapineuse *f*. (*See* **half-brass**)

brassed off ['brɑːst'ɒf] *a P* to be brassed off, en avoir marre/ras-le-bol.

brass-hat ['brɑːs'hæt] *n F Mil* galonné *m*/ galonnard *m*.

brass monkey(s) ['brɑːs'mʌŋkɪ(z)] *n P* it's brass monkey weather/it's a bit brass monkeys, on se les caille/on se gèle les miches/on pèle (de froid). (*See* **balls¹ 4**)

brassy ['brɑːsɪ] *a P* (*impudent*) gonflé/ culotté.

brat [bræt] *n F* enfant* (désagréable)/môme *mf*/moutard *m*; *NAm* brat pack, bande *f* d'ados gâtés et désagréables/la bande des sales gosses.

bread [bred] *n* 1. *P* (*RS = bread and honey = money*) argent*/galette *f*/blé *m*/oseille *f* 2. *P* to be on the bread line, être sans le sou/ claquer du bec/être dans la dèche 3. *F* that's his bread and butter, c'est son gagne-pain/ c'est avec ça qu'il gagne sa croûte.

bread-and-butter ['bredən(d)'bʌtə] *a F* 1. (*politics*) bread-and-butter issues, le prix du bifteck 2. bread-and-butter (letter), lettre *f* de remerciement/de château. (*See* **bread 3**)

breadbasket ['bredbɑːskɪt] *n F* ventre*/ bedaine *f*/brioche *f*; to get one in the bread-basket, prendre un coup* dans le buffet/le gésier.

bread-hooks ['bred'hʊks] *npl P* mains*/ croches *fpl*/paluches *fpl*. (*See* **hook¹ 6**; **meat-hooks**)

break [breɪk] *n F* 1. chance*/coup *m* de pot; that was a lucky break for us, on a eu de la veine/du pot/du cul; a bad break, malchance*, déveine *f*/guigne *f*. (*See* **tough I 4**) 2. to give s.o. a break, (*give s.o. a chance*) donner sa chance à qn; (*help s.o.*) tendre la perche à qn; come on, give me/us a break! arrête ton char!/laisse-moi souffler un peu!/lâche-moi un peu! 3. récréation *f*/récré *f*; a break for lunch, une pause pour le déjeuner; coffee break, pause-café *f* 4. évasion *f* de prison*/cavale *f*; to make a break for it, se faire la malle.

break up ['breɪk'ʌp] *vtr F* break it up!

arrêtez/finissez de vous battre!

breather ['briːðə] *n F* moment *m* de répit/ de repos; give me a breather, laisse-moi tranquille; lâche-moi un peu; arrête ton char! to go out for a breather, sortir prendre l'air.

breeks [briːks] *npl F* (*trousers*) pantalon*/ falzar(d) *m*; jogging breeks, = jogging *m*.

breeze [briːz] *n P* 1. *O* querelle*; there was a bit of a breeze when he got home, il y a eu du grabuge/il s'est fait souffler dans les bronches quand il est rentré 2. it was a breeze, c'était facile/c'était l'enfance de l'art/c'était simple comme bonjour. (See **shoot**[2] 6)

breeze in, out ['briːz'ɪn, 'aʊt] *vi F* 1. (*unexpectedly*) entrer/sortir en coup de vent; (*casually*) entrer/sortir l'air de rien 2. *esp NAm* (*racing*) to breeze in, arriver dans un fauteuil.

breeze off ['briːz'ɒf] *vi NAm F* (*not common*) partir*/se barrer/se débiner.

breeze through ['briːz'θruː] *vtr* faire (un travail) sans difficulté/les doigts dans le nez.

breezy ['briːzɪ] *a F* (all) bright and breezy, plein d'entrain; d'attaque.

brekkers ['brekəz] *n*, **brekky** ['brekɪ] *n F* (= *breakfast*) petit déjeuner/p'tit dèj'.

brick [brɪk] *n F* 1. he's been a (real) brick, c'est le meilleur des potes; be a brick! sois sympa! 2. to drop a brick, faire une bévue*/ faire sa connerie 3. *P* (*drugs*) kilo *m* de marijuana* *ou* de haschisch* présenté sous forme compressée 4. *NAm P* to hit the bricks, partir*/prendre le large/lever l'ancre. (See **come down** 3; **drop**[2] 1; **goldbrick**[1]; **shit**[2] 3; **wall** 4, 5, 6)

brickie ['brɪkɪ] *n F* (*bricklayer*) maçon *m*.

bride [braɪd] *n A P* jeune fille*/gamine *f*; (*girlfriend*) petite amie *f*/nénette *f*/gonzesse *f*.

bridewell ['braɪdwel] *n P* commissariat *m* de police/quart *m*.

brief [briːf] *n P* (*lawyer, esp barrister*) = avocat*/bavard *m*/baveux *m*.

Brighton line ['braɪtn'laɪn] *F see* **bingo 59.**

brill [brɪl] *a* (*short for brilliant*) *F* excellent*/ super/terrible.

bring down ['brɪŋ'daʊn] *vtr & i P* déprimer/attrister/rendre cafardeux; the news really brought him down, la nouvelle ne lui a pas remonté le moral/lui a foutu le cafard. (See **brought down**; **house** 3)

bring off ['brɪŋ'ɒf] *vtr V* masturber*/ branler (qn); faire jouir qn; he brings himself off like that, c'est comme ça qu'il prend son pied.

bring up ['brɪŋ'ʌp] *vi P* = **back up** 2.

brinkmanship ['brɪŋkmənʃɪp] *n F* politique *f* du bord de l'abîme.

briny ['braɪnɪ] *n O F* the briny, l'océan *m*/la Grande Tasse.

Brissie ['brɪzɪ] *Prn Austr F* Brisbane.

Bristol-fashion ['brɪstəlfæʃ(ə)n] *adv & a F* (shipshape and) Bristol-fashion, bien rangé/en ordre/impec/parfaitement comme il faut.

Bristols, bristols ['brɪstəlz] *npl P* (*RS* = *Bristol City's* = *titties*) seins*/nichons *mpl*/ lolos *mpl*; a nice pair of Bristols, une belle paire d'amortisseurs. (See **fit**[1] II 3; **tale** 3; **threepenny-bits**; **trey-bits**)

Brit [brɪt] *n F* Britannique *mf*/britiche *mf*.

bro [brəʊ] *n F* frère*/frangin *m*/frérot *m*.

broad [brɔːd] *n NAm P* (*a*) fille*/femme*/ gonzesse *f*/nana *f*; she's just a dumb broad, c'est une vraie connasse (*b*) prostituée*/pute *f*/grue *f* 2. *pl A* cartes* à jouer; to fake the broads, truquer les cartes/maquiller les brèmes.

brodie, brody ['brəʊdɪ] *n NAm P* (*not common*) échec*/four *m*/fiasc *m*.

broke [brəʊk] *a F* 1. to be broke/dead broke/ flat broke/stony broke, être pauvre*/sans un/ sans le sou/dans la dèche/sans un radis; to be broke to the wide, être fauché (comme les blés) 2. (*gambling*) to go for broke, risquer tout/risquer le paquet.

broker ['brəʊkə] *n P* trafiquant, -ante/ fourgue *m*.

brolly ['brɒlɪ] *n F* 1. parapluie*/pépin *m*/ riflard *m*/pébroque *m* 2. parachute *m*/pépin *m*.

bronco ['brɒŋkəʊ] *n NAm F* cheval sauvage/non dressé.

broncobuster ['brɒŋkəʊbʌstə] *n NAm F* cowboy *m* (*qui dresse des chevaux sauvages*).

bronze [brɒnz] *n P* matières fécales/bronze *m*/merde *f*.

brought down ['brɔːt'daʊn] *pp P* (*drug addict*) déprimé après le flash. (See **bring down**)

brown[1] [braʊn] *V* I *a* to be done brown, se faire entuber/se faire enculer; brown job, coït anal*/baisage *m* à la riche II *n* 1. a bit of brown, coït anal*/baisage *m* à la riche 2. *A* anus*/trou *m* de balle.

brown[2] [braʊn] *vtr V* sodomiser*/enculer (qn); to get browned, se faire enculer.

brown-bag ['braʊnbæg] *vtr & i NAm F* to brown-bag (it), manger*/bouffer des sandwichs/sandwicher.

brown-eye ['braʊnaɪ] *n Austr V* anus*/trou *m* de balle.

brown-hatter ['braʊn'hætə] *n V* homosexuel*/tante *f*/pédé *m*.

brownie ['braʊnɪ] *n* 1. *O V* anus*/trou *m* du cul 2. *V* = **brown-hatter** 3. *F* verre *m* de whisky/de scotch 4. *F* brownie points, prix imaginaire donné pour récompenser une bonne action; bons points.

brown-nose ['braʊnnəʊz] *vtr NAm V* (*to toady*) lécher le cul à (qn).

brown-noser ['braʊnnəʊzə] *n NAm V* lèche-cul *m*.

brown off ['braʊn'ɒf] *vtr P* décourager (qn); to be browned off, avoir le cafard/ broyer du noir; that really browns me off, ça me fiche la déprime/le cafard/le noir.

bruiser ['bruːzə] *n F* boxeur *m*; (*any fighter*) cogneur *m*.

Brum [brʌm] *Prn Br F* Birmingham.

brumby ['brʌmbɪ] *n Austr F* cheval *m* sauvage.

Brummie ['brʌmɪ] *Br F* **I** *Prn* Birmingham **II** *n* habitant, -ante de Birmingham.

brunch [brʌntʃ] *n F* repas *m* tenant lieu de *breakfast* et *lunch*; brunch *m*.

brush [brʌʃ] *n* 1. *P* = **brush-off** 2. *Austr P* jeune femme*/minette *f*/nana *f* 3. *V* pubis féminin/barbu *m* 4. *F* (*a*) to have a brush with, avoir des ennuis/des emmerdes avec (la police, etc) (*b*) he had a brush with him, il s'est bagarré avec lui. (*See* **tar²**; **tarbrush**)

brush-off ['brʌʃɒf] *n F* to give s.o. the brush-off, se débarrasser* de qn/envoyer promener qn/envoyer balader qn; he gave her the brush-off, il l'a envoyée sur les roses/ paître/chier.

brush off ['brʌʃ'ɒf] *vtr F* to brush s.o. off, (*ignore*) snober qn; (*get rid of*) se débarrasser* de qn; he brushed her off with no excuse, il l'a envoyée sur les roses.

bubble ['bʌbl] *n P occ Pej* (*RS* = **bubble-and-squeak** = *Greek*) (*person*) Grec, Grecque.

bubble-and-squeak ['bʌblən(d)'skwiːk] *n* 1. *F* réchauffé *m* (en friture) de pommes de terre et de choux 2. *P* (*RS* = *beak* = *magistrate*): see **beak 1** 3. *P* (*RS* = *week*) semaine *f*.

bubbly ['bʌblɪ] *F* **I** *a* joyeux; rythmé **II** *n F* champagne *m*/champ(e) *m*; a bottle of bubbly, une roteuse. (*See* **champers**)

buck¹ [bʌk] *n* 1. *NAm F* dollar *m*; to make a

fast buck, obtenir/gagner de l'argent rapidement et sans faire de scrupules; to make a few bucks on the side, se faire un peu de fric (au noir)/se faire un petit à-côté 2. *F* to pass the buck, filer la responsabilité à qn/ faire porter le chapeau à qn.

buck² [bʌk] *vi F* to buck against sth, résister à/s'opposer à qch.

bucked [bʌkt] *a O F* ragaillardi/content; enchanté.

bucket ['bʌkɪt] *n F* 1. to kick the bucket, mourir*/lâcher la rampe/casser sa pipe/avaler son bulletin de naissance 2. it's raining buckets, il pleut des cordes/à seaux.

bucket down ['bʌkɪt'daʊn] *vi F* it's bucketing down out there, il tombe des cordes/des hallebardes dehors.

bucket job ['bʌkɪtdʒɒb] *n P* compagnie frauduleuse.

bucket shop ['bʌkɪtʃɒp] *n F* agence *f* de voyages à prix réduits.

Buck House [bʌk'haʊs] *n F* (*Buckingham Palace*) (le palais de) Buckingham *m* (*résidence de la reine d'Angleterre*).

buckle ['bʌkl] *vtr & i P* 1. buckle my shoe: see **bingo 2** 2. to buckle down to sth, se mettre/s'atteler à qch sérieusement; buckle down to your work, lads! au boulot, les gars!

bucko ['bʌkəʊ] *a P Irish* (*term of address*) (me) bucko! mon vieux!

buckshee ['bʌk'ʃiː] *F* **I** *a & adv* gratuit*/ gratis/à l'œil; we got in buckshee, on est entré gratis/sans payer **II** *n* a bit of buckshee, (*extra ration*) du rab.

buck up ['bʌk'ʌp] *vtr & i F* 1. remonter le moral à (qn); come on, buck up! it's not so bad! allons, du courage! ça va pas si mal que ça! 2. se dépêcher*/se grouiller 3. he'd better buck up his ideas a little, il ferait bien de se mettre un peu au point.

bud [bʌd] *n F* 1. *NAm* listen, bud! écoute, mon vieux!/écoute, mec! (*See* **buddy**) 2. to nip sth in the bud, tuer/étouffer qch dans l'œuf.

buddy ['bʌdɪ] *n F* ami*/copain, -ine/pote *m*; they're great buddies, ils sont comme cul et chemise.

buddy-buddy ['bʌdɪbʌdɪ] *a F* to be buddy-buddy, être copains comme cochons/ s'entendre comme larrons en foire.

buddy up ['bʌdɪ'ʌp] *vi NAm F* (*esp university/faculty*) partager une chambre avec qn.

buff [bʌf] *n F* 1. in the buff, tout nu*/à poil 2.

(*enthusiast*) film/opera buff, mordu, -ue/fana *mf* de ciné/d'opéra.

buffalo ['bʌfələʊ] *vtr NAm* F intimider/entortiller/entourlouper (qn).

bug¹ [bʌg] *n* 1. *F* micro clandestin 2. *F* accroc *m*/pépin *m*; a bug in the works, un os/un pépin 3. *F* obsession *f*/marotte *f*; he's been bitten by/he's caught the jogging bug, c'est un mordu/un dingue de jogging 4. *F* (*infection*) microbe *m*/bactérie *f*; I must have picked up a bug, j'ai dû attraper quelque chose/une saloperie 5. *F* as snug as a bug in a rug, (*catchphrase*) super bien (installé) 6. *P* love bugs = crabs (*see* **crab¹** 2). (*See* **big I 1; doodle-bug; firebug; jitterbug; litterbug**)

bug² [bʌg] *vtr & i* 1. *F* installer des micros clandestins dans (une salle, etc); the phone's bugged, le bigophone est (branché) sur table d'écoute 2. *P* to bug s.o., ennuyer* qn/embêter qn/casser les pieds à qn; stop bugging me! m'emmerde pas! fous-moi la paix! what's bugging you? qu'est-ce qui te chiffonne?/qu'est-ce qui te turlupine?

bug-eyed ['bʌgaɪd] *a F* 1. to be bug-eyed, avoir les yeux* en boules de loto; avoir les yeux à fleur de tête 2. bug-eyed monster, monstre *m* atomique.

bugger¹ ['bʌgə] *n* 1. *V* saligaud *m*; he's a filthy bugger! c'est un salaud*/un sale type 2. *P* con *m*/couillon *m*; don't play silly buggers with me! (ne) te paye pas ma tête!/(ne) fais pas le con avec moi!/arrête de déconner! 3. *P* (*affectionately*) individu*/type *m*; a cute little bugger, une gentille petite fripouille; poor little bugger! pauvre petit bonhomme! a silly (old) bugger, un pauvre (vieux) con/une (vieille) andouille; (what a) lucky bugger! le veinard!/il a eu du cul! (*See* **jammy**) 4. *P* (*sth difficult*) that's a real bugger! ça c'est case-couilles!/ça c'est couille! a bugger of a job, une saloperie/un putain de boulot 5. *V I don't give a bugger!* je n'en ai rien à foutre! (*See* **rugger**)

bugger² ['bʌgə] *vtr* 1. *V* bugger (it)! merde (alors)! bugger you! va te faire foutre!/je t'emmerde! 2. *P* that's buggered it! ça a tout foutu en l'air! 3. *P* it's buggered, c'est foutu 4. *V* it's got me buggered, je l'ai dans le dos/le cul 5. *P* well, I'm buggered! ça c'est trop fort!

bugger about, around ['bʌgərə'baʊt, ə'raʊnd] *vi* 1. perdre son temps/ne rien foutre/glander/glandouiller 2. manier/tripoter

qch; stop buggering about with that! arrête de tripoter ça! to bugger about with s.o., peloter qn/mettre la main au panier de qn 3. to bugger s.o. about, faire tourner qn en bourrique.

bugger-all ['bʌgə'rɔːl] *n P* rien*/des clous/que dalle.

buggeration! ['bʌgə'reɪʃ(ə)n] *excl P* tonnerre de Dieu!/bordel de Dieu!

buggered ['bʌgəd] *a P* fatigué*/claqué; I'm buggered, je suis crevé. (*See* **bugger² 3, 4, 5**)

bugger off ['bʌgə'rɒf] *vi V* partir*/foutre le camp; I told him to bugger off, je lui ai dit de foutre le camp.

bugger up ['bʌgə'rʌp] *vtr P* bousiller/saboter; you've buggered it up again! tu l'as encore salopé!/tu nous refais les mêmes conneries!

buggery ['bʌgərɪ] *n P* 1. like buggery! mon œil!/mon cul! can she cook? can she buggery! et pour la bouffe? mon cul!/rien à faire!/que dalle!/zéro! 2. he ran like buggery all the way to the station, il courut à tout berzingue/à toute blinde jusqu'à la gare 3. all to buggery, complètement/jusqu'au trognon 4. *esp Austr V* go to buggery! va te faire voir!/va te faire foutre!

buggy ['bʌgɪ] *a* 1. *NAm P* fou*/timbré/louftingue 2. *F* (= beach buggy, dune buggy) bagnole *f*.

bughouse ['bʌghaʊs] **I** *a NAm P* fou*/cinglé **II** *n P* asile *m* de fous/maison *f* de dingues/cabanon *m*.

bugjuice ['bʌgdʒuːs] *n P* alcool*/casse-gueule *m*/gnôle *f*.

bug off ['bʌg'ɒf] *vi P* partir*/se casser; bug off, will you? fiche le camp!/fiche-moi la paix!

bug out ['bʌg'aʊt] *vi NAm P* 1. se dégonfler/retirer ses marrons du feu 2. s'enfuir*/déguerpir; bug out, kid! tire-toi, mon vieux!

bugs [bʌgz] *a NAm P* fou*/cinglé/dingue.

bulge [bʌldʒ] *n F* 1. *Hum* the battle of the bulge, la bataille du bide/la lutte pour la ligne 2. *Euph* he's got a nice bulge, il est bien équipé/bien monté.

bull [bʊl] *n P* 1. *NAm Austr & occ WInd* policier*/flic *m*/condé *m* 2. (= bullshit) foutaises *fpl*/conneries *fpl*; don't give me all that bull! arrête de déconner!/déconne pas!/arrête ton baratin! bull! quelles conneries!/mon cul! 3. bull and cow, (RS = row) querelle*/corrida *f*. (*See* **rag¹ 4; shoot² 6**)

bulldagger ['bʊldægə] *n O P* = **bull-dyke**.

bulldoze ['bʊldəʊz] *vtr F* intimider/ brutaliser (qn) (*pour lui faire faire qch*).

bulldyke ['bʊldaɪk] *n O P* lesbienne* qui tient le rôle de l'homme/vrille *f*. (*See* **dyke**)

bullet ['bʊlɪt] *n P* 1. capsule *f* contenant de la drogue 2. to give s.o. the bullet, se débarrasser* de qn/sacquer qn/virer qn; he got the bullet, on l'a flanqué/il s'est fait flanquer à la porte 3. *pl* sperme*/semoule *f*; to give s.o. the bullets, envoyer le paquet 4. *pl P Mil & Navy* (*peas*) petits pois.

bullion-fringe ['bʊljən'frɪndʒ] *n F Mil* (*gold braid on epaulettes*) feuilles *fpl* de chêne/graine *f* d'épinards. (*See* **egg 3**)

bull session ['bʊl'seʃ(ə)n] *n NAm F* they were having a bull session, il se taillaient une bavette entre hommes.

bullseye ['bʊlzaɪ] *n F see* **bingo 50**.

bullshine ['bʊlʃaɪn] *n F Euph for* **bullshit¹**.

bullshit¹ ['bʊlʃɪt] *n P* bêtises*/foutaises *fpl*/ conneries *fpl*; to talk bullshit, déconner; that's bullshit, c'est des conneries/c'est de la couille/c'est du bidon; bullshit! mon cul! bullshit artist = **bullshitter 1, 2**.

bullshit² ['bʊlʃɪt] *P* I *vtr* tromper* (qn); he's bullshitting you, il te raconte des conneries II *vi* (*a*) baratiner/dévider/jaspiner (*b*) déconner.

bullshitter ['bʊlʃɪtə] *n P* 1. baratineur, -euse/jaspineur, -euse 2. con *m*, conne *f*/ connard, -arde.

bully ['bʊlɪ] *a F* bully for you! bravo!/ chapeau!

bum¹ [bʌm] I *a esp NAm F* piètre/minable/ moche; a bum deal, un sale coup/un coup en vache; bum steer, faux renseignement*/tuyau crevé; (*drugs*) a bum trip, un mauvais voyage. (*See* **kick¹ 3**; **rap 2**) II *n P* 1. fesses*/postérieur *m*/cul *m*; a kick up the bum, un coup de pied au cul; a pert bum, un petit cul sexy 2. *V* bit of bum, (*heterosexual sex*) coït*/baise *f*; (*sodomy*) enculage *m*/baise *f* à la riche 3. paresseux*/fainéant, -ante/ feignant, -ante; he's a lazy bum, c'est un tire-au-cul; beach bum/ski bum, fana *mf* de la plage/de ski 4. *esp NAm* clochard*/clodo *m* 5. to be on the bum, vivre en clochard*/faire le clodo; (*borrow*) emprunter* qch/taper (qn). (*See* **bum's rush**)

bum² [bʌm] *vtr P* 1. emprunter* (qch)/taper (qn); can I bum a fag/a cig (off you)? t'as une clope à me filer? to bum a lift, faire de l'autostop/du stop; to bum a meal off s.o., se faire payer à manger par qn 2. (*beg*) mendier 3. = **bum around** 4. vivre en clochard*/ faire le clodo.

bum around [bʌmə'raʊnd] *vi P* paresser*/fainéanter/tirer au cul/zoner.

bum-bandit [bʌm'bændɪt] *n V* = **arse-bandit**.

bumboy ['bʌmbɔɪ] *n P* homosexuel*/pédé *m*/enculé *m*.

bumf [bʌmf] *n F* (*short for* **bum-fodder**) 1. (*toilet paper*) papier *m* hygiénique/papier-cul *m*/P.Q. *m*/pécu *m* 2. (*forms, papers, etc*) paperasserie *f*; the taxman sent me all this bumf, le percepteur m'a envoyé toutes ces paperasseries/tout ce papier-cul.

bum flapper ['bʌmflæpə] *n P* mini-jupe fendue sur le côté.

bum-fodder ['bʌmfɒdə] *n O P* = **bumf**.

bumfreezer ['bʌmfriːzə] *n Br P* (*jacket*) pet-en-l'air *m*/rase-pet *m*.

bum-fuck ['bʌmfʌk] *n VV* coït* anal/baise *f* à la riche/enculage *m*.

bum-hole ['bʌm(h)əʊl] *n V* anus*/anneau *m*/rond *m*.

bummed out ['bʌmd'aʊt] *a NAm P* to be bummed out, être déçu/l'avoir mauvaise.

bummer ['bʌmə] *n P* 1. bousillage *m* 2. (*lazy person*) fainéant, -ante/feignant, -ante; (*tramp*) clochard*/clodo *m* 3. (*deception*) déception *f*; (*unpleasant situation*) sale expérience *f*; that party was a real bummer! on s'est rasé/barbé à cette boum! 4. (*failure*) échec *m*/fiasc *m* 5. (*drugs*) mauvais voyage; he was on a bummer, il flippait 6. homosexuel*/pédé *m*/tante *f*.

bump and grind ['bʌmpən(d)'graɪnd] *n F* coït*/carambolage *m*.

bumper ['bʌmpə] *n Austr F* mégot* (de cigarette)/clope *m*.

bumpf, bumph [bʌmf] *n F* = **bumf**.

bump off ['bʌmp'ɒf] *vtr F* tuer*/ descendre/liquider/buter (qn).

bum-robber ['bʌmrɒbə] *n P* (*not common*) homosexuel*/pédé *m*.

bumrush ['bʌmrʌʃ] *n NAm P* attaque *f*/ agression *f*/râble *m*.

bum's rush ['bʌmz'rʌʃ] *n P* to give s.o. the bum's rush, congédier* qn/balancer qn; he got the bum's rush, s'est fait vider/jeter.

bumsucker ['bʌmsʌkə] *n P* lèche-cul *m*/ lécheur, -euse.

bun [bʌn] *n* 1. *P* to have a bun in the oven, être enceinte*/avoir un polichinelle dans le tiroir 2. *NAm O P* to have a bun on, être

ivre*/être soûl 3. *pl NAm* buns, fesses*/miches
fpl/brioches *fpl*; to work one's buns off, bosser
comme un dingue/se décarcasser. (*See* **bust²**
4; **currant-bun**)
bunch [bʌntʃ] *n* 1. *F* a bunch of idiots, une
bande* d'idiots 2. *P* a bunch of fives, (*fist*)
poing *m*/pogne *f*. (*See* **honeybunch**)
bunco ['bʌŋkəʊ] *vtr P* rouler (qn) au jeu
(*surt aux cartes*).
bundle ['bʌndl] *n* 1. *F* grosse somme
d'argent*/liasse *f*/paquet *m*; to make a
bundle, faire sa pelote/son beurre 2. *P* to go a
bundle, s'enthousiasmer/s'emballer; I don't
go a bundle on that, ça (ne) m'emballe pas/ça
(ne) me botte pas tellement 3. *F* a bundle of
nerves, un paquet de nerfs 4. this kid is a
bundle of joy, ce gosse est un amour 5. *Br P*
bagarre*/baston *m or f*; they're always having bundles, ils n'arrêtent pas de se bagarrer/
se bigorner.
bung¹ [bʌŋ] *n Br P* (*bribe*) pot *m* de vin/
graissage *m* de patte.
bung² [bʌŋ] *vtr & i P* 1. jeter*/envoyer;
bung it over here! lance-moi ça par ici! 2.
my nose is bunged up, j'ai le nez bouché/pris
3. to bung s.o., donner un pot de vin à qn/
graisser la patte à qn.
bungalow ['bʌŋgələʊ] *n P* individu bête*/
bas *m* de plafond/andouille *f*.
bung-ho! ['bʌŋ'həʊ] *excl A F* 1. au
revoir!/ciao!/salut! 2. (*cheers!*) à la tienne!
bunghole ['bʌŋ(h)əʊl] *n* 1. *V* anus*/anneau
m 2. *F see* **bingo 50**.
bunk [bʌŋk] *F* I *a NAm* (*unfashionable*)
démodé/ringard/pas cool II *n* 1. = **bunkum**
2. *P* to do a bunk, s'enfuir*/filer/se tirer/se
faire la malle.
bunk in ['bʌŋk'ɪn] *vi P* entrer (quelque
part) sans invitation/resquiller.
bunk off ['bʌŋk'ɒf] *vi P* s'enfuir*/filer/se
tirer/se faire la malle; to bunk off from a
lesson, sécher un cours.
bunkum ['bʌŋkəm] *n F* bêtises*/blagues
fpl/foutaises *fpl*; that's all bunkum! tout ça
c'est du bidon!/de la blague!
bunk-up ['bʌŋkʌp] *n P* to give s.o. a bunk-
up, faire la courte échelle à qn.
bunny¹ ['bʌnɪ] *n* 1. *P* bunny (**girl**), hôtesse
f/entraîneuse *f* 2. *P* (*rare*) prostituée* pour
lesbiennes*/chatte *f* jaune 3. (*rare*) prostitué
pour homosexuels*/micheton *m* 4. *P* bavardage *m*/bavette *f* 5. *P* dupe *f*/cave *m*/navet
m 6. *P* (jeune) femme*/nana *f*/nénette *f*. (*See*
jungle 3)

bunny² ['bʌnɪ] *vi P* bavarder*/(se) tailler
une bavette. (*See* **rabbit²**)
bunny-fuck ['bʌnɪfʌk] *vi VV* faire l'amour*
avec rapidité/fourailler à la une/tirer un coup
vite fait.
bun wagon ['bʌnwægən] *n Can P* car* de
police/panier *m* à salade.
buppie, buppy ['bʌpɪ] *n F* (*black yuppie*)
jeune cadre noir ambitieux et matérialiste.
(*See* **yuppie**)
burbs (the) [ðə'bɜːbz] *n NAm F* (*abbr of
suburbs*) la banlieue.
burk(e) [bɜːk] *n P* individu bête*/gourde *f*/
andouille *f*. (*See* **berk**)
burn¹ [bɜːn] *n* 1. *Br* (*prisons*) tabac*/perle *m*
2. cigarette *f*/clope *m or f*.
burn² [bɜːn] *vtr & i P* 1. *P* (*a*) escroquer*/
arnaquer (*b*) voler*/chaparder 2. *NAm P*
(faire) passer sur la chaise (électrique) 3. *P*
tuer*/descendre/refroidir/flinguer 4. *F* conduire très vite*/foncer/gazer 5. *F* to burn the
candle at both ends, brûler la chandelle par
les deux bouts 6. *F* to burn one's fingers/to get
one's fingers burnt, se brûler les doigts/se
faire échauder 7. *F* to burn one's bridges/
boats, brûler les ponts/ses vaisseaux.
burned out ['bɜːnd'aʊt] *a & pp P* 1.
fatigué*/pompé 2. (être) épuisé/dans un état
d'apathie après avoir cessé de prendre des
drogues 3. ennuyé*/embêté.
burn-up ['bɜːnʌp] *n P* to have a burn-up,
conduire très vite*/foncer/brûler la route.
burn up ['bɜːn'ʌp] *vtr P* to burn up the
tarmac, aller très vite*/brûler le pavé/brûler
la route.
burp¹ [bɜːp] *n F* 1. rot *m* 2. bottom burp,
pet*/fusant *m*.
burp² [bɜːp] *vi F* roter.
burp-gun ['bɜːpgʌn] *n NAm P*
mitraillette*/sulfateuse *f*.
burton ['bɜːtn] *n F* 1. to go for a burton,
(*disappear*) disparaître; (*aviation*) faire un
trou dans l'eau; (*die*) mourir*; he's gone for a
burton, il a eu son compte/il est fichu 2. (*fall
down*) tomber* (par terre)/se casser la figure;
he went for a burton, il s'est étalé.
bus [bʌs] *n F* 1. (*a*) vieille bagnole/
guimbarde *f* (*b*) (*aircraft*) (vieux) coucou 2.
to miss the bus, manquer le coche/rater
l'occasion. (*See* **back II 13**; **back-end**)
bush [bʊʃ] *n* 1. *V* poils *mpl* du pubis
féminin/cresson *m*/gazon *m*/barbu *m* 2. *P*
(*drugs*) marijuana*/foin *m* 3. *F* bush
telegraph, téléphone *m* arabe 4. *Austr F* what

do you think this is, bush week? arrête ton char!/ne la ramène pas avec moi! (*See* **go²** 7)

bushed [bʊʃt] *a P* 1. désorienté/interdit 2. fatigué*/claqué/crevé.

bushel and peck ['bʊʃələn(d)'pek] *n P* (*RS* = *neck*) cou*.

bushie ['bʊʃɪ] *n Austr F* paysan*/péquenot *m*/plouc *mf*.

bushwhack ['bʊʃwæk] *v NAm F* I *vi* (*camp out*) bivouaquer II *vtr* (*ambush*) tendre une embuscade à (qn).

bushwhacker ['bʊʃwækə] *n* 1. *Austr F* paysan*/plouc *mf* 2. *NAm F* qn qui tend une embuscade.

business ['bɪznɪs] *n* 1. *F* to mean business, prendre les choses au sérieux/ne pas rigoler 2. *F* to do one's business, déféquer*/débourrer 3. *F* affaire *f*/histoire *f*; what a filthy business! quelle sale affaire! 4. *F* why he ever married her is nobody's business, Dieu seul sait pourquoi il l'a épousée! 5. *Br P* the business, (*beating*) cogne *f*/torchée *f* 6. *P* attirail* de camé/popote *f*/kit *m* 7. (= *show business, music business, etc*) his father was in the business, son père faisait du show-biz 8. *P* la prostitution/le bisness 9. *Br* the business, (*the very best*) tout ce qu'il y a de mieux; it's the business, c'est le super pied. (*See* **do²** 1; **funny I 2**)

busk [bʌsk] *vi* 1. *F* (*music*) jouer/chanter dans la rue/dans le métro/dans les bars (*pour se faire de l'argent*) 2. *F* (*theatre*) jouer dans une troupe ambulante.

busker ['bʌskə] *n* 1. *F* musicien, -ienne/chanteur, -euse qui se fait de l'argent dans la rue/dans le métro/dans les bars 2. *F* comédien(ne) ambulant(e).

busman ['bʌsmən] *n F* to take a busman's holiday, faire la même chose pendant ses loisirs que pendant son travail.

bust¹ [bʌst] I *a F* 1. cassé/esquinté; my watch is bust, ma montre est fichue/foutue 2. (*a*) sans le sou/fauché (*b*) to go bust, faire faillite/boire un bouillon II *n P* 1. *NAm* exploit *m*/succès *m* spectaculaire 2. réjouissances*/bamboche *f*/bringue *f* 3. arrestation *f*/rafle *f* de police; marijuana bust, arrestation par la police pour usage de marijuana* 4. *Austr* cambriolage *m*/casse *m*.

bust² [bʌst] *vtr P* 1. casser (un racket, etc) 2. arrêter*/agrafer; the club was busted for drugs, la police a fait une descente dans le club pour chercher des stupéfiants; he got busted for possession of cannabis, il a été arrêté pour détention de cannabis* 3. battre*/rosser; to bust s.o.'s ass, casser la gueule à qn 4. to bust a gut/*NAm* to bust one's buns, se décarcasser/se casser le cul. (*See* **shit²** 4)

buster ['bʌstə] *n esp NAm F* homme*/type *m*; listen, buster! écoute, mec!/mon gars!/mon vieux! (*See* **ball-buster**; **blockbuster**; **broncobuster**; **jaw-buster**)

bust in ['bʌst'ɪn] *vtr & i P* 1. to bust s.o.'s face in, casser la figure* à qn/abîmer le portrait à qn 2. to bust in (on s.o.), arriver* comme un chien dans un jeu de quilles 3. to bust in on s.o.'s conversation, s'injecter dans la conversation.

bust open ['bʌst'əʊpən] *vtr P* to bust open a safe, casser un coffre-fort.

bust out ['bʌst'aʊt] *vi P* 1. s'évader/se faire la malle 2. she's busting out all over, elle a des seins* plantureux/(il) y a du monde au balcon.

bust-up ['bʌstʌp] *n F* 1. querelle*/engueulade *f*; to have a bust-up with s.o., avoir une prise de bec avec qn/s'engueuler avec qn 2. rupture *f*/mallette *f* et paquette *f*; they've had a bust-up, ils ont rompu.

bust up ['bʌst'ʌp] *vtr F* 1. abîmer*/bousiller/esquinter (qch) 2. rompre (une amitié)/briser (un mariage).

busty ['bʌstɪ] *a F* à la poitrine proéminente; she's a rather busty lady, (il) y a du monde au balcon.

busy ['bɪzɪ] *n P* (*detective*) enquêteur, -euse/fileur *m*/sondeur *m*; (*police officer*) flic *m*/poulet *m*. (*See* **bizzie**).

butch [bʊtʃ] *a & n P* 1. (*a*) homme* fort et viril/dur *m*/macho *m* (*b*) homosexuel* actif/macho *m*/butch *m* 2. femme*/surt lesbienne* d'apparence *ou* de caractère masculin(e)/viriliste *f*.

butchers ['bʊtʃəz] *n P* (*RS* = *butcher's hook* = *look*) coup d'œil*; to take a butchers at sth, regarder* qch/reluquer qch; let's have a butchers, fais voir.

butt [bʌt] *n NAm F* fesses*/derrière *m*; get your butt out of here! tire ton cul d'ici! he's a pain in the butt, c'est un emmerdeur; it's a pain in the butt, ça me tape sur le système.

butter ['bʌtə] *n F* she looks as though butter wouldn't melt in her mouth, elle fait la Sainte-Nitouche/elle fait la sucrée/on lui donnerait le bon Dieu sans confession. (*See* **bread 3**; **bread-and-butter**)

butterfingers ['bʌtəfɪŋgəz] *n F* malagau-

che *mf*/malapatte *mf*; **to have butterfingers/to be a butterfingers**, avoir la main malheureuse/être brise-tout; **butterfingers!** espèce d'empoté!

butterflies ['bʌtəflaɪz] *npl F* **to have butterflies (in one's stomach/in one's tummy)**, avoir peur*/avoir le trac/avoir les jetons.

butter up ['bʌtə'(r)ʌp] *vtr F* flatter*/pommader/passer de la pommade à (qn).

butters ['bʌtəz] *n P* (*schools*) (*very ugly person*) mocheté *f*/tarderie *f*.

buttfuck¹ ['bʌtfʌk] *n NAm V* 1. coït* anal/baise *f* à la riche 2. homosexuel*/enculeur *m* 3. (*despicable person*) salaud*/trou *m* du cul.

buttfuck² ['bʌtfʌk] *vtr NAm V* sodomiser*/enculer/empaffer.

buttie ['bʌtɪ] *n P* = **butty**.

button¹ ['bʌtn] *n* 1. *P* menton *m*/bichonnet *m*; **right on the button**, (*on target*) pan! dans le mille! 2. *V* clitoris*/bouton *m*. (*See* **belly-button; panic 2**)

button² ['bʌtn] *vtr P* **button your mouth/lip!** button it! (ferme) ton bec!/la ferme!

buttoned up ['bʌtnd'ʌp] *a & pp P* 1. peu communicatif/constipé 2. **it's all buttoned up**, c'est dans le sac/c'est du tout cuit.

buttonhole ['bʌtnhəʊl] *vtr F* accrocher/agrafer/cramponner (qn).

button men ['bʌtn'men] *npl P* agents* *mpl* de police (en uniforme)/habillés *mpl*.

butty ['bʌtɪ] *n P* (*esp N. England*) sandwich *m*; **jam butty**, sandwich *m* à la confiture; **chip butty**, sandwich aux frites.

buy [baɪ] *vtr* 1. *F* (go on,) **I'll buy it**, vas-y, déballe! je donne ma langue au chat; **I'll buy that**, je marche/je suis d'acc/dac! **I hope she buys it**, (*when telling a lie*) j'espère qu'elle va me croire 2. *P* **he bought it/a packet**, (*met with trouble*) il a écopé/il a eu son paquet; (*died*) il a passé l'arme à gauche.

buyer ['baɪə] *n P* receleur*/fourgue *m*.

buzz¹ [bʌz] *n* 1. *F* **to give s.o. a buzz**, (*telephone*) donner/passer un coup de fil à qn 2. *F* (*rumour*) bruit *m*; **there's a buzz going round that you're getting hitched**, paraît que tu vas te marier? 3. *P* plaisir violent/transport *m*; **rock gives me a real buzz**, le rock, ça me branche; **top buzz**, super cool; **it's a buzz**, c'est le pied.

buzz² [bʌz] *vtr F* 1. **to buzz s.o.**, (*telephone*) passer un coup de fil à qn 2. *F* (*of aircraft*) coller/frôler/harceler (un autre avion) 3. *P* (*schools*) **you're buzzing**, (*messing around*) tu rigoles/tu déconnes.

buzzer ['bʌzə] *n* 1. *P* (*rare*) (*pickpocket*) voleur* à la tire/tireur *m*/fourchette *f* 2. *F* téléphone*/ronfleur *m*/bigophone *m*.

buzz off ['bʌz'ɒf] *vi F* s'enfuir*/décamper/filer; **buzz off!** débarrasse!/fiche le camp!/casse-toi!

buzzy ['bʌzɪ] *a P* **buzzy atmosphere**, atmosphère électrisante.

bye(-bye)! ['baɪ('baɪ)] *excl F* salut!/ciao!

bye-byes ['baɪbaɪz] *npl F* (*child's talk*) dodo *m*; **go (to) bye-byes for mummy!** fais dodo pour maman!

BYO ['biːwaɪəʊ] *abbr F* (= *bring your own*) apporter sa bouteille.

C

C, c [siː] *abbr* **1.** *P* (*drugs*) C, big c, (*cocaine*) cocaïne*/coco *f*/neige *f*; C habit, passion *f* d'un toxico pour la cocaïne **2.** (*cancer*) his fight against the Big C, sa lutte contre le cancer.

cabbage ['kæbɪdʒ] *n F Pej* he's a real cabbage, c'est un vrai crétin.

cabbage-head ['kæbɪdʒhed] *n NAm F* individu bête*/gourde *f*/cornichon *m*.

cabbie, cabby ['kæbɪ] *n F* chauffeur *m* de taxi*/taxi *mf*/rongeur *m*.

caboodle [kə'buːdl] *n F* the whole (kit and) caboodle, et tout le Saint-Frusquin/et tout le bataclan/tout le fourbi. (*See* **boiling** II; **shebang 1; shoot¹ 1; shooting-match**)

cack¹ [kæk] *n A P* étron*/caca *m*.

cack² [kæk] *vi A P* (*rare*) déféquer*/caguer/faire caca.

cackhanded ['kæk'hændɪd] *a F* balourd/empoté.

cackle ['kækl] *n P* cut the cackle! assez bavardé!/assez jacté!

cacky ['kækɪ] *a O P* merdeux.

cactus ['kæktəs] *n P* (*drugs*) mescaline *f*/cactus *m* du Mexique.

cad [kæd] *n Br F* salaud*/connard *m*/fumier *m*.

caddy ['kædɪ] *abbr esp NAm F* (*car*) Cadillac *f* (*RTM*).

cadge¹ [kædʒ] *n F* he's always on the cadge, c'est un tapeur chronique/professionnel.

cadge² [kædʒ] *vtr F* emprunter*/taper; faire la manche; to cadge a thousand francs from s.o., taper/torpiller qn de mille francs; to cadge a lift, (réussir à) se faire emmener en voiture/faire du stop.

cadger ['kædʒə] *n F* tapeur, -euse/torpilleur, -euse.

cafe [kæf, keɪf], **caff** [kæf] *n Br P* = café*/troquet *m*; cafèt *f*.

cage [keɪdʒ] *n F* prison*/cage *f*.

cag(e)y ['keɪdʒɪ] *a F* malin*/futé; to be/to act cagey, se boutonner/jouer serré; he's very cagey about his salary, il n'aime pas avouer combien il gagne.

cahoot(s) [kə'huːt(s)] *n F* (*a*) to be in cahoots with s.o., être de mèche/en cheville avec qn (*b*) *NAm* to go cahoots with s.o., partager avec qn.

Cain [keɪn] *Prn P* **1.** to raise Cain, faire du bruit*/faire un boucan de tous les diables **2.** Cain and Abel, (*RS = table*) table *f*; carante *f*.

cake [keɪk] *n* **1.** *F* it's a piece of cake, c'est du gâteau/du nanan **2.** *F* that takes the cake, ça c'est le comble/le bouquet **3.** *NAm P* to grab a piece of cake, faire l'amour*/faire un carton **4.** *F* you can't have your cake and eat it, on ne peut être et avoir été/on ne peut pas tout avoir **5.** *F* the workers are asking for a bigger slice of the cake, les ouvriers revendiquent une augmentation/une plus grosse part du gâteau. (*See* **beefcake; cheesecake; fruitcake; hot 17**)

cakehole ['keɪk(h)əʊl] *n P* bouche*/bec *m*; shut your cakehole! ferme ça!/la ferme!/ferme ton bec!

calaboose, calaboosh [kælə'buːs, kælə'buːʃ] *n NAm P* prison*/bloc *m*/violon *m*/taule *f*.

calendar ['kæləndə] *n P* année* de prison/gerbe *f*.

call¹ [kɔːl] *n F* **1.** to pay a call, uriner*/aller faire sa petite commission **2.** it was a close call, il était moins une. (*See* **shave**)

call² [kɔːl] *vtr F* **1.** to call it quits, abandonner/s'arrêter; let's cut our losses and call it quits, arrêtons les frais et n'insistons pas **2.** to call it a day, mettre fin à qch/s'en tenir là **3.** to call the shots, faire/dicter la loi.

call down ['kɔːl'daʊn] *vtr NAm F* réprimander*/attraper.

call girl ['kɔːl'gɜːl] *n F* (*a*) prostituée*/pute *f* (*b*) prostituée* qui prend ses rendez-vous par téléphone/call-girl *f*.

calling-down ['kɔːlɪŋ'daʊn] *n NAm F* attrapade *f*/savon *m*.

38

camp¹ [kæmp] I *a F* 1. (*a*) affecté/poseur (*b*) qui fait preuve de mauvais goût/de vulgarité (*c*) chichiteux 2. (*a*) efféminé (*b*) homosexuel; **he's very camp**, il fait très pédé/tapette; c'est une affiche (*c*) lesbienne II *n F* manières efféminées (*surt* d'homosexuel)/tantouserie *f*.

camp² [kæmp] *vi P* être homosexuel* *ou* lesbienne*; être de la pédale *ou* de la maison tire-bouton.

camp up ['kæmp'ʌp] *vtr F* to camp it up (*a*) jouer la comédie (*b*) se montrer efféminé/faire la persilleuse/faire l'affiche.

can¹ [kæn] *n* 1. *P* prison*/taule *f*/bloc *m*; to put s.o. in the can, fourrer qn au bloc 2. (*recording, etc*) in the can, en boîte; it's in the can, c'est dans le sac 3. *pl F* casque *m* (à écouteurs) 4. *F* to carry/to take the can for s.o., écoper pour qn/porter le chapeau; I had to carry the can for that, c'est moi qui ai dû payer les pots cassés 5. *P* (*drugs*) deux grammes de marijuana* 6. *esp NAm P* WC*/chiottes *fpl*/pissotière *f* 7. *NAm Euph P* fesses*/pétrousquin *m*; to kick s.o. in the can, botter l'arrière-train de/à qn 8. *F* can of worms, problème *m* difficile à résoudre/sac *m* de nœuds.

can² [kæn] *vtr* 1. *P* (*rare*) emprisonner*/fourrer dedans 2. *esp NAm P* se débarrasser* de (qn)/sacquer/flanquer à la porte 3. *F Mus* enregistrer/mettre en conserve. (*See* **canned** 2) 4. *P* can it! la ferme!/écrase!

canapa ['kænəpə] *n P* (*drugs*) marijuana*/canapa *f*.

canary [kə'nɛərɪ] *n P* dénonciateur*/balance *f*/chevreuil *m*/donneur, -euse; to sing like a canary, tout avouer*/vendre la mèche.

cancer stick ['kænsəstɪk] *n P* cigarette*/cibiche *f*/cancérette *f*.

candle ['kændl] *n F* 1. (*spark plug*) bougie *f* 2. she can't hold a candle to you, elle ne t'arrive pas à la cheville 3. the game's not worth the candle, le jeu n'en vaut pas la chandelle 4. to burn the candle at both ends, brûler la chandelle par les deux bouts. (*See* **Roman 1**)

candy ['kændɪ] *n P* (*drugs*) (*a*) cocaïne*/neige *f* (*b*) héroïne*/blanche *f* (*c*) LSD*/sucre *m* (*d*) drogues* en général/stups *mpl*. (*See* **candyman**; **needle-candy**; **nose-candy**; **rock-candy**)

candyman ['kændɪmæn] *n NAm P* fourgueur *m*/passeur *m* de drogues; dealer *m*.

cane¹ [keɪn] *n P* pince-monseigneur*/

rossignol *m*. (*See* **varnish²**)

cane² [keɪn] *vtr P* 1. to cane s.o., battre*/tabasser qn 2. to cane sth, abîmer*/bousiller qch.

canful ['kænful] *n P* to have (had) a canful, être ivre*/rétamé/schlass.

caning ['keɪnɪŋ] *n F* victoire *f* facile/les doigts dans le nez; he got a real caning, il a été battu à plates coutures; il s'est fait rétamer.

canned [kænd] *a* 1. *P* (*a*) ivre*/soûl; he was completely canned, il était bourré à mort/beurré comme un petit lu (*b*) drogué*/camé/défoncé 2. *F* canned music, musique *f* en conserve 3. *NAm P* balancé/viré 4. canned stuff, opium*/noir *m*. (*See* **stuff¹**)

cannibal ['kænɪbəl] *n V* (*esp Black Sl*) qn qui pratique la fellation* *ou* le cunnilinctus*.

cannibalism ['kænɪbəlɪzm] *n V* (*esp Black Sl*) (*a*) fellation* (*b*) cunnilinctus*.

cannon ['kænən] *n NAm P* voleur *m* à la tire/fourchette *f*/tireur *m*.

canny ['kænɪ] *n Br F* (*esp N. England*) intelligent*/futé; she's a canny lass, elle (n')est pas bête, la nana.

canoe [kə'nuː] *n F* to paddle one's own canoe, mener seul sa barque/voler de ses propres ailes/se débrouiller.

canoodle [kə'nuːdl] *vi O F* (se) bécoter/(se) peloter/se faire des mamours.

canoodling [kə'nuːdlɪŋ] *n O F* pelotage *m*/mamours *mpl*.

Canuck [kə'nʌk] *n F* Canadien(ne) (*surt* français(e)).

cap¹ [kæp] *n* 1. *P* capsule *f* de narcs 2. *F* diaphragme (contraceptif) 3. *NAm P* (*bullet*) balle*/dragée *f*. (*See* **Dutch I 3**; **feather¹ 2**; **Jim cap**; **thinking-cap**)

cap² [kæp] *P* I *vtr* 1. ouvrir *ou* consommer (une capsule de drogue) 2. acheter (des stupéfiants) II *vtr & i NAm* to cap (on) s.o., insulter/humilier qn.

caper ['keɪpə] *n F* (*a*) escapade *f*/farce *f* (*b*) délit *m*/crime *m*/sérieux *m*.

carby ['kɑːbɪ] *n Austr F* carburateur *m*/carbu *m*.

carcass ['kɑːkəs] *n F* drag your carcass over here! radine!/amène ta viande! shift your carcass! (*move!*) bouge-toi!/remue ta graisse!/pousse ton cul!; (*go away!*) débarrasse (le plancher)!/vire de là!

card [kɑːd] *n O F* 1. he's a real card, c'est un drôle d'individu*/de numéro/de phénomène 2. to get one's cards, être renvoyé/se faire virer;

to give s.o. **his cards**, renvoyer qn/sacquer qn/virer qn 3. **to put one's cards on the table**, jouer cartes sur table 4. **it's in the cards/** *NAm* **it's in the cards that ...**, ça se pourrait bien que ... 5. **to play one's trump card**, jouer sa meilleure carte/son atout; **to hold the trump card**, avoir les atouts en main 6. **to throw in one's cards**, abandonner la partie. (*See* **close**; **mark²** 1; **sharp** II)

cardie, cardy ['kɑːdɪ] *n F* (*abbr of cardigan*) gilet *m*/paletot *m*/cardigan *m*.

carhop ['kɑːhɒp] *n NAm F* (*in drive-in*) personne *f* qui sert les repas aux clients (dans leurs voitures)/carhop *m*.

cark (it) ['kɑːk(ɪt)] *vi Austr P* mourir*/clamser/crever.

carn [kɑːn] *n Br P* argent*/fric *m*/pognon *m*.

carpet¹ ['kɑːpɪt] *n* 1. *F* (*a*) **on the carpet**, (*under consideration*) sur le tapis (*b*) **to have s.o. on the carpet**, (*reprimand*) tenir qn sur la sellette 2. *P* (*RS = carpet bag = drag*) trois mois *mpl* de prison*/de taule. (*See* **dirt** 4; **drag¹** 7; **red I** 2)

carpet² ['kɑːpɪt] *vtr F* **to carpet s.o.** = **to have s.o. on the carpet** (**carpet¹** 1 (*b*))

carpetbagger ['kɑːpɪtbægə] *n NAm F* candidat parachuté; aventurier *m*/profiteur *m* politique.

carrier ['kærɪə] *n F* 1. (*drugs*) contact *m*/intermédiaire *mf*/passeur, -euse 2. (= *carrier bag*) sac *m* (en plastique).

carrot(s) ['kærət(s)], **carrot-top** ['kærəttɒp] *n F* rouquin(e)/poil *m* de carotte.

carry ['kærɪ] *vtr F* 1. avoir/posséder de la drogue 2. **he's had as much as he can carry**, il a son compte/il est (bien) plein. (*See* **can¹** 4)

carrying ['kærɪɪŋ] *a F* 1. qui a/qui possède de la drogue 2. *Br* pourvu d'argent*/friqué/chargé.

carryings-on ['kærɪɪŋz'ɒn] *npl F* (*a*) simagrées *fpl*/pitreries *fpl*/chichis *mpl*/clowneries *fpl* (*b*) ébats amoureux/zizi pan-pan *m*.

carry off ['kærɪ'ɒf] *vtr F* **to carry it off** (**well**), bien s'en tirer/réussir son coup.

carry-on ['kærɪ'ɒn] *n P* **what a carry-on!** quel cirque!/quelle comédie!/que d'histoires!

carry on ['kærɪ'ɒn] *vi F* 1. (*a*) **to carry on with s.o.**, fréquenter qn/sortir avec qn/flirter avec qn (*b*) avoir une liaison avec qn 2. faire une scène; **don't carry on like that!** ne fais pas l'idiot!

cars(e)y, carsi ['kɑːzɪ] *n P* = **kazi**.

cart [kɑːt] *n F* **to land s.o. (right) in the cart**,

mettre qn dans le pétrin. (*See* **apple-cart**; **dog-cart**)

cart about, around ['kɑːtə'baʊt, ə'raʊnd] *vtr F* trimbal(l)er (qn/qch).

cart off ['kɑːt'ɒf] *vtr F* **to get carted off to hospital**, être embarqué à l'hosto *m*.

carve [kɑːv] *vtr Br P* massacrer/charcuter (qn) à coups de couteau.

carve-up ['kɑːvʌp] *n Br P* partage *m* du butin.

carve up ['kɑːv'ʌp] *vtr Br P* ruiner les chances de (qn); **they got carved up**, tous leurs projets sont tombés à l'eau.

carz(e)y ['kɑːzɪ] *n P* = **kazi**.

cas [kæʒ] *a NAm P* (*abbr = casual*) 1. (*relaxed*) relax(e)/cool 2. (*good*) chouette/michto.

Casanova [kæsə'nəʊvə] *n F* Casanova *m*/cavaleur *m*/don Juan *m*.

case¹ [keɪs] *n* 1. *F* individu* excentrique; **he's a hard case**, c'est un dur (à cuire); **he's a head case**, c'est un fou/un cinglé 2. *P* casse *f*/fric-frac *m*; **to have/to do a case**, voler*/faire un fric-frac 3. *NAm P* **to get on s.o.'s case**, (*annoy, harass*) taper sur le système à qn/prendre la tête à qn; **get off my case!** laisse tomber!/fiche-moi la paix!/lâche-moi! (*See* **nutcase**)

case² [keɪs] *vtr P* 1. **to case the joint**, aller examiner une maison, une banque, etc avant de la cambrioler*/se rencarder sur la boîte 2. **to get cased**, être inculpé/fargué.

cashed up ['kæʃt'ʌp] *a Austr F* riche*/plein de fric/plein aux as.

cash-in ['kæʃɪn] *n F* affaire *f* qui rapporte; **it's a bit of a cash-in**, ça rapporte pas mal/ça fait du pognon.

cash in ['kæʃ'ɪn] *vtr & i* 1. *P* **to cash in one's chips**, mourir*/lâcher la rampe/poser sa chique 2. *F* **to cash in on sth**, tirer profit de qch.

casting couch ['kɑːstɪŋ'kaʊtʃ] *n F Euph* **she used the casting couch to get a good role in the film**, elle a couché avec le metteur en scène pour avoir un beau rôle dans le film.

cast-iron ['kɑːst'aɪən] *a F* (*a*) **cast-iron case**, affaire *f* inattaquable/dossier *m* en béton (*b*) **cast-iron constitution**, santé *f* de fer; **cast-iron stomach**, estomac *m* d'autruche; **cast-iron alibi**, alibi *m* en béton (armé); **cast-iron jaw**, boxeur *m* difficile à mettre KO.

cast-offs ['kɑːstɒfs] *npl F* 1. vieux vêtements*/vieilles frusques 2. laissés-pourcompte *mpl*; **he's one of her old cast-offs**, c'est une de ses anciennes conquêtes.

casual [ˈkæʒjʊəl] *n F* 1. client *m* de passage 2. *pl* chaussures* *ou* vêtements* de sport.

cat [kæt] *n* 1. *P* (*esp Black Sl*) mec *m*/type *m*; cool cat, mec *m* cool; he's a real cool cat, c'est un type super/un type cool; hey, you cats! eh, les mecs! 2. *P* musicien *m* de jazz 3. *F Pej* femme* (malicieuse)/rosse *f* 4. *F* (= *cat o'nine tails*) fouet *m*/chat *m* à neuf queues 5. jeune homosexuel*/mignard *m*/môme *m* 6. *F* he thinks he's the cat's whiskers, il ne se prend pas pour de la crotte/de la merde. (*See* **bee** 2) 7. *F* to lead a cat and dog life, vivre comme chien et chat 8. *F* it's raining cats and dogs, il tombe des hallebardes; il pleut à vache qui pisse 9. *F* to play cat and mouse with s.o., jouer au chat et à la souris avec qn 10. *F* not enough room to swing a cat, pas la place de se retourner 11. *F* (has) the cat got your tongue? tu as perdu ta langue? 12. *F* you look like something the cat's brought in! t'as l'air dégueulasse!/tu en as une touche! 13. *F* not a cat in hell's chance! rien à faire/des clous! 14. *F* to let the cat out of the bag, vendre la mèche 15. *F* that's put the cat among the pigeons, ça a été le pavé dans la mare. (*See* **copycat; fat I** 5; **fraidy; hellcat; holy** 1; **piss¹** 5; **scaredy-cat; shoot²** 5)

catch¹ [kætʃ] **I** *a F* a catch question, une question-piège/une colle **II** *n* 1. *F* (*husband*) jules *m*/homme *m*; he's a good catch, c'est un beau parti 2. *F* entourloupe(tte) *f*; what's the catch? où est le truc/le piège? 3. *F* it's (a) catch 22 (situation), (il n')y a pas moyen de s'en tirer/de s'en sortir.

catch² [kætʃ] *vtr F* 1. you won't catch me doing that! pas de danger qu'on m'y prenne! don't let me catch you at it again! que je t'y reprenne! 2. you'll catch it! tu vas en prendre pour ton grade! 3. caught napping/with one's trousers down, pris au pied levé/au dépourvu/ sans vert 4. to be caught short, s'oublier/faire pipi dans son froc 5. the age to catch 'em, *see* **bingo** 17 6. to catch s.o. off base, prendre qn au dépourvu 7. *NAm* to catch some z's, dormir*/piquer un roupillon. (*See* **cold II** 1; **packet** 1; **u.v.'s; z's**)

catch on [ˈkætʃˈɒn] *vi F* 1. comprendre/ piger/entraver/percuter; he catches on quick, il pige vite, lui 2. prendre/être en vogue; it'll never catch on! ça ne prendra/ne marchera jamais!

catch out [ˈkætʃˈaʊt] *vtr F* prendre en défaut; he got caught out, il s'est fait

prendre/coincer/pincer; il s'est fait avoir.

cathouse [ˈkæthaʊs] *n esp NAm P* bordel*/ claque *m*/boxif *m*.

catlick [ˈkætlɪk] *Br F* 1. *n* bout *m*/brin *m* de toilette/toilette *f* de chat 2. *a & n* Catho(lique) (*mf*).

catty [ˈkætɪ] *a F* rosse/vache; a catty remark, une vanne/une vacherie.

caution [ˈkɔːʃ(ə)n] *n O F* a proper caution, un drôle de numéro/un drôle de phénomène.

cave [ˈkeɪv] *n O P* (*school*) cave! vingt-deux!/pet! pet!

caveman [ˈkeɪvmæn] *n O* grosse brute; caveman stuff, brutalités *fpl*.

Cecil, cecil [ˈsesl] *n P* (*drugs*) cocaïne*/coke *f*. (*See* **after** 1)

ceiling [ˈsiːlɪŋ] *n F* to go through the ceiling/ to hit the ceiling, se mettre en colère*/sortir de ses gonds/sauter au plafond.

celeb [sɪˈleb] *n F* (*abbr of celebrity*) star *f*/ vedette *f*.

century [ˈsentʃərɪ] *n P* 1. cent livres *fpl* sterling 2. *NAm* century (note), (billet* de) cent dollars *mpl*.

cert [sɜːt] *n F* (*abbr of certainty*) it's a dead cert, c'est du tout cuit/c'est affiché; (*racing*) c'est un gagnant sûr/c'est couru.

cha [tʃɑː] *n F* = **char¹** 1.

chain-gang [ˈtʃeɪngæŋ] *n P* partouze *f* à la bague. (*See* **daisy** 5).

chair [tʃɛə] *n NAm F* 1. chaise *f* électrique; to go to the chair, être grillé 2. chair warmer, rond-de-cuir *m*/gratte-papier *m* 3. (*in pub*) to be in the chair, être celui qui offre une tournée.

Chalfonts [ˈtʃælfɒnts] *npl Br P* (*RS = Chalfont St Giles = piles*) hémorroïdes *fpl*/ émeraudes *fpl*.

chalk [tʃɔːk] *n* 1. *F* better by a long chalk, bien loin le meilleur; not by a long chalk, s'en faut de beaucoup 2. *F* they're like/as different as chalk and cheese, c'est le jour et la nuit.

chalk up [ˈtʃɔːkˈʌp] *vtr & i* 1. *F* mettre sur l'ardoise 2. *P* to chalk up a score = **score²** 1, 2.

champ [tʃæmp] (*abbr of champion*) *F* **I** *n* as *m*/crack *m* **II** *a* = **champion II**.

champers [ˈʃæmpəz] *n F* champagne *m*/ champ'm*/champe *m*.

champion [ˈtʃæmpɪən] *F* (*esp N. England*) **I** *a* (right/proper) champion, excellent*/de première/du tonnerre/impec. (*See* **gatecrasher**) **II** *adv* excellemment/soin-soin/soi-

soi.

chancy ['tʃɑːnsɪ] *a F* 1. (*lucky*) chanceux/
verni 2. (*risky*) risqué; it's a chancy business,
c'est risqué.

change [tʃeɪndʒ] *n F* 1. you won't get much
change out of him, tu n'en tireras pas grand-
chose/tu perds ton temps avec lui 2. it makes
a change, ça change un peu 3. the change of
life, la ménopause/le retour d'âge. (*See* ring²
2)

channel ['tʃæn(ə)l] *n P* (*drugs*) veine dans
laquelle un drogué injecte la drogue.

chap [tʃæp] *n F* individu*/type *m*; poor chap,
pauvre type; he's a queer chap, c'est un drôle
de bonhomme; hello, old chap, salut, mon
pote/vieille branche! listen old chap! écoute,
mon vieux!

chappess [tʃæ'pes] *n F* femme*/gonzesse *f*.

char¹ [tʃɑː] *n F* 1. thé *m*; a cup of char, une
tasse de thé 2. (= *charwoman, charlady*)
femme *f* de ménage/bonniche *f*.

char² [tʃɑː] *vi F* to char/to go out charring,
faire des ménages.

character ['kærɪktə] *n F* he's quite a character, c'est un drôle d'individu*/de numéro.

charas [tʃæ'ræs] *n P* (*drugs*) haschisch*/
chicha *m*/hash *m*.

charge [tʃɑːdʒ] *n P* 1. (*drugs*) (*a*)
marijuana*/douce *f* (*b*) état *m* d'euphorie/trip
m; to go on the charge, planer 2. plaisir *m*/
émotion *f*; to get a charge out of sth, tirer
plaisir de qch/s'en payer une tranche; I got a
charge out of it, ça m'a fait quelque chose.

charged (up) ['tʃɑːdʒd('ʌp)] *a P* drogué*/
défoncé/chargé; to get charged (up), se
camer.

charlie ['tʃɑːlɪ] *P I a* de mauvaise qualité;
de mauvais goût; that suit's a bit charlie, ce
costard est plutôt tocard II *n* 1. a right/proper
charlie, un vrai gugusse 2. charlie's dead, ton
jupon dépasse/tu cherches une belle-mère?
(*See* Anne; snow² 2) 3. (*drugs*) charlie
(coke), cocaïne*/C *f* 4. *NAm* soldat *m ou*
armée *f* du Viêt Cong 5. lesbienne*/gougnotte
f 6. *Austr* prostituée*/poule *f* 7. (*Black Slang*)
blanc *m* 8. *NAm* charlie horse, crampe *f* dans
les muscles des bras ou des jambes. (*See*
good-time 2)

charver¹ ['tʃɑːvə] *n V* coït*/tringlage *m*.

charver² ['tʃɑːvə] *vi V* faire l'amour*/
tringler.

chase around ['tʃeɪsə'raʊnd] *vi F* to
chase around after women, courir les filles/les
jupons/cavaler.

chaser ['tʃeɪsə] *n F* (*glass of whisky, etc.
drunk after beer*) pousse-bière *m*. (*See
petticoat-chaser; skirt-chaser; woman-
chaser*)

chassis ['ʃæsɪ] *n F* (*woman's body*) châssis
m/académie *f*.

chat up ['tʃæt'ʌp] *vtr F* baratiner; draguer;
to chat up a bird, faire du rentre-dedans/du
gringue à une fille*; draguer une nana.

cheapie ['tʃiːpɪ] *n F* 1. it's a cheapie, c'est
de la camelote 2. *pl* cheapies, billets *mpl*
d'avion à prix réduits.

cheapjack ['tʃiːpdʒæk] *n F* camelot *m*;
cheapjack goods, de la camelote.

cheapskate ['tʃiːpskeɪt] *n NAm F* 1.
avare*/grippe-sou *m*/radin *m* 2. vaurien*/bon-
à-rien *m*.

cheat [tʃiːt] *vtr esp NAm F* cocufier/doubler/
faire porter des cornes (à); he's cheating (on)
his wife, il trompe sa femme.

check! [tʃek] *excl NAm* oui*/d'acc!/dac!/
banco!

check out ['tʃek'aʊt] *vtr & i* 1. *P* mourir*/
déposer le bilan/rendre ses clefs 2. *P* partir*/
filer 3. *F* to check s.o./sth out, vérifier qch/se
rencarder sur qn/qch; hey, check out those
chicks! hé, vise-moi ces nanas!

cheddar ['tʃedə] *n F* hard cheddar = hard
cheese (cheese 2)

cheek [tʃiːk] *n F* 1. toupet *m*/culot *m*; he's
got a hell of a cheek/the cheek of the devil, il
a un culot monstre/il manque pas d'air/il est
vachement culotté; bleeding cheek! tu parles
d'un culot! don't give me any of your cheek!
(ne) te fiche pas de moi! it's a damned cheek!
ça c'est se fiche(r) du monde! 2. *pl* fesses*/
fessier *m*/joufflu *m*.

cheeky ['tʃiːkɪ] *a F* effronté/culotté/gonflé;
cheeky little sod! il/tu, etc manque(s) pas
d'air!

cheerio! [tʃɪərɪ'əʊ] *excl F* 1. = cheers! (*a*)
2. à bientôt!/bon courage!/salut!/ciao!/à la
prochaine!

cheers! [tʃɪəz] *excl F* (*a*) à la bonne vôtre!/
à la tienne (Étienne)! (*b*) merci (*c*) salut!/
ciao!

cheerybye! [tʃɪərɪ'baɪ] *excl F* à bientôt!/
bon courage!/salut!/ciao!/à la prochaire!

cheese [tʃiːz] *n* 1. *F* the cheese, (*important
person*) le caïd *m*/la grosse légume. (*See* big
I 1) 2. *F* hard cheese! pas de chance*!/
manque de pot!/quelle guigne! 3. *esp Austr P*
cheese and kisses, (*RS = missis*) épouse*/
bourgeoise *f*/légitime *f* 4. *F* say cheese!

(when taking photograph) souriez!/regardez le petit oiseau!/un beau sourire! 5. P *(sth unpleasant)* dégueulasserie *f*; *(unpleasant person)* dégueulasse *mf*. *(See* **chalk 2**; **cream**[1] **2)**

cheesecake ['tʃiːzkeɪk] *n F* pin-up *f*.

cheesed off ['tʃiːzd'ɒf] *a P* to be/to feel cheesed off, avoir le cafard/en avoir marre.

cheese it ['tʃiːzɪt] *vi NAm P* partir*/se calter; **cheese it! the cops!** vingt-deux, v'la les flics!

cheesy ['tʃiːzɪ] *a* 1. *P* miteux/moche/à la manque/toc; **what a cheesy place!** quel trou! 2. *V* (gland du pénis) recouvert de smegma 3. *F (feet)* qui sentent mauvais/qui tapent.

chemist ['kemɪst] *n P* personne *f* qui falsifie/qui maquille des ordonnances pour un drogué.

cherry ['tʃerɪ] I *a esp NAm P* beau*/choucard; élégant*/rider II *n* 1. *P* virginité*/pucelage *m*/fleur *f*/coquille *f*; **to lose one's cherry**, perdre sa fleur; **to pick a girl's cherry**, déflorer/dépuceler une fille 2. *F* **to take two bites at the cherry/to have another bite at the cherry**, s'y prendre à deux fois/y remordre 3. *NAm F* **cherry pie**, chose *f* facile/jeu *m* d'enfant 4. *Br P (RS = cherrybog = dog)* chien*/clebs *m*.

cherry-ripe ['tʃerɪ'raɪp] *n O P* (a) *(RS = pipe)* pipe *f* (b) *(RS = tripe)* bêtises*/sornettes *fpl*.

chest [tʃest] *n F* **to get sth off one's chest**, déballer ce qu'on a sur le cœur/vider son sac. *(See* **close**; **hair 5)**

chestnut ['tʃesnʌt] *n* 1. *F* **old chestnut**, histoire rabâchée/rengaine *f*; vieille blague/blague éventée 2. *pl O P* testicules*/pruneaux *mpl*.

chesty ['tʃestɪ] *a F* 1. délicat des bronches 2. *(having large breasts)* **she's chesty**, il y a du monde au balcon.

Chevy ['ʃevɪ] *n NAm F Aut* Chevrolet *(RTM) f*.

chew [tʃuː] *vtr P* 1. **to chew the fat/the rag**, bavarder*/se tailler une bavette/discuter le *ou* tailler un bout de gras. *(See* **bite off 2)** 2. *NAm* **to chew s.o.'s ass**, réprimander*/engueuler/passer un savon à qn.

chew off ['tʃuː'ɒf] *vtr F* **to chew s.o.'s head/***NAm* **ears off**, réprimander* qn/passer un savon à qn/allonger les oreilles à qn. *(See* **balls**[1] **7)**

chew out ['tʃuː'aut] *vtr NAm P* to chew s.o. out, réprimander*/engueuler qn.

chew over ['tʃuː'əuvə] *vtr F* to chew it over, réfléchir/ruminer.

chewie, chewy ['tʃuːɪ] *n esp Austr F* chewing-gum *m*.

chi-ack ['tʃaɪæk] *n Austr F* = **chy-ack**.

chib [tʃɪb] *n Br P* (a) couteau*/lame *f* (b) rasoir*/razif *m*.

chi-chi ['ʃiːʃiː] *a F* chichi.

chick [tʃɪk] *n O F* 1. *(child)* môme *mf*/têtard *m* 2. fille*/poulette *f*/pépée *f*; **a good-looking chick**, une jolie nana/minette; **his chick**, sa petite amie/sa gonzesse.

chickabiddy ['tʃɪkəbɪdɪ] *n O F* cocotte *f*; **my little chickabiddy**, mon petit coco/poulet.

chicken ['tʃɪkɪn] I *a P* lâche*; **to turn chicken**, se dégonfler II *n* 1. *F* **she's no (spring) chicken!** elle n'est pas de première jeunesse! 2. *NAm F* **to get up with the chickens**, se lever avec/comme les poules 3. *F* **to count one's chickens (before they are hatched)**, vendre la peau de l'ours (avant de l'avoir tué) 4. *P* poltron*/caneur *m*/dégonfleur *m*/flubard *m*/froussard, -arde 5. *P* (a) gamine *f*/poulette *f*; **to have a chicken dinner**, faire l'amour avec une mineure/déplumer le poulet (b) jeune garçon *m*/gamin *m* susceptible d'être poursuivi par un homosexuel 6. *F* jeu *m* de défi dangereux *(joué par des jeunes)*.

chicken-feed ['tʃɪkɪnfiːd] *n F* 1. quelques sous*/bagatelle *f*/mitraille *f*; **we work there for chicken-feed**, on y travaille pour des clous 2. rien*/des clopinettes *fpl*; **it's just chicken-feed**, c'est de la gnognot(t)e.

chickenhawk ['tʃɪkɪnhɔːk] *n NAm P* homosexuel* qui poursuit les jeunes garçons.

chicken out ['tʃɪkɪn'aut] *vi F* se dégonfler; **he chickened out at the last moment**, il s'est dégonflé/débalonné à la dernière minute.

chicken ranch ['tʃɪkɪn'rɑːntʃ] *n* maison close/bordel *m*.

chickenshit ['tʃɪkɪnʃɪt] *esp NAm P* I *a* poltron*/dégonflé/trouillard II *n* (a) *(anything worthless)* camelote *f*; **it's chickenshit**, ça ne vaut pas un pet (de lapin) (b) rien*/que dalle.

chickie ['tʃɪkɪ] *n NAm F* 1. jeune fille*/minette *f*/nénette *f* 2. *(esp in prisons)* jeune partenaire *m* d'un homosexuel/corvette *f*.

chicklet ['tʃɪklɪt] *n F* jeune femme*/nénette *f*.

chief [tʃiːf] *n* 1. *F* patron*/chef *m*; **the big (white) chief**, le patron*/le grand manitou/le grand chef 2. *O P (drugs)* **the chief**, LSD* 3. *P (schools)* idiot*/andouille *f*/duschnock *m*.

chill[1] [tʃɪl] *n NAm P* 1. **to put the chill on s.o.**, faire la gueule/la tronche à qn **2. to have the chills**, avoir peur*/avoir le trac.

chill² [tʃɪl] **I** *vi esp NAm F* **to chill (out)**, se détendre/être cool; **where do you go to chill!** comment vous vous relaxez! **he's chillin' (out)**, il est cool **II** *vtr P* tuer*/refroidir.

chilled [tʃɪld] *a F* excellent*/super/canon.

chimbley ['tʃɪmblɪ] *n F* (= *chimney*) cheminée *f*/bouffardière *f*.

chime in ['tʃaɪm'ɪn] *vi F* (*interrupt*) couper la parole/placer son mot/mettre son grain de sel; (*agree*) faire chorus.

chimney ['tʃɪmnɪ] *n F* **to smoke like a chimney**, fumer comme un pompier/un sapeur.

chin¹ [tʃɪn] *n* **1.** *F* **to take it on the chin**, encaisser un sale coup/ne pas se laisser abattre **2.** *F* **to keep one's chin up**, tenir bon/tenir le coup; **chin up!** du courage!

chin² [tʃɪn] *vtr Br P* donner un coup de poing (sur le menton) à/balancer un marron à (qn).

china ['tʃaɪnə] *n Br P* (*RS* = *china plate* = *mate*) ami(e)*/pote *m*/copain *m*/copine *f*; **my/me old china**, vieille branche.

chin-chin! ['tʃɪn'tʃɪn] *excl F* **1.** au revoir!/à bientôt! **2.** à la vôtre/à la tienne!/tchin (tchin)!

Chinese ['tʃaɪniːz] *a P* (*drugs*) **Chinese rocks/Chinese N°3**, héroïne*/H *f*/poudre *f*.

chink¹ [tʃɪŋk] *n P* (*money*) pèze *m*; (*change, coins*) ferraille *f*/mitraille *f*.

Chink² [tʃɪŋk] *n P Pej* Chinois *m*/Chinoise *f*/Chinetoque *mf*; *NAm* **Chink joint**, (*place of work, nightclub, etc*) boîte chinoise; (*restaurant*) restaurant Chinois/Chinois *m*.

chinkie, Chinkie, chinky, Chinky ['tʃɪŋkɪ] *a & n P* chinois, -oise/chinetoque (*mf*); **chinky (takeaway)**, bouffe *f* chinetoque (à emporter); (*restaurant*) Chinois *m*.

chinless ['tʃɪnlɪs] *a Pej F* **chinless wonder**, imbécile*/idiot *m* de la haute.

chinwag ['tʃɪnwæg] *n P* bavette *f*/causette *f*; **to have a chinwag**, (se) tailler une bavette.

chip [tʃɪp] *n* **1.** *F* **he's had his chips**, il est cuit/fichu **2.** *F* **when the chips are down**, quand ça se met à chauffer/en cas de coup dur **3.** *F* **to have a chip on one's shoulder**, chercher la bagarre/des crosses *fpl*; **she's always had a chip on her shoulder**, elle en veut à tout le monde **4.** *F* **he's a chip off the old block**, c'est bien le fils de son père. (*See* **cash in 1; chips**)

chip at ['tʃɪp'æt] *vtr O* **1.** *F* critiquer* (qn/qch) **2.** se ficher de (qn).

chip in ['tʃɪp'ɪn] *vtr & i F* **1.** payer* sa part **2.** dire son mot/y aller de son grain de sel.

chipper ['tʃɪpə] *n NAm P* utilisateur, -trice occasionnel(le) de drogues.

chippie ['tʃɪpɪ] *n P* = **chippy II**.

chippy ['tʃɪpɪ] *P* **I** *adv* **to be chippy**, en vouloir à tout le monde **II** *n* **1.** *Br* (= *(fish and) chip shop*) friterie *f*; **let's get sth from the chippy tonight**, allons chercher à manger à la friterie ce soir. **2.** *NAm Austr* (*a*) prostituée*/grue *f*/radeuse *f* (*b*) (*promiscuous woman*) allumeuse *f*/dragueuse *f* **3.** *Br* menuisier *m*.

chips [tʃɪps] *n P* = **chippy II 3**.

chirpy ['tʃɜːpɪ] *adj F* gai/de bonne humeur; **you're very chirpy today**, tu es gai comme un pinson aujourd'hui.

chisel ['tʃɪz(ə)l] *vtr P* tromper*/rouler/ carotter (qn).

chit [tʃɪt] *n F* petit enfant*/mioche *mf*/bout *m* de chou; (*esp in phrase*) **(she's) a mere chit of a girl**, ce n'est qu'une gamine.

chiv¹ [(t)ʃɪv] *n P* **1.** couteau*/surin *m* **2.** rasoir*/rasibe *m*.

chiv² [(t)ʃɪv] *vtr P* blesser* (qn) à coups de couteau/suriner (qn).

chive [(t)ʃɪv] *n & v P* = **chiv¹·²**.

chiv(e)-man ['(t)ʃɪvmæn, 'tʃaɪvmæn] *n P* (*knifer*) surineur *m*.

chocaholic [tʃɒkə'hɒlɪk] *n* fou/folle du chocolat.

chocca, chocka ['tʃɒkə] *a F* = **chock-a-block**.

chock-a-block ['tʃɒkə'blɒk] *a F* plein à craquer/archi-plein/plein comme un œuf.

chocker ['tʃɒkə] *a* **1.** *F* = **chock-a-block 2.** *F* **to be chocker**, en avoir assez*/en avoir jusque là/en avoir ras le bol.

chock-full ['tʃɒk'fʊl] *a F* = **chock-a-block**.

chocolate ['tʃɒklɪt] *n P* **chocolate lover**, homosexuel* blanc qui s'accouple de préférence avec des Noirs. (*See* **coal-burner; queen¹ 2**)

choirboy ['kwaɪəbɔɪ] *n NAm P* **1.** (*naïve male*) tranche *f* de melon; (*young male*) gosselin *m* **2.** (*police*) nouvelle recrue/blanc-bec *m*.

choked(-off) ['tʃəʊkt('ɒf)] *a Br P* ébahi/ muet (de colère, etc); **I was choked when she told me**, j'en suis resté baba quand elle me l'a dit.

choke off ['tʃəʊk'ɒf] *vtr F* (*not common*) se débarrasser* de/envoyer balader (qn).

chok(e)y ['tʃəʊkɪ] *n Br P* prison*/clou *m*/
taule *f*.
chomp [tʃɒmp] *vi F* manger*/croquer.
choo-choo ['tʃuːtʃuː] *n F* (*child's word for
train*) teuf-teuf *m*.
chook [tʃʌk] *n Austr F* poule *f*/poulet *m*.
chop[1] [tʃɒp] *n P* 1. (*a*) to give s.o. the chop,
se débarrasser* de qn/sacquer qn. (*See* **sack**[1]
1) (*b*) to get the chop, être viré/flanqué à la
porte; he's for the chop! qu'est-ce qu'il va
prendre!/son compte est bon! 2. *pl* bouche*/
bec *m*; to smack s.o. round the chops, donner
une bonne claque à qn 3. *Austr* (*share*) part
f/fade *m* 4. *Austr* no chop, minable; not much
chop, qui ne vaut pas grand-chose 5. moto
modifiée à la 'Easy Rider'/chopper *m*. (*See*
lamb[1], **lick**[2] 4)
chop[2] [tʃɒp] I *vtr P* (*sports*) donner un coup
de pied dans les jambes à (qn) II *vi F* to chop
and change, changer d'idée comme de
chemise.
chop-chop ['tʃɒp'tʃɒp] *adv F* vite*/presto/
dare-dare; chop-chop! et que ça saute!/
grouille-toi!
chopper ['tʃɒpə] *n* 1. *V* pénis*/défonceuse *f*
2. *NAm P* mitraillette*/moulin *m* à café/
sulfateuse *f* 3. *P* hélicoptère *m*/hélico *m*/
banane *f* 4. *pl P* dents*/crocs *mpl*/dominos
mpl 5. *P* moto *ou* vélo modifié(e) à la 'Easy
Rider'/chopper *m*.
chow [tʃaʊ] *n F* 1. nourriture*/bouffe *f*/
bectance *f*/boustifaille *f*; chow time, l'heure *f*
de la bouffe. *Pej* chinois, -oise/chinetoque
mf.
chow down ['tʃaʊ'daʊn] *vi F* manger*/
bouffer/croûter.
Chrissie, chrissie ['krɪsɪ] *n F* (=
Christmas) Noël *m*; chrissie present, cadeau
m de Noël.
Christ [kraɪst] *Prn P* 1. Christ (Almighty)!
bon Dieu (de bon Dieu)!/merde alors! 2. for
Christ's sake! pour l'amour de Dieu!/du ciel!
(*See* **Jesus (Christ)!**)
Christmas! ['krɪsməs] *excl Euph P* bon
Dieu!/merde alors!
Christmas tree ['krɪsməstriː] *n P* 1.
(*drugs*) capsule *f* d'amphés multicolore 2.
femme* vêtue d'une façon criarde.
chrome-dome ['krəʊmdəʊm] *n F* homme
chauve*/martien *m*/tête nickelée.
chromo ['krəʊməʊ] *n Austr A P*
prostituée*/pute *f*/racoleuse *f*.
chronic ['krɒnɪk] I *a F* affreux; in-
supportable/empoisonnant/rasoir; she's chron-

ic! elle est imbuvable! she's got chronic taste
in men, question mecs, elle n'a vraiment pas
de goût II *adv P* à haute dose; I've got the
guts-ache something chronic, j'ai un mal de
ventre carabiné.
chuck[1] [tʃʌk] *n P* 1. *NAm* nourriture*/
bectance *f*/bouffe *f* 2. (*of drug addicts during
withdrawal period*) chuck habit, gavage *m*;
chuck horrors, dégoût *m* de la nourriture 3.
to give s.o. the chuck, se débarrasser* de qn/
balancer qn/flanquer qn à la porte; she gave
her bloke the chuck, elle a plaqué son mec 4.
(*term of endearment*) mon petit poulet/mon
poussin.
chuck[2] [tʃʌk] *vtr* 1. *F* jeter*/lancer (qch);
chuck it to me! lance-le moi! 2. *P* se
débarrasser* de (qn); he chucked her, il l'a
plaquée 3. *P* he's chucked the habit, il a
réussi à se faire décrocher 4. *F* chuck it! en
voilà assez*!/ça va comme ça!/laisse béton!
5. *P* acquitter (un accusé). (*See* **dummy 4**)
chuck about, around ['tʃʌkə'baʊt,
'tʃʌkə'raʊnd] *vtr F* 1. to chuck one's money
about/around, jeter son argent* par les fenêtres 2. to chuck one's weight about/around,
faire l'important/faire du volume/de l'es-
brouf(f)e *f*.
chucker-out ['tʃʌkə'raʊt] *n F* videur *m*.
chuck in ['tʃʌk'ɪn] *vtr F* 1. to chuck in one's
job, lâcher son travail*/son boulot 2. to chuck
it in, y renoncer/quitter la partie/lâcher les
dés.
chucking-out ['tʃʌkɪŋ'aʊt] *n F* chucking-
out time, l'heure *f* de la fermeture (des pubs).
chucklehead ['tʃʌklhed] *n NAm F* individu
bête*/andouille *f*/patate *f*.
chuck out ['tʃʌk'aʊt] *vtr F* se débarrasser*
de (qn)/flanquer (qn) à la porte/balancer/
vider (qn).
chuck up ['tʃʌk'ʌp] *vi & tr* 1. *F* to chuck
s.o. up, lâcher qn/plaquer qn 2. *P* vomir*/
dégobiller.
chuff [tʃʌf] *n P* 1. (*esp regional*) individu
bête*/gourde *f*/cruche *f*; to make s.o. look a
chuff, se moquer de qn/se payer la tête de qn
2. anus*/trèfle *m* 3. pet*/louf *m*.
chuffed [tʃʌft] *a F* to be chuffed (pink), être
ravi/être aux anges; I was really chuffed
about it, j'en étais tout content/ravi. (*See*
dead II 3)
chug [tʃʌg] *vtr & i* boire* (de l'alcool)/
écluser (un godet).
chum [tʃʌm] *n F* ami*/pote *m*/copain *m*/
copine *f*; you said it, chum! comme de juste,

Auguste!/c'est toi qui le dis (bouffi)! (*See* **have 4**)

chummy ['tʃʌmɪ] I *a F* amical/bon copain; they were very chummy, ils étaient copains comme cochons II *n P* (*police slang*) suspect, -ecte.

chump [tʃʌmp] *n* 1. *P* tête*, caboche *f*; he's off his chump, il perd la boule 2. *F* individu bête*/nigaud, -aude/cruche *f*; he's a silly chump, c'est un crétin.

chum up ['tʃʌm'ʌp] *vi F* copiner.

chunder ['tʃʌndə] *vi P* vomir*/dégueuler.

chunky ['tʃʌŋkɪ] *a F* trapu; she's a bit on the chunky side, elle est un peu rondelette/elle se porte bien.

Chunnel ['tʃʌn(ə)l] *n F* (= *Channel Tunnel*) le tunnel sous la Manche.

chunter on ['tʃʌntər'ɒn] *vi F* grogner*/maronner.

churn out ['tʃɜːn'aʊt] *vtr F* produire beaucoup de (qch); this author churns out books by the dozen, il pond des bouquins en série, cet auteur.

chute [ʃuːt] *n* 1. *P* to go down/up the chute, ne servir à rien/partir en fumée; down/up the chute, perdu/fichu/foutu 2. *F* (= *parachute*) parachute *m*/pépin *m*.

chutzpah ['χʊtzpɑː] *n F* (*effrontery, cheek*) culot *m*.

chy-ack ['tʃaɪæk] *vtr Austr P* se montrer très insolent envers (qn)/narguer (qn). (*See* **chiack**)

cig(gie) ['sɪg(ɪ)] *n F* cigarette*/cibiche *f*/clope *f or m*.

cinch [sɪntʃ] *n F* certitude *f*; it's a cinch, (*certain, sure*) c'est certain/c'est couru d'avance/c'est du tout cuit; (*easy*) c'est facile/c'est du gâteau.

cinny ['sɪnɪ] *n F* cinéma *m*/cinoche *m*.

circs [sɜːks] *npl F* (*abbr* = *circumstances*) in/under the circs, dans ce cas-là.

circus ['sɜːkəs] *n F* 1. cirque *m*/rigolade *f*; it's just like a circus in here! qu'est-ce que c'est que ce bordel/ce cirque! 2. spectacle *m* érotique/de cul. (*See* **Piccadilly Circus**)

cissy ['sɪsɪ] *n F* = **sissy**.

civvies ['sɪvɪz] *npl F* in civvies, en civelot/en bourgeois; (*police*) en pékin. (*See* **civvy II**)

civvy ['sɪvɪ] I *a F* civil/pékin; in civvy street, dans le civil II *n F* bourgeois, -oise/civil, -ile. (*See* **civvies**)

clack[1] [klæk] *n O P* caquet *m*/jactance *f*.

clack[2] [klæk] *vi P* bavarder*/jacter; this will stop their tongues clacking, ça empêchera les gens de jaser.

clamp-down ['klæmpdaʊn] *n F* contrainte *f*/vissage *m*; there's been a clamp-down on spending, on a mis un frein aux dépenses.

clamp down ['klæmp'daʊn] *vi F* contraindre par la force/freiner/restreindre; to clamp down on sth/s.o., mettre le holà à qch/serrer la vis à qn.

clam up ['klæm'ʌp] *vi F* se taire*/la boucler; she clammed up, elle l'a bouclée.

clang [klæŋ] *vi Br F* = to drop a clanger (**clanger**).

clanger ['klæŋə] *n Br F* to drop a clanger, faire une bévue*/une gaffe.

clap [klæp] *n P* blennorragie*/chaude-lance *f*/chaude-pisse *f*; to have the clap, pisser des lames de rasoir.

clapped out ['klæpt'aʊt] *a F* (*person*) fatigué*/crevé; (*car, etc*) foutu; a clapped-out old banger, un vieux tas de ferraille/de tôle.

clapper ['klæpə] *n F* 1. langue*/bavarde *f* 2. to go like the clappers, aller vite*/à toute berzingue/à toute pompe; to work like the clappers, travailler dur*/comme un fou/comme une bête.

claptrap ['klæptræp] *n F* bêtises*; what a lot of claptrap! c'est un tas de foutaises!

claret ['klærət] *n P* sang *m*/raisiné *m*; to have one's claret tapped, saigner du nez/faire du raisiné.

class [klɑːs] *n F* to have class, avoir de la classe.

classic ['klæsɪk] *a F* you should have seen him, it was absolutely classic, tu l'aurais vu, ça valait le jus/ça payait.

classy ['klɑːsɪ] *a F* (*a*) chic/bon genre (*b*) beau*/badour; that's really classy, ça c'est class.

clean [kliːn] I *a F* 1. to be clean (*a*) (*without a criminal conviction*) être blanc/avoir un casier vierge (*b*) être pauvre*/être raide à blanc (*c*) (*unarmed*) être sans arme (*d*) ne pas prendre de drogues/se tenir clean (*e*) ne pas avoir de drogues *ou* d'objets volés sur soi; the pusher was clean when the cops searched him, le dealer était clean/n'avait rien sur lui quand les flics l'ont fouillé 2. to make a clean breast of it, tout avouer*/se mettre à table. (*See* **nose 3; sweep**[1] **2**) II *adv F* 1. it went clean out of my head, ça m'est complètement sorti de la tête. 2. to come clean, avouer*/lâcher le paquet.

cleaners ['kliːnəz] *npl P* to take s.o. to the cleaners, (*ruin/rob s.o.*) lessiver qn/

nettoyer qn.

clean out ['kliːn'aʊt] *vtr F* (*a*) to clean s.o. out, prendre l'argent* à qn/lessiver qn/ nettoyer qn; to get cleaned out, perdre son argent*/boire un bouillon/se faire plumer (*b*) to be cleaned out, être fauché comme les blés/à sec.

clean-up ['kliːn'ʌp] *n F* 1. clean-up campaign, campagne *f* contre la porno(graphie) 2. *esp NAm* to make a clean-up, faire un gros profit.

clear [klɪə] I *a F* it's (as) clear as mud, c'est la bouteille à l'encre; c'est clair comme du jus de boudin/de chique II *n F* (*a*) to be in the clear, (*out of trouble*) être tiré d'affaire/sorti de l'auberge; (*not involved in a crime*) être blanc (*b*) to put s.o. in the clear, (*help s.o.*) tirer qn d'affaire; (*show s.o.'s innocence*) défarguer qn. (*See* **all-clear**)

clear off ['klɪər'ɒf] *vi F* partir*/prendre le large; clear off! casse-toi!/fiche le camp!

clear-out ['klɪəraʊt] *n* to have a clear-out (*a*) *F* (*tidy up*) faire du rangement/du tri (*b*) *P* déféquer*/déflaquer.

clear out ['klɪər'aʊt] *vi F* 1. to clear s.o. out of sth, (*rob s.o.*) soulager qn de qch/nettoyer qn 2. s'en aller/se tirer; come on, let's clear out! allez, on change de crémerie!

cleavage ['kliːvɪdʒ] *n F* naissance *f* des seins*; her blouse showed a lot of cleavage, son chemisier était très décolleté/laissait voir la naissance des seins/avait un décolleté plongeant.

cleft [kleft] *n V* sexe* de la femme/con *m*/ fente *f*.

clever-clever ['klevəklevə] *a F* malin*/ débrouillard.

cleverclogs ['klevəklɒgz] *n P* petit(e)/ gros(se) malin(e); un Monsieur je-sais-tout. (*See* **dick 4**; **pop² 6**)

click [klɪk] *vi F* (*a*) to click with s.o., (*get friendly*) sympathiser/accrocher avec qn; (*be attracted sexually*) faire une touche (*b*) (*become clear*) and then, suddenly it clicked, et puis tout d'un coup ça a fait tilt.

clickety-click ['klɪkətɪ'klɪk] *F see* **bingo 66**.

cliffhanger ['klɪfhæŋə] *n F* feuilleton *m*, etc à suspense; suspense *m*.

climber ['klaɪmə] *n P* (*cat burglar*) monte-en-l'air *m*.

clinch¹ [klɪntʃ] *n F* étreinte amoureuse/ enlacement *m*.

clinch² [klɪntʃ] *vtr F* that clinches it! ça

coupe court à tout!/c'est le mot de la fin!/ça met un point final!

clincher ['klɪntʃə] *n F* argument décisif; that's a clincher, (*it shut him up*) ça lui a cloué le bec; (*it's the final word*) c'est le mot de la fin.

clinger ['klɪŋə] *n F* (*person*) crampon *m*.

clink [klɪŋk] *n P* 1. prison*/taule *f*/violon *m*; to be in clink, être dedans/à l'ombre; to put s.o. in clink, mettre qn au trou 2. *Br* argent*/ ferraille *f*.

clinker ['klɪŋkə] *n* 1. *NAm P* échec*/four *m*; (*bad film*) navet *m*/naveton *m* 2. *pl V* (*pieces of excrement clinging to hair around the anus*) grommelots *mpl*/grelots *mpl*.

clip¹ [klɪp] *n F* coup*/beigne *f*/taloche *f*; to give s.o. a clip round the ear, flanquer une taloche à qn.

clip² [klɪp] *vtr* 1. *F* flanquer une taloche à (qn) 2. *P* voler*/écorcher/plumer/estamper (qn).

clip-joint ['klɪpdʒɔɪnt] *n F* boîte *f* (de nuit)/ tripot *m* (*qui exploite les clients*).

clippie ['klɪpɪ] *n Br F* receveur, -euse d'autobus.

cliquey ['kliːkɪ] *a F Pej* qui a l'esprit de clan *ou* de chapelle.

clit [klɪt] *n V* clitoris*/clicli *m*/clito *m*/bouton *m*.

cloak-and-dagger ['kləʊk(ə)n'dægə] *a F* clandestin; a cloak and dagger novel, un roman d'espionnage.

clobber¹ ['klɒbə] *n P* (*a*) (*clothing*) vêtements*/frusques *fpl*/hardes *fpl* (*b*) (*belongings*) barda *m*.

clobber² ['klɒbə] *vtr P* battre*/matraquer/ rosser; to get clobbered, être rossé/se faire arranger.

clock¹ [klɒk] *n* 1. *A P* visage*/poire *f* 2. *F* compteur *m*; this car's got 50,000 (miles) on the clock, cette bagnole a 80 000 au compteur 3. *F* to beat the clock, arriver* avant l'heure/ en avance 4. *F* round the clock, vingt-quatre heures sur vingt-quatre; round the clock protection, surveillance permanente.

clock² [klɒk] *vtr P* 1. battre*/tamponner (qn)/abîmer le portrait à (qn); he clocked him one, il lui a collé un marron 2. guetter*/ mater (qn); clock that bloke! vise-moi/ zyeute-moi ce mec-là! 3. prendre une photo de (qn/qch) 4. remettre à zéro (le compteur d'une voiture).

clocking ['klɒkɪŋ] *n NAm P* (*drugs*) vente *f* de crack.

clock up ['klɒk'ʌp] *vtr F* to clock up the miles, rouler vite*/avaler les kilomètres.

clock-watcher ['klɒkwɒtʃə] *n F* employé, -ée qui ne fait que guetter l'heure de la sortie/tire-au-flanc *m*.

clod [klɒd] *n F* = **clodhopper 1**.

clodhopper ['klɒdhɒpə] *n P* 1. *A* paysan*/plouc *m* 2. lourdaud, -aude/balourd, -ourde 3. (*RS=copper=policeman*) agent* de police/poulet *m*/keuf *m* 4. *pl* chaussures*/godasses *fpl*.

clog[1] [klɒg] *n Br P* Hollandais, -aise.

clog[2] [klɒg] *vtr & i Br P* donner un coup de pied/une targette (à).

clogger ['klɒgə] *n Br P* (*esp in football*) joueur déloyal/violent; mauvais joueur.

cloggy ['klɒgɪ] *n Br P* = **clog**[1].

clomp about ['klɒmpə'baʊt] *vi F* = **clump about**.

clone [kləʊn] *n F Pej* (*fashion follower, imitater*) clone *m*.

clonk [klɒŋk] *vtr P* battre*/frapper; to clonk s.o. on the head, assommer qn/endormir qn.

close [kləʊs] *adv F* to play it/one's cards close to the chest, y aller mollo/jouer serré.

close-fisted ['kləʊs'fɪstɪd] *a F* avare*/radin/pingre/dur à la détente.

closet ['klɒzɪt] *a F* secret/caché; he's a closet socialist, il n'avouera jamais qu'il est socialiste; closet queen, homosexuel*/pédé *m* qui ne s'avoue pas.

clot [klɒt] *n F* personne bête*/gourde *f*/patate *f*; you clumsy clot! espèce d'empoté! what a clot! quelle andouille!

cloth cap ['klɒθ'kæp] *a F* (= *working class*) cloth cap ideas, mentalité ouvrière.

cloth-ears ['klɒθɪəz] *n F* sourd*/dur *m*, dure *f* de la feuille; listen, cloth-ears! écoute, sourdingue!

clotheshorse ['kləʊðzhɔːs] *n P* femme* tape-à-l'œil/mannequin ambulant; homme* bien sapé/dandy *m*.

cloud [klaʊd] *n F* 1. to have one's head in the clouds, être dans la lune 2. to be on cloud nine, être au septième ciel/être aux anges.

cloud-cuckoo-land ['klaʊd'kuku:lænd] *n F* pays *m* des rêves/pays des Châteaux en Espagne; you're living in cloud-cuckoo-land, tu te joues des films en couleurs/tu prends tes rêves pour des réalités.

clout[1] [klaʊt] *n* 1. *F* coup*/calotte *f*; to give/fetch s.o. a clout, filer une calotte à qn 2. *F* (*influence*) to have a lot of clout, avoir le bras long.

clout[2] [klaʊt] *vtr F* filer une calotte à (qn).

clover ['kləʊvə] *n F* to be/live in clover, être comme un coq en pâte.

club [klʌb] *n* 1. *F* to join the club, s'acoquiner avec qn; join the club! tu n'es pas le seul!/tope-là! 2. *P* to join the (pudding) club, être enceinte*.

clubbing ['klʌbɪŋ] *n F* to go clubbing, aller dans les clubs/les discos.

cluck [klʌk] *n esp NAm P* dumb cluck, individu bête*/gourde *f*/cruche *f*.

clucky ['klʌkɪ] *a Austr P* 1. (*broody*) en mal d'enfant 2. enceinte*/en cloque.

clue [klu:] *n F* he hasn't a clue, (*no idea*) il n'a pas la moindre idée; (*useless*) il n'est bon à rien/il est nul; (I) haven't (got) a clue! aucune idée!

clue in ['klu:'ɪn] *vtr F* to clue s.o. in, mettre qn au courant/au parfum.

clueless ['klu:lɪs] *a F* qui n'a pas la moindre idée/qui est dans le noir.

clue up ['klu:'ʌp] *vtr F* to clue s.o. up, mettre qn sur la piste/au parfum/à la page; he's very clued up on insurance, il est très calé en assurances.

cluey ['klu:ɪ] *a Austr F* to be cluey about sth, être au courant/au parfum de qch.

clump[1] [klʌmp] *n F* coup*/beigne *f*.

clump[2] [klʌmp] *vtr F* battre*/tabasser (qn).

clump about ['klʌmpə'baʊt] *vi F* marcher lourdement/comme un éléphant.

clunk [klʌŋk] *n NAm F* 1. imbécile*/andouille 2. vieille voiture*/vieux tacot.

c-note ['si:'nəʊt] *n F* (billet* de) cent dollars *mpl ou* cent livres *fpl* sterling.

coal-burner ['kəʊlbɜːnə] *n P* homosexuel* blanc qui s'accouple de préférence avec des Noirs. (*See* **chocolate**; **queen**[1] **2**)

coalie, coaly ['kəʊlɪ] *n O F* charbonnier *m*/carbi *m*.

coast [kəʊst] *n F* the coast's clear, la voie est libre.

coast along ['kəʊstə'lɒŋ] *vi F* se la couler douce/ne pas se fouler.

coasting ['kəʊstɪŋ] *a NAm F* sous l'influence de drogues/défoncé/stone (d).

coat [kəʊt] *n P* (*police slang*) suspect, -ecte.

coating ['kəʊtɪŋ] *n P* réprimande *f*/savon *m*; to give s.o. a coating, sonner les cloches à qn.

cobber ['kɒbə] *n Austr O F* ami*/copain *m*/pote *m*.

cobblers ['kɒbləz] *npl Br P* (*RS = cobblers' awls = balls*) (a) testicules*/balloches *fpl* (b) (that's a load of) cobblers! c'est de la couillonnade/de la couille/des conneries! (*See* **balls**[1]; **load 2**)

cock [kɒk] *n Br* 1. *V* (*a*) pénis*/queue *f*/bite *f* 2. *P* bêtises*/conneries *fpl*; **to talk cock**, déconner/débloquer. (*See* **load 2**; **poppy-cock**) 3. *P* **all to cock**, de traviole 4. *O P* ami*/pote *m*; **well, old cock, eh** bien, mon colon! **wotcher cock!** comment ça gaze, vieille branche? 5. *P* **cock and hen**, (*RS* = *ten*) (*ten pounds*) (billet* de) dix livres *fpl*; (*ten-year prison sentence*) (sapement *m* de) dix longes *fpl*. (*See* **half-cock**)

cock-a-hoop ['kəkɔ'huːp] *a F* fier comme Artaban.

cocked [kɒkt] *a F* **to knock s.o. into a cocked hat**, (*hit*) battre* qn comme plâtre/pulvériser qn; (*astonish*) abasourdir/asseoir qn.

cocker ['kɒkə] *n O P* ami*/pote *m*; **me old cocker**, vieille branche. (*See* **cock 4**)

cockeyed ['kɒkaɪd] *a P* 1. (*idea, etc*) très bête*/dingue/à la noix 2. ivre*/rétamé 3. (*crooked*) de travers/de guingois/de traviole 4. qui louche*/qui a un œil qui dit zut à l'autre/bigleux.

cock-eye(d) bob ['kɒkaɪ(d)'bɒb] *n Austr P* tempête *f ou* cyclone *m* inattendu(e).

cock rag ['kɒk'ræg] *n Austr P* cache-sexe *m* des Aborigènes.

cock-shy ['kɒkʃaɪ] *a V* 1. (*man*) qui n'ose pas se montrer nu devant les autres/qui n'ose pas montrer son pénis* 2. (*woman*) qui a peur des rapports sexuels/bloquée.

cock-sparrow ['kɒk'spærəʊ, 'kɒk'spærə] *n O P* **wotcher, me old cock-sparrow!** salut, vieille branche! (*See* **cock 4**)

cocksucker ['kɒksʌkə] *n V* 1. personne *f* qui fait une fellation* à une autre/suceuse *f* 2. *esp NAm* (*term of abuse*) salaud*/fumier *m*/enculé *m*.

cock-sucking ['kɒksʌkɪŋ] *n V* fellation*/suçade *f*.

cocktail ['kɒkteɪl] *n F* cocktail *m* de drogues.

cock-tease(r) ['kɒktiːz(ə)] *n V* allumeuse *f*/bandeuse *f*/aguicheuse *f*. (*See* **CT**; **prick tease(r)**; **PT**)

cock-up ['kɒkʌp] *n V* **it was one almighty cock-up**, c'était un vrai bordel/une belle salade; **he made a real cock-up of it**, il y a foutu le merdier/il a tout salopé. (*See* **balls-up**)

cock up ['kɒk'ʌp] *vtr V* 1. foutre la merde/foutre le bordel/tout foutre en l'air; **they've** **cocked it up again**, ils y ont refoutu la merde/le bordel 2. *Austr* (*of woman*) s'offrir à (un homme).

cocky ['kɒkɪ] *a F* culotté/gonflé/qui a du toupet; **he's a cocky little sod**, il a un sacré culot.

coco(a) ['kəʊkəʊ] *vtr Br P* (*RS* = *coffee and cocoa* = *I should say so*) **I should coco(a)!** et comment donc!/tu parles (Charles)!

coconut ['kəʊkənʌt] *n Br Pej F* (*Black slang*) noir, -e qui s'insinue dans les bonnes grâces des blancs/Oncle Tom.

cod [kɒd] *vtr O P* duper*/emmener (qn) en bateau/faire marcher (qn).

codger ['kɒdʒə] *n F* **old codger**, (drôle de) vieux bonhomme/vieux décati.

cods [kɒdz] *npl P* testicules*/burettes *fpl*/burnes *fpl*.

codswallop ['kɒdzwɒləp] *n F* bêtises*/foutaises *fpl*; **that's a load of codswallop**, c'est un tas de foutaises. (*see* **load 2**)

co-ed ['kəʊ'ed] *n F* (*abbr* = *co-educational*) (*a*) école *f*/lycée *m*, etc, mixte (*b*) *NAm* étudiante *f* dans un établissement mixte.

C of E ['siːəviː] *abbr F* (= *Church of England*) l'Eglise anglicane.

coffin ['kɒfɪn] *n* 1. *NAm P* (*disciplinary cell*) mitard *m*/(s)chtard *m* 2. *F* **coffin nail**, cigarette*/cibiche *f*/sèche *f*.

cog [kɒg] *n P* **to give it some cog**, accélérer*/crayonner/mettre la gomme.

coin [kɔɪn] *vtr F* 1. **to coin it in**, devenir riche*/faire des affaires en or 2. *Iron* **to coin a phrase**, si je peux m'exprimer ainsi.

coke [kəʊk] *n* 1. *F* Coca(-Cola) *m* (*RTM*) 2. *P* (*drugs*) cocaïne*/coke *f*/reniflette *f*.

coked (up) ['kəʊkt('ʌp)] *a P* drogué*/défoncé (à la cocaïne).

cokehead ['kəʊkhed] *n P* cocaïnomane *mf*/sniffeur, -euse.

cokey, cokie ['kəʊkɪ], **cokomo** [kəʊ'kəʊməʊ] *n NAm O P* cocaïnomane *mf*/sniffeur, -euse.

cold [kəʊld] **I** *a F* 1. **to be out (stone) cold**, être dans les pommes/être KO; **to knock s.o. out cold**, envoyer qn au tapis/mettre qn KO 2. **that leaves me cold**, ça me laisse froid 3. **to give s.o. the cold shoulder**, snober qn/ignorer qn/faire la tête à qn. (*See* **cold-shoulder**) 4. **cold feet**, peur*/frousse *f*; **to get cold feet**, caner/avoir la trouille/avoir le trac/avoir les chocottes 5. **cold fish**, pisse-froid *m* 6. *Fig* **to put in cold storage**, mettre au frigo 7. (*weapon, car*) qu'on ne peut pas identifier.

(*See* **blood 3**; **meat 5**; **stone-cold**; **sweat¹ 4**; **turkey 1**; **water 1**) II *n F* 1. to catch a cold, écoper; (*business, etc*) faire faillite; couler; aller à vau-l'eau 2. to be left out in the cold, être mis de côté/rester sur la touche/rester sur le carreau.

cold-shoulder ['kəʊld'ʃəʊldə] *vtr F* ignorer/snober (qn). (*See* **cold I 3**)

cold turkey [kəʊld'tɜːkɪ] *n See* **turkey 1**.

collar¹ ['kɒlə] *n* 1. *P* arrestation*/piquage *m* 2. *F* the collar and tie brigade, les lesbiennes*.

collar² ['kɒlə] *vtr F* arrêter*/cravater/piquer.

collywobbles ['kɒlɪwɒblz] *npl F* to have the collywobbles (*a*) avoir mal au ventre/au bide; avoir un mal de bide (*b*) avoir la diarrhée*/avoir la chiasse (*c*) avoir peur*/avoir la trouille.

colour, *NAm* **color** ['kʌlə] *n F* let's see the colour of your money, fais voir la couleur de ton fric/où est l'auréole de ton Saint-Fric? (*See* **horse¹ 3**; **off IV 1**)

column-dodger ['kɒləm'dɒdʒə] *n F Mil* tire-au-flanc *m*. (*See* **dodge² 1**)

combo ['kɒmbəʊ] *n* 1. *F* orchestre *m* de jazz 2. *Austr P* Blanc *m* qui cohabite avec une Aborigène.

come¹ [kʌm] *n P* sperme*/jus *m*. (*See* **cum**)

come² [kʌm] *vtr & i* 1. *P* avoir un orgasme*/jouir/venir/prendre son pied; she never comes when they make love, elle ne jouit jamais quand ils font l'amour 2. *F* as dim/daft as they come, bête* comme ses pieds/comme tout 3. *F* you'll get what's coming to you! tu ne perds rien pour attendre!/tu l'as bien cherché! 4. *F* to come it a bit strong, exagérer*/y aller un peu fort/attiger (la cabane) 5. *F* jouer un rôle; to come the heavy husband, faire le mari autoritaire; to come the innocent with s.o., faire l'innocent avec qn; to come it/come (it) hard, exagérer*/y aller fort; don't you come it with me! ne charrie pas avec moi! 6. *F* to come over (all) funny/(all) queer, se sentir tout chose 7. *P* come again? répète un peu?/comment?/quoi donc? 8. *F* how come? comment (que) ça se fait? (*See* **acid 1**; **clean II 2**; **prawn 2**; **think¹**)

come-at-able [kʌm'ætəbl] *a F* accessible/abordable.

comeback ['kʌmbæk] *n F* (*actor*) retour *m* à la scène/à l'écran; (*politician*) retour au pouvoir; to make a comeback, se remettre sur pied/se retaper; he has made several

comebacks, il est remonté plusieurs fois en scène.

comedown ['kʌmdaʊn] *n* 1. *F* what a comedown! (*disappointment, anticlimax*) quelle dégringolade!/quelle douche!/quelle déception! 2. *P* (*drugs*) retour *m* à l'état hors drogue/descente *f*.

come down ['kʌm'daʊn] *vi* 1. *P* revenir à l'état hors drogue/redescendre 2. *V* to come down on s.o., (*fellatio*) faire une fellation* à qn/faire un pompier à qn/tailler une pipe à qn; (*cunnilinctus*) pratiquer le cunnilinctus sur qn/brouter le cresson à qn 3. *F* to come down on s.o. (like a ton of bricks), réprimander* qn/enguirlander qn/tomber sur le dos à qn 4. *F* to come down in the world, déchoir/descendre plusieurs échelons. (*See* **peg 2** (*b*))

comedy ['kɒmɪdɪ] *n F* cut (out) the comedy! finie la comédie!/arrête ton char!/arrête ton cinéma!

come good ['kʌm'gʊd] *vi F* réussir/tenir bon; he's come good, il a apporté la marchandise/il a tenu bon.

come-hither ['kʌm'hɪðə] *a F* a come-hither look, les yeux* doux/un regard aguichant/des yeux couleur besoin.

come off ['kʌm'ɒf] *vtr & i F* 1. avoir un orgasme*/s'envoyer en l'air/prendre son pied 2. come off it! (*don't talk rubbish!*) change de disque!/arrête ton char!/mon œil!

come-on ['kʌmɒn] *n P* to give s.o. the come-on, encourager les avances sexuelles de qn/flirter avec qn/allumer qn/aguicher qn.

come on ['kʌm'ɒn] *vi P* 1. commencer à ressentir les effets d'une drogue/partir 2. flirter/faire des avances sexuelles/aguicher/allumer; he comes on really strong, il en impose 3. come on! (*don't talk rubbish!*) = come off it! (**come off 2**); (*encouraging*) courage! 4. avoir ses règles*/ses affaires.

come out ['kʌm'aʊt] *vi P* (*homosexual*) to come out (of the closet), avouer qu'on est homosexuel/faire son comeout.

come up ['kʌm'ʌp] *vi P* gagner/affurer; to come up on the pools, gagner/ramasser un paquet en pariant sur les matchs de foot.

come-uppance ['kʌm'ʌpəns] *n F* to get one's come-uppance, recevoir ce qu'on mérite/se faire dire ses quatre vérités.

comfy ['kʌmfɪ] *a* (= *comfortable*) *F* confortable/douillet. (*See* **nice II 1**)

commie, commy ['kɒmɪ] *a & n F Pej* communiste (*mf*)/coco (*mf*); commie bastard, salaud *m* de communiste.

commission [kə'mɪʃ(ə)n] *n* P *(protection money)* he pays them commission, il leur verse du fric pour qu'ils le laissent en paix.

comp [kɒmp] *n* F *(abbr of competition)* competition *f*.

compo ['kɒmpəʊ] *n Austr* F *(abbr of (worker's) compensation)* allocation *f* de chômage; prestation *f* d'invalidité.

compree! [kɒm'priː] *excl* F compris!/pigé!

con¹ [kɒn] *n* 1. F *(= convict)* taulard, -arde. *(See* **ex**) 2. F escroquerie*/arnaque *f*/ entourloupe *f*; con game, magouille *f*; con man/con artist, escroc*/arnaqueur *m*/ magouilleur, -euse; it was all a complete con, c'était de l'arnaque à cent pour cent. *(See* **pro** 3)

con² [kɒn] *vtr* F escroquer*/arnaquer/ empaumer/rouler (qn); to con s.o. into doing sth, entourlouper qn; I was conned, je me suis fait avoir/baiser.

conchie, conchy ['kɒntʃɪ] *n O* F *(= conscientious objector)* objecteur *m* de conscience.

condo ['kɒndəʊ] *n NAm* F *(abbr of condominium)* (immeuble *m* en) copropriété *f*.

confab¹ ['kɒnfæb] *n* F causerie *f*/causette *f*; there's a confab going on in there, ça discutaille là-dedans.

confab² ['kɒnfæb] *vi* F bavarder*/tailler une bavette; discutailler.

conflab ['kɒnflæb] *n* F = **confab¹**.

confusion [kən'fjuːʒən] *n WInd* P *(street fight)* bagarre*/baston *m or f* dans la rue.

congrats! [kən'græts] *int* F félicitations!/ bravo!

conk¹ [kɒŋk] *n* P 1. nez*/pif *m*/blair *m* 2. *(less common)* tête*/caboche *f*.

conk² [kɒŋk] *vtr* P to conk s.o., flanquer un gnon à qn/matraquer qn; she conked him on the head, elle lui a flanqué un coup sur la tête.

conk out ['kɒŋk'aʊt] *vi* 1. F *(break down)* tomber en rade/claquer/caler; my car conked out, ma bagnole m'a claqué dans les doigts/ m'a lâché 2. P mourir*/caner/casser sa pipe 3. F s'endormir tout d'un coup; he was so tired he conked out on the sofa, il était tellement crevé qu'il s'est effondré sur le canapé.

connect [kə'nekt] *vi* P trouver à s'approvisionner en drogue/se mettre en contact avec un fourgueur afin de lui acheter de la drogue.

connection [kə'nekʃ(ə)n], **connector** [kə'nektə], **connexion** [kə'nekʃ(ə)n] *n* F *(esp drugs)* contact *m*/fourgueur, -euse/dealer *m*. *(See* **make²** 11)

conshie, conshy ['kɒnʃɪ] *n O* F = **conchie, conchy**.

contract ['kɒntrækt] *n* P engagement *m* à tuer* qn/contrat *m*; to have a contract on s.o., s'être engagé à tuer* qn; contract killing, meurtre *m* sur commande/contrat *m*.

coo! [kuː] *excl* F tiens!/ça alors!

cook¹ [kʊk] *n* F to be head/chief cook and bottle-washer, être l'homme à tout faire/être l'homme-orchestre.

cook² [kʊk] *vtr & i* 1. F what's cooking? quoi de neuf?/qu'est-ce qui se mijote?/qu'est-ce qui se goupille? 2. F to cook the books, truquer/ cuisiner/maquiller les comptes 3. F to cook s.o.'s goose, faire son affaire à qn/régler son compte à qn 4. P = **cook up** 2.

cooked [kʊkt] *a* F très fatigué*/exténué*/ vidé.

cookie ['kʊkɪ] *n* 1. F that's the way the cookie crumbles! c'est la vie (que veux-tu)! 2. *esp NAm* F individu*/type *m*; a tough cookie, un dur (à cuire) 3. P (belle) femme*/ nana (bien carrossée); hot cookie = hot babe (**babe** 2).

cooking ['kʊkɪŋ] *a NAm* P qui marche bien; it's cooking (with gas), ça gaze.

cook up ['kʊk'ʌp] *vtr & i* 1. F to cook up an excuse/a story, (s')inventer une excuse 2. P préparer une drogue en la diluant et en la chauffant/se préparer un fixe.

cool¹ [kuːl] I *a* 1. F *(a)* détendu/relax/cool/ coolos/coulos *(b)* excellent*/canon/géant/ super; that's really cool, c'est le (super-)pied 2. F a cool £1,000, £1000, pas moins 3. F distant/peu émotif/de glace; a cool customer, une personne qui a la tête froide/qui ne se démonte pas 4. F *(jazz)* sobre/relax. *(See* **cat** 1; **hot** 7) 5. P *(drug addict)* to be cool, planer calmement II *adv* F *(a)* to play it cool, ne pas s'énerver/y aller la tête froide; play it cool! pas de panique!/cool, Raoul *(b) esp NAm* stay cool! *(stay calm)* pas de panique!/ t'énerve pas! *(all the best!)* bon courage!/ salut! III *n* F 1. sang-froid *m*; to keep one's cool, ne pas s'énerver/y aller la tête froide 2. to lose one's cool/to blow one's cool, *(get angry)* se mettre en colère*/piquer une crise; *(panic)* paniquer; se démonter.

cool² [kuːl] *vtr* F to cool it, *(calm down)* se calmer; *(relax)* être cool; cool it! t'énerve

pas!/cool, Raoul; (*relationship, etc*) **let's cool it/let's cool things down for a while**, attendons que les choses se calment un peu/si on prenait une certaine distance pendant quelque temps?
cooler ['ku:lə] *n O P* prison*/taule *f*.
cool out, up ['ku:l'aʊt, 'ʌp] *vi F* = **cool it** (**cool²**).
coon [ku:n] *n P* 1. *Pej* Noir(e)*/nègre *m*/bougnoul *m* 2. *NAm* **a coon's age**, longtemps/belle lurette.
co-op ['kəʊɒp] *n F* (*abbr* = *co-operative stores*) société coopérative.
coot [ku:t] *n* 1. *P* individu bête*/gourde *f*; **he's a silly old coot**, c'est un vieux con/une vieille andouille 2. *F* **bald as a coot**, chauve* comme un genou/un œuf.
cootie ['ku:tɪ] *n esp NAm P* pou*/morbac *m*.
cooze [ku:z], **coozie** [ku:zɪ] *n NAm V* 1. femme*/gonzesse *f*/sauterelle *f* 2. sexe* de la femme/abricot *m*.
cop¹ [kɒp] *n* 1. *F* agent* de police/flic *m*/poulet *m*; **bent cop**, (*corrupt*) flic pourri/ripou *m*; **speed/courtesy cop**, motard *m*. (*See* **copper 1**; **fly-cop**) 2. *P* arrestation*/alpague *f*; **it's a fair cop**, on est fait, rien à dire 3. *P* **it's not much cop**, ça ne vaut pas grand-chose/c'est de la camelote 4. *Austr P* (*good deal*) (bon) filon/affaire *f*.
cop² [kɒp] **I** *vtr P* 1. arrêter*/pincer (qn); **to get copped**, se faire pincer/alpaguer 2. recevoir; **I copped a parking ticket**, j'ai chopé une contredanse 3. **to cop it**, (*die*) mourir*/clamser; (*be scolded*) être réprimandé*/prendre un savon 4. **to cop hold of sth**, choper/attraper le bout de qch; **here, cop hold of this!** tiens, attrape ça! 5. **cop a load of this!** (*listen*) écoute-moi ça!; (*look*) vise-moi ça! 6. **to cop on to sth** comprendre/mordre/piger qch 7. *NAm F* **to cop some z's**, dormir*/piquer un roupillon 8. obtenir *ou* acheter (des drogues)/se fournir **II** *vi P* (*accept a bribe*) se laisser acheter; **will he cop?** il se laissera acheter? (*See* **dose 1**; **feel¹**; **needle¹ 1** (*c*); **packet 1**; **plea**; **u.v.'s**; **z's**)
cop-out ['kɒpaʊt] *n P* **it's just one big cop-out**, c'est des craques; c'est pour se défiler tout simplement.
cop out ['kɒp'aʊt] *vi P* 1. se retirer/se dégager/se défiler 2. éviter/éluder/esquiver une question *ou* la responsabilité, etc 3. ne pas tenir une promesse.
copper ['kɒpə] *n* 1. *P* agent* de police/flic *m*; **copper's nark**, indic *m*/mouchard *m*. (*See* **bent 1**) 2. *P* **to come copper**, devenir

indicateur* de police 3. *F* **gros sou**/de la petite monnaie; **he gave the busker a few coppers**, il a donné quelques sous au type qui jouait dans la rue.
copshop ['kɒpʃɒp] *n P* commissariat *m* de police/quart *m*; **he's still down the copshop**, il est toujours au quart.
cop-talk ['kɒptɔ:k] *n P* argot *m* de la police.
cop-wagon ['kɒpwægən] *n P* car* de police/panier *m* à salade. (*See* **Black Maria**)
copycat ['kɒpɪkæt] *n F* **to be a copycat**, faire le singe/singer; **copycat!** espèce de singe!
cor! [kɔ:] *excl* (*a*) *F* ça alors! **cor, she's a knockout!** merde! ce qu'elle est belle!/elle est pas pourrie! *O* **cor love a duck!** grands dieux! (*b*) *P* **cor blimey!** = **gorblimey!**
corked [kɔ:kt] *a P* ivre* mort/blindé.
corker ['kɔ:kə] *n F* 1. (*a*) individu* formidable/chic type *m* (*b*) belle fille/beau morceau (*c*) chose excellente*/super/canon; **the new video's a corker**, le nouveau clip est géant 2. gros mensonge*/bourrage *m* de crâne; craque *f*; **that's a corker**, ça vous en bouche un coin/une surface.
corking ['kɔ:kɪŋ] **I** *a O F* excellent*/épatant/foutral/formid(able) **II** *adv* (*absolutely*) totalement/complètement; **it's corking ridiculous**, c'est complètement con.
corn [kɔ:n] *n F* 1. (*a*) vieille rengaine/scie *f* (*b*) guimauve *f*; **it's pure corn**, c'est de la guimauve/c'est une histoire à l'eau de rose 2. **to step/tread on s.o.'s corns**, toucher qn à l'endroit sensible/marcher sur les pieds de qn; froisser qn.
cornhole¹ ['kɔ:nhəʊl] *n NAm V* (*rare*) anus*/trou *m* de balle; **cornhole palace**, (*homosexual use*) urinoir* public/tasse *f* (à thé).
cornhole² ['kɔ:nhəʊl] *vtr NAm V* (*to have anal sex with*) sodomiser*/empaffer/enculer.
corny ['kɔ:nɪ] *F* (*a*) banal/rebattu (*b*) vieux jeu/ringard (*c*) à l'eau de rose; **this film is so corny**, ce film est tellement cucu(l) (la praline).
corpse [kɔ:ps] *Br F* **I** *vi* (*of actor, singer*) avoir le fou rire sur scène (*pendant une répétition ou une représentation*) **II** *vtr* donner le fou rire à (un acteur, etc).
'cos [kɒz] *conj F* (= *because*) parce que/pasque/because.
cosh¹ [kɒʃ] *n F* matraque *f*/assommoir *m*/goumi *m*.
cosh² [kɒʃ] *vtr F* matraquer*/assommer (qn).

cossie ['kɒzɪ] *n F* (*abbr of* (*swimming*) *costume*) maillot *m* (de bain).

cost [kɒst] *vtr F* I can get it but it'll cost you, je peux l'avoir mais ça sera chérot/ça vous coûtera cher. (*See* **earth 2**)

cottage¹ ['kɒtɪdʒ] *n P* (*homosexual use*) urinoir* public/tasse *f* (à thé)/théière *f*.

cottage² ['kɒtɪdʒ] *vi P* (*homosexual use*) to cottage/to go cottaging, draguer dans les toilettes/dans les tasses; faire les tasses.

cotton¹ ['kɒtn] *n P* (*drugs*) morceau de coton utilisé pour filtrer l'héroïne avant de se piquer; cotton freak, camé(e) qui prépare sa piquouse de cette façon.

cotton² ['kɒtn] *vi O F* (*a*) to cotton to s.o., être attiré par qn/avoir qn à la bonne (*b*) to cotton to sth, approuver/apprécier qch; he doesn't cotton to it much, ça ne le botte pas tellement.

cotton on ['kɒtn'ɒn] *vi F* 1. comprendre/piger/entraver; he cottons on quickly, il pige vite 2. *O* I can't cotton on to him, sa tête ne me revient pas/je ne le sens pas, ce mec.

cotton-picking ['kɒtn'pɪkɪŋ] *a NAm* (*a*) commun/vulgaire (*b*) sacré/satané (*c*) niais/navet; you cotton-picking idiot, tête de nœud!/espèce de nouille!

cotton-wool ['kɒtn'wʊl] *n F* 1. to wrap s.o. in cotton-wool, mettre qn dans du coton/garder qn sous cloche 2. my legs were like cotton-wool, j'avais les jambes en coton/en laine.

couch doctor ['kaʊtʃ'dɒktə] *n F Hum* psychanalyste *mf*/psy *mf*.

couch potato [kaʊtʃpə'teɪtəʊ] *n esp NAm F* paresseux*/cossard, -arde/ramier *m* (*qui passe son temps devant la télé*).

cough [kɒf] *vtr & i Br P* avouer*/accoucher/manger le morceau.

cough up ['kɒf'ʌp] *vi F* 1. payer*/cracher/abouler le fric 2. parler*/dégoiser 3. avouer*/accoucher/manger le morceau.

count [kaʊnt] *n F* to be out for the count, (*unconscious*) avoir son compte/être KO; (*asleep*) être profondément endormi.

counter ['kaʊntə] *n F* to sell sth under the counter, vendre qch au (marché) noir. (*See* **under-the-counter**)

count in ['kaʊnt'ɪn] *vtr F* you can count me in, je marche/je suis partant/je suis de la partie.

count out ['kaʊnt'aʊt] *vtr F* you can count me out, je ne marche pas/je ne suis pas partant/ne comptez pas sur moi.

county ['kaʊntɪ] *a Br F* the county set, l'aristocratie provinciale/la haute bourgeoisie provinciale; she's terribly county, elle fait très aristo/elle fait très snob.

cove [kəʊv] *n O F* individu*; a queer cove, un drôle de pistolet/un drôle de numéro.

Coventry ['kɒvəntrɪ] *n F* to send s.o. to Coventry, (*not to speak to s.o.*) mettre qn en quarantaine.

cover ['kʌvə] *n F* couverture*/couverte *f*/prétexte *m*; you're my cover, tu es mon alibi.

cover-girl ['kʌvəgɜːl] *n F* pin-up *f*/cover-girl *f*.

cover up ['kʌvər'ʌp] *vi F* to cover up for s.o., couvrir qn/prendre les patins de qn.

cow [kaʊ] *n* 1. *P Pej* (*disagreeable woman*) vache *f*/chameau *m*/garce *f*/salope *f*/peau *f* de vache; an old cow, une vieille bique; silly cow! espèce de conne!/connasse! poor cow! pauvre conne! what a cow she is at times, ce qu'elle peut être garce/vache des fois; c'est une vraie peau de vache 2. *Austr* (*disagreeable thing*) it's a fair cow! ce que c'est moche! he's a fair cow! qu'il est moche! 3. *F* till the cows come home, jusqu'à la Saint-Glinglin/quand les poules auront des dents; to wait until the cows come home, attendre la semaine des quatre jeudis. (*See* **bull 3; holy 1; moo-cow**)

cowabunga! ['kaʊə'bʌŋə] *excl F* cri *m* de guerre/de victoire/de joie, enfin.

cowboy ['kaʊbɔɪ] *n Br F* mauvais ouvrier/ouvrier fumiste/fumigo *m*; cowboy electrician, électricien *m* fumiste; cowboy operation, mauvais travail/travail bâclé; cowboy outfit, organisation douteuse/louche/qui sent le roussi.

cow-juice ['kaʊdʒuːs] *n F* lait *m*/lolo *m*.

cowpoke ['kaʊpəʊk], **cowpuncher** ['kaʊpʌntʃə] *n NAm F* cowboy *m*.

crab¹ [kræb] *n F* 1. grognon, -onne/rouscailleur *m*; she's an old crab, c'est une vieille emmerdeuse 2. *pl* poux* du pubis/crabes *mpl*/morpions *mpl*/morbacs *mpl*.

crab² [kræb] *vtr & i P* 1. grogner*/râler 2. to crab the act/deal, mettre des bâtons dans les roues.

crack¹ [kræk] I *a P* (*first-rate*) excellent*/super/canon; a crack team, une équipe du tonnerre. (*See* **cracking 1**) II *n* 1. *V* sexe* de la femme/fente *f*/cramouille *f* 2. *F* blague *f*/vanne *f*; he made a crack about my mother, il a vanné ma mère/il s'est payé la tête de ma mère 3. *F* to have/to take a crack (at sth), (*try sth*) tenter le coup/sa chance **4.** *F* (*person who excels*) as *m*/crack *m*; **crack shot**, tireur, -euse d'élite **5.** *P* renseignement*/tuyau *m*/info *f*; (*gossip*) potins *mpl*; **to give s.o. the crack**, tuyauter qn/mettre qn au parfum; **what's the crack?** quoi de neuf? **6.** *P* (*drugs*) crack *m*. (*See* **paper² 2; whip¹ 1; wisecrack¹**)

crack² [kræk] *vtr & i* **1.** *P* filer/flanquer un coup* à (qn) **2.** *F* **to get cracking**, (*start*) commencer/se mettre au boulot; (*hurry up*) aller vite*/se grouiller; **let's get cracking!** au boulot! **get cracking! magne-toi! 3.** *F* ouvrir; **to crack a safe**, cambrioler/faire un coffre-fort; **to crack a bottle**, ouvrir une bouteille **4. to crack it**, *F* réussir/l'avoir belle; *P* (*of man*) faire l'amour*/s'envoyer en l'air/tringler. (*See* **crib¹ 1; fat II 4; nut¹ 5; stiffie 1; whip¹ 4; wisecrack²**)

crack down ['kræk'daʊn] *vi F* **to crack down on s.o.**, (*reprimand*) tomber sur le paletot à qn/tomber à bras raccourcis sur qn; (*suppress*) serrer la vis à qn; **to crack down on sth**, mettre le frein à qch.

cracked [krækt] *a O F* fou*/cinglé/toqué/fêlé.

cracker ['krækə] *n F* **1.** *O* mensonge*/craque *f* **2. she's a cracker**, elle est formid(able)/c'est un beau morceau/elle n'est pas pourrie **3.** *Austr* **not worth a cracker**, qui ne sert à rien/qui ne vaut pas grand-chose/qui ne vaut pas tripette. (*See* **crib-cracker**)

crackerjack ['krækədʒæk] **I** *a O F* excellent*/formid(able)/sensass **II** *n O F* **1.** (*person*) as *m*/crack *m* **2.** (*thing*) qch d'excellent*/du tonnerre.

crackers ['krækəz] *a P* fou*/cinglé/timbré.

crackhead ['krækhed] *n P* drogué(e) au crack.

cracking ['krækɪŋ] *a F* **1.** excellent*/super/canon; **to be in cracking form**, être en super forme/avoir la frite/avoir la pêche **2. at a cracking pace**, très vite*/en quatrième vitesse.

crack on ['kræk'ɒn] *vi* **1.** *Br F* parler* sans cesse/blablater **2.** *Austr P* **to crack on to s.o.**, faire la connaissance de qn.

crackpot ['kræk'pɒt] *a & n F* fou*/loufoque (*mf*)/cinglé(e) (*mf*).

cracksman ['kræksmən] *n P* (*housebreaker*) cambrioleur*/casseur *m*.

crack-up ['kræk'ʌp] *n F* accident *m*; (*of person*) dépression nerveuse).

crack up ['kræk'ʌp] *vi F* **1.** (*go mad*) perdre la boule/perdre les pédales/être au bout (du rouleau); **I must be cracking up!** ça ne

tourne pas rond chez moi!/je perds la tête! **2.** (*have a mental breakdown*) faire une dépression (nerveuse) **3. it's not all it's cracked up to be**, ce n'est pas aussi bien qu'on le dit/c'est pas aussi sensationnel qu'on le prétend.

cradle-snatcher ['kreɪdlsnætʃə] *n F* vieux marcheur; **he/she is a cradle-snatcher**, il/elle les prend au berceau. (*See* **baby-snatcher**)

crafty ['krɑːftɪ] *a F* (*discreet*) **to have a crafty smoke**, en griller une en douce/en loucedoc; **he's a crafty little beggar**, c'est un petit malin/futé. (*See* **arty-crafty**)

cram [kræm] *vi F* **to cram for an exam**, chauffer/bachoter.

cramp [kræmp] *vtr F* **to cramp s.o.'s style**, ennuyer/gêner qn; **does that cramp your style?** est-ce que ça te défrise?

crank [kræŋk] *n* **1.** *F* excentrique *mf*/original, -ale/loufoque *mf* **2.** *P* (*drugs*) amphétamine*/speed *m*.

crank up ['kræŋk'ʌp] *vi P* (*drugs*) se piquer/se faire un fixe.

cranky ['kræŋkɪ] *a F* excentrique/original.

crap¹ [kræp] *V* **I** *a* mauvais*/bidon; **it's totally crap**, c'est du bidon/de la merde **II** *n* **1.** étron*/merde *f*; **to have a crap**, chier **2.** (*nonsense*) bêtises*/conneries *fpl*/couillonnades *fpl*; **don't give me that crap!** ne me raconte pas des conneries! **I don't have to take that sort of crap from you**, (*unpleasant behaviour*) si tu crois que je vais encaisser ce genre de conneries de ta part; **cut the crap!** déconne pas!/écrase!/fais pas chier! **3.** (*dirt, rubbish*) **it's a load of crap**, tout ça c'est de l'eau de bidet/de la merde/de la saloperie **4. he's full of crap**, il est fort en gueule; c'est un couillon/un connard. (*See* **shoot² 6**)

crap² [kræp] *vi V* déféquer*/chier.

crapola [kræ'pəʊlə] *n NAm V* (*nonsense*) bêtises*/conneries *fpl*; (*dirt, rubbish*) saloperie *f*/merde *f*.

crap on ['kræp'ɒn] *vi P* dire des bêtises*/des conneries/débloquer.

crapper ['kræpə] *n V* WC*/chiottes *fpl*/gogues *mpl*.

crappo ['kræpəʊ], **crappy** ['kræpɪ] *a V* sale* / cracra / crado / cradingue / merdique / dégueulasse; **he's got a really crappy job**, il a un boulot vraiment merdique.

crash [kræʃ] *F* **I** *vtr* = **gatecrash II** *vi O* **to crash (down)**, s'endormir/en écraser/s'enrouspiller.

crashed [kræʃt] *a NAm P* ivre*/rétamé.

crasher ['kræʃə] *n Br F* = **crashing bore**

(**crashing**).

crash-hot [kræʃ'hɒt] *a Austr P* excellent*/
super/canon.

crashing ['kræʃɪŋ] *a F* crashing bore,
casse-pieds *mf*/raseur, -euse de première
(classe).

crash out ['kræʃ'aʊt] *vi P* s'endormir/en
écraser/s'enroupiller.

crashpad ['kræʃ'pæd] *n P* asile *m*
temporaire (*pour dormir*)/gourbi *m*.

crate [kreɪt] *n F* (*a*) (*aeroplane*) zinc *m*/
coucou *m* (*b*) (*car*) vieille voiture*/guimbarde
f/tacot *m*/caisse *f*.

crawl [krɔːl] *vi F* 1. s'aplatir; to crawl all
over s.o., faire de la lèche à qn 2. the place
was crawling with cops, l'endroit grouillait de
flics. (*See* **arse-crawl**; **pub-crawl²**)

crawler ['krɔːlə] *n F* lécheur, -euse de
bottes. (*See* **arse crawler**; **kerb crawler**)

crazy ['kreɪzɪ] *a F* 1. fou*/cinglé; are you
crazy? t'es pas fou*?/ça va pas, la tête? 2.
(*excellent*) terrible/formid(able) 3. enthou-
siaste/passionné/fana(tique); she's crazy
about it, elle en est dingue; he's crazy about
her, il en est toqué. (*See* **man-crazy**; **sex-
crazy**; **stir¹**; **woman-crazy**)

crazyhouse ['kreɪzɪhaʊs] *n P* maison *f* de
fous/asile *m* de dingues.

cream¹ [kriːm] *n* 1. *P* sperme*/blanc *m*/jute
m 2. *V* cream cheese, smegma *m*.

cream² [kriːm] *vtr & i P* 1. *esp NAm*
battre*/filer une raclée à (qn) 2. tuer*/
repasser/descendre (qn) 3. *V* (*a*) (*become
sexually excited*) avoir le gourdin/bander à
mort (*b*) éjaculer*/cracher son venin; to
cream one's jeans, juter dans son froc.

creampuff ['kriːm'pʌf] *n P* (*coward*)
poltron*/dégonflé, -ée.

crease [kriːs] *vtr P* 1. ennuyer*; you crease
me, tu me cours 2. to feel creased, (*be fed up*)
en avoir marre/ras le bol; (*be tired*) être
fatigué*/crevé 3. to crease oneself, (*laugh
uncontrollably*) se rouler par terre/se fendre
la gueule; you crease me up! tu me fais
marrer!

create [kriː'eɪt] *vi P* (*a*) grogner*/rouscailler
(*b*) faire une scène/faire du foin. (*See* **hell 3**)

cred [kred] *Br F* (*abbr of (street)
credibility*) **I** *a* branché **II** *n* branchitude *f*;
he's got cred, il est averti/branché/chébran/
câblé. (*See* **street 6**)

creek [kriːk] *n F* to be up the creek/*V* to be
up shit creek (without a paddle/in a barbed
wire canoe), *F* être dans le pétrin; être

embêté/emmouscaillé; *V* être emmerdé/être
dans les emmerdements/avoir des emmerdes.

creep¹ [kriːp] *n* 1. *F* salaud*/fripouille *f*/
minable *mf*; he's a real creep, c'est une vraie
fripouille 2. *F* (*toady*) lèche-bottes *m*/lèche-cul
m/flagorneur, -euse. (*See* **creeps**)

creep² [kriːp] *vi F* (*to toady*) ramper
(devant qn)/s'aplatir/lécher les bottes à qn.

creeper ['kriːpə] *n P* cambrioleur*/
caroubleur *m* qui travaille la nuit.

creepers ['kriːpəz] *npl Br O F* (*brothel*)
creepers, chaussures* à semelle souple. (*See*
jeepers!)

creeps [kriːps] *npl F* he gives me the creeps,
il me fait peur*/il me donne la chair de poule/
P il me fout les boules; it gives me the
creeps, ça me met les nerfs en pelote.

creepshow ['kriːpʃəʊ] *a F* (*frightening*)
qui fait peur*/qui fout la trouille.

creepy-crawly ['kriːpɪ'krɔːlɪ] **I** *a F*
creepy-crawly feeling, (*pins and needles*)
fourmillement *m*; (*goose pimples*) chair *f* de
poule **II** *n F* vermine *f*; petite bestiole *f*
(rampante).

cretin ['kretɪn] *n F Pej* imbécile*/crétin,
-ine/gland *m*; what a cretin! espèce de
nœud!/quel con!

cretinous ['kretɪnəs] *a F* (*remark, etc*)
bête*/crétin.

crew [kruː] *n F* 1. *Br* (*gang*) bande*/raille *f*
2. *NAm* bande* de jeunes (amis, artistes, etc)

crib¹ [krɪb] *n* 1. *O P* to crack a crib,
cambrioler*/faire un fric-frac/casser un
coffiot. (*See* **crib-cracker**) 2. *F* (*answers
used in exam*) antisèche *f*/pompes *fpl* 3. *NAm
P* maison *f*/cabane *f*/crèche *f*.

crib² [krɪb] *vtr & i F* tricher/empiler.

crib-cracker ['krɪbkrækə] *n O P*
cambrioleur*/casseur *m*. (*See* **crib¹ 1**)

crib-cracking ['krɪbkrækɪŋ] *n O P* cambriolage *m*/casse(ment) *m*.

cricket ['krɪkɪt] *n O F* that's not cricket,
c'est pas de jeu/ça ne se fait pas.

crikey! ['kraɪkɪ] *excl O F* crikey! mince
alors!/fichtre!

crim [krɪm] *n esp Austr P* (= *criminal*)
criminel *m*/taulard *m*.

crimble ['krɪmbl], **crimbo** ['krɪmbəʊ] *n
Br F* (*Christmas*) Noël *m*; crimble pud,
pudding *m* de Noël.

crimp¹ [krɪmp] *n NAm F* to put a crimp in
s.o.'s style, couper les effets à qn; mettre des
bâtons dans les roues de qn.

crimp² [krɪmp] *vtr F* to crimp s.o.'s style,

couper les effets à qn; mettre des bâtons dans les roues de qn.

cringe [krɪndʒ] *vi Br F* to make s.o. cringe, gêner/embarrasser qn.

cringe-making ['krɪndʒ'meɪkɪŋ] *a Br F* gênant/embarrassant.

cripes! [kraɪps] *excl O F* = **crikey!**

cripple ['krɪpl] *n F Pej* idiot(e)*/imbécile *mf*/crétin, -ine; you bloody cripple! espèce d'andouille!

crippler ['krɪplə] *n P* to slip s.o. a crippler, filer un coup bas à qn.

croak [krəʊk] *vtr & i P* 1. tuer*/descendre/liquider (qn) 2. mourir*/crônir/claquer/clamser.

croaker ['krəʊkə] *n P* 1. tueur professionnel/but(t)eur *m* 2. médecin *m*/toubib *m*; *surt* médecin qui prescrit sans scrupules des stupéfiants pour un drogué 3. indicateur*/indic *mf*/flicard *m*.

crock [krɒk] *n* 1. *F* old crock (*a*) vieille voiture*/tacot *m*/guimbarde *f* (*b*) (*old person*) croulant *m*/vieux birbe/vieux jeton 2. *F* cheval* fourbu/rosse *f* 3. *NAm P* crock (of shit), bêtises*/conneries *fpl*/salades *fpl*/vannes *m or fpl*; what a crock! c'est du mou!

crocked [krɒkt] *a P* 1. blessé/amoché 2. *NAm* ivre*/rétamé 3. *NAm* (*angry*) fumasse/furax(e).

crockery ['krɒkərɪ] *n NAm F* dentier *m*/tabourets *mpl*.

crocodile ['krɒkədaɪl] *n F* élèves marchant deux à deux/en rang(s) d'oignons/à la queue leu-leu. (*See* **alligator**)

crook [krʊk] I *a Austr F* 1. (*a*) (*also Dial*) malade*/patraque (*b*) (*worthless*) de mauvaise qualité/de toc (*c*) (*dubious*) craignos/craigneux (*d*) (*dishonest*) malhonnête; he's crook, c'est un flibustier 2. to go crook, se mettre en colère*/piquer une crise; to go crook at s.o./on s.o., réprimander* qn/engueuler qn/passer un savon à qn II *n F* 1. escroc*/arnaqueur *m*/filou *m* 2. voleur*/chapardeur, -euse/faucheur *m*.

cropper ['krɒpə] *n F* to come a cropper (*a*) (*fall*) tomber*/ramasser une pelle/se casser la figure (*b*) (*fail*) tomber sur un bec/faire un bide/faire un four.

crop up ['krɒp'ʌp] *vi F* survenir à l'improviste/surgir; ready for any problems that might crop up, paré à toute éventualité.

cross[1] [krɒs] *n P* escroquerie*/arnaque *f*; on the cross, malhonnêtement/en filouterie.

cross[2] [krɒs] *vtr F* 1. tromper*/trahir/posséder (qn). (*See* **double-cross**) 2. to cross one's heart, jurer ses grands dieux; cross my heart (and hope to die), (*esp child's language*) croix de bois, croix de fer(, si je mens je vais en enfer) 3. to cross one's fingers, faire une petite prière; let's keep our fingers crossed, touchons du bois/croisons les doigts.

crow [krəʊ] *n* 1. *F Pej* old crow, vieille femme*/vieille bique 2. *NAm F* to eat crow, faire des excuses humiliantes 3. *F* stone the crows! ça alors!/merde alors! 4. *F* (*lookout man*) guetteur *m* (*dans une équipe d'arnaqueurs*). (*See* **Jim Crow**)

crowd [kraʊd] *vtr P* casser les pieds à (qn)/s'en prendre à (qn)/chercher noise à (qn); don't crowd me! fiche-moi la paix!

crown[1] [kraʊn] *n P* crown jewels, sexe* de l'homme*/service *m* trois pièces/bijoux *mpl* de famille.

crown[2] [kraʊn] *vtr F* 1. flanquer un coup* sur la tête de (qn)/assommer (qn); if you don't shut up I'll crown you! la ferme, ou je te cogne! 2. and to crown everything ..., et pour comble de malheur/pour couronner le tout; that just about crowns it all, il ne manquait plus que ça.

crucial ['kruːʃəl] *a Br F* 1. (*term of appreciation*) excellent*/canon/géant 2. (*fashionable*) a crucial suit, un costard très à la mode/dernier cri 3. (*necessary*) nécessaire; dangerously crucial, indispensable.

crud [krʌd] *n* 1. *P* salaud*/fumier *m*; you stupid crud, espèce d'andouille!/tête de nœud! 2. *P* saleté*/cochonnerie *f*/crassouille *f* 3. (*nonsense*) it's a load of crud, c'est de la foutaise 4. *V* sperme* séché/foutre *m*.

cruddy ['krʌdɪ] *a P* (*a*) (*unpleasant*) débectant (*b*) (*worthless*) tocard.

cruise ['kruːz] *vi P* (*esp homosexuals*) chercher un partenaire sexuel *ou* un(e) prostitué(e)/draguer.

cruiser ['kruːzə] *n P* 1. homosexuel* qui drague/dragueur *m* 2. *O* prostituée*/marcheuse *f*. (*See* **kerb cruiser**)

cruising ['kruːzɪŋ] *n P* (*esp homosexuals*) la drague; they go there to do some cruising, ils y vont pour draguer les mecs.

crumb [krʌm] *n P* (*a*) salaud*/ordure *f* (*b*) pauvre type *m*.

crumblie, crumbly ['krʌmblɪ] *n Br F* 1. (*old person*) croulant, -ante/vioque *mf* 2. (*parent*) vieux *m*, vieille *f*/vioque *mf*.

crumbs [krʌmz] *excl F* ça alors!/zut!

crummy ['krʌmɪ] *a F* sale*/miteux/moche.

crumpet ['krʌmpɪt] *n* 1. (*a*) *V* (*sex*) to have a bit of crumpet/to get a crumpet, faire l'amour* avec/baiser/s'envoyer une femme (*b*) *P* (*women collectively*) there's some crumpet around, il y a de la fesse; *F* a nice bit of crumpet, (*sexually desirable woman*) un joli lot/un beau morceau/une belle pièce 2. *Austr P* not worth a crumpet, qui ne vaut rien* du tout/que dalle.

crunch [krʌntʃ] *n F* the crunch, le moment critique; when it comes to the crunch..., quand on est au pied du mur.../au moment critique....

crush [krʌʃ] *n F* béguin *m*; to have a crush on s.o., en pincer pour qn/se toquer de qn.

crust [krʌst] *n F* 1. the upper crust, la haute/le gratin/le dessus du panier 2. *Austr P* to earn a crust, gagner sa vie/sa croûte 3. to do one's crust, se mettre en colère*/en rogne/piquer une crise; to be off one's crust, être fou*/toqué/maboul.

crustie, crusty ['krʌstɪ] *n P* membre *m* d'un groupe de jeunes sans-travail sales et mal habillés.

crutch [krʌtʃ] *n P* (*drugs*) béquille *f* (*allumette fendue qui permet de fumer une cigarette de marijuana jusqu'au bout*).

crutch merchant ['krʌtʃ'mɜːtʃənt] *n Austr P* tombeur *m* de femmes/dragueur *m*/chaud lapin.

cry-baby ['kraɪbeɪbɪ] *n F* chialeur, -euse/pleurnicheur, -euse.

cry out ['kraɪ'aʊt] *vi F* for crying out loud! pour l'amour du ciel!

crystal ['krɪstəl] *npl P* (*drugs*) (*a*) méthédrine cristallisée (*b*) *pl* amphétamines*/speed *m* (*c*) héroïne*/poudre *f*.

CT, ct ['siː'tiː] *abbr P* = **cock-tease(r)**. (*See* **prick-tease(r)**; **PT**)

cube [kjuːb] *n P* 1. (*drugs*) (*a*) un gramme de haschisch*/cube *m* (*b*) morphine*/lilipioncette *f*. (*See* **acid 2**) 2. *pl esp NAm* (*dice*) dés*/bobs *mpl*.

cubehead ['kjuːbhed] *n O P* (*drugs*) consommateur, -trice de morceaux de sucre imprégnés de LSD*.

cuckoo ['kʊkuː] *a P* fou*/loufoque/cinglé; you're cuckoo! tu perds la boule!/tu déjantes!

cuff[1] [kʌf] *n* 1. *P* to buy sth on the cuff, acheter qch à crédit/à croume 2. *F* to say sth off the cuff, dire qch au pied levé/à l'improviste 3. *F* coup*/beigne *f*/taloche *f* 4. *pl F*

(= *handcuffs*) menottes*/bracelets *mpl*.

cuff[2] [kʌf] *vtr* 1. *F* to cuff s.o. round the ear, flanquer une taloche/une beigne à qn 2. *P* mettre/passer les menottes à qn.

cum [kʌm] *n P* = **come**[1].

cunt [kʌnt] *n V* 1. sexe* de la femme*/con *m*/chatte *f* 2. *Pej* (*woman*) femme*/femelle *f*/salope *f*; a nice bit of cunt, une nana qui a du chien 3. (*man*) con *m*; he's a prize/first-class cunt, il est archi-con; you silly cunt! espèce de con!/connard! 4. cunt talk, histoires *fpl* de cul/de fesses.

cunt-lapper ['kʌntlæpə] *n V* (*cunnilingus*) brouteur *m* de cresson.

cunt-struck ['kʌntstrʌk] *a V* (*henpecked*) dominé par sa femme/mené par le bout du nez.

cup [kʌp] *n* 1. *F* that's not my cup of tea, ce n'est pas mon truc; that's just her cup of tea, c'est exactement ce qui lui convient; that isn't everyone's cup of tea, ça ne plaît pas à tout le monde 2. *O P* (*homosexuals*) to have a cup of tea, faire l'amour* dans des toilettes publiques/dans les tasses; prendre le thé 3. *F* in one's cups, (*drunk*) dans les Vignes du Seigneur.

cupcake ['kʌpkeɪk] *n NAm F* 1. femme* mignonne/nénette *f* 2. (*eccentric person*) zigoto *m*.

cuppa, cupper ['kʌpə] *n F* tasse *f* de thé.

curl up ['kɜːl'ʌp] *vi F* I just wanted to curl up and die, (*said when very embarrassed*) j'aurais voulu disparaître (sous terre)/rentrer sous terre.

curlies ['kɜːlɪz] *npl P* to have s.o. by the short and curlies, avoir qn à sa merci/à sa pogne.

currant-bun ['kʌrənt'bʌn] *n P* 1. (*RS = sun*) bourguignon *m*/cagnard *m* 2. (*RS = son*) fils *m*/fiston *m*.

curse [kɜːs] *n F* to have the curse, avoir ses règles*/ses affaires *fpl*.

curtains ['kɜːtnz] *npl F* it'll be curtains for you if..., votre compte est bon si...; it was curtains for him, il était fichu.

curvaceous [kɜː'veɪʃəs] *a F* (*woman*) bien balancée/carrossée/roulée.

cushti ['kʊʃtɪ] *a Br P* (*term of approbation*) bien/chouette/formid.

cushy ['kʊʃɪ] *a F* (*easy, comfortable*) a cushy time/number, une planque/un filon; to have a cushy time, se la couler douce; a cushy life, une vie pépère; cushy job, sinécure *f*/fromage *m*.

cuss [kʌs] *n F* 1. individu*; an awkward

cuss, un type pas commode/un mauvais coucheur 2. it's not worth a (tinker's) cuss, ça ne vaut pas un clou; I don't give a tinker's cuss, je m'en fiche pas mal/je m'en moque comme de l'an quarante 3. cuss! (*bad luck!*) pas de chance! (*See* **tinker 2**)

customer ['kʌstəmə] *n F* 1. individu*/type *m*; a queer customer, un drôle de client/de numéro; an awkward customer, un type pas commode/un mauvais coucheur. (*See* **rough I 4**; **tough I 2**) 2. (*of prostitute*) clille *m*/micheton *m*.

cut¹ [kʌt] **I** *a* 1. P (légèrement) ivre*/éméché. (*See* **half-cut**) 2. F cut and dried, tout fait/tout taillé **II** *n F* 1. (*share of profits*) fade *m*/taf(fe) *m*; to get one's cut, toucher son fade/avoir sa gratte 2. he's a cut above the rest, il vaut mieux que les autres 3. (*cards*) to slip the cut, faire sauter la coupe 4. *Mus P* disque *m*/galette *f*; album *m*; extrait musical.

cut² [kʌt] *vtr & i* 1. P to cut and run, (*escape*) se tirer 2. P adultérer/couper (une drogue) 3. F to cut it fine, (*allow little margin of space or time*) compter/calculer trop juste; arriver*/faire qch à la dernière minute 4. F to cut no ice (with s.o.), ne pas faire d'effet; that doesn't cut any ice with me, ça ne me fait ni chaud ni froid 5. F to cut the mustard/to cut it, réussir/cartonner 6. to cut s.o. dead, snober qn/ignorer qn 7. F to cut a class, sécher un cours 8. F to cut corners, économiser*/faire des raccourcis/couper un sou en quatre 9. F it cuts both ways, c'est à double tranchant 10. O F to cut a dash, (*make impression*) faire de l'épate 11. F to cut loose, s'émanciper/couper les amarres 12. F to cut one's teeth on sth, se faire les dents sur qch

13. P mettre fin à qch; cut the crap! arrête de déconner!/déconne pas! 14. *NAm F* to cut (s.o.) a little/some slack, (*make allowances*) se montrer indulgent (envers qn)/être à la coule (avec qn); lâcher du lest avec qn; cut her some slack, laisse-la souffler un peu; lâche-la un peu. (*See* **cackle**; **comedy**; **crap II 2**; **rug 3**; **throat 2**)

cute [kjuːt] *a F* 1. (*person*) (*a*) charmant/gentil; what a cute little baby! quel mignon petit bébé! (*b*) malin*/futé; he's a cute one, il a le nez creux 2. (*thing*) mignon/gentil/chouette; what a cute idea! quelle idée originale/géniale/quelle chouette idée! 3. to play a cute trick on s.o., faire une entourloupette à qn.

cutey, cutie ['kjuːtɪ] *n F* 1. jolie fille/mignonne *f*/poupée *f* 2. malin, -igne/rusé, -ée.

cut in ['kʌt'ɪn] *vtr F* to cut s.o. in, mettre qn dans le coup; we cut him in on the deal, on l'a mis dans le coup.

cut out ['kʌt'aʊt] *vtr & i* 1. F cut it out! ça suffit!/basta! 2. F to have one's work cut out (to do sth), avoir de quoi faire/avoir du pain sur la planche 3. F I'm not cut out for that sort of job, je ne suis pas taillé pour ce genre de boulot 4. F (*exclude*) souffler la place à (qn)/couper l'herbe sous les pieds de (qn). (*See* **fancy¹ 4**)

cut up ['kʌt'ʌp] *vi F* 1. to be/to feel cut up, être affecté/affligé; I was very cut up by his death, sa mort m'a beaucoup secoué 2. to cut up nasty/rough/ugly, (*get angry, unpleasant*) se mettre en colère*/en rogne; se rebiffer/regimber; faire le méchant/être vache.

cylinder ['sɪlɪndə] *n F* to fire on all cylinders, rouler très vite*/à pleins tubes/à pleins gaz.

D

d [diː] (*abbr of decent*) *F* gentil/chic/chouette; that's jolly d of you, c'est sympa de ta part. (*See* **jolly II 2**)

D [diː] (*abbr*) *P* **1.** (*drugs*) (= *dope*) drogue*f*/camé *f* **2.** (= *diamond*) diamant*/diam *m*/caillou *m* **3.** *O Austr* (= *detective*) agent* de la Sûreté/condé *m*.

da [dɑː] *n F* père*/papa *m*/dab *m*; my da, mon vieux/mon vioc. (*See* **dar**)

DA ['diː'eɪ] *abbr* **1.** *P* (= *drug addict*) drogué*/toxico(mane) *mf*/camé, -ée **2.** *NAm F* (= *district attorney*) = procureur *m* de la République/proc(u) *m* **3.** *F* (= *duck's arse*) coiffure *f* des années 50 (*surt des* **Teddy Boys**); = banane *f*.

dab [dæb] **I** *a F* capable/calé/fort(iche); a dab hand, un expert/un as/un crack; he's a dab hand at that, il est doué pour ça/il est calé en ça **II** *n pl P* empreintes digitales; to have one's dabs taken, passer au piano. (*See* **mug¹ 1**)

dabble ['dæbl] *vi F* se droguer* irrégulièrement.

dabbler ['dæblə] *n F* drogué* occasionnel/drogué* du samedi soir.

dad [dæd] *n F* **1.** père*/papa *m*; my dad, mon vieux/mon vioc **2.** un vieux/un pépé/un croulant.

dad(d)a ['dædə] *n F* (*child's word*) père*/papa *m*.

daddio ['dædɪəʊ] *n O P* **1.** = **dad 2** **2.** (*beatnik term*) (*a*) chef *m* d'un groupe de beatniks (*b*) un vieux/un pépé/un croulant.

daddy ['dædɪ] *n F* **1.** = **dad 1** **2.** the daddy (of them all), l'ancien/le maestro; he's the daddy of them all, il les coiffe tous **3.** (*esp prisons*) meneur *m*/chef *m*; I'm the daddy, c'est moi le patron **4.** = **sugar-daddy** **5.** homosexuel* plus âgé *ou* dominant/tante *f*/tata *f*.

daff [dæf] *n F* (*abbr* = *daffodil*) a nice bunch of daffs, un joli bouquet de jonquilles.

daffy ['dæfɪ] *a P* **1.** (*a*) bête*/cruche/nouille (*b*) fou*/timbré/toqué **2.** to be daffy about s.o. = to be daft about s.o. (**daft I 2**).

daft [dɑːft] **I** *a F* **1.** idiot/cruche; he's as daft as a brush/as they come/as they make 'em, il est bête* comme ses pieds/il est con comme un balai; that's a daft idea, c'est ridicule/c'est stupide; c'est une idée à la con/à la noix **2.** to be daft about s.o., être toqué de qn/en pincer pour qn. (*See* **plain**) **II** *adv P* don't talk daft! ne dis pas de conneries!

daftie, dafty ['dɑːftɪ] *n P* individu bête*/cruche *f*/crétin, -ine/cloche *f*.

dag [dæg] *n Austr F* (*person*) (*eccentric*) rigolo *m*/zigoto *m*; (*stupid*) crétin, -ine/con(n)ard, -arde; (*unpleasant*) fumier *m*/salopard *m*.

dagga ['dægə] *n P* (*esp in South Africa*) (*drugs*) cannabis*.

daggy ['dægɪ] *a Austr F* (*stupid*) con/tarte; (*unpleasant*) moche/loquedu.

dago ['deɪgəʊ] *n P Pej* (*greasy*) dago, métèque *mf* (*surt d'origine espagnole ou italienne*)/Rital, -ale/Espingo *mf*.

daily ['deɪlɪ] *n* **1.** *F* femme *f* de ménage **2.** (*abbr of Daily Mail: RS = tail = buttocks*) fesses*/postère *m*; (= *sexual activity*) baisage *m*.

daisy ['deɪzɪ] *n* **1.** *F* qn/qch d'excellent*/d'épatant/d'impec; she's a daisy, c'est une perle; elle est sensass **2.** *F* to be kicking/pushing up the daisies, être enterré/bouffer les pissenlits par la racine **3.** *P* daisy roots/daisies, (*RS* = *boots*) chaussures*/godillots *mpl*/godasses *fpl* **4.** (*a*) homosexuel*/pédé *m* (*b*) homme efféminé/gâcheuse *f* **5.** *P* daisy chain, partouze *f* (à la bague). (*See* **oops-a-daisy!**; **ups-a-daisy!**; **upsy-daisy!**; **whoops-a-daisy!**)

daks [dæks] *npl Austr P* pantalon*/falzar *m*/futal *m*.

dam [dæm] *n F* = **damn¹**.

Dam (the) [ðə'dæm] *Prn F* Amsterdam *m ou f*.

damage ['dæmɪdʒ] *n F* (*expense*) what's the damage? ça fait combien? to stand the damage, payer* l'addition/régler la douloureuse. (*See* **serious**)

damaged ['dæmɪdʒd] *a P* damaged goods, ex-vierge *f*/fille* qui a vu le loup.

dame [deɪm] *n esp NAm F* femme*/fille*/ nana *f*/gonzesse *f*. (*See* **dizzy 2**)

damfool ['dæm'fuːl] I *a F* bête*/stupide/ idiot; damfool idea, idée *f* à la noix/à la con; that damfool driver! ce fichu conducteur! II *n F* individu bête*/imbécile *mf*/crétin, -ine/ connard, -arde; he's a damfool, c'est un sacré idiot.

damfoolery ['dæm'fuːlərɪ], **damfoolishness** ['dæm'fuːlɪʃnɪs] *n F* sacrée imbécillité/foutaises *fpl*/sottises *fpl*/conneries *fpl*.

dammit! ['dæmɪt] *excl F* **1.** zut!/flûte!/nom d'un chien!/merde! **2.** it was as near as dammit, il était moins une; as quick as dammit, aussi sec/illico.

damn¹ [dæm] I *a & adv* = **damned** I, II II *excl* damn! zut!/flûte!/bon sang!/merde! (*See* **damn² 4, 5, 6**) III *n F* **1.** I don't give a damn/I don't care a damn/I don't give a tinker's damn, je m'en moque comme de l'an quarante/je m'en fiche pas mal/je m'en soucie comme de ma première chemise/je m'en tamponne (le coquillard) **2.** it's not worth a damn, ça ne vaut pas un clou/ça ne casse rien. (*See* **tuppenny**)

damn² [dæm] *vtr F* **1.** damn you! va te faire voir (chez les Grecs)!/je t'emmerde! damn him! qu'il aille se faire fiche! **2.** well I'm damned/I'll be damned! ça c'est trop fort!/ça c'est le comble! **3.** I'll be damned if I'll do it! il est hors de question que je le fasse! **4.** damn it! zut!/flûte!/merde! **5.** damn and blast!/ damn it all! nom de nom!/nom d'un chien!/ bon sang!/bordel (de merde)! **6.** damn this car! y en a marre de cette bagnole!

damnable ['dæmnəbl] *a F* maudit/ exécrable.

damnably ['dæmnəblɪ] *adv F* bigrement/ rudement/vachement.

damn-all ['dæm'ɔːl] *n F* rien*; he's doing damn-all, il ne fiche rien/il n'en fout pas une rame; he's done damn-all today, il n'a rien fichu que dalle aujourd'hui/il n'a rien foutu de la journée; I know damn-all about it, je n'en sais fichtre rien/je n'en sais que dalle.

damnation [dæm'neɪʃ(ə)n] *excl F* zut!/ flûte!/merde! *O* what in damnation are you doing here? que diable fais-tu ici?

damned [dæmd] I *a F* **1.** sacré/satané/fichu; these damned taxes, ces fichus impôts! that damned car, cette foutue bagnole! **2.** what a/ it's a damned nuisance! quel empoisonnement!/quelle poisse!/(c'est) la barbe! **3.** he's a damned nuisance! quel enquiquineur!/quel emmerdeur!/quel casse-pieds! **4.** it's a damned shame, c'est une sacrée honte **5.** a damned good idea, une idée hyper chouette/une idée sensass **6.** a damned sight better than..., fichtrement mieux que.../ vachement mieux que.../méchamment mieux que... **7.** it's one damned problem after another, quand ce n'est pas une chose... **8.** a damned fool = **damfool** II II *adv F* **1.** diablement/vachement; it's damned hard, c'est vachement coton/c'est méchamment dur **2.** ...and a damned good job too! ...et c'est pas malheureux! **3.** you're damned right there! tu as carrément raison/tu as fichtrement raison! **4.** pretty damned quick, très vite*/dare-dare/ et que ça saute! (*See* **pdq**) **5.** it'll be damned useful, ça va nous rendre bougrement service.

damnedest ['dæmdɪst] *n F* to do/to try one's damnedest, se décarcasser/travailler d'achar/travailler d'arrache-pied/se faire suer.

damned-well, damn-well ['dæmd'wel, 'dæm'wel] *adv F* **1.** it damned-well serves you right, c'est bien fait pour ta gueule **2.** you can do what you damned-well like! fais ce que tu veux, je m'en fous/je m'en contrefous! **3.** I should damned-well think so! et (il) y a intérêt!/et j'espère bien!

damp [dæmp] *a P* (*woman*) excitée/qui mouille; I'm damp when I see him, je mouille quand je le vois.

damper ['dæmpə] *n F* **1.** douche *f* (froide); to put the damper(s) on sth, jeter un froid sur qch; donner un coup de frein à qch; refroidir l'enthousiasme **2.** to put the damper on s.o., faire taire* qn/clouer le bec à qn/rabattre le caquet à qn.

dance [dɑːns] *n F* to lead s.o. a (merry) dance, donner du fil à retordre à qn/en faire voir de toutes les couleurs à qn. (*See* **song 1**)

d and d ['diːən'diː] *a* (*abbr of drunk and disorderly*) *Euph F* ivre*/paf/pété.

dandruff ['dændrʌf] *n P* walking dandruff, poux*/mies *fpl* de pain à ressorts.

dandy ['dændɪ] *O* I *a esp NAm F* excellent*/ sensas/super; that's (fine and) dandy, c'est chouette II *adv esp NAm F* excellemment; to get along (just) dandy with s.o., s'entendre à merveille avec qn/être copain comme cochon (avec qn) III *n esp NAm F* chose excellente*/perle *f*.

dang¹ [dæŋ] *esp NAm F* I *a* = **damned** I II *n* = **damn¹** III.

dang² [dæŋ] *vtr esp NAm F* = **damn²**.

dangler ['dæŋglə] *n V* 1. pénis*/bout *m*/queue *f* 2. *Austr* exhibitionniste *m*/satyre *m*.

danglers ['dæŋgləz] *npl V* testicules*/balloches *fpl*.

dank [dæŋk] *n NAm P* marijuana*/herbe *f*.

dappy ['dæpɪ] *a P* joyeux/joice.

dar [dɑː] *n F* père*/dab *m*/vieux *m*/vioc *m*. (*See* **da**)

darbies ['dɑːbɪz] *npl Br A P* (*still used occasionally*) 1. menottes*/fichets *mpl*/bracelets *mpl* 2. mains*/pognes *fpl* 3. empreintes digitales.

Darby and Joan ['dɑːbɪən(d)'dʒəʊn] *Prn* 1. *F* vieux ménage; **Darby and Joan club**, club *m* du troisième âge 2. *P* (*RS* = *telephone*) téléphone*/bigophone *m* 3. *P* **on one's Darby and Joan**, (*RS* = *alone*) seulâbre/seulingue.

dare [dɛə] *vtr F* **I dare you!** chiche!

dark [dɑːk] I *a F* **to keep it dark**, garder qch secret; **keep it dark!** motus et bouche cousue! (*See* **horse 1**) II *n* 1. *F* **to be in the dark about sth**, ne pas être dans le coup 2. *P Mil* **in the dark**, au cachot/au violon/à l'ombre. (*See* **shot II 8**)

darkey, darkie, darky ['dɑːkɪ] *n Pej* Noir(e)*/nègre *m*/moricaud(e) *m(f)*. (*See* **strangle; throttle**)

darling ['dɑːlɪŋ] *a F* **that's darling of you!** c'est chouette/c'est sympa de ta part.

darn¹ [dɑːn] I *a & adv F* (*Euph for* **damned** I, II) **that darn car**, cette foutue bagnole!; **it's a darn nuisance**, quelle poisse!/c'est la barbe! (*See* **darned**) II *excl F* (*Euph for* **damn¹** II) zut!/flûte!/crotte!

darn² [dɑːn] *vtr F* (*Euph for* **damn²**) 1. **darn it!** flûte!/zut!/merde! 2. **well I'll be darned!** ça c'est trop fort!/c'est le bouquet!/c'est (un peu) fort de café!

darnation [dɑː'neɪʃ(ə)n] *excl O F* (*Euph for* **damnation**) zut!/flûte!/merde! (*See* **tarnation**)

darned [dɑːnd] *a & adv F* (*Euph for* **damned** I, II) 1. **he's a darned nuisance!** quel casse-pieds!/quel emmerdeur! 2. **you darned idiot!** espèce de nouille!/espèce de

con! 3. **he made a darned good job of it**, il a fait du bien beau travail. (*See* **darn¹** I)

darnedest ['dɑːndɪst] *n F* (*Euph for* **damnedest**) **to do one's darnedest**, faire de son mieux/se décarcasser.

dash¹ [dæʃ] *n F* 1. (= *dashboard*) tableau *m* de bord 2. tentative *f*/essai *m*; **to have a dash at sth**, tenter le coup 3. (*bribe*) pot-de-vin *m*. (*See* **cut²** 10)

dash² [dæʃ] *vtr & i F* 1. partir* rapidement/filer/se débiner; (I) **must dash**, (il) faut que je me tire 2. (*Euph for* **damn²**) **dash it all!** flûte!/zut!

dashed ['dæʃt] *a & adv F* (*Euph for* **damned** I, II) **dashed bad luck, old man!** pas de veine, mon pauvre!/quelle poisse, mon vieux!

date¹ [deɪt] *n F* 1. (*esp with s.o. of the opposite sex*) rendez-vous*/rencard *m*; **I've got a date with him**, j'ai rencard avec lui; **to break a date**, poser un lapin 2. personne *f* (du sexe opposé) avec qui on a rendez-vous*; **my date didn't show up**, mon copain/ma copine ne s'est pas amené(e)/m'a posé un lapin 3. *Austr P* anus*/oignon *m*. (*See* **blind¹** I 1; **heavy** I 2; **hot** 1)

date² [deɪt] *vtr F* **to date s.o.**, donner rendez-vous*/rencard *m* à qn; sortir (régulièrement) avec qn; **he's dating her**, il sort avec elle.

day [deɪ] *n F* 1. **that'll be the day!** ce jour-là, on fera une croix à la cheminée!/on plantera un arbre! 2. **to name the day**, fixer le jour du mariage 3. **to pass the time of day**, bavarder*/jacasser/(se) tailler une bavette 4. **to call it a day**, s'arrêter de travailler/s'en tenir là; **let's call it a day**, ça suffira pour aujourd'hui 5. **this coat's seen better days**, ce manteau a fait son temps 6. **it's not my day**, je me suis levé du pied gauche/c'est un jour à rester couché 7. **at the end of the day**, au bout du compte/en fin de compte 8. **that really made my day!** *Iron* il ne manquait plus que ça! (*improved things*) ça a transformé ma journée/ça m'a remonté le moral 9. **she's thirty if she's a day!** elle a ses trente printemps bien sonnés! (*See* **rainy-day**)

daylight ['deɪlaɪt] I *a F* **it's daylight robbery!** c'est de l'arnaque patentée!/on se fait arnaquer! II *n F* 1. **to be able to see daylight**, commencer à en voir le bout/voir la lumière au bout du tunnel 2. *pl* **to knock/to beat/to bash the living daylights out of s.o.**, battre* qn comme plâtre/flanquer une dérouillée à qn/flanquer une roustée à qn.

daylighting ['deɪlaɪtɪŋ] *n F* travail noir pendant la journée.

dazzler ['dæzlə] *n F* **1.** diamant*/diam *m*/ caillou *m* **2.** (*person*) m'as-tu-vu, -vue/ flambard *m*/frimeur, -euse/qn qui (en) jette.

dead [ded] **I** *a F* **1.** (*a*) (*person*) dead loss, nullité *f*/nullard *m*/crêpe *f*/zéro *m* (*b*) that concert was a dead loss, quel bide/four ce concert!/c'était nul, ce concert; his idea was a dead loss, c'était une idée à la noix/à la con **2.** dead cert/dead cinch, certitude absolue/du sûr et certain; he's a dead cert for the job, il est exactement ce qu'il nous faut pour ce boulot/il est fait pour ce boulot; that horse is a dead cert, ce cheval c'est un tuyau dur comme fer/ c'est du sûr **3.** dead man/dead soldier, bouteille* vide/cadavre *m* **4.** dead duck, échec *m*/faillite *f*/bide *m*; that play is a dead duck, cette pièce a fait un four; he's a dead duck, il est cuit/il est foutu/il est fichu **5.** he's dead from the neck up, il est bête*/il n'a rien dans la tête/il est con comme un balai **6.** dead to the world, (*asleep*) profondément endormi/ dans les bras de Morphée/complètement KO; (*drunk*) ivre* mort/bourré/beurré/rétamé **7.** he's the dead spit of his father, c'est son père tout craché/c'est tout le portrait de son père **8.** to be waiting for dead men's shoes, attendre la mort/le départ de qn (*pour lui prendre sa place*) **9.** (you'll do that) over my dead body! pas question (que tu le fasses)!/il faudra me passer sur le corps (pour faire ça)! **10.** I wouldn't be seen dead wearing that! je ne porterai pas ça même si on me payait! I wouldn't be seen dead with him! plutôt rester vieille fille que sortir avec ce type! **11.** drop dead! écrase!/va te faire voir!/va te faire foutre! (*See* **Anne; charlie 2; cut² 6; dead-and-alive; horse 4; meat 6; ringer 1; set II**) **II** *adv F* **1.** dead boring, très ennuyeux*/barbant/rasant/rasoir au possible **2.** dead broke, fauché comme les blés/sans le sou/sans un/dans la dèche **3.** I was dead chuffed, j'étais tout content/aux anges **4.** dead drunk, ivre* mort/bourré à mort/(s)chlass **5.** dead easy, facile comme bonjour; du gâteau **6.** I was dead lucky, j'ai eu un sacré pot/une de ces veines/une veine de pendu **7.** dead on, (*accurate*) dans le mille **8.** dead right mate! tout juste Auguste/tu l'as dit, bouffi! **9.** dead scared, mort de peur*/de frousse; to be dead scared, avoir peur*/mouiller/avoir les foies/ avoir les chocottes/fluber **10.** dead to rights,

absolument; to catch s.o. dead to rights, prendre qn la main dans le sac/épingler qn sur le fait **11.** to be dead set against sth, être braqué/buté contre qch; to be dead set against s.o., en avoir après qn; to be dead set on doing sth, vouloir faire qch à tout prix.

dead-and-alive ['dedən(d)ə'laɪv] *a F* a dead-and-alive place, un endroit mort *ou* triste; un trou perdu/un bled.

deadbeat ['dedbiːt] *n esp NAm F* **1.** (*poor or homeless person*) crève-la-faim *m*/déchard, -arde/clodo *m* **2.** (*scrounger*) pique-assiette *m*/torpilleur *m* **3.** individu bête*/crétin, -ine/ melon *m*.

dead-end ['ded'end] *a F* **1.** dead-end job, travail*/boulot *m* sans avenir **2.** dead-end kid, jeune délinquant, -ante *surt* des quartiers pauvres qui est sans avenir/voyou *m*/loubard *m*.

deadhead ['dedhed] *NAm F n* **1.** individu bête*/crétin, -ine/melon *m* **2.** personne *f* possédant un billet de faveur pour le théâtre, le train, etc.

deadleg¹ ['dedleg] *n Br F* **1.** (*spineless person*) mollasse *mf*; (*lazy person*) flemmard, -arde **2.** (*numb feeling*) engourdissement *m* de la jambe (*après un coup de genou à la cuisse*).

deadleg² ['dedleg] *vtr Br F* donner un coup de genou à la cuisse à (qn).

deadly ['dedlɪ] **I** *a F* ennuyeux*/rasoir/ casse-pieds **II** *adv F* deadly boring/dull, mortellement ennuyeux*/à mourir d'ennui/ mortellement rasoir.

deadneck ['dednek] *n F* = **deadbeat, deadhead**.

deal¹ [diːl] *n* **1.** *F* to clinch a deal, s'assurer une vente/signer une vente/boucler une affaire; to make a deal, décrocher une affaire; it's a deal! d'accord!/marché conclu! a new deal, un nouveau départ; a phoney deal, une affaire véreuse; dirty deal, mauvais tour/coup bas/sale coup/vacherie *f*. (*See* **raw I 1; square¹ I 1**) **2.** *F* big deal! et alors?/tu parles d'une affaire! no deal! des clous!/rien à faire! **3.** *P* (*drugs*) petite dose (*d'une drogue*)/fixe *m*.

deal² [diːl] *F* **I** *vi* vendre de la drogue/dealer **II** *vtr* she deals dope, elle vend/elle deale de la dope.

dealer ['diːlə] *n F* (*drugs*) trafiquant, -ante/ dealer *m*/revendeur, -euse. (*See* **wheeler-dealer**)

dear [dɪə] *a F* Dear John letter, lettre *f* de rupture d'une jeune fille à son fiancé (qui est à l'armée).

dearie, deary ['dɪərɪ] *n F* 1. (mon petit) chéri/(ma petite) chérie/mon chou/ma puce/ mon lapin 2. (oh) dearie me! (a) douce Mère! (b) see **bingo 3**.

death [deθ] *n F* 1. to feel like death (warmed up), être crevé/se sentir flagada; to look like death (warmed up), avoir l'air d'un cadavre ambulant/être plus mort que vif/être tout patraque 2. his plan died a death, son projet a fait un four/est mort dans l'œuf 3. to bore s.o. to death, faire mourir* qn d'ennui/ barber qn jusqu'à la gauche/raser qn à mort 4. I'm frozen to death, je meurs/je crève de froid 5. we're sick to death of all that, on en a marre/on en a par-dessus la tête/on en a ras le bol de tout ça 6. that car will be the death of me, cette voiture me rendra fou/me donnera des cheveux blancs 7. death seat, (in car) place *f* du mort. (*See* **flog 2; hang on 2; tickle² 3**)

deb [deb] *n F* 1. *Br* (*abbr of debutante*) débutante *f*; deb's delight, parti *m* acceptable pour une débutante 2. *NAm* femme* membre d'une bande.

debag [diːˈbæg] *vtr Br F* déculotter/ défroquer.

debug ['diːˈbʌg] *vtr F* 1. réparer/mettre au point/réviser (un ordinateur, etc) 2. désonoriser/neutraliser des micros clandestins dans (une pièce).

debunk [diːˈbʌŋk] *vtr F* faire descendre (qn) d'un cran; déboulonner.

deck¹ [dek] *n* 1. *F* to hit the deck (a) sortir du lit/sortir du plumard/se dépagnoter (b) tomber à plat ventre 2. *F* to clear the decks, tout préparer/se préparer à agir/être sur le point d'attaquer 3. *P* (*drugs*) petite quantité de drogues/prise *f*; (*dose for injection*) petite dose d'héroïne*.

deck² [dek] *vtr F* envoyer (qn) au tapis/ mettre (qn) KO.

deckman ['dekˈmæn] *n P* (*drugs*) trafiquant *m*/revendeur *m* de cocaïne*.

decorators ['dekəreɪtəz] *npl P* to have the decorators in, avoir ses règles*/repeindre sa grille en rouge. (*See* **painter**)

dee-jay ['diːdʒeɪ] *n F* (*abbr of disc jockey*) présentateur, -trice de disques/disc-jockey *m*.

deep [diːp] I *a F* 1. malin*/fin/roublard/retors 2. to put sth in the deep freeze, mettre qch au frigo. (*See* **end 5, 12; jump² 11**) II *n P* to plough the deep, (*RS = to sleep*) dormir*/ pioncer.

deep six [diːpˈsɪks] *vtr NAm P* 1. (*dispose of*) se débarrasser de/balancer; (*bury*) enterrer 2. (*kill*) tuer*/descendre.

def [def] *a P* excellent*/super/géant.

de facto [deɪˈfæktəʊ] *n Austr F* (*unmarried partner*) concubin, -ine.

deffo ['defəʊ] *adv Br F* (*short for definitely*) c'est certain/(c'est) affiché.

degree [dɪˈgriː] *n F* 1. to be/to feel one degree under, être légèrement malade*/être patraque/ne pas être dans son assiette 2. to give s.o. the third degree, (*interrogate*) cuisiner qn/griller qn; (*hit*) passer qn à tabac.

dekko ['dekəʊ] *n P* let's have a dekko! fais(-moi) voir!/juste un coup d'œil*! have/ take a dekko out of the window! jette un coup d'œil* par la fenêtre!

deli ['delɪ] *n F* (*abbr of delicatessen*) épicerie fine.

delicate ['delɪkət] *a F* to be in a delicate condition, être enceinte*/être dans une situation intéressante.

demo ['deməʊ] *n F* 1. manifestation *f* politique/manif *f* 2. *Mus* cassette *f* de démonstration 3. travail *m* ou ouvrier *m* de démolition.

demob¹ ['diːˈmɒb] *n F* (*abbr of demobilization*) libération *f* militaire/quille *f*; to be due for demob, être de la classe/attendre la quille.

demob² ['diːˈmɒb] *vtr F* (*abbr of demobilize*) démobiliser/libérer/renvoyer dans son foyer.

demolish [dɪˈmɒlɪʃ] *vtr F* manger*/ dévorer; she demolished the whole cake, elle a bâfré tout le gâteau.

dense [dens] *a F* bête*/bouché.

dent [dent] *n F* to make a dent (in sth), commencer à mordre (dans qch); buying the car made a big dent in his savings, avec l'achat de cette voiture, ses économies ont pris une sacrée claque/un sacré coup.

Derby Kelly ['dɑːbɪˈkelɪ] *n P* (*rare*) (*RS = belly*) ventre*/bide *m*/bidon *m*.

der(r)o ['derəʊ] *n F* 1. *Austr* (*tramp, homeless person*) clodo *m* 2. *Br* (*unfortunate person*) pauvre type *m*/déchard, -arde; (*unpleasant person*) salaud*/minable *mf* 3. *Br =* **derry**.

derry ['derɪ] *n Br P* (= *derelict (house)*) (*esp used by tramps, drug addicts, etc*) baraque *f*/cambuse *f*/turne *f*.

des. res. [dezˈrez] *n Br F* (*abbr of desirable residence*) (*used literally and ironically*) résidence *f* superbe/appartement *m ou* maison *f* superbe.

destroyed [dɪ'strɔɪd] *a F* (*completely drunk*) beurré/raide/rétamé; (*drugged*) camé/défoncé.

detox¹ ['diːtɒks] *n F* (*abbr of detoxification*) désintoxication *f*.

detox² [diː'tɒks] *vi F* (*abbr of detoxify*) se faire désintoxiquer.

deuce [djuːs] *n* 1. *A F* (= *devil*) (*expression of annoyance*) zut!/flûte! 2. *O F* (= *devil*) what the deuce! que diable! who the deuce are you? qui diable êtes-vous? 3. *P* deux livres *fpl* sterling/*NAm* deux dollars *mpl* 4. deux années *fpl* de prison/deux berges *fpl*.

deuced [djuːst] I *a O F* satané/sacré; he's a deuced idiot, c'est un sacré imbécile; deuced bad luck old chap! fichue déveine, mon gars! II *adv O F* diablement/diantrement.

devil ['devl] *n F* 1. poor devil! pauvre diable!/pauvre bougre! he's a lucky devil! il a du pot, celui-là! 2. go on, be a devil and have another! allez! laisse-toi tenter et reprends un verre! 3. he's an absolute devil! il est infernal! he's a devil with the ladies, il est terrible avec les femmes/c'est un tombeur de 1ère classe 4. what the devil! que diable! how the devil did you get in? comment diable es-tu entré? how the devil should/would I know? comment veux-tu que je (le) sache? who the devil do you think you are? pour qui tu te prends, à la fin? why the devil didn't you say so? pourquoi tu ne l'as pas dit, bon sang?/mais alors! pourquoi ne l'as-tu pas dit? 5. we had the devil of a job/the devil's own job to find it, ça a été la croix et la bannière pour le trouver/on a eu un mal fou à le trouver; it's the devil of a job/O it's the very devil to wake him up in the morning, c'est la croix et la bannière pour le réveiller le matin; he has the devil of a temper, il a un sale caractère/un caractère de cochon; c'est un mauvais coucheur 6. there'll be the devil to pay, ça va nous coûter cher; ça va barder 7. *O* the devil you will! (il n'en est) pas question!/pas moyen! the devil take it! mince alors! 8. *O* to send s.o. to the devil, envoyer qn au diable/envoyer paître qn; go to the devil! va te faire voir!/va te faire fiche! 9. *O* to go to the devil, mal tourner; his work has gone to the devil, son travail ne vaut pas grand-chose 10. *O* to play the devil with sth, mettre la confusion dans qch/semer la pagaille; this strike will play the devil with trains to London, cette grève va mettre la pagaille dans les trains

pour Londres 11. to work like the devil, travailler* avec acharnement/travailler* comme une bête/bûcher comme un noir 12. to have the luck of the devil, avoir une veine de pendu/de cocu 13. to give the devil his due, rendre justice à (qn) 14. between the devil and the deep blue sea, entre l'enclume et le marteau/entre Charybde et Scylla 15. *O* to raise the devil/to make a devil of a row, faire du bruit/faire du foin/faire du ramdam 16. *A* the Devil's books/playthings, cartes* à jouer/brêmes *fpl* 17. *A* blue devils, le cafard/le bourdon/le blues 18. red devils = reds (**red II 5**).

devilish(ly) ['devlɪʃ(lɪ)] *adv F* diablement/diantrement/extrêmement/vachement.

devo ['diːvəʊ] *n Austr P* (*a*) pervers, -erse (*b*) voyeur *m*.

dewdrop ['djuːdrɒp] *n F Euph* goutte *f* au nez/chandelle *f*.

dex [deks], **dexie** ['deksɪ], **dexo** ['deksəʊ], **dexy** ['deksɪ] *n P* (*drugs*) cachet *m* de dexamphétamine; *pl* dexies/dexos, amphétamines *fpl*/amphés *fpl*.

diabolical [daɪə'bɒlɪkl] *a F* diabolique/satané/affreux/atroce/épouvantable; it's a diabolical liberty! c'est un sacré culot!

dial(-piece) ['daɪəl(piːs)] *n P* visage*/museau *m*/bobine *f*.

diamond ['daɪəmənd] *a Br P* excellent*/doré sur trance/nickel.

diarrhoea, *NAm* **diarrhea** [daɪə'rɪə] *n F* verbal diarrhoea, discours *m* sans fin/clapet *m*/pia-pia *m*.

dib¹ [dɪb] *n P* 1. *esp NAm* portion *f*/part *f*; (*amount of money*) somme *f* d'argent. 2. *Br* cigarette*/clope *f* à moitié fumée (*conservée pour être terminée plus tard*).

dib² [dɪb] *vtr Br P* éteindre une cigarette* à moitié fumée (*pour la terminer plus tard*).

dibs [dɪbz] *n O P* argent*/fric *m*; to have the dibs, être riche*/avoir du fric/être au pèze/être plein aux as.

dice¹ [daɪs] *n F* no dice! pas mèche!/je ne marche pas!/rien à faire!/des clous!

dice² [daɪs] *vi F* to dice with death, faire la course à la mort/jouer avec la mort.

dicey ['daɪsɪ] *a F* hasardeux; it's a bit dicey, c'est plutôt risqué/c'est pas du tout cuit/c'est pas de la tarte.

dick [dɪk] *n P* 1. pénis*/Charles-le-Chauve *m*/Popaul *m*. (*See* **Uncle 2** (*a*)) 2. individu bête*/andouille *f*/crétin, -ine; what a dick! quel nœud!/quel gland! 3. policier*//bourre *m*/

guignol *m*/keuf *m*; a private dick, un privé 4. clever Dick, petit/gros malin, petite/grosse maligne; affranchi, -ie 5. dirty Dick, dégoûtant *m*/sale coco *m* 6. *pl* poux*/morpions *mpl* 7. *O* dictionnaire *m*/dico *m* 8. *esp NAm* rien*/balpeau/que dalle. (*See* **Tom 1**)

dickens ['dɪkɪnz] *n O F* (*Euph for* **devil**) 1. they were making the dickens of a noise, ils faisaient un bruit/un potin du diable 2. we had the dickens of a job to finish it, on a eu un mal fou pour le finir.

dickhead ['dɪk(h)ed] *n P* individu bête*/crétin, -ine/tête *f* de nœud/trouduc *m*.

dickless Tracy ['dɪkləs'treɪsɪ] *n Austr P* femme *f* policier/femme flic.

dick licker ['dɪk'lɪkə] *n V* 1. homosexuel*/pédé *m*/enculé *m* 2. personne *f* qui pratique la fellation*/tailleuse *f* de plumes/suceuse *f*.

dickory dock ['dɪkərɪ'dɒk] *n P* 1. (*RS = clock*) horloge *f*/pendule *f*/tocante *f* 2. (*RS = cock*) pénis*/queue *f*/bite *f*.

dicky ['dɪkɪ] *Br* I *a F* (*a*) malade*/patraque/pas dans son assiette; I feel a bit dicky today, je suis (un peu) mal foutu aujourd'hui; he's got a dicky heart, il a le cœur branlant/qui flanche. (*See* **ticker 1**) (*b*) (*chair, ladder, etc*) pas solide (*c*) (*tricky*) hasardeux/risqué II *n P* = **dicky-dirt**.

dicky bird ['dɪkɪbɜːd] *n Br F* 1. oiseau *m*/zoziau *m*/piaf *m* 2. (*RS = word*) mot *m*; not a dicky bird! pas un mot!/motus (et bouche cousue)!

dicky-dirt ['dɪkɪ'dɜːt] *n P* (*RS = shirt*) chemise*/liquette *f*/limace *f*.

did [dɪd] *n Br P* = **didicoi**.

diddies ['dɪdɪz] *npl A P* seins*/nénés *mpl*.

diddle ['dɪdl] *vtr* 1. *Br F* duper*/rouer/carotter (qn); I've been diddled, je me suis fait avoir 2. *P* faire l'amour* avec (qn)/calcer (qn)/se faire (qn) 3. *P* (*sexually stimulate*) tripoter (une femme).

diddler ['dɪdlə] *n F* escroc*/carotteur, -euse/estampeur *m*.

diddling ['dɪdlɪŋ] *n F* escroquerie*/arnaque *f*.

did(d)lo ['dɪdləʊ] *a & n Br P* fou*/cinglé (, -ée)/louftingue (*mf*).

diddly (shit, squat) ['dɪdlɪ'(ʃɪt, skwɒt)] *n NAm P* (*a*) rien*/nib (de nib) (*b*) (*sth insignificant*) une/de la merde.

diddums ['dɪdəmz] *excl F* (*to a child or ironic*) diddums hurt himself then? on s'est fait bobo, mon petit?

diddy ['dɪdɪ] *Br* I *a F* petit/tout petit/

minuscule; (*cute*) mignon/chou II *n* 1. idiot*/crétin, -ine 2. = **didicoi**.

didicoi ['dɪdɪkɔɪ] *n Br P* (*gypsy or half-gypsy*) romano *mf*/rabouin *m*.

dig¹ [dɪg] *n* 1. *P* dig in the grave, (*RS = shave*) rasage *m* 2. *pl F* digs, logement*/crèche *f*/piaule *f* 3. *F* to have a dig at s.o., (*tease, mock*) vanner/lancer une vanne à qn.

dig² [dɪg] *vtr* 1. *F* (*a*) I dig that! ça me plaît!/ça me botte!/ça me branche! I really dig rock (music), le rock, ça me branche (*b*) aimer* (qn)/avoir qn à la bonne (*c*) comprendre/entraver/piger; you dig? tu piges? (*d*) remarquer; dig that! vise-moi ça!/mate-moi ça! 2. *P* (*not common*) taper sur les nerfs/sur le système à (qn); what's digging you? qu'est-ce qui te turlupine?

digger ['dɪgə] *n O F* Australien, -ienne, kangourou *m*; Néo-Zélandais, -aise, kiwi *m*. (*See* **gold-digger**)

dig in ['dɪg'ɪn] *vtr & i F* 1. manger*/s'empiffrer/bouffer; he dug into a pile of sausages, il attaqua une montagne de saucisses 2. to dig in (one's heels), rester sur ses positions/ne pas broncher/ne pas moufter/se tenir peinard.

dig up ['dɪg'ʌp] *vtr F* dégoter qch; where did you dig that up? où l'as-tu déniché/pêché? (*often humorous*) I wonder where they dug him up from! je me demande où ils ont déniché/été chercher ce type!

dike [daɪk] *n P* = **dyke**.

dildo ['dɪldəʊ] *n P* 1. gode(miché) *m* 2. idiot*/trouduc *m*.

dill [dɪl] *n P* imbécile*/navet *m*/andouille *f*.

dilly ['dɪlɪ] *n F* 1. (*sth remarkable*) qch de chouette/de super; that's a dilly! ça c'est géant! she's a dilly, elle est mignonne (à croquer) 2. *esp Austr* imbécile*/gourde *f*/nouille *f*.

Dilly (the) [ðə'dɪlɪ] *Prn Br F* Piccadilly (à Londres) (*fréquenté par les prostituées, les drogués, etc*).

dilly bag ['dɪlɪ'bæg] *n Austr P* (*small bag or basket*) cabas *m*/lacsé *m*.

dilly-dally ['dɪlɪ'dælɪ] *vi O F* perdre son temps/traînasser/glander.

dim [dɪm] *a F* 1. to take a dim view of sth, ne pas voir qch d'un bon œil 2. bête*/idiot; he's a bit dim, il est bouché/il est concon.

dimbo ['dɪmbəʊ] *n F* idiot*/empaillé, -ée.

dime [daɪm] *n NAm P* pièce *f* de dix cents; dime novel, roman *m* feuilleton/de deux sous; it's a dime a dozen, ça ne vaut pas cher/ça ne vaut pas tripette; **dime-a-dance palace,** bal *m* musette/bastringue *m*/guinche *m*; **dime store,** magasin *m* pas cher/= Prisu *m*; (*drugs*) **dime bag,** paquet *m ou* quantité *f* de drogue qui vaut 10 dollars.

dimmo ['dɪməʊ] *n F* = **dimbo.**

dimwit ['dɪmwɪt] *n F* individu bête*/ andouille *f*/ballot *m*; **what a dimwit!** quel crétin!

dimwitted ['dɪm'wɪtɪd] *a F* bête*/bas de plafond/baluche/ballot.

din-dins ['dɪndɪnz] *n F* (*child's language or Hum*) repas *m*/dinette *f*/miam-miam *m*.

ding [dɪŋ] *n Austr P* = **dinger.**

Ding [dɪŋ] *n Austr P Pej* (*a*) Italien*, -ienne/ Rital, -ale (*b*) Grec(que) *mf*.

dingaling, ding-a-ling ['dɪŋəlɪŋ] *n P* = **ding-dong 4.**

dingbat ['dɪŋbæt] *n P* 1. imbécile*/andouille *f*/crétin, -ine; **you dingbat!** espèce de nouille! 2. *pl Austr* **to have the dingbats/to be dingbats,** avoir le délirium tremens/voir les rats bleus; **to give s.o. the dingbats,** énerver qn/filer le trac à qn.

ding-dong ['dɪŋdɒŋ] *n P* 1. (*shouting match*) pétard *m*/gueulante *f*; (*fright*) luttan-che *f*/carambolage *m* 2. (*rowdy party*) boum *f* 3. imbécile*/gourde *f* 4. pénis*/quéquette *f*/ zizi *m*.

dinge [dɪndʒ] *n esp NAm P occ Pej* Noir(e)*/nègre *m*/négro *m*/moricaud, -aude. (*See* **queen¹ 2**)

dinger ['dɪŋə] *n Austr P* fesses*/pétrousquin *m*/baba *m*; anus*/anneau *m*; **a kick in the dinger,** un coup de pied au cul.

dingleberries ['dɪŋglberɪz] *npl V* = **clink-er 2.**

dink [dɪŋk] *n* 1. *P* individu bête*/nouille *f* 2. *NAm P Pej* Vietnamien, -ienne/Viet *mf* 3. *F* (*acronym of double income, no kids*) mari *m ou* femme *f* dans un couple à deux revenus, sans enfants.

dinkum ['dɪŋkəm] *a Austr F* 1. **fair dinkum,** régulier/réglo/aux petits oignons/vrai de vrai 2. **the dinkum article,** (*genuine*) de l'authentique/du vrai; (*right person*) l'homme/la femme qu'il faut 3. **dinkum Aussie,** Australien, -ienne de naissance/ kangourou *m*.

dinky ['dɪŋkɪ] *F* **I** *a* mignon/chouette/ croquignole **II** *n* 1. *Br* (grosse) voiture*/ (grosse) bagnole *f* 2. = **dink 3.**

dinky-di ['dɪŋkɪ'daɪ] *a Austr F* vrai de vrai/ pur/authentique; **he's a dinky-di Aussie,** c'est

un Australien à 100%/jusqu'au bout des on-gles.

dinky-doo ['dɪŋkɪ'du:] *F See* **bingo 22.**

dip¹ [dɪp] *n* 1. *P* (*pickpocket*) voleur* à la tire/machinette *f*/tireur *m* 2. individu bête*/ crétin, -ine 3. *F* **to take a dip,** faire une petite baignade/faire trempette. (*See* **skinny dip**)

dip² [dɪp] *vtr & i P* 1. mettre en gage/mettre au Mont de Piété/mettre au clou 2. (*pickpockets*) voler* à la tire. (*See* **lid 1** (*a*); **wick 2**)

dippy ['dɪpɪ] *a P* fou*/timbré/toqué/ louf(oque)/dingo.

dipshit ['dɪpʃɪt] *n V* individu bête*/ con(n)ard, -arde/duschnock *m*.

dipso ['dɪpsəʊ] *n F* (*abbr of dipsomaniac*) ivrogne*/soûlot, -ote/soûlard, -arde/poivrot, -ote/alcolo *mf*.

dipstick ['dɪpstɪk] *n P* = **dipshit.**

dirt [dɜ:t] *n* 1. *F* pornographie *f*/porno *m*/ obscénité *f* 2. *P* ragots *mpl*/potins *mpl*/merde *f*; **to dig up the dirt about s.o.,** fouiller la merde de qn; **to dish out the dirt/to throw dirt at s.o./to spread the dirt about s.o.,** déblatérer contre qn/débiner qn; **to have the dirt on s.o.,** savoir des choses pas propres sur qn. (*See* **dish² 4**) 3. *F* **to treat s.o. like dirt,** traiter qn plus bas que terre/traiter qn comme de la merde 4. *F* **to sweep the dirt under** *Br* **the carpet/***NAm* **the rug,** couvrir la vérité/tirer le rideau 5. *F* **to eat dirt,** avaler son amour-propre/avaler des couleuvres 6. *O P* **to do dirt on s.o./to do s.o. dirt,** faire un sale coup/une crasse/des saloperies *fpl* à qn. (*See* **dirty II**) 7. *P* (*prisons*) sucre *m*. (*See* **dicky-dirt**)

dirtbag ['dɜːtbæg] *n NAm P* salaud*/ordure *f*.

dirtbox ['dɜːtbɒks] *n V* anus*/tiroir *m* aux lentilles.

dirt-cheap ['dɜːt'tʃiːp] *a & adv* à vil prix/ pour rien*/pour des clopinettes/pour des clous; **I got it dirt-cheap,** je l'ai eu très bon marché/pour une bouchée de pain/pour trois fois rien.

dirty ['dɜːtɪ] **I** *a* 1. *F* **a dirty business,** (*un-pleasant job*) un sale métier; (*unpleasant situation*) une sale affaire/histoire; **dirty crack,** (*unpleasant remark*) vacherie *f*; **dirty rat/dirty dog,** sale type *m*/sale mec *m*/ salaud *m*; (*sport*) **dirty player,** joueur salaud; **dirty trick,** sale coup *m*/sale tour *m*; **dirty weather,** temps pourri/temps de chien; **I leave all the dirty work to him,** à lui la sale beso-gne; **she gave me a dirty look,** elle m'a regardé d'un sale œil 2. *F* (*lewd*) **dirty joke,** blague cochonne; **dirty old man,** vieux cochon; **dirty weekend,** weekend *m* de débauche/de partouze; **to have a dirty mind,** avoir l'esprit mal tourné/avoir l'esprit cochon; **she's got a really dirty mind!/she's really dirty-minded,** elle ne pense qu'à ça! **to have a dirty mouth,** jurer comme un charretier; être mal embouché 3. *P* **dirty money,** argent* mal acquis/gratte *f*/tour *m* de bâton 4. *P* (*intensifier*) **a dirty great lorry,** un camion maous(se)/un gros bahut; **a dirty big suitcase,** une valoche grande comme un camion 5. *O P* **dirty old Jew:** *see* **bingo 2;** **dirty whore:** *see* **bingo 34 6.** *F* (*police jargon*) (*person*) qui possède de la drogue; (*bag etc*) qui contient de la drogue; **her suitcase was dirty,** il y avait de la came dans sa valise. (*See* **linen 1; mac¹**) **II** *n P* **to do the dirty on s.o.,** jouer un tour de cochon à qn/faire des crasses à qn/chier dans les bottes à qn. (*See* **dirt 6**)

dis [dɪs] *vtr NAm F* (*disparage*) dénigrer/bêcher/couler/débiner (qn). (*See* **diss**)

disappearing [dɪsə'pɪərɪŋ] *a F* **to do a disappearing act,** (*leave*) partir*/s'esquiver/se casser; (*leave without paying*) déménager à la cloche de bois.

disco ['dɪskəʊ] *n F* (*abbr of discotheque*) discothèque *f*/disco *f*/boîte *f*; **disco music,** musique *f* disco/le disco; **to go disco dancing,** (*aller*) danser le disco; **to go to a disco,** aller dans une disco/sortir en boîte.

disgusto [dɪz'gʌstəʊ] *F* **I** *a* dégoûtant/dégueulasse/dégueu **II** *n* (*disgusting thing*) dégueulasserie *f*.

dish¹ [dɪʃ] *n* 1. *F* individu* beau/joli/qui a du chien/qui jette du jus; **he's a real dish,** il en jette/il dégage; **what a dish!** quelle beauté! (*See* **dishy**) 2. *NAm P* (*gossip*) cancans *mpl*/commérages *mpl*/potins *mpl*.

dish² [dɪʃ] *vtr & i P* 1. enfoncer (ses adversaires)/couper l'herbe sous le pied à (qn) 2. duper*/rouler (qn) 3. confondre/dérouter/frustrer; **he dished his chances of getting promoted,** il a gâché/il a foutu en l'air ses possibilités d'avancement 4. *NAm* **to dish the dirt,** (*spread malicious gossip*) potiner; **to dish the dirt on s.o.,** débiner qn/déblatérer contre qn.

dish out ['dɪʃ'aʊt] *vtr F* 1. **to dish out money/the lolly,** payer*/casquer/cracher/allonger 2. **to dish it out,** réprimander*/enguirlander/passer un savon 3. **to dish out

punishment,** assener des coups* à son adversaire/envoyer un marron/envoyer une pêche à qn. (*See* **dirt 2; dish² 4; porridge 2**)

dish up ['dɪʃ'ʌp] *vtr* 1. *F* bien arranger/bien trousser/requinquer; **he dished up some excuse or other,** il a sorti une excuse quelconque; **they just dished up a load of old info in a new form,** ils ont fait un réchauffé de faits bien connus 2. *Austr P* **to look dished up,** avoir l'air fatigué*/lessivé/vanné.

dishwater ['dɪʃwɔːtə] *n F* 1. lavasse *f*; bibine *f*; **this coffee's like dishwater,** ce café c'est du jus de chaussettes 2. **dull as dishwater,** ennuyeux*/chiant comme la pluie. (*See* **ditchwater**)

dishy ['dɪʃɪ] *a F* qui a du chien/qui jette du jus; **she's rather dishy,** elle est plutôt sexy/elle en jette/elle a de la classe; **he's a very dishy guy,** il a de la gueule/il dégage, ce mec. (*See* **dish¹ 1**)

diss [dɪs] *vtr P* (*disparage*) dénigrer/bêcher/couler/débiner (qn). (*See* **dis**)

distance ['dɪst(ə)ns] *n F* (*sport, esp boxing*) **to go the distance,** aller à la limite.

ditch [dɪtʃ] *vtr F* 1. jeter par-dessus bord/larguer/balancer/bazarder 2. **to ditch a car,** (*crash*) se planter en voiture/aller dans le décor; (*scrap*) abandonner*/bazarder une bagnole 3. **to ditch a plane,** amerrir en catastrophe/faire un amerrissage de fortune 4. (*a*) abandonner* (une idée); plaquer/larguer (qn) (*b*) se débarrasser* de/balancer/sacquer/virer (qn).

Ditch (the) [ðə'dɪtʃ] *n F* 1. Shoreditch (*dans l'est de Londres*) 2. l'océan *m* Atlantique/la Mare (aux harengs); **the ditch,** la mer/la grande bleue.

ditchwater ['dɪtʃwɔːtə] *n F* **dull as ditchwater,** ennuyeux*/chiant comme la pluie; **he's as dull as ditchwater,** il est rasoir.

dither ['dɪðə] *n F* **to be all of a dither/to be in a dither,** être dans tous ses états/ne plus savoir où donner de la tête.

dithery ['dɪðərɪ] *a F* agité/nerveux.

ditto ['dɪtəʊ] *adv F* (*the same*) idem.

ditz [dɪts] *n esp NAm P* imbécile*/cruche *f*; (*eccentric person*) zigoto *m*/zigomar *m*.

ditzy ['dɪtsɪ] *a esp NAm P* idiot*/crétin; (*eccentric, mad*) chabraque.

div [dɪv] *n Br P* (*odd person*) zigoto *m*; (*stupid person*) andouille *f*/crétin, -ine.

dive¹ [daɪv] *n F* 1. (*seedy bar or club*) café*/bouge *m*/gargote *f*/boui-boui *m*; **it's a bit of a**

dive, but the music's really good, ça fait un peu boui-boui mais il y a de la bonne musique 2. (*esp boxing*) to take a dive, (*deliberately lose contest*) aller au tapis (*délibérément*)/ s'allonger. (*See* **nosedive¹**)

dive² [daɪv] *vi* V (*cunnilingus*) to dive (into the bushes), faire minette/brouter le cresson. (*See* **muff²** 2; **nosedive²**; **pearl-dive**)

diver ['daɪvə] *n* P voleur* à la tire/pique *m*.

divi ['dɪvɪ] *n* F = **divvy** II.

divvy ['dɪvɪ] I *a Br* P idiot*/crétin; (*eccentric, mad*) chabraque II *n* F (= *dividend*) intérêt *m*/dividende *m*/fade *m*.

divvy up ['dɪvɪ'ʌp] *vi* F partager/aller au fade/faire la motte.

dizzy ['dɪzɪ] *a* F 1. étourdi/écervelé/à tête de linotte 2. a dizzy blonde, une blonde tape-à-l'œil/platinée/vaporeuse; a dizzy dame, une femme* bête*/*Pej* une connasse.

DJ, d.j. ['di:'dʒeɪ] *n* F 1. = **dee-jay** 2. (*abbr of dinner jacket*) smoking *m*.

DM's, d.m.'s ['di:'emz] *npl* F (*abbr of Dr Martens*) = **Doc Martens**. (*See* **bovver-boots**)

do¹ [du:] *n* 1. F réjouissances*/boum *f*; there's a big do on at the Palace tonight, il va y avoir une grande fête au Palais ce soir 2. O P escroquerie *f*/filouterie *f* 3. *pl* F do's, partage *m*/fade *m*/taf *m*; fair do's, une juste part; to give s.o. fair do's, jouer franc jeu avec qn/donner à qn son dû 4. F the do's and dont's, ce qu'il faut faire et ne pas faire 5. F it's a poor do, c'est minable; c'est pas terrible/ça ne casse rien. (*See* **hair-do**)

do² [du:] *vtr* F 1. P (*man*) faire l'amour* avec/ sauter/tomber (qn); *Euph* to do it, to do the business, faire l'amour*/fricoter 2. P sodomiser*/enculer (qn) 3. F to do sth no one else can do for you, déféquer*/couler un bronze/aller où le Roi va à pied 4. P escroquer*/arnaquer/refaire/rouler; to be/to get done, se faire avoir 5. P cambrioler*/ caroubler; to do a place, faire un casse 6. P (*a*) battre*/flauper/tabasser; they did him, ils l'ont passé à tabac; if you don't shut up I'll do you! la ferme! ou je te casse la gueule! (*b*) tuer*/descendre 7. P arrêter*/épingler; to get done by the police, se faire alpaguer/se faire agrafer par la police 8. P (*serve a prison term*) he's doing ten years for GBH, il fait dix ans pour coups et blessures. (*See* **time 1**) 9. F (*to imitate*) he does a very good Groucho Marx, il fait très bien/il imite bien Groucho Marx 10. F visiter; to do Europe, faire

l'Europe 11. P to do drugs, se droguer*/se camer 12. F that'll do! assez!*/ça suffit!/y en a marre!/basta! he'll do me, il me va/ça fait mon blot 13. F that just won't do! (*unacceptable*) ça va pas (du tout) ça! 14. F have nothing to do with it! n'y touchez pas!/ mettez pas le doigt dans cet engrenage! nothing doing! rien à faire!/pas question!/que dalle! lend me a fiver? nothing doing! tu me prêtes cinq livres? rien à faire!/tu peux toujours courir! 15. F done! d'accord*!/dac!/ tope-là! 16. F that's done it! ça a tout gâché!/ ça a tout bousillé! (*See* **tear²**) 17. F do or die, marche ou crève 18. P I'm absolutely done, je suis complètement à plat/à bout/ crevé. (*See* **Bertie; do down; do for; do in; do-it-yourself kit; do out; do over; do up; do with; do without; job 4; number 6; proud; runner 2; thing 10**)

DOA ['di:'əʊ'eɪ] *a* F (*abbr of dead on arrival*) he was DOA, (*dead*) il était mort avant d'arriver à l'hôpital; (*unconscious*) il était complètement KO.

dob in, dob on ['dɒb'ɪn, 'ɒn] *vtr Austr* F dénoncer*/trahir/moucharder/balancer; vendre la mèche.

dobber ['dɒbə] *n Austr* F mouchard, -arde.

doc [dɒk] *n* F (*abbr of doctor*) docteur *m*/ toubib *m*/doc *m*.

dock¹ [dɒk] *n* F in dock (*a*) à l'hôpital/à l'hosto (*b*) (*car, etc*) au garage/en réparation/en rade. (*See* **dickory dock**)

dock² [dɒk] *vtr* F to dock s.o.'s pay, rogner le salaire de qn; to dock £5 off s.o.'s wages, retenir/rogner £5 sur le salaire de qn.

Doc Martens ['dɒk'mɑ:tɪnz] *npl* F (= *Dr Martens*) bottes *ou* grosses chaussures (*portées par des bovver-boys ou des skinheads et autres groupes*) Dr Martens (*RTM*) *mpl*. (*See* **DM's**)

doctor¹ ['dɒktə] *n* F 1. just what the doctor ordered, exactement ce qu'il (me) faut; tout juste ce que recommande la Faculté 2. doctor's orders: see **bingo 9** 3. *Euph* doctors and nurses, jeux sexuels/pelotage *m*. (*See* **couch doctor; horse doctor**)

doctor² ['dɒktə] *vtr* F 1. châtrer/couper; my cat's been doctored, mon chat a été châtré 2. (*wine*) frelater; (*text, etc*) tripatouiller 3. (*accounts*) truquer/maquiller.

doddle ['dɒdl] *n* F it's a doddle, c'est simple comme bonjour/c'est facile comme tout; that exam was a real doddle, j'ai passé cet examen sur une jambe; cet exam, c'était du nougat.

dodge[1] [dɒdʒ] *n F* ruse *f*/astuce *f*/combine *f*; a clever dodge/a good dodge, un bon truc/un filon; the old, old dodge, le coup classique; to be up to all the dodges, connaître tous les trucs/toutes les ficelles; he knows all the tax dodges there are, il connaît toutes les combines pour payer moins d'impôts.

dodge[2] [dɒdʒ] *vtr F* 1. to dodge the column, tirer au flanc/se défiler/tirer au cul 2. to dodge the draft (*a*) *Mil* éviter d'être envoyé outre-mer/se défiler (*b*) (*escape*) faire chibis/se faire la belle. (*See* **column-dodger**; **draft-dodger**)

dodger ['dɒdʒə] *n* (*resourceful*) malin, -igne/débrouillard, -arde/dégourdi, -ie; (*trickster*) roublard, -arde/filou *m*; (*shirker*) tire-au-flanc *m*/tire-au-cul *m*; he's a bit of an artful dodger, il n'a pas les deux pieds dans le même sabot (*b*) *P* artful dodger, (*RS* = *lodger*) locataire *mf*. (*See* **column-dodger**; **draft-dodger**)

dodgy ['dɒdʒɪ] *a F* 1. douteux; it's a dodgy business, c'est une affaire louche/fumeuse/qui sent mauvais 2. délicat/difficile; the whole thing's rather dodgy, we'll have to tread carefully, l'affaire m'a l'air fumeuse, regardons bien où nous mettons les pieds 3. (*stolen*) dodgy merchandise, marchandise volée 4. (*unsafe, dangerous*) that chair's a bit dodgy, don't sit on it, cette chaise est bancale, ne vous asseyez pas dessus.

dodo ['dəʊdəʊ] *n F* (*old-fashioned or reactionary person*) vieux rabâcheur, vieille rabâcheuse/vieux croûton/vieux birbe/vieux débris; dead as a dodo, mort et enterré.

do down ['duː'daʊn] *vtr F* l'emporter sur (qn)/rouler (qn)/refaire (qn).

do for ['duː'fɔː] *vtr* 1. *F* faire le ménage pour (qn) 2. *P* tuer*/descendre/envoyer (qn) en l'air 3. *P* to be done for (*a*) (*have no money*) être ruiné/fauché/dans la dèche/sans un (*b*) (*be ruined*) être fini/fichu/cuit; he's done for, ses carottes sont cuites (*c*) (*be dead*) être mort/fichu; he's done for, il a écopé (*d*) (*be tired*) être fatigué*/sur les genoux/sur les rotules; I'm done for, je suis crevé.

dog[1] [dɒg] *n F* 1. (*person*) vaurien*/sale type *m*/canaille *f*/saligaud *m*; *O* you old dog! canaille!/espèce de salaud! *O* a gay dog, un gai luron/un joyeux drille/un fêtard; *O* a lucky dog, un veinard; *O* a sly dog, un fin renard 2.

pl dogs, pieds*/nougats *mpl*/arpions *mpl*; my dogs are killing me, j'ai les pieds en compote/en marmelade 3. = **dog-end** 4. *pl* the dogs, (*greyhounds*) lévriers *mpl*; (*racing*) courses *fpl* de lévriers; to go to the dogs, mal tourner/aller à la ruine/filer un mauvais coton; his business is going to the dogs, son affaire part à vau-l'eau 5. it's a dog's life, c'est une vie de chien; she's leading him a dog's life, elle lui fait une vie de chien 6. (*a*) dog's breakfast, *occ* dog's dinner, désordre *m*/pagaille *f*; he made a complete dog's breakfast of his lecture, sa conférence était totalement incompréhensible (*b*) dog's dinner, (*display*) étalage *m*; dressed up/got up like a dog's dinner, en grand tralala/sur son trente et un/sapé comme un milord 7. you need some/the hair of the dog (that bit you), bois donc un petit coup, ça te fera passer la gueule de bois 8. he doesn't stand a dog's chance, il n'a pas l'ombre d'une chance 9. *esp NAm* (*worthless thing*) camelote *f*/roustissure *f*; this camera's a dog! c'est de la merdouille cet appareil-photo! 10. (*ugly woman*) cageot *m*/réclamé *m* 11. he's top dog around here, c'est lui qui mène la danse/qui fait la pluie et le beau temps 12. dog in the manger, le chien du jardinier; don't be such a dog in the manger! ne fais pas le rabat-joie! 13. to put on dog, en étaler/poser pour la galerie/frimer/en jeter 14. *Euph* to see a man about a dog, aller aux WC*/uriner*/arroser les fleurs/se payer une ardoise 15. to work like a dog, travailler dur*/trimer/travailler d'arrache-pied 16. to call off the dogs, cesser les hostilités/enterrer la hache de guerre 17. there's life in the old dog yet, il n'est pas près de la fin/il est encore vert 18. love me love my dog, qui m'aime aime mon chien 19. (*RS* = *dog and bone* = *telephone*) téléphone*/bigophone *m*/cornichon *m*. (*See* **cat 7, 8**; **dirty I 1**; **hot 25**; **hounddog**; **shaggy-dog**)

dog[2] [dɒg] *vtr NAm P* 1. abandonner*/larguer; se débarrasser de*/balancer 2. to dog s.o. around, (*pester*) embêter/emmerder qn; (*behave badly towards*) se conduire comme un salopard avec qn; (*snub*) snober qn; (*denigrate*) débiner qn; (*be unfaithful to*) tromper/doubler qn.

dogbreath ['dɒgbreθ] *n NAm F* = **dog's breath, dogsbreath**.

dog-cart ['dɒgkɑːt] *n Austr P* = car* de police/cage *f* à poulets.

dog-collar ['dɒgkɒlə] *n F* faux-col *m*

d'ecclésiastique/col romain; **the dog-collar brigade**, le clergé/les prêtres*/les curetons *mpl*.

dog-end ['dɒgend] *n F* mégot*/orphelin *m*.

dog-fashion ['dɒgfæʃ(ə)n] *adv P* = **doggy-fashion**.

doggie ['dɒgɪ] *n F* = **doggy**.

doggo ['dɒgəʊ] *a & adv* **1.** *F* caché*/planqué; **to lie doggo**, faire le mort/se tenir peinard **2.** *Br P (intoxicated by marijuana)* stone(d) **3.** *NAm P (worthless)* à la noix; *(bad)* moche.

doggone ['dɒgɒn] *NAm F (Euph for damn)* I *a* sacré/satané/fichu/maudit II *excl* **doggone it!** zut!/merde!

doggy ['dɒgɪ] *n F (esp child's word)* chien*/chien-chien *m*/toutou *m*; **doggy bag**, *(in restaurant)* petit sac pour emporter les restes.

doggy-fashion ['dɒgɪ'fæʃ(ə)n] *adv P* **to do it doggy-fashion**, faire l'amour* en levrette. *(See* **dog-fashion***)*

doghouse ['dɒghaʊs] *n F* **in the doghouse**, mis de côté/en quarantaine; **I'm in the doghouse because I forgot his birthday**, il me fait la gueule/la tronche parce que j'ai oublié son anniversaire.

do-gooder ['duː'gʊdə] *n F Pej* redresseur, -euse de torts/dame patronnesse/faiseur, -euse de bonnes œuvres.

dogsbody ['dɒgzbɒdɪ] *n F* subordonné(e)/sous-fifre *m*/lampiste *m*; **I'm the general dogsbody around here**, je suis la bonne à tout faire.

dog's breath, dogsbreath ['dɒgzbreθ] *n NAm* salaud*/ordure *f*/peau *f* de vache.

dog-tag ['dɒgtæg] *n F Mil* plaque *f* d'identité.

dog-tired ['dɒg'taɪəd] *a F* très fatigué/crevé/claqué/lessivé.

do-hickey [duː'hɪkɪ] *n NAm F* **1.** = **doodah 2.** *(pimple, spot)* bouton *m*.

do in ['duː'ɪn] *vtr P* **1.** tuer/assassiner*/liquider/supprimer; **to do oneself in**, se suicider*/se buter/s'envoyer en l'air/se flanquer en l'air **2.** fatiguer/éreinter; **done in**, très fatigué*/claqué/crevé.

doing! ['dɔɪŋ] *excl F* boum!/pan!/vlan! *(See* **doink!***)*

doings ['duːɪŋz] *n F* **1.** machin *m*/truc *m*/fourbi *m*/bidule *m*; **doings over there**, machin là-bas **2.** **the doings**, tout le bataclan/tout le bazar; **I've got the doings**, j'ai de quoi/j'ai ce qu'il faut.

doink! [dɔɪŋk] *excl F* = **doing!**

do-it-yourself kit ['duːɪtjə'selfkɪt] *n V* masturbation*/branlette *f*.

doldrums ['dɒldrəmz] *npl F* **to be in the doldrums**, *(of person)* avoir le cafard/broyer du noir/avoir le blues; *(of business, economy)* être en plein marasme/être en mauvaise posture.

dole [dəʊl] *n F* allocation *f* de chômage *m*/de chômedu *m*; **alloc** *f*/**alloque** *f*.

dole-bludger ['dəʊlblʌdʒə] *n Austr P* faux chômeur, fausse chômeuse; arnaqueur *m* de l'assurance-chômage.

doley, dolie ['dəʊlɪ] *n Austr F* chômeur, -euse/chômedu *m*.

doll [dɒl] *n O F* fille* *ou* jeune femme*/nana *f*/poupée *f*/pépée *f*; **hi doll!** salut bébé!

dollop ['dɒləp] *n F* gros/bon morceau; grosse cuillerée; **a good dollop of jam**, une bonne cuillerée de confiture; **a dollop of beans**, une porcif de haricots.

doll up ['dɒl'ʌp] *vtr F* **to doll oneself up**, se pomponner/se bichonner; **to get all dolled up**, se mettre sur son trente et un.

dolly ['dɒlɪ] *n* **1.** *F* fille*/poupée *f*/pépée *f*. *(See* **doll***)* **2.** *F* = **dolly bird 3.** *P (drugs)* méthadone *f* (dolophine).

dolly bird ['dɒlɪbɜːd] *n O F (attractive and fashionable girl)* (belle) nana/(belle) poupée/nana bien roulée.

D.O.M. [diː'əʊ'em] *n (abbr of dirty old man)* vieux cochon.

dome [dəʊm] *n F* tête*/caboche *f*/boule *f*. *(See* **ivory***)*

done up ['dʌn'ʌp] *a & pp F* **1.** très fatigué*/crevé **2.** ruiné*/fauché/nettoyé **3.** *(a)* maquillé/peinturluré *(b)* habillé avec élégance/bien sapé/bien fringué/tiré à quatre épingles **4.** *(framed)* victime d'un coup monté. *(See* **do up***)*

dong[1] [dɒŋ], **donger** ['dɒŋə] *n V* pénis*/brandon *m*/gland *m*; **to flog the dong**, se masturber*/se taper la colonne.

dong[2] [dɒŋ] *vtr P* donner un coup* violent à/bastonner/sonner.

donk [dɒŋk] *n Austr F* imbécile*/andouille *f*.

donkey ['dɒŋkɪ] *n* **1.** *F* **to talk the hind leg off a donkey**, être bavard* comme une pie/être un moulin à paroles/l'avoir bien pendue **2.** *F* **donkey work**, travail*/turbin *m* **3.** *F* **I haven't seen him in/for donkey's years**, ça fait/il y a une éternité/une paye/un siècle que je (ne) l'ai vu; **donkey's years ago**, il y a une belle lurette **4.** *Br F (clumsy person)* empaillé, -ée/

empaqueté, -ée 5. *Br F* moteur *m*.

donnybrook ['dɒnɪbrʊk] *n F* bagarre*/rififi *m*/corrida *f*.

doodah ['duːdɑː] *n F* truc *m*/machin *m*/ fourbi *m*/bidule *m*/zinzin *m*.

doodle[1] ['duːdl] *n* 1. *P* pénis*/verge *f*/queue *f* 2. *F* (*drawing*) griffonnage *m*.

doodle[2] ['duːdl] *vtr F* griffonner (*d'un air distrait ou en pensant à autre chose*).

doodle-alley ['duːdl'ælɪ] *a O P* = **doolally (tap)**.

doodlebug ['duːdlbʌg] *n A F* 1. vieille voiture*/tacot *m*/guimbarde *f* 2. (*WWII*) bombe volante.

doofer ['duːfə] *n P* = **doodah**.

doojie ['duːdʒɪ] *n NAm P* (*drugs*) héroïne*/ dropou *f*.

dooks [duːks] *npl Austr P* = **dukes**.

doolally (tap) ['duːˈlælɪ('tæp)] *a P* fou*/ cinoque/timbré.

door [dɔː] *n F* 1. to show s.o. the door, mettre/flanquer qn à la porte; virer/balancer qn 2. (*a*) knock at the door: *see* **bingo 4** (*b*) key of the door: *see* **bingo 21**. (*See* **back I 3**)

doormat ['dɔːmæt] *n F* individu* qui se laisse marcher dessus/paillasson *m*.

doornail ['dɔːneɪl] *n F* dead as a doornail, mort et enterré.

doorstep[1] ['dɔːstep] *n F* (*thick slice of bread*) grosse tranche de pain.

doorstep[2] ['dɔːstep] *vtr & i Journ* traîner/ errer devant une maison privée; accoster qn chez lui/chez elle; he doorstepped her for three days, il est resté planté devant sa porte pendant trois jours.

do out ['duːˈaʊt] *vtr F* to do s.o. out of sth, escroquer* qn/arnaquer/rouler/carotter qn.

do over ['duːˈəʊvə] *vtr* 1. *F* (*redecorate*) refaire/retaper 2. *P* (*a*) voler* (qn) (*b*) tromper*/rouler (qn) 3. *P* battre* (qn)/passer (qn) à tabac/tabasser (qn) 4. *P* (*burgle/NAm burglarize*) to do a place over, cambrioler*/ faire un fric-frac/faire un casse; ratisser un endroit.

dope[1] [dəʊp] **I** *a NAm P* excellent*/super*/ canon; a dope magazine, un super magazine/ un magazine branché **II** *n* 1. *P* (*drugs*) drogue *f*/dope *f*/stup *m*/came *f*; marijuana*/ haschisch*; dope addict, camé(e) *m*(*f*)/toxico *mf*/junkie *m*/accro *mf*; dope pusher/peddler, fourgueur *m*/trafiquant, -ante/dealer *m* (de drogue); dope racket, trafic *m* de drogues*; dope ring, bande *f* de trafiquants; to be on

dope/to use dope, se droguer*/se camer/se schnouffer; to push/to peddle dope, revendre de la came/trafiquer 2. *F* (*administered to a horse, etc*) dopant *m*; dope test, contrôle *m* antidoping/antidopage 3. *F* (*a*) renseignement*/tuyau *m*/tubard *m*; the latest dope, les dernières nouvelles/les derniers renseignements*; to give s.o. the latest dope, mettre qn à la page/affranchir qn/mettre qn au parfum (*b*) faux renseignements*/bourrage *m* de crâne (*c*) tuyaux *mpl* sur les courses de chevaux; dope sheet, journal *m* hippique/de turf 4. *F* individu bête*/andouille *f*/nouille *f*; what a dope he is! quel crétin ce type! (*See* **fiend**)

dope[2] [dəʊp] *vtr* 1. *F* (*a*) administrer un narcotique à (qn)/droguer/doper (*b*) mêler un narcotique à (un verre de vin, une cigarette)/ doper (*c*) to dope oneself, se droguer*/se doper; doped (up) to the eyeballs/eyebrows, schnouffé à bloc/camé jusqu'à l'os 2. *F* doper (un cheval, un lévrier) 3. *F* ajouter de l'alcool à (une boisson non alcoolisée)/corser.

dopehead ['dəʊphed] *n NAm P* = **doper**.

dope out ['dəʊpˈaʊt] *vtr esp NAm P* découvrir*/dénicher.

doper ['dəʊpə] *n P* drogué*/camé, -ée/toxico *mf*/junkie *m*.

dope up ['dəʊpˈʌp] *vtr & i P* (*a*) se droguer*/se camer/se doper (*b*) droguer/doper (qn).

dopey ['dəʊpɪ] *a F* 1. bête*/bêta/empoté/ con/cruche 2. abruti (de fatigue) 3. stupéfié/ hébété (par un narcotique).

dopy ['dəʊpɪ] *a F* = **dopey**.

do-re-mi ['dəʊˈreɪˈmiː] *n NAm P* argent*/ fric *m*/oseille *f*/pépettes *fpl*/picaillons *mpl*.

dork [dɔːk] *n P* 1. pénis*/gland *m* 2. imbécile*/gland *m*/crétin, -ine.

dorky ['dɔːkɪ] *n P* bête*/cloche/cucul.

dorm [dɔːm] *n F* (*abbr of dormitory*) dortoir *m*/dort(o) *m*.

Dorothy Dixer ['dɒrəθɪ'dɪksə] *n Austr F* question *f* à un membre du gouvernement, posée par un parlementaire de la majorité.

dose [dəʊs] *n* 1. *P* to get/to catch/to cop a dose, attraper une maladie* vénérienne/ ramasser la (s)chtouille; to have caught/ copped a dose of the clap, être (s)chtouillard/ pisser des lames de rasoir/se faire poivrer/se faire lader 2. *F* like a dose of salts, (*quickly, effectively*) comme une lettre à la poste.

dosed up ['dəʊstˈʌp] *a P* 1. atteint d'une maladie vénérienne*/fadé/poivré/plombé 2. (*horse, greyhound*) dopé; (*unwitting person*) drogué*/défoncé.

dosh [dɒʃ] *n Br P* argent*/fric *m*/pèze *m*.

doss¹ [dɒs] *n P* 1. lit* (*surt dans une pension miteuse*)/pucier *m*/pieu *m* 2. somme *m*/dorme *f*/roupillon *m*; **to have a doss**, dormir*/piquer un roupillon/en écraser.

doss² [dɒs] *vi P* dormir*/pioncer/en écraser.

doss around ['dɒsə'raʊnd] *vi Br P* paresser*/fainéanter/tirer au cul.

dossbag ['dɒsbæg] *n Br P* 1. sac *m* de couchage/sac à viande 2. (*lazy person*) feignant, -ante/tire-au-cul *m*.

doss down ['dɒs'daʊn] *vi P* se coucher*/se plumer; **we can doss down at his place**, on peut pieuter chez lui.

dosser ['dɒsə] *n Br P* (*a*) (*tramp, down-and-out*) clochard*/clodo *m* (*b*) (*North London school slang*) drogué*/junkie *m*/camé, -ée.

doss-house ['dɒshaʊs] *n F* asile *m* de nuit/dortoir *m* à clodos; **their place looks like a real doss-house**, c'est un vrai foutoir chez eux.

dot¹ [dɒt] *n* 1. *F* **on the dot**, à l'heure/à pic/pile/recta 2. *F* **in the year dot**, il y a longtemps/une paye; **it goes back to the year dot**, ça remonte au déluge/à Mathusalem.

dot² [dɒt] *vtr* 1. *P* **to dot s.o. one**, battre* qn/flanquer un gnon à qn/balancer une pêche à qn 2. *F* **to dot and carry one**, boîter (en marchant)/aller clopin-clopant/faire cinq et trois font huit 3. *F* **to dot one's i's and cross one's t's**, faire attention aux détails/à tous les détails; **it's just a case of dotting the i's and crossing the t's**, il ne reste qu'à y mettre la dernière touche/qu'à régler les petits détails.

dottiness ['dɒtɪnɪs] *n F* folie douce/loufoquerie *f*.

dotty ['dɒtɪ] *a F* fou*/cinglé/toqué/maboule; **she's gone a bit dotty**, elle a perdu la boule/elle travaille du chapeau.

double ['dʌbl] **I** *a F* 1. **to do a double take**, y regarder* à deux fois 2. **double talk**, propos ambigus *ou* trompeurs/boniment *m*/double parler *m* 3. **double think**, croyance *f* au pour et au contre 4. **to do the double act**, se marier/signer le bail. (*See* **Dutch III 1**) **II** *adv F* très/super; **it's double cool**, c'est super cool.

double-bagger ['dʌbl'bægə] *n NAm P* (*extremely ugly person*) individu* laid comme un pou/mocheté *f*/trumeau *m*.

double-cross¹ ['dʌbl'krɒs] *n F* (*deception, trick*) entubage *m*/roustissure *f*/arnaque *f*.

double-cross² ['dʌbl'krɒs] *vtr F* tromper*/entuber/doubler; **to be double-**crossed, se faire rouler.

double-crosser ['dʌbl'krɒsə] *n F* faux jeton/entubeur *m*/carambouilleur *m*.

double-quick ['dʌbl'kwɪk] *adv F* au pas de course/en cinq sec; **to do (sth) double-quick/in double-quick time**, faire (qch) fissa/se magner le popotin à faire (qch).

double up ['dʌbl'ʌp] *vi F* 1. **to double up/to be doubled up with laughter**, se tordre (de rire*)/se gondoler/se fendre la pêche; **to double up/to be doubled up with pain**, se tordre de douleur 2. **to double up on a horse**, doubler la mise 3. **to double up with s.o.**, (*share the same bedroom*) partager une chambre avec qn; (*share the same bed*) se doubler.

douche [duːʃ] *n F* surprise *f* désagréable/douche (froide).

dough [dəʊ] *n F* argent*/galette *f*/fric *m*/pognon *m*; **to be in the dough**, être riche*/être au pèze/être bourré aux as; **he throws his dough around**, il dépense sans compter/il jette son argent* par les fenêtres/il flambe son argent*.

doughboy ['dəʊbɔɪ] *n NAm F* (*esp WWI*) soldat* (de 2ème classe) de l'infanterie américaine/biffin *m*/troufion *m*.

doughnut ['dəʊnʌt] *n Austr V* **golden doughnut**, sexe* de la femme*/abricot *m*/moule *f*.

doughy ['dəʊɪ] *a F* (*rare*) riche*/galetteux*/bourré aux as.

do up ['duː'ʌp] *vtr* 1. *P* battre* (qn)/arranger le portrait à (qn)/tabasser (qn)/passer (qn) à tabac 2. (*frame*) monter un coup à (qn)/faire porter le bada à (qn) 3. (*drugs*) (*inject*) se shooter à (l'héroïne)/(*inhale*) sniffer de (la cocaïne). (*See* **done up**)

dove [dʌv] *n F Pol* qn qui s'oppose à la guerre/pacifiste *mf*/colombe *f*. (*See* **hawk**)

do with ['duː'wɪð] *vtr F* **I could do with a drink**, je m'en jetterais bien un (petit) derrière la cravate)/un verre ne serait pas de refus.

do without ['duːwɪ'ðaʊt] *vi F* se l'accrocher/se serrer la ceinture/se taper (sur le ventre).

down¹ [daʊn] **I** *a F* **down drugs**, drogues tranquillisantes/sédatifs *mpl*/calmants *mpl*. (*See* **up¹ I 2**) **II** *adv F* 1. **to be down and out**, être très pauvre*/être dans la dèche/être sans le sou 2. **to be down on s.o.**, (*dislike s.o.*) en avoir à/après qn 3. **to be down on one's luck**, avoir de la malchance*/de la guigne/de la poisse; avoir la cerise 4. **down under,** aux antipodes; en Australie 5. (*a*) (*drugs*) to be **down,** redescendre (*See* **up¹ I 1**) (*b*) to be **(feeling) down,** (*depressed*) avoir le cafard/broyer du noir; avoir le moral à zéro. (*See* **chute 1; drain¹ 1; ground 2; mouth 2; tube 5**) III *n F* 1. to have a down on s.o., (*dislike s.o.*) avoir qn dans le nez/en avoir à/après qn 2. = **downer 1.**

down² [daʊn] *vtr F* 1. faire tomber (qn)/envoyer (qn) au tapis 2. boire*; to **down** a drink, s'envoyer un coup/s'en jeter un derrière la cravate/se rincer la dalle 3. to **down tools,** (*stop work*) cesser le travail; (*go on strike*) se mettre en grève/croiser les bras.

down-and-out ['daʊnən(d)'aʊt] *n F* (*tramp*) clochard*/clodo *m*/déchard, -arde; (*drunkard*) alcoolo *mf*.

downbeat ['daʊnbiːt] *a F* 1. calme/tête froide/coolos/sans avoir l'air d'y toucher; he was rather downbeat about it, il n'avait pas l'air d'y toucher 2. (*person*) déprimé. (*See* **upbeat**)

downer ['daʊnə] *n F* 1. downers, (*drugs*) barbituriques*/barbis *mpl*; sédatifs *mpl*/tranquillisants. (*See* **uppers**) 2. situation déprimante/déconfiture *f*; déprime *f*; to be on a downer, être dans la panade.

downhill ['daʊnhɪl] *adv F* to go downhill, dégringoler/être sur le déclin/être sur la mauvaise pente/filer un mauvais coton.

Downing Street ['daʊnɪŋstriːt] *Prn F see* **bingo 10.**

down-market ['daʊn'mɑːkɪt] *a F* bas de gamme. (*See* **up-market**)

downstairs [daʊn'stɛəz] *adv F* (*in the genital area*) dans les parties; (*in the buttocks*) dans le pont arrière.

doz [dʌz] *n F* (*abbr of dozen*) one doz: see **bingo 12.**

dozen ['dʌzn] *n F* 1. a baker's dozen, treize à la douzaine 2. daily dozen, culture *f* physique 3. dozens of..., une abondance* de.../une flop(p)ée de.../une tripotée de.../une tapée de... (*See* **dime; nineteen; six 3**)

dozy ['dəʊzɪ] *a F* 1. abruti/ballot/demeuré; you dozy twit! espèce d'abruti! 2. *O* paresseux*/flemmard/cossard/feignant.

drabbie ['dræbɪ] *n Br F* (*frump*) femme* mal fagotée; (*bluestocking*) bas-bleu *m*.

drack [dræk] *Austr F* **I** *a* (*unattractive*) moche; a drack sort, une mocheté/un mocheton **II** *n* (*rubbish*) camelote *f*/roustissure *f*.

dracs, **d'racs** [dræks], **D-racks** ['diːræks] *npl O P* cartes* à jouer/brêmes *fpl*.

draft-dodger ['drɑːftdɒdʒə] *n F Mil* réfractaire *m*. (*See* **dodge² 2**)

drag¹ [dræg] *n* 1. *F* vêtements* de travelo; in drag, en travelo; drag club, club *m* de travelos; drag queen, caroline *f*/travelo *m*/trave *m* (*See* **queen¹ 2**) 2. *F* (*a*) individu ennuyeux*/casse-pieds *mf*/raseur, -euse/em-merdeur, -euse/casse-bonbons *m* (*b*) (*thing*) truc ennuyeux*/rasoir/embêtant; what a drag!/it's a real drag! quelle barbe!/c'est la barbe! 3. *P* voiture*/tire *f*/bahut *m*; drag race/racing, course *f* de vieilles voitures* 4. *P* (*a*) bouffée *f* de tabac; to take a drag, tirer une bouffée/un(e) taffe; give us a drag, donne-moi un(e) taffe (*b*) cigarette *f* de marijuana*/joint *m*. (*See* **spit¹ 2**) 5. NAm *P* (*influence*) piston *m*/pistonnage *m* 6. NAm *P* rue *f*/strasse *f*; the main drag, la grand-rue 7. *P* trois mois *mpl* de prison*. (*See* **carpet¹ 2**)

drag² [dræg] *vtr F* to drag one's feet, se faire tirer l'oreille/renâcler/traîner les pieds.

drag-ass ['drægæs] *vi NAm P* 1. (*get moving*) se magner le popotin/le cul 2. (*move slowly, lazily*) traîner les pieds/paresser/tirer au cul.

dragged out ['drægd'aʊt] *a NAm P* fatigué*/crevé/éreinté. (*See* **drag out**)

dragged-up [drægd'ʌp] *a F* 1. (*dressed in drag*) en travelo. See **drag¹ 1**) 2. (*extravagantly dressed*) sur son trente et un.

draggy ['drægɪ] *a O P* ennuyeux*/canulant/rasoir/chiant.

drag in ['dræg'in] *vtr F* amener (qch) comme un cheveu sur la soupe; ramener (qch).

drag on ['dræg'ɒn] *vtr & i F* traîner en longueur/s'éterniser.

dragon ['drægən] *n* 1. *F* (*fierce person, usu old*) *woman*) dragon *m* 2. Hist *F* dragon's teeth, défenses *fpl* anti-tank 3. *P* (*drugs*) green dragon, amphétamine*/amph(é) *f*; to chase the dragon, sniffer *ou* fumer de l'héroïne/chasser le dragon 4. Austr Euph *P* to drain the dragon, uriner*/égoutter son cyclope.

drag out ['dræg'aʊt] *vtr & i F* 1. faire traîner/tirer en longueur 2. to drag sth out of s.o., extirper qch à qn/tirer les vers du nez à qn. (*See* **dragged out**)

drag up ['dræg'ʌp] *vtr* 1. *F* to drag up s.o.'s past, faire ressortir le passé de qn/sortir le squelette du placard/fouiller la merde 2. *P* where were you dragged up? où as-tu été élevé?/d'où sors-tu?/de quel trou est-ce que tu sors? dragged up, élevé à la va-comme-je-te-pousse.

drain¹ [dreɪn] *n F* 1. to go down the drain, échouer*/foirer/tomber à l'eau; it's money down the drain, c'est jeter l'argent* par les fenêtres 2. to laugh like a drain, rire* de bon cœur/se boyauter/se bidonner. (*See* **brain drain**)

drain² [dreɪn] *vtr F* to drain s.o. dry, saigner qn à blanc/plumer qn/tondre la laine sur le dos à qn.

Drain (the) [ðə'dreɪn] *n Br Rail F* (sobriquet *m* de) la ligne *Waterloo and City* (*qui passe sous la Tamise*).

drainpipe ['dreɪnpaɪp] *n F* 1. individu* maigre/asperge *f*/grand sifflet 2. *pl* (= *drainpipe trousers*) pantalon* étroit/fuseau *m*/ (pantalon) tuyau *m* de poêle.

drape [dreɪp] *n F* costume *m*/costard *m*; drapes, vêtements*/fringues *fpl*/nippes *fpl*.

drat [dræt] *excl F Euph for* **damn** (*expression of annoyance*) drat (it)! nom de nom!/ bon sang! drat the child! au diable ce gosse!/ sale môme!

dratted ['drætɪd] *a F* maudit/sacré; this dratted weather! ce fichu temps!/ce temps pourri!

draw¹ [drɔ:] *n* 1. *F* to be quick on the draw, (*with firearm*) être rapide à dégainer son arme/avoir la gâchette facile; (*with answers*) avoir la repartie facile; (*in understanding*) piger au quart de poil 2. *P* cannabis*/herbe *f*/ H *m*.

draw² [drɔ:] *vtr F* 1. to draw s.o., faire parler* qn/tirer les vers du nez à qn 2. taquiner/faire enrager 3. to draw the line, fixer une limite/mettre fin (à qch); I draw the line at that, je n'irai pas jusque là/je me refuse à faire ça. (*See* **blank¹**)

dread [dred] *a WInd P* excellent*/ impressionnant/chié; it's real dread, c'est chié.

dreadlocks ['dredlɒks] *npl WInd P* coiffure *f* rasta/dreadlocks *mpl*.

dream [dri:m] **I** *a F* rêvé/de rêve; to live in a dream world, nager dans le bleu **II** *n* 1. *F* it's a dream, c'est beau*/du tonnerre; she's a dream, c'est la femme rêvée; it goes like a dream, ça marche à merveille/comme dans un rêve 2. *F* he goes about in a dream, il est toujours à rêvasser/à gamberger 3. *F* wet dream, rêve mouillé; carte *f* (de France).

dreamboat ['dri:mbəʊt] *n esp NAm F* (*for girl/woman*) l'homme rêvé; (*for man*) la femme rêvée; (*as term of endearment*) my dreamboat, mon chou/mon trésor.

dream up ['dri:m'ʌp] *vtr F* imaginer/ inventer/gamberger.

dreamy ['dri:mɪ] *a F* exquis/charmant/ ravissant.

dreck [drek] *n P* camelote *f*/gnognot(t)e *f*/ roustissure *f*.

dress down ['dres'daʊn] *vtr F* 1. battre*/ filer une raclée à (qn) 2. réprimander* (qn)/ enguirlander (qn)/assaisonner (qn)/engueuler (qn) comme du poisson pourri. (*See* **dressing-down**)

dressed [drest] *a & pp F* dressed to kill, élégant*/habillé sur son trente et un/en grand tralala/bien bâché/tiré à quatre épingles. (*See* **dressed up 2**)

dressed up ['drest'ʌp] *a & pp F* 1. all dressed up and nowhere to go, laissé(e) pour compte/laissé(e) (sur le carreau)/resté(e) en carafe 2. dressed up to the nines/to the teeth/ to the knocker, élégant*/habillé sur son trente et un/tiré à quatre épingles. (*See* **dressed**)

dressing-down ['dresɪŋ'daʊn] *n F* 1. volée *f* de coups*/raclée *f*/avoine *f* 2. réprimande *f*/savon *m*. (*See* **dress down**)

dressy ['dresɪ] *a F* élégant*/chic/ridère/ rider.

dribs [drɪbz] *npl F* in dribs and drabs, petit à petit/au compte-gouttes.

drift¹ [drɪft] *n F* to catch the drift, tenir le fil/ piger/entraver/saisir; I get your drift, je pige.

drift² [drɪft] *vi P* partir*/décamper/se tailler.

drifter ['drɪftə] *n F* (*a*) personne *f* qui se laisse aller (*b*) vagabond*/clochard*/clodo *m*.

drill [drɪl] *n F* to know the drill, connaître les rouages/connaître la musique/s'y connaître. (*See* **pack-drill**)

drin [drɪn] *n P* (*drugs*) comprimé *m* de Benzédrine* (*RTM*).

drink [drɪŋk] *n* 1. *F* the drink, la mer/la Tasse/la Grande Bleue/la flotte 2. *P* (*bribe*) pot-de-vin *m*; (*tip*) pourliche *m*.

drinkies ['drɪŋkɪz] *npl F* boissons *fpl*/ consommations *fpl*/godets *mpl*; to have drinkies before lunch, prendre/boire l'apéro.

drip [drɪp] *n* 1. *F* (*unassertive person*) mou *m*/molle *f*/nouille *f*; what a drip! quelle nouille!/tête de nœud! 2. *Br P* the drip, (*hire purchase*) location-vente *f*; (*payment by instalments*) paiement *m* en plusieurs fois; on the drip, à crédit/à croume.

dripper ['drɪpə] *n F* goutte-à-goutte *m* (*seringue fabriquée avec un compte-gouttes et une épingle*).

dripping ['drɪpɪŋ] *a Br F* he's absolutely dripping, (*weak, pathetic*) il est mou comme une chiffe.

drippy ['drɪpɪ] *a F* (*unassertive*) mou, molle/nouille.

driver ['draɪvə] *n* 1. *F* to be in the driver's seat, être en position de force/tenir les rênes/diriger les opérations/mener la barque 2. *pl P* (*drugs*) amphétamines*/amphés *fpl*. (*See* **backseat** 1; **nigger-driver**; **pile-driver**; **slave-driver**; **truck-driver**)

droid [drɔɪd] *n NAm F* individu bête*/cornichon *m*/tronche (*plate*).

drone [drəʊn] *n F* individu ennuyeux*/canule *f*/casse-pieds *m*.

drongo ['drɒŋgəʊ] *n esp Austr F* individu bête*/gourde *f*/poire *f*; (*unpleasant*) fumier *m*.

droob [druːb] *n Austr F* (*dull person*) canule *f*/casse-pieds *m*.

drool [druːl] *vi F* to drool over sth/s.o., baver (d'admiration, de plaisir) devant qch/qn.

droolsome ['druːlsəm] *a F* qui fait baver (d'admiration, de plaisir).

droop [druːp] *n P* brewer's droop, affaissement du pénis* dû à l'alcool/le six heures de l'alcoolique; to get brewer's droop, faire flanelle/bander guimauve.

drooper ['druːpə] *n* 1. *F* moustache*/bacchantes *fpl* 2. *pl P* seins* tombants/blagues *fpl* à tabac/tétasses *fpl*.

droopy-drawers ['druːpɪdrɔːz] *n P* 1. jeune femme* négligée/marie-salope *f* 2. *see* **bingo** 44.

drop¹ [drɒp] *n* 1. *P* = **dropsy** 1, 2 2. *F* at the drop of a hat, tout de suite/illico/en un rien de temps/aussi sec 3. *P* (*a*) livraison secrète *ou* illicite (*surt* d'argent) (*b*) *P* (*place for delivery of money, drugs, etc*) cache *f*/planque *f*/planquouse *f*; boîte-aux-lettres *f* (*c*) personne *f* qui vient prendre *ou* qui livre un paquet illicite 4. *P* to have the drop on s.o., (*shoot faster than opponent*) avoir dégainé/avoir tiré plus vite que qn; (*have the advantage*) avoir pris un avantage sur qn 5. *F* a drop in the ocean, une goutte d'eau dans l'océan 6. *P* to have a drop in the eye/to have had a drop too much, être ivre*/avoir bu un (petit) coup de trop/avoir un verre dans le nez/être chargé 7. *F* petit verre d'alcool*/une goutte/un doigt/un chouia.

drop² [drɒp] *vtr & i* 1. *F* to drop s.o. like a hot potato/a hot brick, abandonner* qn/lâcher qn/plaquer qn/laisser tomber qn comme une vieille chaussette 2. *P* (*kill*) abattre/descendre/buter (qn) 3. *F* donner un pourboire* à (qn); we dropped him something, on lui a graissé la patte/refilé la pièce 4. *P* to drop (a bundle), (*gambling, etc*) perdre/paumer de l'argent*; prendre une culotte 5. *P* (*get rid of stolen goods, cheque, etc*) se défarguer de 6. *F* fit to drop, très fatigué*/crevé/éreinté/flagada; he's fit to drop, il a le coup de barre 7. *F* to drop s.o. a line, envoyer/mettre/griffonner un mot à qn 8. *F* to drop sth/to let sth drop, (*stop talking about*) laisser tomber/laisser pisser qch; drop it!/let it drop! c'est marre!/y en a marre!/écrase!/laisse pisser! 9. *P* (*a*) to drop one/one's lunch/one's guts, péter*/louf(f)er/lâcher une perle (*b*) to drop one's load, éjaculer*/arracher son copeau/envoyer la purée 10. *P* prendre une drogue par voie buccale; to drop acid, prendre de l'acide 11. *esp Austr P* battre* (qn)/passer (qn) à tabac. (*See* **bollock** 2; **bomb¹** 6; **brick** 2; **clanger**; **dead** I 11; **shit¹** IV 2 (*a*))

drop in ['drɒp'ɪn] I *vi F* to drop in on s.o., rendre visite à qn en passant/passer chez qn/faire un saut chez qn II *vtr P* to drop s.o. in it, (*put s.o. in bad situation*) mettre qn dans la merde.

drop off ['drɒp'ɒf] *vtr & i F* 1. s'endormir/piquer un roupillon/pioncer 2. to drop s.o. off, déposer qn quelque part 3. to drop off the twig, mourir*/casser sa pipe/dépoter son géranium.

dropout ['drɒpaʊt] *n F* 1. étudiant, -ante qui abandonne ses études 2. qn qui refuse la société/le système; qn qui vit en marge de la société/marginal, -ale; hippie *mf*.

drop out ['drɒp'aʊt] *vi F* 1. abandonner ses études 2. refuser la société/le système; vivre en marge de la société; être un(e) hippie.

dropper ['drɒpə] *n* 1. *F* seringue *f*/shooteuse *f*/pompe *f* 2. *P* passeur, -euse de faux billets *ou* de faux chèques/pastiqueur *m*. (*See* **name-dropper**)

dropsy ['drɒpsɪ] *n O P* 1. pot-de-vin *m*/dessous-de-table *m* 2. pourboire*/pourliche *m*.

drown [draʊn] *vtr F* 1. to drown a drink, mettre trop d'eau dans une boisson/noyer une boisson 2. to drown one's sorrows, noyer son chagrin.

drowning ['draʊnɪŋ] *n Br P* action *f* d'entrer chez une personne âgée en se faisant passer pour un employé du service des eaux.

drube [dru:b] *n Austr F* = **droob.**

druggie, druggy ['drʌgɪ] *n P* drogué*/camé(e) *m(f)*/toxico *mf.*

drughead ['drʌghed] *n NAm P* = **dope-head, doper.**

drum [drʌm] *n* 1. *Br P* logement*/cambuse *f*; to have one's drum done, *(have one's home searched by the police)* avoir une perquisition/avoir une descente dans sa piaule; *(be burgled)* se faire cambrioler/baluchonner. *(See* **screw²** 3) 2. *Austr P* renseignement*/tube *m*/tuyau *m* 3. *F* to beat the drums/the big drum for s.o., faire du battage pour qn/faire du tamtam/battre la grosse caisse pour qn 4. *P* route*/trimard *m*/ruban *m* 5. *P NAm* (= *eardrum*) tympan *m.*

drummer ['drʌmə] *n O P* commis voyageur/roulant *m*/hirondelle *f.*

drumstick ['drʌmstɪk] *n F* 1. pilon *m* (de poulet) 2. *pl* jambes* maigres/flûtes *fpl*/échalas *mpl.*

drum up ['drʌm'ʌp] *vtr F* to drum up business, faire de la réclame/chauffer une affaire.

dry [draɪ] *a* 1. *F* to be dry, avoir soif*/avoir le gosier sec/avoir la pépie; dry as a bone, sec comme un coup de trique 2. *F* not dry behind the ears, blanc-bec/morveux. *(See* **wet¹** I 5) 3. *F* dry run *(a) P* coït* avec préservatif/dérouillage *m* à sec *(b) F (theatre)* répétition *f* d'essai *(c) F (aviation)* manœuvre *f* d'essai 4. *V* dry fuck/dry hump, *Austr* dry root, baisage *m* à sec; to have a dry hump, jouir tout habillé. *(See* **drain²**; **high** I 2; **home** 1; **suck** 2)

dry out ['draɪ'aʊt] *vi P* 1. cuver (son vin)/dessoûler 2. *(drugs)* se désintoxiquer/faire une cure.

dry up ['draɪ'ʌp] *vi F* 1. dry up! tais-toi!/écrase!/ta gueule!/la ferme! 2. *(theatre)* oublier son rôle/sécher/avoir un trou.

DT's ['di:'ti:z] *npl F* delirium tremens *m*/digue-digue *m.*

dub [dʌb] *n* 1. *F (theatre)* doublure *f*/double *m* 2. *NAm P* cigarette*/clope *f.*

dubee ['d(j)u:bi:] *n P (drugs)* cigarette* de marijuana/joint *m*/bombardier *m.*

duby ['d(j)u:bɪ] *n P* = **dubee.**

duchess ['dʌtʃɪs] *n Br F* femme*/*surt* épouse*/bourgeoise *f.*

duck¹ [dʌk] *n F* 1. *(term of affection)* mon poulet/mon chou/mon canard/mon lapin. *(See* **ducks**; **ducky** II) 2. **(Lord) love a duck!** grands dieux!/mazette! 3. **a sitting duck**, une

cible facile 4. **to behave like a dying duck (in a thunderstorm)**, faire la carpe pâmée/faire des yeux de merlan frit 5. **lame duck** *(a)* canard boiteux/épave *f*/éclopé, -ée *(b)* NAm élu, -ue en fin de mandat et non réélu(e); lame duck president, président pendant les derniers mois de sa présidence *(quand son successeur a déjà été élu)* 6. *Mil* véhicule *m* amphibie 7. **it's like water off a duck's back**, c'est comme si on chantait/c'est comme si on pissait en l'air 8. **to play ducks and drakes with one's money**, jeter son argent* par les fenêtres 9. **like a duck (takes) to water**, comme un poisson dans l'eau 10. *(cricket)* **duck (egg)**, zéro (pointé)/chou blanc 11. *NAm* **duck soup**, qch de très facile/du cousu-main/du gâteau 12. **a nice day for ducks/lovely weather for ducks**, beau temps pour les grenouilles 13. **duck tail/duck's arse**, coiffure *f* des années 50 *(surt des* **Teddy Boys**); = banane *f*. *(See* **DA** 3; **dead** I 4; **fuck²** 4)

duck² [dʌk] *vtr F* éviter (qn/qch); passer (qch) à l'as. *(See* **duck out**)

ducket ['dʌkɪt] *n NAm P* liasse *f* de billets* (de banque)/mille-feuille *m.*

duckie ['dʌkɪ] *n F* = **ducky.**

duck out ['dʌk'aʊt] *vi F* to duck out of (doing) sth, s'esquiver/se tirer/se débiner/se dérober/sécher/se défiler. *(See* **duck²**)

ducks [dʌks] *n F* mon chéri/ma chérie/mon chou. *(See* **duck¹** 1; **ducky** II)

ducky ['dʌkɪ] I *a esp Iron* mignon/chou II *n F* 1. mon poulet/ma poupoule/ma cocotte/mon chou 2. **hello ducky!** *(catchphrase)* = **hello sailor!** (**sailor** 2)

dud [dʌd] I *a F* mauvais*/toc(ard)/à la gomme II *n F* 1. obus non éclaté 2. échec*/four *m*/bide 3. faux billet/faux talbin; chèque *m* sans provision/chèque en bois 4. **a dud**, *(person)* un(e) raté(e)/un zéro/une nullité 5. *pl* vêtements*/frusques *fpl*/nippes *fpl*/sapes *fpl*/loques *fpl.*

dude [d(j)u:d] *n NAm F* 1. individu*/mec *m*/type *m*/gars *m*; **bad dude**, *(great guy)* mec super. *(See* **bad** I 11) 2. **dude ranch**, ranch-hôtel *m* de vacances.

dud up ['dʌd'ʌp] *vtr & i F* 1. maquiller (la marchandise, la vérité) 2. se bichonner/se pomponner.

duff¹ [dʌf] I *a F* faux/truqué/à la manque/gnognot(t)eux; **a duff idea**, une idée à la noix; **duff gen/duff info**, *(false information)* tuyau crevé II *n* 1. *P* fesses*/derrière *m*/brioches *fpl* 2. *Br P* **up the duff**, enceinte*/en cloque.

duff² [dʌf] *vtr F (ruin)* rater/bousiller/louper.
duffer ['dʌfə] *n F* individu bête*/nul *m*/
nullard, -arde; he's a **duffer at maths**, c'est
une nullité/il est nul en maths.
duff over, up ['dʌf'əʊvə, -'ʌp] *vtr P* battre* (qn)/tabasser (qn)/passer (qn) à tabac.
dugout ['dʌgaʊt] *n P* officier *m* à la retraite
rappelé en service/rempilé *m*.
duji(e) ['du:dʒɪ] *n NAm P* = **doojie.**
duke [dju:k] *P vi* to **duke it** (out/up), se
battre*/perloter/se torcher/se tabasser.
dukes [dju:ks] *npl P* mains*/poings *mpl*/
paluches *fpl*/pognes *fpl*; **put up your dukes!**
haut les mains!
dullsville ['dʌlzvɪl] *n F* truc *ou* endroit
ennuyeux/mortel/chiant comme la pluie; **this
record is really dullsville**, qu'est-ce qu'il est
rasoir ce disque!
dumb [dʌm] *a (a) F* bête*/bouché/stupide/
cloche (*b*) *P* **dumb ass/cluck/jerk**, individu
bête*/cruchon *m*/gourde *f*/nigaud, -aude (*c*) *F*
to **act/to play dumb**, faire l'idiot (*d*) *F* **dumb
blonde**, blonde vaporeuse/blonde platine. (*See*
broad 1 (*a*); **plain**)
dumbdumb, dum-dum ['dʌm'dʌm] *n* =
dumbo.
dumbell ['dʌmbel] *n esp NAm F* =
dumbo.
dumbo ['dʌmbəʊ] *n P* individu bête*/
andouille *f*/gourde *f*.
dummy ['dʌmɪ] *n 1. P* sourd-muet *m*/
sourde-muette *f 2. P* individu bête*/ballot *m*/
empoté, -ée/empaillé, -ée 3. (*drugs*) dose *f*
d'une drogue de très mauvaise qualité *ou* sans
effet 4. *P* to **chuck a dummy**, (*faint*)
s'évanouir*/tomber dans le cirage/tomber
dans les vapes; (*vomit*) dégueuler/lâcher sa
came 5. *V* to **beat/to flog the dummy**, se
masturber*/secouer la cartouche/se taper la
colonne/se branler.
dummy up ['dʌmɪ'ʌp] *vi P* se taire*/
boucler la trappe/la boucler/ne pas piper.
dump¹ [dʌmp] *n 1. F* endroit *m* sordide/
taudis *m 2. F* to **be fit for the dump**, être bon
pour la casse/bon à mettre au rencart 3. *P* to
have/take a dump, déféquer*/couler un
bronze/(dé)poser une pêche 4. *F* to **be (down)
in the dumps**, avoir le cafard/être dans le
cirage/avoir le noir/avoir le bourdon.
dump² [dʌmp] **I** *vtr F* abandonner*/larguer/
planter/plaquer **II** *vi P* = to **have/take a dump**
(**dump¹** 3)
dumper ['dʌmpə] *n NAm F* individu* qui
tabasse/qui amoche (qn).

dumpling ['dʌmplɪŋ] *n F (short, thickset
person)* patapouf *m*/bouboule *m*/boulot(te)
m(f).
dump on ['dʌmp'ɒn] *vi F (a)* critiquer*/
cartonner (qn); dénigrer/débiner (qn); **you're
always dumping on me!** d'après toi, c'est
toujours de ma faute! tu fais du jardin! (*b*)
NAm (beat up) tabasser/amocher (qn).
dunno [dʌ'nəʊ] *P (= don't know)* dunno!
sais pas!/j'sais pas!/chépa!
dunny ['dʌnɪ] *n Austr F* WC*/chiottes *fpl*/
cabinets *mpl.*
dust¹ [dʌst] *n 1. F* **you couldn't see him for
dust**, il courait comme s'il avait le feu au
derrière 2. *P (drugs)* **happy dust**, narcotique
m en poudre/cocaïne*/amphétamine*/etc;
(**angel**) **dust**, phéncyclidine *f*/PCP *f*; **gold
dust**, héroïne*/H *f*/dropou *f* 3. *P* argent*/
pépettes *fpl*/pèze *m*/blé *m* 4. *F* to **bite the
dust**, (*die*) tomber raide mort/clapser/casser
sa pipe; (*fail*) (*of idea, etc*) tomber à l'eau 5.
F to **lick the dust**, (*toady*) s'aplatir/lécher les
bottes à qn 6. *F* to **throw dust in s.o.'s eyes**,
jeter de la poudre aux yeux de qn 7. *F* to
make s.o. eat one's dust, (*overtake in car or
show one's superiority*) dépasser qn/faire
sentir ses gaz/faire la pige à qn/gratter qn.
(*See* **kick up 2** (*b*))
dust² [dʌst] *vtr 1. NAm Euph P* tuer*/
descendre/effacer 2. *Br P (escape from)*
fausser compagnie à 3. *F* to **dust s.o.'s jacket
for him**, battre* qn/flanquer une raclée à qn/
tanner le cuir à qn.
dustbin ['dʌs(t)bɪn] *n P* **dustbin lids/
dustbins**, (*RS = kids*) enfants*/mioches *mpl*/
moutards *mpl.* (*See* **godfer**)
dust bunnies ['dʌstbʌnɪz] *npl NAm F
(fluff under bed, etc)* moutons *mpl.*
duster ['dʌstə] *n P 1.* (*= knuckle-duster*)
coup-de-poing américain 2. *pl Austr*
testicules*/roubignoles *fpl*/valseuses *fpl.*
dusting ['dʌstɪŋ] *n F* coups*/raclée *f*/
tabassée *f*/trempe *f*/avoine *f.*
dust-off ['dʌstɒf] *n NAm F (Vietnam War)*
hélicoptère *m* d'évacuation.
dust off ['dʌst'ɒf] *NAm F* **I** *vtr (Vietnam
War)* évacuer (des blessés) par hélicoptère **II**
vi partir*/filer/s'éclipser.
dust-up ['dʌstʌp] *n F* bagarre*/coup *m* de
torchon/corrida *f*/baston *m ou f.*
dust up ['dʌst'ʌp] *vtr F* battre* (qn)/passer
(qn) à tabac/filer une avoine à (qn).
Dutch [dʌtʃ] **I** *a F* 1. **Dutch courage,**
courage puisé dans la bouteille 2. **Dutch**

auction, enchère *f* au rabais/vente *f* à la baisse **3. Dutch cap,** (*contraceptive*) diaphragme *m* **4. Dutch comfort,** consolation qui n'en est pas une/piètre consolation **5. to talk to s.o. like a Dutch uncle,** (*be totally honest with s.o.*) dire ses quatre vérités à qn; faire la morale à qn **6. Dutch treat,** sortie *f* où chacun paye sa part. (*See* **Dutch II**) **II** *adv F* **to go Dutch,** payer sa part/partager les frais **III** *n* **1.** *F* **to talk double Dutch,** baragouiner/parler une langue inintelligible; **that's double Dutch to me,** pour moi c'est de l'hébreu/du chinois **2.** *F* **my (old) Dutch,** mon épouse*/ma bourgeoise/ma légitime **3.** *O F* **that beats the Dutch!** c'est le comble!/c'est le bouquet!

Dutchman ['dʌtʃmən] *n F* **if that's so then I'm a Dutchman,** si c'est ainsi je mange mon chapeau/je veux bien être pendu.

duty ['djuːtɪ] *n F* **to do one's duty,** déféquer*/faire la grosse commission.

dweeb [dwiːb] *n* individu bête*/crétin, -ine/ nouille *f*.

dyke [daɪk] *n P* lesbienne*/gouine *f*/gousse *f*/ vrille *f*/goudou *f*. (*See* **bulldyke**)

dykey, dykie ['daɪkɪ] *a P* lesbienne*/qui sent l'ail.

dynamite ['daɪnəmaɪt] *n* **1.** *P* (*drugs*) (*a*) héroïne* extra/cheval *m*/blanche *f*; cocaïne*/ dynamite *f* (*b*) toutes drogues illicites **2.** *F* **she's dynamite!** elle est canon! **3.** *F* **his idea's really dynamite,** c'est une idée sensass/une idée du tonnerre qu'il a eue **4.** *F* **don't touch it, it's dynamite!** n'y touche pas, c'est de la dynamite/c'est explosif/c'est jouer avec le feu!

E

E [i:] *n F* (*abbr of* **ecstasy**) *see* **ecstasy**.

each way [i:tʃ'weɪ] *a Austr Euph* bisexuel/
jazz-tango; **he's a bit each way**, il est un peu
jazz-tango.

eager ['i:gə] *a* 1. *F* **eager beaver**, bourreau
m de travail*/turbineur *m*/bûcheur, -euse/
dingue *mf* du boulot; **to be an eager beaver**,
faire du zèle 2. *P* (*CB*) **eager beaver**, fille* à
la voix sensuelle.

ear [ɪə] *n* 1. *F* **to be all ears**, être tout
oreilles/être tout ouïe 2. *F* **up to one's ears**,
jusqu'au cou/par-dessus la tête; **up to one's
ears in work**, accablé/débordé/submergé de
travail* 3. *F* **to play it by ear**, jouer à
l'oreille/y aller d'instinct/aller au pif(omètre)
4. *P* **to throw s.o. out on his ear**, se
débarrasser* de qn/flanquer qn dehors; **to get
thrown out on one's ear**, se faire flanquer/
foutre dehors 5. *F* **to give s.o. a thick ear**,
donner des coups* à qn/abîmer le portrait à
qn/refaire le portrait à qn 6. *F* **to pin s.o.'s
ears back**, réprimander* qn/enguirlander qn/
sonner les cloches à qn/passer un savon à qn
7. *F* **to turn a deaf ear to sth**, faire la sourde
oreille à qch 8. *F* **to keep one's ear to the
ground**, être/se tenir aux écoutes; être bien
renseigné 9. *pl F* (*CB*) **ears**, poste *m* (de) CB.
(*See* **cloth-ears**; **dry 2**; **flea**; **pig¹ 4**; **wet¹
I 5**)

earache ['ɪəreɪk] *n Br F* bavardage
incessant/clapet *m*/jactance *f*.

earbash ['ɪəbæʃ] *vi P* parler*
incessamment/jacasser.

earbasher ['ɪəbæʃə] *n P* bavard*, -arde/
moulin *m* à paroles/jacasseur, -euse.

earful ['ɪəfʊl] *n P* **to give s.o. an earful**, (*tell
s.o. off*) réprimander* qn/enguirlander qn;
(*be frank with s.o.*) dire ses quatre vérités/
vider son sac à qn; **get an earful of this**,
écoute(-moi) bien/écoute-moi ça.

ear(h)ole¹ ['ɪərəʊl] *n Br F* 1. **to clip s.o.
round the ear(h)ole**, abîmer le portrait à qn/
flanquer une paire de gifles à qn 2. individu

bête*/andouille *f*/gourde *f*. (*See* **plug¹ 2**)

ear(h)ole² ['ɪərəʊl] *Br F* I *vtr* aborder/
agrafer (qn) II *vi* 1. bavarder*/jacasser 2.
écouter aux portes/clocher une conversation.

early ['ɜːlɪ] *a F* 1. **to be an early bird**, se
lever tôt/avec les poules; être matinal 2. **it's
early days yet**, c'est trop tôt pour dire.

earner ['ɜːnə] *n P* 1. (*bribe*) pot-de-vin *m*/
graissage *m* de patte 2. situation
financièrement avantageuse/affure *f*; **at £25 a
day, it's a nice little earner**, £25 par jour, c'est
lucratif/ça (me) fait un peu de fric.

earth [ɜːθ] *n F* 1. **to come back/down to
earth**, revenir sur terre/(re)tomber des nues
2. **to cost the earth**, coûter cher*/coûter les
yeux de la tête 3. **to be down to earth**, avoir
les pieds sur terre/avoir la tête sur les épaules
4. **where on earth is it?** où cela peut-il bien
être? **why on earth did he go?** mais pourquoi
est-il donc parti? (*See* **end 4**)

earthly ['ɜːθlɪ] I *a F* **no earthly use**, sans
aucune/sans la moindre utilité; **for no earthly
reason**, à propos de bottes II *n F* **he hasn't an
earthly**, il n'a pas l'ombre d'une chance.

earwig¹ ['ɪəwɪg] *n Br F* qn qui écoute aux
portes.

earwig² ['ɪəwɪg] *vtr & i Br F* écouter aux
portes; **to earwig a conversation**, clocher une
conversation.

earwigging ['ɪəwɪgɪŋ] *n Br P* réprimande
f/engueulade *f*/shampooing *m*.

easy ['i:zɪ] I *a F* 1. **to be on easy street**, être
riche*/rouler sur l'or 2. **easy money**, argent*
gagné facilement/affure *f* 3. **easy mark**,
personne bête* et crédule/poire *f*/jobard,
-arde/andouille *f* 4. **to take the easy way out**,
(*without any trouble*) bien s'en sortir/s'en
tirer à bon compte; (*commit suicide*) se
suicider*/se balancer (dans la Seine) 5. **easy
meat**, (*easy-going person*) individu*
complaisant/facile; (*easy opponent to beat*)
adversaire peu dangereux *ou* dangereuse 6.
easy as pie, simple comme bonjour/du billard.

(*See* **ABC 1**) 7. easy rider, (*biker*) motocycliste *mf*/motard *m*; (*one who has an easy life*) père peinard; (*promiscuous woman*) Marie-couche-toi-là *f* 8. (*woman*) to be easy on the eye, être bien balancé(e)/bien roulé(e) 9. I'm easy, je ne suis pas difficile, ça m'est égal 10. easy lay, (*usu woman*) femme* qui couche à droite et à gauche/Marie-couche-toi-là *f*; she's an easy lay, elle a la cuisse légère/hospitalière II *adv F* 1. to take it easy, ne pas se fouler la rate/se la couler douce; take it easy, (ne) te tracasse* pas/(ne) t'en fais pas 2. easy now! doucement!/piano! 3. easy does it! vas-y doucement!/vas-y mollo! 4. easy come, easy go, vite gagné, vite perdu; ce qui vient avec le flot s'en retourne avec la marée 5. to go easy on s.o./sth, ménager qn/qch; go easy on him! vas-y doucement avec lui. (*See* **fall 4**)

easy-going ['iːzɪ'gəʊɪŋ] *a F* facile à vivre; he's very easy-going, il n'est pas compliqué/il est super-cool.

eat [iːt] *vtr* 1. *F* what's eating him/her? quelle mouche l'a piqué? qu'est-ce qui le/la chiffonne? qu'est-ce qui le/la turlupine? qu'est-ce qui lui prend? 2. *F* to eat one's words, ravaler ses paroles/retirer ce qu'on a dit 3. *F* to eat one's heart out, se ronger le cœur/se faire du mouron/sécher sur pied 4. *F* he's eating us out of house and home, il mange comme un ogre/comme quatre; il vaut mieux l'avoir en photo que le nourrir! 5. *F* to eat out of s.o.'s hand, manger dans la main de qn; she had him eating out of her hand, il faisait tout ce qu'elle voulait 6. *F* to eat s.o.('s head off), réprimander* qn; she won't eat you! elle ne va pas te manger/bouffer/mordre! 7. *V* (*fellatio*) faire une fellation* à qn/sucer qn; (*cunnilingus*) pratiquer un cunnilinctus* sur qn/brouter le cresson/sucer qn. (*See* **dirt 5**; **shit¹ IV 5**)

eaterie, eatery ['iːtərɪ] *n P* café*/bistroquet *m*.

eat out ['iːt'aʊt] *vtr & i V* to eat (s.o.) out = **eat 7**.

eats [iːts] *npl P* nourriture*/bouffe *f*/boustifaille *f*.

eckies ['ekɪz] *npl Br F* (*short for expenses*) frais *mpl* (de déplacement, etc).

ecofreak, econut ['iːkəʊ'friːk, 'iːkəʊ'nʌt] *n F* écolo *mf* (ramolli(e))/fana *mf* d'écologie.

ecstasy ['ekstəsɪ] *n P* (*drugs*) (*MDMA or methylene dioxy methamphetamine*) ecstasy

f/ecstas(e) *f*. (*See* **adam**; **E**; **Epsom salts**)

edge [edʒ] *n* 1. *NAm P* to have an edge, être légèrement ivre*/être éméché 2. *Austr F* over the edge, qui dépasse les limites 3. *F* to have the edge over s.o., avoir le dessus/l'emporter sur qn.

edged [edʒd] *a NAm P* ivre*/rétamé/blindé.

edgeways ['edʒweɪz], **edgewise** ['edʒwaɪz] *adv F* I couldn't get a word in edgeways, j'arrivais pas à placer un mot/impossible d'en placer une.

edgy ['edʒɪ] *a F* énervé/les nerfs en pelote.

eek [iːk] *n Br P* visage*/balle *f*/frimousse *f*/tronche *f*.

eff [ef] *vi P* (*Euph for* **fuck**) 1. eff off = **fuck off** 2. she was effing and blinding all over the place, elle jurait comme un charretier.

effer ['efə] *n P* (*Euph for* **fucker**) you silly effer! espèce de con/de gland/d'empapaouté!

effing ['efɪŋ] *a P* (*Euph for* **fucking**) 1. (an) effing bastard, (un) espèce de salaud 2. effing this and effing that, une saloperie après l'autre 3. it's an effing nuisance, c'est chiant/c'est emmerdant.

egg [eg] *n* 1. *O F* individu*/mec *m*; bad/rotten egg, vaurien*/sale type *m*/bon *m* à rien; he's a good egg, c'est un mec bien/un bon zigue 2. *O F* good egg! épatant!/bravo! 3. *F Mil* scrambled eggs, (*showing rank*) feuilles *fpl* de chêne/sardines *fpl* 4. *F* as sure as eggs is eggs, couru d'avance/aussi vrai qu'il fait jour/sûr comme deux et deux font quatre 5. *F* don't put all your eggs in one basket, ne mettez pas tous vos œufs dans le même panier 6. *F* don't try to teach your grandmother to suck eggs, ce n'est pas aux vieux singes qu'on apprend à faire la grimace 7. *F* to lay an egg, *NAm* avoir un échec*/faire un four/foirer; *Austr* s'exciter/s'énerver 8. *F* to have egg on one's face, avoir l'air ridicule; he was left with egg on his face, il avait l'air d'un con. (*See* **nest-egg**)

eggbeater ['egbiːtə] *n F* vieille voiture/guimbarde *f*.

egghead ['eghed] *n F* intellectuel, -elle/grosse tête/tête d'œuf/intello *mf*.

ego trip ['iːgəʊtrɪp] *n F* autosatisfaction *f*; he's on an ego trip, il se vante/il jute/il fait le flambard.

ego-trip ['iːgəʊtrɪp] *vi F* (*have a high opinion of oneself*) se gober/le faire à la pose.

eight [eɪt] *n F* 1. to have had one over the eight, être ivre*/avoir bu un coup de trop/en avoir un de trop dans le nez. (*See* **one 1**) 2.

to be behind the eight ball, être en mauvaise posture/dans le pétrin/mal en point.

eighteenpence ['eɪtiːn'pens] *n P* (*RS = (common) sense*) bon sens/sens commun/ jugeotte *f*.

eighty-eights ['eɪtɪ'eɪts] *npl P* (*CB*) (= *love and kisses*) salut!/au revoir!/(grosses) bises!

elbow¹ ['elbəʊ] *n F* 1. to rub elbows with s.o., fréquenter qn/s'acoquiner avec qn 2. elbow grease, huile *f* de coude 3. to lift/to bend the elbow, to get some elbow practice, boire*/lever le coude.

elbow² ['elbəʊ] *vtr Br F* virer (qn); se débarrasser de (qch).

elbow bender ['elbəʊ'bendə] *n Br F* buveur, -euse/pitancheur *m*; ivrogne*/ picoleur, -euse.

elbow out ['elbəʊ'aʊt] *vtr F* écarter/ évincer qn; to be elbowed out, être délogé.

electric [ɪ'lektrɪk] *a P* electric soup, (*drink*) boisson alcoolisée/punch très fort.

electrocuting [ɪ'lektrəkjuːtɪŋ] *n Br P* action *f* d'entrer chez une personne âgée en se faisant passer pour un employé de l'EDF.

elephant ['elɪfənt] *n* 1. *F* white elephant, possession inutile et coûteuse/attrape-poussière *m*; rossignol *m* 2. *O F* pink elephants, rats bleus/éléphants *mpl* roses (*vus par les alcooliques*).

elephant and castle ['elɪfənt(ə)n'kɑːsl] *n O P* (*RS = arsehole*) anus*.

elephants ['elɪfənts] *a P* (*RS = elephant's trunk = drunk*) ivre*.

elevenses [ɪ'levnzɪz] *npl F* pause-café *f*.

el primo [el'priːməʊ] *n NAm P* le meilleur, la meilleure/le numéro un.

'em [əm] *pron F = them*. (*See* **aisle 2; daft I 1; make² 2; set up 1; stick up 1**)

emcee ['em'siː] *vtr F* to emcee a show, présenter/animer un spectacle. (*See* **MC**)

empty ['em(p)tɪ] *a F* to feel empty, avoir faim*/avoir un creux/claquer du bec.

end [end] *n* 1. *P* fesses*/arrière-train *m*. (*See* **rear(-end)**) 2. *V* pénis*/queue *f*/le (gros) bout; to get one's end away/in, faire l'amour*/mettre une brioche au chaud/ tremper son biscuit 3. *F* (*a*) to the bitter end, jusqu'au bout des bouts; that's just the absolute end! il ne manquait plus que cela!/ça c'est le comble!/c'est la fin des haricots! (*b*) he's the end, il est plus que minable 4. *F* to go to the ends of the earth (to do sth), se mettre en quatre/se décarcasser (pour faire qch) 5. *F*

to go off the deep end, se mettre en colère*/se mettre en pétard/piquer une crise 6. *F* to keep one's end up, résister/se défendre/tenir bon 7. *F* to be at a loose end, se tourner les pouces/ avoir du temps à perdre/la couler douce 8. *F* to make ends meet, joindre les deux bouts/ boucler son budget 9. *F* no end of..., une abondance* de.../une flopée de.../une tapée de...; it'll do you no end of good, ça vous fera un bien fou/énormément de bien; he thinks no end of himself, il est prétentieux*/il se gobe 10. *F* three weeks on end, trois semaines d'affilée 11. *F* to get hold of the wrong end of the stick, prendre qch à contresens/saisir le mauvais bout/comprendre de travers/prendre le problème à l'envers 12. *F* to be thrown in at the deep end, subir le baptême du feu 13. *F* he'll come to a sticky end, il finira mal/ça finira mal pour lui. (*See* **back I 2; back-end; beam-ends; dead-end; dog-end; fag-end; jump² 11; tab-end**)

enemy ['enəmɪ] *n A F* the enemy, l'heure *f*/ la montre/la pendule, etc; how goes the enemy? t'as l'heure?

enforcer [ɪn'fɔːsə] *n esp Austr P* tueur professionnel/à gages; voyou*/loubard *m*.

Enzed [en'zed] *n Austr & NZ F* 1. Nouvelle-Zélande *f* 2. Néo-Zélandais(e) *m(f)*.

Enzedder [en'zedə] *Austr & NZ F* Néo-Zélandais(e) *m(f)*.

Epsom salts ['epsəm'sɔːlts] *npl Br P* (*drugs*) = **ecstasy**.

erase [ɪ'reɪz] *vtr P* tuer*/liquider/effacer (qn).

erk [ɜːk] *n Br F* prolo *mf*.

Esky ['eskɪ] *n Austr RTM F* glacière *f*.

Essex man, woman ['esɪks'mæn, -wʊmən] *n Br F* l'homme/la femme (typique) d'Essex (*comté du sud-est de l'Angleterre*); = beauf *m*/Dupont-la-joie *m*.

ethnic ['eθnɪk], **ethno** ['eθnəʊ] *n Austr Euph F* immigrant, -ante.

even ['iːvn] **I** *a F* even Steven(s), quitte; to call it even Steven(s), être quitte; to go even Steven(s), partager fifty-fifty **II** *adv F* to get even (with s.o.), se venger/rendre la pareille à qn; I'll get even with him for that, je lui revaudrai/rendrai ça; il ne perd rien pour attendre.

ever ['evə] *adv F* 1. ever so..., tellement...; ever so much, beaucoup*/vachement 2. did you ever! époustouflant!/par exemple!/ça alors!/sans blague!

evil ['iːvɪl] *a P* excellent*/super/terrible.

ex [eks] *prefix & n F* 1. (*former boyfriend/ girlfriend/husband/wife*) ex *mf* 2. ex-con, ex-prisonnier, -ière.

exec [ɪk'zek] *n Br F* (*abbr of executive*) cadre *m*.

exes ['eksɪz] *npl Br F* = **eckies.**

exhibition [eksɪ'bɪʃ(ə)n] *n F* to make an exhibition of oneself, faire la comédie/se donner en spectacle/se défoncer pour la galerie.

experience [ɪk'spɪərɪəns] *n F* (*drugs*) voyage *m*/trip *m*.

extras ['ekstrəz] *npl F* (*a*) à-côtés *mpl* (*b*) (*food*) (du) rab(iot).

eye [aɪ] *n* 1. *F* easy on the eye, agréable à regarder/de quoi se rincer l'œil. (*See* **easy 8**) 2. *A F* that's all my eye (**and Betty Martin**), tout ça c'est des foutaises/de la blague 3. *F* my eye! mon œil!/mon zob!/mon cul! 4. *F* glad eye, œillade*; to give s.o. the (glad) eye, faire de l'œil à qn/lancer une œillade à qn/ allumer qn 5. *F* to keep an eye on s.o., surveiller qn/avoir qn à l'œil 6. *F* to keep one's eyes open/skinned/peeled, ouvrir l'œil (et le bon)/ne pas avoir ses yeux dans sa poche; keep an eye out for the car, essaie de repérer la bagnole 7. *F* sheep's eyes, des yeux de carpe; to make eyes at s.o., couver qn des yeux/faire les yeux doux à qn 8. *F* to see eye to eye (**with s.o.**), être du même avis (que qn)/être d'accord (avec qn)/voir du même œil; they never see eye to eye (**with each other**), ils ne sont jamais d'accord 9. *F* to turn a blind eye (**to sth**), fermer les yeux (sur qch)/garder les yeux dans le tiroir 10. *F* to be up to one's eyes in sth, être plongé dans qch jusqu'aux yeux/jusqu'aux oreilles; he's in it up to his eyes, il est dans la merde jusqu'au cou. (*See* **ear 2**) 11. *F* a sight for sore eyes, un régal pour les yeux 12. *F* there's more in/ to this than meets the eye, il y a anguille sous

roche 13. *F* private eye, (détective) privé *m*/ fileur *m* 14. *P* that's one in the eye for him! il a été mouché de belle façon!/c'est bien fait pour sa poire! 15. *NAm F* 'eyes only', (*on a letter*) 'confidentiel'/'personnel' 16. *NAm V* round eye, anus*/œuf *m*/pièce *f* de dix sous. (*See* **bingo 1; bird's-eye; drop¹ 6; four-eyes; mud 1; red-eye; shuteye; slap¹ II 1; snake-eyes**)

eyeball¹ ['aɪbɔːl] *n P* 1. (*esp CB*) (*a*) rencontre *f*/visite *f*/rendez-vous* (*b*) to lay an eyeball on s.o., voir qn/regarder qn/avoir qn à l'œil 2. eyeball to eyeball, face *f* à face/tête *f* à tête; (*CB*) visu *m* 3. (*police term*) (*a*) opération *f* de surveillance; to be on eyeball, surveiller (un suspect) (*b*) vue *f*; we have an eyeball on the suspect, le suspect a été repéré/vu. (*See* **dope¹ 1** (*c*); **poxed-up**)

eyeball² ['aɪbɔːl] *vtr P* (*a*) (*esp CB*) rencontrer (qn) (*b*) regarder/mater/zyeuter.

eyebrows ['aɪbraʊz] *npl F* he's hanging on by his eyebrows, il se maintient tout juste/il est sur la corde raide/il tient à un fil. (*See* **dope² 1** (*c*); **poxed-up**)

eyeful ['aɪfʊl] *n P* qch de très beau*/de très intéressant; jolie fille*/belle pépée; to get an eyeful, se rincer l'œil; here, get an eyeful of this! vise-moi ça un peu!/mate-moi ça!

eye-opener ['aɪəʊp(ə)nə] *n F* 1. révélation *f*/surprise *f*; it was a real eye-opener for me, ça m'a vraiment ouvert les yeux 2. (*a*) première boisson de la journée/boisson forte prise à jeun; to have an eye-opener, tuer le ver (*b*) (*drugs*) première piqûre de la journée.

Eyetie ['aɪtaɪ] *n P* Italien*/Rital, -ale/ macaroni *mf*.

eyewash ['aɪwɒʃ] *n F* 1. flatterie *f*/bourrage *m* de crâne/frime *f* 2. baratin *m*/boniment *m*; that's just a load of eyewash! ce ne sont que des foutaises/c'est du bidon!

F

f.a., FA ['ef'eɪ] *abbr of* **Fanny Adams** *or* **fuck-all**; sweet f.a./FA = sweet Fanny Adams *or* sweet fuck-all (**sweet 4**).

fab [fæb] *a* F excellent*/terrible; *excl* fab! chouette!/sensass!/super!

face¹ [feɪs] *n* **1.** F shut your face! ferme ta gueule!/la ferme!/ta gueule! **2.** F to have the face to do sth, avoir le culot/le toupet de faire qch **3.** F to show one's face, montrer (le bout de) son nez; he won't show his face in here again, il ne remettra plus les pieds ici **4.** F to stuff one's face, manger*/s'empiffrer **5.** F to paint one's face, se maquiller*/se ravaler la façade **6.** P célébrité *f*/vedette *f*/caïd *m* *(sort appartenant au* **milieu**) **7.** *Austr* P to be off one's face, être ivre*/bourré; être drogué*/dans les vapes. (*See* **angel-face; back II 13; fungus 1; laugh² 2; puddingface; slap¹ II 1; stare; stuff² 4**)

face² [feɪs] *vtr* F **1.** let's face it/let's face facts, regardons les choses en face/faut bien le dire **2.** *Austr* = **dud up 1**. (*See* **music**)

face-ache ['feɪseɪk], *NAm* **face-case** ['feɪskeɪs] *n* P *(ugly person)* tête *f* à claques; hello, face-ache! salut, mocheté!

face-paint ['feɪspeɪnt] *n* F badigeon *m*/peinture *f*. (*See* **face¹ 5; war-paint**)

facer ['feɪsə] *n* F **1.** *(problem)* pépin *m*/tuile *f* **2.** coup* au visage/torgnole *f*.

face up ['feɪs'ʌp] *vi* F to face up to s.o./sth, affronter qn/qch; tenir tête à qn/qch.

fack [fæk] *vi* P *(Black Sl)* dire la vérité/dire vrai.

facings ['feɪsɪŋz] *npl* F to put s.o. through his facings, *(test s.o.'s intelligence)* éprouver le savoir de qn/voir ce qu'il a dans le crâne; réprimander* qn/laver la tête à qn.

factory ['fæktərɪ] *n* P commissariat *m* de police/quart *m*.

fad [fæd] *n* F marotte *f*/lubie *f*/dada *m*; health food fad, manie *f* des aliments biologiques/naturels.

faddy ['fædɪ] *a* F maniaque/capricieux; she's faddy about her food, elle est difficile sur la nourriture.

fade¹ [feɪd] *n* P **1.** *(Black Sl)* Noir(e)* qui mène la vie d'un Blanc *ou* qui préfère choisir ses ami(e)s parmi les Blancs **2.** *esp NAm* to do a fade, s'enfuir*/s'évaporer.

fade² [feɪd] *vi* P partir*/se barrer/s'évaporer.

faff about, around ['fæfə'baʊt, -ə'raʊnd] *vi Br* F perdre son temps à des bricoles; stop faffing about/around and get on with it! arrête tes conneries et grouille-toi!

fag [fæg] *n* **1.** F cigarette*/sèche *f*/cibiche *f*/clope *f* **2.** P *(a)* homosexuel*/pédé *m*/fiotte *f*/lope(tte) *f* *(b)* fag hag, femme* qui recherche la compagnie des homosexuels* **3.** F what a fag! quelle corvée!

fag-end ['fægend] *n* F mégot*/orphelin *m*.

fageroo [fægə'ruː] *n* P = **fag 1**.

fagged (out) ['fægd('aʊt)] *a* F très fatigué*/vanné/crevé.

faggot ['fægət] *n* **1.** *esp NAm* P homosexuel*/pédé *m*/tante *f* **2.** F *Pej* old faggot, vieille femme*/vieille pouffiasse/vieille bique.

faggotry ['fægətrɪ] *n esp NAm* P les homosexuels*/la pédale.

faggy ['fægɪ] *a* P efféminé/qui fait tapette.

fains! [feɪnz], **fainites!** ['feɪnaɪts], **fainits!** ['feɪnɪts] *excl Br* O F *(schools)* pouce!

fair [fɛə] I *a* F **1.** fair enough! ça va!/d'accord!*/OK! **2.** fair's fair, il faut être juste **3.** *Austr* fair go! fair goes! *(be reasonable, fair)* (allons) sois raisonnable!/déconne pas! (*See* **cop¹ 2; cow 2; dinkum 1; do¹ 3; middling; shake¹ 3; whip¹ 1**) II *adv* P très/absolument/bougrement; I'm fair knackered, je suis complètement à plat/crevé; this fair stumped me, du coup je n'ai su que répondre.

fair-haired ['fɛə'hɛəd] *a NAm* F fair-haired boy = blue-eyed boy (**blue-eyed**).

fair-weather ['fɛəweðə] *a* F fair-weather

friends, amis des beaux jours.

fairy ['fɛərɪ] *n P* 1. homosexuel*/pédé *m*/ tapette *f*; **fairy hawk**, chasseur *m*/casseur *m* de pédés; **fairy lady/queen**, lesbienne*/ gougnotte *f*/gouine *f*; **I look a right fairy dressed up like this**, j'ai l'air d'une vraie tapette avec ces fringues 2. (*football*) joueur ramollo/mou *m*. (*See* **airy-fairy**)

fairyland ['fɛərɪlænd] *n P* le monde des homosexuels*/la pédale/la jaquette; **does he come from fairyland?** il en est? (*See* **pansyland**)

fake off ['feɪk'ɒf] *vi NAm P* (*slip away, thus avoiding work*) s'esquiver/tirer au flanc/se la couler douce/tirer au cul.

fake out ['feɪk'aʊt] *vtr NAm F* **to fake s.o. out**, tromper/duper/avoir qn.

falconer ['fɔːlkənə] *n P* (*con man*) escroc*/ arnaqueur *m*/estampeur *m* (*qui se fait passer pour un aristocrate*).

fall [fɔːl] *vi F* 1. **to fall for a trick**, s'y laisser prendre/tomber dans un piège; **he fell for it**, il s'est fait avoir 2. **to fall for s.o.**, s'amouracher de qn 3. **to fall all over oneself to please s.o.**, se mettre en quatre/se décarcasser pour plaire à qn 4. **it's as easy as falling off a log**, (*very easy*) c'est bête comme chou/c'est du billard. (*See* **backwards 1**)

fall down ['fɔːl'daʊn] *vi F* **to fall down on a job**, échouer*/louper/foirer; rater son coup.

fall-guy ['fɔːlgaɪ] *n F* (*scapegoat*) bouc *m* émissaire/dindon *m* de la farce/couillon *m* (de l'histoire); (*dupe*) pigeon *m*.

fall out ['fɔːl'aʊt] *vi P* 1. *NAm* s'endormir/ s'enrouspiller 2. *Br* échouer*/foirer.

fall through ['fɔːl'θruː] *vi F* (*of plan, etc*) foirer; **it fell through at the last moment**, ça m'a claqué dans les doigts/c'est tombé à l'eau.

falsies ['fɔːlsɪz] *npl F* seins* artificiels/faux nénés/roberts *mpl* de chez Michelin.

family ['fæm(ɪ)lɪ] *a attrib* 1. *O F* **in the family way**, enceinte*/en cloque/dans une situation intéressante 2. *P* **family jewels**, (*male genitals*) bijoux *mpl* de famille.

famished ['fæmɪʃt] *a F* **to be famished**, avoir très faim*/avoir la dent; **I'm absolutely famished**, je crève de faim/j'ai la dalle.

famous ['feɪməs] *a* (*a*) *F* excellent*/ sensass/fameux (*b*) **famous last words!** on verra bien!

famously ['feɪməslɪ] *adv F* fameusement/ rudement; **to get on famously**, s'entendre à merveille.

fan [fæn] *n* 1. *F* fanatique *mf*/fan *mf*/fana *mf*/ mordu, -ue; **fan club**, club *m* de fans; **fan mail**, courrier *m* de fans; **film fan**, cinéphile *mf*/fana de ciné 2. *NAm P* = **fanny 2.**

fancy[1] ['fænsɪ] *a* 1. *P* **fancy man**, (*lover*) amant *m*/gigolo *m*; petit ami; (*pimp*) souteneur*/julot *m* 2. *P* **fancy woman/fancy piece**, prostituée*/pute *f*; (*lover*) maîtresse *f*/ petite amie 3. *P* **fancy pants**, (joli) coco *m*/ minet *m* 4. *F* **cut out the fancy stuff!** (raconte) pas de bêtises!/épargne-moi les détails fumeux!

fancy[2] ['fænsɪ] *vtr F* 1. **fancy!/fancy that!** figurez-vous ça!/ça par exemple! 2. **fancy meeting you!** quelle bonne rencontre! 3. **to fancy oneself**, être satisfait de sa petite personne/se gober/s'en croire; **she really fancies herself**, elle ne se prend pas pour de la crotte 4. **a little of what you fancy does you good**, (*catchphrase*) si ça vous fait envie, ça ne peut pas vous faire de mal (d'en prendre un peu) 5. **do you fancy her?** elle te plaît? **I really fancy him**, je le trouve pas mal du tout/vachement bien; j'ai un faible pour lui.

fanny ['fænɪ] *n* 1. *Br V* sexe* de la femme*/ chatte *f*/minette *f*; **fanny tickler**, lesbienne*/ gouine *f*/gougnotte *f* 2. *NAm P* fesses*/baba *m*/pétrousquin *m*; **to park one's fanny**, s'asseoir/poser son cul 3. *Br P* **fanny merchant**, personne indécise *ou* incompétente/branleur *m* 4. *Br P* **fanny rat**, séducteur *m*/tombeur *m*. (*See* **aunt 1**; **sweet 4**)

fantastic [fæn'tæstɪk] *a F* excellent*/super/ sensass; **that was fantastic**, c'était le pied; **a fantastic concert**, un concert sensationnel/ superbe/génial.

fanzine ['fænziːn] *n esp NAm F* magazine *m* des fans/fanzine *m*.

far [fɑː] *adv F* **far gone** (*a*) fou* à lier (*b*) ivre* mort. (*See* **gone 1**)

Farmer Giles ['fɑːmə'dʒaɪlz] *Prn*, **farmers** ['fɑːməz] *npl Br P* (*RS = piles*) hémorroïdes *fpl*/émeraudes *fpl*.

far-out ['fɑːr'aʊt] *a F* 1. bizarre/avant-garde; (*esp music*) extra-moderne/progressif/ super-branché 2. emballant/enthousiasmant/ bottant; **far out!** (c'est) génial!/(c'est) le pied! **that song is really far-out**, elle est (vachement) cool/super/dingue, cette chanson!

fart[1] [fɑːt] *n V* 1. pet*/perle *f*/perlouze *f* 2. **I don't care a fart**, je m'en fous complètement/ je n'en ai rien à foutre/je n'en ai rien à branler 3. **to stand as much chance as a fart**

in a **wind-storm**, ne pas avoir la moindre chance de réussir/être foutu d'avance 4. **like a fart in a bottle**, agité/nerveux 5. **old fart**, vieux schnoque/croulant, ante/ringard *m*; **he's a silly/boring old fart**, c'est un petit con/un trouduc. (*See* **sparrow-fart**; **traf(f)¹**)

fart² [faːt] *vi V* péter*/cloquer/lâcher une perle. (*See* **traf(f)²**)

fart(-arse) around, about ['faːt(aːs)-ə'raʊnd, ə'baʊt] *vi V* faire le con/déconner.

fart-catcher ['faːtkætʃə] *n V* homosexuel*/pédé *m*/enculé *m*.

fart-hole ['faːt(h)əʊl] *n V* anus*/trou *m* de balle/trou du cul/rondelle *f*/troufignon *m*.

fart-sack ['faːtsæk] *n V* (*a*) sac *m* de couchage/sac à viande (*b*) lit*/plumard *m*/pucier *m*.

fast [faːst] **I** *a F* 1. dévergondé/rapide; **to lead a fast life**, faire les quatre cents coups; **he's a fast worker/a fast one with the girls**, c'est un tombeur de filles/de femmes; c'est un Don Juan/un chaud lapin 2. **fast talk**, boniment *m*/baratin *m*. (*See* **buck¹ 1**; **one 4**) **II** *adv F* **to play fast and loose**, jouer double jeu.

fast food ['faːst'fuːd] *n F* (*hamburgers, pizzas, etc*) fast-food *m*; **we ate in a fast food place**, nous avons pris un truc dans un fast-food.

fastlane ['faːstleɪn] *a F* **fastlane lifestyle**, style *m* de vie du jet set/des mondains.

fast-talk ['faːst'tɔːk] *vtr P* bonimenter/baratiner/faire du baratin à (qn).

fat [fæt] **I** *a* 1. *P* **a fat lot**, rien*/des clous; **a fat lot of good that'll do you!** cela vous fera une belle jambe! **a fat lot I care!** je m'en fiche pas mal!/je m'en moque comme de l'an quarante!/je m'en soucie comme de ma première chemise! **a fat lot you know about it!** comme si vous en saviez quelque chose! **a fat lot of difference it makes to you!** pour ce que ça vous coûte! 2. *P* **fat chance!** y a pas de danger! **a fat chance he's got!** il n'a pas l'ombre d'une chance 3. *F* **a fat salary**, un gros salaire/une bonne paye 4. *esp NAm P* **fat cat**, (*privileged, wealthy person*) rupin, -ine/richard, -arde; **the fat cats**, les gros/les rupins/les richards 5. *NAm P* **fat city**, situation satisfaisante; contentement *m*/super-forme *f*; **in fat city**, en super-forme; **he was in fat city**, ça marchait terrible pour lui; il pétait la forme 6. *F* **one fat lady, two fat ladies**: see **bingo 8, 88** **II** *n F* 1. (*theatre*)

rôle *m* en or 2. *F* **the fat is in the fire**, il y a le feu aux poudres; le torchon brûle 3. *F* **to live off the fat of the land**, vivre grassement/mener la vie de château/vivre comme un coq en pâte 4. *Austr V* **to crack a fat**, être en érection*/bander/avoir la banane/marquer midi. (*See* **chew 1**)

fathead ['fæthed] *n F* individu bête*/imbécile *mf*/enflure *f*/empaqueté *m*/patate *f*/andouille *f*.

fatheaded ['fæthedɪd] *a F* bête*/cloche.

fatso ['fætsəʊ], **fatty** ['fætɪ] *n P* personne grosse*/(gros)/patapouf *m*/gravos(se) *m(f)*/gros plein de soupe.

fave [feɪv] *a Br F* (*short for favourite*) préféré/favori.

faze [feɪz] *vtr F* déconcerter/brouiller l'esprit à/embrouiller (qn).

fear [fɪə] *n F* **no fear!** pas de danger!/jamais de la vie!

fearful ['fɪəfʊl] *a F* effrayant/affreux; **a fearful mess**, un désordre effrayant; **a fearful bore**, un emmerdeur/une emmerdeuse (de première).

feather¹ ['feðə] *n* 1. *F* **birds of a feather**, du pareil au même/du même acabit 2. *F* **a feather in one's cap**, une perle à sa couronne/un bon point; **that's a feather in her cap**, elle peut en être fière 3. *F* **to show the white feather**, laisser voir qu'on a peur*/caner 4. *F* **you could have knocked me down with a feather!** j'en suis resté baba!/les bras m'en sont tombés! 5. *P* lit*/plumard *m*.

feather² ['feðə] *vtr F* **to feather one's nest**, faire sa pelote/faire son beurre/mettre du foin dans ses bottes.

featherbed ['feðəbed] *vtr F* subventionner (excessivement).

featherbedding ['feðəbedɪŋ] *n F* subventionnement excessif; traitement *m* de faveur.

featherbrain ['feðəbreɪn] *n F* individu bête*/tête *f* de linotte; **she's a real featherbrain**, elle n'a rien dans la tête/la cervelle.

featherbrained ['feðəbreɪnd] *a F* bête*/à tête de linotte/écervelé/évaporé; **to be featherbrained**, avoir une cervelle de moineau.

feature ['fiːtʃə] *vi esp Austr P* **to feature with s.o.**, faire l'amour* avec qn/faire une politesse à une femme.

Feds (the) [ðə'fedz] *n US F* (*abbr of Federal Agents*) fonctionnaires chargés de l'application de la loi; agents *mpl* du FBI.

fed up ['fed'ʌp] *a F* (*a*) **to be fed up (to the**

back teeth), en avoir assez*/en avoir ras le bol/en avoir (plus que) marre (b) **I'm fed up with him**, il me tape sur le système; **I'm bloody fed up with it**, j'en ai plein le cul (de ce truc).

feed [fiːd] *n F* 1. **to be off one's feed**, ne pas avoir d'appétit 2. *P (theatre)* comparse *mf/* faire-valoir *m*. *(See* **chicken-feed**)

feel[1] [fiːl] *n P (caress, sexual contact)* tripotage *m/*pelotage *m*; *esp NAm* **to cop a feel**, mettre la main au panier/aller aux renseignements.

feel[2] [fiːl] *vtr* 1. *P* caresser/peloter qn; aller aux renseignements/mettre la main au panier 2. *F* **do you feel like it?** est-ce que ça te chante?/est-ce que ça te dit?/ça t'irait? 3. *P (Black Slang)* **to feel a draught**/*US* **draft**, flairer le racisme (chez qn). *(See* **oats 2**)

feel up [ˈfiːlʌp] *vtr P* **to feel s.o. up** = **feel**[2] 1.

feet [fiːt] *npl see* **foot**[1].

feisty [ˈfaɪstɪ] *a esp NAm F (spirited)* plein d'entrain; *(assertive)* autoritaire; *(quarrelsome)* querelleur.

fella, feller [ˈfelə] *n F (= fellow)* (a) individu*/type *m/*mec *m* (b) amoureux *m/*petit ami; **she brought her latest fella**, elle a ramené le dernier en date/elle s'est pointée avec sa dernière conquête.

fem [fem] *n P* 1. lesbienne* (qui tient le rôle de la femme)/gavousse *f* 2. *(passive homosexual)* tante *f/*tapette *f*.

female [ˈfiːmeɪl] *n F (a)* femme*/fille*; *often Pej* femelle *f (b) (girlfriend)* petite amie/ nana *f*.

femme [fem] *n P* = **fem.**

fence[1] [fens] *n F* 1. receleur*/fourgue *m/* fourgat *m/*lessiveur *m* 2. **to sit on the fence**, ménager la chèvre et le chou 3. *Austr* **over the fence**, qui dépasse les limites/qui n'est pas du tout raisonnable. *(See* **edge 2**)

fence[2] [fens] *vtr F* receler/fourguer.

fence hanger [ˈfenshæŋə] *n NAm F (a)* personne indécise (b) bavard, -arde/commère *f*.

fencing [ˈfensɪŋ] *n F* recelage *m/*lessivage *m/*fourgue *f*.

ferret [ˈferɪt] *n Austr P* **to exercise the ferret**, faire l'amour*/mener le petit au cirque.

fess up [ˈfesʌp] *vi NAm P* avouer*/ accoucher/se mettre à table.

fest [fest] *n esp NAm F* fête *f/*festival *m/*gala *m/*réunion *f*. *(See* **gabfest; gayfest;**

slugfest)

fetch [fetʃ] *vtr F* 1. *(esp of idea)* séduire/ emballer/taper dans l'œil 2. **to fetch a blow at s.o.**, flanquer un coup à qn. *(See* **one 3**)

fetching [ˈfetʃɪŋ] *a F (clothes, personality, etc)* charmant/séduisant/ravissant.

fetch up [ˈfetʃʌp] *vtr & i Br F (esp in North Country)* vomir*/dégobiller.

few [fjuː] *npl F* **to have (had) a few**, être ivre*/avoir un verre dans le nez; **he's had a few too many**, il a pas mal bu/il en a un de trop (dans le nez).

fey [feɪ] *a F* efféminé; **he's a bit fey**, il est un peu pédé sur les bords.

fib[1] [fɪb] *n F* mensonge*/craque *f/*bobard *m*; **that's a big fib**, tu racontes des bobards/c'est du mou.

fib[2] [fɪb] *vi F* mentir*/baratiner/raconter des bobards.

fibber [ˈfɪbə] *n F* menteur, -euse/baratineur, -euse; **you big fibber!** espèce de bidonneur!

fiddle[1] [ˈfɪdl] *n F* 1. violon *m/*crincrin *m/* plumier *m* 2. *(swindle)* combine *f/*fricotage *m/*magouille *f*; **it was all a bit of a fiddle**, tout ça c'était du fricotage/des magouilles; **she's on the/a fiddle**, elle fricote/elle traficote/elle magouille. *(See* **work**[2] **1**) 3. **to be as fit as a fiddle**, se porter comme un charme 4. **to play second fiddle**, jouer un rôle secondaire/jouer un rôle de second *ou* troisième couteau.

fiddle[2] [ˈfɪdl] *vtr & i F* 1. violoner/racler du violon 2. **to fiddle the books**, truquer les comptes; **to fiddle the tax**, rouler le percepteur/maquiller sa feuille d'impôts 3. combiner/fricoter/magouiller/trafiquer.

fiddle about, around [ˈfɪdləˈbaʊt, əˈraʊnd] *vi F (a)* traîner/bricoler/glander/ glandouiller (b) **to fiddle about/around with sth**, *(play with, touch)* tripoter/trifouiller qch.

fiddle-arse about [ˈfɪdlɑːsəˈbaʊt] *vi P* = **fiddle about, around** *(a)*.

fiddlede(e)dee! [ˈfɪdldɪˈdiː] *excl A F* = **fiddlesticks!**

fiddle-faddle! [ˈfɪdlfædl] *excl A F* quelle bêtise*!/quelle blague!

fiddler [ˈfɪdlə] *n F* 1. racleur, -euse de violon/jambonneur *m* 2. fricoteur, -euse/ combinard, -arde/magouilleur, -euse 3. bricoleur, -euse/tripoteur, -euse.

fiddlesticks! [ˈfɪdlstɪks] *excl O F* quelle bêtise*!/quelle blague!

fiddling [ˈfɪdlɪŋ] *n F* 1. raclage *m* de violon 2. combine *f/*fricotage *m/*magouilles *fpl*; **there's been a lot of fiddling going on**, il y a eu beaucoup de fricotage/magouilles là-dessous.

fiddly ['fɪdlɪ] *a* F délicat/minutieux; a fiddly job, un travail délicat; un sac de nœuds.

fidgets ['fɪdʒɪts] *npl* F to have the fidgets, avoir la bougeotte/ne pas tenir en place.

field day ['fiːldeɪ] *n* F umbrella sellers had a field day, ça a été un jour béni/en or pour les marchands de parapluie.

fiend [fiːnd] *n* F emballé *m*/mordu, -ue/fana *mf*; O dope fiend, drogué*/*surt* morphinomane *mf*/toxico *mf*; sex fiend, obsédé sexuel/pineur *m*/queutard *m*.

fifty-fifty ['fɪftɪ'fɪftɪ] *a & adv* F moitié-moitié/afanaf/fifty-fifty; to go fifty-fifty, se mettre de moitié/partager fifty-fifty; a fifty-fifty chance, une chance sur deux. (See **half I 5**)

fig¹ [fɪg] *n* 1. V sexe* de la femme*/figue *f* 2. F I don't care a fig, je m'en moque pas mal/je m'en fiche éperdument 3. O F in full fig, habillé avec élégance; sur son trente et un.

fig² [fɪg] *vtr* P doper (un cheval de course).

figure [fɪgə, *NAm* fɪgjə] *vtr & i esp NAm* F 1. compter sur qch/penser; they don't figure he'll live, on ne pense pas le sauver 2. that figures, ça va de soi/ça s'explique 3. I figure that's OK, ça m'a l'air OK/bon/d'aller.

figure out ['fɪgər'aʊt, *NAm* 'fɪgjər-] *vtr* F 1. calculer/chiffrer; I've figured out how much I need, j'ai calculé combien il m'en faut 2. comprendre; he can't figure it out, ça le dépasse/il (ne) pige pas.

file [faɪl] *n* P voleur, -euse à la tire/tireur, -euse/pique *m*.

filleted ['fɪlɪtɪd] *a Br* P très déçu; when I heard the news, I was filleted, quand j'ai appris la nouvelle, ça m'a foutu un coup (au moral).

fill in ['fɪl'ɪn] *vtr & i* 1. *Br* P to fill s.o. in, battre*/piler/tabasser qn 2. F to fill s.o. in (on sth), mettre qn au courant/au parfum; parfumer qn 3. F to fill in for s.o., remplacer qn (au pied levé).

filly ['fɪlɪ] *n* F (*not common*) jeune fille* fringante/jolie pouliche.

filth, the filth [(ðə)fɪlθ] *n* P la police*/la maison poulaga/la flicaille; then the filth arrived, et puis les flics *mpl*/les poulets *mpl*/les vaches *fpl* se sont amené(e)s; he's filth, c'est un flic/un poulet/un keuf.

filthy ['fɪlθɪ] *a* F 1. (*a*) sale*/cradingue/crado; filthy weather, temps pourri/temps de cochon (*b*) ordurier/obscène; don't be filthy! pas d'obscénités, s'il te plaît! to have a filthy

mind, avoir l'esprit mal tourné; he's got a filthy mind, il ne pense qu'à ça; filthy sod, (*horrible person*) saligaud *m*/salaud *m*/sale cochon, -onne; (*sex maniac*) obsédé, -ée sexuel(lle)/queutard *m*; (*sport*) filthy player, joueur salaud 2. the filthy rich, les (sales) rupins/les pleins aux as; he's filthy (rich), il est pourri de fric. (See **lucre**)

fin [fɪn] *n* P 1. main*/pince *f*/patte *f*. (See **flipper**) 2. bras*/aile *f*/nageoire *f* 3. *NAm* P billet* de cinq dollars.

finagle [fɪ'neɪgl] *vtr* F manigancer/resquiller/magouiller.

finagler [fɪ'neɪglə] *n* F fricoteur, -euse/resquilleur, -euse/combinard, -arde/magouilleur, -euse.

finagling [fɪ'neɪglɪŋ] *n* F combines *fpl*/resquille *f*/magouilles *fpl*.

finals ['faɪn(ə)lz] *npl* F (*university*) examens *mpl* de dernière année.

fine [faɪn] I *a* F 1. bien/parfait; it's all very fine but..., tout cela est bien joli/bien beau mais... 2. one fine day, un beau jour II *adv* F 1. I'm doing fine! je me débrouille bien!/ça va bien! 2. you're doing fine: see **bingo 29**. (See **cut² 3**)

finest ['faɪnɪst] *n* F London's/New York's finest, la police*/la maison poulaga Londonienne/New Yorkaise.

finger¹ ['fɪŋgə] *n* 1. P to put the finger on s.o., dénoncer* qn/balancer qn/donner qn à la police/balanstiquer qn 2. F to pull one's finger out, se secouer/(se) dégrouiller; get/pull your finger out! secoue tes puces!/grouille-toi!/magne-toi! 3. F to put one's finger on it, mettre le doigt dessus 4. F to keep one's fingers crossed, toucher du bois 5. F to lift the little finger, boire*/lever le coude 6. F to have a finger in every pie, être mêlé à tout; to have a finger in the pie, y être pour qch 7. F not to lift a (little) finger (to help s.o.), ne pas lever le petit doigt (pour aider qn) 8. F to lay a finger on s.o., lever la main sur qn/amocher qn; I didn't (even) lay a finger on him! je ne l'ai même pas touché! 9. F to twist s.o. round one's little finger, entortiller qn/faire de qn ce qu'on veut 10. P to give s.o. the finger, (*make an obscene gesture at s.o.*) = faire un bras d'honneur à qn; she was giving me the polite finger, elle me snobait 11. P two fingers!/fingers to you! je t'emmerde! (See **fingers-up**) 12. P finger artist, lesbienne*/gougnot(t)e *f*/gouine *f* 13. *pl* P (*CB*) fingers, cibiste *mf* changeant sans arrêt de canal/cibiste tripotant les boutons de fréquence. (*See* **butterfingers; fruit-basket; green I 5; sticky 2; thumb¹ 1**)

finger² ['fɪŋgə] *vtr* 1. *P* dénoncer*/moucharder/balancer (qn) 2. *V* to finger oneself, (*esp of woman*) se masturber*/se filer une gerbe/s'astiquer le bouton.

finger-fuck¹ ['fɪŋgəfʌk], **finger-job** ['fɪŋgədʒɒb] *n VV* 1. (*woman*) masturbation *f*/gerbe *f* 2. insertion *f* d'un doigt dans l'anus* *ou* le vagin* (de son partenaire).

finger-fuck² ['fɪŋgəfʌk] *v VV* 1. *vi* (*of woman*) se masturber* 2. *vtr* insérer/mettre/enfiler un doigt dans l'anus* *ou* le vagin* de (son partenaire).

finger popper ['fɪŋgə'pɒpə] *n NAm P* (*jazz*) personne *f* qui se défonce en improvisation/qui part sur son tempo.

fingers-up ['fɪŋgəz'ʌp] *n V* geste *m* obscène de dérision/= bras *m* d'honneur.

finish off ['fɪnɪʃ'ɒf] *vtr P* (*prostitutes*) to finish off a client, faire jouir un client.

fink [fɪŋk] *n NAm P* 1. *A* briseur, -euse de grève(s)/jaune *mf* 2. salaud*/fripouille *f*/ordure *f*/fumier *m*; (*untrustworthy*) branleur *m*. (*See* **ratfink**) 3. indicateur*/indic *mf*/donneur, -euse.

finski ['fɪnskɪ] *n NAm F* = **fin 3**.

fire ['faɪə] *vtr* 1. *F* (*dismiss*) sacquer/virer/(qn) 2. *V* to fire in the air, éjaculer* dans le vide/tout balancer sur le ventre/décharger devant la porte.

fire away ['faɪərə'weɪ] *vi F* commencer (à parler)/se lancer; fire away! allez-y!/dites toujours!/racontez!

fireball ['faɪəbɔːl] *n F* individu* dynamique. (*See* **ball¹ 6**)

firebug ['faɪəbʌg] *n F* incendiaire *mf*/pyromane *mf*.

fired-up ['faɪəd'ʌp] *a* 1. en colère*/en rogne 2. (*sexually aroused*) excité/qui bande à zéro.

firewater ['faɪəwɔːtə] *n F* alcool*/gnôle *f*/tord-boyaux *m*.

fireworks ['faɪəwɜːks] *npl F* if you do that again there'll be fireworks! si tu recommences, ça va barder/il y aura du grabuge!

firm, the firm [fɜːm, ðə'fɜːm] *n Br P* 1. bande *f*/gang *m* de criminels/de voleurs, etc 2. amis*/(bande *f* de) copains *mpl*/potes *mpl*.

first [fɜːst] I *a NAm F* to get to first base, *see* **base 1** II *n F Iron* hot coffee! that's a first for British Rail! du café chaud! c'est l'événement/une grande première pour British

Rail!

first-class ['fɜːst'klɑːs], **first-rate** ['fɜːst'reɪt] *F* I *adv* au poil/de première; it's going first-class/first-rate, ça marche super/impec II *a* extra/super; first-class!/first-rate! très bien!/superbe!

first-timer ['fɜːst'taɪmə] *n F* détenu, -ée pour la première fois/nouveau, -elle de la lourde.

fish¹ [fɪʃ] *n* 1. *F* individu*/zèbre *m*; a queer fish, un drôle d'oiseau/de numéro; a poor fish, un(e) paumé(e) 2. *F* to feed the fishes (*a*) avoir le mal de mer/donner à manger aux poissons (*b*) se noyer/boire le bouillon 3. *F* to have other fish to fry, avoir d'autres chats à fouetter 4. *F* to be like a fish out of water, ne pas être dans son élément/être comme un poisson hors de l'eau 5. *F* to drink like a fish, boire* comme un trou 6. *P* (*fresh*) fish (*a*) nouveau, -elle/bleu *m* (*b*) détenue, -ue pour la première fois/nouveau, -elle de la lourde 6. *P* sexe* de la femme/bénitier *m*/nénuphar *m*. (*See* **cold I 5; kettle 2; tin I 4**)

fish² [fɪʃ] *vi F* 1. aller à la pêche/tirer les vers du nez à qn; to fish for compliments, chercher des compliments 2. to fish in troubled waters, pêcher en eau trouble.

fishbowl ['fɪʃbəʊl] *n NAm P* = **fishtank**.

fishtank ['fɪʃtæŋk] *n P* cellule *f* où l'on garde les détenus temporairement. (*See* **tank¹ 2**)

fishy ['fɪʃɪ] *a F* douteux/louche/véreux; it looks a bit fishy, ça ne dit rien de bon/ça n'a pas l'air très catholique.

fist [fɪst] *n P* main*/pogne *f*/paluche *f*. (*See* **hand¹ 2**)

fist-fuck ['fɪst'fʌk] *vtr VV* (*esp homosexual use*) insérer le poing dans l'anus* *ou* le rectum de (son partenaire)/bourrer le cul avec le poing/faire le fist-fucking.

fist-fucker ['fɪst'fʌkə] *n VV* (*esp homosexual use*) homosexuel* qui pratique le fist-fucking/fist-fucker *m*.

fist-fucking ['fɪst'fʌkɪŋ] *n VV* (*esp homosexual use*) fist-fucking *m*.

fistful ['fɪstful] *n NAm P* peine *f* de prison de cinq ans/cinq gerbes *fpl*.

fit¹ [fɪt] I *a F* are you fit? t'es prêt?/tu te sens d'attaque? (*See* **drop² 6; dump¹ 2**) II *n* 1. *F* to have/to throw a fit, piquer une colère*/piquer une crise 2. *F* to have s.o. in fits, faire rire* qn/donner le fou rire à qn 3. *P* fainting fits, (*RS* = *tits*) seins*/nichons *mpl*. (*See* **Bristols; tale 3; threepenny-bits; trey-**

bits) 4. *P* attirail*/artillerie *f* de camé 5. *P* = **fit-up**.

fit² [fɪt] *vtr & i F* that fits/that fits the bill, ça cadre dans le tableau/ça s'explique.

fit-up ['fɪtʌp] *n Br P* complot *m*/coup monté.

fit up ['fɪt'ʌp] *vtr Br P* to fit s.o. up, donner de faux témoignages/monter un coup contre qn/faire porter le bada à qn; **they fitted him up**, il est victime d'un coup monté.

five [faɪv] *n F* 1. repos *m*/pause *f* de cinq minutes; **to take five**, faire la pause/souffler un brin; **take five!** arrêt buffet!/pause-café!/ dételez un peu!/relax(e)! 2. *NAm* (billet* de) cinq dollars *mpl*.

five-finger discount ['faɪv'fɪŋgə-'dɪskaʊnt] *n NAm P* objets/articles volés; (*shoplifting*) vol *m* à l'étalage/achat *m* à la course.

five-O [faɪv'əʊ] *n NAm P* police*/flicaille *f*.

fiver ['faɪvə] *n F* (*a*) cinq livres *fpl* sterling (*b*) billet* de cinq livres *ou NAm* cinq dollars.

fivespot ['faɪvspɒt] *n F* 1. *NAm* billet* de cinq dollars 2. billet* de cinq livres.

fix¹ [fɪks] *n* 1. *P* (*drugs*) (*a*) fixe *m*/piquouse *f*; **to take/give oneself a fix**, se piquer/se faire un shoot/se shooter (*b*) quantité de drogue vendue en paquet/dose *f*/fixe *m*/shoot *m* 2. *F* **my daily fix of caffeine**, ma dose quotidienne de caféine; **she has to have her weekly fix of her favourite television programme**, chaque semaine elle ne manque pas de voir son émission préférée 3. *P* the fix, (*bribe*) pot-de-vin *m*/dessous-de-table *m*; graissage *m* de patte (de la police, etc); **it's a fix**, ça a été truqué/c'est une magouille 4. *F* difficulté *f*/ embêtement *m*; **to be in a fix**, être dans une situation embarrassante; **he's got himself into a real fix**, il est dans un beau pétrin; il s'est mis dans une très sale affaire/dans de sales draps.

fix² [fɪks] I *vtr* 1. *F* (*a*) arranger/mettre en ordre; réparer/rafistoler; **don't worry, I'll fix it**, ne t'en fais pas, je vais m'en occuper/je vais arranger ça; *esp NAm* **fix me a drink!** donne-moi un verre! **how are you fixed moneywise?** (comment) ça va côté argent? (*b*) préparer/décider; *esp NAm* **I'm fixing to go to London**, je compte aller à Londres 2. *P* rendre la pareille à (qn)/régler son compte à (qn); **I'll fix him!** je lui ferai son affaire!/je l'aurai au tournant! 3. *F* soudoyer/suborner (qn); truquer (qch); **the fight was fixed**, le match était truqué II *vi P* s'injecter une drogue/se faire une piquouse/se faire un fixe.

fixed wing [fɪkst'wɪŋ] *n F* avion *m*/coucou *m*.

fixer ['fɪksə] *n P* (*a*) avocat véreux; combinard, -arde (*b*) (*drugs*) revendeur, -euse *m*/trafiquant, -ante (*c*) (*seller of stolen goods*) fourgue *m*.

fixture ['fɪkstʃə] *n F* (*person*) **to be a fixture**, faire partie des meubles; **he's a permanent fixture**, il fait partie du mobilier/du décor.

fizz [fɪz] *n F* champagne *m*/champ *m*.

fizzle ['fɪzl] *n P* échec*/bide *m* (complet).

fizzle out ['fɪzl'aʊt] *vi F* échouer*/ne pas aboutir/finir en queue de poisson/foirer/s'en aller en eau de boudin.

flabbergast ['flæbəgɑːst] *vtr F* abasourdir/ stupéfier; **I was flabbergasted**, j'ai été sidéré/ j'en suis resté baba/j'en suis resté comme deux ronds de flan.

flack [flæk] *n F* = **flak**.

fladge, flage [flædʒ] *n P* (*esp homosexual, sadomasochistic use*) flagellation *f*; **fladge/ flage party**, partie *f* de flagellation.

flag [flæg] *n* 1. *F* **to show the flag**, faire acte de présence 2. *F* **to keep the flag flying**, tenir bon/se défendre 3. *P* **to fly the flag** (*a*) avoir ses règles*/repeindre sa grille en rouge (*b*) être (très) patriote/être chauvin 4. *Austr P* billet* de banque/biffeton *m*.

flag-waver ['flægweɪvə] *n F* patriote exalté(e)/cocardier, -ière/chauvin, -ine.

flag-waving ['flægweɪvɪŋ] *n F* patriotisme *m*/chauvinisme *m*.

flak [flæk] *n F* critique *f*/censure *f* (défavorable); **he had to take a lot of flak from the board**, il a été beaucoup critiqué/il s'est fait allumé par le conseil.

flake [fleɪk] *n* 1. *NAm P* (*drugs*) cocaïne*/ poudrette *f* 2. *NAm P* individu fou*/loufoque *m*/fada *mf* 3. *Austr P* viande *f* de requin; **flake and chips**, requin-frites.

flaked (out) ['fleɪkt('aʊt)] *a F* (*a*) sans connaissance/KO (*surt sous l'effet d'une drogue*) (*b*) très fatigué*/pompé/crevé. (*See* **flakers**)

flake out ['fleɪk'aʊt] *vi F* 1. s'évanouir*/ tourner de l'œil/tomber dans les vapes; perdre connaissance sous l'effet d'une drogue 2. s'endormir/s'enroupiller aussitôt couché.

flakers ['fleɪkəz] *a O P* (**Harry**) **flakers**, très fatigué*/crevé/esquinté/claqué.

flaky ['fleɪkɪ] *a NAm P* fou*/barjot/cinglé/ fada.

flam [flæm] *n F Dial* histoires *fpl*/chiqué *m*/ salades *fpl*.

flame [fleɪm] *n F* an old flame (of hers), une de ses anciennes (conquêtes)/un de ses anciens amoureux. (*See* **shoot down**)

flamer ['fleɪmə] *n NAm P* 1. (*blunder*) gaffe *f*/bourde *f* 2. personne *f* qui fait des gaffes/gaffeur, -euse.

flaming ['fleɪmɪŋ] *a F* (*a*) furax/furibard; a flaming temper, un caractère infernal/un sale caractère; a flaming row, un barouf de tous les diables (*b*) (*Euph for* **bloody**) sacré/fichu/foutu; a flaming idiot, un sacré crétin/le roi des imbéciles; it's a flaming nuisance, c'est sacrément emmerdant/c'est vraiment chiatique; flaming hell! merde alors!

flanker ['flæŋkə] *n P* to do a flanker, jouer un mauvais tour/un tour de cochon.

flannel¹ ['flæn(ə)l] *n F* 1. flatterie *f*/lèche *f* 2. (*empty talk*) verbiage *m*; it was just a load of old flannel, c'était parler pour ne rien dire.

flannel² ['flæn(ə)l] *vtr F* acheter les bonnes grâces de (qn); passer (de) la pommade à (qn).

flap¹ [flæp] *n* 1. *F* affolement *m*/panique *f*; to be in a flap, être dans tous ses états; to get into a flap, paniquer/s'affoler 2. *pl O P* oreilles*/pavillons *mpl*.

flap² [flæp] *vi F* paniquer/s'affoler; stop flapping! (ne) panique pas!

flapdoodle ['flæp'duːdl] *n F* bêtise*/bidon *m*/salades *fpl*.

flapper ['flæpə] *n* 1. *F* (*1920's use*) jeune fille*/gamine *f*/mignonne *f* 2. *P* = **fin 1**. (*See* **flipper**)

flare-up ['fleərʌp] *n F* (*a*) colère bleue (*b*) (*argument, quarrel*) altercation *f*/scène *f* (*c*) bagarre*/grabuge *m*.

flare up ['fleər'ʌp] *vi F* se mettre en colère*/piquer une crise.

flash¹ [flæʃ] I *a F* 1. (*a*) voyant/tapageur; his watch is a bit flash, isn't it? sa montre, c'est un peu tape-à-l'œil, non? *Br* Flash Harry, esbroufeur *m*/m'as-tu-vu/frimeur *m* (*b*) (*glamorous, fashionable*) élégant/chic/nickelé/ridère 2. qui est du milieu/de la pègre II *n* 1. *F* pensée-éclair *f*/idée-éclair *f*/éclair *f* (de génie) 2. *P* exhibition *f* des organes génitaux/des seins 3. *P* argot* des voleurs/argomuche *m* du milieu/jar(s) *m* 4. *P* (*drugs*) sensation *f* de plaisir au moment d'une piqûre/flash *m*. (*See* **rush¹**)

flash² [flæʃ] *vtr & i P* 1. crâner/plastronner/frimer 2. exhiber ses organes génitaux/exhiber ses parties *fpl*/s'exhiber/sortir ses précieuses.

flashback ['flæʃbæk] *n P* (*drugs*) répétition *f* des effets d'une drogue sans nouvelle administration de celle-ci.

flasher ['flæʃə] *n P* exhibitionniste *m*/satyre *m*.

flashy ['flæʃɪ] *a F* voyant/tapageur/tape-à-l'œil/qui jette (du jus).

flat [flæt] I *a F* 1. net/catégorique; that's flat! c'est clair et net!/c'est mon dernier mot!/un point c'est tout! 2. (*penniless*) fauché comme les blés/à sec/raide. (*See* **spin¹ 1**) II *adv F* 1. entièrement/tout à fait/carrément; flat broke, fauché comme les blés/à sec/raide 2. exactement/au poil; in three minutes flat, en trois minutes pile 3. to go flat out, (*at top speed*) aller à fond de train/à pleins gaz/à tout berzingue 4. to fall flat (on its face), (*of joke*) manquer son effet/rater/tomber à plat; (*of play*) faire un four. (*See* **nothing 2**) III *n F* pneu *m* à plat/crevé.

flatfoot ['flætfʊt] *n O F* agent* de police/poulet *m* (*surt en uniforme*).

flatfooted ['flæt'fʊtɪd] *a P* bête*/lourdaud; (*clumsy*) maladroit/empoté.

flathead ['flæthed] *n Austr P* individu *m* bête*/nouille *f*.

flatten ['flætn] *vtr F* 1. (*knock out*) mettre (qn) KO 2. (*humiliate*) écraser (qn)/moucher (qn)/clouer le bec à (qn).

flattener ['flætnə] *n F* coup* d'assommoir/taquet *m*.

flattie, flatty ['flætɪ] *n F* 1. femme* à la poitrine plate/(qui est) plate comme une planche à pain/une planche à repasser 2. *pl* flatties, chaussures *fpl* à talons plats/ballerines *fpl*.

flavour ['fleɪvə] *n F* flavour of the month, chose *f* à la mode; he's not flavour of the month, il n'est pas en odeur de sainteté.

flea [fliː] *n F* to send s.o. away with a flea in his ear, envoyer paître qn/envoyer qn sur les roses.

fleabag ['fliːbæg] *n P* 1. sac *m* de couchage/sac à viande; lit*/sac *m* à puces/pucier *m* 2. personne *f* malpropre/pouilleux, -euse; she's an old fleabag, c'est une vieille cradingue 3. chien*/clebs *m* 4. (*cheap hotel*) hôtel *m* borgne/asile *m* de nuit.

fleabite ['fliːbaɪt] *n F* un rien/une bagatelle/une broutille.

fleabitten ['fliːbɪtn] *a F* sale*/pouilleux/miteux/crassouillard; fleabitten moggy, chat *m* de gouttière/greffier miteux.

flea-house ['fliːhaʊs] *n NAm P* hôtel *m* borgne/asile *m* de nuit/taule miteuse.

flea-market ['fliːmɑːkɪt] *n F* marché *m* aux puces/puces *fpl.*

fleapit ['fliːpɪt] *n F* cinéma miteux; let's go to the local fleapit! si on allait au ciné du quartier?

flea trap ['fliːtræp] *n NAm F* hôtel *m* borgne/asile *m* de nuit.

fleece ['fliːs] *vtr F* estamper/plumer/écorcher (qn); to get fleeced, se faire plumer.

flesh-peddler ['fleʃpedlə] *n F* 1. souteneur*/mangeur *m* de blanc/maquereau *m*/julot *m* 2. prostituée*/raccrocheuse *f*/pute *f*.

flick [flɪk] *n F* (*a*) (*film*) film *m* (*b*) *pl* (*the cinema, films*) cinéma *m*/ciné *m*/cinoche *m*; to go to the flicks, aller au ciné/se payer une toile. (*See* **skinflick**)

flier ['flaɪə] *n F* 1. to take a flier, tomber*/ramasser une bûche/prendre une pelle 2. prospectus *m*. (*See* **high-flier**)

flim-flam[1] ['flɪmflæm] *n F* (*not common*) escroquerie*/filouterie *f*/entubage *m*.

flim-flam[2] ['flɪmflæm] *vtr F* (*not common*) escroquer*/filouter/entuber.

flim-flam man ['flɪmflæm'mæn] *n F* (*not common*) escroc*/filou *m*.

flimsy ['flɪmzɪ] *n* 1. *F* billet* de banque *m*/faffe *m* 2. *Austr* chèque *m*.

fling[1] [flɪŋ] *n Br F* 1. réjouissances*/nouba *f*/bamboche *f*/foire *f*; to have a fling, faire la noce/faire la foire 2. to take a fling, tenter sa chance; to have a fling at sth, tenter le coup/s'essayer la main à qch 3. (*bribe*) pot-de-vin *m*/dessous-de-table *m* 4. liaison amoureuse/chopin *m* (*surt extra-conjugal(e)*); to have a fling, avoir une aventure.

fling[2] [flɪŋ] *vtr Br P* (*bribe*) soudoyer/graisser la patte à (qn).

flip[1] [flɪp] *a* 1. *P* (*flippant*) léger/cavalier; a flip remark, une impertinence/une insolence 2. *F* flip side, (*of record*) revers *m*, face *f* B.

flip[2] [flɪp] *vtr & i* 1. (*also* **flip out**) *P* (*a*) s'emballer; (*drugs*) délirer/flipper; he flipped when he heard the group, il est devenu fou de joie quand il a entendu le groupe (*b*) faire une dépression (nerveuse)/sombrer dans la déprime/flipper 2. *P* to flip one's top/lid/*NAm* noodle/raspberry, se mettre en colère*/piquer une crise/sortir de ses gonds 3. *NAm P* to flip one's lip, bavarder*/jacasser/baver; (*talk nonsense*) dire des bêtises*/dégoiser/radoter.

flipper ['flɪpə] *n NAm P* main*/pince *f*/patte *f*.

flippin(g) ['flɪpɪŋ, -ɪn] *a F* satané/fichu; it's a flippin(g) nuisance, c'est un sacré embêtement; flippin(g) hell! merde alors! what a flippin(g) idiot! quel abruti!/quel crétin!

flit[1] [flɪt] *n* 1. *F* to do a moonlight flit, (*go without paying the rent*) déménager à la cloche de bois 2. *F* (*elopement*) fuite *f* (avec son amant) 3. *NAm P* homosexuel*/pédé *m*.

flit[2] [flɪt] *vi F* 1. = to do a moonlight flit (**flit**[1] 1) 2. (*elope*) s'enfuir* (avec son amant)/se faire enlever.

flivver ['flɪvə] *n Hist P* voiture*/caisse *f*/tacot *m*.

float [fləʊt] *n* 1. tiroir-caisse *m*/caisse *f* 2. (*till money*) encaisse *f*/caisse *f*.

float about, around ['fləʊtə'baʊt, ə'raʊnd] *vi F* there's a rumour floating about (that...), on dit que.../le bruit court que....

floater ['fləʊtə] *n F* 1. ouvrier, -ière itinérant(e) 2. (*cadavre m* d'un(e)) noyé(e)/macchab(ée) *m* 3. étron*/merde *f* qui flotte dans la cuvette 4. *Br* (*a*) saucisse *f* flottant dans de la sauce (*b*) *Austr* pâté *m* en croûte flottant dans de la soupe.

floating ['fləʊtɪŋ] *a F* (*a*) floating on air/on cloud nine, ivre*/dans les vapes (*b*) *O* (*drugs*) high.

flog [flɒg] *vtr* 1. *P* bazarder/refourguer; I flogged it for fifty quid, je l'ai refilé (pour) cinquante livres 2. *F* (*esp idea*) to flog sth to death, rabâcher qch; to flog oneself to death, se crever; he's flogging himself to death, il se tue/se crève au boulot. (*See* **bishop; dong**[1]; **dummy** 5; **horse** 4; **lizard; meat** 3 (*a*))

flogger ['flɒgə] *n Austr P* agent* de police/poulet *m*/keuf *m*.

floor[1] [flɔː] *n* 1. *F* to take the floor (*a*) (*dance*) ouvrir le bal (*b*) (*speech*) prendre la parole 2. *F* to have the floor, (*have the attention*) tenir le crachoir 3. *F* (*driving*) he had his foot on the floor, il appuyait sur le champignon/il mettait le pied au plancher. (*See* **wipe**[2] 1)

floor[2] [flɔː] *vtr F* 1. terrasser (qn)/envoyer (qn) à terre/mettre (qn) KO 2. (*keep quiet*) réduire (qn) au silence; clouer le bec (à qn); (*astonish*) secouer (qn)/laisser (qn) baba; that floored you! ça te l'a coupé!

floosie, floosy, floozie, floozy ['fluːzɪ] *n P* femme* *ou* fille* de mœurs légères/pouffiasse *f*/marie-salope *f*.

flop[1] [flɒp] I *adv F* to go flop = **flop**[2] II *n* 1. *F* (*thing*) échec*/bide *m*; (*person*) raté, -ée; it was a complete flop, c'était le bide complet/un four total 2. *NAm P* (*a*) asile *m* de nuit (*b*) lit*/bâche *f.* (*See* **bellyflop**)

flop² ['flɒp] *vi F* 1. échouer*/faire faillite/
ramasser une pelle; **his film flopped,** son film
a fait un four/un flop 2. (*also* **flop out**)
s'affaisser/s'affaler; **to be ready to flop,** être
fatigué*/claqué/crevé. (*See* **mop**)

flophouse ['flɒphaʊs] *n P* (*dormitory for
vagrants*) asile *m* de nuit/piaule *f* à clodos/
repaire *m* de pouilleux.

floral ['flɔːrəl] *a P* **floral arrangement** =
daisy chain (**daisy 5**).

flounder ['flaʊndə] *n P* **flounder (and dab),**
(*RS = (taxi)cab*) taxi*/rongeur *m*/tac(mard)
m.

flower ['flaʊə] *n* 1. *Hist F* (*late 1960s*) **flower
children/people,** enfants-fleur *mpl*/hippies
mpl; **flower power,** pouvoir *m* des fleurs/
flower power *m* 2. *V* sexe* de la femme/
bégonia *m*. (*See* **wallflower**)

flowery (dell) ['flaʊ(ə)rɪ('del)] *n P* (*RS =
(prison) cell*) cellule *f*/bloc *m*/trou *m*.

flu [fluː] *n F* (= *influenza*) **he's got (the) flu,** il
a la grippe/la crève.

flue [fluː] *n* 1. *V* anus*/pot *m*; **you can stick it
up your flue,** tu peux te le mettre quelque part
2. *P* (*RS = screw*) gardien* de prison/
maton(ne) *m(f)*/gaffe *m*/matuche *m* 3. *F* **up
the flue,** raté/fichu/foutu.

fluence ['fluːəns] *n F* **to put the fluence on**
s.o., persuader qn; hypnotiser qn.

fluff¹ [flʌf] *n* 1. *F* jeune femme*/mousmé(e)
f/gonzesse *f*/nénette *f*/nana *f*; **she's a nice bit
of fluff,** elle est bien roulée/c'est un beau petit
lot/c'est un morceau de choix 2. *F* (*mistake in
pronunciation*) cuir *m*/pataquès *m* 3. *F* (*theatre*) raté *m*.

fluff² [flʌf] I *vtr F* 1. (*theatre*) rater/louper
(son entrée) 2. saboter/bousiller/louper; I
fluffed it, j'ai raté mon coup II *vi Br P* (*Euph
for* **fuck**) **fluff off!** = **fuck off.**

fluke [fluːk] *n F* coup *m* de chance*/veine *f*/
bol *m*/pot *m*; **it was (a) sheer fluke,** c'était un
coup de veine extraordinaire.

fluky ['fluːkɪ] *a F* **fluky shot,** coup heureux;
he won a fluky victory, il a gagné par un
hasard extraordinaire.

flummery ['flʌmərɪ] *n F* bêtises*/balivernes
fpl/blagues *fpl*/sornettes *fpl*.

flummox ['flʌməks] *vtr F* démonter/
éberluer (qn); couper la chique à (qn); I **was
completely flummoxed by his directions,**
après ses explications, j'étais totalement dans
le brouillard.

flunk [flʌŋk] *vtr & i NAm F* 1. se dérober/se

défiler/tirer au flanc 2. se faire recaler/coller/
étendre à un examen; **he flunked high school,**
(*failed final exams*) il a été collé au bac/il a
raté son bac; (*abandoned his studies*) il a
abandonné/laissé tomber ses études.

flunk out ['flʌŋk'aʊt] *vi NAm F* **to flunk out
of high school,** (*fail final exams*) rater son
bac; (*abandon one's studies*) abandonner/
laisser tomber ses études.

flush¹ [flʌʃ] *a F* riche*/plein aux as; **I'm feeling a bit flush today,** j'ai plein de fric/je suis à
l'aise aujourd'hui.

flush² [flʌʃ] *vi P* (*drugs*) faire monter du
sang dans la seringue pour le mélanger à la
drogue avant une piqûre.

flutter ['flʌtə] *n F* 1. **to be all of a flutter,**
être tout chose/être dans tous ses états 2. **to
have a flutter on the gee-gees,** jouer aux
courtines/risquer qch sur les chevaux. (*See*
gee-gee 2; ring¹ 1)

fly¹ [flaɪ] I *a* 1. *F* malin*/rusé/futé/roublard 2.
NAm P élégant/qui a du chic/ridère II *n F* 1.
there are no flies on him, c'est un malin/il
n'est pas né d'hier/il n'est pas tombé de la
dernière pluie 2. (*sing or pl*) braguette *f*; **your
flies are undone,** ta braguette est ouverte 3.
there's a fly in the ointment, (*a problem*) il y
a un cheveu/un hic 4. *Austr* **to have a fly at
sth,** faire un essai/tenter le coup. (*See* **bar-
fly**)

fly² [flaɪ] *vi* 1. (*a*) *F* **to fly high,** voler/viser
haut (*b*) *P* (*drugs*) **flying high,** camé/planant/
high/envapé 2. *P* **to let fly,** (*swear*) lâcher une
volée/une bordée d'injures; (*spit*) cracher*/
glavioter; **to let fly (at s.o.),** (*hit out*) donner
un coup*/balancer un gnon à qn. (*See* **flag 3;
fur; handle 1; kite¹ 2**)

flyboy ['flaɪbɔɪ] *n P* malin* *m*/dégourdi *m*.

fly-by-night ['flaɪbaɪnaɪt, 'flaɪbənaɪt] I *a F*
(*person*) léger/pas sérieux; (*company, etc*)
véreux II *n F* 1. déménageur *m* à la cloche
de bois 2. noctambule *mf*/oiseau *m* de nuit.

fly-cop ['flaɪkɒp] *n P* détective *m*/fileur *m*.

flying eye ['flaɪŋ'aɪ] *n F* hélicoptère *m* qui
survole une ville et donne des renseignements
sur la circulation à une station de radio.

Flynn [flɪn] *Prn see* **in II 3**.

fly-pitch ['flaɪpɪtʃ] *vi O F* vendre à la
sauvette/cameloter.

fly-pitcher ['flaɪpɪtʃə] *n O F* vendeur *m* à la
sauvette/camelot *m*.

fly-pitching ['flaɪpɪtʃɪŋ] *n O F* vente *f* à la
sauvette.

fob [fɒb] *vtr A P* duper*/rouler.

fob off ['fɒb'ɒf] *vtr F* to fob sth off on s.o./to fob s.o. off with sth, refiler qch à qn; to get fobbed off with sth, se faire refiler qch.

fodder ['fɒdə] *n Br F* nourriture*/bouffe *f*.

fog [fɒg] *n F* to be in a fog, être dans le brouillard/ne plus savoir où on en est/être paumé.

fogey ['fəʊgɪ] *n F* (old) fogey, vieille baderne/croulant, -ante/périmé *m*/vieux schnoque; young fogey, ringard, -arde.

foggiest ['fɒgɪst] *a & n F* I haven't the foggiest (idea), je n'en ai pas la moindre idée; not the foggiest! aucune idée!

fog up ['fɒg'ʌp] *vtr F* brouiller (les cartes)/ embrouiller.

fogy ['fəʊgɪ] *n F* = **fogey**.

fold [fəʊld] *vi F* (of company, project, etc) échouer*/faire faillite/tomber à l'eau.

folding ['fəʊldɪŋ] *a P* (the) folding stuff, billets *mpl* de banque/talbins *mpl*.

folks [fəʊks] *npl F* 1. the (old) folks, les parents*/les vieux/les dabes *mpl*; my folks, mes viocs *mpl* 2. hi, folks! salut tout le monde!/salut la compagnie!

folksy ['fəʊksɪ] *a F* (a) la bonne franquette/ sans prétentions/sans chichis (b) sociable/ populaire/sympa.

foodie ['fuːdɪ] *n F* fana *mf* de bouffe; (gourmet) fana de cuisine/bec fin.

fooey! ['fuːɪ] *excl O F* la barbe!/flûte alors! (See **phooey!**)

fool[1] [fuːl] I *a F* bête*/idiot/ridicule. (See **damfool** I) II *n F* stupid fool! espèce d'idiot!/espèce d'imbécile! bloody fool! espèce de con! to play/to act the fool, faire l'idiot/ faire le con.

fool[2] [fuːl] *vtr & i F* 1. faire des bêtises*/des conneries; faire l'idiot/faire l'imbécile 2. to fool s.o., (make fun of) se payer la tête de qn; (cheat) escroquer* qn/empiler qn.

fool about, around ['fuːlə'baʊt, ə'raʊnd] I *vi F* 1. flâner/traînasser/glander/ glandouiller 2. to fool about/around with s.o., flirter/faire des avances à qn; (also NAm to fool around) (commit sexual indiscretion, esp adultery) avoir une liaison/une aventure avec qn II *vtr F* (tease, annoy) taquiner/asticoter/ faire enrager (qn); (make fun of) se payer la tête de (qn).

foot[1] [fʊt] *n F* 1. my foot! mon œil!/et ta sœur! 2. to fall on one's feet, avoir de la chance/du pot; retomber sur ses pattes 3. to find one's feet, voler de ses propres ailes/se dépatouiller 4. to have one foot in the grave,

avoir un pied dans la tombe 5. to put one's foot down, faire acte d'autorité/ne pas se laisser faire; (drive fast) mettre le pied au plancher 6. to put one's best foot forward, allonger/presser le pas; (do one's best) faire de son mieux 7. to put one's foot in it, mettre les pieds dans le plat; he's always putting his foot in it! il n'en rate pas une! 8. to put one's feet up, se reposer/se relaxer/se poser 9. to be carried out feet first, mourir*/s'en aller les pieds devant 10. to be dead on one's feet, être très fatigué*/être à plat 11. to get off/to start off on the wrong foot, être mal parti. (See **cold** I 4; **drag**[2]; **flatfoot**; **pussyfoot**[1]; **six** 1; **sweep**[2] 1; **tanglefoot**)

foot[2] [fʊt] *vtr F* 1. to foot the bill, payer* la note/payer la douloureuse/casquer 2. to foot it, marcher*/aller à pattes/arquer. (See **hotfoot**; **pussyfoot**[2])

football ['fʊtbɔːl] *n P* (drugs) 0,5 grammes d'un narcotique.

footer ['fʊtə], **footie** ['fʊtɪ] *n F* football *m*; let's have a game of footer/footie, allons jouer au foot/taquiner le ballon.

footle about ['fuːtlə'baʊt] *vi F* 1. traînasser/flemmarder/glander 2. faire des bêtises*/des conneries.

footling ['fuːtlɪŋ] *a F* futile/insignifiant; mesquin.

footsie, footsy ['fʊtsɪ] *n F* to play footsie/ footsy with s.o., faire du pied à qn. (See **kneesies**)

foot-slog ['fʊtslɒg] *vi F* marcher* péniblement/arquer/piler du poivre.

foot-slogger ['fʊtslɒgə] *n F* marcheur, -euse/pousse-cailloux *m*.

for [fɔː] *prep F* (a) (in favour of) to be (all) for sth, être tout à fait pour qch; I'm all for it, je suis tout à fait pour/j'en suis très partisan (b) to be (in) for it, être bon pour...; you're for it! ton compte est bon! (See **free** (a); **real** I 1; **what-for**)

force [fɔːs] *n F* (abbr of police force) the force, la police/la rousse; then the force arrived, et puis les flics se sont ramenés.

fork [fɔːk] *n A P* (a) main*/grappin *m*/louche *f* (b) *pl* doigts*/la fourchette du père Adam.

fork out, up ['fɔːk'aʊt, 'ʌp] *vi F* payer*/ casquer/cracher (au bassinet); (large sum) les allonger.

form [fɔːm] *n F* 1. to know the form, savoir ce qu'il faut faire 2. casier *m* judiciaire/ casier/pedigree *m*; has he got any form? est-ce qu'il a un passé? 3. to be off form, ne pas

tenir la forme/ne pas avoir la frite/ne pas
avoir la pêche.

fort [fɔːt] *n F* to hold the fort, garder la
baraque/tenir la position.

forty ['fɔːtɪ] *num a F* to have forty winks,
dormir*/faire un petit somme/piquer un
roupillon.

forty-four ['fɔːtɪ'fɔː] *n P* (*CB*) salut!/
bises!/bye!

fossick ['fɒsɪk] *vi esp Austr F* fureter/
fouiller/farfouiller.

fossicking ['fɒsɪkɪŋ] *n esp Austr F* furetage
m.

fossil ['fɒsɪl] *n F* (*old person*) fossile *m*/
croulant, -ante/vieux schnock; you old fossil!
(espèce de) vieux birbe!

foul [faʊl] *a F* dégueulasse/dégoûtant/infect;
what a foul dump! quel merdier!/quel gourbi!

foul up ['faʊl'ʌp] *vtr F* bousiller/saloper;
that's really fouled everything up, ça a tout
fichu/foutu en l'air. (*See* **snafu**[1,2])

four-by-two ['fɔː'baɪ'tuː] *n P* (*RS = Jew*)
Pej Juif*/feuj *mf.*

four-eyes ['fɔːraɪz] *n P* qn qui porte des
lunettes*/binoclard, -arde/quat'z'yeux *mf.*

four-flusher ['fɔː'flʌʃə] *n P* tricheur *m*/
arnaqueur *m.*

four-letter ['fɔːletə] *a F* four-letter word,
les cinq lettres/le mot de Cambronne (=
merde)/gros mot/mot de cinq lettres; P
four-letterman, (= **shit**) individu*
méprisable/salaud*/salopard *m;* (= **homo**)
homosexuel*/homo *m.*

four-ten ['fɔːten] *n P* (*CB*) (= *10-4*) je
reçois.

fox[1] [fɒks] *n P* (*also CB*) belle femme*/fille*;
beau petit lot/chouette nana; bel homme*/
beau mec/mec qui jette du jus.

fox[2] [fɒks] *vtr F* (*a*) duper*/avoir/rouler (qn)
(*b*) rendre perplexe/mystifier (qn).

foxy ['fɒksɪ] *a P* (*also CB*) foxy lady, belle
femme*/fille; beau petit lot/prix *m* de Diane/
beau morceau; fille bien balancée/bien roulée.

frag [fræg] *vtr NAm P Mil* tuer*/assassiner
(*surt* un compagnon d'armes *ou* un supérieur)
à la grenade (à fragmentation) défensive/
descendre (qn) dans le dos à la grenade.

fragging ['frægɪŋ] *n NAm P Mil* meurtre
déguisé (*surt* d'un compagnon d'armes *ou*
d'un supérieur) à la grenade (à
fragmentation) défensive.

fraidy-cat ['freɪdɪkæt] *n esp NAm F* (*esp
child's word*) to be a fraidy-cat, être lâche/
avoir peur*/avoir la pétoche. (*See* **scaredy-
cat**)

frail [freɪl] *n NAm O P* femme*/nana *f*/
gonzesse *f.*

frame[1] [freɪm] *n P* 1. (*rare, homosexual use*)
hétérosexuel *m* qui plaît aux homosexuels.
(*See* **bait**) 2. (*police jargon*) in the frame,
identifié comme suspect dans un crime.

frame[2] [freɪm] *vtr F* to frame s.o., farguer
qn/faire porter le bada à qn/monter un coup
contre qn; to be framed, être victime d'un
coup monté; I've been framed, c'est un coup
monté contre moi.

frame[3], **frame-up** [freɪm, 'freɪmʌp] *n F*
complot *m*/machination *f*/coup monté. (*See*
fit-up; setup 3)

frat[1] [fræt] *n F* 1. (= *fraternity*) association
f/confrérie *f* d'étudiants 2. *Br* (*schools*) (=
fart) pet*/perle *f.*

frat[2] [fræt] *vi F* 1. fraterniser 2. *Br* (*schools*)
(= **fart**) péter*/lâcher une perle.

frazzle ['fræzl] *n F* 1. to be done to a frazzle,
être trop cuit/être carbonisé/être cramé 2. to
be worn to a frazzle, être très fatigué/à plat/à
bout 3. to beat s.o. to a frazzle, battre qn à
plate(s) couture(s).

freak [friːk] *n* 1. *F* drôle *m* de numéro/
original, -ale/phénomène *m* 2. *P* fervent *m*/
fana *mf*/branché *m*/mordu, -ue; jazz freak,
fana de jazz 3. *P* hippie *mf*/hippy *mf*/freak *m*/
marjo *mf* 4. *P* utilisateur, -trice de drogue/
camé, -ée. (*See* **acid 2**)

freak-out, **freakout** ['friːkaʊt] *n P* 1.
(*drugs*) mauvais trip 2. (*bout of wild
abandon, etc*) boum *f*/surboum *f*/partie *f.*

freak out ['friːkaʊt] *P* I *vi* 1. se
dévergonder/se débaucher 2. (*dance with
abandon*) s'éclater; to freak out to the music,
s'éclater sur la musique 3. devenir fou*/
perdre les pédales/être déboussolé 4. (*drugs*)
perdre tout contrôle mental sous l'effet d'un
hallucinogène/flipper/se défoncer 5. (*be
shocked, scared*) paniquer; (*become angry*)
se mettre en colère*/sortir de ses gonds II *vtr*
(*shock, scare*) bouleverser/faire flipper (qn);
(*mentally unbalance*) rendre (qn) fou*.

freaky ['friːkɪ] *a F* 1. bizarre/saugrenu 2.
(*outstanding*) super/chouette.

Freddy ['fredɪ] *n P* (*drugs*) comprimé *m*
d'éphédrine/Freddie *m.*

free [friː] *a F* (*a*) for free, gratuitement/
gratis/à l'œil/pour pas un rond (*b*) feel free!
je t'en prie!/vas-y!/te gêne pas!/sers-toi! (*See*
show[1] **1**)

freebase ['friːbeɪs] *vi P* (*drugs*) fumer de la

cocaïne* purifiée/fumer du crack. (*See* **base 4**)

freebie ['friːbɪ] *n P esp Journ* (*a*) cadeau *m*; freebie trip, reportage *m* grand luxe (*b*) *pl* freebies, à-côtés *mpl*/bénefs *mpl*/gratte *f*.

free-for-all ['friːfərɔːl] *n F* (*fight, brawl*) mêlée générale/barouf *m*/corrida *f*/castagne *f*.

freeload ['friːləʊd] *vi esp NAm P* parasiter/vivre aux crochets de qn.

freeloader ['friːləʊdə] *n esp NAm P* parasite *mf*/pique-assiette *mf*/tapeur, -euse.

freeloading ['friːləʊdɪŋ] *n esp NAm P* le fait de boire/de manger/de vivre aux frais *ou* aux dépens d'autrui; vie *f* de pique-assiette.

free-wheeling ['friː'wiːlɪŋ] *a F* 1. qui dépense* sans compter/qui jette de l'argent par les fenêtres 2. sans contrainte/sans gêne/en roue libre.

freeze[1] [friːz] *n P* to put the freeze on s.o., snober qn/faire la gueule à qn. (*See* **deep I 2**)

freeze[2] [friːz] *vi F* 1. (*a*) avoir peur*/avoir le sang qui gèle (*b*) être figé sur place/se figer 2. it's freezing cold, ça caille. (*See* **balls**[1] **4**)

freeze out ['friːz'aʊt] *vtr esp NAm F* (*a*) mettre en quarantaine/boycotter (*b*) supplanter (un rival)/évincer (qn).

freeze-up ['friːzʌp] *n F* gel *m* à pierre fendre; the big freeze-up of '76, le grand hiver de '76.

French[1] [frentʃ] I *a* 1. *F* French kiss, baiser* profond sur la bouche/patin *m*/roulée *f*; to give s.o. a French kiss, faire une langue à qn/rouler un patin à qn/rouler une saucisse à qn 2. *F* French letter/*NAm* French safe, capote anglaise/imperméable *m* à Popaul 3. *F* to take French leave, filer à l'anglaise 4. *V* the French way, fellation*; cunnilinctus*; to do it the French way, (*fellatio*) tailler une pipe/faire un pompier à qn; (*cunnilingus*) brouter le cresson/lécher la chatte II *n F* that bloody ...—pardon/'scuse my French! ce sacré... passez-moi l'expression!

french[2] [frentʃ] *vtr & i* 1. *V* faire une fellation* à (qn)/tailler une pipe à (qn); pratiquer le cunnilinctus*/brouter le cresson 2. *F* faire une langue (fourrée) à (qn)/rouler un patin à (qn).

frenchie, frenchy ['frentʃɪ] *n P* = French letter (**French**[1] I 2).

fresh [freʃ] I *a F* 1. *O* légèrement ivre*/éméché/paf 2. (*a*) effronté/culotté; don't get fresh with me! ne la ramène pas avec moi! (*b*) flirteur/coureur/dragueur; he got fresh

with me, il a essayé de me draguer 3. *NAm* excellent*/canon/de première; a really fresh ball game, un match de base-ball de première. (*See* **air 3**) II *adv F* to be fresh out of sth, être complètement en rupture de qch.

fresher ['freʃə] *n F* étudiant, -ante de première année/bizut *m*.

friar ['fraɪə] *n Br P* 1. holy friar, (*RS = liar*) menteur, -euse 2. Friar Tuck, (*RS = fuck*) coït*/baise *f*.

frig [frɪg] *vtr & i* 1. *V* faire l'amour* (avec qn)/baiser/niquer; frig off! fous(-moi) le camp!/va te faire foutre!/va te faire enculer! 2. *V* se masturber*/se branler.

frigging ['frɪgɪŋ] I *a P* (*Euph for* **fucking**) sacré/fichu/foutu; that frigging idiot! ce foutu imbécile!/ce connard!/cet espèce d'enfoiré! it's a frigging nuisance, c'est vachement chiant; frigging hell! putain!/bordel (de merde)! II *n* 1. *V* coït*/baise *f* 2. *V* masturbation*/branlette *f*.

fright [fraɪt] *n F* individu laid*/mocheté *f*/trumeau *m*; you look a fright! t'as l'air dégueulasse!

frighteners ['fraɪtnəz] *npl Br F* to put the frighteners on s.o., (*menace, intimidate*) menacer qn/faire les gros bras à qn.

frightful ['fraɪtfʊl] *a F* affreux/effroyable; a frightful bore, un casse-pieds.

frill [frɪl] *n* 1. *NAm P* jeune fille*/jeune femme*/mousmé *f*/gisquette *f* 2. *F* without any/no frills, sans façons/sans chichis.

frippet ['frɪpɪt] *n O F* femme*/nana *f*.

frisk [frɪsk] *vtr F* fouiller (un suspect, etc).

fritz [frɪts] *n NAm F* on the fritz = on the blink (**blink**).

Fritz [frɪts] *Prn P* (*esp WWII*) Allemand*/fritz *m*/fridolin *m*/frisé *m*.

frog[1] [frɒg] *n Br P* frog (and toad), (*RS = road*) route*/rue *f*/strasse *f*.

Frog[2] [frɒg], **Froggie, Froggy** ['frɒgɪ] *a & n P* Français(, -aise)/Fran(s)quillon, -onne.

front [frʌnt] I *a F* 1. front runner, candidat, -ate en tête/la tête de liste/coureur, -euse de tête 2. front man, homme* de paille; (*drugs, etc*) intermédiaire *m*/agent *m* 3. to have a front seat, être aux premières loges II *n F* 1. activité *ou* individu* qui sert à cacher des activités illicites/couverture *f*/façade *f*/parapluie *m*; paravent *m*/homme* de paille 2. *Br* (*cheek, effrontery*) effronterie *f*/culot *m*/toupet *m* 3. to put on a front, faire le prétentieux*/crâner/faire de l'esbroufe/frimer 4. to put on a bold front, faire bonne contenance/faire bonne figure/réagir avec panache 5. *Br* the front, la grand-rue/la rue principale.

front out ['frʌnt'aʊt] *vi Br P* 1. affronter (qn) avec courage *ou* en faisant du bluff 2. (*also* front off/it) se comporter d'une manière agressive.

frost¹ [frɒst] *n F* 1. (*rare*) échec*/four *m*/bide *m*/fiasc *m* 2. *NAm* rebuffade *f*.

frost² [frɒst] *vtr NAm F* 1. snober (qn) 2. mettre (qn) en colère*/en rogne.

frowst [fraʊst] *n F* renfermé *m*/odeur *f* de renfermé.

frowsty ['fraʊstɪ] *a F* qui sent le renfermé.

fruit [fru:t] *n* 1. *F* hello, old fruit! salut, mon pote!/salut, vieille branche! 2. *esp NAm P* homosexuel*/pédé *m*; **frozen fruit**, homosexuel* frigide; **fruit fly**, *NAm* homosexuel*/pédé *m*; *NAm & Br* (*woman*) femme* qui recherche la compagnie des homosexuels*; **fruit picker**, hétérosexuel *m* qui, de temps en temps, fait l'amour* avec des homosexuels* 3. *F* = **fruitcake 2**.

fruit-basket ['fru:tbɑːskɪt] *n V* sexe* de la femme*/boîte *f* à ouvrage/bonbon *m*; to have one's fingers in the fruit-basket, mettre la main au panier.

fruitcake ['fru:tkeɪk] *n* 1. *NAm P* homosexuel*/pédé *m* 2. *F* individu* excentrique *ou* fou*/cinglé, -ée/dingo *mf*; nutty as a fruitcake, complètement dingue.

fruit-salad ['fru:t'sæləd] *n* 1. *F* rangée *f* de médailles et décorations/batterie *f* de cuisine/ bananes *fpl* 2. *P* (*drugs*) mélange *m* de plusieurs drogues; = cocktail *m*.

fruity ['fru:tɪ] *a* 1. *F* (*voice*) de gorge/ moelleux 2. *F* salace/pimenté/corsé; a fruity joke, blague *f* un peu raide/un peu salée 3. *P* excité/allumé; he was feeling fruity, il bandait/il avait la trique 4. *NAm* excentrique/ bizarre.

fruity-pie ['fru:tɪpaɪ] *n P* listen, fruity-pie! écoute, mon bonhomme/mon pote!

fry [fraɪ] *vtr NAm F* 1. électrocuter (qn) (sur la chaise)/griller (qn)/faire rôtir (qn) 2. punir; he got fried, on lui a passé un savon/on lui a secoué les puces 3. (*Black Slang*) to fry one's hair, se défriser les cheveux. (*See* fish¹ 3)

FTA! ['efti:'eɪ] *excl NAm V* (*abbr of Fuck the Army*) à bas l'Armée!/aux chiottes l'Armée!

fuck¹ [fʌk] *n V* 1. coït*/baise *f*/nique *f*/ tringlage *m*; a good fuck un bon coup/une sa-

crée baise; (*person*) une sacrée baiseuse/un sacré baiseur; a quick fuck, un coup rapide 2. I don't give a fuck, je m'en fous (et m'en contrefous)/j'en ai rien à branler; who gives a fuck! on s'en fout!/rien à branler! 3. what the fuck! qu'est-ce que c'est que cette connerie? what the fuck is going on? qu'est-ce que c'est que ce bordel? 4. get the fuck out of here! casse-toi rapide!/fous le camp! 5. how the fuck did you do that? comment tu as fait ça, bordel? how the fuck should I know? j'en sais rien, moi, merde!/qu'est-ce que tu veux que j'en sache, moi, merde? 6. like fuck! et mon cul!/tiens, mes deux! 7. (*fool*) crétin, -ine/con *m*, conne *f*; you dumb fuck, you've been had! pauvre con, tu t'es fait avoir! 8. *NAm* fuck film, film *m* porno/porno *m*/film de cul. (*See* finger-fuck¹; honey-fuck(ing)).

fuck² [fʌk] *vtr V* 1. faire l'amour* avec (qn)/ baiser (qn)/niquer (qn)/tringler (qn)/enfiler (qn); he'd fuck anything on two legs/with a hole in it, il baiserait n'importe quelle pouffiasse/tout lui est bon pour piner/il s'enverrait même une chèvre 2. fuck me! mon cul!/merde alors! fuck you!/go fuck yourself! va te faire enculer! fuck it! (*damn it!*) merde alors!/et merde! (*that's enough!*) c'est marre!/y en a ras le cul! 3. (I'm) fucked if I know, je n'en sais foutre rien 4. fuck a duck! putain de nom de Dieu!/bordel de merde! 5. it's really fucked! c'est complètement bousillé/naze! (*See* fucked-up) 6. (*tired*) I feel fucked, je suis crevé/vanné 7. *esp NAm* escroquer*/rouler/ carotter; I got fucked by that shopkeeper, j'ai été baisé par ce vendeur/je me suis fait baiser en beauté par ce vendeur. (*See* finger-fuck²; fist-fuck; mind-fuck)

fuckable ['fʌkəbl] *a V* bon(ne) à baiser/ baisable/(pinocu)mettable.

fuck about, around ['fʌkə'baʊt, ə'raʊnd] *vi V* 1. to fuck about/around, traîner (son cul)/traînasser/glandouiller 2. to fuck s.o. about/around, emmerder qn; he's always fucking me about/around, il est toujours en train de me faire chier 3. déconner; to fuck about/around with sth, tripatouiller qch; stop fucking about/around! arrête de déconner!/ fais pas le con!

fuck-all ['fʌk'ɔːl] *n Br V* rien*/que dalle/ peau de balle/des prunes; we get fuck-all out of that, on peut rien en tirer de ce merdier; there's fuck-all to drink here, y'a rien à siffler/avaler dans cette baraque de merde.

(*See* **f.a.**; **sweet 4**)

fuck arse ['fʌkɑːs], *NAm* **fuck ass** ['fʌkæs] *n V* (petit) con, (petite) conne/connard, -arde; merdeux, -euse/ordure *f*.

fucked-up [fʌkt'ʌp] *a V* 1. (*situation*) bordélique; (*thing*) bousillé/naze 2. (*person*) traumatisé/perturbé; (*by drugs or drink*) flippé.

fucker ['fʌkə] *n V* 1. baiseur, -euse 2. (*a*) salaud*/saligaud *m*/trouduc *m* (*b*) **you silly fucker!** espèce de connard/d'enculé/d'enfoiré! (*See* **fist-fucker**)

fuckhead ['fʌkhed] *n V* crétin, -ine/con *m*, conne *f*.

fucking ['fʌkɪŋ] *V I a* 1. sacré/foutu; **it's a fucking nuisance**, c'est vraiment chiant/emmerdant; **he's a fucking cunt/bastard**, (c'est un) espèce de salaud/d'enflure/d'enculé! **you fucking idiot!** (espèce de) connard!/quel crétin!/(espèce d')enculé! **this fucking job is a real pain!** ce putain de boulot/ce job à la con me fout la chiasse!/m'emmerde à crever! **I'll knock your fucking head off!** je vais te rectifier le portrait! 2. **fucking hell!** bordel de Dieu!/bordel de merde! *II adv* a **fucking awful film**, un sacré navet/une vraie connerie de film; **fucking dreadful weather**, saloperie *f*/saleté *f* de temps; une pourriture de temps; **we had a fucking amazing time/a fucking ace time**, on s'en est payé une bonne tranche; *NAm* **fucking A!** c'est vrai!/(je suis) d'accord!/banco!/je marche! *III n V* coït*/baisage *m*/baise *f*. (*See* **fist-fucking**; **honey-fuck(ing)**)

fuck off ['fʌk'ɒf] *vi V* 1. s'enfuir*/mettre les bouts/se tirer; **I'll just fuck off then**, allez, je me casse/barre; **tell him to fuck off**, dis-lui de se barrer/se calter; **fuck off!** va te faire foutre! 2. (*rare*) se masturber*/se branler (la colonne) 3. *NAm* (*not common*) faire le con/déconner.

fuck over ['fʌk'əuvə] *vtr V* (*a*) (*of police*) fouiller (qn); chambouler/bordéliser/retourner; **the cops fucked the place over**, les flics y ont foutu le merdier/mis le bordel (*b*) **to fuck s.o. over**, faire qn/emmerder qn.

fuckpig ['fʌkpɪg] *n Br V* salaud*/crapule *f*/connard, -arde.

fuck up ['fʌk'ʌp] *vtr V* saloper/cochonner/bousiller; foutre la merde/le merdier/le bordel dans (qch); foutre (qch) en l'air; **to fuck s.o. up**, emmerder qn/faire chier qn; **he fucked it up**, il y a foutu le merdier/le bordel. (*See* **snafu**)

fuck-up ['fʌkʌp] *n V* 1. (*disastrous situation*) bordel *m*/merdier *m*; (*blunder, mistake*) couille *f* 2. (*emotionally disturbed person*) individu* perturbé.

fuckwit ['fʌkwɪt] *n Austr V* crétin, -ine/andouille *f*/con *m*, conne *f*.

fuddy-duddy ['fʌdɪdʌdɪ] *n F* vieux croulant, vieille croulante/périmé *m*.

fudge¹ [fʌdʒ] *vtr & i F* mentir*/raconter des bobards *mpl*/des craques *fpl*.

fudge!² [fʌdʒ] *excl* (*Euph for* **fuck**) zut!

fug [fʌg] *n F* forte odeur de renfermé; **what a fug in here!** ça schlingue ici!

full [fʊl] *a P* 1. *Austr* **full** (**as a boot/as a bull's bum**), ivre*/plein (comme une bourrique)/rond 2. intoxiqué par la drogue/chargé/bourré. (*See* **chock-full**)

fun [fʌn] *I a F* marrant/rigolo; **it's the fun thing to do**, c'est ce qu'il y a de plus marrant/c'est la chose à faire; **he's a fun person**, il est rigolo, lui; c'est un marrant/c'est pas un triste *II n F* 1. **like fun**, pas du tout; **did you enjoy yourself? like fun I did!** tu t'es bien amusé? tu parles! 2. **I had fun (and games) getting the car going this morning**, (*difficulty*) j'ai eu du mal/un mal de chien à la faire démarrer ce matin, la bagnole; **there'll be fun and games if we don't get a rise this year**, (*trouble*) ça va barder/il y aura du grabuge si on n'est pas augmentés cette année; *Euph* **to have fun and games with one's secretary**, s'amuser avec sa secrétaire/s'envoyer la secrétaire en douce.

funds [fʌndz] *npl F* argent*/pèze *f*/pognon *m*.

funeral ['fjuːnərəl] *n F* **that's your funeral**, c'est ton affaire/ton problème; **it's not my funeral!** ça ne me regarde pas/c'est pas mes oignons.

fungus ['fʌŋgəs] *n P* (*esp schools*) 1. (*a*) (face) **fungus**, barbe*/moustaches*/poils *mpl* au menton (*b*) **fungus face/features**, barbu *m*; moustachu *m* 2. (*very ugly person*) mocheté *f*/trumeau *m*.

funk [fʌŋk] *n F* 1. *Br* peur*/frousse *f*/trac *m*/trouille *f*; **to be in funk/in a blue funk**, avoir une peur* bleue/avoir la frousse/avoir la trouille. (*See* **acid 2**) 2. *Mus* funk *m* 3. *NAm* mauvaise odeur émise par qn/puanteur *f*.

funky ['fʌŋkɪ] *a F* 1. froussard/trouillard 2. *Mus* funky 3. *NAm* qui sent mauvais/puant/foisonnant.

funny ['fʌnɪ] *I a* 1. *F* **don't (try to) be funny!** c'est pas le moment de plaisanter!/fais pas l'imbécile!/fais pas le con! 2. *F* **funny business**, affaire *f* louche/fricotage *m*; **no funny**

business!/none of your funny tricks! pas
d'histoires, hein!/pas de blagues! 3. *F (ill)* to
feel funny, se sentir tout chose; I came over
all funny, ça m'a fait tout drôle 4. *P* funny
farm/*esp NAm* funny house, asile *m*
(d'aliénés)/maison *f* de fous 5. *P* funny
money, *(counterfeit)* fausse monnaie/faux
billet; *(low denominations)* pièces *fpl* de
petite valeur/mitraille *f*; *(foreign currency)*
devises étrangères; *(enormous wealth)*
énorme fortune *f*/pelote *f* II *n F* 1.
plaisanterie *f*/blague *f*; to make a funny,
plaisanter/blaguer 2. *pl esp NAm* funnies,
(comic strips) bandes dessinées/bédés *fpl*;
(animated cartoons) dessins animés.

fur [fɜː] *n F* to make the fur fly, *(fight)* se battre* avec acharnement/comme des chiffon-
niers; *(quarrel)* se quereller* avec fracas;
this will make the fur fly, ça fera du grabuge;
the fur was flying, ça bardait/il y avait du
grabuge.

furburger ['fɜːbɜːgə] *n esp NAm VV* sexe*
de la femme*/barbu *m*. (*See* **fur pie**;
hairburger)

furphy ['fɜːfɪ] *n Austr P* fausse rumeur/
canulard *m*/ragots *mpl*.

fur pie ['fɜːˈpaɪ] *n V* sexe* de la femme*/
barbu *m*.

fury ['fjʊərɪ] *n F* like fury, *(uncontrollably)*
déchaîné/en fureur; *(at full speed)* très vite*/à

toute pompe; to work like fury, travailler
comme un fou/bosser/boulonner.

fuse [fjuːz] *n F* to blow a fuse, se mettre en
colère*/piquer une crise.

fuss [fʌs] *n F* chichis *mpl*/chinoiseries *fpl*; to
make a fuss/to kick up a fuss, faire des
histoires/en faire tout un plat; it's nothing to
make a fuss about, il n'y a pas de quoi
fouetter un chat.

fusspot ['fʌspɒt], *NAm* **fuss budget**
['fʌsbʌdʒɪt] *n F* individu* qui fait
des histoires; chichiteux *m*; enquiquineur,
-euse.

future ['fjuːtʃə] *n* 1. *F* there's no future in it,
ça n'a pas d'avenir *m*/ça ne servira à rien/ça
ne mènera à rien 2. *P* testicules*/bijoux *mpl*
de famille/roupettes *fpl*.

futz¹ [fʌts] *n NAm V* 1. sexe* de la femme*/
fente *f*/chagatte *f* 2. salaud*/crapule *f*.

futz² [fʌts] *vtr NAm V* faire le con/déconner.

fuzz [fʌz] *n O P* 1. policier*/détective *m*/flic
m/roussin *m* 2. the fuzz, *(collectively)* la
police*/flicaille *f*/rousse *f*; here's the fuzz,
voilà les flics.

fuzzy ['fʌzɪ] *a F (bewildered)* désorienté;
(tipsy) un peu ivre*; my head's a bit fuzzy,
j'ai la tête qui tourne.

f-word (the) [ðiːˈefwɜːd] *n Br F (Euph for
fuck)* to say the f-word, jurer/dire des gros
mots.

G

G [dʒiː] *P* **1. to put in the G** (*a*) (*put pressure on s.o.*) serrer la vis/les pouces à qn (*b*) dénoncer*/balancer/moucharder/donner qn **2.** (*abbr of* **grand**) mille livres *fpl* (sterling); mille dollars *mpl* **3.** gramme *m* (*surt de* cocaïne). (*See* **G-man; grand**)

gab¹ [gæb] *n* **1.** *P* blabla(bla) *m*/jactage *m* **2.** *F* **to have the gift of the gab,** avoir du bagou(t)/savoir baratiner; avoir une fière/ sacrée tapette; **she's got the gift of the gab,** elle a la langue bien pendue/de la tchatche **3.** *P* = **gob¹ 1.**

gab² [gæb] *vi P* bavarder*/bavasser/ blablater/jacter/jaser/tenir le crachoir; **they spend the day gabbing away,** ils/elles passent la journée à jacasser/papoter.

gabber ['gæbə] *n P* bavard*/baratineur, -euse/jacteur *m*.

gabby ['gæbɪ] *a P* bavard/qui a la langue bien pendue.

gabfest ['gæbfest] *n NAm P* (*chat*) converse *f*/jactage *m*/tchatche *f*.

gad, Gad [gæd] *n A F* **by gad!** sacrebleu!/ sapristi!/mes aïeux!

gadabout ['gædəbaʊt] *n F* vadrouilleur, -euse; glandeur, -euse.

gad about ['gædə'baʊt] *vi F* **1.** vadrouiller/se balader/aller par monts et par vaux **2.** courir les filles/le jupon.

gafa (the) [ðə'gæfə] *n Austr P* (*abbr of great areas of f.a.* (*See* **f.a.**)) sale bled *m*/trou perdu.

gaff [gæf] *n P* **1.** logement*/piaule *f*/taule *f*/ crèche *f*; **they did him in his gaff,** ils l'ont arrêté/piqué dans sa piaule. (*See* **drum 1; screw² 3**) **2.** gambling gaff, maison *f* de jeu/ tripot *m* **3. to blow the gaff,** vendre la mèche/ lacher le morceau; **to blow the gaff on,** dénoncer*/donner/balancer (qn); exposer publiquement (un scandale, etc) **4.** *NAm* **to stand the gaff,** être courageux*/encaisser les coups durs/en avoir dans le ventre **5.** bêtises*/ blagues *fpl*/foutaises *fpl*. (*See* **guff¹ 1**) **6.**

café-concert *m*/beuglant *m* **7.** foire *f*.

gaffe [gæf] *n F* bévue*/gaffe *f*; **that was a bit of a gaffe you made there,** t'as fait une gaffe/ tu t'es gour(r)é un peu/tu t'es foutu dedans.

gaffed [gæft] *a NAm P* **gaffed dice,** dés truqués/plats *mpl*.

gaffer ['gæfə] *n F* **1.** patron*/chef *m*/taulier *m*/singe *m* **2.** vieil homme/vieux bonhomme **3.** (*films, TV*) chef électricien.

gag¹ [gæg] *n F* **1.** plaisanterie *f*/blague *f*; **he did it for a gag,** il l'a fait histoire de rigoler/ pour blaguer **2.** canular *m*; **to pull a gag on s.o.,** faire une entourloupette à qn/rouler qn/ mener qn en bateau **3.** (*cinema, etc*) gag *m*.

gag² [gæg] *vi F* **1.** (*theatre*) enchaîner **2.** dire des plaisanteries *fpl*/blaguer; faire des gags **3.** avoir envie de vomir*/de dégueuler.

gaga ['gɑːgɑː] *a F* **1.** (*senile*) gaga; **the old man's completely gaga,** c'est un vieux gâteux **2.** fou*/cinglé/timbré **3.** (*besotted*) **to go gaga over s.o.,** s'enticher de qn/être toqué de qn/ être complètement gaga de qn.

gage [geɪdʒ] *n O P* **1.** whisky *m*/alcool* bon marché/tord-boyaux *m* **2.** tabac*/fume *f* **3.** pipe *f*/bouffarde *f* **4.** (*drugs*) marijuana* **5. to get one's gage up** (*a*) se mettre en colère*/ sortir de ses gonds (*b*) être ivre*/être plein/ avoir sa cuite.

gal [gæl] *n F* jeune fille*/môme *f*/gonzesse *f*/ nana *f*/minette *f*.

galah [gə'lɑː] *n Austr F* individu bête*/ andouille *f*/nave *m*.

gall [gɔːl] *n F* culot *m*/toupet *m*; **he had the gall to do that!** il a eu le culot de faire ça!

gallery ['gælərɪ] *n F* **to play to the gallery,** faire de l'esbroufe/de l'épate.

gallows-bird ['gæləʊzbɜːd] *n F* gibier *m* de potence.

galoot [gə'luːt] *n esp NAm P* **1.** individu*/ mec *m*/client *m*; **old galoot,** vieux schnock **2.** (*stupid*) crétin, -ine/andouille *f*.

galumph [gə'lʌmf] *vi F* galoper lourdement; **to go galumphing around,** marcher comme un éléphant.

gam¹ [gæm] *n* 1. *pl P* jambes*/guibolles *fpl*/ gambettes *fpl* 2. *Br V* fellation*; cunnilinctus* 3. *Austr P* serviette *f* périodique/fifine *f*; tampon *m* périodique.

gam² [gæm] *vi Br V* faire une fellation* *ou* un cunnilinctus*.

game [geɪm] **I** *a* 1. *F* I'm game! OK!/dac!/ ça me botte!/je suis pour! 2. *Br P* (*woman*) qui se prostitue/qui fait le trottoir; she's game, elle fait le bisness **II** *n* 1. *P* to be on the game, racoler*/turbiner/faire le trottoir 2. *F* travail*/boulot *m*; he hasn't been in this game very long, il fait ça depuis très peu 3. *F* I know your little game! je comprends ton petit jeu!/je te vois venir! 4. *F* to have the game sewn up, avoir la partie belle/en main; tenir le bon bout 5. *F* to play the game, jouer le jeu 6. *NAm F* charme *m*/popularité *f*/cote *f* (*surt avec le sexe opposé*) (*See* **army 2**; **badger 1**; **fun II 2**; **play² 2**; **sack¹ 4**; **skin¹ 5** (*a*); **up¹ II 3**)

gammon¹ ['gæmən] *n O P* bobards *mpl*/ boniments *mpl*.

gammon² ['gæmən] *vtr O P* duper*/monter un bateau à (qn)/emmener (qn) en bateau.

gammy ['gæmɪ] *a F* boiteux/bancroche/ tordu; he's got a gammy leg, il a une patte folle.

gamp [gæmp] *n Br O F* parapluie*/riflard *m*/pébroc *m*.

gander ['gændə] *n P* to have/to take a gander, regarder*/jeter un (coup d')œil/ zyeuter; just take a gander (at that)! mate-moi ça!/zyeute-moi ça!

ganef ['gɑːnəf] *n NAm P* voleur*/ chapardeur, -euse.

ganga ['gændʒə] *n P* (*drugs*) marijuana*.

gang bang ['gæŋˈbæŋ] *n P* (*a*) coït* collectif (*plusieurs hommes à tour de rôle avec une femme*)/l'amour *m* en groupe (*b*) viol collectif/baptême *m*/barlu *m*.

gang-bang ['gæŋˈbæŋ] **I** *vtr V* (*a*) baiser (qn) à tour de rôle; (*b*) violer (qn) à tour de rôle **II** *vi NAm P* prendre part aux activités d'un gang/être membre d'un gang.

gangster ['gæŋstə] *n P* (*drugs*) (*a*) mar-ijuana* (*b*) habitué(e) de la marijuana* (*c*) cigarette* de marijuana/joint *m*/stick *m*.

gang up ['gæŋˈʌp] *vi F* to gang up on s.o., former équipe/se liguer contre qn; se mettre d'accord pour tomber qn; they all ganged up on me, ils se sont tous montés contre moi.

ganja(h) ['gændʒɑː], **ganji** ['gændʒɪ] *n P*

(*drugs*) marijuana*. (*See* **bhang; ganga; gunja**)

gannet ['gænɪt] *n Br F* goinfre*/crevard, -arde/morfal, -ale.

garage ['gærɑːʒ] *n Mus* garage *m*.

garbage ['gɑːbɪdʒ] *n* 1. *F* camelote *f*/ rossignols *mpl*/came *f* 2. *P* bêtises*/boniments *mpl*/bobards *mpl*/bidon *m*; don't give me all that garbage! ne me sers pas des conneries!/ arrête de déconner! that's a load of garbage! ce ne sont que des conneries!/c'est de la merde! 3. *P* mauvaise nourriture*/ ragougnasse *f* 4. *P* drogue *f* de mauvaise qualité 5. *P* résidu *m* après cuisson d'une drogue/fond *m* de culot 6. *F* (*computers*) données *fpl* sans signification.

garbo ['gɑːbəʊ] *n Austr F* éboueur *m*/boueux *m*.

garden ['gɑːdn] *n F* 1. to lead s.o. up the garden path, faire marcher qn/faire voir des étoiles en plein midi à qn/(em)mener qn en bateau 2. everything in the garden is lovely, tout va comme sur des roulettes; ça *ou* tout baigne (dans l'huile/dans le beurre). (*See* **bear-garden**)

gargle ['gɑːgl] *n Br & Irish P* boisson *f* alcoolique/gorgeon *m*/coupe-la-soif *m*.

garters ['gɑːtəz] *npl see* **guts 9**.

gas¹ [gæs] **I** *a Austr P* excellent*/terrible/ super **II** *n* 1. *F* bavardage *m* vide/pal(l)as *m*/ baratin *m*/bidon *m*; he's all gas, il parle pour ne rien dire/tout ça c'est du vent; to have a gas, tailler une bavette 2. *esp NAm F* (= *gasoline*) essence *f*/jus *m*; to step on the gas, (*accelerate*) appuyer sur le champignon/ donner plein gaz/foncer; (*hurry*) se dépêcher*/se grouiller/se magner; come on, step on the gas! allez, magne-toi! to run out of gas, devenir fatigué*/fatiguer/être à bout de souffle 3. *P* (*a*) qch d'excellent*/du tonnerre/ de géant; what a gas! c'est le (super-)pied!/ c'est génial! (*b*) rigolade *f*; it was a real gas! c'était une sacrée marrade!/une franche rigolade! we had a real gas, on s'en est payé une bonne tranche 4. *P* a gas meter bandit, (*small-time thief*) un faisandier/un escroc à la petite semaine.

gas² [gæs] *vi F* bavarder*/baratiner/jacter; he never stops gassing, il n'arrête pas de jacasser/bavasser.

gasbag ['gæsbæg] *n F* moulin *m* à paroles/ beau parleur/phrasicoteur *m*.

gash [gæʃ] **I** *a Br P* 1. *A* de rechange/en surplus/en rab(iot) 2. abîmé/naze/pourri **II** *n*

1. *P* rab(iot) *m* 2. *P* femme*/nana *f*/gonzesse *f*
3. *V* sexe* de la femme*/fente *f*/craquette *f*.

gasket ['gæskɪt] *n F* to blow a gasket, se
mettre en colère*/piquer une crise/péter une
durite.

gas out ['gæs'aʊt] *vi P* animer/exciter/
stimuler/émoustiller.

gasp [gɑːsp] *n F* to be at one's last gasp, être
à bout/être au bout du rouleau.

gasper ['gɑːspə] *n P* cigarette*/cibiche *f*/
sèche *f*/pipe *f*.

gassed [gæst] *a O P* légèrement ivre*/gris/
pompette.

gasser ['gæsə] *n P* 1. baratineur, -euse/
phrasicoteur *m* 2. *esp NAm* (*sth impressive*)
une merveille/du canon; (*sth amusing*) bonne
blague/marrade *f*.

gassing ['gæsɪŋ] *n Br P* action *f* d'entrer
chez une personne âgée en se faisant passer
pour un employé du gaz.

gassy ['gæsɪ] *a P* bavard/baratineur/
jacasseur.

gas up ['gæs'ʌp] *vi NAm* 1. *F* faire le plein
(d'essence) 2. *P* animer/exciter/stimuler/
émoustiller.

gat [gæt] *n NAm O P* revolver*/pistolet *m*/
calibre *m*.

Gate (the) [ðə'geɪt] *n Br F* Notting Hill
Gate (*quartier de Londres où a lieu un
Carnaval au mois d'août*).

gatecrash ['geɪtkræʃ] *vtr F* s'inviter à une
réception, une boum, une fête, etc/resquiller/
se glisser à une fête.

gatecrasher ['geɪtkræʃə] *n F* resquilleur,
-euse; **champion gatecrasher**, roi *m* des
resquilleurs.

gatepost ['geɪtpəʊst] *n F* between you and
me and the gatepost, entre nous soit dit/de toi
z'à moi.

gauge [geɪdʒ] *n P* = **gage 3**.

Gawd [gɔːd] *n P* (= *God*) oh my Gawd! ah
mon Dieu!/bon Dieu! Gawd 'elp us!/Gawd
love us! bon diou!/grands dieux!

gawk [gɔːk] *n O F* godille *f*/niais, -aise.

gawky ['gɔːkɪ] *a F* empoté.

gay [geɪ] *a V* F 1. gay deceivers, seins*
artificiels/roberts *mpl* de chez Michelin 2.
homosexuel/pédale/gay *ou* gai/pédé; gay bar,
boîte *f* gay. (*See* **dog¹ 1**)

gayfest ['geɪfest] *n F* réunion *f* d'homo-
sexuels/de pédés.

gaylord ['geɪlɔːd] *n* 1. homosexuel*/gay *m*
2. homme mou/veule.

gazump [gə'zʌmp] *vtr Br F* = revenir sur

une promesse de vente faite à qn pour
accepter une offre plus élevée.

gazunda, gazunder [gə'zʌndə] *n P* pot
m de chambre/jules *m*.

gear [gɪə] I *a Br P* (*esp regional*) excellent*/
du tonnerre/super II *n* 1. *F* biens *mpl*/
possessions *fpl*. (*See* **marriage**) 2. *F* attirail
m/barda *m*/bataclan *m*; he leaves his gear out
everywhere, il laisse traîner ses affaires
partout 3. *F* (*esp fashionable*) vêtements*/
frusques *fpl*/fringues *fpl* 4. *P* drogues*/came
f/stup *m* 5. *P* butin*/rafle *f*/fade *m* 6. *P* marchandise *f* de première qualité/du bath 7. *F*
to be in high gear, péter le feu; to be in low
gear, ne pas avoir la forme/ne pas avoir la
frite 8. *Austr P* fausses dents*/râtelier *m* 9. *P*
gear stick, pénis*/manche *m* à balai/outil *m*.
(*See* **arse I 6**)

geared up ['gɪəd'ʌp] *a & pp F* to be all
geared up for sth, être fin prêt/être
conditionné pour qch.

gee [dʒiː] I *excl esp NAm F* gee (whiz(z))!
ah, dis donc!/mince!/eh ben!/ben mon vieux!
II *n P* 1. = **G 1, 2 2**. *NAm O* individu*/mec
m; front gee, homme *m* de paille/couverture
f; a hip gee, un mec à la coule; un pote/un
régulier 3. *NAm* grosse somme d'argent*.

gee-gee ['dʒiːdʒiː] *n F* 1. (*esp child's
language*) cheval/dada *m* 2. to follow the
gee-gees, jouer aux courtines/suivre les gails/
les canassons. (*See* **flutter 2**)

geek¹ [giːk] *n P* 1. *Austr* coup d'œil*; give us
a geek, fais voir ça 2. *NAm* (*freak*) monstre
m/phénomène *m*; (*disgusting person*)
individu* désagréable/salopard *m*; (*insane
person*) tordu *m*.

geek² [giːk] I *vtr Austr P* regarder*/mater/
zyeuter qch II *vi NAm P* 1. (*also* **geek out**)
se comporter étrangement/faire le dingue 2.
chercher des restes de drogue/*surt* de crack.

gee up ['dʒiː'ʌp] *vtr & i F* 1. (*to a horse*)
gee up! hue!/au trot! 2. *O* he gee-ed them up,
il les a montés l'un contre l'autre/asticotés 3.
préparer/conditionner (qn).

Geez(e)! [dʒiːz] *excl P* (= *Euph for
Jesus!*) bon Dieu!/eh ben ça alors! (*See
Jeeze!*)

geezer ['giːzə] *n P* homme*/type *m*/mec *m*;
he's a silly old geezer, c'est un vieux schnock/
un vieux débris.

gel [gel] *n F* = **gal**.

gelt [gelt] *n P* argent*/pognon *m*/soudure *f*/
fric *m*/flouze *m*.

gen [dʒen] *n F* renseignements*/tuyaux *mpl*/

info *f*; **to give s.o. the gen**, tuyauter qn/mettre qn à la page/rencarder qn; **I need some gen on that business**, il faut me tuyauter sur cette affaire/je veux connaître le papier.

genned up ['dʒend'ʌp] *a & pp* F **to get genned up**, se mettre au courant/se rencarder; **to be all genned up**, être rencardé/être à la page/être au parfum.

gent [dʒent] *n F* (*abbr of gentleman*) 1. **a real gent**, un monsieur/un type bien 2. *pl* **the gents**, WC* pour hommes; **to go to the gents**, aller au petit coin/aux vécés.

genuine ['dʒenjʊɪn] *a F* 1. régulier; **a genuine guy**, un type réglo 2. **the genuine article**, du vrai/de l'authentique/du bath; **it's your genuine article**, c'est pas de la camelote/c'est du vrai de vrai/c'est pas du toc.

gen up ['dʒen'ʌp] *vtr F* **to gen s.o. up**, tuyauter qn/mettre qn au parfum/rencarder qn.

Geordie ['dʒɔːdɪ] *a & n F* 1. originaire (*mf*) *ou* habitant, -ante de la région de Newcastle *ou* Tyneside 2. dialecte parlé dans la région de Newcastle *ou* Tyneside.

George [dʒɔːdʒ] *Prn F* 1. *O* **by George!** sapristi!/mince alors! 2. (*in aircraft*) pilote *m* automatique/Georges *m*.

gerdoing!, gerdoying! [gə'dɔɪŋ] *excl F* boum (badaboum)!/pan!/vlan! (*See* **doing!**; **kerdoing!**)

gerry ['dʒerɪ] *n Br F* (*short for geriatric*) vieux*/croulant, -ante/vioque *mf*.

gertcha! gertcher! ['gɜːtʃə] *excl Br P* (*cockney*) = (*expressing disbelief or mockery*) à d'autres!/arrête ton char!

get¹ [get] *n Br P* = **git II**.

get² [get] *vtr* 1. *F* comprendre/piger/entraver; **I don't get you**, je (ne) pige pas/je te suis pas/je n'entrave que dalle; **get me?/get my drift?/get what I mean?** tu y es?/tu saisis?/tu piges?/compris? 2. *F* **I'll get you for that**! j'aurai ta peau/je t'aurai au tournant/je te louperai pas/tu me le paieras! **I've got him**, je le tiens; **I'll get the bastard!** (*beat up*) je vais lui arranger le portrait à ce salaud! 3. *F* **it gets me when...**, ça m'énerve/ça me crispe/ça m'agace/ça supporte pas quand...; **he really gets my goat/my back up**, il me court (sur le haricot, sur le système)/il me tape sur le système 4. *F* **to get it in the neck**, écoper/en prendre pour son grade 5. *P* **we got trouble**, (= *we have trouble*) on a des emmerdes; **I got rhythm**, (= *I have rhythm*) j'ai du swing; (**you) got a light?**, (= *do you*

have a light?) t'as du feu? 6. *F* **to get ten years**, attraper/prendre dix berges; gerber dix ans 7. *F* **you've got me there**, là tu me la coupes/tu me colles; je donne ma langue au chat 8. *F* émouvoir/secouer/emballer; **this film gets you right there**, ce film te prend aux tripes; ce film te retourne l'estomac 9. *F* tuer*/bousiller/zigouiller; **he always gets his man**, il ne rate jamais son homme/il met toujours dans le mille 10. *F* arrêter*/épingler 11. *F* **to get there**, réussir/arriver/se débrouiller; **we're getting there**, on arrive à la fin/on y arrive; **not to get anywhere**, n'aboutir à rien; **we're getting nowhere**, on tourne en rond/on n'arrive à rien 12. *F* **to get going** (*a*) se dépêcher*/se magner/(se) dégrouiller; **get going!** allez, bouge!/remue-toi! (*See* **hustle¹** 2; **move** 1) (*b*) se mettre au travail*/se mettre en branle 13. *P* **to get behind it**, (*drugs*) être défoncé/être high 14. *P* **to get with it**, se mettre à la mode/dans le vent; être à la coule 15. *P* **to get shot of sth**, se débarrasser de* qch/larguer qch 16. *P* (**you) getting any?** tu baises?/t'as une nana?/t'as un mec? (*See* **case¹** 3; **end** 2; **horn** 1; **hump¹** 2; **jollies**; **knickers**; **leg¹** 10; **needle¹** 1 (*c*); **oats** 1; **rock¹** 5; **tit** 2; **wick** 1)

get about ['getə'baʊt] *vi F* = **get around** 1, 2.

get across ['getə'krɒs] *vtr & i F* faire comprendre/faire piger/éclairer; **I just can't get this across to him**, pas moyen de lui faire piger ce truc.

get along ['getə'lɒŋ] *vi F* 1. **I must be getting along**, il faut que je m'en aille/je me tire 2. **get along with you!** (*expressing disbelief or mockery*) tire-toi! tu charries!/débarrasse (le plancher)!/arrête ton char!/allons donc!/tu me prends pour qui? 3. **to get along with s.o.**, bien s'entendre avec qn 4. se défendre; **I'm getting along fine**, je me défends/je me débrouille.

get around ['getə'raʊnd] *vi F* 1. **it's getting around that...**, le bruit court que... 2. (*travel*) rouler sa bosse/circuler 3. = **get round 1** 4. **to get around to doing sth**, arriver à faire qch 5. circonvenir/surmonter (une difficulté, etc).

get at ['get'æt] *vtr F* 1. (*bribe*) acheter/soudoyer/graisser la patte à (qn) 2. **what are you getting at?** (*what do you mean?*) où voulez-vous en venir? 3. (*annoy*) asticoter/chercher des crosses à (qn); **stop getting at me, will you?** arrête de me les casser/de me courir! **4. I'll get at the bastard,** (*beat up*) je vais lui arranger le portrait à ce salaud.

get-at-able ['get'ætəbl] *a F* accessible/ d'accès facile; **our boss is very get-at-able,** notre patron n'est pas enfermé dans sa tour.

getaway ['getəweɪ] *n F* évasion *f*/la belle/la cavale; **to make a quick getaway,** s'évader*/ s'éclipser/se faire la belle/faire le plongeon; **getaway car,** voiture* de fuite/bagnole *f* de cavale.

get away ['getə'weɪ] *vi* **1.** *F* **get away (with you)!** (*go away!*) dégage!/casse-toi!/fiche-moi la paix!; (*expressing disbelief*) je ne mords pas!/ça ne prend pas! **2.** *F* **to get away with it,** s'en tirer à bon compte; **he won't get away with it,** il ne l'emportera pas au paradis/il ne s'en sortira pas comme ça **3.** *F* **there's no getting away from it,** il n'y a pas moyen d'échapper à ça **4.** *P* **to get it away** = **to get it off** (**get off 4**). (*See* **end 2**)

get behind ['getbɪ'haɪnd] *vtr F* accepter/ croire; **I can't get behind her story,** elle nous fait marcher avec son histoire.

get by ['get'baɪ] *vi F* s'en tirer/faire aller/ s'en sortir; **I get by,** je me débrouille.

get down ['get'daʊn] *F* **I** *vtr* **to get s.o. down,** irriter/déprimer/déconcerter qn; taper sur le système à qn; (*depress*) foutre le cafard/le noir à qn; **what gets me down is his attitude,** ce qui me fout en l'air c'est son attitude; **don't let it get you down!** ne te laisse pas abattre! **II** *vi* **1. to get down to it,** s'y mettre/en mettre un coup; **come on, get down to some work,** allez, au boulot! **2.** *NAm* **come on, get down!** allez, laissez-vous aller!

get off ['get'ɒf] *vtr & i* **1.** *F* **to get off lightly,** s'en tirer à bon compte/bien s'en sortir **2.** *P* **get off!** fous-moi la paix!/arrête ton char! **3.** *F* **to get off with s.o.,** faire une touche **4.** *V* **to get (it) off,** (*climax*) avoir un orgasme*/ prendre son pied/venir/s'éclater; (*make love*) faire l'amour*; (*masturbate*) se masturber*/ se branler; **to get (it) off with a bird/a chick,** s'envoyer/se faire une nana. (*See* **nut¹ 8; rock¹ 5**) **5.** *P* se doper/se défoncer; **heroin really gets him off/he gets off on heroin,** il se défonce à l'héroïne/l'héro c'est son truc pour s'envoyer en l'air **6.** *F* **get it off your chest!** vide ton sac!/accouche!/déballe! **7.** *F* **to tell s.o. where to get off,** réprimander* sévèrement qn/dire à qn ses quatre vérités/ sonner les cloches à qn **8.** *P* **to get off on sth,** prendre son pied avec qch; **I really get off on their music,** leur musique c'est le (super-)

pied/ça me branche.

get on ['get'ɒn] *vi F* **get on with you!** (*be quiet!*) arrête ton char! (*I don't believe you!*) je n'en crois rien!/tu me prends pour qui? (*go away!*) débarrasse (le plancher)!

get onto ['get'ɒntuː] *vtr F* **1.** découvrir*; **I got onto sth really interesting,** j'ai mis le doigt sur un truc vraiment intéressant **2.** se mettre en rapport avec (qn)/contacter (qn) **3.** (*drugs*) **to get onto heroin,** passer à l'héroïne/ à l'héro.

get-out ['getaʊt] *n F* esquive *f*/moyen *m* de sortie.

get out ['get'aʊt] *vi F* **1. to get out from under,** se tirer d'affaire/se dépatouiller **2. to get out while the going's good,** partir* pendant que c'est possible/que la voie est libre.

get over ['get'əʊvə] *vtr F* **1. I can't get over it!** je n'en reviens pas/j'en reste baba!/ ça m'a coupé le souffle! **2. let's get it over with,** finissons-en!

get-rich-quick ['get'rɪtʃ'kwɪk] *a F* **get-rich-quick plan/scheme,** projet qui promet la lune.

get round ['get'raʊnd] *F* **I** *vtr* cajoler/ enjôler; **you can't get round me like that,** tu ne m'auras pas comme ça **II** *vi* = **get around 4**.

get through ['get'θruː] *vtr & i* **1.** *F* **to get through to s.o.,** faire comprendre qch à qn/ faire piger qn **2.** *F* **to get through the month,** boucler son mois/joindre les deux bouts **3.** *P* obtenir des drogues*/se garnir/trouver la cheville/trouver le joint **4.** *F* **to get through some work,** abattre du travail*; **to get through a lot of money,** dépenser* beaucoup d'argent*/bouffer du pognon.

get-together ['gettəgeðə] *n F* réunion amicale/retrouvaille *f*.

get together ['gettə'geðə] *vtr F* **to get it/ one's act/one's head together,** (*get organized*) se ressaisir/s'éclaircir les idées/éclairer sa lanterne.

get-up ['getʌp] *n F* vêtements*/fripes *fpl*/ nippes *fpl*/loques *fpl*; **he was wearing some decidedly peculiar get-up,** il portait des fringues vraiment bizarres/il avait des sapes vraiment pas banales.

get up ['get'ʌp] *vtr* **1.** *V* **to get it up** (*a*) faire l'amour*/s'envoyer en l'air (*b*) (*achieve erection*) réussir à bander; (*have erection*) avoir une érection*/la trique; marquer midi; **he can't get it up,** il arrive pas à bander **2.** *Br P* **to get s.o. up,** (*bribe*) acheter qn/soudoyer qn/graisser la patte à qn; (frame) farguer qn/monter un coup contre qn.

get-up-and-go ['getʌpən(d)'gəʊ] I a F plein d'allant/plein d'entrain/dynamique II n to be full of get-up-and-go, péter le feu/la santé; avoir la frite/la pêche.

ghastly ['gɑːstlɪ] a F abominable/hideux; the weather's ghastly, il fait un temps dégueulasse/pourri; what a ghastly woman! quelle femme* abominable!/quelle sale garce!

gherkin ['gɜːkɪn] n P pénis*/gourdin m; V to jerk one's/the gherkin, se masturber*/se taper la colonne.

ghettoblaster, ghetto box ['getəʊ-'blɑːstə, 'getəʊbɒks] n mini-stéréo f portable.

GI ['dʒiː'aɪ] US F (abbr of government issue) 1. ce qui vient de l'intendance militaire américaine 2. soldat* américain; GI Joe, le bidasse américain pendant la deuxième guerre mondiale.

giddy up! ['gɪdɪ'ʌp] excl F (esp child's language) (to a horse) hue!/au trot! (See gee up 1)

gift [gɪft] n F qch de facile*/du gâteau; it was a real gift, c'était du nougat/du chocolat.

gig¹ [gɪg] n esp NAm 1. F (gadget) machin m/truc m 2. O F réjouissances*/bombe f 3. F (jazz, rock, etc) engagement m d'un soir/gig m; to do/to play a gig, jouer/faire un gig 4. Austr F coup m d'œil 5. Austr P individu bête*/gourde f/crétin, -ine.

gig² [gɪg] vi 1. F jouer dans un groupe (de jazz, de rock) 2. Austr F regarder*/reluquer/ zyeuter 3. P asticoter/faire enrager (qn).

giggle ['gɪgl] n 1. F we did it (just) for a giggle, c'était pour rigoler/on l'a fait histoire de rigoler un peu; it was all a bit of a giggle, on s'est bien marré/on s'en est payé une bonne tranche; what a giggle! quelle rigolade! 2. F to get the giggles, attraper le fou rire 3. P (drugs) giggle smoke/stick/weed, cigarette* de marijuana/joint m/stick m 4. F giggle water, champagne m/champ' m.

giggle-house ['gɪglhaʊs] n Austr F asile m d'aliénés/maison f de fous.

gilbert ['gɪlbət] n Br P green gilbert, see green I 7.

gild [gɪld] vtr P to gild the lily, (of police) exagérer/en rajouter/noircir le tableau.

gills [gɪlz] npl 1. P to be stewed to the gills, être complètement ivre*/avoir sa cuite/être bourré à bloc 2. to be a bit green about the gills, (be frightened) avoir peur*/avoir les

jetons; (feel sick) être sur le point de vomir*/ avoir envie de dégueuler.

gimme! ['gɪmɪ] F (abbr of give me!) donne!/aboule! (See skin¹ 10)

gimmick ['gɪmɪk] n 1. F (trick) attrape f/ tour m/combine f/astuce f/truc m; (advertising) attrape-couillons m/truc publicitaire 2. F (thing) gadget m/truc m/ machin m.

gimmicky ['gɪmɪkɪ] a F plein d'astuces.

gimp [gɪmp] n P (a) individu* boiteux/ bancroche mf (b) individu* bête/andouille f/ crétin, -ine.

gin [dʒɪn] n Austr P Pej femme* aborigène.

ginger ['dʒɪndʒə] n F 1. rouquin, -ine/poil m de carotte 2. to have (a lot of) ginger, avoir de l'entrain m/péter la santé/péter le feu 3. ginger group, groupe m de pression 4. (RS = ginger beer = queer) homosexuel*/pédé m/ tapette f.

ginger up ['dʒɪndʒər'ʌp] vtr F donner de l'entrain/un coup de fouet à.

gink [gɪŋk] n P (a) drôle m de paroissien/de zèbre (b) pauvre type m/couillon m.

gin-mill ['dʒɪnmɪl] n NAm A F = gin-palace.

ginormous [dʒaɪ'nɔːməs] a F colossal/ ma(h)ous/(h)énaurme.

gin-palace ['dʒɪnpæləs] n A F bar mal famé/bouiboui m/troquet m.

gip [dʒɪp] n F to give s.o. gip, faire mal à qn; my rheumatism is giving me gip, mes rhumatismes me font dégueuler/dérouiller.

gippo ['dʒɪpəʊ] n P gitan, -ane/romano mf/ romani mf/manouche mf. (See gyppo)

gippy tummy ['dʒɪpɪ'tʌmɪ] n Br P diarrhée*/courante f.

girl [gɜːl] n P 1. (drugs) (golden) girl, cocaïne*/coco f 2. homosexuel*/tante f 3. working girl, prostituée*/persilleuse f/ gagneuse f. (See bar-girl; B-girl; call girl; cover-girl; glamour-girl; yes-girl)

girlie ['gɜːlɪ] n 1. attrib F fillette f/girl f; girlie show, spectacle m de girls; girlie magazines, presse f de charme; magazines mpl pornos/de cul 2. esp NAm P prostituée*/ fille f 3. Br F (schools) individu* efféminé/ chochotte f.

gis [gɪz] abbr P = giz.

gismo ['gɪzməʊ] n P = gizmo.

git [gɪt] I excl esp NAm P file!/fiche le camp!/décolle! II n P individu bête*/connard, -arde; you stupid git! espèce de con!/tête f de nœud!

give [gɪv] *vtr F* 1. don't give me that! (ne) me raconte pas d'histoires!/de bobards! 2. to give it to s.o., réprimander* qn/passer un savon à qn/sonner les cloches à qn 3. give it all you've got! fais le maxi(mum)!/donne un (bon) coup de collier! 4. to know what gives, être à la page/dans le vent/à la coule; what gives? (*hello!*) salut! (*what's going on?*) qu'est-ce qui se fricote? (*what's new?*) quoi de neuf? 5. avouer*; give! accouche! 6. *V* to give it/her one, faire l'amour* (avec une femme). (*See* **arse I 8; cog; head 13; wellie 1**)

give-away ['gɪvəweɪ] **I** *a F* to sell sth at a give-away price, vendre qch à un prix défiant toute concurrence/pour trois fois rien **II** *n F* 1. article sacrifié 2. a (dead) give-away, geste *m ou* mot *m*, etc qui en dit long.

give over ['gɪv'əʊvə] *vi F* dételer/ s'écraser; give over, will you? laisse tomber, tu veux?/écrase!

giz [gɪz] *abbr P* (= *give us or give me*) donne(-moi); giz a/gizza hand with this! file-moi un coup de main!

gizmo ['gɪzməʊ] *n P* machin *m*/bidule *m*/ truc *m*.

gizzard ['gɪzəd] *n F* that sticks in my gizzard, je ne digère pas ça/ça me reste en travers de la gorge; ça me fout en rogne/ça ne me passe pas.

gizzit ['gɪzɪt] *n Br P* (= *give us it*) (*free hand-out*) cadeau *m* (fait à un client).

glad [glæd] *a F* glad rags, les plus beaux vêtements* de la garde-robe/les nippes *fpl* du dimanche; to put on one's glad rags, se mettre sur son trente et un. (*See* **eye 4**)

gladdie ['glædɪ] *n* (*short for gladiolus*) glaïeul *m*.

glamour-boy ['glæməbɔɪ] *n F* (*a*) séducteur *m*/joli cœur/jeune premier (*b*) beau mâle/beau mec.

glamour-girl ['glæməgɜːl] *n F* (*a*) ensorceleuse *f*/vamp *f* (*b*) beau morceau/prix *m* de Diane/joli lot.

glamour-puss ['glæməpʊs] *n O F* pin-up *f*/ ensorceleuse *f*.

Glasgow hello, Glasgow kiss ['glɑːzgəʊhe'ləʊ, -kɪs] *n Br F* coup *m* de tête/de boule.

glass[1] [glɑːs] *n* 1. *P* diamants*/cailloux *mpl* 2. *F* to have a glass jaw, (*of boxer*) avoir la mâchoire en verre.

glass[2] [glɑːs] *vtr P* taillader (qn) avec un tesson (dans une rixe).

glasshouse ['glɑːshaʊs] *n Br P Mil* prison*/ militaire/caisse *f*.

glassy-eyed ['glɑːsɪ'aɪd], **glazed** [gleɪzd] *a F* ivre*/blindé/bituré/dans les vapes.

glim[1] [glɪm] *n Br P* lampe de poche recouverte de papier (*utilisée dans les cambriolages*).

glim[2] [glɪm] *vi Br P* utiliser une lampe de poche recouverte de papier (*pour un cambriolage*).

glims [glɪmz] *npl A P* 1. yeux*/quinquets *mpl*/lanternes *fpl* 2. lunettes*/bernicles *fpl*/ carreaux *mpl*.

glitch [glɪtʃ] *n F* (*snag, problem*) pépin *m*; (*serious*) emmerdement *m*/galoup *m*/chiasse *f*.

glitz [glɪts] *n F* (*of show business, etc*) brillant *m*/éclat *m*/glamour *m*.

glitzy ['glɪtsɪ] *a F* (*party*) brillant.

glop [glɒp] *vi Br P* boire* de l'alcool/surt de la bière/écluser/soiffer.

glory ['glɔːrɪ] *n F* 1. he's got the glory, (*of prisoner*) il tombe dans la bondieuserie 2. to go to glory, mourir*/casser sa pipe 3. to get all the glory, récolter toute la gloire/ décrocher le pompon 4. glory be! grand Dieu!/Seigneur!

glory-hole ['glɔːrɪhəʊl] *n F* capharnaüm *m*/cagibi *m*.

glossies ['glɒsɪz] *npl F* the glossies, revues *fpl*/magazines *mpl* (sur papier couché) de luxe.

glow [gləʊ] *n NAm F* to have/to get a glow on, être légèrement ivre*/gris/pompette/ éméché/parti.

glue sniffer ['gluː'snɪfə] *n* personne *f*, surt adolescent, -ente qui se drogue en respirant de la colle/sniffeur, -euse.

glue-sniffing ['gluːsnɪfɪŋ] *n P* to go glue-sniffing, se mettre à sniffer de la colle. (*See* **sniff; sniffer**)

glug[1] [glʌg] *n P* boisson *f*/gorgeon *m*.

glug[2] [glʌg] *vi P* boire*/rincer.

G-man ['dʒiːmæn] *n US O F* agent *m* du FBI.

G.M.F.U. [dʒiːemef'juː] *n Br F* (*abbr of grand military fuck-up*) (*disaster*) bordel *m*/ merdier *m*.

gnashers ['næʃəz] *npl P* dents*/crocs *mpl*/ crochets *mpl*.

gnat [næt] *n F* gnat's piss, mauvaise boisson (*surt* bière de qualité inférieure)/bibine *f*/jus *m* de chaussettes/pipi *m* de chat.

go¹ [gəʊ] **I** *a* F en bon ordre/OK; **all systems are go/it's all systems go**, on a le feu vert **II** *n* F **1.** (it's) **no go**, rien à faire/ça ne prend pas/c'est nib/c'est midi/(y a) pas mèche **2.** **to have a go at s.o.**, s'en prendre à qn/dire deux mots à qn/s'accrocher avec qn **3.** **to be always on the go**, avoir la bougeotte/avoir toujours un pied en l'air; **it's all go!** on n'a pas une minute à soi!/ça n'arrête pas! **4.** **have a go!** tente ta chance!/à toi de jouer! **have another go!** remets ça! **5.** **he's got no go in him**, il est ramollo/il est mou comme une chiffe; il n'a pas la frite **6.** **to put some go into it**, y mettre de l'entrain/du cœur **7.** **to give sth a go**, tenter le coup/s'attaquer à qch **8.** **at/in one go**, d'un seul coup/trait; tout d'une haleine **9.** **to be all the go**, faire rage/faire fureur **10.** **(right) from the word go**, dès le départ/tout au début. (*See* **bag² 4**; **touch¹ 2**)

go² [gəʊ] *vtr & i* **1.** F **how goes it?** comment (ça) va? **2.** F **go for it!** lance-toi!/fonce! **3.** P (*drugs*) **to be gone**, être défoncé/planer/être high **4.** F mourir*; **when you've got to go, you've got to go**, quand faut y aller, faut y aller **5.** V **to go**, (*of woman*) être très portée sur les plaisirs sexuels/sur la chose; être baiseuse; **she really goes**, c'est une chaude lapine **6.** P **to go belly-up**, mourir*/bouffer les pissenlits par la racine **7.** *Austr* F **to go bush**, adopter la manière de vivre des campagnards/devenir provincial **8.** F (*say*) dire/faire; **so he goes...**, alors il (me) fait....

go-ahead ['gəʊəhed] **I** *a* F **a go-ahead young man with go-ahead ideas**, un garçon entreprenant qui voit loin; un jeune loup **II** *n* F **to get the go-ahead**, avoir le feu vert.

goalie ['gəʊlɪ] *n* F (*abbr of goalkeeper*) gardien *m* de but/goal *m*.

go along with ['gəʊə'lɒŋwɪð] *vtr* F accepter/approuver (qch); **I'll go along with that**, je suis tout à fait d'accord/je vous suis là-dessus; **I can't go along with that**, je ne suis pas d'accord/je ne marche pas.

goat [gəʊt] *n* F **1.** **to get s.o.'s goat**, ennuyer* qn/irriter qn; **he gets my goat**, il me tape sur le système/il me (les) gonfle **2.** **old goat**, vieux* birbe/vieille bique/vieille baderne/vieux schnock.

gob¹ [gɒb] *n* P **1.** bouche*/gueule *f*; **to keep one's gob shut**, se taire*/la boucler/ne pas piper; **shut your gob!** la ferme! **stick that in your gob and shut up!** fourre-toi ça dans le clapet et boucle-la! **2.** crachat*/glaviot *m*/mol(l)ard *m* **3.** *NAm* marin*/mataf *m*.

gob² [gɒb] *vi* P cracher*/mollarder. (*See* **gob¹ 2**)

gobble ['gɒbl] *vtr* V (*not common*) faire une fellation* à (qn)/sucer (qn)/faire un pompier à (qn).

gobbledegook, gobbledygook ['gɒbldɪguːk] *n* F jargon *m*/charabia *m*/baragouin *m*.

gobbler ['gɒblə] *n* V (*fellator*) suceur, -euse/pipeur *m*.

gobble up ['gɒbl'ʌp] *vtr* *Austr* P arrêter*/agrafer/coffrer (qn).

gobshite ['gɒbʃaɪt] *n* *Br* V salaud*/ducon *m*/trouduc *m*.

gobsmacked ['gɒbsmækt] *a* *Br* P très étonné*/ahuri; **when I heard the price I was gobsmacked**, quand j'ai su le prix, j'en suis resté baba/assis.

gobsmacking ['gɒbsmækɪŋ] *a* *Br* P ahurissant/qui vous coupe le sifflet.

gobstopper ['gɒb'stɒpə] *n* F bonbon dur.

goby ['gəʊbɪ] *n* P (= *go-between*) messager, -ère/intermédiaire *mf*.

go-by ['gəʊbaɪ] *n* F **to give s.o. the go-by**, snober qn/ignorer qn; **to give sth the go-by**, esquiver qch.

God, god [gɒd] *n* **1.** F **by God!** (sacré) nom de Dieu!/grands dieux! **my God!/good God!** bon Dieu (de bon Dieu)! **God Almighty!** Dieu Tout-Puissant! **God only knows**, Dieu seul le sait **2.** P **(the) God man**, prêtre*/l'homme du bon Dieu/cureton *m* **3.** F **the gods**, (*theatre*) le poulailler/le paradis. (*See* **tin I 3**)

godawful ['gɒd'ɔ:fʊl] *a* P répugnant/dégueulasse/puant/infect; **stuck out here in this godawful place**, bloqué dans ce trou perdu/de merde.

god-botherer [gɒd'bɒðərə] *n* *Br* F (*clergyman*) calotin *m*/cureton *m*; (*pious person*) dévot(e) *m*(*f*)/calotin *m*.

goddam ['gɒdæm], **goddamned** ['gɒdæmd] *a* P sacré/satané; **that goddam idiot**, ce sacré imbécile; **the goddamned car's broken down again**, cette saloperie de bagnole est encore tombée en panne/en rade.

goddammit! ['gɒd'dæmɪt] *excl* P sacré nom (de nom)!/merde!/putain!

godfer ['gɒdfə] *n* P (*RS* = *God forbid* = *kid*) enfant*/gosse *mf*/môme *mf*. (*See* **dustbin**)

God-forbid ['gɒdfəbɪd] *n* P (*RS* = *kid*) = **godfer**.

go down ['gəʊ'daʊn] *vi* **1.** F (*universities, etc*) (*a*) finir ses études universitaires (*b*) partir en vacances **2.** F tomber malade*; **to**

go down with sth nasty, attraper/choper la crève 3. *F* my dinner won't go down, mon repas a du mal à passer/ne descend pas 4. *F* it goes down well with the public, ça a été super bien accueilli par le public; that won't go down with me, ça ne prend pas avec moi/je ne vais pas avaler ça; my idea went down like a ton of bricks, mon projet est tombé à l'eau/a fait un bide total/s'est complètement cassé la gueule 5. *esp NAm F* what's going down? que se passe-t-il?/quoi de neuf? it's going down tonight, c'est prévu pour ce soir 6. *F* être mis en prison*/aller en taule; he went down for ten, il a chopé dix ans de prison* 7. *V* to go down on s.o., faire une fellation* à qn/sucer qn/tailler une pipe à qn; pratiquer un cunnilinctus* à qn/sucer qn/brouter le cresson.

God squad (the) [ðə'gɒdskwɒd] *n Br F Pej* forces *fpl*/éléments *mpl* de religion organisée/*surt* de religion évangélique; l'Armée *f* du Salut/Unions chrétiennes universitaires, etc.

goer ['gəʊə] *n P* homme *ou surt* femme très porté(e) sur les plaisirs sexuels/sur la chose; she's a real goer, elle a la cuisse légère/elle ne pense qu'à ça.

gofer ['gəʊfə] *n F* larbin *m*/bonniche *f*.

go for ['gəʊ'fɔː, 'gəʊfə] *vtr F* 1. to go for s.o. (*a*) (*attack*) rentrer dans le chou à qn/tomber sur le poil de qn (*b*) (*argue*) avoir une prise de bec avec qn 2. aller chercher/essayer d'obtenir; let's go for it! allons-y! 3. être fana de/se toquer de; I don't go for that, cela ne m'emballe pas/ça ne me dit pas grand-chose/ça me botte pas tellement 4. everything's going for him/he's really got something going for him, tout va très bien pour lui. (*See* way II 2 (*a*))

go-getter ['gəʊgetə] *n F* battant, -ante.

go-getting ['gəʊgetɪŋ] *a F* énergique/à la redresse.

gogglebox ['gɒglbɒks] *n F* (*television*) télé *f*/téloche *f*/fenestron *m*. (*See* box[1] 2; idiot-box; lantern)

goggle-eyed ['gɒgl'aɪd] *a F* avec les yeux en boules de loto/à fleur de tête.

goggles ['gɒglz] *npl P* lunettes*/pare-brise *m*/bernicles *fpl*.

going ['gəʊɪŋ] *n F* to get out while the going's good, partir* pendant que c'est possible/que la voie est libre/qu'on a le vent en poupe/qu'on en a l'occase; we made good going on that journey, on a bien roulé pendant ce voyage; his speech was a bit heavy going,

son discours traînait en longueur/était plutôt rasoir.

going-over ['gəʊɪŋ'əʊvə] *n F* to give s.o. a going-over (*a*) battre* qn/passer qn à tabac/tabasser qn/amocher qn; the cops gave him a good going-over, les flics lui ont filé une bonne tabassée/l'ont passé à tabac (*b*) réprimander* qn/passer un savon à qn/sonner les cloches à qn (*c*) fouiller qn/faire la barbotte à qn.

goings-on ['gəʊɪŋz'ɒn] *npl F* conduite *f*/manège *m*/manigances *fpl*; such goings-on! en voilà des façons! I've heard of your goings-on, j'en ai appris de belles sur vous; there were some strange goings-on at the cemetery, il se passait des trucs plutôt bizarres/il s'en passait de drôles/il se faisait un drôle de cinéma au cimetière.

gold [gəʊld] *n P* 1. argent*/pèze *m*/flouze *m* 2. (*drugs*) Acapulco gold, marijuana* de bonne qualité/gold *m*. (*See* dust[1] 2)

goldbrick[1] ['gəʊldbrɪk] *n P* 1. *esp Mil* paresseux*/tire-au-flanc *m*/ramier *m* 2. escroquerie *f*/arnaque *f*/estampage *m*.

goldbrick[2] ['gəʊldbrɪk] *vtr & i P* 1. *esp Mil* paresser à son travail/tirer au cul/tirer au flanc/se défiler 2. escroquer*/estamper/arnaquer (qn).

goldbricker ['gəʊldbrɪkə] *n P* = gold-brick[1] 1.

gold-digger ['gəʊld'dɪgə] *n F* aventurière *f*/croqueuse *f* de diamants.

golden ['gəʊld(ə)n] *a* 1. *F* golden disc, disque *m* d'or (*le millionième*) 2. *F* golden opportunity, affaire *f* en or/occasion rêvée 3. *F* excellent*/superbe/doré sur tranche; he's our golden boy, c'est notre chéri à tous/le chouchou de tout le monde; c'est la coqueluche (du bureau, de l'atelier, etc) 4. *P* (*homosexuals, prostitutes*) golden shower, urine *f*/pipi *m*/pisse *f*. (*See* handshake; queen[1] 2)

goldfish-bowl ['gəʊldfɪʃbəʊl] *n F* maison *f* de verre/place *f* publique; it's like living in a goldfish bowl, c'est comme vivre dans une maison de verre.

goldmine ['gəʊldmaɪn] *n F* situation lucrative/mine *f* d'or/filon *m*; the MD doesn't realise he's sitting on top of a goldmine, le P.D.G. ne se rend pas compte qu'il est assis sur une mine d'or.

gollion ['gɒlɪən] *n Austr P* crachat*/graillon *m*/glaviot *m*.

golly[1] ['gɒlɪ] *n P* 1. *Br Pej* Noir(e)*/bougnoul *m*/moricaud, -aude 2. *Austr* = gollion.

golly![2] ['gɒlɪ] *excl O F* (by) golly! mince

alors!/flûte!

gone [gɒn] *a P* 1. parti (sous l'influence de l'alcool* *ou* du hachisch*, etc); **he's really gone,** il est complètement défoncé/il plane. (*See* **go²** 3) 2. **to be gone on s.o.,** être toqué/ amouraché de qn; en pincer pour qn 3. (*pregnant*) **six months gone,** enceinte de six mois. (*See* **far**; **go on 6**)

gonef ['gɒnef] *n NAm P =* **ganef.**

goner ['gɒnə] *n F* 1. (*a*) type fini/foutu (*b*) chose perdue/foutue 2. crevard, -arde/ crevetant *m*; **he was almost a goner,** il a failli mourir/avoir son compte; il revient de loin.

gong [gɒŋ] *n* 1. *F* médaille *f*/banane *f*/ méduche *f* 2. *Austr P* (*drugs*) (*opium*) op *m*/ noir *m*; (*opium pipe*) bambou *m*; **to kick the gong around,** tirer sur le bambou.

gonga ['gɒŋgə] *n P* anus*/anneau *m*/ troufignon *m*; (**you can**) **stick it up your gonga!** tu peux te le mettre/te le fourrer quelque part!/tu peux te le foutre là où je pense! (*See* **stick²** 3)

gonif(f) ['gɒnəf] *n NAm P =* **ganef.**

gonna ['gɒnə, 'gə-] *P = going to.*

gonzo ['gɒnzəʊ] *n P* imbécile*/melon *m*/ dugenou *m*.

goo [gu:] *n F* 1. sentimentalité excessive/à la guimauve/à l'eau de rose 2. substance collante/colle *f*; **I can't get this goo off my hands,** cette saleté de mélasse me colle aux pattes, je ne peux pas m'en débarrasser 3. flatterie *f*/pommade *f*/lèche *f*. (*See* **gooey**)

goober ['gu:bə] *n NAm P* 1. (*pimple*) bouton *m* 2. imbécile*/petit(e) crétin, -ine 3. crachat*/glaviot *m*.

good [gʊd] *a F* 1. (*a*) **good God!/good Lord!** bon dieu! (*b*) **good heavens!** bon sang (de bonsoir)! (*c*) **good grief!** zut alors!/merde alors! (*d*) **good gracious!** eh ben!/purée! (*e*) **good egg!** bath!/super!/bravo! 2. (*prostitute, etc*) **to give s.o. a good time,** faire jouir qn/ régaler qn/faire voir les anges à qn/faire une gâterie à qn. (*See* **hiding 1**; **job 6** (*a*); **nogood**; **set up 3**; **thing 9**)

goodies ['gʊdɪz] *npl F* 1. gourmandises *fpl*/ du nanan 2. les bons *mpl*/les gentils *mpl*; **in his films the goodies always win,** les bons gagnent tout le temps dans ses films. (*See* **baddie**) 3. argent*/fric *m*/flouze *m*.

goodish ['gʊdɪʃ] *a F* 1. assez bon 2. **a goodish while,** assez longtemps; **it's been a goodish time since we met,** ça fait des siècles/une paye qu'on s'est (pas) vus; **it's a goodish way from here,** c'est à un bon bout de

chemin d'ici/ça fait une trotte.

goodness ['gʊdnɪs] *n & excl F* **goodness!** Dieu!/purée!; **goodness me!** oh là là! **goodness gracious (me)!** miséricorde! **for goodness sake!** pour l'amour de Dieu!/du ciel!/par pitié! **thank goodness!** heureusement!/Dieu merci! **goodness (only) knows what I must do,** Dieu sait/va t'en savoir ce que je dois faire. (*See* **honest to goodness**)

goodo! ['gʊdəʊ] *excl F* chic alors!/parfait!/ épatant!/chouette (alors)!

goods [gʊdz] *npl P* 1. (*a*) **a nice bit/piece of goods,** une fille* bien balancée/un beau petit lot/une jolie poupée (*b*) les parties sexuelles/la marchandise; **I like to see the goods before I buy,** j'aime voir la marchandise avant d'acheter. (*See* **damaged**) 2. **the goods,** du vrai de vrai/de la bonne marchandise; **it's the goods,** c'est ce qu'il faut/ça tombe pile 3. **to deliver the goods,** remplir ses engagements/ tenir parole; **she delivered the goods,** elle a couché avec lui/elle a livré la marchandise 4. chose promise/chose due; **he came up with the goods,** il a apporté la marchandise/il a payé ses dettes 5. **to have the goods,** être capable 6. preuves *fpl* de culpabilité 7. drogues *fpl* en général/stups *mpl*/came *f*. (*See* **sample**)

good-time ['gʊd'taɪm] *a P* 1. **good-time girl,** fille* rigolote/pas triste 2. **good-time guy/ Charlie,** (joyeux) viveur *m*/noceur *m*/ bambocheur *m*/joyeux drille.

goody ['gʊdɪ] *n F see* **goodies.**

goody-goody ['gʊdɪgʊdɪ] **I** *a F* bienpensant; **to be all goody-goody,** faire son petit saint/sa sainte-nitouche **II** *excl F* oh, **goodygoody!** chic chic!/chic alors! **III** *n F* (*NAm also* **goody-two-shoes**) **he's/she's a little goody-goody,** c'est un petit saint (de bois)/une sainte-nitouche.

gooey ['gu:ɪ] *a F* 1. collant/visqueux/ poisseux 2. mièvre/à l'eau de rose/sirupeux.

goof¹ [gu:f] *n esp NAm F* individu bête*/ couillon *m*/cave *m*.

goof² [gu:f] *vi* 1. *F* gaffer/faire une bourde/ mettre les pieds dans le plat/se gour(r)er; dire une connerie 2. *F* se trahir/se vendre/se couper 3. *F* rêvasser/regarder* d'un air hébété *ou* vide d'expression 4. *P* (*drugs*) rater/louper une piquouse. (*See* **goofed up**)

goofball ['gu:fbɔ:l] *n esp NAm P* 1. individu bête*/con *m*, conne *f*/andouille *f* 2. individu* bizarre/drôle *m* d'oiseau/drôle de paroissien 3. *pl* (*drugs*) stups *mpl*/came *f*. (*See* **ball¹ 5**) 4. (*drugs*) mélange *m* de barbituriques* et d'amphétamines.

goofed up [guːftˈʌp] *a P* sous l'influence d'un narcotique *ou* d'un barbiturique; bourré/chargé/défoncé/envapé. (*See* **goof up**)

goofer [ˈguːfə] *n P* curieux, -euse/badaud, -aude.

go off [gəʊˈɒf] *vtr & i* 1. *F* détériorer/s'abîmer/tourner; his ideas have gone off recently, depuis quelque temps ses idées sont un peu foireuses. 2. *F* (*a*) to go off s.o., ne plus aimer* qn; I've gone off him, je ne veux plus sortir avec lui/je l'ai plaqué (*b*) to go off sth, ne plus apprécier qch/perdre le goût de qch 3. *P* avoir un orgasme*/décharger/jouir/prendre son pied 4. *F* how did it go off? comment cela s'est-il passé? (*See* **alarming**; **end 5**; **rails**; **rocker 2**)

goof off [ˈguːfˈɒf] *vi NAm P* 1. traînasser/flemmarder/ne rien faire de ses dix doigts/tirer au flanc; se la couler douce 2. faire l'imbécile/le clown.

goof up [ˈguːfˈʌp] *vi esp NAm P* faire une bourde/une gaffe. (*See* **goofed up**)

goofy [ˈguːfɪ] *a F* 1. bête*/stupide/ballot/cruche; (*crazy*) fou*/dingue; he's a bit goofy, il est un peu dingo 2. to be/to go goofy over s.o., être toqué de qn/en pincer pour qn; to be goofy over sth, être mordu de qch; he's goofy over it, il en est dingue 3. *Br* (*teeth*) de lapin.

goog [gʊg] *n Austr F* 1. œuf *m* 2. individu bête*/ballot *m*.

googly [ˈguːglɪ] *n F* to bowl s.o. a googly, coincer qn/poser une question-piège/une colle à qn.

goo-goo [ˈguːguː] *a F* to make goo-goo eyes at s.o., faire les yeux doux à qn.

gook [gʊk] *n esp NAm P* 1. du toc/de la camelote/de la came 2. saleté*/saloperie *f*/crasse *f* 3. sauce visqueuse *ou* assaisonnement visqueux/ratatouille *f* 4. *Pej* (*a*) moricaud, -aude/café *m* au lait (*b*) chinetoque *mf* (*c*) vietnamien, -ienne/niac *m*/niacoué *m*.

gooky [ˈgʊkɪ] *a esp NAm P* gras/collant/poisseux/visqueux.

goolies [ˈguːlɪz] *npl P* testicules*/balloches *fpl*/breloques *fpl*; to kick s.o. in the goolies, filer un coup de pied dans les couilles à qn; to have s.o. by the goolies, avoir qn à sa merci/à sa pogne.

gooly [ˈguːlɪ] *n P* testicule*. (*See* **goolies**)

goon [guːn] *n* 1. *F* (*a*) individu bête*/cornichon *m*/enflé, -ée (*b*) (*zany person*) clown *m* 2. *P* (*thug*) gorille *m*/cogneur *m*/

casseur *m* de gueules.

go on [gəʊˈɒn] *vi F* 1. that's enough to go on with/to be going on with, voilà du pain sur la planche/assez pour le quart d'heure 2. I don't go much on that, ça ne me dit rien/ça me chante pas/je ne suis pas d'accord 3. go on! (*a*) dis toujours! (*b*) go on (with you)! à d'autres!/n'en jetez plus, la cour est pleine!/et ta sœur! 4. discuter le bout de gras; she does go on! impossible de la lui boucler! to go on and on (about sth), déblatérer (sur qch) 5. to be going on (for) forty, friser la quarantaine/aller sur ses quarante piges 6. to be gone on s.o., aimer* qn/s'amouracher de qn/en pincer pour qn.

goop [guːp] *n esp NAm F* individu bête*/couillon *m*/andouille *f*.

goose¹ [guːs] *n F* 1. individu bête*; she's a silly little goose, c'est une petite dinde 2. all his geese are swans, à l'écouter, tout ce qu'il fait tient du prodige. (*See* **cook² 3**)

goose² [guːs] *vtr P* 1. pincer les fesses* à (qn); mettre la main au cul/au panier 2. duper*/faisander/pigeonner/englander (qn).

gooseberry [ˈgʊzb(ə)rɪ] *n Br F* to play gooseberry, faire le chaperon/tenir la chandelle.

goosegog [ˈgʊzgɒg] *n Br F* (= *gooseberry*) groseille verte *ou* à maquereau.

go out [gəʊˈaʊt] *vi F* to go out like a light, (*faint*) s'évanouir*/tourner de l'œil/tomber dans les pommes; (*fall asleep*) s'endormir/se mettre à pioncer.

go over [gəʊˈəʊvə] *vtr & i* 1. passer la rampe/faire son petit effet; that didn't go over too well, ça n'a pas été tellement apprécié 2. *P* battre* (qn); they went over him with an iron bar, ils lui ont arrangé le portrait à coups de barre de fer.

GOP [dʒiːəʊˈpiː] *abbr NAm F* (= *Grand Old Party*) le parti républicain.

gorblimey! [gɔːˈblaɪmɪ] *excl P* sacré nom (de nom)!/merde (alors)! (*See* **blimey!**)

Gordon Bennett! [ˈgɔːdnˈbenɪt] *excl P* doux Jésus!/purée de nous autres!/sacré nom d'une pipe!

gorgeous [ˈgɔːdʒəs] *a F* excellent*/super(be)/terrible/extra; gorgeous weather, un temps superbe; hi, gorgeous! salut ma beauté!/t'as de beaux yeux, tu sais!

gorilla [gəˈrɪlə] *n* 1. *F* (*esp bodyguard*) brute *f*/gorille *m* 2. *P* gangster *m*/tueur *m*/malfrat *m*.

gormless [ˈgɔːmlɪs] *a F* bouché/gourde; you

gormless jerk! espèce de cruche!/ d'andouille!/de patate!

gosh! [gɒʃ] *excl F* mince!/zut!

gospel ['gɒspəl] *n F* that's gospel/it's the gospel truth, c'est la vérité pure/parole d'évangile; croix de bois, croix de fer (si je mens, je vais en enfer).

gospeller ['gɒspələ] *n F* hot gospeller, évangéliste outré/bigot *m* à tous crins.

goss [gɒs] *n Br F* (*short for gossip = rumour*) commérage(s) *m(pl)*/cancans *mpl*/ potins *mpl*.

goth [gɒθ] *n Br P* individu* qui suit le style punk gothique.

go through ['gəʊ'θruː] *vtr F* he's gone through a lot, il en a vu des vertes et des pas mûres/il en a vu de toutes les couleurs.

gotta ['gɒtə] *P* 1. (= *got to*) when you gotta go you gotta go, quand faut y aller, faut y aller 2. (= *got a*) you've gotta lot to go through, t'en verras des vertes et des pas mûres/ce sera pas de la tarte/t'as du chemin à faire.

gourd [gʊəd] *n NAm P* tête*/citrouille *f*; he's out of his gourd, il est tapé/il travaille du chapeau.

gov [gʌv], **governor** ['gʌvnə] *n Br F* 1. (the) gov/(the) governor, le patron*/le singe; le dirlo *m* 2. (the) gov/(the) governor, père*/ le vieux/le paternel 3. (*respectful form of address*) thanks gov! merci chef!

go walkabout [gəʊ'wɔːkəbaʊt] *vi F* rêvasser/planer/gambergeailler.

goy, Goy [gɔɪ] *n F* non-Juif *m*/Gentil *m*/ goy(e) *m*.

grab¹ [græb] *n Br F* 1. (*a*) paye *f*/salaire *m*; grab day, jour *m* de paye/la Sainte-Touche (*b*) (*overtime*) heures *fpl* supplémentaires; heures sup; to do some grab/be on the grab, faire des heures sup(plémentaires) 2. up for grabs, sur le marché/à vendre.

grab² [græb] *vtr* 1. *F* accrocher (qn)/prendre (qn) aux tripes 2. *F* how does that grab you? qu'est-ce que tu en dis?/ça te branche? 3. *F* to grab a bite, avaler un casse-croûte/un morceau sur le pouce; manger en vitesse 4. *P* arrêter*/agrafer/épingler (qn). (*See* **u.v.'s**; **z's**)

grade [greɪd] *n F* to make the grade, réussir/être à la hauteur.

graft¹ [grɑːft] *n P* 1. *NAm* (*bribery*) pot-de-vin *m*/graissage *m* de patte/gratte *f* 2. (*a*) (hard) graft, travail*/grat(t)in *m*/turbin *m*; to put in a bit of hard graft, travailler dur*/

bosser/turbiner (*b*) (*job*) boulot *m* 3. logement* et nourriture*/pension *f*; good graft, bon gîte/bonne bouffe.

graft² [grɑːft] *vi Br P* 1. travailler dur*/ bosser/turbiner 2. (*engage in dishonest financial schemes*) tripoter/magouiller 3. poursuivre des activités criminelles.

grafter ['grɑːftə] *n Br P* 1. (*hard worker*) bosseur, -euse/turbineur, -euse 2. (*dishonest schemer*) magouilleur, -euse/tripatouilleur, -euse 3. criminel, -elle/voleur, -euse/piqueur *m*.

grand [grænd] *n F* (*a*) mille livres *fpl* (sterling) (*b*) mille dollars *mpl*.

grannie, granny ['grænɪ] *n* 1. *F* grand-mère *f*/mémé(e) *f*/mémère *f*/mamie *f* 2. *P* négoce légal qui dissimule des activités illicites; couverte *f*/couverture *f*/couvrante *f* 3. *P* to strangle one's grannie, se masturber*/ s'astiquer la colonne/étrangler Popaul.

grapevine ['greɪpvaɪn] *n F* renseignements* (de bouche à oreille)/téléphone *m* arabe; I heard it on the grapevine, je me le suis laissé dire.

grapplers ['græpləz] *npl P* mains*/grappins *mpl*/pinces *fpl*.

grass¹ [grɑːs] *n* 1. *P* indicateur*/indic *mf*/ mouchard, -arde/donneur, -euse. (*See* **super-grass**). 2. *P* (*drugs*) marijuana*/herbe *f*/ marie-jeanne *f*; to smoke grass, fumer de l'herbe 3. *Austr P* to be on the grass, être en liberté/être largué 4. *F* to be put out to grass, être mis à la retraite.

grass² [grɑːs] *vi P* moucharder/moutonner; to grass on s.o./to grass s.o. up, dénoncer*/ balancer/donner qn.

grasser ['grɑːsə] *n P* indicateur*/indic *mf*/ mouchard, -arde/cafardeur, -euse.

grasshopper ['grɑːshɒpə] *n P* (*RS = copper*) agent* de police/perdreau *m*/flic *m*. (*See* **knee-high**)

grassroots ['grɑːs'ruːts] I *a F* de base/qui émane de la base; grassroots political movement, mouvement *m* politique populaire; grassroots democracy, le populisme II *npl F* 1. région *f* agricole/la brousse 2. le gros (de la troupe)/la base (d'un parti, d'une société, etc) 3. fondation *f*/source *f*/base *f*.

grass-widow ['grɑːs'wɪdəʊ] *n F* femme* dont le mari s'absente régulièrement.

grass-widower ['grɑːs'wɪdəʊə] *n F* mari *m* dont la femme s'absente régulièrement.

graveyard ['greɪvjɑːd] *n F* graveyard shift, équipe *f* (de travailleurs) de nuit.

gravy ['greɪvɪ] *n P* 1. bénéfice*/butin*/bénef *m*/af(f)ure *f*/gratte *f*; **the gravy train**, *(success, easy money, etc)* l'assiette *f* au beurre/le bon filon; **to ride the gravy train**, taper dans l'assiette au beurre 2. **the Gravy**, l'Atlantique *m*/la Grande Tasse 3. **to dish out the gravy**, *(prison sentence)* condamner au maximum.

grease [griːs] *n P* 1. *(a)* *(bribe)* petit cadeau/glissage *m* de pièce/dessous-de-table *m* *(b)* *(protection money)* achat *m* de conscience/prix *m* du silence/amende *f*. *(See* **palm-grease**) 2. *NAm* argent*/fric *m*/beurre *m* 3. **grease monkey**, garagiste *mf*/mécanicien, -ienne/mécano *mf*.

greaseball ['griːsbɔːl] *n NAm P* 1. *Pej* *(Hispanic or Mediterranean)* Rital, -ale/Espingo *mf*/Mexicain, -aine/métèque *mf* *(d'origine espagnole ou italienne)* 2. cuisinier, -ière/cuistot *m*; mécanicien, -ienne/mécano *mf*.

greased [griːst] *a F* **like greased lightning**, très vite*/à plein(s) tube(s)/en quatrième vitesse.

greaser ['griːsə] *n P* 1. *Br O* rocker *m*/rockeur *m* 2. *NAm Pej* = **greaseball 1** 3. jeune homme/jeune voyou (au blouson noir et aux cheveux longs)/blouson noir/loubard *m*/loulou *m* 4. *(toady)* lèche-bottes *m*/lèche-pompes *m*.

grease-up ['griːsʌp] *n Br F* repas cuit à la poêle/*surt* petit déjeuner d'œufs au bacon, etc.

greasy ['griːsɪ, griːzɪ] *a P* 1. flagorneur/lèche-bottes; **he's a greasy old slob**, c'est un vieux lécheur/lèche-cul 2. **greasy spoon**, *(cheap restaurant)* routier *m*/guitoune *f*/bouiboui *m*. *(See* **dago**)

great [greɪt] I *a F* 1. excellent*/terrible/super/génial/sensass; **it's great to be alive**, il fait bon vivre, tout de même; **that's really great**, c'est le (super-)pied; **to have a great time**, s'en payer (une tranche)/s'éclater; **he's a great guy**, c'est un chic type/un type sensass/un mec extra; **he's great at tennis**, il se débrouille vachement bien au tennis/c'est un as du tennis 2. **great Scott! bon dieu!/bon sang!** *(See* **gun¹ 3**; **shake¹ 5**) II *adv F* 1. **I feel great**, j'ai la forme/la pêche/la frite 2. **it was working just great**, ça marchait à merveille/comme sur des roulettes III *n F* **he's one of the all-time greats**, c'est un des grands de toujours/un des plus fameux de tous les temps.

greatest ['greɪtɪst] *n F* **he's the greatest!**

c'est le plus grand/le champion/l'as des as!

grebo, greebo ['griːbəʊ] *n Br P* jeune fana *mf* de musique rock/rocker *m* *(portant cheveux longs et blouson de cuir)*.

greedy-guts ['griːdɪgʌts] *n P* goinfre*/crevard. -arde.

greefa ['griːfə] *n P* *(drugs)* cigarette* de marijuana/joint *m*/stick *m*.

greefo ['griːfəʊ] *n P* *(drugs)* marijuana/herbe *f*.

Greek¹ [griːk] I *a P* **the Greek way**, coït* anal/enculage *m*; **to do it Greek style/to do it like the Greeks**, pratiquer le coït* anal/prendre du petit/tourner la page II *n* 1. *F* **it's all Greek to me**, c'est de l'hébreu/c'est du chinois pour moi 2. *P* coït* anal.

Greek² [griːk] *vtr & i P* pratiquer le coït* anal/prendre du chouette/passer par l'entrée de service.

green [griːn] I *a* 1. *P* *(drugs)* **green ashes**, opium*/dross *m*/op *m* 2. *P* **green and blacks**, capsules *fpl* de barbituriques/vert *m* et noir 3. *F* **to give s.o. the green light**, donner le feu vert à qn 4. *F* *(inexperienced)* novice/inexpérimenté; *(gullible)* crédule/naïf; **he's not as green as he looks**, il n'est pas né d'hier/de la dernière pluie 5. *F* **to have green fingers**/*NAm* **a green thumb**, être un bon jardinier/avoir la main verte 6. *P* **green stuff**, argent*/fric *m*/oseille *f* 7. *Br P* **green gilbert**, morve *f*. *(See* **dragon 3**) II *n* 1. *F* **(do you) see any green (in my eye)?** tu ne m'as pas regardé?/je ne suis pas né d'hier! 2. *P* argent*/fric *m*/oseille *f*. *(See* **greens**)

green-ass ['griːnæs] *a NAm P* = **green I 4**.

greenback ['griːnbæk] *n F* *(a)* *O* billet* d'une livre sterling *(b)* billet* de banque américain.

greenie ['griːnɪ] *n P* 1. *Br O* billet* d'une livre sterling 2. *NAm* bière *f*/mousse *f*.

greenies ['griːnɪz] *npl P* billets *mpl* de banque/talbins *mpl*/fafiots *mpl*.

greens [griːnz] *npl* 1. *F* légumes verts 2. *P* l'amour *m* physique; **to like one's greens**, être porté sur la chose 3. *F* **the Greens**, les écolos *mpl*.

green-welly brigade [griːn'welɪbrɪ'geɪd] *n Br F* = bon-chic-bon-genre/B.C.B.G. *(habillés en anorak et bottes de caoutchouc vert)*.

grefa ['griːfə] *n P* = **greefa**.

gregory ['gregərɪ] *n Br P* *(RS = Gregory Peck = cheque)* chèque *m*.

gremlin ['gremlɪn] *n F* lutin *m* de malheur/ pépin *m*; **the gremlins must have got into my watch, it's ten minutes fast,** il doit y avoir des fourmis dans ma tocante, elle cavale de dix minutes.

grey (the) [ðə'greɪ] *n NAm P Pej (Black Slang)* (homme) blanc *m*.

greyback ['greɪbæk] *n P* pou*/mie *f* de pain à bec.

greybeard ['greɪbɪəd] *n F* vieux *m* de la vieille/vieux routier.

griff ['grɪf] *n F* the griff, renseignement* utile/bon tuyau/bon rencart; **to get the griff on sth,** être affranchi/s'être rencardé sur qch.

grift [grɪft] *vtr esp NAm P* escroquer*/ estamper/faisander.

grifter ['grɪftə] *n esp NAm P* escroc*/ estampeur *m*/faisan(t) *m*.

grill¹ [grɪl] *n F (on fruit machine)* mixed grill, embrouillamini *m*.

grill² [grɪl] *vtr F* to grill s.o., serrer les pouces *mpl* à qn *(pour obtenir un aveu)*/ cuisiner qn.

grilled [grɪld] *a NAm P* ivre*/noir/noircicot.

grim [grɪm] *a F* mauvais*/désagréable/de mauvais augure; **things look grim,** c'est mal barré/ça s'annonce mal; **he's feeling a bit grim,** il a le moral à zéro/il n'a pas la frite/il n'a pas la pêche. *(See* **hang on 2)**

grind¹ [graɪnd] *n* 1. *F* travail* dur et monotone; **the daily grind,** la routine/le train-train quotidien/le métro-boulot-dodo; **to go back to the old grind,** reprendre le collier/se remettre au turbin; **to get down to a bit of hard grind,** travailler dur/bosser/trimer 2. *NAm F* bûcheur, -euse/potasseur *m* 3. *P* coït*/baise *f*/ carambolage *m*/tringlage *m*; **to have a grind,** faire l'amour*/faire un carton/tringler.

grind² [graɪnd] *vtr & i* 1. *F* travailler* dur/ boulonner/trimer/bûcher 2. *P* faire l'amour*/ fourailler/tringler. *(See* **axe¹ 2)**

grinder ['graɪndə] *n F* 1. to put s.o. through the grinder, faire passer un mauvais quart d'heure à qn 2. *pl* dents*/crocs *mpl*/dominos *mpl*.

grip [grɪp] *n* 1. to get a grip on oneself *(a) F* se contenir/se retenir/se contrôler/se ressaisir *(b) V* se masturber*/se faire une pogne/se taper (sur) la colonne 2. *F* to lose one's grip, perdre la tête/les pédales *fpl*.

gripe¹ [graɪp] *n F* 1. plainte *f*/rouspétance *f*; **he's always got a gripe about sth,** il est toujours à rouspéter contre qch; **what gripes does he have against you?** qu'est-ce qu'il te

reproche? **to have/to get the gripes** *(a)* se mettre en rogne/en boule; rouspéter/ ronchonner *(b)* avoir la diarrhée*/la courante 2. geignard, -arde/râleur, -euse.

gripe² [graɪp] *vi F* grogner*/rouspéter/ ronchonner/râler; **he was griping about the bill,** la note lui a fait perdre le sourire/la note trop salée le faisait râler.

griper ['graɪpə] *n F* râleur, -euse/rouspéteur, -euse; mauvais coucheur.

gristletoe ['grɪsltəʊ] *n F (mistletoe)* gui *m*.

grit [grɪt] *n F* 1. cran *m*/battant *m*; **he's full of grit,** il en a dans le ventre 2. *Can Pol* Libéral(e).

gritty ['grɪtɪ] *a Br F* bourru/rude/caustique.

grizzle ['grɪzl] *vi F* 1. pleurnicher/geindre 2. grogner*/rouspéter.

grizzler ['grɪzlə] *n F* 1. pleurnicheur, -euse/ chialeur, -euse 2. geignard, -arde.

grockle ['grɒkl] *n Br P Pej* touriste *mf*/ estivant(e); *surt* caravanier *m*.

grody ['grəʊdɪ] *a NAm P* répugnant/ dégueulasse/débectant.

grog¹ [grɒg] *n P* alcool* (en général); **to be on the grog,** boire* (beaucoup)/caresser la bouteille/biberonner/picoler.

grog² [grɒg] *vi P* boire* (beaucoup)/caresser la bouteille/biberonner/picoler.

groggy ['grɒgɪ] *a F* 1. un peu malade*/ patraque/mal fichu; **to feel a bit groggy,** n'avoir pas la pêche/la frite 2. *(boxing)* groggy/sonné 3. ivre*/paf/éméché/parti 4. **a groggy old table,** une vieille table bancale.

grog shop ['grɒg'ʃɒp] *n F esp Austr (= off-licence)* = débit *m* de boissons/magasin *m* de vins et spiritueux.

groid [grɔɪd] *n F Pej (short for negroid)* Noir(e)/bougnoul *m*.

groin [grɔɪn] *n P (betting ring)* bande noire de parieurs sur un champ de courses.

groove [gruːv] *n O F* 1. spécialité *f*/dada *m*/ rayon *m*; **that's my groove,** ça, c'est mon blot 2. **it's a groove,** c'est chic 3. **in the groove,** en pleine forme/en plein boum; *(jazz)* (orchestre) donnant son plein/faisant des étincelles; **it's in the groove,** *(fashionable)* c'est à la mode/à la coule/dans le vent; *(works well)* ça marche comme sur des roulettes/tout baigne dans l'huile.

groover ['gruːvə] *n F* 1. *O* individu* branché/à la coule/dans le vent 2. bûcheur, -euse/potasseur *m*.

groovy ['gruːvɪ] *a F* 1. *O* excellent*/super/ génial; **that's really groovy,** c'est vachement

bien; c'est super cool **2.** *NAm* ennuyeux/
rasoir/barbant.

grope¹ [grəʊp] *n P* tripotage *m*/pelotage *m*;
to have a quick grope, aller aux
renseignements/mettre la main au panier/
tripoter (qn). (*See* **group-grope**)

grope² [grəʊp] *vtr P* palper les parties de
(qn) sous ses vêtements/peloter (qn)/mettre
la main au panier/faire du rentre-dedans.

gross [grəʊs] *a F* **1.** répugnant/dégueulasse/
débectant **2.** *NAm* (*excessive*) that's gross,
c'est trop.

gross-out ['grəʊsaʊt] *n NAm F* situation *ou*
action répugnante/dégueulasserie *f*.

gross out ['grəʊs'aʊt] *vtr NAm* to gross
s.o. out, répugner/débecter qn.

grot [grɒt] *n Br F* **1.** saleté*/crassouille *f*/
saloperie *f* **2.** individu* sale*/cradingue;
(*disreputable*) craignos *m*.

grotty ['grɒtɪ] *a F* **1.** laid*/moche/tocard/
tarte **2.** outré et inutile.

grouch¹ [graʊtʃ] *n F* **1.** ronchonnage *m*/
rouspétance *f* **2.** râleur, -euse/ronchonneur,
-euse.

grouch² [graʊtʃ] *vi F* grogner*/râler/
ronchonner.

grouch city [graʊtʃ'sɪtɪ] *a NAm F* he's
grouch city, il est super grognon/qu'est-ce
qu'il râle!

groucher ['graʊtʃə] *n F* = **grouch¹ 2.**

ground [graʊnd] *n F* **1.** to run s.o. into the
ground, débiner/démolir qn **2.** that suits me
down to the ground, cela me convient
parfaitement/ça me botte/ça fait mon blot **3.**
to get a scheme off the ground, faire
démarrer un projet; it'll never get off the
ground, cela ne verra jamais le jour/cela ne
démarrera jamais. (*See* **stamping ground**)

grounded ['graʊndɪd] *a esp NAm F*
enfermé à la maison/interdit de sortie
(*comme punition*).

group-grope ['gruːp'grəʊp] *n P* tripotage
m/pelotage *m* en groupe.

groupie ['gruːpɪ] *n* **1.** *F* fan *mf* de groupe
pop/rock; groupie *f* **2.** *P* fille* qui aime faire
l'amour en groupe.

grouse¹ [graʊs] *n F* **1.** plainte *f*/rouspétance
f; grogne *f*/bougonnement *m* **2.** rouscailleur
m/râleur, -euse.

grouse² [graʊs] *vi F* grogner*/marronner/
rouscailler; he's always grousing about something or other, il n'arrête pas de rouspéter/il a
toujours qch à râler.

grouser ['graʊsə] *n F* rouspéteur, -euse/

râleur, -euse.

grub [grʌb] *n P* **1.** nourriture*/boustifaille *f*/
mangeaille *f*/bectance *f*; grub up!/grub's up!
à la bouffe!/à la soupe! **2.** enfant sale*/petite
vermine/petit(e) morveux, -euse.

grubby ['grʌbɪ] *a F* sale*/cracra/crado.

gruel ['gruːəl] *n F* **1.** réprimande *f*/attrapade
f/engueulade *f*/savon *m* **2.** to give s.o. his
gruel, battre* qn (comme plâtre)/filer une
trempe à qn **3.** to take/to get one's gruel,
avaler sa médecine/encaisser/avaler la pilule.

gruelling ['gruːəlɪŋ] *n F* (*a*) passage *m* à
tabac/dérouillée *f*/trempe *f* (*b*) épreuve
éreintante.

grumblebum ['grʌmblbʌm] *n* rouspéteur,
-euse/râleur, -euse.

grunge [grʌndʒ] *n P* **1.** chose répugnante/
dégueulasserie *f*; grunge (fashion/look), mode
f grunge/grunge *m* **2.** personne *ou* chose
ennuyeuse/chiante; rasoir *m*.

grungie, grungy ['grʌndʒɪ] *n P* (jeune)
personne sale et mal habillée.

grunt [grʌnt] *n NAm P* soldat *m*/bidasse *m*.

grunt-and-groan ['grʌntən(d)'grəʊn] *n F*
la lutte/le catch.

grunt-and-groaner ['grʌnt-ən(d)'grəʊnə]
n F lutteur, -euse/catcheur, -euse.

grunter ['grʌntə] *n F* **1.** (*ignorant or
slovenly person*) porc *m* **2.** *Austr* (*sluttish
woman*) salope *f*.

G-string ['dʒiːstrɪŋ] *n F* cache-sexe *m*/
cache-fri-fri *m*.

gubbins ['gʌbɪnz] *n Br F* **1.** accompa-
gnement *m*/garniture *f* (d'un plat) **2.** gadget
m/bidule *m*/truc *m*/machin *m*.

guck [gʌk] *n esp NAm F* = **gook 2, 3.**

guess [ges] *vi F* croire/penser; I guess, je
suppose; I guess that..., il y a des chances
pour que...; you're right, I guess, oui, il me
semble que vous avez raison/tu as sans doute
raison; guess what? devine!/imagine!

guesstimate¹ ['gestɪmət] *n F* estimation *f*
au pifomètre.

guesstimate² ['gestɪmeɪt] *vtr F* estimer/
évaluer/calculer au pifomètre.

guest [gest] *n F* (*also Iron*) be my guest!
fais comme chez toi!/ne te gêne pas!

guff¹ [gʌf] *n* **1.** *F* bêtises*/blagues *fpl*/
foutaises *fpl* **2.** *F* renseignements *mpl*/
information(s) *f(pl)*/info *f*; have you got all
the guff? t'as les infos? **3.** *Br F* pet*/fusant *m*.

guff² [gʌf] *vi Br P* péter*/lâcher une perle.

guide [gaɪd] *n P* drogué* endurci qui en-
traîne les autres/guide *m* de neufs.

guinea ['gɪnɪ] *n Br O F* it's worth a guinea a minute, c'est très amusant*/c'est impayable.

guiver[1] ['gaɪvə] *n Austr F* baratin *m*; to sling the guiver, baratiner.

guiver[2] ['gaɪvə] *vi Austr F* baratiner/faire du baratin.

gum [gʌm] *n F* by gum! mince alors!/nom d'un chien! (*See* **gum-tree**)

gumballs ['gʌmbɔːlz] *npl NAm F* feux clignotants sur le toit d'une voiture de police.

gumption ['gʌm(p)ʃ(ə)n] *n F* bon sens/débrouillardise *f*; to have gumption, avoir de la jugeote; he's got plenty of gumption, c'est un débrouillard/un démerdard; il se débrouille bien.

gumshoe ['gʌmʃuː] *n NAm F* agent* de police habillé en civil/en-bourgeois *m*/hambourgeois *m*/condé *m*.

gum-tree ['gʌmtriː] *n F* (to be) up a gum-tree, (être) dans une impasse/dans le pétrin/dans de beaux draps.

gum up ['gʌm'ʌp] *vtr F* to gum up the works, encrasser les rouages/mettre des bâtons dans les roues/(tout) foutre en l'air.

gun[1] [gʌn] *n* 1. *P* seringue* hypodermique/poussette *f*/shooteuse *f* 2. *F* to jump the gun, brûler le feu/aller plus vite que les violons 3. *F* to go great guns, prospérer/faire un boum; his business is going great guns, son commerce marche à merveille/à plein gaz; the party was going great guns, ça chauffait à la boum/c'était une boum du tonnerre/il y avait une super ambiance à la boum 4. *F* to stick to one's guns, s'accrocher/tenir bon/ne pas en démordre 5. *NAm P* (*a*) voleur*/caroubleur *m*/casseur *m*; voleur, -euse à la tire (*b*) (hired) gun, bandit *m*/gangster *m*/malfrat *m*/porte-flingue *m* 6. *O F* to give sth the gun, accélérer qch/mettre les gaz/mettre la gomme 7. *P Euph* pénis*. (*See* **big I 1**; **burp-gun**; **spike**[2] **3**)

gun[2] [gʌn] *vi F* 1. to be (out) gunning for s.o., pourchasser qn pour se venger de lui/aller à la rebiffe; I'm gunning for you, je t'aurai au tournant/je te revaudrai ça/j'aurai ta peau 2. accélérer/mettre les gaz/mettre la gomme.

gun down ['gʌn'daʊn] *vtr F* fusiller/flinguer/descendre (qn).

gunge [gʌndʒ] *n Br F* saleté*/saloperie *f*/merde *f*.

gunja ['gʌndʒə], **gunny** ['gʌnɪ] *n P* (*drugs*) marijuana*/kif *m*. (*See* **ganja(h)**)

gunk [gʌŋk] *n F* = **gunge**.

gunsel ['gʌnzl] *n NAm P* 1. gangster *m*/malfrat *m*/dur *m* 2. blanc-bec *m*/dadais *m*.

gunship ['gʌnʃɪp] *n Br P* voiture *f* (de police) banalisée.

gunslinger ['gʌnslɪŋə] *n F* vaurien* armé/porte-flingue *m*.

gurk [gɜːk] *vi P* 1. *Br* roter 2. *Austr* péter*/lâcher une perle.

gussie ['gʌsɪ] *n P* (*not common*) homme* efféminé/gâcheuse *f*.

gut [gʌt] *n* 1. *P* to bust a gut to do sth, décarcasser/se crever le cul pour faire qch 2. *F* gut feeling, intuition *f*; gut reaction, réaction viscérale. (*See* **guts**; **rot-gut**)

gutful ['gʌtfʊl] *n P* (*a*) ventrée *f* (*b*) to have (had) a gutful, en avoir ras le bol/en avoir son compte/en avoir plein le cul. (*See* **bellyful**)

gutless ['gʌtlɪs] *a P* to be gutless, être lâche/ne rien avoir dans le bide; a gutless character, un type mou/une chiffe molle/un(e) trouillard, -arde/une lavette.

gut-rot ['gʌtrɒt] *n F* 1. = **rot-gut** 2. mauvaise nourriture*/ragougnasse *f*.

guts [gʌts] *npl* 1. *F* to have guts, être courageux*; avoir des tripes/du cran/de l'estomac; en avoir dans le bide; to have no guts, avoir les foies/les jetons; ne pas en avoir dans le bidon; he's got no guts, il n'a rien dans le ventre; she's got guts, elle a du cran; it takes a lot of guts to do that, il faut beaucoup d'estomac pour faire ça; il faut avoir des couilles/en avoir pour le faire 2. *P* to hate s.o.'s guts, détester* qn/avoir qn dans le nez/ne pas pouvoir blairer qn/ne pas pouvoir pif(f)er qn 3. *V* to drop one's guts, péter*/en lâcher une 4. *P* to knife s.o. in the guts, éventrer qn/mettre les tripes à l'air à qn/crever la paillasse à qn 5. *P* put some guts into it! mets-en un (bon) coup!/magne-toi le train! 6. *P* to sweat one's guts out, travailler* dur/en foutre un coup/se casser les reins/se crever le cul 7. *P* to spew/to spill one's guts (up), vomir*/dégueuler/aller au refil(e)/gerber; (*confess, inform*) avouer*/vider son sac/dégueuler (*See* **spill**) 8. *Austr P* to hold one's guts, se taire*/poser sa chique 9. *P* I'll have your guts for garters! j'aurai ta peau!/je me ferai un porte-monnaie avec tes couilles! 10. *P* du charnu/de l'étoffe *f*/de la substance; the real guts of the problem, l'essentiel *m*/le cœur du problème 11. *P* = **greedy-guts**. (*See* **gut**; **worryguts**)

gutsache ['gʌtseɪk] *n P* (*miserable, contemptible person*) casse-pieds *m*/casse-bonbons *m*/casse-couilles *m*/emmerdeur, -euse/raclure *f*.

gut-scraper ['gʌtskreɪpə] *n P* racleur, -euse de cordes; joueur, -euse de zinzin.

gutsy ['gʌtsɪ] *a Br P* qui a du cran/qui en a dans le ventre; qui a des tripes.

gutted ['gʌtɪd] *a P* très déçu/chagriné; to feel/to be gutted, l'avoir mauvaise; he was gutted, ça lui en a foutu un coup/ça lui a sapé le moral.

gutter ['gʌtə] *n F* 1. the gutter press, la presse à scandales 2. *esp NAm* to have one's mind in the gutter, être obsédé(e)/ne penser qu'à ça/avoir l'esprit mal tourné.

gutty ['gʌtɪ] *a Br P* = **gutsy**.

gutzer ['gʌtsə] *n Austr P* to come a gutzer, (*fall*) tomber*/se casser la figure; (*fail*) tomber sur un bec/faire un bide.

guv [gʌv], **guvnor** ['gʌvnə] *n Br F* = **gov**.

guy [gaɪ] *n* 1. *F esp NAm* (*a*) homme*/type *m*/mec *m*/zigoto *m*; he's a nice guy, c'est un type bien/un mec réglo; a wise guy, (*know-all*) un crâneur/un je-sais-tout; (*crafty person*) un roublard/un mariol(e); a gay guy, un gay/un homo; hi, you guys! salut(, tout le monde)! (*b*) **her guy,** (*boyfriend, husband*) son mec/son jules 2. *P* to do a guy (*a*) s'enfuir*/se tirer/se casser (*b*) donner un faux nom*/un faux blaze. (*See* **fall-guy; great I 1; righteous 1; tough I 1**)

guzunder [gə'zʌndə] *n P* = **gazunda, gazunder**.

gynie ['gaɪnɪ] *n F* (*short for gynaecologist*) gynéco *mf*.

gyp¹ [dʒɪp] *n* 1. *F* = **gip** 2. *NAm P* escroc*/ filou *m*/carotteur, -euse.

gyp² [dʒɪp] *vtr NAm P* to gyp s.o., escroquer* qn/estamper qn/empiler qn/écorcher qn; to be gypped, se faire pigeonner.

gyppo ['dʒɪpəʊ] *n P* = **gippo**.

gyppy tummy ['dʒɪpɪ'tʌmɪ] *n Br P* = **gippy tummy**.

gypsy ['dʒɪpsɪ] *n Br P* danseuse *f*/girl *f* (de music-hall).

H

H [eɪtʃ] *n P* (*drugs*) héroïne*/H *f*/blanche *f*.
habit ['hæbɪt] *n* 1. *F* toxicomanie *f*; to kick the habit, décrocher; off the habit, décamé/désintox(iqué) 2. *P* dose habituelle de drogues.
hack¹ [hæk] *n* 1. *F* journaliste *mf*/journaleux, -euse; **hack writer/literary hack**, pisseur, -euse de copie/pisse-copie *mf*/briseur *m* de nougats 2. *NAm F* (*taxi*) taxi *m*/bahut *m*; (*taxi driver*) chauffeur *m* de taxi/taxi *m* 3. *NAm P* (*Black Slang*) Blanc *m* 4. toux sèche.
hack² [hæk] *vi* 1. *F* conduire un taxi/faire le taxi 2. *P* (*cope*) he can't hack it, il ne s'en sort pas/il est complètement dépassé 3. travailler comme écrivain/écrire.
hack around ['hækə'raʊnd] *vi NAm F* flâner/flânocher/glander.
hacked (off) ['hækt('ɒf)] *a P* 1. en colère*/à cran 2. qui en a assez*/qui en a soupé; qui en a ras le bol/plein le dos.
hacker ['hækə] *n P* 1. *Comptr* pirate *m* 2. (chauffeur *m* de) taxi *m* 3. mauvais ouvrier/fumigo *m*.
hackette [hæ'ket] *n F* (femme) journaliste *f*/femme écrivain.
hack into ['hæk'ɪntuː] *vi Comptr P* to hack into a database, pirater une base de données.
hagbag ['hæg'bæg] *n P* (*CB*) fille* *ou* femme* laide/boudin *m*/mocheté *f*/cageot *m*.
Haggis land ['hægɪslænd] *n P* (*CB*) Écosse *f*.
hair [hɛə] *n* 1. *F* to get in s.o.'s hair, taper sur les nerfs/sur le système à qn 2. *F* to let one's hair down, se laisser aller/ne pas faire de chichis/ne pas se formaliser 3. *P* keep your hair on! calme-toi!/(ne) t'emballe pas! 4. *F* to split hairs, couper les cheveux en quatre 5. *F* get some hair on your chest! conduis-toi en homme!/sors de tes langes! this'll put hair(s) on your chest! (*of medicine, whisky, etc*) ça te fera du bien/te remontera (le moral)! 6. *P* to have s.o. by the short hairs = to have s.o. by the short and curlies (**curlies**). (*See* **dog¹**

7)
hairburger ['hɛəbɜːgə] *n esp NAm V* sexe* de la femme*/barbu *m*/chatte *f*. (*See* **furburger**)
haircut ['hɛəkʌt] *n P* court séjour en prison*.
hair-do ['hɛəduː] *n F* I'm going to have a hair-do, je vais chez le/je vais au coiffeur; je vais me faire couper les douilles *fpl*/les tifs *mpl*.
hairpie ['hɛə'paɪ] *n V* 1. cunnilinctus* 2. = **hairburger**.
hairy ['hɛərɪ] *a P* (*a*) (*difficult*) épineux/duraille/trapu/costaud (*b*) (*frightening*) horrible/à vous faire dresser les cheveux sur la tête; it was a bit of a hairy experience, ça m'a donné une sacrée pétoche/j'ai failli en pisser dans mon froc.
half [hɑːf] I *adv F* 1. not half! et comment!/tu parles!/une paille!/à peine! 2. she didn't half laugh, elle s'est bien tordue de rire/elle s'est marrée, je te dis pas 3. you won't half catch it! qu'est-ce que tu vas prendre! 4. he hasn't half changed, il a drôlement/méchamment changé 5. (*a*) half and half, moitié-moitié (*b*) to go half and half, marcher à cinquante-cinquante/faire moite-moite/faire fifty-fifty/faire afanaf. (*See* **fifty-fifty**) 6. to be only half there, être un peu fou*/être toqué/être un peu timbré. (*See* **shift²** 1) II *n* 1. *F* (*beer*) demi *m* 2. half and half (*a*) *F* panaché *m* de bière brune et blonde (*b*) *P* (*esp prostitutes*) fellation* suivie d'un coït* conventionnel 3. *F* you haven't heard the half of it (yet), faut que je te dise le meilleur!/attends, il y a mieux! 4. *F* my better/other half, ma (douce) moitié.
half-a-crown ['hɑːfə'kraʊn] *n A F* see **bingo 26**.
half-a-dollar ['hɑːfə'dɒlə] *n A P* (= *half-a-crown*) see **bingo 26**.
half-arsed ['hɑːf'ɑːst], *NAm* **half-assed** ['hæf'æst] *a P* mal fait/salopé/bousillé.

half-baked ['hɑːf'beɪkt] *a F* (*a*) inexpérimenté/blanc-bec (*b*) bête*/niais/bêta (*c*) à la noix; *that half-baked idea of yours,* ton idée à la con.

half-brass ['hɑːf'brɑːs] *n O P* femme* facile qui ne fait pas payer ses faveurs. (*See* **brass II 4**)

half-century ['hɑːf'sentʃərɪ] *n P* cinquante livres *fpl*.

half-cock ['hɑːf'kɒk] *n F* to go off at half-cock, mal partir/mal démarrer/rater.

half-cut ['hɑːf'kʌt] *a P* légèrement ivre*/gris/pompette. (*See* **cut¹ I 1**)

half-dead ['hɑːf'ded] *a F* fatigué*/à moitié mort/éreinté.

half-inch ['hɑːf'ɪntʃ] *vtr P* (*RS* = *pinch*) voler*/chiper/chaparder.

half-iron ['hɑːf'aɪən] *n P* qn qui fréquente les homosexuels sans en être. (*See* **hoof¹ 2**)

half-pint ['hɑːf'paɪnt] *n O F* petit* individu/demi-portion *f*.

half-pissed ['hɑːf'pist] *a P* (légèrement) ivre*/paf/parti. (*See* **pissed**)

half-seas-over ['hɑːf'siːz'əʊvə] *a F* (légèrement) ivre*/paf/parti.

half-squarie ['hɑːf'skwɛərɪ] *n Aust P* fille* *ou* femme* de petite vertu/Marie-couche-toi-là *f*.

half-stewed ['hɑːf'stjuːd] *a P* = **half-pissed**. (*See* **stewed**)

halfway ['hɑːf'weɪ] *adv F* 1. to meet s.o. halfway, couper la poire en deux 2. *see* **bingo 45**.

halves [hɑːvz] *adv F* to go halves, y aller moitié-moitié.

ham¹ [hæm] *a F* 1. amateur 2. inférieur/de basse qualité; *NAm* ham joint, gargote *f*.

ham² [hæm] *n F* 1. (*theatre*) pure ham, pièce pleine de clichés et d'emphase 2. (*a*) acteur, -trice amateur (*b*) mauvais(e) acteur, -trice/cabotin, -ine 3. (*radio enthusiast*) amateur *m* de radio.

ham³ [hæm] *F* (*theatre*) I *vtr* to ham it up mal jouer un rôle/cabotiner; déclamer/jouer pour la galerie; *he hams all his parts,* il charge tous ses rôles II *vi* jouer comme un pied.

hamburgers ['hæmbɜːgəz] *npl* (*drugs*) ecstasy *f*.

ham-fisted ['hæm'fɪstɪd], **ham-handed** ['hæm'hændɪd] *a F* maladroit/empoté.

hammer¹ ['hæmə] *n* 1. *NAm P* belle fille*/belle nana/beau petit lot 2. *P* (*CB*) accélérateur *m*/champignon *m* 3. *NAm V*

pénis*/défonceuse *f*/sabre *m*.

hammer² ['hæmə] *vtr* 1. *F* (*Stock Exchange*) déclarer (un agent) en défaut 2. *F* to hammer s.o. into the ground, battre qn à plate(s) couture(s)/tailler qn en pièces 3. *F* to hammer a play/a film, démolir/éreinter une pièce/un film 4. *P* to hammer (and nail), (*RS* = *tail*) suivre (qn)/filer (qn)/prendre (qn) en filature.

hammer back ['hæmə'bæk] *vi P* (*CB*) ralentir/lever le pied. (*See also* **hammer up**)

hammer down ['hæmə'daun] *vi P* (*CB*) accélérer/appuyer sur le champignon/mettre le pied au plancher.

hammered ['hæməd] *a P* ivre*/défoncé/pété.

hammering ['hæmərɪŋ] *n F* 1. volée *f* de coups* 2. (*sports*) défaite *f*/raclée *f*/dérouillée *f* 3. the play took a hammering, la pièce s'est fait esquinter/éreinter.

hammer up ['hæmər'ʌp] *vi P* (*CB*) ralentir/lever le pied. (*See also* **hammer back**)

hammy ['hæmɪ] *a F* outré/chargé/exagéré.

hampton, Hampton Wick ['hæmptən (wɪk)] *n V* (*RS* = *prick*) pénis*. (*See* **wick 1, 2**)

hand¹ [hænd] *F* 1. to keep one's hand in, garder le pied à l'étrier 2. to make money hand over fist, gagner* beaucoup d'argent*/se faire un pognon fou/ramasser du fric à la pelle 3. old hand, vieux *m* de la vieille/vieux routier; he's an old hand (at it), il connaît la musique 4. to be hand in glove with s.o., être comme larrons en foire/comme cul et chemise avec qn. (*See* **big I 5; dab I**)

hand² [hænd] *vtr* 1. *F* you've got to hand it to him! devant lui, chapeau! 2. *P* don't hand me that! raconte pas d'histoires!/arrête tes salades!/arrête ton char(re)! (*See* **plate¹ 3; sweet 3**)

handbag¹ ['hændbæg] *n Br F* (*male escort*) cavalier *m*.

handbag² ['hændbæg] *vtr Br Journ F* (*frustrate*) contrecarrer (qn); faire échouer/torpiller (un projet); (*obstruct*) empêcher/gêner (les mouvements de qn); (*attack*) critiquer*/cartonner/flinguer.

handful ['hændfʊl] *n* 1. *P* (condamnation* à) cinq ans* de prison*; cinq gerbes *fpl*/cinq longes *fpl* 2. *P* cinq livres *fpl* sterling 3. *F* to be a handful, (*esp of child, animal*) donner du fil à retordre/être une peste/être infernal.

hand-job ['hænddʒɒb] *n V* masturbation*;

to give s.o. a hand-job, masturber* qn/branler qn.

handle ['hændl] *n F* 1. to fly off the handle, se mettre en colère*/en rogne/en pétard 2. *F* to have a handle, avoir un titre/avoir un nom à rallonge 3. *F* nom* de famille/prénom *m*/ surnom *m*/blaze *m* 4. *P (CB)* identification personnelle du cibiste/indicatif *m*.

handlebar ['hændlbɑ:] *a attrib F* handlebar moustache, moustache* à la gauloise/bacantes *ou* bacchantes *fpl* en guidon.

hand-me-downs ['hændmɪdaʊnz] *npl O F* vêtements* usagés *ou* d'occasion; frusques *fpl*; my brother's hand-me-downs, les fringues que j'ai héritées de mon frère. (*See* **reach-me-downs**)

hand-out ['hændaʊt] *n F* 1. prospectus *m*/ circulaire *m* publicitaire 2. aumône *f*/charité *f*.

handshake ['hændʃeɪk] *n F* golden handshake, cadeau *m* d'adieu/indemnité *f* de départ.

handsome ['hænsəm] *a Br P* excellent*/de première/nickel.

handwriting ['hændraɪtɪŋ] *n F* style particulier d'un criminel; it's got his handwriting all over it, c'est bien de lui/c'est signé.

handy ['hændɪ] *a Br P* malin*/dégourdi/ fortiche/mariole.

hang[1] [hæŋ] *n F* 1. to get the hang of sth, saisir le truc pour faire qch; when you've got the hang of things, quand vous serez au courant/dans le bain/dans le coup 2. I don't give a hang, je m'en fiche/je m'en fous; j'en ai rien à foutre/à glander; it's not worth a hang, ça ne vaut pas un pet de lapin.

hang[2] [hæŋ] *vtr F* 1. hang it! flûte!/mince alors! 2. hang the expense! au diable l'avarice! 3. I'll be hanged if I'll do that! pas question que je le fasse! I'm hanged if I know! je n'en sais fichtre rien! 4. *NAm F* to hang a ralph/a louie, tourner à droite/à gauche; *Br F* to hang a yooie, faire demi-tour. (*See* **hung**)

hang about, around ['hæŋə'baʊt, ə'raʊnd] *vi* 1. *F* flâner/glander; to keep s.o. hanging about, faire/laisser poireauter qn 2. *F* hang about! minute! (*See* **hang on 1** (*a*))

hanger-on ['hæŋə'rɒn] *n F* dépendant *m*/ parasite *m*; crampon *m*/pique-assiette *mf*.

hang in ['hæŋ'ɪn] *vi esp NAm P* hang in (there)! tiens bon!

hang loose ['hæŋ'luːs] *vi NAm P* se la couler douce; hang loose! cool, Raoul!

hang on ['hæŋ'ɒn] *vi* 1. *F* (*a*) attendre*; hang on! une seconde!/minute! (*telephone*) ne quitte pas! (*b*) poireauter 2. *F* tenir bon; to hang on like grim death, se cramponner/ s'accrocher/ne pas lâcher le morceau 3. *esp NAm P* to hang one on, s'enivrer/se piquer le nez.

hang-out ['hæŋaʊt] *n* 1. *F* logement*/chez-soi *m* 2. *F* rendez-vous*/lieu *m* de réunion; repaire *m* de gangsters 3. *NAm P* hang-out (road), déballage *m* (de la vérité).

hang out ['hæŋ'aʊt] *vi* 1. *F* to hang out for sth, réclamer/exiger qch 2. *F* habiter*/cré-cher/nicher; where do you hang out? où perchez-vous? 3. *F* traîner/glander/ glandouiller; those yobs were hanging out in the bar, ces petits loulous glandaient dans le troquet 4. *P (a)* let it all hang out! fais ta vie!/fais (tout) ce qui te chante! (*b*) *NAm* tout déballer/tout sortir/accoucher. (*See* **hang-out 3**)

hangover ['hæŋəʊvə] *n F* to have a hang-over, avoir la gueule de bois/la GDB. (*See* **hung over**)

hang tough ['hæŋ'tʌf] *vi NAm P* persister/s'obstiner; hang tough! tiens bon!/ accroche-toi, Jeannot!

hang-up ['hæŋʌp] *n F* 1. (*complex*) complexe *m*; to have a lot of hang-ups, être très complexé; he's got a hang-up about driving, il fait un blocage, il ne veut pas conduire 2. (*nuisance*) embêtement *m*/enquiquinement *m*/emmerde *f*. (*See* **hung-up**)

hang up ['hæŋ'ʌp] *vtr F* 1. (*telephone*) raccrocher 2. to hang up one's hat, se marier/se marida 3. to hang s.o. up, planter qn là 4. *NAm* hang up! ça suffit!/ça va comme ça!

hank[1] [hæŋk] *n esp NAm P* to play with hank, se masturber*/se branler/se secouer le bonhomme.

hank[2] [hæŋk] *vi esp NAm P* se masturber*/ se branler/se pignoler.

hankie, hanky ['hæŋkɪ] *n F* (= *handker-chief*) mouchoir*/tire-jus *m*.

hanky-panky ['hæŋkɪ'pæŋkɪ] *n F* 1. (*underhand behaviour*) entourloupe(tte) *f*/ coup fourré 2. (*sexual activity*) batifolage *m*/ galipettes *fpl*/flirt *m*; to go in for a bit of hanky-panky with one's secretary, s'envoyer la secrétaire en douce.

happen[1] ['hæp(ə)n] *adv F* (*regional*) peut-être; happen he will, happen he won't, peut-être bien que oui, peut-être bien que non.

happen[2] ['hæp(ə)n] *vi F* it's all happening,

tout est en marche/tout roule.

happen along ['hæp(ə)nə'lɒŋ] *vi F* arriver* au hasard/entrer en passant.

happening ['hæp(ə)nɪŋ] *F* I *a NAm (fashionable, up-to-date)* branché/dans le coup/câblé; *(exciting)* flashant; it looks well happening, c'est tout à fait dans le coup/c'est vachement branché. *(See* **well***)* II *n* spectacle/événement imprévu *ou* spontané; happening *m*.

happenstance ['hæp(ə)nstæns] *n NAm F* événement fortuit.

happy ['hæpɪ] *a F* 1. légèrement ivre*/paf/pompette 2. happy days! à la (bonne) vôtre! *(See* **bar-happy**; **dust**[1] 2; **shag-happy**; **slap-happy**; **trigger-happy***)*

hard [hɑːd] I *a* 1. *F* a drop of the hard stuff, une goutte d'alcool*/un petit coup de gnôle 2. *F* hard drugs, drogues dures/choucroute *f*. *(See* **soft** I 4) 3. *F* hard lines, malchance*/poisse *f*; hard lines!/hard luck! manque de bol!/pas de pot! *(See* **cheddar**; **cheese** 2) 4. *F* hard tack, biscuits *mpl* de marin 5. *F* hard sell, battage *m* publicitaire. *(See* **soft** I 5) 6. *F* to play hard to get, faire la difficile/faire la Sainte-Nitouche 7. *P* the hard word, *(rejection)* rejet *m*; *(condemnation)* blâme *m*/censure *f* 8. *esp Austr P* to put the hard word on, *(persuade woman to have sex)* (essayer de) persuader une femme de faire l'amour*/faire du rentre-dedans; *(ask for sth difficult)* (essayer de) persuader qn de faire qch (de difficile, de désagréable)/baratiner 9. *NAm P* hard (up), *(person) (tough)* costaud; *(mentally)* dur. *(See* **case**[1] 1; **hard-hat**; **nut**[1] 5) II *n* 1. *P* (= *hard labour*) travaux forcés; **fifteen years' hard**, quinze piges *fpl* des durs 2. *V* = **hard-on** 1.

hard-arse ['hɑːdɑːs], *NAm* **hardass** ['hɑːdæs] *n P (tough person)* dur *m ou* dure *f* à cuire; individu* vachard; saignant *m*.

hard-arsed ['hɑːdɑːst], *NAm* **hardassed** ['hɑːdæst] *a P (tough, severe)* dur/vachard.

hard-baked ['hɑːd'beɪkt] *a F* endurci/dur(aille).

hard-bitten ['hɑːd'bɪtn] *a F* = **hardboiled** 2.

hard-boiled ['hɑːd'bɔɪld] *a F* 1. malin*/coriace; a hard-boiled businessman, un homme d'affaires qui n'est pas né de la dernière pluie 2. dur (à cuire) 3. peu scrupuleux/sans scrupules.

hardcore ['hɑːdkɔː] *a F* 1. inconditionnel; hardcore pornography, pornographie *f* hard 2.

totalement criminel/débauché/etc; he's real hardcore, *(criminal)* c'est un dur du milieu; *(debauched)* c'est un vrai bandeur.

hard-hat ['hɑːdhæt] *n esp NAm F* ouvrier *m* du bâtiment (très à droite politiquement).

hard-liner ['hɑːd'laɪnə] *n Pol F* intransigeant, -ante/faucon *m*/épervier *m*.

hard-nosed ['hɑːd'nəʊzd] *a esp NAm F* réaliste/dur à cuire; qui n'est pas né de la dernière pluie.

hard-on ['hɑːdɒn] *n V* 1. to have a hard-on, être en érection*/bander 2. désir *m*/passion *f*; to have a hard-on for s.o., (en) mouiller pour qn.

hard up ['hɑːd'ʌp] *a F* pauvre*/dans la dèche/fauché/à sec; to be hard up, être raide (comme un passe-lacet).

hardware ['hɑːdwɛə] *n F* armes *fpl*/quincaille(rie) *f*.

hardy ['hɑːdɪ] *a F* hardy annual, vieille histoire/question *f* qui revient régulièrement sur le tapis.

hare [hɛə] *vi F* courir* très vite/cavaler; to hare back home, regagner la maison à toutes jambes/ventre à terre.

haricot (bean) ['hærɪkəʊ(biːn)] *n Austr P (RS = queen)* homosexuel*/folle *f*. *(See* **queen**[1] 2)

hark [hɑːk] *vi F* hark at her! écoute-moi celle-là!

harp[1] [hɑːp] *n F* 1. *A* Irlandais 2. harmonica *m*.

harp[2] [hɑːp] *vi F* he's always harping on the same string, il récite toujours la même litanie/il rabâche toujours la même chose; stop harping on about that! change de disque!/change de refrain!

Harry ['hærɪ] *Prn* 1. *O F* old Harry, le diable; it's giving me old Harry, cela me fait un mal du diable 2. *F* to play old Harry with s.o., engueuler qn/sonner les cloches à qn 3. *O P* Harry bonkers = **bonkers**; Harry flakers = **flakers**; Harry preggers = **preggers**; Harry starkers = **starkers** 4. *Br P (drugs)* héroïne*/héro *f*. *(See* **flash**[1] I 1; **Tom** 1)

has-been ['hæzbiːn] *n F* 1. individu* vieux-jeu; vieux ramolli/vieille ramollie; he's a has-been, c'est un croulant; it's better to be a has-been than a never-was, il vaut mieux ne plus être que n'avoir jamais été 2. vieillerie *f*/vieux machin.

hash[1] [hæʃ] *n F* 1. nourriture*/boustifaille *f*/bectance *f*/bouffe *f* 2. *NAm* ragots *mpl*/potins *mpl*/cancans *mpl* 3. *(drugs)* haschisch*; to smoke hash, fumer du hasch 4. pagaille f/ gâchis m; **to make a hash of it,** tout foutre en l'air/tout faire foirer 5. du rebattu/du rabâché; **don't give me that hash!** garde tes salades!/arrête ton char(re)! 6. **to settle s.o.'s hash** (a) régler son compte à qn (b) clouer le bec à qn.

hash² [hæʃ] vtr F 1. gâcher/bousiller/saloper/bâcler 2. servir de la nourriture*/donner à bouffer à (qn).

hash over ['hæʃ'əʊvə] vi NAm F discuter/ressasser/rabâcher (un problème, une difficulté, etc).

hash-slinger ['hæʃslɪŋə] n NAm F 1. serveur, -euse de gargote/loufiat m 2. mauvais(e) cuisinier, -ière 3. marmiton m.

hash-up ['hæʃʌp] n F (mess, fiasco) boxon m/bordel m/fiasc m.

hash up ['hæʃ'ʌp] vtr F = **hash²** 1.

hassle¹ ['hæsl] n F 1. (inconvenience) emmerde f/pépin m/os m; **all the hassle of filling in the form,** toutes les emmerdes pour remplir le formulaire; **it's a real hassle!** c'est toute une histoire!/c'est vraiment la barbe! 2. (argument) crosse f/embrouille f/corrida f; **the police gave us a lot of hassle,** la police nous a fait des tas d'histoires.

hassle² ['hæsl] F 1. vtr ennuyer*/emmerder (qn); **she keeps hassling me for money,** elle n'arrête pas de m'emmerder pour que je lui donne de l'argent; **don't hassle me!** (ne) m'embête pas!/fiche-moi la paix!/lâche-moi! 2. vi se quereller*/se bouffer le nez.

hassle-free ['hæsl'fri:] a F sans problème(s)/sans emmerde(s).

hat [hæt] n F 1. **old hat,** vieux jeu; **that's old hat,** c'est du déjà vu/c'est vieux comme le monde 2. **to talk through one's hat,** parler* à tort et à travers/délirer 3. **to keep it under one's hat,** garder qch pour soi; **keep it under your hat!** motus (et bouche cousue)!/mets-le dans ta poche avec ton mouchoir dessus! 4. **to pass the hat round,** faire la quête 5. **my hat!** (heavens!) mince alors!/mes aïeux! (sarcastic) mon œil! 6. **hold on to your hat!** gare au choc! (See **brass-hat**; **cocked**; **drop¹** 2; **hard-hat**)

hatch [hætʃ] n F **down the hatch!** à la vôtre! **to put one down the hatch,** s'en jeter un (derrière la cravate)/en mettre un à l'abri de la pluie. (See **booby-hatch**)

hatchet ['hætʃɪt] n F 1. **to bury the hatchet,** se réconcilier/se rabibocher/enterrer la hache de guerre 2. **hatchet man** (a) tueur m (à

gages)/homme m de main (b) celui qui arrange les sales affaires des autres/qui est payé pour laver le linge sale des autres.

haul¹ [hɔ:l] n F a **good haul,** un bon/un beau coup de filet; une bonne récolte.

haul² [hɔ:l] vtr F **to haul s.o. over the coals,** réprimander* qn/engueuler qn; **to get hauled over the coals,** se faire passer un savon. (See **ashes** 2)

haul-ass ['hɔ:læs] vi esp NAm P partir* en vitesse/se tailler/(se) déhotter.

hauler ['hɔ:lə] n NAm F voiture* très rapide/bolide m.

haul in ['hɔ:l'ɪn] vtr F arrêter*/agrafer/épingler/coffrer (qn).

haul off ['hɔ:l'ɒf] vi NAm F lever le bras/faire une pause avant de cogner qn; **I hauled off before I hit him,** je me suis préparé pour le cogner.

haul up ['hɔ:l'ʌp] vi F critiquer* (qn)/débiner (qn)/dénigrer (qn)/casser du sucre sur le dos de (qn).

have [hæv] vtr 1. P **to have it away/off,** faire l'amour*; **to have s.o./to have it away with s.o./to have it off with s.o.,** s'envoyer qn/se faire qn 2. O F **to have it away with sth,** voler* qch/chiper qch 3. O F **to have it away (on one's toes),** s'échapper; **he's had it away over the wall,** il a fait la belle/il s'est fait la paire 4. F **to have had it,** (miss one's chance) rater sa chance/rater son coup; rater le coche; (die) mourir*/claquer; (be exhausted) être fatigué*/crevé; (be broke) être ruiné*; **I've had it,** je suis vanné; **you've had it, chum!** tu es fait, mon vieux!/tu es foutu, mon vieux! **my car's had it,** elle est foutue, ma bagnole; **I've had it (up to here),** j'en ai assez/j'en ai ras le bol/j'en ai plein le cul 5. F **to let s.o. have it,** (hit) battre* qn/filer une avoine à qn; (criticize) critiquer* qn; (reprimand) réprimander* qn/sonner les cloches à qn; dire ses quatre vérités à qn; (settle accounts) régler son compte à qn 6. F duper*/avoir (qn)/rouler (qn); **I've been had,** je me suis fait avoir/on m'a eu 7. F vaincre (qn); **there you have me,** là, tu me la coupes/ça va, je ne dis plus rien/ça va, je me tais 8. F **to have it out with s.o.,** vider une querelle* avec qn/s'expliquer avec qn 9. F **to have it in for s.o./to have a down on s.o.,** en vouloir à qn/en avoir après qn. (See **any** II; **down¹** III 1)

have-nots ['hæv'nɒts] npl F **les dépourvus** mpl/les déshérités mpl; **the haves and the have-nots,** les riches* et les pauvres*/les rupins *mpl* et les purotins *mpl*.

have on ['hæv'ɒn] *vtr F* 1. duper*/faire marcher (qn); he's having you on, il te fait marcher 2. to have sth on, être occupé; I've got nothing on tomorrow, je ne suis pas pris/je n'ai rien demain.

have over ['hæv'əuvə] *vtr Br F* duper*/avoir/rouler (qn).

haves [hævz] *npl see* **have-nots.**

have up ['hæv'ʌp] *vtr F* traduire (qn) en justice; to be had up, passer en jugement; he was had up before the beak, le magistrat l'a convoqué.

hawk [hɔːk] *n* 1. *F Pol* qn qui pousse à la guerre et au chauvinisme; partisan *m* des solutions de force, *surt* dans une guerre; faucon *m*. (*See* **dove; fairy 1; newshawk**) 2. *O P (drugs)* LSD* 3. *P =* **chickenhawk.**

hawkish ['hɔːkɪʃ] *a F Pol* qui pousse à la guerre et au chauvinisme; hawkish policies, politique *f* belliciste/agressive.

hay [heɪ] *n* 1. *F* to hit the hay, se coucher*/se pieuter 2. *P* to have a roll in the hay with s.o., faire une partie de jambes en l'air avec qn. (*See* **roll¹ 2**) 3. *O P (drugs)* (Indian) hay, marijuana*/chanvre (indien) 4. *F* argent*/blé *m* 5. *F* to make hay (while the sun shines), battre le fer pendant qu'il est chaud 6. *F* to make hay of sth, chambarder/bouleverser/démolir qch.

hay-eater ['heɪiːtə] *n P (Black Slang)* Blanc(he) *m(f)*.

hayhead ['heɪhed] *n O P (drugs)* (*a*) usager *m* de la marijuana* (*b*) habitué(e) de la marijuana*. (*See* **hay 3**)

haymaker ['heɪmeɪkə] *n P (boxing)* coup* puissant (*mettant l'adversaire hors de combat*)/knock-out *m*.

hayseed ['heɪsiːd] *n NAm F* paysan*/culterreux *m*/plouc *mf*/bouseux *m*.

haywire ['heɪwaɪə] *a F (machine, etc)* détraqué; (*situation*) embrouillé; (*person*) emballé/excité/cinglé; to go haywire, (*of person*) ne pas tourner rond/perdre la boule/déconner; (*of plan, project*) être loupé/finir en queue de poisson/partir en eau/en jus de boudin; (*of machine*) se détraquer/se mettre à délirer.

haze [heɪz] *vtr NAm F (schools)* brimer; faire des brimades *fpl* à/bizuter (un nouvel élève).

hazing ['heɪzɪŋ] *n NAm F (schools)* brimades *fpl*/bizutage *m*.

head [hed] *n* 1. *F* mal *m* de tête; to have a (bad) head/to have a head on (one), (*have a headache*) avoir mal au crâne; (*have a hangover*) avoir la gueule de bois/la GDB 2. *F* to yell one's head off, gueuler comme un sourd/crier à tue-tête; to talk one's head off, ne pas s'arrêter de parler 3. *F* to be head over heels in love, aimer* qn/être toqué de qn/avoir le béguin pour qn/en pincer pour qn 4. *O P* (*a*) toxicomane *mf*/toxico *mf*/drogué(e)*/camé(e) (*b*) (= *high*) to get a head, planer (*c*) head trip, égocentrisme *m*/égoïsme *m*; (*contemplation, self-exploration*) contemplation *f*/exploration *f* de soi. (*See* **acid 2; cokehead; cubehead; dopehead; hayhead; hophead; juicehead; methhead; pillhead; pothead; smack-head; teahead; weedhead**) 5. *F* to be/go off one's head, être/devenir fou*/perdre la boule; to be soft in the head, être bête*/ramolli. (*See* **get together**) 6. *P* the head/(the) heads, WC*/chiottes *fpl* 7. *F* I need it like (I need) a hole in the head! c'est aussi souhaitable qu'une jambe cassée!/il ne me manque (plus) que ça!/il ne manquait plus que ça! 8. *F* not to (be able to) make head nor tail of sth, ne comprendre goutte/que dalle à qch; I can't make head nor tail of it, je n'y pige que tchi/que couic; you couldn't make head nor tail of it, une truie n'y retrouverait pas ses petits 9. *F* I could do it (standing) on my head, c'est simple comme bonjour 10. *F* to talk s.o.'s head off, étourdir qn/casser les oreilles* à qn 11. *F* to talk off the top of one's head, dire n'importe quoi; I just said that off the top of my head, j'ai dit ça comme ça/j'ai dit ça sans savoir exactement 12. *F* heads will roll, les têtes vont tomber/ce sera le coup de balai/ça va saigner 13. *V* fellation*; head job, pipe *f*/suçade *f*; to give s.o. head/to give s.o. a head job, tailler une pipe/une plume à qn; piper qn 14. *NAm P* gangster *m*/malfrat *m*. (*See* **bighead; bonehead; boofhead; cabbagehead; chew off; chucklehead; deadhead; eat 6; egghead; fathead; flathead; fuckhead; honcho; jughead; knock² 2; knothead; knucklehead; lughead; lunk(head); meathead; musclehead; muttonhead; nail¹ 2; out I 3; pea-head; pinhead; puddinghead; redhead; sap(head); screw² 6; shithead; skinhead; sleepyhead; sore 2; sorehead; squarehead; thickhead; towel head; turniphead; water 2**)

headache ['hedeɪk] *n* 1. *F* ennui *m*/ embêtement *m*/casse-tête *m*; **what a headache you are!** ce que tu peux être casse-pieds! 2. *NAm P* épouse*/bourgeoise *f* 3. *P* **to give s.o. a serious headache,** tuer* qn d'une balle dans la tête/faire sauter la cervelle à qn.

headbanger ['hed'bæŋə] *n* *P* 1. fana(tique) *mf* de rock 2. individu* qui vit dangereusement/qui a un mode de vie frénétique 3. individu bête* *ou* fou*/cinglé, -ée/dingo *mf*/barjot *m*.

headbone ['hedbəʊn] *n* *NAm* *P* (*Black Slang*) crâne *m*/chignon *m*.

headcase ['hedkeɪs] *n* *F* fou*/cinglé, -ée/ dingue *mf*/dingo *mf*/barjot *m*.

header ['hedə] *n* *F* **to take a header,** tomber* par terre/ramasser une pelle; (*esp on motorbike*) se viander.

headhunter ['hedhʌntə] *n* *F* 1. (*media*) chasseur *m* de têtes 2. tueur *m* à gages.

headlamps ['hedlæmps] *npl* *Br*, **headlights** ['hedlaɪts] *npl* *P* (*not common*) seins*/amortisseurs *mpl*/pare-chocs *mpl*.

headlines ['hedlaɪnz] *npl* *F* **to hit the headlines,** devenir célèbre/faire la une/faire les gros titres.

headmerchant ['hedmɜːtʃ(ə)nt] *n* *F* = **headshrink(er)**.

headphones ['hedfəʊnz] *npl* *P* (**set of**) **headphones,** seins*/flotteurs *mpl*; **she's got a nice set of headphones,** elle a une belle avant-scène.

headpiece ['hedpiːs] *n* *F* tête*/cerveau *m*/ ciboulot *m*/cigare *m*.

headshrink(er) ['hedʃrɪŋk(ə)] *n* *F* psychiatre *mf*/psychanalyste *mf*; psy *mf*. (*See* **shrink**)

health [helθ] *n* *F* I **don't do that for (the good of) my health,** je ne fais pas cela pour mon plaisir/pour m'amuser.

heap [hiːp] *n* *F* 1. **to be (struck) all of a heap,** en rester comme deux ronds de flan; **he was struck all of a heap,** ça l'a sidéré/soufflé/ laissé baba 2. (*winner*) **to come out at the top of/on top of the heap,** être au premier rang/ tenir le haut du pavé; (*loser*) **to stay at the bottom of the heap,** être le dernier des derniers/être le der des ders/être la super crasse 3. **a whole heap of nonsense,** un tissu d'âneries 4. vieille voiture*/vieille bagnole/ guimbarde *f* 5. **heaps of...,** une abondance* de.../un tas de.../une tripotée de.../une flopée de.../un rab' de...; **there's heaps of things to do,** il y a tout un tas de choses à faire; **we've**

got heaps of time, on a tout le temps qu'il faut/on n'est pas aux pièces; **he's in heaps of trouble,** il est dans le pétrin/la merde; **heaps better,** beaucoup mieux. (*See* **scrapheap**)

heart [hɑːt] *n* *F* **have a heart!** (ne) parle pas de malheur!/pitié! *Iron* **my heart bleeds for you!/you're breaking my heart!** tu vas me faire pleurer!/tu me fends le cœur! (*See* **purple**)

heart-throb ['hɑːtθrɒb] *n* *F* objet *m* d'amour/béguin *m*; idole *m*.

heart-to-heart ['hɑːttə'hɑːt] *n* *F* **to have a heart-to-heart with s.o.,** parler à cœur ouvert avec qn.

hearty ['hɑːtɪ] *n* *F* 1. athlète *mf* (*opposé à un(e) esthète*) 2. *O Nau* camarade *m*/copain *m*/pote *m*; **me hearties!** les gars!

heat [hiːt] *n* 1. *F* pression *f*/feu *m*; **to turn on the heat,** s'enflammer/s'échauffer; **to put the heat on** (s.o.), faire pression sur qn; (*of police*) aller à la recherche d'un criminel; **the heat is on,** ça commence à chauffer/ça va barder 2. *F* (*police*) interrogatoire* poussé/ cuisine *f*/chansonnette *f* 3. *NAm* *P* police*/ flicaille *f*/renifle *f* 4. *NAm* *P* arme *f*/brelica *m*.

heater ['hiːtə] *n* *NAm* *P* revolver*/feu *m*/ pétard *m*.

Heath Robinson ['hiːθ'rɒbɪnsən] *a* (*machine, contraption*) à la Gaston Lagaffe; à la Géo Trouvetou; (*gadget*) à la noix; **the plumbing's a bit Heath Robinson,** la plomberie laisse beaucoup à désirer.

heave [hiːv] *vi* *F* vomir*/dégueuler; (*retch*) avoir des haut-le-cœur.

heave-ho ['hiːv'həʊ] *n* *P* **to get the (old) heave-ho,** être congédié*/être flanqué à la porte/être lourdé; être plaqué; **to give s.o. the (old) heave-ho,** se débarrasser* de qn/ larguer/sacquer/virer qn; (*jilt*) plaquer qn.

heaven ['hevn] *n* *F* 1. **it's heaven to relax,** c'est super de pouvoir se reposer/c'est bath de pouvoir se reposer 2. **good heavens!** juste ciel!/bonté divine!/zut alors! **heavens above!** nom d'une pipe! **for heaven's sake!** pour l'amour de Dieu! **heaven forbid!** surtout pas!

heavenly ['hevnlɪ] *a* *F* merveilleux; super/ le pied. (*See* **blue[1]** II 1)

heaves [hiːvz] *npl* *F* **to have the heaves,** vomir*/dégueuler; (*retch*) avoir des haut-le-cœur.

heavy ['hevɪ] I *a* 1. *F* (*person*) passionné/ impudique/vicieux. (*See* **petting**) 2. *F* **heavy date,** rendez-vous* sentimental important 3. *F* **to make heavy weather of sth,** faire toute une affaire de qch/faire tout un plat de qch **4.** *P* (*loot*) de valeur; **the heavy mob,** (*police*) la brigade criminelle/la Crime; (*criminal gang*) bande* de voleurs* de grande envergure **5.** *F* heavy stuff, renforts motorisés dans une descente de police **6.** *F* (*theatre, etc*) heavy rôle, rôle *m* du méchant de la pièce **7.** *P* it was a (really) heavy scene, (*drugs*) c'était la grande défonce; (*violence*) il y avait de la bagarre dans l'air; (*situation*) l'atmosphère était très tendue **8.** *P* (*rock*) heavy metal, heavy metal *m*; heavy metal band, groupe *m* de heavy metal **9.** *P* excellent*/très agréable; that's really heavy! c'est le (super-)pied!/ c'est vachement cool! **10.** *P* things started to get heavy, ça allait barder/chier; il y avait de la bagarre dans l'air; he started to get a bit heavy, il avait l'air de chercher la bagarre; don't get heavy with me! (ne) me faites pas chier! **II** *n* **1.** *F* (*boxing*) (= *heavyweight*) (poids) lourd *m* **2.** *P* (*a*) apache *m*/bandit *m* (*b*) assassin* **3.** *F* le méchant dans une pièce *ou* un film **4.** *NAm P* to be in the heavy, avoir beaucoup d'argent*/être riche*/rouler sur l'or **5.** *F* dur *m*/balaise *m*; garde *m* du corps/ gorille *m*; videur *m* (d'une boîte de nuit); *Br* to come the heavy, faire l'autoritaire; faire le méchant/jouer au dur/faire les gros bras.

hebe ['hi:bɪ] *n NAm P* Juif*/youpin, -ine/ youtre *m*. (*See* **heeb**)

heck [hɛk] *n F* (*Euph for* **hell**) **1.** heck! sapristi!/zut!/flûte!/la barbe! what the heck...! que diable...! **2.** a heck of a lot, une abondance*/une grande quantité; un sacré paquet/un tas.

hedge [hɛdʒ] *vtr F* **1.** to hedge one's bets, étaler *ou* protéger ses paris **2.** chercher des échappatoires *fpl*/des faux-fuyants *mpl*; s'échapper par la tangente/tourner autour du pot; stop hedging, dis-le carrément!/allez, accouche!

heeb, heebie ['hi:b(ɪ)] *n NAm P* = **hebe.**

heebie-jeebies ['hi:bɪ'dʒi:bɪz] *npl F* **1.** délirium tremens *m*/digue-digue *f* **2.** angoisse *f*/frousse *f*/trac *m*/peur bleue; to give s.o. the heebie-jeebies, filer la trouille/les chocottes *fpl* à qn; it gives me the heebie-jeebies, (*frightening*) ça me donne la chair de poule; (*repulsive*) ça me dégoûte/ça me débecte.

heel [hi:l] *n* **1.** *F* individu* méprisable/fion *m*/loquedu *m*; to be a (bit of a) heel, friser la canaille; he's a real heel, c'est une vraie pelure **2.** *A P* to have round heels, avoir la cuisse hospitalière. (*See* **roundheel(s)**) **3.** *F*

to cool/to kick one's heels, se morfondre/faire le pied de grue/poireauter. (*See* **head 3**; **kick up 3**; **shitheel**)

heeled [hi:ld] *a NAm P* **1.** = **well-heeled 2.** armé d'un revolver*/enfouraillé.

heft [hɛft] *vtr F* soulever/soupeser (qch).

hefty ['hɛftɪ] *a F* **1.** fort*/costaud/malabar/ balaise **2.** gros/important; a hefty bill, une note de taille/une sacrée douloureuse; a hefty chunk, un morceau imposant.

heifer ['hɛfə] *n NAm Austr P* jeune femme*/ nénette *f*/poulette *f*.

heimie ['haɪmɪ] *n P* = **hymie.**

he-ing and she-ing ['hi:ɪŋn'ʃi:ɪŋ] *n P* partie *f* de jambes en l'air/baisage *m*.

heinie ['haɪnɪ] *n NAm P* fesses*/postère *m*.

Heinz 57 ['haɪnz'fɪftɪ'sevn] *n F* chien* bâtard/corniaud *m*/clébard *m*. (*See* **bingo 57**)

heist[1] [haɪst] *n esp NAm F* (*a*) cambriolage *m*/casse *m* (*b*) hold-up *m*/braquage *m*.

heist[2] [haɪst] *vtr esp NAm F* **1.** cambrioler*/ faire un casse dans (une maison) **2.** voler* (qch).

heister ['haɪstə] *n esp NAm O F* cambrioleur*/casseur *m*/braqueur *m*.

hell [hɛl] *n* **1.** *P* (*a*) go to hell! va te faire voir (chez les Grecs)/va te faire foutre; to hell with it! ras le bol de tout cela!/y'en a marre de tout cela! get the hell out of here! (nom de Dieu) débarrasse le plancher!/fiche-moi le camp d'ici! oh hell! (oh,) bordel!/et merde!/ putain! bloody hell! bordel de merde! hell's bells (and buckets of blood)! sacré nom de nom! would he go? would he hell! partir, lui? penses-tu!/tu parles! hell, I don't know, je n'en sais foutre rien/qu'est-ce que j'en sais moi? like hell (I will)!/the hell I will! tu parles!/ça va pas la tête?/mon œil, oui!/et puis quoi encore?/pas si con! (*b*) what the hell does it matter? qu'est-ce que ça peut bien faire/foutre? what the hell, I've got nothing to lose, et puis merde, je n'ai rien à perdre; what the hell has that got to do with me? qu'est-ce que ça peut me bien foutre? what the hell's going on? qu'est-ce que qui se passe, nom de Dieu? who the hell are you? mais qui êtes-vous donc, nom de Dieu? who the hell do you think you are (anyway)? pour qui te prends tu, nom de nom? what the hell do you think you're doing/playing at? tu maquilles quoi, au juste?/dis donc, tu te crois où? what in hell/in hell's name is that? qu'est-ce que c'est que ce putain de truc? where the hell did you put it? où diable l'as-tu fourré? **why the hell doesn't he belt up?** (est-ce qu')il va la boucler, oui ou merde? (c) **I wish to hell I could remember,** ah purée, si seulement je pouvais me rappeler 2. F **to give s.o. hell,** faire passer un mauvais quart d'heure à qn/en faire voir (de toutes les couleurs) à qn; **to get hell/to have hell to pay,** être réprimandé*; se faire engueuler/incendier; en prendre pour son grade; **there'll be hell to pay!** ça va barder!/ça va chauffer!/il va y avoir du grabuge! 3. F **it was all hell let loose,** c'était infernal; **all hell broke loose,** ça a bardé; **to create/to raise (merry) hell,** (make a noise) faire du boucan/faire un chambard du diable/ faire un foin d'enfer; (make a scene) rouscailler/râler (comme un enragé)/faire une scène de tous les diables; **to play merry hell with sth,** foutre qch en l'air 4. P **in a/in one hell of a mess/state,** dans une pagaille infernale/du tonnerre; **a hell of a/one hell of a nice guy,** un type super sympa/un mec super; **a hell of a price,** un prix salé; **you've got a hell of a nerve/cheek!** tu manques pas d'air!/ tu as un sacré culot!; **it's a hell of a bore/bind,** c'est drôlement embêtant; **a hell of a row,** (noise) un bruit* d'enfer/un vacarme infernal/un de ces boucans; (quarrel) une engueulade maison; **we had a hell of a good time,** on s'est super éclaté 5. F **to do sth for the hell of it,** faire qch histoire de rire/pour s'en payer une tranche 6. F **to play hell with s.o./sth,** en faire voir à qn/cabosser qch; **this weather's playing hell with my leg,** avec ce temps-là, j'ai la jambe qui me fait déguster/ dérouiller 7. F **to feel like hell,** se sentir drôlement pas bien/complètement vaseux/ complètement patraque/au trente-sixième dessous 8. P **sure as hell,** sûr et certain/dans la fouille 9. P **to knock hell out of s.o.,** battre* qn comme plâtre 10. P **all to hell,** démoli/gâché/ coulé 11. F **to go hell for leather,** galoper ventre à terre/courir avec le feu au derrière 12. F **till hell freezes over,** jusqu'à la Saint-Glinglin 13. NAm F **from hell to breakfast,** entièrement/totalement/de A à Z 14. NAm F **to hell and gone,** disparu/passé à l'as; aux antipodes/chez les damnés 15. F **hell's angels,** jeunes voyous mpl (en moto)/blousons noirs/loubars mpl/loulous mpl 16. F **come hell or high water,** advienne que pourra/contre vents et marées. (See **fucking I 2; hellcat; kick up 2** (c); **snowball**[1] **2; sodding; stink**[1] **1**)

hella ['helə] pref NAm F très/super; **hella cool,** super cool.
hellacious [he'leɪʃəs] a NAm F épouvantable/abominable/infernal.
hell-bender ['helbendə] n P bamboche infernale/bamboula f. (See **bender 1**)
hellcat ['helkæt] n F (a) fille* ou femme* pleine d'entrain et de témérité/qui n'a pas froid aux yeux (b) mégère f/sorcière f.
hell-hole ['helhəʊl] n F endroit mal famé/ coupe-gorge m; bouge m.
hellion ['heljən] n NAm F 1. vaurien*/sale type m/fripouille f 2. enfant* terrible/petit diable/gosse infernal(e).
hellishly ['helɪʃlɪ] adv F diablement/ vachement/méchamment.
helluva ['heləvə] P (= hell of a) see **hell 4**.
he-man ['hiːmæn] n F (a) homme fort* et viril/malabar m/un mâle/un mec/un macho (b) un beau mâle.
hemp [hemp] n F (drugs) (Indian) hemp, cannabis*/chanvre (indien).
hen [hen] n F (a) Pej femme*/vieille dinde (b) jeune femme*/poulette f; **hen party,** réunion f de femmes entre elles (surt la veille d'un mariage) (c) (form of address) (regional) ma chère/mon chou (d) NAm **hen fruit,** œuf m. (See **stag 1**)
Henry, henry ['henrɪ] n F (drugs) héroïne*.
hep [hep] a A F = **hip**.
hepcat ['hep'kæt] n A F = **hipster 1** (a), (b). (See also **cat 1**)
herb [hɜːb] n F (drugs) (the) herb, cannabis*/herbe f.
Herbert ['(h)ɜːbət] Prn O F **he's a right little Herbert,** c'est un vrai connard/un vrai crétin.
here [hɪə] adv F 1. **that's neither here nor there,** ça n'a aucun rapport (avec la choucroute)/ça ne change rien à l'affaire/ça n'a rien à voir 2. **here goes!** ça démarre!/ allons-y!/c'est parti (mon kiki)! 3. **here you are,** tenez/prenez-le/et voilà 4. **from here on in,** à partir de maintenant.
her indoors ['(h)ɜːrɪn'dɔːz] n Br P épouse*/bourgeoise f/patronne f; **I've got to get back, her indoors is waiting for me,** il faut que je rentre, la patronne m'attend. (See **indoors**)
herring ['herɪŋ] n F 1. **red herring,** procédé m servant à brouiller les pistes/diversion f 2. **the Herring Pond,** l'océan m Atlantique/la Mare (aux harengs).

het-up ['het'ʌp] *a F* 1. énervé/tracassé/dans tous ses états 2. en colère*/en rogne.

hex¹ [heks] *n F* malédiction *f*/mauvais sort; to put the hex on s.o., jeter un sort à qn.

hex² [heks] *vtr F* jeter un sort à (qn).

hey-diddle-diddle (the) [ðə'heɪdɪdl-'dɪdl] *n Br P* (*RS = the middle*) le milieu/le centre.

hi! [haɪ] *excl F* salut!/bonjour!

hick [hɪk] **I** *a NAm P* 1. rustique/campagnard; a hick town, un patelin/un bled/un trou; a hick operation, organisation mal dirigée 2. ignorant/rustaud **II** *n NAm P* 1. paysan*/péquenaud *m*/plouc *mf* 2. innocent, -ente/couillon *m* 3. *Pej* Portoricain(e) *m(f)*.

hickey ['hɪkɪ] *n NAm F* 1. suçon *m* 2. (*spot*) bouton *m* 3. (*gadget*) machin *m*/truc *m*.

hide [haɪd] *n F* 1. (*skin*) peau *f*/cuir *m*/couenne *f*; to tan the hide off s.o., battre* qn/tanner le cuir à qn 2. to have a thick hide, avoir la peau dure. (*See* **thick-skinned**)

hiding ['haɪdɪŋ] *n F* 1. (good) hiding, volée *f* de coups*/tannée *f*/dérouillée *f* 2. to be on a hiding to nothing, n'avoir rien à perdre et tout à gagner.

hi-fi ['haɪ'faɪ] *abbr F* (*= high fidelity*) (de) haute fidélité/hi-fi.

high [haɪ] **I** *a F* 1. to be (in) for the high jump, en être pour de la casse/être dans de mauvais draps; he's (in) for the high jump, qu'est-ce qu'il va prendre!/son compte est bon 2. to leave s.o. high and dry, laisser qn en plan/laisser tomber qn comme une vieille chaussette 3. to be high (*a*) être ivre*/parti/rétamé/schlass (*b*) (*drugs*) être dans un état d'euphorie/être high/planer/faire un trip/voyager. (*See* **fly²** 1 (*b*); **kite** 3) 4. *NAm* high on sth/s.o., qui a une haute opinion de qch/de qn 5. to have a high old time, faire la fête*/la noce; s'en payer une (bonne) tranche. (*See* **horse** 5; **jinks**; **knee-high**; **muck-amuck**) **II** *n F* to be on a high, être high/planer/faire un trip/voyager.

highbrow ['haɪbraʊ] **I** *a F* intellectuel/intello/calé **II** *n F* intellectuel, -elle/intello *mf*/grosse tête.

highfalutin(g) ['haɪfə'luːtɪn, -ɪŋ] *a F* prétentieux*/bêcheur/ramenard.

high-flier ['haɪ'flaɪə] *n F* ambitieux, -euse/qn qui va aux extrêmes. (*See* **fly²** 1 (*a*))

high muckamuck ['haɪ'mʌkəmʌk] *n NAm F* = **muckamuck**.

highspots ['haɪspɒts] *npl F* to hit the high-spots (*a*) exceller/toucher les hauteurs *fpl*/

toucher sa bille (*b*) s'en payer une tranche/faire la foire/faire la noce.

hightail ['haɪteɪl] *vi F* to hightail it, se dépêcher*/se magner le train; let's hightail it out of here! allez, on se tire!/allez, on change de crémerie!

high-ups ['haɪʌps] *npl F* hauts fonctionnaires/gros bonnets.

highway ['haɪweɪ] *a attrib F* it's highway robbery! c'est du vol manifeste!/c'est de l'arnaque patentée!

high yellow ['haɪ'jeləʊ] *a & n NAm F* (Noir(e)/*surt* Noire) à peau claire.

hike¹ [haɪk] *n P* départ *m*; voyage *m*.

hike² [haɪk] *vi P* partir*/se tailler; partir en voyage.

hillbilly ['hɪl'bɪlɪ] *n NAm F* 1. petit fermier de montagne 2. paysan*/péquenaud *m*/plouc *mf* 3. hillbilly (music), musique montagnarde et rustique/musique bouseuse.

hinky ['hɪŋkɪ] *a NAm P* douteux/louche/fumeux.

hip [hɪp] *a F* 1. (*up-to-date*) branché/câblé/à la coule/dans le vent/à la page; she's hip to what's going down, elle est dans le coup 2. (*cool, detached*) cool/coolos.

hipped [hɪpt] *a NAm P* enthousiaste/passionné/fana(tique).

hippie, hippy ['hɪpɪ] *n F* hippie *mf*/hippy *mf*.

hipster ['hɪpstə] *n O* 1. *F* (*jazz, swing, etc*) (*a*) admirateur, -trice/fana(tique) *mf* du jazz (*b*) individu* branché/dans le vent 2. *F* membre *m* d'un groupe de cools 3. *F* membre *m* de la génération beat. (*See* **hip**)

hister ['haɪstə] *n NAm F* = **heister**.

hit¹ [hɪt] *n* 1. *F* pièce *f*/chanson *f* à succès/tube *m*; summer hit, tube de l'été 2. *F* succès *m* populaire; to make a hit, faire un boum/faire un tabac; she made/scored a big hit with him, elle a fait une grosse impression sur lui/elle lui a tapé dans l'œil 3. *P* (*a*) réussite sexuelle (*b*) *Br* = hit-and miss **1** 4. *P* rendez-vous* de contrebande; moyens *mpl* de contrebande 5. *P* (*a*) dose *f* de drogue*/*surt* de LSD* (*b*) bouffée *f*/touffe *f* d'un joint/de crack (*c*) injection *f* de drogues/piquouse *f*/shoot *m* 6. *P* (*drugs*) to make a hit, (*dilute*) diluer la drogue avant de la vendre; (*obtain*) se procurer de la drogue 7. *P* (*esp contract killing*) meurtre prémédité/meurtre sur commande/contrat *m*; to make a hit, remplir un contrat; tuer*/buter/descendre qn sur commande 8. *P* (*police*) to make a hit, faire une arrestation/mettre la main sur le paletot a qn. (*See* **smash-hit**; **take² 5**)

hit² [hɪt] *vtr* 1. *F* to hit the hundred mark, (*of car, etc*) taper le 160 2. *P* (*drugs*) (*a*) provoquer une forte réaction (*b*) to hit s.o., fournir de la drogue à qn 3. *NAm F* servir à boire à/offrir une boisson à (qn); hit me with a beer, file-moi une bière 4. *F* (*borrow money*) taper/torpiller (qn) pour de l'argent; he hit me for twenty quid, il m'a tapé/torpillé de vingt livres 5. *P* assassiner (qn); the assasin hit his man, le tueur a buté sa victime/a rempli son contrat/a descendu son client 6. *P Mus* commencer à jouer; let's hit it! bon, allez, en avant!/en avant la musique! (*See* **bottle¹ 1**; **brick 4**; **ceiling**; **deck¹ 1**; **hay 1**; **highspots**; **jackpot 1**; **pad¹ 2**; **panic 2**; **pipe 2**; **road 2**; **sack¹ 3**; **sauce¹ 2**; **track 1**; **trail**)

hit-and-miss [hɪtən'mɪs] *n Br P* 1. (*RS = kiss*) baiser *m*/smack *m* 2. (*RS = piss*) urine *f*/pisse *f*.

hitch [hɪtʃ] *vtr & i F* 1. to hitch one's wag(g)on to a star, être dévoré d'ambition/viser très haut 2. to get hitched, se marier/se marida/s'entifler; (*live together*) se maquer. (*See* **unhitched**) 3. to hitch (a ride), se faire emmener en voiture/faire de l'auto-stop/faire du stop.

hitching ['hɪtʃɪŋ] *n F* auto-stop *m*/stop *m*; to go hitching, faire du stop.

hit-man ['hɪt'mæn] *n esp NAm P* tueur *m* (à gages)/meurtrier professionnel.

hit off ['hɪt'ɒf] *vi F* to hit it off with s.o., bien s'entendre avec qn; they don't hit it off, il y a du tirage entre eux.

hit on ['hɪt'ɒn] *vtr NAm P* 1. (*chat up*) draguer/baratiner/faire du rentre-dedans à (qn) 2. brutaliser/maillocher; (*criticize*) maillocher 3. ennuyer/embêter/taper sur l'os à (qn) 4. taper/torpiller (qn) pour de l'argent.

hit-parade ['hɪtpəreɪd] *n F* hit-parade *m*.

hitter ['hɪtə] *n P* 1. individu* énergique/qui pète le feu 2. = **hit-man**.

hive off ['haɪv'ɒf] *vtr & i F* 1. mettre de côté/mettre à l'écart 2. s'enfuir*/se cavaler/se débiner.

hiya! ['haɪjə] *excl F* salut! (*See* **hi!**)

hobo ['həʊbəʊ] *n NAm F* clochard*/clodo *m*/trimardeur *m*.

hock¹ [hɒk] *n F* in hock (*a*) en gage/chez ma tante/au clou (*b*) endetté; he's in hock up to his eyes, il est pourri de dettes (*c*) en prison*/

en taule.

hock² [hɒk] *vtr F* mettre en gage/mettre au clou.

hockshop ['hɒkʃɒp] *n F* mont-de-piété *m*/chez ma tante/le clou.

hocky ['hɒkɪ] *n P* 1. *NAm* mensonges*/blagues *fpl*/salades *fpl*/craques *fpl* 2. saleté*/chiure *f*/merde *f*/crassouille *f* 3. crachat*/glaviot *m*.

ho-dad(dy) ['həʊ'dæd(ɪ)] *n NAm F* 1. individu* farfelu/m'as-tu-vu *m* 2. (*esp hanger-on*) individu* qui aime fréquenter les sportifs sans en être un lui-même; parasite *m* 3. pète-sec *m*/collet monté/constipé *m* 4. individu bête*/crétin *m*/gland *m*/nœud *m*.

hoe [həʊ] *n esp NAm P Pej* (*slut*) marie-salope *f*/pouf(f)iasse *f*; (*tramp*) clocharde *f*.

hoedown ['həʊdaʊn] *n NAm F* 1. danse *f* rustique; bal animé/guinche *f* de pedzouille 2. querelle*/engueulade *f* 3. bagarre*/rixe *f*/rififi *m*/baston *m ou f*.

hog¹ [hɒg] *n* 1. *F* goinfre*/porc *m* 2. *F* to go the whole hog, aller jusqu'au bout/tout risquer/mettre le paquet. (*See* **whole-hogger**; **whole-hoggism**) 3. *NAm P* (*motorbike*) grosse moto/gros cube 4. *P* (*drugs*) phéncyclidine *f*/PCP *f*. (*See* **road-hog**; **speed-hog**)

hog² [hɒg] *vtr F* 1. to hog oneself, se goinfrer/bâfrer 2. monopoliser; to hog the limelight, accaparer la vedette 3. to hog the road, conduire au milieu de la route/conduire comme un âne. (*See* **road-hog**) 4. to hog it, vivre comme un cochon/porc.

hog-tied ['hɒgtaɪd] *a NAm F* réduit à l'impuissance/coincé.

hogwash ['hɒgwɒʃ] *n F* 1. (*tasteless drink*) bibine *f*/lavasse *f* 2. bêtise*/sottise *f*/du pipeau; that's just hogwash! c'est des foutaises!

hoick [hɔɪk] *vi Br P* (se racler la gorge et) cracher*/glaviotter.

hoi polloi ['hɔɪpə'lɔɪ] *n F Pej* the hoi polloi, le peuple/le populo.

hoist¹ [hɔɪst] *n P* 1. cambriolage *m*/casse *m* 2. voleur*/barbot(t)eur, -euse; (*shoplifter*) voleur* à l'étalage/étalagiste *mf*; (*pickpocket*) voleur* à la tire/tireur, -euse. (*See* **heist¹**)

hoist² [hɔɪst] *vtr P* 1. (*a*) cambrioler*/casser (*b*) voler* à l'étalage/faire ou acheter au prix courant (*c*) voler* à la tire. (*See* **heist²**) 2. *Austr* arrêter/coffrer/alpaguer 3. *NAm F* boire* (un verre/*surt* une bière).

hoister ['hɔɪstə] *n P* = **hoist**[1] 2.
hokey-pokey ['həʊkɪ'pəʊkɪ] *n F* 1. = **hokum** 1 2. *NAm* glace *f ou* bonbon *m* de mauvaise qualité.
hokum ['həʊkəm] *n esp NAm F* 1. bêtises*/blagues *fpl*/foutaises *fpl* 2. sentimentalité niaise (dans une pièce, un film, etc); guimauve *f*/mélo *m*.
hold [həʊld] I *vtr* 1. *F* hold everything!/hold your horses!/hold it! arrêtez!/attendez!/(ne) bougez plus!/(ne) faites rien!/minute! 2. *P* to hold (oneself), se masturber*/se branler/se pogner/se palucher II *vi F* posséder des drogues.
holding ['həʊldɪŋ] *a NAm F* qui possède de la drogue; are you holding? t'as de la came?/t'en as?
hold out for ['həʊld'aʊtfɔː] *vtr F* he's holding out for more money, il tient bon pour avoir plus de fric/question fric, il ne veut pas lâcher le morceau.
hold out on ['həʊld'aʊtɒn] *vtr F* faire des cachotteries *fpl* à (qn); he's holding out on us, il nous fait des cachotteries/il nous cache qch.
hole [həʊl] *n* 1. *F* (*sleazy bar*) bouge *m*/bouiboui *m*/caboulot *m*; (*room, house*) taudis *m*/gourbi *m*/piaule *f*; (*town, village*) bled *m*/trou *m* 2. *F* embarras *m*/pétrin *m*/impasse *f*; to be in a hole, être dans une situation difficile/être en rade/être dans le caca 3. *F* to make a hole in one's capital, écorner son capital; taper dans/sur ses économies *fpl* 4. *F* to pick holes in sth, trouver à redire à qch/chercher la petite bête 5. *V* sexe* de la femme*/fente *f*. (*See* **manhole**) 6. *V* anus*/trou *m* de balle. (*See* **arsehole; asshole; bum-hole; bung-hole** 1; **cornhole**[1]; **fart-hole; shit-hole**) 7. *P* the hole, cachot *m* (disciplinaire)/mitard *m*/trou *m* 8. *F* hole in the wall, petite maison; petit magasin/restaurant, etc 9. *F* to burn a hole in one's stomach, manger* *ou* boire* qch de très fort/se brûler l'estomac *m* 10. *NAm P* to go in the hole, s'endetter/s'encroumer 11. *F* to put a hole through s.o./to drill holes in s.o., assassiner* qn/flinguer qn/transformer qn en passoire/trouer la peau à qn 12. *Br Aut F* toit ouvrant. (*See* **cakehole; ear(h)ole**[1]; **glory-hole; head** 7; **hell-hole; keyhole; lu-gholes; nineteenth; rathole; square**[1] I 7; **top-hole**)
hole-and-corner ['həʊlən(d)'kɔːnə] *a F* fait en douce/sous la table; hole-and-corner work, combines *fpl*/magouilles *fpl*.

hole up ['həʊl'ʌp] *vi F* se cacher*/se défiler/se planquer.
holier-than-thou ['həʊlɪəðən'ðaʊ] *a F* to be holier-than-thou, faire la Sainte-Nitouche/le tartuffe.
holler ['hɒlə] *vi P* crier*/gueuler/beugler.
holler-wag(g)on ['hɒləwægən] *n P* voiture-radio *f* de la police.
hollow ['hɒləʊ, 'hɒlə] *adv F* to beat s.o. hollow, battre qn à plate(s) couture(s).
hols [hɒlz] *n(pl) F* (*abbr of holidays*) vacances *fpl*/vacs *fpl*; did you have (a) good hols? t'as passé de bonnes vacances?
holy ['həʊlɪ] *a* 1. *F* holy cow!/holy cats!/holy mackerel!/holy Moses!/holy smoke! sapristi!/saperlipopette!/crénom de nom! *V* holy fuck!/holy shit! merde (alors)!/vingt dieux!/putain de merde! 2. *P Pej* holy Joe (*a*) prêtre*/pasteur *m*/ratiche *m*/ratichon *m*; étudiant, -ante en théologie (*b*) personne dévote/grenouille *f* de bénitier 3. *F* holy terror (*a*) enfant* malicieux/petit diable/affreux, -euse (*b*) individu* importun/bassinant; bassinoire *f* (*c*) individu* qui fait peur/épouvantail *m* 4. Holy Ghost, (*RS = winning post*) poteau *m* (d'arrivée). (*See* **friar 1**)
home [həʊm] *adv F* 1. home and dry, à bon port/sain et sauf 2. *O* my suit's gone home, mon costume n'est plus mettable/a rendu l'âme 3. it's nothing to write home about, ça ne casse rien/ça ne casse pas des briques/ça ne casse pas trois pattes à un canard.
home-bird ['həʊmbɜːd] *n F* he's a home bird, il est casanier; she's a home-bird, elle est casanière/popote/pot-au-feu.
homeboy ['həʊmbɔɪ] *n NAm P* membre *m* d'un gang de voyous (*prêt à défendre son territoire*).
home run [həʊm'rʌn] *n*, **homer** ['həʊmə] *n NAm P* satisfaction *ou* conquête sexuelle; coït*/baise *f*; to score a home run/to make a homer, se faire qn.
homestretch ['həʊm'stretʃ] *n F* dernière étape/dernière ligne droite.
homework ['həʊmwɜːk] *n* 1. to do one's homework (*a*) *F* faire une préparation attentive (*b*) *P Euph* remplir ses obligations conjugales 2. *P* (*a*) pelotage *m*/baisage *m* (*b*) a nice bit of homework, une fille* à la cuisse hospitalière.
homo ['həʊməʊ] I *a P* homo(sexuel) II *n P* homosexuel*/homo *m*/pédé *m*.
hon [hʌn] *n esp NAm F* (= **honey**) listen hon! écoute chéri(e)!

honcho ['hɒntʃəʊ] *n NAm P* (head) honcho, chef *m*/(grand) sachem.

honest to goodness ['ɒnɪst(t)ə'gʊdnɪs] *F* I *a* vrai/réel/authentique II *excl* honest to goodness! je te jure!/j't'assure!

honey ['hʌnɪ] *n F* (*a*) petit(e) ami(e)/chéri(e)/bien-aimé(e); yes, honey! oui, ma puce! (*b*) qch d'excellent*/de bath/de chouette; it's a (real) honey! c'est du nanan! he's a real honey, c'est un vrai chou/un amour; that's a honey of a car, cette bagnole, c'est un petit bijou. (*See* **bee 3**)

honeybunch ['hʌnɪbʌntʃ] *n F* = **honey** (*a*).

honeyfuck ['hʌnɪfʌk] *vi V* 1. faire l'amour* d'une manière romantique/à la douce 2. faire l'amour* avec une fille très jeune/baiser la petite fleur.

honeyfuck(ing) ['hʌnɪfʌk(ɪŋ)] *n V* 1. coït*/crampette *f*/baisage *m* à la douce 2. coït* lent et agréable 3. coït* avec une fille très jeune/baisage *m* de petite fleur.

honeypot ['hʌnɪpɒt] *n P* vagin*/baba *m*.

honk¹ [hɒŋk] *n* 1. *P* vomissement *m*/gerbe *f* 2. *esp Austr F* puanteur *f*/chlipote *f*.

honk² [hɒŋk] *vtr & i* 1. *P* to honk (one's chuff), vomir*/dégobiller/aller au renard/aller au refil(e) 2. *A P* to get honked, s'enivrer/se pinter 3. *esp Austr F* sentir* mauvais/puer/schlinguer.

honked [hɒŋkt] *a*, **honkers** ['hɒŋkəz] *a P* ivre*/rétamé/soûl.

Honkers ['hɒŋkəz] *n Br F* Hongkong *f*.

honkey, honkie, honky ['hɒŋkɪ] *n NAm P Pej* (*Black Slang*) Blanc(he) *m*(*f*).

honky-tonk ['hɒŋkɪ'tɒŋk] I *a F* (*cheap, shoddy*) merdique/tarte/tocard II *n NAm F* 1. cabaret zonard/caboulot *m*/bouiboui *m*/bastringue *m* 2. musique *f* de bastringue.

hooch [hu:tʃ] *n esp NAm F* alcool*/gnôle *f* (*surt* de contrebande).

hood [hʊd] *n P* 1. = **hoodlum** 2. *NAm* (*abbr of neighborhood*) voisinage *m*/quartier *m*.

hoodlum ['hu:dləm] *n esp NAm F* gangster *m*/arcan *m*/malfrat *m*.

hooey ['hu:ɪ] *n P* bêtises*/foutaises *fpl*; that's a lot of hooey! c'est du bidon!

hoof¹ [hu:f] *n* 1. *F* pied*/panard *m*/pinceau *m* 2. *Austr P* horse's hoof, (*RS = poof*) homosexuel*/pédale *f*. (*See* **iron II 2**)

hoof² [hu:f] *vtr F* to hoof it (*a*) aller à pied/à pattes/à pince(s) (*b*) partir*/lever le camp (*c*) danser*/gambiller.

hoofer ['hu:fə] *n F* danseur, -euse/*surt* girl *f* (de music-hall).

hoofing ['hu:fɪŋ] *n F* danse *f*/gambille *f*.

hoo-ha(a) ['hu:ha:] *n F* (*noise*) bruit *m*/ramdam *m*/boucan *m*; (*fuss*) chichis *mpl*; (*mess*) pagaïe *f*; it wasn't worth all the hoo-ha(a), ça valait pas tout ce tapage/c'était vraiment pas la peine d'en faire tout un plat.

hook¹ [hʊk] *n* 1. *F* to get off the hook, débrouiller*/se tirer d'embarras/d'affaire; that lets me off the hook, cela me tire d'affaire; to get s.o. off the hook, tirer qn d'affaire 2. *P* to go off the hooks, mourir*/passer l'arme à gauche/lâcher la rampe 3. *esp NAm F* on one's own hook, sans appui/à son (propre) compte 4. *F* he swallowed it hook, line and sinker, il a tout avalé/il a tout gobé 5. *P* to sling one's hook, partir*/mettre les bouts/foutre le camp 6. *pl F* mains*/croches *fpl*; to get one's hooks on s.o./sth, mettre le grappin sur qn/qch. (*See* **meathooks**) 7. *P* voleur*; *surt* voleur* à la tire/tireur *m* 8. *P* arrestation*/agrichage *m*/alpague *f* 9. *NAm P* to get the hook, (*be sacked*) se faire vider/virer.

hook² [hʊk] *vtr* 1. *P* voler*/chouraver/soulever 2. *P* arrêter*/agrafer/alpaguer/épingler 3. *P* to get hooked for a few quid/*NAm* a few dollars, être estampé/se faire tondre de quelques talbins/quelques sacs (au jeu) 4. *F* to be hooked (on drugs), se droguer*/se camer/se (s)chnouffer/être accro(ché)/être accroch'man 5. *F* to be hooked on s.o., avoir le béguin pour qn/en pincer pour qn 6. *F* to hook a husband, mettre le grappin sur un mari 7. *P* to hook it, s'enfuir*/se tailler/mettre les bouts 8. *P* to hook s.o. one, (*punch*) balancer/flanquer un marron à qn.

hooker ['hʊkə] *n P* 1. prostituée*/raccrocheuse *f*/pute *f* 2. (*pickpocket*) voleur* à la tire/tireur *m*.

hookey ['hʊkɪ] *n esp NAm F* to play hook(e)y, *see* **hooky II**.

hook-shop ['hʊkʃɒp] *n A P* bordel*/clandé *m*/maison *f*.

hook up ['hʊk'ʌp] *vi F* to hook up with s.o., être le complice* de qn; être de mèche/en cheville avec qn.

hooky ['hʊkɪ] I *a Br P* volé/piqué/de provenance douteuse. II *n esp NAm F* to play hooky, faire l'école buissonnière/sécher les cours.

hoon [hu:n] *n Austr P* voyou*/loubard *m*/loulou *m*.

hoop [huːp] *n F* to go through the hoop (*have a hard time*) passer un mauvais quart d'heure; (*be punished*) en prendre pour son grade.

hoop-la ['huːplɑː] *n NAm F* **1.** tapage *m*/chahut *m*/boucan *m* **2.** battage *m* publicitaire.

Hooray (Henry) ['huːreɪ'(henrɪ)] *n F Pej* jeune homme *m* de la haute/B.C.B.G. *m* (tapageur/chahuteur).

hoosegow ['huːsgaʊ] *n NAm F* **1.** commissariat *m* de police/(burlingue *m* de) quart *m* **2.** prison*/bloc *m*/taule *f*.

hoot[1] [huːt] *n F* **1.** rigolade *f*/blague *f*; it's a real hoot, c'est vachement marrant/c'est tordant; he's a real hoot, c'est un marrant/un rigolo **2.** I don't care a hoot/I couldn't give two hoots, je m'en moque/je m'en balance/j'en ai rien à glander/je m'en bats l'œil **3.** it's not worth a hoot, ça ne vaut rien*/ça ne vaut pas un pet de lapin.

hoot[2] [huːt] *vi F* **1.** to hoot with laughter, rire* aux éclats/se bidonner/se tordre de rire **2.** *Austr* sentir* mauvais/puer/schlinguer.

hootch [huːtʃ] *n NAm F* = **hooch.**

hooter ['huːtə] *n Br P* nez*/pif *m*/trompette *f*.

hooters ['huːtəz] *npl NAm P* seins*/ananas *mpl*/doudounes *fpl*.

hoover up ['huːvə'rʌp] *vtr Br F* manger* vite *ou* gloutonnement; dévorer/bâfrer.

hop[1] [hɒp] *n* **1.** *F* danse *f*/sauterie *f*/surboum *f* **2.** *F* a short hop, une courte distance/un pas/un saut; it's only a hop, skip and a jump away, c'est à deux pas d'ici **3.** *F* to catch s.o. on the hop, surprendre qn/prendre qn au pied levé **4.** *F* to be on the hop, être toujours en mouvement/avoir la bougeotte **5.** *P* (*drugs*) (*opium*) noir *m*; (*any drug*) came *f*; hop joint, local *m* où on peut acheter et prendre des drogues.

hop[2] [hɒp] *vtr & i* **1.** *F* hop in! allez hop!/monte!/saute là-dedans! **2.** *F* hop it! file!/fiche le camp!/casse-toi! **3.** *F* to hop on a bus, sauter dans un autobus; to hop off a bus, sauter d'un autobus **4.** *F* hopping mad, très en colère*/en rogne/furax/furibard **5.** *P* to hop into bed with s.o., se foutre au lit avec qn. (*See* **lorry-hop; wag**[1])

hophead ['hɒphed] *n A P* toxicomane *mf*/toxico *mf*.

hopped up ['hɒpt'ʌp] *a P* **1.** stimulé par la drogue/dopé/chargé **2.** *NAm* (*engine*) gonflé/bricolé **3.** (*excited*) excité/survolté.

horn [hɔːn] *n* **1.** *V* pénis*/tige *f* **2.** *V* érection *f*; to have the horn/to get the horn, être en érection*/avoir la trique/bander **3.** *F* (*jazz*) trompette *f*/biniou *m* **4.** *esp NAm F* téléphone*; to get on the horn, passer un coup de bigophone/de biniou. (*See* **blow**[2] **3**)

horn in ['hɔːn'ɪn] *vi esp NAm F* to horn in on s.o.'s conversation, ramener sa fraise/mettre son grain de sel.

hornswoggle ['hɔːnswɒgl] *vtr NAm F* duper/entuber (qn); mener (qn) en bateau.

horny ['hɔːnɪ] *a V* (*a*) être en érection*/avoir le bambou/avoir la canne/avoir le gourdin (*b*) être excité (sexuellement)/avoir une barre/bander à mort (*c*) être obsédé/ne penser qu'à ça.

horrors (the) [ðə'hɒrəz] *n F* to have the horrors (*a*) grelotter de peur*/chier dans son froc (*b*) être en proie au délirium tremens/avoir la digue-digue (*c*) avoir des troubles mentaux dus aux amphétamines/délirer/flipper (*d*) avoir des symptômes dus au sevrage d'héroïne/être cold-turkey/être en manque. (*See* **chuck**[1] **2**)

horse [hɔːs] *n* **1.** *F* he's a dark horse, il cache son jeu/il n'a pas l'air d'y toucher **2.** *F* it's straight from the horse's mouth, (ça vient) de source sûre/c'est un tuyau increvable/de première **3.** *F* a horse of another colour, une autre paire de manches **4.** *F* to flog a dead horse, se dépenser en pure perte **5.** *F* to get on one's high horse, monter sur ses grands chevaux/le prendre de haut **6.** *F* hold your horses! (*calm down*) (ne) t'emballe pas!/mollo! (*wait*) attendez!/arrêtez!/minute! **7.** *NAm F* horse opera, western *m*/film *m* de cowboys **8.** *O P* (*drugs*) héroïne*/cheval *m* **9.** *P* to water the horses, uriner*/changer d'eau son poisson. (*See* **charlie 8; clotheshorse; hoof**[2] **; one-horse; switch**[2])

horse about ['hɔːsə'baʊt], **horse around** ['hɔːsə'raʊnd] *vi F* faire l'imbécile; chahuter/faire le zouave.

horse doctor ['hɔːsdɒktə] *n F* **1.** vétérinaire *mf*/véto *mf* **2.** médecin peu compétent/toubib marron.

horseplay ['hɔːspleɪ] *n F* jeu brutal/chahut brutal.

horse's ass ['hɔːsɪz'æs] *n NAm P* individu* bête*/trouduc *m*.

horseshit ['hɔːsʃɪt] *n NAm V* foutaises *fpl*/conneries *fpl*; that's horseshit! c'est des foutaises!/c'est des conneries!

horse-trading ['hɔːstreɪdɪŋ] *n F* maquignonnage *m*.

hose [həʊz] *vtr NAm* 1. *V* faire l'amour* avec (qn); enfiler/tringler (qn) 2. *P* duper* (qn)/entuber (qn)/mener (qn) en bateau.

hoss [hɒs] *n esp NAm F* (= *horse*) cheval *m*/canasson *m*/bourrin *m*.

hostie ['həʊstɪ] *n Austr F* (= *air hostess*) hôtesse *f* de l'air.

hot [hɒt] *a* 1. *P* chaud de la pince/de la pointe; **to have hot pants**, (*of woman, to be sexually aroused*) avoir le feu aux fesses*/au cul/quelque part; **to be hot for s.o.**, en pincer pour qn/bander pour qn; **hot date**, (*meeting*) rendez-vous/rencard sérieux; (*person*) copin, -ine sexy; bandeur, -euse; **hot mama/hot lay/ hot piece**, femme* passionnée/sexy/qui a le feu au cul; **that's really hot stuff!** (*film, book, etc*) ça fait bander!/c'est super bandant! (*See* **babe 2; cookie 3; number¹ 3; patootie 2; red-hot 1**) 2. *F* **hot pants**, short *m* (sexy) 3. **hot stuff** (*a*) *P* (*man*) chaud lapin; (*woman*) bandeuse *f* (*b*) *P* jeux provocants (*c*) *F* butin* facilement identifiable (*d*) *F* **she's really hot stuff**, elle est sensass/terrible; **he's hot stuff at tennis**, c'est un as au tennis/ un joueur de première 4. *F* **expert** *m*/crack *m* 5. *F* **to be hot under the collar**, être en colère*/être furibard/l'avoir mauvaise 6. *F* énervé/excité/qui a les nerfs en pelote; agité/ dans tous ses états; **to get all hot and bothered**, s'échauffer/se faire du mauvais sang 7. *F* (*jazz*) improvisé avec passion/joué avec chaleur/hot; **hot music**, le jazz/le swing 8. *F* très récent/à la une/sensationnel; **hot tip**, renseignement* sûr/tuyau *m* increvable/tuyau de première; **hot from the press**, dernier cri/ de dernière minute 9. *P* (*a*) (*stolen goods*) recherché par la police/difficile à écouler; **hot car/hot money**, voiture* volée/argent* volé; **hot rock**, bijou fauché (*b*) (*criminal*) recherché par la police pour crime. (*See* **hot 3** (*c*)) 10. (*a*) *NAm P* **hot seat/hot squat**, chaise *f* électrique (*b*) *F* **to be in the hot seat**, être dans une situation difficile/être sur la sellette 11. *F* **to make it hot for s.o.**, faire des difficultés *fpl* à qn/être vache avec qn; **I'll make it hot for him!** ça va chauffer pour lui!/ ça va barder pour son matricule! 12. *F* **to give it to s.o./to let s.o. have it hot (and strong)**, passer un bon savon à qn/sonner les cloches à qn/passer une belle engueulade à qn 13. *F* **to be in hot water**, être dans de mauvais draps/dans la mélasse; **to get into hot water**, se mettre dans le pétrin 14. *F* **that's not so hot!** c'est pas formidable!/c'est pas fameux!

15. *F Iron* **she's had more boyfriends than I've had hot dinners!** elle change de mec plus souvent que moi de chemise! 16. *F* (*esp guessing games*) **you're getting hot**, tu brûles 17. *F* **to sell like hot cakes**, se vendre comme des petits pains 18. *F* (*cards*) **to hold a hot hand**, avoir de bonnes cartes*/un bon jeu/un jeu du tonnerre; **to have a hot streak**, avoir une veine dingue 19. *F* **hot war**, la guerre sanglante (*contraire de* la guerre froide) 20. **hot rod** (*a*) *F* (*souped-up racing car*) bolide *m*; voiture gonflée/bricolée (*b*) *P* pénis*/bite *f*. (*See* **rod 1**) 21. *F* **hot spot**, (*nightclub*) cabaret *m*/boîte *f* de nuit; (*difficult situation*) mauvaise passe/pétrin *m* 22. *V* (*a*) *NAm* **he thinks he's hot shit**, il ne se prend pas pour de la merde (*b*) *Austr* **hot cack**, (*qch*) d'excellent*; **it's hot cack**, c'est pas dégueu/ c'est pas pourri 23. *F* **radioactif**; **hot lab(oratory)**, labo(ratoire) *m* traitant des matières radioactives 24. *NAm F* **hot dog!** hourra!/bravo! (*See also* **hot-dog**) (*See* **air 5; blow² 4; drop² 1; gospeller; potato 3; red-hot; shit¹ I; shit-shot**)

hot-dog ['hɒtdɒg] *vi NAm F* exécuter qch avec succès/faire un tabac.

hotfoot ['hɒtfʊt] *vtr F* **to hotfoot it**, se dépêcher*/mettre les bouts.

hothouse ['hɒthaʊs] *a attrib F* **hothouse plant**, personne délicate/petite nature.

hot-rod ['hɒtrɒd] *vi NAm V* se masturber*/ se mettre à cinq contre un. (*See* **hot 20; rod 1**)

hots [hɒts] *npl NAm P* **the hots**, amour *m*; désir sexuel; **he had the hots for her**, il bandait pour elle/il en pinçait dur pour elle/il avait une barre pour elle.

hotshot¹ ['hɒtʃɒt] *NAm F* **I** *a* excellent*/ terrible; **a hotshot chess player**, un joueur d'échecs super-doué **II** *n* 1. **as** *m*/crack *m*/bête *f* 2. (*drugs*) overdose mortelle (*surt d'héroïne*).

hotshot² ['hɒtʃɒt] *vtr NAm F* (*drugs*) donner une overdose mortelle (*surt d'héroïne*) à (qn).

hotsie, hotsie-totsie¹ ['hɒtsɪ('tɒtsɪ)] *n Br P* = **totsie**.

hotsie-totsie², hotsy-totsy ['hɒtsɪ-'tɒtsɪ] *a NAm O F* = **hunky-dory**.

hotted-up ['hɒtɪd'ʌp] *a F* **hotted-up car**, voiture* au moteur poussé/gonflé/bricolé.

hotter ['hɒtə] *n Br F* individu* qui fait un rodéo (*dans une voiture volée*).

hottie ['hɒtɪ] *n* 1. *F* (= *hot-water bottle*)

bouillotte *f* 2. *NAm P* jolie fille*/belle gosse/ supernana *f*.

hotting ['hɒtɪŋ] *n Br F* rodéo *m*.

hot-wire ['hɒt'waɪə] *vtr F* démarrer (une voiture*) sans la clé/en tripotant les fils d'allumage.

hound-dog ['haʊnd(d)ɒg, *NAm* 'haʊnd(d)ɔːg] *n F* 1. tombeur *m* de femmes/ coureur *m* de jupons/cavaleur *m*/juponneur *m* 2. vaurien *m*/salaud*.

house [haʊs] *n F* 1. (*a*) *O* like a house on fire, (*quickly*) vite*/à toute pompe/à pleins gaz (*b*) to get on like a house on fire, sympathiser/s'entendre comme larrons en foire/être copains comme cochons/être comme cul et chemise 2. on the house, gratuit*/à l'œil/aux frais de la princesse/offert par la maison 3. to bring the house down, faire crouler la salle (sous les applaudissements)/ casser la baraque/faire un malheur 4. *NAm* the big house, la prison*/la taule. (*See* **barrelhouse; blue¹ I 5; bug-house; cathouse; crazyhouse; dog-house; dosshouse; flea-house; flophouse; glasshouse; hothouse; kip-house; madhouse; meat-house; nut-house; powerhouse; rough-house; shithouse; whore-house**)

how [haʊ] I *adv F* 1. any old how, n'importe comment/à la va-comme-je-te-pousse 2. how come? comment est-ce possible?/comment ça?/comment ça se fait? 3. and how! et comment! (*See* **nohow**) II *excl F Hum* (*supposedly used by North American Indians*) how! comment va?/ça va?/ugh!

how-do-you-do ['haʊdjuːduː, 'haʊdjə-duː] *n O F* here's a fine old/a right old how-do-you-do, c'est une mauvaise passe/une sale affaire; *Iron* en voilà du joli!/nous voilà propres!

howdy! ['haʊdɪ] *excl NAm F* salut!/ça va?/ ça gaze?

how-d'ye-do ['haʊdjəduː] *n F* = **how-do-you-do**.

how's-your-father ['haʊzjə'fɑːðə] *n F Euph* a bit of how's-your-father, une partie de jambes en l'air/une partie de traversin.

hoyden ['hɔɪd(ə)n] *n P* (jeune) femme*/ gonzesse *f*/pépée *f*.

hubba-hubba! ['hʌbə'hʌbə] *excl* 1. *Austr* (*referring to pretty girl*) la supernana!/le beau morceau! 2. *NAm* (*showing enthusiasm*) hourrah!/c'est le pied!/super!

hubby ['hʌbɪ] *n F* (= *husband*) mari *m*.

huddle ['hʌdl] *n F* séance/réunion secrète; to go into a huddle, se réunir discrètement.

huff¹ [hʌf] *n Br F* (*esp North of England & Scotland*) to take the huff, s'offusquer/prendre la mouche.

huff² [hʌf] *vi Br P* péter*/lâcher une perle.

hum¹ [hʌm] *n esp Austr P* pet*/fusant *m*.

hum² [hʌm] *vi F* 1. s'animer/chauffer; to be humming, être en pleine activité/boumer 2. sentir* mauvais/schlinguer 3. *esp Austr* péter*/lâcher une perle.

humdinger ['hʌm'dɪŋə] I *F a* a humdinger row, une dispute du tonnerre II *n* 1. *F* qn *ou* qch d'excellent*/du tonnerre; that was a real humdinger! c'était le (super-)pied!/c'était (super) sensass! 2. *Austr P* pet* spectaculaire.

hummy ['hʌmɪ] *a NAm F* 1. excellent*/ épatant 2. heureux/insouciant/relax/à l'aise 3. puant/cocottant.

hump¹ [hʌmp] *n* 1. *F* to get over the hump, surmonter le plus dur (d'un problème, etc) 2. *F* to have/get the hump, être de mauvaise humeur/broyer du noir; to give s.o. the hump, donner le cafard à qn; that gives me the hump, ça me fout le cafard/ça me fiche le moral à zéro 3. *V* (*a*) coït*/baise *f*/crampette *f* (*b*) *esp NAm O* femme*/surt prostituée *f*/ garce *f*; she's good hump, c'est une sacrée baiseuse 4. *NAm F* to get a hump on, se dépêcher*/se dégrouiller/se magner (le train).

hump² [hʌmp] *vtr & i* 1. *V* to hump (s.o.), faire l'amour*/tirer sa crampe/faire une partie de jambes en l'air (avec qn) 2. *F* porter sur le dos (avec difficulté)/se coltiner/ trimbal(l)er; it's not easy humping this case around, c'est pas de la tarte, de se coltiner cette valoche! 3. *NAm F* = to get a hump on (**hump¹** 4).

humpty ['hʌmptɪ] *a Br F* 1. = **humpy** 2. (*sexually aroused*) qui a une barre/qui bande à zéro.

humpy ['hʌmpɪ] *a F* (*a*) en colère* (*b*) grognon/grincheux.

Hun, hun [hʌn] I *a F* allemand*/boche II *n F* (*a*) Allemand*/boche *m* (*b*) soldat* allemand/fritz *m*/frisé *m*.

hunch [hʌntʃ] *n F* intuition *f*/pressentiment *m*; to have a hunch that..., soupçonner que.../ avoir des gourances *fpl* que...; I've got a hunch that..., j'ai comme une petite idée que...; to play a hunch, agir par intuition/aller au pifomètre.

hundred ['hʌndrəd] *n F* 1. a hundred, cent

livres *fpl* sterling; **half a hundred**, cinquante livres sterling **2. a hundred proof**, le meilleur/ vrai/authentique/cent pour cent/garanti pur sucre.

hundred-percenter ['hʌndrədpə'sentə] *n* *F* = **whole-hogger**.

hung [hʌŋ] *a* *P* **1.** *NAm* *A* fâché/irrité/ embêté **2. hung** (like a bull/a horse/a jack donkey), *(man)* bien monté/bien équipé/bien outillé; monté comme un âne/un bourricot/un taureau; **hung like a fieldmouse**, monté comme un serin. (*See* **well-hung**) **3.** = **hung up 1, 2.**

hunger ['hʌŋgə] *n* *NAm* *F* **from hunger**, miteux/pouilleux/toc/moche.

hung over ['hʌŋ'əʊvə] *a* *F* **to be hung over**, avoir la gueule de bois/la GDB. (*See* **hangover**)

hung up ['hʌŋ'ʌp] *a* *F* **1.** (*uptight*) collet monté/vieux jeu; (*neurotic*) obsédé/frustré/ zibé; **he's really hung up about it**, il en fait tout un complexe **2. to be hung up on** s.o., avoir un béguin pour qn; **he's hung up on her**, il en pince pour elle **3.** (*drugs*) en manque. (*See* **hang-up**)

hunk [hʌŋk] *n* *P* (*attractive man*) beau mec/mec bien foutu; **he's a (real) hunk**, il en jette/il jette du jus.

hunkers ['hʌŋkəz] *npl* *F* *esp* *Dial* **on one's hunkers**, accroupi/à croupetons.

hunking, hunkin' ['hʌŋkɪŋ, 'hʌŋkɪn] *a* *P* = **hunky I 1.**

hunky ['hʌŋkɪ] **I** *a* **1.** *P* (*man*) beau/qui a du chien/qui jette du jus; **he's really hunky**, il a de la gueule/c'est un beau mec **2.** *F* = **hunky-dory II** *n* *NAm* *P* immigrant, -ante d'Europe centrale. (*See* **bohunk 1**)

hunky-dory ['hʌŋkɪ'dɔːrɪ] *a* *F* parfait/ ronflant/au poil; **everything's hunky-dory**, ça marche comme sur des roulettes/ça gaze au poil.

hurl [hɜːl] *vi* *esp* *Austr* *F* vomir*/dégueuler.

hurry ['hʌrɪ] *n* *F* **he won't do that again in a hurry**, il ne recommencera pas de sitôt/il (n')est pas prêt de recommencer.

hurry-up ['hʌrɪ'ʌp] *a* *attrib* *O* *F* **hurry-up van/wag(g)on**, car* de police/panier *m* à salade.

hurt [hɜːt] *a* *NAm* *P* (*a*) laid/moche/ mochard/craignos (*b*) qui fait pitié.

hush-hush ['hʌʃ'hʌʃ] *a* *F* très secret/ confidentiel; **it's all very hush-hush!** c'est

ultra-secret!/pas un mot, là-dessus!/c'est top-secret!

hush money ['hʌʃ'mʌnɪ] *n* *P* pot-de-vin *m*/graissage *m* de patte; **to give** (s.o.) **hush money**, acheter le silence (de qn); **he got £500 hush money to keep him quiet**, on lui a acheté son silence (avec) £500.

hush up ['hʌʃ'ʌp] *vtr* *F* étouffer/supprimer (par la censure).

hustle¹ ['hʌsl] *n* *esp* *NAm* *F* **1.** tromperie *f*/ entourloupe *f*/arnaque *f* **2.** bousculade *f*/ grouillement *m*; **to get a hustle on**, se dépêcher*/se grouiller.

hustle² ['hʌsl] *vtr* & *i* *esp* *NAm* *P* **1.** mendier*/faire la manche **2.** (*prostitutes and homosexuals*) racoler*/faire le trottoir/faire le bisness **3.** gagner sa vie par des méthodes louches/magouiller; fourguer/lessiver de la marchandise **4.** (*cards: to obtain a bet under false pretences*) faire la bête **5.** se dépêcher*/ se grouiller.

hustler ['hʌslə] *n* *P* **1.** *esp* *NAm* qn qui ga-gne sa vie par des moyens louches/ débrouillard, -arde/brasseur *m* d'affaires/ magouilleur, -euse *f*. *NAm* (*a*) prostituée*/ bisenesseuse *f* (*b*) (*homosexual prostitute*) tapineur *m*.

hymie ['haɪmɪ] *n* *F* (*offensive*) Juif *m*, Juive *f*/feuj *mf*.

hype¹ [haɪp] *n* **1.** *P* (= *hypodermic syringe*) seringue *f* hypodermique/poussette *f*/shooteuse *f* **2.** *P* (*drugs*) piqûre*/piquouse *f*/shoot *m* **3.** (*drug addict*) drogué*/camé(e) *m(f)*/ toxico *mf* **4.** (*publicity*) grand battage publici-taire; **a big hype**, un grand/gros coup de pub; un matraquage/battage publicitaire monstre.

hype² [haɪp] *vtr* *F* (*publicize*) pousser la vente de (qch) par un grand battage pu-blicitaire; **to hype a rock group**, lancer un groupe de rock à grand renfort de pub.

hyped-up ['haɪpt'ʌp] *a* **1.** *F* (*heavily pu-blicized*) lancé à grand renfort de pub **2.** *F* (*excited*) excité; (*tense*) tendu/contracté **3.** *P* stimulé par la drogue/drogué*/camé.

hypo ['haɪpəʊ] *n* *P* **1.** (*a*) (= *hypochondria*) hypocondrie *f* (*b*) (= *hypochondriac*) hypocondriaque *mf* **2.** = **hype¹ 1, 2.**

hysterics [hɪ'sterɪks] *npl* *F* **to have/to be in hysterics**, se tordre de rire/se marrer/rire à faire pipi dans sa culotte/rire à en pisser dans son froc.

I

I-am [ˈaɪˈæm] *n F* he thinks he's the great I-am, il se prend pour le bon Dieu en personne/il se croit Dieu le Père.

ice¹ [aɪs] *n* 1. *P* diamant(s)*/diam *m*; green ice, émeraude(s) *f(pl)*; ice palace, bijouterie *f* 2. *F* to break the ice, rompre la glace; (*prostitute*) faire le premier client de la journée/dérouiller 3. *F* to cut no ice with s.o., ne pas impressionner qn/ne pas faire d'effet sur qn; that doesn't cut any ice with me, (*I'm not impressed*) ça me laisse froid/de glace; (*I'm not taken in*) ça (ne) marche pas avec moi (ce genre de truc) 4. *F* to put on ice, mettre en veilleuse/au frigo 5. *F* to tread on thin ice, marcher sur des œufs 6. *P* to be on ice, (*certain*) être assuré d'avance/être du tout cuit/être affiché; = to be iced (**ice²** 4) 7. *P* to have ice in one's shoes, avoir peur de s'adonner à la drogue/avoir la hantise des drogues.

ice² [aɪs] *vtr & i P* 1. tuer*/refroidir (qn) 2. feindre d'ignorer (qn)/ne pas s'occuper de (qn)/négliger (qn)/mettre (qn) en quarantaine 3. se taire*/la boucler 4. to be iced, (*in solitary confinement*) être au cachot/au frigidaire.

iceberg [ˈaɪsbɜːg] *n F* 1. (*person*) individu* de glace/glaçon *m* 2. *Austr F* individu* qui nage/qui fait du surf quelle que soit la température de l'eau.

ice creamer [aɪsˈkriːmə] *n Br P Pej* Italien, -ienne/macaroni *mf*.

iceman [ˈaɪsmæn, ˈaɪsmən] *n P* 1. voleur* de bijoux/chopeur *m* de joncaille 2. tueur professionnel/à gages. (*See* **ice¹** 1; **ice²** 1)

icing [ˈaɪsɪŋ] *n F* icing on the cake, ajout *m* inutile/fioritures *fpl*; the rest is just icing on the cake, le reste, c'est pour faire joli.

icky (poo) [ˈɪkɪ(puː)] *a P* 1. d'une sentimentalité excessive/de la guimauve 2. poisseux/visqueux.

ID¹ [ˈaɪˈdiː] *n P* (= *identity (card)*) brèmes *fpl ou* brèmes *fpl*/faffes *mpl*; got any ID on you? fais voir tes faffes!

ID² [ˈaɪˈdiː] *vtr P* to ID s.o., identifier/cerner/repérer qn.

idiot-board [ˈɪdɪətbɔːd] *n F (TV)* pancarte cachée des caméras qui souffle aux acteurs; = téléprompteur *m*.

idiot-box [ˈɪdɪətbɒks] *n F (television (set))* télévision *f ou* téléviseur *m*/télé *f*/téloche *f*. (*See* **box¹** 2; **gogglebox**; **lantern**)

iffy [ˈɪfɪ] *a F* 1. douteux/plein de si/pas gagné d'avance; it's all a bit iffy, c'est pas du tout cuit/du nougat 2. *Br* malhonnête/pas net; he's a bit iffy, il est pas net/c'est un flibustier; they're a bit iffy, (*of stolen goods*) c'est de la marchandise volée/piquée.

Ikey (Mo) [ˈaɪkɪ(ˈməʊ)] *Prn Br P Pej* Juif*/youpin *m*/youtre *m*.

illin' [ˈɪlɪn] *a F* 1. malade*/raide/mal fichu 2. bête*/cul; fou*/détraqué/malade 3. mauvais*/bidon/blèche.

imbo [ˈɪmbəʊ] *n Austr F* imbécile*/crétin, -ine.

in [ɪn] **I** *a attrib F* 1. in joke, plaisanterie *f* pour initiés 2. *O* à la coule/dans le vent; it's the in thing to do, c'est très à la mode de faire ça; it's the in place to go, c'est l'endroit où se faire voir/c'est le dernier endroit chic; it's the in place to eat, c'est le resto où aller **II** *adv* 1. *P* to get it in, faire l'amour*/l'introduire 2. *F* to be (well) in with s.o., être bien avec qn/être dans les petits papiers de qn 3. *F* to be in, *O* (*in vogue*) être dans le vent/à la page/à la coule; (*accepted*) être accepté dans la bonne société/savoir nager; to be like Flynn, avoir de la chance*/du flambeau/du pot 4. *F* to have it in for s.o., (*have sth against s.o.*) en vouloir à qn/avoir une dent contre qn; (*hate s.o.*) détester* qn/avoir qn dans le nez 5. *F* to be in on it, être dans le bain/dans le coup 6. *F* he's in for it! son compte est *n f* bon!/le voilà dans de beaux draps!/il va écoper!/il va en prendre pour son grade! 7. *F* to be all in, être fatigué*/claqué/vidé **III** *n F* 1. to have an in, avoir des relations (bien placées)/avoir le bras long 2. **the ins and outs,** les coins et recoins (d'une affaire)/les tenants et les aboutissants.

in-and-out man [ɪnən'aʊtmæn] *n F* voleur* qui pratique le vol au bonjour (*sans effraction*).

in bother [ɪn'bɒðə] *a Br F* he's in bother, il a des ennuis/des emmerdes. (*See* **bother** II).

incy(-wincy) ['ɪnsɪ('wɪnsɪ)] *a F* **an incy(-wincy) bit of...,** un petit peu* de.../un chouia de.../une pincée de.../une larme de....

indeedy [ɪn'diːdɪ] *adv NAm O F* yes indeedy! bien sûr (que oui)!

India, india ['ɪndɪə] *n O P* (*drugs*) cannabis*/chanvre indien.

Indian ['ɪndɪən] *a* 1. *NAm P* Indian gift, cadeau-hameçon *m*/cadeau-bidon *m*; **Indian giver,** donneur, -euse de cadeaux-hameçons 2. *P* Indian hay/hemp, cannabis*/chanvre indien. (*See* **India**) 3. *F* too many chiefs and not enough Indians, c'est une armée de généraux.

indie ['ɪndɪ] *n Br F* (*a*) marque de disque indépendante (*b*) disque enregistré sous une marque indépendante.

indigo ['ɪndɪɡəʊ] *a esp NAm F* indigo mood, idées noires/cafard *m*/bourdon *m*; **to be in an indigo mood,** avoir les boules.

indoors [ɪn'dɔːz] *adv Br P* chez soi; I left it indoors, je l'ai laissé chez moi/à la maison. (*See* **her indoors**).

in effect [ɪnɪ'fekt] *a & adv Br P* (*Black Slang*) (*in action*) à l'œuvre.

influence ['ɪnflʊəns] *n F* under the influence, sous l'empire de la boisson/dans les vignes (du Seigneur).

info ['ɪnfəʊ] *n F* (*abbr of information*) renseignements*/info *f*/tuyau *m*; he gave me the info, il m'a filé un tuyau/il m'a rencardé/il m'a tuyauté; got any info? t'as du neuf?/t'as une piste?

infra dig ['ɪnfrə'dɪɡ] *adv phr F* indigne/au-dessous de soi/rabaissant.

Injun ['ɪndʒən] *n* 1. *esp NAm F* Indien, -ienne (d'Amérique) 2. *P* honest Injun! vrai de vrai!/vraiment!/sans blague!/je t'assure!

inked, inky [ɪŋkt, 'ɪŋkɪ] *a* (*rare*) ivre*/beurré.

ink-slinger ['ɪŋkslɪŋə] *n F* (*bureaucrat*) gratte-papier *m*/rond-de-cuir *m*.

in-laws ['ɪnlɔːz] *npl F* belle-famille *f*; les beaux-parents *mpl*/les (beaux-)dabs *mpl*.

innards ['ɪnədz] *npl F* ventre*/boyaux *mpl*/tripes *fpl*/cimetière *m* à poulets.

inner ['ɪnə] *a F* the inner man, appétit *m*/ventre*; to look after the inner man, se remplir le buffet/la panse.

innings ['ɪnɪŋz] *n F* 1. to have (had) a good innings, vivre vieux*; he's had a good innings, il a couvert pas mal de chemin/il a fait un bon tour de terrain 2. your innings! à vous de jouer!/à vous le tour!

in-out [ɪn'aʊt] *n V Euph* coït*; to have a bit of the old in-out, se tirer une crampette.

inside I ['ɪnsaɪd] *a F* 1. inside information/dope, tuyaux confidentiels/infos *fpl* de première bourre/tuyaux de première main 2. ['nsaɪd] the inside story, l'histoire *f* authentique/véridique (*racontée par l'un des participants*); témoignage vécu; to know the inside story, connaître les dessous d'une histoire 3. [ɪn'saɪd] inside job, vol, etc, attribué à un membre du personnel (*d'une entreprise*)/coup monté par qn de la maison 4. an inside man, qn de la maison qui aide à monter un coup de l'intérieur; taupe *f* II *adv F* 1. [ɪn'saɪd] en prison*/à l'ombre/au frais; he's been inside, il a fait de la taule 2. ['ɪnsaɪd] inside out (*a*) à fond; to know s.o./sth inside out, connaître qn/qch comme sa poche/à fond; to know Paris inside out, s'y retrouver dans Paris les yeux fermés (*b*) to turn everything inside out, mettre tout sens dessus dessous 3. [ɪn'saɪd] to be inside on sth, connaître les dessous d'une affaire/être bien tuyauté III *n F* 1. [ɪn'saɪd] = **innards**; I laughed so much my insides were all sore, j'ai ri jusqu'à en avoir mal aux côtes/j'ai ri à m'en retourner les tripes 2. ['nsaɪd] to be on the inside, être dans le coup/être du bâtiment IV [ɪn'saɪd] *prep F* to do sth inside (of) an hour, faire qch en moins d'une heure/en un tour d'horloge.

instrument ['ɪnstrʊmənt] *n P* pénis*/outil *m*; to play (with) one's instrument, se masturber*/s'allonger le macaroni.

intended [ɪn'tendɪd] *n O F* un(e) futur(e)/promis(e).

intestinal [ɪntes'taɪnəl] *a NAm F Euph* to have intestinal fortitude, avoir du cran/en avoir dans le bide/avoir des tripes *fpl*.

into ['ɪntuː] *prep F* absorbé par (qch); en proie à (qch); I'm into Russian novels, je suis plongé dans les romans russes; she's heavily into health foods, elle s'est totalement branchée sur/elle donne à fond dans la bouffe-bio; I'm not into that, ça, c'est pas mon truc.

invite ['ɪnvaɪt] *n F* invitation *f*.

Irish ['aɪrɪʃ] I *a F* 1. biscornu; the whole sentence sounds a bit Irish, toute la phrase ne tient pas debout 2. **Irish** confetti, (*stones, rocks, etc thrown at demonstrations*) (gros) cailloux *mpl*/pavés *mpl*, etc (*lancés par des manifestants*) 3. **Irish** banjo, pelle *f* 4. **Irish** apricot/apple/plum/grape, pomme *f* de terre/patate *f* 5. **Irish** wedding, beuverie générale/soûlographie *f* II *n F* to get one's Irish up, se mettre en colère*/se mettre en rogne.

iron ['aɪən] I *n* 1. *P* revolver*/flingue *m*; to carry iron, être armé/enfouraillé. (*See* **shooting-iron**) 2. *F* (eating) irons, couteau *m* fourchette *f* et cuiller *f*; couvert *m* 3. *Br P* = **iron hoof** (**iron** II 2). (*See* **cast-iron**; **half-iron**; **hoof¹** 2; **pumping**) II *a* 1. *A P* iron horse, locomotive *f* 2. *Br P* iron hoof, (*RS* = *poof*) homosexuel*/pédé *m*.

it [ɪt] *pron* 1. *F* du sex-appeal/du chien; he's got it! il jette du jus!/il en a! 2. *F* vermouth (italien); **gin and it**, gin-vermouth *m* 3. *F* you've had it! t'as ton compte!/tu l'as voulu!/tu es fichu! 4. to give it to s.o. (*a*) *P* faire l'amour* avec qn/baiser qn/tringler qn/défoncer qn (*b*) *F* battre* qn/tabasser qn (*c*) *F* réprimander* qn/sonner les cloches à qn 5. *P* to make it with s.o. (*a*) faire l'amour* avec qn/s'envoyer qn (*b*) plaire à qn/faire une touche/avoir le/un ticket 6. *F* he thinks he's really it, il se prend pour le nombril du monde; il ne se prend pas pour de la crotte/pour de la merde 7. *F* to step on it, accélérer/appuyer sur le champignon. (*See* **bad** II; **in**

II **4, 6; with 1** (*a*), (*b*); **with-it**)

itch¹ [ɪtʃ] *n F* 1. the seven-year itch, l'écueil *m* des sept ans* de mariage/la démangeaison de la septième année*; le démon de midi 2. to have an itch to do sth, mourir/crever d'envie de faire qch; I've (got) an itch to do it, ça me démange de le faire.

itch² [ɪtʃ] *vi F* to itch to do sth/to be itching to do sth, être démangé par l'envie de faire qch; mourir d'envie de faire qch; he's itching for trouble, la peau lui démange/ça le démange (de se battre); ça le gratte.

itchy ['ɪtʃɪ] *a F* 1. qui brûle de faire qch 2. to have itchy feet, brûler de partir; (*to be always on the move*) avoir la bougeotte 3. to have itchy fingers, être voleur/chapardeur. (*See* **palm 2**)

item ['aɪtəm] *n F* 1. (*sexual relationship*) liaison *f*/concubinage *m*; (*couple*) couple *m*; they're an item, ils sont ensemble 2. partenaire sexuel(le)/affaire *f*.

itsy-bitsy ['ɪtsɪ'bɪtsɪ] *a F* minuscule/tout petit/riquiqui.

Ivan ['aɪvən] *n F* Russe*/rus(s)kof *m*/ruski *m*.

ivories ['aɪvərɪz] *npl F* 1. dents*/clavier *m*. (*See* **sluice²**) 2. boules *fpl* de billard 3. dés*/doches *mpl*/bobs *mpl* 4. touches *fpl* d'un piano/clavier *m*; to tickle the ivories, jouer du piano/écraser de l'ivoire.

ivory ['aɪvərɪ] *n F* 1. *NAm* ivory dome, intellectuel *m*/grosse tête/tête *f* d'œuf/mandarin *m* 2. ivory tower, tour *f* d'ivoire.

J

J [dʒeɪ] *n* = **jay 1**.

jab¹ [dʒæb] *n* **1.** *F* vaccin *m*/piqûre *f*; **have you had your jabs?** tu les a eues, tes piqûres? **2.** *P* coup *m* de poing/direct *m*.

jab² [dʒæb] *vtr* **1.** *F* vacciner/faire une piqûre à (qn) **2.** *P* envoyer un coup de poing/un direct à (qn).

jabber¹ [ˈdʒæbə] *n F* (*chatter*) jacasserie *f*; (*gibberish*) baragouin *m*.

jabber² [ˈdʒæbə] *F* **I** *vi* (*chatter*) jacasser/ bavarder; (*talk fast*) baragouiner **II** *vtr* bafouiller/bredouiller (une excuse, etc).

jabbering [ˈdʒæbərɪŋ] *n F* = **jabber¹**.

jaboney [ˈdʒæbəʊnɪ] *n NAm P* **1.** (*a*) (*greenhorn*) blanc-bec *m*/bleu *m* (*b*) immigrant(e) *m(f)* (sans expérience)/nouveau, -elle **2.** garde *m* du corps/gorille *m*.

jack¹, Jack [dʒæk] **I** *n* **1.** *P* **on one's jack,** (*RS = Jack Jones = alone*) tout seul/ seulâbre/esseulé *2. F* **every man jack (of them),** tout un chacun/tout le monde **3.** *F* **I'm all right Jack,** ça tourne rond pour bibi; *V* **fuck you, Jack, I'm all right!** je t'emmerde, en tous cas moi ça va! **4.** *P* (*drugs*) (*a*) (*RS = Jack and Jill = pill*) dose *f* de narcotique/surt cachet *m* d'héroïne/cheval *m* (*b*) piqûre*/ piquouse *f* 5. *F* **jack/Jack Tar,** marin*/mataf *m*/marsouin *m* **6.** *F* **before you can say Jack Robinson,** en un clin d'œil/en moins de deux/ avant de pouvoir dire ouf/en deux coups de cuiller à pot **7.** *esp NAm P* argent*/galette *f*; **have ya got some jack?** t'as du fric? **8.** *Br P* **Jack the Ripper,** (*RS = kipper*) hareng saur/ kipper *m* **9.** *P* rien/que dalle; **I worked for three hours and didn't get jack/**V didn't get jack shit, j'ai travaillé pendant trois heures et j'ai eu que pouic!/et tintin! **10.** *P* policier*/flic *m*/poulet *m* **11.** *P* indicateur*/indic *mf*/ mouchard, -arde **12.** *P* **Jack's alive,** (*RS = five*) (*a*) *A* (*billet* de) cinq livres *fpl* sterling (*b*) *see* **bingo 5** **13.** *Br V* anus*/trou *m* du cul; (*buttocks*) fesses*/miches *fpl* **14.** *esp Austr P* maladie vénérienne*/naze *m* **II** *a*

Austr P **to be jack of sth,** (*fed up*) en avoir marre/en avoir ras le bol de qch.

jack² [dʒæk] *vtr P* **1.** = **jack in 1** **2.** coïter*/ baiser/fourailler.

jackaroo [ˈdʒækəˈruː] *n Austr P* jeune (cadre) stagiaire *m* dans un ranch.

jack around [ˈdʒækəˈraund] *P* **I** *vi* (*flirt*) faire du charre/frotter/courir le jupon **II** *vtr* **to jack s.o. around,** enquiquiner/faire suer qn.

jacked off, out [ˈdʒæktˈɒf, -ˈaut] *a P* en colère*/en rogne/en boule; (*annoyed*) à cran.

jacked up [ˈdʒæktˈʌp] *a P* **1.** stimulé par la drogue/drogué/camé **2.** (*excited*) (tout) excité; (*upset*) (tout) retourné/énervé. (*See* **jack up 1**)

jackeroo [ˈdʒækəˈruː] *n Austr P* = **jackaroo**.

jacket [ˈdʒækɪt] *n NAm P* dossier *m*.

jack in [ˈdʒækˈɪn] *vtr P* **1.** abandonner*/ lâcher/balancer/plaquer/laisser tomber; **he's jacked his job in,** il a plaqué/largué son boulot **2. to jack it in,** se taire*/la boucler/la fermer.

jack-in-office [ˈdʒækɪnˈɒfɪs] *n F Pej* fonctionnaire plein(e) de son importance/petit chef.

jack off [ˈdʒækˈɒf] *vi V* se masturber*/ s'astiquer/se polir la colonne.

jackpot [ˈdʒækpɒt] *n F* **1. to hit the jackpot,** gagner le gros lot/décrocher la timbale/taper dans le mille **2.** *NAm* (*mess*) pagaille *f*; **to be in a jackpot,** être dans la merde.

jacksie, jacksy [ˈdʒæksɪ] *n P* fesses*/ miches *fpl*; anus*/trou *m* du cul.

Jack-the-lad [ˈdʒækðəˈlæd] *n Br F* (*young man who is cleverer, more attractive, etc than the rest*) (sacrée/grosse) pointure; bête *f*.

jack up [ˈdʒækˈʌp] *vtr & i* **1.** *P* (*drugs*) to jack (oneself) up, se faire une piquouse/se shooter. (*See* **jacked up 1**) **2.** *P* = **jack in 1** **3.** *P* to jack up the price, corser le prix/saler la note **4.** *F* (*arrange*) organiser/arranger; **don't worry, we'll jack sth up,** ne t'inquiète pas, nous allons nous débrouiller **5.** *Austr F*

136

plaider non-coupable.

jacky ['dʒækɪ] *n Austr P* aborigène *m*.

jag [dʒæg] *n* 1. *P* (*drugs*) (*a*) piqûre*/piquouse *f ou* picouse *f*/shoot *m* (*b*) (*gluesniffing*) snif(fe) *m ou f* 2. *P* to have a jag on (*a*) être drogué*/camé (*b*) être ivre*/rond/noir/rétamé 3. *P* (*binge*) bombe *f*; orgie *f*; to go on a jag, (*take drugs*) se camer à bloc; (*have a party*) faire la noce/la bombe; (*get drunk*) se soûler/prendre une cuite; cocaine jag, orgie *f* de cocaïne*; to go on a culture jag, prendre une indigestion de culture/prendre sa ration de culture/faire une cure de culture 4. *F Aut* Jaguar *f* (*RTM*)/Jag *f*.

jagged [dʒægd] *a esp NAm P* ivre*/rond/noir/rétamé.

jailbait ['dʒeɪlbeɪt] *n P* fille* mineure/faux poids *m*.

jailbird ['dʒeɪlbɜːd] *n F* (*in prison*) taulard, -arde; (*recidivist*) cheval *m* de retour; an old jailbird, un vieux taulard.

jake [dʒeɪk] I *a NAm Austr P* excellent*/impec/de première; things are jake, ça marche/ça gaze/ça roule; *Iron* that's jake! ça c'est la meilleure (de l'année)!/on aura tout vu! II *n* 1. *NAm F* (*cards*) valet *m*/larbin *m*. (*See* **jayboy**) 2. *pl F* WC*/goguenots *mpl*/chiottes *fpl* 3. *Br P* alcool *m* à brûler.

jalop(p)y [dʒə'lɒpɪ] *n F* (vieille) voiture*/(vieux) tacot/(vieille) guimbarde.

jam[1] [dʒæm] *n* 1. *F* it's money for jam, c'est de l'argent* facilement gagné/c'est grassement payé 2. *F* to be in a jam, être dans le pétrin/dans la mélasse/dans la mouise 3. *F* a bit of jam, un coup de chance*; du pot/du bol/du cul 4. *F* do you want jam on it? tu veux (pas) que je te le dore sur tranches, en plus?/tu voudrais pas que je te le mâche, des fois?/la mariée est peut-être pas assez belle pour toi? 5. *Mus F* (*a*) jam (session), séance de jazz improvisée/bœuf *m*; to have a jam (session), faire un bœuf (*b*) séance *f* de rap 6. *NAm F* fête *f*; to have a jam, faire la noce/la bombe 7. *P* (*a*) coït*/baise *f* (*b*) partenaire sexuel(le)/affaire *f* (*c*) vagin*/baba *m* 8. *P* drogue*/surt cocaïne*/confiture *f* 9. *P* (*homosexual use*) hétéro(sexuel) *m*. (*See* **jim-jams**; **rag**[1] 2)

jam[2] [dʒæm] *vtr & i* 1. *Mus F* (*a*) improviser/faire un bœuf (*b*) improviser du rap 2. *NAm F* (*have wild party*) faire la noce/la bombe 3. *NAm P* faire l'amour* (avec qn)/baiser (qn) 4. *NAm F* to jam (it), partir*/décamper 5. *NAm P* (*drugs*) sniffer (de la cocaïne).

jamas ['dʒɑːməz] *npl F* = **jarmas, jarmies**.

jam jar ['dʒæmdʒɑː] *n P* (*RS* = *car*) voiture*/bagnole/caisse *f*.

jammed [dʒæmd] *a NAm P* ivre*/beurré.

jammer ['dʒæmə] *n F* musicien, -ienne qui participe à une séance de jazz improvisée/à un bœuf.

jammies ['dʒæmɪz] *npl F* pyjama *m*/pyj' *m*.

jammy ['dʒæmɪ] *a Br P* qui a de la chance*/qui a du cul/veinard; jammy bugger/sod! quel veinard, celui-là!/il l'a en or!/il a du flambeau! (*See* **bugger**[1] 3; **sod**[1] 2)

jam-packed ['dʒæm'pækt] *a F* archi-plein/archi-comble/bourré à craquer.

jam roll ['dʒæm'rəʊl] *n* (*prisons*) (*RS* = *parole*) liberté conditionnelle.

jam sandwich [dʒæm'sændwɪdʒ] *n P* voiture* de police/voiture pie/bagnole *f* de flics.

jam tart [dʒæm'tɑːt] *n Austr P* 1. fille* *ou* femme*/nana *f*/pépée *f*/poulette *f* 2. pet*/perle *f*.

jam up ['dʒæm'ʌp] *vtr F* to jam up the works = to gum up the works (**gum up**).

jane, Jane [dʒeɪn] *n* 1. *F* fille*/femme*/nénette *f*/nana *f*; a plain Jane, un laideron/un cageot; she's a bit of a plain Jane, ce n'est pas une beauté/c'est pas Raquel Welch 2. *P* petite amie/nénette *f*/gonzesse *f* 3. *P* prostituée*/fille *f*/poule *f* 4. *NAm F* Jane Doe, femme* sans nom *ou* anonyme; Jane Q. Citizen, l'Américaine moyenne 5. *P* WC* pour femmes/chiottes *fpl* à poules 4. *NAm P* vagin*/baba *m*. (*See* **john 1, 5**; **Lady Jane**)

jangle[1] ['dʒæŋgl] *n Br P* bavardage*/jacasserie *f*/jactance *f*.

jangle[2] ['dʒæŋgl] *vi Br P* bavarder*/jacter/tailler une bavette.

jankers ['dʒæŋkəz] *npl Br F Mil* punitions *fpl*/la pelote; to be on jankers, faire la pelote.

Jap [dʒæp] *F Pej* I *a* japonais*/nippon II *n* Japonais*/Nippon, -onne/Jap *mf*/jaune *mf*.

JAP [dʒæp] *n NAm F Pej* (*abbr of Jewish American Princess*) jeune fille* juive *surt* riche et gâtée.

jar[1] [dʒɑː] *n Br* 1. *F* (*beer*) pot *m*; to have/to down a few jars, boire*/s'envoyer quelques verres/quelques godets; let's go and have a jar down the pub, allons prendre un pot au bistrot/allons s'en jeter un au troquet (du coin) 2. *P* faux diamant*/faux diam/caillou *m* de Rennes. (*See* **jam jar**; **jargoon**)

jar² [dʒɑ:] *vtr* P vendre de faux diamants à (qn).

jargoon ['dʒɑ:gu:n] *n* P = **jar¹ 2**.

jarmas, jarmies ['dʒɑ:məz, -ɪz] *npl* F pyjama *m*/pyj' *m*.

jasper ['dʒæspə] *n* NAm P (*Black Slang*) lesbienne*/gavousse *f*.

java ['dʒɑ:və] *n* P café*/caoua *m*/jus *m*.

jaw¹ [dʒɔ:] *n* 1. P bavardage *m*; to have a good jaw, tailler une bonne bavette; hold your jaw!/not so much of your jaw! ta gueule!/la ferme! 2. P pi jaw, bondieuseries *fpl*/sermon *m*/paroles *fpl* de curé/prêchi-prêcha *m* 3. F his jaw dropped, il a fait une drôle de tête/de bobine.

jaw² [dʒɔ:] P I *vi* bavarder*/tailler une bavette II *vtr* engueuler (qn)/enguirlander (qn)/sonner les cloches à (qn).

jawbone ['dʒɔ:'bəun] *vi* NAm P persuader/insister; to jawbone s.o. into paying, faire cracher qn.

jawboning ['dʒɔ:bəunɪŋ] *n* NAm P he needed some jawboning before he paid up, il a fallu insister lourdement pour qu'il raque.

jaw-breaker ['dʒɔ:breɪkə], **jaw-buster** ['dʒɔ:bʌstə] *n* F 1. nom *m* à coucher dehors/mot *m* à vous décrocher la mâchoire 2. bonbon dur.

jawing ['dʒɔ:ɪŋ] *n* P 1. bavardage *m*/jactance *f* 2. to give s.o. a jawing, réprimander* qn/passer un savon à qn/sonner les cloches à qn.

jaw queen ['dʒɔ:kwi:n] *n* V (*homosexual use*) qn qui pratique la fellation*.

jay [dʒeɪ] *n* 1. P (*drugs*) cigarette* de marijuana/joint *m*/stick *m* 2. NAm F individu bête*/nouille *f*/cloche *f*.

jayboy ['dʒeɪbɔɪ] *n* NAm F (*cards*) valet *m*/larbin *m*. (*See* **jake II 1**)

jaywalk ['dʒeɪwɔ:k] *vi* F traverser en dehors des clous/marcher sur la chaussée.

jaywalker ['dʒeɪwɔ:kə] *n* F piéton imprudent.

jazz¹ [dʒæz] *n* 1. F (*lies*) mensonges*/foutaises *fpl*/craques *fpl*/bourres *fpl*; (*empty talk*) baratin *m* 2. F (*things, stuff*) affaires *fpl*/fourbi *m*; ...and all that jazz, et tout et tout/et tout ce qui s'ensuit/et tout le fourbi/et tout le tremblement 3. P (*provocation*) crosse *f*/vanne *f* 4. P (*showiness*) ostentation *f*/luxe tapageur 5. NAm A V (*a*) coït* (*b*) sexe* de la femme*/chatte *f*.

jazz² [dʒæz] *vi* NAm 1. V (*Black Slang*) (*rare*) coïter*/niquer 2. P provoquer/crosser/

chercher des rognes 3. F mentir*/bourrer le crâne/craquer.

jazzed up ['dʒæzd'ʌp] *a* F 1. élégant*/endimanché/sur son trente et un 2. animé/survolté.

jazz up ['dʒæz'ʌp] *vtr* F émoustiller/échauffer/ravigoter/requinquer. (*See* **jazzed up**)

jazzy ['dʒæzɪ] *a* F tapageur/tape-à-l'œil.

jeepers (creepers)! ['dʒi:pəz('kri:pəz)] *excl* NAm O F mon Dieu!/sapristi!

jeez(e)! Jeez(e)! [dʒi:z] *excl* P (*Euph for* **Jesus!**) bon Dieu!/bon sang!

jell [dʒel] *vi* F 1. (*of ideas, etc*) (se) concrétiser/prendre forme 2. bien s'entendre/sympathiser/être sur la même longueur d'ondes/avoir des atomes crochus (avec qn).

jelly ['dʒelɪ] *n* F 1. Br P gélignite *f* 2. to pound s.o. into a jelly, battre* qn comme plâtre/faire de la bouillie de qn.

jellybeans ['dʒelɪbi:nz] *npl* P (*drugs*) amphétamines*.

jelly-roll ['dʒelɪrəʊl] *n* NAm 1. V sexe* de la femme*/bonbon *m*/millefeuille *m* 2. V coït*/baise *f*/partie *f* de jambes en l'air 3. P (*sexual partner*) affaire *f* 4. P amant *m*/jules *m*.

jemima [dʒɪ'maɪmə] *n* F pot *m* de chambre/jules *m*/thomas *m*.

jerk¹ [dʒɜ:k] *n* 1. P individu bête*/(petit) con, (petite) conne/enflé, -ée/connard, -arde/enculé *m*/pauvre type *m*; you stupid jerk! espèce de con! (*See* **dumb** (*b*)) 2. P physical jerks, mouvements *mpl* de gym(nastique).

jerk² [dʒɜ:k] *vtr* V See **gherkin**.

jerk off ['dʒɜ:k'ɒf] *vi* V se masturber*/se branler/se taper sur la colonne.

jerkwater ['dʒɜ:kwɔ:tə] *a* NAm P a jerkwater town, une petite ville/un trou paumé/un bled. (*See* **one-horse**)

jerry, Jerry ['dʒerɪ] *n* F 1. pot *m* de chambre/thomas *m*/jules *m* 2. soldat* allemand*/Fritz *m*/fridolin *m*/frisé *m* 3. les Allemands*/les boches *mpl*.

jerry-built ['dʒerɪbɪlt] *a* F à la manque/à la noix; (construit) en carton/en papier mâché/n'importe comment.

jessie ['dʒesɪ] *n* Br P (*a*) homme* efféminé/gâcheuse *f* (*b*) individu* veule/descente *f* de lit/carpette *f*; he's just a big jessie, il est mou comme une chiffe.

Jesus (Christ)! ['dʒi:zəs('kraɪst)] *excl* P nom de Dieu! *VV* Jesus fucking Christ! putain de merde!/bordel de Dieu!/bordel de merde!/

putain de bordel de merde! **Jesus wept!** nom de Dieu! misère!/bordel! (*See* **jeez(e)!**; **Christ**)

Jesus freak ['dʒiːzəs'friːk] *n F Pej* membre *m* d'un groupe de chrétiens fervents qui mène la vie collective des hippies/illuminé, -ée (de Jésus).

jet [dʒet] *a attrib F* 1. the jet set, les bringueurs *mpl* cosmopolites/le *ou* la jet-set 2. jet job, (*fast racing car*) bolide *m*.

Jew¹ [dʒuː] *n O P* dirty old Jew: see **bingo** 2.

jew² [dʒuː] *vtr P Pej* (*also* **jew down**) duper* (qn)/mettre (qn) dedans/rouler (qn).

jewboy, Jewboy ['dʒuːbɔɪ] *n P Pej* Juif*/youpin *m*.

jewish, Jewish ['dʒuːɪʃ] *a P* 1. *Pej* avare/radin/grippe-sou; he's so jewish, he never buys drinks, il est tellement juif/rat qu'il ne paye jamais un coup 2. Jewish lightning, (*arson*) incendie *m* volontaire 3. Jewish piano, (*cash register*) caisse enregistreuse.

jiff [dʒɪf], **jiffy** ['dʒɪfɪ] *n F* in (half) a jiffy, en un instant/en un clin d'œil/en moins de deux; I'll be back in a jiffy, je reviens dans un instant/une seconde. (*See* **mo**; **sec**; **shake¹** 1; **tick¹** 3)

jig [dʒɪg] *n P* 1. (*thing, object*) machin *m*/truc *m*/bidule *m* 2. = **jigaboo**.

jigaboo [dʒɪgə'buː] *n P Pej* Noir(e)*/bamboula *m*/bougnoul *m*.

jig-a-jig ['dʒɪgə'dʒɪg] *n P* = **jiggy-jig**.

jigger ['dʒɪgə] *n* 1. *A P* prison*/bloc *m* 2. *P* (*rare*) pénis*/queue *f* 3. *NAm F* (*gadget*) truc *m*/machin *m*/bidule *m*.

jiggered ['dʒɪgəd] *a F* 1. *Br* (*exhausted*) crevé/pompé/vanné 2. étonné*/estomaqué/baba; well I'm jiggered! j'en suis comme deux ronds de flan!/je n'en reviens pas!/ça me scie!

jiggery-pokery ['dʒɪgərɪ'pəʊkərɪ] *n F* manigance *f*/attrape *f*/tour *m* de passe-passe; there was a bit of jiggery-pokery going on there, il y avait qch de louche/de pas clair/de pas catholique là-dedans.

jiggy-jig ['dʒɪgɪ'dʒɪg] *n P* coït*/partie *f* de jambes en l'air/zizi-pan-pan *m*.

jill [dʒɪl] *n Br F* (*esp in Liverpool*) femme-agent *f* (de police).

Jim cap ['dʒɪm'kæp] *n NAm P* préservatif*/capote (anglaise).

Jim Crow ['dʒɪm'krəʊ] *n NAm F* (*a*) *Pej* Noir(e)*/bamboula *m*/bougnoul *m* (*b*) la ségrégation raciale et tout ce qui s'y rapporte.

jiminy! ['dʒɪmɪnɪ] *excl F* jiminy cricket! mince (alors)!

jim-jams ['dʒɪmdʒæmz] *npl F* 1. (*a*) les nerfs *mpl* en boule/flip *m*; he's got the jim-jams, il flippe (*b*) délirium tremens *m*/digue-digue *f* 2. pyjama *m*/pyj' *m*.

Jimmy ['dʒɪmɪ] *Prn* 1. *Br P* Jimmy Riddle, (*RS* = **piddle**) pipi *m*; to have a Jimmy Riddle, uriner*/faire pipi; he's gone for a Jimmy Riddle, il est allé pisser/écluser 2. *F* Little Jimmy: see **bingo** 1 3. *F* (*navy*) Jimmy (the one), officier *m* en second à bord d'un navire (de guerre) 4. *F* Écossais *m*; listen Jimmy! écoute, mon pote!/écoute, mec!/écoute, mon gars! 5. *P* (*drugs*) Jimmy (Hix), (*RS* = **fix**) piqûre*/fixe *m*/shoot *m* 6. *NAm P* pénis*/Popaul *m*.

jing-jang ['dʒɪŋdʒæŋ] *n NAm A V* 1. pénis*/zizi *m* 2. sexe* de la femme*/fri-fri *m*.

jingle ['dʒɪŋgl] *n F* argent*/pognon *m*; (*coins, change*) ferraille *f*.

jingo ['dʒɪŋgəʊ] *excl F* by jingo! nom d'une pipe!

jinks [dʒɪŋks] *npl F* high jinks, réjouissances*/noce *f*/bamboche *f*.

jinx¹ [dʒɪŋks] *n F* 1. malchance*/guigne *f*/poisse *f* 2. qn *ou* qch qui porte malheur.

jinx² [dʒɪŋks] *vtr F* porter malchance*/la guigne/la poisse à (qn).

jism ['dʒɪz(ə)m], **jissom** ['dʒɪs(ə)m] *n V* sperme*/jute *m*/foutre *m*.

jitter ['dʒɪtə] *vi F* se trémousser/s'exciter/se démener.

jitterbug ['dʒɪtəbʌg] *n O F* paniquard *m*/trouillard *m*.

jitters ['dʒɪtəz] *npl F* to have the jitters, (*be anxious, afraid*) avoir la frousse/la trouille/les chocottes; to give s.o. the jitters, foutre la trouille/les chocottes à qn.

jittery ['dʒɪtərɪ] *a F* crispé/à cran; to feel jittery, avoir les nerfs en pelote/à fleur de peau; I feel really jittery, j'ai la trouille/le trac.

jive¹ [dʒaɪv] *n* 1. *F* (*deceitful talk, nonsense*) baratin *m*/foutaises *fpl*/conneries *fpl*; don't give me all that jive! arrête de déconner!/arrête ton char(re)!/garde tes salades! *Mus* jive talk, jargon *m* des amateurs de jazz (*surtout les Noirs*). (*See* **jazz** 1) 2. *A P* (*drugs*) marijuana*; jive stick, cigarette* de marijuana/joint *m*/stick *m*.

jive² [dʒaɪv] *P* I *vi* 1. trouver le maillon/éclairer la lanterne 2. bavarder*/bavasser/jacter/dévider le jars II *vtr* to jive s.o., (*tease*) vanner/chercher des crosses à qn; (*deceive*) duper/avoir qn; rouler qn (dans la farine).

jizz [dʒɪz] *n esp NAm V* = **jism.**

joanna [dʒəʊˈænə] *n P* (*RS* = (*Cockney pronunciation of*) *piano*) piano *m*/commode *f*/ armoire *f* à sons.

job [dʒɒb] *n* 1. *F* tout article façonné/ manufacturé *ou* fabriqué; **that new car is a really nice job,** cette nouvelle bagnole, c'est du beau travail/c'est pas de la camelote. (*See* **jet 2**) 2. *P* (*a*) réparation *f*; **he made a good job of it,** il a fait du beau boulot (*b*) (*work*) boulot *m*; **what a dreadful job!** quelle sale boulot! 3. *P* (*a*) vol *m*/coup *m*/fric-frac *m*; **to do/to pull a job,** faire un fric-frac; **they did that bank job/that job on the bank,** ils ont monté le coup de la banque/ils ont opéré la banque (*b*) crime *m*/méfait *m*/coup *m*/ combine *f* 4. *F* **to do a job on s.o.,** tromper*/ arnaquer qn; (*overwhelm, devastate*) écraser/foudroyer qn 5. **to be on the job** (*a*) *F* être au boulot (*b*) *P* être en train de faire l'amour*/d'opérer; (*of prostitute*) être avec un client 6. *F* (*a*) **it's a good job that...,** heureusement que...; **...and a good job too!** c'est pas malheureux! **just the job!** juste ce qu'il faut!/c'est au poil!/c'est pas dommage! (*b*) **to give sth up as a bad job,** laisser tomber qch 7. *F* (*esp child's language*) **to do little small jobs,** faire la petite commission; **to do big jobs,** faire la grosse commission. (*See* **jobbie(s)**; **number¹ 7**) 8. *P* colis *m* de drogues* 9. *F* **to lie/to lay/to fall down on the job,** paresser*/tirer au flanc/s'endormir sur ses lauriers 10. *P* **the blonde job sitting over there,** la petite blonde assise là-bas 11. *P* (*taxi*) client *m* 12. *F* **jobs for the boys,** l'assiette *f* au beurre/distribution *f* des planques/partage *m* du gâteau 13. *F* **to have a job to do sth,** avoir du mal à faire qch; **I had a dreadful job to do that!** j'en ai chié/sué pour faire ça; ça (n')a pas été de la tarte 14. *F* **she had a nose job/boob job,** elle s'est fait arranger/retaper le nez/les seins. (*See* **blow-job**; **brown¹ I**; **finger-job**; **hand-job**; **head 13**; **one-night job**; **pipe-job**; **put-up**; **shack-up**; **skull-job**; **snow-job**; **soup up**)

jobbie(s) [ˈdʒɒbɪ(z)] *n(pl) Br P* (*defecation*) foirade *f*; (*excrement*) merde *f*/ fumerons *mpl*.

jobsworth [ˈdʒɒbzwɜːθ] *n Br F Pej* petit(e) bureaucrate têtu(e)/borné(e).

jock [dʒɒk] *n* 1. *P* pénis*; *pl* testicules*/ roustons *mpl*; **jock itch,** la gratte 2. *F* = **jockstrap** 3. *NAm F* athlète *mf*/sportif, -ive; (*sports fan*) enthousiaste *mf*/fana *mf* de sport 4. *Br F* (*a*) Écossais, -aise (*b*) individu* sans nom/Machin *m*; **does jock there want a drink?** est-ce que Machin là veut prendre un pot? 5. *NAm F* disc-jockey *m.*

jocker [ˈdʒɒkə] *n P* homosexuel*/pédé *m.*

jockey [ˈdʒɒkɪ] *n Br P* 1. client *m* de prostituée*/miché *m*/micheton *m* 2. (*regional*) homme*/gars *m*/type *m* 3. agent* de police/ poulet *m* 4. pilote *m* (d'avion).

jockstrap [ˈdʒɒkstræp] *n F* suspensoir *m*/ soutien-couilles *m*/trousse-couilles *m.*

joe, Joe [dʒəʊ] *n P* 1. café*/caoua *m*/jus *m* 2. homme*/jules *m*/julot *m* 3. *Austr* **Joe Blake,** (*RS* = *snake*) serpent *m* 4. **Joe Gurr,** (*RS* = *stir* = *prison*) prison*/bloc *m* 5. *Br* **Joe Bloggs**/*Br* **Joe Public**/*Br* **Joe Soap** *NAm* **Joe Blow**/*NAm* **Joe Schmo,** l'homme* moyen; l'Anglais/l'Américain moyen; = M. Dupont; *Pej* Tartempion *m* 6. (*also NAm* **Joe Schmo**) (*victim, dupe*) cave *m*/pigeon *m*/têtard *m* 7. *Br* **Joe Soap,** imbécile*/crétin *m*; (*victim, dupe*) cave *m*. (*See* **Gl 2**; **holy 2**; **John 5**; **schmo**; **sloppy 2**)

joey [ˈdʒəʊɪ] *n* 1. *F* clown *m*/pierrot *m* 2. *P* = **joe 6** 3. *P* règles*/doches *fpl* 4. *Austr F* (*a*) jeune kangourou *m* (*b*) bébé *m*/têtard *m* 5. *Austr P* homme* efféminé/gâcheuse *f* 6. *Austr P* hermaphrodite *m ou* sodomite *m* 7. *Br P* paquet introduit illégalement dans une prison; paquet qu'on fait sortir illégalement d'une prison.

john, John [dʒɒn] *n* 1. *esp NAm F* **the john,** WC* pour hommes/chiottes *fpl*/gogues *mpl*. (*See* **jane 5**) 2. *Br P* **John Thomas,** pénis*/Popaul *m*/Charles-le-Chauve *m* 3. *F* **John Barleycorn,** whisky *m* 4. *Austr P* **John (Hop),** (*RS* = *cop*) policier*/flic *m*/poulet *m* 5. *NAm F* **John Doe,** homme* sans nom *ou* anonyme; **John Q. Citizen,** l'Américain moyen/Monsieur Tout-le-monde. (*See* **jane 4**) 6. *NAm F* **John Hancock,** signature *f*/griffe *f* 7. *P* client *m* d'une prostituée*/miché *m*/ micheton *m* 8. *Br P* = **johnnie 3** 9. *P* homosexuel* plus âgé qui protège un jeune homosexuel/tante *f*. (*See* **amy-john**)

johnnie, Johnnie, johnny, Johnny [ˈdʒɒnɪ] *n* 1. *P* jeune homme*/petit gars/ zigoto *m*/zigue *m* 2. *P* homme élégant*/minet *m* 3. *Br P* (**rubber**) **johnnie,** préservatif*/ capote (anglaise)/marguerite *f*. (*See* **rubber**

1) 4. *P* Johnnie Horner, (*RS* = *corner*) coin *m*
(*surt un coin de rue et souv le bistrot du coin*)
5. *F* Johnnie Raw, (*novice, recruit*) bleu *m*/
bleubite *m* 6. *F* = **john 1** 7. *NAm F* Johnny
Reb, soldat *m* sudiste (*guerre de Sécession*);
(*rebel*) rebelle *m*/révolté *m*.

Johnny-come-lately [ˈdʒɒnɪkʌmˈleɪtlɪ]
n F blanc-bec *m*/bleu *m*/bleubite *m*.

Johnny-on-the-spot [ˈdʒɒnɪɒnðəˈspɒt]
n NAm F 1. (*punctual*) qn qui arrive au poil
2. (*ambitious, enthusiastic*) jeune loup *m*;
battant *m*.

johnson [ˈdʒɒnsən] *n NAm P* 1. pénis*/
Popaul *m* 2. fesses*/fouettard *m*; *esp Can*
johnson bar, WC*/chiottes *fpl*.

joint [dʒɔɪnt] *n P* 1. logement*/cambuse *f*/
piaule *f*; a nice joint, une belle cabane. (*See*
case² 1) 2. (*dive*) café/bar mal famé; bouge
m/foutoir *m*; gambling joint, tripot *m* 3.
(*drugs*) cigarette* de marijuana/joint *m*/stick
m 4. *NAm* pénis*/queue *f*/gourdin *m* 5. *NAm*
the joint, la prison*/la taule. (*See* **clip-joint**)

jollies [ˈdʒɒlɪz] *npl F* tout ce qui emballe et
passionne (*surt les plaisirs sexuels*); to get
one's jollies, s'en payer une tranche/goder.

jolly [ˈdʒɒlɪ] *F* I *a* 1. légèrement ivre*/gris/
éméché 2. Jolly Roger, drapeau *m* des
pirates/le pavillon noir. (*See* **bean 7**) II *adv*
1. it's a jolly good job that..., c'est heureux/
heureusement que...; he's jolly glad about it,
il en est drôlement/rudement/vachement
content; it serves him jolly well right! c'est
vachement bien fait pour lui! she's jolly nice,
elle est rudement/vachement bien; I should
jolly well think so! c'est bien ce qui me
semble!/je ne te le fais pas dire!/à qui le dis-
tu? 2. *Br* jolly d, chouette!/super! III *n* 1.
réjouissances*/bombe *f*/boum *f*. (*See* **jolly-
up**) 2. (*marine*) fusilier marin.

jolly along [ˈdʒɒlɪəˈlɒŋ] *vtr F* (*a*) dérider/
ragaillardir (qn) (*b*) faire marcher (qn)
(pour en obtenir qch).

jolly-up [ˈdʒɒlɪʌp] *n F* réjouissances*/
bombe *f*/boum *f*.

jolt [dʒəʊlt] *n P* 1. (*drugs*) cigarette* de
marijuana/stick *m* 2. effets *mpl* primaires
d'une drogue/flash *m* 3. piqûre* d'un
narcotique/fixe *m*/shoot *m* 4. verre *m*
d'alcool*/gorgeon *m*.

jonah [ˈdʒəʊnə] *n Austr F* requin *m*.

jones, Jones [dʒəʊnz] *Prn F* 1. (*drugs*)
usage *m*/habitude *f*/dépendance *f* des drogues.
(*See* **scag**) 2. (*Black Slang*) pénis*/Popaul *m*.

Joneses [ˈdʒəʊnzɪz] *Prnpl F* to keep up

with the Joneses, ne pas se laisser doubler par
ses voisins/ne pas s'en laisser remontrer par
les voisins.

jordan [ˈdʒɔːdn] *n A P* pot *m* de chambre/
jules *m*/thomas *m*.

josh¹ [dʒɒʃ] *n NAm F* plaisanterie *f*/blague *f*.

josh² [dʒɒʃ] *vtr NAm F* taquiner/chiner/
mettre (qn) en boîte.

josher [ˈdʒɒʃə] *n NAm F* blagueur, -euse/
chineur, -euse.

joskin [ˈdʒɒskɪn] *n A F* paysan*/plouc *mf*.

josser [ˈdʒɒsə] *n Br P* imbécile*/crétin, -ine;
(*obnoxious*) fumier *m*/loquedu *m*.

journo [ˈdʒɜːnəʊ] *n F* journaliste *mf*/
journaleux, -euse.

Jove [dʒəʊv] *n O F* by Jove! bon sang!/
sacrebleu! by Jove it's cold! bon Dieu, qu'il
fait froid!

joy [dʒɔɪ] *n F* chance*/veine *f*/pot *m*; any
joy? ça a marché? no joy! pas de chance!/ça
n'a rien donné!/ça n'a pas marché!

joy-juice [ˈdʒɔɪˈdʒuːs] *n P* boisson *f*
alcoolique/coupe-la-soif *m*.

joy-pop¹ [ˈdʒɔɪpɒp] *n P* (*drugs*) emploi
occasionnel (*surt* pour le plaisir) d'une
drogue. (*See* **pop¹ 4**)

joy-pop² [ˈdʒɔɪpɒp] *vi P* (*drugs*) 1. prendre
des stupéfiants à volonté (*surt* pour le plaisir)
sans s'y habituer 2. = **skin-pop**.

joy-popper [ˈdʒɔɪpɒpə] *n P* (*drugs*) 1. qn
qui prend des stupéfiants (à volonté) (*surt*
pour le plaisir) sans s'y habituer 2. = **skin-
popper**.

joy-powder [ˈdʒɔɪpaʊdə] *n P* (*drugs*) morphine*.

joy-ride¹ [ˈdʒɔɪraɪd] *n F* (*a*) équipée *f* en
voiture volée/rodéo *m* (*b*) promenade *f* à
grande vitesse.

joy-ride² [ˈdʒɔɪraɪd] *vi F* (*a*) faire une
équipée en voiture volée/faire un rodéo (*b*)
(*speed*) faire de la vitesse.

joy-rider [ˈdʒɔɪraɪdə] *n F* (*a*) qn qui se
promène en voiture volée (*b*) qn qui fait de la
vitesse.

joy-smoke [ˈdʒɔɪsməʊk] *n P* (*drugs*) (*a*)
marijuana* (*b*) haschisch*.

joystick [ˈdʒɔɪstɪk] *n P* 1. pénis*/cigare *m* à
moustaches/engin *m* 2. (*drugs*) = **joint 3**.

juana [dʒuːˈɑːnə, ˈhwɑːnə], **juane**
[dʒuːˈɑːn, hwɑːn], **juanita** [dʒʊəˈniːtə,
hwɑːˈniːtə] *n P* (*drugs*) marijuana*/marie-
jeanne *f*.

judy [ˈdʒuːdɪ] *n P* 1. fille*/femme*/nénette *f*/
nana *f* 2. *O* to make a judy of oneself, faire le

guignol/le polichinelle.

jug¹ [dʒʌg] *n P* 1. (*RS = jug and pail = jail*) prison*/taule *f*/cage *f*; **to go to jug,** aller en taule; **he's in jug,** il s'est fait enchtiber/il est à l'ombre 2. *pl* seins*/boîtes *fpl* à lait; **juicy jugs,** rotoplots *mpl* 3. *pl* oreilles*/escalopes *fpl* 4. banque *f*; **to screw a jug,** monter un coup contre une banque; braquer/opérer une banque.

jug² [dʒʌg] *P* **I** *vtr* emprisonner*/coffrer/mettre en taule *f*/boucler **II** *vi* **to jug (up),** boire* (beaucoup)/picoler/écluser.

juggins ['dʒʌgɪnz] *n Br F* individu* bête/cruche *f*/nigaud, -aude. (*See* **muggins 1**)

jughead ['dʒʌghed] *n NAm F* individu bête*/cruche *f*/cruchon *m*.

juice [dʒuːs] *n* 1. *F* courant *m* électrique/jus *m* 2. *F* essence *f*/carbure *m*/coco *m*; **to step on the juice,** mettre les gaz 3. *P* sperme*/jute *m*; **to jet the juice,** envoyer la purée/balancer la sauce. (*See* **baby-juice**) 4. *O F* The Juice, la mer du Nord 5. *P* alcool*/gnôle *f* 6. *P* tonus *m*/force *f*/vigueur *f*. (*See* **cow-juice; jungle 4; stew²**)

juiced (up) ['dʒuːst'ʌp] *a* 1. *P* ivre*/chargé/fadé 2. *F* (*car engine*) gonflé/poussé/bricolé 3. *P* (*woman*) excitée sexuellement/qui a le haricot à la portière.

juicehead ['dʒuːshed] *n NAm P* ivrogne*/soûlard, -arde/poivrot, -ote.

juicer ['dʒuːsə] *n NAm* 1. *F* (*film making*) électricien *m*/électro *m* 2. *P* = **juicehead**.

juicy ['dʒuːsɪ] *a* 1. *F* juteux/savoureux 2. *F* lucratif/qui rapporte/bien beurré 3. *P* sexy/séducteur; **she's a juicy bit of stuff,** elle est bien bandante 4. *V* (*female genitals*) qui jute.

juju, ju-ju ['dʒuː:dʒuː] *n P* (*drugs*) cigarette* de marijuana/joint *m*.

jumbo¹ ['dʒʌmbəʊ] *a F* de grande taille/ma(h)ous; **jumbo jet,** (avion) gros porteur/jumbo(-jet) *m*.

Jumbo, jumbo² ['dʒʌmbəʊ] *n F* 1. (nom donné à un) éléphant/Babar 2. jumbo(-jet) *m* 3. *Br* individu* bête/cruche *f*/gourde *f*.

jumbuck ['dʒʌmbʌk] *n Austr F* mouton *m*/bêlant *m*.

jump¹ [dʒʌmp] *n* 1. *P* coït*/partie *f* de jambes en l'air; **to have a jump/to give s.o. a jump** = **jump²** 1 2. *P* **go (and) take a running jump (at yourself)!** va te faire foutre!/va te faire foutre! (*See* **jump² 6**) 3. *F* **to have the jumps,** avoir les nerfs à fleur de peau; avoir la bougeotte/ne pas tenir en place/avoir la danse de Saint-Guy 4. *NAm P* **on the jump,** en

plein coup de feu; **to be on the jump,** ne pas arrêter de courir. (*See* **high I 1**)

jump² [dʒʌmp] *vtr & i* 1. *P* faire l'amour*/faire une partie de jambes en l'air/faire zizi-pan-pan avec (qn); sauter (qn) 2. *P* voler*/faire sauter/faucher; **to jump a drag,** voler* une voiture*/faucher une tire 3. *F* **to jump bail,** se dérober à la justice 4. *F* **to jump ship,** (*of sailor*) déserter (le navire) 5. *F* **to jump the queue,** passer avant son tour/resquiller. (*See* **queue-jumper**) 6. *F* **go (and) jump in the lake!** va te faire voir! (*See* **jump¹ 2**) 7. *F* **jump to it!** et que ça saute! 8. *F* **to jump on s.o.,** réprimander* qn/sonner les cloches à qn/passer un savon à qn 9. *F* **to jump down s.o.'s throat,** rabrouer qn/envoyer paître qn 10. *P* attaquer*/sauter sur le paletot à (qn) 11. *F* **to jump off the deep end,** y aller d'autor/foncer 12. *F* **to jump the broomstick,** se marier/se marida 13. *F* **to jump the lights,** (*of car, driver*) brûler/griller le feu rouge. (*See* **bandwagon; gun¹ 2**)

jumped up ['dʒʌmpt'ʌp] *a F* 1. (*arrogant, pretentious*) prétentieux*/crâneur/esbroufeur 2. (*upstart*) parvenu; **a jumped-up salesman,** un petit péteux de vendeur.

jumper ['dʒʌmpə] *n P* **(you can) stick it up your jumper!** fous ça dans ta poche (et ton mouchoir par-dessus)!/tu sais où tu peux te le mettre! (*See* **queue-jumper; stick² 3**)

jumping ['dʒʌmpɪŋ] *a F* (*party, etc*) en plein boum.

jungle ['dʒʌŋgl] *n* 1. *F* la jungle/endroit *m* de mauvaises mœurs 2. *P* lieu *m* de refuge des vagabonds/la zone 3. *P Pej* **jungle bunny,** Noir(e)*/nègre *m*/bougnoul *m* 4. *P* **jungle juice,** alcool*/gnôle *f*/tord-boyaux *m*.

junk¹ [dʒʌŋk] *n* 1. *F* (*a*) articles variés sans grande valeur/pacotille *f*/gnognote *f*; **this shop sells a load of junk,** ce magasin ne vend que de la camelote; **junk food,** aliment peu nutritif; **to eat junk food,** manger des cochonneries (*b*) effets *mpl* personnels/affaires *fpl*/barda *m*; **get your junk out of here!** ton bazar/ton fourbi de là! 2. *P* (*hard drugs*) drogues *fpl*/stupéfiants *mpl*/came *f*/stups *mpl*; **to be on junk,** se droguer*/se camer 3. *F* bêtises*/foutaises *fpl*/conneries *fpl*; **you do talk a lot of junk!** tu débloques!/tu déconnes! 4. *F* ferraille *f*; **heap of junk,** vieille voiture*/guimbarde *f*/tas *m* de ferraille 5. *F* **junk mail,** courrier *m* publicitaire/pub *f*.

junk² [dʒʌŋk] *vtr esp NAm P* mettre au rebut/au rencart/à la casse/à la poubelle;

balancer.

junker ['dʒʌŋkə] *n NAm P* **1.** (*old car*) tas *m* de ferraille/vieux tacot **2.** (*rare*) = **junkie**.

junkie, junky¹ ['dʒʌŋkɪ] *n P* **1.** (*drugs*) drogué*/toxico(mane) *mf*/junkie *mf*/camé(e)

2. news junkie, qn qui veut toujours connaître les dernières nouvelles/fana *mf* des informations.

junky² ['dʒʌŋkɪ] *a F* qui n'a pas de valeur/ bon à foutre en l'air/de la camelote/(du) toc.

K

K [keɪ] *abbr F* 1. (= *1,000*) mille; salary (of) 35K, salaire de trente-cinq mille (livres, dollars, etc) 2. *Br* titre *m* de chevalier.

kafe [keɪf] *n Br P* = **cafe, caff**.

kale [keɪl] *n P* argent*/blé *m*.

kanga ['kæŋgə] *n esp Austr P* = **kangaroo 2**.

kangaroo [kæŋgə'ruː] *n* 1. *F* kangaroo court, tribunal guignol/irrégulier 2. *P* (*RS* = **screw**) gardien* de prison/gaffe *m*. (*See* **screw¹ 1**)

kaput(t) [kæ'pʊt, kə-] *a F* cassé/fichu; my watch is kaput, ma montre est fichue/foutue; all my plans have gone kaput, tous mes projets sont tombés à l'eau.

kars(e)y, karz(e)y ['kɑːzɪ] *n P* = **kazi**.

Kate and Sidney ['keɪt(ə)n'sɪdnɪ] *n F Hum* (*spoonerism of steak and kidney*) Kate and Sidney pie, tourte *f* à la viande de bœuf et aux rognons.

kayo¹ ['keɪ'əʊ] *n F* (*esp boxing*) = **k.o.¹**.

kayo² ['keɪ'əʊ] *vtr F* (*esp boxing*) = **k.o.²**.

kazi ['kɑːzɪ] *n P* WC*/chiottes *fpl*/gogues *mpl*; kazi paper, papier *m* hygiénique/papier-cul *m*/papier *m* Q.

K-boy ['keɪbɔɪ] *n NAm P* (*cards*) roi *m*/barbu *m*/papa *m*.

kecks [keks] *npl O P* pantalon*/falzar *m*/futal *m*.

keef [kiːf] *n P* (*drugs*) = **kief, kif**.

keen [kiːn] *a NAm O P* excellent*/chouette/bath/super.

keeno, keeny ['kiːnəʊ, -nɪ] *n Br F* (*schools*) individu* enthousiaste; (*swot*) bûcheur, -euse.

keep [kiːp] *vtr F* 1. to keep oneself to oneself, faire bande à part 2. to keep at it, persévérer/s'accrocher à qch/prendre le mors aux dents; to keep s.o. at it, serrer les côtes/la vis à qn. (*See* **hair 3; hat 3; shirt 3**)

keep in ['kiːp'ɪn] *vi F* to keep in with s.o., rester bien avec qn/peaufiner (une relation); to keep in with both sides, ménager la chèvre et le chou/ne pas se mouiller.

keep on ['kiːp'ɒn] *vi F* 1. to keep on at s.o., harceler qn/être sur le dos de qn 2. keep on truckin', continue/faut pas s'arrêter/faut persévérer.

keep out ['kiːp'aʊt] *vi F* you keep out of this! mêle-toi de ce qui te regarde!/occupe-toi de tes oignons!

keeps [kiːps] *npl F* for keeps, pour de bon/pas pour la frime/pour tout le temps.

keep up ['kiːp'ʌp] *vtr F* keep it up! vas-y!/continue!/tu l'auras! keep your pecker up! tiens bon!/te laisse pas abattre! (*See* **end 6; Joneses; pecker 2**)

keester ['kiːstə] *n NAm O P* 1. fesses*/postérieur *m*/derche *m* 2. poche* arrière de pantalon/fouille *f*/profonde *f* 3. valise *f* de camelot/valdingue *f*/valoche *f* 4. coffre-fort *m*/coffiot *m*/jacquot *m*.

kefuffle [kə'fʌfl] *n F* = **kerfuffle**.

keister ['kiːstə] *n NAm O P* = **keester**.

keks [keks] *npl P* = **kecks**.

kelper ['kelpə] *n Br F* habitant, -ante des (îles) Malouines.

kerb-crawl ['kɜːb'krɔːl], **kerb-cruise** ['kɜːb'kruːz] *vi F* accoster un(e) prostitué(e) en voiture; draguer en voiture.

kerb crawler ['kɜːb'krɔːlə], **kerb cruiser** ['kɜːb'kruːzə] *n F* individu* qui accoste les prostitué(e)s en voiture; dragueur *m* en voiture.

kerb crawling, kerb cruising ['kɜːb'krɔːlɪŋ, -kruːzɪŋ] *n F* accostage (de prostitué(e)s) en voiture; drague *f* en voiture.

kerdoing!, kerdoying! [kə'dɔɪŋ] *excl F* boum!/patatras!/vlan! (*See* **gerdoing!**)

kerflooie [kə'fluːɪ] *adv NAm F* to go kerflooie, échouer*/foirer/finir en queue de poisson/faire un bide total.

kerfuffle [kə'fʌfl] *n F* ramdam *m*/agitation *f*/cirque *m*/histoire *f*/affaire *f*; there was all this kerfuffle, c'était toute une histoire.

kermit ['kɜːmɪt] *n Br F* Français, -aise/

Fran(s)quillon, -onne.

kerplunk [kə'plʌŋk] *adv F* to go kerplunk, tomber*/ramasser *ou* prendre un gadin/se ramasser.

kettle ['ketl] *n* 1. *P* montre*; kettle and piece, montre *f* et chaîne/tocante *f* et pendante 2. *F* here's a nice/fine/pretty kettle of fish! en voilà une affaire!/en voilà des histoires!/quelle salade! nous voilà dans de beaux draps/dans un beau gâchis!

Kevin ['kevɪn] *n Br F* homme* vulgaire/ obtus/chauvin, etc; = Dupont-la-Joie *m*/beauf *m*.

key [kiː] *n F* 1. key of the door: see **bingo 21** 2. *NAm P* (*drugs*) kilo *m* (*surt* de marijuana*).

keyed up ['kiːd'ʌp] *a & pp F* gonflé à bloc.

keyhole ['kiːhəʊl] *vi Br F* crocheter une serrure; pénétrer dans un immeuble (pour le cambrioler) en crochetant la serrure.

khazi ['kɑːzɪ] *n P* = **kazi**.

Khyber ['kaɪbə] *n P* (*RS = Khyber Pass = arse*) he can stick it up his Khyber, il peut se le mettre quelque part/il peut se le fourrer là où je pense; a kick up the Khyber, un coup de pied au derrière. (*See* **stick²** 3)

ki [kaɪ] *n P* cacao *m ou* chocolat *m* (*surt* de prison).

kibble ['kɪbl] *n NAm P* nourriture*/bouffe *f*.

kibitz ['kɪbɪts] *vi NAm F* 1. suivre/regarder une partie de cartes en donnant son avis 2. se mêler de ce qui ne vous regarde pas/mettre son grain de sel/ramener sa fraise.

kibitzer ['kɪbɪtsə] *n NAm F* individu* qui donne des conseils non sollicités/qui se mêle de tout; canule *f*.

kibosh ['kaɪbɒʃ] *n F* to put the kibosh on sth, mettre fin/mettre le point final/mettre le holà à qch; that's put the kibosh on that, ça a tout foutu en l'air/ça a tout salopé.

kick¹ [kɪk] *n* 1. *F* (*a*) frisson *m* (de plaisir)/ piquant *m* (d'une chose); to get a kick out of sth, prendre/éprouver du plaisir à qch; prendre son pied/son fade; that's how he gets his kicks, c'est comme ça qu'il prend son pied; he doesn't get much of a kick out of that, ça ne le botte pas tellement; to do sth for kicks, faire qch pour s'amuser/pour prendre son pied (*b*) *NAm* marotte *f*/manie *f*; to be on a health food kick, être accro à la bouffe bio 2. *F* (*drink*) it's got a kick in it, ça vous remonte/ça vous requinque/ça vous donne un coup de fouet 3. *F* (*drugs*) le pied/l'extase *f*; to go on a kick, prendre son pied/aller à la défonce/se

défoncer; bum kicks, mauvaise expérience d'un drogué*/mauvais voyage 4. *F* he's got no kick left in him, il est vidé/lessivé/pompé 5. (*a*) *F* that's better than a kick in the pants, ça vaut mieux qu'un coup de pied au derrière/ça vaut mieux que de se casser une jambe/il vaut mieux entendre ça qu'être sourd (*b*) *P* he's had a kick in the pants/the arse/*NAm* the ass, il s'est fait botter le cul/il s'est fait remonter les bretelles; a kick in the teeth, un coup en vache; that was a kick in the pants/the teeth for my idea, mon idée a été un bide total/je me suis ramassé avec cette idée. (*See* **pants 3**) 6. *A P* poche* (de pantalon)/fouille *f* 7. *P* grogne *f*/rouspétance *f*. (*See* **sidekick**)

kick² [kɪk] *vtr & i* 1. *P* grogner*/bougonner/ rouspéter/ronchonner/râler 2. *F* résister/ruer dans les brancards 3. *P* (*drugs, etc*) he's kicked it, (*he's given up taking drugs*) il a décroché 4. *F* I could have kicked myself, je me serais flanqué des claques/des coups 5. *F* to kick it, mourir*/claquer. (*See* **alive 1**; **bucket 1**; **habit 1**)

kick around ['kɪkə'raʊnd] *vtr F* 1. retourner/ruminer; to kick a few ideas around, lancer quelques idées 2. to kick s.o. around, mener qn à la trique; he kicks his kids around, il mène ses gosses à la trique/ses gosses lui obéissent au doigt et à l'œil 3. rouler sa bosse/bourlinguer; there are lots of people like that kicking around, des gens comme ça, ce n'est pas ça qui manque; I've lost my gloves, but they must be kicking around somewhere, j'ai perdu mes gants, mais ils doivent traîner quelque part. (*See* **gong 2**)

kick ass [kɪk'æs] *vi NAm P* 1. réprimander*; punir; (*severely*) saler 2. créer des ennuis/faire des emmerdes 3. se comporter d'une manière agressive. (*See* **ass-kicker**)

kickback ['kɪkbæk] *n* 1. *F* réaction violente/ coup *m* de boomerang 2. *P* ristourne *f*/ dessous-de-table *m*/pot-de-vin *m*/graissage *m* de patte.

kicker ['kɪkə] *n NAm P* piège *m*/hic *m*/os *m*. (*See* **shitkicker**)

kickers ['kɪkəz] *npl esp NAm F* chaussures*/godasses *fpl*; bottes *fpl*/écrase-merde *fpl*.

kick in ['kɪk'ɪn] *F* I *vi esp NAm* payer sa part/payer son écot II *vtr* to kick s.o.'s head in, battre* qn/passer qn à tabac.

kicking ['kɪkɪŋ] *n Br F* coups*/tabassage *m*.

kick-off ['kɪkɒf] *n F* coup *m* d'envoi/ démarrage *m*; **and you can stop doing that for a kick-off,** et pour commencer tu vas m'arrêter ça/tu vas m'arrêter ce cinéma.

kick off ['kɪk'ɒf] *vi* 1. *F* donner le départ/le coup d'envoi/démarrer 2. *NAm P* partir*/lever l'ancre/se tirer/se tailler 3. *NAm P* mourir*/ claquer/clamser.

kick out ['kɪk'aʊt] *vtr F* (*a*) flanquer (qn) à la porte/balancer/larguer (qn) (*b*) congédier* (qn)/sacquer (qn); **I got kicked out of that job,** je me suis fait virer/balancer de ce boulot-là.

kick-up ['kɪkʌp] *n esp NAm F* chahut *m*/ tapage *m*/chambard *m*.

kick up ['kɪk'ʌp] *vtr* 1. *F* **to kick up a fuss,** faire des chichis/faire des histoires/faire tout un plat 2. (*a*) *F* **to kick up a row/a racket/a shindy/a hullabaloo,** faire beaucoup de bruit*/ faire du boucan/faire du ramdam (*b*) *F* **to kick up a dust,** faire une scène/faire un scandale/faire du foin (*c*) *P* **to kick up hell,** faire un scandale pas possible 3. *F* **to kick up one's heels,** sauter de joie. (*See* **stink¹ 1**)

kick upstairs ['kɪkʌp'stɛəz] *vtr F* **to kick s.o. upstairs,** se débarrasser* de qn en lui donnant une promotion/de l'avancement; mettre qn dans un placard doré.

kid¹ [kɪd] **I** *a F* 1. jeunet/cadet; **my kid sister,** ma sœur cadette 2. enfantin/puéril; **kid stuff,** enfantillage *m*/gaminerie *f*; **it's kids' stuff,** c'est simple comme bonjour/c'est un jeu d'enfant 3. **to handle/to treat s.o. with kid gloves,** (*treat s.o. carefully*) ménager qn/ manier qn comme du verre cassé/prendre des gants avec qn; (*pet s.o.*) dorloter/chouchouter qn **II** *n F* enfant*/gosse *mf*/môme *mf*/moutard *m*; **when I was a kid,** quand j'étais gosse; **our kid,** le benjamin, la benjamine/le cadet, la cadette de la famille; mon petit frangin/ma petite frangine. (*See* **whiz(z)¹ I 1**)

kid² [kɪd] *F* **I** *vtr* faire marcher (qn)/raconter des histoires à (qn); **don't kid yourself!** ne te fais pas d'illusion!/ne te monte pas le bourrichon! **who are you trying to kid?/who do you think you're kidding?** tu te fiches de moi?/tu me prends pour qui? **II** *vi* plaisanter/charrier; **are you kidding?/no kidding?** tu me fais marcher?/tu veux rire ou quoi?/tu déconnes ou quoi? sans blague!/blague à part!/sans déconner!/sans dec'? **stop kidding!** arrête ton char!/arrête tes salades!/arrête tes conneries!

kid along ['kɪdə'lɒŋ] *vtr F* bourrer le crâne à (qn)/envelopper (qn)/monter un bateau à

(qn).

kidder ['kɪdə] *n F* plaisantin *m*/farceur, -euse/blagueur, -euse/loustic *m*.

kiddie ['kɪdɪ] *n F* = **kiddy.**

kiddo ['kɪdəʊ] *n F* (*form of address*) listen, kiddo! écoute mon petit! **are you ready, kiddo?** tu es prêt(e) mon grand *ou* ma grande?

kiddy ['kɪdɪ], **kiddywink** ['kɪdɪwɪŋk] *n F* petit enfant*/mioche *mf*/chiard *m*/gniard *m*. (*See* **kid¹ II**)

kief, kif [kiːf] *n P* (*drugs*) marijuana*/ haschisch*/kif *m*.

kike [kaɪk] *n P Pej* Juif* *m*/youpe *m*/youpin, -ine/youtre *m*.

kiki ['kiːkiː] *n P* homosexuel* passif et actif/ bique *f* et bouc *m*.

kill¹ [kɪl] *n F* 1. assassinat *m*/butage *m*/ saignage *m*/mise *f* en l'air/zigouillage *m* 2. (*a*) descente *f* (d'avion ennemi)/inscription *f* au tableau de chasse (*b*) destruction *f* (d'un navire ennemi) 3. **kill or cure,** remède *m* de cheval/remède héroïque 4. **to be in at the kill,** assister au dénouement. (*See* **set up 2**)

kill² [kɪl] *vtr F* 1. **to kill a bottle,** (*finish off*) sécher/siffler une bouteille; faire cul sec 2. ruiner/enfoncer/couler (qn, qch) 3. (*theatre*) **to kill an audience,** brûler les planches/casser la baraque/faire un tabac 4. (*cigarette*) éteindre/écraser; (*motor*) arrêter; **kill those lights!** coupe-moi ces phares! (*headlights*) coupe-moi ces phares! (*lightbulbs*) éteins-moi ces loupiotes! 5. **to kill time,** tuer le temps/paresser*/flemmarder/ tirer sa flemme/se la couler douce 6. **to kill oneself (with work),** se tuer/se crever à (force de) travailler; *Iron* **don't kill yourself, will you,** ne te fais pas trop mal, surtout! 7. **to kill oneself laughing,** se tordre de rire/se boyauter; **his jokes really kill me,** ses plaisanteries sont tordantes 8. **my feet are killing me,** j'ai les pieds en compote/je ne sens plus mes pinceaux 9. *NAm* **to kill it,** arrêter/ lâcher les pédales. (*See* **dressed**)

killer ['kɪlə] *P* **I** *a* excellent*/super/génial/ extra; **it's a killer band,** c'est un group géant **II** *n* 1. (*joke*) **it was a real killer!** c'était crevant/à se rouler par terre/à mourir de rire! 2. **that job's a real killer!** c'est tuant/ crevant, ce boulot!/on se crève avec ce boulot-là! 3. (*sth superlative, excellent*) **that album's a killer,** cet album est génial.

killing ['kɪlɪŋ] *F* **I** *a* 1. très amusant*/ tordant/crevant/à se rouler par terre/ boyautant; **it's too killing for words,** c'est à

mourir/à crever de rire 2. fatigant/tuant/
crevant; **this job is really killing!** c'est
crevant/chiant, ce boulot! II *n* **to make a killing,** faire de gros profits/affurer/faire son
beurre/un max de bénef.
kind [kaɪnd] *n F* 1. **I don't have that kind of
money,** je n'ai pas des sommes pareilles 2.
these kind of things annoy me, ce genre de
choses, ça m'agace 3. **she's not my kind (of
woman),** cette femme, ce n'est pas mon genre
4. **I'm not that kind (of person),** je ne mange
pas de ce pain-là. (*See* **kind of**)
kinda ['kaɪndə] *adv F* = **kind of.**
kind of ['kaɪndəv] *adv F* 1. **he's kind of
careful with money!** il est plutôt près de ses
sous! 2. **I kind of expected it/I had a kind of
feeling,** j'avais comme un pressentiment/je le
sentais venir/je m'en doutais presque 3. **it's
kind of chilly,** il fait plutôt frisquet.
kingdom-come ['kɪŋdəm'kʌm] 1. *F* le
paradis/le paradouze 2. *P* **to knock s.o. to
kingdom-come,** battre* qn/envoyer qn dans
l'autre monde/foutre une trempe à qn; **shut
your face or I'll knock you to kingdom-come!**
ferme ta gueule ou je te fais une tête au
carré! 3. *P* (*RS = rum*) rhum *m*. (*See* **Tom
4**)
king-size(d) ['kɪŋsaɪz(d)] *a F* géant/
énorme/ma(h)ous; **it was a king-size(d)
problem,** on était dans une sacrée panade.
kink [kɪŋk] *n F* 1. (*person*) maniaque
sexuel(le) 2. perversion sexuelle; (*idiosyn-
crasy*) truc *m*/lubie *f*/manie *f*/dada *m*; **he's
got a kink,** il a des goûts sexuels bizarres;
he's got a kink for young boys, les jeunes
mecs, c'est son truc/il en a que pour les
jeunes mecs.
kinky ['kɪŋkɪ] *a* 1. *F* fantasque/excentrique;
he's really kinky, c'est un drôle de zigoto 2. *F*
bizarre/extravagant; **she wears really kinky
clothes,** elle porte des fringues complètement
dingues; **he asked me to do some very kinky
things,** il m'a demandé de faire des trucs
plutôt bizarres 3. *P* (*a*) qui a des goûts
sexuels spéciaux/bizarres (*b*) homosexuel*/qui
fait pédé.
kip¹ [kɪp] *n P* 1. lit*/pieu *m*/plumard *m*; **he
had to find a kip for the night,** il a dû se
trouver un paddock pour la nuit 2. sommeil
m; **to have a kip,** dormir*/piquer un roupillon
ou un somme/pioncer; **did you get enough
kip?** t'as assez roupillé?
kip² [kɪp] *vi P* 1. se coucher*/se pieuter/se bâcher; **he was kipping on the floor,** il s'était

couché par terre/il pionçait par terre 2.
dormir*/pioncer/roupiller/piquer une bâche.
kip down ['kɪp'daʊn] *vi P* se coucher/se
bâcher/se pieuter; **you can kip down at my
place,** tu peux pioncer à ma taule.
kip-house ['kɪphaʊs] *n P* = **doss-house.**
kipper ['kɪpə] *n* 1. *A P* individu*/type *m*/
client *m* 2. *Austr P* Anglais, -aise*/angliche
mf 3. **kipper season,** (*trading*) morte-saison *f*
4. *V* sexe* de la femme/abricot *m* 5. *P* **to do
s.o. up like a kipper,** tromper*/rouler qn (dans
la farine).
kippered ['kɪpəd] *a Br P* (*person*) terrassé/
foudroyé; **when I heard that, I was kippered,**
quand j'ai entendu ça, ça m'a foutu un coup/
j'en suis resté comme deux ronds de flan.
kipper-feast ['kɪpəfiːst] *n VV*
cunnilinctus*/descente *f* à la cave.
kiss¹ [kɪs] *n F* 1. **the kiss of death,** le coup de
grâce 2. **the kiss of life,** le bouche-à-bouche.
(*See* **French¹ I 1**)
kiss² [kɪs] *vtr F* 1. **to kiss sth goodbye,** faire
ses adieux à qch/en faire son deuil/faire une
croix sur qch; **you can kiss goodbye to your
holidays!** tu peux faire une croix sur tes
vacances 2. **never been kissed:** *see* **bingo 16**
3. **to kiss and be friends/to kiss and make up,**
se réconcilier/se rebecter/faire ami-ami/se
rabibocher. (*See* **arse I 7**)
kiss-ass ['kɪsæs] *n NAm V* 1. (*person*)
lèche-cul *m* 2. lèche *f*/boniments *mpl*. (*See*
arse-kisser, ass-kisser)
kiss ass ['kɪs'æs] *vi NAm V* faire de la
lèche/être lèche-cul.
kisser ['kɪsə] *n P* 1. bouche*/bec *m*/museau
m/micro *m* 2. lèvres*/babines *fpl*/pompeuses
fpl 3. visage*/fiole *f*/trombine *f*/fraise *f*; **he
socked him one right in the kisser,** il lui a
flanqué une pêche en pleine poire. (*See* **arse-
kisser; baby-kisser**)
kissing tackle ['kɪsɪŋ'tækl] *n Br F*
bouche*/bec *m*; lèvres*/pompeuses *fpl*.
kiss-off ['kɪsɒf] *n P* sacquage *m*/limogeage
m/vidage *m*.
kiss off ['kɪs'ɒf] *vtr P* se débarrasser* de/
sacquer/balancer/expédier (qn).
kissy ['kɪsɪ] *a P* sentimental/à l'eau de rose.
kit [kɪt] *n* 1. *F* barda *m*/bataclan *m*/Saint-
Frusquin *m*. (*See* **caboodle**) 2. *F*
vêtements*/frusques *fpl*/sapes *fpl*.
kitchen-sink¹ ['kɪtʃɪn'sɪŋk] *a attrib F*
kitchen-sink novel/play, roman *m ou* pièce *f*
naturaliste/réaliste.
kitchen-sink² ['kɪtʃɪn'sɪŋk] *n F* everything

but the **kitchen-sink**, tout sans exception/y compris la cage aux serins.

kite¹ [kaɪt] *n* 1. *F* avion *m*/coucou *m* 2. *P* chèque *m* sans provision/en bois; **to fly a kite**, émettre un chèque en bois; (*submit for a approval*) tâter le terrain/lancer un ballon d'essai; **kite man**, faussaire *m*/refileur *m* de chèques en bois 3. *F* (**as**) **high as a kite** (*a*) ivre*/parti/beurré/rétamé (*b*) drogué/chargé/envappé/bourré à zéro/défoncé; **he's** (**as**) **high as a kite**, il a du vent dans les voiles/il est dans les vapes.

kite² [kaɪt] *vtr P* **to kite** (**a cheque on**) **s.o.**, donner/filer un chèque sans provision à qn.

kittens ['kɪtnz] *npl F* **to have kittens**, être très en colère*/piquer une crise/avoir un coup de sang; (*be afraid*) avoir peur*/avoir les foies *mpl*/serrer les fesses *fpl*/avoir le trouillomètre à zéro; **he had kittens when he saw how much she had spent**, il a piqué une crise quand il a vu combien elle avait dépensé. (*See* **sex-kitten**)

kitty ['kɪtɪ] *n* 1. *F* chaton *m*/petit(e) chat(te)/mistigri *m* 2. *F* (*cards, etc*) cagnotte *f*/caisse commune *m* 3. *P* prison*/trou *m*/taule *f*/gnouf *m*.

Kiwi, kiwi ['kiːwiː] *n F* Néo-Zélandais, -aise/Kiwi *m*.

klutz [klʌts] *n NAm P* individu bête*/andouille *f*/corniaud *m*.

klutzy ['klʌtsɪ] *a NAm P* bête*/con/balluche.

knacker ['nækə] *vtr P* fatiguer/éreinter/crever (qn); **this job will really knacker you**, ce boulot va vous crever; **it's knackering**, c'est crevant. (*See* **knackered**)

knackered ['nækəd] *a & pp P* **to be knackered**, être fatigué*/crevé/éreinté/naze/vanné; **I'm really knackered after that**, je suis sur les genoux/je suis à ramasser à la petite cuiller; **the car's knackered**, la voiture est naze/bonne pour la casse.

knackers ['nækəz] *npl P* 1. testicules*/balloches *fpl*/noisettes *fpl*/joyeuses *fpl* 2. *excl* **knackers to that!** mon cul (c'est du poulet)!/quelle couillonnade!

knee [niː] *n F* **housemaid's knee**, épanchement *m* de synovie/genou *m* en compote. (*See* **bee 2**)

knee-high ['niː'haɪ] *a F* **to be knee-high to a grasshopper**, être un rase-mottes/être un rase-bitume/être bas-du-cul/avoir le cul près du trottoir; **when I was knee-high to a grasshopper**, quand j'étais haut comme trois pommes.

kneesies ['niːzɪz] *npl F* **to play kneesies with s.o.**, faire du genou à qn. (*See* **footsie**)

knees-up ['niːzʌp] *n F* (*lively dance or party*) java *f*; **to have a knees-up**, faire la java; **they were having a real knees-up in there**, c'était une fête à tout casser/ils s'éclataient carrément là-dedans.

knee-tremble, knee-trembler ['niːtrembl(ə)] *n V* **to do a knee-tremble(r)**, faire l'amour* debout/sabrer à la verticale.

knickers ['nɪkəz] *npl* 1. *P* **to get one's knickers in a twist**, perdre les pédales 2. *excl Br* **knickers!** des foutaises!/des conneries!/mon cul!

knife [naɪf] *n F* **to get one's knife into s.o./to have one's knife in s.o.**, avoir une dent contre qn/être remonté contre qn/en avoir après qn; **she's really got her knife into me**, elle en a après moi/elle m'en veut.

knob¹ [nɒb] *n* 1. *Br V* pénis*/bout *m*/zob *m*/nœud *m*/gourdin *m*; **knob job**, masturbation*/la veuve Poignet; fellation*/pipe *f*/pompier *m*; **knob rot**, blennorragie*/chaude-pisse *f*/chtouille *f*; syphilis*/sifflote *f*/vérole *f* 2. *NAm P* tête*/caboche *f*/ciboulot *m* 3. *P* **with knobs on**, et le pouce/et mèche/et le rab; **and the same to you with brass knobs on**, et ta sœur!/va te faire voir!/j'en ai autant à ton service! 4. *NAm P* seins*/nichons *mpl*.

knob² [nɒb] *vtr Br V* faire l'amour*/baiser/caramboler.

knob-gobbler ['nɒbgɒblə] *n V* 1. homosexuel*/pédé *m*/enculé *m* 2. qn qui fait une fellation* à qn/suceur, -euse/pipeur, -euse.

knock¹ [nɒk] *n Br* 1. *F* critique *f*/éreintement *m*/abattage *m* 2. *F* perte *f* d'argent/pommade *f*; fausse créance; **to take the knock**, essuyer un échec* *ou* une déception/recevoir un coup dans les gencives 3. *F* (*cards*) **it's your knock**, c'est ton tour/c'est ta passe 4. *P* **on the knock**, à crédit/à croume 5. *P* **the knock**, le butin* (du voleur)/la camelote/la prise 6. *F* **the knock**, visite *f* de la police/descente *f* 7. *P* coït*/baise *f*.

knock² [nɒk] *vtr* 1. *F* critiquer*/allumer/maillocher; **don't knock the film before you've even seen it!** ne déglingue pas ce film avant de l'avoir vu! 2. *F* **to knock sth on the head**, battre qch en brèche/mettre le holà à qch; arrêter les frais; **that's knocked his little idea on the head**, son projet est tombé à l'eau/ça a coupé court à son projet 3. *F* **to be knocking 60**, friser la soixantaine 4. *P* **that'll knock 'em cold**, cela va leur en boucher un

coin 5. *P* faire l'amour* avec/baiser/bourrer/
caramboler (qn) 6. *F* to knock for six, (*knock
down*) étendre (qn); (*stun*) abasourdir (qn);
battre (qn) à plate(s) couture(s); ficher (un
projet, etc) en l'air 7. *P* = **knock off 6** 8. *F*
knock at the door: *see* **bingo 4**. (*See*
**feather¹ 4; sideways; spot 3; wall 4;
week**)

knock about, around ['nɒkə'baʊt,
ə'raʊnd] *vi F* 1. vadrouiller/rouler sa bosse/
bourlinguer; he's knocked about a bit, il a
roulé sa bosse 2. to knock about with s.o.,
s'acoquiner avec qn/sortir avec qn/fréquenter
qn; he knocks about with that gang of
hooligans, il fréquente cette bande de voyous.

knock back ['nɒk'bæk] *vtr F* 1. to knock
back a drink, boire*/lamper un verre/écluser
un godet/s'en jeter un derrière la cravate;
knock it back! cul sec! 2. coûter; it knocked
him back a packet, il en a aligné un paquet.

knock-down ['nɒkdaʊn] *n Austr & NAm P*
présentation *f* (d'une personne à une autre);
will you give me a knock-down to him? tu me
présenteras?

knocked off ['nɒkt'ɒf] *a & pp P* volé/
fauché. (*See* **knock off 4**)

knocked out ['nɒkt'aʊt] *a & pp P* 1.
fatigué/vanné/lessivé; I'm really knocked out,
je suis vraiment H.S. 2. épaté/estomaqué/
médusé; I'm really knocked out by that idea,
cette idée m'a coupé le sifflet. (*See* **knock
out**)

knocked up ['nɒkt'ʌp] *a & pp P* 1.
malade*/patraque/flapi/flagada 2. *Austr* très
fatigué*/claqué/vanné 3. *esp NAm* enceinte*/
engrossée/en cloque; she's knocked up, elle a
un polichinelle dans le tiroir/elle a le ballon.
(*See* **knock up**)

knocker ['nɒkə] *n Br* 1. *F* critique *m*
sévère/éreinteur *m* 2. *P* (*door-to-door
salesman*) V.R.P. *m*; (*tout for antiques
dealer*) racoleur *m*; to sell on the knocker,
faire du porte-à-porte 3. *pl P* seins/nichons
mpl/rondins *mpl*/nénés *mpl*/tétons *mpl*; what
a huge pair of knockers! il y a du monde au
balcon! 4. *P* on the knocker, à crédit/à
tempérament/à croume. (*See* **dressed up
2**)

knocking ['nɒkɪŋ] *a* 1. *P* knocking
company, maison *f* de location-vente 2. *P*
knocking shop, bordel*/maison *f* d'abattage/
claque *m* 3. *F* knocking copy, publicité qui
critique un concurrent/publicité comparative.

knock off ['nɒk'ɒf] I *vtr* 1. *P* to knock s.o.

off, caramboler/baiser/tringler/s'envoyer qn;
he's knocking off his secretary, il s'envoie sa
secrétaire 2. *P* knock it off (will you)! (*shut
up!*) basta!/écrase!/la ferme!/boucle-la! 3. *O
F* = **knock back 1** 4. *P* voler*/faucher; to
knock off a bank, faire/monter un coup contre
une banque; did you buy it or did you knock it
off? tu l'as acheté ou piqué? 5. *F* finir vite/
exécuter avec rapidité/liquider/expédier; she
knocked off her letters in no time, elle a bâclé
ses lettres en deux temps trois mouvements/
en cinq secs 6. *P* tuer*/démolir/zigouiller/
refroidir (qn) 7. *F* I'll knock two quid off the
price for you, je vous fais une remise de deux
livres/je vous fais deux livres sur le prix II *vi
F* finir de travailler/dételer; he knocks off at
five, il détèle à cinq heures. (*See* **block 1**)

knockout ['nɒkaʊt] I *a F* 1. knockout drops,
stupéfiant *m* qu'on met dans la boisson de la
victime pour lui faire perdre connaissance
(*dans le but de la dépouiller*)/coup *m*
d'assommoir 2. magnifique/mirobolant; what
a knockout idea! quelle chouette idée!/quelle
idée géniale! II *n F* 1. une merveille/un
phénomène/qch *ou* qn de mirifique; he's a
knockout, il en jette/il jette du jus 2. (*esp
woman*) prix *m* de Diane/femme bien roulée/
belle carrosserie. (*See* **k.o.¹**)

knock out ['nɒk'aʊt] *vtr F* 1. to knock oneself out, se fatiguer/s'esquinter/se culotter;
that work really knocked me out, ce boulot
m'a crevé/m'a mis K.-O. 2. époustoufler/
éblouir/épater/en boucher un coin à (qn); it
really knocked me out when he gave me the
flowers, j'en suis restée baba quand il m'a
donné ces fleurs. (*See* **knock out; k.o.¹**)

knock over ['nɒk'əʊvə] *vtr esp NAm O P*
cambrioler*/casser/faire un fric(-)frac/faire
un casse dans.

knock together ['nɒktə'geðə] *vtr F* =
knock up 1.

knock up ['nɒk'ʌp] *vtr* 1. *F* préparer/
concocter/combiner/bricoler à la hâte;
they've knocked up some sort of an alibi, ils
se sont bricolés/montés un alibi quelconque 2.
Br F (*a*) réveiller/secouer (*b*) tambouriner à
une porte à une heure tardive 3. *esp NAm P*
rendre enceinte*/engrosser/mettre en cloque/
mettre un polichinelle dans le tiroir à 4. *P*
fatiguer/éreinter/crever (qn); that work really knocks you up, ce boulot est vachement
crevant/tuant 5. *F* to knock up £100 a week,
se faire/ramasser cent livres par semaine.

knot [nɒt] *n F* 1. to tie the knot, se marier/se

mettre la corde au cou/se marida 2. to get tied (up) in knots, s'embrouiller/ s'emberlificoter/ne pas s'en sortir/perdre les pédales. (See **topknot**)

knothead ['nɒthed] *n NAm F* = **knucklehead**.

knotted ['nɒtɪd] *a & pp P* get knotted! va te faire voir!/va te faire foutre!

know[1] [nəʊ] *n F* to be in the know, être affranchi/être au parfum/être dans le coup; to put s.o. in the know, affranchir/parfumer/ tuyauter qn.

know[2] [nəʊ] *vtr & i F* 1. I don't want to know, rien à faire/je ne marche pas 2. not that I know of, pas que je sache/à ma connaissance, non; for all I know, (pour) autant que je sache 3. (a) what do you know? quoi de neuf? (b) well, what do you know! sans blague!/sans charre!/sans déconner! 4. don't I know it! à qui le dites-vous! 5. not if I know (anything about) it! pour rien au monde!/pas pour tout l'or du monde! 6. I wouldn't know, je ne saurais dire/j'en sais rien 7. he knows a good thing when he sees one/it, c'est un connaisseur/il sait ce qui est bon/il sait reconnaître un bon cheval 8. you know what you can do with that/where you can put that/where you can stick that/where you can shove that! tu peux te le mettre quelque part/là où je pense/là où tu sais! 9. to know a thing or two/to know what's what, être malin*/être à la coule/être fortiche/être à la hauteur; he knows a thing or two, il (n')est pas bête. (See **score**[1] **1**)

know-all ['nəʊɔːl] *n F* je-sais-tout *mf*; he's a real Mr Know-all, c'est un vrai Monsieur Je-sais-tout.

know-how ['nəʊhaʊ] *n F* (a) savoir-faire *m*/habileté *f* (b) savoir-faire *m* (technique)/ connaissances *fpl* techniques/pratique *f*.

know-it-all ['nəʊɪtɔːl] *n esp NAm F* = **know-all**.

knowledge (the) [ðə'nɒlɪdʒ] *n Br P* examen *m* que doit réussir un chauffeur de taxi (noir) pour avoir l'autorisation d'opérer à Londres.

knuckle[1] ['nʌkl] *n F* near the knuckle, scabreux/grivois; that joke was a bit near the knuckle, cette plaisanterie était plutôt salée.

knuckle[2] ['nʌkl] *vtr P* battre* (qn)/passer (qn) à tabac/amocher (qn).

knuckle down ['nʌkl'daʊn] *vi F* s'y mettre sérieusement; come on, knuckle down to some work! allez, mets-toi au travail!

knucklehead ['nʌklhed] *n F* individu bête*/andouille *f*/ballot *m*.

knuckle sandwich ['nʌkl'sændwɪdʒ] *n P* coup *m* de poing/châtaigne *f*/bourre-pif *m*.

knuckle under ['nʌkl'ʌndə] *vi F* se soumettre/mettre les pouces.

k.o.[1], **KO**[1] ['keɪ'əʊ] *n F* (abbr of knockout) (esp boxing) K.-O. *m*/knock-out *m*.

k.o.[2], **KO**[2] ['keɪ'əʊ] *vtr F* (abbr of knock out) (esp boxing) mettre K.-O./envoyer au tapis/mettre knock-out.

Kojak ['kəʊdʒæk] *n P* agent* de police/flic *m*/keuf *m*.

kook [kuːk] *n NAm P* (eccentric person) excentrique *mf*/chabraque *mf*/louftingue *m*/ (drôle *m* de) zigoto *m*.

kooky ['kuːkɪ] *a NAm F* un peu fou*/ chabraque/louftingue.

kosher ['kəʊʃə] *a F* normal/réglo/qui se fait; it doesn't look very kosher to me, ça n'a pas l'air très catholique.

kowtow ['kaʊtaʊ] *vi F* to kowtow to s.o., s'aplatir/se mettre à genoux devant qn; lécher les bottes à qn/passer la pommade à qn.

kraut, Kraut [kraʊt], **krauthead** ['kraʊthed] *n P Pej* Allemand*/fridolin *m*/ fritz *m*/boche *m*.

Kremlin (the) [ðə'kremlɪn] *n Br F* New Scotland Yard (à Londres); = la P.J./le Quai des Orfèvres.

kudos ['kjuːdɒs] *n F* panache *m*/gloriole *f*; to get all the kudos, récolter toute la gloire/ décrocher le pompon.

kushti ['kʊʃtɪ] *a* = **cushti**.

kvetch[1] [kvetʃ] *n F* (person who complains) râleur, -euse/renaudeur *m*/geignard, -arde.

kvetch[2] [kvetʃ] *vi F* se plaindre/râler/ geindre.

L

la [læ] *n Austr F (abbr of lavatory)* WC*.

LA ['el'eɪ] *abbr F (abbr of Los Angeles)* Los Angeles *m ou f.*

lab [læb] *n F (abbr of laboratory)* labo *m.*

lace curtain ['leɪs'kɜːtn] *n VV (homosexuals)* prépuce *m* d'un homme non circoncis.

laced up [leɪst'ʌp] *a Br F* 1. (*a*) (*person*) très occupé/qui a beaucoup à faire (*b*) it's laced up, c'est dans la poche/c'est du tout cuit 2. (*person*) prude; to be laced up, être collet monté.

lace into ['leɪs'ɪntuː] *vtr F* to lace into s.o., battre*/rosser qn.

lace ups ['leɪs'ʌps] *npl F* chaussures *fpl*/bottes *fpl* à lacets.

lad [læd] *n F* 1. he's a bit of a lad (with the women), c'est un tombeur/c'est un chaud lapin/c'est un sacré dragueur 2. one of the lads, un gai luron/un joyeux compère; to go for a quick drink with the lads, aller prendre un pot avec les potes.

laddie ['lædɪ] *n F* (petit) gars/gamin *m*; listen, (my) laddie! écoute bien, mon petit bonhomme/mon petit gars!

la-de-da, la-di-da, ladidah ['lɑːdɪ'dɑː] *a F* 1. élégant*/(super-)chic/très classe/rider *ou* ridère; it was a very la-di-da gathering, tout le gratin se trouvait là 2. *Pej* she's so la-di-da! elle fait la prétentieuse*/c'est une de ces chochottes; she's got such a la-di-da accent, elle parle avec affectation/elle prend le ton intello-snob/elle parle avec l'accent des beaux quartiers.

ladies ['leɪdɪz] *n F* 1. the ladies, WC* pour dames; where's the ladies? où sont les toilettes?/où est le pipi-room? 2. *Euph* he's not really a ladies' man/he's never been one for the ladies, il préfère les mecs.

Lady Jane ['leɪdɪ'dʒeɪn] *n P* 1. *A* sexe* de la femme*/chatte *f*/pâquerette *f* 2. marijuana*/marie-jeanne *f. (See* fat I 6; lollipop-lady; old 3)

lady-killer ['leɪdɪkɪlə] *n F* bourreau *m* des cœurs/tombeur *m* de filles/play-boy *m*/cavaleur *m.*

lag¹ [læg] *n F* (*a*) forçat *m*/bagnard *m* (*b*) forçat libéré/fagot affranchi; old lag, (*recidivist*) cheval *m* de retour/forçat chevronné.

lag² [læg] *vtr F* 1. (*a*) arrêter*/épingler (*b*) emprisonner*/bloquer/boucler 2. = lag on.

lager lout ['lɑːgəlaʊt] *n Br F* jeune individu* avec un poste bien rémunéré qui se soûle à la bière et se comporte comme un loubard.

lagging ['lægɪŋ] *n P* peine *f* de prison de plus de trois ans; lagging station, prison*.

lag on ['læg'ɒn] *vtr Austr F* dénoncer/moucharder (qn).

lah-di-dah ['lɑːdɪ'dɑː] *a F* = la-de-da.

laid [leɪd] *pp See* lay² 1.

laid back, laidback ['leɪd'bæk] *a P* détendu/relaxe/cool/peinard.

laid up ['leɪd'ʌp] *a & pp F* malade*/alité/mal fichu.

lair [lɛə] *n Austr F* voyou *m*/vaurien *m* à toilette tapageuse; m'as-tu-vu *m*/frimeur *m.*

lairy ['lɛərɪ] *a esp Austr F* voyant/tapageur.

lake [leɪk] *n F* go (and) jump in the lake! va te faire pendre!/va te faire voir!/va voir ailleurs si j'y suis!

lam¹ [læm] *n NAm P* on the lam, (*escaped*) en fuite/en cavale; (*travelling*) en déplacement/en voyage/par monts et par vaux.

lam² [læm] *vtr & i P* 1. battre*/rosser/dérouiller 2. partir* précipitamment/mettre les bouts/se calter/se trisser; (*escape from prison*) faire cavale.

lamb [læm] *n* 1. *O P* lamb (chop), (*RS = pop (See* pop¹ 5)*)*piqûre* de narcotique/piquouse *f*/fixe *m*/shoot *m* 2. *F* (*child*) lapin *m*/agneau *m*; poor little lamb, mon pauvre petit; my little lamb, mon petit poulet/coco/poussin/trésor 3. *NAm F* individu* crédule/gobeur,

-euse/cave *m*/pigeon *m* 4. *F* he took it like a lamb, il s'est laissé faire/il n'a pas rouspété/il l'a pris sans broncher/il l'a encaissé sans rien dire.

lambaste ['læm'beɪst] *vtr F* (*a*) battre*/dérouiller (*b*) critiquer*/maillocher (*c*) engueuler/sonner les cloches à/passer un savon à (qn).

lambasting ['læm'beɪstɪŋ] *n F* (*a*) raclée *f*/frottée *f* (*b*) critique *f*/éreintage *m* (*c*) engueulade *f*/savon *m*.

lamebrain ['leɪm'breɪn] *n esp NAm F* individu bête*/imbécile *mf*/andouille *f*/abruti, -ie.

lamebrained ['leɪm'breɪnd] *a* bête*/cloche.

lam into ['læm'ɪntuː] *vtr P* = **lam² 1**.

lamming ['læmɪŋ] *n P* = **lambasting** (*a*).

lam out ['læm'aʊt] *vi NAm P* = **lam² 2**.

lamp [læmp] *vtr P* 1. regarder*/zyeuter/reluquer/mater 2. *Br* battre*/dérouiller.

lamp-post ['læmppəʊst] *n F* between you (and) me and the lamp-post, tout à fait entre nous/de toi z'à moi/entre nous et la Gare Saint-Lazare. (*See* **gatepost**)

lamps [læmps] *npl P* yeux*/clignotants *mpl*/quinquets *mpl*/lanternes *fpl*/lampions *mpl*.

land [lænd] *vtr F* 1. gagner/obtenir/dénicher/dégot(t)er; he landed himself a really good job, il s'est dégotté un boulot tout ce qu'il y a de bien 2. arriver*/débarquer/s'abouler 3. to land s.o. a blow, flanquer/balancer un coup*/une taloche/une baffe à qn 4. that will land you in prison, cela vous vaudra de la prison*/vous ne couperez pas à la taule. (*See* **muck 3**; **shit¹ IV 2** (*a*))

landed ['lændɪd] *a & pp F* dans le pétrin; to be landed with s.o., avoir qn/rester avec qn sur les bras; I got landed with the washing-up, c'est moi qui ai dû me coltiner toute la vaisselle/qui me suis retrouvé avec la vaisselle (à faire).

land up ['lænd'ʌp] *vi F* (*a*) to land up with nothing, n'aboutir à rien/finir en queue de poisson/finir en eau de boudin (*b*) to land up somewhere, aboutir quelque part; aboutir à qch; to land up nowhere, déboucher sur rien/dans une impasse/dans un cul-de-sac (*c*) to land up in a bar, atterrir finalement dans un bar.

language ['læŋgwɪdʒ] *n F* to speak s.o.'s language, parler le même langage/être sur la même longueur d'ondes que qn.

lantern ['læntən] *n F* idiot's lantern, (*television set*) télé *f*/téloche *f*/fenestron *m*. (*See* box¹ 2; goggle-box; idiot-box)

lap [læp] *n F* 1. to lay sth in s.o.'s lap, coller qch sur le dos de qn/faire porter le chapeau à qn/refiler le morceau à qn; it fell right into his lap, ça lui est tombé tout rôti/tout cru dans la bouche 2. in the lap of luxury, en plein luxe/au sein de l'abondance 3. it's in the lap of the gods, c'est impossible à prévoir/c'est pas sûr/Dieu seul le sait.

lap it up ['læpɪt'ʌp] *vi F* 1. gober/avaler qch/boire du petit lait; he was lapping up all these compliments, il buvait tous ces compliments comme du petit lait/on aurait dit qu'il buvait du petit lait, à écouter ces compliments 2. boire* beaucoup/picoler/biberonner.

lardo ['lɑːdəʊ] *n F* individu* gros/gravos(se) *mf*/gros tas.

large [lɑːdʒ] *n(pl) Br F* mille *m inv*; how much is it? – three large, c'est combien? – trois mille (livres).

lark [lɑːk] *n F* 1. une franche rigolade; talk about a lark!/what a lark!/it was a real lark! quelle rigolade!/quelle bonne blague! 2. he did it for a lark, il l'a fait pour rigoler/histoire de rigoler. (*See* **skylark**)

lark about ['lɑːkə'baʊt] *vi F* faire le zouave/rigoler/faire le pitre; stop larking about and get on with the job! arrête de glandouiller et (mets-toi) au boulot!

larrikin ['lærɪkɪn] *n Austr F* polisson *m*/propre-à-rien *m*/gamin *m* des rues; petit voyou.

larrup ['lærəp] *vtr O F* battre*/rosser.

larruping ['lærəpɪŋ] *n O F* volée *f* de coups*/rossée *f*/raclée *f*/roulée *f*.

lash [læʃ] *n Austr F* 1. to go on a lash, se déchaîner 2. to have a lash at sth, tenter sa chance/tenter le coup.

lashings ['læʃɪŋz] *npl F* une abondance* de.../des tas *mpl* de.../une flopée de...; lashings of cream, une tonne de crème fraîche.

lash out ['læʃ'aʊt] *vi F* 1. lâcher un coup*/décocher des coups* 2. dépenser/larguer son fric; les lâcher/les allonger; I lashed out on a new coat, j'ai fait une petite folie: je me suis payé un nouveau manteau 3. to lash out (at s.o.), invectiver/injurier/emballer (qn); lancer des paroles blessantes (à qn).

lash-up ['læʃʌp] *n P* (*a*) expédient *m*/échappatoire *f*/moyen *m* de fortune; bouts *mpl* de ficelle (*b*) réunion *f* intime/à la bonne franquette; soirée *f* entre copains.

last [lɑːst] *a F* the last word in comfort, le

summum du confort; the last word in socks, des chaussettes dernier cri. (See **leg**[1] 7; **straw 1, 2**)

last-ditch ['lɑːst'dɪtʃ] *a* F ultime; a last-ditch effort, un dernier effort/un baroud d'honneur/le coup de collier final.

latch on ['lætʃ'ɒn] *vi* F comprendre/saisir/piger/entraver.

latch onto, on to ['lætʃ'ɒntuː] *vtr* F obtenir/agrafer/mettre le grappin sur (qch).

latest ['leɪtɪst] *n* F to be up on the latest, être à la page/au courant/à la coule/dans le vent/dans le coup.

lather[1] ['lɑːðə] *n* F to work oneself (up) into a lather (*a*) se mettre en colère*/fulminer/sortir de ses gonds/piquer une crise (*b*) s'inquiéter/se faire du mauvais sang/se faire du mouron.

lather[2] ['lɑːðə] *vtr* F battre*/rosser/tabasser/passer à tabac.

laugh[1] [lɑːf] *n* F 1. that's a laugh! quelle bonne blague!/c'est marrant!/ça paye! 2. to do sth for laughs, faire qch pour rigoler/histoire de rigoler (un peu) 3. he's good for a laugh, il nous fait toujours rire/rigoler 4. the laugh's on you, c'est toi qui as l'air d'une andouille dans l'histoire. (See **belly laugh**)

laugh[2] [lɑːf] *vi* F 1. *Iron* don't make me laugh! ne me fais pas rire*/marrer/rigoler! 2. to laugh on the other side of one's face, rire* jaune/rire* de travers; I soon made him laugh on the other side of his face, je lui ai vite fait passer son envie de rire* 3. to be laughing, se la couler douce/vivre pépère/se les tourner; if you win the pools you'll be laughing, si vous gagnez à la loterie vous pourrez mettre les doigts de pieds en éventail 4. to be laughing all the way to the bank, avoir trouvé le filon/ramasser le fric à la pelle 5. to laugh to oneself, rire* aux anges 6. to laugh one's head off, rire* à se faire mal aux côtes/à en crever; se gondoler/se marrer. (See **drain**[1] 2)

laughing gear ['lɑːfɪŋ'gɪə] *n* Br F bouche*/clapet *m*.

launder ['lɔːndə] *vtr* P laver/blanchir (de l'argent volé); lessiver/laver (une marchandise volée).

lav [læv] *n* F (*abbr of lavatory*) WC*/cabinets *mpl*/cabinces *fpl*; to go to the lav, aller aux vécés *mpl*/aux chiottes *fpl*.

lavatorial [lævə'tɔːrɪəl] *a* F ordurier/cochon; lavatorial humour, humour scatologique/scato.

law, Law [lɔː] *n* F the law, la police*/la rousse; policier*/flic *m*; here comes the law! voilà les flics! I'll have the law on you, je vais vous traîner en justice/devant les tribunaux.

lay[1] [leɪ] *n* 1. P coït*/baise *f*/baisage *m*; to have a lay, coucher avec qn/baiser qn/se faire qn; he's a really good lay, c'est un sacré baiseur; she's an easy lay, elle a la cuisse hospitalière/c'est une Marie-couche-toi-là 2. F pari *m*/mise *f* 3. F to get the lay of the land, tâter le terrain/se rencarder sur qch.

lay[2] [leɪ] *vtr & i* P 1. to lay s.o., faire l'amour* avec qn/coucher avec qn/baiser qn; to lay a girl, s'envoyer une fille; to get laid, s'envoyer en l'air 2. to lay about one, frapper de tous côtés; to lay one on s.o., battre* qn/flanquer une taloche à qn 3. to lay for s.o., attendre qn au tournant/avoir qn dans sa ligne de mire.

lay-down ['leɪ'daʊn] *n* P détention *f* provisoire.

lay down ['leɪ'daʊn] *vtr* to lay s.o. down, tuer*/descendre qn.

lay-in ['leɪ'ɪn] *n* F = **lie-in**.

lay into ['leɪ'ɪntuː] *vtr* F (*a*) attaquer*/tomber sur le poil à/péter la gueule à (qn) (*b*) critiquer*/éreinter (qn); he really laid into me, il m'a filé une engueulade maison.

lay off ['leɪ'ɒf] *vtr & i* 1. P lay off, will you? laisse tomber!/lâche-moi!/écrase! 2. F (*football*) to lay a ball off to s.o., faire une passe à qn 3. P to lay off s.o. (*a*) ficher/foutre la paix à qn; lay off my girlfriend! bas les pattes, c'est ma copine! (*b*) congédier*/bouler/virer qn 4. *Austr* P to lay off with s.o. = to lay s.o. (**lay**[2] 1).

lay on ['leɪ'ɒn] *vtr* F 1. to lay it on thick/with a shovel/with a trowel, flatter*/fayotter/passer de la pommade; exagérer*/y aller fort/charrier/forcer la dose/en rajouter 2. arranger/préparer/amarrer; it's all laid on, tout est bien branché/tout est en règle/tout est en bonnes mains.

lay out ['leɪ'aʊt] *vtr* F 1. assommer/étendre (qn) sur le carreau/mettre qn K.-O./envoyer qn au tapis 2. to lay oneself out (to do sth), se mettre en quatre/se démener/se décarcasser (pour faire qch) 3. to lay out money, dépenser* de l'argent/les allonger/cracher.

lazybones ['leɪzɪbəʊnz] *n* F paresseux*/cossard, -arde/feignant, -ante/feignasse *mf*.

lead[1] [led] *n* 1. F (*a*) to fill s.o. with lead/to pump s.o. full of lead, tirer sur qn/flinguer qn/plomber qn/transformer qn en passoire (*b*) lead greeting card, (*bullet*) balle*/dragée *f*/

praline *f*. (*See* **lead-poisoning**) 2. *F* to swing the lead, tirer au flanc/au cul. (*See* **lead-swinger**) 3. *P* to have lead in one's pencil, être en érection*/avoir la canne/avoir le bambou/avoir une balle dans le canon 4. *P* (*a*) to have lead in one's arse/*NAm* ass, paresser*/tirer au cul/tirer au flanc (*b*) to get the lead out of one's arse/*NAm* ass/*NAm* pants, se dépêcher*/se magner le train/ l'arrière-train; se démerder.

lead² [li:d] *n F* to have a lead on sth, avoir des renseignements* sur qch/avoir un tuyau sur qch; I've got a lead on that stolen car, j'ai un tuyau sur cette bagnole volée.

lead-poisoning ['lɛdpɔɪznɪŋ] *n F* to have lead-poisoning, se faire flinguer/plomber. (*See* **lead¹** 1)

lead-swinger ['lɛdswɪŋə] *n F* paresseux*/ feignant, -ante/tire-au-flanc *m*. (*See* **lead¹** 2)

league [li:g] *n F* not to be in the same league as s.o., ne pas être dans la même catégorie/ne pas arriver à la cheville de qn.

leak¹ [li:k] *n* 1. *P* to go for a leak/to have a leak/to take a leak/*NAm* to spring a leak, uriner*/(aller) pisser un coup/lâcher l'écluse/ lansquiner/égoutter la sardine 2. (*a*) *P* donneur, -euse/mouchard, -arde (*b*) *F* (*of secrets, etc*) fuite *f*.

leak² [li:k] *vtr F* divulguer/laisser filtrer (un secret, etc).

lean and lurch [ˌli:nən'lɜ:tʃ] *n P* (*RS = church*) église *f*.

lean on ['li:n'ɒn] *vtr F* faire pression sur (qn)/serrer la vis à (qn).

leap [li:p] *n F* to take the big leap, se marier/se marida/se mettre la corde au cou.

leaper ['li:pə] *n P* (*drugs*) amphétamine*/ amphets *fpl*.

learn [lɜ:n] *vtr P* I'll learn you! je vais t'apprendre! that'll learn you! ça t'apprendra!

leary ['lɪərɪ] *a F* = **lairy, leery**.

leather¹ ['lɛðə] *n P* 1. to put the leather in, flanquer un coup de pied (à qn). (*See* **boot¹** 2) 2. portefeuille*/lazagne *f*; to snatch leather, voler*/piquer un portefeuille à la tire/ décrocher un portefeuille 3. (*esp homosexuals*) leather brigade/leather merchants, ceux qui portent du cuir/cuirs *mpl*; he's heavily into leather/he's a leather fetishist, c'est un fétichiste du cuir. (*See* **hell** 11; **queen¹** 2)

leather² ['lɛðə] *vtr F* battre*/tanner le cuir à (qn).

leatherboy ['lɛðəbɔɪ] *n P* 1. rocker *m*/

rockeur *m* 2. homosexual* vêtu de cuir/cuir *m*.

leatherneck ['lɛðənek] *n NAm F* fusilier marin/marsouin *m*.

lech¹ [letʃ] *n P* 1. (= *lecher*) obsédé *m*/ débauché *m*/paillard *m*/cavaleur *m* 2. (*a*) (= *lechery*) paillardise *f*/lubricité *f* (*b*) désir ardent et obsédant.

lech² [letʃ] *vi P* to lech after/for/over/on s.o., en pincer pour qn/en mouiller pour qn.

lechy ['letʃɪ] *a Br P* lubrique/débauché.

leery ['lɪərɪ] *a F* 1. méfiant; to be leery of s.o., se méfier de qn/faire gaffe à qn 2. *Br* malin/démerde/marle 3. *Br* de mauvaise humeur/grognon.

leftfooter ['left'futə] *n P* catholique *mf*/ catho *mf*.

left-handed ['left'hændɪd] *a P* immoral.

left-hander ['left'hændə] *n F* gifle donnée de la main gauche.

lefty ['leftɪ] *n F* 1. (*left-handed person*) gaucher, -ère 2. (*of politically leftist views*) gauchiste *mf*/gaucho *mf*.

leg¹ [leg] *n* 1. *F* to show a leg, se lever/sortir du lit/(se) dépieuter/se dépagnoter/montrer le bout de son nez 2. *F* leg show, spectacle *m* de music-hall (*où les girls montrent leurs jambes*) 3. *F* to shake a leg (*a*) danser*/ gambiller (*b*) se dépêcher*/se grouiller 4. *F* he hasn't a leg to stand on, il n'a plus rien à dire/on lui a rivé son clou 5. *F* to pull s.o.'s leg, faire marcher qn/mettre qn en boîte/ monter un bateau à qn/mener qn en bateau. (*See* **leg-pull**) 6. *F* to give s.o. a leg up, (*over a wall, etc*) faire la courte échelle à qn; (*in job, etc*) dépanner qn/donner un coup d'épaule à qn 7. *F* to be on one's last legs (*a*) être très malade*/filer un mauvais coton/avoir un pied dans la tombe/battre de l'aile; my car's on its last legs, ma bagnole est pas loin de rendre l'âme/va pas tarder à rendre l'âme (*b*) être très fatigué*/être flagada/être au bout du rouleau/être pompé/être crevé 8. *F* to stretch one's legs, se dérouiller/se dégourdir les jambes 9. *P* third leg, pénis*/jambe *f* du milieu. (*See* **middle leg**) 10. *P* to get one's leg over/across, to be in a leg over position, (*of man*) faire l'amour*/s'envoyer en l'air/ prendre son pied 11. *F* legs eleven: *see* **bingo** 11. (*See* **donkey** 1; **open²**; **peg-leg**; **show¹** 1)

leg² [leg] *vtr F* to leg it, (*walk*) marcher*/ aller à pinces; (*hurry*) courir*/cavaler; (*leave, escape*) partir*/se cavaler/jouer des flûtes.

leggo! ['le'gəʊ] *excl F* (= *let go!*) lâche (tout)! bas les pattes!

legit [lɪ'dʒɪt] *a F* (= *legitimate*) vrai/authentique; **on the legit,** officiel/légal; **he's legit,** on peut lui faire confiance/il est réglo.

legless ['leglɪs] *a P* ivre*/dans le cirage/bourré comme un coing; **he was completely legless,** il était pété à mort.

legover ['legəʊvə] *n Br P* coït*/partie *f* de jambes en l'air. (*See* **leg¹ 10**)

leg-pull ['legpʊl] *n F* blague *f*/canular *m*/mise *f* en boîte. (*See* **leg¹ 5**)

legshake ['legʃeɪk] *n Austr P* legshake artist, voleur* à la tire/tireur, -euse/fourchette *f*.

legwork ['legwɜ:k] *n F* travail* actif/turbin *m*.

lemon ['lemən] *n* 1. *F* chose *f* sans valeur/à la noix; merdouille *f*; voiture*/bagnole *f* invendable; (*defective car*) mauvais numéro 2. *F* **to feel a (right) lemon,** se sentir un peu bête*/se sentir tout con; rester comme deux ronds de flan 3. *P* femme* laide/cageot *m*/mocheté *f*/remède *m* contre l'amour 4. *P* coup monté/doublage *m*/fumisterie *f* 5. *NAm P* (*not common*) pénis*/robinet *m* d'amour; **to squeeze the lemon,** uriner*/égoutter la sardine/faire pleurer le colosse; se masturber*/s'astiquer (la colonne) 6. *P* **to have a lemon squash,** (*RS = wash*) se laver 7. *pl P* seins*/nénés *mpl*/roberts *mpl*.

length [leŋ(k)θ] *n Br P* 1. pénis*/bout *m* 2. **to give/to slip a woman a length,** faire l'amour* avec une femme/glisser un bout à une femme. (*See* **wavelength**)

lerg(h)i ['lɜ:gɪ] *n Br P* = **lurg(h)i, lurgy.**

les, lez [lez] **I** *a P* (= *lesbian*) lesbienne/qui aime l'ail **II** *n P* (= *lesbian*) lesbienne*/gouine *f*/gougnotte *f*/gousse *f*.

lesbie ['lezbɪ], **lesbo** ['lezbəʊ], **lessie, lezzie** ['lezɪ], **lezo** ['lezəʊ] *n P* lesbienne*/gouine *f*/vrille *f*; **they're a couple of lesbies/lesbos,** c'est deux marchandes d'ail/c'est deux gouines.

letch [letʃ] *n & v P* = **lech¹,².**

letchy ['letʃɪ] *a Br P* = **lechy.**

let-down ['letdaʊn] *n F* déception *f*/déboire *m*.

let down ['let'daʊn] *vtr F* 1. décevoir (qn)/laisser (qn) en panne/laisser (qn) en rade/faire faux bond à (qn) 2. **to let s.o. down gently/lightly,** contrecarrer qn avec ménagement. (*See* **hair 2**)

let in on ['let'ɪnɒn] *vtr F* to let s.o. in on

sth, mettre qn dans le coup/mettre qn au parfum/rencarder qn.

let off ['let'ɒf] *vtr & i P* to let (one) off, péter*/cloquer/lâcher une fusée/lâcher une perle. (*See* **steam 1**)

let on ['let'ɒn] *vi F* 1. to let on (about sth) to s.o., mettre qn au courant/à la page; **don't let on!** motus!/bouche cousue! 2. faire semblant/frimer/chiquer.

let-out ['letaʊt] *n F* excuse *f*; let-out clause, échappatoire *f*.

lettuce ['letɪs] *n P* argent*/blé *m*/galette *f*; billets* (de banque)/fafiots *mpl*. (*See* **kale**)

letty ['letɪ] *n A P* lit*/plumard *m*.

let-up ['letʌp] *n F* with no let-up, sans arrêt/sans pause/sans relâche/sans débrider; **to work ten hours without a let-up,** travailler dix heures d'affilée; **there was no let-up in the rain,** la pluie ne s'arrêtait pas.

let up ['let'ʌp] *vi* 1. *F* cesser/diminuer/relâcher/ralentir; **he just doesn't let up talking,** il n'arrête pas/il n'en finit pas de jacasser 2. *P* to let up on s.o., ficher/foutre la paix à qn; oublier qn.

level¹ ['levl] **I** *a F* to do one's level best, faire de son mieux/en mettre un (vieux) coup/mettre le paquet. (*See* **pegging**) **II** *n F* on the level, honnête/régulier/réglo; **he's on the level,** c'est un mec réglo.

level² ['levl] *vi F* to level with s.o. (*a*) parler franchement à qn; **look, I'm going to level with you,** tenez, je vais être franc avec vous/je vais vous parler franchement (*b*) rendre la pareille/garder un chien de sa chienne.

lez [lez], **lezo** ['lezəʊ], **lezzie** ['lezɪ] *n P* = **les II.**

libber ['lɪbə] *n F* féministe *mf*.

lick¹ [lɪk] *n* 1. *F* we were going at (*a*) great lick/at full lick/at a fair old lick, on allait à pleins gaz/à toute blinde 2. *P* coup*/torgnole *f*/raclée *f* 3. *F* a lick and a promise, un bout/un brin de toilette; une toilette de chat. (*See* **catlick**).

lick² [lɪk] *vtr F* 1. venir à bout de (qch); surmonter (un problème, une difficulté, etc); **it's got me licked,** ça me dépasse 2. to lick s.o. (*a*) battre* qn/rosser qn/passer qn à tabac (*b*) vaincre/écraser qn; **to have s.o. licked,** réduire qn en poussière; **they had us licked,** ils nous ont battus à plate(s) couture(s) 3. to lick sth into shape, finir un travail/boucler une affaire; **to lick s.o. into shape,** former qn/dégrossir qn 4. to lick one's chops, s'en lécher les babines/se (pour)lécher les babines 5.

NAm P (drugs) fumer (du crack). *(See* **arse-lick**; **boot¹ 4**; **bootlick**; **dust¹ 5**; **pants 6**)

licketysplit ['lɪkətɪ'splɪt] *adv NAm F* très vite*/à pleins gaz/à fond de train.

licking ['lɪkɪŋ] *n F* to give s.o. a licking, *(beating)* donner une volée/une raclée à qn; *(to opponent)* vaincre/écraser/laminer qn; **they gave us a dreadful licking**, ils nous ont battus à plate(s) couture(s)/ils nous ont écrabouillés. *(See* **arse-licking**)

lid [lɪd] *n* **1.** *F (a)* chapeau*/galurin *m*/ casquette*/bâche *f*; **to dip one's lid**, soulever son feutre *(b)* casque *m* (militaire *ou* de moto) **2.** *F* **to take/to blow the lid off sth**, faire éclater un scandale **3.** *F* **to put the lid on sth**, tirer un voile sur qch; interdire qch/mettre le holà à qch; mettre qch au placard; **that puts the lid on it!** c'est le comble! **4.** *NAm P (drugs)* deux grammes *mpl* de marijuana* **5.** *F* capote *f* (d'une voiture). *(See* **dustbin**; **flip² 2**; **skidlid**; **tin I 1, 2**)

lie down ['laɪ'daʊn] *vi F (give up, surrender)* abandonner/laisser tomber.

lie-in ['laɪ'ɪn] *n F* to have a lie-in, faire la grasse (matinée).

life [laɪf] *n F* **1.** for the life of me I can't remember, j'ai beau chercher à me souvenir, je n'y arrive pas **2.** to worry the life out of s.o., tourmenter/asticoter qn; to frighten/to scare the life out of s.o., faire très peur* à qn; foutre les jetons/la trouille/les chocottes à qn **3.** he turned up the next day as large as life, il reparut le lendemain comme si de rien n'était; as large as life and twice as natural/ ugly, dans toute sa beauté/grandeur nature; *(person)* en chair et en os **4.** to see life, rouler sa bosse; en voir des vertes et des pas mûres/ être passé par là/en avoir vu de toutes les couleurs **5.** not on your life! pas de danger!/ rien à faire! **6.** to get life, être condamné* à perpétuité/être gerbé à perpète **7.** to get another life, repartir à zéro/recommencer à zéro/ refaire sa vie **8.** I couldn't do it to save my life, même si on me payait, je pourrais pas le faire **9.** *(a)* life begins: *see* **bingo 40** *(b)* life's begun: *see* **bingo 41**. *(See* **dog¹ 5, 17**; **Riley**; **sweet 2**)

lifer ['laɪfə] *n F (a)* condamné, -ée à perpétuité/ench(e)tibé, -ée à perpète *(b) (life sentence)* gerbement *m* à perpète.

lifesaver ['laɪfseɪvə] *n F* planche *f* de salut/ bouée *f* de sauvetage; that cup of coffee was a lifesaver, cette tasse de café m'a redonné vie; you're a lifesaver! tu me sauves la vie!

lift¹ [lɪft] *n F* to give s.o. a lift *(a)* raccompagner/emmener qn; prendre qn en (auto-)stop; can you give me a lift home? tu peux me raccompagner/ramener chez moi (en voiture)? *(b)* remonter le moral à qn.

lift² [lɪft] *vtr F* **1.** voler*/faucher/piquer; he had his wallet lifted, il s'est fait piquer son portefeuille **2.** plagier (un auteur/un livre) **3.** arrêter*/embarquer/pincer (qn) **4.** to lift a glass, boire*/sécher un verre; lever le coude. *(See* **elbow¹ 3**)

lifter ['lɪftə] *n F* voleur*/faucheur *m*. *(See* **shirt-lifter**)

lig [lɪg] *vi Br P* écornifler/parasiter/vivre aux crochets de qn.

ligger ['lɪgə] *n Br P (gatecrasher)* resquilleur, -euse.

light [laɪt] **I** *a F* to be light of sth, avoir qch qui manque; to be (very) light, être à court d'argent*/dans la dèche/sans un **II** *n* **1.** *F* to be out like a light, *(unconscious from drink, drugs or exhaustion)* être dans les vapes/en pleine vape; to go out like a light, s'évanouir*; tomber dans les pommes/dans les vapes/dans le cirage; *(fall asleep)* s'endormir/s'enroupiller aussitôt couché; tourner de l'œil; ...and then the lights went out, ...et puis je me suis évanoui*/j'ai tourné de l'œil **2.** *pl P* yeux*/lanternes *fpl*/clignotants *mpl* **3.** *F* to see the red light *(flashing)*, flairer le danger/voir le voyant passer au rouge **4.** *F* the light of my life, *(RS = wife)* épouse*; *(sweetheart)* bien-aimé(e)/ chéri(e). *(See* **green I 3**; **headlights**; **red-light**; **strike 1**)

lighten ['laɪtn'ʌp] *vi F (relax)* se détendre; *(cheer up)* se dérider; come on, lighten up! allez, rigole un peu!

light-fingered ['laɪt'fɪŋgəd] *a P* qui vole avec facilité/klepto.

light into ['laɪt'ɪntuː] *vtr F* to light into s.o. *(a)* attaquer* qn/tomber (à bras raccourcis) sur qn/agrafer qn *(b)* réprimander* sévèrement/enguirlander/engueuler qn.

lightning ['laɪtnɪŋ] *n F* like (greased) lightning, très vite*/à plein(s) tube(s)/en quatrième vitesse.

lightweight ['laɪtweɪt] *n F* individu* qui ne fait pas le poids/minus *m*/demi-portion *f*.

like¹ [laɪk] **I** *adv* **1.** *P* comme qui dirait; you're one of the family, like, vous êtes comme qui dirait de la famille; he looked angry like, il était comme en colère; he just came up behind me, like, il est venu juste derrière moi, comme ça 2. *F* very like/(as) like as not/like enough, probablement/vraisemblablement II *conj F* 1. (= *as if*) he treated me like I was dirt/a piece of shit, il m'a traité comme si j'étais de la crotte/de la merde; seems like it works, on dirait que ça marche 2. (= *as*) like I said, comme je l'ai (si bien) dit III *n F* the likes of us, des (gens) comme nous/nos semblables/nos pareils.

like² [laɪk] *vtr F* (well,) I like that! elle est bien bonne, celle-là!/en voilà une bonne!/ça par exemple!

likely ['laɪklɪ] *a F* 1. a likely lad, (*fun-loving*) un joyeux gaillard/un joyeux drille/un gai luron; (*promising*) un gars/un mec qui promet 2. (as) likely as not, il y a beaucoup de chance (que...); sans doute 3. not likely! pas de danger!/jamais de la vie! (*See* **bloody II**)

lily ['lɪlɪ] *n NAm P* 1. (*effeminate man*) gâcheuse *f* 2. homosexuel*/tapette *f*.

lily-livered ['lɪlɪlɪvəd] *a F* lâche; froussard/trouillard/foireux.

lily-white ['lɪlɪwaɪt] *a F* blanc(he) comme neige; she's not so lily-white! ce n'est pas un prix de vertu!

limb [lɪm] *n F* out on a limb, (*alone*) en plan; (*in danger*) sur la corde raide.

limey ['laɪmɪ] *n esp NAm P* 1. Anglais, -aise/angliche *mf*/rosbif *mf* 2. *O* matelot *m* anglliche.

limit ['lɪmɪt] *n* 1. *F* that's the limit! c'est le comble!/c'est le bouquet! she's the absolute limit! elle est impossible/chiante! 2. to go the limit (*a*) *F* y aller à fond/mettre le paquet (*b*) *P* (*of girl, woman*) se laisser séduire/céder/lever la jambe 3. *F* the sky's the limit, y a rien d'impossible/tout est possible.

limo ['lɪməʊ] *n F Aut* limousine *f*; stretch limo, limousine super-longue.

limp-wristed ['lɪmp'rɪstɪd] *a F* efféminé; de pédale; he's limp-wristed, il fait tapette/il est pédale.

line¹ [laɪn] *n* 1. *F* what's your line (of business)? quel est votre métier?/vous faites dans quoi? that's not in my line/that's not my line (of country), ce n'est pas mon rayon; that's more in his line, c'est plus dans son genre/dans ses cordes/dans son style; something in that line, quelque chose dans ce genre-là/ce goût-là; all in the line of duty! ça fait partie du boulot! 2. *F* renseignement*/tuyau *m*/rencard *m*; to get a line on sth, reconnaître*/retapisser qch; to get a line on s.o., se rensei-

gner* sur qn/se rencarder sur qn 3. *F* to win all along the line, gagner sur toute la ligne 4. *F* to toe the line, rentrer dans les rangs/marcher au pas 5. *F* to read between the lines, lire entre les lignes 6. *F* to put it on the line, dire en toutes lettres/ne pas mâcher les mots 7. *F* to be out of line, être rebelle/se distinguer; you're way out of line! tu es complètement à côté de la plaque! 8. *F* to come to the end of the line, mourir*/lâcher la rampe 9. *P* (*drugs*) (dose *f* de) cocaïne* à priser/ligne *f*; to do a line, sniffer une ligne. (*See* **drop² 7; hard I 3; headlines; hook¹ 4; main-line¹; pipeline; punch-line; shoot² 4; sweet 3; toot²**)

line² [laɪn] *vi P* (*drugs*) to line (up, out), sniffer de la cocaïne/des lignes.

linen ['lɪnɪn] *n* 1. *F* to wash one's dirty linen in public, laver son linge sale en public 2. *P* linen (draper), (*RS = newspaper*) journal*/canard *m*.

line-shooter ['laɪnʃuːtə] *n F* vantard*/esbroufeur, -euse/baratineur, -euse. (*See* **shoot² 4**)

line-shooting ['laɪnʃuːtɪŋ] *n F* rambin *m*/esbrouf(f)e *f*/baratin *m*. (*See* **shoot² 4**)

lingam ['lɪŋgəm] *n F* pénis*/chibre *m*.

lingo ['lɪŋgəʊ] *n* 1. *F* langue étrangère/baragouin *m*; I shall never get the hang of their lingo, je n'arriverai jamais à parler ce baragouin 2. *P* argot*; to shoot/to sling the lingo, parler l'argot*/dévider le jar(s).

lip [lɪp] *n* 1. *P* effronterie *f*; don't give me/I don't want any of your lip! ne te fiche pas de moi!/ne te paye pas ma tête!/ne la ramène pas! 2. *F* to keep a stiff upper lip, ne pas broncher/garder son courage et faire contre mauvaise fortune bon cœur/serrer les dents. (*See* **flip² 3**)

lippy ['lɪpɪ] I *a P* 1. effronté/culotté/gonflé 2. bavard*/jacasseur II *n F* rouge *m* à lèvres.

lip service ['lɪp'sɜːvɪs] *n V Euph* fellation*.

liquidate ['lɪkwɪdeɪt] *vtr F* tuer*/liquider/effacer.

liquidator ['lɪkwɪdeɪtə] *n esp NAm P* 1. assassin*/tueur *m* à gages/buteur *m* 2. revolver*/flingue *m*/pétard *m*.

liquid lunch ['lɪkwɪd'lʌntʃ] *n F* (*drinking session*) beuverie *f* (*surt à l'heure du déjeuner*).

liquored out, up ['lɪkədaʊt, -'ʌp] *a & pp NAm F* ivre*/cuité/bit(t)uré.

liquorice ['lɪkərɪs] *n P* liquorice stick, clarinette *f*/pibouic *m*/poireau *m*.

lit [lɪt] *a & pp F* légèrement ivre*/éméché; well lit, très ivre*/noir/bourré. (*See* **lit up**)

litterbug ['lɪtəbʌg], **litter-lout** ['lɪtəlaʊt] *n F* qn qui jette des ordures n'importe où/ cochon *m*.

little ['lɪtl] *a* 1. *F* the little woman, mon épouse*/ma bourgeoise 2. *V* little man in a boat, clitoris*/grain *m* de café. (*See* **room 1**)

lit up ['lɪt'ʌp] *a* ivre*/noir/bourré.

live-in lover ['lɪvɪn'lʌvə] *n F* (*unmarried partner*) concubin, -ine.

live it up ['lɪvɪt'ʌp] *vi F* faire la noce/mener une vie de bâton de chaise/faire les quatre cents coups/s'en payer une tranche.

lively ['laɪvlɪ] *a F* look lively (about it)! et que ça saute!/mets-y de l'entrain!/grouille-toi!

liver ['lɪvə] *n F* to have a liver (*a*) être malade* du foie (*b*) être de mauvaise humeur/d'humeur massacrante; être en ro-gne.

liverish ['lɪvərɪʃ] *a F* to feel liverish, avoir une crise de foie.

lizard ['lɪzəd] *n* 1. *NAm P* pénis*/frétillard *m*; to flog/stroke the lizard, se masturber*/ s'astiquer le manche 2. *pl* chaussures* en peau de serpent/en peau de crocodile.

Lizzie ['lɪzɪ] *n O F* (tin) Lizzie, vieille voiture*/tinette *f*.

load [ləʊd] *n* 1. *P* get a load of that! (*listen to this!*) écoute-moi ça!/écoute un peu ça! (*look at this!*) vise-moi ça!/mate-moi ça!/ zyeute-moi ça! 2. *P* a load of baloney/balls/ cobblers/cock/codswallop/crap, un tas de foutaises *fpl*/de conneries *fpl*; you do talk a load of balls at times, ce que tu peux déconner/débloquer des fois. (*See* **muck 2**) 3. *P* to drop one's load, déféquer*/défarguer/ couler un bronze 4. *P* stock illégal de drogues/charge *f* 5. *F* loads of..., une abondance* de.../un paquet de.../une flopée de.../une tapée de... 6. *F* take the load off your feet! assieds-toi!/pose tes fesses!/pose un cul! 7. *F* he's a load of wind, il parle pour ne rien dire/il la ramène pour pas grand-chose 8. *P* sperme*/jus *m*; to shoot one's load, éjaculer*/ envoyer la purée/lâcher sa came 9. *Austr P* maladie* vénérienne/laziloffe *m*.

loaded ['ləʊdɪd] *a* 1. *F* riche*/plein aux as; to be loaded, être plein aux as/avoir le sac/en avoir plein les poches 2. *P* ivre*/beurré/ bourré; drogué*/chargé/défoncé.

loadsamoney ['ləʊdzə'mʌnɪ] *n Br F* (*a*) richesse excessive (*b*) individu* qui affiche/ fait parade de sa richesse; individu* ri-chissime.

loaf [ləʊf] *n Br F* (*RS = loaf of bread = head*) tête*/caboche *f*; use your loaf! fais travailler tes méninges!

lob¹ [lɒb] *n P* pénis*/zob *m*.

lob² [lɒb] *vtr P* 1. jeter*/balancer/ficher en l'air 2. *Austr* to lob somewhere, arriver*/ s'abouler/débouler quelque part; to lob back, revenir/rabouler/(se) radiner.

local ['ləʊkəl] *n F* café* de quartier/bistrot *m* du coin/troquet *m*.

lock-up ['lɒkʌp] *n F* (*a*) prison*/taule *f* (*b*) (*prison cell*) mitard *m*/cellotte *f*.

lock up ['lɒk'ʌp] *vtr F* emprisonner*; met-tre au mitard.

loco ['ləʊkəʊ] *a F* fou*/maboul/dingo.

locoweed ['ləʊkəʊ'wiːd] *n P* (*drugs*) cannabis*/herbe *f*.

lofty ['lɒftɪ] *n F* 1. individu* grand/grande perche/asperge montée 2. *Iron* petit* individu/bas-du-cul *m*.

loid [lɔɪd] *vi P* forcer une porte en faisant passer un morceau de celluloïd/de plastique entre la porte et le chambranle pour dé-bloquer la serrure.

lollie ['lɒlɪ] *n F* = **lolly¹ 4**.

lollipop ['lɒlɪpɒp] *vtr Br P* dénoncer*/ vendre (qn).

lollipop-man, -lady ['lɒlɪpɒp'mæn, -'leɪdɪ] *n F* contractuel(le) qui fait traverser la rue aux enfants aux sorties d'école.

lollop ['lɒləp] *vi F* 1. marcher* lourdement/ comme un éléphant 2. sauter/rebondir/faire des sauts de carpe 3. to lollop around, paresser*/tirer sa flemme.

lolly¹ ['lɒlɪ] *n* 1. *F* argent*/fric *m*/flouze *m*; lay off the lolly! touchez pas au grisbi! 2. *Austr P* un timide/un tiède/un frileux 3. *Austr P* to do the/one's lolly, se mettre en colère/se fâcher 4. *F* (= *lollipop*) sucette *f*; ice(d) lolly, sucette glacée.

lolly² ['lɒlɪ] *vtr Br P* = **lollipop**.

loner ['ləʊnə] *n F* personne *f* qui fait bande à part/qui fait cavalier seul; solitaire *mf*.

lonesome ['ləʊnsəm] *n F* (all) on one's lonesome, tout seul/seulabre/seulingue. (*See* **ownsome**)

long green [lɒŋ'griːn] *n NAm F* argent*/ flouze *m*.

long-tailed ['lɒŋteɪld] *a O P* long-tailed 'uns, billets* de banque.

loo [luː] *n F* WC*/waters *mpl*/gogues *mpl*/ chiottes *fpl*; he's gone to the loo, il est allé au petit coin; loo paper, papier-cul *m*/pécu *m*.

look¹ [lʊk] *n F* to take a long, hard look at sth, examiner qch sur toutes les coutures.

look² [lʊk] *vi F* 1. to look like a million (dollars), être très élégant*/très chic; jeter du jus 2. here's looking at you! à la tienne!/à la bonne vôtre! 3. look here! dis donc! (*See* **nose 7**)

looker ['lʊkə] *n F* belle fille*/beau brin de fille/prix *m* de Diane/joli lot; he's a looker, il est beau mec.

look-in ['lʊk'ɪn] *n F* 1. belle occasion/beau jeu 2. chances *fpl* de succès; he won't get a look-in, il n'a pas la moindre chance 3. coup *m* d'œil rapide/coup de sabord 4. visite-éclair *f*; to give s.o. a look-in, faire un saut chez qn.

lookout ['lʊkaʊt] *n F* 1. guetteur *m*/gaffeur *m* 2. that's your lookout! c'est ton affaire!/tes oignons!/ton truc!/ton problème!

look-see ['lʊk'si:] *n F* coup *m* d'œil*/coup de sabord; let's have a look-see, jetons un coup d'œil/regardons ça un peu.

look up ['lʊk'ʌp] *vi F* business is looking up, les affaires reprennent; things are looking up with him, ses affaires s'améliorent/ses actions remontent.

loon¹ [lu:n] *n F* individu* fou*/fada *mf*/barjot *m*.

loon² [lu:n] *vi F* to loon (about), faire le fou*/le zouave.

loonie ['lu:nɪ] *n Can F* pièce *f* d'un dollar.

loony ['lu:nɪ] *F* I *a* fou*/toqué/cinglé; he's completely loony, il travaille du chapeau/il a perdu la boule/il est complètement siphonné II *n* cinglé(e) *m(f)*/dingue *mf*; are you a complete loony, or what? ça (ne) va pas la tête?/t'es fou ou quoi?/t'es complètement siphonné?

loony-bin ['lu:nɪbɪn] *n P* maison *f* de fous/asile *m* de dingues; to be fit for the loony-bin, être bon/mûr pour Sainte-Anne/pour Charenton.

loony-tune(s) ['lu:nɪtju:n(z)] *a & n* (individu*) fou*/timbré/toqué.

looped [lu:pt] *a NAm P* ivre*/plein/rond; looped to the eyeballs, plein comme une bourrique.

loop-the-loop ['lu:pðə'lu:p] *n P* 1. (*RS = soup*) soupe *f*/rata *m* 2. (*mutual oral sex between two people*) soixante-neuf/69.

loopy ['lu:pɪ] *a F* fou*/dingo/tapé/cinglé/maboul; to go completely loopy, perdre la boule/travailler du chapeau.

loose [lu:s] *F* I *a* détendu/relaxe/cool II *n* to be (out) on the loose, (*be out of control*) être

déchaîné/faire les quatre cents coups; (*lead a fast life*) être en bordée/en virée; mener une vie de bâton de chaise.

loosen up ['lu:sn'ʌp] *vi F* se détendre/se relaxer.

loot [lu:t] *n P* (*a*) argent*/artiche *m*/flouse *m*/pognon *m*/fric *m* (*b*) bénéfice* financier/bénef *m*/gratte *f* (*c*) butin*/fade *m*/taf(fe) *m*.

lorry ['lɒrɪ] *n Euph F* it fell off the back of a lorry, c'est volé/fauché; c'est de l'acheté au prix courant.

lorry-hop ['lɒrɪhɒp] *vi F* faire de l'auto-stop *m* (dans les camions)/faire du pouce aux routiers.

lose [lu:z] *vtr* 1. *P* get lost! va te faire fiche!/va te faire foutre!/va te faire voir!/au bout du quai les ballots! 2. *F* you've lost me! je n'y suis plus/j'ai perdu le fil.

lose out ['lu:z'aʊt] *vi F* perdre/paumer; être perdant.

loud [laʊd] *adv F* for crying out loud! (sacré) nom d'un chien!/nom de nom!

loudmouth ['laʊdmaʊθ] *n F Pej* gueulard, -arde/grande gueule.

loudmouthed ['laʊdmaʊðd] *a F* gueulard/fort en gueule.

louse [laʊs] *n F* vaurien*/saligaud *m*/salope *f*; what a louse! (quelle) peau de vache!

louse up ['laʊs'ʌp] *vtr P* bousiller/gâcher/saloper/louper; I've gone and loused it up again, j'ai encore mis les pieds dans le plat/j'ai tout foutu en l'air/j'y ai refoutu le merdier.

lousy ['laʊzɪ] *a* 1. *F* mauvais*/moche; miteux/pouilleux; lousy weather, temps pourri/dégueulasse; a lousy film, un film merdique/à la con; to feel/to look lousy, être mal fichu/n'avoir pas la frite; to play a lousy trick on s.o., jouer un sale tour/jouer un tour de cochon/faire une vacherie à qn 2. *P* lousy with..., plein de...; the place was lousy with cops, ça grouillait de flics 3. *F* I'm lousy at it, je suis nul/zéro; j'en touche pas une.

love [lʌv] *n F* 1. hello, love! salut! thanks love! merci mon pote!/merci chéri(e)!/merci (mon) coco! 2. for the love of Mike! pour l'amour du ciel! (*See* **bug¹ 6**)

lovebird ['lʌvbɜ:d] *n F* amoureux *m*/amoureuse *f*; young lovebirds, des tourtereaux *mpl*.

love-in ['lʌvɪn] *n O F* festival *m* hippie.

love lumps ['lʌvlʌmps] *npl Br F* seins*/nénés *mpl*.

lover-boy ['lʌvəbɔɪ] *n F* 1. beau* gars/

Adonis *m*/Apollon *m*/jeune premier 2. un don
Juan/coureur *m* de jupons/cavaleur *m*/
tombeur *m* de filles/dragueur *m*.

love juice ['lʌvdʒuːs] *n* V sperme*/jute *m*.

love-weed ['lʌvwiːd] *n* P (*drugs*)
marijuana*/herbe douce.

lovey ['lʌvɪ] *n* F chéri(e)/petit chou/petit
cœur.

lovey-dovey ['lʌvɪ'dʌvɪ] *a* F 1. (*loving*)
(trop) affectueux/amoureux; **to be all lovey-
dovey**, être comme des tourtereaux 2.
(*sentimental*) à la guimauve/à l'eau de rose.

low [ləʊ] *n* F 1. **to be on a low**, avoir la
déprime/broyer du noir 2. (*drugs*) déprime
due à la drogue/flip *m*; mauvaise réaction à
une drogue; **to be on a low**, redescendre;
flipper.

lowbrow ['ləʊbraʊ] I *a* F sans prétentions
intellectuelles/terre à terre II *n* F (*a*)
prolétaire *mf*/prolo *mf*/inculte *mf* (*b*) qn qui
ne s'intéresse pas aux choses intellectuelles/
individu* peu intellectuel.

low-budget [ləʊ'bʌdʒɪt] *a Br* F sordide/
dégueulasse/débectant; **a low-budget restaurant**, un boui-boui.

lowdown¹ ['ləʊ'daʊn] I *a* F méprisable/
moche/dégueulasse; **a lowdown trick**, un sale
tour/une vacherie/un coup rosse II *n* 1. F
renseignements*; **to get the lowdown on s.o.**,
se tuyauter/se rencarder sur qch; **he gave
him the lowdown on it**, il l'a tuyauté/il l'a mis
au parfum/il l'a mis au courant 2. P (*mean
trick*) tour *m* de cochon/coup rosse/sale coup.

low-heel ['ləʊhiːl] *n Austr* P prostituée*/
femme* de trottoir.

low-rent [ləʊ'rent] *a NAm* F = **low-
budget**.

lube [luːb] *n P Aut* lube (job), graissage *m*.

lubricate ['luːbrɪkeɪt] *vtr* F enivrer/soûler
(qn).

lubrication [luːbrɪ'keɪʃ(ə)n] *n* F alcool*/
gnôle *f*.

luck [lʌk] *n* F 1. **you never know your luck**,
on ne sait jamais ce qui vous pend au nez 2.
no such luck! ç'aurait été trop beau!/tu
parles, Charles!/et ben, penses-tu! (*See* **pot-
luck**; **push²** 2)

lucre ['luːkə] *n* F argent*/flouse *m*;
bénéfice*/bénef *m*; **filthy lucre**, (*profit*) gain
m/gratte *f*; (*money, resources*) argent*/
carbure *m*; **to do sth for filthy lucre**, faire qch
rien que pour le fric.

lucy, Lucy ['luːsɪ] *n* 1. *NAm* P sweet lucy,
vin*/pinard *m* 2. *Br* P **Lucy locket**, (*RS* = po-

cket) poche*/fouille *f*.

lug¹ [lʌg] *n P* 1. (*a*) oreille*/cage *f* à miel.
(*See* **lug(h)oles**) (*b*) *NAm* visage*; gueule *f*
(*c*) *pl NAm* mains*/paluches *fpl* 2. (*a*)
homme*/mec *m* (*b*) (*thick-headed*) ballot *m* 3.
NAm (*a*) demande *f* d'argent*/coup *m* de
botte (*b*) (*bribe*) dessous-de-table *m*/gratte *f*/
tour *m* de bâton.

lug² [lʌg] *vtr Austr P* **to lug s.o. for money**,
emprunter* de l'argent à qn/taper qn/bottiner
qn.

lughead ['lʌghed] *n* P individu bête*/ballot
m/cruche *f*.

lug(h)oles ['lʌg(h)əʊlz] *npl Br* P oreilles*/
esgourdes *fpl*; **pin back your lug(h)oles!** ou-
vre tes portugaises!/écarquille tes esgourdes!
(*See* **lug¹** 1 (*a*))

lulu ['luːluː] *n* F (*a*) belle fille*/beau brin de
fille/joli lot (*b*) qch de sensass/de super (*c*) *Br*
= **loo**.

lumber¹ ['lʌmbə] *n Br* P **to be in lumber**, (*in
trouble*) être dans le pétrin/dans de beaux
draps.

lumber² ['lʌmbə] *vtr & i Br* 1. P arrêter*/
agrafer/épingler; **to get lumbered**, se faire
agrafer/alpaguer 2. F **to get lumbered with**
s.o./sth, être chargé/encombré de qn/de qch; **I
got lumbered with the washing up**, je me suis
tapé/je me suis farci/j'ai dû me coltiner la
vaisselle.

lumme! ['lʌmɪ] *excl* F nom de Dieu!/mince
alors!

lummox ['lʌməks] *n* P individu bête*/
cornichon *m*/niguedouille *m*.

lummy! ['lʌmɪ] *excl* F = **lumme!**

lump¹ [lʌmp] *n* F 1. individu bête*/crétin,
-ine/cruche *f*; **you great lump!** espèce
d'empoté! 2. **a big lump of a girl**, une grosse
dondon.

lump² [lʌmp] *vtr Br* F **like it or lump it**, que
ça plaise ou non, c'est le même prix; **you'll
have to lump it**, il faudra l'avaler/il faut
passer par là.

lunchbox ['lʌntʃbɒks] *n Euph* F estomac*/
boîte *f* à ragoût/tiroir *m* (à poulet).

lungs [lʌŋs] *npl* P seins*/rotoplots *mpl*/
doudounes *fpl*; **she's got huge lungs**, il y a du
monde au balcon.

lunk(head) ['lʌŋk(hed)] *n NAm* P = **lughead**.

lurg(h)i, lurgy ['lɜːgɪ] *n Br* F **the dreaded
lurgy**, (*mysterious illnes*) la crève; **he's got
the lurgy**, il a attrapé/chopé la crève.

lurker ['lɜːkə] *n* 1. *Br* P individu* suspect/

louche; (*disreputable*) loubard *m*/loulou *m* **2.** *Austr F* (*petty criminal, fraudster*) faisan(t) *m*/faisandier *m*.

lush¹ [lʌʃ] **I** *a Br F* (*attractive, desirable*) chouette/badour; (*delicious*) délicieux/super bon; **she's a lush piece**, c'est un beau brin de fille/un beau morceau/un joli lot **II** *n esp NAm F* **1.** ivrogne*/poivrot, -ote/soûlard, -arde **2.** soûlerie *f*/bringue *f* **3.** alcool*/gnôle *f*.

lush² [lʌʃ] *vi NAm F* boire* de l'alcool*/ biberonner/siffler/picoler.

lushed [lʌʃt] *a P* ivre*/rond/cuit.

lush-roller ['lʌʃrəʊlə] *n P* voleur* d'ivrognes/(voleur au) poivrier *m*.

lush-rolling ['lʌʃrəʊlɪŋ] *n NAm P* vol *m* au poivrier.

lush up ['lʌʃ'ʌp] *vi F* se soûler/se charger/ se beurrer.

luv [lʌv] *n F* = **love 1**.

luvvie, luvvy ['lʌvɪ] *n F* acteur *m*/actrice *f*.

M

M [em] *abbr* P (*drugs*) morphine*.
ma [mɑː] *n* F mère*/m'man *f*.
Ma Bell ['mɑːˈbel] *n* NAm F (surnom de la) *Bell Telephone Company*; = les Télécoms *fpl*.
mac¹ [mæk] *n* (*abbr of mackintosh*) F imper(méable) *m*; **the dirty mac brigade**, les voyeurs *mpl*; les (vieux) cochons *mpl*; les exhibitionnistes *mpl*.
Mac, mac² [mæk] *n* 1. F Écossais *m* 2. P individu*/mec *m*/gonze *m*. (*See* **mack¹ 3**)
macaroni [mækəˈrəʊnɪ] *n* 1. P Italien*/ macaroni *mf*/Rital, -ale 2. F fil *m*/câble *m* (*surt* électrique) 3. P (*prisons*) excrément *m*/ merde *f*.
machine [məˈʃiːn] *n* P motocyclette *f*/moto *f*/essoreuse.
machine gun [məˈʃiːngʌn] *n* P (*drugs*) seringue *f* hypodermique/shooteuse *f*.
machismo [mætˈkɪzməʊ] *n* F machisme *m*.
macho ['mætʃəʊ] F **I** *a* macho/ phallo(crate); *Iron* **he's terribly macho**, c'est un petit/sale macho **II** *n* macho *m*/ phallo(crate) *m*.
mack¹ [mæk] *n* 1. F = **mac¹** 2. P **Mack (Daddy)**, souteneur*/maquereau *m*/mac *m* 3. P mec *m*/zigoto *m*/gonze *m*.
mack² [mæk] *vi* P rabattre le client (pour une prostituée*)/maquereauter.
Mackay [məˈkaɪ] *n* F = **McCoy**.
mackerel ['mækərəl] *n* P = **mack¹ 2**. (*See* **holy 1**)
mackman ['mækmən] *n* P = **mack¹ 2**.
mad [mæd] **I** *a* F 1. *esp* NAm en colère*; **to be mad at s.o.**, être à cran contre qn/être remonté contre qn 2. **to be mad about s.o./sth**, être fou de qn/raffoler de qch; être dingue de qn/qch; **he's mad about her**, il est fou d'elle/il en pince sec pour elle 3. **like mad** (*a*) comme un enragé/un perdu/un paumé; **to shout like mad**, crier comme un dingue/un sourd (*b*) très vite*; **to run like mad**, foncer/gazer/ courir comme un dératé. (*See* **man-mad**; **sex-mad**; **woman-mad**) **II** *adv* F mad

keen on sth/s.o., emballé par qch/qn.
madam¹ ['mædəm] *n* 1. P (*rare*) **don't come the old madam with me!** ne monte pas sur tes grands chevaux!/(ne) la ramène pas!/pas la peine de jouer à la madame avec moi! 2. F patronne* (de maison de prostitution)/ madame *f*/taulière *f*/maquerelle *f*.
madam² ['mædəm] *vi* A P 1. mentir*/ raconter des craques 2. (*spin a tale*) faire du baratin.
madame [mæˈdɑːm] *n* F **madam¹**.
madhouse ['mædhaʊs] *n* F maison *f* de fous/Charenton; **this place is like a madhouse**, on se croirait à Charenton/à Sainte-Anne/chez les fous.
mag [mæg] *n* (F *abbr of magazine*) magazine *m*/revue *f*; **porny/porno mag**, revue porno/de cul.
maggot ['mægət] *n* P individu* méprisable/ loquedu *m*/ordure *f*.
magic ['mædʒɪk] *a* Br P excellent*/super/ sensass; **magic!** sensass!/super!/le pied!/ formid(able)! **he's really magic, isn't he?** il est super, non?
main line¹ ['meɪnˈlaɪn] *n* P (*drugs*) veine apparente (*pour piqûre intraveineuse*).
mainline² ['meɪnˈlaɪn] *vi* P se faire une injection intraveineuse/se piquer/se piquouser/se shooter/se faire un fixe.
mainliner ['meɪnˈlaɪnə] *n* P drogué* qui se fait des piqûres intraveineuses/piquouseur *m*/ junkie *mf*.
mainman ['meɪnˈmæn] *n* NAm P 1. patron*/chef *m*/boss *m* 2. (*boyfriend, partner*) copain *m*/petit ami 3. (*friend*) copain *m*/pote *m*.
mainstream ['meɪnstriːm] *a* F **it's main-stream**, c'est normal.
make¹ [meɪk] *n* 1. P **easy make**, femme* facile/à la cuisse hospitalière. (*See* **lay¹ 1**) 2. **on the make** (*a*) F âpre au gain/chercheur d'affure; **he's on the make**, il cherche à se faire des petits à-côtés (*b*) P en quête

d'aventures amoureuses/dragueur; he's always on the make, c'est un dragueur/un chaud lapin 3. *NAm P* to get a make on a criminal, identifier/détrancher/tapisser un criminel; we got a make on the stolen car, on a repéré la bagnole volée.

make² [meɪk] *vtr* 1. (*a*) *F* to make it, réussir/cartonner; he's made it, il se la fait belle (*b*) *P* to make (it with) a woman, lever une femme*; he's always trying to make (it with) some chick or other, il est sans arrêt en train de chercher à s'envoyer une nana; they make it two or three times a week, ils font l'amour*/ils baisent deux ou trois fois par semaine 2. *F* he's as sharp as they make 'em, pour un malin, c'est un malin 3. *F* (*earn money*) gagner*; how much do you make? qu'est-ce que/combien tu te fais? 4. *P* voler*/faire/fabriquer (qch) 5. *P* = to get a make on (**make¹** 3) 6. *P* comprendre/piger/entraver (qn/qch) 7. *F* arriver* à/débarquer à (un endroit) 8. *F* do you want to make sth (out) of it? (*do you want to make a fuss?*) tu cherches des histoires, ou quoi?/tu vas pas en faire (tout un) un plat, non? 9. *F* to have it made, se la couler douce/avoir le filon 10. *F* I just made my train, j'ai eu mon train mais ça a été moins une 11. *P* (*drugs*) to make a connection, se ravitailler en drogue; to make speed, obtenir du speed. (*See* **daft I 1**; **side 1**)

make like ['meɪk'laɪk] *vi esp NAm F* faire semblant; make like you're sick, fais comme si tu étais malade.

make out ['meɪk'aʊt] *vi* 1. *F* prospérer/faire des progrès; aller/marcher (bien *ou* mal); how do your children make out at school? comment ça marche/va (pour) vos enfants à l'école? we're making out, on se débrouille/on fait aller 2. *F* subsister; I can make out on bread and water, je peux vivre de pain et d'eau; he earns enough to make out, il se débrouille avec ce qu'il gagne 3. *F* faire semblant/chiquer 4. *NAm P* s'étreindre/s'enlacer passionnément/se peloter 5. *NAm P* to make out with a girl, (*show an interest in*) faire une touche (avec une nana); (*make love to*) se faire/s'envoyer une nana.

make up ['meɪk'ʌp] *vi F* to make up to s.o., (*flatter*) flatter qn/lécher les bottes à qn; (*flirt*) faire des avances *fpl* à qn/flirter avec qn/draguer qn.

malark(e)y [mə'lɑːkɪ] *n F* 1. flatteries *fpl*/boniment *m*/baratin *m* 2. (*nonsense*)

balivernes *fpl*; a lot of malarkey, du pipeau.

mallee ['mælɪː] *n Austr F* to take to the mallee, prendre le maquis.

mam(m)a ['mæmə] *n esp NAm P* 1. fille*/femme*/nana *f*/poupée *f*/chouquette *f*/gonzesse *f*. (*See* **red-hot 1** (*b*)) 2. lesbienne*/gouine *f*.

mammie, mammy ['mæmɪ] *n NAm F* 1. mère*/maman *f* 2. nourrice/nounou noire 3. mammy boy, homme *m* faible/femmelette *f*/chiffe molle.

man [mæn] *n* 1. *F* (why) man, you're crazy! mais mon pauvre vieux, tu es fou*/tu dérailles! 2. *F* he's a big man, (*important*) c'est quelqu'un; (*well-endowed*) il est bien équipé/membré 3. *F* her man, son mari/son homme*/son mec 4. *O F* my young man, (*boyfriend*) mon copain; (*fiancé*) mon futur/mon fiancé 5. *NAm P* the man/the Man (*a*) la police*/ces Messieurs *mpl* (*b*) champion *m* de sport/chanteur *m* de pop, etc (*c*) (*drugs*) fourgueur *m*/dealer *m*; to make the man, acheter des drogues/brancher; to be waiting for the man, (*have withdrawal symptoms*) être en manque/avoir la guenon (*d*) patron*/dab *m*/chef *m*. (*See* **ad-man**; **boss-man**; **busman**; **caveman**; **chiv(e)-man**; **dead I 3, 8**; **dog¹ 14**; **G-man**; **he-man**; **iceman**; **lollipop-man**; **mackman**; **mainman**; **middleman**; **muscle-man**; **old 1, 2**; **one-man**; **penman**; **peterman**; **rod-man**; **sandman**; **screwsman**; **show-man**; **sideman**; **spiderman**; **swagman**; **swordsman**; **tail-man**; **trigger-man**; **yes-man**)

manage ['mænɪdʒ] *vtr F* can you manage a bit more? vous avez bien encore une petite place? I couldn't manage another drop, je ne pourrais plus avaler une seule goutte.

Manc [mæŋk] *a & n Br F* (*abbr of Mancunian*) (habitant, -ante *ou* originaire *mf*) de Manchester.

man-crazy ['mæn'kreɪzɪ] *a F* = **man-mad**. (*See* **woman-crazy**)

mandy ['mændɪ] *n Br P* (*drugs*) cachet *m* de Mandrax (*RTM*) (*somnifère*).

manhole ['mænhəʊl] *n V* sexe de la femme*/fente *f*/con *m*.

manky ['mæŋkɪ] *a Br P* sale et moche/cradingue/crado/dégueulasse.

man-mad ['mæn'mæd] *a F* nymphomane; she's man-mad, elle est nympho. (*See* **woman-mad**)

manners ['mænəz] *npl WInd P* situation *f*/situasse *f*; I'm under heavy manners, c'est le merdier.

Manny ['mænɪ] *Prn Br F* (ville *f* de) Manchester *m ou f*.

manor ['mænə] *n Br P* (*a*) territoire *m*/champ *m* d'action (d'un criminel)/chasse gardée (*b*) secteur couvert par un commissariat de police; **morguey manor**, quartier farci/pourri de flics. (*See* **mystery**; **patch 2**; **plot**)

man-size(d) ['mænsaɪz(d)] *a F* (*a*) gros*/de taille/comaque (*b*) (*strong*) costaud/ma(h)ous; **a man-sized meal**, un repas copieux/abondant; une ventrée.

man up! [mæn'ʌp] *excl NAm P* (*it's the police!*) vingt-deux, (c'est) les flics!

map [mæp] *n* 1. *F* **to put on the map**, populariser/mettre en vedette; **this will put London back on the map**, ça va remettre Londres sous les projecteurs 2. *F* **off the map**, inaccessible/au diable vert/à Trifouillis-les-Oies 3. *Austr P* **to throw a map**, vomir*/aller au refile/aller au renard 4. *P* visage*/boule *f*/bobine *f* 5. *NAm P* chèque *m* 6. *F* **map of France/Ireland/America**, (*stain*) tache *f* sur les draps; carte *f* de France/de géographie; (*patch of vomit*) dégueulis *m*.

maracas [mə'rækəz] *npl P* 1. *esp NAm* seins*/rotoplots *mpl*/roploplots *mpl*/roberts *mpl* 2. (*RS = knackers*) testicules*/noisettes *fpl*/valseuses *fpl*.

Marble Bar ['mɑːbl'bɑː] *n Austr F* **till it rains in Marble Bar**, (*never*) jusqu'à la Saint-Glinglin.

marble orchard ['mɑːbl'ɔːtʃəd] *n* cimetière*/boulevard *m* des allongés.

marbles ['mɑːblz] *npl P* 1. *Austr* **to pass in one's marbles**, mourir*/passer l'arme à gauche/lâcher la rampe 2. **to lose one's marbles**, devenir fou*/perdre le nord/perdre la boule/déménager; **he's lost (all) his marbles**, il a perdu la boule; **he's still got all his marbles**, il a encore toute sa tête 3. testicules*/billes *fpl*/burnes *fpl* 4. argent*/pèze *m*.

marching ['mɑːtʃɪŋ] *n F* **to give s.o. his marching orders**, se débarrasser* de qn/flanquer qn à la porte; envoyer paître qn/envoyer qn dinguer.

mare [mɛə] *n Br P* femme* méprisable/vache *f*.

marge [mɑːdʒ] *n F* (= *margarine*) margarine *f*.

Marine [mə'riːn] *n F* (**go**) **tell that to the Marines!** à d'autres!/et ta sœur!/arrête ton

char(, Ben Hur)!

marjie ['mɑːdʒɪ] *n P* (*drugs*) marijuana*/kif *m*/Marie-Jeanne *f*. (*See* **juana**)

mark¹ [mɑːk] *n F* **to feel up to the mark**, être en train/tenir la forme/péter la santé/avoir la frite; **I don't feel up to the mark**, je ne suis pas dans mon assiette. (*See* **easy I 3**; **tidemark**)

mark² [mɑːk] *vtr Br P* 1. **to mark s.o.'s card**, mettre qn sur ses gardes/faire ouvrir l'œil à qn 2. (*pick out*) (*victim*) chercher *ou* trouver (un *cave*); (*place to burgle*) chercher *ou* trouver (un bon *casse*).

marker ['mɑːkə] *n P* reconnaissance *f* de dette.

mark up ['mɑːk'ʌp] *vtr F* **to mark sth up to s.o.**, mettre qch au crédit de qn.

marriage ['mærɪdʒ] *n P* **marriage gear/prospects**, testicules*/bijoux *mpl* de famille/joyeuses *fpl*.

marrowbones ['mærəʊbəʊnz, 'mærəbəʊnz] *npl P* genoux *mpl*.

marshmallows ['mɑːʃ'mæləʊz] *npl P* 1. seins* 2. testicules*.

marvellous ['mɑːv(ə)ləs] *a F* excellent*/super; *Iron* **marvellous, isn't it?/bloody marvellous!** ça, c'est la meilleure!/voilà bien le bouquet!

Mary, mary ['mɛərɪ] *n* 1. *P* homosexuel* passif/caroline *f*/tapette *f*. (*See* **Mary Ann(e) 2**) 2. *P* lesbienne*/gouine *f* 3. *F* **bloody Mary**, cocktail *m* de vodka et jus de tomate/Marie-Salope *f*.

Mary Ann(e) ['mɛərɪ'æn], **Mary Jane** ['mɛərɪ'dʒeɪn], **Mary Warner** ['mɛərɪ'wɔːnə] *n P* 1. (*drugs*) (*a*) marijuana*/Marie-Jeanne *f* (*b*) cigarette* de marijuana/joint *m* 2. homme* efféminé.

mash [mæʃ] *n Br P* thé *m*.

massage ['mæsɑːʒ] *n Euph F* **massage parlour**, (*brothel*) salon *m* de massages thaïlandais/spéciaux.

massive ['mæsɪv] *a F* excellent*/géant.

master ['mɑːstə] *n F* (*sadomasochism*) partenaire dominant(e)/dominateur, -trice/maître *m*. (*See* **slave¹**)

mat [mæt] *n F* **on the mat** = **on the carpet** (**carpet¹ 1**). (*See* **doormat**; **welcome-mat**)

mate [meɪt] *n F* 1. ami*/copain *m*/pote *m*; **to go for a drink with one's mates**, (aller) prendre un pot avec les potes 2. mec *m*/type *m*/zigoto *m*; **that's too bad, mate!** tant pis pour toi, mon vieux!

matelot ['mætləʊ] *n Br F* **1.** marin*/
matelot *m* **2.** membre *m* de la police fluviale.

matey ['meɪtɪ] I *a F* to be matey, être à tu
et à toi/copiner; they've got all matey now, ils
sont copains comme cochons maintenant II *n*
F = **mate 1, 2.**

mateyness ['meɪtɪnɪs] *n F* copinage *m.*

Matilda [mə'tɪldə] *n Austr F* (*bushman's
swag*) balluchon *m.*

matlo(w) ['mætləʊ] *n F* = **matelot.**

mauler ['mɔːlə] *n Br P* main*/patte *f/*
paluche *f*/pogne *m.*

maybe ['meɪbiː] *adv F* ...and I don't mean
maybe! ...et je ne plaisante pas!/je ne rigole
pas!

max [mæks] *adv F* au maximum.

mazooma, mazuma [mə'zuːmə] *n P*
argent*/pognon *m*/fric *m*/flouse *m.*

MBS [embiː'es] *abbr F* (*Mind, Body and
Soul*) (*drugs*) LSD*.

MC ['em'siː] *vtr P* to MC a show, présenter/
animer un spectacle. (*See* **emcee**)

McCoy [mə'kɔɪ] *n F* the real McCoy (*a*)
boisson *f* de bonne qualité/de la vraie (de
vraie) (*b*) de l'authentique/du vrai de vrai/du
bon d'époque; de la marchandise
irréprochable/du garanti pur sucre; it's the
real McCoy, c'est de l'officiel/c'est pas de la
camelote.

MCP ['em'siː'piː] *abbr P* = **male chauvinist
pig** (*See* **pig**[1] **2**).

MDA ['em'diː'eɪ] *n P* (*drugs*) (*abbr of
methyl diamphetamine*) MDA *m.*

meal [miːl] *n F* to make a meal out of sth,
faire toute une histoire/tout un plat de qch.

meal-ticket ['miːltɪkɪt] *n F* (*prostitute*)
gagne-pain *m*/gagneuse *f*/bifteck *m.*

mean [miːn] *a* **1.** *F* mauvais/méchant/sale;
mean weather, sale temps/temps pourri;
mean job, travail* désagréable/boulot *m*
dégueulasse **2.** *P* a mean bastard/*esp NAm*
a mean son of a bitch, un vrai salaud/une vraie
peau de vache **3.** *F* to feel mean about sth,
avoir honte de qch; I feel really mean about
it, ça m'embête **4.** *P* formid(able)/du
tonnerre; he plays a mean guitar, il touche
(sa bille) à la guitare.

meanie, meany ['miːnɪ] *n F* (*a*)
(*avaricious*) grigou *m*/rat *m*/radin, -ine/
rapiat, -ate (*b*) (*unpleasant*) he's a real
meany, ce qu'il est moche/vache (avec nous).

measly ['miːzlɪ] *a F* **1.** misérable/
insignifiant/de rien du tout; a measly five
quid, cinq malheureuses livres **2.** avare*/

radin/constipé du morlingue.

meat [miːt] *n* **1.** *F* fond *m*/moelle *f*/substance
f **2.** *P* (*sex*) to love one's meat, être porté sur
la chose **3.** *V* (*a*) pénis*; small meat, petit
pénis*/petit bout; to beat/to flog the meat, se
masturber*/secouer le petit homme/se tirer
sur l'élastique (*b*) *Br* meat and two veg, sexe
de l'homme*/service *m* trois pièces **4.** *P*
jouissance *f* d'un homosexuel* **5.** *F* to make
cold meat of s.o., tuer* qn/refroidir qn **6.** *F*
dead meat, cadavre*/viande froide **7.** *Austr F*
as Australian as a meat pie, typiquement
australien/on ne peut plus australien. (*See*
easy I 6; **mincemeat**; **plate**[1] **2**)

meatball ['miːbɔːl], **meathead**
['miːthed] *n P* individu bête*/gourde *f/*
andouille *f*/nouille *f.*

meat-hooks ['miːthʊks] *npl P* grandes
mains*/paluches *fpl*/pognes *fpl.* (*See* **bread-
hooks**; **hook**[1] **6**)

meat-house ['miːthaʊs] *n P* bordel*/
maison *f* d'abattage/claque *m.*

meat market ['miːtmɑːkɪt] *n F* lieu *m* de
rencontre pour personnes en quête de
partenaires; bar *m* pour célibataires.

meat rack ['miːtræk] *n P* lieu *m* de
rencontre pour homosexuels; = les Tuileries
fpl; the meat rack, (*in London*) lieu *m* de
rencontre pour prostitués (*à Piccadilly
Circus*).

meat-show ['miːtʃəʊ] *n P* spectacle *m* de
nu/parade *f* de fesses/spectacle de cul.

meat-wag(g)on ['miːtwægən] *n P* **1.**
ambulance *f* **2.** corbillard*/trottinette *f* à
macchabées **3.** car* de police/panier *m* à
salade.

mebbe ['mebɪ] *adv P* (= *maybe*) ça se
peut/des fois/p'têt ben.

mechanic [mɪ'kænɪk] *n P* tricheur, -euse
aux cartes/fileur *m.*

medals ['medlz] *npl O F* you're wearing
medals today, ta braguette est ouverte;
n'expose pas tes bijoux.

medic(o) ['medɪk(əʊ)] *n F* **1.** médecin *m/*
toubib *m* **2.** étudiant, -ante en médecine/
carabin *m.*

meet [miːt] *n P* **1.** = **gig**[1] **3 2.** rendez-vous*/
rencart *m*; let's arrange a meet, on se donne
rencart/on prend date **3.** (*drugs*) to make a
meet, avoir rendez-vous avec son fourgueur/se
brancher avec un fourgue.

mega ['megə] *a F* (*wonderful*) super/géant/
canon; (*enormous*) gigantesque; (*hugely
successful*) qui a un succès bœuf; mega-rich,

richissime.

megabucks ['megəbʌks] *npl F* énorme somme *f* d'argent; **she's making mega bucks, I'm telling you,** elle se fait un fric pas possible, c'est moi qui te le dit.

megastar ['megəstɑː] *n F* mégastar *f*.

melon ['melən] *n P* 1. *Austr* tête*/caboche *f* 2. *pl* seins*/nichons *mpl*.

mem(sahib) ['mem(sɑːb)] *n Br F* épouse*/ bourgeoise *f*.

mental ['ment(ə)l] *a Br F* **to go mental,** devenir fou*; **you must be mental!** t'es pas un peu secoué? ça va la tête, oui? **mental eunuch,** imbécile*/nigaud *m*/Ducon-la-joie *m*.

me 'n' you [miːən'juː] *n F* (= *menu*) menu *m*.

merch [mɜːtʃ] *n NAm F* marchandise*/came *f*.

merchant ['mɜːtʃənt] *n F* individu*/type *m*/mec *m*/pékin *m*/paroissien *m*. (*See* **speed-merchant**)

merries ['merɪz] *npl Br F* (= *merry-go-rounds*) manèges *mpl*.

merry ['merɪ] *a F* légèrement ivre*/ pompette/éméché; **to get rather merry/a bit merry,** avoir un verre dans le nez. (*See* **hell 3**)

mesc [mesk] *n P* (*drugs*) (*abbr of mescaline*) mescaline*/mesc *f*.

mess [mes] *n* 1. *F* **isn't she a mess!** (*ugly, ridiculous*) ce qu'elle est tarte/tartignolle! 2. *F* **the house is in a real mess,** la maison est un vrai foutoir; **what a mess!** quel gâchis!/quelle pagaille! **his life is in a dreadful mess,** il a fichu sa vie en l'air/il a fait un vrai gâchis de sa vie 3. *F* **to be in a (bit of a) mess,** être dans le pétrin/dans de mauvais draps/dans le caca; **to help s.o. out of a mess,** tirer qn d'un mauvais pas 4. *P* **to make a mess of s.o.,** battre* qn/tabasser qn/amocher qn; faire de la bouillie de qn; **the accident made a dreadful mess of her face,** l'accident lui a bousillé la figure 5. *F* **to make a mess of things/it,** tout gâcher/tout bousiller/tout foutre en l'air; **he always makes a mess of things,** il n'en rate pas une. (*See* **right I 1**)

mess about, around ['mesə'baut, ə'raund] *vtr & i* 1. *F* (*a*) (*play the fool*) faire l'imbécile (*b*) (*waste time*) glander/ glandouiller (*c*) (*tinker*) tripoter 2. *F* **to mess s.o. about,** tourmenter/enquiquiner qn 3. *P* **to mess about with s.o.** (*a*) (*sexually*) peloter/ pelotailler qn; **stop messing around with my wife!** pas de jeux de mains avec ma femme!

(*b*) (*have relations with undesirable person*) s'acoquiner avec qn.

message ['mesɪdʒ] *n F* **to get the message,** comprendre/piger/entraver; **I get the message,** je vous reçois cinq sur cinq; **get the message? tu piges?**

mess-up ['mesʌp] *n F* 1. gâchis *m*/méli-mélo *m*/pagaille *f* 2. malentendu *m*/ embrouillamini *m*/cafouillage *m*.

mess up ['mes'ʌp] *vtr F* 1. salir/bousiller/ saloper 2. abîmer*/amocher/saboter; **he's messed his face up,** il s'est abîmé le portrait; **we're gonna mess your face up,** on va vous arranger joliment le portrait.

Met (the) [ðə'met] *n Br F* (*London Metropolitan Police*) = la Maison poulaga.

metal ['metl] *n P* (*motor trade*) **to move the metal,** vendre des voitures/écouler la marchandise.

metal-man ['metlmæn] *n Mus F* joueur *m* de heavy metal. (*See* **heavy I 8**)

meth [meθ] *abbr* 1. *P* (*drugs*) (= *methedrine*) méthédrine *f*/meth *f* 2. *pl Br F* (= *methylated spirits*) alcool *m* à brûler; **meths drinker,** alcolo *mf*/clodo *m* qui se soûle à l'alcool à brûler.

methhead ['meθhed] *n P* (*drugs*) habitué, -ée de la méthédrine.

metho ['meθəu] *n Austr P* alcool *m* à brûler; **metho drinker,** alcoolo *mf*/clodo *m* qui se soûle à l'alcool à brûler; **to go on the metho,** se soûler à l'alcool à brûler. (*See* **meth 2**)

Mexican green ['meksɪkən'griːn] *n P* (*drugs*) marijuana* du Mexique/de la Mexicaine.

mezz [mez] *n esp NAm P* (*drugs*) cigarette* de marijuana/stick *m*/joint *m*.

MF ['em'ef] *abbr P* = **motherfucker.**

Michael ['maɪkl] *n F* 1. *Hum* **Michael Flyn** = **Mick(e)y Finn** (**mick(e)y 4**) 2. *Br* **to take the Michael** = **to take the mick(e)y** (**mick(e)y 2**).

mick, Mick [mɪk] *n P* 1. *Pej* (*a*) Irlandais *m* (*b*) qn d'origine irlandaise (*c*) Catholique *mf*/catho *mf*. (*See* **Paddy 3**) 2. *Br* **to take the mick** = **to take the mick(e)y** (**mick(e)y 2**).

mick(e)y, Mick(e)y ['mɪkɪ] *n* 1. *P* = **mick, Mick 1** 2. *Br F* **to take the mick(e)y out of s.o.,** faire marcher qn/se payer la tête de qn; **stop taking the mick(e)y!** ne me charrie pas! (*See* **mick(e)y-taker**) 3. *P* pénis*/Popaul *m* 4. *F* **Mick(e)y (Finn)** (*a*) boisson droguée; **to slip s.o. a Mick(e)y Finn**, refiler à qn une boisson droguée (*b*) casse-pattes *m* 5. *P* **to do a mick(e)y**, s'enfuir*/se barrer/déguerpir 6. *Austr F* jeune taureau *m* 7. *Austr P* sexe* de la femme/minet *m*.

Mickey Mouse ['mɪkɪ'maʊs] I *a P* 1. inférieur/du toc; à la noix; **that firm's a real Mickey Mouse outfit**, cette boîte, c'est un truc de rigolos 2. simple/facile/fastoche; **he settled for a Mickey Mouse job instead**, il s'est décidé pour un boulot pépère 3. routinier/train-train 4. (*suspect*) louche/toc II *n P* (*RS = house*) maison *f*.

mick(e)y-taker ['mɪkɪteɪkə] *n F* moqueur, -euse/charrieur *m*/railleur, -euse; **he's a real mick(e)y-taker**, il n'arrête pas de se payer la tête des gens. (*See* **mick(e)y 2**)

middle leg ['mɪdl'leg] *n F* pénis*/jambe *f* du milieu.

middleman ['mɪdlmæn] *n F* (*drugs*) contact *m*/intermédiaire *mf*/passeur, -euse.

middle-of-the-road ['mɪdləvðərəʊd] *a F* modéré/du juste milieu; *Mus* pépère; **the Party has a middle-of-the-road policy**, le parti poursuit une politique modérée *ou* centriste.

middling ['mɪdlɪŋ] *a F* **fair to middling**, pas mal/couci-couça/entre les deux.

middy ['mɪdɪ] *n F* 1. *Austr* verre *m* à bière de taille moyenne 2. *Br* WC*/cabinces *fpl*.

miff¹ [mɪf] *n F* (*a*) mauvaise humeur/rogne *f* (*b*) (*quarrel*) brouille *f*.

miff² [mɪf] *vtr & i F* offenser/vexer; prendre la mouche; **he was a bit miffed by it**, ça l'avait un peu vexé/il avait pas trop apprécié/il appréciait pas trop.

mighty ['maɪtɪ] *adv O F* bigrement/bougrement/fichtrement/vachement; **it's mighty cold**, il fait sacrément froid; **I'm mighty glad to see you**, je suis vachement content de te voir.

mike¹ [maɪk] *n* 1. *P =* **mick 1** 2. *F* **to take the mike = to take the mick(e)y** (**mick(e)y 2**) 3. *F* (*= microphone*) micro *m*; **to chat the mike**, chanter dans le micro 4. *P* **to take a mike at sth**, regarder*/lorgner/mater/tapisser qch 5. *P* **to do a mike = to do a mick(e)y** (**mick(e)y 5**) 6. *P* **to have a mike = mike²** 7. *P* **Mike Malone**, (*RS = telephone*) téléphone*/biniou *m* 8. *P* (*drugs*) (*abbr of microgram*) un microgramme (de LSD). (*See* **love 2**)

mike² [maɪk] *vi P* paresser*/se les tourner/glander/glandouiller/tirer sa cosse.

mile [maɪl] *n F* 1. **you're a mile out/you're miles out/you're miles off course**, (*completely wrong*) tu te plantes complètement/tu es complètement à côté (de la plaque); **you're miles too slow**, tu es mille fois trop lent 2. **I'd go a mile** (*or* **miles**) **for that**, je ferais des kilomètres pour ça/j'irais au bout du monde pour ça 3. **a miss is as good as a mile**, à côté, c'est à côté 4. **to be miles away**, (*daydream*) être ailleurs/être dans la lune/rêvasser 5. **it sticks out a mile/you can see it a mile off/you can see it a mile away**, ça vous crève les yeux/ça se voit comme le nez au milieu de la figure. (*See* **thumb¹ 4**)

milk [mɪlk] *vtr* 1. *F* (*exploit*) dépouiller/écorcher/écrémer (qn) 2. *V* masturber*.

milko ['mɪlkəʊ] *n F* laitier *m*.

milk round (the) [ðə'mɪlkraʊnd] *n Br F* tournée annuelle des institutions d'enseignement supérieur par les employeurs éventuels.

milk run ['mɪlkrʌn] *n F* 1. (*aviation*) vol *m* de routine/vol pépère 2. qch de facile/fastoche/du gâteau.

milktoast ['mɪlktəʊst] *n NAm F* homme* veule/chiffe (molle)/descente *f* de lit.

milk-train ['mɪlktreɪn] *n F* **to catch the milk-train**, rentrer au petit matin.

milky ['mɪlkɪ] *a F* foireux/trouillard; **to turn milky**, avoir peur*/avoir la trouille/avoir les chocottes.

mill¹ [mɪl] *n F* 1. bagarre*/baston *m ou f*/rififi *m* 2. **to go through the mill**, en voir de toutes les couleurs/en voir des vertes et des pas mûres/en baver; **to put s.o. through the mill**, en faire voir à qn.

mill² [mɪl] *vtr F* bourrer de coups*/tabasser/dérouiller/encadrer.

milling ['mɪlɪŋ] *n F* **to give s.o. a milling**, donner une raclée à qn/bosseler qn/filer une toise à qn.

million ['mɪljən] *n F* 1. (*also Iron*) **thanks a million!** merci mille fois! 2. **to feel like a million dollars**, être au septième ciel/être aux nues; **to look like a million (dollars)**, être très élégant*/très chic; jeter du jus 3. *Austr* **gone a million**, dans de mauvais draps/dans le pétrin.

milquetoast ['mɪlktəʊst] *n NAm F =* **milktoast**.

mincemeat ['mɪnsmiːt] *n F* **to make mincemeat (out) of s.o.**, réduire qn en bouillie.

mince-pies ['mɪns'paɪz] *npl P* (*RS = eyes*) yeux*/mirettes *fpl*/calots *mpl*/clignotants *mpl*.

mincers ['mɪnsəz], **minces, mincies**

['mɪnsɪz] *npl* P = **mince-pies**.
mind [maɪnd] *vtr* P protéger/surveiller (qn).
mind-bender ['maɪndbendə] *n* P 1. drogue *f* qui affine l'intelligence; euphorisant *m* 2. problème épineux/difficile; casse-tête *m*.
mind-blower ['maɪndbləʊə] *n* P drogue *f* hallucinogène.
mind-blowing ['maɪnd'bləʊɪŋ] *a* P (*drug*) hallucinogène; (*experience*) ahurissant/ époustouflant/à vous couper le souffle.
mind-boggling ['maɪndbɒglɪŋ] *a* P renversant/à vous couper le souffle; it was a mind-boggling experience, j'en suis resté baba.
mind-bogglingly ['maɪndbɒglɪŋlɪ] *adv* P remarquablement; that film was mind-bogglingly awful, ce film était d'un con pas possible/pas croyable.
minder ['maɪndə] *n* P garde *m* du corps/ ange gardien/gorille *m*.
mind-fuck ['maɪndfʌk] *vtr* P endoctriner (qn)/bourrer le crâne à (qn)/laver le cerveau à (qn).
minge [mɪndʒ] *n* Br V sexe* de la femme/ minou *m*; minge fringe, poils *mpl* du pubis/ barbu *m*/motte *f*/persil *m*.
mingy ['mɪndʒɪ] *a* F = **measly 1, 2**.
mink [mɪŋk] *n* NAm 1. P fille*/gisquette *f*; (*attractive*) nana bien roulée/baisable/ mettable 2. V sexe* de la femme*/chatte *f*.
mint [mɪnt] *n* F to cost a mint (of money), coûter les yeux de la tête; to make a mint, gagner un paquet/une fortune.
mischief ['mɪstʃɪf] *n* F 1. enfant* espiègle/ petit diable/affreux jojo 2. to do oneself some mischief, se faire mal/se blesser*/s'amocher.
misery-guts ['mɪz(ə)rɪgʌts] *n* Br F individu* grognon/rabat-joie *m*.
mish-mash ['mɪʃmæʃ] *n* F méli-mélo *m*.
mishugah [mɪ'ʃʊgə] *a* NAm F fou*/barjot/ cinglé.
miss [mɪs] *n* 1. F to give sth a miss, laisser passer qch/laisser courir qch; sécher (un cours); I think I'll give your plonk a miss, je crois que je vais pas me laisser tenter par ton petit vin/ta piquette. (*See* **mile 3**) 2. P (*drugs*) Miss Emma, morphine*.
missis ['mɪsɪz] *n* F the/my missis, mon épouse*/la bourgeoise/la patronne; I'll have to ask the missis, faut demander à la patronne.
miss out on ['mɪs'aʊtɒn] *vtr* F manquer/ louper/rater (qch); I missed out on my best chance, j'ai raté ma meilleure occasion; he doesn't miss out on a thing, il n'en rate pas

une.
missus ['mɪsɪz] *n* F = **missis**.
missy ['mɪsɪ] *n* O F mademoiselle/ mam'zelle.
mistake [mɪ'steɪk] *n* F ...and no mistake/ make no mistake! ...et tu peux en être sûr!/ pas d'erreur!
mither ['mɪðə] *vi* Br P se plaindre/miauler.
mitt [mɪt] *n* P 1. main*/patte *f*; keep your mitts off! bas les pattes! 2. gant *m* de boxe 3. *pl* menottes*/poucettes *fpl*/bracelets *mpl* 4. to put one's mitts on sth, voler* qch/faire une main tombée sur qch/griffer qch.
mitten ['mɪtn] *n* O F to give s.o. the mitten, abandonner qn/plaquer qn.
mix [mɪks] *vtr & i* F 1. to mix it with s.o., battre* avec qn/s'expliquer avec qn/se castagner 2. to mix things up, remuer les eaux troubles/semer la merde.
mixer ['mɪksə] *n* F 1. he's a good mixer, il est sociable/il se lie facilement; he's a bad mixer, c'est un ours/il est sauvage 2. (*troublemaker*) mauvais coucheur.
mix-up ['mɪksʌp] *n* F 1. confusion *f*/pagaille *f* 2. bagarre*/mêlée *f*/rififi *m*.
miz(z) [mɪz] *a* O P malheureux/tout chose/ cafardeux.
mizzle ['mɪzl] *vi* P 1. s'enfuir*/se cavaler/ mettre les bouts 2. rouspéter/râler/renauder.
mo [məʊ] *n* F (= *moment*) half a mo! une seconde!/minute! (*See* **jiff(y)**; **sec**; **shake¹ 1**; **tick¹ 3**)
m.o. ['em'əʊ] P (*abbr of modus operandi*) = **handwriting**.
moanie-bags ['məʊnɪ'bægz] *n* F geignard, -arde/rouspéteur, -euse.
moaning ['məʊnɪŋ] *a* F a moaning Minnie, un(e) geignard(e)/un(e) rouspéteur, -euse.
mob (the) [ðə'mɒb] *n* F bande* de criminels/flèche *f*/gang *m*. (*See* **heavy I 4**; **swell I 3**)
mobile ['məʊbaɪl] *a* F to get mobile, (*work hard*) travailler* plus vite/se décarcasser/se démancher/se magner le train; (*hurry*) se dépêcher*/se magner/se grouiller/se secouer.
mobster ['mɒbstə] *n* NAm F homme* du milieu/membre *m* de la pègre/dur *m*/truand *m*/arcan *m*/gangster *m*.
mockers ['mɒkəz] *npl* Br F to put the mockers on s.o./sth, (*bring misfortune*) porter la poisse à qn/qch; (*frustrate, spoil*) foutre qch en l'air.
mockie, mocky ['mɒkɪ] *n* NAm P Pej Juif*/youpin, -ine.

mod [mɒd] *n Br F* scootériste *mf*/mod *m*. (*See* **rocker 1**)

mog [mɒg], **moggie, moggy** ['mɒgɪ] *n Br F* chat *m*/matou *m*/greffier *m*.

mojo ['məʊdʒəʊ] *n P* 1. (*spell*) charme *m* 2. (*any object*) machin *m*/truc *m* 3. drogue*/came *f*; *surt* morphine*.

moke [məʊk] *n F* âne *m*/bourricot *m*/martin *m*.

mola ['məʊlə] *n NAm P* homosexuel*/pédé *m*/lope *f*.

moll [mɒl] *n* 1. *O NAm P* jeune femme*/gonzesse *f*/mousmé(e) *f*/nana *f* 2. *Austr P* prostituée*/fille *f* 3. *F* poule *f*/môme *f* d'un gangster.

molly-dooker ['mɒlɪdʊkə] *n Austr F* gaucher, -ère .

molly-shop ['mɒlɪʃɒp] *n P* = **meat-house**.

Molotov cocktail ['mɒlətɒv'kɒkteɪl] *n F* cocktail *m* Molotov.

mom [mɒm] *n esp NAm F* mère*/maman *f*.

moments ['məʊmənts] *npl F* I've had my moments, j'ai eu mes bons moments; moi aussi, j'ai été jeune/j'ai fait les 400 coups.

momser, momzer ['mɒmzə] *n esp NAm P* (*contemptible person*) salaud*/crapule *f*/loquedu *m*.

monarch ['mɒnək] *n Austr F* la police*/les flics *mpl*/les cognes *mpl*/les poulets *mpl*.

Monday ['mʌndɪ] *n F* that Monday morning feeling, le cafard du lundi matin/de l'après-weekend *m*.

Mondayish ['mʌndɪɪʃ] *a F* that Mondayish feeling = that Monday morning feeling (**Monday**); to feel Mondayish, avoir le cafard du lundi.

money ['mʌnɪ] *n F* 1. to be in the money, être riche*/rouler sur l'or/être plein aux as 2. he's the man for my money, c'est juste l'homme qu'il me faut; il a tous mes suffrages 3. to throw good money after bad, (*take risks*) jouer à quitte ou double; (*waste money*) jeter/balancer/foutre l'argent* par les fenêtres 4. I'm not made of money, je ne suis pas cousu d'or; je ne roule pas sur l'or/je ne suis pas Crésus. (*See* **big I 7; funny I 5; rope 1**)

moneybags ['mʌnɪbægz] *n F* individu très riche*/rupin *m*/richard, -arde.

mongrel ['mʌŋgrəl] *n P* 1. *Austr & New Zealand* (*despicable person*) salaud*/loquedu *m* 2. *Austr Pej* métis, -isse.

moni(c)ker ['mɒnɪkə] *n P* nom*/blaze *m*/

centre *m*.

monkey ['mʌŋkɪ] *n* 1. *F* to get one's monkey up, se mettre en colère*/piquer une rogne/prendre la mouche; to get s.o.'s monkey up, mettre qn en colère/en rogne 2. *P* (billet*/fafiot *m* de) cinq cents livres *fpl ou* cinq cents dollars *mpl*/*occ* cinquante livres 3. *P* I don't give a monkey's (toss)! je m'en fous et contrefous!/je n'en ai rien à glander!/je n'en ai rien à foutre! 4. *F* to make a monkey (out) of s.o., se payer la tronche de qn; he made me look a right monkey, il s'est bien foutu de ma poire 5. *F* monkey business (*a*) (*scheme*) fricotage *m*/combine *f*/magouilles *fpl* (*b*) (*underhand dealing*) conduite *f* malhonnête/procédé irrégulier (*c*) (*trickery*) coup fourré/entourloupe *f* (*d*) (*nonsense*) fumisterie *f*; no monkey business! pas de blagues! 6. *P* habitude *f*/besoin *m* de la drogue; la guêpe/la guenon; to get the monkey off, se désintoxiquer/chasser la guenon; to have a monkey on one's back, être drogué*/camé/toxico 7. *F* monkey jacket, veste courte/spencer *m*/rase-pet *m* 8. *F* monkey suit, uniforme *m*; *NAm* smoking *m*/smok *m* 9. *Austr O F* mouton *m*/bêlant *m* 10. *Austr V* sexe* de la femme*/chatte *f*/chagatte *f*. (*See* **balls¹ 4; grease 3**)

monkey about, around ['mʌŋkɪə'baʊt, ə'raʊnd] *vi F* faire des sottises/faire l'imbécile; to monkey about/around with sth, (*touch*) tripoter qch.

monniker ['mɒnɪkə] *n P* = **moni(c)ker**.

Montezuma [mɒntɪ'zuːmə] *n NAm F* Montezuma's revenge, diarrhée*/chiasse *f*/courante *f*/turista *f*.

monthlies ['mʌnθlɪz] *npl F* the monthlies, les règles*; to have the monthlies, avoir ses affaires *fpl*/ses trucs *mpl*/ses histoires *fpl*.

moo [muː] *n P* she's a (right old) moo, c'est une belle vache; silly (old) moo! espèce de vieille bique!/vieille peau de vache!

moocah ['muːkɑː, 'muːkə] *n P* (*drugs*) marijuana*/Marie-Jeanne *f*.

mooch [muːtʃ] *vtr & i P* 1. mendier*/faire la manche 2. voler*/chouraver 3. to mooch about/around, flâner/traîner ses lattes *fpl*/traîner ses guêtres *fpl*; glander 4. emprunter*/taper/sonner.

moocher ['muːtʃə] *n P* 1. mendiant*/mendigot, -ote 2. voleur*/chapardeur, -euse 3. flâneur, -euse/traîne-savates *m*/glandeur, -euse 4. tapeur, -euse/torpilleur, -euse.

moo-cow ['muːkaʊ] *n* 1. *F* (*child's word*)

vache f/meu-meu f 2. P = **cow 1.**

moody ['muːdɪ] Br I n P 1. flatterie f/
boniment m; **cut out the moody!** assez de
baratin!/suffit les boniments! 2. bouderie f; to
throw a moody, bouder/faire la gueule 3. (old)
moody, mensonge*/bobard m/craque f II a P
faux/suspect/véreux; **moody licence,** faux
permis/permis maquillé; **moody gear,** marchandise f bidon/chtrope m.

moola(h) ['muːlɑː, 'muːlə] n, **moolies**
['muːlɪz] npl P argent*/pognon m/fric m/
flouse m.

moon[1] [muːn] n 1. P a moon, un mois de
prison/un marqué 2. F **over the moon,** aux
anges/fou de joie. (See **blue**[1] I 6; **shoot**[2] 8)

moon[2] [muːn] vi P montrer ses fesses*/son
cul; faire voir la lune en plein jour.

moon about, around ['muːnə'baʊt,
ə'raʊnd] vi F lambiner/traînailler/cueillir les
pâquerettes.

moonie [muːnɪ] n F = **moony** II.

moonlight ['muːnlaɪt] vi F faire du
(travail au) noir/travailler au noir.

moonlighter ['muːnlaɪtə] n F qn qui
travaille au noir/travailleur, -euse au noir;
he's a moonlighter, il fait du noir.

moonlighting ['muːnlaɪtɪŋ] n F travail
(au) noir; noir m.

moonshine ['muːnʃaɪn] n F 1. esp NAm
alcool* illicitement distillé ou de contrebande/
gnôle f sous les fagots 2. bêtises*/foutaises
fpl.

moony ['muːnɪ] I a P un peu fou*/toqué/
jeté/secoué/givré II n F (after cult of Rever-
end Moon) mooniste mf.

moosh [muʃ] n P = **mush 1, 2.**

mootah ['muːtɑː], **mooter** ['muːtə] n P
= **moocah.**

mop [mɒp] n F **that's the way the mop flops,**
c'est comme ça que tombent les dés; c'est
ainsi que la roue tourne; c'est comme ça et
pas autrement. (See **cookie 1**; **onion 1**)

mopping ['mɒpɪŋ] n F (police, etc)
mopping-up operations, (opération f de)
nettoyage m.

MOR ['em'əʊ'ɑː] abbr F (= middle-of-the-
road (music)) musique pépère/douce.

moreish ['mɔːrɪʃ] a F **these sweets are very
moreish,** ces bonbons ont un (petit) goût de
revenez-y.

morf [mɔːf] n P (drugs) (= morphine)
morphine*/morph f.

morguey ['mɔːgɪ] a see **manor** (b).

moron ['mɔːrɒn] n P individu bête*/crétin,

-ine; **you moron!** espèce de taré!

mosey along ['məʊzɪə'lɒŋ] vi F aller son
petit bonhomme de chemin/aller mollo.

mosey off ['məʊzɪ'ɒf] vi F s'enfuir*/
décamper/se barrer.

mosquito [mɒ'skiːtəʊ] n P (drugs)
mosquito bite, piqûre* (surt de morphine)/fixe
m/shoot m.

moss [mɒs] n P cheveux*/cresson m/gazon
m.

mossback ['mɒsbæk] n NAm P paysan*/
péquenot m/cul-terreux m.

most(est) ['məʊst(ɪst)] n F **the most(est),**
le super/l'archi (bien)/le plus mieux; **he's the
most,** il est super/sensass; **she's got the mostest,** elle est vachement bien roulée.

mote [məʊt] vi Austr F filer à toute allure/
brûler le pavé/décaniller.

mother ['mʌðə] n 1. F **shall I be mother?** je
vous sers? 2. P **mother's ruin,** gin m 3. P a
(father and) mother of a row, un sacré
barouf/un pétard de tous les diables 4. V =
motherfucker 5. P homosexuel*/tata f.

motherfucker ['mʌðəfʌkə] n NAm VV 1.
(horrible thing) (belle) saloperie/tour m de
salaud; **this motherfucker!** cette saloperie! 2.
(person) con m, conne f/connard, -arde/enculé
m (de sa mère); **you motherfuckers!** bande
d'enculés! 3. (jocular term of address) **listen,
(you) motherfucker!** écoute, mon con!

motherfucking ['mʌðəfʌkɪŋ] a NAm VV
1. (disgusting) pourri/dégueulasse/de merde
2. (annoying) emmerdant/chiant (comme la
pluie).

mother-in-law ['mʌðərɪnlɔː] n F mélange
m de stout (bière brune forte) et de bitter
(bière amère); panaché m nègre.

motor[1] ['məʊtə] n F voiture*/bagnole f/tire
f/caisse f.

motor[2] ['məʊtə] vi Br F **to be motoring,**
faire des progrès/avancer; **we're really
motoring!** ça gaze!/ça marche!

motormouth ['məʊtəmaʊθ] n esp NAm P
baratineur, -euse/jacasseur, -euse.

motser, motza ['mɒtsə] n Austr P (gambling) le gros lot.

mouldy ['məʊldɪ] a F moche(ton)/toc(ard)/
tarte/tartignol(l)e; **mouldy old rubbish,** du
toc/de la came.

mountain ['maʊntɪn] n F 1. **to make a
mountain out of a molehill,** faire d'un œuf un
bœuf/se noyer dans un verre d'eau/faire d'une
merde de chien un pain de sucre 2. a
mountain of a man, un homme* fort/bien

baraqué; une armoire à glace 3. **a mountain
of work**, un tas/une montagne de travail*; un
boulot du diable.

mourning ['mɔːnɪŋ] *n F* to have one's
(finger)nails in mourning, avoir les ongles
sales/en deuil.

mouse [maʊs] *n F* 1. **are you a man or a
mouse?** *(catchphrase)* t'en as ou t'en as pas?
2. fille* *ou* jeune femme* séduisante/gisquette
f/gosseline *f*/souris *f*. (*See* **cat 9; Mickey
Mouse; rat¹ 10**)

mouth [maʊθ] *n* 1. *F* to have a **big mouth**,
être une grande gueule/être fort en gueule.
(*See* **big I 2; blow off II; loudmouth;
shoot off 2**) 2. *F* **to be down in the mouth**,
avoir le cafard/être abattu/être défrisé/être au
36ème dessous 3. *P* indicateur*/indic *mf*/
balance *f*. (*See* **horse 2**)

mouthful ['maʊθfʊl] *n F* 1. **you've said a
mouthful!** tu l'as dit bouffi! 2. to **give s.o. a
mouthful**, en dire à qn de toutes les couleurs/
traiter qn de tous les noms.

mouth off ['maʊð'ɒf] *vi F* 1. to **mouth off
at s.o.** = to **give s.o. a mouthful** (**mouthful
2**) 2. *NAm* *(talk)* parler/l'ouvrir; *(chatter)*
bavasser/tailler une bavette.

mouth on ['maʊð'ɒn] *vi F* discutailler/
pinailler.

mouthpiece ['maʊθpiːs] *n* 1. *F* porte-
parole *m* 2. *P* avocat*/débarbot *m*/bavard,
-arde/babillard, -arde.

move [muːv] *n F* 1. to **get a move on**, se
dépêcher*/se magner; **get a move on!**
grouille-toi! 2. to **be up to every move**, connaître la musique/la connaître dans les coins.

mover ['muːvə] *n P* 1. femme* séduisante/
autichante; **she's a lovely mover**, c'est un
prix de Diane 2. individu* énergique/qui pète
le feu.

mozz [mɒz] *n Austr F* to **put the mozz on
s.o./sth**, *(curse)* jeter un sort à qn/qch;
ensorceler qn/qch; *(bring bad luck)* porter la
poisse à qn/qch.

mozza, mozzer ['mɒzə] *n Br P* chance*/
bol *m*/pot *m*.

mozzie, mozzy ['mɒzɪ] *n F* moustique *m*.

much [mʌtʃ] *adv F* 1. **that's a bit much!**
c'est un peu beaucoup/faut pas pousser
(mémère dans les orties)!/c'est un peu fort de
café! *(it's the limit!)* c'est le comble!/c'est le
bouquet!/faut pas charrier! 2. **it's much of a
muchness**, *(the same)* c'est kif-kif
(bourricot)/c'est blanc bonnet et bonnet
blanc/c'est le même jus/c'est du pareil au

même.

muck [mʌk] *n P* 1. to **make a muck of sth**,
abîmer*/gâcher/bousiller qch 2. **it's a load of
muck**, *(nonsense)* c'est un tas de conneries;
(rubbish) c'est de la saleté*/de la cochonnerie
3. to **land/to drop s.o. in the muck**, mettre qn
dans le pétrin/dans la mouscaille/dans la
merde 4. **common as muck** = **common as
mud** (**mud 6**) 5. **dog muck**, crotte *f* de chien/
sentinelle *f* 6. confusion *f*/pagaille *f* 7. **Lord
Muck**, Monsieur J'en-fous-plein-la-vue; **she**
thinks she's **Lady Muck**, elle ne se prend pas
pour de la crotte/de la merde. (*See* **brass II
1; muckamuck**)

muck about, around ['mʌkə'baʊt,
ə'raʊnd] *vtr & i* 1. *F* traîner/lambiner/
bricoler 2. *F* flâner/traîner ses lattes/
glandouiller 3. *F* to **muck s.o. about**, faire
tourner qn en bourrique 4. *P* to **muck about
with s.o.**, *(touch sexually)* peloter qn; **stop
mucking around, will you?** *(don't touch me!)*
bas les pattes!/jeux de mains, jeux de vilains!
(stop fooling around!) arrête de déconner!/
fais pas le con!

muckamuck ['mʌkəmʌk] *n NAm F* **(high)
muckamuck**, personnage important/grosse
légume/huile *f*/ponte *m*.

mucker ['mʌkə] *n P* 1. ami*/copain, -ine/
pote *m* 2. chute *f*/culbute *f*/bûche *f*; to **come a
mucker**, tomber*/prendre un billet de
parterre/se prendre une pelle. (*See* **cropper**)

muck in ['mʌk'ɪn] *vi F* 1. to **muck in with
s.o.**, crécher avec qn/faire gourbi ensemble 2.
to **muck in together**, *(share)* partager/fader/
aller au pied; *(join in with)* s'actionner/se
dépatouiller ensemble.

muckraker ['mʌkreɪkə] *n Br F* déterreur
m de scandale/fouille-merde *mf*.

muck up ['mʌk'ʌp] *vtr F* abîmer*/gâcher/
bousiller/cochonner; **that's mucked up all our
plans**, ça fout tout en l'air/ça gâche tout.

mucky ['mʌkɪ] *a F* 1. **a mucky eater**, qn qui
mange comme un cochon 2. **a mucky pup**, un
enfant qui fait des saletés/qui se tient mal;
you mucky (little) pup! sale petit cochon!

mud [mʌd] *n* 1. *F* **here's mud in your eye!** à
votre santé!/à la bonne vôtre! 2. *P* *(drugs)*
opium*/noir *m* 3. *NAm P* café*/petit noir/jus
m (de chaussette)/caoua *m* 4. *NAm P* pudding
m au chocolat 5. *NAm P* signes télégra-
phiques brouillés/brouillage *m* 6. *F* **common
as mud**, *(ordinary, not rare)* du tout-venant;
(vulgar) qui traîne partout/dans les ornières;
she's common as mud, des (filles) comme

elle, ça se trouve à la pelle 7. *F* cancan *m*/ déblatérage *m*/débinage *m*; **to throw/to sling mud at s.o.**, éclabousser qn/traîner qn dans la boue 8. *F* **his name is mud**, sa réputation ne vaut pas cher. (*See* **clear I**; **stick-in-the-mud**)

muddler ['mʌdlə] *n F* brouillon, -onne/ individu* pagailleux.

mudslinger ['mʌdslɪŋə] *n F* calomniateur, -trice/médisant, -ante/débineur, -euse.

mudslinging ['mʌdslɪŋɪŋ] *n F* calomnies *fpl*/médisance *f*.

muff¹ [mʌf] *n* 1. *Br F O* échec*/loupage *m*/ ratage *m* 2. *V* sexe* de la femme*/barbu *m*/ chatte *f*/chagatte *f*.

muff² [mʌf] *vtr & i* 1. *Br F O* faire une erreur/rater/louper; **I muffed it**, j'ai raté mon coup/j'ai tout loupé 2. *V* (*cunnilingus*) faire minette/brouter (le cresson). (*See* **pearl-dive**)

muff-diver ['mʌfdaɪvə] *n V* (*cunnilingus*) buveur, -euse de bénitier/lécheur, -euse de minette. (*See* **pearl-diver**)

muff-diving ['mʌf'daɪvɪŋ] *n V* cunnilinctus*/descente *f* au barbu.

mug¹ [mʌg] *n* 1. *P* visage*/fiole *f*; **ugly mug**, gueule *f* d'empeigne; **get your ugly mug out of here!** tire ta sale gueule d'ici! **mug shot**, photo d'un criminel (*prise par `la police ou en prison*); cliché *m* anthropométrique; **mug and dabs**, photo et empreintes digitales; **to have one's mug and dabs taken**, passer au pied 2. *F* dupe *f*/cave *m*//jobard, -arde/vache *f* à lait; **mugs wanted**, on cherche des poires; **to be a mug**, être poire; **to be the mug**, être le couillon/l'avoir dans le baigneur; **what sort of a mug do you take me for?** tu me prends pour un con ou quoi? **it's a mug's game**, c'est un piège à cons/c'est un attrape-couillon; **mug's tax**, impôt *m* sur le revenu/l'impôt des poires.

mug² [mʌg] *vtr F* attaquer*/agresser/ tabasser*/voler*.

mugger ['mʌgə] *n F* 1. agresseur *m*/ cogneur *m* 2. *NAm* acteur, -trice qui grimace pour faire rire.

mugging ['mʌgɪŋ] *n F* (vol *m* avec) agression *f*.

muggins ['mʌgɪnz] *n P* 1. individu bête*/ gourde *f*/cruche *f*/balourd, -ourde 2. (*oneself*) **muggins, here, had to do it**, c'est encore ma pomme/mézigue qui a dû ie faire; c'est encore ma pomme qui s'est fait avoir/qui l'a eu dans le dos.

muggles ['mʌglz] *n P* (*drugs*) marijuana*.

mugg up ['mʌg'ʌp] *vi F* bûcher/piocher/ potasser.

muh-fuh ['məfə] *n NAm P* = **motherfucker**.

mule [mjuːl] *n P* (*drugs*) passeur, -euse/mule *f*.

mulga ['mʌlgə] *n Austr F* cambrousse *f*; **the mulga wire**, le téléphone arabe.

mulled [mʌld] *a Br P* ivre*/pompette.

mullet ['mʌlɪt] *n Austr F* **like a stunned mullet**, ahuri/médusé/baba.

mulligans ['mʌlɪgənz] *npl Austr P* cartes* à jouer/brêmes *fpl*/cartons *mpl*.

mull over ['mʌl'əʊvə] *vtr F* ruminer/ ressasser.

mum [mʌm] **I** *a F* **to keep mum**, se taire*/ne pas moufter/la boucler/l'écraser; **mum's the word!** motus et bouche cousue! **II** *n esp Austr P* **to have mum nature**, avoir ses règles*/ses ours.

mump [mʌmp] *vi P* mendier*/faire la manche/faire la mangave.

munchies (the) [ðə'mʌntʃiz] *npl* faim*; **to feel the munchies**, avoir la dalle/claquer du bec.

munchkin ['mʌntʃkɪn] *n esp NAm F* (*small child*) petit(e) gosse/mignard, -arde; (*dwarf*) rase-bitume *m*.

mung [mʌŋ] *n P* saleté*/crassouille *f*.

murder¹ ['mɜːdə] *n F* 1. **it's (sheer) murder in the rush-hour**, c'est (absolument) épouvantable/un cauchemar aux heures de pointe 2. **to get away with murder**, s'en tirer à bon compte/tirer les marrons du feu; **he could get away with murder**, on lui donnerait le bon Dieu sans confession. (*See* **blue**¹ **I 2**)

murder² ['mɜːdə] *vtr* 1. *P* battre* (qn) comme plâtre/tabasser (qn); **I'll murder you if you don't shut up!** je vais te bousiller, si tu la boucles pas! 2. *F* massacrer/saboter/ assassiner (une chanson, etc) 3. *F* **I could murder a beer/a fag**, je me taperais bien une bière/une clope.

murphy ['mɜːfɪ] *n P* 1. *Br* pomme *f* de terre/patate *f* 2. *NAm* **the murphy**, escroquerie*/arnaque *f*/entourloupe *f*.

musak ['mjuːzæk] *n F* = **muzak**.

muscle-head ['mʌslhed] *n F* individu bête*/truffe *f*.

muscle in ['mʌsl'ɪn] *vi F* 1. se pousser/ jouer des coudes 2. **he muscled his way in**, il s'est introduit de force/il a forcé la porte 3. **to muscle in on a conversation**, s'injecter dans une conversation.

muscle-man ['mʌslmæn] *n F* homme fort*/malabar *m*/costaud *m*/homme* à pogne.

mush [mʌʃ] *n Br P* **1.** (*a*) visage*/frime *f* (*b*) bouche*/goulot *m* **2.** [muʃ] individu*/type *m*/mec *m*; ami*/pote *m*; **listen, mush!** écoute, petit mec!/coco!/mon pote! **3.** parapluie*/pébroc *m*/riflard *m*.

mushy ['mʌʃɪ] *a F* à l'eau de rose/à la guimauve/gnangnan.

music ['mjuːzɪk] *n F* **to face the music**, faire front/braver l'orage/avaler la pilule; **he was left to face the music**, c'est lui qui a payé les pots cassés.

muso ['mjuːzəʊ] *n F* **1.** (bon) musicien, (bonne) musicienne/musico *m* **2.** fan *mf*/fana *mf* de rock, etc.

mustard ['mʌstəd] *a F* capable/malin/dégourdi. (*See* **cut**² **5**)

mutant ['mjuːtnt] *n P* individu* bête/gourde *f*/andouille *f*.

mutt [mʌt] *n P* **1. poor mutt!** le pauvre!/pauv' mec!/pauv' con! **2.** chien* (bâtard)/clébard *m*/clebs *m*/cabot *m* **3.** *Br* **Mutt 'n' Jeff,** (*RS* = *deaf*) sourd*/dur de la feuille.

mutton ['mʌtn] *n* **1.** *F* **mutton dressed (up) as lamb,** vieux tableau/vieille poupée **2.** *P* = **mutt 3.**

muttonhead ['mʌtnhed] *n F* individu bête*/andouille *f*/tête *f* de nœud.

muvver ['mʌvə] *n F* mère*/dabesse *f*.

muzak ['mjuːzæk] *n F Pej* musique *f* de fond/facile à écouter/musiquette *f*.

muzzle¹ ['mʌzl] *n P* bouche*/gueule *f*/tirelire *f*.

muzzle² ['mʌzl] *vtr P* **to muzzle s.o.**, gifler/torgnoler qn; foutre une tarte dans la gueule à qn.

muzzy ['mʌzɪ] *a F* légèrement ivre*/paf/éméché.

mystery ['mɪst(ə)rɪ] *n P* **1.** femme* inconnue dans le pays; **a mystery in the manor,** une nouvelle venue dans le coin **2.** *Austr* **mystery bags,** (*RS* = *snags*) saucisses *fpl*. (*See* **snags**)

N

nab¹ [næb] *n P* (*Black Slang*) agent* de police/flic *m*/keuf *m*.

nab² [næb] *vtr P* 1. (*a*) arrêter*/pincer/ agrafer/cueillir (qn); **the police nabbed the lot of them**, la police les a tous cueillis/ embarqués; **to get nabbed**, se faire pincer/se faire faire (*b*) (*catch in the act*) prendre (qn) sur le fait/la main dans le sac 2. (*a*) voler*/ chiper/chouraver (qch) (*b*) saisir/escamoter (qch).

nadgers ['nædʒəz] *npl A P* **to put the nadgers on** s.o., donner la malchance* à qn/ foutre la poisse à qn; **to give s.o. the nadgers**, ennuyer qn/casser les pieds à qn/courir sur le haricot à qn.

naff [næf] *a P* nul/tocard/moche; **that's a bit naff**, c'est plutôt nul/bidon.

naff off ['næf'ɒf] *vi P* (*Euph for* **fuck off!**) **naff off!** tire-toi!/taille-toi!/casse-toi!/fous le camp!

nag [næg] *n F* cheval*/bidet *m*/canasson *m*; **to follow the nags** = **to follow the gee-gees** (**gee-gee 2**).

nail¹ [neɪl] *n* 1. *F* **to pay (cash) on the nail**, payer cash/payer recta/payer rubis sur l'ongle 2. *F* **to hit the nail on the head**, mettre le doigt dessus/taper dans le mille/tomber juste. (*See* **coffin 2; doornail; tooth 5**)

nail² [neɪl] *vtr P* 1. (*a*) intercepter (qn) (*b*) arrêter*/agrafer (qn); **I got nailed**, je me suis fait pincer 2. demander un prix exorbitant à (qn)/fusiller (qn)/extorquer de l'argent* à (qn) 3. faire l'amour* avec (qn)/aiguiller (qn).

'Nam, Nam [nɑːm] *n NAm P* Vietnam *m*.

namby ['næmbɪ] *n Br F* individu* faible/ lâche; chiffe molle/gonzesse *f*/lavette *f*.

namby-pamby ['næmbɪ'pæmbɪ] *a Br F* (*sentimental*) gnangnan/à l'eau de rose.

name¹ [neɪm] *n F* 1. **to call s.o. names**, injurier* qn/traiter qn de tous les noms 2. **that's the name of the game**, c'est la vie 3. **not a penny to one's name**, sans le sou/sans un/ complètement fauché 4. **what in the name of God/of Heaven are you doing? what in God's/ Heaven's name are you doing?** mais nom d'un petit bonhomme/nom d'un chien/sacré nom d'une pipe/nom de nom, qu'est-ce que tu fais? 5. *NAm* **to take names**, (*act decisively*) agir résolument; (*chastise*) réprimander*/ enguirlander. (*See* **pack-drill; what's-(h)er-name; what's-(h)is-name; what's-its-name; wossname**)

name² [neɪm] *vtr F* **you name it, he's got it!** il a tout ce que tu peux imaginer; **you name it, he's done it!** tout ce que tu peux imaginer, il l'a fait.

name-drop ['neɪmdrɒp] *vi F* truffer sa conversation de noms de personnalités/passer son temps à faire mention des personnalités qu'on connaît; **she's always name-dropping**, à l'entendre on dirait qu'elle connaît le monde entier.

name-dropper ['neɪmdrɒpə] *n F* qn qui passe son temps à faire mention des personnalités qu'il/qu'elle connaît.

nana *n Br* 1. ['nɑːnə] *P* **he's a right nana!** c'est un vrai gugusse! **to feel a right/a proper nana**, se sentir tout bête*; **you silly great nana!** espèce de grande gourde!/espèce de nouille! 2. ['nænə] *F* = **nanna**.

nance [næns], **nancy(-boy)** ['nænsɪ(bɔɪ)] *n Br O P* 1. homosexuel*/tata *f*/folle *f*; **he's a bit of a nancy-boy**, il fait très tapette/il est un peu pédé sur les bords 2. homme* efféminé/ femmelette *f*/chochotte *f*.

nanna ['nænə] *n F* grand-mère/mémé *f*/ mamie *f*.

nap [næp] *vi F* **to be caught napping**, (*taken by surprise*) être pris au dépourvu.

napper ['næpə] *n P* tête*/caboche *f*/ciboulot *m*.

narc¹ [nɑːk] *n NAm P* agent *m* de la Brigade fédérale chargée de la répression du trafic de stupéfiants; = agent des Stups.

narc² [nɑːk] *vtr NAm P* = **nark² 3**.

narco ['nɑːkəʊ] *n NAm P* = **narc¹**.

nark¹ [nɑːk] *n P* 1. *Br* indicateur* de police/
indic *mf*/balance *f*/bordille *f*/mouchard, -arde.
(*See* **copper 1**) 2. = **narc(o)**.

nark² [nɑːk] *vtr P* 1. mettre en colère/mettre
en rogne/prendre à rebrousse-poil; **it really
narks me,** ça me fout en rogne/ça me met en
pétard/ça me met en boule 2. **to get narked,**
se faire arrêter*/agrafer/pincer 3. (*inform
against*) balancer/moucharder/vendre 4. **nark
it!** (*stop it!*) arrête! (*shut up!*) écrase!/la
ferme!/fous-moi la paix!

narked [nɑːkt] *a Br P* (*annoyed*) en rogne/
de mauvais poil.

narky ['nɑːkɪ] *a P* 1. en colère*/en rogne/en
pétard 2. = **sarky**.

nasties ['nɑːstɪz] *npl P* 1. (*drugs*) drogues
fpl/came *f*/dope *f*/stups *mpl* 2. *Br* sous-
vêtements *mpl* (vieux *ou* sales); slip *m* de
bain.

nasty ['nɑːstɪ] *n* 1. *P* organes génitaux;
sexe* de l'homme/de la femme 2. *P* coït*/
baise *f* 3. *F* **video nasty,** vidéo *m* d'épouvante
(*souv* pornographique).

natch! [nætʃ] *excl P* naturellement!/
naturlich!/nature!

natter¹ ['nætə] *n F* baratinage *m*/jactage *m*;
to have a natter, tailler une bavette.

natter² ['nætə] *vi F* bavarder*/jacter/
jacasser/tailler une bavette.

natty ['nætɪ] *a F* 1. *Br* chic/coquet/pimpant;
a natty little outfit, un beau petit ensemble/
costard 2. *WInd* impressionnant/super/cool.

natural ['nætʃrəl] *n F* 1. **never/not in all my
natural,** jamais de la vie 2. **a natural,** qui est
né pour ça/tout trouvé pour ça/qui est fait
pour ça.

naughty ['nɔːtɪ] *n P* coït*/partie *f* de jambes
en l'air; **to have a naughty/to do the naughty,**
faire l'amour*/godiller.

nbg, NBG ['en'biː'dʒiː] *abbr P* (= *no
bloody good*) bon à rien*/bon à nib.

nearly ['nɪəlɪ] *adv F* **nearly there:** *see*
bingo 89.

neat [niːt] *a esp NAm P* formid(able)/
chouette/super; **that's real neat!** c'est extra/
sensass/super!

nebbish ['nebɪʃ] *n P* nullard, -arde; nouille
f/cloche *f*/péteux, -euse.

necessary ['nesɪsərɪ] *n F* **the necessary,**
argent*/galette *f*/beurre *m*/blé *m*; **to do the
necessary,** payer* la note/casquer; **have you
got the necessary?** t'as le fric?

neck¹ [nek] *n F* 1. **to get it in the neck,**

écoper/en avoir pour son compte/trinquer;
he got it in the neck for that, il en a pris
pour son grade 2. (*cheek*) **you've got
a neck!** quel toupet!/quel culot! 3. **to stick
one's neck out,** prendre des risques/se
mouiller/se jeter à l'eau 4. **it's neck or
nothing,** il faut risquer/jouer le tout pour
le tout 5. **to be up to one's neck in work,**
être débordé de travail*/avoir du boulot
par-dessus la tête 6. **to be in sth up to
one's neck,** être submergé de/par qch; être
jusqu'au cou dans qch 7. (*a*) **to break one's
neck to do sth,** se décarcasser/se couper en
quatre pour faire qch (*b*) **I'll break your neck
if you touch it!** si tu y touches, je te casse la
tête/je te fais une tête au carré 8. **to breathe
down/to be on s.o.'s neck,** être sur le dos de
qn/être aux trousses de qn; **to get off s.o.'s
neck,** ficher/foutre la paix à qn 9. **to talk
through the back of one's neck,** dire des
bêtises*/débloquer. (*See* **dead I 5;
deadneck; leatherneck; pain; redneck;
roughneck; rubberneck**)

neck² [nek] *vi F* s'embrasser/se bécoter/se
rouler une pelle; se peloter; **to neck with s.o.,**
peloter qn. (*See* **rubberneck²**)

necking ['nekɪŋ] *n F* bécotage *m*; pelotage
m; **to get down to some serious necking,** faire
un pelotage poussé.

necktie ['nektaɪ] *n NAm F* corde *f* du gibet;
to throw a necktie party, lyncher/pendre/
béquiller qn.

neddy ['nedɪ] *n* 1. *Br F* cheval*/dada *m* 2. *P*
matraque *f*/bidule *m*.

needful ['niːdfʊl] *n F* **the needful** = **the
necessary** (**necessary**).

needle¹ ['niːdl] *n P* 1. *Br* (*a*) **to give s.o. the
needle,** (*annoy*) agacer/enquiquiner qn;
(*provoke*) aiguillonner/inciter qn; (*harass*)
harceler qn; (*tease*) taquiner qn; **he really
gives me the needle,** il me tape sur le
système/il commence à me (les) courir; il
arrête pas de me charrier (*b*) **to get the
(dead) needle for s.o.,** avoir une (sacrée) dent
contre qn (*c*) **to get/to cop the needle,** se mettre en colère*/piquer une crise; **I really got
the needle,** ça m'a vraiment foutu en rogne 2.
to be on the needle, (*habitually injecting*) être
de la piquouse/tenir à la poussette; (*be a drug
addict*) être drogué*/camé/toxico; *NAm*
needle park, lieu fréquenté par les junkies et
où ils se fixent 3. **needle and pin,** (*RS = gin*)
gin *m*. (*See* **piss² 2**)

needle² ['niːdl] *vtr* 1. *F* (*a*) agacer/

asticoter/enquiquiner (qn); **to be needled,** être de mauvais poil (b) aiguillonner/inciter/ tanner (c) harceler/bassiner; **to needle s.o. into doing sth,** pomper (l'air à) qn jusqu'à ce qu'il fasse qch/casser les pieds à qn pour qu'il fasse qch (d) taquiner/canuler **2.** P inoculer/ vacciner.

needle(-)candy ['niːdlkændɪ] n P (drugs) **1.** stupéfiant pris par injection/liqueur f de shooteuse **2.** héroïne*/cheval m.

nellie, Nellie, nelly, Nelly ['nelɪ] n **1.** O P homosexuel*/tante f/tata f **2.** P (weak, ineffectual person) chiffe f/gonzesse f/lavette f **3.** Br F **not on your nellie!** jamais de la vie!/ rien à faire!/tu peux toujours courir!/(il y a) pas de danger!

Nelson ['nelsən] Prn F **Nelson's blood,** rhum m. (See **tear**[1])

nerd [nɜːd] n P **1.** individu* bête*/crétin, -ine/(petit) con, (petite) conne/connard, arde; **he's a real nerd,** c'est un vrai connard **2.** (bookish person) rat m de biblio(thèque); bûcheur, -euse.

nerdy ['nɜːdɪ] a P crétin/déconnant.

nerk [nɜːk] n Br P imbécile*/crétin, -ine/ andouille f.

nerve [nɜːv] n F **1. to get on s.o.'s nerves,** courir/taper sur le système à qn; courir sur le haricot à qn **2. you've got a nerve!** quel culot!/quel toupet! **what a nerve you've got!** t'as un sacré toupet! **I like your nerve!** t'es culotté/gonflé! **that takes a lot of nerve,** faut être gonflé! **3. to have the nerve to do sth,** avoir assez d'audace/de cran/de poil au cul pour faire qch. (See **bundle 3**)

nervy ['nɜːvɪ] a F **1.** énervé; **he's terribly nervy,** il a les nerfs en boule/en pelote/à fleur de peau **2.** esp NAm culotté/gonflé.

nest-egg ['nesteg] n F économies fpl/ argent* mis de côté/pécule m; **to have a nice little nest-egg (tucked away),** avoir un bas de laine bien garni/avoir mis de l'argent à gauche.

nestle ['nesl] n P homosexuel*/pédé m/folle f.

never ['nevə] adv F **1. well I never!** pas possible!/ça par exemple!/j'en reviens pas! **2. never been kissed:** see **bingo 16 3. never fear,** (RS = beer) bière f.

never-never ['nevə'nevə] n Br F **to buy sth on the never-never,** acheter qch à crédit/à croume/à l'œil.

neves [niːvz], **nevis** ['nevɪs] n O P (back-slang = seven) sept; (seven-year sentence) sept gerbes fpl.

new [njuː] a F **1. new boy,** (employee, politician, etc) novice m/bleu m **2. that's a new one on me!** ça vient de sortir!/je ne suis pas au courant! **3. what's new?** quoi de neuf?

Newfie ['njuːfɪ] Prn NAm F (a) Terre-neuvien(ne) m(f) (b) Terre-Neuve f.

newshawk ['njuːzhɔːk], **newshound** ['njuːzhaʊnd] n F journaliste mf/reporter m/ chasseur m de copie.

newt [njuːt] n F **tight/pissed as a newt,** ivre* mort/complètement paf/beurré comme un petit lu/bituré.

newy ['njuːɪ] n Austr F **1.** novice mf/bleu m **2.** qch de nouveau/nouveauté f.

next [nekst] adv P **1. to get next to s.o.,** mettre bien avec qn/se mettre dans les petits papiers de qn **2. next off/next up,** puis/après/ alors.

Niagaras [naɪˈæg(ə)rəz] npl P (RS = Niagara Falls = balls) testicules*/balloches fpl/couilles fpl.

nibble ['nɪbl] n P **to have a nibble,** faire l'amour*/faire un carton.

nibhead ['nɪbhed] n Br F imbécile*/nouille f.

nibs, Nibs [nɪbz] n F (a) gros bonnet/grosse légume/milord m (b) cézig(ue) m; **his nibs,** son altesse.

nice [naɪs] a F **1.** Iron **nice work!** félicitations!/bravo!/chapeau! **2. nice and handy,** bien commode; **nice and comfy,** bien à l'aise **3. nice as pie,** très poli ou gentil; gentil comme un cœur.

nick[1] [nɪk] n **1.** Br P (a) prison*/bloc m/taule f; **he's in the nick,** il est en taule/au violon (b) commissariat m de police/quart m; **they took him down the nick,** ils l'ont emmené au quart/au poste **2.** P **in good nick,** (in a good state) en bon état/impec; (in good form) en forme/d'attaque; **he's in quite good nick for a sixty-year old,** il est encore vert pour un vieux de soixante berges **3.** F **Old Nick,** le diable/le Malin.

nick[2] [nɪk] vtr & i P **1.** voler*/faucher/chiper; **s.o.'s nicked my wallet,** on m'a piqué mon portefeuille **2.** arrêter*/agrafer/cravater/ épingler; **to get nicked,** se faire pincer; **the cops nicked him for that bank job,** les flics l'ont mis en cabane pour ce coup de la banque **3.** (cheat, defraud) arnaquer/niquer; **you were nicked,** tu t'es fait avoir **4.** Austr s'enfuir*/se calter/se trisser; **he nicked off,** il a mis les voiles/les bouts.

nickel ['nɪkl] *n NAm* 1. *F* pièce *f* de cinq cents; **it's not worth a nickel**, ça ne vaut pas tripette 2. *P (drugs)* **nickel bag**, quantité *f* de drogues qui vaut cinq dollars/dose *f* à cinq dollars 3. *P* cinq ans*/cinq berges *fpl*; **a nickel in San Quentin**, cinq gerbes *fpl* à (la prison de) San Quentin.

nicker ['nɪkə] *n P* 1. (billet* *ou* pièce *f* d')une livre sterling; **fifty nicker** = cinquante balles/demi-livre *f*/demi-jambe *f* 2. mégot*/ flèche *m*.

niff¹ [nɪf] *n Br P* 1. puanteur *f*/chlipote *f*; **what a terrible niff!** qu'est-ce que ça (s)chlingue! 2. reniflette *f*; **take a niff at that**, renifle-moi ça.

niff² [nɪf] *vi Br P* puer/(s)chlinguer/cocoter.

niffy ['nɪfɪ] *a Br P* qui sent* mauvais/puant.

nifty ['nɪftɪ] *a* 1. *F* beau*/pimpant/bath/ choucard 2. *P* malin*/débrouillard/dégourdi; **a nifty little motor**, un beau petit bolide; **it's a nifty idea**, c'est génial/c'est super/c'est une idée du tonnerre.

nig [nɪg] *n P Pej* = **nigger 1**.

Nigel ['naɪdʒəl] *Prn F Pej (upper-middle-class male)* = bourge *m*/bour *m*; *(upper-class male)* = B.C.B.G. *m*.

nigger ['nɪgə] *n P Pej* 1. nègre*/bougnoul *m*/bamboula *m* 2. **there's a nigger in the woodpile**, il y a un lézard/un os; **he's the nigger in the woodpile**, c'est un empêcheur de tourner en rond 3. **to work like a nigger**, travailler* comme un nègre/comme une brute/comme une bête; pisser du sang/suer sang et eau 4. *(drugs)* **nigger minstrel**, amphétamine*/amphets *fpl*.

nigger-driver ['nɪgədraɪvə] *n P (brutal overseer)* négrier *m*/garde-chiourme *m*.

nigger-lover ['nɪgəlʌvə] *n NAm P Pej* anti-ségrégationniste *mf*/protecteur, -trice du noir.

niggly ['nɪglɪ] *a F* de mauvaise humeur/ ronchonnard.

night-bird ['naɪtbɜːd] *n F* = **fly-by-night II 2**.

night hawk ['naɪt'hɔːk] *n F* = **night owl**.

nightie ['naɪtɪ] *n F* = **nighty**.

night-night! ['naɪtnaɪt] *excl F* = **nighty-night!**

night owl ['naɪt'aʊl] *n F* oiseau *m* de nuit.

nights [naɪts] *npl F* **to do/to work nights**, être/travailler de nuit/être nuitard/être nuiteux.

nightspot ['naɪtspɒt] *n F* night-club *m*/boîte *f* (de nuit).

nighty ['naɪtɪ] *n F (= nightdress)* chemise *f*/ liquette *f* de nuit.

nighty-night! ['naɪtɪ'naɪt] *excl F* bonne nuit!/'soir!

nignog ['nɪgnɒg] *n P* 1. individu bête*/ niguedouille *mf*; **you silly nignog!** espèce de nouille! 2. *Pej* Noir(e)*/nègre *m*/bougnoul *m*.

nigra ['nɪgrə] *n NAm P Pej* = **nigger 1**.

nimby ['nɪmbɪ] *n F (abbr of 'not in my back yard')* qn qui s'oppose à la construction d'une centrale nucléaire, etc près de chez lui.

nine [naɪn] *n NAm F* pistolet *m*/flingue *m* de neuf millimètres.

nine-bob note ['naɪnbɒb'nəʊt] *n Br P* 1. homosexuel*; **he's bent as a nine-bob note**, c'est une folle tordue/il est pédé comme un phoque 2. qch de faux/du bidon; **it's bent as a nine-bob note**, c'est du bidon/c'est daubé/c'est du toc. *(See* **bent***)*

nineteen [naɪn'tiːn] *n F* **to talk nineteen to the dozen** parler* vite/faire couler le crachoir; bavarder*/bavasser/jaser comme une pie borgne.

nineteenth ['naɪntiːnθ] *a F Hum* **the nineteenth hole**, le bar du golf.

nine-to-five¹ ['naɪntəfaɪv] *n F* **nine-to-five job**, travail*/boulot *m* à plein temps; métro, boulot, dodo *m*.

nine-to-five² ['naɪntəfaɪv] *vi F* travailler de neuf à cinq (heures)/travailler à plein temps/avoir des horaires de bureau.

nine-to-fiver ['naɪntəfaɪvə] *n F* qn qui travaille à plein temps/qui a des horaires de bureau/qui fait le métro, boulot, dodo.

nip¹ [nɪp] *n* 1. *F* **there's a nip in the air**, *(it's cold)* ça pince 2. *F* goutte *f*; **a nip of gin**, une rincette de gin 3. *F* = **nipper 1 4**. *P Pej* Nip, Japonais(e) *m(f)*/Jap *mf*/jaunet *m*.

nip² [nɪp] *vtr & i* 1. *F* **to nip round/over to s.o.'s house**, faire un saut chez qn; **nip along to the shops**, fonce/file à l'épicerie 2. *P* **to nip s.o. for money**, emprunter* de l'argent à qn/ taper qn 3. *P* voler*/barboter/faucher 4. *P (catch in the act)* prendre (qn) la main dans le sac/prendre (qn) en flag/faire (qn) marron en flag.

nip in ['nɪp'ɪn] *vi F* 1. entrer (lestement); **I nipped in to see her**, j'ai fait un saut chez elle 2. **to nip in (smartly)**, tirer avantage d'une situation.

nip off ['nɪp'ɒf] *vi F* partir*/jouer des flûtes/ prendre le large; **he nipped off with the takings**, il a mis les bouts avec la caisse/la recette.

nipper ['nɪpə] *n* 1. *F* gamin, ine/gosse *mf*/ mioche *mf*/moutard *m*/loupiot, -otte; **I've got two nippers**, j'ai deux gosses 2. *pl P* menottes*/bracelets *mpl*.

nipple ['nɪpl] *n F* (*acronym of Northern Irish professional person living in England*) Irlandais, -aise du Nord professionnel(le) résidant en Angleterre.

nippy ['nɪpɪ] I *a F* 1. froid/frisquet/frisco 2. rapide/alerte/vif; **to be nippy**, se dépêcher*/se grouiller; **that's a nippy little car**, c'est une voiture nerveuse/un petit bolide II *n O P* serveuse *f*.

nips [nɪps] *npl Austr P* **to put in the nips/to put the nips into** (s.o.), taper/torpiller (qn) (de qch).

nishte ['nɪʃtə] *n P* rien*/nib.

nit [nɪt] *n F* 1. *Br* individu bête*/crétin, -ine 2. *Austr* **to keep nit**, monter la garde/faire le pet 3. *NAm* rien*/nib. (*See* **nit-nit!**; **nitwit**)

nitery ['naɪtərɪ] *n NAm F* = **nightspot**.

nit-nit! ['nɪt'nɪt] *excl A P* boucle-la!/gare!/ vingt-deux!/acré!

nit-pick ['nɪtpɪk] *vi F* ergoter/chercher la petite bête/couper les cheveux en quatre/ enculer les mouches/chinoiser.

nit-picker ['nɪtpɪkə] *n F* ergoteur, -euse/ enculeur, -euse de mouches.

nitty-gritty ['nɪtɪ'grɪtɪ] *n F* the nitty-gritty, le (fin) fond/le tréfonds (d'une affaire); les faits *mpl* sans fioritures/l'essentiel *m* sans le baratin; **let's get down to the real nitty-gritty**, venons-en aux faits; **no small talk, give me the nitty-gritty!** pas de baratin, du solide!

nitwit ['nɪtwɪt] *n F* = **nit 1**.

nix¹ [nɪks] *esp NAm P* I *excl* nix! pas mèche!/rien à faire! II *n* 1. rien*/nib/que dalle!/peau *f* de balle 2. *O* **to keep nix**, monter la garde/faire le pet/gaf(f)er.

nix² [nɪks] *vtr NAm P* (*forbid*) mettre/ opposer son veto à (qch).

no [nəʊ] I *a F* **long time no see!** ça fait un bail (qu'on s'est vu)! (*See* **fear**; **go¹ II 1**) II *adv F* **no can do**, (*I can't do it*) compte pas sur bibi.

nob¹ [nɒb] *n Br* 1. *P* tête*/caboche *f*/nénette *f*; **so much a nob**, tant par tête de pipe 2. *P* aristo(crate) *mf*; **the nobs**, les rupins *mpl*/les gens *mpl* de la haute/le dessus du panier 3. *V* = **knob¹ 1**.

nob² [nɒb] *vtr Br P* 1. assommer/étourdir (qn) 2. coïter*/niquer.

nobble¹ ['nɒbl] *n Br P* 1. dopage *m* (d'un cheval); (*bribe*) dessous-de-table *m* 2. (*trick*)

entourloupe *f*; (*devious scheme*) combine *f*/ magouille *f*.

nobble² ['nɒbl] *vtr P* 1. doper (un cheval); acheter/soudoyer (qn, un jury); donner un dessous-de-table à (qn)/donner un pot-de-vin à (qn) 2. duper*/entôler 3. enlever/kidnapper.

nobody ['nəʊbədɪ] *n F* **a nobody**, une nullité/un zéro/un rien-du-tout/un(e) minable/ un minus. (*See* **business 4**)

nod [nɒd] *n P* 1. **on the nod** (*a*) ahuri par la drogue/envapé (*b*) *NAm* à crédit/à croume/à l'œil 2. **to get the nod**, être choisi/élu 3. **to give the nod**, donner le feu vert; **it went through on the nod**, la proposition a été adoptée sans discussion.

noddle ['nɒdl] *n F* tête*/ciboulot *m*/caboche *f*; **use your noddle!** fais travailler tes méninges!

noddy ['nɒdɪ] *n Br F* 1. imbécile*/andouille *f* 2. agent* de police/cogne *m*.

nod off ['nɒd'ɒf] *vi F* s'endormir/piquer un roupillon.

nod out ['nɒd'aʊt] *vi F* 1. = **nod off** 2. s'évanouir*/tomber dans les vapes.

noggin ['nɒgɪn] *n Br F* 1. tête*/caboche *f* 2. verre *m* (d'alcool)/pot *m*/demi *m*; **to have a noggin**, prendre un pot.

no-good ['nəʊ'gʊd] *a F* bon à rien; *esp NAm* **he's a no-good son of a bitch**, c'est un bon à rien de connard.

no-gooder ['nəʊ'gʊdə], **no-goodnik** ['nəʊ'gʊdnɪk] *n F* vaurien*/bon-à-rien *m*/ loquedu *m*/minable *mf*.

no-hoper ['nəʊ'həʊpə] *n Austr P* = **nobody**.

nohow ['nəʊhaʊ] *adv P* en aucune façon.

noise [nɔɪz] *n F* **to make the right noises**, savoir se tirer d'affaire/savoir s'en sortir. (*See* **big I 1**)

nonce [nɒns] *n Br P* (*prisons*) violeur *m*; *surt* coupable *m* d'attentat à la pudeur sur des enfants.

non-com [nɒn'kɒm] *n F Mil* (*abbr of non-commissioned officer*) sous-off *m*.

non-drop ['nɒndrɒp] *n P* (*weak, cowardly person*) chiffe molle/lavette *f*; **he's a real non-drop!** il n'a pas de couilles (au cul)!

nong [nɒŋ] *n Austr P* individu bête*/truffe *f*/ andouille *f*/patate *f*.

no-no ['nəʊnəʊ] *n F esp NAm* 1. = **nobody** 2. qch d'interdit; **that's a no-no**, ça ne se fait pas/pas touche à ça; **politics, that's a no-no around here!** la politique, alors là, pas touche!

noodle ['nuːdl] *n F* 1. individu bête*/nouille *f*/andouille *f* 2. *NAm* tête*/tronche *f*. (*See* **flip²** 2)

nookie, nooky ['nʊkɪ] *n Br P* coït*/crampe *f*/crampette *f*; **a bit of nookie,** une partie de jambes en l'air.

noov, noovo ['nuːv(əʊ)] *a & n Br F Pej* nouveau riche.

nope [nəʊp] *adv P* (= *no*) non*.

norgs [nɔːgz], **norkers** ['nɔːkəz], **norks** [nɔːks] *npl Austr P* seins*/rotoplots *mpl*/roberts *mpl*/nichons *mpl*.

north and south ['nɔːθən(d)'saʊθ, 'nɔːfən'saʊf] *n P* (*RS = mouth*) bouche*/goule *f*/trappe *f*.

nose [nəʊz] *n* 1. *F* **to poke one's nose in** (where it's not wanted), fourrer son nez*/mettre son grain de sel/ramener sa fraise 2. *F* **to pay through the nose for sth,** payer* qch une fortune/les yeux de la tête/acheter qch au poids de l'or 3. *P* **to keep one's nose clean,** se tenir à carreau/ne pas se mouiller/se ranger des voitures 4. *P* indicateur* de police/indic *mf*/mouchard, -arde/mouton *m* 5. *F* **to put s.o.'s nose out of joint,** (*make envious*) faire pâlir qn de jalousie/rendre qn vert (de jalousie) 6. *F* **to turn up one's nose (at sth),** faire le dégoûté (devant qch)/faire la petite bouche (sur qch) 7. *F* **to look down one's nose at s.o./sth,** toiser qn/qch/regarder* qn/qch de haut (en bas) 8. *F* **to have a nose (for sth),** avoir le nez creux/avoir du pif 9. *F* **he gets up my nose,** il me fait monter la moutarde au nez/il me tape sur le système 10. *F* **the parson's nose,** le croupion (d'une volaille)/as *m* 11. *esp NAm P* **on the nose,** (*exactly*) pile/juste 12. *Austr F* **on the nose,** qui sent*/mauvais/puant 13. *P* **to rub s.o.'s nose in it,** mettre (à qn) le nez dedans 14. *F* **he can't see any further than/beyond the end of his nose,** (*short-sighted*) il est myope/miro; (*narrow-minded*) il ne voit pas plus loin que le bout de son nez. (*See* **skin¹ 2, 3; toffeenose**)

nose about, around ['nəʊzə'baʊt, ə'raʊnd] *vi F* fureter/fouiner.

nosebag ['nəʊzbæg] *n P* **to put/to tie on the nosebag,** manger*/casser la croûte/se garnir le bocal. (*See* **trough¹,²**)

nose-candy ['nəʊzkændɪ] *n P* (*drugs*) cocaïne*/neige *f*.

nosedive¹ ['nəʊzdaɪv] *n F* baisse *f* (de prix, etc)/plongeon *m*; **oil (prices) took a nosedive,** les prix du pétrole se sont effondrés/ont dégringolé.

nosedive² ['nəʊz'daɪv] *vi F* (*of prices, etc*) dégringoler/s'effondrer.

nose on ['nəʊz'ɒn] *vtr P* dénoncer*/moutonner/bourdiller/cafeter (qn).

nose-rag ['nəʊzræg], **nose-wipe** ['nəʊzwaɪp], **nose-wiper** ['nəʊzwaɪpə] *n P* mouchoir*/tire-jus *m*.

nosey ['nəʊzɪ] *a F* = **nosy.**

nosh¹ [nɒʃ] *n P* 1. nourriture*/bouffe *f*/boustifaille *f* 2. repas *m*/frichti *m*.

nosh² [nɒʃ] *vi P* 1. manger*/boulotter/bouffer/croûter 2. (*steal*) barbot(t)er (qch).

nosher ['nɒʃə] *n P* mangeur, -euse/bouffeur, -euse.

nosherie ['nɒʃ(ə)rɪ] *n P* restaurant *m*/café *m*/bistroquet *m*.

no-show ['nəʊ'ʃəʊ] *n F* passager, -ère *ou* client, -ente qui ne se présente pas.

nosh-up ['nɒʃʌp] *n P* bon repas/bonne bouffe.

nostrils ['nɒstrɪlz] *npl F* **he gets up my nostrils** = he gets up my nose (**nose 9**).

nosy ['nəʊzɪ] *a F* fouineur/fureteur/fouinard; **nosy parker,** fouine *f*/fouille-merde *mf*.

nothing ['nʌθɪŋ] *n* 1. *F* **nothing doing!** rien à faire!/macache (bonbon)!/tu peux toujours courir! 2. *F* **to do sth in nothing flat,** faire qch très vite*/illico (presto)/en cinq sec; **nothing to it!** du nougat!/du gâteau!/du tout cuit! 3. *P* **you don't know nothing,** tu ne sais rien de rien; t'es en retard d'une rame/d'un métro; tu piges que dalle. (*See* **sweet 5; write 1**)

nouve, nouveau ['nuːv(əʊ)] *a & n Br F Pej* = **noov.**

nowt [naʊt] *n Br F* rien*/nib. (*See* **owt**)

nud [nʌd], **nuddy** ['nʌdɪ] *n F* **in the nud/in the nuddy,** tout nu*/à poil/à loilpé/le cul à l'air/en saint Jean.

nudie ['njuːdɪ] *n P* (*a*) film *m ou* revue *f* porno/de cul (*b*) nudie (show), spectacle *m* de strip-tease/de fesses/de cul (*c*) danseuse nue.

'nuff [nʌf] *n F* (*abbr of enough*) assez; **'nuff said,** assez dit/assez parlé.

nuke [njuːk] *vtr P* 1. atomiser 2. détruire/griller; (*defeat*) battre à plate(s) couture(s).

nukes [njuːks] *npl F* armes *fpl*/missiles *mpl* nucléaires; **no nukes!** non au nucléaire!/à bas le nucléaire!/nucléaire: non merci!

number¹ ['nʌmbə] *n F* 1. **your number's up,** ton compte est bon 2. **to look after number one,** penser à mézigue/soigner bibi/tirer la couverture à soi 3. **a hot number** (*a*) une bandeuse; **she's a hot number,** elle est très sexy/elle est bandante; (*attractive*) c'est une belle pièce/elle est bien roulée (*b*) morceau de musique enlevé avec fougue (*c*) article *m* qui se vend bien/article-réclame *m* **4. to have s.o.'s number**, en savoir long sur qn/être rencardé sur qn **5. to have the wrong number**, être sur la mauvaise piste/se gour(r)er **6.** tromperie *f*/arnaque *f*/entourloupe *f*; **to do a number on s.o.**, tromper* qn/rouler qn (dans la farine)/mener qn en bateau **7.** (*child's language*) **to do number one** = **to do little/ small jobs** (**job 7**); **to do number two** = **to do big jobs** (**job 7**) **8.** (*drugs*) cigarette *f* de marijuana*/joint *m* **9.** partenaire sexuel(le) (occasionnel(le))/coup *m* **10.** (*Navy*) **number one**, officier *m* en second à bord d'un navire (de guerre). (*See* **back-number**; **cushy**)

number² ['nʌmbə] *vtr F* identifier (qn); (*denounce*) balancer/vendre (qn).

number-cruncher ['nʌmbə'krʌntʃə] *n F* qn *ou* qch qui calcule; calculatrice *f*/ ordinateur *m*.

nunky ['nʌŋkɪ] *n F* **1.** (*child's word*) oncle *m*/tonton *m* **2.** = **uncle 5.**

nurd [nɜːd] *n P* = **nerd.**

nurk [nɜːk] *n Br P* = **nerk.**

nut¹ [nʌt] *n* **1.** *P* tête*/caboche *f*/ciboulot *m*; **use your nut!** fais travailler tes méninges! *Austr* **to nod the nut**, plaider coupable; **off one's nut**, fou*/timbré/toqué; **to go off one's nut**, devenir fou*/perdre la boule; **he's off his nut**, il travaille du chapeau. (*See* **nuts I 1**) **2.** *P* = **nutcase 3.** *F* (*fanatic*) fana *mf* **4.** *P* **to do one's nut**, se mettre en colère*/sortir de ses gonds/piquer une crise/se mettre en rogne **5.** *F* **he's a hard nut (to crack)**, c'est un têtu/une tête de mule; il n'est pas commode; **it's a hard nut to crack**, (*difficult problem*) c'est un casse-tête chinois/c'est une colle **6.** *F* **she can't play/sing for nuts**, elle joue/chante comme un pied; **he can't drive for nuts**, il conduit comme un manche. (*See* **toffee 1**) **7.** *F* **nuts and bolts**, l'essentiel/les bases *fpl*; **he's a very nuts and bolts sort of person**, il a les pieds sur terre/il ne plane pas **8.** *pl V*

testicules*/couilles *fpl*/noisettes *fpl*; **to get hot nuts**, être en érection*/bander; **to get one's nuts off**, éjaculer*/envoyer la purée; **to have one's nuts cracked**, faire l'amour*/tirer sa chique **9.** *P* **to talk nuts**, dire des bêtises*/des conneries *fpl*; **to talk like a nut**, dérailler/ déconner/débloquer **10.** *NAm P* **she's always (up) on my nuts**, elle fourre toujours son nez dans mes affaires; (*annoy*) elle me tape sur le système. (*See* **peanut**)

nut² [nʌt] *vtr Br P* donner un coup de tête*/ de boule/de caboche/de ciboulot à (qn).

nutcase ['nʌtkeɪs] *n P* fou*, folle/cinglé, -ée/dingue *mf*/barjot *m*; **he's a real nutcase**, il est complètement fou*/barjot/maboul.

nut chokers ['nʌt'tʃəʊkəz] *npl Austr P* caleçon *m*/slip *m*/cal(e)bar *m*/cal(e)cif *m*.

nut-house ['nʌthaʊs] *n P* maison *f* de fous/asile *m* de dingues/Charenton/Sainte-Anne.

nut out, up ['nʌt'aʊt, -'ʌp] *vi* devenir fou*/disjoncter/perdre la boule.

nuts [nʌts] **I** *a P* **1.** fou*/cinglé/dingue; **he's completely nuts**, il est complètement frappé/ fêlé; **you're driving me nuts with all these questions**, tu me rends dingue avec toutes ces questions **2. to be nuts about/on s.o./sth**, être toqué/fana de qn/de qch; être mordu de qn/ qch; **he's nuts about basketball**, c'est un mordu de basket/il est dingue de basket; **he's nuts about her**, il en est dingue/il en pince pour elle. (*See* **nutty**) **II** *excl* **nuts!** zut!/ merde! **nuts to you!** des clous!/flûte!

nutter ['nʌtə] *n P* fou*, folle/toqué, -ée.

nuttiness ['nʌtɪnɪs] *n P* folie *f*/loufoquerie *f*/maboulisme *m*.

nutty ['nʌtɪ] *a P* **1.** fou*/cinglé/loufoque/ maboul. (*See* **fruitcake 2**) **2. to be nutty about s.o./sth** = **to be nuts about s.o./sth** (**nuts I 2**).

nymphet ['nɪm'fet] *n F* nymphette *f*/petite poule/nénette *f*.

nympho ['nɪmfəʊ] *n F* (*abbr of nymphomaniac*) nymphomane *f*/nympho *f*.

O

O [əʊ] *abbr P* (= *opium*) (*drugs*) opium*/op *m*/noir *m*.

oak [əʊk] *n P* (*RS* = *oak and ash* = *cash*) argent*/fric *m*.

oats [əʊts] *npl* 1. *Br P* to get one's oats, être satisfait sexuellement/prendre son pied 2. *F* to feel one's oats, (*be bumptious*) faire l'important/se monter du collet; (*high-spirited*) avoir de l'entrain/avoir la pêche/avoir la frite 3. *F* to be off one's oats, se sentir patraque/tout chose/pas dans son assiette.

obbo [ˈɒbəʊ] *n F* (*Mil, police, etc*) (= *observation*) surveillance *f*; to be on obbo duty, être en planque/planquer; surbiner qn/qch.

obstropolous [ɒbˈstrɒpələs] *a F* bruyant/tapageur.

ochre [ˈəʊkə] *n esp NAm P* argent*/osier *m*/blanc *m*.

ocker [ˈɒkə] *n Austr P* (*boorish male*) plouc *m*/ploum *m*.

OD¹ [ˈəʊˈdiː] *n F* (*abbr of overdose*) dose trop forte (de narcotiques)/overdose *f*.

OD² [ˈəʊˈdiː] *vi F* prendre une overdose; he OD'd on heroin, il a pris/fait une overdose d'héroïne.

oddball [ˈɒdbɔːl] I *a P* excentrique/loufoque/farfelu II *n P* excentrique *mf*/zigoto *m*/drôle *m* d'oiseau/farfelu, -ue.

odds [ɒdz] *npl* 1. *P* odds and sods, objets hétéroclites *ou* dépareillés/bribes *fpl* et morceaux; (*people*) gens *mpl* de tout poil; there were a few odds and sods at the meeting, il (n')y avait pas la foule/il y avait quatre pelés et un tondu à la réunion 2. *F* over the odds, beaucoup trop/bien plus 3. *F* what odds does it make?/what's the odds? qu'est-ce que ça fait?/et après? 4. *P* to shout the odds, se vanter/se faire mousser/ramener sa fraise 5. *F* to be within the odds, être bien possible; that's well within the odds, ça se peut fort bien 6. *F* volumes dépareillés; livres *mpl*

supplémentaires.

odds it [ˈɒdzɪt] *vi Br P* prendre des risques; tenter sa chance.

odds-on [ˈɒdzɒn] *a F* to have an odds-on chance, jouer gagnant; it's an odds-on chance he'll get arrested, il y a gros à parier qu'il va se faire arrêter.

ofay [əʊˈfeɪ] *n NAm P Pej* (*white person*) Blanc, Blanche.

off¹ [ɒf] I *a F* 1. to have an off day, se sentir un peu malade*/ne pas être en train/ne pas avoir la pêche/ne pas être dans son assiette 2. that's a bit off, (*unfair*) ça dépasse les bornes/c'est un peu fort de café/c'est pas sympa; he was a bit off with me, il n'a pas éte sympa avec moi; his attitude was a bit off, il n'y allait pas avec le dos de la cuiller II *prep* 1. *F* (*drugs*) to be off it/off the stuff, ne plus toucher à la drogue 2. *F* off colour, un peu malade*/patraque/mal fichu; (*improper*) scabreux/osé/salé 3. *P* off (of)..., de...; I got it off (of) my brother, je le tiens de mon frère III *n F* ready for the off, prêt à partir*/sur le départ. (*See* **block 1**; **chump 1**; **crust 3**; **face¹ 7**; **head 5**; **nut¹ 1**; **off-the-wall**; **onion 3**; **rocker 2**; **trolley**)

off² [ɒf] *vtr NAm P* tuer*/éliminer/descendre/crounir (qn).

off chance [ˈɒftʃɑːns] *n F* on the off chance that, au cas où; he did it on the off chance, il l'a fait parce qu'on ne sait jamais.

office¹ [ˈɒfɪs] *n P* signal particulier/œillade *f*. (*See* **jack-in-office**)

office² [ˈɒfɪs] *vtr P* (*inform*) rencarder/mettre au parfum.

offie [ˈɒfɪ] *n Br F* (= *off-licence*) magasin *m* de vins et spiritueux.

offish [ˈɒfɪʃ] *a F* (*a*) distant/hautain/snobinard/bêcheur; she was very offish with me, elle me snobait/elle m'ignorait (*b*) mal en train/mal fichu; to feel a bit offish, ne pas avoir la frite.

off-putting [ˈɒfpʊtɪŋ, ɒfˈpʊtɪŋ] *a F*

181

déconcertant/déroutant; **I find all this talk about redundancies rather off-putting,** je trouve toutes ces histoires de licenciements plutôt déprimantes/démoralisantes.

off-side [ɒf'saɪd] *a Br F (unfair)* injuste; that's a bit off-side, c'est pas très sympa.

off-the-wall ['ɒfðəwɔːl] *a NAm P (a)* bizarre/excentrique/loufoque *(b)* fou*/cinglé/tapé/toqué; **she was off-the-wall,** elle était complètement cinglée.

offy ['ɒfɪ] *n Br F (= off-licence)* = **offie.**

oi! [ɔɪ] *excl Br F* holà!/hé!

oik [ɔɪk] *n Br P (vulgar, coarse person)* plouc *mf*/ploum *m*/gougnafier *m.*

oil [ɔɪl] *n F* 1. flatterie *f*/boniment *m*/pommade *f. (See* **palm-oil)** 2. to strike oil, gagner* beaucoup d'argent/trouver le filon 3. *Austr* renseignement* sûr/tuyau *m* de première/tuyau de plomb.

oiled [ɔɪld] *a F (well)* oiled, ivre*/bituré/cuit/dans le cirage.

oil-painting ['ɔɪlpeɪntɪŋ] *n F* she's no oil-painting, elle est laide*/c'est un cageot/elle est moche comme un pou.

oily ['ɔɪlɪ] *a F Pej* onctueux/mielleux. *(See* **rag¹** 9)

oinker ['ɔɪŋkə] *n NAm P* 1. *(vulgar person)* gougnafier *m* 2. policier*/poulet *m.*

OK¹, ok¹, okay¹ ['əʊ'keɪ] *a F* OK/impec/au poil; **an OK guy,** un type bien/un chic type/un mec sympa/un mec réglo.

OK², ok², okay² ['əʊ'keɪ], **oke** [əʊk], **okey-doke** ['əʊkɪ'dəʊk], **okey-dokey** ['əʊkɪ'dəʊkɪ] *adv F* d'accord*/dac/OK/banco; it's OK by me, ça me va; pour moi, ça marche/ça colle.

OK³, ok³, okay³ ['əʊ'keɪ] *n F* accord *m*/approbation *f*/OK *m*; **to give s.o. the OK,** donner le feu vert à qn.

OK⁴, ok⁴, okay⁴ ['əʊ'keɪ] *vtr F* être d'accord avec/approuver; opiner du bonnet; **he OK'd it,** il a fait signe qu'il marchait/qu'il acceptait.

old [əʊld] *a* 1. the old man *(a) F* mari *m*/l'homme *m*/le patron *(b) F* le père*/le pater(nel); **my old man,** mon vieux/mon vioc *(c) F* le patron*/le vieux/le singe/le chef *(d) F* the Old Man, le capitaine d'un navire/le pitaine *(e) P (also* old fellow) pénis*/le petit frère 2. *F* hello, old man! salut, vieille branche!/mon pote! *(See* **thing 8)** 3. *F* old woman/old lady *(a)* épouse*/la moitié/la patronne/la bourgeoise *(b)* mère*/la vieille/la mater(nelle); **my old woman,** ma vieille/ma

vioque *(c)* individu* qui fait des manières/chichiteux, -euse 4. *F* it's the same old story/tune, c'est toujours la même histoire/la même rengaine 5. *F* I met old Fred the other day, j'ai rencontré Fred l'autre jour 6. *F* it's a funny old world (we live in), *(catchphrase)* c'est comme ça/c'est la vie, que veux-tu? 7. *F* put them down any old where, pose-les n'importe où. *(See* **army 2; bean 2; Bill²; boy II 1; chap; crock 1; fogey; fruit 1; Harry 1, 2; hat 1; high I 5; how I 1; how-do-you-do; lag¹** 1 *(b);* **nick¹** 3; **rare; school 2; stick¹** 7 *(b), (c);* **thing 3)**

old-boy ['əʊld'bɔɪ] *n F* the old-boy network, la clique des anciens élèves; **he got his job through the old-boy network,** il a obtenu son boulot grâce au réseau des anciens.

oldie ['əʊldɪ] *n F* 1. vieux*, vieille/viocard, -arde/vioque *mf* 2. (golden) oldie, disque *m ou* chanson *f* pop sorti(e) il y a plus d'un an; vieux film; **that's an oldie,** il est vieux/il est pas tout récent celui-là.

old-timer [əʊld'taɪmə] *n F* un vieux de la vieille/un vieux routier.

Oliver (Twist) ['ɒlɪvə('twɪst)] *n P (RS = fist)* poing*.

ollie ['ɒlɪ] *n Br P (glass ball)* bille *f*; to lose one's ollies, devenir fou*/perdre le nord/perdre la boule.

on [ɒn] I *a P* sexuellement très excité/allumé II *adv F* 1. it's on, ça marche/ça va; **it's not on,** rien à faire/(il n'y a) pas mèche 2. **I'm on,** *(I want to take part)* j'en suis 3. **to be always on at s.o.,** être toujours sur le dos de qn III *prep F* 1. the drinks are on me/this one's on me, j'offre la tournée/c'est moi qui régale 2. *Austr* to be on it, boire*/caresser la bouteille/biberonner/picoler; **he's on it again,** il est (encore) chargé/dans le cirage 3. *Br* to be on one, *(a) (drugs)* être sous l'effet de l'ecstasy/être dans les vapes *(b)* être au courant/au parfum.

once a week [wʌnsə'wiːk] *n P (RS = cheek)* toupet *m*/culot *m.*

once-over ['wʌnsəʊvə] *n F* to give sth/s.o. the once-over *(a)* regarder*/reluquer/mirer qch/qn *(b)* battre* qn/passer qn à tabac/abîmer le portrait à qn.

oncer ['wʌnsə] *n Br P (billet* ou* pièce *f* d')une livre.

one [wʌn] *pron* 1. *F* un verre/un coup; to have (had) one too many, avoir (pris) un coup de trop/en avoir un dans le nez; **one for the road,** le coup de l'étrier. *(See* **eight 1; quick**

1) 2. *F (joke)* that's a good one! elle est bien bonne celle-là! 3. *F (blow)* he landed/fetched him one on the nose, il lui a flanqué un marron/un ramponneau sur le nez 4. *F* he pulled a fast one on me, *(tricked me)* il m'a eu/fait/roulé; il m'a joué un tour de cochon 5. *O F* you are a one! tu es impayable toi! 6. *F* to be a one for sth, être un fana/un mordu de qch; he's a right one for the ladies, c'est un chaud lapin/un chaud de la pince; il est porté sur la chose 7. *F* there's one born every minute, *(catchphrase)* on pend les andouilles sans les compter 8. *F* it's/that's a new one on me! ça m'en bouche un coin! 9. *P* ones and twos, *(RS = shoes)* chaussures*/godasses *fpl* 10. *NAm P* one thou(sand), pire que le plus mauvais/plus que pire. *(See* eye 14; number[1] 2, 7, 10; on III 3; stick[2] 9)*

one-horse ['wʌnhɔːs] *a F* a one-horse town, une petite ville de province/un trou (perdu)/un patelin/un bled.

one-liner ['wʌnlaɪnə] *n F (one-line joke)* un bon mot.

one-man ['wʌn'mæn] *a F* one-man band, homme-orchestre *m* (= *amant parfait ou qn qui fait tout lui-même).*

one-nighter ['wʌn'naɪtə], **one-night job** ['wʌn'naɪt'djɒb] *n P (a) (jazz, rock, etc)* représentation *f* d'un soir/gig *m (b)* rendez-vous sentimental d'un soir/coup *m (c)* client *m* d'une prostituée qui passe la nuit avec elle/clille *m* de nuit/couché *m*; to have/to do a one-nighter, faire un couché. *(See* stand[1] 1)*

one-off ['wʌnɒf] I *a F (a) (TV)* one-off film, film *m* en exclusivité *(b)* one-off title, livre *m* qui ne fait pas partie d'une série/livre à tirage limité II *n (thing)* objet *m* unique; *(person)* personnalité *f* unique; that was a one-off, ça ne se reproduira pas.

oner ['wʌnə] *n* 1. *F (expert)* as *m*/crack *m* 2. *P* coup* d'assommoir *m* 3. *Br P* to down a drink in a oner, faire cul sec; he got it in a oner, *(understood)* il a tout de suite pigé; *(got answer)* il a tout de suite trouvé la solution.

oneser ['wʌnsə] *n Br P* = **oncer**.

one-two ['wʌn'tuː] *n F* the old one-two, coup* sec du gauche suivi d'un direct du droit.

one-up ['wʌnʌp] *vtr NAm* to one-up s.o., l'emporter/renchérir sur qn.

one-upmanship ['wʌn'ʌpmənʃɪp] *n F* l'art de se faire passer pour supérieur aux autres; to practise one-upmanship, écraser les autres/se faire valoir par rapport aux autres.

onion ['ʌnjən] *n* 1. *F* that's the way the onion peels = that's the way the mop flops (mop) 2. *F* to know one's onions, connaître son sujet à fond/connaître son affaire; être à la coule/à la hauteur 3. *P (rare)* tête*/poire *f*; off one's onion, fou*/maboul.

oodles ['uːdlz] *npl F* oodles of..., beaucoup de.../une abondance* de.../des tas de.../un paquet de.../une chiée de ....

oojamaflip ['uːdʒəməflɪp], **oojie** ['uːdʒɪ] *n F* truc *m*/machin *m*/chose *mf*/machin-chose *m*.

oo-la-la! ['uːlɑːˈlɑː] *excl F* ho-là-là!

oomph [umf] *n F* charme *m*/personnalité *f*/sex-appeal *m*/chien *m*; he's got oomph, il jette du jus/il en jette.

oops-a-daisy! ['upsəˈdeɪzɪ] *excl F* hop-là!/youp-là (boum)!

op [ɒp] *n F (abbr of operation)* opération *f*/opé *f*.

open[1] ['əʊp(ə)n] *a F* it's an open and shut case, c'est sûr et certain/c'est du tout cuit/c'est dans le sac/c'est du tout vu/c'est couru d'avance.

open[2] ['əʊp(ə)n] *vtr P* to open one's legs (for s.o.), *(of woman)* faire l'amour*/faire une partie de jambes en l'air (avec qn).

open up ['əʊp(ə)n'ʌp] *vi F* 1. (a) avouer*/manger le morceau *(b)* parler franchement/vider son sac 2. se déchaîner/y aller à fond les manettes 3. *(shoot with a gun, rifle)* tirer*/flinguer/envoyer la purée.

operator ['ɒpəreɪtə] *n P* 1. voleur* (à la tire)/escroc*/filou *m*/empileur, -euse 2. fourgueur *m*/pourvoyeur, -euse de drogues. *(See* smooth)*

oppo ['ɒpəʊ] *n Br F (abbr of opposite (number))* 1. homologue *m*/partenaire *mf* 2. ami*/social *m*.

orchestras ['ɔːkɪstrəz] *npl P (RS = orchestra stalls = balls)* testicules*/couilles *fpl*/balloches *fpl*/roubignoles *fpl*.

organ ['ɔːgən] *n P* 1. pénis*/article *m*/outil *m* 2. organ grinder, sexe* de la femme*/boîte *f* à ouvrage/grippette *f*.

organize ['ɔːgənaɪz] *vtr P* = **wangle**[2].

ornery ['ɔːnərɪ] *a NAm F* désagréable; *(bad-tempered)* rouspéteur/de mauvais poil/en rogne; *(stubborn)* têtu.

OS [əʊˈes] *abbr Austr F (overseas)* à l'étranger; to go OS, partir à l'étranger.

oscar ['ɒskə] *n Br P (RS = Oscar Ashe = cash)* argent*/fric *m*/pèze *m*.

other ['ʌðə] *n P* 1. to have a bit of the other,

faire l'amour*/faire boum/tirer un coup 2. **pull the other one!** (*don't talk nonsense*) à d'autres!/ça prend pas! (*See* **bell¹ 2**; **tother**)

OTT [əʊ'tiː'tiː] *abbr Br P* (= *over the top*) exagéré/excessif/qui dépasse les bornes; **she's gone completely OTT,** elle est vraiment gratinée.

ounce man ['aʊnsmæn] *n NAm P* (*drugs*) petit revendeur (*surt* d'héroïne)/dealer *m*/ fourmi *f*.

out [aʊt] **I** *adv* 1. *F* **out on one's feet,** fatigué/ flapi/flagada 2. *F* (*a*) **to be out of it,** (*not involved*) ne pas être mis dans le coup/être laissé à l'écart; **you're well out of it,** par bonheur, tu n'es pas dans le coup (*b*) **to feel out of it,** (*out of place*) se sentir de trop/ne pas se sentir à sa place 3. *P* **to be out of one's head/one's skull/one's box/one's tree,** être fou*/cinglé/toqué; (*intoxicated by drink or drugs*) être high/dans les vapes; **she's out of it,** elle est dans les vapes 4. *P* **out of sight,** (*also* **outasight**) bœuf/du tonnerre; **that's out of sight!** c'est sensass!/c'est le (super-)pied! (*See* **far-out 2**) 5. *P* **out to lunch,** bizarre/ excentrique/loufoque; (*intoxicated by drink or drugs*) dans les vapes; **to be out to lunch,** travailler du chapeau. (*See* **light II 1**) **II** *a F* **to be out,** (*of homosexual*) s'avouer/vivre ouvertement comme homosexuel* **III** *n F* **to find an out,** se tirer d'affaire/se débrouiller*/se dépatouiller/trouver une porte de sortie. (*See* **get out**; **in III 2**)

outer ['aʊtə] *n Austr F* **to be on the outer,** (*of person*) être pauvre*/dans la dèche; ne pas avoir de chance/ne pas être verni; (*of horse, in races*) ne pas avoir la moindre chance; être un mort.

outfit ['aʊtfɪt] *n* 1. *F* équipe *f*/groupe *m* 2. *F* firme *f*/(maison *f* de) travail *m*; **what an outfit!** quelle boîte!/quelle taule! 3. *P* (*drugs*) attirail *m* de drogué/de junkie.

outlaw ['aʊtlɔː] *n P* membre *m* d'un gang/ loulou *m*.

out of order [aʊtəv'ɔːdə] *a Br F* 1. **to be out of order,** (*in the wrong*) être dans son tort; (*transgress*) violer (une loi, une règle) 2. (*incapacitated by drink or drugs*) rendu incapable/dans les vapes.

outside ['aʊt'saɪd] **I** *n F* **to be on the outside looking in,** ne pas faire partie d'une société *ou* d'un groupe; être un outsider **II** *prep F* **get outside that!** enfile-toi ça!

overcoat ['əʊvəkəʊt] *n F* **wooden/pine over-coat,** cercueil*/redingote *f* de sapin/paletot *m* sans manches; **to fit s.o. with a concrete over-coat,** tuer*/assassiner* qn et l'ensevelir dans du béton.

overspill ['əʊvəspɪl] *n F* ville *f* satellite.

ownsome ['əʊnsəm], **owny-o** ['əʊnɪəʊ] *n F* **on one's ownsome** *or* **owny-o,** tout seul/ seulabre. (*See* **lonesome**)

owt [aʊt] *n Br F* (= *anything*) quelque chose; **I don't do owt for nowt,** je ne fais rien pour rien. (*See* **nowt**)

oyster ['ɔɪstə] *n P* 1. crachat*/glaviot *m*/ huître *f* (bien grasse) 2. *esp NAm* individu* taciturne/qui fait la gueule.

Oz [ɒz] *n Austr P* Australie *f*/pays *m* des kangourous.

ozzy, Ozzy ['ɒzɪ] *n P* 1. hôpital*/host(e)au *m*/hosto *m* 2. *Austr* Australien(ne) *m(f)*/ kangourou *m*. (*See* **Aussie II**)

P

p [piː] *F* **to mind/to watch one's p's and q's,** (*be careful in one's behaviour*) se surveiller/ se tenir convenablement/se tenir à carreau; (*take care over details*) faire bien attention aux détails.

pa [pɑː] *n F* père*/papa *m*.

pace [peɪs] *n F* **to go the pace,** mener une vie de bâton de chaise.

pack¹ [pæk] *n* **1.** *P* (*drugs*) sachet *m* d'héroïne* **2.** *F* **pack of lies,** tissu *m*/tas *m* de mensonges* **3.** *Austr* **to go to the pack,** se détériorer/aller mal; aller à vau-l'eau.

pack² [pæk] *vtr F* **1. to pack a gun/a piece,** être armé/enfouraillé **2. to pack a punch** (*a*) boxer dur/perloter (*b*) (*of drink*) être corsé **3. to send s.o. packing,** envoyer qn dinguer/ paître/promener/sur les roses.

pack-drill ['pækdrɪl] *n F* **no names, no pack-drill,** (*catchphrase*) je ne donnerai pas de nom(s) (pour ne pas avoir d'histoires).

packet ['pækɪt] *n* **1.** *P* **to catch/to cop a packet** (*a*) (*have trouble, bad luck*) écoper/en prendre pour son grade (*b*) (*be imprisoned*) être bouclé/être envoyé en villégiature (*c*) = **to get a dose** (**dose 1**) **2.** *F* **to cost a packet,** coûter cher*/être salé; **it cost me a packet,** coûté bonbon/chaud **3.** *F* (*a*) **to make a packet,** gagner* beaucoup d'argent/prendre le paquet/en ramasser/faire son beurre (*b*) **to lose a packet,** perdre beaucoup d'argent*/ perdre un paquet/prendre une culotte. (*See* **buy 2**)

pack in ['pæk'ɪn] *vtr* **1.** *P* **to pack s.o. in,** cesser de voir qn/plaquer qn **2.** (*a*) *F* **to pack sth in,** cesser de faire qch/larguer qch; **he's packed his job in,** il a plaqué/largué son boulot (*b*) *P* **pack it in!** (*stop it!*) arrête!/laisse tomber! (*shut up!*) écrase!/ta gueule!/la ferme! **3.** *F* (*theatre, etc*) **to pack them in,** faire salle comble.

pack up ['pæk'ʌp] *vtr & i* **1.** *P* **to pack s.o. up** = **to pack s.o. in** (**pack in 1**) **2.** *F* **to pack sth up** = **to pack sth in** (**pack in 2** (*a*), (*b*))

3. *F* arrêter le travail; **come on, let's pack up for today,** allez, on boucle pour aujourd'hui **4.** *F* se détraquer/(commencer à) rendre l'âme **5.** (*a*) *F* partir*/plier bagage/prendre ses cliques et ses claques (*b*) *P* mourir*/lâcher la rampe/rendre ses clefs **6.** *F* tomber en panne/ en rade; **my car's packed up again,** ma bagnole est encore tombée en rade.

pad¹ [pæd] *n* **1.** *F* logement*/piaule *f*; **your pad or mine?** je monte à ta piaule ou tu viens à ma turne? (*See* **crashpad**) **2.** *P* lit*/pieu *m*; **to hit the pad,** se coucher*/se pieuter/se pagnoter.

pad² [pæd] *vtr & i* *F* marcher* (péniblement)/piler du poivre; **to pad it,** aller à pied/arquer/prendre le train onze. (*See* **hoof²**)

paddle ['pædl] *vtr P* = **wallop² 1.**

paddler ['pædlə] *n Austr A P* agent* de police/keuf *m*.

paddles ['pædlz] *npl Austr F* pieds*/ péniches *fpl*/pinceaux *mpl*.

pad down ['pæd'daʊn] *vi F* dormir*/ roupiller.

paddy, Paddy ['pædɪ] *n* **1.** *F* (*a*) (*bad temper*) mauvaise humeur; **he was in a right old paddy,** il était en pétard/en rogne/à cran (*b*) (*rage*) éclat *m* de colère/coup *m* de sang/ coup de raisin **2.** *P* cellule matelassée/ cabanon *m* **3.** (*a*) Irlandais, -aise (*b*) qn d'origine Irlandaise.

paddy-wag(g)on ['pædɪwagən] *n esp NAm F* car* de police/panier *m* à salade.

paddywhack ['pædɪwæk] *n F* **1.** = **paddy 1 2.** (*child's word*) fessée *f*/pan-pan (cucul) *m*.

pain [peɪn] *n F* **pain (in the neck),** individu ennuyeux* *ou* antipathique/raseur, -euse/ casse-pieds *mf*; **he gives me a pain in the neck,** il me tape sur le système; *P* **pain in the arse,** emmerdeur, -euse; **that girl is a real pain,** c'est une emmerdeuse (patentée).

paint [peɪnt] *vtr F* **to paint a picture,** faire

un dessin; **do you want me to paint a picture for you?** je te fais un dessin?/faut te faire un dessin? (*See* **red I 3**)

painter ['peɪntə] *n P* to have the painters in, avoir ses règles*/repeindre sa grille en rouge. (*See* **decorators**)

Pak(k)i ['pækɪ] *n P Pej* Pakistanais(e) *m*(*f*).

pak(k)i-basher ['pækɪbæʃə] *n P* chasseur *m* de Pakistanais; = ratonneur *m*.

pak(k)i-bashing ['pækɪbæʃɪŋ] *n P* chasse *f* aux Pakistanais; = ratonnade *f*.

pal [pæl] *n F* ami*/copain, -ine/pote *m*; **they're great pals**, ils sont copains comme cochons. (*See* **pal up**)

palatic [pə'lætɪk] *a Br P* ivre* mort/bituré/bourré comme un coing.

palaver[1] [pə'lɑːvə] *n F* 1. bavardages *mpl*/palabres *fpl*; baratin *m* 2. embarras *mpl*/chichis *mpl*; **what a palaver!** quelle histoire!

palaver[2] [pə'lɑːvə] *vi F* parler*/palabrer; baratiner.

pal in ['pæl'ɪn] *vi F* = **pal up**.

pally ['pælɪ] *a F* **to be pally with s.o.**, être très copain/lié avec qn; être copain comme cochon avec qn/être comme cul et chemise avec qn.

palm [pɑːm] *n F* 1. **to grease/to oil s.o.'s palm**, graisser la patte à qn 2. **to have an itchy/itching palm**, être grippe-sou/les avoir crochues.

palm-grease ['pɑːmɡriːs] *n P* graissage *m* de patte.

palm off ['pɑːm'ɒf] *vtr F* **to palm sth off on to s.o.**, refiler/coller/cloquer qch à qn.

palm-oil ['pɑːmɔɪl] *n P*= **palm-grease**.

palooka [pə'luːkə] *n esp NAm P* (*a*) (*boxing, etc*) joueur peu compétent/tocard *m* (*b*) (*slow-witted male*) nullité *f*/nouille *f*.

pal out ['pæl'aʊt] *vi F* se brouiller/se fâcher (avec qn).

palsy-walsy ['pælzɪ'wælzɪ] *a esp NAm F* **to be (all) palsy-walsy (with s.o.)**, être bons amis*/être à tu et à toi (avec qn)/être comme cul et chemise (avec qn).

paluka [pə'luːkə] *n P* = **palooka**.

pal up ['pæl'ʌp] *vi F* **to pal up with s.o.**, copiner/se lier avec qn.

pan[1] [pæn] *n* 1. *P* **to go down the pan**, échouer*/tomber à l'eau/foirer. (*See* **drain**[1] 1**) 2. *Br A P* visage*/burette *f*/fiole *f* 3. *F* compte-rendu *m* défavorable/éreintage *m*/flingage *m* (en règle).

pan[2] [pæn] *vtr F* 1. critiquer*/démolir/flinguer (qn/qch) 2. *Cin* prendre (une vue) en

panoramique/faire un pano sur (une vue).

Panama red ['pænəmɑː'red] *n P* (*drugs*) marijuana* de Panama.

panhandle ['pænhændl] *vi NAm F* mendier*/pilonner/faire la manche.

panhandler ['pænhændlə] *n NAm F* mendiant*/mendigot, -ote/piéton *m*.

panic ['pænɪk] *n* 1. *F* **panic stations**, postes *mpl* de combat; **it was panic stations**, c'était la grande panique 2. *F* **to push/to hit the panic button**, (*accelerate*) appuyer sur l'accélérateur/mettre les gaz; (*panic*) être pris de panique/paniquer/avoir les foies/perdre les pédales 3. *P* manque *m* (de drogues).

panicky ['pænɪkɪ] *a F* paniqué/paniquard; **don't get panicky**, ne t'affole pas!/pas de panique!

panning ['pænɪŋ] *n F* = **pan**[1] 3.

pan out ['pæn'aʊt] *vi F* 1. *F* finir/se terminer/aboutir; **it didn't pan out (well)**, ça n'a pas réussi 2. *P* rapporter (de l'argent)/donner 3. *P* **to pan out about sth**, s'étendre sur un sujet.

pansified ['pænzɪfaɪd], **pansy**[1] ['pænzɪ] *a F* (*a*) homosexuel/pédé (*b*) efféminé; **he's a bit pansified**, il fait un peu tapette.

pansy[2] ['pænzɪ] *n F* 1. homosexuel*/tante *f*/pédé *m*/lopette *f* 2. homme efféminé/chochotte *f*/femmelette *f*/gâcheuse *f*.

pansyland ['pænzɪlænd] *n F* le monde des homosexuels*/la pédale/la famille tuyau de poêle. (*See* **fairyland**).

pants [pænts] *npl* 1. *F* (*a*) pantalon*/falzar *m*/futal *m*/fute *m*; *NAm* **easy access**/*V* **fuck me pants**, futal avec la fermeture dans le dos (*b*) caleçon *m*/slip *m*/slibar *m* 2. *P* **to be caught with one's pants down**, être pris au dépourvu/par surprise/sur le tas; se trouver en mauvaise posture 3. *F* **to get a kick in the pants**, être réprimandé* sévèrement; recevoir un coup de pied aux fesses*/quelque part. (*See* **kick**[1] 5**) 4. *P* **to scare the pants off s.o.**, faire peur* à qn/donner la pétoche à qn/foutre les jetons à qn 5. *P* **to tear the pants off s.o.**, (*reprimand*) remonter les bretelles à qn/secouer les puces à qn 6. *P* **to beat/lick the pants off s.o.**, mettre une sacrée volée à qn 7. *F* **she wears the pants around here**, c'est elle qui porte la culotte 8. *P* **to get into s.o.'s pants**, faire l'amour* avec qn/se faire qn. (*See* **ants**; **fancy**[1] 3; **hot** 1, 2; **lead**[1] 4 (*b*); **smarty(-pants)**; **trousers**)

pantsman ['pæntsmən] *n Austr P* séducteur *m*/tombeur *m*/coureur *m*.

pap [pæp] *vi F* prendre des photos.

paper¹ ['peɪpə] *n P* 1. (*theatre*) billets *mpl* de faveur/bif(fe)tons *mpl* 2. (*drugs*) ordonnance *f* 3. (*police*) to put in the papers, démissionner.

paper² ['peɪpə] *vtr* 1. *P* (*theatre*) to paper the house, offrir des billets de faveur pour remplir le théâtre 2. *F* to paper over the cracks, faire du replâtrage/essayer de rafistoler les choses.

paper-hanger ['peɪpəhæŋə], **paper-pusher** ['peɪpəpʊʃə] *n P* faux-monnayeur *m*/morniffleur *m*.

parakeet ['pærəkiːt] *n NAm P Pej* Portoricain(e) *m(f)*.

paralytic [pærə'lɪtɪk] *a F* ivre* mort/bituré; he was completely paralytic, il était rond comme une bille/plein comme une bourrique.

paraphernalia [pærəfə'neɪlɪə] *n Euph* attirail *m* de drogué/de junkie.

pard [pɑːd], **pardner** ['pɑːdnə] *n NAm F* (*a*) associé, -ée/assoce *m*/baron *m* (*b*) ami*/ pote *m*.

park [pɑːk] *vtr F* to park oneself somewhere, se mettre/s'installer quelque part; park your backside down next to me, pose ton cul à côté de moi; park it over there! mets-le/colle-le là! (*See* **ticket 2**)

parker ['pɑːkə] *n F* **nosy parker,** *see* **nosy.**

parking ['pɑːkɪŋ] *n NAm F* = **necking.**

parky ['pɑːkɪ] *a Br F* (*weather*) frais/frisco/ frisquet; it's right parky today, on se les gèle/il fait un froid de canard aujourd'hui.

parlour ['pɑːlə] *n Austr P* bordel*/maison *f* de passe. (*See* **massage**)

parney ['pɑːnɪ] *n Br P* (*rare*) pluie*/flotte *f*/ saucée *f*.

partna ['pɑːtnə] *n NAm F* ami*/copain, -ine intime.

party¹ ['pɑːtɪ] *n F* 1. a certain party, un certain individu*/un loustic/un numéro 2. party pooper, trouble-fête *mf inv*. (*See* **hen** (*b*); **stag 1**)

party² ['pɑːtɪ] *vi P* faire la fête/faire la bringue.

pash [pæʃ] *n F* to have a pash on s.o., aimer* qn/avoir le béguin pour qn/en pincer pour qn/ être mordu de qn.

pass [pɑːs] *n F* to make a pass at s.o., flirter/faire des propositions à qn/draguer qn.

passenger ['pæsɪndʒə] *n F* poids mort.

pass up ['pɑːs'ʌp] *vtr F* refuser (une offre, etc); he passed up the opportunity, il a raté l'occase.

past [pɑːst] *prep F* I wouldn't put it past him, il en est bien capable; he's past it, il est plus cap(able)/il est fichu/il est foutu.

paste [peɪst] *vtr Br F* battre*/rosser/ dérouiller.

pasting ['peɪstɪŋ] *n Br F* to give s.o. a pasting (*a*) coller une raclée à qn/filer une peignée à qn (*b*) (*sport, etc*) battre qn à plate(s) couture(s).

pasture ['pɑːstjə] *n F* to be put out to pasture, être mis à la retraite/au vert.

pat [pæt] *n F* 1. *Austr* on one's pat, tout seul/ seulabre 2. Pat (*a*) Irlandais *m* (*b*) qn d'origine irlandaise.

patball ['pætbɔːl] *n F* tennis mal joué/jeu *m* à la raquette.

patch [pætʃ] *n* 1. *F* she's not a patch on him, elle n'est pas de taille/elle ne lui arrive pas à la cheville 2. *P* (*underworld slang*) territoire *m*/chasse gardée. (*See* **manor**; **plot**) 3. *F* bad patch, malchance*/guigne *f*; we're going through a bad patch, on est dans une mauvaise passe 4. *P* devise inscrite sur le dos des blousons de cuir des "Hell's Angels".

patch up ['pætʃ'ʌp] *vtr F* to patch up a quarrel/to patch it up, se réconcilier/se rabibocher; they've patched things up, ils se sont recollés.

pathetic [pə'θetɪk] *a F* 1. it's pathetic! c'est lamentable!/c'est à pleurer! 2. you're really pathetic! t'es minable!/t'es en dessous de tout!/t'es pitoyable!

patootie [pə'tuːtɪ] *n NAm P* 1. fesses*/ popotin *m* 2. *O* hot patootie, petite amie; blonde incendiaire.

patsy ['pætsɪ] *n P* dupe *f*/victime *f*/gogo *m*/ jobard, -arde/cave *m*.

paw¹ [pɔː] *n P* main*/patte *f*/paluche *f*; paws off!/keep your paws to yourself! bas les pattes!/pas touche! (*See* **southpaw**)

paw² [pɔː] *vtr F* peloter/tripoter (qn, *surt* une femme); tripoter (qch).

pawnee ['pɔːnɪ] *n Br P* (*rare*) = **parney.**

pax! [pæks] *excl Br F* (*schools*) pouce! end of pax, pouce cassé.

pay [peɪ] *vtr P* battre*/rosser/tabasser. (*See* **call¹ 1**; **visit**)

pay dirt ['peɪ'dɜːt] *n Austr F* to strike (bottom on) pay dirt, réussir/toucher au but/ décrocher la timbale *ou* le pompon.

pay-off ['peɪɒf] *n F* 1. règlement *m* de comptes 2. (*bribe*) pot-de-vin *m*/dessous *m* de table.

pay off ['peɪ'ɒf] *vi F* avoir du succès/être

rentable/faire un tabac.

payola [peɪˈəʊlə] *n F* (*bribe, esp to a disc jockey*) ristourne *f*/gratte *f*/pot-de-vin *m*/ dessous *m* de table.

PCP [ˈpiːsiːpiː] *n P* (= *phencyclidine*) (*drugs*) phéncyclidine *m*/PCP *m*.

PD [piːˈdiː] *abbr NAm F* (*police department*) police*/flicaille *f*.

pdq, PDQ [ˈpiːdiːkjuː] *P* (*abbr of pretty damn quick*) très vite*/et plus vite que ça/ dare-dare.

pea-brain [ˈpiːbreɪn] *n F* individu bête*/ crétin, -ine/tête *f* de nœud.

peacenik [ˈpiːsnɪk] *n O F* marcheur, -euse/ manifestant, -ante pour la paix.

peach¹ [piːtʃ] *n* 1. *F* belle* fille/jolie pépée/ beau petit lot; **she's a peach of a girl**, c'est un beau brin de fille 2. *F* qch de super/de sensass; un délice; **it's a peach of a dress**, c'est une super robe; **a peach of an idea**, une idée chouette/sensass 3. *P* indicateur*/indic *mf*/mouchard, -arde.

peach² [piːtʃ] *vi P* dénoncer*/moucharder/ cafarder; **to peach on s.o.**, vendre/balancer/ donner qn.

peachy [ˈpiːtʃɪ] *a NAm F* excellent*/aux pommes/extra.

pea-head [ˈpiːhed] *n NAm P* = **pea-brain**.

peanut [ˈpiːnʌt] *n* 1. *NAm P* (*drugs*) peanut butter, héroïne* 2. *pl F* presque rien*/des clous/des clopinettes/des prunes; **that's peanuts!** ça vaut des clopinettes/ça (ne) vaut pas un rond; **he pays peanuts**, il paie en monnaie de singe/il paie des clous/il les lâche avec un élastique 3. *NAm F* (*theatre*) peanut gallery, poulailler *m*.

pearl-dive [ˈpɜːldaɪv] *vi V* = **muff² 2.**

pearl-diver [ˈpɜːldaɪvə] *n* 1. *V* = **muff-diver** 2. *P* (*washer-up*) plongeur, -euse.

pearlies [ˈpɜːlɪz] *npl F* dents*/dominos *mpl*.

pearly [ˈpɜːlɪ] *a P* pearly gates, graines *fpl* de volubilis (*drogue hallucinogène*). (*See* **blue¹ II 1**)

pears [pɛəz] *npl Austr F* seins*/nénés *mpl*/ roberts *mpl*.

peashooter [ˈpiːʃuːtə] *n P* revolver*/ soufflant *m*. (*See* **shooter**)

peasouper [ˈpiːˈsuːpə] *n F* brouillard *m* (à couper au couteau)/purée *f* de pois.

peck [pek] *F* I *vi* manger* du bout des dents; **to peck at one's food**, pignocher/mangeotter son repas II *vtr* (*kiss*) bécoter/baisoter.

pecker [ˈpekə] *n* 1. *P* pénis*/goupillon *m*/ chibre *m*; **to play with one's pecker**, se

masturber*/s'amuser tout seul/se taper une pignole 2. *F* courage *m*/cran *m*; **to keep one's pecker up**, ne pas se laisser abattre/tenir bon/ tenir le coup.

pecking order [ˈpekɪŋɔːdə] *n F* hiérarchie (sociale).

peckish [ˈpekɪʃ] *a F* **to be/feel peckish**, avoir faim*/claquer du bec/avoir la dalle.

pedigree [ˈpedɪgriː] *n P* casier *m* (judiciaire)/pedigree *m*.

pee¹ [piː] *n P* urine *f*/pipi *m*/pisse *f*; **to have a pee**, uriner*; **to go for a pee**, aller faire pipi/ aller pisser.

pee² [piː] *vi P* 1. uriner*/pisser 2. pleuvoir à torrent/flotter/pisser; **it's peeing down**, il pleut comme vache qui pisse.

peed off [ˈpiːdˈɒf] *a P* = **pissed off.**

peek [piːk] *n P* the peek = **peep 1.**

peeker [ˈpiːkə] *n P* curieux, -euse/indiscret, -ète/voyeur, -euse.

peel [piːl] *vi NAm P* 1. inviter un garçon/une fille à sortir 2. faire l'amour*/baiser.

peeler [ˈpiːlə] *n Br P* (*in Northern Ireland*) agent* de police/flic *m*/poulet *m*.

peel off [ˈpiːlˈɒf] *vtr & i F* **to peel off** (one's clothes), se déshabiller*/se décarpiller/se défringuer. (*See* **banana 1; onion 1**)

pee off [ˈpiːˈɒf] *vi & tr P* = **piss off.**

peep [piːp] *n* 1. *P* the peep, cellule *f*/cellotte *f* de surveillance/surbine *f* 2. *F* I don't want to hear another peep out of you, tâche de ne pas piper/que je ne t'entende plus!

pee-pee¹,² [ˈpiːpiː] *n & vi P* = **pee¹,².**

peepers [ˈpiːpəz] *npl F* yeux *mpl*/mirettes *fpl*/châsses *mpl*/calots *mpl*.

peep freak [ˈpiːpˈfriːk] *n NAm F* = **peeping Tom.**

peeping Tom [ˈpiːpɪŋˈtɒm] *n F* voyeur *m*/ homme* qui se rince l'œil.

pee-slit [ˈpiːslɪt] *n V* sexe* de la femme*/ fente *f*.

peeve¹ [piːv] *n F* ennui *m*/barbe *f*/ emmerdement *m*; pet peeve, barbe *f* de premier ordre/super-emmerde *f*; it's a pet peeve of mine, ça me fout toujours en rogne.

peeve² [piːv] *vtr F* ennuyer*/barber/ empoisonner/faire chier/mettre en rogne.

peeved [piːvd] *a F* fâché/irrité/ennuyé; he was really peeved about it, ça l'a vraiment mis en rogne/ça lui a donné un coup de sang.

peg [peg] *n F* 1. off the peg, prêt-à-porter *m*/ confection *f* 2. (*a*) to take s.o. down a peg (or two), remettre qn à sa place/rabattre le caquet à qn (*b*) to come down a peg, en rabattre/baisser le ton/baisser d'un cran **3.** doigt *m* (de whisky, etc) **4.** *pl* jambes*/bâtons *mpl*/cannes *fpl*. (*See* **square¹ I 7**)

peg away ['peɡə'weɪ] *vi F* travailler* dur/ turbiner/piocher/trimer.

pegging ['peɡɪŋ] *n F* level pegging, à égalité; **it's level pegging,** ils sont à égalité.

peg it ['peɡɪt] *vi F* = **peg out I**.

peg-leg ['peɡleɡ] *n F* (*a*) jambe *f* de bois/ patte *f* de buis (*b*) qn qui a une jambe de bois.

peg out ['peɡ'aʊt] *F* **I** *vi* mourir*/lâcher la rampe/casser sa pipe **II** *vtr* to be pegged out, être très fatigué*/vanné/crevé/claqué.

pelf [pelf] *n Br P* argent*/fric *m*/pèze *m*.

pellet ['pelɪt] *n P* (*drugs*) capsule *f*/ comprimé *m*.

pen [pen] *n NAm F* (= *penitentiary*) prison*/ taule *f*/ballon *m*.

pen and ink ['penən(d)'ɪŋk] *vi Br P* **1.** (*RS = to stink*) puer/(s)chlinguer/taper **2.** (*not common*) (*RS = to drink*) boire*.

pencil ['pensl] *n P* pénis*/bout *m*/pinceau *m*. (*See* **lead¹ 3**)

penguin ['peŋɡwɪn] *n F* penguin suit, habit *m* (de soirée)/queue *f* de pie; **wearing a penguin suit,** déguisé/habillé en pingouin.

penman ['penmən] *n P* faussaire *m*/ maquilleur *m*.

penny ['penɪ] *n F* **1. then the penny dropped,** alors on a compris/pigé; et puis, ça a fait tilt **2. to spend a penny,** aller aux WC*/aller au petit coin **3. a penny for your thoughts,** (*catchphrase*) à quoi tu penses? **4. she cost me a pretty penny,** elle m'en a fait claquer/ écosser. (*See* **bad I 6**)

penny-pincher ['penɪpɪntʃə] *n F* avare *mf*/radin, -ine/rat *m*.

penny-pinching ['penɪpɪntʃɪŋ] *F* **I** *a* avare*/constipé du morlingue **II** *n* avarice *f*/ radinerie *f*; **I'm fed up with all this penny-pinching,** j'en ai ras le bol de ces radineries/ de ces pingreries/de ces histoires de grippe-sous.

pen-pusher ['penpʊʃə] *n F* gratte-papier *m*/rond-de-cuir *m*.

pension ['penʃ(ə)n] *n* **1.** *F* old-age pension: *see* **bingo 65 2.** *P* argent versé à un criminel/un racketteur pour qu'il vous protège.

pen-yen ['pen'jen] *n NAm P* (*drugs*) opium*/op *m*/toufiane *f*/noir *m*.

people ['piːpl] *npl F* **1. the income-tax people,** les gens *mpl* du fisc/les impôts *mpl*/les dégraisseurs *mpl* **2. to know the right people,**

avoir le bras long **3.** famille *f*/parents*; **his people live in the country,** ses vieux *mpl*/ses dabs *mpl* habitent à la campagne **3.** *NAm* the people, les membres *mpl* de son gang/la bande.

pep [pep] *n F* **1. to be full of pep,** être plein d'entrain/péter le feu/péter la santé/avoir la pêche **2. pep pill,** stimulant *m*/remontant *m*/ excitant *m* **3. pep talk,** paroles encourageantes/qui remontent le moral; **she gave me a little pep talk,** elle m'a fait un petit discours* d'encouragement/son baratin m'a requinqué.

peppermint ['pepəmɪnt] *a Br P* (*RS = skint*) très pauvre*/dans la dèche/raide.

peppy ['pepɪ] *a F* plein d'allant et de vitalité; **peppy beat,** rythme fort/dynamique.

pep up ['pep'ʌp] *vtr F* **1. ravigoter (qch) 2.** remonter/ragaillardir (qn).

Perce [pɜːs], **Percy** ['pɜːsɪ] *n P* pénis*/ cyclope *m*/Popaul *m*; **to point Percy at the porcelain,** uriner*/égoutter son colosse/faire pleurer le colosse.

perch [pɜːtʃ] *n F* **to knock s.o. off his perch/ to make s.o. come down from his perch,** (*depose*) détrôner/déboulonner qn; (*force to abandon pretensions*) rabattre le caquet à qn; **to come off one's perch,** (*make concession*) jeter du lest.

perfect ['pɜːfɪkt] *a F* vrai/absolu; **he's a perfect idiot,** c'est un idiot fini; **he's a perfect menace,** c'est un véritable danger public.

perform [pə'fɔːm] *vi P* **1.** déféquer*/ débourrer **2.** faire l'amour*/niquer; **he performs very well,** c'est une sacrée affaire/un sacré baiseur.

period ['pɪərɪəd] *n F* **I'm not going, period!** j'y vais pas, un point c'est tout/c'est marre!

perished ['perɪʃt] *a F* (*very cold*) **I'm perished,** je crève de froid/je me caille.

perisher ['perɪʃə] *n F* **the little perisher!** petite peste!/petit morveux!

perishing ['perɪʃɪŋ] *a F* **1. it's perishing,** il fait un froid de canard/ça caille/on se gèle; **I'm perishing,** je crève de froid/je me caille **2.** sacré/maudit/fichu; **a perishing nuisance,** un sacré embêtement; **you perishing idiot!** espèce de triple idiot!/pauvre cloche!

perks [pɜːks] *npl F* (= *perquisites*) gratte *f*/ affure *f*; les petits à-côtés/les petits bénefs/ avantages *mpl* en nature; **the job does have a few perks,** ce boulot présente des à-côtés intéressants/des avantages non négligeables.

perk up ['pɜːk'ʌp] *F* **I** *vtr* ravigoter/

requinquer (qn) **II** *vi* se ravigoter/se requinquer.

perm¹ [pɜ:m] *n F* 1. (= *permanent wave*) permanente *f* 2. (= *permutation*) permutation *f* (*au loto sportif*).

perm² [pɜ:m] *vtr F* 1. **to have one's hair permed**, se faire faire une permanente 2. (*football pools*) faire une permutation; permuter.

pernickety [pə'nɪkətɪ] *a F* tâtillon/ pointilleux; **to be pernickety about one's food**, être difficile sur la nourriture*.

perp [pɜ:p] *n NAm P* (*abbr of perpetrator*) criminel, -elle/suspect(e).

personals ['pɜ:sənlz] *npl Austr Euph F* sous-vêtements *mpl*/fringues *fpl* de coulisse.

perv(e)¹ [pɜ:v] *n P* 1. pervers(e)/détraqué, -ée 2. voyeur, -euse.

perv(e)² [pɜ:v] *vi P* se comporter comme un(e) pervers(e).

perv-wear ['pɜ:vwɛə] *n P* vêtements *mpl*/ fringues *fpl* sexy *ou* sadomasochistes; fringues de coulisse sexy.

pervy ['pɜ:vɪ] *a P* pervers.

pesky ['peskɪ] *a NAm F* maudit/sacré; **a pesky brat**, un petit morveux/un chiard.

pest [pest] *n F* enquiquineur, -euse/poison *mf*/plaie *f*.

pet [pet] *vi F* se caresser/se peloter. (*See* **petting**)

Pete [pi:t] *Prn F* **for Pete's sake!** pour l'amour de Dieu!/pour l'amour du ciel!/bon sang!

peter ['pi:tə] *n P* 1. coffre-fort *m*/coffiot *m* 2. **Peter (Bell)**, (*RS = (prison) cell*) cellule *f* de prison/cellotte *f*. (*See* **flowery (dell)**) 3. pénis*/Charles-le-Chauve *m*/Popaul *m*.

peterman ['pi:təmən] *n P* perceur *m*/ casseur *m* de coffre-fort.

petting ['petɪŋ] *n F* badinage amoureux/ pelotage *m*; **heavy petting**, attouchements *mpl*; **petting session**, séance *f* de bécotage *m*/ de pelotage *m*. (*See* **pet**)

pew [pju:] *n F* chaise *f*/cadière *f*; **take a pew!** assieds-toi!/pose ton cul!

pewter ['pju:tə] *n P* argent *m* (*métal*).

p.g. ['pi:'dʒi:] *abbr P* (*drugs*) (= *paregoric*) élixir *m* parégorique.

phiz [fɪz], **phizog** ['fɪzɒg] *n P* visage*/ frime *f*/frimousse *f*; **an ugly phiz**, une gueule d'empeigne/une gueule de raie/une sale gueule.

phon(e)y ['fəʊnɪ] **I** *a* 1. *F* faux*/bidon/toc; **it's phon(e)y**, c'est du toc 2. (*a*) *F* contrefait/ falsifié (*b*) *P* **phon(e)y white**, fausses pièces d'argent*/mornifle truquée **II** *n F* (*a*) charlatan *m*/bluffeur, -euse/chiqueur *m*; **he's a phon(e)y**, il est faux comme un jeton (*b*) (*insincere*) **what a phon(e)y he was!** quel baratineur!

phooey! ['fu:ɪ] *excl F* (*disbelief, scorn*) peuh! (*disgust*) pouah!/berk!

phut [fʌt] *adv F* **to go phut**, échouer*/rater/ louper/s'en aller en eau de boudin/claquer.

pi [paɪ] *a P* (= *pious*) bondieusard. (*See* **jaw¹ 2**)

PI [pi:'aɪ] *abbr F* (*private investigator*) détective privé/privé *m*.

pic [pɪk] *m F* (*a*) (*picture*) image *f*; (*photograph*) photo *f* (*b*) **the pics**, le ciné(ma)/le cinoche. (*See* **pix 2**)

Piccadilly Circus ['pɪkədɪlɪ'sɜ:kəs] *Prn F* **it's like Piccadilly Circus!** quel embouteillage!/on se croirait à l'Étoile!/c'est pire que l'Étoile (à six heures du soir)!

piccie ['pɪkɪ] *n F* = **pic** (*a*).

pickle ['pɪkl] *n F* 1. **to be in a pickle**, être dans le pétrin/dans de beaux draps/dans la mouise; **he's got himself into a right old pickle**, il s'est fourré dans un sacré/un beau/ un méchant pétrin 2. (*child*) petit diable/ diablotin *m*.

pickled ['pɪkld] *a F* ivre*/rétamé.

pick-me-up ['pɪkmɪʌp] *n F* remontant *m*/ stimulant *m*.

pick on ['pɪk'ɒn] *vtr F* chercher noise à (qn)/chercher des poux (dans la tête) à (qn)/ être sur le dos à (qn); **stop picking on me!** lâche-moi les baskets!/arrête de me courir sur le haricot!

pick-up ['pɪkʌp] *n* 1. *F* (*a*) rencontre *f* de fortune; personne *f* dont on fait connaissance dans la rue *ou* dans un bar/coup *m* (*b*) client* de prostituée/clille *m*/micheton *m* 2. *F* **to have a pick-up**, être conduit quelque part en voiture 3. *P* drogues* obtenues d'un pourvoyeur; **to make a pick-up**, se garnir/trouver le contact.

pick up ['pɪk'ʌp] **I** *vtr* 1. *F* arrêter/ agrafer/pincer/coffrer 2. *F* (*a*) (*make casual acquaintance*) **to pick up a man/woman**, lever un homme*/une femme*; **he tried to pick me up**, il m'a draguée (*b*) (*of prostitute*) raccrocher/lever (un client); **to pick s.o. up**, faire un levage 3. *F* ramasser/récolter; **to pick up sth nasty**, attraper/choper la crève 4. *F* **to pick up the pieces**, ramasser les morceaux 5. *F* reprendre/corriger (qn) **II** *vi* 1. *F* **to pick up with s.o.**, faire la connaissance de qn 2. *P* obtenir des drogues d'un pourvoyeur 3. *F* to pick up on sth, assimiler/digérer qch 4. *F* (*physically, financially*) se rebecter/se rebéqueter/se remplumer/se refaire.

picky ['pɪkɪ] *a F* difficile/chichiteux; to be picky, chercher la petite bête.

picnic ['pɪknɪk] *n P* occupation *f* agréable et facile/partie *f* de plaisir; it was no picnic, I can assure you, ce n'était pas du gâteau/de la tarte, je vous le promets.

picture ['pɪktʃə] *n F* 1. to put s.o. in the picture, mettre qn au courant/à la page; affranchir qn 2. she's a real picture! c'est une beauté!/elle est ravissante! 3. (*a*) to step into the picture, se montrer/se manifester (*b*) to step out of the picture, s'effacer/se retirer 4. get the picture? compris?/pigé?/tu piges?/vu? (*See* **paint**)

piddle[1] ['pɪdl] *n F* urine *f*/pipi *m*/pisse *f*; I need a piddle, j'ai envie de faire pipi; he's gone for a piddle, il est allé faire pipi.

piddle[2] ['pɪdl] *vi* 1. *F* uriner*/faire pipi/ pisser 2. *P* pleuvoir/flotter.

piddle about, around ['pɪdlə'baʊt, ə'raʊnd] *P* (*a*) paresser*/flâner/glander/ glandouiller (*b*) faire le con/déconner; stop piddling about over there and come here! arrêtez de faire les zouaves et ramenez-vous ici!

piddling ['pɪdlɪŋ] *a F* insignifiant/futile; négligeable; a piddling amount, des nèfles/des clous; you piddling little idiot! espèce de petite andouille/de petit crétin!

pidgin ['pɪdʒɪn] *n F* 1. = **pigeon 2** 2. to talk pidgin, parler petit nègre.

pie [paɪ] *n F* pie in the sky, illusions *fpl*/ (sacrées) illuses. (*See* **apple-pie**; **easy I 6**; **finger**[1] **6**; **fruity-pie**; **fur pie**; **hairpie**; **mince-pies**; **resurrection pie**; **sweetie 1**; **tongue-pie**; **tweety(-pie)**)

piece [pi:s] *n* 1. *P* fille*/femme*; she's a sexy piece, c'est un beau morceau/un beau brin de fille/un beau petit lot; elle est (pinocu)mettable 2. *F* to go to pieces, (*of person*) s'effondrer/s'écrouler; perdre les pédales 3. *P* deux grammes *mpl* d'héroïne *ou* de stupéfiant 4. *F* to pull s.o. to pieces, démolir qn/mettre qn en bouillie 5. *NAm F* arme *f*/revolver*/flingue *m* 6. *F* to give s.o. a piece of one's mind, sonner les cloches à qn/ passer un (bon) savon à qn 7. *F* œuvre *f*/ dessin *m* d'un taggeur. (*See* **ass I 2**; **cake 1, 3**; **headpiece**; **kettle 1**; **mouthpiece**;

pick up I 4; piss[1] 8; ring-piece; tail[1] 4; think-piece; work[1])

pie-eyed ['paɪaɪd] *a F* ivre*/gris/éméché.

piff [pɪf] *n Br F* = **piffle**.

piffle ['pɪfl] *n F* bêtises*/idioties *fpl*/ balivernes *fpl*/conneries *fpl*; to talk piffle, dire des conneries/n'importe quoi; débloquer/ déconner.

piffling ['pɪflɪŋ] *a F* = **piddling**.

pig[1] [pɪg] *n* 1. *F* goinfre*/gueulard, -arde/ morfal, -ale; to make a pig of oneself, se goinfrer/s'empiffrer/bâfrer 2. *F* salaud *m*/ saligaud *m*/vache *f*; you pig! la vache!/ salaud!/sale type! male chauvinist pig, phallo(crate) *m*; he's a real pig towards women, c'est un (sale) phallocrate/un phallo 3. *P* agent* de police/perdreau *m*/flic *m*/vache *f*; the pigs, la flicaille/les vaches 4. *P* (*a*) pig's ear, (*RS = beer*) bière *f* (*b*) pig's ear, désordre *m*/pagaille *f*/gâchis *m*; he made a real pig's ear of it, il l'a bien salopé 5. *P* (*a*) fille*/nénette *f* (*b*) *NAm* fille* laide/cageot *m* 6. *P* in pig, enceinte*/en cloque 7. *F* to buy a pig in a poke, acheter chat en poche 8. *F* pig's breakfast, méli-mélo *m*/fouillis *m*/salade *f* 9. *P* chose *f* difficile; that cupboard was a pig to move, cette armoire a été vachement difficile à déplacer 10. *F* pig Latin, = verlan *m*.

pig[2] [pɪg] *vtr & i P* 1. to pig oneself, se goinfrer/s'empiffrer/bâfrer/bouffer comme un chancre 2. to pig it, vivre comme un cochon/ vivre dans une écurie 3. to pig together, partager la même chambre.

pigeon ['pɪdʒɪn] *n F* 1. dupe *f*/poire *f*/pigeon *m* 2. it's not my pigeon, ça ne me regarde pas/c'est pas mes oignons; that's your pigeon, ça te regarde/c'est ton problème/ton affaire 3. indicateur*/indic *mf*. (*See* **cat 15**; **stool-pigeon**)

pigging ['pɪgɪŋ] *a Br P* (= **fucking**) sacré; take your pigging money and leave! prends ton foutu fric/ta saloperie de fric et tire-toi!

piggish ['pɪgɪʃ] *a F* 1. sale/cochon/crade 2. têtu/entêté.

piggy ['pɪgɪ] *F* I *a* goinfre*/goulu; piggy eyes, les petits yeux de cochon II *n* (*child's word*) 1. cochonnet *m*/cochon de lait/ porcelet *m* 2. petit goret/petit(e) goulu(e) 3. (*a*) doigt *m* (*b*) doigt de pied.

piggyback ['pɪgɪbæk] *n F* to give s.o. a piggyback, porter qn sur le dos *ou* sur les épaules.

piggy-bank ['pɪgɪbæŋk] *n F* (cochon *m*) tirelire *f*.

pig off ['pɪg'ɒf] *vi P* partir*/se tailler; pig off! fous le camp!

pig out ['pɪg'aʊt] *vi P* 1. (*eat excessively*) se goinfrer 2. vivre comme un cochon; (*make a terrible mess*) faire un bordel monstre.

pig-thick [pɪg'θɪk] *a P* très bête*/con comme un balai.

pike [paɪk] *n NAm F* (= *turnpike*) autoroute *f* à péage.

piker ['paɪkə] *n A P* 1. avare *mf*/grigou *m* 2. débiteur, trice/qn qui part sans payer/plante un drapeau.

pikestaff ['paɪkstɑːf] *n F* it's as plain as a pikestaff, c'est clair comme le jour/ça tombe sous le sens.

pile [paɪl] *n F* 1. (*a*) to make a pile (of money), gagner* beaucoup d'argent/en ramasser/faire sa pelote (*b*) to make one's pile, devenir riche*/faire son beurre 2. a pile of work, un tas/une montagne de travail* 3. piles of..., des masses de.../tout un tas de....

pile-driver ['paɪldraɪvə] *n F* coup* d'assommoir/direct *m*/marron *m*/parpaing *m*/taquet *m*.

pile in ['paɪl'ɪn] *vi F* s'empiler dans un véhicule; they all piled into the Mini, ils se sont tous empilés/entassés dans la Mini.

pile into ['paɪl'ɪntuː] *vtr F* to pile into s.o., attaquer* qn/agrafer qn.

pile on ['paɪl'ɒn] *vtr F* to pile it on, exagérer*/y aller fort/charrier. (*See* **agony 2**)

pile-up ['paɪlʌp] *n F* carambolage *m*/emboutissage *m*; a fifty car pile-up on the motorway, un carambolage de cinquante voitures sur l'autoroute.

pill [pɪl] *n* 1. *F* balle *f*/ballon *m* 2. *pl P* testicules*/billes *fpl*/roupettes *fpl* 3. *F* personne *f* désagréable/poison *mf*; it was a bitter pill to swallow, c'était dur à avaler/une pilule difficile à avaler 4. *P* (*drugs*) (*a*) capsule *f* de Nembutal (*b*) boulette *f* d'opium*. (*See* **pill-popper**) 5. *F* to be on the pill, prendre la pilule.

pillhead ['pɪlhed] *n P* drogué(e) aux amphétamines*.

pillock ['pɪlək] *n Br F* imbécile*/andouille *f*/tête *f* de nœud.

pillow biter ['pɪləʊ'baɪtə] *n P* homosexuel* passif/caroline *f*.

pillow-talk ['pɪləʊtɔːk] *n F* confidences *fpl* sur l'oreiller; (*argument*) semonce conjugale/engueulade *f* entre deux draps.

pill-popper ['pɪlpɒpə] *n P* drogué(e) aux amphétamines* *ou* aux barbituriques*.

pimple ['pɪmpl] *n P* 1. pimple and blotch, (*RS* = *Scotch (whisky)*) whisky *m* 2. *pl* pimples, petits seins*/mandarines *fpl*.

pimpsy ['pɪmpsɪ] *a Br P* (*schools*) facile/fastoche.

pin [pɪn] *vtr F* 1. to pin sth on s.o., rendre qn responsable de qch/mettre qch sur le dos de qn; they pinned it on me, j'ai dû porter le chapeau pour eux 2. *NAm* draguer/faire du plat à/faire du gringue à (qn).

pinch¹ [pɪntʃ] *n F* 1. to feel the pinch, tirer le diable par la queue 2. at a pinch, au besoin.

pinch² [pɪntʃ] *vtr F* 1. voler*/chiper/chaparder 2. arrêter*/alpaguer/agrafer; to get pinched, se faire épingler/pincer 3. to be pinched for time/money, être à court de temps/d'argent.

pinching ['pɪntʃɪŋ] *n F* vol *m*/chapardage *m*. (*See* **penny-pinching II**)

pine [paɪn] *n F* pine overcoat = wooden overcoat (**overcoat**).

pineapple ['paɪnæpl] *n F* grenade *f* (à main)/ananas *m*.

pinhead ['pɪnhed] *n P* 1. petite tête*/tête d'épingle 2. ignorant*/nouille *f*.

pink [pɪŋk] *F I a* 1. à tendances socialistes; rose sur les bords 2. *NAm* to get the pink slip, être renvoyé/se faire virer 3. homosexuel*/gay. (*See* **elephant 2; strike 1; tickle² 2**) *II n* to be in the pink, se porter à merveille/comme un charme.

pink-eye ['pɪŋkaɪ] *n Austr P* = **pinko 2**.

pinkie ['pɪŋkɪ] *n* 1. *F* le petit doigt/le riquiqui/le petit didi 2. *P* (*Black Slang*) Blanc *m*, Blanche *f*/fromage *m*.

pink lint ['pɪŋklɪnt] *a P* (*RS* = *skint*) pauvre*/raide.

pinko ['pɪŋkəʊ] *n* 1. *NAm F Pej* personne *f* à tendances socialistes; gauchisant, -ante/gaucho *mf* 2. *Austr P* qn qui boit de l'alcool à brûler/qui carbure à l'alcool à brûler.

pinky ['pɪŋkɪ] *n F & P* = **pinkie**.

pinny ['pɪnɪ] *n F* (= *pinafore*) tablier *m*.

pinpricks ['pɪnprɪks] *npl F* tracasseries *fpl*/asticotages *fpl*.

pins [pɪnz] *F* jambes*/fusains *mpl*/quilles *fpl*; he's not very steady on his pins, il ne tient pas sur ses cannes. (*See* **piss² 2**)

pinta ['paɪntə] *n Br O F* bouteille *f*/pinte *f* de lait.

pint-size(d) ['paɪntsaɪz(d)] *a F* minuscule; rikiki; pint-size(d) person, individu* de petite* taille/demi-portion *f*/rase-bitume *m*.

pin-up ['pɪnʌp] *n F (woman)* belle fille*/pin-up *f*/prix *m* de Diane; *(man)* beau mec; **pin-up mag,** magazine *m* de pin-up.

pip¹ [pɪp] *n F* 1. **to give s.o. the pip** (*a*) déprimer qn/flanquer le cafard à qn (*b*) embêter qn/casser les pieds à qn 2. *Mil* galon *m*/ficelle *f*; **to get one's pip,** recevoir ses galons/arborer la ficelle; **he's just got his third pip,** il vient de recevoir sa troisième ficelle.

pip² [pɪp] *vtr* 1. *P* blackbouler (qn) 2. *F* **the horse was pipped at the post,** le cheval a été battu au poteau (d'arrivée) 3. *F* recaler (un candidat) 4. *P* tuer* *ou* blesser (qn) avec une arme à feu/flinguer (qn).

pipe [paɪp] *n* 1. *F* **put that in your pipe and smoke it!** mets ça dans ta poche et ton mouchoir par-dessus! 2. *P* **to hit the pipe,** fumer de l'opium/y aller du chilom. (*See* **drainpipe; stovepipe**)

pipe down ['paɪp'daʊn] *vi P* (*a*) faire moins de bruit*; mettre un bémol/une sourdine; **pipe down, will you!** baisse un peu ta musique! (*b*) se taire*/la boucler.

pipe-job ['paɪpdʒɒb] *n V* fellation*/pipe *f*; **to give s.o. a pipe-job,** tailler une pipe/faire un pompier à qn. (*See* **blow-job**)

pipeline ['paɪplaɪn] *n F* 1. **to be in the pipeline,** être en cours/en train (de se faire) 2. **to have a pipeline,** avoir une filière/une combine.

piper ['paɪpə] *n NAm P (drugs)* fumeur, -euse de crack.

pipe up ['paɪp'ʌp] *vi F* se faire entendre/l'ouvrir tout d'un coup.

pip out ['pɪp'aʊt] *vi O P* mourir*/faire couic/clamser.

pipsqueak ['pɪpskwiːk] *F* **I** *a* petit/minuscule/insignifiant **II** *n* gringalet *m*/minus *m*/minable *mf*; **a little pipsqueak like you,** un petit avorton/merdeux comme toi.

piss¹ [pɪs] *n P* 1. urine *f*/pisse *f*; **I need a piss,** j'ai envie de pisser; **he's gone for a piss,** il est allé pisser (un coup) 2. *Br* **to take the piss (out of s.o.),** se foutre (de la gueule) de qn; **you're taking the piss!** tu te fous de moi/de ma gueule! (*See* **piss-taker**) 3. **a long streak of piss** (*a*) une perche/un échalas/un individu* long comme un jour sans pain (*b*) qn qui boude/qui fait la gueule 4. bêtises*/foutaises *fpl*/conneries *fpl* 5. *Br* **the piss,** alcool*/boisson *f* (alcoolique)/poivre *m*/gorgeon *m*; **cat's/gnat's piss,** *(inferior drink)* pipi *m* de chat/bibine *f*/pisse *f* d'âne; **to be on the piss,** picoler/se soûler 6. **to be full of/to be all piss and wind/piss and vinegar,** parler pour ne rien dire 7. **to beat the piss out of s.o.,** battre* qn comme plâtre/tabasser qn/passer qn à tabac 8. *Br* **a piece of piss,** qch de très facile/du nougat 9. bière peu forte/bibine *f* 10. sottises *fpl*/conneries *fpl*. (*See* **wind 3**)

piss² [pɪs] *vtr & i* 1. *P* uriner*/pisser/lansquiner 2. **to piss pins and needles,** être atteint de gonorrhée*/avoir la chaude-pisse/pisser des lames de rasoir (en travers) 3. **to piss oneself (laughing),** se tordre les côtes de rire/rire* à s'en mouiller/en pisser dans sa culotte 4. **to piss blood,** suer sang et eau/s'échiner 5. = **piss down** 6. **to piss it out the window,** dépenser* sans compter/claquer son argent/foutre le fric par les fenêtres 7. **to piss against the wind,** pisser en l'air/dans un violon.

piss about, around ['pɪsə'baʊt, ə'raʊnd] *vi V* (*a*) *(waste time)* glander/glandouiller (*b*) *(behave foolishly)* faire le con/déconner; foutre la merde; **stop pissing about, will you!** arrête de déconner, tu veux!

piss-all ['pɪsɔːl] *n P* rien/peau de balle/balpeau; **there's piss-all to do at night round here,** il n'y a rien à foutre/glander ici la nuit; **there's piss-all to drink in the cupboard,** il y a pas une goutte/rien à licher dans le buffet.

piss artist ['pɪsɑːtɪst] *n P* 1. ivrogne*/poivrot, -ote/soûlard, -arde 2. *(fool, idiot)* connard, -arde/con, conne 3. *(bungler)* maladroit, -oite/fouteur, -euse de merde 4. *(braggart)* vantard, -arde/grande gueule.

piss down ['pɪs'daʊn] *vi P* pleuvoir*/pisser; **it's pissing down,** il pleut comme vache qui pisse.

pissed [pɪst] *a P* 1. ivre*; **to get pissed (up),** se soûler/prendre une cuite/se biturer; **they were pissed out of their minds/completely pissed,** ils étaient bourrés à mort/comme des cailles 2. *NAm* = **pissed off.** (*See* **arsehole 3; newt**)

pissed off ['pɪst'ɒf] *a P* 1. **to be pissed off,** en avoir assez*/ras le bol/plus que marre; **I was really pissed off with it all,** j'en avais plein le cul de tout ça 2. très en colère*/furax/fumasse/en boule.

pisser ['pɪsə] *n P* 1. pénis*/queue *f*/pine *f* 2. WC*/pissotière *f*/pissoir *m* 3. con *m*, conne *f*/connard, -arde 4. **to pull s.o.'s pisser,** faire marcher qn/monter un bateau à qn.

pisshead ['pɪshed] *n P* 1. *Br* = **piss-artist** 2. *NAm* salaud*/ordure *f*.

pisshole ['pɪshəʊl] *n Br P (rare)* WC*/pissotière *f*/pissoir *m*.

pissing ['pɪsɪŋ] *a V* **1.** (*intensifier*) it's pissing cold, ça caille dur; he's a pissing nuisance, c'est un raseur/un emmerdeur de première; that was a pissing awful film, c'était un sacré navet, ce film **2.** pissing hell! bordel de merde!

piss it ['pɪsɪt] *vi Br P* réussir/cartonner.

piss off ['pɪs'ɒf] **I** *vi P* s'enfuir*/se tirer/se trisser; piss off! fous le camp! je t'emmerde!/va te faire voir! the little bugger's pissed off, le petit merdeux s'est carapaté/a mis les bouts **II** *vtr* to piss s.o. off, ennuyer* qn/faire chier qn; that really pisses me off! ça me fait vraiment chier! (*See* **pissed off**)

piss on ['pɪsɒn] *vtr P* dénigrer (qn)/débiner (qn)/traiter (qn) comme du poisson pourri; pisser à la raie de (qn).

piss-poor ['pɪs'pɔ:] *a P* **1.** très pauvre*/purotin/déchard **2.** de mauvaise qualité/tocard/de daube/de merde.

pisspot ['pɪspɒt] *n P* **1.** pot *m* de chambre/jules *m*/thomas *m* **2.** saligaud *m*/salaud *m* **3.** ivrogne*/sac *m* à vin/poivrot, -ote/alcolo *mf*.

piss-take ['pɪsteɪk] *n Br P* moquerie *f*/blagues *fpl*; it was a complete piss-take, il/elle se foutait de ma/ta/etc gueule; il/elle se foutait du monde.

piss-taker ['pɪsteɪkə] *n P* moqueur, -euse/charrieur *m*; qn qui se fout du monde. (*See* **mick(e)y-taker; piss¹ 2**)

piss-tank ['pɪstæŋk] *n P* = **pisspot 3**.

piss-up ['pɪsʌp] *n P* beuverie (générale)/soûlerie *f*; he couldn't organize a piss-up in a brewery, il est complètement incompétent/nul; s'il allait à la mer, il la trouverait sèche.

pit [pɪt] *n P* **1.** lit*/pageot *m*/pieu *m* **2.** poche* intérieure d'un vêtement/profonde *f* **3.** endroit *m* sale/dégueulasse; poussier *m* **4.** *pl* the pits, le pire (de tout); it's the pits, c'est nul; this place is the pits (of the Earth), c'est un coin perdu/minable; she's the pits, elle est horrible/quel cageot! (*See* **fleapit**)

pitch¹ [pɪtʃ] *n P* **1.** territoire *m* (d'une prostituée)/chasse gardée *f*. **2.** (*sales*) pitch, discours*/baratin *m*/boniment *m*/(publicitaire); laïus *m*; to make a pitch, bonimenter/faire du boniment/réciter son boniment **4.** *esp NAm* to make a pitch for s.o., draguer qn; faire du rentre-dedans à qn. (*See* **queer² 1**)

pitch² [pɪtʃ] *vi F* to be in there pitching, y aller de tout son soûl/s'en donner à cœur joie. (*See* **fly-pitch; yarn¹**)

pitcher ['pɪtʃə] *n Austr F* bavard*/jacasseur, -euse. (*See* **fly-pitcher**)

pitch in ['pɪtʃ'ɪn] *vi F* **1.** s'empiffrer/s'en mettre plein la lampe **2.** se mettre au travail*/se mettre au boulot/s'y mettre **3.** donner de l'argent*/les allonger.

pitch into ['pɪtʃ'ɪntu:] *vtr F* **1.** attaquer*/tomber sur le poil de (qn)/rentrer dans le lard à (qn) **2.** réprimander*/remonter les bretelles à/secouer les puces à (qn).

pix [pɪks] **1.** *n NAm P* (*not common*) homosexuel*/lopette *f* **2.** *pl F* (= *pictures*) (*a*) ciné(ma) *m*/cinoche *m* (*b*) (*pictures*) images *fpl*; (*photographs*) photos *fpl*. (*See* **pic**))

pixil(l)ated ['pɪksɪleɪtɪd] *a esp NAm F* **1.** un peu fou*/cinglé/barjot **2.** ivre*/bituré/bourré.

P.J.s [pi:'dʒeɪz] *npl* (*abbr of pyjamas*) *NAm F* pyjama *m*/pyj' *m*.

place¹ [pleɪs] *n F* **1.** to go places (*a*) voir du pays et du monde/rouler sa bosse (*b*) réussir (dans la vie)/aller loin **2.** piaule *f*; come for lunch at our place, venez déjeuner chez nous.

place² [pleɪs] *vtr F* I can't place him, je n'arrive pas à le remettre/le situer.

plague¹ [pleɪg] *n F* (*person*) plaie *f*/peste *f*/poison *mf*.

plague² [pleɪg] *vtr F* to plague (the life out of) s.o., harceler qn/rendre la vie impossible à qn.

plain [pleɪn] *adv F* plain daft/dumb, bête* comme ses pieds/complètement borné/con comme la lune.

plank [plæŋk] *n P* **1.** *Br* individu bête*/crétin, -ine/nouille *f* **2.** guitare *f* électrique solide/guitoune *f*.

plant¹ [plɑ:nt] *n P* **1.** (*spy*) taupe *f*; (*from police*) indic *mf*/mouchard, -arde *f* **2.** fabrication *f* de faux témoignage/coup monté **3.** cachette*/lieu sûr/planque *f*/planquouse *f* **4.** (*drugs*) marijuana*/herbe *f*.

plant² [plɑ:nt] *vtr* **1.** *F* to plant sth, cacher* qch/mettre qch en planque; the cops planted a gun/the drugs on him, les flics lui ont collé un canon/de la drogue sur lui **2.** *P* donner/flanquer/foutre (un coup* à qn) **3.** *F* to plant oneself in front of s.o., se planter devant qn; to plant oneself on s.o., s'installer chez qn.

plaster ['plɑ:stə] *vtr P* **1.** battre*/rouer de coups*/flanquer une dérouillée à (qn) **2.** *Mil* to plaster the enemy, bombarder/pilonner l'ennemi.

plastered ['plɑ:stəd] *a P* ivre*/rétamé/blindé/fadé; he was completely plastered, il était bourré à zéro/à mort.

plastering ['plɑ:stərɪŋ] *n F* **1.** volée *f* de coups*/pâtée *f*/raclée *f*/dérouillée *f* **2.** *Mil* bombardement *m* d'artillerie lourde/pilonnage *m*; bombardement de saturation.

plastic ['plæstɪk] *P* **I** *a* (*person*) peu sincère/superficiel **II** *n* disque *m*/galette *f* (de vinyle).

plat [plæt] *n Austr P* individu bête*/andouille *f*.

plate¹ [pleɪt] *n* **1.** *F* to have plenty/a lot on one's plate, avoir du pain sur la planche/avoir largement de quoi faire; I've got far too much on my plate, j'ai du boulot par-dessus les oreilles; j'en ai plus que ma part **2.** *P* plates (of meat), (*RS* = *feet*) pieds*/panards *mpl*/ nougats *mpl*/arpions *mpl* **3.** *F* to give/hand s.o. sth on a plate, le servir sur un plateau/ l'offrir tout rôti.

plate² [pleɪt] *vtr O V* (*oral sex*) faire une fellation à (qn)/faire un pompier à (qn)/sucer (qn).

platter ['plætə] *n P* disque *m*/galette *f* (de vinyle).

play¹ [pleɪ] *n F* to make a play for s.o./sth, user de tout son talent pour obtenir qch *ou* pour séduire qn; faire du gringue/du pa(l)las/ du charme. (*See* **horseplay**)

play² [pleɪ] *vtr & i F* **1.** to play with oneself, se masturber*/jouer de la mandoline/se faire boum/se battre à cinq contre un **2.** don't play games with me! ne te paye pas ma tête!/ne me fais pas marcher!/ne me fais pas tourner en bourrique!/n'essaie pas de me rouler! (*See* **ball¹ 3; cool¹ II** (*a*)**; fool¹ II; footsie; gooseberry; Harry 2; hook(e)y; kneesies; safe II; sucker**)

play about, around ['pleɪə'baʊt, ə'raʊnd] *vi F* **1.** to play about with women, courir le jupon/avoir des aventures; stop playing about with my wife, arrête de tourner autour de ma femme/de faire de l'œil à ma femme **2.** don't play about with me! = don't play games with me! (**play² 2**).

played out ['pleɪd'aʊt] *a* **1.** *F* très fatigué*/vanné/éreinté **2.** *F* vieux jeu/démodé **3.** *F* banal/usé/rebattu.

player ['pleɪə] *n Br P* **1.** (*in Northern Ireland*) terroriste *mf* **2.** spéculateur, -trice **3.** conspirateur, -trice.

play up ['pleɪ'ʌp] *vtr & i F* **1.** my back is playing me up, mon dos m'en fait voir/ déguster **2.** ennuyer*/asticoter/enquiquiner **3.** to play sth up, (*show sth up*) monter qch en

épingle/faire ressortir qch **4.** to play up to s.o. (*a*) flatter* qn/lécher les bottes à qn/ pommader qn (*b*) collaborer avec qn/ baronner qn.

plea [pli:] *n NAm F Jur* to cop a plea, plaider coupable à une faute moins grave afin de recevoir une peine plus légère.

pleb¹ [pleb], **plebby** ['plebɪ] *a P* vulgaire/ popu/populmiche; he lives in a very plebby area, (il) y a du peuple, là où il crèche; il habite un quartier prolo.

pleb² [pleb] *n P* prolo *mf*; the plebs, les prolos/la populace; you're such a pleb! t'es drôlement prolo!

plenty ['plentɪ] *adv F* it's plenty good enough, ça suffit largement; it's plenty big enough, c'est bien assez gros.

plod, the plod [(ðə)'plɒd] *n Br P* (*a*) la police*/la flicaille (*b*) agent* de police/poulet *m* (*c*) enquête policière.

plonk¹ [plɒŋk] *n F* vin* ordinaire/gros rouge/vinasse *f*/décapant *m*.

plonk² [plɒŋk] *vtr F* (*a*) mettre/flanquer/ coller/ficher; to plonk money on a horse, miser sur un cheval* (*b*) laisser tomber lourdement; plonk it down over there, flanque-moi ça dans ce coin.

plonk down ['plɒŋk'daʊn] *vi P* s'asseoir/ se colloquer.

plonker ['plɒŋkə] *n Br P* **1.** pénis*/ défonceuse *f*/dardillon *m*/zob *m*; to pull one's plonker, se masturber*/s'astiquer (la colonne); he got his plonker out, il a sorti son petit frère **2.** individu bête*/tête *f* de nœud/ gland *m* **3.** (*blunder*) gaffe *f*/couille *f* **4.** (*kiss*) patin *m*/pelle *f*.

plonko ['plɒŋkəʊ] *n esp Austr P* ivrogne*/ sac *m* à vin/poivrot, -ote/alcolo *mf*. (*See* **wino**)

plonk off ['plɒŋk'ɒf] *vi P* partir*/se tirer/se casser.

plop [plɒp] *n P* merde*; it's a pile of plop, c'est de la merde.

plot [plɒt] *n P* (*criminals, police*) territoire *m*/champ *m* d'action/chasse gardée. (*See* **manor; patch 2**)

plough¹ [plaʊ] *n O F* échec *m* (à un examen)/plantage *m*.

plough² [plaʊ] *vtr O F* to plough an exam/to be ploughed in an exam, échouer*/être recalé/se planter/être collé à un examen. (*See* **deep II**)

ploughed, *NAm* **plowed** [plaʊd] *a P* ivre*/blindé/bourré (à mort).

plough into, NAm **plow into**
['plaʊ'ıntu:] vtr F to plough into s.o.,
attaquer* qn; rentrer dans le lard/le chou à
qn; to plough into a parked car, emboutir/
(r)entrer dans une voiture en stationnement.

pluck [plʌk] vtr Austr P arrêter*/agrafer/
cueillir (qn).

plug¹ [plʌg] n 1. F publicité f/battage m/
postiche f; pub gratuite 2. P to give s.o. a
plug (in the ear(h)ole), donner*/foutre une
beigne/une baffe à qn 3. P (bullet) balle*/
bastos f/pastille f 4. F cheval* médiocre/
canasson m/bourrin m 5. F (a) to pull the
plug, se suicider*/se décoller (b) to pull the
plug on sth, abandonner l'idée de qch; faire
échouer* qch; to pull the plug on s.o., mettre
qn hors-circuit.

plug² [plʌg] vtr & i 1. F (a) faire de la
réclame/du battage (b) promouvoir/pousser
(qch) 2. P faire l'amour* avec (une femme)/
fourrer 3. P battre*/frapper/rosser (qn) 4. F
= **plug away** 5. P tirer sur/flinguer/flingoter
(qn) 6. to plug in both ways, (be bisexual)
être jazz-tango/marcher à voile et à vapeur.

plug away ['plʌgə'weı] vi F 1. travailler*
dur/turbiner/bûcher 2. s'acharner/s'obstiner;
he was still plugging away at it, il se
décarcassait toujours sur ce travail.

plugger ['plʌgə] n F 1. agent m de
publicité/posticheur m/promoteur, -trice de
vente 2. (hard worker) trimeur m/turbineur,
-euse/bûcheur, -euse/coltineur m.

plug-ugly ['plʌg'ʌglı] a F affreux/craignos/
moche comme un pou.

plum [plʌm] n F plum (job), travail* facile
et bien rétribué/boulot m en or/filon m/
fromage m.

plumb [plʌm] adv F plumb crazy, fou* à
lier/complètement siphonné.

plumbing ['plʌmıŋ] n F to have a look at
the plumbing, aller aux WC*/au petit coin;
faire pipi.

plummy ['plʌmı] a F 1. (job, etc) agréable/
bien payé/en or 2. (voice) (deep) profonde/
caverneuse; (upper-class) de la haute/snob.

plunge¹ [plʌndʒ] n F to take the plunge (a)
prendre le taureau par les cornes/se jeter à
l'eau/plonger (b) se marier/se marida.

plunge² [plʌndʒ] vi F jouer gros jeu/se
mouiller.

plunger ['plʌndʒə] n F joueur, -euse de
grosse mise/ponte m/flambeur, -euse.

plush [plʌʃ], **plushy** ['plʌʃı] a F riche*/
rupin/somptueux; his place is a bit plush, elle

est chic, sa turne; il pète dans la soie.

plute [plu:t] n F (abbr of plutocrat) plouto-
crate m/rupin m.

PNG [pi:en'dʒi:] abbr Br F (persona non
grata) persona non grata f/individu* interdit
de séjour.

po [pəʊ] n F pot m de chambre/jules m. (See
po-faced)

pocket ['pɒkıt] n F to have short arms and
deep pockets/to have a death adder in one's
pocket, être avare*/être constipé du
morlingue/être dur à la détente.

pod [pɒd] n P 1. (drugs) O (a) marijuana*/
thé vert (b) cigarette* de marijuana/stick m/
joint m 2. to be in pod, être enceinte*/être en
cloque/avoir un polichinelle dans le tiroir 3.
ventre*/bidon m/bide m. (See podge 2 (b))

podge [pɒdʒ] n F 1. individu gros*/gravos,
-osse/gras-double m 2. (a) graisse f/pneu m de
secours/poignée f d'amour (b) bedaine f/panse
f/bide m.

podgy ['pɒdʒı] a F rondelet/grassouillet.

poet's day ['pəʊıtsdeı] abbr F & P (= push
off/piss off early tomorrow's Saturday) vendredi m.

po-faced ['pəʊfeıst] a P avec une tête
d'enterrement/de bedeau; po-faced old cow!
sale gueule de vache!

pointy(-)head ['pɔıntıhed] n NAm F
intellectuel, -elle/tête f d'œuf/tronche f.

poison ['pɔızn] n F 1. name your poison!
qu'est-ce que tu veux boire?/qu'est-ce que tu
prends? 2. to put the poison in, empoisonner
l'esprit de qn (contre qn)/semer le venin. (See
rat¹ 5)

poke¹ [pəʊk] n P 1. coït*/baise f/bourre f/
coup m (d'arbalète); to have a quick poke,
faire l'amour*/tirer un coup vite fait/tirer une
petite crampette 2. to take a poke at s.o.,
sonner qn; filer/foutre une taloche à qn 3.
portefeuille*/lazingue m 4. Scot sac m (en
papier) 5. it's better than a poke in the eye,
c'est mieux que rien; il vaut mieux entendre
ça que d'être sourd 6. Br up the poke,
enceinte*/en cloque. (See cowpoke; pig¹ 7;
slowpoke)

poke² [pəʊk] vtr P 1. faire l'amour* avec/
bourrer/filer un coup d'arbalète à (qn) 2. to
poke s.o. = to take a poke at s.o. (poke¹ 2).
(See nose 1)

poke about, around ['pəʊkə'baʊt,
ə'raʊnd] vi F fouiller/farfouiller.

pok(e)y ['pəʊkı] n F prison*/trou m/placard
m. (See hokey-pokey)

pokie ['pəʊkɪ] *n Austr F* (*abbr of poker machine*) machine *f* à sous.

polack ['pəʊlæk] *n P* Polonais, -aise/ pola(c)k *mf*.

pole [pəʊl] *n F* 1. to go up the pole, devenir fou*/perdre la boule 2. to drive s.o. up the pole, rendre qn fou*/faire perdre la boule à qn 3. to be up the pole, avoir tort/se tromper; you're completely up the pole, tu t'es gour(r)é complètement/tu te mets le doigt dans l'œil 4. *Br* up the pole, enceinte*/en cloque 5. I wouldn't touch it with a ten-foot pole, je ne le prendrais/toucherais pas avec des pincettes. (*See* **barge-pole; bean-pole**)

polisher ['pɒlɪʃə] *n P* 1. (*toady*) lèche-bottes *m*/lèches-pompes *m* 2. *Austr* évadé, -ée de prison*/gibier *m* de potence. (*See* **apple polisher**)

polish off ['pɒlɪʃ'ɒf] *vtr F* 1. tuer*/ dégommer/liquider 2. terminer/liquider/ boucler (une affaire); achever/nettoyer (un plat, une bouteille).

pom [pɒm] *n* 1. *F* (*abbr of Pomeranian dog*) loulou *m* (de Poméranie) 2. *Austr P Pej* Anglais*, -aise/angliche *mf*/rosbif *mf*.

pommy, Pommy ['pɒmɪ] *Austr F Pej* I *a* anglais/angliche; pommy bastards, salauds *mpl* d'angliches II *n* = **pom 2**.

ponce[1] [pɒns] *n P* 1. souteneur*/marle *m*/ marlou *m*/mac *m*/julot *m* 2. homme efféminé; he's a bit of a ponce, il fait très tapette 3. (*parasite, borrower*) tapeur *m*/torpilleur *m*.

ponce[2] [pɒns] *vtr & i P* 1. maquer/faire le maquereau/être julot/faire le mac/relever le(s) compteur(s) 2. mendier*/taper*/ torpiller/pilonner; to ponce a fag off s.o., taper qn d'une cigarette*/d'une clope.

ponce about, around ['pɒnsə'baʊt, ə'raʊnd] *vi P* 1. être efféminé/faire des airs (de pédé)/se pavaner 2. (*a*) (*laze about*) glander/glandouiller (*b*) (*play the fool*) faire le con/déconner.

ponce off ['pɒns'ɒf] *vi P* partir*/dégager/ les mettre; ponce off! fous le camp!/casse-toi!

ponce up ['pɒns'ʌp] *vtr P* to get ponced up/to ponce oneself up, se mettre sur son trente et un.

poncy ['pɒnsɪ] *a* 1. *P* a poncy individual, un individu* qui semble se faire entretenir par les femmes/maquereau *m* sur les bords 2. *F* efféminé; a poncy little man, une lopette; a poncy little car, une vraie bagnole de pédé/de tapette.

pond, Pond (the) [pɒnd] *n F* la Mare (aux harengs). (*See* **herring 2**).

pong[1] [pɒŋ] *n P* puanteur *f*/chlipote *f*; what a dreadful pong! ça cocotte/ça (s)chlingue/ça schlipote ici!

pong[2] [pɒŋ] *vi P* sentir* mauvais; puer/ (s)chlinguer/cocotter/schlipoter; your feet really pong! tu chasses des arpions!

pongo ['pɒŋgəʊ] *n P* 1. *Pej* noir*/bougnoul *m* 2. soldat*/bidasse *m* 3. *Austr & New Zealand* Anglais, -aise/angliche *mf*.

pontoon [pɒn'tuːn] *n P* 21 mois *mpl* de prison/de taule.

pony ['pəʊnɪ] *n P* 1. 25 livres *fpl* sterling; it cost me a pony, ça m'a coûté 25 sacs 2. petit verre de liqueur/pousse(-café) *m* 3. *NAm* (*schools*) traduction *f*/traduc *f*/trado *f* (juxtalinéaire).

pony (and trap) ['pəʊnɪən'træp] *P* (*RS = crap*) I *a* that's a bit pony, c'est merdique/ c'est de la merde II *n* to have a pony, déféquer*/chier/poser sa pêche.

poo[1] [puː] *n F* (*child's language*) excrément *m*/caca *m*; to do a poo, faire caca.

poo[2] [puː] *vi F* déféquer*/faire caca.

pooch [puːtʃ], **poochy** ['puːtʃɪ] *n P* chien* (bâtard)/cabot *m*/clebs *m*/clébard *m*.

poodle-faker ['puːdl'feɪkə] *n F* jeune homme* veule/efféminé/maniéré (*qui fréquente des femmes plus âgées*).

poof [puf, puːf], **pooftah, poofter** ['pʊftə] *n P* (*a*) homosexuel*/pédé *m*/tante *f*; he's a poof, il en est/il est de la jaquette/c'est une pédale (*b*) homme* efféminé; I look a right poofter wearing this, j'ai l'air d'une vraie tapette fringué comme ça.

poofy ['pʊfɪ, 'puːfɪ] *a P* efféminé/à tendance homosexuelle/de pédé/qui fait tapette; he was wearing a very poofy looking outfit, ses fringues lui donnaient l'air d'un travelo/d'un pédé.

pooh [puː] *n F* = **poo**[1].

pooh! [puː] *excl F* 1. ça pue! 2. peuh!/quelle affaire!/la belle affaire!

pool [puːl] *vtr Austr F* dénoncer*/ moucharder/balancer (qn).

poon [puːn] *n P* 1. *Austr* individu bête*/niais, -aise/ballot *m*/ducon-la-joie *m* 2. = **poontang**.

poonce [puːns] *n Austr P* homosexuel*/ tapette *f*/pédale *f*.

pooned up ['puːnd'ʌp] *a Austr P* to get pooned up, s'habiller avec élégance/se mettre sur son trente et un.

poontang [puːn'tæŋ] *n P* 1. sexe* de la femme/bonbon *m* 2. femmes* en général/nanas *fpl*.

poop [puːp] *n esp NAm* 1. *P* excrément *m*/merde *f*; **poop chute**, anus*/pot *m* d'échappement/couloir *m* aux lentilles 2. *F* renseignement*/rencard *m*; **hot poop**, dernières nouvelles.

pooped (out) ['puːpt('aʊt)] *a F* très fatigué*/éreinté/vanné.

pooper ['puːpə] *n F* **party pooper**, *see* **party¹** 2.

poo-poo ['puːpuː] *n P* = **poop 1**.

poop-scared [puːp'skɛəd] *a P* qui a peur*/chiasseux/foireux.

poorly ['pʊəlɪ] *a F* malade*/patraque/pas dans son assiette. (*See* **proper**)

poot [puːt] *vi P* péter*/lâcher une perle.

poove [puːv] *n P* = **poof**.

poovy ['puːvɪ] *a P* = **poofy**.

pop¹ [pɒp] *n* 1. *F* **pop (music)**, musique *f* pop/pop *f*; **pop singer**, chanteur, -euse pop; **pop song**, chanson *f* pop; **top of the pops**, palmarès *m*/hit-parade *m*/top cinquante *m*; **pop art**, le pop'art 2. *F* (*a*) père*/papa *m*; vieux *m*/croulant *m* (*b*) vieil homme; **listen pop!** écoute grand-père/pépé! 3. *F* boisson pétillante/gazeuse/avec des bulles 4. *P* (*drugs*) piqûre occasionnelle *ou* pour le plaisir/piquouse *f*/shoot *m*. (*See* **joy-pop¹**; **joy-popper**; **skin-pop**; **skin-popper**) 5. *P* **to take a pop at**, attaquer*/rentrer dans le mou à (qn) 6. *Austr F* **to give sth a pop**, s'attaquer à qch/tenter un essai 7. *F* **to be in pop**, (*pawned*) être chez ma tante/au clou.

pop² [pɒp] *vtr & i* 1. *P* (*drugs*) se faire une piqûre/se piquer/se shooter. (*See* **joy-pop²**; **skin-pop**) 2. *P* (*drugs*) **to pop pills**, prendre des pilules (de LSD*) 3. *F* **to pop the question**, proposer le mariage* (à qn)/demander à qn de l'épouser 4. *P* **to pop (one's rocks)**, avoir un orgasme*/décharger/jouir/prendre son pied 5. *F* mettre en gage/chez ma tante/au clou 6. *P* **to pop one's clogs**, **to pop it**, mourir*/rendre ses clefs/déposer son bilan 7. *P* donner un coup* de poing à (qn); **she popped him one on the chin**, elle lui a flanqué un marron au menton 8. *F* accoucher*/pondre 9. *NAm F* **to pop a vein**, se mettre en colère*/en pétard; péter une durite.

pop along ['pɒpə'lɒŋ] *vi F* 1. aller voir qn/faire un saut chez qn 2. = **pop off 1**.

pop-eyed ['pɒpaɪd] *a F* (*a*) (*having protuberant eyes*) aux yeux exorbités (*b*)

(*surprised*) aux yeux en boules de loto.

pop in ['pɒp'ɪn] *vi F* entrer en passant/pour un instant.

pop off ['pɒp'ɒf] *F* I *vi* 1. partir*/filer/déguerpir 2. mourir*/claquer (subitement) II *vtr* 1. tuer*/but(t)er/estourbir; **to get popped off**, se faire tuer*/descendre 2. **to pop off a gun**, lâcher un coup de fusil.

pop out ['pɒp'aʊt] *vi F* faire un saut dehors/aller faire un petit tour; **I saw him pop out of the house**, je l'ai vu sortir.

pop outside ['pɒpaʊt'saɪd] *vi* uriner*/aller faire pipi.

poppa ['pɒpə] *n esp NAm F* père*/papa *m*. (*See* **pop¹** 2 (*a*))

popper ['pɒpə] *n* 1. *P* (*drugs*) ampoule *f* de nitrite d'amyle*. (*See* **amy**) 2. *F* bouton-pression *m*. (*See* **joy-popper**; **skin-popper**)

poppet ['pɒpɪt] *n F* (*a*) petit(e) chéri(e)/(petit) chou; **she's a poppet**, elle est mimi (*b*) enfant* adorable/chérubin *m*/trésor *m*.

poppy ['pɒpɪ] I *a F* **poppy tune**, mélodie *f*/air *m* pop II *n P* argent*/fric *m*.

poppycock ['pɒpɪkɒk] *n F* bêtises*/idioties *fpl*/fadaises *fpl*; **that's poppycock!** c'est des salades/des conneries!

pop round ['pɒp'raʊnd] *vi F* faire une petite visite à qn/faire un saut chez qn.

popshop ['pɒpʃɒp] *n P* bureau *m* de prêt sur gage(s)/mont-de-piété *m*/clou *m*.

popster, popstrel ['pɒpstə, 'pɒpstrəl] *n F* chanteur, -euse pop.

popsy ['pɒpsɪ] *n* 1. *F* petite amie/petite chérie 2. *P* = **popper 1**.

pop up ['pɒp'ʌp] *vi F* apparaître/surgir/émerger.

pork [pɔːk] *vtr NAm P* faire l'amour* avec (qn)/s'envoyer (qn).

porker ['pɔːkə] *n* 1. *F* (*fat person*) gravos, -osse 2. *P* agent* de police/flic *m*.

pork pie [pɔːk'paɪ] *n Br P* (*RS = lie*) mensonge*/bobard *m*/craque *f*.

porky ['pɔːkɪ] I *a F* 1. gros* et gras/gravos 2. *NAm* très mauvais*/blèche/loquedu 3. *NAm* en colère*/ronchonnant/en rogne II *n P* **porky (pie)** = **pork pie**.

porn [pɔːn], **porno** ['pɔːnəʊ] *n F* porno-graphie *f*, porno *m*; **hard porn**, porno hard/hard *m*; **soft porn**, porno soft/soft *m*; **porn merchant**, qn qui vend *ou* fabrique des produits pornographiques; pornographe *m*; **porno mags**, revues *fpl* pornos/de cul/de fesse.

porn-shop ['pɔːnʃɒp] *n F* boutique* porno/

sex(e)-shop *f*.

porny ['pɔːnɪ] *a P* porno(graphique); **porny books,** livres *mpl* pornos; **porny film,** film *m* porno/de cul; porno *m*.

porridge ['pɒrɪdʒ] *n P* condamnation *f* à la prison; **to dish out the porridge,** condamner à une peine de prison; **to do/to eat porridge,** purger sa peine en prison*/être mis au frais.

port [pɔːt] *n Austr F* valise *f*/valoche *f*.

posh [pɒʃ] *F* **I** *a* élégant*/chic/rupin/de la haute; **posh car,** voiture *f* de luxe; **posh accent,** accent *m* snob/accent de la haute **II** *adv* **to talk posh,** faire des phrases/parler avec un petit accent de la haute/parler pointu.

posh up ['pɒʃ'ʌp] *vtr F* **to posh oneself up,** se pomponner/se bichonner; **all poshed up,** sur son trente et un.

poss [pɒs] *a F* (= *possible*) **it's just poss,** c'est pas impossible/ça se peut bien/on sait jamais; **if poss,** si possible.

posse ['pɒsɪ] *n P* **1.** (*in Jamaica*) gang *m* de criminels; société secrète **2.** bande *f* de jeunes/bande de loubards.

possodeluxe ['pɒsədɪ'lʌks] *n Austr P* dupe *f*/cave *m*/pigeon *m*.

possum ['pɒsəm] *n* **1.** *F* (= *opossum*) **to play possum,** (*pretend*) faire le mort; (*keep low profile*) faire le mort; se faire tout petit **2.** *Austr P* dupe *f*/cave *m*.

posted ['pəʊstɪd] *pp F* **to keep s.o. posted,** tenir qn au courant/au parfum.

postie ['pəʊstɪ] *n F* **1.** facteur *m* **2.** carte postale.

pot[1] [pɒt] *n* **1.** *P* (*drugs*) marijuana*; haschisch*; **pot party,** séance collective au haschisch* *ou* à la marijuana* **2.** *F* (= *pot-belly*) ventre*/bide *m*/bedaine *f*/brioche *f*/gras-double *m* **3.** *F* **to go to pot,** tomber en décrépitude/ aller à la ruine/aller à la dérive/aller à vau-l'eau; **he's gone to pot,** il est fichu; **his plans went (all) to pot,** ses projets sont tombés à l'eau/sont fichus **4.** *F* **pots of money,** des tas d'argent*; **to make pots of money,** gagner gros/faire sa pelote **5.** *F* trophée *m*/coupe *f* **6.** *F pl* (= *potatoes*) pommes *fpl* de terre/patates *fpl* **7.** *F* = **kitty 2 8.** *F* (*bowls*) cochonnet *m*/ petit *m* **9.** *F* verre *m* de bière; **to go for a pot,** aller prendre un pot. (*See* **fusspot; jackpot; pisspot; sexpot; shitpot; stinkpot; tinpot**)

pot[2] [pɒt] *F* **I** *vtr* **to pot a child,** asseoir/ mettre un enfant sur le pot (de chambre) **II** *vi* **to pot at sth,** tirer sur une cible peu éloignée.

potato [pə'teɪtəʊ, pə'teɪtə] *n* **1.** *P* trou *m* dans une chaussette/patate *f* **2.** *F* **small potatoes,** de la petite bière; personnes *ou* choses insignifiantes/racaille *f*/gnognot(t)e *f* **3.** *NAm* **hot potato** (*a*) *F* casse-tête (chinois) (*b*) *F* affaire épineuse (*c*) *P* = **hot patootie** (**patootie 2**) **4.** *Austr P* **potato peeler,** (*RS* = *sheila*) fille*/femme*/nana *f*/gonzesse *f*. (*See* **big I 1; drop**[2] **1; sack**[1] **2**)

pot-boiler ['pɒtbɔɪlə] *n F* œuvre *f* alimentaire.

pothead ['pɒthed] *n P* habitué(e) de la marijuana*; amateur *m* de haschisch*. (*See* **pot**[1] **1**)

pot-licker ['pɒtlɪkə] *n NAm P* chien*/clebs *m*/clébard *m*.

pot-luck ['pɒt'lʌk] *n F* **to take pot-luck,** choisir au hasard/à l'aventure/au pif; y aller au petit bonheur; (*eat*) manger à la fortune du pot.

pot-shot ['pɒtʃɒt] *n F* (*a*) **to take a pot-shot at sth,** faire qch au petit bonheur (la chance)/ faire qch au pif (*b*) **to take a pot-shot at sth/ s.o.,** tirer à l'aveuglette sur qch/qn.

potted[1] ['pɒtɪd] *a F* abrégé; **I gave him a potted version of (the) events,** je lui ai fait un raccourci/un condensé des événements.

potted[2] ['pɒtɪd] *a NAm P* **1.** ivre*/rond/ rondibé/rétamé **2.** drogué*/camé/chargé.

pottie ['pɒtɪ] *n F* = **potty II.**

potty ['pɒtɪ] *F* **I** *a Br* **1.** fou*/toqué/timbré; **to go potty,** devenir fou*/maboul; perdre les pédales/la boule **2. to be potty about/on s.o./ sth,** être mordu de/toqué de qn/qch; en pincer pour qn/qch **3.** minable/insignifiant **II** *n* **pot** *m* de chambre (d'enfant).

pouch [paʊtʃ] *n Austr V* sexe* de la femme*/grip(p)ette *f*/boîte *f* à ouvrage.

poufdah ['pʊfdɑː], **pouff** [pʊf, puːf] *n P* (*not common*) = **poof.**

pound [paʊnd] *vtr P* **1.** faire l'amour* avec/ bourrer/s'envoyer (qn) **2. to pound one's pork/the meat/the pudding,** se masturber*/se taper sur la colonne/secouer la cartouche.

powder ['paʊdə] *n P* **to do/to take a powder** (*a*) déserter (de l'armée)/se débiner (*b*) s'enfuir*/faire chibi(s)/prendre la poudre d'escampette.

powder-room ['paʊdə'ruːm] *n Euph F* WC*/toilettes *fpl* pour dames/pipi-room *m*.

powerhouse ['paʊəhaʊs] *n F* individu* vigoureux et dynamique.

pow-wow ['paʊwaʊ] *n F* palabre *m*/ discussion *f*.

pox [pɒks] *n P* **(the)** pox, syphilis*/la chtouille/le naze/la vérole.

poxed-up ['pɒkst'ʌp] *a P* poxed-up (to the eyeballs/eyebrows), naze(broque)/poivré/plombé.

poxy ['pɒksɪ] *a Br P* (de) camelote/tocard; naze(broque)/vérolé; **it's none of your poxy rubbish**, c'est pas du bidon cette marchandise.

pram [præm] *n Br P* **to be out of one's pram**, être fou*/déménager.

prance about, around ['prɑːnsə'baʊt, ə'raʊnd] *vi F* caracoler; se pavaner/poser; faire le beau/le m'as-tu-vu; **to prance around in the nud**, se balader à poil/à loilpé.

prang[1] [præŋ] *n F* accrochage *m*/emboutissage *m*/pet *m*.

prang[2] [præŋ] *vtr F* emboutir/bousiller (un avion, une auto); **he pranged his car**, il a embouti/cabossé sa tire; sa bagnole a pris un pet.

prat [præt] *n P* 1. fesses*/derche *m*/derjo *m*/pétard *m* 2. sexe* de la femme*/con *m*/conasse *f*/cramouille *f* 3. individu bête*/couillon *m*; **you prat!** espèce de nœud!/connard!/ducon!

prawn [prɔːn] *n P* 1. individu bête*/gourde *f*/andouille *f*; **to look a prawn**, avoir l'air bête/con 2. *Austr O* **to come the raw prawn**, (*deceive*) tromper*/rouler/avoir qn; **don't come the raw prawn with me!** faut pas me la refaire!

preachify ['priːtʃɪfaɪ] *vi F* sermonner/faire la morale.

preachy ['priːtʃɪ] *a F* prêcheur/sermonneur.

preggers ['pregəz] *a P* preggers/*O* Harry preggers, enceinte*/en cloque; **she's preggers**, elle a un polichinelle dans le tiroir/elle est en cloque.

preppie, preppy ['prepɪ] *NAm F* I *a* (*looks, clothes, etc*) = B.C.B.G. II *n* 1. (*student of American preparatory school*) khâgneux, -euse 2. = B.C.B.G. *mf*.

press [pres] *vtr P* **to press the flesh**, serrer la main*/la pince (à qn)/en serrer cinq.

pressie ['prezɪ] *n F* (= *present*) cadeau *m*.

pretty-pretty ['prɪtɪprɪtɪ] *a F* fanfreluché/mignon tout plein; *Pej* affecté/minaudier.

previous ['priːvɪəs] *Br F* I *a* prématuré; présomptueux; **you're a bit previous, aren't you?** tu y vas un peu fort, non? II *n* (= *previous convictions*) casier *m* judiciaire (non vierge)/pedigree *m*; **he's got no previous**, il a un casier judiciaire vierge/il n'a pas de casier; **he's got a lot of previous**, il a un

casier judiciaire bien rempli/il a un pedigree.

prezzie ['prezɪ] *n F* = **pressie**.

priceless ['praɪslɪs] *a F* 1. très amusant*/impayable 2. très bête*/unique.

pricey ['praɪsɪ] *a F* cher*/chérot/coûteux/salé.

prick [prɪk] *n V* 1. pénis*/pine *f*/queue *f* 2. vaurien*/sale coco *m*/couillon *m* 3. **a spare prick**, un pas grand-chose/un bon à rien; **to feel like a spare prick at a wedding**, se sentir inutile/de trop 4. homme bête*/con *m*/connard *m*; **stupid prick!** espèce d'enculé! (*See* **pin-pricks**)

prick-tease[1] ['prɪktiːz] *n V* allumeuse *f*/aguicheuse *f*. (*See* **cock-tease(r)**; **tease**; **teaser 2**)

prick-tease[2] ['prɪk'tiːz] *vtr V* aguicher/allumer/faire bander (qn).

prick-teaser ['prɪk'tiːzə] *n V* = **prick-tease**[1].

printed ['prɪntɪd] *pp P* **to get printed**, se faire prendre les empreintes digitales/passer au piano.

prissy ['prɪsɪ] *a F* (*fussy*) maniaque; (*prudish*) prude/bégueule/collet monté; (*effeminate*) efféminé/chochotte.

privates ['praɪvɪts] *npl F* sexe* de l'homme*/parties *fpl*/service *m* trois-pièces; **a kick in the privates**, un coup de pied dans les couilles/les bijoux de famille/les valseuses.

prize [praɪz] *a F* **a prize idiot**, un ballot de premier ordre/une andouille enracinée/le roi des cons.

pro [prəʊ] *n* 1. *P* (= *prostitute*) prostituée*/professionnelle *f*/pute *f* 2. *F* (= *professional*) professionnel, -elle/pro *mf*; **he's a real pro**, il n'a rien d'un amateur/c'est un vrai pro 3. *F* **the pros and cons**, le pour et le contre.

prob [prɒb] *n F* (*abbr of problem*) **no prob!/no probs!** pas de problème!

prod [prɒd] *n Br F* protestant, -ante.

prog [prɒg] *n Br F* (*abbr of programme*) émission *f* (de télévision, etc).

prole [prəʊl] *n Br F* (*proletarian*) prolo *mf*.

prong [prɒŋ] *n P* pénis*/bite *f*.

pronto ['prɒntəʊ] *adv F* vite*/illico (presto).

proper ['prɒpə] *adv F* vraiment/extrêmement; **proper poorly**, vraiment malade*. (*See* **champion I**)

proposition ['prɒpə'zɪʃ(ə)n] *vtr F* 1. proposer un plan *ou* un projet à (qn) 2. **to proposition a woman**, faire des propositions indécentes à une femme/proposer la botte à une femme/faire du rentre-dedans à une femme.

prop up ['prɒp'ʌp] *vtr F* to prop up the bar, boire dans un bar/être accoudé au zinc/être un pilier de bar *ou* de bistrot.

pross [prɒs], **prossie, prossy** ['prɒsɪ] *n P* prostituée*/pute *f*/putain *f*.

prot [prɒt] *n Austr F* = **prod.**

proud [praʊd] *adv F* to do s.o. proud, faire beaucoup d'honneur à qn/recevoir qn comme un roi/traiter qn comme un pacha; se mettre en frais pour qn; you've done me proud, vous m'avez régalé; to do oneself proud, (*do a good piece of work*) faire un bon travail*/se montrer à la hauteur; (*not to lack for anything*) bien se soigner/ne se priver de rien/ne rien se refuser.

prowl [praʊl] *n F* to be on the prowl, chercher les aventures (amoureuses)/chercher les bonnes fortunes/partir en chasse; *NAm* prowl car, voiture *f* de patrouille (*de police*)/ voiture-pie *f*.

prune [pruːn] *n Br F* individu bête*/ andouille *f*.

pseud [sjuːd] *n P* (*hypocrite*) individu* hypocrite/faux; faux jeton; (*pretentious*) prétentieux, -euse/crâneur, -euse/bêcheur, -euse/frimeur, -euse; he's a real pseud, c'est un faux cul/un faux derche; il est puant/ prétentiard.

pseudo ['sjuːdəʊ] *a F* (*hypocritical*) faux/ hypocrite/faux jeton; (*pretentious*) prétentieux/bêcheur/crâneur/frimeur/poseur.

pseudy ['sjuːdɪ] *a P* = **pseudo.**

psycho ['saɪkəʊ] I *a P* fou*/dérangé/ détraqué/secoué; to go psycho, perdre la boule/débloquer II *n F* 1. psychopathe *mf*/ détraqué, -ée 2. (*a*) psy(chanalyste) *mf* (*b*) psy(chiatre) *mf*.

psych out ['saɪk'aʊt] *vtr & i F* (*a*) perdre les pédales/perdre la tête/débloquer (*b*) avoir peur*/caner/se dégonfler (*c*) démoraliser (qn); faire flancher (qn).

psych up ['saɪk'ʌp] *vtr F* to psych oneself up (for sth), se préparer psychologiquement *ou* mentalement (à faire qch)/se brancher (sur qch)/se brancher (à faire qch).

PT, pt ['piː'tiː] *abbr P* = **prick-tease(r).** (*See* **cock-tease(r); CT**)

pub [pʌb] *n Br F* bar *m*/bistrot *m*/pub *m*.

pubbing ['pʌbɪŋ] *n F* to go pubbing, faire la tournée des bars/des bistrots.

pub-crawl[1] ['pʌbkrɔːl] *n F* tournée *f* des bars/des bistrots.

pub-crawl[2] ['pʌbkrɔːl] *vi F* faire la tournée

des bars/des bistrots.

pub-crawler ['pʌbkrɔːlə] *n F* coureur, -euse de bistrots/vadrouilleur, -euse.

pubes [pjuːbz] *npl P* poils *mpl* du pubis/ gazon *m*/cresson *m*.

public ['pʌblɪk] *n P* (*homosexuals*) to go public, avouer/admettre/oser dire qu'on est homosexuel.

pucker-assed ['pʌkər'æst] *a NAm V* peureux/froussard/pétochard/qui a le trouillo-mètre à zéro/qui chie dans son froc.

pud [pʊd] *n F* (*abbr of pudding*) pudding *m*; dessert *m* (*See* **crimble**).

pudding ['pʊdɪŋ] *n P* to pull one's pudding, se masturber*/s'allonger le macaroni/ s'astiquer (la colonne). (*See* **club 2**; **pound 2**)

puddingface ['pʊdɪŋfeɪs] *n F* visage* empâté.

puddinghead ['pʊdɪŋhed] *n F* individu bête*/gourde *f*/andouille *f*.

puddled ['pʌdld] *a F* fou*/toqué/cinglé.

puff[1] [pʌf] *n* 1. *F* to be out of puff, être essoufflé/à bout de souffle 2. *O F* réclame (tapageuse) 3. *P* = **poof** 4. *Br P* (*life*) la vie; never in my puff, jamais de ma vie. (*See* **creampuff**)

puff[2] [pʌf] *vtr O F* pousser/vanter (des mar-chandises).

puffer(-train) ['pʌfə(treɪn)], **puff-puff** ['pʌfpʌf] *n F* (*child's word*) teuf-teuf *m*/ tchou-tchou *m*.

puffy ['pʌfɪ] *n Br P* cannabis*/herbe *f*.

pug [pʌg] *n P* pugiliste *m*/boxeur *m*.

puka ['puːkə] *n NAm P* sexe* de la femme*/ fente *f*/craquette *f*.

puke[1] [pjuːk] *n P* (*vomit*) vomissure *f*/ dégobillade *f*/dégueulis *m*/Belg dégobillotte *f*; (*vomiting*) vomissement *m*/fusée *f*.

pukeish ['pjuːkɪʃ] *a P* = **pukey.**

puke[2] (up) ['pjuːk('ʌp)] *vi P* vomir*/aller au refil/dégobiller/dégueuler; it makes me want to puke, ça me débecte/ça me fait gerber/c'est dégueulatoire.

pukey ['pjuːkɪ] *a P* (*disgusting*) dégueulasse/débectant/dégueulbif; it's really pukey, c'est vraiment dégueulasse.

pukka ['pʌkə] *a F* authentique/du vrai de vrai; a pukka sahib [saːb], un vrai monsieur/ un vrai gentleman.

pull[1] [pʊl] *n* 1. *P* to be on the pull, chercher un(e) partenaire sexuel(le)/chercher un coup/ draguer 2. *F* influence *f*/piston *m*/bras long 3. *P* arrestation*/agrichage *m*/piquage *m*. (*See* leg-pull)

pull² [pʊl] *vtr* 1. *Br P* (*pick up*) draguer (qn); **to pull a bird,** draguer une nana. (*See* **train 1** (*b*)) 2. *F* **to pull a gun,** sortir un revolver*/dégainer 3. *Br P* arrêter*/agricher/pincer (qn). (*See* **bell¹ 2**; **leg¹ 5**; **one 4**; **plonker 1**; **pudding**; **rank**; **stroke**; **wire 2, 8**; **yarn¹** (*b*)))

pull in ['pʊl'ɪn] *vtr F* arrêter*/embarquer; **the cops pulled him in,** les flics l'ont embarqué/pincé.

pulling ['pʊlɪŋ] *a Br F* **pulling power,** (*usu of men*) attrait sexuel/chien *m*; **he's got pulling power,** il est sexy/baisable.

pull off ['pʊl'ɒf] *vtr* 1. *F* gagner/remporter/décrocher (un prix); **to pull off a deal,** réussir une opération/boucler une affaire 2. *O P* se masturber*/s'astiquer (la colonne).

pull out ['pʊl'aʊt] *vtr & i F* 1. partir*/se tirer 2. (*withdraw*) se retirer 3. **to pull out all the stops,** donner le maximum/donner un coup de collier/mettre le paquet. (*See* **finger¹ 2**)

pump¹ [pʌmp] *n F* cœur *m*/battant *m*/palpitant *m*.

pump² [pʌmp] I *vtr F* **to pump s.o.,** pomper qn (pour avoir des renseignements*)/tirer les vers du nez à qn 2. *NAm P* faire l'amour* avec (qn)/baiser (qn) II *vi Br P* péter*/lâcher une perle. (*See* **lead¹ 1** (*a*))

pumping ['pʌmpɪŋ] *n F* **pumping iron,** (*weightlifting*) haltérophilie *f*/maniage *m* de fonte; (*body building*) gonflette *f*.

pumps [pʌmps] *npl Br F* (*schools*) (*tennis shoes*) tennis *mpl*; (*trainers*) chaussures *fpl* de sport/trainers *mpl*.

punch¹ [pʌntʃ] *n F* 1. énergie *f*/dynamisme *m*/punch *m*/pep *m* 2. **he didn't pull his punches,** (*hit hard*) il n'a pas ménagé son adversaire/il n'a pas pris de gants/il n'y est pas allé de main morte; (*spoke frankly*) il n'a pas mâché ses mots. (*See* **pack² 2**)

Punch² [pʌntʃ] *Prn F* (*a*) (as) **proud as Punch,** fier comme Artaban (*b*) (as) **pleased as Punch,** heureux comme un roi/aux anges.

punch-drunk ['pʌntʃ'drʌŋk] *a F* ivre de coups/abruti (par les coups)/groggy.

punch-line ['pʌntʃlaɪn] *n F* pointe *f* (d'une plaisanterie); chute *f* (d'une histoire).

punch-up ['pʌntʃʌp] *n Br F* bagarre *f*/baston *m ou f*/castagne *f*; **to have a punch-up,** se bagarrer/se castagner.

punk [pʌŋk] *P* I *a* de mauvaise qualité/moche/toc(ard)/tarte II *n* 1. (*contemptible person*) salaud*/crapule *f*/loquedu *m* 2. *A*

homosexuel*/lopette *f* 3. **punk** (**rocker**), punk *mf* 4. qch de toc(ard) *ou* de moche/pacotille *f*/camelote *f*.

punkette [pʌŋ'ket] *n P* punkette *f*.

punter ['pʌntə] *n P* 1. (*horseracing, etc*) parieur, -euse 2. client, -ente; client d'une prostituée/clille *m*/micheton *m* 3. individu* quelconque/type *m*/mec *m*; **the punters,** le public; **the average punter,** l'homme* de la rue.

pup [pʌp] *n F* **to sell s.o. a pup,** escroquer*/entuber/rouler qn. (*See* **mucky 2**)

puppy ['pʌpɪ] *n* (*self-important young man*) freluquet *m*.

purler ['pɜːlə] *n F* **to come a purler,** tomber*/ramasser une bûche/prendre un gadin.

purple ['pɜːpl] *a P* (*drugs*) **purple hearts,** amphétamines*; mélange *m* d'amphétamines et de barbituriques*.

purty ['pɜːrtɪ] *a NAm F* joli/mignon.

push¹ [pʊʃ] *n* 1. *F* **to give s.o. the push,** flanquer qn à la porte/sacquer qn; laisser tomber/plaquer (son/sa petit(e) ami(e)); **she gave him the push,** elle l'a plaqué 2. *F* **at a push,** au besoin; **when it comes to the push,** au moment critique/quand il est question d'agir/au moment de l'exécution; **we could do it at a push,** à la rigueur, ça pourrait se faire/c'est pas impossible/ça se peut bien 3. *Austr P* bande*/gang *m*.

push² [pʊʃ] *vtr F* 1. **to push drugs,** fourguer/dealer de la drogue 2. **to push one's luck,** pousser/aller trop loin/attiger (la cabane)/aller un peu fort; **don't push your luck (too far)!** vas-y mollo! 3. **she must be pushing forty,** elle frise la quarantaine/elle doit aller sur ses quarante printemps 4. **shut up or I'll push your face in!** la ferme ou je te cogne/ou je te casse la gueule/ou je t'écrase le museau! (*See* **queer¹ II 4**)

push around ['pʊʃə'raʊnd] *vtr F* **to push s.o. around,** (*bully*) marcher sur les pieds de qn/mener qn par le bout du nez.

pushed [pʊʃd] *a F* **to be a bit pushed for money/time,** manquer de temps; être à court d'argent; **he's a bit pushed (for time) today,** il est plutôt pressé aujourd'hui.

pusher ['pʊʃə] *n F* 1. (*drugs*) fourgueur *m*/pourvoyeur, -euse/revendeur, -euse/dealer *m*. (*See* **push² 1**) 2. ambitieux, -euse/arriviste *mf*/joueur, -euse de coudes. (*See* **paper-pusher**; **pen-pusher**)

push off ['pʊʃ'ɒf] *vi P* partir*/déguerpir/décamper; **push off!** file!/débarrasse (le plancher)!/fous le camp!/dégage!/du vent!

pushover ['puʃəuvə] *n* **1.** *F* qch de facile/du tout cuit/du gâteau **2.** *P* femme* facile/à la cuisse hospitalière.

pushy ['puʃɪ] *a F* arriviste/plastronneur/ poseur; **he's a pushy little sod!** c'est un crâneur de première!/c'est un prétentiard!/ c'est un de ces puants!

puss [pus] *n* **1.** *F* chat *m*/minou *m*/minet *m*/ minette *f* **2.** *P* visage*/frime *f*/frimousse *f* **3.** *P* bouche*/gueule *f*/goulot *m* **4.** *P* = **pussy 2.** (*See* **glamour-puss; sourpuss**)

pussy ['pusɪ] *n* **1.** *F* = **puss 1 2.** *P* sexe* de la femme/chat *m*/chatte *f*/chagatte *f*/minou *m*; **to chase pussy,** chercher de la fesse; **he's after a bit of pussy,** il ne cherche qu'à baiser/ qu'à tringler **3.** *A F* (= *cat-o'-nine-tails*) fouet *m* (à neuf cordes)/chat *m* à neuf queues **4.** *F* fourrure(s) *f(pl)* **5.** *F* = **pussycat.**

pussycat ['pusɪkæt] *n F* individu* faible/ lavette *f*; individu timide; individu sans malice; **he's just a pussycat,** il ne ferait pas de mal à une mouche.

pussyfoot¹ ['pusɪfut] *n F* qn qui ne veut pas se compromettre/qui tourne autour du pot; **he's a pussyfoot,** il ne veut pas se mouiller.

pussyfoot² ['pusɪfut] *vi F* **1.** marcher* à pas étouffés/sur la pointe des pieds **2.** (*avoid comitting oneself*) ne pas se mouiller/ménager la chèvre et le chou/nager entre deux eaux/ zigzaguer.

pussyfooter ['pusɪfutə] *n F* = **pussyfoot¹.**

pussyfooting ['pusɪfutɪŋ] *n F* l'art *m* de ne pas se mouiller.

pussy-whipped ['pusɪwɪpd] *a NAm F* (*man*) dominé par sa femme *ou* sa petite amie/dont la femme porte la culotte/mené par le bout du nez.

puta ['puːtə] *n NAm P* prostituée*/pute *f*.

put across ['putə'krɒs] *vtr F* **1. to put one across on s.o.,** tromper*/refaire/rouler qn;

they put one across on me, on m'a roulé/je me suis fait avoir **2. to put it across to s.o.,** faire comprendre/piger à qn; éclairer la lanterne à qn.

put away ['putə'weɪ] *vtr* **1.** *P* (*boxing*) mettre (qn) knock-out **2.** *F* **to put it away,** boire *ou* manger beaucoup/(se) morfaler/s'en mettre plein la lampe; **he can't half put it away!** il a une de ces descentes! **3.** *F* emprisonner*/boucler/bloquer; **they put him away,** ils l'ont mis au bloc **4.** *Br P* tuer*/ descendre/dessouder/dézinguer **5.** *F* mettre (de l'argent, etc) de côté. (*See* **rainy**)

put-down ['putdaʊn] *n F* affront *m*.

put down ['put'daʊn] *vtr F* critiquer*/ éreinter/démolir (qn).

put-on ['putɒn] *n F* (*deception, fraud*) **it was all a put-on,** c'était du boniment/de la blague/du chiqué/de la frime.

put on ['put'ɒn] *vtr F* **1. to put it on,** (*pretend*) faire semblant/(en) installer/faire du chiqué; (*exaggerate*) charrier/y aller fort/ faire de la graisse; **he puts it on a bit,** il est un peu crâneur **2. to put s.o. on,** (*deceive*) mener qn en bateau/pigeonner qn/rouler qn **3. who put you on to it?** qui vous a donné le tuyau? **4. to put one on s.o.,** donner un coup* de poing à qn/flanquer un marron à qn/ balancer un gnon à qn. (*See* **bite¹ 1; frighteners; kibosh; mockers; ritz**)

put out ['put'aʊt] **I** *vtr F* déconcerter/ décontenancer/embarrasser (qn) **II** *vi NAm F* (*of woman*) avoir la cuisse hospitalière.

putrid ['pjuːtrɪd] *a F* dégueulasse/ dégueulbif/débectant.

put-up ['putʌp] *a F* **a put-up job,** un coup monté/une magouille/un micmac.

putz [pʌts] *n NAm P* **1.** pénis*/pine *f*/paf *m* **2.** individu bête*/crétin, -ine/andouille *f*.

python ['paɪθ(ə)n] *n P* **to siphon the python,** uriner*/égoutter son colosse.

pzazz [pə'zæz] *n F* (*flair*) punch *m*.

Q

Q [kjuː] *abbr NAm F* prison* de *San Quentin*.

q.t., QT ['kjuː'tiː] *abbr F* **1.** (= *quiet time*) petite prière/méditation *f* **2. on the (strict) q.t.**, (= *quiet*) en douce/discrètement/discrètos/en lousdoc/en loucedé; **to do sth on the q.t.**, faire qch en cachette/à la dérobée/en douce; **I am telling you on the q.t.**, je vous dis ça entre nous; **he fixed it on the QT**, il a arrangé ça en lousdoc.

quack [kwæk] *n P* médecin *m*/toubib *m*/mécano *m*/marchand *m* de mort subite; **I went to see the quack**, je suis allé chez le toubib.

quack-quack ['kwæk'kwæk], **quackers** ['kwækəz] *n Br F* (*child's word*) canard *m*/coin-coin *m*.

quad [kwɒd] *n* **1.** *F* (= *quadrangle*) cour carrée (d'une école, université, etc) **2.** *P* prison*/cabane *f*/bloc *m*/taule *f*/gnouf *m*; **in quad**, au bloc/à l'ombre **3.** *F* (= *quadruplet*) quadruplé(e) **4.** *NAm P* auto *f* à quatre phares *mpl; pl* les quatre phares d'une auto **5.** *P* moto *f* à quatre roues tous terrains.

quail [kweɪl] *n P* (*not common*) femme*/fille*/mousmée *f*/souris *f*.

quandong ['kwændɒŋ] *n Austr P* **1.** individu* louche/voyou *m*/loulou *m* **2.** femme*/gonzesse *f* **3.** prostituée*/pute *f*.

quarter ['kwɔːtə] *n NAm F* pièce *f* de 25 cents.

quean [kwiːn] *n A P* = **queen¹ 1, 2.**

queen¹ [kwiːn] *n* **1.** *F* fille* *ou* femme* séduisante/une beauté/prix *m* de Diane/joli lot **2.** *P* homosexuel* qui joue le rôle de femme/caroline *f*/folle *f*/tante *f*; **an old queen**, une vieille pédale; **dinge queen**, homosexuel* blanc qui préfère les Noirs; **golden shower queen**, homosexuel* qui aime qu'on lui pisse dessus; **leather queen**, fétichiste *m* du cuir/cuir *m*; **size queen**, homosexuel*/pédé *m* qui aime les mecs virils; **xerox queen**, clone *m* **3.** *F* **queen bee**, femme* active/maîtresse-femme *f* **4.** *F* **Queen Anne's dead!** *see* **Anne.**

queen² [kwiːn] *vtr F* **to queen it** (over s.o.), faire la grande dame (avec qn).

queenie ['kwiːnɪ] *n P* (*form of address*) ma petite dame.

queer¹ [kwɪə] **I** *a* **1.** *F* homosexuel/pédé/pédoque; **he's queer as a coot**, il est pédé comme un phoque (*See* **coot**) **2.** *F* **to be in queer street**, (*in bad* (*financial*) *situation*) être dans la mélasse/tirer le diable par la queue/être dans la mouise/être dans la panade **3.** *F* un peu fou*; **queer in the head**, maboul/loufoque/toqué/siphonné/barjot/barge. (*See* **attic; fish¹ 1**) **4.** *P* suspect/louche/pas net; **it's all a bit queer**, ça n'a pas l'air très catholique **5.** *P* faux/contrefait **6.** *O F* **to feel queer**, se sentir tout chose/patraque; **he's feeling a bit queer**, il marche à côté de ses pompes/il n'est pas dans son assiette **II** *n* **1.** *P Pej* pédé *m*/homo *m*/pédale *f*/tante *f* **2.** *P* **in queer**, dans le pétrin/dans la mélasse/dans la mouise/dans de beaux draps **3.** *P* **on the queer**, par des moyens louches/peu honnêtes **4.** *P* monnaie contrefaite/fausse mornifle; **to push the queer**, passer de la fausse monnaie.

queer² [kwɪə] *vtr & i P* **1.** déranger/détraquer; **to queer the pitch**, mettre des bâtons dans les roues; **to queer s.o.'s pitch**, contrecarrer qn/couper l'herbe sous le pied de qn/mettre qch dans les dents de qn **2. to queer oneself with s.o.**, se brouiller avec qn/ne plus être dans les petits papiers de qn/être en suif avec qn **3. to queer for sth**, aimer* qch/en mordre pour qch/en pincer pour qch.

queer-basher ['kwɪəbæʃə] *n P* chasseur *m*/casseur *m* de pédés.

queer-bashing ['kwɪəbæʃɪŋ] *n P* chasse *f* aux pédés/ratonnade *f* contre les pédés.

quesh [kweʃ] *n Br F* (*short for question*) question *f*.

queue-jumper ['kjuːdʒʌmpə] *n F* qn qui passe avant son tour/resquilleur, -euse.

quick [kwɪk] *a F* **1. a quick one** = **quickie 1, 2 2. to do sth in quick order**, faire qch vite*/fissa/à toute vapeur/en moins de deux/en cinq sec. (*See* **double-quick**; **draw**[1]; **pdq**; **uptake** (*a*))

quickie, quicky ['kwɪkɪ] *n* 1. *F* un (petit) verre/un (petit) coup bu en vitesse; to have a quickie, s'en envoyer un/s'en jeter un vite fait; have a quickie? tu prends qch vite fait (sur le gaz)? 2. *P* coït* hâtif; to have a quickie, tirer un petit coup 3. *P* prostituée* rapide/qui fait de l'abattage 4. *F* qch fait rapidement/à la six-quatre-deux/en quatrième vitesse/en deux temps, trois mouvements; du vite-fait 5. *F* question-éclair *f* (*surt dans un jeu de devinette*) 6. *NAm F* grève soudaine/grève sauvage.

quid [kwɪd] *n F* 1. une livre sterling; I paid forty quid for that, je l'ai payé/j'ai craché quatre cent balles 2. to be quids in, avoir de la marge/marcher comme sur des roulettes; he's quids in, il a de la chance*/du pot/du bol/de la bagouse; I'm quids in, tout baigne (dans l'huile) pour moi 3. *Austr* he's not the full quid, (*he's stupid*) il n'était pas derrière la porte le jour de la distribution (d'intelligence).

quidlet ['kwɪdlɪt] *n Br F* = **quid 1**; **quidlets**, argent*/pèze *m*.

quiet ['kwaɪət] *F* I *a* anything for a quiet life! tout ce que tu voudras, mais fiche-moi la paix/fous-moi la paix/lâche-moi les baskets! II *n* on the quiet, en douce/en lousdoc/en loucedé. (*See* **q.t.**)

quiff [kwɪf] *n* 1. *A P* bon tour/tour de passe-passe 2. *A P* conseil *m*/tuyau *m* 3. *NAm P* prostituée*/pute *f*/morue *f* 4. *A V* sexe* de la femme*/baba *m* 5. *P* homosexuel*/pédé *m* 6. *P* pet*/gaz *m*.

quim [kwɪm] *n V* sexe* de la femme*/grip(p)ette *f*/millefeuille *m*/bonbon *m*.

quin [kwɪn] *n F* (= *quintuplet*) quintuplé(e).

quince [kwɪns] *n Austr P* homosexuel*/fiotte *f*/lopette *f*.

quit [kwɪt] *vtr & i* 1. *F* abandonner*/lâcher; he quit while the going was good, il a laissé tomber/il a mis la clef sous la porte au bon moment 2. *P* to quit the scene (*a*) mourir*/lâcher la rampe (*b*) partir*/lever l'ancre.

quitter ['kwɪtə] *n P* lâcheur, -euse/dégonflé, -ée.

quod [kwɒd] *n P* = **quad 2**.

quoit [kɔɪt] *n Austr P* anus*/bagouse *f*.

quote [kwəʊt] *n F* 1. (= *quotation*) citation *f* 2. *pl* (= *quotation marks*) guillemets *mpl*; you can put that in quotes, à mettre entre guillemets/n'oubliez pas les guillemets.

R

rab [ræb] *n P* tiroir-caisse *m*.

rabbit¹ ['ræbɪt] *n* 1. *P Pej* rabbit food, salade *f*/crudités *fpl*/verdure *f* 2. *P* (*RS = rabbit and pork = talk*) bavardage *m*/jactance *f*/jaspinage *m*/blabla *m*; I never heard anyone with so much rabbit, il a une sacrée tapette 3. *F* rabbit punch, le coup du lapin.

rabbit² ['ræbɪt] *vi P* (*RS = rabbit and pork = talk*) to rabbit (on), avoir la langue bien pendue/jacter/blablater; she does go rabbiting on, elle (n')arrête pas de jacasser.

race off ['reɪs'ɒf] *vtr NAm Austr P* séduire/embarquer/taper dans faire du gringue à/taper dans l'œil à (qn).

rack [ræk] *n* 1. *NAm P* lit*/pieu *m* 2. *F* to be on the rack, (*work hard*) bosser/trimer/se crever au boulot.

racked-off [rækt'ɒf] *a NAm F* to be racked-off, en avoir assez*/en avoir marre/en avoir ras le bol.

racket ['rækɪt] *n F* 1. to make a racket, faire du bruit*/du tapage/du ramdam; they were making one hell of a racket, ils faisaient un boucan du diable. (*See* **kick up 2**) 2. coup fourré/combine *f*/magouille *f*/carambouille *f*/arnaque *f*; the drugs racket, le trafic de la drogue; protection racket, racket *m*; what's your racket? à quoi/comment fais-tu ton beurre? (*job*) tu fais/tu es dans quoi? 3. to stand the racket (*a*) payer* les frais/casquer (*b*) (*take the blame*) prendre/se mettre qch sur le paletot 4. to go on the racket = to go on the razzle (**razzle**).

rack off ['ræk'ɒf] *vi Austr P* partir*/décamper; rack off! fiche-moi le camp!

rack (out) ['ræk'aʊt] *vi NAm* se coucher*/se pieuter/se pagnoter.

rad [ræd] *a F =* **radical**.

radical ['rædɪkl] *a F* excellent*/super/canon/géant.

Rafferty rules ['ræfətɪ'ruːlz] *n Austr P* la loi de la jungle/la loi du plus fort; (*to play*) sans règles/de manière sauvage.

rag¹ [ræg] *n* 1. *F* vêtement*; I haven't a rag to wear, je n'ai rien à me mettre/je n'ai plus de sapes; the rag trade, la confection/la *ou* le sape. (*See* **glad**) 2. *P* (jam) rag, serviette *f* hygiénique/fifine *f*; to be on the rag/to have the rag on/to have the rag out, avoir ses règles*/avoir ses ragnagnas/repeindre sa grille en rouge/avoir ses ours (*See* **tam rag**) 3. *F* journal*/canard *m*/torchon *m*/baveux *m*; local rag, feuille *f* de chou du coin 4. *F* any mention of his ex-wife is like a red rag to a bull, dès qu'on parle de son ex-femme il voit rouge 5. *P* to lose one's rag/to get one's rag out, se mettre en colère*/voir rouge/prendre un coup de sang 6. *P* langue*/torchon *m* 7. *F* rag, tag and bobtail, la canaille/la merdaille 8. *F* carnaval *m* d'étudiants 9. *P* oily rag, (*RS = fag = cigarette*) cigarette*/cibiche *f*/sèche *f*/pipe *f* 10. *F* to feel like a wet rag, se sentir mou comme une chiffe/se sentir comme une chiffe molle; se sentir tout ramollo. (*See* **chew 1; nose-rag; snot-rag**)

rag² [ræg] *vtr F* (*a*) brimer (un camarade) (*b*) chahuter (un professeur) (*c*) charrier (qn).

ragbag ['rægbæg] *n F* individu* mal vêtu/mal ficelé/mal fagoté/fringué comme un as de pique; souillon *mf*/loqueteux, -euse.

rage [reɪdʒ] *n Austr F =* **rave-up**.

ragged out, up [rægd'aʊt, 'ʌp] *a NAm F* (*dressed up*) sur son trente et un.

rag-top ['rægtɒp] *n esp NAm F* (voiture *f*) décapotable *f*.

railroad ['reɪlrəʊd] *vtr F* bousculer/tarabuster/houspiller (qn); forcer (qn) (à faire qch); faire pression sur (qn).

rails [reɪlz] *npl F* to go off the rails, dérailler/être détraqué/perdre les pédales.

rain [reɪn] *vi F* it never rains but it pours, (*catchphrase*) un malheur n'arrive jamais seul.

rainbows ['reɪnbəʊz] *npl P* (*drugs*) tuinal

m/barbiturique*/tricolore *m*.

raincheck ['reɪntʃek] *n NAm F* invitation remise/partie remise; **let's take a raincheck (on that)**, ce sera partie remise/pour une autre fois.

rainy ['reɪnɪ] *a F* **to put sth away/by for a rainy day**, garder une poire pour la soif/ mettre qch de côté pour ses vieux jours.

rainy-day ['reɪnɪdeɪ] *a attrib P* (*drugs*) **rainy-day woman**, cigarette* de marijuana/ joint *m*/stick *m*/bombardier *m*.

raise¹ [reɪz] *n V* **to get a raise**, avoir une érection*/bander/l'avoir en l'air/marquer midi.

raise² [reɪz] *vtr V* **to raise it/to raise a beam**, être en érection*/bander/marquer midi.

rake in ['reɪk'ɪn] *vtr F* **to rake it in**, gagner* beaucoup d'argent/(le) ramasser à la pelle/ faire du pèze/faire son beurre/se bourrer; **he's raking it in**, il ramasse un pognon fou.

rake-off ['reɪkɒf] *n F* commission *f*/ristourne *f*/pot-de-vin *m*/dessous *m* de table.

raker ['reɪkə] *n Austr F* **to go a raker**, tomber*/ramasser une bûche/ramasser un gadin/se casser la figure.

rally ['rælɪ] *vi NAm F* faire la noce/la bombe.

ralph [rælf] *vi NAm P* vomir*/gerber/dégobiller/dégueuler (tripes et boyaux). (*See* **hang²** 4)

ram¹ [ræm] *n P* 1. *Austr* = **shill** 2. (*rare*) individu* porté sur le sexe/chaud lapin.

ram² [ræm] *vtr V* 1. faire l'amour* avec (une femme); égoïner/bourrer/sabrer (une femme) 2. avoir un coït* anal avec (qn)/empaffer/ enculer (qn). (*See* **throat 1**)

rambunctious [ræm'bʌŋkʃəs] *a F* tapageur/chahuteur.

ramrod ['ræmrɒd] *n V* pénis*/défonceuse *f*/ gourdin *m*.

r & b, R & B ['ɑːrən'biː] *n Mus F* (= *rhythm and blues*) rhythm and blues *m*/R & B *m*.

R & R ['ɑːrən'ɑː] *n F* 1. *Mus* = **rock-'n'-roll** 1 2. *NAm* (= *rest and recreation*) récréation *f*/récré *f*.

randy ['rændɪ] *a P* sexuellement très excité; **to be randy**, éprouver un désir *ou* une excitation sexuelle intense; (*of man*) bander/ l'avoir en l'air/avoir la trique/avoir le gourdin; (*of woman*) bander/mouiller/avoir le haricot à la portière; **he was really randy for her**, il bandait pour elle/il l'avait en l'air pour elle/elle l'excitait à mort.

rank [ræŋk] *n F* **to pull rank (on s.o.)**, user et

abuser de son rang *ou* de sa position.

rap¹ [ræp] *n* 1. *P* réprimande *f*/punition *f*/ savon *m*/attrapage *m*/engueulade *f*; **to take the rap**, payer les pots cassés; **he had to take the rap**, il a dû trinquer 2. *NAm P* condamnation*/gerbe *m*/gerbement *m*/ sape(ment) *m*/sucrage *m*; **heroin rap**, accusation *f* de possession d'héroïne; **murder rap**, accusation de meurtre; **to beat the rap**, se faire acquitter (en justice)/échapper à la condamnation/faire un coup de nib; **to square a rap**, faire enlever/faire sauter une punition *ou* une amende/défarguer; **a bum rap**, une fausse accusation; **rap sheet**, casier *m* judiciaire/pedigree *m* (*See* **bum¹** I) 3. *P* **not to care a rap**, s'en ficher éperdument/s'en ficher comme de l'an quarante 4. *P* **not to be worth a rap**, ne rien* valoir/ne pas valoir tripette/ne pas valoir un pet de lapin 5. *NAm P* conversation *f*/bavardage *m*/converse *f*; **we had a rap session last night**, on s'est taillé une bavette hier soir 6. *NAm P* **rap club/parlour/ studio**, bar montant 7. *Mus F* rap *m*.

rap² [ræp] I *vtr* 1. *F* **to rap (s.o.) (over the knuckles)**, critiquer*/taper sur les doigts de/ tancer (qn) 2. *P* tuer*/but(t)er/bousiller/ descendre II *vi* 1. *esp NAm P* (*talk*) tailler une bavette/baver/jaspiner 2. *Mus* faire du rap.

rapper ['ræpə] *n Mus F* rappeur *m*.

rapt [ræpt] *a F* ravi/content/joice/jouasse.

rap-top ['ræptɒp] *n NAm F* (voiture *f*) décapotable *f*.

rare [reə] *a F* **we had a rare old time**, on s'en est payé une sacrée tranche/on s'en est donné.

rarin' ['reərɪn], **raring** ['reərɪŋ] *a F* **to be rarin' to go**, piaffer d'impatience/être prêt à ruer/attendre le gong.

raspberry ['rɑːzb(ə)rɪ] *n P* 1. (*RS = raspberry tart = fart*) bruit fait avec les lèvres imitant un pet 2. désapprobation *f*/engueulade *f*/savon *m* 3. (*a*) **to give s.o. a/the raspberry**, dire zut à qn/envoyer paître qn/envoyer chier qn; **his idea was given the raspberry**, son idée a été rejetée dégagée/enterrée (*b*) **to get a raspberry (from s.o.)**, se faire rabrouer/se faire remballer 4. **raspberry (ripple)**, (*RS = cripple*) infirme *mf*/bancroche *mf*. (*See* **flip²** 2)

rasta ['ræstə] *n F* rasta *m*.

rat¹ [ræt] *n* 1. *F* salaud*/sale type *m*/salopard *m*/peau *f* de vache; **you rat!** espèce de salaud!/d'ordure! (*See* **dirty I 1**) 2. *F* indicateur*/donneur, -euse/mouchard, -arde 3.

F briseur, -euse de grève/jaune *mf*/renard *m*
4. *F* **to smell a rat,** sentir qch de louche/
soupçonner anguille sous roche/avoir la puce
à l'oreille/avoir des gourances *fpl* 5. *F* **rat
poison,** alcool* de mauvaise qualité/tord-
boyaux *m*/mort-aux-rats *f* 6. *F* **the rat race,**
(*daily routine*) course *f* au bifteck; (*jungle*)
jungle *f*/foire *f* d'empoigne 7. *F* **to have the
rats** (*a*) être en colère*/en rogne/en suif (*b*)
être en proie au delirium tremens/avoir la
digue-digue 8. *O F* **rats!** flûte!/zut!/crotte!
rats to you! va donc!/sans blague!/mon œil!/
va te faire voir! 9. *F* (*Mil*, *WWII*) **the Desert
Rats,** les Rats *mpl* du Désert (*7ᵉ division
blindée en Afrique du Nord*) 10. *P* **rat and
mouse,** (*RS = house*) maison *f*.

rat² [ræt] *vi F* 1. **to rat on s.o.** (*a*) revenir sur
un marché (*b*) dénoncer*/cafarder/
moucharder/balancer qn; casser le morceau
2. abandonner* ses complices/les lâcher/les
plaquer/les laisser en carafe/les laisser en
frime.

rat-arsed ['rætɑːst] *a P* ivre*/bourré (à
zéro)/poivré.

ratbag ['rætbæg] *n P* 1. salaud*/ordure *f*/
fripouille *f*; **you ratbag!** espèce de salaud!/
sale type!/ordure! 2. *Austr* excentrique *mf*/
original, -ale/numéro *m*.

rate [reɪt] *vtr F* apprécier (qn, un film); **I
really rate him,** je lui donne le tableau
d'honneur/il me botte; **I don't rate him,** je ne
pense pas le plus grand bien de lui/je ne le
sens pas ce mec.

rat-faced ['rætfeɪst] *a P* = **rat-arsed.**

ratfink ['rætfɪŋk] *n P* sale mouchard, -arde/
indic *mf*/balance *f*. (*See* **fink**)

rathole ['ræthəʊl] *n F* = **hole 1.**

rat out ['ræt'aʊt] *vi P* partir*/déguerpir/
détaler/calter; **to rat out on s.o.,** (*abandon*)
lâcher qn/plaquer qn/laisser qn en carafe.

ratted ['rætɪd] *a Br P* ivre*/paf/poivré.

ratter ['rætə] *n F* = **rat¹ 2, 3.**

rattle ['rætl] *vtr F* (*make nervous*)
démonter/décontenancer/ébranler (qn); **it
rattled him,** ça l'a démonté; **he never gets
rattled,** il ne se laisse pas démonter; **don't get
rattled!** pas de panique!

rattle on ['rætl'ɒn] *vi F* (*talk a lot*) **she does
rattle on!** elle (n')arrête pas de jacter!/c'est
un moulin à paroles!

rattler ['rætlə] *n F* 1. train *m*/dur *m* 2. (=
rattlesnake) serpent *m* à sonnettes 3. *Br*
séducteur *m*/tombeur *m*.

rattling ['rætlɪŋ] *a O F* 1. vif/déluré/

d'attaque 2. excellent*/du tonnerre; **a rattling
good book/film,** un film/livre génial/de
première 3. **at a rattling pace,** au grand trot/
au galop/au pas de course.

rat-trap ['rættræp] *n P* bouche*/trappe *f*/
entonnoir *m*/claque-merde *m*. (*See* **trap**)

ratty ['rætɪ] *a* 1. *F* râleur/ronchonneur/
grincheux/rouspéteur/rouscailleur; **to get
ratty,** prendre la mouche; (*of child*) devenir
grognon; **he gets really ratty at times,** ça lui
arrive d'être de mauvais poil/d'être mal
vissé/d'être mal luné 2. *NAm P* (*ugly*)
moche/tarte; (*shabby*) mal soigné/loquedu/
délabré.

raunch [rɔːntʃ] *n NAm F* obscénité *f*.

raunchy ['rɔːntʃɪ] *a F* 1. *NAm O* moche/toc/
tocard/blèche/tartignol 2. grossier/ordurier/
cochon; (*more light-heartedly*) grivois/
scabreux/risqué/salé; (*sexy*) bandant/sexy.
(*See* **ronchie, ronchy**)

rave¹ [reɪv] *n Br F* 1. louange *f* enthousiaste/
concert *m* de louanges/coup *m* d'encensoir; **to
have a rave about sth,** délirer sur qch; **rave
review,** critique élogieuse/dithyrambique; **it's
the latest rave,** c'est la dernière mode/le
dernier cri/en vogue 2. = **rave-up.**

rave² [reɪv] *vi F* 1. s'extasier/baver
d'admiration/être en extase; en rester baba
(d'admiration); **to rave about s.o./sth,** délirer
sur qn/qch 2. faire la java/se marrer (*dans les
clubs, etc*).

raver ['reɪvə] *n Br F* fêtard, -arde/noceur,
-euse; **he's a bit of a raver,** c'est un sacré
noceur; **she's a right little raver,** elle aime
s'éclater/faire la noce.

rave-up ['reɪvʌp] *n F* (*party*) fiesta *f*/nouba
f/rave *m*/boum *f*/surboum *f*; **to have a rave-
up,** faire la nouba/s'éclater/s'en payer une
tranche.

raw [rɔː] *F I a* 1. **raw deal,** sale coup *m*/coup
a vache/vacherie *f*; **it's a raw deal,** (*unfair
treatment*) c'est un coup dur/c'est dur à
avaler; **to give s.o. a raw deal,** (*treat
unfairly*) en faire voir de dures à qn/en faire
voir des vertes et des pas mûres à qn/faire un
sale coup à qn; être vache/moche avec qn 2.
esp NAm risqué/scabreux/cru 3. **a raw hand/a
raw recruit,** un(e) novice/un bleu/un(e) mal
dégrossi(e) **II** *n* **in the raw** (*a*) (*in the nude*) à
poil/en costume d'Adam/d'Ève (*b*) (*coarse*) à
l'état brut/sans fioritures.

ray [reɪ] *n F* **to be s.o.'s little ray of sunshine,**
être le rayon de soleil de qn.

razz¹ [ræz] *n NAm F* dérision *f*/moquerie *f*/

charriage *m*/charre *m*.

razz² [ræz] *vtr NAm F* (*tease*) taquiner (qn)/ se moquer* de (qn)/se payer la tête de (qn)/ mettre (qn) en boîte/emboîter (qn); (*deride*) brimer (qn); (*heckle*) chahuter (qn).

razz(a)matazz ['ræz(ə)mə'tæz] *n* tape-à-l'œil *m*/clinquant *m*/chiqué *m*; **the razzamatazz of show business**, les feux *mpl* de la rampe/le strass et les paillettes du show-biz.

razzle ['ræzl] *n F* **to go on the razzle**, (*have a rowdy party*) faire la bringue/la ribouldingue/ la noce/la tournée des grands ducs/les quatre cents coups.

razzle-dazzle ['ræzldæzl] *n F* (*flashy display*) clinquant *m*/tape-à-l'œil *m*; **to be/to go on the razzle-dazzle**, faire la bringue/la fête/la nouba.

reach [riːtʃ] *n F* **to have a reach impediment**, être avare*/être constipé du morlingue/ avoir un cactus dans la poche.

reach-me-downs ['riːtʃmɪdaʊnz] *npl F* 1. prêt-à-porter *m* 2. vêtements* usagés *ou* d'occasion. (*See* **hand-me-downs**)

read [riːd] *vtr F* 1. **I can read him like a(n open) book**, je le connais comme (le fond de) ma poche/je sais toujours ce qu'il pense 2. comprendre/piger/entraver.

reader ['riːdə] *n P* (*in prisons*) livre *m*/revue *f*/journal *m*/de la lecture.

readies ['redɪz] *npl* argent*/pèze *m*/fric *m*/ trèfle *m*/pépettes *fpl*; **have you got the readies?** t'as le fric/les ronds/les talbins?

ready, the ready [(ðə)'redɪ] *n F* = **readies**.

real [rɪəl] *F* I *adv* 1. **for real**, réel/ authentique/pour de vrai; **it's for real**, c'est du vrai de vrai/pas de la came(lote) 2. *NAm* réellement/véritablement; **that's real nice of you**, c'est vraiment gentil/c'est très gentil de votre part; **I'll see you real soon**, à très bientôt II *a* (*intensifier*) **he's a real jerk**, c'est un vrai con/il est con à 100%.

ream [riːm] *vtr V* **to ream s.o.** (*a*) avoir un coït anal* avec qn; enculer/enviander qn; passer par l'entrée de service (*b*) lécher l'anus* de qn (*avant de faire un coït anal*)/ faire feuille de rose.

ream out ['riːm'aʊt] *vtr NAm P* **to ream s.o. out/to ream s.o.'s ass out**, réprimander* qn sévèrement/passer un savon à qn/ engueulander qn/engueuler qn.

rear(-end) ['rɪər(end)] *n F* fesses*/ postérieur *m*/popotin *m*/derche *m*/pétard *m*/

valseur *m*. (*See* **end 1**)

recap¹ ['riːkæp] *n F* (= *recapitulation*) résumé *m*/récapitulation *f*; **let's do a recap**, faisons le point.

recap² ['riː'kæp] *vi & tr F* (= *recapitulate*) récapituler/faire un résumé (de qch); **to recap the facts**, faire le point.

recce¹ ['rekɪ] *n Br F* (= *reconnaissance*) reconnaissance *f*/exploration *f*/investigation *f*.

recce² ['rekɪ] *vtr Br F* (= *reconnoitre*) faire une reconnaissance/éclairer le terrain/ouvrir la route.

red [red] I *a* 1. *F* communiste/rouge 2. *F* **to roll out the red carpet for s.o.**, faire les honneurs à qn/dérouler le tapis rouge pour qn 3. *F* **to paint the town red**, être en réjouissances*/faire les quatre cents coups/ faire la noce/faire la tournée des grands ducs/ faire la bringue 4. *P* **red devils** = **reds** (**red II 5**) 5. *P* (*drugs*) **red leb**, haschisch *m* du Liban/Liban *m* 6. *V* (*Hell's Angels*) **to get/to earn one's red wings**, pratiquer le cunnilinctus sur une femme pendant ses règles/avoir ses ailes rouges 7. *P* (*prisons*) **red band**, prisonnier*-ière à qui l'on donne certains privilèges. (*See* **herring 1; light II 3; rag¹ 4; tape¹; wing¹ 2**) II *n* 1. *F* communiste *mf*/rouge *mf*/coco *mf* 2. *P* or*/jonc *m* 3. *F* **in the red**, déficitaire/dans le rouge 4. *F* **to see red**, (*be angry*) voir rouge 5. *pl P* (*drugs*) barbituriques*/diables *mpl* rouges/barbis *fpl*. (*See* **red I 4**)

red biddy [red'bɪdɪ] *n Br F* vin* rouge/gros rouge mélangé avec de l'alcool à brûler.

red-eye ['redaɪ] *n P* 1. alcool*/tord-boyaux *m*/gnôle *f*/antigel *m*/schnick *m* 2. vol *m ou* train *m* de nuit.

redhead ['redhed] *n F* rouquin(e)/poil *m* de carotte/rouquemoute *mf*.

red-hot ['red'hɒt] *a F* 1. (*a*) (*enthusiastic*) plein de sève/d'allant; qui pète le feu/qui a du mordant; chauffé à blanc (*b*) avec du sex-appeal; **a red-hot mam(m)a**, (*sexy woman*) une bandeuse/une baiseuse; (*female singer*) une vocaliste plantureuse/une chanteuse de jazz 2. (*very good*) sensass/super 3. **a red-hot communist**, un(e) communiste à tous crins/ un(e) coco 4. très récent/tout chaud/tout brûlant/de dernière heure; **a red-hot tip**, un tuyau sensationnel/de première; **it's red-hot**, ça vient de sortir.

red-lamp ['red'læmp] *a attrib F* = **red-light**.

red-letter ['red'letə] *a attrib F* **red-letter**

day, jour *m* de fête/jour mémorable/jour à marquer d'une pierre blanche.

red-light ['red'laɪt] *a attrib F* **a red-light district**, un quartier à prostituées/un quartier chaud.

redneck ['rednek] *n NAm F* paysan*/plouc *mf*/cul-terreux *m*/bouseux *m*/péquenaud *m*.

reef¹ [riːf] *n F* = **reefer 1.**

reef² [riːf] *vi Austr P* prendre/faucher/ratiboiser/barboter.

reefer ['riːfə] *n* 1. *F (drugs)* (*a*) marijuana* (*b*) cigarette* de marijuana/reefer *m* 2. *Austr P* complice *mf* (d'un pickpocket)/baron *m*/trimballeur *m*.

Reekie ['riːkɪ] *n F* Auld Reekie, Édimbourg.

re-entry [riː'entrɪ] *n O P* fin *f* de voyage d'un drogué/redescente *f (après un trip)*.

ref¹ [ref] *n F (sports)* (= *referee*) arbitre *m*.

ref² [ref] *vtr F (sports)* (= *referee*) arbitrer (un match).

reffo ['refəʊ] *n Austr F Pej* refugié, -ée/immigrant, -ante.

refusenik [rɪ'fuːznɪk] *n* refuznik *mf*.

reg [redʒ] *n Br F* numéro *m* d'immatriculation (d'une voiture).

rego ['redʒəʊ] *n Austr F* = **reg.**

regs [regs] *npl F* (= *regulations*) règlements *mpl*.

rehab ['riːhæb] *n F (abbr of rehabilitation)* réhabilitation *f*; (*of alcoholic, drug addict*) désintoxication *f*; (*of young offender*) rééducation *f*.

reign [reɪn] *vi Austr P* être en liberté/profiter de la fraîche.

rello ['reləʊ] *n Austr F (relative, relation)* parent, -ente.

rent boy ['rentbɔɪ] *n Br P* jeune prostitué/castor *m*/nourrice *f*.

rep [rep] *n F* 1. (= *representative*) représentant, -ante/hirondelle *m* 2. (= *reputation*) réputation *f* 3. (= *repertory (theatre)*) (théâtre *m* de) répertoire *m*; **to be in rep**, faire du théâtre de répertoire; **what's on at the local rep?** qu'est qu'on joue au théâtre municipal?

repeaters [rɪ'piːtəz] *npl P* dés* truqués/matuches *mpl*/dés pipés/bouts *mpl* de sucre.

reptiles ['reptaɪlz] *npl F* 1. chaussures* (*surt* en peau de crocodile, de lézard *ou* de serpent)/crocos *mpl* 2. journalistes *mfpl*/journaleux, -euses; la presse/la menteuse.

result [rɪ'zʌlt] *n Br F* bon résultat; (*in football*) victoire *f*; **to get a result, to get results**, obtenir de bons résultats/arriver à

quelque chose; **we got a result, we got results**, ça a marché/ça a gazé; **we can all kiss the result goodbye**, le fric, on l'aura jamais.

resurrection pie [rezə'rekʃ(ə)n'paɪ] *n F* nourriture* réchauffée/réchauffé *m*.

retard ['riːtɑːd] *n F Pej (retarded person)* arriéré, -ée/handicapé(e) mental(e)/débile *mf*.

revamp [riː'væmp] *vtr F* renouveler/remettre à neuf/retaper; **they've revamped the menu**, ils ont rajeuni le(ur) menu.

reviver [rɪ'vaɪvə] *n F* remontant *m*/apéritif *m*/apéro *m*/tonique *f*.

rhino ['raɪnəʊ] *n* 1. *F (abbr of rhinoceros)* rhino(céros) *m* 2. *Br P* argent*/galette *f*/pèze *m*.

rhubarb ['ruːbɑːb] *n Br P (nonsense)* conneries *fpl*/blabla(bla) *m*; **that's a load of old rhubarb**, tu dis n'importe quoi/c'est des conneries.

rib [rɪb] *vtr F* taquiner/mettre en boîte/mener en bateau (qn); **he was ribbing me**, il se payait ma tronche.

ribbing ['rɪbɪŋ] *n F* **to give s.o. a ribbing**, taquiner qn/mener qn en bateau.

rib-tickler ['rɪbtɪklə] *n F* plaisanterie *f*/rigolade *f*/vanne *f*.

rib-tickling ['rɪbtɪklɪŋ] *a (very funny)* (très) rigolo/marrant/à se tordre de rire/boyautant.

rich [rɪtʃ] *F* I *a* 1. très amusant/rigolo/marrant 2. scabreux/osé/cochon; *Iron* **that's a bit rich!** ça c'est le comble!/c'est un peu fort de café! (*See* **filthy 2**) II *adv* **to strike it rich**, décrocher le gros lot.

Richard, richard ['rɪtʃəd] *n P* Richard (**the Third**) (*a*) (*RS = bird*) oiseau *m*/piaf *m*; (*woman*) nana *f*/gonzesse *f* (*b*) (*RS = turd*) étron*/colombin *m*/rondin *m*.

riddance ['rɪd(ə)ns] *n F* **good riddance (to bad rubbish)**! bon débarras!/ça débarrasse!

ride¹ [raɪd] *n* 1. *P* coït*/baise *f*/crampette *f* 2. *F* **to take s.o. for a ride** (*a*) *NAm* emmener qn en voiture pour le tuer/mettre qn en l'air/faire la peau à qn (*b*) tromper* qn/jouer un sale tour à qn/mener qn en bateau/faire marcher qn/rouler qn 3. *F* **to go along (just) for the ride**, suivre le gros de la troupe/suivre le courant/y aller pour y aller. (*See* **joy-ride¹**)

ride² [raɪd] I *vtr* 1. *P* faire l'amour* avec/baiser/enfiler/grimper 2. *NAm F* **to ride s.o.'s ass**, asticoter qn/enquiquiner qn/courir sur les haricots à qn II *vi F* **to let sth ride**, laisser courir qch; **let it ride!** laisse pisser! (*See*

joy-ride²)
riff [rɪf] n Mus P court motif mélodique de jazz ou de rock/riff m.
rig¹ [rɪg] n NAm 1. P organes génitaux masculins/bijoux mpl de famille/parties fpl 2. P (drugs) équipement m/attirail m (de drogué) (pour se piquer, renifler de la drogue).
rig² [rɪg] vtr F arranger/manigancer/magouiller (à son avantage); to rig an election, truquer une élection.
right [raɪt] I a 1. P (a) to make a right mess of it, tout gâcher/tout bousiller/foutre une vraie pagaille/semer la merde; she made a right cock-up, elle a tout mis en l'air/elle y a foutu le merdier (b) he's a right jerk, c'est un con fini/un idiot intégral (c) she's a right (old) cow, c'est une vraie peau de vache/une salope intégrale. (See **balls-up**; **nana**; **so-and-so 2**; **sucker**) 2. F as right as rain, en parfait état; to feel as right as rain, se porter comme un charme/avoir la frite 3. F to get on the right side of s.o., être bien vu de qn/se mettre dans les petits papiers de qn/se mettre à la bonne avec qn. (See **noise**; **people 2**; **stuff¹ 7**) II adv Austr F she'll be right, tout ira bien/ça ira, mon pote/t'en fais pas, mon pote/on verra bien.
righteous ['raɪtʃəs] a NAm F 1. bien/chic/chouette; a righteous guy, un mec bien/un type réglo 2. grand/large/largeo(t); she made a righteous mess of it, elle a foutu une vraie pagaille.
right-hander ['raɪt'hændə] n P coup m/crochet m du droit; to give s.o. a couple of right-handers, filer une pêche à qn/casser la gueule à qn/passer qn à tabac.
right-ho! ['raɪt'həʊ], **right-o(h)!** ['raɪt'əʊ] excl F oui*!/d'ac(cord)!/OK!/entendu!
right on, right-on ['raɪt'ɒn] a F au poil*/impec; esp NAm P right on! c'est sûr!/c'est vrai!/pas de doute!/vas-y! he was right-on, c'était un mec réglo.
righty-(h)o! ['raɪtɪ'(h)əʊ] excl F = **right-ho!**
rigid ['rɪdʒɪd] a P 1. to bore s.o. rigid, ennuyer* qn au plus haut point/emmerder qn jusqu'à la moelle/scier le dos à qn/prendre la tête à qn/barber qn que c'en est pas possible 2. ivre* mort/bituré/poivré.
rigout ['rɪgaʊt] n F toilette f/tenue f; Pej accoutrement m; pelure f; nippes fpl.
rig out ['rɪg'aʊt] vtr F habiller*/fringuer/

frusquer/loquer/fagoter; to rig oneself out, se harnacher.
rig-up ['rɪgʌp] n F appareil improvisé/installation f de fortune/zinzin m.
rig up ['rɪg'ʌp] vtr F 1. apprêter/préparer/concocter (un repas, une excuse, etc) 2. = **rig out**.
Riley ['raɪlɪ] n F to live the life of Riley, se la couler douce/se la faire belle/vivre comme un coq en pâte.
rim [rɪm] vtr P = **ream**.
ring¹ [rɪŋ] n 1. P anus*/anneau m/bague f/rondelle f; ring twitter/flutter, peur*/frousse f/jetons mpl/chocottes fpl 2. F to run rings round s.o., l'emporter sur qn/surpasser qn.
ring² [rɪŋ] vtr 1. F it rings a bell, cela me dit/me rappelle quelque chose 2. P to ring s.o.'s bell, (bring to sexual climax) faire jouir/faire goder qn 3. F to ring the changes (a) escroquer*/arnaquer; faire du vol au rendez-moi/marcher au rendez (b) écouler de la fausse monnaie/faire la fournaise (c) ressasser (un sujet, etc) 4. F (horseracing) to ring a horse, substituer un cheval à un autre 5. P maquiller (des objets volés).
ring-em ['rɪŋəm] n NAm P police*/flicaille f/volaille f.
ringer ['rɪŋə] n F 1. sosie m; to be a (dead) ringer for s.o., être qn tout craché/être le portrait (tout) craché de qn/être tout le portrait de qn 2. (horseracing) cheval substitué à un autre 3. voiture* volée dont on a changé les plaques minéralogiques.
ring-piece ['rɪŋpiːs] n P = **ring¹ 1**.
ringtail ['rɪŋteɪl] n Austr F poltron*/dégonflard, -arde/dégonflé, -ée.
rinky-dink ['rɪŋkɪ'dɪŋk] a NAm O F (shoddy) toc(ard)/moche.
riot ['raɪət] n F 1. grand succès/boum m (tonnerre)/fureur f; that film's a riot, ça a fait un tabac (monstre), ce film; it was a real riot, on s'en est payé une sacrée tranche/c'était dément 2. (entertaining, amusing person) boute-en-train m/rigolo, -ote/rigolboche m; he's a real riot, that guy, c'est un rigolo/il est impayable, ce type/il est à mourir de rire 3. déchaînement m/tapage m/chahut m/barouf m 4. to read the Riot Act to s.o. (a) avertir/menacer qn (b) réprimander* qn/passer un savon à qn.
rip [rɪp] vi F to let rip, exploser/vider son sac; (motorbike) mettre la poignée dans le coin; let it rip!/let her rip! fonce!/appuie sur le champignon!/mets les pleins gaz! the band

let rip, le groupe s'est arraché; the drummer really let it rip, le batteur a dégagé comme une bête/le batteur s'est défoncé.

rip into ['rɪp'ɪntuː] *vtr F* attaquer* (qn)/ rentrer dans le lard à (qn)/tomber sur le paletot à (qn).

ripoff ['rɪpɒf] *P* I *a* (*goods*) trop cher/chéro; (*person*) avide; a ripoff deal, une magouille II *n* vol *m*/escroquerie *f*/arnaque *f*; (*swindle*) entourloupe *f*/pigeonnage *m*, ripoff artist, voleur*/arnaqueur *m*.

rip off ['rɪp'ɒf] *vtr P* (*a*) voler*/faucher; to get ripped off, se faire tondre/pigeonner/ ratiboiser; you were ripped off, tu t'es fait voler/tu t'es fait avoir (*b*) to rip s.o. off, exploiter/arnaquer/rouler qn; I was really ripped off there, là, je me suis fait baiser en beauté.

ripped [rɪpt] *a P* 1. (*a*) (*drugs*) défoncé/très high/planant/stone(d) (*b*) très ivre*/rétamé/ schlass 2. *NAm* tué/descendu.

ripper ['rɪpə] *a Austr F* = **ripping**.

ripping ['rɪpɪŋ] *a O F* excellent*/ formid(able)/super.

rippy ['rɪpɪ] *a Br F* = **ripping**.

rip-roaring ['rɪp'rɔːrɪŋ] *a P* endiablé/ piaffant; a rip-roaring success, une réussite du tonnerre/un succès fulgurant/un tabac (monstre)/un boum du tonnerre.

ripsnorter ['rɪpsnɔːtə] *n F* personne *f ou* chose *f* remarquable/crack *m*/as *m*; (*man*) type *m* fortiche.

ripsnorting ['rɪpsnɔːtɪŋ] *a F* excellent*/ bœuf/du tonnerre.

rise[1] [raɪz] *n F* to take a/the rise out of s.o./to get a rise out of s.o., mettre qn en pétard/faire monter qn au plafond.

rise[2] [raɪz] *vi* 1. *F* rise and shine! (*catchphrase*) debout les morts! 2. *P* to rise to the occasion, avoir une érection*/bander (quand il faut).

ritz [rɪts] *n F* to put on the ritz, être prétentieux*/se donner des airs/crâner/rouler les mécaniques/rouler les biscotos.

ritzy ['rɪtsɪ] *a F* 1. tape-à-l'œil/voyant/ clinquant; a ritzy tart, une pépée qui en jette/ un beau châssis 2. élégant*/ultra-chic/classe 3. crâneur/esbroufeur/plastronneur.

river ['rɪvə] *n F* 1. to sell s.o. down the river, trahir/vendre/moutonner/donner qn 2. to send s.o. up the river = to send s.o. up (**send up**).

roach [rəʊtʃ] *n P* 1. (*drugs*) (*a*) mégot* de cigarette de marijuana (*b*) cigarette* de marijuana/joint *m* 2. *NAm* salaud*/loquedu

m.

road [rəʊd] *n F* 1. to be on the road, vivre sur les grands chemins/vagabonder/ trimarder/rouler sa bosse 2. to hit the road, partir*/se mettre en route/prendre le large/ lever l'ancre 3. you're in my road, tu es dans mon chemin; get out of the road! dégage! (*See* **middle-of-the-road**; **one 1**)

road-hog ['rəʊdhɒg] *n F* chauffeur *m* qui conduit au milieu de la chaussée/chauffard *m*/écraseur, -euse.

roadie ['rəʊdɪ] *n P* 1. (*rock music*) (*abbr of road manager*) homme *m* à tout faire qui accompagne un groupe en tournée/roadie *m* 2. *NAm* bière *f* /mousse *f*; we can grab some roadies on the way, on peut se prendre une mousse en route.

roast[1] [rəʊst] *n F* (*a*) critique *f* défavorable/ flingage *m* (*b*) calomnie *f*/débinage *m*.

roast[2] [rəʊst] *vtr F* critiquer*/allumer/ flinguer.

roasting ['rəʊstɪŋ] *n F* to give (s.o.) a roast- ing = **roast**[2].

rock[1] [rɒk] *n* 1. *F* (*jazz*) rock *m*. (*See* **rock- 'n'-roll 1**) 2. *F* on the rocks (*a*) (*drink*) servi avec des glaçons (*b*) ruiné*/fauché/nettoyé/à sec (*c*) (*marriage*) à la dérive/à (vau-)l'eau/ qui bat de l'aile (*d*) (*business*) en faillite/dans le bouillon 3. *pl P* diamants*/diams *mpl*/ pierres *fpl*/cailloux *mpl*. (*See* **hot 9** (*a*)) 4. *F* to touch rock bottom, être arrivé au fin fond/ être tout à fait à plat/être dans la dèche 5. *P pl* rocks, testicules*; to get one's rocks off, (*have an orgasm*) avoir un orgasme/s'envoyer en l'air/prendre son pied; (*have a good time*) s'en payer une tranche/prendre son pied. (*See* **pop**[2] **4**) 6. *P* (*drugs*) the rock, cocaïne*/crack *m* 7. *F* the Rock, Gibraltar *m*.

rock[2] [rɒk] *vtr* 1. *F* secouer/ébranler/alarmer 2. *F* to rock the boat, faire des vagues/secouer la barque/la baraque; ruer dans les brancards; faire du grabuge 3. *P* faire l'amour* avec (une femme)/niquer/sauter.

rockbiz ['rɒkbɪz] *n F* l'industrie *f* du rock.

rocker ['rɒkə] *n* 1. *Br* blouson noir sur grosse moto/loubard *m*/loulou *m*/rocker *m*. (*See* **mod**) 2. off one's rocker, fou*/timbré/ loufoque/maboul; échappé de Charenton/de Sainte-Anne 3. *NAm* rocking-chair *f*/fauteuil *m* à bascule.

rocket ['rɒkɪt] *n F* 1. to give s.o. a rocket, réprimander* qn/passer un savon à qn/ engueuler qn/sonner les cloches à qn 2. *pl* rockets, seins*/flotteurs *mpl*/pare-chocs *mpl*.

(See **sky-rocket**)

rockhead ['rɒkhed] *n NAm P* individu bête*/crétin, -ine/andouille *f*.

rock-'n'-roll[1] ['rɒkən'rəʊl] *n F* 1. *Mus* rock-and-roll *m*/rock-'n'-roll *m*/rock *m* 2. *Br* (*RS* = *dole*) allocation *f* de chômage/de chômedu; bureau *m* d'allocation de chômage. (See **rock**[1] 1)

rock-'n'-roll[2] ['rɒkənrəʊl] *vi F* faire du rock-and-roll/danser le rock.

rocky ['rɒkɪ] *a F* (*a*) vacillant/flageolant; a **rocky marriage**, un mariage qui s'effiloche/ qui bat de l'aile (*b*) chancelant/titubant (de boisson *ou* de fatigue).

rod [rɒd] *n P* 1. pénis*/os *m* à moelle/poireau *m*/gourdin *m*. (See **hot 20** (*b*); **hot-rod**) 2. revolver*/calibre *m*/flingue *m*/pétard *m* 3. pardessus*/lardoss *m*/lardingue *m*/pardingue *m*.

rod-man ['rɒdmæn] *n NAm P* gangster *m*/ bandit *m*/voleur* armé/braqueur *m*.

Roger! roger![1] ['rɒdʒə] *excl F* oui*/d'ac!/ OK!

roger[2] ['rɒdʒə] *vtr Br P* faire l'amour*/ baiser/égoïner.

roll[1] [rəʊl] *n* 1. *F* liasse *f* de billets* (de banque)/matelas *m*/millefeuille *m* 2. *P* coït*/ baise *f*/troussée *f*; a **roll in the hay**, une partie de jambes en l'air. (See **hay 2**; **jelly-roll**; **rock-'n'-roll**[1])

roll[2] [rəʊl] *vtr & i* 1. *P* voler*/carotter/ roustir/secouer (*surt* un ivrogne) 2. *F* **to be rolling in it**, être très riche*/être plein aux as/ rouler sur l'or/être rupin/avoir le sac/être au sac 3. *F* **to get rolling**, partir*/(se) déhotter/ décaniller/mettre les voiles 4. *P* faire l'amour* avec (qn)/s'envoyer en l'air/faire un carton 5. *NAm P* conduire/faire de la voiture/ driver; **we were rollin'**, on se promenait en bagnole. (See **aisle 2**; **rock-'n'-roll**[2])

roll along ['rəʊlə'lɒŋ] *vi F* avancer tranquillement/suivre son petit bonhomme de chemin/aller cahin-caha.

Roller ['rəʊlə] *n Br P* = **Rolls**.

rollick ['rɒlɪk] *vtr Br P* engueuler/passer un savon à (qn).

rollicking ['rɒlɪkɪŋ] *n Br P* engueulade *f*/ savon *m*.

rolling ['rəʊlɪŋ] *a Br P* **rolling (in it)**, très riche/plein aux as/qui roule sur l'or.

rollock ['rɒlək] *vtr Br P* = **rollick**.

rollocking ['rɒləkɪŋ] *n Br P* = **rollicking**.

roll on ['rəʊl'ɒn] *vi F* **roll on Christmas!** vivement Noël!

roll out ['rəʊl'aʊt] *vi F* **they rolled out of the pub at closing time**, à la fermeture ils sont sortis du café en titubant. (See **red I 2**)

Rolls [rəʊlz] *n F Aut* Rolls Royce *f* (*RTM*)/ Rolls *f*.

roll-up ['rəʊlʌp] *n P* cigarette* roulée à la main/cibiche *f* maison/*FrC* rouleuse *f*. (See **roll up 2**)

roll up ['rəʊl'ʌp] *vi* 1. *F* arriver*/s'abouler/ débouler/débarquer/se pointer 2. *P* faire une cigarette* de marijuana/rouler un reefer/(se) rouler un joint. (See **roll-up**)

Rolly ['rɒlɪ] *n Br P* = **Rolls**.

roll-your-own ['rəʊljə'rəʊn] *n F* (*a*) machine *f* à rouler les cigarettes*/rouleuse *f* (*b*) = **roll-up**.

roly-poly ['rəʊlɪ'pəʊlɪ] *n F* individu* rondouillard/boudin *m*/gravos, -osse/patapouf *m*/gros lard.

Roman ['rəʊmən] *a P* 1. **Roman candle** (*a*) catholique *mf*/catho *mf* (*b*) *Br* (mort causée par un) accident de parachutisme 2. (= *roaming*) (*a*) **Roman hands**, mains caressantes/baladeuses; mains qui vont aux renseignements (*b*) **Roman eyes**, yeux farfouilleurs.

romp[1] [rɒmp] *n F* 1. **to have a romp on the sofa**, (*have sex*) s'envoyer en l'air sur le canapé; **love romp**, baisage *m*/carambolage *m* 2. chose *f* facile à réaliser/du beurre/du nougat/du gâteau/du cousu main.

romp[2] [rɒmp] *vi F* **to romp home**, (*of horse*) gagner facilement/arriver dans un fauteuil/ gagner haut la main.

ronchie, ronchy ['rɒntʃɪ] *a NAm F* = **raunchy**.

'roo [ruː] *n F* kangourou *m*.

roof [ruːf] *n* 1. *F* **to go through/to hit the roof**, piquer une colère/monter sur ses grands chevaux/sortir de ses gonds/prendre un coup de sang 2. *F* **to raise the roof**, faire du chahut/du chambard/du grabuge.

rook [rʊk] *vtr F* escroquer*/faisander/ pigeonner/rouler/mener en bateau; **he got rooked**, il s'est fait avoir/arnaquer.

rookie ['rʊkɪ] *n F* recrue *f*/débutant, -ante/ blanc-bec *m*.

rooking ['rʊkɪŋ] *n F* **to get a rooking**, payer* trop cher/se faire écorcher/prendre un coup de fusil.

rooky ['rʊkɪ] *n F* = **rookie**.

room [ruːm] *n F* 1. **the smallest room/the little boys' room/the little girls' room**, WC*/le petit endroit/le petit coin 2. (*horseracing*) to go to the rooms, gagner par décision des commissaires à la photo-finish. (*See* **barrack-room; throne-room**)

roost [ruːst] *n F* 1. logement*/niche *f*/ guitoune *f*/cambuse *f* 2. to hit the roost, se coucher*/se zoner/aller au paddock/se plumarder/mettre sa viande dans le torchon.

root[1] [ruːt] *n P* 1. *NAm* (*rare*) cigarette*/ cibiche *f*/clope *f* 2. (*drugs*) marijuana*/ marie-jeanne *f* 3. pénis*/bout *m*/queue *f* 4. *esp Austr* coït*/baise *f*/partie *f* de jambes en l'air 5. (*of man*) partenaire sexuelle/affaire *f*.

root[2] [ruːt] *vi & tr* 1. *Austr P* faire l'amour* avec (une femme)/fourrer/tringler 2. *P Austr P* get rooted! va te faire voir! 3. *F* to root for s.o., applaudir/encourager qn; to root for a cause, soutenir une cause.

rooted ['ruːtɪd] *a Austr P* abîmé/cassé/ naze(broque)/pourri.

rooter ['ruːtə] *n* 1. *F* partisan *m*/fana(tique) *mf*/supporter *m* (d'une équipe, etc) 2. *P Br* (*man*) séducteur *m*/tombeur *m*/bandeur *m*/ chaud lapin; (*woman*) bandeuse *f*.

root-faced ['ruːtfeɪst] *a Austr P* (*person*) maussade.

roots [ruːts] *a P* (*Jamaican*) authentique/ officiel.

rope [rəʊp] *n* 1. *F* it's money for old rope, c'est donné/c'est pour une bouchée de pain 2. *P* tabac*/perlot *m*/trèfle *m*/percal(e) *m* 3. *P* (*drugs*) (*a*) marijuana*/chanvre *m* (*b*) cigarette* de marijuana/stick *m*/joint *m* 4. *F* to know the ropes, être au courant/à la coule/ au parfum/affranchi; savoir nager/connaître la combine/les tenants et les aboutissants 5. *F* to give s.o. plenty of rope, lâcher la bride/ donner du mou à qn; give him enough rope and he'll hang himself, laissez-le faire et il se passera lui-même la corde au cou.

rope in ['rəʊp'ɪn] *vtr F* to rope s.o. in, s'assurer le concours de/recruter qn; they've roped me in on it, ils m'ont mis dans le coup/ m'ont recruté pour leur truc.

rop(e)y ['rəʊpɪ] *a F* minable/toc/tocard; it's a bit rop(e)y, c'est du toc/de la camelote.

rort[1] [rɔːt] *n Austr F* 1. coup monté/fourré; combine bien cuisinée/magouille *f* 2. fiesta *f*/ beuverie *f*/nouba *f*.

rort[2] [rɔːt] *vtr Austr F* tromper*/arnaquer/ rouler/refaire.

rorter ['rɔːtə] *n Austr F* escroc*/arnaqueur *m*/faisan(t) *m*.

rorty ['rɔːtɪ] *a Austr P* (*riotous*) tapageur/ chahuteur; (*wild*) dissolu/dissipé; (*drunken*)

soûl/poivré.

Rory (O'Moore) ['rɔːrɪ(əʊ'mɔː)] *Prn Br P* 1. (*RS = door*) porte *f*/lourde *f* 2. (*RS = floor*) plancher *m*; (on the) Rory, pauvre*/fauché/ sans le sou.

Roscoe, roscoe ['rɒskəʊ] *n NAm O F* revolver*/rigolo *m*.

rosy ['rəʊzɪ] *n P* 1. the rosy, vin* rouge/ pinard *m*/rouquin *m*/picrate *m* 2. ring around the rosy = daisy chain (**daisy 5**) 3. Rosy *or* Rosie (Lee), (*RS = tea*) thé *m*.

rot [rɒt] *n F* bêtises*/sottises *fpl*/salades *fpl*/ bobards *mpl*; what rot! c'est de la blague!/ c'est des foutaises! to talk (utter) rot/a load of rot, dire des bêtises*/des conneries; débloquer/déconner. (*See* **tommyrot**)

rot-gut ['rɒtgʌt] *n F* alcool* de mauvaise qualité/tord-boyaux *m*/gnôle *f*/vitriol *m*.

rotten ['rɒtn] *a F* 1. désagréable/ dégueulasse/débectant/moche/merdique/loque-du; rotten weather, temps *m* de chien/temps pourri/saloperie *f* de temps; a rotten business, une sale affaire; une affaire véreuse/ fumeuse; rotten luck! quelle poisse!/quelle déveine!/pas de veine! you rotten bastard! espèce de pourriture! 2. nul/pourri/toc/tocard 3. malade*/patraque 4. ennuyeux*/barbant/ emmerdant 5. ivre*/chargé/bourré; to get rotten, se noircir/se beurrer/se givrer. (*See* **bastard; sod**[1] **2**)

rotter ['rɒtə] *n O F* vaurien*/fripouille *f*/ charogne *f*/ordure *f*.

rough [rʌf] **I** *a F* 1. a rough diamond, une personne aux dehors grossiers mais bon enfant/un diamant dans sa gangue; he's a rough diamond, ses manières d'ours cachent beaucoup de qualités 2. that's rough! c'est vache!/c'est dur à avaler!/c'est un coup dur! 3. he's had a rough deal, il en a bavé/il a bouffé de la vache enragée/il en a vu (des vertes et des pas mûres); il en a encaissé/il en a chié 4. they're a rough lot, c'est une bande* de sales types/c'est une fine équipe; a rough customer, un mauvais coucheur/un dur à cuire 5. rough and ready (*a*) a rough and ready person, une personne rustre/ péquenaud sur les bords (*b*) a rough and ready method, une méthode sommaire (*c*) a rough and ready piece of work, un ouvrage grossièrement fait/fait à la va-vite/à la va-comme-je-te-pousse 6. rough stuff, brutalités *fpl*/vacheries *fpl*; (*prostitute's term*) sadomasochisme *m*/mutilation *f*, etc.; there'll be some rough stuff tonight, ça va barder/il

va y avoir de la bagarre/il y aura du grabuge/
il y aura du *ou* de la baston ce soir **7. to give
s.o. a rough time,** maltraiter qn/être chien
avec qn/être vache avec qn/en faire voir à qn
8. to feel rough, (*feel ill*) se sentir malade*/
patraque; être mal fichu; (*feel exhausted*) en
avoir sa claque/être rincé; (*have a hangover*)
avoir la gueule de bois/avoir mal aux cheveux
II *adv F* **to sleep rough,** coucher* à la dure/à
la belle étoile; compter les étoiles (*See* **cut
up 2**) **III** *n* 1. *F* **to take the rough with the
smooth,** prendre le bon avec le mauvais/y
aller/à la guerre comme à la guerre/prendre
la vie comme elle vient 2. *P* = **roughneck 3.**
P **to have a bit of rough** = to have a bit on the
side (**side 2**).

rough-house ['rʌfhaʊs] *n F* chahut *m*/
boucan *m*; bagarre*/baston *m ou f*/casse *f*/
corrida *f*; there was a bit of a rough-house, ça
cognait dur.

rough it ['rʌfɪt] *vi F* vivre à la dure.

roughneck ['rʌfnek] *n NAm F* vaurien*/
canaille *f*/voyou *m*/dur *m*/casseur *m*/loubard
m.

rough-trade ['rʌftreɪd] *n P* 1. amant*
homosexuel considéré comme étant vulgaire
et grossier; *quelquefois* homosexuel* violent
2. (*of prostitute*) client/clille grossier *ou*
violent.

rough-up ['rʌfʌp] *n P* violente querelle*/
embrouille *f*/baston *m ou f*.

rough up ['rʌf'ʌp] *vtr P* battre* (qn)/
tabasser (qn)/bourrer (qn) de coups/avoiner
(qn); the cops roughed him up a bit, les flics
l'ont passé à tabac.

roundabouts ['raʊndəbaʊts] *npl F* what
you gain on the swings you lose on the
roundabouts/it's all swings and roundabouts,
(*catchphrase*) il y a des hauts et des bas/à
tout prendre on ne gagne ni ne perd/on
récupère à droite ce qu'on perd à gauche.

roundeye ['raʊndaɪ] *n P* 1. personne *f* de
race blanche/Blanc, Blanche 2. *NAm* anus*/
trou *m* de balle.

roundhead ['raʊndhed] *n Br P* homme
circoncis.

roundheel(s) ['raʊndhiːl(z)] *n NAm P* to
be a roundheel(s), être une femme facile/
avoir la cuisse hospitalière. (*See* **heel 2**)

roundup ['raʊndʌp] *n F* 1. compilation *f*/
résumé *m* (des dernières nouvelles, etc) 2. to
be heading for the last roundup, être près de
mourir*/sentir le sapin/graisser ses bottes.

rouser ['raʊzə] *n P* qch de sensationnel/de

saisissant/un boum.

roust out ['raʊst'aʊt] *vtr F* to roust s.o.
out, se débarrasser* de qn/flanquer qn à la porte/
balancer qn/envoyer balader qn.

row[1] [raʊ] *n* 1. *F* querelle*/embrouille *f*/
crosse *f* 2. *F* chahut *m*/boucan *m* (du diable)/
barouf *m*.

row[2] [raʊ] *vi F* se quereller*/s'attraper/
pétarder/s'engueuler/se voler dans les plumes.

royals ['rɔɪəlz] *npl* 1. *F* the royals, la famille
royale 2. *P* to do the royals, (*to turn Queen's
Evidence*) dénoncer ses complices (*souvent
en échange d'une peine plus légère*)/déballer
le morceau/se mettre à table.

rozzer ['rɒzə] *n Br P* agent* de police/flic *m*/
poulet *m*/poulaga *m*/keuf *m*.

rubadub ['rʌbə'dʌb] *n P* (*a*) (*RS = club*)
club *m*/boîte *f* de nuit (*b*) (*RS = pub*) bar *m*/
bistrot *m*/rade *m*.

rubber ['rʌbə] *n* 1. *P* préservatif*/capote
anglaise/marguerite *f*/imper *m* à Popaul. (*See*
johnnie 3) 2. *pl F* galoches *fpl*/caoutchoucs
mpl 3. *P* (*RS = rubber dub*) = **rubadub**.

rubberneck[1] ['rʌbənek] *n NAm F* (*at scene
of accident, etc*) badaud, -aude/curieux, -euse;
(*tourist*) touriste *mf*.

rubberneck[2] ['rʌbənek] *vi NAm F* (*at
scene of accident, etc*) faire le badaud/bigler;
(*of tourist*) excursionner/visiter.

rubber-stamp[1] ['rʌbə'stæmp] *n F*
fonctionnaire *mf* qui exécute aveuglément les
ordres de ses supérieurs/rond-de-cuir *m*;
béni-oui-oui *m*/lèche-bottes *m*.

rubber-stamp[2] ['rʌbəstæmp] *vtr F* ap-
prouver (qch) sans discussion.

rubbish ['rʌbɪʃ] *vtr F* dénigrer/flinguer/
bêcher/couler (qn, un projet, etc).

rube [ruːb] *n NAm P* paysan*/pedzouille *mf*/
plouc *mf*/péquenaud *m*/glaiseux, -euse.

rub in ['rʌb'ɪn] *vtr F* to rub it in, insister/
remuer le couteau dans la plaie; don't rub it
in/there's no need to rub it in, pas la peine
d'en rajouter.

rub off ['rʌb'ɒf] *vi P* 1. faire l'amour*/
baiser 2. to rub off, (*of woman*) se
masturber*/s'astiquer (le bouton)/se pignoler.

rub-out ['rʌbaʊt] *n P* 1. assassinat *m*/tuerie
f/but(t)age *m*/saignage *m*/coup dur 2. coït*/
baisage *m*/carambolage *m*.

rub out ['rʌb'aʊt] *vtr P* tuer*/but(t)er/
dessouder/effacer/éliminer/refroidir.

rub-up ['rʌbʌp] *n P* masturbation*/pignole
f/branlette *f*/secouette *f*. (*See* **rub up 2**)

rub up ['rʌb'ʌp] *vtr* 1. *F* to rub s.o. up the

wrong way, prendre qn à rebrousse-poil 2. *P* se masturber*/s'astiquer/se battre *ou* se mettre à cinq contre un 3. *P* (*sexually stimulate*) caresser activement (qn)/allumer (qn); (*touch up*) aller aux renseignements/mettre la main au panier/peloter/papouiller.

Ruby (Murray) ['ruːbɪ('mʌrɪ)] *Prn Br P* (*RS = curry*) curry *m*.

ruck[1] [rʌk] *n Br P* bagarre*/baston *m ou f*/ casse *f*/rififi *m*.

ruck[2] [rʌk] *vtr & i P* 1. agacer/énerver/taper sur le système à (qn) 2. se battre*/se bastonner/se rifler/se chiquer (la gueule).

ruckus ['rʌkəs] *n P* chahut *m*/barouf *m*; grabuge *m*.

ructions ['rʌkʃ(ə)nz] *npl F* dispute *f*/ embrouille *f*; **if you come home late there'll be ructions**, si tu rentres tard, tu te feras incendier/tu te feras remonter les bretelles.

ruddy ['rʌdɪ] *a & adv P* (*Euph for* **bloody**) **a ruddy liar**, un sacré menteur/un bourreur de mou; **he's a ruddy nuisance**, il est vachement casse-pieds/il est casse-bonbons/il nous les casse; **you ruddy fool!** espèce de nœud/ d'andouille/d'enfoiré/de branque!

rude [ruːd] *a* 1. *Br F* **rude bits**, seins* *ou* parties (génitales) 2. *P* (*Jamaican*) **rude boy**, membre *m* d'une bande/= loubard *m*/loulou *m*.

rug [rʌg] *n* 1. *P* perruque *f*/moumoute *f* 2. *F* **to pull the rug from under s.o.**('s feet), couper l'herbe sous le pied de qn 3. *P* **to cut a rug**, danser*/gambiller. (*See* **dirt 4**)

rugger ['rʌgə] *n F* le rugby; *Br P* **rugger bugger**, sportif *m* vigoureux *ou* enthousiaste.

rum [rʌm] *a O F* bizarre; **a rum one**, un drôle de type/de zèbre/d'oiseau; **it was a rum do**, c'était un truc plutôt bizarre/c'était un drôle de cinéma.

rumble[1] ['rʌmbl] *n P* bagarre*/rixe *f*/baston *m ou f*; bataille arrangée entre bandes* de voyous.

rumble[2] ['rʌmbl] **I** *vi P* se battre*/se bastonner/se rifler **II** *vtr Br F* flairer/se douter de (qch)/se gourrer/voir venir (qn); **he's rumbled us**, il nous a mis à jour/il a découvert le pot aux roses; **we've been rumbled**, on a deviné notre jeu.

rumbum ['rʌmbʌm] *n P* ivrogne*/poivrot, -ote/soûlard, -arde.

rumbustious [rʌm'bʌstɪəs] *a F* tapageur/ chahuteur.

rummy ['rʌmɪ] **I** *a F* = **rum II** *n P* =

rumbum.

rumpo ['rʌmpəʊ] *n Br P* sexe *m*/baisage *m*/ cul *m*; **a bit of rumpo**, une partie de jambes en l'air.

rumpty-tumpty ['rʌmptɪ'tʌmptɪ] *n*, **rumpy-pumpy** ['rʌmpɪ'pʌmpɪ] *n Br P* = rumpo.

rumpus ['rʌmpəs] *n F* chahut *m*/boucan *m*/ vacarme *m*; **to kick up a rumpus**, faire une scène; **there's gonna be a rumpus**, ça va barder.

run [rʌn] *n F* 1. **to have a run for one's money**, en avoir pour son argent*/pour ses sous 2. **the runs**, diarrhée*/courante *f*/chiasse *f* 3. **to be on the run**, être recherché par la police/être en cavale/faire la belle 4. **dry run**, essai *m*/répétition *f* 5. (*drugs*) = **rush**[1].

runaround ['rʌnəraʊnd] *n F* **to give s.o. the run-around**, donner le change à qn/faire marcher qn/mener qn en bateau.

run down ['rʌn'daʊn] *vtr F* critiquer*/ éreinter/débiner.

run in ['rʌn'ɪn] *vtr F* arrêter*/embarquer/ ramasser/coffrer.

runner ['rʌnə] *n Br P* 1. évadé, -ée (de prison, etc) 2. **to do a runner**, partir*/se débiner/décaniller.

run-out ['rʌnaʊt] *n P* **to have a run-out**, uriner*/écluser.

run out ['rʌn'aʊt] *vi F* **to run out on s.o.**, se défiler/prendre la poudre d'escampette/se débiner.

runt [rʌnt] *n F Pej* avorton *m*/foutriquet *m*/ bas-du-cul *m*; **you little runt!** (espèce de) nabot!/trouduc!/basduc!

runty ['rʌntɪ] *a F* rabougri/riquiqui.

rush[1] [rʌʃ] *n P* 1. (*drugs*) sensation *f* euphorique (*après absorption d'une drogue*); flash *m*/bang *m*/le pied 2. *NAm* = **bumrush**. (*See* **bum's rush**)

rush[2] [rʌʃ] *vtr F* **to rush s.o. for sth**, estamper/refaire/arnaquer qn de qch.

Russky ['rʊskɪ, 'rʌskɪ] *n F* Russe*/popof *m*/ rus(s)kof *m*.

rust-bucket ['rʌst'bʌkɪt] *n P* vieille voiture*/guinde *f*/guimbarde *f*/tacot *m*/tas *m* de ferraille.

rustle up ['rʌsl'ʌp] *vtr F* dénicher/ concocter/dégotter (qch); **she can always rustle up a little something**, elle sait toujours se débrouiller pour faire de quoi bouffer.

Ruth [ruːθ] *Prn Austr P* **to cry Ruth**, vomir*/ dégueuler/aller au refil(e).

S

sab [sæb] *vtr Br F* (*abbr of sabotage*) saboter.

sabbing ['sæbɪŋ] *n Br F* (*abbr of sabotage*) sabotage *m*.

sack¹ [sæk] *n* 1. *F* to get the sack, être congédié*; se faire congédier/renvoyer/ sacquer/lourder; to give s.o. the sack, se débarrasser* de/sacquer/virer/balancer qn; he got (given) the sack, il s'est fait foutre à la porte 2. *F* to look like a sack of potatoes, avoir une drôle de touche; he looks like a sack of potatoes, il est foutu/fringué comme l'as de pique 3. *F* lit*/pieu *m*/plumard *m*; to hit the sack, se coucher*/aller dormir*/se pieuter/se bâcher/se pager; sack time (*a*) temps passé au lit*/temps de pieutage/dorme *f* (*b*) heure *f* du coucher/du plumard/de se pieuter 4. *P* sack game, cour amoureuse/jeux amoureux/ fleurette *f*; sack artist, séducteur *m*/tombeur *m*/chaud lapin.

sack² [sæk] *vtr* 1. *F* to sack s.o. = to give s.o. the sack (**sack¹** 1) 2. *P* (*in Manchester*) (*give up*) abandonner*/laisser tomber; (*cancel*) annuler; I've sacked the E, j'arrête (de prendre de) l'ecstasy.

sack out, up ['sæk'aut, 'ʌp] *vi NAm P* se coucher*/se pieuter.

saddle ['sædl] *vtr & i F* to be saddled with s.o./sth, avoir qn/qch sur le dos; se coltiner qn/qch; I got saddled with all the washing-up, j'ai dû me coltiner/me taper toute la vaisselle.

safe [seif] I *a F* 1. *Br* bien/choucard/ chouette/réglo 2. to be safe/to be on the safe side (*a*) être du bon côté (du manche) (*b*) agir pour plus du sûreté; I'll take an extra £10 (just) to be on the safe side, je prendrai dix livres de plus pour plus de sûreté/au cas où II *adv F* to play (it) safe, ne pas prendre de risques/jouer serré/jouer sur le velours III *n NAm P* préservatif*/capote (anglaise).

safety ['seifti] *n P* préservatif/capote (anglaise).

sail [seil] *n F* to take the wind out of s.o.'s sails, couper l'herbe sous le pied de qn; rabattre le caquet à qn.

sailing ['seilɪŋ] *n F* to be (all) plain sailing, aller tout seul/ne pas faire un pli; it's going to be all plain sailing from now on, ça va aller tout seul/comme sur des roulettes.

sail into ['seil'ɪntu:] *vtr F* (*a*) attaquer*/ assaillir/rentrer dans (la gueule/le lard de) (qn) (*b*) sonner les cloches à/passer un savon à (qn) (*c*) entamer/attaquer (un travail) avec élan (*d*) to sail into a room, entrer majestueusement dans une pièce.

sailor ['seilə] *n* 1. *V* sailor's bride = poupée *f* gonflable; planche *f* à trou 2. *F* hello sailor! (*catchphrase*) salut tata!/salut chochotte!/ coquine va!

sail through ['seil'θru:] *vtr F* terminer (un travail, etc) en moins de deux/faire (qch) en un tour de temps/liquider (qch) en deux coups de cuiller à pot; to sail through an exam, réussir un examen les doigts dans le nez/haut la main.

salami [sə'lɑ:mi] *n NAm P* 1. pénis*/bout *m*/chipolata *m* 2. individu bête*/andouille *f*.

sale [seil] *n P* no sale! pas mèche!/rien à faire!/que dalle!

Sally-Ann ['sælɪ'æn] *n F* = **Sally Army**.

Sally Army ['sælɪ'ɑ:mi] *n F* (= *Salvation Army*) l'Armée *f* du Salut.

salt [sɔ:lt] *n* 1. *F* (old) salt, marin*/vieux loup de mer 2. *Br P* fille*/nénette *f*/gonzesse *f* 3. *NAm P* (*drugs*) héroïne* (en poudre)/poudre *f*/dropou *f*/blanche *f* 4. *P* salt and pepper team, un policier* blanc et un policier noir qui font équipe 5. *F* to be worth one's salt, mériter/ne pas voler sa paye *ou* sa croûte; he's not worth his salt, il ne vaut pas grand-chose; a general worth his salt, un général digne de ce nom (*See* **dose 2**)

salt-cellar ['sɔ:ltselə] *n F* salière *f* (derrière la clavicule).

sam, Sam [sæm] *n P* 1. to stand sam, payer la/une tournée 2. *NAm* agent *m* de la Brigade

217

fédérale des Stupéfiants. (*See* **Uncle 4**)

sambo, Sambo ['sæmbəʊ] *n P Pej* Noir(e)*/nègre *m*/bamboula *m*.

sample ['sɑ:mpl] *vtr F* to sample the goods, (*touch s.o. up*) mettre/coller la main au panier (à qn).

sand [sænd] *n F* 1. sucre *m* 2. *NAm* courage *m*/cran *m*/battant *m*. (*See* **grit 1**)

sandbag ['sændbæg] *vtr NAm F* (*attack*) attaquer/tomber sur le poil à (qn); (*incapacitate*) metre (qn) hors de combat/ neutraliser (qn); (*thwart*) contrarier (qn); déjouer (qn, les projets de qn).

sandboy ['sæn(d)bɔɪ] *n F* (as) happy as a sandboy, gai comme un pinson/heureux comme un poisson dans l'eau.

sandman ['sæn(d)mæn, 'sæn(d)mən] *n* 1. *F* the sandman is coming, le marchand de sable va passer 2. *P* (*drugs*) trafiquant *m*/ dealer *m* (d'héroïne).

sanger ['sæŋgə] *n Austr F* sandwich *m*.

sao [saʊ] *n NAm P* salaud*/fumier *m*/ordure *f*/enflure *f*.

sap(head) ['sæp(hed)] *n esp NAm P* individu bête*/niguedouille *mf*/œuf *m*.

sappy ['sæpɪ] *a F* 1. bête*/ballot/cruche 2. sans expérience/nigaud/bleu.

sarge [sɑ:dʒ] *n F* (= *sergeant*) *Mil* sergent *m*/serre-patte *m*.

sarky ['sɑ:kɪ] *a F* sarcastique/mordant/ ironique/caustique/persifleur; to be sarky with s.o., mettre qn en boîte/chambrer qn; no need to be so sarky! ça va, c'est pas la peine de me chambrer comme ça!

sarnie, sarny ['sɑ:nɪ] *n Br F* sandwich *m*; I forgot my sarnies, j'ai oublié mon casse-croûte.

sashay ['sæʃeɪ] *vi NAm F* marcher d'un air affecté; he sashayed across to the bar, il s'est approché du bar avec une nonchalance affectée.

sass[1] [sæs] *n NAm F* = **sauce**[1] **1**.

sass[2] [sæs] *vtr NAm F* = **sauce**[2] **1**.

sassy ['sæsɪ] *a NAm F* = **saucy 1**.

Saturday ['sætədɪ] *n NAm F* Saturday night special, revolver*/feu *m*/soufflant *m*/calibre *m*/pétard *m*.

sauce[1] [sɔ:s] *n F* 1. effronterie *f*/toupet *m*/ culot *m*; I'll have none of your sauce! pas d'impertinences!/sois poli (si t'es pas joli)! 2. alcool*/goutte *f*; to hit the sauce, picter*/ beaucoup/tomber sur la bouteille/biberonner; to be off the sauce, ne plus boire d'alcool*/être au régime sec. (*See* **apple sauce**)

sauce[2] [sɔ:s] *vtr* 1. *F* faire l'insolent avec/se payer la tête de (qn) 2. *Br P* faire l'amour* avec (qn)/baiser (qn).

saucebox ['sɔ:sbɒks] *n F* effronté, -ée/ malappris, -ise/mal embouché, -ée.

sauced (out) [sɔ:st'aʊt] *a* ivre*/beurré/ cuit/poivré.

saucepan ['sɔ:spən] *n P* saucepan lids, (*RS = kids*) enfants*/mioches *mpl*/mômes *mpl*. (*See* **dustbin**)

saucy ['sɔ:sɪ] *a F* 1. impertinent/effronté/ gonflé/culotté/qui n'a pas froid aux yeux/qui ne manque pas d'air 2. *O* (*smart, attractive*) aguichant/coquet/chic 3. scabreux/osé/épicé/ salé; it's saucy stuff, c'est salé.

sausage ['sɒsɪdʒ] *n* 1. *F* not a sausage, rien* du tout/que dalle 2. *F* (you) silly sausage! gros(se) bête!/gros ballot!/espèce de nouille! 3. *F* sausage dog, teckel *m*/saucisse *f* à pattes 4. *P* sausage and mash, (*RS = cash*) argent*/fric *m*/pognon *m* 5. *P Euph* pénis*/ chipolata *f*; *Austr* sausage grappler, branleur *m*; *Austr* to hide the sausage, faire l'amour*/ baiser.

save [seɪv] *vtr F* save it! arrête ça!/arrête ton char!/écrase!

saver ['seɪvə] *n F* (*horseracing*) pari *m* de protection. (*See* **lifesaver**)

savvy[1] ['sævɪ] *n F* bon sens/jugeot(t)e *f*.

savvy[2] ['sævɪ] *vi O F* savoir/connaître/piger/ con(n)obler; you savvy? tu piges?

sawbones ['sɔ:bəʊnz] *n O F* chirurgien *m*/ charcutier *m*.

sawbuck ['sɔ:bʌk] *n NAm F* billet* de dix dollars.

sawder ['sɔ:də] *n NAm F* soft sawder = **soap**[1] **1**.

sawney ['sɔ:nɪ] *n* 1. *F* Écossais, -aise 2. *P* individu bête*/andouille *f*.

sawn-off ['sɔ:nɒf] **I** *a F* (*person*) petit*/ inachevé **II** *n P* (= *sawn-off shotgun*) fusil *m* à canon scié.

sax [sæks] *n F* (*abbr of saxophone*) saxo(phone) *m*.

say [seɪ] *vi* 1. *F* I'll say! vous avez raison!/et comment donc! 2. *F* you don't say! ça par exemple!/pas possible! 3. *P* says you! que tu dis!/tu parles!/et ta sœur! (*See* **sez you!**) 4. *P* says who? ah ouais?/chiche?

say-so ['seɪsəʊ] *n F* 1. to have the say-so, avoir voix au chapitre; I did it on his say-so, je n'ai fait qu'obéir/j'ai fait ce qu'il m'a dit 2. parole *f*/mot *m*/dire *m*.

scab[1] [skæb] *n F* briseur, -euse de grève/

jaune *mf*.

scab² [skæb] *vi F* briser une grève.

scabby ['skæbɪ] *a P* minable/mesquin/pouilleux.

scag [skæg] *n P* (*drugs*) héroïne*/(s)chnouf *m*/dropou *f*; *NAm* **scag jones**, habitude *f*/dépendance *f* de l'héroïne*.

scale [skeɪl] *vtr & i Austr P* 1. voler*/carotter (qch) 2. ne pas payer (sa part); (*on train*) brûler/griller le dur.

scally ['skælɪ] *n Br P* 1. jeune homme*/gosselin *m* 2. (*criminal*) escroc *m*/arnaqueur *m*; (*hooligan*) loubard *m*/loulou *m* 3. habitant, -ante (des environs) de Liverpool.

scalper ['skælpə] *n F* (*profiteer*) affairiste *mf*/empileur, -euse/arnaqueur *m*/entubeur *m*; (*ticket tout*) revendeur, -euse de billets (au marché noir).

scalping ['skælpɪŋ] *n F* (*profiteering*) affairisme *m*/mercantilisme *m*.

scallywag ['skælɪwæg] *n F* petit(e) polisson(ne)/petit galopin.

scam¹ [skæm] *n NAm P* arnaque *f*/magouille *f*/coup monté/estampage *m*.

scam² [skæm] *vi NAm P* arnaquer.

scamp [skæmp] *n F* you young/little scamp! petit galopin!/petit polisson!

scanties ['skæntɪz], **scants** [skænts] *npl F* culotte *f*/slip *m* (de femme).

scarce [skɛəs] *a F* to make oneself scarce, partir*/s'éclipser/prendre le large.

scaredy-cat ['skɛədɪkæt] *n F* poltron*/lâche *mf*/poule mouillée/dégonflé, -ée/trouillard, -arde/pétochard, -arde. (*See* **fraidy-cat**)

scare up ['skɛər'ʌp] *vtr esp NAm F* chercher et trouver (qch); to scare up a quick snack, dégot(t)er un truc à bouffer.

scarf (up, down, out) ['skɑːf('ʌp, 'daʊn, 'aʊt)] *vi P* (*eat voraciously, devour*) (se) morfaler/s'en mettre plein le col.

scarper ['skɑːpə] *vi P* s'enfuir*/déguerpir/se tailler.

scary ['skɛərɪ] *a F* qui fait peur*/qui file les jetons; a really scary film, un super film d'épouvante.

scat! [skæt] *excl P* décampe!/file!/barre-toi!/casse-toi!

scatterbrain ['skætəbreɪn] *n F* Jean-de-la-lune *m*/étourdi, -ie/écervelé, -ée/tête *f* de linotte.

scatterbrained ['skætəbreɪnd] *a F* étourdi/écervelé/évaporé/à tête de linotte/à cervelle *f* de moineau.

scatty ['skætɪ] *a F* 1. un peu fou*/toqué/maboul 2. (*absent-minded*) farfelu.

scene [siːn] *n* 1. *F* behind the scenes, dans la coulisse/en coulisses 2. *F* action *f*/pratique *f*; it's all part of today's scene, c'est ce qui se fait maintenant; it's a really heavy scene, c'est une galère 3. *P* endroit *m* où les drogués se réunissent/le lieu 4. *F* to make a scene, faire une scène/renauder/rouscailler 5. *F* to make the scene (*a*) arriver*/s'abouler/se pointer; faire acte de présence (*b*) réussir/arriver/y avoir la main 6. *O F* situation*f*/situasse *f*; bad scene, mauvaise posture 7. *F* it's not my scene, ce n'est pas mon genre/c'est pas mon truc 8. *F* to have a scene with s.o., avoir des rapports (sexuels) avec qn.

schizo ['skɪtsəʊ] *a & n F* schizo(phrène) (*mf*); (*crazy*) fou*/maboul(, -oule)/siphonné.

schlemiel [ʃlə'miːl, ʃle'miːl] *n NAm P* (*loser*) nullité *f*/zéro *m*; (*fool*) ballot *m*/gourde *f*; he's a schlemiel, ce n'est pas une lumière.

schlenter ['ʃlentə] *a P* toc/de camelote.

schlep [ʃlep] *vtr P* trimballer/se coltiner/transbahuter.

schlimazel [ʃlɪ'mɑːzl] *n NAm P* qn qui a de la malchance*/poissard *m*/guignard, -arde/qn qui a la scoumoune.

schliver ['ʃlɪvə] *n P* = **chiv¹** 1.

schlock [ʃlɒk] *n NAm P* 1. camelote *f*/daube *f*; (*film, book*) navet *m* 2. (*drugs*) came *f*.

schlong [ʃlɒŋ] *n NAm P* pénis*/trique *f*.

schmal(t)z [ʃmɔːlts, ʃmɒlts] *n F* sensiblerie *f*/sentimentalité doucereuse/guimauve *f*.

schmal(t)zy ['ʃmɔːltsɪ, 'ʃmɒltsɪ] *a F* à l'eau de rose; it's rather smaltzy, c'est de la guimauve.

schmeck [ʃmek], **schmee** [ʃmiː] *n P* 1. odeur *f ou* goût *m* 2. (*drugs*) héroïne/poudre *f*.

schmeet [ʃmiːt] *n NAm P* = **schmeck 2**.

schmier [ʃmɪə] *n P* ristourne *f*/commission *f*/dessous *m* de table/bakchich *m*.

schmo(e) [ʃməʊ] *n P* 1. individu bête*/nigaud, -aude/(du)chnoque *m* 2. individu ennuyeux*/raseur, -euse/casse-pieds *mf*.

schmock [ʃmɒk] *n P* = **schmeck 2**.

schmoose, schmooze [ʃmuːz] *vi P* bavarder*/papoter/ragoter/bavasser.

schmuck [ʃmʌk] *n P* = **prick 1, 2**.

schmutter ['ʃmʌtə] *n P* (*clothing*) fringues *fpl*/frocs *mpl*/frusques *fpl*.

schnockered ['ʃnɒkəd] *a esp NAm P* ivre*/bourré/raide.

schnook [ʃnʊk, ʃnuːk] *n NAm P* 1. = **schmo(e) 1** 2. (*dupe, fall-guy*) pigeon *m*/

cave *m*.

schnorrer [ˈʃnɔːrə] *n P* = **shnorrer**.

schnozz [ʃnɒz], **schnozzle** [ˈʃnɒzl], **schnozzola** [ʃnɒˈzəʊlə] *n P* nez*/pif *m*/ naze *m*/tarin *m*.

schnuk [ʃnʊk] *n NAm P* = **schmo(e) 1**.

school [skuːl] *n F* 1. *esp Austr* personnes réunies pour boire*/groupe *m* de (grands) buveurs 2. the old school tie, la clique des anciens élèves.

schoolboy [ˈskuːlbɔɪ] *n P* (*drugs*) codéine *f*.

schoolie [ˈskuːlɪ] *n Austr F* (= *schoolteacher*) prof *mf*/instit *mf*.

schoolmarm [ˈskuːlmɑːm] *n F* maîtresse *f* d'école; she's a real schoolmarm, c'est une pédante/elle fait sa Julie.

schoolmarmish [ˈskuːlmɑːmɪʃ] *a F Pej* she's very schoolmarmish, elle fait très maîtresse d'école/elle fait très institutrice (en retraite).

schtu(c)k [ʃtʊk] *n Br P* to be in schtuck, être dans le pétrin/dans de mauvais draps/ dans la mélasse/dans la panade. (*See* **shtook; stook**)

schwar(t)z [ʃwɔːts] *n NAm P Pej* Noir(e)*/ nègre *m*/bamboula *m*/bougnoul *m*.

scoff¹ [skɒf] *n Br P* nourriture*/boustifaille *f*/graille *f*.

scoff² [skɒf] *vi Br P* manger*/bouffer/ boulotter/grailler; (*eat a lot*) se goinfrer/s'en mettre plein la lampe.

scoop¹ [skuːp] *n F* 1. coup *m* de chance*/de bol 2. (*press*) nouvelle sensationnelle/ reportage exclusif//scoop *m*.

scoop² [skuːp] *vtr F* 1. avoir un droit exclusif de publication/faire un scoop (sur qch) 2. déjouer les intentions de (qn)/dépasser (qn) en finesse.

scoot [skuːt] *vi F* 1. s'enfuir*/déguerpir (en quatrième vitesse); scoot! dégage!/vire!/du vent! 2. (*go or drive fast*) filer à toute vitesse/aller à fond la caisse.

scope [skəʊp] *vtr NAm P* 1. chercher (qch) 2. regarder*/lorgner/zyeuter.

scorch¹ [skɔːtʃ] *n F* 1. allure effrénée/bride abattue 2. incendie *m* volontaire.

scorch² (**along**) [ˈskɔːtʃ(əˈlɒŋ)] *vi F* conduire comme un fou/aller à un train d'enfer/aller à fond de train.

scorcher [ˈskɔːtʃə] *n F* 1. journée *f* torride; vague *f* de chaleur; it's a scorcher, on se croirait dans un four 2. amateur *m* de vitesse/fou *m*, folle *f* du volant; avaleur *m* de

kilomètres 3. remarque/réplique coupante *ou* sarcastique; riposte cinglante.

score¹ [skɔː] *n* 1. *F* to know the score, être au courant/à la page/dans le coup; what's the score? quoi de neuf? 2. *P* vingt livres *fpl* sterling 3. *P* to make a score = **score² 1, 2** 4. *P* butin*/affure *f* 5. *P* affaire réussie/bien enlevée 6. *esp NAm P* meurtre (prémédité)/ but(t)age *m*/dessoudage *m*; contrat *m*.

score² [skɔː] *vi P* 1. (*drugs*) s'approvisionner/se ravitailler en drogue; se garnir/trouver le joint 2. (*a*) (*of prostitute*) faire un levage/faire un miché (*b*) (*find sexual partner for the night, etc*) faire un levage/ lever qn/emballer qn; did you score last night? t'as emballé hier soir? 3. to score with s.o., être au mieux avec qn/avoir la cote avec qn 4. réussir/se tailler un succès/épater la galerie 5. *esp NAm* tuer*/but(t)er/dessouder/ mettre en l'air (qn).

Scotch [skɒtʃ] *Br F* I *a* to see through Scotch mist, avoir des visions; no money? what's that in your pocket, Scotch mist? (*sarcastic*) pas de fric? qu'est-ce que t'as dans la poche alors, des cailloux? II *n* 1. mirage *m*/fantôme *m*/feu follet, etc 2. *Iron* pluie diluvienne/averse *f*/rincée *f*.

scouse [skaʊs] *Br* I *a* de Liverpool II *n F* patois *m ou* accent *m* de Liverpool.

scouser [ˈskaʊsə] *n F* habitant, -ante *ou* originaire *mf* de Liverpool.

scout [skaʊt] *n NAm F* (**good**) scout, brave homme*/chic type *m*.

scrag [skræg] *vtr P* 1. pendre/garrotter (qn) 2. (*a*) tuer*/tordre le cou à (qn) (*b*) saisir (un adversaire) au collet/attraper (un adversaire) par le colbac 3. *Br* (*schools*) brutaliser/ maillocher; (*tease*) taquiner/asticoter.

scram [skræm] *vi P* partir*/(se) gicler/ficher le camp/détaler; scram! fous le camp!/ dégage!

scran [skræn] *n P* restes *mpl* (de nourriture*)/rogatons *mpl*.

scrap¹ [skræp] *n F* (*a*) querelle*/rixe *f* (*b*) bagarre*/baston *m ou f* (*c*) (*boxing*) match *m*/combat *m*; to have a scrap, se battre/se bagarrer.

scrap² [skræp] I *F vtr* mettre (qch) au rancart; bazarder; envoyer/jeter à la casse II *vi* 1. se quereller*/avoir une prise de bec 2. se battre*/se bagarrer.

scrape¹ [skreɪp] *n* 1. *F* to get into a scrape, se mettre dans un mauvais pas/dans le pétrin; to get out of a scrape, se tirer d'affaire 2. *P* to have a scrape, se raser*/se racler/(la couenne).

scrape[2] [skreɪp] *vtr* 1. *F* to scrape the (bottom of the) barrel, faire les fonds de tiroir 2. *F* to scrape clear of prison, friser la prison* 3. *Austr P* faire l'amour*/baiser/sauter/niquer/tringler.

scrape along ['skreɪpə'lɒŋ] *vi F* s'en tirer péniblement/vivoter/à peine joindre les deux bouts/tirer le diable par la queue.

scrapheap ['skræphiːp] *n F* (*a*) to throw s.o. on the scrapheap, laisser tomber qn comme une vieille chaussette; to be thrown on the scrapheap, (*of person*) être mis au rebut/au placard (*b*) it's fit for/it's only good for the scrapheap, c'est bon à mettre à la poubelle/à balancer pour la casse. (*See* **wind up I**)

scratch [skrætʃ] *n* 1. *P* argent*/pognon *m*/ fric *m* 2. *F* to come up to scratch, se montrer à la hauteur/faire le poids; to bring up to scratch, mettre (qn/qch) à niveau 3. *V* sexe* de la femme*/craquette *f*/cicatrice *f* 4. *F* to start from scratch, partir de zéro.

scratcher ['skrætʃə] *n P* 1. faussaire *mf* 2. allumette *f*/bûche *f*/souffrante *f*/frotte *f*. (*See* **backscratcher**)

scream[1] [skriːm] *n F* 1. she's a scream, elle est rigolotte/désopilante/marrante/impayable; it's a scream, c'est à se tordre/à mourir de rire; c'est à se rouler par terre (de rire) 2. *NAm* (*ice cream*) glace *f*.

scream[2] [skriːm] *vi O F* rire* aux éclats/à gorge déployée/se rouler par terre; he made us scream, il nous a fait (nous) tordre.

screamer ['skriːmə] *n P* 1. = **scream**[1] 1 2. *Pej* homosexuel* qui ne le cache pas 3. *pl* the screamers, diarrhée*/chiasse *f*/courante *f*. (*See* **two-pot screamer**)

screaming ['skriːmɪŋ] *a* 1. *Austr O F* screaming on s.o./sth, remonté contre qn/qch 2. (*also* **screamin'**) *NAm* très bon/ excellent*/extra/chouard/choucard; that pizza's screamin', elle est chouarde cette pizza. (*See* **abdabs**)

screamingly ['skriːmɪŋlɪ] *adv F* screamingly funny, tordant/crevant/à se rouler par terre.

screaming-match ['skriːmɪŋmætʃ] *n F* coups *mpl* de gueule/engueulade *f* maison.

screw[1] [skruː] *n* 1. *Br F* gardien* de prison/ gaffe *m*/gaffre *m*/matuche *m*/maton(ne) *m*(*f*) 2. *V* (*a*) coït*/baisage *m*/baise *f*/tringlage *m*; to have a quick screw, tirer un coup vite fait;

what she needs is a good screw, c'est une mal-baisée (*b*) femme*/fendue *f* (*c*) he's/she's a good screw, il/elle baise bien; c'est un sacré baiseur/une sacrée baiseuse; c'est un bon coup 3. *P* gages *mpl*/salaire *m*; to get a good screw, être bien payé/avoir un bon fromage 4. *F* to have a screw loose, être un peu fou*/être un peu fêlé; she's got a screw loose, il lui manque une case 5. *F* to put the screw(s) on s.o., forcer qn; employer les grands moyens/ la force avec qn 6. *F* cheval*/bidet *m*/ canasson *m* 7. *P* (*a*) clef*/caroub(l)e *f* (*b*) (*passkey*) passe-partout *m*/passe *m*/rossignol *m* 8. *P* coup *m* d'œil*/coup de sabord; take a screw at this! zyeute(-moi) ça!/vise un peu ça!

screw[2] [skruː] I *vtr* 1. *V* faire l'amour* avec (qn)/baiser/niquer/tringler 2. *V* sodomiser*/ enculer/endauffer/encaldosser; he likes screwing men, il aime bien baiser les mecs/il aime bien prendre du chouette 3. *Br P* to screw a gaff/a drum, (*break into a house*) casser une crèche/caroubler une baraque; to go screwing, cambrioler*/faire un casse; to do a screwing job, faire un fric-frac/caroubler. (*See* **screwing 3**) 4. *F* to screw money out of s.o., extorquer/soutirer de l'argent* à qn; taper/torpiller qn 5. *esp Austr P* regarder*/ lorgner/gaffer 6. *F* to have one's head screwed on (the right way), avoir la tête* solide/sur les épaules 7. *NAm P* s'enfuir*/ décamper/se barrer/se débiner 8. *P* duper*/ tromper/entuber 9. *V* screw you!/get screwed! va te faire foutre!/va te faire voir (chez les Grecs)! screw that! j'en ai rien à foutre! 10. *P* (*ruin, spoil*) gâcher/foutre en l'air II *vi V* faire l'amour*/baiser/s'envoyer en l'air.

screwable ['skruːəbl] *a V* baisable/ mettable.

screw around ['skruːə'raʊnd] I *vi* 1. *P* faire le con/déconner 2. *V* faire l'amour*/ baiser avec n'importe qui; être très porté sur la chose/ne penser qu'à ça II *vtr P* to screw s.o. around, enquiquiner/causer des ennuis à qn.

screw-around-town ['skruːə'raʊnd-'taʊn] *n* (*person*) qn porté sur la chose/ baiseur, -euse.

screwball ['skruːbɔːl] *NAm F* I *a* fou*/ tapé/dingue II *n* personne étrange/bizarre/ excentrique/cinglée; he's a bit of a screwball, c'est un drôle de zèbre/de phénomène.

screwed [skruːd] *a P* 1. ivre*/rétamé*/rond/

schlass 2. dupé/roulé/entubé.

screwing ['skru:ɪŋ] *n* 1. *V* coït*/baise *f*/ carambolage *m* 2. *V* (*sodomy*) enculage *m*/ encaldossage *m* 3. *P* cambriolage *m*/ cambriole *f*/fric-frac *m*. (*See* **screw**² I **1, 2, 3**)

screw off ['skru:'ɒf] *vi V* se masturber*/se branler/s'astiquer (la colonne).

screwsman ['skru:zmən] *n P* cambrioleur*/casseur *m*/caroub(l)eur *m*.

screw-up ['skru:ʌp] *n esp NAm P* erreur *f*/ gaffe *f*/gourance *f*/bide *m*.

screw up ['skru:'ʌp] I *vtr* 1. *P* fermer/ boucler/brider 2. *P* gâcher/bousiller/foutre en l'air (qch); **he's screwed it all up again**, il a tout refoutu en l'air; il y a refoutu le merdier; **he screwed up the interview**, il a complètement merdé à l'entretien 3. *F* **to be all screwed up**, (*mistaken*) se tromper/se ficher dedans/se mettre le doigt dans l'œil; (*confused*) avoir les idées confuses/être dans le brouillard; **she's really screwed up**, (*traumatized*) elle est traumatisée/névrosée II *vi P* (*make a mess*) bousiller.

screwy ['skru:ɪ] *a* 1. *F* fou*/cinglé/dingue/ barjot 2. *P* louche/suspect.

scrimshank ['skrɪmʃæŋk] *vi Mil P* tirer au flanc/au cul.

scrimshanker ['skrɪmʃæŋkə] *n Mil P* tireur *m* au flanc/au cul.

scrip(t) [skrɪp(t)] *n P* (*from a doctor*) ordonnance *f* de complaisance (*pour obtenir des drogues*).

scrote [skrəʊt] *n Br P* (*term of abuse*) salaud*/ordure *f*.

scrounge¹ [skraʊndʒ] *n F* 1. = **scrounger 1, 2** 2. **he's always on the scrounge**, c'est un vrai pique-assiette; il ne cherche qu'à vivre aux crochets des autres; **I'm on the scrounge, can you lend me £5**, je suis dans la panade, tu peux pas me refiler cinq livres?

scrounge² [skraʊndʒ] *F* I *vtr* 1. écornifler; taper/torpiller (qn); **to scrounge £5 off s.o.**, taper/torpiller qn de £5 2. voler*/chiper/ chaparder/barbot(t)er II *vi* **to scrounge on s.o.**, vivre aux crochets de qn.

scrounge around ['skraʊndʒə'raʊnd] *vi F* (*a*) rabioter à la ronde (*b*) **to scrounge around for sth**, aller à la recherche de qch/ fouiner.

scrounger ['skraʊndʒə] *n F* 1. pique-assiette *mf*/parasite *mf*/torpilleur, -euse 2. voleur*/chapardeur, -euse/barbot(t)eur, -euse.

scrub [skrʌb] *vtr F* (*a*) **let's scrub it**,

passons l'éponge là-dessus (*b*) effacer/ démagnétiser (une bande).

scrubber ['skrʌbə] *n P Pej* 1. femme* *ou* fille* laide* *ou* peu appétisante/mocheté *f*/ boudin *m* 2. fille* *ou* femme* de mœurs légères/roulure *f*/salope *f*/pute *f*.

scruff [skrʌf] *n F* (*a*) individu* mal soigné *ou* mal fichu/débraillé; **he looks a real scruff**, il est fringué comme l'as de pique (*b*) (*tramp*) clodo *m*.

scrum [skrʌm] *n F* (*pushing, shoving*) mêlée *f*/bousculade *f*.

scrumptious ['skrʌm(p)ʃəs] *a F* (*a*) excellent*/épatant/fameux (*b*) délicieux/ (super) bon.

scrumpy ['skrʌmpɪ] *n Br F* cidre fermier.

scuffer ['skʌfə] *n P* (*regional*) agent *m* de police/flic *m*/condé *m*.

scum [skʌm] *n P* 1. *NAm A* sperme*/blanc *m*/jute *m* 2. = **scumbag 1**.

scumbag ['skʌmbæg] *n P* 1. salaud*/ loquedu *m*; **you scumbag!** espèce de salaud!/ d'ordure!/de salopard! 2. *NAm A* préservatif*/capote (anglaise).

scummy ['skʌmɪ] *a P* méprisable/sans valeur; de salaud; de saloperie/de merde.

scungy ['skʌndʒɪ] *a Austr P* sale*/cracra/ cradingue/dégueu(lasse).

scunner ['skʌnə] *n Br North & Midlands F* salaud*/loquedu *m*/raclure *f*.

scupper ['skʌpə] *vtr F* couler; **that's scuppered all my plans**, ça a fichu en l'air tous mes projets/ça m'a tout foutu en l'air.

scuzz [skʌz] *n NAm P* 1. saleté*/crassouille *f*/saloperie *f* 2. salaud*/fumier *m*/raclure *f*.

scuzzbag ['skʌzbæg], **scuzzball** ['skʌzbɔ:l], **scuzzo** ['skʌzəʊ] *n NAm P* = **scuzz 2**.

scuzzy ['skʌzɪ] *a NAm P* sale*/cradingue/ dégueu(lasse)/dégueulbif.

sea [si:] *n F* **to be all at sea**, être dérouté/ désorienté; avoir perdu le nord; nager (complètement). (*See* **half-seas-over**)

search [sɜ:tʃ] *vtr F* **search me!** je n'en ai pas la moindre idée!/mystère et boule de gomme!/sais pas, moi!

sec [sek] *n F* (*abbr of second*) **just a sec!**/**half a sec!** un moment!/minute! (*See* **jiff(y)**; **mo**; **shake¹ 1**; **tick¹ 3**)

secko ['sekəʊ] *Austr P* I *a* perverti II *n* perverti *m*/vieux salaud/queutard *m*/obsédé sexuel.

seconds ['sekəndz] *npl F* 1. articles défectueux/démarqués 2. portion *f* (de nourriture*) supplémentaire/rab(iot) *m*.

see [siː] *vtr F* see you! au revoir!/salut!/ ciao!/à la revoyure!/à la prochaine!/adios! (*See* **dog¹ 14**; **thing 7**)

seed [siːd] *n F* to go to seed, (*of person*) se décatir/s'avachir/se laisser aller. (*See* **hayseed**)

seedy ['siːdɪ] *a F* **1.** pauvre*/minable/râpé/ usé/élimé **2.** malade*/patraque/pas dans son assiette/mal fichu.

seeing-to ['siːɪŋtuː] *n Br P* raclée *f*/dégelée *f*/tabassage *m*.

see off ['siːˈɒf] *vtr F* (*a*) to see s.o. off, régler son compte à qn (*b*) to see sth off, régler/liquider/conclure qch.

see out [siːˈaʊt] *vtr F* survivre à (qn).

sell¹ [sel] *n F* **1.** (*hoax*) attrape *f*/canular *m*/ farce *f*/tour *m* **2.** déception *f*; the party was a sell, la soirée a été très décevante (*See* **hard I 5**; **soft I 5**)

sell² [sel] *vtr F* **1.** duper* (qn)/avoir (qn)/ mener (qn) en bateau/entuber (qn); you've been sold! on vous a refait! **2.** to sell s.o. short, (*trick*) duper/avoir qn; rabaisser qn; (*denigrate*) débiner qn **3.** to sell sth to s.o./to sell s.o. sth, faire accepter qch à qn; to be sold on s.o./sth, ne jurer que par qn/qch; he's really sold on it, il en est dingue/emballé; il (ne) jure que par ça **4.** to sell oneself, se faire accepter/se faire valoir. (*See* **river 1**)

sell-by date ['selbaɪdeɪt] *n F* it's past its sell-by date, c'est vieux*/périmé.

sellout ['selaʊt] *n F* **1.** trahison *f*/doublage *m* **2.** vente *f* de tous les billets pour un spectacle; séance *f* à guichet(s) fermé(s); this play's a sellout, cette pièce a fait salle comble; this line has been a sellout, cet article s'est vendu à merveille (et il n'en reste plus).

sell out ['selˈaʊt] *vtr F* dénoncer*/vendre/ trahir/balancer/doubler/(qn).

semi ['semɪ] *n F* (= *semidetached house*) maison jumelée/jumelle.

send [send] *vtr F* **1.** emballer/transporter (qn); she sends me! elle me botte!/elle me fait flipper! that really sends me! ça c'est le pied!/ça me botte! **2.** faire partir/faire voyager/faire flipper (qn).

send-off ['sendɒf] *n F* **1.** fête *f* d'adieu/ souhaits *mpl* de bon voyage; we gave him a good send-off, on a bien fêté son départ **2.** inauguration réussie **3.** enterrement *m*.

send-up ['sendʌp] *n F* parodie *f*/mise *f* en boîte.

send up ['sendˈʌp] *vtr F* parodier/se

moquer de; to send s.o. up, mettre qn en boîte.

sent down [sentˈdaʊn] *a Br F* **1.** emprisonné/entaulé/coffré **2.** expulsé/renvoyé (*de l'université*).

sent up [sentˈʌp] *a F* **1.** *NAm* = **sent down 1 2.** *Br* (*imitated, parodied*) mis en boîte.

septic ['septik] *a P* **1.** désagréable/puant **2.** *Austr* septic tank, (*RS = Yank*) Américain*/ Amerlo *m*/Amerloque *m*/Ricain, -aine.

serious ['sɪərɪəs] *a F* grave; he did himself some serious damage/mischief, il s'est blessé gravement/il s'est vachement amoché; serious drugs, drogues dures.

sesh [seʃ] *n Br F* (*abbr of session*) séance *f*; (*esp drinking session*) beuverie *f*. (*See* **session**)

session ['seʃ(ə)n] *n F* longue séance; (drinking) session, beuverie *f*. (*See* **jam¹ 5** (*a*); **petting**)

set [set] I *a & pp F* to be all set, être fin prêt/ être paré II *n F* **1.** to make a dead set at s.o. (*a*) attaquer furieusement qn (à la tribune) (*b*) se jeter à la tête de qn/poursuivre qn de ses avances **2.** (*navy*) (full) set, barbe* et moustaches*.

set about ['setəˈbaʊt] *vtr F* to set about s.o., attaquer* qn/tomber sur le paletot à qn.

set back ['setˈbæk] *vtr F* coûter; the round of drinks set him back twenty quid, la tournée lui a coûté vingt livres; that new car must have set her back a bit, cette nouvelle voiture a dû lui coûter chaud/bonbon/un fric fou.

set-to ['setˈtuː] *n F* bagarre*/torchée *f*/ baston *m ou f*.

setup ['setʌp] *n* **1.** *F* structure *f*/organisation *f*/fonctionnement *m*; it's an odd setup, c'est une drôle de boîte/d'affaire; it's a peculiar setup at their place, c'est bizarrement organisé, chez eux **2.** *F* installation *f*; a nice setup you have here, vous êtes pas mal installé ici/c'est gentil, chez vous **3.** *P* machination *f*/coup monté. (*See* **frame³**)

set up ['setˈʌp] *vtr F* **1.** to set 'em up again, remplir les verres de nouveau/remettre ça/ servir une autre tournée **2.** to set s.o. up for the kill, conditionner qn pour le coup de massue **3.** to set s.o. up, duper*/rouler qn; monter un coup contre qn; they set me up, on a monté un coup contre moi/ils m'ont eu; I've been set up good and proper, on m'a monté le coup/on m'a bien eu.

severe [sɪˈvɪə] *a F* excellent*/super/canon.

sew up ['səʊ'ʌp] *vtr F* it's all sewn up, c'est tout fixé/c'est tout arrangé/c'est dans le sac/ c'est du tout cuit.

sex¹ [seks] *n F* the third sex, homosexuels *mpl*/le troisième sexe/la jaquette.

sex² [seks] *vi Br F* faire l'amour*; they were sexing in the back of a car, il baisaient à l'arrière d'une voiture.

sex-bomb ['seksbɒm] *n O F* allumeuse *f*/ blonde incendiaire.

sex-crazy ['seks'kreɪzɪ] *a F* = **sex-mad**.

sexed up ['sekst'ʌp] *a F* excité/allumé/ aguiché.

sex-kitten ['sekskɪtn] *n F* fille* aguichante/ nana *f* très sexy.

sex-mad ['seks'mæd] *a F* he's sex-mad, il ne pense qu'au sexe/il ne pense qu'à ça/c'est un chaud lapin/il est porté sur la chose.

sexpot ['sekspɒt] *n P* femme* *ou* homme* qui a du sex-appeal/très sexy.

sex-ridden ['seksrɪdn] *a F* porté sur la chose.

sex-starved ['seksta:vd] *a F* en manque (sexuel)/victime de diète sexuelle/frustré/ refoulé.

sexy ['seksɪ] *a F* (*person*) sensuel/chaud/ sexy; (*clothes*) sexy; (*book, film*) érotique; she's sexy, elle est bien bandante.

sez you! ['sez'ju:] *excl P* = says you! (**say 3**).

SF ['es'ef] *abbr F* (= *San Francisco*) San Francisco *m ou f*.

shack [ʃæk] *n F* (*old house*) bicoque *f*.

shack-up ['ʃækʌp] *n* (*living together out- side marriage*) concubinage *m*/maquage *m*.

shack up ['ʃæk'ʌp] *vi P* to shack up with s.o., vivre ensemble *ou* en concubinage/se coller avec qn/se maquer/se mettre à la colle avec qn.

shade ['ʃeɪd] *n* 1. *F* to put s.o. in the shade, laisser qn dans l'ombre/éclipser qn 2. *pl P* lunettes* de soleil/vitraux *mpl* 3. *NAm P* receleur*/fourgue *m*/fourgat *m*.

shadow¹ ['ʃædəʊ] *n F* 1. to put a shadow on s.o., faire suivre qn/faire filer qn/faire filocher qn. (*See* **tail¹ 5**) 2. five-o'clock shadow, barbe du soir.

shadow² ['ʃædəʊ] *vtr F* suivre (qn)/filer (le train à) (qn)/faire la filoche à/filocher (qn).

shady ['ʃeɪdɪ] *a F* louche/équivoque/trouble/ véreux; shady deal, affaire *f* louche/affaire véreuse/magouille *f*.

shaft¹ [ʃɑ:t] *n V* 1. pénis*/ardillon *m*/ défonceuse *f* 2. coït*/baise *f* 3. partenaire

sexuel(le)/affaire *f*.

shaft² [ʃɑ:t] *vtr & i* 1. *V* faire l'amour* (*surt* avec une femme)/niquer 2. *P* escroquer*/ refaire/baiser (qn) 3. *P* (*destroy*) anéantir/ griller (qn).

shag¹ [ʃæg] *n* 1. *V* coït*/baisage *m*/tringlage *m* 2. *V* she's a good shag, c'est une sacrée baiseuse *f*. 3. *P* it's a (bit of a) shag, c'est ennuyeux*/emmerdant/rasoir.

shag² [ʃæg] *vtr V* faire l'amour* avec (qn)/ baiser/tringler. (*See* **arse I 10**)

shag-ass ['ʃægæs] *vi NAm V* s'enfuir*/se carapater/mettre les bouts/foutre le camp.

shagbag ['ʃægbæg] *n* 1. *P* (*shabby, worth- less man*) loufiat *m*/pelure *f*/tocard *m* 2. *V* (*whore*) pute *f*/sac *m* à bites.

shagged (out) ['ʃægd('aʊt)] *a P* très fatigué/éreinté/crevé/HS.

shagger ['ʃægə] *n V* baiseur, -euse.

shaggy-dog ['ʃægɪ'dɒg] *a attrib F* shaggy- dog story, histoire *f* de fous/histoire farfelue/ histoire à dormir debout.

shag-happy ['ʃæg'hæpɪ] *a V* qui pratique avec entrain le baisage/chaud de la pince.

shag-nasty ['ʃæg'nɑ:stɪ] *a P* très désagréable/emmerdant/chiant (comme la pluie).

shag off ['ʃæg'ɒf] *vi V* partir*/décamper; shag off! fous le camp!/file!/dégage!/va faire chier!

shake¹ [ʃeɪk] *n* 1. *F* half a shake! un moment!/une seconde!/minute! 2. *F* in two shakes (of a lamb's tail), en moins de deux/en deux temps trois mouvements/en deux coups de cuiller à pot 3. *F* to give s.o. a fair shake, agir loyalement envers qn/être réglo avec qn; we got a fair shake, on a été réglo avec nous 4. *F* to have the shakes (*a*) avoir peur*/les foies/les jetons/les chocottes (*b*) avoir le délirium tremens 5. *F* no great shakes, rien d'extraordinaire/quelconque/qui ne casse pas des briques/qui ne casse pas trois pattes à un canard. (*See* **handshake**)

shake² [ʃeɪk] *vtr F* 1. *Br* alerter/appeler/ faire venir (qn); you've got to shake him, il faut le faire activer 2. étonner; that'll shake him! ça va lui en boucher un coin!/ça va le faire tiquer! 3. *Austr* voler*/chaparder/ chouraver/secouer. (*See* **leg¹ 3**; **shook**)

shakedown ['ʃeɪkdaʊn] *n* 1. *F* lit* de fortune; hébergement *m* d'une nuit 2. *NAm P* chantage *m*/rançon *f*/chansonnette *f* 3. *NAm P* (*search, frisk*) fouille *f*/barbotte *f*.

shake down ['ʃeɪk'daʊn] *vtr NAm P* 1.

faire du chantage à/rançonner/saigner (qn) 2. fouiller (*surt* un prisonnier)/palper (qn)/ vaguer (qn, un endroit).

shake-up ['ʃeɪkʌp] *n F* 1. remaniement *m*/ réorganisation *f* (du personnel) 2. commotion *f*/bouleversement *m* 3. mélange *m* d'alcool* et de whisky.

shamateur ['ʃæmə'tɜ:] *n F* amateur marron.

shambles ['ʃæmblz] *n F* a shambles, une pagaille; it's a real shambles, their place, c'est un vrai foutoir, leur baraque.

shambolic [ʃæm'bɒlɪk] *a P* en pleine pagaille/bordélique; merdique.

shame [ʃeɪm] *n Br P* to take the shame, endosser la responsabilité/prendre (qch) sur le paletot.

shampers ['ʃæmpəz] *n F* = **champers**.

shampoo [ʃæm'pu:] *n F* = **champers**.

shamus ['ʃeɪməs, 'ʃɑ:məs] *n NAm F* détective privé.

shanghai [ʃæŋ'haɪ] *vtr F* forcer (qn) à un travail désagréable; I was shanghaied into doing it, on m'a forcé à le faire/on m'a forcé la main.

shanks [ʃæŋks] *npl F* 1. jambes*/gambilles *fpl* 2. to ride Shanks's pony/*esp NAm* mare, voyager à pied/aller à pinces/prendre le train onze/y aller pédibus (cum jambis).

shapes [ʃeɪps] *npl NAm P* dés* truqués/plats *mpl*.

shark [ʃɑ:k] *n F* 1. escroc*/arnaqueur *m*/ requin *m*; loan shark, usurier, -ière 2. *NAm* (*talented person*) as *m*/champion, -onne/crack *m* 3. pool shark, débrouillard, -arde/brasseur *m* d'affaires.

sharp [ʃɑ:p] I *a NAm A F* élégant*/coquet/ chic/jojo II *n F* escroc*/arnaqueur *m*; card sharp = **sharper**.

sharper ['ʃɑ:pə] *n F* tricheur* (aux cartes)/ fileur *m*/maquilleur *m*.

sharpish ['ʃɑ:pɪʃ] *adv F* (a bit) sharpish, vite*/(illico) presto/rapidos.

shat upon ['ʃætə'pɒn] *a P* humilié/brimé/ traité comme de la merde. (*See* **shit**[2])

shave [ʃeɪv] *n F* to have a close/narrow shave, l'échapper belle/échapper à un cheveu près; it was a close/narrow shave, ça a été moins une/c'est pas passé loin.

shaver ['ʃeɪvə] *n O F* young shaver, gamin *m*/gosse *m*/môme *m*/moutard *m*.

shebang [ʃɪ'bæŋ] *n* 1. *F* the whole shebang, tout le bataclan/tout le tremblement. (*See* **boiling** II; **caboodle**; **shoot**[1] 1;

shooting-match) 2. *NAm P* cabane *f*/ cambuse *f*.

sheenie, sheeny ['ʃi:nɪ] *n P Pej* (*rare*) Juif*/youpin, -ine.

sheet [ʃi:t] *n* 1. *F* to be three/four sheets in/ to the wind, être ivre*/avoir du vent dans les voiles 2. *A P* billet *m* d'une livre sterling 3. *O P* journal*/feuille *f* (de chou) 4. *P* casier *m* judiciaire (d'un criminel)/pedigree *m*. (*See* **swindle-sheet**)

sheila ['ʃi:lə] *n Austr O F* (jeune) fille*/ (jeune) femme*/nénette *f*/nana *f*/gonzesse *f*/ meuf *f*. (*See* **potato 4**)

shekels ['ʃeklz] *npl P* argent*/fric *m*/pognon *m*/artiche *m*.

shelf [ʃelf] *n F* on the shelf, (*unmarried*) célibataire/laissé(e) pour compte; (*put aside, ignored*) mis(e) de côté/resté(e) au placard.

shelf-kit ['ʃelfkɪt] *n P* seins*/avant-scène *f*/ amortisseurs *mpl*.

shellac(k) [ʃə'læk] *vtr NAm F* 1. battre*/ rosser (qn)/passer (qn) à tabac 2. vaincre/ écraser/écrabouiller (qn).

shellacked [ʃə'lækt] *a NAm P* ivre*/ rétamé/culbuté/déchiré.

shellacking [ʃə'lækɪŋ] *n NAm P* 1. raclée *f*/dégelée *f*/tourlousine *f* 2. (*sports*) défaite *f*/ raclée *f*.

shellback ['ʃelbæk] *n F* vieux marin*/vieux loup de mer.

shell out ['ʃel'aʊt] *vtr & i P* payer*/(les) abouler/casquer/banquer.

shemozzle[1] [ʃɪ'mɒzl] *n P* ennui *m*/ emmerdement *m*/emmerde *f*.

shemozzle[2] [ʃɪ'mɒzl] *vi P* = **skedaddle**.

shenanigans [ʃɪ'nænɪgənz] *npl esp NAm F* manigances *fpl*; he's been having shenanigans with my wife, il a fricoté avec ma femme.

shice [ʃaɪs] P I *vtr* trahir/doubler II *vi* = **welsh**.

shicker ['ʃɪkə] *esp Austr P* I *a* = **shickered** II *n* alcool*/gnôle *f*/antigel *m*; to go on the shicker, biberonner/picoler.

shickered ['ʃɪkəd] *a esp Austr P* ivre*/paf/ éméché/schlass.

shift[1] [ʃɪft] *n F* 1. échappatoire *f*/faux-fuyant *m*/biaisement *m* 2. to get a shift on, se dépêcher*/se magner le train/faire vinaigre.

shift[2] [ʃɪft] *vtr & i* 1. *P* shift! file! bouge-toi! shift your arse/*NAm* ass! pousse ton cul! he didn't half shift! il s'est calté en moins de deux! 2. *F* to shift a pint, écluser un verre*/ s'en jeter un (derrière la cravate) 3. *F* to shift for oneself, se débrouiller/se dépatouiller/se démerder.

shiksa ['ʃɪksə] *n NAm P often Pej* fille* non-juive/goyette *f*.

shill [ʃɪl] *n P* (*con man's confederate, decoy*) avocat *m*/baron *m*/collègue *mf*/roussin *m*; compère *m* dans un tripot de jeux/jockey *m*.

shimmy ['ʃɪmɪ] *n O F* chemise *f*/liquette *f*/ limace *f*.

shindig ['ʃɪndɪg] *n F* 1. querelle*/chambard *m*/raffut *m*/ramdam *m*; to kick up a shindig, faire un boucan du diable/faire du ramdam 2. réunion bruyante/fête *f*/fiesta *f*.

shindy ['ʃɪndɪ] *n F* = **shindig 1**.

shine [ʃaɪn] *n* 1. *F* to take a shine to s.o., (*like*) s'éprendre de qn/s'amouracher de qn/ s'enticher de qn/attraper le béguin pour qn; (*think well of*) avoir qn à la bonne; he's taken a shine to me, je suis dans ses petits papiers 2. *NAm O P Pej* Noir(e)*/nègre *m*/bougnoul *m* 3. *NAm P* = **moonshine 1** 4. *P* = **shindig 1** 5. *F* to take the shine out of s.o., éclipser/dépasser qn. (*See* **bullshine**)

shiner ['ʃaɪnə] *n* 1. *F* œil* poché/au beurre noir; coquard *m* 2. *F* diamant*/diam *m*.

shin(ny) up ['ʃɪn(ɪ)'ʌp] *vtr & i F* to shin(ny) up (a tree), grimper (à *ou* sur un arbre).

ship [ʃɪp] *n F* when my ship comes in, quand il m'arrivera de l'argent*/quand j'aurai décroché le gros lot/quand j'aurai décroché la timbale.

shirt [ʃɜːt] *n F* 1. to put one's shirt on sth, miser le tout pour le tout/parier sa chemise sur qch 2. to lose one's shirt (*a*) tout perdre/ être lessivé (*b*) *NAm* (*lose one's temper*) s'emporter/se mettre en pétard 3. keep your shirt on! (ne) t'énerve pas!/ne t'emballe pas! 4. to have one's shirt out, s'emporter/se mettre en pétard 5. stuffed/boiled shirt, plastronneur *m*.

shirt-lifter ['ʃɜːtlɪftə] *n P Pej* homosexuel*/ pédé *m*; he's a shirt-lifter, il est de la jaquette.

shirty ['ʃɜːtɪ] *a F* to be shirty, être de mauvaise humeur/faire la gueule/être de mauvais poil; to get shirty, se mettre en colère*/en rogne/en pétard.

shit¹ [ʃɪt] **I** *adv V* extrêmement/ complètement/tout à fait; to be shit poor, être vachement pauvre*/être dans la purée; to be shit out of luck, avoir une poisse noire/être dans la merde (jusqu'au cou); to be shit hot at sth, être vachement/foutrement calé en qch (*See* **shit-hot**) **II** *a V* mauvais*/de merde/

merdeux; this is a shit album, c'est un album de merde/merdique 2. *NAm* excellent*/super/ canon. (*See* **shit-hot**) **III** *excl V* shit!/shit me!/shit a brick! merde (alors)!/bordel (de merde)! **IV** *n V* 1. merde*/chiasse *f*; to have/ to go for/to take a shit, (aller) déféquer*/ chier/flaquer//couler un bronze 2. (*a*) to land/ to drop s.o. in the shit, mettre/foutre qn dans la merde (*b*) to be (right) in the shit/to be in deep shit, être emmerdé/dans les emmerdes jusqu'au cou; être dans la merde jusqu'au cou/jusqu'aux yeux 3. (*ill-treatment*) I've had enough shit from him over the years, ça fait des années qu'il me traîne dans la merde 4. (*a*) to scare the shit out of s.o., rendre qn foireux/foutre la chiasse à qn; foutre les jetons/les chocottes à qn. (*See* **shit-scared**) (*b*) to beat the shit out of s.o., battre* qn comme plâtre/passer qn à tabac/passer qn à la machine à bosseler 5. to eat shit, se laisser traîner dans la merde/tout encaisser; eat shit! va te faire enculer! 6. don't talk shit!/that's a load of shit! ne dis pas de conneries!/arrête de déconner! don't give me that shit! fais pas chier! 7. I don't give a shit, j'en ai rien à foutre/à glander/à branler 8. full of shit, mal renseigné/qui dit des conneries/qui déconne; he's full of shit, c'est un déconneur/il déconne à pleins tubes 9. (it's) no shit, c'est la vérité/ sans déconner 10. individu* méprisable/ salaud*/merde *f*/trou-du-cul *m*/trouduc *m*/ loquedu *m*; he's a real shit! tu parles d'un enculé! (*See* **shitbag**) 11. emmerdeur, -euse/ mauvais coucheur/fouteur, -euse de merde/ casse-couilles *mf* 12. (*rubbish*) came(lote) *f*/ de la merde 13. (*drugs*) *O* héroïne*/shit *m*; haschisch*/merde *f*/shit; drogues* en général/ came *f* 14. the shits, diarrhée*/chiasse *f*/ courante *f*; he gives me the shits, (*annoys*) il m'énerve/me fait chier; (*disgusts*) il me débecte 15. when the shit hits the fan, quand la merde me/nous/etc tombera dessus 16. to work like shit, travailler* comme un nègre/se casser le cul; to run like shit, courir comme un dératé/avoir le feu au cul 17. to pick the fly shit out of the pepper, couper les cheveux en quatre. (*See* **bullshit¹**; **creek**; **crock 3**; **horseshit**)

shit² [ʃɪt] *vtr & i V* 1. déféquer*/chier/ débourrer/couler un bronze 2. exagérer*/chier dans la colle; don't shit me! ne me bourre pas le crâne!/ne me bourre pas le mou!/(ne) me prends pas pour un con! 3. to shit a brick/ to shit bricks, paniquer/chier dans son froc/

serrer les fesses 4. **shit or bust**, tout ou rien/ marche ou crève/pisse ou fais-toi éclater la vessie. (*See* **bullshit²**; **shat upon**)

shit-arse ['ʃɪtɑːs], **shit-ass** ['ʃɪtæs] *n V =* **shitbag**.

shitbag ['ʃɪtbæg] *n V* merdaillon *m*/enculé *m*/enfoiré, -ée/merdeux, -euse/merde *f*; **you shitbag!** petit trou-du-cul!

shitcan ['ʃɪtkæn] *vtr V* 1. *Austr* (*denigrate*) bêcher/couler/cracher sur la gueule de (qn) 2. *NAm* se défaire de/balancer/larguer (qch).

shite¹ [ʃaɪt] *n V =* **shit¹** III, IV.

shite² [ʃaɪt] *vi V =* **shit²** 1.

shit-faced ['ʃɪtfeɪsd] *a NAm V* ivre*/ rétamé/dans le cirage.

shit-for-brains ['ʃɪtfə'breɪnz] *n* individu bête*/enfoiré(e) *mf*/trouduc *m*.

shithead ['ʃɪthed], *NAm* **shitheel** ['ʃɪthiːl] *n V =* **shitbag**.

shit-hole ['ʃɪthəʊl] *n V* 1. anus*/trou *m* du cul/trou de balle/rondibé *m* 2. endroit *m* sordide/taudis *m*/foutoir *m*.

shit-hot ['ʃɪt'hɒt] *a P* 1. excellent*/ choucard/du tonnerre/canon 2. enthousiaste/ dynamique.

shithouse ['ʃɪthaʊs] *V* I *n* 1. WC*/chiottes *fpl*/gogues *mpl*/vécés *mpl* 2. = **shit-hole 2** II *a Austr* mauvais*/merdique/de merde.

shitkicker ['ʃɪtkɪkə] *n NAm V* 1. traîne-la-merde *m* 2. paysan*/cul-terreux *m*.

shit-kicking ['ʃɪt'kɪkɪŋ] *a V* sauvage/ primitif/bouseux; **shit-kicking country music**, country music bouseuse.

shitless ['ʃɪtlɪs] *a V* foireux/chiasseux; **to be scared shitless**, avoir les jetons/la chiasse/les chocottes.

shit-list ['ʃɪtlɪst] *n V* liste noire/tableau *m* des mal-vus/liste *f* des hors-petits-papiers. (*See* **stink-list**)

shit off ['ʃɪt'ɒf] *vi V* s'enfuir*/mettre les bouts; **shit off!** calte-toi!/va te faire chier!

shitpot ['ʃɪtpɒt] *n V =* **shitbag**.

shit-scared ['ʃɪt'skɛəd] *a Br V* chiasseux/ foireux; **to be shit-scared** = **to be scared shitless** (**shitless**). (*See* **shit¹** IV 4 (*a*))

shitstick ['ʃɪtstɪk] *n NAm V =* **shitbag**.

shitter ['ʃɪtə] *npl V* **the shitter**, les WC*/les chiottes *fpl*; **the shitters**, la diarrhée*/la chiasse/la courante.

shitty ['ʃɪtɪ] *a V* 1. méprisable/débectant/ dégueulasse/merdique; **they live in some shitty little hole**, ils habitent dans un petit truc merdique; **what a shitty idea!** tu parles d'une idée à la con/à la mords-moi le nœud!

that's a **shitty thing to say**, c'est dégueulasse de dire ça 2. médiocre/merdique; **it's a shitty machine**, cette machine ne vaut rien/c'est de la merde cette machine.

shiv¹ [ʃɪv] *n P =* **chiv¹** 1, 2.

shiv² [ʃɪv] *vtr P =* **chiv²**.

shivers ['ʃɪvəz] *npl F* **to give s.o. the shivers**, donner la tremblote/le frisson à qn.

shivoo [ʃɪ'vuː] *n F* réjouissances*/fête *f*/ bamboula *f*.

shlep [ʃlep] *vtr & i P* 1. porter/traîner/ trimbal(l)er 2. aller/se traîner; **I had to shlep all the way to the shop**, j'ai dû me trimbal(l)er jusqu'au magasin.

shlepper ['ʃlepə] *n P* 1. individu* maladroit/empaillé(e) *mf* 2. (*sluttish or immoral person*) salope *f*.

shliver ['ʃlɪvə] *n P =* **chiv¹** 1, 2.

shlock [ʃlɒk] *n P* (*shoddy goods, etc*) camelote *f*/daube *f*/chtrope *m*/merde *f*.

shlong [ʃlɒŋ] *n NAm P =* **schlong**.

shmarmy ['ʃmɑːmɪ] *a Br F =* **smarmy**.

shmeck [ʃmek], **shmee** [ʃmiː] *n P =* **schmeck**.

shmo(e) [ʃməʊ] *n P =* **schmo(e)** 1, 2.

shmoose, shmooze [ʃmuːz] *vi NAm P* bavarder*/jacter/tailler une bavette.

shnide [ʃnaɪd] *a Br P =* **snide** I 1, 2.

shnorrer ['ʃnɔːrə] *n P* (*cadger, scrounger*) tapeur, -euse/torpilleur, -euse; (*hustler*) arnaqueur *m*.

shocker ['ʃɒkə] *n F* (*person or thing*) horreur *f*/affreux *m*; **you're a shocker!** tu es*/ t'es impossible!

shoestring ['ʃuːstrɪŋ] *n F* **to do business on a shoestring**, faire des affaires avec des moyens financiers très limités; tirer sur la corde.

shonk(er) ['ʃɒŋk(ə)] *n Br P* 1. nez*/pif *m*/ tarin *m* 2. *Pej* Juif*/youpin, -ine.

shook ['ʃʊk] *a Austr F* **to be shook on sth**, être fou*/mordu/dingue de qch; **he was shook on her**, il était amoureux fou d'elle/il en était dingue.

shook up ['ʃʊk'ʌp] *a P* (**all**) **shook up**, ému/secoué/retourné/remué.

shoot¹ [ʃuːt] *n* 1. *F* **the whole (bang) shoot**, tout le bataclan/tout le tremblement. (*See* **boiling** II; **caboodle**; **shebang** 1; **shooting-match**) 2. *P* (*drugs*) piqûre*/ piquouse *f*/fixe *m*/shoot *m*.

shoot² [ʃuːt] I *vtr & i* 1. *P* **shoot!** vas-y!/ accouche!/déballe! 2. *P* **to shoot** (**one's bolt/ wad**) éjaculer*/décharger/dépon(n)er. (*See*

load 8) 3. *F* to get shot of s.o./sth, se débarrasser* de qn/de qch; se défarguer de/ larguer qn/qch 4. *F* to shoot a line, se vanter/ exagérer* son importance/ramener sa fraise; (*sweet-talk*) baratiner; to shoot s.o. a line, jeter de la poudre aux yeux de qn/bourrer le mou à qn. (*See* **line-shooter**; **line-shooting**) 5. *Br P* to shoot the/a cat, vomir*/ aller au refil/écorcher le renard 6. *NAm P* to shoot the bull/the crap/the breeze, bavarder*/ tailler une bavette 7. *F* to shoot the works (*a*) dilapider son argent*/jeter son fric par les fenêtres (*b*) avouer*/manger le morceau/se mettre à table (*c*) jouer/miser/risquer le tout pour le tout; jouer sa chemise (*d*) (*do sth to one's heart's content or put a lot of effort into sth*) y aller à fond/se donner à fond/donner un coup de collier 8. *P* to shoot the moon, (*leave without paying the rent*) déménager à la cloche de bois 9. *F* he has shot his bolt, il a joué sa dernière carte/il n'a plus de dents pour mordre 10. *P* (*drugs*) se piquer*/se shooter/se fixer 11. *P* partir*/filer/se casser II *excl NAm P* shoot! zut!/mince! (*See* **lingo 2**)

shoot down ['ʃuːt'daʊn] *vtr F* to shoot s.o. down (in flames), (*put s.o. in his place*) rabattre le caquet à qn/ramener qn à ses justes proportions/moucher qn; to get shot down in flames, l'avoir dans l'os.

shooter ['ʃuːtə] *n Br P* arme *f* à feu/flingue *m*/pétard *m*/soufflant *m*. (*See* **line-shooter**; **peashooter**; **six-shooter**)

shoot-flier ['ʃuːtflaɪə] *n P* voleur* de montres à l'arraché.

shooting-gallery ['ʃuːtɪŋ'gælərɪ] *n P* (*drugs*) endroit *m* où on se pique/se shoote.

shooting-iron ['ʃuːtɪŋaɪən] *n F* revolver*/ flingot *m*/pétard *m*/feu *m*.

shooting-match ['ʃuːtɪŋmætʃ] *n F* the whole shooting-match = the whole (bang) shoot (**shoot¹ 1**).

shoot off ['ʃuːt'ɒf] *vtr & i* 1. *P* = **shoot² 2** 2. *P* to shoot one's mouth/face off (*a*) révéler un secret/vendre la mèche/se mettre à table (*b*) (*talk a lot*) bavasser/jacter 3. *F* partir*/se tirer/se barrer.

shoot through ['ʃuːt'θruː] *vi Austr F* 1. mourir*/casser sa pipe/faire couic 2. partir*/ se tirer/se casser/mettre les bouts.

shoot up ['ʃuːt'ʌp] *vi P* se piquer*/se shooter/se fixer/se faire un shoot.

shop¹ [ʃɒp] *n* 1. *F* all over the shop, (*untidily*) en vrac/en pagaille/de façon bordélique; (*everywhere*) partout/dans tous

les coins 2. *P* you've come to the wrong shop, vous n'êtes pas au bon guichet/il y a erreur d'aiguillage/vous vous êtes trompé d'adresse 3. *F* to talk shop, parler affaires/parler boutique. (*See* **shop-talk**) 4. *F* to shut up shop, (*sport*) fermer le jeu; (*business*) fermer boutique 5. *P* prison*/boîte *f* 6. *F* top of the shop: *see* **bingo 99**. (*See* **copshop**; **hockshop**; **hook-shop**; **knocking 2**; **molly-shop**; **porn-shop**; **slopshop**; **sweat-shop**; **whore-shop**)

shop² [ʃɒp] *vtr P* 1. dénoncer*/trahir/ balancer/moutonner 2. emprisonner*/mettre en boîte.

shop-talk ['ʃɒptɔːk] *n F* jargon *m* de métier/d'un groupe professionnel, etc. (*See* **shop¹ 3**)

short [ʃɔːt] I *a* 1. *F* to be a bit short, être à court (d'argent*)/être à sec 2. *P* (*prostitutes*) short time, courte séance; passe *f* rapide 3. *P* short arm, pénis*/troisième jambe *f*; (*homosexuals*) short arm bandit, bourrin *m*; short arm heist, viol collectif. (*See* **curlies**; **hair 6**) II *adv F* to be caught short (*a*) (*need to relieve oneself*) être pris d'un besoin pressant; avoir envie de pisser/de chier (*b*) (*not have enough money*) être à court d'argent. (*See* **sell² 2**) III *n F* 1. alcool fort *f* 2. *NAm* petite voiture de sport/petit bolide.

shortarse ['ʃɔːtɑːs] *n V* bas-du-cul *m*/bas-duc *m*/rase-bitume *m*. (*See* **shorty**)

shortchange¹ ['ʃɔːttʃeɪndʒ] *a F* shortchange artist, escroc*/filou *m*/estampeur *m*/ arnaqueur *m*.

shortchange² ['ʃɔːt'tʃeɪndʒ] *vtr F* to shortchange s.o., voler* qn en lui rendant la monnaie (*lui rendre moins qu'il ne lui revient*).

short-eyes ['ʃɔːtaɪz] *n NAm P* coupable *mf* d'attentat à la pudeur sur des enfants.

short out ['ʃɔːt'aʊt] *vi NAm P* se mettre en colère*/piquer une crise/sortir de ses gonds.

shortweight ['ʃɔːtweɪt] *vtr F* estamper (qn) sur le poids.

shorty ['ʃɔːtɪ] *n F* petit individu*/rase-bitume *m*.

shot [ʃɒt] *F* I *a* 1. ivre*/bituré/rétamé/rond 2. très fatigué*/vanné II *n* 1. (*drugs*) piqûre *f*/ piquouse *f*. (*See* **hotshot¹,²**) 2. mesure *f* d'alcool*/dé *m*/rincette *f*/goutte *f* 3. a shot in the arm, un remontant/un stimulant/un coup de fouet 4. to have a shot at sth, essayer qch/ tenter le coup; give it your best shot, fais de ton mieux 5. (*a*) a long shot, un gros risque;

(*horse*) un gros risque; une chance sur mille (*b*) **not by a long shot** = **not by a long chalk** (**chalk 1**) 6. **like a shot** (*a*) très vite*/comme l'éclair (*b*) volontiers/de bon cœur 7. *Austr* **that's the shot!** voilà une idée!/à la bonne heure! 8. **to make a shot in the dark,** deviner au hasard/y aller au pif(omètre); **that was a cheap shot,** je me suis/il/elle s'est mal pris(e). (*See* **pot-shot; shoot² 3**)

shotgun [ˈʃɒtgʌn] *a attrib F* 1. **shotgun agreement,** convention signée sous la contrainte 2. **shotgun wedding,** mariage forcé/régularisation *f* 3. **to ride shotgun,** (*on motorcycle*) monter sur le siège arrière.

shouse [ʃaʊs] *n Austr P* WC*/chiottes *fpl*/ tasses *fpl*/gogues *mpl*.

shout¹ [ʃaʊt] *n F* 1. **it's my shout,** c'est ma tournée 2. **give me a shout when you're ready,** fais signe quand tu es prêt.

shout² [ʃaʊt] *vt Austr P* offrir la tournée à (qn, des amis).

shouting [ˈʃaʊtɪŋ] *n F* **it's all over bar the shouting,** c'est dans le sac/les applaudissements suivront/c'est du tout cuit.

shove [ʃʌv] *vtr* (*a*) *P* **you know where you can shove that!** tu sais où tu peux te le mettre!/tu peux te le mettre quelque part!/tu peux te le mettre là où je pense! (*b*) *V* **you can shove that (right) up your arse!** tu peux te le foutre/carrer au cul!

shove around [ˈʃʌvəˈraʊnd] *vtr F* (*push*) bousculer/ballotter (qn); (*bully*) bousculer/ gendarmer (qn).

shovel [ˈʃʌvl] *n P* (*RS* = *shovel and pick* = **nick** (*See* **nick¹ 1**(*a*)) prison*/taule *f*/bloc *m*.

shovel it down [ˈʃʌvlɪtˈdaʊn] *vi F* se goinfrer/se gaver.

shove off [ˈʃʌˈɒf] *vi* (*a*) *F* partir*/décamper (*b*) *P* **shove off!** fiche le camp!

show¹ [ʃəʊ] *n F* 1. **a show of leg,** un étalage de cuisses; **free show,** strip-tease *m* à l'œil; **it's a free show,** elle a soulevé son capot, on voit le moteur 2. **good show!** bravo!/c'est au poil! **it's a poor show!** c'est lamentable!/c'est minable!/c'est moche!/c'est zone! 3. **to give the show away,** vendre la mèche; débiner le truc 4. (*theatre*) **to stop the show,** faire un tabac/casser la baraque/faire crouler la baraque 5. **to steal the show,** capter l'attention/magnétiser l'assemblée/tirer la couverture à soi 6. **to run the whole show,** faire marcher l'affaire/faire tourner la baraque. (*See* **boss²; leg¹ 2; meat-show**)

show² [ʃəʊ] *vi F* = **show up 1.** (*See* **leg¹**

1)

showbiz [ˈʃəʊbɪz] *n F* l'industrie *f* du spectacle/le showbiz.

showdown [ˈʃəʊdaʊn] *n F* confrontation *f*/ déballage *m* (de ses intentions).

shower [ˈʃaʊə] *n P* (*a*) nullité *f*/nouille *f*; **he's a right shower!** quelle andouille! (*b*) **what a shower!** quelle bande*/quel tas de crétins!

showman [ˈʃaʊmən] *n F* (*jazz*) musicien *m* spectaculaire/showman *m*.

show-off [ˈʃəʊɒf] *n F* individu* qui fait de l'épate *f*/esbroufeur, -euse/poseur, -euse/m'as-tu-vu(e)/plastronneur *m*/frimeur, -euse.

show off [ˈʃəʊˈɒf] *vi F* parader/ plastronner/se donner des airs/faire de l'épate/frimer/se la m'as-tu-vu; **to show off in front of s.o.,** chercher à épater qn.

show up [ˈʃəʊˈʌp] *vtr & i F* 1. arriver/se ramener/se pointer 2. (*a*) révéler (un défaut); dévoiler/démasquer (un imposteur, etc) (*b*) attirer l'attention sur (qn); **he's been shown up,** il est grillé.

shrewdie [ˈʃruːdɪ] *n Austr F* (*shrewd person*) a shrewdie, un(e) petit(e) futé(e)/un malin, une maligne/un mariole.

shrift [ʃrɪft] *n F* **to give s.o. short shrift,** traiter qn sans ménagement; **I got short shrift from him,** il m'a envoyé paître/promener.

shrimp [ʃrɪmp] *n F* petit individu*/avorton *m*/rase-bitume *m*.

shrimper [ˈʃrɪmpə] *n NAm P* fétichiste *mf* du pied.

shrimping [ˈʃrɪmpɪŋ] *n NAm P* léchage *m* (érotique) des doigts de pieds.

shrink [ʃrɪŋk] *n P* psychiatre *mf*/ psychanalyste *mf*/psy *mf*. (*See* **headshrink(er)**)

shtook, shtuk [ʃtʊk] *n Br P* = **schtu(c)k**.

shtum [ʃtʊm] *a P* qui ne parle pas/qui la boucle; **keep/stay shtum!** bouclarès!/écrase!

shtup [ʃtʌp] *vtr NAm P* = **tup**.

shuck [ʃʌk] *n NAm F* **it's not worth shucks,** ça ne vaut pas tripette.

shucks! [ʃʌks] *excl esp NAm F* mince!/zut alors!

shudders [ˈʃʌdəz] *npl F* **to give s.o. the shudders** = **to give s.o. the shivers** (**shivers**).

shuffles [ˈʃʌflz] *npl P* cartes* à jouer/ brèmes *fpl*/cartons *mpl*.

shufty [ˈʃʊftɪ] *n F* regard *m*/coup d'œil*/ coup *m* de châsse/coup de sabord; **to have a quick shufty at sth,** filer un coup de sabord/de saveur à qch/jeter un œil à qch.

shush [ʃʊʃ] *vtr F* faire taire* (qn)/river son clou à (qn)/clouer le bec à (qn).

shut [ʃʌt] *vtr P* to shut it, se taire*/fermer sa boîte/fermer son clapet/la fermer; **shut it!** ta gueule!/la ferme! (*See* **face¹ 1; gob¹ 1; trap**)

shuteye [ˈʃʌtaɪ] *n F* sommeil *m*/somme *m*; to get/to grab some shuteye, dormir*/piquer un roupillon/roupiller.

shutters [ˈʃʌtəz] *npl F* to put the shutters up, se retirer en soi-même/baisser le rideau.

shut up [ˈʃʌtˈʌp] *vtr* (*a*) *F* faire taire* (qn)/clouer le bec à (qn) (*b*) *P* shut up! la ferme!/ferme ça!/ta gueule! (*c*) assassiner*/effacer/liquider (qn).

shy [ʃaɪ] *n A F* 1. jet *m*/lancement *m* 2. tentative *f*/essai *m*.

shyster [ˈʃaɪstə] *n F* homme d'affaires, etc véreux; avocat marron; loquedu, -ue.

sick [sɪk] *a* 1. *F* furieux/furibard/furax 2. *F* déçu/qui l'a mauvaise 3. *F* sick joke, plaisanterie *f* macabre 4. *F* I'm sick (and tired) of it/sick to death of it, j'en ai plein le dos/j'en ai marre/j'en ai ma claque 5. *P* (*drugs*) en manque* 6. *P* sick as a dog, malade comme un chien/à crever 7. *P* to be sick as a parrot, (*disappointed, upset*) être dans un état pas possible/en être malade; (*envious*) être malade/vert (de jalousie) 8. *NAm P* excellent*/chouette/génial/canon.

sickener [ˈsɪkənə] *n F* 1. aventure écœurante 2. spectacle écœurant.

sickie [ˈsɪkɪ] *n Austr F* congé *m* de maladie (*surt quand la maladie est simulée*).

sick-making [ˈsɪkmeɪkɪŋ] *a F* écœurant/dégoûtant/débectant.

sicko [ˈsɪkəʊ] *n esp NAm P* pervers(e) sexuel(le)/obsédé(e) sexuel(le); individu* perturbé mentalement.

sick up [ˈsɪkˈʌp] *vi & tr F* vomir* (qch)/dégobiller/dégueuler.

side [saɪd] *n* 1. *F* to make sth/a bit on the side, se faire des petits à-côtés 2. *P* to have a bit on the side, (*have lover*) (*of man*) avoir une petite amie/une maîtresse; (*of woman*) avoir un petit ami/un amant; (*have casual sex*) faire un petit écart 3. *F* to split one's sides (with) laughing, se tordre de rire*. (*See* **side-splitting**) 4. *Br O F* to put on side, se donner des airs; there's no side to her at all, elle est authentique. (*See* **bed¹ 2; right I 3; safe I 2**)

sideboards [ˈsaɪdbɔːdz], *NAm* **side-burns** [ˈsaɪdbɜːnz] *npl F* favoris *mpl*/pattes

fpl (de lapin).

sidekick [ˈsaɪdkɪk] *n F* 1. ami*/copain, -ine 2. associé, -ée/assistant, -ante/sous-fifre *m*; *Pej* acolyte *mf*.

sideman [ˈsaɪdmæn] *n P* (*jazz*) musicien *m* de pupitre.

side-splitting [ˈsaɪdsplɪtɪŋ] *a F* tordant/désopilant/marrant/crevant/fendant/à se rouler par terre (de rire). (*See* **side 3**)

sideways [ˈsaɪdweɪz] *adv F* to knock s.o. sideways, époustoufler qn/ébahir qn; I was knocked sideways, j'en suis resté assis/j'en suis tombé sur le cul.

siff [sɪf] *n P* = **syph**.

siffo [ˈsɪfəʊ] *n P* = **sypho**.

siffy [ˈsɪfɪ] *n P* = **syphy**.

sight [saɪt] *n F* 1. I can't bear/stand the sight of him, je ne peux pas le voir en peinture 2. (*a*) you (do) look a sight! te voilà bien arrangé!/tu es fichu comme l'as de pique!/tu en as une touche! (*b*) his face was a sight, si vous aviez vu sa tronche! 3. a sight of..., énormément de...; he's a (damn(ed)) sight too clever for you, il est bien trop malin* pour vous. (*See* **damned I 6; out I 4**)

sign off [ˈsaɪnˈɒf] *vi F* conclure/terminer/mettre le point final.

silk [sɪlk] *n Br Jur F* (*King's/Queen's Counsel*) avocat *m* de la Couronne; to take silk, être nommé avocat de la Couronne.

silly [ˈsɪlɪ] *n F* individu bête*/ballot *m*/andouille *f*/nouille *f*.

silvertail [ˈsɪlvəteɪl] *n Austr F* personnage important/gros bonnet/grosse légume/grossium *m*.

simmer down [ˈsɪməˈdaʊn] *vi F* se calmer/ne pas s'emballer.

simp [sɪmp] *n P* (*dimwitted person*) nigaud, -aude/andouille *f*/crétin, -ine.

sin bin [ˈsɪnbɪn] *n Br F* école *f ou* établissement *m* de rééducation (*pour cas difficiles ou désespérés*).

sin-binned [ˈsɪnbɪnd] *a Br F* puni.

sing [sɪŋ] *vi* 1. *P* to sing (like a bird/a canary) (*a*) (*confess*) avouer*/accoucher (*b*) (*inform*) moucharder/vendre la mèche 2. *F* to sing small, se conduire avec humilité.

sing out [ˈsɪŋˈaʊt] *vi F* sing out if you need me, appelez si vous avez besoin de moi.

sink [sɪŋk] *vtr & i F* 1. sink or swim! quitte ou double! to leave s.o. to sink or swim, laisser qn se dépatouiller 2. to sink a pint/a jar, s'envoyer un (demi).

sinker [ˈsɪŋkə] *n F* (= *doughnut*) beignet *m*.

(*See* **hook¹ 4**)

sin-shifter ['sɪnʃɪftə] *n Austr P* prêtre* catholique/cureton *m*.

siphon ['saɪf(ə)n] *vtr P See* **python**.

sir(r)ee [sə'riː] *n NAm F* no sirree! non, monsieur!/non, mon cher! yes sirree! mais oui, mon brave!/ça colle, Anatole!

sissy ['sɪsɪ] *n F* (*a*) (*coward*) poltron*/ dégonflard, -arde/pétochard, -arde (*b*) homme efféminé/chochotte *f*/femmelette *f*/panade *f*.

sit [sɪt] *vi F* to be sitting pretty (*a*) (*have an easy time, a good life*) tenir le bon bout/le filon; avoir la vie belle/se la couler douce (*b*) (*be rich*) rouler sur l'or. (*See* **behind; duck¹ 3; fence¹ 2; tight II**)

sit-down ['sɪtdaʊn] *n P* défécation *f*/flacdal *m*/foirade *f*.

sit-me-down ['sɪtmɪdaʊn] *n F* fesses*/ postère *m*/pont *m* arrière.

sit on ['sɪt ɒn] *vtr F* 1. to sit on sth, ne pas s'occuper de qch/laisser dormir qch/s'asseoir sur qch 2. to get sat on, être réprimandé*/se faire appeler Arthur; to sit on s.o., rabrouer qn/rabaisser le caquet à qn; he won't be sat on, il ne se laisse pas marcher sur les pieds.

sitter ['sɪtə] *n F* 1. = sitting duck (**duck¹ 3**) 2. une certitude/du tout cuit.

sit up ['sɪt'ʌp] *vi F* to sit up and take notice, se réveiller/ouvrir les yeux; I'll make you sit up! tu auras de mes nouvelles!

sit-upon ['sɪtəpɒn] *n F* = **sit-me-down**.

six [sɪks] *n F* 1. to be six feet/foot under, être enterré/bouffer les pissenlits par la racine 2. at sixes and sevens, sens dessus dessous/en pagaille 3. it's six of one and half a dozen of the other, c'est blanc bonnet et bonnet blanc/ c'est kif-kif/c'est du quès. (*See* **knock² 6**)

six-shooter ['sɪks'ʃuːtə] *n F* revolver* (à six coups)/six coups *m*/flingue *m*/pétard *m*.

sixty-four ['sɪkstɪ'fɔː] *n F* the sixty-four (thousand) dollar question (*a*) la question du gros lot/la question super-banco (*b*) la question cruciale.

sixty-nine¹ ['sɪkstɪ'naɪn] *n P* (*mutual oral sex between two people*) soixante-neuf *m*/69.

sixty-nine² ['sɪkstɪ'naɪn] *vi P* faire soixante-neuf.

size [saɪz] *n F* 1. to cut s.o. down to size, rabaisser qn/rabattre le caquet à qn/remettre qn à sa place 2. that's about the size of it, c'est à peu près cela. (*See* **king-size(d); man-size(d); pint-size(d); queen¹ 2**)

sizzler ['sɪzlə] *n F* = **scorcher 1**.

skag [skæg] *n P* = **scag**.

skate [skeɪt] *n* 1. *NAm F* chose *f* facile à faire/jeu *m* d'enfant; it's going to be a skate, ça sera facile comme bonjour/c'est un jeu d'enfant 2. *F* to put/to get one's skates on, se dépêcher*/se grouiller/se magner le train.

skating-rink ['skeɪtɪŋrɪŋk] *n F* crâne *m* chauve*/mouchodrome *m*/boule *f* de billard.

skedaddle [skɪ'dædl] *vi F* s'enfuir*/ficher le camp/filer/se casser/se tailler.

skerrick ['skerɪk] *n Austr F* a skerrick, un peu*/un chouia (de...); not a skerrick..., nib de.../pas une miette de....

skewer ['skjuːə] *n F* (*a*) épée *f* (*b*) baïonnette *f*.

skew-eyed ['skjuːaɪd] *a F* to be skew-eyed, loucher*; avoir un œil qui dit merde/zut à l'autre; bigler/être bigleux.

skew-whiff ['skjuː'wɪf] I *a F* tordu/ biscornu II *adv F* en biais/de traviole/de travers.

skid [skɪd] *vi P* 1. partir*/décamper/se tailler 2. *Br* vivre pauvrement/bouffer de la vache enragée.

skidlid ['skɪdlɪd] *n Br F* casque *m* de moto.

skid marks ['skɪd'mɑːks] *npl P* taches *fpl* d'excrément/de merde sur le slip/sur le calecif.

skid-row ['skɪd'rəʊ] *n esp NAm F* quartier mal famé; bas-fonds *mpl*/zone *f*; a skid-row joint, un boui-boui de la dernière catégorie; he's heading for skid-row, il va finir clochard.

skids [skɪdz] *npl F* 1. to be on the skids, (*of company, marriage, etc*) battre de l'aile/être sur une pente savonneuse/être en perte de vitesse; he's on the skids, il va mal finir 2. to put the skids under s.o./sth, faire échouer* qn/qch; balancer des peaux de banane à qn 3. *Austr* them's the skids, c'est le destin/c'est la vie.

skin¹ [skɪn] *n* 1. *F* to get under s.o.'s skin, ennuyer*/barber/raser qn; he's getting under my skin, il me court sur le(s) haricot(s)/il me tape sur le système 2. *F* it's no skin off my nose, ça ne me touche pas/c'est pas mon problème 3. *O F* skin off your nose! (*toast*) à la bonne vôtre! 4. *F* to have s.o. under one's skin, être entiché de qn/avoir qn dans la peau 5. *P* skin game, escroquerie*/arnaquage *m* 6. *NAm P* billet *m* d'un dollar 7. *P* papier *m* à cigarette 8. *pl P* (*jazz, rock*) batterie *f*/caisse *f* 9. *pl P* pneus *mpl* de voiture 10. *P* gimme some skin! touche là!/tope là! 11. *Br P* skin and blister, (*RS = sister*) sœur *f*/frangine *f* 12. *P* = **skinhead 13** *NAm P* skin flute, pénis*/

clarinette *f*. (*See* **thick 4**)

skin² [skɪn] *vtr F* (*to steal from, strip of money, etc*) carotter/dépouiller/écorcher/ plumer (qn). (*See* **eye 6**)

skinflick ['skɪnflɪk] *n esp NAm F* film *m* porno(graphique)/film de cul/porno *m*.

skinful ['skɪnful] *n P* to have (had) a skinful, être ivre*/tenir une bonne cuite/être dans le sirop.

skinhead ['skɪnhed] *n F* 1. homme* à la tête rasée/individu* qui a une perruque en peau de fesses 2. skinhead *mf*/skin *mf*.

skinner ['skɪnə] *n P* coupable *mf* d'attentat à la pudeur (*surt* sur des enfants).

skinny dip¹ ['skɪnɪ'dɪp] *n esp NAm F* baignade *f* tout nu*/à poil/à loilpé.

skinny-dip² ['skɪnɪ'dɪp] *vi esp NAm F* se baigner tout nu*/à poil/à loilpé.

skin-pop ['skɪnpɒp] *vi P* (*drugs*) se faire une piqûre* intramusculaire.

skin-popper ['skɪnpɒpə] *n P* (*drugs*) qn qui commence à se piquer*/débutant, -ante.

skin-popping ['skɪn'pɒpɪŋ] *n P* (*drugs*) piqûre* intramusculaire.

skint [skɪnt] *a P* très pauvre*/fauché/raide/ sans un.

skip¹ [skɪp] *n* 1. *Br F* fuite *f*/cavale *f* 2. *NAm F* qn qui se dérobe à la justice (*alors qu'il jouit d'une liberté provisoire*) 3. *Br F* = **skipper¹ 1** 4. *Br P* = **skipper¹ 2** 5. *Br F* vieille voiture*/tas *m* de ferraille/tas de tôle.

skip² [skɪp] *vtr* 1. *F* to skip the country, fuir le pays; to skip school, sécher les cours/faire l'école buissonnière 2. skip it! *F* (*leave it!*) laisse courir! *P* (*go away!*) file!/décampe!

skip off ['skɪp'ɒf] *vi Br F* (*leave*) filer/ décamper.

skipper¹ ['skɪpə] *n Br* 1. *F* patron*/chef *m* 2. *P* refuge *m* de clochards *ou* de sans-abris/ baraque *f*/cambuse *f*/turne *f*.

skipper² ['skɪpə] *vi Br P* to skipper/to be skippering, coucher sur la dure/être sans abri/être sur le pavé/compter les étoiles.

skippy ['skɪpɪ] *n NAm P* homosexuel*/ lopette *f*; *surt* homosexuel* efféminé.

skirt [skɜːt] *n P* femme*/jeune fille*/poupée *f*; a nice bit of skirt, une jolie pépée/un beau petit lot; de la fesse; to go out looking for skirt, courir les femmes/cavaler/chercher de la fesse.

skirt-chaser, skirt-hunter ['skɜːttʃeɪsə, 'skɜːthʌntə] *n P* cavaleur *m*/coureur *m* de jupons/chaud lapin.

skite¹ [skaɪt] *n Austr F* vantard*/frimeur *m*/ vanneur *m*.

skite² [skaɪt] *vi Austr F* se vanter/ esbrouf(f)er/en mettre plein la vue/vanner.

skive¹ [skaɪv] *n Br F* there's nothing wrong in having a bit of a skive on Friday after- noons, c'est tout à fait normal de vouloir tirer au flanc/au cul le vendredi après-midi.

skive² (off) ['skaɪv('ɒf)] *vi Br F* s'esquiver/ tirer au flanc/tirer au cul; to skive (off) from school, sécher les cours; he's skiving, il sèche les cours; il tire au flanc/au cul.

skiver ['skaɪvə] *n Br F* tire-au-flanc *m*/tire- au-cul *m*; what a skiver! quel feignant!/quelle feignasse!

skiving ['skaɪvɪŋ] *n Br F* tirage *m* au flanc/ tirage au cul; there's too much skiving here, on tire trop au flanc ici.

skivvies ['skɪvɪz] *npl NAm F* sous-vêtements *mpl* d'homme; caleçons *mpl*/cal(e)cifs *mpl*.

skivvy ['skɪvɪ] *n F* bonne *f* à tout faire/ bonniche *f*.

skulduggery [skʌl'dʌgərɪ] *n F* tripatouillage *m*/magouilles *fpl*/combine *f* louche.

skull¹ [skʌl] *n NAm* 1. *P* tête*/caboche *f*/ ciboulot *m* 2. *V* fellation*/pipe *f*/pompier *m*. (*See* **out I 3**)

skull² [skʌl] *vi Austr P* boire* (de l'alcool)/ biberonner/lever le coude.

skulled [skʌld] *a P* 1. ivre*/bourré/rétamé 2. drogué/stone(d)/dans les vapes.

skull-job ['skʌldʒɒb] *n V* = **skull¹ 2**.

skunk [skʌŋk] *n F* (*contemptible person*) salopard *m*/raclure *f*.

sky [skaɪ] *n P* 1. to see the sky through the trees, faire l'amour* à la campagne; voir/ regarder la feuille à l'envers 2. = **sky- rocket**. (*See* **limit 3**)

skyjack¹ ['skaɪdʒæk] *n F* piraterie aérienne.

skyjack² ['skaɪdʒæk] *vtr F* détourner/pirater (un avion).

skyjacker ['skaɪdʒækə] *n F* pirate *mf* de l'air.

skylark ['skaɪlɑːk] *vi P* (*play around*) rigoler/batifoler/chahuter; (*play jokes*) faire des farces.

sky-pilot ['skaɪpaɪlət] *n P* prêtre*/corbeau *m*/cureton *m*.

sky-rocket ['skaɪrɒkɪt] *n P* (*RS = pocket*) poche*/fouille *f*/glaude *f*.

slab [slæb] *n F* 1. table *f* d'opération/billard *m* 2. dalle *f* funéraire/pierre *f* de macchab.

slack [slæk] *a P* (*in Jamaica*) débauché/qui couche n'importe où.

slag¹ [slæg] *n Br P* 1. vieille prostituée*/ vieille pute 2. fille* *ou* femme* de mœurs légères/putain *f* 3. (*general insult*) individu* méprisable/ordure *f*/trouduc *m*; you slag! ordure!/duchnoque!/enculé!

slagging ['slægɪŋ] *n Br P* slagging (off), critique *f* sévère/flingage *m*/débinage *m*.

slag² **(off)** ['slæg'ɒf] *vtr P* critiquer*/ flinguer/débiner; parents are always slagging off their kids, les vioques bavent toujours sur les jeunes.

slam [slæm] *vtr F* 1. vaincre/écrabouiller/ écraser 2. frapper avec violence/massacrer 3. critiquer* sévèrement/flinguer/débiner/ massacrer.

slammer ['slæmə] *n P* prison*/taule *f*; in the slammer, en taule/au violon/au trou.

slanging-match ['slæŋɪŋmætʃ] *n F* prise *f* de bec/engueulade *f* maison; to have a slanging match with s.o., traiter qn de tous les noms.

slant¹ [slɑːnt] *n* 1. *F* (*a*) point *m* de vue/ manière *f* de voir (*b*) préjugé *m*/biais *m*/point de vue détourné 2. *P* coup d'œil*; take a slant at that! jette un coup de châsse!/vise-moi un peu ça! 3. *F Pej* oriental, -ale/bridé, -ée.

slant² [slɑːnt] *vtr F* fausser (une question, etc); slanted article, article tendancieux/ faussé.

slanter ['slɑːntə] *n Austr P* (*rare*) tour *m*/ ruse *f*/astuce *f*.

slap¹ [slæp] I *adv F* (*a*) directement/tout droit; slap (bang) in the middle, en plein (dans le) milieu/en plein dans le mille/en plein mitan (*b*) brusquement/brutalement/ rudement; she put it slap on the table, elle l'a flanqué sur la table. (*See* slap-bang (-wallop); smack¹ I; wallop¹ I) II *n F* 1. slap in the eye/face, affront *m*/camouflet *m*/ rebuffade *f* 2. *Br* slap and tickle, partie *f* de pelotage *m*; we were having a bit of (the old) slap and tickle, on était en train de se peloter/ de se faire des mamours.

slap² [slæp] *vtr F* slap it on the bill! colle-le sur l'addition!

slap-bang(-wallop) ['slæp-'bæŋ('wɒləp)] *adv F* (*a*) tout à coup/de but en blanc/sans prévenir (*b*) brusquement (*c*) the car went slap-bang(-wallop) into a lamp-post, la voiture a emplafonné un réverbère. (*See* slap¹ I; wallop¹ I)

slap **down** ['slæp'daʊn] *vtr F* réprimander*/rabrouer rudement.

slap-happy ['slæp'hæpɪ] *a F* 1. plein

d'entrain/d'allant/d'humeur joyeuse 2. farfelu/insouciant 3. *NAm* (*punch-drunk*) abruti de coups/ivre de coups/groggy.

slap **together** ['slæptə'geðə] *vtr F* préparer hâtivement/bâcler.

slap-up ['slæpʌp] *a Br F* (*restaurant, etc*) soigné/chic; a slap-up meal, un festin/un repas somptueux. (*See* bang-up)

slash¹ [slæʃ] *n P* to have a slash, uriner*/ pisser/lancequiner; to go for a slash, aller aux WC*/aller pisser un coup.

slash² [slæʃ] *vi Br P* uriner*/pisser.

slate¹ [sleɪt] *n F* 1. on the slate, sur la note/ sur le compte/sur l'ardoise 2. to have a slate loose/missing, être un peu fou*/onduler de la toiture/être fêlé.

slate² [sleɪt] *vtr F* (*a*) réprimander* (qn) vertement/attraper (qn)/passer un savon à (qn)/sonner les cloches (à qn) (*b*) critiquer*/ flinguer/massacrer (un livre, etc).

slater ['sleɪtə] *n F* critique *m* sévère/ abatteur *m*/éreinteur *m*.

slating ['sleɪtɪŋ] *n F* (*a*) verte réprimande/ savon *m* (*b*) critique *f* sévère/flingage *m*.

slats [slæts] *npl P A* (*ribs*) côtes *fpl*/ côtelettes *fpl*.

slaughter¹ ['slɔːtə] *n* 1. *F* défaite *f* sans appel/piquette *f*/coup *m* de Trafalgar/ hécatombe *f* 2. *P* cachette *f*/lieu sûr; planque *f*/placarde *f*/planquouse *f*.

slaughter² ['slɔːtə] *vtr F* battre à plate(s) couture(s)/écrabouiller/filer une piquette à; I'll slaughter you! je vais te massacrer!

slave¹ [sleɪv] *n P* (*sadomasochism*) partenaire passif, -ive/esclave *mf*. (*See* master)

slave² **(away)** ['sleɪv(ə'weɪ)] *vi F* travailler* dur/se crever/s'échiner/bosser comme une bête.

slave-driver ['sleɪvdraɪvə] *n F* garde-chiourme *m*.

slavey ['sleɪvɪ] *n F* = skivvy.

slay [sleɪ] *vtr F* you slay me! tu me fais rigoler!/tu me fais tordre!

sleaze [sliːz] *n P* 1. (*sordidness*) bassesse *f*/ dégueulasserie *f*; (*dirtiness*) crassouille *f*; (*immorality*) débauche *f* 2. (*person*) individu* méprisable/raclure *f*/salaud*/ordure *f*.

sleazebag, **sleazeball** ['sliːzbæg, sliːzbɔːl] *n NAm P* (*very unpleasant person*) merdaillon *m*/trouduc *m*.

sleazo ['sliːzəʊ] *n P* = sleaze 2.

sleazy ['sliːzɪ] *a F* sordide/répugnant/ dégueulasse/débectant/cradingue; a sleazy little joint, un boui-boui/une gargote.

sleep around ['sliːpə'raʊnd] *vi F* coucher avec n'importe qui/fréquenter les lits/coucher à droite et à gauche; **he sleeps around,** c'est un chaud lapin/un chaud de la pince; **she sleeps around,** c'est une bandeuse/une fille à la cuisse hospitalière.

sleeper ['sliːpə] *n F* 1. (*drugs*) somnifère *m*/barbiturique*/barbitos *mpl* 2. (*wrestling, judo*) prise *f* qui met l'adversaire groggy 3. film *m* qui rapporte beaucoup plus qu'on n'escomptait 4. livre *m* qui se vend couramment pendant une longue période sans publicité spéciale 5. (*commerce*) article auquel on découvre soudainement une plus-value jusque-là ignorée 6. wagon-lit *m* 7. (*espionage*) dormant *m*/taupe inactive.

sleeping policeman ['sliːpɪŋpə'liːsmən] *n F* (*on road*) ralentisseur *m*/gendarme couché.

sleep off ['sliːp'ɒf] *vtr F* to sleep it off, cuver son vin.

sleepy-byes ['sliːpɪbaɪz] *n F* (*child's language*) dodo *m*. (*See* **bye-byes**)

sleepyhead ['sliːpɪhed] *n F* endormi, -ie/ (bon(ne)) client(e) du marchand de sable.

slewed [sluːd] *a P* ivre*/blindé/bourré.

slice [slaɪs] *n P* (*not common*) to knock a slice off (a woman), faire l'amour* avec une femme/filer un coup d'arbalète à une femme.

slick [slɪk] *a F* 1. (*a*) malin*/rusé/marle/ démerdard; a slick customer, un faisan(t)/un carambouilleur/un arnaqueur (*b*) (*skilful*) habile/adroit 2. slick talker, beau parleur 3. slick movie/magazine, film/magazine bien fait/bien léché.

slicker ['slɪkə] *n F* escroc* adroit/combinard, -arde; city slicker, roustisseur *m* de ville/ affranchi *m*/mec *m* du milieu.

slide off ['slaɪd'ɒf] *vi F* partir* (sans bruit)/(se) défiler/se débiner.

slime¹ [slaɪm] *n P* 1. flatterie *f*/lèche *f*/ pommade *f* 2. salaud*/ordure *f*/raclure *f*.

slime² [slaɪm] *vtr P* flatter*/cirer les bottes à/pommader.

slimebag, slimeball ['slaɪmbæg, 'slaɪmbɔːl] *n P* = **slime¹** 2.

slimy ['slaɪmɪ] I *n P* lèche-cul *m*/lèche-bottes *m* II *a F* servile/obséquieux/mielleux/lèche-bottes; slimy little creep, lèche-bottes *m*/ lèche-cul *m*.

sling [slɪŋ] *vtr NAm P* to sling it/the bull = to shoot the bull (**shoot²** 6). (*See* **hook¹** 5; **lingo** 2; **mud** 7)

slinger ['slɪŋə] *n P* individu* qui écoule de la fausse monnaie/fourgueur *m*. (*See* **gunslinger**; **hash-slinger**; **ink-slinger**; **mudslinger**)

sling in ['slɪŋ'ɪn] *vtr P* to sling in one's job, lâcher son travail/rendre son tablier.

sling off ['slɪŋ'ɒf] *vi Austr P* to sling off at s.o., charrier qn/mener qn en bateau/raconter un bobard à qn.

sling out ['slɪŋ'aʊt] *vtr P* faire déguerpir/ flanquer dehors/balancer/vider.

slinky ['slɪŋkɪ] *a F* 1. élégant*/classe/rider 2. qui ondule en marchant/ondulant 3. (*clothing*) collant/moulant.

slip¹ [slɪp] *n F* to give s.o. the slip, fausser compagnie à qn/semer qn.

slip² [slɪp] *vtr & i* 1. *F* glisser/filer (qch à qn); he slipped the waiter a couple of quid, il a (re)filé vingt balles au garçon 2. *F* you're slipping, tu perds les pédales/tu baisses/tu te laisses aller/tu dérapes 3. *F* to slip one over on s.o., duper* qn/rouler qn dans la farine 4. *Br P* to slip it to s.o., (*esp of man to woman*) faire l'amour* avec qn/glisser un bout à qn. (*See* **cut¹** II 3; **length** 2)

slippy ['slɪpɪ] *a F* (*a*) glissant (*b*) *Br* (*quick*) you'll have to be pretty slippy about it! il faudra que tu te dépêches/que tu te grouilles! look slippy! grouille-toi!/magne-toi (le train)!

slip-up ['slɪpʌp] *n F* erreur *f*/bévue *f*/gaffe *f*/ bourde *f*.

slip up ['slɪp'ʌp] *vi F* faire une erreur/faire une gaffe/faire une bourde; you slipped up there, tu t'es planté sur toute la ligne.

slit [slɪt] *n V* sexe* de la femme*/fente *f*/ cicatrice *f*. (*See* **pee-slit**)

Sloane (Ranger) [sləʊn('reɪndʒə)] *n F* jeune fille de la bonne société; = B.C.B.G. *f*; she's very Sloane, elle est très comme il faut.

slob [slɒb] *n P* 1. (*a*) a (big) fat slob, un gros (sac à) lard/un gros patapouf (*b*) individu* sale/cracra/cradingue/dégueulasse; you slob! qu'est-ce que t'es dégueulasse! (*c*) rustaud, -aude/plouc *mf* (*d*) (*lazy person*) feignant, -ante/tire-au-cul *m inv* 2. = **slouch**.

slobber ['slɒbə] *vi F* 1. faire du sentimentalisme/larmoyer/s'attendrir 2. baver/avoir la bouche* souillée de nourriture* 3. to slobber over s.o., flatter qn/lécher les bottes à qn 4. to slobber (all) over s.o., (*kiss*) sucer la pomme à qn/faire un baveux à qn.

slog¹ [slɒg] *n F* 1. coup* violent/ramponneau *m*/gnon *m* 2. travail* dur/turbin *m*/boulot *m* 3. marche *f* pénible.

slog[2] [slɒg] *vtr & i F* 1. battre* violemment (qn)/tabasser (qn)/passer (qn) à tabac 2. (*cricket*) marquer des points en frappant fort sur la balle 3. travailler* dur/turbiner/bosser; to **slog away (at sth)**, travailler comme un dingue/bosser comme une bête/se crever (sur qch) 4. = **foot-slog.**

slogger ['slɒgə] *n F* 1. (*boxing*) cogneur *m* 2. travailleur* acharné/turbineur, -euse/ bosseur, -euse/bûcheur, -euse. (*See* **footslogger**)

slop [slɒp] *n F* sentimentalité excessive. (*See* **slops**)

slop about, around ['slɒpə'baʊt, ə'raʊnd] *vi F* patauger/barboter.

slope [sləʊp] *n P* 1. to do a slope = **slope off** 2. *esp Austr* oriental(e)/chinetoque *mf*.

slope off ['sləʊp'ɒf] *vi P* s'enfuir*/se barrer/déguerpir.

slop out ['slɒp'aʊt] *vtr & i P* (*esp in prisons*) vider les seaux hygiéniques/être de corvée des tinettes.

sloppy ['slɒpɪ] *a* 1. *F* sale*/souillon/ cradingue; désordonné/pagailleux/bordélique 2. *F* **sloppy joe**, pull-over *m* très ample; *NAm* sandwich *m* à la viande hachée 3. *NAm P* ivre*/éméché 4. *F* mièvre/larmoyant; **sloppy sentimentality**, sensiblerie *f*/guimauve *f* 5. *F* avec du laisser-aller/sans soin; **sloppy English**, anglais mal parlé/débraillé; **sloppy work**, travail bâclé.

slops [slɒps] *npl F* 1. (*navy*) vêtements*/ uniforme *m*/harnais *mpl* 2. aliments *mpl* liquides/bouillie *f*; (*leftovers*) restes *mpl*/ rabiot *m*.

slopshop ['slɒpʃɒp] *n P* 1. (*second-hand clothes shop*) braderie *f*/décrochez-moi-ça *m* 2. (*navy*) boutique *f* à bord d'un navire de guerre/cambuse *f*.

slosh[1] [slɒʃ] *n P* 1. sensiblerie *f*/ sentimentalité *f* fadasse/guimauve *f* 2. coup*/ gnon *m*/marron *m* 3. boisson *f*/gorgeon *m*.

slosh[2] [slɒʃ] *vtr* 1. *P* flanquer un coup* à (qn)/tabasser (qn) 2. *F* to **slosh paint on/all over the place**, flanquer de la peinture partout/barbouiller de peinture.

sloshed [slɒʃt] *a P* ivre*/gris/pompette/ rond; **completely sloshed**, pété à mort; plein comme un boudin/une vache/un œuf.

slot [slɒt] *n* 1. *P* (*a*) emploi *m*/situation *f*/job *m* (*b*) place *f*; to **finish in third slot**, finir troisième 2. *Austr P* cellule *f* de prison*/ cellotte *f* 3. *V* = **slit** 4. *V* (*homosexual use*) anus*/jaquette *f*.

slouch [slaʊtʃ] *n F* bousilleur, -euse/gâte-métier *m*; **he's no slouch**, il est malin*/il n'est pas empoté.

slow [sləʊ] *adv F* 1. to **go slow**, marcher/ fonctionner au ralenti; faire la grève du zèle 2. to **take it slow**, y aller doucement/y aller mollo/ne pas se précipiter.

slowcoach ['sləʊkəʊtʃ] *n F* traînard, -arde/lambin, -ine.

slowpoke ['sləʊpəʊk] *n NAm F* = **slowcoach.**

slug[1] [slʌg] *n P* 1. balle* (de revolver)/bastos *f*/dragée *f*/valda *f* 2. pièce fausse/fausse mornifle 3. coup*/marron *m*/taloche *f* 4. (*drink*) goutte *f*/coup *m*; to **have a slug**, boire* un coup.

slug[2] [slʌg] *vtr P* 1. battre*/frapper/ tabasser/cogner 2. boire*/s'envoyer/ descendre 3. tirer un coup (de fusil *ou* de revolver*) sur (qn)/fusiller (qn)/flinguer (qn).

slugfest ['slʌgfest] *n NAm P* combat *m* de boxe (*entre boxeurs qui frappent dur*).

slugger ['slʌgə] *n F* boxeur *m* (qui frappe dur)/cogneur *m*.

slug it out ['slʌgɪt'aʊt] *vi F* se battre* en frappant de grands coups*/se rentrer dedans.

slug-up ['slʌgʌp] *n Austr P* = **frame-up.**

sluice[1] [sluːs] *n P* trempette *f*/débarbouillage *m*.

sluice[2] [sluːs] *vtr P* to **sluice one's ivories**, boire*/se rincer la dalle/s'humecter le gosier.

slum [slʌm] *vtr & i* 1. *F* to **go slumming**, fréquenter les bars des bas quartiers/faire la zone 2. *P* to **slum it**, vivre pauvrement/se taper de la vache enragée.

slush [slʌʃ] *n* 1. *F* sensiblerie *f* 2. *P* fausse monnaie/fausse mornifle; **slush fund**, caisse noire; **slush (money) payments**, graissage *m* de patte.

slushy ['slʌʃɪ] *a F* sentimental/fadasse; à l'eau de rose.

sly [slaɪ] *n F* **on the sly**, à la dérobée/en cachette/en loucedoc/en loucedé.

slyboots ['slaɪbuːts] *n F* 1. (*cunning person*) petit malin, petite maligne/finaud, -aude 2. (*mischievous child*) espiègle *mf*/ petit(e) coquin(e); **you old slyboots!** espèce de coquin!

SM ['es'em] *P* (*abbr of sadomasochism*) I *n* sadomasochisme *m* II *a* sadomaso.

smack[1] [smæk] I *adv F* 1. to **hit s.o. smack between the eyes**, frapper qn en plein entre les deux yeux 2. **smack in the middle**, au beau milieu/en plein dans le mille. (*See* **slap**[1] I) II *n* 1. *F* smack in the eye/face = slap in the eye/face (**slap¹ II 1**) 2. *F* to have a smack at sth, essayer de faire qch/tenter le coup 3. *F* to have a smack at s.o., en allonger un(e) à qn 4. *F* = **smacker 1** 5. *P* (*drugs*) héroïne*/ sma(c)k *m*. (*See* **schmeck**)

smack² [smæk] *vtr P* donner un coup de poing/des coups de poing à (qn); cogner (qn).

smack-bang(-wallop) ['smæk'bæŋ-('wɒləp)] *adv F* = **slap-bang(-wallop)**.

smack-botty ['smæk'bɒtɪ] *n F* (*child's language*) panpan-culcul *m*; to give a kid a smack-botty, filer/flanquer une fessée à un gosse. (*See* **botty**)

smack down ['smæk'daʊn] *vtr F* = **slap down**.

smacked out [smækt'aʊt] *a P* (*drugs*) drogué à l'héroïne*/smaké/smashed.

smacker ['smækə] *n* 1. *F* gros baiser sonore/smack *m* 2. *pl P* smackers, livres *fpl* (sterling) *ou* dollars *mpl*.

smackeroo(ny) [smækə'ruː(nɪ)] *n F* = **smacker 1**.

smack-head ['smækhed] *n P* (*drugs*) drogué(e)* (à l'héroïne*)/junkie *mf*/camé(e).

small [smɔːl] *a F* the small print, le texte en petits caractères/l'important *m* du bas de la page. (*See* **potato 2; room 1**)

smalls [smɔːlz] *npl F* sous-vêtements *mpl*/ lingerie *f*/dessous *mpl*/fringues *fpl* de coulisse.

small-time ['smɔːltaɪm] *a F* insignifiant/ médiocre/tocard; a small-time crook, un petit escroc*. (*See* **big-time**)

small-timer ['smɔːltaɪmə] *n F* individu* insignifiant/minus *m*/gagne-petit *m*. (*See* **big-timer 1**)

smarm [smɑːm] *n F Pej* caractère doucereux.

smarm down ['smɑːm'daʊn] *vtr F* to smarm down one's hair, se pommader/se brillantiner/se gominer les cheveux*.

smarmer ['smɑːmə] *n F* flagorneur, -euse/ lèche-bottes *m*/lèche-cul *m*/fayot, -otte.

smarm up to ['smɑːm'ʌptuː] *vtr F* flatter (qn); lécher les bottes à/passer de la pommade à (qn).

smarmy ['smɑːmɪ] *a F* tout sucre tout miel/ mielleux/fayot; smarmy little sod, lèche-cul.

smart [smɑːt] *a F* 1. don't get smart with me! ne fais pas le malin avec moi!/ne la ramène pas! 2. smart guy, malin *m*/fortiche *m*. (*See* **Alec 1**)

smartarse, *NAm* **smartass** ['smɑːtɑːs, -æs] *P* **I** *n* petit malin, petite maligne **II** *a*

malin/fortiche.

smart-arsed ['smɑːtɑːst], *NAm* **smart-assed** ['smɑːtæst] *a P* malin*/fortiche/ démerdard.

smarty-pants ['smɑːtɪpænts] *n F* petit malin, petite maligne/je-sais-tout *mf*.

smash [smæʃ] **I** *adv F* to go smash (*a*) se briser (*b*) (*of firm, bank*) faire faillite/manger la grenouille **II** *n* 1. *F* = **smash-hit** 2. *P* petite monnaie*/ferraille *f*/mitraille *f*.

smashed [smæʃt] *a P* (*a*) ivre*/bituré/ blindé (*b*) défoncé par la drogue*/stone(d)/ raide (def)/smashed.

smasher ['smæʃə] *n F* 1. she's a smasher, c'est une jolie pépée/un beau petit lot; what a smasher! ce qu'elle est belle*/bien roulée! he's a smasher, il est beau mec/il a de la classe 2. qch d'excellent*/de super/de sensass/de génial 3. coup* violent/châtaigne *f*/ marron *m*.

smash-hit ['smæʃ'hɪt] *n F* réussite *f*/gros succès/succès fou; it was a smash-hit, ça a fait un tabac/un malheur; their album was a smash-hit, leur album a fait un tabac monstre.

smash in ['smæʃ'ɪn] *vtr P* to smash s.o.'s face in, casser la gueule à qn/arranger le portrait à qn.

smashing ['smæʃɪŋ] *a Br F* excellent*/ formid(able)/du tonnerre/super/génial; she's smashing! elle est super!/elle est vachement bien! we had a smashing time, c'était vachement bien.

smash up ['smæʃ'ʌp] *vtr P* 1. battre* (qn)/ filer une avoine à (qn)/passer (qn) à tabac 2. he's smashed his car up, il a amoché/bousillé/ plié sa bagnole.

smeg(gy) ['smeg(ɪ)] *n Br P* (*fool*) crétin, -ine/andouille *f*; (*dirty person*) individu* crado/cradingue.

smell [smel] *vi F* sembler louche/ne pas avoir l'air catholique/sentir mauvais; I won't do it, your idea smells, je ne marche pas, ton idée est foireuse. (*See* **rat¹ 4**)

smelly ['smelɪ] *a F* suspect/louche.

smidgen, **smidgeon**, **smidgin** ['smɪdʒən] *n F* un peu*/un chouia/une miette.

smithereens ['smɪðə'riːnz] *npl F* morceaux *mpl*/miettes *fpl*; to smash sth to smithereens, briser qch en mille morceaux/ mettre qch en miettes.

smoke¹ [sməʊk] *n* 1. *F* to go up in smoke, (*disappear*) partir en fumée; (*fail*) tomber à l'eau 2. *F* the Smoke, une grande métropole/la ville; the (Big) Smoke, Londres *m ou f; Austr* the Big Smoke, Sydney *m ou f* 3. *F* tabac*/ fume *f*; a smoke *(a)* cigarette*/cibiche *f*; want a smoke? tu veux une clope? *(b) (drugs)* cigarette* de marijuana*/stick *m* 4. *Austr P* in smoke, *(in hiding)* cache/planqué 5. *NAm P Pej* Noir(e)*/bamboula *m*. (See **giggle** 3; **holy** 1; **joy-smoke**)

smoke[2] ['sməʊk] *P* I *vtr NAm* 1. to smoke s.o. (off, out), faire mieux que qn/gratter qn 2. tuer*/descendre II *vi Austr* partir*/ déguerpir/se barrer.

smoke-o(h) ['sməʊkəʊ] *n Austr F* pause-café *f*/pause-thé *f*; récré *f*.

smoker ['sməʊkə] *n* 1. *F* compartiment *m* fumeurs 2. *Br P* vieille voiture/tas *m* de ferraille 3. *A P* pot *m* de chambre 4. *P (drugs)* fumeur, -euse de cannabis* 5. *V (fellator)* suceur, -euse/pipeur, -euse.

smoko ['sməʊkəʊ] *n Austr P* = **smoke-o(h)**.

smooch[1] [smuːtʃ] *n F* to have a smooch, se bécoter/se peloter *(surt* en dansant).

smooch[2] [smuːtʃ] *vi F* s'embrasser*/se bécoter/se faire des mamours *mpl*/se peloter *(surt* en dansant).

smoocher ['smuːtʃə] *n F* caresseur, -euse/ peloteur, -euse.

smooching ['smuːtʃɪŋ] *n F* caressage *m*/ pelotage *m*/fricassée *f* de museaux *(surt* en dansant).

smoodge [smuːdʒ] *vi,* **smoodger** ['smuːdʒə] *n,* **smoodging** ['smuːdʒɪŋ] *n Austr F* = **smooch**[2], **smoocher, smooching.**

smooth [smuːð] *a F* malin*/débrouillard/ fortiche; **smooth operator,** individu malin*/ démerdard, -arde; bonimenteur *m*/beau parleur.

smoothie, smoothy ['smuːðɪ] *n F* individu* mielleux; **he's a real smoothie,** c'est un beau parleur.

smother ['smʌðə] *n A P* pardessus*/pardoss *m*/pardingue *m*.

smudge [smʌdʒ] *n Br O P* photo *f*/cliché *m*/ portrait *m*.

smudger ['smʌdʒə] *n Br O P* photographe *mf*.

snack [snæk] *n Austr F* qch de facile; **it's a snack,** c'est du gâteau/du nougat/du billard.

snaffle ['snæfl] *vtr P* voler*/barbot(t)er/ chiper.

snafu[1], **SNAFU**[1] ['snæ'fuː] *P (abbr of situation normal, all fucked up)* I *a* en

désordre/en pagaille/bordélisé; amoché/ bousillé II *n* désordre *m*/pagaille *f*/ merdier *m*/bordel *m*.

snafu[2], **SNAFU**[2] ['snæ'fuː] *vtr P* mettre/ foutre la pagaille/le merdier/le bordel dans qch; semer la merde.

snags [snægz] *npl Austr F* saucisses *fpl*.

snakebite ['sneɪkbaɪt] *n P (drink)* mélange *m* de bière blonde et de cidre.

snake-eyes ['sneɪkaɪz] *npl F (dice game)* double un/deux as.

snake off ['sneɪk'ɒf] *vi F* partir*/ s'esquiver/jouer rip.

snakes ['sneɪks] *n Austr P* 1. urine*/pisse *f* 2. WC*/chiottes *fpl*.

snake's hiss [sneɪks'hɪs] *vi & n Austr P (RS* = **piss**) = **piss**[1,2].

snaky ['sneɪkɪ] *a F* trompeur/fourbe.

snap[1] [snæp] *n* 1. *F* vigueur *f*/entrain *m*/ allant *m*/dynamisme *m* 2. *F* qch de facile/du nougat/du tout cuit 3. *Br F (workman's packed lunch)* gamelle *f*/casse-croûte *m* 4. *P* = **amy.**

snap[2] [snæp] *vtr & i F* 1. s'exprimer avec aigreur/parler* d'un ton sec; to snap at s.o./to snap s.o.'s head off, rembarrer, vivement qn 2. *(of person)* perdre la raison; I just snapped, j'ai flippé/j'ai disjoncté 3. to snap into it, s'y mettre sans traîner 4. to snap out of it, se secouer/se ressaisir/se remettre d'aplomb.

snapper ['snæpə] *n* 1. *V* vagin*/baba *m*/ turlu *m* 2. *pl P* dents*/croquantes *fpl* 3. *F* photographe *mf*. (See **whippersnapper**)

snappy ['snæpɪ] *a F* 1. hargneux/bourru/sec 2. look snappy!/make it snappy! 3. snap to it!/grouille-toi!/au trot!/et que ça saute! 3. élégant*/chic(os)/nickelé.

snap up ['snæp'ʌp] *vtr F* 1. to snap up a bargain, sauter sur/saisir une occasion 2. to snap it up, activer le mouvement; snap it up! grouille-toi!/et que ça saute!

snarl [snɑːl] *n F* = **snarl-up.**

snarled up ['snɑːld'ʌp] *a F* embouteillé/ encombré/coincé.

snarl-up ['snɑːlʌp] *n F* embouteillage *m*/ bouchon *m*.

snatch[1] [snætʃ] *n* 1. *V* vagin*/baba *m*/tirelire *f* 2. *V* femmes** en général/nanas *fpl* 3. *P* enlèvement *m*; to put the snatch on s.o., enlever/kidnapper qn 4. *F (bag-snatching)* (vol *m* à la) tire/vol à l'arraché; *(mugging)* vol avec agression; wages snatch, ratissage *m* de la paye.

snatch² [snætʃ] *vtr* 1. *P* enlever/kidnapper 2. *P* voler*/barbot(t)er 3. to snatch a quick one (*a*) F boire* un coup/s'en jeter un vite fait (*b*) *P* faire l'amour* rapidement/tirer un coup vite fait.

snazz [snæz] *n esp NAm F* élégance *f*/chic *m*/donne *f*.

snazzed-up [snæzd'ʌp] *a F* = **snazzy**.

snazzy ['snæzɪ] *a F* (*a*) élégant*/chic(os)/ ridère/rider (*b*) *Pej* criard/voyant/clinquant/ tape-à-l'œil.

sneak¹ [sniːk] *n F* 1. (*esp schools*) cafard, -arde/mouchard, -arde 2. **sneak attack**, attaque sournoise/en dessous; coup *m* en va- che; **sneak preview**, (*of film, play, etc*) banc *m* d'essai/séance privée; **to have a sneak pre- view of**, voir (un film, etc) en avant-première; avoir la primeur de (roman, etc); **sneak thief**, chapardeur, -euse/chipeur, -euse/barbot(t)eur, -euse.

sneak² [sniːk] *vtr & i F* 1. se déplacer furtivement 2. voler*/barbot(t)er/chaparder 3. dénoncer*/moucharder/cafarder.

sneak in ['sniːk'ɪn] *F* I *vtr* introduire/ glisser furtivement (qch dans qch) II *vi* se glisser furtivement/se faufiler; entrer à la dérobée/en douce/en catimini.

sneak on ['sniːk'ɒn] *vtr Br F* (*esp schools*) dénoncer*/caf(e)ter/cafarder/moucharder.

sneak out ['sniːk'aʊt] *F* I *vi* se glisser furtivement/se faufiler hors d'un d'endroit/ s'éclipser II *vtr* sortir (qch) furtivement.

sneaky ['sniːkɪ] *a F* 1. sournois/faux jeton; that was a really sneaky thing to do, c'était vraiment un coup de vache 2. rampant/ servile.

sneeze at ['sniːz'æt] *vtr F* it's not to be sneezed at, ce n'est pas de la petite bière/il ne faut pas cracher dessus.

sneezer ['sniːzə] *n P* nez*/pif *m*/tarin *m*.

snide [snaɪd] I *a F* 1. faux/tocard/à la manque 2. sarcastique/persifleur II *n P* 1. voleur*/filou *m*/truqueur, -euse 2. fausse monnaie/fausse mornifle; bijouterie *f* factice/ toc *m*.

snidy ['snaɪdɪ] *a P* malin*/astucieux/rusé.

sniff [snɪf] *vtr* 1. *P* aspirer/sniffer (une drogue); to sniff glue, sniffer de la colle; to sniff lines, sniffer de la cocaïne*/de la coke/ des lignes. (*See* **line¹** 9) 2. *F* it's not to be sniffed at = it's not to be sneezed at (**sneeze at**).

sniffer ['snɪfə] *n P* 1. nez*/blair *m*/pif *m* 2. (*drugs, glue*) (*person*) sniffeur, -euse.

sniffles ['snɪflz] *npl F* to have the sniffles, être un peu enrhumé. (*See* **snuffles**)

sniffy ['snɪfɪ] *a* 1. *F* arrogant/hautain/ pimbêche 2. *P* = **niffy**.

snifter ['snɪftə] *n O P* petit verre d'alcool*/ goutte *f*; to have a quick snifter, s'en jeter un vite fait.

snip [snɪp] *n F* 1. affaire* avantageuse/ trouvaille *f*/occasion *f*; it's a snip, c'est une occase 2. certitude *f*/affaire* certaine; du nougat/du tout cuit; (*horseracing*) gagnant sûr/grosse cote 3. tailleur *m*/loqueur *m* 4. petit individu*/rase-bitume *m*.

snipe¹ [snaɪp] *n P* mégot*/clope *m*/orphelin *m*.

snipe² [snaɪp] *vtr P* voler*/faucher.

snippy ['snɪpɪ] *a P* insolent/effronté/culotté/ gonflé.

snit [snɪt] *n P* 1. (*obnoxious person*) blaireau *m*/beauf *m*; (*child*) miteux, -euse 2. (*in- significant person*) merdeux, -euse 3. accès *m* de colère*/rogne *f*/crosse *f*.

snitch¹ ['snɪtʃ] *n P* 1. *esp NAm* indicateur* de police/mouchard, -arde; *Br* (*esp schools*) rapporteur, -euse/cafard, -arde 2. nez*/tarin *m*/pif *m*.

snitch² [snɪtʃ] *vi P* dénoncer*/moucharder/ cafarder.

snitcher ['snɪtʃə] *n P* 1. indicateur*/indic *mf*/mouchard, -arde/cafeteur *m* 2. *pl* menottes*/cadènes *fpl*/bracelets *mpl*/poucettes *fpl*.

snob [snɒb] *n A P* cordonnier *m*/bouif *m*/ gnaf *m*.

snockered ['snɒkəd] *a esp NAm P* = **schnockered**.

snoddy ['snɒdɪ] *n A P* soldat*/bidasse *m*/ troufion *m*.

snog¹ [snɒg] *n Br P* (*kissing and cuddling*) pelotage *m*/fricassée *f* de museaux; to have a snog, se peloter.

snog² [snɒg] *vi Br P* s'embrasser*/se bécoter; sucer la pomme/le museau à qn; se peloter.

snogger ['snɒgə] *n Br P* embrasseur, -euse; peloteur, -euse.

snogging ['snɒgɪŋ] *n Br P* pelotage *m*.

snook [snuːk] *n F* to cock a snook at s.o., faire un pied de nez à qn.

snooker ['snuːkə] *vtr F* to snooker s.o., mettre qn dans une impasse; to be snookered, être coincé/dans une impasse.

snooks [snuːks], **snookums** ['snuːkəmz] *n esp Austr F* chéri(e)/cocotte *f*.

snoop[1] [snu:p] *n F* 1. fureteur, -euse/ fouineur, -euse 2. (*a*) inspecteur *m* de police/ sondeur *m* (*b*) détective privé/privé *m*/limier *m*.

snoop[2] [snu:p] *vi F* fureter/fouiner/fourrer le *ou* son nez* partout.

snooper ['snu:pə] *n F* = **snoop**[1] 1, 2.

snoopy ['snu:pɪ] *a F* curieux/fouineur/ fureteur.

snoot [snu:t] I *a F* haut-de-gamme/chic/de luxe; a snoot boutique, un magasin de luxe II *n P* 1. nez*/pif *m* 2. individu* hautain; crâneur, -euse/frimeur, -euse.

snootful ['snu:tful] *n NAm P* to have (had) a snootful, être ivre*/tenir une bonne cuite/en tenir une/avoir un verre dans le nez.

snootiness ['snu:tɪnɪs] *n F* attitude hautaine/arrogance *f*.

snooty ['snu:tɪ] *a F* hautain/orgueilleux/ dédaigneux/frimeur; to be snooty, se donner de grands airs/crâner/frimer.

snooze[1] [snu:z] *n F* 1. petit somme; to have a snooze, piquer un roupillon 2. qch d'ennuyeux/de rasoir; it was a bit of a snooze, c'était plutôt barbant/rasoir.

snooze[2] [snu:z] *vi F* dormir*/roupiller/ pioncer.

snoozer ['snu:zə] *n F* roupilleur *m*/pionceur *m*.

snore [snɔ:] *n F* = **snooze**[1] 2.

snork [snɔ:k] *n Austr P* (*baby*) chiard *m*/ gluau *m*/lardon *m*.

snort[1] [snɔ:t] *n P* 1. petit verre d'alcool*/ goutte *f*; to have a snort, s'en jeter un (derrière la cravate) 2. (*drugs*) dose *f*/ snif(fe) *f ou m*.

snort[2] [snɔ:t] *vtr & i P* (*drugs*) renifler/ sniffer (de la cocaïne*, etc).

snorter ['snɔ:tə] *n* qch d'exceptionnel/du tonnerre; histoire palpitante; *Austr* journée torride. (*See* **ripsnorter**)

snot [snɒt] *n P* 1. morve *f*/chandelle *f* 2. (*obnoxious person, esp child*) morveux, -euse/ merdeux, -euse.

snot-nosed ['snɒtnəuzd] *a P* a snot-nosed kid, un petit morveux/merdeux. (*See* **snotty-nosed**)

snot-rag ['snɒtræg] *n Br P* mouchoir*/tire- moelle *m*/tire-jus *m*.

snotty ['snɒtɪ] I *a P* 1. (*nose*) plein de morve 2. prétentieux*/prétentiard*/puant 3. sale*/crade/cracra/cradingue 4. méprisable/ vache; you snotty little git! petit morveux!/ petite ordure! II *n F* aspirant *m* de Marine/

aspi *m*.

snotty-nosed ['snɒtɪnəuzd] *a P* 1. morveux 2. hautain/dédaigneux/frimeur; she's terribly snotty-nosed, elle joue les grandes dames/elle pète plus haut que son cul.

snout[1] [snaut] *n Br P* 1. nez*/blair *m* 2. (*a*) tabac*/perlot *m* (*b*) cigarette*/sèche *f*; snout baron, prisonnier *m* qui vend du tabac aux au- tres détenus 3. indicateur* de police/indic *mf*/mouchard, -arde.

snout[2] [snaut] *vi Br P* dénoncer*/ moucharder/en becter/en croquer.

snow[1] [snəu] *n* 1. *P* (*drugs*) cocaïne* en poudre/neige *f* 2. *P* pièce *f ou* article *m* en argent; blanc *m*/blanquette *f* 3. *F* neige *f* (sur écran de télévision) *f* 4. *Austr F* snow bunny, jeune fille* qui fréquente les stations de sports d'hiver (et sort avec les skieurs) 5. *NAm F* = **snow-job 1**.

snow[2] [snəu] *vtr & i* 1. *esp NAm P* duper*/ rouler dans la farine/mystifier 2. *F* it's snow- ing down south, ton jupon dépasse; tu cher- ches une belle-mère? (*See* **Anne**; **charlie 2**)

snowball[1] ['snəubɔ:l] *n P* 1. *NAm Pej* Noir(e)*/bougnoul *m*/boule *f* de neige 2. he doesn't stand a snowball's chance in hell, il n'a pas l'ombre d'une chance.

snowball[2] ['snəubɔ:l] *vi F* (*of problems, debts, etc*) faire boule *f* de neige.

snowbird ['snəub3:d] *n P* drogué*/cocaï- nomane *mf*/parfois héroïnomane *mf*.

snowdrop ['snəudrɒp] *vi P* (*esp of fetishist*) voler* le linge/surt la lingerie qui sè- che dans les jardins.

snowdropping ['snəudrɒpɪŋ] *n P* (*esp by fetishist*) vol *m* de linge/surt de lingerie qui sèche dans les jardins.

snow-job ['snəudʒɒb] *n* 1. *NAm F* tromperie *f*/charriage *m*/entourloupe *f*; to give s.o. a snow-job, jeter de la poudre aux yeux à qn/bourrer le mou à qn 2. *V* (*homosexuals*) fellation*/pipe *f*; to give s.o. a snow-job, tailler une pipe à qn/faire un pompier à qn.

snuff[1] [snʌf] *n* 1. *F* up to snuff, malin*/ dégourdi *f* 2. *P* (*drugs*) cocaïne*/renifle(tte) *f* 3. *P* snuff movie, film *m* porno(graphique) dans lequel l'acteur *ou* l'actrice est supposé(e) être réellement tué(e).

snuff[2] [snʌf] *vtr & i P* 1. tuer*/zigouiller/ effacer 2. (*drugs*) aspirer/sniffer (de la cocaïne).

snuff it ['snʌf'ɪt] *vi Br P* mourir*/éteindre son gaz/avaler son bulletin.

snuffles ['snʌflz] *npl F* to have the snuffles, être un peu enrhumé. (*See* **sniffles**)

snuff out ['snʌf'aʊt] *vtr & i P* 1. = **snuff it** 2. tuer*/zigouiller/effacer.

so [səʊ] *adv & conj F* 1. so long! à bientôt!/à tout à l'heure! 2. so what? et après?/et alors?

soak¹ [səʊk] *n P* 1. ivrogne*/poivrot, -ote/ (vieille) éponge 2. ivrognerie *f*/soûlerie *f*/cuite *f* 3. *Austr* averse *f*/rincée *f*.

soak² [səʊk] *vtr & i* 1. *P* boire* beaucoup/ pomper/boire comme un trou *ou* comme une éponge; to get soaked, s'enivrer/prendre une cuite 2. *F* faire payer* trop cher/écorcher/ estamper.

so-and-so ['səʊənsəʊ] *n F* 1. Mr So-and-so/ Mrs So-and-so, Monsieur Un tel/Madame Une telle; Monsieur/Madame Machin(-truc) 2. *Pej* salaud*/sale mec *m*/peau *f* de vache; she's a right old so-and-so, c'est une vraie carne/une vieille bique.

soap¹ [səʊp] *n* 1. *F* flatterie *f*/pommade *f* 2. *NAm F* no soap! = no dice! (**dice¹**) 3. *F* soap (opera), feuilleton *m* sentimental/à l'eau de rose.

soap² [səʊp] *vtr P* = **soft-soap**.

soapy ['səʊpɪ] *F* I *a* doucereux/mielleux/tout sucre tout miel II *n* (*also* **soapie**) = soap (opera) (**soap¹** 3)

s.o.b. ['esəʊ'biː] *abbr P* 1. = **son of a bitch** 2. = shit or bust (**shit²** 4)

sob-act ['sɒbækt] *n P* to put on a/the (big) sob-act, pleurer des larmes de crocodile/la faire aux larmes.

sob-sister ['sɒbsɪstə] *n esp NAm F* journaliste spécialisée dans le mélodrame.

sob-story ['sɒbstɔːrɪ] *n F* histoire larmoyante/au jus de mirettes; he came out with this long sob-story, il s'est amené avec une histoire à faire pleurer dans les chaumières/à nous faire chialer.

sob-stuff ['sɒbstʌf] *n F* sensiblerie *f*/eau *f* de guimauve/mélo *m*.

sock¹ [sɒk] *n* 1. *P* put a sock in it! (*shut up!*) la ferme!/ta gueule!/écrase! 2. *P* coup* de poing/gnon *m*/beigne *f* 3. *F* to pull one's socks up, se reprendre/remonter la pente/faire mieux que ça. (*See* **bobbysocks**)

sock² [sɒk] *vtr P* 1. donner un coup* à (qn)/ flanquer une raclée à (qn)/tabasser (qn); I'll sock you (one), if you don't shut up! la ferme, ou je te refais le portrait! 2. to send it to s.o., (*show what one is made of*) montrer à qn de quel bois on se chauffe; (*show what one can do*) montrer à qn de quoi on est capable; sock

it to me! (*give it to me!*) passe-moi ça!/ flanque-moi ça! (*tell me!*) vas-y!/accouche!/ déballe!

sod¹ [sɒd] *n Br P* 1. (*rare*) sodomite *m*/ enculeur *m* 2. poor sod! pauvre bougre!/ pauv'con! silly sod! espèce d'andouille!/ espèce de con! he's a real sod, c'est un sale con; rotten sod! peau de vache!/salaud!/ ordure!/le fumier! you sods! bande d'enculés!/tas de salauds! (*See* **jammy**) 3. I don't give/care a sod, je m'en fous (comme de l'an quarante); j'en ai rien à branler/à foutre 4. (*nuisance*) that's a real sod! quelle couille!/c'est la chiotte!/quelle chiotte! this door's a sod to open, elle est vachement dure à ouvrir cette porte de merde 5. it's/that's sod's law, tout s'en mêle pour vous emmerder! (*See* **odds 1**)

sod² [sɒd] *vtr Br P* sod you! va te faire foutre!/va te faire voir (chez les Grecs)!/va te faire mettre! sod it! merde alors!/bordel de Dieu!/bordel de merde!

sod about ['sɒdə'baʊt] *vi Br P* 1. faire le con/déconner; stop sodding about! arrête de déconner! 2. paresser*/glander/glandouiller.

sod-all ['sɒd'ɔːl] *n Br P* rien*/que dalle/peau *f* de balle.

sodding ['sɒdɪŋ] *a Br P* (*intensifier*) sacré/ foutu; that's a sodding nuisance! c'est vraiment chiant! you sodding bastard! (espèce de) salaud!/d'enculé! the sodding car, cette saloperie de bagnole/cette putain de bagnole; sodding hell! bordel de Dieu!/bordel de merde!

sod off ['sɒd'ɒf] *vi Br P* partir*/foutre le camp; he just sods off whenever there's work about, il fonce/il se carapate/il fout le camp dès qu'il est question de travailler; sod off, will you! va te faire voir!/va te faire foutre!/ va te faire mettre!

soft [sɒft] I *a F* 1. (*a*) sentimental (*b*) bête*/ niais/nigaud; soft in the head, faible d'esprit (*c*) poltron*/lâche/cave; to go soft, se dégonfler 2. a soft job, un filon/un bon fromage/une planque; to have a soft time (of it), se la couler douce. (*See* **berth 2**) 3. to be soft on s.o., être épris/entiché de qn; he's soft on her, il en est toqué 4. soft drugs, drogues* douces. (*See* **hard I 2**) 5. soft sell, publicité discrète. (*See* **hard I 5**) 6. soft porn, porno *m* soft/soft *m*. (*See* **sawder**; **soft-soap**; **spot 4**; **touch¹ 3**) II *adv F* 1. don't talk soft! ne dis pas de bêtises*! 2. to have it soft, (*have an easy time*) se la couler douce.

soft-pedal ['sɒft'pedl] *vtr & i* F y aller mollo/ne pas trop insister/mettre la pédale douce (sur qch).

softshoe ['sɒftʃuː] *vtr & i* P se comporter d'une façon détournée; **to softshoe one's way out of a situation**, se tirer d'affaire d'une façon détournée.

soft-soap ['sɒft'səup] *vtr* F flatter*/passer de la pommade à/pommader/flagorner (qn); bonimenter/baratiner.

softy ['sɒftɪ] *n* F *(a)* (*not tough*) homme* mou/femme* molle *(b)* (*coward*) lavette *f*/ poule mouillée/dégonflé, -ée/trouillard, -arde *(c)* (*fool*) andouille *f*/nouille *f* *(d)* individu* sentimental à l'excès; **you big softy!** mon gros bébé!

soldier ['səuldʒə] *vi NAm* P (*shirk*) tirer au flanc.

soldier on ['səuldʒə(r)'ɒn] *vi* F persévérer/se défendre/se débattre; **I'll soldier on with this**, je vais m'escrimer là-dessus.

solid ['sɒlɪd] **I** *a* F 1. **five solid hours**, cinq heures d'affilée; **six solid weeks I had to wait**, six bonnes semaines que j'ai dû poireauter 2. excellent*/super/canon **II** *n Br* P (*drugs*) haschisch*/shit *m*.

solitary ['sɒlɪtə(r)ɪ] *n* F régime *m* (d'isolement) cellulaire; **in solitary**, au mitard.

some [sʌm] **I** *a* F 1. excellent*/formid(able); **she's some girl!** elle est sensas(s)!/c'est une fille* formidable!/elle a de la classe!/elle est classe! 2. **some hope!** quelle illusion!/tu parles! **II** *adv* F **to go some**, (*very fast*) y aller plein gaz/gazer; **that's going some, getting there in two hours!** faut pas traîner/ s'amuser pour être là-bas en deux heures! **III** *pron* F **...and then some**, ...et le reste/...et j'en passe.

somebody ['sʌmbɒdɪ, 'sʌmbədɪ] *n* F **he's a somebody**, c'est vraiment quelqu'un/c'est un personnage. (*See* **nobody**)

something ['sʌmθɪŋ] **I** *adv* F très/ beaucoup*; **she went off at him something awful!** elle lui a passé un de ces savons! (*See* **alarming**; **chronic II**) **II** *n* F 1. **that's something like it!** voilà qui est bien!/voilà qui est mieux!/ça au moins, ça vaut le coup! 2. **isn't that something?/that really is something!** c'est pas chouette ça?/ça c'est quelque chose! **it's something else!** c'est au poil!/c'est formide!/c'est géant! **she's something else!** elle est super!/elle est classe!

song [sɒŋ] *n* 1. F **to make a song (and dance) about sth**, faire des histoires/des tas d'histoires pour *ou* à cause de qch; **no need to make a big song and dance over it**, pas de quoi en faire tout un plat 2. F **to buy sth for a song**, acheter qch pour une bouchée de pain 3. P aveu *m*/déboutonnage *m*/accouchage *m*.

sonny ['sʌnɪ] *n* F (mon) petit/(mon) fiston/ mon gars; **look here, sonny Jim**, attention petit gars.

son of a bitch, sonofabitch, sonovabitch ['sʌnəvə'bɪtʃ] *n esp NAm* P 1. salaud*/fils *m* de pute/fils de garce; **you sons of bitches!** bande d'enculés!/tas de salauds! 2. (*thing*) **this car is a real son of a bitch**, c'est une vraie saloperie/une putasserie/une putain de bagnole.

sooty ['sʊtɪ] *n Br* F *Pej* Noir(e)/bougnoul *m*/ noircif *m*.

soppiness ['sɒpɪnɪs] *n* F mollesse *f*/ fadasserie *f*.

soppy ['sɒpɪ] *a* F *(a)* bête*/cucu(l); **you soppy twit!** gros bêta! *(b)* (*person*) mou; (*sentiment*) fadasse *(c)* (*story, etc*) larmoyant/gnangnan.

sore [sɔː] *a* F 1. en colère*/fâché/à cran; **to get sore with s.o.**, en vouloir à qn; **he was really sore about it**, ça l'a foutu en rogne/en pétard 2. **to be like a bear with a sore head**, être d'une humeur massacrante. (*See* **eye 11**; **thumb¹ 4**)

sorehead ['sɔːhed] *n esp NAm* P ronchon, -onne.

sort¹ [sɔːt] *n* 1. F **a good sort**, un brave homme*/un chic type 2. F **out of sorts**, malade*/patraque/pas dans son assiette 3. P fille* *ou* femme*/nénette *f*/nana *f*/gonzesse *f*.

sort² [sɔːt] *vtr Br* P **to sort s.o. (out)**, (*beat up*) battre*/passer qn à tabac; (*have sex with*) (*of man*) faire l'amour* avec qn/glisser un bout à qn.

sorted ['sɔːtɪd] *a Br* P (*person*) satisfait/ content; **I've got a car and some cash, I'm sorted**, j'ai une bagnole et du fric, tout est au poil.

sort of ['sɔːtəv] *adv* F = **kind of**.

so-so ['səusəu] *adv* F couci-couça/entre les deux.

soul [səul] *n* F **poor soul!** pauvre créature!/ pauvre bonhomme!/pauvre bonne femme! le/ la pauvre! **she's a good soul**, c'est une bien brave femme/c'est une bonne âme.

soul brother ['səul'brʌðə] *n esp NAm* F frère *m*/frangin *m* (black).

soul sister ['səʊl'sɪstə] *n esp NAm F* sœur*/frangine *f* (black).

sound off ['saʊnd'ɒf] *vi F* to sound off at s.o., réprimander* qn/engueuler qn/sonner les cloches à qn; to sound off about sth, déblatérer contre qch/rouspéter à propos de qch.

sounds [saʊndz] *n O F* musique *f*/zicmu *f*.

soup [suːp] *n* 1. *F* in the soup, dans le pétrin/la panade 2. *P (a)* nitroglycérine *f (pour faire sauter les coffres-forts) (b)* dynamite *f*. *(See* **duck¹ 11**; **electric**)

soup up ['suːp'ʌp] *vtr F* gonfler (un moteur); a souped-up job, une bagnole gonflée.

soupy ['suːpɪ] *a esp NAm F (a)* sentimental/à l'eau de rose *(b) (voice)* larmoyant.

sourpuss ['saʊəpʊs] *n F* individu* morose/revêche/renfrogné; rabat-joie *m*.

souse¹ [saʊs] *n P (not common)* 1. = **sozzler** 2. ivresse*/cuite *f*/soûlerie *f*.

souse² [saʊs] *vi P* = **sozzle**.

soused [saʊst] *a P* = **sozzled**.

southpaw ['saʊθpɔː] *n F* gaucher, -ère.

sov [sɒv] *n P (abbr of sovereign)* livre *f* sterling.

sozzle ['sɒzl] *vi P* 1. boire* beaucoup/picoler 2. s'enivrer/se charger/se beurrer.

sozzled ['sɒzld] *a P* ivre*/soûl/chargé/beurré/refait.

sozzler ['sɒzlə] *n P* ivrogne*/soûlard, -arde/poivrot, -ote/alcolo *mf*.

sozzling ['sɒzlɪŋ] *n P* ivresse*/poivrade *f*.

SP ['es'piː] *n Br P (abbr of starting price)* 1. *(horseracing)* prix *m* de départ 2. information*/info *f*/tuyau *m*; to give s.o. the SP, mettre qn au parfum/tuyauter qn; give me the SP on this bloke, fais-moi le papier sur ce type.

space cadet, space case ['speɪskə'det, -'keɪs] *n NAm F* individu* excentrique/loufoque.

spaced out ['speɪst'aʊt] *a P (drugs)* drogué*/camé/envapé/chargé; *(eccentric)* loufoque/déjanté; he's really spaced out, il est dans les vapes/parti/déchiré; *(naturally)* il plane.

spac(e)y ['speɪsɪ] *a F* euphorisant/qui fait planer; spac(e)y dope, came *f* qui défonce.

spade [speɪd] *n* 1. *P Pej* Noir(e)*/bougnoul *m* 2. *F* to call a spade a spade, appeler un chat un chat.

spag [spæg] *n F (abbr of spaghetti)* 1. *Br* spaghetti *mpl* 2. *Austr Pej* Italien*/macaroni

mf.

spaghetti-bender, spaghetti-eater [spə'getɪ'bendə, -'iːtə] *n Austr F Pej* = **spag 2**.

spank [spæŋk] *n Br F* = **spanking III**.

spank along ['spæŋkə'lɒŋ] *vi O F* aller vite*/filer/foncer/gazer.

spanker ['spæŋkə] *n F* 1. *O* beau spécimen/qch d'épatant/qch de super 2. *O* cheval* rapide 3. *Br* voiture* de (bonne) qualité/belle caisse.

spanking ['spæŋkɪŋ] *F I a* 1. rapide; to go at a spanking pace, aller à pleins tubes 2. *O* excellent*/épatant *II adv O* brand spanking new, flambant neuf *III n (beating)* raclée *f*/rossée *f*/tabassage *m*.

spanner ['spænə] *n F* to put/to throw a spanner in the works, mettre des bâtons dans les roues.

spare [speə] *I a F* 1. *(a)* to go spare, être furieux/fulminer; to drive s.o. spare, rendre qn furax; he'll go spare when he finds out, il va monter au plafond/il va être fou quand il (l')apprendra *(b)* there's a glass going spare here, il y a un verre qui traîne par ici 2. spare tyre/NAm tire, bourrelet *m* (de graisse)/pneu *m* de secours. *(See* **prick 3)** *II n P* femme(s)* libre(s)/sans partenaire; to have a bit of spare, *(of man)* faire l'amour* à une femme/se faire une nana.

spark [spaːk] *n F* bright spark, qn de très intelligent/lumière *f*; *Iron* andouille *f*/tête *f* de nœud; who's the bright spark who did that! qui c'est, le petit malin qui a fait ça?

sparkler ['spaːklə] *n Br P* mensonge*/craque *f*/vanne *m ou f*.

sparklers ['spaːkləz] *npl F* diamants*/diams *mpl*.

sparko ['spaːkəʊ] *a Br P (fast asleep)* profondément endormi; *(unconscious)* dans les pommes/les vapes; where's Liz? she's sparko, où est Liz? elle pionce *ou* elle est tombée dans les vapes.

spark out [spaːk'aʊt] *adv Br P* to go spark out, s'endormir/s'enroupiller; *(faint)* tomber dans les vapes; tourner de l'œil.

sparks [spaːks] *n F* 1. *(boats, planes)* opérateur, -trice de TSF/radio *m* 2. électricien, -ienne.

sparring-partner ['spaːrɪŋpaːtnə] *n F* époux *m*/épouse*/(chère) moitié.

sparrow-fart ['spærəʊfaːt] *n P* at sparrow-fart, aux aurores/dès la pointe du jour.

spastic ['spæstɪk] *P Pej* **I** *a* bête*/crétin; (*attempt, idea, etc*) minable/nul **II** *n* you spastic! espèce d'enfoiré!/quel nœud!

spat [spæt] *n NAm F* petite querelle*/bisbille *f*/prise *f* de bec.

spaz(z) [spæz] *a & n Pej* = **spastic.**

spazzing ['spæzɪŋ] *n Br P* porte-à-porte *m* en simulant une infirmité (*pour apitoyer le client*).

speakeasy ['spiːkiːzɪ] *n NAm O F* bar clandestin.

spec [spek] *n F* (*abbr of speculation*) on spec, à tout hasard. (*See* **specs**)

specimen ['spesɪmn] *n F* individu*/type *m*; **an odd/a queer specimen,** un drôle de numéro/de client/d'oiseau/de zèbre.

specs [speks] *npl F* (*abbr of spectacles*) lunettes*/bernicles *fpl*/carreaux *mpl*/pare-brise *m*.

speed[1] [spiːd] *n P* (*drugs*) amphétamine*/ speed *m*; **he's on speed,** il est speedé/ speed(y)/défoncé.

speed[2] [spiːd] *vi P* (*drugs*) prendre des amphétamines*/du speed; se speeder; **to be speeding,** être speedé/speed(y).

speedball ['spiːdbɔːl] *n P* (*drugs*) mélange *m* d'héroïne* et de cocaïne*/dada *m*/speedball *m*.

speed-cop ['spiːdkɒp] *n F* motard *m*.

speedfreak ['spiːdfriːk] *n P* (*drugs*) utilisateur, -trice habituel(le) d'amphétamines*/camé, -ée au speed.

speed-hog ['spiːdhɒg] *n F* (*bad driver*) chauffard *m*.

speeding ['spiːdɪŋ] *a P* (*drugs*) speedé/ speed(y).

speed-merchant ['spiːdmɜːtʃənt] *n F* **1.** passionné, -ée de la vitesse/fou *m*, folle *f* du volant **2.** (*bad driver*) chauffard *m*.

speedo ['spiːdəʊ] *n F Aut* (= *speedometer*) compteur *m*.

SPG ['esˌpiːˈdʒiː] *n P* (*abbr of Special Patrol Group*) (*police*) Brigade spéciale.

spic(k) [spɪk] *n P Pej* (*person*) (*Italian*) Rital(e)/macaroni *mf*; (*Hispanic*) Espingo *mf*/espingouin *mf*.

spiderman ['spaɪdəmæn] *n F* ouvrier *m* qui travaille au sommet des immeubles.

spiel[1] [spiːl, ʃpiːl] *n F* boniment *m*/baratin *m*; **he gave me some spiel about having been held up at the airport,** il m'a fait tout un baratin comme quoi il avait été bloqué à l'aéroport.

spiel[2] [spiːl, ʃpiːl] *vi F* avoir du bagou(t);

baratiner/faire du baratin.

spieler ['spiːlə, 'ʃpiːlə] **1.** *P* tricheur* (aux cartes)/fileur *m* **2.** *P* escroc*/arnaqueur *m* **3.** *P* tripot *m* de jeux **4.** *F* beau parleur/ baratineur, -euse/bonimenteur *m*.

spiel off ['spiːlˈɒf, 'ʃpiːlˈɒf] *vtr F* to spiel off a whole list of names, débiter/dégoiser toute une liste de noms.

spiffing ['spɪfɪŋ] *a Br O F* ravissant/ charmant/délicieux.

spifflicate ['spɪflɪkeɪt] *vtr Br F* écraser/ aplatir/fracasser/démolir/écrabouiller (un adversaire).

spiffy ['spɪfɪ] *a F* élégant*/chicos/rider/ ridère.

spike[1] [spaɪk] *n P* (*drugs*) seringue* hypodermique/shooteuse *f*/poussette *f*.

spike[2] [spaɪk] *vtr* **1.** *P* (*drugs*) injecter/ piquer*/picouser/shooter **2.** *F* to spike a drink, ajouter de l'alcool* *ou* une drogue à une boisson non alcoolisée; **to spike coffee with cognac,** corser du café avec du cognac/faire champoreau/faire gloria **3.** *F* to spike s.o.'s guns, priver qn de ses moyens d'action/ contrecarrer qn; **I spiked his guns for him,** je lui ai damé le pion.

spiked [spaɪkt] *a P* (*a*) drogué*/high/défoncé (*b*) spiked drink, boisson droguée/mickey *m*.

spike up ['spaɪkˈʌp] *vi P* (*drugs*) se piquer*/se picouser/se shooter.

spiky ['spaɪkɪ] *a F* susceptible/chatouilleux.

spill [spɪl] *vi F* avouer*/cracher/s'allonger; **he won't spill,** il ne veut pas se mettre à table. (*See* **bean 5; guts 7**)

spin[1] [spɪn] *n* **1.** *F* to be in a flat spin, être paniqué/affolé **2.** *F* to go for a spin, aller se balader (en voiture)/aller faire une virée **3.** *Br F* station *f* de taxis **4.** *F* to give sth a spin, prendre qch à l'essai; **let's give it a spin!** on tente le coup! **5.** *Br P* (*police jargon*) perquisition *f*/barbotte *f*; **let's give him a spin,** on va lui faire une petite descente. (*See* **tailspin**)

spin[2] [spɪn] *vtr & i P* fouiller/vaguer (qn); (*prison*) faire la barbotte; **to spin (a drum),** faire une perquise/une descente.

spit[1] [spɪt] *n* **1.** *F* spit and polish, astiquage *m*/fourbissage *m*; **to give sth a spit and polish,** faire reluire qch/astiquer qch **2.** *P* spit and drag, (*RS* = **fag**) cigarette*/cibiche *f*/sèche *f*. (*See* **fag 1**) **3.** *P* spit and sawdust, (*bar, restaurant*) sans chichis/sans fioritures/à la bonne franquette; **a spit and sawdust place,** un petit boui-boui sympa **4.** *Austr P* to go for the big spit/to do a big spit/to do a long spit, vomir*/dégueuler/gerber/aller au refil(e). (*See* **dead I 7**)

spit² [spɪt] *vi Austr P* 1. avoir (très) soif/ cracher des pièces de dix sous 2. être en colère*/voir rouge/être en pétard.

spit out ['spɪt'aʊt] *vtr F* to spit it out, dire/ accoucher/vider son sac; come on, spit it out! allez, déballe!/accouche!

spiv [spɪv] *n O F* trafiquant *m*/chevalier *m* d'industrie/magouilleur *m*.

splash¹ [splæʃ] *n F* 1. to make a (big) splash, faire sensation/faire de l'épate/faire un effet bœuf 2. jet *m* de siphon; a whisky and splash, un whisky soda.

splash² [splæʃ] *vtr F* 1. annoncer sur cinq colonnes à la une 2. to splash one's money about = **splash out**. (*See* **boot¹ 5**)

splash out ['splæʃ'aʊt] *vtr & i F* dépenser* sans compter/claquer du fric/jeter son fric par les fenêtres; faire une folie; we splashed out on a bottle of plonk, on a claqué notre fric sur une bouteille de pinard; I splashed out £100 on a new dress, j'ai claqué 100 livres sur une nouvelle robe.

splatter movie ['splætə'muːvɪ] *n F* film violent et sanglant.

splay [spleɪ] *n NAm P* (*drugs*) marijuana*.

splendiferous [splen'dɪfərəs] *a O F* splendide/rutilant.

splice [splaɪs] *vtr Br P* faire l'amour* à/ baiser (qn).

spliced [splaɪst] *a & pp F* to get spliced, se marier/se marida.

spliff [splɪf] *n P* (*drugs*) cigarette* de marijuana*/stick *m*/tarpet *m*.

split¹ [splɪt] *n* 1. *F* dénonciateur*/cafard, -arde/mouchard, -arde 2. *P* inspecteur *m* (de police)/condé *m* 3. *P* part *f* (de butin)/gratte *f* 4. *P* allumette *f*/frotteuse *f* 5. *F* (*a*) demi-bouteille *f*/petite bouteille* d'eau gazeuse (*b*) demi-verre *m* de liqueur.

split² [splɪt] *vi* 1. *F* (*a*) (*confess*) vendre la mèche (*b*) to split on s.o., dénoncer*/ cafarder/balancer/donner qn 2. *P* partager (bénéfices, butin, etc)/aller au fade 3. *P* partir*/ficher le camp/mettre les bouts; come on, let's split! allez, on change de crémerie!/ on se casse! 4. *F* splitting headache, mal *m* de tête fou/de première; my head is splitting, j'ai un super mal au crâne. (*See* **side 3**)

split-arse ['splɪtɑːs] *adv F* to run split-arse, courir comme si on avait le feu au derrière.

split beaver ['splɪt'biːvə] *n V* sexe* de la femme*/millefeuille *m*/abricot *m*. (*See* **beaver 2**)

split-up ['splɪtʌp] *n F* 1. querelle*/brisure *f* 2. divorce *m*/séparation légale.

split up ['splɪt'ʌp] *vi F* 1. rompre (avec qn) 2. divorcer/se démaquer.

splodge¹ [splɒdʒ] *n F* tache *f* (de couleur, etc).

splodge² [splɒdʒ] *vtr F* tacher/barbouiller (with, de).

splurge¹ [splɜːdʒ] *n F* (*a*) (*ostentation*) es-brouf(f)e *f*/épate *f*; to make a splurge = **splurge²** (*b*) (*extravagant spending*) folles dépenses; to have a big splurge, faire des folies/dépenser plein de fric.

splurge² [splɜːdʒ] *vi F* faire de l'esbrouf(f)e *f*/de l'épate *f*.

splurge out ['splɜːdʒ'aʊt] *vi F* (*spend extravagantly*) faire des dépenses extravagantes/faire des folies.

spon [spɒn] *n P* = **spondulicks**.

spondulicks, spondulix [spɒn'djuːlɪks] *npl P* argent*/fric *m*/oseille *f*.

sponge¹ [spʌndʒ] *n F* = **sponger**. (*See* **throw in**)

sponge² [spʌndʒ] *vtr & i F* faire le parasite; écornifler/grappiller (un repas, etc); to sponge a drink, se faire offrir une tournée; to sponge on/off s.o., vivre aux crochets de qn.

sponger ['spʌndʒə] *n F* parasite *mf*/ écornifleur, -euse/pique-assiette *mf*.

sponging ['spʌndʒɪŋ] *n F* écorniflage *m*/ tapage *m*.

spoof¹ [spuːf] *n F* (*a*) (*play, film, etc*) satire *f* (*b*) (*trick*) blague *f*/tour *m*/canular *m*; (*dummy, decoy, etc*) attrape *f*; he sent round a spoof memo about redundancies, il a fait passer une circulaire bidon qui parlait de licenciements.

spoof² [spuːf] *vtr & i* 1. *F* parodier/ caricaturer 2. *F* tromper*/filouter/empiler; you've been spoofed, tu t'es fait avoir.

spook¹ [spuːk] *n* 1. *F* fantôme *m*/revenant, -ante/apparition *f* 2. *NAm P* espion, -onne/ agent (secret)/barbouze *m ou f* 3. *NAm P* Noir(e)/bougnoul *m*.

spook² [spuːk] *vtr F* faire peur* à (qn)/ ficher la frousse à (qn).

spooky ['spuːkɪ] *a F* (*a*) hanté (*b*) sinistre/ étrange/zarbi.

spoon [spuːn] *vi A F* se faire des mamours *mpl*/des cajoleries *fpl*.

spoon(e)y ['spuːnɪ] *a A F* sentimental.

sport [spɔːt] *n* 1. *F* a (good) sport, individu*

sympa(thique)/bon type/bonne nature; be a sport! sois sympa! 2. P fille*/petite amie 3. *esp Austr F* ami*/copain *m*/pote *m*; hullo/ g'day sport! salut, mon pote!/salut, vieille branche!

sporting ['spɔːtɪŋ] *a* 1. *F* qui a bon caractère/d'un bon naturel 2. *P* sporting woman, femme* facile/qui a la cuisse légère; Marie-couche-toi-là *f*.

sporty ['spɔːtɪ] *a F* 1. (*person*) sportif 2. (*jacket, etc*) gai; (*car*) sportif; it's a bit too sporty, c'est un peu trop sport.

spot [spɒt] *n* 1. *F* to be in a spot, être dans une situation difficile/être dans le pétrin; he's in a bit of a tight spot, il est dans le mauvaise passe/dans le pétrin 2. *F* to get into a spot of bother, avoir des ennuis *mpl*/être dans de mauvais draps 3. *F* to knock spots off s.o., exceller sur qn/rendre des points à qn/ battre qn à plate(s) couture(s) 4. *F* to have a soft spot for s.o./sth, avoir un faible pour qn/ qch 5. *F* a spot, un (petit) peu*; a spot of whisky, un petit coup de whisky/une goutte de whisky; how about a spot of lunch? si on cassait une petite graine?/si on mangeait un petit qch? 6. *F* on the spot, (*in danger*) en danger/sur la corde raide; (*alert*) alerte/vif/ éveillé; (*immediately*) immédiatement/sur-le-champ/illico presto 7. to put s.o. on the spot, *P* assassiner* qn/descendre qn; *F* mettre qn dans une situation difficile/handicaper qn; *f* (*force to answer difficult questions*) mettre au pied du mur. (*See* **fivespot**; **highspots**; **hot 21**; **Johnny-on-the-spot**; **nightspot**; **tenspot**)

spotlight ['spɒtlaɪt] *vtr F* mettre en vedette.

spot-on ['spɒt'ɒn] *a F* dans le mille/qui fait mouche.

spout[1] [spaʊt] *n P* 1. *O* up the spout, en gage/chez ma tante 2. up the spout, perdu/ raté/fichu/foutu 3. *Br* up the spout, enceinte*/ en cloque; to put a girl up the spout, mettre une fille en cloque.

spout[2] [spaʊt] *vi F* to spout (off), parler*/ dégoiser/déblatérer/débiter; what's he spouting on about now? qu'est-ce qu'il est en train de débiter maintenant?

spread [spred] *n F* 1. repas copieux/ gueuleton *m* 2. middle-age(d) spread, la bedaine/la brioche qui vient avec l'âge; pneu *m* de secours de la quarantaine.

spring [sprɪŋ] I *vtr* 1. *P* faire libérer (qn) de prison*/cautionner (qn) 2. *P* faire évader (qn) de

prison*/arracher (qn) 3. *F* to spring sth on s.o., prendre qn au dépourvu avec qch II *vi F* where did you spring from? d'où sortez-vous? (*See* **leak**[1] 1)

spritz [sprɪts] *vtr F* vaporiser/atomiser; spritz some hairspray on your hair, vaporisez vos cheveux avec de la laque.

sprog [sprɒg] *n Br P* 1. recrue *f*/conscrit *m*/ bleu *m* 2. enfant*/mioche *mf*/moutard *m*.

sprout [spraʊt] *vtr F* to sprout wings, faire une bonne action/une *ou* sa B.A.; s'acheter une conduite/se ranger des voitures.

spruik ['spruːɪk] *vi Austr P* (*of street trader, etc*) faire l'article/faire du baratin/faire la postiche.

spruiker ['spruːɪkə] *n Austr P* 1. (*street trader*) camelot *m* 2. (*talkative person*) baratineur, -euse/jaspineur *m*/jacteur *m*.

sprung on ['sprʌŋɒn] *a NAm P* to be sprung on s.o., (*be infatuated with*) en pincer pour qn/être toqué de qn.

spud [spʌd] *n F* pomme *f* de terre/patate *f*.

spud-basher ['spʌdbæʃə] *n Br F Mil* éplucheur, -euse de pommes de terre.

spud-bashing ['spʌdbæʃɪŋ] *n Br F Mil* corvée *f* de patates/(corvée de) pluches *fpl*.

spug [spʌg], **spuggy** ['spʌgɪ] *n F* moineau *m*/piaf *m*.

spunk [spʌŋk] *n* 1. *V* sperme*/jus *m* 2. *P* courage *m*/cran *m*/estomac *m*; he's got no spunk, il n'a pas de couilles/il n'a rien dans le ventre; to put fresh spunk into sth, ravigoter qch 3. *Austr P* spunk (rat), jeune homme* *ou* jeune femme* sexy/qui en jette.

spunkless ['spʌŋklɪs] *a P* 1. amorphe/ larveux 2. poltron/froussard/sans couilles.

spunky ['spʌŋkɪ] *a F* courageux*/qui en a dans le bide/dans le ventre.

squaddie, squaddy ['skwɒdɪ] *n Br F Mil* soldat*/bidasse *m*.

square[1] [skweə] *F* I *a* 1. a square deal, une affaire* honnête/un coup réglo 2. a square meal, un bon repas 3. to be all square 4. vieux jeu/ démodé/ringard 5. honnête/réglo 6. to get square with s.o., (*get even*) régler ses comptes avec qn; (*settle bills, etc*) être quitte envers qn 7. to be a square peg in a round hole, ne pas être fait/taillé pour qch II *n* 1. to be back to square one, repartir à zéro/revenir à la case départ 2. bourgeois, -oise démodé(e)/ringard *m*; he's a square, il est tout à fait vieux jeu 3. individu* honnête/ réglo; franc *m* 4. on the square, droit/

honnête/comme il faut.

square² [skwɛə] *vtr F* (*a*) soudoyer/acheter/ graisser la patte à (qn) (*b*) obtenir la complicité de (qn); **I've squared it with the boss, j'ai arrangé ça avec le patron; it won't be difficult to square things with him,** je l'ai dans la manche. (*See* **rap¹ 2**)

square-basher ['skwɛəbæʃə] *n Br F Mil* soldat* à l'exercice.

square-bashing ['skwɛəbæʃɪŋ] *n Br F Mil* l'exercice *m*.

squarehead ['skwɛəhed] *n P* 1. Allemand*/boche *m* 2. = **square¹ II 2 3.** *Austr* criminel, -elle en liberté.

squaresville ['skwɛəzvɪl] *n P* société conformiste et bourgeoise.

square up ['skwɛər'ʌp] *vi F* 1. se mettre en posture de combat/se mettre en carante *ou* en quarante 2. **to square up to the facts,** faire face à la réalité/regarder les choses en face 3. **to square up with s.o.,** régler une affaire avec qn; (*get even with s.o.*) régler ses comptes avec qn.

square-wheeler ['skwɛə'wiːlə] *n P* voiture *f* difficile à vendre/rossignol *m*. (*See* **bottler**)

squarie ['skwɛərɪ] *n Austr P* = **square-head 3**. (*See* **half-squarie**)

squat [skwɒt] *n NAm P* 1. = **shit¹ IV 1 2. it's not worth squat,** ça ne vaut rien/ça ne vaut pas un pet.

squawk¹ [skwɔːk] *n P* 1. plainte *f*/ réclamation *f* 2. message *m* (à la) radio.

squawk² [skwɔːk] *vi P* 1. faire des aveux *mpl* (à la police)/se mettre à table 2. se plaindre / rouspéter / ronchonner / rouscailler/ renauder.

squeak¹ [skwiːk] *n* 1. *P* = **squealer 1, 2** 2. *F* **to have a narrow squeak,** l'échapper belle/ revenir de loin 3. *F* **I don't want to hear another squeak out of you,** je ne veux pas entendre le moindre murmure (de ta part)/je ne veux plus t'entendre 4. *Br F* minet, -ette. (*See* **bubble-and-squeak; pipsqueak**)

squeak² [skwiːk] *vi P* = **squeal² 1, 2.**

squeaker ['skwiːkə] *n P* = **squealer 1, 2.**

squeaky-clean ['skwiːkɪ'kliːn] *a F* propre comme un sou neuf; (*person*) blanc/à la réputation sans tache.

squeal¹ [skwiːl] *n P* = **squealer 1, 2.**

squeal² [skwiːl] *vi P* 1. avouer*/manger le morceau/accoucher/vider son sac 2. mou-charder/vendre la mèche; **to squeal on s.o.,** dénoncer*/balancer/cafarder/donner qn.

squealer ['skwiːlə] *n P* 1. dénonciateur*/ cafardeur, -euse/indic *mf*/mouchard, -arde/ donneur, -euse 2. rouspéteur, -euse/ ronchonneur, -euse.

squeeze¹ [skwiːz] *n* 1. *F* (*pressure*) **to put the squeeze on s.o.,** forcer la main à qn 2. *F* **tight squeeze, foule** *f*/cohue *f*; **it was a tight squeeze,** on tenait tout juste 3. *Br P* argent*/ fric *m*/pognon *m* 4. *NAm P* **main squeeze,** petit(e) ami(e) copain, copine 5. *P* soie *f*.

squeeze² [skwiːz] *vtr F* **to squeeze s.o.** = **to put the squeeze on s.o.** (**squeeze¹ 1**). (*See* **lemon 5**)

squeezebox ['skwiːzbɒks] *n F* 1. concertina *f* 2. accordéon *m*.

squelch [skweltʃ] *n Austr P* impair *m*/gaffe *f*/bourde *f*.

squiff [skwɪf] *n Austr F* 1. ivrogne*/ soûlard(e) 2. (*drinking bout*) beuverie *f*/ soûlerie *f*.

squiffy ['skwɪfɪ] *F* 1. légèrement ivre*/paf 2. de travers/biscornu/tordu 3. bête*/cruche.

squillion ['skwɪljən] *n Br F* (*huge number*) mille milliards.

squint¹ [skwɪnt] *n P* coup d'œil*/coup *m* de châsse; **let's have a squint at it!** fais voir! **take a squint at that!** zyeute-moi ça!/vise-moi ça!

squint² [skwɪnt] *vi P* (*a*) regarder*/jeter un coup d'œil* (*b*) **to squint at sth,** regarder* qch de côté/furtivement; zyeuter/mater qch.

squirly ['skwɜːlɪ] *a NAm P* nerveux/agité.

squirt [skwɜːt] *n P* 1. (*obnoxious person*) freluquet *m*/merdaillon *m*; **little squirt!** petit morveux! 2. rafale *f* de mitraillette/purée *f*.

squish [skwɪʃ] *n* 1. *F* boue *f*/mouscaille *f*/ gadouille *f* 2. *P* confiture *f* d'orange.

squishy ['skwɪʃɪ] *a F* détrempé/bourbeux/ gadouilleux.

squit [skwɪt] *n P* 1. = **squirt 1** 2. *pl* diarrhée*/courante *f*/chiasse *f*.

squitters ['skwɪtəz] *npl P* 1. diarrhée*/ courante *f*/chiasse *f* 2. **to have the squitters,** avoir peur*/avoir les foies *mpl*/avoir les jetons *mpl*/faire dans son froc.

stab [stæb] *n F* **to have a stab (at sth),** faire un essai/tenter le coup.

stable-companion ['steɪblkəm'pænjən] *n F* membre *m* d'une même société, bande*, etc.

stack [stæk] **I** *a F* 1. excellent*/super/canon/ génial 2. (*inferior, negative*) minable/nul **II** *adv F* **stack!** (*no way!*) balpeau!/des clous!/ que dalle! **III** *n* 1. *F* (*a*) **to have a stack/**

stacks **of money**, être très riche*/être plein aux as/avoir le sac (b) **to have a stack/stacks of work**, avoir beaucoup de travail*/avoir du pain sur la planche 2. *P* **to blow one's stack** = to blow one's top (**top**[1] II 2) 3. *F Aut* **twin stacks**, double pot *m* d'échappement.

stacked [stækt] *a P* = **well-stacked 1, 2**.

stag [stæg] *n F* 1. célibataire *m*/vieux garçon; **stag party**, réunion *f* pour hommes seulement/P.H.S. *m*; **to have a stag party/ night**, enterrer sa vie de garçon 2. (*Stock Exchange*) (*premium hunter*) loup *m*.

stager ['steɪdʒə] *n F* **an old stager**, un vieux routier/un vieux de la vieille.

staggers ['stægəz] *npl F* **to have the staggers**, chanceler/tituber/avoir du vent dans les voiles.

stakeout ['steɪkaʊt] *n P* 1. lieu sûr/planque *f*/cachette *f*/planquouse *f* 2. maison de criminel, etc, surveillée/embusquée par la police.

stake out ['steɪk'aʊt] *vtr P* surveiller/ embusquer/faire la planque dans (un lieu).

stalk [stɔːk] *n P* pénis*/queue *f*.

stall [stɔːl] *n P* complice *mf* d'un voleur/à la tire/carreur *m*/mur *m*.

stallion ['stæljən] *n F* = **stud**.

stamping ground ['stæmpɪŋɡraʊnd] *n F* lieu *m* que l'on fréquente/coin favori; **that's my old stamping ground**, c'est ici que j'ai usé mes fonds de culotte/c'est mon terrain de chasse/j'ai mes racines dans le coin.

stand[1] [stænd] *n* 1. *F* (*jazz, rock, etc*) (one-night) **stand**, représentation *f* d'un soir 2. *P* **one-night stand**, (*casual sex*) coup *m* 3. *P* **to have a stand**, être en érection*/avoir le bambou. (*See* **one-nighter**)

stand[2] [stænd] *vtr F* 1. **to stand s.o. a drink**, offrir un verre/une tournée à qn; **I'm standing this one**, c'est ma tournée/c'est moi qui paie 2. = **stick**[2] **8**. (*See* **gaff 4**; **racket 3**)

standover ['stændəʊvə] *n Austr P* **standover man/merchant**, extorqueur *m*/racketteur *m*.

stand over ['stænd'əʊvə] *vtr & i Austr F* extorquer de l'argent/faire cracher/faire casquer/mettre à l'amende/racketter.

stand(-)up ['stændʌp] *a NAm F* a **stand(-)up guy**, un mec honnête/réglo.

stand up ['stænd'ʌp] *vtr F* 1. faire attendre* (qn)/faire poireauter (qn) 2. (*fail to meet*) planter là/poser un lapin à (qn).

star [stɑː] *n F* 1. **to see stars**, voir trente-six chandelles 2. **there's a star in the east, ta** braguette est ouverte; on voit le moteur.

stare [stɛə] *vtr F* **it's staring you in the face**, ça (vous) saute aux yeux/ça se voit comme le nez au milieu de la figure.

star-fucker ['stɑːfʌkə] *n V* = **groupie 1**.

starkers ['stɑːkəz] *a P* **starkers**/*O* **Harry starkers**, tout nu*/à poil/à loilpé/cul nul/ défrusqué.

starry-eyed ['stɑːrɪ'aɪd] *a F* extasié/qui voit tout en rose.

stash[1] [stæʃ] *n P* (*drugs*) 1. cachette *f*/lieu sûr/planque *f*/planquouse *f*; **stash man**, carreur *m*/fourgue *m* (*pour des marchandises volées, des drogues, etc*) 2. provision *f* (de drogues).

stash[2] [stæʃ] *vtr P* 1. cacher*/planquer/ planquouser 2. arrêter/finir/lâcher les pédales; **stash it!** arrête!/écrase!

stash away ['stæʃə'weɪ] *vtr P* 1. = **stash**[2] **1** 2. accumuler/amasser/entasser (de l'argent, etc).

stashed [stæʃt] *a F* (**well**) **stashed**, riche*/ plein aux as/friqué/rupin.

state [steɪt] *n Br F* 1. **to be in a (bit of a) state**, être dans tous ses états; **to get into a terrible state**, (*get upset*) se mettre dans tous ses états; (*look terrible*) avoir une tronche/ une touche pas possible 2. **to look a state**, avoir l'air lamentable/pitoyable.

static ['stætɪk] *n NAm P* (*cricitism*) critique *f*/débinage *m*; (*hostile interference*) intrusion *f* hostile.

statistics [stə'tɪstɪks] *npl F* **vital statistics**, mensurations *fpl* d'une femme (*poitrine, taille, hanches*)/(beau) châssis.

stay [steɪ] *vi P* (*maintain an erection*) garder la trique en l'air/marquer midi.

stay loose ['steɪ'luːs] *vi NAm P* = **hang loose**.

steady ['stedɪ] *F* I *adv* **to go steady**, se fréquenter/sortir ensemble II *n* petit(e) ami(e)/l'attitré(e)/régulier, -ière.

steal [stiːl] *n P* 1. (*bargain*) occasion *f*/ occase *f* 2. = **pushover**.

steam [stiːm] *n F* 1. **to let/to blow off steam**, (*use up excess energy*) dépenser son trop-plein d'énergie/se défouler; (*emotionally*) donner libre cours à ses sentiments/se defouler; (*work off anger*) passer sa colère/se défouler 2. **to get up steam**, rassembler toute son énergie; (*get excited*) s'exciter/s'emballer 3. **steam radio**, la TSF des familles/la vieille radio/la radio de l'an quarante.

steamed [stiːmd] *a NAm F* en colère*/en

pétard.

steamed up ['sti:md'ʌp] *a & pp F* to get (all) steamed up (*a*) s'exciter/s'emballer (*b*) se mettre en colère*/mousser/se mettre en pétard.

steamer ['sti:mə] *n Br P* 1. (*from: RS = steam jug = mug*) individu bête*/con *m*, conne *f*/couillon *m* 2. *pl* steamers, bande(s) *f(pl)* d'agresseurs qui entrent dans un magasin/un compartiment, etc en masse pour attaquer leurs victimes.

steaming ['sti:mɪŋ] I *a Br F O* a steaming idiot/twit, un crétin/un couillon achevé/fini II *n* attaque *f* d'une bande d'agresseurs.

steamy ['sti:mɪ] *a F* érotique/chaud/sexy; well steamy, vachement sexy. (*See* **well**)

steep [sti:p] *a F* 1. trop cher*/exorbitant/ excessif/salé 2. (*excessive*) fort/raide; that's a bit steep! c'est un peu fort de café!

steer[1] [stɪə] *n F* renseignement*/tuyau *m*. (*See* **bum**[1] I)

steer[2] [stɪə] *vi P* amorcer les clients (*pour tripot, casino, etc*).

steerer ['stɪərə] *n P* rabatteur, -euse/ racoleur, -euse de clients (*pour bordels, etc*).

step[1] [step] *n* 1. *P* up the steps, (*committed for trial*) renvoyé aux Assises/aux Assiettes 2. *F* all the steps: *see* **bingo 39**. (*See* **doorstep**[1])

step[2] [step] *vi F* 1. to step outside, sortir pour se battre*/aller régler ça dehors 2. *Aut* to step on it, (*accelerate*) accélérer/appuyer sur le champignon; (*hurry up*) se dépêcher*/ se grouiller/se magner; step on it! allez, magne-toi! (*See* **doorstep**[2]; **gas**[1] II 2)

step in ['step'ɪn] *vi F* intervenir; s'interposer.

step on ['step'ɒn] *vtr P* adultérer/couper (une drogue, *surt* cocaïne* *ou* héroïne*).

step-up ['stepʌp] *n F* promotion *f*/ avancement *m*.

stern [stɜ:n] *n F* fesses*/postérieur *m*/ arrière-train *m*.

stew[1] [stju:] *n F* in a stew, (*in a state*) sur des charbons ardents/sur le gril/dans tous ses états; *NAm* en colère*/à cran; to work oneself (up) into a stew, se mettre en colère/en rogne.

stew[2] [stju:] *vi F* to stew in one's own juice, cuire/mijoter dans son jus.

stewed [stju:d] *a P* ivre*/rétamé. (*See* **gills 1; half-stewed**)

stick[1] [stɪk] *n* 1. *Br F* to give s.o. stick, ré- primander* qn/engueuler qn/sonner les clo- ches à qn; (*physical punishment*) flanquer

une dégelée à qn; to take a lot of stick, se faire critiquer/déglinguer; (*be mocked*) se faire mettre en boîte 2. *F* the sticks, (*coun- tryside*) la campagne*/le bled/la cambrousse; (*suburbs*) la banlieue 3. *P* (*drugs*) cigarette* de marijuana*/stick *m*. (*See* **cancer-stick**) 4. *P* pince-monseigneur*/jacques *m* 5. *F* bâton *m* d'agent de police*/matraque *f*/tricotin *m* 6. *V* pénis*/trique *f* 7. *F* (*a*) a queer stick, un drôle de type/de zigoto/de zèbre (*b*) he's a good old stick, c'est un brave zigue (*c*) a dry old stick, un(e) pince-sans-rire 8. *Br P* up the stick, enceinte*/en cloque 9. *NAm F* planche *f* (de surf). (*See* **drumstick; end 11; fiddlesticks; joystick; shitstick; up**[2] 1)

stick[2] [stɪk] *vtr & i* 1. *F* mettre/placer/coller; stick it in your pocket, fourre-toi ça dans la poche 2. *F* to stick to sth, persévérer/ s'accrocher à qch 3. *P* you know where you can stick that, tu sais où tu peux te le mettre!/tu peux te le mettre (là) où je pense! stick it! va te faire voir!/et mon cul c'est du poulet! (*See* **arse I 7; flue 1; gonga; jumper; Khyber**) 4. *F* to get stuck with s.o., avoir qn de collé à soi/avoir qn sur le dos; we're stuck with it, il faut s'y résigner 5. *F* to be stuck on s.o., être amoureux de qn/en pincer pour qn/être entiché de qn 6. *F* to stick with s.o., se cramponner à qn/soutenir qn 7. *F* to make sth stick, faire respecter (un ordre, etc) 8. *F* supporter/endurer/souffrir; to stick it, tenir le coup/tenir bon; I can't stick it any longer, je n'en peux plus; I can't stick him (at any price), je ne peux pas le sentir/le blairer 9. *P* to stick one on s.o., battre* qn/rosser qn/ filer une peignée à qn. (*See* **gun**[1] 4)

stick around ['stɪkə'raʊnd] *vi F* attendre* sur place/poireauter; to stick around the house all day, traîner dans la maison toute la journée; stick around! I'll be back in five minutes, bouge pas! je reviens dans cinq minutes.

stick down ['stɪk'daʊn] *vtr F* 1. stick it down anywhere, collez-le n'importe où. (*See* **stick**[2] 1) 2. to stick sth down in a notebook, inscrire/noter qch dans un carnet.

sticker ['stɪkə] *n F* 1. individu* persévérant 2. problème *m* difficile/colle *f*/casse-tête *m*.

stick in ['stɪk'ɪn] *vtr* 1. *F* to get stuck in, (*start working*) s'y mettre; (*start eating*) se mettre à manger/casser la croûte; let's get stuck in! alors, on s'y met! 2. *V* to stick it in, faire l'amour*/se baguer le nœud.

stick-in-the-mud ['stɪkɪnðəmʌd] I *a F*

(*attitude*) réac/rétro II *n F* he's an old stick-in-the-mud, c'est un vieux réac/il retarde (sur son siècle).

stick out ['stɪk'aʊt] *vi & tr F* 1. to stick out for higher wages, s'obstiner à demander une augmentation de salaire 2. to stick it out, tenir jusqu'au bout 3. she sticks out in all the right places, elle est bien carrossée/elle est bien culbutée/c'est une belle pièce. (*See* **neck¹ 3; thumb¹ 4**)

sticksing ['stɪksɪŋ] *n Br P* (*Black Slang*) (*pickpocketing*) vol *m* à la tire.

stick-up ['stɪkʌp] *n F* vol *m* à main armée/braquage *m*/hold-up *m*.

stick up ['stɪk'ʌp] *F* I *vtr* attaquer* *ou* voler à main armée/braquer; stick 'em up! haut les mains! II *vi* to stick up for s.o., prendre la défense/le parti de qn.

sticky ['stɪkɪ] *a F* 1. (*awkward*) peu accommodant; (*problem*) difficile; is he being sticky about it? est-ce qu'il fait des histoires (à ce sujet)? 2. to have sticky fingers, être voleur/être poisse/ne rien laisser traîner. (*See* **sticky-fingered**) 3. *Br* to be on a sticky wicket, agir lorsqu'il y a peu de chance de réussir/marcher sur un terrain glissant; être dans le pétrin/être dans de mauvais draps.

stickybeak ['stɪkɪbiːk] *n Austr F* curieux, -euse/fouineur, -euse/fouille-merde *mf*.

sticky-fingered ['stɪkɪ'fɪŋɡəd] *a F* qui y met les doigts. (*See* **sticky 2**)

stiff¹ [stɪf] I *a* 1. *P* mort/raidard 2. *P* ivre*/raide 3. *F* that's a bit stiff! c'est un peu fort! (*See* **lip 2**) II *adv F* 1. to bore s.o. stiff, ennuyer qn à mourir/scier (le dos à) qn 2. to be scared stiff, avoir une peur* bleue III *n P* 1. cadavre*/macchab(ée) *m*/refroidi *m* 2. ivrogne*/poivrot, -ote 3. (*very conventional person*) réac *mf* 4. individu*/type *m*/mec *m*; (*esp to be pitied*) pauvre con *m*; working stiff, travailleur*/bosseur *m* 5. lettre de prisonnier passée en fraude 6. cheval* certain de perdre/fer *m* à repasser/mort *m* 7. *NAm* clochard*/clodo *m*/stiff *m* 8. (*failure, flop*) échec *m*/fiasque *m*/flop *m*. (*See* **big I 9; bindle 3**)

stiff² [stɪf] *P* I *vtr* 1. tuer*/refroidir 2. tromper*/arnaquer/rouler 3. ignorer/snober II *vi* échouer*/faire un bide.

stiffener ['stɪf(ə)nə] *n F* boisson alcoolisée/remontant *m*/raide *m*.

stiffie, stiffy ['stɪfɪ] *n Br* 1. *P* (pénis* en) érection*/canne *f*/trique *f*; to crack a stiffie, être en érection*/bander/marquer midi 2. *F*

carte *f* d'invitation.

sting¹ [stɪŋ] *n NAm P* (*confidence trick*) entourloupe *f*/arnaque *f*.

sting² [stɪŋ] *vtr F* to sting s.o. for £50, rouler qn en lui faisant payer 50 livres; to be/to get stung, essuyer le coup de fusil; se faire écorcher/estamper/arnaquer; he stung me for ten quid, il m'a tapé/torpillé de dix livres.

stinger ['stɪŋə] *n F* 1. coup* cinglant/torgnole *f* 2. (*a*) méduse *f* (*b*) torpille *f* 3. (*cocktail*) crème *f* de menthe et cognac.

stink¹ [stɪŋk] *n* 1. *P* (*trouble*) to raise/to kick up a stink, faire de l'esclandre *m*/du grabuge; there's going to be a hell of a stink, il va y avoir du grabuge/ça va chauffer/ça va chier 2. *P* to work like stink, travailler* dur/bûcher/se fouler la rate/bosser.

stink² [stɪŋk] *vi* 1. *P* être un vrai salaud*; he (positively) stinks! c'est un type infect! 2. *F* puer/empester/(s)chlinguer; to stink of money, puer le fric; what do you think of it? – it stinks! qu'en dis-tu? – c'est merdique!/dégueulasse!

stinkbomb ['stɪŋkbɒm] *n F* boule puante.

stinker ['stɪŋkə] *n F* 1. individu* méprisable/salaud*/ordure *f* 2. individu* qui sent* mauvais/qui pue 3. to write s.o. a stinker, (*unpleasant letter*) écrire une lettre carabinée à qn 4. rhume carabiné 5. the English paper was a stinker, on a eu une sale composition d'anglais 6. cigare* *ou* cigarette* bon marché 7. *Austr* = **scorcher 1**.

stinking ['stɪŋkɪŋ] *a* 1. *F* stinking (rich)/stinking with money, très riche*/plein aux as 2. *P* ivre*/blindé 3. *F* puant/empesté; (*disgusting*) dégueulasse 4. *F* stinking weather, temps *m* de cochon/de chien; a stinking cold, un rhume carabiné.

stink-list ['stɪŋklɪst] *n P* to have s.o. on one's stink-list, avoir qn dans le nez/ne pas pouvoir blairer qn. (*See* **shit-list**)

stinko ['stɪŋkəʊ] *a P* = **stinking 2**.

stinkpot ['stɪŋkpɒt] *n O P* saligaud *m*/salopard *m*.

stir¹ [stɜː] *n P* prison*/bloc *m*/taule *f*; in stir, en prison/à l'ombre; stir crazy, fou*/détraqué à force d'être en taule.

stir² [stɜː] *vtr F* to stir it = to stir it up (**stir up**). (*See* **stumps**)

stirrer ['stɜːrə] *n Br F* agitateur, -trice/fomentateur, -trice de difficultés/mauvais coucheur/fouteur, -euse de merde.

stir up ['stɜːr'ʌp] *vtr F* to stir it up, fomenter la discorde/remuer les eaux

troubles/mettre sa merde (quelque part)/
semer la merde.

stitch up ['stɪtʃ'ʌp] *vtr Br P* (faire)
accuser (qn) à tort/farguer (qn)/monter un
coup contre (qn)/faire porter le bada à (qn).

stodge¹ [stɒdʒ] *n Br F* aliment bourratif/
étouffe-chrétien *m*.

stodge² [stɒdʒ] *vi F* manger*
abondamment/se goinfrer/se caler les joues
fpl/s'empiffrer.

stogie ['stəʊgɪ] *n NAm F* cigare*/barreau *m*
de chaise.

stoked [stəʊkt] *a F* excité/exalté.

stoke up ['stəʊk'ʌp] *vi F* manger* de bon
cœur/bouffer.

stomach ['stʌmək] *vtr F* endurer/
supporter/tolérer/digérer; **I can't stomach
that guy**, je (ne) peux pas le gober, ce mec/il
me fait gerber, ce mec.

stone¹ [stəʊn] *n P* (*state of s.o. under the influence of cannabis*) défonce *f*.

stone² [stəʊn] *vtr O Br F* **stone me!**/**stone
the crows!** ça alors!

stone-cold ['stəʊn'kəʊld] *adv F* **I've got
him stone-cold**, je le tiens (à ma merci)/il me
mange dans la main. (*See* **cold I 1**)

stoned [stəʊnd] *a P* (*a*) ivre*/raide (*b*)
drogué*/camé/chargé/stone(d).

stones [stəʊnz] *npl P* 1. testicules*/burettes
fpl/roubignoles *fpl* 2. bijoux *mpl*/cailloux
mpl/joncaille *f*.

stone's throw ['stəʊnzθrəʊ] *n F* **just a
stone's throw from here**, à deux pas d'ici.

stonewall ['stəʊn'wɔːl] *vi F* donner des
réponses évasives; faire de l'obstruction/
répondre à côté; faire la politique de
l'escargot.

stoney ['stəʊnɪ] *a F* = **stony**.

stonker ['stɒŋkə] *n Br P* (*sth stunning*) qch
de super/de sensass/de canon.

stonkered ['stɒŋkəd] *a Austr P* 1. ivre*/
beurré/blindé 2. (*exhausted*) fatigué/claqué/
crevé; (*destroyed*) fini/foutu; **I'm stonkered**,
je suis cuit/foutu/naze; c'est râpé pour moi.

stony ['stəʊnɪ] *a F* **stony (broke)**, archi-
pauvre*/à sec/dans la dèche/fauché comme les
blés.

stooge [stuːdʒ] *n Br F esp Pej* 1. (*police
jargon*) remplaçant, -ante innocent(e) dans
une séance d'identification d'un suspect 2.
individu* trop serviable/ramasse-boulot *m* 3.
(*theatre*) comparse *mf*/faire-valoir *m*.

stook [ʃtʊk] *n Br P* = **schtu(c)k**.

stoolie ['stuːlɪ], **stool-pigeon** ['stuːl-

pɪdʒɪn] *n F* indicateur*/indic *mf*/mouchard,
-arde.

stop by ['stɒp'baɪ] *vtr & i F* rendre visite (à
qn)/entrer en passant/passer chez qn/faire un
saut chez qn.

stopoff ['stɒpɒf] *n F* escale *f*/(point *m*
d')arrêt *m*/halte *f*.

stop off ['stɒp'ɒf] *vi F* faire étape/faire
halte; **to stop off in London**, faire étape à Londres.

stopover ['stɒpəʊvə] *n F* arrêt *m* (au cours
d'un voyage).

stop over ['stɒp'əʊvə] *vi F* interrompre son
voyage/s'arrêter/faire étape.

stopper ['stɒpə] *n F* **to put the stopper on
sth**, mettre fin à qch.

stork [stɔːk] *n F* **a visit from the stork**,
l'arrivée *f* d'un bébé/une visite de la cigogne.

story ['stɔːrɪ] *n F* mensonge*/craque *f*; **to tell
stories**, mentir*/raconter des bobards *mpl*.
(*See* **sob-story**; **tall 2**)

storyteller ['stɔːrɪtelə] *n F* menteur, -euse/
baratineur, -euse/vanneur *m*.

stotious ['stəʊʃəs] *a Br P* ivre*/blindé/
rétamé.

stoush¹ [staʊʃ] *n Austr P* bagarre *f*/castagne
f/rififi *m*/baston *m* ou *f*.

stoush² [staʊʃ] *vtr Austr P* battre* (qn)/
casser la gueule à (qn)/arranger le portrait à
(qn).

stove [stəʊv] *n P Aut* chauffage *m*.

stovepipe ['stəʊvpaɪp] *n* 1. *A F* chapeau*
haut-de-forme/tuyau *m* de poêle 2. *NAm P*
avion *m* de chasse à réaction.

stow [stəʊ] *vtr P* **stow it!** c'est marre!/y en
a marre!/ferme ça!/arrête ton char(re)!

strafe [strɑːf] *vtr F* réprimander*/passer un
savon à (qn)/engueuler (qn).

strafing ['strɑːfɪŋ] *n F* réprimande *f*/bon
savon/engueulade *f*.

straight [streɪt] I *a* 1. *F* (*cigarette, tobacco*)
ordinaire (sans narcotiques); (*alcoholic
drink*) sec/pur/sans eau 2. *P* (*person*)
honnête/réglo/nickel 3. *P* hétérosexuel/hétéro
4. *P* qui ne se drogue pas/qui n'est pas sous
l'influence de drogues 5. *F* **straight man** =
stooge 3. (*See* **straight up**; **ticket 3**) II
adv **to go straight** (*a*) *F* marcher droit/suivre
le droit chemin (*b*) *P* se désintoxiquer/lâcher
la guenon. (*See* **horse 2**) III *n* 1. *P*
hétérosexuel(le)/hétéro *mf* 2. *P* individu*
honnête *ou* réglo (et vieux jeu) 3. *F* **to act on
the straight**, agir loyalement 4. *F* **to follow the
straight**/**to go on the straight and narrow**, se

conduire honnêtement; marcher droit.

straighten ['streɪtn] *vtr* P soudoyer/acheter/graisser la patte à (qn).

straightened-out ['streɪtnd'aʊt] *a & pp* P *Euph* corrompu/pourri/ripou; he got straightened-out, on lui a graissé la patte. (*See* **bent 1**)

straighten out ['streɪtn'aʊt] I *vtr* 1. P to straighten s.o. out = to put s.o. wise (**wise**) 2. F to straighten things out, arranger les choses II *vi* F 1 expect that things will straighten out, je pense que ça va s'arranger.

straight up ['streɪt'ʌp] *a* F honnête/régulier/réglo; straight up! sans blague!/sans déconner!

strain [streɪn] *vtr Austr* P to strain the potatoes, uriner*/lancequiner.

strangle ['stræŋgl] *vtr Austr* P to strangle a darkie, déféquer*/couler un bronze.

strap [stræp] *n Br* P on the strap, à crédit/à croume/à l'œil. (*See* **jock-strap**)

strap-hanger ['stræphæŋə] *n* F voyageur, -euse debout (*dans le métro, le train, etc*).

strapped [stræpt] *a* F to be strapped (for cash), être à court d'argent/être fauché.

straw [strɔ:] *n* F 1. that's the last straw, ça c'est le comble!/c'est la fin des haricots!/il ne manquait plus que ça! 2. it's the last straw that breaks the camel's back, (*catchphrase*) c'est la dernière goutte (d'eau) qui fait déborder le vase.

strawberry ['strɔ:b(ə)rɪ] *n NAm* P prostituée*/raccrocheuse *f* qui se prostitue pour de la drogue.

stray [streɪ] *n* P to have a bit/piece of stray = to have a bit on the side (**side 2**).

streak¹ [stri:k] *n* F 1. a losing streak, une période de malchance*/série noire (au jeu); a winning streak, une période de chance* 2. promenade *f* tout nu*/à poil (en public) 3. a long streak of misery, qn qui boude/qui fait la gueule. (*See* **piss¹ 3; yellow I 1**)

streak² [stri:k] *vi* F 1. se promener *ou* courir tout nu*/à poil (en public) 2. aller à toute vitesse/gazer.

streaker ['stri:kə] *n* F coureur, -euse nu(e) (en public).

street [stri:t] *F* I *n* 1. to be streets ahead of s.o., avoir plusieurs rames d'avance sur qn 2. it's right up your street, ça te connaît/c'est ton rayon/c'est ton truc. (*See* **alley**) 3. the horse won by a street, le cheval a gagné dans un fauteuil 4. it's not in the same street, ce n'est pas du même acabit/du même tonneau 5. to

be on the streets, racoler*/faire le trottoir 6. to have street cred(ibility), être averti/branché/chébran/câblé II *a NAm* = streetwise. (*See* **easy I 1; sunny 1**)

street-suss ['stri:tsʌs] *a* F = **streetwise**.

streetwise ['stri:twaɪz] *a* F averti/branché/chébran/câblé/affranchi.

stretch¹ [stretʃ] *n* P to do a stretch, faire de la prison*/faire une longe/être à l'ombre/être au ballon; he was given a stretch, on l'a mis au trou; to get a twenty-year stretch, tirer vingt piges/longes. (*See* **homestretch**)

stretch² [stretʃ] *vtr* F that's stretching it a bit, c'est un peu tiré par les cheveux.

strewth! [stru:θ] *excl* P (*abbr of God's truth*) sacrebleu!/sapristi!/mince (alors)!

strides [straɪdz] *npl* P pantalon*/falzar *m*/grimpant *m*/futal *m*.

strike [straɪk] *vtr* F strike a light! morbleu! strike me pink! tu m'assois! (*See* **heap 1; rich II; struck**)

strine [straɪn] *n* F la langue *ou* la prononciation australienne.

string [strɪŋ] *n* F 1. to have s.o. on a (piece of) string, mener qn par le bout du nez 2. no strings attached, sans obligations/sans à-côtés/sans os 3. to pull (the) strings, faire jouer le piston. (*See* **apron strings; G-string; shoestring**)

string along ['strɪŋə'lɒŋ] *vtr & i* F 1. (*deceitfully encourage*) tromper*/faire marcher/mener en bateau; they're just stringing you along, ils sont en train de te faire marcher 2. to string along with s.o., accompagner/faire route avec qn.

string out ['strɪŋ'aʊt] *vtr & i* F faire traîner (qch) en longueur. (*See* **strung out**)

string up ['strɪŋ'ʌp] *vtr* F pendre/béquiller (un condamné). (*See* **strung up**)

strip¹ [strɪp] *n* F 1. to tear s.o. off a strip, réprimander* qn/passer un shampooing à qn/sonner les cloches à qn 2. strip show, spectacle *m* de nu/strip-tease *m*; strip poker, strip-poker *m*/strip *m*.

strip² [strɪp] *vtr* F *Mil* faire perdre ses galons *mpl*/dégrader.

stripe [straɪp] *n* F cicatrice *f*/balafre *f*/marquouse *f*.

strip off ['strɪp'ɒf] *vi* F se déshabiller*/se mettre à poil/se désaper.

stripper ['strɪpə] *n* F strip-teaseuse *f*/effeuilleuse *f*; male stripper, strip-teaseur *m*.

stroke [strəʊk] *n* P sale coup *m*/coup (en) vache/coup en traître; to pull a stroke, faire une vacherie/un coup en vache.

strong-arm¹ ['strɒŋɑːm] *a F* strong-arm man, (*strong*) homme fort/fortiche *m*/balèze *m*; (*violent*) dur *m*/saignant *m*; strong-arm tactics, manœuvres *fpl* à la matraque/la manière forte.

strong-arm² ['strɒŋɑːm] *vtr NAm F* forcer (qn) à faire qch/employer la manière forte avec (qn).

strongbox ['strɒŋbɒks] *n Br F* cellule *f* de régime (d'isolement) cellulaire/mitard *m*/ cachot *m*.

stroppy ['strɒpɪ] *a P* de mauvaise humeur/à cran/de mauvais poil; don't get stroppy with me! ne la ramène pas avec moi!

struck [strʌk] *a & pp F* to be/to get struck on s.o., (*c.o.*, aimer* qn/s'enticher de qn/en pincer pour qn/être dingue/toqué de qn; to be struck on sth, être frappé/impressionné par qch; I'm not all that struck on it, ça ne me dit pas grand chose. (*See* **cunt-struck**; **strike**)

strung out ['strʌŋ'aut] *a* 1. *F* tendu/ énervé/qui a les glandes/à cran 2. *P* (*drugs*) drogué*/camé/défoncé; (*suffering from withdrawal*) en manque*; he's strung out, il flippe.

strung up ['strʌŋ'ʌp] *a & pp* 1. *F* to be strung up, être pendu/béquillé. (*See* **string up**) 2. *F & P* = **strung out 1, 2**.

strut [strʌt] *vtr P* to strut one's stuff, (*walk around self-importantly*) parader/frimer/se faire valoir; (*do one's thing*) faire son truc.

struth! [struːθ] *excl P* = **strewth!**

stubby ['stʌbɪ] *n Austr P* petite bouteille de bière/can(n)ette *f*.

stuck [stʌk] *a F* en panne/en rade. (*See* **stick⁴ 2, 4, 5; stick in 1**)

stuck-up ['stʌk'ʌp] *a F* snob; (*conceited*) prétentieux*/crâneur/bêcheur; she's a stuck-up bitch, c'est une crâneuse/une bêcheuse; elle se croit sortie de la cuisse de Jupiter.

stud [stʌd] *n F* mâle *m*/mec *m*/macho *m*; he's a real stud, c'est un sacré pointeur/il jette du jus/c'est un sacré baiseur.

stuff¹ [stʌf] *n* 1. *F* to know one's stuff, être capable/s'y connaître/être à la hauteur/ connaître son truc 2. *F* that's the stuff (to give the troops)! voilà ce qu'il faut (pour remonter la République)! 3. *P* a nice bit of stuff, (*pretty*) une belle pépée/une nana bien carrossée; (*sexy*) une nana autichante; he's a nice bit of stuff, il est classe; his bit of stuff, sa petite amie 4. *P* (*drugs*) drogues*/stups *mpl*/came *f* 5. *P* butin*/camelote *f*/prise *f* 6. *F* to do one's stuff, faire ce qu'on doit/faire son

boulot; go on, do your stuff! allez, au turbin! 7. *NAm F* the right stuff, qualités *fpl* solides; héroïsme *m*. (*See* **green I 6; heavy I 5; rough I 6; sob-stuff; strut; white I 1**)

stuff² [stʌf] *vtr* 1. *V* faire l'amour* avec (qn)/bourrer/égoïner 2. *P* get stuffed! va te faire voir!/va te faire foutre! 3. *Br P* you can stuff it (up your arse)! tu peux te le mettre là où je pense; stuff this job! j'en ai marre de ce boulot! stuff this, I'm going home! et puis merde, je rentre chez moi! 4. *F* to stuff oneself/one's face, manger* abondamment/se goinfrer/s'empiffrer. (*See* **shirt 5**)

stuffing ['stʌfɪŋ] *n F* to knock the stuffing out of s.o. (*a*) battre qn à plate(s) couture(s)/ flanquer une tripotée à qn/étriper qn (*b*) désarçonner/démonter/dégonfler qn; mettre qn à plat.

stuffy ['stʌfɪ] *a F* (*standoffish*) collet monté; (*over-conventional*) vieux jeu; don't be so stuffy, il n'y a pas de quoi se scandaliser.

stum [stʌm] *a P* = **shtum**.

stumer ['stjuːmə] *n P* 1. chose *f* sans valeur/camelote *f*/drouille *f* 2. chèque *m*; *surt* chèque sans provision/chèque en bois 3. bévue*/boulette *f*/bourde *f*; to make a bit of a stumer, faire une gaffe 4. (*esp horse*) perdant *m*/toquard *m* 5. (*worthless individual*) raté, ée/paumé, -ée 6. faillite *f*/banqueroute *f*.

stump [stʌmp] *vtr F* coller (qn)/réduire (qn) à quia; to stump s.o. on sth, faire sécher qn sur qch; that really stumped me, sur le coup je n'ai su que répondre/ça m'a cloué le bec.

stumps [stʌmps] *npl F* jambes*/guibolles *fpl*; to stir one's stumps, se dépêcher*/se décarcasser/se remuer.

stump up ['stʌmp'ʌp] *vi F* payer*/les abouler/cracher/casquer.

stunned [stʌnd] *a NAm P* ivre*/fadé/ rétamé/rond.

stunner ['stʌnə] *n F* (*a*) qn d'irrésistible *ou* de formidable/(*woman*)/prix *m* de Diane (*man*) Apollon *m*; she's a real stunner, elle est vachement belle/c'est un vrai canon (*b*) chose épatante/truc *m* sensas(s).

stunning ['stʌnɪŋ] *a F* (*a*) excellent*/ formid(able)/épatant (*b*) très beau*/ ravissant/irrésistible.

stupe [st(j)uːp] *n NAm P* individu bête*/ cruche *f*/andouille *f*.

stymie, stymy ['staɪmɪ] *vtr F* entraver/ gêner/contrecarrer; I'm completely stymied, je suis dans une impasse/je suis coincé.

sub¹ [sʌb] *n F* 1. to get a sub from/off s.o., emprunter*/faire un emprunt à qn; taper qch à qn 2. (= *sub-editor*) secrétaire *mf* de rédaction 3. (= *submarine*) sous-marin *m* 4. (= *subaltern*) subalterne *mf* 5. (= *substitute*) substitut *m*/remplaçant, -ante 6. (= *subscription*) abonnement *m*/cotisation *f*.

sub² [sʌb] *vtr F* 1. to sub s.o., prêter de l'argent* à qn/financer qn 2. (= *sub-edit*) corriger/mettre au point (un article/des épreuves) 3. (= *substitute*) to sub for s.o., remplacer qn.

substance ['sʌbstəns] *n Br F Euph* cannabis*/haschisch*/marijuana*.

suck [sʌk] I *vtr* 1. *F* suck it and see, (*catchphrase*) essaie et tu verras; suce et tu goûteras 2. *F* to suck s.o. dry, saigner qn à blanc/tondre la laine sur le dos à qn 3. *V* to suck s.o., (*fellatio*) sucer qn/tailler une pipe/ faire un pompier à qn; (*cunnilinctus*) sucer/ brouter le minou à qn. (*See* **egg 6**) II *vi* *NAm P* (*be disgusting, unpleasant, worthless, etc*) être merdique; what do you think of it? – it sucks, qu'en penses-tu? – c'est nul/à chier.

suck around ['sʌkə'raʊnd] *vtr NAm P* to suck around s.o. = to suck up to s.o. (**suck up**).

suckass ['sʌkæs] *n NAm P* lèche-cul *m*/ lèche-bottes *m*.

sucker ['sʌkə] *n F* (*gullible person*) dupe *f*/ poire *f*/nigaud, -aude; there's a sucker born every minute, (*catchphrase*) on pend les andouilles sans les compter; to make a (right) sucker of s.o., faire tourner qn en bourrique; to be played for a sucker, être escroqué*/entubé; he made a right sucker out of you! il t'a eu jusqu'à la gauche! to be a sucker for, ne pas pouvoir résister à; he's a sucker for a beautiful blonde, il est porté sur les belles blondes. (*See* **bumsucker; cocksucker**)

suck-hole(r) ['sʌk'həʊl(ə)] *n Austr P* lèche-cul *m*/lèche-bottes *m*.

suck in ['sʌk'ɪn] *vtr P* escroquer*/carotter/ entuber.

suck off ['sʌk'ɒf] *vtr V* to suck s.o. off, (*fellatio*) sucer qn/faire une pipe à qn; (*cunnilinctus*) sucer qn/brouter le cresson à qn.

suck up ['sʌk'ʌp] *vi F* to suck up to s.o., flatter* qn/faire de la lèche à qn/lécher le cul à qn.

sugar¹ ['ʃʊgə] *n* 1. *P* (*RS = sugar and honey*

= *money*) argent*/galette *f* 2. *F* (*term of endearment*) mon chéri/ma chérie/mon trésor 3. *P* (*drugs*) (*a*) héroïne*/cocaïne*/morphine* (*b*) sugar (lump), LSD*/acide *m*. (*See* **acid 2**) 4. *P* pot-de-vin *m*/dessous *m* de table 5. *P* (*Euph for* **shit**) sugar! zut!/mince (alors)! (*See* **shit III**)

sugar² ['ʃʊgə] *vtr* 1. *F* flatter*/pommader 2. *P* soudoyer/acheter.

sugar-daddy ['ʃʊgədædɪ] *n F* vieux protecteur (*envers une maîtresse*)/ entreteneur *m*/papa-gâteau *m*; she's got a sugar-daddy, elle s'est trouvé un vieux friqué; he's my sugar-daddy, c'est mon papounet.

sugar-hill ['ʃʊgə'hɪl] *n NAm P* quartier *m* des bordels* dans une région habitée par les Noirs.

suit [suːt] *n F* bureaucrate *m*/scribouillard *m*; fonctionnaire *m*/cul *m* de plomb.

summat ['sʌmət, 'sʊmət] *adv & n P* = **something**.

Sunday ['sʌndɪ] *n F* 1. Sunday driver, chauffeur *m* du dimanche 2. (*boxing*) Sunday punch, coup* très violent/à assommer un bœuf.

sundowner ['sʌndaʊnə] *n F* 1. boisson alcoolisée (prise le soir)/gorgeon *m* 2. *Austr* clochard*/cloche *f*/clodo *m*.

sunk [sʌŋk] *a F* ruiné*/perdu/fichu.

sunny ['sʌnɪ] *a F* 1. the sunny side of the street, la vie en rose 2. sunny side up, (*fried egg*) sur le plat.

sunset strip ['sʌnset'strɪp] *n F see* **bingo 77**.

sunshine ['sʌnʃaɪn] *n Br F* (*term of address*) hello, sunshine! (*to man*) salut, mon vieux! (*to woman*) bonjour, ma jolie! *Iron* where do you think you're going to, sunshine? où tu vas comme ça, mon ami?/mon coco?

super ['s(j)uːpə] I *a F* excellent*/super/ épatant II *n Br F* (= *Superintendent* (*of Police*)) commissaire *m* de police/quart *m* d'œil/cardeuil *m*.

super-duper ['s(j)uːpə'd(j)uːpə] *a O F* excellent*/formide/super.

supergrass ['s(j)uːpəgrɑːs] *n P* indicateur* de police/super-indic *mf*. (*See* **grass¹ 1**)

sure [ʃʊə] *F* I *a* (it's a) sure thing, c'est une certitude/c'est sûr et certain/c'est du tout cuit; sure thing! = **sure** II. (*See* **egg 4**) II *excl* sure! sure! naturellement!/bien sûr!/ pour sûr!

sure-fire ['ʃʊə'faɪə] *a F* sûr et certain.

surfie ['sɜːfɪ] *n Austr F* 1. fana *mf* du surf 2.

habitué(e) de la plage.

suss [sʌs] *Br P* **I** *a* suspect/louche; soupçonneux/méfiant; it looks a bit suss to me, ça m'a l'air plutôt louche/c'est pas net, ça **II** *n* 1. to have suss (*a*) (*be suspicious of*) se gourrer (*b*) (*be well-informed*) être à la coule/affranchi; she's got a lot of suss, elle est câblée/affranchie 2. (*also* sus) soupçon *m*/ gourance *f*; *O* sus law, (*police, etc*) loi *f* qui permettait à la police d'arrêter quiconque lui paraissait suspect *ou* qui semblait sur le point de commettre un délit; to get picked up on sus(s), être arrêté sur des présomptions/se faire pincer par gourance.

suss (out) ['sʌs('aut)] *vtr Br P* (*work out*) comprendre/piger; to suss s.o. out, savoir ce que vaut qn/cataloguer qn; to suss sth out, piger qch; he sussed that (out) pretty quick, il a vite pigé le truc.

sussed (out) ['sʌst('aut)] *a Br P* 1. (*person*) affranchi/débrouillard; he's well sussed, il sait ce qu'il veut/il se démerde bien 2. I've got it all sussed (out), j'ai tout arrangé/j'ai tout mis au point.

swaddie, swaddy ['swɒdɪ] *n F* = **squaddie, squaddy**.

swag [swæg] *n F* butin*/camelote *f*/prise *f*.

swagger ['swægə] *a F* (*rare*) élégant*/chic.

swagman ['swægmæn] *n Austr F* clochard*/vagabond *m*.

swallow¹ ['swɒləʊ] *n Br F* boisson *f*/ gorgeon *m*; they went for a swallow, ils sont allés prendre un pot.

swallow² ['swɒləʊ] *vtr F* croire*/gober/ avaler; he won't swallow that, il ne va pas marcher; your story's hard to swallow, elle est difficile à avaler, ton histoire. (*See* **hook¹** 4)

swank¹ [swæŋk] **I** *a F* = **swanky** (*b*) **II** *n F* 1. élégance *f*/chic *m*/coquetterie *f* 2. to put on (the) swank, prendre des airs *mpl*/faire de l'esbrouf(f)e *f*/frimer 3. prétention *f*/épate *f* 4. poseur, -euse/crâneur, -euse/frimeur, -euse.

swank² [swæŋk] *vi F* se donner des airs *mpl*/crâner/faire de l'épate *f*/frimer/en installer.

swanker ['swæŋkə] *n F* = **swank¹ II** 4.

swanky ['swæŋkɪ] *a F* (*a*) prétentieux*/ poseur (*b*) élégant*/flambard/rider/chicos.

swap¹ [swɒp] *n F* (*a*) échange *m*/troc *m* (*b*) objet *m ou* article *m* à échanger *ou* qu'on a échangé; to do a swap, faire un troc; swaps, (*in stamp collecting, etc*) doubles *mpl*.

swap² [swɒp] *vtr & i F* échanger/troquer;

(I'll) swap you! je te l'échange! shall we swap? on fait un échange?

sweat¹ [swet] *n F* 1. travail* pénible/corvée *f*/turbin *m*; it's no sweat, c'est pas dur; no sweat! pas de problème! 2. *Mil* an old sweat, un vieux troupier 3. to work oneself (up) into a sweat = to work oneself (up) into a lather (**lather¹** (*a*), (*b*)) 4. to be in a cold sweat, s'inquiéter/avoir le trac.

sweat² [swet] *F* **I** *vi* 1. to be sweating on the top line, être agité/excité/emballé; être sur des charbons ardents 2. se tracasser*/se casser la nénette/se faire de la bile/se faire un sang d'encre **II** *vtr* 1. to sweat buckets, être en nage 2. *NAm* to sweat s.o. to do sth, forcer qn à faire qch. (*See* **blood** 4)

sweat out ['swet'aut] *vtr F* to sweat it out, prendre son mal en patience/tenir jusqu'au bout. (*See* **guts** 6)

sweatshop ['swetʃɒp] *n F* atelier *m* où les ouvriers sont exploités/vrai bagne.

swe(e)dey ['swiːdɪ] *n P* (*police*) gendarme*/guignol *m*/hirondelle *f*.

Sweeney ['swiːnɪ] *n P* Sweeney Todd/the Sweeney, (*RS = Flying Squad*) la brigade mobile (de la police).

sweep¹ [swiːp] *n F* 1. sweepstake *m* 2. to make a clean sweep, (*change staff, etc*) faire table rase; (*in gambling*) faire rafle/rafler le tout.

sweep² [swiːp] *vtr F* 1. to be swept off one's feet (*a*) être emballé/s'emballer/se montrer chaud pour qn (*b*) être débordé/inondé de travail* 2. to sweep the board, (*in gambling*) faire rafle/rafler le tout; (*be successful*) faire un tabac 3. to sweep (clean), éliminer les micros clandestins dans (une pièce). (*See* **dirt** 4)

sweeper ['swiːpə] *n F* 1. (*football*) arrière volant 2. leave it for the sweeper, ne ramassez rien/laissez pousser.

sweep up ['swiːp'ʌp] *vi F* (*football*) jouer en arrière volant.

sweet [swiːt] *a* 1. *F* to be sweet on s.o., être amoureux de qn/avoir le béguin pour qn/en pincer pour qn 2. *F* you can bet your sweet life! tu peux en mettre la main au feu 3. *F* to hand s.o. a sweet line, flatter* qn/faire marcher qn/faire de la lèche à qn 4. *Br P* sweet Fanny Adams/P sweet FA/V sweet fuck-all, rien*/moins que rien/peau de balle/que dalle/ des prunes/peau de zébi 5. *F* to whisper sweet nothings, dire des mots doux/conter fleurette 6. *NAm F* sweet talk, flatterie *f*/boniment *m*/

pommade *f* 7. *F* facile/lucratif; a sweet job, une planque 8. *F* aimable/accueillant/gentil; sweet (as a nut), (*person*) qui se laisse soudoyer/acheter 9. *Austr F* she's sweet, (*it's OK*) ça va/c'est OK/c'est au poil. (*See* **lucy 1**; **tooth 1**)

sweeten ['swi:tn] *vtr F* (*a*) soudoyer/acheter (qn)/graisser la patte à (qn) (*b*) flatter*/cajoler/pommader (qn).

sweetener ['swi:tnə] *n F* (*a*) pot-de-vin *m* (*b*) pourboire*/pourliche *m*; I had to give him a sweetener, j'ai dû lui graisser la patte/lui refiler la pièce.

sweeten up ['swi:tn'ʌp] *vtr F* = **sweeten**.

sweetie ['swi:tɪ] *n Br* 1. *F* bonbon *m* 2. *F* sweetie(-pie), chéri(e) *m*(*f*)/cocotte *f*; he's a real sweetie(-pie), c'est un cœur/un ange/un chéri 3. *P* (*drugs*) Préludine *f* (*RTM*).

sweets [swi:ts] *npl P* (*drugs*) amphétamines*/bonbons *mpl*.

sweet-talk ['swi:(t)tɔ:k] *vtr NAm F* flatter*/cajoler/enjôler (qn); he tried to sweet-talk his way around me, il a essayé de me passer de la pommade.

sweet-talker ['swi:(t)tɔ:kə] *n F* cajoleur, -euse/enjôleur, -euse.

sweety ['swi:tɪ] *n F* = **sweetie**.

swell [swel] I *a* 1. *O F* élégant*/flambard 2. *O F* excellent*/chouettos/épatant 3. *A P* swell mob, pickpockets bien fringués II *n O F* 1. élégant *m*/suiffard *m*; the swells, les gens *mpl* chics/le grand monde 2. personnage important/grosse légume/grossium *m*.

swellhead ['swelhed] *n NAm F* prétentieux, -euse/crâneur, -euse/frimeur, -euse.

swift [swɪft] *a Br P* that's a bit swift, ce n'est pas juste/ce n'est pas du jeu.

swig¹ [swɪg] *n F* grand trait/lampée *f* (de bière, etc); to take a swig from the bottle, boire à même la bouteille.

swig² [swɪg] *vi F* boire à grands traits/à grands coups; lamper.

swill¹ [swɪl] *n P* (*bad food*) ratatouille *f*/ragougnasse *f*; (*bad drink*) lavasse *f*; this horrible swill, cette saloperie.

swill² [swɪl] *vtr F* boire* (qch) avidement; to swill a beer, lamper/descendre une bière.

swim [swɪm] *n F* in the swim, dans le bain/dans le vent/à la coule; to get back in/into the swim of things, se remettre dans le bain.

swimmingly ['swɪmɪŋlɪ] *adv F* à merveille/comme sur des roulettes.

swindle-sheet ['swɪndlʃi:t] *n P* feuille *f* de frais (professionnels).

swine [swaɪn] *n F* salopard *m*/salaud*/saligaud *m*; you swine! espèce de dégueulasse/de pourri(ture)/d'ordure!

swing¹ [swɪŋ] *n F* 1. to get into the swing of it/of things, se mettre dans le mouvement 2. everything went with a swing, tout a très bien marché 3. in full swing, en pleine activité/en plein boum; the party's in full swing, la soirée bat son plein 4. to take a swing at s.o., balancer un coup de poing à qn. (*See* **roundabouts**)

swing² [swɪŋ] *vtr & i* 1. *O F* (*be up to date*) être dans le mouvement/dans le vent; être dynamique 2. *P* to swing it/a fast one on s.o., duper* qn/refaire qn/tirer une carotte à qn/jouer un tour de cochon à qn 3. *F* être pendu/béquillé; to swing for a crime, être pendu pour un crime 4. *F* to swing a deal, (*bring it off*) mener une affaire à bien; to swing it so that..., arranger les choses de manière (à ce) que... 5. *F* faire balancer (qch) en sa faveur 6. *P* to swing both ways, jouer *ou* miser sur les deux tableaux; *NAm* (*be bisexual*) marcher à voile et à vapeur 7. *Austr P* to swing a bag, racoler*/faire le trottoir. (*See* **lead¹ 2**)

swinger ['swɪŋə] 1. *O F* qn dans le vent/à la coule 2. *pl Austr P* seins*/flotteurs *mpl*. (*See* **lead-swinger**)

swinging ['swɪŋɪŋ] *a O F* (*person*) dans le vent/à la coule; the swinging Sixties, les folles années soixante; swinging party, soirée endiablée.

swipe¹ [swaɪp] *n F* coup* de poing/marron *m*/taquet *m*; coup de bâton; (*in cricket or golf*) coup à toute volée; to take a swipe at s.o., flanquer un marron/une torgnole à qn.

swipe² [swaɪp] *vtr F* 1. donner un coup* de poing *ou* de bâton à; flanquer un marron/une torgnole à (qn) 2. voler*/chiper/piquer (qch à qn).

swish¹ [swɪʃ] I *a F* élégant*/chic/rupin II *n NAm P* homosexuel*/lopette *f*/pédale *f*.

swish² [swɪʃ] *vi NAm P* être efféminé/faire pédé.

switch¹ [swɪtʃ] *n F* to do/to pull a switch, échanger/troquer/chanstiquer.

switch² [swɪtʃ] *vtr F* to switch horses (in midstream), changer son fusil d'épaule (au milieu du combat).

switched on ['swɪtʃt'ɒn] *a & pp F* 1. (*by drugs*) chargé; (*sexually*) allumé 2. à la

switch on) mode/dans le vent/dans le coup. (*See* **switch on)**

switch-hitter ['switʃ'hitə] *n P* bisexuel, -elle/qn qui marche à voile et à vapeur.

switch off ['switʃ'ɒf] *vi F* to switch off (completely), (*of person*) cesser d'écouter/ décrocher.

switch on ['switʃ'ɒn] *vtr F* to switch s.o. on (*a*) éveiller l'intérêt *m ou* la curiosité de qn/brancher qn (*b*) (*sexually*) exciter/ émoustiller/allumer/aguicher/brancher (qn). (*See* **switched on)**

swiz(z)[1] [swiz] *n F* (= **swizzle**[1] **1, 2**) what a swiz(z)! it's a swiz(z)! quelle arnaque!

swiz(z)[2] [swiz] *vtr F* tromper*/rouler; I've been swizzed! on m'a eu!/je me suis fait avoir!

swizzle[1] ['swizl] *n F* **1.** escroquerie*/ filoutage *m*/doublage *m*/estampage *m*/arnaque *f* **2.** déception *f*/déboire *m* **3.** *NAm* cocktail *m*/mélange *m*; **swizzle stick,** fouet *m* à champagne.

swizzle[2] ['swizl] *vtr F* escroquer*/filouter/ doubler/arnaquer.

swoonsome ['swu:nsəm] *a F* beau* à faire pâmer; he's a swoonsome hunk, il est baisable ce mec.

swop [swɒp] *n & v F* = **swap**[1,2].

swordsman ['sɔ:dzmən] *n P* **1.** receleur*/ fourgue *m* **2.** *NAm* cavaleur *m*/coureur *m*/ bandeur *m*.

swot[1] [swɒt] *n F* bûcheur, -euse/potasseur *m*.

swot[2] [swɒt] *vi F* étudier/bûcher/bachoter/ piocher/potasser.

swot up on ['swɒt'ʌpɒn] *vtr F* potasser/ piocher/bûcher (les maths, etc).

syph [sif] *n P* (the) syph, syphilis*/syphilo *f*/ sifflotte *f*/vérole *f*.

syphed up ['sift'ʌp] *a P* atteint de syphilis/ syphilitique/vérolé/nazi.

sypho ['sifəʊ], **syphy** ['sifi] *n P* (*person*) syphilitique *mf*/laziloffe *mf*.

syrup ['sirəp] *n Br P* syrup (of figs), (*RS = wig*) perruque *f*/moumoute *f*.

system ['sistəm] *n F* **1.** the system, le Système **2.** it's all systems go! ça gaze! on démarre!/c'est parti(, mon kiki)!

T

T [tiː] 1. *F* that suits me (down) to a T, cela me va parfaitement/cela me va comme un gant; ça me botte 2. *P* = **tea**.

ta! [tɑː] *excl F* merci!

tab [tæb] *n* 1. *P* cigarette*/cibiche *f*/clop(e) *mf*/sèche *f* 2. *P* oreille*/étiquette *f* 3. *NAm F* note *f*/facture *f*/addition *f* 4. *F* to keep tabs on s.o., surveiller qn/avoir l'œil sur qn/avoir qn à l'œil 5. *P* (*abbr of tablet*) comprimé *m*/ cachet *m*; (*esp drugs*) cachet *m ou* dose *f* de LSD*.

tab-end ['tæb'end] *n F* mégot*/clope *m*.

table ['teɪbl] *n F* to drink s.o. **under the table**, mieux tenir l'alcool que qn; (*deliberately*) faire rouler qn sous la table; **to be under the table**, être ivre*/rouler sous la table.

tache [tæʃ] *n Br F* = **tash**.

tack [tæk] *n F* 1. (*a*) soft tack, pain*/ bricheton *m* (*b*) hard tack, biscuits *mpl* de marin 2. nourriture*/fricot *m*/rata *m* 3. *esp NAm* = **tackiness**. (*See* **brass I** (*a*))

tackiness ['tækɪnɪs] *n esp NAm F* (*shabbiness*) apparence *f* minable; (*bad taste*) mauvais goût/goût douteux; (*vulgarity*) (*of person*) vulgarité *f*.

tackle ['tækl] *n Br P* (wedding) tackle, sexe* de l'homme/boutique *f*/bijoux *mpl* de famille.

tacky ['tækɪ] *a esp NAm F* minable/moche; **tacky joke**, plaisanterie *f*/blague *f* de mauvais goût; **tacky clothes**, vêtements* tocards; **she's really tacky**, elle est très vulgaire.

taco-bender ['tɑːkəʊ'bendə] *n NAm P Pej* Hispano-Américain, -aine; = espingo *mf*.

tad [tæd] *n F* a tad, un peu/un chouïa; **I'm a tad sleepy**, j'ai un peu sommeil/j'ai une petite envie de roupiller.

tadger ['tædʒə] *n Br P* pénis*/queue *f*.

Taff(y) ['tæf(ɪ)] *n F* habitant *m ou* originaire *m* du pays de Galles/Gallois *m*.

tag¹ [tæg] *n F* 1. nom* *ou* surnom *m*/blaze *m* 2. (*theatre*) tag (line), mot *m* de la fin 3. signature *f* de graffiteur *m*; tag *m*. (*See* **dog-tag**)

tag² [tæg] *vtr & i* 1. *esp NAm F* suivre (qn)/ être sur les talons de (qn)/filer le train à (qn)/faire la filoche à (qn) 2. *F* (*to sign graffiti*) tagger/taguer.

tag along ['tægə'lɒŋ] *vi F* suivre; **mind if I tag along?** est-ce que je peux venir avec vous?

tag around ['tægə'raʊnd] *vi F* to tag **around with s.o.**, être accroché à qn/rouler sa bosse avec qn.

tagger ['tægə] *n* (*graffiti artist*) tagger *m*/ tagueur *m*.

tag on to ['tæg'ɒntuː] *vtr F* se joindre à (qn)/s'accrocher à (qn).

tail¹ [teɪl] *n* 1. *P* fesses*/postère *m*/pont *m* arrière; **get your tail out of here!** débarrasse le plancher!/tire ton cul de là! 2. *P* pénis*/ queue *f*/bite *f*/pine *f* 3. *P* sexe* de la femme*/ chagatte *f*/cramouille *f* 4. *P* a piece of tail, un bout de fesses/de cuisse; une femme baisable; **he's after a piece of tail**, il cherche une fille* à baiser/il cherche à se mettre une femme sur le bout 5. *F* (*s.o. following*) fileur *m*; policier*/flic *m* en filature; limier *m*; **to be on s.o.'s tail**, filer (le train à) qn/faire la filoche à qn; **to put a tail on s.o.**, faire suivre qn/faire filer qn/faire la filoche à qn; **we've got a tail**, quelqu'un nous file 6. *F* to sit en s.o.'s tail, (*in car*) = **tailgate** 7. *F* to go top over tail, faire une culbute 8. *F* to turn tail, s'enfuir*/tourner le dos 9. *F* to have one's tail up, (*feel happy*) se sentir très heureux/se sentir pousser des ailes; (*feel positive, good*) être très optimiste/être en pleine forme 10. *F* to keep one's tail up, ne pas se laisser abattre. (*See* **ringtail**)

tail² [teɪl] *vtr F* suivre/épier/filer/filocher (qn). (*See* **hightail**)

tailgate ['teɪlgeɪt] *vtr F* coller (qn); coller au train/au cul de (voiture, etc).

tail-man ['teɪlmæn] *n P* coureur *m* (de jupons)/cavaleur *m*/juponneur *m*.

257

tail-spin ['teɪlspɪn] *n F* to go into a tail-spin, être pris de panique/paniquer.

take¹ [teɪk] *n F* the take, la recette/les revenus *mpl*/le beurre; to be on the take, affurer du pognon/faire son beurre; (*take bribes*) toucher des pots-de-vin.

take² [teɪk] *vtr* 1. *F* to have what it takes, avoir du courage*/du battant; (*be mentally able*) être capable/être à la hauteur; he's got what it takes, il a des couilles; she's got what it takes, (*for job, sexually*) elle a tout ce qu'il faut 2. *F* endurer/encaisser; we can take it, on peut tenir le choc/le coup 3. *F* I'm not taking any of that! je ne gobe rien de tout cela!/ on ne me fera pas croire ça! 4. *F* to take a bath, (*suffer financial loss*) perdre gros/ plonger/faire le plongeon 5. *P* (*drugs*) to take a hit, tirer sur une cigarette* de marijuana* *ou* de haschisch* 6. *P* to take one, (*accept bribe*) toucher des pots-de-vin. (*See* **hit¹** 6; **lamb** 4; **plunge¹**)

take apart ['teɪkə'pɑːt] *vtr F* réprimander* fortement/passer un bon savon à (qn); (*in fight*) démolir (qn).

take in ['teɪk'ɪn] *vtr F* 1. comprendre/piger/ entraver 2. he takes it all in, il prend tout ça pour argent comptant 3. tromper*/ficher dedans/avoir (qn); I've been taken in, je me suis fait rouler/avoir.

takeoff ['teɪkɒf] *n F* imitation *f*/mimique *f*/ caricature *f*.

take off ['teɪk'ɒf] *vtr & i* 1. *F* s'enfuir*/s'en aller/se barrer; take off! fiche le camp!/ déguerpis! 2. *F* imiter/copier/singer 3. *P* (*drugs*) se faire une piquouse/se fixer/se shooter.

take on ['teɪk'ɒn] *vi F* 1. *Br* (*be upset*) s'en faire 2. (*become popular*) prendre.

take out ['teɪk'aʊt] *vtr P* tuer*/descendre/ effacer/liquider (qn).

tale [teɪl] *n* 1. *F* to tell the tale, raconter des boniments *mpl*/faire du baratin 2. *F* to live to tell the tale, survivre/être là pour en parler 3. *P* Tale of Two Cities, (*RS = titties*) seins*. (*See* **Bristols**; **fit¹** II 3; **threepenny-bits** 2; **tit** 1; **titty**; **trey-bits**) 4. *P* sorrowful tale, (*RS = jail*) prison*. (*See* **tall** I 2)

talent ['tælənt] *n Br P* (*people considered sexually*) (*women*) nanas *fpl*/nénettes *fpl*/ minettes *fpl*; (*men*) types *mpl*/mecs *mpl*/gars *mpl*; the local talent, les nénettes/les mecs du coin; he's looking for talent, il cherche de la fesse/un coup.

talk [tɔːk] *vi F* 1. now you're talking!

maintenant tu y es/à la bonne heure!/voilà qui devient intéressant! 2. money talks, l'argent* peut tout 3. talk about luck! tu parles d'une veine! 4. look who's talking! tu peux (toujours) parler, toi! (*See* **Dutch** I 5; **hat** 2; **head** 10, 11; **sweet-talk**)

talkie ['tɔːkɪ] *n O F* (*cinema*) film parlant/ parlé.

talking-to ['tɔːkɪŋtuː] *n F* réprimande *f*/ semonce *f*/savon *m*; to give s.o. a good talking-to, sonner les cloches à qn.

tall [tɔːl] *a F* 1. a tall order, un travail* dur/ un sacré boulot 2. a tall story/*NAm* tale, un mensonge*/un bateau; une histoire à dormir debout; that's a bit of a tall story! elle est bien bonne, celle-là! 3. to walk tall, crâner/se gonfler/se monter le cou.

tammy ['tæmɪ] *n F* (= *tam-o'-shanter*) béret écossais.

tampi ['tæmpɪ] *n O P* (*drugs*) marijuana*.

tam rag ['tæm'ræg] *n Br P* serviette *f* hygiénique/fifine *f*; tampon *m* hygiénique. (*See* **rag¹** 2)

tangle ['tæŋgl] *vi F* to tangle with s.o. (*a*) se brouiller avec qn/se frotter à qn (*b*) embrasser* qn/étreindre qn/serrer qn dans ses bras.

tanglefoot ['tæŋglfʊt] *n F* 1. *NAm* whisky *m* (de mauvaise qualité)/casse-pattes *m*/tord-boyaux *m* 2. *Austr* bière *f*/mousse *f*.

tank¹ [tæŋk] *n P* 1. coffre-fort *m*/coffiot *m*; to blow a tank, faire sauter un coffiot 2. (*a*) prison*/trou *m* (*b*) cellule *f*/cage *f* à poules. (*See* **fishtank**) 3. *Br* voiture* de police*; (*van*) panier *m* à salade 4. *NAm* revolver*/ flingue *m*. (*See* **piss-tank**; **septic** 2)

tank² [tæŋk] *vtr & i Br P* 1. (*overwhelm*) écraser/démolir (qn) 2. to tank along, (*of vehicle, driver, etc*) foncer; all I do is tank up and down the motorway, je ne fais que des va-et-vient à plein gaz sur l'autoroute.

tanked (up) ['tæŋkt(ʌp)] *a P* ivre*/bourré/ chargé/blindé; to get tanked up, se soûler la gueule/se noircir/se bourrer/se piquer le nez.

tank up ['tæŋk'ʌp] *vi P* boire* beaucoup d'alcool/picoler/pinter.

tanner ['tænə] *n Br O F* ancienne pièce de six pennies *ou* 2½ nouveaux pennies.

tanning ['tænɪŋ] *n O F* volée *f* de coups*/ raclée *f*/peignée *f*. (*See* **hide** 1)

tap¹ [tæp] *n F* to be on tap, être (toujours) disponible/être (toujours) à la disposition de qn.

tap² [tæp] *vtr F* demander de l'argent* à/

taper/torpiller (qn). (*See* **claret**)

tap-dance ['tæp'dɑ:ns] *n F* (*evasion*) subterfuge *m*; (*devious manoeuvre*) combine *f*/magouille *f*.

tap-dancer ['tæp'dɑ:nsə] *n F* débrouillard, -arde/démerdard, -arde.

tape[1] [teɪp] *n F* red tape, bureaucratie *f*/paperasserie *f*.

tape[2] [teɪp] *vtr F* to have sth taped, avoir qch bien catalogué/étiqueté/pointé; I've got him taped, j'ai pris sa mesure/je sais ce qu'il vaut.

tapped out ['tæpt'aut] *a NAm P* 1. ruiné*/paumé/dans la dèche 2. fatigué*/crevé.

tapper ['tæpə] *n P* mendiant*/pilon *m*/torpille *f*; (*habitual borrower*) tapeur, -euse.

tar[1] [tɑ:] *n P* (*drugs*) opium*/noir *m*. (*See* **jack**[1] **I 5**)

tar[2] [tɑ:] *vtr F* to be tarred with the same brush, être à mettre dans le même panier/sac.

tarbrush ['tɑ:brʌʃ] *n F* to have a touch of the tarbrush, avoir du négrillon dans les veines/avoir du sang noir.

tarnation! [tɑ:'neɪʃ(ə)n] *excl NAm F* (*Euph for* **damnation**) mince!/mercredi!

tart [tɑ:t] *n P* 1. prostituée*/fille *f*/cocotte *f*/grue *f*/pute *f*; (*promiscuous and vulgar woman*) traînée *f*/pétasse *f*/salope *f* 2. *esp Austr* jeune fille* *ou* femme*/nana *f*/gonzesse *f*; petite amie; his tart, sa nana.

tart about ['tɑ:tə'baut] *vi Br P* 1. se donner des airs/frimer/crâner 2. faire l'imbécile/le con; (*mess about*) glander.

tart up ['tɑ:t'ʌp] *vtr P* (*a*) décorer (qch) avec du tape-à-l'œil; rajeunir/retaper (*b*) to tart oneself up, s'affubler/s'attifer de clinquant/se mettre sur son trente et un.

tarty ['tɑ:tɪ] *a P* to look tarty, (*of woman*) avoir l'air d'une putain/d'une pute; (*of clothes, etc*) être tapageur/tape-à-l'œil.

tash [tæʃ] *n Br F* moustache*/bacchantes *fpl*/moustagache *f*.

tassel ['tæsl] *n O P* pénis*/goupillon *m*.

tasty ['teɪstɪ] *Br P* **I** *a* élégant*/chic; (*good-looking*) bien foutu; a tasty piece, une belle nana/une nana bien carrossée/bien roulée; une belle pièce; a tasty geezer, un mec qui en jette/qui a de la classe **II** *n* boisson* alcoolique/coupe-la-soif *m*.

tat [tæt] *n Br F* (*junk*) camelote *f*.

ta-ta ['tæ'tɑ:] *F* **I** *excl* au revoir/au'voir **II** *n Br O* to go ta-ta's ['tætəz], (*child's word*) faire une petite promenade/sortir en promenade.

tater ['teɪtə], **tatie** ['teɪtɪ] *n P* pomme *f* de terre/patate *f*.

taters ['teɪtəz] *a Br P* to be taters, (*RS = taters in the mould = cold*) avoir froid/être frigo/cailler; it's bleeding taters in here! ça caille/on se les caille ici!

tatty ['tætɪ] *a F* défraîchi; déiabré; miteux*/moche; that's a bit tatty, c'est toc(ard)/c'est moche; a tatty old pair of jeans, un vieux jean délavé/moche/ringard.

tatty-bye! ['tætɪ'baɪ] *excl Br P* au revoir!/au'voir!/salut!.

taurus ['tɔ:rəs] *n P* taurus excretus, (= **bullshit**) bêtises*/foutaises *fpl*/conneries *fpl*.

tax [tæks] *vtr Br P* to tax s.o., voler* qn en lui laissant une partie de son argent*.

tea [ti:] *n P O* marijuana*/herbe *f*; bush tea, concoction *f* d'herbes et de marijuana*. (*See* **cup 1, 2; T 2**)

teach[1] [ti:tʃ] *n* (*abbr of teacher*) prof *mf*.

teach[2] [ti:tʃ] *vtr F* that'll teach you! ça t'apprendra! that'll teach him a thing or two! ça va te dégourdir un peu!

tead-up ['ti:d'ʌp] *a NAm P* drogué* à la marijuana*.

teahead ['ti:hed] *n O P* (*drugs*) habitué, -ée de la marijuana*/fumeur, -euse d'herbe.

tea-leaf ['ti:li:f] *n Br P* (*RS = thief*) voleur*.

team [ti:m] *n F* bande *f*/gang *m* de voyous.

tear[1] [tɪə] *n F* to shed a tear (for Nelson), uriner*/changer d'eau son poisson/égoutter la sardine.

tear[2] [tɛə] *vtr F* that's torn it! ça a tout gâché!/ça a tout bousillé! (*See* **pants 5**)

tear along ['tɛərə'lɒŋ] *vi F* aller très vite*/foncer/brûler le pavé.

tear apart ['tɛərə'pɑ:t] *vtr F* to tear s.o. apart, engueuler qn (comme du poisson pourri).

tear-arse (around) ['tɛərɑ:s(ə'raund)] *vi Br P* courir*/aller de tous les côtés; (*behave recklessly*) faire le casse-cou.

tearaway ['tɛərəweɪ] *n Br F* casse-cou *m*.

tearing ['tɛərɪŋ] *a F* to be in a tearing hurry, avoir le feu au derrière/filer dare-dare.

tearjerker ['tɪədʒɜ:kə] *n F* mélo-(drame) *m*/histoire larmoyante; that film's a real tearjerker, ce film vous arrache les larmes/sortez vos mouchoirs si vous allez voir ce film.

tear off ['tɛər'ɒf] *vtr P* to tear one off/to tear off a piece (of ass), faire l'amour*/tirer un coup/faire un carton.

tearoom ['ti:ru:m] *n P* (*homosexuals*)

urinoir* public/tasse *f* (à thé)/théière *f*.

tease [ti:z] *n P* aguicheuse *f*/bandeuse *f*/ allumeuse *f*. (*See* **cock-tease(r)**; **prick-tease(r)**)

teaser ['ti:zə] *n* 1. *F* casse-tête (chinois) 2. *P* aguicheuse *f*/bandeuse *f*/allumeuse *f*. (*See* **cock-tease(r)**; **prick-tease(r)**)

tec [tek] *n F* (*abbr of detective*) inspecteur *m* (de police)/condé *m*.

tech [tek] *n F* (*abbr of technical college*) lycée *m* technique/L.E.P. *m*.

technicolour ['teknɪkʌlə] *n P* vomissement *m*/renard *m*; **to have a technicolour yawn**, vomir*/gerber/aller au renard.

Ted, ted [ted], **Teddy-boy, teddy-boy** ['tedɪbɔɪ] *n Br F* = blouson noir.

teed off ['ti:d'ɒf] *a P* **to be teed off**, en avoir par-dessus la tête/en avoir ras le bol/en avoir jusque-là.

teensy-weensy ['ti:nsɪ'wi:nsɪ] *a F* = **teeny-weeny**.

teeny ['ti:nɪ] *a F* = **teeny-weeny**.

teenybopper ['ti:nɪ'bɒpə] *n F* minet, -ette.

teeny-weeny ['ti:nɪ'wi:nɪ] *a F* minuscule/ archi-petit; **just a teeny-weeny drop**, juste une toute petite goutte.

teeth [ti:θ] *npl see* **tooth**.

telephone ['telɪfəʊn] *n F* **telephone numbers**, grande quantité d'argent*; **he's talking telephone numbers**, il parle de millions.

tell [tel] *vtr F* **you're telling me!** tu l'as dit bouffi!/et comment! (*See* **another**; **Marine**; **tale 1, 2**)

telling-off ['telɪŋ'ɒf] *n F* réprimande *f*/ engueulade *f*/savon *m*.

tell off ['tel'ɒf] *vtr F* réprimander*/ enguirlander/passer un savon à (qn).

tell on ['tel'ɒn] *vtr F* rapporter sur le compte de (qn); **I'll tell mum on you!** je le dirai à maman!

telly ['telɪ] *n F* (*medium and set*) télé *f*/ téloche *f*.

ten [ten] *n F* 1. **the upper ten**, l'aristocratie *f*/les aristos *mpl*/les cent familles *fpl* 2. *Mus* **the top ten**, le palmarès.

tenderloin ['tendəlɔɪn] *n NAm F* quartier *m* louche/bas-fonds *mpl*/quartier chaud.

ten-four [ten'fɔ:] *n P* (*CB*) je reçois.

tenner ['tenə] *n F* (*a*) dix livres *fpl* sterling (*b*) billet* de dix livres *ou* de dix dollars; **it'll cost you a tenner**, faudra cracher/allonger dix sacs/cent balles.

tenspot ['tenspɒt] *n NAm F* 1. billet* de dix

dollars 2. emprisonnement *m* de dix années/ dix longes *fpl*/dix berges *fpl*/dix piges *fpl*.

terrible ['terɪbl] *a F* excessif/formidable; **terrible prices**, des prix exorbitants/ formidables/dingues/déments; **a terrible talker**, un moulin à paroles.

terribly ['terɪblɪ] *adv F* terriblement/ extrêmement/vachement; **terribly rich**, drôlement riche.

terrific [tə'rɪfɪk] *a F* 1. excellent*/sensass/du tonnerre 2. **a terrific bore**, un(e) sacré(e) casse-pieds.

terrifically [tə'rɪfɪklɪ] *adv F* terriblement/ énormément; **I'm terrifically impressed**, cela m'a fait une énorme impression; **it's terrifically nice of you**, c'est extrêmement gentil de votre part.

terror ['terə] *n F* fléau *m*/cauchemar *m*/peste *f*; **he's a real terror**, c'est un enfant temble/un petit diable. (*See* **holy 3**)

Thames [temz] *Prn F* **he'll never set the Thames on fire**, il n'a pas inventé la poudre/le fil à couper le beurre; il n'a jamais cassé trois pattes à un canard.

that [ðæt] *F* **I** *adv* jusque-là/si; **he's not that clever** ['ðætklevə], il n'est pas si malin* (que ça) **II** *pron* 1. **...and that's that!** un point, c'est tout! **and that was that**, plus rien à dire 2. **...and all that**, ...et tout le reste/...et patati et patata.

thatch [ðætʃ] *n F* **to lose one's thatch**, devenir chauve*/se dégarnir/se déplumer.

them [ðem] **I** *a P* = (*those*) **get up them stairs!** grimpe cet escalier! **give me them pencils!** donne-moi ces crayons! **I know them people**, je connais ces gens-là. (*See* **there 5**) **II** *pron P* (= *those*) **them's my sentiments**, voilà ce que je pense, moi.

there [ðɛə] *adv F* 1. **...so there!** ...et voilà!/et toc! 2. **all there**, malin*/débrouillard; **she's not all there**, elle a un petit grain/elle est un peu marteau; **he's not quite all there**, il est un peu demeuré/il lui manque une case. (*See* **all I 5**) 3. **there you are!** je te l'avais bien dit! 4. **there you go** (*again*)! te voilà reparti!/tu recommences!/tu remets ça! 5. **them there sheep**, ces moutons-là 6. **there you have me**, ça me dépasse 7. **nearly there**: *see* **bingo 89**.

thick [θɪk] *a F* 1. bête*/crétin/gourde; **he's as thick as two short planks**, il est bête* comme ses pieds; **to have a thick head**, être bête*/ être bouché à l'émeri; (*have a hangover*) avoir la gueule de bois/la GDB 2. (*excessive*) that's a bit thick! ça dépasse les bornes!/c'est un peu raide!/c'est un peu fort de café! **3.** to be very thick with s.o., être très lié/être à tu et à toi avec qn; they're as thick as thieves, ils s'entendent comme larrons en foire/ils sont copains comme cochons **4.** to have a thick skin, avoir la peau dure/ne pas être du genre qu'on vexe. (See **ear 5**).

thickhead ['θɪkhed] *n F* individu bête*/andouille *f*/tronche (plate). (See **thick 1**)

thickheaded ['θɪk'hedɪd] *a F* bête*/gourde.

thickie ['θɪkɪ] *n*, **thicko** ['θɪkəʊ] *n Br F* individu bête*/nouille *f*/tronche (plate).

thick-skinned ['θɪk'skɪnd] *a F* to be thick-skinned, avoir la peau dure/ne pas être du genre qu'on vexe. (See **hide 2**; **thick 4**)

thick-skulled ['θɪk'skʌld] *a F* = **thickheaded**.

thigh sandwich ['θaɪ'sændwɪdʒ] *n P* to give s.o. a thigh sandwich, faire éjaculer* qn (en frottant le sexe contre les cuisses).

thin [θɪn] *a F* **1.** to be going a bit thin on top, perdre ses cheveux*/se dégarnir **2.** to have a thin time (of it), s'ennuyer*/s'embêter; (*have a hard time*) manger de la vache enragée **3.** that's a bit thin! c'est peu convaincant! (See **ice¹ 5**; **thin-skinned**)

thing [θɪŋ] *n* **1.** *F* to have a thing about s.o./ sth, avoir qn/qch qui vous trotte dans le ciboulot; she's got a thing about music, (*likes*) la musique, c'est son truc; (*dislikes*) la musique, c'est pas son truc; he's got a thing about her, (*likes*) il en est dingue; (*dislikes*) il ne peut pas la blairer **2.** *F* it's not the (done) thing, ça ne se fait pas **3.** *F* the thing is..., le fait est.../le truc, c'est que ... **4.** *F* just the thing, exactement ce qu'il faut **5.** *F* it's just one of those things, on n'y peut rien **6.** *F* (*a*) to know a thing or two, être malin*/avoir plus d'un tour dans son sac (*b*) I could tell you a thing or two, je pourrais vous en conter/je pourrais vous en dire des vertes et des pas mûres **7.** *F* to see things, avoir des visions/être comme Jeanne d'Arc **8.** *F* individu* quelconque; hello, old thing! bonjour mon vieux!/salut mon pote! he's a nice old thing, c'est un bien brave type; you poor old thing! mon/ma pauvre! le/la pauvre! **9.** *F* (*a*) to be on(to) a good thing, avoir (trouvé) le filon/être sur un bon filon/être sur un bon coup (*b*) he makes a good thing out of it, ça lui rapporte pas mal; il en fait ses choux gras **10.** *F* do your (own) thing! fais ta vie!/fais (tout) ce qui te chante! **11.** *P* pénis*/outil

m/machin *m* **12.** *F* how's things? comment vont les affaires? (*how are you?*) comment (ça) va?

thingamy ['θɪŋəmɪ], **thingamybob** ['θɪŋəmɪbɒb], **thingamyjig** ['θɪŋəmɪdʒɪg], **thingum(a)bob** ['θɪŋəm(ə)bɒb], **thingummy** ['θɪŋəmɪ], **thingy** ['θɪŋɪ] *n F* chose *f*/machin *m*/machin-chose *m*/machin-chouette *m*/truc *m*/bidule *m*/trucmuche *m*.

think¹ [θɪŋk] *n F* you've got another think coming! tu peux toujours courir!/tu te mets le doigt dans l'œil!

think² [θɪŋk] *vi F* I don't think! sûrement pas!/et mon œil!/et ta sœur!

think-in ['θɪŋkɪn] *n O F* colloque *m*/séminaire *m*/groupe *m* d'études.

thinking-cap ['θɪŋkɪŋkæp] *n F* to put one's thinking-cap on, aviser à ce qu'on doit faire/réfléchir à qch; se creuser le cerveau/se remuer la cervelle.

think-piece ['θɪŋkpiːs] *n F Journ* article sérieux/qui fait réfléchir.

thin-skinned ['θɪn'skɪnd] *a F* to be thin-skinned, être trop sensible/être susceptible.

thrash¹ [θræʃ] *n P* réjouissances*/boum *f*/noce *f*/nouba *f*.

thrash² [θræʃ] *vtr F* **1.** battre*/rosser/tabasser (qn) **2.** battre (un adversaire) à plate(s) couture(s).

thrashing ['θræʃɪŋ] *n F* **1.** volée *f* de coups*/raclée *f*/tabassée *f* **2.** défaite *f*/raclée *f*.

thread [θred] *vtr P* (*rare*) faire l'amour* avec/enfiler (une femme).

threads [θredz] *npl P* vêtements*/fringues *fpl*/sapes *fpl*/frusques *fpl*.

three [θriː] *n P* packet of three, préservatifs* (vendus en étui de trois).

threepenny-bits ['θrʌpnɪ'bɪts, 'θrepnɪ-'bɪts] *npl P* **1.** *esp Austr* (*RS* = **the shits**) diarrhée*/chiasse *f*/courante *f* **2.** (*RS* = **tits**) seins*/nénés *mpl*. (See **Bristols**; **fit¹ II 3**; **tale 3**; **tray-bits**; **trey-bits**)

three-piece ['θriːpiːs] *n P* three-piece suite, sexe* de l'homme*/service *m* trois pièces/bijoux *mpl* de famille/panoplie *f*/boutique *f*.

thrill [θrɪl] *n P* (*drugs*) spasme provoqué par l'héroïne*.

throat [θrəʊt] *n F* **1.** to ram/to shove sth down s.o.'s throat, rebattre les oreilles à qn de qch/rabâcher qch à qn; we're always having it rammed down our throats that we've never had it so good, on nous rebat les oreilles en nous répétant que tout est au mieux **2.** he's cutting his own throat, il travaille à sa propre ruine; il creuse sa tombe. (*See* **jump² 9**)

throne [θrəʊn] *n P* siège *m* des WC*/trône *m*.

throne-room ['θrəʊnruːm] *n P* WC*/ cabinets *mpl*/chiottes *fpl*.

throttle ['θrɒtl] *vtr Austr P* to throttle a darkie, déféquer*/couler un bronze.

through [θruː] *F* I *adv* 1. to get through to s.o., faire comprendre/faire piger qch à qn; am I getting through to you? faut te faire un dessin?/tu piges? 2. to be through, (*to have finished*) avoir terminé/en avoir vu la fin; (*be finished, ruined*) être fichu/foutu/au bout du rouleau 3. to be through with s.o., rompre/ couper les ponts avec qn; she's through with him, elle l'a plaqué II *prep* he's been through it, il en a vu de dures/il en a vu des vertes et des pas mûres/il en a bavé/il en a vu de toutes les couleurs.

throw¹ [θrəʊ] *n F* the tickets cost £5 a throw, les billets coûtent £5 chacun.

throw² [θrəʊ] *vtr F* 1. I wouldn't trust him as far as I can throw him, je n'ai pas du tout confiance en lui/je n'ai plus confiance que ça 2. étonner/estomaquer/laisser baba; that threw you! ça te l'a coupé!/ça t'en a bouché un coin! 3. (*sport, etc*) perdre (une course, etc) exprès 4. (*esp boxing*) to throw a fight, se laisser battre volontairement/se coucher 5. to throw a wobbly/a wobbler, (*have a tantrum*) piquer une colère*/piquer une crise. (*See* **bathwater; book¹ 1; mud 7**)

throw about, around ['θrəʊə'baʊt, ə'raʊnd] *vtr F* to throw (one's) money about, dépenser* sans compter/faire valser le fric/ jeter son fric par les fenêtres; he doesn't throw his money about, il n'attache pas son chien avec des saucisses/il est plutôt près de ses sous.

throw in ['θrəʊ'ɪn] *vtr F* to throw in the towel/the sponge (*a*) (*sport*) abandonner la lutte/la partie; jeter l'éponge/se coucher (*b*) s'avouer vaincu/passer les dés. (*See* **end 12**)

throw up ['θrəʊ'ʌp] *vi F* vomir*/gerber/ dégobiller/aller au refil(e)/aller au renard/ refiler la came/dégueuler tripes et boyaux.

thumb¹ [θʌm] *n F* 1. to be all thumbs, être maladroit de ses mains; être malagauche/ empoté 2. thumbs up! bravo!/victoire! to give s.o. (the) thumbs up (sign), faire signe à qn que tout va bien; donner le feu vert à qn; he gave me the thumbs down, il m'a fait signe que ça ne marchait pas; il a rejeté ma proposition 3. to twiddle one's thumbs (and

do nothing), se tourner les pouces 4. it stands/sticks out like a sore thumb, ça saute aux yeux/ça crève les yeux 5. *Br* to be on the thumb, faire de l'auto-stop/du stop. (*See* **green I 5; Tom 4**)

thumb² [θʌm] *vtr F* to thumb a lift/a ride, faire de l'auto-stop/du stop; *Can* faire du pouce; he thumbed it, il y est allé en stop.

thumbsucker ['θʌmsʌkə] *n Br F* (*immature person*) gros bébé.

thumping ['θʌmpɪŋ] *n*, **thump-up** ['θʌmpʌp] *n Br P* (*beating, thrashing*) rossée *f*/tabassée *f*.

thunderbox ['θʌndəbɒks] *n* 1. *Br P* WC*/ cabinets *mpl* 2. *NAm F* = **ghettoblaster**.

thundering ['θʌndərɪŋ] *a F* du tonnerre; to win with a thundering majority, l'emporter avec une majorité écrasante; he's a thundering nuisance, il est assommant au possible; it's a thundering good book, c'est un bouquin à tout casser.

thunder-thighs ['θʌndəθaɪz] *n P* femme* qui a de l'embonpoint/dondon *f ou m*.

tich [tɪtʃ] *n F* = **titch**.

tichy ['tɪtʃɪ] *a F* = **titchy**.

tick¹ [tɪk] *n* 1. *P* individu* embêtant; (*esp younger school pupil*) petite peste/vermine *f* 2. *F* crédit *m*/croume *m*; on tick, à crédit/à croume; I'm buying it on tick, je l'achète à croume 3. *F* moment *m*/instant *m*; hang on a tick!/half a tick! (attends) une seconde!/ minute! (*See* **jiff(y); mo; sec; shake¹ 1**)

tick² [tɪk] *vi F* I'd like to know what makes him tick, je voudrais bien savoir ce qui le pousse/ce qui le fait courir/ses motivations.

ticked off [tɪkt'ɒf] *a esp NAm F* en colère*/ en pétard/en rogne. (*See* **tick off**)

ticker ['tɪkə] *n F* 1. cœur*/palpitant *m*; to have a dicky ticker, avoir le cœur branlant/ qui flanche 2. montre*/pendule *f*/tocante *f*.

ticket ['tɪkɪt] *n* 1. *O F* that's (just) the ticket! voilà qui fera l'affaire!/à la bonne heure! 2. *F* contravention *f*/PV *m*/contredanse *f*; to get a (parking) ticket, attraper/choper un PV/un biscuit/une contredanse 3. *esp NAm F* liste *f* des candidats; to vote a straight ticket, voter pour toute la liste; to vote a split ticket, faire du panachage; the Republican ticket, le ticket républicain 4. *Austr F* to have tickets on oneself, se mettre en avant/se gonfler/ crâner. (*See* **meal-ticket**)

tickety-boo ['tɪkɪtɪ'buː] *a F* excellent*/ parfait/au poil/aux pommes; everything's just tickety-boo, tout baigne (dans l'huile).

ticking-off ['tɪkɪŋ'ɒf] *n F* réprimande *f*/
savon *m*/engueulade *f*; **to get a ticking-off,**
prendre un savon; **to give s.o. a good ticking-
off,** passer un bon savon/sonner les cloches à
qn. (*See* **tick off**)

tickle[1] ['tɪkl] *n Br P* **1.** argent* gagné par des
moyens louches **2.** (*police*) arrestation*
inattendue **3.** (*hint*) allusion *f*/suggestion *f*;
(*inkling*) soupçon *m*/gourance *f*. (*See* **slap**[1]
II 2)

tickle[2] ['tɪkl] *vtr F* **1. to tickle s.o.'s fancy,**
amuser qn **2. to be tickled pink,** être ravi/être
aux anges **3. to be tickled to death,** se tordre
de rire*/se boyauter. (*See* **ivories 4**)

tickler ['tɪklə] *n P* **1.** préservatif* masculin
(*garni de "clous" en caoutchouc pour
accroître la stimulation vaginale*) **2.** martinet
m/fouet *m*. (*See* **rib-tickler**)

tick off ['tɪk'ɒf] *vtr F* réprimander*/
attraper/enguirlander; **to get ticked off,** être
réprimandé*/prendre un savon. (*See* **ticking-
off**)

tick over ['tɪk'əʊvə] *vi F* (*of business, etc*)
aller doucement; **business is ticking over
nicely,** les affaires tournent bien.

tiddle[1] ['tɪdl] *n F* (*child's word*) urine *f*/pipi
m; **to have a tiddle,** faire pipi.

tiddle[2] ['tɪdl] *vi F* (*child's word*) uriner*/
faire pipi.

tiddler ['tɪdlə] *n Br F* **1.** petit poisson/friture
f **2.** petit(e) enfant*/mioche *mf*/gosse *mf*/
môme *mf*/moutard *m* **3.** *O* pièce *f* d'un demi-
penny.

tiddl(e)y ['tɪdlɪ] *Br F* **I** *a* **1.** légèrement
ivre*/pompette/éméché **2.** très petit/minuscule
II *n* **a drop of tiddl(e)y,** un petit coup
d'alcool*/une goutte de gnôle.

tidemark ['taɪdmɑːk] *n Br F* ligne *f* de
crasse autour du cou *ou* sur la baignoire.

tide over ['taɪd'əʊvə] *vtr F* **I borrowed ten
quid to tide me over,** j'ai emprunté cent balles
pour me dépanner.

tidy ['taɪdɪ] *a F* **a tidy sum,** une somme
rondelette; **a tidy fortune,** une jolie fortune.

tie off ['taɪ'ɒf] *vi P* (*drugs*) serrer le bras/la
jambe pour faire sortir une veine.

tie on ['taɪ'ɒn] *vtr P* **to tie one on,** s'enivrer/
se biturer/prendre une cuite/se piquer le nez.

tie up ['taɪ'ʌp] *vtr F* **1. I'm rather tied up at
the moment,** en ce moment je suis pas mal
occupé *ou* pris/j'ai pas mal à faire **2. that ties
up with what I've just said,** cela correspond
à/cadre avec ce que je viens de dire.

tight [taɪt] *F* **I** *a* **1.** ivre*/soûl/pété/raide; **to**

get tight, prendre une cuite. (*See* **newt**) **2.**
avare*/radin/dur à la détente; **he's a bit tight
with his cash,** il est plutôt près de ses sous **3.**
(*money, credit*) resserré/rare; **things are a
bit tight at the moment,** je suis un peu à court
(d'argent)/je suis un peu fauché en ce
moment **4.** *NAm* **to be tight with s.o.,** être très
ami/très copain avec qn. (*See* **squeeze**[1] **2**)
II *adv* **to sit tight,** (*sit still*) ne pas bouger de
sa place; (*not to give in*) ne pas céder.

tight-arse ['taɪtɑːs], *NAm* **tight-ass**
['taɪtæs] *n P* **1.** avare *mf*/rat *m*/grippe-sou *m*
2. *esp NAm* individu* refoulé/coincé/constipé.

tight-arsed ['taɪtɑːst] *a Br P* avare*/radin;
he's a tight-arsed old sod, il est plutôt constipé
du morlingue/il les lâche au compte-gouttes.

tight-assed ['taɪtæst] *a NAm P* refoulé/
coincé/constipé.

tight-fisted ['taɪt'fɪstɪd] *a F* = **tight I 2**.

tightwad ['taɪtwɒd] *n F* avare *mf*/radin,
-ine/grigou *m*/grippe-sou *m*.

tike [taɪk] *n P* = **tyke.**

tile [taɪl] *n F* **1.** *A* chapeau*/bitos *m*; haut-de-
forme *m* **2. to have a tile loose,** être un peu
fou*/onduler de la toiture **3. to be out on the
tiles,** faire la fête/la bombe/la noce; **he spends
his nights on the tiles,** il traîne dehors toute la
nuit.

time [taɪm] *n* **1.** *F* **to do time,** être en
prison*/purger sa peine; **he's done time,** il a
fait de la taule **2.** *NAm P* **to make time with
s.o.,** (*chat up*) draguer qn; (*have sex with*) se
faire qn/s'envoyer qn. (*See* **all-time; big-
time; day 3; good-time; short I 2;
small-time**)

time-bomb ['taɪmbɒm] *n P* (*drugs*)
drogue* (*surt cannabis* *ou* amphétamine*)
enveloppée de papier/de pâte, etc et prise par
la bouche.

timothy ['tɪməθɪ] *n Austr A P* bordel*/boxon
m.

tin [tɪn] **I** *a F* **1. tin hat/lid,** casque *m* (de
soldat) **2. that puts the tin lid on it,** c'est le
comble/c'est la fin des haricots **3. little tin
god,** individu* qui se croit sorti de la cuisse de
Jupiter/frimeur, -euse/poseur, -euse **4. tin fish,**
torpille *f* **II** *n P* (*rare*) argent*/galette *f*/
pognon *m*/fric *m*/braise *f*.

tin-arse ['tɪnɑːs] *n Austr P* qn qui a de la
chance*/veinard, -arde.

tin-arsed ['tɪnɑːst] *a Austr P* qui a de la
chance*/du pot/du cul.

tincture ['tɪŋktʃə] *n Br P* boisson*
alcoolique/carburant *m*.

tinker ['tɪŋkə] *n Br* 1. *F* (*esp child*) (*term of endearment*) petit diable; little tinker, petit coquin 2. *P* I don't care/give a tinker's/a tinker's cuss/a tinker's toss, je m'en fiche/je m'en bats l'œil/je m'en soucie comme de l'an quarante/j'en ai rien à fiche 3. *P* pénis*/quéquette *f*.

tinkle[1] ['tɪŋkl] *n Br* 1. *F* to give s.o. a tinkle, téléphoner/passer un coup de fil *ou* de grelot à qn 2. *P* to have a tinkle, uriner* faire pipi 3. argent*/pèze *m*/pognon *m*.

tinkle[2] ['tɪŋkl] *vi Br F* uriner*/faire pipi.

tinkler ['tɪŋklə] *n Br P* pénis*/quéquette *f*.

tinned [tɪnd] *a F* tinned music, musique *f* en conserve. (*See* **canned 2**)

tinnie, tinny ['tɪnɪ] *n Austr F* boîte *f* de bière/cannette *f*.

tin-pan alley ['tɪn'pæn'ælɪ] *n F* quartier *m* des éditeurs de musique populaire; = le monde de la musique populaire.

tinpot ['tɪn'pɒt] *a F* inférieur/tocard; tinpot ideas, des idées à la noix/bidon.

tinsel town ['tɪnsltaʊn] *n F* Hollywood *m* *ou f*.

tiny ['taɪnɪ] *a F* you must be out of your tiny mind, tu es en train de perdre le peu de raison que tu as/tu es complètement siphonné.

tip [tɪp] *n Br F* endroit *m* en désordre *ou* sordide/taudis *m*; what a tip! quel fouillis!/quel foutoir!/c'est un vrai dépotoir! (*See* **arse I 4**)

tip-off ['tɪpɒf] *n F* renseignement*/avertissement *m*/tuyau *m*; to give s.o. a tip-off, tuyauter qn; the police received a tip-off, la police* a été informée.

tip off ['tɪp'ɒf] *vtr F* avertir/affranchir/mettre dans le coup/tuyauter; he tipped me off, il m'a mis au parfum/il m'a rencardé/tuyauté.

tipple ['tɪpl] *n P* boisson* alcoolisée; whisky is his favourite tipple, le whisky est sa gobette préférée/il carbure au whisky.

tippler ['tɪplə] *n P* ivrogne*/picoleur, -euse.

tiswas ['tɪzwɒz] *n Br F* to be all of a tiswas, ne pas savoir où donner de la tête/être dans tous ses états. (*See* **tizzy**).

tip-top ['tɪp'tɒp] *a F* excellent*/extra/super; in tip-top condition, qui pète la santé/le feu.

tit [tɪt] *n* 1. *V* (*a*) sein*/nichon *m*/téton *m*/néné *m*; to have huge tits, avoir du monde au balcon (*b*) femmes* en général; is there any tit around here? il y a de la fesse dans le coin? 2. *V* to get on s.o.'s tits, taper sur le système à qn; he really gets on my tits, il me

court sur les haricots/il me les casse 3. *P* individu bête*/idiot, -ote/crétin, -ine; you big tit! espèce de connard/de nœud! I must have looked a real tit standing there! qu'est-ce que je devais avoir l'air con/l'air d'un gland planté là! (*See* **arse I 4**; **Tom 3**)

titch [tɪtʃ] *n P* petit* individu/bas-du-cul *m*/rase-bitume *m*/avorton *m*.

titchy ['tɪtʃɪ] *a P* petit/minuscule.

titfer ['tɪtfə] *n P* (*RS = tit-for-tat = hat*) chapeau*/bitos *m*.

titholder ['tɪthəʊldə] *n P* soutien-gorge *m*/soutif *m*.

tit-man ['tɪtmæn] *n P* homme* qui préfère les seins* d'une femme à tout autre partie du corps.

titty ['tɪtɪ] *n V* = **tit 1** (*a*). (*See* **tough I 4**)

titty-bottle ['tɪtɪbɒtl] *n P* biberon *m*.

tizzy ['tɪzɪ] *n F* to be in a tizzy, ne pas savoir où donner de la tête/être dans tous ses états.

toast [təʊst] *n F* to have s.o. on toast, avoir qn à sa merci/tenir qn.

toasted ['təʊstɪd] *a NAm F* ivre*/bourré/pété.

toby ['təʊbɪ] *n P* 1. *A* the toby, la grande route*/le grand trimard 2. secteur couvert par un commissariat de police.

tod, Tod [tɒd] *n Br P* (*RS = Tod Sloan = alone*) on one's tod, tout seul/seulabre/seulingue.

toddle[1] ['tɒdl] *n F* petite promenade/balade *f*; to go for a toddle, aller faire un petit tour.

toddle[2] ['tɒdl] *vi F* trottiner; to toddle along, faire son petit bonhomme de chemin; to toddle off, partir*/lever le camp; toddle off now, there's a good boy! allez, tire-toi, mon petit!

todger ['tɒdʒə] *n Br P* = **tadger**.

to-do [tə'du:] *n F* remue-ménage *m*; what a to-do! quelle affaire!/quelle histoire! to make a great to-do about sth, faire tout un plat de qch.

toe [təʊ] *n F* 1. to tread on s.o.'s toes, marcher sur les pieds de qn/offenser qn/froisser qn 2. to be on one's toes, être alerte/être sur le qui-vive/ouvrir l'œil 3. *Br* to have it (away) on one's toes, s'enfuir*/se débiner/se tirer les pattes (de devant) 4. to turn up one's toes, mourir*/casser sa pipe/sortir les pieds devant 5. *Aut* to put one's toe down, accélérer/appuyer sur le champignon/mettre les gaz.

toe-jam ['təʊdʒæm] *n F* saleté*/crassouille *f* entre les orteils.

toe-job ['təʊdʒɒb] *n P* léchage *m* (érotique)

des doigts de pieds; to do a toe-job on s.o., faire petit salé à qn.

toerag ['təʊræg] *n P* (*term of abuse*) salaud*/con *m*, conne *f*/couillon *m*; you little toerag! petit merdeux!/petit trou-du-cul!

toe-ragger ['təʊrægə] *n Austr P* prisonnier, -ière de courte durée.

toey ['təʊɪ] *a Austr P* inquiet/anxieux/bileux.

toff [tɒf] *n F* aristo *mf*; (*rich*) rupin *m*; the toffs, le gratin.

toffee [tɒfɪ] *n* 1. *F* he can't play for toffee, il joue comme un pied 2. *Br F* (*nonsense*) bidon *m*/conneries *fpl*; (*flattery*) baratin *m*.

toffeenose ['tɒfɪnəʊz] *n F* snob *mf*/crâneur, -euse/poseur, -euse.

toffee-nosed ['tɒfɪnəʊzd] *a F* prétentieux*/snob/snobinard/bêcheur.

together [tə'geðə] *a & adv F* équilibré/peinard/cool/coolos *ou* coulos; he's got it (all) together/he's a very together person/he's got his act together, il est peinard/c'est un père peinard/il se fait jamais de la mousse.

tog out ['tɒg'aʊt] *vtr F* to tog (oneself) out, se mettre sur son trente et un/se saper.

togs [tɒgz] *npl F* vêtements*/nippes *fpl*/frusques *fpl*/fringues *fpl*.

tog up ['tɒg'ʌp] *vtr F* to tog (oneself) up = to tog (oneself) out (**tog out**).

toilet ['tɔɪlɪt] *n P* 1. endroit *m* sordide/taudis *m*/trou *m*; what a toilet! quelle sale baraque!/quel foutoir! 2. his career went into/went down the toilet, sa carrière est foutue/en ruine; the whole plan's gone down the toilet, le projet est tombé à l'eau 3. (*homosexuals*) toilet queen, homosexuel* qui drague dans les WC*/tasseuse *f*.

toilet-talk ['tɔɪlɪttɔːk] *n F* conversation grossière/grivoise/obscène.

toke [təʊk] *n P* 1. *A* pain*/bricheton *m*/larton *m* 2. (*drugs*) (*a*) cigarette* de marijuana*/joint *m* (*b*) bouffée *f*/taffe *f* (d'une cigarette* de marijuana*).

toke (down) ['təʊk'(daʊn)] *vi P* (*drugs*) fumer (une cigarette* de marijuana*).

tokus ['təʊkəs] *n NAm P* fesses*/pétrus *m*/pétrousquin *m*.

Tom, tom [tɒm] *n Br* 1. *F* any Tom, Dick, or Harry, n'importe qui/le premier venu 2. *P* Tom Mix (*a*) (*also* Tom) (*drugs*) (*RS* = *fix*) piqûre* de narcotique/piquouse *f*/fixe *m* (*b*) see **bingo** 6 (*c*) (*RS* = *fix*) difficulté *f*/embêtement *m*/mauvaise passe 3. *P* (*a*) to go for a tom (tit), (*RS* = *shit*) aller déféquer*/aller faire caca/aller couler un bronze (*b*)

Austr the tom tits, the toms, (*RS* = **the shits**) la diarrhée*/la courante/la chiasse. (*See* **shit¹** IV 14)) 4. *P* Tom Thumb, (*RS* = *rum*) rhum *m* 5. *P* prostituée*/pute *f*/tapineuse *f* 6. *P* = **tomfoolery**. (*See* **kingdom-come 3; Uncle 6**)

tomato [tə'mɑːtəʊ, *NAm* tə'meɪtəʊ] *n Austr & NAm F* jolie fille*/pépée *f*/poulette *f*.

tomfoolery [tɒm'fuːlərɪ] *n Br P* (*RS* = *jewellery*) bijoux *mpl*/joncaille *f*.

tommy¹ ['tɒmɪ] *n O F* tommy/Tommy (Atkins), soldat* anglais/Tommy *m*.

tommy² ['tɒmɪ] *vi Austr A P* s'enfuir*/décamper/filer.

tommyrot ['tɒmɪrɒt] *n O F* bêtises*/tissu *m* d'âneries*; that's tommyrot, c'est de la blague/du pipeau.

ton [tʌn] *n* 1. *F* to do a ton, aller très vite/bomber/aller à toute pompe. (*See* **ton-up**) 2. *F* tons of..., une abondance*/une tripotée/une pleine brassée/des tas de...; to have tons of books, avoir beaucoup de livres/avoir des tonnes de livres; to have tons of time, avoir tout son temps (devant soi) 3. *F* (*a*) a ton, cent livres *fpl* sterling (*b*) the ton, cent-soixante *m* (à l'heure) 4. *F* to weigh a ton, peser une tonne/être rudement lourd. (*See* **come down 3**)

tongue [tʌŋ] *vtr V* (*a*) (*cunnilingus*) to tongue (a woman), sucer/brouter/lécher (une femme); faire minette (*b*) (*fellatio*) sucer/faire une pipe/tailler une plume (*c*) (*anilingus*) to tongue s.o. (out), faire feuille de rose (à qn).

tongue-job ['tʌŋdʒɒb] *n* 1. *F* baiser* profond/patin *m*/roulée *f*/baveux *m* 2. *V* cunnilinctus*/descente *f* au barbu. (*See* **French¹ I 1**).

tongue-pie ['tʌŋ'paɪ] *n V* cunnilinctus*/descente *f* au barbu.

tongue-tingling ['tʌŋ'tɪŋlɪŋ] *a F* délicieux*/à s'en lécher les babines.

tonk [tɒŋk] *n P* 1. *Br* coït*/baise *f*/nique *f*/tringlage *m* 2. *Austr* (*a*) homosexuel*/pédé *m*/tapette *f* (*b*) homme* efféminé/gâcheuse *f*/galine *f* (*c*) individu* bête/crétin, -ine/andouille *f*. (*See* **honky-tonk**)

tonker ['tɒŋkə] *n Austr P* = **tonk 2**.

tonking ['tɒŋkɪŋ] *n Br P* coït*/baise *f*/tringlage *m*.

ton-up ['tʌnʌp] *n F* to do a ton-up, faire du cent-soixante à l'heure (*surt* en moto); the ton-up boys/kids, les motards *mpl*/les dingues *mpl* de la moto.

toodle-oo! toodle-pip! ['tuːdl'uː, -'pɪp] *excl O F* au revoir!/ciao!/salut!.

tool [tuːl] *n F* **1.** pénis*/outil *m* **2.** individu bête*/crétin, -ine; you tool! espèce de nœud! he's a real tool! quel connard/quel gland, ce mec! **3.** voleur* à la tire/pickpocket *m*/tireur, -euse/fourchette *f* **4.** *pl* (*drugs*) attirail *m* de camé/artillerie *f*/kit *m* **5.** *NAm* revolver*/flingue *m* **6.** *NAm* femme* sale/souillon *f*; femme* facile/salope *f*/poufiasse *f*.

tool about, around [tuːlə'baʊt, ə'raʊnd] *vi F* paresser*/glandouiller/tirer au flanc.

tool along ['tuːlə'lɒŋ] *vi F* se balader/glander; he was tooling along on the motorway, il roulait pépère sur l'autoroute.

tooled-up [tuːld'ʌp] *a Br P* **1.** armé/enfouraillé/chargé **2.** équipé d'outils pour un cambriolage.

tool up ['tuːl'ʌp] *vi Br P* se munir d'une arme à feu/s'enfourailler/se charger.

toon [tuːn] *n esp NAm F* (*abbr of cartoon*) dessin animé.

toot¹ [tuːt] *n P* **1.** (*drugs*) (*a*) prise *f* (par le nez)/snif(fe) *f ou m* d'une drogue* (*surt de cocaïne* ou d'amphétamine*) (*b*) drogue* prise par le nez/*surt* cocaïne* **2.** *Austr* WC*/téléphone *m*.

toot² [tuːt] *vtr & i P* (*drugs*) absorber (une drogue*/*surt* de la cocaïne* ou de l'amphétamine*) par le nez; sniffer; to toot a line, sniffer une ligne. (*See* **line¹ 9**)

tooth [tuːθ] *n F* **1.** to have a sweet tooth, aimer les sucreries *fpl* **2.** to be long in the tooth, n'être plus jeune/prendre de la bouteille **3.** to get one's teeth into sth, se mettre pour de bon à qch/s'attaquer à qch/se mettre à l'ouvrage/se plonger dans qch **4.** to knock s.o.'s teeth in, battre* qn/rentrer dans le chou à qn/amocher le portrait à qn **5.** to go at it tooth and nail, travailler* avec acharnement. (*See* **dress up 2; fed up** (*a*))

toothy-peg ['tuːθɪpeg] *n F* (*child's word*) dent*/chocotte *f*.

tootle ['tuːtl] *vi F* corner/klaxonner.

tootle along ['tuːtlə'lɒŋ] *vi F* s'en aller/se sauver.

toots [tʊts] *n F* (*to woman*) chérie *f*/poupée *f*; (*to small child*) doudou *m*; hi toots! salut cocotte!

tootsie ['tʊtsɪ] *n F* **1.** = **toots 2.** *pl F* (*child's language*) pieds*/petons *mpl*/pattes *fpl*.

tootsie-wootsies ['tʊtsɪ'wʊtsɪz] *npl F* = **tootsies (tootsie) 2.**

tootsy ['tʊtsɪ] *n F* = **toots; tootsie**.

top¹ [tɒp] *F* **I** *a* excellent*/chouette/super **II** *n* **1.** to go over the top, exagérer*/y aller fort/charrier/forcer la dose **2.** to blow one's top, se mettre en colère*/éclater/sortir de ses gonds/piquer une rage. (*See* **flip² 2**) **3.** (*Irish*) (the) top of the morning (to you!) (je vous souhaite) bien le bonjour! **4.** top of the shop: see **bingo 90.** (*See* **heap 2; rag-top; tail¹ 7; thin 1**)

top² [tɒp] *vtr P* (*a*) *O* pendre/exécuter (*b*) tuer*/descendre (qn); he topped himself, il s'est suicidé*/il s'est foutu en l'air.

top-hole ['tɒp'həʊl] *a O F* excellent*/foutral/au poil/épatant.

topknot ['tɒpnɒt] *n P* tête*/bobèche *f*/plafond *m*.

topnotch ['tɒp'nɒtʃ] *a O F* de premier ordre/de premier rang.

top-off ['tɒpɒf] *n Austr P* dénonciateur*/indic *mf*/donneur, -euse.

top off ['tɒp'ɒf] *vtr & i P* **1.** to top (it) off, finir/achever/terminer (qch) **2.** dénoncer*/servir d'indicateur* de police/en croquer.

topper ['tɒpə] *n F* **1.** le dessus du panier/le bouquet/la crème/le gratin **2.** (chapeau*) haut-de-forme *m*.

topping ['tɒpɪŋ] *a O F* excellent*/formid(able)/épatant.

topping-out ['tɒpɪŋ'aʊt] *n F* cérémonie *f* qui marque la fin de la construction du gros œuvre d'un bâtiment.

tops [tɒps] *n F* the tops, le dessus du panier/la crème/le gratin; he's the tops, il est champion/c'est un as.

torch¹ [tɔːtʃ] *n F* **1.** to carry a torch for s.o., aimer* qn qui ne vous aime pas/porter qn dans son cœur **2.** pyromane *mf*/incendiaire *mf* (*surt qui est payé pour incendier des bâtiments afin de toucher l'assurance-incendie*); torch job, incendie *m* volontaire/criminel.

torch² [tɔːtʃ] *vtr F* incendier/mettre le feu à (qch) (*surt pour détruire des pièces à conviction ou toucher l'assurance-incendie*).

tosh [tɒʃ] *n* **1.** *P* (*regional*) individu*/mec *m*/type *m* **2.** *F* bêtises*/sornettes *fpl*/blague *f*; that's tosh! c'est du bidon!

toss¹ [tɒs] *n Br P* **1.** (*sth worthless, useless*) bistrouille *f*/merdouille *f*/panade *f*; it's a load of toss, c'est de la briquette/ça pisse pas loin **2.** I couldn't give a (monkey's) toss! je n'en ai rien à branler/à glander/à foutre!

toss² [tɒs] *vtr P* **1.** perdre (un match, une course, etc) exprès; (*boxing*) to toss a fight, se coucher 2. fouiller/ratisser (un local) 3. *Austr (esp in sport)* battre (un adversaire).

tosser ['tɒsə] *n Br P (fool)* branleur *m*.

toss-off ['tɒsɒf] *n V* masturbation *f/* branlette *f*/secouette *f*.

toss off ['tɒs'ɒf] *vtr & i* 1. *V* to toss (oneself) off, se masturber*/se branler/s'astiquer la colonne 2. *F* to toss off a pint, boire*/ écluser un godet/s'en jeter un (derrière la cravate).

toss-pot ['tɒspɒt] *n P* 1. ivrogne*/picoleur, -euse/soûlard, -arde 2. *(fool)* crétin, -ine/ branleur *m*; *(incompetent person)* nullard, -arde; *(unpleasant person)* salaud*/loquedu, -ue.

toss-up ['tɒsʌp] *n F* une chance sur deux/ chance égale/pile ou face/kif-kif; it was a toss-up between his car and mine, entre sa tire et la mienne, c'était fifty-fifty.

total ['təʊt(ə)l] *vtr P (write off)* démolir/ bousiller / amocher / déglinguer / écrabouiller (qch).

tote[1] [təʊt] *n F (turf)* totaliseur *m/* totalisateur *m* (des paris)/le pari mutuel/le PMU.

tote[2] [təʊt] *F I vtr* porter/trimballer/ transbahuter; to tote a gun, être armé/chargé II *vi* to tote for business/custom, chercher à faire des affaires/quémander du travail; *(of prostitute)* racoler/tapiner/faire le tapin.

tother, t'other ['tʌðə] *a & pron F (= the other)* l'autre *(mf)*; you can't tell one from tother, ils sont du pareil au même/on ne peut les distinguer l'un de l'autre/ils se ressemblent comme deux gouttes d'eau.

totsie ['tɒtsɪ] *n*, **tottie, totty** ['tɒtɪ] *n Br P* fille*/poupée *f*/nénette *f*.

touch[1] [tʌtʃ] *n* 1. *P* to make a touch/to put the touch on s.o., emprunter* de l'argent à qn/taper qn/torpiller qn 2. *F* soft touch, personne *f* bête* et crédule/dupe *f*/jobard, -arde; he's a really soft touch, c'est un vrai cave/pigeon. *(See* **touch and go***)*

touch[2] [tʌtʃ] *vtr* 1. *P* to touch s.o. for money, emprunter*/taper de l'argent à qn; he touched me for a tenner, il m'a tapé de cent balles 2. *F* to touch lucky, avoir de la chance*/être veinard/avoir du pot/avoir tiré le bon numéro. *(See* **rock**[1] **4**; **wood 1***)*

touch and go ['tʌtʃən'gəʊ] *a F (uncertain)* très incertain/douteux; *(risky)* hasardeux/très risqué; it's touch and go whether we'll have time, c'est pas du tout sûr que nous aurons le temps; it was touch and go whether we would catch the train, on risquait bien/fort de manquer le train; it was touch and go with this project, ce projet ne tenait qu'à un fil; it was touch and go with her, elle a (bien) failli mourir/elle a failli y passer. *(See* **touch**[1] **2***)*

touched [tʌtʃt] *a F* touched (in the head), fou*/toqué/timbré/cinoque.

touch up ['tʌtʃ'ʌp] *vtr P* to touch up a girl, peloter une nana; mettre la main au panier/ aller aux renseignements.

tough [tʌf] *F I a* 1. a tough nut/guy/cookie, un dur (à cuire)/un coriace/un balaise/un saignant 2. he's a tough customer, il est pas très commode/c'est pas un rigolo/c'est un mauvais coucheur* 3. difficile* 4. tough luck/(a) tough break, malchance*/déveine *f*/guigne *f*; that's tough, c'est moche/c'est vache; tough shit! manque de pot!/quel merde! tough titty! pas de chance!/tant pis pour toi! II *n* vaurien*/ voyou *m*/loubard *m*.

toughie ['tʌfɪ] *n F* 1. = **tough** II 2. problème *m* difficile à résoudre/casse-tête *m*.

tout [taʊt] *n Br P (in Northern Ireland)* indicateur*/indic *mf*/donneur, -euse.

towel ['taʊəl] *vtr P* battre*/rosser/dérouiller.

towel head ['taʊəlhed] *n F Pej* arabe *mf/* arbi *m*/bicot *m*/raton *m*.

towelling ['taʊ(ə)lɪŋ] *n P* raclée *f*/peignée *f*/dérouillée *f*.

towel up ['taʊəl'ʌp] *vtr Austr P* = **towel**.

town [taʊn] *n F* 1. to go out on the town *(a)* faire la bombe/la foire/la noce *(b)* dépenser* sans compter/mettre le paquet 2. to go to town, *(make great effort)* se mettre en quatre; they really went to town, *(on doing a job, etc)* ils ont vraiment mis la paquet/fait très fort; *(preparing a party, etc)* ils ont vraiment fait les choses en grand. *(See* **red I 3***)*

town bike ['taʊnbaɪk] *n F* femme* aux mœurs légères/à la cuisse hospitalière; baiseuse *f*. *(See* **bike 4***)*

toyboy ['tɔɪbɔɪ] *n F* jeune amant* d'une femme* plus âgée/gigolo *m*/gosse *m*.

track [træk] *n* 1. *F* to hit the track/to make tracks, partir*/se mettre en route/plier bagage/mettre les bouts/se tailler; to make tracks for home, rentrer chez soi/regagner le bercail; right, must make tracks! bon, faut que je me sauve! 2. *P* tracks, marques *fpl* (de piqûres).

trackmarks ['trækmɑːks] *npl P* = **track 2**.

trad [træd] *F I a (= traditional)* traditionnel; trad jazz, jazz *m* Nouvelle-Orléans et ses dérivés **II** *n* (= *traditional jazz*) jazz traditionnel.

trade¹ [treɪd] *n* 1. *F* to take it out in trade, se faire payer en nature plutôt qu'en argent 2. *P* (*a*) clientèle *f* (d'une prostituée* *ou* d'un homosexuel*); miché *m*/micheton *m*/clille *m* (*b*) partenaire sexuel(le)/affaire *f* 3. *F* he knows all the tricks of the trade, il connaît tous les trucs/toutes les astuces.

trade² [treɪd] *vtr & i F* to trade punches, échanger des coups*/se crêper le chignon.

traf(f)¹ [træf] *n Br P* (*backslang of* **fart¹**) pet*/perle *f*/perlouze *f*.

traf(f)² [træf] *vi Br P* (*backslang of* **fart²**) péter*/cloquer/lâcher une perle.

trail [treɪl] *n F* to hit the trail, partir*/mettre les bouts/se tailler.

train [treɪn] *n* 1. *P* (*a*) coït* collectif/en série; to do a train on s.o., baiser qn à tour de rôle (*b*) to pull a train, (*of woman*) subir un viol collectif/être violée par plusieurs types 2. *F* train surfing, équipée *f* sur le toit d'un train. (*See* **gravy 1**; **milk-train**; **puffer(-train)**)

tramp [træmp] *n P* femme* facile/baiseuse *f*.

trannie, tranny ['trænɪ] *n Br F* 1. (= *transistor radio*) transistor *m*/poste *m* 2. (*homosexual use*) (*a*) transsexuel, -elle (*b*) travesti *m*/trave(lo) *m*.

trap [træp] *n P* 1. bouche*/gueule *f*; shut your trap! ta gueule!/la ferme! to keep one's trap shut, taire sa gueule/la boucler 2. *pl esp NAm Mus* (*drum kit*) batterie *f* (de jazz, etc). (*See* **fleatrap**; **rat-trap**)

trash [træʃ] *n NAm P* 1. mendiant*/clodo *m*/mangave *m* 2. white trash, petits blancs pauvres.

trashed [træʃt] *a NAm F* 1. ivre*/bituré/pété 2. trashed out, très fatigué*/éreinté/lessivé/vanné.

travel-agent ['trævl'eɪdʒənt] *n P* (*drugs*) fournisseur *m* de LSD/dealer* d'acide.

traveller ['træv(ə)lə] *n F* romanichel, -elle/manouche *mf*/romano *mf*.

trawler ['trɔːlə] *n Austr P* car* de police/panier *m* à salade/fourgon *m*.

tray-bits ['treɪbɪts] *npl*, **trays** [treɪz] *npl Austr P* = **threepenny-bits 1**.

tree [triː] *n* 1. *F* up a tree, dans le pétrin/dans de beaux draps/dans la mélasse 2. *F* they don't grow on trees, on n'en trouve pas comme ça si facilement/ça ne court pas les rues 3. *NAm P* to be out of one's tree, (*be crazy*) débloquer/être secoué. (*See* **apple tree**; **Christmas tree**; **gum-tree**)

tremendous [trɪ'mendəs] *a F* 1. énorme/immense; a tremendous decision, une décision très importante 2. formidable; a tremendous time was had by all, on s'est drôlement/follement amusés.

tremendously [trɪ'mendəslɪ] *adv F* énormément/drôlement/vachement.

trendoid ['trendɔɪd] *n P* individu* branché.

trendy ['trendɪ] *F* **I** *a* à la mode/dans le vent/branché/codé; a really trendy restaurant, un resto à la mode/branché **II** *n* individu* branché.

trey-bits ['treɪbɪts] *npl*, **treys** [treɪz] *npl Austr P* = **threepenny-bits 1**.

tribe [traɪb] *n F* tribu *f*/smala(h) *f*; (toute) une kyrielle/une ribambelle (d'enfants).

trick¹ [trɪk] **I** *n* 1. *F* how's tricks? quoi de neuf? 2. *F* he doesn't miss a trick, rien ne lui échappe/il est roublard/il est malin comme pas deux 3. *F* that should do the trick, ça fera l'affaire 4. *P* (*a*) client *m* (d'une prostituée*)/clille *m*/micheton *m*/miché *m* (*b*) coït* tarifé (d'une prostituée*)/passe *f*; to turn a trick, faire une passe 5. *F* to be up to all sorts of tricks, faire les quatre cents coups **II** *a F* sophistiqué; séduisant/giron(d); he bought himself a really trick bike, il s'est acheté une moto super-cool. (*See* **bag¹ 5, 6**; **funny I 2**; **trade¹ 3**)

trick² [trɪk] *vi & tr NAm P* (*of prostitute*) racoler*/faire le truc; to trick a john, monter un client/un micheton; faire une passe.

trick-cyclist ['trɪk'saɪklɪst] *n P* psy(chiatre) *mf*.

triff [trɪf] *a Br F* excellent*/super/canon.

trigger-happy ['trɪgəhæpɪ] *a F* to be trigger-happy, avoir la gâchette facile/flinguer pour un oui pour un non.

trigger-man ['trɪgəmæn] *n F* (*violent man, killer*) but(t)eur *m*/flingueur *m*.

trip¹ [trɪp] *n P* 1. (*drugs*) (*a*) dose *f*/cachet *m* de LSD* (*b*) voyage *m*/trip *m*; to take/to go on a trip, être sous l'effet du LSD*/faire un voyage/triper; faire/prendre un trip 2. état *m* d'esprit; expérience personnelle; she's on a guilt trip, (*she feels guilty*) elle se culpabilise.

trip² [trɪp] *vi P* 1. être sous l'effet du LSD*/faire un voyage/triper 2. *NAm* (*date s.o.*) sortir avec qn. (*See* **trip out**)

tripe [traɪp] *n F* bêtises*/sornettes *fpl*/fichaises *fpl*; that's tripe, c'est du flan/du pipeau.

tripehound ['traɪphaʊnd] *n Br P* vaurien*/charogne *f*/ordure *f*.

trip out ['trɪp'aʊt] *vi & tr P* (*drugs*) être sous l'effet du LSD*/triper; **to be tripped out,** (*under influence of LSD*) triper/voyager; (*in a state of euphoria*) être envapé/être sur sa planète/planer.

trizzer ['trɪzə] *n Austr A P* WC*/chiottes *fpl.*

troll [trəʊl] *vi Br P* marcher*/se balader/se trimbaler/bagoter.

trolley ['trɒlɪ] *n F* off one's trolley= off one's rocker (**rocker 2**).

troppo ['trɒpəʊ] *a Austr P* (*mentally affected by a tropical climate*) he's gone troppo, le soleil lui a trop tapé sur le citron/il a pris un coup de bambou.

trot [trɒt] *n* 1. *F* on the trot, à la suite/coup sur coup; **to win four times on the trot,** gagner quatre fois de suite 2. *F* to keep s.o. on the trot, faire trotter qn/actionner qn 3. *P* the trots, diarrhée*/courante *f*/chiasse *f* 4. *P Pol* (= *trotskyite*) trotskiste *mf*/gauchiste *mf*/gaucho *mf*/stal *mf.*

trot artist ['trɒt'ɑ:tɪst] *n Austr P* avare*/grippe-sou *m* (*qui s'en va aux toilettes pour éviter d'offrir une tournée*).

trotter ['trɒtə] *n P* 1. déserteur *m*/désert *m* 2. évadé, -ée (de prison)/détenu, -ue en cavale 3. *pl* pieds*/trottinets *mpl.*

troub [trʌb] *n Br F* (*abbr of trouble*) = **trub.**

trouble ['trʌbl] *n* 1. *F* to get a girl into trouble, rendre une fille enceinte*/mettre une fille en cloque 2. *P* trouble (and strife), (*RS = wife*) épouse*.

trough¹ [trɒf] *n F* (= *feeding trough*) assiette *f*/tuile *f.*

trough² [trɒf] *vi Br F* manger*/bouffer/gameler.

trouser ['traʊzə] *vtr Br F* (*put in pocket*) empocher; (*steal*) empocher/chiper.

trousers ['traʊzəz] *npl F* she's the one who wears the trousers, c'est elle qui porte la culotte. (*See* **pants 7**)

trouser-snake ['traʊzəsneɪk] *n Austr P* (one-eyed) trouser-snake, pénis*/anguille *f* de calecif.

trout [traʊt] *n P* vieille femme*/vieille bique.

trub [trʌb] *n Br F* (*abbr of trouble*) difficulté *f*/emmerdement(s) *m(pl)*; I'm having a bit of trub, j'ai des emmerdes.

truck-driver ['trʌkdraɪvə] *n P* 1. (*drugs*) amphétamine*/amph *f.* (*See* **driver 2**) 2. lesbienne masculine/gouine *f.*

truckie ['trʌkɪ] *n Austr F* camionneur *m*/routier *m.*

true [tru:] *a NAm F* 1. vrai/authentique 2. loyal/franco/nickel.

trump [trʌmp] *n F* 1. *A* brave homme*/chic type *m*/brave mec *m* 2. to turn up trumps, faire des miracles; he really turned up trumps, il nous a rendu salement service/il a fait des merveilles. (*See* **card 5**)

trusty ['trʌstɪ] *n F* détenu, -ue à qui l'on fait confiance/prévôt *m.*

try-on ['traɪɒn] *n F* (coup *m* de) bluff *m*; it's a try-on, c'est du bluff/de l'esbrouf(f)e.

try on ['traɪ'ɒn] *vtr F* to try it on (with s.o.), bluffer; they're just trying it on, ils bluffent/c'est du bluff; don't (you) try it on with me! (il ne) faut pas me la refaire (à moi)!/(ne) ramène pas avec moi! just (you) try it on! chiche!/essaye pour voir! to try it on with a woman, aller aux renseignements/faire du rentre-dedans; she tried it on with my husband, elle a essayé de lever mon mari.

tub [tʌb] *n F* 1. tub (of lard), individu* gros/gravos, -osse/gros lard 2. (*boat*) rafiot *m*/sabot *m* 3. voiture*/bagnole *f*; camion *m*/gros-cul *m*; autobus *m*/ronibus *m.*

tube [tju:b] *n F* 1. it's my tubes [mɪ'tju:bz], c'est mes bronches 2. the Tube, le Métro/le tube; we came by Tube, nous avons pris le tube 3. the tube, la télé/la téloche. 4. *Austr O* boîte *f* de bière/can(n)ette *f* 5. that's £500 down the tubes, voilà 500 livres foutues en l'air/qui s'envolent en fumée; that's all our efforts gone down the tubes, et voilà tous nos efforts foutus par terre 6. (*surfer's term*) creux formé par une vague déferlante. (*See* **boob tube**).

tubular ['tju:bjʊlə] *a F* excellent*/chouette/super; it's totally tubular, c'est géant/c'est le pied.

tuck [tʌk] *n F* (*schools*) nourriture*/bectance *f*/boustifaille *f.* (*See* **tuckshop**)

tuck away ['tʌkə'weɪ] *vtr F* 1. cacher/mettre à gauche 2. to tuck it away, boire* *ou* manger*; s'en mettre derrière la cravate/s'en mettre jusque-là/se les caler/se taper la cloche.

tucked up [tʌkt'ʌp] *a Br P* 1. en prison*/à l'ombre/au trou 2. trompé/roulé/pigeonné. (*See* **tuck up**)

tucker ['tʌkə] *n Austr F* nourriture*/bectance *f*/boustifaille *f.* (*See* **bib**)

tuckered (out) ['tʌkəd('aʊt)] *a P* fatigué*/éreinté/vanné/lessivé.

tuck-in ['tʌk'ɪn] *n F* bon repas/bon gueuleton; to have a good tuck-in, faire un bon gueuleton/s'en mettre plein la lampe.

tuck in ['tʌk'ɪn] *vi F* manger* de bon cœur/ s'en mettre plein la lampe/se taper la cloche; tuck in! vas-y, mange!/attaque!

tuck into ['tʌk'ɪntuː] *vtr F* to tuck into a meal, manger* un repas à belles dents/faire honneur (à un repas).

tuckshop ['tʌkʃɒp] *n F* (*schools*) annexe *f* de la cantine où se vendent les friandises *fpl.* (*See* **tuck**)

tuck up ['tʌk'ʌp] *vtr P* entuber/rouler/ avoir/pigeonner (qn).

tumble¹ ['tʌmbl] *n P* 1. to have a tumble with s.o., faire l'amour* avec qn/faire une partie de jambes en l'air avec qn 2. arrestation*/emballage *m*/piquage *m*; détention *f*/planque *f.*

tumble² ['tʌmbl] *vtr & i F* 1. to tumble (a woman), culbuter/sauter (une femme) 2. to tumble to sth, (*understand*) piger qch; then he tumbled to it, et puis il a fini par piger.

tummy ['tʌmɪ] *n F* ventre*/bide *m*/bidon *m.*

tummy-ache ['tʌmɪeɪk] *n F* mal *m* de ventre.

tuna ['t(j)uːnə] *n NAm P* femme* *ou* fille*/ morue *f*/poule *f.*

tune [tjuːn] *n F* 1. to be fined to the tune of £80, prendre/ramasser une amende de 80 livres 2. to change one's tune, changer de ton/ de gamme/de note. (*See* **old 4**)

tuned in ['tjuːnd'ɪn] *a P* branché.

tup [tʌp] *vtr Br P* faire l'amour* avec (qn)/ baiser/caramboler.

tuppence ['tʌp(ə)ns] *n O F* (= *twopence*) I don't care tuppence, ça m'est bien égal/je m'en fiche pas mal; it's not worth tuppence, ça ne vaut pas un sou/tripette/un pet de lapin.

tuppenny ['tʌpnɪ] *a O F* (= *twopenny*) I don't give/care a tuppenny damn/V a tuppenny fuck, je m'en fiche complètement/je m'en contrefiche/V je m'en fous pas mal/je m'en branle complètement. (*See* **damn¹ III**)

tuppenny-ha'penny ['tʌpnɪ'heɪpnɪ] *a O F* (= *twopenny-halfpenny*) insignifiant/piètre/ de quatre sous/de rien du tout.

turd [tɜːd] *n P* 1. étron*/colombin *m*/merde *f*/sentinelle *f* 2. saligaud *m*/salaud *m*/fumier *m*/ordure *f*; he's a real turd, c'est un vrai con/un sale type; you turd! (espèce de) salaud! 3. to skin a turd, être avare*/être constipé du morlingue.

turd-burglar ['tɜːdbɜːglə] *n Br V* homosexuel*/amateur *m* de rosette/chevalier *m* de la rosette/amateur *m* de terre jaune.

turf [tɜːf] *n P* territoire *m*/champ *m* d'action (d'une bande de criminels).

turf out ['tɜːf'aʊt] *vtr F* flanquer dehors/ balancer/envoyer dinguer.

turistas [tʊ'rɪstəz] *n NAm P* the turistas, la diarrhée*/la courante/la chiasse/la turista.

turkey ['tɜːkɪ] *n* 1. *P* (*drugs*) cold turkey, sevrage *m* de drogues; to be/have cold turkey, être en manque/flipper/avoir un singe sur le dos; to go (through) cold turkey, faire un sevrage 2. *esp NAm F* to talk turkey (*a*) parler* sérieusement/en venir au fait (*b*) *V* pratiquer la fellation* *ou* le cunnilinctus* 3. *esp NAm P* abruti, -ie/crétin, -ine 4. *esp NAm P* (*failed play, film*) bide *m*/four *m.*

turn [tɜːn] *n F* 1. (*a*) it gave me quite a (nasty) turn, mon sang n'a fait qu'un tour/ça m'a fait quelque chose/tout retourné (*b*) you gave me such a turn! vous m'avez fait une belle peur*!/vous m'avez retourné le sang! 2. she had one of her turns, elle a eu une de ses crises/une de ses attaques.

turned-on ['tɜːnd'ɒn] *a & pp* 1. *F* dans le vent/à la coule/branché 2. *P* (*sexually*) allumé/excité/chauffé; he gets turned on by black leather, le cuir noir c'est son truc/le cuir noir le fait bander.

turn in ['tɜːn'ɪn] *vtr & i F* 1. se coucher*/se pieuter/se mettre au pieu 2. (*hand in*) rendre/ rapporter (qch); (*betray to police*) livrer/ vendre (qn); to turn oneself in (to the police), se constituer prisonnier/se livrer 3. quitter/ abandonner/plaquer (son emploi).

turniphead ['tɜːnɪphed] *n P* individu bête*/cruche *f*/andouille *f.*

turn-off ['tɜːnɒf] *n P* it's a turn-off, c'est dégoûtant/dégueulasse; it was a real turn-off for me, ça m'a foutu les boules; (*sexually*) ça m'a coupé l'envie.

turn off ['tɜːn'ɒf] *vtr P* 1. ennuyer/ emmerder/casser les pieds à (qn) 2. écœurer/ dégoûter (qn); (*sexually*) couper l'envie à; that sort of thing turns me off completely, ces trucs-là, ça me fout les boules; you really turn me off! tu me débectes!

turn-on ['tɜːnɒn] *n P* 1. drogue*/came *f*; my turn-on's cocaine, mon truc c'est la coke 2. qch d'excitant/d'emballant; it's a turn-on! (*exciting*) c'est craquant! that was a real turn-on! c'était le pied! she's a real turn-on, (*sexually*) elle est vachement excitante.

turn on ['tɜːn'ɒn] *vtr & i* 1. *F* emballer/ botter/brancher (qn); that turns me on, ça me botte/ça me branche/c'est comme ça que je prends mon pied 2. *P (drugs)* prendre une drogue*/se camer 3. *P (sexually)* exciter/ allumer/faire bander (qn); **she really turns him on**, elle le fait bander à mort.

turnout ['tɜːnaʊt] *n F* 1. assemblée *f*/foule *f*/assistance *f*; **they had a good turnout at the meeting**, il y avait du monde/du trèpe à la réunion 2. vêtements*/tenue *f*/uniforme *m*.

turn over ['tɜːn'əʊvə] *vtr Br P* 1. voler*/ faucher/piquer; **to turn s.o. over**, refaire qn/ rouler qn/truander qn; **to turn a place over**, faire un cambriolage/un fric-frac/un casse 2. **to turn over a cell**, fouiller une cellule.

turn-up ['tɜːnʌp] *n P* **that's a turn-up (for the book)**, ça c'est une sacrée/une belle surprise!

turn up ['tɜːn'ʌp] *vtr & i F* 1. arriver* (à l'improviste)/débarquer/s'amener; **he turned up ten minutes late**, il s'est amené dix minutes en retard 2. **turn it up!** arrête (les frais)!/c'est fini, oui!/écrase! (*See* **nose 6**; **toe 4**)

turps [tɜːps] *n F* 1. (= *turpentine*) (essence *f* de) térébenthine *f* 2. *Austr* boisson* alcoolique/tord-boyaux *m*/gnôle *f*; **to hit the turps**, écluser/picoler.

tush, tushie ['tʌʃ(i)] *n NAm P* = **tokus.**

tutti-frutti ['tʊtɪ'frʊtɪ] *n esp NAm F* homme* efféminé *ou* maniéré/chochotte *f*/ galine *f*.

tux [tʌks] *n NAm F (abbr of tuxedo)* smoking *m*/smok *m*.

T.V. [tiː'viː] *n F (a)* tra(ns)vestisme *m (b)* travesti *m*/travelo *m*.

twam(my) ['twæm(ɪ)] *n P* = **twat 1.**

twang [twæŋ] *n Austr P (drugs)* opium*/ toufiane *f*/noir *m*.

twat [twæt, twɒt] *n* 1. *V* sexe* de la femme*/con *m*/moule *f* 2. *P* individu bête*/ idiot, -ote/con *m*, conne *f*/connard, -arde; **you great twat!** espèce de nœud*/d'andouille/de couillon!

tweak [twiːk] *vi NAm P (drugs)* être en manque/flipper.

twee [twiː] *a F (a)* gentil/mignon *(b) Pej* maniéré/mignard; **that's terribly twee**, ça fait très cucul (la praline).

tweetie(-pie) ['twiːtɪ('paɪ)] *n F* = sweetie(-pie) **(sweetie 2).**

twenty-five ['twentɪ'faɪv] *n P (rare) (drugs)* LSD*/vingt-cinq *m*.

twerp [twɜːp] *n F* individu bête*/ballot *m*/ crétin, -ine; **what a twerp!** quelle andouille!/ quelle nouille!

twig [twɪg] *vtr & i Br P* comprendre/saisir/ piger/entraver; **now I twig it!** j'y suis maintenant! **and then he twigged!** et puis, ça a fait tilt!

twink [twɪŋk] *n*, **twinkie, twinky** ['twɪŋkɪ] *n NAm P* 1. homosexuel* *ou* homme* efféminé/chochotte *f*/folle *f* 2. individu* mignon*/choupinet.

twirl [twɜːl] *n P* 1. gardien* de prison/maton *m*/matuche *m* 2. clef*/passe-partout *m*/ caroub(l)e *f*.

twirp [twɜːp] *n F* = **twerp.**

twist¹ [twɪst] *n P* 1. **to go round the twist**, devenir fou*/perdre la boule/déménager; **he drives me round the twist**, il me rend fou/ dingue. (*See* **bend¹ 1**) 2. *(drugs)* marijuana*/marie-jeanne *f* 3. *NAm* (jolie) fille* *ou* femme*/(belle) pépée/(jolie) nénette. (*See* **knickers 1**)

twist² [twɪst] *vtr F* 1. escroquer*/frauder/ filouter/arnaquer 2. **to twist s.o.'s arm**, persuader qn/forcer la main à qn; **he likes to have his arm twisted**, il aime se faire prier; **go on! twist my arm!** vas-y toujours!/insiste un peu! je ne dirai pas non. (*See* **finger¹ 9**)

twisted ['twɪstɪd] *a P (drugs)* chargé/ défoncé/camé (jusqu'aux yeux).

twister ['twɪstə] *n F* 1. escroc*/faux jeton/ fripouille *f*/filou *m*/arnaqueur *m* 2. casse-tête (chinois).

twit [twɪt] *n Br F* individu bête*/andouille *f*/ con(n)eau *m*; **you silly twit!** espèce de nœud!/pauvre con, va!

twitcher ['twɪtʃə] *n Br F* observateur, -trice d'oiseaux/ornithologue *mf*.

twitter ['twɪtə] *n F* 1. **to be all of a twitter/in a twitter**, être tout en émoi/être dans tous ses états 2. *(schools, in Scotland)* **to have the twitters**, avoir la tremblote/la trouille. (*See* **ring¹ 1**)

two [tuː] *n F* 1. **to put two and two together**, tirer/en déduire ses conclusions; tirer la leçon de la chose; **he's capable of putting two and two together and getting five**, chez lui deux et deux font cinq, c'est dire s'il est con/il est con comme un balai 2. **all the twos**: *see* **bingo 22.** (*See* **one-two**; **thing 6**)

two and eight [tuː ən(d)'eɪt] *n Br P (RS = state)* 1. nervosité *f*/agitation *f*/cirque *m* 2. individu* désordonné/dépeigné.

two-bit ['tuː'bɪt] *a NAm F* insignifiant/de quatre sous/à la gomme; *(person)* à la noix.

twopenny-halfpenny ['tʌpnɪ'heɪpnɪ] *a F* = **tuppenny-ha'penny.**

two-pot screamer ['tuːpɒt'skriːmə] *n*
Austr P individu* qui ne tient pas l'alcool.

twot [twɒt] *n P* = **twat 1, 2.**

two-time ['tuː'taɪm] *vtr F* **1.** tromper (qn)
(en amour)/doubler (qn) **2.** (*cheat, swindle*)
duper*/tromper.

two-timer ['tuː'taɪmə] *n F* mari *m ou*
femme *f ou* copain *m ou* copine infidèle.

two-timing ['tuː'taɪmɪŋ] *a esp NAm F*
infidèle; **you two-timing bastard!** espèce de
salaud*!

tyke [taɪk] *n P* **1.** *often Pej* natif, -ive du
comté de Yorkshire **2.** vilain chien*/sale cabot
m/clébard *m* **3.** *esp Austr* catholique *mf*/catho
mf **4.** (*small child*) môme *mf*; **you little tyke!**
petit morveux!

typo ['taɪpəʊ] *n F* (=*typographical error*)
coquille *f*.

U

U [juː] *a O F* (= *upper class*) his accent is very U, il a un petit accent de la haute; that's not a terribly U thing to do, ça (ne) fait pas très distingué, ça.

udders ['ʌdəz] *npl P* seins*/boîtes *fpl* à lait/roploplots *mpl*.

u-ie ['juːɪ] *n F* demi-tour *m*; to do/hang a u-ie, faire demi-tour.

umpteen [ʌmp'tiːn] *a F* je ne sais combien; they have umpteen kids, ils ont je ne sais combien de gosses/ils ont une ribambelle de gosses; to have umpteen reasons for doing sth, avoir trente-six raisons de faire qch; I've told you umpteen times, je vous l'ai dit mille fois/x [iks] fois.

umpteenth [ʌmp'tiːnθ] *a F* (é)nième/xième ['iksjɛm].

umpty ['ʌm(p)tɪ] *a O P* un peu malade*/mal fichu/pas dans son assiette/patraque.

'un [ən] *pron F* (= *one*) individu*/quelqu'un/type *m*/mec *m*; a little 'un, un petiot; a wrong 'un, une fripouille/un chenapan/un zigoto.

Uncle, uncle ['ʌŋkl] *n* 1. *Br P* prêteur, -euse (sur gages)/ma tante; at (my) uncle's, chez ma tante/au clou 2. *Br P* (*RS*) Uncle Dick (*a*) (= *prick*) pénis*/Popaul *m*. (*See* **dick 1**) (*b*) (= *sick*) (*also* **uncle**) malade*; he's a bit uncle, il est mal fichu/mal en point 3. *Br P* (*RS*) Uncle (Ned) (*a*) (= *dead*) mort (*b*) (=*bed*) lit* (*c*) (= *head*) tête* 4. *F* Uncle Sam, l'oncle *m* Sam/les États-Unis *mpl* (d'Amérique)/le gouvernement des États-Unis 5. *P* receleur*/fourgue *m* 6. *NAm F* Uncle Tom, Noir *m* qui s'insinue dans les bonnes grâces des Blancs/Oncle *m* Tom 7. *NAm P* organisation chargée de l'application *f* de la loi 8. *NAm F* to say/cry uncle, se rendre; (*schools*) dire/crier pouce 9. *Br P* Uncle Bill/Bob, la police*/la flicaille/la Maison poulaga. (*See* **Bob²**; **Dutch I 5**)

uncool ['ʌn'kuːl] *a P* (*a*) conventionnel/conformiste/ringard (*b*) pas cool; it's uncool to be miserable, c'est pas cool d'être triste.

uncut ['ʌnkʌt] *a P* 1. (*drugs*) (*esp heroin*) pur 2. (*homosexual*) non circoncis.

uncute [ʌn'kjuːt] *a P* pas mignon/moche/pas jojo.

under ['ʌndə] *prep F* to be under the doctor, être en traitement/être sous surveillance médicale. (*See* **weather 1**)

underarm ['ʌndərɑːm] *a Br P* (*a*) louche/pas net/magouilleur (*b*) illégal/illicite.

underchunders ['ʌndətʃʌndəz] *npl Austr P* culotte *f* (de femme); caleçon *m* (d'homme)/cal(e)cif *m*/calbar *m*.

underdaks ['ʌndədæks] *npl Austr P* caleçon *m* (d'homme)/slip *m*/cal(e)cif *m*/calbar *m*.

undergrad ['ʌndə'græd] *n F* (= *undergraduate*) étudiant(e) (de licence).

under-the-counter ['ʌndəðə'kauntə] *a F* au marché noir/en sous-main. (*See* **counter**)

underwhelmed [ʌndə'welmd] *a F* déçu/qui l'a mauvaise.

undies ['ʌndɪz] *npl F* sous-vêtements féminins/lingerie *f*/dessous *mpl*/fringues *fpl* de coulisse.

unearthly [ʌn'ɜːðlɪ] *a F* at an unearthly hour, à une heure impossible/à une heure pas permise; for some unearthly reason, pour une raison absurde. (*See* **ungodly**)

unflappable ['ʌn'flæpəbl] *a F* imperturbable/calme/qui ne s'affole pas/cool.

ungetatable ['ʌnget'ætəbl] *a F* inaccessible; (*place*) paumé.

unglued ['ʌn'gluːd] *a NAm P* frénétique/forcené/affolé/dans tous ses états.

ungodly [ʌn'gɒdlɪ] *a F* at an/some ungodly hour, à une heure impossible/à une heure pas permise.

unhip [ʌn'hɪp] *a P* (*a*) (*not up-to-date*) qui n'est pas à la coule/branché/câblé; ringard (*b*) (*not cool*) qui n'est pas cool.

unhitched ['ʌn'hɪtʃt] *a & pp F* to get unhitched, divorcer/se démaquer/casser le bail. (*See* **hitch 2**)

uni ['ju:nɪ] *n F* université *f*/fac *f*.

unit ['ju:nɪt] *n P* 1. organes génitaux*; *surt* sexe* de l'homme/artillerie *f* 2. partenaire sexuel(le)/affaire *f*.

unload [ʌn'ləʊd] *vi P* 1. déféquer*/défarguer 2. péter*/lâcher une perle.

unlucky ['ʌn'lʌkɪ] *a F* unlucky for some: *see* **bingo** 13.

unmentionables [ʌn'menʃ(ə)nəblz] *npl O Hum F* 1. sous-vêtements *mpl*/fringues *fpl* de coulisse 2. organes génitaux*.

unprintable [ʌn'prɪntəbl] *n F* gros mot/ mot obscène.

unreal [ʌn'ri:l] *a F* (*very good, very bad, unbelievable*) dingue.

unstuck [ʌn'stʌk] *a & pp F* to come unstuck (*a*) (*of project, etc*) s'effondrer/s'écrouler/ tomber à l'eau/partir à vau l'eau (*b*) (*of person*) tomber sur un bec/tomber sur un os/ cafouiller.

unthinkables [ʌn'θɪŋkəblz] *npl Br Hum* = **unmentionables**.

untied [ʌn'taɪd] *a NAm P* = **unglued**.

untogether [ʌntə'geðə] *a F* (*person*) déséquilibré/embrouillé/flippé.

unwashed [ʌn'wɒʃt] *n F Hum* the Great Unwashed, les prolétaires *mpl*/les prolos *mpl*.

up¹ [ʌp] **I** *a F* 1. euphorique/high/défoncé/ planant; to be up, planer/voyager/être sur sa planète 2. up drugs, drogues stimulantes psychiques/stimulants *mpl*/dopants *mpl*. (*See* **down¹ I**; **uppers**) 3. heureux/en pleine forme/qui pète la santé 4. *Austr* up oneself, satisfait de soi-même/suffisant/qui pète plus haut que son cul **II** *adv* 1. *F* to be up against it, avoir la malchance*/la guigne/la déveine/la poisse; we're really up against it now, on a la super-poisse maintenant 2. *F* to be up to sth, fabriquer/mijoter/manigancer qch; what's he up to now? qu'est-ce qu'il mijote? 3. *F* it's all up/the game's up, c'est fichu/c'est cuit/c'est râpé. (*See* **all II 1**) 4. *F* what's up? que se passe-t-il?/qu'y a-t-il?/ça ne va pas? 5. *P* to have it up, être en érection*/l'avoir en l'air. (*See* **move 2**) **III** *n* 1. *F* to be on the up and up (*a*) (*improving*) être en train de faire son chemin /prospérer/faire son beurre; his career is on the up and up, il fait son chemin/il grimpe les échelons (*b*) (*honest*) être honnête/clair/réglo 2. *P* (*drugs*) see **uppers** 3. *F* to give s.o. a quick up and down, jauger qn/se faire une idée de qn. (*See* **high-ups**) **IV** *prep V* up yours! va te faire enculer!/tu peux te le foutre quelque part!/je t'emmerde! (*See*

arse I 7; **creek**; **duff¹ II 2**; **flue 1, 3**; **gonga**; **jumper**; **Khyber**; **poke¹ 6**; **pole 4**; **spout¹ 1, 2, 3**; **stick² 3**)

up² [ʌp] *vtr & i* 1. *F* to up sticks, déménager/ décaniller/bouger ses bois/plier bagages 2. *P* (*a*) se lever d'un bond; then he upped and left, puis il est parti très soudainement/il s'est cassé (*b*) agir avec élan; so I ups and tells him what I think, et je me suis lancé et lui ai dit exactement ce que je pensais/ses quatre vérités 3. *F* augmenter; to up the volume, monter/lever le son/mettre plus fort.

upbeat ['ʌpbi:t] *a F* (*a*) pétillant/fringant/ pimpant (*b*) optimiste. (*See* **downbeat**)

upchuck ['ʌptʃʌk] *vi F* vomir*/dégueuler/ gerber.

upfront [ʌp'frʌnt] *a F* honnête/nickel/réglo.

upholstery [ʌp'həʊlstərɪ] *n P* seins*/ avant-scène *f*/balcon *m*. (*See* **well-upholstered**)

up-market ['ʌp'mɑ:kɪt] *a F* haut de gamme/qui a de la classe; qui vaut très cher. (*See* **down-market**)

upper ['ʌpə] *a F* 1. upper storey, tête*/ cerveau *m*/ciboulot *m*/cafetière *f*; to be weak in the upper storey, avoir une araignée au plafond 2. upper crust, la crème/le gratin/le dessus du panier/la haute/les aristos *mpl*; they're upper crust, ils sont de la haute/c'est des aristos. (*See* **lip 2**; **ten 1**)

uppers ['ʌpəz] *npl* 1. *P* (*drugs*) amphétamines*/amphets *fpl*/amphés *fpl* 2. *F* to be down on one's uppers, être très pauvre*/ être dans la purée noire/être dans la dèche. (*See* **downer 1**)

uppish ['ʌpɪʃ] *a*, **uppity** ['ʌpɪtɪ] *a F* prétentieux*/arrogant/crâneur/hautain; to get uppity, en installer/se croire qn; don't you get uppity with me! ne joue pas les arrogants avec moi!

upriver [ʌp'rɪvə] *a & adv NAm F* en prison*/en taule; he was sent upriver, on l'a mis au frais.

ups-a-daisy! ['ʌpsə'deɪzɪ] *excl F* hoop là!

upset ['ʌpset] *n F* querelle*/engueulade *f*; they had a bit of an upset, ils ont eu une prise de bec.

upsides ['ʌpsaɪdz] *adv F* to be upsides with s.o., être quitte avec qn/rendre la monnaie de sa pièce à qn.

upstage [ʌp'steɪdʒ] *vtr F* reléguer (qn) au second plan/souffler la vedette à (qn).

upstairs [ʌp'stɛəz] *adv F* 1. to have sth upstairs, être intelligent*/avoir du chignon;

he's not got much **upstairs**, c'est pas une lumière **2.** poitrine*/seins*; **she's got plenty upstairs**, il y a du monde au balcon **3.** au ciel; **the man upstairs**, le bon Dieu; **she's gone upstairs**, elle est morte/elle est partie au ciel. (*See* **kick upstairs**)

upstate [ʌp'steɪt] *a & adv NAm F* = **upriver**.

upsy-daisy! ['ʌpsɪ'deɪzɪ] *excl F* = **oops-a-daisy!**

uptake ['ʌpteɪk] *n F* (*a*) **to be quick on the uptake**, comprendre vite/avoir l'esprit vif/avoir la comprenette facile (*b*) **to be slow on the uptake**, avoir la comprenette difficile/être lent à la détente.

uptight ['ʌp'taɪt] *a F* **1.** (*nervous*) tendu/nerveux; **don't get uptight about it!** te fais pas toute cette bile pour ça!/t'en fais donc pas comme ça! **2.** (*inhibited*) coincé; (*on particular occasion*) crispé; **relax, don't be so uptight**, relaxe-toi, ne sois pas aussi crispé **3.** (*conventional*) (*parents, attitude*) dur/strict **4.** (*upset, irritated*) énervé/fâché **5.** *NAm* excellent*/au poil/soi-soi.

urban surfing ['ɜːbən'sɜːfɪŋ] *n F* voyager/rouler a l'extérieur d'une voiture/d'un train, etc.

us [ʌs, əs] *pron F* (= *me*) moi; **give us a kiss!** alors, on m'embrasse?/fais-moi une bise! **let's have a look!** laisse-moi regarder!/fais voir!

u.s. [juː'es] *a Br F* (*object*) inutile/nul; (*person*) bon à rien/nul.

use [juːz] I *vtr* **1.** *F* exploiter/tirer parti de (qn)/abuser de (qn) **2.** *F* prendre plaisir à/profiter de (qch); **I could use a cup of tea**, je ne dirais pas non à une tasse de thé; **I could use a week's holiday**, une semaine de vacances ne me ferait pas de mal II *vi P* se droguer*/se camer.

useful ['juːsfʊl] *a F* efficace/habile/cap(able); **he's pretty useful with his fists**, il sait bien jouer des poings/il sait se servir de ses poings.

user ['juːzə] *n P* drogué*/camé, -ée/toxico *mf*/junkie *mf*.

using ['juːzɪŋ] *a P* drogué*/camé; **he's using again**, il recommence à se camer.

usual ['juːʒʊəl] *n F* **the usual**, ce que l'on a *ou* prend d'habitude/l'ordinaire; **he had his usual, a bottle of red wine**, il siffla son litron quotidien; **the usual?** comme d'habitude?

ute [juːt] *n Austr F* (*abbr of utility vehicle*) camionnette *f*.

u.v.'s [juː'viːz] *npl NAm F* (*abbr of ultra-violet rays*) rayons ultra-violets/soleil *m*; **I'm gonna catch/cop/grab/soak up some u.v.'s on the beach**, je vais me bronzer/me rôtir le cuir sur la plage.

V

v [viː] *a Br F* (*abbr of very*) très; **v. good,** très bien.

vac [væk] *n Br F* (*abbr of vacation*) vacances *fpl*; **the long vac(s),** les grandes vacances.

Vals [vælz], **Valley Girls** ['vælɪgɜːlz] *npl NAm F* culture *f* de la jeunesse californienne (*basée sur les habitudes, le vocabulaire, etc des adolescentes de la région de San Fernando Valley*).

Valspeak ['vælspiːk] *n NAm F* jargon *m*/ argot *m* des *Valley Girls.*

vamoose [və'muːs] *vi P* s'enfuir*/ décamper/riper/s'arracher; **vamoose!** file!/ casse-toi!/fiche le camp!

vamp¹ [væmp] *n Br O F* femme* fatale/ vamp *f.*

vamp² [væmp] *Br O F* **I** *vtr* vamper (un homme); **to vamp it,** s'habiller en/faire la vamp **II** *vi* jouer la femme fatale.

vamp up ['væmp'ʌp] *vtr & i Br F* **1.** rafistoler (qch) **2.** improviser.

varieties [və'raɪətɪz] *npl F* **all the varieties:** see **bingo 57.**

varmint ['vɑːmɪnt] *n A F* **young varmint,** petit(e) polisson(ne)/jeune morpion *m*/mioche *mf.*

varnish ['vɑːnɪʃ] *vtr P* **to varnish one's cane,** (*of man*) faire l'amour*/baiser/ dérouiller son panais.

varsity, Varsity ['vɑːsɪtɪ] *n O F* l'Université *f*/la Faculté/la Fac.

veep [viːp] *n NAm F* = **VIP.**

vegetable ['vedʒtəbl] *n F* handicapé(e) mental(e); **she's just a vegetable,** elle n'a pas toutes ses facultés.

veggie ['vedʒɪ] *n F* végétarien, -ienne.

veg out ['vedʒ'aʊt] *vi F* paresser*/tirer au flanc/glander.

velvet ['velvɪt] *n* **1.** *P* **blue velvet,** drogues* (*mélange de parégorique et d'antihistamine*) **2. black velvet** (*a*) *F* (*drink*) mélange *m* de champagne et de stout/velours *m* (*b*) *P* Noire*/négresse *f* **3.** *F* **to be on velvet** (*a*) jouer sur le velours (*b*) vivre comme un prince/mener la vie de château/se la couler douce **4.** *F* (*a*) bénéfice*/velours *m*/gâteau *m*/ affure *f* (*b*) argent*/galette *f*/galtouse *f.*

Vera Lynn ['vɪərə'lɪn] *n P* (*RS = gin*) gin *m.*

verbal¹ ['vɜːbl] *n P* **1. the verbal,** bavardage *m*/bavette *f*; **they were having a bit of a verbal,** ils taillaient une bavette. (*See* **diarrhoea**) **2.** *Br* (*underworld, etc*) **verbal(s),** témoignage basé sur un aveu prétendument fait à la police; **to put the verbal in/the verbals on s.o.,** (*of police*) impliquer qn dans un crime en citant devant la cour un prétendu aveu.

verbal² ['vɜːbl] *vtr P* (*of police*) impliquer (qn) dans un crime en citant devant la cour un prétendu aveu; **the cops will verbal you,** les flics vont déclarer que tu leur as tout dit.

vet [vet] *n F* **1.** (= *veterinary surgeon*) vétérinaire *mf*/véto *m* **2.** *US* (= *veteran*) ancien combattant. (*See* **Viet Vet**)

vibes [vaɪbz] *npl F* **1.** (*jazz*) vibraphone *m*; **he's on vibes,** il joue du vibraphone **2.** (= *vibrations*) (*also* **vibe**) ambiance *f*/atmosphère *f*; **the vibes are all wrong,** ça ne gaze pas; c'est craignos; **good vibes!** ça gaze!/c'est le pied! **this place gives me bad vibes/a bad vibe,** cet endroit me fait un effet désagréable/ ça craint dans cet endroit; **I get good vibes from it,** ça me branche; **I get a good vibe/ good vibes from him/her,** il/elle me plaît/me botte.

vibrations [vaɪ'breɪʃ(ə)nz] *npl F* = **vibes 2.**

vice [vaɪs] *n F* **1.** (= *vice-president, vice-chairman*) vice-président *m* **2.** (= *vice-chancellor*) recteur *m* (d'une université)/recto *m* **3.** (= *deputy*) substitut *m*/délégué, -ée.

vicious ['vɪʃəs] *a* impressionnant/géant/ canon.

vid [vɪd] *n F* (*abbr of video*) vidéo *f*; vidéocassette *f.*

Viet Vet [vɪet'vet] *n US F* (*abbr of Vietnam Veteran*) ancien *m* du Vietnam.

villain ['vɪlən] *n* 1. *Br P* criminel, -elle/bandit *m*/malfrat *m*; **a small-time villain**, un petit truand/un truand à la mie de pain 2. *F* coquin, -ine/garnement *m*; **you little villain!** petit polisson!/sacré brigand!/petit garnement!

vim [vɪm] *n F* vigueur *f*/force *f*/énergie *f*/vitalité *f*; **to be full of vim**, avoir de la vitalité à revendre/péter le feu.

vine [vaɪn] *n* 1. *P* **the vine** = **the grapevine** (**grapevine**) 2. *NAm F* **clinging vine**, pot-de-colle *m*.

vino ['viːnəʊ] *n P* vin*/gros rouge/pinard *m*/picrate *m*/pivois *m*.

vinyl ['vaɪnɪl] *n F* disque *m*/33 tours *m*; **the album exists on vinyl and cassette**, l'album existe en disque et en cassette.

VIP ['viːaɪ'piː] *n F* (= *very important person*) personnage important/grosse légume/huile *f*; **to give s.o. (the) VIP treatment**, recevoir qn avec tambour et trompettes/dérouler le tapis rouge pour qn.

viper ['vaɪpə] *n NAm P* (*drugs*) drogué* à la marijuana*.

visit ['vɪzɪt] *n F* **to pay a visit**, aller faire pipi/aller faire sa petite commission.

vitamin ['vɪtəmɪn] *n F* (*drugs*) **vitamin A**, LSD*/acide *m*; **ecstasy** *m*; **vitamin C**, cocaïne*; **vitamin E/X** ecstasy.

vitamins ['vɪtəmɪnz] *npl F* cachets *mpl*/cachetons *mpl* de drogue*.

vocab ['vəʊkæb] *n F* (*abbr of vocabulary*) vocabulaire *m*; **vocab book**, carnet *m* de vocabulaire/voca *m*.

vom[1] [vɒm] *n F* (*abbr of vomit*) vomissure *f*/dégueulis *m*.

vom[2] [vɒm] *vi F* (*abbr of vomit*) vomir*/dégueuler/gerber.

W

wack [wæk] *n P* 1. *esp NAm* fou*/fêlé, -ée/
cinglé, -ée/détraqué, -ée/fada *mf* 2. *esp NAm*
excentrique *mf*/farfelu, -ue 3. *Br* (*Liverpool*)
ami*/pote *m*/copain, -ine/poteau *m*.

wacker ['wækə] *n Br P* (*Liverpool*) = **wack
3**.

wacko ['wækəʊ] *a & n P* = **whacko I, II**.

wacky ['wækɪ] *a P* = **whacky**.

wad [wɒd] *n* 1. *Br P* petit pain; (grosse)
tranche de pain/tartine *f*; tea and a wad,
casse-croûte *m* 2. *P* liasse *f* de billets* de
banque/matelas *m*/millefeuille *m* 3. *F*
abondance*/chiée *f* (de...)/tas *m* (de...)/
flop(p)ée *f* (de...) 4. *V* sexe* de l'homme/
boutique *f*. (*See* **tightwad**)

wade in ['weɪd'ɪn] *vi F* se mêler à qch/
intervenir/s'interposer.

wade into ['weɪd'ɪntuː] *vtr F* 1. to wade
into s.o. (*a*) attaquer* qn/rentrer dans le
chou/le lard à qn (*b*) critiquer* qn
sévèrement/flinguer qn 2. to wade into, se
plonger dans (un travail)/s'attaquer à (un
travail)/se mettre à (une tâche).

waffle¹ ['wɒfl] *n F* verbosité *f*/verbiage *m*/
fariboles *fpl*; it's just waffle, c'est du
jaspinage/du pallas.

waffle² (on) ['wɒfl('ɒn)] *vi F* parler pour
ne rien dire; (*in writing*) faire du rem-
plissage; he just waffles on, (il n'a rien à dire
mais) il ne sait pas s'arrêter.

waffler ['wɒflə] *n F* baratineur, -euse.

wag¹ [wæg] *n O F* to hop the wag = **wag²**.

wag² [wæg] *vtr & i F Br* to wag it/*Austr* to
wag (school)/to wag off, (*play truant*) sécher/
faire l'école buissonnière.

wag(g)on ['wægən] *n F* 1. car* de police/
panier *m* à salade 2. to be on the (water)
wagon, ne pas boire d'alcool/être buveur
d'eau/être au régime sec/grenouiller; to be off
the wagon, s'adonner à la boisson/biberonner/
lichailler 3. *NAm* to fix s.o.'s wagon, se
venger sur qn/avoir qn au tournant/garder à
qn un chien de sa chienne. (*See*

bandwagon; cop-wagon; holler-
wag(g)on; meat-wag(g)on; paddy-
wag(g)on)

wake-up ['weɪkʌp] *n P* (*drugs*) première
piqûre de drogues du matin.

wakey(-wakey)! ['weɪkɪ('weɪkɪ)] *excl F*
(*wake up!*) réveille-toi!/debout les morts!
(*get moving!*) secoue-toi!/secoue tes puces!/
dégrouille-toi!

walk [wɔːk] *vtr & i F* 1. (*sports*) to walk it,
arriver dans un fauteuil/gagner les mains
dans les poches/gagner les doigts dans le nez
2. être libre; give us the money and you can
walk, donne-nous le fric et tu es libre/on te
laisse partir 3. disparaître/partir*/ficher le
camp. (*See* **jaywalk**)

walkabout ['wɔːkəbaʊt] *n Austr F* bain *m*
de foule; to go walkabout, prendre un bain de
foule; (*daydream*) rêvasser.

walkaway ['wɔːkəweɪ] *n F* = **walkover**.

walk away ['wɔːkə'weɪ] *vi F* 1. to walk
away with sth, voler*/faucher/chiper/barboter
qch 2. to walk away (with it)/to walk away
with the first prize, gagner les mains dans les
poches/arriver dans un fauteuil; to walk away
from a competitor, semer un concurrent/
laisser un concurrent sur place.

walk off ['wɔːk'ɒf] *vi F* to walk off with sth,
voler* qch/faucher qch.

walk out ['wɔːk'aʊt] *vi F* to walk out on
s.o., (*desert*) abandonner* qn/lâcher qn/
plaquer qn/laisser qn en plan; (*leave in
anger*) quitter qn en rogne/partir en claquant
la porte.

walkover ['wɔːkəʊvə] *n F* victoire *f* facile/
dans un fauteuil/les doigts dans le nez; it was
a walkover, c'était fastoche/du nougat.

walk over ['wɔːk'əʊvə] *vtr F* to walk all
over s.o., agir abominablement envers qn;
traiter qn comme du poisson pourri/plus bas
que terre; if you don't watch him, he'll walk
all over you, si tu fais pas gaffe, il va te marcher sur les pieds.

wall [wɔːl] *n F* **1. to be up the wall,** être fou*/cinglé/dingue/barjot; **to drive/send s.o. up the wall,** rendre qn fou*/dingue; taper sur le système à qn/courir sur le haricot à qn/scier le dos à qn; **the neighbour's baby drives me up the wall,** la voisine me jambonne avec son bébé **2. to go to the wall,** faire faillite/bouffer la grenouille **3. to go over the wall,** s'évader* de prison*/faire la belle/faire cavale **4. to bang/to beat/to hit/to knock one's head against a (brick) wall,** perdre son temps; pisser en l'air/dans un violon; **it's like hitting your head against a brick wall,** ça (ne) vaut vraiment pas la peine/autant aller se coucher **5. he can see through a brick wall,** il a le nez fin/il a le nez creux **6. it's like talking to/you might just as well talk to a brick wall,** autant parler à un sourd/autant parler au mur. (*See* **back II 6**)

walla(h) ['wɒlə] *n Br F* individu*/homme*/type *m*/zèbre *m*/coco *m*; **office walla(h),** scribouillard *m*; **loose walla(h),** magouilleur *m*/combinard *m*.

wall-eyed ['wɔːl'aɪd] *a P* ivre*/raide/rétamé/poivré.

wallflower ['wɔːlflauə] *n* **1.** *F* personne (*surt jeune fille*) qui, à un bal, n'est pas invitée à danser; **to be a wallflower,** faire tapisserie **2.** prisonnier, -ière qui parle toujours de s'évader*.

wallop¹ ['wɒləp] **I** *adv F* slap, bang, wallop! pan, vlan, boum! (*See* **slap-bang(-wallop)**) **II** *n* **1.** *F* gros coup*/beigne *f*/torgnole *f*/pain *m*/gnon *m*; **she gave him a real wallop across the face,** elle lui a flanqué une sacrée beigne à travers la figure **2.** *F* **and down he went with a wallop!** et patatras, le voilà par terre! **3.** *P* (*a*) bière *f*/mousse *f* (*b*) alcool* fort/antigel *m*. (*See* **codswallop**)

wallop² ['wɒləp] *vtr F* **1.** battre* (qn)/rosser (qn)/flanquer une tannée à (qn)/tanner le cuir à (qn) **2.** battre (qn) à plate(s) couture(s).

walloping ['wɒləpɪŋ] *F* **I** *a* énorme/fantastique/phénoménal **II** *adv* **he got a walloping good rise,** il a eu une super augmentation **III** *n F* raclée *f*; **to give s.o. a walloping** (*a*) donner une raclée/une avoine/une peignée à qn (*b*) battre qn à plate(s) couture(s)/battre qn sur toute la ligne.

wally ['wɒlɪ] *n Br P* **1.** (*pickled gherkin*) cornichon *m* (au vinaigre) **2.** individu bête*/cornichon *m*/andouille *f*/nœud *m*; **you wally!** espèce de nœud!/espèce d'enflé! **he's a real wally,** c'est un vrai con(nard)/une tête de nœud.

waltz off ['wɔːls'ɒf] *vi F* partir*/décamper/jouer rip/mettre les adjas; **he's waltzed off with my biro again,** il a encore embarqué mon bic.

wamba ['wæmbə] *n Br P* argent*/fric *m*/pognon *m*.

wampum ['wɒmpəm] *n NAm P* argent*/fric *m*/pèze *m*/flouse *m*.

wang, wanger [wæŋ, 'wæŋə] *n P* pénis*.

wangle¹ ['wæŋgl] *n F* combine *f*/embrouille *f*/truc *m*/magouille *f*/coup fourré.

wangle² ['wæŋgl] *vtr F* **1.** obtenir par subterfuge/carotter/resquiller; **he wangled 20 quid out of me,** il m'a refait/estampé de 20 livres **2.** pratiquer le système D/se débrouiller/se démerder/savoir nager; **I'll wangle it somehow,** je me démerderai; **how did you wangle that?** comment (est-ce que) tu t'es débrouillé pour faire/avoir ça? **3.** (*falsify*) cuisiner (des comptes).

wangler ['wæŋglə] *n F* fricoteur, -euse/carotteur, -euse/magouilleur, -euse.

wangling ['wæŋglɪŋ] *n F* resquillage *m*/carottage *m*.

wank¹ [wæŋk] *n Br V* **to have a wank,** se masturber*/s'astiquer/se branler/se faire une pogne.

wank² [wæŋk] *vi Br V* se masturber*/se branler/secouer le petit homme/s'astiquer (la colonne).

wanker ['wæŋkə] *n Br V* **1.** (*masturbator*) branleur *m* **2. wanker's doom,** masturbation excessive **3.** *Pej* branleur *m*; **you wanker!** espèce d'enculé! **what a wanker!** quel branleur!

wank off ['wæŋk'ɒf] *vi Br V* = **wank²**.

wannabe(e) ['wɒnəbiː] *n* (jeune) ambitieux, -ieuse.

want [wɒnt] *vtr F* **1.** *Iron* **you don't want much, do you!** tu ne doutes de rien!/tu n'as pas froid aux yeux!/tu ne manques pas d'air! **2.** (*a*) **to want in,** vouloir participer à qch/vouloir être du coup; **he wants in,** il veut être dans la course (*b*) **to want out,** vouloir se retirer/retirer ses marrons du feu; **I want out,** je ne suis pas/plus partant.

war [wɔː] *n F* **to be in the wars,** être malmené/être tarabusté; **you really have been in the wars, haven't you?** t'en as vu de toutes les couleurs/bavé/chié, hein?

warb [wɔːb] *n Austr P* personne sale* *ou* désordonnée/souillon *m*/salope *f*/cochon *m*.

warby ['wɔːbɪ] *Austr P* **I** *a* sale*/salingue/crado/craspec **II** *n* = **warb**.

warehouse ['wɛəhaʊs] *vi Br P* organiser *ou* prendre part à une acid-party.

warm [wɔːm] *a F* 1. to be (getting) warm, être sur le point de trouver qch/brûler/chauffer 2. to make things warm for s.o., en faire baver à qn/en faire voir de dures à qn 3. *A* riche*/galetteux/rupin/plein aux as.

war-paint ['wɔːpeɪnt] *n F* maquillage *m*/badigeon *m*/peinture *f*; to put on the war-paint, se maquiller*/ravaler sa façade/se sucrer la gaufre.

warpath ['wɔːpɑːθ] *n F* to be on the warpath, en vouloir à tout le monde; the boss is on the warpath, le patron* est d'une humeur massacrante/est très mal vissé.

wash¹ [wɒʃ] *n* 1. *F* to hold up in the wash, tenir à l'usage 2. *F* to come out in the wash, être dévoilé un jour ou l'autre/se montrer sous son vrai jour; (be all right) se tasser; don't worry, it'll all come out in the wash, t'en fais pas, ça se saura un jour ou l'autre; (be all right) t'en fais pas, ça se tassera 3. *Br P* (drugs) crack *m*. (See **eyewash**; **hogwash**; **whitewash¹**)

wash² [wɒʃ] *vi F* it won't wash with me, cela ne prend pas/cela ne passe pas/je ne marche pas. (See **linen 1**; **whitewash²**)

washed out ['wɒʃt'aʊt] *a F* fatigué*/lessivé.

washed up ['wɒʃt'ʌp] *a F* mis au rancart/fichu en l'air/bazardé; they're all washed up, tout est fini entre eux; our plans are all washed up, nos projets sont tombés à l'eau.

washer-upper ['wɒʃə'rʌpə] *n F* qn qui fait la vaisselle/plongeur, -euse.

washout ['wɒʃaʊt] *n F* 1. échec*/fiasc *m*/bide *m*; the party was a complete washout, la soirée a été un fiasc complet 2. (person) raté, -ée/propre *mf* à rien/nullité *f*/zéro *m*; he's a real washout, c'est un vrai nullard/un raté de première.

Wasp [wɒsp] *n NAm P esp Pej* (= white Anglo-Saxon Protestant) = Américain, -aine blanc(he) protestant(e) d'origine anglo-saxonne.

waste [weɪst] *vtr P* tuer*/effacer/mettre à l'ombre.

wasted ['weɪstɪd] *a P* 1. fatigué*/lessivé/vanné 2. (drugs) drogué*/camé/envapé.

watch [wɒtʃ] *vtr F* watch it! attention!/fais gaffe!

water ['wɔːtə] *n F* 1. to pour cold water on sth, accueillir qch froidement/de façon glaciale 2. to keep one's head above water,

réussir tant bien que mal/ramer; (financially) faire face à ses engagements 3. to hold water, avoir du sens/tenir debout/tenir la route; that doesn't hold water, ça n'a pas de sens/ça ne tient pas debout/ça ne tient pas la route 4. to be in low water, (penniless) être sans le sou/être dans la dèche. (See **bathwater**; **bilge-water**; **dishwater**; **ditchwater**; **duck¹ 7**; **firewater**; **hell 16**; **hot 13**; **jerkwater**; **wag(g)on 2**)

watering hole ['wɔːtərɪŋhəʊl] *n P* bar *m*/café*/troquet *m*.

waterworks ['wɔːtəwɜːks] *npl F* to turn on the waterworks (a) se mettre à pleurer*/ouvrir les écluses *fpl*/gicler des mirettes *fpl*/chialer (b) uriner*/faire pipi/lisbroquer.

wavelength ['weɪvleŋθ] *n F* on the same wavelength, sur la même longueur d'ondes. (See **beam 1**)

wax [wæks] *n O F* accès *m* de colère*/crise *f*/rage *f*/coup *m* de raisin; to be in a wax, être en pétard.

waxy ['wæksɪ] *a O F* en colère/en rogne/en pétard/en boule.

way [weɪ] *F* I *adv* (= away) it was way back in 1900, cela remonte à 1900 II *n* 1. all the way (a) complètement/sans réserve/à bloc/à fond (la caisse); I'll go all the way with you on that, là-dessus, je te soutiendrai jusqu'à la gauche (b) jusqu'à une complète satisfaction sexuelle/jusqu'au septième ciel; to go all the way, le mettre (à qn) jusqu'au bout; she wouldn't let him go all the way, elle voulait pas de ça qu'est bon/elle voulait pas se faire mettre 2. (a) to go for s.o./sth in a big way, s'emballer follement pour qn/qch; he's gone for it in a big way, il en est toqué/dingue/fana (b) to do sth in a big way, mettre les petits plats dans les grands/faire bien les choses 3. to know one's way about/around, être malin*/roublard/démerdard 4. to put s.o. out of the way, se débarrasser* de qn/virer qn/vider qn 5. down our way, chez nous/chez nozigues 6. no way, balpeau/des clous/que dalle/que pouic/peau de balle 7. any way round: see **bingo 69**. (See **family 1**)

way off ['weɪ'ɒf] *a & adv F* dans l'erreur/à côté (de la plaque); you're way off (the mark), tu te plantes complètement.

way-out ['weɪ'aʊt] *a F* 1. original/excentrique 2. dans l'erreur; he was really way-out there, il était complètement à côté de la plaque/il s'était planté sur toute la ligne.

weapon ['wepən] *n P* pénis*/arbalète *f*.

wear [wɛə] *vtr F* he won't wear it, il ne sera pas d'accord/il ne marchera pas; she won't wear that argument, on ne la fera pas gober cet argument.

weasel¹ ['wiːzl] *n F* 1. (*person*) fouine *f*; weasel words, paroles trompeuses/pallas *m* 2. *Br* (*dodge*) combine *f*/magouille *f*.

weasel² ['wiːzl] *vi Br F* (*behave in devious way*) faire des magouilles.

weasel out ['wiːzl'aʊt] *vi F* se défiler; I won't let him weasel out of it, je ne le laisserai pas prendre la tangente.

weather ['weðə] *n F* 1. under the weather (*a*) malade*/patraque (*b*) déprimé/qui n'a pas le moral 2. (*pilot's jargon*) mauvais temps; to run into some weather, rencontrer du mauvais temps/de la turbulence. (*See* **fairweather**; **heavy I 3**)

weave [wiːv] *vi F* to get weaving, s'y mettre/se lancer; get weaving! vas-y!/roule!/ fonce!

wedding tackle ['wedɪŋ'tækl] *n Br F Hum* sexe* de l'homme/bijoux *mpl* de famille.

wedge [wedʒ] *n P* argent*/pognon *m*/galette *f*.

wedged [wedʒd] *a P* riche*/chargé/ galetteux.

wee [wiː] *n & v F* = **wee-wee¹,²**.

weed¹ [wiːd] *n F* 1. (*a*) cigarette*/sèche *f* (*b*) (the) weed, tabac*/perlot *m*/trèfle *m*; to be on the weed, fumer*/bombarder/piper/ cloper 2. marijuana*/chiendent *m*/herbe *f*. (*See* **giggle 3**; **love-weed**) 3. personne malingre/chétive; (*in character*) mauviette *f*; what a weed! quelle mauviette!

weed² [wiːd] *vtr & i Br P* 1. voler*/faucher/ ratisser 2. (*embezzle*) détourner des fonds/ cameloter.

weedhead ['wiːdhed] *n P* (*drugs*) habitué(e) de la marijuana*/fumeur, -euse de marijuana*.

weedy ['wiːdɪ] *a Br F* (*person*) chétif/ malingre.

week [wiːk] *n F* to knock s.o. into the middle of next week, donner à qn un sacré coup*/ envoyer valdinguer qn/mettre un pain à qn/ rentrer dans le portrait à qn.

weekend ['wiːkend] *n P* (*drugs*) to have the weekend habit, toucher à la drogue de temps en temps. (*See* **wet¹ I 2**)

weenie ['wiːnəɪ] *n NAm P* = **wiener, wienie**.

weensy, weeny ['wiːnsɪ, 'wiːnɪ] *a F* minuscule/minus/menu. (*See* **teensy-**

weensy; **teeny-weeny**).

weepie ['wiːpɪ] *n F* = **weepy**.

weeping ['wiːpɪŋ] *a P* weeping willow, (*RS* = *pillow*) oreiller *m*.

weepy ['wiːpɪ] *n F* film/livre, etc larmoyant/à faire pleurer dans les chaumières; mélo *m*.

wee-wee¹ ['wiːwiː] *n F* (*child's word*) pipi *m*; to do a wee-wee/to do wee-wees, uriner*/ faire pipi.

wee-wee² ['wiːwiː] *vi F* (*child's word*) to (go) wee-wee, uriner*/faire pipi.

weigh in ['weɪɪn] *vi F* arriver*/s'amener/ ramener sa fraise.

weight [weɪt] *n* 1. *F* to take the weight off (one's feet), s'asseoir/poser ses fesses* 2. *F* to throw one's weight around, faire l'important/ rouler les mécaniques/les rouler 3. *P* (*drugs*) livre *f* (♭ kg) de drogue (*surt* cannabis*) 4. *NAm P* (*drugs*) narcotiques *mpl*/drogues*. (*See* **chuck about 22**; **lightweight**)

weirdie ['wɪədɪ], **weirdo** ['wɪədəʊ], **weirdy** ['wɪədɪ] *n F* individu* étrange/ excentrique *mf*/olibrius *m*/drôle *m* de coco/ drôle d'oiseau/zigomar *m*.

welch [welʃ] *vi Br F* = **welsh**.

welcher ['welʃə] *n Br F* = **welsher**.

welcome-mat ['welkəm'mæt] *n F* to put out the welcome-mat for s.o., accueillir qn à bras ouverts.

well [wel] *adv Br P* très; well good, très bon/super/canon; a well nice person, une personne très sympa.

well-endowed ['welɪn'daʊd], **well-equipped** ['welɪ'kwɪpt] *a F* 1. (*man*) bien membré/bien monté. (*See* **well-hung**) 2. (*woman*) aux seins* développés/à la poitrine abondante/qui a du monde au balcon. (*See* **well-stacked 2**; **well-upholstered 1**)

well-fixed ['wel'fɪkst], **well-heeled** ['wel'hiːld] *a F* riche*/chargé/galettard/ rupin/plein aux as/au pèze.

well-hung ['wel'hʌŋ] *a P* (*man*) bien membré; bien monté; monté comme un âne/un bourricot/un taureau; she likes her men well-hung, elle les aime bien montés.

wellie¹ ['welɪ] *n Br F* 1. force *f*/impulsion *f*; give it some wellie, mets-y un peu d'effort 2. (*of person*) force *f*/muscles *mpl*; he's got plenty of wellie, il a du biceps 3. renvoi *m*; to get the (order of the) wellie, se faire congédier/sacquer. (*See* **boot¹ 1**) 4. préservatif* (masculin)/marguerite *f*/capote (anglaise).

wellie² ['welɪ] *vtr Br P* 1. congédier/sacquer/mettre à la porte 2. attaquer*/tomber sur le poil de (qn); (*bully*) brutaliser/maillocher; (*defeat*) vaincre/battre.

wellies ['welɪz] *npl F* bottes *fpl* en caoutchouc.

well in ['wel'ɪn] *a Austr F* = **well-fixed**.

well-lined ['wel'laɪnd] *a F* = **well-fixed**.

well off ['wel'ɒf] *a F* 1. to be well off, être riche*/avoir de quoi/être au pèze 2. you don't know when you're well off, vous ne connaissez pas votre bonheur 3. to be well off for sth, être bien pourvu de qch/être à l'aise de qch.

well-oiled [wel'ɔɪld] *a F* = **oiled**.

well-stacked ['wel'stækt] *a F* 1. = **well-fixed** 2. = **well-endowed** 2.

well-upholstered ['welʌp'həʊlstəd] *a F* 1. = **well-endowed** 2. (*See* upholstery) 2. (*plump*) bien rembourré.

welsh [welʃ] *vi Br F* partir* sans payer/poser une ardoise/planter un drapeau/faire jambe de bois; to welsh on s.o., manquer à une obligation envers qn/faire faux bond à qn; to welsh on a bet, ne pas tenir un pari.

welsher ['welʃə] *n Br F* qn qui ne paye pas ses dettes; qn qui manque à ses obligations; voleur*; tricheur*.

welt [welt] *vtr P* (*rare*) battre*/rosser/flanquer une raclée à (qn).

wench [wentʃ] *n F* fille*/môme *f*/gonzesse *f*.

west [west] *adv F* to go west (*a*) *O* mourir*/casser sa pipe/passer l'arme à gauche (*b*) s'user/être fichu/rendre l'âme (*c*) (*of business, etc*) faire faillite/couler (*d*) that's another fiver gone west, encore un faf(f)iot de claqué/encore un dont je ne reverrai pas la couleur.

wet¹ [wet] **I** *a* 1. *F* bête*/crétin; he's a bit wet, il est plutôt bête*/c'est une vraie nouille/il en tient une couche; to talk wet, dire des bêtises 2. *F* wet blanket, rabat-joie *m*/trouble-fête *mf*; *Br* wet weekend, individu* triste/déprimé; flippé, -ée 3. *F Pol* modéré 4. *NAm F* qui a la permission de vendre de l'alcool* 5. *F* to be wet behind the ears, être naïf; she's still a bit wet behind the ears, on lui pincerait le nez qu'il en sortirait encore du lait. (*See* dry 2) 6. *F* sentimental/à l'eau de rose 7. *F* to be all wet, (*be mistaken*) se fourrer le doigt dans l'œil/se gourrer 8. *Austr P* the wet season, règles*/ours *mpl*/coquelicots *mpl* 9. *P* (*woman*) sexuellement excitée/allumée/chauffée. (*See* damp). (*See* dream **II** 3; rag¹ 10) **II** *n F* 1. (*weak, irresolute person*)

chiffe (molle)/lavette *f*; (*foolish*) individu bête*/nouille *f*/andouille *f* 2. *Pol* poule mouillée/modéré, -ée.

wet² [wet] *vtr F* to wet one's pants/to be wetting oneself, avoir peur*/faire dans son froc/mouiller (son froc).

whack¹ [wæk] *n* 1. *F* coup*/taloche *f*/torgnole *f*/pain *m*/beigne *f* 2. *F* to have a whack, tenter le coup/faire un essai 3. *F* part *f*/fade *m*/taf(fe) *m*; to get one's whack, toucher son taf; to earn top whack for a job, gagner le maximum pour un travail; we can offer you £50,000, top whack, nous pouvons vous offrir 50 000 livres, pas plus/dernier prix. 4. *NAm P* (*contract killing*) meurtre *m* sur commande/contrat *m* 5. *P* = **wack 1, 2**.

whack² [wæk] *vtr* 1. *F* battre*/rosser/bourrer de coups*/avoiner 2. *F* battre/vaincre/écraser (un adversaire) 3. *NAm P* tuer*/descendre/liquider.

whacked [wækt] *a F* fatigué*/éreinté/vanné/pompé/lessivé.

whacker ['wækə] *n* 1. *F* = **whopper** 2. *P* = **wack 3** 3. *P* individu* fou*/fêlé/secoué; (*eccentric*) individu farfelu. (*See* bushwhacker)

whacking ['wækɪŋ] *F* **I** *a* énorme/ma(h)ous/bœuf **II** *n* raclée *f*/volée *f* de coups*/avoine *f*.

whacko ['wækəʊ] *P* **I** *a* fou*/fêlé/cinglé **II** *n* fou*/fêlé, -ée/cinglé, -ée **III** *excl O* magnifique!/épatant!/formid!/super!

whack off ['wæk'ɒf] *vi P* se masturber*/se branler/se pignoler.

whack up ['wæk'ʌp] *vtr* 1. *F* to whack up the pace, aller plus vite*/forcer le pas/accélérer la cadence 2. *F* augmenter (les prix, etc) 3. *P* diviser et partager en parts égales; partager le butin* *ou* le gain/fader le butin.

whacky ['wækɪ] *a P* fou*/fêlé/cinglé/secoué; (*eccentric*) farfelu; whacky sense of humour, sens *m* de l'humour farfelu.

whale [weɪl] *n F* we had a whale of a time, on s'est drôlement bien amusé/on a pris notre pied.

wham-bam-thank-you-ma'am ['wæm-'bæm'θæŋkjuː'mæm] *n P* coït* rapide et sans tendresse; coup *m* de queue rapide.

whammy ['wæmɪ] *n esp NAm F* to put the whammy on s.o., jeter un (mauvais) sort sur qn; double whammy, coup dur.

whang, whanger [wæŋ, 'wæŋə] *n P* = **wang, wanger**.

whank [wæŋk] *n & vi* V = **wank**[1,2].

whatcha(ma)callit ['wɒtʃə(mə)'kɔːlɪt], **what-do-you-call-it** ['wɒtdjuː'kɔːlɪt] *n F* machin *m*/chose *f*/machin-chose *m*/machin-chouette *m*/trucmuche *m*.

what-for ['wɒt'fɔː] *n F* to give s.o. what-for, réprimander* qn/laver la tête à qn/flanquer une bonne raclée à qn/passer un savon à qn.

what-ho! ['wɒt'həʊ] *excl O F* 1. eh bien!/ tiens! 2. bonjour! salut!

whatnot ['wɒtnɒt] *n F* = **whatcha(ma)callit**.

what's-(h)er-name ['wɒtsəneɪm] *n F* machin *m*/Madame Machin-Truc/Madame Trucmuche.

what's-(h)is-name ['wɒtsɪzneɪm] *n F* machin *m*/Monsieur Machin-Truc/Monsieur Trucmuche.

whatsit ['wɒtsɪt] *n F* = **whatcha(ma)callit**.

what's-its-name ['wɒtsɪtsneɪm] *n F* = **whatcha(ma)callit**.

wheel[1] [wiːl] *n F* 1. there are wheels within wheels, les rouages (de la chose) sont très compliqués/c'est un sac de nœuds 2. big wheel = big shot (**big I 1**) 3. to take (over) the wheel, prendre la barre/prendre les rênes 4. it greases the wheels, cela fait marcher les affaires 5. *pl* (= *car*) tire *f*/chignole *f*; nice wheels, belle bagnole/caisse. (*See* **wheelman**)

wheel[2] [wiːl] *vi F* to wheel and deal, brasser des affaires (plus ou moins louches)/grenouiller/magouiller.

wheeler-dealer ['wiːlə'diːlə] *n F* brasseur *m* d'affaires (plus ou moins louches)/magouilleur, -euse/grenouilleur *m*.

wheelie ['wiːlɪ] *n Br F* to do a wheelie = rouler sur la roue arrière d'une bicyclette *ou* d'une moto; (*in car*) faire patiner les roues arrières.

wheelman ['wiːlmæn] *n*, **wheels-man** ['wiːlzmæn] *n P* conducteur *m* d'une voiture de fuite/d'une bagnole de cavale.

wheeze [wiːz] *n O F* ruse *f*/artifice *m*/truc *m*; that was a good wheeze, c'était une bonne astuce.

wherewithal ['wɛəwɪðɒːl] *n F* the wherewithal, l'argent*/le nécessaire/les moyens *mpl*; I haven't the wherewithal to buy it, je n'ai pas de quoi l'acheter.

whiff [wɪf] *vi Br P* sentir mauvais*/(s)chlinguer/cocotter.

whiffy ['wɪfɪ] *a Br P* qui sent mauvais/qui

pue; it's a bit whiffy in here, ça (s)chlingue/ ça cocotte là-dedans.

whinge[1] [wɪndʒ] *n F* plainte *f*/jérémiade *f*/ geignements *mpl*.

whinge[2] [wɪndʒ] *vi F* (a) (*of child*) pleurnicher (b) (*complain*) se plaindre/geindre/ miauler/musiquer; *Austr* whingeing pom, Anglais pleurnicheur/pleurnichard.

whingy ['wɪndʒɪ] *a F* pleurnicheur/ geignard/grincheux.

whip[1] [wɪp] *n F* 1. to get a fair crack of the whip, (*have a fair chance*) avoir toutes ses chances; (*have a good go*) avoir sa part/son dû 2. to have/hold the whip hand/*NAm* handle, avoir l'avantage/le dessus/être du côté du manche 3. *Austr* whips of... = tons of... (**ton 2**) 4. to crack the whip, montrer le fouet/faire preuve d'autorité/taper sur la table 5. *Br* =**whipround**.

whip[2] [wɪp] *vtr* 1. *P* voler*/faucher/piquer/ barboter/chour(av)er; someone's whipped my wallet, on m'a piqué mon portefeuille 2. *F* vaincre/battre à plate(s) couture(s); I know when I'm whipped, je sais quand déclarer forfait 3. *F* to whip sth out of sight, cacher qch vite fait/d'un mouvement rapide.

whippersnapper ['wɪpəsnæpə] *n F* 1. freluquet *m*; you young whippersnapper! petit malappris!/petit malotru! 2. jeune homme suffisant/qui fait l'important.

whipround ['wɪp'raʊnd] *n Br F* quête *f*/ collecte *f*; to have a whipround, faire une collecte; let's have a whipround for his widow, faisons passer une enveloppe pour sa veuve.

whip up ['wɪp'ʌp] *vtr F* to whip up a meal, préparer un repas rapidement; faire à manger/faire un morceau vite fait.

whirl [wɜːl] *n F* to give sth a whirl, essayer qch/faire l'essai de qch/tenter le coup.

whirly-bird ['wɜːlɪbɜːd] *n O F* hélicoptère *m*/hélico *m*.

whisker ['wɪskə] *n F* to win by a whisker, gagner dans un mouchoir. (*See* **cat 6**)

whistle[1] ['wɪsl] *n* 1. *F* gorge*/avaloir *m*/ gargoulette *f*/sifflet *m*; to wet one's whistle, boire*/s'humecter le gosier/se rincer la dalle 2. *Br P* whistle (and flute), (*RS* = *suit*) complet *m*/costard *m*/ridère *m* 3. *P* to blow the whistle on sth, révéler qch/débiner le truc; to blow the whistle on s.o., dénoncer*/vendre/ balancer/griller qn; who blew the whistle? qui a vendu la mèche? 4. *P* clean as a whistle = **clean I 1** (*a*), (*c*), (*d*), (*e*). (*See* **wolf-**

whistle)

whistle² ['wɪsl] *vi* 1. *F* you can whistle for it! tu peux toujours courir!/tu peux te fouiller!/tu peux (toujours) te l'accrocher! 2. *P* to whistle in the dark/in the wind, deviner au hasard/y aller au pif(omètre).

whistle-stop ['wɪslstɒp] *n F* 1. *NAm* (*a*) (*railways*) halte *f* (à arrêt facultatif) (*b*) patelin *m*/trou *m*/bled *m* 2. *Pol* whistle-stop tour, tournée électorale rapide (*faite dans un train spécial*).

white [waɪt] I *a* 1. *P* (*drugs*) white lady/ stuff, cocaïne*/coke *f*/(fée) blanche *f*/neige *f*/ bigornette *f*; héroïne*/héro *f*/blanche; white cross, stimulants *mpl*/amphets *fpl*/speed *m* 2. *P* white lightning, (*raw spirit*) alcool* pur illicite/= tord-boyaux *m*; *O* (*drugs*) comprimés *mpl* de LSD* 3. *F* honnête/intègre; to play the white man, bien se conduire/agir en honnête homme; come on, play the white man! allez, sois chic!/allez, fais un bon geste! (*See* angel 22; lily-white; trash 2) II *n A P* 1. cinq livres *fpl* sterling et au-dessus 2. platine *m*/blanquette *f* 3. pièces *fpl* d'argent*/ blanquette *f*. (*See* phon(e)y I 2 (*b*)).

white-slaver ['waɪt'sleɪvə] *n F* souteneur*/ mangeur *m* de blanc/marchand *m* de barbaque/mac *m*.

whitewash¹ ['waɪtwɒʃ] *n F* (*sport*) défaite *f* à zéro.

whitewash² ['waɪtwɒʃ] *vtr F* 1. blanchir/ disculper (qn) 2. (*sport*) to whitewash one's opponents, battre ses adversaires (sans qu'ils aient marqué un point)/écraser ses adversaires.

whitey ['waɪtɪ] *n P Pej* Blanc *m*, Blanche *f*.

whiz(z)¹ [wɪz] I *a attrib* 1. *F* whiz kid, jeune prodige *m*/jeune loup *m* 2. *P* whiz mob, bande* de pickpockets/de tireurs II *n* 1. *esp NAm F* as *m*/crack *m* 2. *F* dynamisme *m*/ entrain *m*/vitalité *f* 3. *Br P* amphétamine(s)*/ amphets *fpl*/speed *m*.

whiz(z)² [wɪz] *vi* 1. *F* aller très vite*/ bomber/gazer/filer à plein tube 2. *P* voler* à la tire/décrocher.

whizzer ['wɪzə] *n P* voleur* à la tire/ fourchette *f*/tireur, -euse.

whizzing ['wɪzɪŋ] *n P* vol *m* à la tire (par une bande de pickpockets).

whodun(n)it [hu:'dʌnɪt] *n F* roman policier/polar *m*.

whole-hogger ['həʊl'hɒgə] *n F* (*a*) qn qui s'engage à fond/jusqu'au-boutiste *mf*/qn qui fonce tête baissée/fonceur, -euse (*b*) partisan

m/supporte(u)r acharné/fan *mf*. (*See* hog¹ 2)

whole-hoggism ['həʊl'hɒgɪzm] *n F* jusqu'au-boutisme *m*.

whoomph [wʊmf] *n F* = oomph.

whoopee ['wʊpi:] I *excl F* whoopee! youpi!/hourrah! II *n O F* to make whoopee (*a*) faire la fiesta/la fête/la noce (bruyamment); bien s'amuser/se marrer (*b*) faire l'amour*.

whoops-a-daisy! ['wʊpsə'deɪzɪ] *excl F* = oops-a-daisy!

whoop up ['wu:p'ʌp] *vtr F* to whoop it up, (*have a good time, celebrate*) faire la noce.

whoosh [wʊʃ] *vi F* aller *ou* rouler *ou* conduire très vite*/à plein(s) gaz.

whop [wɒp] *vtr P* 1. battre*/rosser/avoiner (qn) 2. vaincre/écraser (un adversaire).

whopper ['wɒpə] *n F* 1. qch d'énorme/de colossal; mastodonte *m* 2. gros mensonge*/ monumental bobard/caraco *m*; what a whopper! quelle gonfle!

whopping ['wɒpɪŋ] I *a F* 1. énorme/ ma(h)ous/comaque; a whopping great sandwich, un sandwich comaque 2. whopping lie = whopper 2 II *n P* volée *f* de coups*/rossée *f*/ raclée *f*/dérouillée *f*/trempe *f*.

whore¹ [hɔː] *n P* prostituée/putain *f*/pute *f*; dirty whore: see bingo 34.

whore² [hɔː] *vi P* (*a*) (*of man*) to whore/to go whoring, fréquenter les prostituées (*b*) (*of woman*) se prostituer*/putasser.

whorehouse ['hɔːhaʊs] *n P* maison close*/bordel *m*/boxon *m*/maison (d'abattage).

whoring ['hɔːrɪŋ] *n P* prostitution *f*/bisness *m*/putasserie *f*.

whore-shop ['hɔːʃɒp] *n P* = whorehouse.

wick [wɪk] *n P* 1. to get on s.o.'s wick, taper sur le système à qn/courir sur le haricot à qn/ casser les bonbons à qn/les casser à qn 2. to dip one's wick, faire l'amour*/tremper son biscuit. (*See* hampton)

wicked ['wɪkɪd] *a P* excellent*/canon/géant/ du tonnerre; have you seen my new shoes? — oh, wicked!, t'as vu mes mouvelles pompes? — oh, terrible!/géant!

widdle ['wɪdl] *n & vi Br F* = piddle¹,².

wide [waɪd] *a F* malin*/rusé/roublard/ fortiche; a wide boy, un affranchi/un débrouillard/un fortiche. (*See* berth 1)

widget ['wɪdʒɪt] *n F* objet *m*/machin *m*/truc *m*.

wiener, wienie ['wi:nə, 'wi:nɪ] *n NAm F* 1. = saucisse *f* de Francfort/Francfort *f* 2.

pénis*/merguez *f* 3. (*foolish person*) andouille *f*.

wife [waɪf], **wifey** ['waɪfɪ] *n* F the wife, l'épouse*/la bourgeoise/la bergère/la régulière/la patronne.

wife-swapping ['waɪfswɒpɪŋ] *n* P échangisme *m*.

wigging ['wɪgɪŋ] *n* O F réprimande *f*/engueulade *f*/savon *m*; **to get a good wigging**, se faire réprimander*/se faire laver la tête/se faire passer un savon.

wiggle ['wɪgl] *n esp NAm* F **to get a wiggle on**, se dépêcher*/se dégrouiller/faire vinaigre/faire fissa.

wiggy ['wɪgɪ] *a* fou*/dingue/cinglé; excentrique/chabraque.

wig out ['wɪg'aʊt] *vi* P devenir fou*/dérailler/disjoncter; se mettre en colère*/piquer une crise.

wild¹ [waɪld] *a* F 1. en colère*/furibard/en pétard 2. **to be wild about s.o.**, être emballé pour qn/en pincer pour qn/en mordre pour qn/avoir qn dans la peau/être dingue de qn 3. passionnant/palpitant/captivant; **it'll drive you wild**, ça va t'emballer. 4. *NAm* **wild thing**, coït*/baise *f*/partie *f* de jambes en l'air. (*See* **woolly**)

wild² [waɪld] *vi NAm* P = effectuer, en bande, des actes de violence extrême contre les personnes; agresser/attaquer en bande; (*to run amok*) se déchaîner.

wilding ['waɪldɪŋ] *n NAm* P = actes *mpl* de violence extrême effectués en bande contre les personnes; agression *f*/attaque *f* en bande; (*running amok*) déchaînement *m*.

willie, Willie, willy ['wɪlɪ] *Prn Br* P 1. pénis*/petit frère/quéquette *f*/zizi *m* 2. **to get on s.o.'s willy**, taper sur le système à qn/casser les bonbons à qn. (*See* **wick 1**)

willies ['wɪlɪz] *npl* F **to give s.o. the willies**, donner la chair de poule à qn; foutre la trouille/les jetons à qn; **to have the willies**, avoir peur*/avoir la trouille/avoir les foies/avoir les chocottes.

willie-wellie ['wɪlɪ'welɪ] *n Br* P préservatif (masculin)/capote (anglaise).

wimp [wɪmp] *n* F (*weak, feeble person*) poule mouillée/lavette *f*.

wimpish ['wɪmpɪʃ] *a* F (*attitude, behaviour*) de poule mouillée.

wimp out ['wɪmp'aʊt] *vi* F (*act in feeble way*) faire la poule mouillée/la lavette.

win [wɪn] *vtr & i* 1. F **you can't win (can you)!** (*catchphrase*) tu auras toujours tort! 2.

F **you can't win them all**, (*catchphrase*) on ne peut pas plaire à tout le monde/on ne peut pas contenter tout le monde 3. P voler*/décrocher/soulever.

wind [wɪnd] *n* F 1. O **to raise the wind**, se procurer de l'argent*/rassembler des fonds/récolter le blé 2. **to get the wind up**, avoir peur*/avoir les foies/mouiller (son froc); **to put the wind up s.o.**, faire peur* à qn/ficher la frousse à qn/flanquer la trouille à qn 3. **to be full of wind (and piss)/to be all wind (and water)**, (*useless talk*) parler pour ne rien dire; (*boastful talk*) être vantard/faire le flambard (*See* **piss¹ 6**) 4. **to sail close to the wind** (*a*) friser l'illégalité/l'insolence/l'indécence, etc (*b*) faire des affaires* douteuses/magouiller 5. **there's something in the wind**, il y a anguille sous roche/il se manigance quelque chose. (*See* **bag¹ 2**; **load 7**; **piss² 7**; **sail**; **sheet 1**)

windbag ['wɪndbæg] *n* F (*talkative person*) moulin *m* à paroles; **what a windbag!** il parle pour ne rien dire!/il a une sacrée tapette!

wind-up ['waɪndʌp] *n Br* F (*tease, provocation*) mise *f* en boîte; **he's a real wind-up artist**, c'est un vrai spécialiste de la mise en boîte.

wind up ['waɪnd'ʌp] F I *vi* **to wind up on the scrapheap**, finir sur la paille/dans le caniveau; **to wind up in prison**, finir en prison* II *vtr* (*a*) **to wind up**, finir/terminer (qch); liquider (une société); (*b*) *Br* **to wind s.o. up**, faire marcher qn/mettre qn en boîte; **stop winding her up!** arrête de la taquiner!

windy ['wɪndɪ] *a* F 1. *Br* O **to be windy**, avoir peur*/avoir la trouille/avoir les foies 2. *NAm* (the) **Windy City**, Chicago *m ou f*.

wing¹ [wɪŋ] *n* 1. P bras*/aile *f*/aileron *m* 2. V (*Hell's Angels*) **to get/to earn one's black wings**, faire l'amour* avec un(e) Noir(e)/gagner ses ailes noires; **to earn one's brown wings**, sodomiser* qn/gagner ses ailes brunes. (*See* **red I 6**; **sprout**)

wing² [wɪŋ] *vtr* F **to wing it** (*a*) improviser (*b*) partir*/décamper/lever le pied.

wing-ding ['wɪŋdɪŋ] *n esp NAm* P 1. attaque *f*/crise *f* d'épilepsie/digue-digue *f* (*surt* prétendue crise pour s'attirer de la sympathie*) 2. accès de folie dû aux drogues/flip *m* 3. coup *m* de colère*/rage *f*/coup de raisin 4. **wing-ding (party)**, soirée *f*/fête *f*/surprise-partie *f* 5. chahut *m*/ramdam *m*/barouf *m*.

wing(e)y ['wɪndʒɪ] *a* F = **whingy**.

wink [wɪŋk] *n* F **to tip s.o. the wink**, prévenir

qn/avertir qn/faire signe de l'œil à qn/lancer une œillade à qn. (*See* **forty**)

winkers ['wɪŋkəz] *npl Aut F* clignotants *mpl.*

winkie, winky ['wɪŋkɪ] *n P* 1. *Br* = **winkle** 2. *NAm* fesses*/popotin *m.*

winking ['wɪŋkɪŋ] *n F* (as) easy as winking, simple comme bonjour; like winking, en un clin d'œil/en (un) rien de temps/en cinq sec/ rapidos.

winkle ['wɪŋkl] *n Br P* pénis*/quéquette *f/* zizi *m.*

winkle-pickers ['wɪŋklpɪkəz] *npl Br F* chaussures *fpl* à bout pointu.

winner ['wɪnə] *n F* (a) réussite certaine/ succès assuré; tabac *m* (b) roman *m*, pièce *f*, etc à grand succès.

wino ['waɪnəʊ] *n P* ivrogne*/sac *m* à vin/ poivrot, -ote/alcolo *mf.*

win out ['wɪn'aʊt] *vi F* surmonter les difficultés *fpl*/arriver au but.

wipe[1] [waɪp] *n P* 1. mouchoir*/tire-jus *m* 2. coup*/taloche *f.*

wipe[2] [waɪp] *vtr P* 1. to wipe the floor with s.o., battre qn à plate(s) couture(s)/n'en faire qu'une bouchée 2. battre*/flanquer une raclée à (qn)/filer une purge à (qn) 3. = **wipe out**.

wiped out [waɪpt'aʊt] *a F* 1. très fatigué*/ crevé/lessivé/vanné 2. (*intoxicated by a drink or drugs*) déchiré/défoncé 3. vaincu/battu.

wipe-out ['waɪpaʊt] *n F* échec total/bide *m.*

wipe out ['waɪp'aʊt] *vtr F* tuer*/nettoyer/ ratatiner/lessiver/effacer (qn); the whole lot were wiped out, toute la bande a été zigouillée.

wire[1] ['waɪə] *n* 1. *F* renseignement *m*/tuyau *m*; to give s.o. the wire, donner un tuyau à qn/mettre qn dans le coup/tuyauter qn/mettre qn au parfum 2. *P* to pull one's wire, se masturber*/s'astiquer (la colonne)/s'allonger le macaroni. (*See* **wirepuller**; **wirepulling** 2) 3. *F* a live wire, un individu* énergique; she's a live wire, elle pète le feu 4. *O F* télé-gramme *m*/brême *f* 5. *F* to get in under the wire, arriver* au dernier moment/s'abouler pile/arriver de justesse 6. *F* to get one's wires crossed, se tromper/se gour(r)er/ s'embrouiller/se mettre le doigt dans l'œil 7. *P* voleur* à la tire/fourlineur, -euse/fourchette *f*/tireur, -euse 8. *esp NAm F* to pull (the) wires, tirer les ficelles *fpl*/faire jouer son *ou* le piston.

wire[2] ['waɪə] *vtr & i P* 1. *esp NAm* munir (qn, un policier) d'un micro(phone) 2. (*bug*) installer des micros clandestins/brancher sur table d'écoute.

wired ['waɪəd] *a P* 1. (*drugs*) (a) adonné/ accroché/accro à une drogue (b) défoncé/high 2. nerveux/tendu/à cran.

wirepuller ['waɪəpʊlə] *n* 1. *esp NAm F* intrigant, -ante/magouilleur, -euse/grenouilleur *m*; individu* qui fait jouer son *ou* le piston 2. *P* masturbateur *m*/branleur *m.* (*See* **wire**[1] 2)

wirepulling ['waɪəpʊlɪŋ] *n* 1. *esp NAm F* l'art *m* de tirer les ficelles *fpl*/intrigues *fpl* de couloir *m*/manigances *fpl*/magouilles *fpl* 2. *P* masturbation *f*/branlette *f.* (*See* **wire**[1] 2)

wise [waɪz] *a F* to get wise, (*get informed*) se mettre à la coule/se dessaler; se dégourdir; se mettre à la page; to get wise to sth, s'apercevoir de la vérité/ouvrir les yeux; piger/saisir qch; to get wise to s.o., se rendre compte de/réaliser ce que qn fait; to put s.o. wise, affranchir qn/mettre qn à la page/ tuyauter qn; to put s.o. wise to sth, avertir/ rencarder qn de qch. (*See* **guy** 1)

wiseacre ['waɪzeɪkə] *n NAm O F* (a) petit malin, petite maligne (b) (*know-all*) crâneur, -euse.

wiseass ['waɪzæs] *n NAm P* (*know-all*) crâneur, -euse/je-sais-tout *mf.*

wisecrack[1] ['waɪzkræk] *n F* bon mot/ boutade *f*/blague *f*/vanne *f*; to make a wisecrack, faire/lancer/sortir une vanne.

wisecrack[2] ['waɪzkræk] *vi F* faire de l'esprit/lancer des boutades/lâcher des vannes/vanner.

wise up ['waɪz'ʌp] I *F vi* = to get wise (**wise**) II *vtr* to wise s.o. up = to put s.o. wise (**wise**).

wishing well ['wɪʃɪŋ'wel] *n Austr P* (*RS* = (*prison*) *cell*) cellule *f* de prison/cachot *m*/ mitard *m.*

wishy-washy ['wɪʃɪwɒʃɪ] *a F* (*style, look*) fade/insipide/lavasse; (*person*) qui ne sait pas ce qu'il veut/indécis.

with [wɪð] *prep F* 1. (a) *O* to be with it, être dans le vent/être à la page (b) to get with it, (*wake up*) se réveiller; (*realize what's happening*) ouvrir les yeux/se mettre au parfum 2. I'm not with you, je ne comprends pas/je ne pige pas/je n'y suis pas/je ne vous suis pas.

with-it ['wɪðɪt] *a attrib O F* with-it gear, des vêtements* dernier cri.

witter ['wɪtə] *vi Br F* to witter (on), parler* sans arrêt pour ne rien dire/bavasser/ papoter/jacter.

wittering ['wɪtərɪŋ] *n Br F* bavardage incessant et sans intérêt/blabla(bla) *m*/papotage *m*/jactance *f*.

wizard ['wɪzəd] *a O F* excellent*/épatant/au poil/super/classe; **to be a wizard cook**, être une fée du fourneau.

wizz [wɪz] *n Br P* = **whiz(z)**[1] II 3.

wobbler, wobbly ['wɒblə, 'wɒblɪ] *n Br F* **to throw a wobbler/wobbly**, *(have a tantrum)* piquer une colère*/piquer une crise.

wodge [wɒdʒ] *n F* (a) gros morceau/bloc *m*/quartier *m* (b) liasse *f* (de papiers).

wog [wɒg] *n P Pej* 1. Arabe*/bicot *m*/bougnoul *m*/noraf *m*; barbouillé *m* 2. étranger, -ère 3. *Austr* the wog/wog gut, diarrhée*/chiasse *f*/courante *f* 4. *Br* wog box, mini-stéréo *f* portable.

wolf [wʊlf] *n* 1. *F* coureur *m* de jupons/tombeur *m* de femmes/don Juan *m*/dragueur *m* 2. *P* homosexuel* agressif *ou* débauché *ou* violent 3. *F* lone wolf, homme* qui fait bande à part/qui fait cavalier seul; solitaire *mf*. (*See* loner)

wolf-whistle ['wʊlfwɪsl] *n F* sifflement admiratif (*au passage d'une femme**); **to give a girl a wolf-whistle**, siffler une fille*.

wolly ['wɒlɪ] *n Br P* = **wally** 2.

woman-chaser ['wʊməntʃeɪsə] *n F* coureur *m* de jupons/tombeur *m* de femmes/dragueur *m*.

woman-crazy ['wʊmən'kreɪzɪ], **wo-manmad** ['wʊmən'mæd] *a F* qui a les femmes dans la peau/qui est porté sur la chose/ queutard/qui est chaud de la pince. (*See* man-crazy; man-mad)

womba ['wɒmbə] *n Br P* = **wamba**.

womble ['wɒmbl] *n Br F* individu bête/nouille *f*/andouille *f*.

wonder[1] ['wʌndə] *n F* 1. wonders will never cease! (*catchphrase*) il y a toujours des miracles!/c'est un prodige!/tu m'étonneras toujours! 2. no wonder! pas étonnant!

wonder[2] ['wʌndə] *vi F* I shouldn't wonder, cela ne me surprendrait pas/ça serait pas étonnant!

wonga ['wɒŋgə] *n P* argent*/pognon *m*/pèze *m*.

wonk [wɒŋk] *n NAm P* bûcheur, -euse/potasseur *m*.

wonky ['wɒŋkɪ] *a P* 1. (a) (*machine*) détraqué; (*gadget, switch, etc*) qui débloque; (*picture*) de travers; (*shelf, chair*) branlant (b) (*person*) mal fichu; **to feel wonky**, se sentir patraque 2. *NAm* (*person*) qui travaille beaucoup/bûcheur.

wood [wʊd] *n F* 1. touch wood/*NAm* knock on wood! touche/touchons du bois! 2. you can't see the wood for the trees, (*catchphrase*) on se perd dans les détails; les arbres cachent la forêt.

woodentop ['wʊdntɒp] *n Br P* agent* de police en uniforme/habillé *m*/bourrique *f*.

woodshed ['wʊdʃed] *n F* there's something nasty in the woodshed, on nous cache quelque chose/il y a anguille sous roche.

woof, woofter [wʊf, 'wʊftə] *n Br P* = **poof, poofter**.

wool [wʊl] *n* 1. *F* keep your wool on! = keep your hair on! (hair 3) 2. *F* to pull the wool over s.o.'s eyes, rouler qn (dans la farine). (*See* cotton-wool)

woolly ['wʊlɪ] *a F* (wild and) woolly (a) ignare/inculte/mal léché (b) hirsute/hérissé.

woopsie ['wʊpsɪ] *n Br F* excrément *m*/caca *m*; **to do a woopsie**, faire la grosse commission.

woozy ['wuːzɪ] *a* 1. *F* (*dizzy*) tout chose; to feel a bit woozy, se sentir un peu patraque/être dans le potage 2. *P* ivre*/blindé/chargé.

wop [wɒp] *n P* Italien*/macaroni *mf*/Rital, -ale.

work[1] [wɜːk] *n F* a nasty piece of work, un sale type/une peau de vache/un salopard/une ordure. (*See* cut out 2; homework; legwork; works)

work[2] [wɜːk] *vtr* 1. *F* arranger/manigancer/magouiller/trafiquer; **to work a fiddle**, manigancer une combine/magouiller un sale coup/traficoter 2. *Br P* **to work the oracle** = to put the verbal in/the verbals on s.o. (verbal[1] 2).

workaholic [wɜːkə'hɒlɪk] *n F* bourreau *m* de travail/drogué, -ée de travail.

working girl ['wɜːkɪŋ'gɜːl] *n F* Euph prostituée*/fille *f*.

working over ['wɜːkɪŋ'əʊvə] *n P* **to give s.o. a working over** = to work s.o. over (work over).

work out [wɜːk'aʊt] *vi NAm F* he works out, c'est un dur (à cuire); she really works out! elle est pas timide!/elle se défend bien!

work over ['wɜːk'əʊvə] *vtr P* to work s.o. over, battre* qn/filer une peignée à qn/passer qn à la machine à bosseler; he got worked over by some yobs, il s'est fait bastonner/dérouiller par des loubards.

works [wɜːks] *npl* 1. *P* to give s.o. the works (a) battre* qn/tabasser qn/passer qn à tabac/

flanquer une dérouillée à qn (b) tuer* qn/
zigouiller qn/faire son affaire à qn/avoir la
peau de qn 2. P (drugs) the works, attirail m
de drogué* 3. F the whole works, tout le
bataclan/tout le bazar/tout le tremblement.
(See boiling II; caboodle; gum up;
shebang 1; shoot¹ 1; shoot² 7;
spanner; waterworks)

work up ['wɜːk'ʌp] vtr 1. P (sexually)
exciter/émoustiller/chauffer 2. F mettre (qn)
en colère/échauffer/affoler; don't get worked
up (about it), (ne) t'emballe pas/(ne) te
monte pas le bourrichon/t'excite pas. (See lather¹; sweat¹ 3)

world [wɜːld] n F 1. to feel on top of the
world, être en pleine forme/avoir la frite/avoir
la pêche/tenir une forme olympique 2. out of
this world, mirifique/génial/transcendant/
sensass; it was out of this world! c'était le
pied! 3. to think the world of s.o., estimer
hautement qn/porter qn aux nues; she thinks
the world of him, elle ne jure que par lui. (See
come down 4; dead I 6)

worm [wɜːm] n F (person) (a) lavette f/
mollasson, -onne/chiffe molle (b) raté, -ée/
minable mf.

worry ['wʌrɪ] vi F 1. not to worry! faut pas
s'en faire! 2. I should worry! ce n'est pas mon
affaire!/c'est le cadet de mes soucis!/je m'en
fiche comme de l'an quarante!

worryguts ['wʌrɪgʌts], NAm **worrywart**
['wʌrɪwɔːt] n P bileux, -euse/qn qui se fait de
la bile; don't be such a worryguts, ne te
tracasse pas tant.

worst [wɜːst] n F the worst (a) (awful)
those shoes are the worst, ces pompes sont af-
freuses; she's the worst, elle est vraiment
horrible (b) (excellent) it's the worst, c'est le
pied/c'est classe.

worth [wɜːθ] a F 1. he was pulling for all he
was worth, il tirait de toutes ses forces 2. was
she worth it?: see **bingo 76.**

wossname ['wɒsneɪm] n F = **whatch-
ha(ma)callit** ; **what's(h)is-name**;
what's-(h)er-name.

wotcher! ['wɒtʃə] excl P wotcher mate/
cock! comment ça gaze, vieille branche!

wotsit ['wɒtsɪt] n F = **whatsit.**

wow¹ [waʊ] I excl F wow! oh là là!/wouah!/
wow! II n F succès m formidable/du
tonnerre; tabac m (monstre). (See **pow-
wow**)

wow² [waʊ] vtr F stupéfier/époustoufler/en
mettre plein la vue à/en boucher un coin à

(qn)/laisser (qn) baba.

wowser, wowzer ['waʊzə] n Austr F
rabat-joie m/trouble-fête mf.

wrap¹ [ræp] n F to be under wraps, (of thing,
project, etc) être secret; to keep sth under
wraps, garder qch secret.

wrap² [ræp] vtr F 1. wrap yourself round
that! mange* ou bois* ça!/tape-toi ça!/mets-
toi ça derrière la cravate! 2. he wrapped his
car round a tree, il a encadré un arbre/il s'est
payé un arbre.

wrap-up ['ræpʌp] n P (drugs) paquet m
contenant de la marijuana*.

wrap up ['ræp'ʌp] vtr & i 1. P se taire*/la
fermer/la boucler; wrap up! ta gueule!/la
ferme!/boucle-la!/écrase! 2. F terminer/
achever/boucler; it's all wrapped up, tout est
arrangé/bouclé; c'est dans le sac; that just
about wraps it up for today, c'est à peu près
tout pour aujourd'hui.

wrecked [rekt] a F (intoxicated by drink or
drugs) déchiré/défoncé.

wringer ['rɪŋə] n P to put s.o. through
the wringer, en faire voir des vertes et des
pas mûres à qn/faire passer qn à la cas-
serole/faire passer un mauvais quart d'heure
à qn.

wrinkle ['rɪŋkl] n F 1. truc m/combine f; to
know all the wrinkles, la connaître dans les
coins/connaître toutes les ficelles/en connaître
un rayon 2. (helpful information) tuyau m.

wrinklie, wrinkly ['rɪŋklɪ] n esp Br F (old
person) croulant, -ante/vieux m/vieille f.

write [raɪt] vi F 1. it's nothing to write home
about, cela n'a rien d'extraordinaire/cela ne
casse rien/ça ne casse pas des briques 2. to
write one's name on the lawn, uriner* dehors/
arroser les marguerites.

writer ['raɪtə] n P (drugs) médecin m qui
fait des ordonnances pour des drogues illicites
en échange d'argent*.

write-off ['raɪtɒf] n F perte sèche; my car
was a (complete) write-off, ma voiture a été
complètement démolie/était bonne pour la
casse; he's a write-off, c'est un incapable/un
nullard.

write off ['raɪt'ɒf] vtr F she wrote off her
father's car, elle a bousillé la voiture de son
père; the critics wrote off the play, les
critiques ont démoli la pièce; to write s.o. off,
congédier* qn; ne tenir aucun compte de qn/
éloigner qn de ses pensées; rayer qn.

wrong [rɒŋ] F I a to get on the wrong side
of s.o., se faire mal voir de qn/ne pas être

dans les petits papiers de qn. (*See* **bed**[1] **2**; **end 11**) II *adv* **1. to get s.o. wrong**, mal comprendre qn; **don't get me wrong, I'm not saying ...**, comprenez-moi bien, je ne dis pas ... **2.** *NAm* **to get wrong with s.o.**, se faire mal voir de qn.

wrong'un ['rɒŋən] *n Br F* **1.** criminel, -elle/indésirable *mf* **2.** qch à éviter/

embêtement *m*.

wuss [wʊs] *n F* **1.** *NAm* individu* faible/ mou; poule mouillée/lavette *f*/chiffe molle **2.** (*in Wales*) ami*/copain, -ine; **hello wuss**, salut mon pote.

wussy ['wʊsɪ] *n NAm F* = **wuss 1**.

wuzzy ['wʌzɪ] *a F* **I feel wuzzy**, j'ai la tête qui tourne.

X, Y, Z

X [eks] *n* 1. *F* baiser *m*; give us an x, donne-moi un bisou 2. *P* (*drugs*) ecstasy *m*.
x-out [eks'aʊt] *vtr P* 1. biffer/barrer/rayer (un mot, etc) 2. tuer*/éliminer/effacer.

x-rated [eks'reɪtɪd] *a F* 1. osé/salé; porno(graphique)/de fesse 2. terrifiant/horrifiant/horrifique.

yabber¹ ['jæbə] *n F* bavardage *m*/jactance *f*/blabla(bla) *m*.
yabber² ['jæbə] *vi F* bavarder*/bavasser/jacter; they were yabbering away as usual, ils taillaient leur bavette habituelle.
yack¹ [jæk] *n F* = **yackety-yack**.
yack² [jæk] *vi F* (*a*) bavarder*/jacasser (*b*) (*gossip*) ragoter/papoter.
yacka, yacker ['jækə] *n Austr P* travail*/boulot *m*/turbin *m*.
yackety-yack ['jækətɪ'jæk] *n F* caquetage *m*/jacasserie *f*/blabla(bla) *m*.
yahoo [jə'huː] *n F* brute (épaisse).
yak¹ [jæk] *n F* = **yackety-yack**.
yak² [jæk] *vi F* = **yack²**.
yakka ['jækə] *n Austr F* = **yacka, yacker**.
yammer ['jæmə] *vi F* 1. bavarder*/bavasser/dégoiser 2. grogner*/râler/rouscailler/bougonner.
yancy ['jænsɪ] *a NAm F* = **antsy**.
yang [jæŋ] *n NAm P* pénis*/zob *m*/zébi *m*.
yank¹ [jæŋk] *n F* secousse *f*/saccade *f*/coup sec.
yank² [jæŋk] *vtr* 1. *F* tirer d'un coup sec; to yank the bedclothes off s.o., découvrir qn brusquement 2. *NAm P* to yank s.o. around, (*deceive*) tromper*/duper qn; (*irritate*) ennuyer*/casser les bonbons à/emmerder qn.
Yank³ [jæŋk], **Yankee¹** ['jæŋkɪ] **I** *a F* américain/amerlo(que)/yankee/ricain **II** *n F* 1. habitant, -ante de la Nouvelle-Angleterre *ou* d'un des états du nord des États-Unis 2. Américain*/Amerlo *m*/Amerloque *mf*/Yankee *mf*/Ricain, -aine.
Yankee² ['jæŋkɪ] *n P* (*turf*) pari (cumulatif).

yantsy ['jæntsɪ] *a NAm F* = **antsy**.
yap¹ [jæp] *n P* 1. (*a*) bavardage bruyant/caquetage *m* (*b*) bouche*/goulot *m*/bec *m*/clapet *m* 2. *NAm* paysan*/plouc *mf*/bouseux *m*.
yap² [jæp] *vi P* parler* beaucoup/déblatérer/en dégoiser/jaspiner/bavasser/bagouler.
yapper ['jæpə] *n P* bavard*/jacasseur, -euse/jaspineur *m*/bagouleur *m*.
yapping ['jæpɪŋ] *n P* bavardage *m*/jactance *f*/jaspinage *m*.
yard¹ [jɑːd] *n* 1. *F* he pulled a face a yard long, il a fait une tête de six pieds de long/une gueule longue d'un kilomètre 2. *Br F* the Yard, (= *Scotland Yard*) = P.J. *f* 3. *A P* pénis* 4. *NAm P* cent *ou* mille dollars *mpl* 5. *WInd F* Jamaïque *f*. (*See* **boneyard**)
yard² [jɑːd] *vtr NAm P* to yard (on) one's husband/wife, tromper/doubler son mari/sa femme.
yardbird ['jɑːdbɜːd] *n NAm F* 1. recrue *f* qui effectue des tâches serviles à l'extérieur 2. prisonnier, -ière/taulard, -arde 3. clochard*/clodo *m*/trimardeur *m* (*qui fréquente les dépôts de chemin de fer*).
yardie ['jɑːdɪ] *n WInd F* 1. Jamaïcain, -aine/Antillais, -aise 2. membre *m* d'un gang de criminels.
yarn¹ [jɑːn] *n F* (*a*) histoire merveilleuse/longue histoire (*b*) (*untrue*) histoire *f* à dormir debout/bateau *m*/bobard *m*; to spin/to pitch/to pull a yarn, mentir*/raconter des histoires/bourrer le crâne (à qn); he spun me this long yarn about being short of cash, il m'a fait son charre, soit disant qu'il était raide.

290

yarn² [jɑːn] *vi F* débiter des histoires *fpl*.

yarra ['jærə] *a Austr F* **(stone) yarra**, fou*/loufoque.

yass! [jæs] *excl WInd P* (*showing derision, provocation*) ah ouais?/je t'emmerde!

yatter¹ ['jætə] *n P* bavardage *m*/baratin *m*/blabla(bla) *m*.

yatter² ['jætə] *vi P* bavarder*/baratiner/blablater/tenir le crachoir.

yawn¹ ['jɔːn] *n F* qch d'ennuyeux*/de rasoir/qui fait bâiller (à s'en décrocher la mâchoire)/de chiant (comme la pluie); **this book is one long yawn**, ce livre est drôlement rasoir.

yawn² ['jɔːn] *vi F* vomir*/dégueuler/gerber.

yawp [jɔːp] *vi NAm F* grogner*/râler/rouspéter/renauder.

yeah [jɛə] *adv & excl F* (*a*) oui*/ouais/gi *ou* gy/gygo (*b*) **oh yeah?** et alors?/et après?

year [jɪə] *n F* **to put years on s.o.**, donner du mal à qn/donner des cheveux blancs à qn. (*See* **donkey 3**; **dot¹ 2**)

yecch! [jeχ] *excl NAm F* = **yuck! yuk!**

yecchy ['jeχɪ] *a NAm F* = **yucky, yuky**.

yegg [jeg] *n P* (*rare*) perceur *m* de coffre-fort.

yell [jel] *n Br F* **1.** (*joke*) bonne blague; **it's a yell!** c'est à se tordre (de rire)! **2.** soirée tapageuse; **they had a good yell**, ils se sont bien marrés **3.** **to have a yell**, vomir*/dégueuler.

yellow ['jeləʊ] **I** *a* **1.** *F* lâche/trouillard; **to turn/go yellow**, se dégonfler; **to have a yellow streak**, être un peu trouillard sur les bords **2.** *F* **the Yellow Press**, la presse/les journaux* à scandales **3.** *P Pej* **yellow satin/silk/velvet**, femme* orientale (*en tant que partenaire sexuelle*) **II** *n P* **1.** *Pej* femmes* orientales (*en tant que partenaires sexuelles*) (*See* **yellow I 3**) **2.** *NAm* (*drugs*) **yellows** = **yellow-jackets**.

yellow-bellied ['jeləʊbelɪd, 'jeləbelɪd] *a F* qui a peur*/déballonné/flubard; **to be yellow-bellied**, avoir les foies (blancs)/les chocottes/la chiasse/les copeaux.

yellowbelly ['jeləʊbelɪ] *n F* poltron*/trouillard, -arde/foie blanc/flubard *m*.

yellow-jackets ['jeləʊdʒækɪts] *npl NAm P* (*drugs*) pilules *fpl* à base de barbital/barbituriques*.

yellow-livered ['jeləʊlɪvəd] *a F* = **yellow-bellied**.

yen¹ [jen] *n* **1.** *F* désir ardent et obsédant/appétit *m*; **to have a yen for sth**, ne rêver que de qch/avoir une super envie de qch **2.** *P* = **yen-yen**. (*See* **pen-yen**)

yen² [jen] *vi F* (*not common*) soupirer après/désirer ardemment.

yen shee ['jen'ʃiː] *n P* (*drugs*) opium*/touf(f)iane *f*/op *m*/noir *m*.

yen sleep ['jen'sliːp] *n P* (*drugs*) (*a*) trance *f* (*après avoir fumé de l'opium**) (*b*) sommeil agité (*résultant d'un état de manque*).

yenta, yentl ['jentə, 'jentl] *n P* femme* querelleuse*/(vieille) bique.

yen-yen ['jenjen] *n P* (*drugs*) besoin *m* de la drogue/guêpe *f*/guenon *f*.

yep [jep] *adv & excl P* = **yeah** (*a*).

yer [jɜː] *pron P* (= *you*) tu/vous; **will yer or won't yer?** tu veux ou tu veux pas?

yesca ['jeskə] *n P* (*drugs*) marijuana*/marie-jeanne *f*.

yes-girl ['jesgɜːl] *n P* fille* facile/Marie-couche-toi-là *f*/fille* qui se couche quand on lui dit de s'asseoir.

yes-man ['jesmæn] *n F* individu* qui dit oui à tout/béni-oui-oui *m*.

Yid [jɪd] *n P* **1.** *Pej* Juif*/youtre *m*/youpin, -ine/youde *m* **2.** *Br* supporte(u)r *m* de (l'équipe de football) *Tottenham Hotspurs*.

yike [jaɪk] *n Austr F* **1.** querelle*/engueulade *f*/prise *f* de bec **2.** bagarre *f*/baston *m ou f*/embrouille *f*.

ying-yang ['jɪŋjæŋ], **yinyang** ['jɪnjæŋ] *n NAm P* **1.** (*a*) anus*/oignon *m* (*b*) organes génitaux; sexe* de l'homme/de la femme **2.** = **yoyo¹**.

yippee! [jɪ'piː] *excl F* hourrah!/youpi!

yo! [jəʊ] *excl NAm F* bonjour!/salut!

yob(bo) ['jɒb(əʊ)] *n Br P* (*jeune*) voyou*/loubard *m*/loulou *m*/zonard *m*; **they're just a load of yobs**, c'est rien que des petits loulous.

yodel¹ ['jəʊdl] *n P* vomissures *fpl*/dégueulis *m*.

yodel² ['jəʊdl] *vi P* vomir*/dégueuler/gerber.

yomp [jɒmp] *vi Br F* (*tramp across rough country*) crapahuter/crapaüter.

yonks [jɒŋks] *npl Br F* une éternité/des années*/des berges; **I haven't been there in yonks**, ça fait une paye que je n'y suis pas allé; **that was yonks ago**, ça fait une paye.

yooie ['juːɪ] *n F* = **u-ie**.

york [jɔːk] *vi NAm P* vomir*/aller au renard/dégueuler.

you-and-me ['juːən'miː] *n P* (*RS* = *tea*) (*drink*) thé *m*; (*meal*) goûter *m*.

you-know-what [juːnəʊ'wɒt] *n F Euph* sexe *m*/jeux sexuels; toilettes *fpl*/parties *fpl* du corps, etc; she kicked me in the you-know-what, elle m'a donné un coup de pied là où je pense.

youngblood ['jʌŋblʌd] *n NAm P* jeune noir *m*. (*See* **blood 5**)

yours [jɔːz, juəz] *pron F* 1. what's yours? qu'est-ce que tu prends? 2. yours truly, moi-même/mézigue/bibi/ma pomme. (*See* **up IV**)

yow [jau] *n Austr F* to keep yow = to keep nit (**nit 2**).

yoyo ['jəujəu] *n NAm F* 1. idiot, -ote/individu bête*/gourde *f*/crétin, -ine 2. (*dupe*) pigeon *m*/poire *f*/gobeur, -euse.

yuck!, yuk! [jʌk] *excl F* pouah!/berk!

yucky, yukky ['jʌkɪ] *a F* 1. dégoûtant/dégueulasse/débectant 2. (*sickly*) à l'eau de rose/gnangnan.

yummy ['jʌmɪ] *a F* très bon/délicieux/du nanan; he's dead yummy, il est vachement sexy.

yum-yum! ['jʌm'jʌm] *excl F* du nanan!/miam-miam!

yumyum(s) ['jʌmjʌm(z)] *n F* qch *ou* qn d'irrésistible; partenaire sexuel(le) éventuel(le)/drogue* illicite/somme *f* d'argent*, etc.

yup [kʌp] *adv & excl NAm F* oui*/ouais.

yuppie ['jʌpɪ] *n F esp Pej* (*abbr of young urban professional, young upwardly mobile professional*) = jeune homme* *ou* femme* très matérialiste, à la carrière brillante, prometteuse et hautement rémunératrice; = jeune loup *m*/jeune cadre *m* dynamique.

Z [zed, *NAm* ziː] *n esp NAm P* (*drugs*) = gramme *m* de drogue*/dose(tte) *f*.

za [zɑː] *n NAm F* pizza *f*.

zaftig ['zæftɪg] *a NAm F* = **zoftig**.

zany ['zeɪnɪ] *a F* farfelu/loufoque; a really zany idea, une idée complètement loufoque/farfelue/délirante; zany colours, couleurs *fpl* fantastiques/délirantes.

zap¹ [zæp] *n F* 1. (*in comic books, etc*) paf!/pan! zap, zap and it's done! tac tac et c'est fini! 2. claquement *m*.

zap² [zæp] *F* I *vtr* 1. tuer* d'un coup de feu/zigouiller/flinguer/mettre en l'air 2. (*destroy*) détruire/anéantir; (*criticize severely*) déglinguer/flinguer 3. (*put, send*) zap it in the oven, balance-le/flanque-le au four; we'll zap it across to you by courier, on vous l'enverra vite fait par courrier II *vi* 1. (*change channel on TV*) zapper 2. se dépêcher*/se grouiller; to zap along, aller à pleins tubes.

zapped [zæpt] *a F* fatigué*/crevé/claqué.

zapper ['zæpə] *n* (*TV remote control*) zappeur *m*.

zappy ['zæpɪ] *a F* (*fast*) rapide; (*very responsive*) nerveux; (*stylish, punchy*) énergique/qui a du punch.

Z car ['zedkɑː] *n F* voiture *f* de police/voiture pie.

zeds [zedz] *npl F* sommeil *m*/roupillon *m*. (*See* **z's**)

Zen [zen] *n P* (*drugs*) instant Zen, LSD*.

zero ['zɪərəu] *n F* (*person*) zéro *m*/nullard, -arde.

zero out ['zɪərəu'aut] *vtr & i NAm F* se trouver à court d'argent*; faire faillite; I'm zeroed out, je suis fauché/sans un/dans la dèche.

zilch [zɪltʃ] *n esp NAm F* 1. rien*/zéro/nib/que dalle/(peau de) zob 2. (*person*) zéro *m*/nullard, -arde.

zillion ['zɪljən] *n F* des millions *mpl* (et des millions).

zillionaire [zɪljə'nɛə] *n* individu* immensément riche*/archimillionnaire *mf*.

zine [ziːn] *n F* (*abbr of fanzine*) fanzine *m*.

zing [zɪŋ] *n F* vitalité *f*/vigueur *f*/énergie *f*/dynamisme *m*/ressort *m*.

zingy ['zɪŋɪ] *a F* plein d'entrain *m*/qui pète le feu.

zip¹ [zɪp] *n F* 1. énergie *f*/entrain *m*; put some zip into it! mets-y du nerf!/secoue-toi!/grouille-toi! 2. = **zilch 1**.

zip² [zɪp] *vtr F* to zip it/to zip one's lip, se taire*/la fermer/la boucler.

zip along ['zɪpə'lɒŋ] *vi F* aller très vite*/aller à toute pompe.

zipper ['zɪpə] *n V* (*homosexual use*) zipper dinner/zipper sex, fellation*; pipe vite faite/vite taillée.

zippo ['zɪpəu] *n esp NAm* = **zilch 1**.

zippy ['zɪpɪ] *a F* vif/plein d'allant/dynamique; look zippy! grouille-toi!/magnetoi (le train)!

zit [zɪt] *n P* (*pimple*) bouton *m*; zit doctor, dermato(logue) *mf*.

zizz¹ [zɪz] *n F* (petit) somme/roupillon *m*.

zizz² [zɪz] *vi F* dormir*/faire un (petit) somme/piquer un roupillon.

zoftig ['zɒftɪg] *a NAm F* (*a*) agréable (*b*) voluptueux; succulent; (*woman*) désirable/baisable.

zoid [zɔɪd] *n F* idiot, -ote/crétin, -ine; (*clumsy*) empaillé, -ée/patate *f*.

zombi(e) ['zɒmbɪ] *n F* **1.** zombi *m*/abruti, -ie; I feel like a zombi(e), je me sens complètement abruti **2.** (*UFO*) OVNI *m*.

zomboid ['zɒmbɔɪd] *a* bête*/barjo; (*intoxicated*) qui plane.

zoned (out) ['zəʊnd('aʊt)] *a P* = **zonked (out)**.

zonked (out) ['zɒŋkt('aʊt)] *a P* **1.** (*a*) ivre* mort/cuit/rétamé/bourré (*b*) (*drugs*) drogué*/défoncé à mort/stone(d); he was completely zonked, il était complètement

défoncé/il était défoncé à mort **2.** fatigué*/crevé/claqué/lessivé.

zonko ['zɒŋkəʊ] *a P* = **zonked (out)**.

zoom [zuːm] *n P* (*drugs*) amphétamine*/speed *m*.

zoom up ['zuːm'ʌp] *vi F* to zoom up/to come zooming up, arriver en trombe.

zoot suit ['zuːt'suːt] *n NAm* complet *m* d'homme avec veston long et pantalon large; costume *m* zazou; *Br* (*police term*) sac *m* pour transporter une dépouille mortelle.

z's [ziːz] *npl esp NAm P* to bag/catch/cop/grab some z's, dormir*/faire une ronflette/piquer un roupillon. (*See* **big Z's**; **zeds**)

zulu ['zuːluː] *n Br F Pej* Noir, -e*/bougnoul *m*.

Répertoire Alphabétique
de Synonymes
Argotiques Français

Répertoire Alphabétique
de Synonymes
Argotiques Français

abandonner: balancer; balanstiquer; bouler; caner; chier du poivre (à qn); se coucher; débarquer; faire mallette et paquette à; ficher en l'air; flanquer en l'air; foutre à la porte; foutre dehors/en l'air; lâcher; laisser choir/courir/glisser/tomber; laisser en carafe/en frime/en panne/en plan/en rade; laisser quimper; larguer; mettre une gamelle; mettre (qn) sur la touche; passer les doches; plaquer; scier; semer; virer; zapper.
(*Voir* **débarrasser de, se**)

abîmer: amocher; bousiller; effacer; esquinter; fusiller; niquer; plier; rétamer; saboter; zigouiller.

abject: *voir* **sale.**

abondance *f*: des bottes *fpl*; charibotée *f*; chiée *f*; flop(p)ée *f*; flottes *fpl*; foul(e)titude *f*; des masses *fpl*; max *m*; des mille et des cents; muffée *f*; palanquée *f*; paquet *m*; potée *f*; ribambelle *f*; secouée *f*; tapée *f*; tas *m*; tassée *f*; tinée *f*; tirée *f*; tripotée *f*; un wagon (de).

accord, d': banco; ça biche; ça botte; ça boume; ça colle; ça gaze; ça marche; c'est bon; dac; d'acc; gy; je marche; ji; jy; OK.

accoucher: abouler; chier *ou* faire un lard/un lardon/un môme/un salé; pisser sa/une côtelette; pisser son os; pisser un môme; pondre.

adultère *m*: carambolage *m* en douce; char(re) *m*; coup *m* de canif (dans le contrat); doublage *m*; galoup *m*; impair *m*; mise *f* en double; paille *f*; paillons *mpl*; queues *fpl*.

adversité *f*: cerise *f*; cirage *m*; choux *mpl*; confiture *f*; emmerde *f*; emmerdement *m*; emmouscaillement *m*; guigne *f*; limonade *f*; marmelade *f*; mélasse *f*; merde *f*; merdier *m*; mouise *f*; mouscaille *f*; panade *f*; pétrin *m*; purée *f*; scoumoune *f*; skoumoune *m*.

affaire *f*: balle *f*; blot *m*; boules *fpl*; boulot *m*; combine *f*; commande *f*; coup *m*; filon *m*; flanche *m*; magouillage(s) *m(pl)*; magouilles *fpl*; oignons *mpl*; parcours *m*; truc *m*.

agent *m* **de police:** bédi *m*; bourre *m*; bourrin *m*; cogne *m*; condé *m*; flic *m*; flicard *m*; flikeu *m*; fliquesse *f*; fliquette *f*; guignol *m*; hirondelle *f* de trottoir; kébour *m*; keuf *m*; mannequin *m*; maton *m*; matuche *m*; pélerin *m*; pèlerine *f*; perdreau *m*; poulaga *m*; poulet *m*; royco *m*; schmit(t) *m*; sergot *m*; tige *f*.

agent *m* **cycliste:** cyclo *m*; hirondelle *f* à roulettes/de bitume/du faubourg/de nuit; roulette *f*; tige *f*; vache *f* à roulettes.

agent *m* **en moto:** mobilard *m*; motard *m*.
(*Voir* **policier**)

agression *f*: accrochage *m*; braquage *m*; colletage *m*; cravate *f*; mise *f* en l'air; serrage *m*.

aiguille *f*: *voir* **seringue.**

aimer: s'amouracher de; avoir à la bonne/à la chouette; avoir dans la peau; avoir un/le béguin pour; avoir un/le pépin pour; avoir une toquade pour; bander pour; se coiffer de; en croquer pour; en pincer pour; en tenir pour; s'enticher de; être chipé pour; être pincé/toqué de; être mordu pour; gober; goder pour; l'avoir en l'air pour; raffoler de.

alcool *m*: antigel *m*; camphre *m*; carburant *m*; casse-gueule *m*; casse-pattes *m*; charge *f*; cogne *f*; coupe-la-soif *m*; cric *m*; élixir *m* de hussard; fil *m* en quatre; ginglard *m*; gn(i)aule *f*; gn(i)ole *f*; gnôle *f*; gobelette *f*; gobette *f*; goutte *f*; pousse-au-crime *m*; raide *f*; schnaps *m*; schnick *m*; tafiat *m*; tord-boyau(x) *m*; vitriol *m*.
(*Voir* **boisson; vin**)

alibi *m*: berlanche *f*; berlue *f*; chauffeuse *f*;

coupure *f*; couverte *f*; couverture *f*; couvrante *f*; parapluie *m*; paravent *m*; pébroc *m*; pébroque *m*.

Allemand *m*: boche *m*; chleu(h) *m*; doryphore *m*; fridolin *m*; frisé *m*; fritz *m*; frizou *m*; haricot vert; prusco(t) *m*.

aller, s'en: *voir* **partir**.

amant *m*: coquin *m*; dessous *m*; gigolo *m*; gigolpince *m*; jules *m*; julot *m*; marcel *m*; matou *m*; matz *m*; mec *m*; miché *m*; micheton *m*; régulier *m*.

Américain *m*: amerlo *m*; amerloc *m*; amerloque *m*; amerlot *m*; amerluche *m*; ricain *m*; yankee *m*.

ami, -ie: aminche *m*; cop(a)in *m*; copine *f*; frangin *m*; pote *m*; poteau *m*; social *m*; vieille branche; zig(ue) *m*.

amour, faire l': abattre la quille; aiguiller; aller à la bourre/au cul/au joint; amener le petit au cirque; s'appuyer qn; arracher son copeau/son pavé; asperger le persil; s'astiquer; baiser; baisouiller; besogner; biquer; bit(t)er; bourrer; bourriner; bourriquer; brosser; calecer; caramboler; cartonner; caser; casser la canne; chevaucher; chibrer; coller; coucher avec; cracher dans le bénitier; cramper; culbuter; danser sur le baquet; défoncer; dégraisser son panais; dérouiller (son petit frère/Totor); effeuiller la marguerite; égoïner; (s')embourber; enfiler; enjamber; se l'enfoncer; s'envoyer (qn); (s')envoyer en l'air; le faire; se faire qn; faire la bête à deux dos; faire ça; faire des cabrioles/un carton/criquon-criquette; faire une partie de balayette/d'écarté/de jambes en l'air/de jambons; faire zig-zig/zizi-pan(-)pan; se farcir; filer le coup de guisot; filer un coup d'arbalète/de baguette/de brosse/de patte/de sabre/de tromblon; filer un coup dans les baguettes; flinguer; fourailler; fourrer; foutre un coup d'arbalète/de brosse/de manche; frotter; glisser; en glisser une paire/un bout à; godailler; godiller; goupillonner; grimper; l'introduire à; jouer au bilboquet; jouer de la clarinette baveuse; laisser le chat aller au fromage; limer; se mélanger; la mettre au chaud; le/se mettre; mettre une brioche au chaud; mettre la cheville dans le trou; miser; niquer; passer à la douane; s'en payer un petit coup; pinailler; piner; pinocher; planter; planter le mai; poinçonner; pointer; pousser sa pointe; prendre du mâle; prendre son pied; queuter; ramer; ramoner; sabrer;

sauter; sch(e)nailler; semer sa graine; se taper; tirer; tirer sa chique/son coup/sa crampe/sa crampette; tomber; torcher; torpiller; tremper son biscuit; tringler; trombiner; troncher; trouduculter; verger; voir la feuille à l'envers; yenser; zaiber; zéber.

amphétamine(s) *f(pl)*: amph *m ou f*; amphé(s) *f(pl)*; amphets *fpl*; bonbons *mpl*; speed *m*.

(très) amusant: à (se) crever de rire; astap(e); bidonnant; bolant; boyautant; crevant; drôlichon; fendant; gondolant; gonflant; impayable; mariol(e); mariolle; marrant; pas triste; pilant; pissant; poilant; rigolard; rigolboche; rigouillard; roulant; tire-bouchonnant; tordant; torsif.

an *m*, **année** *f*: balai *m*; berge *f*; carat *m*; gerbe *f*; longe *f*; pige *f*; pigette *f*.

Anglais, -aise: angliche *mf*; britiche *mf*; rosbif *m*.

anus *m*: anneau *m*; baba *m*; bagouse *f*; bague *f*; boîte *f* à pâté; borgne *m*; boutonnière *f*; chevalière *f*; chouette *m*; couloir *m* à/aux lentilles; coupe-cigare *m*; cul *m*; derge *m*; entrée *f* de service; fias *m*; fignard *m*; fignarès *m*; figne *m*; fignedé *m*; fignolet *m*; fion(ard) *m*; foiron *m*; luc *m*; lucarne *f*; motte *f*; œil *m* de bronze; œillet *m*; oignard *m*; oigne *m*; oignon *m*; pastèque *f*; pastille *f*; porte *f* de derrière/de service; pot *m* (d'échappement); petit *m*; petit guichet; rond *m*; rondelle *f*; rondibé *m* (du radada); rosette *f*; terre *f* jaune; trèfle *m*; trou *m* (de balle/du cul); troufignard *m*; troufignon *m*; troufion *m*; turbine *f* à chocolat; tutu *m*; le zéro.

Arabe *mf*: arbi *m*; arbicot *m*; beur *m*; beurette *f*; bic *m*; bicot *m*; bougnoul(e) *m*; crougnat *m*; crouillat *m*; crouille *m*; crouilledouche *m*; figuier *m*; melon *m*; mohamed *m*; rat *m*; raton *m*; rebeu *m*; sidi *m*; tronc *m* (de figuier).

argent *m*: (*pièces et billets*) artiche *m*; aspine *f*; athlète *m*; auber *m*; aubère *m*; barre *f*; bâton *m*; belins *mpl*; beurre *m*; bibelots *mpl*; biscuits *mpl*; blanc *m*; blanquette *f*; blé *m*; boudin *m*; boules *fpl*; braise *f*; brique (lourde); broque *f*; bulle *m*; caire *m*; carbi *m*; carburant *m*; carbure *m*; carme *m*; chips *mpl*; dolluche *m*; douille *f*; ferraille *f*; fifrelin *m*; flouse *m*; flouze *m*; fraîche *f*; fric *m*; galette *f*; galtouze *f*; ganot *m*; grisbi *m*; japonais *m*; kope(c)ks *mpl*; livre *f*;

lovés *mpl*; mitraille *f*; mornifle *f*; nerf *m*;
oseille *f*; osier *m*; pascal *m*; pécune *f*;
pépètes *fpl*; pèse *m*; pésettes *fpl*; petit
format; pèze *m*; picaillons *mpl*; plâtre *m*; pognon *m*; quibus *m*; radis *mpl*; rond(s) *m(pl)*;
rotin *m*; Saint-Fric *m*; soudure *f*; thune *f*;
trèfle *m*; tune *f*.
(*Voir* **billet(s)**)
argot *m*: argomuche *m*; jar(s) *m*; javanais
m; largonji *m*; loucherbem *m*; verlan *m*.
arrestation *f*: agrichage *m*; alpague *f*; coup
m de flan; emballage *m*; piquage *m*; scalp *m*.
arrêter: agrafer; agricher; agriffer;
alpaguer; argougner; arquepincer; baiser;
ceinturer; chauffer; choper; coffrer; coincer;
cravater; crever; croquer; cueillir; donner la
belle; emballer; embarquer; embastiller;
emboîter; embourremaner; empaqueter;
emporter; enchtiber; enchrister; enflaquer;
engerber; entoiler; envelopper; épingler; fabriquer; faire (marron); gaufrer; gauler;
grouper; harponner; lever; mettre/jeter/poser
le grappin sur; mettre la main sur l'alpague
de; paumer; pincer; pingler; piper; piquer;
poisser; quimper; rafler; ramasser; ratisser;
saucissonner; sauter; scalper; scrafer;
secouer; serrer; serrietter; sucrer; tomber.
être arrêté: être alpagué/baisé/bon/bondi/
bonnard/bourru/crevé/dans le sac/fabriqué/
fait/marron/rousti/têtard; se faire bondir; se
faire faire; se faire piger/poivrer.
(*Voir* **emprisonner**)
arriver: abouler/amener sa graisse;
s'abouler; amener sa viande; s'amener;
s'apporter; débarquer; se pointer; (se)
radiner; rambiner; se ramener; rappliquer.
assassin *m*: but(t)eur *m*; flingueur *m*;
metteur *m* en l'air; rectifieur *m*; repasseur
m; saigneur *m*; scionneur *m*; surineur *m*;
tueur *m*.
assassiner: allonger (par terre);
arranger; assaisonner; basculer; bousiller;
but(t)er; canner; chouriner; crever; cronir;
crounir; débarbouiller; décoller; dégringoler;
dégringoler; démolir; déquiller; descendre;
dessouder; dézinguer; ébouser; effacer;
escoffier; estourbir; expédier; faire avaler
son bulletin de naissance à; faire la peau à;
ficher/flanquer/foutre en l'air; finir; flingoter;
flinguer; lessiver; liquider; maraver; mettre
en l'air/à l'ombre; nettoyer; opérer; passer à
la moulinette; percer; planter; plomber;
ratatiner; rectifier; refroidir; repasser;
sacailler; saigner; scrafer; sécher; suriner;

trancher; troncher; zigouiller.
assez (en avoir): arrêter les frais; en
avoir sa claque; en voir jusque-là; en avoir
par-dessus la tête; en avoir plein les bottes/le
cul/les couilles/le dos/les endosses; en avoir
(plus que) marre; en avoir quine; en avoir
ras le bol/la casquette/la coiffe/le cul; en
avoir soupé; se faire chier.
assez!: arrête les frais! barca! basta! ça va
comme ça! c'est class(e)! c'est marre!
écrase! flac! la jambe! n'en jetez plus(, la
cour est pleine)! quine! ras-le-bol! ras-le-cul!
rideau! y en a marre!
attaquer: braquer; chabler; châbler;
harponner; râbler; rentrer dans le chou/le
lard/le mou à; rentrer dedans; sauter dessus;
tomber dessus; tomber sur l'alpague/le
paletot/le poil de; voler dans les plumes.
attendre: arracher le chiendent; croquer le
marmot; espérer après qn; faire le pied de
grue; faire le poireau; se faire poser un lapin;
mariner; maronner; moisir; poireauter;
poser; prendre racine; rester en carafe/en
frime/en plan.
attirail *m* **(d'un drogué):** arsenal *m*;
artillerie *f*; kit *m*; popote *f*.
avare (être): avoir un cactus dans la poche/
dans le portefeuille; avoir un oursin dans la
fouille/des oursins dans le morlingue; avoir
des mites dans son crapaud; être chien; être
dur à la desserre/dur à la détente; être
duraille / grigou / grippe-sou / pignouf / pingre/
radin/raleux/rapiat/rat; être constipé du
morlingue; les lâcher au compte-gouttes; les
lâcher avec un élastique/un lance-pierre; les
planquer; ne pas être large du dos; ne pas les
attacher avec des saucisses; ne pas les sortir;
tondre un œuf.
avocat *m*: bavard *m*; baveux *m*; cravateur
m; débarbot *m*; débarboteur *m*; perroquet
m; pingouin *m*.
avouer: accoucher; s'affaler; s'allonger;
blutiner; bouffer le morceau; casser (le
morceau); cracher (dans le bassin); cracher
le morceau; déballer ses outils; déballonner;
se déboutonner; dégueuler; lâcher le
morceau/le paquet; manger le morceau; se
mettre/passer à table; ouvrir (les vannes);
trouver à qui parler; vider son sac.
bagarre *f*: badaboum *m*; baroud *m*;
barrabille *f*; baston *m* ou *f*; bigorne *f*;
carambolage *m*; casse *f*; castagne *f*;
chambard *m*; chambardement *m*; châtaigne
f; cognage *m*; cogne *f*; corrida *f*; coup *m* de

torchon; crêpage *m* de chignon(s)/de ti-
gnasse(s); crochetage *m*; grabuge *m*; rif *m*;
rififi *m*; sonnage *m*; suif *m*; suiffée *f*; torchée
f.

baiser *m*: canard *m*; mimi *m*; pallot *m*;
patin *m*; pelle *f*; roulée *f*.

balle *f*: (*armes à feu*) bastos *f*; dragée *f*;
pastille *f*; praline *f*; prune *f*; pruneau *m*;
valda *f*.

bande *f*: (*groupe d'individus*) soce *f*; tierce
f.

barbe *f*: barbouze *f*; foin *m*; piège *m* (à
macaronis/à poux).

barbituriques *mpl*: balle *f* de copaille;
barbis *mpl*; barbitos *mpl*.

battre: abîmer (le portrait à); amocher;
aplatir; aquiger; arranger; assaisonner;
astiquer; attiger; avoiner; baffer (la gueule
à); bastonner; battre comme plâtre;
bigorner; bomber la gueule à qn; bosseler;
botter (le cul à); bourrer de coups; brosser;
carder le cuir à; casser la gueule à; castagner; chabler; chicorer; cirer les meubles;
cogner; cornancher; crêper (le chignon/la tignasse à); démolir; dérouiller; emplafonner;
emplâtrer; encadrer; escagasser; étriller;
faire; faire des bricoles à; faire chier des
gaufrettes à; filer *ou* foutre une avoine/une
danse/une pâtée/une toise/une tourlouzine/une
trempe à; flauper; floper; foutre sur la gueule
à; se frotter; se manger; maraver; en mettre
plein la gueule à; mettre la tête au carré à;
moucher; passer à la machine à bosseler;
passer à tabac; passer au tref; passer une
peignée/une raclée/une trempe à; péter la
gueule à; ramponner; rentrer dans le chou/la
gueule/le lard/le portrait à; rentrer dedans;
rosser; rouster; sataner; satonner; scionner;
sécher; secouer la poêle à marrons à; sonner;
suiffer; tabasser; tamponner; tarter;
tatouiller; tisaner; tomber sur le paletot/le
poil à; torgnoler; travailler les côtelettes à;
triquer.

battre, se: s'accrocher; aller à la châtaigne; s'amocher; se bagarrer; se bastonner;
se bigorner; se bouffer le blair; se bûcher;
(se) châtaigner; se chiquer (la gueule); se
chicorer; se colleter; se coltiner; se crêper le
chignon/la tignasse; se crocheter; échanger
des politesses; s'escagasser; s'expliquer; se
filer une/des toise(s); se flanquer/se foutre sur
la gueule; se flanquer/se foutre une peignée;
se frotter; se peigner; se riffer; se rifler; se
torcher.

bavard, -arde: baratineur, euse; bava-
cheur, -euse; bavasseur *m*; bavocheur *m*;
bavocheux *m*; jacasse *f*; jacasseur, -euse;
jacassier, -ière; jacteur, -euse; jaspineur *m*;
mitrailleuse *f*; pie *f*; qui a de la tchatche;
tapette *f*; tchatcheur, -euse; vacciné avec une
aiguille de phono.

bavarder: avoir une platine; baratiner;
bavacher; bavasser; baver; blablater;
caqueter; dégoiser; dépenser beaucoup de
salive; dévider; jaboter; jacasser; jacter;
jasper; jaspiner; ne pas avoir le filet coupé;
palasser; papoter; pomper de l'air; potiner;
rouler; tailler une bavette; en tailler une;
tchatcher; tenir le crachoir; user sa salive.
(*Voir* **parler**)

beau, belle: badour; bath; baveau; bavelle;
beau comme un paf en fleur; bien balancé(e)/
foutu(e); chbeb; choucard; chouettard;
chouette; chouettos; girofle; girond(e); jojo;
juteux; laubé; leaubé; lobé; ridère; riflo;
roulé(e) au moule; schbeb; du tonnerre; urf.

beaucoup: bézef; bigrement; bougrement;
lerche; lerchem; lerchot; un max; un maxi;
(un) rien; vachement; vachté.
(*Voir* **abondance**)

bébé *m*: chiard *m*; gluant *m*; lardon *m*; mignard, -arde; morceau *m* de salé; ourson *m*;
petit salé; têtard *m*.

bénéfice *m*: affure *f*; bénef *m*; beurre *m*;
gants *mpl*; gâteau *m*; gras *m*; gratouille *f*;
gratte *f*; rab(e) *m*; rabiot *m*; velours *m*.

Benzédrine (*RTM*) *f*: *voir* **am-
phétamine(s)**.

bête: andouille; ballot; baluchard; baluche;
banane; barjo(t); bas-de-plafond; bébête; bec
d'ombrelle; bêta; bidon; bille (de clown);
billot; bouché (à l'èmeri); bouffon;
bourrique; branleur; branque; branquignol;
buse; carafon; cave; cavé; cavillon; cloche;
con (à bouffer de la bite); con comme un
balai/comme une bite/comme un comptoir
sans verre/comme un manche/comme des
deux/comme ses pieds; con(n)ard;
con(n)asse; conne; con(n)eau; corniaud;
cornichon; couenne; couillon; crétin; croûte;
cruche; cruchon; cucu; cucul; cul;
déconnant; déplafonné; dorure; ducon(-la-
joie); duschnock; empaffé; empaillé;
empaqueté; emplâtré; emplumé; empoté;
enflé; fada; (fleur de) nave; gland; glandu;
glaude; gourde; gourdiflot; grave; jobard;
lavedu; lourdingue; melon; moule; navet;
neuneu; nière; niguedouille; noix; nono;

nouille; nul (comme pas deux); nunu; oie; panard; patate; peau d'hareng; pied; plat de nouilles; pocheté; poire; pomme; qui n'était pas derrière la porte (le jour de la distribution); qui en tient une couche; saucisse; schnock; serin; taré; tarte; tête de lard; à tête de linotte; tête de nœud; tourte; tranche (de gail/de melon); tranchouillard; tromblon; tronche; trouduc; trou-du-cul; truffe; veau; zozo.

bêtise *f*: de la balançoire; des balançoires *fpl*; du baratin; bidon *m*; blague *f*; bourdes *fpl*; conceté *f*; connerie *f*; couillonnade *f*; déconnante *f*; eau bénite de cour; eau *f* de bidet; fadaise *f*; faribole *f*; fichaise *f*; foutaise *f*; nunucherie *f*; pommade *f*; salades *fpl*; sornettes *fpl*; sottise *f*; trouducuterie *f*.

bévue *f*: boulette *f*; bourde *f*; cagade *f*; caraco *m*; char *m*; connerie *f*; gaffe *f*; galoup(e) *f*.

billet(s) *m(pl)*: biffeton *m*; faf *m*; faf(f)iot *m*; la grosse artillerie; image *f*; papier *m*; talbin *m*; ticket *m*; ticson *m*.

(*Voir* **argent**)

blennorragie *f*: castapiane *f*; chaude-lance *f*; chaude-pince *f*; chaude-pisse *f*; chtouille *f*; coulante *f*; goutte *f* militaire; schtouille *f*.

avoir une blennorragie: être laziloffe; pisser des lames de rasoir.

transmettre la blennorragie: attiger.

blesser: abîmer; amocher; aquiger; aquijer; arranger; attiger; jambonner; maquiller; moucher.

blesser au couteau: faire des boutonnières à; faire la croix des vaches à; mettre les tripes à l'air/au soleil à; piquer; poser un portemanteau dans le dos de; rallonger; saigner; suriner.

bluffer: *voir* **exagérer**.

boire: s'arroser l'avaloir/la dalle; biberonner; chauffer le four; chopiner; dégringoler; écluser (un godet); écraser un grain; s'enfiler un verre; entonner; s'envoyer un coup; en étouffer un; en étrangler un; se gargariser; gorgeonner; se graisser le toboggan; s'humecter les amygdales/le gosier; se jeter une jatte; s'en jeter un (derrière la cravate); lamper; se laver les dents; lever le coude; lécher; lichailler; licher; lipper; se mouiller la dalle/la meule; picoler; pictancher; picter; pictonner; pillaver; pinter; se piquer le nez/la ruche; pitancher; pomper; prendre une tasse; se rincer les amygdales/le bec/le cornet/la dalle/

le fusil/le sifflet; se salir le nez; schnouper; sécher un verre; siffler; siroter; soiffer; sucer; se taper un gorgeon; téter; tututer.

boisson *f* **(alcoolisée):** blanc *m*; carburant *m*; casse-pattes *m*; cerceuil *m*; champ' *m*; gobelette *f*; gobette *f*; jaune *m*; macadam *m*; mandarin *m*; margouillat *m*; mêlé-cass *m*; mominette *f*; plumeau *m*; rincette *f*; riquiqui *m*; soucoupe *f*; valse *f*; velours *m*; voyageur *m*.

(*Voir* **alcool**)

bordel *m*: *voir* **maison close**.

bouche *f*: accroche-pipe; bec *m*; boîte *f* (à mensonges); clapet *m*; claque-merde *m*; dalle *f*; déconophone *m*; égout *m*; entonnoir *m*; gargamelle *f*; gargane *f*; gargue *f*; goule *f*; goulot *m*; gueule *f*; malle *f*; margoulette *f*; micro *m*; museau *m*; porte-pipe *m*; respirante *f*; saladier *m*; salle *f* à manger; tirelire *f*; trappe *f*.

bourreau *m*: charlot *m*; faucheur *m*; grand coiffeur; rectifieur *m*.

bouteille *f*: boutanche *f*; chopine *f*; chopotte *f*; rouillarde *f*; rouille *f*.

bouteille de champagne: roteuse *f*.

bouteille de vin rouge: kil *m*; kilbus *m*; kilo *m*; légionnaire *m*; litron *m*; négresse *f*; pieu *m*; tutute *f*.

bouteille vide: cadavre *m*; macchabée *m*.

boutique *f*: bouclard *m*; boutanche *f*; estanco *m*; magase *m*; magaze *m*.

bras *m*: abattis *m*; aile *f*; aileron *m*; anse *f*; balancier *m*; bradillon *m*; brandillon *m*; manivelle *f*; nageoire *f*.

brave (être): *voir* **courageux (être)**.

bruit *m*: bacchanal *m*; barouf *m*; bastringue *m*; boucan *m*; bousin *m*; chabanais *m*; chahut *m*; chambard *m*; chizbroc *m*; foin *m*; grabuge *m*; musique *f*; pet *m*; pétard *m*; potin *m*; raffut *m*; rafût *m*; ramdam(e) *m*; schproum *m*; tam-tam *m*; zin-zin *m*.

butin *m*: barbotin *m*; bouquet *m*; camelote *f*; fade *m*; pied *m*; prise *f*; taf *m*; taffe *m*.

cacher: car(r)er; mettre en planque; passer au bleu; placarder; planquer; planquouser; plonger.

cacher, se: se carrer; se défiler; se placarder; planquer ses côtelettes; se planquer; se planquouser.

cachette *f*: placarde *f*; planque *f*; planquouse *f*; trou *m*.

cadavre *m*: allongé *m*; can(n)é *m*; croni *m*; macchab *m*; macchabé(e) *m*; refroidi *m*;

viande froide.

café *m*: (*boisson*) caoua(h) *m*; cahoua *m*; jus *m* (de chapeau/de chaussette/de chique); kawa *m*; laféké *m*; laféquès *m*; noir *m*.

café *m*: (*débit*) abreuvoir *m*; bistre *m*; bistro *m*; bistroc *m*; bistroquet *m*; bistrot *m*; caboulot *m*; cafèt *m*; cafeton *m*; estanco(t) *m*; gastos *m*; mastroquet *m*; tapis *m*; troquet *m*.

cambrioler: baluchonner; caroubler; casser; faire une cabane/une cambriole/une case/un casse/un fric-frac; faire du bois; fracasser; fricfraquer; mettre/monter en l'air; travailler au bec de canne.

cambriolage *m*: casse *m*; coup *m* d'arraché.

cambrioleur *m*: bal(l)uchonneur *m*; basset *m*; cambrio *m*; caroubeur *m*; caroubier *m*; caroubleur *m*; casseur *m*; chevalier *m* de la lune; fracasseur *m*; fric(-)frac *m*; lourdeur *m*; marcheur *m*; monte-en-l'air *m*.

(*Voir* **voleur**)

campagne *f*: bled *m*; brousse *f*; cambrousse *f*; parpagne *f*; patelin *m*; trou *m*.

cannabis *m*: voir **marijuana**.

car *m* **de police:** cage *f* à poulets; familiale *f*; panier *m* à salade; voiture *f* de mariée.

caresses *fpl*: chatouilles *fpl*; chouteries *fpl*; mamours *mpl*; papouilles *fpl*; patouilles *fpl*; pattes *fpl* d'araignée; pelotage *m*.

cartes *fpl* **à jouer:** bauches *fpl*; biffetons *mpl*; brèmes *fpl*; cartons *mpl*; papiers *mpl*.

casquette *f*: bâche *f*; bâchis *m*; deffe *f*; gapette *f*; gaufre *f*; gribelle *f*; grivelle *f*; guimpe(tte) *f*.

cercueil *m*: boîte *f* à dominos; caisse *f*; dernier paletot; paletot *m*/redingote *f* de sapin; paletot *m*/pardessus *m* sans manche(s).

chambre *f*: bocal *m*; cambuse *f*; carrée *f*; case *f*; crèche *f*; garno *m*; gourbi *m*; guitoune *f*; piaule *f*; strasse *f*; taule *f*; turne *f*.

chance (avoir de la): avoir de la baraka/ de la bague/de la bagouse/du bol/du cul/du fion/du flambeau/du gluck/du pot/du proze/du vase/de la veine; avoir le cul bordé de nouilles; avoir le godet; avoir l'oignon qui décalotte; avoir (de) la pêche/de la prune; l'avoir large/en or; être bidard/chançard/ cocu/de belle/doré/veinard/verjot/verni.

(*Voir* **malchance**)

chanter: goualer; la pousser; envoyer/ pousser la goualante; y aller de sa goualante.

chapeau *m*: bada *m*; bibi *m*; bitos *m*; bloum *m*; capet *m*; deffe *f*; doul(e) *m*; doulos *m*; galure *m*; galurin *m*; papeau *m*; pétase *m*.

chapeau haut de forme: huit-reflets *m*; lampion *m*; tube *m*; tuyau *m* de poêle.

chaussures *fpl*: bateaux *mpl*; boîtes *fpl* à violon; crocos *mpl*; croquenots *mpl*; écrase-merde *mpl*; flacons *mpl*; godasses *fpl*; godilles *fpl*; godillots *mpl*; grôles *fpl*; grolles *fpl*; lattes *fpl*; peupons *fpl*; pompes *fpl*; ribouis *mpl*; rigadins *mpl*; santiags *fpl*; savates *fpl*; sorlots *mpl*; targes *fpl*; targettes *fpl*; tartines *fpl*; tatanes *fpl*; tiags *fpl*; tiges *fpl*.

chauve (être): avoir une bille de billard/ billard/une boule de billard/le caillou déplumé/le melon déplumé/un mouchodrome/ la tête nickelée/un skating à mouches/un vélodrome à mouches; avoir la casquette en peau de fesse/une perruque en peau de fesse; avoir nib de tif(fes); avoir son genou dans le cou; être chauve comme une bille/un genou/un œuf; être jambonneau/zigué; n'avoir pas d'alfa sur les hauts plateaux; n'avoir plus de cresson sur la cafetière/sur le caillou/sur la fontaine/sur la truffe; n'avoir plus de gazon sur la plate-bande/sur la prairie/sur la terrasse; ne plus avoir de mouron sur la cage.

chemise *f*: bannière *f*; limace *f*; limasse *f*; lime *f*; limouse *f*; limouze *f*; liquette *f*; panais *m*; sac *m* à viande.

cher, chère: ça coûte bonbon/la peau des fesses; chaud; chéro(t); grisol(e); lerche; lerchem; lerchot; salé.

cheval *m*: bique *f*; bourdon *m*; bourrin *m*; canasson *m*; carcan *m*; carne *m*; dada *m*; gail(le) *m*; hareng *m*; rossard *m*; rosse *f*; tréteau *m*.

cheveux *mpl*: crayons *mpl*; cresson *m*; crins *mpl*; douillards *mpl*; douilles *fpl*; gazon *m*; mouron *m*; plumes *fpl*; tiffes *mpl*; tifs *mpl*; tignasse *f*; toison *f*; vermicelles *mpl*.

couper les cheveux: couper les roseaux; déboiser la colline; tiffer; varloper la toiture.

chien *m*: azor *m*; cabot *m*; cador *m*; chien-chien *m*; clébard *m*; clebs *m*; gail *m*; gaille *m*; klébard *m*; klebs *m*; oua(h)-oua(h) *m*; saucisse *f*/saucisson *m* à pattes; toutou *m*.

cigare *m*: barreau *m* de chaise; clou *m* de cercueil; crapulos *m*.

cigarette *f*: baluche *f*; cibiche *f*; cleupon *m*; clope *f* (*rarement m*); cousue *f*; goldo *f*;

grillante *f*; périodique *f*; pipe *f*; pipette *f*; roulée *f*; sèche *f*; taf *f*; taffe *f*; tampax *f*; tige *f*.

(*Voir* **cigarette de marijuana**)

cimetière *m*: boulevard *m* des allongés; champ *m* de navets/d'oignons; champ *m* des clamsés; champ *m*/jardin *m*/parc *m* des refroidis; chez les têtes en os; jardin *m* des claqués; parc *m* des cronis.

clé *f*: caroube *f*; carouble *f*; tournante *f*.

clitoris *m*: berlingot *m*; berlingue *f*; bouton *m* (d'amour/de rose); boutonneau *m*; clicli *m*; cliquette *f*; clito(n) *m*; flageolet *m*; framboise *f*; grain *m* de café; haricot *m*; noisette *f*; praline *f*; soissonnais *m* (rose).

clochard, -arde : cloche *f*; clodomir *m*; clodo(t) *m*; traîne-pattes *m*; traîne-sabots *m*; traîne-savates *m*; traîne-semelles *m*; trimard *m*; trimardeur, -euse; zonard, -arde.

(*Voir* **vagabond**)

cocaïne *f*: bigornette *f*; blanche *f*; C *f*; Caroline *f*; cécil(e) *m*; coco *f*; coke *f*; colombine *f*; dropou *f*; dynamite *f*; fée blanche; Jules *m*; Julie *f*; naph(taline) *f*; naphte *m*; neige *f*; poudrette *m*; respirante *f*; respirette *f*; talc *m*; topette *f*.

cœur *m*: battant *m*; grand ressort; palpitant *m*; (petite) horloge *f*; tocant *m*; toquant *m*; trembleur *m*.

coït *m*: baisage *m*; baise *f*; balayette infernale; bourre *f*; café du pauvre; carambolage *m*; carton *m*; chique *f*; cinq *m* à sept; coup *m*; coup d'arbalète/de tringle; crampe *f*; crampette *f*; nique *f*; partie *f* de balayette/d'écarté/de jambes en l'air/de traversin/de trou du cul; passe *f*; pinette *f*; politesse *f*; pousse-café *m*; queutage *m*; radada *m*; secousse *f*; tringlage *m*; tringlette *m*; troussée *f*; truc *m*; vite-fait *m*; zizi-pan(-) pan *m*.

(*Voir* **faire l'amour**)

coït anal: *voir* **sodomiser**.

coït buccal: *voir* **cunnilinctus; fellation**.

coïter: *voir* **faire l'amour**.

colère *f*, **être en, se mettre en**: attraper le coup de raisin/le coup de sang; attraper une crise; avoir les boules/les glandes; l'avoir à la caille; devenir chèvre; s'emballer; être à cran/à ressaut; être colère; être en boule/en fumasse/en pétard/en renaud/en rif/en rogne/en suif; être fumasse/ furax/furibard; exploser; faire du pet; fumer; maronner; se mettre en renaud; mettre son turbo; monter à l'échelle/au renaud/sur ses grands chevaux; mousser; perdre la bobèche; piquer une crise; péter une durite; (en) prendre un coup de raisin/de sang; râler; rogner; sortir de ses gonds; voir rouge.

complice *mf*: baron *m*; cheville *f*; gaffeur, -euse; roussin *m*.

concierge *mf*: bignole *mf*; cloporte *m*; concepige *mf*; lourdier, -ière; pibloque *mf*; pipelet, -ette.

condamnation *f*: balancement *m*; gerbage *m*; gerbe *f*; gerbement *m*; sape *m*; sapement *m*; sucrage *m*.

condamné, être: cascader; écoper; être bon(nard); être sucré; gerber; morfler; payer; plonger; quimper; saper; tomber; trinquer.

congédier: balancer; balanstiquer; balayer; bordurer; bouler; débarquer; dégommer; envoyer dinguer/paître; envoyer à Chaillot; flanquer/mettre à la porte; gicler; larguer; lessiver; lourder; raousser; raouster; sabrer; sa(c)quer; scier; sortir; valouser; vider; virer.

(*Voir* **débarrasser de, se**)

corbillard *m*: corbi *m*; trottinette *f* (à macchabs).

cou *m*: colbac *m*; colbaque *m*; kiki *m*; sifflet *m*; vis *f*.

coucher, se: aller au dodo/à la dorme/au paddock/au page/au pageot/au pieu/au plumard/au(x) plume(s)/au schlaf/au schloff; (se) bâcher; (se) borgnot(t)er; casser sa came; (se) crécher; faire banette; se filer/se glisser/se mettre dans les toiles; se fourrer au plumard; se grabater; se mettre dans les bâches/dans les bannes; se paddocker; se pageoter; se pager; se pagnot(t)er; se pajoter; se pieuter; se plumarder; se plumer; se sacquer; se zoner.

coup(s) *m*(*pl*): atout *m*; avoine *f*; baffe *f*; baffre *f*; beigne *f*; bénédiction *f*; bourre-pif *m*; calotte *f*; châtaigne *f*; coup *m* de manchette; danse *f*; deuxième degré *m*; direct *m*; emplâtre *m*; flic-flac *m*; fricassée *f*; frictionnée *f*; frottée *f*; gnon *m*; jab *m*; jeton *m*; marron *m*; mornifle *f*; pain *m*; passage *m* à tabac; pâtée *f*; pêche *f*; peignée *f*; pile *f*; prune *f*; pruneau *m*; purge *f*; raclée *f*; ramponneau *m*; ratatouille *f*; rincée *f*; rossée *f*; roulée *f*; tabassage *m*; tabassée *f*; talmouse *f*; taloche *f*; tampon *m*; tamponnage *m*; tannée *f*; taquet *m*; tarte *f*; tatouille *f*; tisane *f*; toise *f*; torchée *f*; torgn(i)ole *f*; tournée *f*; trempe *f*; trempée *f*; tripotée *f*; triquée *f*; troussée *f*; valse *f*.

(*Voir* **battre; recevoir (des coups)**)

courageux, (être): avoir des couilles/du cran/de l'estomac/du poil/des tripes; avoir quelque chose dans le calbar(d)/dans le slip; en avoir; en avoir au cul/dans les bal(l)oches/dans le bide/dans le ventre/entre les quilles; être accroché/culotté; être d'attaque; être gonflé; être un peu là; ne pas avoir froid aux yeux; ne pas manquer d'air.

courir: agiter les badines/les compas; bagot(t)er; se carapater; cavaler; (se) drop(p)er; jouer des flûtes/des guibolles; mettre les bâtons; se tirer des gambettes; tricoter des bâtons/des gambettes; (se) trisser.

couteau *m*: coupe-lard *m*; cure-dent *m*; eustache *m*; lame *f*; lardoir *m*; lingre *m*; outil *m*; pointe *f*; rallonge *f*; rapière *f*; ratiche *f*; saccagne *f*; sorlingue *m*; surin *m*; yatagan *m*.

couverture *f*: *voir* **alibi**.

crachat *m*: glaviot *m*; gluau *m*; graillon *m*; huître *f*; mol(l)ard *m*; postillon *m*.

cracher: glavioter; graillonner; mollarder.

crâne *m*: caillou *m*; caisson *m*; plafond *m*; plafonnard *m*; toiture *f*.

crier: beugler; braire; charronner; goualer; gueuler (au charron); péter; piailler; piauler; pousser des gueulements.

critiquer: abîmer; allumer; aquijer; assassiner; baver sur; bêcher; bousiller; carboniser; cartonner; casser; charrier; chiner; débiner; déglinguer; dégrainer; déshabiller; donner un coup de dent à; éreinter; faire un abattage de; faire du jardin; faire une tinette sur; flinguer; griller; jardiner; jeter de la grêle; jeter la pierre à; vanner.

croire: avaler; couper dedans; donner dedans; encaisser; gober; marcher; mordre à.

cunnilinctus *m*: descente *f* au barbu/à l'étau; gâterie *f*; pèlerinage *m* aux sources; politesse *f*.

faire un cunnilinctus: bouffer la chatte; brouter le cresson; descendre au panier; donner sa langue au chat; faire mimi/minette; faire une descente à l'étau/une langue fourrée/un pèlerinage aux sources; se gougnotter; se gouiner; (se) gousser; lécher; manger; mettre la tête à l'étau; morfier; morfiler; sucer.

danser: dansotter; frotter; gambiller;

gigoter; guincher; en suer une; tortiller des fesses; tricoter des jambes/des gambettes/des pincettes.

débarrasser de, se: balancer; balanstiquer; se décramponner de; se défarguer de; dégommer; envoyer à la gare; envoyer chier/dinguer/paître/promener/se faire voir; laisser choir; larguer; lessiver; lourder; plaquer; sa(c)quer; scier; vider; virer.

(*Voir* **abandonner; congédier**)

débrouiller, se: avoir la combine; la connaître (dans les coins); se débarboter; se défendre; se démerder; se démieller; se démouscailler; se dépatouiller; savoir s'expliquer/nager/se retourner.

découvrir: dégauchir; dégommer; dégot(t)er; dénicher; faire tilt; piger; repérer.

déféquer: aller à la flacdal/chez Flacmann; aller où le Roi va à pied; caguer; chier; couler un bronze; débloquer; débonder; déboucher son orchestre; débourrer (sa pipe); défarguer; déflaquer; déposer sa pêche/une prune; faire caca; faire sa grande commission; faire ses affaires; faire ses grands besoins; faire son gros; flaquer; flasquer; foirer; fuser; ièche; poser un colombin/sa pêche/une prune/un rondin/une sentinelle; pousser le bouchon/son rond; tartir; yèche.

dénoncer: aller au cri; balancer; balanstiquer; bouffer le macaroni; bourriquer; brûler; cafarder; cafeter; cafter; donner; en bouffer; en croquer; fourguer; griller; lâcher le morceau; manger le morceau; moucharder; moutonner; servir de belle; vendre la mèche.

(*Voir* **avouer**)

dénonciateur *m*: balance *f*; balanceur *m*; balanceuse *f*; balançoire *f*; bascule *f*; bordille *m*; bourdille *m*; bourrique *f*; cafard *m*; cafarde *f*; cafardeur *m*; casserole *f*; chevreuil *m*; coqueur *m*; donneur *m*; doul(e) *m*; fileur *m*; indic *m*; mouchard *m*; mouche *f*; mouton *m*; (vieille) salope *f*.

dents *fpl*: chailles *fpl*; chaillottes *fpl*; chocottes *fpl*; crochets *mpl*; crocs *mpl*; doches *fpl*; dominos *mpl*; pavés *mpl*; piloches *fpl*; quenottes *fpl*; ratelier *m*; ratiches *fpl*; tabourets *mpl*; touches *fpl* de piano.

dépêcher, se: s'activer; s'agiter; se dégrouiller; se déhotter; se démerder; se dérouiller; drop(p)er; faire fissa; se grouiller (les miches); se magner le cul/le derche/le derrière/le popotin/le pot/le proze/la raie/la rondelle/le train; manier le pot; en mettre/en filer un rayon; pouloper; se secouer; se trotter.

dépenser: les aligner/les allonger; béquiller; bouffer/claquer/croquer de l'argent; casquer; cigler; décher; les écosser; les faire valser; les lâcher; y aller de ses sous.

dépensier m: claque-fric mf; décheur m; décheuse f.

dés mpl: bobs mpl; doches mpl.

dés truqués: artillerie f; balourds mpl; bouts mpl de sucre; matuches mpl; pipés mpl; plateaux mpl; plats mpl.

déshabiller (se): décapoter; (se) décarpiller; (se) défringuer; (se) défrusquer; (se) déharnacher; (se) délinger; (se) déloquer; (se) dénipper; se dépoiler; (se) désaper; (se) dépiauter; (se) foutre à poil.

détester: avoir à la caille; avoir dans le blair/dans le cul/dans le nez; se mettre (qn) au cul; ne pas avoir à la bonne; ne pas pouvoir blairer/encadrer/encaisser/saquer/sentir; ne pas pouvoir voir en peinture.

diamant m: bauche m; bouchon m de carafe; caillou m; diam(e) m; pierre f.

diarrhée f: cacade f; chiasse f; cliche f; courante f; foirade f; foire f; riquette f; turista f.

difficile: coton; cottard; duraille; duraillon; durillon; duringue; galère; glandilleux; merdique; vache; vicelard; viceloque.

discours m: baratin m; boniment m; laïus m; palas(s) m; parlote f; postiche f; salade f.

dispute f: voir **querelle**.

doigt m: (main) fourchette f; phalangette f; piloir m; salsifis m; (pied) haricot m; racine f; radis m.

donner: abouler; allonger; balancer; balanstiquer; coller; ficher; filer; flanquer; foutre; lâcher; refiler.

dormir: aller à la ronfle; dormailler; dormasser; en écraser (dur); faire dodo/schloff; faire un coup de traversin/une partie de traversin; faire une ronflette; pioncer; piquer une bâche/un chien; piquer/pousser une ronflette/un roupillon; ronfler; roupiller; roupillonner; schloffer; taper de l'œil; zoner.

dormir dehors: compter les étoiles; coucher à la belle étoile/sur la dure; dormir à la dure; la refiler; refiler la comète.

drap m: bâche f; banne f; toile f.

drogué (a): accro; accroché; accroch'man; bourré; branché; camé; chanvré; chargé; dans les vapes; défoncé; déchiré; dynamité; enneigé; en pleine défonce; d'équerre; ensuqué; envapé; fait; flippé; high; parti; pas net; pété; planant; raide (def); sous acide; speedé; stone(d); sur sa planète; touche-piqûre.

drogué, -ée (n): acidulé, -ée; accroché, -ée; branché, -ée; camé, -ée; chevalier m de la piquouze; chnouffé, -ée; dynamité, -ée; enragé, -ée de la shooteuse; fixer m; junkie mf; méca m; priseur m; rouleur, -euse; schnouffé, -ée; seringué, -ée; shitman m; sniffeur m; touche-piqûre m; toxico m.

droguer, se: s'accrocher à une drogue; se camer; carburer à l'héroïne; se charger; se chnouffer; se défoncer; se doper; être de la renifle; faire un trip/un voyage; se faire un fixe/un shoot; se faire sauter les plombs; se fixer; marcher à la dope/à la dynamite; se mettre à la charge; se piquer; se piquouser; popper; se poudrer (le pif); prendre un trip/un voyage; se schnouffer; se shooter; sniffer une ligne/des lignes; se speeder; tirer sur le bambou; tripper; voyager.

drogue(s) f(pl): came f; charge f; chnouff m; choucroute f; défonce f; dopant m; dope f; junk m; marchandise f; méca f; narcs mpl; schnouff(e) m; speedball m; stuff m; stups mpl.

duper: voir **escroquer**.

eau f: baille f; bouillon m; Château-la-Pompe m; flotte f; jus m de grenouille; jus m de parapluie; lance f; lancecaille f; lancequine f; lanscaille f; lansquine f; limonade f; sirop m de canard/de grenouille/de parapluie; tisane f.

échec m: bec m de gaz; bide m; black-boulage m; bouchon m; bûche f; chou blanc; (coup m de) Trafalgar; dèche f; fiasc m; fiasque m; flanelle f; flop m; foirade f; four m; gamelle f; loupage m; nanar m; pelle f; plantage m; planterie f; veste f.

échouer: l'avoir dans l'os; boire la tasse; cafouiller; caguer; se casser le nez; claquer; se cogner le nez; couler; culbuter; s'en aller en eau de boudin; être dans le lac; être en plein baccara; être râpé; être sur la jante; faire baraque; faire chou blanc; faire flanelle; faire la culbute; faire un bide/un four; se faire ramasser; finir dans les choux/en eau de boudin/en queue de poisson; foirer; louper; partir en couille/en jus de boudin; péter dans la main; prendre un bide; (se) prendre une claque/une veste; se prendre une gamelle; ramasser les balais; ramasser un bide/un bouchon/une bûche/une gamelle/une pelle/une veste; se ramasser; se rétamer; rouler sur la jante; tomber à l'eau; tomber dans les choux; tomber en couille; tomber dans le lac/sur un paf; tourner en couille/en jus de boudin.

économiser: arrondir sa pelote; car(r)er; faire son beurre/sa pelote; garer; en mettre à gauche; mettre en petite; planquer; planquouser.

éjaculer: arracher son copeau/son pavé; balancer la/sa purée; balancer la sauce; cracher son venin; décharger; dégorger; égoutter son cyclope; envoyer sa came/la purée/la sauce/la semoule; envoyer son enfant à la blanchisseuse; faire pleurer le cyclope; jeter la purée/son venin; juter; lâcher sa came/une giclée/le jus/sa purée/la semoule/son venin; prendre son taf; tirer une giclée; vider ses burettes/les burnes; y aller du/de son voyage.

(*Voir* **orgasme (avoir un)**).

élégant: badour; chic; chicard; chicos; class(e); classieux; eulpif; flambard; en grand tralala; holpif; qui en jette; qui jette du jus; juteux; minet; rider; ridère; riflo(t); sur son trente et un; tiré à quatre épingles; urf(e).

embrasser (s'): bécoter; coquer un bécot à; faire un bec/un bécot/une bise à; faire une langue fourrée à; se fricasser le museau; galocher; se lécher; lécher les amygdales; se lécher la gueule/la pomme/le museau; rouler une galoche/un patin/des saucisses à; se sucer la couenne; (se) sucer la poire.

emploi *m*: *voir* **travail**.

emprisonner: bloquer; boucler; coffrer; emballer; emplatarder; enchetarder; enchetiber; enchrister; enchtiber; ficher au clou; fourrer au bloc; fourrer dedans; gerber; mettre au bloc/à l'ombre/au frais/au trou; mettre en cage/en taule.

emprunter (de l'argent) à: bottiner; latter; pilonner; relancer; sonner; taper; tartiner; taxer; torpiller.

enceinte (être): s'arrondir; attraper/avoir le ballon; avoir un bébé dans le buffet/un lardon dans le tiroir; avoir avalé le/un pépin; avoir sa butte; avoir un moufflet/un polichinelle dans le tiroir; être dans une situation intéressante; être en cloque; être engrossée; être tombée sur un clou rouillé; se faire

arrondir le devant/le globe; gondoler de la devanture; travailler pour Marianne.

mettre enceinte: coller un gosse à; coller un lardon dans le tiroir; enceintrer; enchoser; encloquer; engrosser; flanquer le ballon à; mettre en cloque.

enfant *m*: bout *m* de chou/de zan; bouture *f*; chiard *m*; crapaud *m*; gamin *m*; gamine *f*; gluant *m*; gnard *m*; gniard *m*; gosse *mf*; gosselin *m*; gosseline *f*; graine *f* de bois de lit; lardon *m*; loupiau *m*; loupiot *m*; loupiotte *f*; marmaille *f*; marmot *m*; marmouset *m*; merdeux, -euse; mignard *m*; mignarde *f*; minot *m*; mioche *mf*; miston *m*; momaque *f*; môme *mf*; momichon *m*; mômichon *m*; momignard, -arde; mômignard, -arde; môminard, -arde; morbac *m*; morbaque *m*; morceau *m* de salé; morpion *m*; mouchacho *m*; moucheron *m*; moucheronne *f*; moufflet *m*; moufflette *f*; moujingue *m*; moustique *f*; moutard *m*; niston *m*; nistonne *f*; ourson *m*; petiot *m*; petiote *f*; petit salé; piaillard, -arde; pisseuse *f*; têtard *m*.

enfuir, s': *voir* **partir**.

ennuyer: assassiner; assommer; barber; bassiner; baver sur les burettes/sur les burnes à; les brouter à; canuler; casser les bonbons/les burettes/les burnes/les couilles/les noix/les pieds/la tête à; la casser à; les casser à; cavaler; les chauffer à; chier dans les bottes de qn; courir qn; courir sur le haricot/sur les osselets à/sur le système à; cramponner; emmerder; emmieller; emmouscailler; empoisonner; enchariboter; enflaquer; enquiquiner; escagasser; faire braire; faire chier; faire mal aux noix à; faire suer; foutre les boules/les glandes à; gonfler; les gonfler à; jamber; peler le jonc à; peler les bonbons à/les peler à; pomper; prendre la tête à; râper les burettes/les burnes à; raser; rompre la tête à; scier; tanner; taper sur le dos/sur le haricot/sur le système.

(*Voir* **assez (en avoir)**)

ennuyeux; personne *ou* **chose ennuyeuse:** à chier; assommant; barbant; barbe; barbifiant; bassin; bassinant; canulant; canule *f*; cassant; casse-bonbons *m*; casse-burettes *m*; casse-burnes *m*; casse-couilles *m*; casse-cul *m*; casse-noisettes *m*; casse-olives *m*; casse-pieds *m*; chiant; chiasse *f*; chiatique *m*; chierie *f*; chiotte *f*; colique *f*; collant comme la glu; colle *f*; crampon; emmerdant; emmerdement *m*; emmerdeur, -euse; ennuyant; gluant; lourd; outil *m*; pompe-l'air *m*; pot *m* de colle; purge *f*; rasant; raseur; rasoir; relou; sciant; scie; tannant.

épouse *f*: baronne *f*; belette *f*; bobonne *f*; boulet *m*; bourgeoise *f*; gerce *f*; gouvernement *m*; greluche *f*; légitime *f*; matos *m*; ma (chère) moitié; particulière *f*; patronne *f*; pouffe *f*; pouf(f)iasse *f*; viande *f*; vieille *f*.

érection *f*, **être en:** arquer; avoir le bambou/la banane/une barre à mine/le bâton/ la canne/la gaule/le manche/le mandrin/la matraque/l'os/le petit pain/le tracassin/le tricotin/la tringle/la trique; avoir du gourdin; avoir les coliques bâtonneuses/cornues; l'avoir dur; l'avoir en l'air; avoir le flageolet à la portière; avoir le piquet (de tête); avoir une balle dans le canon; avoir une bandaison; bander (à mort/à zéro); bandocher; bandouiller; être au garde-à-vous; être triqué; godailler; goder; godiller; lever; marquer midi; pavoiser; redresser; relever; tenir la canne; triquer.

escroc *m*: arnaqueur *m*; arrangemane *m*; arrangeur *m*; bidonneur *m*; bricoleur *m*; cambuteur *m*; carabin *m* de la comète; carambouilleur *m*; carotteur, -euse; carottier, -ière; combinard *m*; embrouilleur, -euse; empileur, -euse; entôleur, -euse; entubeur *m*; estampeur, -euse; faisan *m*; faisandier *m*; faiseur *m*; faux jeton; filou *m*; flibustier *m*; floueur, -euse; fripouillard *m*; fripouille *f*; grenailleur, -euse; musicien *m*; pipeur, -euse; poseur *m*; rangemane *m*; rangeur *m*; requin *m*; resquilleur *m*; rouleur, -euse; roustisseur *m*; truand *m*.

escroquer: arnaquer; arrangemaner; arranger; avoir; baiser; échauder; écorcher; empaumer; empiler; endormir; enfiler; englander; entuber; estamper; fabriquer; faisander; farcir; filouter; flibuster; flouer; mener en bateau/en double; monter le coup à; niquer; opérer; piper; posséder; pigeonner; racketter; rangemaner; refaire; repasser; rouler; roustir; souffler; tirer une carotte à; truander.

escroquerie *f*: arnaquage *m*; arnaque *f*; carabistouille *f*; carambouillage *m*; carambouille *f*; carottage *m*; carotte *f*; coup *m* (d'arnaque); cri sec; doublage *m*; entôlage *m*; entourloupe *f*; entourloupette *f*; entubage *m*; estampage *m*; estampe *f*; fripouillerie *f*; repassage *m*; resquillage *m*; resquille *f*;

trompe-couillon *m*.

estomac *m*: berdouille *f*; bocal *m*; boîte *f* à fressures/à ragoût; bouzine *f*; buffecaille *m*; buffet *m*; burelingue *m*; burlingue *m*; cage *f* (à pain); caisse *f*; cimetière *m* à poulets; coco *m*; cornet *m*; estogom *m*; estom' *m*; estom(m)e *m*; fanal *m*; fusil *m*; garde-manger *m*; gésier *m*; jabot *m*; lampe *f*; lampion *m*; mou *m*; tiroir; tube *m*.

(*Voir* **ventre**)

étonner: aplatir; asseoir; en boucher un coin/une surface à; cisailler; clouer (le bec à); couper la chique/le sifflet à; ébouriffer; épater; époustoufler; esbloquer; escagasser; estomaquer; mastiquer une fissure; scier; souffler.

étonné, être: en avoir la chique coupée; en bâiller; en baver; demeurer/être/en rester baba; être catastrophé; être/en rester comme deux ronds de flan/comme une tomate; en rester assis/sur le cul; tomber du ciel.

étrangler: dévisser le coco/le trognon à; serrer la gargamelle/le kiki/la vis à.

étron *m*: borne *f*; bronze *m*; caca *m*; caille *f*; cigare *m*; colombin *m*; déflaque *f*; factionnaire *m*; merde *f*; orphelin *m*; pêche *f*; prune *f*; rondin *m*; sentinelle *f*.

évader, s': *voir* **partir**.

évanouir, s': quimper; tomber dans le cirage/les frites/les pommes/le sirop/les vapes; tomber en digue-digue; tourner de l'œil.

exagérer: aller mal; attiger (la cabane); blouser; bousculer le pot aux fleurs; broder; charrier/cherrer (dans les bégonias); chier dans la colle; chiquer; cravater; se donner des coups de pied (dans les chevilles); envoyer le bouchon; épicer; esbrouf(f)er; faire de l'esbrouf(f)e/de la graisse/du pallas; en faire une tartine; forcer la dose; se gonfler; gonfler le mou; graisser; grimper aux arbres; en installer; se monter le job; pousser; en pousser une; se pousser du col; pousser le bouchon trop loin; en rajouter; en remettre; vanner; y aller fort.

excellent: à tout casser; au loilpé; aux pommes; baisant; bath; bœuf; canon; ça jette; champion; chié; chouaga; chouard; chouette; chouettos; choupaïa; craquant; délirant; le délire; dément; de première (bourre); doré sur tranche; du tonnerre; épatant; époustouflant; extra; fameux; faramineux; formid(able); formide; foutral; géant; génial; grand; hyper; impec; je te dis pas; je te dis que ça; meumeu; nickel; pallas; pas piqué des hannetons; pas le frère à dégueulasse; pas sale; au poil; pommé; sensass; soi-soi; soin-soin; super; superpied; terrible; trans.

faim (avoir): avoir un creux; avoir les crochets/les crocs/la dalle/la dent; avoir l'estomac dans les talons; avoir les dents longues; les avoir longues; bouffer des briques; se brosser; claquer du bec; la crever; crever la faim/la dalle; danser devant le buffet; se mettre la ceinture; la péter; péter la faim; la piler; la sauter; se sentir l'estomac dans les talons; la serrer; (se) serrer la ceinture; se taper.

fatigué, être: avoir le coup de bambou/de barre/de pompe; avoir son compte; en avoir plein les bottes/sa hotte; n'avoir plus de jambes; être au bout du rouleau; être amorti/à plat/brisé/claqué/crevé/éreinté/esquinté/flagada/flapi/fourbu/foutu/hachès/hachesse/HS/lessivé/mal fichu/naze/pompé/queune/raplapla/vanné/vaseux/vidé; être à ramasser à la petite cuiller; être sur le flanc/sur la jante; être sur les dents/les genoux/les rotules; la piler; rouler sur la jante; sonner le coup de bambou.

faux: bidon; chinetoque; toc; tocard.

fellation f: bonne manière; bouche chaude; boule f de gomme; fantaisie f; gourmandise f; pipe f; plume f; politesse f; pompier m; shampooing m maison/à Charles-le-Chauve; suçade f; suçage m; turlutte f.

faire une fellation: brouter la tige; dévorer; faire boule de gomme; faire une asperge/une pipe/un pompier/un pomplard/une turlutte; se le faire allonger; se faire croquer; jouer de la clarinette baveuse/de la flûte; se laver les dents; manger; pomper (le dard/le nœud/le zob à); prendre en poire; rogner l'os; scalper le mohican; souffler dans la canne/le mirliton; sucer; tailler une flûte/une pipe/une plume.

femme f Péj: belette f; boude m; boudin m; bougresse f; chèvre f; chipie f; connasse f; créature f; donzelle f; fatma f; fatmuche f; femelle f; fendasse f; fendue f; fiasse f; fumelle f; frangine f; garce f; gendarme m; génisse f; gerce f; gisquette f; gniarde f; goncesse f; gonsesse f; gonzesse f; greluche f; grognasse f; guenipe f; harpie f; hourrie f; jeton m; lamdé f; lamedé f; lamfé f; largue f; lesbombe f; lièvre m; limace f; loute f; mefa f; meffe f; mémé f; ménesse f; meuf f;

miquette f; mistonne f; miteuse f; morue f; moukère f; mousmé(e) f; nana f; nénesse f; nénette f; paillasse f; paillasson m; peau f (de vache); pépée f; pétasse f; polka f; pouffiasse f; poule f; poulette f; pouliche f; poupée f; punaise f; rombière f; rouchie f; sagœur f; sauterelle f; sœur f; souris f; tarderie f; tartavelle f; tordue f; typesse f; vache f; viande f.

belle femme: beau châssis; beau linge; beau (petit) lot; belle mécanique/pièce/plante; bien balancée; bien roulée; canon m; corvette f; joli lot; pépée f; pin-up f; poulette f; pouliche f; prix m de Diane; roulée au moule; supernana f.

jeune femme: bergère f; chèvre f; frangine f; garce f; gerce f; gisquette f; gonzesse f; greluche f; grimbiche f; Julie f; lamdé f; lamedé f; lamfé f; louloute f; meuf f; miquette f; mistonne f; môme f; mousmé(e) f; nana f; nénette f; palombe f; pépée f; poule f; poulette f; pouliche f.

(vieille) femme laide: bique f; cageot m; chef-d'œuvre m en péril; grognasse f; guenon f; guenuche f; mémée f; mocheté f; vieille morue; pouffe f; pouf(f)iasse f; prix m à réclamer; remède m d'amour; rombière f; saucisson m; tarderie f; tardingue f; tartavelle f; vieille bique/chèvre/rombière/toupie/vache; vieux trumeau.

fesses fpl: anneau m; arrière-train m; as m de pique; baba m; baigneur m; ballon m; bernard m; bol m; brioches fpl; cadran m (solaire); croupe f; croupillon m; cul m; dédé m; derche m; derge m; derrière m; dossière f; faubourg m; fendu m; fessier m; fouaron m; fouettard m; fouignedé m; foiron m; gagne-pain m; griottes fpl; joufflu m; jumelles fpl; luc m; lune f; meules fpl; miches fpl; mouilles fpl; mouillettes fpl; moutardier m; noix fpl; oignon m; panier m à crottes; pastèque f; pendule f; père-fouettard m; pétard m; petits pains; pétoulet m; pétrousquin m; pétrus m; pont-arrière m; popotin m; postère m; postérieur m; pot m; prose m; prosinard m; proze m; prozinard m; radada m; tafanard m; tal m; tapanard m; train m; troussequin m; tutu m; valseur m; vase m.

fête f: voir **réjouissances**.

figure f: voir **visage**.

(jeune) fille f: branleuse f; caille f; gamine f; gisquette f; gosse f; jeunesse f; jeunette f; minette f; miquette f; momaque f; môme f;

morue *f*; mouchacha *f*; nistonne *f*; pisseuse *f*; quille *f*; tendron *m*; viande *f*.

flatter: baratiner; bonimenter; bourrer la caisse/le crâne/le mou à; caresser dans le sens du poil; casser le nez à coups d'encensoir à; cirer; faire de la lèche à; faire du baratin/ du boniment/du charre/du flan/du plat à; fayoter; gratter la couenne à; jeter de la pommade à; lécher les bottes/le cul à; passer la main dans le dos à; passer (de) la pommade à; peloter; pommader; vaseliner.

fort, être: être balaise/balès/baleste/balèze/ bien balancé/bien baraqué/costaud/fortiche/ mailloche/malabar/maousse; être fort comme un bœuf; être un homme à pogne; être un mec/un macho; se poser là.

fou: azimuté; baisé de la tête; ballot; barge(ot); barjo(t); branque; branquignol; braque; brindezingue; chabraque; chtarbé; cinglé; cinoque; cintré; cucu(l); déjanté; dé-traqué; dingo; dingot; dingue; fada; farfelu; fêlé; flippé; flocard; foldingue; follingue; fondu; frappadingue; frappé; givré; gland; jeté; locdu; loquedu; loubac; louf; loufiat; loufoque; louftingue; maboul(e); malade; marteau; percuté; piqué; ravagé; schtarb; schtarbé; secoué (comme un prunier); sinoc; sinoque; siphonné; sonné; synoque; tapé; timbré; tocbombe; toctoc; toqué; tordu; tou-ché.

devenir fou: décrocher; déménager; dérailler; déjanter; disjoncter; partir du ciboulot; perdre la boule/la boussole/la carte/ le nord/les pédales; piquer/recevoir le coup de bambou.

être fou: avoir une araignée/une chauve-souris/un hanneton au plafond; avoir le coup de bambou; avoir une fêlure/une fissure/un grain; battre la breloque; se décarcasser le boisseau; être bon/fait/mûr pour Sainte-Anne; être cucul (la praline); être dérangé du cigare; être fou à lier; onduler de la coiffe/de la toiture/de la touffe; travailler du bigoudi/du chapeau/du ciboulot/du cigare/de la touffe; yoyoter de la mansarde.

foule *f*: populo *m*; tref *m*; trèfle *m*; trèpe *m*; trèple *m*.

Français (*mf*): franchouillard, -arde.

frère *m*: frangibus *m*; frangin *m*; frelot *m*; frérot *m*; frolot *m*; moré *m*.

fromage *m*: frome *m*; fromegi *m*; frometon *m*; fromgi *m*; fromgom *m*; fromjo *m*; fromtegomme *m*; fromton *m*; puant *m*.

fumer: bombarder; bouffarder; cloper; en

griller une; faire la loco; piper; sécher.

gagner (de l'argent): afflurer; affurer; arrondir sa pelote; en amasser; se bourrer; en ramasser; faire du pèse; faire sa pelote; faire son beurre; faire son oseille; se faire un pognon fou; ferrer la mule; palper; ramasser du fric (à la pelle); se remplir (les poches); se sucrer; tomber sur un champ d'osier; trouver le filon; toucher un joli paquet.

gain *m*: afflure *f*; affure *f*; bénef *m*; beurre *m*; bonus *m*; paquet *m*; velours *m*.

gardien *m* (de prison): gâfe *m*; gaffe *m*; maton *m*; matuche *m*.

gardien-chef *m*: doublard *m*.

gendarme *m*: bédi *m*; hareng (saur); hirondelle bleue; pandore *m*; pèlerin *m*; pèlerine *f*; sansonnet *m*; sauret *m*; schmit *m*.

goinfre (*m*): bâfreur (*m*); (béni-)bouffe-tout (*m*); (béni-)bouftou(t) (*m*); bouffe-la-balle (*m*); bouffe-tout (*m*); bouftou(t) (*m*); crevard (*m*); goulu (*m*); gueulard (*m*); morfal (*m*); morfalou (*m*); piffre (*m*); porc *m*.

gonorrhée *f*: *voir* **blennorragie**.

gorge *f*: avaloir *m*; canon *m* de fusil; colbac *m*; colbaque *m*; cornet *m*; corridor *m*; couloir *m*; courgnole *f*; dalle *f*; entonnoir *m*; garga *f*; gargamelle *f*; gargane *f*; garganelle *f*; gargoine *f*; gargoulette *f*; gargue *f*; goule *f*; goulette *f*; goulot *m*.

gras: *voir* **gros**.

gratuit: au châsse; à l'œil; grat(t)os; pour des clous; pour du beurre; pour la peau; pour que dalle.

grogner: chialer; être en boule/à cran/ comme un crin/en rogne/en suif; groumer; maronner; râler; la ramener; renâcler; renauder; rogner; ronchonner; rouscailler; rouspéter; tousser.

gros: bouboule; boulot(te); dondon; gravos; mahous(s); mahousse; mailloche; malabar; maous(s); maousse; mastard; patapouf; plein de soupe; rondouillard.

guetter: avoir à l'œil; borgnotter; faire le gaffe/le pet/la planque; gaffer; gafouiller; mater; zyeuter.

guillotine *f*: abbaye *f* de Monte-à-regret; bascule *f* (à charlot); bécane *f*; coupante *f*; coupe-cigare *m*; faucheuse *f*; le Grand Ha-choir; machine *f* à raccourcir; Veuve *f*.

être guillotiné: y aller du gadin; cracher dans le panier; épouser la Veuve; éternuer dans le sac/le son; se faire couper le cigare; se faire raccourcir; mettre le nez/la tête à la

fenêtre; tirer sa crampe avec la Veuve.
guitare *f*: bête *f*; gratte *f*; guimauve *f*;
jambonneau *m*; pelle *f*; rape *f*; râpe *f*.
guitare électrique: guitoune *f*.
habile (être): *voir* **malin.**
habiller: fagoter; ficeler; fringuer; frusquer;
harnacher; linger; loquer; nipper; (se)
sabouler; saper.
bien habillé: *voir* **élégant.**
mal habillé: fichu comme quat' sous; la
jeter mal; mal fagoté; mal ficelé; fringué
comme l'as de pique.
habiter: crécher; nicher; percher; pioger.
habits: *voir* **vêtements.**
haschisch *m*: fée verte; H *m*; hasch *m*;
luzerne *f*; merde *f*; savonnette *f*; shit *m*.
héroïne *f*: antigel *m*; blanc *m*; blanche *f*;
boy *m*; brown sugar *m*; cheval *m*; chnouf(fe)
f; dropou *f*; H *f*; héro *m ou f*; jules *m*; junk
m; jus *m*; merde *f*; naphtaline *f*; naphte *f*;
niflette *f*; poudre *m*; schnouf(fe) *f*; sma(c)k
m.
homme *m*: artiste *m*; asticot *m*; birbe *m*;
bougre *m*; client *m*; coco *m*; fias *m*; fiasse *f*;
frangin *m*; frelot *m*; gars *m*; gazier *m*; gnace
m; gniard *m*; gniasse *m*; gnière *m*; gonce *m*;
goncier *m*; gonse *m*; gonsier *m*; gonze *m*;
gonzier *m*; gosselin *m*; gugus *m*; gus *m*;
gusse *m*; indien *m*; jeton *m*; Jules *m*; Julot
m; keum *m*; lascar *m*; loulou *m*; loustic *m*;
matz *m*; mec *m*; mecqueton *m*; mecton *m*;
mironton *m*; miston *m*; moineau *m*; numéro
m; oiseau *m*; paroissien *m*; pékin *m*; péquin
m; pétrousquin *m*; piaf *m*; pierrot *m*; pistolet
m; tartempion *m*; tranche *f*; type *m*; zèbre
m; zig *m*; zigomar(d) *m*; zigoteau *m*; zigoto
m; zigue *m*.
homosexuel *m*: bique *f* et bouc *m*; bourrin
m; caroline *f*; castor *m*; chochotte *f*;
chouquette *f*; corvette *f*; crevette *f*; dallepé *f*;
dep *m*; emmanché *m*; empaffé *m*;
empapaouté *m*; empétardé *m*; emprosé *m*;
encaldossé *m*; enculé *m*; enfiffré *m*; enfoiré
m; englandé *m*; enviandé *m*; fagot *m*; fiotte
f; frégate *f*; gazier *m*; gazoline *m ou f*;
girond *m*; homo *m*; jésus *m*; joconde *f*;
lopaille *f*; lopart *m*; lope *f*; lopette *f*;
mademoiselle *f*; mignard, -arde; minot *m*;
papaout *m*; p.d. *m*; PD *m*; pédale *f*; pédé *m*;
pédéro *m*; pédoc *m*; pédoque *m*; pointeur *m*;
poulette *f*; qui en est; qui est de la bague/de
la jaquette; qui est de la famille tuyau de
poêle; qui en prend; qui file de la jaquette;
rasdep *m*; rivette *f*; schbeb *m*; sœur *f*; tante

f; tantinette *f*; tantouse *f*; tantouze *f*; tapette
f; tata *f*; travelo(t) *m*.
être homosexuel: donner du dos/du
rond; en être; en donner; en lâcher; en prendre; être de la bagouse/de la famille tuyau de
poêle/de la jaquette (flottante)/de la rondelle;
être gay; filer du chouette/du dos/de la
jaquette; mettre sa chemise en véranda;
prendre du dos/du petit; refiler de la bagouse;
travailler de la jaquette.
(*Voir* **sodomiser**)
hôpital *m*: castre *m*; host(e)au *m*; hosto *m*;
planque *f* aux attigés.
idiot (*m*); **ignorant** (*m*); **imbécile**
(*mf*): *voir* **bête.**
indicateur *m*: *voir* **dénonciateur.**
individu *m*: *voir* **homme.**
information *f*: *voir* **renseignement.**
injurier: agonir; baptiser; engueuler;
enguirlander; incendier; rembarrer; traiter
de tous les noms.
(*Voir* **réprimander**)
intelligent; personne intelligente:
bête *f*; calé; débrouillard; démerdard; doué;
fort (en tête); fortiche; grosse tête; tête *f*
d'œuf; tronche *f*.
interrogatoire *m*: blutinage *m*; cuisinage
m; cuisine *f*; musique *f*.
Italien *m*: macaroni *m*; rital *m*.
ivre (être): s'arrondir; avoir une caisse;
avoir sa charge; avoir un coup de chasselas;
avoir du vent dans les voiles; avoir les dents
du fond qui baignent; avoir pris une
bit(t)ure/une cuite; avoir sa cuite/son plumet;
avoir un coup dans l'aile; en avoir un coup
dans la trompette; avoir un verre dans le nez;
se barrer; se bit(t)urer; s'embourber; s'embrouiller; être enjuponné/d'équerre; être à
point; être au pays noir; être allumé/arrondi/
beurré (comme un petit lu/une tartine)/bille/
bit(t)uré /blindé (comme un char)/bourré (à
bloc/à zéro/comme une cantoche)/brinde-
zingue / carroussel / chargé / chicor(e) / chico-
ré/cuit/culbuté (à zéro)/déchiré/défoncé/fa-
briqué / fadé / fait / gelé / givré / ivre-dézingué/
mâchuré / mûr / murdingue / naze / noir/
noircicot / ourdé / paf / parti / pété / pinté / pion/
pionnard / pistaché / poch(e)tronné / poivrade/
poivré/raide/rétamé (à zéro)/rond/rondibé/
saoul/(s)chlass/soûl (perdu)/teinté/torché/
tordu; être dans les brindezingues/dans le
cirage/dans le coaltar/dans les vapes; être en
brosse/pas net; être plein comme un boudin/
une bourrique/un fût/une huître/un œuf/une ou-

tre; être rond comme une barrique/une bille/
un boudin/une boule/une queue de pelle; se
murdinguer; se mûrir; se pionner; se piquer
le nez; se pistacher; prendre la/sa cuite;
prendre une bit(t)ure/une pistache; ramasser
une beurrée/une bit(t)ure; en tenir une
(bit(t)ure/caisse/cuite); tenir une (bonne)
ourdée/son plumet; voir des éléphants roses.
être légèrement ivre: avoir chaud aux
plumes; avoir sa pointe; être ébréché/
éméché/gris/parti/pompette; être en goguette;
être imbibé.
ivresse *f:* beuverie *f;* bit(t)ure *f;* buverie *f;*
caisse *f;* cuite *f;* cuvée *f;* picole *f;* pistache *f;*
pocharderie *f;* poivrade *f;* saoulerie *f;* saoulo-
graphie *f;* soûlardise *f;* soûlographie *f;*
soûlerie *f.*
ivrogne *mf:* alco(o)lo *mf;* bibard *m;* bibart
m; biberon, -onne; éponge *f;* licheur, -euse;
picoleur, -euse; pionnard *m;* pochard, -arde;
pocheron *m;* pochetron *f;* pochetronné, -ée;
poivrot, -ote; qui a la dalle en pente; riboteur,
-euse; sac *m* à vin; saoulard, -arde; saouloir
m; saoulot *m;* soiffard, -arde; soiffeur, -euse;
soûlard, -arde; soûlaud, -aude; soûlographe
m; soûlot *m.*
jambes *fpl:* baguettes *fpl;* bâtons *mpl;*
bégonias *mpl;* béquilles *fpl;* bouts *mpl* de
bois; brancards *mpl;* cannes *fpl;* compas
mpl; flubards *mpl;* fusains *mpl;* fuseaux *mpl;*
gambettes *fpl;* gambilles *fpl;* gigots *mpl;*
gigues *fpl;* guibolles *fpl;* guisots *mpl;*
manivelles *fpl;* nougats *mpl;* pattes *fpl;*
piliers *mpl;* pilons *mpl;* pivots *mpl;* quilles
fpl.
jambes maigres: crayons *mpl;* échalas
mpl; flûtes *fpl;* fumerons *mpl;* pinceaux *mpl;*
pincettes *fpl.*
Japonais, -aise: jap *m;* jaune *m ou f;*
nippon, -on(n)e.
jeter: balancer; balanstiquer; envoyer
dinguer; ficher/foutre en l'air.
journal *m:* babillard *m;* baveux *m;* canard
m; cancan *m;* feuille *f* de chou; menteur *m;*
narca *m;* torchon *m.*
Juif, Juive: Auvergnat *m;* feuj *mf;*
schmoutz *m;* Youde *mf;* Youpe *mf;* Youpin,
-ine; Youpine *f;* Youtre *mf;* Youvance *m.*
laid: belle comme un camion; bléchard; blèche; blèchecaille; craignos; loquedu; miteux;
mochard; moche (à faire peur/comme un
pou); mochetingue; mocheton; pas jojo;
roupie; tarde; tartavelle; tarte; tartignol;
tartouille; tartouse; toc; tocard.

(*Voir* **(vieille) femme laide**)
personne laide: boudin *m;* cageot *m;*
caricature *f;* carnaval *m;* face *f* de crabe/
d'œuf/de rat; gueule *f* à coucher dehors;
gueule d'empeigne/de raie; hideur *f;* mocheté
f; pocheté *f;* qui a une sale/vilaine gueule;
roupie *f;* tarderie *f;* tardingue *f;* tartavelle *f.*
langue *f:* battant *m;* bavarde *f;* baveuse *f;*
clapette *f;* langouse *f;* lavette *f;* membrineuse
f; menteuse *f;* mouillette *f;* patin *m;* platine
m; râpeuse *f;* tapette *f.*
lesbienne *f:* éplucheuse *f* de lentilles;
gavousse *f;* godo *f;* gouchotte *f;* goudou *f;*
gougne *f;* gougnette *f;* gougnot(t)e *f;* gouine
f; gousse *f* (d'ail); mangeuse *f* de lentilles;
marchande *f* d'ail; qui aime/qui tape l'ail;
vrille *f.*
être lesbienne: aimer l'ail; être de la
bottine/de la maison tire-bouton; (se) gougnotter; (se) gouiner; (se) gousser; manger/
sentir/taper l'ail; travailler de la bottine.
lèvre *f:* babine *f;* babouine *f;* badigoince *f;*
bagougnasse *f;* baiseuse *f;* limace *f;*
pompeuse *f.*
lit *m:* bâche *f;* banette *f;* boîte *f* à puces;
champ *m* de manœuvre; dodo *m;* matelas *m;*
nid *m;* paddock *m;* page *m;* pageot *m;* pagne
m; pagnot *m;* panier *m;* pieu *m;* plumard *m;*
plume(s) *f(pl);* pucier *m;* sac *m* à puces;
toiles *fpl.*
logement *m:* bahut *m;* baraque *f;* bocal *m;*
cabane *f;* cagna *f;* cambuse *f;* carrée *f;*
casba(h) *f;* case *f;* crèche *f;* garno *m;* gourbi
m; guitoune *f;* niche *f;* nid *m;* piaule *f;*
planque *f;* strasse *f;* taule *f;* tôle *f;* turne *f.*
loucher: avoir un carreau brouillé; avoir un
œil qui dit merde/zut à l'autre; bigler (en
biais); boîter des calots.
LSD *m:* acide *m;* D *m;* sucre *m.*
lunettes *fpl:* bernicles *fpl;* carreaux *mpl;*
carrelingues *mpl;* faux quinquets; pare-brise
mpl.
maigre: désossé; gremai; long comme un
jour sans pain; maigre comme un clou/une
trique; maigrichon; maigrot; qui n'a que la
peau sur les os; sec comme un coup de
trique; séco(t).
personne maigre: asperge *f;* échalas *m;*
fil *m* (de fer); planche *f* à pain; sac *m* d'os;
sauterelle *f;* séco(t) *m.*
main *f:* agrafe *f;* battoir *m;* croche *f;* cuiller
f; grappin *m;* grattante *f;* griffe *f;* louche *f;*
mimine *f;* palette *f;* paluche *f;* papogne *f;*
patte *f;* pat(t)oche *f;* pince *f* (d'Adam); po-

gne *f*; quintuplée *f*.

maison close: baisodrome *m*; bobi *m*; bobinard *m*; bocard *m*; bocsif *m*; bordel *m*; boui-boui *m*; bouic *m*; boxon *m*; bric *m*; cabane *f*; casbah *m*; chabanais *m*; clac *m*; clandé *m*; claque *m*; claquedent *m*; foutoir *m*; magasin *m* de blanc; maison *f* d'abattage/à gros numéro/de passe; pinarium *m*; pouf *m*; taule *f*; tringlodrome *m*; volière *f*.

malade (être): amoché; avoir une pet de travers; n'avoir pas le moral; être dans les vapes/flagada/flapi/mal fichu/mal foutu/mal vissé; ne pas avoir la frite/la pêche; ne pas être dans un bon jour; pas dans son assiette; pas en train; patraque.

(être) très malade: avoir un pied dans la tombe; battre de l'aile; être cuit/fichu/flambé/foutu/fricassé/frit/paumé; filer un mauvais coton; marcher à côté de ses pompes; sentir le sapin.

maladie vénérienne: *voir* **blennorragie; syphilis.**

malchance *f*: bouillabaisse *f*; bouscaille *f*; cerise *f*; confiture *f*; déveine *f*; guigne *f*; guignon *m*; manque *m* de bol/de fion/de pot/de vase; marmelade *f*; masque *m*; mouise *f*; pestouille *f*; pétrin *m*; poisse *f*; pommade *f*; scoumoune *f*; sirop *m*.

malin: affranchi; à la coule; à la hauteur; à la page; branché; câblé; chébran; dans le train; débrouillard; dégourdi; démerdard; dessalé; ficelle; filou(teur); fortiche; fute-fute; mariole; marle; marloupin; roublard.

manger: aller à la graille; s'appuyer (un repas); becqueter; becter; béquiller; bouffer; boulotter; boustifailler; briffer; casser la croûte/la graine; claper; cléber; criave(r); croquer; croustiller; croûter; dévorer; effacer; s'envoyer; gameler; grailler; grainer; jaffer; lipper; mastéguer; mastiquer; morfier; morfiler; morfiller; morganer; recharger les accus; se remplir le bocal/le cornet/le garde-manger/la lampe; sandwicher; se taper la cloche; tortorer.

manger abondamment: bâfrer; bouffer (à en crever); se bourrer; se caler les amygdales/les babines/les babouines/les badigoinces/les côtes/les joues; se la/ se les caler; s'empiffrer; se faire péter la sous-ventrière; se farcir le chou/la panse; s'en fourrer jusque-là; s'en foutre plein la lampe; s'en jeter/s'en mettre derrière la cravate; s'en mettre jusqu'au menton/jusque-là; s'en mettre plein le fusil/plein la lampe/plein la panse; se goinfrer; gueuletonner; morphaler; prendre une bonne ventrée; se remplir le bide/le buffet; se taper le chou.

maquiller, se: faire un raccord; faire son ravalement; se griffer (la tronche); se peinturlurer (la figure); se plâtrer le visage; ravaler sa façade; se (re)faire la façade; se sabouler; se sucrer la fraise/la gaufre/la tarte.

marchandise *f*: came *f*; camelote *f*; lamedu *m*.

marcher: affûter des pinceaux; aller à pattes; aller par le train d'onze heures; aller pédibus (cum jambis); arpenter le bitume; arquer; bagoter; écraser les paturons; prendre le train onze; prendre la voiture de Saint-Crépin; ripatonner; se trimbaler.

mariage *m*: antiflage *m*; conjungo *m*; entiflage *m*; marida(t) *m*.

se marier: aller au marida(t); s'antifler (de sec); s'entifler (de sec); se marida; prononcer le conjungo; signer un bail.

divorcer: casser le bail.

marijuana *f*: chanvre *m*; chiendent *m*; colombienne *f*; douce *f*; foin *m*; herbe (douce); kif *m*; Marie-Jeanne *f*; pot *m*; thé *m*.

marin *m*: col bleu; loup *m* de mer; marsouin *m*; mataf *m*; matave *m*; mathurin *m*; pompon *m* rouge.

masturber, se: (*homme*) s'achever à la manivelle; s'agiter le poireau; se l'agiter; s'allonger la couenne; se l'allonger; amuser Charlot; s'amuser comme Charlot; s'astiquer; s'astiquer la colonne/le manche; se l'astiquer; se battre le chinois; s'en battre une; se branler; se chatouiller le poireau; se coller un rassis; épouser la veuve Poignet; étrangler le borgne/Popaul/Popol; faire cinq contre un; se faire écrémer; faire glouglouter le poireau; faire juter l'os à moelle; se faire malice tout seul; se faire mousser (le créateur); se faire reluire; faire sauter la cervelle à Charles-le-Chauve; se faire une pogne/une queue; se fréquenter; fréquenter la veuve Poignet; se griffer; se palucher; se pignoler; se polir le chinois/la colonne; se pogner; se secouer le bonhomme; se soulager; se taper la veuve Poignet; se taper (sur) la colonne; se taper une pignole/une queue/un rassis/un ramollo(t)/une sègue; s'en taper une; se tirer son/un coup; se toucher; se tripoter (les couilles).

se masturber: (*femme*) s'astiquer le boilton/le bouton; se branler; se caresser l'hibiscus; se compter les poils; se filer une gerbe; jouer de la mandoline; secouer la cartouche/son grain de café; se soulager; se toucher.

masturbation *f*: branlage *m*; branlée *f*; branlette maison; branlure *f*; paluche *f*; pignole *f*; pogne *f*; ramollo(t) *m*; secouette *f*; sègue *f*; la veuve Poignet.

masturbateur *m*: branleur *m*; branleuse *f*.

mauvais: à la manque; à la noix; bidon; blèche; locdu; loquedu; de merde; merdeux; merdique; moche; du nanar; nul; nullos; nullissime; raté; tarte; tartouse; toc; tocard; zone.

méchant *m*: *voir* **salaud**.

mégot *m*: clope *m*; meg *m*; orphelin *m*.

mendiant, -ante: clodo(t) *m*; frappeur *m*; manchard *m*; mangave *m*; mégot(t)eur, -euse; mégot(t)ier, -ière; mendiche *m*; mendigot *m*; passant *m*; pied-de-biche *m*; pilon *m*; pilonneur *m*; pouilleux *m*; stiff *m*; tapeur, -euse; torpille *f*; torpilleur *m*.

mendicité *f*: manche *f*; mangave *f*; mégotage *m*; pilon *m*; sonnage *m*; tapage *m*; tape *f*; torpille *f*.

mendier: aller à la mangave; faire la manche/le pilon; frapper; marcher à la torpille; mendigoter; pilonner; taper; tirer le pied de biche; torpiller.

menottes *fpl*: bracelets *mpl*; brides *fpl*; cabriolets *mpl*; cadènes *fpl*; cadenettes *fpl*; cadennes *fpl*; cannelles *fpl*; chapelet *m*; ficelles *fpl*; fichets *mpl*; manchettes *fpl*; pinces *fpl*; poucettes *fpl*.

mensonge *m*: balançoire *f*; bateau *m*; bidon *m*; blague *f*; bobard *m*; boniment *m*; bourde *f*; bourrage *m* (de crâne/de mou); du bourre-mou; caraco *m*; char(re) *m*; connerie *f*; craque *f*; cravate *f*; doublage *m*; frime *f*; gonfle *f*; histoire *f* à dormir debout; histoire raide; van(ne) *m*.

mentir: bourrer la caisse/le crâne/le mou; fabuler; monter une galère; raconter des bobards/des craques/des histoires.

merde *f*: *voir* **étron**.

mère *f*: dabe *f*; dabesse *f*; dabuche *f*; daronne *f*; doche *f*; mater *f*; matère *f*; (la) maternelle; rèm *f*; vieille *f*; vioque *f*.

mescaline *f*: mesc *f*.

mitraillette *f*: arroseuse (municipale); arrosoir *m*; joséphine *f*; lampe *f* à souder;

machine *f* à coudre/à percer/à secouer le paletot; mandoline *f*; moulin *m* à café; moulinette *f*; sulfateuse *f*; titine *f*; vaporisateur *m*.

monnaie *f*: ferraille *f*; menouille *f*; mitraille *f*; mornifle *m*; pezette *f*; vaisselle *f* de fouille.

montre *f*: dégoulinante *f*; montrouze *f*; pendule *f*; tocante *f*; toquante *f*.

moquer de, se: acheter; blaguer; chambrer; charrier; chiner; jardiner; la faire à l'oseille; se ficher de; se foutre de; frimer qn; mettre en boîte/en caisse; se payer la cafetière/la gueule/la poire/la tête/la tronche de; vanner.

morphine *f*: lili-pioncette *f*; M *f*; morph *f*.

mouchoir *m*: tire-jus *m*; tire-moelle *m*.

mourir: s'en aller (les pieds devant); avaler son acte/son bulletin/son extrait de naissance; avaler sa chique; l'avaler; boucler sa malle; bouffer du pissenlit/les pissenlits par la racine; cadancher; calancher; calencher; can(n)er; casser sa pipe; la casser; cirer ses bottes; claboter; clam(e)cer; clam(p)ser; clapoter; clapser; claquer; cram(p)ser; crever (la gueule ouverte); crônir; crounir; la déchirer; déchirer son tablier; déposer son bilan; dépoter son géranium; déramer; (la) dessouder; (la) dévisser; dévisser son billard; éteindre sa bougie/son gaz; faire couic; fermer son gaz/son parapluie; glisser; graisser ses bottes; lâcher la bouée/la rampe; se laisser glisser; oublier de respirer; y passer; passer l'arme à gauche; perdre le goût du pain; plier bagage; quimper; remercier son boulanger; rendre ses clefs; sentir le sapin; sortir les pieds devant; souffler sa veilleuse.

moustache(s) *f(pl)*: bac(c)antes *fpl*; bacchantes *fpl*; bacchantes en guidon (de course); baffe *f*; baffi *f*; balai *m* (à chiottes); charmeuses *fpl*; moustagache *f*; ramasse-miettes *m*.

nègre *m*: *voir* **Noir, Noire**.

nez *m*: baigneur *m*; blair *m*; blaireau *m*; blase *m*; blaze *m*; boîte *f* à morve; cep *m*; mufle *m*; naze *m*; pif *m*; piffard *m*; piton *m*; pivase *m*; priseur *m*; reniflant *m*; ronflant *m*; step *m*; tarbouif *m*; tarin *m*; trompette *f*.

nez épaté: patate *f*; pied *m* de marmite; truffe *f*.

grand nez: éteignoir *m*; fer *m* à souder; lampe *f* à souder; quart *m* de brie; step *m* (à trier les lentilles/à repiquer les choux); tasseau *m*; tassot *m*.

nez rouge: aubergine *f*; piment *m*; tomate *f*.

Noir, Noire: bamboula *m*; black *mf*; Blanche-Neige *f*; bougnoul(e) *m*; boule *f* de neige; bronzé, -ée; frisé, -ée; gobi *m*; kebla *mf*; mal blanchi(e); négro *m*; noircicaud *m*; noircico *m*; noyama *m*; radis noir.

nom *m*: blaze *m*; centre *m*.

non!: balpeau! bernique! des clopes! des clopinettes! des clous! des nèfles! des queues! il pleut! macache (et midi sonné)! mon cul, c'est du poulet! mon œil! mon zob! nib! nibe! ouallou! la peau! la peau de mes burnes! peau de balle (et balai de crin)! peau de balle et variété! peau de nœud! peau de zob! que dalle! tu parles (,Charles)! zéro!

nourriture *f*: avoine *f*; becquetance *f*; bectance *f*; bouffe *f*; bouftance *f*; boustifaille *f*; boustiffe *f*; briffe *f*; briffeton *m*; casse-dalle *m*; casse- graine *m*; clape *f*; croustance *f*; croustille *f*; croûte *f*; fébou *f*; frichti *m*; fricot *m*; frip(p)e *f*; graille *f*; graine *f*; grinque *f*; jaffe *f*; mangeaille *f*; mastègue *f*; rata *m*; tambouille *f*; tortore *f*.

mauvaise nourriture: graillon *m*; ragougnasse *f*; rata *m*; ratatouille *f*.

nu: à loilpé; à loilpuche; à oilp(é); à poil; comme un savon; (le) cul à l'air; cul nu; dans le costume d'Adam/d'Eve; en Jésus.

nuit *f*: borgne *f*; borgniot *m*; borgno *m*; borgnon *m*; neuille *f*; noie *f*; noille *f*; sorgue *f*.

œil *m*: agate *f*; bille *f*; calot *m*; carreau *m*; châsse *m*; clignot(ant) *m*; coquillard *m*; lampion *m*; lanterne *f*; lentille *f*; loupe *f*; lucarne *f*; mire *f*; mirette *f*; mironton *m*; neunœil *m*; nœil *m*; œillet *m*; quinquet *m*; yakas *m*.

coup *m* **d'œil**: coup *m* de périscope/de sabord/de saveur.

œil poché: coquard *m*; coquart *m*; coquelicot *m*; œil au beurre noir; œil pavoisé.

œillade (faire une): donner/faire un appel/un coup de châsse/un coup de sabord; jouer des châsses; reluquer.

opium *m*: boue verte; chandoo *m*; dross *m*; fée brune; noir *m*; op *m*; pavot *m*; touffiane *f*.

or *m*: jonc *m*; joncaille *f*.

oreille *f*: anse *f*; cage *f* à miel; cliquette *f*; écoute *f*; écoutille *f*; escalope *f*; esgourde *f*; étagère *f* à mégot; étiquette *f*; feuille *f* (de chou); manette *f*; pavillon *m*; portugaise *f*; soucoupe *f*; zozore *f*.

organes génitaux: *voir* **sexe de l'homme; sexe de la femme**.

orgasme (avoir un): se balancer; briller; déjanter; s'éclater; s'envoyer en l'air; fader; jouir; juter; mouiller; prendre son fade/son panard/son pied/son taf; rayonner; se régaler; reluire; venir; vider ses burettes; y aller du/de son voyage.

oui!: *voir* **accord, d'**.

ouvrier *m*: *voir* **travailleur**.

ouvrir: débâcler; déboucler; débrider; mettre en dedans.

pain *m*: bricheton *m*; briffeton *m*; brignole *f*; brignolet *m*; brignoluche *f*; brutal *m*; lartif (brutal); larton (brutal).

pantalon *m*: bénard *m*; bénouse *m*; bénouze *m*; cotte *f*; culbutant *m*; culbute *f*; false *m*; falzar(d) *m*; fendant *m*; fendard *m*; fendart *m*; froc *m*; fut *m*; futal *m*; fute *m*; grimpant *m*; montant *m*; pante *m*; valseur *m*.

pantalon étroit: fourreau *m*; tuyau *m* de poêle.

papier *m*: balourd *m*; faf(fe) *m*; faf(f)iot *m*; papelard *m*; pelure *f*.

parapluie *f*: paralance *f*; pareflotte *m*; pare-lance *m*; pébroc *m*; pébroque *f*; pèlerin *m*; pépin *m*; riflard *m*.

pardessus *m*: lardeuss *m*; lardingue *m*; lardoss *m*; pardeuss *m*; pardingue *m*; pardoss *m*; pelure *f*.

parents *mpl*: dabs *mpl*; dabes *mpl*; darons *mpl*; paternels *mpl*; vieux *mpl*; viocards *mpl*; vioques *mpl*.

paresser: avoir les bras à la retourne; avoir la cosse/la flème/la flemme/la rame; avoir les pieds en cosses de melon; les avoir à la retourne; les avoir palmées; se branler les couilles; se les branler; buller; se la couler douce; s'endormir sur le mastic; enfiler des perles; feignasser; ne pas en faire/en ficher/en foutre un coup; ne pas en faire/en ficher/en foutre une rame; flânocher; flemmarder; ne pas se fouler la rate; glander; glandocher; glandouiller; peigner la girafe; tirer au cul/au flanc; tirer sa cosse/sa flemme; se tourner les pouces; se les tourner; traîner ses patins/les savates.

paresseux, -euse: cagnard, -arde; cossard *m*; cul *m* seccotine; faignant, -ante; fainéasse *mf*; feignant, -ante; feignasse *mf*; flânocheur, -euse; flemmard, -arde; mollasse *mf*; mollasson, -onne; pousse-mégots *m*; ramier *m*; raoul *m*; raymond *m*; tire(ur)-au-cul *m*; tire(ur)-au-flanc *m*; vachard *m*.

parler: bagouler; baratiner; bavasser;

baver; bonnir; déblatérer; décoincer; dégoiser; dévider; jacasser; jacter; jaspiner; l'ouvrir; tailler une bavette; tenir le crachoir; tortiller de la débagoule; user un litre de salive à l'heure.

(*Voir* **bavarder**)

partir: les agiter; s'arracher; se barrer; (se) caleter; (se) calter; can(n)er; se carapater; se car(r)er; se casser; casser sa canne; se cavaler; changer d'air/de crémerie; chier du poivre; se criquer; débarrasser le plancher; se débiner; déblayer le terrain; décambuter; décamper; décaniller; décarrer; décharger le plancher; se défiler; dégager; déguerpir; (se) déhotter; dériper; se donner de l'air; s'éclipser; s'esbigner; s'esbrousser; escamper; s'évaporer; faire l'adja; faire cassos; faire la valdingue/la valise; faire natchave; (se) faire un patatrot; se faire la belle/la levure/la malle; se faire oublier; ficher le camp; filer; foncer dans le brouillard; foutre le camp; en jouer un air; les jouer; jouer un air de flûte; jouer des flûtes/des fuseaux; jouer (à) la fille de l'air; jouer rip(e); en jouer un air; larguer les amarres/les voiles; lever (l'ancre); lever le camp/le pied/les voiles; mettre les adjas/les baguettes/les bouts/les cannes/les loubés/les voiles; mettre une gamelle; les mettre; se mettre en belle/en cavale; se natchaver; se patiner; se pister; plier bagage; prendre la clef des champs/le large/la poudre d'escampette/la tangente; prendre ses cliques et ses claques; ripatonner; riper; se tailler; se tirer ailleurs; se tirer (des adjas/des flûtes/des ripatons); se tracer; (se) trisser; se trissoter; se trotter; valiser.

partir sans payer: faire jambe de bois; faire une queue; fuser; laisser une feuille de chou; laisser une queue; planter un drapeau; poser une ardoise.

patron, -onne: boss *m*; chef *m*; dab(e) *m*; daron *m*; direlot *m*; dirlingue *m*; dirlot *m*; le grand manitou; latronpem *m*; pompe-la-sueur *m*; singe, -esse; taulier *m*; tôlier *m*.

patronne *f* **(de maison de tolérance):** bordelière *f*; maqua *f*; maquerelle *f*; maquesée *f*; marquise *f*; mère-maca *f*; mère-maquerelle *f*; rombière *f*; taulière *f*; tôlière *f*.

pauvre: à la côte; à la masse; à plat; à sec; cisaillé; couparès; coupé (à blanc); crève-la-faim; dans la chtourbe/la dèche/la limonade/la mélasse/la purée; décavé; déchard; fauché (comme les blés); faucheman; fleur; la tête dans le sac; lavé; lessivé; miteux; mouisard; nettoyé; pané; panné; paumé; purotin; qui traîne les patins/la savate; raide (comme un passe-lacet); raqué; ratiboisé; ratissé; rincé; rôti; sans le sou; sans un; sans un radis; sec; serré; sur la paille/le pavé; tondu; vacant; vidé; de la zone.

pauvreté *f*: bouillabaisse *f*; chtourbe *f*; débine *f*; dèche *f*; mélasse *f*; mistoufle *f*; mouise *f*; mouscaille *f*; panade *f*; purée *f*.

payer: les abouler; les aligner; aller au refil/ au rembour; allonger le tir; les allonger; arroser; banquer; carburer; carmer; casquer; cigler; cracher (au bassinet/dans le *ou* au bassin); décher; douiller; éclairer; envoyer la monnaie/la valse; essuyer le coup de fusil; s'exécuter; se fendre; lâcher les valses lentes; les lâcher; mouiller; raquer; régaler; régler la douloureuse; les sortir; valser; y aller de ses sous.

paysan *m*: boueux *m*; bouseux *m*; cambroussard *m*; croquant *m*; cul-terreux *m*; glaiseux *m*; goyau *m*; goyo(t) *m*; pécore *m*; péd(e)zouille *m*; peigne-cul *m*; péquenaud *m*; péquenot *m*; pétrousquin *m*; petzouillard *m*; petzouille *m*; plouc *m*.

pénis *m*: andouille *f* à col roulé; anguille *f* de calecif; arbalète *f*; asperge *f*; baigneur *m*; baïonnette *f*; baisette *f*; balayette (infernale); baveuse *f*; berloque *f*; bifteck roulé; biroute *f*; bistouquette *f*; bit(t)e *f*; bout *m*; bra(c)quemard *m*; brandon *m*; canne *f*; carabine *f*; Charles-le-Chauve; chibre *m*; chinois *m*; chipolata *mf*; chopine *f*; chopotte *f*; chose *f*; cigare *m* à moustaches; clarinette *f*; colonne *f*; cyclope *m*; dard *m*; dardillon *m*; défonceuse *f*; fifre *m* à grelots; flageolet *m*; frétillante *f*; frétillard *m*; frotteuse *f*; gaule *f*; gland *m*; goupillon *m*; gourde *f* à poils; gourdin *m*; guignol *m*; guiguite *f*; guise *f*; guiseau *m*; guisot *m*; guizot *f*; instrument *m*; jambe *f* du milieu; macaroni *m*; machin *m*; manche *m* (à balai/à couilles); mandrin *m*; marsouin *m*; matraque *f*; mohican *m*; morceau *m*; nœud *m*; os *m* à moelle; outil *m*; paf *m*; panais *m*; papillon *m* du Sénégal; Paupol *m*; le père frappart; pain *m* au lait; petit frère; pine *f*; pointe *f*; poireau *m*; polard *m*; Popaul *m*; Popol *m* (le guignol); quéquette *f*; queue *f*; quille *f*; quique *f*; quiquette *f*; quiqui *m*; sabre *m*; teube *f*; teubi *f*; Totor *m*; tricotin *m*; tringle *f*; trique *f*; verge *f*; vié *m*; vier *m*; zeb *m*; zigouigoui *m*;

zigounette *f*; zizi *m*; zob(i) *m*.

père *m*: dab *m*; dabuche *m*; daron *m*; pater *m*; paternel *m*; vieux *m*; vioque *m*.

pet *m*: flousse *m*; fusant *m*; louffe *f*; louise *f*; pastoche *f*; perle *f*; perlouse *f*; perlouze *f*; vesse *f*.

péter: cloquer; déchirer son false/son froc/ la toile; en écraser un; flouser; flouzer; lâcher une caisse/les gaz/une louise/une perle/ une perlouse; louf(f)er; s'oublier; vesser.

petit individu: astec *m*; astèque *m*; avorton *m*; aztèque *m*; basduc *m*; bas-du-cul *m*; courte-botte *m*; crapaud *m*; crapoussin *m*; demi-portion *f*; fabriqué *m* au compte-gouttes; inachevé *m*; microbe *m*; puce *f*; qui est haut comme trois pommes; raclure *f* de bidet; ras-de-bitume *m*; ras-de-mottes *m*; rasduc *m*; ras-du-cul *m*; rase-bitume *m*; résidu *m* de fausse couche; rikiki *m*; riquiqui *m*.

peu (un): un (petit) bout; un chouia; pas bésef; pas bézef; des clopinettes; pas épais; pas gras; pas lerche; pas lourd; pas lourdingue; une larme; une larmichette; une miette; un poil.

peur *f*: chiasse *f*; chocottes *fpl*; colombins *mpl*; flubes *mpl*; frousse *f*; grelots *mpl*; pétasse *f*; pétoche *f*; pétouille *f*; peur bleue; taf *m*; taffe *m*; trac *m*; tracsir *m*; traczir *m*; traquette *f*; traquouse *f*; tremblote *f*; trouille *f* (bleue).

avoir peur: avoir chaud aux fesses; avoir la boule/les boules/la chaleur/les chocottes/la colique/les colombins/les copeaux/les flubes/ les foies/les jetons/les mouillettes/les moules; avoir les miches/les noix qui font bravo; avoir les pastèques (à mort); avoir le pétoulet/le trouillomètre à zéro; les avoir à zéro; baisser sa culotte; caner; chier dans son froc; se déballonner; se dégonfler; être flubard/ trouillard; fluber; foirer; grelotter; mouetter; les mouiller; serrer les fesses/les miches; trouillotter.

pieds *mpl*: argasses *mpl*; arpions *mpl*; artous *mpl*; nougats *mpl*; panards *mpl*; patins *mpl*; pattes *fpl*; paturons *mpl*; péniches *fpl*; petons *mpl*; pinceaux *mpl*; pinglots *mpl*; pingots *mpl*; pingouins *mpl*; raquettes *fpl*; ribouis *mpl*; ripatons *mpl*; targes *fpl*; targettes *fpl*; tatanes *fpl*; trottinants *mpl*; trottinets *mpl*.

pince-monseigneur *f*: clarinette *f*; dauphin *m*; dingue *f*; dombeur *m*; dur *m*; jacques *m*; jacquot *m*; pied-de-biche *m*;

plume *f*; sucre *m* de pomme.

piqûre *f*: fixe *m*; piquouse *f*; piquouze *f*; shoot *m*.

(se) piquer: (se) faire un fixe/une piquouse/une piquouze/un shoot; (se) fixer; (se) piquouser; (se) piquouzer; (se) shooter. (*Voir* **seringue**)

pleurer: baver des clignotants; chialer; gicler des mirettes/des œillets; miter; ouvrir les écluses/les grandes eaux de Versailles; pisser des châsses.

pluie *f*: bouillon *m*; flotte *f*; lancecaille *f*; lancequine *f*; lanscaille *f*; rincée *f*; saucée *f*.

poche *f*: bacreuse *f*; ballade *f*; farfouillette *f*; fouille *f*; fouillette *f*; glaude *f*; pocket *f*; profonde *f*; vague *f*; valade *f*.

poing *m*: *voir* **main**.

poitrine *f*: armoire *f*; caisse *f*; caisson *m*; coffre *m*; plastron *m*. (*Voir* **seins**)

police *f*: bourre *f*; bourrique *f*; flicaille *f*; flicaillerie *f*; la grive; guignols *mpl*; la Maison Bourreman(e)/Bourremann/Cogne-dur / Parapluie / Pébroc / Poulaga / Poulardin/ Poulemane/Pouleminche; mannequins *mpl*; ces Messieurs; poulaille *f*; poule *f*; raclette *f*; renifle *f*; rousse *f*; volaille *f*.

policier *m*: archer *m* (du Roy); argousin *m*; bleu *m* (de Nanterre); boer *m*; bourre *m*; bourrin *m*; chaussette *f*; cogne *m*; condé *m*; drauper *m*; en bourgeois *m*; flic *m*; flicaillon *m*; flicard *m*; flikeu *m*; guignol *m*; hambourgeois *m*; kébour *m*; keuf *m*; lardu *m*; maton *m*; mec *m* de la rousse; perdreau *m*; poulaga *m*; poulardos *m*; poulet *m*; roussin *m*; royco *m*. (*Voir* **agent** *m* **de police**)

poltron, -onne: baisse-froc *m*; bande-à-l'aise *m*; bandocheur *m*; caneur *m*; capon *m*; chiasseur, -euse; déballonné, -ée; dégonflard, -arde; dégonflé, -ée; dégonfleur, -euse; flubard *m*; foie blanc ; foireux, -euse; froussard, -arde; gonzesse *f*; grelotteur, -euse; lopaille *f*; lopart *m*; lope *f*; lopette *f*; péteux, -euse; pétochard, -arde; poule mouillée; taffeur, -euse; traqueur, -euse; trouillard, -arde.

portefeuille *m*: larfeuil(le); lasagne *m*; lasane *f*; lazagne *f*; lazane *f*; lazingue *m*; morlingue *m*.

portefeuille plein: matelas *m*.

porte-monnaie *m*: artichaut *m*; artiche *m*; crapaud *m*; lasagne *m*; lazingue *m*; morlingue *m*; morniflard *m*; porte-biffetons *m*; porte-faf(f)iots *m*.

pou *m*: crabe *m*; galopard *m*; gau *m*; grain *m* de blé; mie *f* de pain à bec/à roulettes; morbac *m*; morbaque *m*; morfic *m*; morpion *m*; piocre *m*; toto *m*.

pourboire *m*: pourcif *m*; pourliche *m*; poursoif *m*.

préservatif *m*: capote (anglaise); chapeau *m*; imper(méable) *m* à Popaul; marguerite *f*; scaphandre *m* de poche.

prétentieux, être: bêcher; crâner; croire que c'est arrivé; se croire sorti de la cuisse de Jupiter; s'en croire; épater; esbrouf(f)er; être bêcheur/crâneur/esbrouffeur/plastronneur/poseur/prétentiard/snob; faire des chichis/de l'épate/de l'esbrouf(f)e/des magnes; faire du vent; frimer; se gober; se gonfler; en installer; se monter le job; ne pas se prendre pour de la crotte/pour de la merde; ne plus se sentir (pisser); plastronner; pontifier; rouler les épahules/les épaules/les mécaniques.

prêtre *m*: cagne *f*; calotin *m*; coin-coin *m*; corbeau *m*; cureton *m*; radis noir; rase *m*; ratiche *m*; ratichon *m*; sac *m* à carbi/à charbon; sanglier *m*.

prison *f*: ballon *m*; bigne *f*; bing *m*; bloc *m*; boîte *f*; cabane *f*; cage *f*; carlingue *f*; carluche *f*; case *f*; centrouse *f*; centrouze *f*; chetard *m*; ch'tar *m*; chtard *m*; clou *m*; coffre *m*; coquille *f*; gn(i)ouf *m*; grande marmite *f*; grosse *f*; jettard *m*; lazaro *m*; mitard *m*; ombre *f*; ours *m*; placard *m*; ratière *f*; schib *m*; schtard *m*; schtib *m*; schtilibem *m*; séchoir *m*; taule *f*; tôle *f*; trou *m*; violon *m*.

en prison: à l'ombre; au ballon; au bloc; au frais; au frigo; au trou; au violon; bouclé; dedans; en taule; en tôle.

(*Voir* **emprisonner**)

prostituée *f*: allumeuse *f*; amazone *f*; béguineuse *f*; bis(e)nesseuse *f*; barboteuse *f*; boudin *m*; boulonnaise *f*; bourrin *m*; braguette *f*; brésilienne *f*; briquette *f*; caravelle *f*; catin *f*; chamelle *f*; chèvre *f*; chignon émancipé; escaladeuse *f* de braguette; essoreuse *f*; étagère *f*; étoile filante; fille *f*; fin *f* de mois; flibocheuse *f*; frangine *f*; frangipane *f*; gagne-pain *m*; gagneuse *f*; galérienne *f*; garce *f*; girèle *f*; girelle *f*; gisquette *f*; gonzesse *f*; grue *f*; guenon *f*; langouste *f*; langoustine *f*; marcheuse *f*; ménagère *f*; mistonne *f*; morue *f*; moukère *f*; mousmé(e) *f*; nana *f*; pain frais; pépée *f*; persilleuse *f*; pipeuse *f*; ponette *f*; pouffiasse

f; poule *f*; putain *f*; pute *f*; raccrocheuse *f*; racoleuse *f*; radeuse *f*; respectueuse *f*; rivette *f*; rouchie *f*; roulure *f*; sac *m* à bites; souris *f*; tailleuse *f* de plumes; tapin *m*; tapineuse *f*; traînée *f*; trotteuse *f*; trottineuse *f*; truqueuse *f*; turfeuse *f*; volaille *f*; zigouince *f*.

client *m* **de prostituée**: branque *m*; cave *m*; cille *m*; miché *m*; micheton *m*; rivette *f*.

prostituer, se: *voir* **racoler**.

querelle *f*: accrochage *m*; asticotage *m*; attrapade *f*; attrapage *m*; badaboum *m*; barabille *f*; baroud *m*; barouf *m*; barouffe *m*; baroufle *m*; bigorne *f*; bisbille *f*; chicaya *f*; corrida *f*; crosse *f*; engueulade *f*; pétard *m*; prise *f* de bec/de gueule; rif *m*; rififi *m*; rogne *f*; salade *f*; savon *m*; suif *m*; tabac *m*; tapage *m*; torchée *f*.

quereller, se: avoir une prise de bec/de gueule; chercher la cogne/des crosses/des patins/du rif/des rognes/du suif; chercher noise; crosser; se chicorer; s'expliquer (avec).

querelleur: asticoteur; crosseur; mauvais coucheur; pétardier; péteur; râleur; renaudeur; rouspéteur; saladier; suiffeur.

racoler: aller aux asperges; aller au turf; arpenter (le bitume); battre l'antif; en becqueter; becter; brancher; chasser le mâle; dérouiller; se défendre; draguer; emballer; s'expliquer; faire le business/le bitume/la grue/un levage/le macadam/le pavé/le quart/le raccroc/le rade/la retape/le ruban/le tapin/le tas/le trottoir/le truc/le turbin/le turf/la verdure; faire un miché; faire son persil; lever un client; michetonner; en moudre; persiller; putasser; raccrocher; en retourner; tapiner; truquer; turbiner; turfer.

raser, se: se gratter; se gratter/se racler la couenne; se racler.

rasoir *m*: coupe-chou *m*; racloir *m*; rasibe *m*; rasif *m*; razif *m*.

receleur, -euse: fourgat *m*; fourgue *m*; fourgueur, -euse; franquiste *m*; laveur *m*; lessiveur *m*.

recevoir (*des coups ou des insultes*): déguster; dérouiller; écoper; effacer; emplafonner; encaisser; s'enfiler; éponger; étrenner; se faire démolir la façade; se faire étriller; se faire sonner; se manger un coup; palper; en prendre dans les dents; en prendre pour son grade/pour son rhume; en prendre plein la gueule/la tronche; morfler.

recommencer: rebiffer; remettre ça; (y) remordre; repiquer (au truc); replonger.

reconnaître: reconnobler; reconnobrer; redresser; retapisser.

regarder: allumer; bigler; borgnoter; châsser; frimer; gaffer; en jeter un; jeter un œil; lorgner; loucher sur; louquer; mater; matouser; mirer; mordre; rechâsser; reluquer; remoucher; tapisser; viser; zyeuter.

règles *fpl*: affaires *fpl*; Anglais *mpl*; arcagnasses *mpl*; argantes *fpl*; cardinales *fpl*; carlets *mpl*; coquelicots *mpl*; doches *fpl*; histoires *fpl*; kangourou *m*; ours *mpl*; ragnagnas *mpl*; sauce *f* tomate; trucs *mpl*.

avoir ses règles: avoir ses lunes; les Anglais sont arrivés/ont débarqué; faire relâche; pavoiser; recevoir ses cousins; repeindre sa grille en rouge.

réjouissances *fpl*: bamboche *f*; bamboula *f*; bombance *f*; bombe *f*; bordée *f*; boum *f*; bringue *f*; faridon *f*; fiesta *f*; foire *f*; foiridon *f*; java *f*; noce *f*; nouba *f*; renversée *f*; ribote *f*; ribouldingue *f*; riboule *f*; surboum *f*; touzepar *f*; vadrouille *f*; virée *f*.

rendez-vous *m*: rambour *m*; rancart *m*; rembo *m*; rembour *m*; rencart *m*; rendève *m*.

renseignement *m*: duce *m*; info *f*; rancard *m*; rembours *mpl*; rencard *m*; rencart *m*; tubard *m*; tube *m*; tuyau *m*.

renseigner: affranchir; éclairer la lanterne à; embrayer sur; mettre à la page/au parfum/dans le coup; parfumer; rancarder; tuyauter.

réprimander: agonir; agrafer; aligner; assaisonner; attraper; casser; dégommer; dire ses quatre vérités à; donner le bal à; doper; doucher; engueuler (comme du poisson pourri); enguirlander; faire un amphi à; en faire voir des vertes et des pas mûres (à); filer/flanquer un savon à; habiller; incendier; laver la tête à; lessiver; mettre sur le tapis; moucher; passer une bonne engueulade/un (bon) savon à; ramasser; ramoner; remonter les bretelles à; sabouler; secouer (les puces à); sonner les cloches à; souffler dans les bronches à.

être réprimandé: écoper; en prendre pour son grade; recevoir un abattage/une saucée/une savonnée.

revolver *m*: arbalète *f*; arquebuse *f*; artillerie *f*; azor *m*; bagaf *m*; bastringue *m*; brelica *m*; brûle-gueule *m*; brûle-parfum(s) *m*; brutal *m*; calibre *m*; feu *m*; flingot *m*; flingue *m*; pétard *m*; pétoire *f*; pistolache *m*; remède *m*; ribarbère *m*; riboustin *m*; rifle *f*; riflette *f*; rigolo *m*; rigoustin *m*; soufflant *m*; tarpé *m*; tarpet *m*; tic-tac *m*.

riche: bourré (à bloc); calé; chargé; congestionné du morlingue; cousu d'or; flambant; au fric; friqué; galetteux; gonflé; gros; oseillé; péseux; au pèze; plein aux as; qui a du foin dans ses bottes; qui a le matelas; qui a le sac; qui roule dans le fric/sur l'or; rempli; richard; riflo(t); rupin; rupinos; tombé sur un champ d'oseille.

rien: balpeau; des clopinettes; des clous; des prunes; des queues; macache; mégot; de la merde; des nèfles; négatif; nib; niente; nix; pas une broque; la peau; peau de balle/de zébi; pet *m* de lapin; que dalle; que pouic; que t'chi; du vent; zéro.

rire: se bidonner; se boler; se boyauter; se crever; se fendre le bol/la gueule/la pêche/la pipe; se gondoler; se marrer; s'en payer une tranche; pisser dans sa culotte (de rire); se poiler; se pouffer; rigoler; rire à se faire mal aux côtes/à en crever/à s'en mouiller/à ventre déboutonné; se rouler; se taper/s'en taper le cul par terre; se taper/s'en taper le cul au plafond; se tenir les côtes; se tirebouchonner; se tordre (comme une baleine).

route *f*: antif(fe) *f*; bitume *m*; ruban *m*; trimard *m*.

ruiné: *voir* **pauvre**.

rupture *f*: lâchage *m*; largage *m*; malle *f*; mallouse *f*; plaquage *m*; valise *f*; valoche *f*.

Russe *mf*: Popof *mf*; Popov *mf*; Ruscof(f) *m*; Ruski *m*; Ruskof(f) *m*; Russkov *m*.

salaud *m*: affreux *m*; apache *m*; barlou *m*; bon-à-rien *m*; bordille *f*; (sale) bougre *m*; bourdille *f*; canaille *f*; casseur *m*; charognard *m*; charogne *f*; chieur *m*; con *m*; con(n)ard, -arde; connasse *f*; copaille *f*; couillon *m*; crapule *f*; ducon *m*; dur *m*; fils *m* de garce; fils *m* de pute; fripouillard *m*; fripouille *f*; fumier *m*; gale *f*; gouape *f*; gueule *f* de vache; homme *m* de sac et de corde; locdu *m*; loquedu *m*; loubard *m*; loulou *m*; malfrappe *m*; malfrat *m*; marlou *m*; marloupin *m*; mauvaise graine; minable *m*; mufle *m*; ordure *f*; pauvre type *m*; peau *f* de vache; pelure *f*; pourriture *f*; raclure *f*; rien-du-tout *m*; rosse *f*; sale coco *m*/mec *m*/type *m*; saligaud *m*; salopard *m*; salope *f*; teigne *f*; teigneux *m*; trouduc *m*; trou-du-cul *m*; vache *f*; vicelard *m*; zonard *m*.

sale: chiasseux; cochon; cracra; crade; cradingue; crado; crapoteux; crasp; craspec; craspèque; craspet; craspignol; craspouette; craspouillard; débectant; dégueu; dégueulasse; dégueulbif; dégueulpif; merdeux; merdique; minable; miteux; moche; pouilleux; saligaud; salingue; scatologique.

saleté *f:* chiure *f;* cochonnerie *f;* crassouille *f;* crotaille *f;* crotte *f;* merde *f;* merdoie *f;* merdouille *f;* saloperie *f.*

seins *mpl:* amortisseurs *mpl;* ananas *mpl;* avantages *mpl;* avant-postes *mpl;* avant-scène *f;* balcon *m;* ballons *mpl;* blagues *fpl* à tabac; boîtes *fpl* à lait/à lolo; devanture *f;* dodoches *fpl;* doudounes *fpl;* flotteurs *mpl;* globes *mpl;* laiterie *f;* loloches *mpl;* lolos *mpl;* mandarines *fpl;* melons *mpl;* miches *fpl;* du monde au balcon; montgolfières *fpl;* nénés *mpl;* nibards *mpl;* niches *mpl;* nichons *mpl;* œufs *mpl* sur le plat; oranges *fpl;* pare-chocs *mpl;* pelotes *fpl;* roberts *mpl;* rondins *mpl;* roploplots *mpl;* rotoplots *mpl;* rototos *mpl;* tétasses *fpl;* tétés *mpl;* tétines *fpl;* tétons *mpl;* totoches *fpl.*

(*Voir* **poitrine**)

sentir: blairer; renifler.

sentir mauvais: boucaner; chlipoter; chocotter; cocot(t)er; cogner; cornancher; corner; dégager; emboucaner; foisonner; fouetter; plomber; polker; poquer; puer; refouler; renifler; rougnotter; (s)chlinguer; sentir la crevette; taper; trouillotter.

sentir mauvais de la bouche: plomber du goulot; puer du bec; refouler (du goulot); repousser (du goulot); taper du saladier; tuer les mouches à quinze pas.

seringue *f:* hypo *mf;* lance *f;* poussette *f;* shooteuse *f.*

sexe *m* **de la femme:** abricot *m;* as *m* de pique; baba *m;* baigneur *m;* barbu *m;* baveux *m;* bégonia *m;* bénitier *m;* berlingot *m;* bijou *m* de famille; boîte *f* à ouvrage; bonbon *m;* boutique *f;* bréviaire *m* d'amour; centre *m;* chagatte *f;* chat *m;* chatte *f;* cheminée *f;* chignon *m;* cicatrice *f;* con *m;* con(n)asse *f;* crac *m;* cramouille *f;* craque *f;* craquette *f;* crevasse *f;* didi *m;* didine *f;* étau *m;* fendasse *f;* fente *f;* figue *f;* foufoune *f;* foufounette *f;* founette *f;* fri-fri *m;* greffière *f;* grippette *f;* millefeuille *m;* mimi *m;* minet *m;* minou *m;* mistigri *m;* moniche *f;* motte *f;* moule *f;* nénuphar *m;* panier *m* (d'amour); pâquerette *f;* pince *f;* portail *m;* potage *m;* tabernacle *m;* tire-lire *f;* triangle *m* des

Bermudes; turlu *m;* zigouigoui *m.*

sexe *m* **de l'homme:** artillerie *f;* bazar *m;* bijoux *mpl* de famillle; boutique *f;* devant *m;* histoire *f;* marchandise *f;* panoplie *f;* paquet *m;* piège *m* à mémé; service *m* trois pièces.

(*Voir* **pénis; testicules**)

sodomiser: baiser à la riche; caser; casser coco; casser le pot/la rondelle; dauffer; défoncer la pastille/la rondelle; emmancher; empaffer; empaler; empapaouter; empétarder; emproser; encaldosser; enculer; enfirer; englander; entigner; goûter la terre jaune; miser; passer par la porte de derrière; planter; pointer; prendre du bronze/de l'oignon/du petit/du sonore; prendre le thé; prendre par le petit; tourner la page; tremper la soupe; troncher.

sœur *f:* fraline *f;* frangine *f;* frangipane *f;* frelotte *f.*

soif (avoir): avoir la dalle en pente; avoir le gosier sec; avoir la pépie; cracher blanc/des pièces de dix sous; la péter; la sécher.

soldat *m:* bidasse *m;* biffin *m;* deuxième pompe *f;* gribier *m;* grif(e)ton *m;* griveton *m;* grivier *m;* pioupiou *m;* tourlourou *m;* troubade *m;* trouf(f)ion *m;* vert-de-gris *m.*

sou *m:* bourgue *m;* croque *m;* fléchard *m;* kope(c)k *m;* pelot *m;* radis *m;* rond *m;* rotin *m.*

sourd: constipé/dur de la feuille; ensablé des portugaises; sourdingue (comme un pot).

souteneur *m:* Alphonse *m;* barbeau *m;* broche *f;* brochet *m;* brocheton *m;* dos fin/vert; estaf(f)ier *m;* hareng *m;* Jules *m;* Julot *m;* mac *m;* mangeur *m* de blanc/de brioche; maquereau *m;* marchand *m* de barbaque/de bidoche/de viande; marle *m;* marlou *m;* marloupin *m;* mec *m;* mecton *m;* merlan *m;* poiscaille *m;* poiscal *m;* poisson *m;* proxémac *m;* proxo *m;* rabat *m;* rabatteur *m;* sauré *m;* sauret *m.*

être souteneur: être julot; faire le mac/le maquereau; relever les compteurs.

sperme *m:* blanc *m;* came *f;* camelote *f;* crème *f;* foutre *m;* jus *m* de corps/de cyclope; purée *f;* sauce *f;* semoule *f;* venin *m.*

stupéfait: asphyxié; assis; baba; bleu; catastrophé; cisaillé; comme deux ronds de flan; époustouflé; estomaqué; scié; sidéré; soufflé; sur le cul.

suicider, se: s'accrocher; se balancer dans la Seine; se but(t)er; se déramer; s'envoyer en l'air; se faire la peau; se faire sauter la caisse/le caisson; se flanquer en l'air; se flinguer; se foutre en l'air.

syphilis *f*: chtouille *f*; daube *f*; lazziloffe *f*; naze *m*; nazebroque *m*; schtouille *f*; sigma *m*; syphilo *f*; syphlotte *f*; vérole *f*.

avoir la syphilis: être laziloffe/naze(broque); être du syndicat.

tabac *m*: herbe *f*; percale *m*; perle *f*; perlot *m*; pétun *m*; tref *m*; trèfle *m*.

taire, se: avoir la bouche cousue; bonnir lap(e); ne pas en casser une; la boucler; écraser; s'éteindre; s'étouffer; fermer sa boîte/son clapet/sa gueule; la fermer; manger son bifteck; la mettre en veilleuse; (se) mettre un bouchon; ne pas en casser une; ne pas moufter; ne pas piper; poser sa chique; rengracier; taire sa gueule; tirer sa fermeture éclair.

faire taire: boucler la trappe à; brider; clouer (le bec à); mettre un bouchon à; museler; rabattre le caquet à; rembarrer; river le clou à.

tais-toi!: ta bouche! boucle-la! boucle ton égout! ferme-la! la ferme! ferme ta gueule! ta gueule!

taxi *m*: bahut *m*; hotte *f*; loche *m ou f*; rampant *m*; rongeur *m*; sapin *m*; tac *m*; taquemard *m*; tax *m*; tire *f*.

téléphone *m*: bigo(phone) *m*; bigorneau *m*; biniou *m*; cornichon *m*; escargot *m*; grelot *m*; phonard *m*; ronflant *m*; ronfleur *m*; télémuche *m*; tube *m*; turlu *m*; tutu *m*.

testicules *fpl*: balloches *fpl*; balustrines *fpl*; bibelots *mpl*; bijoux *mpl* de famille; billes *fpl*; blosses *fpl*; bonbons *mpl*; breloques *fpl*; burettes *fpl*; burnes *fpl*; claouis *mpl*; clopinettes *fpl*; couilles *fpl*; couillons *mpl*; croquignoles *fpl*; glaouis *mpl*; joyeuses *fpl*; montgolfières *fpl*; noisettes *fpl*; noix *fpl*; olives *fpl*; paire *f*; pendantes *fpl*; pendeloques *fpl*; précieuses *fpl*; rognons *mpl*; roubignolles *fpl*; rouleaux *mpl*; roupes *fpl*; roupettes *fpl*; roupignolles *fpl*; roustons *mpl*; témoins *mpl* à décharge; valseuses *fpl*.

tête *f*: baigneur *m*; bille *f*; binette *f*; bobèche *f*; bobéchon *m*; bobine *f*; bocal *m*; bougie *f*; bouille *f*; bouillotte *f*; boule *f*; bourrichon *m*; boussole *f*; burette *f*; caberlot *m*; caboche *f*; cabochon *m*; cafetière *f*; caillou *m*; carafe *f*; carafon *m*; cassis *m*; chetron *m*; chignon *m*; chou *m*; ciboulot *m*; cigare *m*; citron *m*; citrouille *f*; coco *m*; coiffe *f*; fiole *f*; frite *f*; gadin *m*; gourde *f*; mansarde *f*; mufle *m*; nénette *f*; patate *f*; pêche *f*; plafond *m*; poire *f*; pomme *f*; sinoquet *m*; siphon *m*; terrine *f*; tétère *f*; téterre *f*; théière *f*; tirelire *f*; tomate *f*; toupie *f*; tranche *f*; trogne *f*; trognon *m*; trombine *f*; tronc *m*; tronche *f*.

tirer (*une arme à feu*): canarder; défourailler; envoyer/lâcher la fumée/la purée/la sauce; faire un carton; flingot(t)er; flinguer; révolvériser.

tomber: aller à dam(e); aller valser dans les décors; se casser la figure/la gueule; chuter; faire un valdingue; se ficher/se foutre la gueule en l'air/par terre; se gaufrer; partir à dame; se planter; prendre/ramasser une bûche/un gadin/une pelle/un valdingue; quimper; valdinguer.

tracasser, se: se biler; se cailler; se casser le baigneur/la tête/le tronc; s'en faire; se faire de la bile/des cheveux (blancs)/des crins/du mauvais sang/du mouron/de la mousse/un sang d'encre; se monter le bourrichon; se turlupiner.

travail *m*: bis(e)ness *m*; boulot *m*; bricolage *m*; charbon *m*; coltin *m*; coltinage *m*; flambeau *m*; flanche *f*; gâche *f*; gratin *m*; job *m*; piège *m* à bagnard; placarde *f*; truc *m*; turbin *m*.

travailler dur: bosser (comme une bête/un nègre); boulonner; bûcher; buriner; se cailler; se casser (le cul/le fion); se crever le cul/la paillasse; se décarcasser; en donner (une secousse); s'échiner; s'éreinter; s'esquinter; s'expliquer; en ficher/en foutre un coup/une secousse; mouiller sa chemise/sa liquette/son maillot; pinocher; piocher; pisser du sang; suer (sang et eau); taper dans la butte; travailler comme une bête/un chien/un nègre; trimer; turbiner; usiner.

travailleur, -euse: bête *f* à concours; bosseur *m*; boulot *m*; bûcheur, -euse; piocheur, -euse; prolo *m*; pue-la-sueur *m*; turbineur *m*.

tricher: arnaquer; arrangemaner; avoir; biseauter; doubler; échauder; empalmer; entuber; étriller; faisander; flouer; maquiller; quiller; rangemaner; truander.

tricheur, -euse: arnaqueur, -euse; arrangeman *m*; biseauteur *m*; empalmeur *m*; entôleuse *f*; faisan *m*; faisandier *m*; faiseur *m*; fileur, -euse; floueur, -euse; maquilleur, -euse; rangemane *m*; rangeur *m*.

tromper: arnaquer; arranger; avoir; baiser; balader; bidonner; blouser; bluffer; carotter; charrier; doubler; emmener; empiler; endormir; enfiler; enfler; enfoncer;

entifler; entôler; entuber; envoyer au charbon; faire (à l'oseille); faire monter à l'échelle; faire un tournant à; ficher/foutre dedans; gour(r)er; jardiner; jobarder; maquiller; mettre dedans; monter le job à; monter un bateau à; niquer; posséder; quiller; ranger; refaire; rouler (dans la farine); roustir; serviotter.

trottoir m: bitume m; pavé m; ruban m; turf m.

trouver: voir **découvrir.**

tuer: voir **assassiner.**

uriner: aller faire sa petite commission; arroser les marguerites; changer d'eau son poisson/changer le poisson d'eau; égoutter son colosse/son cyclope/sa sardine; se l'égoutter; faire pipi; faire pleurer le colosse/le costaud/le petit Jésus; faire sa goutte; se faire une vidange; jeter de la lance; jeter sa goutte; lâcher l'eau/l'écluse/un fil; lancecailler; lancequiner; lansquiner; lisbroquer; lispoquer; mouiller une ardoise; ouvrir les écluses; pisser; pisser son coup; prendre une ardoise à l'eau; quimper la lance; renverser la vapeur; tenir l'âne par la queue; tirer un fil; verser de l'eau; (femme) arroser le persil; humecter sa fourrure; mouiller son gazon.

urinoir m: ardoises fpl; lavabe m; pissoir m; pissotière f; pissotoire f; tasse f (à thé); théière f.

vagabond m: cloche f; clodo m; clodomir m; clodot m; grelotteux m; mouisard m; refileur m de comète; traîne-lattes m; traîne-patins m; traîne-pattes m; traîne-sabots m; traîne-savates m; trimard m; vacant m; zonard m.

(Voir **clochard, -arde**)

vagin m: voir **sexe** m **de la femme.**

vantard, -arde: baratineur, -euse; blagueur, -euse; bluffeur, -euse; bourreur m de crâne; chiqueur, -euse; cracheur, -euse; cravateur m; esbrouf(f)eur, -euse; fort m en gueule; frimeur, -euse; fumiste m; grande gueule; gueulard, -arde; musicien m; rambineur, -euse; vanneur, -euse.

vaurien m: voir **salaud.**

ventre m: ballon m; balourd m; baquet m; battant m; bedaine f; bedon m; bide m; bidon m; bocal m; boîte f à ragoût; brioche f; buffecaille m; buffet m; bureau m; burlingue m; caisse f; fusil m; gras-double m; panse f; sac m à tripes; tiroir m (à poulet).

(Voir **estomac**)

veste f: alezingue f; alpague f; alpingue f; cuir m; pelure f; recui m; ted m; teddy m; vestouse f; zomblou m.

vêtements mpl: fringues fpl; frip(p)es fpl; frusques fpl; harnais mpl; linges mpl; loques fpl; nippes fpl; pelure f; sapes fpl; vêtures fpl.

viande f: barbaque f; bidoche f; carne f; charogne f.

vieillir: avoir de la bouteille/du flacon; être bon pour la casse; faire d'occasion; se fossiliser; prendre de la bouteille/du flacon; prendre un coup de vieux; sentir la fin de saison; s'en retourner; vioquir.

vieux: amorti; bibard; bléchard; blèche; croulant; périmé; viocard; vioque.

vieux, vieille: ancêtre m; bonze m; croulant m; (vieux) croûton; fossile m; (vieux) kroumir; mémé f; pépé m; périmé m; PPH m; soixante-dix-huit tours m; vestige m; vieille baderne/croûte/noix; vieux birbe/débris/jeton/rococo; vieux trumeau; vioc m; viocard, -arde; vioquard, -arde; vioque mf; vioquerie f.

vin m: blanc m; brouille-ménage m; brutal m; décapant m; destructeur m; gingin m; gobette f; gorgeon m; du gros (qui tache); gros bleu; gros-cul m; gros rouge; jaja m; petit velours; pichetegorne m; pichtogorme m; pichtogorne m; picolo m; picrate m; picton m; pif m; pinard m; pive m; piveton m; pivois m; reginglard m; reglinguet m; rouquemoute mf; rouquin m; rouquinos m; sens m unique; tutu m; vitriol m.

visage m: balle f; bille f; binette f; bobine f; bougie f; bouille f; bouillotte f; boule f; burette f; cerise f; fiole f; fraise f; frime f; frimousse f; frite f; gargamelle f; gargane f; gaufre f; gueule f; hure f; margoulette f; museau m; poire f; pomme f; portrait m; terrine f; tirelire f; trogne f; trognon m; trombine f; trompette f; tronche f; vitrine f.

vite: à fond de train; à fond la caisse; à fond les gamelles/les manettes; à la vitesse grand V; à plein(s) tube(s); à tout bersingue/berzingue; à toute barre; à toute blinde; à toute bombe; à toute bringue; à toute(s) pompe(s); à toute vibure; comme un zèbre; dare-dare; en cinq sec; en deux coups de cuillère à pot; en moins de deux; en quatrième vitesse; fissa; presto; quatre à quatre; rapide; rapidos; vite fait.

aller vite: aller la poignée dans le coin; avoiner; bomber; bousculer les bornes;

brûler le pavé/la route; dépoter; filer comme un dard; filocher; foncer; gazer; se magner le train; pédaler; rajouter de la sauce; rouler à plein(s) gaz/à toute pompe; tracer; tricoter.

(vieille) voiture: bagnole *f*; bahut *m*; berlingot *m*; bringue *f*; caisse *f*; charrette *f*; chiotte *f*; guimbarde *f*; guinde *f*; hotte *f*; tacot *m*; tape-cul *m*; tinette *f*; tire *f*; tombereau *m*; traîne-cons *m*; tulette *f*.

voler: accrocher; acheter à la foire d'empoigne; arranger; car(r)er; chaparder; chauffer; chiper; choper; chouraver; dégraisser; dégringoler; donner une secousse à; doubler; écorcher; empalmer; empiler; emplafonner; emplâtrer; engourdir; enquiller; escan(n)er; estamper; étouffer; étourdir; fabriquer; faire; faire sauter; faire une main tombée; faucher; gauler; grapper; grappiner; griffer; grincher; lever; pégrer; piquer; plumer; poirer; poisser; raboter; ratiboiser; ratisser; refaire; rincer; roustir; secouer; soulever; sucrer; tirer; toucher.

(*Voir* **cambrioler**)
voleur, -euse: barbotteur, -euse; carotteur, -euse; carottier *m*; carreur *m*; chapardeur, -euse; chipeur, -euse; chopeur, -euse; doubleur *m*; encanneur *m*; faucheur *m*; filou *m*; gauleur *m*; grinche *m*; leveur *m*; pégriot *m*; piqueur *m*; roustisseur *m*, -euse.
(*Voir* **cambrioleur**)
vomir: aller au refil(e)/au renard; bader; débagouler; déballer ses outils; dégobiller; dégoupillonner; dégueuler; fuser; gerber; lâcher sa came/une fusée; refiler (la came); renarder.

voyou *m*: *voir* **salaud**.
WC *mpl*: azor *m*; cabinces *fpl*; cagoinces *mpl*; chiards *mpl*; chiottes *fpl*; débourre *f*; garde-manger *m*; gogs *mpl*; goguenots *mpl*; gogues *mpl*; lieux *mpl*; ouatères *mpl*; petit coin; pipi-room *m*; tartine *f*; tartiss *m*; tartisses *fpl*; tartissoir *m*; tartissoires *mpl*; téléphone *m*; tinettes *fpl*; vécés *mpl*.
yeux *mpl*: *voir* **œil**.

Part 2

French-English

Tableau des Symboles Phonétiques

Voyelles

[i]	pignole snif zizi	[y]	cruche mur ruban truc usine
[e]	chez étriller légume	[ø]	peu feu nœud queue
[ɛ]	chèvre perle pelle resto terre maison	[œ]	peur œuf sœur feuille
		[ə]	le ce quenotte premier
[a]	patte chat tape roile phare	[ɛ̃]	plein machin chien crin
		[ɑ̃]	enfance arranger temps branche sans vent
[ɑ]	gâche paille pâté sable		
[ɔ]	mort bol Popaul	[ɔ̃]	bon tonton monte plomb compte
[o]	pot môme chérot taule		
[u]	tout goût genou coup roue	[œ̃]	un lundi parfum

Consonnes et Semi-Consonnes

[p]	père pain soupe type	[ʒ]	gilet manger gingin cage jeune
[b]	beau bol roberts		
[m]	trumeau main femme	[k]	quart coup klebs fac
[f]	feu bref neuf phrase photo	[g]	gare bague gueule
[v]	voyage grève vrille voir	[ɲ]	campagne gnôle figne niard
[t]	attigé table thune ticket vite	[ŋ]	frotting skating
[d]	dondon danse rondelle coude	[r]	arbre rhume rubis tenir rancart terre
[n]	nougat canne ananas nègre	[ks]	accident action
[s]	sou cirer six scier dessous	[gz]	exister examen
[z]	zéro zézette cuisine basane deuxio	[j]	yeux voyager travailler pied piano
[l]	lait clille aile facile	[w]	noir waters nouer oui
[ʃ]	chat moche miche schnock	[ɥ]	huile reluire aiguille

A

à [a] *prép P* 1. (*s'emploie pour 'de'*) la voiture à mon frère, my brother's car 2. (*s'emploie pour 'chez'*) je vais au coiffeur, I'm going to the hairdresser's. (*Voir* **aller 1, 2**)

abattage [abataʒ] *nm* 1. *Vieilli F* recevoir un abattage, to get told off/to get ticked off 2. *F* rushed work/rush job/quickie; (*livre*) potboiler 3. *F* dynamism; avoir de l'abattage, to be full of go/zest; (*d'un acteur, d'un politicien, etc*) to have charisma; avoir de la graisse d'abattage, to have energy/zest; to be superior 4. *P* faire de l'abattage, (*prostituée*) to get through a succession of clients quickly. (*Voir* **maison 1**)

abatteur, -euse [abatœr, -øz] *n F* abatteur de besogne, hard worker/slogger; workaholic.

abattis [abati] *nm P* arm*; *in pl* limbs; arms*; legs*; tu risques de te casser les abattis si tu sautes, you'll break your legs if you jump; numérote tes abattis! (*avant une lutte*) I'll break every bone in your body!

abattre [abatr] *vtr F* 1. en abattre, to get through a lot of work; to be a glutton for work; to be a workaholic; (*distance*; *Fig*) to cover a lot of ground 2. ne pas se laisser abattre, to eat heartily/to tuck in. (*Voir* **bois 1**)

abbaye [abei] *nf A P* l'abbaye (de Monte-à-Regret/de Monte-à-Rebours/de Saint-Pierre), the scaffold/the guillotine.

abîmer [abime] *vtr F* abîmer qn (a) (*dans la presse, etc*) to run s.o. down/to slate s.o. (b) to beat s.o. up*/to knock s.o. about/to work s.o. over; se faire abîmer, to get beaten up/to get worked over/to get knocked about. (*Voir* **portrait** (*b*))

abonné [abɔne] *F* I *a* être abonné à qch, (*échec etc*) to make a habit of sth II *n* être aux abonnés absents, (*ivre, inconscient*) to be out for the count/blotto; (*sans réaction*) not to react; to show no reaction/no emotion; se mettre aux abonnés absents, (*ne pas réagir*) to switch off.

abouler [abule] I *vtr P* (a) to give/to hand over; aboule ça (ici)! give it here!/let's have it!; abouler le fric, to pay* up/to fork out/to cough up (b) abouler sa graisse/sa viande = s'abouler II *vpr* **s'abouler** *P* to arrive*/to come along; alors, tu t'aboules? well, are you coming?/come on!

aboyeur [abwajœr] *nm* 1. *F* (*théâtre, cirque, etc*) tout/barker 2. *A P* revolver*/shooter 3. (*courses*) individual* who gives racing tips in exchange for a percentage of the profits/tipster.

abricot [abriko] *nm V* female genitals*/fanny/fig.

abruti [abryti] *nm F* 1. drunk/drunkard*/drunken bum 2. fool*/idiot/blockhead; quel abruti! what a clot!/what a moron!

abus [aby] *nm F* (il) y a de l'abus!/y a un peu d'abus! that's going a bit too far!/that's a bit much!

acabit [akabi] *nm F* (*souvent Péj*) des gens de son acabit, people of his sort/people like him; ils sont du même acabit, they're birds of a feather/they're tarred with the same brush.

académie [akademi] *nf F* (*esp femme*) body; avoir une belle académie, to have an attractive body/a shapely figure; to have curves in all the right places; elle a une belle académie, she's well stacked.

accident [aksidɑ̃] *nm F* (a) miscarriage, unplanned pregnancy, etc; ma petite sœur, c'était un accident, my little sister was an afterthought (b) any delicate or embarrassing situation (*eg* bankruptcy, imprisonment, etc) (c) avoir un accident, (*enfant*) to wet one's pants.

accidenter [aksidɑ̃te] *vtr F* to damage (another car, etc) in an accident.

s'accointer [sakwɛ̃te] *vpr F Péj* s'accointer avec qn, to take up with s.o.; to become chummy/pally with s.o.; il s'accointe avec cette femme, he's knocking around with that woman.

accommoder [akɔmɔde] *vtr F* **1.** je vais l'accommoder, I'll soon sort him out/fix him (up) **2.** *(a)* accommoder qn à toutes les sauces, to use s.o. as an odd-job man/as a general factotum *(b)* accommoder qch à toutes les sauces, to use sth for just about everything **3.** accommoder qn au beurre noir, to give s.o. a black eye*.

accordéon [akɔrdeɔ̃] *nm* **1.** *F* en accordéon, *(pare-chocs, etc)* bashed-in/dented/crumpled (up) **2.** *F (Aut, cyclisme)* string of (racing) cars, bikes which close up in a bunch and then become strung out again; faire l'accordéon, to get bunched up/to concertina; rouler en accordéon, *(voitures)* to stop and start **3.** *P (argot policier)* heavy police record/form.

accorder [akɔrde] *vtr F (tomber d'accord)* accorder ses violons, to come to an agreement; *(se concerter)* to agree to tell the same story/to agree on a (version of a) story.

accoucher [akuʃe] *vi F* **1.** to confess*/to come clean; mais accouche donc! come on, out with it!/spit it out!/give!/shoot! faire accoucher un prisonnier, to make a prisoner talk/grass **2.** to be indecisive; to be late; alors, tu viens? t'accouches ou quoi? are you coming? what are you waiting for?

accro [akro] *F (abrév = accroché)* **I** *a* = accroché **II** *n (de jazz, de cinéma)* fanatic/addict; *(drogué)* drug addict*/junkie.

accrochage [akrɔʃaʒ] *nm F (petite dispute)* row.

accroche [akrɔʃ] *nf* **1.** *Vieilli F (publicité)* eye-catching advertisement; *(verbal)* striking (publicity) slogan **2.** *P* l'accroche, *(drogues)* habit/hook; the drug scene/drug addicts (in general) **3.** *Vieilli F* avoir l'accroche de qn, to be loved by s.o.

accroché [akrɔʃe] *a P* être accroché *(a)* to be in debt/in the red *(b)* *(also* rester accroché)* to be arrested*/held for questioning *(c)* to be brave*/to have guts/to have balls *(d)* *(drogues)* to be addicted/hooked/strung out *(e)* to be infatuated* (with s.o.)/to be hung up on (s.o.).

accrocher [akrɔʃe] **I** *vtr* **1.** *F* essayer d'accrocher un mari, to look for a husband **2.** *F* accrocher qn, to buttonhole s.o./to corner s.o. **3.** *F (marketing) (a)* to capture (a market) *(b)* accrocher une affaire, to clinch a deal **4.** *P* se l'accrocher, to be deprived of (sth)/to go without (sth); tu peux te l'accrocher! you can whistle for it!/you can kiss goodbye to

that! **5.** *P* to steal* (sth) **II** *vi P* **1.** to have problems/trouble; les négociations ont accroché, there's been a hitch in the negotiations; ça n'a pas du tout accroché, *(entre deux personnes)* they didn't get on/they didn't click **2.** to begin to take interest; to begin to succeed; les maths, j'accroche pas encore, I'm not getting anywhere with maths **3.** se faire accrocher, to be arrested*/held for questioning **III** *vpr* **s'accrocher** *F* **1.** to hang oneself **2.** to make an effort/to stick at it; il faut t'accrocher si tu veux réussir, you've got to hang in there if you want to succeed; tu peux t'accrocher, you haven't the least chance of succeeding/you'll never make it; *Iron* accroche-toi, Jeannot! *(bon courage)* and the best of luck to you! **3.** *(se dit à l'annonce d'une nouvelle surprenante, etc)* accroche-toi, hold on to your hat/have I got news for you **4.** s'accrocher avec qn *(a) (courses, etc)* to catch up with s.o./to draw level with s.o. *(b)* to have a row with s.o./to pitch into s.o. **5.** s'accrocher à une drogue, to take a drug/to get hooked on a drug.

accrocheur, -euse [akrɔʃœr, -øz] *F* **I** *n* tenacious bore*/leech/clinger **II** *a (a)* stubborn/pig-headed; un vendeur très accrocheur, a very persistent/persuasive salesman *(b)* eye-catching; une pub accrocheuse, an eye-catching ad.

accroch'man [akrɔʃman] *a F* = accroché.

accu [aky] *nm F (abrév = accumulateur)* accumulator; recharger les accus, *(boire)* to have another drink; *(manger)* to have a bite more to eat; *(dormir)* to have a snooze.

accueil [akœj] *nm P Iron (argot policier)* comité d'accueil, welcoming committee.

accuser [akyze] *vtr F* accuser le coup, to react strongly; il a mal accusé le coup, it really hit him hard/the blow really went home.

achar, d' [daʃar] *adv phr P (abrév = acharnement) (a)* travailler d'achar, to work* hard/like mad; to go at it hammer and tongs *(b)* d'achar et d'autor, with insistence. *(Voir* autor, d')

acheter [aʃte] *vtr F* to bribe* (s.o.)/to buy (s.o.) off; acheter la complicité de qn, to buy s.o.'s silence; le flic s'est laissé acheter, the cop didn't object to being bought/bribed.

acide [asid] *nm F* drug(s); *esp* LSD*/acid; prendre de l'acide, to take/to drop acid; être sous acide, to be under the influence of drugs; to be high.

acidulé, -ée [asidyle] *P* (*drogues*) **I** *n* (habitual) user of LSD*/acid head/acid freak **II** *a* trouille acidulée, depression due to LSD*/ acid funk.

acompte [akɔ̃t] *nm* **1.** *F* tiens, mange, c'est un petit acompte, this'll give you a taste of what's to come **2.** *P* prendre un acompte, to have sex* before marriage/to sample the goods.

à-côté [akote] *nm F* extra; à-côtés, (little) extras/perks; a bit on the side; son boulot lui donne la possibilité de faire des petits à-côtés, his job gives him the chance to make a little bit on the side.

acrais! [akrɛ], **acré!** [akre] *int Vieilli P* look out!/watch it!/careful!/mind out! acrais! v'là les flics! beat it! here come the cops!

acteuse [aktøz] *nf P Péj* actress devoid of talent.

action [aksjɔ̃] *nf F* ses actions sont en hausse/en baisse, things are looking up/aren't looking too good for him.

activer [aktive] *vi F* to hurry* up/to get a move on; activons! let's get cracking!/let's make it snappy! activez! get moving!/move it!

Adam [adɑ̃] *Prnm F* dans le/en costume d'Adam, (*homme*) naked*/in the altogether/in one's birthday suit. (*Voir* **Ève**; **fourchette 2**)

adieu, *pl* **-ieux** [adjø] *nm & int F* **1.** faire ses adieux à qch, to kiss sth goodbye; tu peux lui dire adieu! you can kiss it goodbye!/you can say goodbye to that!/you can forget it! **2.** adieu Berthe!/adieu la valise! it's all up!/it's curtains!

adja [adʒa] *nm ou f P* faire l'adja/mettre les adjas/se tirer des adjas, to run away*/to beat it/to clear off/to do a bunk.

adjudant [adʒydɑ̃] *nm F* (*a*) *Mil* coucher avec la femme de l'adjudant, to be put in the guardroom (*b*) domineering person; cette femme, c'est un vrai adjudant, that woman's a real bully.

adjupète [adʒypɛt] *nm P Mil* warrant officer.

ado [ado] *F* (*abrév* = *adolescent*) **1.** *a inv* teenage **2.** *n* teenager; les ados, teenagers.

adresse [adrɛs] *nf F* vous vous êtes trompé d'adresse! you've got the wrong place/you've come to the wrong person (mate)!

afanaf [afanaf] *adv P* half and half/fifty-fifty; faire afanaf, to go halves/to go fifty-fifty/to go even steven/to split (it) down the middle.

affaire [afɛr] *nf* **1.** *F* illegal operation/ business; shady deal **2.** faire son affaire à qn, *F* (*punir, châtier*) to give s.o. what-for; *P* to kill* s.o./to do s.o. in/to bump s.o. off **3.** *F* la belle affaire! so what?/big deal! **4.** *F* ce n'est pas une affaire d'État! it's not a National Emergency! **5.** *F* faire/aller à ses affaires, to defecate*/to go to the loo/to do one's duty **6.** *F* elle a ses affaires, she's got her period*/she's got the curse/it's the (wrong) time of the month **7.** *F* son affaire est claire, I'll settle him/I'll sort him out; I've settled him **8.** *F* montrer son affaire, (*surt enfant*) to show one's 'private property'/= to play mummies and daddies **9.** *F* c'est une affaire, it's a (real) bargain/it's a snip **10.** *F* où en sont tes affaires? how's your love life? **11.** *P* man* *or* woman* who is good in bed/a good lay; c'est une affaire, ce type, that bloke's a really good lay/that guy's fantastic in bed; ce n'est pas une affaire, he's/she's no good in bed **12.** *F* ne pas lâcher l'affaire, to persevere/not to give up/not to give in.

s'affaler [safale] *vpr* **1.** *F* to flop/to slump/to sag; s'affaler dans un fauteuil, to flop into an armchair; ne vous affalez pas! (*à un élève*) sit up (straight)! **2.** *P* to confess*/to come clean/to grass.

affection [afɛksjɔ̃] *nf F* être en retard d'affection, to be hard up (sexually); je suis en retard d'affection, I haven't made love in ages.

affiche [afiʃ] *nf F* affected person; c'est une affiche, he's very camp; faire l'affiche, to show off*/to flaunt oneself; (*homosexuel*) to camp it up; c'est l'affiche, it's just for show.

affiché [afiʃe] *a F* c'est affiché! it's in the bag!/it's a (dead) cert! j'achète la maison, c'est affiché, it's all settled, I'm buying the house.

affirmatif! [afirmatif] *int F* (*esp Mil*) affirmative!/roger!

afflure [aflyr] *nm ou f P* = **affure**.

afflurer [aflyre] *vtr & i P* = **affurer**.

affranchi, -ie [afrɑ̃ʃi] *a & n* **1.** *F* (*a*) totally unscrupulous (person)/nasty piece of work (*b*) (person) who has nothing to learn about sex, vice, etc **2.** *P* (person) who sticks to the code of honour of the underworld. (*Voir* **cicatrice**)

affranchir [afrɑ̃ʃir] *vtr* **1.** *F* affranchir qn, (*informer, avertir*) to put s.o. in the picture/to gen s.o. up/to give s.o. the low-down/to put s.o. in the know/to tip s.o. off **2.** *P* to initiate (s.o.) sexually **3.** *P* to corrupt/to get at/to nobble (s.o.). (*Voir* **couleur 3**)

affreux [afrø] *nm* 1. *F* objectionable person/ nasty piece of work; creep 2. *P* (*esp* white) mercenary (*usu engaged in African conflict*). (*Voir* **jojo II 1**)

affure [afyr] *nm ou f P* 1. profit/gain; faire de l'affure, to find it profitable 2. avoir de l'affure, to have the edge (on/over s.o.).

affurer [afyre] *P* I *vtr* 1. to make a profit out of (sth); faire affurer son fric, to put one's money to good use/to make one's money work 2. to reach/to arrive at; mon fiston affure ses quinze berges, my lad's coming up to fifteen 3. (*courses*) en affurer une, to win a race 4. to make/earn (money); affurer mille balles, to make 1000 francs 5. to obtain/get hold of (sth) II *vi* to make money; to wheel and deal; affurer gros, to make money hand over fist/to rake it in.

affûter [afyte] *vtr* 1. *F* (*sport*) affûter la forme, to get down to some serious training 2. *P* (*voleurs, etc*) to recruit (s.o.) as mercenary for a specific task.

affutiaux [afytjo] *nmpl P* tools.

afghan [afgɑ̃] *nm P* (*drogues*) hashish* from Afghanistan/afghan.

afnaf [afnaf] *adv P* = **afanaf**.

afro [afro] *a inv F* African/afro; elle a une coupe (de cheveux) afro, she's got an afro cut.

agace-cul [agasky] *nm V* penis*/prick.

agace-machin [agasmaʃɛ̃] *nm P* itching/ itchiness.

agacer [agase] *vtr V* agacer le sous-préfet, to masturbate*/to flog the bishop/to flog the mutton.

agates [agat] *nfpl P* eyes*/lamps.

agglo [aglo] *nm* (*abbr* = *aggloméré*) con-glomerate; fibreboard.

agité, -ée [aʒite] *n F* un(e) agité(e) (du bocal), a mad person*/a headcase/a loony.

agiter [aʒite] *P* I *vtr* les agiter, to run away*/to scarper/to beat it II *vpr* s'agiter, to hurry up*/to shake a leg.

agobilles [agɔbij] *nfpl V* testicles*/balls/ bollocks.

agonir [agɔnir] *vtr F* agonir qn d'injures, to hurl abuse at s.o./to let s.o. have it (good and proper)/to eff and blind at s.o.

agrafer [agrafe] *vtr F* 1. to buttonhole (s.o.)/to corner (s.o.) 2. to arrest*/to nab/to nick; il s'est fait agrafer par les flics, he got nicked by the cops 3. to steal*/to hook/to nick.

agreg, agrég [agrɛg] *nf F* (*abbr* = *agréga-*

tion) competitive State exam for teaching posts in French lycées.

agri [agri] *nm F* student at an agricultural college.

agrichage [agriʃaʒ] *nm P* arrest/nicking.

agricher [agriʃe] *vtr*, **agriffer** [agrife] *vtr P* 1. to grab (hold of) (s.o.) 2. to arrest*/to nick (s.o.)/to run (s.o.) in.

agro [agro] *nm F* student at the *Institut national agronomique*.

aguichant [agiʃɑ̃] *a F* seductive/ provocative/inviting/alluring/arousing/sexy.

aguicher [agiʃe] *vtr F* 1. to excite*/to arouse (s.o.)/to lead (s.o.) on/to give (s.o.) the come-on/to prick-tease 2. to excite the curiosity of (s.o.).

aguicheur, -euse [agiʃœr, -øz] *F* I *a* seductive/provocative/alluring/arousing/sexy II *nf* aguicheuse, tease/prick-teaser/cock-teaser.

aidé [ede] *a F* (*personne*) pas aidé, (*laid*) plain/ugly; (*bête*) stupid*/dim/dumb.

aiguiller [eguije] *vtr V* aiguiller une femme, to have sex* with a woman/to screw a woman.

ail [aj] *nm P* aimer/sentir/taper l'ail, manger/ vendre de l'ail, to (appear to) be a lesbian*; marchandes d'ail, lesbians*/gay women/ lesbos/lezzies. (*Voir* **gousse**)

aile [ɛl] *nf* 1. *P* arm*/fin/flipper; battres des ailes, to flail one's arms about 2. *F* battre de l'aile/ne battre que d'une aile, to be in a bad way; l'entreprise ne bat que d'une aile, the business is very shaky/in a bad way 3. *F* voler de ses propres ailes, to stand on one's own two feet 4. *F* en avoir dans l'aile/avoir un coup dans l'aile, to be a bit drunk*/tipsy 5. *F* prendre un virage sur l'aile, (*voiture*) to take a corner on two wheels 6. *P* (*Hell's Angels*) avoir ses ailes brunes, to have anal sex* (with s.o.); avoir ses ailes noires, to have sex* with a Black* (girl); avoir ses ailes rouges, to have sex* with a girl during her period. (*Voir* **plomb 2**; **rogner II**)

aileron [ɛlrɔ̃] *nm P* arm*/fin/flipper.

aimer [eme] I *vtr* 1. *F* j'aime mieux pas, I'd rather not; j'aime autant ça, that sounds more like it; j'aime mieux/j'aime autant te dire que tu ne réussiras pas comme ça! I'm warning you, you won't make it like that! 2. *P* va te faire aimer! get lost!/take a running jump!/get stuffed! II *vpr* s'aimer *F* il s'aime à la campagne, he likes living in the country.

air [ɛr] I *nm* 1. *F* autant cracher/pisser en l'air, it's a sheer waste of time; c'est comme si je crachais en l'air, it's like (I was) talking to a brick wall/I might as well be talking to myself 2. *F* de l'air! go away!/get out of here! 3. *F* se donner/prendre de l'air, changer d'air, jouer (à) la fille de l'air/en jouer un air, to run away*/to clear off. (*Voir* air III 1) 4. *F* ne pas tenir en l'air, (*être fatigué*) to be fit/ready to drop (with tiredness); (*ne vouloir rien dire*) not to make sense/to be meaningless 5. *F* ne pas manquer d'air, to have nerve; to have the cheek of the devil; il ne manque pas d'air! he's a cheeky little sod!/he's got a nerve! 6. *P* fiche(r)/flanquer/foutre (qch) en l'air (*a*) (*abandonner, jeter*) to chuck (sth) away/to chuck (sth) up; elle veut tout foutre en l'air, she wants to chuck it all up/jack it all in (*b*) to ruin/to mess (sth) up; ça a fichu en l'air toutes mes idées, that's completely scuppered/screwed up all my plans (*c*) to kill* (s.o.)/to bump (s.o.) off/*surt NAm* to blow (s.o.) away. (*Voir* **envoyer 3**; **fiche(r) 2**; **foutre I 7** (*c*)) 7. *P* se foutre en l'air, to commit suicide/to do oneself in 8. *P* mettre en l'air, to kill* (s.o.)/*surt NAm* to blow (s.o.) away; to wreck (a place)/to turn (somewhere) upside down/to mess up (a place) 9. *P* avoir de l'air dans son porte-monnaie, être en l'air, to be penniless/broke/skint 10. *F* déplacer de l'air, to bustle around/to rush around (ineffectually) 11. *V* l'avoir en l'air, to have an erection*/to get it up; l'avoir en l'air pour qn, to have the hots for s.o./to be horny/to be randy. (*Voir* **courant 1, 2, 3**; **s'envoyer 3** (*b*); **jambe 18**; **mise**; **pomper I, 2**) II *nm F* 1. (*a*) elle n'a pas l'air d'y toucher/elle a l'air de ne pas y toucher, she looks as if butter wouldn't melt in her mouth (*b*) ça n'a l'air de rien, mais c'est très important, you wouldn't think so to look at it, but it's really very important 2. de quoi j'ai l'air maintenant? I look a right chump now! il a l'air fin, he's been had; il a l'air con/il a plutôt l'air d'un con que d'un moulin à vent, he looks a right idiot/a complete arse/*NAm* ass; avoir l'air con et la vue basse, to look stupid*/dim/daft 3. il vous a dit non, ça en a tout l'air, he said no by the look of things 4. ce vase-là prend un petit air penché, that vase looks as though it's going to go/fall over any moment 5. avoir un faux air de, to appear to be/to seem like (sth) 6. avoir l'air d'avoir deux airs, to have a sly/cunning/shifty look III *nm F* (*mélodie*) 1. en jouer un air/jouer un air de flûte/jouer des flûtes, to run away*/to beat

it/to scarper. (*Voir* **air I 3**) 2. air connu! I've heard that one before! 3. il en a l'air et la chanson, he not only looks it, he is.

aise, à l' [alɛz] *adv F* easily; ça vaut 5,000 francs à l'aise, it's easily worth 5,000 francs; à l'aise, Blaise! easy!/no prob(s)!

album [albɔm] *nm F* (*argot policier*) album de famille, police (photographic) archives.

alco(o)lo [alkɔlo] *nm P* drunkard*/alkie/boozer/wino.

alfa [alfa] *nm F* il n'a plus d'alfa sur les hauts plateaux, (*il est chauve*) he's as bald as a coot/as an egg.

algèbre [alʒɛbr] *nf F* c'est de l'algèbre pour moi, it's all Greek to me.

aligner [aliɲe] *P* I *vtr* 1. les aligner, to pay* up/to fork out/to cough up 2. aligner qn, to reprimand* s.o./to give it to s.o.; se faire aligner, to catch it/to cop it II *vpr* **s'aligner** (*a*) s'aligner avec qn, to take s.o. on/to face up to s.o. (*b*) tu peux (toujours) t'aligner, you're no match for him!/just you try and beat that! (*c*) to confess/admit; tu t'alignes? come on, own up!

aller [ale] *vi* 1. *P* aller au boucher, to go to the butcher's 2. *P* aller en bicyclette, to cycle/to bike (it) 3. *F* aller avec, to match/to go with; les chaussures vont avec, the shoes go with it 4. *F* aller sur ses trente ans, to be nearing thirty/to be nearly thirty 5. *F* to defecate*; qch qui fait aller, laxative/sth that clears you out; tu es allé aujourd'hui? have you been (to the loo) today? 6. *F* (comment) ça va?/comment va la santé? how are you?/how's life?/how's things?/how's tricks? ça va, I'm OK/I'm fine/not so bad/keeping my end up; ça (ne) va pas la tête? are you mad*?/are you off your head?/you need your head examined! où tu vas, toi? are you mad*?/you must be crazy! ça va! all right!/OK! ça va, ça va! all right! all right!/don't go on! ça ira comme ça, we'll leave it at that; ça va comme ça! it's all right as it is! rancard dans une heure? – ça me va, see you in an hour? – suits me/O.K. with me 7. *F* y aller fort, to exaggerate*/to lay it on (a bit thick); aller mal, to exaggerate* a lot/to go OTT 8. *F* y aller de ..., to begin (to do sth)/to decide (to do sth); y aller de ses sous, to put up some money; y aller son baratin, to chatter away/to witter on; il y est allé de ses cent francs, he put in a hundred francs; il y est allé d'une tournée, he stood us a round; elle y est allée de sa petite larme, she had a little

cry **9.** *F* **on y va?** all set?/(are) we off then?
allez-y doucement! go easy!/gently does it!
quand (il) faut y aller, (il) faut y aller, when
you've got to go, you've got to go/there's no
getting away from it **10.** *F* **aller avec une
femme,** to have sex* with a woman **11.** *F* **ça
n'a pas l'air d'aller,** you look as if there's
something wrong; what's the matter?/what's
up? **12.** *F* **ça y va, la manœuvre!** keep going!
13. *F* **je m'en vais vous le dire,** I'm going to
tell you **14.** *F* **s'en aller,** to die*/to go; **il s'en
va du cœur,** he has a serious heart complaint/
his heart is giving out **15.** *P* **faire aller,** to
manage/make do **16.** *P* **faire en aller,** to make
(s.o.) leave*/go away **17.** *P* **s'en être allé,** to
be gone; **elle s'en est allée,** she left/she
scarpered **18. tu peux y aller!** believe (you)
me!/you can take it from me! **cette bagnole
ne vaut rien, tu peux y aller!** this car's worthless, you can take it from me! (*Voir* **caisse
3; chagrin; charbon 1; chemin 2; cri 2,
3; dame I 6** (*a*); **dos 10; doucement 1;
enculer 1; fort** II; **foutre² 6; mal I 3;
malva; mollo(-mollo); pape; se
promener** (*a*); **renseignements; se
rhabiller 1; roi 3**)

aller-retour, aller et retour [alertur,
aleer(ə)tur] *nm F* double slap on the face
(*first with the back of the hand and then the
front*)/a right and a left.

alloc [alɔk] *nf P* = **alloque.**

allongé, -ée [alɔ̃ʒe] *n P* corpse*/stiff; être
aux allongés, (*à l'hôpital*) to be in the mortuary; le boulevard des allongés, the
cemetery/boneyard/bone-orchard.

allonger [alɔ̃ʒe] I *vtr* **1.** *F* **allonger un coup
à qn,** to hit out at s.o.; **allonger une taloche à
qn,** to slap s.o. round the face/to clout s.o.;
allonger qn (par terre), to knock s.o. to the
ground/to knock s.o. flat on his/her face; to
kill* s.o./to knock s.o. off **2.** *F* (**les) allonger,**
to pay* up; **il va falloir que tu les allonges,**
you've got to/you'd better cough up/fork out;
allonger le tir/la sauce, (*délayer un rapport,
etc*) to pad out; (*compléter une somme*) to
pay* the balance; (*augmenter une addition*)
to add a bit extra on a bill. (*Voir* **compas 1;
oreille 2; sauce 2**) II *vpr* **s'allonger** *P* **1.**
to confess*/to come clean/to grass **2.** (*sports*)
(*se laisser battre*) to take a dive.

alloque [alɔk] *nf P* (*abrév* = *allocation*) **1.**
unemployment benefit/dole/*NAm* unemploy-
ment compensation **2.** *pl* family allowance/
child benefit.

allouf [aluf] *nf P* = **alouf.**

allumage [alymaʒ] *nm F* **1. avoir du retard
à l'allumage,** to be slow on the uptake **2.
couper l'allumage,** (*personne*) to switch off
(completely).

allumé [alyme] *a* **1.** *F* mad*/bonkers/loony **2.**
P excited; *esp* sexually excited*/turned on/
randy/horny **3.** *P* (*drogues*) high/stoned/
turned on.

allumer [alyme] *vtr* **1.** *P* to excite* (s.o.)
sexually/to turn (s.o.) on; (*femmes*) to tease/
to prick-tease/to cock-tease **2.** *P* to look out
for/to watch out for; **allume les flics!** keep an
eye out for the fuzz! **allume!** watch out!/look
out! **3.** *P* to shoot* (s.o.)/to fill (s.o.) full of lead
4. *F* to criticize*/to lambaste (s.o.) **5.** *F* **se
faire allumer,** (*attirer l'attention*) to attract
attention/to make oneself conspicuous; (*être
sommé*) to get hauled up.

allumeur [alymœr] *nm A P* associate (of
gambler/swindler, etc)/decoy (man).

allumeuse [alymøz] *nf P* **1.** prostitute*/
hooker (*who attracts clients into brothels*) **2.**
dance/nightclub hostess; bar-girl **3.** tease/
prick-teaser/cock-teaser/PT/CT.

alors [alɔr] *adv F* (*a*) alors, tu viens? are
you coming, then? et (puis) alors?/alors quoi?
and what then?/so what?/what now? (*b*) ça
alors!/non, mais alors! well I'm blowed!/you
don't say!/cor!

alouf [aluf] *nf P* match.

alpague [alpag] *nf P* **1.** jacket/coat **2.** (*a*)
(*dos*) back; **mettre la main sur l'alpague à
qn,** to arrest* s.o./to collar s.o. (*b*) **l'avoir sur
l'alpague,** to be saddled/lumbered (with a
crime, etc) (*c*) **les avoir sur l'alpague,** to
have s.o. breathing down one's neck; **avoir les
flics sur l'alpague,** to have the cops on one's
back **3.** arrest/nicking.

alpaguer [alpage] *vtr P* to arrest* (s.o.); **se
faire alpaguer,** to get arrested/nabbed/nicked;
être alpagué, to be nicked.

alphonse [alfɔ̃s] *nm A F* pimp*/ponce.

alpingue [alpɛ̃g] *nf P* jacket/coat.

Alsaco [alzako] *nm & f F* person from
Alsace/Alsatian.

alu [aly] *nm F* aluminium.

amarrer [amare] *vtr P* **1.** to accost **2.** to
seize/to get hold of/to collar/to nab.

amarres [amar] *nfpl F* **larguer les amarres,**
to go/to leave*/to shove off/to push off.

amazone [amazon] *nf P* high-class
prostitute* operating in a car.

ambulance [ɑ̃bylɑ̃s] *nf F* **on ne tire pas sur

les ambulances/sur une ambulance, you don't hit a man who's down.

âme [ɑm] *nf F* (*a*) **errer comme une âme en peine,** to wander about like a lost soul (*b*) **la mort dans l'âme,** desperate; with a heavy heart (*c*) **je n'ai pas vu âme qui vive,** I haven't seen a soul.

amen [amɛn] *adv F* **dire toujours amen,** to be a yes-man.

amende [amɑ̃d] *nf P* 1. **mettre qn à l'amende,** to take/to force protection money from s.o. 2. (*a*) amount paid by prostitute* to free herself from her pimp (*b*) amount paid by pimp to his predecessor.

amener [amne] I *vtr P* (= *apporter*) to bring (along); **amène une boutanche,** bring a bottle. (*Voir* **fraise 4**(*b*)) II *vpr* **s'amener** *F* to turn up/to put in an appearance/to show one's face; **amène-toi ici!** come (over) here! **il va s'amener dans quelques minutes,** he'll be along in a few minutes; **elle s'est amenée avec trois heures de retard,** she waltzed in/ breezed in three hours late.

américain [amerikɛ̃] *a F* **avoir l'œil américain,** to be able to judge (sth) accurately at a single glance.

Amerloque [amɛrlɔk], **Amerlo(t)** [amɛrlo], **Amerluche** [amɛrlyʃ] *P* I *nm & f* American/Yank/Yankee II *a* American; **amerloque comme l'oncle Sam,** as American as apple pie. (*Voir* **ricain**)

ami, -e [ami] *n F* man* (friend*) *or* boyfriend; *f* woman* (friend*) *or* girlfriend; lover; sweetheart; **sa bonne amie,** his sweetheart; **petit ami,** boyfriend/bloke/guy; **petite amie,** girlfriend/woman*/chick/bird.

amiable, à l' [alamjabl] *adv F* **faire qn à l'amiable,** to rob s.o./to nick s.o.'s wallet using threats but no violence.

ami-ami [amiami] *a F* **faire ami-ami,** to make friends; (*se réconcilier*) to make up.

aminche [amɛ̃ʃ] *nm Vieilli P* friend*/mate*/ pal/buddy.

amocher [amɔʃe] *vtr P* 1. **amocher qch,** to make a mess of sth/to balls sth up; (*bagnole*) to smash up/to wreck 2. **amocher qn,** to beat s.o. up*/to knock s.o. about/to smash s.o.'s face in; **se faire amocher,** to get beaten up/to get done over 3. **il a une patte amochée,** he's got a gammy leg.

amorti [amɔrti] *a F* 1. tired*/done for/flaked out 2. old/past it.

amortisseurs [amɔrtisœr] *nmpl P* breasts*/(big) boobs/knockers; **une belle paire** d'amortisseurs, a nice pair of Bristols.

amour [amur] *nm* 1. *F* **faire l'amour,** to make love; **amour vache,** caveman stuff/ rough stuff 2. *P* **y'a plus d'amour,** it just won't work any longer/it's no good, we just can't make a go of it 3. *F* **quel amour de gosse!** what a cute (little) kid! **tu es un amour** (d'avoir fait ça pour moi), you're an angel/a darling/a love (to have done that for me); **quel amour de robe!** that's a great dress!/that's a dream of a dress! 4. *F* **à vos amours!** (*après un éternuement*) bless you! (*en levant son verre*) cheers!* 5. *F* **vivre d'amour et d'eau fraîche,** to live on love. (*Voir* **gueule II 6; remède 2**)

amph [ɑ̃f] *nf,* **amphés** [ɑ̃fe] *nfpl,* **amphets** [ɑ̃fɛt] *nfpl F* (*abbr* = *amphétamine(s)*) amphetamine(s)*.

amphi [ɑ̃fi] *nm F* (*a*) (*abrév* = *amphithéâtre*) lecture room/hall (*b*) lecture; paper (on a subject); **faire un amphi à qn,** to give s.o. a lecture/a talking to (*c*) (*aviation, Mil*) briefing (*d*) (*à l'hôpital*) mortuary/ morgue.

amphibie [ɑ̃fibi] *nm* 1. suspicious individual*/shady character 2. worker who has several jobs.

ampli [ɑ̃pli] *nm F* (*abrév* = *amplificateur*) amplifier.

ampoule [ɑ̃pul] *nf F* **il ne se fait pas d'ampoules aux mains,** he doesn't overtax himself/he doesn't put himself out much.

amuse-gueule [amyzgœl] *nm F* (*a*) *pl* appetizers/nibbles (*b*) (*théâtre*) warm-up act.

amygdales [ami(g)dal] *nfpl F* 1. **lécher les amygdales à qn,** to give s.o. a French kiss; **se faire lécher les amygdales,** to be kissed on the mouth 2. **s'humecter/se rincer les amygdales,** to have a drink*/to wet one's whistle/to have a (quick) snifter. (*Voir* **caler II 2**)

amyl(e) [amil] *nm P* (*drogues*) amyl nitrate*/amy.

ananas [anana] *nm* 1. *F* hand grenade/ pineapple 2. *pl P* breasts*/melons.

anar [anar], **anarcho** [anarko] *a & n F* (*abbr* = *anarchiste*) anarchist.

Anatole [anatɔl] *Prnm Vieilli F* (*locution populaire*) **ça colle, Anatole!** absoballylu-tely!/absobloodylutely! **ça colle, Anatole?** how's tricks, old man?/how goes it, Joe?/ how's it going, buster?

ancêtre [ɑ̃sɛtr] *nm F* old man/grandad; **alors, l'ancêtre, ça va?** you OK, grandad?

ancien [ɑ̃sjɛ̃] *nm F* antique dealing; **faire**

l'ancien, to be an antique dealer/a second-hand book dealer, etc.

ancre [ᾱkr] *nf F* lever l'ancre, to leave*/to make tracks.

andosses [ᾱdos] *nfpl P* 1. shoulders; back 2. en avoir plein les andosses, to be exhausted*/to be dead beat; (*en avoir assez*) to be sick (and tired) of sth/to have had a bellyful of sth.

andouille [ᾱduj] *nf* 1. *P* fool*/jerk/twerp/ twit/nerd; faire l'andouille, to play the fool; arrête de faire l'andouille! stop acting the goat!/stop arsing about! sacrée andouille!/ espèce d'andouille! (you) bloody fool!/(you) stupid jerk!/(you) stupid idiot! (*Voir* **terrine 2** (*b*)) 2. *F* il est ficelé comme une andouille, his clothes are so tight he can hardly move 3. *F* s'en aller en brouet d'andouille, to fizzle out 4. *F* faire son andouille, to show off*/to swank/to swagger 5. *V* andouille de cal(e)cif/à col roulé, penis*/meat/sausage. (*Voir* **dépendeur**)

âne [ɑn] *nm P* 1. tenir l'âne par la queue, to urinate*/to point Percy at the porcelain 2. être monté comme un âne, (*homme*) to be well-endowed/to be well-equipped/to be well-hung/to be hung like a bull. (*Voir* **bougre 1; monté 3; peau 11; pet 1; pied 11; son II 3**)

ange [ᾱʒ] *nm* 1. *F* faire l'ange, to procure an abortion; faiseur, -euse d'anges, backstreet abortionist 2. *F* un ange passe/un ange a passé, *said after an awkward/embarrassing silence or lull in the conversation* 3. *F* rire aux anges, to have an idiotic grin on one's face; to smile in one's sleep 4. *F* parler aux anges, to talk to oneself 5. *F* être aux anges, (*très heureux*) to be in seventh heaven/to be on cloud nine/to walk on air 6. *F* les anges (*a*) motor-cycle cops (*b*) hell's angels 7. *F* veux-tu être un ange et me passer le pain? be an angel and pass the bread 8. *P* voir les anges, to have an orgasm*/to come; mettre qn aux anges, to give s.o. sexual pleasure/to screw s.o. well/to be a good lay 9. *P* ange blanc, (*infirmière qui fait passer des drogues à un toxicomane*) white angel 10. *F* ange gardien, policeman* guarding a prisoner; (*garde du corps*) bodyguard/guardian angel/ gorilla; anges gardiens, policemen*/(the) cops/(the) fuzz.

Anglais [ᾱglɛ] *nmpl F* avoir ses Anglais, to have one's period(s)*/to come on; les Anglais sont arrivés/ont débarqué, elle a ses anglais,

she's got her period/she's got the curse/she's got the decorators in. (*Voir* **capote**)

anglaise, à l' [alᾱglɛz] *adv phr F* filer à l'anglaise, to take French leave.

anglaiser [ᾱglɛze] *vtr* 1. *P* (*par une prostituée*) to rob/to fleece/to rook (a client) 2. *V* to have anal sex* with (s.o.)/to bugger s.o./ to screw s.o.'s ass 3. *V* to rape (s.o.).

angliche [ᾱgliʃ] *P* I *a* English II *n* un/une Angliche, an Englishman/an Englishwoman; a limey/a Brit.

angoisse [ᾱgwas] *nf F* (c'est) l'angoisse! je te dis pas l'angoisse! bonjour l'angoisse! (*situation*) what a hassle!/what a pain! (*embarrassant*) it was really cringe-making! (*personne*) what a bore!/(s)he's a pain (in the neck)! les vacances/les impôts, c'est l'angoisse! holidays are a real hassle!/income tax, what a hassle! ce type, je te dis pas l'angoisse! that guy will drive me crazy!

anguille [ᾱgij] *nf V* anguille de caleçon/de cal(e)cif, penis*/prick.

anneau, -eaux [ano] *nm V* 1. anus*/ring/ ring-piece/*NAm* roundeye 2. buttocks*/bum/ tail.

annexe [anɛks] *nf F* l'annexe, the local (pub).

antif [ᾱtif] *nm P* battre l'antif (*a*) to pretend to be stupid*/to play the role of dimwit (*b*) to solicit*/to walk the streets.

antifle [ᾱtifl] *nf A P* church.

antifler [ᾱtifle] *P* I *vi* = **s'antifler** II *vpr* s'antifler (de sec), to get married*/hitched/ spliced.

antigel [ᾱtiʒɛl] *nm P* strong spirits*/hard stuff.

antigrippe [ᾱtigrip] *nm F* (*pousse-café*) chaser; (after dinner) liqueur.

antisèche [ᾱtisɛʃ] *nf ou m F* (*à un examen*) crib/*NAm* pony.

apéro [apero] *nm P* aperitif/cocktail; l'heure de l'apéro, cocktail time; venez prendre l'apéro, come for drinks/for cocktails.

aplatir [aplatir] I *vtr F* 1. aplatir qn, to knock (s.o.) down/to flatten (s.o.) 2. aplatir le coup, to forgive/to close one's eyes (to sth) II *vpr* **s'aplatir** *F* 1. to fall flat on one's face/to come a cropper 2. s'aplatir devant qn, to grovel at s.o.'s feet/to crawl to s.o. 3. not to insist; dans ces cas-là, il vaut mieux s'aplatir, when that happens it's best to drop it.

app' [ap] *nm F* (*abrév = appétit*) bon app'! enjoy your meal!/bon appétit! get stuck in!/ *NAm* enjoy!/*NAm* eat hearty!

apparatchik [aparatʃik] *nm F* apparatchik.
appareil [aparɛj] *nm F Hum* dans le plus simple appareil, stark naked*/in the altogether/in one's birthday suit.
appart(e) [apart] *nm*, **appe** [ap] *nm F* flat/*esp NAm* apartment/pad.
appel [apɛl] *nm F* 1. faire des appels à qn, (*des œillades*) to give s.o. the glad eye/to give s.o. the once-over/to give s.o. the come-on 2. faire des appels du pied à qn, to play footsie with s.o. 3. faire des appels de phare, to flash one's headlights at another car 4. appel du peuple, borrowing/loan.
s'apporter [saporte] *vpr P* to arrive*/show up; apporte-toi ici! get yourself over here!
s'appuyer [sapɥije] *vpr P* 1. (*subir, supporter*) to put up with (sth)/to get landed with (sth); s'appuyer qn, to get stuck with s.o./to have to put up with s.o. 2. s'appuyer un boulot, to get stuck with a job; je vais encore m'appuyer la vaisselle, I'm going to be landed with the washing-up again.
aprèm [aprɛm] *nm P* (= *après-midi*) cet aprèm/c't'aprèm, this afternoon/this afto.
après [aprɛ] **I** *adv F* et (puis) après? what of it?/what about it?/so what? **II** *prép P* 1. (*se dit pour 'a' ou 'contre'*) monter après une échelle, to climb a ladder; après le mur, against the wall 2. (*se dit pour 'derrière'*) elle lui a crié après, she called him/shouted at him; il faudra lui courir après, we'll have to run after him.
aquiger, aquijer [akiʒe] *vi P* to hurt/to be painful; les pinceaux m'aquigent, my feet are killing me.
Arabi [arabi] *nm P Péj* = **Arbi**.
araignée [areɲe] *nf F* 1. avoir une araignée au/dans le plafond, to be slightly mad*/to have a screw loose/to be touched in the head 2. avoir des toiles d'araignée, (*objet*) to be seldom used/to sit around unused. (*Voir* **patte 7**)
arbalète [arbalɛt] *nf* 1. *V* penis*/prick/cock; filer un coup d'arbalète, to have sex*/to (have a) screw 2. *Vieilli P* (religious) cross 3. *P* firearm/revolver*/rod.
Arbi [arbi] *nm*, **Arbico(t)** [arbiko] *nm P Péj* Arab/wog. (*Voir* **bicot**)
arbre [arbr] *nm* 1. *F* faire grimper/faire monter qn à l'arbre, to hoax* s.o./to play a practical joke on s.o./to have s.o. on; monter/ grimper à l'arbre, to have/to get one's leg pulled 2. *F* monter à l'arbre, to get angry*/to fly off the handle/to hit the roof 3. *P* grimper

aux arbres, (*en parlant de la déposition d'un témoin ou d'un prévenu*) to exaggerate 4. en bois d'arbre, made of real wood.
arcagnasses [arkaɲas], **arcagnats** [arkaɲa] *nmpl P* period*/the curse. (*Voir* **argagnasses; ragnagnas**)
arcan [arkã] *nm P* (*a*) hooligan*/tough guy/ thug (*b*) crook/shady character.
arche [arʃ] *nm P* buttocks*; tu me fends l'arche, you give me a pain in the arse/*NAm* ass.
archer [arʃe] *nm A P* (*employé par plaisanterie*) archer (du Roy), policeman*.
archi [arʃi] *nm F* (*a*) architect (*b*) student of architecture.
archi- [arʃi] *préf Vieilli F* (très/ extrêmement); archicon, too bloody stupid (for words); archiconnu, overfamous/ tremendously well-known; archicomble/ archiplein, chock-a-block/chocker; archifou, stark staring mad; je suis archifauché, I'm completely skint/cleaned right out; archifaux, completely wrong; archifroid, stone cold; freezing/perishing.
archicube [arʃikyb] *nm F* former student of the *École Normale Supérieure*.
archimillionnaire [arʃimiljɔnɛr] *n & a F* multimillionaire/millionaire many times over/zillionaire.
archipointu [arʃipwɛ̃ty] *nm P* archbishop.
archiriche [arʃiriʃ] *a F* tremendously rich*/ rolling in it/stinking rich.
archisec, -sèche [arʃisɛk, -sɛʃ] *a F* bone-dry.
archisecret, -ète [arʃisəkrɛ, -ɛt] *a F* top secret/very hush-hush.
ardillon [ardijɔ̃] *nm V* penis*/shaft.
ardoise [ardwaz] *nf F* 1. avoir une ardoise chez ..., to have credit with .../to get (things on) tick from ...; inscrire les consommations à l'ardoise, to chalk up the drinks/to put the drinks on the slate; liquider une ardoise, to pay off a debt/to wipe the slate clean; liquider une vieille ardoise, to settle an old score; poser une ardoise, to leave without paying 2. prendre une ardoise à l'eau/se payer une ardoise/mouiller une ardoise, to urinate*/to have a slash/to splash one's boots (in a public urinal).
arêtes [arɛt] *nfpl P* ribs; back; avoir les flics sur les arêtes, to have the cops on one's back.
argagnasses [argaɲas] *nmpl*, **argantes** [argãt] *nfpl P* = **arcagnasses**.
argenté [arʒãte] *a F* rich*/in the money; on

n'est pas très argenté en ce moment, we're a bit broke at the moment; se trouver bien argenté, to be flush. (*Voir* **cuiller 4**)

argomuche [argɔmyʃ] *nm P* slang; jacter/ jaspiner l'argomuche, to talk slang.

argougner [arguɲe], **argouiner** [argwine] *vtr Vieilli P* 1. to get hold of/to grab/to collar 2. to arrest*/to nick.

argousin [arguzɛ̃] *nm Vieilli F* policeman*/ rozzer/bobby.

argus [argys] *nm F* l'argus (de l'automobile), = Glass's Guide; *Péj* ne plus être coté à l'argus, (*personne*) to be old/past it; elle (n')est plus cotée à l'argus, she's past it/she's geriatric.

aria [arja] *nm Vieilli F* fuss/bother; faire des arias, to kick up a fuss; ne faites pas tant d'arias! don't make such a song and dance about it!

aristo [aristo] *nm & f P* aristocrat/nob/toff.

arlequins [arləkɛ̃] *nmpl F* resurrection pie; leftovers.

arlo [arlo] *nm P* worthless piece of bric-à-brac; c'est de l'arlo, it's worthless junk.

arme [arm] *nf F* passer l'arme à gauche, to die*/to peg out/to kick the bucket.

Arménouche [armenuʃ] *a & n P* Armenian.

armoire [armwar] *nf F* 1. armoire (normande)/armoire à glace, hefty fellow/ hulking great brute; c'est une vraie armoire à glace, he's built like a battleship/he's a giant of a man 2. armoire à sons, piano/joanna.

arnaque [arnak] *nf P* swindle*/con; c'est de l'arnaque, it's a con/a rip-off; monter une arnaque, to pull a fast one; faire de l'arnaque, to go in for swindling; to be a con artist/rip-off merchant; attention à l'arnaque! careful you don't get ripped off!

arnaquer [arnake] *vtr P* 1. to swindle*/to do/to diddle/to rook (s.o.) 2. to arrest*/to nab (s.o.); se faire arnaquer par les flics, to get nicked by the cops.

arnaqueur, -euse [arnakœr, -øz] *n P* cheat/swindler*/crook/con artist.

arnau, arno [arno] *a P* very angry*/in a vile temper/hopping mad/fuming.

arpèges [arpɛʒ] *nmpl P* fingerprinting.

arpenter [arpɑ̃te] *vi F* to solicit*/to walk the streets.

arpète, arpette [arpɛt] *nf P Péj* apprentice.

arpinche [arpɛ̃ʃ] *nm P* miser*/skinflint.

arpion [arpjɔ̃] *nm P* 1. foot*/hoof; j'ai mal aux arpions, my dogs are killing me; taper des arpions, to have smelly feet 2. toe.

arquebuse [arkəbyz] *nf P* firearm*/ revolver*/rod.

arquepincer [arkpɛ̃se] *vtr P* to arrest*; se faire arquepincer, to get nabbed. (*Voir* **J't'arquepince**)

arquer [arke] *vi P* to walk*/to hoof it/to go by Shanks's pony; je ne pouvais plus arquer, I couldn't go a step further.

arraché [araʃe] *nm F* 1. vol à l'arraché, practice of robbing (s.o.) by snatching/ grabbing victim's bag, etc suddenly and violently; mugging 2. coup d'arraché, large-scale robbery/burglary.

arracher [araʃe] I *vtr F* 1. ça lui arrache le cœur de ..., it breaks his heart to ... 2. on se l'arrache, he/she/it is in great demand/is all the rage 3. arracher son copeau/en arracher, (*a*) *P* to work*/to grind (*b*) *P* (*prostituée*) to solicit*/to be on the game (*c*) *V* (*homme*) to have an orgasm*/to come; arracher le copeau, to give (s.o.) an orgasm* II *vi P* 1. (*disque, livre, etc*) to be very successful; son dernier simple, il arrache! his latest single is a runaway/smash hit! ça arrache! it's going very well! 2. (*bagnole, moto*) to be very powerful 3. (*chanteur, etc*) to give a powerful performance; le groupe a arraché, the band let rip/pulled all the stops out III *vpr* s'arracher *P* to run away*/to escape (from prison)/ to do a runner.

arrangeman(é) [arɑ̃zman(e)] *a P* (*personne*) who has VD*/the clap.

arrangemaner [arɑ̃zmane] *vtr P* to swindle* (s.o.)/to cheat/to con.

arranger [arɑ̃ze] I *vtr* 1. *F* je l'ai arrangé (de la belle manière), I told him (where to get) off/I fixed him/I sorted him out 2. *F* to swindle*/to cheat/to rook (s.o.) 3. *F* to cook/to doctor (the books, etc) 4. *P* to steal*/to walk off with (sth) 5. *P* to assault/to beat up*; ils l'ont bien arrangé, tes mecs, your blokes gave him a right working over 6. se faire arranger, *F* (*tromper*) to be swindled/ diddled/overcharged; *P* (*blesser*) to get hurt/ to get wounded/to cop a packet; *F* (*réprimander*) to get told off/ticked off; *P* (*tuer*) to get killed/to get done in; *P* (*attraper une maladie vénérienne*) to catch VD*/to cop a dose/to get the clap II *vpr* s'arranger *F* (*a*) ça s'arrangera, it'll turn out all right/it'll sort itself out/it'll all work out; ça s'arrange pas au Moyen Orient, things are getting worse in the Middle East; **laisse-les s'arranger tous les deux,** let them sort it out between themselves (*b*) **tu t'es bien arrangé!** that's a fine mess you've got yourself into! (*c*) **tu pourrais t'arranger un peu!** you could try to smarten yourself up a little!

arrêt-pipi [arɛpipi] *nm F* **faire un arrêt-pipi,** to interrupt one's journey to go to the toilet/to stop for a pee/to have a pit stop.

arrière-saison [arjɛrsɛzɔ̃] *nf F* **sentir l'arrière-saison,** to get old/to be getting past it.

arrière-train [arjɛrtrɛ̃] *nm F* buttocks*/ behind/rear.

s'arrimer [sarime] *vpr F* (*couple*) to live together (*married or unmarried*).

arriver [arive] *vi F* 1. **il croit que c'est arrivé,** he's deluding himself/he lives in a fool's paradise 2. **c'est arrivé,** the penny's dropped 3. **il arrive de son pays/sa campagne,** he's a bit green/he's easily taken in; he's a sucker 4. **arriver comme les carabiniers (d'Offenbach)/arriver après la bataille,** to arrive too late/to miss the boat.

arrondir [arɔ̃dir] I *vtr F* **arrondir ses fins de mois,** to increase one's salary by taking on small jobs/*esp* by prostitution*; to make a bit on the side II *vpr* **s'arrondir** *P* 1. to get drunk* 2. to get pregnant*/to have a bun in the oven.

arrosage [aroza3] *nm F* celebrating (*with drinks*).

arroser [aroze] *vtr F* 1. (*mitrailler*) to spray/to pepper with bullets 2. **se faire arroser,** to get soaked to the skin/to get wet through; **j'ai été bien arrosé,** I got soaking wet 3. to hand out bribes/hush money to (s.o.) 4. to drink while eating; **arroser son déjeuner d'une bouteille de rouge,** to wash down one's lunch with a bottle of red 5. *Mil* **arroser ses galons,** to wet/to christen one's stripes; **arroser un client,** to keep in with a customer by buying him lots of drinks; **ça s'arrose,** this calls for a drink!/let's drink to that! **courage arrosé,** Dutch courage; **café arrosé,** laced coffee. (*Voir* **dalle²**)

arroseuse [arozøz] *nf P* sub-machine-gun; sten gun; tommy-gun; **arroseuse municipale,** police sub-machine-gun.

arsouille [arsuj] I *a P* vulgar/scruffy/tatty; **malgré son air arsouille, il n'est pas si mauvais,** he's not so wild as he looks II *nm P* 1. crook/cheat/swindler* 2. hooligan*/yob(bo).

s'arsouiller [sarsuje] *vpr P* 1. to be a

crook/a scoundrel 2. to be debauched 3. to drink* to excess.

Arthur [artyr] *Prnm F* **se faire appeler Arthur,** to get reprimanded*/told off/ticked off.

artichaut [artiʃo] *nm Vieilli P* purse; wallet/*NAm* pocketbook. (*Voir* **cœur**)

artiche [artiʃ] *nm P* 1. purse; wallet/*NAm* pocketbook 2. money*/bread 3. buttocks*/ behind.

article [artikl] *nm* 1. *F* **faire l'article,** to promote/to plug (a product) 2. *P* **être porté sur l'article,** to be fond of sex*/to like it; to have a one-track mind/to be obsessed; (*femme*) to be a (bit of a) nympho 3. *P* knife/ shiv/chiv 4. *P* revolver*/shooter/piece 5. *P* penis*/tool.

artiflot [artiflo] *nm P Mil* artilleryman/ gunner.

artiller [artije] *vtr P* to have sex* with (s.o.)/to bang (s.o.).

artillerie [artijri] *nf P* 1. loaded dice 2. (collection of) firearms; arsenal; (*arme à feu individuelle*) revolver*/shooter; **balader son artillerie dans ses fouilles,** to carry a gun 3. (*drogues*) **artillerie d'un camé,** drug addict's instruments/artillery 4. simple and copious food 5. *P* male genitals*/block and tackle 6. **sortir la grosse artillerie,** to take strong measures/to bring out the big guns.

artiste [artist] *nm F* character/joker/artist; **c'est triste la vie d'artiste!** life's no joke!

artou, *pl* **-ous** [artu] *nm A P* foot*.

Arverne [arvɛrn] *nm P* = **Auverpin.**

as [as] *nm* 1. *F* (*sports, etc*) star (performer)/ace/whiz(kid); **as du volant,** crack (racing) driver; **ce mec-là, c'est pas un as,** this bloke/guy isn't what you'd call an expert/doesn't seem to know what he's doing 2. *F* **as de pique,** (*volaille*) parson's nose/*surt NAm* pope's nose; *A* (*personne*) buttocks*; (*sexe de la femme*) ace of spades; *F* (*personne*) **fichu comme l'as de pique,** (*contrefait*) deformed; (*mal habillé*) dressed like a scarecrow/dressed (up) anyoldhow 3. *P* **être (plein) aux as,** to be rich*/to be rolling in it 4. *F* **passer qch à l'as,** (*escamoter*) to spirit sth away; (*laisser de côté*) to ignore sth/to leave sth be; **passer à l'as,** to miss an opportunity/a chance; **3000 francs sont passés à l'as,** 3000 francs have disappeared (up) 5. *P* **l'as,** (*dans un restaurant*) table no. 1/no. 1 table 6. *P* alibi*/ let-out. (*Voir* **trèfle 4**)

ascenseur [asɑ̃sœr] *nm F* **renvoyer l'ascenseur,** to return a favour.

asperge [aspɛrʒ] *nf* 1. *F* asperge (montée en graine), tall, thin person*/beanpole 2. *V* penis*/gherkin 3. *pl V* aller/être aux asperges, to be a prostitute*/to solicit*/to be on the game/to walk the streets 4. *pl* stiletto heels/ stilettos.

asphyxier [asfiksje] *vtr F* to steal*/to pinch. (*Voir* **perroquet**)

aspi [aspi] *nm F* (*abbr* = *aspirant*) (*a*) (*marine*) midshipman/middie (*b*) *Mil* officer cadet (*c*) young hopeful.

aspine [aspin] *nm ou f P* money*/dough/ lolly.

aspirateur [aspiratœr] *nm P* aspirateur à pépées, kerb crawler (looking for women).

aspirine [aspirin] *nf F* blanc/bronzé comme un cachet d'aspirine, white as a ghost/sheet.

assaisonner [asɛzɔne] *vtr P* 1. assaisonner qn, to beat s.o. up*/to clobber s.o.; to kill* s.o./to do s.o. in 2. se faire assaisonner, to get beaten up/to get worked over; (*recevoir une lourde peine*) to get a stiff sentence/to get the book thrown at one.

assassiner [asasine] *vtr F* 1. (*a*) to ruin/to make a mess of (sth); elle assassine cette chanson, she's murdering that song (*b*) to bore* (s.o.) to death (de, with) 2. to overcharge (s.o.) (exorbitantly)/to rip (s.o.) off; ses créanciers l'assassinent, his creditors are bleeding him (to death).

asseoir [aswar] I *vtr F* to amaze*/ flabbergast/to floor (s.o.); sa grossièreté m'assoit, I'm staggered by his coarseness. (*Voir* **assis**) II *vpr* **s'asseoir** *F* s'asseoir sur qn, to despise s.o./to ignore s.o.; les ordres du patron, moi, je m'assieds/je m'assois dessus! I don't give a damn about the boss's orders!/ you know what you can do with the boss's orders! (*Voir* **se coucher 3**)

assiette [asjɛt] *nf* 1. *F* il n'est pas dans son assiette, he's feeling out of sorts/below par/ one degree under/off colour 2. *F* l'assiette au beurre, plum (government) job/cushy job; taper dans l'assiette au beurre, to ride the gravy train 3. *pl P* les Assiettes, = the Crown Courts (formerly the Assizes) 4. *F* piquer dans l'assiette de qn, (*vivre aux dépens de qn*) to sponge off s.o.

s'assir [sasir] *vpr P* (*se dit pour 's'asseoir'*) to sit down.

assis [asi] *a F* en être/en rester assis, to be amazed*/flabbergasted/to be gobsmacked/to be struck all of a heap; j'en suis resté assis, it completely staggered me/it floored me/I was

gobsmacked; restez assis! are you sitting down?/are you ready for this? (*Voir* **asseoir** I)

assistance [asistãs] *nf F* help given to a prisoner (*money, clothes, food, etc*).

assister [asiste] *vtr F* to bring (a prisoner) money, clothes, food, etc.

assommant [asɔmã] *a F* deadly boring/ deadly dull.

assommer [asɔme] *vtr F* assommer qn, to bore* s.o. to death/rigid; (*embêter*) to annoy* s.o./to pester s.o. to death.

assumer [asyme] *F* I *vtr* to accept (a situation, etc); to take (sth) on board II *vi* to accept one's responsibilities; j'assume (complètement), I am (totally) responsible for my actions/I accept (totally) my responsibilities.

assurer [asyre] *vi F* 1. to be competent/to be good at (sth); il assure en maths/les maths, il assure, he's good at maths/where maths is concerned, he's no dimwit; il n'assurait pas, faute d'argent de poche, he wasn't managing/ he wasn't making it because he didn't have the cash 2. (*a*) to stay calm/not to be flustered; elle assure toujours, she's always cool, calm and collected (*b*) to be master of a situation/to be in control; il assure, he's cool 3. to have style/to look good; dans ce costard, t'assures un max, you look really stylish in that suit 4. to do what is necessary to achieve sth/to go for sth; to make it.

astape [astap] *a Vieilli P* (*abrév de* à se taper le cul/le derrière par terre) (*Voir* **taper** I 5) c'est astape! it's hilarious!/it's a scream!/it's a riot!

astec [astɛk], **astèque** [astɛk] *nm P* = **aztèque**.

asteure [astœr] *adv P* (= à cette heure) at that moment/then; now.

astibloc [astiblɔk], **astibloche** [astiblɔʃ] *nm P* (*pêche*) maggot/worm.

astic [astik] *nm F* = **astique**.

asticot [astiko] *nm F* 1. engraisser les asticots, to be dead and buried/to be pushing up the daisies/to be food for worms 2. small/ insignificant person; worm; un drôle d'asticot, an odd character/bloke/geezer.

asticotage [astikɔtaʒ] *nm F* teasing/ needling/bugging/pestering/baiting.

asticoter [astikɔte] I *vtr* to tease/needle/ pester; arrête d'asticoter ton frère! stop needling/bugging/pestering your brother! II *vpr* **s'asticoter** *P* to quarrel*/to bicker/to squabble.

astique [astik] *nf F* (*surt Mil*) passer à l'astique, to polish (buttons, etc)/to do fatigues/to do bull.

astiquer [astike] I *vtr* 1. *F* homme bien astiqué, well-groomed/well-turned-out man 2. *P* to thrash/to beat (s.o.) up* 3. *V* s'astiquer la colonne/la gaule, (*homme*) to masturbate*/ to flog the bishop/to flog the dummy; s'astiquer le bouton, (*femme*) to masturbate*/to finger-fuck; astiquer la motte à une nana, to feel up/to touch up/to finger a girl II *vpr* **s'astiquer** *V* 1. to have sex*/to bonk 2. = **astiquer 3.**

astuce [astys] *nf F* 1. joke/wisecrack/pun; une astuce vaseuse, a weak pun/a lousy joke; je ne saisis pas l'astuce, I don't get it 2. gadget/gimmick; voilà l'astuce! that's the trick!/that's how it's done!

athlète [atlɛt] *nm P* 100 franc note.

atomique [atɔmik] *a F* unbelievable/ stupendous.

atout [atu] *nm F* blow*/knock; prendre/ recevoir un atout, (*personne*) to get clouted; (*voiture*) to get a bash/a knock.

atrocement [atrɔsmã] *adv F* excessively/ dreadfully/frightfully; on va se faire atrocement chier, we'll be bored stiff.

attaque, d' [datak] *adv phr F* (*a*) vigor-ously; il y va d'attaque, he goes at it like a bull at a gate/he goes at it hammer and tongs; travailler d'attaque, to work like mad (*b*) on form; être/se sentir d'attaque, to be full of beans/to be on top form; je ne suis pas d'attaque, I don't feel up to it/I feel out of sorts.

attaquer [atake] *vtr F* attaque-moi vers dix plombes, give me a buzz about ten.

attelé [atle] *a P* être attelé (*a*) to be bigamous (*b*) to support two women/to have it off with two women (*esp a wife and a mis-tress*) (*c*) (*souteneur*) to live off the earnings of several prostitutes.

atteler [atle] *vi P* (*souteneur*) to live off the earnings of several prostitutes.

attention [atãsjɔ̃] *nf F* attention aux éplu-chures! watch out for the consequences! attention les yeux! pay attention!/listen care-fully! attention les yeux, il va dire quelque chose, keep your ears open, he's going to say something; il a une bagnole, attention les yeux! some car he's got, it's so flashy you need to shade your eyes!

atterrir [aterir] *vi F* 1. to come back to real-ity; to stop daydreaming 2. (*drogues*) atterrir (après un trip), to come down (after a trip).

attifer [atife] I *vtr F* vise un peu comme elle est attifée! take a look at her get-up!/her outfit! ce gosse est vraiment mal attifé, this kid is really badly dressed II *vpr* **s'attifer** *F* to get oneself up in/to doll oneself up in sth.

attigé, -ée [atiʒe] *a & n P* (*a*) (person) in-fected with VD*; planque aux attigés, VD* clinic (*b*) bashed up/knocked about; être attigé, to get beaten up/done in.

attiger [atiʒe] *P* I *vtr* 1. (*a*) to hit/to wound; il s'est fait attiger, he got hit/he copped it (*b*) to beat (s.o.) up*/to knock (s.o.) about; (*parfois*) to kill (s.o.) 2. to give (s.o.) VD*/a dose/the clap 3. attiger la cabane, to exaggerate*/to shoot a line/to go a bit far II *vi* to exaggerate*/to spin a yarn; n'attiges pas! come off it!/stop having me on!

attrapade [atrapad] *nf*, **attrapage** [atrapaʒ] *nm F* 1. quarrel*/set-to 2. reprimand*/ticking-off.

attrape-con(s), **attrape-couillon(s)** [atrapkɔ̃, -kujɔ̃] *nm inv P* swindle*/hoax*/ con.

attrape-nigaud(s) [atrapnigo] *nm inv F* = **attrape-con(s)**.

attrape-pèze, **attrape-pognon** [atrap-pɛz, -pɔɲɔ̃] *nm inv P* = **attrape-con(s)**.

attrape-poussière(s) [atrappusjɛr] *nm F* useless object that collects dust/white elephant.

attraper [atrape] *vtr F* 1. to reprimand* (s.o.); to come down on (s.o.) like a ton of bricks; se faire attraper, to get told off/to catch it 2. to cheat/to swindle*; se laisser at-traper, to be diddled/to be taken for a ride; je me suis laissé attraper, I was (well and truly) had/done 3. attrape! take that!/put that in your pipe and smoke it! (*Voir* **crève**)

attrape-touristes [atrapturist] *nm inv F* tourist trap.

attributs [atriby] *nmpl P* testicles*/family jewels/marriage prospects.

attriquer [atrike] *vtr P* 1. to appropriate/to acquire (sth) 2. to buy (*esp stolen goods*).

auber [obɛr] *nm P* money*/lolly/dough.

auberge [obɛrʒ] *nf F* 1. n'être pas sorti de l'auberge, to be in a difficult situation/in a tight corner/in danger, etc; on n'est pas (encore) sorti de l'auberge, we're not out of the woods yet 2. il se croit à l'auberge, he treats this place like a hotel.

aubergine [obɛrʒin] *nf P* 1. bishop 2. red nose (from excessive drinking)/bottlenose 3. bottle of red wine 4. *Vieilli* woman traffic warden/*esp NAm* meter maid. (*Voir* **pervenche**)

aubert [obɛr] *nm P* = **auber**.

auge [oʒ] *nf P* plate; passe-moi ton auge que je te serve, hand me your plate/dish so I can serve you.

Auguste [ogyst] *Prnm F* comme de juste, Auguste!/tout juste, Auguste! you('ve) said it, mate!

aussi [osi] *adv P* 1. aussi étrange que ça soit, (*se dit pour 'si...que'*) strange as it may seem 2. aussi jolie comme elle, (*se dit pour 'aussi...que'*) as pretty as her. (*Voir* **sec II 1**)

authentique! [otãtik] *int F* no kidding!/it's the truth! il me l'a dit comme ça, authentique! he told me so himself/in those very words!

autichante [otiʃãt] *af* (*femme*) sexually desirable/sexy; elle est autichante, she's a nice bit of stuff.

autiche [otiʃ] *nf P* faire de l'autiche, to raise a rumpus/to kick up a fuss/to stir up trouble.

auticher [otiʃe] I *vtr P* to excite* (s.o.) sexually/to turn (s.o.) on II *vpr* **s'auticher** *P* to become sexually excited*; to get turned on/to become randy.

auto [oto, ɔto] *nm* 1. *F* (*abbr = autographe*) autograph 2. *P* d'auto, = **d'autor**.

autobus [otɔbys] *nm P* casual prostitute*/pick-up. (*Voir* **suppositoire**)

autor, d' [dɔtɔr, dot-] *adv phr P* faire qch d'autor, (*sans hésiter, avec rapidité*) to do sth on the spur of the moment; **y aller d'autor**, to go it alone; **travailler d'autor et d'achar**, to work* hard (à qch, at sth); to put one's back into it; **d'autor et d'achar/d'autor et de rif/de rif et d'autor**, without more ado. (*Voir* **rif 6**)

autre [otr] *pron F* (*a*) comme dit l'autre, as the saying goes/as they say; as the actress said to the bishop (*b*) l'autre, that one there; qu'est-ce qu'il veut, l'autre? what does *he* want? (*c*) (*riposte*) vous en êtes un autre! and the same to you! (*d*) à d'autres! pull the other one (it's got bells on)!/go and tell that to the marines! (*Voir* **chat 5**)

Auvergnat [ovɛrɲa] *nm P* 1. *Péj* Jew*/four-by-two 2. (*langue incompréhensible*) double Dutch.

Auverpin [ovɛrpɛ̃], **Auverploum** [ovɛrplum] *nm P Péj* native of Auvergne/Auvergnat.

auxi [ɔksi] *nm* (*abbr = auxiliaire*) 1. *F Mil etc* auxiliary 2. *P* (*prison*) trusty.

auxico [ɔksiko], **auxigo** [ɔksigo] *nm* = **auxi**.

auxipatte [ɔksipat] *nm F Mil* = **auxi 1**.

avaler [avale] *vtr* 1. *F* avaler les kilomètres, to eat up the miles 2. *P* avaler son bulletin/son extrait de naissance, *Vieilli* avaler sa chique, l'avaler, to die*/to kick the bucket/to give up the ghost. (*Voir* **consigne; crapaud 1; cuiller 3; disque 3; fumée 3; langue 2; pain 5; parapluie 1; pépin 3**)

avaloir *nm*, **avaloire** *nf* [avalwar] *Vieilli P* throat/gullet; s'arroser l'avaloir, to have a drink*/to wet one's whistle.

avantage [avãtaʒ] *nm* 1. *F* faire un avantage à qn, to be nice to s.o.; fais-moi un avantage, do me a favour 2. *F* à qui ai-je l'avantage? to whom do I have the pleasure of speaking? 3. *pl P* breasts*/charms.

avant-postes [avãpɔst] *nmpl P* breasts*/bristols.

avant-scène [avãsɛn] *nf P* breasts*; elle a une belle avant-scène, she's well stacked/she's a big girl.

avaro [avaro] *nm P* 1. accident/mishap 2. trouble/worry.

avec [avɛk] I *prép P* on l'a fait avec mon frère, my brother and I did it II *adv F* elle a pris mon portefeuille et s'est sauvée avec, she took my wallet and ran off with it; il faudra faire avec, you'll have to make do with what you've got. (*Voir* **ça 3**)

aveux [avø] *nmpl P* passer à la chambre des aveux spontanés, to be put through the third degree/to get the rough stuff.

aviron [avirɔ̃] *nm F* spoon.

avocat [avɔka] *nm P* faire l'avocat/le faire à l'avocat, to act as an accomplice/a decoy. (*Voir* **bêcheur I 4**)

avoine [avwan] *nf P* 1. food*/grub/chow 2. coller/filer/refiler une avoine à qn, to give s.o. a good hiding/a thrashing; to beat s.o. up*/to work s.o. over; (*prostituée*) to flagellate/to whip (a client).

avoiner [avwane] *P* I *vtr* avoiner qn, *voir* **avoine 2** II *vi* to go/travel very fast (*in a powerful car*)/to zoom along.

avoir [avwar] *vtr* 1. *F* to fool (s.o.)/to pull a fast one on (s.o.); se faire/se laisser avoir, to be taken in/to be had/to be conned; on vous a eu! you've been had!/you've been taken for a ride!/you've been done! on ne m'a pas comme ça! you can't fool me!/you won't catch me that way! **il a été bien eu!** he's been well and truly had! **on les aura!** we'll beat them yet!/we'll get them! **2.** F **en avoir,** to have guts/to have balls (*Voir* **couille 1** (*b*)) **3.** F **tu en auras!** you've got it coming to you! **4.** F **je l'ai eu!** I passed (my exam)!/I got it! **5.** F **en avoir par-dessus la tête/plein le dos/assez,** to be fed up*/cheesed off/browned off; **j'en ai jusque-là!** I'm fed up to the (back) teeth! **6.** F **avoir qn à la pitié/à la sympathie,** etc, to play on s.o.'s pity, sympathy, etc **7.** P **avoir une femme,** to have (sex* with) a woman **8.** P **l'avoir,** to have syphilis*. (*Voir* **sec** I **1**; **tournant 1**)

avorton [avɔrtɔ̃] *nm* F *Péj* (*personne*) (little) runt/shorty/shrimp/weed.

azimut [azimyt] *nm* F (*a*) **dans tous les azimuts,** in all directions/all over the shop; left, right and centre; **direction tous azimuts,** facing all ways/*esp NAm* every which way (*b*) **tous azimuts,** (*objet*) multi-purpose.

azimuté [azimyte] *a* P mad*/barmy/crazy*/bonkers.

azor [azɔr] *nm* **1.** *Vieilli* F dog*; (*nom donné aux chiens*) Fido/Rover **2.** A P Mil knapsack/pack **3.** A P revolver*/pistol **4.** P WC*/bog/shithouse **5.** P (*théâtre*) **appeler Azor,** to boo/to hiss.

aztèque [aztɛk] *nm* P *Péj* undersized* man/shrimp of a man/short-arse/(little) runt.

B

baba [baba] I *nm* **1.** *P* buttocks*; **le mettre dans le baba à qn**, to do the dirty on s.o.; **l'avoir dans le baba**, to be badly let down/to get the thin end of the wedge/to come unstuck/to get screwed up; (*être dupé*) to be conned/to be had **2.** *V* female genitals* **3.** *P* **baba (cool)**, (peace-loving) dropout/hippy/ groovy. (*Voir* **carrer I 3**) II *a inv F* amazed*/flabbergasted; **en être/en rester/en demeurer baba**, to be dumbfounded/to be flabbergasted/to be gobsmacked.

babasse [babas] *nf P* pinball; **secouer la babasse**, to play pinball.

babillard [babijar] *nm* **1.** *F* notice board (for job vacancies) **2.** *P* newspaper/daily rag/ scandal sheet **3.** *P* lawyer/brief **4.** *P* chaplain/padre.

babillarde [babijard] *nf P* **1.** letter/line/note **2.** (wrist) watch.

babille [babij] *nf P* = **babillarde 1**.

babin [babɛ̃] *nm Vieilli P* mouth*/chops.

babines [babin] *nfpl F* (*a*) lips; **vous vous en (pour) lécherez les babines**, you'll lick your lips/smack your chops over it (*b*) cheeks. (*Voir* **caler II 2**)

babouin [babwɛ̃] *nm F* pimple on the lip.

babouines [babwin] *nfpl F* = **babines**.

babs [babz] *nm P* = **baba 3**.

baby-foot [babifut] *nm F* miniature *or* table football.

bac [bak] *nm F* (*abrév* = *baccalauréat*) French school-leaving examination (*approx* = A level); **passer son bac**, to sit one's *baccalauréat/*= one's A levels. (*Voir* **bachot**).

bacantes, baccantes [bakɑ̃t] *nfpl F* = **bacchantes**.

baccara [bakara] *nm P* **1.** **avoir baccara**, (*être perdant*) to be on a hiding to nothing/to be sure to lose **2.** **être en plein baccara**, (*avoir des ennuis*) to have a run of bad luck/to have nothing going right; (*être apathique*) to be down in the dumps.

bacchanal [bakanal] *nm F* uproar*/row/ din/racket; **faire un bacchanal de tous les diables**, to kick up a hell of a row/to make the dickens of a noise.

bacchanale [bakanal] *nf F* orgy; drunken revel.

bacchantes [bakɑ̃t] *nfpl F* moustache*; **bacchantes en guidon (de course)**, handlebar moustache.

bâche [baʃ] *nf P* **1.** (*casquette*) cap **2.** (bed) sheet; blanket; **se mettre dans les bâches**, to go to bed*/to hit the sack; **piquer une bâche**, to go to sleep*/to have a kip **3.** *pl* (*au tennis*) net; (*au football*) goal.

se bâcher [səbaʃe] *vpr P* **1.** to cover one's head*/to put on a hat* **2.** to get dressed **3.** to go to bed*/to hit the sack.

bâcheuse [baʃøz] *nf P* landlady (of a lodging-house).

bâchis [baʃi] *nm P* = **bâche 1**.

bachot [baʃo] *nm F* = **bac**; **boîte à bachot**, crammer/cramming school.

bachotage [baʃɔtaʒ] *nm F* cramming/ swotting.

bachoter [baʃɔte] *F* I *vtr* to cram (up) (a subject)/to swot for the *baccalauréat* or other exam II *vi* (*préparer un examen*) to cram/to swot; (*passer le baccalauréat*) to sit the *baccalauréat* exam.

bachoteur, -euse [baʃɔtœr, -øz] *n F* student cramming/swotting (up) for an exam (*esp* the *baccalauréat*); student who works hard/swot.

bâclage [baklaʒ] *nm F* scamping/botching (up) (of work).

bâclé [bakle] *a F* **travail bâclé**, slapdash/ slipshod work; **un travail bâclé**, a botch(ed) job.

bâcler [bakle] *vtr F* to botch (work)/to do (sth) hurriedly and carelessly/to make a hash of (sth).

bada [bada] *nm P* **1.** (*a*) hat/titfer (*b*) **le petit bada rouquinos**, Little Red Riding Hood

2. **porter le bada,** (*prendre la responsabilité*) to take the rap/to carry the can; (*avoir mauvaise réputation*) to have a bad reputation; *esp* to be suspected of being a police informer*; **faire porter le bada à qn,** to get s.o. falsely accused; **on lui a fait porter le bada,** he got a bum rap.

badaboum [badabum] *nm* P brawl/scuffle/ shindy/free-for-all.

baderne [badɛrn] *nf* F *Péj* **une (vieille) baderne,** an old fog(e)y*/an old stick-in-the-mud/an old fuddy-duddy; *Mil* a blimp/a Colonel Blimp.

badigeon [badiʒɔ̃] *nm* F (thick layer of) make-up/face-paint/war-paint. (*Voir* **ripolin**)

badigoinces [badigwɛ̃s] *nfpl* P lips; **se coller du rouge aux badigoinces,** to put on some lipstick.

badines [badin] *nfpl* *Vieilli* P legs*/pins; **agiter les badines,** to run.

Badingues, les [lebadɛ̃g] *Prnmpl* les Batignolles (*district of Paris*).

Badinguet [badɛ̃gɛ] *Prnm* F *Hist* (nickname for) Napoleon III.

badinter [badɛ̃tɛr] *nm* F recidivist.

badour [badur] *a* F 1. (*personne*) attractive/good-looking/handsome/pretty 2. nice/ pleasant.

bâdrage [bɑdraʒ] *nm* *FrC* P nuisance/ annoyance.

bâdrant [bɑdrɑ̃] *a* *FrC* P annoying/ bothersome.

bâdrer [bɑdre] *vtr* *FrC* P to bother/to annoy.

baffe [baf] *nf* P 1. blow*/slap/biff; **coller/ flanquer une baffe à qn,** to slap s.o. (round the face)/to clip s.o. round the ear 2. *Fig* (*atteinte au moral*) slap in the face; **j'ai pris une de ces baffes** I was really traumatized/it affected me deeply. (*Voir* **java 2**).

baffer [bafe] *vtr* P **baffer (la gueule à) qn,** to give s.o. a slap (round the face)/to biff s.o.

baffi [bafi] *nf* *Vieilli* P moustache*.

bafouillage [bafujaʒ] *nm* F (*a*) incoherent speech/babbling (*b*) swallowing of one's words (*c*) nonsense/rubbish/gibberish (*d*) stammering/spluttering/stuttering (*e*) (*moteur*) missing/misfiring/sputtering.

bafouille [bafuj] *nf* P letter/note/line.

bafouiller [bafuje] *vtr & i* F (*a*) to babble (*b*) to swallow one's words (*c*) to talk nonsense/gibberish (*d*) to stammer/to splutter; **bafouiller quelque chose,** to stutter out something (*e*) (*moteur*) to miss/to misfire/to sputter.

bafouillette [bafujɛt] *nf* P short letter.

bafouilleur, -euse [bafujœr, -øz] *n* F (*a*) stammerer/stutterer (*b*) someone who talks nonsense/rubbish.

bafouillis [bafuji] *nm* F = **bafouillage**.

bâfre [bɑfr] *nf* P 1. *A* feed/tuck-in/blow-out 2. *Vieilli* moustache and beard/full set.

bâfrer [bɑfre] P I *vi* to stuff oneself (with food) II *vtr* to wolf/to gobble (one's food) (down); **bâfrer sa mangeaille,** to stuff one's face III *vpr* **se bâfrer,** to stuff oneself (with food).

bâfrerie [bɑfrəri] *nf* P gluttony/gorging/ guzzling.

bâfreur, -euse [bɑfrœr, -øz] *n* P glutton/ hog/pig/greedy-guts/guzzler.

bagage [bagaʒ] *nm* F **plier bagage,** (*partir*) to (pack up and) clear out/to do a bunk; (*mourir*) to die*/to pop off/to snuff it.

bagarrer [bagare] F I *vi* to fight/to battle (pour, for); **il faudra bagarrer pour l'avoir,** you'll have to fight to get it II *vpr* **se bagarrer,** to fight/to brawl/to have a set-to/to have a punch-up.

bagarreur, -euse [bagarœr, -øz] *n* F brawler/rowdy; **c'est un bagarreur/une bagarreuse,** he's/she's a fighter.

bagatelle [bagatɛl] *nf* P *Iron* sex*/love-making; **être porté sur la bagatelle,** to be fond of sex*/to like it a lot/to have a one-track mind; **les bagatelles de la porte,** foreplay/ heavy petting.

bagne [baɲ] *nm* F one's place of work (factory, office, etc); **quel bagne!** what a hole! **un vrai bagne,** a sweatshop; **cette chaleur, quel bagne!** this heat is unbearable.

bagnole [baɲɔl] *nf* F car*/motor/wheels; **c'est une belle bagnole,** she's a nice job/that's a nice motor; **une vieille bagnole,** an old banger/a jalopy/an old heap.

bagot [bago] *nm* P luggage; **faire les bagots,** to steal luggage (from parked cars, railway stations, etc).

bagot(t)er [bagɔte] *vi* P 1. to walk (quickly); to run 2. **comment vont les affaires? – ça bagot(t)e,** how's business? – not so bad.

bagou [bagu] *nm* F glibness (of tongue); **avoir du bagou,** to have a smooth tongue/to have the gift of the gab/to have a touch of the Blarney.

bagougnasses [baguɲas] *nfpl* P lips.

bagouler [bagule] *vi* P to talk/to jabber away nineteen to the dozen.

bagouse [baguz] *nf* 1. *P* ring (worn on finger) 2. *P* luck; **avoir de la bagouse**, to be lucky 3. *P* **l'avoir dans la bagouse**, to be tricked/conned 4. *V* anus*/ring; **être/refiler de la bagouse**, to be a homosexual*/to be one of them.

bagout [bagu] *nm F* = **bagou**.

bagouze [baguz] *nf P V* = **bagouse**.

bague [bag] *nf P* anus*/ring(-piece).

baguenaudage [bagnodaʒ] *nm F* mooching about/loafing around.

baguenaude [bagnod] *nf P* 1. pocket 2. walk/stroll.

baguenauder [bagnode] *vi & pr F* (se) **baguenauder**, to mooch about/to loaf around.

baguette [bagɛt] *nf* 1. *P* **avoir de la baguette**, to be lucky 2. *V* **filer un coup de baguette/filer un coup dans les baguettes à une femme**, to have sex* with/to screw/to lay a woman 3. *F* **cheveux raides comme des baguettes de tambour**, dead straight hair 4. *F* **commander/faire marcher/mener qn à la baguette**, to rule s.o. with a rod of iron 5. *P pl* legs*/drumsticks; **baguettes de tambour**, thin legs; **mettre les baguettes**, to run away*/to beat it/to scarper.

bahut [bay] *nm P* 1. school/lycée 2. (*a*) car * (*b*) taxi (*c*) lorry/truck (*d*) (powerful) motorbike.

bahutage [baytaʒ] *nm P* (*écoles*) (*a*) ragging (*b*) noisy behaviour.

bahuter [bayte] I *vi P* (*écoles*) (*a*) to rag (*b*) to behave noisily II *vpr* **se bahuter** *V* to masturbate*.

bahuteur, -euse [baytœr, -øz] *n P* (*écoles*) 1. rowdy pupil 2. schoolfriend/schoolmate.

baigner [beɲe] *vi F* **baigner dans le beurre/dans l'huile/dans la margarine**, to be functioning perfectly/to go very smoothly/to go like a dream; **tout baigne (dans l'huile)/ça baigne**, everything's fine/hunky-dory.

baigneur [beɲœr] *nm* 1. *P* buttocks*/bum; **l'avoir dans le baigneur**, to be duped/tricked/had; **se casser le baigneur**, to worry 2. *P* body for burial; body of s.o. being buried 3. *P* foetus 4. *P* nose*/snout 5. *V* female genitals*/fanny.

bail [baj] *nm* 1. *F* **il y a un bail/ça fait un bail qu'on ne s'est pas vus!** it's ages/yonks since we met!/we haven't seen each other in donkey's years! 2. *P* **casser le bail**, to get a divorce; to separate.

baille [baj] *nf P* 1. water (of sea, river, etc);

la (**grande**) **baille**, the sea/the drink; **tomber à la baille**, to fall in(to) the drink 2. water (in general) 3. **la Baille**, the *École navale* 4. dilapidated ship/old tub.

bâiller [baje] *vi* 1. to be (wide) open (*Voir* **moule** I 2) 2. **en bâiller**, to be amazed*/staggered.

bain [bɛ̃] *nm* 1. *F* (*a*) **être dans le bain**, (*être dans une situation compromettante*) to be implicated/mixed up in it; (*être au courant*) to be in the know/to be with it (*b*) **se mettre dans le bain**, (*se mettre au courant*) to be informed/in the know; to get genned up; (*s'y mettre*) to get down to it/to get into the swing of things; **mettre qn dans le bain**, to implicate s.o. 2. *F* **envoyer qn au bain**, to send s.o. packing*/to send s.o. off with a flea in his ear/to tell s.o. where he gets off 3. *F* **il a pris tout le bain**, he's been blamed for everything 4. *F* **plaisanterie de garçon de bains**, senseless/stupid joke 5. *F* **c'est un bain qui chauffe**, there's trouble ahead/there's a storm brewing 6. *P* (*a*) **flanquer qn dans le bain**, to accuse s.o./to put s.o. on the spot (*b*) **sortir qn du bain**, to get s.o. out of a fix (*c*) **tremper dans le bain**, to be in it up to one's neck/to be in dead trouble 7. *P* **le Grand Bain**, police archives. (*Voir* **lézard 2**)

bain-marie [bɛ̃mari] *nm P* bidet.

baisable [bɛzabl] *a V* (*femme*) desirable/sexy/screwable.

baisage [bɛzaʒ] *nm V* sex*/love-making.

baisant [bɛzɑ̃] *a P* first-rate/fantastic/super; **peu baisant**, lousy.

baise [bez] *nf* 1. *V* sex*/screw/fuck/lay; **une bonne baise**, a good fuck/screw 2. *P* (*écoles*) detention.

baisé [beze] *a V* **être baisé de la tête**, to be mad*/mental/screwy.

baise-à-l'œil [bɛzalœj] *nf P* (*prostituées*) honest/straight woman/woman not on the game.

baise-en-ville [bɛzɑ̃vil] *nm P* (small) overnight bag; (*sac à main*) man's handbag.

baiser [beze] I *vtr* 1. *V* to have sex*/to have it off/to have it away with (s.o.); to screw/to fuck/to lay (s.o.); to knock (s.o.) off 2. *P* (*a*) to catch (s.o.) red-handed/in the act; **se faire baiser**, to be caught with one's pants down (*b*) to arrest* (s.o.); **se faire baiser**, to get nabbed/nicked 3. *P* to steal*/to knock off/to lift; **il m'a baisée de mon sac à main**, he nicked my handbag 4. *P* to deceive/to fool* (s.o.)/to screw; **se faire baiser**, to be taken in/to be taken for a ride/to be had/to be screwed; **il m'a bien baisé**, he screwed me good and proper **5.** *P* to understand; **je n'y baise rien**, I don't get it/I can't make head nor tail of it **II** *vi* to have sex*/to fuck/to screw; **il baise vachement bien**, he's a good screw/a good lay. (*Voir* **bourgeoise 2; canard 14; couille 7; cygne; épicier 2; hussard; à la hussarde; levrette; papa 1; riche II**).

baiseur, -euse [bɛzœr, -øz] *n V* s.o. who is fond of sex*; fucker; **c'est une sacrée baiseuse!** she's a terrific lay!/she's a fucking good screw! **c'est un sacré baiseur**, he's a real stud.

baisodrome [bɛzɔdrɔm] *nm V* (*lieu où l'on fait souvent l'amour*) (*a*) brothel* (*b*) bedroom; bed (*c*) lovers' lane, etc.

baisoir [bɛzwar] *nm V* = **baisodrome**.

baisoter [bɛzɔte] *vtr F* to kiss (s.o.); to give (s.o.) a peck on the cheek.

baisouiller [bɛzuje] *vtr & i V* to have sex* (with)/to screw (s.o.) (perfunctorily/badly).

baisse-froc [bɛsfrɔk] *nm P* coward*/chicken/yellowbelly. (*Voir* **froc 5**)

bakchich [bakʃiʃ] *nm F* gratuity/tip (as a bribe); baksheesh; backhander.

balade [balad] *nf F* (*a*) stroll/ramble (on foot); **on se fait une petite balade?** come on! let's go for a walk! (*b*) drive/spin/run (in car, etc).

balader [balade] *F* **I** *vi* **envoyer balader qn**, to tell s.o. to clear off/to send s.o. packing*; (*amant*) to jilt/to chuck; **envoyer balader son boulot**, to chuck one's job **II** *vtr* **1.** to take out/to drag around; **balader son chien**, to take one's dog for a walk; **il balade toujours sa valise avec lui**, he always drags that suitcase around with him **2.** *P* **balader qn**, to deceive/fool* s.o.; to lead s.o. on/to have s.o. on **III** *vpr* **se balader** (*a*) to go for a walk/to take a stroll (*b*) to traipse about/to swan around (*c*) **ses affaires se baladent dans la maison**, his things are strewn all over the house.

baladeur, -euse [baladœr, -øz] *a F* **avoir les mains baladeuses**, to have wandering/roaming hands.

balai [balɛ] *nm* **1.** *F* **donner un coup de balai**, to make a clean sweep (of one's staff); to get rid of undesirable people **2.** *F* last bus, tube, etc (at night). (*Voir* **voiture-balai**) **3.** *F* **ramasser les balais**, to come last (in a yacht race, etc); (*échouer*) to fail*/to go down the drain/to come unstuck; **être du balai**, to be the last to arrive **4.** *P* **du balai!** clear off!/hop it!

5. *P* **con comme un balai**, as daft as a brush; **sacré balai!** you bloody fool! **6.** *P* **balai à/de chiottes**, moustache* **7.** *P* year; **il a 50 balais**, he's fifty **8.** (*courses*) **les balais**, (*in steeplechase*) the fences. (*Voir* **balayette; manche I 4; peau 19**)

balaise [balɛz] *P* **I** *a* (*a*) hefty/beefy (*b*) smart/brainy **II** *nm* (*a*) strong/powerfully built/hefty man (*b*) *Iron* smart one/brains; **t'es un balaise, toi!** you're a bright one!/a bright spark!

balançage [balɑ̃saʒ] *nm P* denouncing/informing/grassing.

balance [balɑ̃s] *nf P* **1.** dismissal/sacking **2.** informer*/grass/squealer.

balancé [balɑ̃se] *a F* **bien balancé**, (*personne*) well-built/well-proportioned/well set-up; **elle est bien balancée**, she's got a good figure; she's got curves in all the right places; she's well stacked.

balancement [balɑ̃smɑ̃] *nm P* prison sentence*/stretch.

balancer [balɑ̃se] **I** *vtr F* **1.** (*a*) to throw/to chuck (stones, etc) (*b*) to throw (sth) away/out; to get rid of (sth)/to chuck (sth) away; **elle a tout balancé**, (*en jetant*) she's thrown everything away; (*en abandonnant tout*) she's given it all up **2. balancer un coup de pied à qn**, to kick out at s.o. **3.** to dismiss* (s.o.)/to fire (s.o.)/to sack (s.o.)/to give (s.o.) the push **4.** to give/offer; **balance-moi 1000 balles**, give me 1000 francs **5.** (*a*) to denounce* (s.o.)/grass on (s.o.)/to put the finger on (s.o.); **balancer la cavalerie**, to shop/grass on/blow the gaff on one's accomplices (*b*) **balancer une affaire**, to give information on a deal/to gen (s.o.) up on a deal. (*Voir* **décor 1; fumée 2; grouille; lourde 1; purée 2**) **II** *vi F* **1.** (*musique*) to swing; **ça balance!** it's got rhythm!/it's got a good beat! **2.** (*sur une moto*) to lean over in bends **3.** to become an informer; **il a balancé**, he grassed **III** *vpr* **se balancer 1.** *P* **je m'en balance!** I don't give/care a damn! **il se balance bien de tout ça**, he doesn't give a toss for all that **2. il s'est balancé du 16ème étage**, he chucked himself off the 16th storey.

balanceur, -euse [balɑ̃sœr, -øz] *n F* informer*/squealer/grass.

balançoire [balɑ̃swar] *nf* **1.** *Vieilli F* **de la balançoire/des balançoires**, nonsense*/rubbish; **je ne coupe pas dans tes balançoires**, you can't kid me/I'm not falling for that **2.** *F* **envoyer qn à la balançoire**, to send s.o.

packing*/to get rid of s.o. 3. *P* balançoire à Mickey/à minouche, sanitary towel/*NAm* sanitary napkin 4. = **balance 2**.

balanstiquer [balɑ̃stike] *vtr P* = **balancer I 1, 3, 5** (*a*).

balarguer [balarge] *vtr P* = **balancer I 1, 2, 3**.

balayer [baleje] *vtr F* to dismiss*/to fire/to sack; balayer tout le personnel, to make a clean sweep of the staff. (*Voir* **planche 2**)

balayette [balɛjɛt] *nf V* 1. penis*; dans le dos/dans le cul, la balayette! it's all up!/it's finished! 2. balayette infernale, (*pénis de belle taille*) ramrod/tadger; (*coït*) bonking/screwing.

balayeuse [balɛjøz] *nf F* long hair.

balcon [balkɔ̃] *nm P* (il) y a du monde au balcon, she's well stacked/she's got big knockers; quel balcon! what a pair of beauts/knockers!

baleine [balɛn] *nf F* rire comme une baleine, to laugh uproariously/to fall about (laughing).

baleste [balɛst], **balèze** [balɛz] *a & nm P* = **balaise**.

baliser [balize] *vi P* to be afraid*/to have the wind up.

ballade [balad] *nf P* pocket; faire les ballades à qn, to go through s.o.'s pockets.

balle [bal] *nf* 1. *P* face*/mug; avoir une bonne balle, to look pleasant enough 2. *P* (old *or* new) franc; dix balles, ten francs; t'as pas cent balles? (*formule des mendiants*) can you spare some change (for a cup of tea)? 3. *P* c'est ma balle, that's my affair/my business 4. *P* ça fait ma balle, that suits me down to the ground 5. *F* raide comme balle, like a shot/like (greased) lightning; without beating about the bush 6. *F* (*a*) renvoyer la balle à qn, to give s.o. tit for tat/to give s.o. as good as he gave; to turn the tables on s.o. (*b*) se renvoyer la balle, to pass the buck 7. *F* à vous la balle, (*c'est votre tour*) (it's) your turn; (*c'est à vous qu'on s'adresse*) that (remark, etc) was aimed at you 8. *F* enfant de la balle, s.o. (*esp* actor, circus performer) born into a profession/following in his father's footsteps 9. *P* balle de copaille, barbiturates*/barbs. (*Voir* **peau 19**; **trou 8**)

baller [bale] *vi P* envoyer baller qn, to send s.o. packing*/to give s.o. the push.

ballet [balɛ] *nm P* ballet rose, (sexual) orgy involving under-age girls; ballet bleu, (sexual) orgy involving young boys.

ballochards [balɔʃar] *nmpl P* breasts*.

bal(l)oche [balɔʃ] *nm P* (local) dance.

balloches [balɔʃ] *nfpl V* testicles*/balls/bollocks.

ballon [balɔ̃] *P I nm* 1. buttocks*; enlever le ballon à qn, to give s.o. a kick up the bum/*NAm* butt 2. stomach*; se remplir le ballon, to have a good blow-out/to tuck into one's food 3. faire ballon, (*être privé de qch*) to go without food; to tighten one's belt/to go without; (*être déçu*) to be disappointed; to come away empty-handed 4. faire souffler dans le ballon, to breathalyse (s.o.)/to get (s.o.) to blow into the bag 5. attraper le ballon, to become pregnant*/to get in the family way; avoir le ballon, to be pregnant*/to be in the family way/to be in the club; flanquer le ballon à qn, to get s.o. pregnant*/up the spout; to knock s.o. up 6. prison*/nick; faire du ballon, to do time/to do a stretch/to do bird; mettre qn au ballon, to send s.o. to prison*/to put s.o. inside 7. prison van*/Black Maria 8. (contents of) round wine glass; un ballon de rouge, a glass of red wine II *a* austere/spartan; un régime ballon, a very strict diet III *excl* nothing!/damn all!/sweet FA!

ballonner [balɔne] *vtr P* to imprison*/to put (s.o.) in clink.

ballot [balo] *nm P* fool*/clot/twit/dolt; tu parles d'un ballot! he's a prize idiot!/what an ass! au bout du quai les ballots! get lost*!/go (and) jump in the lake!

balluches [balyʃ] *nfpl P* (*esp forçats*) (pack of) cigarettes/fags.

balluchonner [balyʃɔne] *vtr P* = **baluchonner**.

balluchonneur [balyʃɔnœr] *nm P* = **baluchonneur**.

ballustrines [balystrin] *nfpl V* testicles*/balls.

balmuche! [balmyʃ] *excl Vieilli P* = **balpeau 1**.

baloche [balɔʃ] *nm P* (local) dance.

balourd [balur] *P I a* false/fake/sham; imitation (jewels, etc); phon(e)y II *nm* 1. fool*/idiot/twerp/twit 2. *pl* balourds (*a*) false banknotes (*b*) false identity papers.

balpeau [balpo] *P I excl* (*verlan de peau de balle!*) (*rien*) nothing*!/damn all!/sweet FA! (*rien à faire*) nothing doing!*/no dice! II *nm* faire balpeau, to be disappointed; to come away empty-handed.

Balthazar [baltazar] *nm P* good meal/tuck-in/blow-out/nosh-up.

baltringue [baltrɛ̃g] *a & nm* P good-for-nothing.

baluche [balyʃ] *nm* P (local) dance; **faire les baluches**, to play in dance bands.

baluchonner [balyʃɔne] *vtr* P to pack away (stolen goods) in a bag, etc (during a robbery).

baluchonneur [balyʃɔnœr] *nm* P (small-time) burglar/housebreaker.

bambochade [bɑ̃bɔʃad] *nf* F une bambochade, a bit of a spree.

bambochard [bɑ̃bɔʃar] *nm* F = bambocheur.

bamboche [bɑ̃bɔʃ] *nf* F spree*/good time/bender/binge. (*Voir* **bamboula** II).

bambocher [bɑ̃bɔʃe] *vi* F to go on a spree*/to paint the town red/to live it up/to have a good time*/to have a ball.

bambocheur, -euse [bɑ̃bɔʃœr, -øz] *n* F reveller/hell-bender/hell-raiser/fast liver.

bambou [bɑ̃bu] *nm* 1. F sucer/tirer sur le bambou, to smoke opium*/to suck the bamboo 2. F (*a*) coup de bambou, (*insolation*) sunstroke; (*accès de folie*) sudden attack of madness; piquer le coup de bambou, to get sunstroke; to go mad*; il a le coup de bambou, he's gone mad*/he's gone off his rocker/he's lost his marbles; (*épuisé*) he's tired out/whacked (*b*) c'est le coup de bambou! (*addition, note à payer*) it's daylight robbery! 3. P aller aux bambous, (*forçat*) to be buried 4. P être sous le bambou, to be banned/to be persona non grata somewhere 5. V avoir le bambou, to have an erection*/a hard-on. (*Voir* **sonner 5**)

bamboula [bɑ̃bula] I *nm* P Péj negro* II *nf* F spree*/bender/good time*/binge; faire la bamboula, to have a good time/to live it up/to have a ball/to go out on the town. (*Voir* **bamboche**)

banane [banan] *nf* 1. P military decoration/gong; *pl* bananes, fruit-salad 2. P (big) military helicopter*/chopper 3. F (*cyclisme*) porter la banane, to wear the leader's yellow jersey in the Tour de France 4. F (*coiffure*) rock and roll hairstyle of the 1950s/Teddy-boy cut; duck tail/duck's arse/DA 5. F (car) bumper 6. F skateboard 7. V avoir la banane, to have an erection*/to have a hard-on/to get it up 8. banane! (*insulte*) you fool*!/you berk! (*Voir* **peau 12**)

bananer [banane] *vtr* P se faire bananer, to be deceived/to be conned.

banc [bɑ̃] *nm* 1. F il faut vous remettre sur les bancs, you'd better go back to school 2. P pavement/*NAm* sidewalk; avoir commencé/débuté sur le banc, (*en parlant de la tenancière d'un bordel*) to have begun as a practising prostitute; to have started off on the streets 3. P banc volant, itinerant stallholder. (*Voir* **pied 18**)

banco! [bɑ̃ko] *int* P agreed!*/OK!/you're on!/done!

bancroche [bɑ̃krɔʃ] *a & n* lame/gammy (person).

bandaison [bɑ̃dɛzɔ̃] *nf* V erection*/horn/hard-on.

bandant [bɑ̃dɑ̃] *a* V (*a*) (*surt fille, femme*) desirable/sexually exciting/raunchy; elle est bandante, she's (a bit of) hot stuff/she's a bit of all right/she really gets me going/she's a cracker (*b*) thrilling/stimulating; c'est pas bandant, that's not exactly earth-shattering/it's not exactly a turn-on.

bande [bɑ̃d] *nf* 1. F par la bande, indirectly/in a roundabout way; apprendre qch par la bande, to hear sth on the grapevine 2. F crowd/group/gang; une bande de motards, a gang of bikers/hell's angels 3. V bande de ..., (*insulte*) bunch of ...; bande de cons/bande d'enculés! load of cretins/cunts/piss-artists!

bande-à-l'aise [bɑ̃dalɛz] *nm* V coward*/chicken/yellowbelly.

bander [bɑ̃de] *vi* V 1. (*a*) to have an erection*/to have a hard-on/to get it up; il ne bandait pas, he couldn't get it up; il bandait comme un cerf/un Turc, he had a huge erection*/hard-on; he was really horny/randy (*b*) to feel fruity/horny/randy/turned on (*c*) (en) bander pour qn, to desire s.o. sexually/to be turned on by s.o./to be horny for s.o.; *Fig* to be excited by s.o. (*d*) faire bander, to excite/to thrill; le rock, ça la fait bander, she gets a real buzz from rock music 2. bander mou/ne bander que d'une, to be afraid*/to have the wind up/to have the willies 3. *Hum* bander à part, (*faire bande à part*) to keep (oneself) to oneself. (*Voir* **zéro 6**)

bandeur, -euse [bɑ̃dœr, -øz] *n* V sexually obsessed person/s.o. with a one-track mind/s.o. who can't get enough; (*homme*) randy bugger/devil/sod; a bit of a lecher; (*femme*) a goer/a nympho; quel bandeur, he's continually randy/he's always trying to get his end away.

bandocheur [bɑ̃dɔʃœr] *nm* V coward*/chicken/yellowbelly.

bandouiller [bɑ̃duje] *vi* V to have a small

erection*.

bang [bãg] *nm P* (*drogues*) rush (*after an injection*).

banlieue [bãljø] *nf F Péj* de banlieue, second-rate; tacky; naff.

banlieusard, -arde [bãljøzar, -ard] *F* **I** *n* (*a*) suburbanite (*b*) commuter **II** *a* suburban.

bannes [ban] *nfpl P* (bed) sheets; se mettre dans les bannes, to get between the sheets/to hit the sack.

bannière [banjɛr] *nf P* être en bannière, to be in one's shirt(-tails)/shirt-sleeves. (*Voir* **croix 2**)

banque [bãk] *nf* 1. *P* (jour de) banque, pay day; aller/passer à la banque, to draw one's wages 2. *P* tailler une banque, to bet at cards; faire sauter la banque, to break the bank.

banquer [bãke] *vtr & i P* to pay* (up)/to shell out/to cough up/to stump up.

banquettes [bãkɛt] *nfpl F* (*théâtre*) jouer devant les banquettes, to play to an (almost) empty house.

banquezingue [bãkzẽg] *nm P* banker.

baptême [batɛm] *nm P* (collective) rape/ gang bang.

baptiser [batize] *vtr* 1. *F* to stain (a tablecloth, new clothes) 2. *F* to water down (wine, milk, etc).

Baptiste [batist] *Prnm F* 1. être tranquille comme Baptiste, to be as cool as a cucumber; to feel quite calm and collected; (*enfant*) to be as quiet as a mouse 2. (*cartes, esp belote*) petit Baptiste, trump nine.

se baquer [səbake] *vpr P* to have/to take a bath.

baquet [bakɛ] *nm* 1. *P* stomach*/breadbasket; en avoir dans le baquet, to have guts 2. *V* female genitals*/fruit-basket; danser sur le baquet, to have sex* with a woman/to screw a woman.

barabille [barabij] *nf P* mettre la barabille, to stir up trouble/to stir it up.

baraka [baraka] *nf F* (good) luck.

baraque [barak] *nf* 1. *F* (*a*) hovel/hole (of a place)/dump; quelle baraque! what a dump! il n'y a rien à manger dans cette baraque! there's nothing to eat in this joint! (*b*) place/ pad; à la baraque, at home/at my place 2. *F* (*a*) casser la baraque, to bring the house down/to have 'em rolling in the aisles (*b*) casser la baraque à qn, to ruin s.o.'s plans (*c*) faire baraque, to fail*/to flop 3. *F* toute la baraque, (*tout*) the whole bag* of tricks/the whole bang shoot; (*tout le monde*) the whole

damn lot of them 4. *F* ses copains lui ont monté la baraque avec Rosalie, his mates fixed him up with Rosalie.

baraqué [barake] *a P* bien baraqué, (*homme*) well-built/hefty/beefy; (*femme*) well-built; well-stacked.

baratin [baratẽ] *nm F* (*d'un vendeur*) patter/spiel/sales talk; (*pour draguer*) smooth talk/sweet-talk(ing); faire du baratin (à qn), to spin a yarn/to shoot a line; faire du baratin à une fille, to chat up a girl; avoir du baratin, to be a smooth-talker/to be a fast-talker; c'est du baratin, it's all nonsense*/a lot of hot air.

baratiner [baratine] *F* **I** *vtr* to sweet-talk (s.o.)/to fast-talk; baratiner un client, to give a client one's patter/sales talk/spiel; baratiner une fille, to chat up a girl **II** *vi* (*a*) to talk a lot/to chatter; (*sans sincérité*) to spin a yarn/ to shoot a line (*b*) (*vendeur*) to dish out the sales talk/the patter/the spiel; to fast-talk.

baratineur, -euse [baratinœr, -øz] *n F* glib talker/smooth-talker/fast-talker.

barbant [barbã] *a F* boring/tedious/deadly dull; ce qu'il est barbant! what a bore!/he's a real drag!

barbaque [barbak] *nf P* 1. (poor-quality) meat 2. (human) flesh. (*Voir* **marchand 1**)

barbe [barb] **I** *a F* = **barbant II** *nf F* 1. faire qch au nez et à la barbe de qn, to do sth (right) under s.o.'s nose 2. faire la barbe, to win at cards 3. (*chose ou personne*) bore*; quelle barbe!/c'est la barbe! what a bore!/ what a nuisance!/what a drag!/what a pain! la barbe! shut up*!/shut your mouth!/give it a rest! (*zut!*) damn it!/blast!/hell! 5. *Vieilli* prendre sa barbe, to get drunk*/to get pissed.

barbeau [barbo] *nm P* 1. pimp*/ponce; barbeau à la mie de pain, small-time pimp* 2. s.o. dressed in flashy clothes. (*Voir* **barbillon**)

barbelouzes [barbəluz] *nfpl Vieilli* barbed wire.

barber [barbe] **I** *vtr F* to bore* (s.o.) to tears; barber tout le monde, to bore everyone stiff **II** *vpr* se barber *F* to be bored* (stiff); se barber à cent sous de l'heure, to be bored to tears/to be bored rigid.

barbette [barbɛt] *nf P* coucher à barbette, to sleep (on a mattress) on the floor.

barbichonner [barbiʃɔne] *vi P* to win at cards.

barbifiant [barbifjã] *a F* boring/draggy/ dullsville.

barbifier [barbifje] **I** *vtr Vieilli F* 1. to shave

(s.o.) 2. to bore (s.o.) II *vpr* **se barbifier** *Vieilli F* 1. to (have a) shave 2. to be bored*.

barbillon [barbijɔ̃] *nm P* (*a*) young pimp* (*b*) small-time pimp*. (*Voir* **barbeau 1**)

barbiquet [barbikɛ] *nm P* = **barbillon**.

barbiset [barbizɛ] *nm P* = **barbillon**.

barbotage [barbɔtaʒ] *nm P* stealing/petty thieving/scrounging/pinching/pilfering.

barbote [barbɔt] *nf P* 1. medical examination (*of prostitute*) 2. frisking/body search (*of prisoner in custody*) 3. (police) search (*of premises*).

barboter [barbɔte] *P vtr* 1. to steal*/to swipe/to pinch/to nick (sth) 2. to frisk (a prisoner).

barboteur, -euse [barbɔtœr, -øz] *n P* 1. (petty) thief*/pilferer/scrounger; **c'est un barboteur**, he's got light fingers 2. **barboteuse**, prostitute* who robs her clients.

barbotier, -ière [barbɔtje, -jɛr] *n P* prison officer who searches/frisks prisoners taken into custody.

barbotin [barbɔtɛ̃] *nm A P* proceeds of a theft; loot/haul.

barbottage [barbɔtaʒ] *nm P* = **barbotage**.

barbotte [barbɔt] *nf P* = **barbote 1, 2**.

barbotter [barbɔte] *vtr & i P* = **barboter**.

barbotteur, -euse [barbɔtœr, -øz] *n P* = **barboteur, -euse**.

barbouille [barbuj] *nf P* **la barbouille**, painting (*as an art, trade or hobby*); **être dans la barbouille**, to dabble in painting; to be a (house) painter.

barbouillé [barbuje] *a F* 1. **avoir l'estomac barbouillé**, to have an upset stomach; to feel queasy/funny 2. **avoir le cœur barbouillé/se sentir tout barbouillé**, to feel sick; to be squeamish.

barbouiller [barbuje] I *vtr F* 1. **barbouiller une affaire**, to make a botch(-up) of sth/to botch sth up 2. **ça me barbouille le cœur**, that turns my stomach (over)/that makes me feel sick 3. **barbouiller des toiles**, to mess about with paints and things/to be a bit of an amateur artist II *vpr* **se barbouiller** *P* to make up (one's face).

barbouillette [barbujɛt] *nf V* **faire barbouillette**, to practise cunnilingus*.

barbouilleur, -euse [barbujœr, -øz] *n P Péj* (bad) artist/painter.

barbouse [barbuz] *P* I *nf* beard II *nm ou f* (*a*) secret agent/undercover agent (*b*) member of the secret police.

barbouseux [barbuzø] *a P* (*homme*) bearded.

barbouze [barbuz] *nm ou f P* = **barbouse**.

barbu [barby] *nm* 1. *V* (*a*) female genitals*/ pussy/beaver (*b*) pubic hair. (*Voir* **descente 4**) 2. *F* (*cartes*) king 3. *Mus* orchestral player 4. (*a*) God (*b*) Father Christmas.

barca! [barka] *int P* 1. that's enough!/cut it out! 2. nothing doing!*

barda [barda] *nm P* 1. *Mil* kit/pack 2. things/belongings/gear/stuff; heavy/cumbersome luggage 3. hundred-franc *or* thousand-franc note.

bardane [bardan] *nf P* bed-bug.

barder [barde] *vi P* to take a turn for the worse; **ça barde!** things are warming/hotting up! **ça va barder!** watch out (for trouble)!/ things are going to get rough!/there's trouble brewing!/there'll be some aggro! **ça va barder pour toi!** you're in for it!/you'll cop it! **c'est là que ça a commencé à barder!** and then the fun started! **ça a dû barder!** I bet the fur was flying! **il faut que ça barde!** jump to it!/look lively!/make it snappy! (*Voir* **matricule 2**)

barge [barʒ] *a & n P* = **bargeot, barjo(t)**.

bargeot, barjo(t) [barʒo] *P* (*verlan de jobard*) I *a* mad*/bonkers; **t'es pas barjo(t)?** have you lost your marbles? II *nm* fool*/nut/ nutter.

barlou [barlu] *nm* (*verlan de* **loubar(d)**) (young) hooligan*/yob/yobbo/thug.

barlu [barly] *nm P* 1. boat 2. rape (of a woman) by several men in succession/group rape/gang bang.

barnum [barnɔm] *nm P* 1. uproar/din/ racket 2. **montrer tout son barnum**, (*enfants*) to show one's 'private property'/= to play mummies and daddies 3. (*cirque*) big top.

baron [barɔ̃] *nm P* 1. accomplice/ confederate/decoy; **faire le baron**, to act as decoy 2. *A* rich protector; (sugar-)daddy 3. (*dans une enquête policière*) team member 4. chairman (of large firm) 5. measure/glass of beer (*75 centilitres*).

baronner [barɔne] *vi P* to act as an accomplice/a confederate/a decoy.

baroud [barud] *nm F* (*surt Mil*) fight(ing); **baroud d'honneur**, last stand/last ditch effort.

barouder [barude] *vi F* (*surt Mil*) to fight.

baroudeur [barudœr] *nm P* fighter/ brawler.

barouf(e) [baruf] *nm*, **baroufle** [barufl] *nm P* 1. uproar*/din/racket; **un barouf du dia-**

ble, a hell of a row 2. **faire du barouf,** to kick up a fuss/to cause a rumpus/to make a stink.

barque [bark] *nf F* **mener qn en barque,** to hoax* s.o./to lead s.o. up the garden path.

barrabille [barabij] *nf P* = **barabille.**

barrage [baraʒ] *nm F* **tir de barrage,** obstacles/obstruction (to thwart s.o.'s plans); thwarting of plans.

barraqué [barake] *a P* = **baraqué.**

barre [bar] *nf F* 1. avoir le coup de barre, to be exhausted*/to be fit to drop 2. **coup de barre,** steep (restaurant, hotel) bill; overcharging/fleecing; **c'est le coup de barre,** (*très cher*) it's daylight robbery; I've/you've, etc paid over the odds 3. **manger à la barre fixe,** to eat (next to) nothing 4. **placer/mettre la barre très haut,** to set oneself a difficult target/a very high standard; **placer/mettre la barre plus bas,** to set oneself an easier target 5. **à toute barre,** at top speed/at full tilt 6. avoir barre(s)/sur qn, to have an advantage over s.o./to be one up on s.o./to have the edge on s.o. 7. ten thousand (new) francs 8. **homme de barre,** staunch friend; trustworthy associate; **c'est un homme de barre,** he's straight up 9. **se rafraîchir/rincer les barres,** to (have a) drink* 10. avoir une/la barre avec qn, to make a hit with s.o. (of the opposite sex)/to hit it off with s.o.; avoir une barre pour qn, to be sexually excited* by s.o./to have the hots for s.o. 11. (*a*) barre à mine, (*personne peu sûre*) untrustworthy person (*b*) *V* avoir une barre à mine, to have an erection*/to get a hard-on.

barré [bare] *a F* être bien barré, to be in a good/advantageous position; on est mal barré, things don't look good.

barreau, pl -eaux [baro] *nm P* barreau de chaise, (large) cigar.

se barrer [səbare] *vpr P* to beat it/to run away*/to scram/to clear off; je me barre, I'm making myself scarce.

barreur [barœr] *nm* (*dans un bar, etc*) bouncer.

bas [bɑ] *nm F* bas de laine, savings; avoir un bas de laine bien garni, to have a nice little nest-egg (stashed away).

basane [bazan] *nf* 1. *P* (human) skin/hide; tanner la basane à qn, to tan s.o.'s hide 2. *P* tailler une basane à qn, to make an obscene gesture of contempt/= to put two fingers up at s.o.

bascule [baskyl] *nf P* informer*/grass/ snitch. (*Voir* **botte** II **1**; **Charlot 1**)

basculer [baskyle] *P* **I** *vtr* 1. to kill*/to bump off; il s'est fait basculer, he got bumped off 2. basculer un godet, to knock back a drink **II** *vi* to become a police informer*.

bas-de-plafond [bɑdəplafɔ̃] *nm inv F* fool*/prize idiot/thickhead.

basduc [bɑdyk] *nm,* **bas-du-cul** [bɑdyky] **I** *nm inv P* undersized* person/ short-arse **II** *a P Aut* extra-low/underslung (chassis, etc).

baskets [baskɛt] *nfpl* 1. *F* sneakers/ basketball boots 2. *P* à l'aise/bien dans ses baskets, relaxed/cool (*esp* when in a tight spot) 3. *P* lâcher les baskets à qn, to leave s.o. alone; lâche-moi les baskets! lay off!/get lost!*/get off my back! 4. *P* faire baskets, to leave* without paying; to take French leave.

basoche [bazɔʃ] *nf F Péj* the legal fraternity; termes de basoche, legal jargon.

basset [basɛ] *nm* burglar who breaks into cellars.

bassin [basɛ̃] *nm P* 1. cracher au/dans le bassin = cracher au bassinet (**bassinet**) 2. (*personne*) bore*/pain in the neck.

bassinant [basinɑ̃] *a P* boring.

bassiner [basine] *vtr P* 1. to bore* (s.o.) 2. to pester/to badger (s.o.).

bassinet [basinɛ] *nm P* cracher au bassinet, to pay* up/to cough up/to fork out.

bassinoire [basinwar] *nf* 1. *F* (*chose ou personne*) (*a*) bore* (*b*) pest/nuisance 2. *P* large (old-fashioned) watch.

basta! [basta] *excl P* that's enough (of that)!/cut it out!/give it a rest!

Bastaga, la [labastaga], **Bastoche, la** [labastɔʃ] *Prn P* the Bastille (district) (in Paris).

baston [bastɔ̃] *nm ou f P* fight*/scuffle/ brawl/free-for-all/punch-up.

bastonner¹ [bastɔne] *P* **I** *vi* (*musique, disque*) to be loud/to thump (away); ça bastonne très sec, it's got a strong beat **II** *vtr* to beat up*/to work (s.o.) over.

(se) bastonner² [(sə)bastɔne] *vi & pr P* to fight/to brawl/to have a punch-up.

bastos [bastɔs] *nf P* bullet/slug.

bastringue [bastrɛ̃g] *nm P* 1. (*a*) (seedy) dance-hall (*b*) = pub; café (*with music and dancing*) 2. (*a*) juke box (*b*) noisy dance band 3. uproar*/din/racket/shindy 4. paraphernalia/junk; tout le bastringue, the whole bag* of tricks/the (whole) works 5. building/block of flats 6. vacuum cleaner 7. (*argot des policiers*) revolver*/piece.

bastringuer [bastrɛ̃ge] *vi Vieilli P* 1. to frequent (second-rate/seedy) dance-halls 2. to make a din/a racket/a hell of a noise.

bataclan [bataklɑ̃] *nm F* 1. paraphernalia/ belongings/junk/gear/stuff 2. **tout le bataclan,** the whole lot/the whole works/the whole shooting-match; ... **et tout le bataclan,** ... and all the rest of it.

bataillon [batajɔ̃] *nm F* **inconnu au bataillon,** never heard of him.

bat' d'Af [batdaf] *nm P* 1. (= *bataillon d'Afrique*) French disciplinary battalion (*formerly stationed in North Africa*) 2. (= *bataillonnaire*) young criminal serving in a *bataillon d'Afrique*.

bateau [bato] I *nm F* 1. **monter un bateau à qn,** to hoax* s.o./to have s.o. on/to pull s.o.'s leg/to play a practical joke on s.o. 2. **mener qn en bateau,** to con s.o.; **se laisser mener en bateau,** to allow oneself to be taken in/played for a sucker 3. **du même bateau,** of the same kidney/tarred with the same brush; **des gens du même bateau,** birds of a feather 4. **être dans le même bateau (que qn),** to be in the same boat/fix (as s.o.) 5. **être du dernier bateau,** to be bang up to date 6. **arriver en trois/en quatre bateaux,** to arrive in style/with a great flourish 7. *pl* **bateaux,** big boots*/ clodhoppers 8. **faire (un) bateau,** to (take part in a) gang rape II *a inv P* banal/trite; **un sujet bateau,** a hackneyed subject/the same old thing.

bat(h) [bat] *F* I *a Vieilli* first-rate/first-class/ super/classy; **une bath gonzesse,** a peach of a girl*/a bit of all right; **un bath pantalon,** a snazzy pair of trousers; **t'es bath,** you're a good sort/a great guy; you're straight up/ you're all right; **huit jours de congé, c'est bien bath,** a week's leave — that can't be bad; **bath aux pommes,** tip-top/super-duper. (*Voir* **pieu 1**) II *nm* **c'est du bath,** it's the real thing; it's the genuine article.

bath(e)ment [batmɑ̃] *adv Vieilli F* fabulously/splendidly/terrifically.

bathouse [batuz] *a Vieilli P* = **bat(h) I.**

batifolage [batifɔlaʒ] *nm F* 1. romping/ playing around/larking about 2. flirting; necking/smooching.

batifoler [batifɔle] *vi F* 1. to romp/to play around/to lark about 2. to flirt; to neck/to smooch.

batifoleur, -euse [batifɔlœr, -øz] *n F* 1. s.o. who enjoys larking about/who enjoys having a bit of a lark 2. flirt.

batifouiller [batifuje] *vi P* to get muddled; to be all at sixes and sevens; to be all at sea.

bâtiment [batimɑ̃] *nm F* **il est du bâtiment,** (*du métier*) he's in the trade/he's in the same line (of business); (*expert*) he knows all the tricks of the trade; (*du milieu, de la partie*) he's one of us/he's one of the lads.

bâton [batɔ̃] I *nm* 1. *F* **tour de bâton,** illicit gain/graft/pickings; **savoir le tour du bâton,** to know how to spirit things away (dishonestly) 2. *F* **vie de bâton de chaise,** life of pleasure/ fast living; **mener une vie de bâton de chaise,** to live it up/to have a wild time/to have a ball 3. *P* **un bâton merdeux,** a contemptible and untrustworthy individual; a bastard*/a shit 4. *P* **être sous le bâton** = **être sous le bambou** (**bambou 4**) 5. *F* ten thousand (new) francs 6. *pl P* **bâtons (de cire/de tremplin),** legs*; **mettre les bâtons,** to run away*/to beat it/to scarper 7. *V* **avoir le bâton,** to have an erection*/a hard-on. (*Voir* **merde 13; roue 1**) II *nm P Mil* (= *bataillon*) battalion.

bâtonner [batɔne] *vtr P* to ban (s.o.)/to make (s.o.) persona non grata.

batousard [batuzar] *nm P* = **batouseur.**

batouse [batuz] *nf P* textiles; **faire la batouse,** to sell textiles door to door *or* in open-air markets; to work the markets in textiles.

batouseur [batuzœr] *nm*, **batouzard** [batuzar] *nm*, **batouzeur** [batuzœr] *nm P* (door-to-door) salesman in textiles.

battage [bataʒ] *nm F* publicity; ballyhoo; hard sell; **faire du battage autour d'un livre,** to plug/to push a book; to give a book the hard sell.

battant [batɑ̃] *P* I *a* (*personne*) dynamic/ ambitious II *nm* 1. heart/ticker 2. tongue/ clapper; **avoir un battant,** to have the gift of the gab 3. dynamic/go-ahead individual; **c'est un battant, lui,** he's got plenty of drive/of (get-up-and-)go 4. stomach*; **se remplir le battant,** to have a blow-out/a tuck-in; **n'avoir rien dans le battant,** to have an empty stomach.

battante [batɑ̃t] *nf P* clock; watch; ticker/ tick-tock.

batterie [batri] *nf F* **batterie de cuisine,** array of medals and ribbons (on uniform)/ gongs/fruit-salad.

batteur [batœr] *nm P* 1. (*a*) liar (*b*) hypocrite 2. **batteur (de pavé),** idler/loafer 3. (*argot des policiers*) instigator (*of disturbance, etc*).

batteuse [batøz] *nf P* car battery.

battoir [batwar] *nm A P* (*grande main*) great paw/mitt.

battre [batr] *vtr P* to pretend (to do sth/to be s.o. *or* sth); **battre les dingues**, to pretend to be mad*; **battre la roupillade**, to pretend to be asleep. (*Voir* **beurre 10; cinq 7; dèche 1; Niort; quart 2; sœur 3** (*a*))

bauche [boʃ] *nf P* 1. diamond/sparkler 2. false police identity card 3. playing card; **jeu des trois bauches**, three-card trick.

bavard [bavar] *nm P* 1. defending counsel/lawyer/brief/mouthpiece 2. buttocks*/bottom/behind/bum 3. = **baveux 4.**

bavarde [bavard] *nf P* 1. tongue/clapper 2. letter/note/line.

bavasser [bavase] *vi F* (*a*) to talk without thinking/to go rabbiting on/to natter/to gas/to gossip; **bavasser comme un perroquet**, to chatter away like a parrot/to rattle on (nineteen to the dozen) (*b*) to talk nonsense*/to talk a lot of hot air.

baveau, -elle [bavo, -ɛl] *a P* (*javanais de* **beau, belle**) beautiful/good-looking.

baver [bave] *vtr & i* 1. *F* (*a*) to talk/to chatter; **qu'est-ce que tu baves?** what on earth are you going on about? (*b*) **baver sur qn**, to denigrate s.o./to speak ill of s.o. 2. *F* **en baver** (**des ronds de chapeau**), to have a rough time of it; **j'en ai bavé**, it was (sheer) hell/agony; **en faire baver** (**des ronds de chapeau**) **à qn**, to put s.o. through it/to give s.o. a hard time/to make s.o. sweat (blood) 3. *F* to say (unpleasant things); **je ne veux pas entendre ce qu'il bave**, I don't want to hear him say these things 4. *P* **en baver**, to be amazed*/to be flabbergasted/to be knocked sideways 5. *F* to make (unfortunate) mistakes/to put one's foot in it. (*Voir* **burnes; chapeau 8; clignotants; rouleau 2; roustons**)

bavette [bavɛt] *nf F* **tailler une bavette**, to have a (little) chat* with s.o./to have a natter; (*de façon médisante*) to (have a) gossip.

baveuse [bavøz] *nf P* 1. tongue/clapper 2. talkative woman/chatterbox*/gasbag; (*médisante*) gossip.

baveux [bavø] *nm P* 1. talkative person/gasbag 2. lawyer/brief 3. soap 4. newspaper/rag 5. kiss on the mouth/French kiss. (*Voir* **pallot**)

bavocher [bavɔʃe] *vi P* to talk drivel/to witter on.

bavocheur [bavɔʃœr], **bavocheux**

[bavɔʃø] *nm P* talkative person/gasbag/windbag.

bavure [bavyr] *F* **I** *nf* regrettable error/unfortunate mistake (*esp made by the police*) **II** *a & adv* **sans bavure(s)/net et sans bavure(s)**, *a* clear/precise; impeccable/flawless; *adv* clearly/precisely; impeccably.

baz [baz] *nm P* school; **le Baz Grand**, the *lycée Louis-le-Grand*, in Paris.

bazar [bazar] *nm* 1. *P* **le Bazar**, the Saint-Cyr military school 2. *F* **tout le bazar**, everything/the whole works/the whole bag* of tricks; **vous allez fusiller tout le bazar**, you're going to mess up the whole show/thing 3. *P* untidy flat, room, etc; hole (of a place)/dump; **quel bazar!** what a mess!/what a shambles! 4. *P* belongings/things/gear/stuff/junk; **il a tout son bazar dans sa valoche**, he's got all his clobber stuffed in his suitcase 5. *F* **de bazar**, (of) poor quality/shoddy/tacky 6. *F* (*at a fair*) stall 7. *P* **l'avoir dans le bazar**, to be duped*/conned/tricked.

bazarder [bazarde] *vtr P* 1. to sell (sth) (cheaply); to flog; **j'ai bazardé ma bagnole**, I've sold off/I've flogged my car 2. to get rid of (sth); (*jeter*) to chuck out 3. to denounce* (s.o.)/to sell out on (s.o.)/to shop (s.o.).

b.c.b.g., B.C.B.G. [besebeʒe] (*abrév = bon chic, bon genre*) *F* **I** *a Br* county/*NAm* preppy **II** *nm & f* (*beau cul, belle gueule*) attractive woman*/nice bit of skirt.

BD [bede] *nf F* (*abrév = bande(s) dessinée(s)*) comic strip/comic(s)/cartoon(s)/*NAm* funny/*NAm* funnies; **c'est un fana de BD**, he's nuts about comics. (*Voir* **bédé**)

beau, *pl* **beaux** [bo] *a* 1. *P* **être beau**, to be in a fix*/a mess/a pickle; **nous voilà beaux!** here's a fine mess! (*Voir* **drap 1**) 2. **beau comme un camion**, (*homme*) very handsome/dishy/hunky; **il est beau comme un dieu**, what a dish/a hunk! 3. (*intensif*) (*a*) *F* **il se démène comme un beau diable**, he's like a cat on hot bricks/on a hot tin roof (*b*) *P* **un beau salaud***/a real sod. (*Voir* **belle; jeu 1**)

beau-dab [bodab] *nm P* father-in-law. (*Voir* **dab**) (*pl* beaux-dabs)

beauf(e) [bof] *nm F* (= *beau-frère*) 1. brother-in-law 2. **le beauf(e)**, the average Frenchman (*chauvinistic, racist, reactionary, vulgar, etc*); = Kevin; = Essex man; *a* **il est très beauf(e)**, = he's a real Kevin.

beaujol [boʒɔl] *nm*, **beaujolpif** [boʒɔlpif] *nm*, **beaujolpince** [boʒɔlpɛ̃s] *nm P*

Beaujolais (wine).

beauté [bote] *nf F* **1.** se (re)faire une beauté, to make up (one's face)/to do one's face/to powder one's nose **2.** finir en beauté, to end with a flourish/in a blaze of glory.

beaux-dab(e)s [bodab] *nmpl P* parents-in-law. (*Voir* **dab(e)s**)

beaux-vieux [bovjø] *nmpl P* parents-in-law.

bébé [bebe] *nm F* **1.** (*boisson*) grenadine milkshake **2.** refiler/repasser le bébé (à qn), to pass the buck (on to s.o.); to leave s.o. holding the baby **3.** *Vieilli* bébé Cadum, (*pleurnicheur*) crybaby.

bébête [bebɛt] *a F* silly/babyish/childish; des rires bébêtes, giggling/silly giggles/titters.

bec [bɛk] *nm* **1.** *P* mouth*/gob/kisser/ cakehole; fin bec, gourmet; avoir bon bec/être fort en bec, to have the gift of the gab; clore/ clouer/river le bec à qn, to reduce s.o. to silence/to shut s.o. up*; ça lui clouera le bec, that'll settle his hash; casser du bec, to have bad breath; claquer du bec, to be hungry/ starving/ravenous; donner du bec, to kiss; faire un bec à qn, to give s.o. a peck on the cheek; se refaire le bec, to have a good meal; rincer le bec à qn, to stand s.o. a drink; se rincer le bec, to have a drink*/to wet one's whistle; tenir son bec, to keep quiet/to keep one's trap shut; ferme ton bec! shut up!*/shut your gob!/put a sock in it! **2.** *F (a)* laisser qn le bec dans l'eau, to leave s.o. in the lurch/to ditch s.o./to run out on s.o. *(b)* rester le bec dans l'eau, to be left stranded/to be left in the lurch/to be left high and dry/to be stood up; (*ne pas avoir de réponse*) to be stuck for a reply/to be tongue-tied *(c)* tenir qn le bec dans l'eau, to keep s.o. in suspense/to keep s.o. on a string **3.** *F* donner un coup de bec à qn, to have a dig/a poke at s.o. **4.** *F* faire le bec à qn, to prime s.o. (with what he should say) **5.** *F* avoir une prise de bec avec qn, to have a (violent) quarrel* with s.o./to have an argy-bargy with s.o./to have a slanging match with s.o. **6.** *F* tomber sur un bec, to come up against a snag; to come a cropper* **7.** *F* être bec de gaz, to be deprived of sth/not to have sth. (*Voir* **chlingoter; pisser 12; schlingoter; vesser**)

béca [beka] *nm P* bacillus/germ.

bécamel [bekamɛl] *nm P* (*seconde guerre 1939-45*) (= *bec à mélasse*) grocer.

bécane [bekan] *nf* **1.** *F (a)* bicycle/bike *(b)* moped/motorcycle/motorbike **2.** *F* locomo-

tive/engine **3.** *F (a)* (old-fashioned) typewriter *(b)* printing press *(c)* computer/PC **4.** *A P* guillotine.

bécant [bekã] *nm P* bird/*surt* chicken.

bécasse [bekas] *nf F* silly girl/woman.

bécassine [bekasin] *nf F* silly young girl/ (silly) goose.

because [bikoz] *P* **I** *prép* because of/on account of; je reste ici because le mauvais temps, I'm staying here because of the bad weather; pourquoi ne viens-tu pas? – Because. – Because quoi? – Because d'à cause, why aren't you coming? – Because. – Because what? – Because I'm not **II** *conj* because que, because/'cause/cos; faut pas faire ça because que ça me chatouillerait, you mustn't do that (because) it tickles.

bec-de-cane [bɛkdəkan] *nm P* travailler au bec-de-cane, to burgle/*NAm* to burglarize.

bêchage [beʃaʒ] *nm F* **1.** (*dénigrement*) knocking/running down (of s.o.) **2.** showing off/posing.

béchamel(le) [beʃamɛl] *F* **I** *nf* être dans la béchamel(le), to be in a fix*/in a jam **II** *am* être béchamel, to be pretentious/to show off*/ to pose.

bêche [beʃ] *nf F* faire de la bêche sur qn, to run s.o. down/to criticize s.o.*/to pick s.o. to pieces/to diss s.o.; to look down one's nose at s.o.

bêcher [beʃe] *F* **I** *vtr* to criticize* (s.o.)/to run (s.o.) down/to knock (s.o.)/to get at (s.o.)/to diss (s.o.); to snub (s.o.) **II** *vi* to show off*.

bêcheur, -euse [beʃœr, -øz] **I** *n F* **1.** *(a)* supercilious person/toffee-nosed person/stuck-up person/snob/toffee-nose *(b)* show-off*/poser **2.** hard worker/slogger/plodder **3.** backbiter/ carping critic **4.** (*avocat*) bêcheur = the Public Prosecutor/*NAm* the District Attorney (DA) **II** *a F* **1.** disparaging/carping/critical **2.** supercilious/snobbish/stuck-up/toffee-nosed/ snooty.

béchigne [beʃiɲ] *nf P* (*rugby*) la béchigne, the ball.

bécif [besif] *adv P* = **bessif**.

bécot [beko] *nm F* little kiss; peck; gros bécot, big kiss/smacker; coquer un bécot à qn, to give s.o. a kiss.

bécotage [bekɔtaʒ] *nm F* kissing/necking/ smooching.

bécoter [bekɔte] **I** *vtr F* to give (s.o.) a kiss/a peck **II** *vpr* se bécoter *F* to neck/to smooch; ils étaient en train de se bécoter, they were snogging away.

becquetance, bectance [bɛktɑ̃s] *nf P*
food*/grub/nosh/chow.

becqueter, becter [bɛkte] *vi P* 1. to eat*/
to nosh (away). (*Voir* **fayot** 2) 2. en
becqueter, to be a police informer*/a grass; to
live by prostitution*/to be on the game. (*Voir*
lapin 4)

bedaine [bədɛn] *nf F* (*a*) stomach*/belly
(*b*) (grosse) bedaine, paunch/pot-belly/beer
belly/(beer) gut.

bédé [bede] *nf F* (= *bande(s) dessinée(s)*) =
BD.

bédéaste [bedeast] *n F* comic strip writer.

bédéphile [bedefil] *n F* comics) fan.

bédérock [bederɔk] *a F* of the comic strip
and rock culture.

bédi [bedi] *nm P* gendarme.

bedon [bədɔ̃] *nm F* = **bedaine**.

bedonnant [bədɔnɑ̃] *a F* paunchy/pot-
bellied/beer-bellied.

bedonner [bədɔne] *vi F* to develop a
paunch/to grow paunchy/to get a (beer) gut.

bédouin [bedwɛ̃] *nm P* (*argot des pompes
funèbres*) crucifix/cross.

bégonia [begɔnja] *nm F* 1. *P* charrier/cherrer
dans les bégonias, to exaggerate*/to lay it on
thick/to shoot a line 2. *P* piétiner les bégonias,
(*commettre une bévue*) to put one's foot in it/
to drop a clanger; (*s'ingérer*) to barge in
(where you're not wanted) 3. *V* female
genitals*/fanny.

béguin [begɛ̃] *nm F* (*a*) love/passion/crush;
c'est mon béguin, I've got a crush on him/her
(*b*) avoir le béguin pour qn, to be infatuated*
with s.o./to have a thing on s.o./to be sweet on
s.o./to be crazy about s.o.

béguineuse [beginøz] *nf P* unreliable
prostitute* (*who could easily fall for a client*).

béhème [beɛm] *nf F* BMW (*RTM*) motorbike.

beigne [bɛɲ] *nf P* 1. blow*/clout/slap;
donner/filer/flanquer une beigne à qn, to hit
s.o./to clout s.o.; to beat s.o. up* 2. *pl*
clapping/applause.

beigner [bɛɲe] *vtr P* to hit (s.o.)/to clout
(s.o.)

beignet [bɛɲɛ] *nm P* face*; claquer/tarter
le beignet à qn, to sock s.o. on the jaw.

bêlant [belɑ̃] *nm P* sheep.

bêler [bele] *vtr P Péj* to bleat/to bellyache.

belette [bəlɛt] *nf P* (*a*) woman*/bird (*b*)
wife*/the missis; girlfriend.

belge [bɛlʒ] *nm P* Belgian tobacco; *V* fume!

c'est du belge! = go (and) fuck yourself!
(*said with obscene gesture*).

Belgico [belʒiko] *nm & f P* Belgian.

belins [bəlɛ̃] *nmpl P* money*/dough/readies.

belle [bɛl] *a & nf 1. P* (se) faire la belle/se
mettre en belle, to escape from prison/to
break out of prison/to go over the wall; il s'est
fait la belle, he did a bunk/he bust out (of
prison) 2. *P* (*gangsters, etc*) mener qn en
belle, to kill*/to bump off/to do away with/to
knock off (an accomplice, etc); (*duper*) to
have s.o. on/to take s.o. for a ride 3. *F* l'avoir
belle, to find it easy going 4. *F* la faire belle/se
la faire belle, to have a cushy time/to take it
easy; to go on the spree/to have a good time;
(*avoir le dessus*) to have the advantage (in a
fight) 5. *F* elle est belle femme, she's a big/
fat woman; she's a large lady 6. *F* (= *à la
belle étoile*) coucher à la belle, to sleep in the
open/to sleep rough 7. *F* en faire voir de belles
à qn, to put s.o. through the mill/to put s.o.
through it/to give s.o. a hard time (of it) 8. *F*
il en a fait de belles! he's been up to some
pretty funny things! en conter/en dire de
belles, to say outrageous things; j'en ai
entendu de belles sur ton compte! I've been
hearing some pretty funny things about you!
tu en as fait une belle! you've put your foot
right in it!/you've dropped a real clanger
there!/you've done it now! en voilà une belle!
here's a fine how-do-you-do!/we're in a right
(old) mess now! 9. *P* luck; être de belle, to
be lucky 10. *P* de belle, without trial; without
charges being brought; donner la belle, to
arrest* (s.o.) on suspicion (only); servir de
belle qn, to denounce* s.o./to shop s.o.; to
arrest* s.o. as an administrative measure/on
a technicality. (*Voir* **beau**; **décarrer** 3)

belle-dabesse [bɛldabɛs] *nf*, **belle-
doche** [bɛldɔʃ] *nf P* mother-in-law. (*Voir*
dabesse 1) (*pl* belles-dabesses, -doches)

belle-de-nuit [bɛldənɥi] *nf F* prostitute*.
(*pl* belles-de-nuit)

belle-frangine [bɛlfrɑ̃ʒin] *nf P* (*rare*)
sister-in-law. (*pl* belles-frangines)

belle-mère [bɛlmɛr] *nf F* 1. tu cherches
une belle-mère? your slip's showing/Char-
lie's dead/Queen Anne's dead/it's snowing
down south 2. BMW (*RTM*) motorbike.

bellot, -otte [bɛlo, -ɔt] *Vieilli F* I *a* pretty/
dainty/cute II *n* mon bellot/ma bellotte, my
little cherub.

ben [bɛ̃] *adv P* (= *bien*) eh ben! well!/why!
ben oui! why, yes!/well, of course! ben quoi?

so what?

bénard [benar] *nm P* (men's) trousers/*esp NAm* pants.

bénarès [benarɛs] *nm Vieilli P* opium*.

bène [bɛn] *nm P* = **bénard**.

bénédiction [benediksjɔ̃] *nf* 1. *F* il pleut que c'est une bénédiction! it's raining cats and dogs!/it's bucketing down! 2. *P* beating (-up)*/working over.

bénef [benɛf] *nm P* profit/gain; c'est tout bénef, it's all profit; petits bénefs, perks.

Ben Hur [bɛnyr] *Prnm F Voir* **char 1**.

béni-bouffe-tout, béni-bouftou(t) [benibuftu] *nm inv P* glutton*/hog/ greedyguts.

béni-oui-oui [beniwiwi] *nm inv F* yes-man/rubber stamp.

bénissage [benisaʒ] *nm F* blarney/soft soap.

bénisseur, -euse [benisœr, -øz] *a & n F* glib (individual); oily/greasy/slippery (person); (s.o.) who pays empty compliments.

bénitier [benitje] *nm* 1. *V* female genitals*; cracher dans le bénitier, to have sex* 2. *P* client's tip to a prostitute*.

bénouse, bénouze [benuz] *nm P* 1. = **bénard 2.** (men's or women's) briefs.

benzine [bɛ̃zin] *nf F* petrol/*NAm* gas.

béqueter [bekte] *vi P* = **becqueter**.

béquille [bekij] *nf P* 1. *pl* béquilles, legs*/ stumps 2. (*langage des policiers*) last-minute argument.

béquiller [bekije] *vtr P* 1. to eat*/to nosh 2. to spend (one's) money/to splash out.

berceau [bɛrso] *nm F* les prendre au berceau, to like (very) young boys/girls; to cradle-snatch/to go in for cradle-snatching; il/elle les prend au berceau, he's/she's a cradle-snatcher.

berdouille [bɛrduj] *nf A P* 1. stomach*/ belly/gut 2. mud.

Bérézina [berezina] *nf P* calamity/disaster/ catastrophe.

berge [bɛrʒ] *nf P* (*surt pl*) year; tirer dix berges à l'ombre, to do a ten-year stretch; avoir trente berges, to be thirty (years old).

bergère [bɛrʒɛr] *nf* 1. *F* last card in the pack 2. *P* woman*; ma bergère, my wife*/my old lady/my old woman 3. pimp's* first (regular) mistress.

berlingot [bɛrlɛ̃go] *nm* 1. *F* (old) banger/ jalopy/old crock 2. *P* (car, motorbike) engine 3. *V* virginity/maidenhead/cherry 4. *V* clitoris; allonger le berlingot, to practise

cunnilingus* 5. *P* stolen goods.

berlingue [bɛrlɛ̃g] *nm* = **berlingot**.

berlue [bɛrly] *nf* 1. *F* illusion; avoir la berlue, to have hallucinations/to be deluded/to be seeing things; j'ai cru avoir la berlue en le voyant revenir, I thought my eyes were deceiving me when I saw him returning; se faire des berlues, to labour under a delusion/ to kid oneself 2. *P* blanket; taper la berlue, to roll dice on a blanket 3. *P* front (for some illegal activity); cover-up.

(se) berlurer [(sə)bɛrlyre] *vi & pr F* to delude oneself/to kid oneself/to imagine things.

bernicles [bɛrnikl] *nfpl Vieilli F* spectacles/ specs.

bernique! [bɛrnik] *excl Vieilli F* nothing doing!*/not a chance!/no dice!

bersingue [bɛrzɛ̃g] *nm P* = **berzingue**.

Bertha [bɛrta] *Prnf* la grosse Bertha (a) *F* Big Bertha (*the German heavy gun that shelled Paris in WWI*) (b) *Péj* a fat woman*.

berzingue [bɛrzɛ̃g] *nm P* à tout berzingue, (a) with great force; jouer de la musique à tout berzingue, to play (music) very loudly (b) at top speed/at full tilt; donner à tout berzingue, to go flat out.

bésef [bezɛf] *adv P* much/a lot/many; y en a pas bésef, there's not much of it.

bésiclard [beziklar] *nm F* man/boy wearing glasses; four-eyes.

besicles [bəzikl] *nfpl F* spectacles/specs.

besogner [bəzɔɲe] *vi P* (a) (*pour un homme*) to have sex* (b) (*en parlant d'un homme qui masturbe une femme*) to finger-fuck.

besoins [bəzwɛ̃] *nmpl F* (a) faire ses besoins, to defecate* (b) faire ses petits besoins, to urinate*/to spend a penny (c) faire ses besoins, (*chien, chat, etc*) to do its business.

bessif [besif] *adv P* 1. under coercion/under compulsion; forced 2. necessarily/of course.

bestiau [bɛstjo] *nm F* animal.

bêta, -asse [bɛta, -as] *F* I *a* stupid*/dim/ gormless; elle est jolie mais bêtasse, she's pretty but clueless II *n* fool*/dimwit/dope; gros bêta, you silly twit!/you berk! c'était pour te taquiner, gros bêta! I was only teasing, stupid!

bête [bɛt] I *nf* 1. *F* (*personne*) une bonne bête, a good sort; une mauvaise bête, a spiteful character 2. *F* chercher la petite bête, to be over-critical/to pick holes/to nitpick 3. *F* faire la bête, *(au jeu)* *(perdre)* to lose; *(feindre la maladresse)* to pretend to play badly *(in order to deceive other players)*; to pretend to be stupid **4.** *P* faire la bête à deux dos, to have sex*/to hump **5.** *F* crack player/ace/ wiz(ard); *surt* star pupil; c'est la/une bête, (s)he's the expert/(s)he's brilliant **6.** *F* guitar **7.** *F* bête de scène, actor/comedian etc who give his/her all **8.** *F Péj* bête à concours, *Br* swot; *NAm* grind/wonk **9.** *F* travailler/bosser comme une bête, to slave away/to slog one's guts out. *(Voir* **poil 9**; **tour I 5**) **II** *a* **1.** bête à manger du foin/bête à pleurer/bête comme un âne/bête comme une oie/bête comme ses pieds, very stupid*/thick (as two short planks) **2.** bête comme chou/comme tout, very easy*/ dead easy*/as easy as pie; c'est bête comme chou, I could do it standing on my head; it's a cinch/a doddle **3.** pas si bête! I'm not such a fool* (as all that)! *(absolument pas)* not likely!/not if I can help it!/no chance! **4.** ses bêtes d'idées, his daft/silly ideas; ce bête de voyage, that stupid journey. *(Voir* **chou 10**; **pleurer 2**)

béton [betɔ̃] **I** *nm F* **1.** faire du béton, to become established (in a place, etc); *(football)* to pack the defence/to play defensively **2.** en béton, solid/cast-iron; un alibi en béton, a cast-iron alibi **II** *vi P (verlan de tomber)* laisse béton! lay off!/drop it!/give it a rest!

bétonner [betɔne] *vtr F* to make (an argument) unassailable/foolproof.

betterave [betrav] *nf P* **1.** bottle of red wine **2.** dupe/mug/sucker.

beuark! [bœrk] *int* = **beurg! beurk!**

beuglant [bøglɑ̃] *nm P* music hall/nightclub/cabaret (club), etc.

beuglante [bøglɑ̃t] *nf P* **1.** cabaret singer **2.** song (bawled out in unison) **3.** yell/bawling; pousser une beuglante, to shout one's head off.

beugler [bøgle] *P* **I** *vi* to yell/to bawl/to holler **II** *vtr* beugler une chanson, to bawl/to bellow out a song.

beur, beurette [bœr(ɛt)] *nm & f F* young second generation North African *(born in France)*.

beurg! beurk! [bœrg, bœrk] *int* yuk!

beurre [bœr] *nm* **1.** *F* comme dans du beurre, with the greatest of ease; c'est rentré comme dans du beurre, it went in with no trouble at all **2.** *F* c'est du beurre!/c'est un (vrai) beurre! it's very easy* (to do)!/it's dead simple!/it's a cinch! **3.** *F* money*;

profit; y aller de son beurre, to spend (one's money) freely/to throw one's money about; faire son beurre, to make stacks of money*/to make one's pile/to make a packet/to feather one's nest **4.** *F* ça fait mon beurre, that suits me down to the ground **5.** *F* du beurre dans les épinards, welcome bonus; ça mettra du beurre dans les épinards, that'll make life (a bit) more comfortable (for me)/that'll make life easier (for me) **6.** *F* au prix où est le beurre, the way things are going these days; with the cost of living today **7.** *F* pour du beurre, for nothing/in vain; compter pour du beurre, to count for nothing; jouer pour du beurre, to play for nothing/for love **8.** *F* promettre plus de beurre que de pain, to make exaggerated promises **9.** *P* pas plus de ... que de beurre en broche/que de beurre en branche/que de beurre au cul/que de beurre aux fesses, nothing at all/damn all/sweet FA in the way of ... **10.** *F* battre le beurre, to speculate on a rising and falling market; to bull and to bear (the market) **11.** on ne peut pas avoir le beurre et l'argent du beurre, you can't have your cake and eat it (too). *(Voir* **accommoder 3**; **assiette 2**; **baigner**; **bique I 1** *(b)*; **œil 20**; **pédaler 2**)

beurré [bœre] *a P* drunk*/smashed/ plastered/canned; beurré comme un petit lu/ une tartine, complètement beurré, dead drunk*/pissed as a newt/totally plastered.

beurrée [bœre] *nf P* ramasser/en avoir une beurrée, to be dead drunk*; il a pris une sacrée beurrée, he's had a skinful.

se beurrer [səbœre] *vpr* **1.** *F* to make one's pile/to make a packet/to feather one's nest. *(Voir* **beurre 3**) **2.** *P* to get drunk*/canned/ pissed.

beuverie [bøvri] *nf F* drinking session/ binge/booze-up.

bézef [bezɛf] *adv P* = **bésef**.

bi [bi] *F* **I** *a* (= *bisexuel*) bisexual/bi/AC-DC **II** *nm Vieilli* **(grand)** bi, (= *bicyclette*) pennyfarthing.

bibard [bibar] *nm P* **1.** old soak/old boozer/ old wino **2.** old fog(e)y*/old fuddy-duddy.

bibelot [biblo] *nm P* **1.** burglar's tool; skeleton key **2.** *pl* *(a)* coins *(b)* jewellery **3.** *pl* testicles*.

biberon, -onne [bibrɔ̃, -ɔn] *F* **I** *a* tippling/boozing **II** *n* **1.** drunkard*/heavy drinker/wino/alky/boozer/soak **2.** bottle **III** *nm F* je ne les prends pas au biberon, I'm not a baby-snatcher/I don't go in for cradle-snatching. (*Voir* **berceau**)

biberonner [bibrɔne] *vi F* to drink*/to tipple/to booze/to go on the booze/to hit the bottle.

bibi [bibi] *nm* 1. *F* (*à un enfant*) **fais bibi à papa**, give daddy a kiss! 2. *F* (woman's) hat 3. *P* **un simple bibi**, a private (soldier) 4. *P* I/me/myself/yours truly; **pour bibi ça!** that's mine!/bags I (that)! **pas pour bibi!** not for me! **ça tourne rond pour bibi, bibi lui s'en tire**, I'm all right Jack 5. *P* burglar's tool; skeleton key.

bibiche [bibiʃ] *nf P* (*terme d'affection*) **ma bibiche!** my darling*!/my sweetie!/honey!/my pet!

bibine [bibin] *nf P* tasteless drink/dishwater/gnat's piss.

bibli [bibli] *nf*, **biblio** [biblio] *nf F* (= *bibliothèque*) library.

bic [bik] *nm P Péj* Arab/wog. (*Voir* **bicot**)

bica [bika] *nm*, **bicarré** [bikare] *nm F* fourth-year student in a class preparing for the *grandes écoles* or in a *grande école*.

bicause [bikoz] *prép of conj P* = **because**.

biche [biʃ] *nf* 1. *F* (*terme d'affection*) **ma biche!** my darling*!/my pet!/my love! 2. *P* transvestite prostitute. (*Voir* **pied-de-biche**)

bicher [biʃe] *vi* 1. *F* **ça biche?** how goes it?/how's tricks?/how's things?/everything OK? **ça biche!** everything's fine/OK; not so bad; (*d'accord*) agreed!/it's a deal! **ça biche entre eux**, they get on very well together/they hit it off well 2. *P* to be delighted; **ça me fait bicher**, that does my heart good; **bicher comme un pou (dans la crème fraîche)**, to be as pleased as Punch.

bichette [biʃɛt] *nf F* (*terme d'affection*) **ma bichette!** my (little) darling*!/my (little) pet!

bichon, -onne [biʃɔ̃, -ɔn] *n F* = **bichette**.

bichonner [biʃɔne] *vtr F* to mollycoddle (s.o.); **bichonner sa bagnole**, to take great care of one's car; to be nuts/daft about one's car.

bichonnet [biʃɔnɛ] *nm P* chin.

bichot(t)er [biʃɔte] I *vi F* = **bicher 1** II *vtr P* to steal*/to swipe/to pinch.

biclo [biklo] *nm*, **biclou** [biklu] *nm P* bicycle/bike.

bico [biko] *nm P Péj* = **bicot**.

bicoque [bikɔk] *nf F* (*a*) poky little house; shanty/shack/dump (*b*) **nous avons une bicoque à la campagne**, we've got a small place in the country.

bicot [biko] *nm P Péj* Arab/wog. (*Voir* **Arbi**,

Arbico(t))

bidard [bidar] *a Vieilli P* lucky.

bidasse [bidas] *nm P* private (soldier)/squaddie.

bide [bid] *nm* 1. *P* (*a*) stomach*/belly; **gras du bide**, fat/pot-bellied; **avoir du bide**, to be paunchy; **prendre du bide**, to get a pot-belly/to get a beer gut; **s'en mettre plein le bide/se remplir le bide**, to stuff oneself (*b*) **en avoir dans le bide**, to have guts/to have what it takes; **il n'a rien dans le bide**, he's got no guts/no balls 2. *F* (*surt théâtre*) **faire un bide**, to be a flop/a washout.

bidet [bidɛ] *nm F* **eau de bidet**, something worthless/cheap/contemptible; **il ne se prend pas pour de l'eau de bidet**, he thinks he's really something/he thinks he's the cat's whiskers/he thinks no small beer of himself; *V* **raclure de bidet**, (little) runt/shorty.

bidochard [bidoʃar] *nm P* pimp*/ponce/mack.

bidoche [bidoʃ] *nf P* (*a*) (poor-quality) meat (*b*) human flesh. (*Voir* **marchand 1**)

bidon [bidɔ̃] *P* I *a* false/fake/phon(e)y; **une maladie bidon**, a fake illness II *nm* 1. (*a*) (*brocante*) fake *or* doubtful article/object (*b*) **c'est du bidon**, (*faux*) it's a fake/a phon(e)y; (*des bêtises*) it's (a load of) rubbish/codswallop/crap/balon(e)y; **c'est pas du bidon**, it's the gospel/honest truth 2. **faire le bidon de boiter**, to pretend to have a limp 3. (= **bide 1**) **se remplir le bidon**, to fill one's belly/to stuff one's face.

bidonnage [bidɔnaʒ] *nm P* careless/unprofessional job; botched job.

bidonnant [bidɔnɑ̃] *a P* very comical/screamingly funny; **c'est bidonnant!** it's a real scream!

bidonner [bidɔne] I *vtr P* 1. to deceive/to take (s.o.) in/to trick (s.o.) 2. **bidonner un travail**, to do a job carelessly/unprofessionally; to do a botched job II *vpr* **se bidonner** *P* to laugh* uproariously/to split one's sides laughing/to crease one's head off/to crease oneself.

bidonneur [bidɔnœr] *nm P* 1. cheat/swindler*/crook; liar 2. careless/unprofessional worker; botcher.

bidouillage [bidujaʒ] *nm P* (*a*) tinkering/repair job (*b*) faking (of antiques) (*c*) *Mus* **bidouillage sonore**, sound effects.

bidouiller [biduje] *vtr P* (*a*) to patch (sth) up (*b*) to tinker with (sth).

bidule [bidyl] *nm P* 1. gadget*/contraption/

thing; thingamy/whatsit/what-do-you-call-it/ thingamybob; (*personne*) what's-his-name*/ thingy 2. (policeman's, etc) truncheon.

biduleur [bidylœr] *nm P* potterer/tinkerer/ do-it-yourselfer.

bien suce [bjɛ̃sys] *adv F* (= *bien sûr*) of course/natch.

bière [bjɛr] *nf F* 1. ce n'est pas de la petite bière, (*d'une personne*) he's a big shot/a VIP; (*d'une chose*) it's not to be sneezed at; it's no joke 2. ne pas se prendre pour de la petite bière, to have a high opinion of oneself/to think no small beer of oneself.

bif [bif] *nm P* (beef)steak.

biffe [bif] *nf P* la biffe (*a*) the junk business; (*chiffonniers*) junk collectors (*b*) *Mil* the infantry.

biffeton [biftɔ̃] *nm P* 1. (railway, theatre, etc) ticket 2. (*prisons*) (short) letter/note (passed secretly) 3. banknote. (*Voir* **porte-biffetons**) 4. (doctor's, etc) certificate; **piquer un biffeton**, to inflict injuries on oneself in order to obtain discharge from the armed forces, to claim insurance, etc 5. *pl* playing cards.

biffetonner [biftɔne] *vi P* to pass messages; to write messages/notes.

biffin [bifɛ̃] *nm P* 1. rag-and-bone man/junk collector/junk dealer 2. *Mil* infantryman/footslogger.

bifteck, biftèque [biftɛk] *nm* 1. *F* faire du bifteck, to get saddle-sore 2. *P* gagner son bifteck, to earn one's living; la lutte/la course au bifteck, the rat race; défendre son bifteck, to look after one's own bread and butter/to look after number one 3. *P* prostitute* profitable to her pimp*/good earner/good meal-ticket 4. *P* the human body; manger son bifteck, to swallow one's tongue/to keep quiet 5. *P* bifteck roulé, penis*/meat 6. *P* les Biftecks, the English*/the British/the Brits. (*Voir* **rosbif**) 7. *F* il est bifteck moins cinq, it's nearly dinnertime.

bifton [biftɔ̃] *nm P* = **biffeton**.

biftonner [biftɔne] *vi P* = **biffetonner**.

bigler [bigle] *P* I *vtr* (*a*) to (have a) squint at (s.o./sth); to take a gander/a butcher's at (s.o./sth) (*b*) **bigler qn en biais**, to give s.o. the glad eye/to eye s.o. up II *vi* to squint.

bigleux, -euse [biglø, -øz] *a & n P* 1. squint-eyed/cockeyed (person) 2. short-sighted (person); elle est complètement bigleuse, she's very short-sighted/she's as blind as a bat.

bigne [biɲ] *nm P* prison*; au bigne, in prison; bigne à perpète, life sentence.

bignol(l)e [biɲɔl] *nm & f P* concierge.

bignolon [biɲɔlɔ̃] *nm P* detective.

bigo [bigo] *nm F* = **bigophone**.

bigophone [bigɔfɔn] *nm F* (tele)phone*/ blower; donner/filer/passer un coup de bigophone à qn, to give s.o. a ring/a buzz/a bell; to get on the blower to s.o.

bigophoner [bigɔfɔne] *vi F* bigophoner à qn, to (tele)phone s.o./to give s.o. a buzz.

bigorne [bigɔrn] *nf P* 1. fight*/battle 2. *A* slang; jaspiner le bigorne, to speak slang.

bigorneau, *pl* **-eaux** [bigɔrno] *nm F* 1. = **bigophone** 2. microphone/mike 3. *Mil Péj* infantryman/footslogger.

bigorner [bigɔrne] I *vtr P* 1. (*battre*) to beat (s.o.) up*/to work (s.o.) over; (*tuer*) to kill* (s.o.)/to do (s.o.) in 2. to damage/to injure; il s'est fait bigorner sa bagnole, s.o.'s smashed up/into his car II *vpr* **se bigorner** *P* to fight/to come to blows/to have a set-to.

bigornette [bigɔrnɛt] *nf Vieilli P* (*drugs*) cocaine*/coke/nose-candy.

bigoudi [bigudi] *nm P* travailler du bigoudi, to be slightly mad*/to be touched (in the head)/to have a screw loose.

bigre! [bigr] *excl Vieilli F* gosh!/crikey!

bigrement [bigrəmɑ̃] *adv Vieilli F* very/ extremely/awfully; il fait bigrement froid, it's jolly cold; c'est bigrement embêtant, it's a blessed nuisance; vous avez bigrement raison! you're dead right!

bijou, *pl* **-oux** [biʒu] *nm* 1. *F* mon bijou, my darling*/my precious/my pet 2. *A V* bijou de famille, female genitals* 3. *V* bijoux de famille, testicles*/rocks; male genitals*/ family jewels/crown jewels.

bijouterie [biʒutri] *nf F* (professional) strong man's equipment/weights.

bilan [bilɑ̃] *nm P* déposer son bilan, to die*/to cash in one's chips.

bilboquet [bilbɔkɛ] *nm P* 1. jouer au bilboquet (avec qn), to have a sexual relationship (with s.o.)/to have it off (with s.o.) 2. bilboquet merdeux, homosexual* suffering from a venereal disease.

bile [bil] *nf F* se faire de la bile, to worry/to fret/to get into a tizzy; to get all hot and bothered; ne te fais pas de bile! don't worry! épancher sa bile, to let off steam. (*Voir* **cailler** II 1)

se biler [səbile] *vpr F* (= *se faire de la bile*) il ne se bile pas, he doesn't get worked up/he's not easily upset; ne te bile pas! (ne t'inquiète pas) don't worry! (doucement) easy does it!/ take it easy!

bileux, -euse [bilø, -øz] F I a (addicted to) worrying/fretting; il n'est pas bileux, (calme) he's a cool one/a cool customer; (détendu, qui ne s'en fait pas) he's easy-going/happy-go-lucky II n worrier/worryguts/ fretter.

billancher [bijɑ̃ʃe] vi P to pay* (up).

billard [bijar] nm 1. F c'est du billard, it's very easy*/it's a pushover/it's a piece of cake; it's all plain sailing; c'est pas du billard, it's no cinch/it takes a lot of doing 2. F operating table; monter/passer sur le billard, to have an operation/to be operated on 3. F straight and flat road 4. P dévisser son billard, to die*/to snuff it.

bille [bij] I nf 1. F head*/nut; face*/mug; avoir une drôle de bille, to look odd/peculiar; il a une bille de billard, he's as bald* as a coot 2. F bille (de clown), fool*/blockhead/moron 3. F retirer/reprendre ses billes, to pull out of a deal 4. F bille en tête, directly/straight; entrer dans une pièce, bille en tête, to walk straight into a room 5. toucher sa bille, to be good/great at (sth); to be ace/a whizz at (sth) 6. pl V testicles*/balls II a 1. stupid*/daft/ cretinous; qu'est-ce qu'il est bille! he's such a moron! 2. drunk*/blotto/stewed.

billet [bijɛ] nm F 1. je te donne/fiche/flanque/ fous mon billet que ..., (you can) take my word for it that .../(you can) take it from me that ...; you can bet your boots/your bottom dollar/your life that ...; I'll bet you what you like that ... 2. prendre/ramasser un billet de parterre, to come a cropper/to fall flat on one's face/to take a header.

billot [bijo] nm Vieilli P fool*/idiot/imbecile/ dope.

bin [bɛ̃] adv P (= bien) c'est bin beau, it's really beautiful.

binaise [binɛz] nf P (= combinaison (louche)) shady scheme/crooked deal/fiddle/ racket. (Voir **combine 1**)

binette [binɛt] nf F head*/nut; face*/mug.

bing [biŋ] nm P = **bigne**.

bingre [bɛ̃gr] nm P executioner.

biniou [binju] nm 1. P wind instrument; accordion, organ, trumpet, etc 2. P automatic (pistol); jouer un air de biniou, to fire an automatic 3. P (tele)phone*; filer un coup de biniou, to make a phone call 4. V (rare) (a) female genitals* (b) penis*; jouer un air de

biniou/souffler dans le biniou, to have oral sex*/a blow-job.

binoclard, -arde [binɔklar, -ard] n F person who wears glasses/four-eyes.

binôme [binom] nm F (school) room-mate; workmate.

bin's, binz [binz] nm, **bintz** [bints] nm P disorder/mess/clutter/shambles; quel bin's dans sa piaule! his/her room is a tip!

bio [bio] F 1. nf (= biographie) écrire une bio, to write a biography 2. a inv (= biologique) organic; des légumes bio, organic vegetables.

bique [bik] I nf 1. (a) F (nanny) goat (b) P c'est du beurre de bique, it's worthless*/ useless/not much cop/no great shakes; de la crotte de bique, rubbish/tripe; c'est de la crotte de bique, it's rubbish(y)/trash(y) 2. P old horse/nag 3. F Péj une vieille bique, an old hag/an old cow/an old trout 4. P bique et bouc, passive and active homosexual*/kiki. II nm P Péj Arab/wog.

biquer [bike] vtr & i V to have sex* (with) (s.o.).

biquet [bikɛ] nm F (terme d'affection) mon biquet, my darling*/my pet.

biquette [bikɛt] nf F = **biquet**.

birbasse [birbas] nf P (rare) old hag/old bag/old bat.

birbe [birb] nm P old man; vieux birbe, old fogey*/old fuddy-duddy.

biribi [biribi] nm Mil P = **bat' d'Af 1**.

biroute [birut] nf 1. V penis* 2. P windsock 3. P (traffic) cone.

bisbille [bisbij] nf F petty quarrel/tiff; être en bisbille avec qn, to be at odds/at logger-heads with s.o.

Biscaille [biskaj] Prnm P (Bicêtre) 1. old people's home (at Bicêtre, outskirts of Paris) 2. flea market (at Bicêtre).

biscoteaux, biscot(t)os [biskoto] nmpl P 1. biceps; rouler les/jouer des biscoteaux, to swagger/to throw one's weight around 2. calves (of leg).

biscotte [biskɔt] prep & conj P = **because**.

biscuit [biskɥi] nm 1. F (a) les biscuits, money*/bread (b) ne pas (s')embarquer/ partir sans biscuit(s), to get clued up in advance/to do one's homework; avoir des biscuits, to be clued up/to know the score 2. P (parking) ticket; coller un biscuit à qn, to book s.o./to give s.o. a ticket; choper un biscuit, to get booked/to get a ticket 3. P c'est du biscuit, it's easy*/it's a cinch 4. V tremper son biscuit, to have sex*/to dip one's wick.

bise [biz] *nf F* kiss (on the cheek); (*à un enfant*) fais la/une bise à ..., (go and) kiss ...; fais une bise à maman, give mummy a kiss; grosse bise, big kiss/smacker; se faire la bise, to kiss each other on both cheeks.

bis(e)ness [biznɛs] *nm P* 1. work; job 2. (shady) business/job/racket 3. (*a*) confusion/muddle; quel bis(e)ness! what a mess! (*b*) en faire tout un bis(e)ness, to make a big fuss/a song and dance about it 4. (*prostitution*) faire son/le bis(e)ness, to solicit*/to be on the game.

bis(e)nesseuse [biznɛsøz] *nf P* prostitute*/hooker/tart.

bisnesser, biznesser [biznɛse] *vi P* to engage in shady practices/to clinch shady deals.

bisou [bizu] *nm F* = **bise**.

bisquant [biskã] *a F* annoying/irritating; ce que c'est bisquant! what a nuisance!

bisque [bisk] *nf F* bad temper*/irritation; avoir la bisque, to be peeved; to be in a bad mood; prendre la bisque, to take umbrage.

bisquer [biske] *vi F* to be in a bad mood; to be annoyed/irritated/riled; to sulk; faire bisquer qn, to rub s.o. up the wrong way; (*écoliers*) bisque! bisque! rage! yah boo sucks!

bistouille [bistuj] *nf P* 1. coffee laced with brandy (*or some other spirit*) 2. poor-quality spirits/rotgut 3. worthless thing; c'est de la bistouille, it's not worth tuppence.

bistouquette [bistukɛt] *nf V* penis*.

bistral [bistral] *nm*, **bistre** [bistr] *nm*, **bistro** [bistro] *nm*, **bistroc** [bistrɔk] *nm*, **bistroquet** [bistrɔke] *nm*, **bistrot** [bistro] *nm F* 1. = public house/pub/bar (*esp where snacks are served*); le bistrot du coin, the local. (*Voir* **troquet**) 2. (*a*) = publican/bartender (*b*) *Vieilli* wine merchant.

bistrote [bistrɔt] *nf F* = landlord's wife.

bistrotier, -ière [bistrɔtje, -jɛr] *n F* landlord/landlady of a *bistrot*.

bistrouille [bistruj] *nf P* = **bistouille**.

bisut(h) [bizy] *nm*, **bisut(h)age** [bizytaʒ] *nm*, **bisut(h)er** [bizyte] *vtr F* = **bizut(h), bizutage, bizuter**.

bitard [bitar] *nm*, **bitau**, *pl* **-aux** [bito] *nm P* hat*/titfer. (*Voir* **bitos**)

bite [bit] *nf V* 1. penis*/prick/cock; il a une grosse bite, he's well-endowed/well-hung; he's got a huge tool 2. bite à Jean-Pierre, (policeman's) truncheon; cosh 3. con à bouffer de la

bite/con comme une bite, very stupid*/thick as two short planks/dead from the neck up 4. rentrer la bite sous le bras, to return empty-handed. (*Voir* **sac 20; sous-bite**)

biter [bite] *vtr* 1. *V* to have sex* with/to have it off with (s.o.) 2. *P* (*comprendre*) je n'y bite rien, I can't make head nor tail of it; it's all Greek to me.

bitonner [bitɔne] *vi P* to be undecided/to be in two minds.

bitos [bitos] *nm P* hat*/titfer; bitos à la reculette, hat tilted at the back of the head.

bitte [bit] *nf V* = **bite**.

bitter [bite] *vtr V & P* = **biter**.

bitture [bityr] *nf P* 1. drunkenness; prendre/ramasser une bitture, to get drunk*/canned/plastered; une bonne bitture, a skinful; qu'est-ce qu'il tient comme bitture! he's had a skinful!/he's blind drunk!/he's completely plastered! 2. à toute bitture, at top speed/flat out/at full blast.

bitturer [bityre] I *vtr P* to make (s.o.) drunk*/to get (s.o.) pissed II *vpr* se bitturer *P* to get drunk*/pissed; se bitturer au pastis, to get pissed on pastis.

bitume [bitym] *nm P* pavement; (*a*) raser le bitume, to be very short/to be a short-arse (*b*) arpenter/faire/polir le bitume, to be a prostitute*/to walk the streets; elle arpente le bitume du Boul' Mich, her beat is the Boulevard St Michel. (*Voir* **calouser**)

biture [bityr] *nf*, **(se) biturer** [(sə)bityre] *vtr & pr P* = **bitture, (se) bitturer**.

bizet [bizɛ] *nm P* (*rare*) small-time pimp*.

bizness [biznɛs] *nm*, **biznesseuse** [biznɛsøz] *nf P* = **bis(e)ness, bis(e)nesseuse**.

bizutage [bizytaʒ] *nm F* initiation (of freshman); ragging.

bizuter [bizyte] *vtr F* to rag (a freshman).

bizut(h) [bizy] *nm F* first-year student/freshman/fresher (in a *grande école*).

bla(-)bla((-)bla) [blablabla)] *nm F* (*a*) blah(-blah)/yackety-yack; claptrap/boloney (*b*) padding (of a speech, etc)/waffle.

blablater [blablate] *vi P* to talk nonsense*; to blather/to blether; ces politiciens passent leur temps à blablater, politicians do talk a lot of bilge.

black [blak] *F* I *a* black (person, music, culture) II *nm & f* Black*.

blackboulage [blakbulaʒ] *nm F* blackballing/rejection.

blackbouler [blakbule] *vtr F* to blackball/

to reject; to fail (examinee); to turn down (candidate); **je me suis fait blackbouler à l'oral,** I failed my oral.

blackie [blaki] *nm F* = **black** II.

blafarde [blafard] *nf A P* **la blafarde** (*a*) death (*b*) the moon.

blague [blag] *nf* 1. *F* tall story/hoax/humbug/bunkum; **tout ça c'est de la blague!** that's all bunkum!/that's all rot!/that's a load of nonsense! **ne racontez pas de blagues!** you're having me on!/pull the other one! **quelle bonne blague!** my Aunt Fanny! 2. *F* joke; **sans blague?** really?/you're joking!/no kidding? **blague à part,** seriously/joking apart; **blague dans le coin, il faut que tu le fasses,** joking apart/seriously though, you must do it; **quelle blague!** what a joke! **faire une blague à qn,** to fool* s.o.; **il m'a fait une sale blague,** he played a dirty trick on me; **prendre qch en blague/à la blague,** to take sth as a joke; **il prend tout à la blague,** he's always got his tongue in his cheek; he's never serious about anything 3. *P* **blagues à tabac,** (woman's) flabby breasts*/droopers.

blaguer [blage] *F* I *vi* (*a*) to talk nonsense*/to talk through one's hat (*b*) to talk with one's tongue in one's cheek (*c*) **blaguer avec qch,** to make light of sth/not to take sth seriously; **ne blague pas avec ce flingue,** don't fool around with that gun (*d*) to joke; (**c'est**) **assez blagué!** that's enough of that! II *vtr* **blaguer qn,** to make fun of s.o./to pull s.o.'s leg/to tease s.o.

blagueur, -euse [blagœr, -øz] *F* I *a* bantering/ironical/mocking II *n* joker/leg-puller; tease(r); **c'est le blagueur de la bande,** he's the joker of the group.

blair [blɛr] *nm P* 1. nose*/conk/hooter; **il a un drôle de blair,** I don't like the look of him 2. **je l'ai dans le blair,** I can't stand him/he gets up my nose 3. **en avoir un coup dans le blair,** to be drunk*/to have (had) a skinful.

blaire [blɛr] *nm P* = **blaireau 2.**

blaireau, *pl* **-eaux** [blɛro] *nm P* 1. nose* 2. middle-aged man* who thinks he's up to date/in the know/with it; square 3. unpleasant character.

blairer [blɛre] *P vtr* **je** (**ne**) **peux pas le blairer,** I can't stand/stick/stomach him (at any price); **je le blaire bien,** I don't dislike him.

blanc, *f* **blanche** [blɑ̃, blɑ̃ʃ] I *a* 1. *F* **dire tantôt blanc tantôt noir,** to say first one thing and then another 2. *P* empty 3. **être blanc,** to

have a clean (police) record 4. *F* **je suis blanc,** I'm innocent; **je ne te vois pas blanc,** you're (in) for it. (*Voir* **bonnet 1; foies 2**) II *nm* 1. *F* **se bouffer le blanc des yeux,** to have a terrific row 2. *F* **chauffer qn à blanc,** to bring s.o. up to scratch 3. *F* white wine; **prendre un coup de blanc/un petit blanc,** to knock back a glass of white wine 4. *P* silver 5. *P* cocaine*/snow 6. *P* heroin*/H 7. (*langage des policiers*) police report (*typed on a white sheet*) 8. *pl F* (painter's) white overalls 9. *V* sperm/semen*/spunk 10. *P* **magasin de blanc,** brothel*/massage parlour. (*Voir* **raide I 1; saigner 1**) III *nf P* (*drogues*) 1. cocaine*/snow 2. heroin*/H.

blanc-bleu [blɑ̃blø] *a & n P* totally trustworthy (person).

blanc-cass [blɑ̃kas], **blanc-cassis** [blɑ̃kasis] *nm P* (*boisson*) white wine and blackcurrant liqueur *or* syrup. (*Voir* **kir**)

blanchecaille [blɑ̃ʃkɑj] *nf P* 1. laundress; washerwoman 2. laundry; washing.

Blanche-Neige [blɑ̃ʃnɛʒ] *Prnf F Péj* negro*/snowball.

blanchi [blɑ̃ʃi] *nm P Péj* **un mal blanchi,** a negro*.

blanchiment [blɑ̃ʃimɑ̃] *nm F* laundering (of money).

blanchir [blɑ̃ʃir] *vtr* 1. *F* to clear (s.o.) (of an accusation, etc)/to whitewash (s.o.) 2. *F* **blanchir de l'argent,** to launder money.

blanchisseur [blɑ̃ʃisœr] *nm P* (prisoner's) counsel/lawyer/brief. (*Voir* **blanchir 1**)

blanchisseuse [blɑ̃ʃisøz] *nf* 1. *P* customer who doesn't buy and says 'I'll come again' (*je repasserai*); **cette blanchisseuse a une ardoise dans tous les bistrots,** he's got a slate in every pub 2. *V* **envoyer son enfant à la blanchisseuse,** to ejaculate*/to come (off) in the sheets.

blanchouillard [blɑ̃ʃujar] *a P* 1. white 2. = **blanc I 3, 4.**

blanco [blɑ̃ko] *P* I *a* (*a*) pale; **la frousse l'a fait tourner blanco,** he went white with fear/he was scared shitless (*b*) innocent (of a crime) II *nm* glass of white wine.

blanquette [blɑ̃kɛt] *nf Vieilli P* (*a*) silver (*b*) coins.

blanquiste [blɑ̃kist] *nm P* = **blanco II.**

blard [blar] *nm P* shawl.

blase [blaz] *nm P* = **blaze.**

blaser [blaze] *vtr P* to call/to name.

blavard [blavar] *nm,* **blave** [blav] *nm,* **blavec** [blavɛk] *nm* handkerchief*.

blavin [blavɛ̃] *nm P* scarf.
blaze [blɑz] *nm P* 1. (*a*) name/monicker (*b*) nickname 2. nose* 3. (*brocante*) mark/hallmark/signature.
blé [ble] *nm F* 1. être pris comme dans un blé, to be caught like a rat in a trap 2. money*/bread; j'ai plus de blé, I've no bread left/I'm skint. (*Voir* **fauché 1**)
bléchard [bleʃar], **blèche** [blɛʃ] *a P* 1. ugly; elle est rien blèche! isn't she a fright! (*Voir* **gerber 1**) 2. old/decrepit 3. (*a*) shameful/scabby/mean/nasty (*b*) bad/rotten.
bled [blɛd] *nm* 1. *F* (*a*) place/locality; sale bled, God-forsaken place/hole/dump/*NAm* boondocks; quel sale bled! what a dump! en plein bled, at the back of beyond/in the sticks (*b*) home town; mon bled c'est Nantes, I come from Nantes 2. *P Mil* (*première guerre 1914–18*) no-man's-land; monter sur le bled, to go over the top.
bleu [blø] I *a F* 1. une colère bleue, a dreadful rage; piquer/se mettre dans une colère bleue, to flare up/to hit the roof 2. avoir une peur bleue, to be scared stiff; ça m'a donné/fichu une peur bleue, it frightened the life out of me/it scared me to death 3. une envie bleue, an overwhelming desire 4. j'en suis resté bleu, I was flabbergasted. (*Voir* **rat 1** (*b*)) II *nm F* 1. passer qch au bleu, to conceal sth; to hush sth up 2. n'y voir que du bleu, to be fooled*; le flic n'y a vu que du bleu, the cop didn't twig/was none the wiser/didn't smell a rat 3. (*a*) (*f* bleue) beginner/novice; greenhorn (*b*) *esp Mil* raw recruit/rookie 4. petit bleu/gros bleu, coarse/poor quality red wine 5. (= *bleu caporal*) un paquet de bleu, a packet of cheap pipe tobacco 6. un bleu/des bleus (de travail/de chauffe), overalls/dungarees/boiler suit 7. bleu (de Nanterre), police* officer responsible for rounding up tramps (*and taking them to a centre at Nanterre*) III *nf F* la grande bleue, the sea/*esp* the Mediterranean (sea).
bleubite [bløbit] *nm P* (*a*) beginner/novice/greenhorn (*b*) *esp Mil* raw recruit/rookie.
bleues [blø] *nfpl F* un paquet de bleues, a packet of Gauloises (*RTM*) (cigarettes).
bleusaille [bløzaj] *nf P* (*a*) novice/beginner; *Mil* raw recruit/rookie (*b*) la bleusaille, the raw recruits/the awkward squad.
blinde [blɛ̃d] *nm P* share (of loot)/cut/whack/split; après le coup chacun a reçu son blinde, we all got our cut after we'd pulled the job.

blindé [blɛ̃de] *a* 1. *F* (*endurci*) je suis blindé, I'm hardened to it; blindé contre qch, immune/impervious/hardened to sth; je suis blindé contre les injures, you can't insult me 2. *P* blindé, drunk*/plastered/blotto; il était blindé comme un char du matin au soir, he was completely pissed from morning to night 3. *P* être blindé, to have cheek/nerve; il est blindé celui-là! he's got a nerve!
blinder [blɛ̃de] I *vtr P* to give (s.o.) VD*; cette pute m'a blindé, that whore gave me a dose/I copped a dose from that tart II *vpr* se **blinder** *P* to get blind drunk*/to get pissed.
bloblote [blɔblɔt] *nf P* avoir la bloblote (*a*) to be afraid*/to be all of a tremble/to have the jitters (*b*) to have the shivers/the shakes (*c*) to have a fever/to be feverish.
bloc [blɔk] *nm* 1. *P* prison*/clink/jug; police cell; mettre/flanquer/fourrer qn au bloc, to send s.o. to prison*/to put s.o. in the nick 2. *F* gonflé à bloc (*a*) keyed up (*b*) full of zip/full of vim; les joueurs étaient gonflés à bloc avant le match, the players were full of beans before the match (*c*) cocksure 3. *F* ça gaze à bloc, things are going like a house on fire.
bloche [blɔʃ] *nm P* maggot.
blonde [blɔ̃d] *nf P* 1. lager 2. *FrC* girlfriend.
bloqué [blɔke] *a F* être bloqué, to have a psychological block.
bloquer [blɔke] *vtr* 1. *P* to send (s.o.) to prison*/to put (s.o.) inside 2. *P* bloquer une pêche, to receive a blow*/to get one in the kisser 3. (*écoles*) (se) bloquer une sale note, to get/cop a bad mark.
blosses [blɔs] *nfpl A V* testicles*.
blot [blo] *nm* 1. *F* (agreed, contract) price; acheter qch à bas blot, to buy sth on the cheap; faire un blot à qn, to knock sth off the price for s.o. 2. *P* personal business/job/work; c'est mon blot, (*c'est mon travail*) it's my business; it's in my line (of business); (*c'est mon affaire*) that's my affair; ce n'est pas ton blot, it's none of your business; c'est pas mon blot, it's not my cup of tea; ça fait mon blot, that suits me fine 3. *P* en avoir son blot, to have had enough/one's fill (of sth) 4. *P* c'est le même blot, it makes no odds/it's as broad as it's long/it's much of a muchness; que ça te plaise ou pas, c'est le même blot, like it or lump it.
bloum [blum] *nm*, **bloumard** [blumar] *nm Vieilli P* (outlandish) hat.

blouse [bluz] *nf* P blouse de plâtrier, (priest's) surplice.

blouser [bluze] *vtr* F to fool*; to cheat*/to deceive; to take (s.o.) in/to put one over on (s.o.); **se faire blouser**, to be taken in/to be had/to be conned.

blouson [bluzɔ̃] *nm* F **blouson noir** (*a*) teenage delinquent/young hooligan*/teddy-boy/ yobbo (*b*) biker/hell's angel.

blues [bluz] *nm* F the blues; **avoir/traîner un blues d'enfer**, to have the blues/to be down in the dumps.

blueseux, -euse [bluzø, -øz] *a* F depressed/blue.

bluffer [blyfe] *vtr* F to fool*/to trick/to bluff (s.o.); to have (s.o.) on.

blutinage [blytinaʒ] *nm* P questioning (of prisoner); third degree.

blutiner [blytine] *vi* P to confess*/to come clean (*after questioning*).

bob [bɔb] *nm* F bob(sleigh).

bobard [bɔbar] *nm* F (*a*) nonsense*/bosh/ rot; **des bobards (à la noix/à la gomme)**, rubbish/balderdash/bilge (*b*) tall story; *Vieilli* **bobard dans le coin**, seriously; **envoyer des bobards à qn**, to make a dirty crack about s.o.; **monter un bobard**, to shoot a line; **monter un bobard à qn**, to pull s.o.'s leg.

bobèche [bɔbɛʃ] *nf Vieilli* P head*/nut; **se monter la bobèche**, to kid oneself; **se payer la bobèche de qn**, to fool* s.o./to have s.o. on; **perdre la bobèche**, to lose one's head/one's cool.

bobéchon [bɔbeʃɔ̃] *nm Vieilli* P head*; **monter le bobéchon à qn**, to fool* s.o./to have s.o. on.

bobi [bɔbi] *nm*, **bobinard** [bɔbinar] *nm* P brothel*/whorehouse/knocking shop.

bobine [bɔbin] *nf* P 1. head*/nut; face*/ mug; **il a une drôle de bobine**, I don't like his face/I don't like the look of him 2. **être/rester en bobine**, (*personne*) to be alone/on one's tod; (*objet*) (*en gage*) to be in hock; (*voiture*) (*en panne*) to be broken down.

bobinette [bɔbinɛt] *nf* P 1. = **bobine 1** 2. illegal dice game; three-card trick; **taper la bobinette**, to play dice; to do the three-card trick.

bobino [bɔbino] *nm* P magnetic tape.

bobo [bobo] *nm* F (*mot enfantin*) (*a*) pain/ sore/bump/bruise/cut; **j'ai bobo**, it hurts; **ça fait bobo**, it hurts/it aches; **ça te fait bobo?** does it hurt?/is it sore? **avoir un bobo au doigt**, to have a sore finger (*b*) **y a pas de bobo**, no harm's been done; nothing's broken.

bobonne [bobɔn] *nf* F (*épouse*) the missus/ the old lady/the trouble and strife; *Vieilli* (*terme d'affection*) **oui ma bobonne**, yes (my) love/(my) pet/honeybunch/ducky.

bobs [bɔb] *nmpl* P 1. dice; **piper les bobs**, to cheat at dice; to load/to stack the dice; **manier les bobs**, to play dice; **pousser les bobs**, to throw the dice/to roll the bones 2. **lâcher les bobs**, to cry off/to drop out/to quit/to call it quits.

boc [bɔk] *nm* P = **bocard 1**.

bocal, pl -aux [bɔkal, -o] *nm* P 1. (= *local*) premises/building; room; house/place/pad; **les flics l'ont cueilli à son bocal**, the cops/the fuzz picked him up at his place 2. **un échappé de bocal**, undersized* person/little squirt/shortarse 3. stomach*/belly; **s'en faire crever le bocal**, to eat* and drink greedily/to stuff one's face/to stoke up 4. head*/nut 5. **mettre/ tremper le poisson dans le bocal**, to have sex*/to dip one's wick.

bocard [bɔkar] *nm* P 1. brothel* 2. disorder/mess.

boche [bɔʃ] *a & n* P *Péj* German*/jerry/ kraut.

bocsif [bɔksif], **bocson** [bɔksɔ̃] *nm* P = **boxif, boxon 1**.

boer [bɔɛr] *nm* F police* officer in charge of policing taxis.

bœuf (*f occ* **bœuve**) [bœf, bœv] **I** *a* F tremendous/amazing/fantastic/great (success etc); **faire un effet bœuf**, to have a huge impact **II** *nm* F 1. **travailler comme un bœuf**, to work like a horse/a Trojan 2. (**on fait ce qu'on peut,**) **on n'est pas des bœufs!** we're only human! 3. **avoir un bœuf sur la langue**, to (have been paid to) keep one's mouth shut 4. **faire du bœuf à la mode**, to get saddle-sore 5. income; **faire son bœuf**, to earn one's living/one's bread and butter; to carve out a lucrative career for oneself 6. (*musiciens*) **faire un bœuf**, to have a jam (session)/to jam 7. **enlever le bœuf!** it's ready/done/finished! we're ready to roll!

bœuf-carottes [bœfkarɔt] *nm* P member of the *Inspection générale des services*/= member of the Police Complaints Authority; **la maison bœuf-carottes** = the Police Complaints Authority.

B.O.F., bof[1] [beɔɛf, bɔf] *nm* F spiv/black marketeer (*originally, in WWII, the French profiteers in beurre, œufs, fromages*).

bof[2] [bɔf] *int* F (*pour exprimer le mépris,*

l'indifférence, l'ironie, la lassitude, le doute, etc) (a) pooh!/pah!/bah! (b) who cares!/you don't say!/big deal! (c) (I) dunno.

boilton [bwaltɔ̃] nm V (peu usuel) = **bouton 1**.

boire [bwar] vtr F il y a à boire et à manger (là-dedans), (vin, etc) it's got bits in it/it's food as well as drink; (film, livre, etc) it has its good points and its bad points/there's a bit of everything in it; (situation) there are pros and cons; on boit de bons coups mais ils sont rares! the drink's good but my glass is empty!/any chance of a refill? (Voir **lait 1**; **tasse 1, 2**; **trou 4**)

bois [bwa] nm 1. F abattre du bois, to work* hard/to slog away 2. F homme de bois, dull/lifeless man 3. F je leur ferai voir de quel bois je me chauffe, I'll show them (what I'm made of) 4. F ils ne se chauffent pas du même bois, they've got nothing in common 5. F il est du bois dont on fait les flûtes, you can twist him round your little finger 6. F casser du bois, (avion) to crash on landing; (voiture) to crash one's car 7. F on n'est pas de bois, I'm not made of wood/I'm only human 8. F touche(z) du bois! touch wood!/NAm knock on wood! 9. F chèque en bois, dud/rubber cheque 10. F langue de bois, (surt en politique) speech full of jargon/obscure words 11. furniture; être dans ses bois, to have a place of one's own; se mettre dans ses bois, to set up home/to buy one's own furniture 12. P mettre les bois, to run away*/to clear off/to beat it 13. P tirer sur le bois mort, to row 14. P faire du bois (a) (en avion) to crash on landing (b) to break a door down 15. P (cocu) il lui pousse du bois/des bois, his horns are sprouting 16. scier du bois, to play the cello. (Voir **cloche I 4**; **gueule I 4** (a); **sirop 2**; **visage 2**)

boîte [bwat] nf 1. P (a) uncomfortable/poky little room; quelle boîte! what a dump!/what a hole! (b) place of work, etc (eg school, office, shop, factory, café); aller à la boîte, to go to work/school, etc; je travaille dans une boîte d'informatique, I work for a computer company; sale boîte, rotten hole/crummy dump 2. F boîte (de nuit), nightclub/nightspot; aller/sortir en boîte, to go (night-)clubbing/to go out on the town/to go down the clubs 3. P prison*; Mil guardroom/cells; mettre qn à la boîte, to put s.o. inside/in the can; bouffer de la boîte, to be put away 4. P boîte (à mensonge(s)), mouth*; ferme ta boîte!

shut your trap! 5. F (a) mettre qn en boîte, to pull s.o.'s leg/to take the mickey (out of s.o.) (b) (musique, cinéma, TV) mettre en boîte, to record/to can; c'est dans la boîte, it's in the can 6. F Aut (boîte de vitesse) gearbox 7. F (églises) confessional 8. P boîte à chocolat/à dominos/à violon, coffin/box; F boîte à cancans, (personne) gossip/chatterbox; (lieu) gossip-shop; P boîte aux claqués/aux dégelés/aux refroidis, mortuary/morgue; boîte à conneries, television*/gogglebox/idiot-box; P boîte a ragoût, stomach*/breadbasket; P boîtes à lait/à lolo, breasts*/jugs. (Voir **lolo 3**); P boîte à morve, nose*/conk; V boîte à ouvrage/aux lettres, vagina*/box; F (théâtre) boîte à sel, box office; F boîte à vice, sly dog/sly customer. (Voir **bachot**)

boitout [bwatu] nm, **boit-sans-soif** [bwasɑ̃swaf] nm, **boit-tout** [bwatu] nm P drunkard (who drinks all his earnings); tippler/lush/alky.

bol [bɔl] nm 1. F prendre un bon bol d'air pur, to fill one's lungs with fresh air 2. P luck; un coup de bol, a bit of luck/a stroke of luck; avoir du bol, to be lucky/in luck; to have a lucky break; manquer de bol, to be unlucky/out of luck; manque de bol! bad luck!/hard luck!/rotten luck! 3. F cheveux coupés au bol/une coupe-au-bol, pudding-basin haircut 4. P buttocks*/backside; j'en ai ras le bol, I'm fed up (to the back teeth) with it/I've had a basinful of it/I've had it up to here (Voir **ras**) 5. P il en fait un bol, it's boiling hot/it's stifling 6. P il ne se casse pas le bol, he's not worried.

bolcho [bɔlʃo] Vieilli F I a communist/commie/red/lefty II nm & f communist/commie/red/lefty.

bombance [bɔ̃bɑ̃s] nf Vieilli F feast(ing)/carousing; faire bombance, to go on a binge/a spree; (manger) to feast.

bombarder [bɔ̃barde] vtr & i 1. F to pitchfork (s.o.) into a job; on l'a bombardé ministre, he's been made a minister out of the blue 2. P to smoke (a lot); il bombarde toute la journée, he chain-smokes all day long; qu'est-ce qu'elle bombarde! she smokes a hell of a lot!/she's a heavy smoker! 3. P (boxe) to give (one's opponent) a pasting/to hit (one's opponent) all over the ring.

bombardier [bɔ̃bardje] nm P (drogues) marijuana cigarette*/bomber.

bombe [bɔ̃b] nf F 1. (a) arriver en bombe/comme une bombe/à toute bombe, to turn up unexpectedly/out of the blue (b) entrer en bombe/comme une bombe/à toute bombe, to come bursting in 2. feast/spree/binge/good time; faire la bombe, to go out on a spree/on a binge; s'offrir une bombe carabinée/une bombe à tout casser, to have a rare old time/ to have a ball/to have a wild time; passer la nuit en bombe, to make a night of it; un lendemain de bombe, the morning after the night before.

bomber [bɔ̃be] I *vi* P to drive fast/to bomb along; on a bombé pour arriver à l'heure, we had to step on it/to belt along/to do a ton to get there in time II *vtr* 1. P bomber la gueule à qn, to beat* s.o. up/to bash s.o.'s face in/to bash s.o.'s head in 2. *F* to spraypaint III *vpr* se bomber P 1. se bomber de qch, to do/to go without sth 2. tu peux (toujours) te bomber! nothing doing!*/get lost!*/go (and) jump in the lake!/go take a running jump!

bombido [bɔ̃bido] *nm*, **bombita** [bɔ̃mbita] *nf* P (*drogues*) (*a*) amphetamine*/ bam (*b*) mixture of amphetamine* and heroin* for injection/bombida.

bon, *f* **bonne** [bɔ̃, bɔn] *a & nf F* 1. être bon, (*être trompé*) to be duped/hoaxed/ swindled/conned; to be done/to be had; (*être fini, ruiné*) to be done for/to be a goner; to be in for it; (*être arrêté*) to be arrested/to get nicked/to get done; être bon pour ..., to be due for (sth unpleasant)/to be in for ...; on est bon pour rentrer à pied, (*obligés*) we're in for walking home/we'll just have to walk back; (*disposés*) we're game for walking home 2. ne pas être bon, to refuse/not to agree; j'suis pas bon! I'm not having any (of it/that)! 3. (*personne*) être bon à rien/à lap(e), to be a dead loss/a hopeless case 4. y a bon! OK! 5. c'est tout bon! it's perfect/A1/wicked! 6. avec dix minutes de bon, with ten minutes to spare/in hand 7. une bien bonne, a good joke/a good one; elle est (bien) bonne, celle-là! that's a good one, that is!/I like that! en voilà une bonne! that's a good 'un! tu en as de bonnes! you've got some funny ideas!; you've got a weird sense of humour!; it's all very well for you to talk! 8. avoir qn à la bonne, to like s.o./to have a liking for s.o./a soft spot for s.o.; to take a shine to s.o.; ne pas avoir qn à la bonne, to have a down on s.o.; la garder bonne à qn, to have a grudge against s.o./to have it in for s.o. 9. prendre qch à la bonne, to take sth in good part 10. (*brocante*) bon d'époque, authentic/the genuine article. (*Voir* **ferte; lap(e); romaine 2**)

bona [bɔna] *nm*, **bonap** [bɔnap] *nm*, **bonaparte** [bɔnapart] *nm P* 500-franc note.

bon app'! [bɔnap] *int F* (*bon appétit*) enjoy your meal!/bon appétit!/*NAm* enjoy!

bonbon [bɔ̃bɔ̃] I *nm* 1. *pl V* (*drogues*) *esp* amphetamines* *ou* LSD*/candy/sweets 2. *V* clitoris*/clit 3. *pl V* testicles*; casser les bonbons à qn, to bore* s.o. to death/to give s.o. a pain in the arse/to get on s.o.'s tits 4. *P* bonbon à liqueur, boil; bonbon anglais, small spot/zit. (*Voir* **peler** I; **ras 2**) II *adv* coûter bonbon, to be expensive/to cost a lot.

bondieu [bɔ̃djø] *P* I *int* bondieu (de bondieu)! God almighty!/good God! II *nm* quel bondieu d'imbécile! what a bloody fool!

bondieusard, -arde [bɔ̃djøzar, -ard] *P Péj* I *n* sanctimonious/churchy person II *a* sanctimonious/churchy/pi.

bondieuserie [bɔ̃djøzri] *nf P Péj* 1. churchiness/sanctimonious devotion 2. *pl* church ornaments/devotional objects (in bad taste)/religious knickknacks.

bondir [bɔ̃dir] *vi* 1. *A P* se faire bondir, to be arrested/to get run in 2. *F* to get angry*/ crazy/mad; ça va le faire bondir! he'll go nuts/he'll hit the roof!

bonheur [bɔnœr] *nm F* 1. faire qch au petit bonheur, to do sth in a slapdash manner; il fait les choses au petit bonheur, he's slaphappy 2. au petit bonheur la chance! here's chancing it!/here's trusting to luck! 3. tu ne connais pas ton bonheur! you don't know how lucky you are!

bonhomme [bɔnɔm], *pl* **bonshommes** [bɔ̃zɔm] *nm* 1. *F* (*a*) man*/chap/fellow/ bloke/guy; connaître son bonhomme, to have s.o. sized up/weighed up (*b*) (*mari*) old man/ bloke/guy 2. *F* soldier 3. *F* il va son petit bonhomme de chemin, he's just going/ trundling/footling along in his own little way; (*en voiture*) he's just tootling along 4. *F* nom d'un petit bonhomme! gosh!/wow!/good heavens! 5. *F* (*théâtre*) entrer dans la peau du bonhomme, to get into the skin of the character 6. *F* salut, (mon) bonhomme! hello, old man!/wotcher, cock! 7. *V* erect penis*.

boni [bɔni] *nm F* = **bénef.**

boniche [bɔniʃ] *nf P Péj* = **bonniche.**

boniment [bɔnimɑ̃] *nm F* 1. patter/sales talk/spiel/fast talk(ing) (of showman, tout, etc) 2. du boniment *ou* des boniments (à la graisse (d'oie)/à la graisse de chevaux de bois/à la graisse de hareng saur/à la noix/à la peau de toutou), nonsense*/rubbish/twaddle/ claptrap/piffle/bilge 3. avoir qn au boniment, to deceive* s.o./to kid s.o. along/to put one across s.o. 4. faire du boniment à qn, to try to get round s.o./to try to coax s.o.; to fast-talk s.o./to sweet-talk s.o.; faire du boniment à une femme, to chat a woman up/to sweet-talk a woman.

bonimenter [bɔnimɑ̃te] *F* I *vi* to hand out the sales talk II *vtr* bonimenter qn = faire du boniment à qn (**boniment 4**).

bonimenteur, -euse [bɔnimɑ̃tœr, -øz] *n F* 1. tout; spieler 2. flatterer*/soft-soap artist.

bonir [bɔnir] *vi & tr P* 1. to talk/to speak/to tell/to say; personne n'en a boni une, no one uttered a word 2. to hand out the sales talk. (*Voir* **salade 3**)

bonisseur [bɔnisœr] *nm P* cheapjack/street hawker; il a un p'tit job de bonisseur aux Galeries Lafayette, he makes a living hawking outside the *Galeries Lafayette*.

bonjour [bɔ̃ʒur] *nm* 1. *F* c'est simple comme bonjour, it's as easy* as ABC/as pie 2. *F* avoir le bonjour, to come too late/to arrive when it's all over 3. *P* bonjour d'Alfred, (*pourboire*) tip; *Iron* si tu crois ça t'auras le bonjour d'Alfred/de Clara, if you believe that then you're more stupid than I thought 4. *F Iron* bonjour les dégâts! wait for the mess! bonjour la soirée! it's going to be a long evening! 5. *P* vol au bonjour, burglary committed without breaking in (*the door, etc being left open*) 6. *F* connaître qn comme ça, bonjour bonsoir, to have a nodding acquaintance with s.o.

bonnard [bɔnar] *a P* (*a*) simple-minded/ naive/easily conned (*b*) être (fait) bonnard = être bon (**bon 1**).

bonne [bɔn] *a & nf Voir* **bon**.

bonnet [bɔnɛ] *nm* 1. *F* c'est bonnet blanc et blanc bonnet, it's six of one and half a dozen of the other/it's as broad as it's long 2. *F* avoir la tête près du bonnet, to be quick-tempered/to fly off the handle easily/to have a short fuse 3. *F* parler à son bonnet, to talk to oneself 4. *F* bonnet de nuit, wet blanket; c'est une histoire triste comme un bonnet de nuit, that story's as cheerful as the grave 5. *F* jeter son bonnet par-dessus les moulins, to throw caution to the winds 6. *F* gros bonnet, important person*/big shot/big noise/bigwig 7. *F* (*cuisine*) bonnet d'évêque, parson's nose 8. *P* (= **bonneteau**) three-card trick 9. *P* il ne se casse pas le bonnet, he doesn't worry about

anything/he's not worried.

bonneteau [bɔnto] *nm P* three-card trick.

bonneteur [bɔntœr] *nm P* dealer of the three-card trick.

bonniche [bɔniʃ] *nf P Péj* maid/skivvy; je ne suis pas ta bonniche, who was your servant last?

bonnir [bɔnir] *vtr & i P* = **bonir**.

bonnisseur [bɔnisœr] *nm P* = **bonisseur**.

bonsoir [bɔ̃swar] *nm F* tout est dit, bonsoir! there's nothing more to be said!/there's an end of it!/and that's that!

bonze [bɔ̃z] *nm F* 1. (*personnage important*) big shot/bigwig 2. vieux bonze, old fog(e)y*/ old dodderer/old fossil.

book [buk] *nm F* bookmaker/bookie; book marron, welsher.

boom [bum] *nf F* (young people's) party; (*grandes écoles*) end-of-term/end-of-year party. (*Voir* **boum II**)

bord [bɔr] *nm F* sur les bords, slightly/a bit; menteur sur les bords, a bit of a liar; il est un peu empaffé/pédé/tapette sur les bords, he's a bit camp/a bit of a poofter/a bit poofy.

bordée [bɔrde] *nf F* courir/tirer une bordée, être en bordée, to go on a spree*/on a binge/on a bender; to go on a pub-crawl.

bordel [bɔrdɛl] *nm* 1. *F* brothel*/ whorehouse/knocking shop 2. *P* shambles; quel bordel! what a bloody mess! ça va être le bordel, it's going to be hell; semer le bordel, to raise hell; foutre le bordel (quelque part), to bollocks sth up/to cock sth up/to balls sth (up) 3. *P* et tout le bordel, and all the rest 4. *P* bordel (de Dieu)!/bordel de merde! damn and blast it!/bloody hell!/sodding hell! faut être raisonnable, bordel! for Christ's sake be reasonable!

bordelaise [bɔrdəlɛz] *nf P* partie de bordelaise, heavy petting session.

bordéleux [bɔrdelø] *a P* (*rare*) = **bordélique**.

bordelier, -ière [bɔrdəlje, -jɛr] *n F* brothel-keeper.

bordélique [bɔrdelik] *P* I *a* in a mess/in a shambles/shambolic; tu es très bordélique, you're a real slob; c'est bordélique, ce truc, this thing's a real bastard*/a real sod; it's a real cock-up II *n* un(e) bordélique, a slob.

bordille [bɔrdij] *nf P* 1. (*personne*) nasty piece of work/(rotten) bastard*/(real) sod/son of a bitch 2. police informer*/stoolie/grass 3. trash/rubbishy goods/crap/junk.

bordurer [bɔrdyre] *vtr P* se faire bordurer/

être borduré, to be prohibited (*by the police or by the underworld*) from frequenting certain specified places; to be made persona non grata; (*médecin*) to be struck off (the register); **le patron l'a borduré de son établissement**, the landlord's banned him from the premises.

borgne [bɔrɲ] *P* I *nm* 1. penis*; **étrangler le borgne**, to masturbate*/to beat the meat 2. *A* buttocks*/bum II *nf* night; **profiter de la borgne pour disparaître**, to slip off into the night.

borgnesse [bɔrɲɛs] *nf P Péj* one-eyed girl *or* woman.

borgnio [bɔrɲo] *nm*, **borgnon** [bɔrɲɔ̃] *nm P* night.

borgnoter [bɔrɲɔte] *P* I *vtr* **borgnoter qn**, (*observer*) to gaze intently at s.o.; (*épier*) to keep a sharp lookout for s.o. II *vi* to go to bed*.

borne [bɔrn] *nf F* kilometre; **bousculer les bornes**, to speed along; to eat up the miles; **se taper cinq bornes à pied**, to walk five kilometres/to do five kilometres on foot.

bornioler [bɔrnjɔle] *vtr P* to darken (a room, etc)/to shut out the light in (a room).

bosco, boscot, -otte [bɔsko, -ɔt] *P* I *a* hunchbacked/humpbacked II *n* (*a*) hunchback (*b*) **rigoler/rire/se tordre comme un bosco**, to laugh* uproariously.

boss [bɔs] *nm F* 1. boss/guv'nor/chief 2. leader (of gang, etc)/big shot/top man.

bossant [bɔsɑ̃] *a A F* very funny*/priceless.

bosse [bɔs] *nf F* 1. **avoir la bosse de qch**, to have a knack/a flair for sth 2. (*a*) **rouler sa bosse (un peu partout)**, to knock about/to be a rolling stone; **j'ai roulé ma bosse**, I've been around (*b*) **allons, roule ta bosse!** come on, get a move on!/on your bike! 3. (*cyclisme*) hill/slope/incline. (*Voir* **demander 1**)

bosseler [bɔsle] *vtr P* to beat up*/to lay into (s.o.)/to set about (s.o.); **machine à bosseler**, fist/bunch of fives; **passer qn à la machine à bosseler**, to beat s.o. up*/to work s.o. over.

bosser [bɔse] *vi P* 1. to work* hard/to slave/ to slog (away); **bosser comme un nègre**, to work* very hard/to work like a nigger/to slog one's guts out 2. *A F* to have lots of fun/to have a whale of a time.

bosseur [bɔsœr] *P* I *a* hard working II *nm P* hard worker/swot/plodder/slogger.

bossoirs [bɔswar] *nmpl P* (large prominent) breasts*.

bossu [bɔsy] *nm P* **petit bossu**, coffee laced with brandy.

botte [bɔt] I *nf F* (*a*) wad of 100 notes (*b*) (*postiers*) bunch of letters (tied together) (*c*) (il) **y en a des bottes**, there's stacks/heaps/ loads of them II *nf* 1. *P* **avoir les bottes à bascule**, to be drunk* 2. *F* **j'en ai plein les bottes**, (*fatigué*) I'm exhausted*; (*excédé*) I'm fed up (to the back teeth)/I'm pissed off (with it, them) 3. *P* **filer un coup de botte à qn**, to tap/touch s.o. (for a loan, money, etc); to be on the cadge 4. *F* **cirer/graisser ses bottes**, (*se préparer à partir*) to prepare for a journey; (*à mourir*) to prepare for the next world 5. *F* **cirer/lécher les bottes à qn**, to toady to s.o./to suck up to s.o./to lick s.o.'s boots 6. *P* **être à la botte de qn**, to be a slave to s.o./to obey s.o. unquestioningly 7. *P* **proposer la botte à qn**, to make amorous advances to s.o./to try to get off with s.o.; **dès la première rencontre il leur proposait la botte**, he used to try and get them into bed right from the word go 8. *F* **sortir dans la botte**, to graduate brilliantly from the *École polytechnique*. (*Voir* **bottier**) 9. *F* **y laisser ses bottes**, to die* with one's boots on 10. *V* **chier dans les bottes de qn**, to annoy* s.o./to get on s.o.'s wick/to give s.o. a pain in the arse/*NAm* ass 11. *P* **faire dans les bottes de qn**, to disturb/to interfere with s.o.; to be a nuisance to s.o./to get in s.o.'s hair 12. *F* **à propos de bottes**, apropos of nothing at all; without rhyme or reason; **chercher querelle à qn à propos de bottes**, to pick a quarrel with s.o. over nothing/over a trifle. (*Voir* **foin 1**)

botter [bɔte] *vtr F* 1. **botter (le derrière/les fesses/P le cul à) qn**, to kick s.o.'s buttocks/to give s.o. a boot up the behind/to give s.o. a kick in the pants 2. to suit; **ça me botte**, that suits me fine/down to the ground/to a T; I really like/fancy/dig that. (*Voir* **fouettard 2**)

bottier [bɔtje] *nm F* s.o. who graduates brilliantly from the *École polytechnique*. (*Voir* **botte II 8**)

bottine [bɔtin] *nf P* 1. lesbians* (in general); lesbianism; **travailler dans/être de la bottine**, to be a lesbian*/a les/a dyke 2. **filer un coup de bottine à qn**, to tap/touch s.o. for money; to be on the cadge.

bottiner [bɔtine] *vtr P* **bottiner qn**, to tap/to touch s.o. (for money, etc); to cadge off s.o.

bouboule [bubul] *nm & f F* fat person/ fatso/(fat) slob.

bouc [buk] *nm P* 1. **planquer son bouc**, to take shelter 2. **qu'est-ce qui pue? c'est le bouc!** *insult addressed to bearded man* 3. *F* =

book. (*Voir* **bique I 4**)

boucan [bukɑ̃] *nm F* uproar/din/hullabaloo; faire un boucan infernal/du tonnerre/de tous les diables, to make a hell of a row; to kick up a fuss.

bouche [buʃ] *nf* 1. *F* en avoir à bouche que veux-tu, to have plenty/to have one's fill 2. *F* être sur sa bouche/être porté sur la bouche, to be fond of one's food 3. *F* dire qch la bouche en cœur, to say sth with a simper 4. *F* il en avait la bouche pleine/plein la bouche, he could talk of nothing else/he was full of it 5. *F* (motus et) bouche cousue! mum's the word!/don't breathe a word (of it)! 6. *P* ta bouche (bébé, t'auras une frite)! shut up!*/belt up!/give it a rest!/put a sock in it! 7. *V* bouche chaude, fellatio*. (*Voir* **cul 12**)

bouché [buʃe] *a F* être bouché, to be stupid*; être bouché à l'émeri, to be as thick as two short planks.

bouchée [buʃe] *nf F* 1. ne faire qu'une bouchée de ..., to make short work of (s.o., sth)/to make mincemeat of (s.o.)/to wipe the floor with (s.o.) 2. mettre les bouchées doubles, to work at double speed; to do a job in double quick time 3. pour une bouchée de pain, for a trifle/for a song/for a mere nothing.

boucher [buʃe] *vtr P* en boucher un coin/une surface à qn, to amaze* s.o./to floor s.o./to flabbergast s.o.; ça vous en bouche un coin! that's flummoxed you!

bouchon [buʃɔ̃] *nm* 1. *P* the youngest child in a family/the baby of the family 2. *F* (*terme d'affection*) mon petit bouchon, my love/pet/sweetie 3. *F* (*marine*) bouchons gras, engine-room artificers 4. *P* prendre du bouchon, to age/to be getting on in years; avoir du bouchon, to be quite elderly 5. *F* traffic jam; hold-up/tailback 6. *F* bouchon (de carafe), large stone/large diamond/sparkler 7. *F* c'est plus fort que de jouer au bouchon (avec des queues de radis), that's the (absolute) limit!/that beats everything! 8. *P* envoyer le bouchon/pousser le bouchon (un peu loin), pousser le bouchon trop loin, to exaggerate*/to go a bit (too) far 9. *P* mettre un bouchon à qn, to shut s.o. up; (se) mettre un bouchon, to shut up*/to wrap up; mets un bouchon! belt* up!/put a sock in it! 10. *F* être payée au bouchon, (*entraîneuse de bar*) to be paid according to the number of (champagne) bottles consumed by the client(s).

bouclage [buklaʒ] *nm P* imprisonment.

bouclard [buklar] *nm P* shop.

bouclarès [buklarɛs] *a inv P* 1. closed; le tripot du coin est bouclarès, the local gambling joint has been closed down 2. (*personne*) locked up.

boucle [bukl] *nf* 1. *F* se serrer la boucle, to tighten one's belt/to go without (food) 2. *F* grande Boucle, the Tour de France (cycle race).

boucler [bukle] *vtr* 1. *F* se boucler la ceinture/se la boucler, to tighten one's belt/to do without 2. *P* to send (s.o.) to prison*/to lock (s.o.) up; se faire boucler, to get put inside 3. *F* boucler son budget, to make ends meet 4. (*a*) *F* to close; bouclez la lourde! shut the door! (*b*) *P* boucle-la! shut up!*/belt up!/shut it!/shut your trap! la boucler, to keep quiet/to keep one's trap shut; ça vous la boucle! that's got you! (*c*) *F* boucler une affaire, to settle/to clinch a matter; c'est une affaire bouclée, it's all sewn up (*d*) *F vi* il n'y a plus qu'à boucler, we'll have to close down/to shut up shop.

boude [bud] *nm Vieilli P* ugly woman/fright. (*Voir* **boudin 2** (*c*))

bouder [bude] *vi F* 1. bouder à la besogne, to be workshy 2. bouder contre son ventre, to cut off one's nose to spite one's face.

boudin [budɛ̃] *nm* 1. *P* (*pneu*) tyre 2. *P* (*a*) woman of easy virtue/easy lay/pushover (*b*) old prostitute* (*c*) ugly/frumpish woman; fright; fat woman 3. *P* girl(friend) 4. *pl F* fat/podgy fingers 5. *P* (*a*) roll of coins (*b*) prostitute's earnings 6. avoir du boudin, (*au jeu*) to have the master cards 7. *P* être plein/rond comme un boudin, to be blind drunk*/to be plastered 8. *F* faire du/son boudin, to have the sulks 9. *P* boudin blanc, penis*/sausage. (*Voir* **eau 5**; **jus 1** (*a*))

bouée [bue] *nf P* lâcher la bouée, to die*/to kick the bucket.

bouffarde [bufard] *nf F* (old) pipe; tirer sur sa bouffarde, to smoke one's pipe.

bouffarder [bufarde] *vtr F* to smoke (a pipe)/to puff at (one's pipe).

bouffe [buf] *nf P* 1. food*/grub/nosh/chow; faire la bouffe, to do the cooking; se faire la/sa bouffe, to make/rustle up something to eat 2. meal/eating; se faire une (petite) bouffe, to have a meal (*esp* at restaurant); c'est l'heure de la bouffe! grub's up! une grande bouffe, a blow-out.

bouffer [bufe] *I vtr & i* 1. *P* (*a*) to eat* (*b*) to eat greedily; bouffer à en crever, to stuff oneself/one's face (with food); j'ai bien bouffé, that was a bloody good meal (c) **bouffer de l'essence**, (voiture) to be heavy on/ to drink petrol; NAm to be a gas guzzler (d) **bouffer du kilomètre**, to eat up the miles (e) **bouffer du curé/du juif**, etc, to be violently anticlerical/antisemitic, etc 2. P to spend (freely)/to blow/to run through/to get through a lot of money 3. P **en bouffer**, to be a police informer*/to grass/to nark 4. V **bouffer la chatte**, to practise cunnilingus*/to eat hairpie II vpr **se bouffer** F (a) to be eaten; ces biscuits se bouffent vite, these biscuits go down quickly (b) **se bouffer le nez**, to quarrel*/to bicker/to row; to have a go at each other. (Voir **bite 3; boîte 3; brique 2; clou 7; lion; morceau 2; rat 10; vache II 4**)

bouffetance [buftɑ̃s] nf P food*/grub/nosh.

bouffi [bufi] nm P tu l'as dit, bouffi! (locution) you've said it!

bouffon [bufɔ̃] nm F fool*/twit/berk/jerk.

bouftou(t) [buftu] nm P glutton/greedy-guts.

bougeotte [buʒɔt] nf F avoir la bougeotte, to be restless/to have the fidgets/to have ants in one's pants; (voyager sans cesse) to be always on the move.

bougie [buʒi] nf P face*/dial/mug; tirer une drôle de bougie, to look astonished.

bougnat [buɲa] nm, **bougne** [buɲ] nm F 1. native of Auvergne/Auvergnat 2. coalman/coal merchant 3. (a) small bistrot/pub (b) keeper of a small bistrot.

bougnette [buɲɛt] nf P stain/spot.

bougnoul(e) [buɲul] nm P Péj 1. Arab/wog 2. negro* 3. half-breed.

bougre, f **bougresse** [bugr, bugrɛs] P I n 1. person/individual; **un bon bougre**, a good sort/a nice guy; **un mauvais bougre**, an ugly customer; **un sale bougre**, a rotter/a rotten sod/a bastard*; **un pauvre bougre**, a poor devil; **pauvre bougre!** poor sod! **bougre d'imbécile!/bougre d'âne!** (you) bloody fool! 2. **bougre de temps**, filthy weather 3. f **bougresse**, big/strapping woman II int **bougre!** hell!/heck! **bougre que ça fait mal!** Christ, that hurts!

bougrement [bugrəmɑ̃] adv P damn(ed)/darn(ed) / damnably / devilishly / hellishly/ bloody; **il fait bougrement froid**, it's bloody cold.

boui-boui [bwibwi] nm P 1. brothel*/knocking shop 2. (low, sleazy) dive (for eating or entertainment); honky-tonk joint;

dingy café/greasy spoon. (pl **bouis-bouis**)

bouic [bwik] nm Vieilli P = **boui-boui**.

bouif, bouiffe [bwif] n P cobbler.

bouillabaisse [bujabɛs] nf P être dans la bouillabaisse, to be in a fix*/in a pickle.

bouille [buj] nf P 1. face*/mug; avoir une bonne bouille, to have a friendly face/to look like a friendly sort of person 2. **(bonne) bouille**, (potential) victim (of a confidence trick, etc)/mug/sucker 3. old steam locomotive.

bouillie [buji] nf F (a) c'est de la bouillie pour les chats, it's a worthless jumble/a hopeless muddle/a dog's dinner (b) **mettre qn/qch en bouillie**, to smash s.o./sth to pieces; to beat s.o./sth to a pulp.

bouillon [bujɔ̃] nm 1. P water; tomber dans le/au bouillon, to fall into the water/into the drink; boire/prendre un/le bouillon, (se noyer) to drown; (subir une perte d'argent) to sustain a heavy financial loss; to come unstuck (in a business venture)/to be ruined 2. F cheap, popular restaurant 3. F bouillon d'onze heures, poisoned drink 4. pl F bouillons, unsold copies (of a newspaper, a book)/returns/remainders.

bouillonner [bujɔne] vi F (journaux, etc) to remain unsold; ce canard bouillonne à 15% (de son tirage), 15% of this newspaper's print run remains unsold. (Voir **couvercle**)

bouillotte [bujɔt] nf P 1. head*/nut 2. = **bouille 3**.

bouisbouis [bwibwi] nm P = **boui-boui**.

boul' [bul] nm F (boulevard) avenue; le Boul' Mich', the boulevard Saint-Michel (in the Latin Quarter of Paris).

boulange [bulɑ̃ʒ] nf 1. F bakery trade; il travaille dans la boulange, he's a baker 2. P la Grande Boulange/la Boulange aux faffes, the Bank of France 3. counterfeit money.

boulanger [bulɑ̃ʒe] nm 1. F le Boulanger, the devil/Old Nick 2. P remercier son boulanger, to die*.

boulangère [bulɑ̃ʒɛr] nf P prostitute* supporting a fancy man; meal-ticket.

boule¹ [bul] nm F = **boul'**.

boule² [bul] nf 1. P head*/nut; perdre la boule, to go mad*/to go round the bend/to go off one's head; un coup de boule, a (head-)butt (in the chest or stomach); boule de billard/à zéro, bald head; il a une boule de billard, he's as bald as a coot. (Voir aussi **zéro I 6**) 2. A F Mil boule (de son), ration loaf 3. F boule (dans la gorge), lump in one's throat 4. *P* day in prison*/in detention 5. *F* football 6. *F* (*brocante*) important sale; **faire une boule**, to make a big sale 7. *P pl* **boules**, money*; (*affaires*) business; financial affairs; **remonter les boules de qn**, to sort out s.o.'s shaky financial affairs 8. *F* **avoir les yeux en boules de loto**, to be goggle-eyed/bug-eyed; to have eyes like saucers 9. *F* **boule de feu, boule de fer**, cross my heart (and hope to die). (*Voir* **croix 6**) 10. *P* **avoir des boules de gomme dans les zozos/dans les portugaises**, to be deaf 11. *P* (*courses*) **arriver dans les boules**, to be one of the first three past the (winning) post 12. *F* **se mettre en boule**, to get angry*/to blow one's top; **ça me met (les nerfs) en boule**, that gets my goat/that makes me livid; **il me met en boule**, he gets my back up 13. *P* **avoir les boules**, (*avoir peur*) to be afraid*/to be scared shitless; (*être irrité*) to be pissed off; (*être prêt à exploser*) to be fuming/boiling with rage; **avoir la boule**, (*être énervé*) to be nervous/worried; (*avoir peur*) to have the jitters 14. *P* **foutre les boules à qn**, to annoy* s.o./to give s.o. a pain in the arse/to get on s.o.'s tits; (*angoisser*) to fill s.o. with anguish; **ça me fout les boules de la voir dans cet état**, I can't stand seeing her in this state 15. *F* **la boule noire lui tombe toujours**, nothing ever turns out well for him; he is dogged by bad luck 16. *V* **faire boule de gomme**, to have oral sex*. (*Voir* **mystère 1**)

boule-de-neige [buldənɛʒ] *nm Vieilli P Péj* Black*/nigger.

bouler [bule] *vtr F* 1. **envoyer bouler qn**, to send s.o. packing/to tell s.o. where he gets off 2. (*théâtre*) **bouler un rôle**, to fluff (one's lines).

boulet [bulɛ] *nm* 1. *P* wife*/ball and chain 2. *P Péj* **boulet Bernot**, Black*.

boulette [bulɛt] *nf F* mistake*/blunder/ boob; **grosse boulette**, howler; **faire une boulette**, to boob/to drop a brick/to drop a clanger.

boulevard [bulvar] *nm F* **les événements du boulevard**, life in town; **faire un boulevard**, to wander/to stroll up and down a boulevard/ an avenue. (*Voir* **allongé**)

bouliner [buline] *vtr P* **bouliner un mur/un plafond**, (*pour voler*) to make a hole in a wall/a ceiling.

boulon [bulɔ̃] *nm F* **serrer les boulons**, to be in control of/to be firm with the staff, etc; to rule with a firm hand; **resserrer les boulons**, to take things in hand; to take firm control (of a company, etc).

boulonnaise [bulɔnɛz] *nf F* prostitute* working in the Bois de Boulogne (*in Paris*).

boulonner [bulɔne] *vi F* to work* hard/to slog away.

boulonneur, -euse [bulɔnœr, -øz] *a & n* hard-working (person); *n* grafter/slogger.

boulot¹ [bulo] *nm* 1. *F* work; job; drudgery/grind/slog; **quel est/c'est quoi son boulot**? what's his job? **quel sale boulot!** what a crummy job! **s'atteler/se mettre au boulot**, to pitch in/to get down to it; **au boulot!** get cracking! **du boulot tout cuit**, an easy* job, a cushy number; **parler boulot**, to talk shop; **être boulot(-)boulot**, to be hard-working/to be a slogger/a grafter 2. *F* worker 3. *P* business; **c'est ton boulot**, that's your business!/ that's your look-out! 4. *P* burglary/job.

boulot², -otte [bulo, -ɔt] *a & n F* podgy/ dumpy/plump (person); **petit boulot** (d'enfant), little dumpling.

boulotter [bulɔte] *P* **I** *vtr* 1. to eat* 2. **boulotter une fortune**, to squander a fortune **II** *vi Vieilli* **ça boulotte!** **ça boulotte?** = **ça biche!** **ça biche?** (**bicher 1**).

boum [bum] **I** *nm* 1. *F* (*grande animation*) **en plein boum**, in full swing; **être en plein boum**, to be in full swing; (*avoir beaucoup de travail*) to be up to one's neck in work/to have plenty on one's plate 2. *F* **faire un boum**, (*faire sensation*) to cause a sensation; (*avoir du succès*) to be a success/a hit; to be going great guns 3. *V* (*a*) **faire boum**, to have sex* (*b*) **se faire boum**, to masturbate* **II** *nf* (young people's) party. (*Voir* **surboum**)

boumer [bume] *vi F* 1. to go well; **ça boume?** how's tricks?/how's it going? 2. **où ça boume**, where it's at.

bouquet [bukɛ] *nm* 1. *F* (**ça**) **c'est le bouquet!/v'là le bouquet!** that's the absolute limit!*/that's the last straw!/that takes the cake! 2. (*a*) *F* gift/present/tip to a prostitute* (*b*) *P* pay-off (to police informer*, etc) 3. *V* **mettre les pieds en bouquet de violettes**, to have an orgasm*/to climax. (*Voir* **doigt 10**)

bouquin [bukɛ̃] *nm F* book.

bouquiner [bukine] *vi F* to read (for pleasure)/to browse through books.

bouquineur, -euse [bukinœr, -øz] *n F* bookworm.

bour [bur] *a & n F* = **bourge**.

bourbier [burbje] *nm F* **être dans le bourbier**, to be in a fix*/to be in a mess/to be in a pickle; **se tirer d'un bourbier**, to get out of a scrape/a mess.

bourde [burd] *nf F* **1.** lie/fib/story; **débiter/ raconter des bourdes,** to tell fibs/stories; to have s.o. on **2.** mistake*/boob/bloomer; **faire une bourde,** to put one's foot in it/to drop a clanger.

bourdille [burdij] *nf P* = **bordille.**

bourdon [burdɔ̃] *nm P* **avoir le bourdon,** to be/to feel depressed*; to have the blues/to feel down in the mouth/to be down in the dumps.

bourge [burʒ] *F* **I** *a* bourgeois/middle-class; *Péj* philistine **II** *n* (*bourgeois*) middle-class person; *Péj* philistine/person with middle-class values.

bourgeois [burʒwa] *nm P* **1.** *A* boss; **et le pourboire, mon bourgeois?** what about something for myself, guv'nor? **2. en bourgeois,** (*policier*) in plain clothes; **les en bourgeois,** plain-clothes detectives.

bourgeoise [burʒwaz] *nf* **1.** *P* **ma bourgeoise,** the wife*/the missis/her indoors/ the old lady **2.** *V* **baiser à la bourgeoise,** to have sex* in the missionary position.

bourgeron [burʒərɔ̃] *nm A P* (priest's) surplice.

bourgue[1] [burg] *nm A P* **1.** (*pièce de cinq centimes*) sou **2.** minute.

bourgue[2] *nm A*, **bourguignon** [burgiɲɔ̃] *nm P* the sun.

bourguignotte [burgiɲɔt] *nf F Mil* steel helmet; tin hat.

bourin [burɛ̃] *nm P* = **bourrin.**

bourlingue [burlɛ̃g] *nf F* wandering from place to place; journey with no set destination.

bourlinguer [burlɛ̃ge] *vi F* (*a*) to work hard* for little profit (*b*) to be a rolling stone; **bourlinguer de par le monde/un peu partout,** to knock about the world.

bourlingueur, -euse [burlɛ̃gœr, -øz] *F* **I** *a* adventurous **II** *n* adventurer/rolling stone; **c'est un grand bourlingueur,** he's knocked about a bit.

bourrage [buraʒ] *nm F* **bourrage de crâne/ de mou,** eyewash; *surt Pol* propaganda; brainwashing. (*Voir* **crâne 1**)

bourratif, -ive [buratif, -iv] *a F* very filling/stodgy (food).

bourre [bur] **I** *nm P* policeman*/cop/copper **II** *nf P* **1. la bourre,** the police*/the fuzz **2.** *pl* lies **3. être à la bourre,** to be (running) late/ behind time/behind schedule; (*être pressé*) to be in a hurry **4. de première bourre,** excellent*/first-rate/top-quality/super **5.** *Iron*

bonne bourre! have a good time with your lady friend!/if you can't be good, be careful! **6.** struggle/rivalry; **se tirer la bourre/des bourres,** (*concurrents*) to compete with one another; to have a closely fought match **7. être en pleine bourre,** to feel fit*/to be fighting fit/to be in cracking form.

bourré [bure] *a P* **1.** rich*; **bourré aux as/ bourré de fric,** loaded/stinking rich **2.** drunk*/ sloshed/tight; **bourré comme un coing/une cantine/une caille,** dead drunk*/stewed to the eyeballs/pissed as a newt; **il est complètement bourré,** he's legless. (*Voir* **cantoche 2**).

bourre-mou [burmu] *nm P* nonsense*/ eyewash.

bourre-pif [burpif] *nm inv P* punch on the nose*.

bourrer [bure] **I** *vtr* **1.** *F* **bourrer un élève de latin,** to cram a pupil with Latin **2.** *F* **il est bourré de complexes,** he's one mass of complexes **3.** *F* to thrash (s.o.)/to beat (s.o.) up*; **bourrer qn de coups,** to give s.o. a (good) hiding/to give s.o. a belting; **bourrer la gueule à qn,** to bash s.o.'s face in; (*boxe*) **il le bourrait de coups de gauche,** he was plugging away at him with his left **4.** *V* to have sex* with (s.o.)/to screw (s.o.) **II** *vi F* **1.** to accelerate; to speed along/to belt along **2.** (*surenchérir*) to make a higher bid/to bid higher. (*Voir* **caisse I 1; crâne 1; mou III 2**) **III** *vpr* **se bourrer** *F* **1.** to make a packet (of money) **2. se bourrer (la gueule),** to get drunk*/plastered/sloshed/legless.

bourre-toujours [burtuʒur] *nm inv P* road-hog/speed merchant.

bourreur [burœr] *nm F* **bourreur de crâne/ de mou,** s.o. who fills people full of lies/ propaganda; brainwasher.

bourriche [buriʃ] *nf P* = **bourrichon.**

bourrichon [buriʃɔ̃] *nm P* head*; **monter le bourrichon à qn,** to excite s.o./to get s.o. worked up; **se monter le bourrichon,** to get excited/to work oneself up (into a state).

bourrin [burɛ̃] *nm P* **1.** (*a*) horse/nag **2.** (*a*) prostitute* (*b*) woman of easy virtue/easy lay (*c*) unattractive woman*/girl* (*d*) sexually obsessed man*; randy bugger; lecher **3.** policeman*/cop/pig **4.** motorbike.

bourriner [burine] *vi P* (*a*) to chase after women/to chase skirt (*b*) to have sex*/to screw around.

bourrique [burik] *nf* **1.** *F* idiot*/ass/ ignoramus **2.** *F* stubborn/pig-headed person; mule **3.** *P* policeman*/cop/pig **4.** *P* police informer*/copper's nark; grass 5. *F* **faire tourner qn en bourrique**, to drive s.o. crazy/ round the bend; **il m'a fait tourner en bourrique avec ses questions**, he drove me up the wall with his questions 6. *P* **plein/soûl comme une bourrique**, dead drunk*/(as) pissed as a newt.

bourriquer [burike] *vtr* 1. *P* to inform on* (s.o.)/to rat on (s.o.) 2. *V* to have sex* with (s.o.) 3. *F* (*ordinateur*) to make a calculation.

Bourrmann [burman] *nm P* **la maison Bourrmann**, the police*/the cops/the boys in blue.

bourru [bury] *a P* 1. **être (fait) bourru**, to be arrested* 2. **faire qn bourru**, to catch s.o. in the act/red-handed.

bouscaille [buskaj] *nf Vieilli P* mud; **être dans la bouscaille**, to be in a fix*/to be in a mess/to be in a pickle. (*Voir* **mouscaille 1**)

bousculée [buskyle] *af P* **elle est bien bousculée**, she's got curves in all the right places.

bousculer [buskyle] *F* I *vtr* **bousculer le pot au fleurs**, to exaggerate*/to come it (a bit) strong II *vpr* **ça ne se bouscule pas**, it's not exactly crowded/there's not much of a crowd. (*Voir* **portillon**)

bouseux [buzø] *P* I *a* hick/rustic II *nm Péj* peasant*/country bumpkin/yokel/hick.

bousillage [buzijaʒ] *nm* 1. *F* bungling/ botching 2. *F* bungled/botched work; bungle/ botch-up/cock-up 3. *F* smashing up/wrecking 4. *P* (*a*) killing/murdering (*b*) **bousillage en série**, war 5. *P* tattooing.

bousille [buzij] *nf P* (*a*) tattooing (*b*) tattoo/tattoo marks.

bousiller [buzije] *vtr* 1. *F* **bousiller qch**, to bungle*/to botch sth; **du travail bousillé**, a botched job/a botch-up; **tu vas tout bousiller**, you're going to louse everything up 2. *F* to smash up/to wreck/to crash/to prang (a car, a plane, etc); **il l'a complètement bousillée, sa bagnole**, he's written off his car/his car's a complete write-off 3. *P* to adulterate (drugs) 4. *P* **bousiller qn**, to kill* s.o./to do s.o. in/to bump s.o. off; **se faire bousiller**, to get bumped off 5. *P* to tattoo.

bousilleur, -euse [buzijœr, -øz] *n* 1. *F* bungler/botcher 2. *P* tattooist.

bousin [buzɛ̃] *nm Vieilli P* 1. seedy/sleazy café *or* pub 2. brothel*/knocking shop 3. (*a*) bear garden/bedlam (*b*) uproar*/racket/ shindy/rumpus.

boussole [busɔl] *nf F* head; **perdre la**

boussole, to go mad*/dotty; to lose one's head.

boustifaille [bustifaj] *nf P* food*/grub/nosh.

boustifailler [bustifaje] *vi P* to eat* (and drink) (greedily).

boustiffe [bustif] *nf P* = **boustifaille**.

bout [bu] *nm* 1. *F* **c'est le bout du monde**, (*d'un lieu*) it's a god-forsaken hole/a dump; (*d'un prix, etc*) it's the outside limit; **s'il a huit mille francs c'est (tout) le bout du monde**, he's got eight thousand francs at the outside/at the very most; he's lucky if he's got eight thousand francs to his name 2. *F* **faire un bout de conduite à qn**, to set s.o. on his way/to go part of the way with s.o. 3. *F* **tenir le bon bout**, (*être près de réussir*) to be on the right track; to be close to winning/succeeding 4. *F* **en connaître un bout**, to know a thing or two/to know the score 5. *F* **prendre le bout de bois**, (*d'un véhicule*) to take the wheel 6. *F* **mettre les bouts (de bois)**, to run away*/to do a bunk. (*Voir* **mettre 3**) 7. *F* (*a*) **un petit bout de femme**, a mere slip of a woman (*b*) **un petit bout de chou**, a little mite/a little nipper 8. *P* **bouts de sucre**, loaded dice 9. *F* penis*/end/knob; **se l'envoyer sur le bout/se mettre une femme sur le bout**, (*en parlant d'un homme*) to have sex*/to have it off/to get one's end away (with a woman). (*Voir* **connaître** I; **discuter**; **glisser** II 3; **tailler** I 2)

boutanche [butɑ̃ʃ] *nf P* bottle.

bouteille [butɛj] *nf F* 1. **prendre de la bouteille**, to be getting on/to be past one's prime/to be long in the tooth 2. **c'est la bouteille à l'encre**, it's a hopeless mess/ muddle; it's as clear as mud 3. **aimer la bouteille**, to be fond of the bottle/to like a drink.

boutéon, bouthéon [buteɔ̃] *nm P Mil* 1. dixie 2. (*seconde guerre 1939-45*) cookhouse rumour.

boutique [butik] *nf* 1. *F* (seedy, crummy) place/hole; **quelle boutique!** what a dump! 2. *F* **parler boutique**, to talk shop 3. *F* **toute la boutique**, the whole bag of tricks/the whole works 4. *P* male *or* female genitals*; **montrer sa boutique**, (*homme*) to expose oneself/to flash.

bouton [butɔ̃] *nm* 1. *V* (*sexe de la femme*) **bouton (de rose)**, clitoris*/clit; **avoir le bouton qui fait robe à queue**, to be sexually excited*/ to be hot/to be horny; **arroser le bouton**, to ejaculate*/to come outside; **s'astiquer/se chatouiller le bouton**, to masturbate*/to play with oneself/to finger oneself; **lécher le bouton**, to indulge in cunnilingus* **2.** *F* **donner/filer des boutons (à qn)**, to irritate/to aggravate s.o.; to get on s.o.'s nerves; **ça me donne des boutons**, that gets on my wick **3.** *F* **s'en jeter un derrière le bouton de col**, to knock back a drink/to knock one back **4.** *F* **cirer toujours le même bouton**, to be always harping on the same string. (*Voir* **tire-bouton**)

boutonnière [butɔnjɛr] *nf* **1.** *F* **faire une boutonnière à qn**, to slash s.o. (with knife, razor, etc) **2.** *V* (*rare*) female genitals*/slit/hole **3.** *V* anus*/ring hole.

bouture [butyr] *nf* child*/brat/kid.

bouzillage [buzijaʒ] *nm F P* = **bousillage**.

bouzille [buzij] *nf P* = **bousille**.

bouziller [buzije] *vtr F P* = **bousiller**.

bouzin [buzɛ̃] *nm P* = **bousin**.

bouzine [buzin] *nf P* **1.** stomach*/belly **2.** old car*/old banger/old jalopy **3.** steam engine **4.** computer.

boxif [bɔksif] *nm*, **boxon** [bɔksɔ̃] *nm P* **1.** brothel*/whorehouse/knocking shop **2.** shambles/mess; **quel boxon!** what a shambles! **3.** (*juron*) **faut être raisonnable, boxon!** for Christ's sake be reasonable!

boxonneux [bɔksɔnø] *a P* shambolic.

boy [bɔj] *nm P* (*drogues*) heroin*/boy/H.

boyau, *pl* **-aux** [bwajo] *nm P* **1.** **aimer qn comme ses petits boyaux**, to love s.o. dearly **2.** **avoir le boyau de la rigolade/avoir le boyau rigolard**, to want to burst out laughing.

boyautant [bwajotɑ̃] *a P* screamingly funny*; **c'est boyautant!** it's a real scream!

se boyauter [səbwajote] *vpr P* to laugh* uproariously/to crease oneself (with laughter)/to piss oneself (laughing).

bracelets [braslɛ] *nmpl P* handcuffs*/cuffs.

braco [brako] *nm P* poacher.

bradillon [bradijɔ̃] *nm P* arm*/fin.

braguette [bragɛt] *nf P* prostitute* who works in doorways.

braire [brɛr] *vi F* **1.** to weep/to cry/to bawl **2.** to protest loudly/to complain **3.** **faire braire qn**, to annoy* s.o./to bore* s.o./to get on s.o.'s tits.

braise [brɛz] *nf P* money*/cash/dough.

bran [brɑ̃] *nm A P* shit/muck.

brancards [brɑ̃kar] *nmpl* **1.** *P* legs*/pins **2.** *F* **ruer dans les brancards**, to protest*/to kick out/to rebel/to refuse to do sth **3.** *P* **sortir des brancards**, to leave one's wife*/to walk out on one's wife.

branchant [brɑ̃ʃɑ̃] *a F* exciting/fantastic; **c'est un album très branchant**, it's an album that really knocks you out.

branche [brɑ̃ʃ] *nf* **1.** *F* **avoir de la branche**, to look distinguished **2.** *P* **ma vieille branche**, my old friend*/my old pal; **salut, vieille branche!** hello, old bean!/wotcher cock! (*Voir* **beurre 9**)

branché [brɑ̃ʃe] *F* **I** *a* (*a*) **être branché**, to be with it/to be up-to-date/to be in/to be trendy; **Londres est une ville branchée**, London's a with-it place/the in-place/a turned-on place (*b*) knowledgeable/well-informed; **être branché football**, to know all there is to know about football/to be a football fanatic; **être branché cinéma**, to be a film buff **II** *n* **un(e) branché(e)**, a trendy; a hip guy/girl*.

brancher [brɑ̃ʃe] **I** *vtr F* **1.** **brancher qn avec qn**, to put s.o. in touch with s.o. **2.** **brancher qn sur un sujet**, to get s.o. onto/to get s.o. started on a subject; **il faut que je le branche sur cette affaire**, I must get him interested in this business **3.** to give (s.o.) a buzz/to turn (s.o.) on; **le reggae, ça me branche mais le disco, ça ne me branche pas du tout!** reggae really turns me on but disco's not my scene at all; **la peinture, ça te branche?** are you into painting? **elle le branche**, she excites him/she turns him on **4.** (*racoler*) to pick (s.o.) up; **il a branché une nana au café**, he picked up a bird in the pub **II** *vpr* **se brancher F 1.** **se brancher avec qn**, to get in touch/in contact with s.o. **2.** **se brancher sur une conversation**, to tune into a conversation.

brancherie [brɑ̃ʃri] *nf F* those in the know/the in crowd/the trendies.

branchitude [brɑ̃ʃityd] *nf F* state of being turned on/tuned in; hipness.

branco [brɑ̃ko] *nm P* stretcher bearer.

brandillon [brɑ̃dijɔ̃] *nm P* arm*/fin.

brandon [brɑ̃dɔ̃] *nm P* penis*/prick.

branlée [brɑ̃le] *nf V* **1.** (*raclée*) **attraper/prendre une branlée**, to take a beating*/a hiding/a thrashing **2.** masturbation*/tossing off/wanking.

branler [brɑ̃le] **I** *vi F* **ça branle dans le manche**, it's not going too well; it's a bit dicey/a bit tricky **II** *vtr* **1.** *F* **qu'est-ce qu'il branle?** what's he up to? **2.** *P* **n'en avoir rien à branler**, not to give a damn/a monkey's (about sth); **qu'est-ce que j'en ai à branler?** what the hell/what the fuck has it got to do with me? **3.** *V* **se les branler/se branler les couilles**, not to work at all/to do damn all/to do fuck all/to sit on one's arse and do nothing 4. *V* to masturbate (s.o.); elle a dû le branler dans la bagnole, she had to toss him off in the car III *vpr* **se branler** 1. *P* s'en branler/se branler de qch, not to give a damn/a monkey's (about sth); je m'en branle, I don't give a toss/a fuck 2. *V* to masturbate*/to toss off/to wank/to jerk off.

branlette [brɑ̃lɛt] *nf V* masturbation*; se faire une petite branlette, to masturbate*/to have a quick toss.

branleur [brɑ̃lœr] *nm V* (*a*) *Péj* young boy (*b*) incompetent fool*/jerk; c'est un branleur de 1ère, he's a real wanker/jerk.

branleuse [brɑ̃løz] *nf V* 1. *Péj* young girl 2. masturbator; c'est une bonne branleuse, she's got a good wrist action/she tosses off well.

branlocher [brɑ̃lɔʃe] *vtr & i* = **branler**.

branque [brɑ̃k] *P* I *nm* 1. fool*/simpleton/dope 2. eccentric*/crackpot/loony 3. prostitute's client/punter/john II *a* mad*/crazy/bonkers/round the twist.

branquignol [brɑ̃kiɲɔl] *P* = **branque** I 1, 2, II.

braquage [brakaʒ] *nm F* armed attack/armed robbery/hold-up/stick-up/heist.

braque [brak] I *a F* mad*/crackers/nutty II *nm P* clapped-out engine (of car, etc).

braquemard, braquemart [brakmar] *nm Vieilli V* penis*; dérouiller son braquemard, to have sex*.

braquer [brake] *vtr F* 1. to hold (s.o.) up at gunpoint) 2. braquer une banque, to hold up a bank 3. braquer qn, to antagonize s.o./to get s.o.'s back up; être braqué contre qn, to be stubbornly opposed to s.o.; être braqué contre qch, to be dead set against sth.

braquet [brakɛ] *nm F* changer de braquet, to change tactics.

braqueur [brakœr] *nm F* armed robber/hold-up man/blagger.

bras [bra] *nm F* 1. avoir les bras retournés/à la retourne, to be lazy/to be a layabout. (*Voir* **retourne, retourné** 2) 2. gros bras, (*homme fort*) strong man; (*homme influent*) influential man; faire/jouer les gros bras, to try to intimidate (s.o.) with a show of strength; avoir le bras long, to be very influential/to have friends in the right places 3. bras cassé, pathetic individual*/poor bugger/poor sod 4. être le bras droit de qn, to be s.o.'s right-hand man 5. avoir des yeux qui se croisent les bras, to be cross-eyed/to (have a) squint 6. faire un bras d'honneur à qn, to make an obscene

gesture at s.o./= to put two fingers up at s.o. (= up yours!). (*Voir* **lourd** I 1; **sac** 18; **tomber** II 1)

brasser [brase] *F* I *vtr* brasser de l'argent, to handle large amounts of money II *vi* dans ce milieu, on brasse pas mal, in these circles you get to meet lots of people.

bravo [bravo] *int P* faire/crier bravo, to be dead scared. (*Voir* **miches** 1 (*b*))

break [brɛk] *nm F* pause/break.

brêle [brɛl] *nm P* 1. motorbike 2. obstinate person/mule; (*comme terme d'injure*) cretin/moron.

brelica [brelika] *nm P* (*verlan de* **calibre**) revolver*/pistol/shooter.

brelique-breloque [brəlikbrəlɔk] *adv F* higgledy-piggledy/anyoldhow/anywhichway.

breloque [brəlɔk] *nf* 1. *F* watch *or* clock 2. *F* mon cœur bat la breloque, (*bat vite*) my heart is racing; (*fonctionne mal*) my heart is playing me up 3. *pl P* testicles*/bag of tricks.

brème, brême [brɛm] *nf P* 1. playing card; taper les brèmes, to play cards; maquiller les brèmes, to mark/to fake the cards 2. identity card; policeman's card; business card; prostitute's card; (*informatique*) punched/perforated card; être en brème, (*d'une prostituée*) to be registered/to be a registered prostitute 3. telegram.

brésilienne [breziljɛn] *nf* transsexual prostitute.

Bretagne [brətaɲ] *Prnf F* neveu/nièce/oncle/tante à la mode de Bretagne, first cousin once removed.

bretelles [brətɛl] *nfpl F* 1. remonter les bretelles à qn, to reprimand* s.o./to dress s.o. down/to tell s.o. where to get off 2. avoir qn sur les bretelles, to (have to) put up with s.o.

Breton [brətɔ̃] *nm P* coup de tête de Breton, head-butt (in the face or stomach).

brevet [brəvɛ] *nm P* faire passer le brevet colonial à qn, to introduce s.o. to sodomy/to initiate s.o.

bréviaire [brevjɛr] *nm P* 1. book 2. (*argot des policiers*) (Paris) street guide.

bric [brik] *nm P* (licensed) brothel*.

bricard [brikar] *nm P Mil* lance sergeant.

bricheton [briʃtɔ̃] *nm P* bread.

bricolage [brikɔlaʒ] *nm F* (*a*) pottering about/tinkering/doing odd jobs; un mordu du bricolage, a do-it-yourself/DIY enthusiast; a keen do-it-yourselfer (*b*) bad work/botch(ed) job; c'est du bricolage! it's a bodge-up!

bricole [brikɔl] *nf F* 1. trifles/odd jobs/odds

and ends; **s'occuper à des bricoles**, to potter about (the house/the garden/the office, etc); to do odd jobs **2.** *pl (a) (ennuis)* problems; **il va lui arriver des bricoles**, he's going to get into (serious) trouble *(b)* **faire des bricoles à qn**, to treat s.o. brutally; to beat s.o. up violently.

bricoler [brikɔle] **I** *vtr* **1.** *F* to knock together (a piece of furniture, etc); to tinker with (a car engine, etc) **2.** *P* **bricoler une femme**, to feel a woman (up)/to touch up a woman **3.** *P* **bricoler le chemin**, to lurch along the road (in a drunken state) **II** *vi F* to potter about/to do odd jobs.

bricoleur, -euse [brikɔlœr, -øz] *F* **I** *a* handy (person) **II 1.** *n* handyman/potterer/ tinkerer/do-it-yourselfer **2.** *nm* man* without a steady job/odd-job man; *(qui travaille mal)* bad worker/cowboy **3.** *nm* petty criminal/ small-time crook.

bricolo [brikɔlo] *nm* = **bricoleur II**.

bride [brid] *nf P* **1.** *(a)* chain *(b)* lock **2.** **se mettre la bride**, to tighten one's belt/to go without.

bridé, -ée [bride] *n F Péj* oriental *or* asiatic person/slant.

brider [bride] *vtr* **1.** *F* to check/to restrain (s.o.); to keep a tight rein on (s.o.); to clamp down on (s.o.) **2.** *P* to close (a door, a shutter, etc).

briefer [brife] *vtr F* to gen (s.o.) up.

briffe [brif] *nf P* food*/grub/chow; meal; **aller à briffe**, to (go and) eat*.

briffer [brife] *vtr & i P* to eat* *(esp* greedily).

briffeton [briftɔ̃] *nm P (a)* bread *(b)* snack; food*/grub.

briffeur, -euse [brifœr, -øz] *n P* greedy eater/greedyguts.

brigadier [brigadje] *nm* **1.** *F (théâtre)* the stick with which one gives the three knocks *(just before the curtain rises)* **2.** *P* **brigadier d'amour**, middle finger.

brignol(e) [briɲɔl] *nm*, **brignolet** [briɲɔlɛ] *nm*, **brignoluche** [briɲɔlyʃ] *nm P* bread.

brillant [brijɑ̃] *a F* **pas brillant, ça!** that's not too good!/that's not so hot!/it's not up to much!

briller [brije] *vi V* to have an orgasm*/to come.

brin [brɛ̃] *nm F* **1.** **un brin de causette**, a bit of a chat; **un brin de toilette**, a quick wash/a catlick/a lick and a promise; **aller prendre un brin d'air**, to go for a breather **2.** **un beau brin**

de fille, a nice-looking girl **3.** = **bran**. *(Voir* **salade 4**)

brindezingue [brɛ̃dzɛ̃g] *P* **I** *a* **1.** drunk*/ blotto/stewed **2.** mad*/loony/cracked **II** *nm* **1.** *Vieilli* **être dans les brindezingues**, to be drunk* **2.** mad* person/crackpot.

bringue [brɛ̃g] *nf P* **1.** binge; **faire la bringue**, to go on a spree*/on a binge **2.** **grande bringue**, *(femme)* gangling/lanky girl *or* woman **3.** old car*/old jalopy **4. à toute bringue**, at top speed/at full tilt.

bringuer [brɛ̃ge] *vi P* = **faire la bringue (bringue 1)**.

bringueur [brɛ̃gœr] *nm P* reveller/hell-raiser.

brioche [brijɔʃ] *nf* **1.** *F* mistake*/blunder/ boob **2.** *F* paunch; **avoir de la brioche**, to be paunchy/pot-bellied; **prendre de la brioche**, to develop a paunch/a pot-belly/a beer belly **3.** *F* **partir/se barrer en brioche**, to neglect oneself/to go to pieces/to go to pot **4.** *F* **tortiller de la brioche**, to dance **5.** *pl P* brioches, buttocks* **6.** *P* **mettre une brioche au chaud**, to have sex* with a woman/to have it off with a woman **7.** *P* **brioche infernale**, (male) homosexuality.

brique [brik] *nf P* **1.** ten thousand (new) francs; **brique lourde**, one million (new) francs **2.** **manger/bouffer des briques**, to go without food/to live on air. *(Voir* **casser I 3**; **poil 10**)

briquer [brike] **I** *vtr F* to clean thoroughly; to polish; to scrub **II** *vpr* **se briquer** *F* to have a wash (and brush-up).

briquet [brikɛ] *nm F* **battre le briquet**, to knock one's ankles together when walking.

briquette [brikɛt] *nf* **1.** *P* trifle; **c'est de la briquette**, it's not worth a fig **2.** *F* = **poussière 1** **3.** *P* young prostitute* (who does not take her job seriously).

brisant [brizɑ̃] *nm P* wind.

briscard [briskar] *nm F* = **brisquard**.

briser [brize] *vtr P* **1.** **il me les brise**, he gets on my bloody nerves; **ça me les brise**, it gets on my tits **2.** **se la briser**, to run away*/to clear off/to scarper.

briseur [brizœr] *nm F* **briseur de nougats**, pestering journalist/hack.

brisquard [briskar] *nm F* old soldier/old campaigner/veteran.

brisque [brisk] *nf F Mil* **1.** long-service badge/stripe; war-service chevron **2.** **une vieille brisque**, an old campaigner.

Britiche [britiʃ] *a & n F* British (person);

Brit.

broc [brɔk] *nm P* (= *brocanteur*) second-hand/antique dealer.

brocasse [brɔkas] *nf P* (*a*) second-hand goods (*b*) junk/scrap.

broche [brɔʃ] *nm P* pimp*/ponce.

brochet [brɔʃɛ] *nm P* pimp*/ponce.

brocheton [brɔʃtɔ̃] *nm P* young pimp*.

broco [brɔko] *nm P* = **broc**.

broder [brɔde] *vi F* to exaggerate*/to lay it on thick.

bronzaille [brɔ̃zaj] *nf F* bronze goods (*sold by second-hand dealer*).

bronze [brɔ̃z] *nm* 1. *P* couler/mouler un bronze, to defecate*/to have a shit 2. *V* prendre du bronze, (*homosexuels*) to sodomize*/to brown 3. *P* c'est du bronze, it's solid (stuff). (*Voir* œil 25)

bronzé [brɔ̃ze] I *a F* bronzé comme un cachet d'aspirine/comme un petit-suisse/comme un lavabo, very pale/white as a sheet II *n P Péj* Black*/darky/high yellow.

broque [brɔk] *nf P* 1. minute 2. small change; vingt balles et des broques, twenty francs plus (a bit) 3. pas une broque, nothing*/not a sausage 4. de la broque, dud/worthless* stuff; junk/trash.

broquille [brɔkij] *nf P* = **broque**.

brosse [brɔs] *nf P* prendre une brosse, to get drunk*/plastered; être en brosse, to be drunk*/plastered.

brosser [brɔse] I *vtr* 1. *P* se brosser le ventre, to go hungry/to have an empty belly 2. *V* to have sex* with (s.o.) 3. *V* to give (s.o.) an orgasm*/to make (s.o.) come II *vpr* se **brosser** *P* to have to go without (food, etc); tu peux te brosser! you can whistle for it!/go screw yourself!

broue [bru] *nf FrC P* froth; faire/péter de la broue, to show off*/to talk big.

brouette [bruɛt] *nf F* semelles en cuir de brouette, wooden soles.

brouillamini [brujamini] *nm F* confusion/disorder/tangle.

brouillard [brujar] *nm* 1. *F* je suis dans le brouillard/je n'y vois que du brouillard, I'm very hazy about it/I can't make head nor tail of it 2. *P* (*a*) être dans le brouillard, to be drunk*/tipsy/sozzled/fuddled (*b*) chasser le brouillard, to clear one's head/to brush away the cobwebs (with an alcoholic drink); to take (a) hair of the dog (that bit you) 3. *P* s'évanouir/foncer dans le brouillard, to run away*/to skedaddle/to clear off. (*Voir*

foncer 3)

brouillé [bruje] *a F* être brouillé avec les dates, to be unable to remember dates/to be hazy about dates; être brouillé avec les chiffres, to be hopeless at figures.

brouille-ménage [brujmenaʒ] *nm P* red wine.

brousse [brus] *nf F* au fin fond de la brousse, at the back of beyond/*NAm* out in the boondocks.

brouter [brute] I *vtr & i* 1. *V* brouter le cresson/le minou, (*cunnilinctus*) to have oral sex*/to eat hairpie 2. *V* brouter la tige, (*fellation*) to have oral sex*/to suck cock/to give (s.o.) a blow-job 3. *P* les brouter à qn, to get on s.o.'s tits/on s.o.'s bloody nerves 4. *P* (*d'un moteur*) to judder II *vpr* se **brouter** *V* (*entre femmes*) to indulge in mutual cunnilingus*; elles se broutent, they're a couple of lesbians*/they're sucking each other off.

brouteur [brutœr] *nm V* brouteur de cresson, cunt-lapper/cunt-sucker.

brouteuse [brutøz] *nf V* lesbian*.

broutille [brutij] *nf F* trifling matter/trifle/(mere) fleabite; *pl* chicken-feed; c'est de la broutille, it's not worth worrying about.

brown sugar [braunʃugar] *nm P* (*drogues*) low-quality heroin* (*containing 33% pure heroin*).

brûlé [bryle] *a F* il est brûlé, he has lost his reputation/his credit/his influence; he's done for/he's ruined; (*trahi*) he has been betrayed; (*espion*) his cover's (been) blown.

brûle-gueule [brylgœl] *nm inv*, **brûle-parfum(s)** [brylparfœ̃] *nm P* firearm/revolver*/heater.

brûler [bryle] *vtr* 1. brûler qn, *F* to ruin s.o.'s reputation/credit; *P* to kill* s.o. 2. *F* brûler un espion, to uncover/expose a spy 3. *F* brûler le pavé/la route, to tear along the road (at full speed)/to burn up the road/to scorch the road/to do a ton. (*Voir* dur II 1; planche 2)

brutal [brytal] *nm P* 1. strong wine; eau-de-vie 2. low-quality bread 3. revolver*/piece 4. (*métro*) underground/tube. (*Voir* lartif; larton)

brute [bryt] *nf F* = **bête** I 5.

bu [by] *a P* il est bu, he's drunk*.

bûche [byʃ] I *nf* 1. *F* fool*/blockhead/prize idiot; ne reste pas planté là comme une bûche, don't just stand there like a dummy/a lemon 2. *P* (safety) match 3. *P* bad card (in gambling games) 4. *F* ramasser une bûche, to fall/to come a cropper II *nf F* hard work/ swotting/slogging (away).

bûcher [byʃe] I *vtr & i F* to work* hard (at)/to slog away (at); to swot (at); **bûcher un examen**, to swot/to mug up for an exam; bûcher toute la journée, to slave away/to slog away all day II *vtr P* to thrash/to beat (s.o.) up*; to kill* III *vpr* **se bûcher** *P* to fight/to come to blows/to have a set-to/to scrap.

bûcheur, -euse [byʃœr, -øz] *a & n F* hard-working (person); *n* grafter/slogger.

bucolique [bykɔlik] *nf P* prostitute* who picks up her clients in parks.

buffecaille [byfkɑj] *nm Vieilli P* = **buffet 1**.

buffet [byfɛ] *nm* 1. *P* (*a*) stomach*/belly; piquer qn au buffet, to knife s.o. in the guts; se remplir le buffet, to have a good tuck-in/a good nosh(-up); en avoir dans le buffet, (*être brave*) to have guts/balls; n'avoir rien dans le buffet, to have an empty belly; (*être lâche*) to have no guts (*b*) uterus; avoir un bébé dans le buffet, to be pregnant*/to have a bun in the oven 2. *Vielli F* danser devant le buffet, to have nothing to eat*/to go hungry*. (*Voir* **plomber I 2**)

buis [bɥi] *nm P* 1. avoir reçu un coup de buis, to be exhausted*/to be bushed 2. recevoir/prendre un coup de buis, to be the victim of circumstances 3. patte de buis, wooden leg 4. racine/dent de buis, yellow tooth.

buissonnière [bɥisɔnjɛr] *af F* faire l'école buissonnière, to play truant/*esp NAm* hook(e)y.

bull [byl] *nm F* (= *bulldozer*) dozer.

bulle [byl] I *nm Vieilli P* money* II *nf P* 1. coincer/écraser la/sa bulle, (*paresser*) to be idle/to laze about/to take it easy/to skive (off); (*dormir*) to go to sleep*/to get some shut-eye; (*se reposer*) to have a rest 2. (*écoles*) se ramasser une bulle, to get nought (in an exam, etc) 3. *Iron* (*écoles*) faire sa bulle, to do sth bloody stupid. (*Voir* **chier 4**)

buller [byle] *vi P* (*paresser*) to be idle/to laze about.

bullshiterie [bulʃitri] *nf P* (*a*) nonsense/ bullshitting (*b*) shambles/bloody mess.

bureau, *pl* **-eaux** [byro] *nm* 1. *F* bureau des pleurs, complaints office/department

2. *P* stomach*.

burelingue [byrlɛ̃g] *nm P* = **burlingue**.

burette [byrɛt] *nf* 1. *P* face* 2. *V* penis* 3. *pl V* testicles*/balls (*a*) vider ses burettes, to ejaculate*/to come/to get one's nuts off (*b*) casser/râper les burettes à qn, baver sur les burettes à qn, to annoy* s.o./to give s.o. a pain in the arse/to get on s.o.'s tits.

buriner [byrine] *vi P* to work* hard; to swot.

burineur [byrinœr] *nm P* hard worker; swot.

burlain [byrlɛ̃] *nm P* office worker.

burlingue [byrlɛ̃g] *nm P* 1. stomach* 2. office 3. desk.

burnes [byrn] *nfpl V* testicles*/balls/nuts; casser/râper les burnes à qn, baver sur les burnes à qn, to bore s.o. to death/to give s.o. a pain in the arse/to get on s.o.'s tits/to get on s.o.'s wick; se vider les burnes, to ejaculate*/ to come off/to shoot one's load.

burnous [byrnu(s)] *nm F* faire suer le burnous, to slavedrive/to exploit/to sweat (cheap labour).

bus [bys] *nm F* (= *autobus*) bus.

buse [byz] *nf F* fool*/idiot/dimwit; triple buse, extremely stupid* person/a real thickie.

business [biznɛs] *nm P* = **bis(e)ness**.

buter [byte] I *vtr P* to kill* (s.o.); se faire buter, to get bumped off II *vpr* **se buter** *P* to commit suicide*/to do oneself in.

buteur [bytœr] *nm P* killer*/hit man.

buttage [bytaʒ] *nm P* murder.

butte [byt] *nf* 1. *P* avoir sa butte, to be pregnant* 2. *P* killing/murdering/bumping off; massacre; violent death 3. *F* (*a*) la Butte, Montmartre (*b*) les Buttes, les Buttes-Chaumont (*district in Paris*) (*c*) aller à la Butte, to go to the races/to go racing.

butter [byte] *vtr*, **butteur** [bytœr] *nm P* = **buter, buteur**.

buvable [byvabl] *a F* bearable/tolerable/ acceptable/passable; un type pas buvable, an impossible character/an insufferable individual. (*Voir* **potable**)

buveton [byvtɔ̃] *nm F* blotter/blotting pad; blotting paper.

buveur [byvœr] *nm F* (*écrivain, journaliste, etc*) buveur d'encre, ink-slinger; pen-pusher.

Byzance [bizɑ̃s] *Prn* c'est Byzance, it's excellent*/ace/champion/wicked.

C

ça [sa] *dem pron neut* **1.** *F* **rien que ça?** is *that* all? **rien que ça!** no kidding! **2.** *F* **les gonzesses, il faut que ça jase!** these birds will natter! **c'est ça ta bagnole?** (is) that your car?/these your wheels? **3.** *P* **avec ça!** get along with you!/(a load of) rubbish!/tell that to the marines! **4.** *F* (*a*) **elle est grande et mince avec ça,** she's tall, and, what's more, slim (*b*) **avec ça que ...,** as if ...; **avec ça qu'on vous le permettrait!** as if they'd let you! **avec ça qu'il n'a pas triché!** don't say he didn't cheat! **5.** *F* **avoir de ça,** to have what it takes; to have plenty of money*; (*femme*) to have sex appeal; *Vieilli* to have intelligence*/courage, etc **6.** *P* (*a*) **comme ça tu déménages?** so you're moving out, are you? **il a dit comme ça qu'il regrettait bien,** he said just like that (that) he was very sorry (*b*) **les avoir comme ça,** to be scared*/to have the wind up **7.** *F* **allons, pas de ça!** now then, none of that! **8.** *P* **c'est pas tout ça,** that's all very well ... **9.** *P* **faire ça,** to have sex*/to make love/to do it; **ne penser qu'à ça,** to be obsessed by it/to have a dirty mind/*NAm* to have one's mind in the gutter. (*Voir* **aller 6**; **alors** (*b*))

cabane [kaban] *nf* **1.** *F* (small) ramshackle house/flat; **cabane à lapins,** dump/shack **2.** *P* **faire une cabane,** to burgle a house/a home; **faire de la cabane,** to be a burglar **3.** *P* **prison*; être en cabane,** to be in clink/in the nick; **il a passé trois ans en cabane,** he did three years in the nick/*NAm* in (the) stir; **cabane bambou,** military prison* **4.** *P* brothel*. (*Voir* **attiger 3**)

cabanon [kabanɔ̃] *nm F* lunatic asylum/loony bin; **il est bon à mettre au cabanon,** they ought to lock him up/he's off his head.

cabèche, cabêche [kabɛʃ] *nf Vieilli P* head*/nut/bonce.

caberlot [kabɛrlo] *nm P* **1.** small country pub **2.** head*/nut.

cabestron [kabɛstrɔ̃] *nm Vieilli P* mug/sucker/fall guy.

cabinces [kabɛ̃s] *nmpl Vieilli P* WC*/the bog(s).

câblé [kable] *a F* (*à la mode*) hip/trendy.

caboche [kabɔʃ] *nf F* **1.** head*/nut; **mets-le-toi dans la caboche!** get that into your thick skull! **2. avoir la caboche dure,** (*être bête*) to be slow on the uptake/to be thick; (*être têtu*) to be stubborn as a mule/to be pigheaded.

cabosse [kabɔs] *nf F* bruise/bump; **se faire une cabosse,** to get a bump.

cabot [kabo] *nm P* **1.** dog/pooch/mutt; **sale cabot!** dirty dog/hound! **2.** = **cabotin 3.** *Mil* corporal **4.** foreman.

cabotin, -ine [kabɔtɛ̃, -in] *n F* (*a*) inferior/third-rate actor *or* actress; ham (*b*) show-off*.

cabotinage [kabɔtinaʒ] *nm F* (*a*) inferior acting/hamming (*b*) histrionics; showing off.

cabotiner [kabɔtine] *vi F* (*a*) to act badly/to ham (*b*) to play-act (*c*) to play to the gallery.

caboulot [kabulo] *nm F* seedy *or* grotty pub/dive.

cabrette [kabrɛt] *nf F* (*danse*) waltz (*with an accordion band*).

cabri [kabri] *nm P* = **cabriolet.**

cabriole [kabrijɔl] *nf F* **1. faire une cabriole,** to come a cropper **2. faire la cabriole,** to swing/to go with the tide **3. faire des cabrioles,** to have sex*/to sleep around.

cabriolet [kabrijɔlɛ] *nm P* handcuff*/cuff.

caca [kaka] *nm F* (*langage enfantin*) **1.** excrement*/number two/big job/poo/poo-poo; **faire caca,** to do a poo/to do poo-poo's; **tu as fait caca?** (*à un enfant*) have you done your duty?/have you done (your) big jobs?/have you been? **jette ça, c'est (du) caca,** throw that away, it's nasty/dirty; **caca boudin!** (*excl enfantine*) oh, poo! **2. mettre à qn le nez dans son caca,** to put s.o. (firmly) in his place/to rub s.o.'s nose in it.

cacade [kakad] *nf P* diarrhoea*/the shits.

cacafouiller [kakafuje] *vi A P* =

cafouiller.

cacasse [kakas] *nf V* aller à la cacasse, to have sex*/to have it off.

cache-fri-fri [kaʃfrifri] *nm inv P* G-string. (*Voir* **fri-fri**)

cachemire [kaʃmir] *nm F* (waiter's) tea towel/*NAm* dish towel/cloth; duster; **un coup de cachemire sur le piano**, a quick wipe over the counter.

cache-pot [kaʃpo] *nm inv P* (pair of) knickers.

cachet [kaʃɛ] *nm P* sum of money paid by a prostitute* to her pimp*. (*Voir* **bronzé**)

cacheton [kaʃtɔ̃] *nm P* (*a*) fee (of private teacher, actor, etc); **courir le cacheton**, (*artiste/comédien*) to look for work/a job (*b*) = **cachet** (*c*) pill/tablet.

cachetonner [kaʃtɔne] *vtr & i P* to receive a fee; **cachetonner un acteur**, to pay an actor his fee.

cachetonneur, -euse [kaʃtɔnœr, -øz] *n* mediocre actor/actress looking for a job/a part.

cachotterie [kaʃɔtri] *nf F* faire des cachotteries à qn, to keep/to hold things back from s.o.; to hold out on s.o.

cachottier, -ière [kaʃɔtje, -jɛr] *a & n F* secretive/cagey (person); **quel cachottier vous faites!** well, you are a sly one!

cacique [kasik] *nm F* candidate who comes first in the entrance exam for the *École normale supérieure*; candidate who comes first in an exam.

cactus [kaktys] *nm P* 1. problem/hitch/ nuisance 2. **avoir un cactus dans la poche/ dans le portefeuille**, to be a miser*/to have short arms and deep pockets.

cadancher [kadɑ̃ʃe] *vi P* to die*.

cadavre [kadavr] *nm F* 1. **il y a un cadavre entre eux**, they are linked by a crime; **il y a un cadavre dans le placard**, it's a bit of a mystery/we haven't got to the bottom of it 2. empty (wine) bottle/empty/dead man/dead soldier 3. unlucky gambler/jinxed player.

cadeau, *pl* **-eaux** [kado] *nm* 1. *F* ton frère, c'est pas un cadeau! your brother's a real bore/a real pain (in the arse)! **il ne lui a pas fait de cadeau**, (*il ne l'a pas épargné*) he didn't spare him; (*il n'a pas donné d'indication*) he didn't help him/a fat lot of use he was to him; **je te fais cadeau du reste**, I'll spare you the details 2. *P* un petit/p'tit cadeau, prostitute's fee.

cadenassé [kadnase] *a F* buttoned up/mum.

se cadenasser [səkadnase] *vpr F* to keep a secret/to keep mum/to button (up) one's lip.

cadène [kadɛn] *nf P* chain necklace.

cadènes [kadɛn] *nfpl*, **cadenettes** [kadnɛt] *nfpl*, **cadennes** [kadɛn] *nfpl P* handcuffs*/cuffs.

cadet [kadɛ] *nm F* c'est le cadet de mes soucis, that's the least of my worries.

cadière [kadjɛr] *nf P* chair.

cador [kadɔr] *nm P* 1. dog*/hound 2. top dog/big shot/boss* 3. expert/ace.

cadran [kadrɑ̃] *nm F* faire le tour du cadran, to sleep twelve hours or more/to sleep round the clock.

cadre [kadr] *nm P* painting/canvas.

cafard, -arde [kafar, -ard] I *n F* 1. smug, sanctimonious person 2. sneak; tell-tale* II *nm F* avoir le cafard, to be depressed*/to have the blues/to be down in the dumps; **avoir un coup de cafard**, to be a bit down/to be feeling (a bit) blue; **il fiche le cafard à tout le monde**, he gets everyone down.

cafardage [kafardaʒ] *nm F* sneaking; tale-telling.

cafarde [kafard] *nf P* moon.

cafarder [kafarde] *F* I *vi* 1. to sneak; to snitch/to tell tales/to tell on s.o. 2. to feel depressed*/to have the blues II *vtr* cafarder qn, to sneak/to split/to snitch on s.o.

cafardeur, -euse [kafardœr, -øz] *n F* sneak; tell-tale*.

cafardeux, -euse [kafardø, -øz] *F* I *a* depressed*/down in the dumps/browned off; temps cafardeux, depressing/miserable weather II *n* miserable person/miseryguts; **quel cafardeux!** what a misery!

caf'conc', caf'conce [kafkɔ̃s] *nm A P* (= *café-concert*) kind of old-time music hall; café providing evening entertainment by artistes.

café [kafe] *nm P* prendre le café du pauvre/ des pauvres, to have sex* (*after a meal at home, instead of coffee*)/to make one's own entertainment. (*Voir* **fort 2**)

café-couette [kafekwɛt] *nm F* (*en Bretagne*) bed and breakfast/b. & b.

cafèt [kafɛt] *nf F* (*abrév* = *cafétéria*) coffee bar/café/caff.

cafeter [kafte] *vtr & i P* = **cafarder**.

cafeteur, -euse [kaftœr, -øz] *n P* = **cafardeur, -euse**.

cafetière [kaftjɛr] *nf P* 1. head*/nut/skull; travailler de la cafetière, to be mad*/to be round the bend; **un coup sur la cafetière**, a thump on the head; **en prendre un coup sur la cafetière**, to be on a downer; **se payer la cafetière de qn**, to make fun of s.o./to take the mickey out of s.o.; **bouillir de la cafetière**, to be overflowing with ideas 2. sneak; tell-tale*. (*Voir* **cresson 1** (*a*))

cafeton [kaftɔ̃] *nm P* 1. pub 2. coffee; je prendrais bien un petit cafeton, I could do with a coffee.

cafouillage [kafujaʒ] *nm F* mess/muddle/ shambles/snafu; (*moteur, etc*) missing/ misfiring.

cafouiller [kafuje] *vi F* to get into a mess/to make a mess of things; to muddle; to be all at sixes and sevens; to go to pieces; (*moteur, etc*) to miss/to misfire/to work in fits and starts; (*orateur*) (*bafouiller*) to talk incoherently/to burble/to splutter; (*dire des sottises*) to talk nonsense*/to talk a lot of hot air.

cafouilleux [kafujø] *a F* ham-fisted/ bungling.

cafouillis [kafuji] *nm F* muddle/mess/ shambles.

cafouine [kafwin] *nf P* excrement*/dung.

cafter [kafte] *vtr & i P* = **cafarder**.

cafteur, -euse [kaftœr, -øz] *n P* = **cafeteur, -euse**.

cagade [kagad] *nf P* mistake*/blunder; faire une cagade, to slip up/to goof/to make a mess of things.

cage [kaʒ] *nf* 1. *P* prison*/coop/pen; mettre qn en cage, to send s.o. to prison*/to put s.o. in the can; cage à poules, (communal) prison cell/cage; cage à poulets, police van/Black Maria 2. *F* cage à lapins, tiny room/flat etc; poky hole/box/doll's house/rabbit hutch; (*immeuble d'habitation*) tenement flats 3. *Vieilli P* cage à poules = space behind glass doors in entrance hall of certain hotels from where prostitutes solicit 4. *F* cage à poules/à écureuil, climbing frame (in playground) 5. *F* cage (à pain), stomach*/breadbasket 6. *F* cage à miel, ear*/lughole 7. *F* (*football*) goal (area)/box; le goal n'est pas sorti de la cage, the goalie didn't come out of the box.

cageot [kaʒo] *nm F* unattractive/ugly woman *or* girl.

cagibi [kaʒibi] *nm F* 1. hut/shelter 2. lumber-room/cubby-hole/glory-hole; *Péj* poky little room.

cagna [kaɲa] *nf P* room/pad/place/crash-out.

cagnard, -arde [kaɲar, -ard] I *a Vieilli F* idle/lazy* II *n* 1. *Vieilli F* lazybones/good-for-

nothing 2. *nm P* sun/currant bun.

cagne [kaɲ] I *nf P* 1. broken-down horse/old nag 2. (*curé*) (parish) priest 3. *Vieilli* avoir la cagne, to feel lazy* II *nf P* (*écoles*) second-year arts class preparing for the entrance exam to the *École normale supérieure*. (*Voir* **khâgne**)

cagner [kaɲe] *vi Vieilli P* to shirk/to swing the lead/to skive (off).

cagneux, -euse [kaɲø, -øz] *n P* student in a *cagne* (**cagne II**).

cagoinces, cagouinces, cago(u)in-sses [kagwɛ̃s] *nmpl P* WC*/bog(s).

caguer [kage] *vi P* 1. to defecate*/to (have a) crap 2. to fail*/to go down the pan.

cahin-caha [kaɛ̃kaa] *adv F* se porter cahin-caha, to be so-so/to be fair to middling; vivre cahin-caha, to scrape a living/to get by; leur ménage va cahin-caha, they get by somehow/they struggle along.

caïd [kaid] *nm* 1. *P* leader (of gang, etc)/ boss*/big chief/big shot/hot shot; comme un caïd, like a leader/cleverly 2. *F* ace/expert/ champion.

caïdat [kaida] *nm P* the big bosses/= the mafia; (*surt en prison*) the barons.

caille [kɑj] I *nf F* girl*/chick; ma (petite) caille! (*à un enfant, une femme*) my pet! II *nf P* 1. excrement*/cack 2. avoir qn/qch à la caille, to hate* the sight of s.o./sth; to hate s.o.'s guts 3. l'avoir à la caille, to be furious; to be put out 4. être à la caille, to be unlucky. (*Voir* **œil 20**)

cailler [kɑje] I *vtr & i P* on caille/ça caille/il caille, it's bloody cold/it's (bloody) freezing/ it's brass-monkey weather/it's (cold) enough to freeze the balls off a brass monkey; je caille, I'm perishing II *vtr* 1. se cailler le sang/le raisin/la bile, to get worried stiff 2. cailler (le sang/le raisin à) qn, to worry s.o./to make s.o. anxious III *vpr* se cailler *P* to be (freezing) cold; je me (les) caille, I'm bloody freezing/I'm perishing.

caillou, *pl* **-oux** [kaju] *nm P* 1. (*a*) head*/ nut/bonce; *souv* bald head; ne pas avoir un poil sur le caillou, to be bald* as a coot (*b*) intelligence*; il en a dans le caillou, he's got brains 2. *Vieilli* se sucer le caillou, (*couple*) to kiss/to neck 3. battre le caillou, (*paresser*) to loaf about (the streets); (*chercher du travail*) to walk the streets in search of a job 4. (*brocante*) stone object/ornament 5. precious stone, *surt* diamond/sparkler/rock; caillou de Rennes/du Rhin, false diamond.

caïman [kaimɑ̃] *nm F* senior master at the *École normale supérieure*.

caisse [kɛs] **I** *nf* 1. *P* head*; **bourrer la caisse à qn**, to stuff s.o.'s head full of lies, empty talk, etc; to lead s.o. up the garden path; **ne me bourre pas la caisse!** don't give me that rubbish! 2. *P* stomach*; **n'avoir rien au fond de la caisse**, to be starving/ravenous 3. *P* chest; **être malade/souffrir de la caisse**, to be consumptive/to have a weak chest; **il s'en va/il part de la caisse, il a la caisse qui se fait la malle**, his lungs are giving up the ghost/giving out 4. *Vieilli* **P la caisse d'épargne**, mouth* 5. *P Mil* prison*; **faire de la caisse**, to be in clink 6. *P* coffin/box 7. *P* (*à l'église*) confessional (box) 8. *F* (*a*) **passer à la caisse**, to get paid; (*illégalement*) to be paid off; (*être congédié*) to be sacked (*b*) **faire la caisse**, to rob the till (*c*) **caisse noire**, slush fund; *NAm* boodle/graft 9. *F* car*/banger/crate; (*moto*) motorbike; **caisse à savon**, (any) vehicle; **aller à fond la caisse**, to go all out/to do a ton 10. *P* **lâcher une caisse**, to fart*/to let off 11. *P* **prendre une caisse**, to get drunk*/stewed; **avoir/tenir une caisse**, to be drunk*/sloshed/stewed 12. *Iron P* **voyez caisse!** (*s'adresse à qn qui reçoit des coups*) you can really defend yourself! 13. *F* percussion section (in an orchestra) 14. *F* **mettre qn en caisse**, to pull s.o.'s leg 15. *F* **rouler sa caisse**, to swagger/to throw one's weight around **II** *nm P* **c'est du caisse**, it's six of one and half a dozen of the other; it makes no odds/it's much of a muchness; **c'est jamais du caisse**, it's never the same.

caiss(e)mar [kɛsmar] *nm Vieilli P* cashier.

caisson [kɛsɔ̃] *nm P* 1. head*; **se faire sauter le caisson**, to blow one's brains out 2. stomach*/breadbasket.

calanche [kalɑ̃ʃ] *nf Vieilli P* death; (**une) calanche V. P.**, (= *voie publique*) (a) death on the public highway/the roads.

calancher [kalɑ̃ʃe] *vi P* to die*/to snuff it.

calbar [kalbar] *nm P* (men's) underpants; **il a rien dans le calbar**, he's got no guts/balls.

calbombe [kalbɔ̃b] *nf P* (*a*) *Vieilli* candle (*b*) lamp; (electric) lightbulb/light/torch; *Aut* headlight; **tenir la calbombe** = **tenir la chandelle** (**chandelle 11**).

calcer [kalse] *vtr V* **calcer une nana**, to have sex* with/to screw a girl.

calcif [kalsif] *nm P* (men's) underpants; **filer un coup dans le calcif**, to have sex*/to get one's leg over. (*Voir* **anguille**)

calculé [kalkyle] *a F* **c'est calculé pour**, it's specially designed/worked out; it's custommade.

caldif [kaldif] *nm F* (*écoles*) (= *calcul différentiel*) differential calculus.

cale [kal] *nf* 1. *F* **être à fond de cale**, to be penniless*/to be on one's uppers 2. *P* **être de la cale 2**, to be (a) homosexual* 3. *P* **mettre une nana en cale**, to get a girl pregnant*/*esp NAm* to knock a girl up. (*Voir* **se lester**)

calé [kale] *a F* 1. **être calé en qch**, to be well informed about sth/to be good at sth; **être calé en maths**, to be good at maths; **c'est un type calé**, he's a bright/clever bloke 2. difficult/complicated/awkward/dodgy 3. **ça c'est calé!** that's crafty!/that's clever! 4. (= *recalé*) **être calé**, to fail (an exam) 5. *A* rich*/well-off/well-to-do.

calebar [kalbar] *nm P* = **calbar**.

calebasse [kalbɑs] *nf P* 1. head*/nut; **un coup sur la calebasse**, a thump on the head 2. face*/mug.

calebombe [kalbɔ̃b] *nf P* = **calbombe**.

calecif [kalse] *vtr V* = **calcer**.

calecif [kalsif] *nm P* = **calcif**.

caleçon [kalsɔ̃] *nm P* prisoner's parcel.

cale-dent(s) [kaldɑ̃] *nm P* snack.

calencher [kalɑ̃ʃe] *vi P* = **calancher**.

calendes [kalɑ̃d] *nfpl F* **renvoyer qn/qch aux calendes grecques**, to put s.o./sth off indefinitely.

calendo(t) [kalɑ̃do] *nm,* **calendos** [kalɑ̃dos] *nm P* camembert cheese.

caler [kale] **I** 1. *vtr & i* (*voiture, moteur*) to stall; **caler le moteur**, to stall the engine 2. *vi* to back down/to climb down/to give up; to get cold feet; **je cale**, I give up **II** *vtr* 1. **caler un malade sur des coussins**, to prop a patient up on cushions 2. **se caler les amygdales/les babines/les babouines/les badigoinces/les côtes/les joues, se les caler**, to eat* heartily/to stuff oneself/to feed one's face/to get stuck in; **se caler du fromage**, to eat* some cheese; **ça cale l'estomac**, it fills you up **III** *vpr* **se caler** *F* to settle comfortably (in an armchair, etc).

(se) caleter [(sə)kalte] *vi & pr P* = **calter**.

caleur, -euse [kalœr, -øz] *n P* 1. idler/loafer/shirker/skiver 2. coward*/funk/fraidy cat.

calfouette [kalfwɛt] *nm P* = **calbar**.

calibre [kalibr] *nm P* 1. pistol/revolver*/shooter 2. **ils sont du même calibre**, (*ils se valent*) one is just as good *or* bad as the other/there's nothing to choose between them.

calmer [kalme] *F* **I** *vtr* to knock out (an opponent) **II** *vpr* **se calmer** on se calme! calm down! don't panic!

calmos [kalmos] *adv F* calmly; **calmos!** don't panic!

calot [kalo] *nm P* 1. *pl* eyes*; **rouler/ribouler des calots**, to roll one's eyes (in amazement)/ to goggle; **boiter des calots**, to squint 2. (*de verre*) marble.

calotin [kalɔtɛ̃] *F Péj* **I** *nm* (*a*) priest/ clergyman*; **ces fichus calotins**, these blasted priests (*b*) (over-zealous) churchgoer/bigot **II** *a* churchy.

calotte [kalɔt] *nf F* 1. box on the ear/clout/ cuff/smack/slap; **flanquer une calotte à qn**, to give s.o. a clout; **se prendre une calotte**, to get boxed round the ears 2. *Péj* **la calotte**, the clergy/the priesthood/the cloth.

calotter [kalɔte] *vtr P* to steal*/to nick.

calouse [kaluz] *nf P* leg*; **jouer des calouses**, to walk.

calouser [kaluze] *vtr P* **calouser le bitume**, to walk along the street/to pound the pavement.

calpette [kalpɛt] *nf P* (wagging) tongue (of a gossip).

(se) calter [(sə)kalte] *vi & pr P* to run away*/to clear off; **je suis pressé, je calte**, I'm in a hurry, (I) must dash/I've got to split; **je t'ai dit d'calter**, I told you to get lost; **caltez, volaille(s)!** buzz off!/get lost!

calva [kalva] *nm F* (*boisson*) calvados.

cam [kam] **I** *a inv P* (= *camouflé*) (*surt Mil*) camouflaged **II** *nm P* (= *camelot*) street trader/hawker; **faire cam**, to hawk/to trade.

Camarde [kamard] *nf Vieilli F* (*surt littéraire*) **la Camarde**, death; **épouser la Camarde**, to die*/to meet one's maker.

camaro [kamaro] *nm A P* friend*/comrade/ pal/buddy.

cambouis [kãbwi] *nm P* (*a*) **le Cambouis** = *l'Intendance Militaire* = *approx* the Royal Army Service Corps (*now part of the Royal Corps of Transport*) (*b*) **un cambouis**, a member of the *Intendance Militaire*.

cambrio [kãbrio] *nm P* (*abrév* = *cambrioleur*) burglar/housebreaker.

cambriole [kãbrijɔl] *nf Vieilli P* housebreaking/burgling.

Cambronne [kãbrɔn] *Prnm F* **le mot de Cambronne = merde!** (*qv*); = four-letter word. (*Voir* **mot**)

cambrousard, -arde [kãbruzar, -ard], **cambroussard, -arde** [kãbrusar, -ard]

P **I** *a* countrified **II** *nm* peasant*/yokel/*esp NAm* hick.

cambrouse [kãbruz] *nf*, **cambrousse** [kãbrus] *nf P* (*campagne*) country; **au fin fond de la cambrousse**, at the back of beyond; **se paumer en pleine cambrousse**, to get lost in the middle of nowhere.

cambuse [kãbyz] *nf P* 1. untidy house *or* room *or* workshop, etc; hovel/dump/hole 2. seedy *or* sleazy pub; dive.

cambut [kãby] *nm P* **travailler au cambut**, to substitute/to switch imitation jewellery for real/false money for good, etc; to pull a switch.

cambuter [kãbyte] *P* **I** *vtr & i* = **travailler au cambut** (**cambut**); **cambuter un portefeuille**, to substitute a wallet full of paper, etc for one full of money; to switch wallets **II** *vi* to change (places, appearance, etc); (*humeur*) to alter/change.

cambuteur [kãbytœr] *nm P* person who makes the switch/the exchange in a *cambut*. (*Voir* **cambut**)

came [kam] **I** *nm P* (= *camelot*) street trader/hawker **II** *nf* 1. *P* (*a*) drugs*/junk/ dope; **priseur, -euse de came**, junkie/junky (*b*) cocaine* 2. *P* (*a*) goods/merchandise/stuff (*b*) shoddy goods/junk/trash; *esp* fake *or* dubious articles/merchandise 3. **lâcher sa came/refiler la came**, *V* to ejaculate*/to come; *P* to vomit*/to throw up.

camé, -ée [kame] *P* (*drogues*) **I** *n* drug addict*/dope addict/junkie/junky **II** *a* under the influence of drugs*/high (on drugs*)/doped up/stoned; **il était camé jusqu'aux yeux**, he was bombed out of his mind.

camée [kame] *nm F* (*spectacles*) cameo role.

camelote [kamlɔt] *nf* 1. *F* (*a*) goods/ merchandise; **fais voir ta camelote!** let's have a look at your stuff; **c'est de la bonne camelote**, it's good stuff (*b*) cheap shoddy goods; junk/trash; **c'est de la camelote**, it's rubbish/trash; it's rubbishy/trashy 2. *P* (*butin de voleur*) loot 3. *V* sperm.

camembert [kamãbɛr] *nm P* 1. traffic policeman's raised platform 2. circular machine-gun loader 3. any circular box *or* loader.

se camer [sǝkame] *vpr P* to take drugs*; to be a drug addict*; to get high/stoned (on drugs); **il se came à l'héro**, he's on heroin*/he gets high on H.

camion [kamjɔ̃] *nm P* girl* *or* woman* with

large breasts*/big tits.

camoufle [kamufl] *nf A P* candle; lamp; (electric) light/torch.

camp [kɑ̃] *nm F* ficher/P fiche/P foutre le camp, to run away*/to clear off/to beat it; to bugger off; **fiche(z)(-moi) le camp!** hop it!/ get lost!* **fous(-moi)/foutez(-moi) le camp!** sod off!/bugger off!/piss off!/fuck off! **on lève le camp**, let's split.

campagne [kɑ̃paɲ] *nf P* **1.** (*surt prostituée*) **aller à la campagne**, to go to prison* **2. emmener qn à la campagne**, to hold s.o. in contempt.

campêche [kɑ̃pɛʃ] *nm A P* (bois de) campêche, inferior wine/plonk.

camphre [kɑ̃fr] *nm P* **1.** *Vieilli* strong spirits*/rotgut **2.** (*argot des policiers*) **sentir le camphre**, (*d'un dossier*) to have remained too long in the archives; (*d'une manifestation*) to be turning nasty/violent.

camplouse [kɑ̃pluz] *nf*, **campluche** [kɑ̃plyʃ] *nf P* = **cambrous(s)e**.

campo(s) [kɑ̃po] *nm Vieilli F* holiday/day off/free time; **avoir campo**, to have a day off (from school, work).

camtar [kamtar] *nm P* (*camion*) lorry/ truck.

canadienne [kanadjɛn] *nf P* une canadienne en (peau de) sapin, a coffin/a wooden overcoat/a pine overcoat.

canard [kanar] *nm* **1.** *F* marcher comme un canard, to waddle **2.** *F* trempé comme un canard, drenched (to the skin)/like a drowned rat **3.** *F* il fait un froid de canard, it's freezing cold **4.** *F* mon petit canard, my darling*/ ducks/ducky **5.** *F* false rumour; hoax* **6.** *F* newspaper/rag/scandal sheet; **acheter un canard**, to buy a paper **7.** *F* difficult customer **8.** *F* social climber **9.** *F* (*musique*) false note; **il a fait un canard**, he hit a wrong note **10.** *F* a lump of sugar dipped in brandy or coffee **11.** *F* (*médecine*) speculum **12.** *P* horse/nag **13.** *F* kiss on the mouth **14.** *V* baiser qn en canard, to have sex* with s.o. dog(gie)-fashion/from behind. (*Voir* **patte 8; sirop 3**)

canarde [kanard] *nf P* settling of accounts.

canarder [kanarde] *F vtr* to take pot-shots at people/to snipe at s.o.; to kill s.o. (in this way).

canardeur [kanardœr] *nm F* sniper.

canasson [kanasɔ̃] *nm P* horse/nag.

cancan [kɑ̃kɑ̃] *nm P* newspaper/rag.

cancérette [kɑ̃sɛrɛt] *nf F* cigarette*/cancer stick.

cancre [kɑ̃kr] *nm F* (*écoles*) dunce/duffer/ dud.

cané [kane] *a P* **1.** exhausted*/worn out **2.** dead.

caner [kane] *vi P* **1.** (*a*) to be afraid*/to have the jitters; **ne pas caner**, to keep one's pecker up (*b*) to be a coward*/to show the white feather; to climb down/to chicken out **2.** to die*/to kick the bucket **3.** to leave*/to clear off **4.** to give up. (*Voir* **décaner**)

canette [kanɛt] *nf F* **1.** small beer bottle; **tu veux/bois une canette?** want a beer? **2. toucher sa canette**, to be good/great (at sth); to be ace/a whizz (at sth).

caneur, -euse [kanœr, -øz] *P* **I** *a* cowardly*/yellow-bellied/chicken **II** *n* coward*/quitter.

canevas [kanva] *nm* **1.** *F* broder le canevas, to embroider a story **2.** *P* (*boxe*) canvas; **envoyer qn au canevas**, to floor s.o.

caniche [kaniʃ] *nm & f F* ce n'est/c'est pas fait pour les caniches, it's not there as an ornament, it's meant to be used.

canif [kanif] *nm F* donner un coup/des coups de canif dans le contrat (de mariage), to be unfaithful (to one's husband, wife).

canne [kan] *nf* **1.** *P* casser sa canne, (*partir*) to leave*/to beat it; (*s'endormir*) to go to sleep*/to crash out; (*mourir*) to die*/to peg out **2.** *pl P* legs*/pegs/pins; **mettre les cannes** (en vitesse), to run away*/to clear off; **être sur les cannes/avoir les cannes en vermicelle**, to be exhausted*/to be out on one's feet **3.** *V* penis*/rod/prick; **avoir la canne**, to have an erection/to have a hard-on; **souffler dans la canne à qn**, to fellate* s.o./to give s.o. a blowjob; **casser la canne**, to have sex*/to have it off/to get one's end away.

cannelles [kanɛl] *nfpl P* handcuffs*/ bracelets.

canner [kane] *P vi* = **caner 2, 3**.

canon [kanɔ̃] **I** *nm* **1.** *P* glass of wine **2.** *P* canon de fusil, throat **3.** *P* balle dans le canon, suppository **4.** *V* avoir une balle dans le canon, to have an erection*/to have a loaded gun/to have a hard-on **5.** *P* beautiful girl* *or* woman*/smasher/bombshell **II** *a F* excellent*/super/cool/ace; **une fille canon**, a bombshell.

canonnier [kanɔnje] *a & nm F* (*football*) (joueur) canonnier, high goalscorer.

canotier [kanɔtje] *nm P* travailler du canotier, to be mad*/to be off one's rocker.

canou [kanu] *nm Belg V* female genitals*.

cantalou(p) [kɑ̃talu] *nm Vieilli P* native of Auvergne/Auvergnat.

cantiner [katine] *vtr & i P (prisons)* to buy (goods) in the prison shop.

cantoche [kɑ̃tɔʃ] *nf P* 1. canteen 2. bourré comme une cantoche, completely drunk*/ stewed to the eyeballs. (*Voir* **bourré 2**)

canulant [kanylɑ̃] *a F* boring.

canular, canulard[1] [kanylar] *nm F (histoire invraisemblable)* tall story; (*farce*) practical joke/hoax*/leg-pull; (*d'étudiants*) rag; **monter un canular à qn**, to hoax* s.o.

canulard[2] *nm P* male nurse.

canularesque [kanylarɛsk] *a F* histoire canularesque, hoax/leg-pull.

canule [kanyl] *nf F (personne, chose)* bore*/ pest/pain.

canuler [kanyle] *vtr & i F* 1. to bore* (s.o.)/ to be a pest (to s.o.) 2. (*d'un client d'une prostituée*) to haggle (over the fee).

caoua [kawa] *nm P* coffee. (*Voir* **kawa**)

cap [kap] *a F (abrév = capable)* t'es pas cap, you haven't got it in you.

capa [kapa] *nf F (abrév = capacité)* votre capa en droit, your law diploma.

caperlot [kapɛrlo] *nm Mil P* lance corporal.

capet [kapɛ] *nm P* hat.

capist(r)on [kapist(r)ɔ̃] *nm Vieilli P (Mil, marine)* captain.

capital [kapital] *nm P* virginity/ maidenhead; **entamer le (petit) capital**, to deflower a virgin/to pick a girl's cherry/to be the first; **entamer son capital**, to lose one's virginity/to lose one's cherry.

capitonnée [kapitɔne] *af F* elle est bien capitonnée, she's nice and plump/cuddly/well padded/well stacked.

capo [kapo] *nm F Mil (= caporal)* corporal/ corp. (*Voir* **kapo**)

capot [kapo] *a inv P* être capot, to lose at cards.

capote [kapɔt] *nf P* capote anglaise, condom*/French letter/frenchie/rubber (johnnie).

capsule [kapsyl] *nf P (casquette)* cap.

caquer [kake] *vi P* to defecate*/to (have a) crap.

caquet [kakɛ] *nm F* noisy chatter/gossiping/ prattle; **rabattre le caquet à qn**, to shut s.o. up/to take s.o. down a peg (or two).

caquetage [kak(ə)taʒ] *nm F* noisy chatter(ing)/prattling/cackle/gossip(ing).

caqueter [kak(ə)te] *vi F* to chatter*/to prattle/to cackle.

cara [kara] *nm Vieilli P (abrév = caractère)* character; **un mauvais cara**, a bad temper.

carabin [karabɛ̃] *nm F* medical student/ medic(o).

carabinade [karabinad] *nf F* medical students' rag.

carabine [karabin] *nf V* penis*.

carabiné [karabine] *a F* very strong/ intense/a whale of a .../a father and mother of a ...; splitting (headache); stinking (cold); stiff (drink, bill, etc); **une guigne carabinée**, an extraordinary run of bad luck; **une noce carabinée**, a rare old binge/a real piss-up; **prendre une cuite carabinée**, to get totally drunk*/to get absolutely plastered/to get pissed as a newt; **un toupet carabiné**, a hell of a nerve/a bloody cheek.

carabiner [karabine] *vi F (jeux d'argent)* to lay an occasional stake.

carabistouille [karabistuj] *nf P* swindle*/ swindling/fiddle/racket.

caraco [karako] *nm P* 1. lie*/fib/whopper 2. rudeness/rude remark/lack of good manners.

carafe [karaf] *nf* 1. *P* head*/nut 2. *P* fool*/ idiot/twit/nurd 3. *P* mouth*/trap; **en carafe**, (*à court de mots*) at a loss for words; (*sans ressources*) short of cash; **rester en carafe**, to be left in the lurch/to be left high and dry; to be left out of it/to be left out in the cold; **ils m'ont laissé en carafe**, they left me high and dry/ they left me in mid air; they left me out of it; **tomber en carafe**, (*voiture*) to break down; **ma bagnole est (tombée) en carafe**, my car conked out on me. (*Voir* **bouchon 6**)

carafon [karafɔ̃] *nm P* 1. (*a*) head*/nut (*b*) (*cerveau*) il n'a rien dans le carafon, he's got no brains 2. fool*/idiot/nurd.

carambolage [karɑ̃bɔlaʒ] *nm* 1. *F Aut* (multiple) pile-up/crash 2. *P* fight*/punch-up/ scrap 3. *V* sex*/bump and grind.

caramboler [karɑ̃bɔle] *vtr* 1. *F* to run/to crash/to plough into (a car); **cinquante voitures se sont carambolées sur l'autoroute**, there was a fifty car pile-up on the motorway 2. *V* to have sex* with (s.o.).

carambouillage [karɑ̃bujaʒ] *nm*, **carambouille** [karɑ̃buj] *nf F* fraudulent conversion (for cash, of goods bought on credit).

carambouilleur [karɑ̃bujœr] *nm F* swindler*/fiddler/con man.

caramel [karamɛl] *nm P (drogues) (abcès provoqué par une piqûre avec une aiguille non stérilisée ou par des drogues impures)* ab/AB/

ABC.

carante [karɑ̃t] *nf P* 1. (*a*) table (*b*) (illicit) street-vendor's folding table 2. se mettre en carante, (*en colère*) to get angry*/to blow one's top; (*devenir méchant*) to turn nasty/to cut up rough; (*en position de combat*) to square up (for a fight). (*Voir* **quarante**)

carapatage [karapataʒ] *nm P* hurried departure/quick exit.

se carapater [səkarapate] *vpr P* to run away*/to skedaddle/to split/to make a quick exit/to make tracks.

caraque [karak] *nf A P* dirty slut.

carat [kara] *nm* 1. *F* un con à vingt-quatre/à trente-six carats, a prize idiot 2. *P* age; year; un môme de treize carats, a kid of thirteen; prendre du carat, to grow old/to get long in the tooth 3. *P* jusqu'au dernier carat, (right) up to the last moment/up to the minute; dernier carat, at the latest.

caravelle [karavɛl] *nf P* high-class prostitute*.

carbi [karbi] *nm P* 1. coal/black stuff 2. coalman/coalie/coaly 3. aller au carbi/(aller) bosser au carbi, (*surt pour un criminel*) to do unpleasant manual work/to get down to some hard work (for a change) 4. money*/brass. (*Voir* **sac 17**)

carboniser [karbɔnize] *vtr P* (*a*) carboniser qn, to ruin s.o.'s reputation/to discredit/to malign s.o.; to run s.o. down/to roast s.o. (*b*) carboniser un coup, to frustrate an attempt/to put the kibosh on sth.

carburant [karbyrɑ̃] *nm P* 1. (alcoholic) drink*/juice/lubrication 2. money*/dough/lolly.

carbure [karbyr] *nm P* 1. = **carburant 2** 2. petrol/*NAm* gas.

carburer [karbyre] *vi P* 1. *Vieilli* to pay* up/to shell out 2. to work efficiently/to function well; ça carbure, it's going fine/it works like a treat; carburer sec, to drive very fast/to do a ton 3. carburer à la bière/à l'héroïne, to drink beer*/to take heroin* 4. to think (hard)/to turn over in one's mind; carbure un peu! think it over!

carcan [karkɑ̃] *nm Vieilli P* (*courses*) bad horse/nag/hack.

carder [karde] *vtr P* to scratch (s.o.). (*Voir* **cuir 4**)

cardinal [kardinal] *nm P* a *kir* made with red wine. (*Voir* **kir**)

cardinoche [kardinɔʃ] *nm F* = **cardinal**.

carer [kare] *P* = **carrer**.

caricature [karikatyr] *nf F* ugly person/figure of fun; quelle caricature! what a fright!

carlingue [karlɛ̃g] *nf P* 1. prison*/clink/stir 2. (*seconde guerre 1939–45*) la Carlingue, the Gestapo.

carluche [karlyʃ] *nf P* prison*/clink/stir.

carme [karm] *nm A P* money*.

carmer [karme] *vtr & i Vieilli P* to pay* up/to cough up.

carmouille [karmuj] *nf Vieilli P* (*rare*) payment/settling up.

carnaval [karnaval] *nm F* (*personne*) figure of fun/guy/clown; c'est un vrai carnaval, he looks a real clown.

carne [karn] *nf*, **carogne** [karɔɲ] *nf P* 1. tough/inferior meat 2. old horse/nag/hack 3. bad-tempered, cantankerous person; swine; (*femme*) bitch; vieille carne, (*femme*) old bag.

caroline [karɔlin] *nf P* (*a*) (passive) homosexual* (*b*) transvestite/TV.

carottage [karɔtaʒ] *nm F* (*a*) swindling/cheating/diddling (*b*) (petty) theft/nicking/swiping.

carotte [karɔt] *nf F* 1. hoax*/swindle*; tirer la/une carotte à qn, (*tromper*) to try to hoax* s.o./to try to pull the wool over s.o.'s eyes; to diddle/to trick s.o. (out of sth); to do/to con s.o.; (*faire avouer*) (to try) to make s.o. talk/to make s.o. spill the beans 2. (*a*) (*billard*) jouer/tirer la carotte, to leave nothing on the table (*b*) (*tennis*) drop shot 3. les carottes sont cuites, it's all up; ses carottes sont cuites, he's done for/he's had it/he's had his chips 4. *Mus* soprano saxophone 5. sign outside a tobacconist's (shop). (*Voir* **poil 10**)

carotter [karɔte] **I** *vtr F* 1. to steal*/to pinch/to nick 2. carotter qch à qn/qn de qch, to do/to swindle*/to diddle s.o. out of sth; to con sth off s.o./to con s.o. out of sth 3. *Mil* carotter le service, to dodge duty; carotter une permission, to wangle some leave 4. to hide (an object) in the rectum **II** *vi P* (*a*) (*jeux d'argent*) to play for trifling/piddling stakes (*b*) to jump the queue/to gate-crash.

carotteur, -euse [karɔtœr, -ǿz] *n*, **carottier** [karɔtje] *nm* 1. *F* cheat/swindler*/trickster/con artist/wangler 2. *F* malingerer*/shirker/skiver 3. *P* queue-jumper/gate-crasher.

caroube [karub] *nf P* = **caroroble**.

caroubeur [karubœr] *nm*, **caroubier** [karubje] *nm P* = **caroubleur**.

carouble [karubl] *nf P* **1.** duplicate key (used for robbery); skeleton key/screw **2.** forcing open of door (*to commit a burglary*) **3.** lock **4.** beating up*/working over.

caroubler [karuble] *vtr P* **1.** to break into (a house, etc) with a duplicate *or* skeleton key **2.** to beat (s.o.) up*/to give (s.o.) a going over **3.** to steal*/to swipe/to pinch.

caroubleur [karublœr] *nm P* burglar/ screwsman; picklock.

carpe [karp] *nf F* **1. faire la carpe,** (*de fatigue*) to pass out with exhaustion; (*de plaisir*) to pass out in (sheer) ecstasy/to go into seventh heaven **2. faire des yeux de carpe** (**pâmée**), to show the whites of one's eyes **3. regarder qn avec des yeux de carpe,** to make sheep's eyes at s.o.

carpette [karpɛt] *nf P* weak/feeble/flabby/ spineless individual.

carrante [karɑ̃t] *nf A P* = **carante 1.**

carre [kɑr] *nf P* **1.** hiding place; **mettre qch à la carre,** to stash sth away **2.** reserve; **mettre à la carre,** to save up **3.** total stakes (at poker, etc).

carré [kare] **I** *nm P* **1.** second-year student in a *grande école* **2.** four of a kind (at poker); **carré de valets,** four jacks **3.** (*TV*) **carré blanc,** sign indicating a programme is unsuitable for children; *Fig* **elle est tellement laide, faudrait mettre le carré blanc,** she's so ugly, she ought to be censored **II** *a F* **tête carrée,** stubborn person. (*Voir* **tête 16**).

carreau, *pl* **-eaux** [karo] *nm* **1.** *P* eye*; **affranchir le carreau,** to keep a look-out/to watch out for (s.o., sth); **avoir un carreau brouillé,** to have a squint in one eye; **avoir un carreau à la manque,** to be blind in one eye **2.** *P* (*a*) monocle; lens (*b*) *pl* **carreaux,** glasses/ specs/goggles **3.** *P* **en avoir un coup dans les carreaux,** to be drunk*/to be smashed out of one's head **4.** *P* (*a*) **le Petit Carreau,** the magistrates' court (= court of summary jurisdiction) (*b*) **le** (**Grand**) **Carreau,** the Crown Court (formerly the Assize Court) **5.** *F* **coucher/laisser qn sur le carreau,** to lay s.o. out/to flatten s.o./to send s.o. sprawling **6.** *F* **rester sur le carreau,** (*tué*) to be lying dead*/ cold; to be killed on the spot; (*blessé*) to be seriously wounded; to be laid out cold; (*éliminé*) to be out of the running **7.** *F* **se tenir à carreau,** to take every precaution/to be on one's guard; to lie low.

carrée [kare] *nf F* (*a*) (*chambre*) room/flat; pad (*b*) *Mil* barrack room.

carrelingue [karlɛ̃g] *nm P* **1.** lens (of spectacles) **2.** *pl* glasses/specs.

carrément [karemɑ̃] *adv F* absolutely/ totally; **il y est allé carrément,** he made no bones about it/he didn't beat about the bush; **dire les choses carrément,** not to mince one's words; **il est carrément chiant, ce mec!** that guy's a real pain (in the neck)!

carrer [kare] *P* **I** *vtr* **1.** to conceal/to stash (sth) away **2.** to steal*/to swipe/to lift (sth) **3.** to place/to put (sth) somewhere; to plonk (sth) down; **tu peux te le carrer dans le train/ le cul/le baba,** you know where you can stick that/you can stick that up your arse/*NAm* ass **II** *vpr* **se carrer** to run away*/to beat it/to skedaddle.

carreur [karœr] *nm P* **1.** shoplifter **2.** stakeholder (at poker, etc).

carreuse [karøz] *nf P* shoplifter.

carriole [karjɔl] *nf F* ramshackle old car*/ jalopy.

carrosse [karɔs] *nm Vieilli F* **rouler carrosse,** to live in great style. (*Voir* **roue 3**)

carrossée [karɔse] *af F* **elle est bien carrossée,** she's got a good figure/she's got everything in all the right places/she's well stacked.

carrosserie [karɔsri] *nf F* (*personne*) build; **elle a une sacrée carrosserie,** she's well built.

Carrousel (**le**) [ləkaruzɛl] *Prnm F* the *Salle des pas perdus* in the law courts in Paris.

carroussel [karusɛl] *a inv P* drunk*/tipsy.

carte [kart] *nf* **1.** *F* **perdre la carte,** (*être désorienté*) to lose one's bearings; (*être nerveux*) to get flustered **2.** *F* **c'était la carte forcée,** it was (a case of) Hobson's choice **3.** *F* **connaître/voir le dessous des cartes,** to be in the know/to have the low-down on sth **4.** *F* **fille en carte,** registered prostitute; *Fig* **être en carte,** to be on file; to be qualified; to be under contract **5.** *P* **carte de France/de géographie,** sperm stain(s) left on sheet (after sex*); wet dream.

carton [kartɔ̃] *nm* **1.** *F* **rester/dormir dans les cartons,** to be shelved/pigeonholed **2. faire un carton,** *F* (*tirer sur qch*) to fire at a target; (*sur qn*) to fire at s.o./to take a pot shot at s.o./to use s.o. for target practice; *F* (*avoir du succès*) to be a success/a hit; (*écoles*) to get a very good mark/grade (*in maths, etc*); *V* (*posséder une femme, brièvement*) to have sex* with a woman/to have a quick screw/a quickie; (*d'une prostituée*) to get a client; *F* (*avoir un accident, en course automobile*) to crash 3. *P* playing card; **battre les cartons,** to shuffle; **taper le carton,** to play cards 4. *P de carton,* worthless 5. *F* **prendre un carton,** to be badly beaten; (*écoles*) to get a bad mark.

cartonner [kartɔne] *vtr & i P* 1. *A* (*a*) to play cards (*b*) to be a compulsive card-player 2. to break wind/to fart* 3. (*a*) to fire at (s.o.) (*b*) to hit the target (*c*) *Fig* to be very successful/to hit the bullseye; (*écoles*) **cartonner en maths,** to get a very good mark/ grade in maths 4. to travel/drive/go very fast 5. to have a serious car *or* motorbike accident 6. *V* to have sex* with (a woman)/to screw (a woman) 7. to criticize severely/to slate 8. = **prendre un carton** (**carton 5**).

cartonnier [kartɔnje] *nm P* cardsharp.

cartouche [kartuʃ] *nf V* **secouer la cartouche,** to masturbate*.

cartouse [kartuz] *nf P* card.

cas [ka] *nm F* 1. **c'est bien le cas de le dire!** you said it!/and how!/you can say that again! 2. **pas la peine d'en faire cas,** (it)'s not worth worrying about 3. **c'est un cas, ce mec!** that guy's unbelievable! I don't believe this guy! 4. **au cas où,** [okazu] just in case.

casaque [kazak] *nf F* **tourner casaque,** to make an about-face (in one's opinions, etc); (*politique, etc*) to change sides/to rat.

casaquin [kazakɛ̃] *nm F* 1. **tomber sur le casaquin à qn,** to beat s.o. up*/to clobber s.o. 2. **avoir qch dans le casaquin,** to be ill; **donner sur le casaquin,** (*vin*) to go to one's head.

casba(h) [kazba] *nf P* house/pad/joint; *esp* brothel*.

cascader [kaskade] *vi P* to serve a prison sentence*/to do time/to do bird.

case [kaz] *nf P* 1. house/pad; **faire une case,** to burgle a house 2. **il a une case de moins/ une case vide/une case qui manque, il lui manque une case,** he's mad*/barmy/bonkers; he's not all there; he's got a screw loose/ missing 3. **revenir/retourner à la case départ,** to go back to square one; **retour à la case départ!** we're back to square one! 4. prison*/ nick; **bouffer de la case,** to serve a prison sentence*/to do time.

caser [kaze] **I** *vtr* 1. *F* **caser qn,** to fix s.o. up with a job; **il est bien casé,** he's got a good job/he's got himself fixed up nicely 2. *F* **elle a trois filles à caser,** she's got three daughters to marry off 3. *V* (*a*) to have sex* with (s.o.)/ to screw (s.o.); **va te faire caser!** fuck off! (*b*) to sodomize* (s.o.) **II** *vpr* **se caser** *F* 1. to settle down/to find somewhere to live 2. to

find a job/to get fixed up with a job 3. to get married*/to settle down.

cash [kaʃ] *adv F* **payer/casquer cash,** to pay cash (down); **100 balles cash,** 100 francs (cash) on the nail/on the barrel.

casier [kazje] *nm F* (= *casier judiciaire*) police record/form; **avoir un casier vierge/ne pas avoir de casier,** to have a clean record; **avoir un casier,** to have form.

casimir [kazimir] *nm P* waistcoat.

casin(gue) [kazɛ̃(g)] *nm P* bar/pub/ restaurant, etc.

casque [kask] **I** *nm* 1. *F* **Casques bleus,** (*de l'ONU*) the Blue Berets 2. *P Vieilli* (*a*) **avoir/ prendre son casque,** to be drunk*/to get drunk*/to get tanked up (*b*) **avoir le casque,** to have a hangover; **j'en ai dans le casque,** I've got a bit of a head (from drinking) **II** *nf P* **donner le coup de casque,** (*payer*) = **casquer 1**; (*conclure le baratin*) to wrap up the sales talk.

casquer [kaske] *vtr & i* 1. *F* to pay* up/to cough up/to foot the bill; **casquer qn,** to pay* s.o.; **faire casquer qn de vingt francs,** to touch s.o. for twenty francs 2. *P* = **cascader.**

casquette [kaskɛt] *nf* 1. *P* **avoir une casquette en peau de fesse,** to be bald* 2. *P* (*courses*) **ramasser les casquettes,** to come in last 3. *P* **prendre une casquette,** to be/to get drunk*; to get tanked up; **avoir une casquette en plomb/en zinc,** to have a hangover/to have a bit of a head 4. *F* **en avoir ras la casquette,** to be fed up*/to have had it up to here 5. *F* **avoir plusieurs casquettes,** (*rôles, fonctions*) to have several jobs/roles/responsibilities, etc 6. *F* **en avoir sous la casquette,** to have brains/to be brainy.

casqueur, -euse [kaskœr, -øz] *n* 1. *F* the person who pays up/forks out/foots the bill 2. *P* cashier.

cass [kas] *nm F* (*cassis*) blackcurrant. (*Voir* **blanc-cass; mêlé-cass**)

cassage [kasaʒ] *nm F* **cassage de gueule,** punch-up.

cassant [kasɑ̃] *a F* (*a*) boring*/deadly; **c'est cassant,** it's a drag (*b*) tiring; **c'est pas (très) cassant!** it's not exactly tiring/it won't kill you!

casse [kas] **I** *nm P* 1. burglary/break-in; **faire un casse,** to burgle a place/to do a place over 2. robbery/heist **II** *nf F* 1. **vendre une voiture à la casse,** to sell a car for scrap; **envoyer une voiture à la casse,** to send a car to the scrapyard; **être bon pour la casse,** to be fit (only) for the scrap-heap **2.** bloody fight*/ brawl/punch-up **3.** breaking/breakage/damage; **il y aura de la casse**, something will get broken; (*des ennuis*) there'll be trouble/ ructions/some rough stuff; **faire de la casse** (*faire du bruit*) to kick up a row/a rumpus; (*faire des dégâts*) to smash a place up/to do a place over **4.** *Mil* casualties/losses.

cassé [kɑse] *a* **1.** *F* **qu'est-ce qu'il y a de cassé?** what's all the trouble/hoo-ha about? **qu'est-ce qu'il y a encore de cassé?** what's the trouble now? **il y a quelque chose de cassé**, there's been a spot of bother **2.** *F* **c'est cassé**, (*d'une liaison*) it's over **3.** *P* drunk*/smashed.

casse-bonbons [kɑsbɔ̃bɔ̃] *nm inv*, **casse-burnes** [kɑsbyrn] *a & nm inv V* (*personne*) a bastard*/a sod; (*chose*) a bastard*/a sod; **il est plutôt casse-bonbons**, he's a bit of a pain.

casse-cou [kɑsku] *nm inv F* reckless person/daredevil.

casse-couilles [kɑskuj] **I** *nm inv V* pest/ bloody nuisance/pain in the arse **II** *a inv* annoying; **c'est casse-couilles**, it's a pain (in the arse)/it's a drag.

casse-croûte [kɑskrut] *nm inv* **1.** *F* **casse-croûte de cheval**, straw hat **2.** *P* **se mettre au casse-croûte**, to turn informer*.

casse-cul [kɑsky] *nm inv P* pest/bloody nuisance/pain in the arse.

casse-dal(l)e [kɑsdal] *nm inv P*, **casse-graine** [kɑsgrɛn] *nm inv F* **1.** snack **2.** = food counter (in pub, etc); snack bar.

casse-gueule [kɑsgœl] *P* **I** *nm inv* **1.** strong spirits*/rotgut **2.** (*endroit*) hot spot; (*boîte, etc*) (low) dive/crummy joint **3.** danger *or* dangerous spot; (*attraction foraine*) dangerous ride; (*entreprise*) risky/*Br* dodgy undertaking; daredevil act(ion); dicey/*Br* dodgy business **II** *a inv* (*endroit*) dangerous; (*entreprise*) risky/*Br* dodgy; **acrobaties casse-gueule**, dangerous acrobatics.

cassement [kɑsmã] *nm P* = **casse I**.

casse-noisettes [kɑsnwazɛt] *nm inv V* **1.** (*forains*) lion's, etc jaw **2.** (*femme*) **faire casse-noisettes**, to contract the vaginal muscles (*during lovemaking*)/to squeeze s.o.'s nuts.

casse-olives [kɑsɔliv] *nm inv V* = **casse-bonbons**.

casse-pattes [kɑspat] *P* **I** *nm inv* **1.** strong spirits*/rotgut **2.** rough wine **3.** (*cyclisme*) breakneck descent **II** *a inv* (*escalier, etc*)

tiring/exhausting.

casse-pieds [kɑspje] *F* **I** *nm inv* (*personne*) (crashing) bore*/pest/nuisance/ pain in the neck **II** *a* (*chose*) **c'est rudement casse-pieds**, it's a hell of a bore*/of a bind; it's enough to give you a pain in the neck. (*Voir* **pied 15**)

casse-pipe [kɑspip] *nm P* war; dangerous area; **aller au casse-pipe(s)**, (*guerre*) to go to war/to the front line; (*moto*) to ride very fast/to do a ton. (*Voir* **pipe 2**)

casse-poitrine [kɑspwatrin] *nm inv P* = **casse-pattes 1**.

casser [kɑse] **I** *vtr* **1.** *P* **casser une turne**, to break into (and burgle) a place; **casser un coffre-fort**, to break open a safe; *vi* **casser**, to burgle **2.** *F* to break up (a car, etc) for scrap **3.** *F* **ça ne casse pas des briques/ça ne casse pas trois pattes à un canard/ça ne casse rien**, there's nothing extraordinary about that/it's nothing to write home about/it's no great shakes; **il ne casse rien**, he's no great shakes/ he's no big deal **3.** *F* **à tout casser**, (*à toute vitesse*) at full speed/without restraint; (*beaucoup*) a hell of a .../a helluva ...; no end of a .../the devil of a .../a father and mother of a ...; **un film à tout casser**, a fantastic film/a great movie; **une bringue à tout casser**, a hell of a bender; **une attaque à tout casser**, an all-out attack; **se faire applaudir à tout casser**, to bring the house down; **cet objet vaut 1000 balles à tout casser**, this article is worth 1000 francs at the very most/at the outside **4.** *P* to say/to blurt out (sth); **ne pas en casser une**, not to say a word/to say nothing/to keep mum **5.** *F* **casser qn**, to criticize* s.o./to cut s.o. to pieces **6.** *P* **casser sa pipe/la casser**, to die*/to kick the bucket/to snuff it **7.** *P* **la/les casser à qn**, to bore* s.o. stiff/to give s.o. a pain in the neck/to get on s.o.'s tits; **tu me les casses!** you're a bore*!/you're getting up my nose!/ stop bugging me! **8.** *P* **casser du flic/du bougnoul**, to beat up* some cops/some wogs **II** *vpr* **se casser** *P* **1.** to run away*/to beat it/to split/*Br* to push off; **on se casse?** let's split/ let's blow **2.** **se casser la gueule**, to fall*/to come a cropper; to have an accident **3.** **ne pas se casser le cul/la tête/le bonnet, ne rien se casser/ne pas se casser**, not to put oneself out; (*ne pas s'inquiéter*) not to worry; **il ne se casse pas**, he doesn't put himself out much; he's not worried; **il ne s'est pas cassé pour m'aider**, he didn't overstrain himself/bust a gut to help me; **je me suis cassé (le tronc/le**

cul) à lui trouver cette adresse, I really went out of my way/bust a gut to find him that address. (*Voir* **bail 2; baraque 2** (*a*), (*b*); **bec 1; bois 6; bonbon 3; bonnet 9; burette 3** (*b*); **burnes; canne 1; cou 2; couille 1** (*a*); **croûte 1; cul I 1** (*c*), **17; figure 1; fion 5; goulot** (*c*); **graine 1; gueule II 2; melon 2; morceau 1, 2, 3; nénette 4; nez 9; œuf 4; oreille 4; patte 3, 8; pied 15; pot 16, 17; reins 2, 3; rondelle 1; sucre 3; tête 5, 6**)

casserole [kasrɔl] *nf P* 1. police informer*/copper's nark 2. tinny (old) piano 3. (*voiture*) ramshackle old banger 4. large old-fashioned (silver) watch 5. worthless individual/washout/layabout 6. low-class prostitute*/cheap whore/tart 7. (*a*) passer qn à la casserole, (*tuer*) to kill* s.o.; passer une nana à la casserole, (*violer*) to rape/to gang-bang a girl; (*faire l'amour brutalement*) to screw/to lay a girl (*b*) passer à la casserole, (*être tué*) to get killed/bumped off; (*subir un revers*) to suffer a setback/to have a rough time (of it); (*femme*) to get raped/gang-banged; to be laid/screwed 8. (*au théâtre, cinéma*) projector; spotlight 9. sth that ruins s.o.'s reputation; avoir une casserole au derrière, to have one's reputation sullied; accrocher une casserole au derrière de qn, to (try to) ruin s.o.'s reputation 10. chanter comme une casserole, to sing (very) out of tune.

casseur [kɑsœr] *nm* 1. *P* burglar/housebreaker 2. *P* violent individual; (*manifestant*) destructive demonstrator 3. *P* (*bravache*) swaggerer 4. *F* scrap dealer.

cassis [kasis] *nm P* 1. head*/nut/block 2. *Vieilli* cassis de lutteur/de déménageur, rough red wine.

cassos [kasos] *adv* faire cassos, to leave*/to split.

cassure [kasyr] *nf P* old actor.

castagne [kastaɲ] *nf P* 1. brawl/free-for-all; aller à la castagne, to have a punch-up 2. blow*; coller/flanquer/foutre une castagne à qn, to fetch s.o. a clout; to clobber/to thump s.o. 3. war.

castagner [kastaɲe] I *vtr & i P* to punch/hit; ça castagne, there's a punch-up going on; they're having a punch-up II *vpr* se castagner *P* to scuffle/to brawl; to have a punch-up.

castagneur [kastaɲœr] *nm P* violent individual/brawler.

castapiane [kastapjan] *nf Vieilli P* VD*/gonorrhoea/the clap.

castor [kastɔr] *nm P* 1. sexually virile man 2. male prostitute* 3. homosexual*/homo.

castrole [kastrɔl] *nf P* saucepan.

casuel [kazɥɛl] I *nm P* (*surt prostituées*) faire le casuel, to hire a room by the hour II *a P* (*verrerie, etc*) easily broken/fragile.

cat [kat] *nm F* jazz musician/cat.

cata [kata] F I *nf* (*abrév = catastrophe*) catastrophe/disaster II *nm* (*abrév = catamaran*) catamaran.

catalogue [katalɔg] *nm P* penal code.

catalogué [kataloge] *a & pp F* c'est catalogué! it's in the bag!/it's a (dead) cert*!

cataloguer [kataloge] *vtr F* cataloguer qn, to size s.o. up/to suss s.o. out; celui-là, je l'ai catalogué, I've got him sussed out/I know where I stand with that one.

catapulter [katapylte] *vtr F* catapulter qn, to send s.o. off to a distant place.

catas [katas] *nf F* = **cata I**.

catastrophe [katastrɔf] *nf F* 1. en catastrophe, (*en hâte*) panic stations/in a mad rush; (*immédiatement*) immediately/as a matter of the utmost urgency 2. c'est une vraie catastrophe, ce type-là! that guy's a disaster.

catastrophé [katastrɔfe] *a F* 1. (*plan, projet*) come to grief; (*avion, etc*) wrecked 2. amazed*/flabbergasted/stunned/knocked all of a heap.

catastropher [katastrɔfe] *vtr F* 1. to wreck (sth) 2. to amaze*/flabbergast (s.o.)/to knock (s.o.) sideways/to shatter (s.o.).

catho [kato] *a & n F* (*abrév = catholique*) Catholic.

catholique [katolik] *a F* straight; in order; genuine/kosher; ce n'est pas (très) catholique, I don't like the look/the sound of it; it looks/sounds fishy; c'est un peu plus catholique, that's more like it; il n'est pas catholique, he's a bit phoney/he's not altogether aboveboard/he's a bit shady.

catiche [katiʃ] *nf Vieilli P* prostitute*/whore/hooker/tart.

en catimini [ɑ̃katimini] *adv phr F* on the sly.

catin [katɛ̃] *nf Vieilli P* = **catiche**.

causailler [kozaje] *vi Vieilli F* to indulge in small talk/to chatter* (away)/to natter on.

causant [kozɑ̃] *a F* chatty/talkative; il n'est pas causant, he doesn't have much to say for himself/he doesn't waste his words.

causer [koze] *vi F* to talk/to chat; dire qch

pour **causer**, to talk for the sake of it; **je disais ça pour causer, moi,** I was just talking for the sake of it; it's not important. (*Voir* **cul I 25**).

causette [kozɛt] *nf F* little chat; **faire un bout/un brin de causette avec qn,** to have a little chat/*Br* a natter with s.o.

cautère [kotɛr] *nm F* **c'est un cautère sur une jambe de bois,** it's no earthly use/it's about as much use as an umbrella in a heatwave.

cavale [kaval] *nf P* escape (*esp* from prison)/getaway; **faire cavale,** to escape; **être en cavale,** to be on the run.

cavaler [kavale] **I** *vi* **1.** *F* (*a*) to run very fast/to go like the clappers; **cavaler cher,** to run hard (*b*) to run away* **2.** *P* to run after women/to chase skirt **II** *vtr P* **cavaler qn,** to bore*/to pester s.o.; **tu me cavales (sur l'os)!** you're getting on my wick! (*Voir* **ciboulot**) **III** *vpr* **se cavaler** *P* to run away*/to clear off/to make a smart getaway/to make a run for it.

cavalerie [kavalri] *nf P* **1.** loaded dice/crooked dice; **envoyer la cavalerie,** to substitute loaded dice **2. de la grosse cavalerie,** run-of-the-mill assortment/collection (of books, etc); **c'est de la grosse cavalerie,** it's the heavy stuff **3. la cavalerie de Saint-Georges,** English money/British gold (for subsidizing troops, for bribing the enemy, etc) **4.** false cheque, etc. (*Voir* **balancer I 5** (*a*))

cavaleur [kavalœr] *nm P* womanizer*/Don Juan/Casanova/skirt-chaser/ladies' man/wolf.

cavaleuse [kavaløz] *nf P* pushover/easy lay/tramp; **ce n'est qu'une petite cavaleuse,** she'll go after anything in trousers/she'll go to bed with anybody.

cave [kav] **I** *nm P* **1.** outsider (*ie* anyone not belonging to the **milieu**) **2.** (*a*) (*dupe*) fall-guy/mug/sucker (*b*) fool*/idiot/twerp/clot **3.** prostitute's (paying) customer; client of a brothel; punter. (*Voir* **descente 4**) **II** *a P* (*personne*) **1.** (looking) old/the worse for wear/decrepit **2. ce qu'il est cave!** (*dupe*) what a mug/a sucker (he is)!; (*idiot*) what a fool!/what a clot!

cavé [kave] *nm* = **cave I 2.**

caver [kave] *vtr P* to swindle*/to cheat/to diddle; **être cavé/se faire caver,** to be done.

cavette [kavɛt] *nf* **1.** *P* woman* *or* girl* not belonging to the **milieu**; *esp* prostitute* without a pimp* **2.** *F* stupid* girl/dumb cluck.

caviar [kavjar] *nm F* **passer au caviar** =

caviarder.

caviardage [kavjardaʒ] *nm F* (*censure*) censoring; (*passage supprimé*) censored passage (of book, newspaper article, etc).

caviarder [kavjarde] *vtr F* to censor/to blue-pencil (a passage in a book, newspaper, etc).

cavillon, -onne [kavijɔ̃, -ɔn] *n P* fool*/little twerp.

cavouse, cavouze [kavuz] *nf P* cellar.

cavu [kavy] *nm P* buttocks*.

ce (cet), cette, *pl* **ces** [sə (sɛt), sɛt, se *or* se] *unstressed dem a* (*a*) *F* **eh bien, et cette jambe?** well, how's that leg of yours? **et ce café, garçon?** what about that coffee, waiter? **ce cher Thomas!** good old Thomas! **cette question!** what an absurd question!/what a thing to ask! (*b*) *P* **sur ce, salut!** OK fine, see you later! (*c*) *F* **je lui ai écrit une de ces lettres!** I wrote him such a letter! **vous avez de ces expressions!** the expressions you come out with! **j'ai une de ces faims!** I'm starving!/I'm ravenous! **elle a une de ces têtes!** (*elle est fatiguée, malade*) she looks awful! (*elle est laide*) she's as ugly as sin!

cédule [sedyl] *nm P* schedule/timetable.

ceinture [sɛ̃tyr] *nf* **1.** *F* **se mettre/se serrer la ceinture, faire ceinture,** (*se priver*) to tighten one's belt/to go without; (**c'est**) **ceinture, mon vieux!/tu peux te mettre la ceinture, mon vieux!** you've had it, chum!/you can say goodbye to that, mate! **2.** *P* **s'en mettre/s'en donner plein la ceinture,** to eat* heartily/to have a good tuck-in/a good blow-out **3.** *P* (*langage des policiers*) **boucler la ceinture,** to watch out for pickpockets/to keep an eye on pickpockets on the buses **4.** *F* **accrochez/attachez vos ceintures!** get ready!/fasten your seatbelts/hold on! **5.** *F* **humour en dessous de la ceinture,** coarse/crude humour; smutty jokes.

ceinturer [sɛ̃tyre] *vtr P* to arrest*/to nab/to collar (s.o.).

cell′ [sel] *nm*, **cello** [selo] *nm*, **cellulo** [selylo] *nm F* (*abrév* = *celluloïd*) celluloid (*used in photography, film, etc*).

cellotte [selɔt] *nf P* **1.** (prison) cell* **2. faire de la cellotte** = **faire de la cellule** (**cellule**).

cellule [selyl] *nf P* **faire de la cellule,** to go into hiding (from the police)/to go underground.

cencul [sɑ̃ky] *nm Vieilli P* vice-principal (of *lycée*).

cendar [sɑ̃dar] *nm P* ashtray.

cent [sɑ̃] *num a F* 1. je vous le donne en cent, I'll give you a hundred guesses/(I bet) you'll never guess (it) 2. le numéro cent, (*à l'hôtel, etc*) the WC*/the loo. (*Voir* **balle 2**; **coup 12**; **mille 1**)

centrale [sɑ̃tral] *nf F* 1. (= *maison, prison centrale*) = county jail 2. (= *École centrale*) = (university level) State school of engineering.

centre [sɑ̃tr] *nm* 1. *P* name/handle/mon(n)icker 2. *V* female genitals*.

centriot [sɑ̃trijo] *nm P* nickname.

centrouse, centrouze [sɑ̃truz] *nf F* (= *maison, prison centrale*) = county jail.

cerbère [sɛrbɛr] *nm F* (*a*) bad-tempered concierge (*b*) c'est un vrai cerbère, he's a grumpy old sod.

cerceau, *pl* **-eaux** [sɛrso] *nm* 1. *F* avoir le dos en cerceau, to be round-shouldered 2. *F* steering wheel (of car) 3. *P* rib.

cercle [sɛrkl] *nm P* cercle (de barrique), rib.

cercleux [sɛrklø] *F* I *nm* club-man; man about town II *a* clubbish.

cercueil [sɛrkœj] *nm F* cocktail of beer, Picon and grenadine.

cérébral [serebral] *nm F* intellectual/thinker.

cerf [sɛr, sɛrf] *nm* 1. *F* (*a*) athletic type (*b*) good horseman 2. *F* se déguiser en cerf, to run away*/to take to one's heels/to hare off 3. *V* bander comme un cerf, to be horny/randy/ready for it.

cerise [s(ə)riz] *nf* 1. *F* le temps des cerises, happy bygone days 2. *P* bad luck; avoir la cerise, to have (a run of) bad luck/to be down on one's luck; porter/ficher/foutre la cerise à qn, to bring s.o. bad luck/to put a jinx on s.o. 3. *P* head* 4. *P* face*; se taper la cerise, to eat* heartily/to feed one's face 5. *P* se (re)faire la cerise, (*après une maladie*) to pick oneself up/to get back on one's feet 6. *P* ramener sa cerise, (*se donner des airs*) to show off*/to throw one's weight around; (*rouspéter*) to grumble*/to grouse/to bellyache; (*arriver*) to turn up/to put in an appearance 7. *P* ma cerise, me/yours truly.

certals [sɛrtal] *nmpl A P* (= *certificats de licence*) diploma/degree.

certif [sɛrtif] *nm F* (*abrév* = *certificat d'études primaires*) certificate.

césarienne [sezarjɛn] *nf P* faire une césarienne, to steal* a wallet *or* purse, etc, by slitting a pocket *or* bag, etc, with a razor blade, etc.

césarin [sezarɛ̃] *pron m P* he/him(self)/his nibs.

césarine [sezarin] *pron f P* she/her(self).

ceusses [søs] *dem pron m P* (les) ceusses qui, (= *ceux qui*), those who.

cézig [sezig] *pron m P* he/him(self)/his nibs.

cézigos [sezigo] *pl pron m P* they/them(selves).

cézigue [sezig] *pron m P* he/him(self)/his nibs.

chabanais [ʃabanɛ] *nm P* 1. *Vieilli* noise/row/din/racket/uproar 2. *A* brothel*/knocking shop.

chabler [ʃable], **châbler** [ʃable] *P* I *vtr* chabler qn, to attack* s.o./to set about s.o.; to beat s.o. up*/to knock s.o. about II *vi* ça va chabler, there's going to be trouble/a riot/some aggro.

chabraque [ʃabrak] *P* I *a* (*a*) mad*/bonkers (*b*) (*femme*) (*laide*) ugly; (*facile*) loose(-living)/easy; (*distraite*) scatterbrained II *nf* (*a*) ugly woman/fright (*b*) trollop/slut (*c*) scatterbrain.

chafouin, -ine [ʃafwɛ̃, -in] *a & n F* weasel-faced/foxy-looking/sly-looking (person).

chagatte [ʃagat] *nf V* (*javanais de* **chatte**) female genitals*/cunt/pussy.

chagrin [ʃagrɛ̃] *nm P* aller au chagrin, to go to work; (*porter plainte*) to lodge a complaint.

chahut [ʃay] *nm F* 1. (*a*) noise/din/uproar*; faire du chahut/en faire un chahut, to kick up a row (*b*) horse-play/playing about 2. rag/ragging.

chahutage [ʃaytaʒ] *nm F* 1. horseplay/playing about 2. (*a*) ragging (of teacher) (*b*) teasing (of girl) 3. (*a*) booing (of a play, etc) (*b*) (*sports*) barracking.

chahuter [ʃayte] *F* I *vi* 1. to kick up a row/to make a racket 2. to indulge in horseplay/to lark about 3. (*a*) to boo (*b*) to barrack 4. vol chahuté, bumpy flight II *vtr* 1. to knock (things) about/to send (things) flying 2. to bump/to knock into (s.o.) 3. (*a*) cha-huter un prof, to rag a teacher (*b*) to tease (a girl).

chahuteur, -euse [ʃaytœr, -øz] I *a F* rowdy/disorderly/unruly II *n* (*a*) *F* rowdy; hooligan*/yob (*b*) *P* chahuteur de mac-chabées, undertaker's assistant.

chaille [ʃaj] *nf P* tooth.

Chaillot [ʃajo] *Prn F* envoyer qn à Chaillot, to send s.o. packing*/to send s.o. off with a flea in his ear.

chaîne [ʃɛn] *nf F* entre Martin et Sophie, c'est la chaîne, Martin and Sophie are inseparable.

chair [ʃɛr] *nf F* 1. un(e) marchand(e) de chair fraîche, a white-slaver 2. hacher qn menu comme chair à pâté/réduire qn en chair à pâté, faire de qn de la chair à saucisses, to make mincemeat of s.o. (*Voir* **cuir 4**)

chaise [ʃɛz] *nf F* avoir le cul entre deux chaises, to be in an awkward position/to fall between two chairs. (*Voir* **barreau**)

chaland [ʃalɑ̃] *nm Vieilli F* customer/ punter; c'est un drôle de chaland, he's a queer customer/an odd bod.

chaleur [ʃalœr] *nf P* 1. avoir la chaleur, to be afraid*/to be scared stiff; avoir des chaleurs*/to be apprehensive 2. être en chaleur, (*personne*) to be sexually excited*/to have the hots.

chaleureux [ʃalœrø] *a Vieilli P* afraid*/ scared/cowardly/chicken.

chambard [ʃabar] *nm F* 1. disorder*/ shambles; quel chambard! what a mess! 2. row/din/racket; faire du chambard, to kick up a rumpus.

chambardement [ʃabardəmɑ̃] *nm F* upheaval/upset; general reshuffle; le grand chambardement, the revolution.

chambarder [ʃabarde] *F vtr* 1. (*a*) to ransack (a room, etc); tout chambarder, to turn everything upside down (*b*) chambarder les plans de qn, to upset s.o.'s apple cart/to mess up s.o.'s plans 2. to reorganize/to rearrange.

chambardeur, -euse [ʃabardœr, -øz] *n F* 1. hooligan*/yob 2. revolutionary.

chambouler [ʃabule] *vtr F* = **chambarder 1**.

chambrer [ʃabre] *vtr F* to tease*/to make fun of/to poke fun at (s.o.); to make a fool* of (s.o.); chambrer qn à froid, to take the mickey out of s.o. (while keeping a straight face).

chambreur, -euse [ʃabrœr, -øz] *F a & n* être (un) chambreur, to be a tease/to take the mickey.

chameau, pl -eaux [ʃamo] I *nm* 1. *P* (*homme*) beast/brute/sod/*NAm* son of a bitch/ bastard*; (*femme*) bitch/(old) cow; ratbag; la chameau! (*parfois*) the bitch! un vieux chameau, an old so-and-so; un petit chameau, (*enfant*) a little rascal/a little pest 2. *F* il est sobre comme un chameau, he never drinks 3. *P* (*boules*) slide for spotting loaded balls 4. *P* gynaecological (examination) couch II *a P* ce

qu'il/qu'elle est chameau! what a bastard* he/she is!

chamelle [ʃamɛl] *nf P Péj* 1. (*femme*) bitch/(old) cow 2. prostitute*/(old) bag.

champ [ʃɑ̃] *nm F* 1. se sauver à travers champs, to dodge a question/an issue; to change the subject 2. fou à courir les champs, (as) mad as a hatter/as daft as a brush 3. le champ est libre, the coast is clear/it's all clear 4. horse racing; aller au champ, to go to the races/to go racing; faire le champ, to take and bring back the punters; jouer le champ, to play the field/to bet across the board 5. les Champs, the Champs-Élysées (in Paris); (*champs de courses*) racecourses 6. le champ de manœuvre, (fam) the bed 7. champ d'oignons, cemetery*/boneyard. (*Voir* **clamsé(e)** II; **clef 2**; **refroidi**)

champ' [ʃɑ̃p] *nm*, **champe** [ʃɑ̃p] *nm*, **champerlot** [ʃɑ̃pɛrlo] *nm P* champagne*/ champers/bubbly.

champignard [ʃɑ̃piɲar] *nm P* mushroom.

champignon [ʃɑ̃piɲɔ̃] *nm F* 1. *Aut* accelerator (pedal); appuyer sur/écraser le champignon, to step on the gas/to step on it/to put one's foot down (on the floor) 2. le champignon, dry rot.

champion [ʃɑ̃pjɔ̃] *a inv F* excellent*/ champion.

chançard, -arde [ʃɑ̃sar, -ard] *F* I *a* lucky/ jammy II *n* lucky person/lucky blighter; quel chançard! lucky devil!

chance [ʃɑ̃s] *nf F* 1. (ça c'est) pas de chance! that's hard luck!/tough luck! (il) y a des chances! most likely!/more likely than not! joue ta chance! have a go! 2. la faute à pas de chance, nobody's fault.

chancetiquer [ʃɑ̃stike] *P* I *vi* to totter/ wobble/stagger II *vtr* (*bouleverser*) to upset/ overturn; to turn upside down.

chancre [ʃɑ̃kr] *nm F* glutton; manger/ bouffer comme un chancre, to eat*/to stuff oneself like a pig.

chancrer [ʃɑ̃kre] *vi F* to eat*/to stuff oneself like a pig.

chandelier [ʃɑ̃dəlje] *nm* 1. *F* être sur le chandelier, to be in a prominent position; mettre qn sur le chandelier, to put s.o. in the limelight 2. *P* nose*.

chandelle [ʃɑ̃dɛl] *nf* 1. *F* souffler sa/la chandelle, to die*/to snuff it 2. *A F* allons, la chandelle brûle, come on, there's no time to lose 3. *F* je vous dois une fière chandelle, I owe you more than I can repay; you've saved my life 4. *F* dandelion clock 5. *P* (trickle of) snot/candle; **une chandelle lui pend au nez,** his nose is running/he's got a candle 6. *P* bottle 7. *P* single-column article (in newspaper) 8. *P Aut* spark plug 9. *F (tennis)* lob; **faire des chandelles,** to lob 10. *F* **en voir trente-six chandelles,** to see stars *(after a blow on the head, etc)* 11. *F* **tenir la chandelle,** *(aider des amoureux)* to act as a go-between or decoy in a love affair; to act as look-out in a love affair; *(être de trop)* to play gooseberry; *NAm* to feel like a fifth wheel; *(mari ou épouse)* to turn a blind eye (to the other's extramarital activities) 12. *P* prostitute who works from a fixed patch.

changer [ʃãʒe] *vi* 1. *P* **change pas de main (je sens que ça vient),** go on!/don't stop! 2. *P* **changer d'eau son canari,** to urinate*/to see a man about a dog 3. *F* **plus ça change et plus c'est pareil/la même chose,** the more it changes, the more it stays the same; things never change; it's more of the same. *(Voir* **disque 1; olive 2; poisson 5)**

chanson [ʃãsɔ̃] *nf F* 1. **chansons (que tout cela)!** nonsense!/rubbish! 2. **c'est toujours la même chanson,** it's always the same old story; **on connaît la chanson!** I've/we've heard that one before!/I've/we've heard it all before. *(Voir* **air III 3)**

chansonnette [ʃãsɔnɛt] *nf P* 1. *(a)* (interrogatoire à la) **chansonnette,** harsh questioning (by police, etc)/(the) third degree/grilling *(b)* **avoir qn à la chansonnette/le faire à la chansonnette/ pousser sa chansonnette,** to lead s.o. up the garden path/to have s.o. on 2. blackmail.

chanstique [ʃãstik] *nm P* 1. fraudulent exchange/switch 2. unpleasant circumstances/situation; trouble/aggro 3. *(changement)* change.

chanstiquer [ʃãstike] **I** *vtr & i P* 1. to change/transform; to turn upside down 2. to substitute/to switch imitation jewellery for real/false money for good, etc; to pull a switch 3. to take a turn for the worse 4. *(brocante)* to restore carelessly/quickly **II** *vpr* **se chanstiquer** *P* **se chanstiquer en ...,** to turn/to change into ....

chanter [ʃãte] **I** *vtr F* **qu'est-ce que vous me chantez là?** what's this fairy tale you're telling me?/what are you rabbiting on about? **II** *vi* 1. *F* **si ça vous chante,** if you feel like it/if you fancy it; **je le ferai si ça me chante,** I'll do it if it suits me 2. *F* **c'est comme si je**

chantais, I'm just wasting my breath/I might as well be talking to myself 3. *F* **faire chanter qn** to blackmail s.o.; **faire chanter qn sur un autre ton,** to make s.o. change his tune 4. *F* **chanter plus haut,** to make a better offer/to go a bit higher/to up the bidding 5. *Vieilli P* to turn informer*/to squeal/to grass/to shop 6. to protest (loudly). *(Voir* **casserole 10)**

chanterelle [ʃãtrɛl] *nf F* **appuyer sur la chanterelle,** to hammer a point home/to rub it in.

chanvre [ʃãvr] *nm F (drogues)* **chanvre (indien),** hashish*/(Indian) hemp/hash.

chanvré [ʃãvre] *a F (drogues)* high on hash(ish)*/stoned.

chapardage [ʃapardaʒ] *nm P* stealing/ pilfering/pinching; **menus chapardages,** petty thefts/pilfering.

chaparder [ʃaparde] *vtr P* to steal*/to pilfer/to pinch/to have light fingers.

chapardeur, -euse [ʃapardœr, -øz] *P* **I** *a* thieving/pilfering/pinching **II** *n* petty thief*/ pilferer.

chapeau, *pl* **-eaux** [ʃapo] *nm* 1. *F* **chapeau!** *(a)* well done!/bravo!/congrats!/ hats off! *(surt TV)* **un coup de chapeau à ...!** hats off to ...! *(b) Iron* great!/blinking marvellous! 2. *A P* **chapeau de paille,** transportation with hard labour 3. *P* **perdre son chapeau de paille,** *(jeune homme)* to lose his virginity 4. *P* **porter le chapeau,** *(assumer une responsabilité)* to take on (a) responsibility; to carry the can; *(avoir mauvaise réputation)* to have a bad reputation 5. *P* **travailler du chapeau,** to be mad*/off one's rocker 6. *P* **(ne) t'occupe pas/t'occupes du chapeau de la gamine!** mind your own business! 7. *F (a) Aut* **prendre un virage sur les chapeaux de roue(s),** to screech round a bend (at full speed) *(b)* **démarrer/partir sur les chapeaux de roues,** to plunge straight into (an argument/enterprise, etc); to go for it 8. *F* **en baver des ronds de chapeau,** to be under pressure 9. *P* **petit chapeau,** condom*/French letter/rubber/johnnie.

chapeauter [ʃapote] *vtr F* 1. to be in charge of/to be the head of (a department, etc) 2. to write an introductory paragraph to (an article, etc) 3. **chapeauter qn,** to give s.o. a (helping) hand/to put a word in for s.o.

chapelet [ʃaplɛ] *nm* 1. *F* **défiler/dévider son chapelet,** to speak one's mind/to have one's say 2. *F* **un chapelet d'injures,** a string of insults/a stream of abuse 3. *P* handcuffs*/

cuffs.

Chapelouze [ʃapluz] *Prn P* la Chapelouze, the La Chapelle district (in Paris).

chapiteau, *pl* **-eaux** [ʃapito] *nm P* head*.

chaque [ʃak] *pron F* (= *chacun*) c'est quinze francs chaque, they cost fifteen francs each.

char [ʃar] *nm P* = **charre**; arrête ton char (Ben Hur) = arrête ton charre (**charre 1**).

charabia [ʃarabja] *nm F* 1. Auvergnat dialect 2. gibberish/gobbledygook.

charançons [ʃarɑ̃sɔ̃] *nmpl P* gonococci (*bacteria causing gonorrhoea*).

charbon [ʃarbɔ̃] *nm P* 1. aller au charbon, (*travail de façade*) to have a job as a front for one's normal shady activities; (*travail régulier*) to have a trade/a profession/an occupation; (*travail pénible*) to do unpleasant *or* hard work; to take on a difficult task 2. envoyer qn au charbon, to mislead s.o./to lead s.o. up the garden path. (*Voir* **sac 17**)

charcutage [ʃarkytaʒ] *nm P* 1. bungled surgical operation/cock-up/butchery 2. charcutage électoral, gerrymandering.

charcuter [ʃarkyte] *vtr P* charcuter un malade, to operate clumsily on a patient/to hack a patient about/to butcher a patient.

charcutier [ʃarkytje] *nm P Péj* surgeon/butcher.

Charenton [ʃarɑ̃tɔ̃] *Prn F* c'est un pensionnaire de Charenton/il faut l'envoyer à Charenton, he's mad*/he ought to be locked up/they ought to put him in the loony bin; un échappé de Charenton, a madman/a loony/a nutter; on se croirait à Charenton, it's absolute bedlam/an absolute madhouse (*from Charenton, a town near Paris with a mental hospital*).

charge [ʃarʒ] *nf* 1. F il en a sa charge, (*il en a assez*) he's had as much as he can take; (*il est gros*) he's very fat 2. F (*a*) faire une charge à qn, to play a (nasty) trick on s.o. (*b*) faire la charge de qn, to take s.o. off/to take the mickey (out of s.o.) 3. F il est à charge, vraiment! he's a real pain (in the neck)! 4. P (*a*) (*drogues*) (any) stimulant *or* drug; dope/junk; alcohol*/booze; se mettre à la charge, to fill oneself up with drugs*; avoir sa charge, to be drunk* *or* drugged*/charged (up); prendre une charge, to get drunk*/stewed (*b*) (*sports*) (*dopage*) doping.

chargé [ʃarʒe] *a P* être chargé (*a*) to be armed/to pack a gun (*b*) to be drunk*/bombed (out)/smashed (*c*) to be high on drugs/stoned/bombed (out) (*d*) to be rich*/loaded.

se charger [səʃarʒe] *vpr P* 1. to arm oneself (with gun) 2. to get drunk*/plastered 3. to take a drug/to get stoned; (*sports*) to take drugs/to dope oneself.

charibotage [ʃaribɔtaʒ] *nm P* adverse criticism/flak.

chariboter [ʃaribɔte] *vi P* 1. to exaggerate*/to lay it on thick/to go a bit far 2. to work without method/to muddle on 3. to make a mess/a muddle.

Charlemagne [ʃarləmaɲ] *Prnm F* faire Charlemagne, to stop gambling when one is winning/to quit when the going's good (*without allowing one's opponent to play a return game*).

charlemagner [ʃarləmaɲe] *vi F* = faire Charlemagne (**Charlemagne**).

Charles [ʃarl] *Prnm F* tu parles, Charles! now you're talking!

Charles-le-Chauve [ʃarlləʃov] *nm V* penis*/John Thomas; faire sauter la cervelle à/de Charles-le-Chauve, to masturbate*/to flog the bishop. (*Voir* **shampooing 2**)

Charlot [ʃarlo] *Prnm* 1. *A P* public executioner; la boutique de Charlot/la bascule à Charlot, the guillotine 2. *F* (*cinéma*) Charlie Chaplin 3. *F* clown; quel charlot! what a clown! 4. *P* worthless individual/poor bugger; faire le charlot, to try to be clever 5. *V* amuser Charlot/s'amuser comme Charlot, (*homme*) to masturbate*/to play with oneself.

charlotte [ʃarlɔt] *nf P* wire cutters (*used by burglars*).

charme [ʃarm] *nm F* 1. se porter comme un charme, to be in the best of health/to be as fit as a fiddle 2. faire du charme, to turn on the charm 3. chanteur de charme, crooner.

charmeuses [ʃarmøz] *nfpl P* moustache*/tickler.

charmingue [ʃarmɛ̃g], **charmouille** [ʃarmuj] *a P* charming.

charnelle [ʃarnɛl] *nf P Péj* girl* (regarded as a sex object)/bit of fluff.

charnière [ʃarnjɛr] *nf F* nom à charnière, double-barrelled name; name containing the nobiliary particle *de*.

charognard [ʃarɔɲar] *nm P* rotter*/louse/skunk/sod.

charogne [ʃarɔɲ] *nf P* bastard*/sod.

charre [ʃar] *nm P* 1. exaggeration; bluff; sans charre? no kidding?/you're not having me on? c'est pas du charre! I'm not kidding! arrête ton charre! come off it!/pull the other one! 2. mocking; lie; méchant charre, dirty trick; **il te raconte des charres**, he's telling you a pack of lies **3. faire du charre (à une femme)**, to flirt (with a woman)/to chat up (a woman) **4. faire des charres à son mari/sa femme**, to be unfaithful to one's husband/one's wife; to two-time one's husband/wife.

charrette [ʃarɛt] *nf* **1.** *P* mass redundancy **2.** *F* car*/crate **3. être/se mettre en charrette**, to be late; **être/faire charrette**, to work hard*/ to finish an urgent piece of work **4. des charrettes de ...**, masses of .../loads of ...; **des chaises comme ça, on en voit des charrettes!** I've seen masses of chairs like these!

charriage [ʃarjaʒ] *nm P* **1.** con(fidence) trick **2.** leg-pulling; **passer qn au charriage**, to pull s.o.'s leg **3.** exaggeration/line-shooting **4.** *Vieilli* brutal attack; **charriage à la mécanique**, throttling/garotting (*in order to rob s.o.*).

charrier [ʃarje] **I** *vtr P* to poke fun at s.o./to take s.o. for a ride/to kid s.o.; **se faire charrier**, to have one's leg pulled **II** *vi* **1.** to joke; **sans charrier!** no kidding!/joking apart!/pull the other one! **2.** to exaggerate*/to overstep the mark/to lay it on a bit thick; **faut pas charrier!** that's going a bit far!/that's too much! (*Voir* **bégonia 1**)

charrieur, -euse [ʃarjœr, -øz] *n P* joker/ leg-puller; **c'est un charrieur**, he's always having people on; he's a bit of a joker.

charron [ʃarɔ̃] *nm P* **aller/crier/gueuler au charron**, (*ameuter*) to cause a disturbance/to raise Cain/to raise hell/to scream blue murder; (*protester*) to protest.

charronner [ʃarɔne] *vi P* = **aller au charron** (**charron**).

chasse [ʃas] **I** *nf* **1.** *F* chasse; **chasse au mari**, husband hunting; **chasse aux soldes**, bargain hunting **2.** *P* peloton de chasse, punishment squad/jankers brigade **3.** *P* être en chasse, to (try to) pick up/to get off with (women) **II** *nm F* (*abrév* = *chasse-neige*) snowplough.

châsse [ʃas] *nm P* **1.** eye*; **cligner du châsse vers qn**, to wink at s.o.; **donner un coup de châsse(s) à qn**, to look at* s.o.; to give s.o. the glad eye; **avoir les châsses en portefeuille**, to have bags under one's eyes; to have swollen eyes; **pisser des châsses**, to cry* **2. au châsse**, free/for nothing/on the house. (*Voir* **godille** (*a*))

chasse-coquin [ʃaskɔkɛ̃] *nm P* verger.

chasselas [ʃasla] *nm P* **avoir un coup de chasselas**, to be drunk*/blotto.

chasser [ʃase] *vi F* (*a*) to flirt (*b*) **elle chasse au mari**, she's on the look-out/on the hunt for a husband (*c*) **elle chasse le mâle**, she's on the prowl for a man. (*Voir* **brouillard 2** (*b*))

châsser [ʃase] *vtr P* to look* at/to clock.

chasseur [ʃasœr] *nm P* **chasseur de pigeons**, person who recruits clients for pornographic cinemas and theatres.

châssis [ʃasi] *nm* **1.** *F* **c'est un beau châssis**, she's got a great figure/body; **vise le châssis!** get a load of that!/*NAm* check the chick out! **2.** *pl P* eyes* *or* eyelids; **fermer les châssis**, to go to sleep*.

chat [ʃa] *nm* **1.** *P* (*a*) clerk of the court (*b*) examining magistrate (*c*) **chat fourré**, judge **2.** *V* female genitals*/pussy. (*Voir* **chatte 2**) **3.** *V* **laisser le chat aller au fromage**, (*en parlant d'une femme*) to have sex*/to have a screw **4.** *F* **avoir un chat dans la gorge**, to have a frog in one's throat **5.** *F* **avoir d'autres chats à fouetter**, to have other fish to fry **6.** *F* **il n'y a pas de quoi fouetter un chat**, it's nothing to make a fuss/a song and dance about **7.** *F* **c'est pas fait pour les chats**, it's not there as an ornament, it's meant to be used. (*Voir* **chien II 3**) **8.** *F* **écriture de chat**, illegible scrawl **9.** *F* (*terme d'affection*) **mon (petit) chat**, my (little) darling*/my (little) pet/my (little) love. (*Voir* **chatte 1**) **10.** *F* (non,) **c'est le chat!** it must have been the cat!/it was Mr Nobody I suppose! **11.** *F* (il n'y a) **pas un chat**, not a (living) soul **12.** *F* **être comme chat sur braise**, to be like a cat on hot bricks/ on a hot tin roof. (*Voir* **bouillie** (*a*))

châtaigne [ʃatɛɲ] *nf P* **1.** blow*/punch/ clout; **recevoir/ramasser une châtaigne**, to get beaten up **2.** (*a*) brawl/punch-up/scrap/ fisticuffs; **aller à la châtaigne**, to have a brawl/a scrap (*b*) (*sports*) **jouer la châtaigne**, to play dirty/rough **3.** electric discharge; **j'ai pris une châtaigne**, I got an electric shock.

châtaigner [ʃatɛɲe] *P* **I** *vtr* to hit/to punch/ to sock (s.o.) **II** *vi & pr* (**se**) **châtaigner** to exchange blows/to trade punches.

château, pl -eaux [ʃato] *nm* **1.** *P* hospital **2.** *P* (*brocante*) good antique/good piece **3.** *F* **Château-Lapompe**, (drinking) water*/Adam's ale.

chatouille [ʃatuj] *nf F* **faire des chatouilles à qn**, to tickle s.o.; **craindre les chatouilles**, to be ticklish.

chatouiller [ʃatuje] **I** *vtr* **1.** *F* **chatouiller les côtes à qn**, to give s.o. a thrashing **2.** *P*

chatouiller une serrure, to pick a lock **II** *vi F Aut* to accelerate in fits and starts. (*Voir* **dame** 5)

châtré [ʃɑtre] *a P* weak/spineless.

chatte [ʃat] *nf* 1. *F* (petite) chatte, darling*/ pet 2. *V* female genitals*/pussy. (*Voir* **bouffer** 4; **chat** 2)

chaud [ʃo] **I** *a* 1. *F* tenir les pieds chauds à qn, to keep s.o. on the go 2. *F* avoir la main chaude, to have a run of luck (at gambling) 3. *F* enthusiastic/game; il n'est pas chaud pour le projet, he's not keen on the project 4. *F* cela ne lui fait ni chaud ni froid, it's all the same to him/he doesn't care about it one way or the other 5. *F* ça va vous coûter chaud, (*ça sera cher*) it'll cost you/you'll have to pay through the nose for it; (*vous en souffrirez*) you'll pay/suffer for it 6. *F* il fera chaud! nonsense!*/never! il fera chaud quand elle commencera à bosser! that'll be the day when she starts working! 7. *F* (*cri des garcons de café/de restaurant*) chaud (devant)! excuse me!/'scuse me!/mind your backs! 8. *F* difficult/tricky/dodgy/dicey; risky; on y va pas, c'est chaud, we're not going there, it's too risky/it's hot 9. *P* (*personne*) wary/on the lookout 10. *P* unsettled/troubled (times) 11. *P* lustful/hot; être chaud de la pince/de la pointe, to be highly sexed/to be hot stuff/to be a randy devil. (*Voir* **lapin** 5) **II** *nm F* 1. avoir les pieds au chaud, to have a cushy job 2. je crève de chaud, I'm boiling (hot) 3. il a eu chaud (aux fesses), (*peur*) he was scared stiff/he got a nasty fright; (*échappé belle*) he had a narrow escape/a close shave 4. *V* la mettre au chaud, (*du point de vue de l'homme*) to have sex* (with a woman)/to have it off (with a woman).

chaud-chaud [ʃoʃo] *a inv* ne pas être chaud-chaud, = **chaud I** 3.

chaude-lance [ʃodlɑ̃s] *nf*, **chaude- pince** [ʃodpɛ̃s] *nf*, **chaude-pisse** [ʃodpis] *nf P* VD*/clap; il a la chaude-pisse, he's got the clap; elle m'a donné la chaude- pisse, she gave me a dose (of the clap).

chaudron [ʃodrɔ̃] *nm* 1. *F* worn-out musical instrument, *esp* tinny old piano 2. *P* écurer son chaudron, to confess*/to come clean.

chauffage [ʃofaʒ] *nm F* cramming (for an exam).

chauffard [ʃofar] *nm F* (*mauvais con- ducteur*) road-hog; speed merchant; maniac; (*qui provoque un accident et ne s'arrête pas*) hit-and-run driver.

chauffer [ʃofe] **I**. *vtr* 1. *F* chauffer qn (en vue d'un examen), to cram s.o. for an exam; chauffer un examen, to swot for an exam 2. *F* il faut chauffer l'affaire, we must strike while the iron is hot 3. *F* chauffer un livre/un écrivain, to promote/to plug a book/a writer 4. *F* chauffer qn (à blanc), (*exciter*) to get s.o. worked up; (*provoquer*) to rouse/to incite s.o. (*Voir* **blanc II** 2); chauffer une nana, to get a woman sexually excited*/to get a woman going; (*théâtre*) chauffer une scène, to ginger up a scene; chauffer une salle/l'auditoire, to warm the place up/to get the audience going 5. *P* to steal*/to pinch; on m'a chauffé mon portefeuille, someone's pinched my wallet/ *NAm* my pocketbook 6. *P* to arrest*/to nick; se faire chauffer, to get nicked 7. *P* to catch (s.o.) red-handed 8. *P* les chauffer à qn, to bore* s.o. to death/to give s.o. a pain in the neck **II** *vi* 1. *F* ce n'est pas pour vous que le four chauffe, it's not for you 2. *P* ça chauffe! things are hotting up!/things are getting a bit heated! ça va chauffer! there's going to be trouble!/there's trouble brewing!/sparks are going to fly! 3. *F* (*jazz*) ça chauffe, it's getting hot/it's beginning to swing. (*Voir* **bain** 5)

chausser [ʃose] *vtr F* ça me chausse (bien), that suits me fine/that suits me down to the ground.

chaussette [ʃosɛt] *nf P* 1. *Aut* tyre 2. chaussettes à clous, (*grosses chaussures*) hobnailed boots; (*policiers*) policemen* 3. mettre les chaussettes à la fenêtre, (*femme*) not to have an orgasm*/not to come. (*Voir* **jus** 2)

chausson [ʃosɔ̃] *nm P* prostitute*.

chaussure [ʃosyr] *nf F* 1. trouver chaussure à son pied, (*ce qui convient*) to find exactly what one is looking for; (*qn à marier*) to find a husband*/a wife*; (*son égal*) to meet one's match/one's equal 2. avoir un pied dans deux chaussures, to have two strings to one's bow 3. une chaussure à tout pied, something quite ordinary/commonplace.

chauve [ʃov] *nm V* chauve à col roulé, penis*/John Thomas.

chbeb¹ [ʃbɛb] *a Vieilli P* great/super. (*Voir* **schbeb¹**)

chbeb², chebeb [ʃ(ə)bɛb] *nm P* good- looking young homosexual. (*Voir* **schbeb²**)

chébran [ʃebrɑ̃] *a & n P* (*verlan de* **branché**) = **branché**.

chef [ʃɛf] *nm F* (*patron*) chief/boss/guvnor; d'acc chef! OK, chief/guv! un vrai chef, (*as*) a champion/an ace/the greatest; **comme un chef**, perfectly.

chef-d'œuvre [ʃɛdœvr] *nm Péj* chef-d'œuvre en péril, ugly person/fright; *esp* ugly old woman/old bat; **c'est un chef-d'œuvre en péril**, (s)he's no oil painting/(s)he looks like the back of a bus.

chelem [ʃlɛm] *nm P* **être grand chelem**, to be penniless*/flat broke.

chemin [ʃ(ə)mɛ̃] *nm F* 1. **chemin des écoliers**, longest way round 2. **il n'y va pas par quatre/par trente-six chemins**, he goes straight to the point/he doesn't beat about the bush; **on vous cherche par les quatre chemins**, they're looking for you all over the place 3. **être toujours sur les chemins/par voie et par chemin**, to be always on the go 4. **être en chemin de famille**, to be pregnant*/in the family way.

cheminée [ʃ(ə)mine] *nf P* 1. large glass of red wine; = pint *or* half-pint of beer 2. **grande cheminée**, tall girl.

chemise [ʃ(ə)miz] *nf* 1. *F* **je m'en moque/m'en fiche comme de ma première chemise**, I couldn't care less*/I don't give two hoots (about it) 2. *P* **compter ses chemises**, to be (sea)sick. (*Voir* **cul 10; mouiller II 2**)

chêne [ʃɛn] *nm A P* man; **faire suer un chêne**, to kill* a man. (*Voir* **sueur**)

chenillon [ʃ(ə)nijɔ̃] *nm P* ugly girl*/woman*; slut.

chenu [ʃ(ə)ny] *a & nm Vieilli P* excellent*; **c'est du chenu**, that's first-rate.

chéquard [ʃekar] *nm F (Péj surt Pol)* bribed backer (of an undertaking); influence peddler.

chèque [ʃɛk] *nm F* **chèque en bois**, rubber cheque.

chèqueton [ʃɛktɔ̃] *nm P* cheque.

cher, *f* **chère** [ʃɛr] *a & adv* 1. *F* **je l'ai eu pour pas cher**, I got it (on the) cheap 2. *P* **je ne vaux pas cher**, I feel unwell*/I don't feel up to much 3. *F* **ne pas donner cher de (la peau de) qn**, not to bet much on s.o.'s chances; **je ne donnerais pas cher de sa peau**, I wouldn't bet much on his chances/on him 4. *F* **ne pas valoir cher**, (*personne*) to be a bastard*; **il ne vaut pas cher, ce mec**, that guy's a worthless bastard/a no-gooder. (*Voir* **cavaler I 1** (*a*))

chercher [ʃɛrʃe] *vtr* 1. *F* to blame (s.o.)/to pick on (s.o.); **tu l'as cherché!** you asked for it! **tu me cherches, et tu vas me trouver!** you're asking for it, and you'll get it if you're not careful! **il me cherche**, he's trying to pick

a quarrel with me 2. *P* **aller en/les chercher**, to look for a lucrative deal/to look for a way to make a fast buck 3. *P* **où vas-tu chercher ça?/qu'est-ce que tu vas chercher?** where did you get that idea from?/where did you dig that one up?/what are you getting at? 4. *F* **ça va chercher dans les trois mille francs**, that costs/that's worth/that'll fetch about three thousand francs; **elle va sûrement chercher dans les quarante berges**, she must be (at least) forty if she's a day 5. *F* **ça va chercher loin**, that can have serious consequences; **ça ne va pas chercher loin**, it won't come to much. (*Voir* **bête 2; crosse 1** (*a*); **pou 5**)

chérer [ʃere] *vi P* = **cherrer**.

chéro(t) [ʃero] *a F* rather dear/too dear/pric(e)y; **mille balles, c'est chéro(t)**, a thousand francs, that's a bit steep.

cherrer [ʃere] *P* **I** *vi* to exaggerate*/to shoot a line/to talk big; **ne cherre pas!** come off it! **II** *vtr* to attack violently. (*Voir* **bégonia 1**)

chetard [ʃ(ə)tar] *nm P (rare)* = **chtar 1**.

chetron [ʃətrɔ̃] *nf P (verlan de* **tronche***)* head*/nut.

cheval, *pl* **-aux** [ʃəval, ʃfal, -o] *nm* 1. *F* **grand cheval**, woman* who is too tall; **cette femme, c'est un vrai cheval**, what a horsy-looking woman she is 2. *F* **mémoire de cheval**, excellent memory; **fièvre de cheval**, raging fever; **remède de cheval**, drastic remedy/kill or cure remedy 3. *F* **c'est son cheval de bataille**, he flogs this subject to death; it's his hobby horse/his stock answer 4. *F* **c'est pas le mauvais cheval**, he's not a bad (old) sort 5. *F* **c'est un cheval à l'ouvrage/de labour/pour le travail**, he works like a Trojan 6. *F* **ça ne se trouve pas sous le pas d'un cheval**, it's not easily come by; it doesn't grow on trees 7. *P* **cheval de retour**, (*récidiviste*) old lag 8. *P* **becqueter/dîner/manger avec les chevaux de bois**, to go without food/to go dinnerless 9. *P* (*drogues*) heroin*/horse 10. *F* (*a*) **être à cheval sur qch**, to be insistent about sth/to be a stickler for sth (*b*) **monter sur ses grands chevaux**, to get on one's high horse 11. *F* **faire du cheval sur un tonneau**, to be bow-legged/to have bandy legs 12. *P* **à un cheval près**, as near as dammit 13. **j'en parlerai à mon cheval**, (*réponse donnée quand on ne veut pas faire qch*) later, later; I'll see about it later. (*Voir* **boniment 1; torchon 8**)

chevalier [ʃəvalje] *nm* 1. *F* **chevalier d'industrie**, swindler*/crook 2. *F* **les chevaliers de la gaule**, the knights of the rod/

the angling fraternity 3. *P* chevalier de la guirlande, convict 4. *P* chevalier de la lune, burglar 5. *P* chevalier de la rosette/du prépuce-cul, homosexual* 6. *P* chevalier de la piquouse, morphine addict*/junkie.

chevalière [ʃəvaljɛr, ʃfal-] *nf P* anus*/ring.

cheveu, *pl* **-eux** [ʃ(ə)vø] *nm* 1. *P* avoir mal aux cheveux, to have a hangover/to feel a bit fragile 2. *F* il y a un cheveu, there's a snag/a hitch (somewhere); there's a fly in the ointment 3. *P* avoir un cheveu sur la langue, to (have a) lisp 4. *F* se faire des cheveux (blancs), to worry oneself sick/to go grey with worry 5. *F* se prendre aux cheveux, to come to blows/to have a set-to 6. *F* argument tiré par les cheveux, far-fetched argument 7. *F* venir comme un cheveu/comme des cheveux sur la soupe, to be most inappropriate/out of place; to be quite uncalled-for; arriver comme un cheveu sur la soupe, to arrive at an awkward moment/to turn up like a bad penny 8. *F* couper les cheveux en quatre, to split hairs 9. *F* ne tenir qu'à un cheveu, to depend on very little/to hang by a thread 10. *F* à un cheveu, as near as dammit.

cheville [ʃ(ə)vij] *nf F* 1. se donner des coups de pied dans les chevilles, to blow one's own trumpet 2. ça va les chevilles? (*se dit à qn qui se vante*) you're getting too big for your boots!/who the hell do you think you are! 3. il ne vous arrive/monte/vient pas à la cheville, he's not a patch on you/he's not in the same league as you 3. complicity; être/se mettre en cheville avec qn, to be in collusion/in cahoots/in league with s.o. 4. vivre en cheville avec qn, to cohabit/to shack up with s.o.

se cheviller [səʃ(ə)vije] *vpr F* se cheviller avec qn = être/se mettre en cheville avec qn (**cheville 3**).

chevilleur, -euse [ʃ(ə)vijœr, -øz] *n P* go-between; stooge/decoy.

chèvre [ʃɛvr] *nf P* 1. (*a*) *Péj* girl* or woman* (*b*) girl or woman of easy virtue; pushover/easy lay 2. devenir chèvre, to be exasperated/enraged; to go mad with rage.

chevreuil [ʃəvrœj] *nm P Péj* informer*/grass/squealer.

chez [ʃe] *prep P* 1. non, mais chez qui? no damn fear!/not bloody likely*!/not if I know (anything about) it!/you must be joking! 2. *F* c'est bien de chez nous! that's typically French.

chiadé [ʃjade] *a P* carefully made/neat/smart.

chiader [ʃjade] *P* I *vi* to work hard*/to swot; j'ai chiadé en latin, I did well in Latin II *vtr* 1. j'ai chiadé mon thème, I worked hard* on/I made a good job of my prose 2. to do (a job) carefully/with care.

chiadeur, -euse [ʃjadœr, -øz] *n P* hard worker; swot.

chialer [ʃjale] *vi F* 1. to cry*; to snivel; se mettre à chialer, to turn on the waterworks 2. to complain/to moan.

chiale-toujours [ʃjaltuʒur] *nm*, **chialeur, -euse** [ʃjalœr, -øz] *n F* 1. cry-baby; sniveller 2. moaner/grizzler.

chiant [ʃjɑ̃] *a V* irritating/sickening/bloody annoying; il est chiant, ce type! that bloke/that guy is a bloody nuisance!/a real pain (in the arse/*NAm* ass)!

chiard [ʃjar] *nm P Péj* (small) child*/kid/brat.

chiasse [ʃjas] *nf V* 1. avoir la chiasse, to have diarrhoea*/the runs; (*peur*) to be afraid*/to have the willies/to be shit-scared; ça me fout la chiasse, it gives me the willies 2. quelle chiasse! what a bloody/sodding nuisance! what a bloody drag!

chiasseux, -euse [ʃjasø, -øz] *V* I *a* 1. dirty/filthy/cruddy 2. cowardly/yellow (-bellied) II *n* coward*/yellow-belly.

chiatique [ʃjatik] *a V* irritating/bloody annoying; qu'est-ce qu'elle est chiatique celle-là! she's a real pain in the arse/*NAm* ass!

chibi(s) [ʃibi] *nm P* faire chibi(s), to escape/to do a bunk.

chibre [ʃibr] *nm V* penis*; un chibre mol, a limp prick.

chibrer [ʃibre] *vtr V* (*peu usuel*) to have sex* with (s.o.).

chic [ʃik] I *a F* c'est un chic type, he's a nice guy/a great bloke II *excl F* chic (alors)! fine!/great!/neat! III *adv F* faire qch de chic, to sham/to bluff.

chicandier, -ière [ʃikɑ̃dje, -jɛr] *P* I *a* quarrelsome II *n* quarrelsome person/awkward customer.

chicaya [ʃikaja] *nf P* quarrel*/argy-bargy.

chicha [ʃiʃa] *nm P* (*drogues*) (*verlan de haschisch*) hashish*.

chiche [ʃiʃ] I *a F* t'es pas chiche de le faire! you haven't got the guts to do it! II *excl F* 1. chiche! you just try it!/I dare you! 2. chiche (que tu ne le feras pas)! (I) bet you can't!/(I) bet you don't! chiche (que je le fais)! (I) bet you I can!/(I) bet you I will!

chichi [ʃiʃi] *nm* F fuss/to-do/carry-on; **en voilà du chichi!** what a fuss!/what a carry-on! **faire des chichis,** (*compliquer les choses*) to make/to kick up a fuss; (*faire l'important*) to put on airs; **des gens à chichis,** overpolite *or* gushing people; **un type à chichis,** a prig/a poseur; **toutes sortes de chichis,** all kinds of complications/of snags.

chichite [ʃiʃit] *nf* P vague illness; imaginary illness.

chichiteur, -euse [ʃiʃitœr, -øz], **chichiteux, -euse** [ʃiʃitø, -øz] *a & n* F affected/snobbish; prissy/priggish; fussy; **c'est une femme chichiteuse,** she's a fusspot.

chicor [ʃikɔr] *a* P drunk*/blotto.

chicore¹ [ʃikɔr] *nf* P fight*/punch-up.

chicore² [ʃikɔr] *a* P = **chicor.**

chicorée [ʃikɔre] *nf* P 1. reprimand*/slating/telling-off 2. **être chicorée,** to be drunk*/blotto 3. **défriser la chicorée,** to flirt extensively with a woman; to (try to) get off with a woman.

chicorer [ʃikɔre] P I *vtr* to hit/sock (s.o.) II *vpr* **se chicorer** (*a*) to quarrel*/to row (*b*) to fight/to have a punch-up.

chicos [ʃikos] *a* P elegant/smart.

chié [ʃje] *a* P 1. **c'est chié!** (*bien, parfait*) it's bloody good!/it's fucking amazing! (*mauvais, horrible*) it's bloody awful!/it stinks! 2. **elle est chiée de dire ça,** she's got a nerve, saying that/she's really going OTT.

chie-dans-l'eau [ʃidãlo] *nm inv* V sailor/tarry arse.

chiée [ʃje] *nf* V 1. loads/masses; **une chiée de ...,** a great quantity* of .../lots of .../oodles of .../lashings of .../bags of .../loads of .../stacks of ...; **y en pas des chiées,** they don't grow on trees 2. eleven; **j'en ai une chiée,** I've got eleven.

chien [ʃjɛ̃], *f* **chienne** [ʃjɛn] I *a* 1. F **être chien** (**avec qn**), to be mean*/stingy/tight-fisted (with s.o.); **être chien comme tout,** to be as mean as they come/as they make 'em 2. F **être chien avec qn,** to be rotten to s.o./to be hard on s.o./to give s.o. a rough time II *n* 1. F **il n'attache pas ses chiens avec des saucisses,** he's a skinflint/he's as mean as they come 2. F *Journ* **faire les chiens écrasés,** to be a hack reporter/to write fillers; to be in charge of the accident column 3. F **c'est pas fait pour les chiens,** it's not there as an ornament, it's meant to be used. (*Voir* **chat 7**) 4. F **garder à qn un chien de sa chienne,** to have a grudge against s.o.; to have it in for s.o. 5. F **avoir du chien,** to have charm; to be attractive/fascinating; **il a du chien,** he's really got something/he's a real charmer 6. F **faire le chien couchant auprès de qn,** to fawn/to crawl to s.o. 7. F (*locution populaire*) **les chiens aboient, la caravane passe,** = I don't care what Mrs Grundy says 8. F (*a*) **être malade comme un chien,** to be as sick as a dog (*b*) **avoir un mal de chien à faire qch,** to have the devil of a job to do sth; **se donner un mal de chien,** to take great pains (with/over sth) 9. F **métier de chien,** difficult and unpleasant job; **vie de chien,** dog's life; **elle m'a fait mener une vie de chien,** she led me a dog's life; **quelle chienne de vie!** what a miserable life! **quel temps de chien!** what filthy weather! **être d'une humeur de chien,** to be in a vile mood/a filthy temper*; **avoir un caractère de chien,** to be a nasty/vile person; to be a nasty piece of work; **parler à qn comme à un chien,** to treat s.o. like dirt 10. P **cette chienne de musique!** that bloody music! 11. F **un coup de chien,** (*manifestation violente*) a sudden violent riot/clash/flare-up; (*marine*) a sudden squall 12. F **mon chien,** my darling*/my pet 13. F **piquer un chien,** to take a nap 14. P underling/subordinate/dogsbody; **chien du commissaire,** secretary in a police station; *Mil* **chien de quartier,** (company) sergeant major; **chien du bord,** second officer 15. P (*eau-de-vie*) brandy 16. P **chien vert,** jack of spades. (*Voir* **mordre 1**; **quille 4**)

chienchien [ʃjɛ̃ʃjɛ̃] *nm* F 1. (*langage enfantin*) doggie/doggy; bow-wow 2. darling*/pet; **le chienchien à sa mémère,** mummy's little boy/little darling/little pet.

chiendent [ʃjɛ̃dã] *nm* 1. F snag/difficulty/hitch 2. F **arracher le chiendent,** to be kept hanging about; to be stood up 3. F **ça pousse comme du chiendent,** it grows like a weed 4. P (*drogues*) marijuana*/grass/hay; **fumer le chiendent,** to smoke grass.

chienlit [ʃjɛ̃li] *nf* F (*pagaille*) mess/shambles.

chiennerie [ʃjɛnri] *nf* 1. F (*a*) (*action malhonnête*) filthy/dirty trick (*b*) (*avarice*) meanness/tightfistedness 2. P male chauvinism 3. P difficulty/trouble; **quelle chiennerie!** what a bloody bore/drag!

chier [ʃje] *vi* V 1. to defecate*/to shit/to crap; **to have a crap/a shit** 2. **il y en a à chier partout,** there's plenty of it; **un repas à chier partout,** a huge meal/a blow-out 3. **une gueule à chier dessus,** a repulsive face/a face like the back(-end) of a bus **4. ça chie!/ça va chier (dur)!/ça va chier des bulles (carrées)!/ça va chier des flammes!** now the shit's going to fly!/now the shit's going to hit the fan!/now there'll be one hell of a stink! **5. va chier!** get stuffed! **faire chier qn,** to annoy* s.o./to get on s.o.'s wick/to give s.o. a pain in the arse/*NAm* ass; **tu me fais chier!/(ne) me fais pas chier!/fais-moi pas chier!** you make me sick!/ you get on my bloody nerves!/don't give me that crap!/you're a pain in the arse! **envoyer chier qn,** to tell s.o. to bugger off/to piss off/to sod off; **va te faire chier!** bugger off!/sod off!/piss off! **se faire chier (sérieux/ méchamment),** to be bored stiff/to be really pissed off; **qu'est-ce qu'on se fait chier ici!** God! it's bloody boring here!/this place really pisses me off! **6. faire chier des gaufrettes à qn,** to abuse s.o.; to beat s.o. up/to beat the shit out of s.o. **7. ça chie pas!** it doesn't matter a fuck! **8. y a pas à chier (faut que ça chie),** there are no two bloody/frigging ways about it **9. à chier,** (*mauvais*) no (bloody) good/rotten/hopeless; (*agaçant, insupportable*) annoying/irritating; **il est vraiment à chier!** he's useless! he's a pain in the arse/ *NAm* ass! **10. chier dans sa culotte/dans son froc,** to be afraid*/to be shit-scared/to be scared shitless **11. en chier,** to go through an unpleasant experience; **elle en a chié, elle,** she's had a really rough/shitty time of it **12. ne pas se faire chier (à faire qch),** not to bother with (doing) sth; **je vais pas me faire chier (à faire ça),** I can't be fagged (to do it). (*Voir* **botte** II **10; colle 5; colonne 1; matricule 2; pendule 3; poivre** I **2; pot 14**)

chierie [ʃiri] *nf V* trouble/a bloody nuisance/a drag; **quelle chierie!** what a bloody drag! **la vie est une chierie,** life is fucking awful.

chie-tout-debout [ʃitudbu] *nm & f inv V* tall thin person*/long streak of piss.

chieur, -euse [ʃjœr, -øz] *n V Péj* **1.** (*personne ou animal*) one who shits a lot **2.** (*personne*) stinker/bastard*/shit **3.** *Péj* **chieur d'encre,** ink-slinger/pen-pusher/hack.

chiffe [ʃif] *nf F* **1. une chiffe (molle),** a spineless individual/a drip/a wet/a wimp; **être mou comme une chiffe,** to be a drip/a wimp **2. la chiffe,** the rag-and-bone business; the junk business.

chiffon [ʃifɔ̃] *nm* **1.** *F* **parler/causer chiffons,** to talk (about) clothes/to talk dress/to talk fashion **2.** *P* handkerchief.

chiffonner [ʃifɔne] *vtr F* to worry/to annoy* (s.o.); **ça me chiffonne,** that gets me/that bothers me; **qu'est-ce qui le chiffonne?** what's eating/bugging him?

chifforton [ʃifɔrtɔ̃] *nm P* rag-and-bone man; junk dealer.

chiftir(e) [ʃiftir] *nm P* **1.** rag **2.** = **chifforton.**

chignole [ʃiɲɔl] *nf F* **1.** old car*/banger/ jalopy; any vehicle **2.** (any sort of) machine.

chignon [ʃiɲɔ̃] *nm* **1.** *P* head*/nut/bonce; **avoir du chignon,** to be intelligent/to have brains; **elle n'a rien sous le chignon,** she's an idiot/a brainless twit **2.** *V* female genitals*/ beaver; **chignon émancipé,** prostitute*. (*Voir* **crêpage; crêper**)

chine [ʃin] *nf P* **1.** cadging/scrounging; **tabac de chine,** cadged tobacco **2.** peddling/hawking (of junk); **aller à la chine,** to peddle/hawk (junk); **marchand à la chine,** street hawker **3.** teasing/leg-pulling/ragging; **passer qn à la chine,** to make fun of s.o./pull s.o.'s leg.

chiner [ʃine] I *P vi* **1.** to hawk one's goods about **2.** (*a*) to look for antiques *or* junk (to buy) (*b*) to hunt for bargains/to go bargain hunting II *vtr* **1.** *F* to criticize* (s.o.) severely/to pull (s.o.) to pieces/to run (s.o.) down **2.** *F* to make fun of (s.o.)/to pull (s.o.'s) leg/to have (s.o.) on **3.** *P* to cadge/to scrounge (sth).

chinetoc, chinetoque [ʃintɔk] I *nm & f & a F* Chinese/chink; (any) Asiatic/slant; **bouffe chinetoc,** Chinese/chinky food II *nm P* bungler/botcher.

chineur, -euse [ʃinœr, -øz] *n P* **1.** (*emprunteur*) cadger **2.** pedlar/hawker; second-hand dealer **3.** bargain hunter **4.** practical joker/leg-puller.

chinois [ʃinwa] I *a F* (*objet, chose*) over-elaborate/complicated/involved II *nm* **1.** *F* fellow/guy/bloke/chap* (*esp* a stranger) **2.** *F* **c'est du (vrai) chinois (pour moi),** it's all Greek to me/it's double Dutch to me **3.** *V* penis*; **se battre/se polir le chinois,** to masturbate*/to toss off.

chinoiserie [ʃinwazri] *nf F* unnecessary complication; complicated formality; **chinoiseries administratives,** red tape.

chioteur [ʃjɔtœr] *nm P* (*langage des policiers*) corrupt(ible) policeman*/bent cop.

chiotte [ʃjɔt] *nf P* **1.** *Péj* (old) car*/jalopy/ banger **2. c'est la chiotte/quelle chiotte!** it's a deadly bore/what a drag! **3.** *pl* WC*/bog/*NAm* can/shithouse; *Mil* **la corvée des chiottes,** latrine fatigue **4. aux chiottes!** (*allez-vous en*) go to hell! (*jetez-le*) chuck it away! **aux chiottes, le patron!** to hell with the boss!/ screw the boss! **5. avoir un goût de chiottes,** to have bad taste/to be vulgar. (*Voir* **courant 3**)

chipage [ʃipaʒ] *nm F* stealing; scrounging.

chipé [ʃipe] *a Vieilli F* être chipé pour qn, to be infatuated* with s.o./to have a crush on s.o.

chiper [ʃipe] *vtr F* 1. to steal*/to pinch/to nick/to swipe (qch à qn, sth from s.o.) 2. to catch/to cop (a cold, a disease).

chipette [ʃipɛt] *nf P* ça ne vaut pas chipette, that's worthless*/it's not worth a sausage.

chipeur, -euse [ʃipœr, -øz] *F I a* thieving; scrounging II *n* petty thief*/sneak thief/ pilferer; scrounger III *nm* man who steals another man's girl.

chipolata [ʃipɔlata] *nm or f P* penis*/ sausage.

chipotage [ʃipɔtaʒ] *nm F* 1. haggling/ quibbling (over trifles) 2. time-wasting; fiddling about.

chipoter [ʃipɔte] *F I vi* 1. to haggle/to quibble (over trifles) 2. to nibble/to pick at one's food 3. to waste time/to dilly-dally/to shilly-shally II *vtr* ça me chipote, it bothers me.

chipoteur, -euse [ʃipɔtœr, -øz] *F I n* 1. time-waster/s.o. who shilly-shallies 2. haggler/quibbler/nit-picker II *a* 1. time-wasting 2. hair-splitting/nit-picking/picky 3. choosy/fastidious.

chips [ʃips] *nmpl P* 20 and 50 franc notes.

chique [ʃik] *nf* 1. *F* c'est clair comme du jus de chique, it's as clear as mud 2. *P* avaler/ poser sa chique, to die*/to kick the bucket 3. *F* avoir la chique (*a*) to chew (a quid of) tobacco (*b*) to have a gumboil/a swollen cheek 4. *F* ça ne vaut pas une chique, that's worthless*/it's not worth a brass farthing 5. *F* se sentir mou comme une chique, to feel listless/like a wet rag; il est mou comme une chique, he's a drip/he's wet/he's a bit of a wimp 6. *F* (*a*) couper la chique à qn, to cut s.o. short/to cramp s.o.'s style/to cut in on s.o.; (*déconcerter*) to amaze*/flabbergast/ stump s.o.; en avoir la chique coupée, to be amazed*/flabbergasted (*b*) couper la chique à quinze pas, to have (very) bad breath 7. *V* pousser sa chique, to defecate*/to crap 8. *V* tirer sa chique, to have sex*/to have it off/to get one's end away; cracher sa chique, to

ejaculate*/to shoot one's load.

chiqué [ʃike] *nm F* 1. sham/fake/phoney; c'est du chiqué, it's phoney/fake/bluff; it's a put-up job; tout ça, c'est du chiqué, that's all bluff/a put-up job; c'est pas du chiqué, it's straight from the horse's mouth; it's the real McCoy; le/la faire au chiqué, to sham/to make-believe; to put on an act/to bluff 2. fuss/to-do; faire du chiqué, to put on airs/to swank/to show off*; un faiseur de chiqué, a show-off*.

chiquement [ʃikmɑ̃] *adv F* (*avec élégance*) smartly/stylishly; (*avec fair-play, etc*) nicely/decently.

chiquer [ʃike] *P I vi* 1. to pretend/to sham; to make-believe; chiquer à ..., to pretend to be ...; sans chiquer, sincerely 2. to discuss/ quibble; to hesitate; il (n')y a rien à chiquer/ il (n')y a pas à chiquer (contre), there's no getting away from it!/there's no two ways about it! ne rien vouloir chiquer, to refuse to discuss sth; elle veut rien chiquer, she doesn't want to know; she's (already) made up her mind II *vtr* 1. *A* to eat*/to get stuck into (one's food) 2. to hit/beat/punch; se chiquer (la gueule), to fight*/to have a punch-up.

chiqueur, -euse [ʃikœr, -øz] *n P* 1. pretender/phoney 2. swank/show-off* 3. crook's associate.

chirdent [ʃirdɑ̃] *nm F* (*chirurgien-dentiste*) dental surgeon.

chizbroc [ʃizbrɔk] *nm P* scandal; (*bruit*) racket/row; (*bagarre*) set-to/punch-up.

chlaff(e) [ʃlaf] *nm ou f P* aller au chlaff(e)/à (la) chlaff(e), to go to bed*; faire chlaff(e), to sleep*; to be asleep/sleeping. (*Voir* **schlaff(e)**)

chlass(e) [ʃlas] *I a P* (*ou* **chlâsse**) drunk*/ sozzled II *nm P* knife; dagger; chiv. (*Voir* **schlass(e) I, II**)

chleu(h) [ʃlø] *a & n P* (*seconde guerre 1939–45*) German*/Jerry.

chlingoter [ʃlɛ̃gɔte], **chlinguer** [ʃlɛ̃ge] *vi P* to stink*/to pong; chlingoter du bec, to have foul breath. (*Voir* **schlingoter**)

chlipote [ʃlipɔt] *nf P* sickening smell.

chlipoter [ʃlipɔte] *vi P* to smell; ça chlipote ici, there's a terrible smell in here.

chloff(e) [ʃlɔf] *nm ou f P* = **chlaff(e)**.

chmoutz [ʃmuts] *nm P Péj* Jew*/Yid. (*Voir* **schmoutz**)

chnaps [ʃnaps], **chnique** [ʃnik] *nm F* inferior whisky *or* brandy; cheap spirits*/ rotgut. (*Voir* **schnaps, schnick**)

chniquer [ʃnike] *vi P* to stink*/to pong.

chnoc, chnoque [ʃnɔk] *P* **I** *a* mad*/ bonkers; gaga **II** *nm* fool*/blockhead/ schmo(e)/schmuck; **un vieux chnoc**, a silly old fool/a doddering old idiot/an old fart. (*Voir* **schnock, schnoque**)

chnouf(fe) [ʃnuf] *nf P* (*drogues*) heroin*/H/junk. (*Voir* **schnouf(fe)**)

chnouffé, -ée [ʃnufe] *n P* (*drogues*) heroin* addict/dope addict/junkie. (*Voir* **schnouffé**)

se chnouffer [səʃnufe] *vpr P* (*drogues*) to take heroin*; to be a heroin* addict/a junkie; to take dope. (*Voir* **se schnouffer**)

choc [ʃɔk] **I** *a inv F* amazing; **prix choc**, drastic reductions **II** *nm* **tenir le choc**, (*objet*) to last; (*personne*) to endure (sth); to survive; **prof de choc**, dynamic teacher.

chochoter [ʃɔʃɔte] *vi P* to put on airs.

chochoteuse [ʃɔʃɔtøz] *af P* affected; finicky; genteel/(would-be) refined.

chochotte [ʃɔʃɔt] **I** *nf* 1. *F* **ma chochotte**, my darling*/my pet 2. *P Péj* lah-di-dah woman; (*homme*) pouf/fairy; **petite chochotte, va!** you stuck up so-and-so! **fais pas ta chochotte**, stop mincing about/ stop simpering **II** *a P* lah-di-dah/affected/mannered; (*homme*) camp.

choco [ʃɔko] *nm F* chocolate.

chocolat [ʃɔkɔla] *a inv P* 1. (*a*) **être/faire chocolat**, to be done out of sth; to get swindled/rooked/cheated out of sth (*b*) **demeurer/rester chocolat**, to be left in the lurch; to be left stranded 2. **c'est du chocolat**, it's easy (as pie) 3. **avoir la gueule en chocolat/être chocolat**, to be drunk*/sozzled 4. **médaille en chocolat**, (worthless) award/gong.

chocotter [ʃɔkɔte] *vi P* 1. to be afraid*/to tremble with fear/to have the willies 2. to stink*/to pong.

chocottes [ʃɔkɔt] *nfpl P* 1. teeth*/ivories/ gnasher/choppers 2. **avoir les chocottes**, to be afraid*/to get the wind up/to have the jitters; **donner/flanquer/foutre les chocottes à qn**, to put the wind up s.o.

choir [ʃwar] *vi F* **laisser choir** (qn/qch), to drop/to get rid of/to dump (s.o./sth); **laisser choir ses potes**, to let one's mates down.

choléra [kɔlera] *nm P* disagreeable individual/nasty piece of work/poisonous character; (*chose, affaire*) nasty business.

chôme [ʃom] *nf P* unemployment/dole.

chômedu, chôm'du [ʃomdy] *nm P* (*a*) unemployed worker/person out of work; **être/**

faire chômedu, to be unemployed/on the dole (*b*) unemployment/dole; **être au chômedu**, to be unemployed/out of work/on the dole.

chômeur [ʃomœr] *nm P* glass of mineral water.

choper [ʃɔpe] *vtr P* 1. to steal*/to pinch/to nick/to swipe (qch à qn, sth from s.o.) 2. to catch/to cop; **il a chopé un rhume**, he caught a cold; **choper le train**, to catch the train 3. to arrest*; **se faire choper**, to get nabbed/done. (*Voir* **biscuit 2**)

chopeur, -euse [ʃɔpœr, -øz] *P* **I** *a* thieving; scrounging **II** *n* petty thief*/sneak thief/ pilferer; scrounger.

chopin [ʃɔpɛ̃] *nm P* 1. bit of luck/lucky break; windfall/godsend; **faire un (beau) chopin**, to clinch a good deal/to do a good piece of business 2. (love) conquest/catch; **faire un (beau) chopin**, to make a good catch; to find a wealthy lover/a wealthy mistress 3. *Vieilli* beautiful girl*; **cette fille, c'est un chopin**, that girl is a real beauty 4. infatuation for/crush on (a girl/woman).

chopine [ʃɔpin] *nf P* 1. *F* small bottle (of wine, etc); **tu viens boire une chopine?** coming for a drink? 2. *V* (large) penis*/chopper.

chopiner [ʃɔpine] *vi P* to drink* heavily/to booze/to hit the bottle.

chopotte [ʃɔpɔt] *nf P* = **chopine**.

chose [ʃoz] **I** *a inv F* **être/se sentir tout chose/un peu chose**, to feel unwell*/out of sorts/under the weather; **vous avez l'air tout chose**, you look upset/as if something's happened/as if something's gone wrong **II** *nm & f F* 1. **Monsieur Chose/Madame Chose**, Mr/ Mrs What-do-you-call-it; Mr/Mrs Thingummy; Mr What's-his-name/Mrs What's-her-name 2. **v'la/voilà autre chose!** well, that's a turn-up for the books! **III** *nm & f* (*Euph pour remplacer des mots vulgaires*) 1. **je vais te botter le chose**, I'll kick you up the you-know-where; **il a sorti son chose**, he's got his thingy out 2. **être porté sur la chose**, to be fond of sex*/to like it/to like a bit of nooky.

chou, pl -oux [ʃu] **I** *nm* 1. *P* head*/nut; **en avoir dans le chou**, to be intelligent/to have brains; **se casser le chou**, to take a lot of trouble (over sth); **rentrer dans le chou à qn**, to attack s.o./to beat s.o. up*; **travailler du chou**, to be mad*/crazy/bonkers; **avoir le chou farci**, to have worries/to worry; **se monter le chou**, to get excited/to get (all) worked up 2. *F* **mon (petit) chou**, (my) darling*/my precious (one); **mon petit chou en sucre/en susu-**

cre, sweetie-pie; **c'est un vrai chou!** he's a perfect darling! (*Voir* **chou** II; **choute**) 3. *P* **être/arriver dans les choux,** to be late; (*courses*) to be amongst the last; **tomber/finir dans les choux,** (*plan, projet*) to fail/to come to grief; to be up the spout; (*courses*) **laisser les autres dans les choux,** to leave the rest of the field standing; **faire chou blanc,** to fail completely/to draw a (complete) blank; (*dans un jeu*) to fail to score 4. *F* **aller planter ses choux,** to retire and go and live in the country 5. *F* **faire ses choux gras,** to make one's pile/ to feather one's nest; **faire ses choux gras de qch,** to make a handsome profit out of sth 6. *F* **faites-en des choux et des raves,** do just what you like with it/you can please yourself what you do with it 7. *P* **se taper/se farcir le chou,** to have a good tuck-in/to have a good blow-out 8. *F* **chou pour chou,** word for word; taking one thing with another; **répondre à qn chou pour chou,** to answer s.o. pat; **faire/marcher chou pour chou,** to reciprocate; *V* to take part in a homosexual orgy (*where partners swap roles*) 9. *F* **c'est chou vert et vert chou,** it's much of a muchness/it's six of one and half a dozen of the other 10. *F* (*a*) **c'est bête comme chou,** it's as easy* as winking/as falling off a log (*b*) **il est bête comme chou,** he's extremely stupid*/as thick as two (short) planks 11. *F* **manger les choux par les trognons,** to be dead and buried/to be pushing up the daisies. (*Voir* **feuille 1, 2**; **ramer** I) II *a* **ce que tu es chou!** you're a perfect darling! **ce serait chou!** that'd be great!/nice! **c'est chou!** it's divine! (*Voir* **chou I 2**)

chouaga [ʃwaga] *a,* **chouard** [ʃwar] *a P* excellent*/first-rate/super/wicked.

chouaye [ʃwaj] *adv P* = **chouïa.**

choubiner [ʃubine] *P* I *vtr* to heat II *vi* ça choubine, everything's going well/going great guns; we're doing fine.

choubinette [ʃubinɛt] *nf P* small stove.

choucard(e) [ʃukar(d)] *a P* (*a*) = **chouaga** (*b*) (*personne*) good-looking; (*chose*) nice-looking/good-quality.

chouchou, *f* **chouchoute** [ʃuʃu, -ut] *n F* darling*/favourite/pet; **le chouchou de/à** (sa) **maman,** mummy's blue-eyed boy/mummy's little boy; **la chouchoute de/à** (son) **papa,** daddy's darling (girl); **le chouchou du prof**(esseur), teacher's pet.

chouchouter [ʃuʃute] *F* I *vtr* to pet/to caress/to fondle (s.o.); to pamper/to coddle (a child) II *vpr* **se chouchouter,** to have a

cushy time.

choucroute [ʃukrut] *nf* 1. *F* petite choucroute, curly head of hair 2. *P* hard drug. (*Voir* **pédaler 3**)

choucrouté [ʃukrute] *a F* coiffure choucroutée, curly hairstyle.

chouette [ʃwɛt] I *a F* 1. excellent*/first-rate/great/smashing; **c'est chouette!** that's great! **une chouette cravate,** a snazzy tie; *Iron* **tu as l'air chouette avec ton chapeau,** you look something else in that hat 2. nice/pretty/ good-looking/cute 3. honest/straight/decent; **c'est un chouette mec,** he's a straight guy 4. **être chouette,** to be duped/hoaxed/to be played for a sucker; to be done/had; **se faire chouette,** to be taken in/taken for a ride II *adv phr F* **avoir qn à la chouette,** to like s.o./to have a soft spot for s.o.; to take a liking to s.o. III *excl F* **chouette** (**papa**)!/**chouette papa, maman fume!** super!/great!/ smashing!/wicked! IV *nm* 1. *V* anus*; **prendre du chouette,** to be an active homosexual*; **donner/filer du chouette,** to be a passive homosexual* 2. *P* real name (*as opposed to assumed name*); **marcher sous son chouette,** to travel under one's real name; to use one's real name 3. *pl P* genuine identity papers.

chouettement [ʃwɛtmɑ̃] *adv F* excellently/splendidly/fabulously.

chouettos [ʃwɛtos] *a F* excellent*/great/ super/marvellous; **c'est vraiment chouettos,** it's really terrific.

chouf [ʃuf] *nm P* surveillance/spying.

chou-fleur [ʃuflœr] *nm* 1. *F* **avoir les oreilles en chou-fleur,** to have cauliflower ears 2. *pl P* **choux-fleurs,** haemorrhoids/*NAm* hemorrhoids/piles.

chouïa [ʃuja] *P* I *nm* tad; **un chouïa de ...,** a little .../a small quantity of ... II *adv A* 1. pas chouïa, not much 2. **vas-y chouïa!** go easy!/ steady on!

chouilla [ʃuja] *nm,* **chouille** [ʃuj] *nm P* = **chouïa** I.

choupaïa [ʃupaja] *a inv P* = **chouaga, chouard.**

choupette [ʃupɛt] *nf F* tuft of baby's hair tied with a bow.

choupinet, -ette [ʃupinɛ, -ɛt] *a F* sweet/ cute.

chouquette [ʃukɛt] *nf P* 1. affected young woman 2. (*a*) homosexual* (*b*) effeminate young man (*with exaggeratedly affected mannerisms*)/fairy/poofter; **il fait très chouquette,** he's rather camp.

chourave [ʃurav] *P* **I** *nf* thieving **II** *a* stolen/hot; bagnole chourave, hot car.

chouravé [ʃurave] *a P* slightly mad*/bats.

chouraver [ʃurave] *vtr P* to steal*.

chouraveur [ʃuravœr] *nm P* thief.

chourer [ʃure] *vtr P* = **chouraver**.

chourin [ʃurɛ̃] *nm Vieilli P* knife; dagger.

chouriner [ʃurine] *vtr Vieilli P* to knife (s.o.)/to stab (s.o.) (to death); to cut (s.o.) up.

chourineur [ʃurinœr] *nm Vieilli P* knifer/chiv(e)-man.

choute [ʃut] *nf F* ma choute, (my) darling*/my dear little girl. (*Voir* **chou I 2**)

chouter [ʃute] *vtr F* = **chouchouter**.

chouterie [ʃutri] *nf F* caress(ing)/fondling; cuddling.

chpile [ʃpil] *nm P* gambling; avoir beau chpile, (*beau jeu*) to have/to hold a good hand (at cards); (*réaliser facilement*) to find it easy/to have no difficulty; il avait beau chpile à faire cela, it was a walkover/all plain sailing for him. (*Voir* **schpile**)

chpiler [ʃpile] *vi P* to gamble. (*Voir* **schpiler**)

chpileur [ʃpilœr] *nm P* gambler. (*Voir* **schpileur**)

chproum [ʃprum] *nm P* **1.** scandal/(scandalous) gossip/dirt; faire du chproum, to cause a scandal **2.** din/row/racket; faire du chproum, to kick up a row **3.** *Vieilli* anger; aller au chproum, to lose one's temper/to flare up/to hit the roof. (*Voir* **schproum(e)**)

chrono [krɔno] *nm F* (= *chronomètre*) stopwatch; il faisait du 260 chrono, (= *au chronomètre*) he was doing (a speed of) 260 km per hour.

chroumer [krume] *vi P* (*a*) to steal* (*b*) to thieve from cars in a police pound.

chtar [ʃtar] *nm P* **1.** prison*/stir/clink; disciplinary cell. (*Voir* **schtar(d)**) **2.** blow*/smack/sock/clout **3.** (*marque*) dent; la voiture est pleine de chtars! the car's all dented!

chtarbé [ʃtarbe] *a P* mad*/crazy/bonkers.

chtib(e) [ʃtib] *nm P* prison*. (*Voir* **schtar(d), schtib(e)**)

ch'timi [ʃtimi] *nm P* native of northern France/northerner. (*Voir* **schtim(m)i**)

chtouillard [ʃtujar] *nm P* person who has (got) VD*/the clap. (*Voir* **schtouillard**)

chtouille [ʃtuj] *nf P* VD*/the clap; ramasser la chtouille, to cop a dose; flanquer la chtouille à qn, to give s.o. a dose. (*Voir* schtouille)

chtourbe [ʃturb] *nf P* **1.** poverty; être dans la chtourbe, to be down on one's uppers **2.** trouble/(spot of) bother; dans la chtourbe, in a fix*/a jam.

chtrasse [ʃtras] *nf P* room in a hotel, etc, used by a prostitute. (*Voir* **strasse 1**)

chtrope [ʃtrɔp] *nm P* (*brocante*) bad merchandise/bad-quality goods (*despite its appearance*).

chtuc [ʃtyk] *nm P* small piece/bit; juste un chtuc, just a smidgen.

chut-chut [ʃytʃyt] *adv phr F* à la chut-chut, in strict confidence/on the QT/hush-hush.

chute [ʃyt] *nf F* point de chute, meeting place/rendezvous.

chuter [ʃyte] *vi F* to fall/to come a cropper*; (*pièce*) to be a flop; (*fille, femme*) to go wrong/to allow herself to be seduced; (*cartes*) to lose; chuter de trois levées, to be three tricks down.

cibiche [sibiʃ] *nf P* cigarette*/fag/ciggy.

ciboule [sibul] *nf P* **1.** = **ciboulot 2.** entrer en ciboule, (*dans une course*) to come in first.

ciboulot [sibulo] *nm P* head*/noddle/nut; intelligence*/brains; il en a dans le ciboulot, he's got brains; se creuser le ciboulot, to rack one's brains; il travaille du ciboulot, he's got a screw loose; tu me cours/tu me cavales sur le ciboulot, you get on my nerves/on my wick; you send me up the wall.

cicatrice [sikatris] *nf F* female genitals*/gash/slit; une affranchie de la cicatrice, a girl who has lost her virginity.

ci-devant [sidvã] *nm & f inv F A* old fog(e)y*/has-been/back-number.

cidre [sidr] *nm P* **1.** water **2.** ça ne vaut pas un coup de cidre, it's absolutely worthless*/it's not worth a sausage.

ciel [sjɛl] *nm* **1.** *F* tomber du ciel, (*aubaine*) to be a godsend; (*abasourdi, foudroyé*) to be thunderstruck/gobsmacked **2.** *F* il ne l'emportera pas au ciel, he won't get away with it **3.** *P* approcher du ciel à reculons, to be guillotined **4.** *P* monter au ciel/atteindre le septième ciel, to have an orgasm*/to climax/to come.

Cifelle [sifɛl] *Prn F* la tour Cifelle, the Eiffel Tower (in Paris).

ciflard [siflar] *nm P* (French) dried sausage. (*Voir* **sauciflard**)

cigare [sigar] *nm* **1.** *P* head*/nut; avoir mal au cigare, to have a headache; y aller du cigare, to risk one's neck; to stick one's neck out; **travailler du cigare/être dérangé du cigare**, to be mad*/nuts/off one's block; **se remettre le cigare à l'endroit**, to pull oneself together; **couper le cigare à qn**, to guillotine s.o.; (*interrompre*) to interrupt s.o./to cut in on s.o. (talking) 2. *P* intelligence*/brains; **avoir du cigare**, to be brainy 3. *V* piece of excrement/turd; **avoir le cigare au bord des lèvres**, to have an urgent need to defecate 4. *V* **cigare à moustaches**, penis*.

cigler [sigle] *vtr & i P* to pay* (up)/to settle.

cigogne [sigɔɲ] *nf* 1. *F* tall, thin girl or woman; beanpole 2. *P* **la Cigogne**, the Palais de Justice; the Préfecture de police (*the headquarters of the Paris police*).

cigotin [sigɔtɛ̃] *nm P* = **cigue 1**.

cigue [sig] *nm P* 1. **avoir un cigue**, to be twenty years old; **il doit avoir deux cigues et un peu de mornifle**, he must be forty-two or forty-three years old 2. *Vieilli* twenty francs.

ciguer [sige] *vtr & i P* = **cigler**.

cil [sil] *nm P* 1. **avoir les cils cassés**, to feel very sleepy; **plier les cils**, to go to sleep 2. **jeter un cil à qn**, to make eyes at s.o.

cimetière [simtjɛr] *nm P* 1. **rendre le cimetière bossu**, to be buried 2. **cimetière à poulets**, stomach*/belly.

ciné [sine] *nm F Br* cinéma/pictures/flicks/ *NAm* movies; **aller au ciné**, to go to the pictures.

cinéma [sinema] *nm F* 1. **c'est du cinéma**, it's unbelievable; it's just show/it's all put on/ it's all an act; **faire tout un cinéma/faire son cinéma**, to make a fuss/a song and dance about something 2. **se faire du cinéma**, to have delusions/to imagine things 3. **faire du cinéma**, to be a malingerer/to put on an act.

cinémateux, -euse [sinematø, -øz] *a F* cinematographic; cinema/film (*production, etc*).

cinglé, -ée [sɛ̃gle] *a & n P* mad* (person); **il est raide cinglé**, he's stark raving mad/a complete nut/a nutter.

cinoche [sinɔʃ] *nm P* 1. cinema; **le cinoche du coin**, the local fleapit; **aller au cinoche**, to go to the flicks/the pictures/*NAm* the movies 2. **se faire du cinoche**, to have delusions/to imagine things.

cinochier [sinɔʃje] *P* I *a* cinematographic/of the cinema II *nm* film-goer/film buff.

cinoque [sinɔk] *a & nm & f P* = **cinglé(e)**.

cinq [sɛ̃, sɛ̃k] *num a inv & nm inv* 1. *F* **il était moins cinq**, it was a narrow escape/a near thing/a close shave 2. *F* **en cinq sec**,

immediately*/in no time (at all)/in five seconds flat/in a couple of shakes 3. *F* **faire cinq et trois font huit**, to limp/to dot and carry one 4. *F Euph* **le mot de cinq lettres/les cinq lettres** = **merde** (*qv*); = four-letter word (*Voir* **Cambronne**); **dire les cinq lettres**, to use bad language/to use four-letter words; **répondre en cinq lettres à qn/dire cinq lettres à qn**, to tell s.o. to go to hell/to tell s.o. where to go/to tell s.o. where to get off 5. *P* **en serrer cinq (à qn)**, to shake hands (with s.o.); **je t'en serre cinq**, put it there! (*Voir* **écraser II 2**) 6. *P* **les cinq à sept**, clandestine lovers; **un cinq à sept**, a quick one/a quick screw/a quickie (in daytime) 7. *V* **se battre/se mettre à cinq contre un**, to masturbate*/to give (oneself/ s.o.) a hand job/to toss off 8. *F* **je vous reçois cinq sur cinq**, receiving you loud and clear; *Fig* I get you/I see what you mean 9. *F* **à cinq du**, (= *à cinq heures du matin*) at five in the morning/at five am.

cinq-en-cinq [sɛ̃kɑ̃sɛ̃k] *nm F* **un vigoureux cinq-en-cinq**, a hearty handshake.

cinquante-pour-cent [sɛ̃kɑ̃tpursɑ̃] *nm P* **mon cinquante-pour-cent**, the wife*/my better half.

cintième [sɛ̃tjɛm] *nm P* (*cinquième*) fifth; **j'habite au cintième**, I live at number five.

cintre [sɛ̃tr] *nm P* (*vélo*) handlebar; **couché sur le cintre**, leaning over the handlebar.

cintré [sɛ̃tre] *a P* **être cintré**, to be mad*/ nuts.

cipal, -aux [sipal, -o] *nm Vieilli P* (= *garde municipal*) member of the police in Paris *or* the local police.

cipale [sipal] *nf P* 1. (*chemins de fer* = *voie principale*) main line 2. (*municipalité*) municipality.

cirage [siraʒ] *nm F* **être dans le cirage**, (*avoir des ennuis*) to be in a fix*/in a jam/in Queer Street; (*être dans le noir, le vague*) to be in the dark/to be all at sea/to be in a complete daze; (*être évanoui*) to have fainted/to be unconscious; (*ne pas comprendre*) not to be able to make head or tail (of sth); (*être déprimé*) to be depressed*/ to have the blues; (*aviation*) to be flying blind; (*être ivre*) to be drunk*; **être en plein cirage**, to be dead drunk*/completely blotto.

circuit [sirkɥi] *nm F* 1. **être dans le circuit**, to be informed/in the know; **être hors circuit/ ne plus être dans le circuit**, to be out of touch/ to be out of it 2. **se faire un circuit**, to go on a pub-crawl/to do a tour of the nightclubs; to go pubbing/nightclubbing.

cirer [sire] *vtr F* 1. (*écoles*) **cirer un garçon,** to give a boy the bumps 2. **cirer les meubles,** to beat up* one's wife 3. (je n'en ai) **rien à cirer!** I don't give a damn/a monkey's! (*Voir* **botte II 4, 5**)

cirque [sirk] *nm* 1. *P Hum* Chamber of Deputies 2. *P* (*agitation*) commotion/fuss/ scene/to-do; (*désordre*) chaos/bear garden; **faire tout un cirque/son cirque** = **faire son cinéma** (**cinéma 1**) 3. *V* **mener le petit au cirque,** to have sex*.

cisaillé [sizɑje] *a P* 1. penniless*; **complètement cisaillé/cisaillé à zéro,** stony broke 2. amazed*/dumbfounded/flabbergasted.

cisailler [sizɑje] *vtr P* 1. to fleece* (s.o.) (at gambling)/to clean (s.o.) out/to take (s.o.) to the cleaners 2. to amaze*/to dumbfound/to flabbergast* (s.o.)/to knock (s.o.) sideways 3. to demoralize/to cause (s.o.) to lose heart.

ciseaux [sizo] *nmpl V* **faire petits ciseaux/ faire les ciseaux,** to insert simultaneously the index and middle fingers in the anus and vagina.

citoyen [sitwajɛ̃] *nm F* bloke/guy; **un drôle de citoyen,** a strange fellow/a queer customer.

citron[1] [sitrɔ̃] *nm P* head*/nut; intelligence*/ brains; **se creuser/se presser/se casser le citron,** to rack one's brains; **se lécher le citron,** to kiss.

citron[2], **Citron** *nf Vieilli P Aut* Citroën (*RTM*) (car).

citrouille [sitruj] *nf P* head*/nut/bonce.

civ(e)lot [sivlo] *nm P* civilian/civvy; **en civ(e)lot,** in civvies/in civvy clothes.

clabaud [klabo] *nm F* = **clabaudeur, -euse.**

clabaudage [klaboda3] *nm F* scandalmongering/malicious gossip/backbiting.

clabauder [klabode] *vi F* 1. **clabauder sur/ contre qn,** to say malicious things/to gossip about s.o. 2. = **claboter.**

clabauderie [klabodri] *nf F* malicious gossip.

clabaudeur, -euse [klabodœr, -øz] *n F* scandalmonger/backbiter.

claboter [klabɔte] *vi P* to die*/to peg out/to snuff it; **être/avoir claboté,** to be dead/to have died.

clac [klak] *nm* = **claque II 1, 2.**

clair [klɛr] *a F* **être clair,** (*dans un état normal*) to be clear-headed; to be neither drunk* nor drugged; (*avoir la conscience tranquille*) to have a clear conscience; (*savoir où on va*) to be sure of oneself. (*Voir* **eau 3; pavé 5**)

clairon [klɛrɔ̃] *nm P Mil* (automatic) rifle.

clam(e)cer [klamse] *vi P* = **clamser.**

clampin, -ine [klɑ̃pɛ̃, -in] *n F* 1. individual*, *esp* loafer/layabout/skiver 2. (young) show-off*/boaster.

clampiner [klɑ̃pine] *vi F* to hang about/to loaf about/to mooch around.

clamsé(e) [klamse] **I** *a* dead/cold/done for **II** *n* corpse*/stiff; **champ des clamsés,** cemetery/boneyard.

clamser, clampser [klamse, klɑ̃pse] *vi P* to die*/to kick the bucket/to snuff it.

clandé [klɑ̃de] **I** *nm P* clandestine *or* illegal brothel*; illegal gambling joint **II** *nf P* prostitute* working in a clandestine/an illegal brothel*.

clandès [klɑ̃dɛs] *nm P* (*seconde guerre 1939–45*) black market.

claouis [kla(u)wi] *nmpl V* testicles*/goolies; **casser/râper les claouis à qn,** to bore* the balls off s.o./to give s.o. a pain in the arse/to get on s.o.'s tits.

clape [klap] *nf P* 1. food/nosh 2. meal.

claper [klape] *vi P* to eat*/to stuff oneself.

clapet [klapɛ] *nm P* mouth*; **fermer/boucler son clapet,** to shut* up/to pipe down; **elle a un de ces clapets!** she never stops talking!

clapier [klapje] *nm F Péj* small (untidy) house *or* flat/dump/hole; rabbit hutch; *pl* **clapiers,** back streets/slums; **ça a fait jaser dans les clapiers,** it was the talk of the slums.

clapoter [klapɔte] *vi P* = **claboter.**

clapser [klapse] *vi P* to die*.

claquant [klakɑ̃] *a F* tiring/exhausting/ killing.

claque [klak] **I** *nf* 1. *F* **une tête à claques,** (*visage*) an unpleasant/unprepossessing face; (*individu*) a cheeky-looking blighter; **c'est une tête à claques,** he's just asking for it 2. *P* **il en a sa claque,** (*il est épuisé*) he's on his last legs/he's dead beat/he's all in; (*il en a eu assez*) he's fed up to the back teeth with it/ he's had (more than) enough of it 3. *P* (*se*) **prendre une claque,** to fail/to suffer a setback. (*Voir* **cliques**) **II** *nm P* 1. brothel*/ whorehouse 2. gambling den.

claqué [klake] **I** *a* (*a*) *F* exhausted*/clapped out/shattered (*b*) *P* dead **II** *nm P* corpse*; **le jardin des claqués,** the cemetery/the boneyard; **la boîte aux claqués,** the mortuary.

claquedent [klakdɑ̃] *nm Vieilli P* 1. = **claque** II **1, 2** 2. half-starved person/ miserable wretch.

claquefaim [klakfɛ̃] *nm A P* = **claquedent 2.**

claque-fric [klakfrik] *nm & f Vieilli P* spendthrift.

claque-merde [klakmɛrd] *nm ou f P* mouth*; **ferme ton/ta claque-merde!** shut up!*/shut your face!

claquer [klake] I *vi P* (*a*) to die*; (*entreprise*) to go to pieces/to go bust; (*machine, appareil*) to pack up/to conk out/to go phut; **le moteur m'a claqué dans les mains,** the engine died on me; **ce plan m'a claqué dans la main/ dans les doigts,** the plan failed/fell apart II *vtr F* 1. to exhaust*/to wear (s.o.) out 2. to spend* freely/to squander/to blow; **il claque tout son fric avec des putes,** he blows all his money on prostitutes. (*Voir* **bec 1**; **polichinelle 2** (*b*)) III *vpr* **se claquer** *F* (*a*) to tire oneself out/to work oneself to death/to kill oneself (with work)/to shatter oneself (*b*) **se claquer un muscle,** to pull/to strain a muscle.

clarinette [klarinɛt] *nf* 1. *A P Mil* rifle 2. *P* (burglar's) jemmy/*NAm* jimmy 3. *V* penis*; **jouer de la clarinette baveuse,** (*coïter*) to have sex*; (*faire une fellation*) to fellate* (s.o.)/to give (s.o.) a blow-job.

class [klas] *adv & a P* = **classe** II, III.

classe [klas] I *nf F* 1. (*a*) être de la classe, to be due for *Mil* demob(ilization), (*retraite*) retirement, etc (*b*) date of liberation; **vive la classe!** freedom at last! 2. *Vieilli* **avoir la classe/une sacrée classe,** (*élégance*) to be elegant*/to dress smartly; **elle a de la classe,** she's got class/she's pretty classy. (*Voir* **classe III**) II *adv P* enough; **j'en ai classe (et archiclasse),** I'm fed up* with it/I've had (more than) enough of it/I'm fed up to the back teeth with it; **c'est classe!** that'll do!/ that's enough!/give it a rest! **attends que ça soit classe!** wait till it's over! III *a F* être classe, to be elegant*/smart; **elle est classe,** she's got class/she's pretty classy; **c'est classe,** it's (dead) smart.

classé [klase] *a F* **c'est un homme classé,** he's been sized up/sussed out.

classieux, -euse [klasjø, -øz] *a F* elegant*/smart.

classique [klasik] *a F* **le coup classique,** the same old trick/the usual stunt; **c'était le coup classique!** it was classic!

classiques [klasik] *nmpl P* **avoir ses** classiques, to have a period*/to have the monthlies.

clavier [klavje] *nm P* set of false teeth.

clé [kle] *nf* = **clef.**

clean [klin] *a F* straight/clean-living; **elle a un look clean,** she has a clean-living/straight image.

clébard [klebar] *nm*, **cleb(s)** [klɛb(s)] *nm P Péj* dog*/hound/tyke/pooch/mutt.

cléber [klebe] *vtr P* to eat*.

clef [kle] *nf* 1. *F* **mettre la clef sous la porte/ sous le paillasson,** to sneak off/to do a moonlight flit/to do a bunk 2. *F* **prendre la clef des champs,** to run away*/to beat it; (*déménager à la campagne*) to take to the country; **avoir la clef des champs,** to be free to roam 3. *P ...* **à la clef,** ... into the bargain/... with something tacked on (to it); **dîner avec du champagne à la clef,** dinner with champagne thrown in 4. *P* **rendre ses clefs,** to die*/to cash in one's chips. (*Voir* **nager 3**; **portail**)

Cléopâtre [kleɔpɑtr] *Prnf* 1. *P* **elle croit avoir le nez de Cléopâtre!** she thinks she's something (big)/the bee's knees! 2. *V* **faire Cléopâtre,** to fellate* s.o./to suck cock.

cleps [klɛps] *nm P* = **cleb(s).**

clerc [klɛr] *nm F* **faire un pas de clerc,** (*faire une erreur*) to make a mistake* (through inexperience); (*agir à tort*) to make a wrong move.

clergeon [klɛrʒɔ̃] *nm F* altar boy.

cleupon [kløpɔ̃] *nm P* (*verlan de* **clope**) cigarette*/fag.

cliche [kliʃ] *nf P* 1. diarrhoea*; **avoir la cliche,** to have diarrhoea*/to have the runs 2. **avoir la cliche,** to be afraid*/to have the wind up/to be in a blue funk.

cliché [kliʃe] *nm P* ugly face*/ugly mug.

clicher [kliʃe] *vtr P Phot* to take a picture/to film; **cliche celle-là!** get that shot!/take that one!

clicli [klikli] *nm V* clitoris*/clit.

client [klijɑ̃] *nm* 1. *F* (*a*) man*/chap/fellow/ guy; **un sale client,** an ugly customer; **un drôle de client,** a weird sort of bloke/an odd bod (*b*) (*dupe*) fall guy/mug/sucker 2. *P* **merci, je ne suis pas client,** no thanks, you can count me out.

clignotants [kliɲɔtɑ̃] *nmpl*, **clignots** [kliɲo] *nmpl P* eyes*/blinkers; **baver des clignotants,** to cry one's eyes out.

clille [klij] *nm P* client/customer/punter (*esp* of prostitute); **clille de nuit,** all-nighter.

clinoche [klinɔʃ] *nf P* clinic/nursing home.

clinquaille [klɛ̃kɑj] *nf P* money*/cash.

clique [klik] *nf F Péj* gang/crowd/shower; **ramener sa clique,** to bring along all one's mates/buddies.

cliques [klik] *nfpl F* **prendre ses cliques et ses claques,** to pack up and clear out/to make off smartly.

cliquette [klikɛt] *nf* 1. *P pl* ears*; **avoir du miel dans les cliquettes,** to be deaf/hard of hearing 2. *V* clitoris*/button.

clito [klito] *nm V* clitoris*/clit.

clochard, -arde [klɔʃar, -ard] *n F* tramp*/bum/down-and-out/*NAm* hobo.

cloche [klɔʃ] **I** *nf* 1. *F* (*a*) tramp*/beggar; **c'est une cloche,** he's a down-and-out (*b*) **la cloche,** vagrancy; tramps/down-and-outs (*in general*); **être de la cloche,** to be a tramp/a beggar/a down-and-out; **être à la cloche,** to have nowhere to sleep/to be homeless 2. *P* stupid* person; **quelle cloche!** what a clot! **pauvre cloche!** you poor dope!/you silly jerk! 3. *P* **sonner les cloches à qn,** to reprimand* s.o. severely/to tell s.o. off in no uncertain manner; **se faire sonner les cloches,** to be severely reprimanded*/to get a rocket 4. *F* **déménager à la cloche (de bois),** to leave* without paying/to do a moonlight flit 5. *F* **qui n'entend qu'une cloche n'entend qu'un son,** there are two sides to every question; **un (tout) autre son de cloche,** a quite different way of looking at things 6. *F* **avoir des cloches aux mains,** to have blistered hands 7. *P* **se taper/se tasser la cloche,** to eat* heartily/to have a good nosh/to stuff oneself **II** *a P* 1. ugly 2. stupid*; **ce que t'es cloche!** what a dope/twit you are! **avoir l'air cloche,** to look daft; **ça fait cloche,** that looks idiotic.

clocher [klɔʃe] **I** *vi F* to go wrong; **qu'est-ce qui cloche?** what's the trouble? **il y a quelque chose qui cloche,** there's something the matter/something wrong; there's something not quite right **II** *vtr P* to listen (to)/to hear; **il a cloché quelqu'un qui entrait,** he heard someone coming in.

clochettes [klɔʃɛt] *nfpl P* **avoir des clochettes au cul,** (*personne*) to be dirty/filthy.

clodo [klɔdo] *nm, Vieilli* **clodomir** [klɔdomir] *nm P* tramp/beggar/down-and-out/bum.

clone [klɔn] *nm P* (*homosexuels*) xerox queen.

clop(e) [klɔp] *P* **I** *nm* cigarette* end/fag-end; cigar butt **II** *nf* (*plus rare au masculin*) cigarette*/fag/cig(gy). (*Voir* **piqueur 2**)

cloper [klɔpe] *vtr & i P* (*a*) to smoke (*b*) to smoke (marijuana*/pot); to be on the weed.

clopin-clopant [klɔpɛ̃klɔpɑ̃] *adv F* **aller clopin-clopant,** to limp along; to hobble about; **commerce qui va clopin-clopant,** business that has its ups and downs.

clopinettes [klɔpinɛt] *nfpl P* (*a*) **des clopinettes,** nothing*/damn-all/sod-all (*b*) **des clopinettes!** nothing doing!*/no dice!/balls!

cloporte [klɔpɔrt] *nm & f P* doorkeeper/hall porter; caretaker/janitor/concierge.

cloque [klɔk] *nf P* 1. fart 2. **être en cloque,** to be pregnant*/to be in the family way; **mettre une femme en cloque,** to get a woman pregnant/to get a woman in the family way/to put a woman in the (pudding) club.

cloquer [klɔke] *P* **I** *vtr* 1. (*a*) (*donner*) to give/to hand over/to fork out; (*bazarder*) to sell off/to flog (*b*) (*mettre, poser*) to put; (*lancer*) to bung/to chuck; to land (a blow) (*c*) **cloquer le naze,** to catch syphilis*/to cop a dose of syph; **cloquer le naze à qn,** to give s.o. syphilis*/to give s.o. a dose of syph 2. **se cloquer qch,** to treat oneself to sth; **se cloquer un godet,** to knock back a drink **II** *vi* to fart* **III** *vpr* **se cloquer** 1. to place/to plonk oneself (somewhere) 2. **se cloquer à poil,** to strip naked* 3. **je m'en cloque,** I couldn't care less*/I don't give a damn/I couldn't give a fart.

clou [klu] *nm* 1. *F* chief attraction/star turn/climax/highlight; **le clou de la soirée,** the high point/the highlight of the evening 2. *P* pawnshop/uncle's; **mettre qch au clou,** to pawn sth; **ses bagues sont au clou,** her rings are in hock 3. *F* old/worn-out machine *or* instrument; **vieux clou,** old crock; (*vélo*) boneshaker; (*voiture*) banger/heap/wreck 4. *Mil* cells/clink/glasshouse; **ficher qn au clou,** to run s.o. in/to put s.o. in the cooler 5. *pl P* tools; **boîte à clous,** toolbox 6. *P* (*a*) **des clous!** nothing*!/damn all!/sweet FA! **pour des clous,** for nothing at all (*b*) **des clous!** not (bloody) likely!*/no (blooming) fear!/nothing doing!*/not on your nelly! 7. *P* **bouffer des clous,** to go without food/to live on air 8. *P* **river son clou à qn,** to silence s.o.; **ça lui a rivé son clou,** that shut him up 9. *P* **il ne fiche pas/n'en fiche pas un clou,** he doesn't do a stroke (of work)/he does damn-all 10. *P* **ça ne vaut pas un clou,** it's worthless*/it's not worth a tinker's cuss; **je n'en donnerais pas un clou,** I wouldn't give a penny for it 11. *F* **arriver sur le clou,** to arrive on the dot/to be dead on time 12. *P* **clou de cercueil,** small cigar. (*Voir* **rouillé**)

clouer [klue] *vtr P* 1. **clouer qn,** to reduce s.o. to silence/to shut s.o. up* 2. (*brocante*) **clouer un objet,** to keep an object in reserve (*for client who hasn't got the immediate cash*). (*Voir* **bec 1**)

coaltar [koltar] *nm P* 1. thick cheap red wine/plonk 2. **être dans le coaltar,** to be in a mess/in the soup; to be in a tight spot; (*ivre*) to be drunk*/pissed; (*ne pas avoir les idées claires*) to be muddle-headed.

cocard [kɔkar] *nm P* black eye*/shiner.

coccinelle [kɔksinɛl] *nf F* (*petite voiture Volkswagen*) Beetle (*RTM*).

coche [kɔʃ] *nm F* 1. **manquer/rater/louper le coche,** to miss one's chance/to miss the boat/to miss the bus 2. **faire la mouche du coche,** to buzz around self-importantly.

cocher [kɔʃe] *nm P* 1. (*aviation*) pilot 2. (*musique*) conductor.

cochon, -onne [kɔʃɔ̃, ɔn] I *nm F* 1. swine/dirty pig/filthy beast; **quel cochon!** what a swine!/what a bastard!* **c'est un cochon,** (*il raconte des histoires immondes*) he's got a filthy mind 2. **jouer un tour de cochon à qn,** to play a dirty/rotten trick on s.o. 3. (*a*) **travail de cochon,** botch job/slapdash piece of work (*b*) **il est adroit comme un cochon avec sa queue,** he's ham-fisted; he's all fingers and thumbs 4. **être copains comme cochons,** to be as thick as thieves/to be great mates/to be great buddies 5. **cochon qui s'en dédit,** it's a deal 6. **jouer un pied de cochon à qn,** to leave s.o. in the lurch 7. **nous n'avons pas gardé les cochons ensemble!** don't take liberties (with me)!/don't try it on with me! **je n'ai pas gardé les cochons avec lui!** he has no right to try it on with me! (*Voir* **cuivre**) 8. **plein/soûl comme un cochon,** dead drunk*/pissed as a newt 9. **quel cochon de temps!** what filthy weather! II *nf F* slut III *a F* 1. swinish/dirty/disgusting/filthy; dirty/smutty (story); obscene (joke); porn/blue (film) 2. **ça, c'est cochon!** that's a dirty/a rotten trick! that's a rotten thing to do! 3. **c'est pas cochon,** that's excellent*!/that's not at all bad! **mille francs, c'est pas cochon!** a thousand francs, that's pretty good!/that's better than a poke in the eye (with a blunt stick)!

cochonceté [kɔʃɔ̃ste] *nf P* 1. smutty joke 2. dirty trick.

cochonnaille [kɔʃɔnaj] *nf F* (*charcuterie*) pork; cooked meats (*bought at a pork butcher's*).

cochonner [kɔʃɔne] *vtr F* to bungle*/to botch (up)/to make a mess of (a piece of work, etc).

cochonnerie [kɔʃɔnri] *nf F* 1. (*a*) filthiness/filth; **faire des cochonneries,** (*des saletés*) to make a mess (*b*) **dire des cochonneries,** to talk smut/obscenities; **raconter des cochonneries,** to tell dirty stories/filthy jokes; **il fait des cochonneries avec la voisine,** he's up to no good with the woman next door 2. rubbish/trash/junk; **elle vend des cochonneries,** she sells junk 3. vile food/pigswill 4. **faire une cochonnerie à qn,** to play a dirty/rotten trick on s.o.; to do the dirty on s.o.

cocker [kɔkɛr] *nm P* **les avoir en oreilles de cocker,** to feel limp after making love/to feel shagged out.

cocktail [kɔktɛl] *nm F* (*a*) mixture of drugs (*eg* cocaine* and heroin*, barbiturates* and amphetamines*)/cocktail (*b*) (*alcool*) **avaler un sacré cocktail,** to drink a hell of a mixture/to mix all sorts of drinks (at a party, etc).

coco [koko, kɔ-] I *nm* 1. *Vieilli P* head*/nut; **dévisser le coco à qn,** to strangle s.o.; **avoir le coco fêlé,** to be mad*/to be off one's nut/to be as nutty as a fruit-cake 2. *P* stomach*; **se remplir le coco,** to eat* heartily/to stuff oneself/to have a good blow-out; **en avoir plein le coco,** to have a bellyful 3. *F* (*mot enfantin*) (*a*) cock/hen/chicken (*b*) egg/eggie 4. *F* communist; **les cocos,** the commies/the reds 5. *F* (*a*) (*type*) **un (drôle de) coco,** a strange fellow/an odd bod/a queer customer; **un vilain coco/un sale coco,** a nasty piece of work; *Iron et Péj* **c'est un gentil/un beau/un joli coco!** he's a nice one! (*b*) (*Péj ou amical*) **je te le répète encore une fois, coco,** I'll say it once again, old bean/mush/mate (*c*) **mon (petit) coco,** my darling*/my pet 6. *P* petrol; **mettre le coco,** to hurry* up/to step on the gas II *nf Vieilli P* (*drogues*) cocaine*/coke/snow/flake.

cocorico [kɔkɔrikɔ] *F* I *int* three cheers for France! II *nm* French victory cheer; **faire cocorico/pousser des cocoricos,** to give a victory cheer (for France).

cocoter [kɔkɔte] *vi P* to stink*/to pong.

cocotier [kɔkɔtje] *nm* 1. *F* **gagner le cocotier,** to win the big prize/to hit the jackpot 2. *F* **il descend de son cocotier,** he's a bit of a fool* 3. *F* **grimper au cocotier,** to fly into a temper/to hit the roof 4. *F* **radio cocotier,** bush telegraph.

cocotte [kɔkɔt] *nf* **1.** *F* (*mot enfantin*) cock/hen/chicken/cock-a-doodle(-doo) **2.** *F* horse; hue, cocotte! gee up!/giddy up, neddy! **3.** *F* ma (petite) cocotte, my darling*/my pet/*esp NAm* honey(bunch)/sweetie(-pie) **4.** *P* (*a*) kept woman* (*b*) prostitute*/tart/floozie.

cocotte-minute [kɔkɔtminyt] *nf P* prostitute* who gets through a succession of clients quickly.

cocotter [kɔkɔte] *vi P* to stink*/to pong.

cocu [kɔky] *nm P* **1.** cuckold **2.** avoir une chance/une veine de cocu, to have the devil's own luck; cocu! you lucky devil! **3.** et bien cocu qui s'en dédit! it's a deal!

cocuage [kɔkya3] *nm P* cuckoldry.

cocufier [kɔkyfje] *vtr P* **1.** to be unfaithful to/to cuckold (one's husband) **2.** to seduce the wife of (s.o.).

codé [kɔde] *a P* fashionable/trendy/up-to-date/with it/in the know.

cœur [kœr] *nm F* **1.** (*a*) joli cœur, effeminate man/pansy (*b*) faire le joli cœur, to put on airs (and graces) **2.** avoir le cœur bien accroché, to have a strong stomach **3.** courage; avoir du cœur au ventre, to have plenty of guts; donner du cœur au ventre à qn, to buck s.o. up/to put fresh heart into s.o.; ça vous remettra du cœur au ventre, that'll buck you up **4.** avoir un cœur d'artichaut, to fall in love with every pretty girl/handsome boy one meets **5.** dîner/déjeuner par cœur, to go without food **6.** mettre cœur sur carreau, to vomit*.

coffiot [kɔfjo] *nm P* safe/strongbox.

coffioteur [kɔfjɔtœr] *nm P* safe-breaker.

coffre [kɔfr] *nm F* chest/lungs/wind; avoir du coffre, to have a powerful voice.

coffrer [kɔfre] *vtr P* to imprison*; faire coffrer qn, to put s.o. away inside; to run s.o. in; se faire coffrer, to get nicked.

cogiter [kɔ3ite] *vi Iron* to cogitate/to think.

cogne [kɔɲ] *P* **I** *nm* (*agent de police, gendarme*) policeman*/copper/cop **II** *nf* police station*/cop shop.

Cogne-dur [kɔɲdyr] *attrib P* la Maison Cogne-dur, the police*/the cops.

cogner [kɔɲe] **I** *vtr F* **1.** (*a*) to strike/to hit/to thump (s.o.); to knock (s.o.) about; se faire cogner par la police, to get beaten up/done over by the police; il cogne sa femme, he knocks his wife about; ça va cogner, there's going to be trouble (*b*) *vi* il cogne dur, he's a hard hitter/he hits hard **2.** se cogner une corvée, to lumber oneself with a thankless job; je me suis cogné(e) le ménage comme toujours, as usual, I ended up having to do the cleaning/housework (*c*) *Journ* se cogner une manif, to cover/to report (on) a demo **3.** se cogner la tête contre les murs, to bang one's head against a brick wall **II** *vi F* **1.** to stink*/to pong **2.** ça cogne, the sun is beating down; it's pretty hot **III** *vpr* **se cogner 1.** *F* to come to blows/to have a fight*/to have a punch-up; ils se sont cognés, they had a punch-up/a fist-fight **2.** *V* to have sex*/to have a bang; se cogner qn, to bonk s.o. **3.** *P* se cogner de qch, to do without sth **4.** *P* je m'en cogne, I couldn't care less*/I don't give a damn.

cognoter [kɔɲɔte] *vi P* to stink*/to smell/to pong (to high heaven).

coiffe [kwaf] *nf F* **1.** head*/nut; en avoir ras la coiffe, to be fed up* (to the back teeth) with sth/to have had one's fill of sth **2.** onduler de la coiffe, to be mad*/nuts/bonkers.

coiffer [kwafe] **I** *vtr* **1.** *F* to control/to be at the head of (an organization, etc); coiffer un service, to head a department **2.** *F* (*sports*) to overtake; coiffer d'une courte tête, to beat by a short head; se faire coiffer au poteau, to be pipped at the post **3.** *F* coiffer son mari, to be unfaithful to one's husband **4.** *F* coiffer Sainte-Catherine, (*jeune fille*) to reach (the age of) 25 and remain unmarried **5.** *P* to arrest* (s.o.); je me suis fait coiffer par les flics, I got nicked/nabbed by the fuzz **II** *vpr* **se coiffer** *F* se coiffer de qn, to become infatuated* with s.o.; se coiffer de qch, to go for sth in a big way.

coiffeur [kwafœr] *nm F* le grand Coiffeur, the executioner.

coin [kwɛ̃] *nm F* **1.** il m'a flanqué un coup sur le coin de la gueule, he hit me in the face*/in the kisser **2.** connaître dans les coins, to know sth inside out **3.** dans le coin, in these parts/round here; est-ce que le patron est dans le coin? is the boss about/around? il habite dans le coin, he lives (a)round here **4.** le petit coin, the smallest room/the loo/NAm the bathroom; aller au petit coin, to go to the loo/NAm the bathroom **5.** aller la poignée dans le coin, (*motocycliste*) to go at a terrific speed/to do a ton **6.** se la prendre dans les coins, to have sex*/to have a quick screw/to have a quickie in strange places **7.** regard en coin, sidelong glance; sourire en coin, half smile. (*Voir* blague 2; boucher)

coincé [kwɛ̃se] *a* **1.** *F* in a fix*/in a jam/stymied/up a gum-tree **2.** *F* uneasy/stiff/not relaxed (*in a sexual situation*); sex-shy; (*complexé*) hung-up 3. *P* (*homosexuels*) homo/pédé coincé, closet queen.

coincer [kwɛ̃se] I *vi P* to stink*/to pong II *vtr F* coincer qn, (*duper*) to corner s.o.; (*arrêter*) to arrest* s.o./to nick s.o./to nab s.o. III *vpr* **se coincer** *V* se coincer les couilles, to get one's balls in a twist (*esp by wearing tight trousers*). (*Voir* **bulle II 1**)

coinceteau [kwɛ̃sto] *nm P* (*a*) (little) corner; district/manor; dans le coinceteau, in these parts/round here (*b*) sheltered spot.

coincoin [kwɛ̃kwɛ̃] *nm P* 1. holder of the *Palmes académiques* 2. priest*.

coing [kwɛ̃] *nm P* gelée de coing, difficult situation/fix/trouble.

coinsteau, coinsto(t) [kwɛ̃sto] *nm P* = **coinceteau**.

coke [kɔk] *nf P* (*drogues*) cocaine*/coke.

col [kɔl] *F* I *nm* 1. se hausser/se pousser du col, to swank/to show off*/to put on airs 2. col(-)bleu, (*marin*) sailor/bluejacket; (*ouvrier*) blue-collar worker 3. col(-)blanc, white-collar worker 4. faux col, head (*of froth on glass of beer*) II *nf Journ* (*abrév = colonne*) column; article sur trois cols, three-column article. (*Voir* **rabat 2**)

colbac, colbaque [kɔlbak] *nm P* 1. neck; sauter au colbac de qn, to grab (hold of) s.o. 2. throat.

colère [kɔlɛr] *a F* être colère, to be angry*/to blow up.

colibar [kɔlibar] *nm P* (*a*) parcel/package (*b*) (*argot des prisons*) (food) parcel.

colibri [kɔlibri] *nm P* untrustworthy acquaintance/rat/double-crosser.

colique [kɔlik] *nf* 1. *F* (*personne ou chose*) bore*; quelle colique! what a drag!/what a bind! 2. *F* avoir la colique, to be afraid*/to have the wind up/to be in a blue funk 3. *V* avoir des coliques bâtonneuses, to have an erection*/to have a hard-on.

colis [kɔli] *nm* 1. *F* girl* 2. *P* prisoner (*esp bound hand and foot with a rope*) 3. prostitute* 'posted' elsewhere/abroad by her pimp*.

collabo [kɔlabo] *nm P* (*surt seconde guerre 1939–45*) collaborator.

collage [kɔlaʒ] *nm F* cohabitation (*of unmarried couple*)/living together.

collant [kɔlɑ̃] I *a F* (*personne*) hard to get rid of; clinging; ce qu'il est collant! he's a real pain in the neck! II *nm P* thief*/sticky-fingers.

collante [kɔlɑ̃t] *nf F* letter giving notice of the date and place/notification of an examination.

colle [kɔl] *nf* 1. (*écoles*) *F* (*a*) oral test (*b*) detention; ficher une colle à qn, to keep s.o. in; attraper deux heures de colle, to be kept in for two hours/to get two hours' detention 2. *F* poser/teaser; poser/pousser une colle à qn, to ask s.o. a sticky question/to stump s.o. 3. *F* faites chauffer la colle! (*en entendant qch se casser*) that's right/go on, smash the place up/smash everything! 4. *F* (*mariage à la*) colle, cohabitation (*of unmarried couple*)/living together; ménage à la colle, unmarried couple (living together); être/se marier/vivre à la colle, to live together/to live in sin/to be shacked up with s.o. 5. *V* chier dans la colle, to exaggerate*/to bullshit. (*Voir* **pot 1**)

coller [kɔle] I *vtr F* 1. (*a*) to give/to land (a blow, etc); coller son poing dans la figure de qn/coller une tarte à qn, to bash s.o. in the face/to sock s.o. on the jaw (*b*) to put/to place/to shove/to stick; colle ça dans un coin, stick it/plonk it/dump it in a corner; Mil coller qn au mur, to stand s.o. up against a wall and shoot him (*c*) coller qch à qn, to foist/to palm off sth on (to) s.o.; coller un gosse à une femme, to get a woman pregnant*/to put a woman in the club. (*Voir* **colloquer**) 2. coller qn, to follow s.o. (about)/to stick to s.o. like glue 3. (*écoles*) coller un élève, to keep a pupil in/to put a pupil in detention; (*à un examen*) to fail/to plough; être collé, to be failed/ploughed; j'ai été collé à l'exam, I flunked (the exam) 4. to stump/to floor (s.o.) II *vi* 1. *F* ça colle! (*d'accord*) agreed!*/OK! (*c'est logique*) that figures!/that makes sense! ça colle? how's tricks?/how goes it? (*Voir* **Anatole**); ça ne colle pas, there's something wrong/there's something not quite right; that's no good; ça ne colle pas avec lui, I can't get on with him/we don't exactly hit it off; we don't see eye to eye 2. *F* (*cyclisme, etc*) to keep close up behind the pacemaker; coller derrière, (*voiture*) to stay on s.o.'s tail/to tailgate 3. *F* elle lui colle au train/au cul, (*suivre*) she tags on to him/she clings on to him like a leech; (*importuner*) she drives him mad/she gets on his nerves III *vpr* **se coller** *F* 1. se coller avec qn, to live with s.o./to shack up with s.o. 2. se coller qn/qch, to get stuck/landed/lumbered with s.o./sth 3. je m'en colle, I couldn't care less*/I don't give a damn 4. s'y coller, to get down to work.

collet [kɔlɛ] *nm* 1. *F* être collet monté, to be straight-laced/priggish; elle est très collet monté, she's a bit of a prig, really 2. *P* (*brocante*) collet rouge, (*à Paris*) chief auctioneer at the general auction rooms.

colletar [kɔltar] *nm P* = **coaltar**.

colleter [kɔlte] I *vtr F* to embrace/to hug (s.o.) II *vpr* **se colleter** *A F* = **se coltiner** II 2.

colletin [kɔltɛ̃] *nm P* = **coltin**.

colleur, -euse [kɔlœr, -øz] *n F* 1. (*écoles*) examiner 2. bore*/pest/pain.

collier [kɔlje] *nm* 1. *F* (*a*) donner un coup de collier, to make a special effort/to put one's back into it; il est franc du collier, he's a hard worker/he won't give you any trouble (*b*) reprendre le collier, to go back to work/to get back into harness (*after holiday, illness, etc*); reprendre le collier de misère, to go back to the grindstone/to get back to (the) drudgery 2. *P* collier de corail, haemorrhoids/piles.

collimateur [kɔlimatœr] *nm F* avoir qn dans le/son collimateur, to keep an eye on s.o./a close watch on s.o.

colloquer [kɔl(l)ɔke] *F* I *vtr* colloquer qch à qn, to foist/to palm off sth on(to) s.o. II *vpr* **se colloquer** to sit down/to plonk oneself down.

colo [kɔlo] *nm or f F* (= *colonie de vacances*) children's holiday camp/summer camp/summer school; en colo, at a holiday camp.

colombier [kɔlɔ̃bje] *nm F* 1. revenir au colombier, to come back home/to come back to the nest 2. (*théâtre*) le colombier, the gods.

colombienne [kɔlɔ̃bjɛn] *nf P* (*drogues*) marijuana*.

colombin [kɔlɔ̃bɛ̃] *nm* 1. *V* turd; poser un colombin, to defecate*/to (have a) crap; *Mil* être de colombin, to be on latrine fatigue 2. *P* avoir les colombins, to be afraid*/to be shit-scared; foutre les colombins à qn, to scare s.o. shitless 3. *P* des colombins! not bloody likely!*/nothing doing!*/nuts!

colon [kɔlɔ̃] *nm P* 1. colonel/the old man 2. friend*/mate; mon pauvre colon! poor old chap!/poor blighter! ben, mon colon! well, old cock!

colonne [kɔlɔn] *nf V* 1. on dirait qu'il a chié la colonne Vendôme (et qu'elle lui pend encore au cul!), he thinks he's the cat's whiskers; he thinks the sun shines out of his arse 2. penis*/shaft; se taper (sur)/se polir la colonne, to masturbate*/to jerk off. (*Voir*

astiquer 3)

coloquinte [kɔlɔkɛ̃t] *nf P* head*; ça lui a tapé sur la coloquinte, it drove him barmy/nuts.

colosse [kɔlos] *nm* 1. *V* égoutter son colosse/faire pleurer le colosse, to urinate*/to siphon the python 2. *F* être bâti comme un colosse, to be built like a horse/to be a giant of a man.

coltin [kɔltɛ̃] *nm P* hard work/graft.

coltiner [kɔltine] I *vtr P* to carry/lug (a heavy load) II *vpr* **se coltiner** 1. *F* se coltiner qch, to take on sth disagreeable; to get landed/stuck/lumbered with sth; c'est moi qui vais me coltiner toute cette vaisselle? have I really been lumbered with all that washing-up? 2. *P* se coltiner (avec qn), to have a fight*/a punch-up (with s.o.).

comac [kɔmak], **comaco** [kɔmako] *a P* 1. very big/huge/whopping 2. broad-shouldered/hefty/beefy; athletic(-looking).

combien [kɔ̃bjɛ̃] *nm inv F* le combien sommes-nous? what's the date? il y a un car tous les combien? how often does the bus run? tu es arrivé (le) combien? where did you come (in your race)?

combientième [kɔ̃bjɛ̃tjɛm] *a & n F* nous sommes le combientième aujourd'hui? what's the date today? tu as été reçu (le) combientième à l'examen? where did you come in the exam?

combinard [kɔ̃binar] *P* I *nm* racketeer/spiv/smart Alec II *a* slick (operator).

combine [kɔ̃bin] *nf* 1. *F* (*a*) racket/shady scheme/fiddle/trick; une bonne combine, a good wheeze/scheme; il a une combine pour entrer sans payer, he knows a way of getting in without paying; gagner beaucoup d'argent au moyen de la combine, to make a lot of money by fiddling; tu es de la combine? are you in on it?/are you with us? je ne marche pas dans tes combines, I'm not falling for your fancy tricks; connaître les combines, to be in the know; mettre qn dans la combine, to put s.o. wise/to bring s.o. in on it; jouer une combine sûre, to be on(to) a sure thing (*b*) knack; (il) faut savoir la combine pour faire marcher ma radio, to get my radio to work you've got to have the knack 2. *P* (= *combinaison*) (woman's) slip.

combiner [kɔ̃bine] I *vtr F* to contrive/to cook up/to concoct/to dream up; elle combine un sale coup, she's plotting something nasty/she's planning a dirty trick II *vpr* **se**

combiner *F* ça ne se combine pas bien, it doesn't look good/right.

comble [kɔ̃bl] *nm F* ça, c'est le comble/un comble! that's the limit!*/that's the last straw!/that takes the cake!/that takes the biscuit!/that beats everything!

comédie [kɔmedi] *nf F* 1. c'est une vraie comédie! it's a laugh a minute! 2. c'est toujours la même comédie pour garer la voiture, it's always a real palaver trying to park the car 3. faire la comédie/faire une de ces comédies, to make a scene/to kick up a fuss 4. jouer la comédie, to sham/to play-act/ to put on an act.

comète [kɔmɛt] *nf F* tirer des plans sur la comète, to dream up wild schemes; to build castles in the air/in Spain. (*Voir* **refiler I** 2; **renifler I** 5)

comingue [kɔmɛ̃g] *nf P* commission/ percentage; tu prends combien de comingue? how much do you get on it?

comm' [kɔm] *nf P* = **comingue**.

commande [kɔmɑ̃d] *nf F* 1. illegal operation/shady deal(ings); fraud 2. une drôle de commande, a strange/funny business 3. connaître la commande, to be in the know 4. louper la commande, to miss one's chance/ the boat/the bus.

comme [kɔm] **I** *adv F* 1. comme ci comme ça, (fair to) middling; so-so 2. c'est tout comme, it comes to (much) the same thing; il est nommé? – non, mais c'est tout comme, has he been appointed? – no, but as good as 3. ... comme qui dirait ..., ... so to speak .../... as you might say ... 4. j'ai comme une idée qu'il va venir ce soir, I've a sort of idea that he'll come tonight 5. drôle comme tout, terribly funny*; rire comme tout, to split one's sides laughing 6. à ce moment j'ai comme perdu la tête, at that moment I sort of lost my head 7. ce n'est pas mal comme film, it's not a bad film 8. (= *comment*) il y est arrivé Dieu sait comme, he managed it, God (alone) knows how; voilà comme il est, that's just like him/that's him all over 9. naturellement/comme de juste et comme de bien entendu! absolutely! (*Voir* **autre** (*a*)) **II** *nf P* (= *commission*) commission/ percentage. (*Voir* **comingue**)

comment [kɔmɑ̃] *adv F* et comment! and how!/not half!/you bet!/rather!/you said it! ils ont été battus, et comment! they were well and truly beaten/they were beaten and how!

commiss [kɔmis] *nf P* = **comme II**.

commission [kɔmisjɔ̃] *nf F* (*langage des enfants*) faire une/sa petite commission, to urinate*/to do a wee-wee/to go wee-wee(s)/to do (a) number one; faire une/sa grosse commission, to defecate*/to do number two(s)/to do big jobs.

commode [kɔmɔd] *nf P* piano/joanna.

communard [kɔmynar] **I** *nm P* (*boisson*) red wine and blackcurrant liqueur *or* syrup **II** *a P* pif communard, red nose*/bottle-nose.

compagnie [kɔ̃paɲi] *nf F* 1. gathering/ group (of people); salut la compagnie! hi/ hello everyone! hi gang! 2. ... et compagnie, ... et cetera.

compal [kɔ̃pal] *nf P* (*écoles*) = **compo**.

compas [kɔ̃pa] *nm* 1. (*souvent au pl*) *P* legs*; allonger le(s) compas, to walk briskly; agiter les compas, to run/to beat it; jouer des compas, to run away*/to skedaddle 2. *F* avoir le compas dans l'œil, to have a good eye (*for measurements or distances*).

compère [kɔ̃pɛr] *nm F* tout se fait par compère et compagnie, it's all a put-up job.

complet [kɔ̃plɛ] *a F* (ça) c'est complet (alors)! that's the limit!*/that's all we needed!

complet-veston [kɔ̃plɛvɛstɔ̃] *nm P* se faire tailler un complet-veston, to get beaten* up.

compo [kɔ̃po] *nf*, **compote¹** [kɔ̃pɔt] *nf P* (*écoles*) composition/essay; test paper/ revision test.

compote² *nf F* 1. mettre/réduire qn en compote, to beat s.o. to a pulp; to make mincemeat of s.o. 2. j'ai la tête/les jambes en compote, my brains have gone to mush/my legs feel like jelly 3. pédaler dans la compote, to make slow progress/to find the going difficult.

compotier [kɔ̃pɔtje] *nm F* agiter les pieds dans le compotier, to put one's foot in it/to drop a brick.

comprenette [kɔ̃prənɛt] *nf F* understanding; avoir la comprenette un peu dure, to be a bit slow on the uptake/to be a bit slow to catch on.

comprenoire [kɔ̃prənwar] *nf F* = **comprenette**.

compte [kɔ̃t] *nm F* 1. il a son compte/il en a pour son compte, (*mort, fichu*) he's done for/ he's had it; he's a gonner; (*ivre*) he's drunk*/ he's had a skinful; j'ai eu mon compte, I've had enough; son compte est bon, he's for it/ he'll get what's coming to him 2. en avoir son compte, to get told off/to get hauled over the coals 3. être laissée pour compte, (femme) to be left on the shelf 4. tu te rends compte! would you believe it!/can you imagine! 5. rendre des comptes, to vomit* 6. comptes d'apothicaire, (very) detailed accounts (every penny haggled over).

comptée [kɔ̃te] nf P prostitute's earnings (to be handed over to her pimp*). (Voir **compteur 2**)

compte-gouttes [kɔ̃tgut] nm inv P fabriqué au compte-gouttes, in very small quantities; (personne) undersized*/short-arsed.

compteur [kɔ̃tœr] nm P 1. avoir un compteur à gaz dans le dos, to be hunchbacked 2. relever le compteur, (souteneur) to collect a prostitute's earnings. (Voir **comptée**).

con [kɔ̃] I nm V 1. female genitals*/cunt; avoir le con en joie/être chaude du con, to feel randy/to have the hots/to be asking for it 2. fool*; stupid* bastard*/silly bugger/(silly) cunt/silly fucker; le roi des cons, a complete ass/a bloody idiot/a real jerk; (quelle) bande de cons! what a load of (bloody) idiots!/what a load of cretins! si les cons volaient, tu serais chef d'escadrille, you really are a prat! pauvre con! poor sod! espèce de con!/tête de con! you bloody fool!/you silly sod!/you stupid* bugger! faire le con/jouer au con, to play the bloody fool; to fart around; to pretend to be stupid*/to act daft; va pas faire le con là-dedans! don't go arsing about in there! arrête de faire le con! stop pissing about! ... à la con, bloody silly .../cockeyed ...; idée à la con, lousy idea/bloody stupid idea; boulot à la con, lousy job; piège à cons, swindle*/hoax; mug's game 3. se retrouver comme un con, to find oneself alone in a ridiculous situation; je me suis retrouvé comme un con, I felt a real wally/jerk. (Voir **attrape-con(s)**) 4. contemptible person/creep/rotten bastard*/nasty piece of work/cunt/son of a bitch II a inv V (a) il est con comme la lune/comme un (manche à) balai/comme un panier/comme une valise, he's as stupid* as they come/as daft as a brush; he's a bloody idiot/he's a prize cunt. (Voir **manche I 1**) (b) elle est rien con, ton histoire! your story is all balls/is a load of cobblers! c'est trop con! it's too bloody silly for words! c'est drôlement con! it's a load of crap!/it's fucking rubbish! pas si con! (chose) not such a bad idea!/a bloody good idea!

(personne) he/she/I, etc ain't such a fool! (Voir **bite 3**; **traîne-cons**)

conard, -arde [kɔnar, -ard] n & a V = **connard**.

conasse [kɔnas] nf V = **connasse**.

concal [kɔ̃kal] nm P exam(ination).

concentre [kɔ̃sɑ̃tr] nf P (= concentration) gathering/group/band (of motorcyclists, etc); bikers' rally.

concepige [kɔ̃spiʒ] nm & f P concierge/caretaker.

conceté [kɔ̃ste] nf P crass stupidity; bloody nonsense*/bollocks/bullshit.

concierge [kɔ̃sjɛrʒ] nm & f F 1. quel(le) concierge! what a chatterbox! c'est une vraie concierge, he's/she's a terrible gossip 2. (ne) fais pas la concierge! don't be nosy! 3. journal de concierge, popular (news)paper/= tabloid.

concours [kɔ̃kur] nm F concours Lépine, the cours Albert-1er and the cours La Reine (in Paris) (frequented by homosexuals).

condé [kɔ̃de] nm P 1. plain-clothes detective 2. (a) police permit (b) police protection; avoir le/du condé, to be authorized to carry on a more or less illicit activity (in return for information) 3. scheme/wheeze (for making easy money with minimum risk)/fiddle 4. (tuyau) information*/tip(-off).

condice, condisse [kɔ̃dis] nf P = **conditionnelle**.

conditionnelle [kɔ̃disjɔnɛl] nf F = conditional discharge (of prisoner if work is found for him/her).

conduite [kɔ̃dɥit] nf F (s')acheter une conduite, to turn over a new leaf/to mend one's ways. (Voir **Grenoble**)

coneau [kɔno] nm & a V = **connard** I, II.

confiture [kɔ̃fityr] nf 1. F de la confiture aux cochons, caviar(e) for the general 2. F mettre/réduire qn en confiture, to pound s.o. to a jelly/to make mincemeat of s.o. 3. P être dans la confiture, to be in a fix*/to be in a jam 4. P opium*/tar 5. V passive homosexuality.

confortables [kɔ̃fɔrtabl] nmpl F carpet slippers.

confrérie [kɔ̃freri] nf P la grande confrérie, (cocus) cuckolds/deceived husbands (in general); (homosexuels) homosexuals* (in general)/pansyland.

cônir [konir] vtr P to kill*/to bump off.

conjungo [kɔ̃ʒœ̃go] nm F (a) marriage; prononcer le conjungo, to tie the knot (b) mon conjungo, my husband*/my wife*/my better half.

connaissance [kɔnɛsɑ̃s] *nf F* girlfriend; boyfriend; lover.

connaître [kɔnɛtr] I *vtr F* en connaître un bout/un rayon, to know a lot; to be in the know; to be an old hand (at it); to know the score; to know a thing or two; ça me connaît, I know all about that/you can't teach me anything about that; I'm an old hand/a dab hand at that; that's right up my street; je ne connais que ça/que lui! I know that/him only too well!/don't I know it/him! (*Voir* **bout 4; musique 1; rayon 2**) II *vpr* **se connaître** *F* il s'y connaît, he's an expert/a dab hand; he knows his stuff/he knows what it's all about.

connard, -arde [kɔnar, -ard] I *n* fool*/ stupid bastard/silly bugger/silly cow II *a* stupid*/bloody silly.

connasse [kɔnas] *nf V* 1. female genitals*/ cunt 2. = **con** I 2 3. (*a*) *pl Péj* women* (*in general*)/bitches (*b*) stupid bitch/silly cow/ silly old bag 4. freelance prostitute (*not protected by a pimp*).

conne [kɔn] *V* I *nf* stupid bitch/silly cow II *af* bloody stupid*/daft as they come.

conneau [kɔno] *nm & a V* = **connard** I, II.

connement [kɔnmɑ̃] *adv V* like a bloody fool.

connerie [kɔnri] *nf P* bloody nonsense*/ boloney/balls/crap; quelle connerie! balls!/ what (a load of) crap!/cobblers! arrête tes conneries! cut the crap! faire une connerie, to do sth bloody stupid; il a encore fait une connerie, he's fucked it up again; c'est des conneries, it's all cock/it's a load of balls; (ne) dis pas de(s) conneries, don't talk cock/ balls/crap.

con(n)obler [kɔnɔble], **con(n)obrer** [kɔnɔbre] *vtr P* to know.

connu! [kɔny] *pp & excl F* = ça me connaît (**connaître** I).

conomètre [kɔnɔmɛtr] *nm P* faire péter le conomètre, to be extremely stupid*/to be bloody silly.

conscrard [kɔ̃skrar] *nm P* (*argot de l'École polytechnique*) conscript.

conscrit [kɔ̃skri] *nm F* (*a*) novice/greenhorn (*b*) (*argot de l'École normale supérieure*) first-year student.

conséquent [kɔ̃sekɑ̃] *a F* big/important; homme conséquent, bigwig; affaire conséquente, important piece of business.

consigne [kɔ̃siɲ] *nf F* avaler/manger la consigne, to forget one's orders/one's instruc-

tions; to disregard one's orders/one's instructions.

conso [kɔ̃so] *nf P* = **consomme**.

consolation [kɔ̃sɔlasjɔ̃] *nf* 1. *Vieilli F* brandy; spirits*; un petit verre de consolation, a little drop of comfort 2. *P* fellatio* *or* masturbation* instead of sex*.

consomme [kɔ̃sɔm] *nf F* (= *consommation*) drink (in a café, etc).

constipé [kɔ̃stipe] *a* 1. *F* miserly*. (*Voir* **morlingue**) 2. *F* (*a*) serious-minded (*b*) sullen (*c*) uneasy/embarrassed/strained 3. *V* être constipé de l'entre-jambes/du calbard, to be unable to get an erection*/a hard-on. (*Voir* **feuille 1**)

contact [kɔ̃takt] *nm F* (*personne*) contact/ connection/informant (*esp for drugs*).

content [kɔ̃tɑ̃] *nm Vieilli P* avoir son petit content, to have sex*.

contrat [kɔ̃tra] *nm F* (*d'un tueur*) contract; (*assassinat*) contract killing.

contre [kɔ̃tr] *adv F* against/agin; je suis contre, I'm against it.

contrecarre [kɔ̃trəkar] *F* 1. *nm ou f* faire un(e) contrecarre à qn, to put obstacles in s.o.'s way/to thwart s.o. 2. *nf* rivalry.

contrecoup [kɔ̃trəku] *nm F* foreman/boss.

contredanse [kɔ̃trədɑ̃s] *nf F* police summons/(parking) ticket; flanquer une contredanse à qn, to book s.o./to give s.o. a ticket.

contrefiche [kɔ̃trəfiʃ] *nm F* = **contrecoup**.

se contrefiche(r) [səkɔ̃trəfiʃ(e)] *vpr,* **se contrefoutre** [səkɔ̃trəfutr] *vpr P* je m'en fiche et (je) m'en contrefiche!/je m'en fous et (je) m'en contrefous! I couldn't care less!*/I couldn't care bloody less!/I couldn't give a toss!

contremarque [kɔ̃trəmark] *nf Vieilli F* une contremarque pour Bagneux/pour Pantin, a doctor's prescription.

contremouche [kɔ̃trəmuʃ] *nf P* smuggling.

contrer [kɔ̃tre] *vtr F* to thwart/to cross (s.o.).

convalo [kɔ̃valo] *nf P* convalescence/sick leave.

converse [kɔ̃vɛrs] *nf P* conversation.

convoi [kɔ̃vwa] *nm F* être du même convoi, to be in the same boat.

convoque [kɔ̃vɔk] *nf P* summons.

cool [kul], **coolos** [kulos] *a P* 1. relaxed/ cool; il est très cool, ce mec, he's a really cool guy/he's really laid-back; **il est pas très cool ton père,** you're father's a bit uptight; **cool, Raoul,** relax/let's not get excited/don't panic **2.** *Péj* limp. (*Voir* **raoul**)

coopé [kɔpe] *nf F* **1.** (*abrév* = *coopérative*) co-operative stores/co-op **2.** (*abrév* = *coopération*) aid to developing countries; = Voluntary Service Overseas.

coordonnées [kɔɔrdɔne] *nfpl F* **donnez-moi vos coordonnées,** give me your address and phone number/give me your details.

cop [kɔp] *nm P* = **copain.**

copaille [kɔpaj] *nf P* despicable person/good-for-nothing/heel/louse. (*Voir* **balle 9**)

copain [kɔpɛ̃] *nm F* friend*/pal/mate/buddy; **être bons copains,** to be good pals/to be mates; **les petits copains,** those who stick together; = the old boy network. (*Voir* **cochon I 4; copine**)

copeaux [kɔpo] *nmpl P* **avoir les copeaux,** to be afraid*; **foutre les copeaux à qn,** to put the wind up s.o. (*Voir* **arracher I 3**)

copie [kɔpi] *nf P Journ* **pisser de la copie/sa copie,** to churn it out; **pondre de la copie,** to write copy to order; **pisseur, -euse de copie,** hack writer. (*Voir* **pisse-copie**)

copier [kɔpje] *vtr F* **1. celle-là, tu me la copieras!** you won't catch me (out) again!/I'll know better next time!/I'll pay you back for that! **2. je la ferai copier, celle-là!** well, I like that!/that's a good one, that is!

copinage [kɔpinaʒ] *nm F* pally/chummy relationship; palliness/chumminess; **dans ce milieu ça ne marche que par copinage,** around here, it's who you know that matters/what counts around here is who you're friendly with.

copine [kɔpin] *nf F* (female) friend/girlfriend. (*Voir* **copain**)

copiner [kɔpine] *vi F* **copiner avec qn,** to become friendly with s.o./to be great mates with s.o.; to pal up/to be pally with.

copinerie [kɔpinri] *nf F* = **copinage.**

coq [kɔk] *nm F* **des mollets de coq,** thin legs*/matchsticks.

coquard, coquart [kɔkar] *nm P* black eye*/shiner.

coquelicot [kɔkliko] *nm P* **1.** = **coquard 2. elle a ses coquelicots,** she's got a period*/she's got the curse.

coqueluche [kɔklyʃ] *nf F* **être la coqueluche de qn,** to be s.o.'s idol/great favourite/darling.

coquetier [kɔktje] *nm F* cup; **gagner/**emporter **le coquetier,** to win (the) top prize/to hit the jackpot.

coquette [kɔkɛt] *nf* **1.** *V* penis*/cock/prick **2.** *F* **faire sa (grande) coquette,** (*se faire prier*) to play hard to get; to be difficult to persuade.

coquetterie [kɔkɛtri] *nf P* **avoir une coquetterie dans l'œil,** to squint.

coqueur [kɔkœr] *nm Vieilli P* informer*/squealer/grass.

coquillard [kɔkijar] *nm P* eye*; **je m'en bats/je m'en tamponne/je m'en tape le coquillard,** I couldn't care less*; I don't give a damn; to hell with it.

coquin [kɔkɛ̃] *nm* **1.** *F Hum* (*a*) husband (*b*) fancy man **2.** *F* (*en Provence*) **coquin de sort!** hang it!/blow it!/damn it! **3.** *P* strong wine.

cor [kɔr] *nm F* **1.** he-man **2. emmaillotté dans un cor de chasse,** bandy-legged.

corbaque [kɔrbak] *nm P* crow; rook; raven.

corbeau, pl -eaux [kɔrbo] *nm P* **1.** priest* (*in a cassock*)/black coat **2.** body-snatcher/ghoul **3.** (*personne*) bird of ill omen **4.** writer of (anonymous) poison-pen letters **5.** rapacious person/shark.

corbi [kɔrbi] *nm P* (*abrév* = *corbillard*) hearse.

corde [kɔrd] *nf F* **1. être au bout de sa corde,** to be at the end of one's tether; **être à la corde,** to be penniless* **2. être sur la corde raide,** to be in a dangerous situation/to walk the tightrope **3. sauter à la corde,** (*se priver*) to tighten one's belt/to go without (food); to go/to do without **4. se mettre la corde au cou,** to get married*/to tie the knot/to get hitched/to get spliced **5. se mettre la corde pour ...,** to give up all hope of ... **6. ça sent la corde,** it looks suspicious/I don't like the look of it **7. tenir la corde,** to hold an advantage/to have the edge **8. il y va de la corde,** it's a hanging matter; **il ne vaut pas la corde pour la prendre,** he's not worth the rope to hang him with; **il a de la corde de pendu dans sa poche,** he has the devil's own luck **9. il pleut/il tombe des cordes,** it's raining cats and dogs; it's bucketing down **10.** *Aut* **prendre un virage/un tournant à la corde,** to cut a corner close/to hug the bend **11. ce n'est pas/ça ne rentre pas dans mes cordes,** it's not in my line/it's not my cup of tea; **c'est tout à fait dans mes cordes,** it's right up my street/it suits me fine.

cormoran [kɔrmɔrɑ̃] *nm P Péj* Jew*.

cornac [kɔrnak] *nm F* (tourist) guide. (*Voir* **cornaquer**)

cornanche [kɔrnɑ̃ʃ] *nf P* mark made on (playing) card (*by cardsharp*).

cornancher [kɔrnɑ̃ʃe] *P* I *vtr* 1. (*a*) to beat up*/to brain (s.o.) (*b*) to kill* 2. to mark (a playing card) II *vi* to stink*.

cornaquer [kɔrnake] *vtr F* to guide/to shepherd (tourists). (*Voir* **cornac**)

cornard [kɔrnar] *nm F* deceived husband/ cuckold.

corner [kɔrne] *vi* 1. *F* les oreilles ont dû lui corner, his ears must have been burning 2. *P* to stink*.

cornes [kɔrn] *nfpl F* 1. montrer les cornes, to show fight 2. faire les cornes à qn, to jeer at/to mock/to make a face at s.o. 3. porter des cornes, to be a cuckold/to wear horns; faire porter des cornes à qn, to cuckold s.o.

cornet [kɔrnɛ] *nm P* 1. throat/gullet; se rincer le cornet, to have a drink*/to wet one's whistle 2. stomach*; se mettre qch dans le cornet/se remplir le cornet, to eat* heartily/to have a good tuck-in.

cornette [kɔrnɛt] *nf F* 1. woman whose husband is unfaithful to her 2. (Catholic) nun.

corniaud [kɔrnjo] *nm P* fool*/clot/twit.

corniche [kɔrniʃ] *nf P* class preparing for Saint-Cyr military school.

cornichon [kɔrniʃɔ̃] *nm* 1. *P* novice/ greenhorn 2. *P* fool*/jerk 3. *P* telephone*/ blower; un coup de cornichon, a (phone) call/ a ring/a buzz 4. *P* student preparing for Saint-Cyr military school.

Cornouailles [kɔrnwaj] *Prnf Vieilli F* aller en Cornouailles, to be a cuckold/to wear horns.

corps [kɔr] *nm F* 1. il faut voir ce qu'il a dans le corps, we'll have to see (*de quoi il est fait*) what he's made of/what he's got in him, (*ce qui le pousse*) what makes him tick 2. c'est un drôle de corps, he's a strange creature/an odd bod.

corrida [kɔrida] *nf P* free-for-all/punch-up; quelle corrida! what a carry-on/what a to-do! ça a été une vraie corrida, there was a lot of trouble/aggro; c'est la corrida dans le métro à cette heure-ci, it's a real hassle in the tube at this time of day.

corser [kɔrse] *I vtr F* 1. corser une note, to charge extortionately/to stick sth (extra) on the bill 2. corser un problème, to make a problem harder to solve 3. *Journ* corser la sauce, to add spice to/to liven up a story

II *vpr* **se corser** *F* ça se corse/l'affaire se corse, (*d'une enquête, etc*) the plot thickens; (*dans la vie*) things are getting serious.

Corsic [kɔrsik] *nm & f,* **Corsico** [kɔrsiko] *nm P* Corsican.

corsif [kɔrsif] *nm P* corset.

cortausse [kɔrtos] *nf P* beating*/severe thrashing/good hiding.

corvette [kɔrvɛt] *nf P* 1. seductive/sexy girl* 2. young homosexual*.

cossard [kɔsar] *P* I *a* lazy*/idle II *nm* lazybones/lazy bum/lazy slob.

cosse [kɔs] *nf P* laziness; avoir la cosse/ avoir les pieds en cosses de melon, to be/to feel lazy*; tirer sa cosse, to (sit around and) do nothing/to laze about/to do damn-all/to be a couch potato.

cossu [kɔsy] *a F* rich*/well-off/well-to-do/ flush.

costard [kɔstar] *nm P* man's suit; costard-cravate/costard trois pièces, three piece suit (and tie)/suit, waistcoat and tie; le look costard-cravate, the well-dressed man/gent; se faire tailler un costard, to get beaten up.

costaud, -aude [kɔsto, -od], **costeau** [kɔsto], **costo, -ote** [kɔsto, -ɔt] *F* I *a* hefty/beefy/strapping (individual); (*moralement*) tough; solidly built (structure); tough (material, etc); solid/intense (argument); ça c'est costaud! (*boisson*) that's strong!/that's got a kick in it! je ne me sens pas costaud, I don't feel too good/I feel a bit out of sorts II *n* strong/hefty/strapping person; (*moralement*) tough person; c'est du costaud, it's sturdily made.

costume [kɔstym] *nm P* se faire faire/se faire tailler un costume en bois, to die*/to get fitted for a wooden overcoat. (*Voir* **Adam**; **Ève 2**; **sapin 1**)

cote [kɔt] *nf F* (*a*) reputation; avoir une grosse cote, to be highly thought of (*b*) favouritism/popularity; avoir la cote, to be popular; avoir une drôle de cote, to be extremely popular.

côte [kot] I *nf F* 1. avoir les côtes en long, to be lazy* 2. se tenir les côtes (de rire), to laugh* uproariously/to split one's sides laughing 3. chatouiller/tanner les côtes à qn, to give s.o. a good hiding 4. serrer les côtes à qn, to keep s.o. at it; to keep s.o. up to scratch 5. Côtes du Rhône (wine). (*Voir* **caler II 2**) II *nf F* être à la côte, to be penniless*/to be on one's beam ends.

cotelard [kɔtəlar] *a P* = **cottard**.

côtelette [kotlɛt, kɔ-] *nf* 1. *pl P* ribs (of person); **sauver ses côtelettes**, to save one's skin; **travailler les côtelettes à qn**, to beat s.o. up*/to lay into s.o. 2. *pl Vieilli F* muttonchop whiskers 3. *P* (*taxis Parisiens*) (*a*) disciplinary commission (*b*) temporary withdrawal of (taxi driver's) licence 4. *V* **pisser/sortir sa côtelette**, to give birth (to a baby); **pisseuse de côtelettes**, fertile woman; woman who is always giving birth. (*Voir* **planquer I 1** (*a*))

coton [kɔtɔ̃] **I** *a F* difficult; complicated; **c'est coton**, it's a tough/tricky job; it's a bit tricky **II** *nm* 1. *P* trouble/difficulty; **il va y avoir du coton**, there's going to be trouble; **avoir un sacré coton pour ...**, to have the devil of a job to ... 2. *F* **filer un mauvais/un sale/un vilain coton**, to be in a bad way (*in health or business*) 3. *F* **élevé dans le/dans du coton**, mollycoddled 4. *F* fog/mist; (*aviation*) clouds 5. *F* **se sentir tout en coton**, to feel flabby. (*Voir* **jambe 6**)

cottard [kɔtar] *a P* 1. hefty/husky/beefy/brawny 2. (*chose, problème*) difficult/tough.

cotte [kɔt] *nf P* (*bleu*) (workman's) overalls/dungarees.

cou [ku] *nm F* 1. **monter le cou à qn**, to kid s.o./to have s.o. on 2. **casser le cou à qn**, to beat s.o. up*/to give s.o. a going-over. (*Voir* **casse-cou**; **jambe 1** (*a*))

couchage [kuʃaʒ] *nm P* sex*.

couche [kuʃ] *nf P* **en avoir une couche/en tenir une couche**, to be an absolute fool*/a complete idiot/really thick; **il en a/il en tient une couche!** he's really dumb!/he's a real thickie!

couché, coucher[1] [kuʃe] *nm P* (*prostitution*) (*a*) whole night spent with a prostitute* (*b*) **avoir/faire un couché**, (*prostituée*) to have an all-night client/an all-nighter.

coucher[2] *F* **I** *vi* **coucher avec qn**, to have sex* with s.o./to sleep with s.o./to go to bed with s.o.; **coucher à droite et à gauche/avec n'importe qui**, to sleep/to screw around; to be an easy lay/a pushover **II** *vtr* **avoir un nom à coucher dehors**, to have a name which is very difficult to pronounce. (*Voir* **adjudant** (*a*); **tête 22**) **III** *vpr* **se coucher** 1. *F* **va te coucher!** get lost!*/clear off! 2. *F* (*sports*) to abandon/pull out (of a match, etc); (*boxe*) to take a dive 3. *P* **elle se couche quand on lui dit de s'asseoir**, she'll go to bed with any Tom, Dick or Harry; she's an easy lay/

a pushover.

coucherie [kuʃri] *nf P* sex*.

coucheur [kuʃœr] *nm F* **c'est un mauvais coucheur**, he's a cantankerous so-and-so/a bloody-minded sod/an awkward customer.

couci-couça [kusikusa], **couci-couci** [kusikusi] *adv F* so-so; **ça va couci-couça**, I'm fair to middling/I'm not doing too badly.

coucou [kuku] *nm* 1. *F* (*vieux véhicule, vieille machine*) (*avion*) old plane/crate; (*voiture*) (old) banger/jalopy/heap 2. *Vieilli P* watch/tick-tock.

coucouche [kukuʃ] *int F* **coucouche (panier)!** (*à un chien*) go to your basket!/lie down! **coucouche!** (*à une personne*) don't move!/calm down!/don't panic!

coude [kud] *nm F* 1. **avoir mal au coude**, to be/to feel lazy 2. **lâche-moi le coude!** stop bothering me! 3. **lever le coude**, to lift the elbow/to booze. (*Voir* **doigt 6**; **huile 1**; **se moucher 1**)

couenne [kwan] *nf* 1. *P* skin; **gratter la couenne à qn**, to flatter* s.o./to scratch s.o.'s back; **se gratter/se racler la couenne**, to have a shave; **se sucer la couenne**, to kiss 2. *P* fool*/twit/clot; **quelle couenne!** what a twerp!/what a nurd!

couic [kwik] *nm F* 1. **faire couic**, to die*/to croak/to give one's last gasp 2. **je n'y comprend/je n'y pige que couic**, I don't see/understand/get it at all; I can't make head or tail of it; I haven't the foggiest.

couillard [kujar] *a V* having large testicles*/big-balled/well-hung/well-equipped.

couille [kuj] *nf V* 1. testicle*/ball; (*a*) **j'en ai plein les couilles**, I've had it up to here/I'm fucking fed up* (with it)/I'm pissed off (with it); **casser les couilles à qn**, to bore* s.o. rigid/to give s.o. a pain in the arse; **tu me casses les couilles/tu me fais mal aux couilles**, you give me (the) balls-ache/you piss me off (*b*) **avoir des couilles au cul**, to have guts/to have spunk/to have (a lot of) balls; **il n'a pas de couilles**, he's got no balls/no bottle; he's a non-drop (*c*) **c'est des couilles** (**en barre/en bâtons**)! (*sans intérêt*) that's balls!/that's bollocks!/that's a load of balls! (*sans valeur*) it's worthless junk!/it's crap! **mes couilles!** balls!/bollocks! 2. **une couille molle**, a wet/a drip/a wimp/a non-drop 3. **partir/tomber/tourner en couille**, to fail*/to go down the drain/to go to pot/to go downhill 4. **ça, c'est couille!** that's a bugger!/that's a bastard! 5. **je me ferai un porte-monnaie avec**

tes couilles! I'll have your guts for garters! **6. se faire des couilles en or,** to make a lot of money*/to get rich*/to make a packet **7. à couilles rabattues,** intensely/energetically; **baiser qn à couilles rabattues,** to make love to s.o. often and all over the place; to be always at it/on the go **8.** mistake*; **faire une couille,** to make a balls-up/a cock-up **9.** (serious) problem/trouble; **il lui est arrivé une couille,** he got into trouble; he was in deep shit. (*Voir* **branler II 3; peau 22** (*a*))

couiller [kuje] *vtr P* to deceive*/to swindle*; **il s'est fait couiller,** he got done/had.

couillibi [kujibi] *nm P* fool*/twit/clot.

couillon [kujɔ̃] *P* I *a* stupid*/thick/dim; **être couillon comme la lune,** to be as thick as two short planks/to be a bloody idiot/to be a real jerk; **c'est drôlement couillon!** that's a load of cobblers! **c'est trop couillon!** it's too fucking daft for words! II *nm* (*a*) fool*/jerk/cretin; **espèce de couillon!** you bloody fool!/you silly fucker!/you stupid cunt! **faire le couillon,** to arse about/to fart about/to piss about. (*Voir* **attrape-couillon(s)**) (*b*) (et) **couillon qui s'en dédit,** and to hell with anyone who says otherwise!

couillonnade [kujɔnad] *nf P* (*a*) nonsense*/rubbish/boloney/crap/shit; **quelle couillonnade!** what a load of tripe!/(what) balls!/ballocks!/bullshit! **dire des couillonnades,** to talk cock/to bullshit (*b*) **faire une couillonnade,** to make a mistake*/to put one's foot in it; **il en a fait une couillonnade,** he's made a balls(-up)/a cock(-up) of it; **en voilà une couillonnade!** what a bloody stupid thing to do!

couillonner [kujɔne] *P* I *vtr* (*a*) to make a fool/a sucker of (s.o.); to make a monkey out of (s.o.); **je me suis fait couillonner,** I've been had/I've been done (*b*) to make a balls(-up) of (sth); **du travail couillonné,** ballsed-up work/a balls-up II *vi* to fool around*/to arse about/to fart around/to piss about.

couillonnerie [kujɔnri] *nf P* = **couillonnade**.

couiner [kwine] *vi F* **1.** to cry*/to snivel/to whine/to whimper **2.** (*freins, pneus*) to squeal/to screech.

couineur [kwinœr] *nm F* driver who toots his horn incessantly.

coulage [kulaʒ] *nm F* **1.** waste/wasting **2.** (*dans une entreprise*) petty theft (*by staff*).

coulant [kulɑ̃] I *nm P* **1.** ripe cheese/*esp* camembert **2.** *Vieilli* milk II *a F* easy-going;

homme coulant en affaires, man who takes things in his stride.

coulante [kulɑ̃t] *nf V* **1.** diarrhoea*/the runs **2.** VD*/gonorrhoea*/clap.

coule [kul] *nf F* (*a*) **être à la coule,** (*au courant*) to be in the know/to know what's what/to know the score/to be with it; (*indulgent*) to be easy-going/laid-back (*b*) **mettre qn à la coule,** to put s.o. wise/to show s.o. the ropes/to teach s.o. the tricks of the trade (*c*) **se mettre à la coule,** to get wise/to wise up (**de,** to)/to get with it.

coulé [kule] *a F* **c'est un homme coulé,** he's finished/done for/washed up; he's had it.

couler [kule] *F* I *vtr* **1.** to discredit/to bring disgrace on (s.o.)/to ruin; **ce scandale l'a coulé,** this scandal has brought about his downfall/this scandal has brought him down **2. se la couler douce,** to take it easy*/to have a good time/to have it easy. (*Voir* **bronze 1**) II *vi* (*d'une entreprise, etc*) to go bankrupt/to go bust; **l'éditeur a coulé,** the publisher went bust/down the tubes.

couleur [kulœr] *nf F* **1.** lie/fib; **monter une couleur,** to lie*/to fib **2. annoncer la couleur,** to have one's say/to state one's case; to show one's hand/to lay one's cards on the table; (*faire son choix de boisson*) to state one's choice of drink/to name one's poison; **faut pas changer de couleur,** don't mix your drinks **3. affranchir/donner la couleur à qn, ouvrir à la couleur,** to put s.o. in the know/to put s.o. wise; **ne pas être à la couleur,** not to be in the know **4. défendre ses couleurs,** to stick up for oneself **5. en dire de toutes les couleurs à qn,** to give s.o. a piece of one's mind; **on m'en dit de toutes les couleurs sur votre compte,** I've heard all sorts of (bad) things about you **6. en voir de toutes les couleurs,** to have a rough time of it; **en faire voir de toutes les couleurs à qn,** to lead s.o. a song and dance; **en avoir vu de toutes les couleurs,** to have been through the mill/to have had a rough time of it. (*Voir aussi* **voir II 1**) **7. je n'en ai pas encore vu la couleur,** I've seen no sign of it yet.

couloir [kulwar] *nm V* **couloir à/aux lentilles,** anus*/arse(-hole)/*surt NAm* ass (-hole).

coulos [kulos] *a P* = **coolos**.

coup [ku] *nm F* **1. avoir/piger le coup pour faire qch,** to have the knack of doing sth **2. coup de rouge,** glass of red wine; **boire un coup,** to have a drink; **il a bu un coup de trop,**

he's had a drop too much/one too many 3. un sale coup, a dirty trick; ça, c'est un sale coup! what a dirty trick! c'est encore un coup de ton ami, it's another of your friend's tricks; coup dur, awkward/difficult situation; trouble; coup fourré, (délit) offence; (situation malhonnête) fraud/shady operation; (coup déloyal) dirty trick. (Voir aussi coup 14) 4. écraser le coup, to hush sth up; to let bygones be bygones/to say no more about it 5. en avoir un coup, to be mad*/insane 6. être au coup, to be in the know 7. être aux cents coups, to be worried stiff 8. faire un coup, to clinch a lucrative deal which leads to nothing 9. être dans le coup, (participer à qch) to be in on sth/to be involved; (être au courant) to be in the know/to know what's going on; (être à la mode) to be up to date/to be with it; mettre qn dans le coup, to put s.o. in the picture; (impliquer) to get/bring s.o. in on it; se mettre dans/sur le coup, to be in on sth/to be involved 10. expliquer le coup, to explain the situation/to gen s.o. up 11. faire le coup à qn, to play a trick on s.o.; si on cherche à vous faire le coup ..., if people try it on with you ... 12. faire les quatre cents coups, to lead a reckless life 13. en jeter un coup/en mettre un (vieux) coup, to put some guts/some vim/ one's back into it; to buckle down to it; mets-y un coup! give it everything you've got! 14. (a) monter un coup, (cambriolage, entreprise plus ou moins délictueuse, etc) to set up/to pull (off) a job (b) monter un coup contre qn, to frame s.o.; un coup monté, a frame-up/a put-up job (c) monter le coup à qn, to (try to) deceive* s.o./to kid s.o./to have s.o. on; ne me monte pas le coup! don't give me that! se monter le coup, to kid oneself 15. tenir le coup, to stick it out/to be able to take it 16. tenter le coup, to chance it/to chance one's arm/to have a bash (at it)/to have a stab (at it); ça vaut le coup, it's worth a try; ça ne vaut pas le coup, it's not worthwhile/it's not worth 17. marquer le coup, to mark/celebrate the occasion 18. prendre un coup de vieux/en prendre un coup, to age (suddenly)/to start to look old 19. coup de queue/de guiseau/de traversin, sex*/(a) screw/(a) bonk 20. sexual partner/lover; (occasionnel) one-night stand; c'est (un) bon coup, (s)he's a good screw/a good lay; (d'un sportif, etc) (s)he's a good player; j'ai vu un de mes anciens coups, I saw an ex-lover of mine/one of my ex-lovers. (Voir aile 4; balai 1; bambou 2; barre 1, 2; blanc II 3; boule² 1; carreau 3; châsse 1; chien 11; cidre 2; deux 1; épaule 1; feu 7; ficher 1, 3; fil 9; filet 2; foudre; fourchette 1, 3; foutre I 9; François; fusil 1, 4; gueule 1 3; lapin 3; masse II 1, 2; massue; nez 5 (b); patte 2, 9; pied 11, 12, 14, 23; pompe 1, 4 (b); pot 12; pouce 1; sabord 2; sabre 2; serviette; tampon 1; tirer 6; torchon 6; Trafalgar; tromblon 3; trompette 3; veine)

couparès [kuparɛs] a P penniless*/broke.

coupé [kupe] a P être coupé (à blanc), to be penniless*/to be skint.

coupe-chiasse [kupʃjas] nm P (dispensing) chemist/pharmacist.

coupe-choux [kupʃu] nm inv 1. (a) P bayonet/pig-sticker (b) F cut-throat (razor) 2. Vieilli F frère coupe-choux, lay brother.

coupe-cigare [kupsigar] nm P 1. guillotine 2. anus*.

coupe-lard [kuplar] nm inv knife.

coupe-la-soif [kuplaswaf] nm F (alcoholic) drink*/thirst-quencher; snifter.

couper [kupe] F I vtr 1. couper qn, to interrupt s.o./to cut s.o. short 2. la couper à qn, to silence s.o./to reduce s.o. to silence; ça te la coupe! that stumps you!/that shuts you up!/ beat that if you can! II vi 1. couper à qch, to avoid/to dodge sth; ne pas y couper, not to (be able to) dodge (a task, etc); il ne coupera pas au service militaire, he won't get out of his military service 2. couper dans le pont/ couper dedans, to fall into the trap; je ne coupe pas dedans, I'm not falling for that 3. Fig to stop thinking about sth/to switch off; quand je rentre du bureau je coupe, when I get back from the office I switch off/I relax. (Voir chique 6; effet 1; sifflet; truc 3) III vpr se couper to contradict oneself (after having told a lie); to give oneself away; to let the cat out of the bag.

couperet [kuprɛ] nm F passer au couperet, to get the axe/the chop.

coupe-tif(fe)s [kuptif] nm inv F hairdresser/barber.

Coupolard [kupɔlar] nm F member of the French Academy.

coupure [kupyr] nf F 1. excuse/alibi/cover-up; connaître la coupure, to be aware of the cover-up; to be in the know; trouver une coupure, to produce an alibi/to find a way out 2. confidential piece of information*/tip-off 3. la coupure! I'm not falling for that!

courailler [kuraje] *vi F* (*a*) to run here and there/to run around (*b*) to run after women/girls; to chase skirt.

courailleur [kurajœr] *nm F* = **coureur.**

courant [kurã] *nm* 1. *F* **courant d'air,** rumour/leak; indiscretion 2. *F* **se déguiser en courant d'air,** to make oneself scarce/to do a bunk 3. *P* **faire courant d'air avec les chiottes,** to have foul breath.

courante [kurãt] *nf P* diarrhoea*/the runs/the trots.

courette [kurɛt] *nf F* (*poursuite*) chase; **faire une courette à qn,** to pursue s.o./to be on s.o.'s trail; **faire qn à la courette,** to catch up with s.o./to catch s.o. up.

coureur [kurœr] *nm F* **coureur de femmes/de filles/de jupes/de jupons,** womanizer*/skirt-chaser/wolf/Casanova.

coureuse [kurøz] *nf P* (*a*) girl*/woman* of easy virtue; loose woman; easy lay/pushover (*b*) prostitute*/tart/hooker.

courge [kurʒ] *nf P* fool*/clot/berk/twit/wally/prat.

courir [kurir] **I** *vi* 1. *F* (*a*) **elle est toujours à courir,** she's always gadding about (*b*) to run after women/to chase skirt; **il ferait mieux de travailler au lieu de courir,** it'd be better if he did some work instead of running after women 2. *F* **il est bien loin s'il court encore,** he left ages ago 3. *F* **tu peux (toujours) courir!** nothing doing!*/no way! **laisse courir!** drop it!/give it a rest!/forget it! 4. *P* **tu me cours sur le haricot/sur l'os,** you get up my nose/you get on my wick 5. *F* **ne pas courir après qch,** not to be overfond of sth; **je ne cours pas après le vin rouge,** I can take or leave red wine; **il ne court pas après le boulot,** he's not a workaholic/he's not overfond of work **II** *vtr* 1. *F* **courir les filles,** to chase after girls/to go chasing after skirt 2. *P* **courir qn,** to get on s.o.'s nerves/to bug s.o. (*Voir* **gueuse; poste II; système**)

courrette [kurɛt] *nf F* = **courette.**

courrier [kurje] *nm F* (*cartes*) Jack/knave.

cours [kur] *nm F* **ne pas avoir cours,** to be unacceptable; **ça n'a pas cours,** it's unacceptable/intolerable; it won't do.

course [kurs] *nf F* 1. **être à bout de course,** (*personne*) to be exhausted*/worn out/done in 2. **être dans la course,** to be in the know/to be with it; **il n'est plus dans la course/il est hors course,** he's out of it/he's not in the running (any more)/he's behind the times 3. **résultat des courses ...,** the long and the short of it is

.... (*Voir* **bifteck 2; échalote 3; oignon 6**)

courser [kurse] *vtr F* **courser qn,** to chase s.o./to run after s.o.

court-circuit [kursirkɥi] *nm P* 1. sudden stabbing pain; **avoir un court-circuit dans le gésier/dans le palpitant,** to get a shock 2. *pl* **courts-circuits,** infidelities; harassment/hassles.

court-circuiter [kursirkɥite] *vtr F* **court-circuiter qn,** to by-pass s.o.

courtille [kurtij] *nf P* 1. **de la courtille, on the short side (in length) 2. **être un peu de la courtille,** to be short of cash/to be hard up.

courtines [kurtin] *nfpl P* (*courses*) **les courtines,** (horse)racing/the races; **jouer aux courtines,** to have a bet on the horses/to have a flutter (on the gee-gees); **flamber aux courtines,** to gamble heavily at the races.

courtineur [kurtinœr] *nm P* taxi driver whose clients are mainly racegoers.

court-jus [kurʒy] *nm P* 1. short-circuit 2. = **court-circuit 1.** (*Voir* **penseuse**)

couru [kury] *a F* **c'est couru (d'avance),** it's a cert*/a cinch; **c'était couru,** it was bound to happen.

couscous-pommes frites [kuskus-pɔmfrit] *a & adv* (*d'un mariage ou d'un couple mixte franco-maghrébin*) mixed (*where one of the spouses/partners is North African, the other French*).

cousin [kuzɛ̃] *nm F* 1. **un cousin à la mode de Bretagne,** a distant relation/a sort of relation 2. **ils sont grands cousins,** they're great friends/they hit it off well 3. **le roi n'est pas son cousin,** he thinks he's the cat's whiskers/the bee's knees 4. **recevoir ses cousins,** to have a period*/to have friends to stay.

cousu, -ue [kuzy] *F* **I** *a* **cousu d'or,** rich*/rolling in it **II** *nf* **une (toute) cousue,** a machine-made cigarette* **III** *nm* **c'est du cousu main,** (*certain*) it's a cert*/a cinch/a sure bet/a sure thing; (*parfaitement réalisé*) it's beautifully made/it's a work of art.

couteau, *pl* **-eaux** [kuto] *nm F* 1. **second/troisième couteau,** (*théâtre*) supporting part/role; (*truand*) petty criminal (*who is not taken seriously*) 2. **grand couteau,** top surgeon.

coûter [kute] *vi F* **pour ce que ça vous coûte!** as if it made any difference to you! (*Voir* **œil 17** (*a*); **peau 15**)

couture [kutyr] *nf F* 1. **battre qn/un adversaire à plate(s) couture(s),** to beat s.o. hollow/to slaughter an opponent 2. **sous**

toutes les coutures, from all sides/from every angle 3. **gêné aux coutures**, stiff/awkward/ill at ease; (*en difficultés financières*) in financial difficulties/short of cash.

couvercle [kuvɛrkl] *nm P* **bouillonner/ fermenter/frissonner du couvercle**, to be mad*/to flip one's lid.

couvert [kuvɛr] *nm F* 1. **mettre le couvert**, to prepare for a game of poker 2. **remettre le couvert**, to begin again/to start all over again; *surt* to make love again.

couverte [kuvɛrt] *nf F* 1. blanket; **passer qn à la couverte**, to toss s.o. in a blanket 2. = **couverture 1**.

couverture [kuvɛrtyr] *nf F* 1. cover-up/ front; **son métier n'était qu'une couverture**, his profession was just a blind; **servir de couverture à qn**, to front for s.o. 2. responsibility taken by a superior (*in the police, etc*) 3. **tirer la couverture à soi**, to take the lion's share/to look after number one.

couvrante [kuvrɑ̃t] *nf P* = **couverte**.

coxer [kɔkse] *vtr P* to arrest*/to nick.

crabe [krab] *nm* 1. *F* shady character. (*Voir* **panier 2**) 2. *P* prison warder/screw 3. *P Mil* (*a*) corporal (*b*) (*seconde guerre 1939-45*) old tank 4. *P* **un vieux crabe**, (*vieillard*) an old-timer; (*vieillard grincheux*) a pig-headed/ crabby old fool* 5. *F pl* crab-lice/crabs/ walking dandruff 6. *F* cancer; **avoir le crabe**, to have cancer 7. *F* staple remover.

crac [krak] *nm V* female genitals*/slit/crack.

crachat [kraʃa] *nm F* 1. **se noyer dans un/ dans son crachat**, to make a mountain out of a molehill 2. (*a*) decoration/medal/gong (*b*) ribbon/star/Grand Cross (*of an order*).

craché [kraʃe] *a F* (*a*) **c'est son père tout craché**, he's the (dead) spit/the spitting image of his father (*b*) **c'est lui tout craché!** that's him all over!/that's just like him! (*Voir* **portrait** (*a*))

cracher [kraʃe] I *vi* 1. *F* **il ne faut pas cracher dessus**, it's not to be sneezed/sniffed at; **il ne crache pas sur le pinard**, he doesn't turn his nose up at plonk 2. *F* **cracher blanc**, to be very thirsty/to be parched 3. *P* to pay* (up)/to cough up. (*Voir* **bassin 1; bassinet**) 4. *P* to confess*/to spit it out/to spill the beans 5. *F* **cracher dans la soupe**, to run down the job that gives one a living/to bite the hand that feeds you 6. *F* **ça crache (fort)!** (*musique*) it's great/wicked! what a beat! it's got a great beat! II *vtr P* 1. to pay* up/to cough up; **j'ai dû cracher mille francs**, I had to cough up/

fork out a thousand francs 2. to confess*; **crache-le!** out with it! (*Voir* **morceau 2**) 3. to drop (s.o.) (off); **je l'ai crachée chez elle en passant**, I dropped her (off) at her place 4. **cracher le marmot**, to give birth. (*Voir* **air I 1; bénitier 1; feu 3; sac 11; son II 2; venin**) III *vpr* **se cracher** *F* (*accident*) to crash/to have an accident (*in one's car, etc*).

cracheur, -euse [kraʃœr, -øz] *n P* show-off*/swank.

crachoir [kraʃwar] *nm F* 1. **tenir le cra-choir**, to monopolize the conversation/to do all the talking/to hold the floor 2. **tenir le crachoir à qn**, to play up to s.o.

crachouiller [kraʃuje] *vi F* to be always spitting; to splutter.

crack [krak] *nm* 1. *F* (*a*) crack player/ace/ wizz (*b*) star pupil 2. *P* (*drogues*) crack (cocaine).

cracra [krakra], **crade** [krad], **cradeau** [krado], **cradingue** [kradɛ̃g], **crado** [krado], **cradoc** [kradɔk], **crados** [krados] *a inv P* dirty/lousy/filthy/crummy/ grotty.

craigneux, -euse [krɛɲø, -øz], **crai-gnos** [krɛɲos] *P* I *a* (*a*) dubious/shady/ worrying; ugly; **c'est craignos!** it's difficult; it's dangerous; (*démodé*) it's out of date/ square; (*affreux*) it's dreadful/it's awful; it stinks; it sucks (*b*) (*personne*) dubious/ unreliable; **il est craignos**, he's a shady character/I don't like the look of him/he's shifty II *n* (*personne*) (*douteuse*) shady/shifty character; (*imbécile*) wally/prat; (*démodée*) square.

craindre [krɛ̃dr] *P* I *vi* 1. to be wanted by the police/to be on the run 2. to be incompetent/useless; **il craint en maths**, he's useless at maths 3. **ça craint** = **c'est craignos** (**craignos I** (*a*)) II *vtr* **ça craint le soleil/le jour**, it's stolen merchandise; **tu crois que ça craint le soleil/le jour, cette télé?** do you think this telly's hot? (*Voir* **jour 4; soleil 3**)

crais! (crais!) [krɛ(krɛ)] *excl Vieilli P* look out! (*Voir* **acrais!**)

cramé [krame] *nm P* (*a*) **ça sent le cramé**, there's a smell of burning/there's something burning (*b*) **le cramé**, the burnt bit (*on a piece of meat, etc*).

cramer [krame] *P* I *vtr & i* to burn/to go up in smoke; **toute la baraque a cramé**, the whole place went up in flames; **attention, tu vas cramer le tapis!** careful, you'll burn the carpet! II *vpr* **se cramer** to burn oneself; se cramer les doigts, to burn one's fingers.

cramouille [kramuj] *nf* V female genitals*/pussy.

crampe [krɑ̃p] *nf* P 1. tirer sa crampe, (*s'enfuir*) to run away*/to do a bunk/to split; (*coïter*) to have sex*/to have it off 2. = **crampon, -onne** I.

crampette [krɑ̃pɛt] *nf* P tirer une crampette, to have sex*/to have it off.

crampon, -onne [krɑ̃pɔ̃] F I *n* (tenacious) bore*; limpet II *a* ce qu'il est crampon! what a bore*/drag he is!

cramponnant [krɑ̃pɔnɑ̃] *a* F pestering; tu es cramponnant avec ta politique! you're becoming a real pest with your politics!/your politics are a real drag!

cramponner [krɑ̃pɔne] *vtr* F cramponner qn, to bore* s.o./to pester s.o./to cling to s.o. (like a leech).

cram(p)ser [krɑ̃mse] *vi* P to die*.

cran [krɑ̃] *nm* 1. F avoir du cran, to have guts 2. F baisser d'un cran, to come down a peg (or two) 3. F être à cran, to be on the point of losing one's temper/to be ready to explode; j'avais les nerfs à cran, my nerves were on edge; P ça l'a foutu à cran, that made him see red 4. F il ne me lâche pas d'un cran, he won't leave me for a moment/I can't shake him off 5. P Mil dix (jours de) cran, ten days' CB/confined to barracks 6. F cran (d'arrêt), flick knife/NAm switchblade (knife).

crânage [krɑnaʒ] *nm* F snootiness.

crâne [krɑn] *nm* 1. F bourrer le crâne à qn, to stuff s.o.'s head (up) with lies, etc; to (try to) lead s.o. up the garden path; to brainwash s.o.; ne me bourre pas le crâne! don't give me that (stuff)!/don't give me that old story! (*Voir* **bourrage; bourreur**). 2. F crâne de piaf, (*prétentieux*) = **crâneur** I; (*imbécile*) fool*/imbecile/bird-brain 3. P (*argot policier*) faire un crâne, to make an arrest. (*Voir* **lessivage 2**)

crânement [krɑnmɑ̃] *adv* F 1. il s'en est acquitté crânement, he did it without batting an eyelid 2. elle est crânement belle, she's ravishing/gorgeous.

crâner [krɑne] *vi* F to swank/to swagger/to show off*.

crâneur, -euse [krɑnœr, -øz] F I *n* (*personne*) show-off*/swank; toffee-nose; faire le crâneur, to swank/to show off* II *a* swaggering/showy; il est un peu crâneur, he puts it on a bit/he's a bit of a show-off*.

crapahu [krapay] *nm* Mil F land exercises.

crapahuter [krapayte] *vi* F 1. Mil (*a*) to go on land exercises (*b*) to yomp/to trudge (*over difficult terrain*) 2. to go on a walking trip/to go hiking/to hike.

crapaud [krapo] *nm* 1. F avaler un crapaud, (*se forcer de faire qch de désagréable*) to force oneself to do a very unpleasant task; (*avaler un affront*) to swallow an insult 2. F child*/kid/brat 3. F crapaud de murailles, stonemason 4. P (*personne*) un vilain crapaud, a toad/a creep 5. Vieilli P purse 6. Vieilli P padlock 7. F faire des yeux de crapaud mort d'amour, to show the whites of one's eyes/to look like a dying duck in a thunderstorm 8. F la bave du crapaud n'atteint pas la blanche colombe, you can say what you like, my conscience is clear.

crapautard [krapotar] *nm* P small purse; constipé du crapautard, miserly*.

crape, crâpe [krap, krɑp] *nf* P = **crapule**.

crapoteux, -euse [krapotø, -øz] *a* P dirty/filthy/crummy/grotty.

crapoussin [krapusɛ̃] *nm* Vieilli P undersized* person/shrimp; dwarf; freak.

crapser [krapse] *vi* P = **cram(p)ser**.

crapulados [krapylados] *nm* P = **crapulos**.

crapule [krapyl] *nf* F rotter/nasty piece of work/bastard*/sod; crook; (*collectif*) scum.

crapulerie [krapylri] *nf* F dirty trick.

crapuleuse [krapyløz] *a* P se la faire crapuleuse, to go on a spree*/on the razzle; to paint the town red.

crapulos [krapylos] *nm* P cheap cigar.

craquant [krakɑ̃] *a* P (*a*) excellent*/great/super/wicked/magic (*b*) adorable/cute.

craque [krak] *nf* 1. F (*a*) lie*/fib/whopper (*b*) tall story 2. V female genitals*/crack/slit.

craquer [krake] I *vtr* P (faire) craquer une crèche, to burgle a house/to do a place over II *vi* F 1. plein à craquer, (*plein*) chock-full/chock-a-block/chocker; (*riche*) rich*/flush 2. to tell lies/fibs 3. (*personne*) (*a*) (*s'effondrer*) to crack up; j'étais sur le point de craquer, I was at breaking point/I was about to crack up (*b*) (*de plaisir*) to be in ecstasy (over sth) (*c*) (*de désir*) craquer pour qch/qn, to fall for sth/s.o.; c'est plus fort que moi, je craque! I really can't resist (it)!

craquette [krakɛt] *nf* V female genitals*/crack/slit.

craqueur, -euse [krakœr, -øz] *n* F fibber.

craquos [krakos] P I *a* = **craquant** II *nm*

spot/pimple/*NAm* zit.

se crasher [səkraʃe] *vpr F* = **se cracher** (**cracher III**)

crasp' [krasp], **craspec** [kraspɛk], **craspect** [kraspɛ], **craspèque** [kraspɛk], **craspet** [kraspɛ], **craspignol** [kraspiɲɔl], **craspouillard** [kraspujar] *a P* filthy/crummy/grotty.

crasse [kras] *nf F* faire une crasse à qn, to play a dirty trick on s.o./to do the dirty on s.o.

crasserie [krasri] *nf Vieilli F* 1. = **crasse** 2. avarice.

crasseux, -euse [krasø, -øz] *n P* comb.

crassouillard [krasujar] *a P* filthy/crummy/grotty.

crassouille [krasuj] *nf P* filth/dirt.

cravacher [kravaʃe] *vi F* to slog/to work like mad (*to finish sth*).

cravacheuse [kravaʃøz] *nf F* flagellator.

cravate [kravat] *nf* 1. *F* showing off; c'est de la cravate! it's all bluff!/it's just for show! arrête tes cravates! stop boasting!/stop showing off! 2. *F* faire une cravate à qn, to put a neck-hold/a stranglehold on s.o. 3. *Vieilli F* cravate (de chanvre), hangman's rope 4. *P* s'en jeter un derrière la cravate, to knock back a drink/to put one down the hatch/to sink one 5. *P* cravate à Charlot/à Gaston/à Gustave, sanitary towel/*NAm* napkin.

cravaté [kravate] *nm F* manager/boss; les cravatés, the management.

cravater [kravate] I *vtr* 1. *F* cravater qn, to kid/to hoodwink s.o.; to take s.o. for a ride 2. *F* to get (s.o.) in a neck-hold/a stranglehold 3. *P* to arrest*/to nab/to collar (s.o.); se faire cravater, to get nabbed 4. *P* to steal*/to pinch/to nick; on m'a cravaté ma carte de crédit, someone's swiped my credit card II *vi F* to exaggerate*/to shoot a line; to boast.

cravateur [kravatœr] *nm F* bluffer; boaster.

cravetouse [kravtuz] *nf P* (neck)tie.

crayon [krɛjɔ̃] *nm P* 1. (financial) credit; avoir du/un crayon, to have credit/to have an account (with s.o.) 2. *pl* hair; se faire tailler les crayons, to get a haircut 3. *pl* legs*; s'emmêler les crayons, to trip; (*moralement*) to get confused/to get one's knickers in a twist 4. *P* walking stick.

crayonner [krɛjɔne] *vi P Aut* to accelerate/to put one's foot down; crayonne, Lulu! (*remark aimed at slow driver in front*) get a move on!

cré [kre] *a inv P* (*abrév* = *sacré*) cré nom de

nom! hell! cré bon Dieu! (Jesus) Christ!

créature [kreatyr] *nf F* person/individual*; c'est une bonne créature, he's a good sort; une belle créature, a beautiful woman.

crebleu! [krəblø] *excl P* (*abrév* = *sacrebleu*) damn it!

crèche [krɛʃ] *nf P* room; house/digs/pad.

crécher [kreʃe] *vi P* to live; où que tu crèches? where do you hang out?

crédié! [kredje], **crédieu!** [kredjø] *excl P* (*abrév* = *sacré nom de Dieu!*) (God) damn it (all)!

crédo [kredo] *nm P* (financial) credit; faire du crédo, to give credit.

crémaillère [kremajɛr] *nf F* pendre la crémaillère, to have/to give a house-warming (party); à quand la crémaillère? when's the house-warming (going to be)?

crème [krɛm] I *nm F* (= *café crème*) un crème, a (small) white coffee; un grand crème, a large white coffee II *nf* 1. *F* (*a*) la crème, the cream (of society)/the (social) elite/the upper crust (*b*) the best; c'est la crème des hommes, he's the best of men/he's one of the best 2. *F* easy job; c'est de la crème, it's a piece of cake; there's nothing to it; c'est pas de la crème, it's no easy matter; it's no walk-over 3. *P* faire une crème, (*courses*) to do a sweep(stake) 4. *V* sperm/juice.

crémerie [kremri] *nf F* (*a*) dwelling (place)/living quarters/pad; changer de crémerie, to move on/to push off; allez, on change de crémerie, come on, let's get out of here!/let's high-tail it out of here! (*b*) *Vieilli* small restaurant (serving light meals)/café.

crénom! [krenɔ̃] *excl P* (*abrév* = *sacré nom de Dieu!*) = **crédié!**

crépage [krepaʒ] *nm F* crêpage de chignons, fight*/set-to (between women).

crêpe [krep] *nf* 1. *F* se retourner comme une crêpe, to change one's opinion completely; to do an about-face; to change sides; je l'ai retourné comme une crêpe, I soon changed his mind for him 2. *F* s'aplatir comme une crêpe, to fall flat on one's face 3. *F* faire la crêpe, (*voiture*) to turn turtle 4. *F* fool*/idiot 5. *P* flat cap.

crêper [krepe] *vpr F* se crêper (le chignon), (*femmes*) to fight/to have a set-to/to tear each other's hair out.

cresson [krɛsɔ̃] *nm* 1. (*a*) *P* hair/thatch; il n'a plus de cresson sur la fontaine/sur la cafetière/sur le caillou, he's lost his hair/he's bald* (b) V (femme) pubic hair; **arroser le cresson**, (pour un homme) to have sex* 2. P money*; **le cresson ne pousse pas sans effort**, money doesn't grow on trees 3. P **idem au cresson**, ditto; same difference. (Voir **brouter I 1**; **marguerite 2**)

cressonnière [krɛsɔnjɛr] nf V = **cresson 1** (b).

crétin, -ine [kretɛ̃, -in] F I n fool*/cretin/ moron; **quelle bande/quel tas de crétins!** what a shower!/what a bunch of morons! II a stupid*/cretinous/moronic.

creuser [krøze] I vtr F 1. **ça vous creuse** (l'estomac)/**ça (vous la) creuse**, it gives you an appetite/it makes you feel peckish 2. **se creuser la tête/le cerveau/la cervelle/le ciboulot/le citron**, to rack one's brains II vpr **se creuser** F **se creuser sur un problème**, to rack one's brains/to puzzle over a problem.

creux [krø] F I nm **avoir un creux (dans l'estomac)**, to feel empty/peckish/ravenous II a **avoir le nez creux**, to be shrewd/far-seeing.

crevaison [krəvɛzɔ̃] nf P 1. death 2. exhaustion/extreme fatigue; **quelle crevaison!** what a slog!/what a fag!

crevant [krəvɑ̃] a P 1. exhausting*/killing/ murderous; **ce boulot, c'est vachement crevant**, this job really kills you/is really knackering 2. very funny*/side-splitting/ killing; **c'était crevant**, it was a real scream/ it was (absolutely) priceless.

crevard, -arde [krəvar, -ard] a & n P 1. hungry/starving (person); **c'est un crevard**, he's got hollow legs/he never stops eating 2. unhealthy/sickly (person) 3. dying (person).

crevasse [krəvas] nf V female genitals*/ crack/slit.

crève [krɛv] nf P illness/cold/flu, etc; (mort) death; **attraper/choper la crève**, to catch one's death (of cold); (mourir) to die*.

crevé [krəve] a P 1. dead 2. exhausted*/dead tired/shattered/shagged-out/knackered.

crève-la-faim [krɛvlafɛ̃] nm inv F half-starved person; down-and-out.

crever [krəve] I vi 1. F to have a puncture 2. F **crever de rire**, to laugh* uproariously 3. P (personne) to die*/to snuff it; **crever la gueule ouverte**, (de faim) to die* of hunger; (abandonné) to die* alone/abandoned by all; **qu'il crève!** to hell with him! **tu peux (toujours) crever!** get stuffed! **marche ou crève!** do or die! **crever d'ennui**, to be bored to death/bored out of one's mind; **je crève de chaleur**, I'm baking/boiling; **crever de faim**,

to be starving/famished; to be dying of hunger II vtr 1. P **crever la faim/la crever/crever/crever la dalle**, (avoir très faim) to be starving/ famished; (être dans la misère) to be destitute/down-and-out 2. F **crever qn**, to work/to flog s.o. to death; to knacker s.o. (Voir **tempérament 3**) 3. F **ça (vous) crève les yeux**, it's staring you in the face/it's right under your nose/it sticks out a mile 4. P to arrest*/to bust (s.o.). (Voir **tas 2**) 5. P to wound (s.o.). 6. P **crever (la gueule à) qn**, to kill* s.o./to do s.o. in III vpr **se crever** 1. F to knock oneself out/to bust a gut (with work); **se crever au travail**, to work oneself to death/ to work oneself into the ground/to kill oneself with work; **je me suis crevé là-dedans pendant dix ans**, I slaved away/flogged my guts out there for ten years 2. P to fight (to the death)/to slaughter one another 3. P **se faire crever**, to get killed 4. F **se crever (de rire)**, to laugh* uproariously/to kill oneself (laughing)/to split one's sides laughing/to piss oneself laughing. (Voir **cul I 17**; **paillasse 1, 2**; **peau 13**)

crevette [krəvɛt] nf 1. P young homosexual*/bum-boy; (qui se prostitue) rent boy 2. F **sentir la crevette**, (personne) to smell/to have B.O.

cri [kri] nm 1. F **le dernier cri**, the latest fashion/the in-thing; **c'est le dernier cri**, it's all the rage 2. F uproar; vehement protest; **faire du cri/aller au cri**, to kick up a fuss/to make a (terrible) scene 3. P **aller au cri**, to denounce/to inform on/to grass 4. P pretence/ bluff; **cri sec**, swindle*/racket/sting 5. V **la bête a lâché son cri**, (moment of) ejaculation.

criave(r) [krijav(e)] vtr & i P to eat*.

cric [kri(k)] nm P (poor-quality) brandy/ rotgut.

cricri [krikri] nm F (insecte) cricket.

crime [krim] nm P **avoir du crime/ne pas manquer de crime**, to have cheek/nerve.

Crime (la) [lakrim] Prn F (= la brigade criminelle) (police) the Crime squad.

crin [krɛ̃] nm F 1. (a) **être comme un crin/ être à crin/être de mauvais crin**, to be in a bad temper/in a disagreeable mood; to be like a bear with a sore head; to be cantankerous (b) **se faire des crins**, to get (all) upset/to work oneself up (into a state) 2. **à tout crin/à tous crins**, diehard/fanatical/out-and-out/ thoroughgoing (revolutionary, etc) 3. **avoir qn dans le crin**, to be infatuated* with s.o./to be gone on s.o. 4. pl hair/thatch; **se faire tailler**

les **crins**, to have one's hair cut. (*Voir* **peau 19**)

crincrin [krɛ̃krɛ̃] *nm F* string instrument; *surt* violin/fiddle; racler le **crincrin**, to scrape on the fiddle.

se criquer [sǝkrike] *vi P* to run away*/to clear off/to skedaddle/to scarper.

crise [kriz] *nf F* 1. (*a*) piquer une/sa **crise**, (*de nerfs*) to throw a fit; to have hysterics; (*de rage*) to fly into a rage/to blow one's top/to fly off the handle/to do one's nut (*b*) faire prendre une **crise** (*de nerfs*) à qn, to drive/send s.o. up the wall 2. hilarity/mirth; quelle **crise**! it was so funny!/what a laugh!

crispant [krispɑ̃] *a F* irritating/annoying/aggravating; ce que tu es **crispant**! what a pain (in the neck) you are!/you get on my wick!

cristi! [kristi] *excl P* (*abrév* = *sacristi!*) curse it!/damn it!/(damn and) blast it!

crob [krɔb] *a P* = **crobe**.

crobar(d) [krɔbar] *nm P* sketch/drawing; tu veux que je te fasse un petit **crobar(d)**? do I have to spell it out for you?

crobe [krɔb] *a P* (= *microbe*) tiny/titchy.

croc [kro] *nm F Voir* **crocs**.

crocher [krɔʃe] I *vtr* 1. *F* to grab; je l'ai **croché** amicalement, I took his arm in a friendly manner 2. *F* to arrest*/to nab 3. *P* to pick (a lock) II *vpr* se **crocher** *Vieilli P* = **se crocheter**.

croches [krɔʃ] *nfpl Vieilli P* hands*/hooks.

crochet [krɔʃɛ] *nm F* 1. vivre aux **crochets** de qn, to live off s.o./to sponge off s.o. 2. *pl* = **crocs 1, 2**.

se crocheter [sǝkrɔʃte] *vpr Vieilli P* se **crocheter** (avec qn), to come to blows (with s.o.)/to have a set-to (with s.o.)/to have a barney (with s.o.).

crochu [krɔʃy] *a F* il a les doigts **crochus**/il a les pattes **crochues**/il les a **crochues**, (*il est voleur*) he's light-fingered/he's got sticky fingers; (*il est avare*) he's miserly*/grasping/tight-fisted.

croco [krɔko] *nm F* crocodile (skin); un larfeuil en **croco**, a crocodile(-skin) wallet.

crocs [kro] *nmpl*, 1. *F* teeth*/fangs/gnashers; avoir mal aux **crocs**, to have toothache; se laver les **crocs** au roquefort, to have foul breath 2. *F* avoir les **crocs**, to be starving/ravenous.

croire [krwar] I *vtr F* 1. je vous **crois!**/j'te **crois!** you bet!/sure!/rather! 2. que tu **crois!** that's what *you* think! 3. t'as qu'à **croire!** not

a bit of it! you can believe that if you want to! j'aime mieux le **croire** que d'y aller voir, I have my doubts but I'll take your word for it 4. faut le voir pour le **croire**, seeing is believing; I'll believe it when I see it 5. **croire** au père Noël, to be naive/gullible. (*Voir* **arriver 1**) II *vpr* se **croire** *F* il se **croit** (beaucoup)/s'en **croit**, he thinks a lot of himself/he thinks he's the bee's knees.

croître [krwatr] *vi F* cela ne fait que **croître** et embellir, (it's getting) better and better! *Iron* it's getting worse and worse.

croix [krwa] *nf* 1. *F* mettre une **croix** dessus, to consider it over and done with/to write sth off 2. *F* c'est la **croix** et la bannière, it's the devil of a job 3. *F* il faut faire une **croix** (à la cheminée), put out the flags!/mark it with a red letter! 4. *P* (*dans le milieu*) **croix** des vaches, cross-shaped scar made on the cheek *or* forehead of a traitor; faire la **croix** des vaches à qn, to mark s.o.'s cheek with a knife-scar *or* razor-cut (*for informing on one's associates to the police, etc*) 5. *P* gagner la **croix** de bois, to be killed in action 6. *F* **croix** de bois, **croix** de fer(, si je mens je vais en enfer), cross my heart (and hope to die). (*Voir* **boule 9**) 7. *P* fool*/ignoramus/twit 8. *P* (*prostituées*) demanding client.

cromi [krɔmi] *nm P* (*verlan de* **micro**) microphone/mike.

croni, crôni [krɔni, kro-] *P* I *nm* corpse*; le parc des **cronis**, the cemetery*/the bone orchard II *a* dead.

cronir, crônir [krɔnir, kro-] *P* I *vtr* to kill*/to do in/to bump off (s.o.) II *vi* to die*/to snuff it.

croquant [krɔkɑ̃] *nm F Péj* 1. peasant*/clodhopper/yokel/country bumpkin 2. insignificant man/nonentity.

croquante [krɔkɑ̃t] *nf P* mouth*/cakehole/gob. (*Voir* **tabourets**)

croque [krɔk] I *nm F* 1. (*croque-monsieur*) toasted cheese and ham sandwich 2. = **croque-mort** 3. *Vieilli* pas un **croque**, not a cent/not a brass farthing II *nf P* food*/eats/nosh.

croque-mort [krɔkmɔr] *nm F* undertaker; avoir une figure de **croque-mort**, to have a face like an undertaker. (*pl* **croque-morts**)

croquemuche [krɔkmyʃ] *nm P* = **croque-mort**.

croqueneaux [krɔkno] *nmpl*, **croquenots** [krɔkno] *nmpl P* big boots*/beetle-crushers.

croquer [krɔke] I *vtr* 1. *P* to eat*/to scoff/to tuck into; croquer un sandwich en moins de rien, to wolf down a sandwich in no time 2. *P* to squander (one's money, etc); to blue/to get through (money) 3. *P* croquer une poulette, to have/to get a girl*/a bird 4. *P* to arrest*/to nab (s.o.) 5. *F* elle est jolie/mignonne à croquer, she's as pretty as a picture; she's a sweetie 6. *V* (*fellation*) se faire croquer, to be sucked off. (*Voir* **marmot 2**) II *vi P* 1. to eat*/to tuck in; croquer avec une côtelette dans le genou, to fast 2. en croquer (*a*) to be a police informer*/to grass (*b*) to accept money *or* a gift in return for a favour; to take bribes (*c*) to watch an erotic show; to be a Peeping Tom/a voyeur 3. en croquer pour qn, to be infatuated* with s.o./to have a crush on s.o.

croqueur [krɔkœr] *nm F* croqueur de femmes, womanizer*/Don Juan/wolf.

croqueuse [krɔkøz] *nf F* 1. prostitute*/tart 2. une croqueuse de diamants, an expensive mistress/a gold-digger.

croquignol [krɔkiɲɔl] *F a* = **croquignolet**.

croquignoles [krɔkiɲɔl] *nfpl V* testicles*/nuts.

croquignolet, -ette [krɔkiɲɔlɛ, -ɛt] *a F* (*souv Iron*) dainty/dinky/sweet/cute.

croquis [krɔki] *nm F* tu veux que je te fasse un (petit) croquis? do I have to spell it out for you?

crosse [krɔs] *nf* 1. *F* (*a*) chercher des crosses à qn, to pick a quarrel with s.o. (*b*) prendre les crosses de qn, to stick up for s.o. 2. *F* se mettre/*P* se foutre en crosse, to get angry* 3. *F* lever/mettre la crosse en l'air, to surrender/to show the white flag/to lay down one's arms 4. *P* autant/au temps pour les crosses! start again!/back to square one!

crosser [krɔse] *P* I *vtr* 1. to criticize* (s.o.)/to tell (s.o.) off; to pick a quarrel* with (s.o.) 2. to beat/to punch (s.o.) II *vpr* **se crosser** *P* to wrangle; to scuffle.

crosseur [krɔsœr] *nm P* quarrelsome man.

crotte [krɔt] I *nf* 1. *F* ma (petite) crotte! my darling!* 2. *P* c'est-il oui ou crotte? is it yes or no?/are you going to or not? (*Voir* **merde** I 17) 3. *P* être à la crotte, to be depressed*/to feel low/to have the hump 4. *P* il n'y a pas de quoi se rouler dans la crotte, it's no laughing matter/it's not *that* funny 5. *P* ce n'est pas de la crotte, it's not rubbish 6. *F* elle ne se prend pas pour de la crotte, she thinks she's really something/she thinks the sun shines out of her

arse. (*Voir* **bique** I 1 (*b*); **panier 8**) II *excl Vieilli P* (*Euph de* **merde**!) shit!/damn (and blast) it!

crotter [krɔte] *vi P* to defecate*/to crap.

crougnat [kruɲa] *nm,* **crouilla(t)** [kruja] *nm,* **crouille** [kruj] *nm,* **crouilledouche** [krujduʃ] *nm P Péj* Algerian/North African/Arab*/wog.

croulant [krulɑ̃] *P* I *nm* back-number/has-been; les croulants, (*surt parents*) the old people/the (old) folk(s)/the wrinklies; c'est un croulant, he's an old crock/a wrinklie; he's past it II *a* (*personne*) (*a*) old/ancient (*b*) old-fashioned/square/not with it.

croum(e) [krum] *nm P* credit (with a shop/a store, etc); à croum(e), on tick/on the cuff.

crouni [kruni] *nm & a P* = **croni**.

crounir [krunir] *vtr & i P* = **cronir**.

croupanche [krupɑ̃ʃ] *nm P* croupier.

croupe [krup] *nf F* (*surt femme*) buttocks*/behind/rear/rump; tortiller de la croupe, to wiggle/to sway one's hips (*when walking*).

croupion [krupjɔ̃] *nm F* 1. (*a*) = **croupe** (*b*) se décarcasser le croupion, to put oneself out/to go to a lot of trouble 2. (*cuisine*) parson's nose.

croupionner [krupjɔne] *vi F* to wiggle/to sway one's hips (*when walking*).

croustance [krustɑ̃s] *nf P* food*/grub/nosh.

croustillant [krustijɑ̃] *a F* (*a*) spicy/fruity (story, etc) (*b*) (*fille, femme*) sexy; une petite femme croustillante, a sexy little piece/number.

croustille [krustij] *nf Vieilli P* = **croustance**.

croustiller [krustije] *vi Vieilli P* to eat*/to nosh.

croûte [krut] *nf F* 1. food; casser une croûte, to have a snack/a bite/something (to eat); casser la croûte, to eat*/to nosh; viens casser la croûte avec moi, come and have a bite to eat with me; à la croûte! let's eat!/grub's up!/come and get it! 2. gagner sa croûte, to earn one's living/one's bread and butter/to make a living. (*Voir* **miches 2** (*b*)) 3. badly painted picture/daub 4. (*a*) (*imbécile*) wally; quelle croûte! what a berk/a wally! (*b*) une vieille croûte, an old fossil/buffer.

croûter [krute] *vi P* to eat*/to feed (oneself, one's face)/to nosh; de quoi croûter, something to eat/a bite (to eat); tu vas croûter ça, take a bite of that/get that down you.

croûtier [krutje] *nm F* bad artist.

croûton [krutɔ̃] *nm F* 1. = **croûtier** 2. (vieux) croûton, old fossil/old stick-in-the-mud 3. *Vieilli* s'ennuyer comme un croûton de pain derrière une malle, to be bored* stiff/rigid; to be bored* to tears.

crouya [kruja] *nm P Péj* = **crougnat**.

cruche [kryʃ] I *nf F* fool*/idiot/twit/ass; être bête comme une cruche, to be thick/dense II *a F* stupid*; jamais je n'ai vu des gosses si cruches, I've never seen such dumb kids.

cube [kyb] *nm* 1. *F* (*écoles*) third-year student in a class preparing for the *grandes écoles* or in a *grande école*; (*élève qui redouble une deuxième fois*) pupil repeating a class for the second time 2. *P* gros cube, 500 cc plus motorbike; les gros cubes, the big bikes/heavy metal.

cuber [kybe] *vi* 1. (*écoles*) *F* to stay down for the third year 2. *P* (*revenir cher*) to mount up/to work out expensive; ça cube/ça finit par cuber, it's expensive/pric(e)y; it mounts up.

cucu(l) [kyky] I *nm F* le (petit) cucu(l), the buttocks*/bottom/backside/behind. (*Voir* **pan(-)pan**) II *a F* stupid*/idiotic/goofy/daft; ce qu'il est cucu(l)! what a fool* he is!/he's daft; il est cucu(l), ce film, this film's stupid; gentille, mais un peu cucu(l), nice enough, but a bit daft/*Br* dotty/nutty. (*Voir* **praline 4**)

cueille [kœj] *nf P* (*de police*) raid/bust/comb-out.

cueillir [kœjir] *vtr* 1. *F* (*a*) to arrest*; to round up (suspects); se faire cueillir, to be arrested/rounded up/hauled in/picked up (by the police) (*b*) cueillir qn (au passage), to buttonhole s.o.; se faire cueillir, to get nabbed/caught 2. *F* où as-tu cueilli ça? where did you dig that up from? 3. *F* to collect (s.o.)/to pick (s.o.) up; je passerai te cueillir demain soir, I'll come and pick you up tomorrow evening 4. *P* (*théâtre*) se faire cueillir, to get booed/hissed off the stage; to get the bird.

cuiller, cuillère [kɥijɛr] *nf* 1. *F* en deux/trois coups de cuiller à pot, in less than no time/in two shakes (of a lamb's tail) 2. *F* être à ramasser à la petite cuiller, (*blessé*) to be badly hurt/smashed up; (*épuisé*) to be exhausted*/all in; (*déprimé*) to be down in the dumps; on l'a ramassé à la petite cuiller, he was scraped off the pavement 3. *Vieilli F* avaler sa cuiller, to die* 4. *F* argenté comme une cuiller de bois, penniless*/completely broke 5. *F* (*tennis*) servir à la cuiller, to serve

underhand 6. *P* hand*; serrer la cuiller à qn, to shake hands with s.o.; serre-moi la cuiller! put it there! (*Voir* **dos 10**)

cuir [kɥir] *nm* 1. *F* leather jacket; (*aviation*) (leather) flying suit; *pl* leathers 2. *P* un cuir/un fétichiste du cuir, s.o. who is into leather/a leather merchant; (*homosexuels*) a leather queen 3. *F* (*a*) faire un cuir, to make an incorrect/false liaison (*eg il a fait une erreur* [ilafɛzynɛrœr]) (*b*) il parlait sans cuirs, his way of speaking didn't give him away 4. *F* skin/hide; tanner/carder le cuir à qn, to give s.o. a good hiding/to tan s.o.'s hide; se rôtir le cuir, to sunbathe; il a le cuir épais, he's thick-skinned; jurer entre cuir et chair, to swear under one's breath.

cuirasse [kɥiras] *nf P* (*poitrine*) chest.

cuire [kɥir] *vi F* on cuit dans cette pièce, it's boiling hot in this room; this room's like an oven. (*Voir* **dur I 1**; **dur II 2**; **jus 8**; **œuf 10**)

cuisinage [kɥizinaʒ] *nm F* questioning/interrogation/grilling/sweating (of prisoner, suspect) (*with the object of forcing a confession*).

cuisine [kɥizin] *nf F* 1. = **cuisinage** 2. underhand scheming/wangling/(dirty) tricks; les petites cuisines du métier, the little tricks of the trade; la cuisine parlementaire, parliamentary intrigue 3. secret of manufacture; avoir sa petite cuisine, to have one's (own) way of doing things. (*Voir* **batterie**)

cuisiner [kɥizine] *vtr F* 1. to question/to interrogate/to grill/to sweat (a prisoner, a suspect); to pump (s.o.) 2. to cook up/to concoct (a scheme of revenge, etc); cuisiner une nomination pour qn, to pull the wires/to pull a few strings in order to get s.o. an appointment.

cuisse [kɥis] *nf* 1. *F* se croire/croire qu'on est sorti de la cuisse de Jupiter, to think a lot of oneself/to have a high opinion of oneself; elle se croit sortie de la cuisse de Jupiter, she thinks she's really something/she thinks she's God's gift/she thinks she's the bee's knees 2. *P* avoir la cuisse hospitalière/facile/gaie/légère, to be an easy lay/a pushover.

cuistance [kɥistɑ̃s] *nf P* 1. cookery/cooking 2. kitchen.

cuisteau, *pl* **-eaux** [kɥisto] *nm*, **cuistot, -ote** [kɥisto, -ɔt] *n P* cook.

cuit [kɥi] *a* 1. *P* drunk*/plastered/stewed 2. *F* un conservateur cuit et recuit, a dyed-in-the-wool Conservative/a true blue Tory **3. F il a son pain cuit**, he's (financially) all right for the rest of his life; he's comfortably off **4. F** (a) (*personne*) ruined/done for/finished; **je suis cuit**, I'm done for/I've had it (b) (*chose*) ruined/kaput; **ça c'est cuit**, that's had it/that's bitten the dust **5. F c'est du tout cuit**, it's a cert*/it's a cinch/it's a walkover; it's all settled/it's in the bag; **ce n'est pas du tout cuit**, it's not all plain sailing; it's no pushover **6. ça (ne) va pas te tomber tout cuit (dans le bec)**, it won't be handed to you on a plate; you've got to work for it/earn it.

cuite [kμit] *nf P* drunkenness; drunken bout; **prendre la/sa/une cuite, prendre une bonne/ une forte cuite**, to get drunk*/canned/ plastered; **avoir sa cuite**, to be dead drunk*/to be as pissed as a newt; **il a sa cuite**, he's completely smashed; **tenir une (bonne/forte) cuite**, to be plastered/to have (had) a skinful; **cuver sa cuite**, to sleep oneself sober/to sleep it off; **le lendemain de cuite**, the morning after the night before. (*Voir* **tenir 2**)

se cuiter [səkμite] *vpr P* to get drunk*/ canned/paralytic/plastered/pissed/stewed.

cuivre [kμivr] *nm F* **nous n'avons pas fait les cuivres ensemble!** don't take liberties (with me)!/don't try it on with me! (*Voir* **cochon 7**)

cul [ky] **I** *nm P* **1.** (a) backside/buttocks*/ bottom/bum/*NAm* butt/arse/*NAm* ass; **un coup de pied au cul**, a kick up the arse; **cul par- dessus tête**, head over heels/arse over tip/arse over tits/A over T; **faire tête à cul**, to go flying/to come a cropper*; **il en est tombé/il en est resté sur le cul**, he was flabbergasted/ knocked sideways (b) **trou du cul**, anus*/arse- hole; **tu peux te le mettre/foutre au cul**, you can shove it/stick it up your arse; you know where you can stick it (c) **ne pas se manier le cul**, to sit on one's arse and do nothing; to do fuck-all/to do piss-all; **casser le cul à qn**, to bore* s.o. rigid/to give s.o. a pain in the arse/ to get on s.o.'s tits **2.** stupid* person/fool*/ prat/arsehole/*NAm* asshole; **un vieux cul**, a silly old bugger; **quel cul!** what a bloody fool!/what an arsehole! **c'est un vrai cul**, he's a right wally/a real nurd **3. mon cul!** my foot!/my arse! (*Voir* **poulet 2**) **4. avoir du cul**, to be lucky; **avoir le cul bordé de nouilles**, to be extremely lucky/to have the luck of the devil; **quel cul (il a)!** what amazing luck (he has)!/what a lucky blighter (he is)! **5. un gros cul**, (*camion*) a heavy goods vehicle (HGV)/a

long-distance lorry/a juggernaut; (*chauffeur*) an HGV driver/a long-distance lorry-driver/a trucker **6. avoir qn au/dans le cul**, se mettre qn au cul, to despise s.o. utterly/to hate s.o.'s guts **7. en avoir plein le cul**, to be fed up* (with it)/to be sick and tired (of it)/to be pissed off (with it); **l'avoir dans le cul**, to be unlucky; to have had it; **il l'a dans le cul**, he's had it; that's screwed/fucked him up; that's him buggered **8. avoir chaud au cul**, (*manquer avoir un accident de justesse*) to have only just avoided an accident; to have a narrow escape; **j'ai eu chaud au cul!** that was close!/that was a close shave! **9. être à cul**, (*être au plus bas*) to be at one's lowest point/ to be in a miserable state; to be ruined; **met- tre qn à cul**, to put s.o. down **10. être (comme) cul et chemise/être copains comme cul et chemise**, to be great buddies/mates; to be as thick as thieves **11. faire cul sec**, to down one's drink in one (go); **cul sec!** bottoms up!/down the hatch! **12. avoir/faire la bouche en cul de poule**, to purse one's lips; to pull a face/to pout **13. lécher le cul à qn**, to flatter* s.o./to lick s.o.'s arse/*NAm* to brown- nose s.o. (*Voir* **lèche-cul**) **14. ça lui pend au cul (comme un sifflet de deux ronds)**, he's got it coming to him/he's (in) for it **15. pisser au cul à qn**, to despise s.o.; **je lui pisse au cul!** two fingers to him!/he can go to hell!/he can get stuffed **16. rire comme un cul**, to laugh without opening one's mouth **17. se casser/se crever le cul**, to work* hard/to slog away (at it)/to work one's arse off **18. traîner son cul/ tirer au cul**, to shirk/to swing the lead/to skive off. (*Voir* **tire-au-cul**) **19. péter plus haut que son cul**, (*être vaniteux*) to be bigheaded/ conceited **20. se taper le cul par terre**, to roar with laughter/to be in stitches/to split one's sides laughing; **pas de quoi se taper le cul par terre!** it's no laughing matter! (*Voir* **astape**) **21. il chante comme mon cul**, he can't sing for toffee/for nuts **22. avoir le cul sur selle**, (*à cheval*) to be in the saddle; (*toujours assis*) to be always sitting down; **cul seccotine**, one who never leaves his/her chair; lazybones **23.** (a) **faux cul**, (*malhonnête*) deceitful/shifty person; shady customer; hypocrite; (*traître*) traitor/double-crosser (b) **cul béni**, cleric; practising Catholic; bigot **24. papier cul**, toilet paper/loo paper/bum-fodder **25. cause à mon cul, ma tête est malade**, bugger off/sod off, I don't want to know; (*je ne te crois pas*) go and tell that to the marines!/(you're talking a load of) balls! 26. (*a*) sex*; **aller au cul,** to have sex*/to have a bonk/a screw; **il ne pense qu'au cul,** he's sex-mad/he's got sex on the brain/that's all he ever thinks about (*b*) pornography/porn; **histoires de cul,** dirty stories; **bouquin de cul,** dirty book; **revue de cul,** tits and bum/porn magazine; **film de cul,** blue/porn movie. (*Voir* **basduc, bas-du-cul; beurre 9; chaise; clochettes; couille 1** (*b*); **cul-de-plomb; cul-terreux; feu 1, 6; (se) magner; pied 14; poil 2, 4**) II *a* *P* stupid*/daft/silly; **ce qu'il est cul!** what a bloody twerp (he is)!/what a nerd!

culbutant [kylbytɑ̃] *nm, Vieilli* **culbute¹** [kylbyt] *nf P* trousers*/*NAm* pants.

culbute² *nf F* **faire la culbute,** (*personne*) to come a cropper*; (*gouvernement*) to fall/to collapse; (*entreprise*) to fail/to go bankrupt/to go bust; (*faire une bonne affaire* (*en doublant le prix d'achat*)) to make a scoop/to make a huge profit/to make a killing; (*doubler la mise*) to double one's stakes.

culbuté [kylbyte] *a P* 1. **culbuté (à zéro),** (dead) drunk*/(completely) canned/smashed 2. **bien culbutée,** (*d'une femme*) with a nice/ attractive figure.

culbuter [kylbyte] I *vtr* 1. *P* to convince (s.o.)/to win (s.o.) over 2. *V* **culbuter une femme,** to have sex* with a woman/to lay a woman II *vi F = faire la culbute* (**culbute²**).

culbuteur [kylbytœr] *nm P* **culbuteur de femmes,** womanizer*/ladykiller/wolf/Don Juan/ Casanova.

cul-de-plomb [kydplɔ̃] *nm P* 1. (dispensing) chemist's assistant 2. pen-pusher/petty bureaucrat 3. **c'est un cul-de-plomb,** he's a lazy swine/he sits on his behind all day and does damn-all.

culeter [kylte] *vtr V* to have sex* with (s.o.).

culot [kylo] *nm F* 1. impudence*; **avoir du culot,** to be cheeky; to have plenty of cheek/of nerve; **avoir un culot monstre/un culot infernal/un sacré culot,** to have a hell of a cheek/to have the cheek of the devil; **vous en avez du culot!** you've got a nerve! **tu ne manques pas de culot!** you're a cool one!/ you've got a (bloody) cheek! **y aller au culot/ le faire au culot,** to bluff 2. (*dernier*) last chick hatched/last animal born (of litter); baby of the family; (*écoles*) **culot (d'une promotion)** = wooden spoon/booby prize.

culotte [kylɔt] *nf* 1. *P* drunkenness; **avoir sa culotte,** to be drunk* 2. *F* **prendre/ramasser une culotte,** to lose heavily (at cards, etc)/to

come a cropper*/to come unstuck 3. *F* **trembler/**P **faire/**V **chier dans sa culotte,** to be afraid*/to be scared stiff/to have the wind up; to wet/to piss oneself; to shit oneself 4. *P* **baisser sa culotte (devant qn),** to be a coward*/to refuse to fight/to show the white feather 5. *F* **c'est la femme qui porte la culotte,** it's the wife who wears the trousers 6. *F* **jouer ses culottes,** to stake everything one has 7. *F* **je m'en moque comme de ma première culotte,** I couldn't care less; I don't give a damn 8. *F* **une vieille culotte de peau,** an old dugout/a Colonel Blimp 9. *F* (*certains ordres religieux*) **porter la culotte de zinc,** to conform to a rigorous discipline.

culotté [kylɔte] *a F* 1. impudent*/cheeky; **elle est culottée comme tout,** she's got a hell of a nerve/a bloody cheek; *Iron* **vous n'êtes pas culotté, vous!** you don't want much, do you! 2. brave/game 3. (*livre, etc*) well-thumbed; rather the worse for wear.

se culotter [səkylɔte] *vpr P* 1. to get drunk* 2. to wear oneself out.

culte [kylt] *a F* **un film/livre culte,** a cult film/book.

cul-terreux [kytɛrø] *nm F Péj* peasant*/ clodhopper/country bumpkin/hick/yokel. (*pl* **culs-terreux**)

cumulard [kymylar] *nm F Péj* pluralist; holder of several (paid) jobs (etc)/ moonlighter.

cumuler [kymyle] *vi F* **il cumule,** he has more than one (paid) job/he's a moonlighter/ he's moonlighting.

cunu [kyny] *nm P* (*écoles*) arithmetic; counting.

cunuter [kynyte] *vtr & i P* (*écoles*) to count (numerically).

curaillon [kyrajɔ̃] *nm F Péj* young priest; **petit curaillon de village,** (petty) parish priest.

curé [kyre] *nm F* **avoir affaire au curé et aux paroissiens,** to be between the devil and the deep blue sea. (*Voir* **bouffer I 1** (*e*))

cure-dent(s) [kyrdɑ̃] *nm* 1. *F* **venir en cure-dent(s),** to turn up at the end of a dinner/to gate-crash an evening party 2. *P* knife 3. *P* (*langage des policiers*) failed police investigation.

curée [kyre] *nf F* **la curée,** the rat race; **se ruer à la curée (des places),** to join the rat race; **être âpre à la curée,** to be on the make.

cureton [kyrtɔ̃] *nm F Péj* (parish) priest.

curetot [kyrto] *nm*, **curetosse** [kyrtos] *nm P* = **cureton**.

curieux [kyrjø] *nm P* 1. examining magistrate 2. police superintendent 3. father confessor.

cuterie [kytri] *nf P* stupidity/stupid nonsense.

cuti [kyti] *nf F* (*a*) (*médecine*) (*abrév* = *cuti-réaction*) skin test (*b*) **virer sa cuti**, to change one's way of life radically; to change one's mind; to lose one's virginity; to become homosexual, etc.

cuvée [kyve] *nf P* drinking bout/drunken orgy/binge/bender/piss-up.

cuver [kyve] I *vtr F* 1. **cuver son vin**, to sleep off the effects of wine/to sleep oneself sober/to sleep it off 2. **cuver sa colère**, to work off one's anger; to simmer down II *vi P* to laze about.

cyclard [siklar] *nm F* cyclist.

cyclo [siklo] *nm F* 1. policeman on a bicycle 2. (*abbr* = *cyclomoteur*) moped.

cyclope [siklɔp] *nm V* penis*; **faire pleurer le cyclope/égoutter son cyclope**, to urinate*/to have a slash/to take a leak; (*jouir*) to have an orgasm*/to ejaculate*/to come.

cygne [siɲ] *nm V* **baiser une femme en cygne**, to have sex* with a woman with her legs over her partner's shoulders/in the wheelbarrow position.

cynoque [sinɔk] *a P* mad*/crackers/bonkers. (*Voir* **sinoc, synoque**)

Cyrard [sirar] *nm F* cadet at the Saint-Cyr military school.

D

D [de] *nm F* le système D, (= *système dé-brouille ou système démerde*) resourceful-ness; wangling; fiddling.

dab, dabe[1] [dab] *nm P* 1. father*/dad/pa; mon vieux dab, my old man. (*Voir* **beau-dab(e)**; **dab(e)s**; **grand-dab(e)**) 2. the boss*/the governor; le Grand Dab, God.

dabe[2] *nf P* 1. mother*/mum/ma/old lady 2. (*d'un couvent*) mother superior 3. mistress. (*Voir* **dab(e)s**)

dab(e)s [dab] *nmpl P* mes dab(e)s, my parents/the old folk(s)/my folks/mum and dad/ma and pa. (*Voir* **beaux-dab(e)s**)

dabesse [dabɛs] *nf P* = **dabe**[2]. (*Voir* **belle-dabesse**)

dabuche [dabyʃ] *nf P* = **dabe**[2].

dac! d'ac(c)! [dak] *int F* agreed!*/OK!/ roger! t'es d'ac? OK with you? pas d'ac! nothing doing! no way!

dache, Dache [daʃ] *nm P* (*a*) à dache, far away/miles away/at the back of beyond (*b*) envoyer qn à dache, to send s.o. packing*/to send s.o. off with a flea in his ear; va (le dire) à Dache!/va-t'en chez Dache! go to hell!

dada [dada] *nm* 1. *F* (*langage enfantin*) horse/gee-gee 2. aller à dada, *F* (*langage en-fantin*) to ride a cock-horse; to ride a horse/to ride a gee-gee; *Vieilli V* to have sex* with a woman/to ride a woman. (*Voir* **radada**) 3. *F* hobby/fad; chevaucher/enfourcher son dada, to get on to one's pet subject/one's hobby-horse 4. *P* (*drogues*) mixture of heroin* and cocaine*.

dadais [dadɛ] *nm F* silly/awkward boy; espèce de grand dadais! you great gawk of a boy!

daf, d'Af [daf] *nm P* = **bat' d'af**.

dal, dalle[1] [dal] *adv P* que dalle, nothing* at all/damn-all/sweet FA; je n'y entrave/n'y pige que dalle, I don't get it/I can't see what it's all about/I can't make head or tail of it; j'ai fichu que dalle aujourd'hui, I've done damn all today.

dalle[2] *nf P* 1. throat/gullet; s'arroser/se mouiller/se rincer la dalle, to (have a) drink*/to wet one's whistle; avoir la dalle en pente, to have a permanent thirst/to like a drink 2. avoir la dalle/une de ces dalles, to be hungry*.

dallepé [dalpe] *nf P* (*verlan de pédale*) homosexual*/queer/poof.

dam [dam] *nf P* aller à dam; envoyer à dam, *Voir* **dame 6**.

dame [dam] **I** *nf* 1. *F* faire la (grande) dame, to put on airs/to be all lah-di-dah 2. *P* vot' dame, your wife*/your good lady/your missis 3. *P* ma petite dame = missis/honey/ love/lovey/ducky/ducks 4. *P* une dame blan-che, a bottle of white wine 5. *F* dame de pique, pack of cards; chatouiller/taquiner/ faire valser la dame de pique, to play cards/to be fond of playing cards 6. *P* (*a*) aller à dame, to fall/to come a cropper* (*b*) envoyer qn à dame, to send s.o. sprawling; *Fig* to spurn s.o. 7. *P* entrer en dame avec qn, to strike up a conversation with s.o. **II** *int F* (*ré-gional*) dame ouais! I should say so!

dame-pipi [dampipi] *nf F* (female) lavatory attendant. (*pl* **dames-pipi**)

damer [dame] *F* **I** *vtr* 1. damer qn, to send s.o. sprawling 2. damer le pion à qn, to out-wit s.o./to go one better than s.o.; (*mauvais tour*) to play a trick on s.o. **II** *vi* to fall (over)/to come a cropper*.

damner [dɑne] *vtr F* faire damner qn, to drive s.o. crazy/to drink; cela ferait damner un saint, it's enough to make a saint swear.

danse [dɑ̃s] *nf* 1. *P* thrashing/beating*; donner/filer une danse à qn, to give s.o. a good hiding; ramasser une danse, to get a good belting 2. *F* ouvrir la danse, to start the ball rolling/to get things under way; voilà la danse qui va commencer, now we're in for it/the fun's just starting; there'll be fireworks.

danser [dɑ̃se] **I** *vtr Vieilli P* la danser, to get a good hiding; tu vas la danser! you'll catch

430

it!/you're in for it! **II** *vi* F 1. **faire danser qn,** to lead s.o. a dance/to give s.o. a hard time (of it) 2. **il ne sait sur quel pied danser,** he doesn't know which way to turn; he's all at sea; **avec lui on ne sait jamais sur quel pied danser,** you never know where you are with him. (*Voir* **buffet 2; empêcheur**)

danseuse [dɑ̃søz] *nf* F **pédaler/rouler en danseuse,** (*à vélo*) to ride standing (up) on the pedals.

dard [dar] *nm* 1. V penis*/shaft/prick; **avoir du dard,** to be (very) sexually excited*; to be randy/horny. (*Voir* **pomper I 3**) 2. **filer comme un dard,** to go very fast/like the clappers.

dardillon [dardijɔ̃] *nm* V penis*/prick; **avoir le dardillon,** to have an erection*.

dare-dare [dardar] *adv* F double-quick/like a shot/like the clappers/at the double/toot sweet; **accourir dare-dare,** to come charging up.

dargeot [darʒo] *nm,* **dargif** [darʒif] *nm* P buttocks*; **faire fumer le dargeot à qn,** to give s.o. a good hiding.

daron [darɔ̃] *nm* P 1. father*/old man 2. boss*/(big white) chief 3. *pl* **les darons,** parents/the old folk(s).

daronne [darɔn] *nf* P mother*/old lady.

darrac, darraque [darak] *nm* 1. *Vieilli* P hammer 2. V penis*/tool/hammer.

datte [dat] *nf* P 1. **ne pas en faire/fiche(r) une datte,** to do nothing/to (sit on one's behind and) do damn-all 2. **des dattes!** nothing doing!*/it's no go!/no dice! *Vieilli* **ça c'est comme des dattes,** that's impossible.

daube [dob] *nf* P **c'est de la daube,** it's worthless*/it's not worth a sausage.

daubé [dobe] *a* P (*meubles, etc*) fake(d)/imitation.

dauf(f)er [dofe] *vtr* V **dauf(f)er qn,** to have anal sex* with s.o./to sodomize* s.o./to bugger s.o.

dauphin [dofɛ̃] *nm* P 1. *Vieilli* pimp*/ponce 2. (burglar's) jemmy/*NAm* jimmy.

dé [de] *nm* 1. P **lâcher les dés,** to throw in the towel/to throw in the sponge/to call it a day 2. P **passer les dés,** to make peace/to make a peace offering 3. V **dé à coudre,** anus*.

deal [dil] *nm* P (*drogues*) deal.

dealer[1] [dilœr] *nm* P (*drogues*) (*drug*) dealer/pusher.

dealer[2] [dile] P **I** *vtr* **dealer de la drogue,** to sell drugs*/to deal in drugs* **II** *vi* 1. to sell/to deal in drugs*; to be a dealer 2. to bargain/to haggle.

deb [dɛb] *a* P = **débile**.

débâcher [debaʃe] **I** *vi* P to pack up and leave **II** *vpr* **se débâcher** P to get up/to get out of bed.

débâcler [debakle] *vtr* P **débâcler la lourde,** to open the door.

débagoulage [debagulaʒ] *nm* P 1. *Vieilli* vomiting 2. (*orateur*) spouting (forth).

débagoule [debagul] *nf* P **tortiller de la débagoule,** to spout (forth)/to spiel.

débagouler [debagule] P **I** *vi* *Vieilli* to vomit* **II** *vtr* 1. to bring up (food)/to throw up 2. to spout (nonsense, sales talk, etc).

déballage [debalaʒ] *nm* 1. P (*femme*) **vaut mieux pas qu'il la voie au déballage,** it's best if he doesn't see her first thing before she puts her make-up on; **être volé au déballage,** (*d'un homme*) to find the wrapping better than the goods; **gagner/perdre au déballage,** (*d'une femme*) to look more attractive unclothed and without make-up/clothed and made-up 2. F (*aveu*) confession/outpouring.

déballer [debale] *vtr & vi* (*a*) F to confess*; **allez, déballe!** come on, own up! P **déballer ses outils,** (*avouer*); to confess*/to come clean; (*se déculotter*) to pull one's pants down; F **déballer (ce qu'on a sur le cœur),** to get it off one's chest (*b*) F **déballer ses connaissances,** to tell all one knows; **il a tout déballé sur la table,** he put all his cards on the table. (*Voir* **paquet 10**)

déballonné [debalɔne] *nm* P coward*/quitter.

se déballonner [sədebalɔne] *vpr* P 1. to confess*/to come clean 2. to lose courage/to funk it/to back out/to chicken out.

débander [debɑ̃de] *vi* 1. P to be afraid* 2. V to lose one's erection/to shrink/to go limp; **cela m'a fait débander rapide,** it was like a cold shower/it really put me off 3. P to cease/to stop going; **sans débander,** to keep going/to keep it up.

débarbe [debarb] *nm,* **débarbot** [debarbo] *nm* P defence lawyer/mouthpiece.

débarboter [debarbɔte] **I** *vtr* P **débarboter qn,** to act as counsel for the defence for s.o./to be s.o.'s mouthpiece **II** *vpr* **se débarboter** P to get by/to manage; to shift for oneself.

débarbot(t)eur [debarbɔtœr] *nm* P = **débarbe**.

débarbouiller [debarbuje] **I** *vtr* 1. F to get (s.o.) out of a scrape 2. P to kill*/to wipe out **II** *vpr* **se débarbouiller** F 1. **qu'il se**

débarbouille, let him sort it out for himself/let him shift for himself 2. **le temps se débarbouille**, the weather's clearing up.

débarcade [debarkad] *nf P* release (from prison); discharge.

débardeur [debardœr] *nm F* (man's) vest/undershirt.

débardot [debardo] *nm P* = **débarbe**.

débarquement [debarkəmã] *nm P* start of a period*.

débarquer [debarke] I *vtr F* **débarquer qn**, to dismiss* s.o./to give s.o. the sack; **il faut le débarquer!** he's got to go! II *vi* 1. *F* **débarquer chez qn**, to drop in on s.o.; **elle a débarqué hier soir**, she turned up last night 2. *F* **il débarque**, he's a novice; he's a bit green; **tu débarques?** where have *you* been? 3. *P* **ils ont débarqué**, she's got her period*/she's got the curse. (*Voir* **Anglais**)

débarrasser [debarase] *vtr F* **débarrasser le plancher**, to leave*/to clear out.

débauche [deboʃ] *nf F* **faire une (petite) débauche (de table)**, to make a pig of oneself.

débauchée [deboʃe] *nf F* knocking-off time (after a day's work).

débaucher [deboʃe] *F* I *vi* to knock off (after a day's work) II *vtr* **est-ce que je peux te débaucher et t'inviter au cinéma?** can I tempt you with a film? **c'est lui qui m'a débauché hier soir**, (*il m'a emmené au cinéma, etc*) he led me astray last night III *vpr* **se débaucher** *F* **laissez là vos livres et débauchez-vous un peu**, put your books away and have a bit of fun/let yourself go a little.

dèbe [dɛb] *a P* = **débile**.

débectage [debɛktaʒ] *nm P* disgust/revulsion.

débectant [debɛktã] *a P* disgusting/revolting/sickening/nauseating.

débecter [debɛkte] *P vtr* to disgust/to revolt/to sicken; **ça me débecte**, I can't stomach that/it makes me sick; **il me débecte**, he makes me (want to) puke.

débile [debil] *a F* idiotic/feeble/moronic; **il est complètement débile**, he's an absolute moron.

débinage [debinaʒ] *nm P* disparagement*/knocking/slamming/running down (of s.o.).

débine [debin] *nf F* 1. poverty; **être dans la débine**, to be penniless*/to be down on one's luck/to be on one's beam-ends; **tomber dans la débine**, to go broke/to fall on hard times 2. rout/disorderly retreat.

débiner [debine] *P* I *vtr* 1. to disparage*/to run down/to knock (s.o.) 2. to denounce (s.o.); **débiner le truc**, to give the game away/to spill the beans/to let the cat out of the bag II *vi & vpr* **(se) débiner** 1. to leave*/to scram/to clear off/to hop it 2. to be a shirker; **il se débine toujours**, he's always getting out of doing sth; he's always shirking his responsibilities.

débineur, -euse [debinœr, -øz] *n P* backbiter/knocker.

débiter [debite] *vtr F* **débiter une histoire**, to spin a yarn; **débiter des sottises**, to talk rubbish.

déblayer [debleje] *vtr & vi* 1. **déblayer le terrain**, *F* to pave/to clear the way; to lay the groundwork (for negotiations, etc); to clear the decks; *P* (*partir*) to run away*/to beat it/to scarper/to do a bunk; **déblaie!** hop it!/push off!/scram! 2. *F* (*théâtre*) **déblayer (un rôle)**, to emphasize the main speeches in a role by rushing through the others.

débleuir [deblœir] *vtr F* **débleuir qn**, to open s.o.'s eyes (to life)/to teach s.o. a thing or two/to put s.o. straight.

débloquer [deblɔke] *vi P* 1. to defecate*/to have a crap 2. to talk rubbish/to talk cock/to talk crap; to be off one's rocker; **tu débloques!** you're off your head/you're out of your mind! **son grand-père commence à débloquer**, his grandfather's going gaga 3. (*machine, etc*) to be out of order/on the blink; **la télé débloque**, the telly's on the blink.

déboisé [debwaze] *a P* bald*.

déboiser [debwaze] I *vtr P* **se faire déboiser la colline**, to get one's hair cut II *vpr* **se déboiser** *P* to lose one's hair/one's thatch.

débouclage [debuklaʒ] *nm P* 1. breaking open (of a door, a till, etc); blowing (of a safe) 2. release (of a prisoner).

déboucler [debukle] *vtr P* 1. to break open (a door, safe, till, etc) 2. to release (a prisoner).

déboucleur [debuklœr] *nm P* burglar; safe-breaker.

débouler [debule] *vi* 1. *F* (*cyclisme*) to start/move off suddenly 2. *F* to arrive suddenly/to drop in/to turn up 3. *P* **débouler de la cocotte**, to talk rubbish/crap.

déboulonnage [debulɔnaʒ] *nm*, **déboulonnement** [debulɔnmã] *nm F* dismissal (from a post)/sacking/firing.

déboulonner [debulɔne] *vtr F* to dismiss*/to fire/to sack.

débourre [debur] *nf V* WC*/craphouse.

débourrer [debure] I *vi V* to defecate*/to
have a crap/to have a clear-out II *vtr P* to
despise (s.o.)/to run (s.o.) down. (*Voir* **froc
3**)

débousille [debuzij] *nf P* elimination/
removal of a tattoo.

déboussolé [debusɔle] *a & n F* confused/
bewildered person; **être tout déboussolé**, to
have lost one's bearings/to be all at sea.

déboutonnage [debutɔnaʒ] *nm F* unload-
ing of one's mind/opening up of one's heart.

déboutonné [debutɔne] *a F* 1. **manger à
ventre déboutonné**, to eat* heartily/to gorge/to
stuff oneself (with food) 2. **rire à ventre
déboutonné**, to laugh* uproariously/to split
one's sides laughing.

se déboutonner [sədebutɔne] *vpr F* to
unburden one's mind/to open up (one's
heart)/to get it off one's chest.

se débrailler [sədebraje] *vpr F* to loosen
one's clothing; **l'atmosphère se débraille**,
things are getting a bit too relaxed.

débrayer [debreje] *vi F* (*se mettre en
grève*) to down tools; (*à la fin de la journée*)
to down tools/to knock off.

débridage [debridaʒ] *nm P* = **débouclage 1**.

débrider [debride] I *vtr P* 1. = **déboucler
1** 2. to draw (a gun, a knife) II *vi* 1. *F*
travailler huit heures sans débrider, to work
eight hours non-stop/at a stretch 2. *P* to draw
a gun/a knife, etc 3. *P* (*langage des policiers*)
to open fire suddenly/without warning.

débringué [debrɛ̃ge] *a P* slovenly.

débris [debri] *nm P* **un vieux débris**, an old
fogey*/an old dodderer/an old wreck.

débrouillard, -arde [debrujar, -ard] *F* I
a resourceful*/canny/smart II *n* resourceful
person; **c'est un débrouillard**, he's got his wits
about him/he's got plenty of gumption/he's a
smart lad/he can look after himself.

débrouillardise [debrujardiz] *nf*, **débrouille** [debruj] *nf F* resourcefulness/
smartness; wangling/fixing. (*Voir* **D**)

débrouiller [debruje] I *vtr F* **débrouiller
qn**, to get s.o. out of a jam/a mess; **débrouiller
qch**, to clear up a mess/sort out a muddle II
vpr **se débrouiller** *F* to shift for oneself/to
get by/to manage; **qu'il se débrouille!** let him
look after himself!/let him sort himself out!
savoir se débrouiller, to know one's way
around; **se débrouiller tant bien que mal**, to
muddle through; **se débrouiller pour avoir**

qch, to wangle sth; **débrouillez-vous!** that's
your look-out! (*faites comme vous voulez*)
you'll just have to manage; **se débrouiller sur
le voisin**, to pass the buck/the baby.

debs [debz] *a P* = **débile**.

dec [dek] *vi P* (*abrév* = **déconner**) **sans
dec!** no kidding!/no shit!

dèc [dɛk] *nm P* police officer*/copper/filth.

déca [deka] *nm F* **un déca**, (= *un café
décaféiné*) a (cup of) decaffeinated coffee/a
decaf.

se décalcifier [sədekalsifje] *vpr F Hum*
(*homme*) to take one's (under)pants off. (*Voir*
calcif)

décalqué [dekalke] *a F* **c'est son père tout
décalqué**, he's the spitting image of his
father; he's a chip of(f) the old block.

décambuter [dekɑ̃byte] *vi P* 1. (*a*) to
come out/to emerge (*b*) to go out/to exit 2. to
run away*/to beat it/to scarper.

décamper [dekɑ̃pe] *vi F* to run away*/to
bolt/to make oneself scarce/to clear out;
décampe! clear off!/buzz off!/beat it! **il a
décampé**, he's done a bunk/he's scarpered.

décaner [dekane] *vi P* to die*. (*Voir* **caner
2**)

décanillage [dekanijaʒ] *nm P* hurried
departure/flight.

décaniller [dekanije] *vi P* = **décamper**.

décapant [dekapɑ̃] *F* I *nm* poor quality
wine/plonk II *a* (*vin*, etc) harsh.

décapiter [dekapite] *vtr F* to open/to un-
cork (a bottle).

décapotable [dekapɔtabl] *a P* (*femme*)
fond of taking off her clothes/ready and will-
ing.

décapoter [dekapɔte] *vi P* to take one's hat
off.

se décarcasser [sədekarkase] *vpr F* (*a*)
to go to a (hell of a) lot of trouble/to put oneself out/to bend over backwards; **je me suis
décarcassé pour vous procurer ce billet**, I
really put myself out to get you this ticket (*b*)
to wear oneself out/to flog oneself to death.

décarpillage [dekarpijaʒ] *nm P* 1. sorting
out (of the proceeds of a robbery) 2.
undressing/stripping; **au décarpillage, elle
n'était pas belle**, she wasn't a pretty sight
with no clothes on.

décarpiller [dekarpije] *vtr P* 1. to sort out/
to make a list of (the proceeds of a robbery)
2. to undress (*esp* a woman) 3. to draw (a
gun).

décarrade [dekarad] *nf P* departure; (*éva-*

sion) escape/flight/exit (from prison, etc).

décarrer [dekare] *vi P* 1. to go out/to (make an) exit 2. (*a*) to run away*/to make oneself scarce/to take off (*b*) to escape (*esp* from prison)/to go on the run 3. décarrer de belle, to be released without trial/to beat the rap.

se décartonner [sədekartəne] *vpr P* to grow old/to be getting on in years.

décati [dekati] *a F* (*a*) faded/wilted/old and worn; elle n'est pas trop décatie, she's not so dusty/she's worn quite well (considering) (*b*) (*visage*) wrinkled.

(se) décatir [(sə)dekatir] *vi & pr F* to show the effects of age; elle commence à (se) décatir, she's beginning to lose her looks.

décavage [dekava3] *nm P* ruin/bankruptcy.

décavé [dekave] *a F* 1. (*a*) (*personne riche*) ruined/done for/bankrupt (*b*) penniless*/(stony) broke 2. visage décavé, drawn/pinched/haggard face.

décesser [desese] *vtr & i F* (*se dit pour cesser*) il ne décesse pas de se plaindre, he never stops complaining.

déchanter [deʃɑ̃te] *vi F* to change one's tune; il a fallu déchanter, it was time to lose all our illusions.

déchard, -arde [deʃar, -ard] *a & n P* hard-up (individual)/penniless* (person); down-and-out.

décharge [deʃar3] *nf V* ejaculation/come; témoins à décharge, testicles*/balls.

décharger [deʃar3e] *vi V* to ejaculate*/to shoot one's load. (*Voir* **plancher¹ 2**)

dèche [dɛʃ] *nf P* 1. poverty; être dans la dèche/être dans une dèche noire/tomber dans la dèche/battre la dèche, to be penniless*/to be down on one's uppers/to be on one's beam-ends/to be stony broke 2. failure*/flop/washout 3. surplus/excess.

décher [deʃe] *vtr P* (*a*) to pay* (up)/to dish out/to fork out (*b*) to spend (*c*) to pay for (something).

décheur, -euse¹ [deʃœr, -øz] *a & n P* spendthrift/big spender.

décheux, -euse² [deʃø, -øz] *a P* penniless*/stony broke/flat broke.

déchiré [deʃire] *a P* 1. drunk*/pissed 2. high on drugs.

déchirer [deʃire] *vtr P* la déchirer/déchirer son tablier, to die*. (*Voir* **false**; **toile 2**)

deck [dɛk] *nm P* = **dèc**.

déclouer [deklue] *vtr F* déclouer qch, to redeem sth/to take sth out of pawn.

décocter [dekɔkte] *vi V* to defecate*/to

have a crap.

décoiffer [dekwafe] *vi P* (*d'une voiture, entreprise, etc*) to work well/to go well; ça décoiffe! it's going like a bomb!

décoincer [dekwɛ̃se] *vi P* 1. to move/to budge 2. to talk/to chat*/to jabber.

décoller [dekɔle] I *vi* 1. F il ne décolle pas d'ici, he won't budge/he's staying put 2. F six heures sans décoller, six hours without a break/at a stretch 3. P (*couple (marié)*) to separate 4. P elle a drôlement décollé depuis sa maladie, she's got terribly thin/she's gone to pieces/she doesn't look too good since her illness 5. F to get high (on music, drugs, etc) II *vtr P* to kill* III *vpr* se décoller P to commit suicide.

décompte [dekɔ̃t] *nm F* trouver du décompte à qch, to be disillusioned by sth/to be disappointed in sth.

déconnade [dekɔnad] *nf P* mucking about/bullshitting.

déconnage [dekɔna3] *nm P* nonsense*/rubbish/tripe/cock/balls/crap/*surt NAm* bull (shit).

déconnant [dekɔnɑ̃] *a P* stupid*/moronic/cretinous.

déconnante [dekɔnɑ̃t] *nf P* stupidity/nonsense/rubbish.

déconnecter [dekɔnɛkte] *vi F* to isolate oneself; to cut off all links.

déconner [dekɔne] *vi P* déconner (à pleins tubes)/déconner plein pot, to talk absolute nonsense*/to talk cock; déconne pas!/arrête de déconner! cut the crap!/don't give me that bull/shit/crap/balls! (*ne fais pas de bêtises*) don't do anything stupid!/don't piss about! (*ne plaisante pas*) stop arsing about! tu déconnes! what on earth are you talking about? sans déconner, c'était super, no fooling, it was great; sans déconner! no kidding!/no shit!

déconneur, -euse [dekɔnœr, -øz] *n V* s.o. who talks cock/bullshitter; (*plaisantin*) s.o. who arses about; quel déconneur, ce mec! what a load of balls/crap that guy comes out with! he never stops arsing about!

décon(n)ographe [dekɔnɔgraf] *nm P* teleprinter/*NAm* teletypewriter.

décon(n)omètre [dekɔnɔmɛtr] *nm P* 1. (*a*) radio (set) (*b*) television (set)/(idiot-)box/(goggle)box 2. telephone*/blower 3. microphone/mike 4. = **décon(n)ophone**.

décon(n)ophone [dekɔnɔfon] *nm P* mouth*; fermer son décon(n)ophone, to shut one's trap.

décontract' [dekɔ̃trakt] *F I a* (= décontracté) relaxed; veste décontract', casual jacket II *adv* quietly/casually.

décoqueter [dekɔkte] *vi V* = **décocter**.

décor [dekɔr] *nm F* **1.** entrer/rentrer/foncer/aller/valser dans le décor, (*voiture*) to run/to smash into a wall, house, etc; to leave the road; balancer/envoyer qn dans le décor, to send s.o. flying **2.** cela ne fera/ferait pas mal dans le décor, that will/would suit me down to the ground **3.** l'envers du décor, the other side of the picture/of the coin.

se décramponner [sədekrɑ̃pɔne] *vpr F* **1.** to shake s.o. off **2.** to break up a relationship/to break up with s.o.

décrasser [dekrase] I *vtr F* décrasser qn, to knock the rough edges off s.o./smarten s.o. up/to lick s.o. into shape II *vpr* **se décrasser** *F* (*devenir plus sophistiqué*) to lose one's rough edges; to smarten up.

décrassing-room [dekrasiŋrum] *nm P* bathroom.

décroche [dekrɔʃ] *nf P* (*drogues*) stopping taking drugs/kicking the habit.

décrocher [dekrɔʃe] I *vtr* **1.** *F* (*a*) to get/to hook/to land; décrocher le grand succès, to make a big hit; décrocher le gros lot, to hit the jackpot; ils ont décroché le contrat, they landed the contract (*b*) to wangle; il a décroché une bonne position, he's wangled himself a nice job; décrocher une augmentation, to wangle/to land a rise **2.** *F* to redeem (sth)/to take (sth) out of pawn. (*Voir* **tableau 2**; **timbale 1**) II *vi* **1.** *P* (*langage des policiers*) to abandon an investigation **2.** *F* to retire (from one's job) **3.** *P* (*drogues*) to stop taking drugs/to knock off the dope/to kick the habit III *vpr* **se décrocher** *P* = **décrocher** II **3**.

décrochez-moi-ça [dekrɔʃemwasa] *nm inv F* **1.** cheap second-hand garment; reach-me-down/hand-me-down; cast-off **2.** cheap second-hand clothes shop; elle s'habille au décrochez-moi-ça, she gets her clothes from jumble sales/from the Oxfam shop.

(se) décrotter [(sə)dekrɔte] *vtr & pr F* **1.** = **(se) décrasser** **2.** se décrotter le nez, to pick one's nose.

décuiter [dekɥite] I *vtr P* to sober (s.o.) up II *vpr* **se décuiter** *P* to sober up.

déculottée [dekylɔte] *nf P* **1.** heavy defeat; prendre la/une déculottée, to get thrashed/to get clobbered **2.** heavy loss (at gambling).

déculotter [dekylɔte] I *vtr P* déculotter sa pensée, to speak openly/freely II *vpr* **se**

déculotter 1. *P* to speak openly/freely **2.** *F* to grovel.

dedans [dədɑ̃] *adv* **1.** *F* mettre/P fiche(r)/flanquer/fourrer/foutre qn dedans, (*tromper*) to bamboozle s.o./to take s.o. in/to have s.o. on; *surt Mil* (*mettre en prison*) to imprison s.o./to put s.o. inside/to put s.o. away; être dedans, to be in prison*/to be inside **2.** *F* rentrer dedans à qn, (*attaquer*) to pitch into s.o./to lay into s.o./to go for s.o.; je vais lui rentrer dedans, I'm going to give him what for **3.** *P* (*a*) entrer/rentrer dedans qch, to knock/to crash/to bash/to smash into sth (*b*) mettre une porte (en) dedans, to break a door down/to break in **4.** *F* mettre les pieds dedans, to put one's foot in it; je me suis foutu dedans, I really boobed there **5.** *F* marcher dedans, to tread in (a dog's, etc) excrement/to put one's foot in some dog-shit/to tread in something nasty. (*Voir* **défourailler 1**; **donner 6**; **rentre-dedans**)

dédouaner [dedwane] I *vtr F* dédouaner qn, (*blanchir*) to clear s.o.'s name; dédouaner un voleur, to rehabilitate a thief II *vpr* **se dédouaner** *F* to redeem oneself.

def [dɛf] *a P* (*abrév* = *défoncé*) *Voir* **raide I 6**.

défarguer [defarge] I *vtr P* to clear (s.o.) of a charge/to put (s.o.) in the clear/to get (s.o) off the hook II *vi V* to defecate/to (have a) crap III *vpr* **se défarguer** *P* **1.** se défarguer de qch, to get rid of sth (incriminating) **2.** to exonerate oneself (and put the blame on s.o. else).

défargueur [defargœr] *nm P* witness for the defence.

se défausser [sədefose] *vpr P* = **se défarguer** (**défarguer III 1**).

défaut [defo] *nm F* (il) y a comme un défaut/(il) y a a qu'un petit défaut, there's a snag/a hitch.

se défendre [sədefɑ̃dr] *vpr* **1.** *F* to get along/to hold one's own/to manage; je me défends pas mal, I'm getting along quite nicely/I'm doing fine; il se défend au tennis, he's quite good at tennis **2.** *F* elle se défend bien, she wears (her age) well/she doesn't do badly for her age **3.** *P* (*prostituée*) to solicit*/to go on the game.

défense [defɑ̃s] *nf P* **1.** swindle; racket **2.** avoir de la défense = **se défendre 1**.

déferrer [defere] I *vtr F* déferrer qn (des quatre pieds), to disconcert s.o./to put s.o. out II *vpr* **se déferrer** *F* c'est un mec qui ne se déferre pas facilement, he's a bloke who's not easily put out.

deffe [dɛf] *nf P* cap/beret.

se défiler [sədefile] *vpr F* 1. to run away*/to clear off/to beat it 2. to back out (of sth unpleasant)/to duck out (of sth) 3. to hide.

défilocher [defilɔʃe] *vtr P* défilocher les haricots verts à qn, to make a fool of s.o.

déflaque [deflak] *nf V* excrement*/shit.

déflaquer [deflake] *vi V* to defecate*/to shit.

défonce [defɔ̃s] *nf P* 1. (*par la drogue*) trip/ high; être en pleine défonce, to be on a trip; il était entre deux défonces, he was between highs 2. drugs*/dope.

défoncé [defɔ̃se] *a P* (*a*) drunk*/pissed (*b*) (*drogué*) high/stoned/bombed/tripping; il était complètement défoncé, he was stoned out of his mind/he'd completely flipped.

défoncer [defɔ̃se] I *vtr P* 1. (*drogues*) to make (s.o.) high/to give (s.o.) hallucinations 2. to have sex* with (s.o.)/to screw (s.o.) II *vpr* **se défoncer** 1. *P* to get drunk*/pissed 2. *P* to get high/stoned on drugs 3. *V* to have sex* 4. *P* (*passer du bon temps*) to have a whale of a time 5. *V* se faire défoncer la rondelle, to be sodomized*/to get one's ass fucked 6. *P* (*faire un grand effort*) to sweat blood.

défonceuse [defɔ̃søz] *nf V* penis*/chopper/ tool; être amputé de la défonceuse, to be impotent.

déforme [defɔrm] *nf P* être (un peu) en déforme, to be (temporarily) out of luck (*esp* at gambling).

défourailler [defuraje] *vtr & i P* 1. to draw (a gun, knife, etc); défourailler dedans, to pull the trigger/to shoot/to fire; to let s.o. have it 2. to get out of prison*.

défrimer [defrime] *vtr P* 1. to stare at (s.o.)/to look (s.o.) straight in the eye 2. to recognize (s.o.).

défringuer [defrɛ̃ge] I *vtr P* to undress (s.o.) II *vpr* **se défringuer** *P* to undress/to get undressed/to take one's clothes off.

défrisé [defrize] *a F* avoir l'air défrisé, to look down in the mouth/put out.

défrisement [defrizmɑ̃] *nm F* disappointment.

défriser [defrize] I *vtr F* to annoy* (s.o.); to disappoint (s.o.)/to put (s.o.) out; ça m'a beaucoup défrisé, that really got me down II *vpr* **se défriser** *F* to lose heart; to feel put out.

se défroquer [sədefrɔke] *vpr P* to pull

one's trousers/pants down.

défrusquer [defryske] I *vtr P* to undress (s.o.) II *vpr* **se défrusquer** *P* to undress/to get undressed/to take one's clothes off.

défunter [defœ̃te] *vi P* to die*/to kick the bucket.

dég [deg] *a P* = **dégueulasse**.

dégager [degaʒe] *vi P* 1. to stink*/to whiff 2. to fart*/to let off 3. to leave*/to clear off/to clear out; allez, dégage! get lost*!/buzz off!/ scram! 4. to make a strong impression; elle dégage, she's really something/she's a bit of all right.

dégaine [degɛn] *nf F* (*allure*) gait; (*attitude*) behaviour/manner; vise la dégaine! look at the way he/she walks!

dégauchir [degoʃir] *vtr* 1. *F* dégauchir qn, to smarten s.o. up/to knock the rough edges off s.o./to lick s.o. into shape 2. *P* to find/to get (a flat, etc).

dégelée [deʒle] *nf P* beating*/thrashing/ good hiding.

se dégeler [sədeʒle] *vpr F* (*personne*) to become less reserved/to thaw (out)/to loosen up.

déglingue [deglɛ̃g] *nf P* (mental) breakdown/collapse; elle était à la limite de la déglingue, she nearly had a breakdown (over it).

déglingué [deglɛ̃ge] *a P* drunk*/pissed.

déglinguer [deglɛ̃ge] *vtr* 1. *F* to put out of order/to knock to pieces/to smash up/to bust up/to make a mess of; ma moto est toute déglinguée, my motorbike's falling to pieces 2. *P* to kill* 3. *P* to criticize*/to slate.

dégobillade [degɔbijad] *nf P* vomit/spew/ puke.

dégobillage [degɔbijaʒ] *nm P* vomiting/ spewing/puking.

dégobiller [degɔbije] *vtr & i P* to vomit*/to throw up/to chuck up/to spew up/to puke (up).

dégobillis [degɔbiji] *nm P* vomit/spew/ puke.

dégoiser [degwaze] *vtr & i F* (en) dégoiser, to talk* a lot/to rattle on/to rabbit on; to spout; dégoiser tout, to shoot one's mouth off; dégoise! speak up! dégoiser sur qn/qch, to run s.o./sth down; to go on about s.o./sth.

dégommage [degɔmaʒ] *nm F* dismissal/ sacking/firing.

dégommer [degɔme] *vtr F* 1. to dismiss* (s.o.)/to give (s.o.) the sack; se faire dégommer, to get the sack/the push 2. (*vider*) to kick (s.o.) out 3. to beat/to lick (s.o. at a game) 4. to reprimand* (s.o.)/to tear (s.o.) off a strip; **qu'est-ce qu'elle va dégommer!** she's really going to cop it!/she'll get hauled over the coals!

dégonflage [degɔ̃flaʒ] *nm F* backing down/backing out/climbing down/getting cold feet/chickening out.

dégonflard, -arde [degɔ̃flar, -ard] *P I a* cowardly*/yellow/chicken **II** *n* coward*/ yellow-belly/quitter/chicken.

dégonfle [degɔ̃fl] *nf F* = **dégonflage**.

dégonflé, -ée [degɔ̃fle] *a & n P* = **dégonflard, -arde**.

dégonflement [degɔ̃fləmɑ̃] *nm F* debunking (of hero, etc).

dégonfler [degɔ̃fle] **I** *vtr F* to debunk (hero) **II** *vpr* **se dégonfler** *P* 1. to climb down/to back out/to have cold feet/to funk it/to chicken out/to lose one's bottle; **tu vas pas te dégonfler?** you're not going to chicken out?/ (have you) lost your bottle? 2. to confess*/to come clean/to get it off one's chest.

dégonfleur, -euse [degɔ̃flœr, -øz] *a & n P* = **dégonflard, -arde**.

dégorger [degɔrʒe] *vi V* to ejaculate*/to come/to shoot one's load.

dégot(t)er [degɔte] **I** *vtr F* 1. to find/to pick up/to dig up/to spot/to hit (up)on; **il a dégot(t)é ça chez un antiquaire,** he unearthed that in an antique shop; **je l'ai dégot(t)é chez sa mère,** I ran him to ground at his mother's 2. (*a*) **dégot(t)er qn,** to oust s.o./to supplant s.o./to knock s.o. off his perch (*b*) **dégot(t)er qn/qch,** to get the better of s.o./sth; to lick/to beat s.o./sth; **il vous dégot(t)e,** he's too clever for you/he's got you beat **II** *vi P* (*a*) **elle dégot(t)e bien,** (*elle a de l'allure*) she looks good/I like the look of her; **elle dégot(t)e mal,** she looks scruffy; **qu'est-ce qu'elle dégot(t)e!** she's got something about her all right! (*b*) **ça dégot(t)e!** (*ça fait bonne impression*) it looks good/great!

dégoulinade [degulinad] *nf F* drip/trickle (of paint, wine, etc).

dégoulinage [degulinaʒ] *nm F* dripping/ trickling.

dégoulinante [degulinɑ̃t] *nf P* 1. clock; watch 2. run of bad luck.

dégouliner [deguline] *vi F* to trickle (down)/to drip (slowly, drop by drop).

dégourdi [degurdi] *a F* **il n'est pas très dégourdi,** he's not very bright/he's not really on the ball/he's a bit slow on the uptake; **dégourdi comme un manche,** stupid*/thick (as

two short planks)/dumb.

dégourdir [degurdir] **I** *vtr F* **dégourdir qn,** to sharpen s.o.'s wits; to put s.o. wise; **son séjour à Paris l'a dégourdi,** his stay in Paris has taught him a thing or two **II** *vpr* **se dégourdir** *F* (*a*) to grow smarter/to get with it/to wise up (*b*) to lose one's innocence/to learn a thing or two.

dégourrer [degure] *vtr P* 1. to disgust; to dishearten 2. to slander/to malign.

dégoûtance [degutɑ̃s] *nf P* = **dégoûtation**.

dégoûtant [degutɑ̃] *nm F* 1. vulgar/coarse individual 2. voyeur; **un vieux dégoûtant,** a dirty old man.

dégoûtation [degutasjɔ̃] *nf P* disgusting thing.

dégoûté [degute] *a F* fastidious/finicky; fussy/choosy/picky; squeamish; **ne faites pas trop le dégoûté,** don't be too squeamish/don't turn your nose up at it! *Iron* **vous n'êtes pas dégoûté(e)!** you don't want much, do you!

dégrafer [degrafe] **I** *vi P* to run away*/to sling one's hook **II** *vpr* **se dégrafer** *P* to give up/to withdraw; to cry off.

dégrainer [degrɛne] *P* **I** *vtr* to disparage* (s.o.)/to run (s.o.) down **II** *vi* to slander/to malign.

dégraissage [degrɛsaʒ] *nm F* mass redundancy.

dégraisser [degrɛse] **I** *vi F* to initiate mass redundancies/to lay off staff; **il faut dégraisser,** we've got to make some cutbacks/ layoffs **II** *vtr V* **dégraisser son panais,** (*homme*) to have sex*/to dip one's wick.

dégraisseur [degrɛsœr] *nm P* tax collector.

degré [dəgre] *nm F* **deuxième degré,** beating up*/working over.

dégréner [degrene] *P* **I** *vtr* 1. to seduce (s.o.); to get round (s.o.) 2. = **dégrainer I** **II** *vi* 1. (*faire grève*) to come out on strike/to down tools 2. = **dégrainer II** **III** *vpr* **se dégréner** = **dégréner II** 1.

dégringolade [degrɛ̃gɔlad] *nf F* 1. fall/ tumble; **faire une dégringolade,** to come a cropper*; **quelle dégringolade après sa dernière situation!** what a comedown after his last job! **la dégringolade du franc,** the collapse of the franc 2. decadence.

dégringoler [degrɛ̃gɔle] **I** *vtr & i F* to fall down/to tumble down; **il a dégringolé l'escalier,** he came tearing/clattering down the stairs **II** *vi F* (*a*) (*personne*) to come down in the world (*b*) (*affaires, etc*) to

slump/to collapse/to go to pieces III *vtr* 1. *P*
to steal*/to nick 2. *P* to kill* (s.o.) 3. *P* to lend
(money) 4. *P* to drink heavily*/to knock back
(a drink).

dégrossi [degrosi] *a F* un (individu) mal dégrossi, a boor/a lout.

dégrossir [degrosir] I *vtr F* dégrossir qn, to
smarten s.o. up/to lick s.o. into shape II *vpr*
se dégrossir *F* to have the rough edges
knocked off one; to smarten up/to acquire polish.

(se) dégrouiller [(sə)degruje] *vi & vpr F*
to hurry* (up)/to get a move on/to get cracking; allez, dégrouillez-vous! come on, get a
move on!/come on, get your finger out!

dégueu [degø] *a P* = **dégueulasse I**;
(c'est) pas dégueu! that's not bad!/that's
pretty good!/that's great!

dégueulade [degølad, -gœ-] *nf P* vomit/
spew/puke.

dégueulasse [degølas, -gœ-] *P* I *a* (*a*) (*ré-
pugnant*) disgusting/repulsive/sickening; (*de
mauvaise qualité*) lousy/crappy/rotten; (*sale*)
filthy; un type dégueulasse, a creep (*b*)
(c'est) pas dégueulasse! that's not (half)
bad!/that's pretty good! II *nm & f* disgusting/
repulsive person; louse; creep; c'est un
dégueulasse! he's a rotten bastard/sod! petit
dégueulasse! you filthy little beast!

dégueulasser [degølase] *vtr P* to make
dirty/to stain (sth).

dégueulasserie [degølasri, -gœ-] *nf P* (*a*)
vile/disgusting thing/action (*b*) faire une
dégueulasserie à qn, to behave tactlessly
towards s.o./to treat s.o. shabbily.

dégueulatoire [degølatwar, -gœ-] *a P*
revolting/sickening/sick-making/puke-making.

dégueulbi(f) [degølbi(f), -gœ-], **dégue-
ulebite** [degølbit, -gœ-] *a V* = **dégueulasse I**.

dégueulée [degøle, -gœ-] *nf P* 1. vomit/
spew 2. une dégueulée (d'injures), a torrent
of abuse.

dégueulement [degølmã -gœ-] *nm P*
vomit(ing)/spew(ing).

dégueuler [degøle, -gœ-] *vtr & i P* 1. to
vomit*/to throw up/to puke (up)/to spew/to
chuck up 2. to speak/to say; dégueule! out
with it!/spit it out! dégueuler sur qn, to
criticize* s.o./to say rotten things about s.o.

dégueulis [degøli, -gœ-] *nm P* vomiting/
spewing/puking.

dégueuloir [degølwar] *nm P* mouth*/gob.

dégueulpif [degølpif, -gœ-] *a V* =

dégueulasse I.

deguin, degun [dəgɛ̃] *pron*, **dégun**
[degɛ̃] *pron P* (*quiconque*) someone/anyone/
anybody; je dois rien à deguin, I don't owe
anyone anything.

se déguiser [sədegize] *vpr F* se déguiser
en courant d'air, to disappear/to do a disappearing act/to fade.

déguster [degyste] *P* I *vtr* déguster des
coups, to get beaten up/roughed up; qu'est-ce
qu'on a dégusté! we didn't half catch/cop it!
II *vi* 1. to get beaten up 2. to get killed *or*
wounded 3. to suffer like hell/to go through
hell.

se déhancher [sədeɑ̃ʃe] *vpr F* to sway/to
wiggle one's hips when walking.

déharnacher [dearnaʃe] *vtr P* to undress
(a woman).

dehors [dəɔr] *P* I *nm* faire le dehors,
(*prostituée*) to walk the streets/to be a streetwalker II *adv* il est con dehors comme
dedans, he really is as stupid*/dumb/thick as
he looks.

déhotter [deɔte] *P* I *vtr* 1. to eject (s.o.)/to
throw (s.o.) out/to turn (s.o.) out 2. =
dégot(t)er I 1 II *vi* to leave*/to split/to beat
it III *vpr* **se déhotter** *P* 1. = **déhotter** II 2.
to hurry up/to get moving/to get a move on/to
get cracking.

Deibler [deblɛr] *Prn F* coupe à la Deibler,
short haircut baring the neck.

déj [deʒ] *nm F* (= *déjeuner*) le petit déj,
breakfast/brekkers.

déjante [deʒɑ̃t] *n P* madness/looniness/
nuttiness.

déjanté [deʒɑ̃te] *a P* 1. mad*/cracked/off-
the-wall/loopy 2. (*marginal*) marginal; *n* c'est
un déjanté, he's a drop-out.

déjanter [deʒɑ̃te] *vi P* 1. (*jouir*) to come
(*sexually or after taking a drug*) 2. to go
mad*; to become an alcoholic/a drug addict*,
etc; to sink into alcoholism/poverty, etc; to
end up in the gutter; to drop out.

déjeté [deʒte, deʃte] *a F* (= *décati*) il/elle
n'est pas déjeté(e), he's/she's well preserved.

delacroix [dəlakrwa] *nm P* 100-franc note.

délirant [delirɑ̃] *a F* great/wicked/ace.

délire [delir] *F* I *nm* (c'est) le délire (total)!
it's great/wicked/far out! II *a inv* c'est total
délire! it's great/wicked/far out!

délirer [delire] *vi F* = **dérailler**.

déloquer [delɔke] I *vtr P* to undress (s.o.)
II *vpr* **se déloquer** *P* to undress/to get
undressed/to strip off.

délourder [delurde] *vtr P* to open (a door).
(*Voir* **lourde 1**; **lourder 1**)

démancher [demɑ̃ʃe] I *vtr F* démancher
un complot, to upset a plot II *vpr* **se démancher** *F* se démancher pour obtenir qch, to go
to a lot of trouble/to put oneself out to get sth.
(*Voir* **trou 8**)

demander [dəmɑ̃de] *vtr F* 1. il ne demande
que plaies et bosses, he's always asking for
trouble 2. je vous demande un peu! I ask
you!/did you ever! 3. faut pas lui en
demander (trop)! it's no use getting him to do
it!/you mustn't ask too much of him! (*Voir*
heure 1)

démangeaison [demɑ̃ʒɛzɔ̃] *nf F* j'avais
une démangeaison de le faire, I was itching to
do it.

démanger [demɑ̃ʒe] *vi F* (*a*) la langue lui
démangeait, he was itching to speak; la main
lui démangeait, he was itching/dying for a
fight (*b*) gratter qn où ça le démange, to
toady to s.o./to scratch s.o.'s back.

démantibuler [demɑ̃tibyle] I *vtr F*
démantibuler qch, (*démonter*) to take sth to
pieces/to bits; (*casser*) to break sth up/to
smash sth to pieces II *vpr* **se démantibuler**
F to come to pieces/to break up/to fall apart.

se démaquer [sədemake] *vpr P* (*couple*)
to separate/to break up/to split up.

déménager [demena ʒe] *F* I *vi* 1. to be
mad*; il déménage! he's off his head!/he's
round the bend! 2. to clear off/to do a bunk;
faire déménager qn, to chuck s.o. out; allez,
déménagez! hop it!/scram! 3. de la moutarde
qui déménage, mustard that takes the top of
your head off; musique qui déménage, powerful music; ça déménage un max! that's really
great!/that's really something! (*Voir* **cloche**
I **4**) II *vtr* déménager la maison, (*cam-
brioleurs*) to strip the house (of its contents).

dément [demɑ̃] *a F* extraordinary/
fantastic/wicked.

démerdard, -arde [demɛrdar, -ard] *P* I *a*
resourceful*/crafty/shrewd; il n'est pas
démerdard, he's hopeless II *n* resourceful*
person; c'est un démerdard, he's a shrewd
customer/there are no flies on him/he's a
crafty sod/he knows a trick or two; c'est un
démerdard à rebours, he's a clumsy bugger.

démerde [demɛrd] *P* I *a* = **démerdard** I
II *nf* (*système*) démerde, resourcefulness;
wangling. (*Voir* **D**)

démerder [demɛrde] *P* I *vtr* to sort out (a
mess); to clear up (a confusion); démerder

qn, to get s.o. out of a mess/out of the shit II
vpr **se démerder 1.** (*a*) to get by/to manage
(to get along)/to make out; je me démerde, I
get by/I'm doing fine (*b*) to get out of a mess/
out of the shit; savoir se démerder, to know
how to get out of trouble/to know how to look
after oneself; se démerder pour obtenir qch,
to wangle sth; démerde-toi! get (yourself) out
of that then!/sort it out yourself! 2. to hurry*
up/to get one's arse into gear/to move it;
allez, démerde-toi! come on, get your finger
out!/come on, shift your arse!

démerdeur, -euse [demɛrdœr, -øz] *P* I *a*
= **démerdard** I II *nm* lawyer/(defending)
counsel.

demi [dəmi] *nm F* glass of beer/= a half(-
pint); deux demis, s'il vous plaît! two halves,
please! demi direct, = half(-pint) of draught
beer.

demi-cercle [dəmisɛrkl] *nm P* pincer qn au
demi-cercle, to arrest* s.o./to nab s.o.

demi-cigue [dəmisig] *nm Vieilli P* ten
francs; ten-franc note. (*Voir* **cigue 2**) (*pl
demi-cigues*)

demi-jambe [dəmiʒɑ̃b] *nf,* **demi-jetée**
[dəmiʒəte] *nf,* **demi-livre** [dəmilivr] *nf P*
fifty francs; fifty-franc note. (*pl* demi-jambes,
-jetées, -livres)

demi-molle [dəmimɔl] *a phr P* être/l'avoir
en demi-molle, to be unenthusiastic/not over-
keen/half-hearted.

demi-plombe [dəmiplɔ̃b] *nf P* half an
hour. (*Voir* **plombe**) (*pl* demi-plombes)

demi-porkesse [dəmipɔrkɛs] *nf P* =
demi-portion. (*pl* demi-porkesses)

demi-portion [dəmipɔrsjɔ̃] *nf F* undersized* person / half-pint / shorty / short-ass*/
shrimp/weed/dead loss. (*pl* demi-portions)

demi-sac [dəmisak] *nm P* (*a*) *Vieilli* five
hundred francs (*b*) five thousand francs. (*pl*
demi-sacs)

demi-sel [dəmisɛl] *nm P* 1. petty criminal/
small-time crook (*despised by the underworld*) 2. petty/small-time pimp*; part-time
pimp*. (*pl* demi-sels)

demi-sigue [dəmisig] *nm P* = **demi-
cigue**. (*pl* demi-sigues)

demi-tour! [dəmitur] *int P* hop it!/clear
off!/beat it!

démo [demo] *nm & f F* demonstration
cassette/record/tape; demo.

démoduler [demɔdyle] *vtr P* démoduler
qn, to silence s.o./to shut s.o. up.

demoiselle [dəmwazɛl] *nf P* 1. (*régional*)

comment va votre demoiselle? how's your daughter? 2. shy man; **il est comme une demoiselle au piano**, he's as gentle as a lamb/ as nice as pie 3. *(courses)* filly.

démolir [demɔlir] *vtr F* 1. to beat (s.o.) up*/to do (s.o.) over/to smash (s.o.) up 2. to ruin (s.o.'s reputation); to slate (s.o., sth).

démolissage [demɔlisaʒ] *nm F* severe criticism*/slating/roasting/panning.

démonté [demɔ̃te] *a (a) F* temporarily without a car *(b) P (souteneur)* temporarily without a woman to live off.

démonter [demɔ̃te] *vtr F* to unnerve/to upset; **la nouvelle m'a complètement démonté**, I was really cut up/put out by the news; **il ne se démonte pas pour si peu**, he's not so easily put out/thrown.

démouler [demule] *vi F (dans un hôtel, un wagon-lit, etc)* to make up a bed/to turn down a bed.

se démouscailler [sədemuskɑje] *vpr P =* **se démerder** (**démerder II 1**). *(Voir* **mouscaille**)

démouscailleur, -euse [demuskɑjœr, -øz] *a & n P =* **démerdard, -arde I, II.**

démurger [demyrʒe] *vi P* to leave*/to run off (in a hurry).

déniaiser [denjɛze] *vtr F* 1. to teach (s.o.) the ways of the world/to teach (s.o.) a thing or two 2. to initiate (s.o.) sexually; **elle s'est fait déniaiser**, she's lost her virginity*/she's learnt a thing or two.

dénicher [deniʃe] *F* I *vtr* to find/to discover; **où as-tu bien pu dénicher ce vieux tacot?** where the devil did you dig up that old banger/crate? **se dénicher un aparte**, to find a flat/*NAm* an apartment. *(Voir* **filon 2**) II *vi* **dénicher sans tambour ni trompette**, to move off quietly/without attracting attention.

dénicheur, -euse [deniʃœr, -øz] *n F* searcher/unearther (of objects); **dénicheur de talent(s)**, talent scout; headhunter.

se dénipper [sədenipe] *vpr P* to undress/to get undressed.

dent [dɑ̃] *nf* 1. *F* **avoir la dent**, to be hungry*; **j'ai une de ces dents!** I'm so hungry I could eat a horse! 2. *F* **avoir les dents longues**, to be very hungry*; to be famished/ starving; *(être ambitieux)* to be very ambitious; to be greedy/grasping; **avoir les dents qui rayent le parquet**, to be extremely ambitious/to be driven 3. *F* **avoir de la dent**, *(personne)* to be still young 4. *F* **avoir mal aux dents**, *(cheval)* to be prevented from winning/to be pulled/to be nobbled 5. *F (a)* **avoir la dent dure**, to be biting/sarcastic *(b)* **donner un coup de dent à qn**, to criticize* s.o. severely/to have a go at s.o. *(c)* **avoir/ conserver/garder une dent contre qn**, to bear s.o. a grudge/to have it in for s.o. 6. *F (a)* **être sur les dents**, to be exhausted*; *(surmené)* to be under pressure *(from work or business)*/to be overworked *(b)* **mettre qn sur les dents**, to work s.o. to death/to knock s.o. up 7. *P* **avoir les dents du fond qui baignent**, to be drunk*/ boozed (up)/sloshed. *(Voir* **buis 4**; **poule 5**)

dentelle [dɑ̃tɛl] *nf F* 1. **avoir les pieds en dentelle**, *(avoir mal aux pieds)* to have sore feet; *(refuser)* to refuse to agree to sth; to refuse to budge; to sit tight 2. **faire dans la dentelle**, to be extra careful/to wear kid gloves; **il ne fait pas dans la dentelle**, he goes in feet first/he just dives straight in.

dentiste [dɑ̃tist] *nm P* **aller au dentiste**, to look for food/for something to eat.

dep [dɛp] *nm P (verlan de* **pédé**) homosexual*/pansy.

se dépagnoter [sədepaɲɔte] *vpr P* to get out of bed/to show a leg/to rise and shine.

dépannage [depanaʒ] *nm F* tiding over/ helping out; **tu pourrais pas me faire un petit dépannage?** could you just give me a hand?/ could you do me a small favour?

dépanner [depane] *vtr F* **dépanner qn**, to tide s.o. over/to help s.o. out; to bail s.o. out; to get s.o. out of a difficulty/a hole; **j'ai oublié mon portefeuille, tu pourrais pas me dépanner?** I've forgotten my wallet, do you think you could drop me a few quid/a few bucks?

déparler [deparle] *vi F* 1. to talk nonsense*; to ramble; to become incoherent/inarticulate through drink 2. **il ne déparle pas**, he never stops talking.

départ [depar] *nm F* **piquer un départ**, to make a quick exit; to shoot off/to beat it.

dépatouiller [depatuje] *P* I *vtr* to get (s.o.) out of a fix*/a mess/a jam **se dépatouiller** *vpr* to get out of a fix*/a mess/a jam.

dépendeur [depɑ̃dœr] *nm F* **dépendeur d'andouilles**, tall and lanky man.

déphasé [defɑze] *a F* disoriented; **je suis un peu déphasé aujourd'hui**, I'm just not with it today; **il est complètement déphasé**, he's completely out of touch (with reality).

dépiauter [depjote] I *vtr F* 1. to skin (a rabbit, etc) 2. to take (sth) to pieces 3. to pull (a book, a play, an article, etc) to pieces II *vpr* **se dépiauter** *P* to undress/to strip/to peel (off).

(se) dépieuter [(sə)depjøte] *vi & vpr P* to get out of bed/to show a leg.

déplaner [deplane] *vi P* (*drogues*) to come down (*after a drug trip*).

déplanquer [deplãke] I *vtr P* (*a*) to take (sth) out of its hiding place (*b*) to take (sth) out of pawn II *vi P* (*a*) to come out of hiding (*b*) to leave prison III *vpr* **se déplanquer** *P* to come out of hiding.

déplâtrer [deplatre] *vtr P* (*brocante*) to manage to sell/to manage to flog (an object) (*originally bought at too high a price*).

déplumé [deplyme] *F a* bald*; c'est un mec d'une trentaine d'années un peu déplumé, he's a balding thirty. (*Voir* **melon 1**)

se déplumer [sədeplyme] *vpr* 1. *F* to go bald*/to lose one's thatch 2. *P* to get out of bed.

se dépoiler [sədepwale] *vpr P* to undress/to get undressed/to strip off.

dépoitraillé [depwatraje] *a F Péj* with one's shirt, etc all undone (at the front).

dépoivrer [depwavre] *vi P* to lay off the booze/to be on the waggon.

dépon(n)er [depɔne] I *vtr P* (*a*) to bore (s.o.) rigid (*b*) **être dépon(n)é**, to be dejected/depressed II *vi V* to defecate*/to drop one's load.

déposer [depoze] *vtr P* **déposer son bilan**, to die*/to cash in one's chips.

dépoter [depɔte] I *vtr* (*a*) *F* (*chauffeur de taxi*) to drop off (a passenger) (*b*) *F* to exhume (a body). (*Voir* **géranium**) II *vi P* to go fast/at full tilt.

dépotoir [depɔtwar] *nm F* **ma classe est le dépotoir de l'école**, I've got the dregs of the school in my class; *V* **son cul, c'est un vrai dépotoir**, she's been laid by just about everyone.

dépouille [depuj] *nf P* stealing/theft (of s.o.'s money, clothes, etc); mugging.

dépouiller [depuje] *vtr P* to steal (s.o.'s money, clothes, etc); to mug (s.o.).

déprime [deprim] *nf F* nervous depression; **il est en pleine déprime**, he's got the blues/he's really low.

déprimer [deprime] *vi F* to have the blues/to be really low/to be down in the dumps.

dépucelage [depys(ə)laʒ] *nm F* deflowering (of a virgin); **son dépucelage c'était à 14 ans**, his/her first time was at 14; he/she had it for the first time at 14.

dépuceler [depys(ə)le] *vtr F* (*a*) to deflower (a virgin); **il s'est fait dépuceler par une pute**, he had it with a prostitute the first time (*b*) to open (a new packet of cigarettes, etc); to cut (the pages of a book); to christen (a bottle of wine, etc) (*c*) **dépuceler qch**, to help oneself to sth for the first time.

déquiller [dekije] *vtr P* to kill*/to bump off.

der [dɛr] *n F* (*abrév = dernier(s), -ière(s)*) 1. le/la der (des der), (*le dernier*) the last (of all); (*le plus bas*) the lowest of the low; **viens boire le der des der**, let's have a last drink/let's have one for the road; **la der des der**, the war to end all wars 2. (*belote*) **dix de der**, last trick (*worth ten points*). (*Voir* **tierce 2**)

dérailler [deraje] *vi F* 1. (*machine*) to go on the blink 2. (*personne*) to talk drivel/to rave.

déramer [derame] I *vi P* to die* II *vpr* **se déramer** *P* to commit suicide/to do oneself in.

dératé [derate] *nm F* **courir comme un dératé**, to run like mad/like the clappers.

derche [dɛrʃ] *nm*, **derge** [dɛrʒ] *nm P* 1. buttocks*; **papier à derche**, toilet paper/bumfodder; **avoir le feu au derche**, to be in a tearing hurry; **se magner le derche**, to get a move on 2. **un faux derche**, (*faux jeton*) a shifty/shady customer; (*hypocrite*) a hypocrite; (*traître*) a traitor/a double-crosser.

dergeot [dɛrʒo] *prep & adv P* = **derjo**.

dérive [deriv] *nf F* wandering/nomadic life; **il a fait trois ans de dérive**, he drifted/bummed around for three years.

derjo [dɛrʒo] *prep & adv P* behind; **le jardin est derjo**, the garden's at the back.

dernière [dɛrnjɛr] *F* I *nf* 1. **tu connais (pas) la dernière?** (*dernière nouvelle*) have you heard the latest? (*dernière blague*) have you heard the latest joke?/have you heard this one? 2. (*courses*) **toucher la dernière**, to back the winner of the last race II *a* **la dernière ligne droite**, the home stretch.

dérober [derɔbe] *vi F* 1. to run away*/to make oneself scarce; **je ne pouvais pas dérober**, I couldn't slip off on the quiet 2. not to keep one's word/not to honour one's commitments 3. (*prostituée*) to let down her pimp* by giving up prostitution*.

dérondir [derɔ̃dir] I *vtr P* to sober (s.o.) up II *vpr* **se dérondir** *P* to sober up/to get over one's drink.

dérouillade [derujad] *nf*, **dérouille** [deruj] *nf*, **dérouillée** [deruje] *nf P* beating(-up)*/belting/thrashing/working over;

prendre une/la **dérouillade**, to get a good hiding/belting; flanquer une dérouillée à qn, to do s.o. over/to knock the hell out of s.o.

dérouiller [deruje] I *vtr P* to beat (s.o.) up*/to clobber (s.o.)/to thrash (s.o.)/to work (s.o.) over. (*Voir* **frère 5**; **panais**) II *vi P* 1. to get beaten up*; to be killed* *or* wounded; to be punished/to catch it; to suffer like hell/to go through hell; qu'est-ce qu'il va dérouiller! he won't half cop it!/he's going to have a really hard time! qu'est-ce que j'ai dérouillé! I really went through hell! 2. (*a*) (*dans un magasin*) to make the first sale of the day (*b*) (*prostituée*) to pick up the first client of the day III *vpr* **se dérouiller** *P* se dérouiller les jambes, to stretch one's legs.

dérouler [derule] *vi P* to (go on a) pub-crawl/to go pub-crawling.

derrière [dɛrjɛr] *nm F* buttocks*/behind/backside/bottom/*NAm* fanny; se lever le derrière le premier, to get out of bed on the wrong side; *P* péter plus haut que son derrière, (*être vaniteux*) to be conceited/big-headed; elle pète plus haut que son derrière, she thinks she's really something/the bee's knees; se taper le derrière par terre/sur le coin d'un meuble, to laugh* uproariously/to be in stitches; il n'y a pas de quoi se taper le derrière par terre, there's nothing to be jubilant about. (*Voir* **astap(e)**; **botter 1**; **feu 1**; **se magner**)

désaper [desape] I *vtr P* to undress (s.o.) II *vpr* **se désaper** *P* to undress/to get undressed.

désargenté [dezarʒɑ̃te] *a F* penniless*.

désargenter [dezarʒɑ̃te] *vtr F* to clean (s.o.) out of money; ces dépenses m'ont complètement désargenté, these expenses have completely cleaned me out.

descendre [desɑ̃dr] I *vtr P* 1. to kill*; se faire descendre, to get bumped off/done in 2. faire descendre, to abort (an unborn child) 3. to debunk; descendre qn en flammes, to shoot s.o. down in flames 4. to down/to knock back (a drink) II *vi* 1. *F* mon dîner ne descend pas, my dinner won't go down 2. *P* (*police*) to raid a house 3. *F Iron* descendez, on vous demande! (*said to s.o. who is falling* (*over*) enjoy your trip!

descente [desɑ̃t] *nf* 1. *P* capacity for downing drink(s) (*surt* alcohol); big swallow; avoir une bonne descente, to hold one's drink 2. *P* descente de lit, individual who would stoop to anything 3. *F* (*a*) descente (de

police), (police) raid/bust (*b*) raid by gang of thieves 4. *V* descente à la cave/au barbu/au lac, cunnilingus*/pearl-diving/muff-diving.

désert [dezɛr] *nm P* deserter.

déshabillage [dezabijaʒ] *nm F* severe criticism*/dressing down; slating (of play, etc).

déshabiller [dezabije] *vtr* 1. *F* déshabiller qn, (*faire ouvrir son cœur à qn*) to lay bare s.o.'s soul/s.o.'s innermost thoughts; (*critiquer qn*) to criticize* s.o. severely/to give s.o. a dressing-down; déshabiller une pièce, to slate a play 2. *P* to strip down (a stolen car).

désinto(x) [dezɛ̃tɔks, -to] *nf P* (= *une cure de*) *désintoxication*) detox(ification)/treatment for alcoholism *or* drug addiction; faire une désinto(x), to dry out.

désordre [dezɔrdr] *a P* 1. disorganized/untidy 2. *Iron* ça fait désordre, (*d'une affaire dévoilée qui fait scandale, d'un échec*) it's messy.

désossé [dezose] *a F* (*personne*) thin.

désosser [dezose] *vtr F* (*a*) to break up/to strip down/to dismantle (a car, etc) (*b*) to dissect (a book, etc).

dessalé, -ée [desale] *F* I *a* sharp/wide awake*/with it II *n* man/woman of the world; someone who has learnt a thing or two.

dessaler [desale] I *vtr F* dessaler qn, to put s.o. wise/to teach s.o. a thing or two/to open s.o.'s eyes II *vpr* **se dessaler** *F* to learn a thing or two/to learn the facts of life/to get with it/to wise up.

desserre [desɛr] *nf F* forking out; être dur à la desserre, to be mean*/tight-fisted/stingy.

dessin [desɛ̃] *nm F* veux-tu que je te fasse un dessin?/faut (te) faire un dessin? do I have to draw a picture for you?/do you want a diagram?

dessouder [desude] *P* I *vtr* to kill*/to bump off/to do in II *vi & vpr* dessouder/se (la) dessouder, to die*/to peg out.

dessous [dəsu] *nm* 1. *F* avoir le dessous, to get the worst of it/to be defeated 2. *F* il y avait là un dessous que je ne comprenais pas, there was some mystery about it that I didn't understand 3. *F* être dans le troisième/le trente-sixième dessous, to be in a very bad situation; (*sans argent*) to be penniless*/to be down and out; (*avoir perdu sa réputation*) to be completely discredited; (*déprimé*) to be depressed*/down in the dumps 4. *P* pimp's second woman 5. *P* prostitute's fancy man 6.

F dessous de table, bribe/underhand commission/kickback/backhander. (*Voir* **carte 3**)

dessus [dəsy] *F* I *adv* elle m'est tombée dessus (comme une furie), she went off at me something alarming II *nm* le dessus, the best/the pick of the bunch.

destroy [dɛstrɔj] *F* I *a* 1. destructive/destroying; musique destroy = punk music 2. (*vêtements*) un jean destroy, punk jeans/torn and dirty jeans II *nm* smashing/wrecking; faire un destroy, to smash everything up (for the sake of it).

destructeur [dɛstryktœr] *nm F* red wine/plonk/vino.

détail [detaj] *nm F* faut pas faire de détail, we musn't be sparing/we must use every means at our disposal/it's no use skimping.

dételer [detle] *vi* 1. *F* to settle down/to retire (after a hectic life) 2. *F* to ease off/to stop working; travailler dix heures sans dételer, to work for ten hours without letting up/to work non-stop for ten hours 3. *P* to leave one's wife*/to walk out on one's wife; to get a divorce/to get unhitched.

détente [detãt] *nf F* être dur à la détente, (*être avare*) to be mean*/tightfisted/stingy; (*ne pas comprendre facilement*) to be a bit dim/to be slow on the uptake.

déterré [detere] *a F* avoir une mine/une figure/une tête de déterré, to look drawn and haggard/to look ghastly/to look like a living corpse/to look like death (warmed up).

détrancher [detrãʃe] I *vtr P* 1. to notice/to spot (s.o.) 2. détrancher qn, to distract s.o.'s attention II *vpr* se détrancher *P* 1. to look round; to turn round 2. to change one's bet at the last moment.

détraqué [detrake] *a F* mad*; être un peu détraqué, to have a screw loose/to be a bit nutty/to be nuts.

détraquer [detrake] *vtr F* détraquer (le cerveau à) qn, to drive s.o. mad/nuts.

détréper [detrepe] *vi P* (*camelots, etc*) to get rid of unlikely customers.

détroncher, se détroncher [(sə)detrõ-ʃe] *vtr & pr* = **(se) détrancher**.

deuche [døʃ] *nf*, **deudeuche** [dødøʃ] *nf F* (*Aut = deux chevaux*) Citroën 2CV (*RTM*).

deuil [dœj] *nm* 1. *F* avoir les ongles en deuil, to have dirty fingernails 2. *F* faire son deuil de qch, to resign oneself to (the loss of) sth/to kiss sth goodbye 3. *P* aller au deuil/porter le deuil, to lodge a complaint (*esp* with the

police) 4. *P* danger; porter le deuil, to warn of a danger; il y a du deuil, it's dangerous/risky.

deusio [døzjo] *adv P* secondly.

deux [dø] *num a inv & nm* 1. *F* en moins de deux, very quickly*/in no time at all/in two shakes (of a lamb's tail)/in two ticks; en deux coups les gros, immediately*/there and then/before you could say Jack Robinson 2. *F* ça fait deux, that's two (completely) different things 3. *P* être bête/nul/con, etc comme pas deux, to be as silly/dumb as they come 4. *F* se casser en deux, (*après un coup*) to double up after a blow; (*de rire*) to double up with laughter 5. *F* il était moins deux, it was a close shave/a narrow shave/a near thing 6. *P* (*souteneur*) faire le coup de deux, to live off two women. (*Voir* **attelé**) 7. *V* de mes deux! balls!/bollocks! tiens, de mes deux! not bloody likely!*/not effing likely!/not sodding likely!

deuxio [døzjo] *adv P* secondly.

deux-pattes [døpat] *nf P* = **deuche**.

deuzio [døzjo] *adv P* secondly.

dévalisé [devalize] *a F* être dévalisé, (*magasin*) to be sold right out of stock/to be cleaned out.

devant [dəvã] *nm* 1. *F* se faire arrondir le devant, to become pregnant* 2. *F* bâtir sur le devant, to develop a paunch/to get pot-bellied/to get a beer belly 3. *P* male *or* female genitals*/goods.

devanture [dəvãtyr] *nf* 1. *F* lécher les devantures, to go window-shopping 2. *P* faire la devanture, to carry out a smash-and-grab raid 3. *F* se faire refaire la devanture, to have a face-lift; (*se faire abîmer la figure*) to get one's face bashed in 4. *P* breasts*/boobs. (*Voir* **gondoler** I)

déveinard [devɛnar] *nm F* (*a*) gambler, etc, whose luck is out (*b*) consistently unlucky man.

déveine [devɛn] *nf F* (run of) bad luck; avoir la déveine/être en déveine/être dans la déveine, to be out of luck/down on one's luck; to hit a bad patch.

dévider [devide] *vtr F* to reel off/to ad-lib (a story, etc); dévider le jars, to talk slang.

dévierger [devjɛrʒe] *vtr P* to open/uncork (a bottle).

dévisser [devise] I *vtr P* 1. to injure (s.o.) (seriously) 2. to kill* (s.o.) 3. to find/to unearth/to dig up 4. dévisser le mironton, to have a miscarriage. (*Voir* **billard 4; trou 8**) II *vi* 1. *P* to die*/to peg out 2. *F* (*alpiniste*) to lose one's hold/to slip/to fall **III** *vpr* **se dévisser** 1. *F* **nom qui se dévisse**, double-barrelled name; name with the nobiliary particle *de* 2. *P* **to leave*/to make tracks/to beat it** 3. *P* **to die***.

dévorer [devɔre] *vtr V* **to eat/to go down on** (s.o.).

dévoreuse [devɔrøz] *nf P* **hot stuff/red-hot mamma/hot number.**

dézinguer [dezɛ̃ge] *vtr P* 1. **dézinguer qch**, to smash sth up/to demolish sth 2. **dézinguer qn**, to kill* s.o./to bump s.o. off.

diam [djam] *nm P* **diamond**; *pl* **diam's**, sparklers/rocks/ice.

diap [djap] *nf F* = **diapo**.

diapason [djapazɔ̃] *nm F* (*a*) **monter le diapason**, to raise one's voice (*b*) **baisser le diapason à qn**, to take s.o. down a peg (or two).

diapo [djapo] *nf F* (*abrév* = *diapositive*) slide/transparency.

diche [diʃ] *nf P* (*écoles*) headmistress.

dico [diko] *nm F* 1. **dictionary** 2. **passe-moi le dico**, look out, it's the cops!

didine [didin] *nf V* **female genitals*/cunt.**

didis [didi] *nmpl F* **fingers.**

didite [didit] *nf P* (*courses*) **faire didite**, to back/to have a bet on a horse that dead-heats.

Dieu [djø] *nm & int* 1. *F* **Dieu merci!** thank goodness! **mon Dieu!/grand Dieu!** heavens (above)!/dear me! **mon Dieu, mon Dieu!** good heavens!/really! **mon Dieu oui!** why, yes! **mon Dieu non!** well, no! **mon Dieu je n'en sais rien!** I'm sure I don't know! **pour l'amour de Dieu!** for goodness' sake!/for heaven's sake! **Dieu sait si j'ai travaillé**, God knows, I've worked hard enough; **qu'est-ce que j'ai fait au bon Dieu (pour mériter ça)**? what did I do to deserve *this*? 2. *P* (*jurons*) **bon Dieu (de bon Dieu)!/Dieu de Dieu!/(sacré) nom de Dieu!** God almighty!/my God!/Christ!/Jesus (Christ)!/Jeez(e)! **ce sacré bon Dieu d'idiot!** this goddam idiot! **ce n'est pas Dieu possible!** it ain't ruddy (well) possible!

digérer [diʒere] *vtr F* **to swallow/to stomach** (an insult, etc); **je ne digère pas ça**, I can't take/swallow/stomach/that (sort of thing).

digeste [diʒɛst] *a F* (*nourriture*) **easily digestible.**

digue [dig] *adv P* **que digue**, nothing* at all/damn all/sweet FA.

dig(ue)-dig(ue) [digdig] *nf P* (*a*) (*épilepsie*) epilepsy; (*delirium tremens*) DTs (*b*) **tomber en dig(ue)-dig(ue)**, to faint.

dimanche [dimɑ̃ʃ] *nm F* **il est né/il est venu au monde un dimanche**, he was born tired; **c'est tous les jours dimanche!** every day's a holiday!/this is the life! **s'habiller en dimanche**, to dress in one's Sunday best.

dinde [dɛ̃d] *nf F* (*a*) (*fille*) **petite dinde**, little goose/little softy; **quelles dindes que mes élèves cette année!** what a hopeless bunch of girls I've got in my class this year! (*b*) stupid woman; **prendre le thé avec un tas de vieilles dindes**, to take tea with a lot of old hens/old trouts (*c*) **plumer la dinde**, to play the guitar.

dindon [dɛ̃dɔ̃] *nm F* **fool*/clot/prize idiot**; **être le dindon de la farce**, to be the victim of a joke/to be the fall-guy/to be the mug.

dîne [din] *nf Vieilli P* **meal**; **food**; **aller à la dîne**, to go and eat.

dingo [dɛ̃go] *P* **I** *a* (*a*) **mad*/bonkers/crackers** (*b*) (*bizarre*) weird/screwy **II** *n* **mad person*/crackpot/screwball**; **on va te mettre chez les dingos!** you'll get locked up in/sent to the loony bin!

dingue[1] [dɛ̃g] *P* **I** *a* (*a*) **mad*/bonkers/crackers/nuts** (*b*) (*bizarre*) weird/screwy; (*incroyable*) **unbelievable/incredible/terrific**; **il fait une chaleur dingue**, it's unbelievably hot (*c*) **être dingue de qn**, to be infatuated* with s.o./to be potty about s.o.; **elle en est dingue (de ce type)**, she's nuts/crazy about him **II** *n* **crackpot/nutcase/screwball/loony/nutter**; **la maison/la baraque aux dingues**, the madhouse/the loony bin. (*Voir* **battre**)

dingue[2] *nf P* (burglar's) **jemmy/*NAm* jimmy.**

dingue[3] *nf P* (a) malaria (b) flu.

dinguer [dɛ̃ge] *vi P* (*a*) **envoyer dinguer qch**, to fling sth out/to chuck sth away (*b*) **envoyer dinguer qn**, (*l'éconduire*) to send s.o. packing*/to tell s.o. to get lost; (*le repousser*) to send s.o. sprawling (**contre**, against); to send s.o. flying.

dinguerie [dɛ̃gri] *nf* **madness**; **loony action**; **crazy behaviour**; **faire des dingueries**, to do mad*/crazy things.

dire [dir] *vtr F* 1. **à qui le dites-vous?** you're telling me!/as if I didn't know!/don't I (just) know it! 2. **c'est dire**, that's saying something; **ce n'est/c'est pas pour dire, mais ...**, you can say what you like, but ...; there's no getting away from it ... 3. **ce n'est rien/c'est peu de le dire!** and no mistake!/you bet! **ce n'est pas tout de le dire!** it's easier said than done! 4. **y a pas à dire**, there's no denying it/there's no getting away from it/there's no two ways about it 5. je ne lui ai pas envoyé dire, I told him (so) straight (to his face)/I let him have it straight 6. c'est moi qui vous le dis! (you can) take my word for it!/need I say more?/say no more! 7. qu'il dit, says he; so he says; que tu dis! that's what *you* say!/sez you! 8. je te/vous dis pas! je te/vous dis que ça! you can imagine (it)! j'ai vu une nana, je te dis pas/je te dis que ça! I saw this bird, well, you can imagine what she looked like/ what she was like! 9. moi, ce que j'en dis..., je dis/je disais ça comme ça, I was just talking for the sake of it; I wasn't saying anything important 10. on dit ça! that's what *you* say! 11. qu'on se le dise! you have been warned! 12. je ne te le fais pas dire! that's exactly what I think! (*Voir* **autre** (*a*); **comme I 3**)

direct [dirɛkt] *nm P* blow*/punch; un direct à l'estomac, a punch in the stomach.

directo [dirɛkto] *adv F* directly/straight away; je viendrai directo, I'll come at once.

dirigeoir [diriʒwar] *nm P* handlebars (of bicycle).

dirlingue [dirlɛ̃g] *nm*, **dirlo** [dirlo] *nm P* (= *directeur*) 1. headmaster 2. director.

disciplote [disiplɔt] *nf P Mil* discipline; compagnies de disciplote, (= *Bat' d'Af*) disciplinary companies (*stationed formerly in North Africa*).

disco [disko] *nf F* (*abrév* = *discothèque*) disco; musique disco, disco music; danser disco, to dance disco; to go disco dancing; se fringuer disco, to wear disco clothes/to dress disco.

discrétos [diskretos] *adv P* discreetly/on the QT.

discutailler [diskytaje] *vi F* (*a*) to argue the toss/to argufy/to quibble (*b*) to chatter/to natter away; to rabbit on.

discuter [diskyte] *vtr F* discuter le bout (de gras), to talk about things in general; to have a good old natter/chinwag.

disjoncter [disʒɔ̃kte] *vi F* (*a*) to go mad*/to lose one's marbles (*b*) to get angry*/to blow one's top.

disputailler [dispytaje] *vi F* to wrangle/to bicker/to squabble (sur, about).

disputaillerie [dispytajri] *nf F* (petty) squabble; bickering.

disputailleur, -euse [dispytajœr, -øz] *F* I *a* fond of bickering; cantankerous II *n* squabbler.

disputer [dispyte] *vtr F* disputer qn, to tell s.o. off/to tick s.o. off.

disque [disk] *nm* 1. *F* changer de disque, to change the subject; change(z) de disque! put another record on!/give it a rest! 2. *F* siffler au disque, to ask for sth in vain/to whistle for it 3. *P* avaler le disque, to take Holy Communion 4. *V* anus*; casser le disque, to have anal sex*/to sodomize; se faire casser le disque, to be buggered/arse-fucked/*NAm* ass-fucked; to get one's arse/*NAm* ass fucked.

disserte [disɛrt] *nf F* (*écoles*) (= *dissertation*) essay.

distingué [distɛ̃ge] *nm F* large glass of beer (*one litre*).

distinguo [distɛ̃go] *nm F* distinction; faire le distinguo, to make a subtle distinction.

distribe [distrib] *nf* 1. *F Mil* (= *distribution*) issue (of army rations) 2. *P* = **distribution**.

distribution [distribysjɔ̃] *nf P* beating (up)*/thrashing/working over.

dix [dis] *num a inv & nm inv* 1. *F* ça vaut dix! that's excellent*!/ten out of ten! (*histoire, etc*) that's a good one!/it's hilarious! 2. *F* je vous le donne en dix, I'll give you ten guesses; you'll never guess 3. *P* piquer le dix, (*prisonnier*) to pace up and down (in one's cell) 4. *F* marcher à la dix heures dix, to walk with one's feet turned out/with one's feet at a quarter to three 5. *V* dix (sous/ronds), anus*. (*Voir* **der 2**)

DKV [dekave] *a F* = **decavé**.

doc [dɔk] *F* I *nm* doctor/doc/medico II *nf* = **docu**.

doche [dɔʃ] *P* I *nf* mother*. (*Voir* **belle-doche**) II *nmpl* les doches, parents III *nfpl* 1. (*a*) dice; passer les doches, to give in/up (*b*) domino; boîte à doches, domino box 2. menstruation/period*; avoir ses doches, to have a period*/to be on the rag/to have the curse.

docu [dɔky] *nm F* (*a*) document(s)/info (*b*) documentary (film).

dodo [dodo] *nm F* (*a*) sleep/bye-bye(s); faire dodo, to go bye-byes (*b*) bed; aller à dodo/aller au dodo/aller faire dodo, to go to bed/to go to beddy-byes.

dodoches [dodɔʃ] *nfpl P* breasts*/boobs.

dogue [dɔg] *nm F* être d'une humeur de dogue, to be in a vile mood/in a filthy temper; to be like a bear with a sore head.

doigt [dwa] *nm F* 1. être comme les doigts de la main, to be hand in glove 2. mon petit doigt me l'a dit, a little bird told me (so) 3. faire qch les doigts dans le nez/*V* les doigts dans le cul, to do sth effortlessly/standing on one's head/with one's eyes shut; **gagner/arriver les doigts dans le nez,** to win by a mile/to win hands down/to leave the rest standing **4.** il n'a pas remué le petit doigt, he didn't do a thing/he didn't budge **5.** (a) cela se voit au doigt et à l'œil, it's obvious/it's as plain as day (b) obéir à qn au doigt et à l'œil, to be at s.o.'s beck and call (c) mener son personnel au doigt et à l'œil, keep a tight rein on one's staff **6.** se mettre/se fourrer/se ficher/se foutre le doigt dans l'œil (jusqu'au coude), to be completely wrong/to be (very) wide of the mark/to be barking up the wrong tree **7.** il s'en mord les doigts, he bitterly regrets it/he's kicking himself **8.** (a) y mettre les doigts, to steal*/to put one's hand in the till (b) y mettre les quatre doigts et le pouce, to grab (sth) **9.** (a) doigt d'honneur, obscene gesture; faire un doigt d'honneur à qn, to show a finger at s.o. (b) faire un doigt de cour, to flirt **10.** avoir les doigts de pied en éventail/en bouquet de violettes, (paresser) to laze about/to relax totally/to do absolutely nothing; (avoir un orgasme) to come **11.** avoir les mains pleines de doigts, to be all thumbs. (Voir **crochu; mordre 8; taper I 4**)

se doigter [sədwate] vpr P (femme) to masturbate*/to finger oneself/to play with oneself.

dolluche [dɔlyʃ] nm P dollar/buck.

domb [dɔb] a P = **dombi**.

dombi [dɔbi] a P (verlan de **bidon**) c'est dombi! it's (a load of) rubbish/crap!

dominos [dɔmino] nmpl P **1.** (jeu de) dominos, teeth*/ivories/choppers; avoir mal aux dominos, to have toothache **2.** (drogues) Durophet capsules/dominoes. (Voir **boîte 8**)

dondon [dɔdɔ] nf F grosse dondon, big lump of a girl/of a woman; big fat wench.

donne [dɔn] nf P **1.** alms **2.** generosity; être de la donne, to be generous; (être à court d'argent) to be out of pocket; ne pas être de la donne, to be a miser*/to be miserly.

donné [dɔne] **I** a & pp F c'est donné, (pas cher) it's dirt cheap/it's a gift **II** nm F (coup sûr) safe operation/low-risk business.

donner [dɔne] **I** vtr **1.** P donner qn, to denounce* s.o./to inform on s.o. **2.** F je vous le donne en mille, you can have as many guesses as you like/I bet you'll never guess **3.** F on vous en donnera! you don't want much, do you! **4.** F se la donner, to be wary/suspicious (of); se la donner de qn, to mistrust s.o./to

suspect s.o./to have one's suspicions about s.o. **II** vi F **1.** j'ai donné, I've already thought about that/I'm not worrying about that any more **2.** j'ai déjà donné, I've had enough of that/I don't want anything more to do with that **3.** donner dedans, to fall for it/to walk right into a trap **4.** ça donne (un max)! that's great/that's really something! **III** vpr se **donner** F **1.** to be kind/to show kindness (towards s.o.) **2.** se donner la main, to be of equal value; elles se donnent la main, there's not much to choose between them **3.** s'en donner, (s'amuser) to have a good time; (faire beaucoup d'efforts) to take great trouble (over sth). (Voir **air I 3**)

donneur, -euse [dɔnœr, -øz] n P (police) informer*/(copper's) nark/grass.

donzelle [dɔzɛl] nf F Péj girl*/young woman*/chick/bird (who puts on airs).

dopant [dɔpɑ̃] nm F narcotic/drug*.

dope [dɔp] nf F (a) drugs*/dope (b) doping; marcher à la dope, to dope oneself.

doper [dɔpe] F **I** vtr **1.** to dope **2.** to reprimand*/to blow up/to haul over the coals **II** vpr se doper to dope oneself.

doré [dɔre] a F **1.** lucky **2.** doré sur tranche, excellent*.

dorer [dɔre] vtr V se faire dorer, to be buggered; va te faire dorer! get stuffed!

dorme [dɔrm] nf P sleep/shuteye; aller à la dorme, to go to bed*/to hit the sack.

dort-en-chiant [dɔrɑ̃ʃjɑ̃] nm inv V slowcoach/NAm slowpoke/dawdler/weary Willie.

dorto [dɔrto] nm F (écoles) (= dortoir) dormitory/dorm.

dorure [dɔryr] nf F fool*/moron.

doryphore [dɔrifɔr] nm F (seconde guerre 1939–45) German* soldier/Jerry.

dos [do] nm **1.** P dos d'azur/vert, pimp*/ponce **2.** F j'en ai plein le dos, I'm sick of it/I'm fed up* with it/I've had it up to here; il me scie le dos, I've had (more than) enough of him; he bores me rigid **3.** F avoir qch sur le dos, to be saddled with s.o.; mettre qch sur le dos de qn, to saddle s.o. with sth **4.** F avoir bon dos, to take the blame for s.o. else **5.** se mettre qn à dos, to make an enemy of s.o. **6.** F l'avoir dans le dos, to be duped/to be played for a sucker/to be had **7.** P les avoir sur le dos, to have the police* on one's track. (Voir **pied 16; reins 4**) **8.** F se n'ai rien à me mettre sur le dos, I haven't anything fit to wear/I haven't a stitch to put on **9.** F (a) elle est toujours dans mon dos, she's always nagging at me/finding fault with me; she's always on my back (*b*) elle est toujours sur mon dos, she watches every move I make (*c*) elle me tombe toujours sur le dos, she's always jumping down my throat 10. *F* il n'y va pas avec le dos de la cuiller, he doesn't mince his words/he makes no bones about it/he doesn't go in for half measures; he goes the whole hog/he stops at nothing 11. *F* passer la main dans le dos à qn, to flatter* s.o.; se passer la main dans le dos, to pat oneself on the back 12. *P* filer/donner/prendre du dos, to be a homosexual 13. *P* faire un enfant dans le dos de qn, to betray s.o.'s confidence 14. *F* être mort dans le dos, to be frozen to death/perished with (the) cold. (*Voir* **bête** I **4**; **large 2**; **singe 4**; **sucre 3**)

dose [doz] *nf* 1. *P* j'en ai eu une dose/j'en ai eu ma bonne dose, I've had more than my (fair) share of it 2. *P* en avoir/en tenir une dose, to be an absolute fool*/to be as stupid as they come 3. *P* en prendre une bonne dose, to enjoy oneself immensely 4. avoir sa dose, (*battu*) to have been badly beaten up; (*mort*) to be dead 5. *F* forcer la dose, to overdo it/to go too far; to pile on the agony 6. *P* (*drogues*) dose/fix.

dossière [dosjɛr] *nf P* 1. buttocks*; jouer de la dossière, to wiggle/to waggle one's behind (when walking); remuer la dossière, to hurry* (up)/to get cracking/to move it 2. underpants with a slit in the back 3. prendre/refiler de la dossière, to be a homosexual* 4. avoir de la dossière, to have amazing luck/to have the luck of the devil.

douane [dwan] *nf P* passer à la douane, to have sex* (standing up) in a doorway.

douanier [dwanje] *nm A P* glass of absinth(e).

doublage [dublaʒ] *nm P* 1. (*trahison*) double-cross(ing) 2. (*prostitution*) maintaining of two pimps* by one prostitute*.

doublard [dublar] *nm P* 1. pimp's second woman 2. prostitute's second lover 3. loaded dice.

doublarde [dublard] *nf P* = **doublard 1**.

double [dubl] *nm P* 1. = **doublard 3** 2. mener/faire mettre qn en double, to dupe s.o./to con s.o.; se laisser mener en double, to allow oneself to be played for a sucker.

doublé [duble] *nm* 1. *P* (*second coït*) second bonk/screw (*immediately after the first one*) 2. *F* faire un doublé, to give birth to twins.

doubler [duble] *vtr P* 1. to double-cross (s.o.) 2. to be unfaithful to (one's husband, one's wife, one's lover) 3. to beat (s.o.) to it; to gazump (s.o.).

double-six [dubl(ə)sis] *P* I *nm* jouer/rendre le double-six à qn, to be more than a match for s.o. II *nfpl* molars.

double-zéro [dublazero] *nm F* c'est un double-zéro, he's a dead loss/he's useless. (*pl* doubles-zéros)

doublure [dublyr] *nf P* 1. figurehead/man of straw 2. les doublures se touchent, I'm penniless*/flat broke/skint 3. = **doublard 1**.

douce [dus] I *nf* 1. *P* (*drogues*) marijuana*/grass 2. *Vieilli V* se faire/se foutre une douce, to masturbate*/to toss oneself off II *adv phr F* en douce, discreetly/quietly/on the quiet/on the QT; (*en confidence*) between you, me and the gatepost; il a filé en douce, he slipped off quietly; vas-y en douce! easy does it! (*Voir* **couler 2**; **glisser** II **1**)

doucement [dusmã] *adv F* 1. vas-y doucement avec l'alcool, go easy on the booze 2. ça m'a fait doucement rigoler, I had a good laugh over it.

doucettement [dusɛtmã] *adv F* (*a*) gently; quietly (*b*) cautiously.

douche [duʃ] *nf F* 1. prendre une douche, to get a soaking/to get soaked (to the skin) 2. douche écossaise, succession of good and bad news/experiences, etc; ups and downs/blowing hot and cold 3. je lui ai passé une bonne douche, I gave him a good telling-off/I let him have it (good and proper).

doucher [duʃe] *vtr F* 1. *F* se faire doucher, to get a soaking (from the rain) 2. to reprimand* (s.o.)/to tell (s.o.) off/to bawl (s.o.) out 3. to disappoint (s.o.).

doudou [dudu] *nf F* West Indian woman.

doudounes [dudun] *nfpl P* breasts*/boobs.

douillard, -arde [dujar, -ard] *F* I *a* (*personne*) 1. soft/cuddly/cosy 2. rich*/loaded/rolling in it 3. with a good thatch (of hair)/well-thatched II *n* 1. soft person 2. rich* person/moneybags 3. well-thatched person.

douille [duj] *nf P* 1. (*a*) money*/cash/dough (*b*) payment/forking out 2. *pl* douilles, hair/thatch; se faire faucher les douilles, to have a haircut/to get one's hair cut; fausses douilles, wig.

douiller [duje] *vtr & i P* to pay* (for); to fork out/to cough up; ça douille! (*c'est cher*) that's pric(e)y! (*ça rapporte*) it's profitable/it pays.

douillettes [dujɛt] *nfpl V* testicles*/goolies.

doul(e) [dul] *nm P* 1. hat*/titfer 2. police informer* 3. **porter le doul(e)**, to be (suspected of being) a police informer*.

douleur [dulœr] *nf F* 1. **la douleur**, irritating person/pain (in the neck) 2. **comprendre sa douleur**, to realize one's disappointment/to be mortified 3. *pl* rheumatism; **j'ai des douleurs**, my rheumatism is playing me up.

doulos [dulos] *nm P* 1. = **doul(e) 1, 2, 3** 2. *pl* hair.

douloureuse [dulurøz] *nf F* **la douloureuse**, the bill/*esp NAm* the check (in hotel, restaurant, etc)/the damage/the bad news.

doux [du] *adv F* **filer doux**, to give in/to climb down/to knuckle under.

douze [duz] *nm F* **faire un douze**, to make a mistake*/to boob.

drage [draʒ] *nf P* **faire la drage**, to sell herbal remedies.

dragée [draʒe] *nf P* bullet; **envoyer une dragée**, to fire a bullet/to shoot.

drague [drag] *nf* 1. *P* = **drage** 2. *F* chatting up men and women; **alors, la drague, ça marche?** so, how's your love life? **il y a de la drague dans l'air**, someone's getting the come-on; **champion de la drague**, expert at chatting up women.

draguer [drage] *vtr & i F* to try to pick up/chat up/get off with men, women; (*hommes*) to chase skirt; (*homosexuels*) to cruise/to go cruising; **il est toujours en train de draguer les filles**, he's always trying to get off with the girls/with some chick or other.

dragueur, -euse [dragœr, -øz] *n P* chat-up merchant; (*homme*) skirt-chaser; (*femme*) flirt; (*homosexuels*) s.o. who's cruising/who's trying to get off with s.o. else; **c'est une sacrée dragueuse**, she's always chatting up the men.

drap [dra] *nm F* 1. **être/se mettre dans de beaux draps**, to be in a fix*/in a fine (old) mess/in a pickle; **nous voilà dans de beaux draps!** we're really up the creek! 2. **tailler en plein drap**, (*gaspiller*) to be wasteful/extravagant; (*faire comme on veut*) to do just as one pleases.

drapeau, -eaux [drapo] *nm* 1. *F* **mettre son drapeau dans sa poche**, to conceal one's opinions/to keep one's mouth shut 2. *P* unpaid debt; **planter un drapeau**, (*s'endetter*) to get into debt; (*partir sans payer*) to leave without paying the bill.

drauper, draupère, dreauper [droper] *nm P* (*verlan de* **perdreau**) policeman*.

dresser [drese] *vtr F* **dresser qn**, to discipline s.o./to bring s.o. to heel/to make s.o. toe the line; **ça le dressera!** that'll teach him!/that'll put him in his place!

driver [drive] *vtr F* 1. to drive (a car, etc) 2. to accompany (s.o.); to show (s.o.) the way 3. to advise (s.o.) 4. to run (a business) 5. (*proxénète*) to supervise (a prostitute).

droico, droit-co [drwako] *nm F* (*abrév = droit commun*) s.o. found guilty of a civil offence (*as opposed to a criminal offence*).

droitier [drwatje] *a & nm* right-wing (student)/(student) of the far right.

drôle [drol] I *a F* (*a*) **se sentir tout drôle**, to feel queer/(a bit) funny/off colour/all peculiar (*b*) **vous êtes drôle!** qu'auriez-vous fait à ma place? don't be funny! what would you have done in my place? (*c*) **un drôle de coco/de mec/de numéro/de paroissien/de type**, a queer fish/an odd bod/a strange chap/a weird bloke/a funny fellow; **une drôle d'odeur**, a peculiar smell; **quelle drôle d'idée!** what a funny idea! II *adv P* 1. **ça m'a fait tout drôle de te voir là**, I felt very odd/it gave me a funny feeling seeing you there 2. **ça va lui faire tout drôle**, he'll/she'll get a shock/the shock of his/her life; he'll/she'll get a bit of a shock.

drôlement [drolmã] *adv F* awfully/terribly/terrifically; **il fait drôlement froid**, it's jolly cold; **nous sommes drôlement amusés**, we had a smashing/fabulous time; **elle est drôlement bien**, she's gorgeous; **il a drôlement décollé**, he hasn't half changed; **et drôlement!** and how!

drôlet, -ette [drolɛ, -ɛt], **drôlichon, -onne** [droliʃɔ̃, -ɔn] *a F* funny/odd/queer/quaint.

droper [drope] *P* I *vi* to hurry (up)*/to get a move on/to step on it II *vtr* (*amener*) to drop (s.o.) off.

dropou [dropu] *nf P* (*verlan de* **poudre**) (*drogues*) heroin*/cocaine*.

dropper [drope] *vi P* = **droper**.

dross [drɔs] *nm P* (*drogues*) residue in opium pipe/green mud.

drouille [druj] *nf P* (*a*) worthless goods; shoddy goods; trash/rubbish (*b*) second-hand goods; sale goods.

drouilleur [drujœr] *nm P* buyer of clearance lines.

duce [dys] *nm P* (*a*) (agreed) signal/sign (*to warn s.o.*); **faire un duce**, to make a sign (*b*) (*renseignement*) tip-off; **faire le duce à qn**, to tip s.o. off*/to give s.o. a tip-off.

duch(e)nock [dyʃnɔk], **duch(e)noque** [dyʃnɔk], **ducon** [dykɔ̃], **duconneau** [dykɔno], **duconnard** [dykɔnar], **duconno** [dykɔno], **duconnoso** [dykɔnoso], **duconnosof** [dykɔnɔsɔf] *nm* P fool*/idiot/nit(wit)/twit/berk/jerk; silly sod; stupid bugger. (*Voir* **schnock**)

Ducon-la-joie [dykɔ̃laʒwa] *nm* P happy fool*/happy bugger.

dugenou [dyʒ(ə)nu]   *nm*   P   = **duch(e)nock**.

Dupont-la-joie [dypɔ̃laʒwa] *nm* P (caricature of) the average Frenchman (*chauvinistic, racist, reactionary, vulgar, etc*); = Kevin; = Essex man.

dur [dyr] I *a* 1. *F* **être dur à cuire**, to be a tough nut (to crack); **il est dur à cuire**, he's a tough cookie 2. *F Iron* **il n'est pas dur!** he doesn't want much!/he's got a nerve! 3. *P* **il n'est pas dur à piger**, he's quick on the uptake/he twigs on quickly/he cottons on quickly 4. *P* **c'est dur-dur!** it's a (bloody) pain (in the neck); **c'est plutôt dur-dur**, it's a bit of a pain/a hassle; **t'es dur, là**, you're a pain (in the neck) 5. *V* (*a*) **l'avoir dur**, to have an erection*/to have a hard-on/to get it up (*b*) **l'avoir dur pour qn/en avoir dur pour qn**, to desire s.o. sexually/to be turned on by s.o./to be horny for s.o. (*Voir* **desserre; détente; dure; feuille 1; lâcher 2; respirer 1**) II *nm* 1. *P* train; underground train/tube (train); **prendre le dur**, to go by train/by tube; **brûler/griller le dur**, to travel (on a train, on the tube) without paying 2. *F* **un dur (de dur)**, a tough guy/a hard nut; **un dur à cuire**, a hard-boiled man; **jouer au dur/jouer les durs (de durs)**, to play the tough guy 3. *P* (burglar's) jemmy/*NAm* jimmy 4. *P* gold coins 5. *P* **les durs**, hard labour 6. *Vieilli P* **un**

verre de dur, a glass of spirits*/a drop of the hard stuff. (*Voir* **dure**) III *int F* **oh! dur!** oh, blast (it)! **dur-dur!** what a pain!

duraille [dyraj] *a* P difficult/tough; **se lever tôt, c'est duraille**, it's a job to get up early.

dure [dyr] *nf F* 1. ground; **coucher sur la dure**, to sleep on the ground 2. (*a*) **en dire de dures à qn**, to give s.o. a good telling-off/to bawl s.o. out (*b*) **il en a vu de dures**, he's had a bad/a hard/a rough time (of it); he's been through the mill (*c*) **en faire voir de dures à qn**, to give s.o. a bad/hard/rough time (of it); to put s.o. through it 3. **une dure à cuire**, a hard-boiled woman 4. *adv phr* **à la dure**, violently; **il a été élevé à la dure**, he was brought up the hard way. (*Voir* **dur I, II**)

durer [dyre] *vi F* 1. *Péj* **est-ce qu'il dure toujours?** is he still alive? 2. (*a*) **nous n'y pouvons plus durer**, we can't hold out/stick it out any longer (*b*) **il ne peut pas durer en place**, he can't stay put (a minute); he's like a cat on hot bricks/on a hot tin roof.

durillon [dyrijɔ̃], **durillot** [dyrijo], **duringue** [dyrɛ̃g] *a* P hard/tough/difficult.

durite [dyrit] *nf P* **péter une durite**, to get angry*/to blow a gasket.

duschnock [dyʃnɔk]   *nm*   V   = **duch(e)nock**.

duvet [dyvɛ] *nm F* 1. sleeping bag 2. **coucher sur le duvet**, to live in the lap of luxury.

dynamite [dinamit] *nf* 1. *F* **n'y touche pas, c'est de la dynamite!** don't touch it, it's dynamite! 2. *P* (*a*) very strong drug *or* drink/dynamite/knock-out (*b*) very high-quality drug (*c*) cocaine*; **marcher à la dynamite**, to be on drugs*/to dope oneself.

dynamité, -ée [dinamite] *P* I *a* high on drugs* II *n* drug addict*/junkie.

E

eau, *pl* **eaux** [o] *nf F* **1. marin d'eau douce,** landlubber **2. il y a de l'eau dans le gaz,** (*ça va mal aller*) there's trouble brewing; there's going to be trouble; (*il y a un problème*) there's a snag in it somewhere **3.** (*a*) **clair comme l'eau de vaisselle,** as clear as mud (*b*) **clair comme de l'eau de roche,** perfectly clear/crystal clear **4. mettre de l'eau dans son vin,** to moderate one's opinions; to go easy/to ease off; to tone it down a bit **5. tomber à l'eau, tourner/s'en aller/finir/partir en eau de boudin,** (*projet, etc*) to fall through/ to fizzle out/to come to nothing/to end (up) in smoke **6. il n'a pas inventé l'eau chaude/tiède,** he's not very bright; he'll never set the Thames on fire **7.** (*a*) **eau plate,** ordinary (drinking) water (*b*) **eau à ressort/à pédale,** fizzy water/soda water (*c*) **eau d'affe,** brandy **8. avoir les eaux basses,** to be short of cash/ out of funds; **les eaux sont basses,** there's a lack of funds; I'm/he's/she's hard up *or* short of cash **9. à l'eau de rose,** (*sentimental*) milk-and-water; schmaltzy; gooey (sentimentality)/sugary/sticky/soppy **10. un imbécile de la première eau/de la plus belle eau,** an out-and-out fool*/a complete idiot **11. dans ces eaux-là,** approximately/thereabouts; **c'était en 1982, dans ces eaux-la,** it was in 1982, or thereabouts; **ça m'a coûté 2000 balles, dans ces eaux-là,** it cost me about £200; **ça doit se trouver vers Paris, dans ces eaux-là,** it must be somewhere near Paris. (*Voir* **bec 2; bidet; changer 2; épée 2; olive 2; poisson 5; revenir 3**)

ébaubi [ebobi] *a F* amazed*/flabbergasted.

ébaubir [ebobir] *vtr F* to amaze*/to flabbergast*.

éberlué [eberlɥe] *a F* amazed*/ flabbergasted/dumbfounded.

ébouriffant [eburifɑ̃] *a F* breathtaking/ startling.

ébouriffer [eburife] *vtr F* to amaze* (s.o.)/ to take (s.o.'s) breath away.

ébouser, ébouzer [ebuze] *vtr P* to kill*/to assassinate/to do in/*surt NAm* to blow away.

ébrécher [ebreʃe] *vtr F* **1.** to damage (reputation) **2.** to make a hole in (one's capital).

écailler [ekɑje] *vtr* to swindle*/to fleece (s.o.)/to clean (s.o.) out/to rip (s.o.) off.

échalas [eʃala] *nm F* **1.** tall/thin person; beanpole; **il est sec comme un échalas,** he's very skinny **2.** *pl* long/skinny legs*.

échalote [eʃalɔt] *nf P* **1.** anus* **2.** *pl* ovaries; **se faire dévisser les échalotes,** to have one's ovaries removed **3. pratiquer la course à l'échalote,** to make s.o. run by holding him/ her by the collar and the seat of his/her trousers; (*en voiture*) to tailgate; to have a car chase, driving very close to the car in front.

échangisme [eʃɑ̃ʒism] *nm P* wife-swapping/swapping partners (*in orgy*).

échangiste [eʃɑ̃ʒist] *nm & f P* s.o. who takes part in wife-swapping sessions.

échasses [eʃas] *nfpl F* **marcher/être monté sur des échasses,** to have long/skinny legs*.

échassier [eʃasje] *nm F* tall/thin person.

échassière [eʃasjɛr] *nf P* prostitute* (who sits at the bar)/bar-girl/hostess.

échauder [eʃode] *vtr F* to swindle*; **se faire échauder/être échaudé,** to get fleeced/to get one's fingers burnt/to be taken for a ride/ to be ripped off.

échauffer [eʃofe] *vtr F* **échauffer la bile/les oreilles à qn,** to anger s.o./to rub s.o. up the wrong way.

échelle [eʃɛl] *nf F* **1. monter/grimper à l'échelle,** (*se laisser tromper*) to be taken in/ to fall for something; (*se mettre en colère*) to get angry*/to flare up; **faire monter qn à l'échelle,** (*tromper*) to kid s.o./to have s.o. on; (*mettre en colère*) to make s.o. angry/to get s.o.'s blood up; **c'est pas vrai, vous voulez me faire monter à l'échelle!** I don't believe it, you're pulling my leg!/you're having me on! **2. après ça, il en peut/il n'y a plus qu'à tirer l'échelle, that's the limit*/there's no point in carrying on; **après lui, on peut/il n'y a plus qu'à tirer l'échelle,** after what he's done we may as well give up.

s'échiner [seʃine] *vpr F* to work* oneself to death/to work oneself into the ground/to wear oneself out; **s'échiner à qch,** to slave away at sth/to slog one's guts out; **s'échiner à faire qch,** to break one's back doing sth.

échouer [eʃwe] *vi F (personne) (aboutir)* **il a échoué sur un banc de jardin public,** he ended up on a park bench.

éclairer [eklɛre, -ere] *vtr & i P (a)* **éclairer (la dépense),** to pay* up/to foot the bill *(b) (jeux d'argent)* **éclairer (le tapis),** to stake one's money/to lay it on the line; **les éclairer,** to show the colour of one's money.

éclatade [eklatad] *nf,* **éclate** [eklat] *nf,* **éclaterie** [eklatri] *nf F* intense pleasure; whale of a time/ball.

éclaté [eklate] *nm F* **un éclaté de la vie,** s.o. who enjoys himself/who has a really good time.

s'éclater [seklate] *vpr F* **1.** *(drogues)* to have psychedelic visions/to trip **2.** to have a wild/a really good time*; to have a ball (at a party, etc); **s'éclater comme une bête,** to freak out **3.** to have an orgasm*/to come.

s'éclipser [seklipse] *vpr F* to run away*/to make oneself scarce/to do a disappearing act; **je me suis éclipsé(e) avant la fin,** I sneaked/ *NAm* snuck out before the end.

écluse [eklyz] *nf* **lâcher/ouvrir les écluses,** *F* to start crying/to turn on the waterworks; *P (aussi:* **lâcher l'écluse)** to urinate*/to splash one's boots/to (have a) piddle/to take a leak.

écluser [eklyze] *P* **I** *vtr* **écluser un verre/un godet,** to knock back/to sink a drink; to put one down the hatch/to have a swig **II** *vi* to urinate*.

écolo [ekɔlo] **1** *nm & f F (= écologiste)* ecologist/ecofreak **II** *a (= écologique)* green.

éconocroques [ekɔnɔkrɔk] *nfpl P* savings/economies.

écopage [ekɔpaʒ] *nm F* **1.** blow*/wound **2.** reprimand*/telling-off/slating.

écoper [ekɔpe] *vi F (a)* to catch it/to cop it/ to get it in the neck; **écoper de six mois de taule,** to cop six months inside; **il va écoper,** he's (in) for it/he's got it coming to him/he'll cop it/he's for the high jump; **il a salement écopé,** he got the book thrown at him *(b)* to be hit/wounded.

écopeur [ekɔpœr] *nm F* victim; c'est

toujours moi l'écopeur, I'm always the one who gets it in the neck/who takes the rap.

à écorche-cul [aekɔrʃ(ə)ky] *adv phr P (a)* **monter à écorche-cul,** to ride bareback; **descendre une pente à écorche-cul,** to go down a slope on one's backside *(b)* **il n'est venu qu'à écorche-cul,** we had to drag him here.

écorcher [ekɔrʃe] *vtr F* **1.** to murder (a language, etc) **2.** to overcharge/to fleece*; **il écorche ses clients,** he makes them pay through the nose/he rips them off **3.** ça t'écorchera pas le derrière, it won't bite you/it won't kill you. *(Voir* **renard 3)**

écorcheur, -euse [ekɔrʃœr, -øz] *n F* s.o. who overcharges/fleecer/extortioner.

écorniflage [ekɔrniflaʒ] *nm F* cadging/ scrounging/sponging.

écornifler [ekɔrnifle] *vtr F* to cadge/to scrounge (money, etc); to sponge; **écornifler une clope à qn,** to scrounge a fag off s.o.

écornifleur, -euse [ekɔrniflœr, -øz] *n F* cadger/scrounger/sponger.

écosser [ekɔse] *vi P* **1.** to pay* up/to shell out **2.** to spend lavishly; **elle m'en a fait écosser,** she cost me a pretty penny **3.** to work* hard; to do one's job **4.** to be a prostitute*/to solicit*/to be on the game.

écoutilles [ekutij] *nfpl P* ears*/lugholes.

écrabouillage [ekrabujaʒ] *nm,* **écrabouillement** [ekrabujmɑ̃] *nm F* crushing/squashing.

écrabouiller [ekrabuje] *vtr F* to crush/to squash; to reduce (s.o./sth) to a pulp; to make mincemeat of (s.o.); *(vaincre)* to thrash (s.o.).

écrase-merde [ekrazmɛrd] *nf ou nmpl P* big boots*/beetle-crushers.

écraser [ekraze] **I** *vi P* **1.** écrase! shut* up!/ put a sock in it!/give it a rest!/lay off! **2.** en écraser, to be a prostitute*/to be on the game **3.** en écraser, to sleep like a log **4.** = **s'écraser 2 5.** = **s'écraser 3 II** *vtr* **1.** *P* en écraser une (en lousdoc), to let out a silent fart. *(Voir* **perle 4)** **2.** *P* je t'en écrase cinq, I shake your hand **3.** *F* écraser l'affaire, to hush something up. *(Voir* **champignon 1; coup 4; grain 3** *(a)*; **ivoire; planète 1; tomate 8)** **III** *vpr* **s'écraser** *P* **1.** *(une affaire)* to blow over **2.** to give in **3.** to keep silent; not to denounce s.o./sth.

écraseur, -euse [ekrazœr, -øz] *n F* rotten driver; road-hog.

écrémer [ekreme] *vtr F* **1.** to take the best of/the cream of (a collection); to cream off (a collection) 2. to deprive/rob (s.o.) of his/her most treasured possession.

écroulé [ekrule] *a F* écroulé de rire, doubled up with laughter.

ecstasy [ɛkstazi] *nf P* (*drogues*) ecstasy/E.

écu [eky] *nm F* avoir des écus, to be rich*/to have pots of money*.

écumer [ekyme] *vtr F* 1. écumer la marmite/les marmites, to scrounge/to sponge/to be a hanger-on 2. écumer les bars, to go bar-hopping/to go on a pub-crawl.

écumeur, -euse [ekymœr, -øz] *n F* écumeur de marmite, scrounger/sponger/ freeloader; hanger-on.

écumoire [ekymwar] *nf F* 1. transformer en écumoire, to riddle with bullets 2. avoir la tête comme une écumoire, to be scatterbrained/to have a brain like a sieve.

écureuil [ekyrœj] *nm F* cyclist circling a racing track.

écurie [ekyri] *nf F* 1. entrer comme dans une écurie, to come in without saying hallo/to barge in 2. sentir l'écurie, to be eager/in a hurry to get back home 3. c'est une vraie écurie, it's a real pigsty.

édicule [edikyl] *nm F* (public) convenience/ street urinal.

édredon [edrədɔ̃] *nm P* faire l'édredon, (*prostituée*) to steal* from a client while he is asleep.

effacer [efase] I *vtr P* 1. to kill*/to wipe out/ to blow away 2. to destroy/to smash up (sth) 3. to receive/to cop (a blow) 4. to polish off/to knock back (food, drink). (*Voir* **gomme 2**) II *vpr* s'**effacer** *P* to die*.

effaroucher [efaruʃe] *vtr P* to steal*.

effet [efɛ] *nm F* 1. ça m'a coupé mes effets, it took the wind out of my sails 2. ça m'a fait un drôle d'effet, it gave me quite a turn 3. si c'est ça (tout) l'effet que ça te fait! if that's the way you feel about it! 4. faire des effets de cuisse, (*surt autostoppeuse*) to catch the driver's eye by showing/flashing one's legs.

effeuillage [efœjaʒ] *nm F* striptease.

effeuiller [efœje] *vtr F* effeuiller la marguerite, (*flirter, draguer*) to flirt (with s.o.)/to chat up (s.o.); to make sexual advances (to s.o.); (*faire un strip-tease*) to do a striptease.

effeuilleuse [efœjøz] *nf F* striptease artist/ stripper.

égoïner [egɔine] *vtr* 1. *P* égoïner qn, to evict s.o.; to throw/to kick/to boot s.o. out 2. *V* to have sex* with (s.o.).

égorger [egɔrʒe] *vtr Vieilli F* to ruin/to bleed dry (a creditor).

égout [egu] *nm P* mouth*/trap/kisser/gob.

éjecter [eʒɛkte] *vtr F* (*a*) to throw out/to chuck out/to kick out (sth) (*b*) to dismiss*/to fire/to sack (s.o.); to give (s.o.) the push.

élastique [elastik] *nm F* il les lâche avec un élastique, he's really stingy/he's as mean as hell; he doesn't like to part with his money.

éléphant [elefɑ̃] *nm F* 1. landlubber 2. il a une mémoire d'éléphant, like an elephant he never forgets 3. comme un éléphant dans un magasin de porcelaine, like a bull in a china shop 4. voir des éléphants roses, to be drunk* *or* under the influence of drugs*; to be floating on cloud nine.

élixir [eliksir] *nm P* élixir de hussard, hard liquor.

emballage [ɑ̃balaʒ] *nm P* arrest/nabbing/ nicking.

emballarès [ɑ̃balarɛs] *a P* arrested/nicked/ run in.

emballé [ɑ̃bale] *a F* (mad) keen/ enthusiastic; emballé pour qch, (mad) keen on sth. (*Voir* **emballer 1**)

emballement [ɑ̃balmɑ̃] *nm F* (*a*) burst of enthusiasm; sudden craze (*b*) burst of energy (*c*) passing fancy.

emballer [ɑ̃bale] I *vtr* 1. *F* to excite/to thrill (s.o.); to fire (s.o.) with enthusiasm; ça ne m'emballe pas, I can't work up much enthusiasm for that; that doesn't exactly do a lot for me; il ne m'emballe pas, I don't go much/a bundle on him; être emballé par qn/ qch, to be (mad) keen on s.o./sth; to get carried away by sth 2. *P* (*a*) to arrest* (s.o.)/ to run (s.o.) in/to nick (s.o.) (*b*) to put (s.o.) in prison*/in the nick; se faire emballer, to get run in 3. *P* to reprimand* (s.o.)/to tell (s.o.) off/to tell (s.o.) where he/she gets off; se faire emballer, to get told off 4. *P* (*a*) to chat up/to sweet-talk/to get off with (s.o.)/to pick (s.o.) up; emballer une nana/*vi* emballer, to get off with/to pull a bird/a chick II *vpr* s'**emballer** *F* 1. (*par enthousiasme*) to be carried away/to get excited; (*par colère*) to get worked up (into a state); ne vous emballez pas! cool it!/don't get excited!/don't get worked up!/keep your hair on! il s'emballe pour un rien, he gets (all) worked up over nothing 2. s'emballer pour qn, to fall madly in love with s.o./to fall for s.o.

emballes [ɑ̃bal] *nfpl P* faire des emballes, to make/to kick up a fuss.

emballeur [ãbalœr] *nm P* **1.** policeman* **2.** emballeur (de refroidis), undertaker.

s'embaquer [sãbake] *vpr P* to lose/to be a loser (*at the races, at gambling, etc*).

embarbouiller [ãbarbuje] **I** *vtr F* to confuse/to muddle (s.o.) **II** *vpr* **s'embarbouiller** *F* to get muddled/confused/(all) mixed up.

embarquer [ãbarke] *vtr* **1.** *F* il m'a embarqué dans l'avion, he put me on the plane/he saw me onto the plane **2.** *F* embarquer qn dans sa voiture, to give s.o. a lift (in one's car) **3.** *F* être embarqué dans une sale histoire, to be mixed up in/to be involved in some nasty/dirty business **4.** *P* to arrest* (s.o.)/to run (s.o.) in; se faire embarquer par les flics, to get picked up by the cops **5.** *P* embarquer une nana, to get off with/to pick up/to pull a girl/a chick/a bird **6.** *P* to steal*/to make away with/to filch **7.** *P* = **emballer I 1.**

embarras [ãbara] *nm F* faire de l'embarras/des embarras, to make a fuss/a song and dance (about sth); ne fais pas tant d'embarras! don't make such a song and dance about it! un faiseur/une faiseuse d'embarras, a fusspot.

embastiller [ãbastije] *vtr P* se faire embastiller, to be arrested*/to get run in.

embellemerdé [ãbɛlmɛrde] *a P* saddled with a troublesome mother-in-law.

embellie [ãbɛli] *nf F* **1.** stroke of luck; profiter de l'embellie, to make hay while the sun shines **2.** good deal/bargain.

emberlificoter [ãbɛrlifikɔte] *vtr F* **1.** to tangle (s.o.) up (in an argument, etc); to involve (s.o.) in difficulties/to get (s.o.) mixed up in something **2.** to get round (s.o.)/to take (s.o.) in/to sweet-talk (s.o.).

emberlificoteur, -euse [ãbɛrlifikɔtœr, -øz] *n F* hoaxer/duper; sweet-talker/soft-soaper.

embêtant [ãbɛtã] *F* **I** *a* annoying/aggravating; tiresome/boring; qu'il est embêtant, celui-là! what a pest!/what a pain!/he's a real nuisance! c'est bien embêtant! it's a real nuisance! **II** *nm* l'embêtant c'est que ..., the annoying thing is that .../the problem is that ....

embêté [ãbɛte] *a F* (*a*) bored*/fed up* (*b*) worried; je suis bien embêté, I've got a problem.

embêtement [ãbɛtmã] *nm F* **1.** nuisance/annoyance/aggravation/bother; worry **2.**

chercher des embêtements, to look for trouble; avoir des embêtements, to be in a fix*.

embêter [ãbɛte] **I** *vtr F* (*a*) to annoy*/to be a nuisance to (s.o.); ne l'embête pas! stop pestering him!/leave him alone!/stop bugging him! il m'embête, he gets on my nerves; I've got no time for him; ça m'embête de ..., (ça m'ennuie) I can't be bothered to ...; (ça me gêne) I wish I didn't have to ...; ça m'embête d'arriver en retard, I hate being late (*b*) to bore* **II** *vpr* **s'embêter** *F* (*a*) to be bored*; s'embêter comme une carpe/s'embêter ferme/s'embêter un bon coup/s'embêter à crever/s'embêter à mourir/s'embêter à cent sous de l'heure/s'embêter à cent francs de l'heure, to be bored stiff/rigid; to be bored to death/to tears (*b*) *Iron* il ne s'embête pas, celui-là! you don't have to worry about him, he does pretty well for himself/his first priority is for number one; he's got a lot of nerve!

embistrouiller [ãbistruje] *vtr P* to annoy*/to pester.

embobeliner [ãbɔbline], **embobiner** [ãbɔbine] *vtr F* to get round (s.o.)/to take (s.o.) in/to lead (s.o.) up the garden path; se laisser embobeliner, to let oneself be hoodwinked/be taken in.

emboiser [ãbwaze] *vtr P* to get (a woman) pregnant*/to put (a woman) up the spout/*surt NAm* to knock (a woman) up.

emboîtage [ãbwataʒ] *nm F* (*théâtre*) booing/hissing; cat calls.

emboîter [ãbwate] *vtr* **1.** *F* (*théâtre*) to boo/to hiss/to give (s.o.) the bird; se faire emboîter, to get the bird **2.** *P* (*a*) to arrest* (*b*) to send to prison*.

emboucané [ãbukane] *a P* fed up*/pissed off.

emboucaner [ãbukane] *P* **I** *vtr* **1.** to irritate/to annoy*; tu m'emboucanes, you get on my tits/you're a pain in the arse/*NAm* ass **2.** to stink (the place) out **3.** to poison **II** *vi* to stink*/to pong.

embouché [ãbuʃe] *a F* mal embouché, (*grossier*) foul-mouthed; (*de mauvaise humeur*) in a foul mood.

embourber [ãburbe] *P* **I** *vtr* to have sex* with (a woman)/to bed (a woman) **II** *vpr* **s'embourber** **1.** to tolerate/to put up with (sth) **2.** s'embourber une femme, to have sex* with a woman; ils se sont embourbés, they had it away/they had it off **3.** to get drunk*/

sloshed.

embourremaner [ɑ̃burmane] *vtr P* to put in prison*.

embrasser [ɑ̃brase] *vtr F* embrasser un platane, to hit a tree/to wrap a car round a tree.

embrayer [ɑ̃breje] I *vi F* 1. to begin to understand 2. to begin to explain (sth) 3. to start work/to get cracking/to get down to it II *vtr P* embrayer une nénette, to have sex*/to have it off with a girl*.

embringuer [ɑ̃brɛ̃ge] I *vtr F* se laisser embringuer dans qch, to get involved/mixed up in sth II *vpr* **s'embringuer** *F* 1. s'embringuer dans qch, to get involved/mixed up in sth 2. s'embringuer mal, to get off to a bad start.

embrouillamini [ɑ̃brujamini] *nm F* confusion/disorder*/muddle.

embrouille [ɑ̃bruj] *nf P* 1. disorder*/muddle/jumble/mess/confusion; ça ficherait l'embrouille, things would get (very) complicated 2. shady transaction; faire une embrouille à qn, to do the dirty on s.o. 3. conflict; fight; illegal situation 4. problem/difficulty; misunderstanding; un sac d'embrouilles, a muddle; il a eu une embrouille avec les flics, he got into trouble/he got mixed up with the cops 5. l'Embrouille, the French Stock Exchange/the Bourse.

s'embrouiller [sɑ̃bruje] *vpr P* to begin to get drunk*/to get fuddled (with drink).

embrouilleur, -euse [ɑ̃brujœr, -øz] *n* 1. *F* muddler 2. *P* shady dealer.

embusqué [ɑ̃byske] *nm F* (*a*) slacker/lead-swinger/skiver (*b*) shirker (from call-up or active service)/column-dodger.

embusquer [ɑ̃byske] I *vtr P* to arrest*; se faire embusquer, to get nabbed II *vpr* **s'embusquer** *F* to shirk active service/to dodge the column.

éméché [emeʃe] *a F* slightly drunk*/merry/tipsy.

émécher [emeʃe] *vtr F* émécher qn, to get s.o. slightly drunk*/merry/tipsy.

émeraudes [emrod] *nfpl P* (= *hémorroïdes*) piles.

emmanché [ɑ̃mɑ̃ʃe] *nm & a V* 1. (passive) homosexual*/fairy/*surt NAm* fag(got)/poof/queer 2. (*imbécile*) berk/cretin; espèce d'emmanché! (you) stupid prick!/you jerk!

emmancher [ɑ̃mɑ̃ʃe] I *vtr V* to have anal sex* with (s.o.)/to sodomize* (s.o.)/to bugger (s.o.); se faire emmancher, to get one's arse/

NAm ass fucked II *vpr* **s'emmancher** 1. *V* to have anal sex* together/to arse-fuck/*NAm* ass-fuck/to shaft each other 2. *P* to start; s'emmancher mal, (*affaire*) to get off to a bad start.

s'emmêler [sɑ̃mele] *vpr P* s'emmêler les pédales/les pieds, to get into a muddle/to get tied up in knots. (*Voir* **crayon** 3; **pinceau** 3)

emmener [ɑ̃mne] *vtr P* 1. (*trahir*) to betray (s.o.); (*tromper*) to take (s.o.) for a ride/to string (s.o.) along 2. je t'emmène à la campagne! go to hell!

emmerdant [ɑ̃mɛrdɑ̃] *a P* (bloody) annoying; bloody/damned boring; ça c'est emmerdant! it's a bloody nuisance!/that's a bastard! tu es emmerdant, you're a pain in the neck/you're a real drag.

emmerdation [ɑ̃mɛrdasjɔ̃] *nf Vieilli P* = **emmerdement**.

emmerde [ɑ̃mɛrd] *nf P* bother/trouble; drag; avoir des emmerdes, to have problems/to be in deep trouble/to be up shit creek; faire des emmerdes à qn, to be a bloody nuisance to s.o./to be nothing but trouble for s.o.

emmerdé [ɑ̃mɛrde] *a P* être emmerdé, to be in the shit; il est emmerdé jusqu'au cou, he's right in the shit/he's up to his neck in shit.

emmerdement [ɑ̃mɛrd(ə)mɑ̃] *nm P* bloody/damned nuisance; (*gros problème*) glitch; quel emmerdement! what a bloody/sodding mess! j'ai des emmerdements, I've got problems/I'm in trouble; il a des emmerdements avec sa femme, he's having a bit of bother with his wife/he's got wife-trouble.

emmerder [ɑ̃mɛrde] *P* I *vtr* 1. (*ennuyer*) to bore (s.o.) to death/to bore the pants off (s.o.)/to bore the tits off (s.o.) 2. (*importuner*) emmerder qn, to get on s.o.'s nerves/s.o.'s wick; to bug/to pester s.o.; tu m'emmerdes à la fin, you're getting on my tits/you're getting up my nose; je l'emmerde! he can just go and get stuffed!/bugger him!/he can fuck off!/sod him! les voisins? je les emmerde! the neighbours? they can just piss off!/sod the neighbours! II *vpr* **s'emmerder** 1. to be bored to tears/out of one's tiny mind; to be bored to death; to be really pissed off; s'emmerder à cent sous de l'heure, to be bored out of one's skull/shitless/rigid; qu'est-ce qu'on s'emmerde ici! God! it's boring here!/we're bored out of our tiny minds in this place! 2. **ne pas s'emmerder**, not to worry about anything; to be doing very nicely thank you; **tu t'emmerdes pas toi!** you're doing very nicely for yourself! (*tu n'es pas gêné*) you've got a nerve!

emmerdeur, -euse [ɑ̃mɛrdœr, -øz] *n P* bloody nuisance/pest; **c'est un emmerdeur**, he's a bloody bore; he's a real headache; he's a pain in the arse/*NAm* ass.

emmieller [ɑ̃mjɛle] *vtr F* (*Euph de* **emmerder**) to annoy*/to irritate; **tu m'emmielles!** you little so-and-so (I'd like to strangle you)!

emmouscailler [ɑ̃muskɑje] *vtr P* (*rare*) = **emmerder**.

émos [emos] *nf Vieilli P* emotion; excitement; shock/turn.

émotion [emosjɔ̃] *nf F* fright/shock; **ça m'a fait une émotion**, it was a bit of a shock; it gave me quite a turn.

émotionnant [emosjɔnɑ̃] *a F* moving (story, etc); exciting; thrilling.

émotionner [emosjɔne] **I** *vtr F* (*émouvoir*) to move/to affect (s.o.); (*exciter*) to thrill (s.o.); (*attendrir*) to upset (s.o.) **II** *vpr* **s'émotionner** *F* to get excited/to get worked up/to get into a state*.

empaffé [ɑ̃pafe] *P* **I** *a* (*a*) effeminate/poofy/queer (*b*) troublesome **II** *nm* **1.** (*a*) effeminate man; pansy/fairy (*b*) homosexual*/poof(ter)/*surt NAm* fag(got)/queer **2.** (*imbécile*) fucking idiot/jerk; (*gêneur*) sodding nuisance.

empaffer [ɑ̃pafe] *vtr V* **empaffer qn**, to have anal sex* with/to sodomize*/to bugger s.o.; to screw s.o.'s arse/*NAm* ass; **qu'il aille se faire empaffer!** screw him! (*Voir* **paf II 2**)

empaillé, -ée [ɑ̃pɑje] *F* **I** *a* stupid*/dim (-witted); (*maladroit*) clumsy **II** *n* (*a*) fool*/dope/dimwit (*b*) (*maladroit*) clumsy clot.

empalmer [ɑ̃palme] *vtr F* **1.** to steal*/nick **2.** to palm (card, coin, etc).

empalmeur [ɑ̃palmœr] *nm F* cardsharp(er).

empapaouter [ɑ̃papaute] *vtr P* = **empaffer**.

empaqueté [ɑ̃pakte] *a & nm P* = **empaillé I, II**.

empaqueter [ɑ̃pakte] *vtr P* **1.** to arrest* **2.** to send to prison* **3.** to fool (s.o.).

empaumer [ɑ̃pome] *vtr* **1.** *F* to dupe/to hoax*/to pull a fast one on (s.o.); **se faire empaumer/se laisser empaumer**, to be tricked/conned/taken in **2.** *P* to arrest*; **se**

faire empaumer, to get caught/nabbed.

empêché [ɑ̃peʃe] *a F* **il est empêché de sa personne/il a l'air empêché**, he's awkward/he doesn't know what to do with himself.

empêcher [ɑ̃peʃe] *vtr F* **n'empêche**, all the same; so what? makes no odds/same difference.

empêcheur [ɑ̃peʃœr] *nm F* **un empêcheur de danser/de tourner en rond**, a spoilsport/a wet blanket/a real drag; **c'est un empêcheur de tourner en rond**, he's the nigger in the woodpile.

empégaler [ɑ̃pegale] *vtr P* to pawn/to hock. (*Voir* **pégal(e)**)

empeigne [ɑ̃pɛɲ] *nf P* **1.** **gueule d'empeigne**, ugly face*/ugly mug **2.** **marcher sur les empeignes**, to be down at heel/to be down on one's uppers.

empétardé [ɑ̃petarde] *nm P* (active) homosexual*.

empétarder [ɑ̃petarde] *vtr P* **empétarder qn**, to have anal sex* with s.o.; to screw/to fuck s.o.'s arse/*NAm* ass.

s'empiffrer [sɑ̃pifre] *vpr F* to eat* greedily/to pig oneself/to stuff one's face.

empiler [ɑ̃pile] *vtr F* to swindle*/to con/to cheat/to do/to rook (s.o.); **se faire empiler**, to get done/to be had/to get ripped off.

empileur, -euse [ɑ̃pilœr, -øz] *n F* swindler*/cheat/fraud/trickster/con man.

emplacarder [ɑ̃plakarde] *vtr P* to send to prison*.

emplafonner [ɑ̃plafɔne] *vtr P* **1.** (*frapper de la tête*) to head-butt (s.o.) **2.** (*voiture*) to collide with/to run (smack) into/to smash into (another vehicle) **3.** to receive/to take (a blow).

emplâtre [ɑ̃plɑtr] *nm* **1.** *F* spineless person; **c'est un emplâtre**, he's got no backbone **2.** *F* food that lies heavy on the stomach/stodgy food **3.** *F* (*a*) **mettre un emplâtre à sa fortune**, to patch up one's fortune (*b*) **c'est mettre un emplâtre sur une jambe de bois**, it's not the slightest use/it's no earthly use. (*Voir* **cautère**) **4.** *P* blow*/punch/wallop; **coller un emplâtre sur la figure de qn**, to slap s.o. round the face.

emplâtrer [ɑ̃plɑtre] *vtr P* **1.** to lay into (s.o.)/to beat (s.o.) up*; to head-butt (s.o.) **2.** = **emplafonner 2 3.** to get one's hands on (some money) (*more or less legally*) **4.** **se faire emplâtrer**, (*brocanteur*) to get lumbered with worthless goods; (*payer trop cher*) to be overcharged (for an object).

empoisonnant [ɑ̃pwazɔnɑ̃] *a F* annoying/ irritating/aggravating; **c'est empoisonnant,** it's a damned nuisance.

empoisonné [ɑ̃pwazɔne] *a F* fed up*/sick and tired; **être empoisonné par qch,** to be plagued by/with sth; to be driven crazy/up the wall by sth.

empoisonnement [ɑ̃pwazɔnmɑ̃] *nm F* **quel empoisonnement que cette femme!** what a pest/pain that woman is! **cette affaire ne me donne que des empoisonnements,** I've had nothing but trouble from that business.

empoisonner [ɑ̃pwazɔne] **I** *vtr F* to bore*/to annoy*/to bug/to pester (s.o.); to drive (s.o.) up the wall **II** *vpr* **s'empoisonner** *F* (*a*) to get bored sick (*b*) to be driven up the wall (by s.o./sth).

empoisonneur, -euse [ɑ̃pwazɔnœr, -øz] *n F* deadly/crashing bore*; nuisance/pest; pain in the neck.

emporter [ɑ̃pɔrte] *vtr Vieilli P* **se faire emporter,** to get arrested/run in (*by the police*). (*Voir* **morceau 4; paradis 2**)

empoté, -ée [ɑ̃pɔte] *F* **I** *a* clumsy/ awkward; **être empoté comme un casse-pot,** to be a clumsy clot; to be all thumbs **II** *n* (*a*) clumsy clot (*b*) dimwit/thickie; **espèce d'empoté!** you great idiot!/you dumb cluck!

emprosé [ɑ̃proze] *nm P* = **empaffé II.**

emproser [ɑ̃proze] *vtr P* = **empaffer.**

emprunt [ɑ̃prœ̃] *nm F* **emprunt forcé,** (*chantage*) blackmail; (*racket*) racket.

en [ɑ̃] *pron F* **1. en sortir,** to be out (of prison) **2. il en est,** he's a homosexual*/he's one of them; he's a policeman*/a cop.

en-bourgeois [ɑ̃burʒwa] *nm inv P* plain-clothes policeman.

encadrer [ɑ̃kadre] *vtr* **1.** *F* **il a encadré un arbre,** he wrapped his car round a tree **2.** *P* **je ne peux pas l'encadrer,** I can't stand (the sight of) him/I can't stick him **3.** *P* to hit (s.o.) (repeatedly) in the face/about the head.

encaisser [ɑ̃kese] *vtr & i* **1.** *F* (*a*) (*boxeur, etc*) **encaisser un coup,** to take a blow; **il a encaissé,** he took a hiding; **il sait encaisser,** he can take a punishment/he can take it (*b*) **l'encaisse sans broncher,** he grins and bears it; **j'ai encaissé,** I put up with it **2.** *P* **je ne peux pas l'encaisser,** I can't stand (the sight of) him/I can't stick him. (*Voir* **salade 6**)

encalbécher [ɑ̃kalbeʃe] *vtr P* (*rare*) to head-butt (s.o.).

encaldosser [ɑ̃kaldose] *vtr P* **1.** *A* to grab (s.o.) from behind **2. se faire encaldosser,**

(*sodomiser*) to be screwed from behind; to get one's arse/*NAm* ass fucked/balled.

encarrade [ɑ̃karad] *nf P* entry; entering.

encarrer [ɑ̃kare] *vtr & i P* **1.** to enter; to let (s.o.) in **2.** to send (s.o.).

enceint(r)er [ɑ̃sɛ̃t(r)e] *vtr P* to make pregnant*/to put (s.o.) up the spout/*surt NAm* to knock (s.o.) up.

enchariboter [ɑ̃ʃaribɔte] *vtr P* (*rare*) **1.** to bore* (s.o.) **2.** to annoy*/to bug/to pester (s.o.).

enchaudelancer [ɑ̃ʃodlɑ̃se] *vtr Vieilli P* **enchaudelancer qn,** to give s.o. VD*/the clap. (*Voir* **chaude-lance**)

enchetarder [ɑ̃ʃtarde], **enchetiber** [ɑ̃ʃtibe] *vtr P* (*peu usuel*) to put in prison*; **se faire enchetarder,** to get put inside/away.

enchoser [ɑ̃ʃoze] *vtr P* **1.** to get pregnant*/ to put (s.o.) up the spout/*surt NAm* to knock (s.o.) up **2.** = **emmerder I 1, 2.**

enchrister [ɑ̃kriste], **enchtiber** [ɑ̃ʃtibe] *vtr P* to send to prison*/to put away.

encloquer [ɑ̃klɔke] *vtr P* to get (s.o.) pregnant*/to put (s.o.) up the spout/*surt NAm* to knock (s.o.) up.

encoinsta [ɑ̃kwɛ̃sta] *nm,* **encoinsto** [ɑ̃kwɛ̃sto] *nm P* door wedge (*used by burglars to force a door*).

encordé [ɑ̃kɔrde] *nm F* Franciscan monk/ friar.

encorné [ɑ̃kɔrne] *nm F* deceived husband/ cuckold.

encorner [ɑ̃kɔrne] *vtr F* to deceive/to cuck-old (a husband).

encrister [ɑ̃kriste] *vtr P* = **enchrister.**

encroumé [ɑ̃krume] *a P* in debt.

s'encroumer [sɑ̃krume] *vpr P* to get into debt.

encroûtant [ɑ̃krutɑ̃] *a F* soul-destroying (occupation, etc).

encroûté [ɑ̃krute] *F* **I** *a* (stuck) in a rut/set in one's ways; **qu'est-ce que tu peux être encroûté!** what a stick-in-the mud you are! **vieux bonhomme encroûté,** old fogey/stick-in-the-mud **II** *nm* (**vieux, vieil**) **encroûté,** old fogey*/(old) stick-in-the-mud.

s'encroûter [sɑ̃krute] *vpr F* to get into a rut/to get stuck in one's ways/to stagnate/to become an old fogey*.

enculade [ɑ̃kylad] *nf V* = **enculage 1.**

enculage [ɑ̃kylaʒ] *nm* **1.** *V* anal sex*/bum-fuck **2.** *P* **enculage de mouches,** quibbling/ hair-splitting/nit-picking.

enculé [ɑ̃kyle] *nm V* **1.** homosexual*/homo/

fag(got)/queer 2. (*terme d'injure*) fool*/stupid bugger/silly sod/bloody fool/stupid bastard*/ silly fucker; **bande d'enculés!** (what a) load of cretins!/(what a) load of bloody idiots!

enculer [ãkyle] *vtr* 1. *V* (*a*) **enculer qn,** to have anal sex* with s.o./to sodomize* s.o./to bugger s.o./to screw s.o.'s arse/*NAm* ass; to butt-fuck (s.o.); **va te faire enculer!** bugger off!/sod off!/fuck off!/go fuck yourself! (*b*) *vi* to be a homosexual* 2. *P* **enculer les mouches,** to quibble/to split hairs/to nit-pick 3. *P* = **baiser 4.**

enculeur [ãkylœr] *nm* 1. *V* = **enculé** 2. *P* **enculeur de mouches,** quibbler/hair-splitter/ nit-picker.

endauffer [ãdofe] *vtr V* = **endoffer.**

endêvé [ãdɛve] *a Vieilli F* angry*/furious; provoked/aggravated.

endêver [ãdɛve] *vi F* **faire endêver qn,** to torment s.o./to drive s.o. wild/to get s.o.'s goat.

endoffer [ãdofe] *vtr V* to have anal sex* with (s.o.)/to screw (s.o.) from behind/to bugger (s.o.). (*Voir* **dauf(f)er**)

endormant [ãdɔrmã] *a F* dull/boring/ deadly.

endormeur, -euse [ãdɔrmœr, -øz] *n* 1. *F* crashing bore* 2. *F* cajoler/sweet-talker 3. *P* thief.

endormi [ãdɔrmi] *nm P* magistrate/judge/ beak.

endormir [ãdɔrmir] I *vtr* 1. *F* to bore* (s.o.) stiff 2. *F* to cajole/to sweet-talk (s.o.) 3. *F* (*boxe*) to knock out (an opponent) 4. *P* to kill* II *vpr* **s'endormir** *F* **s'endormir sur une affaire,** to let sth drag on/to sit on sth. (*Voir* **mastic 2; rôti I**)

endosses [ãdos] *nfpl P* 1. shoulders; back 2. **en avoir plein les endosses,** (*être fatigué*) to be exhausted*/to be dead beat; (*en avoir assez*) to be sick (and tired) of it/to have had a bellyful of it/to be browned off with it.

endroit [ãdrwa] *nm* 1. *F* **le petit endroit,** WC*/the loo/the smallest room/*NAm* the john 2. *P* **le bon endroit,** (the) buttocks*.

enfance [ãfãs] *nf F* **c'est l'enfance de l'art,** it's very easy*/it's child's play.

enfariné [ãfarine] *a F* **avoir la langue/la bouche/la gueule enfarinée/le bec enfariné,** to look all innocent.

enfer [ãfɛr] *nm F* 1. **c'est l'enfer,** it's intolerable/it's hell/it's the pits; **des gens comme lui, c'est l'enfer,** people like him are just hell 2. **il va à une vitesse d'enfer,** he goes

bloody fast; **c'était une soirée d'enfer,** it was a fantastic party/a hell of a party; **j'ai une idée/un plan d'enfer,** I've got a great idea. (*Voir* **look**)

enfifré [ãfifre] *nm P* homosexual*/poof/ fag(got)/queer.

enfifrer [ãfifre] *vtr P* to have anal sex* with (s.o.)/to bugger (s.o.).

enfilade [ãfilad] *nf F* run of bad luck.

enfilé [ãfile] *nm P* = **enfifré.**

enfiler [ãfile] I *vtr* 1. *F* to arrest* (a criminal) 2. *V* to have sex* with (s.o.); **enfiler une nana,** to lay/to screw/to make a girl; **va te faire enfiler!** get stuffed!/go screw yourself! (*Voir* **perle 3**) II *vpr* **s'enfiler** 1. *V* to have sex*/to make love; **s'enfiler une nana,** to screw/to bonk/to make a girl 2. *F* (*a*) to knock back/to down (a drink); **s'enfiler un bon dîner,** to have a slap-up meal (*b*) (*avoir à supporter*) to get stuck/landed with (a task); **s'enfiler une corvée,** to take on a rotten job.

enflaquer [ãflake] *vtr A P* 1. to arrest* 2. to put in prison* 3. to bore*.

enfle [ãfl] *a P* swollen; **mon doigt est enfle,** my finger's swollen.

enflé [ãfle] *nm F* fool*/clot/jerk; **espèce d'enflé!** you (blinking) idiot!/you dope!

enfler [ãfle] *vtr P* 1. to swindle*/to cheat (s.o.)/to double-cross (s.o.) 2. to get (s.o.) pregnant*/to put (s.o.) in the club/to knock (s.o.) up.

enflure [ãflyr] *nf F* = **enflé.**

enfoiré [ãfware] *V* I *nm* 1. homosexual*/ poof/*surt NAm* fag(got)/queer 2. (*imbécile*) **espèce d'enfoiré!** you stupid bugger!/you (stupid) prick!/you silly sod!/*surt NAm* you dumb shit! II *a* stupid*/dozy-arsed.

enfoirer [ãfware] *vtr V* to have anal sex* with (s.o.)/to screw (s.o.) from behind/to bugger (s.o.).

enfoncé [ãfõse] *a P* (*a*) beaten/licked (*b*) cheated/swindled/rooked.

enfoncer [ãfõse] I *vtr* 1. *F* to get the better of (s.o.)/to beat (s.o.) hollow/to lick (s.o.); **enfoncer qn dans les grandes largeurs,** to beat s.o. hollow/to hammer s.o. into the ground; **ça enfonce tout!** that beats everything!/that's got them all licked! 2. *P* (*a*) to accuse (s.o.)/to put the finger on (s.o.)/to blow the gaff on (s.o.) (*b*) to crush/to overwhelm (s.o.) 3. *F* **enfoncer une porte ouverte,** to come out with/ to state the obvious II *vpr* **s'enfoncer** 1. *P* **s'enfoncer dans sa merde,** to be going downhill/to be on a bummer 2. *F* **s'enfoncer**

qch dans le **crâne**, to beat sth into one's head/ to get sth into one's head.

enfonceur, -euse [ãfõscœr, -øz] *n F* c'est un enfonceur de porte(s) ouverte(s), he's got a gift for stating the obvious. (*Voir* **enfoncer 3**)

enfouiller [ãfuje] *vtr P* to pocket.

enfouraillé [ãfuraje] *a P* armed with/ carrying/packing a gun.

s'enfourailler [sãfuraje] *vpr P* to arm oneself with a gun/to pack a gun.

enfourner [ãfurne] I *vtr* 1. *F* enfourner une affaire, to start sth up/to get sth going/to get sth off the ground 2. *F* to gobble (sth) up; to shove (sth) down/to stuff (sth) into one's mouth, throat 3. *P* enfourner un enfant à une femme, to make a woman pregnant*/to put a bun in the oven/*surt NAm* to knock a woman up II *vpr* **s'enfourner** *F* 1. to get into a fix*/ to get mixed up in sth 2. s'enfourner dans une **impasse**, to go down a blind alley.

engailler [ãgaje] *vtr Vieilli P* to deceive/to take in/to con.

engeance [ãʒãs] *nf F* mob/crew; quelle engeance! what a collection (of yobs, etc)!/ what a crew! triste engeance! what a pathetic crew!

engelure [ãʒlyr] *nf P* (*personne*) (damned) nuisance/pain in the neck.

engerber [ãʒɛrbe] *vtr P* to arrest*.

engin [ãʒɛ̃] *nm V* penis*/tool.

englandé [ãglãde] *nm V* homosexual*/poof/ fag(got).

englander [ãglãde] *vtr* 1. *V* to have anal sex* with (s.o.)/to bugger (s.o.) 2. *P* to swindle*/to cheat/to diddle; se **faire** englander, to get rooked.

engliche[1] [ãgliʃ] *a P* English.

Engliche[2] *nm & f P* Englishman*/English-woman/Brit.

engourdir [ãgurdir] *vtr P* to steal*.

engrainer [ãgrɛne] *vtr P* to take on/to sign on (a worker).

engrais [ãgrɛ] *nm P* money*.

engraisser [ãgrɛse] *vtr P* engraisser qn, to support/keep s.o.; to give regular amounts of money to s.o.; c'est **elle** qui l'engraisse, (*prostituée et son souteneur*) she's his meal-ticket; se **faire** engraisser, to be kept.

engrosser [ãgrose] *vtr P* to get (s.o.) pregnant*/to get (s.o.) (into trouble)/*surt NAm* to knock (s.o.) up.

engrosseur [ãgroscœr] *nm P* man who gets women pregnant*/gets girls into trouble/

knocks girls up.

engueulade [ãgœlad] *nf P* (*a*) severe reprimand*/(good) telling-off/bawling out/ bollocking; prendre/recevoir une engueulade, to get a rocket/to get a real bollocking; envoyer une lettre d'engueulade à qn, to write s.o. a stinker/a stinking letter (*b*) slanging match; avoir une engueulade avec qn, to have a slanging match/a huge row with s.o. (*Voir* **maison 3**)

engueuler [ãgœle] I *vtr P* 1. to reprimand*/to bawl out; se **faire** engueuler, to get bawled out/to get a rocket/to get a (right) bollocking 2. to insult. (*Voir* **poisson 3**) II *vpr* **s'engueuler** *P* s'engueuler (ferme), to have a slanging match; s'engueuler avec qn, to have a (flaming) row with s.o.

enguirlander [ãgirlãde] *vtr F* to reprimand* (s.o.)/to tell (s.o.) off/to give (s.o.) a (good) dressing-down; se **faire** enguirlander, to get torn off a strip/to get a rocket.

énième [enjɛm] *a F* pour la énième fois, for the umpteenth time/for the nth time.

enjamber [ãʒãbe] *vtr V* enjamber une femme, to have sex* with a woman/to ride a woman; to get one's leg over.

enjambeur [ãʒãbœr] *nm V* womanizer*/ highly-sexed male/lecher.

enjuponné [ãʒypɔne] *a P* drunk*/pissed/ stewed.

enneigé [ãneʒe] *a P* high on cocaine*.

ennuyant [ãnɥijã] *a F* boring/deadly.

enquiller [ãkije] I *vtr & i P* to enter; se **faire** enquiller dans une affaire, to get involved in sth/dragged into sth II *vpr* **s'enquiller** *P* to enter/to get in.

enquilleuse [ãkijøz] *nf P* woman thief*/ shoplifter who hides stolen goods between her legs.

enquiquinant, -ante [ãkikinã, -ãt] *a F* infuriating/irritating; il est enquiquinant, he's a pain in the neck/he gets up my nose.

enquiquinement [ãkikinmã] *nm F* (*a*) bore*/(terrible) nuisance/pest (*b*) pestering; quel enquiquinement! what a flipping/flaming/ darned nuisance!

enquiquiner [ãkikine] I *vtr F* to bore*; to irritate/to annoy*/to aggravate/to pester/to bug; je suis bien enquiquiné, I've got problems II *vpr* **s'enquiquiner** *F* s'enquiquiner (de qn/qch), to be/to get bored (with s.o/sth)/fed up/tired (of s.o./sth).

enquiquineur, -euse [ãkikinœr, -øz] *F* I

a infuriating/irritating **II** *n* (*personne*) (terrible) nuisance/pain in the neck.

enragé, -ée [ɑ̃raʒe] *F* **I** *a* (*a*) vie enragée, wild/energetic life (*b*) enthusiastic (sportsman, etc); joueur enragé, inveterate gambler/fanatic; un facho enragé, an out-and-out fascist **II** *n* un(e) enragé(e) du football, a football fanatic/a football nut; (*politique*) les enragés, the extremists. (*Voir* vache **II** 4)

enrouler [ɑ̃rule] *vi F* (*cyclisme*) to pedal in an easy, relaxed manner.

s'enroupiller [sɑ̃rupije] *vpr P* to fall asleep/to flake out.

enseigne [ɑ̃sɛɲ] *nf F* nous sommes tous logés à la même enseigne, we're all in the same boat.

ensoutané [ɑ̃sutane] *a & nm F* (priest) in a cassock.

ensuqué [ɑ̃syke] *a Vieilli P* 1. exhausted*/tired out/weary 2. dazed/stupefied; (*drogué*) bombed (out).

entamer [ɑ̃tame] *vtr F* entamer son capital, to lose one's virginity*.

entasseur, -euse [ɑ̃tɑsœr, -øz] *n F* miser*; hoarder.

entendu [ɑ̃tɑ̃dy] *a F* comme de (juste et de) bien entendu, naturally/of course; that goes without saying.

enterrement [ɑ̃tɛrmɑ̃] *nm F* 1. avoir une tête/une gueule d'enterrement, to have a face as long as a fiddle; to look really down/gloomy; ne fais pas cette tête d'enterrement! don't look so miserable!/don't be such a misery! 2. c'est un enterrement de première classe, that (thing) has been shelved for good; c'est l'enterrement de tous mes projets, that's killed off all my plans.

enterrer [ɑ̃tere] *vtr F* 1. enterrer sa vie de garçon, to have a stag party/a stag night 2. il nous enterrera tous, he'll outlive the lot of us.

entifler [ɑ̃tifle] *P* **I** *vi* to enter/to breeze in; to barge in **II** *vtr* 1. entifler qn, to marry s.o. 2. to deceive*/to take (s.o.) in 3. to take/to go down (a road) **III** *vpr* s'entifler *P* 1. = entifler **I** 2. *Vieilli* to get married*.

entoiler [ɑ̃twale] *vtr P* to arrest*; se faire entoiler, to get nicked/run in.

entôlage [ɑ̃tolaʒ] *nm P* (*surt en parlant d'une prostituée*) stealing from/robbing/fleecing (a customer).

entôler [ɑ̃tole] *vtr P* (*surt en parlant d'une prostituée*) to rob/to steal (from)/to swindle*/to diddle; entôler un clille, to fleece*/to pull a fast one on one's customer.

entôleuse [ɑ̃toløz] *nf P* prostitute* who robs/fleeces/swindles a customer.

entonner [ɑ̃tɔne] *F* (*rare*) **I** *vtr* to knock back (a drink) **II** *vi* to booze/to tipple/to drink* like a fish.

entonnoir [ɑ̃tɔnwar] *nm P* 1. mouth*/gob 2. entonnoir à musique, ear* 3. hard drinker/drunkard*/boozer.

entortiller [ɑ̃tɔrtije] *vtr F* entortiller qn, to wheedle s.o./to cajole s.o./to get round s.o.; elle sait l'entortiller, she can twist him round her little finger.

entortilleur, -euse [ɑ̃tɔrtijœr, -øz] *n F* wheedler/cajoler/sweet-talker.

entourloupe [ɑ̃turlup] *nf F* = entourloupette.

entourlouper [ɑ̃turlupe] *vtr F* entourlouper qn, to play a mean/rotten/dirty trick on s.o.; to swindle* s.o.

entourloupette [ɑ̃turlupɛt] *nf F* mean/rotten/dirty trick. (*Voir* maison **3**)

entournures [ɑ̃turnyr] *nfpl F* être serré/gêné aux entournures, (*mal à l'aise*) to be awkward/ill at ease; (*financièrement*) to feel the pinch.

entraîneur [ɑ̃trɛnœr] *nm F* decoy.

entraîneuse [ɑ̃trɛnøz] *nf F* hostess/bar-girl.

entraver [ɑ̃trave] *vtr P* to understand/to twig; je n'entrave/je n'y entrave que couic/que dalle/que pouic, I don't get it; I can't make head or tail of it; I haven't the foggiest/the faintest.

s'entre-cogner [sɑ̃trəkɔɲe] *vpr F* to have a fight/a punch-up.

entrée [ɑ̃tre] *nf* 1. *F adv phr* d'entrée, from the outset/from the very beginning/from the word go 2. *V* entrée des artistes, anus*/back door. (*Voir* service **4**)

entrejambes [ɑ̃trəʒɑ̃b] *nm P* en avoir dans l'entrejambes, to be well hung/to have a nice bulge.

entremichon [ɑ̃trəmiʃɔ̃] *nm P* the cleft separating the two buttocks.

entrêper [ɑ̃trɛpe], **entréper** [ɑ̃trepe] *vtr P* (*camelot, etc*) to attract/to pull in (a crowd).

entreprendre [ɑ̃trəprɑ̃dr] *vtr F* to try to convince/persuade (s.o.).

entripaillé [ɑ̃tripaje] *a F* fat.

entrouducuter [ɑ̃trudykyte] *vtr V* to have anal sex* with (s.o.)/to bugger (s.o.)/to fuck (s.o.'s) ass.

entubage [ãtybaʒ] *nm* P swindling/doing/conning; swindle/con.

entuber [ãtybe] *vtr* 1. P to swindle*/to do/to con; to dupe/to have on; se faire entuber, to be taken for a ride/to be had/to get ripped off 2. V to have anal sex* with (s.o.)/to sodomize* (s.o.)/to bugger (s.o.).

entubeur [ãtybœr] *nm* P swindler*/crook/con artist.

envapé [ãvape] *a* P under the influence of drugs; doped (up)/charged (up).

enveloppe [ãvlɔp] *nf* F bribe*; passer une enveloppe à qn, to bribe s.o./to grease s.o.'s palm; marcher à l'enveloppe, to take a bribe/to go on the take.

envelopper [ãvlɔpe] *vtr* P 1. to dupe/to hoax* (s.o.); se faire envelopper, to be taken in/to be taken for a ride/to be conned 2. to arrest*; se faire envelopper, to get nicked 3. to steal*/to pinch.

envers [ãver] *adv phr* P les avoir à l'envers, to be lazy*/to sit about doing nothing.

enviandé [ãvjãde] *nm* V = **enculé**.

enviander [ãvjãde] *vtr* V to have anal sex* with (s.o.)/to bugger (s.o.).

envie [ãvi] *nf* F (*surt langage enfantin*) avoir envie, to want to (do) wee-wee/to want a wee.

envoyer [ãvwaje] I *vtr* 1. P les envoyer/envoyer la monnaie, to pay up*/to cough up/to shell out. (*Voir* **soudure 2**) 2. P en envoyer une, to take one's turn to tell a story, etc 3. P (*a*) envoyer qn en l'air, (*tuer*) to kill* s.o./*surt NAm* to blow s.o. away; (*faire tomber*) to send s.o. flying; to floor s.o. (*b*) ça, c'est envoyé! well said! that's got him!/that's stumped him!/that's floored him! (*Voir* **bain 2**; **balader I**; **bouler 1**; **chier 5**; **dinguer**; **dire 5**; **foutre I 7** (*a*), (*b*); **fraise 5**; **fumée 2**; **paître**; **(se) promener**; **rose II 2**) II *vpr* **s'envoyer** 1. P to wolf down/to scoff/to guzzle (food); to knock back (a drink); s'envoyer un verre (de vin) (derrière la cravate), to knock back a drink/a glass of wine 2. P s'envoyer la vaisselle, to tackle the washing-up; to get landed/stuck with the washing-up; s'envoyer tout le boulot, to get on with/to get landed with the whole job 3. V (*a*) s'envoyer qn, to have sex* with s.o.; s'envoyer une nana, to have it off with/to have it away with/to lay/to screw a girl/a bird/a chick (*b*) s'envoyer en l'air, (*faire l'amour*) to have sex*/to have it off/to have it away; (*jouir*) to have an orgasm*/to come; (*se droguer, s'enivrer*) to get high (on drugs,

drink, etc); (*se suicider*) to commit suicide*/to do oneself in.

épahules [epayl] *nfpl* P shoulders; rouler des épahules, to swagger/to throw one's weight around.

épais [epɛ] *a* P 1. ça fait pas épais! that's not much/a lot! 2. *Vieilli* j'en ai épais (sur le cœur), I regret it terribly.

épaisseur [epesœr] *nf* F se tirer d'épaisseur, to manage to get out of a scrape.

éparpiller [eparpije] *vi* P en éparpiller de première, to sleep like a log.

épatamment [epatamã] *adv* F splendidly/wonderfully/admirably.

épatant [epatã] *a* F 1. excellent*/first-rate/splendid/wonderful; c'est un type épatant, he's a great guy; ce n'est pas bien épatant, it's nothing to write home about 2. *int* épatant! (that's) fine/great!

épate [epat] *nf* F swank/swagger; faire de l'épate, (*prendre de grands airs*) to show off*/to swank/to put on airs; (*étonner*) to create a sensation/to make a splash; on l'a fait à l'épate, it was done to make an impression; un faiseur d'épate, a show-off.

épaté [epate] *a* F amazed*/flabbergasted/dumbfounded.

épatement [epatmã] *nm* F astonishment/amazement.

épater [epate] *vtr* F to amaze*/to flabbergast; rien ne l'épate/il ne se laisse pas épater, he isn't easily flummoxed; épater la galerie, to impress (the) onlookers/to show off*/to play for the gallery.

épaule [epol] *nf* F 1. donner un coup d'épaule à qn, to help s.o. (out)/to give s.o. a helping hand/to give s.o. a push in the right direction 2. faire qch par-dessus l'épaule, to do sth in a perfunctory manner 3. regarder qn par-dessus l'épaule, to look down one's nose at s.o. 4. rouler les épaules, to swagger.

épauler [epole] *vtr* F épauler qn, to help s.o. (out)/to give s.o. a helping hand/to give s.o. a leg-up; to back s.o. up.

épée [epe] *nf* F 1. expert/ace 2. coup d'épée dans l'eau, wasted/fruitless effort; c'est un coup d'épée dans l'eau, it's come to nothing.

épicemar(d) [epismar] *nm* P grocer.

épicerie [episri] *nf* F changer d'épicerie, to make a change (of surroundings, etc)/to move on/to get a change of air. (*Voir* **crémerie** (*a*))

épicier [episje] *nm* 1. F *Péj* c'est un épicier, (*il n'aime que l'argent*) he's a money-grubber

2. *V* baiser qn en épicier, to make love to s.o. without enjoyment/mechanically.

épinards [epinar] *nmpl P* 1. aller aux épinards, to be kept by a prostitute*; (*ouvrier*) to earn one's living/one's bread 2. plat d'épinards, (*mauvais tableau*) bad landscape painting; (*bouse de vache*) (fresh) cowpat. (*Voir* **beurre 5**; **graine 4**)

épingle [epɛ̃gl] *nf* 1. *F* tiré à quatre épingles, in one's Sunday best/dressed up* to the nines 2. *F* tirer son épingle du jeu, to get out of a tough situation unharmed/to get out while there's still time 3. *F* monter qch en épingle, (*exagérer*) to make too much of sth 4. *Vieilli V* ramasser des épingles, to have anal sex*. (*Voir* **pelote 7**)

épingler [epɛ̃gle] *vtr F* 1. épingler qn, to arrest* s.o.; se faire épingler, to get nicked/nabbed 2. to catch (s.o.) out.

éplucheur, -euse [eplyʃœr, -øz] *n* 1. *F* fault-finder 2. *P* éplucheuse de lentilles, lesbian*.

épluchures [eplyʃyr] *nfpl F* attention aux épluchures! watch your step!/mind how you go!

époilant [epwalɑ̃] *a F* surprising/astonishing.

éponge [epɔ̃ʒ] *nf* 1. *P* lung; avoir les éponges mitées/bouffées aux mites, to have tuberculosis/TB 2. *F* passons l'éponge (là-dessus), let's say no more about it; let bygones be bygones 3. *F* drunk(ard)*/soak 4. *P* nymphomaniac/nympho.

éponger [epɔ̃ʒe] *vtr* 1. *F* éponger un retard, to make up for lost time 2. *P* éponger qn, to clean s.o. out (at gambling, etc)/to take s.o. to the cleaners 3. *P* to suffer/to put up with (a jibe, a snide remark, etc) 4. *V* (*prostituée*) to give sexual satisfaction to (a client).

époques [epɔk] *nfpl F* avoir ses époques, to have a period*/to have the curse; elle a ses époques, it's her time of the month.

époustouflant [epustuflɑ̃] *a F* amazing/staggering/stunning/terrific.

époustoufler [epustufle] *vtr F* to amaze*/to astound/to flabbergast.

épouvantail [epuvɑ̃taj] *nm F* 1. bogey/bugbear/bugaboo 2. quel épouvantail! what a fright!/what a mess!

équerre [ekɛr] *nf F* d'équerre, (*honnête*) honest/straight; (*soûl*) drunk*/half-seas-over; (*drogué*) high/charged.

éreintage [erɛ̃taʒ] *nm F* = **éreintement 2**.

éreintant [erɛ̃tɑ̃] *a F* exhausting/back-breaking/gruelling/killing (work, etc); c'est éreintant! it really takes it out of you!

éreinté [erɛ̃te] *a F* exhausted*/fagged (out)/bushed/whacked/shattered.

éreintement [erɛ̃tmɑ̃] *nm F* 1. exhaustion 2. (*critique*) savage attack/slating/panning; éreintement avec des fleurs, damning with faint praise.

éreinter [erɛ̃te] I *vtr F* 1. to exhaust*/to tire (s.o.) out/to shatter (s.o.) 2. to criticize* (author, s.o.'s character, etc) unmercifully; to slate/to pan/to roast/to pull to pieces (author, book, performance, etc) II *vpr* s'**éreinter** *F* 1. to exhaust* oneself/to tire oneself out 2. s'éreinter à qch, to slave away/to slog away at sth.

ergotage [ɛrgɔtaʒ] *nm F* quibbling/hair-splitting/nit-picking.

ergoter [ɛrgɔte] *vi F* to quibble/to split hairs; tu ne vas pas ergoter pour si peu, don't be so finicky/choosy/picky.

ergots [ɛrgo] *nmpl F* monter/se dresser sur ses ergots, (*se montrer menaçant*) to show one's teeth.

erreur [ɛrœr] *nf P* 1. (y a) pas d'erreur! that's right!/you're (so) right!/and no mistake!/no doubt (about it)! 2. erreur d'aiguillage, misfiling (of document, etc); misdirecting (of visitor, etc).

s'esbigner [sɛzbiɲe] *vpr P* to clear off/to scarper/to do a bunk.

esbrouf(f)ant [ɛzbrufɑ̃] *a F* amazing/astounding/staggering/unheard-of.

esbrouf(f)e [ɛzbruf] *nf F* (a) showing off; faire de l'esbrouf(f)e, (*épate*) to show off*/to put on airs; (*bluff*) to bluff; to shoot a line (b) vol à l'esbrouf(f)e, pocket-picking by hustling one's victim.

esbrouf(f)er [ɛzbrufe] *vtr & i F* (a) = faire de l'esbrouf(f)e (**esbrouf(f)e** (a)) (b) esbrouf(f)er qn, to impress s.o./to take s.o. in/to bluff s.o. (by putting on airs, by blustering).

esbrouf(f)eur, -euse [ɛzbrufœr, -øz] *F* I *a* (a) swanky/swanking (b) hectoring/hustling II *n* (a) swank/show-off* (b) hustler (c) bluffer (d) *Vieilli* pickpocket* who hustles his/her victim; snatch-and-grab thief.

escagassant [ɛskagasɑ̃] *a P* (*régional*) annoying/irritating.

escagasser [ɛskagase] *vtr P* (*régional*) 1. to damage/to spoil (sth) 2. to beat (s.o.) up*/to do (s.o.) over 3. escagasser qn, to annoy*/to plague s.o.; to get up s.o.'s nose.

escaladeuse [ɛskaladøz] *nf* P escaladeuse de braguette, prostitute*/tart; (*femme portée sur les plaisirs sexuels*) sex-mad woman/hot piece.

escalope [ɛskalɔp] *nf* P 1. rouler une escalope à qn, to give s.o. a French kiss 2. *pl* escalopes, ears* 3. *pl* feet*.

escampette [ɛskãpɛt] *nf* F prendre la poudre d'escampette, to run away*/to do a bunk/ to take to one's heels.

escargot [ɛskargo] *nm* P (*rare*) telephone*.

escoffier [ɛskɔfje] *vtr* A P to kill*/to bump off.

s'escrimer [sɛskrime] *vpr* F s'escrimer à faire qch, to wear oneself out/to knock oneself out doing sth; to bite off more than one can chew.

esgourde [ɛsgurd] *nf* P ear*; écarquillez vos esgourdes! pin back your lugholes!

esgourder [ɛsgurde] *vtr* P (*entendre*) to hear; (*écouter*) to listen to.

espadoches [ɛspadɔʃ] *nfpl*, **espagas** [ɛspaga] *nmpl* P (= *espadrilles*) rope-soled sandals/espadrilles.

espèce [ɛspɛs] *nf* (*Péj: pour renforcer une injure*) espèce de ...: F cet/cette espèce d'idiot, that silly fool*/that stupid idiot; P espèce de crétin!/espèce d'imbécile!/espèce d'andouille!/espèce de con! you bloody fool! espèce de salaud! you bloody swine!/you bastard!

espérer [ɛspere] *vi* F espérer après qn, to wait for s.o.

espingo [ɛspɛ̃go], **espingouin** [ɛspɛ̃gwɛ̃] P I *a* Spanish II *nm* (*a*) Spanish (language) (*b*) Spaniard*/dago/wop.

esquimau, *pl* **-aux** [ɛskimo] *nm* F chocice.

esquintant [ɛskɛ̃tã] *a* F exhausting/backbreaking (work, etc).

esquinté [ɛskɛ̃te] *a* F 1. exhausted*/all in/ shattered/dead beat 2. (*santé, etc*) ruined.

esquintement [ɛskɛ̃tmã] *nm* F 1. exhaustion 2. thrashing/beating/good hiding.

esquinter [ɛskɛ̃te] I *vtr* F 1. to exhaust* (s.o.)/to tire (s.o.) out/to wear (s.o.) out/to knock (s.o.) up 2. (*a*) to kill* (s.o.)/to do (s.o.) in (*b*) to smash up (sth); to spoil/to damage; s'esquinter les yeux, to ruin one's eyes; s'esquinter la santé, to do in one's health; esquinter une voiture, to flog a car (to death)/ to run a car into the ground; to smash up/to wreck a car. (*Voir* **tempérament 3**) II *vpr* s'esquinter F 1. to tire/to wear oneself out

(à faire qch, doing sth) 2. to get spoilt/ damaged; votre voiture s'esquinte en plein air, your car's getting ruined standing in the open.

essence [esãs] *nf* P essence de panards, sweat on feet.

essorer [esɔre] *vtr* P 1. essorer qn, to clean s.o. out (of money)/to squeeze s.o. dry 2. (*prostituée*) to give sexual satisfaction (to a client).

essoreuse [esɔrøz] *nf* P 1. prostitute* 2. noisy motorbike.

estaf(f)ier [ɛstafje] *nm* P pimp*/ponce.

estampage [ɛstãpaʒ] *nm* F (*a*) swindling/ fleecing (*b*) swindle/con.

estampe [ɛstãp] *nf* 1. P = **estampage** 2. F *Euph Hum* venez voir mes estampes japonaises, come up and see my etchings!

estamper [ɛstãpe] *vtr* F estamper qn, to swindle* s.o./to fleece s.o./to diddle s.o./to do s.o.; se faire estamper, to be done/rooked/ ripped off.

estampeur, -euse [ɛstãpœr, -øz] *n* F swindler*/fleecer/shark; small-time crook.

estanco [ɛstãko] *nm* P 1. shop 2. (*café*) = pub/bar.

estogom [ɛstɔgɔm], **estom'** [ɛstɔm] *nm* P 1. stomach* 2. le faire à l'estom', to put it over on s.o./to pull a fast one on s.o.; faire qch à l'estom', to show a lot of guts 3. avoir de l'estom'/avoir bon estom', (*courage*) to be brave*/to have guts; (*toupet*) to have plenty of cheek/a lot of nerve.

estomac [ɛstɔma] *nm* 1. F avoir l'estomac dans les talons, (*avoir faim*) to be famished/ ravenous; (*avoir peur*) to be afraid*/to be in a blue funk 2. F avoir de l'estomac, (*courage*) to have guts; (*toupet*) to have plenty of cheek/a lot of nerve 3. F le faire à l'estomac à qn, to pull a fast one on s.o. 4. P avoir l'estomac bien accroché, to have a strong stomach.

estomaquer [ɛstɔmake] *vtr* F estomaquer qn, to amaze*/to flabbergast/to dumbfound s.o.; ça m'a estomaqué(e), it took my breath away/I was really staggered/I was gobsmacked.

estome [ɛstɔm] *nm* P = **estogom, estom'**.

estourbir [ɛsturbir] *vtr* P to kill* (s.o.)/to bump (s.o.) off.

établi [etabli] *nm* 1. F office/place of work; aller à l'établi, to go to work 2. P (*prostituées*) bed 3. gaming table.

étagère [etaʒɛr] *nf P* **1.** étagère à mégot, ear* **2.** prostitute* who solicits from her window.

étalage [etalaʒ] *nm P* faire l'étalage, (*prostituée*) to display oneself and let the client make his choice.

étaler [etale] **I** *vi F* (en) étaler, to show off*/ to swank/to put on airs **II** *vpr* **s'étaler** *F* **1.** to go sprawling/to come a cropper* **2.** to show off*/to swank/to put on airs **3.** to confess*.

état [eta] *nm F* (*a*) *Iron* être dans un bel état, to be in a nice mess (*b*) être dans tous ses états, to be in a terrible state*/all worked up; se mettre dans tous ses états, to get all steamed up/het up.

état-major [etamaʒɔr] *nm F* (*boisson*) wine and lemon.

étau [eto] *nm V* female genitals*/snatch; mettre la tête à l'étau/faire une descente à l'étau, to practise cunnilingus*.

éteignoir [etɛɲwar] *nm* **1.** *F* (*personne*) killjoy/wet blanket **2.** *P* big nose* **3.** *P* top hat **4.** *P* c'est un vrai éteignoir de concupiscence, she's as ugly as sin; she's a cock-freezer/a passion-killer.

étendre [etɑ̃dr] *vtr* **1.** *F* étendre qn à un examen, to fail/to plough/to flunk s.o. in an exam; se faire étendre à un examen, to fail/to flunk an exam; se faire étendre, (*au jeu*) to lose **2.** *P* to kill*; se faire étendre, to get killed/to be done in.

s'éterniser [setɛrnize] *vpr F* **1.** s'éterniser chez qn, to outstay one's welcome **2.** pas la peine d'éterniser là-dessus, no point in crying over spilt milk.

éternuer [etɛrnɥe] *vi A P* éternuer dans le sac/dans le son, to be guillotined.

Étienne [etjɛn] *Prnm F* à la tienne, Étienne! cheers!*/good health!

étincelles [etɛ̃sɛl] *nfpl F* faire des étincelles, (*être brillant*) to sparkle with wit; ça va faire des étincelles, there'll be fireworks/trouble; it's bad news.

étiquette [etikɛt] *nf P* ear*.

étoffe [etɔf] *nf F* avoir de l'étoffe, to have what it takes.

étoile [etwal] *nf* **1.** *P* étoile filante, part-time prostitute* **2.** *pl F* voir les étoiles en plein midi, to see stars (as the result of a blow, etc).

étonner [etɔne] *vtr F Iron* tu m'étonnes! you don't say! as if I didn't know!

étouffage [etufaʒ] *nm P* stealing/pinching/ nicking.

étouffer [etufe] **I** *vtr* **1.** *F* ce n'est pas l'intelligence qui l'étouffe, he's not over-burdened with brains; ce n'est pas la modestie qui t'étouffe, modesty isn't exactly your strong point **2.** *F* étouffer le coup, to let bygones be bygones/to say no more about it/to forget old scores **3.** *F* étouffer qch dans l'œuf, to nip sth in the bud **4.** *F* en étouffer un, to knock back a drink **5.** *F* (*courses*) étouffer un cheval, to pull a horse **6.** *P* to steal*/to pinch/ to nick **II** *vi P* to drink* during office hours.

étourdir [eturdir] *vtr P* to steal*.

étrangler [etrɑ̃gle] *vtr P* en étrangler six, to knock back six drinks one after the other. (*Voir* **pierrot 3**)

étrangleuse [etrɑ̃gløz] *nf P* (neck)tie.

être [ɛtr] *vi F* **1.** en être (comme un phoque), to be a homosexual*/to be one of them; être pour hommes/être pour femmes, to be a homosexual*/a lesbian*; to be gay **2.** en être, to belong to the police* **3.** l'être, to be a cuck-old **4.** y être, to understand; tu y es? d'you get me?/are you with me? j'y suis, I get the picture.

étrenne [etrɛn] *nf F* (*a*) avoir l'étrenne de qch, to be the first to use sth (*b*) n'en avoir pas l'étrenne, to get sth second-hand; to get s.o.'s cast-offs.

étrenner [etrene] *vi F* **1.** tu vas étrenner! you'll catch it!/you'll get it (in the neck)! **2.** (*brocante, etc*) to make the first sale of the day.

étrillage [etrijaʒ] *nm F* overcharging/ fleecing.

étriller [etrije] *vtr F* **1.** to overcharge/to fleece* (s.o.); to rip (s.o.) off; on s'est fait étriller à cet hôtel, we got well and truly stung at that hotel **2.** étriller qn aux échecs, to wipe the floor with s.o. at chess **3.** se faire étriller, to get beaten up*/thrashed.

étripage [etripaʒ] *nm F* (*adversaires, etc*) slaughter/tearing each other's guts out.

s'étriper [setripe] *vpr F* (*adversaires, etc*) to slaughter one another/to tear each other's guts out.

étron [etrɔ̃] *nm P* (*excrément*) turd; **poser un étron**, to defecate*/to have a crap.

étuve [etyv] *nf F* sweltering (hot) room; quelle étuve! it's like an oven in here!

eulpif [ølpif] *a Vieilli P* smart/stylish/natty.

eustache [østaʃ] *nm F* (clasp) knife/pig-sticker.

euzigs, euzigues [øzig] *pron P* them/ themselves.

évaporé, -ée [evapɔre] *F* **I** *a* (*personne*) featherbrained/irresponsible/flighty/giddy; **une blonde évaporée**, a dumb blonde **II** *n* **c'est une petite évaporée**, she's a featherbrain/a scatter-brain.

s'évaporer [sevapɔre] *vpr F* to vanish (into thin air)/to make oneself scarce.

Ève [ɛv] *Prnf F* **1. je ne le connais ni d'Ève ni d'Adam**, I don't know him from Adam **2. dans le/en costume d'Ève**, (*femme*) naked*/in the altogether/in one's birthday suit. (*Voir* **Adam**)

évident [evidɑ̃] *a F* **c'est pas évident**, it's not easy; (*certain*) it's not certain.

exam [egzam] *nm F* (= *examen*) exam.

excuser [ɛkskyze] *vtr F Iron* **excusez-moi/je m'excuse de vous demander pardon**, oh, I *do* beg your pardon!/I'm *frightfully* sorry!

s'exécuter [segzekyte] *vpr F* **1.** to pay* up **2.** to toe the line.

exhibo [egzibo] *nm F* (= *exhibitionniste*) dirty old man/flasher.

exister [egziste] *vi F* **ça n'existe pas!** that's stupid!/that's absolute tripe!; I don't believe it!

exo [egzo] *F* **I** *nm* (*écoles*) (= *exercice*) exercise **II** *nf* (*exonérée*) theatre ticket free of entertainment tax.

expédier [ɛkspedje] *vtr F* **1.** to kill*/to do (s.o.) in/to bump (s.o.) off **2.** to ruin/to do for (s.o.) **3.** (*a*) **je l'ai expédié**, I got rid of him (*b*) to polish (sth) off; **s'expédier un verre**, to knock back a drink **4. c'est de l'expédié**, that was a quickie/a quick one!

expliquance [ɛksplikɑ̃s] *nf P* explanation.

expliquer [ɛksplike] **I** *vtr F* **je t'explique pas!** I'll leave it to your imagination! you can imagine (it)! **II** *vpr* **s'expliquer** *vpr* **1.** *F* **s'expliquer avec qn**, to have it out (man to man) with s.o.; **nous allons nous expliquer**, we'll sort this out together/we'll fight it out **2.** *P* (*argot du* **milieu**) to turn to pros-titution/to become a prostitute*/to go on the game.

exploser [ɛksploze] *vi P* to have an orgasm*/to go off.

expo [ɛkspo] *F* **I** *nm* (= *exposé*) (*au lycée*) **faire un expo**, to give a talk (**sur**, on) **II** *nf* (= *exposition*) exhibition/show.

s'exterminer [sɛkstɛrmine] *vpr F* to work* one's guts out/to flog oneself to death (**à faire qch**, doing sth).

extra [ɛkstra] *F* **I** *a* excellent*/out of this world/something else/fantastic/terrific/great; **c'est extra!** that's great!/far out! **II** *nm* **c'est de l'extra**, it's extra-special; **s'offrir un petit extra**, to give oneself a small treat.

F

fabriquer [fabrike] *vtr* 1. *F* to do/to be up to/to cook up; qu'est-ce que tu fabriques? what(ever)/what on earth are you up to? qu'est-ce que tu as fabriqué avec mes clopes? what on earth/what the hell have you done with my fags? qu'est-ce qu'il peut bien fabriquer, maintenant? what the heck is he up to now?/what's his game, this time? 2. *P* fabriquer qch, to steal*/to pinch/to nick sth; je me suis fait fabriquer mon portefeuille, my wallet got nicked 3. *P* to swindle*/to cheat/to diddle/to con; je me suis fait fabriquer, I've been done/had/taken for a ride 4. *P* to arrest*; être fabriqué/se faire fabriquer, to get arrested/nicked; il s'est fait fabriquer pour excès de vitesse, he got done/he was busted for speeding; he got a speeding fine. (*Voir* **tas 2**)

fabuler [fabyle] *vi F* to lie/to tell fibs.

Fac, fac [fak] *nf F* (= *la Faculté*) la Fac, (the) University; quand j'étais à la fac/en fac, when I was at university/at uni/at college/*surt NAm* in school.

façade [fasad] *nf F* face; se faire démolir la façade, to get one's face smashed up; se ravaler la façade/ravaler sa façade, to put on make-up/to make oneself up; (*chirurgie esthétique*) to have plastic surgery done on one's face/to have a face-lift.

face [fas] *nf P* (*insulte*) face de crabe/de rat/d'œuf, etc, rat-face/ugly mug.

facho [faʃo] *a & n P* fascist; right-wing(er)/reactionary.

facile [fasil] *adv F* easily; il y en aura dix facile, there will be at least ten.

factionnaire [faksjɔnɛr] *nm P* relever un factionnaire, to have a drink (at the bar). (*Voir* **sentinelle 1**)

fada [fada] *F* (*surt Dial du midi*) I *a* stupid*/screwy/crazy II *nm* fool*/nutter/crackpot.

fadasse [fadas] *a F Péj* dull/insipid; cette couleur est un peu fadasse, this colour is a bit wishy-washy.

fade [fad] *nm* 1. *P* share (of loot, etc)/cut/whack/split; avoir/toucher son fade, to get one's share/cut; y aller de son fade/payer son fade, to pay one's whack/to chip in with one's share 2. *P* avoir son fade, (*avoir son compte*) to have one's fair share (of illness, beating up, bad luck, etc); (*après avoir trop bu*) to be drunk* 3. *V* prendre son fade, to have an orgasm*/to come.

fadé [fade] *a P* 1. (*facture, etc*) excessive/steep/stiff; c'est fadé, it beats them all/it takes the biscuit 2. être fadé (*a*) to have had (more than) one's fair share (of illness, bad luck, etc); avec trois rhumes, déjà, je suis drôlement fadé, *Iron* what with three colds already, my luck's really in/s.o.'s got it in for me (*b*) to be drunk*/tight/pissed (*c*) to be ill; *surt* to have VD*/to have the clap/to have copped a dose (*d*) il est fadé dans son genre, he's a prize specimen.

fader [fade] *P* I *vtr* 1. to give (s.o.) his share/whack/cut (of the loot, etc); avec ça je ne serai pas fadé, that's not a fair whack/*Iron* whatever will I do with all that! 2. to sentence; le juge l'a fadé, the judge gave him a heavy (prison) sentence/threw the book at him 3. to ruin/to spoil/to make a mess of 4. se faire fader, to get VD*/to get the clap/to cop a dose II *vi* 1. to succeed 2. to pay one's share/one's whack 3. to have an orgasm*/to come III *vpr* **se fader** 1. to share out 2. to help oneself to (sth) 3. to put up with (s.o., sth); to get landed with (an unpleasant task).

faf¹ [faf] *a & n F* fascist; right-wing(er)/reactionary.

faf², faffe [faf] *nm P* 1. *pl* identity papers; maquiller les faffes, to fake/to forge identity papers; taper aux faffes, to check s.o.'s (identity) papers 2. piece of paper 3. banknote/flimsy.

fafiot [fafjo] *nm Vieilli P* 1. banknote/flimsy. 2. (piece of) paper 3. *pl* identity papers.

faflard [faflar] *nm P* passport.

465

fagot [fago] *nm* 1. *F* une bouteille de vin de derrière les fagots, a bottle of wine reserved for a special occasion; un repas de derrière les fagots, an extra-special meal 2. *F* un fagot d'épines, a surly individual/a crosspatch 3. *P* ex-convict/ex-con 4. *F pl* les fagots, the wood-wind (instruments).

fagotage [fagɔtaʒ] *nm F* ridiculous way of dressing/get-up/rig-out.

fagoté [fagɔte] *a F* (mal) fagoté, badly dressed/dowdy/frumpish; femme mal fagotée, frump/scarecrow.

fagoter [fagɔte] I *vtr F* to dress (s.o.) like a scarecrow/badly; to rig/deck out (s.o.) II *vpr* **se fagoter** *F* to dress badly/like a scare-crow; to rig/deck oneself out; comme les jeunes se fagotent de nos jours! what dread-ful clothes young people wear these days!

faiblard [fɛblar] *a F* (a bit) weak/weakish; ce vin est un peu faiblard, this wine tastes like it's been watered down.

faible [fɛbl] *a P* 1. tomber faible, to faint/to pass out 2. tomber faible sur qch, to steal* sth/to knock sth off.

faim [fɛ̃] *nf F* 1. j'ai une de ces faims!/je crève de faim! I'm starving!/I'm ravenous! 2. il fait faim, I feel peckish/I'm getting hungry 3. il s'est jeté dessus comme la faim sur le monde, he threw himself into it unhesitatingly/like nothing on earth/like a man possessed.

fainéasse [fɛneas] *a & n P* = **feignant, -ante**.

faire [fɛr] I *vtr & i* 1. *F* se laisser faire, to be/to get taken in; on ne me la fait pas! you can't fool me! faut pas me la faire! don't try it on with me! on t'a fait, you've been had/ you've been done; someone's pulled a fast one over on you; tu es fait, mon vieux! you've had it, mate! (*Voir* **marron** II **3**) 2. *F* ça fait chic/riche, it looks smart/posh 3. *F* la faire (à qn) à la vertu/à l'innocence, to put on a virtuous/an innocent act (for s.o.'s benefit). (*Voir* **oseille 2**) 4. *F* (*a*) to charge; combien ça fait le demi? how much is a half (of beer)? (*b*) to be worth; une bagnole qui fait six mille francs, a car that is worth six thousand francs 5. *F* savoir y faire, to know the score/to be with it/to get by 6. *F* faire troisième/ quatrième, to come third/fourth 7. *F* faire avocat, to study law 8. *F* (*âge*) to look; il faisait dans les vingt ans, he looked about twenty; elle fait très jeune, she looks very young (for her age) 9. *F* j'ai de quoi faire,

I've got my work cut out 10. *F* ça commence à bien faire! that's enough of that!/this is getting beyond a joke! 11. *F* faire l'Europe/ l'Autriche, to do Europe/Austria 12. *F* faut le faire! that's pretty amazing! deux ans au chômage, faut le faire! unemployed for two years, it's not as easy as you think! 13. *F* faire (ses besoins), to defecate*/to relieve oneself/to go; le gosse a fait dans sa culotte, the kid's done it in his pants 14. *F* c'est bien fait pour vous! it serves you right!/you asked for it! 15. *F* être fait, to be arrested; il était fait comme un rat, they had him cornered. (*Voir* **marron** II **2**; **tas 2**) 16. *P* être fait, to be drunk* *or* under the influence of drugs*; to be charged 17. *P* to beat (s.o.) up*/to do (s.o.) over 18. *P* to steal*; on m'a fait ma montre, someone's pinched/nicked my watch 19. *P* to seduce/to make/to have (s.o.) 20. *P* (*prostituée*) faire un client/un micheton, to pick up and have sex* with a client; to do/to turn a trick; en faire, to be a prostitute*/to be on the game 21. *F* fais voir! let's have a look! II *vi F* faire avec, to make do III *vpr* **se faire** 1. *F* ne pas s'en faire, not to worry; faut pas s'en faire!/t'en fais pas! don't worry (yourself) about it! *Iron* faut pas s'en faire surtout! feel free! don't mind me! 2. *P* se faire qn (*a*) to put up with s.o.; il faut se le/la faire! he's/she's a real pain (in the neck)! (*b*) to have sex* with s.o.; il se l'est faite, he got laid/he got his end away 3. *P* se faire du fric/du pognon, to make money*/to earn money*. (*Voir* **belle 1, 4**)

faisan [fəzɑ̃, fɛzɑ̃] *nm P* = **faisandier**.

faisandé [fəzɑ̃de, fɛ-] *a F* 1. fake/bogus/ phon(e)y 2. corrupt/decadent (literature, style, etc).

faisander [fəzɑ̃de, fɛ-] *vtr P* to swindle*/to cheat/to con.

faisandier [fəzɑ̃dje, fɛ-] *nm P* unscrupulous person/swindler*/crook/shark/con man.

fais-dodo [fɛdodo] *nm F* dance/disco.

faiseur [fəzœr] *nm F* fraud/swindler*/shark. (*Voir* **ange 1**; **embarras**)

falot [falo] *nm P Mil* court-martial; passer au falot, to be court-martialled.

false [fals] *nm*, **falzar(d)** [falzar] *nm P* (pair of) trousers*/surt *NAm* pants/strides/ keks/duds; déchirer son false, to fart* (loudly).

fameusement [famøzmɑ̃] *adv Vieilli F* famously/marvellously; on s'est fameusement amusé(s), we had a great time.

fameux, -euse [famø, -øz] *a F* excellent*/first-rate; **un fameux menteur,** a hell of a liar; **une fameuse canaille,** an out-and-out/a downright bastard*; **ce n'est pas fameux,** it's not up to much/it's no great shakes; **pas fameux, ton boulot!** you're job's nothing to write home about.

famille [famij] *nf F* **des familles,** simple/without pretension; **on va se faire un repas des familles,** we'll make ourselves a nice little meal. (*Voir* **tuyau 4**)

fan [fan] *nm F* fan; **club des fans,** fan club; **courrier des fans,** fan mail; **fan de foot,** football fan/nut.

fana [fana] *F* **I** *a* enthusiastic/(dead) keen; **il est fana,** he's got it on the brain **II** *nm & f* fan; **fana de cinéma,** film buff; **un fana du flipper,** a pinball fanatic; **fana de rock,** rock freak.

fanal, *pl* **-aux** [fanal, -o] *nm Vieilli P* stomach*.

fandard [fãdar] *nm P* = **fendard**[1].

fanfan [fãfã] *nm & f F* (= *enfant*) small child*/little boy/little girl.

fanfare [fãfar] *nf P* **c'est un sale coup pour la fanfare,** it's a hell of a blow.

fantabosse [fãtabos] *nm Vieilli P Mil* infantryman/foot soldier/foot-slogger.

fantaise [fãtɛz] *nf F* (= *fantaisie*) fancy/imagination; **de fantaise,** fanciful/imaginary.

fantaisie [fãtezi] *nf P* fellatio*.

fantassin [fãtasɛ̃] *nm P* crab louse.

fantoche [fãtɔʃ] *P* **I** *a* fanciful/far-fetched **II** *nf* **1.** (*fantaisie*) fancy/notion **2.** = **fantaisie.**

fanzine [fãzin] *nm F* fanzine.

faramineux, -euse [faraminø, -øz] *a F* phenomenal/colossal; amazing/staggering; **prix faramineux,** steep/sky-high price(s); **un rhume faramineux,** a stinking cold.

farci [farsi] *a P* fake(d); **dé farci,** loaded dice.

farcir [farsir] **I** *vtr* **1.** *P* to deceive*/to trick/to con/to do the dirty on (s.o.) **2.** *P* to riddle (s.o.) with bullets/to fill (s.o.) with lead **II** *vpr* **se farcir 1.** *P* **se farcir qch** (*a*) to treat oneself to sth (*b*) **se farcir un sandwich,** to have a sandwich (*c*) to put up with sth; **ce bouquin, il faut se le farcir!** this book is such a drag/is really heavy going! (*d*) to steal* sth/to knock sth off **2. se farcir qn** (*a*) *P* to put up with s.o./to be stuck with s.o. (*b*) *P* (*vaincre*) to beat s.o.; (*humilier*) to humiliate s.o./to put s.o. down (*c*) *V* to have sex* with s.o./to screw s.o.; **il se la farcirait bien,** he'd love to make

it with her; **se la farcir en vitesse,** to have a quick one/a quickie **3.** *P* **se farcir deux mois de cabane,** to spend two months in prison*/in the nick. (*Voir* **chou I 7; panse 2** (*b*); **zizique**)

fard [far] *nm F* **piquer un fard,** to blush/to go red.

farfadet [farfadɛ] *nm P* foetus.

farfelu, -ue [farfəly] *F* **I** *a* weird/nutty/crazy* **II** *nm & f* crazy* person/nut/nutter/weirdo.

farfouillement [farfujmã] *nm F* rummaging (about); groping.

farfouiller [farfuje] *vtr & i F* to rummage (about) (in, among); to grope (about, for, in); **farfouiller (dans) les affaires de qn,** to mess around with s.o.'s things; to meddle in s.o.'s business.

fargue [farg] *nm P* criminal charge/accusation; indictment.

farguer [farge] *vtr P* to charge/to accuse; to indict.

fargueur [fargœr] *nm P* witness for the prosecution.

faridon [faridɔ̃] *nf Vieilli F* **1. faire la faridon,** to go on a spree*/on a binge/on a bender **2. être à la faridon,** to be penniless*/flat broke.

farine [farin] *nf F* **1. ce sont des gens de (la) même farine,** they're birds of a feather; they're all the same **2. rouler qn dans la farine,** to make a complete fool of s.o. **3. se les rouler dans la farine,** to laze about/to skive off.

farniente [farnjɛnte] *nm F* (pleasurable) idleness.

fastoche [fastɔʃ] *a P* easy.

fatma [fatma] *nf*, **fatmuche** [fatmyʃ] *nf P Péj* Arab woman* *or* any woman*.

faubert [fobɛr] *nm P* (*marine*) **passer le faubert en ville,** to swan around in town.

faubourg [fobur] *nm P* buttocks*/backside.

fauche [foʃ] *nf P* **1.** (petty) theft/stealing/nicking; (*dans les magasins*) shoplifting **2.** poverty; pennilessness.

fauché [foʃe] *a F* **1.** penniless*/flat broke; **fauché comme les blés,** flat broke/stony broke/*NAm* stone-broke **2. avec toi on n'est pas fauché,** you really disappoint me!/you're a bit of a let-down!

faucheman [foʃman] *a P* = **fauché 1.**

faucher [foʃe] *vtr* **1.** *F* to steal*/to swipe/to nick; **qui a fauché mes clopes?** who's pinched my fags? **2.** *P* to guillotine (s.o.) **3.** *F* to clean (s.o.) out (at gambling).

faucheur [foʃœr] *nm Vieilli P* 1. thief 2. executioner.

faucheuse [foʃøz] *nf P* 1. death/the Reaper 2. guillotine.

fauchman(n) [foʃman] *a P* = **fauché 1.**

faune [fon] *nf F* la faune des cafés de Montparnasse, the regular crowd of the cafés of Montparnasse/the Montparnasse set.

fauter [fote] *vi Vieilli F (fille, femme)* to allow herself to be seduced/to go astray; ma chienne a fauté, my dog's found herself a boyfriend.

fauteuil [fotœj] *nm F* arriver dans un fauteuil, *(cheval, etc)* to win easily/to romp home/to win hands down/*Br* to walk it.

faux [fo] *a F* 1. *Péj (hypocrite)* false/devious/shifty; il est faux comme un jeton, he's a phoney. *(Voir* **jeton 1**) 2. avoir tout faux, to be completely wrong/off the mark 3. pour de faux, pretending/for fun/for a laugh.

faux-col [fokɔl] *nm F* head (of froth on glass of beer).

faux-derche [foderʃ] *nm P* deceitful person/shifty customer; hypocrite; double-crosser; phoney.

fav' [fav] *nm F (courses)* favourite.

faveur [favœr] *nf P* fellatio*.

favouille [favuj] *nf P (javanais de* **fouille**) pocket.

fax [faks] *nm F* 1. fax 2. fax number.

faxer [fakse] *vtr F* to fax.

fayot [fajo] *nm P* 1. kidney bean/haricot bean 2. aller becqueter des fayots, to go to prison*/to do bird 3. re-enlisted soldier *or* sailor; faire fayot, to re-enlist 4. *Mil* warrant officer; *(marine)* naval officer 5. *(qui fait du zèle)* swot; eager beaver; *(flagorneur)* bootlicker/toady/creep.

fayotage [fajɔtaʒ] *nm P Péj* bootlicking/toadying; sucking up (to one's boss, etc).

fayoter [fajɔte] *vi P* to toady (to s.o.)/to suck up (to s.o.)/to bootlick; tu es toujours à fayoter, salaud! you're always sucking up to your boss, you creep!

fébou [febu] *nf P (verlan de* **bouffe**) food*/grub.

féca [feka] *nm P (verlan de* **café**) coffee.

fée [fe] *nf P (drogues) (a)* la fée blanche, cocaine* *(b)* la fée brune, opium* *(c)* la fée verte, hashish*.

feignant, -ante [fɛɲɑ̃, -ɑ̃t], **feignard, -arde** [fɛɲar, -ard], **feignasse** [fɛɲas] *P* I *a* idle/lazy* II *n* idler/loafer/lazybones.

feignasser [fɛɲase] *vi P* to laze about/to loaf about/to lounge about/to idle away one's time.

feinter [fɛ̃te] *vtr F* to deceive*/to dupe (s.o.)/to pull a fast one on (s.o.)/to take (s.o.) in; t'es bien feinté! you've been had/you've been taken for a ride.

fêlé [fele] *F a* slightly mad*/cracked; il a le cerveau fêlé/la tête fêlée, he's a bit cracked/he's got a screw loose/he's a bit funny in the head.

felouse, felouze [fəluz] *nm P Hist* Algerian soldier *(during 1954–62 Algerian war)*.

fêlure [felyr] *nf F* avoir une fêlure, to be slightly mad*/a bit cracked/a bit touched (in the head).

femelle [fəmɛl] *nf F Péj* woman*/female; ce n'est qu'une femelle, after all, she's only a woman.

femme [fam] *nf* 1. *F* une petite femme, a lady friend/a bit of skirt/a bit of fluff/a bit of stuff 2. *F* bonne femme, *(épouse)* wife*/old lady/missus; *(femme)* woman; *pl* les bonnes femmes, women *(in general)* 3. *F (cartes)* queen 4. *P (marine)* femme du capitaine, inflatable doll *(used for erotic purposes)*.

femmelette [famlɛt] *nf F (femme)* weak woman/weakling; *(homme)* weakling/sissy; *(homme efféminé)* effeminate man/nancy-boy.

fendant¹ [fɑ̃dɑ̃] *a P* very funny*/killing/side-splitting.

fendant² [fɑ̃dɑ̃] *nm,* **fendard¹** [fɑ̃dar] *nm P* (man's) trousers/pants.

fendard² [fɑ̃dar] *a P (personne)* who enjoys laughing; il est fendard lui! he's always laughing/he's always cheerful.

fendasse [fɑ̃das] *nf* 1. *V* female genitals*/crack 2. *Péj* woman*/female.

fend-la-bise [fɑ̃labiz] *nm P* someone in a tearing hurry.

se fendre [səfɑ̃dr] *vpr F* 1. to be generous; to splash out (on sth); to shell out/to fork out/to cough up; il ne s'est pas fendu, *(peu généreux)* he wasn't exactly what you'd call generous; *(ça ne lui a rien coûté)* it didn't break him/it didn't cost him a penny 2. se fendre la gueule/la pêche/la pipe/la prune, to laugh* one's head off/to crack up/to crease oneself.

fendu [fɑ̃dy] *nm P* 1. = **fendant²** 2. buttocks*/backside.

fenestron [fɛnɛstrɔ̃] *nm P* television*/goggle-box.

fenêtre [fənɛtr] *nf* 1. *F* il faut passer par là ou par la fenêtre, there's nothing else for it/ there's absolutely no choice 2. *F* jeter son argent par les fenêtres, to throw one's money away/down the drain 3. *Vieilli P* mettre la tête/le nez à la fenêtre, to be guillotined 4. *F* se mettre à la fenêtre, to try to see one's opponent's cards 5. *P* boucher une fenêtre à qn, to punch s.o. in the eye 6. *P* faire la fenêtre, *(prostituée)* to solicit* from the window. *(Voir* **chaussette 3***)*

fenêtrière [fənɛtrijɛr] *nf P* prostitute* who solicits from her window.

fente [fɑ̃t] *nf V* female genitals*/crack/slit.

fer [fɛr] *nm* 1. *F* mauvais/sale fer, dangerous fellow/ugly customer/heavy 2. *P* fer à repasser, *(courses)* bad horse/also-ran 3. fer à souder, large nose*/hooter 4. *pl P* fers, tools used for safe-breaking.

fer-blanc [fɛrblɑ̃] *nm F* en fer-blanc, worthless*/shoddy/tinpot.

fermer [fɛrme] *vtr P* ferme ta boîte/ta gueule/ta malle! ferme ça!/ferme-la!/la ferme! shut up!*/belt up!/shut it!/shut your face!/shut your trap!

fermeture [fɛrmətyr] *nf P* fermeture! tu me cours! shut* up! you get on my nerves!

ferraille [fɛrɑj] *nf F* coins/small change; je lui ai donné toute ma ferraille, I gave him all my small change.

ferré [fɛre] *a F* être ferré sur un sujet, to be well up in *or* on sth/to know a subject inside out.

ferte [fɛrt] *nf P* la bonne ferte, fortune-telling; dire la bonne ferte, to tell fortunes.

fesse [fɛs] *nf P* 1. *pl* les fesses, buttocks*/ bottom/bum/*esp NAm* butt/arse/*esp NAm* ass; poser ses fesses, to sit down (on one's back-side); pousse tes fesses (de là)! move up a bit!/shift your arse/*NAm* ass! 2. serrer les fesses, to be afraid*/to get the wind up/to have the jitters/to have cold feet; il est parti en serrant les fesses, he went off with his tail between his legs 3. avoir chaud aux fesses, *(avoir peur)* to have a nasty fright; *(avoir la police à ses trousses)* to have the police hot on one's track 4. n'y aller que d'une fesse, to be hesitant/indecisive; to set about sth half-heartedly; n'être assis que d'une fesse, *(être énergique)* to be always on the go; *(être nerveux)* to be very nervous 5. prendre ses fesses à poignée, to run like hell/to get the hell out (of somewhere) 6. occupe-toi de tes fesses! mind your own bloody business! 7.

mes fesses! my arse/*surt NAm* my ass! poli comme mes fesses, downright/bloody rude; cette bagnole de mes fesses! that bloody/ bleeding car! 8. women/crumpet/skirt/a bit of the other; y a de la fesse, there's some skirt/ crumpet knocking around 9. *(a)* magasin de fesses, brothel* *(b)* pain de fesse, money earned by prostitution *or* pornography *(c)* pornography/porn/tits and bums; magazine/ revue de fesses, porno/porny/dirty magazine/ mag; un film de fesses, a dirty/porny film; a blue movie; *surt NAm* a porno flick/a skin flick *(d)* histoire de fesses, sordid affair; *(blague)* dirty story/joke. *(Voir* **beurre 9**; **feu 1, 6**; **peau 15, 20** *(d)))*

fessier [fɛsje] *nm F* buttocks*/behind/arse/ *surt NAm* ass.

festonner [fɛstɔne] *vi Vieilli F (ivrogne)* to stagger about/to lurch about.

fête [fɛt] *nf* 1. *F (a)* être à la fête, to be as pleased as Punch/to be over the moon *(b)* il n'était pas à la fête, he was having a rough time (of it)/things weren't going too well for him 2. *P* faire sa fête à qn, to beat s.o. up*/to work s.o. over; ça va être ta fête! you'd better watch out!/you're in for it!/you'll get what's coming to you! 3. *F* il n'a jamais été/il ne s'est jamais vu à pareille fête, he never had such a good time/he never enjoyed himself so much 4. *F* faire la fête, to have a good time*/to live it up/to have a ball/to get one's rocks off. *(Voir* **salle 3**)

feu [fø] *nm* 1. *F* avoir le feu quelque part/au derrière/*P* au cul/aux miches/aux fesses, to be in a tearing hurry/in a huge rush; to have ants in one's pants; il courait comme s'il avait le feu au derrière, you couldn't see him for dust; he went like greased lightning. *(Voir* **train 2**) 2. *F* donner le feu vert à qn, to give s.o. the go-ahead/the green light; avoir/ recevoir le feu vert, to get the green light 3. *P* cracher/péter le feu, to be full of go/to be full of beans 4. *F* il (n')y a pas le feu (au lac), there's no hurry!/no need to panic!/take your time! il y a le feu sur le pont? what's the big hurry?/what's the great rush? 5. *P* revolver*/ gun/shooter/piece 6. *P* avoir le feu au tambour/au cul/aux fesses, *(d'une femme)* to feel sexy/randy/horny 7. *F (dans un restaurant)* coup de feu, busy period/busiest time.

feuille [fœj] *nf* 1. *P* ear*/lug/(hole); feuilles de chou, big ears; être dur de la feuille/être constipé des feuilles, to be hard of hearing/to be a bit deaf; avoir les feuilles (de chou) ensablées, (*être un peu sourd*) to be hard of hearing; (*ne pas comprendre*) not to take it in/to be a bit slow; *Mus* jouer à la feuille, to play by ear; jouer les feuilles mortes, to have no ear for music/not to be musical 2. *F* feuille de chou, newspaper/rag 3. *P* regarder/voir la feuille à l'envers, to have sex* in the open air; to have a roll in the hay 4. *V* faire feuille de rose (à qn), to have anal sex*/to lick (s.o.'s) anus*/to ream (s.o.'s) ass 5. *F* glisser dans les feuilles, to confide a secret. (*Voir* **millefeuille**)

feuj [føʒ] *P* (*verlan de juif*) I *a* Jewish II *n* Jew*/Yid.

fias [fjas] *nm P* (*souvent Péj*) man*/fellow/ bloke/guy.

fiasc, fiasque [fjask] *nm F* (= *fiasco*) failure*/fiasco/flop.

fiasse [fjas] *P* (*souvent Péj*) I *nm* = **fias** II *nf* girl*/bird/chick/tart.

ficelé [fisle] *a F Péj* dressed up*/got up; mal ficelé, untidily dressed; elle est ficelée comme quat' sous, she *does* look a mess/she looks like a sack of potatoes. (*Voir* **andouille 2**)

ficeler [fisle] *vtr P* to follow/tail/shadow (s.o.).

ficelle [fisɛl] I *a F* cunning/wily/smart II *nf* 1. *F* une grosse/vieille ficelle, an old hand/a wily (old) bird; a smooth operator 2. *F* (*a*) (*truc*) on voit bien la ficelle, it's easy to see how it's done; la ficelle est un peu grosse, that's too obvious; I'm not falling for that (*b*) connaître les ficelles, to know the ropes/to know the tricks of the trade (*c*) tirer les ficelles, to pull the strings/to run the show 3. *F Mil* (*galon*) (NCO's *or* officer's) stripes/gold braid 4. *F* casser la ficelle, to get a divorce/to get unhitched 5. *pl P* handcuffs*/bracelets 6. *F* bootlace tie 7. *F* tirer sur la ficelle, to exaggerate*/to stretch it a bit.

fichaise [fiʃɛz] *nf F* nonsense*/rubbish/ garbage/trash; tout ça c'est des fichaises, that's a load of rot/bull/garbage.

fiche, ficher [fiʃ, fiʃe] I *vtr F* 1. (= *faire*) ne pas en ficher un coup/une secousse/une ramette, ne rien fiche(r)/ne pas en ficher lourd, to do nothing/to skive off; je n'ai rien fichu/je n'en ai pas fichu une aujourd'hui, I haven't done a thing/a stroke all day (*Voir* **dal, dalle¹**; **rame 2**); qu'est-ce que ça fiche? what does it matter?/who the hell cares? j'en ai rien à fiche, I don't give a damn 2. (= *mettre*) fiche(r) qn dedans, (*tromper*) to fool* s.o./to take s.o. in; (*en prison*) to put s.o. in-

side; fiche(r) qn dehors/en l'air, to give s.o. the sack/to fire s.o.; to give s.o. his cards/ the push (*Voir* **air I 6**); fiche(r) qn à la porte, to throw/to chuck s.o. out; ça fiche tout par terre/en l'air, that ruins everything/that messes everything up 3. (= *donner*) ficher un coup à qn, to hit s.o./to clout s.o./to thump s.o.; fiche-moi la paix! leave me alone!/clear off!/get lost!/shove off! qu'est-ce qui m'a fichu un imbécile pareil? what have I done to be landed with such an idiot? ça me fiche la déprime, that depresses me/it gives me the blues; ça m'a fichu un coup! it hit real(ly) hard! qu'est-ce qui m'a fichu ça? how did I end up with that? 4. va te faire fiche! get the hell out of here!/clear off!/go to hell! envoyer qn faire fiche, to send s.o. packing/to tell s.o. to clear off; envoyer qch faire fiche, to chuck sth up/to pack sth in; fiche(r) le camp, to beat it/to do a bunk; fiche-moi le camp! buzz off!/ clear off!/get lost! 5. je t'en fiche! nothing of the sort!/not a bit of it!/not at all!/not flipping likely! vingt-cinq ans je t'en fiche, elle a quarante ans et mèche! twenty-five, my foot — she's forty if she's a day! 6. ça la fiche mal, that makes a lousy impression II *vpr* **se ficher** *F* 1. se ficher par terre, (*se jeter par terre*) to fling oneself on the ground/to the ground; (*tomber*) to go sprawling/to come a cropper* 2. (*a*) se fiche(r) de qn, to make fun of s.o./to pull s.o.'s leg/to take the mickey out of s.o.; vous vous fichez de moi, you're having me on/you're kidding me (*b*) se fiche(r) de qch, to poke fun at sth; ça, c'est se fiche(r) du monde! well, of all the nerve!/what a (damned) cheek! je m'en fiche (pas mal)!/ce que je m'en fiche! I don't give a damn!/I couldn't care less!*/a fat lot I care! je me fiche bien de ce qu'on pense de moi, I couldn't care less what they think of me; il se fiche du quart comme du tiers, he doesn't give a damn for anything/anybody; je m'en fiche et m'en contrefiche/je m'en fiche comme de l'an neuf/ comme de l'an quarante/comme de ma première chemise/comme d'une guigne/ comme un poisson d'une pomme, I couldn't care less*!/I couldn't give a damn!/I couldn't give a monkey's!/I don't care two hoots! 3. se ficher dedans, to make a mistake*/to put one's foot in it; il s'est fichu dedans, he boobed 4. il peut se le ficher quelque part! he knows where he can stick it!/he can stick it up his arse/*NAm* ass!

fichets [fiʃɛ] *nmpl P* handcuffs*.

fichtre! [fiʃtr] *int Vieilli F* **1.** (*exprime l'étonnement, l'admiration*) good heavens!/ good Lord!/well I never! **2.** (*exprime la contrariété, la douleur*) damn!/blast!/hell!/ Jeez! **3.** (*intensif*) fichtre oui! rather!/I should say so! fichtre non! no fear!/I should think not! je le sais fichtre bien! don't I know it!/I know it too damn well! je n'en sais fichtre rien! I'm damned if I know! ça n'est fichtre pas agréable de ..., it's no joke to .../it's no fun to ....

fichtrement [fiʃtrəmã] *adv Vieilli F* (*intensif*) extremely/awfully/terribly; hellishly; il a fichtrement raison, he's dead right! c'est fichtrement bien, it's damn(ed)/*NAm* darned good; c'est fichtrement loin, it's a hell of a long way/a damned long way.

fichu [fiʃy] *a F* **1.** rotten/awful; quel fichu temps! what filthy/lousy weather! une fichue idée, a ridiculous/stupid/lousy idea; un fichu embêtement, a flipping/damn/*NAm* darn nuisance **2.** il est fichu, he's done for/he's had it/it's all up with him; c'est de l'argent (de) fichu, it's money down the drain; ma montre est fichue, my watch has bitten the dust/has had it/is bust **3.** fichu de, likely to/capable of; il est fichu de partir avant que j'arrive, it's just like him to leave before I get there/it's on the cards that he'll leave before I get there; il n'est même pas fichu de faire ça, he isn't even up to/capable of doing that **4.** (a) être mal fichu, (*mal fabriqué*) to be badly made/put together; (*fatigué*) to feel tired*; (*malade*) to feel unwell*/under the weather; (*mal habillé*) to be badly dressed/badly turned out (*Voir* **as 2; sou 1**); elle n'est pas mal fichue, (*bien habillée*) she's quite well turned out/quite smart; (*jolie*) she's not bad-looking (b) être bien fichu, (*bien fabriqué*) to be well made; (*bien habillé*) to be well dressed/well turned out; (*beau*) to be good-looking.

fichûment [fiʃymã] *adv Vieilli F* extremely/awfully/terribly; c'est fichûment gentil à vous de m'écrire, it's jolly nice of you to write to me.

fiérot [fjero] *F* **I** *a* (a) stuck-up/snooty (b) cocky **II** *nm* stuck-up/cocky person; faire le fiérot, to swagger (around).

fiesta [fjɛsta] *nf F* celebration/party; faire la fiesta, to go out on the town/to live it up/to have a ball.

fieu, *pl* **-eux** [fjø] *nm* (*surt Dial*) son/sonny; lad; c'est un bon fieu, he's a good sort/a nice chap.

fifi [fifi] *nm F* sparrow.

fifille [fifij] *nf F* little girl*; la fifille à son papa, daddy's little girl.

fifine [fifin] *nf P* sanitary towel/*NAm* napkin.

fifre [fifr] **I** *indef pron P* que fifre, nothing* at all/not a damn thing/sweet FA **II** *nm V* fifre à grelots, penis*.

fifrelin [fifrəlɛ̃] *nm F* cela ne vaut pas un fifrelin, it's not worth a (brass) farthing; je n'ai pas un fifrelin, I'm broke/I haven't a penny to my name.

fifti, fifty [fifti] *nm F* half; faire fifti, to go halves/fifty-fifty.

fifti-fifti, fifty-fifty [fiftififti] *adv F* half and half/fifty-fifty.

figaro [figaro] *nm* **1.** *F Hum* barber **2.** *Vieilli P* faire figaro, (*garçon de café*) not to get a tip.

fignard [fiɲar] *nm*, **fignarès** [fiɲarɛs] *nm*, **figne** [fiɲ] *nm*, **fignedé** [fiɲde] *nm*, **fignolet** [fiɲɔlɛ] *nm P* (a) buttocks*/arse/ surt *NAm* ass (b) anus*/arsehole/*surt NAm* asshole.

figue [fig] *nf* **1.** *F* faire la figue à qn, to make an obscene gesture of contempt at s.o. (by putting the thumb between the fingers) **2.** *V* female genitals*/cunt **3.** *pl V* testicles*/nuts; avoir les figues molles, to feel sexually unexcited/to be limp/to droop. (*Voir* **mi-figue**)

figuier [figje] *nm P Péj* tronc de figuier, Arab/wog.

figure [figyr] *nf F* **1.** (a) casser la figure à qn, to push/to smash s.o.'s face in; to beat s.o.'s head in (b) se casser la figure, (*tomber*) to come a cropper*; (*avoir un accident*) to smash oneself up (in an accident, etc) **2.** se payer la figure de qn, (*se moquer*) to take the mickey out of s.o./to pull s.o.'s leg/to have s.o. on **3.** faire triste figure, to look out of place/ out of one's element/like a fish out of water.

fil [fil] *nm F* **1.** *Vieilli* avoir le fil, to be wide awake/to be all there/to be with it **2.** avoir un fil à la patte, (*être tenu par un engagement*) to have commitments/to be tied down; (*avoir une maîtresse*) to be lumbered (with a mistress); se mettre un fil à la patte/se laisser attacher un fil à la patte, to get married*/to get hitched/to tie the knot **3.** donner du fil à retordre à qn, to give s.o. a lot of trouble/to make life difficult for s.o.; il vous donnera du fil à retordre, you'll have your work cut out with him/he'll give you a big headache **4.** il n'a pas inventé le fil à couper le beurre, he won't set the Thames on fire/he won't set the world on fire/he's no superman/he's nothing special 5. **avoir des jambes comme des fils de fer**, to have legs like matchsticks 6. **elle est mince comme un fil**, she's as thin as a rake 7. **sécher sur le fil**, to be stood up 8. *Vieilli* **fil en quatre**, strong brandy/rotgut/hard stuff 9. **être au bout du fil**, to be on the phone; to be at the other end of the line; **donner/passer un coup de fil à qn**, to give s.o. a ring/a tinkle/a buzz. (*Voir* **glisser** II 2; **lâcher** 4; **tirer** I 7)

filaturer [filatyre] *vtr F* to shadow/to tail (s.o.).

filer [file] I *vtr* 1. *F* to give/to hand over/to pass; **file-moi une pipe**, slip me a fag; **en filer une bonne à qn**, to clout s.o./to give s.o. a good thump. (*Voir* **avoine** 2; **coton** II 2; **danse** 1; **doux**; **raclée** 1; **roustasse**; **sabre** 2; **toise**; **train** 7; **trempe**) 2. *P* **filer qn**, to tail/to shadow s.o. 3. *P* **filer de la drogue**, to sell drugs/to deal II *vi* 1. *F* **filer (en vitesse)**, to run away*/to beat it/to clear off; **filez!** clear off!/get lost*! **filer comme une flèche**, to shoot off/to dash off/to zoom off; **faut que je file**, must dash/fly; **il fila sur l'Amérique avec l'argent**, he skipped off to America with the money; **filer en douceur**, to slip away/to slope off. (*Voir* **anglaise**; **dard** 2) 2. *V* **en filer**, to be a passive homosexual*. (*Voir* **chouette** IV 1) III *vpr* **se filer** *F* to get in/to enter; **elle s'est filée dans les toiles**, she went to bed/she slipped between the sheets.

filet [file] *nm F* 1. **elle n'a pas le filet coupé**, she's got the gift of the gab/she's a real chatterbox 2. **coup de filet**, (police) raid/bust.

filetouze [filtuz] *nm P* (= *filet*) string bag.

fileur, -euse¹ [filœr, -øz] *n F* 1. shadow(er)/tail 2. racecourse spy (*in search of winning tips*).

fileuse² [filøz] *nf P* s.o. (*man or woman*) who informs criminals of possible burglaries to be committed.

filière [filjɛr] *nf F* **passer par/suivre la filière**, (*personne*) to work one's way up (from the bottom); (*demande d'emploi, etc*) to go through the usual (official) channels.

fille [fij] *nf* 1. *F* **elle est bonne fille**, she's rather naive 2. *F* prostitute*; **elle a des manières de fille**, she's a bit of a tart/a slut 3. *F* **courir les filles**, to be a womanizer*/a skirt-chaser/a bit of a lecher.

fillette [fijɛt] *nf P* half-bottle (of wine).

filochard [filɔʃar] *a P* resourceful*/smart/canny.

filoche [filɔʃ] *nf P* shadowing/tailing; **pren-**

dre qn en filoche/prendre la filoche de qn, to shadow/to tail s.o.

filocher [filɔʃe] *P* I *vtr* to shadow/to tail (s.o.) II *vi* to speed (along)/to belt along/to zip along.

filon [filɔ̃] *nm F* 1. (*a*) cushy job/cushy number/soft option; **les meilleurs filons**, the plum jobs/jobs for the boys (*b*) **avoir le filon**, to be sitting pretty; **j'ai un bon filon pour avoir des vidéos gratuites**, I know where I can get free videos easily 2. money-spinner; **trouver le filon/trouver un bon filon/dénicher le bon filon**, to strike it rich/to strike it lucky/to strike oil.

fils [fis] *nm F* 1. boy/lad/chap/fellow; **c'est un bon fils**, he's a good sort (of chap) 2. **fils à papa**, daddy's boy; **fils d'archevêque**, daddy's boy with an influential father/whose father pulls strings for him. (*Voir* **pute** 1)

fin [fɛ̃] I *nf* 1. *F* **tu es stupide à la fin!** you really are stupid! **il m'énerve, à la fin!** he's beginning to get on my nerves! 2. *P* **une fin de mois**, a part-time prostitute*. (*Voir* **arrondir** I) 3. *F* **sentir la fin de saison**, to (begin to) feel old. (*Voir* **haricot** 3) II *a F* good; **une blague fine**, a subtle joke; *Iron* **j'avais l'air fin**, I looked a right idiot/a proper Charlie; *Iron* **qu'est-ce que c'est fin!** oh, very funny! (*Voir* **mouche** 5; **partie** 3 (*b*)) III *adv F* completely/absolutely; **fin soûl**, dead drunk*/plastered.

finasser [finase] *vi F* to resort to trickery; to pull a fast one; **finasser avec qn**, to play tricks on s.o.

fini [fini] *a F* 1. **un menteur fini**, an out-and-out liar; **un imbécile fini**, a complete/a downright idiot 2. **il est fini**, he's had it.

finir [finir] I *vtr P* 1. to kill*/to do in/to erase 2. **finir un client/son partenaire sexuel**, to bring a client/one's partner to orgasm*/to a climax; to bring off/to finish off a client/one's partner II *vpr* **se finir** 1. to finish off getting drunk* 2. **se finir (à la main)**, (*masturbation*) to finish oneself off/to bring oneself off.

fiole [fjɔl] *nf P* 1. head*/bonce; **se payer la fiole de qn**, to make a fool of s.o./to have s.o. on/to pull s.o.'s leg 2. face*/mug; **j'en ai soupé de ta fiole!** I'm fed up with you!/I'm tired of looking at your ugly mug!/I've had (just about) enough of you! 3. self; **ma fiole**, myself; me; **sa fiole**, himself/herself; him/her.

fion [fjɔ̃] *nm* 1. *F* **donner le coup de fion à qch**, (*mettre la dernière main*) to give/to put the finishing touch(es) to sth; (*nettoyer*) to clean/to tidy sth up 2. *F* avoir le fion pour faire qch, to have the knack of doing sth 3. *P* coup de fion, stroke of luck; avoir du fion, to be lucky; avoir un fion du tonnerre, to have the luck of the devil 4. *P* bastard*/scumbag/son of a bitch 5. *V* anus*/arsehole/*NAm* asshole/ring; se casser le fion à faire qch, to put a lot of effort into doing sth/to put oneself out to do sth; ils nous rabâchent le fion avec leurs histoires, we've had it up to here with their problems.

fiotte [fjɔt] *nf P* 1. *(a)* effeminate man/pansy *(b)* homosexual*/poof(ter)/fairy/fag(got) 2. *(insulte)* man*/fellow; espèce de fiotte! you jerk!

fissa [fisa] *adv P* faire fissa, to be quick about it/to get a move on/to look sharp/to get one's finger out.

fissure [fisyr] *nf P* mastiquer une fissure, to amaze*/to stagger.

fissurer [fisyre] *vi P* to be on the point of cracking up/to be near breaking point.

fiston [fistɔ̃] *nm F* son; youngster; **(mon)** fiston, my lad/my boy/sonny.

fistot [fisto] *nm F* first-year naval cadet.

fistule [fistyl] *nf P* avoir de la fistule, to be lucky/to get a lucky break.

fix(e) [fiks] *nm F (drogues)* un fix(e), an injection*/a fix; se faire un fix(e), to shoot up.

fixé [fikse] *a F* être fixé, to know where one stands/to know the score.

se fixer [səfikse] *vpr P (drogues)* to (have a) fix/to shoot up.

flac [flak] *nm P* (il) y en a flac! that's enough!/I've had it up to here!/I'm sick to death of it!

flacdal(le) [flakdal] *P* I *a* 1. *(personne)* soft/spineless/gutless/weedy 2. worthless II *nm* 1. soft/spineless/gutless/weedy person 2. defecation; aller à flacdal, to defecate*/to go for a crap.

Flacmann [flakman] *Prn P* aller chez Flacmann, to defecate*/to go for a crap. *(Voir* flaquer 1)

flacon [flakɔ̃] *nm* 1. *F (a)* prendre du flacon, to be getting on (in years) *(b)* avoir du flacon, to be past one's prime/to be a bit long in the tooth; plaisanterie qui a du flacon, vintage joke; hoary old joke/chestnut 2. *pl P* boots/shoes; déboucher les flacons, to take off one's shoes.

fla(-)flas [flafla] *nmpl F* faire des fla(-)flas, to put on airs/to be affected.

flag [flag] *nm P* être pris en flag/se faire piquer en flag, (= *en flagrant délit*) to be caught red-handed/in the act; to be caught with one's trousers/pants down.

flagada [flagada] *a inv F (personne)* exhausted*/fagged (out)/whacked; *(jambes)* like jelly; se sentir tout flagada, to feel limp (with tiredness).

flagda [flagda] *nm P* kidney bean/haricot bean.

flagelle [flaʒɛl] *nf P* (sexual) flagellation/flag/fladge.

flageolet [flaʒɔlɛ] *nm V* penis*/stalk; avoir le flageolet à la portière, to have an erection*/to have it up; se faire souffler dans le flageolet, to have fellatio*/to have a blow-job.

flagre [flagr], **flague** [flag] *nm P =* **flag**.

Flahute [flayt] *nm & f P (a)* Fleming *(b) (cyclisme)* les Flahutes, Belgian racers.

flambante [flɑ̃bɑ̃t] *nf Vieilli P* une flambante, a match/a light.

flambard [flɑ̃bar] *nm F* show-off*/swank; faire le flambard, to show off*/to swank.

flambe [flɑ̃b] *nf P (a)* gambling *(b)* (any) gambling game.

flambé [flɑ̃be] *a P (a) (au jeu)* ruined/done for/cleaned out/taken to the cleaners *(b)* il est flambé, he's had it/he's had his chips/he's done for.

flambeau [flɑ̃bo] *nm P* avoir du flambeau, to be lucky *(esp* at gambling).

flamber [flɑ̃be] *vi F* 1. to gamble heavily. *(Voir* **courtines)** 2. to squander/to spend heavily; c'est de l'argent flambé, it's money down the drain.

flambeur [flɑ̃bœr] *nm F* heavy gambler.

flan [flɑ̃] *nm P* 1. à la flan, *a phr* not serious; *adv phr* in a slapdash fashion; tes idées à la flan, you and your lousy ideas; travail fait à la flan, work/job done anyoldhow 2. au flan, at random/on the spur of the moment; j'ai dit ça au flan, I said that off the top of my head; il est venu au flan, he came on the off chance 3. coup de flan, *(crime)* unpremeditated crime; pilfering/shoplifting; *(arrestation)* arbitrary arrest 4. du flan! I promise!/cross my heart! 5. c'est du flan! it's a load of rubbish/hooey/codswallop! 6. faire du flan, to tell lies/to con s.o./to have s.o. on 7. en rester comme deux ronds de flan, to be amazed*/flabbergasted; elle en est restée comme deux ronds de flan, she couldn't believe it/she was gobsmacked.

flanc [flɑ̃] *nm* 1. *F* être sur le flanc, to be exhausted*/to be all in; ce boulot m'a mis sur le flanc, this job has worn me out 2. *F* se battre les flancs, to waste energy and achieve nothing/to beat one's head against a brick wall 3. *P* tirer au flanc, to shirk/to skive/to swing the lead; tireur au flanc, skiver/shirker.

flanche [flɑ̃ʃ] *nm P* 1. crime; job/business; monter un flanche, to plan a burglary, etc/to pull a job 2. gambling den; aller au flanche, to go gambling 3. (salesman's) patter.

flancher [flɑ̃ʃe] *vi F* 1. (*a*) (*faiblir*) to flinch/to give in (*b*) (*abandonner*) to quit/to back out; ce n'est pas le moment de flancher! don't give up now! 2. (*d'une voiture, etc*) to pack up.

flancheur [flɑ̃ʃœr] *nm P* (heavy) gambler.

flanelle [flanɛl] *nf P* 1. bad customer/client (*who doesn't spend his/her money*); faire flanelle, to be an unprofitable customer (in a café, a brothel, etc) 2. failure*/flop; faire flanelle, (*paresser*) to loaf around/to mooch about; (*être impuissant*) to be impotent; (*échouer*) to fail*/to flop.

flâneuse [flɑnøz] *nf F* chair.

flanquer [flɑ̃ke] I *vtr F* to throw/to chuck; flanquer qch par terre, to fling/to chuck/to plonk sth (down) on the ground/on the floor; flanquer une gifle à qn, to slap s.o. round the face/to clout s.o. round the ears; flanquer un coup de pied à qn, to kick s.o.; flanquer qn à la porte, (*faire sortir*) to turn/to turf s.o. out; to throw/to chuck s.o. out; (*sacquer*) to give s.o. the sack/to fire s.o./to give s.o. the push; flanquer la trouille à qn, (*faire peur*) to put the wind up s.o.; flanquer la chtouille à qn, to give s.o. VD*/the clap/a dose. (*Voir* air I 6) II *vpr* se flanquer *F* se flanquer par terre, (*se jeter par terre*) to fling oneself to the ground; (*tomber*) to fall (over)/to fall flat on one's face/to come a cropper*.

flanquette [flɑ̃kɛt] *nf F* (= *franquette*) à la bonne flanquette, simply/without ceremony; venez dîner chez nous, ce sera à la bonne flanquette, come for dinner, you'll have to take pot luck with us/it won't be anything special.

flapi [flapi] *a F* (*personne*) exhausted*/fagged out/washed out/shattered.

flaquedalle [flakdal] *a & nm P* = **flacdal(le)**.

flaquer [flake] *vi P* 1. to defecate* 2. = **flancher 1**.

flash [flaʃ] *nm P* 1. (*drogues*) flash/bang (experienced by drug addicts) 2. violent emotion *or* sensation.

flashant, -ante [flaʃɑ̃, -ɑ̃t] *a P* 1.

(*drogues*) that gives one a flash 2. that gives intense pleasure; c'est une fille flashante, she really turns men on.

flasher [flaʃe] *vi P* 1. (*drogues*) to get a flash 2. to fall (sur, for); j'ai flashé sur cet apparte, I (really) fell for the flat; il a flashé sur elle dès qu'il l'a vue, he fell for her the moment he saw her 3. to experience intense pleasure.

flasquer [flaske] *vi Vieilli P* to defecate*.

flauper [flope] *vtr P* to beat*/to thrash (s.o.).

flèche [flɛʃ] I *nm P* 1. je n'ai pas un flèche, I haven't got a farthing/a cent/a bean 2. trick/wangle II *nf* 1. *P* (policeman's) partner; faire flèche, to team up 2. *P* La Flèche, the underworld 3. *P* trick/dodge/fiddle.

(se) flécher [(sə)fleʃe] *vi & vpr P* to team up/to gang up/to work together.

flémard, flemmard, -arde [flemar, -ard] *P* I. *a* lazy*/idle/work-shy II *n* idler/slacker/loafer.

flémingite [flemɛ̃ʒit] *nf P* laziness; il a une flémingite aiguë, he's very lazy/he's a real slacker/he's a lazy sod.

flemmarder [flemarde] *vi P* to loaf/to idle/to slack; to laze around/to sit around doing nothing.

flemme [flɛm] *nf P* laziness/slacking; il a la flemme, he's feeling lazy/he doesn't feel like work(ing); j'ai la flemme de lire, I don't feel like reading/I can't be bothered to read; ça me donne la flemme, I can't be bothered (with it); tirer sa flemme, to idle away one's time/to (sit and) do nothing/to bum around.

fleur [flœr] I *nf* 1. *F* s'envoyer des fleurs, to give oneself a pat on the back/to blow one's own trumpet 2. *F* arriver comme une fleur, to arrive innocently/naively confident/without any qualms 3. *F* être fleur bleue, to be sentimentally amorous/(a bit of a) romantic 4. (*a*) *F* gift/present; tip (*b*) *P* pay-off (to police informer*, etc) (*c*) *P* cut/whack; share (of the loot) 5. *F* faire une fleur à qn, (*service*) to do s.o. a favour/a service; (*cadeau*) to give s.o. a present 6. (*a*) *F* la fleur des pois, the pick of the bunch/the cream of the crop (*b*) *P* une fleur des pois, a homosexual* 7. *P* perdre sa fleur (d'oranger), (*fille, femme*) to lose one's virginity*/one's cherry. (*Voir* **macadam 1; nave 2** (*b*); **paf II 3**) II *a P* être fleur, to be penniless*/broke.

flibocheuse [flibɔʃøz] *nf P* greedy prostitute* (*who won't miss an opportunity to* *earn some money).*

flibuster [flibyste] *vtr & i P* to swindle*/to be on the fiddle; to steal*/to nick (sth).

flibusterie [flibystri] *nf P* swindling; stealing/nicking.

flibustier [flibystje] *nm P* swindler*/crook; thief*.

flic [flik] *nm P* policeman*/cop/copper/rozzer/ *NAm* bull; **flic de la route,** speed cop; **v'là les flics,** here are the cops/the fuzz. (*Voir* **pavé 5**)

flicage [flika3] *nm P* 1. police surveillance 2. surveillance of the staff/employees by the management.

flicaille [flikɑj], **flicaillerie** [flikɑjri] *nf P* the police*/the cops/the fuzz/*NAm* the bulls.

flicard [flikar] *nm P Péj* 1. policeman* 2. informer*; snout/grass.

flic-flac [flikflak] *nm F* two slaps in the face/a right and left.

flikeu [flikø] *nm P* = **flic.**

flingage [flɛ̃ga3] *nm P* 1. shooting (of s.o.); killing (of s.o.) with a gun 2. slating (of s.o.).

flingot [flɛ̃go] *nm P* rifle/shotgun.

flingoter [flɛ̃gɔte] *vtr P* = **flinguer I 1.**

flingue¹ [flɛ̃g] *nm P* (a) firearm/gun/ revolver*/shooter/rod (b) rifle/shotgun.

flingue², flingué [flɛ̃ge] *a P* penniless*/ bust/broke/cleaned out.

flinguer [flɛ̃ge] **I** *vtr P* 1. to kill* (s.o.)/to gun (s.o.) down/to shoot (s.o.) dead/to bump (s.o.) off 2. to criticize severely*/to pull to pieces/to slate 3. to break/destroy/demolish 4. to have sex* with/to lay/to screw (a woman) **II** *vpr* **se flinguer** *P* 1. to shoot oneself/to commit suicide*/to blow one's brains out 2. **s'il n'y a pas de quoi se flinguer!** it's enough to drive you mad!

flingueur [flɛ̃gœr] *nm P* (trigger-happy) killer.

flip [flip] *nm* 1. *P* (*après avoir absorbé une drogue*) depression 2. *F* (*angoisse*) flipping out/freaking out 3. *F* = **flipper I.** (*Voir* **superflip**)

flippant [flipɑ̃] *a* 1. *P* (*drogues*) mindblowing 2. *F* demoralizing; frightening; **c'est flippant,** it makes you want to flip out/freak out.

flippé [flipe] *a* 1. *P* (*drogues*) high (on a drug) 2. *F* a bit mad*/screwy; **t'es complètement flippé!** you're completely off your rocker! 3. *F* depressed/blue.

flipper I [flipɛr, flipœr] *nm F* pinball (machine)/pin table **II** [flipe] *vi* 1. *P*

(*drogues*) (a) to flip out/to freak out/to get high/to be on a trip (b) to have withdrawal symptoms/to go cold turkey 2. *F* to be depressed*/down/blue.

fliqué [flike] *a P* (*personne, immeuble*) under (police) surveillance.

fliquer [flike] *vtr P* to carry out police surveillance on/to police; **fliquer des employés,** to keep an eye on employees; **une société fliquée,** a police state.

fliquesse [flikɛs], **fliquette** [flikɛt] *nf P* policewoman.

flop [flɔp] *nm F* (*théâtre, etc*) failure/flop; **sa pièce a fait flop,** his play flopped.

floper [flɔpe] *vtr P* = **flauper.**

flop(p)ée [flɔpe] *nf P* 1. large quantity/ lashings/oodles/tons (of sth); crowd (of people); **elle a toute une flop(p)ée de gosses,** she's got a whole bunch of kids 2. *Vieilli* thrashing/beating.

flottard [flɔtar] **I** *a F* watery/thin (sauce, etc); **du café flottard,** watery coffee/ dishwater/gnat's piss **II** *nm F* naval cadet.

flotte [flɔt] *nf F* 1. (a) (sea, river) water; tomber dans la flotte, to fall into the water/ into the drink (b) (drinking) water*; boire de la flotte, to drink water/to have a drink of water (c) rain; il tombe de la flotte, it's raining/it's pouring (with rain) 2. (thin, watery) soup, sauce, coffee, etc 3. **la Flotte,** the Naval Academy 4. *pl* **des flottes de ...,** large numbers of .../crowds of ...; oodles/ lashings/tons of ....

flotter [flɔte] *v impers F* **il flotte,** it's raining/it's pouring (with rain).

flotteurs [flɔtœr] *nmpl P* breasts*/boobs.

flouer [flue] *vtr & i F* 1. to cheat at gambling 2. to swindle*/to con (s.o.) (**de qch,** out of sth); **on m'a floué,** I've been had/done.

flouerie [fluri] *nf F* (a) swindle*/con (trick) (b) swindling/cheating.

floueur, -euse [fluœr, -øz] *n F* 1. cheat (at gambling) 2. swindler*/con man/con artist.

flouse [fluz] *nm P* money*/cash/dough/bread.

flouser [fluze] *vi P* to fart*.

flousse [flus] *nf P* fart.

flouze [fluz] *nm P* = **flouse.**

flubard [flybar] **I** *nm P* 1. *Vieilli* (tele)phone* 2. *pl* **flubards,** legs* 3. coward* **II** *a P* frightened; cowardly*.

fluber [flybe] *vi P* to be afraid*.

flubes [flyb] *nmpl P* **avoir les flubes,** to be afraid*; to be a coward*/to be chicken; **ficher/flanquer/foutre les flubes à qn,** to put the wind up s.o.

fluo [flyo] *a inv F* (= *fluorescent*) fluorescent; **chemise vert fluo**, fluorescent green shirt.

flurer [flyrε] *vtr* **flurer le pet**, to try to pick quarrels.

flûte [flyt] **I** *int P* damn!/blast (it)!/damn and blast!/blow it! **II** *nfpl* 1. *P* legs*/pins; **jouer/se tirer des flûtes**, to run away*/to beat it/to clear off 2. *V* **jouer de la flûte/tailler une flûte**, to perform fellatio*.

fofolle [fɔfɔl] *a & nf F* foolish/silly/daft (woman/dog). (*Voir* **foufou**)

foie [fwa] *nm* 1. *F* **avoir les jambes en pâté de foie**, to have cotton-wool legs 2. *P* **avoir les foies**/*Vieilli* **avoir les foies blancs**, to be afraid*/to be scared to death.

foin [fwɛ̃] *nm* 1. *F* money*; **quand il n'y a plus de foin dans le râtelier**, when the money runs out; **faire ses foins**, to make money; **mettre du foin dans ses bottes**, to make a lot of money*/to make one's pile; **avoir du foin dans ses bottes**, to be rich*/well heeled 2. *Vieilli F* beard; **le foin de la journée**, five-o'clock shadow 3. *P* **faire du foin**, (*du bruit*) to make a din/a (hell of a) noise/a racket; (*un scandale*) to protest vehemently/to kick up a fuss/to make a scene; **faire un foin de tous les diables**, to make a terrific din; (*scandale*) to make a great song and dance (about sth)/to make a big stink (about sth)/to raise hell 4. *P* **coucher dans les foins**, to have a roll in the hay 5. *P* tobacco/baccy 6. *P* (*drogues*) marijuana*/hay. (*Voir* **bête II 1**)

foirade [fwarad] *nf P* 1. **avoir la foirade**, to have diarrhoea*/the runs/the trots; (*avoir peur*) to be afraid*/to have the jitters/to be shitting oneself 2. disaster/failure*/fiasco/flop; **c'est une vraie foirade**, it's a complete washout/flop.

foirailleur, -euse [fwarɑjœr, -øz] *n P* small-time reveller.

foire [fwar] **I** *nf P* **avoir la foire** = **avoir la foirade** (**foirade 1**) **II** *nf F* 1. crowd/crush 2. bedlam/bear-garden/madhouse 3. **faire la foire**, to go on a spree*/a binge; to let one's hair down/to paint the town red/to live it up/to have a ball/to get one's rocks off 4. **foire d'empoigne**, free-for-all; rat-race 5. **la foire est sur le pont!** we've got to get a move on!/we must get cracking!

foirer [fware] *vi* 1. *P* = **avoir la foirade** (**foirade 1**); **foirer dans son fourreau**, to be shit-scared. (*Voir* **froc 3**) 2. *P* to defecate* 3.

F to fail*/to flop/to come unstuck/to fall through.

foireur [fwarœr] *nm P* reveller.

foireux, -euse [fwarø, -øz] *P a & n* (*a*) (person) suffering from diarrhoea*/the runs (*b*) frightened/in a funk/jittery; **c'est un foireux**, he's scared/chicken (*c*) **pièce foireuse**, play that flopped; **c'est un plan foireux**, the plan's doomed to fail.

foiridon [fwaridɔ̃] *nf,* **foirinette** [fwarinεt] *nf F* **faire la foiridon**, to go on a spree*/on a binge; to live it up.

foiron [fwarɔ̃] *nm P* buttocks*; **avoir le foiron flottant**, to wiggle one's hips (*when walking*).

fois [fwa] *nf* 1. *F* **non mais des fois!** well, I like that!/don't make me laugh!/what d'you take me for?/do you mind! 2. *P* **des fois**, sometimes/now and then; **des fois que vous le verriez/si des fois vous le voyez**, if by any chance you (should) happen to see him/just in case you (happen) to see him; **vous n'auriez pas des fois ...?** you haven't by any chance got ...?/you wouldn't happen to have ...?

foisonner [fwazɔne] *vi P* to smell bad/to stink*/to pong.

foldingue [fɔldɛ̃g] *a & n P* = **folingue**.

folichon [fɔliʃɔ̃] *a F* **ce n'est pas folichon**, it's not much fun/it's not very exciting.

folies [fɔli] *nfpl F* (*a*) **faire des folies**, to be extravagant/to splurge; **quel magnifique cadeau, vous avez fait des folies!** what a lovely present, you really shouldn't have done it! **ne faites pas de folies!** don't put yourself out! (*b*) **les folies de la jeunesse**, the follies of youth; **faire des folies**, to have a wild time/to have one's fling (*c*) **faire des folies (de son corps)**, (*fille, femme*) to sleep around.

folingue [fɔlɛ̃g] *a & n P* (slightly) mad*/loony/nutty (person).

folkeux, -euse [fɔlkø, -øz] *n* folk musician/singer.

folklo [fɔlklo] *a F* eccentric*/offbeat/weird (and wonderful); (*vieux jeu*) old-fashioned.

folklore [fɔlklɔr] *nm F* **leur idée, c'est du folklore!** their idea can't be taken seriously/is daft!

folle[1] [fɔl] *nf P* homosexual*/queen. (*Voir* **fou**).

follingue [fɔlɛ̃g] *a & n P* = **folingue**.

foncer [fɔ̃se] *vi F* 1. to speed along/to tear along/to belt along 2. to throw oneself enthusiastically into sth/to charge into sth; **les flics ont foncé dans la foule**, the cops made a charge at the crowd; **quand je le vois, j'ai envie de lui foncer dedans,** each time I see him, he makes me so mad I could kill him **3. foncer dans le brouillard,** to go blindly ahead/ to forge ahead regardless.

fonceur, -euse [fɔ̃sœr, -øz] *n F* dynamic/ aggressive/go-ahead person.

fondant [fɔ̃dɑ̃] *nm P* (*drogues*) abscess caused by an unsterilized needle *or* by impure drugs/ab/AB/ABC.

fondre [fɔ̃dr] *vi F* (se faire) **fondre,** to get thin/to slim; to train down; **tu as drôlement fondu,** you've really lost weight/got thin.

fondu [fɔ̃dy] **I** *a P* mad*/nuts/round the bend/bonkers **II** *nm F* **1.** mad person*/loony/ headcase **2.** passionate admirer/fan **3. faire un fondu,** to drop out of circulation/to do a disappearing act.

fontaine [fɔ̃tɛn] *nf F* **ouvrir la fontaine,** to start crying/to turn on the waterworks. (*Voir* **cresson 1** (*a*))

fonte [fɔ̃t] *nf F* (weightlifter's) weights and barbells; **manier la fonte,** to do weighlifting/ weight training; to pump iron.

foot [fut] *nm F* football; **jouer au foot,** to play football. (*Voir* **baby-foot**)

forçat [fɔrsa] *nm F* **les forçats de la route,** the competitors in the *Tour de France* cycle race.

forcé [fɔrse] *a F* **c'est forcé!** it's inevitable!/ it's (just) got to happen!/there's no way round it!

forcir [fɔrsir] *vi F* to get fat; to put on weight.

format [fɔrma] *nm F* **1. petit format,** 100-franc note; **grand format,** 500-franc note **2. ce type-là, c'est du grand format,** he's a big guy.

forme [fɔrm] *nf F* **être en pleine forme/avoir la forme** (olympique), to be in fine form/in the peak of condition; to be up to scratch; **tenir la forme,** to keep in trim.

formid [fɔrmid] *a F* = **formidable I** (*a*).

formidable [fɔrmidabl] **I** *a F* (*a*) great/ super/terrific; **c'est formidable!** well I never! **elle est formidable,** she's fantastic/smashing/a smasher; **c'est un type formidable,** he's a great bloke/a really nice guy (*b*) incredible; **c'est tout de même formidable!** it's a bit much all the same!/that's the limit! **c'est formidable qu'elle ne puisse arriver à comprendre ça!** it's incredible (that) she can't understand that! **II** *nm F* **un formidable** = a pint (of beer).

formide [fɔrmid] *a F* = **formidable I** (*a*).

fort [fɔr] **I** *a F* **1.** clever/good (en, at) **2. c'est un peu fort** (de café/en vinaigre)! that's a bit much/a bit steep! **c'est** (un peu) **trop fort!**/ **c'est plus fort que tout!** that's going too far!/ that's too much!/that's a bit thick! **3. en voilà une forte!/elle est forte, celle-là!** well I never!/that takes the cake!/that beats everything! **4. c'est plus fort que moi!** I (simply) can't help it! (*Voir* **bouchon 7**; **cuite**; **gueule I 2**; **thème 1**) **II** *adv F* **1.** (*a*) (y) aller fort, to exaggerate*/to lay it on (a bit) thick/to overdo it (*b*) **je ne vais pas fort,** I'm not feeling very well/I don't feel too good **2. faire fort,** to do brilliantly well in an undertaking/in a venture. (*Voir* **aller 7**)

fortiche [fɔrtiʃ] *F* **I** *a* (*a*) (*malin*) smart; (*doué*) clever/smart (*b*) (*robuste*) strong/ hefty/brawny **II** *n* (*a*) (*personne maligne*) smart/cunning person; smart aleck; (*personne douée*) smart/clever person; **il est fortiche,** he knows what's what/he's on the ball; **c'est une fortiche,** she's no dimwit/she's as smart as they come (*b*) strong/hefty/ brawny person; **un fortiche,** a tough guy/a heavy.

fortif(e)s [fɔrtif] *nfpl A P* (*abrév* = *fortifications*) **les fortif(e)s,** the old defence works around Paris (*formerly an habitual resort of criminals*). (*Voir* **laffes**)

fortune [fɔrtyn] *nf F* **être en quête de bonnes fortunes,** (*hommes*) to be on the make/after a bit; (to be trying) to get off with/to pull a girl/a woman.

fosse [fos] *nf F* **avoir un pied dans la fosse,** to have one foot in the grave.

fossé [fose] *nm F* **sauter le fossé,** (se *résoudre à qch*) to take the plunge; (se *marier*) to get married*.

fossile [fosil, fo-] *F* **I** *nm* **un vieux fossile,** an old fossil/an old fogey/(an old) has-been/an old fuddy-duddy **II** *a* fossilized/antiquated (ideas, etc).

se fossiliser [səfosilize, -fo-] *vpr F* to become an old fossil/fossilized; to get past it/ to have had it.

fou, folle² [fu, fol] *a F* **1.** tremendous/ enormous/fantastic; **un argent fou,** pots/ loads/bags of money; **un monde fou,** a terrific/a huge crowd; **j'ai un mal fou à apprendre cette langue,** I'm having a really tough time with this language; **c'est un succès fou,** it's a smash hit/a tremendous success **2.** mad*/crazy; **t'es** (pas) **fou?** are you mad?/ you must be out of your mind! **3.** (*a*) **c'est fou**

ce que ..., it's amazing/extraordinary how ...;
c'est fou ce que c'est cher! it costs the earth!
c'est fou ce qu'on s'amuse! we're having a
fantastic time! c'est fou ce qu'elle est drôle!
she's a real scream! (*b*) c'est fou, New York!
New York is fantastic!

fouchtra [fuʃtra] *a & nm* P (native, in-
habitant) of Auvergne.

foudre [fudr] *nf* F le coup de foudre, love at
first sight.

fouettard [fwɛtar] *nm* 1. (*a*) F le père
Fouettard, the bog(e)yman (*b*) F un père
fouettard, a very strict father 2. P buttocks*;
botter le fouettard à qn, to give s.o. a boot up
the backside/arse/*surt NAm* ass 3. P l'avoir
dans le (père) fouettard, to be swindled*/
done/had/diddled; se le faire mettre dans le
(père) fouettard, to get the worst of it/to come
off second best 4. P s.o. who enjoys (sexual)
flagellation; passive flagellant.

fouetter [fwete] *vi* P 1. to stink* (to high
heaven); ça fouette ici, it stinks in here 2. to
be afraid*/to get the wind up. (*Voir* **chat 5,
6**)

foufou [fufu] *a & nm* F silly/foolish/daft/
crazy (person, dog). (*Voir* **fofolle**)

foufoune(tte) [fufun(ɛt)] *nf* V female
genitals*/pussy/twat.

fouignedé [fwiɲəde] *nm* P (*a*) buttocks*/
arse/*surt NAm* ass (*b*) anus*/arsehole/*surt
NAm* asshole.

fouille [fuj] *nf* P 1. pocket; en avoir plein les
fouilles, to be rich*/flush/loaded 2. l'avoir dans
la fouille, to have it all sewn up; c'est dans la
fouille, it's in the bag 3. être une fouille
percée, to be a spendthrift/to spend money
like water. (*Voir* **vaisselle 1**)

fouille-merde [fujmɛrd] *nm & f inv* P 1.
scandalmonger/muck-raker; *surt* journalist/
hack/hackette 2. (private) investigator.

fouiller [fuje] I *vtr* V to have sex* with
(s.o.)/to screw (s.o.)/to have it off with (s.o.)
II *vpr* se fouiller P 1. se fouiller (de qch), to
(make) do without (sth)/to go without (sth) 2.
tu peux te fouiller (si tu as des poches)! (you
can) go jump in the lake!/get stuffed!/get
knotted!

fouillette [fujɛt] *nf* P 1. pocket*. (*Voir*
fouille 1) 2. frisk; body search.

fouillouse [fujuz] *nf* P pocket*. (*Voir*
fouille 1)

Fouilly-les-Chaussettes [fujilɛʃosɛt],
Fouilly-les-Coucous [fujilɛkuku] *Prn* F
= **Fouilly-les-Oies** (*a*).

Fouilly-les-Oies [fujilɛzwa] *Prn* F (*a*)
imaginary out-of-the-way place; one-horse
town/hick town; = Much-Binding-in-the-
Marsh/*NAm* Podunk. (*Voir* **Tripatouille-les-
Oies**) (*b*) sortir de Fouilly-les-Oies, to come
from the back of beyond/the sticks; *NAm* to
come from the backwoods/the boondocks/the
boonies; *Austr* to come from the backblocks.

fouinard, -arde [fwinar, -ard] I *a* F
inquisitive/nosy/snoopy II *nm & f* F snoop(er).

fouinasser [fwinase] *vi* P = **fouiner 1**.

fouine [fwin] *nf* F 1. à tête de fouine,
weasel-faced/ferret-faced; c'est une vraie
fouine, he/she is very nosy/a nosy parker 2.
snooping/prying.

fouin(e)darès [fwindarɛs] *nm* P 1. anus* 2.
buttocks*.

fouiner [fwine] *vi* F 1. to ferret (about)/to
nose about/to snoop; fouiner dans les affaires
d'autrui, to poke one's nose into other people's
affairs 2. (*aux puces, etc*) to hunt for
bargains, etc.

fouineur, -euse [fwinœr, -øz] F I *a & n* =
fouinard II *n* bargain hunter.

foulant [fulɑ̃] *a* F tiring/exhausting/back-
breaking; ce n'est pas bien foulant, it's a bit
of a doddle/a soft option, really.

se fouler [səfule] *vpr* F 1. to take pains
(over sth)/to put oneself out (to do sth well) 2.
il ne se foule pas/il ne se foule pas la rate/il ne
se la foule pas, he takes it easy/he doesn't
exactly kill himself working/he doesn't overdo
things; il n'a pas à se fouler, he doesn't have
to flog himself to death/he's onto a cushy
number. (*Voir* **méninges** (*a*); **poignet 1**)

foultitude [fultityd] *nf* F une foultitude de
..., a crowd/mass of ...; bags/heaps/loads/
masses/piles of ....

founette [funɛt] *nf* V = **foufoune(tte)**.

four [fur] *nm* F (*théâtre, etc*) failure/
disaster/flop; faire un four, to flop; (*pour un
voleur*) to steal an empty wallet; la pièce a
fait un four, the play was a flop/the play
flopped; un four noir, a complete washout.

fouraille [furaj] *nf* P firearm/shooter/piece.

fourailler [furaje] I *vtr & i* V to have sex*
(with) (s.o.)/to screw (s.o.) (very quickly);
fourailler à la une, to have a quick in-and-out
job/a quickie; to bunny-fuck II *vi* P to use a
firearm/to fire a gun.

fourbi [furbi] *nm* F 1. *Mil* kit/gear 2.
belongings/gear/clobber/stuff 3. (*a*) rubbish;
mess; bits and pieces; je vais me débarrasser
de tout ce fourbi, I'm going to get shot of all

this junk/I'm going to chuck this lot out (b) (et) **tout le fourbi**, the whole works/the whole (kit and) caboodle; **habillé en jean, blouson noir et tout le fourbi**, dressed in jeans, black (leather) jacket, the lot/the whole works/you name it! (c) (truc) thingummy/gadget 4. peculiar/funny business; **un fourbi arabe**, one hell of a mess; **un sale fourbi**, a rotten job; **c'est tout un fourbi**, it's quite a business.

fourche [furʃ] nf 1. F **faire qch à la fourche**, to do sth anyoldhow 2. F **traiter qn à la fourche**, to treat s.o. roughly/badly 3. P (voleur à la) **fourche**, pickpocket*.

fourchette [furʃɛt] nf 1. F **il a un bon coup de fourchette/c'est une bonne fourchette**, he's got a good/healthy appetite 2. F **manger avec la fourchette du père Adam**, to eat with one's fingers; **à la fourchette**, with the hand(s) 3. P **donner le coup de fourchette à qn**, to poke s.o. in the eyes (with the index and second fingers) 4. P pickpocket*; **vol à la fourchette**, pickpocketing/dipping.

fourgat [furga] nm P = **fourgue**.

fourgue [furg] nm P 1. (a) receiver (of stolen goods)/fence (b) (drogues) pusher/dealer*/(the) man 2. (a) receiving (of stolen goods) (b) (drug) dealing.

fourguer [furge] vtr P 1. (a) to buy (stolen goods) (b) to sell/to flog (stolen goods) (c) to sell (sth) on the cheap 2. to inform on*/to grass on (s.o.); to shop (s.o.) 3. (drogues) to push/to deal.

fourgueur, -euse [furgœr, -øz] n P = **fourgue**.

fourlineur, -euse [furlinœr, -øz] n A P pickpocket*/dip.

fourmi [furmi] nf 1. F **avoir des fourmis dans les pattes**, to have pins and needles in one's legs; **j'ai des fourmis dans le pied**, my foot has gone to sleep 2. F **une fourmi blanche**, a busy and thrifty person/eager beaver 3. P (rare) **une fourmi rouge**, a woman traffic warden 4. P (drogues) (small-scale) pusher/dealer*.

fourneau, pl **-eaux** [furno] nm A P fool*.

fournée [furne] nf F batch/contingent (of tourists, etc).

fourré [fure] a F **être toujours fourré chez qn**, to be never off s.o.'s doorstep/to be constantly (calling) at s.o.'s house; **être toujours fourré avec qn**, to hobnob with s.o. (Voir **langue 9**)

fourreau, pl **-eaux** [furo] nm P trousers*/surt NAm pants. (Voir **foirer 1**)

fourrer [fure] I vtr 1. F (a) to cram/to stuff/to stick/to shove; **il a fourré la lettre dans sa poche**, he shoved the letter into his pocket; **fourre-toi ça dans la tête**, get that into your head (b) to place/to put; **il ne sait pas où il a fourré ses clés**, he doesn't know where he put his keys; **fourrez tout ça par terre!** dump all that lot on the ground! 2. F **fourrer qn dedans**, (tromper) to cheat* s.o./to have s.o. on/to take s.o. in; (mettre en prison) to put s.o. behind bars/to put s.o. inside 3. F **fourrer son nez partout**, to poke/to stick one's nose into everything; **fourrer le nez dans les affaires des autres**, to poke one's nose in other people's business 4. V to have sex* with (s.o.)/to screw (s.o.)/to stuff (s.o.). (Voir **doigt 6**; **tiroir 3**) II vpr **se fourrer** F 1. (a) **je ne savais où me fourrer**, I (was so embarrassed that I) didn't know where to hide/where to put myself (b) **où est-il allé se fourrer?** where on earth has he got to?/what has he got himself into? (c) **se fourrer dans un guêpier**, to get mixed up in a nasty business 2. **chercher quelque trou où se fourrer**, to be looking for a job (without much hope of success) 3. **se fourrer dans la conversation**, to butt in 4. **s'en fourrer jusque-là**, to gorge oneself/to have a blow-out/to stuff one's face.

fourrure [furyr] nf V **humecter sa fourrure**, (femme) to urinate*/to (have a) piss.

foutaise [futɛz] nf P 1. rubbish/nonsense*/rot/bull(shit); **tout ça c'est de la foutaise/des foutaises**, that's a load of bullshit/Br a load of old cobblers 2. **on s'est quitté(s) pour des foutaises**, we split up for no real reason/for sod all.

fouteur [futœr] nm V **fouteur de merde**, piss artist.

foutoir [futwar] nm P 1. messy room, house, etc; pigsty/dump; **quel foutoir!** what a (bloody) shambles! 2. brothel*/knocking shop.

foutral, -als [futral] a Vieilli P extraordinary/amazing.

foutre¹ [futr] V I nm semen*/spunk/jism/cum II int **foutre!** fuck (it)!/sod (it)!/bugger (it)!/shit! **je n'en sais foutre rien**, I know sod all about it/I haven't got a fucking clue.

foutre² I vtr 1. P (mettre) **foutre qch par terre**, to chuck/to fling sth on the ground; **foutre qn dehors/à la porte**, to kick s.o. out/to give s.o. the boot/to give s.o. the push; V **ta lettre, tu peux te la foutre quelque part!** you know what you can do with your letter!/you can stick your letter up your arse/surt NAm ass 2. *P* (*donner*) **foutre un coup de pied à qn**, to give s.o. a kick up the arse/*surt NAm* ass; **ça m'a foutu le trac**, it gave me the creeps/the willies; **elle m'a foutu la honte**, (*d'elle*) I was ashamed of her; (*de moi*) she made me ashamed of myself; **je t'en foutrai, moi!** I'll teach you a lesson you'll never forget!; what do you take me for! 3. (*faire*) **il ne fout rien de la journée**, he just sits on his arse/ass all day long; he does bugger all; he just sods/bums around; **qu'est-ce que tu fous?** what the hell are you doing? **qu'est-ce qu'elle peut bien foutre là-dedans?** what the fuck is she doing in there? 4. *V* **qu'est-ce que ça peut me foutre?/qu'est-ce que j'en ai à foutre?/j'en ai rien à foutre**, what the fuck's it got to do with me?/I don't give a fuck/a shit/a fart! **rien à foutre!** nothing doing!*/not a chance in hell!/not a sodding chance! 5. *V* **foutre le camp**, to fuck off/to bugger off/to sod off/to piss off; **foutez le camp!** fuck off!/piss off!/sod off! 6. *V* **fous-moi la paix!** fuck off!/piss off!/sod off!/bugger off!/lay off!/stop bugging me!/stop pissing me about! **va te faire foutre!** fuck off!/go fuck yourself!/screw you!/fuck you!/go screw yourself! **qu'il aille se faire foutre**, he can piss off/*Br* get stuffed 7. *V* (*a*) **envoyer qn faire foutre**, to tell s.o. to fuck off (*b*) **envoyer qch faire foutre**, to pack sth in (*c*) **tout foutre en l'air**, to bugger/to fuck/to screw everything up; **ça a tout foutu en l'air**, that's ballsed/*NAm* balled/bollocksed it up nicely (*d*) **foutre qn dedans**, to mislead s.o.; to land s.o. in the shit 8. *P* **ça la fout mal**, that makes a lousy impression/that looks really bad 9. *P* **en foutre un coup**, to work hard*/to work one's balls off/*surt NAm* to work one's tail off 10. *P* **foutre la merde/le merdier dans qch**, to make a balls-up/a cock-up of sth; to balls sth up 11. *V* **foutre qn**, to have sex* with s.o./to fuck s.o./to screw s.o. II *vpr* **se foutre** *P* 1. **se foutre par terre**, (*se jeter par terre*) to fling oneself on the ground; (*tomber*) to fall flat on one's face/to come a cropper* 2. (*a*) **se foutre de qn**, (*se moquer de*) to poke fun at s.o./to pull s.o.'s leg/to have s.o. on; (*embêter*) to mess s.o. about/around; **est-ce que vous vous foutez de moi?** are you trying to make me look stupid? **tu te fous de ma gueule?** are you taking the piss (out of me)?/what the hell do you take me for?/I'm not a complete arsehole/*surt NAm* asshole! (*b*) **se foutre de qch**, not to give a damn/shit about sth; **il s'en fout comme de l'an quarante/**

comme de sa première chemise, il s'en fout pas mal/complètement, il s'en fout et s'en contrefout, he couldn't give a damn/a shit/a fuck; **je me fous bien de ce qu'on pense de moi**, I don't give a damn what they think of me/they can think what they bloody well like about me; **tu te fous du monde ou quoi?** who the fuck do you think you are? **ça, c'est se foutre du monde!** well, what a bloody/damn cheek/nerve! he's/she's/they've got a bloody nerve! 3. **se foutre dedans**, to put one's foot in it/to boob; **alors là, il se fout dedans/le doigt dans l'œil!** well, he's bloody wrong then! 4. **se foutre à faire qch**, to begin to do sth 5. **s'en foutre plein la lampe**, to stuff one's face/to have a good blow-out/to pig out. (*Voir* **air I 7; doigt 6; gueule II 2, 4**)

foutrement [futr(ə)mɑ̃] *adv P* very/extremely; **c'est foutrement loin**, it's a bloody long way/it's damn far; **être foutrement con**, to be bloody stupid/damn thick; to be a fucking idiot.

foutriquet [futrikɛ] *nm Vieilli P* insignificant person/nobody/little squirt/little runt.

foutu [futy] *a P* 1. (*a*) **être mal foutu**, (*appareil*, *etc*) to be badly made/designed; (*personne*) (*malade*) to feel unwell*/under the weather; (*fatigué*) to feel (bloody) tired*/shagged/knackered; (*mal habillé*) to be badly/untidily dressed; (*laid*) to be ugly; **ce stylo est très mal foutu**, this biro is useless; **je suis vraiment mal foutu aujourd'hui**, I feel really lousy/I feel bloody awful today; **elle n'est pas mal foutue, cette nana**, she's not at all bad(-looking), that bird/chick (*b*) **être bien foutu**, (*chose*) to be well made; (*personne*) (*bien habillé*) to be well dressed; (*beau*) to be good-looking; **c'est bien foutu, ce petit truc**, it's not bad, this little thingamyjig; **il est vachement bien foutu, ce mec**, he's a damn good looker/he's really dishy, that guy/bloke 2. rotten/awful/lousy; **quel foutu temps!** what bloody awful/foul/lousy weather! **quelle foutue idée!** what a bloody stupid/pathetic/useless idea! **dans un foutu état**, in a terrible state; **un foutu imbécile**, a bloody idiot/a fucking idiot 3. **il est foutu**, he's done for/he's had it; **c'est un type foutu**, he'll never get anywhere/he's finished; **la réunion est foutue**, the meeting's screwed up/buggered up; **ma montre est foutue**, my watch is bust/buggered; **c'est de l'argent (de) foutu**, it's money down the drain; **ce n'est pas la peine d'essayer, c'est foutu d'avance,**

there's no point in trying/what's the use of trying, it's already fucked (up) **4. foutu de**, likely to/capable of; **il n'est même pas foutu de faire son lit**, he can't even make his own bed; **elle n'est même pas foutue de me le dire en face**, she hasn't the guts to say so to my face; **il est foutu de partir avant que j'arrive**, he's bound to leave before I get there; **elle est bien foutue de le faire**, she's quite capable of doing it; I wouldn't put it past her.

fracasser [frakase] *vtr Vieilli P* to burgle/*NAm* to burglarize.

fracasseur [frakasœr] *nm P* burglar.

fraîche¹ [frɛʃ] *nf P* **1.** money*/cash/dough **2. une fraîche**, a bottle/carafe of water.

fraîchement [frɛʃmɑ̃] *adv F* **ça va fraîchement ce matin**, it's a bit cool this morning; **accueillir qn fraîchement**, to give s.o. a cool welcome/reception.

frais¹, fraîche² [frɛ, frɛʃ] I *a* **1.** *F* **frais comme l'œil/comme une rose**, as fresh as a daisy; **il n'est pas frais ce matin**, he doesn't look too hot this morning **2.** *P* **me voilà frais!/je suis frais (comme un porc)!** I'm in a fix*/I'm in a right old mess!/I'm really up the creek! **II** *nm F* **mettre au frais**, to imprison*/to put away; (*mettre à l'abri*) to put out of circulation/in a safe place.

frais² *nmpl F* **1. arrêter les frais**, to give up/to throw in the sponge/the towel **2. aux frais de la princesse**, at the expense of the taxpayer/the government; on the firm; on expenses; on the house/buckshee.

fraise [frɛz] *nf* **1.** (*a*) *F* **aller aux fraises**, (*voiture*) to go off the road (by accident); (*Hum, Euph: amoureux*) to go for a walk in the woods (*b*) *P* **allez aux fraises!** get lost*!/go jump in a lake!/get knotted! **2.** *P* **sucrer les fraises**, to tremble/to have the shakes **3.** *P* **face*/mug**; **se sucrer la fraise/se refaire la fraise**, to make up/to powder one's nose; **un coup en pleine fraise**, a punch in the kisser **4.** *P* (*a*) **ramener sa fraise**, (*faire l'importun*) to butt into the conversation/to put in one's oar (*b*) **(r)amener sa fraise**, (*arriver*) to turn up/to put in an appearance/to show one's face; **(r)amène ta fraise!** come here! **5.** *P* **envoyer qn aux fraises/sur les fraises**, to send s.o. packing*/to send s.o. off with a flea in his ear.

fraline [fralin] *nf P* = **frangine**.

framboise [frɑ̃bwaz] *nf V* clitoris*/clit.

franc, *f* **franche** [frɑ̃, frɑ̃ʃ] *a F* safe/without risk; **c'est pas très franc**, it's a bit tricky/dodgy; **franc du collier**, trustworthy/

dependable.

la Franchecaille [lafrɑ̃ʃkaj] *Prnf P* France.

franchouillard, -arde [frɑ̃ʃujar, -ard] *F Péj* **I** *a* (*a*) French (*b*) chauvinistically French **II** *n* (*a*) French chauvinist (*b*) average Frenchman/Frenchwoman **III** *nm* French (language).

franco [frɑ̃ko] **I** *a P* **1.** (*personne*) loyal/dependable **2.** = **franc II** *adv F* readily/unhesitatingly; **y aller franco**, to go straight to the point/to come right out with it; **vas-y franco!** go right ahead!

François [frɑ̃swa] *Prnm Vieilli P* **faire le coup du père François à qn**, to strangle s.o./to throttle s.o.; to garrotte s.o.

francouillard [frɑ̃kujar] *nm P* (*argent*) franc.

frangibus [frɑ̃ʒibys] *nm P* brother/bruvver/bro'.

frangin [frɑ̃ʒɛ̃] *nm P* **1.** brother/bruvver/bro' **2.** fellow*/chap/bloke/guy **3.** friend*/mate **4.** monk/friar **5.** *pl* **les frangins**, (the) freemasons.

frangine [frɑ̃ʒin] *nf P* **1.** sister/sis **2.** (*a*) girl*/bird/chick/sister (*b*) woman*/*surt NAm* dame/broad **3.** prostitute*/hooker/tart **4.** mistress **5.** lesbian*/lezzy/dyke **6.** nun.

fransquillon, -onne [frɑ̃skijɔ̃, -ɔn] *P* **I** *a* French/frog/frogge **II** *n* Frenchman/Frenchwoman; **les Fransquillons**, the frogs/the froggies.

frappadingue [frapadɛ̃g] *a P* mad*/bonkers/barmy/nuts.

frappe [frap] *nf P* hooligan*/thug/yob/yobbo; **c'est une petite frappe**, he's a dirty/nasty little bastard*.

frappé [frape] *a P* mad*/crazy/loony/nuts.

frapper [frape] **I** *vtr P* **frapper qn**, to tap/to touch s.o. for money; to cadge (off s.o.)/to be on the cadge **II** *vpr* **se frapper** *F* to get flustered/to get into a state/to get worked up/to get into a flap; **(ne) vous frappez pas!** don't panic!/don't flap!/stay cool!

frayer [freje] *vi F* **frayer avec qn**, to associate with s.o.; **je ne fraye pas avec eux**, I don't mix with them.

freak [frik] *nm F* freak.

frégate [fregat] *nf P* young passive homosexual*.

frégaton [fregatɔ̃] *nm F* naval commander.

frein [frɛ̃] *nm F* **mâcher/ronger son frein**, (*personne*) to champ at the bit/to be raring to go.

frelot [frəlo] *nm P* (younger/kid) brother.

frelote [frəlɔt] *nf P* (younger/kid) sister.

fréquenter [frekɑ̃te] I *vtr F* fréquenter qn, (*sortir avec qn*) to go out with s.o. II *vpr* **se fréquenter** *V* to masturbate*/to toss off/to play with oneself.

frère [frɛr] *nm* 1. *F* friend*/mate/buddy; (*surt argot des noirs*) (soul) brother; t'es un frère, you're a real pal/a brick; you're all right/OK 2. *F* (*a*) qu'est-ce qu'ils veulent, ces frères-là? what do those blokes/guys want? (*b*) vieux frère! old chap!*/my old mate! 3. *F* c'est pas le frère à dégueulasse, it's excellent*/first-rate/scrumptious 4. *F* frère trois-points, freemason 5. *P* petit frère, penis*/John Thomas; **dérouiller son petit frère**, to have sex*/to get one's end away.

frérot [frero] *nm F* (little/kid) brother.

frétillante [fretijɑ̃t] *nf P* tail.

fric [frik] *nm F* money*/bread/dough/lolly; être bourré de fric/être au fric, to be rich*/ loaded/rolling in it; **il pue le fric**, he's stinking rich; **se faire du fric**, to make money*/to earn one's living; **aboule ton fric!** cough up!/fork out! ça m'a coûté un max de/plein de fric, it cost me a fortune/a hell of a lot.

fricassée [frikase] *nf F* 1. thrashing/beating up* 2. **fricassée de museaux**, kissing and cuddling; necking.

fricasser [frikase] *F* I *vtr* to squander/to blow (one's money) II *vpr* **se fricasser le museau**, to kiss and cuddle; to have a necking session.

fric-frac [frikfrak] *nm P* 1. burglary/ housebreaking; break-in; **faire un fric-frac**, to break in/to burgle/*NAm* to burglarize/to heist; ils sont allés faire un fric-frac quelque part, they've gone off to do a job some place 2. burglar/cracksman. (*pl* fric-frac(s))

fricfraquer [frikfrake] *vi P* = faire un fric-frac (**fric-frac 1**)

frichti [friʃti] *nm P* food*/grub/nosh/chow; meal; être de frichti, to be in charge of the cooking/to be chief cook.

fricot [friko] *nm F* 1. grub/nosh/chow; cooking; meal; **faire le fricot**, to do the cooking/to make the grub 2. work/job; *surt* profitable/ fruitful activity.

fricotage [frikɔtaʒ] *nm F* fiddling/ underhand practice(s)/shady dealing; c'est du fricotage, it's a shady business.

fricoter [frikɔte] *vtr & i* 1. *F* to cook; elle fricote bien, she's a good cook 2. *Vieilli F* to squander/to blow/to run through (money) 3. *F*

(*a*) to plot/to cook up; to wangle; je me demande ce qu'il fricote, I wonder what he's cooking up; qu'est-ce que tu fricotes? what are you up to? (*b*) to engage in (small-scale) shady dealings/to be on the fiddle 4. *P* (*Euph sexuel*) ils fricotent ensemble ces deux-là, those two are sleeping together/knocking around together.

fricoteur, -euse [frikɔtœr, -øz] *n F* dishonest dealer/wangler/fiddler; (*profiteur*) profiteer.

frictionnée [friksjɔne] *nf P* thrashing/going over/roughing up/beating* up.

Fridolin [fridɔlɛ̃] *nm P* German*/Jerry/ Fritz/Kraut.

fri-fri [frifri] *nm V* female genitals*; **cache fri-fri**, G-string.

frig [friʒ] *nm F* mortuary/morgue.

frigo [frigo] I *a F* il fait frigo, it's freezing (cold) II *nm F* refrigerator/fridge/*NAm* ice box; **mettre un projet au frigo**, to put a project into cold storage/to shelve a project.

frigorifié [frigɔrifje] *a F* être frigorifié, (*personne*) to be frozen stiff/to be frozen to death.

frimant, -ante [frimɑ̃, -ɑ̃t] *n P* (*théâtre*) bit-player/extra/walker-on.

frime [frim] *nf F* 1. (*a*) sham/pretence/put-on; c'est de la frime, it's all put on; that's just a lot of eyewash/hokum (*b*) **faire qch pour la frime**, to do sth for appearances' sake/for show 2. (*a*) head*; face* (*b*) appearance/looks/(facial) expression 3. (*théâtre*) faire une frime/faire de la frime, to have walk-on parts/to be an extra/to play bit parts 4. en frime, face to face; **laisser qn en frime**, to abandon s.o./to leave s.o. high and dry/to leave s.o. in the lurch.

frimer [frime] *F* I *vi* 1. to pretend; to put on an act/a show; to show off*; **arrête de frimer**, stop showing off 2. bien frimer, to look good; mal frimer, to look shoddy; **il frime mal**, he doesn't look good 3. ça frime, it makes an impression/it's impressive II *vtr* 1. to look at*/to stare at 2. frimer l'orgasme, to pretend to have an orgasm/to pretend to come 3. frimer qn, to scoff at s.o./to make a monkey out of s.o.

frimeur, -euse [frimœr, -øz] *nm F* show-off*/poseur/poser.

frimousse [frimus] *nf F* cute/sweet little face.

fringale [frɛ̃gal] *nf F* hunger; **avoir la fringale**, to be ravenous/starving.

fringue [frɛ̃g] *nf P* clothing trade/industry; faire dans la fringue, to be in the clothing trade. (*Voir* **fringues**)

fringuer [frɛ̃ge] I *vtr P* to dress (s.o.); bien/ mal fringué, well/badly dressed; fringué en jean, wearing jeans II *vpr* **se fringuer** *P* to get dressed (up); to do oneself up/to doll oneself up; il s'est bien fringué pour sortir, he's got himself up all ready to go out.

fringues [frɛ̃g] *nfpl P* clothes*/clobber/togs/ gear; fringues de coulisse, underwear. (*Voir* **fringue**)

frio [frio] *a P* il fait frio, it's freezing (cold)/ it's brass monkey weather.

fripe [frip] *nf* 1. *P* food*/grub/nosh/chow; faire la fripe, to rustle up some food 2. (*a*) clothing trade/industry (*b*) *pl F* **fripes**, second-hand clothes.

fripouille [fripuj] *nf F* rotter/swine/bastard*.

friqué [frike] *a F* rich*/loaded/rolling in it.

friquet [frikɛ] *nm P* (*prison*) informer*.

frire [frir] *vtr F* rien à frire! (*rien à faire*) nothing doing!*/not on your nellie! (*rien à manger*) not a bite to eat.

Frisco [frisko] *Prn F* San Francisco/Frisco.

frisé, -ée [frize] *n P Péj* (*non-Blanc*) nignog/spade.

Frisé [frize] *nm*, **Frisou**, *pl* **-ous** [frizu] *nm F* German* (soldier)/Jerry.

frisquet [friskɛ] *a F* chilly/nippy/parky; il fait frisquet, there's a nip in the air/it's a bit chilly.

fristiquer [fristike] *vi P* to have a bite to eat*; to have a meal.

frit [fri] *a F* on est frits, we've had it/we're done for/our goose is cooked.

frite [frit] *nf P* 1. face*; head; vise un peu la frite qu'il a! just take a dekko at his face! 2. (*forme*) il a la frite, he's in form/in great shape; t'as pas la frite? don't you feel too good? ça va te donner la frite, that'll perk you up 3. (painful) flick of the fingers on the buttocks 4. *pl Vieilli* tomber dans les frites, to faint*/to pass out. (*Voir* **bouche 6**)

Fritz [frits] *P* I *a* German* (soldier)/Jerry II *nm* (*a*) German*/Jerry/Fritz/Kraut; les Fritz, Jerry/the Jerries (*b*) le fritz, (the) German (language).

Frizou, *pl* **-ous** [frizu] *nm F* German* (soldier)/Jerry.

froc [frɔk] *nm* 1. *P* trousers*/pants 2. *P* déchirer son froc, to fart* loudly 3. *V* chier/ débourrer/faire/foirer/lâcher tout dans son froc, to be afraid*/to be shit-scared/to be scared shitless 4. *V* pisser dans son froc, to piss oneself laughing. (*Voir aussi* **pisser I 10**) 5. *P* baisser son froc, to humiliate oneself/to eat humble pie 6. *pl P* clothes*.

frocard [frɔkar] *nm Vieilli P* 1. monk/ clergyman 2. trousers*/pants.

frolot [frɔlo] *nm P* (younger/kid) brother.

from [frɔm] *nm P* cheese.

fromage [frɔmaʒ] *nm* 1. *F* cushy job/easy number/soft option; il est dans un de ces fromages, he's onto a really cushy number/ he's got a really cushy job; un gentil petit fromage, a nice little earner 2. *F* faire de ça un fromage/en faire tout un fromage, to kick up a fuss about nothing/to make a song and dance about nothing 3. *P* juryman/ jurywoman; les douze fromages, members of the jury 4. *pl P* fromages, feet* 5. *P* circular machine-gun loader 6. *P* white cap 7. *P Péj* white person. (*Voir* **chat 3**)

frome [frɔm] *nm*, **fromegi** [frɔmʒi] *nm*, **frometon** [frɔmtɔ̃] *nm*, **fromgi** [frɔmʒi] *nm*, **fromgom** [frɔmgɔm] *nm*, **fromjo** [frɔmʒo] *nm*, **fromtegom** [frɔmtəgɔm] *nm*, **fromton** [frɔmtɔ̃] *nm P* cheese. (*Voir* **os 1**)

frotte [frɔt] *nf P* 1. la frotte, scabies/the itch 2. la Frotte, the Hôpital Saint-Louis (*in Paris*).

frottée [frɔte] *nf F* (*a*) thrashing/beating/ good hiding (*b*) defeat.

frotter [frɔte] I *vtr* 1. *Vieilli F* to thrash (s.o.)/to give (s.o.) a good hiding; frotter les oreilles à qn, to reprimand* s.o./to chew s.o.'s ears off 2. *V* to have sex* with (s.o.) II *vi P* 1. to flirt 2. to dance close together/to smooch (*esp in the slow numbers*) III *vpr* **se frotter** 1. *F* se frotter à qn, to come up against s.o./to tangle with s.o.; faut pas s'y frotter! don't get involved!/don't meddle! 2. *P* to dance close together/to smooch (*esp in the slow numbers*).

frotteuse [frɔtøz] *nf* 1. *P* (safety) match 2. *V* penis*/rod 3. *P* dancing.

frotti-frotta [frɔtifrɔta] *nm P* sexy dancing/smooching.

frottin [frɔtɛ̃] *nm P* faire une partie de frottin/faire un frottin, to have a game of billiards.

frotting [frɔtiŋ] *nm P* dance hall.

froussard, -arde [frusar, -ard] *a & n P* cowardly* (person)/chicken; c'est un froussard/il est froussard, he's a (bit of a) coward*.

frousse [frus] *nf P* fear/fright; avoir la

frousse, to be afraid*/to be scared stiff; **ficher/flanquer/foutre la frousse à qn,** to put the wind up s.o./to give s.o. the willies.

fruit [frɥi] *nm* F **fruit sec,** student who has failed to qualify for a profession/dropout; failure*/dead loss/washout.

frusqué [fryske] *a* P dressed; **frusqué de/en noir,** dressed in/wearing black.

frusquer [fryske] I *vtr* P to dress/to clothe (s.o.) II *vpr* **se frusquer** P to get dressed/to put one's clothes on.

frusques [frysk] *nfpl* P clothes*; **mettre ses belles frusques,** to put one's glad rags on; **de vieilles frusques,** cast-offs; **apportez vos frusques de foot,** bring (along) your football clobber/gear; **enfile tes frusques,** get dressed.

frusquin [fryskɛ̃] *nm* P = **Saint-Frusquin** (*a*), (*b*).

fuite [fɥit] *nf* F **la fuite** (*a*) *Mil* demob(ilization); (*écoles*) the holidays (*b*) indiscretion; revelation of a secret/leak.

(se) fuiter [(sə)fɥite] *vi & vpr* P to run away*/to scarper/to do a bunk.

fumant [fymɑ̃] *a* F wonderful/amazing/brilliant/terrific/sensational.

fumante [fymɑ̃t] *nf* P sock.

fumasse [fymas] *a* P to be angry*/fuming/ *surt NAm* mad/sore.

fume [fym] *nf* F (*a*) smoking (*b*) tobacco.

fumée [fyme] *nf* 1. danger; tricky situation; **y a de la fumée,** there's trouble 2. **balancer/ envoyer la fumée,** P to shoot (a firearm)/to fire; V to ejaculate*/to shoot (one's load) 3. V **avaler la fumée,** (*fellation*) to give (s.o.) a blow-job/to give (s.o.) head.

fumelle [fymɛl] *nf Vieilli P* woman*/female.

fumer [fyme] *vi* F 1. to fume/to be fuming/to rage 2. **ça fume!** things are warming up!/ things are hotting up! **ça va fumer!** there'll be fireworks!/there'll be trouble! (*Voir* **belge**; **pompier 1; sapeur**)

fumeron [fymrɔ̃] *nm* 1. *Vieilli F* heavy smoker/chain-smoker 2. *pl* P (*a*) legs*/pins (*b*) **avoir les fumerons,** to be afraid*/to have the jitters.

fumette [fymɛt] *nf* P **la fumette,** smoking/ blowing (marijuana*, etc).

fumier [fymje] *nm* P despicable person/ bastard*/louse/shit/*surt NAm* son of a bitch; **espèce de fumier!** you bastard*!/you sod!

fumiste [fymist] F I *nm* (*a*) *Vieilli* practical joker/hoaxer (*b*) fraud/phon(e)y II *a* **il est un peu fumiste,** he's a bit of a phon(e)y.

fumisterie [fymistəri] *nf* F practical joke/ hoax*; **tout ça, c'est de la fumisterie!** that's a load of hooey!/it's a real con!

fun [fœn] *a & nm* fun.

funérailles! [fyneraj] *int* F (*dans le Midi*) oh, **funérailles!** oh blast!/oh no!/help!

furax(e) [fyraks], **furibard** [fyribar] *a* P furious/livid/hopping mad.

fusain [fyzɛ̃] *nm* P 1. (cassocked) priest 2. *pl* (*a*) **fusains,** legs* (*b*) **avoir les fusains,** to be afraid*/to have the wind up.

fusant [fyzɑ̃] *nm* P fart.

fuseaux [fyzo] *nmpl* F legs*; **il peut à peine se tenir sur ses fuseaux,** he can hardly keep on his pins; **jouer des fuseaux,** to run away*/ to leg it/to scarper.

fusée [fyze] *nf* P vomit(ing); **lâcher une fusée,** to vomit*/to throw up/to puke; (*péter*) to fart*/to let off.

fuser [fyze] *vi* P 1. to defecate*/to crap 2. to vomit*/to puke 3. to leave without paying.

fusil [fyzi] *nm* 1. F **coup de fusil,** exorbitant charge/overcharging/fleecing; **essuyer le/ recevoir un coup de fusil,** to be fleeced/ rooked/stung/ripped off 2. F **changer son fusil d'épaule,** to change one's tack 3. F stomach*/ breadbasket; **se coller qch dans le fusil,** to stuff oneself/to stuff one's face 4. V **fusil à trois coups/à trois trous,** three-way lady (*ie a prostitute who allows her clients to use her vagina, mouth and anus*).

fusiller [fyzije] *vtr* F 1. to bungle*/to mess up/to make a botch-up of (sth); **fusiller sa bagnole,** to smash up one's car; to run one's car into the ground 2. to fritter away/to blow (one's money); **se faire fusiller,** to lose at gambling; **fusiller une fortune au jeu,** to gamble away a fortune 3. to overcharge/to fleece*/to rook (s.o.); to rip (s.o.) off 4. (*a*) **fusiller qn du regard,** to look daggers at s.o. (*b*) (*Journ*) **être fusillé par des photographes,** to be bombarded by photographers. (*Voir* **pavé 1**)

futal [fytal] *nm*, **fute** [fyt] *nm* P trousers*/ *surt NAm* pants/breeks; slacks; jeans.

fute-fute [fytfyt] *a* P smart/clever/sharp/on the ball; **elle n'est pas fute-fute,** she's not too bright.

G

gabarit [gabari] *nm* F (*souv Péj*) des gens de son gabarit, people of his sort/people like him; ils sont du même gabarit, they come from the same mould.

gabelou [gablu] *nm* F *Péj* customs officer.

gabouiller [gabuje] *vi* P to make a mistake*/to boob/to slip up.

gâche [gɑʃ] *nf* P une bonne gâche, a cushy job/a cushy number/a soft option.

gâcher [gɑʃe] I *vi* P 1. to work*/to slog (away) 2. to waste II *vtr* F gâcher le métier, to undercut.

gâchette [gɑʃɛt] *nf* F avoir la gâchette facile, to be trigger-happy; c'est une bonne gâchette, he's/she's a good shot.

gâcheuse [gɑʃøz] *nf* P 1. effeminate young man/poofter 2. pretentious *or* affected woman*.

gadiche [gadiʃ] *nf* = **gadin 2**.

gadin [gadɛ̃] *nm* P 1. head*/nut 2. fall; prendre/ramasser un gadin, to take a header/ to come a cropper/to fall flat on one's face 3. y aller du gadin, to be condemned to death *or* to a heavy prison sentence.

gadjo [gadʒo] *nm* F 1. (*pour les gitans*) s.o. who is not a gypsy/gadjo 2. fool*/nurd.

gadoue [gadu] *nf* P 1. mud/slime 2. je suis dans une belle gadoue! I'm in a right (old) mess! 3. excrement*/shit.

gadouille [gaduj] *nf* P 1. mud/slime 2. mess/disorder*/jumble/muddle.

gadzarts [gadzar] *nm inv* F (= gars des Arts) student *or* former student of an *École des Arts et Métiers*, *esp* the *École Nationale Supérieure des Arts et Métiers*.

gaffe¹ [gaf] *nm* P 1. (*a*) look-out man (*b*) faire gaffe, to take care; to be on the look-out/to be on one's guard; fais gaffe! look out!/watch it!/(be) careful!/mind (out)! fais gaffe à Marcel! watch out for yourself with Marcel!/be on your guard with Marcel! 2. prison warder/screw. (*Voir* **os 10**; **osselets 1**)

gaffe² *nf* 1. F mistake*/gaff/boob; faire une gaffe, to make a mistake*/to drop a clanger/to put one's foot in it/to boob 2. P avaler sa gaffe, to die*/to snuff it/to kick the bucket.

gaffer [gafe] I *vi* P to act as look-out (man) II *vtr & i* P to look (at)*/to observe; gaffe un peu! have a butcher's!/take a dekko!/get a load of this! III *vi* F to make a mistake*/to boob/to drop a clanger/to put one's foot in it IV *vpr* se gaffer P se gaffer de qn, to mistrust s.o.; se gaffer de faire qch, to be careful not to do sth.

gaffeur, -euse [gafœr, -øz] I *nm* P look-out man II *n* F blunderer; c'est un gaffeur, he's a blundering fool/he's always putting his foot in it.

gafouiller [gafuje] *vi* P = **gaffer II**.

gaga [gaga] F I *a inv* senile/gaga/doddering II *nm* old dodderer/old fogey*.

gagne-pain [gɑɲpɛ̃] *nm inv* P 1. woman's buttocks/bum 2. = **gagneuse**.

gagneur [gɑɲœr] *nm* F ambitious and successful (young) man; winner.

gagneuse [gɑɲøz] *nf* P (*a*) well-paid prostitute* (*b*) prostitute who is a good earner (for her pimp)/good meal-ticket.

gai [ge] *a* un peu gai, slightly drunk*/merry/ tipsy.

gail, gaille [gaj] *nm* P 1. horse/nag 2. dog/ mutt.

galapiat [galapja] *nm Vieilli* F (*a*) loafer/ layabout/good-for-nothing (*b*) rough/tough; un petit galapiat, a young tough/hooligan*.

gale [gal] *nf* F obnoxious person; (*homme*) creep/bastard*/nasty piece of work/*surt NAm* son of a bitch; (*femme*) bitch/cow.

galère [galɛr] F I *nf* difficult/painful/ intolerable situation; c'est la galère, it's hell/ it's a real pain; il est en retard? quelle galère! he's late? what a drag/a pain! II *a* c'est galère, it's awful/a pain; it's a bad scene.

galérer [galere] *vi* F 1. to be having/to have

a hard time; ça **galère**, things are going badly/nothing's going right 2. to throw oneself into a project without achieving any results 3. to be bored; to have no aim in life; **elle galère**, she doesn't know what she wants to do.

galerie [galri] *nf* F (group of) people watching/spectators.

galérien [galɛrjɛ̃] *nm* F **mener une vie de galérien**, to lead a dog's life.

galérienne [galɛrjɛn] *nf* F prostitute* who solicits in shopping centres.

galetouse, galetouze [galtuz] *nf* P 1. = **galette** 1 2. mess tin/dixie.

galettard [galɛtar] *a* P rich*/loaded/rolling in it.

galette [galɛt] *nf* 1. P money*/bread/dough; **avoir de la galette**, to be rich*/loaded; **épouser la grosse galette**, to marry into money 2. F **plat comme une galette**, as flat as a pancake 3. F spool of film 4. F **galette (de vinyle)**, record/LP; compact disc.

galetteux, -euse [galɛtø, -øz] *a* P = **galettard**.

galine [galin] *nf* P effeminate young man*/ poofter.

galipette [galipɛt] *nf* F 1. somersault; **faire la galipette**, to turn a somersault 2. **faire des galipettes** (*a*) to be up to one's tricks/to lark about (*b*) to have sex* (with s.o.)/to have a bit of fun.

galoche [galɔʃ] *nf* 1. P **vieille galoche**, old fogey* 2. F **menton en galoche**, nutcracker chin 3. P kiss; **rouler une galoche (à qn)**, to kiss (s.o.) passionately on the mouth/to give (s.o.) a French kiss.

galocher [galɔʃe] *vtr & i* P = **rouler une galoche (à qn)** (**galoche 3**).

galon [galɔ̃] *nm* F (*a*) **arroser ses galons**, to celebrate one's promotion (*b*) **prendre du galon**, to be promoted; to move up in the world/to climb the ladder.

galonné [galɔne] *nm* P *Mil* (non-commissioned) officer.

galopard [galɔpar] *nm* P louse/cootie.

galopeuse [galɔpøz] *nf* F second hand (of clock, watch).

galopin [galɔpɛ̃] *nm* F small glass (= *approx* ¼ litre) of beer.

galoup [galu] *nm*, **galoupe** [galup] *nm* P 1. ungentlemanly/unscrupulous behaviour/ dirty trick; breach of trust; **faire un galoup à qn**, to do the dirty on s.o. 2. infidelity/ unfaithfulness; **sa femme lui a fait un galoup,**

his wife was unfaithful to him 3. serious problem/glitch.

Galpi [galpi] *Prn* P (*verlan de* **Pigalle**) the Pigalle quarter (*in Paris*).

galtouse, galtouze [galtuz] *nf* P = **galetouse, galetouze.**

galuche [galyʃ] *nf* P Gauloise (*RTM*) cigarette.

galure [galyr] *nm*, **galurin** [galyrɛ̃] *nm* P hat*; titfer/lid; **porter le galure/le galurin**, to be wrongly accused/to get the blame/to take the rap.

gamahuche [gamayʃ] *nf* V fellatio* and cunnilingus*.

gamahucher [gamayʃe] *vi* V to have oral sex*; to have fellatio* and cunnilingus*.

gamberge [gɑ̃bɛrʒ] *nf* P 1. thought/ reflection; daydream; **à la gamberge**, on second thoughts 2. dawdling; idling.

gambergeailler [gɑ̃bɛrʒaje] *vi* P to daydream; to have one's head in the clouds.

gamberger [gɑ̃bɛrʒe] *vtr & i* P 1. (*a*) to think (deeply)/to reflect (on); to meditate (on) (*b*) to imagine/to get into one's head (**que ..., that...**) (*c*) to daydream; to have one's head in the clouds 2. to dawdle; to idle 3. to psych oneself up; **gamberger un match**, to psych oneself up for a match.

gambette [gɑ̃bɛt] *nf* P leg*; **jouer/tricoter des gambettes**, to run away*/to beat it/to leg it.

gambille [gɑ̃bij] *nf* P 1. (*a*) dance/hop (*b*) dancing 2. *pl* **gambilles**, legs*.

gambiller [gɑ̃bije] *vi* P to dance (to a lively rhythm)/to prance about/to jig about.

gamelle [gamɛl] *nf* 1. F **manger à la gamelle**, to eat simply/to eat out of a tin; *Mil* to eat in the mess 2. F **s'accrocher une gamelle**, to go without (food, etc) 3. P **ramasser/(se) prendre une gamelle**, to fall down/to come a cropper*; (*échouer*) (*projet, etc*) to fail/to fall through/to go down the drain 4. P **mettre une gamelle**, (*renoncer*) to give up; (*partir*) to leave*/to make tracks 5. P **à fond les gamelles**, very quickly*/like mad/like greased lightning.

gamin [gamɛ̃] *nm* F 1. (*a*) boy/lad/kid/ nipper; **un gamin de neuf ans**, a kid of nine (*b*) son; **mon gamin va aller en Angleterre**, my son's/my boy's going to England 2. **il est très gamin, (*homme*)** he's very childish.

gamine [gamin] *nf* 1. F (little) girl*/kid/ nipper (*b*) daughter 2. F **elle est très gamine**, she's very childish; **elle est encore gamine,**

she's still just a child **3.** *P* **t'occupe du chapeau de la gamine!** mind your own business!

gamme [gam] *nf F* **toute la gamme!** the whole (damn) lot (of them)!/the whole caboodle!

ganache [ganaʃ] *nf Vieilli* **1.** *P* (lower) jaw **2.** *F (a)* **vieille ganache,** fool*/idiot/clot/dumb cluck *(b)* old man*/old dodderer.

gandin [gɑ̃dɛ̃] *nm P (jeu de cartes)* jack/knave.

gano(t) [gano] *nm P (a)* booty/loot *(b)* bag of money *(c)* purse.

gapette, gâpette [gapɛt, gɑ-] *nf P (casquette)* cap.

garage [garaʒ] *nm* **1.** *F* dead-end job; **mettre/ranger (qn/qch) sur une voie de garage,** to shelve (s.o./sth) **2.** *P* (prostitute's term for a) hotel room.

garce [gars] *P* **I** *nf (a)* bitchy girl* *or* woman*; **sa mère est une de ces garces,** her mother is a real bitch/cow *(b)* **fils de garce!** son of a bitch! *(c)* **une belle garce,** hot stuff/a bit of all right *(d)* prostitute*/tart/scrubber *(e)* **quelle garce de vie!** what a hell of a life!/what a bloody awful life! **II** *a* bitchy; **ce qu'elle peut être garce!** what a bitch/a cow she can be! she can be really bitchy when she wants!

garde-à-vous [gardavu] *nm P* **être au garde-à-vous/avoir le gourdin au garde-à-vous,** to have an erection*/a hard-on.

garde-manger [gard(ə)mɑ̃ʒe] *nm inv P* stomach*/breadbasket.

garde-mites [gard(ə)mit] *nm inv F Mil* stores orderly.

gare [gar] **I** *nf F* **à la gare!** scram!/hop it!/beat it!/clear off!/on your bike! **envoyer (qn) à la gare,** to send (s.o.) packing/to get rid of (s.o.) **II** *int F* **gare!** watch out! **gare à tes pattes,** mind your legs*/feet*!

garé [gare] *a P* **1.** **être garé en double file,** to wait for a prostitute* who is busy with another client **2.** **garé des voitures,** secluded/living a secluded life.

garer [gare] **I** *vtr F* to put by/to stash away (money, etc) **II** *vpr* **se garer** *F* **1.** **se garer des voitures,** to settle down/to calm down **2.** **gare-toi de mon chemin!** steer clear of me!/keep out of my way!/get out of my way!

gargamelle [gargamɛl] *nf*, **gargane** [gargan] *nf P* **1.** *(a)* throat/gullet; **serrer la gargamelle à qn,** to strangle/throttle s.o. *(b)* mouth* **2.** face*/mug.

se gargariser [səgargarize] *vpr F* **se gargariser de qch,** to delight/revel in sth.

gargoine [gargwan] *nf P* throat; **se rincer la gargoine,** to drink*/to wet one's whistle.

gargue [garg] *nf P (a)* mouth* *(b)* throat/gullet.

garni [garni] *a P* **elle est bien garnie,** she's well upholstered/well stacked.

garno(t) [garno] *nm P (a)* lodgings/digs *(b)* hotel *(esp used by prostitutes)*.

garouse [garuz] *nf P* (railway) station.

gars [gɑ] *nm F* **1.** boy/young man/lad/laddie; **un beau gars,** a fine/handsome young man; **bonjour, mon petit gars!** hello, young fellow/son(ny) **2.** man*/chap/guy/fellow; **eh les gars!** hey, (you) lads/guys! **un brave gars,** a good sort.

gaspard [gaspar] *nm P* **1.** rat **2.** **avaler le gaspard,** to receive Holy Communion.

gastos [gastos] *nm P* restaurant/eatery; pub/café.

gastro [gastro] *n P (CB) (a)* restaurant/café *(b)* meal; **gastro liquide,** drink; **gastro solide,** meal.

gâteau [gɑto] *F* **I** *nm* **1.** **partager le gâteau,** to share/to split the profits/the loot; **avoir sa part de gâteau,** to get a share (of the profit); **se disputer le gâteau,** to quarrel over who should get (a share of) the profits **2.** **c'est du gâteau!** it's easy!*/it's a piece of cake!/it's a walkover! **II** *adj inv* **papa gâteau,** *(qui cède à ses enfants)* over-indulgent father/grandfather; *(qui gâte les enfants des autres)* friend of the family who spoils the children; **marraine gâteau,** fairy godmother.

gâterie [gɑtri] *nf V (a)* fellatio*/blow-job *(b)* cunnilingus*.

gau [go] *nm P* louse/cootie.

gauche [goʃ] **I** *adv phr F* **en mettre à gauche,** to save/to put money by; **avoir un peu d'argent à gauche,** to have something put by for a rainy day **II** *nf F* **aller jusqu'à la gauche,** to go right on to the (bitter) end/to go the whole hog; **ils nous ont eu jusqu'à la gauche,** they cheated us right, left and centre. *(Voir* **arme; pied 1; porter II)**

gaucho [goʃo] *a & n inv P Pol* leftist/lefty/Trot.

gaufre [gofr] *nf P* **1.** (peaked) cap **2.** face*; **se sucrer la gaufre,** to put on one's make-up/to make up **3.** **prendre/ramasser une gaufre,** to fall flat on one's face/to come a cropper* **4.** mistake*/error; **faire une gaufre,** to boob. *(Voir* **moule II)**

gaufrer [gofre] I *vtr P* to arrest*; se faire gaufrer, to be caught in the act/with one's pants down II *vpr* **se gaufrer** *P* 1. to give oneself a treat; **on s'est bien gaufré!** we did ourselves proud; we had a rare old time 2. to fall flat on one's face/to come a cropper*.

gauldo [goldo] *nf P* = **galuche**.

gaule [gol] *nf V* penis*/rod; avoir la gaule, to have an erection*/to have a stiff(y). (*Voir* **chevalier 2**)

gaulée [gole] *nf P* beating* (up)/thrashing.

gauler [gole] *vtr* 1. *P* to arrest*/to pinch/to nab; se faire/se laisser gauler, to get nicked 2. *P* to steal*/to pinch/to knock off; il s'est fait gauler son vélo, he had his bike nicked 3. *V* to have sex* with (s.o.)/to knock (s.o.) off.

gauluche [golyʃ] *nf P* = **galuche**.

gavousse [gavus] *nf P* (*javanais de* **gousse**) lesbian*/lezzy/dyke.

gay [gɛ, ge] *a & nm F* gay; une boîte gay, a gay night-club.

gaye [gaj] *nm P* = **gail**.

gaz [gaz] *nm F* 1. (à) plein(s) gaz, *Aut* with one's foot down/on the floor; (*à toute vitesse*) at full speed/flat out/at a hell of a pace; ouvrir/mettre les gaz, to step on the gas/to put one's foot on the floor 2. éteindre/fermer son gaz, to die*/to snuff it 3. avoir des gaz, to suffer from flatulence/from wind; lâcher un gaz, to break wind/to fart. (*Voir* **bec 7**; **compteur 1**; **eau 2**)

gazer [gaze] *vi* 1. *F* to move at top speed/to belt along/to go like the clappers 2. *F* to go smoothly; alors, ça gaze? how goes it?/how's tricks? (everything) all right?/OK? ça gaze! everything's OK!/we're doing fine! gazer au poil/à bloc, to go (off) without a hitch 3. *P* ça va gazer! there'll be trouble!/there'll be fireworks!/there's trouble brewing! 4. *F* gazer avec qn, to love s.o.; ça ne gaze plus entre eux, they don't get on any more/they don't love each other any more.

gazier [gazje] *nm P* 1. geezer/bloke/guy 2. homosexual*.

gazoline [gazɔlin] *nm ou f P* passive homosexual.

gazon [gazɔ̃] *nm* 1. *P* hair/thatch; n'avoir plus de gazon sur la plate-bande/sur la prairie/sur la terrasse, to be as bald* as a coot; se faire tondre le gazon, to get one's hair cut 2. *V* pubic hair/fringe/pubes; mouiller son gazon, (*femme*) to urinate*.

GDB [ʒedebe] *nf P* (*abrév* = *gueule de bois*) avoir la GDB, to have a hangover.

géant [ʒeɑ̃] *a F* c'est géant! it's fantastic!/wicked!

gégène [ʒeʒɛn] *P* I *nf* 1. electricity generator 2. torture by electric shock II *nm Mil* general III *a* = **génial**.

gelé [ʒ(ə)le] *a P* 1. gelé (à zéro), (dead) drunk*/(completely) canned/plastered 2. mad*/cracked/loony.

se geler [sə ʒ(ə)le] *vpr P* se geler (les couilles/les miches), to freeze (one's balls/bum off)/to freeze to death.

gencives [ʒɑ̃siv] *nfpl P* jaw(s); un coup dans les gencives, a punch on the jaw.

gendarme [ʒɑ̃darm] *nm F* 1. (*a*) (*hareng saur*) red herring/Billingsgate pheasant (*b*) (Swiss) flat, dry sausage 2. chapeau de gendarme, (two-pointed) paper hat 3. gendarme couché, (*sur la chaussée*) sleeping policeman 4. bossy woman/battleaxe/martinet; faire le gendarme, to boss people about; la peur du gendarme, fear of being caught 5. dormir en gendarme, to sleep with one eye open.

se gêner [sə ʒene] *vpr F* 1. (*a*) faut pas se gêner, no need to ask (*b*) *Iron* il ne se gêne pas! he's not backward in coming forward! (ne) vous gênez pas! don't mind me – make yourself at home! 2. (si) je vais me gêner!/avec ça que je vais me gêner! you bet (your sweet life) I will!/you (just) see if I don't!

génial [ʒenjal] *a F* great/fantastic/marvellous; c'est un mec génial, he's a great bloke/guy; une idée géniale, a fantastic/an amazing idea; t'es génial! (*tu as résolu le problème*) you're a genius!

génisse [ʒenis] *nf P* cow/bitch (of a woman).

genou, *pl* **-oux** [ʒ(ə)nu] *nm F* 1. faire (un appel) du genou, = to play footsy (under the table) 2. être sur les genoux, to be exhausted*/ready to drop/flaked out 3. bald head; avoir son genou dans le cou, to be (as) bald* as a coot.

genre [ʒɑ̃r] *nm P* (*brocante*) cette chaise est un genre de Louis XV, this chair is a fake Louis XV/is imitation Louis XV.

géo [ʒeo] *nf F* (*écoles*) geography.

Georges [ʒɔrʒ] *nm F* (*aviation*) George (*automatic pilot*).

géranium [ʒeranjɔm] *nm P* dépoter son géranium, to die*/to drop off the twig.

gerbe [ʒɛrb] *nf* 1. *P* (*verlan de* **berge**) year in prison 2. *P* (prison) sentence*/stretch/rap 3. *V* (*femme*) masturbation*/finger-fuck/

finger-job; se **filer une gerbe**, to bring oneself off 4. P vomiting/puking; **avoir la gerbe**, to feel sick/NAm nauseous.

gerbement [ʒɛrbəmɑ̃] nm P judgement; sentence*.

gerber [ʒɛrbe] P I vi to vomit*/to throw up; **blèche à gerber**, as ugly as sin II vtr (a) to be sentenced to; **il a gerbé sept ans**, he's copped a seven-year stretch/he's doing seven years (b) to sentence; to imprison; **il est gerbé**, he's doing time/he's inside.

gerbeux, -euse [ʒɛrbø, -øz] a P sickening/nauseating.

gerbier [ʒɛrbje] nm P 1. judge/magistrate/beak 2. member of the jury.

gerbique [ʒɛrbik] a P = **gerbeux, -euse.**

gerboise [ʒɛrbwaz] nf P = **giton.**

gerce [ʒɛrs] nf P 1. Vieilli prostitute* 2. young girl* or woman* 3. wife*/the missis.

gérer [ʒere] vtr F **gérer une situation/sa vie**, to manage a situation/to organize one's life.

gervais [ʒɛrvɛ] nm P = **demi-sel.**

gésier [ʒezje] nm P stomach*/gut(s); **recevoir un coup dans le gésier**, to get one in the breadbasket; **ça m'est resté sur le gésier**, I couldn't stomach it. (Voir **court-circuit 1**)

gi! [ʒi] int P yes!/yeah!/OK!/roger! (Voir **gy**)

gibier [ʒibje] nm P **manger le gibier**, (prostituée) to keep (back) part of her earnings (from her pimp).

giclée [ʒikle] nf 1. F burst (of machine-gun fire) 2. V (spurt of) semen*/sperm*/spunk/come; **lâcher/tirer une giclée**, to ejaculate*/to come/to shoot one's load; **giclée de grenouille**, swallowing of sperm*. (Voir **grenouille 3**)

gicler [ʒikle] P I vi 1. (arme à feu) to go off 2. (personne) to run away*/to beat it; **allez, gicle!** go on, hop it!/scram! 3. to be dismissed*/fired II vtr (faire sortir) to throw (s.o.) out. (Voir **mirettes**)

gicleur [ʒiklœr] nm P mouth*; **ferme ton gicleur!** shut up!*/shut your trap!

gidouille [ʒiduj] nf P 1. stomach*/belly 2. navel/belly-button 3. spiral.

gifle [ʒifl] nf F **une tête à gifles = une tête à claques** (**claque I 1**).

gig [ʒig] nm F (jazz, rock, etc) gig/one-night stand.

gigal, pl **-aux** [ʒigal, -o] nm Vieilli P 1. roofer/slater 2. plumber.

gigo! [ʒigo] int P = **gi!**

gigolette [ʒigɔlɛt] nf Vieilli P 1. young girl* 2. (young) floozy/tart/scrubber; easy lay.

gigolo [ʒigɔlo] nm F 1. gigolo/fancy man

2. (cartes) jack.

gigolpince [ʒigɔlpɛ̃s] nm P = **gigolo 1.**

gigot [ʒigo] nm F 1. thigh; buttock 2. pl gigots, legs*.

gigoter [ʒigɔte] vi F 1. to wriggle about; **ne gigote pas!** don't fidget! 2. to dance/to shake a leg.

gigoteur, -euse [ʒigɔtœr, -øz] n F dancer.

gigue [ʒig] nf F 1. (grande) gigue, tall girl/beanpole 2. pl Vieilli gigues, legs*.

gilboque [ʒilbɔk] nm P billiard table.

gilet [ʒilɛ] nm F **pleurer dans le gilet de qn**, to pour out one's troubles to s.o./to cry* on s.o.'s shoulder.

gileton [ʒiltɔ̃] nm, **gilton** [ʒiltɔ̃] nm P waistcoat; (veste en laine) cardigan/cardy.

gingin [ʒɛ̃ʒɛ̃] nm Vieilli F common sense; **avoir du gingin**, to have gumption.

girafe [ʒiraf] nf P 1. Cin (micro) boom 2. **peigner la girafe**, to waste one's time; (ne rien faire) to do damn all.

girèle, girelle [ʒirɛl] nf Vieilli P prostitute*.

giries [ʒiri] nfpl P 1. complaining/whining/bellyaching; **assez de giries!** stop moaning! 2. affectation; **faire des giries**, to put on airs.

girofle [ʒirɔfl] a Vieilli P good-looking.

giroflée [ʒirɔfle] nf P **une giroflée (à cinq feuilles/à cinq branches)**, a slap round the face.

girond [ʒirɔ̃] I a P (surt femme) good-looking; easy on the eye; **ce qu'elle est gironde!** she's a bit of all right! II nm P (passive) homosexual*.

gisquette [ʒiskɛt] nf P (a) woman*/bird/NAm dame/NAm broad (b) girl*/bird/chick/judy/tart.

giton [ʒitɔ̃] nm F (young, passive) homosexual*/catamite.

givré [ʒivre] a P 1. drunk*/sozzled/plastered 2. mad*/nuts/bonkers; **il est complètement givré**, he's completely off his rocker.

glace [glas] nf P **passer devant la glace**, to stand a round (of drinks); (dans une affaire) to be the loser; **se bomber devant la glace**, to be done out of one's share. (Voir **armoire 1**)

glagla [glagla] a inv P **être glagla**, to be freezing cold; adv phr **je les ai à glagla**, it's freezing; it's cold enough to freeze the balls off a brass monkey/it's brass monkey weather. (Voir **miches 1** (b))

glaglater [glaglate] vi P to be cold/freezing to death.

glaise [glɛz] *nf P* earth/ground; **il couche sur la glaise,** he sleeps on the bare ground.

glaiseux [glɛzø] *nm P* peasant*/hick/yokel/ country bumpkin.

glamour(eux) [glamur(ø)] *a F* glamorous.

gland [glɑ̃] **I** *nm* 1. *P* fool*/clot/nit/twit 2. *V* penis*; **se taper sur le gland,** to masturbate*; **effacer le gland,** to have sex*/to have it away **II** *a P* stupid*/daft.

glander [glɑ̃de] *P* **I** *vi* to fritter away one's time; to hang/to moon/to mooch about *or* around; to footle about; to mess around **II** *vtr* to do; **qu'est-ce que tu glandes aujourd'hui?** what are you up to today? **j'en ai rien à glander,** I couldn't care less (about it).

glandes [glɑ̃d] *nfpl P* **avoir les glandes,** to be angry*/annoyed/pissed off; *(déprimé)* to have the blues/to flip; **ça me fout les glandes!** *(ça irrite)* it gets on my tits; *(ça démoralise)* it gives me the creeps/the willies!

glandeur, -euse [glɑ̃dœr, -øz] *n P* idler/ moocher/layabout; **quel glandeur, ce mec!** what a lazy so-and-so that bloke is!/what a skiver!

glandilleux, -euse [glɑ̃dijø, -øz] *a P* difficult/dangerous/chancy/risky/dic(e)y/tick- lish.

glandouiller [glɑ̃duje] *vi P* 1. = **glander I** 2. to wait/to hang about/to kick one's heels.

glandouilleur, -euse [glɑ̃dujœr, -øz] *n P* = **glandeur, -euse.**

glandouilleux, -euse [glɑ̃dujø, -øz] *a P* = **glandilleux, -euse.**

glandu [glɑ̃dy] *nm P* fool*/clot/dimwit.

glaouis [gla(u)wi)] *nmpl V* = **claouis.**

glass(e) [glas] *nm P* 1. (drinking) glass 2. drink/snifter/snort; **payer un glass(e) à qn,** to buy/to stand s.o. a drink.

glaude [glod] *P* **I** *nf* pocket **II** *nm* fool*/ blockhead **III** *a* stupid*/dimwitted.

glauque [glok] *a F* dreadful/awful; **il est glauque ce film,** that film stinks/sucks.

glaviot [glavjo] *nm P* 1. gob (of spit/ phlegm) 2. **se noyer dans un glaviot,** to make a mountain out of a molehill.

glavioter [glavjɔte] *vi P* to spit/to gob.

glisse [glis] *nf P* **faire de la glisse à qn,** to do s.o. out of his share of the loot; to hold out on s.o.

glisser [glise] **I** *vi P* **se laisser glisser,** to die* *(from natural causes or as the result of an illness)*/to peg out **II** *vtr* 1. *F* **glisser qch en douce à qn,** to tell s.o. sth in confidence/ confidentially 2. *P* **glisser un fil,** to urinate*/to

splash one's boots/to have a slash 3. *V* **glisser une femme, en glisser une paire/un bout à une femme,** to have sex* with/to slip it to/to screw a woman.

globe [glɔb] *nm* 1. *P* stomach*; **se faire arrondir le globe,** to become pregnant*/to join the (pudding) club 2. *F* **globes arrondis,** (plump) breasts*.

gluant [glyɑ̃] *nm P* 1. baby 2. soap.

gluau [glyo] *nm P* gob (of phlegm).

gluc(k) [glyk] *nm P* luck.

gnace [ɲas] *nm P* = **gniasse 1.**

gnaf [ɲaf] *nm P* cobbler.

gnangnan [ɲɑ̃ɲɑ̃] *F* **I** *a inv* spineless/ flabby/soppy/drippy/wet **II** *nm & f* (a) spine- less person/sissy/wet/drip (b) dawdler/ slowcoach **III** *nm* **du gnangnan,** drivel/ rubbish.

gnard, -arde [ɲar, ɲard] *n P* = **gniard, -arde.**

gnaule [ɲol] *nf P* = **gnole.**

gnaupe [ɲop] *nf P* (smoker's) pipe.

gniaf(fe) [ɲaf] *nm P* = **gnaf.**

gniangnian [ɲɑ̃ɲɑ̃] *a & n F* = **gnangnan.**

gniard, -arde [ɲar, ɲard] *n P* 1. child*/ brat/kid/nipper 2. (a) man*/bloke/guy (b) woman*/female/*NAm* dame.

gniasse [ɲas] *nm P* 1. man*/fellow/bloke/ guy 2. **mon gniasse,** I/me/yours truly; **ton gniasse,** you; **son gniasse,** he/him; **vos gniasses,** you/you lot.

gniaule [ɲol] *nf P* = **gnole.**

gnière [ɲɛr] *nm P* 1. man*/fellow/bloke/guy; **qui c'est ce gnière?** who is this guy? 2. fool*/ cretin; *(maladroit)* clumsy clot.

gniol(l)e [ɲol] *nf P* = **gnole.**

gniouf [ɲuf] *nm P* = **gnouf.**

gnognot(t)e [ɲɔɲɔt] *nf P* 1. trash/rubbish/ junk/tripe/crap; **c'est de la gnognot(t)e,** it's a load of rubbish; **ça, ce n'est pas de la gno- gnot(t)e!** that's really something! 2. trifle; **ça, c'est de la gnognot(t)e,** that's peanuts/ that's just chicken-feed.

gnole, gnôle [ɲol] *nf P* brandy; spirits*/ rotgut/hard stuff/hooch/firewater; **un coup de gnole,** a wee dram/a drop of the hard stuff.

gnon [ɲɔ̃] *nm P* 1. blow*/sock/thump/biff; **filer/prendre un gnon à qn,** to take a swipe at s.o.; **se prendre un gnon,** to get biffed; **sa ba- gnole a pris un gnon,** his car took a bash; **his car got bashed in/smashed up** 2. *(marque)* *(sur un objet)* mark/dent; *(sur le corps)* bruise/scratch, etc; **sa voiture est pleine de gnons,** her car's all dented; **il a un gnon sur le**

bras, he's got a bruise on his arm.

gnouf [ɲuf] *nm P* (*a*) prison*/clink/cooler/ jug (*b*) police station*/cop (*c*) cell in a police station; lock-up (*d*) *Mil* guardroom.

go (tout de) [tudəgo] *adv phr F* tout de go, without ceremony/all of a sudden; répondre tout de go, to answer straight off.

Gob' [gɔb] *Prn P* les Gob', the Gobelins quarter (*in Paris*).

gobelette [gɔblɛt] *nf P* = **gobette**.

gobelot(t)er [gɔblote] *vi F* to tipple/to drink*/to hit the bottle/to go on the booze.

gobe-mouches [gɔbmuʃ] *nm inv F* (*personne*) simpleton/dope.

gober [gɔbe] **I** *vtr* 1. *F* gober des mouches, to stand gaping; to have a vacant/stupid expression on one's face 2. *F* to swallow; il a gobé tout ce qu'on lui a dit, he fell for it hook, line and sinker; et tu crois que je vais gober tout ça? you really think I'm going to fall for that? (*Voir* **morceau 5**) 3. *P* to have a strong liking for (s.o.)/to go for (s.o.) in a big way; je ne peux pas le gober, I can't stand/ stick him **II** *vpr* **se gober** *F* to have a big opinion of oneself/to fancy oneself; elle se gobe, she thinks she's really something/she thinks the sun shines out of her arse/*NAm* ass.

se goberger [səgɔbɛrʒe] *vpr F* to do one-self well/proud.

gobette [gɔbɛt] *nf P* 1. drink/booze; drinking/boozing; payer la gobette, to pay for the drinks 2. (*en prison*) wine ration.

gobeur, -euse [gɔbœr, -øz] *F* **I** *n* simpleton/sucker/mug; c'est un gobeur, he's very gullible/he'll swallow anything; gobeur de fausses nouvelles, stupidly credulous person **II** *a* il est très gobeur, he's very gullible/he'll swallow anything; he's easily taken in.

gobi [gɔbi] *nm P Péj* Black*/coon/nigger.

gobilleur [gɔbijœr] *nm P* examining magistrate.

godaille [gɔdaj] *nf Vieilli F* feast/blow-out/ tuck-in/nosh-up.

godailler [gɔdaje] *vi* 1. *P* (*festoyer*) to have a blow-out; to go on a binge 2. *P* to laze about/to mooch about/to hang around 3. *V* to have an erection*/to have a hard-on 4. *V* to have sex*/to screw around.

godailleux, -euse [gɔdajø, -øz] *a P* (very) sexually excited*/randy/horny.

godant [gɔdã] *a P* sexually exciting/ arousing/hot; un film godant, a film which really gets you going.

godasse [gɔdas] *nf P* shoe; (*qui n'est pas élégante*) clodhopper.

gode [gɔd] *nm P* 1. = **godemiché** 2. = **godet**.

godelureau, -eaux [gɔdlyro] *nm F Péj* dandy/*NAm* dude.

godemiché [gɔdmiʃe] *nm P* dildo.

goder [gɔde] *vi* 1. *P* to be (very) sexually excited*; to be ready for it; goder pour qn, to be horny/randy for s.o.; to want s.o.; faire goder qn, to give s.o. a sexual thrill/to turn s.o. on; un film qui fait goder, a film which really gets you going/turns you on 2. *V* to have an erection*/to have a hard-on.

godet [gɔdɛ] *nm P* 1. (drinking) glass 2. glass(ful)/drink/jar; basculer/écluser/s'envoyer/se cloquer/se taper un godet, to knock back a drink 3. avoir le godet, to be lucky/to have all the luck.

godeur, -euse [gɔdœr, -øz] *a P* (very) sexually excited*/horny/randy/hot.

godiche¹ [gɔdiʃ] *nf P* fever/*esp* malaria.

godiche², godichon, -onne [gɔdiʃɔ̃, -ɔn] *F* **I** *a* (*a*) stupid*/silly/thick/dumb; je ne suis pas si godiche que j'en ai l'air, I'm not as dumb as I look/I wasn't born yesterday (*b*) (*empoté*) awkward/gawky; clumsy/ham-fisted **II** *n* quelle godiche, cette fille! what a lump (of a girl)!

godille [gɔdij] *nf F* à la godille (*a*) crooked/ askance; un coup de châsse à la godille, side-ways look/glance (*b*) without method; travailler à la godille, to work without method/anyoldhow.

godiller [gɔdije] *vi V* 1. to have an erection*/to have a hard-on/to get it up 2. to have sex*.

godilleur, -euse [gɔdijœr, -øz] *n V* highly-sexed man/woman; hot stuff; easy lay/ good screw; (*homme*) pussy chaser/cunt chaser.

godillot [gɔdijo] *P* **I** *nm* (big) boot/shoe; clodhopper **II** *a Pol* faithful/unconditional; parti godillot, (political) party which follows the government line on everything; *nmpl* les godillots, the party faithful.

gogo [gogo] **I** *nm F* sucker/mug **II** *adv phr F* whisky à gogo, whisky galore; avoir de l'argent à gogo, to have money to burn.

gogol [gɔgɔl] *a & nm P* = **gol**.

gogueneau, -eaux [gogno] *nm*, **goguenot** [gogno] *nm P* 1. chamber pot*/ po/jerry 2. *pl* goguenots = **gogues**.

gogues [gɔg] *nmpl P* WC*/loo/bog/*surt NAm*

can/*surt NAm* john.

goguette [gɔgɛt] *nf F* être en goguette, to be (a bit) tight/merry.

goinfrade [gwɛ̃frad] *nf F* (bean)feast/blow-out/tuck-in/nosh-up.

goinfre [gwɛ̃fr] *nm F* glutton*/greedyguts/guzzler/pig.

se goinfrer [səgwɛ̃fre] *vpr F* 1. (*a*) to drink like a fish (*b*) to eat like a pig/to make a pig of oneself 2. to make a lot of money*/to coin it in/to make a pile.

gol [gɔl] *P* (= *mongolien*) I *a* stupid*/thick/moronic II *nm* moron/cretin/nurd/jerk.

goldo [gɔldo] *nf P* Gauloise (*RTM*) cigarette.

gomme [gɔm] *nf* 1. *F* à la gomme, trashy/rubbishy/useless/hopeless; une idée à la gomme, a pathetic/useless idea; histoire à la gomme, pointless story; individu à la gomme, hopeless person/dead loss 2. *P* gomme à effacer le sourire, (*matraque*) cosh; (policeman's) rubber truncheon 3. *P* tyre 4. *P* mettre la gomme, (*accélérer*) to get a move on/to pull out all the stops/to step on it; *Aut* to put one's foot down 5. *P* remettre la gomme, to have another go; to have another drink/game of cards; to make love again, etc.

gommé [gɔme] *a F* blanc gommé, white wine sweetened with syrup.

gommeux, -euse [gɔmø, -øz] *P* I *a* (*a*) flashy/overdressed (*b*) pretentious/snooty/snobbish II *n* (*a*) flashy dresser/overdressed person (*b*) member of high society/nob/toff; (*homme*) fop/dandy/*NAm* dude.

gonce [gɔ̃s] *nm P* (*rare*) = **gonze** I.

goncesse [gɔ̃sɛs] *nf P* (*rare*) = **gonzesse**.

goncier [gɔ̃sje] *nm P* (*rare*) = **gonze** I.

gondolant [gɔ̃dɔlɑ̃] *a F* very funny*/side-splitting/priceless/a scream.

gondole [gɔ̃dɔl] *nf P* door.

gondoler [gɔ̃dɔle] I *vi P* gondoler de la devanture, to be pregnant*/to be in the (pudding) club II *vpr* **se gondoler** *F* to laugh* uproariously/to double up with laughter/to split one's sides laughing.

gonds [gɔ̃] *nmpl F* sortir de ses gonds, to get angry*/to fly off the handle/to blow one's top.

gone [gɔn] *nm*, **gonesse** [gɔnɛs] *nf F* (*Dial lyonnais*) 1. child*/brat/kid 2. fellow/man*/guy/bloke.

gonflaga [gɔ̃flaga] *a P* = **gonflé 1, 2**.

gonflant [gɔ̃flɑ̃] *a F* 1. = **gondolant** 2. intolerable/exasperating; il est gonflant, lui, he's a real pain (in the arse/*NAm* ass).

gonfle [gɔ̃fl] *nf F* 1. swelling; avoir la gonfle, to be swollen/to have a swelling 2. lie*/tall story/whopper.

gonflé [gɔ̃fle] *a F* 1. courageous; full of guts/balls 2. cheeky; t'es gonflé! you've got a nerve/a cheek! 3. gonflé à bloc, (*personne*) keyed up; (*en pleine forme physique*) full of beans/raring to go; (*sûr de soi*) sure of one-self; *Aut* moteur gonflé, hotted-up/souped-up engine.

gonfler [gɔ̃fle] I *vi F* to exaggerate*/to shoot a line/to lay it on a bit thick; to bluff II *vtr* 1. *F Aut* gonfler un moteur, to hot up/to soup up an engine 2. *P* gonfler qn/les gonfler à qn, to annoy* s.o./to get on s.o.'s tits/to get under s.o.'s skin 3. *P* gonfler une femme, to get a woman pregnant*/to put a woman in the club/to put a woman up the spout/*surt NAm* to knock a woman up.

gonflette [gɔ̃flɛt] *nf F* body building; pumping iron.

gonfleur [gɔ̃flœr] *nm F* bluffer.

gong [gɔ̃g] *nm F* être sauvé par le gong, to have a narrow escape/to be saved by the bell.

gonze [gɔ̃z] *P* I *nm* man*/fellow/chap*/guy/bloke/dude II *nf* = **gonzesse**.

gonzesse [gɔ̃zɛs] *nf P* 1. woman*/girl*/bird/chick/lady 2. (*homme*) coward*/cissy/patsy.

gonzier [gɔ̃zje] *nm P* = **gonze** I.

goret [gɔrɛ] *nm F* dirty child*; grubby/mucky little brat/filthy little pig; manger comme un goret, to eat* like a pig.

gorgeon [gɔrʒɔ̃] *nm F* 1. mouthful/gulp (of wine, etc) 2. glassful; se taper un gorgeon, to knock back a drink.

se gorgeonner [səgɔrʒɔne] *vpr P* to drink*/to booze/to tipple; to get drunk*/pissed.

Gorgonzola [gɔrgɔ̃zɔla] *nm F* avoir les dents plombées au Gorgonzola, to have bad breath.

gorille [gɔrij] *nm F* 1. bodyguard/strong-arm man/henchman/gorilla 2. bearded and hairy tramp*.

gosier [gozje] *nm F* avoir le gosier en pente, to have a permanent thirst; avoir le gosier sec, to be dry/parched/thirsty; s'humecter le gosier, to have a drink/to wet one's whistle.

gosse [gɔs] *nm & f* 1. *F* child*/kid/brat/nipper 2. *F* young man/girl; ma gosse, my girlfriend 3. *F* c'est une belle gosse, she's a smashing girl; il est beau gosse, he's good-looking 4. *F* gosse de riche, rich man's son; spoilt (rich) brat/rich kid 5. *pl FrC P* testicles*.

gosselin [gɔslɛ̃] *nm F* **1.** small child* **2.** young man*.

gosseline [gɔslin] *nf F* little girl*.

goualante [gwalɑ̃t] *nf P* (popular) song; envoyer la goualante/pousser une goualante/y aller de sa goualante, to sing a song.

gouale [gwal] *nm P* **1.** blackmail **2.** faire du gouale, to kick up a row/to make a big fuss.

goualer [gwale] *vtr & i P* **1.** to sing (loudly) **2.** faire goualer qn, to blackmail s.o.

goualeur, -euse [gwalœr, -øz] *n P* **1.** (noisy) singer **2.** blackmailer.

gouape [gwap] *nf P* hooligan*/yob(bo)/thug/ nasty piece of work/bastard*.

gouapeur [gwapœr] *nm Vieilli P* layabout/ (lazy) bum.

goudou [gudu] *nf P* lesbian*/les/lez/dyke.

gouge [guʒ] *nf F* je n'ai pas une gouge, I'm broke/I haven't got a penny.

gougnafier [guɲafje] *nm F* bad worker/ cowboy; c'est du travail de gougnafier/tu as fait ça comme un gougnafier, you've messed/ buggered it up; it's a cowboy job.

gougne [guɲ] *nf*, **gougnot(t)e** [guɲɔt] *nf P* = **gouine**.

gougnot(t)er [guɲɔte] I *vtr & i P* to be a lesbian*/to be gay/to be a dyke; to have a lesbian relationship (with another woman) II *vpr* se gougnot(t)er *P* to practise lesbianism; les deux filles se gougnottaient, the two girls were having it away/bringing themselves off.

gouine [gwin] *nf P* lesbian*/dyke/les/lez.

se gouiner [səgwine] *vpr P* to practise lesbianism.

goujon [guʒɔ̃] *nm* **1.** *F* (personne) avaler le goujon, (croire) to swallow/to take the bait; (mourir) to die*/to croak **2.** *F* taquiner le goujon, to fish (for sth/information) **3.** *Vieilli P* young (inexperienced) pimp*.

goule [gul] *nf P* **1.** (big) mouth* **2.** throat.

goulée [gule] *nf F* **1.** big mouthful/gulp **2.** tirer une goulée, to have a puff (of a cigarette)/to take a drag.

goulot [gulo] *nm P* (a) throat/gullet; se rincer le goulot, to have a drink*/to wet one's whistle (b) taper/repousser du goulot, to have bad breath (c) casser le goulot à une bouteille, to open a bottle and drink it. (Voir refouler (b))

goumi [gumi] *nm P* rubber cosh/truncheon.

goupiller [gupije] I *vtr P* to arrange/to wangle/to fix (sth); goupiller un truc, to cook

sth up; to knock sth together II *vpr* se goupiller *F* to happen/to work (out); se goupiller bien, to turn out well/to go off all right; ça se goupille mal, it's going badly.

goupillon [gupijɔ̃] *nm V* penis*; mouiller le goupillon, to have sex*/to get one's end away.

goupiner [gupine] *P* I *vi* to work* (more or less honestly) II *vtr* to steal*/to knock off/to pinch.

gourance [gurɑ̃s] *nf*, **gourante** [gurɑ̃t] *nf P* **1.** mistake*/bloomer/boob **2.** doubt; avoir des gourances, to be suspicious/to smell a rat.

gourbi [gurbi] *nm F* **1.** (a) dirty/untidy lodgings or house; digs/pad; slum/hovel/dump (b) *Mil* funk hole/foxhole/dugout **2.** faire gourbi, (prisonniers, etc) to muck in together; (couple, surt d'homosexuels) to live together/to shack up together.

gourde [gurd] I *a F* stupid*/gormless/ dimwitted II *nf F* fool*/dimwit/dope.

gourdin [gurdɛ̃] *nm V* (a) penis*/chopper/ shaft; avoir le gourdin, to have an erection* (b) avoir du gourdin, to womanize/to be a skirt-chaser/to be on the make; avoir du gourdin pour une femme, to be turned on by a woman/to have the hots for a woman.

goure [gur] *nf P* fraud/con/deception; vol à la goure, con(fidence) trick.

gourer [gure] I *vtr P* to cheat/to trick/to con/to take in/to pull a fast one on (s.o.) II *vpr* se gourer *P* **1.** (a) to be wrong; to make a mistake*/to boob; il s'est gouré, he boobed/ he slipped up **2.** se gourer de qn, to mistrust s.o./to be suspicious of s.o.; je m'en gourais, I thought as much.

gourmandise [gurmɑ̃diz] *nf V* fellatio*.

gourrer [gure] *vtr*, **se gourrer** [səgure] *vpr P* = **gourer**, **se gourer**.

gousse [gus] *nf P* gousse (d'ail), lesbian*.

se gousser [səguse] *vpr P* to practise lesbianism.

goût [gu] *nm P* oublier le goût du pain, to die*/to kick the bucket; ôter/faire passer le goût du pain à qn, to kill* s.o./to do s.o. in/to bump s.o. off.

goutte [gut] *nf* **1.** *F* nip (of brandy, etc); boire la goutte, to have a nip/a snort; veux-tu de la goutte? do you want a drop of the hard stuff? il aime la goutte, he's fond of a nip **2.** *F* il a bu la goutte, (il s'est noyé) he (was) drowned; (il a perdu de l'argent) he suffered a heavy loss/he caught a packet **3.** *F* se noyer dans une goutte d'eau, to make a mountain out of a molehill **4.** *P* goutte militaire, chronic gonorrhoea*/clap.

gouzi-gouzi [guziguzi] *nm F* tickling; **faire gouzi-gouzi à qn,** to tickle s.o.

goyau, -aux, goyo(t) [gwajo] *nm P* 1. peasant*/clodhopper/hick 2. (cheap) prostitute*/old slag/scrubber.

grabasse [grabas] *a P* drunk*/tight.

se grabater [səgrabate] *vpr P* to go to bed*/to hit the hay/to hit the sack.

grabuge [graby3] *nm F* quarrel*; row/ rumpus; **faire du grabuge,** to kick up a shindy/to create; **il va y avoir du grabuge,** there'll be trouble/there's gonna be some aggro.

gradaille [gradɑj] *nf P Mil* officers and NCOs.

grade [grad] *nm F* **en prendre pour son grade/prendre qch pour son grade,** to be severely reprimanded*/to get hauled over the coals; **il en a pris pour son grade!** he got what was coming to him!/he asked for it!

graf [graf] *nm F* graffito *or* graffiti.

graffiter [grafite] *vtr F* to spray graffiti on/ to cover with graffiti; **des murs tout graffités,** graffiti-covered walls.

graille [grɑj] *nf P* food*/grub/nosh; **aller à la graille,** to (go and) eat*/to nosh; **à la graille!** grub's up!

grailler [grɑje] *vi P* to eat*/to nosh.

graillon [grɑjɔ̃] *nm P* 1. smell of fried food *or* burnt fat 2. gob (of phlegm).

graillonner [grɑjɔne] *vi F* to hawk up/to cough up phlegm/to gob (noisily).

grain [grɛ̃] *nm* 1. *F* **être dans le grain,** to be in clover 2. *F* **avoir un grain,** to be slightly mad*; **il a un grain,** he's not quite right in the head/he's a bit cracked/he's a bit nuts 3. *F* (*a*) **écraser un grain,** to have a glass of brandy/to have a snort (*b*) **avoir son grain,** to be slightly drunk*/to be a bit tight 4. *P* **grain de blé,** louse 5. *V* **grain de café,** clitoris*; **secouer son grain de café,** to finger oneself/to bring oneself off. (*Voir* **sel 1**)

graine [grɛn] *nf* 1. *F* food*/grub; **casser la graine,** to have a bite (to eat) 2. *F* **en prendre de la graine,** to profit from s.o.'s example/to take a leaf out of s.o.'s book 3. *F* **monter/ pousser en graine,** (*personne*) to grow older; to go to seed; (*femme*) to be left on the shelf 4. *F Mil* **graine d'épinards,** gold braid on senior officers' epaulettes/scrambled eggs 5. (*a*) *F* **c'est de la mauvaise graine,** he's a bad lot (*b*) *F* **graine de bois de lit,** newborn baby (*c*) *F* **graine de bagne,** jailbird (*d*) *P* **graine de con,** fool*/cretin/bloody fool 6. *P* **semer sa graine,** (*d'un homme*) to have sex*/to sow one's wild oats.

grainer [grɛne] *vtr & i F* to eat*/to have a bite (to eat)/to nosh.

graissage [grɛsaʒ] *nm F* **graissage de patte,** bribe*/palm-greasing/backhander; kickback.

graisse [grɛs] *nf* 1. *P* money*/bread/dough 2. *P* **faire de la graisse,** to exaggerate*/to lay it on thick 3. *P* **traîner sa graisse,** to hump one's fat (around); **amène ta graisse!** drag your carcass/your butt over here! **tire tes graisses!** get out of my way!/shift your arse/*NAm* ass! 4. *P* cheating (at cards, etc) 5. *P* **graisse d'abattage,** force/muscle power. (*Voir* **boniment 2**)

graisser [grɛse] **I** *vi P* to exaggerate*/to boast/to lay it on thick **II** *vtr F* **graisser la patte à qn,** to bribe s.o.; to grease/to oil s.o.'s palm; to make s.o. an offer he can't refuse. (*Voir* **botte II 4**)

grand [grɑ̃] *F* **I** *a* excellent*; **c'est grand!** it's ace/great/wicked! **II** *n* 1. **faire qch tout seul comme un(e) grand(e),** to (manage to) do sth all by oneself/like a grown-up 2. **jouer dans la cour des grands,** to play in the big league; to be/become a big-league player.

grand-chose [grɑ̃ʃoz] *nm & f F* **un/une pas grand-chose,** a good-for-nothing; a poor sort; (*femme*) an easy lay/a bit of a tramp.

grand-dab(e) [grɑ̃dab] *nm P* grandfather/ grandad. (*Voir* **dab(e)**) (*pl* **grands-dab(e)s**)

grand-duc [grɑ̃dyk] *nm F* **faire la tournée des grands-ducs,** to go on a spree*/to go out on the town/to go clubbing.

grand-mère [grɑ̃mɛr] *nf P* (*instrument de musique*) double bass.

grappe [grap] *nf P* **lâcher la grappe à qn,** to leave s.o. alone/to lay off s.o.

grappillage [grapijaʒ] *nm F* (*a*) (*d'argent*) making something on the side (*b*) (*petits vols*) pilfering.

grappiller [grapije] *vtr & i F* (*a*) (*voler*) to fiddle; to make something/to make a bit on the side (*b*) (*voler*) to pilfer.

grappin [grapɛ̃] *nm* (*a*) *P* hand*/hook (*b*) *F* **mettre le grappin sur qch/qn,** to lay one's hands on sth/s.o./to get one's hooks into sth/ s.o./to grab sth/s.o. (*c*) *F* **mettre/poser le grappin sur qn,** to arrest* s.o./to pull s.o. in/to nick s.o.

gras, *f* **grasse** [grɑ, grɑs] **I** *a F* (*a*) **être gras à lard,** to be fat/porky (*b*) **être gras du**

bide/du genou, to be fat/paunchy; to have a (beer) gut (c) **il n'y (en) a pas gras/y a pas gras**, there's not much (of it)/that's not a lot (d) **se la faire grasse**, to live like a lord/to live off the fat of the land **II** *nm* P profit; **faire du gras**, to make a profit (*Voir* **discuter**)

gras-double [grɑdubl] *nm* F paunch/pot belly/beer belly/spare tyre.

gratin [gratɛ̃] *nm* F **le gratin** (a) high society/the upper crust; **il fréquente le gratin**, he mixes with the nobs; **faire gratin**, to pretend to be from the upper crust (b) the best/the pick of the basket/the cream.

gratiné [gratine] *a* F excessive/over the odds/over the top; **une addition gratinée**, an enormous/a huge bill; a rip-off; **prendre une cuite gratinée**, to get really plastered/rolling drunk*; **c'est gratiné!** it's a bit much! **elle est gratinée, elle!** she really goes too far!

grat(t)os [gratos] *adv* F free/gratis; **travailler grat(t)os**, to work for nothing.

gratouille [gratuj] *nf* F 1. itch 2. (*musique*) maraca.

gratouiller [gratuje] F **I** *vtr* to scratch **II** *vi* to itch.

grattante [gratɑ̃t] *nf* P 1. hand*/mitt/paw 2. *Vieilli* match(stick).

gratte [grat] *nf* 1. F (*profits illicites*) pickings/rake-off/profits on the side; **faire de la gratte**, to get a rake-off/to make a bit on the side 2. F **des grattes**, last savings/scrapings off the bottom of the barrel 3. P *Méd* scabies/the itch 4. P scratching (oneself) 5. P *Mus* guitar; **jouer de la gratte**, to play the guitar/to strum on the guitar 6. P (*aide-mémoire*) crib/*NAm* pony.

gratte-couenne [gratkwan] *nm* P barber/men's hairdresser.

gratte-papier [gratpapje] *nm inv* F *Péj* civil servant; pen-pusher. (*pl* **gratte-papier(s)**)

gratter [grate] **I** *vtr* F 1. (*auto, vélo*) to pass/to overtake (a competitor, another car, etc) 2. *Péj* **gratter le papier**, to scribble/to be a pen-pusher 3. to scrape together (a sum of money); **gratter les fonds de tiroir**, (*rassembler ses dernières économies*) to scrape the bottom of the barrel; **il n'y a pas grand-chose à gratter**, you won't make much out of that **II** *vi* 1. F **un verre de qch qui gratte**, a glass of sth strong/of sth with a kick in it 2. P to work* hard/to graft/to slog (away); **je gratte de 9 à 5**, I slave away from 9 to 5 3. P to write; **il arrêtait pas de gratter**, he was writing like mad/scribbling away 4. F **en gratter**, (*être*

expert) to be an expert in one's subject; (*se plaire*) to enjoy doing sth. (*Voir* **couenne 1**; **jambon 1**; **jambonneau**; **pavé 3**) **III** *vpr* **se gratter 1**. F to hesitate/to think it over/to weigh up the pros and cons 2. P **se gratter de qch**, to go without sth; **tu peux (toujours) te gratter!** nothing doing!/you can whistle for it!/not on your nelly! 3. P **se faire gratter** (a) to get a shave/to get shaved (b) to get overtaken/to be passed (by another car, etc). (*Voir* **gratter I 1**)

gratteur, -euse [gratœr, -øz] *n* F (bad) violinist/fiddler; guitarist.

grattiche [gratiʃ] *nf* F scabies/the itch.

grattin [gratɛ̃] *nm* F 1. = **gratin 2. aller au grattin**, to go to work.

grattoir [gratwar] *nm* F razor.

grattouiller [gratuje] *vtr & i* F = **gratouiller**.

grattouse [gratuz] *nf* F = **grattiche**.

grave [grav] *a* P 1. stupid*/cretinous; **vous êtes graves, les mecs!** you're a bunch of morons 2. annoying; **c'est grave, ça!** what a bore/hassle!

Gravelotte [gravlɔt] *Prn* P **ça tombe comme à Gravelotte**, (*ça arrive*) it's coming from all sides; (*il pleut*) it's coming down in sheets.

gravos, -osse [gravo, -os] *P* (*javanais de* **gros, grosse**) **I** *a* (big and) fat; tubby **II** *n* fat person/fatty/fatso.

grec [grɛk] *nm* P 1. card-sharper; **faire le grec**, to manipulate the cards, to work the broads 2. **va te faire voir/foutre par/chez les Grecs!** go to hell!/piss off!/get stuffed!

à la grecque [alagrɛk] *adv phr Vieilli* P vol **à la grecque**, con(fidence) trick/con.

greffier [grefje] *nm* F cat*/pussy(cat)/mog(gy).

greffière [grefjɛr] *nf* V female genitals*/pussy.

grelot [grəlo] *nm* 1. F **faire sonner son grelot**, to draw attention to oneself/to blow one's own trumpet 2. F **attacher le grelot**, to take the initiative 3. P **avoir les grelots**, to be afraid*; to have the shakes/the willies; **filer/flanquer/foutre les grelots à qn**, to put the wind up s.o. 4. F (tele)phone*/blower; **filer du grelot**, to (tele)phone*; **passer un coup de grelot à qn**, to give s.o. a ring/a tinkle 5. *pl* F testicles*/nuts 6. *pl* V (*morceaux d'excrément collés aux poils de l'anus*) clinkers/dingleberries. (*Voir* **fifre II**)

grelotte [grəlɔt] *nf* P **avoir la grelotte**, to be

afraid*/to be in a blue funk/to have the wind up.

grelotter [grǝlɔte] *vi P* to be afraid*/to have the shakes.

greluche [grǝlyʃ] *nf P* (young) woman*; *surt Péj* wife*/the little woman.

greluchon [grǝlyʃɔ̃] *nm P* prostitute's lover.

grenadier [grǝnadje] *nm F* tall/masculine woman.

Grenoble [grǝnɔbl] *Prn F* faire à qn la conduite de Grenoble, (*congédier*) to give s.o. his marching orders/to give s.o. the (order of the) boot; (*rendre la vie difficile*) to make it hot for s.o./to give s.o. a rough time.

grenouillage [grǝnujaʒ] *nm F* 1. (*a*) wangle; shady deal; fiddle (*b*) wangling/shady dealing(s)/wheeling and dealing 2. scandalmongering/malicious gossip.

grenouillard [grǝnujar] *nm F* 1. teetotaller 2. cold-water fiend.

grenouille [grǝnuj] *nf* 1. *F* grenouille de bénitier, excessively pious person/bigoted churchwoman 2. *F* (*a*) (frog-shaped) money box (*b*) club money/funds (of a society, etc); manger/bouffer la grenouille, (*s'approprier une caisse, etc*) to make off with the cash/the cash box/the kitty; to dip one's hand in the till; (*faire faillite*) to go bankrupt 3. *V* grenouilles de bidet, (*langage des policiers*) visible traces of semen*; cum stains. (*Voir* giclée 2)

grenouiller [grǝnuje] *vi F* 1. to drink water 2. to be on the fiddle; to go in for shady dealing/to wheel and deal 3. to go in for malicious gossip/to spread rumours; to bitch.

grenouilleur, -euse [grǝnujœr, -øz] *n F* shady dealer/fiddler/fixer.

greumai [grømɛ] *a P* (*verlan de maigre*) thin.

gribier [gribje] *nm Vieilli P* = **griveton**.

griffard [grifar] *nm F* (pussy)cat*/mog(gy).

griffe [grif] *nf* 1. *F* donner un coup de griffe à qn, to have a dig at s.o. 2. *F* hand*; serrer la griffe à qn, to shake hands with s.o. 3. *F* foot*; aller à griffe, to go on foot; to use/to go by Shanks's pony; taper des griffes, to have smelly feet 4. *P* la Griffe, the Army; military service 5. *P* = **griveton**.

griffer [grife] I *vtr F* (*a*) to seize/to catch/to grab (*b*) griffer un bahut, to catch a taxi II *vpr* se griffer 1. *P* se griffer (la tronche), to put on one's make-up 2. *V* to masturbate*/to finger oneself.

griffeton [griftɔ̃] *nm*, **grifton** [griftɔ̃] *nm P* = **griveton**.

grigou, *pl* **-ous** [grigu] *nm F* miser*/skinflint/tight-ass.

grigri [grigri] *nm F* charm worn as a pendant.

gril [gri(l)] *nm F* être sur le gril, to be on tenterhooks; to be like a cat on hot bricks/*NAm* on a hot tin roof.

grillante [grijɑ̃t] *nf P* cigarette*/fag/gasper.

grille [grij] *nf P* 1. grille d'égout, set of false teeth/dentures 2. repeindre sa grille en rouge/au minium, to have a period*/to have the painters in/to have the decorators in/to have the reds.

griller [grije] I *vtr* 1. *F* griller une cigarette/*P* en griller une, to smoke a cigarette*/to have a smoke 2. *F* to oust/supplant (a rival, etc); griller qn, (*sports*) to race past s.o.; to leave s.o. standing; to pip s.o. at the post 3. *F Aut* griller le feu rouge, to shoot/to jump the lights 4. *P* (*a*) to criticize* (s.o.)/to run (s.o.) down/ to knock (s.o.)/to pick (s.o.) to pieces (*b*) to denounce* (s.o.)/to put the finger on (s.o.)/to squeal on (s.o.) 5. *P* (*a*) il est grillé, (*dévoilé*) he's been found out/his game's up; his cover's been blown; (*rayé*) he's done for/he's had it (*b*) c'est une affaire grillée/c'est grillé, it's fallen through/it's up the creek/it's no go. (*Voir* dur II 1) II *vpr* se griller *P* to lose one's reputation/one's credit/one's influence; to be discredited/done for/ruined; se griller auprès de qn, to blot one's copybook with s.o.

grillot [grijo] *nm P* 1. *Vieilli* unscrupulous opportunist 2. compromising document.

grimbiche [grɛ̃biʃ] *nf P* young woman*/babe/chick.

grimoire [grimwar] *nm Vieilli P* police record.

grimpant [grɛ̃pɑ̃] *nm P* trousers*/pants/strides.

grimpe [grɛ̃p] *nf F* rock climbing/mountain climbing.

grimper [grɛ̃pe] *vtr V* 1. to have sex* with (s.o.)/to jump (s.o.)/to ride (s.o.) 2. grimper un client, (*prostituée*) to be with a client/to turn a trick. (*Voir* arbre 1)

grimpette [grɛ̃pɛt] *nf V* (*prostituées*) time spent with a client/trick.

grimpouzer [grɛ̃puze] *vtr V* = **grimper 1**.

grinche [grɛ̃ʃ] *P* I *nm* thief*/burglar II *nf* theft/burglary; vivre de la grinche, to live by thieving.

grincher [grɛ̃ʃe] *vtr Vieilli P* to steal*/to pinch/to nick.

gringue [grɛ̃g] *nm P* 1. être en gringue, to flirt 2. jeter/faire du gringue à qn, to make a pass at s.o./to give s.o. the come-on/to chat s.o. up/to try to pick s.o. up.

gringuer [grɛ̃ge] *vtr P* to flirt/to make a pass at (s.o.)/to try it on with (s.o.)/to (try and) make out with (s.o.).

grinque [grɛ̃k] *nf P* food*/grub/nosh.

griottes [grijɔt] *nfpl P* buttocks*/bum/*surt NAm* butt/(pressed) hams/buns.

grippe-sou, *pl* **-sou(s)** [gripsu] *nm F* miser*/skinflint/tight-ass.

grippette [gripɛt] *nf* 1. *F* (mild) flu 2. *V* female genitals*/snatch.

gris [gri] *a F* slightly drunk*/tipsy; **un peu gris,** a bit high/tight.

grisbi [grizbi] *nm P* money*/bread/dough/ackers; **(ne) touchez pas au grisbi!** lay off the lolly!/hands off the dough!

grisol, *f* **-ol(l)e** [grizɔl] *a P* (*cher*) dear/expensive/pric(e)y.

grive [griv] *nf P* 1. the police*/the cops/the law 2. (*a*) the army (*b*) military service; **faire sa grive,** to do one's military service/to do one's stint in the army.

grivelle [grivɛl] *nf F* (*casquette*) cap.

griveton [grivtɔ̃] *nm P* soldier/infantryman/foot-slogger. (*Voir* **griffeton**)

groggy [grɔgi] *a F* groggy.

grognasse [grɔɲas] *nf P Péj* 1. (old) woman*; old bag/old bat/old bitch 2. low-class prostitute*/tart.

grognasser [grɔɲase] *vi P* to grumble*/to bitch.

grogne [grɔɲ] *nf F* grumbling/grousing/bitching.

groin [grwɛ̃] *nm P* 1. ugly mug 2. nose/snout.

grôle [grol] *nm Vieilli P* louse.

grolle [grɔl] *nf P* boot/shoe; **traîner ses grolles à Paris,** (*y aller*) to go to Paris/to drag oneself to Paris; (*y être*) to hang around in Paris.

grolles [grɔl] *nmpl ou fpl P* **avoir les grolles,** to be afraid*/to have the willies; **fiche/foutre les grolles à qn,** to put the wind up s.o.

grommelots [grɔmlo] *nmpl V* = **grelots 6.**

groove [gruv] *nm P* **avoir le groove,** to be up-to-date/with it/trendy.

gros, *f* **grosse** [gro, gros] **I** *n F* 1. (*a*) large/fat person; **un gros plein de soupe,** a well-fed type/big fat lump (*b*) **eh bien, mon gros!** well, old man! 2. rich/influential person; **les gros,** the nobs; the big shots 3. **du gros qui tache/du gros rouge,** coarse red wine/plonk/vino 4. **faire son gros,** to defecate*/to do a number two **II** *nf P* prison*; **faire de la grosse,** to do time; **deux ans de grosse,** a two-year stretch. (*Voir* **bonnet 6; cul I 5; légume 1; maison 5; panse 1; papa 2**)

gros-cul [groky] *nm P* 1. shag (tobacco) 2. heavy lorry/juggernaut/HGV 3. large motor-bike 4. mediocre wine/plonk. (*pl* **gros-culs**)

grossium [grosjɔm] *nm P* important businessman/big shot/big bug/bigwig.

grosso merdo [grosomɛrdo] *adv* (= *grosso modo*) roughly (speaking).

grouille [gruj] *nf P* **à la grouille,** all over the place; **les balancer/les jeter à la grouille,** to spend* money like water/to live like a lord.

(se) grouiller [(sə)gruje] *vi & vpr F* to hurry* (up)/to get a move on/to get cracking; **allez, grouille(-toi)!** get a move on!/move it!/pull your finger out! **dis-lui de se grouiller,** tell him to step on it/to put a jerk in it. (*Voir* **miches 1** (*c*); **tomate 7**)

grouillot [grujo] *nm & f F* (*a*) errand boy/messenger boy (*b*) subordinate/underling/minion (*c*) apprentice.

groumer [grume] *vi P* to grumble*/to grouse/to gripe.

groumeur, -euse [grumœr, -øz] *a P* grumpy.

grouper [grupe] *vtr P* 1. to arrest*/to pull (s.o.) in; **se faire grouper,** to get nicked 2. to seize/to grab (sth) 3. **être groupé,** to be in love.

groupie [grupi] *nf F* groupie.

groupiste [grupist] *nm & f F* (*théâtre*) s.o. who looks after the generating unit.

grue [gry] **I** *nf* (*a*) *P* prostitute*/hooker/tart (*b*) *F* **grande grue,** great gawk of a woman **II** *a F* **une jeune femme très grue,** a very flashy young woman. (*Voir* **pied 9** (*b*))

guenon [gənɔ̃] *nf* 1. *F* ugly woman*/fright 2. *P* (*drogues*) withdrawal symptoms; **avoir la guenon,** to be in need of drugs/to be strung out/to be waiting for the man; **chasser la guenon,** to get the monkey off (one's back).

guenuche [gənyʃ] *nf F* = **guenon 1.**

guêpe [gɛp] *nf* 1. *F* (*a*) nagging woman/nagger (*b*) (*homme*) persistent bore*/pain in the neck 2. *F* artful/crafty person; **pas folle, la guêpe!** I'm/she's/he's nobody's fool! 3. *P* = **guenon 2.**

guérite [gerit] *nf* (*églises*) *F* confessional

(box).

guêtres [gɛtr] *nfpl F* **1.** tirer ses guêtres, to run away*/to clear off/to beat it **2.** traîner ses guêtres (partout) (*a*) to loaf about/to mess around/*NAm* to goof off (*b*) to travel a lot; **il a traîné ses guêtres dans tous les coins,** he's been all over (the world)/he's been everywhere.

guette-au-trou [gɛtotru] *nm & f inv P* obstetrician; midwife.

gueugueule [gœgœl] *P* **I** *nf* pretty face **II** *a* (*fille, femme*) attractive/good-looking; **ça c'est gueugueule!** she's a good looker!/that's a bit of all right!

gueulante [gœlɑ̃t] *nf P* uproar*/din; **pousser une gueulante,** (*colère, douleur*) to shout/to yell/to bawl; to yell one's head off/to shout one's mouth off; to kick up a stink/to raise the roof; (*chanter*) to bawl/to belt out a song; (*acclamer*) to give an almighty cheer/one hell of a cheer.

gueulard, -arde [gœlar, -ard] *F* **I** *a* (*a*) noisy/loud-voiced/loudmouthed; (*couleurs*) loud/gaudy (*b*) (*gourmand*) greedy **II** *n* (*a*) loudmouth/bigmouth (*b*) glutton*/greedyguts (*c*) noisy baby; screaming kid/brat **III** *nf P* loudspeaker/loudhailer; Tannoy (*RTM*).

gueulardise [gœlardiz] *nf P* gluttony/greediness.

gueule [gœl] *nf* **I** *P* (*bouche*) **1.** (vas-tu fermer) ta gueule!/ferme ta gueule!/tais ta gueule! shut up!*/belt up! shut your mouth/trap/gob/face! **2.** aller de la gueule, to spout/to rabbit on; être fort en gueule, to be loudmouthed/to shoot one's mouth off; c'est une grande gueule, he's got far too much to say for himself/he's got a big mouth but he does nothing; it's all words and no action with him; avoir de la gueule, to have the gift of the gab **3.** des coups de gueule, shouting/bawling/slanging match; donner de la gueule/donner un coup de gueule/pousser un coup de gueule, to shout one's mouth off; jeter des injures à pleine gueule, to bawl out abuse **4.** (*a*) se soûler/se péter la gueule, to get drunk*/pissed; avoir la gueule de bois, to have a hangover (*b*) une fine gueule, a gourmet; être de la gueule/être porté sur la gueule, to be fond of eating and drinking; s'en mettre plein la gueule/se taper la gueule/se tasser la gueule, to stuff one's face (*c*) en prendre plein la gueule, to be full of admiration for (sth); to be very attracted by (s.o.) **5.** arracher/emporter la gueule, (*alcool, épices, etc*) to

burn one's throat/to take the roof off one's mouth **II** *P* (*visage*) **1.** avoir une bonne gueule, to look a good sort; avoir une sale gueule, (*être laid*) to have an ugly mug; (*avoir mauvaise mine*) to look rotten; (*être déprimé*) to look down in the mouth; (*être antipathique*) to look like a nasty customer/a nasty piece of work; il a été arrêté pour délit de sale gueule, he was arrested because they didn't like his face/the look of him; avoir la gueule de l'emploi, to have a face that suits the job; gueule d'empeigne/gueule de raie/gueule à coucher dehors (avec un billet de logement dans sa poche), repulsive face/ugly mug; gueule de vache, brute/martinet. (*Voir* **chier 3**) **2.** bourrer/casser la gueule à qn, rentrer dans la gueule à qn/foutre sur la gueule à qn, to bash s.o.'s head in/to beat s.o. up*/to work s.o. over; ils se sont foutus sur la gueule, they had a punch-up; se casser la gueule, (*tomber*) to fall*/to come a cropper/to fall flat on one's face; (*se battre*) to fight/to have a punch-up/to have a scrap; il s'est fait cassé la gueule, he got his face smashed in/he got beaten up/he got worked over; je vais lui en mettre plein la gueule, I'm going to do him some serious damage/I'm going to work him over; il en a pris plein la gueule (pour pas un rond), (*physiquement*) he got badly beaten up*/he got done over; (*moralement*) he had a really hard time; gueule noire, (coal) miner **3.** faire la gueule/tirer une gueule, to sulk/to pull a long face; il m'a fait la gueule, he's given me the cold shoulder; faire une gueule d'enterrement/de faire-part, to look gloomy/depressed. (*Voir aussi* **tirer I 5**) **4.** se payer/se foutre de la gueule de qn, to make fun of s.o./to poke fun at s.o./to have s.o. on/to pull s.o.'s leg; tu te fous de ma gueule, ou quoi? are you taking the piss, or what? non mais, elle se fout de la gueule du monde! she's got a bloody nerve! **5.** se fendre la gueule, to laugh* uproariously/to split one's sides laughing **6.** gueule d'amour, womanizer*/skirt-chaser/Casanova **7.** ma gueule, (*terme d'affection*) (my) darling*/(my) love **8.** ma gueule/ta gueule, etc, me/you, etc; c'est pour ma gueule, it's for me **9.** bien fait pour ma/ta/sa gueule, serves me/you/him *or* her right! (*Voir* **tournant 2**) **III** *F* (*air*) look; avoir de la gueule, to have a certain something; (*personne*) to have an air about one; ça a de la gueule, non? it's beautiful/that's really something, isn't it? ce chapeau a une drôle de gueule, that's a weird sort of hat; **cette bagnole a de la gueule,** that's some car/that car's really got something. (*Voir* **crever I 3, II 6; enfariné; ramener I**)

gueulement [gœlmɑ̃] *nm P* shout/yell; **il a poussé un gueulement de souffrance,** he let out a yell of pain; **pousser des gueulements,** to make a hell of a din/to kick up a row; to shout one's mouth off.

gueuler [gœle] *P* **I** *vi* 1. to shout/to bawl/to holler; **gueuler comme un sourd,** to yell one's head off; **faire gueuler la radio,** to turn the radio on full blast; **sa télé gueule toujours,** his telly/TV is still *or* always blaring away 2. to protest (noisily); **arrête de gueuler!** stop bitching!/stop bellyaching! 3. **couleurs qui gueulent,** loud/gaudy colours **II** *vtr* to bawl out (a song, orders, etc). (*Voir* **charron**)

gueuleton [gœltɔ̃] *nm P* lavish meal/feast/ nosh-up/tuck-in/blow-out; **tu parles d'un gueuleton/c'était un gueuleton à tout casser,** that was one hell of a blow-out; **nous avons fait un bon petit gueuleton/on s'est tapé un bon petit gueuleton,** we did ourselves proud/ we had a damn good meal.

gueuletonner [gœltɔne] *vi P* to eat* heartily/to have a good blow-out/to have a good tuck-in.

gueuloir [gœlwar] *nm* 1. *F* (*a*) mouth* (*b*) throat 2. *P* = **gueulard, -arde III**.

gueusaille [gøzɑj] *nf F* rabble/riff-raff/ scum.

gueuse [gøz] *nf* 1. *Vieilli F* **courir la gueuse,** to chase skirt/to go out looking for a bit (of the other)/to be on the make 2. *P* **la gueuse,** death/the (Grim) Reaper.

gugus [gygys] *nm P* = **gus(se)**.

guibolles [gibɔl] *nfpl P* legs*; **jouer des guibolles,** to run away*/to scram; **il (ne) tient pas sur ses guibolles,** he's a bit shaky on his pins.

guichet [giʃɛ] *nm* 1. *F* (**il est trop tard,**) **les guichets sont fermés!** nothing doing!*/no go!/ (it) can't be done!/no can do! 2. *V* **le (petit) guichet,** anus*/ring/hole.

guignard, -arde [giɲar, -ard] *F* **I** *a* unlucky **II** *n* unlucky person.

guigne [giɲ] *nf F* bad luck; **avoir la guigne,** to be down on one's luck/to be jinxed; to have a run of bad luck; **ficher/flanquer/fourrer/ porter la guigne à qn,** to bring s.o. bad luck/to jinx s.o.; **il porte (la) guigne,** he's bad luck/a jinx. (*Voir* **porte-guigne**)

guignol [giɲɔl] *nm* 1. *F* eccentric/crank/nut;

faire le guignol, to play the fool 2. *P* (*gendarme*) = policeman*/cop/bobby 3. *P law* court; magistrates' court; **passer au guignol,** to appear/to be up before the beak 4. *F* (*théâtre*) prompt box.

guignon [giɲɔ̃] *nm F* bad luck; **c'est un abonné au guignon,** he's got rotten luck/he's got a jinx on him.

guiguite [gigit] *nf P* (*mot enfantin*) penis*/ willie.

guili-guili [giligili] *nm F* **faire guili-guili à un gosse,** to tickle a kid under the chin.

guillotine [gijɔtin] *nf P* 1. **guillotine sèche,** solitary (confinement) 2. (*courses*) results board.

guimauve [gimov] **I** *nf F* 1. (*a*) sloppy/ sentimental/icky poetry *or* song; schmaltz; **c'est de la guimauve, ta chanson,** your song's really soppy (*b*) **guimauve blonde,** insipid writing 2. guitar **II** *adv P* **bander guimauve,** to be impotent/not to be able to get it up.

guimbarde [gɛ̃bard] *nf F* (vieille) guimbarde, ramshackle (old) car*/jalopy/ (old) banger/(old) crock.

guimpe [gɛ̃p] *nf*, **guimpette** [gɛ̃pɛt] *nf P* (peaked) cap.

guinche [gɛ̃ʃ] *nm P* (*a*) (public) dance/hop/ bop (*b*) (seedy) dance hall.

guincher [gɛ̃ʃe] *vi P* to dance/to bop/to jive.

guincheur, -euse [gɛ̃ʃœr, -øz] *n P* dancer.

guindal, *pl* **-als** [gɛ̃dal] *nm P* = **godet 1, 2**.

guinde [gɛ̃d] *nf P* car*/motor/jam-jar.

guise [giz] *nm* = **guisot**.

guiser [gize] *vtr V* **guiser qn,** to have sex* with s.o./to get one's leg over.

guisot [gizo] *nm* 1. *P* leg* 2. *V* penis*; **filer le coup de guisot,** to have sex*/to have it off.

guitare [gitar] *nf* 1. *F* **c'est toujours la même guitare,** it's (always) the same old story 2. *F* **avoir une belle guitare,** (*fille, femme*) to have big/shapely hips 3. *P* bidet. (*Voir* **sac 18**)

guitoune [gitun] *nf P* 1. (*a*) house/home/ pad (*b*) *Mil* dugout/shelter 2. (camping) tent 3. electric guitar.

guizot [gizo] *nm* = **guisot**.

gun [gœn] *nm P* (*drogues*) hypodermic syringe*/gun/hypo.

gus(se) [gys] *nm P* 1. fellow/guy/chap*/ bloke; **qu'est-ce que c'est que ce gus(se)?** who's that character? 2. eccentric* person/ crank/nut.

gy [ʒi] *int & adv* P yes/yeah/OK/roger; **faire gy de la tête**, to nod (in agreement).

gym [ʒim] *nf* P 1. gymnastics; **il m'a fait faire une drôle de gym**, he really put me through my paces 2. **au pas de gym**, at the double.

H

Les mots qui commencent par un h aspiré sont indiqués par un astérisque.
Words beginning with an aspirate h are shown by an asterisk.

*H [aʃ] *nm* P **1.** heroin*/H **2.** hashish*/hash; fumer du H, to smoke hash/dope.

habillé [abijɛ] *P* **I** *nm* uniformed policeman*; les habillés, the boys in blue **II** *a* il est habillé d'une peau de vache/d'une salope, he's not to be trusted/he's a con artist/he's a nasty piece of work.

habitant [abitɑ̃] *nm* P vermin; louse/cootie; avoir des habitants, to have lice/worms, etc.

hachès, hachesse [aʃɛs] *a* P (= hors service) (a) (personne) exhausted*/worn out/dead beat; unwell*/out of sorts/rough; drunk*/paralytic/legless (b) (chose) unusable/useless.

*hachoir [aʃwar] *nm* F le Grand Hachoir, the guillotine.

hafnaf [afnaf] *adv* P = **afanaf**.

haine [ɛn] *nf* P deep hatred/hostility towards society/the police, etc; avoir la haine, to be full of hatred/mad with hatred (esp for the establishment); donner la haine à qn, to fill s.o. with hatred (for the establishment).

*hallebardes [albard] *nfpl* F il pleut/il tombe des hallebardes, it's raining cats and dogs/it's tipping down/it's chucking it down.

halluciné, -ée [alysine] *nm & f* F lunatic/nutcase/crackpot.

*hambourgeois [ɑ̃burʒwa] *nm* F (= en bourgeois) plain-clothes policeman*/CID officer. (Voir **bourgeois 2**)

hameçon [amsɔ̃] *nm* F mordre à l'hameçon, (personne) to rise to the bait.

*hanneton [antɔ̃] *nm* F **1.** avoir un hanneton dans le plafond/dans la boîte à sel, to have a bee in one's bonnet; c'est un vrai hanneton, he's completely scatterbrained **2.** pas piqué des hannetons, (frais) fresh/well preserved; (excellent) excellent*/first-rate/not (half) bad; un rhume pas piqué des hannetons, one hell of a cold; il a reçu une raclée qui n'était pas piquée des hannetons, he got a hiding he won't forget in a hurry. (Voir **ver 2**)

*hard [ard] *a & nm* F hard (porn/rock, etc).

*hardeux, -euse [ardø, -øz] *a* F hard/aggressive; who likes hard rock.

*hareng [arɑ̃] *nm* P **1.** pimp*/ponce **2.** (a) Vieilli skinny horse/nag/hack (b) sec comme un hareng, as thin as a rake **3.** hareng (saur), gendarme/Br = police constable **4.** F serrés comme des harengs, packed together like sardines. (Voir **boniment 2**; **mare**; **peau 21**)

*harengère [arɑ̃ʒɛr] *nf* F Péj fishwife.

*haricot [ariko] *nm* **1.** P courir/taper sur le haricot à qn, to bore* s.o. rigid/to give s.o. a pain (in the arse); to get on s.o.'s wick/up s.o.'s nose **2.** P des haricots! nothing*/chicken-feed/not a sausage/zilch; travailler pour des haricots, to work for peanuts **3.** P c'est la fin des haricots, that's the bloody limit*/that's the last straw; it's all up/we've had it **4.** F (a) toes; feet*; marcher sur les haricots à qn, to tread on s.o.'s feet (b) (jambes en) haricots verts, skinny and bow legs* **5.** P les haricots verts, (pendant l'Occupation) the Germans*/the Krauts/the Jerries **6.** V clitoris*; avoir/mettre le haricot à la portière, (femme) to be (very) sexually excited*/randy/horny **7.** P aller manger des haricots, to go to prison* **8.** P hôtel des haricots, municipal prison. (Voir **défilocher**)

*harnacher [arnaʃe] **I** *vtr* F to rig out/to dress up (s.o.) **II** *vpr* se harnacher F to rig oneself out/to get togged up; elle s'était harnachée en cow-boy pour attirer la clientèle, she got dressed up in cowboy gear to attract custom.

*harnais [arnɛ] *nmpl P* clothes*/gear/togs; mettre les harnais, to put one's glad rags on.

*harpe [arp] *nf P* jouer de la harpe, to escape (from prison) by sawing the bars off (the window).

*harper [arpe] *vtr P* = **harpigner I**.

*harpigner [arpiɲe] **I** *vtr P* to take/to seize/to grab **II** *vpr* **se harpigner** *F* to come to blows/to have a punch-up.

*harpion [arpjɔ̃] *nm P* foot*. (*Voir* **arpion**)

*harponner [arpɔne] *vtr P* 1. to arrest*/to nail/to nick; se faire harponner, to get nabbed/done 2. (*happer*) to stop/to corner (s.o.); se faire harponner, to get buttonholed.

*hasch [aʃ] *nm P* (*drogues*) hashish*/hash; ils fumaient du hasch, they were smoking dope.

*haut [o] *adv & nm F* 1. aller par haut et par bas, to be sick and have diarrhoea* 2. le prendre de haut, to put on airs/to be condescending (towards s.o.); le porter haut, to have a high opinion/to think a lot of oneself.

*haute [ot] *nf P* la haute/les gens de la haute, high society/the upper classes/the upper crust; un gars de la haute, a toff; il a un petit accent de la haute, his accent is very U/he has a very classy accent/he talks posh.

*hauteur [otœr] *nf F* (*a*) être à la hauteur, (*personne*) to be capable/to know one's stuff; (*chose*) to be up to the mark/up to scratch; je ne me sentais pas à la hauteur, I didn't feel up to it; dîner à la hauteur, first-class/slap-up meal (*b*) ça, c'est à la hauteur! that's the ticket!/sock it to them!

hebdo [ɛbdo] *nm F* (= *hebdomadaire*) weekly (paper/magazine).

hélico [eliko] *nm F* helicopter*/chopper.

hénaurme [henorm] *a F* enormous/ginormous.

Henriette [ɑ̃rjɛt] *Prnf P* (*drogues*) heroin*/henry.

herbe [ɛrb] *nf* 1. *P* manger l'herbe par la racine, to be dead and buried/to be pushing up the daisies 2. *F* sur quelle herbe avez-vous marché? what's the matter with you?/what's eating you?/what's bugging you? 3. *P* brouter l'herbe, (*jockey*) to be unseated/to come a cropper* 4. *P* tobacco 5. *P* marijuana*/grass/weed; fumer de l'herbe, to smoke grass 6. *F* une mauvaise herbe, a bad lot/a no-gooder.

héro [ero] *nm P* (*drogues*) heroin*.

hétéro [etero] *a & n F* (= *hétérosexuel*) heterosexual/hetero.

heure [œr] *nf F* 1. je (ne) te demande pas l'heure (qu'il est)! I wasn't talking to you!/mind your own business! je t'ai demandé l'heure qu'il est? I didn't ask for your opinion!/who asked you? 2. à l'heure qu'il est, now; in this day and age 3. l'heure H, zero hour 4. s'embêter/s'emmerder à cent sous de l'heure, to be bored* stiff/rigid/to death 5. faire l'heure, to be punctual 6. l'heure du berger, right time/moment for making love 7. ouvriers de la onzième heure, latecomers/workers who are always late. (*Voir* **bouillon 3; quart 3**)

heureux, -euse [œrø, ørø, -øz] *a F* il vit comme un imbécile heureux, he's as happy as a pig in muck.

*hic [ik] *nm F* voilà le hic! that's the snag/the problem.

*hideur [idœr] *nf F* quelle hideur! (*surt femme*) what a hideous sight!/what a fright!

hier [iɛr, jɛr] *adv F* il est né d'hier, he's still very green/he's a bit wet behind the ears; je ne suis pas né d'hier, I wasn't born yesterday/what sort of a mug do you take me for?

*high [aj] *a F* (*drogues*) high.

hippie, hippy [ipi] *a & n F* hippie/hippy.

hirondelle [irɔ̃dɛl] *nf F* 1. hirondelle (bleue), gendarme/*Br* = police constable; hirondelle de trottoir, policeman*/cop; hirondelle à roulettes/de bitume/du faubourg/de nuit, cycle cop 2. gatecrasher (at cocktail parties, *Th* dress rehearsals, etc) 3. avoir une hirondelle dans le soliveau, to have bats in the belfry/to have a screw missing 4. les hirondelles volent bas, there's trouble brewing 5. hirondelle d'hiver, hot chestnut seller 6. (*seconde guerre 1939–45*) hirondelle de cimetière, bomb.

histoire [istwar] *nf* 1. *F* c'est toujours la même histoire, it's the same old story; c'est dingue, cette histoire-là, the whole thing's daft; c'est de l'histoire ancienne, it's ancient history 2. *F* c'est toute une histoire, it's a long story; (*c'est compliqué*) it's one hell of a business/it's no end of a job 3. *F* la belle histoire! is that all?/so what? 4. *F* fib/story; tout ça c'est des histoires! that's a load of rubbish!/*NAm* a bunch of hooey! tu racontes des histoires! you're pulling my leg!/you're having me on! une histoire à dormir debout, a tall story/a cock-and-bull story 5. *F* (*a*) faire des histoires/faire un tas d'histoires, to kick up a fuss/a rumpus; il a fait toute une histoire pour avoir cette bagnole, he kicked up one hell of a fuss to get that car; **pas d'histoires!** don't let's have any bother!/come off it! **en voilà une histoire!** what a lot of fuss!/what a carry-on!/what a song and dance!; (*c'est incroyable*) that's quite a story (*b*) **avoir des histoires avec qn,** to be in s.o.'s black books/to be at loggerheads with s.o.; (*il*) **faut éviter d'avoir des histoires,** we've got to stay out of trouble (*c*) **chercher/faire des histoires à qn,** to make trouble for s.o.; **s'attirer des histoires,** to get into trouble; **cela s'est passé sans histoires,** it went like a dream/without a hitch **6.** *F* what's-its-name*/thingummy/ thingumajig / whatcha(ma)callit / whatsit; **qu'est-ce que c'est que cette histoire?** what's that (thing)? **7.** *F* **histoire de rire/de s'amuser/de se marrer,** just for a joke/just for fun/just for the fun of it/for laughs; **ils ont volé cette tire, histoire de rigoler,** they stole that car for kicks; **j'y suis allé, histoire de faire qch,** I went just for the sake of (having) sth to do **8.** *F* **il a été renvoyé pour une histoire de femme,** he got the sack over some business with a woman/for carrying on with some woman **9.** *Vieilli P* **avoir ses histoires,** to have a period*/to have the curse **10.** *pl P* male genitals*/private parts/privates.

hiviau, hivio [ivjo] *nm P* winter.

holpif [ɔlpif] *a P* smart/stylish/natty.

*homard [ɔmar] *nm* **1.** *F* **rouge comme un homard,** (*d'embarras*) (as) red as a beetroot; (*après un coup de soleil*) as red as a lobster **2.** *P* Englishman*.

homasse [ɔmas] *a F* (*femme*) mannish/butch.

homme [ɔm] *nm* **1.** *P* (*a*) husband; boyfriend; lover; **mon homme,** my man; my husband (*b*) pimp* **2.** *F* (*a*) **je suis votre homme,** I'm your man (*b*) **ça c'est un homme!** that's what I call a man! **3.** *F* **dépouiller le vieil homme,** to turn over a new leaf **4.** *P* **être sous l'homme,** (*prostituée*) to be with a client/to be on the job. (*Voir* **barre 8; poids 2** (*a*))

hommelette [ɔmlɛt] *nf P* feeble man/ (little) weed/wimp.

homme-orchestre [ɔmɔrkɛstr] *nm F* **1.** one-man band **2.** man of many talents. (*pl* **hommes-orchestres**)

homo [ɔmo] *a & nm F* homosexual*/homo.

*honte [ɔ̃t] *nf F* (*c'est*) **la honte,** it doesn't look good/it looks bad; it's dreadful; it stinks; it sucks; **se payer la honte,** to be humiliated/to look silly/to look a right mug.

*honteuse [ɔ̃tøz] *nf P* homosexual* who denies his true sexual feelings/who has not come out; closet queen.

horizontale [ɔrizɔ̃tal] *nf Vieilli P* prostitute*/tart/hooker; **elle fait l'horizontale,** she earns her money on her back.

horloge [ɔrlɔ(ʒ)] *nf* **1.** *P* **la Grosse Horloge,** the Conciergerie (prison, in Paris) **2.** *F* **la petite horloge,** the heart; **il a l'horloge détraquée,** he's got a dicky/a bad heart.

horreur [ɔrœr] *nf* **1.** *P* (*a*) obscenity; repulsive sexual behaviour; **il me proposa des horreurs,** he asked me to do sth really disgusting; **dire des horreurs,** to say obscene things (*b*) bizarre sexual behaviour (appreciated by partner) **2.** *P* **musée des horreurs,** unpleasant/nasty faces **3.** *F* **le lycée, c'est l'horreur!** school is the pits! **ce mec, c'est l'horreur!** that guy is gross/the pits!

host(e)au, hosto [ɔsto] *nm P* **1.** hospital **2.** *A Mil* prison*/glasshouse.

*hotte [ɔt] *nf P* **1.** (*a*) car*/motor/jam-jar (*b*) taxi/cab **2. en avoir plein la hotte,** to be exhausted*/to be worn out.

*hotu [oty] *a & nm* down-at-heel/shabby-looking (individual).

*hourdé [urde] *a* **1.** *F* stupid*/idiotic/daft **2.** *P* drunk*/stoned.

*houri(e) [uri] *nf P souv Péj* woman*.

housard [uzar] *nm P* hole in a wall (*esp used for an escape*).

houst(e)! [ust] *int P =* **oust(e)!**

HP [aʃpe] (*abrév = hôpital*) *F* hospital.

HS [aʃɛs] (*abrév = hors service*) *P =* **hachès, hachesse.**

*hublot [yblo] *nm P* **1.** lens (of pair of spectacles) **2.** *pl* **hublots,** eyes*/peepers; **il a les hublots ensablés,** he hasn't woken up yet.

huile [ɥil] *nf* **1.** *F* **huile de bras/de coude,** elbow grease **2.** *P* important person*/VIP/ bigwig; **les huiles,** the big shots/the top brass; **être/nager dans les huiles,** to have influence/to know the right people/to have pull/to have clout **3.** *P* money* **4.** *P* **filer de l'huile,** to die in peace (having had the last rites). (*Voir* **baigner; pédaler 2; tronche 3**)

*huit [ɥit] *nm F* **faire des huit,** (*surt ivrogne*) to stagger/to lurch about (*often while urinating*).

huître [ɥitr] *nf P* **1.** fool*/mug/clot **2.** gob (of spit).

*huit-reflets [ɥir(ə)flɛ] *nm inv F* top hat/topper.

*huppé [ype] *a F* **1.** rich*/loaded/rolling in

it; **c'est quelqu'un de très huppé,** he's got pots/bags of money **2.** belonging to the smart set; posh/classy; **les gens huppés,** the nobs/the toffs.

*hure [yr] *nf P* **1.** head*/nut **2.** face*/mug; **se gratter la hure,** to (have a) shave.

*hurf(e) [œrf] *a P* elegant/posh/classy/ snazzy. (*Voir* **urf**)

*hussard [ysar] *adv phr F* **en hussard,** un- ceremoniously; *V* **baiser qn en hussard,** to make love to s.o. without preliminaries/to do away with the preliminaries/to get down to it. (*Voir* **élixir**)

à la *hussarde [alaysard] *adv phr V* **baiser/prendre qn à la hussarde,** to make love to s.o. without preliminaries/to get down to it.

hyper [ipɛr] *F* **I** *adv* very/extremely/ completely **II** *a* excellent*/terrific/super/great.

hypo [ipo] *nm ou f P* (*drogues*) hypodermic (needle*)/hypo/dropper.

à l'hypocrite [alipɔkrit] *adv F* **le feu est passé au rouge à l'hypocrite,** the light changed to red without warning.

hypokhâgne [ipokaɲ] *nf P* preparatory class to get into **khâgne.** (*Voir* **khâgne**).

hystérique [isterik] *a & nf F* nymphoma- niac/nympho.

hystéro [istero] *a & n F* nervous/neurotic (person); bag of nerves; (*délirant*) raving.

I

i [i] *pron F* (= *il*) (*souvent prononcé 'i' devant une consonne*) **i** peut pas venir, he can't come; **qu'est-ce qu'i veut?** what does he want? **ton père, i va venir?** will your father be coming? **i fait pas chaud!** it's rather cold; **i va tomber, ce truc,** that thing's going to fall off. (*Voir* **y**)

ici [isi] *adv F* **je vois ça d'ici,** I can see it from here.

icidé [iside], **icigo** [isigo], **icite** [isit] *adv P* here.

idée [ide] *nf F* **1. il y a de l'idée,** you may have sth there; (*chose*) it's got a certain something **2.** very small quantity; **une idée d'ail,** just a hint of garlic **3. se faire des idées,** to imagine things; **je me suis fait des idées noires,** I was imagining all sorts of things/the worst; **ne vous faites pas d'idées,** don't get ideas (into your head) **4. j'ai dans l'idée que tu me roules,** I've got the feeling you're having me on **5. a-t-on idée de ...?** who ever heard of ...?/who would have thought it! **6. avoir de la suite dans les idées,** to be persistent; **il a de la suite dans les idées,** he doesn't give it a rest/give up.

idem [idɛm] *adv F* **idem au cresson,** the same thing; **elle a vingt ans et son ami idem,** she's twenty and so's her boyfriend.

idiot [idjo] *adv F* **bronzer idiot,** to find nothing better to do than lie on the beach and sunbathe; **voyager idiot,** to travel without appreciating the country (like a dumb tourist).

ièche [jɛʃ] *vi V* (*verlan de* **chier**) to defecate*/to shit; **se faire ièche,** to be bored/to get pissed off; **c'est ièche,** it's bloody awful/it's shit(ty).

illico [iliko] *adv F* **illico (presto),** immediately*/right away/straight away/at once; **je suis sorti illico,** I left pronto/pretty sharpish.

illuse [ilyz] *nf F* (*abrév = illusion*) **se faire des illuses,** to get ideas/to imagine things.

image [imaʒ] *nf P* banknote; **grande image,** 100-franc *or* 500-franc note.

imbibé [ɛ̃bibe] *a P* (slightly) drunk*/tipsy.

imbitable [ɛ̃bitabl] *a P* incomprehensible; **c'est imbitable,** it's gibberish; it's all Greek. (*Voir* **biter 2**)

imbuvable [ɛ̃byvabl] *a F* (*personne*) insufferable/unbearable; (*film, etc*) (unbearably) awful/dreadful.

impair [ɛ̃pɛr] *nm F* (*a*) mistake*; **faire un impair,** to make a bloomer/a gaffe/a goof; to put one's foot in it/to boob (*b*) **faire un impair à qn,** to play a dirty trick on s.o./to do the dirty on s.o.

impasse [ɛ̃pas] *nf F* (*écoles*) part of syllabus not learnt for an exam; **faire l'impasse/une impasse sur l'allemand,** to give German a miss (*when revising for an exam*).

impayable [ɛ̃pɛjabl] *a F* very funny*/priceless; **vous êtes impayable!** you're a (real) scream!/*NAm* you're a riot!

impec [ɛ̃pɛk] *F* **I** *a* impeccable/perfect; **c'est impec!** great!/smashing!/amazing! **II** *adv* impeccably; **ça marche? – impec!** is it working? – like a dream!

imper [ɛ̃pɛr] *nm F* (*abrév = imperméable*) raincoat/mac.

importer [ɛ̃pɔrte] *vi F* **n'importe quoi!** what utter rubbish/drivel! **dire n'importe quoi,** to talk a load of drivel/bull.

impossible [ɛ̃pɔsibl] *a F* **1.** (*personne*) impossible; **vous êtes impossible!** you're the (bitter) end! **2. à une heure impossible,** at an ungodly/unearthly hour; **rentrer à des heures impossibles,** to come home at all hours (of the night) **3.** (*proverbe*) **impossible n'est pas français,** everything's possible/there's no such word as impossible.

in [in] *a inv F* **être in** (*a*) (*être dans le coup*) to be on sth (*b*) to be in fashion; **s'habiller in,** to wear the latest fashion.

incendier [ɛ̃sɑ̃dje] *vtr F* **incendier qn,** to reprimand* s.o. severely/to blow s.o. up/to tear s.o. off a strip; **se faire incendier**, to catch it/ to get a rocket.

inco [ɛ̃ko] *a P* (*a*) (= *incorrigible*) incorrigible/hopeless/past praying for (*b*) (= *inconnu*) unknown.

incollable [ɛ̃kɔlabl] *a F* (*personne*) unbeatable; who can't be floored/faulted; **il est incollable sur l'histoire du cinéma**, you can't catch him out/beat him when it comes to films; he knows all there is to know about films.

incon [ɛ̃kɔ̃] *a & n P* (*Pol, etc*) (= *inconditionnel*) unwavering (supporter); **c'est un incon du jazz**, he's a jazz fanatic/buff.

inconnoblé [ɛ̃kɔnɔble], **inconobré** [ɛ̃kɔnɔbre] *a P* unknown.

incontournable [ɛ̃kɔ̃turnabl] *a F* (*inévitable*) unavoidable; (*film*) unmissable; (*livre*) which must be read; (*personne*) unavoidable/that can't be avoided/that one can't get away from.

s'incruster [sɛ̃kryste] *vpr F* to wear out/to overstay one's welcome; **quand on l'invite il s'incruste**, whenever he's invited he seems to take root/you just can't get rid of him; **je ne vais pas m'incruster ...**, don't let me/I mustn't take up any more of your time.

incurable [ɛ̃kyrabl] *a P* condemned to death.

indéboulonnable [ɛ̃debulɔnabl] *a P* (*personne*) undismissable/who can't be sacked/who is a permanent fixture.

indécrottable [ɛ̃dekrɔtabl] *a F* incorrigible/hopeless/past praying for; **un tire-au-flanc indécrottable**, a hopeless skiver/a lazy bum.

indérouillable [ɛ̃derujabl] *a P* too ignorant to learn (a job, etc); **c'est un maladroit indérouillable**, he's a very clumsy/a hopeless worker.

indic [ɛ̃dik] *nm & f P* (*abrév = indicateur*) police informer*/(copper's) nark/stool pigeon/ grass.

indien [ɛ̃djɛ̃] *nm P* man*/bloke/guy/geezer.

indigestion [ɛ̃diʒɛstjɔ̃] *nf F* **j'en ai une indigestion**, I'm fed up* (to the back teeth) with it/I'm sick and tired of it.

indisposée [ɛ̃dispoze] *af F Euph* **être indisposée**, to have a period*/to have the curse.

infectados [ɛ̃fɛktados] *nm P* cheap cigar/ stinkweed.

infichu [ɛ̃fiʃy] *a P* incapable/useless.

info [ɛ̃fo] *nf P* (*presse*) (*abrév = information*) information/info.

infourgable [ɛ̃furgabl] *a P* unsaleable/ unfloggable; **c'est infourgable ce truc**, you can't flog this thing anywhere/you can't give it away.

infoutu [ɛ̃futy] *a P* = **infichu**.

ino [ino] *a P* (*abrév = inoccupé*) unemployed.

inox [inɔks] *nm F* (= *inoxydable*) (*acier*) inox, stainless steel.

inquiète (t') [tɛ̃kjɛt] *int P* (= *ne t'inquiète pas*) don't worry (about that).

insinuante [ɛ̃sinɥɑ̃t] *nf P* (*drogues*) syringe*/hypo.

installer [ɛ̃stale] *vi P* **en installer**, to show off*/to swank; **il en installe un max, mais c'est du bidon**, he puts on a bold front, but it's all a bit of a sham.

installeur [ɛ̃stalœr] *nm F* show-off*/swank.

insti(t), -ite [ɛ̃sti(t)] *n F* (*abrév = instituteur, -trice*) (school)teacher/teach.

instrument [ɛ̃strymɑ̃] *nm V* penis*/tool.

insupporter [ɛ̃sypɔrte] *vtr F* **ce type m'insupporte**, I can't stand/stomach that bloke/guy.

intégrer [ɛ̃tegre] *vi F* (*écoles*) **intégrer à une grande École**, to get into a *grande École*; **intégré à la Normale**, admitted to the *École Normale*.

intello [ɛ̃telo] *F* **I** *a* intellectual **II** *n* intellectual/highbrow/egghead.

inter [ɛ̃tɛr] *nm & f* 1. *P* tout/steer(er)/hustler 2. *F* interpreter.

interdit [ɛ̃tɛrdi] *a F* **interdit de séjour**, barred/banned (*from pub, restaurant, etc*).

interpeller [ɛ̃tɛrpele] *vtr F* **ça m'interpelle**, I'm shocked/gobsmacked; (*ça m'émeut*) I'm deeply moved.

intox(e) [ɛ̃tɔks] *nf F* 1. brainwashing; **ce n'est pas de l'information mais de l'intox(e)**, that's not objective info, that's plain propaganda 2. intoxication (through alcohol, drugs).

intoxico [ɛ̃tɔksiko] *nm & f F* drug addict*/ junkie.

introduire [ɛ̃trɔdɥir] *vtr* 1. *F* **l'introduire à qn**, to hoax s.o./to take s.o. in/to kid s.o. (along); **se la laisser introduire/se la faire introduire**, to let oneself be taken in/to be had 2. *P* **l'introduire à qn**, to have sex with s.o.*/to screw s.o.

invalo [ɛ̃valo] *nm & f F* invalid.

les Invaloches [lɛzɛ̃valɔʃ], **les Invalos** [lɛzɛ̃valo] *Prn P* the Invalides (quarter) (*in Paris*).

inventaire [ɛ̃vɑ̃tɛr] *nm Mus F* faire l'inventaire, to play arpeggios.

invitation [ɛ̃vitasjɔ̃] *nf F* invitation à la valse, (unwelcome) invitation to pay (the bill).

invite [ɛ̃vit] *nf F* invitation/invite.

invivable [ɛ̃vivabl] *a F* avec sa pipe il devient invivable, he's impossible to live with/he gets on my nerves smoking that pipe.

iroquois [irɔkwa] *nm F* young man*/punk wearing a Mohican hairstyle.

iroquoise [irɔkwaz] *nf F* Mohican hairstyle.

isoloir [izɔlwar] *nm F* (public) urinal.

Italboche [italbɔʃ] *nm*, **Italgo** [italgo] *nm*, **Italo** [italo] *nm Vieilli P Péj* Italian*/Eyetie/wop.

itou [itu] *adv P* too/also/likewise; et moi itou! (and) me too!

Ivan [ivɑ̃] *Prn P* Russian*/Russkie; les Ivans, the Russians/the Commies.

IVG [iveʒe] *nf F* (*abrév* = *interruption volontaire de grossesse*) termination of pregnancy/abortion; elle en est à sa 3ème IVG, that's her third abortion.

ivoire [ivwar] *nm F* écraser de l'ivoire/taquiner l'ivoire, to play the piano/to tickle the ivories.

ivre-dézingué [ivrədezɛ̃ge] *a P* dead drunk*/pissed as a newt/paralytic.

J

J [ʒi] *nmpl & fpl F* (*seconde guerre 1939–45*) les **J3**, (*d'après l'abréviation que portaient les cartes de rationnement des adolescents en France à l'époque*) teenagers/young people.

jab [ʒab] *nm P* punch in the stomach.

jabot [ʒabo] *nm F* **1.** stomach*/belly; **se remplir le jabot**, to stuff oneself/to have a good blow-out **2.** **faire jabot/enfler le jabot/ gonfler le jabot**, to put on airs/to strut.

jabotage [ʒabotaʒ] *nm F* chatter*/ nattering/jabbering/jaw/yackety-yack.

jaboter [ʒabote] *vi F* **1.** to chatter*/to jabber/to rabbit **2.** to eat*/to fill one's belly/to stuff oneself/to pig oneself.

jaboteur, -euse [ʒabotœr, -øz] *n F* chatterbox*/gasbag/windbag.

jacasse [ʒakas] *nf F* chatterbox*; **ma concierge est une vieille jacasse**, my concierge is a real old gasbag.

jacasser [ʒakase] *vi F* to chatter*; **vous êtes là pour travailler, pas pour jacasser**, you're here to work, not to have a good natter; **assez jacassé!** put a sock in it!/stop gassing!

jacasserie [ʒakas(ə)ri] *nf F* (*a*) (endless) chatter*/jabbering/prattling/nattering (*b*) gossip.

jacasseur, -euse [ʒakasœr, -øz] *n*, **jacassier, -ière** [ʒakasje, -jɛr] *n F* (*a*) chatterbox*/prattler; gasbag (*b*) gossip.

jacot [ʒako] *nm P V* = **jacques**.

jacques [ʒak] *nm*, **jacquot** [ʒako] *nm* **1.** *P* (burglar's) jemmy/*NAm* jimmy **2.** *P* safe/ peter **3.** *V* penis*/John Thomas **4.** *V* dildo **5.** *P* (*mollet*) calf **6.** *F* **faire le jacques/le Jacques**, to play the fool/to fool about/to act dumb **7.** *P* taxi meter/clock.

jactance [ʒaktɑ̃s] *nf P* chat(tering)*/ jabber(ing); **avoir de la jactance**, to have the gift of the gab; **ce type, c'est le roi de la jactance**, that bloke's got the gift of the gab.

jacter [ʒakte] *vi P* **1.** to talk* (at great length)/to gas; to (go) rabbit(ing) on **2. jacter sur qn**, to speak badly of s.o./to slander/*NAm*

to badmouth s.o.; **la concierge jacte sur tous les locataires**, the caretaker goes on about all the tenants **3.** (*argot policier*) to confess*/to come clean/to nark.

jacteur, -euse [ʒaktœr, -øz] *P I a* talkative/prattling/gossipy **II** *n* chatterbox*/ gasbag/windbag.

jaffe [ʒaf] *nf P* (*repas*) meal; (*nourriture*) food*/grub/nosh; **à la jaffe!** grub's up!

jaffer [ʒafe] *vi P* to eat*.

Jag [ʒag] *nf F Aut* Jaguar (*RTM*)/Jag.

jaja [ʒaʒa] *nm P* (red) wine/plonk; **écluser un jaja**, to knock back/to down a glass of vino.

jalmince [ʒalmɛ̃s] *P I a* jealous/green **II** *nm & f* jealous person **III** *nf* jealousy.

jalmincerie [ʒalmɛ̃s(ə)ri] *nf P* jealousy.

jambard [ʒɑ̃bar] *nm Vieilli P* (*personne*) bore*; pain (in the neck/in the arse/*NAm* the ass).

jambe [ʒɑ̃b] *nf* **1.** *F* (*a*) **prendre ses jambes à son cou**, to take to one's heels/to show a clean pair of heels (*b*) **jouer des jambes**, to run away*/to do a bunk/scarper **2.** *F* **se dérouiller les jambes**, to stretch one's legs **3.** *F* **tenir la jambe à qn**, to buttonhole/to corner s.o./to keep s.o. talking **4.** *F* **tirer dans les jambes de qn**, to play a dirty trick on s.o./to do the dirty on s.o.; to make life difficult for s.o. **5.** *F* (*a*) **faire la belle jambe**, to show off*/to swank/to strut about (*b*) **ça vous fera une belle jambe!** a fat lot of good that'll do you!/that won't get you very far! **6.** *F* **avoir les jambes en coton/en pâté de foie**, to feel weak/wobbly on one's legs; **j'ai les jambes comme du coton**, my legs feel like (they're made of) jelly/cotton-wool; **je n'ai plus de jambes**, I'm exhausted*/dead on my feet **7.** *F* (*a*) **avoir les jambes en manches de veste/ avoir des jambes Louis XV**, to be bow-legged/ bandy-legged (*b*) **avoir des jambes comme des allumettes**, to have legs like matchsticks/ to have skinny legs **8.** *F* **en avoir plein les jambes**, to be exhausted*/worn out/bushed/

whacked **9.** (*a*) *P* s'en aller sur une jambe, to go without a final drink; tu ne vas pas rentrer chez toi sur une jambe? you're not going to refuse a nightcap?/you must have one for the road (*b*) *F* ça se fait sur une jambe, you can do that standing on one leg; it's as easy as falling off a log; il a fait ses six semaines sur une jambe, he did those six weeks standing on his head/those six weeks were a walkover for him **10.** *F* (*a*) faire qch par-dessous/par-dessus la jambe, to do sth/to work in a slipshod manner; travail fait par-dessous/par-dessus la jambe, botched work (*b*) traiter qn par-dessous/par-dessus la jambe, to treat s.o. badly/in an offhand manner; to be offhand with s.o. **11.** *F* se mettre/être dans les jambes de qn, to get/to be (always) under s.o.'s feet **12.** *P* en aurai-je la jambe mieux faite? what good's that going to do me?/shall I be any the better for it? **13.** *P* ça vaut mieux qu'une jambe cassée/que de se casser la jambe, it's better than a kick in the pants/than a poke in the eye **14.** *P* la jambe! put a sock in it!/you're getting on my wick!/stop being (such) a pain! **15.** *P* faire jambe de bois, to leave without paying/to do a flit; il a disparu en faisant jambe de bois, he left without paying the rent/he did a moonlight (flit) **16.** *Vieilli P* one hundred francs. (*Voir* **demi-jambe**) **17.** *V* lever la jambe, (*femme*) to be a pushover/to be an easy lay/to open one's legs for anyone **18.** *V* une partie de jambes en l'air, a bit of slap and tickle/a bit of how's your father/a bit of the other; faire une partie de jambes en l'air, to have sex*/to have a screw/to have a fuck/to have a bit of the other **19.** *V* jambe du milieu/troisième jambe, penis*/middle leg/third leg. (*Voir* **rond III** 1)

jamber [ʒɑ̃be] *vtr Vieilli F* jamber qn, to annoy* s.o./to get up s.o.'s nose.

jambon [ʒɑ̃bɔ̃] *nm* **1.** *P* gratter/racler du/le *jambon*, to play the guitar/the banjo, etc **2.** *pl* *P* jambons, thighs; *V* partie de jambons, = **partie de jambes en l'air (jambe 18).**

jambon-beurre [ʒɑ̃bɔ̃bœr] *nm F* (buttered) ham roll *or* sandwich.

jambonneau, *pl* **-eaux** [ʒɑ̃bɔno] *nm P* = **jambon 1, 2.**

jambonner [ʒɑ̃bɔne] **I** *vi P* to play the guitar/the banjo, etc **II** *vtr* **1.** *A P* jambonner le blair à qn, to thump/to bash s.o. on the nose **2.** *F* = **jamber.**

jante [ʒɑ̃t] *nf F* **1.** se trouver sur les jantes, to be penniless*/to be down on one's uppers **2.**

être/rouler sur la jante, (*cyclisme; après plusieurs coïts, un effort intense*) to be exhausted*/to be all in; (*échouer*) to flop.

Jap [ʒap] *nm & f P* Jap/Nip.

japonais [ʒapɔnɛ] *nmpl Vieilli P* money*; les japonais ont tourné le coin/sont pas laga, I haven't a bean.

japonaise [ʒapɔnɛz] *nf F* drink consisting of milk mixed with grenadine or strawberry syrup/= milkshake.

jaquette [ʒakɛt] *nf* **1.** *F* tirer qn par la jaquette, to buttonhole s.o./to stick to s.o. like a leech **2.** *P* jaquette flottante, homosexual*; il est/il file/il refile de la jaquette (flottante), he's a homosexual*/he's gay/he's one of them.

jar [ʒar] *nm P* = **jars.**

jardin [ʒardɛ̃] *nm* **1.** *F* faire du jardin, to criticize s.o./to knock s.o./to get at s.o./to make digs at s.o.; (*calomnier*) to slander (s.o.) **2.** *P* aller au jardin, to work a swindle*/a fiddle; to be on the fiddle.

jardiner [ʒardine] *vtr Vieilli P* **1.** to fool* (s.o.)/to lead (s.o.) up the garden path **2.** *P* to tease*/to make fun of (s.o.).

jars [ʒar] *nm P* (thieves', etc) slang/cant; dévider/jaspiner le jars, to talk slang/to talk the lingo.

jasante [ʒazɑ̃t] *nf A P* prayer.

jaser [ʒaze] *vi P* **1.** to chatter*/to prattle/to jabber; ces deux vieilles commères passent leur temps à jaser, those two old gossips/windbags do nothing but gas **2.** (*médire*) to gossip; ça va faire jaser, it'll set tongues wagging **3.** to divulge* a secret/to inform on s.o./to talk; en face des poulagas, il va jaser, when he sees the cops, he's going to give us away/grass/talk **4.** *A* to pray.

jaspin [ʒaspɛ̃] *nm*, **jaspinage** [ʒaspinaʒ] *nm P* chatter(ing)*.

jaspiner [ʒaspine] *P* **I** *vtr* to speak (a language); il jaspine bien l'anglais, he speaks English well **II** *vi* to talk/to chatter*/to natter; qu'est-ce qu'il jaspine bien! what a good talker he is!

jaspineur [ʒaspinœr] *nm P* **1.** chatterbox*/gasbag/windbag **2.** lawyer/barrister/brief.

jaune [ʒon] **I** *nm & f f* **1.** strikebreaker/blackleg/scab **2.** *Vieilli* sa femme le peint en jaune, his wife is unfaithful/is seeing another man/has got s.o. on the side **3.** aniseed aperitif/pastis **II** *nm & f p Péj* Jaune, yellow-skinned person/Chink(ie). (*Voir* **terre**)

jaunet [ʒonɛ] *nm P* **1.** gold coin **2.** = **jaune 3 3.** = **jaune II.**

jaunisse [ʒonis] *nf F* **en faire une jaunisse,** to be mad with jealousy/to be green with envy; (*en faire un plat*) to make a fuss/a song and dance about sth.

java [ʒava] *nf P* **1.** (*fête*) rave-up; **faire la java,** to have a good time*/a rave-up/a ball; to live it up; **être/partir en java,** to go on the razzle/to go out on the tiles **2.** beating up*/ hammering/thrashing; **java des baffes,** beating* up/the third degree; **filer une java à qn,** to give s.o. a going-over/to work s.o. over.

javanais [ʒavanɛ] *nm F* (*argot consistant à introduire dans un mot les syllabes* **av** *ou* **va:** *donc* **jardin** *devient* **javardavin, jeudi** *devient* **javeudavi**) = form of slang; **c'est du javanais,** (*c'est incompréhensible*) it's double Dutch.

jazz-tango [dʒaztɑ̃go] *a P* **être jazz-tango,** to be bisexual/bi/AC-DC.

Jean [ʒɑ̃] *Prnm F* **en saint Jean,** naked*/as God made us/in one's birthday suit.

jean-fesse [ʒɑ̃fɛs] *nm inv A* = **jean-foutre.**

jean-foutre [ʒɑ̃futr] *nm inv P Péj* (*a*) unreliable person/good-for-nothing (*b*) bastard*/ nasty piece of work/sod (*c*) fool*/twit/nurd.

jean-le-gouin [ʒɑ̃ləgwɛ̃] *nm inv P* sailor*.

Jean-nu-tête [ʒɑ̃nytɛt] *nm inv V* penis*/ John Thomas.

je-m'en-fichisme, j'men-fichisme [ʒmɑ̃fiʃism] *nm F* couldn't-care-less attitude.

je-m'en-fichiste, j'men-fichiste [ʒmɑ̃fiʃist] *nm & f F* person who couldn't care less about anyone or anything.

je-m'en-foutisme, j'men-foutisme [ʒmɑ̃futism] *nm P* couldn't-give-a-damn attitude.

je-m'en-foutiste, j'men-foutiste [ʒmɑ̃futist] *nm & f P* person who doesn't give a damn/a shit about anyone or anything.

je-sais-tout [ʒ(ə)sɛtu] *a & n inv* know-all; **un Monsieur Je-sais-tout,** Mr Know-all/Mr Know-it-all/(Mr) Clever-Dick.

jèse [ʒɛz] *nm P* Jesuit. (*Voir* **jèze**)

jésuite [ʒezɥit] *a F Péj* hypocritical.

jésus [ʒezy] *nm* **1.** *F* (*terme d'affection*) **mon jésus,** my (little) darling* **2.** *P* effeminate young man*; (young) passive homosexual* **3.** *V* erect penis* **4.** *P* **le petit Jésus en culotte de velours,** delicious drink* *or* meal.

jetard [ʃtar] *nm P* = **ch'tar.**

jeté [ʒ(ə)te] *a F* **1.** (*a*) mad*/crazy; **il est complètement jeté avec ses idées modernistes,** he's completely nuts about all these modern ideas (*b*) demoralized (*c*) drunk* **2.** useless/good for nothing **3. bien**

jeté! well said!

jetée [ʒ(ə)te] *nf Vieilli P* hundred francs. (*Voir* **demi-jetée**)

jeter [ʒəte, ʃte] *vtr* **1.** *F* to throw (s.o.) out/to chuck (s.o.) out; **se faire jeter,** to get thrown out **2.** *P* (*a*) **(en) jeter,** to make a good impression; **ça jette!** it's really something!/ it's brilliant! **en jeter à qn,** to impress s.o.; **elle en jette!** she's got what it takes!/she's got class!/she's really something! **elle en jette, ta bagnole!** that's a really classy car you've got!/that's some car you've got there! (*b*) **la jeter mal,** to make/to give a bad impression **3.** *F* **n'en jetez plus, la cour est pleine,** stop it!/ give it a rest!/pack it in! **4.** *P* **s'en jeter un,** to have a drink/to have one; **s'en jeter un dernier,** to have one for the road **5.** *P* **jeter de la grêle,** to criticize*/to run down/to slate. (*Voir* **coup 13; cravate 4; jus 6; pierre I 1; purée 2; tête 15; venin**)

jeton [ʒətɔ̃, ʃtɔ̃] *nm* **1.** *F* **un faux jeton,** a hypocrite **2.** *P* man*/bloke; woman*/female; **un vieux jeton,** an old person; an old fogey*/a has-been/a back-number; **beau jeton,** pretty girl*/nice bit of stuff **3.** *P* punch/blow*; **prendre un jeton en pleine poire,** to get biffed/clouted/socked right on the kisser **4.** *P* **dent** (on car, etc); **sa voiture est pleine de jetons,** his car's all dented **5.** *P* **avoir les jetons,** to be afraid*/to get the jitters; **donner/filer/flanquer les jetons à qn,** to put the wind up s.o./to give s.o. the willies; **ça me fout les jetons,** it gives me the creeps/it scares me shitless **6.** *P* **prendre/se payer un jeton (de mate),** (*volontairement*) to be a voyeur/a peeping Tom; (*volontairement ou non*) to watch an erotic/a porny display.

jeu, pl jeux [ʒø] *nm F* **1.** (*a*) **vous avez beau jeu,** now's your chance (*b*) **il avait beau jeu à faire cela,** it was easy for him to do that; he had every opportunity to do that **2. jouer bon jeu bon argent,** (*honnêtement*) to play it straight; (*sérieusement*) to mean business; **y aller bon jeu bon argent,** to come/to go straight to the point **3. faire le grand jeu à qn/jouer le grand jeu,** to give s.o. the works **4. nous sommes à deux de jeu,** two can play at that game; **ce n'est pas du jeu,** that's not fair/that's not on **5.** (*a*) **cacher son jeu,** to keep one's cards close to one's chest; **serrer son jeu,** to take no risks/to play it close to the chest (*b*) **elle cache bien son jeu,** (*hypocrite*) she looks as though butter wouldn't melt in her mouth. (*Voir* **épingle 2**)

jeudi [ʒødi] *nm F* la semaine des quatre jeudis, never; when pigs have wings/when Hell freezes (over); **tu risques d'attendre jusqu'à la semaine des quatre jeudis,** you'll end up waiting till the cows come home; **il vous le paiera la semaine des quatre jeudis,** it'll be a miracle if he pays you for it.

jeunabre, jeunâbre [ʒœnabr, -abr] *P I a* young/youngish II *nm & f* youngster.

jeune [ʒœn] *a F* 1. son jeune homme, her young man/her boyfriend 2. not enough; **c'est un peu jeune/ça fait un peu jeune,** (*quantité*) it's a bit on the short side/on the small side; (*argent*) that's a bit tight/stingy; (*temps*) that's cutting it a bit fine.

jeunesse [ʒœnɛs] *nf F* une jeunesse, a girl*/a (little) bit of fluff.

jeunet, -ette [ʒœnɛ, -ɛt] *Vieilli F I a* young/youngish; on the young side II *n* un jeunet/une jeunette, a young boy/girl; a mere lad/a slip of a girl.

jeunot, -otte [ʒœno, -ɔt] *F I a* young/youngish; on the young side II *nm* youth/(young) lad.

jèze [ʒɛz] *nm P* Jesuit. (*Voir* **jèse**)

jinjin [ʒɛ̃ʒɛ̃] *nm P* 1. red wine/plonk/vino 2. il n'a rien dans le jinjin, he's empty-headed/he's got nothing up there/he's a bit dim.

job I [dʒɔb] *nm F* (*a*) job/work/employment (*b*) temporary job; **c'est un job d'étudiant,** it's not a job for life/it's only temporary (*c*) alibi*/cover/front (for illegal activity) II [ʒɔb] *nm F Vieilli* (*a*) **monter le job à qn,** (*tromper*) to pull s.o.'s leg/to have s.o. on/to take s.o. in/ to take s.o. for a ride (*b*) **se monter le job,** (*se faire des illusions*) to imagine things/to kid oneself; (*s'énerver*) to get excited/to work oneself up/to go off the deep end.

jobard, -arde [ʒɔbar, -ard] *F I n* 1. mug/ sucker 2. madman/madwoman/nutter/nut II *a* gullible/naive.

jobarder [ʒɔbarde] *vtr* (*rare*) *F* jobarder qn, to hoax* s.o./to take s.o. for a ride/to have s.o. on.

jobarderie [ʒɔbard(ə)ri] *nf,* **jobardise** [ʒɔbardiz] *nf F* gullibility; **c'est de la jobarderie,** it's a mug's game; **commettre une jobarderie,** to let oneself be taken in/to be had.

jobré [ʒɔbre] *a P* mad*; **il est complètement jobré,** he's completely nuts/he's off his head.

jockey [ʒɔkɛ] *nm* 1. *F* faire jockey/être au régime jockey, to be on a strict diet/on a starvation diet 2. *P* decoy in gambling joint, etc/*NAm* shill(aber).

joice [ʒwas] *a P* happy/cheerful/pleased/ joyful; **il est tout joice,** he's as happy as a clam; **t'es pas joice?** what's wrong, not happy? (*Voir* **joisse; jouasse**)

joint [ʒwɛ̃] *nm* 1. *F* trouver le joint pour faire qch, to hit on the right way of going about sth; to discover the trick/the knack of doing sth; to come up with the answer 2. *P* (*drogues*) marijuana* cigarette/joint; **fumer/ tirer un joint,** to smoke a joint.

joisse [ʒwas] *a P* = **joice**.

jojo [ʒoʒo] *F I a* 1. (*a*) nice/pleasant; **c'est pas très jojo,** it's not very/terribly nice (*b*) pretty/good-looking; **sans maquillage elle n'est pas tellement jojo,** without all that make-up she's not such a pretty sight 2. me voilà jojo! I'm in a fix*/I'm in a fine old mess! II *nm* 1. **affreux jojo,** (*enfant*) horrible (little) brat/kid; (*personne provocatrice*) s.o. who stirs things up 2. **faire son jojo,** to behave puritanically/to be all goody-goody/to be holier-than-thou.

joker [ʒɔkɛr] *nm F* jouer/sortir son joker, to play one's joker/trump card.

joli [ʒɔli] *F I a Iron* fine/nice; **je serais joli!** a fine mess I'd be in! **c'est pas joli,** it's a poor show; **tout cela c'est bien joli, mais ...,** that's all very well, but ... II *nm* c'est du joli! a nice mess (it is)!/it's a disgrace! **il a encore fait du joli!** a fine mess he's made of it again! (*Voir* **coco 5** (*a*); **cœur 1**)

joliment [ʒɔlimɑ̃] *adv F* (*intensif*) very/ extremely; **joliment amusant,** awfully funny; **il danse joliment bien,** he's a jolly good/a great dancer; **il a joliment raison!** he's dead right! **on s'est joliment amusé(s),** we had a great time/a really good time.

jonc [ʒɔ̃] *nm* 1. *P* gold (*ingot or coin*) 2. *P* peler le jonc à qn, to annoy* s.o.; **tu me pèles le jonc!** you get on my bloody nerves!/you get up my nose!

joncaille [ʒɔ̃kaj] *nf P* gold jewellery.

jongler [ʒɔ̃gle] *vi F* to do without/to be deprived of (sth); **faire jongler qn de qch,** to do s.o. out of what is due to him.

Jordonne [ʒɔrdɔn] *Prn F* (= j'ordonne) **c'est un monsieur/une madame Jordonne,** he's/she's bossy/a real bossy-boots.

jordonner [ʒɔrdɔne] *vtr F* to boss (s.o./ people) about.

jornaille [ʒɔrnaj] *nf,* **jorne** [ʒɔrn] *nm A P* day; daytime.

joséphine [ʒozefin] *nf P* submachine gun/

tommy gun.

jouasse [ʒwas] *a P* = **joice.**

jouer [ʒwe] *vtr P* 1. jouer qn, to fool* s.o. 2. les jouer, to run away*/to clear off/to beat it 3. où t'as vu jouer ça? where did you get that idea from?/are you mad? (*Voir* **air I 2; châtaigne 2** (*b*); **clarinette 3; compas 3; con I 2; feuille 1; flûte II; fuseaux; guibolles; harpe; jambe 1** (*b*); **rip; violon 1**)

joufflu [ʒufly] *nm P* buttocks*/bum/cheeks/ *NAm* ass/*NAm* butt.

jouge [ʒuʒ] *adv phr P* en moins de jouge, very quickly*/immediately/in no time (at all)/ as quick as a flash.

jouir [ʒwir] *vi* 1. *F* (*Iron; par antiphrase*) ça l'a fait jouir! I bet he enjoyed that! quand je me suis mis le marteau sur les doigts j'ai joui, I was overjoyed/ecstatic/over the moon when I hit my fingers with the hammer 2. *P* to have an orgasm*/to come.

jouissance [ʒwisɑ̃s] *nf P* orgasm*/climax.

jouissif, -ive [ʒwisif, -iv] *a F* very pleasurable; orgasmic.

joujou [ʒuʒu] *nm P* faire joujou avec qn, to have sex* with s.o.

jour [ʒur] *nm* 1. *F* long comme un jour sans pain, (*personne*) tall and thin 2. *F* demain il fera jour, tomorrow's another day 3. *F* avoir ses jours, (*femme*) to have a period*/to have the curse/to come on 4. *P* ça craint le jour, (*marchandises volées*) that stuff's hot 5. *F* (= *plat du jour*) dish of the day 6. *F* des jours avec et des jours sans, good days and bad days; lucky days and unlucky days. (*Voir* **craindre II**)

jourdé [ʒurde] *nm,* **journaille** [ʒurnaj] *nf P* day.

journaleux, -euse [ʒurnalø, -øz] *nm & f F Péj* journalist/hack.

journanche [ʒurnɑ̃ʃ] *nf,* **journe** [ʒurn] *nm ou f P* day.

joyeuses [ʒwajøz] *nfpl V* testicles*/nuts.

joyeux [ʒwajø] *nm A P Mil* soldier serving in a *bataillon d'Afrique*. (*Voir* **bat' d'Af**)

JT [ʒite] *nm F TV* (= *journal télévisé*) the news; = the 9 o'clock *or* 10 o'clock news.

J't'arquepince [ʒtark(ə)pɛ̃s] *a P* (ces messieurs de) la maison J't'arquepince, the police*/the cops/the fuzz.

jucher [ʒyʃe] *vi A F* où juchez-vous? where do you live?/where do you hang out?

jugeot(t)e [ʒyʒɔt] *nf* 1. *F* common sense/ gumption/savvy; avoir de la jugeot(t)e, to

know what's what 2. *P* passer en jugeot(t)e, to stand for trial.

juif [ʒɥif] *nm* 1. *F* le petit juif, the funnybone 2. *P Péj* miser*; faire qch en juif, to do sth in secret/secretly; to do sth without sharing it with others.

juivoler [ʒɥivɔle] *vtr Vieilli P Péj* to overcharge/to rip off.

Jules, jules [ʒyl] *Prn & nm P* 1. chamber pot*/jerry 2. (*a*) lover/fancy man; boyfriend/ bloke/guy (*b*) husband*; mon jules, my hubby/my old man 3. man*/chap/bloke/guy 4. pimp*/ponce 5. se faire appeler Jules, to get reprimanded*/torn off a strip. (*Voir* **Arthur**)

Julie, julie [ʒyli] *Prn & nf* 1. *F* faire sa julie, to be a prude/prudish/all goody-goody 2. *P* woman*; wife*/old lady; mistress 3. *P* (*drogues*) julie du Brésil, cocaine*.

Julot, julot [ʒylo] *Prn & nm P* 1. = **jules** 2. (petit) julot casse-croûte, petty/small-time crook/thief.

jumelles [ʒymɛl] *nfpl P* buttocks*/bum/*NAm* ass.

junk¹ [dʒœk] *nm P* (*drogues*) heroin*/H.

junk² [dʒœnk], **junkie, junky** [dʒœki] *nm & f P* (*drogues*) drug addict*/junkie.

jupé [ʒype] *a P* drunk*.

jupon [ʒypɔ̃] *nm F* woman*/girl*/(bit of) skirt; courir le jupon, to run after girls *or* women/to chase skirt/to be on the make; amateur de jupon, womanizer.

juponné [ʒypɔne] *a P* drunk*.

jus [ʒy] *nm* 1. *P* (*a*) (dirty) water; c'est clair comme du jus de boudin/de chique, it's as clear as mud; jus de grenouille, water (*as a drink*); jus de parapluie, (rain)water; tomber au jus, to fall in the water/the drink (*b*) tourner/partir en jus de boudin, (*projet, etc*) *Voir* **eau 5** 2. *P* coffee; jus (de chapeau/de chaussette/de chique), watery coffee/ dishwater/cat's piss; au jus! coffee time!/ coffee's up! *Mil* c'est du dix au jus, only ten days to demob; premier jus, lance corporal/ *US* private first cass; deuxième jus, private 3. *P* (*a*) electric current*/juice; mettre le jus, to switch on (*b*) petrol/juice/gas; donner du jus, to step on the gas/to step on it; à plein jus, at full throttle 4. *P* être au jus, to be informed/in the know 5. *P* long (boring) speech; faire un jus, to spout on (at length) 6. *P* avoir du jus, to be smart/elegant; to have class; jeter du jus, to make a good impression; (*avoir de la classe*) to look classy/to have class 7. *P* ça vaut le jus, it's worth it/it's worth the effort; y mettre du jus, to put one's back into it 8. *F* cuire/mariner/mijoter dans son jus, to stew in one's own juice 9. *F* un français pur jus, a hundred percent Frenchman/a typical Frenchman 10. *F* c'est le même jus, it's the same thing; c'est jus et verjus, it's six of one and half a dozen of the other 11. *P* jus de sarment, wine 12. *P* nitroglycerine/soup 13. *P* (*drogues*) heroin*/cocaine* 14. *P Péj* jus de réglisse, negro/Black* 15. *V* semen*/sperm/ spunk; lâcher le jus, to ejaculate*/to shoot one's load. (*Voir* court-jus; tire-jus)

jusqu'auboutisme [ʒyskobutism] *nm F* extremist attitude; (*politique*) hardline policy.

jusqu'auboutiste [ʒyskobutist] *nm & f F* 1. (*extrémiste*) whole-hogger/all-outer; (*politique*) hardliner 2. (*fidèle à un parti, des principes*) diehard/last-ditcher/bitter-ender.

jusque [ʒysk(ə)] *prép F* en avoir jusque-là, to have had enough (of sth)/to be fed up* to the back teeth (with sth)/to have had it up to here.

juste [ʒyst] *a & adv F* 1. ç'a été juste! it was a tight squeeze! arriver un peu juste, to cut it a bit fine 2. comme de juste (et de bien entendu), of course/obviously.

justice [ʒystis] *nf F* des cheveux raides comme la justice, dead straight hair.

jutant [ʒytɑ̃] *nm F* large pimple; il a un jutant sur le pif, he's got a big juicy spot/*NAm* zit on the end of his nose.

jute [ʒyt] *nm V* semen*/sperm/spunk.

juter [ʒyte] *vi* 1. *P* to hold forth/to spout on 2. *P* = jus 6 3. (*être rentable*) to pay/to be profitable 4. *V* to ejaculate*/to shoot (one's load).

juteux, -euse [ʒytø, -øz] *P* I *a* (*a*) smart/classy/tarted up (*b*) profitable; affaire juteuse, juicy bit of business II *nm Mil* (company) sergeant major.

JV [ʒive] *abrév P* (*argot policier = jeune voyou*) young hooligan*/juvenile delinquent/young hoodlum.

K

kaki [kaki] *nm P* (*prostitution*) discount granted to the client.

kangourou [kãguru] *nm* 1. *F* Australian*/Aussie 2. *pl P* (*règles*) period/the curse 3. *P* (*prostitution*) undecided client.

kapo [kapo] *nm Vieilli Mil* (*seconde guerre 1939-45*) (*surveillant dans un camp de concentration*) German corporal. (*Voir* **capo**)

kasba(h) [kazba] *nf P* house/pad/joint.

kawa [kawa] *nm P* (a cup of) coffee.

kebla [kəbla] *a & n P* (*verlan de* **black**) Black (person).

kéblo [keblo] *a P* (*verlan de* **bloqué**) être kéblo, to have a psychological block.

kébour [kebur] *nm P* 1. *Vieilli Mil* kepi/peaked cap 2. policeman*/copper/rozzer.

képa [kepa] *nm P* (*drogues*) (*verlan de* **paquet**) dose of cocaine*/fix.

képi [kepi] *nm P Mil* 1. ramasser les képis, to be promoted as a result of the death of one's superior(s)/to step into dead men's shoes 2. (*églises*) képi à moustaches, biretta.

kès [kɛs] *nm P* c'est du kès, it's six of one and half a dozen of the other; it makes no odds/it (all) comes to the same thing/it's much of a muchness; c'est jamais du kès, it's never the same. (*Voir* **quès**)

keuf [kœf] *nm P* (*verlan de* **flikeu**) policeman*/copper.

keufé [køfe] *a P* (*personne, immeuble*) under (police) surveillance.

keum [køm] *nm P* 1. (*verlan de* **mec**) man*/guy/bloke/geezer 2. (*verlan de* **manque**) (*drogues*) être keum, to suffer from withdrawal symptoms*; to have cold turkey.

keupon [køpɔ̃] *n P* (*verlan de* **punk**) punk.

keusse [køs] *nm P* (*verlan de* **sac**) one hundred francs; hundred-franc note.

khâgne [kaɲ] *nf P* second year arts class preparing for the entrance exam to the *École normale supérieure*. (*Voir* **cagne** II)

khâgneux, -euse [kaɲø, -øz] *n P* student in a *khâgne*.

kid [kid] *nm F* child*/kid/brat; des hordes de kids, hordes of kids.

kidnappinge [kidnapɛ̃ʒ] *nm P* kidnap(ping).

kif¹ [kif] *nm P* (*drogues*) marijuana* (mixed with tobacco)/kif/keef/kief.

kif² *nm*, **kif-kif** [kifkif] *a inv P* c'est kif-kif (bourricot *ou* le même sac)/c'est du kif, it's all the same/it's six of one and half a dozen of the other/it makes no odds/it's as broad as it's long.

kifer [kife] *vi P* to get a high/a kick; ça me fait kifer, I get a high from it.

kiki [kiki] *nm P* 1. (*a*) Adam's apple (*b*) windpipe; serrer le kiki à qn, to throttle s.o.; to wring s.o.'s neck 2. (child's) penis*/willie. (*Voir* **quiqui**) 3. c'est parti, mon kiki! here we go!/off we go!/here goes!

kil [kil] *nm*, **kilbus** [kilbys] *nm*, **kilo¹** [kilo] *nm P* un kil de rouge = a bottle of plonk/vino; payer un kil à qn = to stand s.o. a pint.

kilo² [kilo] *nm* 1. *P* a thousand francs 2. *P* (*lycée*) prendre un kilo, to be punished/to get detention 3. *V* déposer un kilo, to defecate*/to have a crap 4. *pl P* des kilos, many/a large amount/a packet; y en a pas des kilos, there aren't many of those.

kiné [kine] *F* I *nf* (= *kinésithérapie*) physiotherapy; une séance de kiné, a physio (session) II *nm & f* (= *kinésithérapeute*) physiotherapist/physio.

kino [kino] *nm Vieilli F* cinema; j'vais au kino, I'm going to the flics/to the pictures.

kir [kir] *nm F* (*boisson*) white wine and blackcurrant liqueur *or* syrup.

kit [kit] *nm P* (*drogues*) drug addict's instruments*/artillery (for shooting up).

kiwi [kiwi] *nm F* New Zealander/kiwi.

klébard [klebar] *nm*, **kleb(s)** [klɛb(s)] *nm P* dog*/hound/pooch/mutt. (*Voir* **clébard**, **cleb(s)**)

klepto [klɛpto] *a & n F* (*abrév* = *kleptomane*) kleptomaniac; light-fingered (person).

knockout [knɔkut, nɔkaut], **KO** [kao] *a P* (*a*) exhausted*/knocked out/done in/shattered (*b*) drunk*/pissed/paralytic (*c*) (*drogues*) stoned/high.

kopeck [kɔpɛk] *nm F* 1. (*a*) ne plus avoir un kopeck (en poche), to be penniless*/broke; je n'ai pas un kopeck, I haven't got a penny/I'm skint (*b*) *pl* kopecks, money*/bread/dough 2. ça ne vaut pas un kopeck, it's not worth a farthing.

kroum(e) [krum] *nm P* = **croum(e)**.

kroumir [krumir] *nm P* (vieux) kroumir, old fogey*/blimp/old fossil.

kyrielle [kirjɛl] *nf F* toute une kyrielle d'enfants, a whole hoard/tribe of children/kids; il leur a lancé à la figure toute une kyrielle d'injures, he shouted a whole stream *or* torrent of abuse at them/he was effing and blinding at them.

L

là [la] *adv* 1. *F* (*a*) (*personne*) être (**un peu**) **là**, to have authority/to make one's presence felt; **comme menteur il est/se pose un peu là**, he's a pretty good liar! **elle est un peu là**, she makes her presence felt; (*on ne peut éviter de la voir*) you can't miss her! (*b*) (*chose*) être **un peu là**, to be the real McCoy 2. *F* **tout est là**, that's the whole point; **la question n'est pas là**, that's not the point 3. *P* **ils sont pas là**, (*il n'y pas d'argent*) there's no money (left) in the kitty; I'm penniless*/skint 4. *P* **je l'ai là**, I don't give a damn about him/I've had him up to here. (*Voir* **jusque**; **se poser 1, 2**)

labo [labo] *nm F* laboratory/lab.

lac [lak] *nm* 1. *F* (*a*) être/tomber **dans le lac**, (*personne*) to be done for/to be in the soup/to be up the creek; (*projet, etc*) to be a failure/a flop; to fall through; **je suis dans le lac**, I'm sunk; **l'affaire est dans le lac**, it fell through/it came to nothing 2. *V* female genitals*. (*Voir* **descente 4**)

lâchage [laʃaʒ] *nm F* dropping/running out on (s.o., a friend); jilting/chucking/throwing over (of boyfriend, girlfriend, etc).

lâcher [laʃe] *vtr* 1. *F* (*a*) **lâcher son boulot**, to throw up/to chuck one's job; **lâcher la politique**, to give up/to drop politics (*b*) **lâcher qn**, (*amant*) to let s.o. down; to drop/to chuck s.o./to run out on s.o.; (*ami, etc*) to walk out on s.o./to leave s.o. in the lurch (*c*) **lâche-moi/lâche-nous un peu, tu veux?** leave me/us alone, will you? lay off, will you? 2. *F* **les lâcher**, to pay* up/to fork out; **être dur à les lâcher/les lâcher au compte-gouttes**, to be mean/stingy; **il ne les lâche pas**, he's really tight-fisted/he's a mean sod 3. *P* **en lâcher un(e)**, to let out a fart 4. *P* **lâcher un fil**, to urinate*/to have a slash. (*Voir* **baskets 3; bouée; dé 1; écluse; élastique; froc 3; fusée; gaz 3; morceau 2; paquet 3, 10, 11; pédale 3; perle 4; perlouse 2; rampe 1; valse 1; vent 4**)

lâcheur, -euse [laʃœr, -øz] *n F* unreliable person/s.o. who lets you down; **quitter; c'est un lâcheur**, he's unreliable.

lacrymo [lakrimo] *nf F* (= *grenade lacrymogène*) tear gas grenade.

lacsatif [laksatif] *nm*, **lacsé** [lakse] *nm*, **lacsif** [laksif] *nm P* (*largonji de sac*) 1. handbag 2. 100-franc note; one hundred francs. (*Voir* **sac 1**)

lacson [laksɔ̃] *nm P* package; **lacson de pipes**, cigarette packet.

ladé [lade] *adv P* (*a*) there (*b*) here.

laféké [lafeke] *nm*, **laféquès** [lafekɛs] *nm P* (*largonji de café*) (cup of) coffee.

laffes, lafs [laf] *nfpl A P* **les laffes**, the old defence works around Paris (*formerly an habitual resort of criminals*). (*Voir* **fortif(e)s**)

laga [laga], **lago** [lago], **laguche** [lagyʃ] *adv P* = **ladé**.

laine [lɛn] *nf F* 1. **tondre/manger la laine sur le dos de qn**, to fleece s.o. 2. **jambes de laine**, weak/wobbly legs* 3. woollen garment; **il fait froid, prends ta laine**, it's cold, take your woolly.

laissez-passer [lesepase] *nm F* 500-franc note.

lait [lɛ] *nm* 1. *F* (*a*) **boire du petit lait**, (*personne*) to take it all in eagerly/to lap it up; **avaler qch comme du petit lait**, to be tickled pink by sth (*b*) (*boisson*) **ça se boit comme du petit lait**, it slips down nicely 2. *P* **lait de chameau/de panthère/de tigre**, pastis. (*Voir* **pain 7; soupe 2; vache II 3**)

laiterie [lɛtri] *nf P* breasts*/boobs/knockers.

laitue [lɛty, le-] *nf* 1. *P* novice prostitute*; under age prostitute 2. *V* female genitals*/fruit-basket 3. *V* (*femme*) pubic hair/minge fringe/pubes; **mouiller sa laitue**, to urinate*.

laïus [lajys] *nm F* speech/lecture; **faire/piquer un laïus**, to speechify/to hold forth; **on a eu droit à son laïus**, we had to sit and listen to his lecture; **ce n'est que du laïus**, it's just talk/waffle/a lot of hot air.

laïusser [lajyse] *vi F* to make a (long) speech; to speechify/to hold forth.

lambda [lɑ̃bda] *a P* ordinary/commonplace; le pékin lambda, the man in the street/Mr Average.

lambin, -ine [lɑ̃bɛ̃, -in] *F* **I** *a* slow/ dawdling **II** *n* slowcoach/*NAm* slowpoke/ dawdler.

lambiner [lɑ̃bine] *vi F* to dawdle/to take one's time (about sth); to footle around/to mess about.

lamdé [lamde] *nf P (largonji de dame)* (a) lady (b) wife*/old lady.

lame [lam] *nf P* 1. knife/chiv 2. *(dans le milieu)* brave and loyal man* 3. pisser des lames de rasoir (en travers), to experience pain when urinating/to piss pins and needles; to have VD*/to have the clap.

lamedé [lamde] *nf P* = **lamdé**.

lamedu [lamdy] *nm P* goods.

lamefé [lamfe] *nf P* = **lamfé**.

lamer [lame] *vtr P* to stab/to knife/to stick (s.o.).

lamfé [lamfe] *nf P* (a) woman* (b) wife*/old lady.

laminoir [laminwar] *nm F* faire passer qn au laminoir, to give s.o. a hard time (of it)/to put s.o. through the mill.

lampe [lɑ̃p] *nf P* 1. stomach*; s'en mettre/ s'en coller/s'en foutre/s'en taper plein la lampe, to eat* heartily/to have a good blow-out/to (have a good) tuck-in/to pig oneself 2. lampe à souder, *(avions)* turbojet; *Mil* machine gun/tommy gun; *(grand nez)* big nose*/conk/nozzle.

lampée [lɑ̃pe] *nf F* swig (of wine, etc); vider un verre d'une lampée, to down a drink in one go.

lamper [lɑ̃pe] *vtr F* to gulp down/to swig (down)/to knock back (a drink).

lampion [lɑ̃pjɔ̃] *nm* 1. *F* crier sur l'air des lampions, to chant (slogan, etc) 2. *P* eye* 3. *P* s'en mettre un coup dans le lampion, to drink*/to take a swig; to knock one back 4. *P* = **lampe 1**.

lampiste [lɑ̃pist] *nm F (subalterne)* underling; *(dupe)* scapegoat/fall guy/mug; s'en prendre au lampiste, to bully/to take it out on one's subordinate(s).

lanarqué [lanarke] *nm P (largonji de canard)* difficult customer.

lance [lɑ̃s] *nf P* 1. rain 2. water; boire de la lance, to have a drink of water 3. urine; jeter de la lance, to urinate*/to have a slash 4.

tears 5. *(drogues)* syringe*/hypo.

lancé [lɑ̃se] *a F* slightly drunk* and talkative.

lancecaille [lɑ̃skaj] *nf P* (a) water (b) liquid (c) rain.

lancecailler [lɑ̃skaje] *vi P* to urinate*.

lance-parfum [lɑ̃sparfœ̃] *nm inv P* machine gun/tommy gun.

lance-pierres [lɑ̃spjɛr] *nm P* 1. rifle 2. il les lâche/les envoie au lance-pierres, he's tight with his money; you have to drag the money out of him 3. être nourri avec un lance-pierres, to be on a strict diet; manger avec un/au lance-pierres, to bolt down one's food *(esp a small amount)*.

lancequinade [lɑ̃skinad] *nf P* steady downpour (of rain).

lancequine [lɑ̃skin] *nf P* (a) rain (b) water (c) urine.

lancequiner [lɑ̃skine] *vi P* 1. to rain; lancequiner à pleins tubes, to rain cats and dogs/to chuck it down/to piss down 2. *Vieilli* to weep/to cry one's eyes out 3. to urinate*/to piss.

lancer [lɑ̃se] *vi F* ma dent me lance, my tooth's giving me stabbing pains/shooting pains; my tooth's giving me hell.

lanciner [lɑ̃sine] *vtr Vieilli F* to bore* (s.o.).

langouse [lɑ̃guz] *nf P* tongue; filer une langouse à qn, to give s.o. a French kiss.

langouste [lɑ̃gust], **langoustine** [lɑ̃gustin] *nf P* 1. prostitute* 2. mistress.

langue [lɑ̃g] *nf* 1. *F* langue verte, slang 2. avaler sa langue, *P* to die*; *P (bâiller)* to yawn one's head off; *F* tu as avalé/perdu ta langue? has the cat got your tongue? 3. *F* avoir la langue bien pendue, to have the gift of the gab 4. *F* donner/jeter sa langue au(x) chat(s), *(réponse à une devinette)* to give up; je donne ma langue au chat! go on, I'll buy it!/I give up! 5. *F* s'en mordre la langue, to regret bitterly having spoken; to kick oneself 6. *F (personne)* tirer la langue, to be very thirsty; *(être dans le besoin)* to have one's tongue hanging out (for sth); *(se donner du mal)* to huff and puff; *(être épuisé)* to show signs of exhaustion/to be near the end of one's tether 7. *F* faire tirer la langue à qn, to keep s.o. waiting/hanging about 8. *F* il n'a pas la/sa langue dans sa poche, he's a great talker/he's never at a loss for words/he's never stuck for sth to say 9. faire une langue (fourrée) à qn (a) *P* to give s.o. a French kiss (b) *V (cunnilinctus)* to suck s.o.('s cunt)/to go down on s.o. 10. *V* donner sa langue au chat, to eat fur pie. (*Voir* **bœuf** II 3; **cheveu** 3)

languetouse, languetouze [lãgətuz] *nf*, **languette** [lãgɛt] *nf* 1. *P* tongue. (*Voir* **langouse**) 2. *V* (*rarement*) clitoris*/clit.

lanlaire [lãlɛr] *adv Vieilli F* envoyer qn se faire lanlaire, to send s.o. packing*/to tell s.o. to get lost.

lanscaille [lãskaj] *nf P* = **lancecaille**.

lanscailler [lãskaje] *vi P* = **lancecailler**.

lansquine [lãskin] *nf*, **lansquiner** [lãskine] *vi P* = **lancequine, lancequiner**.

lanterne [lãtɛrn] *nf* 1. *P* window 2. *P* eye*. (*Voir* **pisser** I 3) 3. *P* stomach*; se taper sur la lanterne, to be hungry* 4. *F* lanterne rouge, back marker/last man in the race; *Rugby* wooden spoon; (*à l'école*) bottom of the class 5. *F* (*a*) éclairer sa lanterne, to explain one's point (of view) (*b*) éclairer la lanterne de qn, to put s.o. straight.

lanterner [lãtɛrne] *F vi* to waste (time)/to dilly-dally/to dawdle; **faire lanterner qn**, to keep s.o. waiting.

lanvère [lãvɛr] *nm P* back slang.

lap(e) [lap] *nm & adv P* nothing*; que lap(e), nothing* at all/damn all/sweet FA; bonnir lap(e), not to utter a word; to keep mum; je n'y pige que lap(e), I can't make head or tail of it; un bon à lap(e), a good-for-nothing/a layabout.

lapin [lapɛ̃] *nm* 1. *F* (*a*) c'est un rude/un fameux/un fier/un sacré lapin, he's a great bloke/guy; he's quite a guy/lad; he's smart; he's got plenty of nerve; he's a Jack the lad (*b*) un drôle de lapin, a queer customer/an odd character 2. *F* mon petit lapin, my darling*/my dear/my pet 3. *F* rabbit punch; *Med* whiplash injury; faire le coup du lapin à qn, to kill s.o. (by a blow to the neck from behind) 4. *P* poser un lapin à qn, to fail to turn up/to stand s.o. up; becqueter du lapin, to be let down/to be stood up 5. *P* un chaud lapin, a highly-sexed man/a Casanova/a don Juan/a bit of a lad/a randy sod 6. *P* sentir le lapin, to smell fuggy/sweaty. (*Voir* **peau 10**; **pet 1**)

lapine [lapin] *nf* 1. *F* woman with many children 2. *P Péj* lapine de couloir, maid(servant); chambermaid.

lapiner [lapine] *vi P Péj* (*femme*) to keep on having children/to have one child after another/to breed like a rabbit.

lapinisme [lapinism] *nm F* 1. excessive fertility (*in a woman*) 2. population explosion.

lapinoche [lapinɔʃ] *nm*, **lapinski** [lapinski] *nm*, **lapinskoff** [lapinskɔf] *nm P* rabbit/bunny(rabbit).

lapp(e) [lap] *nm & adv P* = **lap(e)**.

laps [laps] *nm P* rabbit/bunny(rabbit).

lapuche [lapyʃ] *nm & adv P* = **lap(e)**.

laquépem [lakepɛm] *nm P* (*largonji de* **paquet**) packet.

larbin [larbɛ̃] *nm F* (*souv Péj*) servant/flunkey; waiter (in a café); je ne suis pas ton larbin! I'm not your servant!

larbine [larbin] *nf F* (*rare*) (*souv Péj*) maid.

larbinos [larbinos] *nm P* flunkey.

lard [lar] *nm* 1. *F* (se) faire du lard, to become fat (through idleness); to (sit around and) get fat; être gras à lard, to be as fat as a pig 2. *P* un gros lard, (*personne*) a big fat slob; tête de lard, pig-headed idiot 3. *P* rentrer dans/sauter sur le lard à qn, to attack s.o./to go for s.o. 4. *P* prendre tout sur son lard, to assume complete responsibility/to take the rap/to carry the can 5. *F* ne pas savoir si c'est du lard ou du cochon, not to know whether to take s.o. seriously; not to understand what s.o. is saying; je ne sais pas si c'est du lard ou du cochon, I can't make head or tail of it 6. *P* skin; se frotter le lard, to stroke oneself; se gratter le lard, to have a scratch; se racler le lard, to have a shave. (*Voir* **saloir**)

larder [larde] *vtr P* larder qn, to get on s.o.'s nerves.

lardeuss(e) [lardøs] *nm*, **lardingue** [lardɛ̃g] *nm P* overcoat.

lardoire [lardwar] *nf F* 1. sword 2. knife/chiv.

lardon [lardɔ̃] *nm P* young child*/kid/brat; avoir un lardon dans le tiroir, to be pregnant*/to have a bun in the oven; coller un lardon dans le tiroir, to make pregnant*; faire un lardon, to have a baby.

lardoss(e) [lardos] *nm P* overcoat.

lardu [lardy] *nm P* 1. police station* 2. police superintendent 3. policeman*; les lardus, the police*/the cops/the fuzz.

larf [larf], **larfeuil(le)** [larfœj] *nm P* wallet.

larfou [larfu] *nm P* (*verlan de* **foulard**) scarf.

large [larʒ] I *nm F* 1. être au large, to be rich*/well off; en ce moment, on n'est pas au large, we're a bit broke/things are a little tight, at the moment 2. pas large du dos, miserly*/tight-fisted 3. prendre le large/tirer au large, to run away*/to clear off/to beat it **II** *a F* l'avoir large, (*avoir de la chance*) to be lucky; (*avoir de l'influence*) to have a lot of clout. (*Voir* **mener**)

largement [larʒəmɑ̃] *adv F* il en a eu largement (*assez*), he's had (more than) enough.

largeo(t) [larʒo] *a F* widish/broadish.

largeur [larʒœr] *nf F* dans les grandes largeurs, thoroughly/with a vengeance/in a big way.

largonji [larɔ̃ʒi] *nm P* butchers' slang (*in which words are altered by substituting l for the first letter and adding the original first letter and é, em, i, oque, uche, etc, to the end; thus* largonji = jargon).

largue [larg] *nf A P* prostitute*/tart.

largué, -ée [large] *a & n P* il est largué/ c'est un largué, things are getting too much for him; je suis larguée, I don't understand any of it/it's beyond me.

larguer [large] *vtr P* 1. to set (s.o.) free/to release (a prisoner, etc) 2. to give (s.o.) up; to drop (s.o.); tu devrais larguer cette môme, you should chuck/ditch/dump that girl 3. to dismiss*/sack (s.o.) 4. to give/to hand over (sth); to throw sth out; j'ai largué toutes mes vieilles frusques, I've chucked out all my old clothes. (*Voir* **amarres**)

Laribo [laribo] *Prnm* the hôpital Lariboisière (*in Paris*).

larme [larm] *nf F* 1. le faire aux larmes, to cry/to turn on the waterworks; y aller de sa (petite) larme, to shed a little tear 2. prendre une larme de rhum dans son café, to have a drop of rum in one's coffee.

larméleauté [larmelote] *nm P* (*largonji de* marteau) hammer.

larmichette [larmiʃɛt] *nf P* very small quanity; une larmichette de rhum, a tiny drop/a wee dram of rum.

larron [larɔ̃] *nm F* s'entendre/s'accorder comme larrons en foire, to be as thick as thieves.

larteaumic [lartomik] *nm P* (*largonji de* marteau) hammer.

lartif [lartif] *nm P* bread; lartif brutal, brown bread.

larton [lartɔ̃] *nm P* bread; larton brutal, brown bread; larton savonné, white bread.

lartonnier [lartɔnje] *nm P* baker.

larve [larv] *nf F* spineless person/wet/drip/ worm; ce type, c'est une larve, he's such a little worm; ce week-end j'ai été une vraie

larve, I was a real lazy sod this weekend.

larzac [larzak] *F* **I** *a* ecological/green **II** *n* ecologist/green.

lasagne [lazaɲ] *nf*, **lasane** [lazan] *nf P* 1. letter/note 2. wallet/*NAm* billfold.

lascar [laskar] *nm P* smart/streetwise character; c'est un sacré lascar, he's really streetwise; un rude lascar, a tough guy/a tough customer; c'est un drôle de lascar, he's a queer customer/he's a bit of a rogue.

lastique [lastik] *nm F* (*élastique*) elastic (band).

Latin [latɛ̃] *Prnm F* le Latin, (= le Quartier latin) the Latin Quarter (*in Paris*). (*Voir* **le Quartier**)

latino [latino] *a & n F* Latin-American (person).

latronpem [latrɔ̃pɛm] *nm P* (*largonji de* patron) boss*/chief.

latte [lat] *nf P* 1. boot; shoe; un coup de latte, a kick/a boot (up the arse/*surt NAm* ass); filer un coup de latte (à qn), to borrow/ cadge (money off s.o.) 2. foot 3. traîner ses lattes quelque part, to go somewhere; to stay/ hang around a place. (*Voir* **traîne-lattes 2**) 4. marcher à côté de ses lattes, to be penniless*/to be down on one's uppers; (*faire n'importe quoi*) to behave/act stupidly; to muck about 5. ski 6. deuxième latte, private (soldier).

latter [late] *vtr P* 1. to kick/to boot (s.o.) 2. to tap (s.o. for money).

lattoche [latɔʃ] *nf P* boot; shoe.

laubé, laubiche [lobe, lobiʃ] *a P* (*largonji de* beau) beautiful.

lauchem [loʃɛm] *a P* (*largonji de* chaud) hot.

lavabe [lavab] *nm F* (= lavabo) WC*/ lavatory/loo.

lavable [lavabl] *a P* (*marchandise volée*) easy to get rid of/easy to sell; (*argent illicite*) easy to launder.

lavage [lavaʒ] *nm F* 1. pawning 2. selling-off; faire un lavage de, to sell off (*esp* one's personal belongings or stolen goods) 3. lavage de cerveau, brainwashing. (*Voir* **tête 8**)

lavasse [lavas] *nf F* (*boisson*) tasteless stuff/dishwater/cat-lap; du café! c'est de la lavasse! (you call that) coffee! it's dishwater!/it's gnat's piss!

lavdu [lavdy] *a & nm P* = **lavedu**.

lavé [lave] *a P* (*brocante*) lot lavé, batch (of goods) whose best pieces have been removed.

lavedu [lavdy] *P* **I** *a* stupid*/dim/thick **II** *nm*
(*a*) victim of a swindle/fall guy/mug/sucker
(*b*) fool*/idiot/clot.

lavement [lavmɑ̃] *nm P* **1.** (*personne*)
bore*/drag **2.** **comme un lavement**, suddenly/
without apparent motive; **partir comme un
lavement**, to run away*/to be off like a shot;
elle est pressée comme un lavement, she's in
a terrible hurry/she's rushed off her feet.

laver [lave] *vtr* **1.** *F* to launder (money);
laver un chèque, to forge a cheque (by alter-
ing it) **2.** *F* to sell (cheap *or* at a loss)/to sell
off (*esp* one's own belongings or stolen
goods)/to turn (sth) into cash **3.** *F* (*brocante*)
laver un lot, to remove the best pieces from a
batch (of goods) **4.** *F* **se laver le bout du nez**,
to give oneself a cat's lick **5.** *V* **se laver les
dents**, (*fellation*) to give (a man) a blow-job/
head. (*Voir* **pied 13**; **tête 8**)

lavette [lavɛt] *nf P* **1.** tongue **2.** spineless
person/drip/washout/wimp; **son mari, c'est
une vraie lavette**, her husband's a real drip.

laveur [lavœr] *nm P* receiver (of stolen
goods)/fence.

lavougne [lavuɲ] *nf P* laundry/washing;
jour de lavougne, wash day.

lavure [lavyr] *nf F* **lavure (de vaisselle)** =
lavasse.

laxé [lakse] *nm P* 100-franc note; one
hundred francs. (*Voir* **lacsé 2**)

laxon [laksɔ̃] *nm P* linen.

lazagne [lazaɲ] *nf*, **lazane** [lazan] *nf P* =
lasagne.

lazaro [lazaro] *nm P* (*a*) prison* (*b*) military
prison (*c*) cell in a police station.

laziloffe [lazilɔf] *P* **I** *a* infected with VD*/
syphilitic/poxy/syphy **II** *nm* syphilis*/
gonorrhoea*/pox/clap.

lazingue [lazɛ̃g] *nm P* wallet/*NAm* billfold.

leaubé, leaubiche [lobe, lobiʃ] *a P* =
laubé, laubiche.

léchage [leʃaʒ] *nm F* **léchage de vitrines**,
window-shopping; **léchage de bottes**, bootlick-
ing.

léchard, -arde [leʃar, -ard] *n P* flatterer*/
bum-licker/arse-crawler/*NAm* ass-crawler.

lèche [lɛʃ] *nf P* flattery*/arse-licking/*NAm*
ass-licking; **faire de la lèche à qn**, to flatter*
s.o./to suck up to s.o.; to lick s.o.'s boots/s.o.'s
arse/*NAm* s.o.'s ass.

léché [leʃe] *a F* **c'est du travail léché**, that's
a good job done/a careful job.

lèche-bottes [lɛʃbɔt] *nm inv P* flatterer*/
bootlicker/toady.

lèche-cul, lèche-motte [lɛʃky, -mɔt] *nm
inv V* flatterer*/arse-licker/*NAm* ass-licker/
NAm brown-noser.

lèche-pompes [lɛʃpɔ̃p] *nm inv P* =
lèche-bottes.

lécher [leʃe] **I** *vtr* **1.** *F* il s'en léchait les
doigts/les pouces/les babines, he was smacking
his lips/licking his chops over it **2.** *F* **lécher les
vitrines**, to go window-shopping. (*Voir*
devanture 1) **3.** *F* **lécher un tableau**, to paint
a picture with care/with great attention to
detail **4.** *P* **lécher les bottes/les pieds de qn**, to
lick s.o.'s boots/to creep; *V* **lécher le cul de qn**,
to suck up to s.o.; to arse-lick/*NAm* to ass-lick
(s.o.) **5.** *V* to perform cunnilingus* on. (*Voir*
amygdales 1) **II** *vpr* **se lécher** *F* to kiss.

lèche-train [lɛʃtrɛ̃] *nm inv P* flatterer*/
arse-licker/*NAm* ass-licker/toady.

lécheur, -euse [leʃœr, -øz] *n P* flatterer*/
bootlicker/bumlicker/*surt NAm* apple-polisher.

lèche-vitrine(s) [lɛʃvitrin] *nm F* window-
shopping; **faire du lèche-vitrine(s)**, to go
window-shopping.

lecture [lɛktyr] *nf P* **être en lecture**,
(*prostituée*) to be with a client/to be on the
job.

léger [leʒe] *nm P* **faire du léger/faire dans le
léger**, (*agir avec tact*) to be tactful; (*ne pas
prendre de risque*) to do sth without taking
any risks/chances.

légitime [leʒitim] *nf P* **ma légitime**, my
wife*/the missis/the boss/her indoors.

légobiffin [legobifɛ̃] *nm Mil P* soldier of the
Foreign Legion; legionary. (*Voir* **biffin 2**)

légume [legym] *nf P* **1.** (**grosse**) **légume**,
important person*/VIP/bigwig/big shot; *Mil*
high-ranking officer; **les grosses légumes**, the
top people; *Mil* the top brass/the brass hats **2.**
perdre ses légumes, (*femme*) to have a
period*; (*être incontinent*) to be incontinent/to
wet oneself/to shit oneself (*from fright or
senility*).

légumier [legymje] *nm P* VIP's car.

lentilles [lɑ̃tij] *nfpl P* **mangeuse de lentilles**,
lesbian*. (*Voir* **couloir**; **éplucheur, -euse
2**)

Léon [leɔ̃] *Prnm F* **vas-y, Léon!** have a go,
Joe!

léotard [leotar] *nm F* leotard.

lerche [lɛrʃ], **lerchem** [lɛrʃɛm], **lerchot**
[lɛrʃo] *P* **I** *adv* **il n'y avait pas lerche de
crème sur le gâteau**, there wasn't much
cream on the cake; **c'est pas lerche**, that's not
much; **ça vaut pas lerche**, it's not worth much

II *a & adv* dear/expensive/pric(e)y; **ça coûte lerchem**, it's expensive/pricey; **une brique pour ça, c'est lerche**, a million for that, it's a bit much/that's a bit steep.

lesbombe [lɛsbɔ̃b] *nf* A P woman*; mistress.

lessivage [lɛsivaʒ] *nm* F 1. selling-off. (*Voir* **lavage** 2) 2. **lessivage de crâne**, brainwashing.

lessive [lɛsiv] *nf* F 1. selling-off. (*Voir* **lavage** 2) 2. heavy loss (at cards, etc)/clean-out 3. beating(-up)*/dusting/thrashing 4. **une lessive pour les prisonniers politiques**, an amnesty for political prisoners.

lessivé [lɛsive] *a* 1. F ruined (financially)/cleaned out/taken to the cleaner's 2. P exhausted*/completely washed out/shattered/dead beat 3. P **il est lessivé**, he's had it/he's done for/he's out of the running.

lessiver [lɛsive] *vtr* F 1. to sell/to flog 2. to launder (money) 3. to kill* (s.o.)/to wipe (s.o.) out 4. to ruin (financially)/to clean (s.o.) out/to take (s.o.) to the cleaner's; **je me suis fait lessiver au poker**, I got cleaned out at poker 5. to dismiss*/to sack. (*Voir* **tête 8**)

lessiveur [lɛsivœr] *nm* P receiver (of stolen goods)/fence. (*Voir* **laveur**)

lessiveuse [lɛsivøz] *nf* P 1. steam locomotive 2. machine gun.

lest [lɛst] *nm* F **lâcher du lest**, to make small concessions/allowances; *NAm* to cut some slack.

se lester [səlɛste] *vpr* F **se lester (l'estomac/la cale)**, to eat* heartily/to have a good feed/to stuff oneself.

lettre [lɛtr] *nf* F 1. **faire des lettres/être en lettres**, to study arts subjects 2. **passer comme une lettre à la poste**, to go smoothly/without any problems/without a hitch/like clockwork 3. **c'est pour moi lettres closes**, it's a mystery to me. (*Voir* **cinq 4**)

leudé [lœde] *nm* P (*largonji de* **deux**) two-franc coin.

leur [lœr] *nm* F **ils continuent à faire des leurs**, they're still getting up to their old tricks; **ils ont encore fait des leurs**, they've been up to their old tricks again. (*Voir* **sienne 1**)

leur(s) zig(ue)s [lœrzig] *pron* P they/them/themselves.

levage [ləvaʒ] *nm* P (*homme ou femme*) picking up (of man or woman in the street, etc); (*prostituée*) soliciting; **faire un levage**, (*prostituée*) to make a pick-up/to get a trick.

lever [ləve] **I** *vtr* P 1. to arrest* (s.o.)/to pick (s.o.) up/to run (s.o.) in 2. to steal*/to lift 3. **lever un mec**, (*femme*) to pick up a bloke/guy (in the street, in a bar, etc); (*prostituée*) to make a pick-up/to get a trick; **lever une femme**, (*homme*) to pick up/to get off with/to make out with a woman. (*Voir* **ancre; coude 3; jambe 17; pied 5; torchon 9**) **II** *vi* P 1. to leave*/to kick off/to leg it/to split 2. to have an erection*; **quand je vois ses miches, je lève**, I get a hard-on when I see her tits **III** *vpr* **se lever** F **se lever de là**, to move onto/push off (somewhere else).

leveur [ləvœr] *nm Vieilli* P thief*/tea leaf; pickpocket.

leveuse [ləvøz] *nf* P prostitute*.

lévier [levje] *nm* F (*évier*) sink.

levrette [ləvrɛt] *nf* V **baiser qn en levrette**, to have sex*/to make it doggie-fashion/doggie-style (with s.o.).

levure [ləvyr] *nf* P **pratiquer/se faire la levure**, to run away*/to make a quick exit/to do a bunk.

lézard [lezar] *nm* F 1. idler/lounger/layabout 2. **faire le lézard/prendre un bain de lézard** = **lézarder 2** 3. problem/difficulty/hitch; **il y a un lézard**, there's a hitch; **y a pas de lézard**, no problem!

lézarder [lezarde] *vi* F 1. to idle/to laze about/to lounge about 2. to sunbathe/to bask in the sun/to soak up the sun.

liard [ljar] *nm Vieilli* F 1. **il n'a pas un liard**, he's penniless*; he hasn't a penny to his name 2. **couper un liard en deux/en quatre**, to be very stingy/tightfisted.

Liban [libã] *nm* P (*drogues*) Lebanese hashish*.

lichailler [liʃaje] *vi* P to drink*/to tipple/to booze.

lichedu [liʃdy] *nm* P (*personne*) bore*/drag/pain.

licher [liʃe] P **I** *vtr* 1. to lick/to slobber; **se licher la gueule/la pomme/le museau**, to kiss/to snog 2. to knock back (a drink, etc) **II** *vi* to drink* heavily/to booze/to tipple.

lichette [liʃɛt] *nf* P thin, small slice (of bread, meat, etc)/nibble/taste.

licheur, -euse [liʃœr, -øz] *n* P 1. heavy drinker/tippler/boozer 2. s.o. who likes kissing/who is fond of kissing.

lieute [ljøt] *nm* F (*Mil, marine, etc*) lieutenant/lieut.

lieux [ljø] *nmpl* F WC*; **où sont les lieux?** where's the loo/*NAm* the bathroom?

lièvre [ljɛvr] *nm* 1. *F* il a une mémoire de liè-vre, he's got a memory like a sieve 2. *F* c'est vous qui avez levé le lièvre, you started it 3. *F* c'est là que gît le lièvre, that's the crucial point/the crux of the matter 4. *F* prendre le lièvre au gîte, to catch s.o. napping 5. *F* courir deux/plusieurs lièvres à la fois, to try to do two things/too many things at once 6. *F* nous courons le même lièvre, we're both after the same thing 7. *P* (*homme*) smart/ streetwise character 8. *P* (*langage de pro-xénète*) nervous/uncontrollable prostitute* 9. *F* (*courses, etc*) front runner/pacemaker; il a fait le lièvre sur le 1ᵉʳ tour, he set the pace on the first lap.

ligne [liɲ] *nf* 1. *F* tirer à la ligne, (*journaliste, écrivain*) to pad out an article 2. *F* c'est dans ma ligne! that's right up my street! c'est bien dans sa ligne! that's him all over! 3. *P* (*drogues*) line (of cocaine*); sniffer une ligne, to do a line; sniffer des li-gnes, to snort coke. (*Voir* **sniffer 1**)

ligodu [ligɔdy], **ligoduji** [ligɔdyʒi] *int P* (*largonji de* **gigo**) (*peu usuel*) yes/OK.

ligote [ligɔt] *nf P* (length of) cord/rope (*esp for tying s.o. up*).

ligoter [ligɔte] *vtr P* to read.

lili-pioncette [lilipjɔ̃sɛt] *nf P* (*drogues*) morphine*/Miss Emma.

limace [limas] *nf P* 1. shirt/dicky dirt 2. *pl* limaces, lips.

limande [limɑ̃d] *nf* 1. *P* slap in the face 2. *P* prostitute* 3. *F* être plate comme une limande, (*femme*) to be as flat as a pancake/ as a board 4. *F* faire la limande, to bow and scrape/to crawl/to kowtow 5. *P* (*motos*) rouler en limande, to ride crouched forwards on one's bike.

limasse [limas] *nf*, **lime¹** [lim] *nf P* = **limace 1**.

lime² [lim], **limé** [lime] *a & pp F* un (verre de) blanc lime/limé, (a glass of) white wine diluted with lemonade.

limer [lime] I *vtr & i V* limer (qn), (*homme*) to have sex* (with s.o.), (*usu slowly*)/to grind/ to have a bit of in and out/to get one's end away II *vpr* se **limer** *V* to masturbate*/to jack off/to jerk off.

limier [limje] *nm F* sleuth/bloodhound.

limite [limit] *nf F* 1. (*a*) à la limite, if needs be/if really necessary (*b*) à la limite, je dirais que ce mot est grossier, I'd go so far as to say that this word is crude 2. c'est limite, it's touch and go; ce mec, il est limite, he'll just

about do.

limogeage [limɔʒaʒ] *nm F* (*a*) *Mil* superseding/bowler-hatting (of a senior offi-cer) (*b*) dismissal (of a government official, etc).

limoger [limɔʒe] *vtr F* (*a*) *Mil* to supersede (a senior officer) (*b*) to dismiss (a govern-ment official, etc).

limonade [limɔnad] *nf* 1. *F* être dans la limonade, (*dans la misère*) to be penniless*/to be down and out; (*tenir un bar*) to keep a (small) bar/to be in the (drinks) trade 2. *P* tomber dans la limonade, to fall into the water/into the drink.

limonadier [limɔnadje] *nm F* publican/ barkeeper/keeper of a small pub.

limouse, limouze [limuz] *nf P* 1. shirt/ dicky dirt 2. file (for smoothing metal).

linge [lɛ̃ʒ] *nm F* 1. (il) faut laver son linge sale en famille, don't wash your dirty linen in public 2. avoir du linge, to be well dressed/to have a good wardrobe 3. du beau linge, (*personne élégante*) a good-looker/a bit of all right; (*gens distingués*) fashionable society/ (the) jet set.

lingé [lɛ̃ʒe] *a F* être bien lingé, to be well dressed.

linger [lɛ̃ʒe] I *vtr F* to dress/to rig out II *vpr* se **linger** *F* to get dressed up*/togged up.

lingre [lɛ̃gr] *nm P* = **lingue 1**.

lingue [lɛ̃g] *nm P* 1. knife/chiv 2. (= *lingot*) gold bar/ingot.

linguer [lɛ̃ge] *vtr P* to stab (s.o.) with a knife.

lino [lino] I *nm F* linoleum/lino II *F* (*a*) *nf* Linotype (machine) (*b*) *nm & f* Linotype operator/linotypist.

linotte [linɔt] *nf F* tête de linotte, empty-headed person; scatterbrain.

lion [ljɔ̃] *nm F* c'est un lion! he's as brave as a lion! avoir mangé/bouffé du lion, to be very energetic; (*agressif*) to be very aggressive; se défendre comme un lion, to do well/to succeed by being very energetic.

liquette [likɛt] *nf P* shirt/dicky dirt. (*Voir* **mouiller II 2**)

liquider [likide] *vtr* 1. *F* to get rid of (s.o., sth); to spend (money) quickly 2. *P* to kill* (s.o.)/to liquidate (s.o.)/to wipe (s.o.) out; se faire liquider, to get done in/bumped off.

lisbroquer [lisbrɔke] *vi P* to urinate*/to (have a) piss.

Lisette [lizɛt] *Prnf F* pas de ça, Lisette! (let's have) none of that!/come off it!

lispoquer [lispɔke] *vi P* = **lisbroquer**.

lissépem [lisepɛm] *vi P* (*largonji de* **pisser**) to urinate*/to piss/to pee.

lisses [lis] *nfpl P* stockings; **lisses en soie noire**, black silk stockings.

litanies [litani] *nfpl F* (*aéronautique*) checklist; **débiter les litanies**, to run through the checklist.

litron [litrɔ̃] *nm P* litre (of wine); **il ne tient pas son litron**, he can't take his drink/he can't hold his liquor.

livre [livr] *nf F* 100-franc note.

lixdré [liksdre] *a & nm P* (*largonji de* **dix**) ten.

lobé [lɔbe] *am P* good-looking. (*Voir* **laubé**)

locdu [lɔkdy] *a & n P* = **loquedu**.

loche [lɔʃ] I *nm or f P* (*a*) taxi-driver/cabby (*b*) taxi/cab II *nf P* ear*.

loco [lɔko] *nf F* (*abrév* = *locomotive*) engine/loco; **faire la loco**, to smoke like a chimney.

loffe [lɔf] *a F* = **loufoque I**.

loge [lɔʒ] *nf F* **être aux premières loges**, to have a ringside seat/to have a grandstand view.

loger [lɔʒe] *vtr P* (*police*) to track (s.o.) down; **loger une voiture**, to track down the owner of a car. (*Voir* **enseigne**)

loi [lwa] *nf F* 1. **avoir la loi**, (*dans le milieu*) to have the upper hand 2. **faire la loi**, to lay down the law; **les enfants ne font pas la loi ici!** kids don't run this place!

loific [lwafik] *nm P* (*largonji de* **foie**) liver.

à loilpé¹ [alwalpe], **à loilpuche** [alwalpyʃ] *a phr P* (*largonji de* **à poil**) naked*/starkers.

au loilpé² [olwalpe] *a & adv phr P* (*largonji de* **au poil**) very good; very well; excellent.

loinqué [lwɛ̃ke] I *adv P* far off/a long way away; **c'est loinqué?** is it far? **au loinqué**, in the distance II *nm P* (*largonji de* **coin**) corner.

lolo [lolo] *nm* 1. *F* (*mot enfantin*) milk 2. *F* **c'est du lolo!** it's nice! 3. *P pl* **lolos**, breasts*/tits/Bristols/jugs. (*Voir* **boîte 8**)

loloches [lɔlɔʃ] *nmpl P* breasts*/tits/Bristols. (*Voir* **soutien-loloches**)

long, *f* longue [lɔ̃, lɔ̃g] *F* I *a* **les avoir longues**, (*avoir très faim*) to be ravenously hungry*; (*être très ambitieux*) to be extremely ambitious II *adv phr* **de longue**, uninterruptedly/on end/ceaselessly II *nm* 1. cigar 2. **avoir les côtes en long**, to be lazy/bone idle 3. **y aller de tout son long**, to go at it

hammer and tongs. (*Voir* **bras 2**; **jour 1**; **nez 14**)

longe [lɔ̃ʒ] I *nf P* year (of prison sentence); **il me reste cinq longes à tirer**, I've got five years left to do II *nf F* **marcher sur sa longe**, to get into a fix*/to get (all) tied up.

longuet, -ette [lɔ̃gɛ, -ɛt] *a F* rather long/longish (book, time, etc); (a bit) on the long side.

longueur [lɔ̃gœr] *nf F* **être sur la même longueur d'ondes**, to be on the same wavelength; **être sur une autre longueur d'ondes**, to be way off beam/to be way out.

look [luk] *nm F* look/image; **soigner son look**, to pay attention to/to cultivate one's image; **je vais changer de look**, I'm going to change my image; **elle a un look d'enfer**, she looks absolutely stunning.

looké [luke] *a F* **être looké punk**, to have a punk image.

lopaille [lɔpaj] *nf*, **lopard** [lɔpar] *nm*, **lope** [lɔp] *nf*, **lopette** [lɔpɛt] *nf P* 1. homosexual*/pansy/queer/*NAm* fag(got) 2. coward*/chicken/patsy; **cette lopette s'est carapatée dès le début de la bagarre**, the little sissy pissed off as soon as the fighting started.

loque [lɔk] *nf* 1. *F* (*personne*) **être comme une loque/n'être qu'une loque**, to be as limp as/to feel like a wet rag; to be a wreck; **l'alcool a fait de lui une loque**, alcohol has turned him into a wreck 2. *pl P* **loques**, clothes*/clobber/gear.

loqué [lɔke] *a P* dressed/togged up.

loquedu, -ue [lɔkdy] *P* I *a* 1. (*a*) worthless*/rotten (*b*) ugly/revolting 2. lazy*/bone idle 3. mad*/bonkers/crackers II *nm* 1. good-for-nothing/layabout/bum 2. mean(-looking)/dangerous *or* unpleasant man; bastard*/nasty pice of work/*NAm* son of a bitch III *nm & f* mad person*/crackpot/nutcase.

loquer [lɔke] I *vtr P* to dress II *vpr* **se loquer** *P* to get dressed/to put one's clothes on.

lorgne [lɔrɲ] *nf P* (*cartes*) ace.

loser [luzœr] *nm F* loser.

lot [lo] *nm* 1. *F* **gagner/décrocher le gros lot**, to strike it lucky; to hit the jackpot 2. *P* **un beau petit lot/un joli lot**, (*fille, femme*) a dish/a bit of all right/a nice bit of stuff.

loub [lub] *nm P* = **loubar(d)**.

loubac [lubak] *a A P* mad*/bonkers.

loubar(d) [lubar] *nm P* (young) hooligan*/yob/yobbo/thug/lout/*NAm* hoodlum; **des loubards de banlieue**, (young) thugs/hooligans who terrorize people in the suburbs/= hell's angels/ bikers.

loubarde [lubard] *nf F* = **loupiot(t)e²**.

loubé [lube] *nm P* (*largonji de* **bout**) 1. a small amount/a wee bit/a smidgen 2. **mettre les loubés**, to run away*/to clear off.

loubiat [lubja] *nm P* bean.

(en) loucedé [ālusde], **(en) loucedoc** [ālusdɔk] *adv phr P* (*largonji de* **en douce**) on the quiet/on the q.t./on the sly; **lorgner qn en loucedoc**, to eye s.o. up/to give s.o. the glad eye.

louche [luʃ] *nf P* hand*/flipper/mitt/paw; **serrer la louche à qn**, to shake hands with s.o.; **filer la louche à qn**, to give s.o. a helping hand/to lend a hand; **mettre la louche au panier**, to feel up/to touch up a woman.

louchébem, louchébème [luʃebɛm] *nm P* = **loucherbem 1, 2**.

loucher [luʃe] *vi F* **loucher vers/sur qch**, to look longingly at sth/to have one's eyes on sth/to eye sth (up) (with a view to stealing it).

loucherbem, loucherbème [luʃerbɛm] *nm P* 1. butcher 2. form of **largonji**, but more complex.

louchon, -onne [luʃɔ̃, -ɔn] *n A P* cross-eyed person; squint-eyes.

louf¹ [luf], **loufetingue** [luftɛ̃g] *a & n F* = **loufoque**.

louf² **louffe** [luf] *nm P* fart; **lâcher un louffe**, to (let out a) fart*.

louf(f)er [lufe] *vi P* to (let out a) fart*.

loufiat [lufja] *nm* 1. *P* waiter (in a café) 2. *P* rotter; boor; slob.

loufoque [lufɔk] *F* (*largonji de* **fou**) I *a* (*personne*) mad*/cracked/bonkers/a bit touched (in the head)/nuts; (*histoire, etc*) crazy/daft II *nm & f* crackpot/crank/ screwball/nut/nutter.

loufoquerie [lufɔkri] *nf F* (*a*) eccentricity; barminess/craziness (*b*) crazy act.

louftingue [luftɛ̃g] *a & n F* = **loufoque**.

louise [lwiz] *nf P* **lâcher une louise**, to (let out a) fart*.

louisette [lwizɛt] *nf F* the guillotine.

Louis-Quinze [lwikɛ̃z] I *Prn F* **avoir des jambes (à la) Louis-Quinze**, to have bandy legs/to be bandy(-legged) II *nf A P* **une Louis-Quinze**, an elegant mistress.

loulou, louloute¹ [lulu, -ut] I *nm & f F* **mon loulou/ma louloute**, my dear/darling*/love II *nm P* (young) hooligan*/yob(bo)/*NAm* hoodlum; **je me suis fait voler par une bande de loulous**, I was robbed/mugged by a gang of thugs.

louloute² [lulut] *nf P* flighty young woman*.

loup [lu] *nm* 1. *F* **mon petit loup!/mon gros loup!** my darling!*/my pet!/my love! 2. *F* (*a*) mistake*/miscalculation (*b*) **ça marche pas, y a un loup quelque part**, there must be something wrong (with it) because it isn't working 3. *F* (*dans un texte*) gap/omission 4. *F* (*théâtre*) fluff/fluffed entrance 5. *F* **un vieux loup de mer**, an old sea dog/an old salt 6. *F* **elle a vu/connu le loup**, she's lost her virginity*/her cherry; she's fallen off the apple tree 7. *F* **loup rouge**, noticeable person; **j'ai été repéré comme un loup rouge**, I stuck out a mile and they spotted me.

loupage [lupaʒ] *nm F* (*a*) bungling (*b*) botched work; failure/flop; **le repas fut un loupage complet**, the meal was a total flop.

loupe [lup] *nf F* idleness/laziness/slackness.

loupé [lupe] *F a* (*a*) (*travail*) botched/ bungled (*b*) (*fichu*) **pas besoin de s'en faire, c'est loupé**, there's no point in getting all het up about it, it's up the spout; **la soirée est loupée**, the party's a flop.

louper [lupe] *F* I *vi* to misfire; to go haywire; **ça n'a pas loupé**, that didn't miss/ that hit the mark; that's what happened, sure enough II *vtr* (*a*) to bungle*/to botch (a piece of work); to make a mess of sth; **il a loupé son coup**, he botched it/he messed it up (*b*) to miss (one's turn/train/opportunity); to fail/ *NAm* to flunk (exam); (*théâtre*) to fluff (one's lines, entrance); (*aviation*) **louper son atterrissage**, to crash-land; **cette affaire m'a fait louper les vacances**, that business put paid to/messed up/wrecked my holidays (*c*) **il n'en loupe pas une!** he's always opening his big mouth! **je ne vais pas le louper, je vais lui dire ce que je pense de lui**, I won't let him get away without telling him what I think of him. (*Voir* **coche 1**; **commande 4**)

loupiot, -ot(t)e¹ [lupjo, -ɔt] *n F* small child*/brat/kid.

loupiot(t)e² [lupjɔt] *nf F* (*a*) small light; torch; flashlight (*b*) electric light (bulb).

louquer [luke] *vtr F* to look at/observe; **louque un peu ça, mon vieux!** take a look at that, mate!

lourd [lur] I *a F* 1. **avoir le bras lourd/être lourd**, to be rich*/loaded 2. **être lourd**, to be stupid*/thick/dim; **ce qu'elle est lourde!** she's so dumb, she can't take a hint! II *adv F* **il n'en reste pas lourd**, there's not much left/ there aren't many left; **je ne donnerais pas**

lourd de ..., I wouldn't give much for ...; **gagner lourd**, to earn good money; **je ne suis pas payé lourd**, I'm not paid much; **je n'en fais pas lourd**, I don't exactly overwork III *nm* 1. *F* rich man 2. *P* peasant*/yokel/hick.

lourdage [lurdaʒ] *nm P* redundancy; dismissal.

lourde [lurd] *nf P* 1. door; **balancer la lourde**, to break down the door; **boucler la lourde**, to shut the door; **casser la lourde/ mettre la lourde en dedans**, to burgle/*NAm* to burglarize/to break in; **mettre qn à la lourde**, to show s.o. the door/to kick s.o. out 2. strong drug/powerful narcotic.

lourder [lurde] *vtr P* 1. to shut (a door); to shut (s.o.) in; **lourder une boutique**, to shut up shop 2. to get rid of (sth); **je lourde tous mes disques**, I'm getting rid of all my records 3. **lourder qn**, (*évincer*) to show s.o. the door/to throw s.o. out/to kick s.o. out; (*congédier*) to dismiss* s.o./to give s.o. the push.

lourdier, -ière [lurdje, -jɛr] *n P* doorkeeper/concierge/caretaker.

lourdingue [lurdɛ̃g] *a P* 1. stupid*/thick/ dim 2. (*a*) heavy; **c'est drôlement lourdingue à trimbal(l)er**, it's bloody heavy to lug around (*b*) **en avoir lourdingue sur la conscience**, to have a load on one's mind.

(en) lousdé [ɑ̃lusde], **(en) lousdoc** [ɑ̃lusdɔk] *adv phr P* = **(en) loucedé, (en) loucedoc.**

loustic [lustik] *nm F* 1. joker/comedian; **faire le loustic**, to fool around/to act the goat 2. bloke/*surt NAm* guy; **c'est un drôle de loustic**, he's a strange bloke/*surt NAm* guy; he's an oddball.

loute [lut] *nf F* 1. women* (*in general*)/ chicks 2. **ma loute**, my darling*/my love.

lové [lɔve] *nm P* 1. money*/loot/bread 2. (*verlan de vélo*) bicycle/bike.

à la loyale [alalwajal] *adv phr F* without cheating; **se battre à la loyale**, to fight cleanly.

luc [lyk] *nm P* (*inversion de* **cul**) anus*; buttocks*.

le Lucal [ləlykal], **le Luco** [ləlyko] *Prnm*

F the Luxembourg gardens (*in Paris*).

lucarne [lykarn] *nf V* **lucarne enchantée**, anus*/round eye.

luisant [lɥizɑ̃] *nm*, **luisard** [lɥizar] *nm P* sun.

lundi [lœ̃di] *nm F* **faire/fêter ie lundi**, to take Monday off; **faire lundi**, to take the day off. (*Voir* **Saint-Lundi**)

lune [lyn] *nf* 1. *P* buttocks*/bum/*NAm* butt; **faire voir la lune (en plein jour)**, to show one's buttocks/to moon 2. *F* whim; mood; **il est dans une bonne/mauvaise lune**, he's in one of his good/bad moods 3. *F* **avoir (un quartier de) la lune dans la tête**, to be mad*/loony/ moonstruck 4. *F* **être dans la lune**, to be starry-eyed/to be wool-gathering/to be miles away/to be day-dreaming/to have one's head in the clouds 5. *F* **tomber de la lune**, to be unaware of what's going on/to look blank 6. *F* **faire voir la lune à qn en plein midi/en plein soleil**, to fool s.o./to lead s.o. up the garden path 7. *F* **je vous parie la lune que ...**, I bet you anything you like that ... 8. *V* **se faire taper dans la lune**, to be sodomized*/to get one's ass fucked 9. *pl P* **avoir ses lunes**, to have one's period/the curse. (*Voir* **chevalier 4; con II** (*a*))

luné [lyne] *a F* **être bien/mal luné**, to be in a good/bad mood.

lunette [lynɛt] *nf P* round opening; lunette (of guillotine); **mettre la tête à la lunette**, to be guillotined.

luron, -onne [lyrɔ̃, -ɔn] *n F* **c'est un gai/un joyeux luron**, he's one of the lads; he's a bit of a lad; he's quite a. lad; **c'est une sacrée luronne**, she's quite a girl.

lustucru [lystykry] *nm F* 1. fool*/nurd 2. (**le père**) **Lustucru**, the bogeyman 3. **lustucru?** (= *l'eusses-tu cru?*) can you believe it?

luttanche [lytɑ̃ʃ] *nf P* (*a*) wrestling (*b*) contest/fight/struggle.

luxurieux [lyksyrjø] *a F* (*par erreur pour luxueux*) luxurious.

luzerne [lyzɛrn] *nf P* (*drogues*) hashish*/ hemp.

M

M [εm] *nf P* 1. (= **merde**) turd/crap 2. (*drogues*) morphine*/shit.

maboul, -oule [mabul] *P* I *a* mad*/crazy/ nuts/round the bend/bonkers II *n* loony/ nut(ter)/crackpot.

maboulisme [mabulism] *nm*, **maboulite** [mabulit] *nf P* madness.

mac [mak] *nm P* pimp*/ponce/mack.

maca [maka] *nf P* = **maquerelle**.

macab [makab] *nm P* corpse*/stiff. (*Voir* **macchab**)

macache [makaʃ] *int Vieilli P* (c'est) macache (et midi sonné)!/macache bono!/macache bonbon! not (bloody) likely*!/no fear!/nothing doing!/not on your nelly!

macadam [makadam] *nm P* 1. fleur de macadam, prostitute*/streetwalker; faire le macadam, to solicit*/to walk the streets/to be on the game 2. fake industrial accident; piquer un macadam, to feign/to fake an industrial accident (*in order to claim insurance, etc*) 3. English ale/bitter.

macadamiste [makadamist] *nm & f P* s.o. who fakes an industrial accident (*in order to claim insurance, etc*).

macaron [makarɔ̃] *nm* 1. *F* (*a*) rosette (of a decoration) (*b*) (*insigne*) badge (on official car) 2. *F* (*voiture*) steering wheel; manier le macaron, to take the wheel; c'est un as du macaron, he's a champion driver 3. *P* blow*/ punch/clout; filer un macaron à qn, to clout s.o.

macaroni [makarɔni] I *nm & f P* Italian*/ Eyetie/wop II *nm* 1. *V* penis*; s'allonger/se griffer le macaroni, to masturbate* 2. *P* telephone wire/spaghetti 3. *P* shadowing/tailing (*by police*) 4. *pl P* macaronis, long, thin legs*.

macchab [makab] *nm*, **macchabée** [makabe] *nm P* corpse*/stiff. (*Voir* **chahuteur** II (*b*); **trottinette 2**)

mâcher [mɑʃe] *vi F* 1. mâcher de haut, to eat without appetite 2. mâcher à vide, to live on daydreams. (*Voir* **frein**)

machin [maʃɛ̃] *n* 1. *F* (*a*) (*personne*) (monsieur, madame) Machin, (Mr, Mrs) what's-his-name/what's-her-name/what-d'you-call-him/what-d'you-call-her/thingy; machin, Thingum(m)ybob/thingy (*b*) (*chose*) what's-its-name* / thing(amy) / whatcha(ma)callit whatsit/wossname/thingy; contraption/gadget (*c*) *Péj* vieux machin, old fogey*; espèce de vieux machin! you old fool! 2. *P* penis*/tool/ thingy/instrument.

machin-chose [maʃɛ̃ʃoz] *nm*, **machin-chouette** [maʃɛ̃ʃwɛt] *nm F* = **machin** (*b*).

machine [maʃin] *nf* 1. *F* thing/gadget/ contraption 2. *F* (*fille, femme*) what's-her-name/what-d'you-call-her/thingy 3. *F* machine à confetti, ticket punch 4. *F* vehicle/plane/ bike/machine 5. *P* machine à coudre/à percer, (*mitrailleuse ou mitraillette*) (sub)machine gun/tommy gun; machine à ramer/à battre/à secouer le paletot, (*mitrailleuse*) machine gun 6. *pl V* machines, testicles*. (*Voir* **bosseler**; **raccourcir**)

machiner [maʃine] *vi Vieilli F* to do/to be up to; qu'est-ce que tu machines? what are you up to?/what are you plotting?

machinette [maʃinɛt] *nf P* pickpocket*; vol à la machinette, pickpocketing by salesperson who has accomplices outside the shop.

machino [maʃino] *nm F Th TV etc* (= *machiniste*) stagehand/scene shifter.

machin-truc [maʃɛ̃tryk] *nm F* = **machin** (*b*). (*Voir* **truc 2**)

macho [maʃo] *F* I *a inv* (*comportement, etc*) male chauvinist II *nm* male chauvinist/ *Péj* male chauvinist pig.

mâchouiller [mɑʃuje] *F* I *vtr & i* to eat without appetite II *vtr* to chew away at (sth).

macquecé(e) [makse] *nf P* (woman) brothel owner; madam(e).

macreuse [makrøz] *nf F* avoir du sang de macreuse, to be cool, calm and collected.

macrotin [makrɔtɛ̃] *nm P* = **maque-**

526

reautin.

madame [madam] *nf F* 1. (woman) brothel owner/madam(e) 2. jouer à la madame, to put on airs (and graces).

madame-pipi [madampipi] *nf P* (lady) WC*/lavatory attendant. (*Voir* **pipi 1**)

Madeleine [madlɛn] *Prnf F* pleurer comme une Madeleine, to cry one's eyes out/to cry buckets.

mademoiselle [madmwazɛl] *nf F* 1. homosexual*/queen 2. (woman) brothel owner's deputy.

maganer [maganɛ] *vtr FrC P* 1. to beat (s.o.) up*/to work (s.o.) over/to do (s.o.) in 2. to damage/to bash (up)/to prang (a car).

magase, magaze [magaz] *nm P* shop/store.

se magner [səmaɲe] *vpr P* se magner (le cul/le derche/le derrière/les fesses/le fion/le mou/le popotin/la rondelle/le train), to hurry* up/to get a move on/to get cracking/to pull one's finger out/to stir one's stumps.

magnes [maɲ] *nfpl P* faire des magnes, (*se donner des airs*) to put on airs/to show off*; (*compliquer les choses*) to kick up a fuss.

magnéto [maɲeto] *nm F* (= *magnétophone*) tape recorder; (= *magnétoscope*) video recorder.

magnificat [magnifikat, maɲifika] *nm F* le magnificat est plus long que les vêpres, your slip's showing/Charlie's dead.

mago [mago] *nm P* shop/store.

magot [mago] *nm F* hoard/pile (of money); (*économies*) savings/nest egg; avoir un joli magot, to have a nice little nest egg put by; épouser un gros magot, to marry into money.

magouillage [maguijaʒ] *nm P* wangling/wheeling and dealing; faire des magouillages, to scheme; magouillages électoraux, pre-election plotting.

magouille [maguij] *nf P* (*a*) wangle/shady deal(s); faire des magouilles, to scheme (*b*) wangling/shady dealing(s)/wheeling and dealing (*c*) il y a de la magouille, I'm being cheated here; s.o.'s having me on/not playing straight.

magouiller [maguije] *P* **I** *vtr* to scheme/to plot; il magouille un mauvais coup, he's cooking up a dirty trick/he's up to no good **II** *vi* to wangle/to wheel and deal/to get up to some shady business/to (work a) fiddle; il magouille pour se faire bien voir du patron, he's scheming to get into the boss's good books **III** *vpr* **se magouiller** qu'est-ce qui se magouille?

what's going on?/what's cooking?

magouilleur, -euse [magujœr, -øz] **I** *n F* wangler/shady dealer/wheeler-dealer/fiddler **II** *a* shady/underhand; pratiques magouilleuses, shady/underhand dealings.

mahomet [maɔmɛ(t)] *nm P* the sun.

mahous(s), mahousse [maus] *a P* = **maous(s), maousse.**

maigrichon, -onne [mɛgriʃɔ̃, -ɔn], **maigriot, -otte** [mɛgrijo, -ɔt] *a F* thin/skinny (person).

mailloche [majɔʃ] *a P* big/strong/hefty/beefy.

main [mɛ̃] *nf* 1. *F* passer la main, to give up/not to insist 2. *F* homme de main, hired assassin/hired gun 3. *P* faire une main tombée, to steal*/to nick; (*caresser le postérieur*) to pat s.o.'s bottom/to touch s.o. up 4. *P* être en main, (*prostituée*) to be with a client/to be on the job; (*femme ou jeune fille*) to have a boyfriend/to have a bloke/to be attached. (*Voir* **baladeur; chaud I 2; doigt 1, 11; dos 11; malheureux 4; palmé II; panier 8; péter 8; sac 9; tour I 3**)

se maintenir [səmɛ̃tnir] *vpr F* ça va? – ça se maintient, how goes it? – so-so/not so bad/bearing up.

maire [mɛr] *nm F* passer devant (monsieur) le maire, to get married*/to get hitched.

mairie [meri] *nf F* se marier à la mairie du 21ᵉ (arrondissement)/se marier derrière la mairie, to live together.

maison [mɛzɔ̃] *nf* 1. *F* brothel*; maison de passe, hotel, etc., used by prostitutes and their clients/call joint; maison d'abattage, cheap brothel/cathouse; travailler en maison, (*prostituée*) to work in a licensed brothel 2. *P* la maison tire-bouchon/tire-bouton, (the world of) lesbians*/lesbianism/gay women 3. *P* exceptional; huge; first-rate; fantastic; une bagarre maison, an almighty row/one hell of a fight; une châtaigne maison, a hell of a clout; une engueulade maison, a real ticking-off/a right bollocking; une entourloupette maison, a filthy trick 4. *F* la (Grande) Maison, the police*; the headquarters of the (Paris) police/the Central Police Headquarters 5. *F* c'est gros comme une maison, (*très évident*) it sticks out a mile/it sticks out like a sore thumb/it's bloody obvious. (*Voir* **J't'arquepince; parapluie 5; pébroc 2; poulaga; tire-bouton**)

major [maʒɔr] *nm F* 1. (*université*) first in one's year/top of the year 2. army doctor/

surgeon.

mal [mal] I *adv* F 1. (*a*) pas mal, not (at all) bad; il (n')est pas mal ce tableau, this picture's quite good; elle (n')est pas mal, she's quite good-looking/not (at all) bad (*b*) je m'en fiche pas mal! a fat lot I care! I couldn't care less! (*c*) il en était pas mal fâché, he wasn't half cross about it/it really bugged him 2. (*a*) pas mal de ..., quite a lot of .../quite a bit of .../a good deal of ...; quite a few ...; y a pas mal de choses à faire, there's quite a lot/a hell of a lot of things to do (*b*) j'ai pas mal envie de rester, I've a good mind/half a mind to stay (*c*) nous sommes pas mal à dîner ce soir, we're rather a lot for dinner this evening 3. tu vas mal, toi! you're exaggerating!/ you're stretching it a bit! (*Voir* **aller 7**) 4. se trouver mal sur qch, to appropriate sth/to make off with sth 5. ça fait mal, it gives a (really) bad impression/it doesn't look good; (*ça fait bon effet*) it looks good/it's bad; ça va faire mal, there's going to be trouble 6. ça me ferait mal! I'd be amazed (if what you're saying is true); you're talking a lot of nonsense! ça te ferait mal de fermer la porte? would you *mind* closing the door? do you think you could manage to close the door? (*Voir* **blanchi; foutre[2] I 8**) II *nm* 1. F il n'y a pas de mal/P y a pas d'mal, don't mention it! 2. F (*a*) se donner un mal de chien pour faire qch, to bend over backwards to do sth (*b*) sans se faire de mal, without taking too much trouble/without overdoing it.

malabar [malabar] F I *a* strapping/hefty/ beefy/butch II *nm* 1. hefty chap/strapping fellow/beefy guy/muscleman 2. 500-franc note.

malade [malad] F I *a* 1. vous voilà bien malade! poor chap!/poor thing!/poor you! 2. t'es pas (un peu) malade? have you gone mad*?/you must be out of your (tiny) mind!/ are you off your rocker? 3. il en est malade, he's really upset about it/he's worried sick about it. (*Voir* **pouce 7**) II *nm* (travailler) comme un malade, (to work) like mad.

maladie [maladi] *nf* F 1. il en fera une maladie, he'll have a fit (when he finds out); he's not going to be very happy about it 2. maladie de neuf mois, pregnancy 3. disease (*affecting flora or fauna*); l'orme a la maladie, the elm is diseased/has got Dutch elm disease 4. avoir la maladie de, to be obsessed with (cleanliness, etc).

malaga [malaga] *nm Vieilli P* un malaga de

boueux, a glass of red wine.

malagauche [malagoʃ] F I *a* awkward/ clumsy/ham-fisted II *nm* & *f* awkward person/clumsy clot/butterfingers.

malaise [malɛz] *nm P* il y a (comme) un malaise, there's a hitch/a snag.

à la mal-au-ventre [alamalovɑ̃tr] *adv phr F* (*pantalon*) with pockets at the front.

mal-baisé(e) [malbeze] *nm & f V* (sexually) frustrated person; une mal-baisée, an unsatisfied woman*/wife*.

malchançard [malʃɑ̃sar] *nm F* unlucky person/unlucky blighter.

maldonne [maldɔn] *nf F* (il) y a maldonne, there's (been) a mistake somewhere; something's wrong somewhere; (*malentendu*) there's been a misunderstanding.

mâle [mɑl] *nm V* aller au mâle/prendre du mâle/se farcir du mâle, (*femme*) to have sex*/to get laid.

mal-en-pattes [malɑ̃pat] *nm inv F* c'est un mal-en-pattes, he's a clumsy oaf; he's all fingers and thumbs.

malfrappe [malfrap], **malfrat** [malfra], **malfrin** [malfrɛ̃] *nm P* 1. (*gangster*) gangster/crook 2. (*voyou*) hooligan*/thug/yob.

malheur [malœr] *nm F* 1. *Iron* le beau malheur!/le grand malheur! there's no harm in that!/what's all the fuss about? 2. jouer de malheur, to be out of luck 3. (ne) parle pas de malheur! God forbid!/have a heart! 4. ces formulaires de malheur! these blasted forms! 5. (*a*) faire un malheur, to do something desperate; to commit murder; s'il entre ici je fais un malheur! if he comes in here I'll do something desperate/I'll kill him/I'll kill myself (*b*) faire un malheur, (*théâtre, etc*) to be a hit/a huge success.

malheureux, -euse [malœrø, -øz] *a F* 1. trivial/paltry; vous faites des histoires pour cinq malheureux francs! you're making all this hoo-ha over a measly five francs! 2. te voilà enfin, ce n'est pas malheureux! here you are at last, and a good job too! 3. si c'est pas malheureux!/c'est-y pas malheureux! isn't it a shame!/it's a crying shame!/it's too bad! 4. avoir la main malheureuse, (*malchanceux*) to be unlucky; (*maladroit*) to be clumsy/ awkward/ham-fisted. (*Voir* **pierre I 2**)

malice [malis] *nf* 1. F la belle malice! there's nothing very clever in that! 2. P se faire malice tout seul, to masturbate*. (*Voir* **sac 13**)

malin [malɛ̃] F I *a* (*a*) *Iron* c'est malin! that

is clever (of you)! (*b*) **c'est pas malin**, that's not very difficult/there's nothing very clever in that **II** *nm* (*a*) **un malin/un petit malin/un gros malin**, a smart guy/a smart Alec(k) (*b*) **faire le/son malin**, to try to be clever/smart; to show off*.

malle [mal] *nf* **1.** *P* mouth*; **boucle/ferme ta malle!** shut up!*/shut your trap!/pack it in! **2.** *P Mil* guardroom; **grosse malle**, prison* **3.** *P* **faire sa malle**, to die*/to snuff it **4.** *F* **faire la malle à qn**, to walk out on s.o./to leave s.o. in the lurch **5.** *F* (**se**) **faire la malle**, to run away*/to scarper/to do a bunk **6.** *F* **porter sa malle**, to be hunchbacked/to have a hump **7.** *F* **malle à quatre nœuds**, handkerchief (containing one's savings, etc).

maller [male] *vtr & i P* **1.** to run away*/to scarper/to do a bunk **2.** to leave (s.o.)/to dump (s.o.). (*Voir* **malle 5**)

mallette [malɛt] *nf F* **faire mallette et paquette**, to (pack one's bags and) clear out; **faire mallette et paquette à qn**, to walk out on s.o./to leave s.o. in the lurch.

mallouser, mallouzer [maluze] *vtr & i P* = **maller**.

malpoli [malpɔli] *a F* impolite.

maltouze [maltuz] *nf A P* **pastiquer la maltouze**, to smuggle.

malva [malva] *adv P* (*verlan de va mal*) it's going badly; **aller chez malva**, (*événement, situation*) to go badly/to be bad; (*personne*) to be in poor health; **il va chez malva**, he's not doing so well/he's going to the dogs.

mama [mama] *nf F* mother with a large family/with many children.

mamelu, -ue [mamly] *a & nf P* (woman) with large breasts; **c'est une grosse mamelue**, she's got huge tits.

mamie [mami] *nf F* grandmother/gran/grannie/granny/nana.

mamours [mamur] *nmpl F* **faire des mamours à qn**, to fondle/to caress s.o.; **se faire des mamours**, to kiss and cuddle/*Vieilli* to canoodle/to bill and coo.

manchard [mɑ̃ʃar] *nm P* **1.** beggar **2.** s.o. who performs on the street for money/busker.

manche [mɑ̃ʃ] **I** *nm* **1.** *P* fool*; **c'est un manche**, he's a (clumsy) clot/a twit; **il raisonne comme un manche**, he can't think straight; **il conduit comme un manche**, he's a hopeless driver; he can't drive for toffee/for nuts; **il se débrouille/s'y prend comme un manche**, he goes about things in an idiotic way; (*maladroitement*) he goes about things

in a cockeyed/ham-fisted way; **il est con comme un manche**, he's a real twit/a real jerk. (*Voir* **dégourdi**) **2.** *F* **être du côté du manche**, to be on the strongest/the winning side **3.** *F* **tomber sur un manche**, to come up against/to hit a snag **4.** *V* **manche** (**à balai/à couilles**), penis*/rod; **avoir le manche**, to have an erection*/a stiff(y)/a rod. (*Voir* **branler** I) **II** *nf F* **1.** (*a*) **la manche**, begging; beggary (*b*) **faire la manche**, (*mendier*) to beg/to go on the cadge; (*chanter, etc dans les rues*) to busk (*c*) **faire la/une manche à qn**, to go round with the hat for s.o./to have a whip-round for s.o. **2.** **avoir qn dans sa manche**, to enjoy s.o.'s confidence/trust; to have s.o. in one's pocket. (*Voir* **jambe 7** (*a*); **paire 1**)

manchette [mɑ̃ʃɛt] *nf F* **1.** **mettre des manchettes pour faire qch**, to make elaborate preparations before doing sth **2.** *pl* handcuffs*/cuffs **3.** **coup de manchette**, blow with the forearm.

manchot [mɑ̃ʃo] *a F* **1.** **il n'est pas manchot**, (*adroit*) he's clever with his hands; (*il peut le faire lui-même*) he's got hands, hasn't he? **2.** **bandit manchot**, (*machine à sous*) one-armed bandit.

manchouillard [mɑ̃ʃujar] *a & nm P* one-armed/one-handed (man).

mandagat [mɑ̃daga] *nm P* (= *mandat*) money order/postal order.

mandale [mɑ̃dal] *nf P* slap round the face; **filer/allonger une mandale à qn**, to give s.o. a clout.

mandarin [mɑ̃darɛ̃] *nm F* aperitif made with mandarin extract.

mandarines [mɑ̃darin] *nfpl P* small breasts*/pimples.

mandibules [mɑ̃dibyl] *nfpl P* jaws; **claquer des mandibules**, to be hungry*/to be peckish; **jouer (la polka) des mandibules**, to eat*/to nosh; **se faire les mandibules sur qch**, to chew sth.

mandole [mɑ̃dɔl] *nf P* = **mandale**.

mandoline [mɑ̃dɔlin] *nf* **1.** *P* (*a*) bludgeon/cosh made out of a bag filled with sand (*b*) machine gun **2.** *P* (*a*) round bedpan (*b*) bidet **3.** *V* **jouer de la mandoline**, (*femme*) to masturbate*/to play with oneself/to finger oneself.

mandrin [mɑ̃drɛ̃] *nm V* penis*; **avoir le mandrin**, to have an erection*.

manettes [manɛt] *nfpl P* **1.** ears*/lugs **2.** pedals (of bicycle); **appuyer/pousser sur les manettes**, to pedal away **3.** **à fond les**

manettes, very quickly*/at full throttle/at full speed 4. **perdre/lâcher les manettes**, to lose all self-control/to get flustered/to get all balled up.

mangave [mɑ̃gav] *P* I *nf* begging/beggary; **il est à deux doigts de la mangave**, he's within an inch of the gutter/he's almost been reduced to begging II *nm* beggar.

mangeaille [mɑ̃ʒɑj] *nf F* food*/grub/nosh. (*Voir* **bâfrer** II)

mange-merde [mɑ̃ʒmɛrd] *nm inv P* miser*/skinflint.

manger [mɑ̃ʒe] I *vtr & i* 1. *F* **manger une peine**, (*faire de la prison*) to do time/to do a stretch; **il a mangé cinq piges**, he did a five-year stretch 2. *P* **en manger**, to live by illicit earnings; (*d'un policier*) to be corrupt/bent; **en manger** (**du pain de fesse**), to live by prostitution*/to be on the game 3. *V* to have oral sex* (with) (s.o.)/to eat (s.o.) 4. *F* **manger à la table qui recule**, to go without food II *vpr* **se manger** *P* 1. **se manger un coup**, to get hit/to get biffed 2. **se manger qn**, to beat s.o. up*/to do s.o. over. (*Voir* **bête** II 1; **boire**; **consigne**; **morceau 1, 2**; **pif 7**; **pissenlit**; **poisson 1**; **pouce 2**; **râtelier 1**)

mangeur [mɑ̃ʒœr] *nm* 1. *F* **mangeur de curés**, violently anticlerical person 2. *P* **mangeur de crucifix**, sanctimonious hypocrite 3. *P* **mangeur de blanc**, pimp*/ponce; white slaver.

mangeuse [mɑ̃ʒøz] *nf P* **mangeuse d'hommes/mangeuse de santé**, highly-sexed woman/hot lay/easy lay/nympho.

se manier [səmanje] *vpr P* = **se magner**.

manière [manjɛr] *nf* 1. *F pl* (*a*) **faire des manières**, to be affected/to put on airs; **pas tant de manières!** come off it! (*b*) **en voilà des manières!** fine manners you have, I must say!/that's a nice way to behave!/talk about manners! 2. *V* **bonne manière**, fellatio*.

manieur [manjœr] *nm F* **manieur de fonte**, weightlifter.

manif [manif] *nf P* (*abrév* = *manifestation*) (public) demonstration/demo.

manigance [manigɑ̃s] *nf F* (*a*) scheme/plot; underhand dealing/undercover deal/fiddle; fiddling; (*b*) *pl* underhand practices/wire-pulling.

manigancer [manigɑ̃se] I *vtr F* to scheme/to plot; to wangle/to work (sth) underhand; **qu'est-ce qu'il manigance?** what's he up to?/

what's his (little) game?/what's he cooking up? II *vpr* **se manigancer** *F* **je me demande ce qui se manigance**, I wonder what's going on; I wonder what's cooking; **il se manigance quelque chose**, there's something in the wind.

manip(e)s [manip] *nfpl F* (*écoles*) (= *manipulation*) practical work (*esp in chemistry, physics*).

manitou [manitu] *nm F* **le** (**grand**) **manitou**, the big shot; (*patron*) the big boss/the big white chief/the big noise.

manivelles [manivɛl] *nfpl P* 1. pedals (of bicycle) 2. legs*/pins 3. arms*/fins.

mannequins [mankɛ̃] *nmpl P* policemen*/coppers/pigs/boys in blue.

mannezingue [manzɛ̃g] *nm P* publican/landlord; bartender.

manoche [manɔʃ] *nf F* (French card game of) *manille*.

manouche [manuʃ] *P* I *nm & f* gipsy/gippo II *nm* Romany/gipsy lingo.

manque [mɑ̃k] *nm P* 1. (*drogues*) **être en** (**état de**) **manque**, to suffer from withdrawal symptoms*/to need a fix; to have/to be in cold turkey 2. **manque de bol/de pot!** hard luck!/bad luck! 3. (*personne ou chose*) **à la manque**, (*à qui ou à quoi on ne peut faire confiance*) unreliable. (*Voir* **nière 3**); (*médiocre, de mauvaise qualité*) poor/worthless*/useless/third-rate; **un(e) modéliste à la manque**, a would-be dress designer; **un artiste à la manque**, a second-rate artist; **une idée à la manque**, a hopeless/half-baked idea.

manquer [mɑ̃ke] *vtr F* (**il ne**) **manquait plus que ça!** that's the last straw!

mansarde [mɑ̃sard] *nf F* head*/skull/attic.

maous(s), maousse [maus] *a P* (*a*) huge/enormous/massive/whacking/great (*b*) (*personne*) hefty/tremendously strong.

maq [mak] *nm P* = **maquereau**.

maqua [maka] *nf P* = **maquerelle**.

maque [mak] *nm P* = **maquereau**.

maqué [make] *a P* **être maqué avec qn**, to be living (in sin) with s.o./to be shacked up with s.o.

maquer [make] I *vtr P* to exploit (s.o.)/to swindle* (s.o.)/to con (s.o. out of sth) II *vpr* **se maquer** *P* **se maquer avec qn**, to live (in sin) with s.o./to shack up with s.o.

maquereau, pl -eaux [makro] *nm P* pimp*/ponce/mack.

maquereautage [makrotaʒ] *nm P* living off a prostitute*/procuring/pimping.

maquereauter [makrote] *vi P* to procure/ to live off the earnings of a prostitute*/to pimp.

maquereautin [makrotɛ̃] *nm P* (a) young inexperienced pimp* (b) small-time pimp*.

maquerellage [makrɛlaʒ] *nm P* = **maquereautage**.

maquerelle [makrɛl] *nf P* (mère) maquerelle, (woman) brothel owner; madam(e).

maquillage [makijaʒ] *nm* 1. *F* (a) (de documents, etc) forging/faking; fiddling; doctoring (b) disguising (of stolen or second-hand car) 2. *P* marking (of playing cards) 3. *P* self-inflicted injury (in order to claim insurance, etc).

maquille [makij] *nf F* = **maquillage 1** (b), **2.**

maquiller [makije] I *vtr F* to fake up (a picture, etc); to forge/to doctor (a cheque); to fiddle (the accounts); to distort/to cover up (the truth); to disguise (a stolen or second-hand car); ils ont maquillé la voiture, they did a paint-job on the car; qu'est-ce que tu maquilles? what are you up to? (*Voir* **brème 1; faf², faffe 1**) II *vpr* se maquiller *P* to inflict a wound, an injury on oneself (in order to claim insurance, etc).

maquilleur, -euse [makijœr, -øz] *n F* cheat/swindler*; forger (of cheques); fiddler (of accounts); disguiser (of stolen or second-hand cars) cardsharp(er).

marabout [marabu] *nm P* naval chaplain.

marasquin [maraskɛ̃] *nm P* blood.

maraude [marod] *nf P* taxi en maraude, cruising taxi (looking for clients outside taxi ranks, illegal in France).

marauder [marode] *vi P* (taxi) to cruise around (looking for clients).

maraudeur [marodœr] *nm P* cruising taxi (driver) (looking for clients).

marave [marav] *vtr P* = **maraver**.

maravédis [maravedi(s)] *nm Vieilli F* je n'ai pas un maravédis, I'm penniless*/I haven't a brass farthing.

maraver [marave] *vtr P* 1. to beat up*/to batter (s.o.) 2. to kill*/to bump off/to wipe out (s.o.).

marca(t) [marka] *nm P* market. (*Voir* **supermarca(t)**)

marcel [marsɛl] *nm P* 1. boyfriend/lover 2. string vest.

marchand [marʃɑ̃] *nm F* 1. marchand de barbaque/de bidoche/de viande, pimp dealing

in the white-slave trade/white-slaver 2. marchand de lacets, gendarme 3. marchand de participes, teacher/schoolmaster/pedant 4. marchand de puces, junk dealer; old-clothes man 5. marchand de sommeil, (small) hotel keeper (who hires out rooms at exorbitant prices) 6. marchand de soupe, proprietor of a poor/a seedy restaurant; *Fig* businessman only interested in making a profit; ce n'est qu'un marchand de soupe, he's only in it for the money 7. être le mauvais marchand de qch, to be the loser by sth.

marchande [marʃɑ̃d] *nf F* 1. *F* marchande de plaisir/d'amour, prostitute* 2. *P* marchande d'ail, lesbian*/les/dyke.

marchandise [marʃɑ̃diz] *nf* 1. *F* vanter/ étaler/faire valoir sa marchandise, to make the most of oneself; (fille, femme) to show off the goods/her charms; to show what she's got 2. *P* male genitals*/bag of tricks/the goods 3. *P* excrement*/shit/crap; mettre les pieds dans la marchandise, to tread in the shit 4. *P* drugs*/the goods.

marcher [marʃe] *vi F* 1. to accept/to agree (to sth); je marche (avec vous)!/ça marche! I'm on!/agreed!/count me in! je ne marche pas! nothing doing!*/(you can) count me out! je ne marche pas à moins de 100 francs, nothing doing under 100 francs; ça n'a pas marché, it didn't work/it didn't come off 2. to believe everything one is told/to be gullible; il a marché, he fell for it/he swallowed it; il n'a pas marché, he wasn't having any 3. faire marcher qn, to fool s.o./to pull s.o.'s leg/to lead s.o. up the garden path; on vous a fait marcher, you've been had 4. marcher dedans, to tread in some shit/to tread in it 5. marcher au café/au whisky, etc, to drink/take (a lot of) coffee/whisky, etc; to guzzle coffee/whisky, etc all day long. (*Voir* **dix 4; latte 4; ombre 3; pompe 5**)

marcheur [marʃœr] *nm* 1. *Vieilli F Péj* vieux marcheur, dirty old man 2. *P* housebreaker/burglar.

marcheuse [marʃøz] *nf* 1. *F* (théâtre) walker-on/extra; rôle de marcheuse, walk-on part/bit part 2. *P* prostitute*/streetwalker.

marchis [marʃi] *nm P Mil* = **margis**.

marcotin [markɔtɛ̃] *nm P* month. (*Voir* **marqué II**)

marde [mard] *nf FrC P* (= **merde**) 1. shit/ crap 2. fou comme la marde, crazy*/nuts/ crackers 3. mange de la marde! piss off!/ bugger off!/drop dead!

mardeux [mardø] *nm FrC P* (= **merdeux**) shit/creep/jerk/bastard*.

mardoche [mardɔʃ] *nm P* Tuesday.

mare [mar] *nf* la Mare (aux harengs), the (Herring) Pond/the Atlantic. (*Voir* **pavé 7**)

margis [marʒi] *nm P Mil* (= *maréchal des logis*) sergeant (*in the cavalry or artillery*)/ sarge.

margotin [margotɛ̃] *nf*, **margoton** [margotɔ̃] *nf P* woman of easy virtue/easy lay/pushover.

margouillat [marguja] *nm P kir* made with red wine.

margoulette [margulɛt] *nf P* face*/mug; casser la margoulette à qn, to smash s.o.'s face in/to spoil s.o.'s beauty for him.

margoulin [margulɛ̃] *nm F* 1. (*bourse*) petty speculator 2. dishonest tradesman/ swindler*/shark 3. black marketeer/spiv 4. bungler/botcher/bodger; il a fait ça comme un margoulin, he bungled/botched it.

marguerite [margərit] *nf* 1. *P* condom*/ French letter/*NAm* rubber 2. *P* **une marguerite**, a white hair; **avoir des marguerites dans le cresson**, to have some white hairs (on one's head)/to have some silver threads among the gold. (*Voir* **effeuiller**)

Marianne [marjan] *Prnf F* the (French) Republic; **travailler pour Marianne**, to be expecting (a baby).

marida [marida] I *nm P* marriage/holy deadlock; **aller au marida**, to get married*/ hitched II *a inv P* married/hitched/spliced.

se marida [səmarida] *vpr P* se marida avec qn, to get married* to s.o.; je me suis marida, I've got hitched.

Marie-Chantal [mariʃɑ̃tal] *Prnf F* c'est une Marie-Chantal, she's a rich, empty-headed little snob/a Mayfair nitwit/= a Sloane ranger/a bright young thing.

Marie-couche-toi-là [marikuʃtwala] *nf inv P* woman of easy virtue/pushover/easy lay/scrubber/tart.

mariée [marje] *nf* 1. *F* la mariée est trop belle, it's too good to be true; il se plaint que la mariée est trop belle/il trouve la mariée trop belle, he doesn't know how lucky/how well off he is 2. *P* pint of beer (with lots of head) 3. *P* voiture de la mariée, police *or* prison van*/Black Maria.

marie-jeanne [mariʒan] *nf P* (*drogues*) marijuana*/Mary Jane.

marie-louise [marilwiz] *nf P* fart. (*Voir* louise)

Marie-pisse-trois-gouttes [maripistrwagut] *nf inv P* very young girl*.

Marie-salope [marisalɔp] *nf* 1. *F* mud dredger 2. *P* slut/scrubber/tart 3. *P Mil* field kitchen 4. *F* (*boisson*) bloody Mary.

marine [marin] I *nf P* travailler pour la marine, to be constipated II *nm F* (*pantalon*) bell-bottoms with pockets on the front.

mariner [marine] *P* I *vi* to wait/to hang about/to kick one's heels II *vtr* mariner qn, to make s.o. wait/to let s.o. stew.

mariol(e), mariolle [marjɔl] *F* I *a* 1. clever/smart/cunning 2. pleasant/amusing; c'est pas mariole, it's not much fun II *nm* faire le mariol(e), to show off*.

marjo, margeot [marʒo] *nm & f P* (= *marginal*) drop-out; hippie; second-class citizen.

marle [marl] *P* I *a* = **mariol(e)** I 1 II *nm* pimp*/ponce.

marlou [marlu], **marloupin** [marlupɛ̃] *nm P* 1. procurer/pimp*/ponce 2. lout/ hooligan/*Br* yob(bo).

marloupinerie [marlupinri] *nf*, **marlouserie** [marluzri] *nf P* sly trick/ cunning dodge.

marmaille [marmaj] *nf F* (noisy) children/ kids/brats; la marmaille sortait de l'école, the kids were coming out of school; rue pleine de marmaille, street swarming with (noisy) kids.

marmelade [marməlad] *nf F* (*a*) en marmelade, in a frightful mess; quelle marmelade! what a mess!/what a shambles! (*b*) avoir les pieds en marmelade, to have very sore feet*; mettre qch en marmelade, to pound sth to a jelly/to a pulp; mettre qn en marmelade, to make mincemeat of s.o./to beat s.o. to a pulp.

marmitage [marmitaʒ] *nm P Mil* heavy bombardment/heavy shelling/pounding.

marmite [marmit] *nf* 1. *Vieilli P Mil* heavy shell 2. *P* prostitute* supporting her pimp*; meal-ticket. (*Voir* **écumer 1**; **écumeur**)

marmiter [marmite] *vtr P* 1. *Vieilli Mil* to bombard (trenches, etc) with heavy shells 2. (*prison*) se faire marmiter, to get caught infringing regulations.

marmot [marmo] *nm F* 1. kid/brat/nipper. (*Voir* **cracher II 4**) 2. croquer le marmot, to be kept waiting/to be kept hanging about; to cool/kick one's heels 3. beurrer le marmot, to console/to comfort.

marmouset [marmuzɛ] *nm F* 1. undersized* person/shorty/shrimp/pipsqueak 2. kid/nipper 3. foetus.

marner [marne] *vi P* to work* hard/to slog (away).

marneur, -euse [marnœr, -øz] *n P* hard worker/grafter.

maronner [marɔne] *vi* 1. *F* to grumble*/to grouse 2. *F* to be very angry*/to throw a fit 3. *P* to wait around/to hang about/to kick one's heels.

marotte [marɔt] *nf F* hobby; (*manie, folie*) fad; avoir une marotte, to have a bee in one's bonnet.

marquat [marka] *nm P* market.

marqué [marke] I *a F* c'est un homme marqué, he's a marked man II *nm P* month; tirer six marqués, to do a six-month stretch (*in prison*).

marquer [marke] *F* I *vtr* 1. to mark (a playing card) 2. to scar (s.o.'s face) 3. marquer un point, to have the advantage. (*Voir* **coup 17**; **midi 4**) II *vi* 7. marquer mal/bien, to give/to make a bad/a good impression.

marquet [markɛ] *nm P* = **marqué II**.

Marquis [marki] *nm F* (*locution populaire*) après vous, Marquis − non, après vous, Prince, after you, Claude − no, after you, Cecil.

marquise [markiz] *nf* 1. *P* madam(e) (of a brothel) 2. *F Iron* tout va très bien, Madame la Marquise! oh yes, things couldn't be going better!/everything's just fine!

marquotin [markɔtɛ̃] *nm P* month.

marquouse [markuz] *nf P* 1. mark (on a playing card) 2. scar.

marquouser [markuze] *vtr P* 1. to mark (playing card) 2. to tattoo.

marrade [marad] *nf F* fun (and games)/lark.

marraine [marɛn] *nf P* female witness for the prosecution.

marrant [marɑ̃] I *a & nm F* 1. funny*; il est marrant! he's a (real) scream! c'est un marrant, celui-là, that guy's a total laugh/a gas; il n'est pas marrant, he's a drip; he's as dull as ditchwater/he's not much fun 2. (*étrange*) odd/funny/strange/funny peculiar; vous êtes marrant, vous alors! you're the limit! II *nm V* anus*.

marre [mar] *adv P* 1. (*a*) (en) avoir marre de qch/en avoir marre, to be fed up* with sth/to have had enough of sth/to be cheesed off with sth/to be sick of sth; (il) y en a marre!

I've had a bellyful of it/a basinful of it! j'en ai marre, I'm fed up (to the back teeth) with it/I've had it up to here (*b*) (en) avoir marre de qn, to be fed up with s.o./to be bored* stiff with s.o./to be sick of s.o./to be browned off with s.o. 2. c'est marre!/en voilà marre!/un point, c'est marre! and that's all there is to it!/enough said!/and that's that!/enough's enough.

se marrer [səmare] *vpr F* to laugh* uproariously/to split one's sides laughing/to kill oneself laughing; elle se marrait un bon coup, she was in stitches; tu me fais marrer, you make me laugh; (*je ne te crois pas*) that's a laugh; you can't kid me; on va se marrer, we're going to have a good time/a ball.

marron [marɔ̃] I *nm P* (*a*) blow*/clout/thump/wallop; coller/flanquer/foutre un marron à qn, to fetch/to land s.o. a clout; fous-lui un marron! thump him!/give him one! (*b*) secouer la poêle à marrons à qn, to beat s.o. up*/to give s.o. a going-over/to knock the living daylights out of s.o. II *a* 1. *F* (*négociant,* *marchand*) unlicensed/clandestine; médecin/avocat marron, quack doctor/lawyer 2. *P* être (fait/paumé) marron, to be caught in the act/in flagrante delicto/red-handed 3. *P* être marron, to be disappointed; sans l'argent, je suis marron, without the money, I've had it. (*Voir* **tas 2**) III *nm P* victim/mug/sucker/fall guy/patsy.

marronnier [marɔnje] *nm F Journ* seasonal article on an event that takes place every year.

Marsiale [marsjal] *Prnf P* Marseille(s); un(e) de la Marsiale, a native of Marseille(s)/someone from Marseilles.

marsouin [marswɛ̃] *nm* 1. *F* marine/*NAm* leatherneck 2. *F* sailor.

marteau [marto] I *a F* mad*; il est un peu marteau, he's not all there, he's a bit cracked/he's a bit nutty; elle est complètement marteau, she's completely off her rocker II *nm F* avoir un coup de marteau, to be (slightly) mad*.

martien [marsjɛ̃] *nm F* bald man.

Martigue(s) [martig] *P* I *Prnf* Marseille(s) II *a & n* (native) of Marseille(s).

maso [mazo] *F* (= *masochiste*) I *a* masochistic II *nm & f* masochist. (*Voir* **sado**)

massacrant [masakrɑ̃] *a F* être d'une humeur massacrante, to be in a vile/a foul mood; to be in a filthy temper.

massacre [masakr] *nm F* 1. il a une tête de massacre, he's got an unpleasant/a horrible face; he's no oil painting 2. *(théâtre, etc)* faire un massacre, to be a smash hit.

massacrer [masakre] *vtr F* (a) to bungle*/ to botch/to bodge/to make a hash of (sth) (b) to murder (a piece of music); to murder/to massacre (a language) (c) to ruin (clothes) (d) to beat (s.o.).

massacreur, -euse [masakrœr, -øz] *n F* bungler/botcher/bodger.

masse [mas] I *nf F* des masses de ..., masses of ...; (il n')y en a pas des masses, there isn't/aren't an awful lot; avoir des livres en masse, to have masses of books II *nf F* 1. coup de masse, exhaustion/extreme tiredness; *(note très élevée)* stiff/steep (restaurant/ hotel) bill; overcharging/fleecing/daylight robbery/rip-off 2. recevoir le coup de masse, to get a violent emotional shock 3. être à la masse, *(abruti)* to be dazed/disorientated; *(déséquilibré)* unbalanced; *(sans argent)* penniless*/broke 4. prisoner's pay *(given to him/her on his/her release)* 5. *(caisse commune)* fund/kitty.

masser [mase] *vi P* to work* hard/to keep at it.

massue [masy] *nf F* coup de massue, *(choc émotif)* staggering blow/shattering news/ bombshell; *(note très élevée)* stiff/steep (restaurant/hotel) bill; overcharging/fleecing/ daylight robbery/rip-off.

mastard [mastar] *a P* very big/enormous/ huge/whacking (great).

mastègue [mastɛg] *nf P* (a) food* (b) meal.

mastéguer [mastege] *vi P* (a) to eat* (b) to chew.

mastic [mastik] *nm P* 1. muddle; tu parles d'un mastic! talk about a mess! 2. s'endormir sur le mastic, péter dans/sur le mastic, to abandon a job/to give up on a job/to drop one's work 3. faire le mastic, *(garçon de café)* to sweep up/to clean up 4. bouder le mastic, to pick at one's food.

masticotte [mastikɔt] *nf P* avoir une bonne masticotte, to have the gift of the gab.

mastiquer [mastike] *vtr P* to eat*.

mastoc [mastɔk] *a inv F* *(personne)* heavy/ loutish/lumpish; *(construction)* clumsy; *(machine)* bulky; *(bifteck)* thick.

mastodonte [mastɔdɔ̃t] *nm F* (a) *(véhicule)* juggernaut (b) *(personne)*

colossus/hulking great brute (c) *(chose)* whopper.

mastroquet [mastrɔkɛ] *nm P* (a) publican; keeper of a pub *or* wine bar (b) *(bistro)* bar/pub. *(Voir* **troquet)**

m'as-tu-vu, -vue [matyvy] *n inv F* show-off*/swank; faire le m'as-tu-vu, to prance around; to camp it up.

mat [mat] *a F* (a) exhausted*/dead beat (b) finished; c'est mat, it's all over.

mat' [mat] *nm P* morning; à quatre plombes du mat', at four am/four in the morning.

matador [matadɔr] *nm F* *(milieu)* tough guy; big shot; magnate.

mataf [mataf] *nm P* sailor*.

mataguin [matagɛ̃] *nm P* *(javanais de matin)* morning.

matave [matav] *nm P* = **mataf.**

mate [mat] *nm P* = **mat'.**

matelas [matla] *nm P* 1. well-filled wallet/ wad (of banknotes); avoir le matelas, to be rich*/to have a well-filled wallet 2. hoard (of money); savings/nest egg.

matelassier [matlasje] *nm P* *(courses)* racegoer/punter who bets very large sums.

mater¹ [mate] *P* I *vtr* (a) to watch closely/to keep an eye on (s.o./sth) (b) to look at*/to take a dekko at/to have a gander at (s.o./sth); mate-moi ça! get a load of that! II *vi* 1. to be on the lookout/to watch 2. to be a peeping Tom/a voyeur. *(Voir* **jeton 5)**

mater², matère [matɛr] *nf P* = **maternelle.**

matérielle [materjɛl] *nf F* la matérielle, the necessities of life; gagner/faire sa matérielle, to make a living/to keep the wolf from the door.

maternelle [matɛrnɛl] *nf Vieilli P* mother*/mater; la maternelle, my old lady.

mateur [matœr] *nm P* voyeur/peeping Tom.

math(s) [mat] *nf(pl) F* maths/*NAm* math; fort en math(s), good at maths/*NAm* math.

matheux, -euse [matø, -øz] *n F* *(quelquefois Péj)* keen mathematician/maths wizard; *(étudiant(e))* maths/*NAm* math student.

mathurin [matyrɛ̃] *nm F* sailor.

matière [matjɛr] *nf F* avoir de la matière grise, to be clever/brainy/smart.

maton [matɔ̃] *nm P* 1. policeman* 2. (male) prison warder/screw.

matonne [matɔn] *nf P* (female) prison warder/screw.

matos [matos] *nm P* 1. (= *matériel)*

equipment/gear; (*utilisé par des musiciens*) musical instruments/drum kit/amplifiers/mikes, etc 2. girlfriend/wife*/companion.

matou [matu] *nm P* lover/fancy man/boyfriend.

matouser, matouzer [matuze] *vtr & i P* = **mater.**

matraquage [matrakaʒ] *nm F* (*à la télévision, la radio*) matraquage (publicitaire), constant bombardment of adverts.

matraque [matrak] *nf* 1. *F* coup de matraque, barefaced overcharging (in restaurant, etc) 2. *P* mettre la matraque, (*cartes*) to lay the winning card(s); (*prendre des mesures radicales*) to take drastic measures; to use forceful tactics 3. *P* avoir la matraque, (*cartes*) to hold a winning hand 4. *V* penis*; avoir la matraque, to have an erection*.

matraquer [matrake] **I** *vtr* 1. *F* to overcharge/to fleece/to rip off (a customer) 2. *P* to inflict a stiff penalty on (s.o.); to punish* (s.o.) severely 3. *F* la radio matraque cette chanson toute la journée, the radio churns out that song all day long **II** *vi P* to take drastic measures; to use forecul tactics.

matraqueur [matrakœr] *nm P* dirty player (*at football, etc*).

matricule [matrikyl] *nm P* 1. annoncer son matricule, to fart 2. ça va barder/ça va chier, pour ton matricule! you're (in) for it!/you've got it coming to you!/you'll cop it!

matuche [matyʃ] *nm P* 1. = **maton 1, 2** 2. *pl* matuches, (loaded) dice.

matz [mats] *nm P* 1. husband*/old man 2. chap*/guy/bloke.

la Maub' [lamob] *Prnf F* place Maubert; (*quartier*) the Maubert district (*in Paris*). (*Voir* **la Mocobo**)

mauresque [mɔrɛsk] *nm F* (*boisson*) pastis and barley water.

mauvaise [movɛz] *af F* l'avoir/la trouver mauvaise, to be indignant/annoyed/disappointed/fed up.

mauviette [movjɛt] *nf F* (*a*) frail-looking/sickly-looking/puny individual; elle mange comme une mauviette, she doesn't eat enough to keep a sparrow alive (*b*) (*moralement*) drip/wet; quelle mauviette tu fais! you're such a drip!

MAV [emave] *abrév P* (*tatouage, graffiti*) (= *mort aux vaches*) death to the pigs!

max [maks] *nm P* (= *maximum*) (*a*) il en a pris un max, he copped the maximum (*b*) il déconne un max, he's a real joker; ça lui plaît

un max, he likes it a lot/he likes it loads; il assure un max, he does everything perfectly/he's totally competent (*c*) j'en ai vu un max, de ces films, I've seen lots/loads of those films (*d*) on sera 20 au max, there'll be 20 of us at the most.

maxé(e) [makse] *nf P* brothel owner; madam(e). (*Voir* **macquecé(e)**)

maxi [maksi] **I** *nm F* maxi (coat, etc); la mode du maxi, the maxi fashion **II** *nf F* maxi (skirt) **III** *nm P* (= *maximum*) (*a*) je suis bon pour le maxi/je vais écoper le maxi, I'm sure to get the maximum sentence (*b*) (*surt Aut; Fig*) donner/taper le maxi, to go all out/to step on it/to put one's foot down (*c*) ça lui plaît un maxi, he likes it a lot/he likes it loads (*d*) on sera 20 au maxi, there'll be 20 of us at the most. (*Voir* **max**)

maximum [maksimɔm] *nm F* au grand maximum, at the very most/at the absolute maximum. (*Voir* **max**)

mazette [mazɛt] *Vieilli* **I** *nf F* c'est une mazette, he's hopeless (at games, at sport); (*sans énergie*) he's a spineless individual/he's a dead loss **II** *int F* mazette! (*admiration, étonnement*) good Lord!/well I never!/my goodness!

mec [mɛk] *nm P* 1. *Vieilli* pimp*/ponce 2. (*a*) fellow*/guy/chap/bloke; un drôle de mec, an odd character/a funny bloke; un sale/vilain mec, a nasty piece of work; un petit mec, a little twerp; pauv' mec! poor sod! t'es un pauv' mec! you're a jerk/a sod/a bastard*! c'est un bon mec, he's a nice bloke/an ace guy; t'as raison, mec! you're right, mate! (*b*) le mec des mecs/le grand Mec, God (*c*) tough guy; un mec à la redresse, a thug (*d*) husband*; boyfriend; lover; mon mec, my man/my bloke/my guy. (*Voir* **rousse 1**)

meca [məka] *nf P* (*verlan de* **came**) drugs*/dope/junk.

méca [meka] *n P* (*verlan de* **camé**) drug addict*/dope addict/junkie.

mécanique [mekanik] *nf* 1. *F* gadget 2. *pl P* shoulders; rouler les mécaniques, to swagger/to strut 3. *F* c'est de la belle mécanique, (*voiture*) that's a nice-looking machine/that's a lovely piece of machinery; (*femme*) she's got a great chassis.

mécano [mekano] *nm F* mechanic/grease monkey.

méchamment [meʃamɑ̃] *adv P* very/extremely/fantastically/terrifically; un type méchamment bien, a hell of a nice guy.

méchant [meʃɑ̃] I *a* 1. *F* pas méchant, harmless; ce n'est pas bien méchant, there's no (great) harm in it/it's not too serious; ce n'est pas méchant, ça va chercher dans les 50 francs, it's not too bad, about 50 francs or so 2. *P* great/terrific/fantastic; une méchante dégaine, a snappy look; une méchante gueule de bois, a terrific hangover; une méchante victoire, a resounding victory II *nm F* faire le méchant, to be/to turn nasty; to be difficult.

mèche [mɛʃ] I *nf F* (*a*) vendre la mèche, to divulge a secret*/to give the game away/to let the cat out of the bag/to spill the beans/to blow the gaff (*b*) découvrir la mèche, to get wind of a secret; to uncover the plot II *nf inv F* 1. être de mèche avec qn, to be in collusion/in league/in cahoots with s.o.; to be hand in glove with s.o. 2. et mèche, (*et plus*) and a bit more (besides)/and the rest; (*et demi*) and a half; elle a trente ans et mèche, she's thirty if she's a day/she's the wrong side of thirty; (*trente ans et demi*) she's thirty and a half. (*Voir* **toutim(e)** (*b*)) 3. (il n'y a) pas mèche, not a (ghost of a) chance/nothing doing*/no way 4. on n'y voit (pas) mèche, you can't see a thing.

mécol, mécolle [mekɔl] *pron P* I/me/myself/yours truly. (*Voir* **mézig**)

mecton [mɛktɔ̃] *nm P* (*petit mec*) man*/bloke/guy; *Péj* twerp/jerk. (*Voir* **mec**)

médaille [medaj] *nf F* 1. porter la médaille, (*assumer la responsabilité*) to carry the can 2. médaille en chocolat, (worthless) award/gong.

médicale [medikal] *nf P* sortir en médicale, to be released (from prison) on medical grounds/to get a medical discharge.

médoche [medɔʃ] *nf*, **méduche** [medyʃ] *nf P* (religious) medal; decoration.

Méduse [medyz] *Prnf F* c'est la tête de Méduse, it's petrifying/paralysing.

meetinge [mitɛ̃ʒ] *nm P* (*surt Pol*) meeting/rally/meet.

mefa [mɛfa], **meffe** [mɛf] *nf P* (*verlan de* **femme**) girl*/woman; bird/chick/*NAm* broad.

mégachiée [megaʃje] *nf V* une mégachiée de ..., a fantastic quantity of .../loads and loads of .... (*Voir* **chiée**)

mégalo [megalo] *a & n F* megalomaniac.

mégaphone [megafɔn] *nm P* exhaust (pipe) (*esp of motorbike*).

mégot [mego] *nm P* 1. (*a*) cigarette end*/butt/fag-end/dog-end; boîte à mégots, ashtray (*b*) cigar stump (*c*) cigarette*/fag/cig 2. nothing*/damn all. (*Voir* **étagère 1**)

mégot(t)age [megotaʒ] *nm P* 1. (*mesquinerie*) scrimping (and scraping); mener une vie de mégot(t)age, to spend one's life scrimping and scraping 2. idle talk/pointless discussion.

mégot(t)er [megote] *vi P* 1. *A* to go around picking up cigarette ends* 2. (*a*) to live meanly/to scrimp/to skimp (*b*) ne pas mégot(t)er sur qch, not to be stingy/mean with sth 3. to quibble 4. to be an amateur/to work as an amateur.

mégot(t)eur, -euse [megotœr, -øz], **mégot(t)ier, -ière** [megotje, -jɛr] *n P* 1. person who picks up cigarette ends*; down-and-out/bum/tramp 2. useless/pathetic person; dead loss/failure.

mélanco [melɑ̃ko] *a P* melancholy/mournful/gloomy.

se mélanger [səmelɑ̃ʒe] *vpr P* to have sex*.

mélasse [melas] *nf F* être dans la mélasse, (*avoir des ennuis*) to be in a fix*/to be in a jam/to be up a gum-tree; (*être dans la misère*) to be penniless*/to be broke/to be cleaned out.

mêlé-cass [melekas] *nm F* vermouth *or* brandy and cassis (*blackcurrant liqueur*); voix de mêlé-cass, thick/hoarse/husky voice (*of a drunkard*).

mêler [mele] I *vtr F* vous avez bien mêlé les cartes! a nice mess you've made of it! II *vpr* **se mêler** *F* de quoi je me mêle! what's it got to do with you?/who asked you? mêlez-vous de vos oignons! mind your own business!

mêle-tout [mɛltu] *nm & f inv F* busybody/nosy parker.

méli-mélo [melimelo] *nm F* mish-mash/hotchpotch/muddle/jumble (of facts, etc); quel méli-mélo!, what a mess!/what a balls-up! (*pl* mélis-mélos)

mélo [melo] I *nm F* (= *mélodrame*) melodrama/blood-and-thunder drama/tear-jerker II *a F* (= *mélodramatique*) melodramatic/over-the-top.

melon [məlɔ̃] *nm P* 1. head*; avoir le melon déplumé, to be bald (as a coot) 2. brain; se casser le melon, to rack one's brains; (*s'inquiéter*) to worry 3. *Péj* Arab*/wog 4. freshman (at Saint-Cyr). (*Voir* **cosse**)

membre [mɑ̃br] *nm P* (= *membre viril*) penis*/member.

membré [mɑ̃bre] *a P* (*homme*) bien membré, well-hung/well-equipped; **mal membré,** with a small penis*.

même [mɛm] I *adv* 1. *F* mais tout de même! but dash it all!/but hang it all! 2. *F* ah! tout de même, vous voilà! so you've turned up at last! 3. *P* je l'avais prévenu, même que je lui avais écrit, I told him − I even wrote to him II *nm P* c'est du même/c'est pas du même, it's the same/it's not the same. (*Voir* **pareil** I)

mémé [meme] *nf F* 1. grandma/granny/nan(n)a 2. old woman/old dear; ça fait mémé cette robe! that dress makes you look like an old woman! (*Voir* **orties**)

mémère [memɛr] I *nf F* 1. grandma/granny/nan(n)a 2. mother/mummy; **un petit chien-chien à sa mémère,** mummy's little doggie-woggie 3. *Péj* une grosse mémère, a blowsy middle-aged *or* elderly woman II *a F* old-fashioned/dowdy (dress, etc). (*Voir* **orties**)

ménage [menaʒ] *nm F* 1. homosexual liaison (between two males or two females) 2. (unmarried) couple.

ménagère [menaʒɛr] *nf P* prostitute* who solicits in the morning (*dressed like a housewife doing her shopping*).

mendès [mɛ̃dɛs] *nm P* (*a*) milk (*b*) glass of milk.

mendiche [mɑ̃diʃ] *nm,* **mendigo(t)** [mɑ̃digo] *nm P* beggar/tramp*/down-and-out.

mendigoter [mɑ̃digɔte] *vtr & i P* to beg.

mener [m(ə)ne] *vtr F* ne pas en mener large, to be in a tight spot; to have one's heart in one's boots; il n'en menait pas large, he'd had the fear of God put into him. (*Voir* **barque; bateau** I 2; **belle** 2; **cirque** 3; **double** 2)

ménesse [menɛs] *nf P* 1. woman* 2. (*compagne*) wife*; mistress; girlfriend; lover.

mengave [mɑ̃gav] *nf P* begging/beggary. (*Voir* **mangave**)

Ménilmuche [menilmyʃ] *Prnm P* Ménilmontant (*in Paris*).

méninges [menɛ̃ʒ] *nfpl F* (*a*) se casser/creuser/se fatiguer/se masturber/se retourner/se torturer les méninges, to rack one's brains; il ne se fatigue/foule pas les méninges, he doesn't exactly overwork/overtax his brain; casse-toi les méninges!/fais (un peu) travailler tes méninges! use your loaf! (*b*) on a visité des musées pour se stimuler les méninges, we did a few museums/we got a bit of culture.

méningite [menɛ̃ʒit] *nf F* il ne s'est pas donné une méningite, he didn't exactly over-tax his brain.

menotte [mənɔt] *nf F* (child's) little hand.

mentale [mɑ̃tal] *nf,* **mentalité** [mɑ̃talite] *nf F* (*a*) avoir une bonne mentale, (*dans le milieu*) to stick by the rules/to follow accepted beliefs, etc (*b*) avoir une mauvaise/une sale mentale, (*dans le milieu*) not to stick by the rules/to reject accepted beliefs, etc (*c*) *Iron* belle mentalité!/jolie mentalité! what a nice mind you've got!/what a charming way of looking at things you have!

menteur [mɑ̃tœr] *nm P* newspaper/rag.

menteuse [mɑ̃tøz] *nf P* 1. tongue/clapper 2. newspapers/the press.

méquer [meke] *vtr P* to order (s.o.) about.

mer [mɛr] I *a P* (= *merveilleux*) marvellous/great/super. (*Voir* **mérovingien**) II *nf F* 1. ce n'est pas la mer à boire, it's no big deal 2. tenir la mer, (*voiture*) to hold the road well.

mercanti [mɛrkɑ̃ti] *nm F* profiteer/shark.

mercenaire [mɛrsənɛr] *nm F* travailler comme un mercenaire, to work* like a horse (for next to nothing); to work for peanuts.

mercuro [mɛrkyro] *nm F* mercurochrome (*RTM*).

merdaille [mɛrdɑj] *nf P* 1. dirty brats/ragamuffins 2. riff-raff; scum.

merdailleux [mɛrdɑjø] *nm,* **merdaillon** [mɛrdɑjɔ̃] *nm P* 1. dirty (little) brat/street arab/street urchin 2. dirty dog/dirty beast; skunk; stinker/shit.

merde [mɛrd] I *nf P* 1. excrement*/shit/*surt NAm* crap 2. une merde/de la merde, (*chose*) crap; (*personne*) a turd/a shit; c'est de la merde, (*ce qu'il vient de dire/d'acheter etc*) that's/it's (a load of) shit/crap 3. traiter qn comme une merde, to treat s.o. like dirt; laisser tomber qn comme une merde, to drop s.o. like a piece of shit 4. traîner qn dans la merde, to treat s.o. like dirt; to drag s.o. through the mire 5. il fait sa merde/il ne se prend pas pour une merde, he thinks he's really something/he thinks he's the cat's whiskers/the bee's knees; he thinks the sun shines out of his arse 6. il a de la merde dans les yeux, (*il a de mauvais yeux*) he can't see a thing; (*il n'a pas d'imagination*) he can't see further than his nose 7. avoir qn à la merde, to hate/to loathe s.o. 8. (*a*) être dans la merde (jusqu'au cou/jusqu'aux yeux), to be in a (hell of a) fix*/to be in the shit/to be in it up to one's bloody neck/to be up shit creek (without a paddle); on n'est pas dans la merde, tiens! we're really up the creek now!/we're in a bloody mess! (*b*) mettre/foutre qn dans la merde, to land/to drop s.o. in the shit 9. serious problem; **il lui est arrivé une merde**, he's got a problem/he's in the shit 10. c'est la merde, life is shitty; *NAm* this/it sucks; (*situation inextricable*) now the shit's really hit the fan/it's a bloody mess 11. merde pour ..., to hell with ...; merde pour le boulot! stuff the job! 12. foutre/semer la merde, to cause chaos and confusion 13. il y a de la merde au bout du bâton, it's a terrible state of affairs; it's a shitty set-up 14. de merde, shitty/crappy; une idée de merde, a shitty idea; une voiture de merde, a crappy car 15. avoir un œil qui dit merde à l'autre, to be cross-eyed/to (have a) squint 16. (*drogues*) hashish*/shit 17. (c'est-il) oui ou merde? (is it) yes or no? (*Voir* **crotte I 2**) 18. mouche à merde, (house)fly/bluebottle 19. ça sent la merde, it stinks (to high heaven). (*Voir* **foutre² I 10**; **rampe 3**) II *int P* (*a*) merde (alors)!/merde et contre-merde!/et puis merde!/merde de merde!/bon Dieu de merde! shit!/bugger it!/damn and blast it!/Christ! merde alors, je ne m'attendais pas à ça, oh shit, I didn't expect that (*b*) ah! merde, ce que c'est beau! shit! it's bloody beautiful!/Christ! it's really nice! (*c*) **je te dis merde**, (*bonne chance*) = break a leg! (*Voir* **bordel 4**)

merder [mɛrde] *vi P* to fall through/to come to nothing/to fizzle out; j'ai complètement merdé à l'examen, I completely screwed up the exam/I completely ballsed the exam.

merdeux, -euse [mɛrdø, -øz] *P* I *a* (*a*) dirtied/soiled (*b*) filthy/nasty/shitty (situation, etc); elle se sent merdeuse, she feels shitty II *n* (*personne*) 1. dirty swine; bugger; shit; *f* dirty bitch; un petit merdeux, a little squirt/a little shit; une petite merdeuse, a stuck-up little bitch 2. child*/brat/sprog III *nm* faire le merdeux, to have a very high opinion of oneself; il fait le merdeux, he thinks the sun shines out of his arse. (*Voir* **bâton 3**)

merdier [mɛrdje] *nm P* (*a*) je suis dans un sacré merdier, I'm in a hell of a fix/I'm really in the shit (*b*) on n'est pas encore sorti de ce merdier, we're not out of the shit yet (*c*) foutre le merdier quelque part, to balls sth up (*d*) qu'est-ce que c'est que ce merdier? what the hell is this bloody mess? (*Voir* **foutre² I 10**)

merdique [mɛrdik] *a P* 1. very difficult; ce problème de math est complètement merdique, this maths/*NAm* math problem is

bloody difficult/a real bastard/a real sod 2. of poor quality; not up to the mark; c'est plutôt merdique comme système, it's a really shitty/crappy system; ce film est complètement merdique, this film is trash/shit/really crappy.

merdouille [mɛrduj] *nf P* 1. (*saleté*) dirt/shit 2. serious/unfortunate situation; être dans la merdouille, to be in the shit 3. worthless object/crap.

merdouiller [mɛrduje], **merdoyer** [mɛrdwaje] *vi P* to flounder/to be all at sea/to get all tied up; to get into a bloody mess; to make a balls-up/a cock-up.

mère [mɛr] *nf* (*a*) *F* (*quelquefois Péj*) la mère Thomas, old Mrs Thomas/old mother Thomas (*b*) *P* et dites donc, la petite mère! well, missis!/well, ducks!/well, old girl!

mère-maca [mɛrmaka] *nf P* (= *mère maquerelle*) madam(e) of a brothel. (*pl* mères-maca)

mère-pipi [mɛrpipi] *nf P* (female) lavatory attendant. (*pl* mères-pipi)

mère-poule [mɛrpul] *nf F* overindulgent mother/mother hen.

mérinos [merinos] *nm P* laisser pisser le mérinos, to bide one's time/to wait till the moment is ripe/to let things take their (normal) course.

merlan [mɛrlɑ̃] *nm* 1. *P* hairdresser/barber 2. *P* pimp*/ponce 3. *P* faux merlan, petty criminal/small-time operator/small-timer 4. *F* faire des yeux de merlan frit, (*lever les yeux au ciel*) to roll one's eyes heavenwards/to show the whites of one's eyes; to look like a dying duck in a thunderstorm; faire des yeux de merlan frit à qn, to look gooey-eyed at s.o.

merle [mɛrl] *nm F* 1. jaser comme un merle, (*personne*) to chatter like a magpie/to go rabbiting on 2. (*a*) un fin merle, a cunning person/a crafty specimen (*b*) un vilain merle/*Iron* un beau merle, a nasty piece of work; an awkward customer; siffle, beau merle! just wait till I get you!/I'll get you in the end!

merlette [mɛrlɛt] *nf P* prostitute* soliciting on behalf of another.

merluche [mɛrlyʃ] *nf P Péj* 1. woman* 2. wife*.

mérovingien [merɔvɛ̃ʒjɛ̃] *a P* = **mer I**.

mesquine [mɛskin] *a P* (*personne*) small/frail; il est mesquine, he's puny.

messe [mɛs] *nf F* 1. dire/tenir/faire des messes basses, to carry on a conversation in an undertone; je n'aime pas les messes basses, I don't like people whispering to each other 2. **je ne répète pas la messe pour les sourds/je n'aime pas chanter la messe pour les sourds,** I don't like having to say the same thing twice.

messieurs-dames [mesjødam] *nmpl F* bonjour, messieurs-dames, good morning sir, madam; morning all! **entrez messieurs-dames,** come in, sir, madam; come in, ladies and gentlemen.

métallo [metalo] *nm F* metallurgist; metal-worker; steel-worker.

météo [meteo] *F* **I** *nm & f* meteorologist/weather man; *TV* **Monsieur météo,** the weather man **II** *nf* (*a*) weather forecast/report; **la météo est bonne,** the weather forecast is good (*b*) weather centre; Met office (*c*) bad weather; **la météo a fait que le match a été annulé,** the match was cancelled because of the (bad) weather.

métèque [metɛk] *nm F Péj* foreigner; dago; wog; wop.

métier [metje] *nm F* 1. **il est du métier,** he's in the same line (of business)/he's in the trade; **il a du métier,** he knows what he's doing/he knows all the tricks of the trade/he knows all the angles 2. **vous faites là un vilain métier!** that's a dirty game you're playing 3. **faites votre métier!** mind your own business!/get on with your own job! 4. **quel métier!** what a life!

mètre [mɛtr] *nm F* **piquer un cent mètres,** to run away*/to beat it/to clear off.

métral [metral] *nm P* underground/*NAm* subway/metro.

métro [metro] *nm* 1. *P* one gramme of cocaine* 2. *P* **avoir un métro de retard,** to be slow to understand things/to be slow on the uptake 3. *F* (*locution populaire*) **métro, boulot, dodo,** = work, rest and no play; the daily grind/the daily routine.

mettable [mɛtabl] *a P* desirable/sexy; screwable; **une femme mettable,** an easy lay; **elle est mettable,** she's a bit of all right.

metteur, -euse [mɛtœr, -øz] *n F* **metteur en l'air,** killer/assassin; murderer/murderess.

mettre [mɛtr] **I** *vtr* 1. *P* (*a*) **le/la mettre à qn, mettre qn,** to have sex* with s.o.; **se faire/se laisser mettre,** to get laid; **va te faire mettre!** (*insulte*) get stuffed! (*b*) **mettre une fille en perce,** to deflower a girl/to pick a girl's cherry 2. *F* (*boxe*) **les mettre avec qn,** to have a bout with s.o. 3. *P* **les mettre,** to make oneself scarce/to do a bunk. (*Voir* **adja; air I 8;**

bâton I 6; bocal 5; boîte 3, 5; bout 6; caisse I 14; canne 2; coup 9, 13; dedans 1; doigt 6, 8; paquet 6; veilleuse 2, 3, 4; voile 2) **II** *vpr* **se mettre** *F* 1. to have sex*/to make love 2. **se mettre qch/s'en mettre jusque-là,** to eat* heartily/to tuck in/to have a blow-out/to make a pig of oneself. (*Voir* **lampe 1**) 3. **se mettre avec qn/se mettre ensemble,** to cohabit/to shack up with s.o.; **ils se sont mis ensemble,** they're living together 4. **il se met bien,** he does himself well/he does himself proud 5. **se mettre qch quelque part,** not to give a damn about sth. (*Voir* **bain 1** (*b*); **bout 9; ceinture 1; cul 1** (*b*); **s'ôter; table 2**)

meubles [mœbl] *nmpl F* **faire partie des meubles,** (*personne*) to be part of the furniture/to be a permanent fixture. (*Voir* **cirer 2**)

meuf [mœf] *nf P* (= *verlan de* **femme**) girl*/woman*; bird/chick/*NAm* broad; **sa meuf,** his old lady.

meule [mœl] *nf P* 1. (motor)bike 2. *pl* **meules,** buttocks*/buns/*NAm* fanny 3. *pl* teeth* 4. **mouiller la meule,** to have one's first drink of the day.

meumeu [mømø] **I** *a P* excellent*/first-rate/super **II** *nf F* (*langage enfantin*) cow/moo-cow.

meunier [mønje] *nm F* cockroach.

meurt-de-faim [mœrdəfɛ̃] *nm inv,* **meurt-la-faim** [mœrlafɛ̃] *nm inv F* down-and-out; **recevoir un salaire de meurt-de-faim,** to get paid starvation wages/to be on the breadline.

meurt-de-soif [mœrdəswaf] *nm inv F* heavy drinker/alky/(real) boozer/thirsty mortal.

mézig [mezig], **mézigo** [mezigo], **mézigue** [mezig] *pron P* I/me/myself/yours truly. (*Voir* **tézig(ue), cézig(ue)/sezig(ue), no(s)zig(ue)s, vo(s)zig(ue)s, euzig(ue)s/leur(s)zig(ue)s**)

miam-miam! [mjamjam] *int F* yum-yum!

miauler [mjole] *vi F* (*personne*) to grouse/to whine/to bellyache.

miché [miʃe] *nm P* (*a*) prostitute's client*/trick/meal-ticket/john; **faire un miché,** to solicit a client/to turn a trick (*b*) homosexual prostitute's client/trick (*c*) passenger/fare (*in a taxi*); customer (*in a bar, etc*).

miches [miʃ] *nfpl P* 1. (*a*) buttocks*/buns/bum/*NAm* butt/*NAm* fanny; **pincer les miches à une femme,** to pinch a woman's bottom/to goose a woman (*b*) **poser ses miches**, to sit down (on one's backside)/to plonk one's arse down somewhere; **serrer les miches**, to be on one's guard/to be wary; **avoir les miches à zéro/avoir les miches à glagla/avoir les miches qui font bravo**, to be dead scared/to be in a blue funk/to be scared shitless; to have cold feet; **avoir chaud aux miches**, to have a nasty fright; **il est parti en serrant les miches**, he went off with his tail between his legs; **on se caille les miches**, it's freezing/it's brass monkey weather (*c*) **se grouiller les miches**, to hurry up*/to get a move on/to stir one's stumps (*d*) **occupe-toi de tes miches!** mind your own bloody business! **2.** (*a*) breasts*/boobs/Bristols (*b*) **gagner sa croûte avec ses miches**, (*femme*) to prostitute oneself/to earn a living on one's back.

michet [miʃɛ] *nm*, **micheton** [miʃtɔ̃] *nm* *P* = **miché**.

michetonner [miʃtɔne] *vi P* **1.** to pay s.o. to have sex*; to pay a prostitute*/a homosexual* to have sex* **2.** (*femme*) to prostitute oneself (on a casual basis).

michetonneuse [miʃtɔnøz] *nf P* (*a*) (part-time) prostitute* (*b*) kept woman.

michette [miʃɛt] *nf P* (*rare*) lesbian prostitute.

michto [miʃto] *a P* **c'est michto**, it's fine.

mickey [miki] *nm P* **1.** (*personne médiocre*) nonentity/dead loss **2.** adulterated drink/Mickey Finn **3.** **petit Mickey**, (any) cartoon character; **faire des petits Mickeys**, to draw strip cartoons/comic strips. (*Voir* **balançoire 3**)

micmac [mikmak] *nm F* **1.** (= **manigance**) intrigue/scheming/funny business; (*résultat*) put-up job **2.** jumble/mess.

micro [mikro] *nm* **1.** *F* microphone/mike; **micro caché/clandestin**, bug; **parler au micro**, to talk into the mike **2.** *P* mouth*; **ferme ton micro!** shut up!*

microbe [mikrɔb] *nm F* **1.** **attraper un microbe**, to catch a bug; **garde tes microbes!** keep your germs to yourself! **2.** undersized*/person/little runt; **écrase-toi, microbe!** push off, you little squirt!

midi [midi] *nm* **1.** *F* **ne pas voir clair en plein midi**, to be blind to the obvious/the facts **2.** *F* **chercher midi à quatorze heures**, to look for difficulties where there are none; to complicate the issue/things **3.** *F* **c'est midi (sonné)!** it's (all) finished!/that's it!/it's all up! not likely!*/no fear! **4.** *V* **marquer midi**,

to have an erection*/to get it up. (*Voir* **étoile 2**)

mie [mi] *I nf P* **1.** **une mie de pain**, someone with no go (in him/her) **2.** **à la mie de pain**, worthless*/no good/not worth a damn **3.** (*a*) **mie de pain à bec**, louse/cootie (*b*) **mie de pain à ressorts/mécanique**, flea *II nf A F* (*fille, femme*) loved one/lady love.

miel [mjɛl] *I nm F* **c'est du (pur) miel**, it's (dead) easy*/it's a piece of cake. (*Voir* **cage 6**; **cliquette 1**) *II int P* **miel!** (*Euph pour* **merde**) damn!/blast!/damn and blast!/sugar!

miette [mjɛt] *nf F* **1.** small quantity; **ne pas en perdre une miette**, to see everything/to let nothing escape one **2.** **et des miettes**, and the rest/and a bit more besides.

mi-figue [mifig] *a phr F* **mi-figue, mi-raisin**, neither one thing nor the other; half of one thing and half another.

mignard, -arde [miɲar, -ard] *I a F* small/frail/puny *II n* **1.** *F* baby **2.** *F* small child*/kid **3.** *P* young homosexual*.

mignonnettes [miɲɔnɛt] *nfpl P* photographs sold in the streets (*of Paris, etc*) purporting to be 'dirty postcards', but which are usually inoffensive.

mijoter [miʒote] *I vtr F* **mijoter un complot**, to hatch a plot; **qu'est-ce que tu mijotes dans ton coin?** what are you hatching up over there?/what are you cooking up? **il mijote des conneries**, he's up to no good *II vpr* **se mijoter** *F* **qu'est-ce qui se mijote?** what's up?/what's going on? **je sais qu'il se mijote quelque chose**, I know there's something in the wind.

milieu [miljø] *nm F* **le milieu/les gens du milieu**, the (French) underworld; gangland.

mille [mil] *nm inv F* **1.** **il a des mille et des cents**, he's got pots of money* **2.** **mettre/taper dans le mille**, (*avoir du succès*) to be successful/to come out on top; (*deviner juste*) to be spot on/to score a bull's-eye/to hit the nail on the head/to get it in one. (*Voir* **donner 2**)

millefeuille [milfœj] *nm* **1.** *P* **c'est du millefeuille**, it's dead easy*/it's a cinch **2.** *V* female genitals*/crumpet/fur pie **3.** *P* wad of ten 100-franc notes.

mille-pattes [milpat] *nf P* (*CB*) lorry/truck/HGV/juggernaut/rig.

milliasse [miljas] *nf Vieilli F* millions and millions; enormous quantity*; huge sum (of money).

millimètre [milimɛtr] *nm F* 1. **faire du millimètre**, (*être avare*) to be close-fisted/stingy/tight-fisted 2. **faire qch au millimètre**, to do sth with great precision.

milord [milɔr] *nm Vieilli F* immensely rich* man.

mimi [mimi] I *a F* sweet/darling/precious/cute; **c'est mimi**, it's sweet/cute II *nm* 1. *F* (*a*) **mon petit mimi**, my darling*/my pet. (*Voir* **mimine 1**) (*b*) (*baiser*) kiss; **fais mimi à ta maman**, give mummy a kiss (and a cuddle) 2. *F* pussy(cat*) 3. *V* female genitals*/pussy/*Br* fanny; **faire mimi**, to perform cunnilingus*/to eat hairpie.

mimine [mimin] *nf* 1. *F* **ma petite mimine**, my darling*/my pet. (*Voir* **mimi II 1** (*a*)) 2. *pl P* **mimines**, hands*.

minable [minabl] *F* I *a* (*personne*) shabby/seedy-looking/tatty; (*meubles, voiture, etc*) shabby(-looking)/tatty/grotty/crummy; **un salaire minable**, a crummy wage/a pittance/peanuts II *n* (*personne*) hopeless/useless individual; dead loss; **un tas de minables**, a pathetic bunch/a useless lot.

mince! [mɛ̃s] *int F* (*a*) (ah!) **mince alors!** (*surprise*) well, I'll be blowed!/just fancy that!/well I never!/good Lord!/crikey!/you don't say! (*irritation*) drat!/blast!/damn! (*b*) **mince de rigolade!** what a lark!/what a giggle! **mince de déception!** what a shame!

mine [min] *nf F* 1. **faire mine de rien**, to look as if nothing had happened; **mine de rien**, **il t'a tiré les vers du nez!** he pumped you so casually, you didn't know he was doing it! **mine de rien, il est pas si con que ça!** you wouldn't think it, but he's not as dumb as he looks! **mine de rien et bouche cousue!** mum's the word! 2. *Iron* **nous avons bonne mine maintenant!** *don't* we look foolish! **t'as bonne mine!** get away with you!/go on!/I'm not impressed! **j'ai bonne mine maintenant que je lui ai dit le contraire**, I'm going to look good, now that I've told him something (quite) different.

minet, -ette [minɛ, -ɛt] *n* 1. *F* **mon minet/ma minette**, my darling*/my pet 2. *F* fashionable young man *or* young woman/trendy; **t'as vu la minette là-bas!** look at her over there! what a cracker! 3. *F* pussy(cat*)/kitty 4. *V* female genitals*/pussy; **faire minette**, to perform cunnilingus*/to pearl-dive.

mini [mini] *F* I *a inv* mini; **la mode mini est de retour**, the mini is back (in fashion) II *nf* 1. mini(skirt)/mini(dress) 2. *Aut* mini (*RTM*)

III *adv* **s'habiller mini**, to wear a miniskirt/minidress.

minot [mino] *nm* 1. *F* child*/kid/brat/nipper 2. *P* young homosexual*.

minou [minu] *nm* 1. *F* pussy(cat*)/mog(gy) 2. *F* **mon minou**, my darling/my pet 3. *V* female genitals*/pussy.

minouche [minuʃ] *nf F* darling/pet.

minouse [minuz] *nf P* (pair of) (woman's) pant(ie)s/briefs/knickers.

minus [minys] *nm inv*, **minus habens** [minysabɛ̃s] *nm inv F* 1. fool*/clot/twit/moron; **c'est un minus**, he's not very bright/he's moronic 2. freshman/fresher; *quelquefois* = **bizut(h)**.

minute [minyt] I *nf P* **se poser là cinq minutes**, (*personne*) to be hefty/on the beefy side II *int F* **minute** (**papillon**)! just a minute!/hold on!/hang on!/half a mo!/not so fast!/hold your horses!

mioche [mjɔʃ] *nm & f F* 1. small child*/mite/kiddy; **bande de mioches**, band of little urchins/of tiny tots 2. **faire descendre le mioche**, to bring about an abortion.

miquette [mikɛt] *nf* woman*; girl*/chick.

mirante [mirɑ̃t] *nf P* mirror.

miraud [miro] *a P* = **miro**.

mirer [mire] *vtr P* to look (closely) at; **mire un peu celle-là!** get a load of/take a dekko at her!

mirettes [mirɛt] *nfpl P* eyes*/peepers; **gicler des mirettes**, to cry; **en mettre plein les mirettes à qn**, to impress s.o./to dazzle s.o.

mirifique [mirifik] *a F* excellent*/marvellous/terrific/fabulous.

mirifiquement [mirifikmɑ̃] *adv F* excellently/marvellously/terrifically/fabulously.

mirliton [mirlitɔ̃] *nm V* **souffler dans le mirliton** (**à qn**), to fellate* (s.o.)/to give (s.o.) a blow-job/to give (s.o.) head.

miro [miro] *a P* myopic/short-sighted; **il est complètement miro**, he's as blind as a bat.

mirobolant [mirɔbɔlɑ̃] *a F* stupendous/astounding/splendiferous/staggering news (etc).

mironton [mirɔ̃tɔ̃] *nm F* odd character/strange individual; **un drôle de mironton**, an odd bod/a weirdo. (*Voir* **dévisser I 4**)

mise [miz] *nf F* **mise en l'air**, (violent) action against s.o. who will not give in to blackmail; (*détroussage*) robbing/mugging (of s.o.); (*hold-up*) hold-up; (*cambriolage*) burglary. (*Voir* **air I 8**)

miser [mize] *vtr* 1. *F* on ne peut pas miser là-dessus, you can't count on it/bank on it. (*Voir* **tableau 3** (*a*)) 2. *V* miser qn, to have sex* with s.o./to lay s.o./to ball s.o. 3. *V* va te faire miser! get stuffed!

misère [mizɛr] *nf F* 1. cent francs? une misère! a hundred francs? a mere trifle! 2. quelle misère! what a (rotten) life! 3. ça vous tombe dessus comme la misère sur le pauvre monde, it happens to you before you know what's going on/it comes like a bolt from the blue 4. faire des misères à qn, to tease s.o. unmercifully/to put s.o. through it. (*Voir* **collier 1** (*b*))

miso [mizo] *F* I *a* misogynous II *nm* misogynist/woman hater.

mistigri [mistigri] *nm* 1. *F* (pussy)cat/puss/ moggy 2. *V* female genitals*/pussy.

miston [mistɔ̃] *nm P* 1. boy/kid; (*individu*) bloke/guy 2. prostitute's client/trick/john/ meal-ticket.

mistonne [mistɔn] *nf P* 1. woman*; girl* 2. mistress/lover.

mistouflard [mistuflar] *nm P* pauper/ down-and-out.

mistoufle [mistufl] *nf* 1. *P* poverty; être dans la mistoufle, to be down-and-out/to be very hard up 2. *F* faire des mistoufles à qn, to pester/to annoy*/to tease s.o.

mistron [mistrɔ̃] *nm P* (*cartes*) (game of) *trente et un*.

mitaines [mitɛn] *nfpl F* 1. boxing gloves; croiser les mitaines, to box; to have a punch-up 2. y aller avec des mitaines, to go at it with kid gloves 3. dire qch sans mitaines, to say sth bluntly; to blurt sth out; je n'ai pas pris de mitaines pour lui dire, I didn't mince my words with him.

mita-mita [mitamita] *nm P* compromise; even split; faire un mita-mita, to split (sth) down the middle/to split (sth) fifty-fifty.

mitan [mitɑ̃] *nm P* 1. middle/centre; au mitan de la place, in the centre of the square; en plein mitan, smack in the middle/a bull's-eye 2. = **milieu**.

mitard [mitar] *nm P* 1. disciplinary cell/ punishment cell (in prison)/cooler 2. police cell.

mitarder [mitarde] *vtr F* se faire mitarder, to be put in solitary confinement/to get solitary/to get put in the cooler.

mite [mit] I *nf P* j'ai la mite à l'œil/aux yeux, my eyes are (all) gummed up II *nm P* = **mitard**. (*Voir* **éponge 1**)

miter [mite] *vi P* to cry/to grizzle/to snivel.

miteusement [mitøzmɑ̃] *adv F* shabbily (dressed).

miteux, -euse [mitø, -øz] *F* I *a* shabby/ seedy(-looking)/down-at-heel; tatty/crummy/ grotty (furniture, etc); ragged/tattered (clothes) II *n* (*a*) shabby person/ragbag (*b*) *Péj* child*/kid/brat (*c*) person/*esp* woman easily given to tears/cry-baby.

mitonnard [mitonar] *nm P* = **mitan 1, 2**.

mitraille [mitraj] *nf F* small change/small coins.

mitrailler [mitraje] *vtr F* les photographes mitraillent les délégués, the photographers are clicking away at the delegates.

mitrailleuse [mitrajøz] *nf P* 1. chatterbox*/babbling brook 2. automatic stamping machine.

mixte [mikst] *nm F* mixed sandwich/cheese and ham sandwich.

mob [mɔb] *nf F* (*abrév = Mobylette* (*RTM*)) light motorcycle; moped/put-put.

mobilard [mɔbilar] *nm F* (= *gendarme mobile*) policeman belonging to a special mobile squad.

mochard [mɔʃar] *a P* = **moche**.

moche [mɔʃ] *a F* (*a*) ugly; moche comme un pou/moche à faire peur/moche à pleurer, as ugly as sin; ce qu'il est moche! he's really ugly!/he's got a face like the back of a bus! (*b*) rotten/lousy; la pluie pendant les vacances, c'est moche, it's rotten/foul if it rains when you're on holiday; c'est moche ce qu'il a fait, that's a lousy/nasty trick he played; qu'en dis-tu? − c'est moche! what do you think of it? − it's lousy!/it stinks!/*NAm* it sucks! être moche avec qn, to treat s.o. badly/to be rotten to s.o. (*c*) poor/shoddy (work); c'est moche, le travail que t'as fait, it's pretty abysmal/awful, the work you did.

mochement [mɔʃmɑ̃] *adv F* (*a*) in an ugly way (*b*) in a rotten/lousy way (*c*) poorly/ shoddily.

mocheté [mɔʃte] *nf F* (*a*) ugly woman/ fright/hag/(old) bag; c'est une mocheté, celle-là! she's as ugly as sin/she's got a face like the back of a bus! (*b*) ce costume! a-t-on jamais vu une mocheté pareille? have you ever seen such a lousy suit?

mochetingue [mɔʃtɛ̃g], **mocheton, -onne** [mɔʃtɔ̃, -ɔn] *a P* = **moche**.

moco, Moco [mɔko] *nm & f P* (*méridional*) southerner; native/inhabitant of Toulon *or* of Provence.

la Mocobo [lamɔkɔbo] *Prnf F* = the place Maubert; (*quartier*) the Maubert district (*in Paris*). (*Voir* **la Maub'**)

les mœurs [lemœrs] *nfpl P* (= *la brigade (de la police) des mœurs*) the vice squad. (*Voir* **mondaine**)

mohamed [mohamɛd] *nm P* 1. *Péj* Arab*/ wog 2. sun.

mohican [mɔikɑ̃] *nm V* penis*; scalper le mohican, to perform fellatio*/to give a blow-job.

moinaille [mwanɑj] *nf F Péj* monks (*in general*).

moineau, *pl* **-eaux** [mwano] *nm F* (*a*) *Vieilli* un drôle de moineau, a strange fellow/a funny old bird; un sale moineau/un vilain moineau, a bad lot/a nasty piece of work (*b*) c'est un épouvantail à moineaux, he's/she's a real scarecrow; he's/she's enough to frighten off the birds (*c*) avoir une cervelle de moineau, to be featherbrained/empty-headed. (*Voir* **perchoir**)

moins [mwɛ̃] *F* **I** *adv phr* (*a*) tu n'es pas malade, au moins? I hope you're not ill/ you're not ill, are you?/I can take it you're not ill? (*b*) c'est bien le moins! it's the least he/ she can do! **II** *prep* il était moins une/moins deux/moins cinq, it was a near thing/a close shave/a close call/a narrow escape. (*Voir* **deux 5**)

mois [mwa] *nm F* 1. treizième mois, month's salary paid as a bonus; Christmas bonus 2. oublier les mois de nourrice, to pretend to be younger than one really is/to be mutton dressed up as lamb 3. avoir ses mois, to have a period*; elle a ses mois, it's her time of the month. (*Voir* **trente-six II 2**)

moisi [mwazi] *a F* pas moisi, strong/robust.

moisir [mwazir] *vi F* (*a*) to hang about/to be kept waiting (indefinitely); on ne va pas moisir ici, let's not hang about here/let's go (*b*) moisir en prison, to rot in prison; on moisit à travailler dans ce bureau, you stagnate/vegetate working in this office.

moite [mwat] *a P* 1. les avoir moites, to be afraid*/to be in a blue funk/to wet oneself/to be shitting oneself 2. être moite, to say nothing/to keep quiet/to stay mum.

moite-moite [mwatmwat] *adv* (= *moitié-moitié*) faire moite-moite, to split (sth) down the middle/to split (sth) fifty-fifty.

moiter [mwatɛ] *vi P* to be afraid*/to wet oneself/to be pissing oneself. (*Voir* **moite 1**)

moitié [mwatje] *nf F* 1. ma (chère/douce) moitié, my wife*/my husband*/my better half 2. c'est pas la moitié d'un con, (*il est très intelligent*) he's not stupid/he's no dumb bum.

mol(l)ard [mɔlar] *nm P* gob (of spit *or* phlegm).

mol(l)arder [mɔlarde] *vi P* to spit/to gob/to hawk up phlegm.

mollasse [mɔlas], **mollasson, -onne** [mɔlasɔ̃, -ɔn] *F* **I** *a & n* soft/flabby/spineless/ gutless (person); (*paresseux*) slow/lazy (person) **II** *n* un(e) grand(e) mollasse/un(e) grand(e) mollasson(ne), a great lump (of a man/woman).

molleton [mɔltɔ̃] *nm P* calf (of leg).

molletonné [mɔltɔne] *a F* (*personne*) fearful/nervous; (*inhibé*) inhibited.

mollo(-mollo) [mɔlo(mɔlo)] *adv P* y aller mollo(-mollo), to act cautiously; vas-y mollo(-mollo)! (take it) easy!/easy does it!/ easy now!

mollusque [mɔlysk] *nm F* c'est un mollusque, he's got no go in him; he's got no backbone/he's a drip/he's a bit wet; avancer comme un mollusque, to be very slow/ sluggish.

molosse [mɔlɔs] *P* **I** *a* huge/colossal (man) **II** *nm* huge man; colossus/giant.

moltegomme [mɔltəgɔm] *nm*, **moltogomme** [mɔltɔgɔm] *nm P* = **molleton**.

momaque [mɔmak] *nf P* little girl.

môme [mom] **I** *nm & f F* child*/kid/brat; young boy/young girl*/youngster; il est encore tout môme, he's still only a kid **II** *nm P* 1. faire couler/faire descendre un môme, to bring about an abortion; pisser un môme, to give birth (to a baby) 2. taper un môme, to kill* a child **III** *nf P* 1. woman*; une jolie môme, a nice bit of stuff/a nice piece of skirt/ a nice bit of crumpet 2. (*a*) (*petite amie*) girl-friend (*b*) (gangster's, pimp's) moll.

momi [mɔmi] *nf P* = **mominette**.

momichon [mɔmiʃɔ̃] *nm*, **momignard, -arde** [mɔmiɲar, -ard], **mômignard, -arde** [momiɲar, -ard], **mominard, -arde** [mɔminar, -ard], **môminard, -arde** [mominar, -ard] *nf P* child*/kid/brat/ nipper.

mominette [mɔminɛt] *nf P* small glass of pastis.

monacos [mɔnako] *nmpl A P* money*/ dough.

la mondaine [lamɔ̃dɛn] *nf* P *(police)* the vice squad. (*Voir* **les mœurs**)

monde [mɔ̃d] *nm* 1. *F* (*a*) en faire (tout) un monde, to make a lot of fuss/to make a song and dance about it (*b*) se faire un monde de qch, to make a mountain out of a molehill 2. *F* se croire le centre du monde, to think no small beer of oneself/to think one is the cat's whiskers 3. *F* ça (alors), c'est un monde! well, that's the limit*/the last straw! 4. *F* (*a*) se moquer/se ficher/P se foutre du monde, not to give a damn about anyone/anything; elle se fout du monde, she's got a bloody/damn cheek/nerve! ils se foutent du monde, they don't give a toss; c'est se moquer du monde! it's the height of impertinence! (*b*) vous vous moquez du monde! you're joking! 5. *F* c'est le monde à l'envers! what *is* the world coming to! it's a mad/crazy world (we live in)! (*Voir* **balcon**)

moniche [mɔniʃ] *nf* V female genitals*.

monnaie [mɔnɛ] *nf* F 1. commencer à rendre la monnaie, to begin to grow old; rendre la monnaie, to be old and ugly 2. payer qn en monnaie de singe, to fob s.o. off/to let s.o. whistle for his money 3. par ici, la monnaie! give me the money!/come on, cough up!/give!

monseigneur [mɔ̃sɛnœr] *nm* F (burglar's) jemmy/*NAm* jimmy.

monsieur [məsjø] *nm* F 1. faire le (gros) monsieur, to act big 2. un joli/un vilain monsieur, a bad lot/a nasty piece of work.

monstre [mɔ̃str] *F* I *a* huge/enormous/ mammoth; whopping/whacking (great); travail monstre, mammoth task; un sandwich monstre, a huge sandwich/a whopper II *nm* 1. te voilà, petit monstre! there you are, you little devil/monster! 2. quel monstre, cette bagnole! what a powerful beast that car is!

mont [mɔ̃] *nm* F promettre monts et merveilles à qn, to promise s.o. the earth.

montage [mɔ̃taʒ] *nm* P frame-up/put-up job/fit-up; (police) trap.

montagne [mɔ̃taɲ] *nf* F se faire une montagne de qch, to make a mountain out of a molehill; c'est la montagne qui accouche d'une souris, what a lot of fuss about nothing!

montant [mɔ̃tɑ̃] *a* P bar montant, cafe/bar used for prostitution*/frequented by prostitutes*; serveuse montante, barmaid who also works as a prostitute* in a room above the bar.

monte [mɔ̃t] *nf* P *(prostituées)* time spent with a client/trick.

monté [mɔ̃te] *a* 1. *F* il était monté, he was (all) worked up; his blood was up; il est monté contre moi, he's furious with me; he's got a down on me. (*Voir* **tête 14**) 2. *F* slightly drunk*/tipsy/merry 3. *P* être bien monté/monté comme un âne/monté comme un bourricot/comme un taureau, (*homme*) to be well developed/well equipped/well hung/hung like a bull; (*très viril*) to be highly sexed/to have plenty of sexual drive. (*Voir* **collet 1; coup 14**)

montée [mɔ̃te] *nf* P 1. (*drogues*) high 2. = **monte.**

monte-en-l'air [mɔ̃tɑ̃lɛr] *nm inv* F cat burglar.

monter [mɔ̃te] I *vi* F 1. faire monter qn, (*mettre qn en colère*) to take a rise out of s.o./to make s.o.'s blood boil/to get s.o. all worked up 2. (*prostituée*) to have sex* with a client/to turn a trick; tu montes, chéri? do you want a good time, love? (*Voir* **cheval 10** (*b*); **échelle 1; soupe 2**) II *vtr* 1. *F* monter qn contre qn, to set s.o. against s.o./to egg s.o. on against s.o. 2. *P* monter un client, (*prostituée*) to have sex* with a client/to turn a trick 3. *P* to have sex* with (s.o.)/to ride (s.o.). (*Voir* **baraque 4; bateau I 1; bourrichon; cou 1; coup 14; tête 14**) III *vpr* se monter *F* to flare up/to fly off the handle/to lose one's cool; elle se monte pour un rien, she gets all worked up over nothing; elle s'est montée contre lui, she's got it in for him.

montgolfière [mɔ̃gɔlfjɛr] *nf* 1. *P* nymphomaniac/nympho 2. *pl V* testicles* 3. *pl V* breasts*/boobs.

Montparno [mɔ̃parno] *Prnm F* (*quartier*) the Montparnasse quarter; (*boulevard*) the boulevard du Montparnasse (*in Paris*).

Montretout [mɔ̃trətu] *Prnm F* aller à Montretout, to have a medical (examination) (*esp for a prostitute*).

montrouze [mɔ̃truz] *nf Vieilli P* watch/ ticker.

Mont Valo [mɔ̃valo] *Prnm F* Mont Valérien (*near Paris*).

moral [mɔral] *nm F* avoir le moral, to be in high spirits/to feel on top of the world; *Iron* eh ben, t'as le moral! well, you're optimistic! you think it's all fine and dandy! avoir le moral à zéro, to be right down in the dumps; to be really depressed*/low/down; remonter le moral à qn, to cheer s.o. up/to buck s.o. up.

morbac, morbaque [mɔrbak] *nm P*

1. crab (louse)/pubic louse 2. child*/brat.

morceau, -eaux [mɔrso] *nm F* 1. manger/casser un morceau, to have a bite (to eat)/to have a snack. (*Voir* **pouce 2**) 2. **bouffer**/casser/cracher/lâcher/manger le morceau, to confess*/to come clean; (*dénoncer*) to turn informer*/to grass. (*Voir* **bouffer I 3**) 3. casser le morceau à qn, to give s.o. a piece of one's mind/to let s.o. have it straight 4. emporter/enlever le morceau, to succeed; to win out; to get one's own way 5. gober le morceau, to swallow the bait/to rise to the bait/to fall for it (hook, line and sinker) 6. **un beau/un joli morceau**, (*fille, femme*) a nice bit of stuff/a bit of all right.

morcif [mɔrsif] *nm P* (= **morceau**) piece/morsel.

mordante [mɔrdɑ̃t] *nf P* (*lime*) file.

mordicus [mɔrdikys] *adv F* stubbornly/tooth and nail; **défendre mordicus son opinion**, to stick to one's guns.

mordre [mɔrdr] *vtr & i* 1. *F* quel chien l'a mordu? what's biting him?/what's bugging him?/what's got into him? 2. *P* to understand; **tu mords?** (do you) get it? **il ne mord pas à l'espagnol**, he can't get on with Spanish/he hasn't taken to Spanish; **je ne peux pas y mordre**, it's beyond me 3. *F* **mords-le!** (*formule d'encouragement à deux personnes qui se bagarrent*) come on! go for the jugular! 4. *F* **ça ne mord pas**, (*ce n'est pas dangereux*) (don't worry,) it won't bite (you) 5. *F* **c'est à se les mordre**, (*très drôle*) it's very funny*!/it's a scream! (*ridicule*) it's laughable/it's crazy 6. *P* **mordre à qch**, to be convinced by sth; **je ne mord pas à ces histoires**, I don't believe any of these stories 7. *P* to look at* (s.o./sth) closely; **mords(-moi-ça)!/mordez(-moi-ça)!** just look at that!/take a dekko at that!/get a load of that! 8. *adv phr P* ... **à la mords-moi le doigt/le chose/le nœud/l'œil**, (*de façon ridicule*) ridiculously; (*de façon risquée*) in a risky/dodgy way; hit-or-miss; **un pianiste à la mord-moi le doigt**, an amateur pianist. (*Voir* **doigt 7; pouce 6; truc 3**)

mordu, -ue [mɔrdy] *F* **I** *a* (*a*) être mordu de théâtre, to be mad on/(dead) keen on the theatre; **mordu de foot**, crazy/mad/nuts about football (*b*) être mordu (pour qn), to be madly in love (with s.o.) **II** *n* enthusiast/fan; **c'est un mordu de flipper/de jogging**, he's pinball/jogging crazy; he's nuts/crazy about pinball/jogging; he's a pinball/jogging fanatic/nut; he's been bitten by the pinball/jogging bug.

morfal(e) [mɔrfal] *nm P* = **morfalou**.

morfaler [mɔrfale] *P* **I** *vi* to stuff oneself (with food)/to (make a) pig (of) oneself **II** *vtr* to wolf (one's food) (down); **morfaler sa mangeaille**, to shovel food into one's mouth **III** *vpr* **se morfaler** 1. to stuff oneself (with food)/to (make a) pig (of) oneself 2. to claim the biggest share (for oneself); **il s'est morfalé les bijoux**, he kept the jewellery for himself 3. to do sth unpleasant; **je me suis morfalé la vaisselle**, I got landed with the washing-up.

morfalou [mɔrfalu] *nm P* glutton*/greedy-guts/pig.

morfic [mɔrfik] *nm P* = **morpion 1**.

morfier [mɔrfje], **morfiler** [mɔrfile], **morfiller** [mɔrfije] *vtr & i* 1. *P* to eat* 2. *V* to perform cunnilingus* (on)/to go down (on)/to eat.

morfler [mɔrfle] *P* **I** *vtr* 1. to get/to cop (a beating/a bullet/a punishment/a prison sentence, etc); **morfler le maxi**, to get the maximum sentence 2. to convict/to sentence (s.o.); to punish (s.o.) **II** *vi* 1. (*objet*) to get damaged; (*personne*) to get beaten up/hit; **faire morfler qn**, to put s.o. through it/to give s.o. the works 2. to get a heavy sentence.

morgane [mɔrgan] *nf P* salt.

morganer [mɔrgane] *vtr P* 1. to eat*; to chew; to bite 2. to denounce* (s.o.)/to blow the whistle on (s.o.).

moricaud, -aude [mɔriko, -od] *F Péj* **I** *a* dark-skinned/dusky/swarthy **II** *n* Black*/darkie/wog/spade.

morlingue [mɔrlɛ̃g] *nm P* purse; wallet; **congestionné du morlingue**, with plenty of money/well-heeled/well-stacked; **être constipé du morlingue/avoir des oursins dans le morlingue**, to be miserly*/stingy/tight-fisted/tight-assed.

morniflard [mɔrniflar] *nm P* purse.

mornifle [mɔrnifl] *nf P* 1. (*a*) money* (*b*) small change 2. slap (in the face); **flanquer/allonger une mornifle à qn**, to land s.o. a backhander. (*Voir* **cigue 1**)

mornifleur [mɔrniflœr] *nm P* counterfeiter/forger.

morph [mɔrf] *nf P* (*drogues*) (= *morphine*) morphine*/morf.

morphino [mɔrfino] *nm & f P* (= *morphinomane*) morphine* addict/junkie.

morpion [mɔrpjɔ̃] *nm* 1. *F* crab (louse)/pubic louse 2. *P* child*/brat 3. *F* (*jeu*) =

noughts and crosses/*NAm* tick-tack-toe.

mort [mɔr] I *a F* 1. c'est mort/elle est morte, (*c'est fini*) it's all over (and done with); (*sans espoir*) it's hopeless; (*bouteille*) it's empty/ dead; (*journée terminée*) let's call it a day/ that's another day's work done; (*plus d'argent*) there's no more cash/there's nothing left in the kitty 2. (*chaussures etc*) worn out; useless; (*batterie*) flat. (*Voir* **dos 14**) II *nm F* 1. la place du mort, the front passenger seat/*surt NAm Austr* the death seat 2. faire le mort, to lie low (and say nothing); (*cartes*) to be dummy III *nf F* c'est pas la mort! it's not all *that* difficult! (*Voir* **vache II 2**) IV *adv phr P* à mort, extremely; freiner à mort, to jam on the brakes; *V* bander à mort, to have a terrific erection*/hard-on.

mortibus [mɔrtibys] *a P* dead/stiff/cold.

morue [mɔry] *nf P Péj* 1. prostitute*/tart/ slut 2. woman*/girl*; vieille morue, old bag/ old bat/old trout.

morveux, -euse [mɔrvø, -øz] *F* I *a* snotty-nosed/with a runny nose II *n* 1. (annoying) child*/brat; (*plus âgé*) snot/little jerk 2. les morveux veulent moucher les autres, it's like Satan reproving sin; quand on est morveux on se mouche, do your own dirty business.

moscoutaire [mɔskutɛr] *nm & f Vieilli F Péj* communist/commie/bolshie.

mot [mo] *nm F* 1. pas un mot à la reine mère! mum's the word!/keep it under your hat! 2. mot de cinq lettres, (= **merde**) = four-letter word. (*Voir* **Cambronne**) 3. (petit) mot/mot d'écrit, short letter/note/a few lines.

motal [mɔtal] *nf P* motorbike.

motard [mɔtar] *nm F* 1. motor-cyclist; biker/bikie 2. police motor-cyclist/cycle cop.

moto [mɔto] *nf F* motorbike/bike; casque de moto, helmet/skid-lid.

motobécane [mɔtɔbekan] *nf F* (light) motorcycle/bike.

motocyclard [mɔtɔsiklar] *nm F* (*a*) = **motard 1, 2** (*b*) dispatch rider.

motorisé [mɔtɔrize] *a F* êtes-vous motorisé? have you got a car/transport? are you mobile?/have you got wheels?

motte [mɔt] *nf* 1. *P* faire la motte, to go halves/to go dutch 2. *V* anus* 3. *V* (*a*) female genitals*/beaver/cunt (*b*) female pubis/mons veneris. (*Voir* **astiquer 3**)

motus [mɔtys] *int F* motus (et bouche cousue), mum's the word!/keep it under your hat!

mou, *f* **molle** [mu, mɔl] I *a F* 1. flabby/ spineless/wet (individual) 2. pâte molle/cire molle, person you can twist round your little finger. (*Voir* **chiffe; chique 5**) II *adv P y* aller mou, to act cautiously; vas-y mou! mind how you go!/easy does it!/go easy!/take it easy! III *nm P* 1. (*a*) stomach*/belly (*b*) rentrer dans le mou à qn, to attack s.o./to beat s.o. up*/to work s.o. over 2. bourrer le mou à qn, to have s.o. on/to lead s.o. up the garden path; c'est du mou! it's a lot of eyewash!/it's a load of bull! (*Voir* **bourre-mou**) 3. les mous, the lungs.

mouchacha [mutʃatʃa] *nf F* young girl*/ chick.

mouchacho [mutʃatʃo] *nm F* young boy/ nipper.

mouchard [muʃar] *nm F* 1. (*a*) sneak/telltale (*b*) police informer*/snout/grass/stool pigeon 2. spyhole (in door, prison cell, etc) 3. (*dans un camion, etc*) tachograph/spy in the cab.

mouchardage [muʃardaʒ] *nm F* sneaking/grassing/squealing; mouchardage électronique, telephone tapping; bugging.

moucharde [muʃard] *nf Vieilli P* moon.

moucharder [muʃarde] *vtr F* to sneak (on) (s.o.); to denounce* (s.o.)/to grass on (s.o.).

mouche [muʃ] *nf F* 1. (= **mouchard 1**) faire la mouche, to turn informer 2. quelle mouche vous pique? what's eating you?/ what's bugging you?/what's got into you? 3. tuer les mouches au vol/à quinze pas, to have bad breath 4. attraper/compter les mouches, (*femme*) to think of something else while making love 5. c'est une fine mouche, he's/ she's a crafty little so-and-so; he's/she's a sharp customer. (*Voir* **coche 2; enculer 2; merde I 18**)

moucher [muʃe] I *vtr* 1. *F* moucher qn, to tell s.o. off/to put s.o. (firmly) in his place; se faire moucher, to get put in one's place; il a été mouché de belle façon, he really got told where to get off 2. *P* moucher (la gueule à) qn, to beat s.o. up*/to work s.o. over; se faire moucher, to get injured/damaged. (*Voir* **morveux II 2** II *vpr* se moucher 1. *F* il ne se mouche pas du coude/du pied, (*il est prétentieux*) he thinks an awful lot of himself; (*il demande trop cher*) he's asking too much (for it)/he's not cheap 2. *P* je m'en mouche! I couldn't care less!*/I don't give a damn!

mouchique [muʃik] *a P* 1. ugly/hideous 2.

disreputable; notorious.

mouchodrome [muʃɔdrom] *nm P* bald* head/skating rink.

mouchoir [muʃwar] *nm F* 1. le mouchoir d'Adam, one's fingers 2. (*sport*) arrivée dans un mouchoir, close finish; arriver dans un mouchoir, to make a close finish. (*Voir* **poche II 3**)

moudre [mudr] *vtr P* en moudre, (*cycliste*) to pedal hard; (*être prostituée*) to be a prostitute*; to be/to go on the game.

mouetter [mwɛte] *vi P* to be afraid*/to wet oneself.

la Mouffe [lamuf] *Prnf F* the rue Mouffetard (and district) (*in Paris*).

mouflet, -ette [muflɛ, -ɛt] *n P* child*/kid/ sprog.

moufter [mufte] *vi P* to talk/to blab; (*protester*) to protest/to complain; ne pas moufter/ne rien moufter, to keep mum/shtum.

mouillé [muje] *a* 1. *F* il est mouillé dans cette affaire, he's in it up to his neck 2. *P* il fait mouillé, it's wet/it's raining. (*Voir* **poule 4**)

mouiller [muje] I *vi P* 1. (en) mouiller pour qn, to be sexually excited* by s.o./to have the hots for s.o.; elle en mouille pour lui, he turns her on/she has the hots for him 2. *P* (*femme*) to have an orgasm*/to come; *Fig* to get immense pleasure (from sth)/to be exhilarated (by sth) 3. *F* ça mouille, it's raining II *vtr* 1. *P* mouiller qn, to compromise s.o./to implicate s.o. 2. *P* mouiller sa chemise/sa liquette/son maillot, to work hard*/to make a lot of effort/to peg away/to sweat blood 3. *P* mouiller le goupillon, to have sex*/to dip one's wick III *vtr & i P* mouiller (son froc), to be afraid*/to have the willies/to be scared stiff/to have the wind up/to be in a blue funk. (*Voir* **dalle² 1; meule 4**) IV *vpr* **se mouiller** *F* to compromise oneself; to implicate oneself (in a shady business, deal, etc); (*prendre parti*) to stick one's neck out/to get one's feet wet; il ne veut pas se mouiller, he doesn't want to get mixed up in it.

mouilles [muj] *nfpl P* buttocks*.

mouillette [mujɛt] *nf P* 1. tongue 2. aller à la mouillette = **se mouiller** 3. *pl* buttocks*; avoir les mouillettes, to be afraid*/to have the willies.

mouisant [mwizɑ̃] *nm P* (*écoles*) poverty-stricken student.

mouisard [mwizar] *a P* poverty-stricken/ down-and-out/penniless.

mouise [mwiz] *nf P* 1. poverty; être dans la mouise, to be penniless*/to be very hard up/to (have) hit hard times; (*avoir des ennuis*) to be in trouble/in the shit 2. bad luck.

moujingue [muʒɛ̃g] *P* I *a* small/child-size II *nm* 1. child*/kid/brat/sprog 2. tricoter le moujingue, to bring about an abortion.

moukala [mukala] *nm P* revolver*/gun/ piece/shooter.

moukère [mukɛr] *nf P* (*a*) *Péj* North African woman (*b*) woman*/bint (*c*) wife* (*d*) mistress (*e*) prostitute*/surt NAm hooker/tart.

moulana [mulana] *nm P* sun.

moule [mul] I *nf* 1. *P* (*a*) (*personne molle*) drip/wet/wimp (*b*) fool*/twerp/dope/jerk 2. *V* female genitals*; avoir la moule qui bâille, to be sexually excited*/randy/horny 3. *P* avoir les moules, to be afraid*/to have the wind up/ to have the willies; foutre les moules à qn, to frighten s.o.; ça me fout les moules, it gives me the willies 4. *P* avoir de la moule, to be very lucky II *nm P* moule à gaufre(s), fool*/ prize idiot/jerk.

mouler [mule] *vtr & i P* 1. (en) mouler, to be a prostitute*/to solicit*/to be on the game 2. to leave (s.o., sth) behind/to abandon (s.o., sth) 3. mouler (un bronze), to defecate*/to have a crap.

moulin [mulɛ̃] *nm* 1. *F* engine (of car, plane, etc) 2. *F* moulin (à paroles), (*bavard*) chatterbox*/gasbag/windbag 3. *P* moulin à café, (sub)machine gun 4. *P* profitable business; avoir un moulin qui tourne/des moulins qui tournent, to have a profitable source of income.

mouliner [muline] *vi* 1. *F* (*cycliste*) to pedal along at a steady pace 2. *F* to chatter*/ to talk (away) nineteen to the dozen 3. *P* = (en) mouler (**mouler 1**).

moulinette [mulinɛt] *nf P* 1. submachine gun; tommy gun 2. (*a*) passer qn à la moulinette, (*tuer*) to kill* s.o./to liquidate s.o.; (*interroger*) to grill s.o. (*b*) passer qch à la moulinette, to destroy sth/to wipe sth out.

moulu [muly] *a F* exhausted*/dead beat; moulu (de coups), black and blue/aching all over.

moumoute [mumut] *nf P* 1. wig 2. sheepskin jacket/Afghan jacket.

mouniche [muniʃ] *nf V* female genitals*.

mouquère [mukɛr] *nf P* = **moukère**.

mourir [murir] *vi* 1. *F* c'est à mourir de rire, it's very funny*/it's absolutely killing 2. *P* plus beau que moi, tu meurs! nothing doing!/no way!/not if I know anything about it!

mouron [murɔ̃] *nm P* **1.** se faire du mouron, to get worried/to worry oneself sick/to get into a state*; te fais pas de mouron pour moi! don't worry about me! **2.** hair; *(poils)* hairs; ne plus avoir de mouron sur la cage, to be as bald* as a coot **3.** c'est pas du mouron pour ton serin, it's not for you.

(se) mouronner [(sə)murɔne] *vi & pr P* to worry oneself sick.

mouscaille [muskɑj] *nf* **1.** *P* mud/dirt/ gunge **2.** *V* excrement/shit/crap **3.** *P* être dans la mouscaille, to be in a fix*/to be up to one's neck in it/to be in the shit **4.** *P* avoir qn à la mouscaille, to hate s.o.'s guts.

mousmé(e) [musme] *nf P (a)* young woman* *(b)* mistress.

moussante [musɑ̃t] *nf Vieilli P* beer/ale/ lager.

mousse [mus] *nf P* **1.** *Vieilli* = **mouscaille 2 2.** se faire de la mousse, to worry oneself sick **3.** beer/lager.

mousseline [muslin] *nf P (drogues)* morphine*.

mousser [muse] *vi* **1.** *F* to be angry*/to flare up/to blow one's top/to fly off the handle **2.** faire mousser qn, *F* to make s.o. lose his temper/flare up; *F (vanter)* to crack s.o. up/to build s.o. up (to be pretty amazing); *V (masturber)* to masturbate* s.o./to cream s.o. off **3.** *(a) F* se faire mousser, to show off*/to blow one's own trumpet; to think one is the cat's whiskers *(b) V* se faire mousser le créateur, to masturbate*/to bring oneself off/ to cream one's jeans.

mousseux [musø] *nm P* soap.

moussu [musy] *a P* hairy.

moustachue [mustaʃy] *nf P (homosexuels)* masculine/butch/macho homosexual.

moustagache [mustaga] *nf P (javanais pour moustache)* moustache/*NAm* mustache.

moustique [mustik] *nm F (personne insignifiante)* weed; *(enfant)* brat/nipper.

moutard [mutar] *nm F* small boy/kid/ nipper; *pl* les moutards, the kids.

moutarde [mutard] *nf F* **1.** la moutarde lui est montée au nez, he lost his temper/he went off the deep end **2.** c'est (comme) de la moutarde après dîner, it's like closing the stable door after the horse has bolted; it's come a day after the fair **3.** s'amuser à la moutarde, to waste one's time on trifles. *(Voir* **pesant)**

moutardier [mutardje] *nm* **1.** *A F* il se croit le premier moutardier du pape, he's grown too big for his boots **2.** *P* buttocks*/ arse/*NAm* ass.

mouton [mutɔ̃] *nm* **1.** *F* un mouton à cinq pattes, something very rare; chercher le mouton à cinq pattes, to look for the impossible **2.** *F (dans les prisons)* (police) spy **3.** *pl F* moutons, fluff/*NAm* dust bunnies *(under bed, etc)*.

moutonner [mutɔne] *vtr F* to spy on/to inform against (a fellow prisoner).

moyen [mwajɛ̃] *nm P* **1.** tâcher moyen de faire qch, to try to do sth **2.** il n'y a pas moyen de moyenner, nothing doing*!/not a chance (in hell)!/no go!

m'sieu [msjø] *nm F (= monsieur)* mister/ Mr; sir.

m'sieurs-dames [msjødam] *nmpl F =* **messieurs-dames**.

mud [myd] *nm P (drogues)* opium*/mud.

Muette [myɛt] *nf F Mil* la grande Muette, the Army.

muf(f)e [myf] *nm P =* **mufle 1, 2**.

muffée [myfe] *nf P* **1.** prendre une (bonne) muffée, to get drunk*/to tie one on; avoir la muffée/une muffée, to be dead drunk*/to be (completely) plastered. *(Voir* **tenir 2)** **2.** y en a une muffée, there's tons of it/there's any amount of it.

mufle [myfl] *nm P* **1.** nose*/beak/schnozzle **2.** head*/bonce/conk **3.** bastard*/nasty piece of work/*surt NAm* son of a bitch; espèce de mufle! what a slob/lout/jerk!

muflée [myfle] *nf P =* **muffée**.

mule [myl] *nf P* **1.** *(drogues)* small-time (drug) dealer **2.** ferrer la mule, to make illicit profits* (when buying for others); to make a bit on the side; *(se laisser corrompre)* to take a bribe (for obtaining an interview for s.o.) **3.** charger la mule, to get drunk*/loaded. *(Voir* **tête 4)**

munitions [mynisjɔ̃] *nfpl F* provisions.

mur [myr] *nm* **1.** *F* faire le mur, to slip out/ away; to skive off; *Mil* to go over the wall **2.** *F* être logé entre quatre murs, to be in prison*/inside **3.** *F* se heurter contre un mur, to come up against a brick wall **4.** *F* c'est pire que (de) parler à un mur, it's like talking to a brick wall **5.** *F (il) y a de quoi se taper la tête contre les murs, it's enough to drive you up the wall **6.** *P* pickpocket's accomplice (who acts as a shield while the theft is carried out) **7.** *P* faire les pieds au mur, to express one's satisfaction/to show one's contentment.

mûr [myr] *a P* drunk*/stewed/pissed. (*Voir* **vert I 2**)

muraille [myrɑj] *nf F* être logé entre quatre murailles, to be in prison*/inside. (*Voir* **mur 2**)

se murdinguer [səmyrdɛ̃ge] *vpr P* = **se mûrir.**

mûre [myr] *nf Vieilli P* blow*/punch; sock (in the face).

se mûrir [səmyrir] *vpr P* to get drunk*.

muscu [mysky] *nf F* (= *musculation*) body building.

museau, -eaux [myzo] *nm F* face*; joli petit museau, sweet/cute little face; vilain museau, ugly mug; se poudrer le museau, to powder one's face/one's nose. (*Voir* **fricassée 2**)

museler [myzle] *vtr F* to shut (s.o.) up.

musette [myzɛt] *nf P* qui n'est pas dans une musette, which is worth it/which is something; un petit rouge qui n'est pas dans une musette, a nice little red wine worth taking some trouble over; il a reçu une raclée qui n'était pas dans une musette, he got a hiding he won't forget in a hurry.

musicien [myzisjɛ̃] *nm P* 1. flatterer* 2. crook/underhand dealer 3. *pl* **musiciens,** beans.

musico(s) [myziko(s)] *nm P* musician.

musique [myzik] *nf* 1. *F* connaître (un peu) la musique, to know what's what/to know the score/to be up to all the tricks 2. *P* jouer/monter une musique à qn, to spin s.o. a yarn/to tell s.o. stories 3. *P* blackmail 4. *F* réglé comme du papier à musique, as regular as clockwork 5. *F* (*a*) faire de la musique, to kick up a row/to make a fuss; (*b*) baisse un peu ta musique! pipe down, will you! 6. *F* c'est une autre musique, that's another matter/that's a different kettle of fish.

musiquette [myzikɛt] *nf* 1. *F Péj* piped music/muzak (*RTM*) 2. *P* blackmail.

must [mœst] *nm F* must; l'informatique c'est un must, data processing is a must.

la Mutu [lamyty] *Prnf F* the Palais de la Mutualité (*in Paris*).

mystère [mistɛr] *nm F* 1. mystère et boule de gomme! I haven't a clue!/search me! 2. y a pas de mystère, quoi! it's as simple as that!/there's no two ways about it!

N

na! [na] *int F* (*mot d'enfants*) so there!/ya
boo sucks! **j'irai pas, na!** I'm not going, so
there!/I'm not going and that's that!

nada [nada] *adv P* **1.** no **2.** nothing*.

nage [naʒ] *nf F* **être (tout) en nage,** to be
bathed in sweat/dripping with sweat.

nageoire [naʒwar] *nf P* **1.** *pl A* **nageoires,**
sidewhiskers/sideboards **2.** arm*/fin/flipper **3.**
avoir des nageoires, to be a pimp/a mackerel.

nager [naʒe] *vi F* **1.** (*ne pas comprendre*)
nager (dans l'encre), to be out of one's depth;
je nage complètement, I'm all at sea; **en
maths, il nage complètement,** he's completely
lost/he's hopeless at maths **2. savoir nager,** to
know the ropes/to be clued up; to know the
score **3. il nage comme un caillou/comme un
chien de plomb/comme une clef,** he swims like
a brick.

nana [nana] *nf P* **1.** (*a*) woman*/girl*/bird/
chick; **la vraie nana,** the goods (*b*) girlfriend;
sa nana, his bird/his chick/his woman **2.**
prostitute*. (*Voir* **peau 3; supernana**)

nanan [nanɑ̃, nɑ̃nɑ̃] *nm Vieilli F* **c'est du
nanan!** (*c'est bon*) yum-yum! (*c'est facile*)
it's a piece of cake!/it's a walkover!/it's a
doddle!

nanar [nanar] *a & nm P* **1.** worthless object;
c'est (du) nanar, (*laid*) it's ugly; (*sans
valeur*) it's worthless*/it's no good/it's useless
2. (*film, pièce*) flop/*NAm* turkey; **ce film est
un vieux nanar,** this film is a load of old
rubbish/a dead loss.

Nantoche [nɑ̃tɔʃ] *Prn F* Nanterre (*suburb
of Paris*).

nap [nap] *nm F* (= *napoléon*) (*rare*) (*a*) (*à
l'origine*) twenty-franc gold piece (*bearing the
effigy of Napoleon*) (*b*) (any) gold piece.

N.A.P. [nap] *a & n F* (*abrév* = Neuilly-
Auteuil-Passy) = preppy/Sloane Ranger.

naph [naf] *nf P* = **naphtaline**.

naphtalinard [naftalinar] *nm P Mil* retired
army officer recalled to active duty/dugout/
retread.

naphtaline [naftalin] *nf,* **naphte** [naft] *nf
Vieilli P* (*drogues*) cocaine*/coke.

napo [napo] *nm* **1.** *P* Neapolitan **2.** *F* = **nap**.

nappe [nap] *nf F* **1. mettre la main sur la
bonne nappe,** to strike it rich **2. trouver la
nappe mise,** to marry into a fortune.

napy, *pl* **napies** [napi, -iz] *a & n F* =
N.A.P.

narc [nark] *nm P* (*drogues*) narcotic; *pl*
narcs, drugs/dope/junk.

narca [narka] *nm P* (*verlan de* **canard**)
newspaper/rag.

nardu [nardy] *nm P* police superintendent/
super.

narines [narin] *nfpl F* **en prendre plein les
narines,** (*être touché*) to be cut/stung; **prends
ça dans les narines,** serves you right!

narzo [narzo] *nm P* (*verlan de* **zonard**) layabout; yob/yobbo/hooligan*.

nase [naz] I *nm P* **1.** nose* **2.** = **naze¹ 3** II *a
P* = **naze² 1, 2.**

naseau, -eaux [nazo] *nm P* (*a*) nose* (*b*)
pl nostrils.

nasi [nazi] *a P* = **nazi.**

nasque [nask] *nf P* drunkenness; **prendre
une nasque,** to get drunk*; **ils ont pris une
nasque de première,** they got completely
pissed/plastered/smashed.

nasse [nas] *nf F* **tomber dans la nasse,** to fall
into a trap; to get stymied.

natchave [natʃav] *a P* **1.** shaky; (*dent*)
loose **2. faire natchave,** to run away*/to beat
it.

se natchaver [sənatʃave] *vpr P* to run
away*/to beat it/to scram/to skedaddle.

nattes [nat] *nfpl F* **faire des nattes,** to get
into a tangle/to get muddled/to get tied up in
knots/to lose the thread (of one's ideas).

nature [natyr] I *nf F* **1. disparaître/
s'évaporer/se perdre dans la nature,** to vanish
into thin air **2.** *Aut* **partir/se retrouver dans la
nature,** to run/to smash into a wall, tree, etc
3. envoyer/expédier qn dans la nature, to

send s.o. packing*/to turf s.o. out 4. **lâcher qn dans la nature**, to give s.o. his head/to give s.o. a free rein 5. **c'est une (vraie) force de la nature**, he's as strong as an ox; he's a giant of a man 6. **c'est une nature**, he's a real personality 7. **c'est une petite nature**, he's a bit wet/a bit of a drip 8. **il n'est pas aidé par la nature**, he's stupid* (from birth)/he's a natural idiot II *a inv F* 1. **ça fera plus nature**, that'll look more natural 2. *(personne) (a)* natural/open/frank/uninhibited *(b) (naïf)* gullible/easily taken in 3. *(boisson, etc)* neat III *adv P (naturellement)* naturally/of course.

naturlich(e) [natyrliʃ] *adv P (naturellement)* naturally/of course/natch.

(se) navaler [(sə)navale] *vi & vpr P (a)* to run (at full pelt) *(b)* to run away*/to beat it. *(Voir* **cavaler 1** *(a))*

navdu [navdy] *nm P* = **navedu**.

nave [nav] *nm P* 1. *(individu n'appartenant pas au* **milieu**) outsider 2. *(a)* victim of a swindle*/fall guy/mug/sucker *(b)* **(fleur de) nave**, fool*/idiot/twerp/clot 3. *(film, etc)* flop/ *NAm* turkey/tripe/rubbish.

navedu [navdy] *nm P* 1. someone/ somebody/an invidual 2. = **nave 2**.

navet [navɛ] *nm* 1. *F* trashy/third-rate novel; *(film)* flop/third-rate film/*NAm* turkey/ tripe; *(pièce)* pure ham 2. *P* **des navets!** nothing doing!/not bloody likely*! 3. *P* idiot/clot 4. *P* **se creuser le navet**, to rack one's brains 5. *P* **le champ de navets**, the cemetery* 6. *P* **il a du sang de navet**, he's anaemic; *(poltron)* he's got no guts/no spunk.

naveton [navtɔ̃] *nm P* 1. fool*/idiot/twerp/ clot 2. = **navet 1**.

naviguer [navige] *vi F (a)* to move around/ to travel about (from one place to another); **elle a beaucoup navigué**, she's knocked about a bit/she's been around/she's seen the world *(b)* **il sait naviguer**, he can take care of himself.

naze¹ [naz] *nm P* 1. nose* 2. syphilis*/syph/ pox; **il a chopé le naze**, he's copped a dose (of syph) 3. *(langage des motocyclistes)* bad *or* drunken driver. *(Voir* **cloquer I 1** *(c))*

naze² [naz] *a P* 1. syphilitic/syphed up/poxy 2. *(personne)* exhausted*/shattered; *(machine, voiture, etc)* done for/clapped out; **ma moto est complètement naze**, my bike's packed up 3. mad*/cracked 4. drunk*/pissed.

nazebroque [nazbrɔk] *a P* = **naze² 1, 2**.

nazi [nazi] *P* I *a* syphilitic/syphed up II *nm* = **naze¹ 2**.

naziqué [nazike] *a P* syphilitic/syphed up/ poxy.

naziquer [nazike] *vtr P* to infect (s.o.) with syphilis*/to give (s.o.) a dose.

nécro [nekro], **nécrops** [nekrɔps] *nf P (a)* post-mortem/autopsy *(b) Journ (notice nécrologique)* obituary/obit.

nèfles [nɛfl] *nfpl P* **des nèfles!** *(rien)* nothing/zilch; *(pas du tout)* nothing doing!/no (blooming) fear!/not bloody likely*!

négatif [negatif] *adv F* no/negative.

négifran [neʒifrɑ̃] *nf P (verlan de* **frangine)** sister/sis.

nègre [nɛgr] I *nm* 1. *P Péj* Black* (man)/ nigger *NAm* nigra 2. *F* ghost (writer); devil (of barrister); (general) dogsbody; **il me faut un nègre**, I want s.o. to do the donkey work 3. *F* **fais comme le nègre!** *(continue!)* carry on(, sailor)!/keep it going!/don't stop! 4. *F* **parler petit nègre**, to talk pidgin French 5. *P* **c'est un combat de nègres dans un tunnel**, *(on ne le voit pas bien)* you can't see it very clearly/you can't make it out; *(on ne le comprend pas)* it's as clear as mud/you can't make head or tail of it 6. *V Péj* **noir comme dans le trou du cul d'un nègre**, as black/dark as a nigger's/ *Austr* an abo's arsehole. *(Voir* **bosser 1)** II *a inv F* **propos nègre blanc**, double talk.

négresse [negrɛs] *nf P* 1. bug, flea 2. bottle of red vintage wine; **éternuer sur/étouffer/ étrangler/éventrer une négresse**, to down/to knock back a bottle of vino 3. *(dans un restaurant)* deep frier/*Br* chip pan.

négrier [negrije] *nm F* owner of sweatshop; *(employeur)* slave-driver.

négro [negro] *nm P Péj* Black*/negro/ nigger.

neige [nɛʒ] *nf P (drogues)* cocaine*/snow/ white stuff.

neiger [neʒe] *vi F* **il a neigé sur sa tête**, he's got white hair.

nénés [nene] *nmpl P* breasts*/tits/knockers/ boobs/Bristols; **des nénés de chez Michelin**, falsies.

nénesse [nenɛs] *nf P (a)* woman* *(b)* wife*.

nénette [nenɛt] *nf P* 1. (young) woman*/ girl*/chick/bird; **nénette ronronnante**, sex kitten; **vas-y, nénette! attagirl! 2. head* 3. **travailler de la nénette**, to be mad*/off one's rocker 4. **se casser la nénette**, to make an effort; *(réfléchir)* to think hard/to rack one's brains; *(s'inquiéter)* to worry; **il ne se casse pas la nénette**, he doesn't exert himself/he doesn't put himself out 5. **en avoir par-dessus**

la nénette, to have had enough; **j'en ai par-dessus la nénette,** I'm sick and tired of it/I've had it up to here/I've had a bellyful of it 6. rag used for polishing car.

nénuphar [nenyfar] *nm V* female genitals*.

nerf [nɛr] *nm* 1. *F* **taper sur les nerfs à qn,** to get on s.o.'s nerves 2. *F* **mets-y du nerf!** [nɛr(f)] put some go/some guts/some vim into it! 3. *Vieilli P* money*; **je n'ai pas un nerf (dans la fouille),** I'm penniless*/I haven't got a bean. (*Voir* **pelote 2**)

nervi [nɛrvi] *nm F* gangster/hoodlum from Marseilles.

nespasien [nɛspazjɛ̃] *nm F Hum* person who makes excessive use of *n'est-ce pas?* in speaking/= a 'you-knower'.

net [nɛt] *a F* **pas net,** (*suspect*) suspicious/fishy/shady; (*marginal*) (on the) fringe; (*ivre*) drunk*/gone/merry; (*drogué*) high/spaced out; (*un peu fou*) batty/dotty/not quite all there.

nettoyage [nɛtwajaʒ] *nm F* 1. nettoyage (à sec), cleaning out (financially) 2. nettoyage **d'une maison,** (*par un cambrioleur, etc*) stripping bare (of a house) 3. rifling (of s.o.'s pockets) 4. (*Mil, police, etc*) mopping-up (operation) 5. killing/wiping out.

nettoyer [nɛtwaje] *vtr F* 1. nettoyer qn (à sec), to clean s.o. out (financially)/to take s.o. to the cleaners; **je suis nettoyé,** I'm cleaned right out/I'm completely broke 2. nettoyer **une maison,** (*cambrioleur, etc*) to strip a house bare 3. nettoyer un homme, to rifle a man's pockets 4. (*Mil, police, etc*) to mop up 5. to kill* (s.o.) off/to eliminate (s.o.)/to wipe (s.o.) out/to blow (s.o.) away; **il s'est fait nettoyer,** he got bumped off 6. nettoyer une **assiette/un verre,** to clean out a plate/to lick a plate clean; to empty a glass.

neuf [nœf] *a F* **quoi de neuf?** what's the news?/what's new? **rien de neuf,** (there's) no news.

neuille [nœj] *nf P* night.

Neuneu[1] [nønø], **Neuneuille** [nønœj] *Prn F* Neuilly-sur-Seine (*suburb of Paris*); **aller à la fête à Neuneu,** to dress up/to put on one's best bib and tucker.

neuneu[2] [nønø] *a inv F* stupid*/silly; **c'est un peu neuneu,** it's a bit daft.

neunœil [nœnœj] *nm P* = **nœil.**

neveu, *pl* **-eux** [nəvø] *nm F* **un peu, mon neveu!** not half!/you bet!/I should jolly well think so! (*Voir* **Bretagne**)

nez [ne] *nm* 1. *F* **ça lui pend au nez,** he's got

it coming to him; he's (in) for it 2. *F* **ton nez bouge/remue!** you're fibbing! 3. *F* **je l'ai dans le nez,** I can't stand him; *Br* he gets up my nose 4. *F* **si on lui pressait/pinçait/tordait le nez il en sortirait du lait,** on lui presserait/pincerait le nez qu'il en sortirait encore du lait, he's still wet behind the ears; he's still a bit green 5. *F* (*a*) **se salir/se piquer le nez,** to get drunk*/to hit the bottle/to go on the booze (*b*) **avoir un (petit) coup dans le nez/avoir un coup de trop dans le nez/avoir le nez piqué/avoir le nez sale,** to be drunk*. (*Voir* **verre 1**) 6. *F* (en) **faire un nez/faire un drôle de nez/faire un sale nez,** to look disgruntled; to pull a long face; **vise un peu le nez qu'il fait!** just look at the face he's pulling! 7. *F* **se promener le nez au vent,** to be on the lookout for opportunities *or* bargains 8. *F* **à vue de nez,** at first sight/at a guess/at a rough estimate; **faire qch à vue de nez,** to do sth in a rough and ready way. (*Voir* **pifomètre**) 9. *F* **se casser le nez,** (*trouver porte close*) to find nobody at home (*when calling at a house*); (*échouer*) to fail (in business), to come a cropper 10. *F* **se bouffer le nez,** to quarrel*/to wrangle; to be constantly arguing/to be always getting at each other 11. *F* **avoir le nez creux/avoir le nez fin/avoir du nez,** (*avoir de l'intuition*) to be shrewd/*esp NAm* cute/smart; to have a flair/a nose for a bargain 12. *F* **ça va nous retomber sur le coin du nez (comme un sifflet de deux ronds/de deux sous),** we're sure to get the blame for it; we'll have to carry the can for it 13. *F* **ça se voit comme le nez au milieu de la figure,** it's bloody obvious/it's as plain as the nose on your face 14. *F* **avoir le nez trop long,** to be (too) nosy/to be a nosy parker 15. *P* **saigner du nez,** to be afraid*/to have the wind up/to be in a blue funk. (*Voir* **caca 2; doigt 3; fourrer I 3; laver 4; passer I 5; pleuvoir 2; pointer I 2; ver 3**)

niac [njak], **niacoué** [njakwe] *a & nm P Péj* Indochinese; viet; chink.

niaiser [njɛze] *vi FrC P* to waste one's time/to mess around/to loaf about.

niaiseux, -euse [njɛzø, -øz] *a FrC F* stupid*/dumb/dense/thick.

niak [njak] *a & nm P Péj* = **niac.**

niard [njar] *nm P* 1. child*/kid/brat 2. man*/chap*/fellow/bloke/guy. (*Voir* **gniard, -arde**)

nib [nib] *adv & pron inv Vieilli P* nothing*; **nib!** my foot!/get lost*!/nothing doing! **nib de nib/nib de rien,** nothing at all/sweet Fanny

Adams; **nib de fric**, no money*; **un bon à nib**, a good-for-nothing/a layabout; **nib de tif(fe)s**, bald.

nibards [nibar] *nmpl P* breasts*.

nibé! [nibe] *excl A P* silence!/quiet!

nicdouille [nikduj] *a & nm & f F* = **niguedouille.**

(se) nicher [(sə)niʃe] *vi & vpr F* to live; **où nichez-vous?** where do you hang out? **Malte, où est-ce que ça se niche?** where the hell is Malta on the map?

niches [niʃ] *nmpl P* breasts*.

nichons [niʃɔ̃] *nmpl P* breasts*/tits/boobs; **faux nichons**, falsies.

nickel [nikɛl] *a P* **1.** clean; **c'est nickel(-nickel)!/c'est drôlement nickel!** it's superclean/it's spick and span/it's as clean as a new pin **2.** honest; **ce type est nickel**, that guy's straight.

nickelé [nikle] *a F* **1. avoir les pieds nickelés**, to refuse to agree to sth/to refuse to budge/to sit tight; *(avoir de la chance)* to be lucky **2. tête nickelée**, bald(-headed)* man/baldy.

niçois [niswa] *P* **I** *a* **être niçois**, *(au poker, etc)* not to increase one's stake/to stand pat/to stay put **II** *nm* watchman/security officer *(working for private company)*.

nième [ɛnjɛm] *a* **1.** *F* **pour la nième fois**, for the umpteenth time/for the nth time **2.** *P* **être nième**, [njɛm] to suffer from withdrawal symptoms*/to need a fix/to be (in) cold turkey.

nien [njɛ̃] *nm*, **nienne** [njɛn] *nf P* yearning for drugs; withdrawal symptoms/cold turkey.

niente [njɑ̃t] *P* **I** *adv* nothing/nix **II** *nf* *(personne)* nonentity/nothing/nobody.

nière [njɛr] *nm P* **1.** chap*/fellow/bloke/guy **2.** fool*/cretin; *(maladroit)* clumsy clot **3.** accomplice/confederate; **un nière à la manque**, an unreliable accomplice. *(Voir* **gnière)**

niflette [niflɛt] *nf P* *(drogues)* cocaine*/coke/nose-candy. *(Voir* **reniflette)**

niguedouille [nigduj] *F* **I** *a* stupid*/idiotic **II** *nm & f* fool*/idiot/imbecile.

niole [njɔl] *nf*, **niôle** [njol] *nf P* brandy/spirits*/rotgut/hard stuff/hooch/firewater; **un coup de niole**, a wee dram/a drop of the hard stuff. *(Voir* **gnole)**

Niort [njɔr] *Prn P* **aller à Niort/battre (à) Niort**, to swear blind that one is innocent; to refuse to confess to a crime.

nippé [nipe] *a F* dressed/rigged out/togged up.

nipper [nipe] **I** *vtr F* *(habiller)* to rig (s.o.) out/to tog (s.o.) up/to kit (s.o.) out/to get (s.o.) up (in sth) **II** *vpr* **se nipper** *F* to rig oneself out/to tog oneself up/to get oneself up (in sth).

nippes [nip] *nfpl F* clothes*/gear/clobber.

nique [nik] *nf* **1.** *F* **faire la nique à qn**, to cock a snook at s.o./to thumb one's nose at s.o. **2.** *V* sex*/bonking/nookie.

niquedouille [nikduj] *a & nm & f F* = **niguedouille.**

niquer [nike] *P* **I** *vtr* **1.** to have sex* with (s.o.)/to screw (s.o.)/to have it off with (s.o.); **va te faire niquer!** fuck off!/bugger off! **2. se faire niquer par qn**, to be taken in/to get done/to be conned/to get screwed by s.o. **3.** to damage; **j'ai niqué le magnéto**, I've wrecked the video (recorder) **II** *vi* to have sex*/to have a bonk.

niston, -onne [nistɔ̃, -ɔn] **I** *n P* **1.** child*/kid; boy/girl. *(Voir* **fiston) 2.** *(prisons)* passive homosexual* **II** *a P* = **niçois I.**

nitouche [nituʃ] *nf F Voir* **Sainte-Nitouche.**

niveau [nivo] *nm F* **(au) niveau (des) finances ça ne va pas trop mal**, as far as (the) finances are concerned/moneywise, things aren't too bad.

nobler [nɔble] *Vieilli P* **I** *vtr* to know/to be acquainted with (s.o.) **II** *vpr* **se nobler** to be called/named; **comment tu te nobles?** what's your name?

noblesse [nɔblɛs] *nf P* **la noblesse**, the (French) underworld/gangland. *(Voir* **milieu)**

nocdu [nɔkdy] *a P* ugly.

noce [nɔs] *nf* **1. faire la noce**, *F* to have a good time*/to live it up/to have a ball/to go on a binge/to go on the razzle; *P* *(devenir prostituée)* to become a prostitute*/to go on the game; **usé par la noce**, worn out with living it up **2.** *F* **il n'avait jamais été à pareille noce**, he'd never had such a good time/he was having the time of his life/he'd never had it so good; *Iron* he'd never seen such a shambles/such an unholy mess **3.** *F* **être à la noce**, to be happy; **je n'étais pas à la noce**, I was feeling very uneasy/I wasn't at all happy; I was having a bad time/a rough time; it was no picnic.

nocer [nɔse] *vi F* to have a good time*/to live it up/to have a ball/to go on the razzle.

noceur, -euse [nɔsœr, -øz] *n F* dissipated/debauched person; reveller/fast liver/hell-raiser.

nœil [nœj] *nm P* eye*/blinker.

nœud [nø] *nm* 1. *P* tête de nœud, fool*/berk/ *Br* dickhead/*NAm* asshole 2. *V* penis*/knob; se baigner le nœud, to have sex*/to dip one's wick/to get one's end away. (*Voir* **malle 7; mordre 8; peau 19; pomper I 3**)

nœud-pap [nøpap] *nm* *F* (= nœud papillon) bow tie/dicky (bow).

noïe [nɔj] *nf*, **noille** [nɔj] *nf P* night.

noir [nwar] I *a P* 1. drunk*; complètement noir, dead drunk*/plastered/sloshed/blotto 2. être noir, to have a black police record/to have form. (*Voir* **œil 20; série 1**) II *nm* 1. *F* avoir le noir/broyer du noir/voir tout en noir, to be depressed/to have the blues/to be down in the dumps 2. *F* (petit/grand) noir, (small/large cup of) black coffee; noir-chic, coffee with chicory 3. *F* black market; acheter qch au noir, to buy sth on the black market; faire du noir, to be a black marketeer; travailler au noir, to moonlight 4. *P* (*drogues*) opium*/black stuff/tar 5. *P* être dans le noir, not to understand clearly/to be in the dark (*concerning a criminal investigation*) 6. *P* porter le noir, (*joueur*) to be dogged by bad luck/to be a loser.

noircicaud, noircico [nwarsiko] *P* I *a* 1. drunk*/plastered/sloshed 2. black II *nm* Black (man); coloured man; darkie.

noircif [nwarsif] *nm F* le noircif = **noir** II 3.

noircir [nwarsir] I *vtr F* 1. noircir du papier, to write something down 2. noircir le tableau, to take a gloomy view/to look on the black side (of things) II *vpr* **se noircir** *P* to get drunk*/to have one over the eight.

noire [nwar] *nf* (*rare*) 1. *P* night 2. (*quelquefois nm*) *P* opium*/black stuff/tar.

noirot [nwaro] *nm P* taxi-driver/cabbie who finishes his shift late in the evenings. (*Voir* **nuiteux**).

noisettes [nwazɛt] *nfpl V* 1. testicles*/nuts 2. en avoir chaud aux noisettes, to have had a close shave/a close call.

noité [nwate] *a P* être bien noité, to have a shapely posterior; elle est salement bien noitée, she's got a pert bum/a real cute ass.

noix [nwa] I *nf* 1. *P* fool*/clot/nit(wit)/nurd 2. *P* vieille noix, old fogey*/old codger; *Hum* old fruit/old bean/old thing/old chap* 3. *P* head*/nut 4. *P* à la noix (de coco), worthless*/useless/lousy/crappy/shitty; des boniments à la noix, empty talk/eyewash/bull; excuses à la noix, trivial excuses; un film à la noix, a dreadful/an awful film; une idée à la noix, a useless/pathetic/lousy idea; un travail à la noix, a trashy piece of work 5. *V pl* testicles*/nuts; tu me casses les noix/tu me fais mal aux noix, you get on my nerves/you're getting on my tits/you give me (the) balls-ache 6. *P* buttocks*; une belle paire de noix, a shapely posterior/a cute ass; serrer les noix, (*être sur ses gardes*) to be on one's guard/to watch it; (*ne pas bouger ou céder*) to sit tight; (*avoir peur*) to be afraid*/to have the wind up/to have the jitters; il a les noix qui font bravo, he's got the wind up/he's lost his bottle; il est parti en serrant les noix, he went off with his tail between his legs II *a inv P* avoir l'air noix, to look an absolute fool*; ce que tu es noix! you're hopeless!

nom [nɔ̃] *nm F* 1. petit nom, first name 2. nom de nom!/nom d'un nom!/nom d'un chien!/nom d'un (petit) bonhomme!/nom d'une pipe!/nom de deux!/nom d'un tonnerre!/tonnerre de nom! good heavens!/my goodness!flipping heck!/blimey!/for heaven's sake!/blow it!/hang it (all)! nom de Dieu! my God!/Jesus (Christ)!/Christ (Almighty)!/Jeez!/damn!/bloody hell! 3. ça n'a pas de nom! it's unspeakable! it's incredible! (*Voir* **charnière; coucher² II; se dévisser 1; rallonge 1; tiroir 1; tonnerre I 2**)

nombril [nɔ̃bri] *nm F* 1. il se prend pour le nombril du monde, he thinks he's God's gift (to mankind)/he thinks he's the bee's knees 2. décolletée jusqu'au nombril, (*femme*) showing everything she's got/showing a lot of cleavage.

nonnette [nɔnɛt] *nf F* bandaged finger/dolly.

nono¹ [nɔno] *a inv F* zone nono, (*en France, entre 1940 et 1942*) unoccupied zone.

nono² [nɔno] *nm FrC F* fool*/idiot/nurd.

nonosse [nɔnɔs] *nm F* (*mot enfantin*) bone.

Noraf [nɔraf] *nm P Péj* = **Nordaf(e)**.

nord [nɔr] *nm F* perdre le nord, (*s'égarer*) to lose one's bearings; (*paniquer*) to lose one's head/to get (all) confused/to go (all) to pieces.

Nordaf(e) [nɔraf] *nm P Péj* Arab of *or* from North Africa.

Normale Sup [nɔrmalsyp] *Prnf F* (= l'école normale supérieure) = university level college which prepares students for senior posts in teaching and other professions.

Normand, normand [nɔrmɑ̃] *F* I *a* (faire le) trou normand, (to have a) glass of Calvados (*between two courses of a meal*) II *nm* 1. donner/faire une réponse de Normand/

répondre en Normand, to give an evasive/non-committal answer 2. c'est un fin Normand, he's a shrewd fellow 3. (et) Normand qui s'en dédit! and to hell with anyone who says otherwise!

Norm' Sup' [nɔrmsyp] *Prnf F* = **Normale Sup.**

noszig(ue)s [nozig] *pron P* we/us/ourselves. (*Voir* **mézig(ue), tézig(ue), cézig(ue), sézig(ue), vo(s)zig(ue)s, euzig(ue)s, leur(s) zig(ue)s**)

notaire [nɔtɛr] *nm F* c'est comme si le notaire y avait passé, his word is as good as his bond.

note [nɔt] *nf F* 1. donner la note, to call the tune 2. chanter sur une autre note/changer de note, to change one's tune 3. piquer une bonne/une mauvaise note, to get a good/a bad mark 4. forcer la note, to exaggerate; (*faire du zèle*) to overdo it. (*Voir* **saler 1**)

nôtres [notr] *nfpl F* nous avons bien fait des nôtres, we've played quite a few tricks of our own/we had a few things up our sleeves.

nouba [nuba] *nf P* faire la nouba, to have a good time*/to go on a bender/to paint the town red/to live it up/to have a ball.

nougat [nuga] *nm P* 1. du nougat/un vrai nougat/du vrai nougat, an easy job/a cushy number; c'est du nougat, it's easy*/a walkover/a doddle 2. loot; toucher son nougat, to get one's share/one's whack/one's cut (of the proceeds, profits, etc) 3. *pl* nougats, feet*.

nougatine [nugatin] *nf P* de la nougatine, an easy job/a cushy number; c'est de la nougatine, it's easy*/a walkover/a doddle.

nouille [nuj] *nf* 1. *F* idiot/dope; c'est une nouille, he's/she's an idiot/a drip; quelle nouille!/espèce de nouille! what a jerk/drip/nurd! ce que c'est nouille, ton idée! what a pathetic idea! 2. *pl P* (*CB*) interference/background fizz/garbage. (*Voir* **cul I 4**)

nounou [nunu] *nf F* (*mot enfantin*) nanny.

nounours [nunurs] *nm F* (*mot enfantin*) 1. teddy (bear) 2. fur coat.

nourrice [nuris] *nf F* (*brocante*) objet en nourrice, object held in trust by another dealer.

nourrisson [nurisɔ̃] *nm F Iron* (any) dependant; another mouth to feed.

nouvelles [nuvɛl] *nfpl F* (*a*) j'ai de vos nouvelles! I've heard about your goings-on! (*b*) goûtez ça, vous m'en direz des nouvelles, taste this, I'm sure you'll like it; just you taste that/get a load of that(, and tell me what

you think about it)! (*c*) vous aurez de mes nouvelles, you haven't heard the last of this; I'll give you something to think about; I'll give you what-for!

nouzailles [nuzaj] *pron P* = **noszig(ue)s.**

novo [novo] *nm F* smart young snob.

noyaux [nwajo] *nmpl F* rembourré avec des noyaux de pêche, (*siège*) hard and lumpy.

noye [nɔj] *nf P* night.

noyé [nwaje] *a F* 1. (*vin, pastis, etc*) watered down/drowned 2. (*personne*) out of one's depth/hopelessly at sea.

nozig(ue)s [nozig] *pron P* = **noszig(ue)s.**

nuitard [nɥitar] *nm P* worker (post-office worker, policeman, etc) on night shift.

nuiteux [nɥitø] *nm P* worker, *esp* taxi-driver, on night shift.

nul, *f* **nulle** [nyl], **nullard, -arde** [nylar, -ard] *F* I *a* useless/hopeless/pathetic II *n* (*a*) stupid* person/dunce/dummy/thickie (*b*) hopeless person/washout/dead loss.

nullissime [nylisim] *a F* totally useless/hopeless/pathetic.

nullité [nylite] *nf F* (*a*) stupid person/dunce (*b*) hopeless person/washout/dead loss.

nullos [nylos] *a F* useless/worthless/trashy.

numéro [nymero] *nm F* 1. (*a*) un (drôle de) numéro, an eccentric* (person)/a weirdie/a weirdo; (*bizarre*) an odd/strange/funny person; an odd bod; (*drôle*) an amusing person/a funny bloke (*b*) un vieux numéro, an old stick-in-the-mud/a back-number/a has-been/an old fogey* (*c*) *Vieilli* je connais son numéro, I know his sort/I've got his number/I've got him sized up 2. ... numéro un, best/A1; tenue numéro un, best clothes; ennemi public numéro un, public enemy number one 3. il aime faire son (petit) numéro, he likes going through his old routine/he likes going through with his (little) act 4. *Vieilli* (maison au) gros numéro, brothel*/knocking shop/whorehouse 5. numéro cent, WC*/loo 6. je retiens votre numéro! (*menace*) you haven't heard the last of this!/I've got your number! 7. filer le bon numéro, (à qn), to give (s.o.) a valuable piece of information/a good tip 8. tirer le bon numéro, to draw the winning ticket/to be lucky; j'ai tiré un bon numéro, I did well when I married him/her; I picked a winner (when I married him/her).

nunu(che) [nyny(ʃ)] *a P* silly/daft/goofy; (*infantile*) babyish/soppy.

nunucherie [nynyʃri] *nf P* silliness/goofiness; babyishness/soppiness.

O

obligado [ɔbligɑdo] *adv*, **obligeman** [ɔbliʒman] *adv P* faire qch obligado, to do sth under compulsion/to be forced into doing sth.

obsédé, -ée [obsede] *n F* sex maniac.

occase [ɔkɑz] *nf P* 1. opportunity; profiter de l'occase, to make the most of it; louper/rater l'occase, to miss the chance/to miss out on it; je ferai ça à l'occase, I'll do it if I get the chance 2. bargain/good buy/snip 3. d'occase, second-hand; bagnole d'occase, used car; tuyaux d'occase, stale news.

occasion [ɔkɑzjɔ̃] *nf P* faire d'occasion, to look old/shopworn.

l'occup(e) [lɔkyp] *nf P* (*seconde guerre 1939–45*) (the) German occupation.

s'occuper [sɔkype] *vpr P* 1. to live by one's wits/to manage/to get by 2. t'occupe! mind your own business! (*Voir* **oignon 4**)

œil, *pl* **yeux** [œj, jø] *n* 1. *Vieilli F* taper de l'œil, to sleep*/to grab some shuteye 2. *F* taper dans l'œil de/à qn, to take s.o.'s fancy 3. *F* tourner de l'œil, to faint*/to pass out 4. *F* (*a*) battre de l'œil, to feel sleepy/drowsy (*b*) je m'en bats l'œil, I don't care a hoot/I don't give a damn 5. *F* (*a*) à l'œil, free/gratis*/on the house/buckshee; entrer à l'œil, to get in for nothing (*b*) avoir l'œil, to be given credit/tick 6. *F* il a les yeux plus grands que le ventre/que la panse, he has eyes (that are) bigger than his stomach/belly; he's bitten off more than he can chew 7. *F* jeter un œil, to have a glance/a look; risquer un œil, to take a peep/to have a look-see 8. *F* (*a*) faire les yeux doux à qn, to make (sheep's/goo-goo) eyes at s.o. (*b*) faire de l'œil à qn, to give s.o. the glad eye/to eye s.o. up; to wink at s.o. 9. *F* faire les gros yeux à qn/regarder qn d'un œil noir, to give s.o. a black look 10. *F* en mettre plein les yeux à qn, to bluff s.o./to hoodwink s.o. 11. (*a*) *F* l'avoir dans l'œil, to be duped/to be done (in the eye) (*b*) *P* se mettre le doigt dans l'œil (jusqu'au coude), to be completely mistaken/to be right up the pole/to be on the wrong track; to stick one's foot in it 12. *F* (et) mon œil! my foot!/my Aunt Fanny! 13. *F* faire qch pour les beaux yeux de qn, to do sth for the love of s.o. 14. *F* il n'a pas les yeux dans sa poche, (*il est observateur*) he's very observant; he keeps his eyes skinned/peeled; (*il sait se débrouiller*) he's got his wits about him/he knows the score/he's very clued up 15. *F* (*a*) ouvrir l'œil (et le bon), to be on the lookout/to keep an eye on things; to keep one's eyes peeled; to keep a weather eye open (*b*) avoir/tenir qn à l'œil, avoir l'œil sur qn, to keep an eye/a close watch on s.o. 16. *F* avoir l'œil, to be observant; avoir l'œil américain, to be able to judge (sth) at a glance/to see everything at a glance 17. *F* coûter les yeux de la tête, to cost the earth/to cost a packet 18. *F* il n'a pas froid aux yeux, he's got plenty of nerve/he's not backward at coming forward 19. *F* ouvrir des yeux ronds, to be wide-eyed (with amazement)/to be amazed*/flabbergasted 20. *F* avoir un œil à la caille/un œil poché/un œil au beurre noir, to have a black eye*/a shiner 21. *F Vieilli* ça a de l'œil, that looks good/smart; it's got sth; ça manque d'œil, it lacks style/sth 22. *F* être très sur l'œil, to be very strict 23. *F* ne dormir que d'un œil, to catnap 24. *F* se rincer l'œil, to get an eyeful (*of a woman's charms, a pornographic film, etc*) 25. *V* œil de bronze, anus*/round eye. (*Voir* **bras 5; carpe 2; crapaud 7; doigt 5, 6; frais¹ 1; merde I 6, 15; merlan 4; pisser I 3; trou 7; zut** (*d*))

œillet [œjɛ] *nm* 1. *V* anus* 2. *pl P* œillets, eyes*; gicler des œillets, to cry*/to weep/to cry one's eyes out.

œuf [œf], *pl* **œufs** [ø] *nm* 1. *P* espèce d'œuf! silly fool*! fais pas l'œuf, don't behave like an idiot 2. *P* aux œufs, excellent*/first-class 3. *F* avoir l'œuf colonial, to be potbellied/to have a gut/to have a beer belly 4. *P* casser son œuf, to have a miscarriage 5. *P* œufs sur le plat, flat breasts*/pimples; **elle a des œufs sur le plat**, she's as flat as a board/as a pancake **6.** *P* **l'avoir dans l'œuf**, to be duped/hoaxed/conned/had **7.** *F* **marcher (comme) sur des œufs**, to tread/to skate on thin ice **8.** *P* **plein comme un œuf**, (*très plein*) chock-full/chock-a-block/chocker; (*repu*) satiated/full; (*ivre*) dead drunk*/as high as a kite **9.** *F* **c'est comme l'œuf de Colomb**, it's easy once you've thought of it **10.** *P* **va te faire cuire un œuf!** get lost*!/go to hell!/go and boil your head! **11.** *P* **tondre un œuf**, to be a miser*/a skinflint **12.** *F* **tête d'œuf**, intellectual/egghead.

offense [ɔfɑ̃s] *nf F* **y a pas d'offense!** don't mention it!/that's quite all right!

officemar [ɔfismar] *nm P* officer.

officiel [ɔfisjɛl] *F* **I** *a* genuine/authentic **II** *nm* **de l'officiel**, the real McCoy/the real thing/the genuine article **III** *int* (c'est) **officiel!** (it's) no joke!/straight up!/there's no getting away from it!/it's for sure!

oie [wa] *nf F* **1. une oie blanche**, a naive young girl* **2. ne faites pas l'oie!** don't be silly!/don't be an idiot!/don't be such a silly goose! **3. envoyer qn ferrer des oies**, to send s.o. on a fool's errand. (*Voir* **boniment 2**)

oignard [waɲar] *nm*, **oigne** [waɲ] *nm* **1.** *V & P* = **oignon 2 2.** *pl P* feet*.

oignon [ɔɲɔ̃] *nm* **1.** *F* **en rang d'oignons**, strung out in a row/single file **2.** *V* anus*; *P* buttocks*/arse/*NAm* ass; **tu peux te le carrer à l'oignon!** you can stick it up your arse/*NAm* ass! **3.** *P* luck; **avoir de l'oignon/avoir l'oignon qui décalotte**, to have all the luck **4.** *F* **c'est pas tes/leurs, etc oignons**, it's none of your/ their, etc business; **occupe-toi/mêle-toi de tes oignons!** mind your own business! **5.** *F* **aux petits oignons**, excellent*/first-class/first-rate; **soigner qn aux petits oignons**, to treat s.o. with loving care/with kid gloves/*Iron* harshly **6.** *P* **pratiquer la course à l'oignon**, = **pratiquer la course à l'échalote** (**échalote 3**) **7.** *P* (*courses*) also-ran/hack/stumer **8.** *Vieilli F* pocket watch. (*Voir* **champ 7**)

à oilp(é) [awalp(e)] *adv phr* (= **à poil**) naked*/starkers/in one's birthday suit.

oiseau, *pl* **-eaux** [wazo] *nm* **1.** *F* **un drôle d'oiseau**, an odd sort of chap/a strange bird/a queer fish; **qui c'est cet oiseau?** who's that guy/geezer? **un vilain oiseau**, a shady customer; a nasty piece of work **2.** *Vieilli F* **aux oiseaux**, excellent*/super **3.** *P* **donner des noms d'oiseaux à qn**, to insult s.o./to call s.o. rude names.

oiselle [wazɛl] *nf Vieilli F* naive young girl*.

oison, -onne [wazɔ̃, -ɔn] *n Vieilli F* credulous person; mug/sucker.

olive [ɔliv] *nf* **1.** *P* bullet/slug **2.** *P* **changer d'eau ses olives/changer l'eau des olives**, to urinate*/to go and see a man about a dog/to splash one's boots **3.** *pl V* testicles*/goolies/nuts.

olkif [ɔlkif], **olpette** [ɔlpɛt], **olpiche** [ɔlpiʃ], **olpif** [ɔlpif] *a inv P* smart/stylish/natty.

olrette [ɔlrɛt] *adv P* (*courses*) all right/OK.

ombre [ɔ̃br] *nf* **1.** *P* **être à l'ombre**, to be in prison*/to be inside; **mettre qn à l'ombre**, to put s.o. away; (*tuer*) to kill* s.o./to wipe s.o. out **2.** *F* **il y a une ombre au tableau**, there's something wrong somewhere; there's a fly in the ointment **3.** *P* **marcher à l'ombre**, to keep a low profile/to stay out of the way; **marche à l'ombre!** stay away!/keep away!

ombrelle [ɔ̃brɛl] *nf P* **avoir un bec d'ombrelle**, to be repugnant/to have a nasty look.

omelette [ɔmlɛt] *nf* **1.** *F* **faire une omelette**, to smash things up/to do some damage **2.** *P* **omelette soufflée**, pregnant* woman.

on [ɔ̃] *pron F* (*souvent utilisé au lieu de* tu *ou* vous, *au pluriel ou au singulier, surtout dans les phrases exclamatives ou interrogatives*) **on se calme!** calm down!/keep cool! **alors, on se fout du monde?** are you trying to take the mickey (out of me)?

onduler [ɔ̃dyle] *vi P* **onduler de la coiffe**, to be mad*/to have a screw loose. (*Voir* **toiture; touffe 1**)

onze [ɔ̃z] *num a inv F* **prendre le train onze/le train d'onze heures**, to walk*/to go on foot/ to go by Shanks's pony/to foot it. (*Voir* **bouillon 3**)

op [ɔp] *nm P* (*drogues*) opium*.

opé [ɔpe] *nf F* (= *opération*) (police) operation.

opérer [ɔpere] *vtr P* **1. opérer qn**, (*tuer au revolver*) to shoot s.o. (dead)/to drill holes in s.o.; (*escroquer, tromper*) to cheat/to swindle*/to diddle/to do/to con s.o. **2. opérer un moteur**, to take an engine apart (for repair); **opérer une banque**, to raid a bank; **opérer des pneus**, to slash tyres.

or [ɔr] *nm F* **1. or noir**, oil/black gold **2. c'est de l'or en barres**, it's as safe as the Bank of England/as safe as houses **3. c'est en or**, it's easy*/it's a piece of cake **4. un caractère**

d'or/en or, a lovely nature; **j'ai une femme en or**, my wife's a real treasure/is worth her weight in gold; **une idée en or**, a marvellous/great/fantastic idea; *(théâtre)* **un rôle en or**, a great/marvellous part; **une occasion en or**, an opportunity not to be missed; a (great) bargain 5. **l'avoir en or**, to be lucky 6. **rouler sur l'or**, to be rich*/to be rolling in it. *(Voir* **cousu** I; **pont 2***)*

orange [ɔrɑ̃ʒ] I *nf* 1. P **balancer/payer une orange à qn**, to hit/to slap s.o. 2. P **avoir des oranges sur l'étagère**, to have small breasts* II *nm* F **l'orange**, amber traffic light; **prendre l'orange bien mûr**, to jump the lights.

ordure [ɔrdyr] *nf* V utterly despicable person; **ordure!** you shit(bag)!/you rat! *(femme)* you bitch!

oreille [ɔrɛj] *nf* F 1. **il s'est (bien) fait tirer l'oreille/il s'est fait un peu tirer l'oreille**, he needed quite a bit of persuading/he took a lot of coaxing; **il ne s'est pas fait tirer l'oreille**, he didn't need to be asked twice 2. **allonger les oreilles à qn**, to reprimand s.o./to chew s.o.'s head off 3. **fendre l'oreille à**, to put (an officer, official, etc) on the retired list 4. **casser les oreilles à qn**, to deafen s.o. (with noise); to drive s.o. mad (with questions, etc) 5. **dormir sur ses deux oreilles**, to sleep* soundly/like a log; **vous pouvez dormir sur vos deux oreilles**, you can sleep easily in your bed. *(Voir* **cocker**; **échauffer**; **frotter** I 1*)*

orges [ɔrʒ] *nfpl* F **faire ses orges**, to make one's pile/one's stack.

orme [ɔrm] *nm* F **donner à qn un rendez-vous sous l'orme**, to make s.o. wait till doomsday/till the cows come home.

orphelin [ɔrfəlɛ̃] *nm* 1. P *(a)* cigarette end*/dog-end *(b)* cigar stump 2. F odd item (book, plate, etc) from a set 3. V turd.

orphelines [ɔrfəlin] *nfpl* V testicles*.

orteil [ɔrtɛj] *nm* F **avoir les orteils en éventail**, to experience immense satisfaction. *(Voir* **doigt 10***)*

orties [ɔrti] *nfpl* F **faut pas pousser mémé/mémère dans les orties!** don't overdo it!/don't push your luck (too far)!

os [ɔs, *pl* o] *nm* 1. F difficulty/snag/hitch; **il y a un os (dans le frometon)**, there's (been) a hitch; **tomber sur un os**, to come up against a snag; **ça va être l'os**, there's an unexpected hitch 2. F *(a)* **c'est un os**, he's a dangerous customer *(b)* **c'est un os dur à ronger**, it's a hard nut to crack 3. F **ça vaut l'os!** that's worthwhile!/it's worth it! 4. F **c'est le même**

os, it all comes down to the same thing in the end 5. F *(a)* **se casser les os**, to fall*/to come a cropper *(b)* **casser/rompre les os à qn**, to beat s.o. up*/to work s.o. over 6. V anus*; *(a)* **l'avoir dans l'os**, *(échouer)* to fail*/to fall flat on one's face; *(être trompé)* to be diddled/to be taken in/to be done/to be had *(b)* **jusqu'à l'os**, totally/completely/utterly 7. P money*; **avoir de l'os**, to have money*/to have the wherewithal; **gagner son os**, to earn one's living 8. P **chez les têtes en os**, in the cemetery*/in the boneyard 9. **os à moelle**; P nose*; V penis*; **faire juter l'os à moelle**, P to use one's fingers instead of a handkerchief; V to masturbate*/to cream off; V **rogner l'os (à qn)**, to perform fellatio* (on s.o.)/to give (s.o.) a blow-job 10. F **mes os/tes os**, etc, me/you, etc; **amène tes os**, come (over) here/drag your carcass over here; **fais gaffe à tes os**, be careful/watch it/take care. *(Voir* **cavaler** II; **courir** I 4; **paquet 7**; **pisser 8**; **sac 3**; **taper** II 2 *(b))*

oseille [ozɛj] *nf* P 1. money*; **faire son oseille**, to get rich* 2. **la faire à l'oseille à qn**, to (try to) pull a fast one (over) on s.o./to make a sucker (out) of s.o.; *(se moquer)* to take the mickey out of s.o.

oseillé [ozeje] *a* P rich*/loaded.

osier [ozje] *nm* P money*; **avoir un champ d'osier**, to be very rich*/to be rolling in it.

osselets [ɔslɛ] *nmpl* P 1. **mes/tes osselets**, me/you; **fais gaffe à tes osselets**, be careful/watch it/take care 2. **courir sur les osselets à qn**, to annoy* s.o./to get s.o.'s back up; **ne me cours pas sur les osselets**, stop pestering me/bugging me.

ost(e)au, osto [ɔsto] *nm* P hospital. *(Voir* **host(e)au, hosto***)*

ostiner [ɔstine] *FrC* F I *vi* to contradict/to go on saying the opposite II *vpr* **s'ostiner** 1. to be stubborn 2. to argue/to bicker.

ostrogot(h) [ɔstrɔgo] *nm* F rough/uncouth man; boor; **quel ostrogot(h)!** what a savage! **un drôle d'ostrogot(h)**, a weirdo.

s'ôter [sote] *vpr* F **ôte-toi de là (que je m'y mette)!** get out (of here)!/get out of the way!

oua(h)-oua(h) [wawa] *nm* F *(mot d'enfant)* dog*/bow-wow/doggy(-woggy).

ouais! [wɛ] *int* F *(oui)* yeah! *Iron* oh yeah!

ouallou! [walu] *int* P nothing doing*!/no chance!/no way!/not bloody likely*!

ouatères [watɛr] *nmpl* F WC*/loo/*NAm* john.

oubli [ubli] *nm* F **marcher à l'oubli**, to feign

ignorance/to pretend one doesn't know.

oublier [ublije] **I** *vtr F* **1.** oublier de respirer, to die*/to snuff it. (*Voir* **goût**) **2.** oublie-moi! leave me alone! **II** *vpr* **s'oublier** *F* **1.** (*enfant, chien etc*) to urinate*/to forget oneself/to wet oneself **2.** to fart*.

oubliettes [ublijɛt] *nfpl F* mettre/jeter qch aux oubliettes, to consign sth to oblivion/to shelve sth indefinitely; to neglect sth.

ouf! [uf] *int F* ouf! phew! avant de pouvoir dire ouf! before you could say Jack Robinson; il n'a pas eu le temps de dire ouf! he didn't even have time to catch his breath.

oui-da! [wida] *int Vieilli F* yes, indeed!/yes, of course!/*NAm* yes, sirree!

ouiouine [wiwin] *nf P* sanitary towel/*NAm* napkin.

ouistiti [wistiti] *nm P* **1.** the boss's son **2.** skeleton key.

ourdé [urde] *a P* drunk*; ourdé à zéro, blind drunk*.

ourdée [urde] *nf P* il tient une bonne ourdée, he's dead drunk*/he's pissed out of his mind/ he's completely plastered.

s'ourder [surde] *vpr P* to get drunk*/pissed.

ours [urs] *nm* **1.** *F* one's own work; literary *or* artistic production; *esp* manuscript that has gone the rounds (of the publishers)/that has been repeatedly rejected **2.** *P Mil* glasshouse **3.** *P* avoir ses ours, to have one's period*/to have the curse **4.** *F* ours mal léché, uncouth individual; quel ours! what a boor!

oursin [ursɛ̃] *nm P* avoir des oursins dans le morlingue, to be miserly*/to be close-fisted/to have short arms and deep pockets.

ousque, ous'que [uskə] *adv P* (= *où est-ce que*) where; ous'qu'il est? where is he? c'est là ousque je suis né, that's where I was born.

oust(e)! [ust] *int P* allez oust(e)! (*allez-y*) come on!/get a move on!/look sharp! (*allez-vous en*) hop it!/scram!/get out of my road!

outil [uti] *nm* **1.** *P* (annoying) individual/ bore*/nuisance; un drôle d'outil, a clumsy clot/a tool **2.** *P* (*a*) knife (*b*) gun (*c*) *pl* weapons **3.** *V* penis*/tool **4.** *P* déballer ses outils, (*avouer*) to confess*/to open up; (*vomir*) to vomit/to spew (one's guts out); (*faire de l'exhibitionnisme*) to take one's trousers off and expose one's genitals/to flash; remballer ses outils, to put one's trousers (back) on again.

outillé [utije] *a P* bien outillé, (*homme*) well-equipped/well-hung/well-endowed.

outiller [utije] *vtr P* to knife/to stab (s.o.).

ouverture [uvɛrtyr] *nf P* avoir l'ouverture retardée, to be slow on the uptake.

ouvrage [uvraʒ] **I** *nm P* (*cambriolage, coup*) job. (*Voir* **boîte 8**) **II** *nf F* c'est de la belle ouvrage, that's a nice piece of work; *Iron* that's a nice mess (you've got us into).

ouvrier [uvrije] *nm P* **1.** burglar/ housebreaker **2.** skilful and hard worker.

ouvrir [uvrir] *vtr P* **1.** ouvrir sa gueule/ l'ouvrir, to talk*/to open one's mouth; (*avouer*) to confess*/to open one's trap/to open up **2.** ouvrir les grandes eaux de Versailles, to start crying/weeping*/ blubbering.

ovale [ɔval] *nm P* avoir un bel ovale, (*fille, femme*) to have a shapely posterior/a cute ass.

overdose [ɔvœrdoz] *nf F* (*drogues*) overdose; overdose d'affection, too much affection.

P

pac [pak] *nm P* = **pac(k)son**.

pacha [paʃa] *nm F* 1. mener une vie de pacha/faire le pacha, to (sit back and) take it easy; to lead an easy life; to live like a lord 2. (*marine*) le pacha, the captain/the old man.

packson [paksɔ̃] *nm*, **pacqsif** [paksif] *nm*, **pacqson** [paksɔ̃] *nm*, **pacque** [pak] *nm*, **pacqueson** [paksɔ̃] *nm*, **pacsif** [paksif] *nm*, **pacson** [paksɔ̃] *nm P* 1. parcel/package 2. (*courses*) toucher le packson, to make a lot of money/to make a packet 3. pack(et) of cigarettes *or* tobacco 4. mettre le pacsif, to make an effort/to try hard 5. (*drogues*) sachet *m*/dose *f* of heroin*.

paddock [padɔk] *nm P* bed*; être au paddock, to be in bed.

(se) paddocker [(sə)padɔke] *vpr & vi P* to go to bed*/to hit the hay/to hit the sack/to crash out.

padoc [padɔk] *nm P* = **paddock**.

(se) padoquer [(sə)padɔke] *vpr & i P* = **(se) paddocker**.

paf [paf] **I** *a inv P* drunk*; complètement paf, dead drunk*/plastered/pissed/sloshed **II** *nm* 1. *P* tomber sur un paf, to hit a snag; (*échouer*) to fail*/to come unstuck 2. *V* penis*/prick 3. *P surt Iron* beau comme un paf (en fleur), handsome/dishy; elegant/all tarted up. (*Voir* **terrine 2** (*b*))

se paffer [səpafe] *vpr P* to get drunk*.

pagaïe [pagaj] *nf*, **pagaille** [pagaj] *nf F* 1. muddle/jumble/confusion/chaos; quelle pagaïe! what a mess!/what a shambles! en pagaïe, in disorder/in a mess; une belle pagaïe, an absolute muddle/a right old shambles; c'est la pagaïe dans la cuisine, the kitchen looks like a bomb's hit it 2. il y en a en pagaïe, there's lots/loads of it; there are masses of them; avoir de l'argent en pagaïe, to have bags of money*/to be rolling in it.

pagailleur, -euse [pagajœr, -øz] *n F* muddler/messer.

pagailleux [pagajø] *a F* (*a*) in a muddle/in

a mess/in a shambles; shambolic; cluttered (up) (*b*) (*personne*) untidy/messy.

pagaye [pagaj] *nf F* = **pagaïe**.

page¹ [paʒ] *nf* 1. *F* être à la page, (*à la mode*) to be up-to-date/to be with it; (*au courant*) to be in the know/in the picture; mettre qn à la page, to bring s.o. up-to-date; to put s.o. in the picture/to gen s.o. up; se mettre à la page, to keep up with the times 2. tourner la page, *F* (*passer l'éponge sur qch*) to let bygones be bygones; *F* (*changer de conduite*) to turn over a new leaf; *V* to be a homosexual*; *V* (to turn over one's sexual partner in order) to have anal sex*/to screw from behind.

page² *nm*, **pageot** [paʒo] *nm P* bed*; aller/se filer/se mettre au page, to go to bed*/ to hit the hay/to hit the sack.

se pageoter [səpaʒɔte] *vpr P* to go to bed*/to hit the sack/to crash out.

pager [paʒe] **I** *vi P* to sleep*/to have a kip/to get some shuteye **II** *vpr* **se pager** *P* to go to bed*.

pagne [paɲ] *nm*, **pagnot** [paɲo] *nm P* bed*.

se pagnoter [səpaɲɔte] *vpr P* to go to bed*/to get into bed/to turn in/to crash out/to hit the sack.

pagouze [paguz] *nf P* salary; wages; pay.

paie [pɛj] *nf F P* = **paye**.

paillarde [pajard] *nf F* bawdy/dirty/coarse story *or* joke etc; chanter des paillardes, to sing dirty songs/rugby songs.

se paillarder [səpajarde] *vpr F* (*a*) to have a good time*/to have a ball (*b*) to have a good laugh.

paillasse [pajas] *nf P* 1. stomach*/belly; crever/trouer la paillasse à qn, to knife s.o. in the guts 2. se crever la paillasse à (faire) qch, to work oneself to death doing sth 3. (*a*) (cheap) prostitute*/tart (*b*) easy lay/ pushover/scrubber/tart.

paillasson [pajasɔ̃] *nm* 1. *P* (*a*) = **paillasse 3** (*b*) mener une vie de paillasson, to lead a fast/debauched life 2. *F Péj* servile person/doormat 3. *F* old tennis racket. (*Voir* **clef 1**)

paille [pɑj] *nf* 1. *F* être sur la paille, to be in extreme poverty/to be down-and-out 2. *F* voilà une paille que je t'ai pas vu! it's ages since I last saw you! 3. *F Iron* il demande un million: une paille! he's asking a million: a mere trifle!/that's peanuts!/that's chicken-feed! 4. *Vieilli F* avoir/tenir une paille, to be drunk* 5. *P* passer la paille de fer, to play music/to busk (from table to table) in a restaurant *or* night club. (*Voir* **chapeau 2, 3**)

paillon [pɑjɔ̃] *nm Vieilli P* faire un paillon/des paillons à son mari/à sa femme, to be unfaithful to one's husband*/wife*; to cheat on one's husband*/wife*; to have a bit on the side.

pain [pɛ̃] *nm* 1. *F* avoir du pain sur la planche, to have one's hands full/to have a lot on one's plate 2. *F* bon comme (du) bon pain/bon comme le pain, (*personne*) good-hearted/good-natured 3. *F* je ne mange pas de ce pain-là, I don't go in for that sort of thing/I'd rather starve (than get involved in that) 4. *F* se vendre/partir comme des petits pains, to sell/to go like hot cakes 5. *F* avaler le pain à cacheter, to take Holy Communion; il n'a pas inventé les pains à cacheter, he'll never set the Thames/the world on fire 6. *P* blow*/punch; coller/flanquer/foutre un pain (sur la gueule) à qn, to hit s.o. in the face/to sock s.o. on the jaw 7. *V* pain au lait, penis*/stick; avoir le petit pain, to have an erection* 8. *pl V* petits pains, buttocks*/buns 9. *V* pain blanc/frais/des Jules, prostitution/pimps' bread and butter; money earned by prostitution; manger du pain blanc, to procure/to live off a prostitute's earnings/to pimp; pain frais, prostitute*/meal-ticket (*from the point of view of the pimp*) 10. *P* pain dur, unimportant/uninteresting business 11. *F* ça (ne) mange pas de pain, there's no (financial) risk/it's nothing (to worry about); (*facile*) it's not difficult to do/it's no hassle 12. *P Mus* wrong note. (*Voir* **cuit 3**; **fesse 9** (*b*); **goût**; **planche 4**)

paire [pɛr] *nf* 1. *F* ça, c'est une autre paire de manches, that's another story/that's a different kettle of fish/that's a whole new ball game 2. *P* (*a*) se faire la paire, to run away*/to clear off/to do a bunk/to beat it (*b*) dîner à la paire, to leave without paying for one's meal 3. *P* avoir une paire de lunettes contre le soleil, to have two lovely black eyes 4. *F* les deux font la paire, (*personnes*) they make a fine pair/they're two of a kind 5. *F* une belle paire de fesses, (*de femme*) a nice piece of ass; (*d'homme*) nice buns 6. *P* cette bonne paire! what a joke!/that's a good one! 7. *F* une paire chaude, (*saucisses*) two hot frankfurters 8. *V* testicles*; avoir une belle paire/en avoir une paire, to have guts/to have balls/to have spunk. (*Voir* **glisser II 3**)

paître [pɛtr] *vi F* envoyer paître qn, to send s.o. packing*/to tell s.o. to get lost/to tell s.o. where to go; je l'ai envoyé paître, I sent him packing.

paix [pɛ] *nf P* ficher/foutre la paix à qn, to leave s.o. alone/in peace; fiche-moi/fous-moi la paix! leave me alone!/stop bugging me!/get lost*!/go to hell!/piss off!

pajot [paʒo] *nm P* = **pageot**.

se pajoter [səpaʒɔte] *vpr P* = **se pageoter**.

pakistoche [pakistɔʃ] *a & n P Péj* Pakistani/Paki.

pakson [paksɔ̃] *nm P* = **packson**.

palace [palas] *a P* excellent*/first-rate*. (*Voir* **palas, pallas**)

palanquée [palɑ̃ke] *nf P* une palanquée de ..., lots*/loads/lashings/oodles of ....

palas [palas] *P* I *a* (*chose*) excellent*/first-rate*/great; nice; beautiful; une idée palas, a great/smart/fantastic idea; c'est palas ici, it's really nice here II *nm* 1. (*boniment*) patter/hot air/gas/yackety-yak; du palas (en tartine), boloney/bull(shit)/eyewash 2. faire (au) palas, to swank/to show off* 3. (*a*) faire du palas à qn, to try to get round s.o./to try and coax s.o./to fast-talk s.o. (*b*) faire du palas à une femme, to chat a woman up/to sweet-talk a woman/to try to get off with a woman.

palasser [palase] *vi P* (*a*) to ad-lib (*b*) to gas/to yack/to rabbit (on)/to bunny.

palasseur [palasœr] *nm P* compulsive talker/windbag/gasbag.

pâle [pɑl] *a P* 1. ill/sick; *Mil* se faire porter pâle, to go sick/to report sick 2. être pâle des genoux, to be exhausted*/on one's knees.

paletot [palto] *nm P* 1. dernier paletot/paletot de sapin/paletot sans manches, coffin/wooden overcoat; se faire faire un paletot sans manches/un paletot de sapin, to die*/to put on a wooden overcoat 2. tomber/sauter sur le paletot à qn, to sail into s.o./to jump (on) s.o. 3. prendre tout sur le paletot, to carry the can/to take the rap **4. avoir qn sur le paletot**, to be saddled with s.o.; **il a les flics sur le paletot**, he's got the cops on his heels/on his back/breathing down his neck; he's on the run from the cops **5. mettre la main sur le paletot à qn**, to arrest* s.o./to collar s.o. **6. secouer le paletot à qn**, to reprimand* s.o./to tear s.o. off a strip. (*Voir* **machine 5**)

palette [palɛt] *nf P* **1.** hand*/mitt **2.** shoulder-blade.

pâlichon, -onne [pɑliʃɔ̃, -ɔn] *a F* palish/rather pale; (*personne*) peaky/sickly.

pallaque [palak] *nf P* prostitute*.

pallas [palas] *a & nm P* = **palas**.

pallot [palo] *nm P* kiss on the mouth; **pallot baveux**, French kiss.

palmé, -ée [palme] **I** *n F* holder of the *Palmes académiques* **II** *a F* **avoir les mains palmées/P les avoir palmées**, to be workshy.

palombe [palɔ̃b] *nf P* woman*; girl*; bird/chick.

palper [palpe] **I** *vtr P* **1.** to receive/to earn/to win (money); **qu'est-ce qu'on a pu palper comme pognon!** we were raking it in/making money hand over fist! **j'ai jamais palpé aux courses**, I've never won anything on the horses **2.** to search (s.o./sth); **se faire palper**, to be searched **II** *vpr* **se palper** *F* **tu peux te palper!** nothing doing!*/you've got another thing *or* think coming!/(you can) take a running jump!/you can go (and) fly a kite!

palpitant [palpitɑ̃] *nm P* heart/ticker. (*Voir* **court-circuit**)

palpouser [palpuze] *vtr P* = **palper**.

paltoquet [paltɔkɛ] *nm F* (*a*) nonentity; (pompous) idiot (*b*) *A* boor.

paluche [palyʃ] *nf P* hand*/mitt/paw; **écraser les paluches**, to shake hands; **s'emmêler les paluches**, to play (the piano, etc) badly/to keep hitting (the) wrong notes.

palucher [palyʃe] **I** *vtr P* to finger/to fondle/to caress/to feel up/to touch up (a woman) **II** *vpr* **se palucher 1.** *P* to imagine/to kid oneself **2.** *P* to be happy/pleased **3.** *V* to masturbate*/to take oneself in hand.

pana [pana] *nm P* = **panne 3, 4**.

panache [panaʃ] *nm F* **1. avoir son panache**, to be slightly drunk*/to be a bit tight/to be rather tiddly **2. faire panache**, (*cycliste, cavalier*) to take a header; (*voiture*) to turn a somersault/to overturn; **faire un panache complet**, to turn right over/to turn turtle.

panade [panad] *nf* **1.** *F* **être dans la panade**, to be in a fix*/to be in the soup; (*être dans la misère*) to be penniless*/to be down-and-out **2.** *P* spineless individual/drip/wet.

panais [panɛ] *nm V* penis*/root; **dérouiller/planter/tremper son panais**, to have sex*/to dip one's wick. (*Voir* **dégraisser II**)

Panam(e) [panam] *Prnm P* Paris.

panard [panar] *nm* **1.** *P* foot*/hoof; *pl* plates (of meat); **avoir les panards enflés**, to have swollen feet **2.** *P* **j'en ai plein les panards**, I'm sick and tired of it/I'm cheesed off with it **3.** *P* share (of booty)/cut/whack/split. (*Voir* **fade 1**) **4.** *P* pleasure; **quel panard!** great!/terrific!/fantastic! **prendre son panard**, *V* to have an orgasm*/to come; *P* to get a kick (out of sth) **5.** *P* = **panne 3, 4**. (*Voir* **essence**)

pandore [pɑ̃dɔr] *nm A F* policeman*.

pane [pan] *nf A F* = **panne 4, 6**.

pané [pane] *a A P* = **panné**.

panet [panɛ] *nm V* = **panais**.

panetot [panto] *nm P* = **paletot**.

panier [panje] *nm* **1.** *F* **panier à salade**, police *or* prison van/*Br Vieilli* Black Maria*/*surt NAm* paddy waggon **2.** *F* **c'est un panier de crabes**, they're always fighting amongst themselves/they're all at each other's throats **3.** *P* job lot (of books, etc) **4.** *P* sidecar (of motorbike) **5.** *F* **on peut les mettre dans le même panier**, they're all as bad as each other **6.** *F* **panier percé**, spendthrift; **c'est un panier percé**, he spends money like water **7.** *F* **le dessus du panier**, the pick of the bunch; the cream; **le fond du panier**, the bottom of the barrel; the dregs **8.** *P* **panier à crottes**, buttocks*/bottom/ass; **mettre la main au panier**, to feel/to pinch a (woman's) bottom; to goose (a woman); to feel (a woman) up/to touch (a woman) up **9.** *V* female genitals*/cunt; **descendre au panier**, to have oral sex*/with a woman/to go down on a woman; **se faire défoncer le panier**, to have sex*/to have it away/to get balled. (*Voir* **con II** (*a*); **coucouche**)

paniquard [panikar] *F* **I** *a* scare-mongering/alarmist **II** *nm* scare-monger/alarmist.

panne [pan] *nf F* **1.** (*personne*) **être en panne**, to be/to get stuck; to have come to a standstill; **rester en panne devant une difficulté**, to be/get stuck over a problem **2.** (*a*) **laisser qn en panne**, to leave s.o. in the lurch/to let s.o. down (*b*) **elle est en panne de cigarettes**, she's (run) out of cigarettes (*c*) **avoir une panne d'oreiller**, to oversleep **3.** (*théâtre*) small part/bit part **4.** worthless*/

useless object, etc; (*tableau*) daub; (*brocante*) unsaleable object/= white elephant; (*personne*) hopeless/useless individual; **son patron le traite comme de la panne,** his boss treats him like dirt/badly **5.** lapse of memory **6.** *A* poverty; **dans une panne noire,** terribly hard up/stony broke.

panné [pane] *a A F* penniless*/flat broke/ down-and-out.

pano [pano] *nm Cin F* (= *panoramique*) **pano sur un petit groupe de fans,** pan on a small group of fans.

panoplie [panɔpli] *nf P* (*armes individuelles*) weapons; (*organes génitaux*) male genitals*/block and tackle/goods; **sortir sa panoplie,** to display one's weapons; (*faire de l'exhibitionnisme*) to expose oneself/to flash.

panouillard [panujar] *nm P* (*théâtre*) bit actor.

panouille [panuj] *nf P* **1.** fool*/dimwit/ moron **2.** (*théâtre*) small part/bit part.

pan(-)pan [pɑ̃pɑ̃] *nm F* **faire pan(-)pan (cucul) à un enfant,** to smack a child's bottom/to give a child a smack-botty. (*Voir* **zizi 1**)

panse [pɑ̃s] *nf* **1.** *F* stomach*/belly; **grosse panse,** paunch*/pot-belly/(beer) gut **2.** *P* (*a*) **se faire crever la panse,** to get knifed in the guts (*b*) **bouffer à s'en faire crever la panse/ se farcir la panse/s'en mettre plein la panse,** to eat greedily*/to stuff one's guts/to blow one's guts out **3.** *Vieilli F* **il n'a pas fait une panse d'a,** he hasn't done a stroke of work/ he's done damn all. (*Voir* **œil 6**)

pansu, -ue [pɑ̃sy] *a & n F* paunchy*/tubby/ pot-bellied (person).

pante¹ [pɑ̃t] *nm P* **1.** fellow*/chap/bloke/guy; **un drôle de pante,** an odd character/an odd-ball **2.** mug/sucker.

pante² [pɑ̃t] *nm F* (= *pantalon*) trousers/*surt NAm* pants/strides/duds.

panthère [pɑ̃tɛr] *nf P* **1. ma panthère,** my wife*/the missis **2. lait de panthère,** pastis.

pantouflard [pɑ̃tuflar] *F* **I** *a* stay-at-home **II** *nm* **1.** stay-at-home/home-bird **2.** officer who has taken a civilian job; civil servant who has joined the private sector.

pantoufle [pɑ̃tufl] *nf F* **1.** (*personne*) dead loss/washout; **quelle pantoufle!** he's hopeless! **2. il joue comme une pantoufle,** he can't play for nuts/for toffee **3. raisonner comme une pantoufle,** to talk through one's hat **4.** civilian job **5.** (*a*) sum of money which may be

demanded from any graduate of a *grande école* who does not remain in the service of the state (*b*) group of graduates of a *grande école* who do not remain in the service of the state.

pantoufler [pɑ̃tufle] *vi F* **1.** to talk through one's hat/to talk cock **2.** (*a*) to take it easy/to put one's feet up (*b*) to lead a quiet life **3.** (*officier*) to take a civilian job; (*fonctionnaire*) to join the private sector.

pantoute [pɑ̃tut] *adv FrC P* not at all/no way.

pantre [pɑ̃tr] *nm P* = **pante¹ 1, 2.**

Pantruchard, -arde [pɑ̃tryʃar, -ard] *n P* Parisian.

Pantruche [pɑ̃tryʃ] *Prnm P* Paris.

panuche [panyʃ] *nf P* **être dans la panuche** = être dans la panade (**panade 1**).

pap [pap] *nm F Voir* **nœud-pap.**

papa [papa] *nm F* **1.** middle-aged man (without much energy); **allez, papa!** come on, old mate! **à la papa,** in a quiet/simple/homely way; **faire l'amour/baiser à la papa,** to make love in a slow, leisurely fashion; *Aut* **aller à la papa,** to potter along; **on a fait le voyage à la papa,** we took it nice and easy **2. un gros papa,** a banknote of any large denomination **3. de papa,** old-fashioned/behind the times/ antiquated; **le football de papa,** football as it used to be played **4.** (*cartes*) **les quatre papas,** the four kings. (*Voir* **fils 2; gâteau II**).

papaout [papau(t)] *nm P* homosexual*.

pape [pap] *nm F* **aller à Rome sans voir le pape,** to lose (a game, etc) narrowly. (*Voir* **téléphoner 2**)

papeau [papo] *nm P* hat*/titfer.

papelard [paplar] *nm F* **1.** (*a*) (piece of) paper (*b*) letter (*c*) (official) document (*d*) **c'est du papelard,** it's not serious/you can't take this seriously **2.** *pl* (*a*) identity papers (*b*) business papers (*c*) (news)papers.

papier [papje] *nm* **1.** *F* (*journalisme*) **faire un papier,** to write copy/to do an article/to do a piece (*for a newspaper*) **2.** *F* **avoir un bon papier/avoir le papier,** to have a good record/ a good reputation **3.** *F* **connaître le papier,** to be well informed (**de,** about) **4.** *F* (*courses, etc*) **faire le papier,** to study form; **faire son papier,** to make out one's bet **5.** *F* **papier à douleur,** unpaid bill **6.** *F* **un papier,** a hundred-franc note **7.** *F* **rayez ça de vos papiers,** don't count on it/(you can) forget it **8.** *F* **être dans les petits papiers de qn,** to be in s.o.'s good books **9.** *P* (*séquence de cartes*) run 10. *F* job lot of newspapers *or* books 11. *P* passer qn au papier de verre, to shave s.o.'s hair very close. (*Voir* **cul 24**; **musique 4**)

papillon [papijɔ̃] *nm* 1. *P* papillon d'amour, crab (louse)/pubic louse 2. *F* (parking) ticket 3. *P* papillon du Sénégal, penis*. (*Voir* **minute II**)

papognes [papɔɲ] *nfpl P* hands*.

papotage [papɔtaʒ] *nm F* (*a*) chattering; gossiping (*b*) chatter/gossip.

papoter [papɔte] *vi F* to gossip; to chatter*; to rabbit on.

papouille [papuj] *nf P* caress/tickle/squeeze/cuddle; faire des papouilles à qn, to hug and squeeze s.o.

papouiller [papuje] *vtr P* to caress/to cuddle/to hug/to squeeze (s.o.).

pap's [pap] *nmpl F* (= *papiers d'identité*) (identity) papers.

pâquerette [pɑkrɛt] *nf* 1. *F* cueillir les pâquerettes, to wander about idly/to moon about/to waste time 2. *F* aller aux pâquerettes, (*voiture*) to run off the road 3. *F* au ras des pâquerettes, at the lowest level; son humour reste/vole au ras des pâquerettes, his sense of humour is pretty basic/low 4. *V* female genitals*. (*Voir* **tige 2**)

Pâques [pɑk] *nm F* 1. remettre qch à Pâques ou à la Trinité, to put sth off indefinitely 2. faire Pâques avant les Rameaux, to consummate a marriage before the ceremony/to have sex* before marriage/to jump the gun.

paquesif [paksif] *nm*, **paqueson** [paksɔ̃] *nm P* = **pacsif, pacson**.

paquet [pakɛ] *nm* 1. *F* avoir son paquet, to get one's (just) deserts; recevoir son paquet, to be reprimanded*/to catch it/to get a bawling out; (*être congédié*) to be dismissed*/to get the sack; il a eu son paquet, I told him what I thought of him 2. *F* faire son paquet/faire ses paquets, to pack up (and go); to pack one's bags 3. *F* lâcher/donner son paquet à qn, to let fly at s.o./to let s.o. have it/to give s.o. a piece of one's mind 4. *F* risquer le paquet, to risk it/to chance it; to stick one's neck out 5. *F* toucher un joli paquet, to make/to win a packet 6. *F* (y) mettre le paquet, to go all out/to pull out all the stops/to give it all one's got 7. *F* (*personne*) quel paquet! what a lump! (*mal habillé*) what a frump! être fichu comme un paquet de linge sale, to be got up like a guy/done up like a dog's dinner; c'est un paquet d'os, he's/she's (nothing but) a bag

of bones; he's/she's all skin and bones; c'est un paquet de nerfs, he's a bundle of nerves 8. *P* male genitals*/privates 9. *P* stock *or* supply of (illegal) drugs 10. *P* lâcher/déballer/sortir le paquet, to confess*/to spill the beans/to blow the gaff 11. (*a*) *P* lâcher/envoyer le paquet, to shoot/to fire (a gun); ils lui ont lâché le paquet dans le dos, they emptied their guns into him (*b*) *V* envoyer/lâcher son paquet, to have an orgasm*/to ejaculate*/to shoot one's load 12. *V* paquet de tabac, woman's pubic hair/beaver.

para [para] *F* I *nm Mil* (= *parachutiste*) paratrooper/para II *n* = **parano** III.

parachuter [paraʃyte] *vtr F* to pitchfork (s.o.) (into a job, etc).

parade [parad] *nf Vieilli P* défiler (dur) à la parade, to die*.

paradis [paradi] *nm F* 1. (*théâtre*) le paradis, the gods 2. vous ne l'emporterez pas en paradis! you won't get away with it!/I'll get even with you!

paradouze [paraduz] *nm P* paradise.

paralance [paralɑ̃s] *nm P* umbrella*/brolly.

parano [parano] *F* I *a* paranoid; il est parano, he's paranoid/obsessed II *nf* paranoia; elle fait de la parano, she's being paranoid; arrête ta parano! stop being paranoid! III *nm & f* paranoid person.

parapluie [paraplɥi] *nm* 1. *F* il a l'air d'avoir avalé son parapluie, he's very stiff and starchy/P he looks as though he's got a poker up his arse 2. *P* porter le parapluie, to bear the responsibility/to carry the can/to take the rap 3. *P* fermer son parapluie, to die* 4. *P* alibi*/cover/front 5. *P* la Maison Parapluie, the police*; the cop shop. (*Voir* **sirop 3**)

paravent [paravɑ̃] *nm F* (*personne*) screen/decoy/cover (*eg to divert the suspicions of a jealous husband, etc*).

pardessus [pardəsy] *nm P* pardessus de sapin, coffin/wooden overcoat; se faire faire un pardessus de sapin, to die*. (*Voir* **paletot 1**)

pardeuss(e) [pardøs] *nm P* overcoat.

pardi! [pardi] *int F* of course! naturally!

pardingue [pardɛ̃g] *nm P* overcoat.

pardon! [pardɔ̃] *int P* 1. pardon! t'y vas fort! steady on! 2. (*admiration, etc*) le père était déjà costaud, mais alors le fils, pardon! the father was a hefty bloke, but as for the son, well! pardon! c'est pas de la camelote, excuse me! it's far from being trash.

pardoss(e) [pardos] *nm* P overcoat.

paré [pare] *a* P 1. ready 2. protected from hardship; in a comfortable (financial) situation.

pare-brise [parbriz] *nmpl* P spectacles/specs/glasses.

pare-choc(s) [parʃɔk] *nmpl* P large breasts*/big knockers.

pare-flotte [parflɔt] *nm inv* P umbrella*.

pareil [parɛj] P I *nm* c'est du pareil au même, it all comes to the same thing/it's much of a muchness/it's as broad as it's long II *adv* (et) moi pareil! so do I!/me too!

pare-lance [parlɑ̃s] *nm* P umbrella*.

parenthèses [parɑ̃tɛz] *nfpl* 1. F avoir les jambes en parenthèses, to be bow-legged/bandy-legged 2. P pisser entre parenthèses, to experience pain when urinating.

parfum [parfœ̃] *nm* P être au parfum, to be well informed/to be in the know/to know the score; **mettre qn au parfum**, to give s.o. information* about sth/inform s.o. about sth/to put s.o. in the know/to wise s.o. up/to tip s.o. off/to put s.o. in the picture/to gen s.o. up/to give s.o. the lowdown.

parfumer [parfyme] *vtr* P = mettre au parfum (**parfum**).

Parigot, -ote [parigo, -ɔt] *a & n* P Parisian.

Paris-beurre [paribœr] *nm* F ham sandwich.

parlant [parlɑ̃] *nm Cin* F (*film*) talkie.

parler [parle] I *vi* F 1. tu parles(, Charles)! (*je suis d'accord*) now you're talking!/that's more like it!; you're telling me!/you bet!/not half!/rather! (*absolument pas*) what a hope!/no chance!/you have to be joking!/what do you take me for?/oh yeah? 2. (*a*) **bonne cuisinière, tu parles!** elle n'est pas fichue de faire cuire un œuf! good cook my foot! she can't even boil an egg! (*b*) **tu parles d'une occasion!** talk about an opportunity! **tu parles d'une rigolade!** talk about a lark!/it was a right giggle! 3. trouver à qui parler, to meet one's match 4. to confess*/to cough up II *vpr* **se parler** A F *Dial* to be courting.

parlot(t)e [parlɔt] *nf* F gossip/chitchat/natter.

paroisse [parwas] *nf* F 1. changer de paroisse, (*déménager*) to move (house); (*changer de café*) to change one's local (pub) 2. porter des chaussettes de deux paroisses, to be wearing odd socks.

paroissien [parwasjɛ̃] *nm* F man*/chap*/fellow/bloke/guy; c'est un drôle de paroissien, he's a strange character/an odd bloke/a funny guy.

parole [parɔl] *nf & int* 1. F parole (d'homme)! word of honour!/cross my heart! ma parole! upon my word!/well I never! 2. P porter la bonne parole, to make a punitive expedition to an establishment that refuses to cooperate in a racket.

parpagne [parpaɲ] *nf* P aller à la parpagne, to go into the country(side).

parpaing [parpɛ̃] *nm* P punch/thump (in the face).

parrain [parɛ̃] *nm* P 1. lawyer/barrister/counsel 2. (male) witness (for the prosecution) 3. (*plaignant*) plaintiff 4. (*dans le milieu*) important person*/big shot/big-time operator; (*mafia*) godfather.

partant [partɑ̃] *nm* F je suis partant, (you can) count me in; je ne suis pas partant, (you can) count me out.

parti [parti] *a* F (un peu) parti, slightly drunk*/tipsy/woozy; à moitié parti, half-seas-over/half-gone; complètement parti, sloshed/plastered/stoned.

partie [parti] *nf* 1. F vous avez la partie belle, now's your chance/the ball's in your court 2. P une partie de traversin, a nap/a snooze/forty winks; (*coït*) sex*/bonking 3. P (*a*) partie carrée, (sex) orgy involving two couples/P foursome; = wife-swapping (*b*) partie fine, (sex) orgy 4. F ce n'est pas une partie de plaisir! it's no picnic! 5. F les parties, male genitals*/private parts/privates 6. F (*boum*) party/bop. (*Voir* **bordelaise**; **jambe 18**)

partousard, -arde [partuzar, -ard] P I *a* debauched; orgiastic II *n* person who takes part in an orgy.

partouse [partuz] *nf* P (collective sex) orgy; daisy chain; partouse à la bague, daisy chain; partouse carrée, orgy for two couples/foursome; = wife-swapping.

partouser [partuze] *vi* P to take part in an orgy.

partouzard, -arde [partuzar, -ard] *a & n* P = **partousard, -arde**.

partouze [partuz] *nf* P = **partouse**.

partouzer [partuze] *vi* P = **partouser**.

pas [pɑ] I *nm* F 1. mettre qn au pas, to make s.o. toe the line/to bring s.o. to heel 2. sauter le pas, to take the plunge II *adv* 1. P (*a*) pas? = n'est-ce pas? tu m'écriras, pas? you'll write (to me), won't you? (*b*) y a pas, there's no denying it/there's no getting away from it/ there's no two ways about it (c) **pas vrai?** that not so?/(am I) right? **c'est foutu ton truc, pas vrai?** it's all screwed up, isn't it?/you've ballsed it! go on, admit it! (d) **pas si fort, la radio!** turn that radio down! 2. *F* **il connaît Londres comme pas un,** he knows London better than anyone; **il est menteur comme pas un,** he's a terrible liar 3. *F* **il est pas mal, ce mec-là,** he's not at all bad, that bloke/he's a pretty good-looking guy.

pascal [paskal] *nm F* 500-franc note.

passant [pasɑ̃] *nm P* itinerant beggar.

passe [pas] **I** *nf* 1. *F* **vous êtes en bonne passe,** you're in a strong position/everything's going right for you; **être dans une mauvaise passe,** to be in a fix/in a tight corner 2. *P* period of time spent with a prostitute* and paid for by the client/trick; **chambre de passe,** bedroom (*esp* in a hotel) let by the hour; **hôtel de passe,** hotel which lets out rooms by the hour to prostitutes; **maison de passe,** brothel*/whorehouse/call joint/knocking shop; **passe bourgeoise,** straightforward sex with a prostitute*/a quick (in and out) job/a quickie; **être en passe,** (*prostituée*) to be with a client/to be on the job; **faire une passe,** to do/to turn a trick; **faire la passe,** (*hôtelier*) to let out rooms to prostitutes (by the hour) 3. *P* **passe anglaise,** gambling game with dice; **rouler la passe,** to shake the bones 4. *P* commission (*on a financial deal*) **II** *nm F* 1. passkey/skeleton key/master key 2. passport.

passé [pase] *nm F* **avoir un/du passé,** to have had dealings with the law/to have form.

passe-lacet [paslasɛ] *nm F* **raide comme un passe-lacet,** penniless*/broke to the wide.

passer [pase] **I** *vi* 1. *F* **il faut passer par là ou par la porte/par la fenêtre,** it's a case of Hobson's choice/there's no alternative/love it or leave it/like it or lump it 2. *F* (a) **y passer,** to die*; **il a bien failli y passer,** he nearly kicked the bucket (b) *F* **y passer,** to have to go through with (sth); **tout le monde y passe,** it happens to everyone/we all have to go through (with) it; **j'y ai passé/j'y suis passé,** I've been through it 3. *F* **passer sous une voiture,** to be run over by a car 4. *F Fig* **passer sur le ventre de qn,** to brush s.o. aside/to push s.o. out of one's way 5. *F* **l'occasion lui est passée sous le nez,** he/she just missed the opportunity 6. ·*F* **le/la sentir passer,** to experience sth painful/traumatic, etc; to have a hard time of it/to go through

the mill 7. *P* **le faire passer,** to bring about a miscarriage **II** *vtr* 1. *F* **il passera pas l'hiver,** he's dying/he's on his last legs 2. *F* **qu'est-ce que je vais lui passer!/qu'est-ce qu'il va se faire passer!** I shan't half tell him off!/he won't half cop it! (*Voir* **arme; as 4; banque 1; casserole 7; dé 2; fil 9; main 1; piano 3; pogne 1; pommade 1; PPH; savon; suif 1; tabac 1** (a)**; travers 3**)

passe-sirop [pasiro] *nm inv P* telephone mouthpiece.

passeur, -euse [pasœr, -øz] *n F* smuggler (of drugs, refugees, etc); **passeur fourmi,** drug dealer*/pusher.

passion [pasjɔ̃] *nf F* sexual perversion; **un homme/une femme à passions,** a sex(ual) pervert/a perve.

passoire [paswar] *nf F* 1. **sa mémoire est une passoire,** she has a memory like a sieve 2. **c'est une passoire,** (*gardien de but*) he lets them all through 3. **transformer qn en passoire,** to riddle s.o. with bullets 4. **il a bronzé à travers une passoire,** he's got freckles/he's covered in freckles.

pastaga [pastaga] *nm P* pastis.

pastèque [pastɛk] *nf P* 1. = **pastille 2** 2. **avoir les pastèques (à mort),** to be afraid*/to be scared shitless/to get the wind up.

pastille [pastij] *nf P* 1. bullet 2. anus*; **être de la pastille,** to be a homosexual*/one of them; **se faire défoncer la pastille,** to get one's arse/*NAm* ass screwed 3. *Vieilli* **lâcher une pastille,** to fart* 4. **se faire dorer la pastille,** to spend some pleasant days/to have a good time 5. **venir en pastilles de Vichy,** to gate-crash a dinner party 6. (*CB*) microphone/mike/lollipop.

pastiquer [pastike] *vtr & i P* to smuggle. (*Voir* **maltouze**)

pastiquette [pastikɛt] *nf P* = **passe I 2, 3.**

pastiqueur, -euse [pastikœr, -øz] *n P* smuggler.

pastis [pastis] *nm F* muddle/mess/confusion; fix/trouble; **être dans le pastis,** to be in a fix*/ in a jam; **être dans un drôle de pastis,** to be in an awful mess/a real fix.

pasto [pasto] *nm P* blind alley/dead end/cul-de-sac.

patachon [pataʃɔ̃] *nm F* **mener une vie de patachon,** to lead a wild life/to live it up.

patafioler [patafjɔle] *vtr P* to fill/stuff (sth) (de, with).

patapouf [patapuf] *nm F* **gros patapouf,** fat*

lump (of a man/woman); fatso/fatty/fat slob.
pataquès [patakɛs] *nm F* confusion; faire
un pataquès, to cause a scandal.
patate [patat] *nf* 1. *F* potato/spud/tater 2. *P*
head*; avoir qch sur la patate, to have something on one's mind; en avoir gros/lourd sur
la patate, to have plenty to be worried about/
to be very upset; (*avoir des remords*) to feel
remorse/to feel guilty 3. *A P* peasant* 4. *P* (*a*)
fat person*/fatso (*b*) fool*/clot/twit 5. *P* large
nose*/beak 6. *P* blow*/punch/wallop/clout 7. *F*
hole in sock 8. *P* awkward situation; problem;
danger; sentir la patate, to sound fishy/to
smell a rat 9. *F* tennis ball which doesn't
bounce.
patati [patati] *adv F* et patati et patata, and
so on and so forth/blah-blah-blah.
patatras [patatra] *int F* crash! et patatras
le voilà par terre! and down he went with a
wallop!
patatrot [patatro] *nm P* faire (un) patatrot/
se faire le patatrot/faire son patatrot, to run
away*/to beat it/to do a bunk/to scarper; faire
un patatrot à qn, to chase (after) s.o.
pâte [pɑt] *nf F* 1. une bonne pâte, a kind and
simple soul 2. tomber en pâte, to fall over*/to
come a cropper; (*s'évanouir*) to faint*/to pass
out. (*Voir* **mou I 2**)
pâté [pɑte] *nm V* boîte à pâté, anus*/shit-
hole.
pâtée [pɑte] *nf* 1. *F* food*/grub/swill 2. *F*
beating*/thrashing/good hiding; son père lui a
collé une pâtée maison, his father beat the living daylights out of him.
patelin [patlɛ̃] *nm F* (*a*) native village/
birthplace (*b*) village/small place; ce n'est
qu'un petit patelin! it's a tiny place! quel sale
patelin! what a dump!/what a hole!
patente [patɑ̃t] *nf FrC F* (*truc*) thing/
whatchamacallit.
pater [patɛr], **paternel** [patɛrnɛl] *nm F*
father*/the old man/pater/pop; les paternels,
my parents/the old folk.
patin [patɛ̃] *nm P* 1. kiss (on the mouth);
rouler un patin (à qn), to give s.o. a French
kiss 2. *pl* patins, shoes; traîner ses patins, to
loaf around 3. chercher des patins (à qn), to
pick a quarrel* (with s.o.) 4. prendre/porter
les patins de qn, to stick up for s.o. (in a
quarrel or fight) 5. faire le patin, to shoplift.
patinage [patinaʒ] *nm F* pawing (s.o.)/
monkeying about (with s.o.)/touching (s.o.)
up.
patiner [patine] I *vtr F* to paw (*esp* a

woman)/to monkey about with (s.o.)/to touch
up (s.o.) II *vpr* se patiner *P* to run away*/to
beat it.
pâtissemar [patismar] *nm P* pastrycook/
pastry chef; confectioner.
patoche [patɔʃ] *P* I *nf* hand*/paw II *a* pas
patoche, (it's) not a success/(it's) no good.
patouillard [patujar] *nm F* (*maritime*)
(old) tub.
patouille [patuj] *nf* 1. *F* mud/slush/goo 2. *P*
gentle caress/squeeze/cuddle.
patouiller [patuje] I *vi F* to splash/to
flounder (in the mud) II *vtr P* = **patiner**.
patouilleux, -euse [patujø, -øz] *a F* (*a*)
muddy/slushy (*b*) choppy (sea).
patraque [patrak] I *a F* unwell*/out of
sorts; je me sens tout patraque, I feel a bit
under the weather; avoir le cœur patraque, to
have a dicky heart II *nf* 1. *P* (wrist)watch 2.
Vieilli F broken-down machine.
patriotard [patriɔtar] *F Péj* I *a* jingoistic II
nm blatant patriot/flag-waver/jingoist.
patron [patrɔ̃] *nm F* le patron, the boss*/the
(big white) chief; (*mon mari*) my husband*/
my old man; (*commissaire de police*) police
superintendent; chief commissioner of (the
Paris) police; (*chef de clinique*) chief consultant (of hospital); (*commandant de bord
d'un avion*) captain.
patronne [patrɔn] *nf F* la patronne, the
proprietress/the boss; (*ma femme*) my wife*/
the missis/the old lady.
patte [pat] *nf F* 1. leg*; aux pattes! let's
go!/let's get out of here! à quatre pattes, on
all fours; être court sur pattes, to have short
legs; aller à pattes, to go on foot/to leg it;
traîner la patte, (*boiter*) to limp along;
(*rester en arrière*) to lag behind; jouer des
pattes/se tirer les pattes (de devant)/tricoter
des pattes, to run away*/to clear off/to beat it;
il retombe toujours sur ses pattes, (*personne*)
he always falls/lands on his feet; se fourrer
dans les pattes de qn, to get under s.o.'s feet
2. hand*/paw/mitt; bas les pattes! hands off!/
keep your paws to yourself!/paws off! avoir
le coup de patte/avoir de la patte, to be clever
with one's hands/to have the knack (for it);
(*peintre*) to have talent 3. casser les pattes à
qn/tirer dans les pattes de qn, to put a spoke
in s.o.'s wheel/to give s.o. a bad time 4. se
faire faire les pattes/être fait aux pattes, to be
caught/to get nabbed; to be taken prisoner/to
be run in 5. faire qch aux pattes, to steal*/to
pinch/to nab sth 6. (*a*) marcher sur trois

pattes, (*d'un moteur*) to work on three (out of four) cylinders (*b*) *Aut* une deux-pattes, a two horsepower car/*esp* a Citroën (*RTM*) 2 CV (*Voir* **deuche**; **deudeuche**) 7. (*a*) pattes d'araignée/de mouche(s), (*écriture*) spidery handwriting; (*doigts longs*) long, thin fingers (*b*) faire des pattes d'araignée à qn, to caress s.o.'s body (*esp* the genitals) delicately with the tips of one's fingers 8. ça ne casse pas trois pattes à un canard, there's nothing extraordinary about that; il n'a jamais cassé trois pattes à un canard, he won't set the world on fire 9. donner un coup de patte à qn, to have a (sly) dig at s.o. 10. patte d'éph', (*pantalon*) bell-bottomed trousers/bell-bottoms (*Voir* **graissage**; **graisser** II)

patuche [patyʃ] *nf P* licence (to exercise a trade *or* profession); se faire inscrire à la patuche, to take out a licence.

paturons [patyrɔ̃] *nmpl P* feet*; écraser les paturons, to walk*; jouer des paturons, to run away*/to skedaddle.

(se) paumaquer [(sə)pomake] *vtr & vpr P* = **paumer** I, II.

paumard, -arde [pomar, -ard] *n P* loser.

paumé, -ée [pome] I *a P* lost; il est complètement paumé, he hasn't got a clue; un bled paumé, a godforsaken dump II *n P* loser/drop-out.

paumer [pome] I *vtr P* 1. (*a*) to lose (money at gambling) (*b*) to lose (an object, one's hair, etc) 2. to arrest*; *Vieilli* paumer qn marron, to catch s.o. red-handed; se faire paumer, to get nabbed 3. (*a*) to steal*/to pinch/to swipe; se faire paumer, to be diddled 4. to catch (an illness, a disease) 5. to waste (one's time). (*Voir* **rat 3**) II *vpr* se paumer *P* 1. to get lost/to lose one's way 2. to go down in the world/to go to the dogs/to become a down-and-out/to drop out.

Paupol [popɔl] *Prnm V* = **Popaul**.

pauvreté [povrəte] *nf F* se jeter là-dessus/ sur les biscuits comme la pauvreté sur le monde, to jump unhesitatingly at sth/to do sth like there was no tomorrow.

pavé [pave] *nm F* 1. fusiller le pavé, to blow one's nose with one's fingers 2. malheureux comme un pavé de bois, as unhappy as can be; (*dans la misère*) utterly destitute 3. gratter le pavé, to be desperately poor; to scrape a living from the gutter; to be on the breadline 4. battre le pavé, to loaf about the streets/about town; to tramp the streets (in search of work, etc) 5. clair comme un pavé dans la gueule

d'un flic, perfectly clear/patently obvious 6. il n'a plus de pavé dans la cour, he's toothless/ he hasn't got a tooth left in his head 7. un pavé dans la mare, a (nice) bit of scandal 8. ten thousand francs (one million old francs) 9. prendre le haut du pavé, to lord it (over s.o.); ici, c'est lui qui tient le haut du pavé, he's the big white chief around here 10. battre/faire le pavé, to be a prostitute*/a streetwalker; to be on the game. (*Voir* **brûler 3**)

paver [pave] *vtr F* 1. avoir le gosier pavé, to have a cast-iron throat 2. la ville en est pavée/les rues en sont pavées, you can find it/ them everywhere; it's/they're common as dirt.

paveton [pav(ə)tɔ̃] *nm P* paving stone; être sur le paveton, to be in the gutter/on the breadline.

pavillons [pavijɔ̃] *nmpl P* ears*/flaps/ flappers.

pavoiser [pavwaze] *vi* 1. *F* to rejoice/to crow/to put out the flags 2. *P* (*a*) to have a black eye (*b*) *Vieilli* (*boxe*) to be bleeding from the nose 3. *P* to show off*/to parade oneself/to swagger 4. *P* to have an erection* 5. *P* to have a period*/to fly the flag 6. *P* to get into debt.

pavot [pavo] *nm P* buttocks*.

pavoule [pavul] *nf P* (*javanais de* **poule**) prostitute*.

pavton [pavtɔ̃] *nm P* = **paveton**.

pavute [pavyt] *nf P* (*javanais de* **pute**) prostitute*.

pax [paks] *nm P* air passenger.

paxon [paksɔ̃] *nm P* = **packson 5**.

payant [pejɑ̃] *a F* profitable; c'est payant, it's worth it.

paye [pɛj] *nf* 1. *F* c'est une mauvaise paye, he's a bad/a slow payer 2. *P* ça fait une paye/ il y a une paye qu'on s'est vus, it's been ages/ donkey's years since we met; il y en a pour une paye, it'll take ages/years.

payer [peje, pɛ-] I *vi F* ça paye, it's profitable/it brings in a good return; (*c'est drôle*) it's very funny*/priceless/a laugh a minute II *vtr F* 1. s'en payer (une tranche), to have a good time*/a good laugh/a ball 2. tu me le paieras!/tu vas me payer ça! you'll pay for this!/I'll get my own back (on you) for this! 3. se payer qch, to treat oneself to sth; (*tolérer qch*) to have to put up with sth 4. (*expier*) to pay for (sth); je suis payé pour le savoir, I've learned (it) the hard way/I know it to my cost; *Fig* je l'ai payé cher, I paid dearly for it. (*Voir* **figure 2**; **monnaie 2**; **place 2**; **poire 7**; **portrait** (*c*); **tête 9**; **toile 3**)

pays[1] [pei] *nm F* 1. battre du pays, to wander from one's subject; to ramble/to waffle (on) 2. il est bien de son pays! well, he *is* green!

pays[2], **payse** [pei, peiz] *nm & f F* fellow-countryman/-countrywoman; nous sommes pays, we're from the same parts/the same place/the same village.

paysage [peiza3] *nm F* ça fait bien dans le paysage, it's just right there/it looks good there.

PBI [pebei] *abrév F* (= *pas de bouches inutiles*) (we will have) no unwelcome guests!

pd, PD [pede] *nm P* (= *abrév pédé*(*raste*)) homosexual*/queer/poof(ter)/fag(got). (*Voir* **pédé**)

p.-d. [pede] *nm F* (*abrév* = *porte-documents*) briefcase; document case.

peau, *pl* **peaux** [po] *nf* 1. *F* bouffer à s'en faire crever la peau du ventre, to eat* an enormous amount/to stuff one's guts/to pig oneself 2. *F* manger la peau sur le dos à qn, to starve s.o. 3. *F* une nana en peau, a girl in a low-cut dress/showing a lot of cleavage 4. *F* faire peau neuve, to turn over a new leaf 5. *F* la peau lui démange, he's itching for trouble 6. *F* (*a*) avoir qch dans la peau, to be moved by an irresistible impulse; qu'est-ce qu'elle a dans la peau? what makes her tick? (*b*) avoir qn dans la peau, to be infatuated* with s.o./to be crazy about s.o.; il l'a dans la peau, he's madly in love with her/he's got her under his skin 7. *F* se sentir mal dans sa peau, to feel uncomfortable; c'est un garçon mal dans sa peau, he's all mixed up; se sentir bien dans sa peau, to feel very much at ease 8. *F* avoir la peau trop courte, to be lazy* 9. *F* traîner sa peau, to loaf about 10. *F* communiste en peau de lapin, would-be communist 11. *F* peau d'âne, diploma 12. *F* peau de banane, plot (against s.o.)/trap (set to catch s.o. out); se prendre une peau de banane, (*projet, disque, etc*) to fail*/to flop 13. *P* (*a*) avoir/crever/faire/trouer la peau à qn, to kill* s.o./to bump s.o. off; j'aurai sa peau! I'll get him! se faire crever la peau, to get killed/bumped off (*b*) se faire la peau, to commit suicide*/to do oneself in (*c*) risquer sa peau, to risk one's life 14. *P* il ne sait pas quoi faire de sa peau, he doesn't know where to put himself 15. *P* ça coûte la peau des fesses, it's very expensive/it costs an

arm and a leg 16. *P* travailler pour la peau, to work for nothing*; to have one's trouble for nothing; il n'a eu que la peau, he got nothing (out of it)/he didn't get a sausage 17. *P* porter/pousser à la peau à qn, to excite s.o. sexually/to turn s.o. on/to work s.o. up 18. *P* péter dans sa peau, to be too big for one's boots 19. *P* la peau!/peau de balle (et balai de crin)!/peau de balle et variété!/peau de nœud!/peau de zob(i)! nothing*/nix; (*absolument pas*) nothing doing*!/my Aunt Fanny!/ no fear!/nuts! la peau de mes burnes! no chance!/no dice!/no way! (*Voir* **balpeau** I; **zébi**) 20. *P* (*a*) vieille peau, ageing prostitute*; (*vieille femme*) old trout/old bag/old hag (*b*) peau (de chien), (*fille*) tart/scrubber (*c*) une peau de vache, (*homme*) a bastard*/a lousy bum/a sod/*surt NAm* a son of a bitch; (*fille, femme*) a bitch/a cow; sa mère est une vraie peau de vache, her mother is a real cow (*d*) une peau de fesses, a nasty piece of work/a despicable character; peau de fesses/de con/d'andouille! (you) scum! 21. *P* une peau d'hareng, a useless individual/a drip/a wet; quelle peau d'hareng! what a jerk! 22. *P* (*a*) (*maritime*) peau de couille, oilskin (*b*) peau de bête, fur coat 23. *P* (*a*) peau de saucisson, inferior merchandise; junk/rubbish (*b*) en peau de lapin/de toutou, useless/worthless*; trashy/rubbishy; à la peau de toutou, (*mal fait*) botched/bungled. (*Voir* **tanner 1**; **zébi**)

peaufiner [pofine] I *vtr F* (*fignoler*) to polish up/to add the final touches to (a piece of work) II *vpr* **se peaufiner** *F* to make up/to do one's face; to put on one's make-up/one's war-paint.

peau-rouge [poru3] *nm Vieilli F* hooligan*/hoodlum/rough/lout/thug/yob; ces peaux-rouges terrorisaient tout le quartier à la nuit tombée, those yobbos terrorized the whole neighbourhood at night.

peausser [pose] *vi P* to (go to) sleep*/to kip down/to crash out.

pébroc, pébroque [pebrɔk] *nm P* 1. umbrella*/brolly. (*Voir* **sirop 3**) 2. la Maison Pébroc, the police* 3. alibi*; avoir le pébroc, to have an alibi.

pêche [pɛʃ] I *nf P* aller à la pêche, to look for (sth) without method/in a haphazard way; (*être au chômage*) to be out of work II *nf* 1. *P* blow*; balancer/filer/flanquer/foutre une pêche à qn (en pleine poire), to punch s.o. in the face/to take a swing at s.o. (*Voir aussi* **poire I**

8 (*b*)) **2.** *P* (*a*) face* (*b*) head*; **sucer la pêche à qn**, to kiss s.o.; **se fendre la pêche**, to laugh* uproariously/to kill oneself laughing; **nous nous fendions la pêche**, we were in stitches **3.** *P* **avoir la pêche/une pêche d'enfer/une pêche terrible**, to be in high spirits/to feel on top of the world **4.** *P* **avoir (de) la pêche**, to be lucky **5.** *V* **poser/déposer une pêche/sa pêche**, to defecate*/to drop one's load.

pêchecaille [pɛʃkaj] *P* **I** *nf* fishing **II** *nm* fisherman/angler.

pêcher [peʃe] *vtr F* **où as-tu pêché ça?** where did you get hold of that?/where did you pick that up?/who told you that?

pécole [pekɔl] *nf P* gonorrhoea*/the clap.

pécore [pekɔr] **I** *nf F* (*a*) silly girl/woman; *surt NAm* dumb cluck/dumb broad (*b*) stuck-up girl/woman **II** *nm P* peasant*/yokel.

pécu [peky] *nm P* **1.** toilet paper/bum-fodder **2.** written report.

pécufier [pekyfje] *vi P* **1.** to write a report, etc **2.** (*discourir*) to speechify.

pécune [pekyn] *nf Vieilli P* money*.

pédale [pedal] *nf* **1.** *F* **perdre les pédales**, to lose all self-control/to lose one's head/to get flustered/to get all balled up; **tu perds les pédales**, you're slipping/you're cracking up; **il a perdu les pédales**, he's going mad/nuts; he's lost his marbles; **s'emmêler/se mélanger/ s'embrouiller les pédales**, to get all mixed up; **je m'emmêle les pédales**, I can't think straight **2.** *P* homosexual*/queer/poof/poove/ *surt NAm* fag(got); **c'est une pédale**, he's a homo/he's gay; **la pédale**, gay men (*in general*)/pansyland; **être de la pédale**, to be a queer/to be gay/to be one of them **3.** *F* **lâcher les pédales**, to give up/to throw in the towel.

pédaler [pedale] *vi P* **1.** to rush along, to go full blast **2.** **pédaler dans l'huile/dans le beurre**, to go smoothly/without a hitch; to make good progress **3.** **pédaler dans la choucroute/dans la semoule/dans le couscous/ dans le yaourt**, to find the going difficult/to make slow progress; (*s'embrouiller*) to be all mixed up/confused.

pédé [pede] *nm P* homosexual*/queer/*surt NAm* fag(got)/poof/poove; **pédé comme un phoque**, queer as a coot.

pédesouille, pédezouille [pedzuj] *nm & f P* = **pedzouille**.

pédibus [pedibys] *adv F* **pédibus (cum jambis)**, on foot.

pedigree, pédigrée [pedigre] *nm P* police record (of criminal)/pedigree/form/ *NAm* rap sheet.

pédoc, pédoque [pedɔk] *nm P* homosexual*/gay.

pedzouille, pédzouille [pɛdzuj, pe-] *nm & f P* peasant*/country bumpkin/yokel/hick/ rube.

pégal(e) [pegal] *nm A P* pawnshop.

pègre [pɛgr] *P* **I** *nm* thief*/swindler*/crook/ gangster **II** *nf* the underworld.

pégrer [pegre] *vtr P* **se faire pégrer**, to get nabbed/nicked.

pégriot [pegrijo] *nm P* petty thief*/pilferer; small-time crook; (young) delinquent/ hooligan*.

peigne [pɛɲ] *nm P* **1.** (burglar's) crowbar/ jemmy/*NAm* jimmy **2.** **sale comme un peigne**, very dirty/filthy/disgusting.

peigne-cul [pɛɲky] *nm*, **peigne-derche** [pɛɲdɛrʃ] *nm P* (*personne*) creep/yob/lout/ jerk. (*pl* **peigne-culs, peigne-derches**)

peignée [pɛɲe] *nf F* thrashing/beating*(- up); **filer une peignée à qn**, to give s.o. a good thrashing/hiding.

peigner [pɛɲe] **I** *vtr F* **peigner la girafe**, to waste one's time **II se peigner** *vpr F* (*surt entre femmes*) to (have a) fight/scrap; to tear each other's hair out.

peigne-zizi [pɛɲzizi] *nm P* (*personne*) creep/yob/lout/jerk. (*pl* **peigne-zizis**)

peinard, -arde [pɛnar, -ard] *P* **I** *a* **boulot peinard**, cushy job/soft option; **père peinard**, easy-going man; easy rider; **vie peinarde**, easy life/soft option; **être peinard**, to have it easy*/to have a bit of peace/to play it cool; to be laid-back; **on sera bien peinards ici**, we'll be OK here/we'll get a bit of peace here; **rester/se tenir peinard**, to take things easy/to lie doggo/to keep one's nose clean; to be careful/to take care; **tiens-toi peinard**, keep quiet/take it easy/stay cool/play it cool **II** *nm* easy-going man; **faire qch en (père) peinard**, to be in no hurry to do sth/to take it easy*; **il est sorti en peinard**, he slipped out quietly/on the quiet **III** *adv* quietly/in peace; **je voudrais lire peinard**, I want to read in peace.

peinardement [pɛnardəmɑ̃] *adv P* (*a*) quietly/slyly/on the sly/on the quiet/on the QT (*b*) in a leisurely fashion (*c*) without any fuss.

peinardos [pɛnardos] *P* **I** *a* easy*/cushy/ soft; easy-going/laid-back **II** *adv* in a leisurely fashion.

peine-à-jouir [pɛnaʒwir] *nm & f inv P* **1.** s.o. who has difficulty in reaching orgasm/ frigid person **2.** driver who takes his/her time driving off; driver who can't drive off smoothly.

peinture [pɛtyr] *nf F* 1. je ne peux pas le voir en peinture, I can't bear the sight of him; I hate the sight of him; I can't stick him 2. *Péj* make-up/war-paint; pot de peinture, outrageously made-up woman*/girl*; woman/girl caked in make-up.

peinturlurer [pɛtyrlyre] *F* I *vtr* to paint (a building, etc) in all the colours of the rainbow II *vpr Péj* se peinturlurer (la figure), to put on make-up/the war-paint.

pékin [pekɛ̃] *nm F* civilian; en pékin, in civvies/in civvy street.

pelé [p(ə)le] *nm F* il n'y avait que trois pelés et un tondu, there were only a few odd bods/a few odds and sods there.

peler [p(ə)le] I *vtr P* peler les bonbons/les peler à qn, to annoy* s.o./to get up s.o.'s nose II *vi & vpr P* peler de froid/se les peler, to be very cold/to be freezing (cold); je pèle (de froid), I'm freezing (cold). (*Voir* **jonc 2**)

pèlerin [pɛlrɛ̃] *nm* 1. *F* (long-distance) traveller 2. *F* man*/chap/fellow/bloke/type 3. *P* policeman* 4. *P* umbrella*/brolly.

pèlerinage [pɛlrinaʒ] *nm V* faire un pèlerinage aux sources, to perform cunnilingus* (on a woman)/to go down on s.o.

pèlerine [pɛlrin] *nf Vieilli P* policeman* (in Paris).

pelle [pɛl] *nf* 1. *F* ramasser/(se) prendre une pelle, to fall off (a horse, a bicycle, etc)/to take a spill; *Fig* to fail*/to fall flat on one's face 2. *P* rouler une pelle à qn, to give s.o. a French kiss 3. *F* à la pelle, in big quantities/in large numbers/in profusion; remuer l'argent à la pelle, to be very rich*/to be rolling in it 4. *P* en prendre plus avec son nez qu'avec une pelle, to be smelly/to stink*/to pong 5. *P* guitar; gratter la pelle, to play the guitar/to strum on the guitar.

pello [pɛlo] *nm P* = **pellot**.

pelloche [pɛlɔʃ] *nf P Phot* (roll of) film.

pellot [pɛlo] *nm*, **pélo(t)** [pelo] *nm P* sans un pélot, penniless*; je n'ai pas un pélot, I'm flat broke/I haven't got a bean.

pelotage [p(ə)lɔtaʒ] *nm P* cuddling; (heavy) necking/petting; pawing; feeling up/touching up; partie de pelotage, necking session/snogging session; y a du pelotage! she's a bit of all right; pas de pelotage avant le mariage! no sampling the goods!

pelote [p(ə)lɔt] *nf* 1. *F* fortune; faire sa pelote, to make one's pile/to feather one's nest; ça me fait ma pelote, that suits me very well 2. *F* avoir les nerfs en pelote, to be on edge/jumpy/jittery; mettre les nerfs en pelote à qn, to set s.o.'s nerves on edge 3. *P Mil* la pelote, the defaulters' squad; faire la pelote, to do punishment drill 4. *P* envoyer qn aux pelotes, to send s.o. packing*/to send s.o. away with a flea in his ear; va aux pelotes! go to hell!/screw you! 5. *pl P* testicles*/balls 6. *F* une pelote d'épingles, a bad-tempered person/a prickly individual.

peloter [p(ə)lɔte] I *vtr* 1. *P* peloter une nana, to cuddle a girl; to neck with/to feel up to touch up a girl; to paw a girl/to maul a girl about 2. *F* to flatter* (s.o.)/to butter (s.o.) up/to suck up to (s.o.) II *vpr* se peloter *P* to pet/to neck/to snog; ça se pelote là-dedans, there's some (heavy) petting/there's a real snogging session going on in there.

peloteur, -euse [p(ə)lɔtœr, -øz] *n* 1. *P* cuddler/(heavy) necker/snogger/petter 2. *F* flatterer*/backscratcher/sweet-talker.

pelousard, -arde [p(ə)luzar, -ard] *n F* racegoer/horseracing enthusiast.

pelure [p(ə)lyr] *nf* 1. *F* overcoat/fur coat/jacket; enlever sa pelure, to take one's coat, etc off 2. *P* stupid* person/fool*/bonehead; (*méprisable*) heel/scumbag 3. *P* prepared statement (in writing)/(press) hand-out 4. *pl P* pelures, tyres (of racing cycle).

pénard, -arde [penar, -ard] *a & nm P* = **peinard**.

penco [pɑ̃ko] *nm & f P* (*écoles*) boarder.

pendantes [pɑ̃dɑ̃t] *nfpl P* 1. earrings 2. testicles*; un coup de pied dans les pendantes, a kick in the balls/goolies.

pendard [pɑ̃dar] *nm A F* rogue/rotter/good-for-nothing.

pendeloques [pɑ̃dlɔk] *nfpl*, **pendentifs** [pɑ̃dɑ̃tif] *nmpl V* testicles*/danglers.

pendouiller [pɑ̃duje] *vi P* to hang loosely/to dangle.

pendule [pɑ̃dyl] *nf* 1. *F* taximeter/clock 2. *F* remonter la pendule à qn contre qn d'autre, to work s.o. up against s.o. else 3. *P* en faire/en chier une pendule, to make a big fuss about nothing 4. *P* remettre les pendules à l'heure, to straighten/sort things out.

pénible [penibl] *F* I *a* (*personne*) difficult; ce qu'il est pénible! he's a real nuisance/a pain in the neck! ce qu'elle est pénible! she's impossible/she's the limit! II *n* (*personne*) nuisance/pain in the neck.

péniche [peniʃ] *nf P* 1. shoe 2. foot*.

péno [peno] *nm P* (*football;* = *pénalty*) penalty.

pensarde [pɑ̃sard] *nf P* (*peu usuel*) head*; **il en a dans la pensarde**, he's got brains/he's an egghead.

penscu [pɑ̃sky] *nm & f P* (*écoles*) boarder.

pense-bête [pɑ̃sbɛt] *nm F* memory jogger/ aide-mémoire.

penser [pɑ̃se] *vtr & i F* 1. (*a*) **penses-tu!/ pensez-vous!/tu penses!/vous pensez!** not (bloody) likely*!/not on your (sweet) life!/ don't you believe it! **est-ce qu'il a donné un bon pourboire? – tu penses!** did he give a good tip? – you must be/you have to be joking! (*b*) **tu n'y penses pas!/vous n'y pensez pas!** (surely) you don't mean it!/you're not serious!/you've got to be joking! 2. **bande de ce que je pense!** you shower of so-and-sos! **marcher dans ce que je pense**, to tread in dog's muck; **il peut se le mettre où je pense**, you know where he can stick/stuff it!/you know what he can do with it! **il lui a flanqué un coup de pied (là) où je pense**, he booted him up the you-know-where 3. **il ne pense qu'à ça**, he's got a one-track mind/a dirty mind.

penseuse [pɑ̃søz] *nf P* head*; **court-jus dans la penseuse**, migraine.

pensio [pɑ̃sjo] *nm & f F* (*écoles*) boarder.

pente [pɑ̃t] *nf* 1. *P* **avoir la dalle/le gosier en pente**, to have a perpetual thirst/to be a heavy drinker/to be a real boozer; **avoir sa pente**, to be drunk*/juiced up 2. *F* **être sur la pente du mal**, to be going downhill/to the dogs; **être/ glisser sur une mauvaise pente**, to be in a bad way/to be going downhill/to be on a slippery slope/to be on a downward path.

pépé [pepe] *nm F* 1. granddad/grandpa 2. old man/granddad/old geezer.

pépée [pepe] *nf P* (*a*) girl*/doll/bird/chick/ *NAm* broad; **une belle pépée**, a nice bit of stuff/fluff; **quelle jolie pépée!** she's a bit of all right! (*b*) *Péj* dolly-bird/dolly-girl (*c*) **courir les pépées**, to chase skirt; to chat up/to try to get off with the girls.

pépère [pepɛr] I *nm F* 1. grandfather/ grandpa/granddad 2. easy-going old codger/ old softy; **c'est un gros pépère**, he's a big old softy II *a F* (*a*) **une somme pépère**, a nice fat sum (of money); **un gueuleton pépère**, a good blow-out; **un sandwich pépère**, a huge/ whopping great sandwich (*b*) **un petit coin pépère**, a cosy little spot/a snug little corner; **un petit boulot pépère**, a cushy job/a cushy

billet/a soft option (*c*) (*personne*) easy-going/ laid-back III *adv F* 1. **jouer pépère**, to play nicely/not to play rough 2. *Aut* **rouler pépère**, to jog along/to tootle along.

pépète, pépette[1] [pepɛt] *nf P* **de la pépète/des pépètes/pépettes**, money*/lolly/ dough/bread.

pépette[2] *nf P* = **pépée.**

pépie [pepi] *nf F* **avoir la pépie**, to be thirsty/parched.

pépin [pepɛ̃] *nm* 1. *F* hitch/snag; **avoir un pépin**, to be in trouble/in difficulties; to hit a snag/to have a spot of bother; **j'ai eu un pépin sur la route**, (*panne*) I broke down on the road; (*accident*) I had an accident/I crashed the car 2. *F* **avoir le pépin pour qn**, to be infatuated* with s.o./to have a crush on s.o. 3. *P* **avoir avalé le/un pépin**, to risk becoming pregnant* *ou* to be pregnant* 4. *P* umbrella*/ brolly 5. *P* parachute. (*Voir* **timbale 2**)

pépinière [pepinjɛr] *nf F* nursery (of young actors, up-and-coming ballet dancers, etc); breeding ground (of anarchists, etc).

pépon [pepɔ̃] *nf P* (*verlan de* **pompe**) pépons, shoes; sneakers/pumps.

péquenaud, péquenot [pekno] *nm*, **péquenouille** [pekɔnuj] *nm P* peasant*/ clodhopper/country bumpkin/hick.

péquin [pekɛ̃] *nm F* civilian. (*Voir* **pékin**)

percal(e) [pɛrkal] *nm P* tobacco/baccy/ snout; **il se fume bien, ton percal**, that's a nice bit of baccy you've got there.

percée [pɛrse] *nf F* illegal frontier-crossing.

percer [pɛrse] *P* I *vtr* **percer qn**, to kill* s.o.; to put a bullet/a knife through s.o. II *vi* (*cyclisme*) to have a puncture.

perche [pɛrʃ] *nf F* 1. **une grande perche**, a tall, thin person*/a beanpole 2. **tendre la perche à qn**, to give s.o. a helping hand/to help s.o. out.

percher [pɛrʃe] *F* I *vi* to live/to hang out; **où perchez-vous?** where do you hang out? **je perche au troisième**, I live (up) on the third floor; **où ça perche, ce trou-là?** where on earth is this place? II *vtr* **percher un vase sur une armoire**, to perch/stick a vase on top of a wardrobe III *vpr* **se percher** tâchez de vous percher de manière à dominer la foule, try and find somewhere so that you can see over the heads of the crowd.

perchoir [pɛrʃwar] *nm F* **perchoir à moineaux**, bow tie/dicky bow/dicky/butterfly bow.

perco [pɛrko] *nm F* (coffee) percolator.

percuté [pɛrkyte] *a P* mad*/bonkers/ touched (in the head).

percuter [pɛrkyte] *vi P* to understand/to cotton on; quand il va percuter, ça va faire mal, when he gets the message, there's going to be trouble.

perdre [pɛrdr] *vtr F* 1. elle l'a perdu, she's lost her virginity*/she's lost her cherry/she's lost it 2. il n'en a pas perdu une, he saw everything/he didn't miss a thing.

perdreau, *pl* **-eaux** [pɛrdro] *nm P* (a) plain-clothes policeman; detective (b) policeman*.

perdu [pɛrdy] *a F* 1. soûl perdu, completely drunk*/plastered/blotto 2. folle perdue, conspicuous homosexual*/raging queen/raving poofter.

père [pɛr] *nm* 1. *F* petit père, old chap/*NAm* old buddy 2. *P* le père presseur, the taxman 3. *V* (a) le père frappart, penis* (b) repartir avec son père frappart sous le bras, to return empty-handed 4. *F* croire au père Noël, to believe in Father Christmas/in fairies; to delude oneself. (*Voir* **fouettard 1, 3**; **François**; **peinard I, II**)

perfect(o) [pɛrfɛkt(o)] *nm F* leather jacket.

perfo [pɛrfo] *nf F* 1. card punch 2. punch card operator/girl.

périf [perif] *nm P* (= (*boulevard*) *périphérique*) (Paris) ring road.

périmé [perime] *nm F* (*personne*) back-number/old fogey*/old has-been/old fart.

périodique [perjɔdik] *nm P* filter(-tip) cigarette*.

périph [perif] *nm P* = **périf**.

périscope [periskɔp] *nm F* un coup de périscope, a discreet look/glance (at sth/s.o.).

perle [pɛrl] **I** *nf* 1. *F* (*personne*) jewel/gem/ pearl/treasure 2. *F* (*écoles, etc*) howler/gem; c'est une perle, it's a peach 3. *F* enfiler des perles, to waste time/to idle one's time away/ to footle about; (*s'ennuyer*) to be bored/to twiddle one's thumbs 4. *P* lâcher/laisser tomber une perle, to (let out a) fart*/to blow off; écraser une perle, to fart* silently 5. *P* prostitute* who will perform unnatural acts/ who is game for anything **II** *nm P* = **perlot**.

perlot [pɛrlo] *nm P* tobacco/baccy/snout.

perloter [pɛrlɔte] *vi P* (*boxe*) to pack a punch.

perlouse, perlouze [pɛrluz] *nf P* 1. pearl 2. fart; lâcher une perlouse, to (let out a) fart*/to blow off/to let (one) off.

perm(e) [pɛrm] *nf P* (= *permission*) *Mil* leave; pass.

pernaga [pɛrnaga] *nm*, **perniflard** [pɛrniflar] *nm*, **pernifle** [pɛrnifl] *nm Vieilli P* Pernod (*RTM*).

péronnelle [perɔnɛl] *nf F* silly halfwit (of a girl)/silly goose/*NAm* dumb chick.

le Pérou [ləperu] *Prnm F* gagner le Pérou, to make a fortune; ce n'est pas le Pérou, (*ce prix*) that's cheap; (*ce travail*) it's not exactly a fortune/it's not very much (money); it's not highly paid; (*cet objet*) it's not worth very much; pas pour tout l'or du Pérou, not for all the tea in China.

à perpète [apɛrpɛt] *adv phr P* for ever (and ever)/for life; jusqu'à perpète, till the cows come home; être condamné à perpète, to get a life sentence/to get life; il habite à perpète, he lives at the back of beyond; c'est à perpète-les-alouettes, it's miles away.

perquise [pɛrkiz] *nf P* (= *perquisition*) house search (by police)/raid.

perroquet [pɛrɔkɛ] *nm* 1. *F* pastis with mint; *Vieilli* absinthe; étrangler/étouffer un perroquet, to drink a glass of pastis with mint or absinthe 2. *P Mil* sniper. (*Voir* **soupe 1**)

perruche [pɛryʃ, pe-] *nf F* talkative woman/chatterbox*/gas bag/windbag.

perruque [pɛryk, pe-] *nf* 1. *F* une vieille perruque, an old fogey*/an old has-been 2. *P* hair; il a une perruque en peau de fesse, he's as bald* as a coot 3. *P* faire de la perruque, to do sth on the side/on the quiet; to moonlight.

perruquemar [pɛrykmar] *nm P* hairdresser/barber.

persil [pɛrsi] *nm P* 1. aller au persil/faire son persil, (*prostituée*) to walk the streets/to go on the game; (*homme*) to pick up a prostitute* 2. aller au persil, to go to work 3. pubic hair; (*femme*) arroser le persil, to urinate*.

persiller [pɛrsije] *vi P* (*prostituée*) to walk the streets/to solicit*/to go on the game.

persilleuse [pɛrsijøz] *nf P* prostitute*/pro/ hooker.

perso [pɛrso] *a & adv F* (*abrév* = *personnel(lement)*) (*sport d'équipe*) être perso/jouer perso, to play on one's own without involving the other members of the team.

pervenche [pɛrvɑ̃ʃ] *nf F* = traffic warden.

pesant [pəzɑ̃] *nm F* valoir son pesant de cacahuètes/de moutarde, (*histoire, blague, etc*) to be very funny*/to be worth a guinea a minute.

pescal(e) [pɛskal] *nm P* 1. fish 2. (*maque-*

reau) pimp*/mac.

pèse [pɛz] *nm* P = **pèze**.

pèse-brioches [pɛzbrijɔʃ] *nm inv* P bathroom scales.

pesetas [pezeta] *nfpl*, **pésettes** [pezɛt] *nfpl* P money*.

pessigner [pesiɲe, pɛ-] *vtr* P pessigner une lourde, to break down a door.

peste [pɛst] *nf* F *(surt enfant)* pest/damn nuisance; petite peste, little pest/little horror.

pestouillard, -arde [pɛstujar, -ard] *a & n* P unlucky (person).

pestouille [pɛstuj] *nf* P bad luck.

pet [pɛ(t)] *nm* P 1. fart; faire/lâcher un pet, to (let out a) fart*/to blow off; vouloir tirer des pets d'un âne mort, to try to get blood out of a stone; pas un pet, not at all/never; ça ne vaut pas un pet (de lapin), it's absolutely worthless*/it's not worth a monkey's fart; il n'a pas un pet [pɛt] de bon sens, he hasn't got an ounce of common (sense) 2. *(a) Vieilli* il va y avoir du pet, there's trouble brewing; there's going to be trouble; *(scandale)* there's going to be a nice bit of scandal *(b)* faire du pet, to be furious/angry*; to blow a fuse 3. danger; il n'y a pas de pet, it's OK/there's no danger; pet! le voilà! look out! he's coming! fare le pet, to keep a look-out/to be on the watch 4. fleurer/flurer le pet à qn, to pick a quarrel* with s.o. 5. aller au pet/porter le pet, to kick up a row/a fuss; to cause a scandal; *(donner l'alerte)* to sound the alarm; *(porter plainte)* to lodge a complaint (with the police) 6. comme un pet sur une toile cirée, quickly and discreetly; filer/partir comme un pet sur une toile cirée, to run away*/to scarper/to take to one's heels/to sling one's hook/to do a bunk 7. avoir un pet de travers, to feel unwell* 8. [pɛt] *(a)* traffic/road accident; crash; avoir un pet, to have an accident/a crash *(b)* dent; ta voiture a pris un pet, your car's had a bash.

pétanqueur [petɑ̃kœr] *nm* P homosexual*/ queer/fag(got).

pétant [petɑ̃] *a* P à cinq heures pétantes, on the stroke of five/at five sharp/at five on the dot.

Pétaouchnok, Pétaouchnoque [petauʃnɔk] *Prn* F (imaginary) faraway place.

pétarader [petarade] *vi* P to be very angry*/to be hopping mad.

pétard [petar] *nm* 1. F row/din/uproar*; il va y avoir du pétard, there's going to be a hell

of a row; faire du pétard, to kick up a row/to raise a stink; to cause a scandal; un coup de pétard, a rumpus/a racket/a hullabaloo 2. P buttocks*/behind/bum/*NAm* butt; se manier/se magner le pétard, to hurry*/to get a move on/ to get cracking/to shift one's arse/*NAm* to shift one's fanny 3. P gun/firearm/revolver*/ shooter 4. F *(a)* être en pétard, to be very angry*/to be in a flaming temper/*surt NAm* to be really mad; se mettre/se foutre en pétard, to get angry*/to blow one's top/to do one's nut; mettre qn en pétard, to make s.o. angry*/to put s.o. in a huff/to get up s.o.'s nose *(b)* être en pétard avec qn, to have quarrelled with s.o./to be on bad terms with s.o.; elles sont en pétard, they're not talking (to each other) 5. P = **pet 3** 6. P *(drogues)* marijuana cigarette*/joint/reefer.

pétarder [petarde] *vi* F to kick up a row/to make a big stink/to kick up one hell of a fuss.

pétardier, -ière [petardje, -jɛr] P I *a (a)* quarrelsome/argumentative *(b)* noisy/rowdy II *n (a)* bickerer/squabbler/awkward customer *(b)* noisy individual/noisy sod *(c)* scandalmonger.

pétasse [petas] *nf* P 1. fear/fright/funk; avoir la pétasse, to be afraid*/to be in a blue funk 2. *Péj* woman*/bint 3. part-time *or* new prostitute*/tart/scrubber/floozy.

pète [pɛt] *nm ou f* P = **pet 8** *(b)*.

pété [pete] *a* P drunk* *or* drugged*; complètement pété, *(ivre)* rat-arsed; *(drogué)* bombed (out).

pétée [pete] *nf* 1. P big quantity/loads/ masses 2. P drunkenness; il a pris une pétée, he got completely plastered 3. V *(a)* tirer une pétée, to have sex*/to get one's end away *(b)* filer une pétée, to have an orgasm*/to come (off).

pet-en-l'air [pɛtɑ̃lɛr] *nm inv* F (man's) short indoor jacket; bum-freezer.

péter [pete] I *vi* 1. F *(chaise, etc)* to break/to give way; *(corde, etc)* to snap; la tête me pète, my head feels as if it's going to burst 2. F il faut que ça pète ou que ça dise pourquoi, it's got to work/it has to happen (come what may) 3. P to break wind/to fart* 4. P elle me fait péter les boutons de braguette, she really turns me on/gets me going; she makes me (feel) randy/horny; she gives me a rise/a hard-on 5. P envoyer péter qn, to tell s.o. to clear off; elle l'a envoyé péter, she told him to go to hell/to piss off 6. P péter dans la soie, to live in the lap of luxury 7. P manger à s'en faire péter la sous-ventrière, to eat* till one is ready to burst/to stuff one's guts/to really pig oneself; rire à se péter la sous-ventrière, to laugh uproariously/to split one's sides laughing 8. P péter dans la main à qn, to let s.o. down/to fail to keep one's promise to s.o. 9. P to kick up a (hell of a) row/to make a big fuss; ça va péter (sec)! there's going to be a hell of a stink!/there's going to be a big bust-up! 10. P to complain/to lodge a complaint II vtr 1. F péter le feu/du feu/des flammes, to be bursting with energy/to be full of beans; péter la santé, to be bursting with health 2. P péter la faim/la péter, to be ravenously hungry*; viens au restau, je la pète, let's go for a bite to eat, I'm starving 3. P péter la gueule à qn, to bash* s.o. up/to bash s.o.'s face in 4. P péter une lourde, to break down a door. (*Voir* conomètre; cul I 19; derrière; mastic 2) III vpr se péter P 1. se péter la gueule, to do oneself an injury; to come a cropper*; (*s'enivrer*) to get drunk*/plastered 2. se péter (la tête), to blow one's mind (on drugs).

pète(-)sec [pɛtsɛk] *nm inv F* disciplinarian/martinet.

péteur, -euse[1] [petœr, -øz] I *n P* 1. farter 2. ill-mannered oaf/lout/boor 3. coward* II *nf P* motorbike.

péteux, -euse[2] [petø, -øz] *P* I *n* (*a*) coward*/yellowbelly; c'est un petit péteux, he's yellow (*b*) snob/show-off* II *a* (*a*) cowardly*/yellow/in a funk (*b*) pretentious/snobby/snooty.

petiot, -ote [pətjo, -ɔt] *a & n F* tiny/wee/titchy/diddy (child); un petiot/une petiote, a tiny tot.

petit [pəti] I *a & nm* 1. *F* un petit coup de rouge, a nice drop of red wine; s'en jeter un petit (blanc), to down a glass of (white) wine 2. *F* salut, petite tête! hello, mate! 3. *F* faire des petits, (*argent*) to increase; to bear interest 4. *P* anus*; prendre/donner/envoyer/lâcher/refiler du petit, to have anal sex*/to go in by the back door; prendre qn par le petit, to sodomize* s.o. II *nm & f F* bonjour, mon petit/ma petite, good morning, my dear. (*Voir* cirque 3; coin 4; endroit 1; frère 5; noir II 2; salé II)

petite [pətit] *nf P* 1. mettre en petite, to put by/to save; j'ai un peu de pèze en petite, I've got something put away for a rainy day 2. une petite, a small glass of pastis 3. (*drogues*) prendre une petite, to take a fix (*esp* of heroin*).

petit-nègre [pətinɛgr] *nm F* parler petit-nègre, to talk pidgin French.

pétochard, -arde [petɔʃar, -ard] *P* I *a* cowardly*/yellow/chicken II *nm & f* coward*/yellow-belly/chicken.

pétoche [petɔʃ] *nf P* fear/(blue) funk; avoir la pétoche, to be afraid*/to have the wind up/to be scared shitless.

pétoire [petwar] *nf F* 1. (child's) peashooter 2. gun/firearm/revolver*/popgun 3. moped/put-put.

peton [pətɔ̃] *nm F* (*mot enfantin*) tiny foot/tootsie(-wootsie).

pétouille [petuj] *nf P* = **pétoche**.

pétoulet [petulɛ] *nm P* buttocks*.

pétrin [petrɛ̃] *nm F* être dans le pétrin/dans un beau pétrin, to be in a fix*/in the soup/up the creek/in a tight spot; se mettre dans le pétrin, to get into a fix*/into a mess; mettre qn dans le pétrin, to get s.o. into a fix*/to land s.o. in a fine mess; to drop s.o. in it; un beau pétrin!/un joli pétrin! here's a fine mess!

pétrole [petrɔl] *nm Vieilli F* hard liquor/strong spirits*/rotgut.

pétrolette [petrɔlɛt] *nf F* small motorbike.

pétrousquin [petruskɛ̃] *nm P* 1. *Vieilli* = **pedzouille** 2. buttocks*/bum/*NAm* butt/*NAm* fanny; tomber sur son pétrousquin, to sit down with a bump/to land up on one's arse/*NAm* ass 3. civilian/civvy.

pétrus [petrys] *nm Vieilli P* buttocks*.

petzouille [pɛtzuj] *nm P* = **pedzouille**.

peu [pø] *adv & nm F* 1. un peu(, mon neveu)! rather!/not half!/you bet!/I should say so! 2. c'est un peu bien! that's jolly good!/that's really great! 3. ça, c'est un peu fort! that's a bit much! 4. pas qu'un peu, completely; elle est pas qu'un peu tapée, she's completely mad*/nuts 5. ah! non, très peu (pour moi)!/ah! non, très peu de ce genre! not for me!/not blooming likely!/I'm not having any!/count me out! 6. viens un peu! come here! 7. un peu beaucoup, far too much.

peuchère! [pøʃɛr] *int F* (*Dial du Midi*) blast!/strewth!

peuple [pœpl] *nm F* il y avait du peuple, there was quite a crowd/there were a lot of people.

peuplier [pøplije] *nm P* en cuir de peuplier, wooden/made of wood; chaussures en cuir de peuplier, clogs.

peupons [pøpɔ̃] *nfpl P* (*verlan de* pompes) shoes. (*Voir* pompe 4).

peur [pœr] *nf F* vous n'avez pas peur! you've got a nerve!/you don't want much, do you?/ you're not backward in coming forward, are you? (*Voir* **bleu I 2**)

pèze [pɛz] *nm P* money*/dough/bread/lolly; être au pèze, to be very rich*/to be rolling in it; un vieux tout à fait au pèze, a stinkingly rich old man; fusiller son pèze, to blow a hole in one's money/to blow one's dough.

pezette [pəzɛt] *nf P* coins/change.

pfui! [pfɥi] *int F* phooey!

PG [peʒe] *nm F* (*abrév = prisonnier de guerre*) prisoner of war/POW.

phalanges [falɑ̃ʒ] *nfpl P* hands*.

phalangettes [falɑ̃ʒɛt] *nfpl P* fingers.

phalzar [falzar] *nm P* (pair of) trousers*/ *NAm* pants. (*Voir* **false, falzar(d)**)

pharamineux, -euse [faraminø, -øz] *a F* staggering; fantastic/colossal. (*Voir* **faramineux**)

pharmaco [farmako] *nm & f P* (= *pharmacien*) chemist.

pharo [faro] *nm F* (= *pharaon*) faro (*card game*).

philo [filo] *nf F* (*écoles*) philosophy.

philosophailler [filozofaje] *vi F Péj* to philosophize.

phonard [fonar] *nm Vieilli P* 1. telephone* 2. (male) telephonist/(telephone) operator.

phonarde [fonard] *nf Vieilli P* (female) telephonist/(telephone) operator.

phono [fono] *nm Vieilli F* (= *phonographe*) gramophone.

phoque [fok] *nm P* 1. les avoir à la phoque, to be lazy*/to be workshy 2. homosexual*. (*Voir* **être 1**)

phosphorer [fosfore] *vi P* to think (hard).

photographier [fotografje] *vtr F* photographier qn, to identify s.o.; se faire photographier, to be spotted.

phrasicoter [frazikote] *vi F* to speechify/to hold forth/to waffle.

phrasicoteur [frazikotœr] *nm F* speechifier/spouter/waffler.

PHS [peaʃɛs] *nm F* (= (*réunion*) *pour hommes seulement*) stag party/stag dinner; stag night.

piaf [pjaf] *nm P* 1. (*a*) sparrow (*b*) (any) bird 2. un drôle de piaf, a strange individual/a queer bird 3. (*rare*) policeman*. (*Voir* **crâne 2**)

piaillard, -arde [pjajar, -ard] *F* I *a* squawking/screeching/squealing (child) II *n* (*enfant*) squaller/squealer/squawker.

piailler [pjaje] *vi F* to squawk/to screech/to squeal.

piailleur, -euse [pjajœr, -øz] *a & n F* = **piaillard, -arde**.

piane-piane [pjanpjan] *adv F* very slowly/ very softly/nice and gently; vas-y piane-piane! gently does it!/easy does it!/go easy!

piano [pjano] *nm P* 1. *F* piano du pauvre/piano à bretelles, accordion 2. *P* (*drogues*) piano du pauvre, hashish* 3. *P* (flat) top (on which fingerprints are taken); passer au piano/jouer du piano, to have one's fingerprints taken; touche de piano, fingerprint 4. *P* (*comptoir de café*) bar. (*Voir* **zinc 1**) 5. *P* (front) teeth*/ ivories; il n'a plus de ratiches dans son piano, he's got no teeth left 6. *P* vendre un piano à qn, to give s.o. a lot of patter/to spiel to s.o.

piano-piano [pjanopjano] *adv F* = **piane-piane**.

pia-pia [pjapja] *nm F* chatter/natter.

piastre [pjastr] *nf FrC F* dollar.

piaule [pjol] *nf P* room/pad/digs; ma piaule, my pad.

se piauler [səpjole] *vpr P* to go home/to turn in/to make tracks.

pibloque [piblɔk] *nf P* (*gardienne*) caretaker/*surt NAm* janitor.

pibouic [pibwik] *nm P Mus* clarinet.

à pic [apik] *adv phr F* arriver/tomber à pic, to come/to happen at the right moment; (*au dernier moment*) to come/to happen in the nick of time; ça tombe à pic, it couldn't have come at a better time/it worked out just right.

picaillon [pikajɔ̃] *nm P* (*a*) money*/cash; j'ai plus un picaillon, I haven't got a penny (*b*) *pl* picaillons, small change; cash; money*; avoir des picaillons, to be rich*/to be rolling in it.

pichet [piʃɛ] *nm P* wine.

pichoun [piʃun] *a F* small/little/tiny/wee/ titchy. (*Voir* **pitchoun**)

pichpin [piʃpɛ̃] *nm P* = **pitchpin**.

pichtegorme [piʃtəgorm] *nm*, **pichtegorne** [piʃtəgorn] *nm*, **pichtogorme** [piʃtogorm] *nm*, **pichtogorne** [piʃtogorn] *nm P* ordinary (red) wine/plonk/vino.

pick-up [pikœp] *nm P* (*langage des policiers*) picking up of prostitutes*.

picole [pikol] *nf P* drinking/boozing.

picoler [pikole] *vi P* to drink* heavily/to hit the bottle/to tipple/to (go on the) booze; je me suis mis à picoler, I hit the bottle/I went on the booze.

picoleur, -euse [pikolœr-, øz] *nm & f P*

(heavy) drinker/drunk(ard)*/tippler/boozer; c'est un grand picoleur, he's a real boozer/he can't half knock it back.

picolo [pikɔlo] *nm P* ordinary wine/plonk/vino.

picote [pikɔt] *nf P* pockmarks (*on face*).

picotin [pikɔtɛ̃] *nm F* pas un picotin, not a bean/not a cent.

picouse [pikuz] *nf P* = **piquouse.**

picouser [pikuze] *vtr P* = **piquouser.**

picrate [pikrat] *nm P* poor-quality wine/plonk/vino.

pictance [piktɑ̃s] *nf P* alcoholic drink/liquor.

pictancher [piktɑ̃ʃe] *vi P* to drink* heavily/to hit the bottle/to go on the booze/to tipple.

pictancheur [piktɑ̃fœr] *nm P* heavy drinker/drunk(ard)*/tippler/boozer.

picter [pikte] *vi P* = **pictancher.**

picton [piktɔ̃] *nm P* ordinary red wine; boire un coup de picton, to knock back some wine.

pictonner [piktɔne] *vi Vieilli P* = **picoler.**

pie [pi] *nf F* chatterbox*; jaser comme une pie, to chatter* away (nineteen to the dozen); elle est bavarde comme une pie (borgne), she's a terrible chatterbox*/she's got the gift of the gab.

pièce [pjɛs] *nf* 1. *F* on n'est pas aux pièces, we're not in any hurry/there's no rush 2. *F* belle pièce, beautiful woman*/sexy bird 3. *F* mettre qn en pièces, to slander s.o./to pull s.o. to pieces 4. *P* pièce de dix ronds/pièce de dix sous, anus*; il a perdu sa pièce de dix ronds/de dix sous, he's a homosexual*/he's queer 5. *P* cracher des pièces de dix sous, to be very thirsty/to be parched 6. *P* pièce humide, syringe*/hypo; artilleur de la pièce humide, male nurse. (*Voir* **service 3**)

pied [pje] *nm* 1. *F* se lever du pied gauche, to get out of bed on the wrong side; je suis parti du pied gauche avec lui, we started off on the wrong foot/I got off to a bad start with him 2. *F* (*a*) faire du pied à qn, (*pour avertir*) to give s.o. a kick; (*par jeu*) to play footsie with s.o. (*b*) faire un/des appel(s) du pied à qn, to sound s.o. out (*esp* in order to make peace with s.o.). (*Voir* **genou 1**) 3. *F* mettre les pieds dans le plat, to make a mistake*/to put one's foot in it/to drop a brick/to drop a clanger 4. *F* il ne sait sur quel pied danser, he doesn't know which way to turn/he's in a real quandary 5. *F* (*a*) lever le pied, to abscond/to bolt/to flit/to welsh; un financier qui lève le pied, a fly-by-night (*b*) lever le pied, (*ralentir*)

to slow down 6. *F* se tirer des pieds, to run away*/to beat it/to clear off 7. *F* sortir/s'en aller les pieds devant, to die*/to go out feet first 8. *F* ça lui fera les pieds! that'll serve him right!/that'll teach him (a lesson)! c'est bien fait pour tes pieds! it serves you right! s'il arrive quelque chose c'est pour mes pieds! if something happens, I'm the one who suffers/who gets it (in the neck)! 9. *F* (*a*) sécher sur pied, to be bored to death/to be bored rigid (*b*) faire le pied de grue, to be kept waiting/to be kept hanging about/to kick one's heels; on m'a laissé faire le pied de grue dans la salle d'attente, I was left to sweat it out in the waiting room 10. *F* faire un pied de nez à qn, to thumb one's nose at s.o./to cock a snook at s.o. 11. *F* c'est le coup de pied de l'âne, that's the unkindest cut of all 12. *F* il ne se donne pas des coups de pied, he's always giving himself a pat on the back; he's always blowing his own trumpet 13. *A P* (aller) se laver les pieds, to be sentenced to hard labour 14. *P* il y a des coups de pied au cul qui se perdent, some people are past praying for; there's no hope for some people 15. *P* casser les pieds à qn, (*ennuyer*) to bore* s.o. stiff; (*agacer*) to annoy* s.o.; il me casse les pieds, he's a terrible bore*/he bores me rigid/he's a real drag; he drives me mad/he gets on my wick; il me casse les pieds pour que je fasse quelque chose, he's on my back to get me to do something 16. *P* avoir les pieds dans le dos/dans les reins/dans le râble, to have the police* on one's track/on one's tail. (*Voir* **dos 7**; **reins 4**) 17. *P* j'en ai (mon) pied, I'm fed up with it/I've had it up to here 18. *P Mil* pied de banc, NCO (*esp sergeant*) 19. *P* (*a*) fool*/idiot; quel pied! what a twerp!/what a jerk! (*b*) il joue comme un pied, he can't play for nuts/for toffee; il conduit comme un pied, he's a bloody awful driver 20. *P* aller au pied, to share out the spoils; avoir son pied, to have one's share 21. *P* (*a*) kick/thrill; prendre son pied, to enjoy oneself; to get a kick out of sth/to get one's rocks off; j'ai pris mon pied, it was a real gas/I got a real kick (out of it)/it really turned me on; c'était le pied! it was great/fantastic/a gas!/it really blew my mind! (*Voir* **superpied**) 23. *V* prendre son pied, to have an orgasm*/to come 23. *P* coup de pied de Vénus, dose of VD*/the clap. (*Voir* **bête II 1**; **bouquet 3**; **chaud I 1, II 1**; **chaussure 1, 2, 3**; **dentelle 1**; **doigt 10**; **lécher 4**; **se moucher 1**; **mur 7**; **nickelé 1**;

quelque part 2; retourné 1)
pied-de-biche [pjedbiʃ] *nm* P 1.
(burglar's) jemmy/*NAm* jimmy 2. (*mendiant*)
beggar (going from house to house); (*représentant*) door-to-door salesman; tirer le
pied-de-biche, to beg from house to house; to
sell door to door. (*pl* pieds-de-biche)
pied-de-figuier [pjedfigje] *nm* P *Péj*
Arab/wog. (*pl* pieds-de-figuier)
pied-noir [pjenwar] *nm & f* F Algerian-born
Frenchman/Frenchwoman. (*pl* pieds-noirs)
piège [pjɛʒ] *nm* P 1. piège (à poux/à
macaronis), beard 2. bookmaker/bookie 3.
prison* 4. piège à nichons, bra/titholder 5.
piège à filles, attractive man*/good-looker;
(*voiture*) stylish nice-looking car (*used to attract women*); V piège à mémé, male
genitals*/goods 5. piège à bagnard, work/hard
graft. (*Voir* con I 2)
piéger [pjeʒe] P I *vi* to be a bookmaker; to
take bets II *vtr* se faire piéger, to be had/to be
conned.
pierre [pjɛr] I *nf* 1. F jeter la pierre à qn, to
criticize* s.o./to run s.o. down 2. F
malheureux comme les pierres, bitterly
unhappy/thoroughly miserable 3. F pierre de
taille, miser*/skinflint 4. *pl* P jewels/
sparklers/stones II *Prnm* F Pierre et Paul,
Pierre, Paul et Jacques, Tom, Dick and
Harry.
pierreuse [pjɛrøz] *nf* P low-class
prostitute*/streetwalker.
pierrot [pjɛro] *nm* 1. F (*oiseau*) sparrow 2.
F un drôle de pierrot, a strange fellow*/an odd
chap 3. P étrangler un pierrot, to drink/to
knock back a glass of white wine.
piétaille [pjetaj] *nf* P *Mil* la piétaille, the
rank and file/the infantry/footsloggers/PBI (=
poor bloody infantry).
piétard [pjetar] *nm* P pedestrian.
piéton [pjetɔ̃] *nm* P 1. traffic policeman* 2.
tramp/*surt NAm* hobo.
pieu, *pl* **pieux** [pjø] *nm* P 1. bed; se mettre
au pieu, to go to bed*/to kip down/to crash
out/to hit the hay; bath au pieu, good in bed/
(a) good screw 2. litre of red wine 3.
(*courses*) finishing post.
pieuter [pjøte] I *vi* P to (go to) sleep*/to hit
the sack II *vpr* se pieuter P to go to bed*.
pieuvre [pjœvr] *nf* F (*personne*) parasite/
limpet/leech/hanger-on.
pif [pif] *nm* P 1. (large) nose*/conk/hooter 2.
ça lui pend au pif, he's got it coming to him;
he's (in) for it; qui sait ce qui nous pend au

pif? who knows what's in store for us? 3. je
l'ai dans le pif, I can't stand him/he gets up
my nose 4. (*a*) se salir/se piquer le pif, to get
drunk* (*b*) avoir un (petit) coup dans le pif/
avoir un coup de trop dans le pif/avoir le pif
sali/avoir le pif piqué, to be drunk* 5. (*a*)
intuition/flair (*b*) au pif, at a rough guess;
faire qch qu pif, to do sth by guesswork 6. se
casser/se cogner le pif, to find nobody at home
(*when calling at a house*) *or* to be shown the
door/to be thrown out 7. se manger/se bouffer
le pif, to quarrel*; to be always getting at
each other; to fight/to scrap 8. wine/plonk.
(*Voir* communard II)
pif(f)er [pife] I *vtr* P je (ne) peux pas le
piffer, I can't stand (the sight of) him/I can't
stomach him/he gets up my nose II *vpr* se
piffer P ils ne peuvent pas se piffer, they
can't stand each other/they hate each other's
guts.
piffomètre [pifɔmɛtr] *nm* P = **pifomètre.**
piffre [pifr] *nm* P glutton*/greedy person/
greedy-guts.
se piffrer [səpifre] *vpr* P to eat* greedily/to
gorge oneself/to stuff one's guts/to pig oneself.
pifomètre [pifɔmɛtr] *nm* P au pifomètre, at
a rough estimate/at a rough guess; calculer
au pifomètre, to guesstimate; aller au pifomètre, to play it by ear; en politique, c'est le
pifomètre qui compte, in politics, having a
nose for things is all-important.
pige [piʒ] *nf* P 1. year (of age, of prison
sentence); il a 45 piges, he's 45; à 30 piges, at
30; pour soixante piges il n'est pas mal, he's
not bad for sixty 2. faire la pige à qn, to go
one better than s.o./to leave s.o. standing 3.
freelance journalism; être payé à la pige, to
be paid by the line.
pigeon [piʒɔ̃] *nm* F 1. loger comme/avec les
pigeons, to live in an attic 2. (*person*) sucker/
mug/*NAm* fall guy/*NAm* patsy; plumer un
pigeon, to fleece a mug/a sucker 3. il fait un
croquis comme un pigeon avec sa queue! he
can't draw for nuts!
pigeonneau, *pl* **-eaux** [piʒɔno] *nm* F
(*personne*) mug/sucker/*NAm* fall guy.
pigeonner [piʒɔne] *vtr* F to swindle*/to
cheat; to dupe/to take (s.o.) in; to fleece; je
me suis laissé/fait pigeonner, I've been had/
done.
pigeonnier [piʒɔnje] *nm* F (*théâtre*) the
gods.
piger [piʒe] *vtr & i* P 1. to understand*; il
n'a pas pigé, it hasn't registered with him/he

hasn't twigged/the penny hasn't dropped; **je n'y ai rien pigé,** I couldn't make head or tail of it; **tu piges?** get it?/you dig? **je pige,** I get it; I get the drift; **piger rapidement,** to be quick on the uptake; **tu piges la combine?** do you see what they're up to?/do you see their little game? **je ne pige rien aux maths,** I haven't a clue about maths/maths is like double Dutch to me 2. to look* at/to have a butchers at (sth); **pige-moi ça!** just look at that!/get a load of that!/take a butcher's at that! 3. (a) **piger un rhume,** to catch a cold (b) **piger cinq ans de prison,** to cop a five-year stretch 4. to spot (the winner of a race) 5. **se faire piger,** to get nabbed. (*Voir* **dal, dalle**[1])

pigette [piʒɛt] *nf* P **depuis pas mal de pigettes,** for a number of years. (*Voir* **pige 1**)

pigiste [piʒist] *nm & f* F = journalist paid at a rate per line; freelance journalist/freelance(r).

pignole [piɲɔl] *nf* V masturbation; **se taper une pignole,** to masturbate*/to toss oneself off.

se pignoler [səpiɲɔle] *vpr* V to masturbate*/to toss oneself off.

pignouf [piɲuf] *nm* P 1. lout/yob(bo)/layabout/hooligan*/thug 2. miser*/skinflint/tight-ass.

pile [pil] I *nf* F 1. thrashing; **donner/flanquer une pile à qn,** to give s.o. a thrashing/to beat s.o. up*; (*prendre le dessus*) to get the better of s.o./to beat s.o. (in a race, etc) 2. **prendre/recevoir une pile,** to suffer a crushing defeat II *adv* F in the nick of time/bang on time; **s'arrêter pile,** to stop dead/to come to a dead stop; **arriver pile,** to arrive on the dot; **vous tombez pile,** you've come just at the right moment/you timed it just right; **à six heures pile,** on the dot of six.

piler [pile] F I *vtr* 1. to thrash (s.o.)/to beat (s.o.) up*; **être à piler,** to deserve/to need a good hiding; **notre équipe s'est fait piler,** our team was licked/got thrashed 2. **la piler,** (*être très fatigué*) to be exhausted/bushed; (*avoir faim*) to be famished II *vi* to stop dead/to come to a dead stop; to brake abruptly/to slam on the brakes. (*Voir* **poivre 1**)

pilier [pilje] *nm* 1. F *Péj* **pilier de bar/de café/de bistrot,** frequenter of pubs; *esp NAm* barfly; **c'est un vrai pilier de bar,** he's always propping up the bar/he seems to live in the pub 2. *pl* P fat/solid/sturdy legs*; **être ferme sur ses piliers,** to be steady on one's pins.

pillaver [pilave] *vtr* P to drink*.

pills [pils] *nmpl* P (*drogues*) LSD* pills.

piloches [pilɔʃ] *nfpl* P teeth*/choppers/grinders.

piloirs [pilwar] *nmpl* P fingers.

pilon [pilɔ̃] *nm* P 1. beggar/bum; **faire le pilon,** to beg 2. (a) foot* (b) wooden leg*.

pilonner [pilɔne] *vi* P to beg/to sponge.

pilonneur [pilɔnœr] *nm* P beggar/bum.

pilule [pilyl] *nf* F 1. **dorer la pilule,** to sugar the pill 2. **avaler la pilule,** to bite the bullet 3. **prendre une/la pilule,** to have a crushing defeat/to take a hammering/to be beaten hollow; **l'équipe de foot a pris une pilule,** the football team got thrashed.

piment [pimɑ̃] *nm* P nose*.

pinaillage [pinajaʒ] *nm* P quibbling/hair-splitting/nit-picking.

pinailler [pinaje] *vi* P to quibble/to split hairs; to be finicky/picky; **pinailler sur les détails,** to quibble over details.

pinailleries [pinajri] *nfpl* P = **pinaillage**.

pinailleur, -euse [pinajœr, -øz] *n* P quibbler/hair-splitter/nit-picker; finicky person/fusspot.

pinard [pinar] *nm* F wine/plonk/vino.

pinardier, -ière [pinardje, -jɛr] P I *n* wholesale wine merchant II *nm* tanker transporting wine.

pinarium [pinarjɔm] *nm* P room where one makes love.

pince [pɛ̃s] *nf* 1. P hand*/paw/mitt; **serrer la pince à qn,** to shake hands with s.o.; **serre-moi la pince!** tip us your fin/your flipper! **pince d'Adam,** hand/fingers used for eating 2. P foot*; **à pince(s),** on foot; **aller à pinces/se taper la route à pinces,** to foot it/to hoof it/to leg it 3. F (burglar's) jemmy/*NAm* jimmy 4. *pl* P handcuffs*/cuffs; **gare la pince!** mind you don't get nabbed/pinched! 5. P slow motorbike rider 6. V (**un**) **chaud de la pince,** (*homme*) hot stuff/randy sod; skirt-chaser 7. P **bonne pince,** opportunity/chance; **bonne pince!** good luck! well done!

pinceau, *pl* **-eaux** [pɛ̃so] *nm* 1. P foot*; **avoir les pinceaux en fleurs/en bouquets de violettes,** to stretch out one's toes with tiredness *or* when having an orgasm 2. P **aller se laver les pinceaux,** to be sentenced to hard labour 3. P **s'embrouiller/s'emmêler les pinceaux,** to get into a muddle/to get tied up in knots; (*penser*) not to think clearly/to be confused 4. V penis*.

pince-cul [pɛ̃sky] *nm* P (a) rowdy party/dance/*NAm* shindig (b) (low-class) dance hall/dive. (*pl* pince-cul(s))

pincée [pɛ̃se] *nf F* large sum (of money); toucher la pincée, to hit the jackpot.

pince-fesses [pɛ̃sfɛs] *nm inv P* = **pince-cul**.

pincer [pɛ̃se] *vtr F* 1. to arrest*; se faire pincer, to get nabbed/nicked/pinched; il s'est fait pincer en sautant de la fenêtre, the police collared him as he jumped out of the window 2. en pincer pour qch, to be expert at sth 3. en pincer pour qn/être pincé pour qn, to be infatuated* with s.o./to be crazy about s.o./to have a crush on s.o. 4. to understand/to see; tu pinces? get it? (*Voir* **nez 4**)

pincettes [pɛ̃sɛt] *nfpl* 1. *F* il n'est pas à prendre avec des pincettes, (*il est de mauvaise humeur*) he's like a bear with a sore head; (*il est sale*) I wouldn't touch him with a bargepole/*NAm* with a ten-foot pole 2. *P* legs*; remuer les pincettes, to dance; affûter ses pincettes, to prepare to run away*/to beat it/to clear off.

pine [pin] *nf V* penis*/cock/prick; il est revenu avec la pine sous le bras, (*il a échoué dans une tentative amoureuse*) he didn't make out/he didn't score (with her).

piné [pine] *a P* successful.

piner [pine] *vtr & i V* to have sex* (with) (s.o.)/to have it away (with) (s.o.)/to screw (s.o.)

pinette [pinɛt] *nf V* (*rare*) sex*/quickie/ quick screw.

pineur, -euse [pinœr, -øz] *n V* (*homme*) hot stuff/randy sod; (*femme*) hot stuff/randy sod/nympho.

pingler [pɛ̃gle] *vtr P* to arrest*/to collar/to nab/to cop/to nick. (*Voir* **épingler 1**)

pinglots [pɛ̃glo] *nmpl*, **pingots** [pɛ̃go] *nmpl P* feet*.

pingouin [pɛ̃gwɛ̃] *nm P* 1. Spaniard*. (*Voir* **espingouin**) 2. *pl* feet* 3. lawyer (*wearing a gown*) 4. (habillé) en pingouin, (*homme*) in evening dress/in a penguin suit 5. (*a*) (*individu*) bloke/guy (*b*) (*compagnon*) (boy)friend.

pingre [pɛ̃gr] *F* I *a* miserly*/mean/stingy; il est pingre comme tout, he's as mean as can be II *nm & f* miser*/skinflint/tightwad.

pingrerie [pɛ̃grəri] *nf F* stinginess/ meanness.

pinoche [pinɔʃ] *a P* excellent*/super/first-rate.

pinocher [pinɔʃe] *vtr & i* 1. *P* (*homme*) to be promiscuous/to sleep around/to screw

around 2. *F* to quibble/to split hairs; to be finicky/picky.

pinocumettable [pinɔkymɛtabl] *af V* (*femme*) screwable.

pinte [pɛ̃t] *nf Vieilli F* se faire/s'offrir/se payer une pinte de bon sang, to have a good time/a good laugh; se payer une pinte de nostalgie, to get a good dollop of nostalgia.

pinté [pɛ̃te] *a P* dead drunk*/smashed/ plastered/pissed.

pinter [pɛ̃te] *P* I *vi* to tipple/to booze II *vtr* to swill/to knock back (beer, wine) III *vpr* **se pinter** to get drunk*.

pin-up [pinœp] *nf inv F* (*en photo*) pin-up (girl); (*jolie fille*) dolly-bird.

piochage [pjɔʃaʒ] *nm F* hard work; swotting.

pioche [pjɔʃ] *nf F* hard work/slog/grind. (*Voir* **tête 4**)

piocher [pjɔʃe] I *vtr F* to study hard at (sth)/to swot at (sth); piocher son espagnol, to mug up one's Spanish II *vi* (*a*) *F* to study hard/to swot (*b*) *F* il faut tout le temps piocher, it's a constant grind (*c*) *P* pioche (dans le plat)! dig in!

piocheur, -euse [pjɔʃœr, -øz] *n F* hard worker/swot/slogger.

piocre [pjɔkr] *nm P* louse.

pioger [pjɔʒe] *vi P* to live; où est-ce qu'il pioge? where does he hang out?

piôle [pjol] *nf P* = **piaule**.

pion [pjɔ̃] I *nm* 1. *F* (*écoles*) = prefect (*paid to supervise pupils*); *NAm* = monitor 2. *P* pas le plus petit pion, not a cent/not a bean; je ne donnerais pas le plus petit pion pour l'acheter, I wouldn't give a penny for it. (*Voir* **damer I 2**) II *a P* drunk*/plastered/smashed.

pioncer [pjɔ̃se] *vi P* to sleep/to kip down/to doss down; to get some kip/some shuteye; pioncer ferme, to be fast asleep/to be dead to the world; pioncer un bon coup, to have a good snooze/a good kip.

pionceur [pjɔ̃sœr] *am P* être pionceur, to be a sleeper/a snoozer.

pion(n)ard [pjɔnar] *nm P* drunk(ard)*/ boozer/tippler.

se pion(n)arder [səpjɔnarde] *vpr P* to get drunk*.

pionne [pjɔn] *nf F* (*écoles*) = prefect (*paid to supervise pupils*); *NAm* = monitor.

se pion(n)er [səpjɔne] *vpr P* to get drunk*.

pioupiou, *pl* **-ous** [pjupju] *nm Vieilli P* (young) infantryman/foot soldier.

pipard [pipar] *nm P* pipe-smoker.

pipe [pip] *nf* 1. *Vieilli P* cigarette*/cig(gy)/ fag. (*Voir* **lacson**) 2. *P* casser sa pipe, to die*/to kick the bucket/to snuff it. (*Voir* **casser I** 6) 3. *P* se fendre la pipe, to laugh* uproariously/to split one's sides laughing/to laugh one's head off; nous nous fendions la pipe, we were in stitches 4. *A P* prendre la pipe, to get badly caught out/to come to grief/ to come a cropper; to lose out on a deal/to get stung 5. *P* musical note; faire des pipes, to play music 6. *V* fellatio*; faire/tailler une pipe à qn, to give s.o. a blow-job/to blow s.o./to suck s.o. off/to suck s.o.'s cock/to give s.o. head; prise de pipe, blow-job/head; une bouche à tailler des pipes, a real cock-sucker's mouth. (*Voir* **nom 2; tête 10**)

pipeau [pipo] *nm F* c'est du pipeau, it's nonsense/rubbish; it doesn't bear thinking about.

pipelet, pipelette [piplɛ, piplɛt] *n F* (*a*) porter/caretaker (of block of flats, etc) (*b*) pipelette, nosy and gossipy person/nosy parker.

piper [pipe] **I** *vtr* 1. *Vieilli P* to arrest*; se faire piper, to get nabbed/nicked 2. *P* je (ne) peux pas le piper, I can't stand/stick/ stomach/bear him (at any price); he really gets up my nose 3. *V* piper qn, to give s.o. fellatio*/to blow s.o./to give s.o. a blow-job/to suck s.o. off **II** *vi P* 1. to be a pipe-smoker 2. to speak; il n'a pas pipé, he didn't say a word/a dicky-bird.

piperlot [pipɛrlo] *nm P* (pipe) tobacco.

pipette [pipɛt] *nf P* 1. cigarette* 2. vol à la pipette, stealing petrol (from cars) by siphoning it off 3. (*Suisse*) ça ne vaut pas pipette, that's worthless*/it's not worth a sausage. (*Voir* **tripette**)

pipeur, -euse [pipœr, -øz] *n V* (*a*) fellator/cock-sucker/head artist/dick-licker (*b*) pipeuse, prostitute* specializing in fellatio*.

pipi [pipi] *nm* 1. *F* urine*/wee(-wee); faire pipi/faire un petit pipi, to urinate*/to wee-wee/to piddle/to pee; aller faire pipi, to spend a penny/to pay a call/to go for a pee; j'ai envie de pipi/d'aller faire pipi, I want to go to the loo/*NAm* the bathroom/*NAm* the john; il a fait pipi dans sa culotte, he's wet himself/he's had an accident; il y a du pipi de chien sur le tapis, the dog's made a puddle/the dog's weed/the dog's pissed on the carpet. (*Voir* **dame-pipi; madame-pipi**) 2. *P* du pipi de chat, (*boisson*) poor-quality wine, etc/cat's piss/gnat's piss; ce café, c'est du pipi de chat,

this coffee's like dishwater/this coffee is as weak as piss.

pipi-room [pipirum] *nm inv F* WC*; où sont fourrés les pipi-room? where the hell is the loo/*NAm* the john in this place?

Pipo [pipo] *P* **I** *Prnf* la Pipo, the *École polytechnique* (in Paris) **II** *nm & f* a student at the *École polytechnique*.

piquage [pikaʒ] *nm F* 1. arrest 2. (*prostituée*) picking up of client. (*Voir* **piquer 4**)

pique [pik] **I** *nf F* être à cent piques au-dessus de qn, to be vastly superior to s.o./to be ten times better than s.o.; il est à cent piques au-dessous de son frère, he isn't a patch on his brother **II** *nm P* thief/pickpocket. (*Voir* **as 2; dame 5**)

piqué, -ée [pike] *F* **I** *a* mad*/cracked/nuts/ screwy/loony **II** *n* crackbrained person/ nutter/loony; c'est une vieille piquée, the old girl's a bit touched in the head/she's an old loony. (*Voir* **hanneton 2; ver 2**)

pique-assiette [pikasjɛt] *nm & f inv inv F* scrounger/sponger/parasite/*NAm* freeloader/ hanger-on.

pique-fesse [pikfɛs] *nf inv P* nurse.

pique-gâteau [pikgɑto], **pique-gaufrette** [pikgofrɛt] *nm inv Vieilli P* nose*.

pique-lard [piklar] *nm inv P* flick knife.

pique-pouces [pikpus] *nm*, **pique-prunes** [pikpryn] *nm inv Vieilli P* tailor.

piquer [pike] *vtr* 1. *F* faire piquer son chien, to have one's dog put down/put to sleep 2. *F* to steal*/to pinch/to swipe (qch à qn, sth from s.o.); piquer les troncs, to steal from the church collecting boxes; je ne l'ai pas volé, je l'ai piqué sur un chantier, I didn't steal it, I found it lying around; il a fallu qu'on pique une tire pour y aller, we had to nick a car to get there 3. *P* piquer des clopes, to pick up cigarette* ends 4. *P* to arrest*; se faire piquer, to get nabbed; il s'est fait piquer, he got nicked/picked up 5. *P* to tattoo; se faire piquer, to get tattooed 6. *P* to stab/to knife (s.o.) 7. *F* piquer les cartes, to mark the cards 8. *F* piquer les pneus, to slash the tyres 9. *F* piquer un cent mètres, to sprint (off)/to go into a sprint 10. *F* piquer une tête, to take a header/to dive. (*Voir* **assiette 4; bambou 2** (*a*)**; chien II 13; crise 1** (*a*)**; départ; dix 3; fard; hanneton 2; macadam 2; mouche 2; nez 5; roupillon; sèche²; soleil 1; tas 4; truc 5**) **II** *vpr* se piquer *F* to take drugs; to give oneself a fix/to fix (up)/ to shoot up; **il se pique**, he's a drug addict/a junkie/a fixer.

piquet [pikɛ] *nm V* **avoir le piquet (de tente)**, to have an erection*.

piqueton [piktɔ̃] *nm P* ordinary red wine. (*Voir* **picton**)

piquette [pikɛt] *nf P* 1. cheap (and nasty) wine/plonk 2. **ça n'était pas de la piquette**, that was no small matter 3. **prendre/ramasser une piquette**, (*au jeu, etc*) to get thrashed/ licked/hammered 4. slaughter/bloodbath.

piqueur [pikœr] *nm P* 1. (*a*) pickpocket/dip (*b*) thief; **piqueur de troncs**, man who steals from a church collecting box 2. **piqueur de clopes**, man who goes around picking up cigarette* ends.

piquouse [pikuz] *nf P* (*drogues*) shot/ injection*/fix/shoot; **faire une piquouse à qn**, to give s.o. a fix; **se faire une piquouse**, to give oneself a fix/to shoot up. (*Voir* **chevalier 6**)

piquouser [pikuze] *vtr P* **piquouser qn**, to give s.o. an injection/a jab/a shot/(*drogues*) a fix.

piquouze [pikuz] *nf P* = **piquouse**.

piquouzer [pikuze] *vtr P* = **piquouser**.

piratage [pirataʒ] *nm F* (*informatique*) hacking.

pirate [pirat] *nm F* **pirate informatique**, hacker.

pirater [pirate] *vtr F* to record/to copy fraudulently (records, films, videos, etc); to hack (computer programs); **des cassettes piratées**, pirated cassettes.

pire [pir] *adv P* 1. **tant pire!** (= *tant pis!*) never mind!/it can't be helped! 2. **plus pire**, (= *pire*) worse/worser.

pirouette [pirwɛt] *nf F* **répondre par des pirouettes**, to sidestep/to dodge the question; to give a facetious answer.

piscine [pisin] *nf F* 1. **en pleine piscine**, in a frightful mess 2. **la Piscine**, = French counterespionage headquarters; = MI5.

pissant [pisɑ̃] *a P* very funny*.

pissat [pisa] *nm P* **pissat (d'âne)**, poor-quality wine, etc; cat's piss/gnat's piss.

pisse [pis] *nf P* piss; **c'est de la pisse d'âne, ta bière!** your beer's as weak as piss!

pisse-copie [piskɔpi] *nm & f inv P* hack (writer)/hackette. (*Voir* **copie**)

pissée [pise] *nf P* (*a*) downpour (of rain) (*b*) **une bonne pissée**, a good piss.

pisse-froid [pisfrwa] *nm inv P* (*personne*)

cold fish; wet blanket.

pissement [pismɑ̃] *nm P* pissing/peeing.

pissenlit [pisɑ̃li] *nm P* **manger/bouffer les pissenlits par la racine**, to be dead and buried/to be pushing up the daisies.

pisser [pise] I *vtr & i* 1. *P* to urinate*/to piss/to pee; **avoir envie de pisser**, to want to (have a) piss/to be bursting (for a pee); **il est allé pisser un coup**, he's gone for a piss/a slash; **pisser dans sa culotte**, to wet one's pants/knickers 2. *P* **une bouteille qui pisse**, a leaking bottle 3. *P* **pisser des châsses/de l'œil/ de la lanterne**, to cry (one's eyes out) 4. *P* **pisser entre parenthèses**, to feel pain when urinating/to piss pins and needles 5. *P* **laisse pisser!** let it ride!/forget it! 6. *P* **ne plus se sentir pisser**, to be terribly conceited 7. *P* **en faire pisser à qn**, to put s.o. through it/to put s.o. through the mill 8. *Vieilli V* **pisser des os**, to give birth (to a baby) 9. *V* **envoyer pisser qn**, to tell s.o. to piss off 10. *V* **faire pisser qn**, to make s.o. piss himself laughing; **il nous raconte des blagues à en pisser dans son froc/ dans sa culotte**, his jokes are so good you piss yourself laughing 11. *P* (*pluie*) **ça pisse dur/il pleut comme (une) vache qui pisse**, it's pissing down/it's bucketing down/it's chucking it down 12. *P* **avoir autant d'effet que pisser dans la mer**, to stand as much chance as a fart in a windstorm; **c'est comme si je pissais sur un bec de gaz**, I might as well save my breath; it's a sheer waste of time; it's like banging your head against a brick wall 13. *P* **ça pisse pas loin**, (*sans intérêt*) it's boring; (*pas efficace*) it's useless 14. *F* (*sang*) to pour out; **ça pisse le sang**, (*blessure*) it's pouring blood/the blood is pouring out. (*Voir* **copie**; **côtelette 4**; **cul 15**; **froc 4**; **lame 3**; **mérinos**; **môme II 1**; **raie 2**; **sang 7**; **violon 4**) II *vpr* **se pisser** *V* to piss oneself/to kill oneself laughing.

pissette [pisɛt] *nf P* 1. *Aut* windscreen washer 2. fire-hose nozzle.

pisseur, -euse¹ [pisœr, -øz] *P* I *n* **c'est un pisseur**, he keeps disappearing for a piss/for a pee; he's got a weak bladder II *nf* **pisseuse** (*a*) baby girl; young girl*; little brat (*b*) young woman*/chick. (*Voir* **copie**; **côtelette 4**)

pisseux¹, -euse² [pisø, -øz] *a P* (*a*) smelling of urine/piss/pee (*b*) stained with urine/ piss-stained/pee-stained (*c*) (*couleur*) faded/ washed-out/wishy-washy; **jaune pisseux**, dingy yellow.

pisseux[2] *nm P* 1. inexperienced young man; je vais pas laisser ce petit pisseux me donner des conseils, I'm not going to let that little runt/jerk give me advice 2. clumsy and dirty/scruffy worker who bungles everything; espèce de pisseux! you jerk!/you clumsy idiot!

pisse-vinaigre [pisvinɛgr] *nm inv P* 1. miser*/skinflint 2. grumbler/grouser/groucher.

pissoir [piswar] *nm P* urinal/pisshouse/loo/ *NAm* can/*NAm* john/(*homosexuels*) cottage.

pissoter [pisɔte] *vi P* to be for ever pissing.

pissotière [pisɔtjɛr] *nf P* (public) urinal/ (*homosexuels*) cottage; (*homosexuels*) **faire les pissotières**, to go cruising in urinals/to go john-cruising/to go cottaging.

pissouse, pissouze [pisuz] *nf P* = **pisseuse**[1].

pistache [pistaʃ] *nf P* **prendre/ramasser une pistache**, to get drunk*; **il a une belle pistache**, he's dead drunk/he's pissed out of his mind.

se pistacher [səpistaʃe] *vpr P* to get drunk*/pissed.

pistage [pistaʒ] *nm F* (*police, etc*) shadowing/tracking/tailing (of suspect).

pistard [pistar] *nm F* (*cyclisme*) track racer.

piste [pist] *nf F* **être en piste**, to be in the running.

pister [piste] I *vtr F* 1. to track/to trail (s.o.); to shadow/to tail (a suspect, etc) 2. **pister des clients**, to tout for customers (for a nightclub, hotel, etc) II *vpr* **se pister** *F* to run away*/to clear off.

pisteur [pistœr] *nm F* 1. (nightclub, etc) tout 2. (police) spy/tail/shadow.

pistoche [pistɔʃ] *nf F* (*écoles*) **la pistoche**, the (swimming) pool/the baths.

pistolache [pistɔlaʃ] *nm P* pistol/revolver*.

pistole [pistɔl] *nf F* cell (in prison).

pistolet [pistɔlɛ] *nm F* 1. **un drôle de pistolet**, an odd (sort of) chap/a strange bloke/a queer fish 2. (*urinal*) bedpan.

piston [pistɔ̃] *nm* 1. *F* string-pulling; **avoir du piston**, to get s.o. to use his influence on one's behalf; to know the right people; to have friends in the right places; to have clout; **il est arrivé à coups de piston**, he succeeded because he knows the right people/ through the old boy network; **faire obtenir une place à qn au piston**, to pull a few strings/ wires in order to get s.o. a job 2. *F Mus* (*a*) cornet (*b*) cornet-player 3. *P Mil etc* (= *capiston*) captain 4. *P* **Piston**, *École centrale des arts et manufactures*; **piston**, student at the *École centrale*.

pistonnage [pistɔnaʒ] *nm F* string-pulling/ wire-pulling/clout/pull.

pistonner [pistɔne] *vtr F* **pistonner qn**, to use one's influence/one's clout to help s.o.; to pull strings/wires for s.o.; to back s.o.; **il s'est fait pistonner**, he got s.o. to pull strings for him.

pistonneur, -euse [pistɔnœr, -øz] *n F* influential backer; friend at court/string-puller.

pitaine [pitɛn] *nm* (= *capitaine*) *P* (*a*) *Mil* captain/cap (*b*) (sea) captain/cap'n/the Old Man.

pitancher [pitɑ̃ʃe] *vtr P* = **pictancher**.

pitancheur [pitɑ̃ʃœr] *nm P* = **pictancheur**.

pitchoun [pitʃun], **pitchounette** [pitʃunɛt] *a F* small/little/tiny/wee/titchy. (*Voir* **pichoun**)

pitchpin [pitʃpɛ̃] *nm P* **c'est du (vrai) pitchpin**, it's easy*/it's a sure bet/it's a doddle. (*Voir* **pichpin**)

piton [pitɔ̃] *nm P* (big) nose*.

pive [piv] *nm*, **piveton** [pivtɔ̃] *nm P* (*a*) wine/vino (*b*) poor-quality wine/plonk.

pivois [pivwa] *nm P* = **pive**.

pivoter [pivɔte] *vi F* **faire pivoter qn**, to boss s.o. about.

pivots [pivo] *nmpl F* legs*.

pivre [pivr] *nm P* = **pive**.

PJ [peʒi] *nf F* (*abrév=Police Judiciaire*) **la PJ**=CID (*Criminal Investigation Department*).

placage [plakaʒ] *nm F* = **plaquage**.

placard [plakar] *nm P* 1. prison*; **foutre qn au placard**, to throw/to bung s.o. in jail/in clink 2. **être/rester au placard**, to be pushed aside/to be put on the shelf; **mettre au placard**, to put (sth) aside; to cover up (a story); to push (s.o.) aside/to neutralize (s.o.) 3. (*homosexuels*) **sortir du placard**, to come out of the closet; **faire sortir qn du placard**, to out s.o. 4. sum of money paid to pimp* for the purchase of a prostitute*.

placarde [plakard] *nf P* 1. public square 2. **une bonne placarde**, (*au marché*) a good pitch 3. (cushy) job 4. **louer des placardes**, to book seats 5. hide-out/hide-away/hiding place/ hidey-hole.

placarder [plakarde] I *vtr P* 1. to place/to find a job for (s.o.); to place (a prostitute*) (in a brothel) 2. to hide (sth)/to stash (sth) away **II** *vpr* **se placarder** *P* 1. to find a good pitch (*for selling goods*) 2. to hide/to go into hiding.

placardier [plakardje] *nm P* tout.

place [plas] *nf P* 1. place d'armes, stomach* 2. c'était à payer sa place, I wouldn't have missed it for anything.

placé [plase] *a F* (*a*) il a le cœur bien placé, his heart is in the right place (*b*) elle a des rondeurs bien placées, she comes out in (all) the right places.

placer [plase] *vtr F* en placer une, to be able to have one's say; ne pas pouvoir en placer une, to be unable to get a word in (edgeways); je peux en placer une, oui? would you just let me speak?

placeur [plasœr] *nm P* tout.

placoter [plakote] *vi FrC F* to gossip/to chatter*/to gas.

plafond [plafɔ̃] *nm F* 1. head*; se crever/se défoncer/se faire sauter le plafond, to blow one's brains out 2. être bas de plafond, to be stupid*/thick/dim/dumb. (*Voir* **bas-de-plafond**) 3. sauter au plafond, (*de joie*) to jump for joy; (*de rage*) to flare up/to blow one's top/to hit the roof. (*Voir* **araignée 1**)

plafonnard [plafɔnar] *nm P* = **plafond 1**.

à plaga [aplaga] *adv phr P* = **plat II 1**.

plaie [plɛ] *nf F* (*personne*) pest/menace; quelle plaie! what a nuisance! (*Voir* **demander 1**)

plaisir [plezir] *nm F* au plaisir! goodbye!/ nice seeing you!/see you (again)!

plan [plã] *nm* 1. *F* laisser qn en plan, to leave s.o. stranded/to leave s.o. in the lurch/to walk out on s.o./to ditch s.o.; laisser qch en plan, to leave sth unfinished/to leave off in the middle of sth/to drop sth; rester en plan, to be stranded/to be left in the lurch/to be left out in the cold/to be ditched/to be left high and dry 2. *P* il n'y a pas plan!/y a pas plan! (there's) nothing doing!/it's no go! y a plan pour sortir d'ici? is there any way out of here? 3. *P* metal tube containing precious objects, etc, hidden in the rectum 4. *F* plan/project; alors, t'as un plan? well, have you got an idea/ something in mind? on se fait un plan ciné? shall we go to the flicks/*surt NAm* the movies? plan galère, bad/rotten idea 5. *P* (*drogues*) (*a*) 1 gram measure (*b*) organization of the distribution of drugs; faire un plan, to organize a supply of drugs (*c*) dose (of a drug); elle attend après un plan, she's waiting for her supply of heroin* 6. *P* lie; faire un

plan, to try to trick s.o./to do the dirty on s.o.

planant [planã] *a F* (*musique, drogue, alcool, etc*) that makes one feel high; cool/ far-out.

planche [plãʃ] *nf F* 1. (*a*) (*écoles*) blackboard; passer à la planche, to go up to the blackboard (*b*) oral (test) 2. (*théâtre*) brûler des planches, to act with fire; to put a lot into one's performance; balayer les planches, to act in the curtain-raiser 3. il y a du travail sur la planche, there's plenty of work to be done/ there's a lot to do. (*Voir* **pain 1**) 4. une vraie planche à pain, a flat-chested woman; être plate comme une planche à pain/à repasser, to be as flat as a board/as a pancake 5. s'habiller de quatre planches/être entre quatre planches, to be dead (and buried)/to be wearing a wooden overcoat/to be six foot under 6. *Aut* mettre le pied sur la planche, to accelerate/to put one's foot down/to step on the gas.

plancher¹ [plãʃe] *nm F* 1. le plancher des vaches, dry land/terra firma 2. débarrasser/ décharger/vider le plancher, to clear out/to beat it; videz(-moi) le plancher! get lost*!/ beat it!/hop it!/scram! 3. rouler (le pied) au plancher/mettre le pied au plancher, to drive with one's foot on the floor/to drive flat out.

plancher² *vi F* (*écoles*) to be called up to the blackboard (*for questioning, etc*); il a dû plancher devant un parterre de spécialistes, he had to present a report to a group of experts.

plané [plane] *a F* faire un vol plané, to fall (heavily)/to come a cropper*/to pitch down (headfirst)/to nosedive.

planer [plane] *vi F* (*a*) to be under the influence of a drug; to feel exhilarated (*after taking a drug*); (*drogues*) to be high/to be stoned (*b*) (*être particulièrement bien*) to be/ feel on top of the world; to be on cloud nine; (*rêvasser*) to daydream; planer à trois mille mètres, to have one's head in the clouds; planer complet, (*personne*) to be away off course/to go adrift.

planète [planɛt] *nf P* 1. écraser la planète, (*avion*) to crash 2. (*drogues*) être sur sa planète, to be high/to be stoned.

plan-plan [plãplã] *a P* slow/easy(-going)/ leisurely/laid-back; amour plan-plan, gentle/ leisurely/tender lovemaking. (*Voir* **plon-plon**)

planque [plãk] *nf* 1. *F* soft/cushy job; safe berth; soft option; ce fut une ruée pour la distribution des planques, there was a rush to find jobs for the boys; **une bonne planque si on a de la veine!** nice work if you can get it! **son nouveau boulot, c'est la planque,** he's got a dead cushy new job/his job's a real doddle 2. *P (a)* hiding place/hide-out/hide-away/hidey-hole *(b) Mil* funk hole 3. *P* savings/nest egg/stash 4. *P (prostituées)* sum of money put on one side for a prostitute's own use and held back from her pimp 5. *P* police surveillance/obbo/stakeout; **la police était en planque devant la maison,** the police were staking out the house; **la baraque était en planque,** the police had the place staked out; **il y a un flic qui fait la planque devant l'immeuble,** there's a cop on watch in front of the building. *(Voir* **attigé** *(a))*

planqué [plɑ̃ke] *a & nm P (a)* (person) in hiding *(b)* slacker/skiver/lead-swinger; *(c) Mil* shirker (from call-up *or* active service)/column-dodger; funker.

planquer [plɑ̃ke] *P* I *vtr* 1. *(a)* to hide (sth)/to stash (sth) (away); **il a planqué la came dans ses chaussettes,** he stashed the dope in his socks; **planquer ses côtelettes,** to hide *(b)* to plant (money) by *(c)* to plant (stolen goods) 2. to place/to put/to stick/to shove (sth somewhere) II *vi* to put somewhere under surveillance/to stake out a place/to keep somewhere under observation III *vpr* **se planquer** 1. *(a) (s'abriter)* to take cover/shelter; to hide (oneself) *(b)* to go into hiding/to go to ground/to lie low; **elle s'est planquée chez des amis,** she's hiding out/she's lying low with (some) friends 2. to park oneself/to plonk oneself down (somewhere) 3. to find oneself a cushy job.

planquouse [plɑ̃kuz] *nf P* = **planque**.

planquouser [plɑ̃kuze] *vtr P* = **planquer** I.

plantage [plɑ̃taʒ] *nm P* 1. error/mistake 2. failure/flop.

plante [plɑ̃t] *nf P* 1. **une belle plante,** a fine specimen (of humanity); *(femme)* a nice bit of stuff 2. error/mistake; **faire une plante,** to make a mistake.

planté [plɑ̃te] *a F* **ne la laissez pas plantée là,** don't leave her standing there; **ne reste pas planté là! dis qch!** don't just stand there like a stuffed dummy, say sth!

planter [plɑ̃te] I *vtr* 1. *F* **planter là qn,** to leave s.o. in the lurch; *(abandonner)* to desert s.o./to walk out on s.o.; *(amant)* to jilt s.o.; **je ne vous planterai pas là,** I won't let you down

2. *F* to put/to stick/to shove; **planter ses miches sur une chaise,** to plonk one's arse/*NAm* ass/*NAm* fanny down on a chair 3. *P* to stab (s.o.)/to knife (to death) 4. *V (a)* to have sex* with (a woman)/to screw (a woman) *(b) (homosexuels)* to have anal sex* with (s.o.); **il aime bien planter les mecs,** he likes screwing men 5. *P* **planter qn de 5000 francs,** not to pay back the 5000 francs owed to s.o.; **il m'a planté de 600 francs,** he hasn't paid me back the 600 francs he owes me. *(Voir* **chou** I 4; **drapeau** 2) II *vpr* **se planter** *F* 1. *Aut* to go off the road (into a ditch, etc) 2. *(théâtre)* to forget one's lines/to get stuck 3. to make a mistake*/to go wrong (in one's calculations, etc) 4. to fail; **il s'est planté à l'examen,** he failed/he flunked the exam.

planterie [plɑ̃tri] *nf P* = **plantage**.

planton [plɑ̃tɔ̃] *nm F* **faire le planton,** to hang about (waiting).

plaquage [plakaʒ] *nm F* chucking/ditching/dumping/jilting *(esp* of lover); **alors, toi et ton mec, c'est un plaquage en règle?** so it's all over/finished between you two, is it?/so you've really chucked/ditched him, have you?

plaqué [plake] *nm F* **c'est du plaqué,** it's false/phon(e)y/fake.

plaquer [plake] *F* I *vtr* 1. *(a)* to leave (s.o.) in the lurch/to ditch (s.o.) *(b)* to jilt (s.o.); **elle a plaqué son mari,** she's walked out on her husband; **il l'a plaquée, son mec,** her bloke's dropped her/chucked her/given her the push 2. **avoir envie de tout plaquer,** to feel like chucking everything up/packing everything in II *vi* to give up; to throw in the sponge/the towel.

plaquouse [plakuz] *nf F* (red) spot/patch/blotch (on the skin).

plaquouser [plakuze] *vtr & i F* = **plaquer**.

plastoc, plastoque [plastɔk] *nm P* plastic.

plastron [plastrɔ̃] *nm F (poitrine)* chest.

plastronner [plastrɔne] *vi F* to pose/to strut/to show off*/to put on airs/to swagger.

plastronneur, -euse [plastrɔnœr, -øz] *n F (personne) (a)* show-off*/swank/pose(u)r *(b)* stuffed shirt.

plat [pla] I *nm* 1. *F* **mettre les petits plats dans les grands,** to spare no expense/to go to town on (sth) 2. *F* **en faire (tout) un plat (à qn),** to make a great fuss/a song and dance about sth (to s.o.); to pile it on; **il n'en a pas fait un plat,** he made no bones about it 3. *P* **il en fait un plat!** it's boiling hot!/it's a real scorcher! **4.** *P* **faire du plat à qn,** to sweet-talk s.o./to chat s.o. up/to try to get off with s.o./to try and make out with s.o. **5.** *P* **plat de nouilles,** fool*/idiot/twerp/drip **6.** *pl P* **plats,** faked dice **7.** *F* **puiser dans le plat,** to help oneself/to dig in. (*Voir* **œuf 5; pied 3; repiquer II 2**) **II** *adv phr F* **1.** **être à plat,** to be exhausted*/all in; (*déprimé*) to be depressed; (*sans le sou*) to be completely broke; *Aut* to have a flat (tyre); **j'étais complètement à plat,** I was completely run down; (*déprimé*) I was really low; (*sans le sou*) I was really broke; **cette maladie l'a mis à plat,** this illness has really knocked him out **2.** **mettre à plat,** (*faire des économies*) to save (up)/to put by/to stash away (money).

plates-bandes [platbɑ̃d] *nfpl F* **marcher sur/piétiner les plates-bandes de qn,** to poach on s.o.'s preserves/to poke one's nose into s.o.'s business; **(ne) marchez pas sur mes plates-bandes,** mind your own business/keep out of my patch.

platine [platin] *nf Vieilli P* tongue; **avoir une fameuse platine,** to have the gift of the gab; **quelle platine!** what a gasbag!/what a windbag!

plato [plato] *nm P* platonic love.

plâtrage [plɑtraʒ] *nm F* **c'est du plâtrage, tout ça,** that's (all) a load of rubbish/hooey.

plâtre [plɑtr] *nm* **1.** *F* **essuyer les plâtres,** to be the first to try out sth new; **on a dû essuyer les plâtres au début,** we had a few teething troubles in the beginning **2.** *P* money*; **être (plein) au plâtre,** to be rich*; **se faire un petit plâtre,** to make a little bit on the side.

plâtrée [plɑtre] *nf F* huge helping of food.

se plâtrer [səplɑtre] *vpr F* **se plâtrer (le visage),** to plaster one's face with make-up/to put on one's war-paint.

plat-ventre [plavɑ̃tr] *nm inv F* **1.** heavy fall; (*natation*) belly-flop **2.** *Fig* **faire un plat-ventre,** to come a cropper/to fall flat on one's face.

plein [plɛ̃] **I** *a F* drunk*; **plein comme un boudin/une bourrique/un fût/une huître/un œuf/une outre/un Polonais/une vache,** dead drunk*/drunk as a lord/tight as a drum/high as a kite/pissed as a newt. (*Voir* **andosses 2; as 3; botte 2; cul I 7; dos 2; plâtre 2; tube 8**) **II** *nm P* **faire le plein,** to eat* heartily/to stoke up **III** *adv P* **tout plein,** very much/a lot; **tout plein de gens,** any number of people/loads of people; **y avait plein de fric dans le portefeuille,** there was plenty of

money*/bread/dough in the wallet/*NAm* billfold; **elle est mignonne tout plein,** she's terribly sweet; she's a real sweetie. (*Voir* **œil 10; pot 19**)

pleur [plœr] *nm F* **bureau des pleurs,** complaints office; **allez vous plaindre ailleurs, ici ce n'est pas le bureau des pleurs!** go and complain somewhere else!

pleurer [plœre] *vi F* **1.** **pleurer pour avoir qch,** to demand sth; **je veux ça ou je pleure!** give it (to) me or I'll scream! **2.** (*a*) **il est bête à pleurer,** he's unbelievably stupid*/he's as thick as two short planks (*b*) **c'est bête à (en) pleurer,** (*facile*) it's as easy* as winking; (*idiot*) it's quite idiotic. (*Voir* **colosse 1; cyclope; vache II 6**)

pleurnichard, -arde [plœrniʃar, -ard] *n F* crybaby/sniveller/whiner.

pleuvasser [plœvase], **pleuviner** [plœvine] *v impers F* to drizzle.

pleuvoir [plœvwar] *v impers* **1.** *F* **il pleut tant qu'il peut,** it's raining hard/it's pelting down. (*Voir* **corde 9; hallebardes; seau 1; vache II 6**) **2.** *Vieilli P* **un nez dans lequel il pleut,** a turned-up nose/a pug-nose **3.** *P* **il pleut!** (*absolument pas!*) not (bloody) likely!*/not on your life! (*attention!*) watch it!/look out! **4.** *F Iron* **il va pleuvoir!** you don't say!/how amazing! well, strike a light! **5.** *F* (*a*) **elle ramasse du fric comme s'il en pleuvait,** she's raking it in (*b*) **à la manif, il y avait des flics comme s'il en pleuvait,** there were police absolutely everywhere/you couldn't move for cops at the demo.

pleuvoter [plœvɔte] *v impers F* = **pleuvasser.**

pli [pli] *nm F* **1.** **ça (ne) fait pas un pli,** (*c'est parfait*) that's fine/perfect; (*il n'y a pas de difficulté*) it's all plain sailing; (*c'est évident*) (there's) no doubt about it; (*c'est fatal*) it's/it was bound to happen **2.** **mettre qn au pli,** to make s.o. toe the line/to bring s.o. to heel **3.** **les enfants prennent aisément de mauvais plis,** children easily get into bad habits.

plié [plije] *a F* **plié (de rire),** doubled up (with laughing)/creased up.

plier [plije] *P* **I** *vtr* to smash up/to wreck/to crash (a car, an aeroplane, etc) **II** *vi* (*entreprise, etc*) to fail/to go under/to go down the chute.

plomb [plɔ̃] *nm* **1.** *F* **ça te mettra du plomb dans la tête,** that'll steady you down a bit/knock some sense into you **2.** *F* **avoir du plomb dans l'aile,** (*être malade*) to be ill/to be in a bad way; (*avoir des ennuis*) to be in difficulties; (*être atteint dans sa réputation*) to have one's reputation tarnished **3.** *F* **cul de plomb**, (*dispensing*) chemist's assistant; (*petit bureaucrate*) pen-pusher/clerk; (*personne paresseuse*) lazybones **4.** *P* discount made to a prostitute* by a hotel keeper **5.** *P* **se faire sauter les plombs**, to get high on drink*/drugs*.

plombard [plɔ̃bar] *nm P* plumber.

plombe [plɔ̃b] *nf P* hour; **il est cinq plombes**, it's striking five now/it's five o'clock; **à cinq plombes pile**, on the dot of five; **ça fait une plombe que j'attends**, I've been waiting a whole hour/a solid hour.

plombé [plɔ̃be] *a P* infected with syphilis/syphy/pox-ridden/poxy.

plomber [plɔ̃be] **I** *vtr P* **1.** to infect (s.o.) with syphilis*/to give (s.o.) the pox/to give s.o. a dose; **se faire plomber**, to cop a dose (of the pox); **il s'est fait plomber**, he's got syph **2.** to shoot (s.o.)/to fill (s.o.) with lead/to drill (s.o.) full of holes; **elle l'avait plombé, le mec, avec son propre flingue**, she'd shot the bloke/*surt NAm* guy with his own gun; **se faire plomber** (**le buffet**), to get shot/pumped full of lead **II** *vi P* **1.** *A* (*heure*) to strike **2.** *Vieilli* to stink*/to pong; **plomber du goulot**, to have bad breath; **ça plombe dans cette baraque**, it stinks in here **3.** to weigh/to be heavy; **elle plombe cette valise**, that suitcase weighs a bit.

plombier [plɔ̃bje] *nm F* **1.** one who places bugs (*in a room, etc*); (*au téléphone*) phone-tapper **2.** (*policier spécialiste de l'écoute clandestine*) snooper/eavesdropper.

plonge [plɔ̃ʒ] *nf F* washing-up (*esp* in restaurant); **j'ai dû faire la plonge dans un resto à Paris pour gagner le fric nécessaire**, I had to be a washer-up/I had to wash dishes in a Parisian restaurant to get the money together.

plongeon [plɔ̃ʒɔ̃] *nm F* **faire le plongeon**, (*se décider*) to make up one's mind (to do sth)/to take the plunge; (*s'incliner*) to bow deeply/to give a low bow; (*perdre beaucoup d'argent*) to lose a great deal of money/*NAm* to take a bath.

plonger [plɔ̃ʒe] *vi* **1.** *F* to do the washing-up/to wash dishes (*esp* in restaurant) **2.** *F* to lose a great deal of money/*NAm* to take a bath **3.** *P* **il a plongé**, he's been sent to prison*/sent down; he's been put inside/away **4.** *P* to make an important decision/to take

the plunge.

plongeur, -euse [plɔ̃ʒœr, -øz] *nm & f F* washer-up/bottle-washer (*esp* in restaurant).

plon-plon [plɔ̃plɔ̃] *a P* = **plan-plan**.

plote [plɔt] *nf P* **envoyer qn aux plotes** = **envoyer qn aux pelotes** (**pelote 4**).

plouc, plouk [pluk] *P* **I** *nm & f* **1.** peasant*/country bumpkin/*NAm* hick **2.** stupid* person/fool*/twit/nit/clot/cloth-head **II** *a* stupid*/dumb.

ploum [plum] *nm P* **1.** = **plouc I 1 2.** native of Auvergne/Auvergnat. (*Voir* **Auverploum**)

plouque [pluk] *nm P* = **plouc I 1, 2.**

plouquesse [plukɛs] *nf P* peasant*/country bumpkin. (*Voir* **plouc I 1**)

pluche [plyʃ] *nf F* **la pluche**, peeling (of vegetables); *Mil etc* **les pluches**, spud-bashing.

pluie [plɥi] *nf F* **1.** **il n'est pas né/tombé de la dernière pluie**, he wasn't born yesterday; there are no flies on him **2.** **en mettre un à l'abri de la pluie**, to down a drink/to knock one back **3.** **faire la pluie et le beau temps**, to be the boss/to rule the roost; **c'est lui qui fait la pluie et le beau temps ici**, he's the big white chief around here.

plumaison [plymɛzɔ̃] *nf F* fleecing/ripping off (of s.o.).

plumard [plymar] *nm P* bed*; **aller au plumard/se fourrer au plumard**, to go to bed*/to hit the hay/to hit the sack/to crash out; **être doué au plumard**, to be good in bed.

se plumarder [səplymarde] *vpr P* to go to bed*/to turn in/to hit the hay/to hit the sack/to kip down/to crash down.

plume [plym] **I** *nm P* bed*; **il est resté au plume, le veinard!** he stayed in bed, the lucky devil! **II** *nf* **1.** *F* (**y**) **laisser des plumes**, to lose money (*esp* at gambling); **il y a laissé des plumes/il a perdu des plumes**, he lost out on it/he didn't get off scot-free/he got his fingers burnt **2.** *F* **craindre pour ses plumes/avoir chaud aux plumes**, to go about in fear of one's life **3.** *F* **voler dans les plumes à qn**, to attack s.o./to go for s.o. **4.** *F* **passer à la plume**, to get beaten up; **passer qn à la plume**, to beat s.o. up*/to work s.o. over **5.** *pl F* bed* **6.** *pl F* hair; **perdre ses plumes**, to go bald*/to lose one's thatch **7.** *P* wing (of aircraft) **8.** *P* (burglar's) jemmy/*NAm* jimmy **9.** *V* fellatio*; **tailler une plume (à un mec)**, to give head to/to blow/to suck off/to give a blow-job to (a bloke/a guy); **ce qu'il préfère, c'est qu'on lui taille une plume**, he really gets off when you give him a blow-job/he likes you to suck him off.

plumeau, *pl* **-eaux** [plymo] *nm* 1. *F* **un vieux plumeau,** an old stick-in-the-mud/an old fuddy-duddy 2. *P* (*boisson*) cocktail of mandarin(e) aperitif and champagne*; **avoir son plumeau,** to be (slightly) drunk*/tipsy 3. *P* (*a*) **va chez Plumeau!** go to hell!/get lost*! (*b*) **envoyer qn chez Plumeau,** to chuck/to turf s.o. out. (*Voir* **Plumepatte**) 4. *V* **foutre un coup de plumeau à (une femme),** to have sex* with/to screw/to fuck (a woman).

plumée [plyme] *nf* 1. *F* fleecing/ripping off (of s.o.) 2. *P* thrashing/beating-up/(good) hiding.

Plumepatte [plympat] *Prn P* **envoyer qn chez Plumepatte,** to chuck/to turf s.o. out. (*Voir* **plumeau 3** (*b*))

plumer [plyme] I *vtr F* to fleece* (s.o.); **se faire plumer,** to get fleeced/cleaned out; **je me suis fait plumer,** I got done/had; I was taken for a ride; I got diddled. (*Voir* **pigeon 2**) II *vpr* **se plumer** *P* 1. to fight/to have a set-to 2. to go to bed*/to hit the sack.

plumet [plyme] *nm P* **avoir son plumet,** to be (slightly) drunk*/tiddly.

plumier [plymje] *nm P* violin/fiddle.

pluviner [plyvine] *v impers F =* **pleuvasser.**

PLV [pεεlve] *abrév F* (*tatouage, graffiti*) (= *pour la vie*) for ever (and ever)/for life.

pneu [pnø] *nm F* 1. **pneu de secours,** (*bourrelet de graisse autour de la taille*) spare tyre 2. **viande à pneu,** careless/reckless pedestrian.

pochard, -arde [poʃar, -ard] *n P* drunk(ard)*/boozer/alkie.

pocharder [poʃarde] *Vieilli* I *vtr P* to make (s.o.) drunk* II *vpr* **se pocharder** *P* to get drunk*.

pocharderie [poʃardəri] *nf Vieilli P* boozing/heavy drinking.

pochardise [poʃardiz] *nf Vieilli P* habitual drinking/drunkenness/boozing.

poche [poʃ] I *nm F* (= *livre de poche*) paperback II *nf F* 1. **c'est dans la poche,** it's a cert*/it's in the bag 2. **faire les poches de qn,** to pick s.o.'s pockets; to go through s.o.'s pockets 3. **mettez ça dans votre poche (et votre mouchoir (par-)dessus)!** put that in your pipe and smoke it! 4. **s'en mettre plein les poches,** to make a fortune 5. **mettre qn dans sa poche,** to twist s.o. round one's little finger; **il te mettrait dans sa poche,** he'd make

mincemeat of you/he'd have you for breakfast/he'd wipe the floor with you 6. **en être de sa poche,** to be out of pocket (by it)/to lose out; **j'y ai été de ma poche,** I had to pay* up/to cough up. (*Voir* **se fouiller 2**; **langue 8**; **œil 14**)

pocher [poʃe] *vtr F* **pocher l'œil à qn/P pocher qn,** to give s.o. a black eye*; *P* **la ferme, ou je te poche un œil,** if you don't belt up I'll give you a black eye/I'll sock you one.

pochetée [poʃte] *nf P* 1. ugly person/*surt* ugly woman* 2. fool*/prize idiot/twit/twerp/ berk; **il en a une pochetée,** (*ivre*) he's completely drunk*/plastered; (*bête*) he's as daft as a brush/he's a complete arse(hole)/ *surt NAm* ass(hole).

pocheton [poʃtɔ̃] *nm,* **pochetron** [poʃtrɔ̃] *nm P* drunk(ard)*/boozer/alkie.

poch(e)tronné, -ée [poʃtrɔne] *P* I *a* drunk*/plastered II *n* drunk(ard)*/boozer/ alkie.

pocket [pɔkεt] *nf F* pocket; (c'est) **in the pocket,** it's in the bag.

poème [pɔεm] *nm F* (*a*) **c'est un poème!** it's a beaut(y)!/it's priceless! (*b*) **c'est tout un poème,** (*personne*) he's quite a character; (*situation*) it's quite a carry-on.

pogne [pɔɲ] *nf* 1. *P* hand*/mitt; **passer la pogne,** to give up/to hand over (to s.o.); **serrer la pogne,** to shake hands 2. *Vieilli P* **avoir les pognes retournées,** to be lazy/to be bone idle 3. *P* (*a*) grip; **un homme à pogne/de pogne,** (*fort*) a strong man/a muscleman; (*autoritaire*) a masterful man (*b*) **être à la pogne de qn,** to be under s.o.'s thumb; **je l'ai à ma pogne,** I have him in my power. (*Voir* **poigne**) 4. *P* **prendre la pogne,** to take the initiative 5. *P* **y mettre la pogne,** to steal*/to nick/to pinch sth 6. *V* **se faire une pogne,** to masturbate*/to take oneself in hand/to give oneself a hand-job.

se pogner [səpɔɲe] *vpr V* to masturbate*/ to take oneself in hand/to give oneself a hand-job/to toss oneself off.

pognon [pɔɲɔ̃] *nm P* money*/lolly/bread/ dough; **avoir du pognon/***Vieilli* **être au pognon,** to be rich*/to be rolling in it/to have plenty of dough.

poids [pwa] *nm F* 1. **faire le poids,** to have the necessary experience; **il ne fait pas le poids,** he isn't up to it/he's not up to scratch 2. (*a*) **avoir du poids,** to have influence; to carry weight; **c'est un homme de poids,** he's important/he's a big noise/he's a bigwig (*b*)

prendre du poids, to age/to grow old 3. avoir/
faire le poids, to have come of age; faux
poids, under-age prostitute*; under-age girl*
who looks older than she is 4. un poids mort,
(*personne*) a dead loss; (*employé*) someone
who does not pull his weight/a passenger 5.
(*drogues*) faire du poids, to adulterate drugs
with other harmless substances in order to
make a profit. (*Voir* **sanctuaire**)

poigne [pwaɲ] *nf F* (*a*) (hand-)grip/grasp;
un homme à poigne, (*fort*) a strong man/a
muscleman; (*autoritaire*) a firm-handed/
masterful man; montrer de la poigne, to be
equal to the situation; il manque de poigne, he
lacks grip (*b*) energy; avoir de la poigne, to
be full of vim. (*Voir* **pogne 3** (*a*))

poignée [pwaɲe] *nf* 1. *F* poignée(s)
d'amour, (*bourrelet de graisse autour de la
taille*) spare tyre 2. *P* aller la poignée dans le
coin, (*en moto*) to go/to travel very fast; to go
full pelt.

poignet [pwaɲe] *nm* 1. *P* ne pas se fouler le
poignet, to take it easy*/to raise no sweat 2. *P*
se casser le poignet/les poignets sur qch, to
steal* sth/to pinch sth/to whip sth 3. *V* la
veuve Poignet, masturbation*; épouser/
fréquenter/se taper la veuve Poignet, to
masturbate*/to toss off/to jack off/to be
married to the five-fingered widow.

poil [pwal] *nm* 1. *P* à poil, naked*/starkers/in
the altogether/in one's birthday suit; se
mettre/se foutre à poil, to strip 2. *F* (*a*) au
poil! super!/great!/fantastic! ça me va au
poil, that suits me down to the ground/that
suits me to a T; au (petit) poil/au quart de
poil, dead accurate/spot on/right on the
button; à un petit poil près/P au poil du cul
près/à un poil de grenouille près, very
accurate/as near as dammit; down to the last
detail; un poil plus vite, a tiny bit/fraction
faster (*b*) j'ai eu mon train, mais d'un poil! I
caught my train, but only just! (*c*) de tout
poil, of all sorts; voitures de tout poil, all
sorts of cars 3. *F* avoir un poil dans la main,
to be workshy/to be bone idle 4. *P* avoir du
poil au cul, to have courage*; il a du poil au
cul, he's got guts/balls; avoir le poil de (faire
qch), to have the guts to (do sth) 5. *F* n'avoir
plus un poil de sec, to be very worried; to be
scared stiff/to have the wind up 6. *F* chercher
des poils sur l'œuf, to split hairs 7. *F* mood/
temper; être de bon/mauvais poil, to be in a
good/bad mood 8. *P* (*a*) tomber sur le poil de
qn, to attack* s.o./to lay into s.o./to go for s.o.

(*b*) avoir la police sur le poil, to be hunted by
the police/to have the police on one's back 9.
F (*a*) reprendre du poil (de la bête), to pick
up/to perk up/to get back on one's feet (after
an illness or a setback) (*b*) reprendre du poil
de la bête, to take a hair of the dog (that bit
you) 10. *F* poil de brique/poil de carotte/poil
de Judas, redhead/carrot-top/ginger 11. *F*
(re)faire le poil à qn, to diddle s.o. out of his
money/to fleece* s.o./to rip s.o. off 12. *V*
compter les poils, (*femme*) to masturbate*/to
touch oneself up.

poilant [pwalɑ̃] *a P* screamingly funny*/
killing; c'était poilant, it was a real killer.

se **poiler** [səpwale] *vpr P* to laugh*
uproariously/to split one's sides laughing/to kill
oneself laughing/to piss oneself (laughing).

poil-poil [pwalpwal] *adv F* ça colle poil-poil,
that's just the job/that's just what we need/
that'll do the trick/that'll do nicely.

à poilpuche [apwalpyʃ] *adv P* naked*/
starkers. (*Voir* **poil 1**)

poilu [pwaly] I *a P* 1. brave/courageous*/
gutsy/balls(e)y. (*Voir* **poil 4**) 2. c'est poilu,
(*parfait*) it's super/great; (*drôle*) it's
extremely funny*/killing II *nm F* 1. French
soldier (*1914–1918*) 2. man*/bloke/guy.

poinçonner [pwɛ̃sɔne] *vtr V* poinçonner
une fille, to have sex* with a girl/to screw a
girl.

point [pwɛ̃] *nm* 1. *F* un point, c'est tout! and
that's that!/and that's all there is to it!/and
there's an end to it!/period!/full stop! 2. *F*
être mal en point, to be in a bad way; être
plus mal en point, to be worse off 3. *F*
commencer à rendre des points, to age/to
grow old 4. *P* franc 5. *P* avoir un point de
côté, to be sought by the police/to be on the
run 6. point noir, *F* (*sur la route*) black spot;
V anus*/ring hole 7. *P* à point, drunk*/stewed.
(*Voir* **chute**)

pointe [pwɛ̃t] *nf* 1. *F* s'asseoir sur la pointe
des fesses, to sit on the edge of a chair 2.
Vieilli F avoir sa pointe, to be (slightly)
drunk* 3. *P* (*a*) être de la pointe, to like
women; to be a womanizer*/a skirt-chaser (*b*)
être chaud/dur de la pointe, (*homme*) to like
sex*; to be continually randy/horny (*c*)
tomber pour la pointe, to be arrested* for a
sexual offence; les mecs de la pointe, the sexual offenders/sex maniacs (*serving a prison
sentence*) (*d*) il est porté sur la pointe bic,
(*homosexuel*) he likes (to screw) Arabs 4. *V*
pousser sa pointe, to have sex* 5. *P* knife.

pointé [pwɛ̃te] *a P* rester pointé, to remain in custody (of the police). (*Voir* **zéro I 2**)

pointer [pwɛ̃te] I *vtr* 1. *V* (*a*) to have (*esp* anal) sex* with (a woman) (*b*) (*homosexuel actif*) to have anal sex*/to screw (s.o.'s) ass/ to go in by the back door 2. *P* pointer son nez, to turn up/to show up II *vi V* to have sex*/to get it up III *vpr* **se pointer** *P* (*personne*) to turn up/to appear on the scene/to show up.

pointeur [pwɛ̃tœr] *nm* 1. *P* (*a*) great womanizer*/Don Juan/*V* cunt-chaser (*b*) (*prisons*) rapist/sex offender 2. *V* active homosexual*.

pointu [pwɛ̃ty] *a F* expert; c'est pointu, it's very specialized; être pointu sur qch, to be an expert on sth.

pointure [pwɛ̃tyr] *nf P* une (sacrée/grosse) pointure, an unusual person/a special person.

poire [pwar] I *nf* 1. *Vieilli F* faire sa poire (anglaise), to put on airs/to give oneself airs; to fancy oneself 2. *F Fig* garder une poire pour la soif, to put something by for a rainy day 3. *F Fig* couper la poire en deux, (*faire la moyenne entre deux quantités*) to split the difference; (*transiger*) to compromise 4. *F* la poire est mûre, the moment is ripe 5. *F ma* poire, I/me/myself/yours truly; c'est bien fait pour sa poire! serves him/her right! (*Voir* **pomme I 11**) 6. *P* mug/sucker; une poire blette, a complete sucker/a real mug; est-ce que tu me prends pour une poire? what sort of a sucker do you take me for? l'impôt des poires, the mugs' tax (*ie* income tax); être la poire, to be the mug/the fall guy 7. *P* head*; se payer la poire de qn, (*tromper*) to swindle* s.o./to play s.o. for a sucker; (*se moquer de*) to ridicule s.o./to take the mickey out of s.o. 8. *P* face*/mug (*a*) sucer la poire à qn, to kiss s.o.; je les ai vus en train de se sucer la poire, I saw them snogging away (*b*) une pêche en pleine poire, a blow on the mouth/one right in the kisser. (*Voir aussi* **pêche II 1**) (*c*) il a une bonne poire, he looks a nice sort of bloke/ guy; he looks nice enough II *a P* être poire, to be over-indulgent; to be a mug/a sucker.

poireau, *pl* **-eaux** [pwaro] *nm* 1. *P* mug/ sucker/easy mark 2. *P* faire le poireau = **poireauter** 3. *F* le Poireau, decoration (*le Mérite agricole*) awarded to farmers, etc 4. *V* penis*; s'agiter/se chatouiller/faire glou-glouter le poireau, to masturbate*/to flog the bishop 5. *V* souffler dans le poireau à qn, (*fellation*) to give s.o. a blow-job/to suck s.o. off 6. *P Mus* clarinet.

poireauter [pwarote] *vi P* to be kept waiting/to be kept hanging about/to kick one's heels; faire/laisser poireauter qn, to keep s.o. waiting/to keep s.o. hanging about; j'ai poireauté deux heures après l'autobus, I hung around for two hours waiting for the bus to turn up.

poirer [pware] *vtr P* to catch/to nab (s.o.); se faire poirer, to get nabbed/nicked; je me suis fait poirer à pomper à l'examen, I got caught cheating in the exam.

poiscaille [pwaskɑj] *nm P* 1. fish 2. pimp*/ sweet man/mack.

poison [pwazɔ̃] *nm & f P* (*personne*) pest; cet enfant est un petit poison, this child's a little horror; (*chose*) damn nuisance/drag; quel poison ce travail! what a bind this work is!

poissarde [pwasard] *nf Vieilli F* vulgar/ foul-mouthed woman; langage de poissarde, Billingsgate; parler comme une poissarde, to talk common/to talk like a fishwife/to talk Billingsgate.

poisse [pwas] I *nf F* 1. bad luck; tough luck; avoir la poisse, to be unlucky; to have bad/ tough luck; porter (la) poisse à qn, to bring s.o. bad luck; jour de poisse, bad day (at the races, etc); quelle poisse! just my luck!/what rotten luck! (*Voir* **porte-poisse**) 2. bore*/ fag; quelle poisse! what a bind! c'est vraiment la poisse! it's a real drag! II *nm P* 1. pimp* 2. hooligan*/good-for-nothing/ layabout/yob(bo) 3. thief*/sticky-fingers/tea leaf.

poisser [pwase] *vtr P* 1. *Vieilli* to steal*/to pinch/to swipe 2. to arrest*; se faire poisser, to get nabbed/nicked/run in 3. to bore* (s.o.) stiff/rigid; tu me poisses avec tes problèmes, you're a real pain with all your problems; poisse Dudule! go and tell that to somebody else, I don't want to know.

poisson [pwasɔ̃] *nm* 1. *F* donner à manger aux poissons, to be seasick/to feed the fishes 2. *F* gros poisson, big businessman/big shot 3. *P* engueuler qn comme du poisson pourri, to tell s.o. off/to tear s.o. off a strip/to bawl s.o. out/to give s.o. a bollocking 4. *Vieilli P* pimp* 5. *P* changer d'eau son poisson/changer le poisson d'eau, to urinate*/to take a leak/to splash one's boots 6. *F* noyer le poisson, to tire out one's opponent. (*Voir* **bocal 5; se ficher 2** (*b*); **queue 4**)

poitrine [pwatrin] *nf F* poitrine de vélo, flat and narrow chest.

poitringle [pwatrɛ̃gl] *a* *P* tubercular/ consumptive.

poivrade [pwavrad] *P* I *nf* 1. boozing; en avoir une poivrade, to be drunk*/boozed up/ juiced up 2. drunk(ard)*/boozer II *a*=**poivré 1**.

poivre [pwavr] I *nm* 1. *F* piler du poivre, to go on a tiring walk; (*médire de qn*) to speak ill of s.o./to run s.o. down; (*s'ennuyer à attendre qn*) to kick one's heels (while waiting for s.o.) 2. *P* chier du poivre, (*abandonner qn*) to leave s.o. in the lurch; (*échapper à la police*) to escape from the police; to throw the police off the scent 3. *P* brandy 4. *P* syphilis*/pox II *a P* = **poivré 1**.

poivré [pwavre] *a P* 1. drunk*/plastered/ smashed/sozzled 2. infected with syphilis*/ syphed-up/pox-ridden/syphy; il était poivré, he had syph/he was a sypho 3. expensive; la note est poivrée, the bill is a bit steep/a bit excessive.

poivrer [pwavre] I *vtr P* 1. to make (s.o.) drunk 2. to infect (s.o.) with syphilis*/to give (s.o.) a dose; se faire poivrer, to cop a dose (of the pox)/to get syph 3. se faire poivrer, to get arrested*/busted/nicked II *vpr* **se poivrer** *P* to get drunk*/plastered/smashed/stoned; se poivrer la gueule, to get drunk*/pissed/ plastered; ils sont là-bas en train de se poivrer la gueule, they're over there getting steadily sloshed/stoned (out of their tiny minds).

poivrier [pwavrije] *nm P* thief* who robs drunks/*NAm* lush-roller; vol au poivrier, robbing of drunks/*NAm* lush-rolling.

poivrot, -ote [pwavro, -ɔt] *n P* drunk(ard)*/*surt NAm* lush/alkie/wino/boozer.

se poivroter [səpwavrɔte] *vpr P* to get drunk*/pickled/sozzled.

poix [pwa] *nf F* avoir de la poix aux mains, to have sticky fingers (when it comes to money).

pok [pɔk] *nm F* (*cartes*) poker; taper un pok jusqu'à l'aube, to play poker till dawn.

Pola(c)k, Polaque [pɔlak] *nm & f P Péj* Pole/Polack.

polar [pɔlar] *nm F* detective novel/thriller/ whodunnit.

polard [pɔlar] *nm V* penis*/stick/shaft/pole.

police [pɔlis] *nf P* faire ses polices, (*prostituée*) to report regularly (for a health check).

polichinelle [pɔliʃinɛl] *nm* 1. *F* (*a*) figure of fun; faire le polichinelle, to act the buffoon/to lark about (*b*) mener une vie de polichinelle, to have a good time*/to lead a fast life/to go the pace (*c*) un secret de polichinelle, an open secret 2. *P* (*a*) avoir un polichinelle dans le tiroir, to be pregnant*/to have a bun in the oven/*surt NAm* to be knocked up (*b*) claquer le polichinelle, to have a miscarriage.

politesse [pɔlitɛs] *nf* 1. *P* faire une politesse à une femme, to give (sexual) pleasure to a woman/to do a woman a favour 2. *V* faire une politesse à un homme, to give a man a blowjob; to do a man a favour.

politicailler [pɔlitikaje] *vi F* to indulge in political manoeuvring/*NAm* maneuvering.

politicaillerie [pɔlitikajəri] *nf F* political manoeuvring/*NAm* maneuvering; peanut politics.

politicard [pɔlitikar] *nm F* political manoeuvrer/*NAm* maneuvrer/bad politician.

polka [pɔlka] *nf P* 1. woman*/bird/*NAm* dame/*NAm* broad 2. pimp's woman. (*Voir* **mandibules**)

pollope! [pɔlɔp] *int P* = **polope!**

polochon [pɔlɔʃɔ̃] *nm F* bolster; bataille (à coups) de polochons, pillow fight; partie de polochon, nap/snooze; dormir avec son polochon, to sleep alone/to sleep with one's pillow.

Polonais [pɔlɔnɛ] *nm F* soûl comme un Polonais, dead drunk*/as drunk as a lord.

polope! [pɔlɔp] *int P* 1. look out!/watch out!/careful! 2. nothing doing!/no dice!/you'll be lucky!/not bloody likely*!

poltron [pɔltrɔ̃] *nm Vieilli P* fart.

poly [pɔli] *nm F* (*étudiants*) duplicated course material.

polychiée [pɔliʃje] *nf V* = **chiée**.

polycope [pɔlikɔp] *nm F* = **poly**.

pomaquer [pɔmake] *vtr P* to lose (money, one's hair, etc).

pommade [pɔmad] *nf F* 1. flattery*/soft soap; passer (de) la pommade à qn, to flatter s.o./to butter s.o. up; to lay it on thick 2. être dans la pommade, to be in a fix*/in a jam.

pommadin [pɔmadɛ̃] *nm Vieilli P* hairdresser/barber.

pomme [pɔm] I *nf* 1. *F* quand j'étais haut comme trois pommes, when I was just a kid/ when I was knee-high to a grasshopper 2. *F* tomber dans les pommes, to faint*/to pass out 3. *F* simpleton/mug/sucker; l'autre pomme, that idiot/jerk; pauvre pomme! poor sucker! c'est une pomme à l'eau/à l'huile, he's/she's a real clot/twerp/jerk/nurd 4. *P* aux pommes, excellent*/first-rate; **c'est aux pommes!** it looks good!/*Austr* she'll be apples! **une nana aux pommes,** a good-looking bird/chick; a doll **5.** *P* **pomme de terre,** hole in one's sock **6.** *P* head*/nut **7.** *P* face*/mug **8.** *P* **ma pomme,** I/ me/myself/yours truly; (*également:* **ta pomme, sa pomme, votre pomme, nos pommes, vos pommes, leurs pommes**). (*Voir* **sucer 2; sucre 7**) **II** *a P* simple/naive/ green; **bonne pomme,** indulgent.

pommé [pɔme] *a F* (*a*) absolute/complete/ utter (fool, etc) (*b*) downright/out-and-out (blunder, etc) (*c*) excellent*/first-rate; slap-up (meal).

pompage [pɔpaʒ] *nm V* fellatio*/blow-job/ head.

pompard [pɔpar] *nm P* = **pompelard.**

pompe [pɔp] *nf* **1.** *F* **avoir le/un coup de pompe,** to be exhausted*/fagged out/ shattered/shagged out/pooped; **j'ai le coup de pompe (de onze heures),** I've got that sinking feeling **2.** *F* **à toute(s) pompe(s),** very quickly*/at full speed/as fast as possible/flat out **3.** *F* **faire des pompes,** to do push-ups/ press-ups **4.** *P* (*a*) *pl* **pompes,** shoes; **j'ai des pompes aspirantes,** my shoes have got holes in them/my shoes let in water (*b*) **un coup de pompe au derrière,** a kick up the backside **5.** *P* **marcher à côté de ses pompes,** (*rêvasser*) to daydream; (*ne pas se sentir bien*) to be/ feel out of sorts; (*agir bêtement*) to do sth stupid; to act in an illogical way **6.** *P Mil* **soldat de deuxième pompe**/*nm* **deuxième pompe,** *Br* squaddie/*US* grunt. **7.** *P* (*écoles, etc*) (*aide-mémoire*) crib **8.** *P* (*drogues*) syringe. (*Voir* **château 3**)

pompé [pɔpe] *a P* exhausted*/pooped/ shattered/fagged (out).

pompe-l'air [pɔplɛr] *nm inv F* s.o. who gets on other people's nerves/pain in the neck.

pompelard [pɔp(ə)lar] *nm P* fireman/fire fighter.

pompe-la-sueur [pɔplasɥœr] *nm inv F* (*patron d'entreprise, etc*) workhorse; slave-driver.

pomper [pɔpe] **I** *vtr* **1.** *F* to exhaust* (s.o.); **je suis pompé,** I'm shattered/fagged/pooped **2.** *F* to annoy*; **tu me pompes l'air,** you're wearing me out/you're getting on my nerves/I'm getting fed up with you; **elle me pompe, cette nana!** she's a real drag/pain, that girl! **3.** *V* **pomper (le dard/le nœud/le zob à) qn,** to fellate* s.o./to suck s.o. off/to give s.o. head/to give s.o. a blow-job **II** *vi* **1.** *P* **pomper (dur),**

to drink* heavily/to (go on the) booze/to tipple **2.** *F* to copy (**sur qn,** from s.o.)/to crib/to cheat.

pompette [pɔpɛt] *a F* slightly drunk*/ tipsy/half-seas-over.

pompeur, -euse [pɔpœr, -øz] *n F* copier/ cribber.

pompeuses [pɔpøz] *nfpl P* lips; **elle a des pompeuses à tailler des pipes,** she's got a real cock-sucker's mouth.

pompier [pɔpje] *nm* **1.** *F* **fumer comme un pompier,** to smoke like a chimney **2.** *V* **faire un pompier (à qn),** to fellate* (s.o.)/to suck (s.o.'s) cock/to give (s.o.) head.

pomplard [pɔplar] *nm* **1.** *P* fireman/fire fighter **2.** *V* fellatio*; **faire un pomplard à qn,** to give s.o. a blow-job/to give s.o. head/to suck s.o. off.

pompon [pɔpɔ̃] *nm F* **1.** *Vieilli* **avoir son pompon,** to be slightly drunk*/tipsy/half-seas-over **2. avoir/décrocher le pompon,** to get the better of s.o.; **à lui le pompon!** he's the winner!/he's way ahead (of everyone else)! **3. ça, c'est le pompon!** that's the limit*!/that's the last straw!

pondeuse [pɔ̃døz] *nf F Hum* **c'est une bonne pondeuse,** she's got lots of children/she breeds well/she breeds like a rabbit.

pondre [pɔ̃dr] **I** *vtr F Journ etc* to produce/ to give birth to/to turn out (an article, a poem, a speech, etc); **il les pond en série,** he churns them out by the dozen **II** *vtr & i P* to give birth (to) (a child).

pon(n)ette [pɔnɛt] *nf P* (*a*) gangster's moll; pimp's woman (*b*) (young) part-time prostitute*.

pont [pɔ̃] *nm F* **1.** (*jour chômé entre deux jours fériés*) **faire le pont,** to take the intervening working day(s) off; to take an extra day off; (*en fin de semaine*) to make a long weekend of it **2. faire un pont d'or à qn,** to make s.o. a lucrative offer to entice him to change his job; to give s.o. a golden hello; **on lui a fait un pont d'or,** they made it worth his while/they made him an offer he couldn't refuse **3. pont arrière,** buttocks*/rear end.

ponte [pɔ̃t] *nm* **1.** *F* important person*/big shot **2.** *P* gambler/punter; **un gros ponte,** a heavy gambler **3.** *P* (big) drugs trafficker/ dealer*.

pontifier [pɔ̃tifje] *vi F* to pontificate/to lay down the law.

Pont-Neuf [pɔ̃nœf] *Prn F* **être solide comme le Pont-Neuf,** to be as strong as an ox/to be as fit* as a fiddle.

Popaul [pɔpɔl] *Prnm V* Popaul (le guignol), penis*/John Thomas; égoutter Popaul, to urinate*/to take a leak; étrangler Popaul, to masturbate*/to beat the meat/to flog the bishop; imperméable à Popaul, condom*/rubber/mac.

poper [pɔpe] *vtr & i P* (*drogues*) to inject (a drug)/to pop/to shoot up.

la Popinque [lapɔpɛ̃k] *Prnf F* (the area around) the rue Popincourt (*in Paris*).

Popof [pɔpɔf] *a & n P* Russian; les Popofs, the Russians*/the Russkies/the Reds.

Popol [pɔpɔl] *Prnm V* = **Popaul**.

popote [pɔpɔt] **I** *a inv F souvent Péj* stay-at-home; elle est vachement popote, she's never out of the kitchen; she's always busy about the house **II** *nf* 1. *F* (*a*) faire la popote, to do the cooking (*b*) *Mil etc* canteen; (*mess*) officers' mess (*c*) faire popote (ensemble), to mess together 2. *P* drug addict's instruments*/artillery/arsenal.

popotier [pɔpɔtje] *nm F* canteen manager; *Mil* mess officer/manager.

popotin [pɔpɔtɛ̃] *nm P* (*a*) buttocks*/bottom/*NAm* fanny/*NAm* butt (*b*) (se) remuer/se trémousser le popotin, to dance/to shake a leg (*c*) tortiller du popotin, to swing/to wiggle one's hips (when walking) (*d*) se manier/se magner le popotin, to hurry* (up)/to get a move on/to get one's arse in(to) gear; magne-toi le popotin! get a move on!/shift your arse!/*NAm* shift your ass!/pull your finger out!

Popov [pɔpɔv] *a & n P* = **Popof**.

popu [pɔpy] *F* **I** *a* popular; common/vulgar **II** *nmpl* les popu, people occupying the cheap seats (in a stadium).

populo [pɔpylo] *nm F* (*a*) the (common) people/*Péj* the rabble/the riff-raff/the hoi polloi (*b*) crowd/mob; c'est plein de populo là-dedans, it's really packed/chocker in there.

poque [pɔk] *nf FrC P* bruise/bump; dent (*on car*).

poquer [pɔke] *vi P* to stink*/to pong/to whiff.

poquette [pɔkɛt] *nf F* = **pocket**.

porcelaine [pɔrsəlɛn] *nf F* bidet.

porcherie [pɔrʃəri] *nf F Fig* pigsty/shambles.

porcif(e) [pɔrsif] *nf P* (*a*) portion/part (*b*) portion of food (for one person).

porno [pɔrno] *F* **I** *a* pornographic/porno/porny/blue/dirty; blague porno, dirty/porny

joke; film porno, blue/porno movie/film; revue porno, dirty/porny mag(azine) **II** *nm* 1. le porno, pornography/porn; (*cinéma porno*) porn/blue films/*NAm* movies; lire des pornos, to read porny/dirty books, magazines, etc; porno doux/dur, soft/hard porn 2. cinema specializing in porn films. (*Voir* **hard**; **soft**)

portail [pɔrtaj] *nm V* female genitals*; essayer la clef dans le portail, to rape s.o.

porte [pɔrt] *nf F* 1. à la porte! out!/get out! (*Voir* **fiche(r)** 2; **flanquer** I) 2. *Fig* vous êtes trompé de porte, you've come to the wrong place 3. trouver porte de bois, to find nobody at home 4. aimable comme une porte de prison, like a bear with a sore head 5. c'est la porte à côté, it's only a hop, skip and a jump from here/it's just round the corner 6. entre deux portes, hurriedly/very quickly 7. se ménager une porte de sortie, to give oneself a let-out/a safety clause 8. il n'était pas derrière la porte le jour de la distribution, he wasn't there when God gave out common sense/he's not terribly bright/he's not all there 9. *P* porte de derrière/de service, anus*; *V* passer par la porte de derrière, to have anal sex*. (*Voir* **bagatelle**; **clef** 1; **enfoncer** I 3)

porté [pɔrte] *a F* 1. c'est bien porté, it's the right thing to do; c'est mal porté, it's bad form 2. être porté sur sa bouche/sa gueule, to think only of food and drink; être porté sur la bouteille, to like a drink; to be a bit of a boozer/an alkie. (*Voir* **article** 2; **bagatelle**; **chose** III 2; **truc** 7)

porte-biffetons [pɔrt(ə)biftɔ̃] *nm inv*, **porte-fafiots** [pɔrt(ə)fafjo] *nm inv P* wallet. (*Voir* **biffeton** 3; **fafiot** 1)

porte-coton [pɔrt(ə)kɔtɔ̃] *nm inv*, **porte-couteau** [pɔrt(ə)kuto] *nm F* second fiddle; dogsbody (*pl* porte-couteau(x)).

porte-cravate [pɔrt(ə)kravat] *nm inv P* neck.

porte-feu [pɔrt(ə)fø] *nm inv P* = **porte-flingue**.

portefeuille [pɔrt(ə)fœj] *nm F* 1. lit en portefeuille, apple-pie bed 2. ferme ton portefeuille, c'est moi qui paie, your fly's un-done; you're showing your medals 3. œil en portefeuille, black eye*/shiner.

porte-flingue [pɔrt(ə)flɛ̃g] *nm inv P* bodyguard/henchman/gorilla. (*Voir* **flingot**)

porte-guigne [pɔrt(ə)giɲ] *nm inv F* (*personne*) jinx/jonah/bad luck. (*Voir* **guigne**)

porteluque [pɔrt(ə)lyk] *nm Vieilli P* wallet.

portemanteau [pɔrt(ə)mɑ̃to] *nm* 1. *P* shoulders 2. *P* avoir un portemanteau dans le dos, to be stabbed in the back/between the shoulders 3. *V* avoir un portemanteau dans le pantalon, to have an erection*/a hard-on.

portemince [pɔrt(ə)mɛ̃s] *nm P* wallet.

porte-monnaie [pɔrt(ə)mɔnɛ] *nm V* porte-monnaie à moustaches, female genitals*/cunt/beaver.

porte-pipe [pɔrt(ə)pip] *nm inv P* mouth*; en avoir un coup dans le porte-pipe, to be drunk*/to be juiced up.

porte-poisse [pɔrt(ə)pwas] *nm inv F* (*personne*) jinx/jonah/bad luck. (*Voir* **poisse I 1**)

porter [pɔrte] I *vtr F* 1. en porter, (= *porter des cornes*) to be a cuckold; elle lui en fait porter depuis des années, she's been unfaithful to him/she's had a bit on the side/she's had a fancyman for years 2. ce bruit me porte sur les nerfs, that noise gets on my nerves. (*Voir* **culotte 5**; **deuil 3, 4**; **pet 5**) II *vi P* porter à gauche, to be manly/macho III *vpr* **se porter** *P* un(e) ... qui se porte bien, a rare old ...; recevoir un savon qui se porte bien, to get a telling-off one won't forget in a hurry.

porteur [pɔrtœr] *nm P* accomplice.

porte-viande [pɔrt(ə)vjɑ̃d] *nm inv P* (first-aid) stretcher. (*Voir* **viande 1, 2**)

portigue [pɔrtig] *nm & f P* Portuguese.

portillon [pɔrtijɔ̃] *nm F* ça se bouscule au portillon, he's spluttering/he can't get his words out (fast enough)/he's having trouble getting his words out.

porto(s) [pɔrto(s)] *a & nm P* Portuguese.

portrait [pɔrtrɛ] *nm P* face*; (*a*) le portrait tout craché de son vieux, the dead spit/the spitting image of his old man (*b*) abîmer/arranger/esquinter le portrait à qn, to spoil s.o.'s beauty (for him)/to smash s.o.'s face in; il s'est abîmé le portrait, he's messed his face up; se faire abîmer le portrait, to get one's face bashed in/to get worked over; rectifier/rentrer dans le portrait à qn, to hit s.o. hard in the face/to sock s.o. on the jaw/to smash s.o.'s face in/to lay into s.o. (*c*) se payer le portrait de qn, to make fun of s.o.; to take the mickey/the piss out of s.o. (*Voir* **se refaire 1** (*a*)).

portugaises [pɔrtygɛz] *nfpl P* ears*; dessable tes portugaises! pin back your lugholes! avoir les portugaises ensablées, to be deaf/hard of hearing.

pose [poz] *nf F* la faire à la pose, to show off*/to be a bit of a pose(u)r/to put on airs.

poser [poze] I *vi* 1. *F* faire poser qn, to keep s.o. waiting/hanging about 2. *F* je ne pose pas à l'ange, I don't pretend to be an angel 3. *P* to work the three-card trick II *vtr* 1. *F* ça vous pose, it gives you status/standing; it makes you look big/good 2. *P* poser ça là, to down tools; to stop work(ing). (*Voir* **chique 2**; **lapin 4**; **pêche II 5**) III *vpr* **se poser** *P* 1. se poser là, to be excellent*/first-class; to be up to scratch/up to it; comme gaffeur il se pose là, when it comes to putting one's foot in it he takes some beating 2. il se pose (un peu) là, (*il est fort*) he's a hefty bloke/he's a giant; (*il est idéal*) he's just right for the job.

poseur [pozœr] *nm P* card-sharper who works the three-card trick.

posséder [pɔsede] *vtr F* to fool* (s.o.)/to pull a fast one on (s.o.); to diddle/to con (s.o.); je me suis fait posséder, I've been had.

possible [pɔsibl] *a F* (*a*) possible! it's (quite) possible/very likely/(it) could well be (*b*) pas possible! impossible!/you can't mean it!/you don't say!/no way! (*c*) il est pas possible, ce mec! (*insupportable*) that guy's a pain (in the neck/in the arse); (*super*) that guy's great/really cool!

poste [pɔst] I *nm F* 1. toujours solide/fidèle au poste, still going strong/still alive and kicking 2. radio II *nf Vieilli F* aller un train de poste/courir la poste, to hurry* (up)/to get a move on.

postère [pɔstɛr], **postérieur** [pɔsterjœr] *nm F* buttocks*/posterior/backside/behind/bum/*NAm* butt/*NAm* fanny.

postiche [pɔstiʃ] *nf* 1. *F* (*esp* door-to-door salesman's) spiel; sales talk; il travaille à la postiche, he's got a good line in sales talk/patter/fast talk; faire la postiche, to draw a crowd (with sales patter) 2. *P* faire une postiche à qn, to pick a quarrel with s.o.; sa femme va lui faire une postiche, his wife's going to give him hell.

posticheur [pɔstiʃœr] *nm F* door-to-door salesman, etc/fast-talker.

postillon [pɔstijɔ̃] *nm* 1. *F* envoyer/lancer des postillons, to splutter (when speaking) 2. *V Vieilli* donner le postillon/faire postillon, to insert the index finger into s.o.'s anus*/to finger-fuck.

postillonner [pɔstijɔne] *vi F* to splutter (when speaking).

pot [po] *nm* **1.** *F* **pot de colle,** boring person/ bore*/pain in the neck; **c'est une julie pot de colle, cette nana,** she's a damned nuisance/I can't shake her off/I can't get rid of her **2.** *F* **c'est le pot au noir,** it's a wretched business; it's a hopeless muddle **3.** *F* **être invité à un pot,** to be invited for a drink/for a jar/for drinks; **allons boire/prendre un pot,** let's go and have a drink **4.** *F* **payer les pots cassés,** to be left holding the baby/to carry the can/to take the rap **5.** *F* **c'est le pot de terre contre le pot de fer,** he's more than met his match **6.** *F* **tourner autour du pot,** to shilly-shally/to beat about the bush **7.** *F* **sourd comme un pot,** as deaf as a post **8.** *F* **découvrir le pot aux roses** [potoroz], to find out what's been going on; to get to the bottom of sth; **quand le pot aux roses sera découvert,** when the balloon goes up/when the news breaks **9.** *A F* **être à pot et à rot,** to be bosom friends **10.** *F* **faire son pot,** to make a fortune/to make one's pile **11.** *F* **pot à tabac,** short and tubby/stocky person **12.** *P* luck; **un coup de pot,** a stroke of luck/a lucky break; **avoir le pot/du pot,** to be lucky/in luck; to have a lucky break; **manquer de pot,** to be unlucky/out of luck; **manque de pot!/pas de pot!** hard luck!/rotten luck!/bad luck!/too bad! **elle a vraiment pas de pot,** she has no luck at all; **un pot de cocu/un pot d'enfer/un pot du tonnerre,** the luck of the devil **13.** *P* (*au jeu*) **le pot,** the kitty/the pot **14.** *P* **bousculer le pot de fleurs/***V* **chier dans le pot,** to exaggerate*/to shoot a line **15.** *P* buttocks*/ bum/arse/*NAm* ass/*NAm* fanny; **se manier le pot/se magner le pot,** to hurry* (up)/to shift one's arse/to pull one's finger out/to get one's arse/*NAm* ass in(to) gear **16.** *P* **casser le pot à une jeune fille,** to rob a girl* of her virginity*/to take a girl's cherry **17.** *V* anus*; **pot d'échappement,** arsehole/*NAm* asshole/ poop chute/exhaust pipe; **casser le pot,** to have anal sex*; **se faire casser le pot,** to be buggered/to have one's arse/*NAm* ass fucked **18.** *P* **j'en ai plein le pot,** I'm fed up* with it/ I'm sick and tired of it **19.** *P* **plein pot,** at full speed/like the clappers; **démarrer plein pot,** to zoom off. (*Voir* **cuiller 1; yaourt**)

potable [potabl] *a F* bearable/tolerable; **un bouquin qui est tout juste potable,** a book which is just about readable; **travail potable,** average sort of work. (*Voir* **buvable**)

potache [potaʃ] *nm F* schoolboy/schoolkid (*attending a collège or lycée*).

potage [potaʒ] *nm* **1.** *A F* **pour tout potage,** altogether/all in all/all told **2.** *F* **servir/verser le potage à la seringue,** to serve parsimoniously/to give small helpings **3.** *P* **être dans le potage,** (*être abruti*) to be utterly confused/to be all at sea/to be in a daze; (*être dans une mauvaise situation*) to be in a fix/in a jam; to be up the creek/*V* up shit creek **4.** *V* female genitals*/crumpet.

potard [potar] *nm P* chemist; chemist's assistant; pharmacy student.

potasser [potase] *F* **I** *vtr* to study hard at (sth)/to swot up (sth)/to cram for (sth); **potasser son espagnol,** to mug up one's Spanish; **potasser un examen,** to work hard* for an exam **II** *vi* to study hard/to swot/to cram.

potasseur [potasœr] *nm F* hard worker/ swot/slogger.

pot-auf [potof] *nm F* (= *pot-au-feu*) = boiled beef with vegetables.

pot-au-feu [potofø] **I** *nm inv* **1.** *F* **faire aller le pot-au-feu,** to keep the pot boiling **2.** *F* stay-at-home woman **3.** *P* prostitute* supporting a pimp*/meal-ticket **II** *a inv F* stay-at-home (woman).

pot-de-vin [podvɛ̃] *nm F* bribe*/hush money/backhander; **donner un pot-de-vin à qn,** to grease s.o.'s palm/to make it worth s.o.'s while. (*pl* **pots-de-vin**)

pote [pot] *nm & f P* friend*/mate/pal/buddy; **écoute-moi, mon pote!** listen, mate/buddy! **il est allé boire un coup avec les potes,** he went for a drink with the lads/with his mates/with his buddies.

poteau, *pl* **-eaux** [poto] *nm* **1.** *F* **poteau (d'exécution),** execution post (*for s.o. about to be shot*); **mettre qn au poteau,** to put s.o. against the wall (and shoot him) **2.** *P* = **pote 3.** *F* **avoir des (jambes comme des) poteaux,** to have legs like tree trunks.

potée [pote] *nf Vieilli F* **une potée de ...,** a large quantity* of ...; heaps/loads/piles of ...; **j'en ai une potée,** I've got masses/tons/pots.

potin [potɛ̃] *nm F* **1.** row/uproar*/rumpus; **un potin d'enfer/de tous les diables,** a hell of a racket/the devil of a row; **faire du potin,** to kick up a row/a racket; (*faire un scandale*) to make a fuss/to make trouble **2.** (*a*) (piece of) gossip/scandal; **ça a fait du potin,** it made quite a stir (*b*) *pl* **potins,** gossip/scandal/tittle-tattle.

potiner [potine] *vi F* to gossip/to talk scandal/to tittle-tattle.

potinier, -ière [potinje, -jɛr] *Vieilli F* **I** *a* gossipy **II** *n* gossip(er)/scandalmonger/

gossipmonger/gossip-shop.

potiron [pɔtirɔ̃] *nm F* member of the jury (of an Assize Court).

potron-ja(c)quet [pɔtrɔ̃ʒakɛ] *nm,* **potron-minet** [pɔtrɔ̃minɛ] *nm A F* dès potron-ja(c)quet/dès potron-minet, at the crack of dawn.

pou, *pl* **poux** [pu] *nm* 1. *F* sale comme un pou, filthy/filthy dirty 2. *F* laid/moche comme un pou, as ugly as sin 3. *F* fier/orgueilleux comme un pou, as proud as a peacock 4. *F* écorcher un pou pour en avoir la peau, to be very miserly*/stingy 5. *P* chercher des poux (dans la tête) à qn, to pick a quarrel* with s.o. (about nothing). (*Voir* **bicher 2; piège 1**)

pouacre [pwakr] *a & nm & f F* 1. *A* unwashed/dirty/filthy (person) 2. mean/ miserly*/stingy (person).

se poualer [səpwale] *vpr P* = **se poiler.**

poubelle [pubɛl] *nf F* 1. ramshackle old car*/old crock/jalopy/heap; où as-tu garé ta poubelle? where did you park your old heap of junk/that old pile of scrap metal? 2. motor-bike.

pouce [pus] *nm* 1. *F (a)* donner un coup de pouce à qn/à qch, to give s.o./sth a push; to in-fluence s.o.; avoir un coup de pouce, to have influence/to have friends in the right places/to have pull *(b)* donner le coup de pouce à qch, to give the finishing touches to sth/to finish sth off *(c)* filer le coup de pouce, (*commerçant*) to give short weight/to jiggle the scales; (*augmenter le prix*) to raise the price/to up the ante 2. *F* manger sur le pouce, to have a (quick) snack/a (quick) bite (to eat); lire un livre du pouce, to skim through a book 3. *F* se tourner les pouces, to twiddle one's thumbs/to idle around; ne pas se fouler le pouce/les pouces, to take it easy*/to laze about 4. *F* met-tre les pouces, to give in/to surrender/to knuckle under; (*écoles*) pouce! pax!/give in!/ truce! 5. *F* et le pouce, and the rest; (*un peu plus*) and a bit over/and a bit more 6. *F* s'en mordre les pouces, to bitterly regret it/to kick oneself 7. *F* être malade du pouce, to be miserly*/tight-fisted 8. *FrC F* faire du pouce/ voyager sur le pouce, to hitch(-hike)/to thumb a lift 9. *F* tenir/serrer les pouces pour qn, to keep one's fingers crossed for s.o./to wish s.o. luck. (*Voir* **lécher I 1**)

poucettes [pusɛt] *nfpl P* handcuffs*.

poudre [pudr] *nf* 1. *F* il n'a pas inventé la poudre, he won't set the Thames on fire 2. *F*

Fig jeter de la poudre aux yeux de qn, to dazzle/impress s.o.; c'est de la poudre aux yeux, it's only window-dressing; it's just bluff/it's all eyewash 3. *F Fig (a)* être vif comme la poudre, to be volatile *(b)* cette affaire sent la poudre, it's a dodgy business/ the balloon could go up at any moment 4. *P* (*drogues*) heroin*. (*Voir* **escampette**)

poudrée [pudre] *nf P* road/highway.

se poudrer [səpudre] *vpr P* se poudrer (le pif), to take heroin* *or* cocaine*; to sniff cocaine.

poudrette [pudrɛt] *nf P* (*drogues*) cocaine*/snow.

pouet-pouet [pwɛpwɛ], **pouette-pouette** [pwɛtpwɛt] *a Vieilli P* 1. so-so; fair to middling 2. c'est pouet-pouet, it doesn't look too good; it's pretty uncertain.

pouf [puf] I *nm P* 1. *Vieilli* faire (un) pouf, to go off without paying (one's bill, one's debt) 2. brothel*/whorehouse/knocking shop II *nf P* = **pouf(f)iasse.**

pouffe [puf] *nf,* **pouf(f)iasse** [pufjas] *nf P* 1. *Péj (femme)* slag/slut; une grande pouf(f)iasse, a (great) fat cow/Br a fat slag 2. *Péj (amie)* girlfriend/female/surt Austr tart; (*épouse*) wife*/the missis/the old woman 3. immoral woman*/slut/scrubber 4. (low-class) prostitute*/cheap hooker/cheap tart.

pouic [pwik] *adv P* que pouic, nothing*/not a damn thing. (*Voir* **entraver**)

pouilladin [pujadɛ̃], **pouillasson** [pujasɔ̃] *nm P* down-and-out/no-hoper/NAm bum.

pouilleux, -euse [pujø, -øz] *F* I *a (a)* dirty *(b)* wretched/miserable/lousy II *n (a)* dirty/louse-ridden person *(b)* tramp/beggar/ NAm bum.

poulaga [pulaga] *nm P* policeman*/cop; (plain-clothes) detective; la Maison poulaga, the police*/the fuzz.

poulaille [pulaj] *nf P* la poulaille *(a)* the police*/the law/the fuzz *(b)* (*théâtre*) people/ audience who frequent the **poulailler.**

poulailler [pulaje] *nm F (théâtre)* the gods/ NAm peanut gallery.

poulardin [pulardɛ̃] *nm,* **poulardos** [pulardos] *nm P* = **poulaga.**

poule [pul] *nf* 1. *P (a)* woman*/bird/chick/ tart/NAm broad *(b)* kept woman; sa poule, his little bit of fluff/stuff; his mistress *(c)* prostitute*; poule de luxe, high-class prostitute; call girl 2. *F* ma (petite) poule! my pet!/my darling*! 3. *P (a)* la poule, the police*/the fuzz; **aller à la poule**, to lodge a complaint (with the police); **il a la poule au cul**, he's got the cops on his back/breathing down his neck (b) **la fausse poule**, bogus policemen*/phon(e)y cops **4.** F **une poule mouillée**, (personne) a wet/a drip/a wimp **5.** F **quand les poules auront des dents**, when pigs have wings/when the cows come home **6.** F **comme une poule qui a trouvé un couteau**, amazed*/gobsmacked/speechless **7.** F **ce n'est pas à la poule à chanter devant le coq**, a wife should not tell her husband what to do. (Voir **cage 1, 3, 4**)

Pouleman(n) [pulman], **Poulemince** [pulmɛ̃s], **Pouleminche** [pulmɛ̃ʃ], **Pouleminse** [pulmɛ̃s] nm P **la Maison Pouleman(n)** (a) the police*/the cops (b) Police headquarters.

poulet [pulɛ] nm **1.** F (terme d'affection) **mon (petit) poulet**, my pet/(my) sweetie/ sweetheart/surt NAm sugar **2.** P **mon cul, c'est du poulet!** (refus) not (bloody) likely*!/ no way!/not sodding likely!/you've got to be joking! (réponse à un refus) get lost*!/bugger off!/nuts (to you)! **3.** A P love letter/billet doux **4.** P policeman*/copper/cop; (plainclothes) detective. (Voir **cage 1**)

poulette [pulɛt] nf F (a) (young) girl*/ pretty young thing; bird/chick/doll (b) **ma poulette**, my darling*/my pet.

pouliche [puliʃ] nf **1.** F = **poulette 2.** P prostitute/prostitute*; **pouliche faux-poids**, under-age girl who looks older than she is; jailbait; under-age prostitute*; chicken dinner.

Poulman(n) [pulman] nm P = **Pouleman(n)**.

pouloper [pulɔpe] vi P to hurry up*/to get a move on; to rush around.

poulot, -otte [pulo, -ɔt] n F (à un enfant) (my) pet/(my) darling*/(my) love.

poupée [pupe] nf F girl*/bird/chick/(baby) doll.

poupoule [pupul] nf F **ma poupoule**, my darling*/my pet.

pour [pur] I prép F **1.** **c'est pour de bon/pour de vrai**, I mean it/I'm serious/it's for real **2.** **moi, je suis pour**, I'm (all) for it **3.** **c'est étudié pour**, it's specially designed/it's made for that purpose **4.** **être pour hommes**, to be a homosexual*; **être pour femmes**, to be a lesbian* II nm Vieilli P **c'est du pour!** it's a pack of lies!/it's a load of crap! **c'est pas du pour!** it's the gospel truth!

pourcif [pursif] nm P (pourboire) tip.

pourliche [purliʃ] nm P (pourboire) tip.

pourri [puri] I a F **1.** (machine, etc) in bad repair/broken; **la batterie est pourrie**, the battery's had it **2.** (surt enfant) thoroughly spoilt **3.** **être pourri d'argent**, to be very rich*/to be stinking rich **4.** **il n'est pas pourri**, he's fighting fit* **5.** **elle n'est pas pourrie**, she's not bad/she's a bit of all right/she's a nice bit of stuff **6.** **c'est pas pourri ça!** it's pretty good!/it's a bit of all right!/it's not bad! II nm P **1.** swine/Br sod/rotter/creep; **vieux pourri!** you swine!/you bastard*! **bande de pourris!** you sods!/you (lousy) bastards! **2.** Belg idler/loafer/lazybones/layabout.

pourriture [purityr] nf F rotter/bastard*; **vieille pourriture!** you swine!/(you) creep!

poursoif [purswaf] nm P (pourboire) tip.

pourvoyeur, -euse [purvwajœr, -øz] n F (drogues) dealer*/pusher.

pouské [puske] nm P (argot des gitans) revolver*/gun.

pousse-au-crime [pusokrim] nm inv P strong wine; strong spirits*; mother's ruin.

pousse-au-vice [pusovis] nm inv P aphrodisiac.

pousse-ballon [pusbalɔ̃] nm inv F poor football player/ball pusher.

pousse-bière [pusbjɛr] nm inv F (boisson) (beer) chaser.

pousse-café [puskafe] nm inv F **1.** (afterdinner) liqueur **2.** sex* immediately after a meal.

pousse-cailloux [puskaju] nm inv F infantryman/foot-slogger.

pousse-canule [puskanyl] nm inv P male nurse/medical orderly.

pousse-dehors [pusdəɔr] nm inv F (alcoholic) drink taken early in the morning; early-morning nip.

pousse-mégots [pusmego] nmpl inv F (personne) good-for-nothing/layabout.

pousser [puse] F I vtr **en pousser une**, to sing a song. (Voir **goualante**) II vi to exaggerate*; to overdo it; **faut pas pousser!** that's a bit much!/that's (going it) a bit strong! (Voir **bouchon 8**; **orties**; **vacomme-je-te-pousse (à la)**) III vpr se **pousser pousse-toi!** move up!/shove up!

poussette [pusɛt] nf F **1.** (cyclisme) help given to a cyclist (in a race) by pushing him/ her **2.** (drogues) syringe/hypo **3.** (par un commerçant) jiggling of the scales.

poussier [pusje] nm P = **pucier 2**.

poussière [pusjɛr] nf F **1. cela m'a coûté**

dix francs et des poussières, it cost me ten francs plus/ten and a bit francs 2. *Mus* faire des poussières, to play some false notes. (*Voir* rentrer 2)

poussin [pusɛ̃] *nm F* 1. mon poussin, my pet/my darling*/my little chickabiddy 2. (*armée de l'air*) (first-year) officer cadet.

PPH [pepeaʃ] *abrév & nm P* (= passera pas l'hiver) un PPH, an old man (*or s.o. considered to be 'ancient' by the younger generation*)/a wrinklie/an old fart.

(au) p.p.p.d.c. [opepepedese] *adv P* (*abrév = au plus petit poil du cul*) (*a*) absolutely super!/really great! (*b*) dead accurately/spot on/right on the button.

P.Q. [peky] *abrév & nm P* = **pécu.**

praline [pralin] *nf* 1. P blow*/punch/wallop 2. P bullet/slug 3. V clitoris*; avoir la praline en délire, to be extremely randy/to be on the point of orgasm 4. P ça paraît un peu (cucul) la praline, it seems a bit nutty/daft/*Br* dotty; il fait un peu cucul la praline, he's a bit of a twit/he's a bit cuckoo.

pratiquement [pratikmɑ̃] *adv F* almost/nearly.

pravise [praviz] *nf*, **pravouse** [pravuz] *nf Vieilli P* (*drogues*) dose of cocaine* or morphine*.

précaution [prekosjɔ̃] *nf F Euph* prendre ses précautions, to practise coitus interruptus.

prêchi-prêcha [prɛʃiprɛʃa] *nm inv F* sermonizing/preachifying.

précieuses [presjøz] *nfpl P* testicles*/family jewels.

Préfectance [prefɛktɑ̃s] *nf P* (= Préfecture) (Paris) police headquarters.

prem [prɛm, prɔm], **prems** [prɔms] *a & nm & f F* (*écoles*) (the) first; je suis prem(s) en maths, I'm top in maths.

première [prɔmjɛr] *a phr P* de première, excellent*/first-class; un mec de première, a really great bloke/guy. (*Voir* bourre II 4)

prendre [prɑ̃dr] I *vtr* 1. F (*a*) qu'est-ce que tu vas prendre! you're (in) for it!/you'll catch it! qu'est-ce que j'ai pris! I didn't half catch/cop it! (*b*) en prendre pour 6 mois, to be sentenced to 6 months' imprisonment/to get 6 months 2. F j'en prends et j'en laisse, I'm taking that with a pinch of salt; avec lui, il faut en prendre et en laisser, you can't believe everything he says/you've got to take what he says with a pinch of salt 3. *Vieilli F* en prendre, to get rich*/to make a pile 4. F où prends-tu ça? how do you make that out?/

where do you get that idea from? 5. F to challenge (s.o.) (to a game) 6. P prendre la tête à qn, to get on s.o.'s tits/wick 7. P (*homosexuels*) celui qui en prend, passive partner. (*Voir* grade) II *vi F* ça ne prend pas (avec moi)! that won't work with me!/it won't wash with me! ce truc-là prend toujours, that trick always works/it's a sure bet.

presse [prɛs] *nf P* être sous presse, (*prostituée*) to be with a client/to be on the job.

presto [prɛsto] *adv F* immediately*/pronto/pdq. (*Voir* illico; subito)

prétentiard, -arde [pretɑ̃sjar, -ard] *Vieilli F* I *a* pretentious II *n* pretentious/conceited person; quel prétentiard! what a conceited little jerk!/he really does think a lot of himself!

preu(m) [prø(m)] *a & nm inv F* (*écoles*) (the) first; top.

prévence [prevɑ̃s] *nf P* (= detention préventive) detention on suspicion/detention awaiting trial; mettre en prévence, to take into custody/to hold (s.o.) (on suspicion).

prévette [prevɛt] *nf P* = **prévence.**

prévôt [prevo] *nm P* (*en prison*) privileged prisoner.

priante [priɑ̃t] *nf P* prayer.

primeur [primœr] *nf* 1. F virginity*/maidenhead 2. P very young prostitute (*esp* under-age).

primo [primo] *adv P* firstly.

prise [priz] I *af P* être prise, to be pregnant* II *nf P* 1. (*drogues*) small quantity of cocaine* sniffed up the nose/snort of coke 2. stench/stink/pong; prendre une prise, to be overwhelmed by a filthy stench 3. thief's loot. (*Voir* bec 5)

priseur¹, -euse [prizœr, -øz] *nm & f P* priseur, -euse de cocaïne/de coke, cocaïne*/coke sniffer.

priseur² [prizœr] *nm P* nose*/conk.

privé [prive] *nm F* private detective*/(private) dick.

prix [pri] *nm F* 1. un prix de Diane, a very pretty girl*/woman*; a smasher/a bit of all right/a nice bit of stuff 2. un prix à réclamer, an ugly woman; cette fille, c'est un vrai prix à réclamer, she'll never be a candidate for Miss World 3. ce n'est pas un prix de vertu, she's/he's no angel 4. acheter au prix courant, to shoplift. (*Voir* beurre 6)

pro [pro] *nm & f F* (= professionnel, -elle) pro.

probloc, probloque [prɔblɔk] *nm & f P*

1. landlord/landlady (of rented flat/*NAm* apartment, etc); le **probloc** réclame son loyer, the landlord's asking for the rent 2. problem/hitch. (*Voir* **proprio**; **propriote**)

probzi [prɔbzi], **probzo** [prɔbzo] *nm P* maths problem.

proc [prɔk] *nm*, **procu** [prɔky] *nm P* (= *procureur de la République*) = public prosecutor.

prof [prɔf] *nm & f F* (*écoles, etc*) (= *professeur*) (*a*) master/mistress; le/la prof de maths, the maths teacher (*b*) prof de fac(ulté) prof(essor); lecturer.

professionnelle [prɔfɛsjɔnɛl] *nf F* prostitute*/pro.

profiter [prɔfite] *vi F* (*enfant, plante, etc*) to thrive/to grow; ça lui a bien profité, ces vacances, his holiday did him a world of good.

profonde [prɔfɔ̃d] *nf F* pocket; en avoir plein les profondes, to be rich*/loaded.

projo [prɔʒo] *nm P* (*cinéma, etc*) (= *projecteur*) projector.

prolo [prɔlo] *nm & f P* (= *prolétaire*) proletarian/prole; tes fringues font prolo, you look like a real pleb in those clothes.

prolongé [prɔlɔ̃ʒe] *a F* jeune fille prolongée, girl who is taking a long time to get married; old maid.

promenade [prɔmnad] *nf F* (*a*) easy job/cinch/doddle (*b*) promenade (de santé), easy victory/walkover.

se promener [səprɔmne] *vpr F* (*a*) envoyer promener qn, to send s.o. packing*/to tell s.o. to clear off; va te promener! get out!/go jump in the lake!/go take a running jump! (*b*) envoyer tout promener, to give everything up/to chuck everything.

promis, -ise [prɔmi, -iz] *nm & f Vieilli F* fiancé(e)/intended/betrothed.

promo [prɔmo] *nf F* (= *promotion*) 1. (*écoles*) year/class; la promo de '68, the class of '68 2. (*marketing, etc*) (sales) promotion; en promo, on (special) offer.

prompto, pronto [prɔ̃to] *adv P* immediately*/pronto.

prono [prɔno] *nm F* (*sport*) (= *pronostic*) forecast/prediction.

propé [prɔpe] *nf A F* (= *propédeutique*) first year of university course.

propre [prɔpr] *F* I *a* nous voilà propres! we're in a fine (old) fix*!/this is a nice mess we've got ourselves into! II *nm* ça, c'est du propre!/en voilà du propre! well, that's a real

mess!/that's a complete shambles!

proprio [prɔprijo] *nm P* (= *propriétaire*) proprietor/owner/landlord. (*Voir* **probloc, probloque**; **propriote**)

propriote [prɔprijɔt] *nf P* (*rare*) proprietress/owner/landlady. (*Voir* **probloc, probloque**; **proprio**)

prose [proz] *nm*, **prosinard** [prɔzinar] *nm P* = **proze, prozinard**.

protal [prɔtal] *nm F* (*écoles*) head teacher (*of lycée*). (*Voir* **proto, provo**)

protescul [prɔtəsky] *nm P Péj* Protestant.

proto [prɔto] *nm F* (*écoles*) head teacher (*of lycée*). (*Voir* **protal**; **provo**)

prout [prut] *nm P* 1. fart*; lâcher un prout, to (let out a) fart 2. prout (ma chère)! (*lancé à un inverti*) ooh, ducky/ducks!

prouter [prute] *vi P* to fart*.

prouteur, -euse [prutœr, -øz] *a P* afraid*/frightened; cowardly/yellow.

prove [prɔv] *nf*, **provise** [prɔviz] *nf P* (= *provision*) chèque sans prove, dud cheque/bouncer.

provisoire [prɔvizwar] *nf P* être en provisoire, to be (out) on conditional discharge.

provo [prɔvo] *nm F* (*écoles*) head (of lycée). (*Voir* **protal**; **proto**)

provoc [prɔvɔk] *nf F* (= *provocation*) provocation.

proxémac [prɔksemak] *nm Vieilli*, **proxo** [prɔkso] *nm P* pimp*/procurer.

proze [proz] *nm*, **prozinard** [prɔzinar] *nm P* 1. buttocks*; se magner le proze, to get a move on/to pull one's finger out; l'avoir dans le proze, to be cheated/had/done 2. luck; faut avoir du proze pour faire ça, you need a bit of luck to do that.

prune [pryn] *nf* 1. *F* aux prunes, last summer *or* next summer; (*jamais*) never 2. *F* pour des prunes, for nothing*/for peanuts; ça compte pour des prunes, that doesn't count for anything; je ne veux pas me déranger pour des prunes, I'm not going to put myself out for nothing 3. *P* des prunes! not (bloody) likely*!/no fear!/nothing doing!/not on your life!/no chance! 4. *Vieilli P* bullet/slug 5. *P* blow*; slap; avoir de la prune, to pack a punch; (*avoir de la chance*) to be lucky 6. *P* (*contravention*) se faire coller une prune, to be booked/to get a ticket 7. *Vieilli P* avoir sa prune, to be drunk* 8. *pl V* prunes, testicles*/nuts.

pruneau, *pl* **-eaux** [pryno] *nm* 1. *P* bullet.

(*Voir* **prune 4**) 2. *P* blow*. (*Voir* **prune 5**) 3. *P* des pruneaux! not (bloody) likely*! (*Voir* **prune 3**) 4. *F* pour des pruneaux, for nothing*. (*Voir* **prune 2**) 5. *pl V* testicles*. (*Voir* **prune 8**) 6. *A P* quid of tobacco.

prunelle [prynɛl] *nf F* jouer de la prunelle, to make (sheep's) eyes (at s.o.)/to flutter one's eyelashes.

Prusse [prys] *Prnf F* 1. travailler pour le roi de Prusse, to work for nothing*/for love 2. aller voir le roi de Prusse, to go to the loo/to spend a penny/to have a look at the plumbing.

pseudo [psødo] *nm F* 1. c'est du pseudo, it's pseudo/fake/phon(e)y/bogus 2. pseudonym.

psy [psi] *F* I *nm & f* 1. (= *psychiatre*) psychiatrist/shrink 2. (=*psychiatrique*) mental patient/psycho II *nf* (=*psychologie*) psychology.

puant [pɥɑ̃] I *nm P* abscess caused by an unsterilized needle or by impure drugs; ab/AB/ABC II *nm P* cheese III *a F* objectionably conceited/bumptious.

pub [pyb] *nf F* (= *la publicité*) publicity; (= *une publicité*) advertisement/ad(vert); faire de la pub, to advertise; il est dans la pub, he's in advertising.

puce [pys] *nf F* 1. marché aux puces/les puces, flea market. (*Voir* **marchand 4**) 2. undersized* person/little squirt/shrimp 3. charmer ses puces, to have a drink before going to bed/to have a nightcap 4. chercher des puces, to go through sth with a fine-tooth comb 5. chercher des puces à qn, to provoke s.o. 6. avoir la puce à l'oreille, to be uneasy/suspicious; ça m'a mis la puce à l'oreille, it made me suspicious/I smelled a rat 7. secouer ses puces, to stretch oneself (out) 8. secouer les puces à qn, to tell s.o. off 9. saut de puce, quick flight (*in an aircraft*)/hop 10. (*cartes*) les puces, the three aces 11. (*terme d'affection*) ma puce, my darling*/my pet/my love 12. faire les puces/faire la puce travailleuse, to engage in lesbian practices for the benefit of a voyeur.

puceau, *pl* **-eaux** [pyso] *nm F* (male) virgin.

pucelage [pys(ə)laʒ] *nm F* virginity*.

pucelle [pysɛl] *nf F* (female) virgin.

pucier [pysje] *nm* 1. *F* junk dealer in a flea market 2. *P* bed*/fleabag/sack; dix heures de pucier, ten hours' kip.

pue-la-sueur [pylasɥœr] *nm inv P* manual worker. (*Voir* **pompe-la-sueur**)

pull [pyl] *nm F* pullover/jumper.

punaise [pynɛz] *nf* 1. *F* punaise de sacristie, bigoted churchwoman 2. woman*/bird/female 3. *F & Dial* oh, punaise! goodness! (*plus fort*) blast it! 4. *P* (*1939–45*) punaises vertes, German soldiers/Jerries. (*Voir* **soufflet 2**)

punch [pœnʃ] *nm F* dynamism; manquer de punch, to lack punch.

punk [pœ̃k] *F* I *a* punk (*music, etc*) II *n* punk.

punkette [pœ̃kɛt] *nf* female punk/punkette.

punkitude [pœ̃kityd] *nf F* punk condition *or* appearance *or* attitude.

pur, *f* **pure**[1] [pyr] *n F Pol etc* an uncompromising person/diehard.

pure[2] [pyr] *nf P* (*drogues*) heroin* with a high degree of purity.

purée [pyre] *nf* 1. *P* balancer la purée, to fire/to shoot a gun, etc 2. *V* balancer/envoyer/jeter/lâcher la/sa purée, to ejaculate*/to come (off)/to shoot one's load 3. *F* être dans la purée, to be penniless*/broke/skint; être dans la purée noire, to be on one's beam ends/in a real fix* 4. *F* purée de pois, (*brouillard*) peasouper 5. *A P* drink of absinthe 6. *P* purée! hell!/blast!/darn! (*surprise*) wow!

purge [pyrʒ] *nf P* 1. thrashing/good hiding; coller/donner/filer une purge à qn, to beat s.o. up*/to work s.o. over; prendre la purge, to get beaten up; (*sports*) to get thrashed/licked/hammered 2. intolerable person; quelle purge! what a pain (he/she is)!

purotin [pyrɔtɛ̃] *nm P* person living in abject poverty; down-and-out/loser.

pus [py] *adv P* (= *plus*) y a pus! (= *il n'y en a plus*) (it's) no go!

pusher [puʃœr] *nm & f P* (*drogues*) dealer*/pusher.

putain [pytɛ̃] *P* I *nf* 1. (*a*) prostitute*/whore/tart (*b*) enfant de putain!/fils de putain! you son of a bitch! 2. cette putain de guerre! this bloody war! leur putain de bagnole! their bloody/*NAm* goddamn/sodding car! 3. petite putain! you little sod! II *int* (bloody) hell!/blast!/dammit! putain de bordel de merde! sodding/pissing/fucking hell!/bugger it!/sod it!

putasse [pytɑs] *nf V* prostitute*/whore.

putasser [pytɑse] *vi V* to be a prostitute*/to solicit*/to be on the game; il envoie sa femme putasser, he sends his wife out on the game.

putasserie [pytɑsri] *nf V* 1. whoring; living as a prostitute* 2. smut(tiness)/filth; quelle putasserie! how disgusting!

putassier, -ière [pytasje, -jɛr] *P* I *a*

whorish/tarty; **langage putassier**, filthy/dirty language; **avoir un air putassier**, to look like a whore/a tart; **avoir des manières putassières**, to act like a whore/a tart **II** *nm* whoremonger/woman-chaser/rake.

pute‹ [pyt] *nf* 1. *V* prostitute*/whore/hooker/ tart; **la pute!** (*elle m'a menti*) the bitch! **fils de pute!** you son of a bitch! **à la pute**, tarty/whor- ish 2. *P* (*cartes*) **les putes**, (the) four queens.

pyj' [piʒ] *nm F* (*abrév = pyjama*) jimjams/ jammies.

pyjama [piʒama] *nm F* **faire du pyjama**, to stay at home (in order to save money); (*aller à la campagne*) to go to the country (to re- cuperate); (*se cacher*) to hide out/to lie low/to hole up (*in the country, abroad, etc*).

Q

Q.H.S. [kyaʃɛs] *nm F* (*abrév = quartier de haute sécurité*) (*dans une prison*) top/high-security wing.

quand-est-ce [kɑ̃tɛs] *nm F* welcome round of drinks offered by new employee to his/her colleagues.

quarante [karɑ̃t] *nf P* **1.** (*a*) table (*b*) (illicit) street-vendor's folding table/fly-pitcher's stand **2. se mettre en quarante,** (*en colère*) to get angry*/to blow one's top; (*devenir méchant*) to turn nasty/to cut up rough; (*en position de combat*) to square up (for a fight). (*Voir* **carante 1, 2; se ficher II 2** (*b*))

quarante-quatre [karɑ̃tkatr] *nm inv* **1.** *F* (*médecin à ses patients*) **dites quarante-quatre!** say ninety-nine!/say ah! (*Voir* **trente-trois**) **2.** *Vieilli P* **un quarante-quatre maison,** a good kick in the pants.

quart [kar] *nm* **1.** *P* (*a*) police station; **il est au quart,** he's down the station/the cop shop (*b*) **quart** (**d'œil**), police superintendent **2.** *F* **faire/battre son quart, être de quart,** (*prostituée*) to walk her beat **3.** *F* (*a*) **passer un mauvais/un fichu/un sale quart d'heure,** to have a rough time of it/to go through some awkward moments; **faire passer un mauvais quart d'heure à qn,** to give s.o. a bad time/to put s.o. through it (*b*) **le quart d'heure de Rabelais,** the hour of reckoning (*c*) **pour le quart d'heure,** for the time being **4.** *F* **les trois quarts du temps,** most of the time **5.** *F* **partir au quart de tour,** to set off at an easy pace **6.** *P* **quart de brie,** big nose*/conk **7.** *P* **quart de beurre,** gold bar/ingot. (*Voir* **se ficher II 2** (*b*); **poil 2** (*a*); **tiers**)

Quartier [kartje] *Prnm F* **le Quartier,** (= *le Quartier latin*) the Latin Quarter (*in Paris*). (*Voir* **Latin**)

quat' [kat] *nm inv F* (= *quatre*) four; **un de ces quat',** one of these days. (*Voir* **quatre**)

quat'crans [katkrɑ̃] *nm P Mil* very strict NCO. (*Voir* **cran 5**)

quatre [katr] *nm inv F* **un de ces quatre (matins),** one of these days.

quatre-z-yeux [katrəzjø], **quat'zyeux¹** [katzjø] *nmpl F* **entre quatre-z-yeux,** in private/between you and me; between you, me and the gatepost/lamp-post.

quat'zyeux² [katzjø] *a & nm P Péj* bespectacled (person)/four-eyes.

quebri [kəbri] *nf P* (*verlan de* **brique**) ten thousand (new) francs.

quelque chose [kɛlkəʃoz] *indef pron m inv* **1.** *F* **prendre quelque chose,** to get a bashing/to cop it; **tu vas prendre quelque chose!** you'll catch it! (*Voir* **grade**) **2.** *F* **il a quelque chose,** there's something the matter with him **3.** *F* **vous y travaillerez quelque chose comme deux ans,** you'll be at it for about two years **4.** *F* **il lui manque un petit quelque chose,** he's slightly lacking somewhere; he's got a screw loose **5.** *F* **aller faire quelque chose,** to go to the loo/NAm the bathroom **6.** *F* **c'est quelque chose, ça, tout de même!** that's really intolerable!/this won't do at all! **7.** *P* **quelque chose de bien,** extremely/very; **il s'est viandé, quelque chose de bien,** he had a serious accident/he didn't half do himself some damage.

quelquefois [kɛlkəfwa] *adv F* in case; **quelquefois qu'il serait arrivé,** in case he'd arrived.

quelque part [kɛlkəpar] *adv* **1.** *F* **aller quelque part,** to go to the WC*/the loo/NAm the bathroom **2.** *F* **donner à qn un coup de pied quelque part/mettre le pied quelque part,** to give s.o. a kick up the backside; **tu veux mon pied quelque part?** do you want my foot up your backside? **3.** *P* **je l'ai quelque part!** I don't give a damn about him! **je les ai quelque part!** you know where you can stick 'em! **quant à ton offre généreuse, moi je me la mets quelque part,** as for your generous offer, you can stick it; **il peut se le/la mettre quelque part!** he can stuff it (up his arse)! **les**

ordres du patron, moi je me les mets quelque part, I don't give a toss about the boss's orders.

quelqu'un [kɛlkœ̃] *indef pron* **1.** *F* elle se croit déjà quelqu'un, she thinks she's really something; **ils sont quelqu'un dans leur village**, they're somebodies/big fish in their own village **2.** *P* c'est quelqu'un, ça alors! (*c'est extraordinaire*) that's (really) something!/how amazing! (*c'est anormal*) how odd!/that's odd!

quène [kɛn] *a P* = **queune.**

quenotte [kənɔt] *nf F* (*langage enfantin*) tooth/toothy-peg.

quenottier [kənɔtje] *nm F* dentist.

quèque [kɛk] *a & adv F* (= *quelque*) quèque chose = **quelque chose;** quèque part = **quelque part.**

quéquette [kekɛt] *nf P* **1.** (child's) penis*/ willie/wee-wee **2.** (condemned) rapist/sex offender.

quès [kɛs] *nm P* **1.** c'est du quès, it's six of one and half a dozen of the other/it makes no odds/it's as broad as it's long/it's much of a muchness; **c'est jamais du quès**, it's never the same **2.** en quès, (= *en question*) in question; **la bagnole en quès**, the car in question. (*Voir* **kès**)

qu'est-ce que [kɛskə] *interr pron* **1.** *P* (= *combien*) (*a*) qu'est-ce que vous êtes de personnes ici? how many of you are there here? (*b*) (*excl*) qu'est-ce qu'il fait beau! isn't the weather gorgeous! qu'est-ce qu'on rigole! what a laugh! **2.** *F* (= *pourquoi*) qu'est-ce que tu avais besoin d'aller lui dire ça? what did you want to go and say that to him for?

qu'est-ce qui [kɛski] *interr pron F* **1.** (= *ce qui*) je vous demande un peu qu'est-ce qui lui prend? whatever's got into him! **2.** (= *qui*) je ne savais pas qu'est-ce qui était là, I didn't know who was there.

question [kɛstjɔ̃] *nf F* **1.** question boulot, je me débrouille, as far as work goes, I get on all right **2.** question de dormir, j'ai passé une nuit blanche, as far as sleep goes, I didn't get a wink all night **3.** c'te question!/quelle question! what a thing to ask! **4.** la question (super-)banco/à cent balles, the sixty-four thousand dollar question.

quétaine [ketɛn] *a FrC P* **1.** old-fashioned/ dated; past it **2.** cheap and nasty/rubbishy.

queue [kø] *nf* **1.** *V* penis*/cock/prick; se faire/se taper une queue, to masturbate*/to beat the dummy. (*Voir* **coup 19**) **2.** *F* il s'en

retourna la queue entre les jambes/la queue basse, he went off with his tail between his legs **3.** *P* faire des queues à son mari/à sa femme, to be unfaithful to one's husband/ wife; to cheat on one's husband/wife; to have a bit on the side **4.** *F* (*a*) *Aut* faire une queue de poisson à qn, to cut right in front of s.o. (*b*) finir en queue de poisson, to come to nothing/ to fizzle out/to peter out **5.** *F* pas la queue d'un/d'une, not a sign of one/not a blessed one/not a sausage; n'en avoir pas la queue d'un, to be penniless*/skint **6.** *P* des queues(, Marie)! no way!/nothing doing! **7.** *F* pour des queues de cerises/de prunes, for nothing/for peanuts **8.** *F* ajouter des queues aux zéros, to cook the books **9.** *F* n'avoir ni queue ni tête, to be pointless; une histoire sans queue ni tête, a story that one cannot make head or tail of/a real cock-and-bull story **10.** *P* (*prisons*) queue de cervelas, daily walk in the prison yard/ exercise period **11.** *F* tenir la queue de la poêle, to be in charge/to run the show/to rule the roost **12.** *F* laisser une queue, to pay only part of a bill; to settle only part of a debt **13.** *P* rond comme une queue de pelle, dead drunk*/(completely) pissed/smashed/plastered **14.** *V* faire queue de rat, to fail to have an orgasm*; il a fait queue de rat, he went limp/ he didn't come/he couldn't manage it/he didn't get his rocks off. (*Voir* **un I 2**)

queue-de-vache [kødvaʃ] *a inv F* cheveux queue-de-vache, mousy(-coloured) hair.

queune [køn] *a P* exhausted*/dead beat/ shagged out.

queuner [køne] *vi P* to have sex*/to bonk/to screw.

queutage [køtaʒ] *nm V* fornication/ screwing/fucking.

queutard [køtar] *V* **I** *nm* (*obsédé sexuel*) womanizer*/wolf/randy bugger/cunt-chaser; c'est un queutard, he's sex-mad/he'd screw anything on two legs **II** *a* sexually obsessed/ sex-mad/cunt-struck.

queuter [køte] *vtr V* to have sex* with/to screw/to fuck (s.o.).

quibus [kɥibys] *nm P* money*/the readies/ the wherewithal.

qui c'est qui [kisɛki] *P* = **qui est-ce qui.**

qui est-ce qui [kiɛski] *interr pron m sing F* je ne sais pas qui est-ce qui vous a dit ça, I don't know who told you that.

quillard [kijar] *nm F Mil* soldier who is about to be *or* who has just been demobbed.

quille [kij] *nf* 1. *F* la quille, *Mil* demobilisation/demob; à nous la quille! civvy street here we come! 2. *P* leg*/pin; il ne tient pas sur ses quilles, he's a bit shaky on his pins; jouer des quilles, to run away*/to skedaddle/to leg it; être sur ses quilles, to be in good health/in fine form; en avoir entre les quilles, to be brave*/to have balls/to have guts 3. *F* être planté comme une quille, to be rooted to the spot 4. *F* être reçu comme un chien dans un jeu de quilles, to be given a chilly welcome; to be made as welcome as a dog on a putting green 5. *P* quille (à la vanille), girl*.

quiller [kije] I *vtr P* to cheat*/to trick/to swindle*/to con (s.o.) II *vi P* to run away*/to beat it/to leg it.

quimper [kɛ̃pe] *P* I *vi* 1. (*a*) to fall/to take a header (*b*) (*être dupé*) to be done/to be taken for a ride 2. to be sentenced; quimper chéro, to get a stiff sentence/to get the book thrown at one 3. laisser quimper qn, to abandon s.o./to drop s.o./to ditch s.o.; laisse quimper, drop it/forget it 4. to faint*/to keel over II *vtr* 1. to seduce/to get off with (a woman) 2. quimper la lance, to urinate*/to (have a) piss.

quincaille [kɛ̃kaj] *nf* **quincaillerie** [kɛ̃kajri] *nf F* 1. row of medals/decorations 2. jewellery/jewels 3. (*informatique*) hardware 4. weapons/firearms; hardware/ironmongery.

Quincampe [kɛ̃kãp] *Prnf F* la Quincampe, the rue Quincampoix (*in Paris*).

quine [kin] *adv P* j'en ai quine, I'm fed up* with it/I've had enough (of it)/I've had it.

quinquets [kɛ̃kɛ] *nmpl P* eyes*/lamps/ peepers; ouvrir/allumer ses quinquets, to look carefully/to observe/to keep one's eyes peeled; rouler/ribouler des quinquets, to roll one's eyes (with amazement)/to goggle/to gawp; faux quinquets, spectacles/glasses/specs.

quinquin [kɛ̃kɛ̃] *nm P* petit quinquin, native of northern France.

quinte [kɛ̃t] *nf P* avoir quinte, quatorze et le point, to be infected with several strains of VD*.

quique [kik] *nf*, **quiquette** [kikɛt] *nf P* penis*/prick.

quiqui [kiki] *nm P* 1. (*a*) Adam's apple (*b*) windpipe; serrer le quiqui à qn, to throttle s.o.; to wring s.o.'s neck 2. (child's) penis*/ willie/wee-wee. (*Voir* **kiki**)

quoi [kwa] I *rel & interr pron* 1. *P* de quoi? you what?/what was that?/what did you say?/ did you say something? non, mais, de quoi j'me mêle? it's none of your business! 2. *F* t'es fou, ou quoi? are you crazy or something? 3. *F* avoir de quoi, to be comfortably off/to be worth a bob or two; il a de quoi, he's not short of a bob or two 4. *F* (*a*) (il n'y a) pas de quoi! don't mention it!/a pleasure!/cheers! (*b*) il n'y a pas de quoi être fier, that's nothing to be proud of/nothing to crow about II *int F* enfin, quoi, c'est la vie! well, such is life! il est mort, quoi! he's dead and that's that!

R

rab [rab] *nm P* extra; a bit more; a drop more; **y a du rab,** there's second helpings/ (some) seconds/(some) extras; **tu n'as pas une clope en rab?** can you spare a cig?/can I bum a fag? **un petit rab?** would you like a drop more? **faire du rab,** to work overtime/to do a bit extra. (*Voir* **rabiot**)

rabat [raba] *nm F* 1. tout (*working for a nightclub/a brothel, etc*) 2. **rabat de col/de cop(e),** discount; refund; **faire un rabat de col/de cop(e),** to give a discount/a refund.

rabatteur [rabatœr] *nm F* = **rabat 1.**

rabatteuse [rabatøz] *nf F* procuress.

rabattre [rabatr] *vi P* to return/to come back. (*Voir* **caquet**)

rabe [rab] *nm P* = **rab.**

rabibochage [rabibɔʃaʒ] *nm F* (*a*) patching up/botching up (of sth) (*b*) patching up (of a quarrel)/making it up.

rabibocher [rabibɔʃe] I *vtr F* (*a*) to patch (sth) up/to botch (sth) up/to make (sth) do (*b*) to patch up (a quarrel); to make/patch things/it up between (two people) II *vpr* **se rabibocher** *F* to become reconciled/to make it up/to patch things up/to kiss and make up.

rabiot [rabjo] *nm P* 1. (*a*) second helping; seconds/leftovers; **en rabiot,** going begging; **qui veut du rabiot?** who wants some more/ seconds? (*b*) illicit profits*/pickings/graft; **se faire du rabiot,** to make a bit on the side 2. (*a*) extra work; **faire du rabiot,** to work overtime/to do a bit extra (*b*) *Mil* extra period of service (owing to imprisonment, etc).

rabiotage [rabjɔtaʒ] *nm P* 1. fiddling 2. scrounging.

rabioter [rabjɔte] *P* I *vi* 1. to make illicit profits*/to fiddle/to make a bit on the side 2. to scrounge surplus food, etc II *vtr* 1. to scrounge; to wangle; *Mil* **j'ai rabioté deux jours de perm,** I've wangled two extra days' leave 2. to take part of someone else's share; **rabioter une somme sur le compte de qn,** to appropriate/to take an amount from s.o.'s account.

rabioteur, -euse [rabjɔtœr, -øz] *n P* 1. person who makes a bit on the side/fiddler 2. scrounger; wangler.

râble [rɑbl] *nm F* 1. (*a*) (*dos*) back (*b*) (*épaules*) shoulders 2. **il m'a sauté sur le râble/il m'est tombé sur le râble,** he jumped on me; (*importuner*) he cornered me/he buttonholed me.

râbler [rɑble] *vtr P* to attack* (s.o.)/to go for (s.o.)/to set about (s.o.).

rabouin, -ine [rabwɛ̃, -in] I *n P* gipsy/ gippo II *nm A P* **le Rabouin,** the Devil/Old Nick.

rac(c)a! [raka] *int* (*marque la colère*) grrrr!

raccord [rakɔr] *nm F* **faire un raccord,** to touch up one's make-up/to freshen up (one's face).

raccourcir [rakursir] *vtr Vieilli P* to guillotine/to behead/to top (s.o.); **la machine à raccourcir,** the guillotine.

raccroc [rakro] *nm F* **faire le raccroc,** to tout; (*prostituée*) to solicit*/to walk the streets/to hustle.

raccrocher [rakrɔʃe] I *vtr & i F* 1. to tout (for custom); (*camelot, vendeur, etc*) to stop (s.o. in the street, etc); (*prostituée*) to accost (passer-by)/to hustle 2. to recover (sth)/to get hold of (sth) again/to latch on to (sth) (again) 3. (*cyclisme*) to pull out of a competition; *Fig* to give up II *vpr* **se raccrocher** *F* (*au jeu, etc*) to recoup one's losses.

raccrocheuse [rakrɔʃøz] *nf F* prostitute*/ streetwalker/hooker.

race [ras] *nf F* **quelle (sale) race!** what a collection!/what a pathetic bunch!/what a load of jerks!

racho(t) [raʃo] *P* (=*rachitique*) I *a* 1. (*personne*) rickety; (*malingre*) puny/feeble; **il est racho(t) du ciboulot,** he's got a pea-sized brain 2. (*portion*) small/mean; **c'est un peu racho(t) comme portion!** that helping's a bit on the small side! II *n* puny person/weed.

racine [rasin] *nf* F **prendre racine,** (*personne*) to cling like a leech/like a limpet; to take root.

racket [rakɛt] *nm* F (*a*) racket; **faire du racket,** to run a racket (*b*) racketeering.

racketter [rakɛte] *vtr* F to extort money from (s.o.)/to subject (s.o.) to a protection racket.

racketteur [rakɛtœr] *nm* F racketeer.

raclé [rakle] *a* F penniless*/(flat) broke.

raclée [rakle] *nf* F **1.** thrashing/good hiding; **donner/filer/flanquer/**P **foutre une raclée à qn,** to give s.o. a good hiding/to beat s.o. up*/to work s.o. over; **prendre la raclée,** to get a hiding; **recevoir sa raclée en homme,** to take one's punishment like a man **2.** (*sports, etc*) (decisive) defeat (in a game)/good hiding; **ils ont pris une sacrée raclée en demi-finale,** they got hammered/thrashed/licked in the semi-final.

racler [rakle] I *vtr* F **racler les fonds de tiroir,** to scrape the (bottom of the) barrel II *vpr* **se racler** P to (have a) shave; **se faire racler,** to get shaved. (*Voir* **couenne 1**)

raclette [raklɛt] *nf* P **1.** squad car; (**coup de**) raclette, police raid/round-up; bust **2.** *Aut* windscreen wiper.

racloir [raklwar] *nm* P razor.

raclure [raklyr] *nf* P despicable individual/scum(bag)/louse/son of a bitch; V **raclure de pelle à merde,** shit/bastard*/mother-fucker; V **raclure de bidet,** undersized* person/short-arse.

raconter [rakɔ̃te] *vi* F **j'te raconte pas!** you can imagine!/you can work it out for yourself!

radada [radada] *nm* P **1.** buttocks* **2.** **aller au radada,** to have sex*/to make love/to have it away. (*Voir* **rondibé**)

radar [radar] *nm* F **aujourd'hui j'avance/je marche au radar,** I'm like a zombie today/I'm on auto-pilot today.

rade [rad] I *nm* P **1.** (*comptoir*) bar; (*débit*) bar/pub; **allez, on va boire un coup au rade,** come on, let's go to the pub for a drink **2.** road/street; pavement; **faire le rade,** (*prostituées, etc*) to solicit*/to tout for custom; to hustle II *nf* F (*a*) **demeurer/rester en rade,** (*abandonné*) to be left in the lurch/high and dry/standing; (*à l'écart*) to be left out of it/to be left out in the cold; **laisser qn en rade,** to leave s.o. in the lurch/high and dry; to leave s.o. out of it/to leave s.o. out in the cold (*b*) **sa bagnole est tombée en rade,** his/her car's broken down/conked out.

radeuse [radøz] *nf* P prostitute*/streetwalker/hooker.

radin, -ine [radɛ̃, -in] P I *a* mean*/stingy/tight-fisted/penny-pinching II *n* miser*/skinflint/tight-ass/penny-pincher.

radiner [radine] I *vi* P to arrive*/to turn up/to show up/to blow in; (*en hâte*) to rush over; (*revenir*) to rush back/to dash back II *vpr* **se radiner** P **alors, tu te radines!** so you decided to show up! **il s'est radiné à huit heures,** he showed up/rolled up at eight.

radinerie [radinri] *nf* P miserliness/stinginess/tight-fistedness/penny-pinching.

radio [radjo] *nf* F **avoir un physique de radio,** to be unattractive/to lack charm.

radioteur [radjotœr] *nm* F radio broadcaster.

radis [radi] *nm* **1.** F **sans un radis,** penniless*; **je n'ai pas un radis,** I'm (stony) broke/I haven't got a bean; **je ne dépense pas un radis de plus,** I'm not spending a penny more **2.** F **ça ne vaut pas un radis,** it's worthless*/it's not worth a sausage/*NAm* a dime **3.** P **des radis!** nothing doing!/no fear!/not (bloody) likely*!/no way! **4.** P *Péj* **radis noir,** priest* **5.** *pl* F (*a*) feet* (*b*) toes. (*Voir* **bouchon 7**)

radoter [radɔte] *vtr* F **qu'est-ce qu'il radote?** what's he rambling/drivelling on about?

raffolement [rafɔlmɑ̃] *nm* F infatuation (de, with).

raffoler [rafɔle] *vi* F (*a*) **raffoler de qn,** to be infatuated* with s.o./to be gone on s.o./to have a thing about s.o. (*b*) **raffoler de qch,** to be mad (keen) on sth/to be nuts about sth; **je n'en raffole pas,** I'm not crazy about it.

raffut [rafy] *nm* F noise/din/row/racket; **faire du raffut,** to kick up a row; (*faire un scandale*) to kick up a fuss/a stink; **un raffut du diable/de tous les diables,** a devil of a row/one hell of a row.

rafiau, *pl* **-aux** [rafjo] *nm*, **rafiot** [rafjo] *nm* F (*bateau*) (*vieux*) rafiau, old tub.

rafistolage [rafistɔlaʒ] *nm* F patching up/botching up; **ça n'ira pas loin, c'est du rafistolage,** it won't last long, it's just a makeshift/patched-up job.

rafistoler [rafistɔle] *vtr* F (*a*) to patch up/to botch up (*b*) to get (sth) going again; **leur ménage s'est rafistolé,** they've patched things up/they're having another go at it.

ragaga [ragaga] *nm* P **faire du ragaga,** to waste one's time (doing something useless)/to piss about/to fart about.

rageant [raʒɑ̃] *a F* infuriating.

rager [raʒe] *vi F* cela me fait rager! it's infuriating!/it makes me mad!/it makes my blood boil!

ragnagnas [raɲaɲa] *nmpl P* avoir ses ragnagnas, to have one's period*/to have the curse.

ragot [rago] *nm F* (a) piece of ill-natured gossip/tittle-tattle (b) *pl* ragots, ill-natured gossip/tittle-tattle.

ragoter [ragɔte] *vi F* to gossip maliciously/to tittle-tattle.

ragougnasse [raguɲas] *nf F* poor-quality food/pigswill.

raidard [rɛdar] *a P* penniless*/(stony) broke.

raide [rɛd] I *a* 1. *P* drunk*/tight/stoned/ plastered 2. *P* être raide, to be penniless*; raide comme une barre/raide à blanc/raide comme la justice/raide comme un passe-lacet, stony broke/skint 3. *F* (a) une histoire raide, a tall story/a tale that's a bit hard to swallow; il en raconte de raides, he's always spinning some yarn or other/some cock-and-bull story (b) il lui a dit des trucs assez raides, he made some pretty suggestive remarks to her (c) ça c'est un peu raide!/elle est raide, celle-là! that's a bit far-fetched/a bit hard to swallow/a bit thick! (d) il en a vu de(s) raides, he's had some strange experiences/he's seen a thing or two/he's been around 4. *F* être sur la corde raide, to be on a tightrope 5. *P* (*surt Mil*) se (faire) porter raide, to report sick 6. *P* (*surt drogues*) high/stoned; être raide def, to be stoned/bombed out of one's mind 7. *V* être raide, to have an erection*/to be as stiff as a poker. (*Voir* **balle 5**; **défoncé**) II *adv F* être raide fou, to be raving mad*/to be (stark staring) bonkers III *nm P* 1. boire du raide, to drink neat spirits 2. hundred-franc note.

raidillard [rɛdijar] *nm Vieilli P* ten-franc note.

raidillon [rɛdijɔ̃] *am Vieilli P* 1. drunk 2. penniless*.

raidir [rɛdir] *vi P* 1. to die* 2. se faire raidir, (*au jeu*) to get cleaned out.

raie [rɛ] *nf* 1. *F* crease of the buttocks* 2. *P* pisser à la raie à qn, to despise s.o.; je te/vous pisse à la raie! two fingers to you! 3. *P* taper dans la raie/miser la raie (à qn), to sodomize* (s.o.).

raiguisé [rɛgize] *a P* (*au jeu*) cleaned out.

rail [raj] *nm P* (*drogues*) dose/line (of cocaine).

raille [raj] *nf P* gang/crew (of louts).

raisin [rɛzɛ̃] *nm P* 1. blood/claret 2. wine/ plonk 3. avoir du raisin, to be courageous*/to have guts; prendre un coup de raisin, to get angry*/mad.

raisiné [rɛzine] *nm P* = raisin 1, 2.

rajouter [raʒute] *vtr F* en rajouter, to lay it on thick; n'en rajoute pas! don't exaggerate!/ come off it!

râlant [rɑlɑ̃] *a F* maddening/infuriating.

râler [rɑle] *vi F* to grumble*/to grouse/to gripe; râler en silence, to fume; ça me fait râler de voir ce gaspillage, it really makes me fume/see red/makes my blood boil to see all this waste; laisse-le râler, let him moan; elle râle contre notre retard, she's moaning about our being late.

râleur, -euse[1] [rɑlœr, -øz] *F* I *a* il est terriblement râleur, he's always grumbling/ bellyaching/griping about something II *n* grumbler/grouser/bellyacher.

râleux, -euse[2] [rɑlø, -øz] *a P* mean*/ stingy/tight-fisted.

ralléger [raleʒe] *vi P* to turn up/to show up/ to breeze in/to blow in; (*revenir*) to get back.

rallonge [ralɔ̃ʒ] *nf* 1. *F* nom à rallonge, double-barrelled name 2. *F* additional/extra time *or* payment, etc; une rallonge de trois jours, an additional/extra three days; *F* demander une rallonge (au patron), to ask for a rise/*surt NAm* a raise 3. *P* (flick) knife/ switchblade/shiv.

rallonger [ralɔ̃ʒe] *vtr P* to stab/to knife (s.o.).

ramarrer [ramare] *vi P* to meet up (with s.o.) again.

ramasse [ramɑs] *nf F* (*sports*) être à la ramasse, to lag behind.

ramasser [ramɑse] I *vtr* 1. *P* to arrest* 2. *P* se faire ramasser, to be arrested*/to get picked up/to get nicked (by the police); (*subir un échec*) to fail*/to fall flat on one's face; (*écoles*) to fail an exam/to flunk 3. *F* ramasser un rhume, to catch/to pick up a cold 4. *F* (se) ramasser un PV/une contredanse, to get a ticket. (*Voir* **billet 2**; **bûche I 4**; **cuiller 2**; **culotte 2**; **gadin 2**; **pelle 1**; **traînard**; **valdingue II 2**; **veste 1**) II *vpr* se ramasser *P* to fall (down)/to come a cropper*; *Fig* to fail*/to fall flat on one's face.

ramassis [ramɑsi] *nm F Péj* (a) untidy heap/pile/jumble (of things) (b) bunch/crowd (of people).

ramastiquer [ramastike] *vtr P* = ramasser I.

rambin [rɑ̃bɛ̃] *nm P* 1. faire du rambin à qn, to flatter* s.o./to butter s.o. up; (*faire la cour*) to make up to s.o./to try and get off with s.o./ to sweet-talk s.o. 2. excuse; **marcher au rambin**, to try to make amends/to wriggle out (of it)/to try to get out (of it).

rambiner [rɑ̃bine] *P* I *vtr* 1. rambiner le coup, to reach a peaceful settlement/to sort things out; ça devrait rambiner vos affaires, that should put things straight for you 2. rambiner qn, to become reconciled with s.o./to patch things up with s.o. 3. to put new life into (s.o.)/to cheer (s.o.) up/to buck (s.o.) up II *vi* 1. to arrive/to turn up 2. to apologize 3. to become reconciled/to make peace; il vaut mieux rambiner, it's better to patch things up III *vpr* **se rambiner** = rambiner le coup; (**rambiner I 1**).

rambineur, -euse [rɑ̃binœr, -øz] *n P* 1. peace-maker/patcher-up (of quarrels) 2. flatterer*/fast-talker.

rambot [rɑ̃bo] *nm P* = **rembo(t)**.

rambour [rɑ̃bur] *nm P* = **rembour**.

ramdam [ramdam] *nm P* uproar*/noise/din/ row/racket; faire du ramdam, to make a din/ to kick up a row; (*rouspéter*) to grumble*/to bellyache; (*protester*) to protest; arrêtez ce ramdam! stop this racket!/cut it out!

rame [ram] *nf P* 1. avoir la rame, to be lazy*/bone idle 2. ne pas (en) faire/fiche(r)/ foutre une rame, to sit around and do nothing; to footle about; il n'en fout pas une rame, he doesn't do a stroke; he does damn-all/fuck-all/piss-all; he just pisses around.

ramée [rame] *nf P* = **rame 2**.

ramenard, -arde [ramnar, -ard] *P a* pretentious/self-important.

ramener [ramne] I *vtr P* ramener sa gueule/la ramener, (*intervenir dans une conversation*) to butt into the conversation/to stick in one's oar; (*rouspéter*) to grumble*/to grouse/to gripe/to bellyache; (*protester*) to protest; (*faire le prétentieux*) to show off*/to think a lot of oneself/to come the acid. (*Voir* **fraise 4**) II *vpr* **se ramener** *F* to arrive*/to turn up/to roll up/to show up/to blow in; alors, tu te ramènes? are you coming, then?

rameneur, -euse [ramnœr, -øz] *a P* = **ramenard, -arde**.

ramer [rame] I *vtr F* il s'y entend comme à ramer des choux, he hasn't a clue/he hasn't got the slightest; he doesn't know which end of a cow you get the milk from II *vi* 1. *P* (bien) ramer, to work* hard/to slog away 2. *P*

to get tired* 3. *Vieilli V* to have sex*/to dip one's wick/to get one's end away.

ramier [ramje] *P* I *a* lazy II *nm* lazybones/ (lazy) bum.

ramolli, -ie [ramɔli] *F* I *a* soft (in the head)/half-witted II *n* dodderer.

se ramollir [sǝramɔlir] *vpr F* to go/to get soft (in the head).

ramollo(t) [ramɔlo] I *a F* il est un peu ramollo(t), he's gone a bit soft in the head/a bit gaga II *nm* 1. *F* un vieux ramollo(t), a dodderer/a has-been/an old fogey*/an old fuddy-duddy 2. *V* masturbation*; se taper un ramollo(t), to masturbate*.

ramoner [ramɔne] *vtr* 1. *P* to reprimand* (s.o.)/to haul (s.o.) over the coals/to bawl (s.o.) out; je l'ai ramoné de la belle façon, I didn't half tell him off 2. *P* (*au jeu*) to clean (s.o.) out/to take (s.o.) to the cleaners 3. *V* ramoner une femme, to have sex* with a woman/to screw a woman.

rampant [rɑ̃pɑ̃] *nm* 1. *F* (*aviation*) les rampants, the ground staff/the kiwis 2. *P* taxi/cab.

rampe [rɑ̃p] *nf* 1. *P* lâcher la rampe, to die*/to kick the bucket 2. *F* (*a*) tenir bon la rampe, to be in good health/be still going strong (*b*) tiens bon la rampe! look after yourself!/keep your pecker up!/*surt NAm* hang in there! 3. *P* il y a de la merde après la rampe, there's been a (serious) dispute/the shit hit the fan.

ramper [rɑ̃pe] *vi F* 1. to drive slowly/to crawl 2. (*se soumettre*) to crawl/to grovel (devant qn, to s.o.).

ramponneau, *pl* **-eaux** [rɑ̃pɔno] *nm P* blow*; flanquer un ramponneau à qn, to thump/to hit s.o. (*esp* in a fight).

ramponner [rɑ̃pɔne] *vtr P* to thump/to hit (s.o.).

rancard [rɑ̃kar] *nm P* = **rencard**.

rancarder [rɑ̃karde] *P* = **rencarder I, II**.

rancart [rɑ̃kar] *nm F* mettre/filer/flanquer au rancart, to discard/to shelve (sth); to retire (officer, official); nous avons filé son projet au rancart, we've got rid of/got shot of/ slung out his idea; elle est au rancart, she's on the shelf.

rangé [rɑ̃ʒe] *a F* être rangé des voitures, to retire from active life; *esp* to be a reformed character/to have settled down; ce voleur est rangé des voitures, this thief* has reformed/ gone straight.

rangeur [rɑ̃ʒœr] *nm A P* swindler*/cheat/

con artist.

ranquiller [rɑ̃kije] *vtr & i F & P* = **renquiller.**

rantanplan [rɑ̃tɑ̃plɑ̃] *nm P* faire qch au
rantanplan, to use bluff/to try it on.

raoul [raul] *nm P* 1. person with old-
fashioned *or* out-dated ideas/square 2. good-
for-nothing/nonentity. (*Voir* **cool 1**)

raousse! [raus] *int P* get out!

raousser [rause] *vtr P* to turf (s.o.) out.

raouste! [raust] *int P* = **raousse!**

raouster [rauste] *vtr P* = **raousser.**

rap [rap] *nm F Mus* rap.

rapapillotage [rapapijɔtaʒ] *nm*, **rapa-
pilloter** [rapapijɔte] *vtr*, **se rapapillo-
ter** *vpr F* = **rabibochage, rabibocher, se
rabibocher.**

rape, râpe [rap, rɑp] *nf P Péj* guitar.

râpé [rɑpe] *a P* c'est râpé, it's no good/it's
done for/it's had it/it's a flop.

râper [rɑpe] *vtr* 1. *Vieilli P* les râper à qn, to
bore* s.o. rigid; il me les râpe, he's a dreadful
bore*/he's a real pain 2. *V* to have sex* with
(a woman)/to have it away with (a woman).

rapiat, -ate [rapja, -at] *F* **I** *a* miserly*/
stingy/tight **II** *n* miser*/skinflint.

rapide [rapid] *F* **I** *nm* c'est un rapide, he's
quick on the uptake/he's smart/he catches on
quick; there are no flies on him **II** *adv* rapide
vite fait, quickly/swiftly.

rapido(s) [rapido(s)] *adv P* very quickly*/at
the double/quick as a flash/pdq/pronto.

rapière [rapjɛr] *nf Vieilli P* knife/dagger.

rapiérer [rapjere] *vtr Vieilli P* to knife/to
stab/to stick (s.o.).

raplapla(t) [raplapla] *a F* (*personne*)
exhausted*; washed out/frazzled.

rapper [rape] *vi F Mus* to rap.

rappeur [rapœr] *nm F Mus* rapper.

(se) rappliquer [(sə)raplike] *vi & pr P* to
return/to rush back/to dash back; rappliquer à
la maison, to make tracks (for home); il a
rappliqué à minuit, he rolled in at midnight;
rappliquer sur qn, to make a bee-line for
s.o.

rapport [rapɔr] *nm* 1. *F* rapport à ...,
because of .../on account of .../about ...; je ne
dirai rien, rapport à ton père, I won't say anything because of your father 2. *F* (*surt écoles*)
faire des rapports, to be a sneak/to tell tales
3. *P* (*prostituée*) être d'un bon rapport, to be
a good earner/a good meal-ticket (*for her
pimp*).

rapporter [rapɔrte] *vi F* to (be a) sneak/to

be a telltale; il est toujours à rapporter, he's
always telling tales; rapporter sur le compte
de qn, to tell on s.o.

rapporteur, -euse [rapɔrtœr, -øz] *n F*
telltale/sneak.

râpure [rɑpyr] *nf P* bore*/drag; awful grind.

raquedal [rakdal] *nm P* miser*/skinflint.

raquer [rake] *vi P* to pay* up/to cough up;
c'est moi qui ai dû raquer, I had to fork out/
shell out the cash; ils se feront raquer
jusqu'au dernier sou, they'll screw you for
every penny you've got.

raquette [rakɛt] *P* 1. foot* 2. = **racket.**

rare [rar] *a F* unexpected/surprising; tu crois
qu'elle viendra? – ça serait rare, do you
think she'll come? – I'd be surprised (if she
did); ça n'aurait rien de rare, that wouldn't
be anything out of the ordinary.

rarranger [rarɑ̃ʒe] *vtr P* se faire rarranger,
(*duper*) to be swindled/diddled/overcharged;
(*blesser*) to get hurt/wounded; (*contracter
une maladie vénérienne*) to catch VD*/to cop
a dose.

ras [rɑ] *a P* en avoir ras le bol/le bonbon/la
coiffe, to be fed up* (to the back teeth) (with
it)/to have had one's fill (of it); j'en ai ras le
bol, I've had it up to here; ras la guerre!
down with war! (*Voir* **bol 4**; **pâquerette 3**;
ras-le-bol)

rasant [razɑ̃] *a F* (very) boring (person,
speech, etc); qu'il est rasant, ton vieux! your
old man's a real bore*/drag/pain!

rasdep [razdep] *nm P* (*verlan de pédéraste*)
homosexual*/homo.

rase [raz] *nm P* 1. priest* 2. prison chaplain.

rase-bitume [razbitym] *P* **I** *a inv* quotidien
rase-bitume, tabloid/popular newspaper; rag;
les quotidiens rase-bitume, the gutter press **II**
nm undersized* person/(little) runt/pipsqueak.

rase-pet [razpɛ] *nm inv P* (*veston*) rase-pet,
(man's) short jacket; bum-freezer.

raser [raze] *F* **I** *vi* demain on rase gratis,
that'll be the day! **II** *vtr* to bore* (s.o.); ça
me rase, this bores me to tears/this bores me
rigid **III** *vpr* **se raser** to be bored* (stiff).

raseur, -euse [razœr, -øz] *n F* (*personne*)
bore*; ce qu'elle est raseuse! she's a real
pain/drag!

rasibe [razib] *nm P* razor.

rasibus [rɑzibys] *F* **I** *adv* (*a*) couper
rasibus, to cut it close/fine (*b*) la balle m'est
passée rasibus de l'oreille, the bullet grazed
my ear **II** *int* (*a*) rasibus! nothing doing! (*b*)
... et puis rasibus! ... and then it was all over!

rasif [razif] *nm P* razor.

ras-le-bol [rɑlbɔl] *P* I *nm* 1. j'en ai/(il) y en a ras-le-bol (de tes histoires), I'm fed up (with your nonsense)/I'm sick to the back teeth (of your nonsense) 2. complete dissatisfaction *or* disgust; exasperation; 68 dans les facs, c'était le ras-le-bol, students in '68 had just about had enough (of everything); le ras-le-bol des jeunes, the dissatisfaction of the young II *int* enough! tu ne vas pas recommencer! ras-le-bol! don't start that again! enough's enough! (*Voir* **bol 4**; **ras**)

ras-le-cul [rɑlky] *nm P* = **ras-le-bol**.

rasoir [razwar] *F* I *a* boring; ce que c'est rasoir! what a bore/bind/drag! II *nm* (*personne*) bore*/drag; quel rasoir! what a pain in the neck!

rassis [rasi] *nm V* se coller/se taper un rassis, to masturbate*.

rasta¹ [rasta] *nm & f P* (= *rastafari*) rastafarian/rasta; musique rasta, rasta music; coiffure rasta, dreadlocks.

rasta² *nm*, **rastaque** [rastak] *nm*, **rastaquouère** [rastakwɛr] *nm F Péj* flashy foreign adventurer (*esp* from South America).

rat [ra] *nm* 1. *F* (*a*) voir les rats, to have persecution mania (*b*) voir les rats bleus, to see pink elephants/to have the DT's/to have the screaming abdabs 2. *P* c'est un rat, he's a miser*; *a* être rat, to be miserly*/mean/stingy; ce qu'il est rat! what a skinflint! 3. *F* être fabriqué/fait/paumé comme un rat, to be caught out/to be cornered/to be done for/to be caught like a rat (in a trap) 4. *F* s'embêter/s'ennuyer/s'emmerder comme un rat mort, to be bored* stiff 5. *F* mon petit rat, my darling*/my pet 6. *F* rat de bibliothèque, bookworm 7. *F* rat d'église, constant churchgoer 8. *F* rat (d'hôtel), hotel thief 9. *F* petit rat (d'Opéra), young ballet pupil (used as an extra) 10. *P* il a bouffé du rat, you can't see him for dust 11. *F Péj* face de rat, repulsive face/rat-face/ratbag.

rata [rata] *nm P* (*a*) (*nourriture, repas*) grub/nosh/chow; nous avons eu un maigre rata, we had a lousy meal; ne pas s'endormir sur le rata, to be alert/wide awake; not to fall asleep on the job (*b*) bean *or* potato stew. (*Voir* **ratatouille 1**)

ratage [rataʒ] *nm F* botching/bungling/messing up.

ratatiner [ratatine] *vtr P* 1. to kill*/to bump off 2. to destroy/to smash up 3. to beat (s.o.) up*/to work (s.o.) over.

ratatouille [ratatuj] *nf P* 1. (*a*) stew (*b*) poor-quality food/pigswill 2. thrashing/beating-up*/pasting.

ratatouiller [ratatuje] *vi P* (*moteur*) to miss/to misfire/to splutter.

rate [rat] *nf F* se dilater la rate, to have a good laugh/to split one's sides laughing. (*Voir* **se fouler 2**)

raté, -ée [rate] *n F* (*personne*) failure*/dud/washout.

râteau, *pl* **-eaux** [rɑto] *nm P* comb; tu devrais te donner un coup de râteau, you should put a comb through your hair.

râtelier [rɑtəlje] *nm F* 1. manger au râtelier de qn, to live at s.o.'s expense/to scrounge off s.o.; manger/bouffer à deux râteliers, manger/bouffer à tous les râteliers, to serve several causes or work for several people with only profit in mind; to take one's profit where one finds it; to make the most of what comes along; il mange à tous les râteliers, it's all grist to his mill 2. remettre ses armes au râtelier, to leave the service 3. (set of) false teeth/dentures. (*Voir* **foin 1**)

rater [rate] *vtr F* il n'en rate pas une! he's always putting his foot in it!/he's always making a mess of things!

ratiboiser [ratibwaze] *vtr P* 1. (*a*) ratiboiser qch à qn, to do s.o. out of sth; to nick/to pinch sth from s.o. (*b*) ratiboiser sur les notes de frais, to fiddle the expenses 2. (*surt au jeu*) to fleece (s.o.)/to clean (s.o.) out/to take (s.o.) to the cleaners; je suis complètement ratiboisé, I'm flat broke/*Br* stony broke/*Br* skint 3. se faire ratiboiser la colline/les tif(fe)s, to get a haircut.

ratiche¹ [ratiʃ] *nf P* 1. knife/chiv/shiv 2. *pl* ratiches, teeth*/gnashers.

ratiche² *nm*, **ratichon** [ratiʃɔ̃] *nm P Péj* priest*.

ratichonne [ratiʃɔn] *nf P Péj* mother superior (*of a convent*).

ratier [ratje] *nm P* prisoner.

ratière [ratjɛr] *nf F* prison*/nick/slammer.

ration [rasjɔ̃] *nf F* 1. avoir sa ration, to have had one's share/fill (of sth); ça va, j'ai eu ma ration de critiques, that'll do! I've had my share of criticism/I've had enough criticism for one day 2. avoir sa ration, (*pour une femme*) to be satisfied sexually/to have had a good screw.

ratissage [ratisaʒ] *nm F* les flics étaient en train de faire un ratissage du quartier, the cops were combing the area/doing a house-to-house search.

ratissé [ratise] *a P* 1. ruined/done for 2. penniless*/broke/cleaned out.

ratisser [ratise] *vtr* 1. *F* to search/to comb (a district); **la police a ratissé tout le quartier**, the police searched/combed the entire district 2. *P* to fleece* (s.o.)/to clean (s.o.) out/to take (s.o.) to the cleaners 3. *F* **ratisser large**, to gather as many elements as possible; *Pol* to get as many votes as possible; *vi* **pour obtenir une majorité, le parti a dû ratisser large**, to obtain a majority, the party had to cast its net as wide as possible.

raton [ratɔ̃] *nm P Péj* North African; Arab*/wog.

raton(n)ade [ratɔnad] *nf P (a) (à l'origine) (surt en Algérie)* punitive raid against the Arabs; Arab-bashing *(b) (par extension)* brutal action *or* attack by a majority group against ethnic minorities; *Br* = Paki-bashing.

ratonner [ratɔne] *vi P* to take part in attacks against ethnic minorities; *Br* = to go Paki-bashing.

raton(n)eur [ratɔnœr] *nm P* person who takes part in attacks against ethnic minorities; *Br* = Paki-basher.

raugmenter [rɔgmɑ̃te] *P* I *vtr* to increase/to put up the price of (sth) II *vi (les prix)* to increase/to go up.

ravagé [ravaʒe] *a & n F* mad* (person); **il est complètement ravagé!** he's quite mad*!/he's nuts! **c'est une ravagée**, she's a loony/a crackpot.

ravageuse [ravaʒøz] *a & nf P* (souris) ravageuse, seductive and flirtatious woman*.

ravalement [ravalmɑ̃] *nm F Péj (maquillage)* make-up; *(chirurgie esthétique)* plastic surgery; face-lift; **elle fait son ravalement**, she's putting on her make-up/her war-paint.

ravaler [ravale] *vtr F* 1. *(brocante)* to take back (an unsold object) 2. *Voir* **façade.**

rave [rɛiv] *nf P* rave(-up).

ravelin [ravlɛ̃] *nm F* second-hand/used car.

ravelure [ravlyr] *nf P* ageing woman*/(old) bat.

ravigotant [ravigɔtɑ̃] *a F* refreshing/invigorating; **un verre de calva ravigotant**, a revitalizing glass of calvados.

ravigoter [ravigɔte] *vtr F* to cheer (s.o.) up/to buck (s.o.) up; **un petit verre va le ravigoter**, a drop of spirits will put new life into him/will perk him up.

ravissant [ravisɑ̃] *nm F* sissy/pansy.

ravito [ravito] *nm Vieilli F* (= *ravitaillement*) food supplies/stocks; **aller au ravito**, to go shopping.

raymond [rɛmɔ̃] *nm P* = **raoul.**

rayon [rɛjɔ̃] *nm F* 1. **c'est mon rayon**, that's right up my street/that's just my cup of tea; **c'est pas mon rayon**, *(ça ne me concerne pas)* that's nothing to do with me/that's none of my business; *(ça n'est pas dans mes compétences)* that's not in my line/that's not in my department 2. **en connaître un rayon**, to know a lot; to be in the know; to be an old hand (at it); to know the score; to know the ropes; **elle en connaît un rayon (sur la question)**, she's well clued up (on the subject) 3. **en filer un rayon**, to put some vim/one's back/a jerk into it; to go all out; **il en a mis un rayon**, he pulled out all the stops/he really got down to it.

razif [razif] *nm P* razor.

razis [razi] *nm P* = **rase 1, 2.**

réac [reak] *a & nm & f F Pol* (= *réactionnaire*) reactionary.

rébecca [rebɛka] *nm P* **faire du rébecca**, *(protester)* to kick up a fuss/a row; **(il) va y avoir du rébecca**, there'll be trouble/ructions; there'll be a hell of a row; **il a fait du rébecca pour avoir ça**, he kicked up a real fuss to get that.

rebectage [rəbɛktaʒ] *nm P* 1. getting back to normal (health, etc); getting back on one's feet (financially, etc) 2. reconciliation/making it up 3. petition for a reprieve.

rebectant [rəbɛktɑ̃] *a P (a)* appetizing *(b)* encouraging.

rebecter [rəbɛkte] *P* I *vtr* 1. to buck (s.o.) up 2. to reconcile (people) II *vi* 1. to become reconciled/to make it up 2. to buck up/to start feeling better III *vpr* **se rebecter** 1. to pick up (physically, financially) 2. to become reconciled/to make it up.

rebecteur [rəbɛktœr] *nm P* doctor/doc/medico.

rebelote [rəbəlɔt] *int F* here we go again.

rebéqueter [rəbɛkte] *v P* = **rebecter I, II, III.**

rebeu [rəbø] *nm P (verlan de* beur*)* 1. Arab 2. = **beur.**

rebiffe [rəbif] *nf F* 1. vengeance 2. **aller à la rebiffe**, to be up in arms about sth.

rebiffer [rəbife] *F* I *vi* **rebiffer (au truc)**, to begin again; to have another go/another shot (at sth). *(Voir* **repiquer II 3)** II *vpr* **se**

rebiffer to strike/hit back; **se rebiffer contre qch,** to be up in arms against sth/to kick against sth/to hit back at sth.

rebiquer [rəbike] *vi F* **elle a les cheveux qui rebiquent,** her hair sticks up.

rebondir [rəbɔ̃dir] *vi P* **envoyer rebondir qn,** to send s.o. packing/to tell s.o. to clear off/to give s.o. the push.

récal [rekal] *a P* (= *récalcitrant*) recalcitrant/rebellious/obstinate/bolshie.

recalage [rəkalaʒ] *nm F* failure/flunking (*in an exam*).

recalé, -ée [rəkale] *a & n F* failed (candidate); **les recalés,** the failures/the flunkers.

recaler [rəkale] I *vtr F* **1.** to fail* (s.o. in an exam); **être recalé/se faire recaler (au bac/en maths),** to fail/to flunk (the baccalaureat/(in) maths) **2.** *Vieilli* to set (s.o.) up again/to put new life into (s.o.); to set (tradesman, etc) on his feet again II *vpr* **se recaler** *Vieilli F* to get back on one's feet again/to get a new lease of life/to recover one's health.

recaser [rəkɑze] *F* I *vtr* **1.** to find another job for (s.o.) **2.** to rehouse/to resettle (s.o.) II *vpr* **se recaser** elle cherche à se recaser, she's looking for a new job; (*se remarier*) she's looking for a new husband/a replacement.

recharger [rəʃarʒe] *vtr & i F* **recharger (les wagonnets),** to refill (glasses) (for another round of drinks); to set them up again.

réchauffage [reʃofaʒ] *nm F* dishing up/rehashing (of sth old as new).

réchauffante [reʃofɑ̃t] *nf P* wig.

réchauffé [reʃofe] *nm F* rehash/stale news; **c'est du réchauffé,** we've heard that (news, joke, etc) before; that's ancient history/that's old hat; (*politique*) it's the same old thing.

rechoper [reʃɔpe] *vtr P* to catch (s.o.) again; to get another go at (s.o.); **je le rechoperai au tournant,** I'll find a way of getting even with him.

récidiver [residive] *vi F* to do it again.

récluse [reklyz] *nf P* (= *réclusion*) imprisonment.

reco [rəko] *nf F Mil* (= *reconnaissance*) recce.

se recoller [sərəkɔle] *vpr P* to be reconciled/to make up; **ils se sont recollés,** they've made it up/they've patched things up.

reconnobler [rəkɔnɔble], **reconnobrer** [rəkɔnɔbre] *vtr Vieilli P* (= *reconnaître*) to recognize.

récré [rekre] *nf F* (*écoles*) (= *récréation*) recreation/playtime/break.

recta [rɛkta] *F* I *a inv* **1.** punctual; **ils sont recta et font un gros travail,** they arrive on the dot and get through a lot of work **2.** trustworthy/honest; **il est pas recta, le mec,** that guy's not to be trusted/there's something fishy about that guy II *adv* (*a*) **payer recta,** to pay on the nail; **arriver recta,** to arrive punctually/on the dot (*b*) immediately; **j'y suis allé recta,** I went there straight away/first thing.

rectifier [rɛktifje] *P* I *vtr* **1.** to break **2.** to kill*; **se faire rectifier,** to get bumped off/done in **3.** to fleece*/to rip off II *vpr* **se rectifier** to get drunk*/to get pissed. (*Voir* **portrait** (*b*))

rectifieur [rɛktifjœr] *nm P* killer; executioner.

recui [rəkɥi] *nm P* (*verlan de* **cuir**) leather jacket.

récupération [rekyperɑsjɔ̃] *nf F* scrounging/cadging.

récupérer [rekypere] *vtr F* to scrounge/to cadge.

redescendre [rədesɑ̃dr] *vi P* (*drogues*) come down (*after the effects of the drug have ended*).

rédimer [redime] *vtr P* **1.** to kill*/to bump off **2.** to destroy/to smash **3.** to beat (s.o.) up*/to work (s.o.) over.

redingote [rədɛ̃gɔt] *nf P* **redingote de sapin,** coffin/wooden overcoat.

redresse [rədrɛs] *nf P* **c'est un type à la redresse,** (*débrouillard*) he knows just what he's doing/he's on the ball/he knows the score/he's got his wits about him; (*énergique*) he's a strong/tough guy/he's got guts.

redresser [rədrɛse] *vtr P* **1.** to look* at/to take a dekko at (s.o./sth) **2.** to recognize/to identify/to spot.

reefer [rifɛr] *nm F* (*drogues*) marijuana cigarette*/reefer.

refaire [rəfɛr] I *vtr F* **1.** **à refaire!** (*au café, au pub, etc*) same again! **2.** to swindle*/to do/to diddle (s.o.); **on t'a refait,** you've been done; **être refait,** to be had; **je suis refait de vingt francs,** I've been done out of twenty francs; **il ne faut pas me la refaire!** don't try it on with me! II *vpr* **se refaire** *F* **1.** (*a*) **se refaire (le portrait),** to get back on one's feet (physically)/to pick up again; **il s'est bien refait,** he's made a good recovery (*b*) **à mon âge on ne peut pas se refaire,** at my age you can't change your ways; **tu ne me referas pas!** you won't change me! **2.** to retrieve/to recoup one's losses; to make/to stage a comeback. (*Voir* **cerise 5**)

réfectionner [refɛksjɔne] *vtr F* to do up (a house, etc).

refil(e) [rəfil] *nm P* **1.** aller au refil(e), to vomit*/to throw up; (*rembourser*) to pay* up; to pay back; (*dénoncer*) to denounce/to grass **2.** faire un refil(e), to make a loan **3.** returned goods/article (*to a shop*).

refiler [rəfile] I *vtr P* **1.** (*a*) refiler qch à qn, to give sth (back) to s.o./to pass sth on to s.o./to slip s.o. sth; elle m'a refilé ses vieilles fringues, she handed her old clothes down to me (*b*) refiler qch à qn, to fob/to palm sth off on s.o.; se faire refiler qch, to get fobbed/palmed off with sth; il m'a refilé sa grippe, he gave me his flu **2.** refiler la comète/la refiler, to sleep (out) in the open. (*Voir* **tubard¹**) II *vi P* en refiler, to be a homosexual*/to be one of them. (*Voir* **comète**; **jaquette 2**; **petit I 4**)

réformette [refɔrmɛt] *nf F* small and insignificant reform.

refouler [rəfule] *vi P* (*a*) to stink* (*b*) refouler (du goulot), to have foul breath.

refourgue [rəfurg] *nf P* selling of stolen goods to a receiver/a fence.

refroidi [rəfrwadi] *nm P* corpse*/stiff; champ/jardin/parc des refroidis, cemetery*/bone-orchard; musée des refroidis, mortuary/morgue. (*Voir* **boîte 8**)

refroidir [rəfrwadir] *vtr P* to kill* (s.o.)/to make cold meat of (s.o.)/to bump (s.o.) off.

refus [rəfy] *nm F* ce n'est pas/c'est pas de refus, I won't say no to that/I don't mind if I do.

se refuser [sərəfyze] *vpr F* il ne se refuse rien, he does himself proud; he doesn't stint himself.

régalade [regalad] *nf F* **1.** (*a*) treating (s.o.)/doing (s.o.) proud (*b*) treat **2.** boire à la régalade, to pour a drink down one's throat without the bottle touching one's lips.

régalant [regalɑ̃] *a F* cela n'est pas régalant, that's no joke/that's not at all funny*/what's so funny* about that?

régaler [regale] I *vi F* to stand treat; c'est moi qui régale, it's my treat/it's my shout/this one's on me II *vtr P* to pleasure (a woman) (sexually) III *vpr* se régaler **1.** *F* to feast (de, on); se régaler de qch, to treat oneself to sth; on s'est bien régalé(s), we thoroughly enjoyed it/we had a great time; (*nous avons bien mangé*) we had a slap-up meal; we did ourselves proud **2.** *V* to have an orgasm*.

regardant [rəgardɑ̃] *a F* (*économe*) careful (with one's money); stingy.

regarder [rəgarde] *vtr F* **1.** regardez-moi ça! just look at that!/get a load of that! **2.** (non, mais) tu ne m'as pas regardé!/tu m'as bien regardé? what do you take me for?/d'you think I'm a mug? **3.** ça te regarde! mind your own damn business!

régime [reʒim] *nm F* régime jockey, strict diet/starvation diet.

reginglard [rəʒɛ̃glar] *nm A F* new wine (*esp* a local wine with a somewhat sharp taste).

reglinguet [rəglɛ̃gɛ] *nm A F* = **reginglard**.

réglo [reglo] *P* I *a inv* (*a*) (*personne*) straight/on the level; c'est un type réglo, he's an all-right guy/he's straight-up/he's on the level (*b*) (*papiers*) in (good) order; ce n'est pas très réglo, it's a bit dodgy; un contrat réglo, a bona fide contract II *adv* il s'est conduit réglo avec moi, he's acted straight with me/he was on the level with me.

regonfler [rəgɔ̃fle] *vtr F* to cheer (s.o.) up/to buck (s.o.) up/to bolster (s.o.) up; to put new life into (s.o./sth); il est regonflé à bloc, he's back on top of the world/he's back to his old self again; ça m'a regonflé, that's put me back on my feet.

régule [regyl], **régulier, -ière¹** [regylje, -jɛr] *a P* = **réglo** I.

régulière² *nf P* **1.** ma régulière, the wife*/the missis/the old lady; the woman I live with/my better half/my old lady; my steady girlfriend **2.** à la régulière, without cheating/honestly/straight up.

reine [rɛn] *nf P* homosexual* who prostitutes himself/queen. (*Voir* **tante 1**)

reins [rɛ̃] *nmpl* **1.** *F* il a les reins solides, he's a man of substance **2.** *F* il ne se cassera pas les reins à travailler, he won't kill himself working **3.** *F* casser les reins de qn, to break s.o./to ruin s.o. **4.** *P* les avoir dans les reins, to have the police* on one's track. (*Voir* **dos 7**; **pied 16**) **5.** *P* être chaud des reins, to be highly sexed/randy/horny. (*Voir* **chaud I 11**) **6.** *F* avoir qch sur les reins, to be saddled/landed with sth **7.** *F* tour de reins, lumbago; se faire un tour de reins, to rick one's back.

relâche [rəlɑʃ] *nf P* faire relâche, to have one's period*.

relance [rəlɑ̃s] *nf P* **1.** aller à la relance, to bring home an unfaithful wife; (*prostituée*) to solicit; (*chercher à s'informer*) to try to get information about sth/to try to get the low-down on sth 2. **venir à la relance,** to try to start an old affair again.

relarguer [rəlarge] *vtr P* to release/to set free.

relax(e) [rəlaks, rilaks] *F* I *a* relaxed; **elle est très relax,** she's very easy-going/laid-back II *adv* calmly/gently III *nf* **relaxe,** rest(ing) IV *int* **relax(e)(, Max)!** calm down!/stay cool!

relègue [rəlɛg] *nf P* transportation (*of criminal*).

relever [rəlve] *P* I *vtr* **relever le compteur/la relever,** (*d'un proxénète*) to take one's share of the prostitute's earnings II *vi* *V* to have an erection*.

se relooker [sərəluke] *vpr F* to change one's look/one's appearance/one's image.

se reloquer [sərələke] *vpr P* to get dressed again/to put one's clothes back on.

relou [rəlu] *a P* (*verlan de* **lourd**) boring*; il est relou, he's a pain (in the neck).

reluire [rəlɥir] *vi* 1. *F* **manier la brosse à reluire,** to flatter* s.o./to soft-soap s.o. 2. *V* to have an orgasm*/to get one's rocks off.

reluisant [rəlɥizɑ̃] *a F* **cela n'est pas très reluisant,** it's not all that wonderful.

reluquer [rəlyke] *vtr F* 1. to eye (stranger, s.o.'s fortune, etc); **reluquer les filles,** to eye (up)/to ogle the girls 2. **reluquer qch,** to covet sth/to have one's eye on sth.

rèm [rɛm] *nf P* (*verlan de* **mère**) mother*/ (the) old lady/(the) old girl.

remballer [rɑ̃bale] *vtr F* = **rembarrer.** (*Voir* **outil 4**)

rembarrer [rɑ̃bare] *vtr F* to rebuff/snub (s.o.); to put (s.o.) (firmly) in his place; **se faire rembarrer,** to get rebuffed/snubbed; to be put in one's place.

rembiner [rɑ̃bine] I *vtr * *vi P* = **rambiner** I, II II *vpr* **se rembiner** *P* = **se rambiner** (**rambiner** III).

rembo(t) [rɑ̃bo] *nm P* rendezvous/meeting/ date.

rembour [rɑ̃bur] *nm P* 1. appointment/ meeting/date/rendezvous; **on avait rembour chez lui,** we had a meeting/we'd arranged to meet at his place 2. *pl* information/gen; **il nous a fourni tout un tas de rembours sur elle,** he gave us a whole load of info/a hell of a lot of info/the low-down on her 3. **aller au rembour,** to pay* up; to pay back/to settle up.

rembrayer [rɑ̃breje] *vi F* to start work again.

remède [rəmɛd] *nm* 1. *P* revolver*/ persuader 2. *P* **un remède d'amour/un remède contre l'amour,** (*femme laide*) a woman as ugly as sin/a perfect fright/an eyesore; (*femme désagréable*) an old bitch/an old slag 3. *F* **remède de cheval,** drastic remedy/kill or cure remedy; **remède de bonne femme,** old wives' remedy.

remettre [rəmɛtr] *vtr F* 1. (*a*) **remettons ça!** let's have another go!/let's begin again! **remettons(-nous) ça!** (*boisson*) let's have another drink!/let's set 'em up again! (*b*) **voilà qu'elle remet ça!** she's at it again! 2. **en remettre,** to exaggerate*/to lay it on (a bit) thick.

remise [rəmiz] *nf F* **être sous la remise,** to be on the shelf.

remiser [rəmize] I *vtr P* 1. **remiser qn (à sa place),** to put s.o. (firmly) in his place/to take s.o. down a peg or two 2. to superannuate (s.o.)/to put (s.o.) out to grass 3. to give (s.o.) up/to drop (s.o.)/to chuck (s.o.)/to walk out on (s.o.) II *vi F* 1. to take it easy*/to slow up/to ease up 2. to settle down (after a merry life).

remontant [rəmɔ̃tɑ̃] *nm F* pick-me-up/ bracer/tonic.

remonte [rəmɔ̃t] *nf P* procuring girls for brothels; talent hunting.

remonter [rəmɔ̃te] *P* I *vtr* **remonter qn,** to find s.o.'s trace/to find s.o. II *vi* **faire remonter,** to acquire/get hold of (sth); **en faire remonter,** to straighten out one's finances.

remoucher [rəmuʃe] *vtr P* 1. to tell (s.o.) off/to put (s.o.) firmly in his place; **se faire remoucher,** to get told off/to get sat on 2. to recognize/to identify; to spot.

rempilé [rɑ̃pile] *nm F Mil* re-enlisted soldier.

rempiler [rɑ̃pile] *vi F Mil* to re-enlist; (*pour un emploi*) to sign on again.

se remplir [sərɑ̃plir] *vpr F* 1. **se remplir (les poches),** to get rich*/to make a packet 2. **se remplir le bide,** to eat* copiously/to stuff oneself.

se remplumer [sərɑ̃plyme] *vpr F* (*personne*) 1. to pick up again (physically *or* financially) 2. to put on weight (again).

remue-fesses [rəmyfɛs] *nm inv P* (any kind of) dance.

renâcler [rənakle] *vi F* to show reluctance (in doing sth); to hang back; **renâcler à la besogne,** to be workshy; **il a accepté en renâclant,** he accepted grudgingly.

renâcleur [rənaklœr] *nm F* shirker.

renard [rənar] *nm* 1. *F* strikebreaker/blackleg/scab 2. *F* tirer au renard, to malinger/to be workshy 3. *P* aller au renard, *Vieilli* écorcher le renard/piquer un renard, to vomit*/to throw up.

renarder [rənarde] *vi P* to vomit*/to throw up.

renaud [rəno] *nm P* 1. être à renaud, to be very angry* (contre qn, with s.o.); to be in a foul temper*/to be hopping mad; to see red; se mettre en renaud/monter au renaud, to get very angry*/to fly off the handle; filer/mettre qn à/en renaud, to make s.o. furious 2. violent protest/row; y a du renaud, there's a hell of a row (going on); chercher du renaud à qn, to pick a quarrel* with s.o./to have a bone to pick with s.o.

renaude [rənod] *nf P* faire de la renaude = **renauder**.

renauder [rənode] *vi P* to grumble*/to complain/to beef/to bellyache.

renaudeur, -euse [rənodœr, -øz] *n P* grumbler/griper/bellyacher.

rencard [rākar] *nm P* 1. information*/gen/info/low-down 2. appointment/meeting/date; elle a rencard avec son mec, she's got a date with her bloke/she's meeting her bloke.

rencarder [rākarde] *P* I *vtr* 1. rencarder qn, to give s.o. the information/to gen s.o. up/to fill s.o. in/to put s.o. wise 2. to make an appointment/a date with (s.o.)/to arrange to meet (s.o.) II *vpr* se **rencarder** to get the info/to get genned up (on sth); je me suis rencardé sur le patron, I got the low-down on the boss.

rencardos [rākardɔs] *nm P* = **rencard 2**.

rencart [rākar] *nm P* = **rencard**.

rencontre [rākɔ̃tr] *nf F* le faire à la rencontre, to jostle s.o. in order to steal from him/her; (*en parlant d'un policier*) to pretend that it is a chance meeting.

se rencontrer [sərākɔ̃tre] *vpr F* comme on se rencontre! it's a small world! comme cela se rencontre! how lucky!/how things do happen! les grands esprits se rencontrent! great minds think alike!

rendève [rādɛv] *nm P* rendezvous.

rendez(-moi) [rāde(mwa)] *nm inv P* vol au rendez(-moi), theft which involves giving change for a (bank)note which one then takes back surreptitiously/ringing the changes.

rendre [rādr] *vtr* 1. *F* ça rend! it works!/it does the trick! ça n'a rien rendu, it was a waste of time 2. *P* rendre ses clefs, to die*/to

check out. (*Voir* **tripes 2**)

rengaine [rāgɛn] *nf F* c'est toujours la même rengaine, it's (always) the same old story; c'est sa rengaine, he's always harping on that subject.

rengainer [rāgene] *vtr F* rengainer son compliment, to save one's compliments/to keep one's compliments to oneself.

rengracier [rāgrasje], **rengrâcir** [rāgrasir] *vi P* 1. to back down/to (beat a) retreat/to give up 2. to cool down/to calm down.

renifle [rənifl] *nf P* 1. la renifle, the police*/the fuzz 2. (*drogues*) cocaine*; être de la renifle, to take/to sniff cocaine/coke.

renifler [rənifle] I *vtr* 1. *P* je (ne) peux pas le renifler, I can't bear/stick/stomach him (at any price) 2. *F* il sait renifler une bonne affaire, he's got a (good) nose for a bargain 3. *P* renifler le coup, to sense (the) danger; to smell a rat 4. *P* se faire renifler, to get found out 5. *P* renifler la comète, to sleep in the open air II *vi* 1. *F* renifler sur qch, to sniff at/to turn one's nose up at sth 2. *P* ça renifle, it stinks/pongs.

reniflette [rəniflɛt] *nf P* (*drogues*) cocaine*/nose-candy.

renquiller [rākije] I *vtr F* to put (sth) back in one's pocket; renquille ton argent, c'est moi qui paie, put your money away, it's on me/this one's on me II *vi* 1. *P Mil* to re-enlist 2. *P* to come back/to return.

renseignements [rāsɛɲmā] *nmpl P* aller aux renseignements, to feel a woman's bottom/to goose a woman/to touch a woman up.

rentes [rāt] *nfpl P* tu penses à mes rentes, chéri? (*prostituée à son client*) how about a little present?

se rentoiler [sərātwale] *vpr P* to put on weight again/to put weight back on.

rentre-dedans [rātrədədā] *nm P* faire du rentre-dedans à une femme, to make amorous advances to/to make a pass at a woman; to get off with/to make out with a woman.

rentrer [rātre] *vi F* 1. les jambes me rentrent dans le corps, I'm exhausted*/I can hardly keep on my feet 2. faire rentrer qn dans la poussière/en terre/cent pieds sous terre, to reprimand* s.o. severely/to tell s.o. where he gets off; (*humilier*) to humiliate s.o./to drag s.o. through the mud 3. rentrer dans qn, (*attaquer*) to pitch into s.o./to go for s.o./to have a go at s.o. (*Voir* **chou I 1**;

dedans 2, 3 (*a*); **lard** 3; **mou** III **1** (*b*); **portrait** (*b*))

renversant [rɑ̃vɛrsɑ̃] *a F* staggering/ stunning/amazing/astounding (news, etc).

renversée [rɑ̃vɛrse] *nf P* change of attitude/change of opinion/about-turn/*NAm* about-face; **faire la renversée**, to change (one's) opinion.

renverser [rɑ̃vɛrse] *vi P* 1. to go on a spree*/to paint the town red 2. to change one's attitude towards s.o./to turn hostile towards s.o. (*Voir* **vapeur**)

rèp [rɛp] *nm P* (*verlan de* **père**) father*/ (the) old man/(the) guv'nor.

repapilloter [rəpapijɔte] I *vtr F* to re-concile (people); to make it up II *vpr* **se repapilloter** *F* se repapilloter avec qn, to become reconciled with s.o./to make it up with s.o.

réparouze [reparuz] *nf P* repair; repairing.

repassage [rəpɑsaʒ] *nm P* 1. murder/ killing/bumping off/doing in 2. swindling/ cheating/diddling; double-crossing.

repasser [rəpɑse] I *vtr P* 1. to kill*/to murder/to bump off/to do in 2. *Vieilli* to swindle*/to cheat/to diddle; to double-cross; **il s'est fait repasser**, he got done; (*au jeu*) he got taken to the cleaners II *vi F* **vous pouvez toujours repasser!** you've got another thing/ think coming! **pour ça, tu repasseras!** you've got a hope!/no chance!/nothing doing*!/no way! (*Voir* **planche 4**)

repaumer [rəpome] *vtr P* to lose (sth) again.

repiquer [rəpike] I *vtr P* 1. to re-arrest; **se faire repiquer**, to be recaptured 2. to take back/to grab back II *vi* 1. *F* to recuperate/to get back on one's feet again 2. *F* **repiquer à un plat**, to have a second helping 3. *P* **repiquer (au truc)**, to begin again; to have another go/another shot; (*reprendre une vieille habitude*) to go back to one's old ways; *Mil* to re-enlist; **repiquer au tapin**, to go back on the game.

replonger [rəplɔ̃ʒe] *vi P* to begin again; to have another go/another try; (*reprendre une vieille habitude*) to go back to one's old ways; **elle a replongé à la cigarette**, she's started smoking again.

répondant [repɔ̃dɑ̃] *nm* avoir du répondant, *F* to have money put by (for a rainy day); *P* (*femme*) to be overweight.

repousser [rəpuse] *vi P* to stink*/to smell foul; **repousser (du corridor)**, to have bad

breath. (*Voir* **goulot** (*b*))

repoussoir [rəpuswar] *nm F* c'est un repoussoir, he's/she's terribly ugly/an eye-sore; he's/she's got a face like the back of a bus.

représentation [rəprezɑ̃tasjɔ̃] *nf F* être toujours en représentation, to be always try-ing to impress/showing off/putting on an act.

requimpe [rəkɛ̃p] *nf Vieilli P* full-length coat.

requimpette [rəkɛ̃pɛt] *nf Vieilli P* (short) jacket.

requin [rəkɛ̃] *nm F* tough dealer*/shark.

requinquant [rəkɛ̃kɑ̃] *F* I *nm* tonic/pick-me-up/reviver II *a* (drink, etc) that bucks you up/perks you up.

requinquer [rəkɛ̃ke] I *vtr F* 1. (*a*) to smarten (s.o.) up/to spruce (s.o.) up (*b*) to give (a place) a face-lift/to posh up (a place) 2. to buck (s.o.) up; **ça vous requinque**, (*boisson*) it's got a kick in it II *vpr* **se requinquer** *F* 1. (*a*) to smarten oneself up (*b*) to get a new set of clothes 2. to buck up/ perk up (after an illness).

résiné [rezine] *nm P* = **raisin 1, 2**.

respectueuse [rɛspɛktɥøz] *nf Vieilli P* prostitute*/tart.

respirante [rɛspirɑ̃t] *nf P* mouth*.

respirer [rɛspire] *vtr P* 1. dur à respirer, incredible/hard to swallow 2. to tolerate/bear (s.o.); **je ne peux pas la respirer**, I can't stick her.

respirette [rɛspirɛt] *nf P* (*drogues*) cocaine*/nose-candy.

resquillage [rɛskijaʒ] *nm F* gate-crashing; getting in without paying; (*dans le métro, etc*) fare-dodging.

resquille [rɛskij] *nf F* faire de la resquille = **resquiller**.

resquiller [rɛskije] *vtr & i F* to gate-crash; to get in/sneak in without paying; (*dans le métro, etc*) to dodge paying one's fare.

resquilleur, -euse [rɛskijœr, -øz] *n F* 1. uninvited guest/gate-crasher; **roi des resquilleurs**, champion gate-crasher 2. (*dans une queue*) queue-jumper; (*dans le métro, etc*) fare-dodger.

ressaut [rəso] *nm P* 1. **mettre/foutre qn en/à ressaut**, to get on s.o.'s nerves/to drive s.o. mad/to get s.o.'s goat 2. **faire du ressaut/aller au ressaut**, to rebel/to revolt/to be up in arms (about sth).

ressauter [rəsote] *vi P* (*a*) to protest/to rebel/to be up in arms (*b*) **faire ressauter qn**, to provoke s.o. (to anger)/to make s.o. blow his stack.

ressauteur [rəsotœr] *nm* P rebel/agitator; barrack-room lawyer.

ressent [rəsɑ̃] *nm* P warning/danger; **aller au ressent/porter le ressent**, to alert the police*.

se ressentir [sərəsɑ̃tir] *vpr* P (*a*) **s'en ressentir pour qch**, to feel fit for sth/to feel up to sth; **je ne m'en ressens pas de faire ça**, I don't feel up to doing that (*b*) **s'en ressentir pour qn**, to have a liking for s.o./to be keen on s.o./to be struck on s.o.

restau [rɛsto] *nm* F restaurant; **restau-U**, university restaurant/canteen. (*Voir* **RU**)

rester [rɛste] *vi* F **y rester**, to die*; to be killed (on the spot); **cette fois, tu vas y rester!** this time your number's up!/you've had it this time! (*Voir* **carafe 3; flan 7; plan 1**)

restif [rɛstif] *nm* P restaurant.

resto [rɛsto] *nm* F restaurant.

resucé, -ée [rəsyse] F **I** *a* stale (news, etc) **II** *nf* resucée (*a*) rehash (of book, etc) (*b*) **une resucée**, a drop more; (**on en boit**) **une petite resucée?** (how about) another little drink?/ how about another?

retailler [rətɑje] *vi* P to hesitate/to pull back.

rétamé [retame] *a* P 1. drunk*/tight/canned; **il était complètement rétamé**, he was completely pissed 2. (*machine*) out of order/ broken; **la téloche est rétamée**, the telly's knackered/wrecked 3. penniless*/skint/flat broke.

rétamer [retame] **I** *vtr* P 1. to clean (s.o.) out (at gambling)/to take (s.o.) to the cleaners 2. to break/wreck/knacker (sth); **elle a rétamé la bagnole**, she wrecked the car **II** *vpr* **se rétamer** P 1. to fall down*/to come a cropper 2. to flunk/to fail*; **je me suis rétamé à mon exam**, I flunked my exam 3. to get (completely) drunk*/to get totally pissed/to get canned.

retape [rətap] *nf* F 1. (*a*) (*prostituée*) **faire (de) la retape**, to solicit*/to hustle/to be on the game; **être à la retape**, to be on the beat (*b*) **faire (de) la retape**, to tout (around)/to hustle; to go scouting for customers, volunteers, etc 2. cheap/vulgar publicity.

retaper [rətape] **I** *vtr* F 1. (*a*) to patch up/to do up (an old house, etc); to repair/to fix (up) (in a perfunctory way); to straighten (bed) (*b*) **se retaper les cheveux**, to straighten one's

hair 2. to buck (s.o.) up/to cheer (s.o.) up; **prends ça, ça te retapera**, drink that, it'll set you up (again); **se retaper le moral**, to buck up/to (begin to) feel better 3. to fail (a candidate in an exam) **II** *vpr* **se retaper** F 1. to perk up (after an illness)/to get back on one's feet/to get back to one's old self 2. to recover from a financial setback/to get back on one's feet.

retapissage [rətapisaʒ] *nm* P **passer au retapissage**, to submit to an identification parade.

retapisser [rətapise] *vtr* P to identify/to recognize; **il a été retapissé par les flics**, he was spotted/clocked by the cops.

retenir [rət(ə)nir] *vtr* F (*a*) **je te retiens!** I'll get my own back on you for that!/I shan't forget you in a hurry! (*b*) **je la retiens, celle-là**, I'll get my own back for that! (*c*) **pour le tact, je te retiens!** talk about tact!

se retirer [sərətire] *vpr* P to practise coitus interruptus.

retourne [rəturn] *nf* F **avoir les bras à la retourne/P les avoir à la retourne**, to be lazy*/to be (bone) idle; to be workshy. (*Voir* **bras 1**)

retourné [rəturne] *a* 1. P **avoir les pieds retournés**, to be lazy*. (*Voir* **bras 1**) 2. F **être tout(e) retourné(e)**, to be all of a dither/to be all shook up.

retourner [rəturne] **I** *vtr* 1. F (*bouleverser*) to shake/to shock (s.o.); **ça m'a tout retourné(e)**, that gave me quite a turn. (*Voir* **crêpe 1; vapeur**) 2. *vi* P **en retourner**, to take to prostitution/to go on the game. (*Voir* **sang 6**) **II** *vpr* **s'en retourner** F 1. to grow old/to age 2. **elle ne s'en retourne pas du tout**, she's not interested in it at all/she couldn't care less about it.

rétro [retro] F **I** *nm* 1. (= *rétroviseur*) driving mirror/rear-view mirror 2. pre-1960s style **II** *a inv* pre-1960s-style (film, dress, fashion, etc).

retrousser [rətruse] *vtr* P 1. to earn (money) (*esp* dishonestly); **il en a retroussé**, he made a penny or two 2. **elle en retrousse**, she lives on her charms.

se retrouver [sərətruve] *vpr* F 1. **s'y retrouver**, (*rentrer dans ses frais*) to recover one's expenses/to break even 2. **on se retrouvera**! I'll get my own back!/I'll get even (with you)!

reum [rœm] *nf* P = **rèm**.

reunoi [rønwa] *a* P (*verlan de* **noir**) black.

reup [rœp] *nm P* = **rèp.**

réussi [reysi] *a F Iron* c'est réussi, ça! a nice mess you've made of that!/very clever!

réussir [reysir] *F* I *vi* les huîtres ne me réussissent pas, oysters don't agree with me; I'm allergic to oysters; les vacances, ça ne lui a pas réussi, his holiday/vacation didn't do him any good II *vtr* réussir son coup, to do the trick/to bring it off; je n'ai pas réussi mon coup, I didn't bring it off.

revenant [rəvnɑ̃] *nm F* stranger; quel revenant vous faites!/mais c'est un revenant! hello, stranger!/look who's back from the dead!

revendre [rəvɑ̃dr] *vtr F* 1. en revendre à qn, to outwit s.o.; to take s.o. in 2. avoir de qch à revendre, to have plenty to spare; on en a à revendre, we've got loads going begging/ we've got more than enough of it.

revenez-y [rəvnezi] *nm inv F* 1. un revenez-y de tendresse, a renewal of affection 2. il m'a joué un vilain tour, mais je l'attends au revenez-y, he played a dirty trick on me, but (just) wait till he tries it again! 3. avoir un (petit) goût de revenez-y, (*plat, etc*) to taste moreish.

revenir [rəvnir] *vi* 1. *F* je n'en reviens pas! I just can't get over it!/well, I never!/that's amazing! 2. *F* n'y revenez plus! don't do it again! 3. *F* le voilà revenu sur l'eau, he's found his feet again; cette question est revenue sur l'eau/sur le tapis, this question has cropped up again 4. *P* (= *venir*) je reviens de le voir, I've just seen him.

réverbère [reverber] *nm P* être sous les réverbères, (*femme, prostituée*) to be on the streets.

reviens [rəvjɛ̃] *nm F* mon livre s'appelle reviens! make sure you give my book back to me!

réviso [revizo] *nm & f F Pol* revisionist.

revoici [rəvwasi] *prép F* me revoici! here I am again!/(it's) me again! me revoici sans le sou! here I am — broke again! nous revoici à Noël, it's Christmas again.

revoilà [rəvwala] *prép F* le revoilà! there he is again!

revoyure [rəvwajyr] *nf P* à la revoyure! so long!/(I'll) be seeing you!/see you!

revue [rəvy] *nf F* 1. nous sommes de revue, we'll meet again (before long) 2. je suis encore de la revue, I've had all this trouble for nothing; (*être trompé*) I've been swindled again/I've been had again.

rez-de-chaussée [redʃose] *nm inv F Journ* article in the lower half of the page.

se rhabiller [sərabije] *vpr F*. *F* il peut aller se rhabiller, (*comédien, joueur médiocre*) = don't call us, we'll call you 2. *P* se faire rhabiller, to be swindled/done/had.

rhume [rym] *nm P* en prendre pour son rhume, to be reprimanded*/to get hauled over the coals; qu'est-ce qu'il a pris pour son rhume! he didn't half get told off!/he didn't half cop it!

ribambelle [ribɑ̃bɛl] *nf F* long string (of names, insults, etc); toute une ribambelle de gosses, a whole swarm/crowd/bunch of kids.

ribarbère [ribarbɛr] *nm A P* revolver*.

ribote [ribɔt] *nf Vieilli F* binge/bender/ booze-up; faire (la) ribote, to go on a spree*/ on a bender; to have a booze-up; être en ribote, to be drunk*/tight.

ribouis [ribwi] *nm Vieilli P* 1. boot; shoe (*esp* poor quality) 2. foot* 3. cobbler.

ribouldingue [ribuldɛ̃g] *nf Vieilli P* spree; faire la ribouldingue, to go on a spree*/to paint the town red.

ribouldinguer [ribuldɛ̃ge] *vi Vieilli P* = faire la ribouldingue (**ribouldingue**).

riboule [ribul] *nf P* partir en riboule, to go on a spree*/to go out on the town.

ribouler [ribule] *vi F* ribouler des calots/des quinquets, to roll one's eyes (in amazement)/ to goggle.

riboustin [ribustɛ̃] *nm P* revolver*.

ricain, -aine [rikɛ̃, -ɛn] *a & nm & f P* American*/Yank(ee); Ricains, Americans/ Yanks.

ric-à-rac [rikarak], **ric et rac** [rikerak] *F* I *a* il est ric-à-rac, he's very strict II *adv* (*a*) punctually (*b*) strictly/rigorously (*c*) to the last penny; payer ric-à-rac, to pay on the nail (*d*) barely/narrowly; c'était ric-à-rac, it was touch and go/a bit tight.

richard, -arde [riʃar, -ard] *n F* rich* person/moneybags; c'est un gros richard, he's rich*/he's rolling in it/he's absolutely loaded.

riche [riʃ] I *a F* (*a*) excellent*; une riche idée, a splendid idea; comme offre ce n'est pas riche, it's not much of an offer (*b*) ça fait riche! it looks posh! II *adv phr V* baiser qn à la riche, to have anal sex* with s.o./to brown s.o.

ric-rac [rikrak] *a & adv F* = **ric-à-rac.**

rideau [rido] I *nm P* 1. tomber en rideau, (*voiture*) to break down/to conk out 2. faire rideau/passer au rideau, to be done out of sth

II *int* P **rideau!** (that's) enough!/that'll do!/
cut it out!

rider, ridère [raidɛr] *P* I *a* smart/elegant/
distinguished-looking; well-dressed II *nm* (*a*)
elegantly dressed man (*b*) (man's) snazzy
suit.

ridicule [ridikyl] *nm* F bag/handbag.

rien [rjɛ̃] I *indef pron* F (*a*) **ce n'est pas rien!**
that's quite something! (*b*) **pour trois fois
rien,** for next to nothing (*c*) **il sait deux fois
rien,** he knows nothing about anything; he's
dead ignorant (*d*) *Iron* **rien que ça!** is that all!
(*e*) **c'est rien de le dire!** you bet! II *adv* P (*intensif*) very/not half; **il est rien laid!** he's as
ugly as sin! **elle est rien belle!** she's a
stunner!/she's a bit of all right! **elle est rien
chic!** she's right smart!/*Br* she isn't half
smart! **ce serait rien chouette!** that'd be
great! **il fait rien froid!** it ain't half cold!/it's
bloody cold! **il est rien salaud,** he's a real
sod/a filthy bastard*/a son of a bitch.

rien-du-tout [rjɛ̃dytu] F I *nf inv* woman of
easy virtue/pushover/tart II *nm inv* a nobody/
a nothing*.

rif(e), riff(e) [rif] *nm* P 1. (*a*) fire; **coquer/
mettre/coller le rif(e) à qch,** to set fire to sth
(*b*) light (from a lighter); **t'as du rif(e)?**
(have you) got a light? 2. (*a*) argument/
quarrel*; **chercher du rif(e) à qn,** to pick a
quarrel with s.o. (*b*) fight/brawl/punch-up (*esp*
between rival gangs); **ils cherchent le rif,**
they're looking for trouble/for action 3. *Mil*
war(fare); front; firing line; **aller/monter au
rif(e),** to go off to war; to get into the thick of
the fighting; to get into the firing line 4.
mettre qn en rif(e), to make s.o. angry*/to get
s.o.'s goat (up) 5. revolver*/shooter 6. **de rif
(et d'autor),** without more ado. (*Voir*
d'autor; sirop 9)

rif(f)auder [rifode] *vtr* P (*a*) to set fire to/to
burn (*b*) to cook/to heat up (food).

se riffer [sərife] *vpr* P = **se rifler.**

rififi [rififi] *nm* P scuffle/brawl/free-for-all;
faire du rififi, to fight/to have a punch-up;
chercher le rififi, to look for trouble/for aggro.

riflard¹ [riflar] *nm* F umbrella*/brolly.

riflard² [riflar] *a* P = **riflo(t).**

rifle [rifl] *nm* P = **rif 1, 2, 3, 4, 5.**

rifler [rifle] P I *vtr* 1. to set fire to (sth)/to
burn (sth) 2. to pick a quarrel* with (s.o.) 3.
to shoot (s.o.) with a revolver II *vpr* **se rifler**
to fight/to have a punch-up.

riflette [riflɛt] *nf* P *Mil* war(fare); front
(line); **partir pour la riflette,** to go off to war;

to get into the thick of the fighting; to get into
the firing line; **on en a marre de la riflette,**
we're sick of the fighting. (*Voir* **rif 3**)

riflo(t) [riflo] *a* P 1. rich*/plush 2. elegant/
expensively dressed; snazzy; **avoir des goûts
de riflo(t),** to have expensive tastes.

rigodon [rigɔdɔ̃] *nm* F backward
somersault/backward flip.

rigolade [rigɔlad] *nf* F fun/fun and games/
lark; **une partie de rigolade,** a bit of fun/a bit
of a laugh; a rare old time; **tout ça, c'est de
la rigolade,** that's just tomfoolery/that's just
for fun; **prendre qch à la rigolade,** to laugh
sth off; **il prend tout à la rigolade,** he won't
take anything seriously/he thinks it's all one
big joke; **ce n'est pas de la rigolade,** it's no
laughing matter/there's nothing to laugh
about; **c'est de la rigolade/c'est une vraie
rigolade,** (*facile*) it's child's play/it's a cinch;
(*amusant*) it's a right giggle/a real joke. (*Voir*
boyau 2).

rigolard, -arde [rigɔlar, -ard] F I *a* (*a*)
funny*/comical (*b*) full of fun; fond of a joke/a
lark. (*Voir* **boyau 2**) II *n* joker; **c'est un
rigolard,** he likes a laugh/a joke.

rigolboche [rigɔlbɔʃ] *a & n* P = **rigolo I,
II.**

rigoler [rigɔle] *vi* F (*a*) to laugh*/to joke; **tu
rigoles!** you're joking!/you're kidding!/you're
not serious, are you? *Iron* **tu me fais rigoler!**
you slay me!/you make me laugh! **ne me fais
pas rigoler,** don't make me laugh! **pour
rigoler,** for fun/for a laugh; **je ne rigolais pas,**
I was serious/I wasn't kidding/it's no joke;
histoire de rigoler un coup, it's good for a
laugh/for a joke (*b*) to have fun/to enjoy oneself; **ils ont bien rigolé hier soir,** they had a
good time/a good laugh last night.

rigoleur, -euse [rigɔlœr, -øz] F I *a* fond of
a laugh/a joke/a lark II *n* joker; **c'est un
rigoleur,** he's always ready with a joke/he
likes a laugh.

rigolo, -ote [rigɔlo, -ɔt] F I *a* (*a*) funny*/
comical; **c'était d'un rigolo!** it was a
scream!/it was too funny for words!/it was a
(real) killer! **ce n'était pas rigolo,** it was no
joke; **c'est rigolo!** what a lark!/what a giggle!
(*b*) odd/peculiar/surprising; **tiens, c'est rigolo
ce truc-là,** that thing's a bit odd/a bit funny
(*c*) **fille rigolote,** good-time girl II *n* (*a*) joker/
comedian; **c'est un rigolo, ton père,** your
father's a real scream (*b*) (*fumiste*) phoney/
fraud III *nm* *Vieilli* 1. revolver*/gun/shooter/
piece 2. (burglar's) jemmy/*NAm* jimmy.

rigouillard [rigujar] *a A P* = **rigolo I** (*a*).

rigoustin [rigustẽ] *nm Vieilli P* revolver*/gun.

rikiki [rikiki] *a & nm F* = **riquiqui**.

rilax(e) [rilaks] *a P* = **relax(e)**.

rima [rima] *nm P* (*verlan de mari*) husband*/the old man.

rincé [rɛ̃se] *a P* 1. exhausted*/washed out 2. ruined/cleaned out (at gambling).

rince-cochon [rɛ̃skɔʃɔ̃] *nm inv P* white wine and mineral water drunk to relieve a hangover; = hair of the dog.

rincée [rɛ̃se] *nf F* 1. heavy shower; **j'ai pris une rincée**, I got caught in a downpour/I got soaked 2. *Vieilli* thrashing/beating*(-up).

rince-gueule [rɛ̃sgœl] *nm inv P* (after dinner) liqueur *or* spirits.

rincer [rɛ̃se] *vtr* 1. *F* to drench; **se faire rincer**, to get drenched/soaked (in the rain) 2. *P* to clean (s.o.) out (at gambling); **se faire rincer**, to get cleaned out/to get taken to the cleaners 3. *P* to stand (s.o.) a drink; **c'est lui qui rince**, the drinks are on him/he's buying; **se faire rincer**, to be offered a drink 4. *Vieilli P* to thrash (s.o.)/to beat (s.o.) up* 5. *P* **se rincer les amygdales/le bec/la dalle**, to have a drink; to wet one's whistle; to knock back a drink. (*Voir* **œil 24**)

rincette [rɛ̃sɛt] *nf P* nip of brandy, etc (*put into emptied cup or glass*).

rinçure [rɛ̃syr] *nf F* **de la rinçure** (**de bouteilles/de bidet**), poor quality *or* weak wine/beer; dishwater/cat's piss/gnat's piss.

ringard [rɛ̃gar] *P* **I** *a* (*démodé*) old-fashioned/behind-the-times/passé **II** *n* 1. mediocre actor/ham 2. (*personne*) good-for-nothing; nonentity 3. person with old-fashioned *or* out-of-date ideas, etc; square/fuddy-duddy.

ringardise [rɛ̃gardiz] *nf P* old-fashioned ideas; squareness.

ringardiser [rɛ̃gardize] *P* **I** *vtr* to ridicule (sth, s.o.) by accusing it/him/her of being old-fashioned **II** *vi* to be old-fashioned/square.

ringardisme [rɛ̃gardism] *nm P* = **ringardise**.

ringardos [rɛ̃gardos], **ringue** [rɛ̃g] *a & n P* = **ringard**.

ringuer [rɛ̃ge] *vtr & i P* = **ringardiser**.

rip [rip] *nm P* **jouer rip**, to make off/to run away*/to skedaddle.

ripaille [ripɑj] *nf F* feast/spread/tuck-in; **faire ripaille**, to have a good blow-out.

ripailler [ripɑje] *vi F* to feast/to have a good blow-out.

ripailleur, -euse [ripɑjœr, -øz] *n F* carouser/reveller/merrymaker.

(se) ripatonner [(sə)ripatɔne] *vi & vpr P* 1. to walk*/to go by Shanks's pony/to foot it 2. to run away*/to beat it/to blow/to hop it.

ripatons [ripatɔ̃] *nmpl P* 1. *Vieilli* (old, well-worn) boots/shoes 2. feet*/dogs/tootsies; **jouer des ripatons/se tirer des ripatons**, to run away*/to leg it.

ripe [rip] *nm P* = **rip**.

riper [ripe] *vi P* to leave*/slip away/to slope off; **allez ripez!** clear off!

ripincelle [ripɛ̃sɛl] *nm P Mil* = **riz-pain-sel**.

ripolin [ripɔlɛ̃] *nm P* make-up/face-paint/war-paint.

ripou, *pl* **-oux** [ripu] *P* (*verlan de* **pourri**) **I** *a* 1. corrupt/bent 2. **elle n'est pas ripou**, she's not bad/she's a bit of all right **II** *n* corrupt policeman*/bent cop.

riquiqui [rikiki] *F* **I** *a* (*portion, etc*) undersized/puny/measly; **il est tout riquiqui**, he's only pint-sized **II** *nm* 1. undersized* person/little squirt/shrimp/little runt 2. (the) little finger/pinkie 3. mixture of brandy and liqueur; **un petit verre de riquiqui**, a little drop of spirits/a wee dram.

rire [rir] *vi F* **c'était pour de rire**, it was only for fun/it was only (done) for a laugh.

rital, *mpl* **-als**, *fpl* **-ales** [rital], **ritalo** [ritalo] *P Péj* **I** *a* Italian **II** *nm & f* Rital, -ale, Italian*/Eyetie/Wop.

ritournelle [riturnɛl] *nf F* **c'est toujours la même ritournelle**, it's always the same old story.

rivette [rivɛt] *nf P* 1. (*a*) prostitute*/hooker (*b*) prostitute's client*/john 2. *Vieilli* male prostitute.

rixer [rikse] *vi P* (*CB*) to stop transmitting/QRX.

riz-pain-sel [ripɛ̃sɛl] *nm inv P Mil* soldier in the French Army Service Corps.

roberts [rɔbɛr] *nmpl P* breasts*/boobs/tits; **roberts de chez Michelin**, falsies; **une belle paire de roberts**, a nice pair of knockers.

robine [rɔbin] *nf FrC P* methylated spirits/meths.

robinet [rɔbinɛ] *nm* 1. *F* **tenir le robinet**, to hold the purse-strings 2. *F* **ouvrir le robinet**, to start crying/to turn on the waterworks 3. *F* **fermer le robinet**, to shut up*/to put a sock in it 4. *F* **un robinet (d'eau tiède)**, (*personne*) a drivelling bore* 5. *V* **robinet (d'amour)**, penis*.

robineux [rɔbinø] *nm FrC P* drunk(ard)*/wino/alkie/meths drinker.

rockab' [rɔkab] *nm* (*abrév* = *rockabilly*) *F* rockabilly.

rocker [rɔkɛr] *nm*, **rockeur, -euse** [rɔkœr, -øz] *n F* 1. (*musicien*) rock musician; (*enthousiaste*) rock (music) fan 2. rocker.

rodéo [rɔdeo] *nm P* (*dans une voiture volée*) joy-ride/hotting.

rôdeuse [rodøz] *nf F* prostitute*/streetwalker/hooker/hustler.

rognard [rɔɲar] *a F* angry*/in a temper.

rogne [rɔɲ] *nf F* 1. bad temper*; être en rogne, to be in a bad temper/in a huff; se mettre/se ficher/*P* se foutre en rogne, piquer la/une rogne, to get angry*/to get hot under the collar/to get shirty; mettre/ficher/*P* foutre qn en rogne, to make s.o. angry*; ça me fiche en rogne, that makes me see red/that really makes me mad 2. chercher rogne/des rognes à qn, to pick a quarrel* with s.o.

rogner [rɔɲe] I *vi F* to grumble*/to grouse/to gripe II *vtr F* rogner les ailes à qn, to clip s.o.'s wings. (*Voir* **os 9**)

rognon [rɔɲɔ̃] *nm* 1. *F* kidney 2. *pl V* testicles*/nuts/balls.

rognonnement [rɔɲɔnmɑ̃] *nm F* grumbling*/grousing/griping.

rognonner [rɔɲɔne] *vi F* to grumble*/to grouse/to gripe.

rognure [rɔɲyr] *nf P* (low-class) prostitute*/slag/cheap tart.

rogomme [rɔgɔm] *nm P* spirits*/liquor/booze; voix de rogomme, husky/beery voice (of a drunkard).

roi [rwa] *nm F* 1. un morceau de roi, a pretty woman*/a dish/a tasty piece 2. travailler pour le roi de Prusse, to work for nothing/to do sth for love/to get nothing out of it 3. aller où le roi va à pied/va seul/va en personne, aller voir le roi de Prusse, to go to the WC*/to the loo/*NAm* the bathroom; to have a look at the plumbing 4. (*a*) le roi des fromages/des vins, a really good cheese/wine (*b*) roi des resquilleurs, champion gate-crasher; le roi de la pizza/des pizzas, the king of pizzas; le roi des imbéciles, a complete idiot*/a prize idiot; c'est le roi des cons, he's a complete arsehole/*NAm* asshole; he's a real nurd/jerk; le roi des salauds, a real bastard*/a real sod.

romaine [rɔmɛn] *nf P* 1. (drink of) rum mixed with barley water and iced water 2.

être bon comme la romaine, (*bienveillant*) to be too kind for words; (*destiné à être victime*) to be done for/to be sure to get it in the neck.

romance [rɔmɑ̃s] *nf P* piquer une romance, to go to sleep*/to go to bed*.

romani [rɔmani], **romano** [rɔmano] *nm & f F Péj* gipsy/romany/gippo.

rombier [rɔ̃bje] *nm P* fellow*/chap/guy/bloke.

rombière [rɔ̃bjɛr] *nf P Péj* (*a*) woman* (*b*) pretentious and ridiculous (middle-aged) woman (*c*) une vieille rombière, an old hag/an old bag/an old trout/an old bat (*d*) wife*/the missus.

roméo [rɔmeo] *nm F* (= *rhum et eau*) rum and water (drink).

rom'pol' [rɔmpɔl] *nm F* (= *roman policier*) detective novel/thriller/whodunnit.

rompre [rɔ̃pr] *vtr P* ça me les rompt, it gets on my (bloody) nerves/on my tits. (*Voir* **tête 6**)

ronchon [rɔ̃ʃɔ̃] *nm & f inv F* grumbler/grouser.

ronchonnement [rɔ̃ʃɔnmɑ̃] *nm F* grumbling*/grousing/griping.

ronchonner [rɔ̃ʃɔne] *vi F* to grumble*/to grouse/to gripe.

ronchonnot [rɔ̃ʃɔno] *a F* grumbling/grousing/griping.

rond [rɔ̃] I *a P* drunk*; rond comme une barrique/comme une bille/comme un boudin/comme une boule/comme une queue de pelle, dead drunk*/as high as a kite; il est fin rond, he's as pissed as a newt II *adv P* ça ne tourne pas rond, it's not working properly; there's sth wrong/up; elle ne tourne pas rond, she's potty/crackers; she's off her head; she's a bit touched III *nm* 1. *F* faire des ronds de jambe, to crawl/to bow and scrape 2. *P* (en) être/(en) rester comme deux ronds de flan, to be amazed* / flabbergasted / dumbfounded / gobsmacked (by sth) 3. *P* (*a*) il n'a pas un rond, he's penniless*/he's completely broke; j'ai plus un rond sur moi, I'm completely skint; je l'ai eu pour pas un rond, I got it for nothing (*b*) des ronds, money*/dosh; avoir trois ronds, to have some money/to have a bit of cash 4. *P* il n'est pas ambitieux pour un rond/pour deux ronds, he's not the least bit ambitious 5. *F* faire des ronds dans l'eau, to be idle/to twiddle one's thumbs 6. *V* le rond/la pièce de dix ronds, anus*/ring/ring-piece/round eye; donner/prendre/(re)filer du rond, to be a homosexual*/to be an arse-bandit; pousser son rond, to defecate/to have a crap. (*Voir* **baver 2; chapeau 8**)

rond-de-cuir [rɔ̃dkɥir] *nm F* (*a*) clerk (*esp* in government service); pen-pusher; vieux rond-de-cuir, old stick-in-the-mud (*b*) bureaucrat. (*pl* ronds-de-cuir)

rondelle [rɔ̃dɛl] *nf V* 1. anus*/ring/ring-piece/round eye; se manier/se magner la rondelle, to hurry* (up)/to pull one's finger out/to shift one's arse/*NAm* ass; être de la rondelle, to be a homosexual*/to be an arse-man/*NAm* ass-man; casser la rondelle, to have anal sex*/to go in by the back door; casser/défoncer la rondelle à qn, to sodomize* s.o. 2. baver sur les rondelles à qn, to get on s.o.'s nerves/on s.o.'s tits; to give s.o. a pain in the arse.

rondibé [rɔ̃dibe] *nm V* rondibé (du radada), anus*/ring/ring-piece.

rondin [rɔ̃dɛ̃] *nm* 1. *V* turd; poser un rondin, to defecate*/to (have a) crap 2. *pl P* breasts*/ tits.

rondir [rɔ̃dir] I *vtr P* to make (s.o.) drunk*/ to tie one on (s.o.) II *vpr* se rondir *P* to get drunk*/to have one over the eight.

rondouillard, -arde [rɔ̃dujar, -ard] *F* I *a* (small and) fat; plump/chubby/podgy/dumpy II *n* fat person*/fatso/fatty.

ronflaguer [rɔ̃flage] *vi P* 1. to snore 2. to sleep.

ronflant [rɔ̃flɑ̃] *nm P* 1. nose*/conk 2. telephone*/blower/buzzer.

ronfle [rɔ̃fl] *nf P* sleep; aller à la ronfle, to go to sleep*.

ronfler [rɔ̃fle] *vi P* 1. (*a*) to sleep (*b*) ronfler avec qn, to sleep with s.o./to go to bed with s.o. 2. ça ronfle, it's going well.

ronflette [rɔ̃flɛt] *nf P* sleep/snooze/doze/nap; faire/piquer/pousser une ronflette, to have forty winks/to get some shuteye.

ronfleur [rɔ̃flœr] *nm P* 1. telephone*/blower 2. envoyer le ronfleur à qn, to tip s.o. off/to give s.o. the low-down.

ronflon [rɔ̃flɔ̃] *nm P* = **ronflette**.

rongeur [rɔ̃ʒœr] *nm P* (*a*) taximeter/clock (*b*) taxi-driver/cabbie (*c*) taxi/cab.

ronibus [rɔnibys] *nm P* bus.

roots [ruts] *a inv F* c'est roots, it's genuine/ it's the genuine article.

roploplo(t)s [rɔplɔplo] *nmpl P* breasts*/ tits/knockers.

Rosalie [rozali] *nf P Mil* bayonet/toothpick/ (meat) skewer.

rosbif [rɔzbif] *P Péj* I *a* English II *nm & f* Englishman*/-woman; Brit; limey; les rosbifs, the Brits.

rose [roz] I *a F* 1. ce n'est pas bien rose, cette histoire-là, it's a pretty horrific story 2. elle n'avait pas la vie bien rose, she didn't have an easy time of it; her life wasn't exactly a bed of roses; ce n'est pas rose tous les jours! life isn't exactly a bed of roses, you know II *nm F* voir la vie en rose/voir tout en rose, to see everything through rose-coloured spectacles III *nf* 1. *F* ça sent pas la rose/les roses, that doesn't smell at all nice; that smells nasty/that stinks 2. *F* envoyer qn sur les roses, to send s.o. packing*/to tell s.o. to clear off 3. *F* ce n'était pas des roses, it wasn't all plain sailing. (*Voir* **bouton 1; eau 9; feuille 4; pot 8**)

roseaux [rozo] *nmpl P* se faire couper les roseaux, to have one's hair cut.

rosette [rozɛt] *nf V* anus*; amateur de rosette, (active) homosexual*. (*Voir* **chevalier 5**)

rossard [rosar] I *a P* 1. lazy*/idle 2. spiteful/catty/bitchy II *nm P* = **rosse II 1**.

rosse [rɔs] I *a P* (*a*) objectionable/beastly/ nasty/horrid (person); professeur rosse, swine of a teacher (*b*) low-down/rotten/lousy (trick, etc) II *nf P* 1. (*homme*) beast/swine/ rotter; (*femme*) bitch/beast 2. *Vieilli* (*mauvais cheval*) old nag.

rossée [rose] *nf F* une (bonne) rossée, a beating*(-up)/a thrashing/a good hiding.

rosser [rose] *vtr F* rosser qn, to thrash s.o./ to beat s.o. up*/to give s.o. a good hiding; to lick s.o./to hammer s.o.

rosserie [rosri] *nf F* 1. nastiness/rottenness/ bitchiness 2. (*a*) (*mauvaise action*) nasty/ dirty/rotten trick; double-cross; faire une rosserie à qn, to do the dirty on s.o. (*b*) (*parole*) snide/spiteful/catty/bitchy remark.

rossignol [rosiɲɔl] *nm F* 1. unsaleable article/white elephant/piece of junk; vieux rossignols, old (unsaleable) stock; écouler/ passer un rossignol à qn, to sell s.o. a pup; on vous a refilé un rossignol, you've been had/ done 2. skeleton key/picklock/screw 3. noise/ squeak; il y a un rossignol dans la voiture, the car's making a funny noise.

rot [ro] *nm P* belch/burp; faire/lâcher un rot, to belch/to burp; faire faire son rot à un bébé, to burp a baby/to get a baby's wind up.

rotations [rɔtasjɔ̃] *nfpl P* avoir des rotations, to belch/to burp.

roter [rɔte] *vi P* 1. to belch/to burp 2. **en roter**, to have a rough/tough time of it/to go through the mill; (*être plein d'admiration*) to be full of admiration (**pour qch**, for s.o.).

roteuse [rɔtøz] *nf P* bottle of champagne*.

rôti [roti] I *nm F* **s'endormir sur le rôti**, (*au travail*) to dawdle over one's work/to fall asleep on the job; (*en amour*) to be half-hearted in one's love-making/to have one's mind on other things/to fall asleep on the job II *a* 1. *P* **être rôti**, (*compromis*) to be done for; to have lost one's reputation/one's credit; **c'est rôti**, there's no hope/it's hopeless/it's no go 2. *F* **attendre que qch tombe tout rôti**, to wait for sth to be handed to one on a plate/to wait for sth to drop in one's lap.

rotin [rɔtɛ̃] *nm F* **je n'ai pas un rotin**, I'm penniless*/flat broke; I haven't got a bean.

rôtissoir [rotiswar] *nm*, **rôtissoire** [rotiswar] *nf P* crematorium.

rotoplo(t)s [rɔtɔplo] *nmpl P* breasts*/tits/ knockers.

rototos [rɔtɔto] *nmpl P* 1. breasts*/knockers 2. **faire des rototos**, to belch/to burp.

rotules [rɔtyl] *nfpl F* **être sur les rotules**, to be exhausted*/to be on one's last legs/to be fagged out; **mettre qn sur les rotules**, to exhaust* s.o./to wear s.o. out.

roubignolles [rubiɲɔl] *nfpl V* testicles*/ balls/nuts; **j'en ai plein les roubignolles**, I'm fed up* to the back teeth (with it)/I've had a bellyful (of it).

roublard, -arde [rublar, -ard] *F* I *a* crafty/cunning/wily (person); **elle est roublarde**, she's up to every trick II *n* crafty person; wily/cunning devil; **un fin roublard**, a cunning old fox; **c'est un roublard**, he knows a trick or two; he's a wily old bird/he's a crafty (old) beggar.

roublarderie [rublardəri] *nf F* = **roublardise 1**.

roublardise [rublardiz] *nf F* 1. (*caractère*) cunning/craftiness 2. (*acte*) piece of cunning/ of trickery; sly/crafty/cunning trick.

rouchie [ruʃi] *nf P* 1. (low-class) prostitute*/cheap tart/scrubber/floozy 2. woman*/bird.

roucouler [rukule] *vi P* (*dans une vente publique*) to look carefully at an article/to examine an article for a long time.

roudoudou [rududu] *nm F* = coloured toffee (*licked out of a mould*).

roue [ru] *nf F* 1. **mettre des bâtons dans les roues**, to put a spoke in s.o.'s wheel; to throw a spanner in the works 2. (*cyclisme*) **prendre la roue de qn/être dans la roue de qn/sucer la roue de qn**, to follow s.o. closely/to get right behind s.o./to be on s.o.'s tail 3. **la cinquième roue du carrosse**, an entirely useless person *or* thing/NAm fifth wheel; (*dans une entreprise*) passenger 4. **roue de secours**, helpful thing *or* person; right-hand man 5. **en roue libre**, laid-back; free-wheeling 6. **prendre un virage sur les chapeaux de roue**, to go round a bend at full speed.

rouflaquette [ruflakɛt] *nf F* kiss curl.

rouge[1] [ruʒ] *nm* 1. *F* **un coup de rouge**, a glass of red wine; **gros rouge**, coarse red wine/plonk 2. *nm & f F* red/communist/ commie 3. *P* **faire rouge**, to shed blood 4. *P* **mettre le rouge**, (*courses*) to announce the start of a race (and stop the betting); (*s'arrêter de faire qch*) to stop (doing sth); (*rompre avec qn*) to break off with s.o.; (*faire un scandale*) to create a disturbance; **le rouge est mis**, you can't back out now/there's no going back.

rouge[2] [ruʒ] *nf P* the Legion of Honour.

rougeole [ruʒɔl] *nf P* **avoir la rougeole**, to be a member of the Legion of Honour.

rougnotter [ruɲɔte] *vi P* to stink*/to pong/ to whiff.

rouillarde [rujard], **rouille** [ruj] *nf P* bottle (of wine, etc.).

rouillé [ruje] *a P* **être tombée sur un clou rouillé**, to be pregnant*.

rouiller [ruje] *vi P* (*prostituée*) to be without work/without a client; to be resting.

roulant [rulɑ̃] I *a F* very funny* (joke, sight, etc); **c'est roulant!** it's a scream!/it's a killer! **il est roulant!** he's a real scream! II *nm* 1. *F* travelling/door-to-door salesman 2. *P* taxi/cab.

roulante [rulɑ̃t] *nf* 1. *F Mil* field kitchen 2. *P* car* 3. *pl P* **roulantes**, (game of) bowls.

rouleau, *pl* **-eaux** [rulo] *nm* 1. *F* **être au bout du son du rouleau**, to be exhausted*/worn out; (*à bout de ressources*) to be at the end of one's tether; (*près de la mort*) to be on one's last legs; **c'est le bout du rouleau pour lui**, it's all up with him/it's curtains for him 2. *pl V* **rouleaux**, testicles*; **avoir mal aux rouleaux**, to have VD*; **baver sur les rouleaux à qn/ casser les rouleaux à qn**, to get on s.o.'s nerves/on s.o.'s wick/on s.o.'s tits; to give s.o. a pain in the arse/NAm ass 3. *F* **changer de rouleau**, to change the subject; **change(z) de rouleau!** put another record on!

roulée [rule] I *af F* **bien roulée**, (*femme*)

with a good figure/with curves in all the right places/well-stacked **II** *nf* **1.** *F* hand-rolled cigarette*/roll-up **2.** *P* kiss on the mouth/ French kiss **3.** *Vieilli P* donner une roulée à qn, to beat s.o. up*/to work s.o. over.

rouler [rule] **I** *vtr* **1.** *F* rouler qn, to swindle*/to rook/to diddle/to do s.o.; se faire rouler, to be conned/done/had; il m'a roulé de mille francs, he did me out of a thousand francs; rouler qn dans la farine, to make a fool* of s.o./to string s.o. along **2.** *Vieilli F* rouler les cafés, to go from one café/bar to another; to go pub-crawling **3.** *F* en rouler une, to (hand-)roll a cigarette* **4.** *P* se les rouler, to (sit about and) twiddle one's thumbs/to have a cushy time/to do damn all **5.** *P* les rouler, to throw one's weight around. (*Voir* **bosse 2**; **caisse 15**; **escalope 1**; **mécanique 2**; **patin 1**; **pelle 2**; **saucisse 4**) **II** *vi F* **1.** ça roule, (ça va) it's going fine/ things are going well/everything's OK; (*d'accord*) OK/fine (by me); ça roule? how goes it?/how's tricks?/everything OK? ça roule entre eux, they get on (very) well together/they hit it off well **2.** rouler (un peu partout), to knock about (the world)/to be a rolling stone; j'ai roulé, I've been around/I've knocked about (a bit)/I've been places. (*Voir* **bosse 2**) **3.** to throw the dice/to roll the bones **4.** to talk a lot/too much; to shoot one's mouth off; to sound off. (*Voir* **danseuse**; **jante 2**; **or 6**) **III** *vpr* se rouler *F* se rouler par terre, to laugh* uproariously/to fall about laughing; il y a de quoi se rouler par terre, it's a real scream/a killer. (*Voir* **crotte I 4**)

roule-ta-bille [rultabij], **roule-ta-bosse** [rultabɔs] *nm inv F* (*personne*) rolling stone/ drifter.

rouletaille [rultɑj] *nf P* (game of) roulette.

roulette [rulɛt] *nf* **1.** *F* dentist's drill **2.** *F* ça marche/ça va comme sur des roulettes, every-thing's going/working smoothly; things are going like clockwork/like a house on fire **3.** *P* les roulettes, les vaches à roulettes, *Vieilli* policemen* on bicycles/cycle cops; (*on motor-bikes*) police motorcyclists/cycle cops.

rouleur, -euse [rulœr, -øz] **I** *n F* **1.** cheat/ diddler/con artist/swindler*; s.o. who always gets the best of the bargain **2.** (*personne*) (*a*) rolling stone/drifter (*b*) rouleur de cafés/de cabarets, pub-crawler **3.** s.o. who talks too much/who shoots his mouth off **4.** rouleur (de mécaniques), s.o. with superior airs/conceited person; show-off*/pose(u)r **5.** hashish*

smoker/pot smoker **II** *nf P* prostitute*/tart **III** *nf P* **1.** machine for rolling cigarettes **2.** *FrC* hand-rolled cigarette*/roll-up **IV** *a F* conceited/boastful.

roulottage [rulɔtaʒ] *nm F* stealing from parked vehicles.

roulotte [rulɔt] *nf F* vol à la roulotte, steal-ing from parked vehicles; voleur à la roulotte, thief* who steals from parked vehicles.

roulot(t)er [rulɔte] *vi F* = **rouler II 1, 4**.

roulottier [rulɔtje] *nm F* thief* who steals from parked vehicles.

roulure [rulyr] *nf P Péj* (*a*) loose woman*/ slut (*b*) prostitute*/tart/slut.

roupane [rupan] *nf P* **1.** (*a*) (woman's) dress (*b*) lawyer's *or* judge's gown **2.** (town) policeman's uniform.

roupe [rup] *nf*, **roupette** [rupɛt] *nf* **1.** *P* car wheel **2.** *pl V* testicles*/balls.

roupie [rupi] *nf P* **1.** *Vieilli* drop of running mucus/snot; dewdrop; avoir la roupie, to have a runny nose **2.** de la roupie de sansonnet/de singe, worthless* stuff/rubbish/tripe; c'est de la roupie de sansonnet, it's strictly for the birds; it's a load of old rubbish.

roupignolles [rupiɲɔl] *nfpl V* testicles*.

roupillade [rupijad] *nf F* nap/doze/snooze/ forty winks.

roupiller [rupije] *vi F* to (go to) sleep*/to have a kip/to get some shuteye.

roupilleur, -euse [rupijœr, -øz] *F* **I** *a* sleepy/drowsy **II** *n* sleeper/snoozer.

roupillon [rupijɔ̃] *nm F* sleep/nap/snooze; faire/piquer un roupillon, to have forty winks/ to grab some shuteye/to have a kip.

roupillonner [rupijɔne] *vi F* = **roupiller**.

rouquemout(t)e [rukmut] *P* **I** *a* red-haired/ginger(-haired) **II** *nm & f* redhead/ carrot-top **III** *nm* (rough) red wine/plonk.

rouquin, -ine [rukɛ̃, -in] **I** *a F* red-haired/ carroty(-haired)/ginger(-haired) **II** *nm & f F* redhead/carrot-top/copper-nob **III** *nm P* (rough) red wine/plonk.

rouquinos [rukinos] *a P* red-haired/ ginger(-haired). (*Voir* **bada 1** (*b*))

rouscaille [ruskɑj] *nf P* (*a*) (*protestation*) complaint/grouse/beef (*b*) (*action de protester*) grumbling*/bellyaching/beefing/ bitching.

rouscailler [ruskɑje] *vi P* to grumble*/to grouse/to bitch/to gripe/to bellyache/to beef.

rouscailleur, -euse [ruskɑjœr, -øz] *P* **I** *a* grouchy/(always) grumbling* **II** *n* grumbler/ grouser/bellyacher/grump.

rouspétance [ruspetɑ̃s] *nf F* grumbling*/grousing/griping/bellyaching.

rouspéter [ruspete] *vi F* to grumble*/to grouse/to gripe/to bellyache.

rouspéteur, -euse [ruspetœr, -øz] *F* **I** *a* grumpy/grouchy **II** *n* grumbler/grouser/griper/bellyacher.

rouspignolles [ruspiɲɔl] *nfpl V* testicles*. (*Voir* **roubignolles**)

Rousqui [ruski] *nm P* = **Rousski**.

rousse [rus] *nf P* 1. la rousse, the police*/the law/the fuzz; mec de la rousse, prefect of the Paris police; = police commissioner 2. faire de la rousse = **rousser**.

rousser [ruse] *vi P* to grumble*/to grouse/to gripe/to bellyache.

roussi [rusi] *nm F* ça sent le roussi, (*ça va mal aller*) there's trouble brewing; there's danger ahead; we're in for a rough time; (*c'est louche*) it's dubious/fishy.

roussin [rusɛ̃] *nm P* 1. policeman* 2. partner in a crime.

Rousski [ruski] *nm P* Russian*/Russki.

roustasse [rustas] *nf,* **rouste** [rust] *nf,* **roustée** [ruste] *nf P* beating*(-up)/severe thrashing/good hiding; (*défaite*) defeat/hammering/licking; **filer/flanquer une roustée à qn,** to beat s.o. up*/to give s.o. a good hiding/to thrash s.o.

rouster [ruste] *vtr P* to thrash (s.o.)/to beat (s.o.) up*.

rousti [rusti] *a P* 1. done for/ruined; c'est rousti, it's all up 2. être rousti, to be arrested*/nicked.

roustir [rustir] *vtr P* 1. to swindle* (s.o.)/to cheat (s.o.)/to diddle (s.o.) 2. to steal*/to rob.

roustisseur, -euse [rustisœr, -øz] *n P* 1. cheat/swindler*/con artist 2. sponger/scrounger.

roustissure [rustisyr] *nf P* de la roustissure/des roustissures, worthless* stuff/trash/junk/tripe.

roustons [rustɔ̃] *nmpl V* testicles*/balls; baver sur les roustons à qn, to get on s.o.'s nerves/on s.o.'s wick; to give s.o. a pain in the arse.

routard [rutar] *nm P* traveller on foot; hiker.

routier [rutje] *nm F* **vieux routier,** old campaigner/old trouper/old stager/old hand.

royalement [rwajalmɑ̃] *adv F* (a) s'amuser royalement, to enjoy oneself immensely/to have a whale of a time (b) je m'en fiche royalement, I couldn't care less* (about it)/I couldn't give two hoots (for it).

royco [rwako] *nm P* policeman*/copper.

RU [ɛry *ou* ry] *nm F* (*abrév = restaurant universitaire*) university restaurant/canteen. (*Voir* **restau**)

ruban [rybɑ̃] *nm P* 1. road; se taper un bon bout de ruban, to walk a fair way/quite a distance 2. pavement; **faire le ruban,** (*prostituées*) to walk the streets/to hustle; **il a mis sa femme sur le ruban,** he sent his wife out on the game/on the streets.

rubaner [rybane] *vi P* (*prostituées*) to walk the streets/to be on the game/to hustle.

rubis [rybi] *nm F* faire rubis sur l'ongle, to drink to the last drop; payer rubis sur l'ongle, to pay cash on the nail.

ruche [ryʃ] *nf P* 1. nose* 2. se taper la ruche, to eat* heartily/to tuck it away 3. se péter la ruche, to get drunk*/pissed.

rudement [rydmɑ̃] *adv F* c'était rudement bon, it was jolly/awfully/damned good; je suis rudement fatigué, I'm dog-tired/I'm dead beat; vous avez rudement bien fait, you certainly did the right thing.

ruine-babines [ryinbabin] *nm inv FrC F* mouth organ/harmonica.

rupin, -ine [rypɛ̃, -in] *P* **I** *a* (a) luxurious/plush (b) (filthy) rich*/loaded/flush **II** *n* rich* person; c'est un rupin, he's rolling in it; les rupins, the rich, the well-off.

rupiner [rypine] *vi P* 1. (*écoles*) to do well (in an exam); il a rupiné, he's done a good paper; he's given a good answer 2. ça rupine, everything's fine/OK.

rupinos [rypinos], **rupinskoff** [rypɛ̃skɔf] *a A P* elegant/smart.

Ruski [ruski, ry-], **Rus(s)kof(f)** [ruskɔf, ry-], **Russkov** [ruskɔv, ry-] *nm P* Russian*/Russky/Ivan.

S

sabbat [saba] *nm F* **faire un sabbat de tous les diables**, to make an awful lot of noise/a hell of a row; **c'est le sabbat déchaîné**, it's (all) hell let loose.

sable [sɑbl] *nm F* **1.** (*a*) **être (mis) sur le sable**, to be left high and dry/in the lurch (*b*) **être sur le sable**, (*démuni*) to be penniless*/to be down-and-out; (*sans travail*) to be out of work; **mettre qn sur le sable**, to ruin s.o. **2.** **aller dans le sable**, (*train*) to go off the rails/to be derailed.

sabler [sɑble] *vtr F* **sabler le champagne**, to celebrate with champagne/to break open a bottle of champagne.

sableur, -euse [sɑblœr, -øz] *n Vieilli F* hard drinker/drunkard*/boozer.

sabord [sabɔr] *nm* **1.** *Vieilli F* **mille sabords!** shiver my timbers! **2.** *pl P* **les sabords**, eyes*/peepers; **coup de sabord**, searching glance; **donner un coup de sabord à qch**, to give sth the once-over.

sabot [sabo] *nm* **1.** *F* **je vous vois/je vous entends venir avec vos gros sabots**, I can see what you're after; it's pretty obvious what your little game is/I can see you coming a mile off **2.** *F* (*a*) bungler/botcher (*b*) **travailler comme un sabot**, to botch/to bodge one's work; to bungle* sth; to botch/to louse things up (*c*) **jouer comme un sabot**, to play very badly/to be a hopeless player; **il joue comme un sabot**, he can't play for toffee/to save his life **3.** *F* **raisonner comme un sabot**, to talk through one's hat **4.** *F* **dormir comme un sabot**, to sleep* like a log **5.** *F* **il ne reste pas/il n'a pas les deux pieds dans le même sabot**, (*il ne reste pas sans rien faire*) he doesn't remain idle for long/he gets on with the job; (*il est au courant*) he knows what's what; he knows the score; there are no flies on him **6.** *P* old *or* useless article; useless rubbish/junk; dud violin; old tub (of a ship); ramshackle old car*, bicycle, etc **7.** *P* **casser le sabot à une jeune fille**, to deflower a girl/to

pick a girl's cherry.

sabotage [sabɔtaʒ] *nm F* (*a*) botching/bodging/bungling (of work) (*b*) botched piece of work.

saboter [sabɔte] *F* **I** *vi* to botch one's work **II** *vtr* to botch/to bodge/to bungle* (work); to make a bad job of (sth)/to louse (sth) up; to murder (a song, etc).

saboteur, -euse [sabɔtœr, -øz] *n F* bungler/botcher/bodger.

sabouler [sabule] **I** *vtr Vieilli F* to torment/to harass (s.o.) **II** *vpr* **se sabouler** *F* **1.** to dress up (in fine clothes)/to get togged up (in one's best) **2.** to make oneself up/to put on the war-paint.

sabre [sɑbr] *nm* **1.** *F* **le sabre et le goupillon**, the Army and the Church **2.** *V* penis*; **filer le/un coup de sabre**, to have sex*/to get one's end away.

sabrer [sɑbre] *vtr* **1.** *F* to bungle*/to botch/to bodge/to make a mess of (sth) **2.** *F* to make drastic cuts in/to cut great chunks out of (a play, a manuscript, etc) **3.** *F* to criticize* (s.o.)/to run (s.o.) down/to knock (s.o.) **4.** *P* **sabrer une fille**, to have sex* with a girl; **il la sabre**, he's knocking her off; **sabrer qn à la verticale**, to give s.o. a knee trembler/to give s.o. a stand-up job/to have it (off) standing up **5.** *P* to kill*/to eliminate/to knock off/to bump off; (*licencier, renvoyer*) to sack (s.o.)/to throw (s.o.) out.

sabreur [sɑbrœr] *nm* **1.** *F* bungler/botcher/bodger; **sabreur (de besogne)**, slapdash worker **2.** *P* fornicator.

sac [sak] *nm* **1.** *P* (*a*) ten francs (*b*) **avoir le sac/être au sac**, to be (stinking) rich*/to have stacks (of money); **ils ont le sac/il y a le sac**, they've got pots of money/they're absolutely loaded; **avoir la tête dans le sac**, to be penniless*/broke (*c*) **faire/gagner son sac**, to make one's pile (*d*) rich* person; **épouser un sac/le gros sac**, to marry a rich girl/to marry (into) money **2.** *F* **sac à viande**, (*chemise*) shirt; *(sac de couchage)* sleeping bag 3. *F* sac d'os, *(personne)* bag of bones 4. *F* un sac de nœuds/d'embrouilles, a muddle; faire un sac de qch, to dramatize sth/to make a mountain out of a molehill 5. *F (boxe)* travailler le sac, to practise with the punchbag 6. *F* sac percé, spendthrift 7. *P (a)* sac à vin, drunkard*/ boozer/(old) soak/alkie *(b)* homme de sac et de corde, out-and-out scoundrel 8. *F (a)* mettez ça dans votre sac! put that in your pipe and smoke it! *(b) Péj* je les mets dans le même sac, as far as I'm concerned they're all the same *(c)* nous sommes tous dans le même sac, we're all in the same boat 9. *F* prendre qn la main dans le sac, to catch s.o. red-handed/in the act/with his hand in the till 10. *F (a)* l'affaire est dans le sac/c'est dans le sac, it's a (dead) cert*/it's in the bag *(b)* être dans le sac, *(personne)* to be arrested*/to get nicked; *(chose)* to be useless/broken/out of order 11. *Vieilli F* cracher/éternuer dans le sac, to be guillotined 12. *F* habillé/ficelé/fichu comme mon sac, dressed like a guy/tramp/ scarecrow 13. *F* sac à malice, bag of tricks; avoir un nouvel expédient dans son sac à malice, to have another card up one's sleeve; c'est un sac à malice, he's always got something else up his sleeve 14. vider son sac, *F* to get it off one's chest/to make a clean breast of it; *(avouer)* to come clean; *P* to empty one's bowels/to have a clear-out 15. *P* il a reçu une raclée qui n'était pas dans un sac, he got a hiding he won't forget in a hurry 16. *P* stomach* 17. *P* sac à charbon/à carbi, priest* 18. *P* avoir un bras/une guitare dans le sac, to have had an arm/a leg amputated; *(infirme)* to be crippled in the arm/the leg 19. *P* avoir son sac, to have had (more than) enough 20. *V* sac à bites, prostitute*. *(Voir* **embrouille 4; tour I 1)**

sacail [sakaj] *nf P =* **sac(c)agne**.

sac(c)agne [sakaɲ] *nf P* 1. knife/chiv/ sticker; donner un coup de sac(c)agne à qn, to stab s.o. 2. fight with knives.

sac(c)agner [sakaɲe] *vtr P* to stab/to knife/to chiv (s.o.).

sachem [saʃɛm] *nm F* **(grand)** sachem, important person*/big cheese/big white chief.

sachet [saʃɛ] *nm P* sock.

sacouse [sakuz] *nm P* handbag.

sacquer [sake] *F* I *vtr* 1. to dismiss* (s.o.)/ to sack (s.o.)/to give (s.o.) the sack; être sacqué, to get the sack 2. *(noter sévèrement)* to be a tough marker of (student) 3. je ne peux pas les sacquer, I hate their guts 4. sacquer la route, to leave the road (by accident) II *vi (d'un professeur)* to be a tough marker.

sacré [sakre] *a P* damn(ed)/bloody/*NAm* goddam(n); votre sacré chien, that bloody dog of yours/your damned dog; sacré imbécile! you bloody fool! une sacrée voiture, a hell of a car; il a un sacré pot, he's damn lucky/he's got the luck of the devil; c'est un sacré menteur, he's one hell of a liar/a bloody liar; sacré nom de Dieu! (God) damn it (all)! sacré nom d'un chien!/sacré nom de nom! damn and blast (it)!/bloody hell! *(Voir* **baiseuse)**

sacrément [sakremɑ̃] *adv P* damn(ed)/ bloody; il fait sacrément froid, it's damn(ed) cold/bloody cold/jolly cold; elle a sacrément bien répondu, she gave a damn *or* bloody good answer.

sacrer [sakre] *vi Vieilli F* to curse and swear/to eff and blind.

sado [sado] *F (= sadique)* I *a* sadistic II *n* sadist.

safran [safrɑ̃] *nm Vieilli P* aller au safran, to throw one's money away/to chuck one's money about.

sagœur [sagœr] *nf P (javanais de* **sœur)** *(a)* any girl* or woman* *(b)* friend/sister.

sagouin, -ine [sagwɛ̃, -in] *n F* slovenly individual/filthy pig/slob; *(femme)* slut; *(homme)* swine/slob; vieux sagouin, revolting old man.

saïdi [saidi] *nm Vieilli P Péj* North African/ Arab* *(esp* living in France); wog. *(Voir* **sidi 1)**

saignant [sɛɲɑ̃] *P* I *a* tough/full of grit II *nm* tough guy/toughie.

saignée [seɲe] *nf F* faire une saignée à qn, to extort money from s.o./to bleed s.o.

saigner [seɲe] *vtr* 1. *F* to extort money from (s.o.); ils l'ont saigné à blanc, they've cleaned him out/bled him white 2. *P (a)* to kill* (s.o.) with a knife/to stab (s.o.) to death *(b)* ça va saigner! there's trouble brewing!/ there's going to be trouble!/there'll be some aggro! *(Voir* **barder)**

saindoux [sɛ̃du] *nm P Mil* corporal/corp.

saint [sɛ̃] *F* I *a* toute la sainte journée, the whole blessed day II *nm (a)* prendre un air de petit saint, to look as though butter wouldn't melt in one's mouth *(b)* c'est un petit saint (de bois), he's a little prig *(c)* mieux vaut s'adresser à Dieu qu'à ses saints, it's better to go straight to the top.

saint-bernard [sɛ̃bɛrnar] *nm inv F* c'est un vrai saint-bernard, he's a good Samaritan.

Saint-Crépin [sɛ̃krepɛ̃] *nm F* 1. prendre la voiture de Saint-Crépin, to walk*/to go by Shanks's pony 2. tout son saint-crépin, all one's worldly goods.

Saint-Cyr [sɛ̃sir] *Prnm F (d'après l'école militaire de Saint-Cyr)* il ne faut pas être sorti de Saint-Cyr pour ..., you don't have to be a genius to ....

Sainte-Anne [sɛ̃tan] *Prn (jadis hôpital psychiatrique à Paris) F* être bon/fait/mûr pour Sainte-Anne, to be raving mad*/to be fit for the loony-bin; un échappé de Sainte-Anne, a nutcase/a loony/a nutter.

Sainte-Barbe [sɛ̃tbarb] *nf F* 1. c'est la Sainte-Barbe, it's an awful bore/a real drag. (*Voir* **barbe II 3**) 2. *Vieilli* faire sauter la Sainte-Barbe, to put fire to/to light the powder keg; faites sauter la Sainte-Barbe! let everything go to hell!

Sainte-Ginette [sɛ̃tʒinɛt] *nf F* the Sainte-Geneviève library (*in Paris*).

sainte-nitouche [sɛ̃tnituʃ] *nf F* elle fait la sainte-nitouche/elle a l'air d'une sainte-nitouche/elle a un air de sainte-nitouche, she looks as if butter wouldn't melt in her mouth.

Sainte-Touche [sɛ̃ttuʃ] *nf F* pay day.

Saint-Fric [sɛ̃frik] *nm P* money*/dough/ackers.

saint-frusquin [sɛ̃fryskɛ̃] *nm P (a)* tout le saint-frusquin, the whole bag of tricks*/the whole (damn) lot/the whole (kit and) caboodle (*b*) tout son saint-frusquin, all one's worldly goods.

Saint-Ger [sɛ̃ʒɛr] *Prn F* the Saint-Germain-des-Prés district (*in Paris*).

Saint-Glinglin [sɛ̃glɛ̃glɛ̃] *nf F* à la Saint-Glinglin, never (in a month of Sundays); when pigs (begin to) fly; jusqu'à la Saint-Glinglin, till the cows come home; till hell freezes over.

Saint-Jean [sɛ̃ʒɑ̃] *F* I *nm* en Saint-Jean, naked*/in the altogether/in one's birthday suit II *nf* employer toutes les herbes de la Saint-Jean, to leave no stone unturned.

Saint-Lago [sɛ̃lago] *Prn Vieilli P* (the prison of) Saint-Lazare.

Saint-Lundi [sɛ̃lœ̃di] *nf F* faire la Saint-Lundi, to take Monday off. (*Voir* **lundi**)

Saint-Martin [sɛ̃martɛ̃] *nf Vieilli F* c'est (toujours) la même Saint-Martin, it's (always) the same thing.

Saint-Trou-du-cul [sɛ̃trudyky] *nf V* jusqu'à la Saint-Trou-du-cul, = jusqu'à la Saint-Glinglin (**Saint-Glinglin**).

saint-truc [sɛ̃tryk] *nm P* tout le saint-truc, the whole bag of tricks*/the whole (kit and) caboodle/the works.

salade [salad] *nf* 1. *F* jumble/mix-up/hotchpotch; *Journ* bad copy/messy article; en salade, mixed up; mettre tout en salade, to mix everything up/to get things into a muddle/to throw everything into confusion; quelle salade! what a mess!/what a muddle! 2. *F* vendre sa salade, to try and persuade (s.o.) to accept a project, etc; (*chanter en public*) to sing (a song) in public; (*écoles*) to give a lesson/to lecture 3. *F* sales talk; vendre qch avec beaucoup de salade, to hand out the sales patter/spiel/talk in order to sell sth 4. *Vieilli P* faire brin de salade, to leave without paying; to welsh 5. *P* difficulty/problem/trouble; il m'est arrivé une salade, I'm in trouble/in a fix; elle a eu des salades avec les flics, she's been in trouble with the police; faire des salades, to make trouble/to complicate things 6. *pl P* lies; nonsense*; tout ça c'est des salades! that's a lot of poppycock! encaisser des salades, to swallow it; je ne veux plus encaisser ses salades, I don't want to listen to him/her any more; arrête tes salades! shut up*!/belt up!/give it a rest! (*Voir* **panier 1**)

saladier [saladje] *nm P* 1. troublemaker/stirrer 2. mouth*; taper du saladier, to have foul breath 3. fast-talker/line-shooter; glib salesman.

saladière [saladjɛr] *nf P* = **saladier 1**.

salamalec [salamalɛk] *nm F* salaam; bowing and scraping; faire des salamalecs à qn, to bow and scrape to s.o.; to kowtow to s.o.

salaud [salo] *P* I *nm* 1. *Vieilli* dirty/filthy individual; slut; petit salaud! you dirty little beast! 2. bastard*/swine/sod; (*femme, rare*) bitch; un beau salaud, a dirty/filthy bastard; a shit; dis, mon salaud! (*affectueusement*) listen, you old bugger! petit salaud! you little bastard! espèce de salaud! you rotten swine!/you bastard! enfant de salaud, son of a bitch; le dernier des salauds/un salaud de première/le roi des salauds, a real bastard*/a real sod; ça c'est un tour de salaud, that's a lowdown/dirty trick. (*Voir* **roi 4**) II *a* rotten; un mec salaud, a bastard*; ce qu'il est salaud! what a bastard*!

sale [sal] *a F* 1. (*a*) rotten/nasty/dirty/filthy;

c'est un sale boulot, it's a rotten job; sale type, bastard*/swine/nasty piece of work; il a une sale gueule, he looks really mean/he looks like a nasty piece of work; (*malade*) he looks rotten; ne fais pas cette sale gueule! take that look off your face! ah la sale bête! (*cet animal*) bloody animal! (*cette personne*) the beast!/the rotten thing! sale fasciste! filthy Fascist!/Fascist pig! c'est une sale affaire, it's a dirty business; il m'a joué un sale tour/un sale gag, he did the dirty on me (*b*) rotten/beastly (weather) 2. c'est pas sale! it's pretty good!/it's not bad at all! (*Voir* coup 3)

salé [sale] I *a F* (*a*) spicy (story); blue/dirty (joke); en raconter des salées, to tell smutty stories *or* jokes (*b*) (*prix*) exorbitant/stiff (*c*) (*peine de prison*) stiff/(unduly) severe II *nm P* 1. un (petit) salé/un morceau de salé, a (newborn) baby; a little brat; avoir un (petit) salé dans le tiroir, to be pregnant*/to have a bun in the oven 2. *P* faire petit salé (à qn), to lick (s.o.'s) toes/to give (s.o.) a toe job.

salement [salmã] *adv P* (very) badly; être salement amoché, to be terribly/badly beaten up; j'ai salement besoin d'argent, I'm badly in need of money; être salement fatigué, to be exhausted*/to be dead beat; salement difficile, bloody difficult; ça va nous rendre salement service, it'll be bloody useful.

saler [sale] *vtr* 1. *F* to overcharge/to fleece*/to rip off (customers); saler la note, to stick it on/to bump up the bill; on nous a salés, we were stung/we had to pay through the nose 2. *P* saler qn, to be harsh with s.o./tough on s.o.; on l'a salé, he got a stiff sentence/they threw the book at him.

saleté [salte] *nf* 1. *F* (*a*) dirty trick; faire une saleté à qn, to do the dirty on s.o. (*b*) smutty remark; blue/dirty joke 2. *P* rotten bastard*/rotten sod/nasty piece of work/*NAm* son of a bitch.

salière [saljɛr] *nf F* hollow above the collar bone/salt cellar.

saligaud, -aude [saligo, -od] *n P* = salaud I.

salingue [salɛ̃g] *P* I *a* (*physiquement et moralement*) dirty/filthy II *n* filthy/disgusting person; un vieux salingue, a dirty old man.

salir [salir] *vtr P* tu la salis! you're exaggerating!/you're laying it on (a bit) thick! (*Voir* nez 5)

salisson [salisɔ̃] *nf F Dial* dirty/untidy young girl.

salive [saliv] *nf F* 1. perdre/gaspiller/user sa

salive, to waste one's breath 2. dépenser beaucoup de salive, to talk a lot*/to gas/to bang on 3. avaler/ravaler sa salive, to be stumped (for an answer).

salle [sal] *nf* 1. *P* salle à manger, (inside of the) mouth*; salle à manger démontable, set of false teeth 2. *P* des plaisanteries de salle de garde, dirty/blue jokes 3. *V* salle des fêtes, vagina*. (*Voir* tabourets)

saloir [salwar] *nm P* mettre le lard/la viande au saloir, to go to bed*.

salon(n)ard, -arde [salɔnar, -ard] *n F* social climber; s.o. who frequents social functions (in the hope of making profitable contacts).

salopard [salɔpar] *nm P* (dirty) bastard*/swine/sod/*NAm* son of a bitch. (*Voir* salaud 2)

salope [salɔp] *nf P* 1. bitch/cow; slut/tart; cette petite salope, that little slut/bitch; c'est une vieille salope ce type, that guy's a real bastard*/louse; (*indicateur*) that guy's a grass 2. prostitute*/tart.

saloper [salɔpe] *vtr P* to botch/to bungle*/to make a mess of (sth); to muck (sth) up/to bugger (sth) up.

saloperie [salɔpri] *nf P* 1. = salaud I 2. (*a*) filth/filthiness; saloperie de temps! filthy/disgusting weather! (*b*) dire des saloperies, to talk smut/filth (*c*) faire une saloperie à qn, to play a dirty trick on s.o./to do the dirty on s.o. 3. rubbish/trash; c'est de la vraie saloperie, it's absolute rubbish/junk 4. botched piece of work/bungle/botch-up.

salopiaud [salɔpjo] *nm*, **salopiot** [salɔpjo] *nm P* = salaud I.

salsifis [salsifi] *nmpl P* 1. fingers; une poignée de salsifis, a punch/a bunch of fives 2. toes.

salut! [saly], *Vieilli* **salutas!** [salytas] *int F* (*a*) salut (la compagnie)! (*bonjour*) hello/hi (everybody/everyone/*surt NAm* you guys)! (*au revoir*) so long/cheers/bye (everybody)! (*b*) bonjour, salut! hello, how are you? (*c*) et puis salut! right, that's it!/I quit!/I've had it!

sana [sana] *nm F* sanatorium/san.

sanctuaire [sãktɥɛr] *nm F* peser qch au poids du sanctuaire, to examine sth thoroughly.

sandos [sãdo] *nm F* = sans-dos.

sandwich [sãdwi(t)ʃ] *nm F* être pris en sandwich, to be caught/stuck/jammed/sandwiched (between two things, two people).

sandwicher [sãdwi(t)ʃe] I *vtr F* to sandwich; **il était sandwiché entre deux femmes,** he was sandwiched between two women II *vi* F to have a sandwich meal/to have a snack/to snack.

sang [sã] *nm* 1. F **prendre un coup de sang,** (*avoir une attaque d'apoplexie*) to have a stroke; (*se mettre en colère*) to become very angry*/to hit the roof; **il a failli crever d'un coup de sang,** he nearly bust a blood vessel 2. F **avoir du sang dans les veines,** to have guts; **il n'a pas de sang dans les veines,** he's gutless 3. F **avoir qch dans le sang,** to be mad*/crazy/nuts about sth; **il l'a dans le sang,** he's got it/it's in his blood 4. F (*a*) **se faire du mauvais sang/se cailler le sang/se faire du sang noir,** to worry/to fret; **ne vous faites pas de mauvais sang à mon sujet,** don't worry your head about me (*b*) **se dévorer/se manger/se miner/se ronger/se tourner le(s) sang(s),** to worry oneself sick 5. F **suer sang et eau,** to sweat blood 6. F **ça m'a tourné/retourné les sangs,** it gave me quite a turn/it upset me no end 7. P **pisser du sang,** (*saigner beaucoup*) to bleed like a stuck pig; (*travailler dur*) to sweat one's guts out; **pisser le sang,** to have a hard time (of it); **faire pisser le sang à qn,** to give s.o. a hard time 8. P (*a*) **bon sang (de bon sang/de bon soir)!/bon sang de bon Dieu!** damn and blast (it)!/(bloody) hell! (*b*) **bon sang d'imbécile!** you bloody fool! (*Voir* **navet 6; pinte; pisser I 14**)

sanglier [sãglije] *nm* P *Péj* priest*.

se sanguiner [səsãgine] *vpr* P to get drunk*.

sans [sã] *prép* 1. F **pourquoi porter des lunettes si tu (y) vois sans?** why wear glasses if you can see without? 2. P **des lettres de lui? voilà trois mois qu'on est sans,** letters from him? we haven't had any for three months. (*Voir* **un I 2**)

sans-châsses [sãʃas] *a* P blind. (*Voir* **châsse 1**)

sans dec' [sãdɛk] *adv phr* P (= sans déconner) no kidding/no fooling/no shit.

sans-dos [sãdo] *nm inv* F high stool/bar stool.

sans-le-sou [sãlsu] F I *a inv* penniless*/broke II *n inv* penniless* person; **c'est un sans-le-sou,** he's broke.

sans-loches [sãlɔʃ] *a* P deaf. (*Voir* **loche II**)

sans-mirettes [sãmirɛt] *a* P blind. (*Voir* **mirettes**)

sansonnet [sãsɔnɛ] *nm A P* gendarme. (*Voir* **roupie 3**)

sans-soin [sãswẽ] *n inv* F careless person.

Santaga [sãtaga] *Prnf* F **la Santaga,** the Santé prison (*in Paris*). (*Voir* **santoche II**)

santé [sãte] *nf* F 1. **avoir une petite santé,** to have poor health/to be delicate; **soigner sa petite santé,** to mollycoddle oneself; **comment va la santé?** how's things?/how's tricks? 2. **il a une santé!/il a de la santé!** he's got a nerve!/I like his cheek! 3. **se refaire une santé,** to improve one's financial situation/to have a healthier bank balance. (*Voir* **mangeuse**)

santiags [sãtjag] *nfpl* F (*bottes mexicaines*) Mexican (style) boots/cowboy boots.

santoche [sãtɔʃ] I *nf* P (state of) health II *Prnf* F **la Santoche,** the Santé prison (*in Paris*). (*Voir* **Santaga**)

santonner [sãtɔne] *vtr* P = **sataner.**

saoul [su], **saoulard** [sular], **saouler** [sule], *etc* = **soûl, soûlard, soûler,** *etc.*

sape [sap] I *nf* F *Mil* **la sape,** army engineers/sappers II *nm* P (*inculpation*) charge/indictment; (*condamnation*) conviction/sentence; **sape de gonzesse,** light sentence III *nf* P 1. **la sape,** (*habillement*) clothing; (*industrie*) the clothing industry/rag trade 2. *pl* **sapes,** clothes*/gear/threads.

sapé [sape] *a* P **bien sapé,** well-dressed.

sapement [sapmã] *nm* P = **sape II.**

saper [sape] I *vtr* P to convict/to sentence (s.o.); **être sapé,** to be sentenced II *vpr* **se saper** P to get dressed.

saperlipopette! [saperlipɔpɛt], **saperlotte!** [saperlɔt] *int Vieilli* F good heavens!/gad!

sapeur [sapœr] *nm* F **fumer comme un sapeur,** (*personne*) to smoke like a chimney. (*Voir* **tablier 2**)

sapin [sapẽ] *nm* 1. F (*costume de*) **sapin,** coffin; **sentir le sapin,** to have one foot in the grave; **toux qui sent le sapin,** churchyard cough 2. P taxi/cab. (*Voir* **paletot 1; pardessus; redingote**)

saprelotte! [saprəlɔt], **sapristi!** [sapristi] *int Vieilli* F good heavens!/gad!

saquer [sake] *vtr & i* F = **sacquer I.**

sarbacane [sarbakan] *nf P* rifle.

sarcif [sarsif] *nm*, **sarcigol** [sarsigɔl] *nm* P sausage/banger.

sarco [sarko] *nm* P coffin.

sardine [sardin] *nf* 1. F *Mil* NCO's stripe 2. *pl A P* **les sardines,** the fingers 3. V **égoutter la/sa sardine,** to urinate*.

sardoche [sardɔʃ] *nf P* sardine.

sarrasin [sarazɛ̃] *nm P (typographie)* non-union worker; blackleg.

sarrasiner [sarazine] *vi P (typographie)* to work at non-union rates.

satané [satane] *a F (intensif)* blasted/damn(ed)/confounded/cursed; **satané temps!** beastly/filthy weather!

sataner [satane] **I** *vtr P* **sataner qn,** to beat s.o. up*/to knock the stuffing out of s.o./to work s.o. over **II** *vpr* **se sataner** *P* to (have a) fight/to have a set-to/a punch-up; to set about each other.

saton [satɔ̃] *nm P* blow*; *esp* kick.

satonner [satɔne] *vtr & vpr P =* **sataner.**

saturer [satyre] *vi F* to have had enough (of sth); **je travaille depuis 6 heures, je commence à saturer,** I've been working for the last 6 hours, I've just about reached saturation point; **les histoires de la famille royale, je sature un peu,** I've had all I can take of stories about the royal family!

satyre [satir] *nm F* 1. sex maniac; dirty old man 2. flasher.

sauc' [sos] *nm P =* **sauciflard.**

sauce [sos] *nf* 1. *F (a)* rain; shower; **recevoir une sauce,** to get soaked *(b)* blood; **sauce tomate,** period*/curse 2. *F* **rallonger la sauce,** to pad out a book; to spin out a story 3. *F* **on le met à toutes les sauces,** he's given all kinds of different jobs to do; **je ne sais à quelle sauce le mettre,** I don't know what use to make of it/of him 4. *F* **un repas à trente francs sans la sauce,** a thirty-franc meal without extras/with no frills 5. *F (a)* **gâter la sauce,** to spoil the whole business/the whole show *(b)* **qu'il en boive la sauce,** he'll have to put up with the consequences 6. *F* **être dans la sauce,** to be in a fix*/to be in the soup 7. *F Mus* **faire de la sauce,** to improvise 8. *F Aut* petrol; diesel (oil); **mettre (toute) la sauce,** to step on the gas; **rajouter de la sauce,** to accelerate/to put one's foot down 9. **balancer/envoyer la sauce,** *P* to fire (a gun, a burst of machine-gun fire, etc); *V* to ejaculate*/to shoot one's load. *(Voir* **accommoder 2;** **allonger 2)**

saucée [sose] *nf F* 1. downpour; **attraper/prendre une saucée,** to get drenched/to get soaked (to the skin) 2. reprimand*/telling-off/rocket.

saucer [sose] *vtr F* 1. to drench/to soak (to the skin); **l'orage nous a saucés,** we got wet through in the storm; **se faire saucer,** to get drenched/to get soaking wet 2. to reprimand*/to tell (s.o.) off/to blow (s.o.) up; **se faire saucer,** to get a rocket.

sauciflard [sosiflar] *nm P* (French) dried sausage.

saucisse [sosis] *nf* 1. *F Mil (a)* observation balloon; barrage balloon *(b)* trench mortar shell 2. *F* **il ne les attache pas avec des saucisses,** he's very mean. *(Voir* **chien II 1)** 3. *P* fool*/idiot/silly sausage 4. *P* **rouler une saucisse (à qn),** to kiss (s.o.) on the mouth/to give (s.o.) a French kiss 5. *F* **saucisse à pattes,** dachshund/sausage dog.

saucisson [sosisɔ̃] *nm* 1. *P =* **saucisse 3** 2. *P Mus* second-rate piece *or* song; piece of music frequently played/broadcast 3. *F* **elle est toujours ficelée/serrée comme un saucisson,** she's always bulging/bursting out of her clothes 4. *F* **saucisson à pattes,** dachshund/sausage dog. *(Voir* **peau 23** *(a))*

saucissonné [sosisɔne] *a F* dressed in tight-fitting clothes/got up like a sausage; **saucissonnée dans son collant,** poured into her tights.

saucissonner [sosisɔne] **I** *vtr* 1. *F* to tie up like a sausage 2. *F Fig* to carve up/chop up (an area, etc) into regular plots; *TV* **saucissonner une émission par des annonces publicitaires,** to intersperse a programme with advertisements **II** *vi F* to have a snack/to picnic; **nous avons saucissonné dans le train,** we had a snack on the train.

saucissonneur [sosisɔnœr] *nm F* picnicker.

saumâtre [somatr] *a F* 1. *(personne)* bitter/sour 2. **je la trouve saumâtre,** I think that's a bit much; I don't find that at all funny/I think it's in very bad taste.

saumure [somyr] *nf P* sea/the briny.

sauré [sore] *nm*, **sauret** [sorɛ] *nm P* 1. pimp*/ponce/mack/sweet man 2. *Vieilli* gendarme.

saut [so] *nm F* 1. **faire le (grand) saut,** to make a decision/to take the plunge 2. **faire le saut en l'air,** to be hanged/to swing 3. **faire un saut chez qn,** to pop round to s.o.'s house/to drop in on s.o.

saute-au-crac [sotokrak] *nm inv V* **c'est un saute-au-crac,** he's obsessed/he's got a one-track mind; he's cunt-struck; he'd screw anything in a skirt. *(Voir* **crac)**

saute-au-paf [sotopaf] *nf inv V* nymphomaniac/nympho; **c'est une saute-au-paf,** she'd jump into bed with anyone. *(Voir* paf II 2)

saute-dessus [sotdəsy] *nm* (strong) complaint; **faire du saute-dessus**, to complain in the strongest possible terms.

sautée [sote] *nf F* **grande sautée**, tall, thin person*; beanpole.

sauter [sote] I *vtr* 1. *F* **je la saute**, I'm starving/ravenous 2. *P* to arrest*; **se faire sauter**, to get nabbed/nicked 3. *P* to have sex* with (s.o.)/to have/to jump; **elle s'est fait sauter**, she got laid/screwed/jumped II *vi* 1. *F* **se faire sauter la cervelle**, to blow one's brains out 2. *F* **et que ça saute!** jump to it!/ make it snappy!/step on it! 3. *P* **sauter du train en marche**, to practise coitus interruptus/to withdraw (before ejaculation). (*Voir* **caisson 1**; **fossé**; **pas I 2**)

sauterelle [sotrɛl] *nf F* 1. woman* 2. tall, thin person/beanpole.

sauteur, -euse [sotœr, -øz] I *n F* unreliable person/waverer II *nm P* womanizer*; **un sacré sauteur**, a really good lover/a hell of a good lay III *nf P* 1. bottle of champagne* 2. flea 3. (*a*) prostitute*/tart (*b*) easy lay/ pushover; **une sacrée sauteuse**, a good screw.

sauvage [sovaʒ] I *a F* **grève sauvage**, wildcat strike II *nm P* 1. (*surt criminel*) lone wolf/loner 2. **se mettre en sauvage**, to strip (right) off.

à la sauvette [alasovɛt] *adv phr F* ready to cut and run/ready to beat it quickly; (*camelots*) **vendre à la sauvette**, to sell goods in the street illicitly/without having a licence.

savate [savat] *nf F* 1. clumsy person/ bungler/botcher; **quelle savate!** what a clumsy clot! **comme une savate**, abominably/ very badly 2. **traîner la savate**, to be down at heel/down on one's uppers/on one's beamends.

savater [savate] *vtr F* to kick (s.o.).

saveur [savœr] *nf P* **coup de saveur**, (searching) glance; **donner un coup de saveur à qch**, to take a butcher's at sth/to get an eyeful (of sth).

savoir [savwar] *vtr F* 1. **je n'ai pas à le savoir**, I don't want to know/it's got nothing to do with me 2. **est-ce que je sais(, moi)?** allez/ **va-t'en savoir!** don't ask me!/I haven't a clue!/no idea! 3. **tu sais quoi?** (you) know what?/guess what? 4. **il en sait des choses**, he knows a thing or two/he knows what's what/ he's got his wits about him.

savon [savɔ̃] *nm F* (severe) reprimand*; **donner/flanquer/passer un savon à qn**, to re-

primand* s.o./to tear s.o. off a strip/to bawl s.o. out; **recevoir un savon**, to be reprimanded*/to catch it/to get a rocket.

savonnage [savɔnaʒ] *nm F* reprimand*/ telling-off/bawling-out.

savonner [savɔne] *vtr F* **savonner (la tête à) qn**, to reprimand* s.o./to tell s.o. off/to give s.o. a (good) dressing-down; **se faire savonner (la tête)**, to get told off.

savonnette [savɔnɛt] *nf F* 1. *Aut* bald tyre 2. (*drogue*) hashish*.

saxo [sakso] *nm F* saxophone/sax.

sbire [zbir] *nm F Péj* 1. (officious) policeman*/pig 2. (*voyou*) thug 3. *A* prison warder/screw.

scalp [skalp] *nm P* arrest.

scalper [skalpe] *vtr P* to arrest*/to nick. (*Voir* **mohican**)

scaphandre [skafɑ̃dr] *nm P* **scaphandre de poche**, (contraceptive) sheath/condom*/ rubber/johnnie.

scato [skato] *a F* (*abrév* = *scatologique*) dirty; **plaisanterie scato**, dirty joke; **humour scato**, lavatory humour.

schbeb[1] [ʃbɛb] *a Vieilli P* great/super. (*Voir* **chbeb**[1])

schbeb[2], **schebeb** [ʃ(ə)bɛb] *nm P* good-looking young homosexual*. (*Voir* **chbeb**[2])

schizo [skizo] *a & n F* (*abrév* = *schizophrène*) schizo.

schlaff(e) [ʃlaf] *nm ou f P* **aller au schlaff(e)/à (la) schlaff(e)**, to go to bed*; **faire schlaff(e)**, to sleep; to be sleeping. (*Voir* **chlaff(e)**)

schlague [ʃlag] *nf P* whip/cane (*as corporal punishment*); caning/flogging; **dix coups de schlague**, ten strokes of the cane.

schlaguer [ʃlage] *vtr P* to flog.

schlass(e) [ʃlɑs] I *a P* drunk*/sozzled/tight II *nm P* knife; dagger; chiv. (*Voir* **chlass(e) I, II**)

schlingoter [ʃlɛ̃gɔte], **schlinguer** [ʃlɛ̃ge], **schlipoter** [ʃlipɔte] *vi P* to stink*; **schlingoter du bec**, to have foul breath. (*Voir* **chlingoter, chlinguer, chlipoter**)

schlof(f), schloffe [ʃlɔf] *nm ou f P* = **schlaff(e)**.

schloffer [ʃlɔfe] *vi P* to sleep*.

schmecter [ʃmekte] *vi P* to stink*/to pong.

schmilblick [ʃmilblik] *nm P* enigma/ mystery; **faire avancer le schmilblick**, to unravel the mystery/to try to get to the bottom of it.

schmitt [ʃmit] *nm Vieilli P* gendarme.

schmoutz [ʃmuts] *nm P Péj* Jew*/Yid. (*Voir* **chmoutz**)

schnaps [ʃnaps] *nm,* **schnick** [ʃnik] *nm F* (inferior) brandy/rotgut. (*Voir* **chnaps, chnique**)

schnock, schnoque [ʃnɔk] *P* I *a* mad*/ bonkers; gaga II *nm* fool*/blockhead/NAm schmo(e)/schmuck; **vieux schnock**, silly old fool/old dodderer/old goat. (*Voir* **chnoc, chnoque**)

schnouf(fe) [ʃnuf] *nf P* (*drogues*) heroin*/ H/junk. (*Voir* **chnouf(fe)**)

schnouffé, -ée [ʃnufe] *n P* (*drogues*) heroin* addict/dope addict/junkie. (*Voir* **chnouffé**)

se schnouffer [səʃnufe] *vpr P* (*drogues*) to take heroin*; to be a heroin addict/a junkie; to take dope. (*Voir* **se chnouffer**)

schnouper [ʃnupe] *vi P* to drink*/to booze/ to hit the bottle.

schpile [ʃpil] *nm P* gambling; **avoir beau schpile**, (*beau jeu*) to have/to hold a good hand (at cards); (*réaliser facilement*) to find it easy/to have no difficulty; **il avait beau schpile à faire ça**, it was a walkover/all plain sailing for him. (*Voir* **chpile**)

schpiler [ʃpile] *vi P* to gamble. (*Voir* **chpiler**)

schpileur [ʃpilœr] *nm P* gambler. (*Voir* **chpileur**)

schproum(e) [ʃprum] *nm P* 1. scandal/ (scandalous) gossip/dirt; **faire du schproum(e)**, to cause a scandal 2. din/row/ racket; **faire du schproum(e)**, to kick up a row 3. *Vieilli* anger; **aller au schproum(e)**, to lose one's temper/to flare up/to hit the roof. (*Voir* **chproum**)

schtarb [ʃtarb], **schtarbé** [ʃtarbe] *a P* mad*/loopy/mental.

schtar(d) [ʃtar] *nm,* **schtib(e)** [ʃtib] *nm,* **schtilibem** [ʃtilibɛm] *nm P* prison*/stir; disciplinary cell/cooler. (*Voir* **chtar 1; chtib(e)**)

schtim(m)i [ʃtimi] *nm P* native of northern France/northerner. (*Voir* **ch'timi**)

schton [ʃtɔ̃] *nm P* blow*/punch/slug. (*Voir* **jeton 3**)

schtouillard [ʃtujar] *nm P* person with VD*/the clap. (*Voir* **chtouillard**)

schtouille [ʃtuj] *nf P* VD*/(the) clap; **ramasser la schtouille**, to cop a dose; **flanquer la schtouille à qn**, to give s.o. a dose. (*Voir* **chtouille**)

schwartz [ʃvarts] *nm P* (*argent*) money*

earned by moonlighting/on the black market; undeclared income; (*dessous de table*) bribe/ backhander.

sciant [sjɑ̃] *a F* boring; **il est sciant**, he's a damn nuisance; he's a terrible bore.

scie [si] *nf F* 1. *Vieilli* (*chose ou personne*) bore*/bind; nuisance; **quelle scie!** what a bore!/what a bind! 2. monotonous/incessant repetition of a word/phrase, etc.

Sciences-Po [sjɑ̃spo] *nfpl F* = *École supérieure des Sciences politiques.*

scier [sje] *vtr* 1. *P* (*a*) to dismiss*/to get rid of (s.o.) (*b*) to jilt/to throw over/to chuck (s.o.) 2. *F* **scier qn**, to amaze*/stagger s.o.; **être scié**, to be dumbfounded/gobsmacked; **ça m'a scié**, I was staggered/gobsmacked 3. *F* **scier une entreprise (à la base)**, to cause a business to collapse/to ruin a business 4. *F* to annoy*/bore/pester (s.o.). *Voir* **bois 16; dos 2**)

scion [sjɔ̃] *nm P* 1. knife/chiv/sticker; dagger; **donner un coup de scion à qn**, to stab s.o. 2. penis*.

scionner [sjɔne] *vtr Vieilli P* to stab/to knife/to chiv (s.o.).

sciure [sjyr] *nf F* **avoir de la sciure dans le tronc**, to be a fool*/an idiot; to be dead from the neck up.

score [skɔr] *nm P* prison sentence*/time.

scoubidou [skubidu] *nm P* 1. contraption/ gadget 2. (*stérilet*) coil/loop.

scoumoune [skumun] *nf P* persistent bad luck.

scrafer [skrafe] *vtr P* 1. to arrest*/ apprehend 2. to kill*/to blow away.

se scratcher [səskratʃe] *vpr F* to crash/to have an accident (*in one's car, etc*).

scribe [skrib] *nm F Péj* clerk/pen-pusher.

scribouillage [skribujaʒ] *nm F* (*a*) scribbling (*b*) work written in poor/slapdash style; scribble.

scribouillard, -arde [skribujar, -ard] *n F* 1. *Péj* clerk/pen-pusher 2. (any) writer; *esp* journalist/hack.

scribouiller [skribuje] I *vi F* (*a*) to be a pen-pusher (*b*) to scribble; to write in poor/ slapdash style II *vtr P* to write (a letter, etc).

scribouilleur, -euse [skribujœr, -øz] *n F* second-rate writer.

scro(n)gneugneu, *pl* **-eux** [skrɔɲøɲø] *nm F* (*a*) cantankerous old soldier; Colonel Blimp (*b*) *int* grumble, grumble ...!/moan, moan ...!

scroum [skrum] *nm P* = **schproum(e).**

seau, *pl* **seaux** [so] *nm F* 1. il pleut/il tombe à (pleins) seaux, il tombe des seaux, it's raining hard/it's raining cats and dogs/it's bucketing down/it's pelting down 2. être dans le seau, to be in a fix*/to be in the soup.

Sébasto [sebasto] *Prnm F* le Sébasto, the boulevard de Sébastopol (*in Paris*). (*Voir* **Topol**)

sec, *f* **sèche**[1] [sɛk, sɛʃ] I *a F* 1. l'avoir sec, (*avoir soif*) to be very thirsty/parched. (*Voir* **gosier**); (*être dépité*) to be indignant/ annoyed 2. (*surt écoles*) rester sec, to be stumped (for an answer) 3. consultation sèche, free consultation. (*Voir* **cri 4**) II *adv F* 1. aussi sec, immediately*/straight away/right away 2. quinze mille balles sec, fifteen thousand quid net/exactly 3. boire sec, to drink* a lot/to knock it back 4. *adv phr* être à sec, (*ne plus trouver les mots*) to run out of words/ideas; to dry up; (*être sans argent*) to be penniless*/to be broke/to be skint; mettre qn à sec, to clean s.o. out/to take s.o. to the cleaners. 5. en cinq sec, very quickly*/in two shakes (of a lamb's tail)/in (next to) no time. (*Voir* **péter I 9**)

sécateur [sekatœr] *nm P Péj* baptisé au sécateur, Jewish*.

séchage [seʃaʒ] *nm F* (*écoles*) failure (*at an exam*).

sèche[2] *nf* 1. *F* (*écoles*) piquer une sèche, to be stumped/to dry up (*at an oral exam*) 2. *P* cigarette*/fag/cig(gy); griller une sèche, to smoke a fag; piquer une sèche, to cadge/to bum a fag.

séché [seʃe] *a P* dead*; il est séché, he's a goner/he's had it/he's done for.

sécher [seʃe] I *vtr* 1. *F* sécher un verre/un pot, to knock back/to swig (down) a drink 2. *F* (*a*) (*écoles*) sécher un cours, to miss/to skip/ to skive off a lecture (*b*) sécher une réunion, to cut a meeting 3. *F* sécher un candidat, to fail a candidate 4. *P* sécher qn, (*tuer*) to kill* s.o./to bump s.o. off; (*assommer*) to knock s.o. out/to clobber/to clout s.o. 5. *P* la sécher, to be very thirsty/parched II *vi F* to be stumped/to be floored; to dry up (*esp in an exam*). (*Voir* **fil 7; pied 9; tas 3**)

séchoir [seʃwar] *nm P* prison.

séco [seko] *a & nm F* = **sécot**.

secor [səkɔr] *a & nm & f P* (*verlan de corse*) Corsican.

sécot [seko] *F* I *a* lean/lanky/skinny; *Fig* dry II *nm* un petit sécot, a skinny little bloke/*surt NAm* guy.

secoué [səkwe] *a F* 1. secoué (comme un prunier), mad*/cracked/mental 2. secoué de jazz, mad keen on jazz.

secouée [səkwe] *nf F* 1. *Vieilli* reprimand*/ telling off 2. great quantity*; il y en avait une secouée, there were heaps/loads/tons of them.

secouer [səkwe] I *vtr* 1. *F* to shake (s.o.) up/to make (s.o.) sit up and listen 2. *F* to re-primand* (s.o.)/to tear (s.o.) off a strip; (*pousser à agir*) to rouse (s.o.) to action. (*Voir* **paletot 6; puce 7, 8**) 3. *P* to steal* 4. *P* to arrest* 5. *P* j'en ai rien à secouer! I don't give a damn!/I couldn't care less!/I don't give a toss! II *vpr* se secouer *F* to get a move on/to get moving; to shake oneself out of it/to snap out of it; secoue-toi!/secouez-vous! get cracking!/look alive!/make it snappy!

secouette [səkwɛt] *nf V* (act of) masturbation*/wanking/tossing off.

secousse [səkus] *nf* 1. *F* en donner/en mettre/*P* en foutre une secousse, to work* hard/to (really) get down to it; il n'en fiche pas une secousse, he doesn't do a stroke (of work)/he doesn't do a hand's turn 2. *P* theft; donner une secousse à qch, to steal sth 3. *V* sex*/bump and grind.

la Sécu [laseky] *nf F* (*abrév = la Sécurité sociale*) = the National Health Service (NHS).

seg [sɛg] *nm Vieilli F* 1. (*écoles*) second/ junior master 2. (*marine*) executive officer.

sègue [sɛg] *nf V* masturbation*/wank/hand-job; se taper une sègue, to toss off/to jack off/ to wank.

seins [sɛ̃] *nmpl P* 1. tu me fais mal aux seins! you get on my (bloody) nerves!/you get on my tits! 2. se tâter le sein, to worry (about one's health); arrête de te tâter le sein, stop worrying about it/don't let it get you down.

sel [sɛl] *nm F* 1. mettre/mêler son grain de sel, y aller de son grain de sel, to butt in; il met son grain de sel dans tout, he's always sticking his nose into what doesn't concern him 2. (*a*) *Iron* c'est fin comme du gros sel, very clever! (*b*) cela ne manque pas de sel, it's quite clever/witty really.

select, sélect [selɛkt] *a F* select/high-class/posh (gathering); le monde sélect, high society.

self [sɛlf] *nm F* self-service store *or* restaurant.

sellette [sɛlɛt] *nf F* être sur la sellette, to be on the carpet; mettre/tenir qn sur la sellette, to have s.o. on the carpet.

semelle [s(ə)mɛl] *nf F* ça ne leur arrive pas à la semelle, it doesn't begin to compare with them/it's not a patch on them.

semer [səme] *vtr F (a)* to get rid of (s.o.)/to shed (s.o.)/to shake (s.o.) off/to give (s.o.) the slip; semer une connaissance, to drop an acquaintance *(b)* *(courses)* to leave (a competitor) behind/to outdistance (s.o.). *(Voir* **graine 6; merde I 12)**

semi [səmi] *nm F* (= *(camion) semi-remorque)* semitrailer/*NAm* semi.

semou [səmu] *nf P (verlan de* **mousse)** beer.

semoule [səmul] *nf* 1. *P* être dans la semoule, to be confused/muddled/befuddled. *(Voir* **pédaler 3)** 2. *V* envoyer/balancer la semoule, to ejaculate*/to shoot one's load.

sens [sɑ̃s], **sensass** [sɑ̃sas] *a inv F* sensational/terrific/smashing/super; un type sensass, a great bloke/*surt NAm* guy.

sens unique [sɑ̃synik] *nm* glass of red wine.

sent-bon [sɑ̃bɔ̃] *nm inv,* **senti-bon** [sɑ̃tibɔ̃] *nm inv F* scent/perfume; sentir le sent-bon, to smell nice.

sentiment [sɑ̃timɑ̃] *nm F* le faire au sentiment à qn/avoir qn au sentiment, to appeal to s.o.'s emotions/to win s.o. over by appealing to his feelings; vous ne m'aurez pas au sentiment, that won't work with me/you won't get me that way.

sentinelle [sɑ̃tinɛl] *nf P* 1. relever une sentinelle, to have a drink at the bar 2. turd *(on the pavement, etc).* *(Voir* **factionnaire)**

sentir [sɑ̃tir] *F* I *vtr* je ne peux pas le sentir, I can't bear/stand/stick (the sight of) him; I just can't stomach him. *(Voir* **blairer; passer I 6))** II *vi* ça ne sent pas bon, ça sent mauvais, I don't like the look of it/it's (a bit) fishy; it stinks III *vpr* **se sentir** tu ne te sens plus? have you taken leave of your senses?/ have you gone mad*?

séraille [seraj] *nf P* passer/passage en séraille = passer/passage en série **(série 2).**

serbillon [sɛrbijɔ̃] *nm Vieilli P* 1. faire/ envoyer le serbillon à qn = faire/envoyer le serre à qn **(serre 1)** 2. = **serre 2.**

sergot [sɛrgo] *nm Vieilli P* policeman*.

série [seri] *nf* 1. *F* série noire, run of bad luck; chapter of accidents 2. *P* passer en série, *(femme)* to be raped by several men in succession/to be gang-banged; passage en série, group rape/gang-bang.

sérieux [serjø] I *nm* 1. *F* litre glass of beer

2. *P* aggravated offence/crime II *adv F* se-riously; elles se sont battues sérieux, they had a hell of a fight/they fought tooth and nail.

serin [s(ə)rɛ̃] *F* I *a* stupid*/idiotic (person) II *nm* fool*/nitwit/nit/twit. *(Voir* **mouron 3)**

seringue [s(ə)rɛ̃g] *nf P* 1. *(a)* firearm; rifle; pistol *(b)* submachine gun 2. *Mus* trombone 3. tall woman*/beanpole 4. *(a)* bad/second-rate singer *(b)* chanter comme une seringue, to sing out of tune/off key 5. coup de seringue, sudden feeling of tiredness; sinking feeling. *(Voir* **potage 2)**

seringué, -ée [s(ə)rɛ̃ge] *n P (drogues)* heroin* addict/junkie/mainliner.

seringuer [s(ə)rɛ̃ge] *vtr P* seringuer qn, to shoot s.o./to riddle s.o. with bullets/to fill s.o. with lead.

serpent [sɛrpɑ̃] *nm* 1. *F* un serpent à lunettes, person wearing spectacles; four-eyes 2. *P* gob (of spit, phlegm) 3. *F Journ* serpent de mer, stock article; = silly season story.

serpillière [sɛrpijɛr] *nf P* (girl's, woman's) dress.

serre [sɛr] *nm P* 1. faire/envoyer le serre à qn, to warn s.o. (by a signal); to give s.o. the tip-off/to tip s.o. the wink 2. *(guet)* lookout/ watch; faire le serre, to be on the lookout.

serré [sɛre, se-] *a F* 1. penniless*/broke 2. *A* miserly*/tight(-fisted). *(Voir* **entournures)**

serrer [sɛre, se-] I *vtr P* 1. to arrest*; se faire serrer, to get nabbed/nicked 2. to force (s.o.) into a corner with a view to robbing (him/her) 3. to strangle (s.o.) 4. to exaggerate*/to overstate (sth) 5. se la serrer, *(serrer la main)* to shake hands; *(se priver)* to tighten one's belt/to go without (food). *(Voir* **ceinture 1; cinq 5; fesse 2; gargamelle; jeu 5** *(a)***; kiki 1** *(b)***; pince 1; pouce 9; sifflet; vis)** II *vpr* **se serrer** *F* 1. to tighten one's belt 2. se serrer les coudes, to back one another up.

sert [sɛr] *nm P* = **serre.**

servi [sɛrvi] *a & pp P* être servi, *(arrêté)* to be arrested*; *(incarcéré)* to be sent to prison*.

service [sɛrvis] *nm* 1. *F* faire du service, to be over-zealous/to be over-keen; être service service, to be finicky/pernickety/a stickler for rules and regulations; to go by the book 2. *F* j'en ai autant à ton service! the same to you with knobs on! 3. *P suite;* service trois pièces, male genitals*/three-piece suite 4. *V* entrée de service, anus*/back door.

serviette [sɛrvjɛt] *nf P* coup de serviette,

(police) raid/bust.

servietter [sɛrvjɛte] *P* **I** *vtr* to arrest*/to nab/to nick **II** *vi* to round up suspects, etc in a police raid.

serviotter [sɛrvjɔte] *vtr P* to swindle*/to pull a fast one on/to set up (s.o.).

seug [sœg] *nm P* = **seg 1, 2.**

seulabre, seulâbre [sœlɑbr] *a P* alone/on one's tod.

seulet, -ette [sœlɛ, -ɛt] *a F* alone/lonely; je suis bien seulette, I'm all on my own/on my lonesome.

seulingue [sœlɛ̃g] *a P* = **seulabre.**

sexy [sɛksi] *a F* sexy; elle est sexy, she's a sexy girl/a bit of all right/a nice bit of stuff/a sexy piece.

sézig, sézigue [sezig] *pron P* him(self)/her(self)/oneself; his nibs. (*Voir* **cézig(ue), mézig(ue), no(s)zig(ue)s, vo(s)zig(ue)s, euzig(ue)s, leur(s) zig(ue)s**)

shake [ʃek] *nm F* milkshake/shake.

shampooing [ʃɑ̃pwɛ̃] *nm* 1. *P* passer un shampooing à qn, to reprimand* s.o./to give s.o. a dressing-down/to give s.o. a rocket 2. *V* shampooing maison/shampooing à Charles-le-Chauve, fellatio*/blow-job.

shit [ʃit] *nm P* (*drogues*) hashish*/shit.

shitman [ʃitman] *nm P* hashish* smoker/pot smoker/pothead.

shoot [ʃut] *nm P* (*drogues*) injection*/shot/fix; se faire un shoot, to shoot up/to fix (up).

shooté [ʃute] *nm P* (*drogues*) drug addict*/junkie/fixer.

se shooter [səʃute] *vpr P* (*drogues*) to inject oneself with a drug/to shoot up/to fix (up).

shooterie [ʃutri] *nf P* (*drogues*) place where drug addicts go to shoot up/shooting gallery.

shooteuse [ʃutøz] *nf P* (*drogues*) hypodermic needle*/hyp(e)/hypo/dropper; enragé de la shooteuse, heroin* addict/junkie/fixer.

sidateux, -euse [sidatø, -øz], **sidatique** [sidatik] *F Péj* **I** *a* suffering from Aids **II** *n* Aids sufferer/victim.

sidérant [siderɑ̃] *a F* staggering/shattering (piece of news, etc).

sidéré [sidere] *a F* amazed*/dumbfounded/staggered/flabbergasted; j'en suis resté sidéré, I was completely shattered (by the news).

sidérer [sidere] *vtr F* to amaze*/to dumbfound/to flabbergast/to stagger (s.o.)/to strike (s.o.) all of a heap/to shatter (s.o.).

sidi [sidi] *nm P Péj* Arab*/wog; (*native of N Africa living in France*).

siècle [sjɛkl] *nm F* il y a un siècle que je (ne) vous ai pas vu, I haven't seen you for ages/for yonks.

sienne [sjɛn] *nf F* 1. faire des siennes, to be up to one's tricks; il a encore fait des siennes, he's been up to his tricks again; la voiture fait des siennes, the car's not working properly/up to its tricks again. (*Voir* **leur**) 2. y aller de la sienne, to make one's contribution (of stories, songs, etc)/to join in.

sifflard [siflar] *nm P* (French) dried sausage. (*Voir* **sauciflard**)

sifflé! [sifle] *int P* rubbish!/boo!

siffler [sifle] *vtr* 1. *P* to swig/to knock back (a drink) 2. *P* siffle-le! come on, out with it!/shoot!/give! 3. *F* se faire siffler (par la police), to be pulled up (by the police) 4. *F* siffler une fille, to give a girl a wolf-whistle/to wolf-whistle at a girl.

sifflet [siflɛ] *nm P* throat; couper le sifflet à qn, to cut s.o.'s throat; (*faire taire*) to shut s.o. up; to take the wind out of s.o.'s sails; (*ahurir*) to take s.o.'s breath away; serrer le sifflet à qn, to strangle s.o./to throttle s.o./to wring s.o.'s neck; se rincer le sifflet, to wet one's whistle*/to knock one back. (*Voir* **nez 12**)

sifflot(t)e [siflɔt] *nf P* syphilis*/syph.

sigler [sigle] *vtr & i Vieilli P* = **cigler.**

signé [siɲe] *a & pp F* c'est signé, it's easy to guess who did that/it's clear to see who's behind that/it's written all over it.

sigue [sig] *nm Vieilli P* = **cigue.**

silencieux [silɑ̃sjø] *nm* 1. *A P* (murderer's) knife/chiv 2. *V* se taper un silencieux, to masturbate*.

singe [sɛ̃ʒ] *nm* 1. *F* ugly person; fright; scarecrow 2. *P* le singe, the boss/the guv'nor 3. *P* (tinned) corned beef/bully beef 4. *P* (*drogues*) avoir un singe sur le dos, to have withdrawal symptoms/to have a monkey on one's back 5. *F* passenger in a sidecar. (*Voir* **monnaie 2**)

singesse [sɛ̃ʒɛs] *nf P* boss.

sinoc, sino(c)que [sinɔk], **sino(c)qué** [sinɔke] *a P* mad*/bonkers. (*Voir* **synoque**)

sinoquet [sinɔkɛ] *nm P* 1. head* 2. mad person*/crackpot.

siouplaît, siouplé [sjuple] = *s'il vous plaît.*

siphon [sifɔ̃] *nm P* head*.

siphonné [sifɔne] *a F* mad*/crazy/nuts/

crackers; **il est complètement siphonné,** he's absolutely nuts/as nutty as a fruit cake.

siphonner [sifɔne] *P* **I** *vtr* to drive (s.o.) mad* **II** *vi* to talk through one's hat/to talk rubbish/to talk cock.

sirop [siro] *nm P* **1.** alcoholic drink; **avoir un coup de sirop,** to be drunk*; to have had a drop too much/one too many; **sortir du sirop,** to sober up **2. sirop de bois tordu, wine 3. sirop (de grenouille(s)/de canard),** water*/Adam's ale; sea; **aller au sirop,** to fall into the water/the drink; **sirop (de parapluie/de pébroc/de pébroque),** rain(water) **4. tomber dans le sirop,** to faint/to pass out **5. je l'ai eu au sirop,** I led him up the garden path; I put one over on him **6. ça ne vaut pas un coup de sirop,** that's worthless*; it's not worth a sausage **7. être dans le sirop,** to be in a fix*/in a jam/in a spot of bother; **(ne rien comprendre)** to be confused/muddled; **elle est en plein dans le sirop,** she's in trouble; she hasn't a clue what's going on **8.** gambling den/joint; dive **9.** *(drogues)* **sirop de rif,** speedball **10.** (human) blood *(from a wound)* **11. sirop de corps d'homme,** sperm/semen*/love juice/come.

siroter [sirɔte] *vtr F* to sip (wine, coffee, etc).

sita [sita] *nm Vieilli F (à Paris)* dust cart *(from 'Société industrielle de transports automobiles').*

situasse [sitɥas] *nf P (= situation)* social position/status.

situation [sitɥasjɔ̃] *nf F* **être dans une situation intéressante,** to be pregnant*/to be in an interesting condition.

situer [sitɥe] *vtr F* **situer qn,** to size s.o. up/to suss s.o. out.

six-à-neuf [sizanœf] *nm P* sixty-nine *(simultaneous oral sex by two partners).* *(Voir* **soixante-neuf)**

à la six-quatre-deux [alasiskatdø] *adv phr F* **faire qch à la six-quatre-deux,** to do sth in a slapdash manner; to dash sth off; to do sth all anyhow; **travail à la six-quatre-deux,** slapdash work.

skating [sketiŋ] *nm F* **un skating à mouches,** a bald head*/a skating rink.

sked [skɛd]**, skeud** [skød] *nm P (= verlan de disque)* record/disc/album.

skin(head) [skin(ɛd)] *nm & f F* skinhead.

slalom [slalɔm] *nm F* **faire du slalom entre les voitures,** to dodge in and out among the cars; **conduire à Paris c'est un drôle de slalom,** driving in Paris is one hell of an obstacle race.

slibar [slibar] *nm P* (man's) underpants.

sma(c)k [smak] *nm P (drogues)* heroin*/smack.

sma(c)ké [smake] *a P (drogues)* high on heroin*/smacked out.

smala(h) [smala] *nf F* large family; **elle est partie au bord de la mer avec toute sa smala(h),** she's gone off to the seaside with all her tribe.

smashed [smaʃt] *a P (drogues)* = **sma(c)ké.**

smicard, -arde [smikar, -ard] *n F* person receiving the *SMIC (= salaire minimum interprofessionnel de croissance)*/worker on (statutory) minimum wage/minimum wage earner.

smok [smɔk] *nm F (= smoking)* dinner jacket/*NAm* tuxedo.

snack(-bar) [snak(bar)] *nm P* snack bar.

snif¹ [snif] *int F* snif, **il est parti!** boohoo, he's gone!

snif², sniffe [snif] *nf ou m P (drogues)* **1.** cocaine*/(nose-)candy **2.** *(prise de cocaïne, etc)* snort (of cocaine*, etc).

sniffer [snife] *vtr & i* **1.** *P* to take drugs *(esp* cocaine*) nasally; to sniff/to snort (coke); **sniffer de la colle,** to sniff glue. *(Voir* **ligne 3) 2.** *F* to cry/to blub.

sniffette [snifɛt] *nf P (drogues) (petite prise de drogue)* small snort (of cocaine*, etc).

sniffeur, -euse [snifœr, -øz] *n P* (glue-) sniffer; cocaine snorter/sniffer.

snob [snɔb] *a F* smart/posh; **ça fait très snob,** that's very posh/very with it/very U.

snobinard, -arde [snɔbinar, -ard] *F Péj* **I** *a* stuck-up/snobbish **II** *n* stuck-up/snobbish type.

snobinette [snɔbinɛt] *nf F Péj* pretentious/stuck-up young woman; little snob.

soce [sɔs] *nf P (= société)* gathering; gang; **bonsoir la soce!** (good)night all!

social [sɔsjal] *nm P* friend*/mate/pal/buddy.

socialo [sɔsjalo] *a & n F* socialist/lefty.

sœur [sœr] *nf P* **1.** *(a)* girlfriend; mistress *(b)* any girl* or woman* friend/sister; **c'est une sœur,** she's a real friend **2.** effeminate young man/pansy **3.** *(a) (to which the answer is often* **elle bat le beurre (et quand elle battra la merde tu lécheras le bâton))** mind your own business!/get lost!/take a running jump! *(b)* **et ma sœur, elle en a!** pull the other one *(= leg),* it's got bells on!

sœurette [sœrɛt] *nf F* **1.** little sister **2.**

girl*/woman*; **alors, sœurette?** what's on, honey?/how about it, love?

soft [sɔft] *a & nm F* soft (porn, etc).

soie [swa] *nf P* **avoir qn sur la soie,** to have s.o. on one's track/on one's trail. (*Voir* **péter I 6**)

soif [swaf] *nf F* 1. **il fait soif!** it's thirsty weather!/it's thirsty work! 2. **jusqu'à plus soif,** to the very end.

soiffard, -arde [swafar, -ard] *F* I *a* boozy (person) II *n* heavy drinker/drunk(ard)*/ boozer.

soiffer [swafe] *vi F* (*a*) to drink* heavily/to (hit the) booze (*b*) to drink in one gulp/to gulp it down.

soiffeur, -euse [swafœr, -øz] *n Vieilli F* heavy drinker/drunk(ard)*/boozer.

soigné [swaɲe] I *a P* excellent*/first-class/ first-rate*; **une raclée soignée,** a hell of a beating*; **un rhume soigné,** a rotten cold/a stinker II *nm F Iron* **voilà du soigné!** that's a fine piece of work!

soigner [swaɲe] *vtr F* 1. **soignez-le bien (, pas d'indulgence)!** give him the works!/ give him the full treatment! 2. **il faut te faire soigner!** you must be mad*!/you need your head examined! 3. **soigner l'addition,** (*dans un restaurant, etc*) to bump up the bill; **ils nous ont soignés,** they ripped us off.

soin-soin [swɛ̃swɛ̃], **soi-soi** [swaswa] *F* I *a inv* excellent*/great/first-rate/super II *adv* excellently/superbly/beautifully/marvellously.

soissonnais [swasɔnɛ] *nm V* **soissonnais** (rose), clitoris*.

soixante-dix-huit tours [swasɑ̃tdizɥitur] *nm inv F* old person/wrinklie.

soixante-neuf [swasɑ̃tnœf] *nm P* sixty-nine (*simultaneous oral sex by two partners*). (*Voir* **six-à-neuf**)

sokète [sɔkɛt] *nf Belg F* **faire une sokète,** to have a nap/to get a bit of shuteye/to have a kip.

soleil [sɔlɛj] *nm* 1. *F* **piquer un soleil,** to blush/to flush 2. *F* **user le soleil,** to laze about 3. *P* **ça craint le soleil,** (*marchandises volées*) those goods are hot/that stuff's hot. (*Voir* **jour 4**) 4. *F* slice of lemon in a grog 5. *P* a million francs.

solide [sɔlid] *nm F* **chercher le solide,** **songer/viser au solide,** to have an eye to the main chance/to look to the main chance.

solo [sɔlo] *a & adv F* alone/on one's own; **travailler solo,** to work on one's own; **le cambrioleur était solo,** the burglar was alone.

sombre [sɔ̃br] *a F* **un sombre imbécile/ crétin,** a complete fool*/a prize idiot/a real cretin.

son [sɔ̃] I *poss a F* **il/ça sent son policier d'une lieue,** you can tell he's a detective a mile away; he's got detective written all over him II *nm* 1. *P* **les son et lumière,** the old folks/the old fogeys/the wrinklies; **il est tout à fait son et lumière,** he's past it 2. *Vieilli P* **cracher/éternuer dans le son,** to be guillotined 3. *Vieilli F* **faire l'âne pour avoir du son,** to pretend to be stupid in order to find sth out. (*Voir* **boule 2**)

sondeur [sɔ̃dœr] *nm P* police inspector without a specific area of duty.

sonnage [sɔnaʒ] *nm P* borrowing; tapping (for money); cadging.

sonnanche [sɔnɑ̃ʃ] *nf P* bell.

sonné [sɔne] *a* 1. *F* mad*/cracked/nutty 2. *F* (*a*) stunned (by a blow)/groggy (*b*) (*boxe*) punch-drunk 3. *P* sentenced/condemned; **il est sonné,** he's had it.

sonner [sɔne] *vtr P* 1. **sonner qn,** beat* s.o. up/to work s.o. over; (*cogner la tête*) to stun s.o. by banging his head against a wall/on the pavement, etc; **se faire sonner,** to get a good thrashing 2. to give (s.o.) a heavy sentence 3. **sonner qn,** to borrow money from s.o./to tap s.o. for money 4. **on ne vous a pas sonné(e)!** who asked you (to butt in)?/mind your own business! 5. **sonner le coup de bambou,** to be stunned by some bad news; (*être fatigué*) to be exhausted*/bushed/whacked. (*Voir* **cloche I 3**)

sonneur [sɔnœr] *nm F* 1. **dormir comme un sonneur (de cloches),** to sleep like a log; **ronfler comme un sonneur,** to snore like a pig 2. brawler.

sono [sɔno] *nf F* (= *sonorisation*) PA (system); (*de discothèque, etc*) sound system; **la sono était pourrie,** the sound (system) wasn't working/the PA (system) was up the creek.

sonore [sɔnɔr] *nm V* anus*; **le mettre au sonore,** to have anal sex*.

Sophie [sɔfi] *Prnf F* **faire sa Sophie,** (*fille*) to show off*/to put on airs; (*être difficile*) to make a fuss.

sorbonnard, -arde [sɔrbɔnar, -ard] *F Péj* I *a* pedantic; **esprit sorbonnard,** niggling turn of mind II *n* student *or* lecturer at the Sorbonne.

sorbonne [sɔrbɔn] *nf P* head*; **je paumerai la sorbonne,** I'll lose my head.

sorcier [sɔrsje] *a F* ce n'est pas (bien) sorcier, there's nothing very difficult about that!/you don't have to be a magician to do that!

sorcière [sɔrsjɛr] *nf F* une vieille sorcière, an old hag/an old trout/an old witch.

sorgue [sɔrg] *nf P* evening; night.

sorlots [sɔrlo] *nmpl A P* boots; shoes.

sort [sɔr] *nm F* faire un sort à un repas, to eat up/to make short work of a (whole) meal; faire un sort à une bouteille de vin, to polish off a bottle of wine.

sortable [sɔrtabl] *a F* presentable; il n'est pas sortable, you can't take him (out) anywhere.

sortie [sɔrti] *nf F* 1. outburst/tirade; faire une sortie à/contre qn, to pitch into s.o./to lash out at s.o.; elle est capable de n'importe quelle sortie devant les gens, she's capable of saying anything in front of other people 2. ils sont de sortie, they're missing/they're nowhere to be found. (*Voir* **porte 7**)

sortir [sɔrtir] **I** *vtr F* 1. to dismiss*/to expel (s.o.); se faire sortir, to get thrown out/ chucked out 2. to say/to come out with (a remark, etc); il nous en a sorti une bien bonne, (*plaisanterie*) he came out with a good one. (*Voir* **paquet 10**) **II** *vi* 1. *F* d'où sortez-vous? (*vous ne savez rien?*) don't you (even) know that?/where have you been all this time? (*en voilà une tenue!*) where are your manners?/ where were you brought up? 2. *F* (= *venir de* ...) (*a*) sortir de faire qch, to have just done sth; je sors de le voir, I've just seen him (*b*) merci (bien)! je sors d'en prendre, no thank you! once is enough/I've had quite enough of that (already), thank you!/you won't find me doing that again (in a hurry)! 3. *F* je ne sors pas de là/je n'en sors pas, I stick to that; that's my firm conviction; you won't make me change my mind; il n'y a pas à sortir de là, you can't get away from that/there's no getting away from it 4. *F* j'ai trop à faire, je n'en sors pas, I'm completely swamped/ ploughed under (with work) 5. *P* en sortir/ sortir du trou, to leave prison*/to be released (from prison). (*Voir* **trou 2**) 6. *P* il me sort par les pores/les yeux, I can't stand him 7. *P* (*a*) sortir avec une femme, to sleep with a woman (*b*) sortir avec (une fille/un garçon), to go out with/to go steady with/to date (a girl/a boy) 8. *F* c'est nouveau, ça vient de sortir, this is the latest thing, idea, etc; this is the latest trend/this is really with it; this is the latest discovery/invention/decision, etc. (*Voir* **aller 10**) **III** *vpr* **s'en sortir** *F* to make ends meet/to get by.

sossot, -otte [sɔso, -ɔt] *a P* stupid*/daft/ twittish.

sou [su] *nm F* 1. fichu comme quatre sous, dressed like a guy/any old how; je n'en donnerais pas quatre sous, I wouldn't give you a thank-you for it 2. en être/en rester comme deux sous de frites, to be flabbergasted* 3. être près de ses sous, to count every penny 4. être sans le sou, to be penniless*; il n'a pas le premier sou, he hasn't a penny to his name 5. (*a*) il n'est pas ambitieux pour deux sous/pour un sou, he's not in the least ambitious (*b*) il n'a pas pour deux sous de courage, he hasn't an ounce/a scrap of courage. (*Voir* **aller 7**)

soua-soua [swaswa] *a inv & adv P* = **soin-soin**.

soucoupe [sukup] *nf* 1. *F* soucoupe volante, flying saucer 2. *P* (*dans un café*) drink*.

soudure [sudyr] *nf* 1. *F* faire la soudure, to make ends meet; (*financièrement*) to bridge the gap/to tide (one) over 2. *P* money*; envoyer la soudure, to pay* up/to fork out.

soufflant, -ante [suflɑ̃, -ɑ̃t] **I** *a F* amazing/astounding; ça, c'est soufflant, it's breathtaking **II** *nm P* revolver*; pistol.

souffle [sufl] *nm F* impudence/cheek; il ne manque pas de souffle! he's got a nerve/a flipping cheek!

soufflé [sufle] *a F* 1. être soufflé, to be flabbergasted*/dumbfounded/struck all of a heap 2. impudent/cheeky; t'es soufflé toi! you've got a nerve!

souffler [sufle] **I** *vtr F* 1. souffler qn, to take s.o. aback/to flabbergast* s.o.; son culot nous a soufflés, his cheek took our breath away/ staggered us 2. souffler qch à qn, (*prendre*) to pinch sth from s.o.; (*en trompant*) to swindle* s.o. out of sth **II** *vi F* 1. tu peux souffler dessus, you can whistle for it; il croit qu'il va y arriver en soufflant dessus, he thinks he can do it just like that/without having to do anything 2. souffler aux oreilles de qn, to have a quiet word with s.o./to have a word in s.o.'s ear about sth. (*Voir* **canne 3; chandelle 1; mirliton**)

soufflerie [sufləri] *nf P* lungs.

soufflet [suflɛ] *nm* 1. *pl F* soufflets, lungs 2. *P* soufflet à punaises, concertina/accordion.

souf(f)rante [sufrɑ̃t] *nf Vieilli P* (sulphur-tipped) match.

souk [suk] *nm P* shambles; faire le souk/faire

un sacré souk, to have a wild party; qu'est-ce que c'est que ce souk? what on earth's going on here? − it's an absolute mess!

soûl [su] *a* F drunk*. (*Voir* **bourrique 6**; **cochon 8**; **Polonais**).

soulager [sulaʒe] I *vtr* 1. F soulager qn de qch, to steal* sth from s.o./to relieve s.o. of sth 2. V soulager qn, to bring s.o. to orgasm*/ to bring s.o. off/to help s.o. out II *vpr* **se soulager** 1. F to urinate* *or* defecate*/to relieve oneself 2. V to masturbate*/to bring oneself off.

soûlant [sulɑ̃] *a* P boring/tedious; il est soûlant, his talking makes my head spin.

soûlard, -arde [sular, -ard] *n* P drunk(ard)*/boozer/alkie; un vieux soûlard, an old soak.

soûlardise [sulardiz] *nf* P drunkenness.

soûlaud, -aude [sulo, -od] *n* P = **soûlard, -arde**.

soûler [sule] I *vtr* F soûler qn, to make/to get s.o. drunk* II *vpr* **se soûler** F to get drunk*; ils se sont soûlés la gueule, they got pissed; se soûler de paroles, to become intoxicated by the sound of one's own voice.

soûlerie [sulri] *nf* P 1. drunkenness 2. drinking bout*/binge/booze-up/piss-up.

soulever [sulve] *vtr* F 1. to steal*/to lift (s.o.'s purse, etc) 2. to seduce/to get off with (a woman) 3. ça me soulève le cœur, that turns my stomach/disgusts me.

souliers [sulje] *nmpl* F être dans ses petits souliers, to be in an awkward/embarrassing situation.

soûlographe [sulɔgraf] *nm & f* P = **soûlard**.

soûlographie [sulɔgrafi] *nf* P = **soûlerie 1**.

soûlot [sulo] *nm* P = **soûlard**.

soupapes [supap] *nfpl* P lungs.

soupe [sup] *nf* 1. F soupe au perroquet, bread soaked in wine 2. F monter/s'emporter comme une soupe au lait, to fly off the handle/to go off the deep end; il est très soupe au lait, he flares up easily/he's always flying off the handle 3. F *surt Mil* grub/nosh/chow; être de soupe, to be on cookhouse fatigue; à la soupe! grub's up!/come and get it! aller à la soupe, to (go and) have dinner/a meal; *Fig* to look for power *or* financial gain 4. F manger la soupe à la grimace, to be in the doghouse (*after a quarrel, etc*); recevoir la soupe à la grimace, to get a poor welcome 5. F trempé comme une soupe, drenched (to the skin)/like

a drowned rat 6. F un gros plein de soupe, very fat man/fatso 7. F (*théâtre*) servir la soupe, to play small roles/to take bit parts 8. F (*ski*) soft snow 9. P par ici la bonne soupe! (*qch de désagréable*) come and get it! (*qch d'avantageux*) that's the way to make money! 10. V piece of bread left in public urinal by a sexual pervert. (*Voir* **cheveu 7**; **cracher I 5**; **marchand 6**)

souper [supe] *vi* F j'en ai soupé, I'm fed up* (with it/him/her, etc); I've had enough/a bellyful (of it/him/her, etc). (*Voir* **fiole 2**)

soupeur [supœr] *nm* V sexual pervert who eats bread soaked in urine*.

sourdine [surdin] *nf* F mettre la sourdine, to shut up*/to pipe down/to put a sock in it.

sourdingue [surdɛ̃g] *a & n* P deaf (person).

souricière [surisjɛr] *nf* 1. F police trap 2. P police station/lock-up.

sourire [surir] *nm* 1. P sourire de la vache, knife cuts in both cheeks starting from the corner of the mouth (*used on prostitutes who give information to the police, etc*) 2. F sourire Gibbs, broad (toothy) grin/toothy smile. (*Voir* **croix 4**; **gomme 2**)

souris [suri] *nf* 1. P (*esp* young) woman*/ bird/chick 2. F petite souris, busy little old lady; mousy little woman 3. F souris de sacristie, bigoted churchwoman 4. P souris d'hôtel, (female) hotel thief.

sous-bite [subit] *nm* P Mil (*sous-lieutenant*) second lieutenant; (*sous-officier*) non-commissioned officer/NCO. (*pl* sous-bites)

sous-cul [sukyl] *nm inv* P (*a*) seat mat/ bottom mat (*b*) (padded) cushion (to sit on).

sous-fifre [sufifr] *nm* F underling/second fiddle/dogsbody. (*pl* sous-fifres)

sous-lieute [suljøt] *nm* F Mil second lieutenant. (*pl* sous-lieutes)

sous-mac [sumak] *nf* P chief assistant to brothel keeper; brothel hostess. (*pl* sous-macs)

sous-main [sumɛ̃] *adv phr* F en sous-main, secretly/behind the scenes.

sous-maq [sumak] *nf P* = **sous-mac**.

sous-marin [sumarɛ̃] *nm* P 1. swindler*/ crook/shark 2. worker sent to spy on other workers *or* who has secret motives for working in his job; s.o. who does not appear on the payroll 3. converted van used for police surveillance. (*pl* sous-marins)

sous-maxé [sumakse] *nf P* = **sous-mac**.

sous-off [suzɔf] *nm* F Mil non-commissioned officer/non-com/NCO. (*pl* sous-offs)

sous-tasse [sutɑs] *nf P* innocent client who pays for a nightclub hostess's drinks. (*pl* sous-tasses)

sous-ventrière [suvɑ̃trijɛr] *nf P* manger à se/s'en faire péter la sous-ventrière, to eat till one is fit to burst.

sous-verge [suvɛrʒ] *nm inv P* underling/ second fiddle/(*general*) dogsbody.

soutien-loloches [sutjɛ̃lɔlɔʃ] *nm inv P* bra/tit-holder. (*Voir* **loloches**)

soutif [sutif] *nm P* = **soutien-loloches**.

souvent [suvɑ̃] *adv P* plus souvent! no fear!/not (bloody) likely*!/not on your life! plus souvent que j'irai! you won't catch me going!/no way am I going!

soviétique [sɔvjetik] *a F* c'est soviétique, it's old-fashioned; it's tacky; it's badly organized; there's a queue/you have to queue.

spé [spe] *nm P* = **spécial** I.

'spèce [spɛs] *nf P* 'spèce de ... = espèce de ....

spécial, *pl* **-aux** [spesjal, -o] I *nm P* 1. filer/prendre du spécial, (*homme*) to be a homosexual* 2. faire le spécial, (*femme*) to be a backside special II *a* 1. *F* c'est un peu spécial, it's rather odd/queer 2. *P Euph* mœurs spéciales, homosexuality; avoir des goûts spéciaux, to have homosexual tendencies/to be that way inclined.

spécialo [spesjalo] *nm F* specialist.

speed [spid] *P* (*drogues*) I *a inv* = **speedé, speedy** II *nm* amphetamine*/speed.

speedball [spidbɔl] *nm P* (*drogues*) heroin* and cocaine* mixture/speedball.

speedé [spide]**, speedy** [spidi] *a P* être speedé, (*drogues*) to be on amphetamines*/ speed; to be speeding; (*nerveux*) to be very excited/nervous/strung out; il bosse trop, il est complètement speedé, he works so much he's like a bag of nerves/it's like he's on speed.

speeder [spide] *P* (*drogues*) I *vtr* to make (s.o.) high on speed II *vpr* **se speeder** to take speed/to get high on speed.

splitté [splite] *a F* split up/separated.

sport [spɔr] *nm F* 1. il va y avoir du sport!/ nous allons voir du sport! now we're going to see some fun/some action! now for the fireworks! 2. c'est du sport, it's difficult (and dangerous).

square [skwɛr] *a inv & n F* 1. (*jazz, drogues*) (person who is) uninitiated/not part of the scene 2. (*démodé, ringard*) square/ fuddy-duddy (person).

squatter [skwate] *vtr F* to usurp/take over

(a flat, a room, etc); elle m'a squatté mon bureau, she's taken over my office/she's moved into my office (without so much as a by-your-leave); on peut squatter cette chambre? can I/we have this room?

stal [stal] *nm & f F* (= *stalinien*) Stalinist; (*communiste*) commie/red/= trot.

steak [stɛk] *nm P* gagner son steak, to earn one's living. (*Voir* **bifteck 2**)

step [stɛp] *nm P* nose*; step à trier les lentilles/à repiquer les choux, big nose/big conk.

steupo [støpo] *nm P* (*verlan de poste*) car radio.

stick [stik] *nm P* (*drogues*) marijuana* cigarette/joint.

stiff [stif] *nm P* tramp*/dosser/*NAm* bum/ stiff.

stomba [stɔ̃ba] *nf P* (*verlan de* **baston**) fight/punch-up/fisticuffs.

stone(d) [stɔn(d)] *a P* (*drogues*) drugged*/ stoned.

stop [stɔp] *nm F* faire du stop, to hitch(-hike)/to thumb (a lift); to backpack; aller à Paris en stop, to hitch (it)/to thumb it to Paris; un camion nous a pris en stop, we hitched/thumbed a lift on a lorry/*NAm* a truck.

stoppeur, -euse [stɔpœr, -øz] *n F* hitch-hiker/hitcher; backpacker.

stoqué [stɔke] *a FrC F* être stoqué sur qn, to have a crush on s.o./to be nuts about s.o./to have a thing about s.o.

store [stɔr] *nm P* eyelid; baisser les stores, to close one's eyes.

strasse [strɑs] *nf P* 1. (*a*) room (*b*) room in a hotel, etc, used by a prostitute* 2. street; road; être en strasse, (*taxi*) to wait at the taxi rank.

stripteaseuse [striptizøz] *nf F* stripper/ *NAm* nudie.

stresser [strɛse] *vi F* 1. to be anxious/ nervous; je stresse un max à l'approche des exams, I'm really nervous about the exams 2. to be afraid*/to funk it.

stropia [strɔpja] *nm P* cripple (*real or sham*).

stuff [stœf] *nm P* (*drogues*) drugs*/dope/ junk/stuff.

stup [styp] *nm P* (*drogues*) narcotic; *pl* stups, drugs/dope/junk; la Brigade des stups/ les stups, (*police*) the Drug(s) Squad.

suant [sɥɑ̃] *a P* boring.

suante [sɥɑ̃t] *nf P* week.

sub [syb] *nm P* (*verlan de bus*) bus.

subito [sybito] *adv F* subito (presto), (*subitement*) all of a sudden; (*immédiatement*) immediately*/at once/pronto/in a jiffy.

subodorer [sybɔdɔre] *vtr F* (*personne*) to suspect/to get wind of (sth); to sense (danger, etc); **il a subodoré quelque chose,** he smelt a rat.

subtiliser [syptilize] *vtr F* to steal*/to sneak/to swipe; **ils m'ont subtilisé ma montre,** they've pinched my watch.

suçade [sysad] *nf,* **suçage** [sysaʒ] *nm V* fellatio*.

sucer [syse] *vtr* 1. *F* sucer qn (jusqu'au dernier sou/jusqu'à la moelle des os), to suck s.o. dry/to bleed s.o. white/to take s.o.'s last penny 2. *P* sucer la pomme/le museau à qn, to kiss s.o. (*Voir* **caillou 2**; **poire I 8** (*a*)) 3. *P* to drink* (wine, etc); **il ne suce pas des glaces/que des glaces,** he drinks* like a fish/ he's a boozer 4. *F* **ma voiture suce l'essence,** my car consumes a lot of petrol/my car's a gas guzzler 5. *V* (*fellation, cunnilinctus*) to suck (s.o.) off/to go down on (s.o.)/to eat (s.o.).

sucette [sysɛt] *nf P* (*CB, etc*) microphone/ mike/lollipop.

suceuse [sysøz] *nf V* woman* who practises fellatio*.

suçon [sysɔ̃] *nm F* love-bite/hickey.

sucrage [sykraʒ] *nm P* 1. arrest 2. conviction; (prison) sentence; stretch/rap/time.

sucre [sykr] *nm* 1. *F* **c'est du sucre,** (*facile*) it's easy*/it's a cinch/it's a doddle; (*le meilleur*) it's great/it's the best 2. *F* **un vrai sucre,** a pet/a poppet/a honey 3. *F* **casser du sucre sur le dos/sur la tête de qn,** to speak ill of s.o./to run s.o. down/to knock s.o. 4. *F* **il a été tout sucre (et) tout miel,** he was as sweet as could be; he was all honey 5. *P* (*drogues*) (*a*) LSD*/sugar (lump) (*b*) heroin*/cocaine* *or* morphine* in powdered form; sugar 6. *F* (*théâtre*) **recevoir son morceau de sucre,** to be applauded the moment one first appears on stage 7. *Vieilli P* sucre de pomme, jemmy/ *NAm* jimmy. (*Voir* **bout 8**)

sucrée [sykre] *nf F* faire la sucrée, to put on demure airs; **elle fait la sucrée,** she acts as though butter wouldn't melt in her mouth.

sucrer [sykre] I *vtr P* 1. to arrest*; se faire sucrer, to get nabbed 2. to remove/to withdraw (sth); to cut (a text, an article); **on lui a sucré son permis,** he's had his driving licence taken away. (*Voir* **fraise 2, 3**) II *vpr* **se sucrer** *F* (*a*) to get rich*; to feather one's nest

(*b*) to take the lion's share. (*Voir* **gaufre 2**)

sucrette [sykrɛt] *nf F* aller à la sucrette, to compromise with one's conscience; to accept a bribe.

suée [sɥe] *nf P* 1. fright/scare 2. hard work/ sweat/grind/slog.

suer [sɥe] I *vi F* faire suer qn, (*embêter*) to annoy*/to plague s.o.; **tu me fais suer!** you get on my nerves!/you're a pain in the neck! II *vtr P* 1. **en suer une,** to (have a) dance 2. **faire suer le burnous,** to exploit *or* overwork people; to use sweated labour. (*Voir* **sang 5**)

sueur [sɥœr] *nm P* sueur de chêne, thief who will kill if necessary. (*Voir* **chêne**)

suif [sɥif] *nm P* 1. reprimand*; **donner/ flanquer/passer un suif à qn,** to reprimand* s.o./to tear s.o. off a strip 2. **chercher du suif,** to be looking/to be out for a fight; **chercher du suif à qn,** to pick a quarrel* with s.o.; **être en suif,** to be on bad terms (**avec qn,** with s.o.) 3. uproar; **faire du suif,** to kick up a row 4. scandal 5. **se faire du suif,** to worry/to fret 6. **faire en suif,** to cheat (*at cards, etc*) 7. **jeter du suif,** to be elegantly dressed; to put on one's glad rags.

suiffard [sɥifar] *Vieilli P* I *a* elegant/smart II *nm* cheat (*at cards, etc*). (*Voir* **suif 6**)

suiffée [sɥife] *nf P* beating*/thrashing/good hiding.

suiffer [sɥife] *vtr P* to give (s.o.) a good beating*/thrashing.

suisse [sɥis] *nf F* boire en suisse, to drink on one's own (*without treating the company*); **faire suisse,** to drink on one's own; (*être égoïste*) to be selfish/not to share with others.

de suite [dəsɥit] *adv phr F* (= *tout de suite*) at once/immediately.

sulfater [sylfate] *vtr P* sulfater qn, to shoot/ to kill* s.o. with a (sub)machine gun/*NAm* chopper.

sulfateuse [sylfatøz] *nf P* (sub)machine gun/*NAm* chopper.

sultane [syltan] *nf P* mistress.

sup [syp] *a inv F* (= *supplémentaire(s)*) supplementary/extra; **une heure sup,** an hour's overtime; **faire des heures sup,** to do overtime.

super [sypɛr] *F* I *a* excellent*/super/terrific/ great II *nm Aut* (= *supercarburant*) four-star (petrol)/*NAm* premium *or* hi-test gas.

super- [sypɛr] *préf F* (*hors de commun*) (*avant nom*) super-; (*avant adjectif*) ultra-; **super-professeur/bombe,** super-teacher/bomb; **super-chic,** ultra-chic.

super-banco [sypɛrbãko] *a F* la question super-banco, the sixty-four thousand dollar question.

supercagnotte [sypɛrkaɲɔt] *nf F* (*de loterie, etc*) jackpot.

super-class [sypɛrklas] *a inv F* excellent*/ fantastic/really great/amazing/far out.

superflic [sypɛrflik] *nm P* supercop.

superflip [sypɛrflip] *nm P* deep/severe depression; flipping out/freaking out. (*Voir* **flip 1, 2**)

supermarca(t) [sypɛrmarka] *nm F* supermarket. (*Voir* **marca(t)**)

supernana [sypɛrnana] *nf P* beautiful girl* *or* woman*; gorgeous bird/sexy number. (*Voir* **nana 1** (*a*))

superpied [sypɛrpje] *nm P* c'était le superpied, it was absolutely fantastic/out of this world; I/we had a wild time. (*Voir* **pied 21**)

suppositoire [sypozitwar] *nm F* suppositoire à autobus, small car. (*Voir* **autobus**)

supprimer [syprime] I *vtr F* supprimer qn, to kill* s.o./to liquidate s.o./to remove s.o./to bump s.o. off II *vpr* **se supprimer** *F* to commit suicide*/to top oneself.

sûr [syr] *F* I *a* c'est sûr et certain, it's absolutely certain/it's a dead cert*; c'est du sûr, it's a good tip/it's good info; **pour sûr!** sure!/of course! **pour sûr que c'est pas facile!** of course it's not easy! **bien sûr?** you really mean it? **(bon sang, mais) c'est bien sûr!** of course, why didn't I think of it before! II *adv* surely; **pas sûr!** perhaps not!

surbine [syrbin] *nf Vieilli P* 1. observation cell 2. (police) surveillance.

surbiner [syrbine] *vtr P* (*surt police*) to keep (s.o.) under surveillance; to watch/to keep a close eye on (s.o.).

surboum [syrbum] *nf F* party. (*Voir* **boum II**)

Sûrepige [syrpiʒ] *nf P* (= *Sûreté*) Criminal Investigation Department/CID; *approx* = New Scotland Yard.

surface [syrfas] *nf* 1. *F* refaire surface, (*personne*) to surface (*after long silence, scandal, etc*) 2. *F* en boucher une surface à qn; *Voir* **boucher** 3. *P* il a de la surface, he's comfortably off/he's not short of a penny or two.

surgé [syrʒe] *nm*, **surgeot** [syrʒo] *nm*, **surgo** [syrgo] *nm F* (= *surveillant général*) vice-principal/deputy head(master); senior master.

surin [syrɛ̃] *nm P* knife/dagger/chiv.

suriner [syrine] *vtr P* to knife (s.o.); to stab (s.o.) to death; to chiv(e) (s.o.).

surineur [syrinœr] *nm P* knifer/chive-man/ knife merchant.

surpatte [syrpat] *nf F* = **surboum**.

surprenante [syrprənãt] *P* I *nf* illegal and faked lottery II *adv phr* à la surprenante, unawares/by surprise.

surtout [syrtu] *conj phr F* surtout que ..., (e)specially as ....

survé [syrve] *nm F* = **surgé**.

survolté [syrvɔlte] *a F* (*a*) (*surexcité*) excited/worked up/(all) het up (*b*) une affaire survoltée, a souped-up job.

survolter [syrvɔlte] *vtr F* survolter une foule, to get a crowd worked up.

susucre [sysykr] *nm F* (*langage enfantin*) sugar.

swing [swiŋ] *a inv Vieilli F* hip/with it; une jeune fille swing, a with-it chick; les gens swing, hip cats; une robe swing, a fashionable dress.

swing(u)er [swiŋge] *vi F Mus* to swing.

sympa [sɛ̃pa] *a F* (*abrév* = *sympathique*) (*personne*) likeable/nice; elle est très sympa, cette prof, that teacher's really nice/very friendly.

synchro [sɛ̃kro] *a inv F* (= *synchronisé*) in sync; pas synchro, out of sync.

syndicat [sɛ̃dika] *nm P* être du syndicat, to have syphilis*.

synoque [sinɔk] *a P* mad*/crackers/ bonkers. (*Voir* **cynoque**; **sinoc**)

syphilo [sifilo] *P* I *nf* syphilis*/syph II *nm* person suffering from syphilis*; syphilitic/ sypho.

syphlotte [siflɔt] *nf P* syphilis*/syph/siff/ (the) pox.

système [sistɛm] *nm F* taper/courir sur le système à qn, to get on s.o.'s nerves/on s.o.'s wick. (*Voir* **D**)

T

tabac [taba] *nm F* 1. (*a*) (*surt police*) passer qn à tabac, to beat s.o. up*/to work s.o. over/ to do s.o. over; to handle s.o. roughly; passage à tabac, beating* up/working over/ rough handling; les flics l'ont passé à tabac, the cops worked him over/beat him up (*b*) il y a du tabac, we're in for a spot of bother/we're up against it; there's going to be some aggro/ action/trouble (*c*) faire un tabac, to kick up a fuss/to make a song and dance about sth; (*théâtre*) to be a success/a hit; ce film a été son premier tabac, that film was his first box-office success/his first hit 2. c'est le même tabac, it's the same thing; ce n'est pas le même tabac, that's quite a different matter/ *NAm* that's a whole new ball game 3. *Vieilli* tabac de Chine, OP (= other people's) tobacco. (*Voir* **blague 3**; **paquet 12**; **pot 11**)

tabassage [tabasaʒ] *nm F* beating* up (of s.o.)/going-over/working over/doing over; fight*/punch-up; third degree.

tabassée [tabase] *nf F* beating* (up)/(good) thrashing/pasting; fight*/punch-up; trouble/ aggro.

tabasser [tabase] *F* I *vtr* to beat (s.o.) up*/ to work (s.o.) over/to give (s.o.) a going-over; to give (s.o.) the third degree II *vpr* **se tabasser** to beat* each other up.

tabellion [tabeljɔ̃] *nm F Hum* limb of the law; lawyer.

table [tabl] *nf* 1. *F* sous la table, secretly/ under the table 2. *P* se mettre/passer à table, (*avouer*) to confess*/to come clean; (*dénoncer*) to grass/to snitch; to shop s.o.; manger à la grande table, to be a police* informer/a copper's nark/a snout. (*Voir* **manger 4**)

tableau, -eaux [tablo] *nm F* 1. vieux tableau, (*vieille femme*) painted old hag/mutton dressed (up) as lamb 2. décrocher ses tableaux, to pick one's nose 3. (*a*) jouer/miser sur les deux tableaux, to lay odds both ways/ to hedge (one's bets); jouer/miser sur le même tableau, to put all one's eggs in one basket (*b*) gagner sur tous les tableaux/sur les deux tableaux, to win all along the line/on all counts 4. cela fera bien dans le tableau/ cela ne ferait pas mal dans le tableau, that will/would suit me down to the ground 5. voir le tableau, to understand/to get the picture. (*Voir* **ombre 2**)

tablettes [tablɛt] *nfpl F* mettre/noter qch sur ses tablettes, to make a note of sth; rayez cela de vos tablettes, you can forget that.

tablier [tablije] *nm* 1. *F* rendre son tablier, to leave (one's job)/to give in one's notice/to ask for one's cards 2. *V* tablier de forgeron/de sapeur, (woman's) pubic hair/mount of Venus 3. *F* ça lui va comme un tablier à une vache, it looks ridiculous on him/her. (*Voir* **déchirer**)

tabourets [taburɛ] *nmpl P* teeth*/choppers; n'avoir plus de tabourets dans la salle à manger/dans la croquante, to have no teeth.

tac [tak] *nm P* taxi/cab.

tache [taʃ] *P* I *nf ou m* (*personne*) nonentity/complete dud; c'est un(e) tache, he's a poor sod II *nf* c'est la tache, it's worthless/useless.

tachon [taʃɔ̃] *nm P* = **tache I**.

tacmard [takmar] *nm P* = **tac**.

tacot [tako] *nm* 1. *F* (ramshackle) old car*/ banger/old crock/jalopy; quel tacot! what a wreck!/what a heap! 2. *P* (*aussi* **taco**) taxi/ cab.

taf [taf] *nm P* 1. fear/funk; avoir le taf, to be afraid*/to get the wind up 2. share (of the loot)/cut; aller au taf, to share out the spoils/ to divvy up 3. (*a*) aller au taf, to go to work (*b*) faire le taf, (*prostituée*) to solicit*/to be on the job 4. prendre son taf, to ejaculate*/to come/to shoot one's load; to have an orgasm* 5. c'est pas mon taf, it's not my strong point.

tafanar(d) [tafanar] *nm P* buttocks*/arse/ *esp NAm* ass.

taffe [taf] *P* I *nm* = **taf** II *nf* 1. *Vieilli* cigarette*/fag 2. puff/drag on a cigarette.

taffer [tafe] *vi P* to be afraid*/to get the wind up.

taffeur [tafœr] *Vieilli P* I *a* cowardly*/yellow II *nm* coward*/chicken/yellowbelly.

tag [tag] *nm F* (*signature du dessinateur de graffiti*) tag; faire des tags, to tag; to cover with graffiti.

tagger¹ [tagɛr] *nm F* (*dessinateur de graffiti*) tagger.

tagger², taguer [tage] *vi F* (*tracer des tags*) to tag/to cover with graffiti.

tagueur [tagœr] *nm F* = **tagger¹**.

taille [tɑj] *nf P* faire sa taille, to earn one's daily bread.

tailler [tɑje] I *vtr* 1. *F* tailler de la besogne à qn, to make work for s.o. 2. *P* tailler le bout de gras/en tailler une avec qn, to have a chat*/a chinwag/a natter with s.o.; to chew the fat with s.o. (*Voir* **bavette**) 3. *P* tailler la route, (*partir*) to beat it/to clear off. (*Voir* **basane 2**; **drap 2**; **pipe 6**; **plume II 9**) II *vpr* **se tailler** *P* (*partir*) to split/to beat it.

tailleuse [tɑjøz] *nf V* tailleuse de plumes, prostitute* who practises fellation*.

tala [tala] *F* I *n* (*militant*) Roman Catholic student (*esp at the École normale supérieure*) (*from* "ceux qui vont à la messe") II *a* sanctimonious.

talbin [talbɛ̃] *nm P* banknote/greenback; quelques talbins, a few quid.

talmouse [talmuz] *nf Vieilli F* blow*/punch/ wallop.

talochage [talɔʃaʒ] *nm F* slapping (round the face); clouting (on the head).

taloche [talɔʃ] *nf F* slap (round the face); clout (on the head); filer une taloche à qn, to slap s.o. round the face.

talocher [talɔʃe] *vtr F* talocher qn, to slap s.o. (round the face); to clout s.o. (on the head); to box s.o.'s ears.

talon [talɔ̃] *nm P* avoir les talons courts, (*femme*) to be an easy lay/a pushover. (*Voir* **estomac 1**)

tam [tam] *nm P* = **tam-tam**.

tambouille [tɑ̃buj] *nf P* (*cuisine*) cooking/ cookery; (*plat, etc*) chow/nosh/grub; faire la tambouille, to make/to get (the) grub; quelle tambouille! what muck!

tambour [tɑ̃bur] *nm F* 1. raisonner comme un tambour (mouillé), to talk through one's hat/to talk drivel 2. marcher comme un tambour, to fall for it (like a mug) 3. il n'y a

pas de quoi faire passer le tambour de ville, it's nothing to make a song and dance about; it's nothing to write home about. (*Voir* **feu 6**)

tampax [tɑ̃paks] *nm ou f P* filter-tip(ped) cigarette*.

tampon [tɑ̃pɔ̃] *nm F* 1. fist; coup de tampon, violent blow*/punch/thump; coups de tampon, brawl/punch-up 2. *Mil* orderly/ batman.

tamponnage [tɑ̃pɔnaʒ] *nm*, **tamponnement** [tɑ̃pɔnmɑ̃] *nm F* beating*-up/good hiding.

tamponner [tɑ̃pɔne] I *vtr* 1. *F* tamponner qn, to beat s.o. up*/to give s.o. a good hiding/ to knock s.o. about 2. *P* tamponner une nana/ une nénette, to have sex* with a girl; se faire tamponner, (*fille*) to get laid II *vpr* **se tamponner** 1. *F* to come to blows/to have a punch-up 2. *P* je m'en tamponne, I couldn't care less*; I don't give a damn; to hell with it. (*Voir* **coquillard**)

tamponnoir [tɑ̃pɔnwar] *nm P* sanitary towel/*NAm* napkin; rag.

tam-tam [tamtam] *nm F* (*a*) (vulgar/loud) publicity (*b*) row/fuss/ballyhoo; faire du tam-tam (à propos de qch/autour de qch), to make a great fuss/to make a great ballyhoo/to kick up a rumpus (about sth).

tandem [tɑ̃dɛm] *nm F* pair (of criminals, etc); duo/couple/twosome.

tangent, -ente [tɑ̃ʒɑ̃, -ɑ̃t] I *a* 1. *P* c'est tangent, it's as near as dammit; (*critique*) it's touch and go 2. *F* être tangent à un examen, to fail an exam narrowly II *n F* candidate who came very near the pass mark/borderline case III *nf F* 1. invigilator (at an exam) 2. sword (*of student at the École polytechnique*) 3. prendre la tangente/s'échapper par la tangente/filer par la tangente, to go off at a tangent; to dodge the question/to wriggle out (of sth); (*partir*) to make a quick getaway/to beat it.

tango [tɑ̃go] *nm F* (*boisson*) beer and grenadine syrup/(sort of) shandy.

tannant [tanɑ̃] *a P* boring; annoying/ irritating; il est tannant, he drives me mad; he's a pest/a (damned) nuisance.

tannée [tane] *nf F* thrashing/(good) hiding/ tanning.

tanner [tane] *vtr* 1. *F* tanner (la peau à) qn, to thrash s.o./to tan the hide off s.o./to give s.o. a (good) hiding. (*Voir* **côte I 3**; **cuir 4**) 2. *F* tanner les oreilles à qn au sujet de qch, to din/to drum sth into s.o. 3. *P* (*harceler*) to pester/to badger (s.o.); (*ennuyer*) to bore* (s.o.); (*irriter*) to annoy*/to irritate (s.o.); to drive (s.o.) up the wall/mad.

tant [tɑ̃] *adv* 1. *F* il pleut tant qu'il peut, it's raining like anything/it's raining cats and dogs; il cognait tant qu'il pouvait, he was hitting as hard as he could 2. *F* vous m'en direz tant! you don't say!/really? 3. *F* un Docteur Tant pis, a pessimist; un Docteur Tant mieux, an optimist 4. *P* tant qu'à (*a*) (= *quant à*) as for; tant qu'à ça, je m'en fous, as for that, I don't give a damn (*b*) (= *pendant que*) tant que vous y êtes, prenez-en deux, take two, while you're about it. (*Voir* **pire 1**)

tante [tɑ̃t] *nf P* 1. homosexual*/fairy/queen/ *Br* poof(ter)/*surt NAm* fag(got)/nancy-boy 2. espèce de tante! (*insulte*) you poofter! 3. ma tante, (*mont-de-piété*) uncle's/the pawnbroker's (shop); chez ma tante, at the pawnbroker's/in hock 4. si ma tante en avait, elle s'appellerait mon oncle, if my aunt had balls she'd be my uncle 5. (*CB*) Tante Victorine, television (set)/TV. (*Voir* **Bretagne**)

tantine [tɑ̃tin] *nf F* auntie/aunty.

tantinette [tɑ̃tinɛt] *nf* = **tante 1**.

tantouse, tantouze [tɑ̃tuz] *nf P* = **tante 1**.

tapage [tapaʒ] *nm P* cadging; tapping/ touching (of s.o. for money).

tapanard [tapanar] *nm Vieilli P* buttocks*.

tapant [tapɑ̃] I *a F* arriver tapant/à l'heure tapante, to arrive dead on time/bang on time/ on the dot II *nm P* (smelly) cheese.

tape [tap] *nf P* failure/setback/knock; quelle tape! what a flop! recevoir/prendre une tape, to flop.

tapé [tape] *P* I *a* 1. mad*/bonkers/cracked 2. excellent*/first-rate; une réponse tapée, a smart answer; ça, c'est (bien) tapé! that's a good one!/nice work! II *n* mad person*/loony/ crackpot.

tape-à-l'œil [tapalœj] *F* I *a inv* flashy/ showy/loud/tarty II *nm* du tape-à-l'œil, flashy stuff; c'est du tape-à-l'œil, it's all for show.

tapecul, tape-cul [tapky] *nm F* 1. car* (*with poor suspension*)/rattletrap/boneshaker 2. train that stops at every station 3. faire du tapecul, to trot (on horseback).

tapée [tape] *nf F* great quantity*/large number (of things, people); une tapée de marmots, a swarm of brats; j'en ai une tapée, I've got heaps/tons/plenty.

taper [tape] I *vtr F* 1. taper la carte/le carton, to play cards; taper une belote/en

taper une, to play/to have a game of *belote* 2. *F Aut* taper du 200, to clock 200 kilometres an hour; to hit the 200 mark 3. *F* taper qn de cent francs, to tap/to touch s.o. for a hundred francs; to cadge a hundred francs off s.o. 4. *F* se faire taper sur les doigts, to take the rap 5. *P* se taper/s'en taper le cul par terre/le cul au plafond, to split one's sides laughing/to kill oneself laughing. (*Voir* **astape**; **colonne 2**; **faffe 1**; **gueule I 4** (*b*); **lampe 1**; **môme II 2**; **tête 20**) II *vi* 1. *F* (*soleil*) to beat down; ça tape! it's a scorcher! 2. *F* (*a*) taper sur qn, (*critiquer*) to knock s.o./to have a go at s.o.; on lui a tapé dessus, they pitched into him (*b*) taper sur l'os (à qn), to annoy* (s.o.) (*c*) *Mil* taper sur un objectif, to strafe a target 3. *P* to stink*; ça tape ici! what a stink! taper des pieds, to have smelly feet*. (*Voir* **nerf 1**; **œil 1, 2**; **système**; **tas 4**; **ventre 4**) III *vpr* **se taper** 1. *F* (*a*) se taper de qn, to make fun of s.o./to poke fun at s.o. (*b*) je m'en tape, I couldn't give a damn (about it) 2. *F* se taper de qch, to be deprived of sth/to (have to) do without sth 3. *F* se taper qch (*a*) to treat oneself to sth (nice); se taper un double whisky, to treat oneself to a double whisky. (*Voir* **cloche I 7**; **gueule I 4** (*b*); **gueuleton**) (*b*) to have to do sth (unpleasant); se taper 20 kilomètres à pied, to have to do 20 kilometres on foot; se taper le ménage, to get landed/lumbered with the housework 4. *P* tu peux te taper! nothing doing*!/no way!/you can whistle for it!/take a running jump! 5. *V* se taper une femme, to have sex* with/to lay/to screw a woman. (*Voir* **colonne 2**)

tapette [tapɛt] *nf P* 1. homosexual*/fairy/ pansy/*Br* poof(ter)/nancy-boy/*surt NAm* fag(got); c'est une vraie tapette, he's a real fairy; bar à tapettes, gay bar 2. tongue/ clapper; avoir une fière/une sacrée tapette, avoir une de ces tapettes, to be a dreadful chatterbox*/to talk the hind leg off a donkey.

tapeur, -euse [tapœr, -øz] *n F* 1. (third-rate) pianist 2. cadger/sponger/scrounger.

tapin [tapɛ̃] *nm P* 1. (*a*) prostitution*/the game; faire le tapin/aller au tapin/descendre sur le tapin, to solicit*/to be on the game/to walk the streets (*b*) prostitute*/hooker 2. work/job; aller au tapin, to go to work.

tapinage [tapinaʒ] *nm P* prostitution; être au tapinage, to solicit*/to be on the game.

tapiner [tapine] *P* I *vi* (*prostituée*) to walk the streets (looking for clients)/to solicit*/to be on the game; to be on the job **II** *vtr & i* to work (**qch**, at sth).

tapineur [tapinœr] *nm P* male prostitute*.

tapineuse [tapinøz] *nf P* prostitute*/streetwalker/hooker.

tapir [tapir] *nm F* (*écoles*) 1. private lesson 2. pupil who takes private lessons.

tapis [tapi] **I** *a P* être tapis, to be penniless*/to be broke **II** *nm* 1. *F* discussion de marchands de tapis, haggling 2. *F* sur le tapis, on the carpet/under consideration 3. *P* amuser le tapis, to say amusing things; (*attirer les badauds*) to attract passers-by with sales patter/spiel; (*au jeu*) to stake small sums/small amounts of money 4. *P* seedy nightclub/dive/gambling joint. (*Voir* **revenir 3**)

tapis-franc [tapifrɑ̃] *nm A P* = **tapis 4**.

tapissage [tapisaʒ] *nm P* identification; passer au tapissage, to submit to an identification parade.

tapisser [tapise] *vtr P* to identify/to recognize/to clock (s.o.); il s'est fait tapisser par les flics, he was spotted by the cops/the cops got a make on him.

tapisserie [tapisri] *nf F* faire tapisserie, to be a wallflower (at a dance); to sit on the sidelines.

tapuscrit [tapyskri] *nm F* typed manuscript.

taquemart [takmar] *nm P* taxi/cab. (*Voir* **tac**)

taquet [takɛ] *nm Vieilli F* blow*/punch; prendre un taquet dans la gueule, to get a clout on the jaw.

taquiner [takine] *vtr F* taquiner le goujon, to angle/to do a bit of fishing; taquiner la muse, to write the odd bit of verse; taquiner la dame de pique, to play cards.

tarabistouille [tarabistuj] *nf F* confused situation/muddle; quelle tarabistouille! what a muddle/mess!

tarabuster [tarabyste] *vtr F* (*a*) to annoy*/to worry/to pester/to bug (s.o.) (*b*) se tarabuster l'esprit, to rack one's brains.

taratata! [taratata] *int F* nonsense*!/bunkum!/fiddlesticks!

taraudée [tarode] *nf F* thrashing/beating*(-up)/pasting/(good) hiding.

tarauder [tarode] **I** *vtr* 1. *F* to thrash/to beat (up)*/to lay into (s.o.) 2. *V* se faire tarauder le bouton, (*cunnilinctus*) to be sucked (off) **II** *vi P* tarauder à sec, to be very thirsty/to be parched.

tarbouif [tarbwif] *nm P* nose*/hooter.

tarde [tard] *nf P* night; à/sur la tarde, towards evening/towards nightfall.

tarderie [tardri] *nf P* une (vraie) tarderie, (*femme très laide*) an old hag/an old bag; (*objet*) a really ugly object/piece; an eyesore; cette robe c'est une vraie tarderie, that dress is a real eyesore/a perfect mess.

tardillon, -onne [tardijɔ̃, -ɔn] *n Vieilli F* last child/baby (of the family).

tardingue [tardɛ̃g] *a & nf P* ugly (woman).

taré, -ée [tare] *F* **I** *a* (*idiot*) cretinous **II** *n* cretin/moron.

tarebouif [tarbwif] *nm P* = **tarbouif**.

targe [tarʒ] *nf*, **targette** [tarʒɛt] *nf P* 1. foot*/hoof; (coup de) targette, (*coup de pied*) kick 2. shoe/boot; 3. coup de targette, loan; filer un coup de targette à qn, to borrow from s.o./to cadge off s.o./to touch s.o. (for sth).

tarif [tarif] *nm F* maximum penalty (for crime, etc); trois mois de prison, c'est le tarif, three months in prison is what it'll cost you.

tarin [tarɛ̃] *nm P* 1. nose*/beak/*Br* conk 2. se casser/se cogner le tarin, to find nobody at home (when calling at a house); (*échouer*) to fail (in business); to come a cropper* 3. avoir qn dans le tarin, to detest s.o.; je l'ai dans le tarin, he gets up my nose 4. se salir/se piquer le tarin, to get drunk*; to hit the bottle; avoir un (petit) coup dans le tarin/avoir un coup de trop dans le tarin/avoir le tarin sali, to be drunk*.

tarpé [tarpe] *nm*, **tarpet** [tarpɛ] *nm P* (*verlan de* **pétard**) 1. marijuana cigarette*/joint/reefer 2. firearm/revolver*/shooter.

tartavelle [tartavɛl] *a & nf P* ugly (woman).

tarte [tart] **I** *a F* 1. (*personne*) stupid*/daft/ridiculous 2. ugly; lousy/crummy; ridiculous; un film tarte, a rotten/stupid film; chapeau tarte, ridiculous hat **II** *nf* 1. *F* tarte à la crème, (*théâtre, etc*) custard pie (*thrown at s.o.*); (*lieu commun*) cliché/commonplace/truism 2. *F* c'est de la (vraie) tarte, it's easy*/it's a piece of cake; c'est pas de la tarte, it's not easy; it's quite difficult; la vie c'est pas de la tarte, life's not always a bed of roses 3. *P* slap/smack 4. *P* se fendre la tarte, to laugh* a lot/to be in stitches 5. *F* (*personne*) idiot/berk.

Tartempion [tartɑ̃pjɔ̃] *nm F Péj* (*personne*) thingummy/what's-his-name/so-and-so; un quelconque Tartempion, some bloke or other/any Tom, Dick or Harry.

tarter [tarte] *vtr P* tarter qn, to slap s.o.'s

face; to punch s.o. in the face.

tartignol(le) [tartiɲɔl] *a P* = **tarte I 1, 2**.

tartinage [tartinaʒ] *nm P* borrowing/ cadging/scrounging.

tartine [tartin] *nf* 1. *F* long, rambling speech, letter, article, etc; screed; il m'a débité toute une tartine, he came out with this really long story; he lectured me at great length/he seemed to go on for ever; en faire une tartine/faire des tartines sur qch, to waffle on about sth 2. *P* shoe/boot 3. *P* foot*; aller à tartine, to go on foot 4. *pl P* WC*/(the) john/(the) lav. (*Voir* **palas II 1**)

tartiner [tartine] I *vi* 1. *F* to ramble (on)/to waffle (on)/to be long-winded (*orally or in writing*) 2. *P* to borrow (*esp money*) II *vpr* se **tartiner** *P* 1. je m'en tartine! I couldn't care less*!/I don't give a damn!/I don't give a monkey's! 2. se tartiner qch/qn, to have to do sth unpleasant/to have to deal with sth/s.o.; to get landed with sth/s.o.

tartinier [tartinje] *nm F* long-winded/ rambling speaker *or* writer.

tartir [tartir] *vi* 1. *P* envoyer tartir qn, to tell s.o. to get lost/to bugger off; to give s.o. the bum's rush 2. *P* se faire tartir, to be bored* stiff/to be fed up to the back teeth 3. *V* to defecate*/to (have a) shit/to (have a) crap.

tartiss [tartis] *nm*, **tartisses** [tartis] *nfpl*, **tartissoir** [tartiswar] *nm*, **tartissoires** [tartiswar] *nfpl V* WC*/craphouse/crapper/ shithouse.

tartissure [tartisyr] *nf V* stain/dirty mark (of excrement on underclothes).

tartouillard [tartujar], **tartouille** [tartuj] *a P* = **tarte I 1, 2**.

tartouse [tartuz], **tartouzard** [tartuzar], **tartouze** [tartuz] *a P* = **tarte I 1, 2**.

tas [tɑ] *nm F* 1. sur le tas, immediately*/ straight away 2. prendre qn sur le tas, to catch s.o. in the act/red-handed; être crevé/ fabriqué/fait marron/piqué sur le tas, to be caught in the act/to be caught red-handed 3. sécher sur le tas, to wait in vain/to be stood up 4. piquer/taper dans le tas, to help oneself; to take one's choice/to take one's pick 5. faire le tas, (*prostituée*) to solicit*/to walk the streets/to be on the game; to hook/to hustle 6. ugly girl*/woman*; quel tas! what an eyesore (she is)!/what a fright! 7. tas de ferraille/de boue/de tôle, broken-down car*/old banger/ wreck/heap (of scrap metal) 8. large quantity*; un tas de mensonges, a pack of lies; (il) y en a des tas (et des tas), there's heaps

(and heaps)/bags (and bags)/loads (and loads) of them; j'ai un tas de choses à faire, I've (got) loads of things to do; quel tas de gens! what a collection!/what a crew! tas de crétins! bunch of idiots! tas de salauds! you bastards! 9. tirer dans le tas, (*groupe de gens*) to shoot/ fire indiscriminately (at a group).

tasse [tɑs] *nf* 1. *F* (a) Vieilli la grande tasse, the sea/the drink/the briny/Davy Jones's locker; boire (à) la grande tasse, to be drowned at sea (b) boire une/la tasse, to get a mouthful (*when swimming*); il a bu une/la tasse, he nearly drowned 2. *F* (*échec*) failure*/flop/ bomb; boire la tasse, to come a cropper*/to fail/to come unstuck/to go under; c'est la tasse, it's useless/worthless 3. *P* en avoir sa tasse, to be (thoroughly) fed up* (with sth)/to have had it (up to here) 4. *P* tasse (à thé), street urinal (*esp one frequented by homosexuals*)/cottage/tea room(s); faire les tasses, to cottage/to go cottaging/to go john-cruising 5. *P* drink; glass of wine; prendre une tasse, to have a drink 6. *P* tasse (à café), small moped (*less than 50 cm³*).

tassé [tɑse] *a F* (a) full/complete/whole; livre de 1000 pages bien tassées, book with a good/of at least 1000 pages; deux heures (bien) tassées, two whole/solid hours; elle a 50 ans bien tassés, she's at least 50 (years old) (b) un whisky bien tassé, a stiff whisky; un café bien tassé, a strong coffee.

tasseau, *pl* -**eaux** [tɑso] *nm P* = **tassot**.

tassée [tɑse] *nf F* large quantity*. (*Voir* **tas 8**)

tasser [tɑse] I *vtr P* 1. qu'est-ce que je lui ai tassé! I gave him what for!/I didn't half let him have it! 2. qu'est-ce qu'il s'est tassé au dîner! he didn't half put it away at dinner! (*Voir* **cloche I 7**; **gueule I 4** (*b*)) II *vpr* se **tasser** *F* 1. to settle down; to blow over; (tout) ça se tassera/finira (bien) par se tasser, it will (all) sort itself out; it'll all come out in the wash; tout finira par se tasser, everything will come out all right in the end 2. je m'en tasse, I couldn't care less*/ I don't give a monkey's.

tasseuse [tɑsøz] *nf P* homosexual* who frequents urinals/who hangs about in loos/ *NAm* johns (*looking for partners*).

tassot [tɑso] *nm P* nose*; se sécher le tassot, to blow/to wipe one's nose.

tata [tata] *nf* 1. *F* (*mot enfantin*) auntie/ aunty 2. *F* Madame Tata, Mrs Busybody 3. *P* homosexual*/queen/fairy/*Br* poof.

tatane [tatan] *nf P* 1. boot; shoe; **filer un coup de tatane dans les burnes à qn**, to kick s.o. in the balls 2. foot* 3. laziness.

tâter [tate] I *vi F* 1. **en/y tâter**, to be competent (at sth)/to know a thing or two (about sth) 2. **il a tâté de la prison**, he's done time/he's been inside II *vtr P* **va te faire tâter!** get lost*!/beat it!/go play with yourself! III *vpr* **se tâter** *F* **se tâter** (avant de faire qch), to think it over/to weigh up the pros and cons (before doing sth).

tâteuse [tatøz] *nf P* skeleton key.

tati [tati] *nf F* = **tata 1**.

tatoué [tatwe] *nm P* **un tatoué**, a tough guy.

tatouille [tatuj] *nf P* (a) thrashing/beating*(-up) (b) defeat/licking.

tatouiller [tatuje] *vtr P* (a) to thrash/to beat (s.o.) up* (b) to defeat/to lick.

taulard, -arde [tolar, -ard] *P* I *n* prisoner; convict; **vieux taulard**, old lag/jailbird II *a* **mes Noëls taulards**, the Christmases I spent in prison*/in clink.

taule [tol] *nf P* 1. prison*; **en taule**, in the nick; **aller en taule**, to go to prison; **faire de la taule**, to do time/to do a stretch; **il a fait de la taule**, he's been inside/he's done bird; *Mil* **six semaines de taule**, six weeks' detention/six weeks in the glasshouse; **la Grande Taule**, the Central Police Headquarters 2. (a) house; (*voleurs*) drum/gaff; **rappliquer à la taule**, to return home/to make tracks (b) room/pad 3. brothel*/knocking shop 4. workplace; office/factory, etc.

taulier [tolje] *nm P* 1. landlord; proprietor/owner/keeper (of pub, lodging house, brothel, etc) 2. boss*/guv'nor/chief.

taulière [toljɛr] *nf P* brothel owner/madam(e).

taupe [top] *nf* 1. *F* **partir pour le/s'en aller au royaume des taupes**, to die* 2. *F* (a) *Mil* **guerre de taupes**, mine warfare (b) (*espionnage*) mole 3. *F* (*écoles*) (a) second-year class preparing for the *École polytechnique* (b) special maths/*NAm* math class 4. *P* **vieille taupe**, old hag/old bag/old bat.

taupin [topɛ̃] *nm F* (*écoles*) (a) student reading for the *École polytechnique* (b) student in special maths/*NAm* math class.

tax [taks] *nm P* taxi/cab.

taxer [takse] *vtr P* 1. to steal*/to nick/to swipe 2. to borrow.

taxi [taksi] *nm* 1. *F* taxi/cab driver; **il est taxi**, he's a cabbie 2. *F* (*véhicule*) car; plane

3. *P* agent/go-between 4. *P* prostitute*.

tchatche [tʃatʃ] *nf P* 1. **avoir de la tchatche**, to have a smooth tongue/to have the gift of the gab 2. conversation/chat.

tchatcher [tʃatʃe] *P* I *vi* (*baratiner*) to shoot a line/to spiel II *vtr* to speak/talk; **tchatcher anglais**, to speak English.

tchatcheur, -euse [tʃatʃœr, -øz] *P* I *a* talkative/chatty II *n* s.o. with the gift of the gab/smooth talker.

t'chi [tʃi] *adv phr P* **que t'chi**, nothing* at all/damn all/sweet FA/sod-all.

tchin-tchin! [tʃintʃin] *int F* cheers*!/chin-chin!/bottoms up!

tchouch [tʃutʃ] *nm* (*camelots*) free gift/bonus.

tebi [tɛbi] *nf*, **tébi** [tebi] *nf P* (*verlan de* **bite**) penis*/cock/prick/tool.

técolle [tekɔl] *pron P* you.

ted, teddy [tɛd(i)] *nm* jacket embroidered in the back.

tefu, téfu [tefy] *nf P* (a) motorbike/bike (b) mobylette/moped.

téhon [teɔ̃] *nf P* (*verlan de* **honte**) shame.

teigne [tɛɲ] *nf P* = **teigneux 1**.

teigneux [tɛɲø] *nm P* 1. nasty individual/rat/*Br* nasty piece of work/rotter/louse 2. **j'en mangerais sur la tête d'un teigneux**, I (simply) adore it.

teint [tɛ̃] *nm F* **bon teint**, authentic/genuine/kosher; (*convaincu*) staunch; **catholique bon teint**, staunch catholic.

teinté [tɛ̃te] *a P* drunk*/sloshed.

teintée [tɛ̃te] *nf P* (a) drunkenness (b) binge.

télé [tele] *nf F* (a) television/TV/telly/*NAm* tube; **je l'ai vu à la télé**, I saw it on the box (b) television set/TV/telly/gogglebox/idiot-box.

télégraphe [telegraf] *nm Vieilli* (a) *F* **faire le télégraphe**, to wave one's arms about; to gesticulate (wildly) (b) *P* **faire le télégraphe à qn**, to warn s.o. (by a signal); to give s.o. the tip-off/to tip s.o. off*.

télémuche [telemyʃ] *nm P* telephone*/blower.

téléphone [telefɔn] *nm* 1. *F* **téléphone arabe**, grapevine/bush telegraph; **par le téléphone arabe**, on the grapevine 2. *P* WC; **aller au téléphone**, to go to the toilet/to go pay a call.

téléphoner [telefɔne] *vtr & i* 1. *F* **c'était téléphoné**, it was easy to see what was coming; you could tell a mile off what was going to happen next 2. *P* **téléphoner au pape**, to defecate* 3. *V* **téléphoner dans le ventre (à**

qn), *(fellation)* to give (s.o.) head/to give (s.o.) a blow-job.

télévise [televiz] *nf F* = **télé.**

téloche [telɔʃ] *nf P* = **télé.**

tème [tɛm] *nm P* faire tème = faire thème (**thème 2**).

tempérament [tɑ̃peramɑ̃] *nm* 1. *F* avoir du tempérament, to be highly sexed/to be hot-blooded 2. *P* tu en as un tempérament! you've got a nerve! 3. *P* se crever/s'escrimer/ s'esquinter/se tuer le tempérament, to wear oneself out/to knock oneself out (doing sth); to ruin one's health.

température [tɑ̃peratyr] *nf F* prendre la température, to see how things stand/to suss things out.

temps [tɑ̃] *nm F* 1. il fera beau temps quand je ferai cela, it'll be a long time before I do that 2. en deux temps trois mouvements, immediately*/in no time/in two shakes (of a lamb's tail) 3. prendre/se payer/s'en payer/ passer du bon temps, to have a good time/to have fun. (*Voir* **tirer 4**)

tendeur [tɑ̃dœr] *nm P* highly-sexed man; womanizer*/Casanova/skirt-chaser.

tendre [tɑ̃dr] *nm F* avoir un tendre pour qn, to have a soft spot for s.o.

tendron [tɑ̃drɔ̃] *nm* 1. *Vieilli F* young and innocent girl 2. *P (homosexuels)* se faire un tendron, to have sex* with a young boy/to have a chicken dinner.

tenir [tənir] *vtr* 1. *F* tenir un bon rhume, to have a stinking cold 2. *P* tenir une bonne cuite, en tenir une bonne, to be drunk*/to have one tied on; qu'est-ce qu'il tient (comme cuite/comme muffée)! he's dead drunk*!/he's completely sozzled! 3. *P* en tenir/en tenir une (couche), to be an absolute fool*/to be very stupid*. (*Voir* **couche**). 4. *F* tenir la route, *(argument, etc)* to make sense/to hold water 5. *F* en tenir pour qn, to be infatuated* with s.o./to have a crush on s.o./to fancy s.o. (*Voir* **air I 4**; **crachoir 1, 2**; **mer II 2**)

Tentiaire [tɑ̃sjɛr] *nf P* la Tentiaire, (= *système/administration pénitentiaire*) penitentiary system.

terre [tɛr] *nf V* terre jaune, anal sex*/ sodomy/buggery; *(anus)* anus*/brownie. (*Voir* **rentrer 2**)

terre-neuve [tɛrnœv] *nm F* faire le terre-neuve, to help lame ducks.

terreur [tɛrœr] *nf F* gangster/thug; jouer les terreurs, to act tough/to play the tough guy.

terrible [tɛribl] **I** *a F* terrific/extraordinary/ fantastic/great/out of this world; c'était pas bien terrible, it wasn't anything special; c'est un type terrible, he's terrific/incredible **II** *adv F* fantastically/terribly; ça chauffe terrible, it's going really well/it's really great/it's going great guns.

terriblement [tɛribləmɑ̃] *adv F (intensif)* terribly/dreadfully; terriblement en retard, terribly/dreadfully late.

terrine [tɛrin] *nf P* 1. face*/mug; se fendre la terrine, to laugh* a lot/to split one's sides laughing; on se fendait la terrine, we were in stitches 2. head* *(a)* souffrir de la terrine, to have headaches *(b)* terrine de gelée d'andouille!/terrine de gelée de paf!/terrine de gelée de con! you bloody fool!/you stupid* bugger!/you arsehole!/*NAm* you asshole!

têtard [tɛtar] *nm P* 1. child*/kid/brat 2. drunkard*/heavy drinker/boozer/alkie 3. être têtard, *(être la dupe)* to be a mug/a sucker; to be the fall guy/the patsy; faire qn têtard, to dupe s.o./to take s.o. in; to make a sucker out of s.o. 4. horse fit only for the knacker's yard.

tétasses [tetas] *nfpl P* (large, pendulous) breasts*/big tits.

tête [tɛt] *nf* 1. *F (a)* une (grosse) tête, an intellectual/a highbrow/an egghead *(b)* faire/ avoir la grosse tête, to think oneself more important than one is/to have a swelled head 2. *F* faire la tête, to sulk/to make a face; faire sa tête, to give oneself airs; (en) faire une tête, to pull a long face; to look glum/grim; faire une drôle de tête, to look quite put out 3. *F* c'est une tête de bois, he's a blockhead/he's wood/dead from the neck up 4. *F* c'est une tête de cochon/de mule/de pioche/*P* de lard, he's/she's pigheaded; he's/she's as stubborn as a mule 5. *F* se casser la tête, to rack one's brains; te casse pas la tête! it's not worth bothering about!/don't bother! *Iron* don't strain yourself!/don't overdo it! 6. *F* casser/ prendre/rompre la tête à qn, to annoy*/to pester s.o.; to get on s.o.'s nerves 7. *F* j'en ai par-dessus la tête! I've had enough (of it)!/ I'm fed up (with it)!/I've had it up to here! *(travail)* I'm snowed under with it!/I'm up to my eyes in it! 8. *F* laver/lessiver/savonner la tête à qn, to reprimand* s.o. severely/to tear s.o. off a strip; lavage de tête, reprimand*/ ticking-off/bawling-out 9. *F* se payer la tête de qn, *(se moquer)* to take the mickey out of s.o.; *(tromper)* to fool s.o./to pull a fast one on s.o. 10. *F* tête de pipe, picture (of s.o.) *(eg in a newspaper)*; avoir une tête de pipe, to have a funny face/to look odd 11. *F* **avoir qch derrière la tête**, to have a secret plan/to have sth up one's sleeve 12. *F* **tête d'oreiller**, (= *taie d'oreiller*) pillowcase/pillowslip 13. *F* **avoir une bonne tête**, to look a decent (sort of) chap; (*avoir la tête sur les épaules*) to have one's head screwed on the right way 14. *F* **monter la tête à qn**, to work on s.o.'s feelings/s.o.'s emotions; to poison s.o.'s mind; to work s.o. up (contre, against); **il avait la tête montée**, he was (all) worked up; his blood was up 15. *F* **jeter qch à la tête de qn**, to foist sth on s.o. 16. *P* **faire/filer une (grosse) tête/une tête au carré à qn**, (*gifle*) to box s.o.'s ears/to give s.o. a thick ear; (*correction*) to give s.o. a good hiding/thrashing 17. *P* **tomber sur la tête**, to go mad*/crackers/bonkers; **il est tombé sur la tête**, he's mad*/he was dropped on his head when he was young; **je ne suis pas tombé sur la tête**, I'm not daft 18. *F* **être bien/mal dans sa tête**, to feel great/down in the dumps 19. *P* **tête d'imbécile!** (you) idiot!/*Br* (you) clot!/(you) thickhead! 20. *P* **se taper la tête**, to eat* heartily/to have a good tuck-in/to have a good blow-out 21. *P* (*terme d'affection*) **petite tête**, young fellow/young lad; **comment ça va, petite tête?** how goes it, my boy/laddie? 22. *P* **avoir une tête à coucher dehors** (avec un billet de logement dans sa poche), to have a very ugly face*/to have a face that would stop a clock 23. *P* **tête de cire**, bald-headed person*/baldie. (*Voir* **aller 6; claque 1; cul I 1, 25; enterrement 1; gifle; linotte 1; nickelé 2; nœud 1; œil 17; œuf 12; prendre I 6; sac 1** (*b*)**; un III; veau 2**)

téter [tete] *vi F* to drink* heavily/to booze/to knock it back/to swill it down.

tétère [teter] *nf*, **téterre** [teter] *nf Vieilli P* head*.

tétés [tete] *nmpl P* breasts*/tits/titties.

tétines [tetin] *nfpl P* (pendulous) breasts*.

tétonnière [tetɔnjer] *a & nf F* big-bosomed (woman).

tétons [tetɔ̃] *nmpl P* breasts*/tits/titties.

teube [tøb] *nf*, **teubi** [tøbi] *nf V* (*verlan de* **bite**) penis*/prick.

teuch [tœʃ] *nm P* (*drogues*) (*verlan de* **shit**) hashish*/shit.

teuche [tœʃ] *nf P* (*verlan de* **chatte**) female genitals*/pussy/beaver.

teuf-teuf [tœftœf] *nm F* 1. (*mot d'enfant*) train/puffer (train)/puff-puff/chuff-chuff/chuffer 2. (*a*) (*mot d'enfant*) car*/brum-brum (*b*) ramshackle old car*/banger/jalopy.

tévé [teve] *nf F* (*a*) television/telly/TV (*b*) television set/TV set/telly. (*Voir* **télé**)

texto [teksto], **textuel** [tekstɥel], **textuo** [tekstɥo] *adv P* word for word; verbatim.

tézig(ue) [tezig] *pron P* you/yourself. (*Voir* **mézig(ue), cézig(ue), sézig(ue), no(s)-zig(ue)s, vo(s)zig(ue)s, euzig(ue)s, leur(s) zig(ue)s**)

thala [tala] *a & n F* = **tala**.

thé [te] *nm P* 1. **marcher au thé**, to drink* heavily/to be a drunk(ard); (*drogues*) to smoke marijuana*/grass 2. **prendre le thé**, to be a homosexual*; (*copuler*) to have anal sex*. (*Voir* **tasse 4; théière 2**)

théâtreux, -euse [teatrø, -øz] *n F Péj* actor/actress with little talent; actor/actress of sorts.

théière [tejer] *nf P* 1. head* 2. = tasse (à thé) (**tasse 4**)

thème [tem] *nm* 1. *F* **c'est un fort en thème**, he's a swot/a bit of an egghead 2. *P* **faire thème**, to keep mum; to keep one's trap shut (and mind one's own business).

thé-partouse [tepartuz] *nm P* homosexual* orgy. (*Voir* **partouse**)

thésard, -arde [tezar, -ard] *n F* student preparing a thesis/PhD student.

Thomas, thomas [tɔma] *nm P* chamberpot*/jerry.

thunard [tynar] *nm P* = **thune** (*a*).

thunarder [tynarde] *vi P* 1. to pinch and scrape 2. to play for small stakes/for peanuts.

thune [tyn] *nf P* (*a*) *A* five francs *or* five-franc piece (*b*) money*/dosh; **se faire de la thune**, to make some money*; **je me suis retrouvé sans une thune**, I found myself penniless*; **je n'en donnerais pas deux thunes**, I wouldn't give tuppence for it.

thunette [tynet] *nf P* = **thune** (*a*).

tiags [tjag] *nfpl F* = **santiags**.

tiber [tibe] *vtr P* to bore*/to bug.

à tic [atik] *adv phr F* **prendre qn à tic**, to take a dislike to s.o.

ticket [tike] *nm P* 1. *Vieilli* **un drôle de ticket**, an odd character/a strange person*/a strange (sort of) chap/a funny bloke/a queer fish 2. **prendre un ticket**, to watch a pornographic show; to watch an erotic/a porny display. (*Voir* **jeton 5**) 3. (*a*) 1000 (old) franc note (*b*) 10 (new) franc note 4. **faire un ticket**, to make discreet advances; to make a pass (at s.o.); **avoir un ticket avec qn**, to make a hit with s.o. (*of the opposite sex*)/to get off with s.o./to make off with s.o. (*Voir* **touche 1**)

tickson, ticson [tiksɔ̃] *nm P* 1. (railway, theatre, etc) ticket 2. = **ticket 3** 3. faire un tickson avec qn = avoir un ticket avec qn (**ticket 4**).

tic-tac [tiktak] *nm P* revolver*.

tiédasse [tjedas] *a F* lukewarm/tepid.

tienne [tjɛn] *poss pron f F* 1. à la (**bonne**) tienne! cheers*!/here's mud in your eye!/skol! 2. tu as encore fait des tiennes! you've been up to your usual (stupid) tricks again!

tierce [tjɛrs] *nf P* 1. gang (*of criminals, etc*) 2. avoir tierce, belote et dix de der, to be fifty (years old).

tiers [tjɛr] *nm F* (*a*) devoir au tiers et au quart, to owe money right and left (*b*) consulter le tiers et le quart, to consult all and sundry (*c*) je me moque du tiers comme du quart, I don't give a damn about anyone or anything.

tiffes [tif] *nmpl P* = **tifs**.

tiffier [tifje], **tifman** [tifman] *nm P* hairdresser/barber.

tifs [tif] *nmpl P* hair/thatch. (*Voir* **nib**)

tige [tiʒ] I *nf* 1. *F* (*aviation*) les vieilles tiges, the very first pilots/veteran pilots 2. *F* des tiges de pâquerettes, thin, spindly legs*/matchsticks 3. *P* cigarette* 4. *P* shoe; boot II *nm P* 1. policeman* 2. convicted person doing community service instead of serving a prison sentence. (*Voir* **brouter I 2**)

tignasse [tiɲas] *nf F* shock/mop (of hair).

tilleul [tijœl] *nm F* (*boisson*) red and white wine mixed.

tilt [tilt] *adv P* faire tilt, (*comprendre tout d'un coup*) to click; (*avoir une inspiration soudaine*) to have an inspiration/a sudden thought; et puis tout à coup, ça a fait tilt, and then, suddenly, it clicked; tilt! click!

timbale [tɛ̃bal] *nf F* 1. décrocher la timbale, to hit the jackpot 2. avoir un pépin dans la timbale, to be slightly mad*/to have a screw loose.

timbre, -ée [tɛ̃br] *nm F* head*; avoir le timbre fêlé/avoir un coup de timbre, to be slightly mad*/to be a bit cracked/to have a screw missing.

timbré, -ée [tɛ̃bre] *F* I *a* 1. slightly mad*/cracked/dotty/potty 2. du papier timbré, (*assignation*) a summons; (*communication*) an (unpleasant) official communication II *n* mad person*/crackpot/headcase.

tinche [tɛ̃ʃ] *nf P* faire la tinche, to make a collection/to pass the hat around; faire la/une tinche à qn, to go round with the hat for s.o./to have a whip-round for s.o. (*esp for a prisoner*).

tinée [tine] *nf Vieilli P* large quantity*/lots/bags; il y en a une tinée, there's tons of it.

tinette [tinɛt] *nf P* 1. (*a*) old car*/(old) banger/jalopy (*b*) old motorbike 2. faire une tinette sur qn, to criticize* s.o./to knock s.o./to drag s.o.'s name through the mud 3. *pl* tinettes, WC*/loo/*NAm* john.

tintin [tɛ̃tɛ̃] *F* I *nm* faire tintin, to (have to) go without; to be done out of sth; to get nothing* II *int* tintin! nothing doing*!/no go!/not a hope!

tintouin [tɛ̃twɛ̃] *nm F* 1. din/racket/shindig 2. worry/trouble/bother; se donner du tintouin, to go to a lot of trouble; elle me donne bien du tintouin, she's a headache; quel tintouin ces gosses! what a worry the kids are!

tiquer [tike] *vi F* to wince; il n'a pas tiqué, he didn't turn a hair; sans tiquer, without batting an eyelid; cela le fera tiquer! that'll shake him!/that'll give him a jolt! tiquer sur qch, to react unfavourably to sth/to jib at sth.

tir [tir] *nm F* allonger le tir, to pay/to fork out more than anticipated.

tirage [tiraʒ] *nm F* 1. difficulty/trouble; il y a du tirage entre eux, they don't hit it off 2. le premier tirage, the first time/the first go/the first shot.

tiraillement [tirajmã] *nm F* disagreement/wrangling/friction.

tiraillerie [tirajri] *nf F* wrangling/friction.

tirailleur [tirajœr] *nm F* freelance (journalist).

tirants [tirã] *nmpl P* stockings.

tire [tir] *nf* 1. *F* (vol à) la tire, pickpocketing; voleur à la tire, pickpocket*/dip/dipper; faire la tire, to be a pickpocket/to pick pockets 2. *P* car*.

tire-au-cul [tiroky] *nm inv P*, *F* **tire-au-flanc** [tiroflã] *nm inv* malingerer*/lazy bastard*/lazy sod/skiver/lazy bum/lead-swinger.

tirebouchonnant [tirbuʃɔnã] *a F* very funny*/hilarious/killing (joke, etc).

se tirebouchonner [sətirbuʃɔne] *vpr F* to laugh* uproariously/to crease oneself/to double up with laughter.

tire-bouton [tirbutɔ̃] *nm P* la maison tire-bouton, (the world of) lesbians*/lesbianism;

un ménage tire-bouton, a couple of lesbians.

se tireboutonner [sətirbutɔne] *vpr P* (*lesbiennes*) to have sexual relations/to have sex*.

tirée [tire] *nf F* long distance (still to be covered); il y a encore une bonne/sacrée tirée, there's still a long haul/trek ahead 2. une tirée de ..., lots of .../heaps of .../loads of ....

tire-fesses [tirfɛs] *nm inv F* drag lift/ski tow/ski lift.

tire-gosse [tirgɔs] *nf & nm P* = **tire-môme(s)**.

tire-jus [tirʒy] *nm inv P* handkerchief*/nose-wipe/snot-rag.

à tire-larigot [atirlarigo] *adv phr F* boire à tire-larigot, to drink* heavily/like a fish; s'en donner à tire-larigot, to drink/to eat to one's heart's content; to have one's fill; il y en a à tire-larigot, there are/is enough to keep any-one happy; *P* baiser à tire-larigot, to have non-stop sex*.

tirelire [tirlir] *nf* 1. *P* face* and mouth*/mug; se fendre la tirelire, to laugh (all over one's face) 2. *P* head*/bonce 3. *P* stomach*/belly/guts 4. *A V* female genitals*.

tire-moelle [tirmwal] *nm inv P* handkerchief*/snot-rag/nose-rag.

tire-môme(s) [tirmom] *P* I *nf* midwife II *nm* obstetrician.

tire-pognon [tirpɔɲɔ̃] *nm inv Vieilli F* one-arm(ed) bandit/fruit machine.

tirer [tire] I *vtr* 1. *F* être tiré à quatre, to be worried stiff 2. *P* to steal*/to pinch/to swipe/to knock off (sth); tirer qn, to rob s.o. 3. *F* six mois à tirer, six months to go/to do/to get through; en voilà encore un(e) de tiré(e)! that's another year (day, month, etc) gone! 4. *P* tirer de la prison/tirer son temps, to serve a prison* sentence/to do time/to do bird; tirer sept ans, to get seven years/to do a seven-year stretch; deux longes à tirer, two years to do 5. *P* tirer la gueule, (*objet*) to be badly made/to be botched; sa robe tire la gueule, her dress looks terrible 6. *V* (*a*) se tirer son/un coup, to masturbate*/to toss off (*b*) tirer son/un coup, (*homme*) to have sex*/to get one's end away; tirer une femme, to have sex* with a woman/to screw a woman 7. *P* tirer un fil, to urinate*. (*Voir* bambou 1; couverture 3; crampe 1; crampette; cul 18; échelle 2; ficelle II 2 (*c*), 7; flanc 3; ligne 1; renard 2; ver 3) II *vpr* se tirer 1. *F* to come to an end; ça se tire, the end's in sight; it's nearly

finished; it'll soon be over now; ça s'est bien tiré; did everything go off well?/did every-thing turn out all right? 2. *P* (*personne*) to run away*/to beat it/to clear off/to make tracks; bon, faut que je me tire, right, must go!/OK, I'm off! tirez-vous de là! hop it!/clear off! (*Voir* flûte II 1; patte 1; pied 6; ripatons 2)

tireur, -euse [tirœr, -øz] I *nm & f F* pickpocket*. (*Voir* tire 1) II *nm P* tireur au cul/*F* tireur au flanc = **tire-au-cul, tire-au-flanc**.

tiroir [tirwar] *nm* 1. *F* nom à tiroir, double-barrelled name *or* name with a handle to it 2. *P* tiroir (à poulet), stomach*. (*Voir* lardon; polichinelle 2 (*a*); salé II 1) 3. *P* fourrer un corps dans le tiroir, to place a corpse* in the coffin/to box a corpse.

tisane [tizan] *nf P* 1. severe thrashing/beating*; filer une tisane à qn, to beat s.o. up* 2. water; tomber dans la tisane, to fall in the water.

tisaner [tizane] *vtr P* tisaner qn, to give s.o. a thrashing/to beat s.o. up*.

tisanier [tizanje] *nm P* male nurse.

titi [titi] *nm P* 1. street arab/cheeky urchin/cocky little kid 2. titi négro = pidgin (English).

titine [titin] *nf P* machine gun.

toboggan [tɔbɔgɑ̃] *nm P* se graisser le toboggan, to drink* heavily/to booze/to hit the bottle.

toc [tɔk] I *a inv* 1. *F* worthless*/sham/rubbishy/trashy 2. *F* être un peu toc, to be slightly mad*/to be a bit touched 3. *P* ugly; unpleasant/horrid II *nm* 1. *F* fake/sham/imitation (gold, jewellery, etc); bijoux en toc, imitation jewellery; c'est du toc! it's a sham!/it's phon(e)y!/it's rubbish!/it's junk! 2. *P* marcher/vivre sous un toc, to go about with false identity papers; to live under a false name 3. *P* manquer de toc, to lack self-confidence/to lack nerve; (*manquer d'à-propos*) to be slow on the uptake; il ne manque pas de toc, (*courage*) he's got guts; (*aplomb*) he's pretty sure of himself III *int P* (et) toc! so there!/put that in your pipe (and smoke it)!

tocade [tɔkad] *nf F* = **toquade**.

tocant [tɔkɑ̃] *nm F* = **toquant**.

tocante [tɔkɑ̃t] *nf F* = **toquante**.

tocard, -arde [tɔkar, -ard] *P* I *a* = **toc** I II *n* (*a*) (*courses*) (*mauvais cheval*) (rank) outsider; stumer (*b*) (*personne*) hopeless case/dead loss.

tocasse [tɔkas], **tocasson** [tɔkasɔ̃] *a P* = **toc** I.

tocbombe [tɔkbɔ̃b] *a inv*, **toctoc** [tɔktɔk] *a inv P* mad*/daft/dotty/potty.

tocs [tɔk] *nmpl P* false (identity) papers.

toile [twal] *nf* 1. *F* se mettre/se filer/se fourrer/se glisser dans les toiles, to go to bed*/to get between the sheets 2. *P* déchirer (de) la toile, to fart* loudly 3. *P* se faire/se payer une toile, to go to see a film; to go to the cinema/the flicks 4. *P* enlever les toiles d'araignée, to seduce a serious woman.

toise [twaz] *nf P* thrashing/good hiding; filer une toise à qn, to beat s.o. up*/to clobber s.o.; se filer des toises, to fight/to have a punch-up.

toison [twazɔ̃] *nf F* mop/shock (of hair).

toiture [twatyr] *nf P* head*; onduler de la toiture, to be mad*/to have a screw loose; varloper la toiture, to have a haircut/to get one's barnet cut.

tôlard, -arde [tolar, -ard] *a & n P* = **taulard, -arde** I, II.

tôle [tol] *nf P* = **taule** (*all senses*).

se tôler [sətole] *vpr P* to laugh* uproariously.

tôlier [tolje] *nm P* 1. = **taulier 1, 2** 2. superintendent of police.

tôlière [toljɛr] *nf P* = **taulière**.

tomate [tɔmat] *nf* 1. *F* être (rouge) comme une tomate, to be as red as a beetroot 2. *P* (*boisson*) pastis with grenadine 3. *P* rosette of the Legion of Honour 4. *P* big red nose* 5. *P* fool*/idiot/twit; avoir l'air tomate, to look stupid* 6. *P* en être/en rester comme une tomate, to be flabbergasted* 7. *P* grouille-toi la tomate! hurry up!/get a move on!/move it! 8. *P* écraser des/ses tomates, to have a period*/the curse. (*Voir* **sauce 1** (*b*))

tombeau, *pl* **-eaux** [tɔ̃bo] *nm F* 1. il me mettra/conduira au tombeau, he'll outlive me; (*il me tuera*) he'll be the death of me 2. c'est un vrai tombeau, (*personne*) his lips are sealed/he won't breathe a word about it 3. à tombeau ouvert, at breakneck speed.

tomber [tɔ̃be] I *vtr P* 1. (*vaincre*) to beat/throw (an opponent) 2. to have sex* with (a woman)/to lay (a woman); il les tombe toutes, they all fall for him; he's a real Casanova/a real ladies' man/a wolf 3. tomber qn, (*prostituée*) to pick s.o. up/to score/to turn a trick. (*Voir* **veste 3**) II *vi* 1. *F* les bras m'en tombent, I'm flabbergasted*/amazed 2. *F* laisser tomber qn, to drop/ditch s.o.; (*lui*

faire faux bond) to let s.o. down; to hang s.o. up 3. *F* laisse tomber! forget it!/drop it!/give it a rest! 4. *F* qu'est-ce qui/qu'il tombe! it's pouring!/it's raining cats and dogs! 5. *F* être tombé du lit, to have got up at the crack of dawn 6. *P* (*a*) to be arrested* (*b*) to be condemned (*c*) to be sentenced 7. *F* to allow oneself to be corrupted. (*Voir* **bec 6**; **dessus I**; **eau 3**; **manche I 3**; **paletot 2**; **poil 8** (*a*); **pomme 2**; **tête 17**)

tombeur [tɔ̃bœr] *nm F* tombeur (de femmes/de filles), womanizer*/lady-killer/wolf/Don Juan/Casanova.

tondre [tɔ̃dr] *vtr F* 1. to fleece* (s.o.); to take (s.o.) to the cleaners/to clean (s.o.) out; se faire tondre (la laine sur le dos), to get fleeced 2. se faire tondre, to get one's hair cut 3. j'ai d'autres chiens à tondre, I've got other fish to fry. (*Voir* **œuf 11**)

tondu [tɔ̃dy] *a F* être tondu (à zéro), to be penniless*/cleaned out. (*Voir aussi* **zéro I 6**)

tonneau, *pl* **-eaux** [tɔno] *nm F* 1. du même tonneau, of the same kind; alike; ce sont des gens du même tonneau, they're birds of a feather; c'est du même tonneau, it's much of a muchness; it's six of one and half a dozen of the other 2. faire un tonneau, (*voiture*) to flip/to roll over; to turn turtle. (*Voir* **cheval 9**)

tonnerre [tɔnɛr] *F* I *nm* 1. être fait comme un coup de tonnerre, to be badly made 2. ... du tonnerre, wonderful/terrific/great; il fera un médecin du tonnerre/du tonnerre de Dieu/du tonnerre du diable/de tous les tonnerres, he'll make a bloody good/a fantastic doctor; un repas du tonnerre (de Dieu), a fantastic/terrific/stupendous meal; un nom du tonnerre de Dieu, a hellishly difficult name to pronounce 3. au tonnerre de Dieu, a long way away/very distant II *int* tonnerre!/tonnerre de Dieu!/tonnerre de chien!/mille tonnerres (de Brest)! by thunder!/heavens above!/good heavens! III *adv phr* le tonnerre, extremely well; very fast. (*Voir* **nom 2**)

tonton [tɔ̃tɔ̃] *nm* 1. *F* uncle 2. *P* homosexual* 3. *P* (*CB*) Tonton Victor, television (set)/TV.

tonus [tɔnys] *nm F* energy/dynamism.

top [tɔp] *a inv F* top (top), top quality/(very) best/up-market; mannequin top top, top model; être au top niveau, to be the best (in one's job)/to be (an) expert (at sth); to be top manager/top executive, etc.

topaze [tɔpaz] *nm P* grafter.

topo [tɔpo] *nm F* (*a*) *Journ* (popular) article (*b*) exposé/report/rundown; **faire le topo sur la situation/expliquer le topo**, to give a rundown on the situation; **elle veut déménager chez moi; tu vois le topo?** she wants to move in with me; d'you see the problem (I've got)? **c'est toujours le même topo**, it's always the same old story.

Topol [tɔpɔl] *Prnm F* **le Topol**, the boulevard de Sébastopol (*in Paris*). (*Voir* **Sébasto**)

toquade [tɔkad] *nf F* (passing) craze/fad; infatuation; **avoir une toquade pour qn**, to be infatuated* with s.o./to have a crush on s.o.

toquant [tɔkɑ̃] *nm F* heart/ticker.

toquante [tɔkɑ̃t] *nf F* watch/ticker. (*Voir* **tocante**)

toquard, -arde [tɔkar, -ard] *a & n P* = **tocard**.

toqué, -ée [tɔke] *F* I *a* 1. (slightly) mad*/cracked/round the bend; **il est un peu toqué**, he's a bit touched in the head/he's got a screw loose/he's a bit of a nutcase 2. **être toqué de qn**, to be infatuated* with s.o./to have a crush on s.o./to be nuts about s.o.; **il est toqué de la télé**, he's got telly on the brain II *n* (*fou*) nut/crackpot/*Br* nutter.

se toquer [sətɔke] *vpr F* **se toquer de qn**, to become infatuated* with s.o.; to be crazy*/nuts about s.o.

toques [tɔk] *nmpl P* = **tocs**.

torché [tɔrʃe] *a* 1. (*a*) *F* **bien torché**, well done/(pretty) good (*b*) (*bâclé*) botched/bungled 2. drunk*/boozed (up).

torche-cul [tɔrʃky] *nm inv P* (*a*) toilet paper/loo paper/bog paper/bumf (*b*) *Péj* (*texte*) (piece of) trash (*fit only for use as toilet paper*) (*c*) third-rate *or* boring newspaper/rag.

torcheculatif, -ive [tɔrʃkylatif, -iv] *a P* relating to the gutter press.

torchée [tɔrʃe] *nf P* 1. fight*/scrap 2. beating*/thrashing/good hiding 3. advanced drunkenness.

torcher [tɔrʃe] I *vtr* 1. *F* to dash off/to knock off (an article, etc); to do (sth) in a hurry; **elle a bientôt torché son rapport**, she soon got through her report 2. *P* **ce bouquin est drôlement bien torché**, this book's damn well written 3. *F* to botch/to mess up (a job, a piece of work etc) 4. *P* **se faire torcher**, to get a good hiding; to get beaten up II *vpr* **se torcher** *P* 1. to fight/to have a punch-up 2. **se torcher** (**le derrière/le cul**), to wipe one's

backside/bum/arse/*NAm* ass; **je m'en torche** (**le cul**)! I don't give a damn!/I couldn't give a toss! **tu peux te torcher!** take a running jump!/go (and) jump in the lake! 3. to get drunk*/tanked up.

torchon [tɔrʃɔ̃] *nm* 1. *P* slovenly woman/slut; **être fait comme un torchon**, to be dressed like a slut 2. *P* (*a*) sheet (*b*) bed. (*Voir* **viande 1**) 3. *F* (*journal*) rag 4. *F* (*texte mal écrit*) mess; (*texte sans valeur*) badly written article/rubbish/trash 5. *F* **il ne faut pas mélanger les torchons et les serviettes**, we mustn't get our values mixed 6. *P* **coup de torchon** (*a*) fight*/punch-up; **se donner/se filer/se flanquer un coup de torchon**, to fight/to have a set-to/to have a bit of an argy-bargy (*b*) (*en mer*) sudden (and violent) gust of wind (*c*) (police) raid/bust 7. *F* **le torchon brûle** (**chez eux**), they don't hit it off (together)/they're always at each other's throats/they lead a cat and dog life 8. *V* **être à cheval sur un torchon**, to have a period*/to have the rag out/to be on the rag 9. *Vieilli P* (*théâtre*) **lever le torchon**, to raise the curtain.

torchonner [tɔrʃɔne] *vtr F* = **torcher 3**.

tordant [tɔrdɑ̃] *a F* very funny*/creasing/side-splitting.

tord-boyaux [tɔrbwajo] *nm P* (*eau-de-vie*) rotgut; (*fabriqué maison*) jungle juice.

se tordre [sətɔrdr] *vpr F* **se tordre** (**de rire**)/**rire à se tordre**, to laugh* a lot/to split one's sides laughing/to fall about (laughing); **c'était à se tordre**, it was a (perfect) scream/a real killer; **il y a de quoi se tordre**, it's screamingly funny.

tordu, -ue [tɔrdy] I *a* 1. *F* **être** (**complètement**) **tordu**, to be (quite) mad*/loony/nuts 2. *F* (*personne*) (*physiquement*) twisted/bent 3. *P* drunk*/legless/tight 4. *P* **avoir la gueule tordue**, to be as ugly as sin. (*Voir* **sirop 2**) II *n* 1. *F* **c'est un tordu/une tordue**, he's/she's (quite) mad*/*Br* a nutter/a loony; **les tordus**, the lunatic fringe 2. *P* **qui c'est ce tordu?** who's that geezer? **des tordus sans intérêt**, a bunch of dreary gits; **c'est une tordue**, she's a slut/a slag.

torgnole [tɔrɲɔl] *nf P* blow*/punch/clout/slap (round the face).

torgnoler [tɔrɲɔle] *vtr P* **torgnoler qn**, to slap s.o. round the face; to hit s.o. (on the head)/to give s.o. a clout.

tornif [tɔrnif] *nm P* handkerchief*/nose-wipe/snot-rag.

torpille [tɔrpij] *nf P* (*a*) professional beggar (*b*) begging; **marcher à la torpille**, to live by begging.

torpiller [tɔrpije] *vtr* **1.** *F* to torpedo (s.o.'s plans, etc) **2.** *P* to borrow money from (s.o.)/ to tap (s.o.) for money/to cadge off (s.o.) **3.** *P* to destroy the reputation of (s.o.'s) **4.** *V* to have sex* with (s.o.).

torpilleur [tɔrpijœr] *nm P* **1.** scrounger/ cadger/sponger **2.** beggar **3.** door-to-door salesman **4.** (en) **faire/en chier un torpilleur**, to attach too much importance to sth; to over-do sth; to make a fuss about sth.

torrieu! [tɔrjø] *int FrC P* damn and blast!/ bloody hell!

torsif [tɔrsif] *a P* very funny*.

tortillard, -arde [tɔrtijar, -ard] **I** *a P* lame/limping **II** *nm* **1.** *F* (*a*) local railway (*b*) milk train (*that stops at every station*) **2.** *P* espresso coffee **III** *P n* lame person/cripple.

tortiller [tɔrtije] **I** *vtr Vieilli P* to wolf down/ to bolt down/to make short work of (food); **tortiller des courants d'air**, to have nothing to eat* **II** *vi P* **1.** **tortiller des fesses/du cul**, to wiggle one's hips; (*danser*) to dance **2.** to quibble; **il n'y a pas à tortiller (du cul pour chier droit dans une bouteille)**, it's got to be done/it's no good trying to wriggle out of it/ there's no getting away from it; (*c'est évident*) it's quite clear/it's obvious/it's as plain as the nose on your face. (*Voir* **croupe**; **débagoule**)

tortore [tɔrtɔr] *nf P* (*a*) food*/grub/nosh (*b*) (art of) cooking.

tortorer [tɔrtɔre] *P* **I** *vtr* to eat*/to nosh **II** *vi* to cook/to do the cooking.

tôt [to] *adv F* **c'est pas trop tôt!** and about time too!

total [tɔtal] *adv F* **1.** **ils se sont chamaillés et, total, les voilà brouillés**, they've had a row and, to cut a long story short, they're no long-er on speaking terms **2.** completely/totally; **c'est total chiant**, it's a complete bore/it's bloody annoying.

totale [tɔtal] *nf P* **1.** *Med* total hysterectomy **2.** **c'est la totale!** that's the (bloody) limit! (*maximum d'ennuis*) it's a real hassle!

toto [tɔto] *nm* **1.** *P* (head) louse/*NAm* cootie **2.** *F* **vas-y, toto!** attaboy!

totoches [tɔtɔʃ] *nfpl P* breasts*/boobs.

Totor [tɔtɔr] *nm V* penis*; **dérouiller Totor**, to have sex*/to get one's end away.

toubib [tubib] *nm F* doctor/doc/quack/ medico; *Mil* MO (= *medical officer*).

toubibaille [tubibaj] *nf F Péj* la toubibaille, the medical fraternity.

touche [tuʃ] *nf* **1.** *F* **faire une touche avec qn**, **avoir une/la touche avec qn**, to make a hit with s.o. (*of the opposite sex*)/to get off with s.o./to click with s.o./to make out with s.o.; **essayer de faire une touche avec qn**, to make a pass at s.o./to try to get off with s.o. **2.** *F* **rester sur la touche**, to stay on the sidelines/ out in the cold; **mettre qn sur la touche**, to leave s.o. behind/out in the cold **3.** *P Péj* appearance/look(s); **je n'aime pas sa touche**, I don't like the look of him; **quelle (drôle de) touche!** what a sight!/what a mess! **il a une drôle de touche!** what a strange-looking character!/what a weirdo! **4.** *P* **touches de piano**, teeth*/ivories **5.** *P* puff at/on a cigar-ette; drag **6.** *P* injection*/shot/jab (of a drug, etc) **7.** *V* **se faire une touche**, to masturbate*/ to play with oneself.

touché [tuʃe] *a Vieilli P* (slightly) mad*/(a bit) touched in the head.

touche-à-tout [tuʃatu] *F* **I** *a* (*a*) (person) who can't keep his hands off things (*b*) meddling/interfering **II** *nm & f* (*a*) meddler/ busybody (*b*) Jack-of-all-trades.

touche-pipi [tuʃpipi] *nm P* **jouer à touche-pipi**, (*enfants*) to play mummies and daddies/ doctors and nurses; (*se caresser*) to have a (heavy) petting session; not to go all the way.

touche-piqûre [tuʃpikyr] *F* **I** *a* drugged*/ stoned/high **II** *nm* drug addict*/junkie.

toucher [tuʃe] **I** *vi F* **1.** **toucher à (un métier, etc)**, to practise (a craft, etc); **elle touche à la trompette**, she plays the trumpet; **toucher à mort**, to be very talented/gifted **2.** **pas touche!** don't touch!/mustn't touch!/hands off! **II** *vtr P* to steal* (sth); to rob (s.o.). (*Voir* **air II 1** (*a*); **fade 1**) **III** *vpr* **se tou-cher 1.** *V* to masturbate*/to play with oneself **2.** *P* **se toucher (la nuit)**, to delude oneself. (*Voir* **bille 5**; **canette 2**)

à touche-touche [atuʃtuʃ] *adv phr* **rouler à touche-touche**, (*voitures*) to go (along)/to travel bumper to bumper.

touffe [tuf] *nf P* **1.** **onduler/travailler de la touffe**, to be mad*/to have a screw loose **2.** pubic hair **3.** puff/drag (on a cigarette).

touf(f)iane [tufjan] *nf P* (*drogues*) opium*.

touiller [tuje] *vtr F* to stir (washing, liquid, etc); to mix (salad); to shuffle (cards).

toupet [tupɛ] *nm F* impudence*/cheek; **quel toupet!** what a cheek!/what a nerve! **il a eu le toupet de faire ça**, he had the cheek/the gall/

the nerve to do that.

toupie [tupi] *nf F* vieille toupie, (silly) old bag/old bat/old trout.

tour [tur] I *nm* 1. *F* avoir plus d'un tour dans son sac, to have more than one trick up one's sleeve 2. *F* faire un petit tour, to urinate*/to go and see a man about a dog/to pay a call 3. *F* en un tour de main, as quick as a flash/like lightning 4. *F* quand viendra mon tour, when my turn comes (to die)/when my number's up 5. *P* tour de bête, promotion by seniority. (*Voir* bâton I 1; cadran; cochon I 2; sale 1 (*a*)) II *nf F* la Tour pointue/la Tour de l'Horloge, the Paris Police headquarters.

tourlousine, tourlouzine [turluzin] *nf P* (*a*) blow*/punch/clout (*b*) thrashing/beating*(-up)/good hiding.

tournailler [turnɑje] *F vi* (*a*) to keep wandering round and round/to prowl (around) (*b*) tournailler autour d'une femme, to hang around/to bother a woman.

tournanche [turnɑ̃ʃ] *nf P* = **tournée 1**.

tournanché [turnɑ̃ʃe] *a P* une petite brune bien tournanchée, a shapely little brunette/a little brunette with a lovely figure.

tournant [turnɑ̃] *nm F* 1. avoir/choper/pincer/rattraper qn au tournant, to arrest* s.o.; (*se venger*) to get one's own back on s.o.; attendre un concurrent au tournant, to be waiting for (an opportunity to catch) a rival; je l'aurai au tournant! I'll get even with him yet! 2. sur le tournant de la gueule, (right) in the face; il lui a foutu un coup de poing sur le tournant de la gueule, he punched him right in the face/in the kisser 3. (*a*) savoir prendre le tournant, to know how to adapt oneself to a situation (*b*) être dans un sale tournant, to be in a fix*/to be in a (right old) mess 4. faire un tournant à qn, to play a dirty trick on s.o./to do the dirty on s.o.

tournante [turnɑ̃t] *nf P* key.

tourne [turn] *nf F* (*cartes*) turned-up card (*indicating trumps*)/turn-up.

tournebouler [turnəbule] *vtr F* to upset (s.o.)/to mix (s.o.) up/to put (s.o.'s) head in a whirl.

tournée [turne] *nf* 1. *F* payer/offrir une tournée, to stand a round (of drinks); to pay for/to stand drinks all round; c'est ma tournée, it's my round/my shout; the drinks are on me; c'est la tournée du patron, the drinks are on the house 2. *P* thrashing; flanquer une tournée à qn, to thrash s.o./to beat s.o. up*/to give s.o. a good hiding. (*Voir*

grand-duc)

tourner [turne] I *vi P* 1. to become; tourner hippie, to become a hippy 2. (*drogues*) to pass the marijuana cigarette*/the joint around (*Voir* œil 3) II *vtr V* tourner la page; (*Voir* page¹ 2).

tournicoter [turnikɔte] *vi F* to wander round and round/to hover (round).

tourniquer [turnike] *F vi* = **tournicoter**.

tourniquet [turnikɛ] *nm P Mil* passer au tourniquet, to be court-martialled.

tourte [turt] I *a F* stupid*/thick/dense/dumb; elle est jolie mais plutôt tourte, she's pretty but rather thick II *nf F* fool*/clot/thickie.

tourtières [turtjɛr] *nfpl P Mus* cymbals.

tousser [tuse] *vi Vieilli F* 1. to grumble*/to grouse; to protest 2. *Iron* il n'est pas poivré, non, c'est que je tousse! he's not drunk, oh no – not much! tu ne connais pas la rue Madeleine? – non, c'est que je tousse! j'y demeure, do you happen to know the rue Madeleine? – do I know it? I only live there! 3. (*moteur*) to backfire/to splutter.

tout [tu] *F* I *pron* 1. et tout et tout, and all the rest of it/and so on and so forth 2. il a tout du délégué d'atelier, he's the epitome of a shop steward 3. drôle comme tout, very funny*; rire comme tout, to laugh* a lot/like anything; il est bête comme tout, he's really stupid*/a real moron II *nm* ce n'est pas le tout, ça! that's a long way from what's wanted/that's not good enough!

tout-fou [tufu] *F* I *am* mad*/crazy II *nm* (prize) idiot/nutcase.

toutim(e) [tutim] *nm P* (*a*) (tout) le toutim(e), the whole lot/the (whole) works/the whole bag* of tricks (*b*) et tout le toutim(e)/(le) toutim(e) et la mèche, and so on and so forth.

tout-le-monde [tuləmɔ̃d] *nm F* Monsieur Tout-le-monde, the man in the street/the average man/Mr Average/Joe Public.

toutou [tutu] *nm F* (*a*) (*surt mot d'enfant*) dog/doggie/doggy/bow-wow; viens, mon toutou! come on, little doggy (*b*) filer comme un toutou, to let oneself be easily led; to be as meek as a lamb. (*Voir* boniment 2; peau 23 (*b*))

Tout-Paris [tupari] *nm F* Parisian smart set; il connaît son Tout-Paris à fond, he knows everybody who is anybody in Paris.

à tout-va [atuva] *adv phr F* abundantly/copiously.

touze(par) [tuz(par)] *nf P* (*verlan de*

partouze) (collective sex) orgy.

toxico [tɔksiko] *nm & f P* (= *toxicomane*) drug addict*/dope addict/junkie.

trac [trak] *nm F* fear/fright/funk; (*théâtre*) stage fright; (*avant un examen*) (examination) nerves; **avoir le trac/se prendre de trac,** to be afraid*/to have the wind up; **filer le trac à qn,** to put the wind up s.o. (*Voir* **traquer**)

tracassin [trakasɛ̃] *nm* 1. *F* **avoir le tracassin,** to worry/to fret 2. *V* **avoir le tracassin,** to have an erection* (*esp on waking up*).

tracer [trase] I *vi P* to move quickly/to get a move on; to speed/to belt along; **allez, trace!** come on, get a move on! II *vpr* **se tracer** *P* to leave* hurriedly/to clear off/to scarper.

tracsir [traksir] *nm,* **traczir** [trakzir] *nm P* = **trac.**

traduc [tradyk] *nf F* (*écoles*) (= *traduction*) translation.

Trafalgar [trafalgar] *Prnm F* **un (coup de) Trafalgar,** a difficult and violent situation; (*bataille*) a punch-up; (*échec*) a failure*/bomb; (*désastre*) a sudden catastrophe/an unexpected disaster.

trafiqué [trafike] *a F* **moteur trafiqué,** souped-up engine.

trafiquer [trafike] *vtr P* **qu'est-ce que tu trafiques?** what the hell are you up to?

train [trɛ̃] *nm* 1. *P* buttocks*/bum/NAm butt; **un coup de pied/de pompe dans le train,** a kick up the arse/NAm ass. (*Voir* **se magner, se manier**) 2. *P* **avoir le feu au train,** to be in a tearing hurry/in a great rush; to have ants in one's pants. (*Voir* **feu** 1) 3. *P* **se crever/se casser le train,** to work* hard/to flog oneself to death 4. *F* **être en train,** to be tipsy; **il était un peu en train,** he'd had a drop (too much) 5. *F* **être dans le train,** to be up-to-date/to be in the swim/to be with it 6. *F* **prendre le train en marche,** to jump/climb on the bandwagon 7. *P* **filer le train à qn/coller qn au train/coller au train de qn,** to follow s.o. closely/to trail s.o./to dog s.o.('s footsteps) 8. *F* uproar*/noise/din/row; **faire du train/faire un train de tous les diables,** to kick up (a hell of) a row 9. *P* **faire le petit train,** (*hétérosexuel ou homosexuel*) to take part in an orgy/a daisy chain. (*Voir* **onze**)

traînailler [trɛnɑje] *F* I *vtr* **traînailler la jambe,** to drag one's leg II *vi* 1. (*errer*) to wander (aimlessly) about; to loaf around; (*être lent*) to dawdle 2. (*parler lentement*) to drawl.

traînard [trɛnar] *nm P* **faire/ramasser un traînard,** to fall down*/to come a cropper.

traîne [trɛn] *nf P* 1. **être à la traîne,** to be late; to lag behind; **arriver à la traîne,** to turn up late 2. **être à la traîne,** to be short of money*/of cash.

traîne-cons [trɛnkɔ̃] *nm* car*/banger.

traînée [trene] *nf P* (low-class) prostitute*/(cheap) floozy/slut/(cheap) tart.

traîne-lattes [trɛnlat] *nm inv,* **traîne-patins** [trɛnpatɛ̃] *nm inv P* 1. tramp/hobo/bum 2. person in dire poverty/down-and-out.

traîner [trene] *vi F* **ça traîne les rues,** it's/they're not unusual; you see it/them everywhere.

trainers [trɛnœrz] *nmfpl F* (*chaussures*) trainers.

traîne-sabots [trɛnsabo] *nm inv,* **traîne-savates** [trɛnsavat] *nm inv,* **traîne-semelles** [trɛnsəmɛl] *nm inv F* = **traîne-lattes** 1, 2.

traîneur [trɛnœr] *nm F* (*peu usuel*) **traîneur de cafés,** pub-crawler.

traineux [trɛnø] *nm FrC F* untidy/messy/sloppy person.

trainglot [trɛ̃glo] *nm P Mil* soldier in the French Army Service Corps.

train(-)train [trɛ̃trɛ̃] *nm F* **le train(-)train (quotidien) de la vie,** the ordinary humdrum daily routine; the daily grind; **rien qui sort du train(-)train des événements ordinaires,** nothing out of the ordinary; **aller son petit train(-)train/s'en aller de son train(-)train habituel,** to jog along/to trundle along (in one's own little way).

trait [trɛ] *nm F* **faire des traits à sa femme/à son mari,** to be unfaithful/to cheat on one's wife/one's husband.

tralala [tralala] *nm F* 1. **faire du tralala,** to make a great show/to splash out; **sans tralala,** without fuss/without standing on ceremony 2. **être sur son tralala/en grand tralala,** to be all dressed up/to be dressed up to the nines 3. **et tout le tralala,** and all the rest/and so on and so forth.

tram [tram] *nm F* tramway.

tranche [trɑ̃ʃ] *nf* 1. *F* **s'en payer une tranche,** to have the time of one's life/to have a great time/to have a ball; **s'en payer une (bonne) tranche,** to let oneself go/to let one's hair down 2. *P* fellow*/bloke; **tranche (de gail/de melon)/pauvre tranche,** (*idiot*) fool*/idiot/jerk; **fausse tranche,** s.o. who doesn't keep his/her promises; unreliable person;

faire la tranche, to play the fool/to act the goat; en avoir une tranche, to be as daft as they come. (*Voir* **couche**) 3. *P* = **tronche 1, 2.**

tranche-montagne [trɑ̃ʃmɔ̃taɲ] *nm F* boaster/show-off*; d'un air de tranche-montagne, blusteringly.

trancher [trɑ̃ʃe] *vtr & i* 1. *V* trancher (une femme), to have sex* (with a woman) 2. *P* to kill*/to rub out/to liquidate. (*Voir* **troncher**)

tranchouillard [trɑ̃ʃujar] *nm P* fool*/idiot/jerk.

trans [trɑ̃s] *a Vieilli P* excellent*/sensational/out of this world.

transbahutement [trɑ̃sbaytmɑ̃] *nm F* transferring; transporting; épuisé par le transbahutement de ses bagages, worn out with carting/humping his luggage around.

transbahuter [trɑ̃sbayte] I *vtr F* to shift/to lug/to hump around/to cart around; transbahuter une armoire, to shift a wardrobe; impossible de transbahuter tout ce bazar! it's just impossible to shift all this stuff! si je n'avais pas à me transbahuter! if only I didn't have to move/to shift! transbahuter des touristes d'un musée à l'autre, to shepherd tourists from one museum to another II *vpr* **se transbahuter** *F* to shift oneself (about)/to traipse around.

transfo [trɑ̃sfo] *nm F* (= *transformateur*) transformer.

transparent [trɑ̃sparɑ̃] *a F* tu n'es pas transparent, you're (standing) in my light; you'd make a better door than a window.

transpiration [trɑ̃spirasjɔ̃] *nf P* passer à la transpiration, to (have a) dance.

transpoil [trɑ̃spwal] *a P* = **trans.**

tran(-)tran [trɑ̃trɑ̃] *nm F* = **train-train.**

trapanelle [trapanɛl] *nf F* (*aviation*) glider.

trappe [trap] *nf P* mouth*; boucle la trappe! shut up*!/shut your trap!

trapu [trapy] *a F* (*a*) (*personne*) clever/brainy; être trapu en math, to be bright at maths/*NAm* math (*b*) difficult; ce problème est trapu, that's a sticky problem.

traque [trak] *nf F* chase; chasing (of criminal) (*by police*); manhunt.

traquer [trake] *vi F* to be afraid*; (*théâtre*) to get stage fright. (*Voir* **trac**)

traquette [trakɛt] *nf P* avoir la traquette/prendre les traquettes, to be afraid*/to get the wind up. (*Voir* **trac**)

traqueur, -euse [trakœr, -øz] *F* I *a* cowardly*/chicken/yellow II *n* coward*/

chicken/bottler.

traquouse [trakuz] *nf P* = **traquette.**

trav [trav] *nm P* = **trave.** (*Voir aussi* **travs**)

travail [travaj] *nm P* 1. faire un petit travail, (*cambrioleur*) to break into/to do a safe 2. aller au travail, (*prostituée*) to go (out) on the beat/on the game 3. et voilà le travail! well, that's done/we can wrap that up/that's a good job done!

travailler [travaje] I *vi P* aller travailler, (*prostituée*) to go (out) on the beat/on the game II *vtr F* travailler qn au corps, to use strong-arm tactics with s.o. (*Voir* **canotier; chapeau 5; chou I 1; touffe 1**)

travailleuse [travajøz] *nf P* une bonne travailleuse, a prostitute* profitable to her pimp; good earner/good meal-ticket.

trave [trav] *nm,* **travelo** [travlo] *nm P* (*travesti*) drag queen/TV.

travers [travɛr] *nm F* 1. prendre par le travers, to take a short cut 2. être en plein travers, to be dead out of luck 3. passer au/à travers, to miss an opportunity; (*être privé*) to have to do without (sth); (*vendeur, prostituée*) not to have a customer.

de traviole [dətravjɔl] *adv phr P* crooked/(all) on one side/lopsided/askew/skew-whiff; son chapeau était tout de traviole, his hat was all askew; il comprend tout de traviole, he always gets hold of the wrong end of the stick; le monde va de traviole, the world's all cock-eyed/all upside down.

travs [trav] *nmpl P* (= *travaux forcés*) les travs (à perpète), penal servitude (for life).

tref [trɛf] *nm P* 1. = **trèfle 1, 3, 4** 2. *Vieilli* passer qn au tref, to beat s.o. up*/to work s.o. over.

trèfle [trɛfl] *nm P* 1. *Vieilli* tobacco/baccy 2. crowd/mob 3. money*/lolly/dough 4. (as *m de*) trèfle, anus*/arsehole/*NAm* asshole.

tremblement [trɑ̃bləmɑ̃] *nm F* tout le tremblement, the whole bag of tricks*/the whole shooting-match/the (whole) works/the whole kit and caboodle.

trembleur [trɑ̃blœr] *nm F* heart/ticker.

tremblote [trɑ̃blɔt] *nf P* avoir la tremblote, (*avoir peur*) to have the jitters; (*avoir de la fièvre*) to have the shivers/the shakes.

trempe [trɑ̃p] *nf,* **trempée** [trɑ̃pe] *nf P* beating*/thrashing/good hiding; filer une trempe à qn, to beat s.o. up*/to work s.o. over/to clobber s.o.

tremper [trɑ̃pe] *vi P* tremper dans un coup,

to be involved in a crime; to be a party to/an accessory to a crime. (*Voir* **bain 6** (*c*); **biscuit 4**)

trempette [trãpɛt] *nf* F quick bath; faire trempette, to have a soak (in the bath).

trente [trãt] *nm inv* F se mettre sur son trente et un, to put one's glad rags on/to get (all) dolled up/to get dressed up to the nines.

trente-six [trãtsi(s), -siz] F I *a inv* 1. umpteen; avoir trente-six raisons de faire qch, to have umpteen reasons for doing sth 2. faire les trente-six volontés de qn, to dance attendance on s.o./to be at s.o.'s beck and call II *nm inv* 1. le trente-six = the CID 2. tous les trente-six du mois, once in a blue moon. (*Voir* **chandelle 10**; **chemin 2**)

trente-sixième [trãtsizjɛm] *a & nm inv* F umpteenth. (*Voir* **dessous 3**)

trente-trois [trãttrwa] *nm inv* F dites trente-trois! say ninety-nine!/say ah! (*Voir* **quarante-quatre 1**)

trèpe [trɛp] *nm*, **trèple** [trɛpl] *nm* P crowd/mob.

trésor [trezɔr] *nm* 1. F mon trésor, (my) darling*/(my) treasure; sa secrétaire est un vrai trésor, his secretary is a real treasure 2. F il a dépensé des trésors pour cette affaire, he spent a fortune over this business.

tréteau, *pl* **-eaux** [treto] *nm* P horse/nag.

triage [trijaʒ] *nm* P à chaque triage, each time; le premier triage, the first time; plusieurs triages, several times.

triangle [triãgl] *nm* 1. F (*cache-sexe*) G-string 2. V triangle (des Bermudes), female genitals*/beaver/slit.

tricard [trikar] P I *nm* (*interdit de séjour*) persona non grata II *a* excluded/sent to Coventry; mettre qn tricard, to send s.o. to Coventry/to make s.o. persona non grata.

triche [triʃ] *nf* F trick; trickery; cheating (*esp* at cards); c'est de la triche, that's cheating; that's not fair.

trichoter [triʃɔte] *vi* F to cheat/to fiddle.

trichoterie [triʃɔtri] *nf* F cheating/fiddling.

tricoter [trikɔte] *vi* F to walk* fast; (*pédaler*) to pedal; tricoter des jambes/des gambettes/des pincettes, to dance. (*Voir* **moujingue II 2**)

tricotin [trikɔtɛ̃] *nm* V penis*; avoir le tricotin, to have an erection*. (*Voir* **trique 3**)

tric-trac [triktrak] *nm* P shady deal.

trifouillage [trifujaʒ] *nm* F 1. rummaging (about) 2. fiddling about; meddling; tampering.

trifouiller [trifuje] *vtr & i* F 1. to rummage about (in a drawer, etc) 2. to fiddle about/to mess about; to tamper with (sth).

Trifouillis-les-Oies [trifujilezwa] *Prn* F = **Tripatouille-les-Oies.**

trimard [trimar] *nm* P 1. road/highway; faire le trimard/être sur le trimard, to be on the road; to be a tramp 2. vagrancy.

trimarder [trimarde] *vi* P to be on the road; to be a tramp.

trimardeur, -euse [trimardœr, -øz] *nm & f* P 1. tramp/vagrant/vagabond/*NAm* hobo/bum 2. itinerant worker.

trimbal(l)age [trɛ̃balaʒ] *nm*, **trimbal(l)ement** [trɛ̃balmã] *nm* F carting about/lugging about (of parcels, etc); trailing around (of children, etc).

trimbal(l)er [trɛ̃bale] I *vtr* 1. F to cart about/to lug about; il trimbal(l)e toujours sa famille avec lui, he always has his family in tow; trimbal(l)er sa viande, to trail (around)/*US* to schlep 2. F qu'est-ce qu'il trimbal(l)e! what a fool*/what a clot (he is)! II *vpr* se trimbal(l)er F to wander around; to drag oneself along/to trail (around); se trimbal(l)er jusqu'à la gare, to trail/*US* to schlep over to the station; je ne vais pas me trimbal(l)er en ville, I'm not trailing/*US* schlepping into town.

trime [trim] *nf* P drudgery/slog; hardship; une vie de trime, a hard life/a rotten life.

trimer [trime] *vi* F to work* hard/to slog away (at sth); quand on a trimé toute une vie, when one has slaved away all one's life; faire trimer qn, to keep s.o. at it/to keep s.o.'s nose to the grindstone.

trimeur [trimœr] *nm* F hard worker/slogger/drudge.

tringlage [trɛ̃glaʒ] *nm* V sex*/bonking.

tringle [trɛ̃gl] I *a* P silly II *nf* 1. P se mettre la tringle, to go without/to tighten one's belt 2. *Vieilli* P travailler pour la tringle, to work for (next to) nothing/for peanuts 3. V penis*/rod; avoir la tringle, to have an erection*; il est de la tringle, he likes sex*/he's continually randy/he's got a one-track mind; un coup de tringle, (*coït*) a screw/a fuck.

tringler [trɛ̃gle] I *vtr* V to have sex* with/to screw/to fuck/to lay (a woman); se faire tringler, to get laid II *vpr* se tringler P to cause oneself to abort/to give oneself an abortion.

tringlette [trɛ̃glɛt] *nf* V (*coït*) (quick) screw/fuck.

tringleur [trɛ̃glœr] *nm*, **tringlomane**

[trɛ̃glɔman] *nm V* man* who is fond of sex*; fucker/screwer.

tringlodrome [trɛ̃glɔdrom] *nm V* = **baisodrome**.

tringlot [trɛ̃glo] *nm P Mil* = **trainglot**.

trinquée [trɛ̃ke] *nf F* drinking (in company); j'aime la trinquée au bistrot avec les potes, I like having a drink at the pub with friends.

trinquer [trɛ̃ke] *vi* 1. *F* to drink* (*esp* heavily); to booze; on a trinqué ensemble, we had a few (together) 2. *P* (*subir un désagrément*) to get the worst of sth/to get it in the neck/to cop it; to get a punishment/a thrashing/a prison sentence, etc; to take the rap; trinquer de six mois de taule, to get six months inside; s'en tirer sans trinquer, to get off scot-free.

trinqueur [trɛ̃kœr] *nm F* drunkard*/(heavy) drinker/tippler/boozer.

trip [trip] *nm P* 1. (*drogues*) trip (*esp* on LSD*); faire un trip, to get high; redescendre d'un trip, to come down from a trip/to stop tripping 2. (*situation imaginée*) fantasy 3. c'est pas mon/son trip, it's not my/his/her scene; I'm/he's/she's not into that sort of thing; it doesn't turn me/him/her on.

tripaille [tripɑj] *nf F* (*intestins*) innards/guts.

tripatouillage [tripatujaʒ] *nm F* tampering/fiddling with (text, accounts, etc).

Tripatouille-les-Oies [tripatujlezwa] *Prn F* (imaginary) out-of-the-way place; one-horse town; = Much-Binding-in-the-Marsh/*NAm* Podunk. (*Voir* **Fouilly-les-Oies**)

tripatouiller [tripatuje] *vtr F* to tamper/to fiddle with (text, accounts etc).

tripatouilleur, -euse [tripatujœr, -øz] *nm P* fiddler/tamperer.

Tripatouillis-les-Oies [tripatujilezwa] *Prn F* = **Tripatouille-les-Oies**.

tripe [trip] *nf F* 1. *F* avoir la tripe républicaine, to be an out-and-out republican 2. *pl P* tripes, guts/innards; rendre/dégueuler tripes et boyaux, to vomit*/to be as sick as a dog/to spew one's guts out; je sentais mes tripes se retourner, I felt my stomach heaving; mettre les tripes au soleil/à l'air à qn, to rip/open s.o. up (with a knife, etc) 3. *P* courage/guts; avoir des tripes, to have guts; il manque de tripes, he's got no guts 4. *P* (*théâtre*) jouer avec ses tripes, to play a role/a part with gut feeling/to put one's guts into sth.

triper [tripe] *vi P* (*drogues*) to take a trip

(*esp* on LSD*)/to trip.

tripette [tripɛt] *nf F* ça ne vaut pas tripette, that's worthless*/it's not worth a sausage.

tripeur, -euse [tripœr, -øz] *n P* (*drogues*) tripper (*esp* on LSD*).

tripotage [tripɔtaʒ] *nm F* 1. messing about/fiddling about (de, with) 2. underhand/shady/crooked deal; tripotages, shady dealings; tripotages électoraux, election fiddles; tripotage financier, market jobbery; tripotages de caisse, tampering with/fiddling the cash.

tripotailler [tripɔtaje] *v F Péj* = **tripoter** I, II III.

tripotée [tripɔte] *nf P* 1. thrashing/(good) hiding/belting/beating*(-up); flanquer une tripotée à qn, to knock s.o. about 2. une tripotée de ..., a large number/quantity* of ...; lots of .../crowds of ....

tripoter [tripɔte] I *vi F* 1. to mess about/to fiddle about; tripoter dans un tiroir, to rummage about in a drawer 2. to engage in underhand deals/shady deals/shady business; tripoter dans l'immobilier, to get involved in some shady property deals II *vtr F* 1. to mess about with/to fiddle with (sth); ne tripote pas mes outils! don't play around with my tools! 2. qu'est-ce que vous tripotez là? what are you getting up to (there)? 3. to deal dishonestly/shadily with (money) 4. tripoter qn, to paw s.o./to touch s.o. up/to grope s.o.; ne me tripotez pas comme ça! don't paw me like that! III *vpr* se **tripoter** *V* to masturbate*/to play with oneself.

tripoteur [tripɔtœr] *nm F* 1. man who touches up women/groper 2. shady dealer/fiddler; swindler*/shark.

tripoteux [tripɔtø] *nm FrC F* = **tripoteur** 1.

triquard [trikar] *nm P* = **tricard** I.

trique [trik] *nf* 1. *P* prohibition from entering specified areas/ban(ning) order/bar. (*Voir* **tricard**) 2. *F* cudgel/heavy stick; avoir recours à la trique, to use the big stick; mener qn à la trique, to rule s.o. with a rod of iron; *F* maigre comme une trique/sec comme un coup de trique, as thin as a rake 3. *V* penis*/shaft/rod; avoir la trique, to have an erection*/a hard-on/a stiffy.

triquée [trike] *nf Vieilli P* thrashing/beating*(-up)/belting; filer une triquée à qn, to give s.o. a (good) hiding.

triquer [trike] I *vtr P* 1. to ban/bar (s.o.) from specified areas; to make (s.o.) persona

non grata 2. to beat up*/to thrash (s.o.) II *vi*
V to have an erection*/a hard-on; to get it up.

(se) trisser [(sə)trise] *vi & vpr* P to run*
very fast; (*s'enfuir*) to run away*/to beat it/
NAm to hightail it/to clear off.

triste [trist] *a* F c'était vraiment pas triste, it
was really funny.

tristounet, -ette [tristunɛ, -ɛt] *a* P sad/
gloomy/dreary.

trogne [trɔɲ] *nf* F face*; une trogne d'ivrogne, a beery mug.

trognon [trɔɲɔ̃] I *a inv* F dear/nice/sweet;
ce qu'il/qu'elle est trognon! what a cute little
boy/girl! II *nm* 1. F darling*/pet/poppet/
sweetie 2. F jusqu'au trognon, (*jusqu'au bout*)
to the (bitter) end; (*complètement*) well and
truly; up to the neck; avoir qn jusqu'au trognon, to take s.o. in completely 3. P head*; se
casser le trognon, to rack one's brains; y aller
du trognon, to risk one's neck; dévisser le trognon à qn, to strangle s.o. 4. P face*/mug.

trôleur [trolœr] *nm* F (= *contrôleur*) ticket
inspector.

trombe [trɔ̃b] *nf* F entrer/sortir en trombe,
to burst in/out (like a whirlwind); to dash in/
out.

trombine [trɔ̃bin] *nf* P (a) head*/bonce/nut
(b) face*/mug.

trombiner [trɔ̃bine] *vtr* V trombiner une
femme, to have sex* with/to bonk a woman.

tromblon [trɔ̃blɔ̃] *nm* 1. P (any) unwieldy
or old-fashioned-looking firearm 2. P (vieux)
tromblon, fool*/idiot 3. V (filer un) coup de
tromblon, (to have) sex*.

tromblonard [trɔ̃blɔnar] *nm* P face*; se
casser le tromblonard, to fall flat on one's
face/to come a cropper*.

tromboner [trɔ̃bɔne] *vtr* V tromboner une
femme, to have sex* with/to bonk a woman.

tromé [trɔme] *nm* P (*verlan de métro*)
underground/metro/tube.

trompe-couillon [trɔ̃pkujɔ̃] *nm inv* P 1.
deception/fraud/con 2. drinking glass containing less than it appears.

trompe-la-mort [trɔ̃plamɔr] *nm & f inv* F
(a) death dodger (b) aged, sick person (c)
(*volontaire*) daredevil.

trompette [trɔ̃pɛt] *nf* 1. F c'est la
trompette du quartier, he's/she's the local
gossip 2. P face* 3. P nose*/hooter; en avoir
un coup dans la trompette, to be drunk*/
pissed/loaded.

trompinette [trɔ̃pinɛt] *nf* P small nose*.

tronc [trɔ̃] *nm* 1. P head*; se casser le tronc,

to worry; il (ne) se casse pas le tronc, he
doesn't think; (*il ne se fait pas de souci*) he's
not worried 2. P se taper le tronc, to eat*
heartily/to have a good tuck-in/a good blow-
out 3. P Péj tronc (de figuier), Arab*/wog.
(*Voir* **sciure**)

tronche [trɔ̃ʃ] *nf* P 1. head*; filer un coup de
tronche à qn, to (head-)butt s.o.; se casser la
tronche, to rack one's brains; se payer la
tronche de qn, to make fun of s.o./to take the
mickey out of s.o. 2. face*/mug; se taper la
tronche, to eat* heartily/to feed one's face 3.
tronche (à l'huile), fool*/twerp/clot; tronche
plate! (you) cloth-head! 4. clever/brainy
person; c'est une tronche, elle, she's very
brainy.

troncher [trɔ̃ʃe] *vtr & i* 1. V troncher (une
femme), to have sex* (with) (a woman) 2. P to
kill*/to rub out/to liquidate. (*Voir* **trancher**)

troncheur [trɔ̃ʃœr] *nm* V man who has sex/
screw(er)/fucker.

trône [tron] *nm* F lavatory/loo seat/throne; il
est sur le trône, he's (sitting) on the throne/
he's on the loo.

trop [tro] *a inv* F être trop, to be
unbelievable/amazing/incredible; (*excessif*) to
be too much; il est trop ce mec! that guy's unreal!

troquet [trɔkɛ] *nm* P (a) A (*patron de café*)
= publican; keeper of a pub or wine bar.
(*Voir* **mastroquet**) (b) (*petit café*) = pub/
(wine) bar; une tournée de troquets, a pub-
crawl.

trot [tro] *nm* F au trot, at the double; allez-y,
et au trot! go on, and be quick about it!

trotte [trɔt] *nf* F distance/stretch/run; il y a
une (bonne) trotte d'ici là/ça fait une (bonne)
trotte, it's a good way from here; faire une
bonne trotte, to go a good long way (to see
s.o., etc); tout d'une trotte, at a stretch/
without stopping.

trotter [trɔte] I *vi* F elle est toujours à
trotter, she's always on the go II *vpr* se
trotter P (a) to go (away)/to be off/to make
tracks (b) to run away*/to clear off (in a
hurry).

trotteuse [trɔtøz] *nf* P prostitute*/
streetwalker/*esp NAm* hooker.

trottinet [trɔtinɛ] *nm* P foot*.

trottinette [trɔtinɛt] *nf* 1. F (small) car;
runabout 2. P trottinette à macchabs,
hearse/meat wag(g)on.

trottineuse [trɔtinøz] *nf* P = **trotteuse**.

trottoir [trɔtwar] *nm* F 1. faire le trottoir,

(*prostituée*) to solicit*/to walk the streets/to be a streetwalker; to hook/to hustle; **fille de trottoir**, streetwalker; **elle fait le trottoir**, she's on the game **2.** (*théâtre*) **le grand trottoir**, the classical repertory (of the French stage).

trou [tru] *nm* **1.** F *Péj* (*village, etc*) hole; **habiter un petit trou** (**mort/paumé/perdu**), to live in a dead-and-alive hole/dump; **elle n'est jamais sortie de son trou**, she's never been out of her own backyard **2.** P prison*/nick/clink/jug; **on l'a mis au trou**, they put him away/he was put inside **3.** P grave; **on l'a mis dans le trou**, they buried him; **être dans le trou**, to be dead and buried **4.** F (*a*) **trous de nez**, nostrils (*b*) **boire comme un trou**, to drink like a fish; P **avoir un trou sous le nez**, to be a heavy drinker **5.** F **boucher un trou**, to pay off a debt; **faire un trou pour en boucher un autre**, to rob Peter to pay Paul; **cela servira à boucher un trou**, that will do as a stopgap/that'll (help to) tide us over **6.** F **faire son trou**, to get on (in the world); to make a name for oneself **7.** F **ne pas avoir les yeux en face des trous**, (*être mal éveillé*) to be (still) half asleep; (*mal observer*) not to look carefully; P **t'as donc pas les yeux en face des trous?** can't you see?/are you blind? **8.** V (*a*) **trou du cul/trou de balle**, anus*/arsehole/*NAm* asshole; **un vieux trou de balle**, an old fogey*; (**petit**) **trou du cul!** (you) bloody fool*!/(you) jerk!/(you) arsehole!/*NAm* (you) asshole! **jusqu'à la Saint-trou-du-cul**, till doomsday/till the cows come home; **avoir le trou du cul qui fait bravo**, to be very frightened/in a blue funk; to be shit-scared/to be scared shitless; **se démancher/se décarcasser/se dévisser le trou du cul** (**pour faire qch**), to make every effort/to go all out (to do sth); to shift one's arse/*NAm* ass (*b*) **ça ne te fera pas un trou au cul**, there's no danger/you don't risk anything (*c*) **partie de trou du cul**, sex*/bump and grind **9.** P (*aviation*) **il a fait un trou dans l'eau**, he's gone for a burton **10.** F **trou normand**, glass of Calvados (*drunk between two courses of a meal*) **11.** P (*drogues*) **se faire des trous**, to shoot up/to fix/to fill oneself full of holes.

troubade [trubad] *nm* A P private/ (infantry) soldier/squaddie.

trouduc [trudyk], **trou-du-cul** [trudyky] *nm* V bloody fool*/jerk/nurd; **petit trouduc!** you arsehole/*NAm* asshole!

trouduculier, -ière [trudykylje, -jɛr] *a* V

pornographic.

trouducuter [trudykyte] *vtr* V to have sex* with/to lay/to fuck (a woman).

troufignard [trufiɲar] *nm* V anus*/ arse(hole).

troufigner [trufiɲe] *vi* V to stink*.

troufignon [trufiɲɔ̃] *nm* V anus*/ arse(hole)/*NAm* ass(hole).

troufion [trufjɔ̃] *nm* P **1.** (infantry) soldier/ private/squaddie **2.** fool*/jerk/nurd.

trouillard, -arde [trujar, -ard] P I *a* cowardly*/windy/yellow(-bellied) II *n* coward*/funk/chicken/bottler.

trouille [truj] *nf* P fear; **avoir la trouille**, to be afraid*/to have the wind up; **flanquer/ ficher/foutre la trouille à qn**, to put the wind up s.o./to scare the pants off s.o.; **une trouille bleue/verte/noire**, a blue funk; **tu n'as pas la trouille!** you've got a nerve!/you're not backward in coming forward!

trouiller [truje] *vi* P to be afraid*/to get the wind up/to lose one's bottle.

trouillomètre [trujɔmɛtr] *nm* P **avoir le trouillomètre à zéro**, to be in a blue funk/to be scared stiff/to be scared shitless.

trouilloter [trujɔte] *vi* P **1.** to stink*/to pong **2.** to be afraid*/to have the heebie-jeebies/the willies.

trousse-couilles [truskuj] *nm inv* P (men's) underpants*/nut chokers.

troussée [truse] *nf* P **1.** beating(-up)*/ dusting **2.** (*coït en vitesse*) quick screw/ quickie.

troussequin [truskɛ̃] *nm* P buttocks*/bum/ *surt NAm* butt.

trousser [truse] *vtr* **1.** F **il est toujours à trousser les jupons**, he's always chasing after women/he's forever chasing skirt **2.** V (*coïter en vitesse*) to have a quick scew/a quickie with (a woman); **elle s'est fait trousser**, she got laid **3.** F to get through/to polish off (work, business, a meal).

trousseur [trusœr] *nm* F **trousseur de jupons**, womanizer*/skirt-chaser/ladies' man.

truand [tryɑ̃] *nm* F (*escroc*) crook; (*gangster*) gangster.

truander [tryɑ̃de] F I *vtr* to swindle*/to con/to do (s.o.); **se faire truander**, to be swindled/to get done II *vi* to cheat; **truander à un examen**, to cheat in an exam.

truc [tryk] *nm* **1.** F (*a*) trick/dodge/wheeze/ caper; **les trucs du métier**, the tricks of the trade (*b*) knack; **avoir le truc**, to have the knack; **prendre/attraper le truc pour faire**

qch, to get the hang of it 2. (*a*) *F* (*chose*) what's-its-name* / thingummy(jig) / thingy; passe-moi ce truc-là, give me that thing/that whatchamacallit (*b*) *P* (*personne*) thingy/ what's-his-name*/thingummybob (*c*) *F* **j'ai un truc à te dire**, I've got something to tell you; **il y a un tas de trucs à faire**, there's loads of things to do (*d*) *F* **c'est mon truc**, (*ça m'intéresse*) it's right up my street/I'm into that; **ça, c'est pas mon truc**, that's not my (sort of) thing at all/I'm not into that 3. *F* **couper dans le truc**, to be swindled/conned; **mordre dans le truc**, to fall into a trap/to fall for it 4. *F* **lâcher/débiner le truc**, to let the cat out of the bag 5. *P* **piquer au truc**, to have a go/a shot; **repiquer au truc**, to have another shot 6. *P* prostitution; **faire le truc**, to solicit*/to be on the game 7. *P* **être porté sur le truc**, to be fond of sex*/to like it a lot/to have a one-track mind.

trucider [tryside] *vtr F* to kill*/to bump off/ to do away with (s.o.).

trucmuche [trykmyʃ] *nm P* (*chose*) what's-its-name*/thingy/thingummyjig; (*personne*) what's-his-name*/thingy.

truffe [tryf] *nf P* 1. (bulbous) nose* 2. idiot*/twit/clot/nurd/jerk.

trumeau, -eaux [trymo] *nm F* 1. ugly woman* 2. **vieux trumeau**, old person; old geezer; old bat.

truqué [tryke] *a F* faked/rigged/fixed; **c'est truqué**, it's a con/a fix.

truquer [tryke] *vtr F* to fake/to fix/to fiddle/ to rig; to cook (accounts); **il avait truqué les cartes**, he'd fixed the cards; **truquer une élection**, to rig an election.

truqueur [trykœr] *nm P* 1. (sexual) black-mailer 2. dealer in fake antique furniture.

truqueuse [trykøz] *nf A P* (low-class) prostitute*/(cheap) tart/(cheap) floozy.

truster [trœste] *vtr F* to monopolize (s.o./ sth/n) to keep (s.o./sth) to oneself.

tsoin-tsoin [tswɛ̃tswɛ̃] *a inv F* = **soin-soin**.

tubard¹ [tybar] *nm P* 1. (*renseignement*) tip/low-down/gen; **refiler un tubard à qn**, to give s.o. a tip/to put s.o. onto sth hot 2. stallholder/salesman, -woman (*who sells his/ her wares in the undergound*).

tubard², -arde [tybar, -ard] *F* (= *tuberculeux*) I *a* suffering from TB II *nm & f* person suffering from TB/TB case.

tubardise [tybardiz] *nf F* tuberculosis/TB.

tube [tyb] I *nm* 1. *Vieilli F* top hat/topper 2. *Vieilli P* stomach* 3. *P* (*métro*) underground/

tube 4. *P* telephone*/blower; **filer/passer un coup de tube à qn**, to give s.o. a bell/a buzz/a tinkle 5. *P* = **tubard¹** 1 6. *P* (*a*) = **tubardise** (*b*) = **tubard²**, **-arde** II 7. *F* hit song/record; **tube de l'été**, summer hit/chart-topper 8. *P* **à plein(s) tube(s)**, completely/ totally; full blast; **débloquer/déconner à plein(s) tube(s)**, to talk utter nonsense*/a load of rubbish/(a load of) shit; to bullshit 9. *F* (*de vélo*) tubular tyre II *a P* = **tubard²**, **-arde** I.

tuber [tybe] *vtr P* (*renseigner*) to give (s.o.) a good tip; (*courses*) to sell (s.o.) tips.

tubeur [tybœr] *nm P* (*courses*) tipster.

tuile [tyil] *nf* 1. *F* piece of bad luck; (un-expected) mishap/accident/blow; **quelle tuile!** what a blow!/what a drag! **une tuile imprévue**, a bolt from the blue; **il lui est arrivé une sale tuile**, he's had a terrible blow 2. *P* ten thousand francs.

tulette [tylɛt] *nf P* car*/motor.

tune¹ [tyn] *nf P* = **thune**.

tune² [tyn] *a & n P* Tunisian.

tunnel [tynɛl] *nm P* **être dans le tunnel**, to be in a fix*/in trouble/in a hole.

turbin [tyrbɛ̃] *nm P* 1. work*/slog/grind/ graft; **aller au turbin**, to go to work; **se remettre au turbin**, to get back to the daily grind/the slog 2. (*cambriolage, etc*) job; **aller au turbin**, to pull (off) a job 3. **faire un vache turbin/un drôle de turbin à qn**, to do the dirty on s.o./to play a dirty trick on s.o. 4. prostitu-tion; **aller au turbin**, to go on the game 5. event; **qu'est-ce que c'est que ce turbin?** what's going on?/what's happening?/what's up?

turbine [tyrbin] *nf V* **turbine (à chocolat)**, anus*.

turbiner [tyrbine] *vi P* 1. to work* hard/to flog oneself (to death)/to slog away at sth 2. (*prostituée*) to solicit*/to be on the game.

turbineuse [tyrbinøz] *nf P* prostitute*.

turbo [tyrbo] *nm F* 1. **mettre son turbo**, to get angry*/to blow a fuse/to blow one's top 2. **mettre/enclencher le turbo**, to get a move on/ to step on the gas.

turf [tyrf] *nm P* 1. prostitution; prostitute's beat; **(fille de) turf**, prostitute*; **aller au/sur le turf**, **faire le turf**, to go on the beat/the game; to walk the streets 2. (*a*) place of work; workshop/office, etc (*b*) work/job; **c'est pas mon turf**, it's none of my business/nothing to do with me.

turfer [tyrfe] *vi P* (*prostituée*) to solicit*/to be on the game/to hustle.

turfeuse [tyrføz] *nf P* prostitute*.

turista [turista] *nf P* diarrhoea*/the turistas.

turlu [tyrly] *nm* 1. *P* telephone* 2. *V* vagina*.

turlupiner [tyrlypine] *vtr F* to bother/to worry/to annoy*; **qu'est-ce qui te turlupine?** what's eating you?/what's bugging you?

turlute [tyrlyt] *nf V* fellatio*; **faire une turlute à qn,** to give s.o. a blow-job/to give s.o. head.

turne [tyrn] *nf P* (*chambre, logement*) room/digs/place/pad; (*maison*) (untidy/ messy) house.

tutoyer [tytwaje] *vtr F* **se faire tutoyer,** to get reprimanded*/told off/ticked off/hauled over the coals.

tutu [tyty] *nm* 1. *P* (*vin ordinaire*) wine/ plonk/vino 2. *P* telephone*; **passer un coup de tutu,** to make a phone call 3. *P* (*langage enfantin*) bottom/botty.

tutute [tytyt] *nf P* bottle of wine/plonk/vino.

tututer [tytyte] *vi P* to drink*/to booze/to tipple.

tuyau, *pl* **-aux** [tɥijo] *nm* 1. *F* tip/hint/info; **avoir des tuyaux,** to be in the know; **il m'a donné/filé quelques tuyaux sur l'affaire,** he gave me the low-down/some gen/a few tips on that business; **tuyau crevé,** wrong information/rotten tip; **c'est un tuyau increvable,** it's straight from the horse's mouth 2. *P* (*courses*) tip/cert; **marchand de tuyaux,** tipster; **un tuyau de première main,** a dead cert 3. *P* (*a*) *A* **tuyau de poêle,** top hat/topper (*b*) (pantalon) **tuyau de poêle,** drainpipe trousers/drainpipes 4. *P* **la famille tuyau de poêle,** couples who swap partners/who practise wife-swapping; (*homosexuels*) homosexuals (*in general*)/pansyland.

tuyauter [tɥijote] *vtr F* **tuyauter qn,** to inform s.o./to give s.o. a tip/to put s.o. in the know/to gen s.o. up/to give s.o. the low-down; **être bien tuyauté,** to be in the know.

tuyauterie [tɥijotri] *nf P* digestive and respiratory systems.

type [tip] *nm P* man*/bloke/chap/guy; **un chic type,** a great guy/bloke; **un sale type,** a bastard*/a sod/*surt NAm* a son of a bitch; *Péj* **t'es un pauvre type!** you bastard*!/you sod!

typesse [tipɛs] *nf P surt Péj* woman*/ female/chapess.

typo [tipo] *F* **I** *nf* typography **II** *nm* (*typographe*) typo.

typote [tipɔt] *nf F* (*typographe*) typo.

U

u [y] *a F* (= *universitaire*); cité u = (students') hall(s) of residence/campus. (*Voir* **restau**)

un, une [œ̃, yn] *F* **I** *num a & n* **1.** il était/c'était moins une, it was a narrow escape/a close shave/a near thing; s'en tirer à moins une, to have a narrow squeak **2.** être sans un/ne pas avoir la queue d'un, to be penniless*/to be (dead/stony) broke **3.** ne faire ni une ni deux, not to hesitate/not to think twice about it; il n'a fait ni une ni deux, he didn't hesitate (for a moment)/he made no bones about it **4.** l'un(e) dans l'autre, taking one thing with another/on average/by and large **5.** et d'un(e)! so much for that (one)!/that settles that! (d'abord) et d'une, to begin with/for a start/to kick off with **6.** (*a*) *Journ* la une, the front page/page one; cinq colonnes à la une, front page spread/banner headline; événement qui fait la une, front-page news/news which hits the headlines (*b*) *TV* la Une, (*première chaîne*) the first channel; = BBC1 **7.** de deux choses l'une, it's one thing or the other/either ..., or ... **II** *indef pron* tu n'en as même pas une de voiture, you haven't even got a car **III** *indef art* **1.** il a fait une de ces têtes, you should have seen his face! tu m'as fait une de ces peurs! you gave me such a fright! **2.** vous en êtes un autre, (*idiot, etc*) (and) the same to you too (with knobs on) **IV** *indef pron avec 'en'* en boucher un à qn, (*coin*) to flabbergast* s.o.; en griller/s'en fumer une, (*cigarette*) to smoke a cigarette*; en allumer une, (*cigarette*) to light up; en tenir une, (*cuite*) to be drunk*/pissed as a newt; ne pas en ficher/*V* foutre une (rame), to do damn-all/fuck-all; je n'ai pas pu en placer une, (*parole*) I couldn't get a word in edgeways. (*Voir* **bander 2**; **bonir 1**; **pas II 2**; **rater**; **suer II 1**)

unif [ynif] *nm F* uniform.

unique [ynik] *a F* il est unique! he's priceless! he's the (absolute) limit! voilà qui est unique! who ever heard such nonsense!

unité [ynite] *nf P* ten thousand (new) francs.

urf [œrf] *a inv Vieilli P* smart/posh/snazzy.

urger [yrʒe] *vi F* to be urgent; ça urge! it's urgent!/it can't wait!/it's got to be done quickly! y a rien qui urge, there's no great hurry.

user [yze] *vtr* **1.** à user le soleil, for ever; (*toute la journée*) all day long **2.** user un litre de salive à l'heure, to talk a lot*/nineteen to the dozen.

usine [yzin] *nf P* **1.** aller à l'usine, to go to work **2.** *Aut* usine à gaz, carburettor **3.** qu'est-ce que c'est que cette usine? what sort of a place/dump is this?

usiner [yzine] *P vi* (*a*) to work* hard/to slog (away); ça usine ici! we're hard at it in here! (*b*) en usiner, (*prostituée*) to go on the beat/to be on the game.

utilité [ytilite] *nf F* (*théâtre*) small/minor part; jouer les utilités, (*théâtre*) to play bit parts; *Fig* to play second fiddle/a minor role (in an enterprise, etc).

V

va [va] *excl P* **1.** (*précédant une injure*) va donc, eh, connard/petit con! get lost, you little jerk/nurd! **2.** (*intensif*) je t'aime bien, va! of course I love you! **3.** va pour ..., OK for .../it's OK with me; va pour le prix, the price is fine.

vacant [vakɑ̃] *a P* penniless*/broke.

vacciné [vaksine] *a* **1.** *F* être vacciné avec une aiguille de phono, to talk* a lot/to chatter* away (nineteen to the dozen) **2.** *F* to be hardened/immune (to sth); tu peux y aller, je suis vacciné! do what you like, it won't affect me! **3.** *F* être majeur et vacciné, to know all about the birds and the bees/to know what's what/to know the score **4.** *V* elle est vaccinée au pus de génisse, she's lost her virginity*/her cherry.

vachard [vaʃar] *a P* **1.** (*a*) mean/nasty/rotten; ce que tu peux être vachard, des fois! you can be a real bastard* at times! (*b*) difficult; il est plutôt vachard, ce problème, it's a bit of a bastard/sod this problem **2.** lazy*/bone idle.

vachardise [vaʃardiz] *nf P* laziness.

vachasse [vaʃas] *nf P Péj* (large, ugly) woman*/slob/bag/(fat) cow.

vache [vaʃ] *a P* **1.** (*personne*) mean/nasty/rotten; ce qu'il peut être vache, he can be a real bastard*/a rotten swine; elle est vache, sa femme, his wife's a real bitch/cow; il a été vache comme tout avec moi, he was really mean/rotten to me **2.** (*chose*) rotten/nasty; un coup vache, a dirty trick; ça, c'est vache! that's a filthy trick! that's rotten! **3.** difficult; il est vache ce problème, this problem's a sod **4.** important; un vache de travail, an important job. (*Voir* **amour 1**) II *nf* **1.** *P* (*homme*) bastard*/swine/sod; (*femme*) bitch/cow; sale vache! you bastard!/you filthy swine!/you sod! bande de vaches! you swine!/you lousy bastards! **2.** *P* policeman*/cop; les vaches, the cops/the fuzz/*NAm* the bulls; mort aux vaches! down with the cops!/death to the fuzz! vache à roulettes, motor-cycle cop **3.** *P* vache à lait, mug/sucker **4.** *P* manger/bouffer de la vache enragée, to rough it/to have a hard time of it **5.** *F* le plancher des vaches, dry land/terra firma **6.** *F* il pleut comme (une) vache qui pisse, it's chucking it down/it's pissing down **7.** *P* plein comme une vache, dead drunk*/loaded/pissed **8.** *F* regarder (qn) comme une vache regarde passer le train, to gape/gawp at (s.o.) **9.** *P* coup en vache, an underhand trick/a dirty trick; faire un coup en vache à qn, to do the dirty on s.o. **10.** *P* (*excl*) oh la vache! damn!/blast!/hell!/sod!; (*admiration*) blimey!/ I'll be damned!/wow!/Christ! **11.** *P* une vache de problème, one hell of a problem/a really sticky problem; une vache de moto, one hell of a (motor)bike/a really amazing bike/a mean bike. (*Voir* **gueule II 1**; **peau 20** (*c*))

vachement [vaʃmɑ̃] *adv F* **1.** (*très*) c'est vachement bon, it's damned/bloody good; j'ai vachement soif, I'm bloody thirsty/I could really do with a drink; t'es vachement con, you're a bloody idiot*; il a vachement vieilli, he's got a helluva lot older looking **2.** *Vieilli* in a mean way; il m'a répondu vachement, he replied nastily.

vacherie [vaʃri] *nf P* **1.** (*action*) dirty/mean/rotten trick; (*remarque*) nasty remark; faire une vacherie à qn, to play a nasty trick on s.o./to do the dirty on s.o.; dire des vacheries à qn, to be bitchy/nasty to s.o. **2.** unpleasant situation/event; quelle vacherie! what a bummer! cette vacherie de temps! this bloody/*NAm* goddamn weather! **3.** difficulty/snag; y a une vacherie, there's a hitch/a snag.

vachetement [vaʃtømɑ̃] *adv P* = **vachement**.

vachté [vaʃte] *adv P* = **vachement 1**.

va-comme-je-te-pousse [vakɔmʒtəpus] *adv phr F* à la va-comme-je-te-pousse, anyoldhow/all anyhow/in a slapdash way.

vacs [vak(s)] *nfpl F* (= *vacances*) holidays/ hols/vacation/vac.

va-de-la-gueule [vadlagœl] *nm P* bigmouth/loudmouth.

vadrouille [vadruj] *nf F* ramble/stroll; être en vadrouille, to rove/to roam/to wander about; partir en vadrouille, to go out for a bit of a wander/a bit of fun.

(se) vadrouiller [(sə)vadruje] *vi & vpr F* to rove/to roam/to wander about; to knock around.

vadrouilleur, -euse [vadrujœr, -øz] *n F* rover/wanderer/gadabout/gallivanter.

vague [vag] *nf P* pocket.

vaguer [vage] *vtr P* vaguer qn, to go through s.o.'s pockets/to frisk s.o.

vaisselle [vɛsɛl] *nf* 1. P vaisselle de fouille, pocket money; se faire un peu de vaisselle de fouille, to make a bit of pocket money/to get oneself a bit of cash together 2. V (*lesbiennes*) laver la vaisselle, to have cunnilingus*.

valade [valad] *nf P* pocket.

valda [valda] *nf P* 1. bullet/slug 2. *Vieilli* green traffic light.

valdingue [valdɛ̃g] *P* I *nf* 1. suitcase/case; faire la valdingue, (*s'en aller*) to pack up/to clear off/to make tracks 2. la Grande Valdingue, death II *nm* 1. (*cartes*) jack 2. faire/ramasser un valdingue, to come a cropper*/to fall flat on one's face.

valdinguer [valdɛ̃ge] *vi P* 1. to fall down*/ to come a cropper*/to go sprawling/to fall flat on one's face 2. (*a*) envoyer valdinguer qn, (*congédier*) to send s.o. packing*/to send s.o. off with a flea in his ear/to tell s.o. to get lost; (*faire tomber*) to send s.o. spinning/reeling (*b*) envoyer valdinguer ses affaires, to send everything flying.

valise [valiz] *nf F* 1. (se) faire la valise, to run away*/to pack up/to clear off; (*rompre*) to break up/to split up with one's boyfriend *or* girlfriend 2. avoir des valises sous les yeux, to have rings/bags under one's eyes. (*Voir* con II (*a*); malle)

valiser [valize] *vtr & i F* (*a*) to run away*/to pack up (*b*) to walk out on (s.o.) (*c*) to throw/ to boot/to kick (s.o.) out.

valoche [valɔʃ] *nf P* 1. (suit)case 2. = valise.

valouse [valuz] *nf P* = valoche 1.

valouser [valuze] *vtr P* (*a*) to walk out on (s.o.) (*b*) to throw (s.o.) out; il l'a valousée, he kicked her out/booted her out/got rid of her.

valse [vals] *nf* 1. P envoyer la valse, to give money*/to pay* up; lâchez-les, valse lente! pay* up! 2. P inviter qn à la valse, to ask s.o. to step outside (for a fight); filer une valse à qn, to beat s.o. up*/to thrash s.o. 3. F la valse du personnel/des ministres, constant changes of staff/the ministerial merry-go-round 4. F beer and peppermint.

valser [valse] *vi F* 1. to throw/to fling/to chuck; envoyer valser qn, to send s.o. packing*/to tell s.o. to buzz off; envoyer valser qch, to send sth flying 2. faire valser l'argent/les faire valser, to spend money like water.

valseur [valsœr] *nm P* 1. buttocks*/arse/ *NAm* ass 2. filer du valseur, to wiggle one's hips (when walking); (*être homosexuel*) to be a homosexual* 3. trousers*/*NAm* pants/ strides/duds.

valseuses [valsøz] *nfpl V* testicles*/balls/ nuts.

valtouse [valtuz] *nf P* (suit)case.

vamper [vɑ̃pe] *vtr F* to vamp/to seduce; elle essayait de le vamper, she was flirting with him/she was trying to get off with him.

vanne [van] *nf ou m P* 1. (nasty) crack/dig/ jibe; lancer une vanne à qn, to make a dig at s.o./to knock s.o.; faire/lancer des vannes, to make snide remarks 2. joke; (*farce*) practical joke/prank 3. spot of bother/trouble.

vanné [vane] *a P* exhausted*/dead beat/ shagged out/knackered.

vanner [vane] *P* I *vtr* to exhaust*/to tire out/to shatter/to knacker II *vi* 1. to boast*/to brag/to talk big 2. to make a (nasty) crack/to knock/to have a dig (at s.o./sth) 3. to joke/to crack jokes III *vpr* se vanner to become exhausted*; se vanner à la bourre, to have too much sex*/too much of the other/to shag one's arse off.

vanneur, -euse [vanœr, -øz] *n P* boaster/ bragger/show-off*/loudmouth.

vanterne [vɑ̃tɛrn] *nf P* window.

vape [vap] *nf P* 1. être (complètement) dans les vapes/être en pleine vape, to be dopey/ woozy/in a daze (*esp* after drugs *or* drink *or* when tired, etc); (*rêver*) to have one's head in the clouds 2. tomber dans les vapes, to faint/to pass out 3. doubt/suspicion; sentir/ renifler/respirer la vape, to suspect sth fishy/ to smell a rat.

vapé [vape] *a P* dopey/woozy/in a daze.

vapeur [vapœr] *nf P* retourner/renverser la

vapeur, to change sides *or* to go back on one's decision/to backpedal. (*Voir* **voile 3**)

vaporisateur [vapɔrizatœr] *nm Vieilli P* machine gun/tommy gun.

variétoche [varjetɔʃ] *nf P Péj* variety show.

varlot [varlo] *nm P* customer who buys nothing (in a shop) and annoys the staff in the process/browser.

vase [vaz] *P* **I** *nf* 1. rain 2. water **II** *nm* 1. *Vieilli* (*a*) anus* (*b*) buttocks* 2. luck; avoir du vase, to be lucky/jammy.

vaseliner [vazline] *vtr F* to flatter*/to butter (s.o.) up.

vaser [vaze] *vi P* to rain.

vaseux, -euse [vazø, -øz] *a F* 1. unwell*/under the weather/off-colour; se sentir vaseux, to feel unwell*; (*après avoir trop bu*) to have a hangover 2. des idées vaseuses, woolly ideas; explication vaseuse, confused/muddled explanation; plaisanterie vaseuse, off-colour/unsavoury joke.

vasouillard, -arde [vazujar, -ard] *a F* (*propos, explication, idée, etc*) woolly/airy-fairy/muddled; (*personne*) dopey/muddle-headed.

vasouiller [vazuje] *vi F* to struggle/to flounder; ça vasouille depuis hier, things haven't been going well since yesterday.

va-te-faire-fiche [vatfɛrfiʃ] *adv phr F* à la va-te-faire-fiche, anyoldhow/in a slapdash way.

va-te-laver [vatlave] *nm ou f P* slap/blow*; flanquer un(e) va-te-laver à qn, to slap s.o. round the face/head.

veau, *pl* **veaux** [vo] *nm P* 1. pleurer comme un veau, to cry one's eyes out/to blubber 2. (*a*) (tête de) veau, fool*/clot/clod/*NAm* dumb cluck; (*abruti*) lump/lout (*b*) tête de veau, bald man/baldie 3. prostitute* (who doesn't put herself out too much) 4. (*courses*) outsider; (*mauvais cheval*) nag 5. slow vehicle/jalopy/banger/heap/crate.

vécés [vese] *nmpl F* WC*/loo/*NAm* bathroom/*NAm* john.

veilleuse [vɛjøz] *nf* 1. *F* éteindre/souffler sa veilleuse, to die*/to snuff it 2. *F* mettre qch en veilleuse, to shelve sth/to keep sth on the back burner 3. *P* la mettre en veilleuse, to shut up*/to button one's lip; mets-la en veilleuse! put a sock in it!/pipe down! 4. *F* se mettre en veilleuse, to keep a low profile/to drop out of circulation/to lie low.

veinard, -arde [vɛnar, -ard] *F* **I** *a* lucky/

jammy **II** *nm & f* lucky person/lucky devil; le veinard! (the) jammy so-and-so/(the) jammy sod!/the lucky beggar!

veine [vɛn] *nf F* luck; coup de veine, stroke of luck/lucky break; pas de veine! bad luck!/hard luck! avoir de la veine, to get a lucky break/to hit lucky; il a de la veine, he's a lucky devil/a jammy so-and-so. (*Voir* **cocu 2**)

vélo [velo] *nm F* bicycle/cycle/bike.

vélodrome [velɔdrɔm] *nm F* un vélodrome à mouches, a bald head*/a skating rink.

velours [vəlur] *nm P* 1. profit/winnings/takings; jouer sur le velours, to stake only part of one's winnings/to play on (the) velvet; rouler sur le velours, to be winning/on a winning streak 2. c'est du/un velours, it's very easy*/a piece of cake 3. (*boisson*) black velvet.

vendange [vãdãʒ] *nf P* (*butin d'un cambriolage*) loot/swag/takings.

vendanger [vãdãʒe] *vi P* to burgle/*NAm* to burglarize/to steal*.

vendre [vãdr] *vtr F* to denounce* (s.o.)/to shop (s.o.)/to squeal on (s.o.)/to grass on (s.o.). (*Voir* **piano 6**)

vendu [vãdy] *nm F* double-crosser/rat/grass/*surt NAm* fink; va donc, eh, vendu! you traitor!/you rat!

venin [vənɛ̃] *nm V* cracher/filer/jeter/lâcher son venin, to ejaculate*/to come/to shoot one's load.

vent [vã] *nm* 1. *F* du vent, nothing*; c'est du vent, it's all hot air/wind/nonsense; envoyer du vent, to tell lies/tall stories 2. *P* du vent! clear off!/buzz off!/get lost*! 3. *F* jouer du vent, to run away*/to clear off 4. *F* lâcher un vent, to fart/to break wind/to blow off 5. *F* faire du vent, to fuss about without much effect 6. *F* avoir du vent dans les voiles, to be drunk* 7. *F* être dans le vent, to be with it/to know where it's at/to be trendy.

ventilateur [vãtilatœr] *nm P* helicopter*/chopper.

ventre [vãtr] *nm F* 1. avoir qch dans le ventre/en avoir dans le ventre, to have guts/to have balls/*NAm* to be ballsey; savoir ce que qn a dans le ventre, to see what sort of stuff s.o. is made of 2. prendre du ventre, to get a potbelly/a gut 3. se serrer le ventre, to tighten one's belt 4. taper sur le ventre à qn, to dig/to poke s.o. in the ribs 5. tu me fais mal au ventre! you make me feel sick!/you make me (want to) puke! (*Voir* **passer I 4**)

ventrée [vãtre] *nf Vieilli F* une ventrée, a

bellyful.

Vénus [venys] *Prn P* recevoir un coup de pied de Vénus, to get VD*/to cop a dose.

ver [vɛr] *nm F* 1. nu comme un ver, stark naked*/starkers 2. pas piqué des vers, (*frais*) fresh/well preserved; (*excellent*) first-rate*/ not (half) bad/one hell of a .... (*Voir* **hanneton** 2) 3. tirer les vers du nez à qn, to worm sth out of s.o./to winkle sth out of s.o./to pump s.o. 4. tuer le ver, to take the hair of the dog/an eye-opener/an alcoholic pick-me-up.

verdâtres [vɛrdɑtr] *nmpl A P* (*seconde guerre 1939–45*) German* soldiers/Jerries.

verdine [vɛrdin] *nf P* gypsy's caravan.

verdure [vɛrdyr] *nf P* faire la verdure, (*prostituée*) to solicit in a park.

vergeot, verjot [vɛrʒo] *a Vieilli P* lucky/ jammy.

verlan, verlen [vɛrlɑ̃] *nm F* back slang.

vermicelles [vɛrmisɛl] *nmpl P* hair/barnet.

verni [vɛrni] *a P* lucky; être verni, to be lucky/to get a break; il est verni, he's a jammy devil.

vérole [vɛrɔl] *nf P* 1. syphilis*/syph*; attraper/choper la vérole, to get the pox 2. problem/difficulty; quelle vérole! what a drag! 3. comme la vérole sur le bas clergé (breton), like a bolt from the blue.

vérolé [vɛrɔle] *a P* 1. syphilitic; il est vérolé, he's got the pox 2. (*appareil*) damaged/poxy; cette chaise est vérolée, this chair is moth-eaten.

verre [vɛr] *nm F* 1. avoir un verre de trop/ avoir un verre dans le nez, to have had one too many/one over the eight; boire un petit verre, to have a drink (*of alcohol*)/a snort/a snifter 2. manier qn comme du verre cassé, to handle s.o. with kid gloves 3. se noyer dans un verre d'eau, to make a mountain out of a molehill; une tempête dans un verre d'eau, a storm in a teacup.

Versailles [vɛrsaj] *Prn P* et lycée de Versailles, (= *et vice versa*) and vice versa. (*Voir* **ouvrir** 2)

Versigo [vɛrsigo] *Prn P* Versailles.

vert [vɛr] I *a P* (*a*) tricked/deceived; être vert, to be conned (*b*) furious/angry*/mad; il en était vert, he was as mad as hell II *nm F* se mettre au vert, to go to the country to re-cuperate; (*pour se cacher*) to hide out/to lie low/to hole up (*in the country, abroad, etc*) III *nf* verte *P* 1. spicy/saucy/smutty story en raconter des vertes et des pas mûres, to tell spicy/smutty/dirty jokes; en avoir vu des

vertes et des pas mûres, to have been through the mill/to have been through a lot; en faire voir des vertes et des pas mûres à qn, to give s.o. a bad time/a hard time 2. *A* absinth(e).

verts-de-gris [vɛrdəgri] *nmpl A P* (*seconde guerre 1939–45*) German* soldiers/Jerries.

vesse [vɛs] *nf F* (silent and smelly) fart/ s.b.d.

vesser [vɛse] *vi F* to fart*/to blow off; vesser du bec, to have bad breath.

vessie [vɛsi] *nf F* prendre des vessies pour des lanternes, to be easily taken in/to believe that the moon is made of green cheese; il vous ferait prendre des vessies pour des lanternes, he'd talk black into white/he'd pull the wool over your eyes.

veste [vɛst] *nf F* 1. failure*/setback; ramasser/se prendre une veste, to fail*/to come a cropper 2. retourner sa veste, to change one's colours/one's tune 3. tomber la veste, to take one's coat off/to slip off one's jacket.

vestiaire [vɛstjɛr] *nm P* second-hand clothes/clothing (*given by charities to the homeless*).

véto [veto] *nm & f F* (= *vétérinaire*) veter-inary surgeon/vet; *NAm* animal doctor.

veuve [vœv] *nf* 1. *F* la Veuve, the guillotine 2. *P* fréquenter/se taper la veuve poignet, to masturbate*/to flog the bishop/to beat the dummy.

viandage [vjɑ̃daʒ] *nm P* accident.

viande [vjɑ̃d] *nf P* 1. (human) body/carcass; bouge ta viande! move your carcass!/shift! amène ta viande! drag your carcass over here!/get your arse/*NAm* ass over here! met-tre la viande dans le torchon, to get into bed/ between the sheets. (*Voir* **porte-viande**) 2. viande froide, corpse/stiff 3. *P* girl*/woman*; bird/chick; wife*/the missis; sa viande, his girlfriend/old lady/bit of stuff. (*Voir* **mar-chand 1; pneu 2; sac 2; saloir**)

se viander [səvjɑ̃de] *vpr P* (*en voiture, en moto*) to come a cropper*/to smash oneself up/to break one's neck.

vibure [vibyr] *nf F* à toute vibure, very quickly*/at full speed/like greased lightning.

vice [vis] *nm F* 1. il a du vice/c'est une boîte à vice, he's a sly/crafty/sharp customer; he's a smart alec; (*en affaires*) he's a shark 2. *Vieilli* aller au vice, to visit a prostitute*.

vicelard, -arde [vislar, -ard], **viceloque** [vislɔk] *P* I *a* 1. (*personne*) (*a*) sly/cunning

(b) depraved 2. difficult; **il est vicelard ce problème**, this problem's a sod **II** n (a) sly/cunning person/sharp 'customer (b) sex maniac; (voyeur) peeping Tom; (exhibitionniste) flasher; **un vieux vicelard**, a dirty old man.

vicelot [vislo] nm P = **vicelard II**.

vidage [vidaʒ] nm F 1. dismissal/sacking (from job) 2. chucking out (of pub, etc).

vidange [vidãʒ] nf P **faire la/une vidange**, to urinate*/to take a leak.

vidangeur [vidãʒœr] nm F official who empties parking meters.

vidé [vide] a F 1. exhausted*/tired out/worn out/all in/dead beat; **c'est un homme vidé**, he's played out 2. penniless*/broke/cleaned out 3. dismissed/sacked/fired.

vider [vide] vtr F 1. **vider les lieux/le plancher**, to beat it/to make oneself scarce 2. to dismiss* (s.o.)/to give (s.o.) the sack 3. to exhaust* (s.o.)/to wear (s.o.) out 4. to ruin (s.o.)/to clean (s.o.) out/to squeeze (s.o.) dry 5. to throw out/to boot out/to chuck out (s.o.); **se faire vider**, (licencier) to be dismissed/sacked/fired; (mettre dehors) to get thrown out/booted out/chucked out (of a club, a café, etc). (Voir **sac 14**)

videur [vidœr] nm F chucker-out/bouncer.

videuse [vidøz] nf P backstreet abortionist.

vie [vi] nf 1. F **faire la vie/mener la vie**, to live it up/to have a good time 2. F **faire toute une vie**, to make a scene/to kick up a fuss 3. F **enterrer sa vie de garçon**, to give a stag party 4. F **une vie de chien**, a dog's life.

vieille [vjɛj] nf F 1. **la vieille**, mother*/the old lady 2. **ma vieille**, (vieille femme; femme quelconque) old girl.

vier [vje] nm Vieilli P penis*.

viergeot, -otte [vjɛrʒo, -ɔt] n Vieilli F virgin.

vieux [vjø] F **I** nm 1. father*/the old man/the guv'nor 2. **mes vieux**, my parents/my (old) folks 3. **mon vieux**, old chap*/(my) old mate/(my) old pal 4. (patron) boss/chief/guv'nor 5. **prendre un coup de vieux**, to age/to get old **II** a (intensif) **vieux con/crétin, va!** (you) old idiot!/(you) old bastard*!/you plonker!

vif [vif] nm F **être pris sur le vif**, to be caught in the act/to be caught red-handed.

vigne [viɲ] nf F **être dans les vignes du Seigneur**, to be drunk*/well away/loaded.

vilain [vilɛ̃] nm F **il y aura/il va y avoir du vilain**, there's going to be some trouble/there's some trouble brewing.

villégiature [vileʒjatyr] nf P **être en villégiature**, to be in prison*/in clink.

Villetouse [viltuz] Prn P **La Villette** (quarter in Paris).

vinaigre [vinɛgr] nm F 1. **faire vinaigre**, to hurry* up/to get a move on 2. **ça tourne (au) vinaigre**, things have taken a turn for the worse 3. **crier au vinaigre**, to get angry*; (appeler à l'aide) to call for help/to scream blue murder.

vinasse [vinas] nf F (poor quality) wine/cheap plonk.

vingt-deux [vɛ̃dø] int F **vingt-deux!** watch out!/watch it! **vingt-deux, v'là les flics!** beat it, here come the cops!

vioc [vjɔk], **viocard, -arde** [vjɔkar, -ard] a & nm & f P = **vioque, vioquard, -arde**.

violette [vjɔlɛt] nf F (a) gift/present; **faire une violette à qn**, to do s.o. a favour (b) (pourboire) tip. (Voir **doigt 10**; **fleur 5**)

violon [vjɔlɔ̃] nm 1. P prison*/jug/clink; **être au violon**, to be in the nick; **jouer du violon**, to escape (esp from prison)/to do a bunk (by sawing the bars off the window) 2. P **boîte à violon**, coffin 3. F **payer les violons**, to pay the expenses/to pay the piper 4. F **c'est comme si je pissais dans un violon**, it's like talking to a brick wall.

vioquard, -arde [vjɔkar, -ard] P **I** a old/aged/ancient **II** n old person/old-timer/wrinklie.

vioque [vjɔk] P **I** a old/aged/ancient **II** n 1. old person/old-timer/wrinklie 2. **mes vioques**, my parents/my (old) folks; **mon/ma vioque**, my old man/lady.

vioquerie [vjɔkri] nf P old person/wrinklie.

vioquir [vjɔkir] vi P to age/to get old.

vipère [vipɛr] nf P **vipère broussailleuse**, penis*.

virage [viraʒ] nm F **choper qn au virage**, to get one's own back on s.o. (Voir **tournant 1**)

virée [vire] nf F trip/run/outing (in a car, etc); (dans les cafés) = Br pub-crawl/NAm barhopping; **faire une virée**, to go for a run/on an outing; (dans les cafés) Br to go on a pub-crawl/NAm to barhop.

virer [vire] **I** vtr F to dismiss*/to sack/to fire; **se faire virer**, to get the boot/to get kicked out. (Voir **cuti** (b)) **II** vi P 1. to change one's opinion; to change sides 2. to become; **il a viré barjot**, he went mad*/off his rocker.

virolo [virɔlo] nm P bend (in road).

vis [vis] nf **serrer la vis à qn**, F to put the screw(s) on s.o./to pressurize s.o.; P to strangle s.o.

visage [vizaʒ] *nm F* **1.** épouser un visage, to marry a pretty face **2.** trouver visage de bois, to find nobody at home.

viscope [viskɔp] *nf F* (*casquette à visière*) peaked cap.

vise-au-trou [vizotru] *nm & f inv P* obstetrician; midwife.

viser [vize] *vtr P* to look at/to clock; vise-moi ça!/vise un peu ça! get a load of that!/just take a dekko at that!

vision [vizjɔ̃] *nf F* avoir des visions, to kid oneself/to delude oneself/to fantasize.

visite [vizit] *nf F* avoir de la visite, to have a period*/to have visitors.

vissé [vise] *a P* être bien vissé, to be in a good mood; être mal vissé, to be in a filthy temper/in a vile mood.

visser [vise] *vtr F* **1.** to treat (s.o.) severely/to put the screw(s) on (s.o.) **2.** être vissé sur sa chaise, to be glued to one's seat; il y semble vissé, it looks as though there's no shifting him.

visu [vizy] *nm P* (*CB*) meeting/eyeball; se faire un visu, to lay an eyeball (on one another)/to eyeball (one another).

vite fait [vitfɛ] *adv phr F* quickly/in no time; on a tout rangé vite fait (bien fait), we tidied everything away in no time; on va prendre un pot vite fait, let's go and have a quick drink/a quick one; tirer un (coup) vite fait, to have a quick poke/a quick screw/a quick in-and-out job/a quickie.

vitesse [vitɛs] *nf F* à la vitesse grand V, very fast/like the clappers/like a shot.

vitrine [vitrin] *nf F* face*/dial/map.

vitriol [vitrijɔl] *nm P* (*vin médiocre*) plonk; (*alcool médiocre*) rotgut.

vivoter [vivɔte] *vi F* to live frugally/to live from hand to mouth/to rub along; usine qui vivote, factory that is just managing to keep going/that is just keeping its head above water.

vivre [vivr] *vi F* **1.** apprendre à vivre à qn, to teach s.o. (some) manners/a lesson **2.** se laisser vivre, to take it easy/to take it as it comes.

voile [vwal] *nf* **1.** *F* avoir du vent dans les voiles, to be (slightly) drunk*/to be tipsy/to be merry **2.** *P* mettre les voiles, to run away*/to scarper/to do a bunk **3.** *P* marcher/être à voile et à vapeur, to be bisexual/bi; to be AC-DC/ambidextrous; to swing both ways.

voir [vwar] **I** *vtr* **1.** *P* va voir ailleurs/va-t'en

voir si j'y suis! get lost*!/take a running jump! va te faire voir (par/chez les Grecs)! get stuffed!/go screw yourself! **2.** *F* en voir (de toutes les couleurs), to be treated roughly/to have a rough time (of it); en faire voir (de toutes les couleurs) à qn, to make s.o.'s life a misery; (*le faire tourner en bourrique*) to lead s.o. a merry dance **II** *vi F* (il) faudrait voir à voir! (*il ne faut pas exagérer*) that's going it a bit strong! **III** *adv P* dites voir! just tell me!/get on with it! écoutez voir! just listen to this!/get a load of this! montre voir! give us a look! regarde voir! just take a look/a dekko!

voiture-balai [vwatyrbalɛ] *nf F* last bus, tube, etc (at night).

volaille [vɔlɑj] *nf* **1.** *A P Péj* woman*; *esp* prostitute* **2.** *P* la volaille, the police*/the cops. (*Voir* **poulet 4**)

volée [vɔle] *nf F* thrashing/hiding/beating*.

voler [vɔle] **I** *vtr P* il ne l'a pas volé, he asked for it/it serves him right **II** *vi P* **1.** voler dans les plumes, to attack s.o./to go for s.o./to fly at s.o. **2.** (*a*) il vole bas, he's not very intelligent*/not a very bright spark; he's morally reprehensible/his moral standards are pretty low (*b*) ça vole bas/pas haut, (*histoire, humour*) it's not very funny/good; it's not much to write home about.

volet [vɔlɛ] *nm F* mettre les volets à la boutique, to die*/to shut up shop.

volière [vɔljɛr] *nf A P* brothel*.

volo [vɔlo] *nf F* (= *volonté*) à volo, at will/ad lib; as you like.

voltigeur [vɔltiʒœr] *nm F* **1.** (*locution populaire*) à tout à l'heure, voltigeur! – à bientôt, mon oiseau! see you later, alligator! – in a while, crocodile! **2.** messenger/courier.

volume [vɔlym] *nm F* **1.** faire du volume, to throw one's weight around **2.** écrire des volumes, to write reams.

vo(s)zig(ue)s [vozig] *pron P* you/yourselves.

vôtre [votr] *poss pron* à la (bonne) vôtre, cheers*!/good health!

vouloir [vulwar] **I** *vi* (*en signe d'accord*) je veux! and how!/I should say so! qu'est-ce qu'il fait froid! – je veux! it's so bloody cold! – you're too right!/not half!/I should say so! **II** *vtr* en vouloir, to be ambitious/keen.

vouzailles [vuʒaj] *pron P* = **vo(s)zig(ue)s**.

voyage [vwajaʒ] *nm* **1.** *F* gens du voyage, itinerants/travellers; (*forains*) stallkeepers (*at a fair*) **2.** *P* (*drogues*) trip (*caused by*

LSD); **faire un voyage**, to take a trip/to trip; **il est du/il fait un voyage**, he's on a trip/he's tripping 3. *F* **ne pas être déçu du voyage**, to have had a very nice experience 4. *V* orgasm*; **emmener qn en voyage**, to give s.o. an orgasm*/to make s.o. come.

voyager [vwajaʒe] *vi P (drogues)* to get high/to trip.

voyageur [vwajaʒœr] *nm P* small glass of white wine.

vrai [vrɛ] I *a F* 1. **pas vrai?** right?/OK? **c'est pas vrai!** (oh) no!/it's not possible! 2. **il est pas vrai, celui-là**, this guy's incredible/weird/not for real II *nm F* 1. genuine/loyal/reliable, etc person; **c'est un vrai de vrai**, he's a genuine criminal 2. **c'est pour de vrai**, it's for real.

vrille [vrij] *nf* lesbian*/les/dyke.

vu, vue [vy] I *a F* 1. **c'est tout vu**, it's all settled; **vu?** agreed? **c'est bien vu?/c'est vu?** OK?/all right?/got it?/all clear? 2. **on aura tout vu!** wonders will never cease! 3. **ni vu ni connu!** keep it under your hat!/mum's the word! (*Voir* **m'as-tu-vu**) II *nf P* 1. **à vue de nez**, at a rough guess/roughly 2. **en mettre plein la vue à qn**, to hoodwink s.o./to have s.o. on.

vulgos [vylgos] *a P* vulgar/coarse/crude.

vurdon [vyrdɔ̃] *nm P* gypsy's caravan.

W, X, Y, Z

wagon [vagɔ̃] *nm F* (tout) un wagon de/des wagons de livres, a large number of/masses of/loads of/cratefuls of books.

wagonnière [vagɔnjɛr] *nf A P* prostitute*.

waterloo [watɛrlo] *nm F* 1. disaster; scandal 2. en plein waterloo, dead out of luck.

waters [watɛr] *nmpl F* WC*/toilet/loo/*NAm* john. (*Voir* **ouatères**)

watrin [watrɛ̃] *nm P* (pair of) trousers.

weekendard [wikɛndar] *nm F* weekend holiday-maker/weekender.

whisky [wiski] *nm P* whisky soviétique, (glass of) red wine.

X, x [iks] *F I nm* 1. (*a*) un X, a student at the *École polytechnique* (*b*) un fort en x/une tête à x, a gifted mathematician/s.o. who is good at maths 2. je vous l'ai dit x fois, I've told you a thousand times/any number of times 3. avoir les jambes en x, to be knock-kneed 4. classé X, (*film, histoire, etc*) X-rated **II** *nf* l'X, the *École polytechnique* (*in Paris*).

y [i] I *adv F* (*a*) ah, j'y suis! ah, now I understand!/I've got it!/I'm with you! vous y êtes! you've got it!/you've hit the nail on the head! tu y es? (*tu comprends?*) do you get it?/have you twigged? (*tu es prêt?*) are you ready? vous n'y êtes pas du tout, you're wide of the mark/you're not very warm (*b*) il n'y est plus, he's not all there (*c*) je voudrais (bien) t'y voir! I'd like to see *you* do it!/see if you can do it better! **II** *pron inv P* (= *lui*) dites-y que je suis venu, tell him I've come; demandez-y s'il en a, ask him if he's got any. (*Voir* **dire 4**) **III** *pers pron P* (= *il, ils*) he; they; y chiale, he's blubbering; y chialent, they're blubbering; c'est-y pas vrai? isn't that right/so?

ya [ja] *nm P* = **yatagan**.

yakas [jaka] *nmpl P* eyes*.

yaouled [jaulɛd] *nm P* (young) Arab* (*esp of the Arab community in Paris*).

yaourt [jaurt] *nm F Aut* pot de yaourt, bubble car. (*Voir* **pédaler 3**)

yatagan [jatagã] *nm P* knife/chiv.

yèche [jɛʃ] *vi V* = **ièche**.

yeuter [jøte] *vtr P* = **zyeuter**.

yeux [jø] *nmpl Voir* **œil**.

yéyé [jeje] *F I a inv* (*années 60*) pop; chanteur, -euse yéyé, pop singer; chanson yéyé, pop song **II** *nm* le yéyé, pop music.

yéyette [jejɛt] *nf F* pop-mad teenager.

youde [jud] *P Péj* **I** *nm & f* Jew*/yid **II** *a* Jewish.

youdi [judi] *nm P Péj* Jew*/yid.

youpin, -ine [jupɛ̃, -in], **youtre** [jutr] *P Péj* **I** *nm & f* Jew*/Jewess/yid/sheeny **II** *a* Jewish.

youvance [juvãs] *nm P Péj* Jew*/yid/heeb.

youvoi [juvwa] *nm P* (*verlan de voyou*) hooligan*/yob(bo).

youyou [juju] *nm & f P* Yugoslav.

yoyo [jɔjo] *nm P* (*prostitution*) succession of clients/tricks.

yoyoter [jɔjɔte] *vi P* yoyoter de la mansarde/de la toiture, to be slightly mad*/to have a screw loose/to have bats in the belfry.

Yvans [ivã] *nmpl P* Russians*/Russkies.

zacharie [zakari] *nm* P skeleton.

zaiber [zebe] *vtr & i* V (*verlan de* **baiser**) to have sex*/to screw/to have it away (with (s.o.).

zan [zã] *nm* P liquorice.

zanzi(bar) [zãzi(bar)] *nm* P dice game played in bars.

zappé [zape] *a* F zappy/dynamic.

zapper [zape] *vtr* F zapper un projet, to abandon/dump/shelve a project.

zarbi [zarbi] *a* P (*verlan de* **bizarre**) eccentric*/strange/odd.

zazou [zazu] F *Vieilli* I *a* hep II *n* hepcat.

zeb [zɛb] *nm* V penis*.

zéber [zebe] *vtr* V = **zaiber**.

zébi [zebi] *nm* V penis*; peau de zébi, nothing*/damn all/sod all.

zèbre [zɛbr] *nm* F 1. (*individu*) character/bloke/*surt NAm* guy; un drôle de zèbre, a weird character/an oddball/a funny guy; qu'est-ce que c'est que ces zèbres-là? who are those jokers? faire le zèbre, to play the fool 2. (*CB*) name/handle.

zef [zɛf] *nm* F wind/breeze.

zèle [zɛl] *nm* F faire du zèle, to be an eager beaver; to overdo it; pas de zèle! don't overdo it!

zep [zɛp] *nm* P (*verlan de* **pèze**) money*/brass/dough/the ready.

zeph [zɛf] *nm* F = **zef**.

zéphir(e), zéphyr(e) [zefir] *nm* A P soldier of the **bat' d'Af**.

zéro [zero] I *nm* 1. F (*personne*) (*a*) un vrai zéro/un zéro à gauche/un zéro en chiffre/un zéro fini, a nonentity/a complete washout/a dead loss/a nobody/*surt NAm* a no-no (*b*) c'est un pur zéro (dans l'équipe), he's just a passenger (in the team)/he's just there for the ride 2. F (*écoles*) un zéro pointé, a nought/a zero (in exam, etc) 3. F être à zéro/avoir le moral à zéro, to be depressed*/to be low/to feel down/to be down in the dumps 4. F partir de/à zéro, to start from scratch 5. P les avoir à zéro, to be afraid*/to be in a blue funk/to be scared shitless 6. P au zéro/au triple zéro, completely/totally; être tondu à zéro/avoir la boule à zéro, to have very close-cropped hair/to have a close-cropped head; bander à zéro, to be/to get highly excited; (*sexuellement*) to have a big erection* 7. P le zéro, the anus* II *int* P nothing doing! (*aucun résultat*) nothing! zilch! zéro pour la question! no way!/not bloody likely*!/not on your life!

zetou [zətu] *nf* P (*abrév* = **zetoupar**) = **zetoupar**.

zetoupar [zetupar] *nf* P (*verlan de* **partouze**) orgy.

zézette [zezɛt] *nf* A P tot of absinth(e).

ziber [zibe] *vtr & i* P ziber qn de qch, to do s.o. out of sth/to screw s.o. for fun.

zic [zik], **zicmu** [zikmy] *nf* P (*verlan de musique*) music.

zieuter [zjøte] *vtr* P = **zyeuter**.

zig [zig] *nm Vieilli* P fellow/chap*; un bon zig, a decent sort of bloke/a great guy; un drôle de zig, a weirdo/a screwball/a queer fish.

zigomar [zigɔmar] *nm*, **zigoteau, zigoto** [zigɔto] *nm Vieilli* P 1. odd character; c'est un drôle de zigomar, he's a queer customer. (*Voir* **zig**) 2. faire le zigoto, to play the fool/to show off*; fais pas le zigoto! don't try it on with me!

zigouigoui [zigwigwi] *nm* 1. V (*a*) penis* (*b*) female genitals* 2. P thing/thingummy.

zigouiller [ziguje] *vtr* P 1. to kill*/to murder (*esp* by cutting s.o.'s throat); toute la bande a été zigouillée, the whole lot of them were wiped out 2. to damage/break (sth); le gosse a zigouillé la radio, the kid's broken the radio.

zigounette [zigunɛt] *nf* P penis*.

zigouzi [ziguzi] *nm* P 1. object/thing/thingummy 2. faire des zigouzis à qn, to caress/paw s.o.; (*chatouiller*) to tickle s.o.

zigue [zig] *nm* P = **zig**.

ziguer [zige] *vtr* P ziguer qn, to clean s.o. out/to take s.o. to the cleaners (*at cards, etc*).

zig-zig [zigzig] *nm* P faire zig-zig, to have sex*/to bonk.

zinc [zɛ̃g] *nm* F 1. bar/counter (of public house); prendre un verre sur le zinc, to have a drink at the bar 2. (*surt vieil avion*) plane/crate; vider le zinc, to bale out. (*Voir* **culotte 9; piano 9**)

zinzin [zɛ̃zɛ̃] F I *nm* 1. noise/row/uproar*/rumpus 2. thingummy/what's-its-name*/what-do-you-call-it 3. violin/fiddle II *a* mad*/cracked/nuts/loopy.

zizi [zizi] *nm* 1. V penis*; female genitals*; faire zizi pan(-)pan, to have sex* 2. P whatsit/what's-its-name*/thingummy.

zizique [zizik] *nf* P music; se farcir de la zizique, to go to a concert; en avant la zizique! here we go!/off we go!/let it rip!

zob [zɔb] *nm* V 1. penis*. (*Voir* **pomper I 3**) 2. (mon) zob! my arse!/*NAm* my ass!/my foot!/nuts!/balls! (*Voir* **peau 19**)

zobi [zɔbi] *nm V* penis*. (*Voir* **peau 19**)

zomblou [zɔ̃blu] *nm P* (*verlan de blouson*) jacket; (*plus léger*) blouson.

zonard, -arde [zonar, -ard] *n P* 1. homeless person/down-and-out 2. hooligan*/yob/thug (*from the suburbs*); delinquent. (*Voir* **narzo**)

zone [zon] *F* I *nf* 1. la Zone, slum area/shanty town (*on the outskirts of any large town*); être de la Zone, (*sans abri*) to be homeless; (*sans argent*) to be desperately poor 2. dirty/messy place; **quelle zone!** what a dump! 3. c'est la zone, it's not done/it's non-U/it's naff II *a* useless/rubbishy; c'est zone, ce truc, this thing's useless.

zoner [zone] I *vi P* 1. (*paresser*) to hang about/to drift/to mooch about/*surt NAm* to bum around; (*se promener*) to stroll (around) 2. (*homosexuels*) to cruise/to go cruising 3. to live *or* to sleep; où est-ce que tu zones? where d'you live?/where's your pad? where do you crash out? 4. to be homeless/to be a tramp II *vpr* **se zoner** *P* to go to bed*/to turn in.

zonerie [zɔnri] *nf P* wandering/drifting.

zonga [zɔ̃ga] *nm P* (*verlan de* **gazon**) (*drogues*) marijuana*/grass.

zou! [zu] *int F* allez zou! shoo!/hop it!

zouave [zwav] *nm F* faire le zouave, to play the fool/to fool about.

zoulou [zulu] *nm, f* **zoulette** [zulɛt] *P* 1. rapper 2. (*abusivement*) member of an urban gang.

zouzou [zuzu] *nm P* = **zouave**.

zozo [zozo] *nm Vieilli F* 1. mug/sucker 2. fool*/idiot/nit(wit)/*Br* twit.

zozores [zɔzɔr] *nfpl P* ears*.

zozoter [zɔzɔte] *vi F* to lisp.

zut [zyt] *int F* (*a*) zut (alors)! damn!/dash it!/darn it!/blow it!/hang it all! (*b*) (et puis) zut! rubbish!/fiddlesticks! zut pour vous! go to blazes!/get lost*! dis-lui zut de ma part! tell him to go to hell! (*c*) I can't be bothered! (*d*) avoir un œil qui dit zut à l'autre, to be cross-eyed/to (have a) squint.

zyeuter [zjøte] *vtr P* to have a look at (sth)/*Br* to take a butcher's/*Br* to have a dekko/to have a squint at (sth); zyeute-moi ça! get a load of that!/get an eyeful of that!

Index of
English Slang Synonyms

Index of
English Slang Synonyms

afraid, to be: *see* **coward, to be a.**

agreed!: ace; all right; check! done! fair enough! fucking A! I'll buy it! I'll go along with that! I'm game! I'm on! it's OK by me! OK! ok! okay! okey-doke! okey-dokey! right-ho! right-o(h)! right on! righty-(ho)! Roger! roger! that suits me to a T! yeah! yep! you're on!

alibi: blind; cover; front.

amaze, to: to blindside; to bowl over; to floor; to jigger; to knock all of a heap/down with a feather/flat/out/sideways; to flabbergast; to shake; to shatter; to stagger; to strike all of a heap; to stun; to take the wind out of s.o.'s sails; to throw; to wow.

amazed: banjanxed; blown away; bowled over; choked(-off); filletted; floored; gobsmacked; jiggered; kippered; knocked all of a heap; knocked out; knocked sideways; shattered; staggered; stunned; thrown.

American: septic tank; Yank; Yankee.

amphetamines: A; bam; blackbirds; black and tan; black and white (minstrel/nigger); blues; bombida; bombido; candy; chalk; crank; Christmas tree; crystals; dex; dexie; dexo; dexy; double blue; drivers; forwards; garbage; green dragon; greenies; happy dust; jelly beans; jolly beans; leaper; lid popper(s); lift pill; nigger minstrel; peach; root; sparkle plenty; speed; speedball; sweeties; thrust; truck drivers; uppers; uppies; wake-up; (old lady) white; white cross; whitey; whiz(z); wizz; zoom.

amyl nitrite *or* **nitrate:** amy; amyl; amys; aroma; pearls; poppers; popsy; snapper.

anal sex, (to have): to be done brown; brown job; to brown; to butt fuck; chain gang; to cornhole; daisy chain; to do; to do it dog-fashion /doggy-fashion/dogways; to do it Greek style/like the Greeks/the Greek way; to earn one's brown wings; to finger fuck; to fist fuck; fist-fucking; floral arrangement; to get one's brown wings; to Greek; to have a cup of tea; to Oscar; to ram; to ream; to ream s.o.'s (ass) out; to screw; to tongue s.o. out.

angry: aer(e)ated; crocked; fired up; fuming; furious; hacked off; het-up; hopping mad; humpty; humpy; jacked off/out; livid; mad; pissed off; porky; red-assed; sick; smoky; sore; steamed; ticked off; wild.

angry, to be, to get: to be hot under the collar/in a huff/in a stew/in a wax; to blow a fuse/a gasket; to blow one's lid/one's stack/one's top/one's wig; to blow up; to burn; to cop the needle/the spike; to cut up nasty/rough/ugly; to do one's block/crust/lolly/nut; to flare up; to flip one's lid/one's noodle/one's raspberry/one's top; to fly off the handle; to fly up in the air; to freak out; to get all steamed-up/all worked up; to get one's blood up/one's dander up/one's gage up/one's Irish up/one's monkey up; to get one's rag out; to get mad/narked/shirty; to get the needle/the spike; to go ape; to go apeshit; to go off crook; to go spare; to go through the ceiling/the roof; to go up in the air; to have a fit; to have kittens; to have the rats; to hit the ceiling/the roof; to lose one's rag/shirt/wool; to nearly have a baby; to pop a vein; to see red; to short out; to spit; to throw a fit/a wobbler/a wobbly; to wig out.

(*See* **temper**)

annoy, to: to aggravate; to be a pain in the arse/ass/neck; to be (up) on s.o.'s nuts; to bug; to crease; to devil; to dig; to dog s.o. around; to faze; to fool s.o. about/around; to get s.o.'s back up; to get s.o.'s goat; to get in s.o.'s hair; to get on s.o.'s case/tits/wick/willy; to get up s.o.'s nose; to get under s.o.'s skin; to give s.o. balls ache; to give s.o. a pain in the arse/ass/neck; to give s.o. the nadgers/the pip/the shits; to gripe s.o.; to hit on s.o.; to jack s.o. around; to needle; to peeve; to pester; to plague; to play up; to piss s.o. off; to razz; to ride; to scrag; to tread on s.o.'s toes; to turn off; to yank s.o. around.

anus: ace; 'Aris; Aristotle; 'Arris; 'arris; arse; arsehole; ass; asshole; backdoor; back passage; brown; brown eye; brownie; bumhole; bung-hole; chuff; coit; cornhole; date; ding; dinger; dirtbox; fart-hole; flue; gig; gonga; hole; jack; jacksie; Khyber; poop chute; poop hole; quoit; ring; ring hole; ringpiece; roundeye; shit-hole; slot; tokus; yinyang.

Arab: towel head; wog.

arm: fin; flipper; wing.

arrest, to: to bag; to bust; to collar; to cop; to do; to get; to gobble; to grab; to haul in; to hoist; to hook; to knock off; to lag; to lift; to lumber; to make a hit; to nab; to nail; to nick; to pick up; to pinch; to pluck; to pull in; to put the snatch on; to rap; to run in; to snatch; to tag; to touch; to yank.

(*See* **imprison, to**)

arrested, to be, to get: to be *or* to get busted/done/nabbed/narked/nicked/picked up/run in; to have an accident.

arrive, to: to blow along; to blow in; to breeze in; to get in under the wire; to land; to lob in; to make the scene; to pop in/to pop up; to roll along; to roll up; to show up; to turn up (out of the blue); to weigh in.

attack s.o., to: to crack down on; to go for; to lay into; to light into; to pile into; to rip into; to sail into; to set about; to wade into; to walk into.

Australian: Aussie; Ozzie; Wallaby.

bag of tricks, the whole: (and) all that jazz; all the rest of it; and what have you; the whole bang shoot; the whole boiling; the whole kit (and caboodle); the whole set-up; the whole shebang; the whole shooting match; the whole works.

bald-head(ed person), bald man: baldie; baldy; billiard-ball; chrome-dome; skating rink; as bald as a coot/an egg.

barbiturates: barbies; barbs; blue heavens; double blue; downers; goofball; goofers; green and blacks; mandy; peanuts; phenie; purple hearts; rainbows; red birds; red devils; red jackets; reds; sleeper;

stumbler; yellow-jacket.

bastard: animal; basket; bee; beggar; bitch; bleeder; bugger; buttfuck; cad; cheese; cocksucker; crud; crumb; dag; der(r)o; dirtbag; dogbreath; dog's breath; dogsbreath; effer; (old) fart; fatherfucker; fink; four-letter man; fucker; fuckpig; geek; gink; gobshite; heel; jerk; josser; maggot; MF; momser; momzer; mongrel; mother; motherfucker; muhfuh; nasty piece of work; no-gooder; nogoodnik; pig; pisshead; pisspot; punk; quandong; rat; ratbag; ratfink; roach; roughneck; sao; schmuck; scrote; scum (bag); scunner; scuzz; scuzzbag; scuzzball; scuzzo; shit; shit-ass; shit-bag; shite; shit-head; shitheel; shitpot; shitstick; skunk; slag; slob; so-and-so; s.o.b.; sod; sonofabitch; son of a bitch; sonovabitch; stinker; stinkpot; swine; toerag; tosspot; tough; tripehead; turd; tyke; worm; wrong'un.

(*See* **hooligan**)

beating(-up): belting; dusting; hammering; hiding; kicking; knuckle sandwich; lambasting; larruping; licking; milling; paddy-whack; pasting; seeing-to; shellacking; smack-botty; spank(ing); tanning; third degree; thrashing; towelling; walloping; whacking; whopping; working over.

beat up, to: to bash (about); to bash s.o.'s face/head in; to bash the living daylights out of s.o.; to bat; to batter; to beat hollow; to beat the living daylights out of s.o.; to beat the piss/the shit out of s.o.; to belt; to brain; to bust (s.o.'s ass); to cane; to chin; to clobber; to clock; to clonk (s.o. on the head); to clout; to clump; to cream; to crown; to deck; to do; to dong; to do over; to dot (s.o. one); to do up; to duff up; to dump on s.o.; to dust s.o.'s jacket (for him); to dust up; to flatten; to floor; to give it to s.o.; to give s.o. a (good) going-over; to give s.o. a belt/a licking/a milling/a thick ear/a walloping/a working over; to give s.o. the horrors/the once-over; to go over; to have a scrap; to hook s.o. one; to kick s.o.'s head in; to knock s.o.'s block off/s.o.'s teeth in; to knock hell out of s.o.; to knock s.o. silly/for six; to knock s.o. to kingdom come; to knock s.o. in the middle of next week; to knock the bejesus/the living daylights/the stuffing out of s.o.; to knuckle; to KO; to lace into; to lambaste; to lam (into); to lamp; to larrup; to lather; to lay into; to lay one on s.o.; to leather; to let s.o. have it; to mug; to murder; to paste; to pay;

to plaster; to plug; to pop; to pound s.o. into a jelly; to put one on s.o.; to put the boot in; to put the leather in; to rough up; to rub out; to scrap; to shellac(k); to skelp; to slam; to slaughter; to slog; to slug; to smack; to smash s.o.'s face in; to smash up; to sort out; to stick one on s.o.; to stoush; to swipe; to take a swipe at s.o.; to tan s.o.'s hide; to thrash; to total; to towel; to whip; to whop; to wipe the floor with; to work over.

bed: doss; feather(s); flea-bag; flop; hay; kip; letty; pit; rack; sack; shake-down; Uncle Ned.

bed, to go to: to doss (down); to get between the sheets; to go to kip; to hit the hay; to hit the pad; to hit the roost; to hit the sack; to kip (down); to rack out; to sack out; to shake down; to turn in.

(*See* **sleep, to go to**)

Benzedrine (*RTM*): bean; benny; benz; copilots; drin; (old lady) white.

betray, to: see **divulge a secret, to**.

Black: ace of spades; boogie; coon; darkey; darkie; darky; dinge; fade; golly; groid; high yellow; jig; jigaboo; Jim Crow; jungle bunny; nig; nigger; nignog; nigra; pongo; Sambo; schwartz; shine; smoke; snowball; sooty; spook; soul brother; soul sister; spade; Uncle Tom; wog; youngblood.

Black Maria: see **prison van**.

bloody (*euphemisms or substitutes for*): bally; blanketty; blasted; blazing; bleeding; blessed; blinking; blithering; blooming; damned; darn; darned; deuced; dratted; effing; flaming; flipping; frigging; fucking; goddamn; goddamned; motherfucking; pigging; ruddy; sodding.

blow: backhander; bang; bash; belt; biff; bonk; clip (round the ear); clump; conk; crack; cuff; facer; finisher; flattener; fourpenny one; haymaker; lefthander; righthander; slog; slug; smasher; sock; swipe; thump; wallop; whack; wipe.

boots, big: beetle-crushers; boats; bovver-boots; canal boats; clodhoppers; daisy-roots; DM's; Doc Martens; tugboats.

bore, to: to bore s.o. to death/to tears; to bore s.o. rigid/stiff; to bore the balls off s.o.; to bore the hind legs off a donkey; to give s.o. a pain in the arse; to get on s.o.'s tits; to yank s.o. around.

(*See* **annoy, to**)

bore: bind; buttonholer; clinger; clinging vine; crasher; crashing bore; drag; drone;

droob; fixture; grunge; gutsache; hanger-on; pain in the butt/neck; (bloody) nuisance; pest; plague; schmo; schmock; schmoe; sticker; zombie.

bored, to be: to be bored rigid/stiff; to be bored to death/to tears; to be chocker.

(*See* **depressed**)

boring: deadly; draggy; dullsville; groovy; killing; rotten; a snooze; yawny.

boss: bossman; chief; gaffer; gov; (the) governor; guv; (the) guv'nor; mainman; the man; the old man; skip; skipper.

brave: see **courage, to have; courageous, to be**.

breasts: apples; balloons; bazookas; bazooms; beauties; boobies; boobs; bouncers; bristlers; bristols; bubbies; bumpers; cans; charms; diddies; droopers; dumplings; falsies; fainting fits; gay deceivers; globes; hammocks; headlamps; headlights; hooters; jugs; knobs; knockers; lemons; love lumps; lungs; maraccas; marshmallows; melons; ninnies; norgies; norgs; norkers; norks; pancakes; pears; pimples; pippins; rockets; rude bits; (set of) headphones; shakers; shelf-kit; swingers; tale of two cities; threepenny bits; tits; titties; udders; upholstery; upstairs.

bribe: backhander; bung; commission; dash; dirty money; drink; drop; dropsy; earner; fix; grease; hush money; kickback; loot; lug; nobble; oil; palm-grease; palm-oil; pay-off; payola; schmier; straightener; sugar; sweetener; (the) take; taste; velvet.

bribe, to: to bung; to fling; to get s.o. up; to grease s.o.'s palm; to nobble; to square; to straighten; to sugar; to sweeten.

bribe, to accept a: to be on the take; to cop; to get a backhander; to make a bit on the side; to take one.

(*See* **profits, illicit**)

brothel: bawdy house; bed house; blue house; cat house; chicken ranch; honky-tonk; hook shop; knocking shop; massage parlour; meat-house; molly-shop; parlour; red-light house; shebang; stew; timothy; whorehouse; whore-shop.

bungle, to: to arse up; to balls (up); to bitch (everything up); to blow; to bodge up; to bog up; to bollix (up); to bollocks; to boob; to botch; to bugger up; to cock up; to fluff it; to foul (things) up; to fuck; to goof up; to gum up (the works); to hash (up); to jigger up; to knock up; to louse (things) up; to make a balls/a balls-up/a ball-up/a bog/a bollocks/a cock-up/a mess/a muck of; to mess up; to muck up; to muff.

buttocks: Aristotle; 'Arris; 'arris; arse; ass; backside; behind; bot; bottom; botty; bum; buns; butt; can; cheeks; daily; Daily Mail; ding; dinger; dish; duff; end; fan; fanny; heinie; jack; jacksie; johnson; Keester; posterior; prat; rear(-end); sit-me-down; sit-upon; stern; tail; tokus; tush(ie); winkie; winky.

cannabis: blow; charas; charash; dagga; draw; (Indian) hay; (Indian) hemp; (the) herb; India; india; locoweed; maconha; manicure; mutah; puffy; substance; ton.

(*See* **marijuana**)

car: banger; Beetle; bomb; boneshaker; bottler; buggy; bus; caddy; chevvy; clunk; crate; crock; dinky; doodle-bug; drag; egg beater; heap (of junk); Jag; jalopy; jam-jar; Junker; Limmo; limo; motor; palm-tree; rap-top; Roller; Rolly; Rolls; rust-bucket; skip; square-wheeler; (tin-)Lizzie; tub; wheels; (old) wreck.

cat: kitty; mog; moggie; moggy; puss.

cemetery: bone-orchard; bone-yard; marble orchard.

cert, it's a: *see* **easy, very.**

chamber-pot: daisy; gazunda; gazunder; guzunder; jemima; jerry; jordan; latrine-bucket; latrine-pail; pisspot; po; pottie; potty; smoker; thunder-mug; tinkler.

champagne: Bolly; bubbly; cham(p); champers; fizz; giggle-water; shampers; the widow.

chap, old: buddy; chum; fruity-pie; old bean; old fruit; old man; old pal; old thing.

(*See* **man**)

chat; chattering: bunny; cackle; chinfest; chinwag; clack; clackety-clak; confab; ear-ache; gabfest; gas(sing); hot air; jabber(ing); jangle; jaw; natter(ing); patter; prattling; rabbit; verbal (diarrhoea); wittering; yabber; yack; yackety-yack; yak; yap; yapping; yatter.

chat, to; chatter, to: to bang on; to bunny; to chew the fat/the rag; to clack; to confabulate; to crack on; to ear(h)ole; to have a bull session/a bunny/a chinwag/a confab/a natter; to gas; to gossip; to jabber; to jangle; to jaw; to jive; to natter (on); to poodle on; to prattle; to rabbit (on); to schmoose; to schmooze; to spout (off); to talk away nineteen to the dozen; to talk the hind

leg off a donkey; to witter (on); to yabber; to yack; to yak; to yammer; to yap; to yatter.

(*See* **talk a lot, to**)

chatterbox: babbling brook; bag of wind; blabbermouth; earbasher; flapjaw; gabber; gasbag; gasser; motormouth; to have the gift of the gab.

cheat, to: *see* **fool, to; swindle, to. cheated, to be:** *see* **fooled, to be; swindled, to be.**

cheers!: bottoms up! bung-ho! cheerio! chin chin! down the hatch! good health! happy days! here's looking at you! (here's) mud in your eye! skin off your nose!

child: ankle-biter; brat; chick; chit; dustbin (lid); godfer; God forbid; holy terror; kid; kiddie; kiddy; mischief; mite; munchkin; nip; nipper; saucepan lid; (young) shaver; snork; sprog; tiddler; toddler; (tiny) tot; tyke.

Chinese: ABC; Chink; chinkie; Chinkie; chinky; Chinky; gook; slant.

cigarette: burn; cancer-stick; cig; ciggie; ciggy; coffin-nail; drag; dub; fag; faggeroo; gage; gasper; oily-rag; roll-up; roll-your-own; root; smoke; spit and drag; tab; twirl.

(*See* **marijuana cigarette**)

cigarette-end: bumper; dead soldier; dog-end; fag-end; nicker; roach (of marijuana cigarette); old soldier; snipe; tab-end.

clergyman: bible-basher; bible-puncher; black coat; devil-dodger; dog-collar brigade; God-botherer; God man; holy Joe; Joe; sin-shifter; sky-pilot.

clitoris: button; clit.

(*See also* **female genitals**)

clothes: cast-offs; clobber; drag; drapes; duds; gear; get-up; glad rags; hand-me-downs; kit; rags; rig-out; rig-up; schmutter; slops; threads; togs; turnout; vines.

cocaine: base; bernice; bernies; Big C; big bloke; blow; C; candy; Cecil; cee; Charlie (coke); coke; crack; flake; dynamite; girl; happy/heaven/gold dust; jam; nose-candy; powder; (the) rock; snow; talc; vitamin C; wash; white cross; white stuff; whizz-bang.

coffin: concrete/pine/wooden overcoat.

condom: bag; French letter; French safe; frenchie; frenchy; Jim cap; John; (rubber) johnnie; mac; mack; packet of three; rubber; safe; scumbag; skin; wellie; willie-wellie.

confess, to: *see* **divulge a secret, to. corpse:** blob; cold meat; dead meat; dead 'un; floater; goner; stiff.

courage, to have; courageous, to be: to be balls(e)y; to be game; to have backbone; to have balls; to have bottle; to have grit; to have guts; to have (plenty of) go; to have intestinal fortitude; to have spunk; to have what it takes; to keep one's pecker up; to stand the gaff.

coward: bottler; chicken; cissy; creampuff; fraidy cat; Jessie; milktoast; milquetoast; namby; non-drop; patsy; quitter; ringtail; scare-baby; scaredy-cat; sissy; yellowbelly.

coward, to be a; cowardly, to be: to back down; to be chickenshit; to be dead scared/in a blue funk/(a bit) green about the gills / gutless / jittery / panicky / poop-scared/ pucker-assed/scared shitless/scared stiff/shit-scared/spunkless/windy/yellow/yellow-bellied; to be shitting oneself/wetting oneself; to bottle; to bug out; to chicken out; to fink; to freeze; to funk it; to get cold feet/the wind up; to go soft; to have a yellow streak; to have butterflies (in one's stomach/tummy); to have the chills/the collywobbles/the heebie-jeebies/the horrors/the jim-jams/the jitters/the screaming-meemies/the shakes/the squitters/ the willies; to have no guts; to have ring-flutter; to hit the panic button; to lose one's bottle; to nearly have a baby/kittens; to psych out; to punk out; to push the panic button; to shit a brick/bricks; to show the white feather; to turn chicken/milky; to wet oneself/one's pants.

crazy: *see* **mad.**

criticism, (severe): backbiting; bitching; coating; cutting up; dressing-down; flack; flak; knocking; lambasting; lamming; panning; razz; roast; roasting; running down; slagging (off); slamming; slating; static.

(*See* **reprimand**)

criticize, to (severely): to backbite; to bad-mouth; to bitch; to chip at; to crab; to cut up; to cut to pieces; to dis(s); to do dirt on; to dog around; to drag s.o.'s name through the mud; to dump on s.o.; to give s.o. a coating/a dressing down; to give s.o. stick; to hammer; to handbag; to have a dig at; to have a go at; to haul up; to hit on s.o.; to jump on s.o.; to jump down s.o.'s throat; to knock; to lambaste; to lash; to lay into; to pan; to pick on; to pull to pieces; to put down; to put the poison in; to rap over the knuckles; to razz; to roast; to run down; to

run into the ground; to slag off; to slam; to slate; to snap at s.o.; to snap s.o.'s head off; to tear to pieces; to wade into.

(*See* **reprimand, to (severely)**)

cropper, to come a: *see* **fall (down/over).**

cunnilingus: cannibalism; gam; hairpie; kipper feast; muff-diving; pearl diving; tongue-job; tongue-pie.

to practise cunnilingus: to dive into the bushes; to eat; to eat fur-pie/hairpie; to eat out; to French; to gam; to go down on; to muff; to pearl-dive; to suck (off); to talk turkey; to tongue; to whistle in the dark.

person who practises cunnilingus: cannibal; cunt-lapper; muff-diver; pearl-diver.

darling: angel-face; chickabiddy; cutie; dearie; deary; duck; ducks; ducky; hon; honey; honeybunch; lamb; love; lovey; pet; poppet; precious; sweet; sweetie; sweetie-pie; sweety; sweety-pie; treasure.

dead (to be): cold; done for; pushing up the daisies; six feet under; stiff; to be with one's fathers; to have bought a packet; to have bought it; to have had it.

(*See* **die, to**)

dealer: *see* **drugs; swindler.**

deceive, to: *see* **fool, to.**

defecate, to: to cack; to crap; to do big jobs; to do number two(s); to do one's duty; to do a poo; to do sth no one else can do for you; to drop one's load; to go for a crap/a shit/a pony (and trap)/a tom tit; to go to the bog/to the loo; to have a clear-out/a crap/a dump/a shit/a shite; to perform; to poo; to relieve nature; to relieve oneself; to shit; to strangle a darkie; to take a dump; to throttle a darkie.

denounce, to: *see* **divulge a secret, to; inform on, to.**

depressed: blue; brassed off; browned off; cheesed off; chocker; chuffed; creased; cut up; down; downbeat; down in the doldrums/in the dumps/in the mouth; gutted; low.

to be depressed: to be in an indigo mood/in low water; to be on a bummer/on a downer/on a low; to feel grim; to flip; to have the blues/the hip/the hump/the mizzers/the pip.

detective: *see* **police.**

diarrhoea: Bali/Bangkok belly; Bombay cruds; collywobbles; Delhi belly; gippy tummy; the gripe; Montezuma's revenge; the runs; the screamers; shitters; the shits; threepenny-bits; the toms; the tom tits; the trots; the turistas; the wog; wog gut.

die, to: to be carried out feet first; to be on the way out; to bite the dust; to cark (it); to cash in one's chips; to check out; to choke; to come to the end of the line; to conk out; to cop it; to croak; to drop off the twig; to get fitted for a wooden overcoat; to give up the ghost; to go; to go belly up; to go for a burton; to go off the hooks; to go out feet first; to go to glory; to go west; to kick it; to kick off; to kick the bucket; to meet one's maker; to pack up; to pass in one's marbles; to peg out; to pip out; to pop one's clogs; to pop off; to quit it; to quit the scene; to shoot through; to shut up shop; to slip the painter; to snuff it; to snuff out; to sprout wings; to take a leap into the great unknown; to take off; to turn up one's toes.

(*See* **dead (to be)**)

dismiss, to: to axe; to boot (out); to bounce; to can; to chuck out; to ditch; to fire; to give s.o. the air/the arse/the axe/the bird/the boot/the bullet/the bum's rush/the chop/the chuck/the (old) heave-ho/the one-two/the order of the boot/the pink slip/the push/the sack/the shaft/the shove/the tin-tack; to give s.o. his/her cards/marching orders/walking orders; to kick out; to kiss off; to lay off; to pack s.o. in/out; to pitch s.o. out; to pull rank on s.o.; to put the skids under; to roust out; to sack; to shaft; to show s.o. the door; to sling out; to throw s.o. out (on his ear); to turf out; to wellie; to write s.o. off.

(*See* **packing, to send s.o.**)

dismissed, to be: to be fired; to be thrown out on one's ear; to get the air/the axe/the bird/the (order of) the boot/the bullet/one's cards/the chop/the hook/the kick/the push/the sack/the shove/the tin-tack/(the order of) the wellie; to get one's marching orders/one's walking orders; to get kicked out.

disparage, to: *see* **criticize, to (severely)**.

disparagement: *see* **criticism, (severe)**.

divulge a secret, to: to belch; to blab (one's mouth off); to be a blab(ber)mouth; to bleat; to blow the gaff; to blurt it out; to come clean; to cough up; to dob in; to fess up; to give the game/show away; to let the cat out of the bag; to nark; to open up; to peach (on s.o.); to pool; to put the squeal in; to sell s.o. down the river; to shice; to shoot one's face/

mouth off; to shoot the works; to sing (like a canary); to snitch; to spill one's guts/the beans; to squawk; to squeal; to talk.

(*See* **inform on, to**)

dog: bitser; bow-wow; doggy; Heinz 57; hound; mutt; pooch; pot-licker; tyke.

done for: it's all over with s.o.; it's all up with s.o.; it's curtains for s.o.; to have bought it; caput; come unstuck; dished; down-and-out; finished; a goner; gone to pot; the game's up; kaput; to have had it; to have had one's chips; s.o.'s number is up; sunk; up a gum tree; wiped out.

(*See* **fix, to be in a**)

dress up, to: to doll up; to dud up; to ponce oneself up; to posh oneself up; to put on one's best bib and tucker; to put on one's glad rags; to put on one's Sunday best; to rig out; to spruce (oneself) up; to tart oneself up; to titivate; to tog oneself up.

dressed up, all: all dolled up; all poshed up; all togged up; done up like a spiced pig; dressed (fit) to kill; dressed like a dog's dinner; dressed up/got up to the nines/to the teeth/to the knocker; in full fig; in one's best bib and tucker; in one's glad rags; in one's Sunday best; in one's monkey-suit; jazzed up; la-di-da(h); looking the business; looking (like) a million dollars; natty; posh; ritzy; sharp; slinky; snappy; snazzy; swish; tarted up; tasty.

drink, (heavily) to: to bash it; to be on the booze/on the bottle/on the grog/on it/on the piss; to booze; to chug; to down a pint/a few jars; to drink like a fish; to get bevvied; to get some elbow practice; to get tanked up; to glop; to glug; to go on the beer/the booze/the bottle/the grog/the shicker; to go for a pot; to grog; to have a bevvy/a few jars/a liquid lunch/one for the road/a slug/a snort; to hit the booze/the bottle/the sauce; to hoist a beer/a glass; to jug (up); to keep the damp out; to knock one back; to lap it up; to lift the little finger; to lubricate (one's throat); to lush; to pen and ink; to shift a pint; to sink a pint; to skull; to slug; to sluice one's ivories; to snatch a quick one; to souse; to sozzle; to sup up; to swig; to tank up; to tie one on; to tie on a load; to toss off a pint; to wet one's whistle.

(alcoholic) drink: amber fluid; amber nectar; black and tan; black velvet; booze; brownie; bugjuice; electric soup; firewater; gage; gargle; glug; greenie; grog; (the) hard stuff; hoo(t)ch; joy-juice; juice; jungle-juice;

lubrication; moonshine; mother-in-law; never-fear; plonk; (the) piss; rat poison; red-biddy; red-eye; roadie; rot gut; sauce; shicker; snakebite; stinger; swallow; tanglefoot; tasty; tiddl(e)y; tincture; turps; varnish; Vera Lynn; vino; wallop.

alcoholic drink, an: bevvy; bracer; drappie; drappy; drop (of the hard stuff); eye-opener; snifter; snort; snorter; (a drop of) tiddl(e)y; tincture; tot; wee dram.

inferior drink: bilge(-water); cat-lap; cat's piss; dishwater; gnat's piss; hogwash; swill; washing-up water.

drugged: *see* **drugs, under the influence of**.

drugs: D; dope; dynamite; junk; gear; hop; jam; mojo; nasties; shit; schlock; stuff; substance; turn on; vitamins.

drugs, to use: to be on dope/on junk/on the needle/on speed/on a trip; to blast; to blow; to chase the dragon; to crank up; to dabble; to do a line; to do drugs; to do up; to dope up; to fix (up); to freebase; to get off (on dope); to go on a jag; to have the weekend habit; to jam; to jolt; to joy-pop; to lick; to line (up/out); to mainline; to pop (pills); to shoot up; to skin-pop; to snuff; to speed; to spike (up); to switch on; to take; to take off; to toke; to toot; to trip (out); to turn on; to use; to wag out.

drugs, under the influence of: blasted; blocked; bombed (out); boxed; brought down; canned; charged up; coasting; cooked up; crashed out; destroyed; doggo; dosed up; flipped (out); floating (on cloud nine); flying high; freaked out; full; funked out; geed up; geezed up; gone; gowed up; to have a jag on; high; hooked; hopped up; hyped up; jacked up; junked up; knocked out; lit up; loaded; off/on the habit; on; on dope/on one/on speed/on a trip; out of it; out of one's box/head/skull/tree; out of order; out to lunch; potted; ripped; schnockered; skulled; smacked up; smashed; snowed; spaced out; speeding; spiked; stoned; strung out; switched on; tead-up; tripped out; turned on; twisted; up; using; wasted; wiped out; wired; wrecked; zomboid; zoned; zonked (out); zonko.

drugs, to have withdrawal symptoms from: to be cold turkey; to be hung up/sick/strung out; to be waiting for the man; to have a chinaman/a monkey on one's back; to have the chuck habit/the horrors; to need a fix; to tweak; yen sleep; yen-yen.

drug addict: AD; ad; cokehead; cotton freak; crackhead; cubehead; DA; dabbler; dip; dope addict; dope fiend; dopehead; doper; dosser; druggie; druggy; drughead; fixer; freak; goof; hard-liner; hay-head; head; hophead; hyp(e); hypo; joy-popper; junkie; mainliner; pillhead; pill-popper; piper; pothead; skin-popper; smackhead; snowbird; speedfreak; tea blower; tea head; user; viper; voyager; weedhead.

drug addict's equipment/instruments: artillery; biz; (the) business; fit; gimmick; joint; layout; machinery; outfit; paraphernalia; rig; tools; works.

needle/syringe: dropper; hyp(e); hype-stick; hypo; jabber; machine gun; nail; point; spike.

injection: dig; fix; hyp(e); hypo; jab; jab-off; jag; Jimmy (Hix); jolt; mosquito bite; ping; pop; shoot; skin-popping; Tom Mix; wake-up.

drugs, dealer of: bagman; candyman; carrier; Chino; connection; connector; connexion; dealer; deckman; dope peddler/pusher; fixer; junkie; kickman; the man; mule; operator; ounce man; powder monkey; pusher; sandman; travel-agent; viper.

drunk, (to be): arseholed; bagged; barrelled up; bevvied; blind (drunk); (Harry) blinders; blitzed; blotto; boiled; bombed (out); boozed (up); bottled; boxed; Brahms'n' Liszt; canned; corked; crashed; crocked; cut; dagged; d and d; dead drunk; dead to the world; destroyed; edged; elephants; far gone; floating on cloud nine; full (as a boot/as a bull's bum); fuzzled; fuzzy; gaged; gassed; geezed up; glassy-eyed; gone; grilled; groggy; half-cut; half-pissed; half-seas over; half-stewed; hammered; happy; to have a jag on; helpless; high (as a kite); honked; honkers; inked; inky; in one's cups; in the bag; jagged; jammed; jolly; juiced up; knocked out; legless; liquored up; lit (up); loaded; lubricated; lushed (up); merry; mulled; muzzy; off one's face; out of it; out of one's box/head/skull/tree; out of order; out to lunch; palatic; paralytic; pickled; pie-eyed; pissed (up); pissed as arseholes/as a newt; pixilated; plastered; potted; ploughed; rat-arsed; rat-faced; ratted; rigid; ripped; rorty; rotten; sauced (out); schnockered; screwed; shellacked; shickered; shot; skulled; slewed;

sloppy; sloshed; smashed; snaped; soaked; soused; sozzled; spifflicated; sprung; squiffy; steaming; stewed; stiff; stinking (drunk); stinko; stoned; stotious; stunned; tanked up; teed up; three/four sheets in/to the wind; tiddl(e)y; tight (as a newt); tipsy; toasted; trashed; under the influence; under the table; well away; well lit; well-oiled; whittled; wiped out; woozy; wrecked; zomboid; zoned (out); zoned; zonko.

drunk(ard): alkie; alko; alky; bar-fly; boozer; dipso; dosser; elbow-bender; juice-head; juicer; lush; piss-artist; pisspot; piss-tank; rumbum; rumhound; rummy; rumpot; soaker; souse; sozzler; squiff; tank; tippler; toss-pot; wino.

dumbfound, to: *see* **flabbergast, to**.

dupe, to: *see* **fool, to**.

dupe: *see* **fool**.

ears: ear-holes; flappers; flaps; jugs; lobs; lugholes; lug'oles; lugs; tabs.

easy, very: a (dead) cert; child's play; a cinch; cushy; dead easy; a doddle; as easy as ABC/as pie/as falling off a log/as winking; a gift; in the bag; jammy; kid's stuff; like falling off a log; money for jam/for old rope; nothing to it; a piece of cake; a piece of piss; pimpsy; plain sailing; a pushover; a romp; a snack; a snap; a snip; a steal; a sure bag; a sure thing; a walkover.

easy, to take it: to be sitting pretty; to bludge; to bugger about/around; to coast along; to diddle away one's time; to dilly dally; to doddle it; to fake off; to goof off; to hang loose; to have a cushy/an easy/a soft time of it; to kill time; to lay up; to lead a soft life; to live the life of Riley; to lollop around; to loosen up; to mess about/around; to mooch about/around; to piddle about/around.

eat (greedily), to: to binge; to chomp; to chow down; to demolish; to dig in; to eat like a horse/a pig; to feed one's face; to fill one's belly; to get stuck in; to gorge; to have a (good) blow-out/a (good) feed/a (good) tuck-in; to hog it; to hoover up; to make a pig of oneself; to pig out; to put on the nosebag; to scarf (down/out/up); to scoff; to shovel it down; to stodge; to stoke up; to stuff one's face/one's guts/oneself; to tie on the nosebag; to trough; to tuck in; to tuck it away; to wolf.

eccentric (person): card; case; caution; character; cupcake; crank; dag; ditz; div; freak; fruitcake; funny; goofball; goon; kook; kooky; oddball; odd specimen; out-to-lunch; queer cove/cuss/customer/fish/specimen; rat-bag; rum one; screwball; space cadet; space case; spaced out; wacky; weirdie; weirdo; weirdy.

ecstasy: *see* **MDMA**.

ejaculate, to: to come (off); to cream (one's jeans); to drop one's load; to fire; to fire in the air; to fire blanks; to get one's nuts off; to jet the juice; to shoot (one's bolt/load/ wad).

English: Brit; limey; Pom; Pommy; pongo.

erection, to have an: to be horny/hot/ randy; to be as stiff as a poker; to crack a fat/a stiffie; to get it up; to get the jack; to get hot nuts; to get a raise; to have a bar on/a beat on/a bone-on/a hard-on; to have a biggie/ a bone/a boner/a horn/a rod/a stand/a stiff/a stiffy; to have the hots; to have lead in one's pencil; to have a loaded gun; to have it up; to raise a beam; to raise it; to rise to the occasion; to stay.

(*See* **penis**)

exaggerate, to: to be a bit much; to bull-shit; to come it (a bit) strong; to come the acid; to gild the lily; to go a bit (too) far; to go OTT/over the top; to jazz; to lay it on thick; to lay it on with a shovel/with a trowel; to overdo it; to pile it on; to shit; to soup up; to spin a yarn; to stretch it a bit far; to talk big.

excellent: ace; amazing; awesome; bad; bang-up; beaut; a bit of all right; a bitch; bonzer; boss; brill; the business; cas; champion; chilled; classy; corking; crack; crackerjack; crash-hot; crucial; cushti; daisy; dandy; def; diamond; dope; dread; ducky; evil; fab; famous; fantastic; far-out; first class; first rate; fresh; a gas; gear; gold-en; gorgeous; great; groovy; handsome; hot-shot; hunky-dory; jake; keen; killer; lush; magic; massive; mega; natty; neat; nifty; not at all bad; OK; out of sight; out of this world; peachy; radical; really great; right-eous; ripper; ripping; rip-snorting; screamin'; screaming; scrumptious; sensa-tional; severe; shit; shit-hot; sick; smashing; solid; something else; spanking; stack; stun-ning; super; superduper; superfly; ten out of ten; terrific; tickety-boo; tip-top; top; top-buzz; top-flight; top-hole; top-line; top-notch; topping; triff; (totally) tubular; uptight; vicious; whizzo; wicked; wizard; the worst. (*See* **first-rater**)

excite, to (sexually): to cock tease; to give s.o. the come-on; to lead on; to prick tease; to switch on; to turn on; to work up.

excited, sexually: damp; fired up; fruity; to have the hots; horny; hot; humpty; juiced (up); randy; sex crazy; sexed up; sex mad; shag-happy; switched on; turned on; wet; worked up.

excrement: big jobs; bronze; cack; crap; floater; hocky; jobbie(s); macaroni; muck; plop; poo; poop; poo-poo; pony (and trap); Richard; shit; turd; woopsie.

exhaust, to: to bust a gut; to conk out; to knacker; to knock up; to take it out of s.o.; to wear out.

exhausted, to be: to ache/to be aching all over; all in; beat; buggered; burned out; bushed; busted; clapped out; cooked; creased; dead-beat; dead-tired; dead on one's feet; dished up; done for/in/up; to drag-ass; dragged-out; to drop; fagged out; fit to drop; flaked out; flat out; frazzled; fucked; half-dead; (Harry) flakers; to have had it; jiggered; knackered; knocked out; knocked up; at one's last gasp; on one's last legs; out on one's feet; pegged out; played out; pooped (out); ready to drop/flop; rooted; shagged; shot; sold out; stonkered; tapped out; trashed out; tuckered; used up; washed out; whacked; whipped; wiped out; worn to a frazzle; zapped; zonked (out); zonko.

exhausting: back-breaking; fagging; gruelling; killing; knackering; murderous; shattering; tiring.

expletives: balls! blast it! begob! begorra! bleeding hell! blimey! bloody hell! blow it! blow me! bollocks! bother! botheration! buggeration! bugger it! bugger you! bull! by George! by God! by Golly! by gum! by jiminy! by jingo! by Jove! Christ (Almighty)! Christmas! cor blimey! crumbs! dammit! damn! damn and blast! darn! darnation! darn it! dash (it all)! doggone it! drat it! flipping hell! for Christ's sake! for crying out loud! for goodness sake! for heaven's sake! for Pete's sake! for the love of Mike! fuck! fuck a duck! fucking hell! fuck it! fuck me! fudge! Gawd 'elp us! Gawd love us! Geez(e)! glory be! God Almighty! goddamm it! good God! good gracious! good grief! good heavens! good Lord! goodness! goodness me! goodness gracious me! gorblimey! Gordon Bennett! gosh! great Scott! hang it! hang up! heaven forbid! heck! hell! hell's bells (and

buckets of blood)! holy cats/cow/fuck/mackerel/Moses/shit/smoke! jeez(e)! Jeez(e)! Jesus (Christ)! Jesus fucking Christ! Jesus wept! like buggery! lord love a duck! lumme! lummy! my foot! my Gawd! my God!; my hat! pissing hell! shit! shit a brick! shite! shit me! shoot! shucks! sodding hell! sod it! stone me! stone the crows! strewth! strike a light! strike me pink! struth! sugar! tarnation! well, I'm blowed/buggered! what the deuce/the devil/the heck!

eye, a black: an eye in mourning; a painted peeper; a shiner; (both eyes) to have one's eyes in full mourning.

eye, to give s.o. a black: to black s.o.'s eye; to bung s.o.'s eye up; to put s.o. in mourning.

eyes: baby blues; bins; bin(n)s; blinkers; glims; lamps; lights; mince-pies; mincers; minces; peepers.

face: boat (race); chevy (chase); clock; coupon; dial; dial-piece; eek; kisser; lug; map; mug; mush; muzzle; pan; phiz; phizog.

fail, to: to bomb; to catch a cold; to come unstuck; to be washed up; to fall down on a job; to fall flat on one's face; to fall out; to fall through; to fizzle out; to flop; to fold; to go down like a ton of bricks; to go down the drain/the pan; to go kaput; to go kerflooie; to go phut; to go smash; to go to the dogs/to the wall; to go up the flue; to lay an egg; to pull the plug (on sth/s.o.); to put the skids under sth; to stiff.

to fail s.o. in an examination: to flunk; to pip; to plough.

failure: belly-flop; bomb; brodie; brody; bummer; bust; clinker; dead duck; dead loss; dud; fizzle; fivver; flop; flopperoo; frost; muff; oil-can; stiff; washout.

faint, to: to black out; to chuck a dummy; to flake out; to nod out; to go out like a light; to go spark out; to keel over; to hum; to pass out.

fall (down/over), to: to come a cropper/a gutzer/a mucker/a purler; to fall flat on one's face; to go for a burton; to go kerplunk; to go sprawling; to take a flier; to take a header. (See **fail, to**)

fart, to: to backfire; to blow off; to drop a bomb/one/one's guts/one's lunch; to frat; to guff; to gurk; to huff; to hum; to let (one) off; to poot; to pump; to traf(f).

fart: bottom burp; chuff; frat; guff; hum; humdinger; jam tart; quiff; traf(f).

fat person: blimp; dumpling; fatso; lardo; podge; porker; roly-poly.

father: da; dad(da); daddio; daddy; (the) gov; (the) governor; guv; (the) guv'nor; the old man; pa; pop; poppa.

fed up, to be: to be brassed off; to be chocker; to be chuffed; to be jack (of sth); to be peed off; to be pissed off; to be poxed off; to be sick (and tired) of sth; to be sick of the whole layout; to be teed off; to have had a basinful/a bellyfull/a gutful; to have had it up to here.

(*See* **bored, to be**)

feet: beetle-crushers; dogs; hoofs; paddlers; plates of meat; tootsies; tootsie-wootsies; tootsy; trotters.

fellate s.o., to; to have fellatio: to blow; to eat (out); to gam; to French; to give (s.o.) head; to give (s.o.) a blow-job/a head-job/a pipe-job; to gobble; to go down on (s.o.); to plate; to root; to suck cock; to suck off; to talk turkey; to tongue.

fellatio: blow-job; cannibalism; cock-sucking; the French way; gam; head; head-job; knob job; lip service; pipe job; root; skull(-job); snow job; zipper dinner.

fellator: cannibal; cock-sucker; dick licker; gobbler; jaw queen; knob-gobbler; rooter.

fellow: *see* **chap, old; man.**

female genitals: ace of spades; ass; beaver; box; bush; (the) business; cleft; clout; cookie; cooze; coozie; crack; crease; crumpet; cunt; doughnut; fanny; fig; fish; fish bowl; fish tank; flower; flue; fruit basket; furburger; fur pie; futz; gash; gig; gig factory; glue pot; goods; hairburger; hairpie; hole; honeypot; jam; jane; jazz; jelly-roll; jing-jang; keester; kipper; Lady Jane; little man in a boat; manhole; mick(e)y; minge; mink; monkey; muff; nasty; organ grinder; pee slit; piece of ass; poontang; pouch; prat; puka; puss; pussy; quiff; quim; rude bits; scratch; slit; slot; snapper; snatch; split beaver; split tail; tail; twack; twammy; twat; yinyang.

fight: aggro; bother; bovver; bundle; confusion; dust-up; hoe-down; mill; mix-up; punch-up; rough-house; rough stuff; rough-up; row; ruck; rumble; scrap; set-to; stoush; yike.

(*See* **quarrel**)

first-rate: *see* **excellent.**

first-rater: ace; beaut; the business; corker; cracker; daisy; dandy; dilly; dish; dream; dreamboat; el primo; eyeful; fizzer; gas; gasser; the greatest; hot cack; hotshot; humdinger; hunker; knockout; looker; the mostest; peach; rattler; rip-snorter; smasher; stunner; whacker; whammy; whopper; wow.

fit, (to feel): to be as fit as a fiddle/as right as rain; to be full of beans/full of get up and go/full of pep/full of piss and vinegar/full of vim; to be fighting fit; to be in cracking form/ in fat city/in good nick/in high gear/in the pink; to be up to the mark; to be zingy/zippy; to feel chipper; to feel on top of the world; to have (a lot of) ginger; to have lead in one's pencil.

fix, to be in a: to bat on a sticky wicket; to be for the high jump; to be gone a million; to be in a fine old/right old how-do-you-do; a pretty kettle of fish; to be in a bad patch/in a bad way/in a hole/in a hot spot/in a jackpot/in a jam/in a mess/in a pickle/in a scrape/in a (tight) spot; to be in hot water/in schtu(c)k/in stook; to be in the muck/in the shit/in the soup; to be on the hook; to be over a barrel; to be stuck up a gum tree; to be up shit creek without a paddle/up the creek/up the smoke; to be under heavy manners.

(*See* **done for; penniless**)

flatter, to: to apple-polish; to be all over s.o.; to blarney; to bootlick; to brown-nose; to butter s.o. up; to creep; to flannel; to hand s.o. a sweet line; to kiss ass; to lay it on thick; to lay it on with a trowel; to lick s.o.'s boots; to play up to s.o.; to polish the apple; to scratch s.o.'s back; to shine up to; to slime; to slobber over (s.o.); to smarm up to s.o.; to soft-soap; to spiel; to suck around; to suck up to s.o.; to sugar s.o. up; to sweeten s.o. up; to sweet-talk; to tell the tale.

flatterer: apple-polisher; arse crawler; arse-creeper; arse-kisser; arse-licker; ass crawler; ass-kisser; ass-licker; back-scratcher; backslapper; bootlicker; brown-noser; bum-sucker; cock-sucker; crawler; creep; flanneller; greaser; kiss-ass; oddball; pink-eye; polisher; slick customer; slim(e)y; smarmer; soft-soap artist; spieler; suckass; suck-holer; sweet-talker; toady.

flattery: apple-polishing; apple-sauce; arse-crawling; arse-licking; back-scratching; blarney; butter; eyewash; flannel; goo; moody; mush; oil; sawder; slime; snow-job; soft soap; spiel; sugar; sweet-talk.

fleece, to: *see* **swindle, to.**

fogey, old: back number; blimp; has been; old codger; old crock; old dodderer; old dodo; old dug-out; old fart; old fossil; old fuddy-duddy; old geezer; old goat; old stick-in-the-mud.

food: chow; chuck; din-dins; dub; eat; extras; fodder; grub; hash; kibble; moosh; nosh; resurrection pie; scoff; seconds; slops; stodge; swill; tack; tuck; tucker; victuals.

fool: airhead; arse; ass; arsehole; asshole; barmpot; berk; Berkeley Hunt; bimbo; bird brain; blithering idiot; blockhead; bohunk; bonehead; boob(y); boof-head; bungalow; bunny; cabbage-head; (proper) Charley; chinless wonder; chowderhead; chucklehead; chuff; chump; clit; clodhopper; cloghead; clot; clunk; coot; cretin; cripple; cuckoo; cunt; daftie; dafty; dag; damfool; deadbeat; deadhead; deadneck; dick; dickhead; diddy; dildo; dill; dilly; dimbo; dimmo; dimwit; dingbat; ding-dong; dink; dip; dipshit; dipstick; ditz; div; donk; dope; dork; dozy-arsed bastard; dozy twit; drip; droid; drongo; droob; drube; duffer; dumb ass/bunny/cluck/fuck/jerk; dumbdumb; dumbell; dumdum; dumbo; dummy; dumpling; dweeb; ear(h)ole; easy mark; (silly) fart; fathead; featherbrain; fuckhead; fuckwit; galah; gimp; gonzo; goober; goose; headbanger; Herbert; Hooray Henry; horse's ass; imbo; jay; jerk; joe; Joe Schmo; Joe Soap; josser; jughead; juggins; jumbo; Jumbo; klutz; knucklehead; lamb; lughead; lummox; lump; lunkhead; meatball; meathead; mental eunuch; moron; motherfucker; mug; muggins; musclehead; mush; mutant; muttonhead; nana; nebbish; nerd; nerk; nibhead; nignog; nincompoop; nit; nitwit; noddy; nong; noodle; nurd; palatic; patsy; pea-brain; pea(-)head; pigeon; pillock; pinhead; piss-artist; pisser; plank; plat; plonker; poon; poonce; possodeluxe; possum; prat; prick; prize idiot; prune; puddinghead; pumpkinhead; putz; Richard Cranium; rockhead; salami; sap(head); sawney; scatterbrain; shit-for-brains; schlemiel; schlemihl; schmo; schmock; schmoe; schnook; shower; silly (sausage); simp; smeg(gy); soft touch; spare; spastic; steamer; steaming idiot; stupe; sucker; thickhead; thickie; thicko; tit; tonk; tool; tosser; toss-pot; turkey; turniphead; twat; twerp; twirp; twit; wally; wanker; wet; widget; wolly; womble; yap; yo-yo; zoid; zombie.

fool s.o., to: to bitch (s.o. out of sth); to bite; to blindside; to bullshit s.o.; to cattle; to cod; to diddle; to do (s.o. out of sth); to do a job on s.o.; to do s.o. down; to do the dirty on s.o.; to do a number on s.o.; to dope s.o.; to double cross; to do s.o. up like a kipper; to euchre s.o.; to fake s.o. out; to fox s.o.; to goof s.o.; to goose s.o.; to have s.o. on; to have s.o. over; to hornswoggle; to hose; to jew s.o. (down); to jive s.o.; to kid s.o. (along); to lead s.o. up the garden path; to make s.o. look a chuff/a right monkey; to make a monkey/a sucker out of s.o.; to play games with s.o.; to play s.o. for a sucker; to pull a fast one on s.o.; to pull a gag on s.o.; to pull s.o.'s leg; to pull the wool over s.o.'s eyes; to pull s.o.'s pisser; to put the bite on s.o.; to put it/one across s.o.; to sell s.o. a pup; to spoof; to string s.o. along; to suck s.o. in; to swing a fast one on s.o.; to take s.o. in; to take s.o. for a ride;to take the Michael/the mickey/the mick/the mike/the piss; to take a rise out of s.o.; to tuck s.o. up; to two-time.
(*See* **swindle, to**)

to fool around: to fart(-arse) about/around; to footle about; to fuck about/around; to horse about/around; to jack around; to lark about; to mess about/around; to monkey about/around; to muck about/around; to piddle about/around; to play about/around; to ponce about/around; to skylark; to sod about/around.

foot: *see* **feet**.

French (person): Frog; Froggie; Froggy; Kermit.

friend: bud; buddy; chum; cobber; cock; cocker; cock-sparrow; mainman; mate; mucker; old China; oppo; pal; pard; pardner; partna; side-kick; sport; wuss.

funny, very: creasing; a gas; a guinea a minute; a hoot; a killer; killing; priceless; rib-tickling; rich; a riot; a scream; screamingly funny; side-splitting; rollicking; too funny for words.

gadget: *see* **what's-its-name**.

German: Fritz; Heinie; Hun; Jerry; Kraut; Krauthead; squarehead.

get lost!: beat it! bollocks to you! bugger off! bugger you! buzz off! damn you! drop dead! frig off! fuck off! get knotted/rooted/screwed/stuffed! get the hell out of here! get your tail out of here! git! go (and) jump in the lake! go and play marbles! go fly a kite! go fuck/screw yourself! go tell it to the Marines; go to blazes/to buggery/to hell! hop it! knackers (to that)! knickers! lay off! leggo! naff off! not on your nellie! nuts (to you)! on your bike! piss off! ponce off! push off! put that in your pipe and smoke it! rats to you! save it! scat! scoot! scram! screw you! screw that! shag off! skip it! sod off! stick it! stow it! stuff it! two fingers! up your gig! up yours! vamoose! (you can) stick it up your flue/up your gonga/up your jumper! you can shove that right up your arse! you know what you can do with that! you know where you can shove/stick that!

girl: babe; baby; bimbo; bint; bird; bit of all right/crumpet/fluff/skirt/stuff/tail; bobby-dazzler; bobby soxer; broad; brush; bunny; chick; chickie; chicklet; corker; cracker; crumpet; cunt; cupcake; cutie; cutey; dame; dish; doll; dolly; dolly-bird; eager beaver; female; filly; flapper; fluff; flychick; fox; foxy lady; frail job; frill; gal; gel; girlie; hammer; heifer; hottie; jail bait; jam tart; Jane; Judy; lovely; lulu; mamma; mink; moll; mouse; nice bit of cunt/goods/homework/stuff; peach (of a girl); piece (of ass/goods); pin-up; potato peeler; quail; queen; raver; salt; scrubber; sex kitten; sheila; shiksa; smasher; sort; sugar; tart; tomato; totsie; tottie; totty; twist; wench.

gonorrhoea: clap; jack; knob rot; load.

to have gonorrhoea: to be dosed up; to cop/to catch/to get a dose; to get dosed up; to have the clap; to piss pins and needles.

glutton: greedy guts; guzzler; hog; pig; piggy; (walking) dustbin.

goodbye!: bung ho! bye! cheers! chin chin! see you! so long! ta-ta! tatty-bye! toodle-oo! toodle-pip!

good time: ball; bash; bat; beanfeast; beer-up; bender; blast; blinder; binge; booze-up; do; fling; fuck-about; gas; gig; hell bender; high jinks; jag; jam; jollies; jolly (-up); knees-up; lark; piss-about; piss-up; rage; rave(-up); shivoo; thrash; whing-ding; wing-ding; yell.

to have a good time: to barhop; to beat it up; to be on cloud nine; to be on the loose; to be out on the tiles/the town; to blow one's mind; to get a kick out of sth; to get off on sth; to get one's jollies; to get one's rocks off; to go on a binge/on the racket/on the razzle(-dazzle); to go to town; to have a ball/a high old time/a rare old time/a whale of a time; to hit the high spots; to jam; to lead a fast life; to live it up; to make whoopee; to paint the town red; to party; to push the boat out; to rally; to rave; to whoop it up.

gratis: buckshee; for free; freebie; on credit; on the cuff; on the house; on the nod; on tick.

grudge against, to have a: to crowd s.o.; to give s.o. the finger; to have a down on s.o.; to have a monkey on one's back; to have it in for s.o.; to have/to get one's knife into s.o.; to put the freeze on s.o.; to send s.o. to Coventry.

grumble, to: to beef; to belly-ache; to bitch; to bleat; to brass off; to chunter on; to crab; to create; to gripe; to grizzle; to grouch; to grouse; to have a beef about sth; to kvetch; to mither; to mizzle; to moan and groan; to whinge; to yap; to yawp.

grumbling: belly-aching; beefing; griping; grousing; ratty.

hand(s): breadhooks; bunch of fives; daddle; darbies; dooks; dukes; fin; fist; flapper; flipper; forks; grappling hooks; hooks; lugs; mauler; meat hooks; mitt; oliver twist; paw.

handcuffs: bracelets; cuffs; darbies; pinchers; snitchers; stringers.

handkerchief: billy; hankie; hanky; nose-rag; nose-wipe(r); sniffer; sniff rag; snitch rag; snot-rag; wipe(r).

hashish: afghan; block; brick; charas; chunks; cube; hash; hemp; muggles; red Leb; shit; solid; substance.

(*See* **cannabis**)

hat: cadie; cady; kelly; lid; sky-piece; stovepipe; tile; titfer; topper.

head: attic; bean; beezer; block; bonce; brain box; chump; conk; crown; cruet; crumpet; dome; gourd; headpiece; loaf; lolly; melon; napper; nob; noddle; noggin; noodle; nut; onion; sconce; skull; think-box; thinker; think-piece; top-knot; Uncle Ned; (upper) storey.

helicopter: chopper; copter; dust-off; whirly-bird.

heroin: Big H; birdie-powder; boy; candy; Chinese No 3; Chinese rocks; courage pills; crap; crystal; doojie; duji(e); dynamite; elephant; gold dust; H; Henry; horse; jack; junk; needle(-)candy; peanut butter; rocks; rock-candy; salt; scag; scat; s(c)hmeck; s(c)hmee(t); schmock; scot; shit; skag; smack; speedball (*heroin and cocaine*); stuff; sugar; white cross; white stuff; (old lady) white.

hoax: blarney; booby-trap; bunk(um);

catch; clap-trap; cock-and-bull story; eye-wash; flummery; gag; guff; hanky-panky; hooey; humbug; jiggery-pokery; leg-pull; number; plant; sell; spoof; swizz; swizzle; take-in; take-on; yarn.
(*See* **swindle**)

hoax, to: *see* **fool, to; swindle, to.**

homosexual: angel; arse-bandit; ass-bandit; arse-man; ass man; aunt; auntie; aunty; bait; beef-bandit; brown-hatter; brownie; bum-bandit; bum-boy; bummer; bum-rubber; butch; cat; catch; chickenhawk; chocolate lover; coal-burner; cock-handler; cock-pusher; cock-sucker; cornholer; cream-puff; cruiser; daddy; daisy; dick licker; dirt track rider; drag queen; fag; faggot; fairy; fart-catcher; fem; femme; fist fucker; flit; flower; flute(r); four-letter man; freak; fruit; fruit-cake; fruit fly; gay; gaylord; gingerbeer; girl; gobbler; gonif; gonof; gonoph; gooser; gussie; haricot (bean); hawk; homo; hoof; hustler; iron hoof; jocker; joey; kiki; knob-gobbler; lilly; limp-wrist; lizzie; leatherboy; maricon; Mary; mola; mother; mutton fancier; nance; nancy-boy; nellie; nelly; nestle; nine-bob note; oddball; pansy; pillow biter; pitch; pix; ponce; poof; pooftah; poofter; poonce; poove; popcorn; poufdah; pouff; punk; quean; queen; queenie; queer; quiff; quince; rough-trade; screamer; shirt-lifter; short-arm bandit; sissy; skippy; sod; softy; sonk; steamer; sweet; swish; third-sexer; toilet queen; tonk(er); treacle; turd-burglar; turd-snipper; twink; twinkie; twinky; wolf; woof(ter).

homosexual (*adj*): bent (as a nine-bob note); camp; gay; ginger; kinky; lacy; left-handed; light-footed; limp-wristed; pansified; pink; poofy; poncy; possodeluxe; queer (as a coot).

to be a homosexual: to be one of them.

hooligan: biker; good-for-nothing; goon; gorilla; greaser; homeboy; hood; hoodlum; hoon; lager lout; layabout; lout; nasty piece of work; outlaw; punk; quandong; .rough; rude boy; scally; ted; teddy-boy; thug; tough guy; yob; yobbo.

hungry, to be: to be empty; to be famished; to feel the munchies; to be/to feel peckish; to be ravenous; to be starving.

hurry (up), to: to ball the jack; to barrel ass; to beetle (along/off); to be nippy; to buck up; to burn; to burn up the tarmac; to do sth double-quick/in double-quick time; to get a hump on/a hustle on/a move on/a shift on/a wiggle on; to get going; to get one's skates on; to get weaving; to give sth the gun; to go flat out; to have a burn-up; to look lively/snappy; to make it snappy; to pull one's finger out; to put one's foot/toe down; to run like blazes; to shift; to shift one's carcass; to shake a leg; to snap it up; to step on it; to step on the gas; to stir one's stumps; to tear along; to whack up the pace; to whizz; to whoosh; to zap along; to zip along.

husband: better half; catch; hubby; old man; other half.

idiot: *see* **fool.**

immediately: *see* **quickly, very.**

important person: big Brother; big bug; big cheese; big gun; biggy; big hitter; big man; big noise; big shot; big-time operator; big-timer; big white chief; bigwig; boss of the show; the brass; brass-hat; fat cat; (high) muckamuck; high-up; Mr Big; (his) nibs; nob; the nobs; silvertail; somebody; top brass; top dog; tycoon; VIP.

imprison, to: to bang up; to bolt up; to box; to cage; to can; to clap in jail; to jug; to lag; to lock up; to nick; to put away; to put in the can/in clink; to send down/up; to shop.
(*See* **arrest, to**)

impudence: back-chat; brass; buck; cheek; face; gall; lip; mouth; neck; nerve; once-a-week; sass; sauce.

impudent, to be: to be brassy/cheeky/cocky / cool / flip / fresh / gutsy / lippy / nervy / sassy/saucy/snippy; to be a cool hand/a cool one/a cool customer; to have a hell of a cheek/nerve; to have a neck/a nerve; to sauce s.o.

individual: *see* **chap; man.**

infatuated, to be: to be bats about; to be batty over; to be crazy about/over; to be dippy about; to be gone on; to be goofy over; to be head over heels; to be hipped/hooked on; to be hot for; to be hung up on; to be mad/nuts/nutty about; to be potty about; to be sold on; to be sent; to be shook/soft/sprung on; to be swept off one's feet by; to be sweet on; to be struck on; to be wild about; to carry a torch for; to dig; to fall for; to fancy; to go crazy/gaga over; to go for sth in a big way; to have a pash on; to have a soft spot for; to have a thing about; to have it bad for; to have s.o. under one's skin; to le(t)ch for/about; to queer for; to rave; to take a shine to; to think the world of.

inform on, to; informer, to be an: to bleat; to blow the gaff on; to blow the whistle on; to come copper; to do a Bertie; to do the Royals; to finger; to fink; to grass; to lag on s.o.; to lollipop; to lolly; to narc; to nark; to turn nark; to nose on s.o.; to number; to put in the G; to put the finger on; to rat on s.o.; to sell out; to shop s.o.; to skunk; to sneak on s.o.; to snitch; to snout; to split on s.o.; to squeal on s.o.; to tell on; to top off; to turn snitch.

(*See* **divulge a secret, to**)

information: dope; gen; guff; (hot) tip; lowdown; oil; poop; SP; steer; tip-off.

information, to give: to give s.o. the lowdown/the SP/the wire; to put s.o. in the picture; to put s.o. on to sth; to put s.o. wise; to tip s.o. off; to tip s.o. the wink.

informer, (police): canary; copper's nark; croaker; dobber; finger; fink; grass; grasser; nose; peach; plant; rat; sneak; snitch; snout; split; squealer; stooger; stoolie; stool-pigeon; supergrass; top-off; tout; Uncle.

intelligence: brains; common; grey matter; gumption; horse-sense; savvy.

Irish: bog-trotter; harp; Mick; Paddy; Pat.

Italian: dago; ding; Eyetie; greaseball; ice creamer; macaroni; spag; spaghetti bender/eater; spic(k); wop.

Japanese: Jap; Nip.

Jew: four-by-two; hebe; heeb; heimie; hymie; Ikey (Mo); Jaybird; Jewboy; kike; mockie; mocky; sheenie; sheeny; shonk; Yid.

kill (s.o.), to: to ace; to blow away; to bump off; to burn; to chill; to cream; to croak; to deep six; to do for; to do in; to drill holes in s.o.; to dust; to erase; to fill full of lead; to fit with a concrete overcoat; to get; to give the works; to gun down; to hit; to ice; to kiss off; to knock off; to lay s.o. down; to liquidate; to make a hit; to off; to pip; to plug; to polish off; to pop off; to put a hole through (s.o.); to put away; to put on the spot; to rap; to rip off; to rub out; to score; to scrag; to shut up; to smoke; to snuff; to stiff; to take for a ride; to top; to waste; to wipe out; to X-out.

killer: croaker; head hunter; hit-man; hitter; iceman; liquidator; red man; torpedo; trigger man.

(*See* **suicide, to commit**)

laugh uproariously, to: to be doubled-up; to be in fits (of laughter); to be in hysterics/in stitches; to be tickled pink/to death; to crease oneself; to double up; to hoot; to kill oneself laughing; to laugh like a drain; to laugh one's head off; to piss oneself laughing; to scream; to split one's sides laughing; to wet oneself.

lazy, to be: to be bone-idle; to be born tired; to be a bummer/a couch potato/a lazybones/a lazy bum/a slob; to be dozy; to be workshy; to bum around; to doss around; to drag-ass; to fuck about; to have lead in one's arse; to soldier; to tool about/around; to veg out.

(*See* **easy, to take it; malinger, to**)

leave, to: *see* **run away, to.**

legs: drumsticks; gams; matchsticks; pegs; pins; shanks; stalks; stilts; stumps.

lesbian: amy-john; bull-dagger; bull-dyke; butch; charley; diesel; dike; dyke; dykey; dykie; fairy lady; fairy queen; fanny tickler; fem; femme; finger artist; jasper; kinky; les; lesbie; lesbo; lessie; lez; lezo; lezzie; Marge; Mary; minty; queer; quim queer; tootsie; truck driver.

less, couldn't care: I couldn't care/I don't give a bean/a damn/a fart/a fig/a fuck/a hang/a monkey's/a rap/a sausage/a tinker's cuss/a (tinker's) toss/tuppence/a tuppenny damn/a tuppenny fuck/two hoots.

lie: corker; cracker; crock of shit; fairy tale; fib; jazz; jive; (old) moody; pork pie; porky (pie); rouser; sparkler; story; tall story; tall tale; whopper; yarn.

lie, to: to be full of wind; to fib; to jazz; to jive; to madam; to pitch/to pull/to spin a yarn; to tell stories.

(*See* **fool (s.o.), to**)

life, to lead a soft: *see* **easy, to take it.**

limit! that's the: that beats the Dutch; that beats everything; that's a bit much/a bit off/a bit rich/a bit steep/a bit thick! that's all we needed! that's the absolute limit! that's the bloody limit! that's the last straw! that takes the biscuit/the cake!

look at, to: to bad eye; to clock; to dig; to do a double take; to eyeball; to gander; to geek; to get an eyeful/a load of; to gig; to give s.o. the glad-eye/the once-over; to goof at; to have a butcher's/a dekko/a gander/a look-see/a mike/a shufty/a squint at; to keep one's eyes open/peeled/skinned; to keep tabs on; to lamp; to lay an eyeball on; to make (goo-goo) eyes at; to scope; to screw; to squint; to take a dekko/a gander/a screw/a slant at.

look: butcher's; eyeball; flash; gander; geek; gig; glad-eye; look-see; once-over; shufty; squint.

LSD: acid; blue heaven; candy; the chief; D; MBS; sugar; trip; twenty-five; vitamin A; (instant) zen.

mad: bananas; barking (mad); barmy; bats; batty; bonkers; bug-house; buggy; bugs; cracked; crackers; crackpot; crazy; cuckoo; daft; did(d)lo; dippy; ditzy; divvy; doolally (tap); doodle-alley; dotty; far gone; flaky; gaga; goofy; illin'; kooky; loco; loony; loony tunes; loopy; mental; mishugah; moony; not quite all there; nutty (as a fruit cake); off one's block/chump/head/nut/onion/rocker/trolley; off-the-wall; out to lunch; pixilated; plumb crazy; potty; psycho; puddled; queer (in the attic); scatty; schizo; screwy; stark raving bonkers; touched; unglued; wacko; wacky; whacko; whacky; wig; yarra.

to be/to go mad: to be living in cloud-cuckoo land; to be off one's crust; to be out of one's box/head/gourd/pram/skull/tree; to be out to lunch; to be weak in the upper story; to crack up; to freak out; to go haywire; to go off the hooks/off the rails; to go round the bend/round the twist; to go up the pole/up the wall; to have bats in the belfry/attic; to have a screw/a slate/a tile loose; to lose one's marbles/one's ollies; to nut out/up; to wig out.

mad person: crackpot; flake; fruitcake; geek; headbanger; headcase; loon; loony (tunes); nut; nutcase; nutter; screwball; wacko; wacky; whacko; whacky.

male genitals: block and tackle; bulge; crown jewels; family jewels; goods; marriage prospects; meat and two veg; nasty; privates; rig; rude bits; three-piece suite; (wedding) tackle; yinyang.

malinger, to: to bludge; to dodge the column; to goldbrick; to have lead in one's arse; to scrimshank; to shirk; to skive (off); to skrimshank; to swing the lead; to swing it.

malingerer: bludger; column-dodger; dodger; goldbrick; lead-swinger; scrimshanker; shirker; skiver; skrimshanker; slowcoach; slowpoke.

man: article; baby; beggar; bimbo; bird; blighter; bloke; bod; body; bugger; buster; cat; cookie; dude; egg; Essex man; fella; feller; fox; galoot; gee; geezer; gent; get; gink; git; goof; guy; hunk; jockey; joe; Joe; John; joker; josser; Kevin; lug; mac; mate;

merchant; mush; stiff; talent; turky; wallah.

marijuana: alfalfa; baby; bambalacha; bang; bhang; bo-bo; boo; brick; canapa; charge; dank; duros; dynamite; fu; gage; ganga; gangster; ganjah; ganji; gauge; (Acapulco) gold; gow; grass; greefo; green; grefa; griffo; gunji; gunny; (Indian) hay; joy-smoke; juana; juane; juanita; keef; kief; kif; Lady Jane; love-weed; (sweet) lucy; M; marjie; marjorie; Mary; Mary Ann(e); Mary Jane; Mary Warner; Mexican red; moocah; mootah; mooter; muggles; Panama red; plant; pot; root; rope; salt and pepper; splay; stum; substance; tampi; tea; weed; weed-tea; yesca.

marijuana cigarette: ace; African woodbine; birdwood; bomber; burn; drag; dubee; duby; gangster; giggle smoke weed; greefa; grefa; griffa; gyve; jay; jive stick; joint; jolt; joystick; ju; ju-ju; kickstick; killer; mezz; muggles; number; pod; pot; rainy-day woman; reef; reefer; roach; rope; sausage; smoke; spliff; stick (of gage/of tea); toke; twist.

married, to get: to do the double act; to get hitched; to get hooked; to get spliced; to jump the broomstick/the hurdle; to take the big leap/the plunge; to tie the knot.

masturbate, to: to ball off; to bash the bishop; to be married to the five-fingered widow; to beat off; to beat the dummy/the meat; to blow; to bring oneself off; to cream off; to diddle; to finger oneself; to finger fuck; to flog the bishop/the dong/the dummy/one's donkey; to frig; to fuck off; to get a grip on oneself; to get (it) off; to have a ball-off; to hank; to hold oneself; to hot-rod; to jack off; to jap off; to jerk off; to jerk one's gherkin; to milk; to play with oneself/with one's instrument/with one's pecker; to play with hank; to pound one's pork; to pound the meat/the pudding; to pull off; to pull one's plonker/one's pudding/one's wire; to rub off; to rub up; to screw off; to squeeze the lemon; to strangle one's grannie; to stroke the lizard; to toss (oneself) off; to varnish the cane; to wank (oneself) off; to whack off; to whank.

masturbation: do-it-yourself; finger job; finger fuck; hand job; knob job; one off the wrist; rub-up; toss(-off); wank; whank; wire-pulling.

masturbator: hand artist; sausage grappler; wanker; whanker; wire-puller.

MDMA: adam; big brown ones; disco

biscuits; E; ecstasy; Epsom salts; hamburgers; vitamin E/X; X; xtc.

mescaline: cactus; mesc; peyote.

mess, in a: *see* **fix, in a**.

miser: cheapskate; meanie; meany; penny-pincher; piker; skinflint; tight-arse; tight-ass; trot artist; trotter.

miserly: assy; careful (with one's money); close-fisted; jewish; mean; measly; mingy; penny-pinching; snotty; stingy; tight; tight-arsed; tight-assed; tight-fisted.

to be miserly: to have a reach impediment; to have a death adder in one's pocket; to have short arms and deep pockets; to skin a turd; to throw one's money about like a man with no arms.

mistake: ball-up; balls(-up); bish; bloomer; blooper; bodge-up; bog-up; boner; boob; booboo; clanger; cock-up; flamer; fuck-up; gaffe; howler; plonker; screw-up.

to make a mistake: to ball it; to balls sth up; to be off base; to be (way) off beam; to be up the pole; to boob; to clang; to drop a bollock/a brick/a clanger/a stumer; to get one's wires crossed; to goof off; to make a balls(-up)/a ball-up/a bodge-up/a booboo/a cock-up/a gaffe/a goof/a (right) mess/a slip-up; to put one's foot in it; to screw (sth) up; to slip up.

money: ackers; alfalfa; bank; bar; beans; bees and honey; beer tokens/vouchers; bit; bluey; bob; boodle; brass; bread; buck; bundle; carn; century (note); chink; clink; C-note; cock and hen; copper(s); daughter; dibs; dimmock; do-re-mi; dosh; dough; dross; ducket; dust; earners; filthy lucre; fin; finski; five; fiver; five spot; folding stuff; font; funds; funny money; G; gee; gelt; gilt; gold; goodies; gorilla; grand; greenback; grease; greenies; green stuff; half-a-dollar; jack; jack's alive; jingle; kale; lettuce; lolly; long green; looka; loot; marbles; mazooma; mazuma; moola(h); moolies; monkey; (the) necessary; (the) needful; nest-egg; nicker; once; oner; Oscar (Ashe); pelf; poppy; quid; quidlet; quiff; readies; (the) ready; rhino; sausage and mash; sawbuck; scratch; shekels; sobs; sov; spondulicks; squeeze; sugar; tenner; ten-spot; tin; velvet; wamba; wedge; white; (the) wherewithal; womba; wonga.

mood, to be in a bad: *see* **angry, to be**.

morphine: birdie-powder; block; cube; joy-powder; Miss Emma; mojo; morf; morph; snow; white cross; white stuff; whizz-bang.

mother: ma; mamma; mom; mum; muvver; (my) old girl; (my) old lady; (my) old woman.

moustache: dropper; (face) fungus; handlebar moustache; tash; tickler.

mouth: bazoo; box of dominoes; cakehole; chops; gob; kisser; kissing tackle; laughing gear; mush; muzzle; north and south; puss; rat-trap; satch; satchel mouth; trap; yap.

naked: in one's birthday suit; in the altogether; in the buff; in the raw; stark bollock-naked; starkers; without a stitch on.

negro: *see* **Black**.

nonsense: all my eye (and Betty Martin); apple sauce; balderdash; ballyhoo; baloney; balls; bilge; blah-blah; blarney; blather; blether; bollocks; boloney; bosh; bull; bullshine; bullshit; bumf; bum-fodder; bunkum; cherry ripe; claptrap; cock; codswallop; crap; crapola; a crock (of shit); crud; eyewash; fanny; fiddlesticks; flam; flapdoodle; flim-flam; flummery; fudge; gammon; garbage; guff; hocky; hogwash; hokey pokey; hokum; holly-golly; hooey; horse shit; hot air; jazz; junk; malarkey; moonshine; much; mush; piff; piffle; pigwash; piss; poppycock; rhubarb; rot; shit; spoof; squit; stuff (and nonsense); swill; taurus excretus; toffee; tommy rot; tosh; trash; tripe; twaddle; waffle.

to talk nonsense: to be full of shit; to crap on; to flip one's lip; to jive; to shuck; to shoot one's mouth off; to spoof; to talk a lot of junk; to talk a load of rot; to talk like a nut; to talk nuts/piffle/rot/shit; to talk out of one's arse; to talk through the back of one's neck; to talk wet.

nose: beak; beezer; bill; boko; conk; hooter; horn; neb; nozzle; s(ch)nozz; schnozzle; schnozzola; schonk(er); sneezer; sniffer; snitch; snoot; snout.

not (bloody) likely!; nothing doing!: balls! can't be done! count me out! no chance! no can do! no dice! no fear! no go! no sale! no soap! no such luck! no way! not a chance in hell! not a sodding chance! not a hope! not effing likely! not sodding likely! not on your life/on your nellie/on your sweet life! not if I know anything about it! stack! take a running jump!

(*See* **get lost!**)

nothing: bugger-all; chicken feed; chicken-

shit; damn all; dick; diddly (shit/squat); FA;
Fanny Adams; fat lot; fleabite; fuck-all; jack
(shit); nishte; nit; nix; not a droob; not a
sausage; nowt; piss-all; sod-all; sweet FA;
sweet Fanny Adams; sweet fuck-all; zilch.

nothing doing!: *see* **not (bloody) likely!**

opium: black stuff; can; canned stuff; chef;
dopium; dreams; dream wax; gong; gow;
green ashes/mud; hop; ice-cream; mud; O;
pen-yen; poppy; tar; twang; yen shee.

opium pipe: bamboo.

oral sex: *see* **cunnilingus; fellatio.**

orgasm, to have an: to come; to come
off; to cum; to finish off; to get (it) off; to get
one's rocks off; to go off; to pop (one's
rocks).
(*See* **ejaculate, to**)

packing, to send s.o.: to bounce s.o.; to
choke s.o.; to give s.o. the air/the brush off/
the bum's rush/his marching orders/the raspberry; to railroad; to send s.o. to the devil; to
send s.o. off with a flea in his ear; to sling
out; to tell s.o. where he gets off; to tell s.o. to
fuck off/to piss off/to sod off.
(*See* **dismiss s.o., to**)

paunch: beer belly; beer gut; belly; bread
basket; corporation; Derby Kelly; pod;
podge; pot; pot-belly; tub; tummy.
(*See* **stomach**)

pawn, to; in pawn: to dip; to hock; to
lumber; to put in hock/in pop; to put up the
spout; at my uncle's; at the hockshop; in
hock; in pop; up the spout.

pay (up), to: to ante (up); to brass up; to
chip in; to cough up; to dab down; to dish
out; to do the necessary; to foot the bill; to
fork out; to pay cash on the nail; to pitch
in; to plonk out; to shell out; to splash out; to
stand sam; to stand the racket; to stump up.

PCP: (angel) dust.

peasant: bushie; bushwhacker; chew-bacon;
clod; clodhopper; country bumpkin; hayseed;
hick; hillbilly; jaybird; joskin; mossback;
redneck; rube; shitkicker; swedey; yap.

penis: bayonet; bazooka; bone; bozack;
(the) business; chopper; cock; dangler; dick;
dickory dock; dicky; dingaling; dingdong;
dong; donker; donkey; doodle; dork; end;
gear stick; gherkin; gun; hammer; Hampton
(Wick); hot rod; instrument; jack; jigger;
Jimmy; jing-jang; jock; johnson; John
Thomas; joint; jones; Jones; joystick; knob;
leg; lemon; lingam; lizard; lob; meat;

Mick(e)y; middle leg; nob; (the) old man;
one-eyed trouser snake; organ; pecker;
peenie; pencil; Perce; Percy; persuader;
peter; pisser; plonker; poker; prick; prong;
putz; ramrod; rig; rod; roger; root; salami;
sausage; schlong; schmuck; shaft; short-
arm; skin flute; stalk; stick; stiffy; tadger;
tail; tassel; thing; thingy; third leg; tinker;
todger; tonk; tool; twinkle; Uncle Dick;
wally; wanger; weapon; weeny; whang(er);
widget; wiggy; willie; willy; winkie; winkle;
winky; yang; yard.

penniless: boracic (lint); broke; broke to
the wide; cleaned out; dead broke; down on
one's uppers; flat; hard-up; in low water; in
queer street; light; on one's ass; on one's
beam ends; on the bread line; on the outer;
on the rory; peppermint; pink lint; piss-poor;
played out; shit poor; short; skint; stony
(broke); tapped out.

to be penniless: to feel the pinch; not to
have a bean/a brass farthing/a cent/a sausage.
(*See* **fix, to be in a**)

period, to have a: to be on the rag; to
come on; to fall off the roof; to fly the flag;
flowers; to have the curse; to have the monthlies; to have mum nature; to have the
decorators/the painters in; to have one's relations to stay; to have the rag on/out; to have
the reds; joey; the wet season.

pervert, to be a: dirty old man; to have a
dirty/filthy mind; filthy sod; flasher; to be
kinky; perve; secko; sex fiend; sexo; sicko.

pimp: bludger; bully; easy rider; fancy
man; flesh peddler; hustler; mack; mackerel; mackman; ponce; white slaver.

pocket: cly; keester; kick; Lucy locket; pit;
poke; sky-rocket.

police: Babylon; babysnatchers; the beast;
boys in blue; bulls; button men; (the) cops;
five-O; (the) Force; (the) filth; (the) fuzz;
(the) heat; the heavy mob; (the) law; (the)
Man; the Met; mob; monarch; New York's
finest; old Bill; PD; pigs; the plod; ring-em;
SPG; sweeney; Uncle.

policeman, (uniformed): blue-bottle;
bobby; cop; copper; flatfoot; flattie; flatty;
fuzz; jockey; man in blue; old Bill; pig;
swedey; woodentop.

policeman, policewoman (*general
term*): bear; beast; bizzie; bobby; bogey;
bull; busy; clod hopper; cop; copper; dickless
Tracy; fed; filth; fuzz; grasshopper; Jack;
Jill; jockey; Kojak; nab; noddy; oink; old

Bill; paddler; peeler; pig; plod; porker; rozzer; scuffer; swedey.

detective: dick; eye; fly-ball; fly-bob; fly-bull; fly-cop; fly-dick; fly-mug; gumshoe; private eye; Richard; snoop; tail; tec.

police station: bridewell; cop shop; factory; hoosegow; lock-up; nick; warehouse.

(*See* **prison van**)

pregnant, to be: to be clucky/expecting; to be in a delicate condition/in the club/in the family way/in pool/in poke/in trouble/in the pudding club; to be knocked up/preggers; to be up the duff/the poke/the pole/spout; to have a bun in the oven.

to make pregnant: to get in the club/in the family way/into trouble; to knock up; to put up the duff/up the spout.

priest: *see* **clergyman**.

prison: the big house; bird; boob; cage; can; CB; calaboose; calaboosh; chok(e)y; clink; cooler; glasshouse; hoosegow; jail; jankers; jigger; Joe Gurr; the joint; jug; klink; lock-up; (the) nick; pen; pokey; quad; quod; shop; shovel; slammer; slams; sneezer; stir; tank.

to be in prison: to be banged up; to be behind bars; to be bolted up; to be in bird; to be inside; to be tucked up; to be upriver/upstate; to do bird; to do time.

(*See* **imprison, to**)

prison cell: bing; bird-cage; the block; chok(e)y; coffin; cooler; flowery dell; hole; lock-up; Peter (Bell); slot; think tank; wishing well.

prisoner: body; con; first-timer; fresh fish; jailbird; jaybird; (old) lag; lifer; polisher; toe-ragger; yardbird.

prison sentence: bender; bird-lime; bit; carpet (bag); drag; fistful; five fingers; five spot; haircut; handful; hard (labour); lagging; neves; nevis; nickel; pontoon; porridge; rap; spot; stretch; ten-spot; ticket; time; wooden one.

prison van: Black Maria; bun wag(g)on; cop-wag(g)on; hurry-up wag(g)on; jam sandwich; meat wag(g)on; milk sandwich; paddy-wag(g)on; tank wag(g)on.

prison warder: flue; fuzz; kangaroo; screw; twirl.

profits, illicit: bit on the side; commission; earner; graft; gravy; perks; pickings; rake-off.

(*See* **bribe**)

prostitute: alley cat; bag(gage); band; bat; blister; brass; broad; bunny; call-girl; chippy; chromo; cruiser; doxy; endless belt; fancy woman; flat-backer; flesh peddler; floosie; floosy; floozie; floozy; forty-four; fruit; hello-dearie; hooker; hustler; jane; Jane; joy-girl; low-heel; meal ticket; moll; pig-meat; possum; pro; pross; prossie; prossy; prostie; prosty; puta; quandong; quickie; quicky; scrubber; shagbag; slag; street-walker; tart; tom; tomato; tramp; trollop; wench; whore; working girl.

prostitute's client: casual; jockey; john; one-nighter; one-night job; punter; rough-trade; trade; trick.

prostitution: the business; the game; the turf; whoring.

(*See* **solicit, to**)

pub: battle-cruiser; beer joint; boozer; clip-joint; joint; local; nightspot; nineteenth hole; rubadub; rubbity; watering hole.

quantity, a great: bags; a barrel of; dozens of; ever so much; heaps; a hell of a lot; lashings; loads; lots; lousy with; no end of; oodles; piles; pots; squillion; stacks; tons; umpteen; wad; zillion.

quarrel: argle-bargle; argy-bargy; barney; breeze; bull and cow; donnybrook; dust-up; flare-up; hassle; hoedown; rhubarb; row; ruck; ructions; rumpus; scrap; screaming match; slanging match; split-up; up-and-downer; upper-and-downer; yike.

to quarrel: to argufy; to be bolshy/obstropolous; to go for s.o.; to hassle; to have an argy-bargy with s.o.; to make the fur fly; to pal out; to pick a bone with s.o.; to queer oneself with; to row; to tangle; to yike.

(*See* **fight**)

quickly, very: as quick as dammit; as soon as dammit; asap; at a cracking pace; at a fair old lick; at a fast mince; before you can say Jack Robinson; chop chop; to fire on all cylinders; hubba hubba; in a jiff; in a jiffy; in a twinkling; in nothing flat; in quick order; in two shakes (of a lamb's tail); in two ticks; licketysplit; like the clappers; like fury; like greased lightning; like a house on fire; like mad; like a shot; like a streak of piss; nippy; pdq; pretty damn quick; pronto; (a bit) sharpish.

ready, absolutely: all buttoned up; all set; all sewn up; all shipshape; all taped; all teed up; all wrapped up.

reprimand: bawling out; blowing-up; calling-down; coating; dressing-down; earwigging; rap; raspberry; roasting; rocket; rollicking; rollocking; slating; strafing; talking-to; telling-off; ticking-off; wigging.

reprimand, to: to ball out; to bawl out; to bite s.o.'s head off; to blow s.o. up; to call down; to carpet; to chew s.o.'s ass/balls/ears/head off; to chew s.o. out; to come down on s.o. like a ton of bricks; to cuss; to dish it out; to dress down; to eat s.o.'s head off; to give (s.o.) a balling out/a bawling out/a bollocking/a coating/a going-over/a jawing/a mouthful/a kick in the pants/a piece of one's mind/a rocket/stick/what-for; to give it to s.o. (hot and strong); to go crook; to haul s.o. over the coals; to have s.o. on the carpet/on the mat; to jaw s.o. out; to jump on s.o.; to kick ass; to lambaste; to let s.o. have it; to lead off at; to light into; to pitch into; to play old Harry with; to put s.o. through his facings; to read the riot act; to ream s.o./s.o.'s ass out; to rollick; to rollock; to send s.o. away with a flea in his ear; to sit on s.o.; to slapdown; to slate; to strafe; to take names; to tear s.o. off a strip; to tell s.o. where to get off; to tick s.o. off; to wipe the floor with s.o.

reprimanded, to be: to be on the carpet; to carry the can; to catch it; to cop it; to get a bawling-out/a bollocking/a talking-to/a telling-off/a ticking-off/a wigging; to get fried; to get a kick in the pants/a lot of stick/a slice of tongue-pie; to get hauled over the coals; to get hell; to get one's ass chewed out/one's head bitten off.

resourceful: all there; cagey; clever-clever; cleverclogs; a clever Dick; clever guts; cute; deep; dodgy; downy; fly; know-all; know-it-all; mustard; nifty; shrewd; slick; smart; smart-arsed; smart-assed; snak(e)y; snide; snidey; swift; wide; wise.

resourceful person: cleverclogs; clever Dick; clever guts; dodger; finagler; flyboy; know-all; know-it-all; shrewdie; slyboots; smart arse; smart ass; smarty pants; smooth operator.

to be resourceful: to be up to every move; to be on the ball; to be/to get on with it; to get wise; to have the suss; to know a thing or two; to know all the tricks of the trade/all the wrinkles; to know the drill/the ropes; to know one's p's and q's; to know one's way about; to know what's what; to wise up.

revolver: artillery; barker; biscuit; gat; heat; heater; iron; nine; pea-shooter; persuader; piece; rod; roscoe; Saturday night special; sawn-off; shooter; shooting-iron; six-shooter; squirter; tank; tool.

rich: cashed up; doughy; filthy rich; flush; in the money; loaded; plush; rolling (in it); stinking (rich); stinking with money; wedged; well-fixed; well-heeled; well-lined; well-off; well-stacked.

to be rich: to bank; to be in the chips/in the heavy/in the money; to be on easy street; to be worth a packet; to coin it in; to feather one's nest; to have a barrel of money/stacks (of money); to make a bomb; to make a packet; to make one's pile; to make money hand over fist; to rake it in; to stink of money.

ropes, to know the: *see* **resourceful, to be**.

rot: *see* **nonsense**.

rot, to talk: *see* **nonsense, to talk**.

rotten: awful; beastly; cheesy; chronic; corny; crap; crappo; crappy; crummy; daggy; disgusto; doggo; dud; foul; ghastly; gross; illin'; lousy; low-budget; low-rent; mingy; mouldy; mucky; no bloody good; the pits; poxy; pukeish; pukey; putrid; rancid; rinky-dink; ropey; shit; shithouse; shitty; shocking; shoddy; spastic; stack; stinking; u.s.; the worst.

rotter: *see* **bastard**.

run away, to: to Adam and Eve; to amscray; to beat it; to belt off; to blow; to bog off; to bolt; to breeze off; to bugger off; to bug off/out; to bunk off; to buzz off; to check out; to cheese it; to clear off; to clear out; to dash; to do a bunk/a disappearing act/a fade/a guy/a mick(e)y/a mike/a runner/a slope; to drag-ass; to drift; to dust off; to fade; to flit; to fuck off; to get moving/rolling; to go through; to hare off; to haul-ass; to have it away for the hurry-up; to have it (away) on one's toes; to hightail it; to hike; to hit the bricks/the road/the track/the trail; to hive off; to hook; to hotfoot it; to jam (it); to kick off; to lam (out); to leg it; to make oneself scarce; to make tracks; to mizzle; to mosey off; to nick off; to nip off; to pack up; to pee off; to piss off; to pig off; to plonk off; to ponce off; to pop off; to pull out; to push off; to quit the scene; to rack off; to rat off; to run out on s.o.; to scarper; to scoot; to scram; to screw; to shag-ass; to shag off; to ship out; to shit off; to shoot (off/through); to shove off; to skedaddle; to skid; to skip off;

to slide off; to slope off; to smoke; to sneak out; to sod off; to split (out); to take a powder; to take stoppo; to take off; to toddle off/along; to tommy; to tool off; to turn tail; to vamoose; to waltz off; to wing it.

Russian: commie; commy; Ivan; red; Russky.

sack, to: *see* **dismiss, to**.

sailor: jack; Jack tar; tar; jolly; leather-neck; matelot; matlow; pongo; (old) salt; shellback.

Scotsman: Jimmy; Jock; Mac; Sawney.

self-conceited, to be: *see* **show off, to**.

semen: baby-juice; bullets; come; cum; cream; crud; hocky; jism; jissom; jizz; juice; load; love juice; scum; spunk.

sentence: *see* **prison sentence**.

sex, to have: to ball; to bang; to be at it; to bed; to be in a leg-over position; to be on the job; to biff; to boink; to bonk; to bone; to bunny fuck; to charver; to crack it; to diddle; to dig; to dip one's wick; to do (it); to do a knee-trembler; to do the business/the naughty; to feature with s.o.; to finger fuck; to frig; to fuck; to futz; to get into s.o.'s pants; to get (it) in; to get (it) off; to get it up; to get one's ashes hauled; to get one's leg over; to get one's black/red wings; to give s.o. the bullets; to give it/her one; to give it to s.o.; to give a length; to give s.o. a thigh sandwich; to go to bed with; to go enders with (a woman); to go the naughty; to grab a piece of cake; to grind; to have a bang/bayonet practice/a chicken dinner/a bit of crumpet/a bit of the other/a bit on the side/a bit of spare/a bit of stray/a dry fuck/a dry hump/a grind/a jump/a lay/a naughty/a nibble/a poke/a quick one/a quickie/a romp/a screw/a shag/a taste/a wham-bam; to have it; to have s.o.; to have it away with; to have it off with; to have one's ashes hauled/banana peeled/nuts cracked; to have a roll in the hay/a tumble; to hide the sausage; to honeyfuck; to horse; to hose; to hump; to jack s.o.; to jam; to jazz; to jerk; to join the mounties; to knob; to knock off; to knock a slice off; to lay; to make it; to make love; to make out; to nail; to nob; to nut; to open one's legs for s.o.; to peel; to perform; to plant; to plug; to poke; to pork; to pound; to pull; to pull a train; to pump; to put the hooks on s.o.; to ram; to ride; to rock; to roger; to roll; to root; to rub off; to score a homer/a homerun; to scrape; to screw; to see the sky

through the trees; to sex; to shaft; to shag; to skip; to sleep about/around/with s.o.; to slip it to s.o.; to slip s.o. a length; to snatch a quick one; to sort s.o. out; to splice; to stick it in; to stuff; to tear it off; to tear off a piece of ass; to thread; to trick; to tup; to varnish one's cane; to wham; to work; to yard.

sex: bang; bed; belt; bit of bum/of crumpet/of tail; bit of the other; bit on the side; bonk(ing); bump and grind; business; charver; daily; daisy chain; dry fuck; dry hump; finger-fuck; Friar Tuck; fuck; fucking; gash; grind; half and half; heing and sheing; homer; homerun; how's your father; honey-fucking; hump; in-out; jam; jazz; jelly-roll; jig-a-jig; jig-jig; jing-jang; jump; knee-trembler; knock; lay; legover; love romp; naughty; nookie; nooky; pull; quick one; quickie; ride; roll; root; rub-out; rumpo; rumpty-tumpty; screw; screwing; shaft; shag; slap and tickle; snatch; thrash; tonk(ing); wham-bam; wild thing.
(*See* **anal sex; oral sex**)

sexual intercourse, (to have): *see* **sex (to have)**.

shirt: dicky dirt; flesh-bag; shift; shimmy.

show off, to: to be too big for one's boots; to be big-headed; to big-note oneself; to be snotty-nosed/uppity; to ego trip; to fancy one-self; to gam; to go on an ego trip; to play to the gallery; to put on the dog/a front/the ritz; to shoot a line; to skite; to splurge; to strut one's stuff; to swank; to talk big; to think no end of oneself; to think one is the bee's knees/the cat's whiskers/the big I am/hot shit/really it; to throw one's weight around; to toss (one-self) off; to walk tall.

show off: bighead; bit-note man; blow-hard; dazzle-dasher; four-flusher; ho-daddy; lair; line-shooter; piss-artist; pisshead; poser; skite; swank; swanky; swellhead.

shut up, to: to belt up; to button one's mouth/lip; to dummy; to hold one's guts; to ice; to keep mum; to keep one's gob shut; to keep one's trap shut; to pipe down; to shush; to squelch; to wrap up.

shut up!: belt up! button your lip/your mouth! can it! cheese it! chuck it! cut the cackle! cut it out! cut out the fancy stuff! cut the crap! drop dead! drop it! dry up! give it a rest! knock it off! nark it! none of your lip! pack it in! pack it up! pipe down! put a sock in it! shut your face/your gob/your row! shut it! stow it! turn it up! wrap it up!

(*See* **get lost!**)

silence s.o., to: to choke s.o. off; to give s.o. a clincher; to put the damper on; to put the kibosh on s.o.; to score off s.o.; to settle s.o.'s hash; to shut s.o. up; to sit upon s.o.; to squash s.o.

sleep, to go to: to bag some z's; to be out like a light; to catch/to cop some z's; to crash down/out; to doss down; to drop off; to fall out; to get some shut-eye; to go out like a light; to go (to) bye-byes; to go spark out; to go to kip; to grab some shut-eye/some z's; to have forty winks/a kip/a nap/a snooze; to hit the sack; to nod off; to pad down; to plough the deep; to zizz.

sodomize, to: *see* **anal sex (to have)**.

solicit, to: to be on the game/on the streets/on the turf; to go (john) cruising; to hustle; to kerb crawl; to kerb cruise; to mack; to peddle ass; to score; to swing a bag; to tote; to trade; to trick (a john); to turn a trick; to walk the streets; to whore.

Spaniard: dago; greaseball; spic(k); wop.

spectacles: bins; glims; goggles.

spend, to: to blow; to get through; to go to town; to lay out; to play ducks and drakes with one's money; to piss away (one's money); to run through; to shoot the works; to splash out; to throw good money after bad; to throw money down the drain; to throw one's money about.

spirits, strong: *see* **(alcoholic) drink**.

spree, to be/to go on a: *see* **good time, to have a**.

state, in a: all of a dither; all of a doodah; all of a flutter; all of a jitter; all at sea; all shook up; dithery; edgy; flummoxed; nervy; rattled; uncool; uptight.

to be in a state: to be in a flap/in a lather/in a stew/in a tizwas/in a tizzy; to be rattled/strung-up; to flap; to go off the rails; to go to pieces; to go into a tail-spin; to have the fidgets/the jitters/the twitters; to sweat; to work oneself up into a lather.

steal, to: to bag; to bone; to case a joint; to dip; to do over; to do a case/a job/a villainy; to finger; to half-inch; to have it away with; to heist; to hoist; to hook; to jump; to knock off; to knock over; to lift; to make (away with); to move; to nab; to nick; to nip; to pinch; to pull a job; to put one's mitts on sth; to reef; to ring the changes; to rip off; to roll; to scale; to screw a gaff; to scrounge; to shop; to snaffle; to snatch; to sneak; to snipe;

to snitch; to snowdrop; to stick up; to swipe; to take off; to trouser; to turn over; to walk away with; to walk off with; to weed; to whip; to whizz; to win.

stolen: bent; dodgy; (fell) off the back of a lorry; hooky; hot; iffy; knocked off.

(*See* **theft; thief**)

stink, to: to honk; to hoot; to hum; to niff; to be niffy; to be nifty; to pen and ink; to pong; to whiff; to be whiffy.

stomach: beer-belly; beer-gut; bread-basket; belly; Derby Kell(ly); lunch box; tummy.

(*See* **paunch**)

stupid, extremely: chuckle-headed; cretinous; (as) daft/dim as they come; daffy; daggy; dead from the neck up; dense; dilly; dim; dimwitted; dippy; ditzy; divvy; dopey; dorky; dozy; drippy; dumb; fat; fatheaded; featherbrained; flatheaded; goofy; gormless; half-baked; jerky; illin'; klutzy; lame-brained; nerdy; obtuse; pig-thick; plain daft/dumb; priceless; sappy; slow on the uptake; spastic; squitty; thick; thick as a plank/as two short planks; thickheaded; thickskulled; wet; wrongheaded; zomboid.

suicide, to commit: to blow one's brains out; to hump oneself off; to do away with one-self; to do oneself in; to pull the plug; to top oneself.

suit, to: that suits me down to the ground; that suits my book; that suits me to a T; that's just what the doctor ordered; that's right up my street; that's just my cup of tea; that's right up my alley.

swank, to: *see* **show off, to**.

swank(er): *see* **show off**.

swindle, to: to be on a fiddle; to burn; to chisel; to con; to cross; to diddle; to do a number on s.o.; to do out of; to do s.o. up like a kipper; to fit up; to fleece; to flimflam; to fob; to frame; to frig; to fuck; to gazump; to goldbrick; to graft; to grift; to gyp; to have s.o. over; to jive s.o.; to nick; to pull a fast one; to rip off; to rook; to rort; to rush; to scam; to screw; to sell a pup; to set up; to shaft; to sharp; to skin; to slip one over on s.o.; to snow; to stiff; to sting; to string along; to swizz(le); to take s.o. for a ride; to twist; to tuck up; to wangle; to weasel; to work a fiddle; to yank s.o. around.

swindle: (the old) army game; the badger game; clip-game; cross; daylight robbery; fiddle; fit-up; fix; flim-flam; frame-up; goldbrick(er); hustle; the murphy; nobble; number; racket; ramp; razzle-dazzle; ripoff; rort; scam; sell; skin game; snow(-job); sting; swizz; swizzle; wangling; weasel.

swindler: chiseller; con artist; con man; crook; diddler; double-crosser; fiddler; fixer; flimflammer; frigger; gazumper; grafter; griffer; gyp; highbinder; kite man; racketeer; ripoff artist; rorter; scalper; shark; sharp; sharpie; shortchange artist; skin artist; spieler; twister; wangler; welsher.

syphilis: jack; knob rot; load; pox; siff; syph.

to have syphilis: to be dosed up; to be a sypho/a syphy; to be poxed up/siffy/syphy/syphed up.

talk a lot, to: *see* **chat, to.**

talkativeness: *see* **chat; chattering.**

tall, thin person: bag of bones; bean-pole; big gawk; drain pipe; flag-pole; long streak of piss; string-bean.

tease, to: *see* **annoy, to.**

teeth: choppers; dominoes; fangs; gnashers; grinders; ivories; mashers; pearlies; snappers; toothy-pegs.

telephone: bell; blower; buzzer; Darby and Joan; dog and bone; horn; Mike Malone.

to telephone: to give s.o. a bell/a buzz/a tinkle; to get on the blower to s.o.

television: boob tube; box; goggle-box; idiot box; idiot's lantern; telly; the tube.

temper, to be in a bad: to be crabby/niggly/shirty/stroppy; to be in a right old paddy; to be like a bear with a sore head; to have one's shirt out; to be on the warpath; to throw a moody.

(*See* **angry, to be**)

testicles: apples; bag of tricks; balls; ballocks; bollix; bollocks; chestnuts; cobblers; cods; danglers; dusters; futures; goolies; jocks; knackers; maracas; marbles; marriage gear/prospects; marshmallows; Niagaras; nuts; orchestras; pills; rocks; stones; two-piece.

theft: bag-snatching; bust; crib-cracking; five-finger discount; heist; hoist; snatch; snow-dropping; sticksing.

thief: bag-snatcher; cracksman; creeper; crib-cracker; crook; file; ganef; gonef; grafter; heister; hoist; hoister; hook; hooker; in-and-out man; lifter; snide; tealeaf; welcher; welsher; yegg.

tired: *see* **exhausted.**

tramp: bindle stiff; bo; bum; bummer;

der(r)o; dosser; down-and-out; drifter; fink; floater; hobo; scruff; stiff; sundowner; swagman; yardbird.

trousers: bags; breeks; daks; drainpipes; kecks; keks; pants; slacks; strides.

umbrella: brolly; gamp; gingham; mush.

underpants; underwear: drawers; jockeys; nasties; nut chokers; personals; scanties; scants; skivvies; underchunders; unmentionables; unthinkables.

undersized (person): half-pint; knee-high to a grasshopper; lightweight; lofty; pint-sized; pipsqueak; runt; sawn-off; short-arse; shorty; shrimp; snip; tich; titch.

unwell, to be/to feel: to come over (all) funny/(all) queer; crook; dicky; funny; groggy; illin'; knocked-up; laid-up; liverish; off-colour; off one's oats/one's feed; offish; to have an off day; on one's last legs; one degree under; out of sorts; poorly; queer; rough; seedy; shaky; sick as a parrot; umpty; uncle (Dick); under the weather; wonky.

uproar: barney; bear garden; circus; hoo-ha(a); hoop-la; hullabaloo; kerfuffle; kick-up; racket; rough-house; row; ruck(us); rumpus; scream; shemozzle; shindig; shindy; (a big) stink.

to make an uproar: to be bolshy/obstropolous/rowdy; to kick up a dust/fuss/row; to make the fur fly; to play old Harry; to raise Cain; to raise (merry) Hell; to raise hell/a big stink.

urinate, to: to do wee-wees; to do number one; to do small jobs; to diddle; to go to the gents/the loo; to go for a leak/for a piddle/for a piss/for a strain; to have a Jimmy Riddle/a leak/a pee/a piss/a run-out/a slash/a squirt/a tinkle/a wee-wee; to have a look at the plumbing; to let fly; to pay a call/a visit; to pee; to piddle; to piss; to point Percy at the porcelain; to pop outside; to see a man about a dog; to shed a tear for Nelson; to siphon the python; to slash; to snake's hiss; to splash one's boots; ·to spring/to take a leak; to squeeze the lemon; to tiddle; to tinkle; to turn on the waterworks; to water the horses; to widdle; to write one's name on the lawn.

urine: hit and miss; pee; piddle; piss; snakes; snake's hiss; wee; wee-wee.

vagina: *see* **female genitals.**

VD: *see* **gonorrhea; syphilis.**

virginity: cherry; maidenhood.

to lose one's virginity: to fall off the

apple tree; to lose one's cherry.

vomit, to: to barf; to be as sick as a dog; to boot; to chuck a dummy; to chuck up; to chunder; to cry Ruth; to feed the fishes; to fetch up; to gag; to go for the big spit; to have a technicolour yawn; to have the heaves; to have a yell; to heave (one's guts up); to honk (one's chuff); to hurl; to puke (up); to ralph; to shoot the cat; to sick up; to spew (one's guts up); to throw a map; to throw up; to upchuck; to vom; to yawn; to yodel; to York.

walk, to: to foot it; to foot-slog; to go for a toddle; to hoof it; to leg it; to pad it; to ride Shank's pony/Shank's mare; to troll.

WC: bathroom; bog; can; carsi; carsy; cottage; craphouse; crapper; dike; dub; dunny; (the) Gents; Jane; (the) john; karsi; karzy; khazi; (the) ladies; lav; (the) little boy's/girl's room; (the) loo; middy; pisser; pisshouse; powder-room; privy; shit-house; the shitter; shouse; (the) smallest room; snakes; tea house; tea room; throne room; thunderbox; trizzer.

weep, to: to be a cry-baby; to blub; to grizzle; to put on a/the (big) sob-act; to turn on the waterworks.

what's-his-name; what's-her-name: doings; jock; thing; thingamy; thingum(e)bob; thingummy; what-do-you-call-him/her; wossname.

what's-its-name: do-hickey; (the) doings; doo-da; doodah; doofer; doojigger; gimmick; gismo; gizmo; gubbins; hickey; jig; jigger; mojo; oojamaflip; oojie; thingamy; thingamybob; thingamyjig; thingum(e)bob; thingummy; thingy; whatcha(ma)callit; what-do-you-call-it; whatnot; whatsit; widget; wossname.

wife, (my): my ball and chain; my better half; cheese and kisses; duchess; headache; her indoors; (the) light of my life; the little woman; (the) main squeeze; mem(sahib); the missis; the missus; my old duchess; my old Dutch; my old girl; my old lady; my old woman; my other half; my sparring partner; my trouble and strife. (*See* **husband**)

woman: article; beast; bimbo; bird; body; broad; cat; chappess; cookie; cooze; coozie; dame; fem; female; floosie; floosy; floozie; floozy; hen; hoyden; jam tart; Judy; mamma; potato peeler; quandong; queen; sheila; skirt; talent.

Pej: baggage; bat; bicycle; bike; bint; bitch; boiler; cow; crow; drabbie; droopy-drawers; gash; grunter; hagbag; hellcat; hoe; scrubber; shagbag; tart; town bike; tramp; tuna.

attractive woman: bit of all right; bit of stuff; cookie; crumpet; cupcake; fox; foxy lady; hot lay/mamma/piece/stuff; mover; nice bit of stuff; nympho; piece of ass/crumpet/skirt; sex bomb; sexpot; twist.

(ugly) old woman: old bag; old bat; old biddy; old crow; old faggot; old trout.

(*See* **girl**)

womanizer, (to be a): a bit of a lad; Casanova; to be cunt-struck; fast worker; to be a fast one with the girls; filthy sod; gash-hound; hound-dog; jelly-roll; lady-killer; one for the ladies; petticoat chaser; ram; skirt-chaser; skirt-hunter; smoothie; smoothy; tail-man; wolf.

work hard (at), to: to be an eager beaver; to be on the wrack; to be snowed under; to bust a gut; to dig; to do one's damnedest/darnedest; to flog oneself to death; to get down to a bit of hard grind; to go at it tooth and nail; to grind; to kill oneself with work; to knock oneself out; to peg away; to piss blood; to plug away; to put in a bit of hard graft; to shag one's arse off; to slog (away); to sweat blood; to sweat one's gust out; to work like the devil; to work like a dog/a nigger; to work like shit/like stink; to work one's buns off.

worthless: chickenshit; crap; crappy; cruddy; a dead loss; diddly (shit); doggo; duff; fit for/good for the scrap heap; measly; mouldy; nbg; NBG; no bloody good; no earthly use; no great shakes; not much cop; not worth a cracker/a crumpet/a damn/a nickel/a rap; not worth shucks/tuppence; poxy; shitty; tin-pot; the pits; tuppenny-ha'penny; trashy; a washout.